D1474411

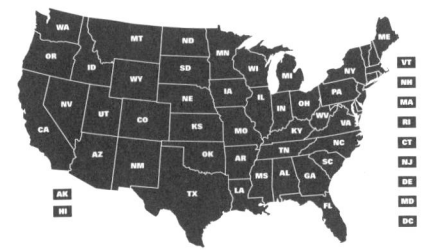

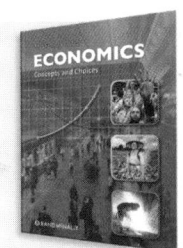

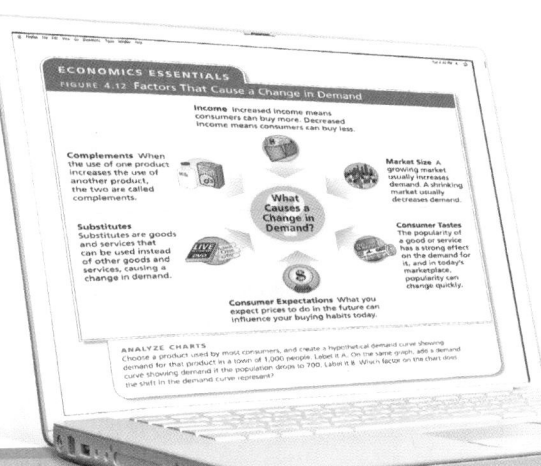

Teacher's Edition

McDougal Littell

ECONOMICS

Concepts and Choices

McDougal Littell

Acknowledgments
1B Courtesy of James E. Benjamin **35B, 507B** Courtesy of Casey P. Wright **67B, 379B** Courtesy of (William) Fremd H.S. **95B** Courtesy of Brother Peter Hannon **161B, 285B** Courtesy of Lisa Herman-Ellison **223B** Courtesy of Steve Lueck **189B, 443B, 471B** Courtesy of Shyrl L. Smiley **315B, 347B** Courtesy of Carrie Aaron-Young **255B, 407B, 541B** © Alan Magayne-Roshak/University of Wisconsin, Milwaukee

Acknowledgments begin on page R79.
ISBN-13: 978-0-618-81523-4 ISBN-10: 0-618-81523-6

Printed in Canada.
3 4 5 6 7 8 9-TBQC-10 09 08

McDougal Littell

ECONOMICS

Concepts and Choices

WHERE GREAT LESSONS BEGIN

McDougal Littell equips you with the tools you need to get students thinking economically and to help them apply what they learn in class to real life.

ECONOMIC CONCEPTS AND CONNECTIONS

Integrated print and technology capture your students' attention and help them connect to real-world economic concepts.

FLEXIBLE RESOURCES

Easy-to-use instructional tools reduce your preparation time and enable you to teach the way you want to teach.

TARGETED ASSESSMENT

Custom-built testing and remediation tools help you save time as you keep every student on a path to understanding and achievement.

ECONOMIC CONCEPTS AND CONNECTIONS

Integrated print and technology capture your students' attention and help them connect to real-world economic concepts.

FIGURES 4.8 AND 4.9 CHANGE IN DEMAND

FIGURE 4.8 DECREASE IN DEMAND

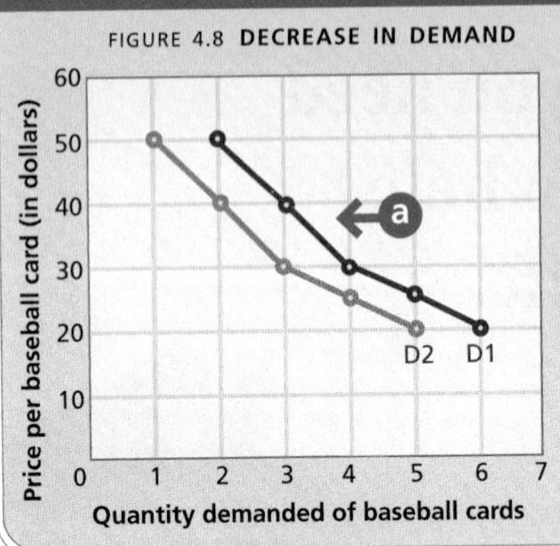

FIGURE 4.9 INCREASE IN DEMAND

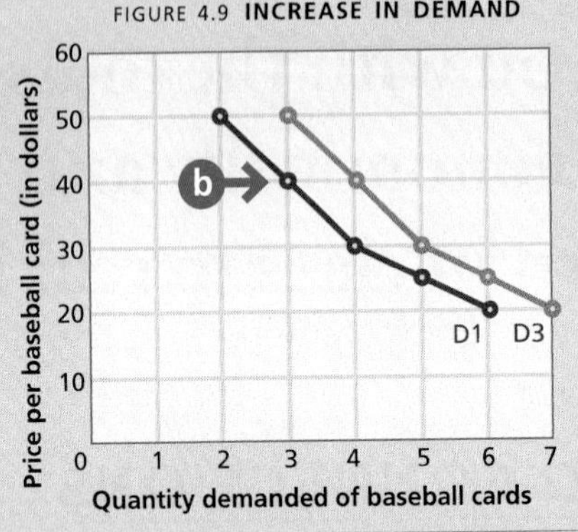

When a **change in demand** occurs, the demand curve shifts.

ⓐ As Figure 4.8 shows, a shift to the left (D2) indicates a decrease in demand.

ⓑ As Figure 4.9 shows, a shift to the right (D3) indicates an increase in demand.

ANALYZE GRAPHS

1. In Figure 4.8, how has demand for baseball cards changed at each of these prices: $20, $30, and $40?
2. In Figure 4.9, how has demand for baseball cards changed at each of these prices: $30, $40, and $50?

Animated Economics

Use an interactive version of shifting demand curves at **ClassZone.com**

Animated Economics

Interactive charts and graphs help engage your students, showing how economic concepts apply in changing conditions.

Available at 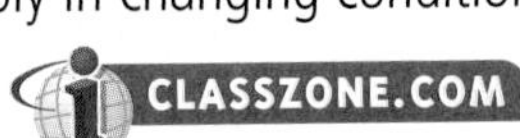

ECONOMICS ESSENTIALS

FIGURE 4.12 Factors That Cause a Change in Demand

Income Increased income means consumers can buy more. Decreased income means consumers can buy less.

Complements When the use of one product increases the use of another product, the two are called complements.

Market Size A growing market usually increases demand. A shrinking market usually decreases demand.

What Causes a Change in Demand?

Substitutes Substitutes are goods and services that can be used instead of other goods and services, causing a change in demand.

Consumer Tastes The popularity of a good or service has a strong effect on the demand for it, and in today's marketplace, popularity can change quickly.

Consumer Expectations What you expect prices to do in the future can influence your buying habits today.

ANALYZE CHARTS

Choose a product used by most consumers, and create a hypothetical demand curve showing demand for that product in a town of 1,000 people. Label it A. On the same graph, add a demand curve showing demand if the population drops to 700. Label it B. Which factor on the chart does the shift in the demand curve represent?

Economics Essentials

Eye-catching graphs and illustrations summarize important economic concepts in every chapter.

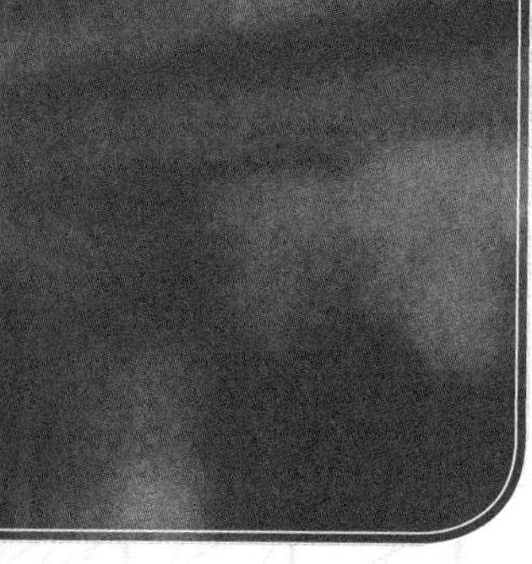

Case Study

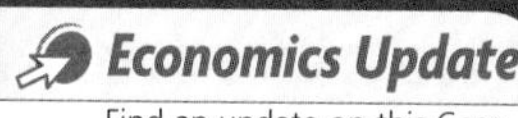

Economics Update
Find an update on this Case Study at **ClassZone.com**

Fueling Automobile Demand

Background Automobiles make up a huge portion of the American economy. In recent years the demand for automobiles and all the services connected with them has accounted for approximately one-fifth of all retail sales. Over the past decade, the total number of automobiles, including light trucks and SUVs (Sport Utility Vehicles), sold has been over 16 million units.

Car dealers are constantly looking for ways to sustain and increase demand for their product. Paul Taylor, chief economist of the National Automobile Dealers Association, observed, "The key to sales of 16.9 million will be the continued strong economy and sustained incentives." Incentives are awards designed to lure potential buyers into an automobile showroom and encourage sales. Manufacturers have tried everything from giving away mountain bikes to zero percent financing.

What's the issue? How does demand affect your selection of a vehicle? Study these sources to discover how the law of demand and the factors that affect demand shape the market.

B. Political Cartoon

Brian Duffy, a cartoonist with the *Des Moines Register,* drew this cartoon about the rising price of gasoline.

Thinking Economically Which of the factors that cause a change in demand does this cartoon address? Explain your answer.

CASE STUDIES

Diverse points of view show how economic concepts apply to real-life scenarios. **Economics Updates** assure that case studies remain current and relevant.

Online Summary

Complete the following activity either on your own paper or online at **ClassZone.com**

Choose the key concept that best completes the sentence. Not all key concepts will be used.

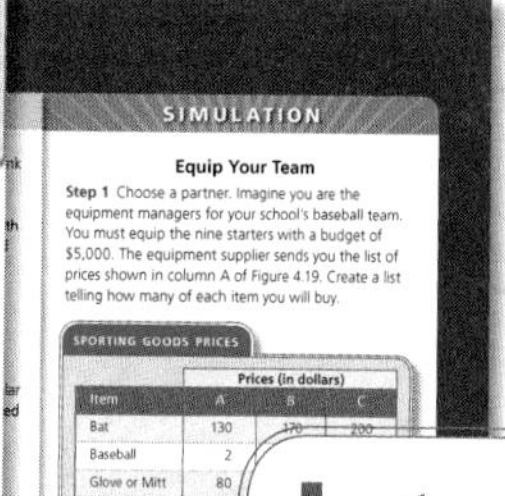

change in demand
change in quantity demanded
demand
demand curve
demand schedule
elastic
elasticity of demand
income effect
inelastic
inferior goods
law of demand
market demand curve
market demand schedule
normal goods
substitutes
substitution effect
total revenue
total revenue test
unit elastic

__1__ is the desire for a product and the ability to pay for it. According to the __2__, when price decreases, demand rises, and when price increases, demand falls.

Demand can be displayed in a table called a __3__ or on a graph called a __4__. A __5__ is a table that shows how much demand all consumers in a market have. When that same information is displayed on a graph, it is called a __6__.

The different points on a demand curve show a __7__. A __8__ occurs when consumers are willing to buy different amounts of a product at every price. The six factors that change demand are income, market size, consumer expectations, consumer taste, complement, and __9__.

The term __10__ describes how responsive consumers are to price changes. Demand that changes significantly when prices change is __11__. Demand that doesn't change significantly when prices change is __12__. The dividing line between the two is where demand is __13__.

__14__ is calculated by multiplying price by quantity sold.

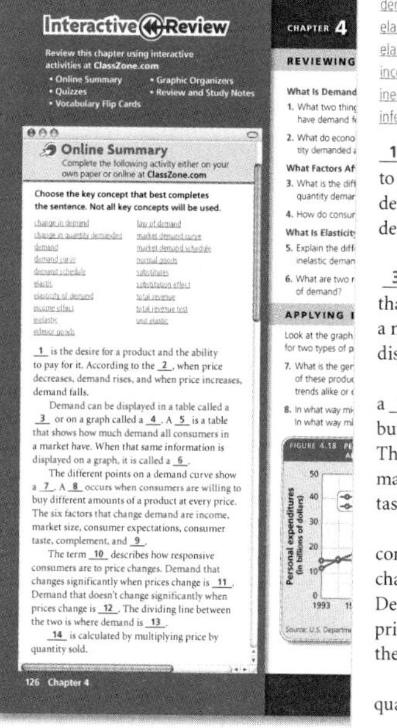

Interactive Review

A hands-on environment enables students to review chapter material through custom-built activities, games, and quizzes.

Available at  CLASSZONE.COM

FLEXIBLE RESOURCES

Easy-to-use instructional tools enable you to reduce your preparation time and teach the way you want to teach.

Resources2Go™

One USB drive contains your complete print resources, giving you a fast and easy way to access and edit your lessons and resources.

- Complete Teacher's Edition
- All print ancillaries and transparencies

Lesson Plans

McDougal Littell
ECONOMICS
Concepts and Choices

- Time-saving resources and strategies
- Inclusion strategies for every section
- Tips for substitute teachers
- Correlated to NCEE Standards

NCEE Student Activities

McDougal Littell
ECONOMICS
Concepts and Choices

- Adapted from NCEE publications including *Capstone* and *Economics in Action*
- One activity per chapter
- Apply economics to real-world subjects
- Activities range from personal finance to global issues

Lesson Plans

Lesson plans for every section help you build engaging lessons for your students.

NCEE Student Activities

Real-life activities help students develop economic literacy in accordance with NCEE standards.

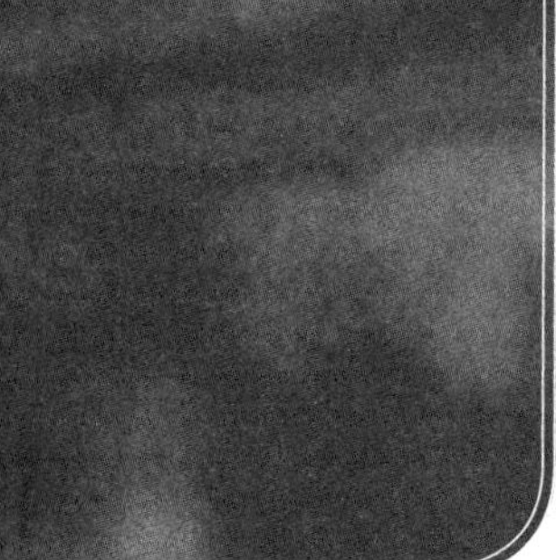

A. Online Article

Vera Wang's new collection demonstrates the relationship of cause and effect in the marketplace. At first, Wang responded to an unmet demand for more fashionable wedding attire. Now she has created demand by expanding into other product categories.

Very Vera Wang

In June 2005, Vera Wang won the CFDA (Council of the Fashion Designers of America) Womenswear Designer of the Year. On May 27, 2006, Wang was awarded the André Leon Talley Lifetime Achievement Award from the Savannah College of Art and Design.

Demand for the sophisticated Wang style has spread beyond weddings. Recently, Wang has expanded her product line to include ready-to-wear dresses, perfume, accessories, and home fashions. Wang has expanded her brand name through her fragrance, jewelry, eyeware, shoe and houseware collections. She has also penned the book Vera Wang on Weddings.

On August 24, 2006, clothing chain Kohl's announced that it would carry clothing and handbags designed by Wang. The collection will be available in Kohl's department stores as well as kohls.com, and will include sportswear, jewelry,

ECONOMICS PACESETTER

Vera Wang: Designer in Demand

In this section, you've learned about the law of demand. You've also seen demand in action in some hypothetical situations. The story of fashion designer Vera Wang, however, provides a real-world example of demand at work.

When they married, Mariah Carey, Jennifer Lopez, and several other stars turned to Wang for their wedding dresses. What explains the demand for this one woman's gowns?

Responding to Demand

Vera Wang had worked in the fashion industry for more than 15 years by the time she started planning her own wedding in 1989. So she was frustrated when she couldn't find the type of sophisticated bridal gown she wanted. She knew that many modern brides were savvy career women who preferred designer clothing. Yet, no one was making wedding dresses for those women.

The next year, Wang decided to fill that unmet demand. She created her own line of gowns featuring elegant sleeveless styles rather than the hooped skirts, puffed sleeves, and lace flounces that had dominated wedding-dress designs before.

Changing Styles Vera Wang wanted to change traditional wedding dress styles that, she thought, made brides look "like the bride on top of a cake, very decorated."

Soon celebrities such as Uma Thurman were choosing Vera Wang wedding gowns. This generated publicity, and demand for Wang's creations grew. In response, other designers began to create sleeker wedding dresses, and the style spread. Vera Wang is now considered to be one of the country's most influential designers of wedding gowns.

Demand for the sophisticated Wang style has spread beyond weddings. In recent years, Wang has expanded her product line to include ready-to-wear dresses, perfume, accessories, and home fashions.

Price Range for Vera Wang Wedding Gowns: about $2,000 to $20,000

Economics Update Find the latest on Vera Wang's business at **ClassZone.com**

APPLICATION Analyzing Cause and Effect

D. In what ways did Vera Wang respond to consumer demand? In what ways did she generate consumer demand?

104 Chapter 4

Economics Update

Online statistics and reports keep your students at the forefront of the latest economic news and information.

Available at  CLASSZONE.COM

Economics Concepts Transparencies

McDougal Littell

ECONOMICS

Concepts and Choices

- Ready-to-use overheads f
- Present key economics c
- Apply economics concep
- Reinforce concepts for v

The Presentation Toolkit

Interactive lessons connect your students to economics through activities, multimedia presentations, and more.

- Economics Concepts Transparencies
- Power Presentations DVD-ROM features:
  - Animated Economics
  - Activity Maker
  - Interactive Review
  - SmartGrapher
  - Automatic Updates
- Economics Video Series on DVD

Custom-built testing and remediation tools help you save time as you keep every student on a path to understanding and achievement.

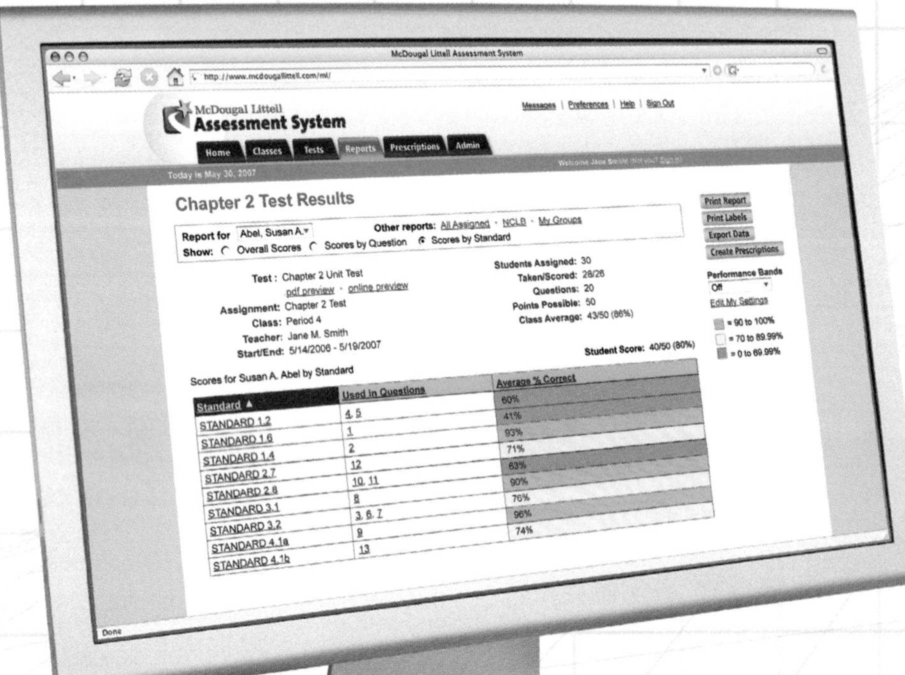

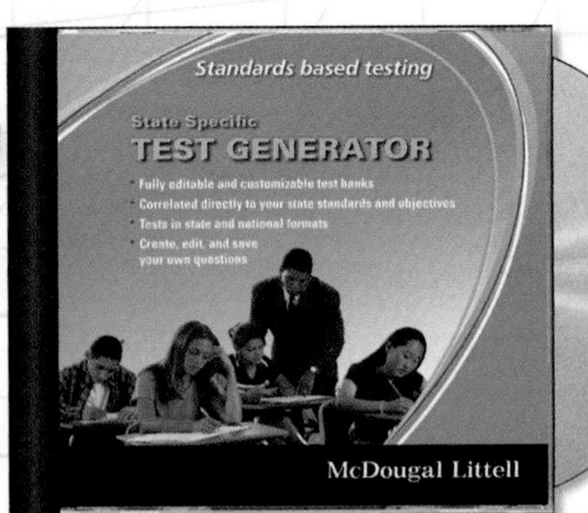

The McDougal Littell State-Specific Test Generator CD-ROM includes thousands of editable test questions correlated to your state standards.

McDougal Littell Assessment System

This flexible, Web-based program enables you to use assessment as a teaching tool, giving you a fast and seamless way to:

Test
Unique testing is custom-built to your state standards.

Score
Automatic scoring gives you results in minutes.

Report
Diagnostic reports show you what standards were missed.

Reteach
Personalized remediation helps you target reteaching.

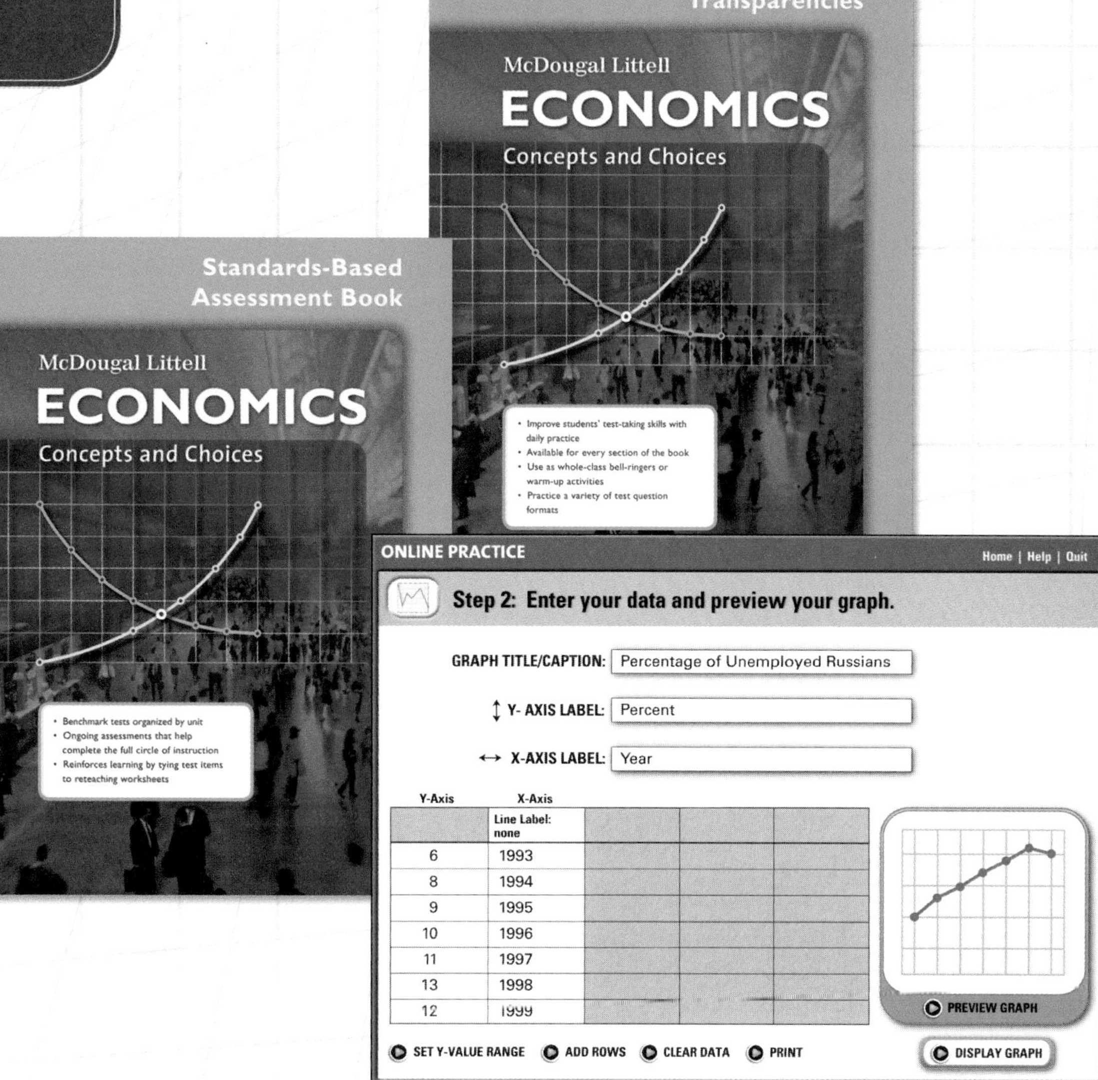

Assessment and Reteaching Package

A wealth of direct, daily, and differentiated resources ensures that students master important economic concepts.

Direct

Test preparation strategies right in the Pupil's Edition

Daily

Test practice transparencies for each section of every chapter

Differentiated

Standards-based options and online practice for all learners

McDougal Littell

ECONOMICS

Concepts and Choices

WHERE GREAT LESSONS BEGIN

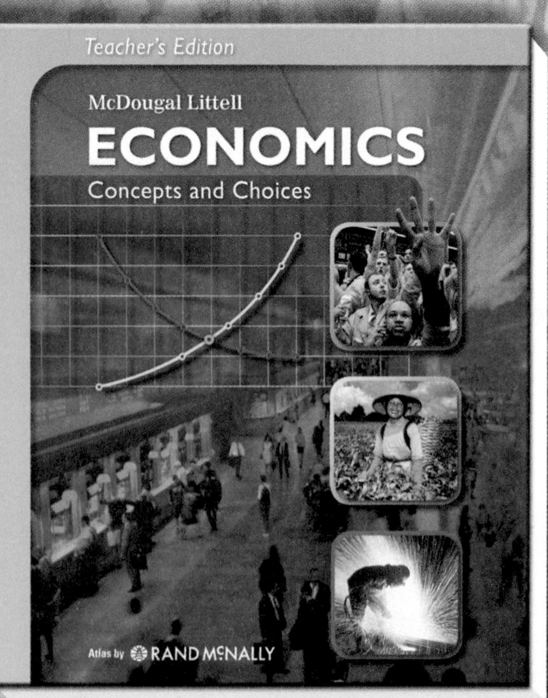

Pupil's Edition

Teacher's Edition

Resource Manager
- Lesson Plans
- Unit Resource Books
- Consumer and Personal Finance Activities

Presentation Toolkit
- Power Presentations DVD-ROM
- Economics Video Series on DVD
- Economics Concepts Transparencies

Assessment and Reteaching Package
- McDougal Littell Assessment System
- McDougal Littell Test Generator
- Standards-Based Assessment Book
- Daily Test Practice Transparencies
- Online Test Practice

Student Workbooks
- Reading Study Guide
- Reading Study Guide with Additional Support
- Test Practice and Review Workbook
- NCEE Student Activities

Technology
- ClassZone.com
- eEdition DVD-ROM with Audio
- eEdition Plus Online with Audio
- EasyPlanner DVD-ROM
- Resources2Go™ USB Drive

McDougal Littell

ECONOMICS

Concepts and Choices

McDougal Littell

ECONOMICS

Concepts and Choices

McDougal Littell

Senior Consultants

Senior Consultants

Sally Meek has been teaching Economics, AP Microeconomics, and AP Macroeconomics in the Plano Independent School District in Plano, Texas since 1987. She has served as an AP Economics reader since 1998, and is currently a Lead Consultant for AP Economics at Summer Institutes for universities across Texas and a member of the AP Economics Test Development Committee. Additionally, Ms. Meek serves on the National Assessment of Educational Progress Economics Steering Committee and as a test item writer. She served as President of the Global Association of Teachers of Economics and addressed the National Summit on Economic and Financial Literacy in 2005. In 2004, Ms. Meek co-founded the North Texas TINSTAAFL Society and was on the National Council on Economic Education (NCEE) Virtual Economics 3.0 Design Committee. She has received the Southwest College Board Advanced Placement Special Recognition Award and the GATE Distinguished Service Award. Ms. Meek earned her B.A. in political science at the University of Texas at Dallas and her M.Ed. in Secondary Education with a content emphasis on Economics from the University of North Texas.

John Morton is Senior Program Officer for the Arizona Council on Economic Education. He taught economics for 31 years at the high school and university levels. Mr. Morton founded and directed the Center for Economic Education at Governors State University in Illinois for 15 years and founded and served as president of the Arizona Council on Economic Education for 4 years. He served as vice president for program development at the National Council on Economic Education (NCEE) for 5 years. He has authored or co-authored more than 80 publications and chaired the advisory board of *The Wall Street Journal Classroom Edition* from 1991 to 2000. Mr. Morton has won the Leavey Award from the Freedoms Foundation, as well as the Bessie B. Moore Service Award and the John C. Schramm Leadership Award from NCEE and the National Association of Economic Educators. He earned his M.A. from the University of Illinois and pursued postgraduate work at the University of Chicago.

Mark C. Schug is Professor and Director of the University of Wisconsin-Milwaukee Center for Economic Education and served as a Senior Fellow for the National Council for Economic Education from 2002–2005. He has taught for over 35 years at the middle school, high school, and university levels. Dr. Schug has written and edited over 180 publications. Additionally, he edited *The Senior Economist* for the National Council on Economic Education (NCEE) from 1986–1996. Dr. Schug often speaks and writes about economic and financial education, market-based reforms in education, and issues in urban schools, and has addressed local, state, national, and international groups. Similarly, he has done training programs for teachers in several states across the nation. Dr. Schug earned his Ph.D. from the University of Minnesota.

Acknowledgments begin on page R79.
ISBN-13: 978-0-618-59403-0 ISBN-10: 0-618-59403-5

Printed in Canada.
1 2 3 4 5 6 7 8 9-TBQC-10 09 08 07 06

iv

Teacher Consultants

The following educators provided ongoing review during the development of the program.

Sheri Perez
Mesa Community College
Mesa, Arizona

Bill Smiley
Leigh High School (retired)
San Jose, California

Sandra K. Wright
Adlai E. Stevenson High School
Lincolnshire, Illinois

Douglas Young
Croton-Harmon High School
Croton-on-Hudson, New York

Content Reviewers

The content reviewers evaluated the text for depth, accuracy, and clarity in the use of economics concepts.

Joanne Benjamin
Board of Directors, California Council on Economic Education
President, California Association of School Economics Teachers
San Bernardino, California

Joseph Calhoun
Assistant Director, Stavros Center for Economic Education
Florida State University
Tallahassee, Florida

R. J. Charkins
Executive Director, California Council on Economic Education
San Bernardino, California

Sarah E. Culver
Director, UAB Center for Economic Education
University of Alabama-Birmingham
Birmingham, Alabama

Beth S. Eckstein
Director, Center for Economic Education College of Business, East Carolina University
Greenville, North Carolina

Gail A. Hawks
Director, Center for Economic Education
Miami-Dade Community College
Miami, Florida

Gary A. Hoover
Associate Professor of Economics
University of Alabama
Tuscaloosa, Alabama

Mary Anne Pettit
Associate Director, Office of Economic Education
Southern Illinois University-Edwardsville
Edwardsville, Illinois

Dennis Placone
Director, Clemson University Center for Economic Education
Clemson University
Clemson, South Carolina

Jennifer Thomas
Senior Director of Operations, Florida Council on Economic Education
Largo, Florida

Teacher Reviewers

The following teachers and administrators reviewed the text for its appropriateness for use in high school economics programs.

Julie Barker
Pittsford Mendon High School
Pittsford, New York

Michael D. Bruce
William Fremd High School
Palatine, Illinois

Brett Burkey
Spanish River High School
Boca Raton, Florida

Jan Collins
Franklin High School
Elk Grove, California

Melanie Craven
Nanuet Senior High School
Nanuet, New York

Lisa Herman-Ellison
Kokomo High School
Kokomo, Indiana

Rebecca L. Johnson
Raoul Wallenberg Traditional High School
San Francisco, California

Kathleen Ryan Johnston
Rufus King High School
Milwaukee, Wisconsin

Romano Luchini
Encina High School
Sacramento, California

Robert Mira
West Lafayette High School
West Lafayette, Indiana

Michael Noto
Brighton High School
Rochester, New York

Nick Petraccione
K-12 Supervisor
Bethlehem Central School District
Delmar, New York

Elida Petrella-Yocum
Indian Creek High School
Wintersville, Ohio

Heather Price
Eau Gallie High School
Melbourne, Florida

David Sweeney
Dryden High School
Dryden, Michigan

Rick Sydor
C.K. McClatchy High School
Sacramento, California

Gerald Taylor
SEED School
Washington, D.C.

v

ECONOMICS: Concepts and Choices

Contents

MACROECONOMICS

UNIT 5 Measuring and Monitoring Economic Performance

MACROECONOMICS

UNIT 6 The Role of Government in the Economy

UNIT 7 The Global Economy

Consumer and Personal Finance

Reference Section

Economics Updates

For current economic data and news, go to **ClassZone.com**

Economics Updates (continued)

Animated Economics

For interactive graphs and lessons, go to **ClassZone.com**

YOUR ECONOMIC CHOICES

ECONOMICS: Concepts and Choices

Economics Pacesetters

Global Perspectives

Economics Skillbuilders

Math Challenges

x

Graphs, Charts, Tables, and Maps

xi

Graphs, Charts, Tables, and Maps (continued)

xiii

Economic Atlas and Statistics

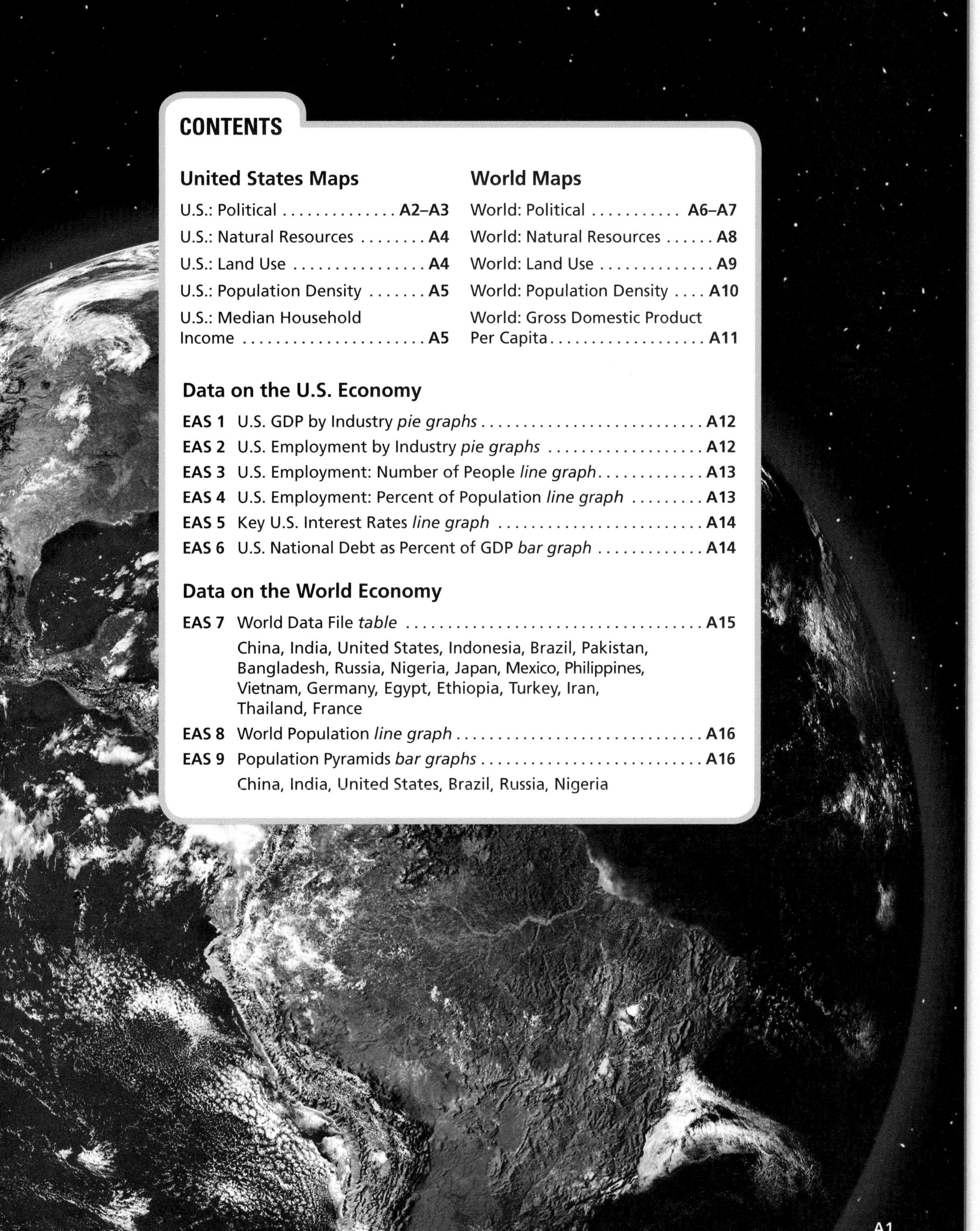

CONTENTS

United States Maps

World Maps

Data on the U.S. Economy

Data on the World Economy

A1

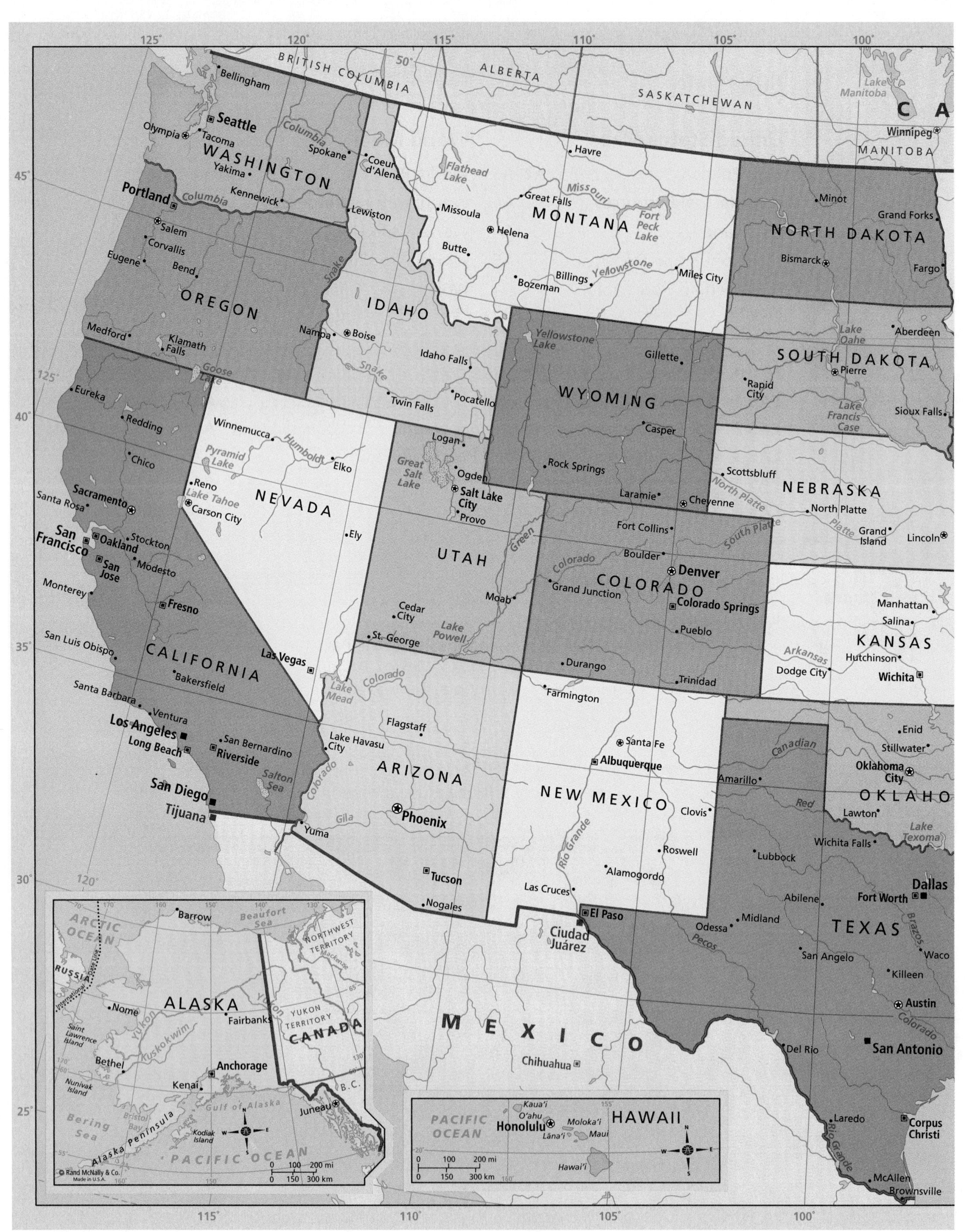

BRITISH COLUMBIA
ALBERTA
SASKATCHEWAN
MANITOBA
CA
Lake Manitoba
Winnipeg
WASHINGTON
Bellingham
Seattle
Olympia
Tacoma
Spokane
Yakima
Kennewick
Coeur d'Alene
OREGON
Portland
Salem
Corvallis
Eugene
Bend
Medford
Klamath Falls
IDAHO
Lewiston
Nampa
Boise
Idaho Falls
Twin Falls
Pocatello
MONTANA
Havre
Great Falls
Missoula
Helena
Butte
Bozeman
Billings
Miles City
Flathead Lake
Fort Peck Lake
NORTH DAKOTA
Minot
Grand Forks
Bismarck
Fargo
SOUTH DAKOTA
Aberdeen
Pierre
Rapid City
Sioux Falls
Lake Oahe
Lake Francis Case
WYOMING
Yellowstone Lake
Gillette
Casper
Rock Springs
Laramie
Cheyenne
NEBRASKA
Scottsbluff
North Platte
Grand Island
Lincoln
CALIFORNIA
Eureka
Redding
Chico
Sacramento
Santa Rosa
San Francisco
Oakland
San Jose
Stockton
Modesto
Monterey
Fresno
San Luis Obispo
Bakersfield
Santa Barbara
Ventura
Los Angeles
Long Beach
San Bernardino
Riverside
San Diego
Tijuana
Salton Sea
Goose Lake
NEVADA
Winnemucca
Elko
Reno
Carson City
Lake Tahoe
Pyramid Lake
Ely
Las Vegas
Lake Mead
UTAH
Logan
Ogden
Salt Lake City
Provo
Great Salt Lake
Cedar City
St. George
Moab
Lake Powell
COLORADO
Fort Collins
Boulder
Denver
Grand Junction
Colorado Springs
Pueblo
Durango
Trinidad
KANSAS
Manhattan
Salina
Hutchinson
Dodge City
Wichita
ARIZONA
Flagstaff
Lake Havasu City
Phoenix
Yuma
Tucson
Nogales
NEW MEXICO
Farmington
Santa Fe
Albuquerque
Clovis
Roswell
Alamogordo
Las Cruces
OKLAHOMA
Enid
Stillwater
Oklahoma City
Lawton
Lake Texoma
TEXAS
Amarillo
Wichita Falls
Lubbock
Abilene
Fort Worth
Dallas
Midland
Odessa
El Paso
San Angelo
Waco
Killeen
Austin
San Antonio
Del Rio
Laredo
Corpus Christi
McAllen
Brownsville
MEXICO
Ciudad Juárez
Chihuahua
Columbia
Snake
Missouri
Yellowstone
Humboldt
Green
Colorado
Gila
Rio Grande
Pecos
Brazos
Canadian
Red
Arkansas
North Platte
South Platte
Platte
125°
120°
115°
110°
105°
100°
45°
40°
35°
30°
25°
50°
ALASKA
ARCTIC OCEAN
Beaufort Sea
Barrow
NORTHWEST TERRITORY
YUKON TERRITORY
CANADA
RUSSIA
Nome
Fairbanks
Anchorage
Bethel
Kenai
Juneau
B.C.
Saint Lawrence Island
Nunivak Island
Bering Sea
Bristol Bay
Alaska Peninsula
Kodiak Island
Gulf of Alaska
PACIFIC OCEAN
Yukon
Kuskokwim
0 100 200 mi
0 150 300 km
© Rand McNally & Co. Made in U.S.A.
HAWAII
PACIFIC OCEAN
Kaua'i
O'ahu
Honolulu
Moloka'i
Lāna'i
Maui
Hawai'i

United States: Political
National capitals
State capitals
Towns
Population
Over 1,000,000
250,000 – 1,000,000
Under 250,000
International boundary
State boundary
0 100 200 300 Miles
0 100 200 300 400 Kilometers
MINNESOTA
WISCONSIN
MICHIGAN
IOWA
ILLINOIS
INDIANA
OHIO
PENNSYLVANIA
NEW YORK
VERMONT
NEW HAMPSHIRE
MAINE
MASSACHUSETTS
CONN.
R.I.
NEW JERSEY
DELAWARE
MARYLAND
WEST VIRGINIA
VIRGINIA
KENTUCKY
TENNESSEE
NORTH CAROLINA
SOUTH CAROLINA
GEORGIA
ALABAMA
MISSISSIPPI
LOUISIANA
ARKANSAS
MISSOURI
FLORIDA
ONTARIO
QUÉBEC
NEW BRUNSWICK
ATLANTIC OCEAN
GULF OF MEXICO
BAHAMAS
Gulf of Maine
Lake Superior
Lake Michigan
Lake Huron
Lake Erie
Lake Ontario
Lake Champlain
Georgian Bay
Lake Nipigon
Lake of the Woods
Lake Winnipeg
Lake Okeechobee
Kentucky Lake
Isle Royale
Long Island
Washington D.C.
New York
Philadelphia
Chicago
Detroit
Houston
Boston
Atlanta
Miami
Montréal
Ottawa
Toronto
Nassau
© Rand McNally & Co.
Made in U.S.A.

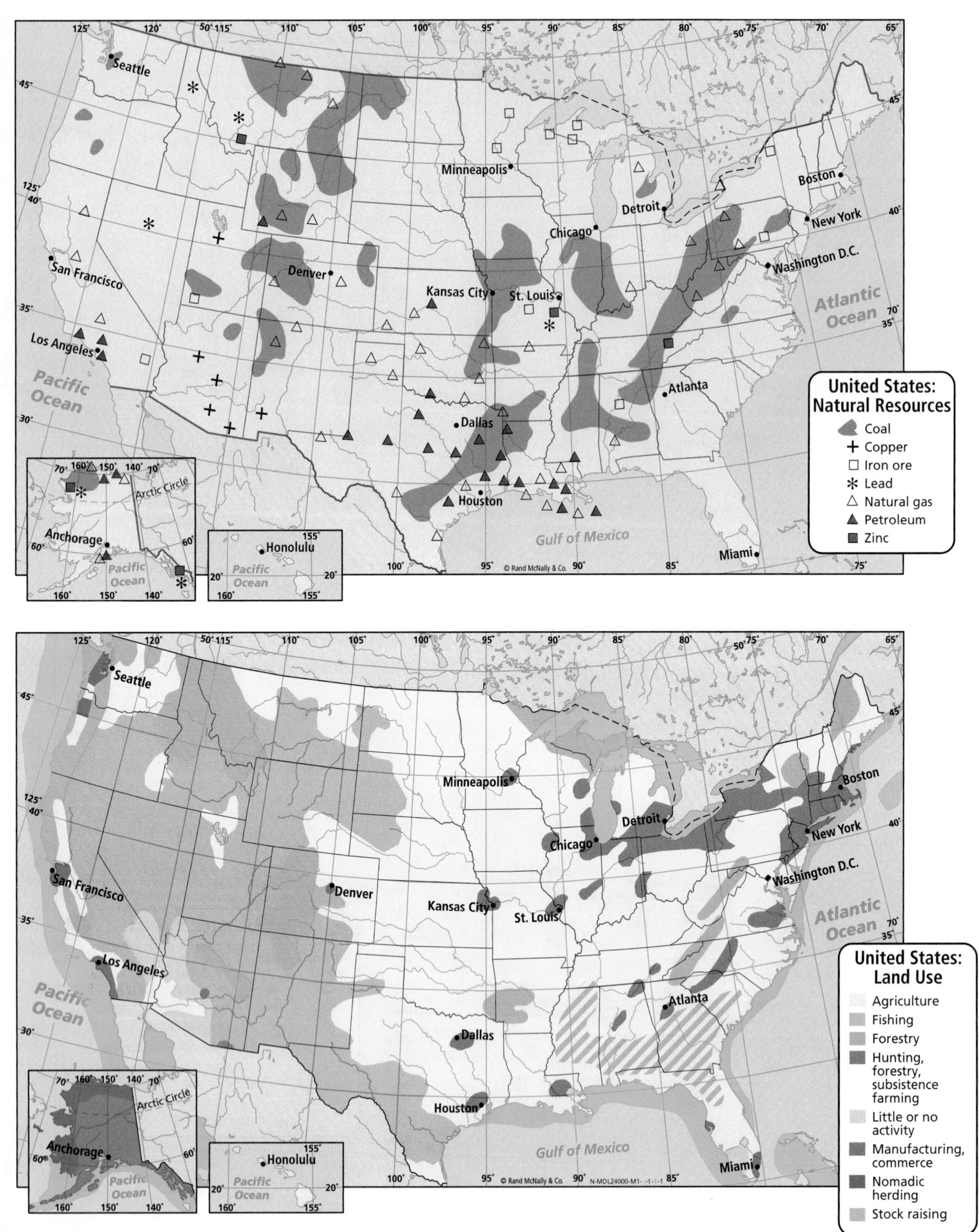
United States: Natural Resources
Coal
Copper
Iron ore
Lead
Natural gas
Petroleum
Zinc
Seattle
Minneapolis
Boston
Detroit
Chicago
New York
Washington D.C.
San Francisco
Denver
Kansas City
St. Louis
Atlantic Ocean
Los Angeles
Pacific Ocean
Atlanta
Dallas
Houston
Gulf of Mexico
Miami
Anchorage
Arctic Circle
Honolulu
© Rand McNally & Co.
United States: Land Use
Agriculture
Fishing
Forestry
Hunting, forestry, subsistence farming
Little or no activity
Manufacturing, commerce
Nomadic herding
Stock raising
N-MDL24000-M1- -1-1-1

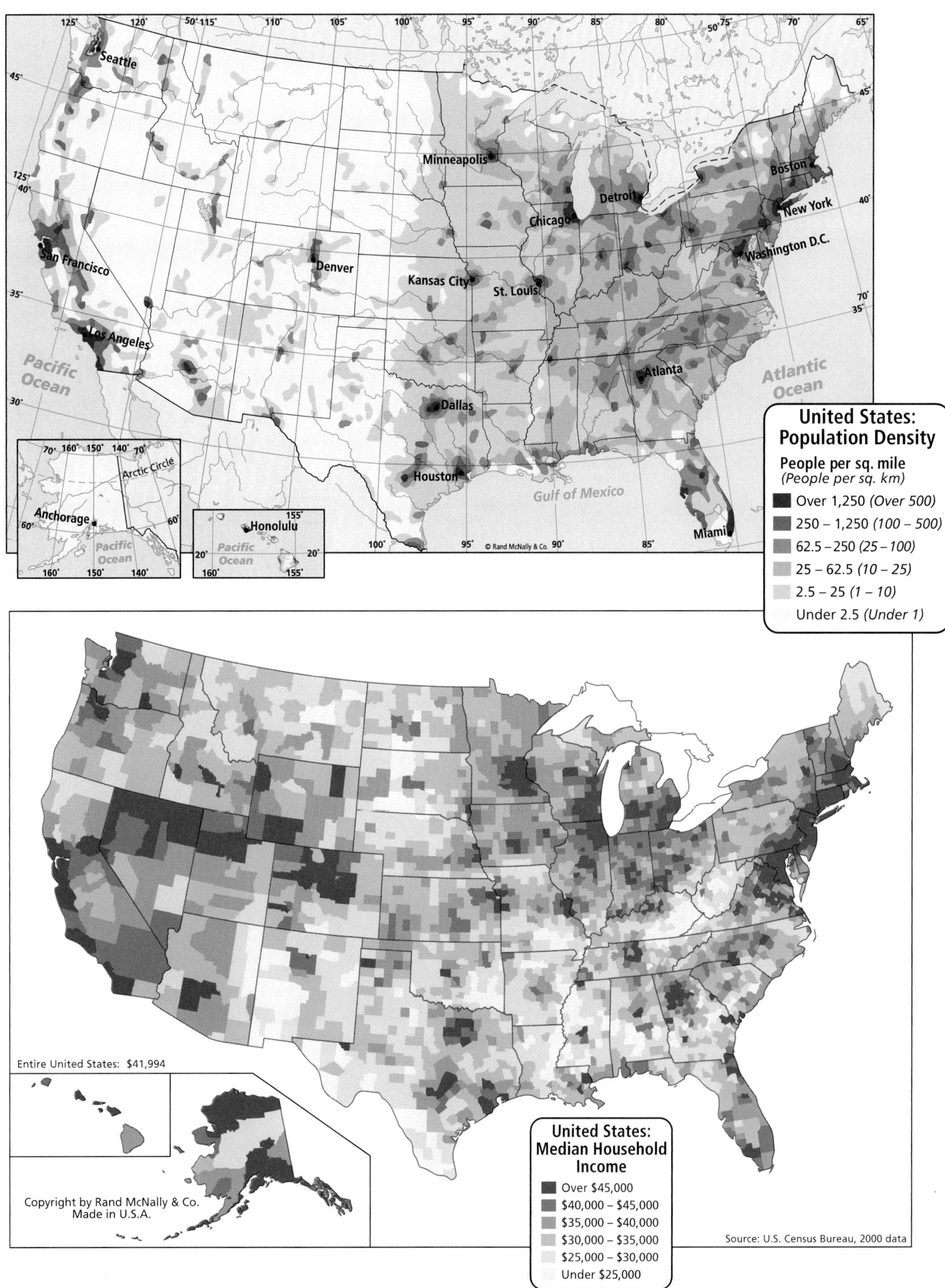
Seattle
Minneapolis
Boston
Detroit
New York
Chicago
San Francisco
Denver
Washington D.C.
Kansas City
St. Louis
Los Angeles
Pacific Ocean
Atlantic Ocean
Atlanta
Dallas
Houston
Gulf of Mexico
Miami
Arctic Circle
Anchorage
Honolulu
© Rand McNally & Co.
United States: Population Density
People per sq. mile
(People per sq. km)
Over 1,250 (Over 500)
250 – 1,250 (100 – 500)
62.5 – 250 (25 – 100)
25 – 62.5 (10 – 25)
2.5 – 25 (1 – 10)
Under 2.5 (Under 1)
Entire United States: $41,994
Copyright by Rand McNally & Co.
Made in U.S.A.
United States: Median Household Income
Over $45,000
$40,000 – $45,000
$35,000 – $40,000
$30,000 – $35,000
$25,000 – $30,000
Under $25,000
Source: U.S. Census Bureau, 2000 data

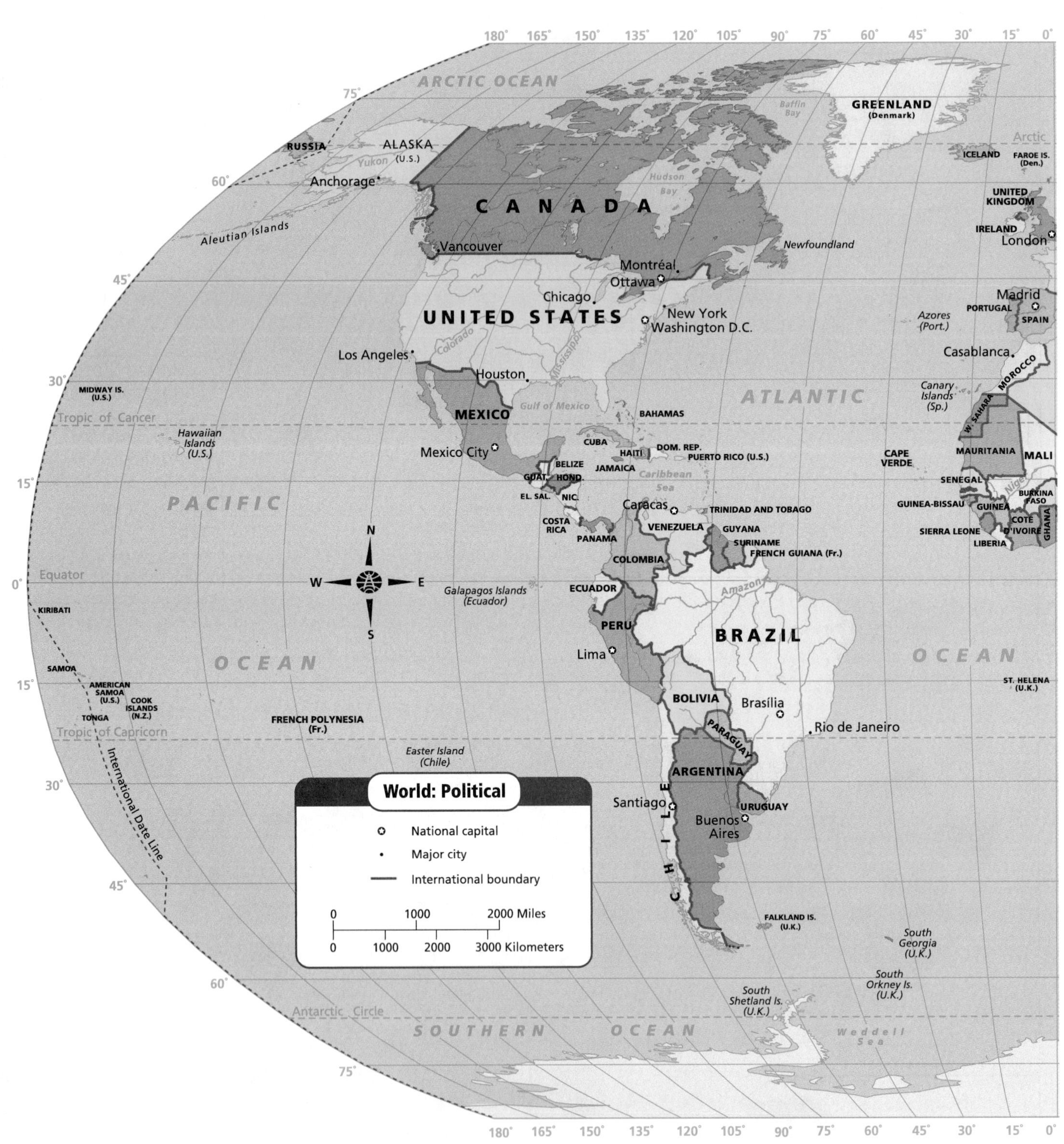
World: Political
National capital
Major city
International boundary
0
1000
2000 Miles
0
1000
2000
3000 Kilometers
ARCTIC OCEAN
PACIFIC
OCEAN
ATLANTIC
OCEAN
SOUTHERN
OCEAN
GREENLAND
(Denmark)
ALASKA
(U.S.)
RUSSIA
Anchorage
Aleutian Islands
CANADA
Vancouver
Montréal
Ottawa
Chicago
UNITED STATES
New York
Washington D.C.
Los Angeles
Houston
MEXICO
Mexico City
Gulf of Mexico
BAHAMAS
CUBA
HAITI
DOM. REP.
PUERTO RICO (U.S.)
JAMAICA
BELIZE
GUAT.
HOND.
EL SAL.
NIC.
COSTA RICA
PANAMA
Caribbean Sea
Caracas
TRINIDAD AND TOBAGO
VENEZUELA
GUYANA
SURINAME
FRENCH GUIANA (Fr.)
COLOMBIA
ECUADOR
PERU
Lima
BRAZIL
Brasília
Rio de Janeiro
BOLIVIA
PARAGUAY
ARGENTINA
Santiago
Buenos Aires
URUGUAY
CHILE
FALKLAND IS.
(U.K.)
South Georgia
(U.K.)
South Orkney Is.
(U.K.)
South Shetland Is.
(U.K.)
Weddell Sea
Antarctic Circle
Hudson Bay
Baffin Bay
Newfoundland
ICELAND
FAROE IS.
(Den.)
UNITED KINGDOM
IRELAND
London
Madrid
PORTUGAL
SPAIN
Azores
(Port.)
Casablanca
MOROCCO
Canary Islands
(Sp.)
W. SAHARA
MAURITANIA
MALI
CAPE VERDE
SENEGAL
GUINEA-BISSAU
GUINEA
BURKINA FASO
SIERRA LEONE
CÔTE D'IVOIRE
GHANA
LIBERIA
ST. HELENA
(U.K.)
MIDWAY IS.
(U.S.)
Hawaiian Islands
(U.S.)
Tropic of Cancer
Equator
Tropic of Capricorn
KIRIBATI
SAMOA
AMERICAN SAMOA
(U.S.)
COOK ISLANDS
(N.Z.)
TONGA
FRENCH POLYNESIA
(Fr.)
Galapagos Islands
(Ecuador)
Easter Island
(Chile)
International Date Line
Yukon
Colorado
Mississippi
Amazon
Niger
N
S
E
W
180° 165° 150° 135° 120° 105° 90° 75° 60° 45° 30° 15° 0°
75° 60° 45° 30° 15° 0° 15° 30° 45° 60° 75°

ARCTIC OCEAN
RUSSIA
KAZAKHSTAN
MONGOLIA
CHINA
INDIA
PACIFIC OCEAN
INDIAN OCEAN
SOUTHERN OCEAN
ANTARCTICA
AUSTRALIA
INDONESIA
JAPAN
NEW ZEALAND
© Rand McNally & Co.

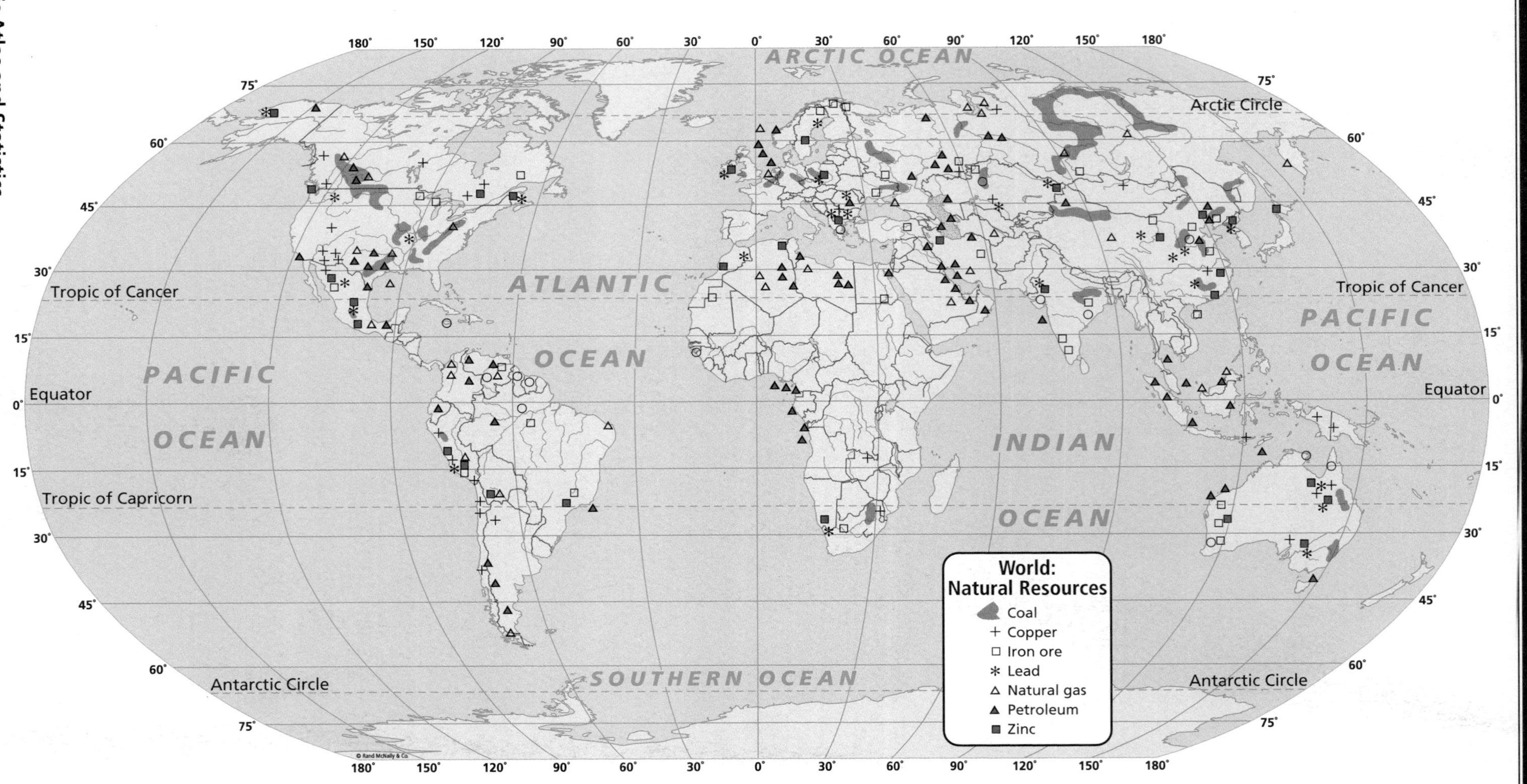

World:
Natural Resources
Coal
Copper
Iron ore
Lead
Natural gas
Petroleum
Zinc
ARCTIC OCEAN
PACIFIC OCEAN
ATLANTIC OCEAN
INDIAN OCEAN
SOUTHERN OCEAN
Arctic Circle
Tropic of Cancer
Equator
Tropic of Capricorn
Antarctic Circle

World: Land Use

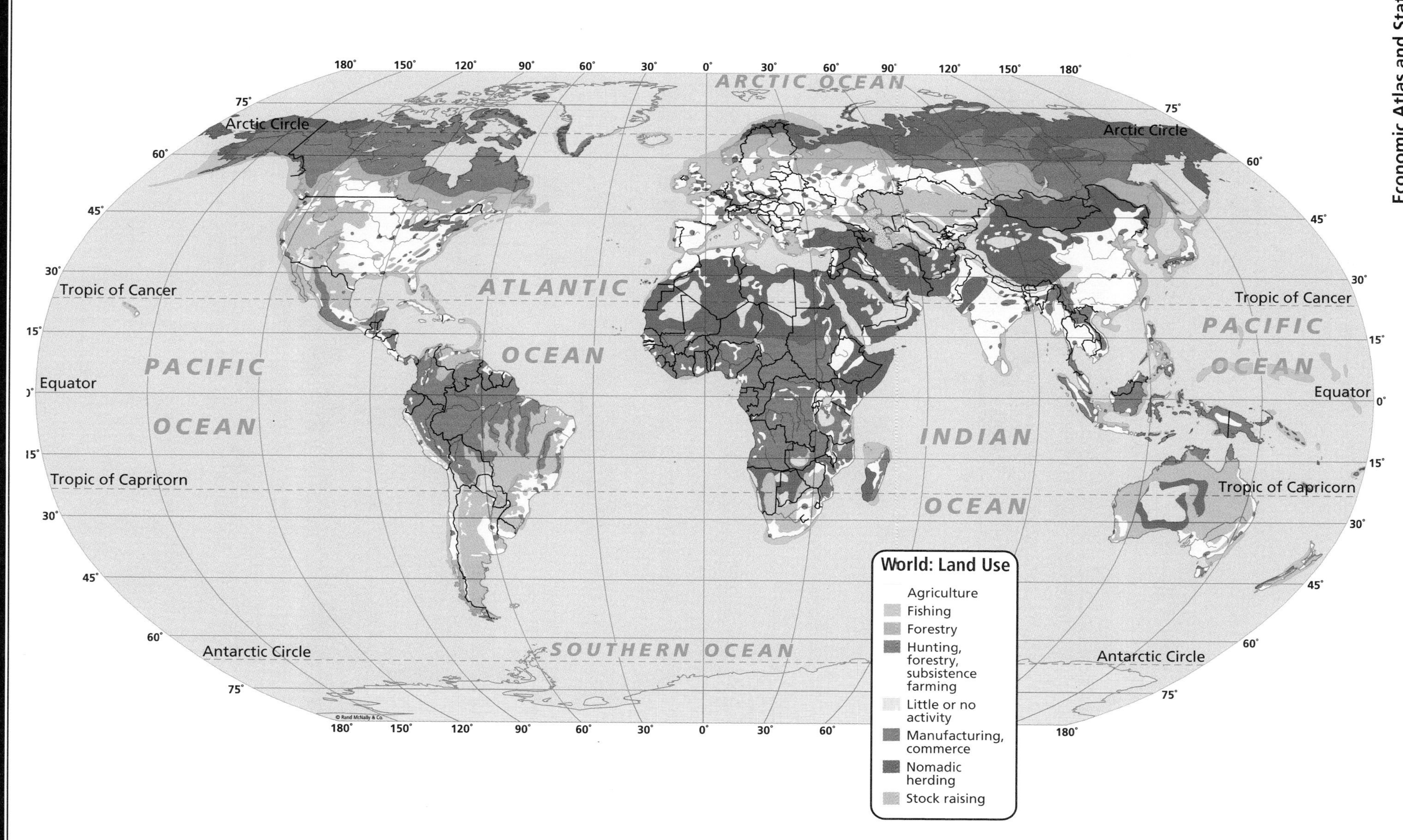

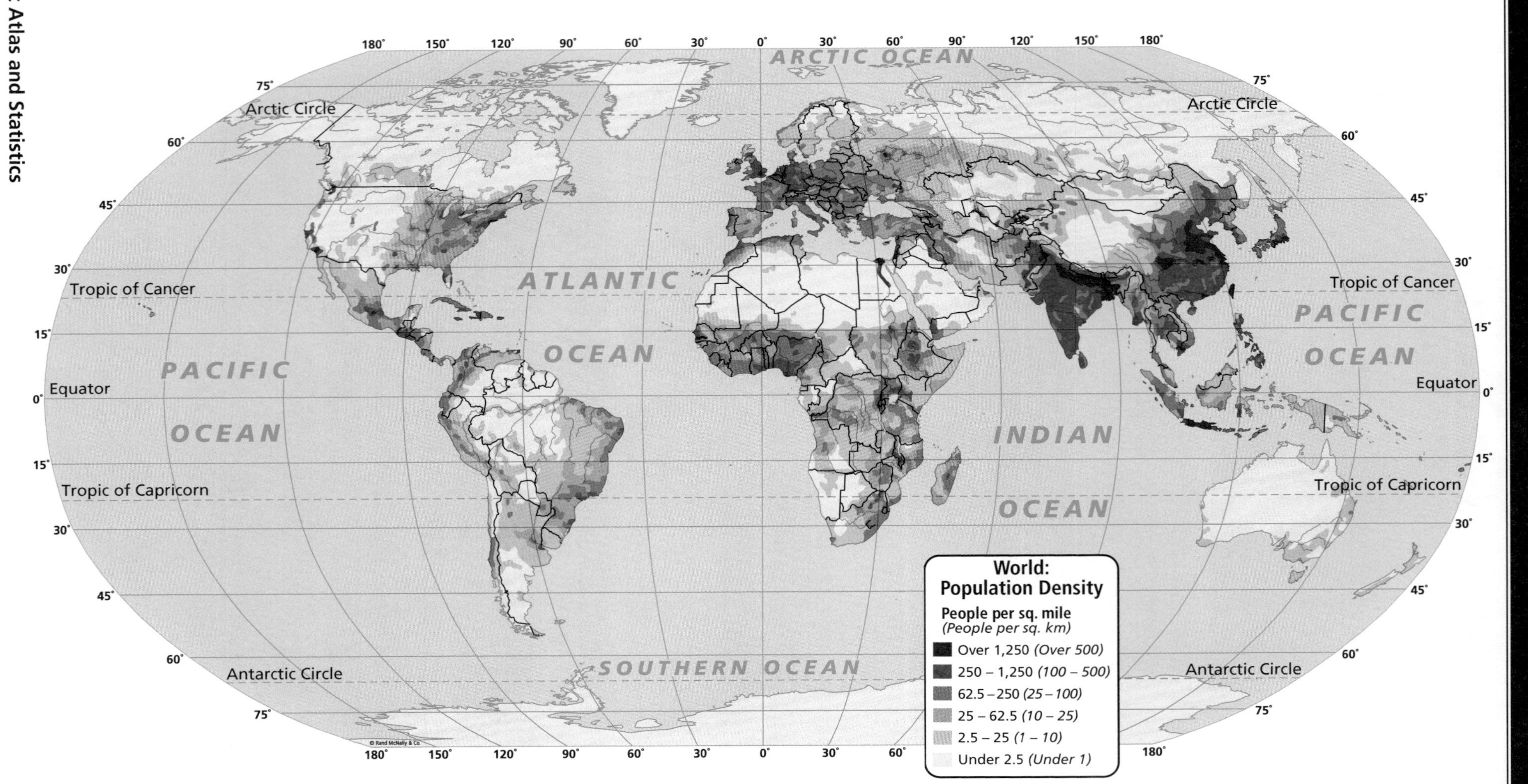
ARCTIC OCEAN
Arctic Circle
Arctic Circle
Tropic of Cancer
Tropic of Cancer
ATLANTIC
OCEAN
PACIFIC
OCEAN
PACIFIC
OCEAN
Equator
Equator
INDIAN
OCEAN
Tropic of Capricorn
Tropic of Capricorn
SOUTHERN OCEAN
Antarctic Circle
Antarctic Circle
World:
Population Density
People per sq. mile
(People per sq. km)
Over 1,250 (Over 500)
250 – 1,250 (100 – 500)
62.5 – 250 (25 – 100)
25 – 62.5 (10 – 25)
2.5 – 25 (1 – 10)
Under 2.5 (Under 1)

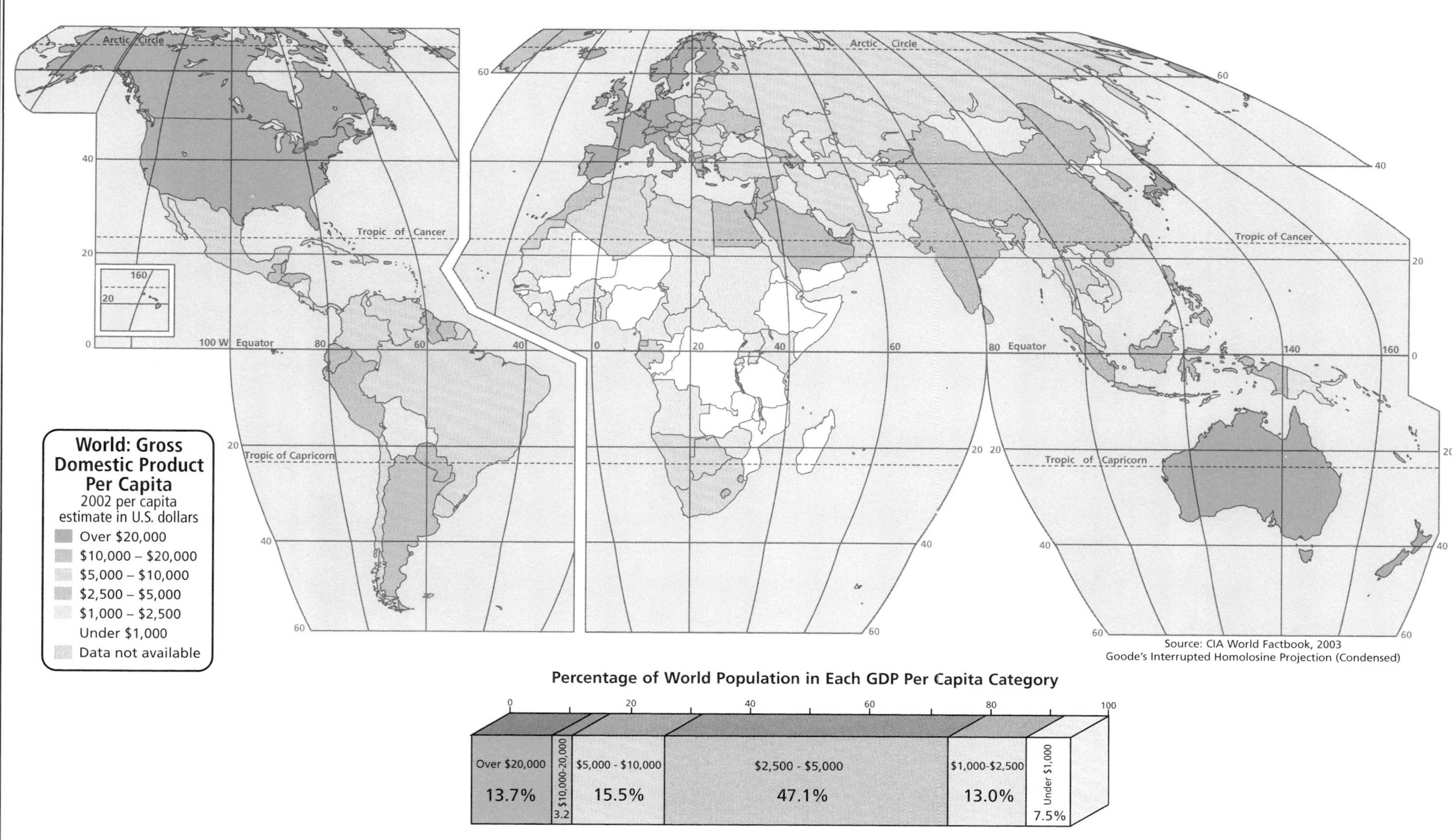
World: Gross Domestic Product Per Capita
2002 per capita estimate in U.S. dollars
Over $20,000
$10,000 – $20,000
$5,000 – $10,000
$2,500 – $5,000
$1,000 – $2,500
Under $1,000
Data not available
Arctic Circle
Tropic of Cancer
Equator
Tropic of Capricorn
Source: CIA World Factbook, 2003
Goode's Interrupted Homolosine Projection (Condensed)
Percentage of World Population in Each GDP Per Capita Category
Over $20,000
13.7%
$10,000-20,000
3.2
$5,000 - $10,000
15.5%
$2,500 - $5,000
47.1%
$1,000-$2,500
13.0%
Under $1,000
7.5%

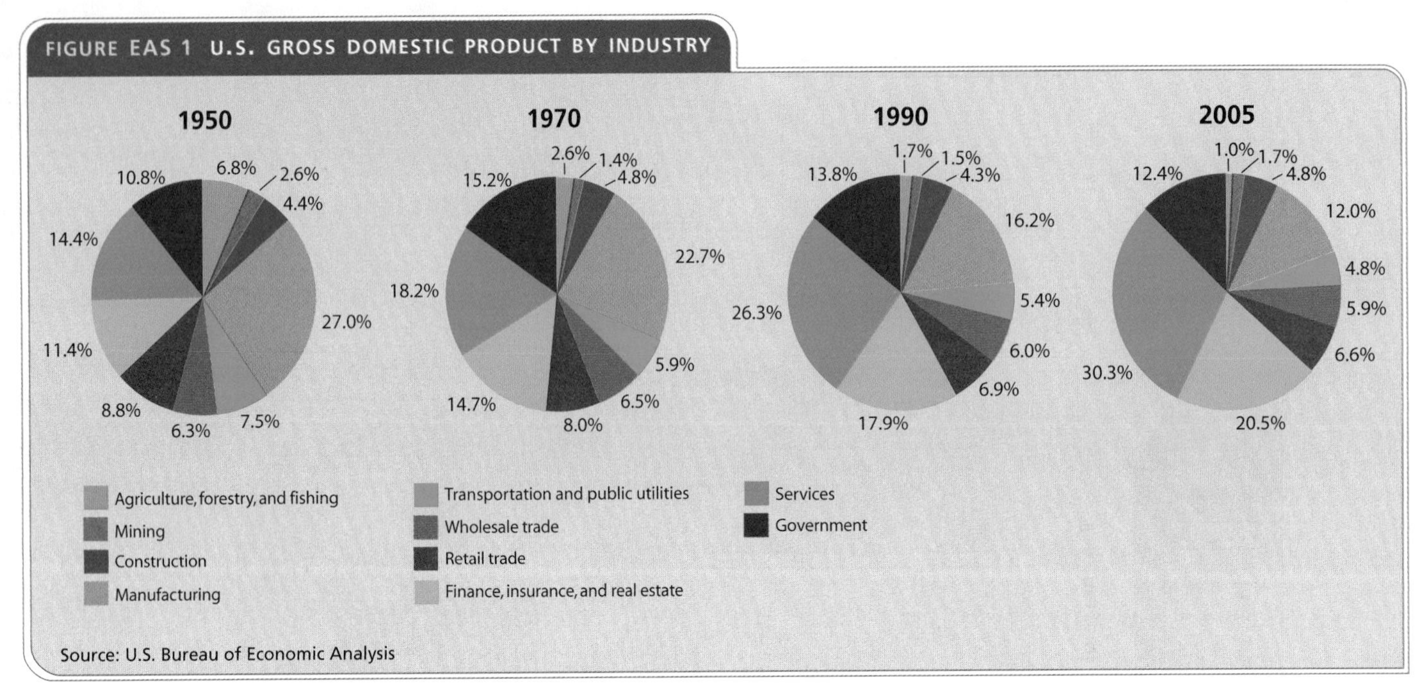
FIGURE EAS 1 U.S. GROSS DOMESTIC PRODUCT BY INDUSTRY
1950
10.8%
6.8%
2.6%
4.4%
14.4%
27.0%
11.4%
8.8%
6.3%
7.5%
1970
2.6%
1.4%
15.2%
4.8%
22.7%
18.2%
5.9%
14.7%
6.5%
8.0%
1990
1.7%
1.5%
13.8%
4.3%
16.2%
26.3%
5.4%
6.0%
6.9%
17.9%
2005
1.0%
1.7%
12.4%
4.8%
12.0%
4.8%
5.9%
6.6%
30.3%
20.5%
Agriculture, forestry, and fishing
Mining
Construction
Manufacturing
Transportation and public utilities
Wholesale trade
Retail trade
Finance, insurance, and real estate
Services
Government
Source: U.S. Bureau of Economic Analysis

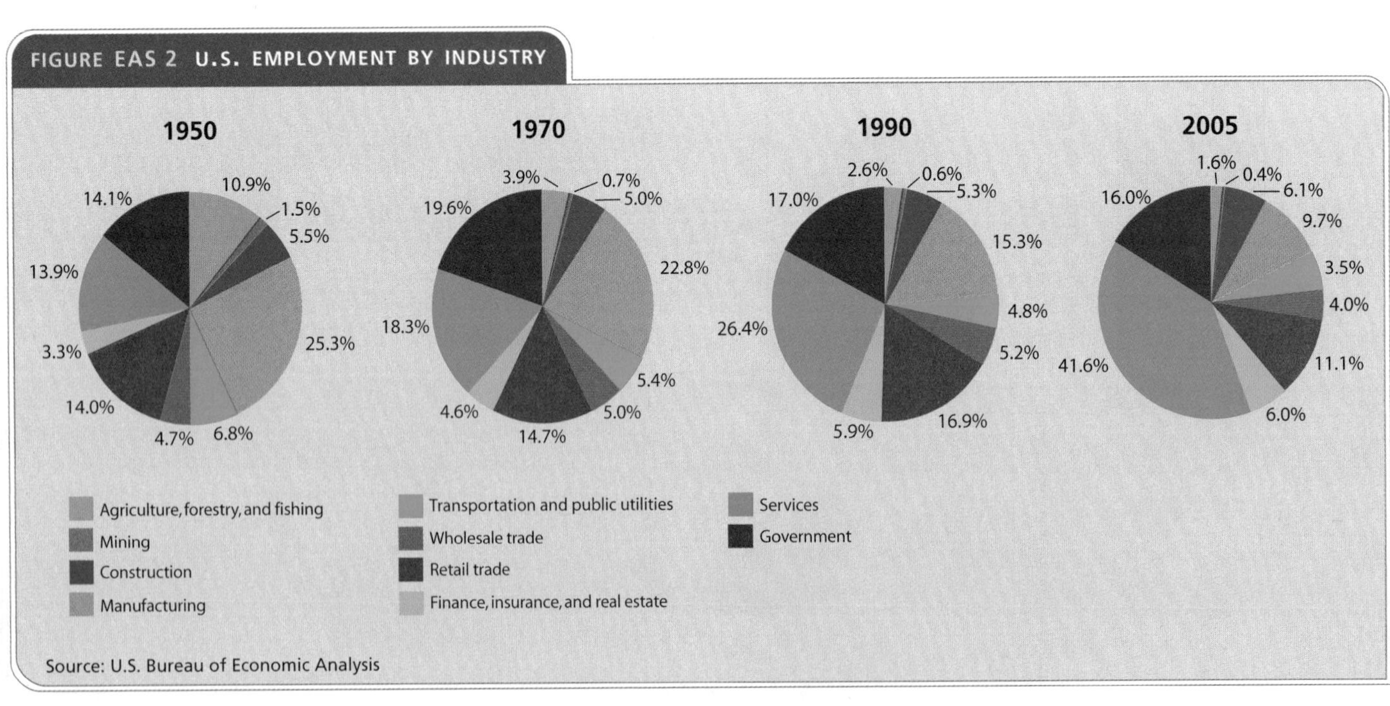
FIGURE EAS 2 U.S. EMPLOYMENT BY INDUSTRY
1950
14.1%
10.9%
1.5%
5.5%
13.9%
25.3%
3.3%
14.0%
4.7%
6.8%
1970
3.9%
0.7%
5.0%
19.6%
22.8%
18.3%
5.4%
4.6%
5.0%
14.7%
1990
2.6%
0.6%
5.3%
17.0%
15.3%
26.4%
4.8%
5.2%
5.9%
16.9%
2005
1.6%
0.4%
6.1%
16.0%
9.7%
3.5%
4.0%
41.6%
11.1%
6.0%
Agriculture, forestry, and fishing
Mining
Construction
Manufacturing
Transportation and public utilities
Wholesale trade
Retail trade
Finance, insurance, and real estate
Services
Government
Source: U.S. Bureau of Economic Analysis

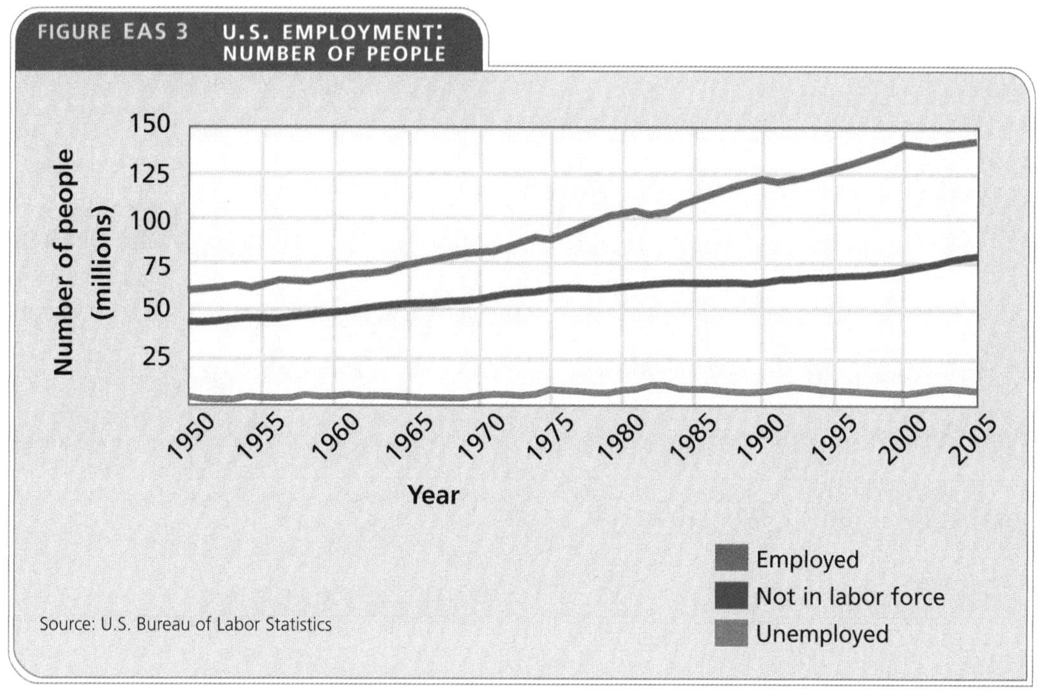
FIGURE EAS 3
U.S. EMPLOYMENT: NUMBER OF PEOPLE
Number of people (millions)
150
125
100
75
50
25
1950
1955
1960
1965
1970
1975
1980
1985
1990
1995
2000
2005
Year
Employed
Not in labor force
Unemployed
Source: U.S. Bureau of Labor Statistics

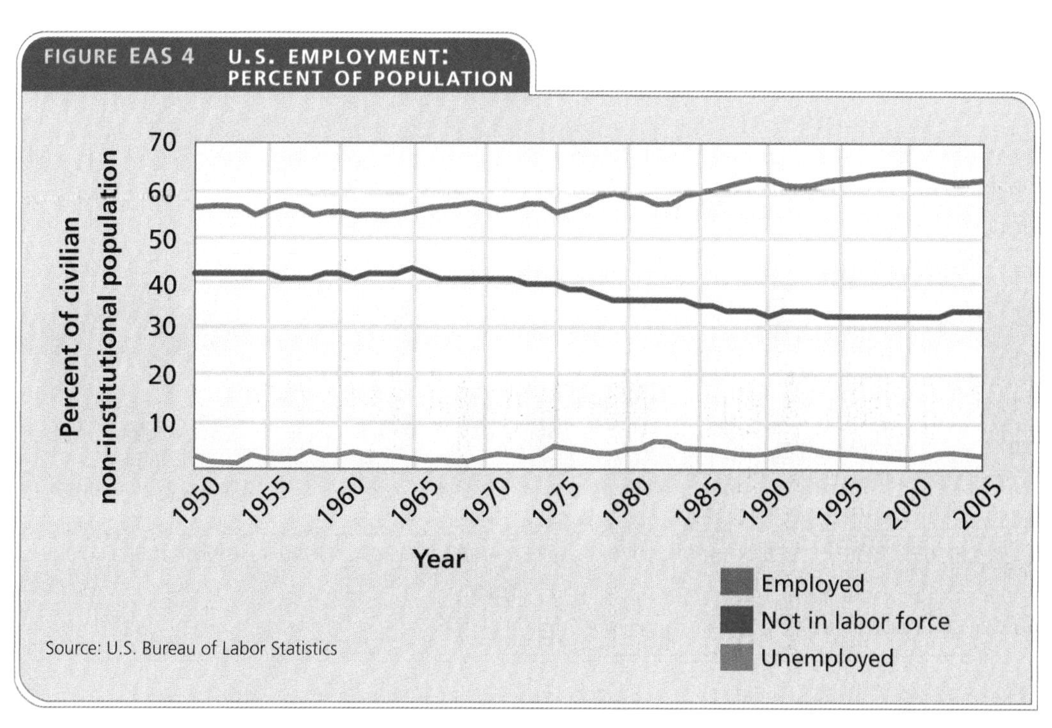
FIGURE EAS 4
U.S. EMPLOYMENT: PERCENT OF POPULATION
Percent of civilian non-institutional population
70
60
50
40
30
20
10
1950
1955
1960
1965
1970
1975
1980
1985
1990
1995
2000
2005
Year
Employed
Not in labor force
Unemployed
Source: U.S. Bureau of Labor Statistics

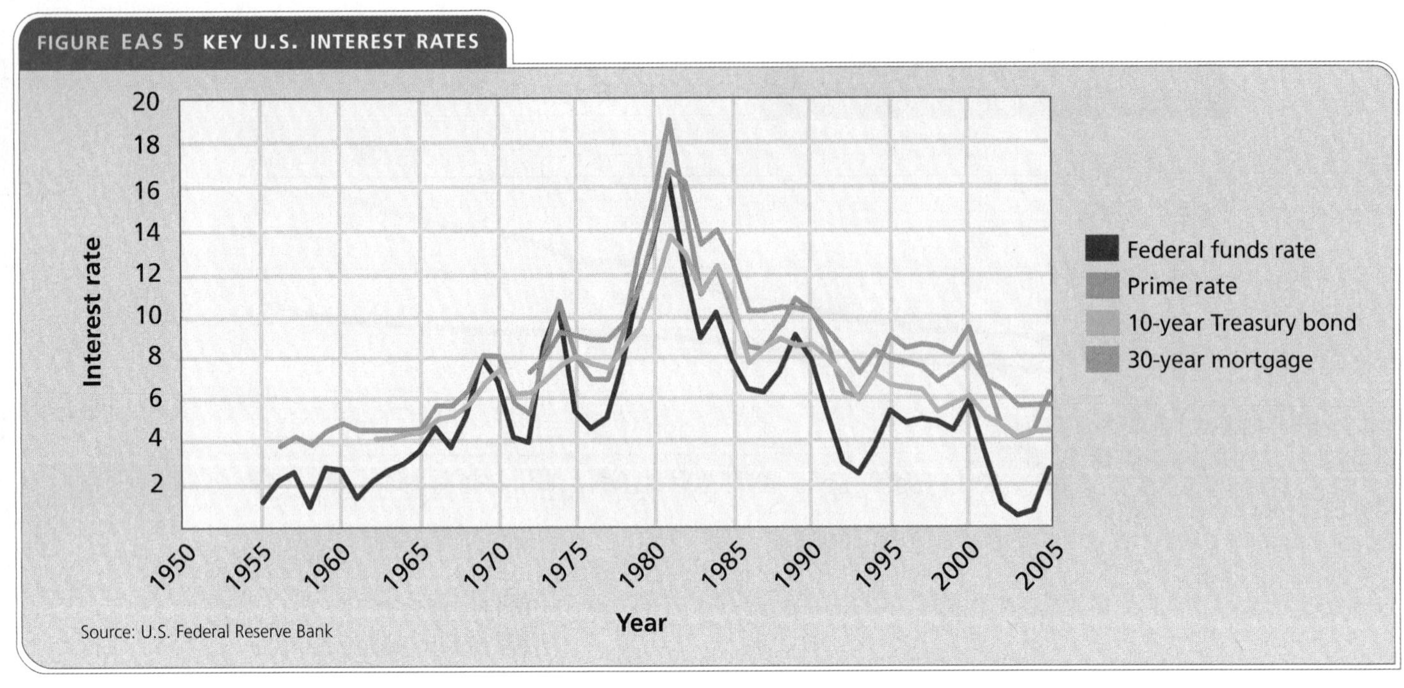
FIGURE EAS 5 KEY U.S. INTEREST RATES
Interest rate
20
18
16
14
12
10
8
6
4
2
1950
1955
1960
1965
1970
1975
1980
1985
1990
1995
2000
2005
Year
Federal funds rate
Prime rate
10-year Treasury bond
30-year mortgage
Source: U.S. Federal Reserve Bank

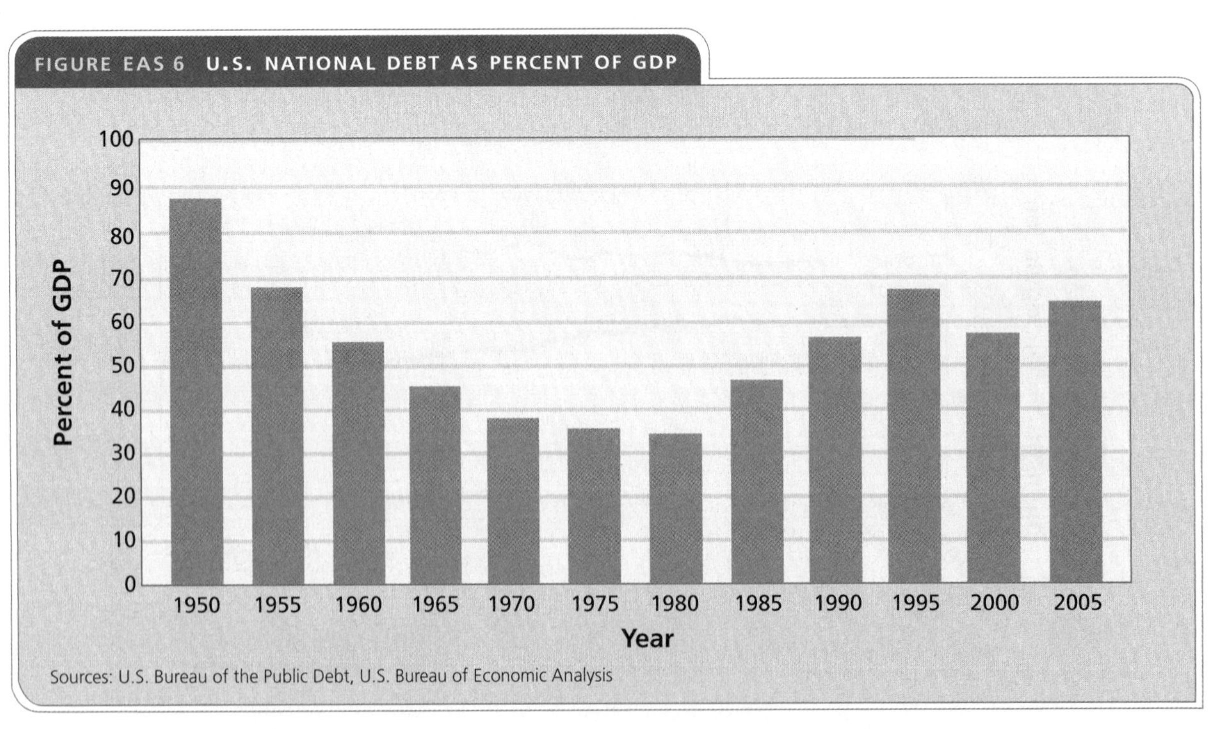
FIGURE EAS 6 U.S. NATIONAL DEBT AS PERCENT OF GDP
Percent of GDP
100
90
80
70
60
50
40
30
20
10
0
1950
1955
1960
1965
1970
1975
1980
1985
1990
1995
2000
2005
Year
Sources: U.S. Bureau of the Public Debt, U.S. Bureau of Economic Analysis

FIGURE EAS 7 World Data File

Country	Population	Percent urban / rural	Unemployment rate	GDP (in billions of U.S. dollars)	GDP per capita (in U.S. dollars)	National debt (as percent of GDP)	Inflation rate
China	1,303,701,000	37 / 63	9.0	2,234.1	1,709	24.4	1.8
India	1,103,596,000	28 / 72	8.9	772.0	705	53.8	4.0
United States	296,483,000	79 / 21	5.1	12,455.8	42,000	64.7	3.4
Indonesia	221,932,000	42 / 58	11.8	281.3	1,283	49.9	10.5
Brazil	184,184,000	81 / 19	9.8	795.7	4,320	51.6	6.9
Pakistan	162,420,000	34 / 66	6.6	111.0	728	53.8	9.3
Bangladesh	144,233,000	23 / 77	2.5	60.8	400	44.5	7.0
Russia	143,025,000	73 / 27	7.6	763.3	5,349	12.9	12.6
Nigeria	131,530,000	44 / 56	2.9	99.1	678	11.0	17.9
Japan	127,728,000	79 / 21	4.4	4,567.4	35,757	158.0	–0.6
Mexico	107,029,000	75 / 25	3.6	768.4	7,298	17.4	4.0
Philippines	84,765,000	48 / 52	8.7	98.4	1,168	72.3	7.6
Vietnam	83,305,000	26 / 74	2.4	51.4	618	48.2	8.2
Germany	82,490,000	88 / 12	11.7	2,791.7	33,854	67.3	2.0
Egypt	74,033,000	43 / 57	9.5	89.5	1,265	104.7	11.4
Ethiopia	77,431,000	15 / 85	no data	11.2	153	no data	6.8
Turkey	72,907,000	65 / 35	10.2	362.5	5,062	68.0	8.2
Iran	69,515,000	67 / 33	11.2	192.3	2,767	28.9	12.1
Thailand	65,002,000	31 / 69	1.8	173.1	2,659	47.6	4.5
France	60,742,000	76 / 24	9.9	2,126.7	33,918	66.2	1.9

Sources: International Monetary Fund, Population Reference Bureau, U.S. Central Intelligence Agency; data from 2005 and earlier

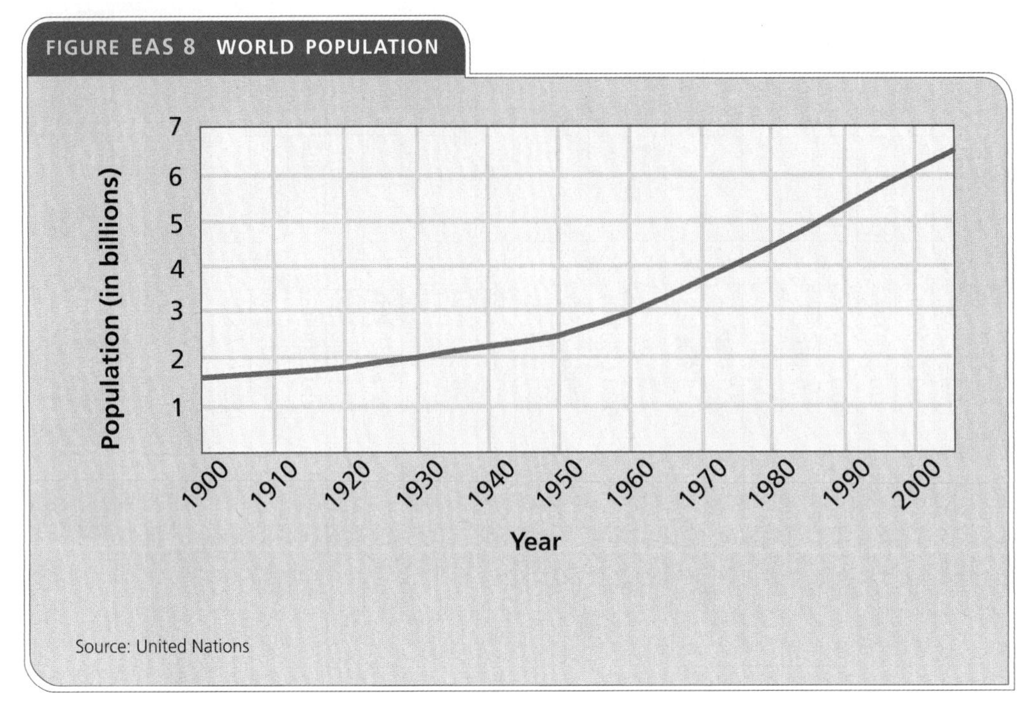

FIGURE EAS 8 WORLD POPULATION

Population (in billions)
7
6
5
4
3
2
1
1900
1910
1920
1930
1940
1950
1960
1970
1980
1990
2000
Year

Source: United Nations

FIGURE EAS 9 POPULATION PYRAMIDS

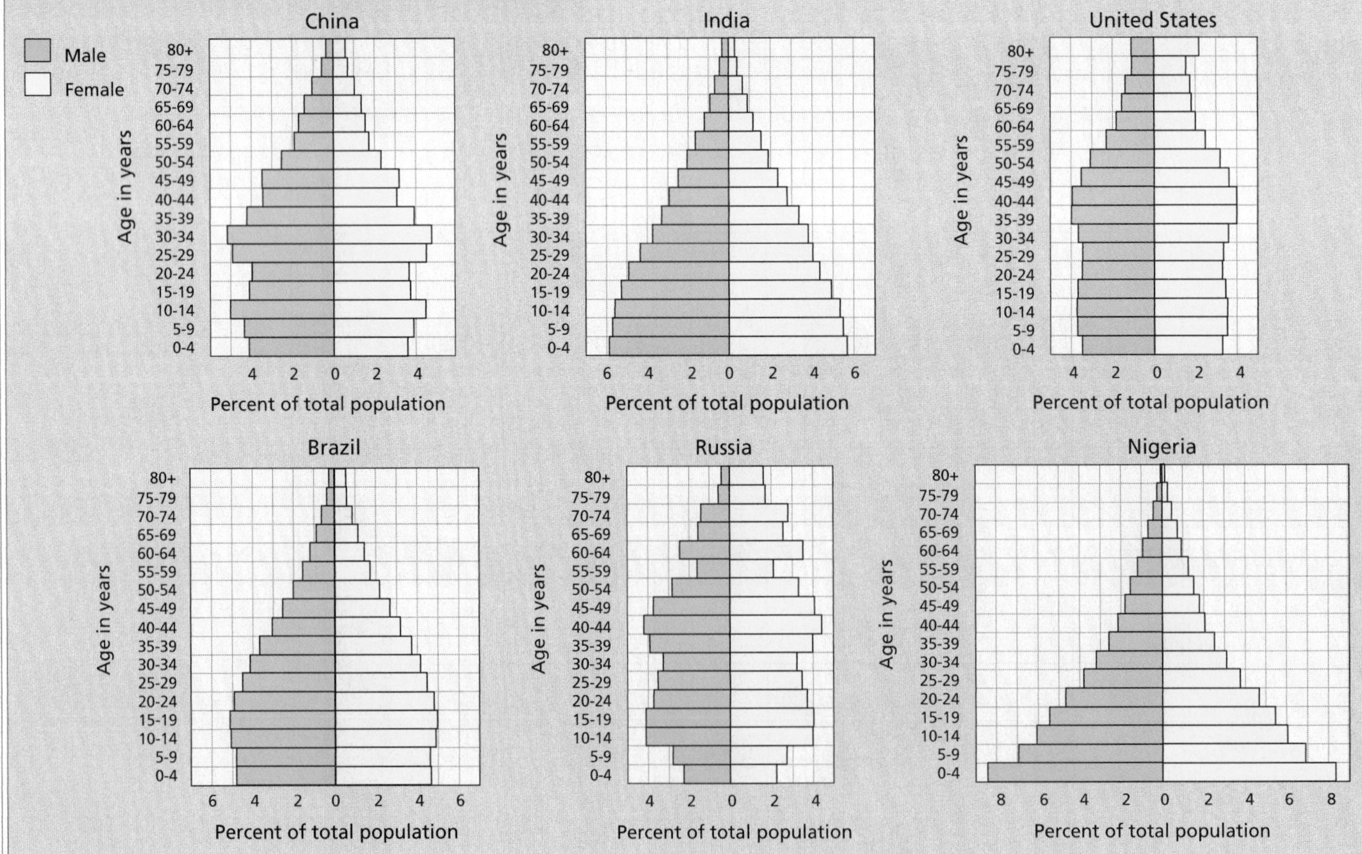

Male
Female
China
India
United States
Brazil
Russia
Nigeria
Age in years
80+
75-79
70-74
65-69
60-64
55-59
50-54
45-49
40-44
35-39
30-34
25-29
20-24
15-19
10-14
5-9
0-4
Percent of total population

Source: U.S. Census Bureau, 2000 data

STRATEGIES FOR TAKING STANDARDIZED TESTS

This section of the textbook helps you develop and practice the skills you need to study economics and to take standardized tests. Part 1, **Strategies for Studying Economics,** takes you through the features of the textbook and offers suggestions on how to use these features to improve your reading and study skills.

Part 2, **Test-Taking Strategies and Practice,** offers specific strategies for tackling many of the items you will find on a standardized test. It gives tips for answering multiple-choice and extended-response questions. In addition, it offers guidelines for analyzing charts and line, bar, and pie graphs that often accompany these questions. Each strategy is followed by a set of questions you can use for practice.

CONTENTS for Strategies for Taking Standardized Tests

STRATEGIES FOR TAKING STANDARDIZED TESTS

Part 1: Strategies for Studying Economics

Reading is the central skill in the effective study of economics or any other subject. You can improve your reading skills by using helpful techniques and by practicing. The better your reading skills, the more you will understand what you read. Below you will find several strategies that involve built-in features of *Economics: Choices and Concepts.* Careful use of these strategies will help you learn and understand economics more effectively.

Preview Chapters Before You Read

Each chapter begins with a two-page chapter opener. Study these pages to help you get ready to read.

1. Read the chapter title and section titles for clues to what will be covered in the chapter.
2. Read the **Concept Review,** which reviews previous learning important to understanding chapter content. Then study the **Key Concept,** which focuses on the main idea explored in the chapter. Finally, read the **Why the Concept Matters** explanation and question. These help place the chapter's main idea in a real-world context.
3. Study the chapter-opening photograph and caption. These provide a visual illustration of the chapter's main idea.

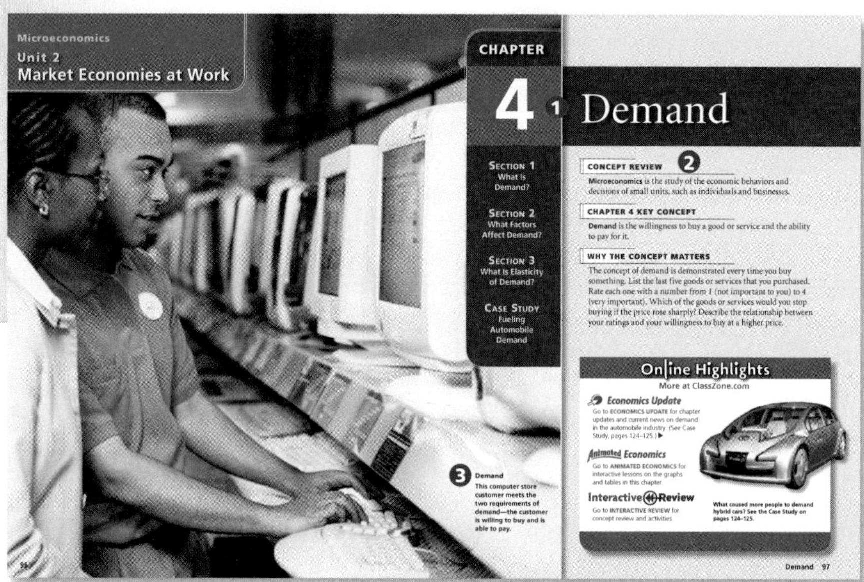

Preview Sections Before You Read

Each chapter consists of three or four sections. These sections explain and build on the **Key Concept.** Use the section openers to help you prepare to read.

1. Study the information under **Objectives.** This bulleted list tells you the key points discussed in the material you are about to read.
2. Preview the **Key Terms** list. This list identifies the vocabulary you will need to learn in order to understand the material you are about to read. Use the **Taking Notes** graphic to help you organize information presented in the text.
3. Notice the structure of the section. **Blue** heads label the major topics; **red** subheads signal smaller topics within a major topic or illustrative examples of the major topic. Together, these heads provide you with a quick outline of the section.
4. Read the first paragraph under **Key Concepts.** This links the content of the section to previous chapters or sections.

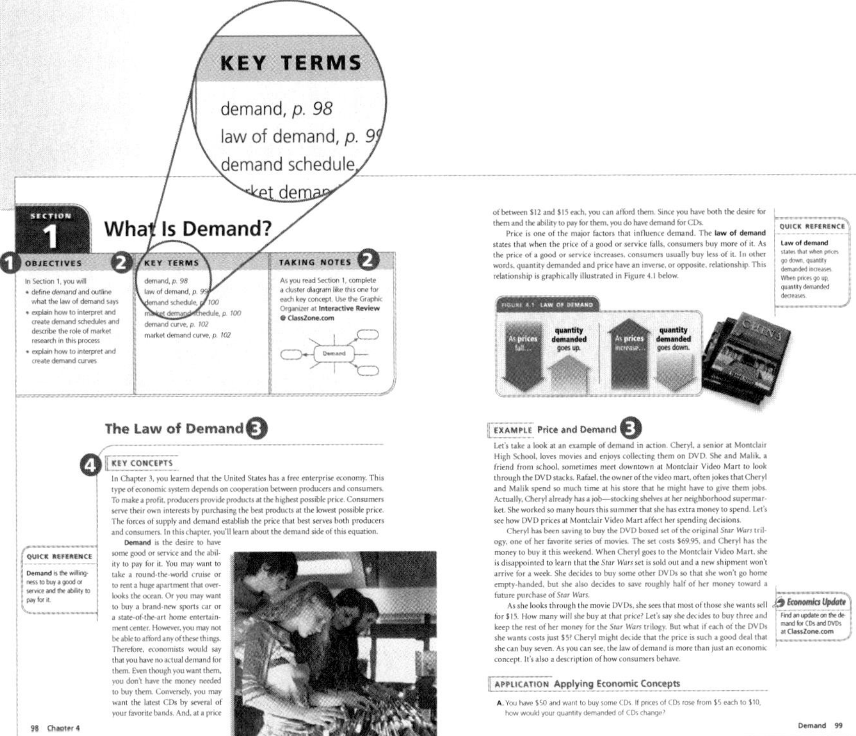

STRATEGIES

Use Active Reading Strategies As You Read

Now you are ready to read the chapter. Read one section at a time, from beginning to end.

1. Read to build your economic vocabulary. Use the marginal **Quick Reference** notes to reinforce your understanding of key economic terms.
2. Use special features and illustrations to reinforce and extend your understanding of content and to apply your knowledge. Study features such as Your Economic Choices, which applies economic concepts to a real-world situation. Look closely at the **figures,** which illustrate economic concepts in table, chart, or graph form. Answer the accompanying **Analyze** questions to test your understanding of the visual and the concept it illustrates.
3. At natural breaks in the section, ask yourself questions about what you have just read. Look for **APPLICATION** headings at the bottom of pages and answer the questions or complete the activities. These provide you with opportunities to apply the knowledge you have gained from your reading.

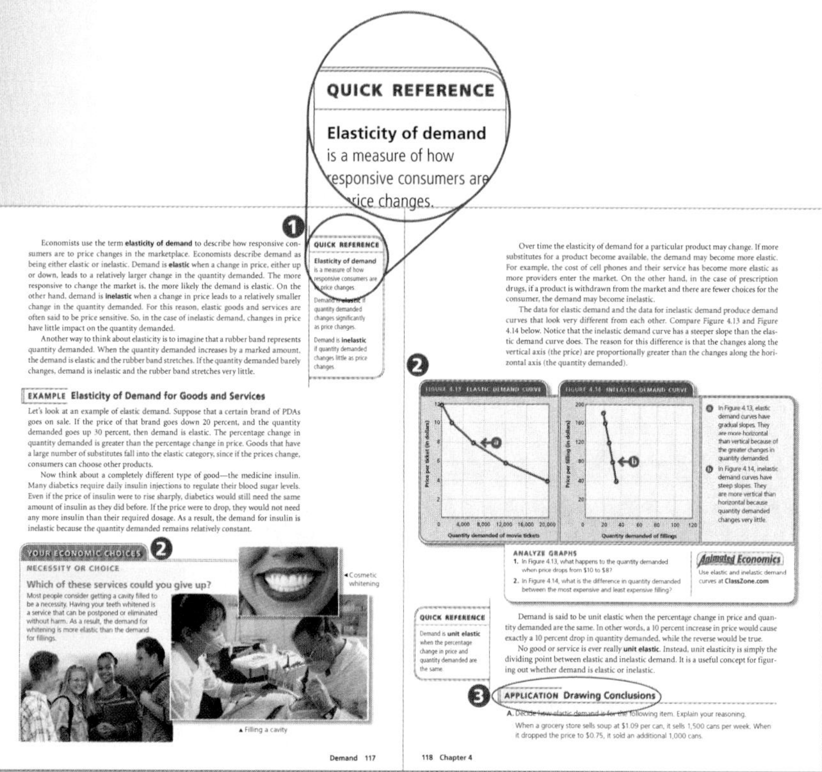

QUICK REFERENCE
Elasticity of demand is a measure of how responsive consumers are to price changes.
1
2
3
APPLICATION Drawing Conclusions

STRATEGIES FOR TAKING STANDARDIZED TESTS

Review and Summarize What You Have Read

When you finish reading a section, review and summarize what you've read. If necessary, go back and reread information that was not clear the first time through.

1. Look again at the **blue** heads and red heads for a quick summary of the major points covered in the section.
2. Study any tables, charts, graphs, and photographs in the section. These visual materials often convey economic information in condensed form.
3. Complete all the questions in the **Section Assessment.** This will help you think critically about the material you have just read.

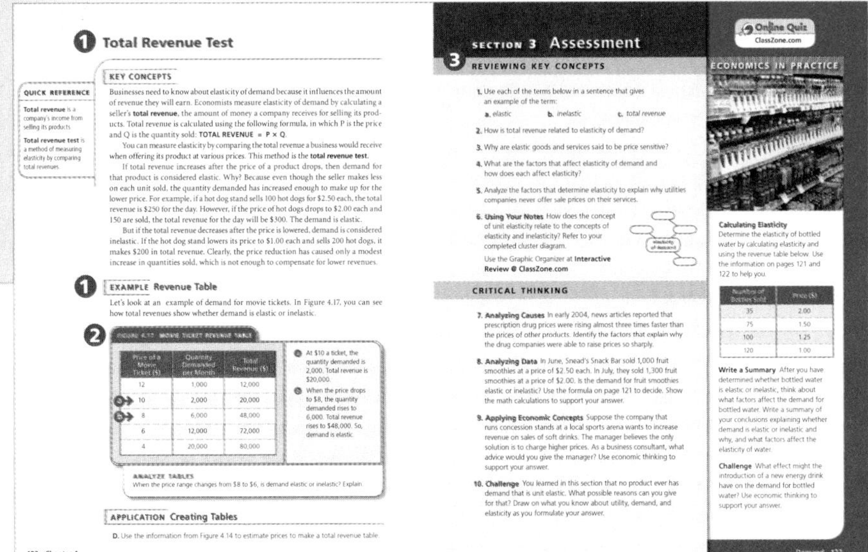

1 Total Revenue Test

QUICK REFERENCE

Total revenue is a company's income from selling its products.

Total revenue test is a method of measuring elasticity by comparing total revenues.

KEY CONCEPTS

Businesses need to know about elasticity of demand because it influences the amount of revenue they will earn. Economists measure elasticity of demand by calculating a seller's **total revenue**, the amount of money a company receives for selling its products. Total revenue is calculated using the following formula, in which P is the price and Q is the quantity sold: **TOTAL REVENUE = P × Q.**

You can measure elasticity by comparing the total revenue a business would receive when offering its product at various prices. This method is the **total revenue test.**

If total revenue increases after the price of a product drops, then demand for that product is considered elastic. Why? Because even though the seller makes less on each unit sold, the quantity demanded has increased enough to make up for the lower price. For example, if a hot dog stand sells 100 hot dogs for $2.50 each, the total revenue is $250 for the day. However, if the price of hot dogs drops to $2.00 each and 150 are sold, the total revenue for the day will be $300. The demand is elastic.

But if the total revenue decreases after the price is lowered, demand is considered inelastic. If the hot dog stand lowers its price to $1.00 each and sells 200 hot dogs, it makes $200 in total revenue. Clearly, the price reduction has caused only a modest increase in quantities sold, which is not enough to compensate for lower revenues.

1 EXAMPLE Revenue Table

Let's look at an example of demand for movie tickets. In Figure 4.17, you can see how total revenues show whether demand is elastic or inelastic.

2 FIGURE 4.17 MOVIE TICKET REVENUE TABLE

Price of a Movie Ticket ($)	Quantity Demanded per Month	Total Revenue ($)
12	1,000	12,000
10	2,000	20,000
8	6,000	48,000
6	12,000	72,000
4	20,000	80,000

A At $10 a ticket, the quantity demanded is 2,000. Total revenue is $20,000.

B When the price drops to $8, the quantity demanded rises to 6,000. Total revenue rises to $48,000. So, demand is elastic.

ANALYZE TABLES
When the price range changes from $8 to $6, is demand elastic or inelastic? Explain.

APPLICATION Creating Tables

D. Use the information from Figure 4.14 to estimate prices to make a total revenue table.

122 Chapter 4

SECTION 3 Assessment

3 REVIEWING KEY CONCEPTS

1. Use each of the terms below in a sentence that gives an example of the term:
   a. *elastic* b. *inelastic* c. *total revenue*
2. How is total revenue related to elasticity of demand?
3. Why are elastic goods and services said to be price sensitive?
4. What are the factors that affect elasticity of demand and how does each affect elasticity?
5. Analyze the factors that determine elasticity to explain why utilities companies never offer sale prices on their services.
6. **Using Your Notes** How does the concept of unit elasticity relate to the concepts of elasticity and inelasticity? Refer to your completed cluster diagram.

   Use the Graphic Organizer at **Interactive Review @ ClassZone.com**

CRITICAL THINKING

7. **Analyzing Causes** In early 2004, news articles reported that prescription drug prices were rising almost three times faster than the prices of other products. Identify the factors that explain why the drug companies were able to raise prices so sharply.
8. **Analyzing Data** In June, Snead's Snack Bar sold 1,000 fruit smoothies at a price of $2.50 each. In July, they sold 1,300 fruit smoothies at a price of $2.00. Is the demand for fruit smoothies elastic or inelastic? Use the formula on page 121 to decide. Show the math calculations to support your answer.
9. **Applying Economic Concepts** Suppose the company that runs concession stands at a local sports arena wants to increase revenue on sales of soft drinks. The manager believes the only solution is to charge higher prices. As a business consultant, what advice would you give the manager? Use economic thinking to support your answer.
10. **Challenge** You learned in this section that no product ever has demand that is unit elastic. What possible reasons can you give for that? Draw on what you know about utility, demand, and elasticity as you formulate your answer.

Online Quiz
ClassZone.com

ECONOMICS IN PRACTICE

Calculating Elasticity
Determine the elasticity of bottled water by calculating elasticity and using the revenue table below. Use the information on pages 121 and 122 to help you.

Number of Bottles Sold	Price ($)
35	2.00
75	1.50
100	1.25
120	1.00

Write a Summary After you have determined whether bottled water is elastic or inelastic, think about what factors affect the demand for bottled water. Write a summary of your conclusions explaining whether demand is elastic or inelastic and why, and what factors affect the elasticity of water.

Challenge What effect might the introduction of a new energy drink have on the demand for bottled water? Use economic thinking to support your answer.

Demand 123

STRATEGIES FOR TAKING STANDARDIZED TESTS

Part 2: Test-Taking Strategies and Practice

Using Strategies For.... Multiple Choice

Explain to students that they will do best on test questions by thinking them through carefully and by applying test-taking strategies, such as the following.

1. In question 1, *most* is a key word, but before that is meaningful, you must recognize *command* as an even more important word. With that word, you can call to mind the characteristics of that kind of economy and eliminate nations you know to have a market economy, including Japan. A second step is to recognize the qualifier that *most* adds and evaluate the degree to which each of the remaining choices has a command economy.
2. The strategy of eliminating alternatives known to be incorrect, such as letter C in question 2, will quickly narrow the choices. The second strategy of watching out for such absolute words as *all*, *must*, and *always* will help point to B, the correct answer.
3. For alternative D, "All of the above," to be correct, all of the other alternatives must be correct. When dealing with questions that have "All of the above" as an alternative, be sure to test each alternative before choosing.
4. If you read question 4 too quickly, you may miss the negative construction. Only that choice that is NOT a factor of production—in this case letter C—is correct.

General Test-Taking Tips
Share these tips with your students.

- Get plenty of sleep the night before a test.
- Get your supplies ready the night before so the morning can be calm.
- Use strategies that help fight nervousness.
- Engage your mind in the task. Good tests are actually learning tools!

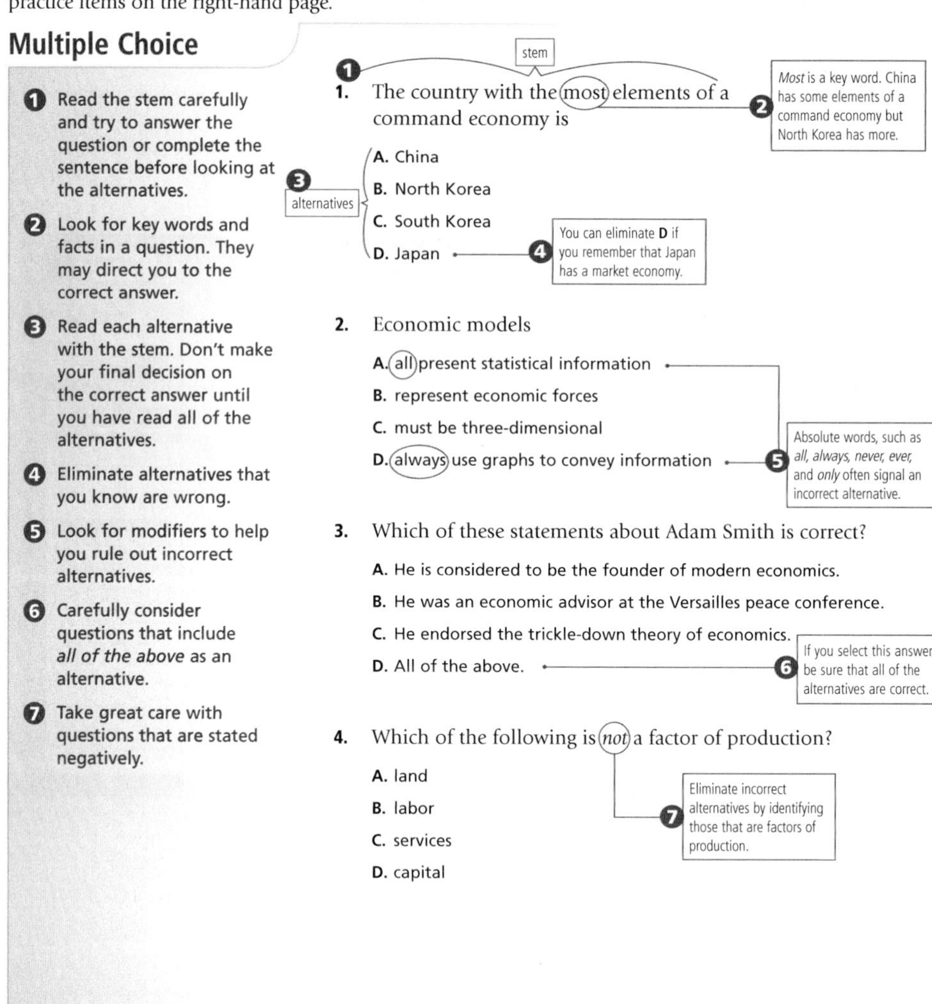

STRATEGIES

Part 2: Test-Taking Strategies and Practice

You can improve your test-taking skills by practicing the strategies discussed in this section. First, read the tips on the left-hand page. Then apply them to the practice items on the right-hand page.

Multiple Choice

1. Read the stem carefully and try to answer the question or complete the sentence before looking at the alternatives.
2. Look for key words and facts in a question. They may direct you to the correct answer.
3. Read each alternative with the stem. Don't make your final decision on the correct answer until you have read all of the alternatives.
4. Eliminate alternatives that you know are wrong.
5. Look for modifiers to help you rule out incorrect alternatives.
6. Carefully consider questions that include *all of the above* as an alternative.
7. Take great care with questions that are stated negatively.

answers: 1 (B), 2 (B), 3 (D), 4 (C)

1. The country with the most elements of a command economy is
   A. China
   B. North Korea
   C. South Korea
   D. Japan

2. Economic models
   A. all present statistical information
   B. represent economic forces
   C. must be three-dimensional
   D. always use graphs to convey information

3. Which of these statements about Adam Smith is correct?
   A. He is considered to be the founder of modern economics.
   B. He was an economic advisor at the Versailles peace conference.
   C. He endorsed the trickle-down theory of economics.
   D. All of the above.

4. Which of the following is not a factor of production?
   A. land
   B. labor
   C. services
   D. capital

stem
alternatives
Most is a key word. China has some elements of a command economy but North Korea has more.
You can eliminate **D** if you remember that Japan has a market economy.
Absolute words, such as *all, always, never, ever,* and *only* often signal an incorrect alternative.
If you select this answer, be sure that all of the alternatives are correct.
Eliminate incorrect alternatives by identifying those that are factors of production.
STRATEGIES FOR TAKING STANDARDIZED TESTS

S6

English Learners

Understanding Vocabulary
Make sure students understand the following terms and concepts in the sample questions on these pages.

Strategies
Multiple Choice
Question 2 *statistical*: data in numerical form
forces: trends with the ability to create change

Practice
Multiple Choice
Question 1 *consolidation*: joining of two or more businesses
Question 2 *discrimination*: unfair treatment
Question 4 *reserves*: supply on hand

Directions: Read each question carefully and choose the best answer from the four alternatives.

1. Which of the following is *not* a type of business consolidation?

A. vertical merger
B. franchise
C. conglomerate
D. multinational corporation

2. Wage rates are influenced by

A. supply and demand
B. discrimination
C. government actions
D. all of the above

3. As of 2005, the euro had been adopted by

A. the United Kingdom
B. all the European countries
C. some European countries
D. every member of the European Union

4. The central bank of the United States

A. has no cash reserves
B. is the U.S. Treasury
C. does not lend money
D. was established by the Federal Reserve Act

Thinking It Through

Share the following explanations with students as they discuss the strategies they used to answer the practice questions.

1. In this question, the task is to find the item that is a counter example of a business consolidation. A is easy to eliminate because it uses the word merger, a common word for a business consolidation. The word *conglomerate* in C is also used outside of economics, so that might be the next easiest to eliminate. That narrows the choice to between B and D, and your knowledge of economics can eliminate D. B is the correct answer.
2. With this type of question, you must test each alternative. In this case, alternatives A, B, and C are all correct, so D is the correct answer.
3. In this question, the qualifiers hold the key to finding the correct answer. They range from *one* nation adopting the euro to *all* European nations adopting it. Often you can eliminate the extremes and in this case you can narrow the choice to between C and D. D is another absolute, and although it might be correct, you need to use your knowledge of the status of the European Union to choose C.
4. In question 4, your knowledge of economics will tell you that A, B, and C are all incorrect. Therefore, D is the correct answer.

Strategy Items

Item	Skill Tested
1	Comparing and Contrasting Economic Information
2	Creating and Interpreting Economic Models
3	Drawing Conclusions
4	Explaining an Economic Concept

Practice Items

Item	Skill Tested
1	Applying Economic Concepts
2	Analyzing Cause and Effect
3, 4	Explaining an Economic Concept

Using Strategies For... Charts

Explain to students that they will do best on test questions by thinking them through carefully and by applying test-taking strategies, such as the following.

1. To answer question 1, you need to recognize the key words in the stem: *greatest* and *2003*. Run your finger down the 2003 column to find the largest number. The correct answer is A, the United States.
2. The key words in question 2 are *decline* and *2002*. There is once again an "express lane" way to answer this question. Negative numbers express a decline in GDP. Alternatives A, B, and C can be eliminated since alternative D, Japan, is the only country with a negative number in the 2002 column.

General Test-Taking Tips

Share these tips with your students.

- Skim through the test before you start answering questions to determine the types and number of questions.
- Budget your time according to what you learn when you skim.

Charts

Charts present information in a visual form. Economics textbooks use several types of charts, including tables, flow charts, Venn diagrams, circular flow charts, and infographics. The chart most commonly found in standardized tests, however, is the table. This organizes information in columns and rows for easy viewing.

1. Read the title and identify the broad subject of the chart.
2. Read the column and row headings and any other labels. These will provide more details about the subject of the chart.
3. Note how the information in the chart is organized.
4. Compare and contrast the information from column to column and row to row.
5. Try to draw conclusions from the information in the chart.
6. Read the questions and then study the chart again.

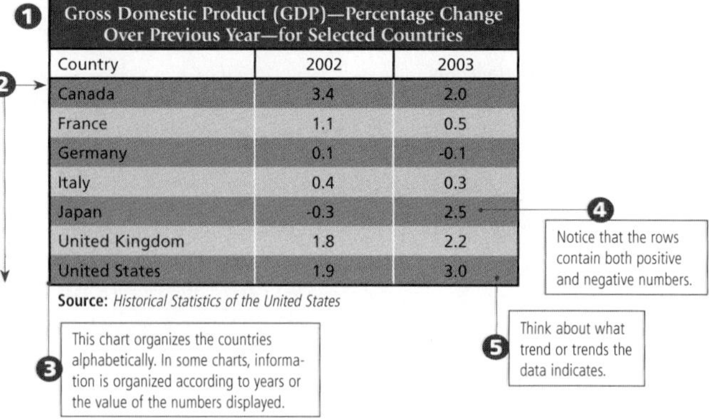

Gross Domestic Product (GDP)—Percentage Change Over Previous Year—for Selected Countries

Country	2002	2003
Canada	3.4	2.0
France	1.1	0.5
Germany	0.1	-0.1
Italy	0.4	0.3
Japan	-0.3	2.5
United Kingdom	1.8	2.2
United States	1.9	3.0

Source: *Historical Statistics of the United States*

1
2
3 This chart organizes the countries alphabetically. In some charts, information is organized according to years or the value of the numbers displayed.
4 Notice that the rows contain both positive and negative numbers.
5 Think about what trend or trends the data indicates.

6

1. The country that had the greatest percentage change in GDP in 2003 was

   A. the United States

   B. the United Kingdom

   C. Japan

   D. Canada

2. In 2002, which country experienced a decline in GDP?

   A. France

   B. Italy

   C. Germany

   D. Japan

answers: 1 (A), 2 (D)

English Learners

Understanding Vocabulary

Make sure students understand the following terms and concepts in the sample questions on these pages.

Strategies
Charts
Question 2 *decline*: drop off

Practice
Charts
Question 1 *refined copper*: copper extracted from the ore using water
Question 2 *constant*: unchanging

Directions: Use the chart and your knowledge of economics to answer questions 1 through 4.

Refined Copper Production for Selected Countries (in thousands of metric tons)						
Year	North America			South America		
	Canada	Mexico	United States	Brazil	Chile	Peru
1986	493.4	72.3	1,479.9	166.0	783.7	225.6
1987	491.1	128.4	1,541.6	201.7	795.0	224.8
1988	528.7	140.9	1,852.0	185.9	852.9	174.7
1989	515.2	155.8	1,953.8	207.8	1,071.0	224.3
1990	515.8	157.1	2,017.4	201.7	990.8	181.8
1991	538.0	190.1	2,000.0	141.4	1,012.8	244.1
1992	539.3	191.0	2,140.0	158.0	1,242.3	251.1
1993	561.6	197.8	2,250.0	161.1	1,093.2	261.7
1994	527.5	199.5	2,230.0	170.0	1,080.0	253.0
1995	560.0	207.5	2,280.0	165.0	1,288.8	282.0

Source: *2003 Industrial Commodity Statistics Yearbook,* United Nations

1. Which country produced the most refined copper in the years shown?

A. Canada
B. Mexico
C. the United States
D. Chile

2. From 1986 to 1988, Mexico's copper production

A. remained fairly constant
B. nearly doubled
C. decreased slightly
D. almost tripled

3. Which North American country showed an increase in copper production each year from 1987 through 1995?

A. Canada
B. Mexico
C. the United States
D. all of the above

4. Brazil's copper production was greatest in

A. 1995
B. 1994
C. 1990
D. 1989

STRATEGIES FOR TAKING STANDARDIZED TESTS

Thinking It Through

Share the following explanations with students as they discuss the strategies they used to answer the practice questions.

1. The key words in question 1 (*most* and *years shown*) require you to look for overarching trends reflecting the entire time period covered in the chart. A quick glance shows that only one nation, the United States (C), has had enough copper production to be expressed in quadruple digits in every single year covered.

2. Question 2 requires focusing in two ways: on Mexico only, and on the years between 1986–1988. Some of the alternatives also require the skill of estimating. Answers A and C can be quickly eliminated because the growth in production is clear. So the task is to decide whether 140.9 is nearly double or triple 72.3. Round off the numbers for easy multiplying. Multiplying 70 by 3 results in 210, while multiplying 70 by 2 results in 140, so B is the correct answer.

3. The key term *North American* allows you to disregard the right half of the chart and concentrate on the left. The key terms *increase, each year,* and *1987–1995* set you on the task of checking each column for any time period when the production declined. Both Canada (A) and the United States (C) had at least one year when production declined, which also eliminates D. Only Mexico (B) had steady growth.

4. In question 4, the stem focuses on the terms *Brazil* and *greatest*. To find the answer, identify the largest number in Brazil's column and follow it leftward to see that it corresponds to the year 1989 (D).

Strategy Items

Item	Skill Tested
1, 2	Interpreting Tables; Synthesizing Economic Data

Practice Items

Item	Skill Tested
1, 2, 3, 4	Interpreting Tables; Synthesizing Economic Data

Using Strategies For... Line Graphs

Explain to students that they will do best on test questions by thinking them through carefully and by applying test-taking strategies, such as the following.

1. Sometimes rephrasing the statement into a question can clarify your focus. Question 1, for example, can be rephrased to: What was the first year in which nuclear energy generation was more than 80 percent of capacity? Check the graph to find the year, then find the letter of that year among the alternatives (B).
2. The strategy of looking for trends will help you answer Question 2. A quick glance at the line showing nuclear energy generation reveals two noteworthy exceptions to the general steady rise: a decline from 1995–1997 and a sharp rise from 1997–1999. Seeing that trend will help you quickly find the correct answer (C).

General Test-Taking Tips

Share these tips with your students.

- Use practice tests, such as the one you are taking now, to find out your strengths and weaknesses in test taking.
- Focus on your weaknesses as you develop a plan to improve your test-taking abilities.

Line Graphs

Line graphs display information in a visual form. They are particularly useful for showing changes and trends over time.

1. Read the title of the graph to learn what it is about.
2. Study the labels on the vertical and horizontal axes to see the kinds of information presented in the graph. The vertical axis usually shows what is being graphed, while the horizontal axis indicates the time period covered.
3. Review the information in the graph and note any trends or patterns. Look for explanations for these trends or patterns.
4. Carefully read and answer the questions. Note if questions refer to a specific year or time period, or if they focus on trends or explanations for trends.

answers: 1 (B), 2 (C)

1 Nuclear Generation of Electricity in the United States

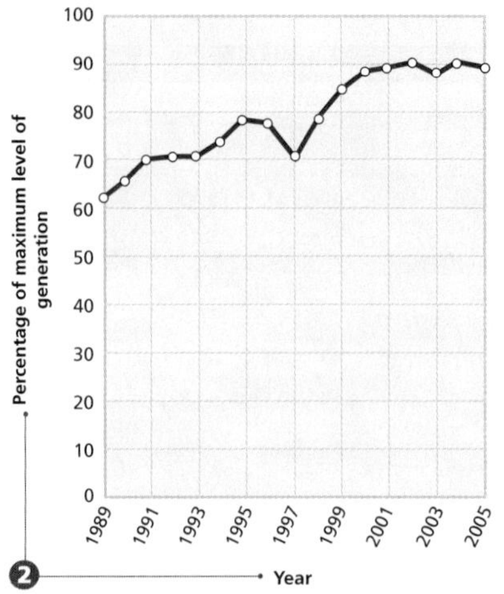

3 One likely explanation for increase in electricity generated is an increase in demand.

Source: U.S. Energy Information Administration

4

1. Nuclear generation of electricity first exceeded 80 percent of maximum capacity in
   A. 1994
   B. 1995
   C. 1998
   D. 1999

2. During which time period did the percentage of maximum capacity increase the most?
   A. 1989–1991
   B. 1993–1995
   C. 1997–1999
   D. 1999–2002

English Learners

Understanding Vocabulary
Make sure students understand the following terms and concepts in the sample questions on these pages.

Strategies
Line Graphs
Question 1 *generation*: creation
exceeded: was greater than
maximum: highest level possible

Practice
Line Graphs
Question 2 *spike*: sudden rise
fluctuation: wave-like change

Directions: Use the graph and your knowledge of economics to answer questions 1 through 4.

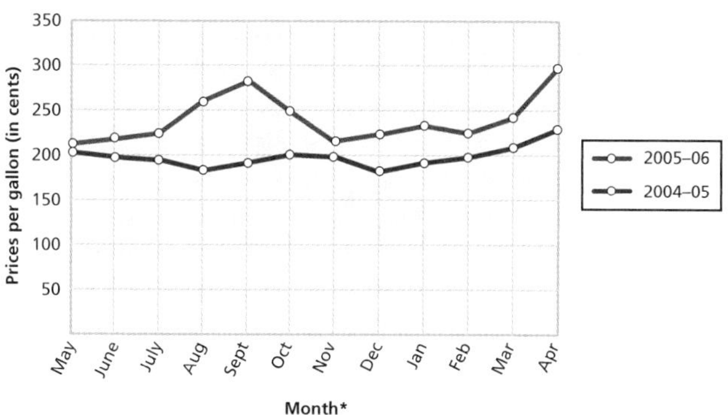

*Survey taken last week of month
Source: U.S. Energy Information Administration

1. During which period did the price of regular gasoline rise toward its peak?
   - **A.** May–August 2004
   - **B.** November 2004–February 2005
   - **C.** August–November 2005
   - **D.** February–April 2006

2. Which of the following statements most accurately describes the information shown in the graph?
   - **A.** Gas prices were stable during both 12-month periods.
   - **B.** There was a severe spike in price during each 12-month period.
   - **C.** The price of gas was always higher in 2005–2006.
   - **D.** The price of regular gas fluctuated more during 2004–2005.

3. During which period was the price of gasoline lowest?
   - **A.** in December 2004
   - **B.** in December 2005
   - **C.** in May 2004
   - **D.** in May 2005

4. In 2005–2006, the price of gasoline per gallon
   - **A.** nearly reached $3.00
   - **B.** dropped from close to $3.00 to less than $2.20
   - **C.** fluctuated more than in 2004–2005
   - **D.** all of the above

Strategy Items

Item	Skill Tested
1, 2	Interpreting Graphs

Practice Items

Item	Skill Tested
1	Interpreting Graphs
2	Drawing Conclusions; Synthesizing Economic Data
3, 4	Interpreting Graphs

Thinking It Through

Share the following explanations with students as they discuss the strategies they used to answer the practice questions.

1. Question 1 asks you to identify a specific time period in which gasoline prices rose toward their *peak,* a key word. With the key word in mind, you can look for the highest price represented and a rise toward it, both of which point to the period from February to May 2006 (D). Checking the other alternatives confirms this choice, since they all include declines, do not approach the peak, or both.
2. Question 2 could be answered even if there were no prices on the vertical axis. Looking for trends and patterns based solely on the graph lines themselves is the strategy to use for this question. You can eliminate A because of the spike and decline in 2005–2006. You can eliminate B because you can see that there are no severe spikes in the levels for 2004–2005. You can eliminate D because the line for 2004–2005 is actually less jagged than that for 2005–2006. Alternative C, therefore, is the correct answer.
3. The key word in question 3 is *lowest.* Your task, then, is simply to find the lowest point on the lines and trace it to its time period. That makes answer A the obvious and correct choice.
4. Question 4 is an *all of the above* type, so each alternative must be tested. It also focuses only on the line for 2005–2006, so you can disregard the other line as you test each answer, paying most attention to the vertical axis indicating prices. A, B, and C are true, so D is the correct answer.

Using Strategies For... Bar and Pie Graphs

Explain to students that they will do best on test questions by thinking them through carefully and by applying test-taking strategies, such as the following.

1. Since the purpose of bar graphs is to make information readily understandable in a graphic way, finding the answer to Question 1 requires no more than recognizing the key word, *most,* and finding the largest bar. A, B, and D are far smaller than C, the Gulf Coast, which is the correct answer.
2. Once again the key word, *largest,* will point you to the correct answer. The largest slice of the pie is easy to see; matching it to the correct category in the key will give the final answer. In this case, the answer is A.

General Test-Taking Tips

Share these tips with your students.

- Remember the time budget you set for each part of the test. If you find yourself stuck on one question and using up your time, move on.
- If there is time left when you have finished all the questions you know, go back and try to complete the ones you skipped.
- If there is no penalty for guessing, attempt an answer to every question.

STRATEGIES

Bar and Pie Graphs

A bar graph allows for comparisons among numbers or sets of numbers. A pie, or circle, graph shows relationships among the parts of a whole. These parts look like slices of a pie. The size of each slice is proportional to the percentage of the whole that it represents.

1. Read the title of the graph to learn what it is about.
2. For a bar graph, study the labels on the vertical and horizontal axes to see the kinds of information presented in the graph. Note the intervals between amounts or years.
3. Study the legend, if there is one. The legend on a bar graph provides information on what is being graphed. The legend on a pie graph shows what each slice of the pie represents.
4. Look at the source line and evaluate the reliability of the information in the graph.
5. Study the data on the graph. Make comparisons among the slices of a pie graph. Draw conclusions and make inferences based on the data.
6. Read the questions carefully and use any words to reject incorrect alternatives.

answers: 1 (C), 2 (A)

1 U.S. Imports of Crude Oil and Petroleum Products by Region

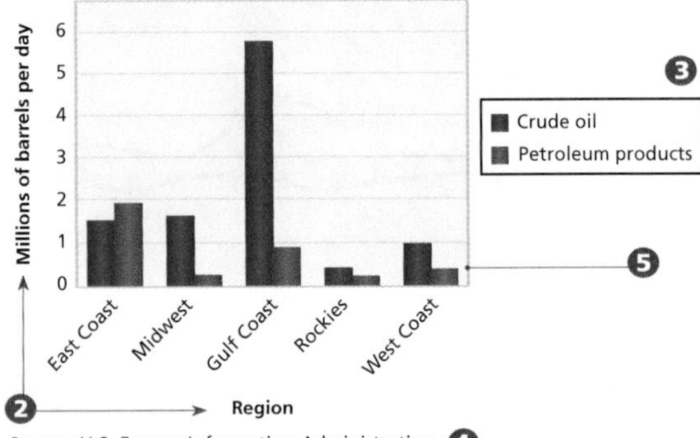

Source: U.S. Energy Information Administration 4

6 1. Which region of the United States imported the most crude oil per day during 2004?

A. East Coast
B. West Coast
C. Gulf Coast
D. Midwest

1 Components of M1

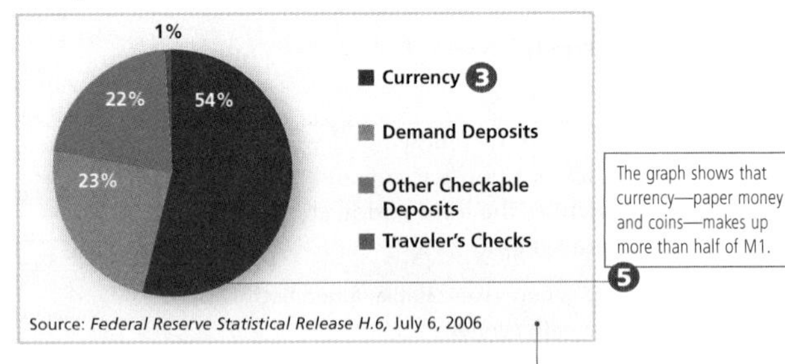

Source: *Federal Reserve Statistical Release H.6,* July 6, 2006

The graph shows that currency—paper money and coins—makes up more than half of M1.

6 2. What is the largest component of M1?

A. currency
B. demand deposits
C. other checkable deposits
D. traveler's checks

4 Statistics from government agencies, such as the Federal Reserve, tend to be reliable.

S12

STRATEGIES FOR TAKING STANDARDIZED TESTS

English Learners

Understanding Vocabulary

Make sure students understand the following terms and concepts in the sample questions on these pages.

Strategies
Bar and Pie Graphs
Question 1 *imports*: goods or services produced in one country and purchased by another
Question 2 *component*: part, segment

Practice
Bar and Pie Graphs
Question 2 *fluctuation*: wave-like change

PRACTICE

Directions: Use the graphs and your knowledge of economics to answer questions 1 through 4.

New Jobs Added to the U.S. Economy

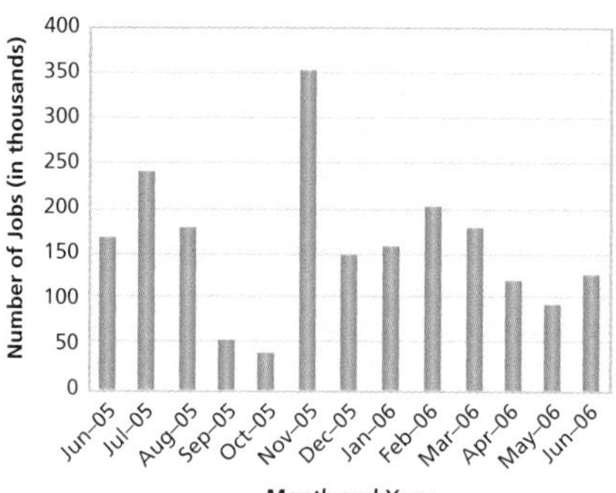

Source: U.S. Department of Labor

Electricity Generation by Energy Source

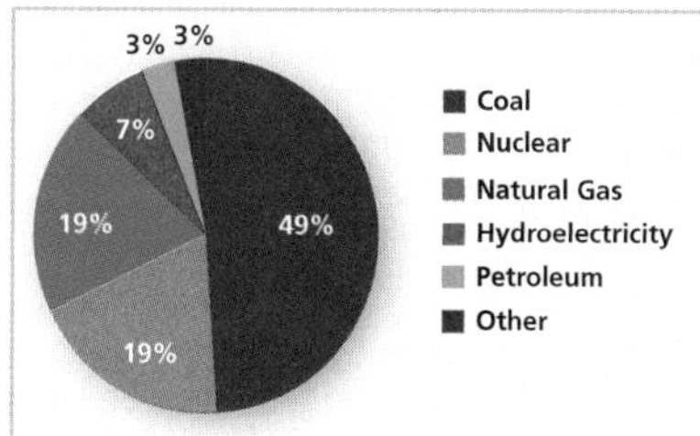

Source: Energy Information Administration, *Electric Power Monthly,* June 2006

1. When was the greatest number of jobs added to the economy?

A. July 2005
B. November 2005
C. February 2006
D. March 2006

2. Which statement is supported by information in the graph?

A. The graph shows that there were greater fluctuations in job creation in the later months of 2005 than there were in the early months of 2006.
B. More jobs were added to the economy in all of 2005 than in all of 2006.
C. The graph shows a steady upward trend in the number of jobs added to the economy.
D. More jobs were added to the economy between January and June of 2006 than between June and December of 2005.

3. Which source of fuel generated nearly half of all electric power?

A. coal
B. natural gas
C. nuclear
D. petroleum

4. Which single source generated the least amount of electricity?

A. coal
B. natural gas
C. nuclear
D. petroleum

STRATEGIES FOR TAKING STANDARDIZED TESTS

S13

Thinking It Through

Share the following explanations with students as they discuss the strategies they used to answer the practice questions.

1. Like the first strategy question, Question 1 can be easily answered by noting the key word, *greatest,* and looking for the biggest bar, which corresponds to November of 2005 (B).
2. Question 2 requires you to draw conclusions from the data. Testing each conclusion will show that: 1) A is the correct answer; 2) B can be eliminated because the graph does not even show all of 2005 and all of 2006; 3) C can be eliminated because the bars show no clear trend; and 4) D can be eliminated because the huge number of jobs added in November of 2005 tips the balance in favor of the second half of 2005.
3. Question 3 asks you to look for a slice of the pie that fills nearly half the pie and then check the key to identify it. The answer is obviously A.
4. Question 4 requires very careful reading. At first glance, it would appear that two wedges of the pie could be the correct answer, since they both represent the same percentage. However, the question asks for the *single* source, which eliminates the "other" category and points to D as the correct answer.

Strategy Items

Item	Skill Tested
1, 2	Interpreting Graphs

Practice Items

Item	Skill Tested
1	Interpreting Graphs
2	Drawing Conclusions; Synthesizing Economic Data
3, 4	Interpreting Graphs

Using Strategies For... Extended Response

Explain to students that they will do best on test questions by thinking them through carefully and by applying test-taking strategies, such as the following.

1. Question 1 requires you to use your knowledge of economic principles to complete a graph showing a change in demand. However, there are two parts to the question. One is to establish the relationship between CDs and CD players, since it is the price of CD players that is known to be rising. The other is to determine how to draw the changed demand curve. Since CDs and CD players are complementary goods, a rise in the price of one will result in a decline in demand for both. With a decline in demand, the curve shifts to the left.
2. To answer Question 2, clarify the task, which includes two parts: 1) write a brief description of the changes; and 2) explain why they occurred. The sample answer provided shows a good model of responding to both parts of the question in complete sentences and also keeping the response brief.

General Test-Taking Tips

Share these tips with your students.

- Use complete sentences in writing extended responses.
- Treat the extended response as you would an essay. Check to be sure it is well organized and free from errors that could interfere with getting your message across.

Extended Response

Extended-response questions usually focus on an exhibit of some kind—a chart, graph, or diagram, for example. They are more complex than multiple-choice questions and often require a written response.

Some extended-response questions ask you to complete the exhibit. Others require you to present the information in the exhibit in a different form. Still others ask you to write an essay, a report, or some other extended piece of writing. In most standardized tests, exhibits have only one extended-response question.

1. Read the title of the exhibit to get an idea of the subject.
2. Carefully read the extended-response questions. (Question 1 asks you to complete the graph by drawing and labeling a new demand curve. Question 2 asks you to write a brief explanation of what is shown in the completed graph.)
3. Study and analyze the exhibit.
4. If the question requires an extended piece of writing, jot down ideas in outline form to get started.

❶ **Shifts in Demand**

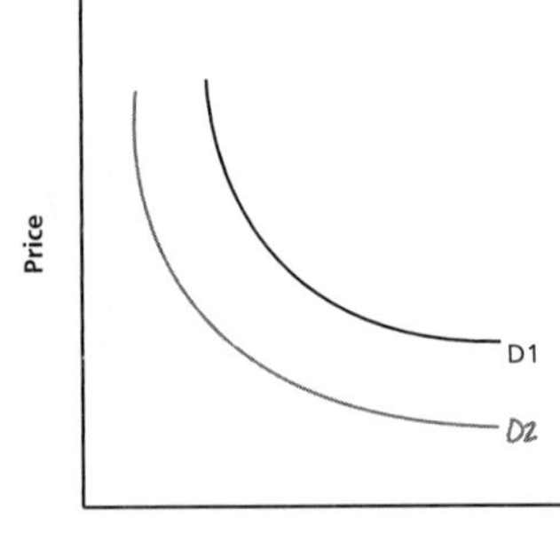

❷
1. The graph above shows the demand for CDs. How would demand for CDs change if the price of CD players rose? Draw a new demand curve to reflect this change. Label the new curve D2.
2. Write a brief explanation of why demand for CDs changed in this way.

❹ **Sample Response** CDs and CD players are used together, so they are complements. If demand for one changes, demand for the other will change in the same way. If the price of CD players rises, then demand for CD players and CDs will decrease and the demand curve shifts to the left.

S14

English Learners

Understanding Vocabulary
Make sure students understand the following terms and concepts in the sample questions on these pages.

Strategies
Extended Response
Question 1 *reflect*: show

Practice
Extended Response
Question 1 *macroeconomic equilibrium*: the point where aggregate demand equals aggregate supply
aggregate supply: the sum of all the supply in the economy

Directions: Use the graph and your knowledge of economics to answer questions 1 and 2.

Shifts in Aggregate Supply

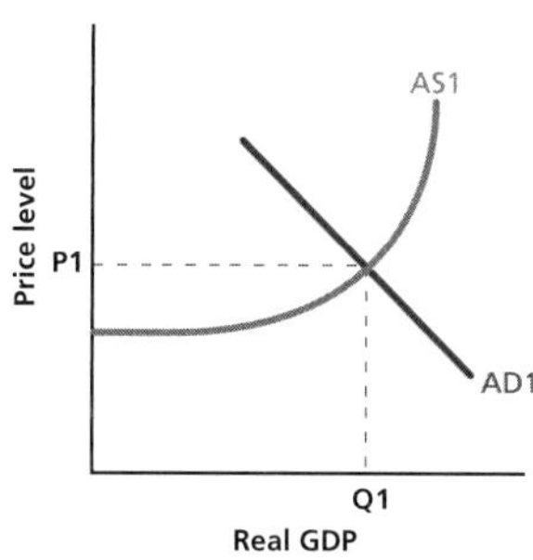

1. The graph above shows an economy at its macroeconomic equilibrium. Copy this graph onto a separate sheet of paper. On the graph, chart how the aggregate supply curve and macroeconomic equilibrium would change if interest rates went up.
2. Write a brief description of these changes and explain why they occurred.

Strategy Items

Item	Skill Tested
1	Interpreting Graphs; Creating and Interpreting Economic Models
2	Applying Economic Concepts

Practice Items

Item	Skill Tested
1	Interpreting Graphs; Creating and Interpreting Economic Models
2	Applying Economic Concepts

Thinking It Through

Share the following explanations with students as they discuss the strategies they used to answer the practice questions.

1. Taking care to understand the question completely may be the most important strategy for extended response. Break the question down into all its parts. Question 1, for example, asks you to: 1) copy the graph on a separate sheet of paper; 2) chart how aggregate supply and macroeconomic equilibrium would change with higher interest rates. When making your graph, use standard naming conventions, in this case labeling the new aggregate supply curve AS2, for example.

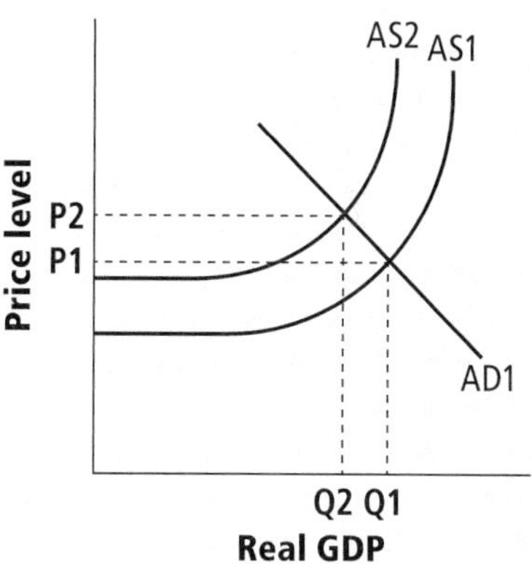

2. **Sample Response** The aggregate supply shifts to the left to AS2, marking a decrease in aggregate supply and establishing a new macroeconomic equilibrium where the price level (P2) is higher and the level of real GDP (Q2) is lower. Rising interest rates increase the cost of borrowing money and, therefore, the cost of doing business. Because of this, businesses will cut production, resulting in a decrease in aggregate supply.

Planning Guide

Resources 2Go Complete print resources all on one USB drive allow you to customize lessons.

Section Titles and Objectives	Unit 1 Resource Book and Workbooks		Assessment Resources
1 Scarcity: The Basic Economic Problem pp. 4–11 • Explain how the economic definition of scarcity differs from the common definition • Understand why scarcity affects everyone • Learn three economic questions that societies face because of scarcity • Describe the four factors of production and how they are used	**Unit 1 Resource Book** • Reading Study Guide, pp. 1–2 • RSG with Additional Support, pp. 3–5 • RSG with Additional Support (Spanish), pp. 6–8	**NCEE Student Activities** • Scarcity, Opportunity Cost and Production Possibilities Curves, pp. 1–4	**Unit 1 Resource Book** • Section Quiz, p. 9 • Reteaching Activity, p. 10 **Test Generator CD-ROM** **Daily Test Practice Transparencies,** TT1
2 Economic Choice Today: Opportunity Cost pp. 12–17 • Understand why choice is at the heart of economics and explain how incentives and utility influence people's economic choices • Consider the role of trade-offs and opportunity costs in economic choices • Demonstrate how to do a cost-benefit analysis	**Unit 1 Resource Book** • Reading Study Guide, pp. 11–12 • RSG with Additional Support, pp. 13–15 • RSG with Additional Support (Spanish), pp. 16–18 • Economic Simulations: One Thing or Another, pp. 47–48	**NCEE Student Activities** • Scarcity, Opportunity Cost and Production Possibilities Curves, pp. 1–4	**Unit 1 Resource Book** • Section Quiz, p. 19 • Reteaching Activity, p. 20 **Test Generator CD-ROM** **Daily Test Practice Transparencies,** TT2
3 Analyzing Production Possibilities pp. 18–23 • Describe what a production possibilities curve is and how it is constructed • Explain what economists learn from using production possibilities curves • Analyze how production possibilities curves show economic growth	**Unit 1 Resource Book** • Reading Study Guide, pp. 21–22 • RSG with Additional Support, pp. 23–25 • RSG with Additional Support (Spanish), pp. 26–28	• Math Skills Worksheet: Making a Production Possibilities Curve (PPC), p. 49	**Unit 1 Resource Book** • Section Quiz, p. 29 • Reteaching Activity, p. 30 **Test Generator CD-ROM** **Daily Test Practice Transparencies,** TT3
4 The Economist's Toolbox pp. 24–33 • Demonstrate how and why economists use economic models and statistics, charts, tables, and graphs • Compare macroeconomics to microeconomics and positive economics to normative economics	**Unit 1 Resource Book** • Reading Study Guide, pp. 31–32 • RSG with Additional Support, pp. 33–35 • RSG with Additional Support (Spanish), pp. 36–38 • Economic Skills and Problem Solving Activity, pp. 41–42	• Readings in Free Enterprise: The First Modern Economist, pp. 43–44 • Case Study Resources: The Real Cost of Expanding O'Hare Airport, pp. 45–46 **Test Practice and Review Workbook,** pp. 23–24	**Unit 1 Resource Book** • Section Quiz, p. 39 • Reteaching Activity, p. 40 • Chapter Test, (Forms A, B, & C), pp. 51–62 **Test Generator CD-ROM** **Daily Test Practice Transparencies,** TT4

Integrated Technology

No Time? To focus students on the most important content in this chapter, use Economics Concepts Transparencies, CT2, "Analyzing Choices," available in Resources 2Go.

Teacher Presentation Options

Presentation Toolkit

Power Presentation DVD-ROM

- Lecture Notes
- Interactive Review
- Media Gallery
- Animated Economics
- Review Game

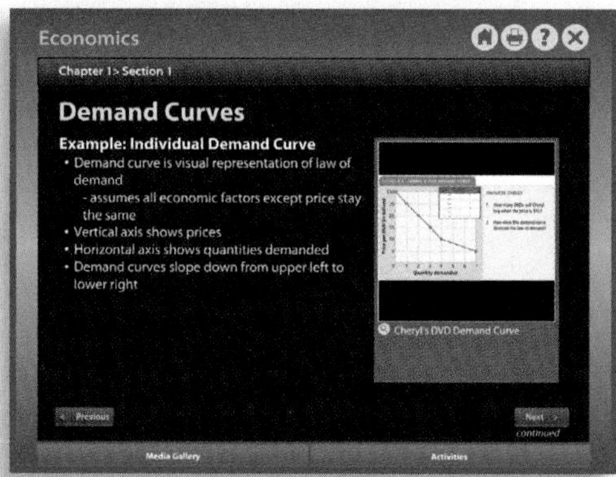

Economics Concepts Transparencies

- Four Factors of Production, CT1
- Analyzing Choices, CT2
- Production-Possibility Table and Curve, CT3
- Revenue Bar Graph and Pie Chart, CT4

Electronic Books

eEdition DVD-ROM

eEdition Online

Daily Test Practice Transparencies, TT1, TT2, TT3, TT4

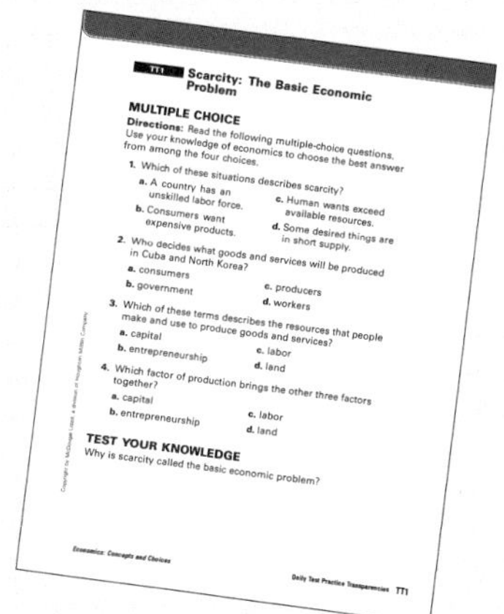

TT1 Scarcity: The Basic Economic Problem

MULTIPLE CHOICE

Directions: Read the following multiple-choice questions. Use your knowledge of economics to choose the best answer from among the four choices.

1. Which of these situations describes scarcity?
   a. A country has an unskilled labor force.
   b. Consumers want expensive products.
   c. Human wants exceed available resources.
   d. Some desired things are in short supply.
2. Who decides what goods and services will be produced in Cuba and North Korea?
   a. consumers
   b. government
   c. producers
   d. workers
3. Which of these terms describes the resources that people make and use to produce goods and services?
   a. capital
   b. entrepreneurship
   c. labor
   d. land
4. Which factor of production brings the other three factors together?
   a. capital
   b. entrepreneurship
   c. labor
   d. land

TEST YOUR KNOWLEDGE

Why is scarcity called the basic economic problem?

Economics: Concepts and Choices

Daily Test Practice Transparencies TT1

Animated Economics

- Graphing the Production Possibilities Curve, p. 19
- What We Learn From PPCs, p. 20
- Changing Production Possibilities, p. 22
- Types of Graphs, p. 26

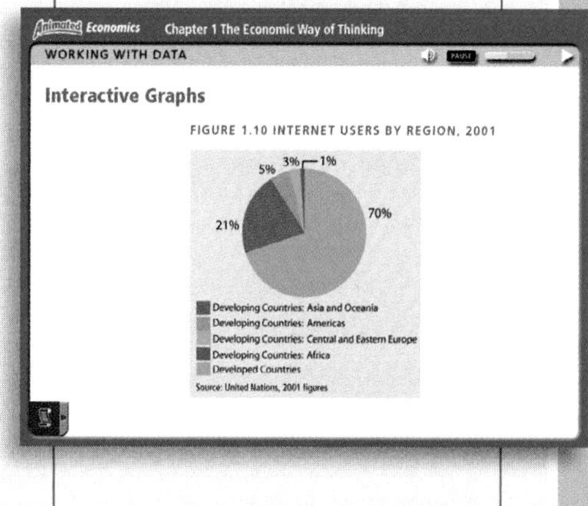

Online Activities at ClassZone.com

Economics Update

- Computer Ownership in the United States, p. 5
- Foreign Aid, p. 25
- Adam Smith, p. 30
- The Real Cost of Expanding O'Hare Airport, p. 32

Animated Economics

- Interactive Graphics

Activity Maker

- Vocabulary Flip Cards
- Review Game

Research Center

- Graphs and Data

Interactive Review

- Online Summary
- Quizzes
- Vocabulary Flip Cards
- Graphic Organizers
- Review and Study Notes

SMARTGrapher

- Create a PPC, p. 23
- Using Graphs, p. 31
- Create a Graph, p. 35

Teacher-Tested Activities

Name: Joanne Benjamin (ret.)

School: Los Gatos High School

State: California

Teacher-Tested Activities

At the beginning of this chapter, look for my classroom-proven idea for teaching economics concepts and thinking.

Resources for Differentiated Instruction

Struggling Readers

Teacher's Edition Activities

- Use Heading Structure and Graphics, p. 8
- Use Signal Words, p. 10
- Find Main Ideas, p. 14
- Map the Text, p. 22
- Use Text Features, p. 30
- Make a Before-and-After Chart, p. 32

Unit 1 Resource Book

- RSG with Additional Support, pp. 3–5, 13–15, 23–25, 33–35 (A)
- Reteaching Activities, pp. 10, 20, 30, 40 (B)
- Chapter Test (Form A), pp. 51–54 (C)

ClassZone.com

- Animated Economics
- Interactive Review

Test Generator CD-ROM

- Chapter Test (Form A)
- Chapter Test (Form A), in Spanish

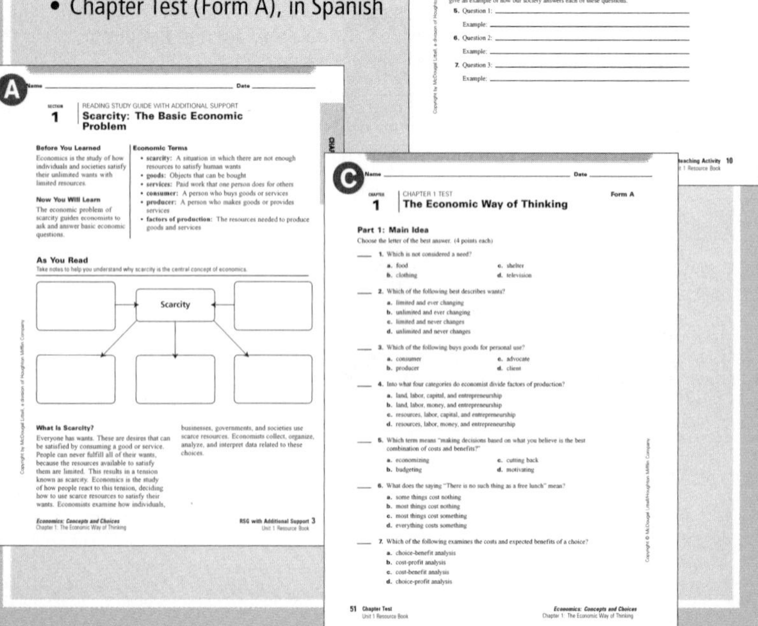

B — Section 1, Reteaching Activity: Scarcity: The Basic Economic Problem

A — Section 1, Reading Study Guide with Additional Support: Scarcity: The Basic Economic Problem

C — Chapter 1 Test, Form A: The Economic Way of Thinking

English Learners

Teacher's Edition Activities

- Relate Words to One Another, p. 8
- Personal Dictionary: Hyphenated Words, p. 14
- Use Economic Terms in Writing, p. 21
- Make Oral Presentations, p. 26
- Determine Meaning from Prefixes, p. 28

Unit 1 Resource Book

- RSG with Additional Support (Spanish), pp. 6–8, 16–18, 26–28, 36–38 (A)

Test Generator CD-ROM

- Chapter Test (Forms A, B, & C), in Spanish (B)

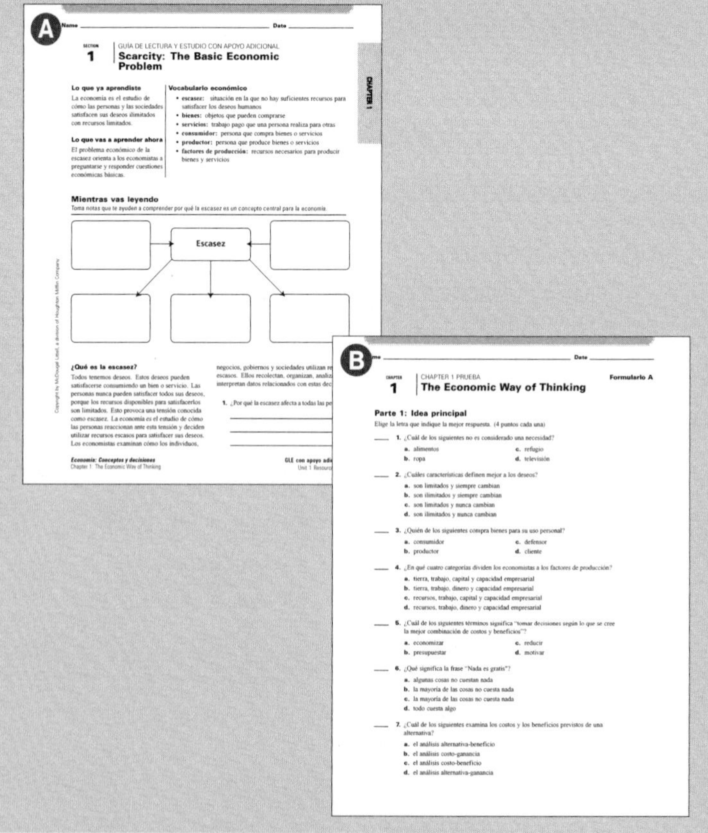

A — Section 1, Guía de lectura y estudio con apoyo adicional: Scarcity: The Basic Economic Problem

B — Chapter 1 Prueba, Formulario A: The Economic Way of Thinking

Inclusion

Teacher's Edition Activities

- Relate to Everyday Life, p. 6
- Relate to Personal Experience, p. 16
- Use Manipulatives, p. 19
- Extend an Activity, p. 21
- Extend an Activity, p. 22
- Make 3-D Graphs, p. 26
- Listen and Visualize, p. 30

Lesson Plans

- Modified Lessons for Inclusion, pp. 1–4 (A)

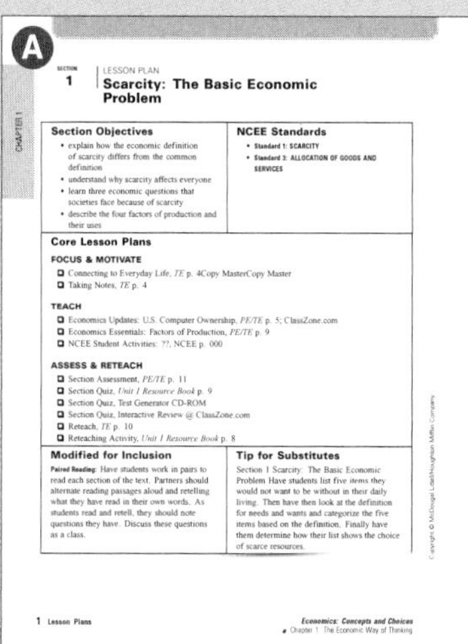

SECTION 1 LESSON PLAN
Scarcity: The Basic Economic Problem

Section Objectives | NCEE Standards

Core Lesson Plans

FOCUS & MOTIVATE

TEACH

ASSESS & RETEACH

Modified for Inclusion | Tip for Substitutes

Gifted and Talented

Teacher's Edition Activities

- Evaluate Teens' Economic Power, p. 6
- Write a Cause-and-Effect Analysis, p. 10
- Do a Cost-Benefit Analysis, p. 16
- Use Math Skills, p. 19
- Relate to Current Economic Events, p. 28
- Conduct Research, p. 32

Unit 1 Resource Book

- Readings in Free Enterprise: The First Modern Economist, pp. 43–44 (A)
- Case Study Resources: The Real Cost of Expanding O'Hare Airport, pp. 45–46 (B)

NCEE Student Activities

- Scarcity, Opportunity Cost, and Production Possibilities Curves, pp. 1–4 (C)

ClassZone.com

- Research Center

Test Generator CD-ROM

- Chapter Test (Form C)
- Chapter Test (Form C), in Spanish

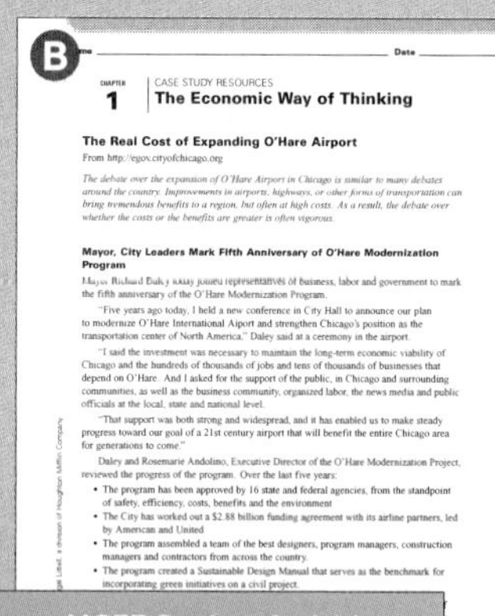

CHAPTER 1 CASE STUDY RESOURCES
The Economic Way of Thinking

The Real Cost of Expanding O'Hare Airport

Mayor, City Leaders Mark Fifth Anniversary of O'Hare Modernization Program

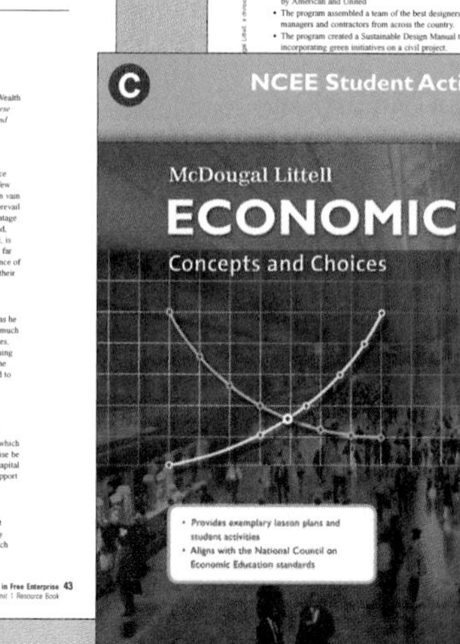

CHAPTER 1 READINGS IN FREE ENTERPRISE
The Economic Way of Thinking

The First Modern Economist

Individual Self-Interest

Self-Interest Benefits Society

Profit Motive

Monopoly

Readings in Free Enterprise 43

Focus & Motivate

Objective

Understand how scarcity requires choices by both individuals and society and describe some of the tools economists use.

Why the Concept Matters

Explain that scarcity and choice are the fundamental principles of economics—that everything else grows out of them. Students usually have many personal examples of economic scarcity, such as a long list of things they would like to have but cannot afford. Encourage them to offer some examples for discussion. After a few have been discussed, have students consider the other key realm in which scarcity is a fact of life: time. Ask students to offer examples of choices they make with their time. *(Possible answers: decisions on which electives to take, what extracurricular activities to be involved in, and so on)* Point out that the economic way of thinking extends far beyond the study of economics and applies to all areas of life.

Analyzing the Photograph

Focus the attention of students on the photograph. Have them discuss the lunch choices they make, giving reasons for their choices. Encourage students to understand that some of the reasons are not economic in the financial sense of the word. Some might involve ways to save time or taste preferences. Also ask students to give examples of other kinds of choices evident in the photograph. *(Possible answers: which clothes to wear, whom to sit with, hairstyles, jewelry)*

Unit 1

Economics and Choice

Scarcity and Choices
Economics is about making choices. Even such an ordinary task as deciding what to have for lunch involves economic choice. Should you spend $5 on a hot meal, $3 on a sandwich, or should you save your money and bring lunch from home?

2

CONTENT STANDARDS

NCEE STANDARDS

Standard 1: Scarcity
Students will understand that
Productive resources are limited. Therefore, people cannot have all the goods and services they want; as a result, they must choose some things and give up others.

Students will be able to use this knowledge to
Identify what they gain and what they give up when they make choices.

Benchmarks
Students will know that
- Scarcity is the condition of not being able to have all of the goods and services that one wants. It exists because human wants for goods and services exceed the quantity of goods and services that can be produced using all available resources. *(pages 4–5)*
- Productive resources are the natural resources, human resources, and capital goods available to make goods and services. *(pages 8–9)*
- Choices involve trading off the expected value of one opportunity against the expected value of its best alternative. *(pages 12–16)*

CHAPTER

1

The Economic Way of Thinking

CONCEPT REVIEW

Economics is the study of how individuals and societies satisfy their unlimited wants with limited resources.

CHAPTER 1 KEY CONCEPT

Scarcity is the situation that exists because wants are unlimited and resources are limited.

WHY THE CONCEPT MATTERS

You confront the issue of scarcity constantly in everyday life. Look again at the caption on page 2. Suppose you have $20 to cover the cost of lunches for the week. How will you use your limited funds to meet your wants (lunch for Monday through Friday)? What if you stayed late at school twice a week and bought a $1 snack each day? How would this affect your lunch choices? Identify one or two other examples of scarcity in your everyday life.

Online Highlights

More at ClassZone.com

Economics Update
Go to ECONOMICS UPDATE for chapter updates and news on the cost of expansion plans at O'Hare Airport in Chicago. (See Case Study, pages 32–33).

Animated Economics
Go to ANIMATED ECONOMICS for interactive lessons on the graphs and tables in this chapter. ▶

Interactive Review
Go to INTERACTIVE REVIEW for concept review and activities.

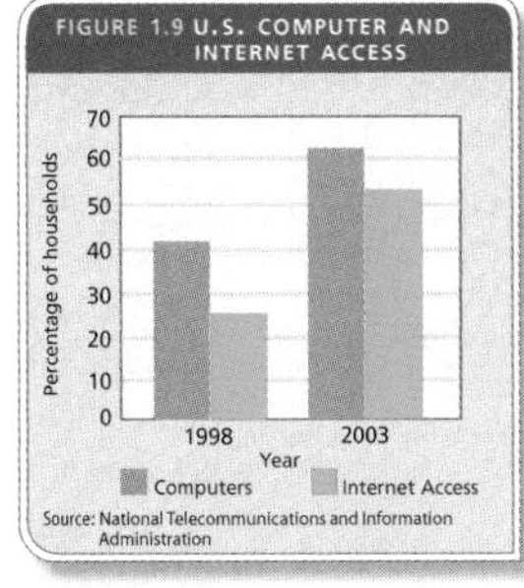

How do economists use graphs? See Section 4 of this chapter.

From the Classroom

Joanne Benjamin, Los Gatos High School (retired)

OPPORTUNITY COST

Explain to students that every time you make a choice, you experience opportunity cost. Opportunity cost is what you give up in order to get what you want. The cost of the decision may not be monetary. A cost could be lack of contact with one friend when choosing to hang out with another.

Ask students to write on a piece of paper the two things he or she would most like to do this coming Friday evening. Then ask students to think about the alternatives and to complete a decision-making grid.

Alternative 1	Alternative 2
Benefits	Opportunity Cost

After they have completed the grid, ask each student to make a choice and to explain the cost of his or her decision.

Previewing Chapter Technology at ClassZone.com

Economics Update Students will find references to online articles or statistics that update information in the pupil edition on pages 5, 25, and 30.

Animated Economics Students will find interactive lessons related to materials on pages 19, 20, 22, and 26.

Interactive Review Students will find additional section and chapter assessment support for materials on pages 11, 17, 23, 31, and 34.

TEACHER MEDIA FAVORITES

Books

- Friedman, David. *Hidden Order: The Economics of Everyday Life.* New York: Harper Collins, 1996. Offers a clear-cut approach to why people make the choices they do and strategies for making the right ones.
- Landsburg, Steven E. *The Armchair Economist.* New York: The Free Press, 1995. Demonstrates the economic way of thinking in everyday experiences, answering such questions as why tickets for rock concerts are not more expensive and why movie popcorn is so expensive.
- Winter, Harold. *Trade-Offs: An Introduction to Economic Reasoning and Social Issues.* Chicago, IL: University of Chicago Press, 2005. Provides analytic tools to understand the costs and benefits of public policy issues and the importance of recognizing trade-offs.

Videos/DVDs

- *The Invisible Hand: Economics in Daily Life.* 22 minutes. Learning Seed, 2004. Explores basic economic ideas, using everyday examples.
- *Economics U$A: Scarcity and Resources.* 30 minutes. The Annenberg/CPB Collection, 2002. Uses historical examples to demonstrate how society allocates resources.

Internet

Visit **ClassZone.com** to link to

- a variety of chapter-specific, content-reviewed sites
- updates on data and topics presented throughout the chapter sections and Case Study
- updates to the Power Presentations

1 Plan & Prepare

Section 1 Objectives

- explain how the economic definition of scarcity differs from the common definition
- understand why scarcity affects everyone
- learn three economic questions that societies face because of scarcity
- describe the four factors of production and their uses

2 Focus & Motivate

Connecting to Everyday Life Explain that this section—and all of economics in one way or another—focuses on scarcity. Ask students to discuss what the word *scarcity* means to them. *(In the discussion, lead students toward the idea of the gap between available resources and human wants.)*

Taking Notes Remind students to take notes as they read by completing a cluster diagram that shows scarcity as the central concept of economics. They can use the Graphic Organizer at **Interactive Review @ ClassZone.com**. A sample is shown below.

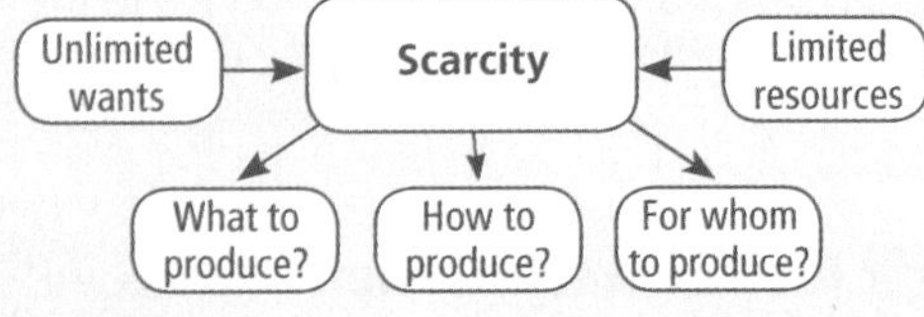

SECTION 1

Scarcity: The Basic Economic Problem

OBJECTIVES

In Section 1, you will

- explain how the economic definition of scarcity differs from the common definition
- understand why scarcity affects everyone
- learn three economic questions that societies face because of scarcity
- describe the four factors of production and their uses

KEY TERMS

wants, *p. 4*
needs, *p. 4*
scarcity, *p. 4*
economics, *p. 4*
goods, *p. 5*
services, *p. 5*
consumer, *p. 5*
producer, *p. 5*
factors of production, *p. 8*
land, *p. 8*
labor, *p. 8*
capital, *p. 8*
entrepreneurship, *p. 9*

TAKING NOTES

As you read Section 1, complete a cluster diagram showing how scarcity is the central concept of economics. Use the Graphic Organizer at **Interactive Review @ ClassZone.com**

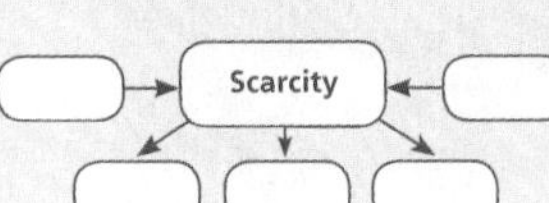

What Is Scarcity?

QUICK REFERENCE

Wants are desires that can be satisfied by consuming a good or a service.

Needs are things that are necessary for survival.

Scarcity exists when there are not enough resources to satisfy human wants.

Economics is the study of how individuals and societies satisfy their unlimited wants with limited resources.

KEY CONCEPTS

Have you ever felt you wanted a new cell phone, a car, a new pair of running shoes, or the latest MP3 player? You are not alone. Consumers have many economic wants. **Wants** are desires that can be satisfied by consuming a good or service. When making purchases, people often make a distinction between the things they need and the things they want. Some things that people desire, like a house or an apartment, are more important than other things, like a flat-screen television. **Needs** are things, such as food, clothing, and shelter, that are necessary for survival.

People always want more, no matter how much they have already. In fact, wants are unlimited, but the resources available to satisfy them are limited. The result of this difference is **scarcity**, the situation that exists when there are not enough resources to meet human wants. Scarcity is not a temporary shortage of some desired thing. Rather, it is a fundamental and ongoing tension that confronts individuals, businesses, governments, and societies. Indeed, it is so basic to human experience that a social science has developed to understand and explain it. That social science is **economics**, the study of how people choose to use scarce resources to satisfy their wants. Economics involves

1. **examining** how individuals, businesses, governments, and societies choose to use scarce resources to satisfy their wants
2. **organizing, analyzing, and interpreting data** about those economic behaviors
3. **developing theories and economic laws** that explain how the economy works and to predict what might happen in the future.

SECTION 1 PROGRAM RESOURCES

ON LEVEL

Lesson Plans

- Core, p. 1

Unit 1 Resource Book

- Reading Study Guide, pp. 1–2
- Economic Simulations, pp. 47–48
- Section Quiz, p. 9

STRUGGLING READERS

Unit 1 Resource Book

- Reading Study Guide with Additional Support, pp. 3–5
- Reteaching Activity, p. 10

ENGLISH LEARNERS

Unit 1 Resource Book

- Reading Study Guide with Additional Support (Spanish), pp. 6–8

INCLUSION

Lesson Plans

- Modified for Inclusion, p. 1

GIFTED AND TALENTED

NCEE Student Activities

- Scarcity, Opportunity Cost, and Production Possibilities Curves, pp. 1–4

TECHNOLOGY

eEdition DVD-ROM

eEdition Online

Power Presentation DVD-ROM

Economics Concepts Transparencies

- CT1 Four Factors of Production

Daily Test Practice Transparencies, TT1

ClassZone.com

Shortages and Scarcity Shortages often are temporary. Movie tickets may be in short supply today, but in a few days' time they may be easy to come by. Scarcity, however, never ends because wants always exceed the resources available to satisfy them.

PRINCIPLE 1 People Have Wants

Choice is central to the use of scarce resources. People make choices about all the things they desire—both needs and wants. You might think of food as a need, because it is necessary for your survival. Nevertheless, you make choices about food. What do you want for dinner tonight? Will you cook a gourmet creation or heat up a frozen dinner? Or will you treat yourself to a meal at your favorite restaurant? You make choices about other needs too. For example, consider the choices you make about the clothes you wear.

Wants are not only unlimited, they also are ever changing. Twenty-five years ago, for example, few Americans owned a personal computer. Today, however, few Americans can imagine life without computers and computer-related technology.

PRINCIPLE 2 Scarcity Affects Everyone

Because wants are unlimited and resources are scarce, choices have to be made about how best to use these resources. Scarcity, then, affects which goods are made and which services are provided. **Goods** are physical objects that can be purchased, such as food, clothing, and furniture. **Services** are work that one person performs for another for payment. Services include the work of sales clerks, technical support representatives, teachers, nurses, doctors, and lawyers. Scarcity affects the choices of both the **consumer**, a person who buys goods or services for personal use, and the **producer**, a person who makes goods or provides services.

APPLICATION Applying Economic Concepts

A. Identify five wants that you have right now. Describe how scarcity affects your efforts to meet these wants.

See answer in Teacher's Edition. ▶

Economics Update

Find an update about computer ownership in the United States at **ClassZone.com**

QUICK REFERENCE

Goods are objects, such as food, clothing, and furniture, that can be bought.

Services are work that one person does for another.

A **consumer** is a person who buys or uses goods or services.

A **producer** is a maker of goods or a provider of services.

❸ Teach

What Is Scarcity?

Discuss

- What is the economic way of thinking? *(recognizing that all human behavior involves choice, and that choices can be analyzed and understood logically)*
- How does scarcity affect consumers? producers? governments? *(Consumers must make choices about what to buy and save; producers must make choices about how and what to produce; governments must make choices about how to spend public money.)*

Economics Update

At **ClassZone.com,** students will see updated information on the demand for computers.

APPLICATION

Answer *Student responses will vary, but will include such things as a new MP3 player, new shoes, tickets to a music concert, an automobile, and so on. Most students will note that their wants are unlimited but their resources are scarce, so they have to make choices among their wants.*

LEVELED ACTIVITY

Assess Opportunity Costs

Time 30 minutes ◑

Objective Students will demonstrate an understanding of the opportunity costs of economic choice. (Opportunity cost is discussed in Section 2.)

Basic

You have won $1,000 in a contest. Create a three-column chart. In the first column, list how you would spend the money. You can divide it up any way you like. In the second column, write a gain from each choice. In the third column, write what you would give up with each choice.

On Level

You have won $1,000 in a contest. Make a list of possible uses for that money. Then draw up a plan for spending it, dividing it in any way that you like. Write a paragraph explaining the trade-offs involved in your choices and identifying the opportunity costs.

Challenge

You have won $1,000 in a contest. Make a list of possible uses for that money. Then draw up a plan for spending it, dividing it in any way you like. Write an essay explaining your motivation for each choice, as well as the trade-offs and opportunity costs.

Scarcity Leads to Three Economic Questions

Discuss

- What is the role of scarcity in each of the three economic questions? *(What will be produced—scarcity of resources in the broadest sense limits what can be produced, so choices have to be made. How will it be produced—scarcity of production factors requires choice. For whom will it be produced—scarcity means that all people cannot have all their wants met, so some distribution systems need to be developed.)*
- Are efficient methods absolute or relative? In other words, if a method of production is efficient in one place, will it also necessarily be efficient in another? *(no, because a region's resources will determine what is or is not efficient, as in the example in the photographs on page 7)*

Scarcity Leads to Three Economic Questions

KEY CONCEPTS

If you have ever had to decide whether something you want is worth the money, then you have experienced scarcity firsthand. Scarcity in the lives of individual consumers—the gap between their unlimited wants and limited resources—is all too easy to understand. Scarcity, however, also confronts producers and whole societies. Indeed, scarcity requires every society to address three basic economic questions: What will be produced? How will it be produced? For whom will it be produced?

QUESTION 1 What Will Be Produced?

To answer the first fundamental economic question, a society must decide the mix of goods and services it will produce. Will it produce mainly food, or will it also produce automobiles, televisions, computers, furniture, and shoes? The goods and services a society chooses to produce depend, in part, on the natural resources it possesses. For example, a country that does not possess oil is unlikely to choose to produce petroleum products. Resources, however, do not completely control what a country produces. Japan does not possess large amounts of the iron ore needed to make steel. Yet Japan is a leading producer of automobiles, whose construction requires a great deal of steel.

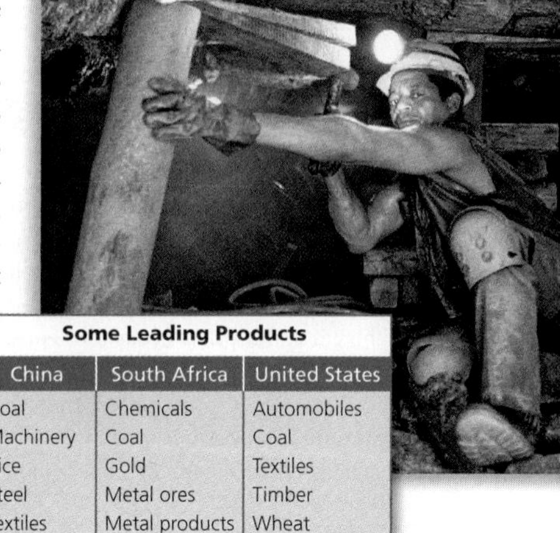

Some Leading Products

China	South Africa	United States
Coal	Chemicals	Automobiles
Machinery	Coal	Coal
Rice	Gold	Textiles
Steel	Metal ores	Timber
Textiles	Metal products	Wheat

What to Produce? The availability of natural resources, such as gold, influences what the country of South Africa produces.

Some countries, including the United States, resolve the issue of what goods and services to produce by allowing producers and consumers to decide. For example, if consumers want cars with automatic transmissions, automobile companies would be unwise to make only cars that have manual transmissions. In other countries—Cuba and North Korea, for example—the consumer plays little or no part in answering this question. Rather, the government decides what goods and services will be produced.

This first fundamental economic question involves not only what to produce, but also how much to produce. To answer this, societies must review what their wants are at any time. A country at war, for example, will choose to produce more weapons than it would during peacetime.

DIFFERENTIATING INSTRUCTION

Inclusion

Relate to Everyday Life

Within a small group, have three pairs of students talk through the choices involved in shopping for, cooking, and sharing an evening meal. Each pair should focus on one of the stages and its related economic question. For example, one pair will talk through shopping for the meal, thereby addressing the question "What to produce." The second pair will concentrate on how to produce it, depending upon available supplies. The third pair will talk through the sharing of the meal.

Gifted and Talented

Evaluate Teens' Economic Power

Group students and have them create a presentation on the power of teenagers in the American economy. Direct students to use their personal experience to determine ways in which teenagers are significant economic decision-makers. Have them address these questions in their presentation: Which economic question do they play the greatest role in answering? In what categories of goods and services are teenagers an economic force? What influences teenagers' economic choices?

How to Produce For some societies, using a large amount of human labor is the most efficient way to produce food (left). For other societies, using a lot of machinery is a more efficient method of production (right).

QUESTION 2 How Will It Be Produced?

Once a society has decided what it will produce, it must then decide how these goods and services will be produced. Answering this second question involves using scarce resources in the most efficient way to satisfy society's wants. Again, decisions on methods of production are influenced, in part, by the natural resources a society possesses.

In deciding how to grow crops, for example, societies adopt different approaches. Societies with a large, relatively unskilled labor force might adopt labor-intensive farming methods. For this society, using many workers and few machines is the most efficient way to farm. The United States, however, has a highly skilled work force. So, using labor-intensive methods would be an inefficient use of labor resources. Therefore, the United States takes a capital-intensive approach to farming. In other words, it uses lots of machinery and few workers.

QUESTION 3 For Whom Will It Be Produced?

The third fundamental economic question involves how goods and services are distributed among people in society. This actually involves two questions. Exactly how much should people get and how should their share be delivered to them?

Should everyone get an equal share of the goods and services? Or should a person's share be determined by how much he or she is willing to pay? Once the question of how much has been decided, societies must then decide exactly how they are going to get these goods and services to people. To do this, societies develop distribution systems, which include road and rail systems, seaports, airports, trucks, trains, ships, airplanes, computer networks—anything that helps move goods and services from producers to consumers in an efficient manner.

APPLICATION Analyzing Cause and Effect

B. Why does the basic problem of scarcity lead societies to ask the three fundamental economic questions?

because every society faces the problem of having too few resources to meet unlimited wants

International Economics

Cuba's Command Economy
After U.S. business interests were forced out following the 1959 revolution, the Cuban economy realigned itself with the Soviet Union (now Russia). Cuba arranged a sugar-for-oil exchange that helped fuel economic growth. In the early 1990s, the Cuban economy suffered a major shock when the Soviet Union collapsed. Although Cuba maintains most aspects of a command economy today, it has opened its doors to foreign investment and continues to have widespread access to health care and education.

Rubric

	Understanding of Concepts	Presentation of Information
4	excellent	clear and complete
3	good	mostly clear
2	fair	sometimes clear
1	poor	unclear

SMALL GROUP ACTIVITY

Creating a Simple Product

Time 45 minutes

Task Answer the basic economic questions by creating a simple product.

Materials Needed two boxes of colored markers, 24 paper plates, 12 pencils, two staplers, two rolls of transparent tape, 4 scissors, instruction sheets (see below)

Activity

- Set up two groups. One group will be given half the materials and an instruction sheet that reads "Make as many as you can of whatever product you think will appeal to buyers in your age group." The second group will be given an instruction sheet that reads "Government Orders: Make six pencil cases. See the teacher for supplies."
- Let the first group work on its own. When the second group comes to you for supplies, give them only the paper plates, pencils, and scissors. If they need more supplies, they have to figure out that they need to ask you for more. When they ask for something to hold the product together, give them either the stapler or the tape, not both.
- Allow 30 minutes to create the products.
- Have each group display what they have produced and discuss how they answered the first two economic questions.
- Discuss how each group would determine who gets the product.
- Have students compare and contrast the two methods of producing goods.

See Rubric in side column above.

The Factors of Production

Discuss

- What is the main difference between land and capital as a factor of production? *(Land includes only natural things; capital refers to only human-made things.)*
- Which of the factors of production is most important? *(Answers will vary, but the discussion should lead to the idea that no matter which factor students choose, all four factors are important and necessary.)*

More About . . .

Capital: Nothing Ventured . . .
In economics, there are other kinds of capital besides physical, or real capital, and human capital. One of these other kinds of capital is *venture capital,* financial resources invested in businesses considered too risky for mainstream investing. Venture capitalists—the persons who invest capital in business ventures—expect that two of every ten companies they invest in will be failures, six will be marginally successful, and the remaining two will be so successful that they will more than make up for any losses. The phenomenal growth of dot-com companies in the 1990s led to an expansion in venture capitalism, which is often associated with technology enterprises.

Presentation Options

Review the relationship between scarcity and production by using the following presentation options:

 **Power Presentations DVD-ROM**
Using the Display Tool, you can examine the three basic economic questions.

 **Economics Concepts Transparencies**
- CT1 Four Factors of Production

The Factors of Production

QUICK REFERENCE

Factors of production are the resources needed to produce goods and services.

Land refers to all natural resources used to produce goods and services.

Labor is all of the human effort used to produce goods and services.

Capital is all of the resources made and used by people to produce goods and services.

KEY CONCEPTS

To understand how societies answer the first two basic questions—what to produce and how to produce it—economists have identified the **factors of production**, or the economic resources needed to produce goods and services. They divide the factors of production into four broad categories: land, labor, capital, and entrepreneurship. All of these factors have one thing in common—their supply is limited.

FACTOR 1 Land

In everyday terms, the word *land* usually refers to a stretch of ground on the earth's surface. In economic terms, however, **land** includes all the natural resources found on or under the ground that are used to produce goods and services. Water, forests, and all kinds of wildlife belong in the category of land. So, too, do buried deposits of minerals, gas, and oil.

FACTOR 2 Labor

The word *labor* usually brings to mind images of hard physical work. In economic terms, however, its meaning is far broader. **Labor** is all the human time, effort, and talent that go into the making of products. Labor, then, is not only the work done by garbage collectors, factory workers, and construction workers. It also includes the work of architects, teachers, doctors, sales clerks, and government officials.

FACTOR 3 Capital

When you hear the word *capital,* you probably think of money. In economic terms, however, **capital** is all the resources made and used by people to produce and distribute goods and services. Tools, machinery, and factories are all forms of capital. So are offices, warehouses, stores, roads, and airplanes. In other words, capital is all of a producer's physical resources. For this reason capital is sometimes called physical capital, or real capital.

While businesses invest in real capital, workers invest in human capital—the knowledge and skills gained through experience. Human capital includes such things as a college degree or good job training. When workers possess more human capital, they are more productive.

Human Capital Education increases your human capital and makes you more productive in the workplace.

DIFFERENTIATING INSTRUCTION

Struggling Readers

Use Heading Structure and Graphics
Help students recognize the clues that reveal the key points and organization of the material in this section. Point out that each main heading begins with a Key Concepts introduction that raises the most important points. Then, explain that the subheads (here they identify the factors of production) signal the important ideas. Also point out that a graphic may represent main ideas, as Figure 1.1 does. In addition, the Quick Reference tabs in the margins provide definitions for key words.

English Learners

Relate Words to One Another
Point out the parts of the word *entrepreneurship.* Explain that it is from the Old French word *entreprendre,* which means to undertake. Point out the prefix, the root, and the suffix. *Entre* means between or across; *preneur* is from *prendre,* which means to take; and *ship* is an English suffix meaning state of being. "Ship" always signals a noun form of the word. Mention that *entrepreneur* is closely related to the word *enterprise,* another key economic term.

ECONOMICS ESSENTIALS

FIGURE 1.1 Factors of Production

Land All the natural resources found on or under the ground that are used to produce goods and services are considered land.

Labor All the human time, effort, and talent that go into the production of goods and services are considered labor.

Entrepreneurship The combination of vision, skill, ingenuity, and willingness to take risks that is needed to create and run new businesses is called entrepreneurship.

Capital All the physical resources made and used by people to produce and distribute goods and services are considered capital. So, too, are the knowledge and skills that make workers more productive.

ANALYZE CHARTS

Two new businesses have opened in your neighborhood—a coffee bar called Lou's Café and a health club called BodyPower. Construct your own Economics Essentials diagram to show how the four factors of production are used in one of these businesses.

FACTOR 4 Entrepreneurship

The fourth factor of production, entrepreneurship, brings the other three factors together. **Entrepreneurship** is the combination of vision, skill, ingenuity, and willingness to take risks that is needed to create and run new businesses. Most entrepreneurs are innovators. They try to anticipate the wants of consumers and then satisfy these wants in new ways. This may involve developing a new product, method of production, or way of marketing or distributing products. Entrepreneurs are also risk takers. They risk their time, energy, creativity, and money in the hope of making a profit. The entrepreneurs who build a massive shopping mall or who open a new health club do so because they think they could profit from these business ventures. The risk they take is that these enterprises might fail.

QUICK REFERENCE

Entrepreneurship involves the vision, skills, and risk-taking needed to create and run businesses.

APPLICATION Applying Economic Concepts

C. Think of a product that you recently purchased. How do you think the four factors of production were used to create this product?

See answer in Teacher's Edition. ▶

Economics Essentials: Figure 1.1

Ask students how people come into possession or control of each of the factors of production. One way to frame the discussion is to ask: If you wanted to start a business, could you pull together all the factors of production? If not, why not? *(Discussion will yield a variety of answers but may center on the need for assets with which to begin building.)* Ask students to discuss whether entrepreneurship is only a natural gift, only a skill that can be developed (and if so, how), or some combination of the two. *(Possible answer: Students may suggest that entrepreneurship can be developed through modeling the behavior of successful entrepreneurs in an enterprise.)*

Analyze

Have students present and discuss their own Economics Essentials diagrams.

APPLICATION

Answer *Student responses will vary, but probably will note the following:*

Land: natural resources, such as metals, needed to make product.

Labor: work needed to make, transport, and sell product.

Capital: factories, machinery used in making product; warehouses, trucks, transportation networks used to store and transport product; stores where product sold.

Entrepreneurship: skills, effort, and energy used to bring all other factors together.

INDIVIDUAL ACTIVITY

Identifying the Factors of Production for a New Product or Service

Time 30 minutes ◑

Task Identify the factors of production for a new product or service

Materials Needed paper, pen, colored markers

Activity

- Ask students to think of a new product or service that they would like to have in their lives. It can be realistic (a computer that offers homework help) or fanciful (a food that tastes like French fries but has the nutrition of broccoli).
- Have students identify the specific factors of production needed to manufacture this product or provide the service.
- Have students create a visual showing how the factors of production would be used.
- Give each student a few minutes to present his or her new product or service and the visual showing factors of production needed for its creation.
- Ask students to reflect on what they learned from the activity.

Rubric

	Understanding of Concepts	Presentation
4	excellent	clear and complete
3	good	mostly clear
2	fair	sometimes clear
1	poor	unclear

Analyzing Cause and Effect

1 Plan & Prepare

Objectives

- identify the causes and effects of scarcity
- understand that an effect can become a cause in a chain of events or conditions

2 Focus & Motivate

Remind students that in the summer of 2006, gas prices were still high after a spring of rapidly rising prices. Ask students to consider (or remember) what effect the high gas prices had on individual consumers—people just like them. For example, how might travel plans have been affected? *(They may have been postponed until gas prices fell.)* How might the high gas prices have affected consumer decisions about which vehicles to purchase? *(Consumers may have leaned toward more fuel-efficient cars or even motorcycles.)* Point out that each cause creates a ripple of effects. For example, postponed travel plans (the effect of high gas prices) might have caused a downturn in business for hotels or tourist attractions.

3 Teach

The skills-instruction focus here is on two things: (1) the strategy of asking *why* questions as a way to isolate causes; (2) the signal words associated with effects. Ask students to think of as many words and phrases as they can that signal effects, and write them on the board. *(Sample answers: because, therefore, consequently.)* The instruction also covers the transformation of an effect to a cause in a chain of events. Remind students not to assume that just because an event happened before another event that it caused the event. Ask them to give examples of this logical fallacy. *(Sample answer: Just because you come down with a cold after being outside without a coat does not mean that being coatless caused your cold; colds are caused by germs.)*

For additional practice see **Skillbuilder Handbook**, page R20.

THINKING ECONOMICALLY
Answer

Have students discuss their cause-and-effect chain diagrams.

ECONOMICS SKILLBUILDER

For more on cause and effect, see the Skillbuilder Handbook, page R20.

Analyzing Cause and Effect

Causes are the events that explain why something happens and **effects** are what happens. An effect can become the cause of other effects, resulting in a chain of events or conditions. Identifying causes and effects helps economists understand how economic conditions occur. Use the strategies below to help you identify causes and effects using a graphic organizer.

Identify causes by using the word *why* to formulate questions about the topic of the passage. Example: *Why did oil become more scarce in 2003? Why did this situation continue?* The answers you find will be the causes.

Turmoil Reduces Oil Supply

Oil is a scarce resource, but events in the Middle East have made it more so. The invasion of Iraq in 2003 by U.S.- and British-led coalition forces led to an almost immediate shutdown of Iraq's oil exports, thereby reducing the availability of crude oil by some 1.8. million barrels per day. Unrest in Nigeria, Africa's largest oil producer, further added to global scarcity. More than two years later, in part due to continued unrest in the Middle East, oil production was still sluggish. One result of the continued scarcity was a rise in energy prices. Increased energy prices in turn caused shipping costs to rise. The increased costs of shipping led shippers to seek more economical means of transport. Some shippers have decreased their use of planes and trucks. Instead, they have turned to less fuel-dependent modes of transport. One example is the use of double stacked railroad cars that can carry two shipping containers stacked one on top of the other.

Identify effects by looking for results or consequences. These are sometimes indicated by words such as *led to, brought about, thereby,* and *as a result.*

Look for cause-effect chains, where an effect may be the cause of another event and so on.

Diagram the causes and effects in a flowchart like this one.

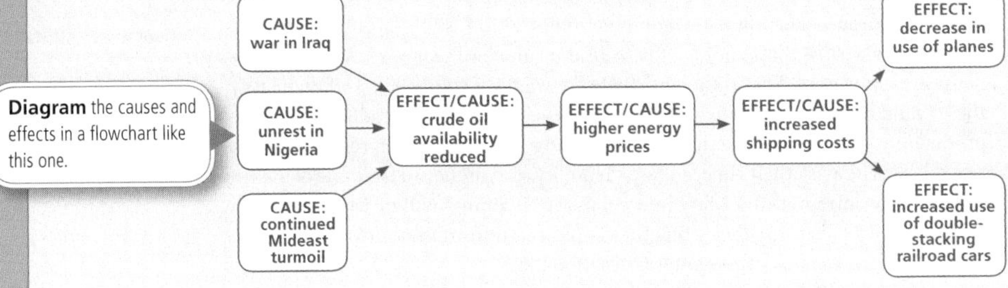

THINKING ECONOMICALLY **Analyzing Causes and Effects**

Locate and read an economics-related article in a current affairs magazine, such as *Time, Newsweek,* or *U.S. News & World Report.* Make a diagram to summarize the causes and effects discussed in the article.

DIFFERENTIATING INSTRUCTION

Struggling Readers

Use Signal Words

The skills instruction points out signal words for cause and effect, but students can improve their comprehension by using signal words of other types as well. Help students identify the transitional signal words in the passage that have not already been identified and explain their purpose. *(further—shows idea is being extended; more than two years later—shows passage of time; still—shows continuation of problem; in turn—shows chain of causes and effects; instead—shows contrast)*

Gifted and Talented

Write a Cause-and-Effect Analysis

Have students reflect on some of the economic choices that they have made in the past week by free writing about things they bought or decided not to buy. Then, have them use their notes to write a short essay explaining the causes behind their choices, as well as the effects of their choices on themselves, their family, and others. Have students read their essays to the class.

SECTION 1 Assessment

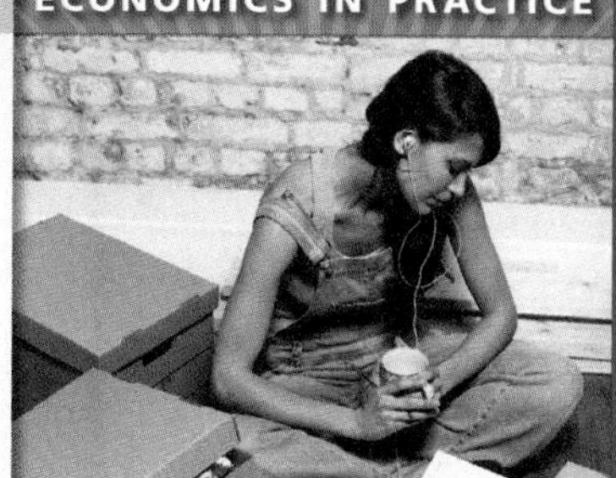

REVIEWING KEY CONCEPTS

1. Explain the relationship between the terms in each of these pairs:
   a. *wants* *scarcity* **b.** *consumer* *producer* **c.** *factors of production* *entrepreneurship*
2. What is the difference between needs and wants? Explain how a need may also be a want.
3. How does scarcity affect consumers? Producers?
4. What services that individuals or businesses provide do you use every day?
5. Describe how the owners of a computer repair store might use the four factors of production to run their business.
6. **Using Your Notes** How does scarcity affect methods of production? Refer to your completed cluster diagram.

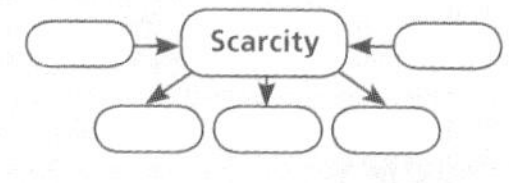

Use the Graphic Organizer at **Interactive Review @ ClassZone.com**

CRITICAL THINKING

7. **Drawing Conclusions** Many high schools throughout the United States have faced a serious shortage of math and science teachers. Many prospective teachers choose to go into business and industry because of higher salaries. In some communities, businesses are "loaning" employees who want to teach part-time to schools to fill the math and science teacher gap. Does this scenario illustrate scarcity? Why or why not?
8. **Applying Economic Concepts** Consider the following entrepreneurs: Lucy, who runs an organic farm, and Ron, a sports superstar who owns several restaurants. Describe how they may have used entrepreneurship to establish and run their businesses.
9. **Writing About Economics** Select a 10-minute period of time in your day-to-day life—when you are in the cafeteria at lunchtime, for example. Analyze how scarcity affects your activities during this time period. Write your analysis in a paragraph.
10. **Challenge** At one time or another, you have probably made a choice about how to use your scarce resources that you later regretted. For example, you may have purchased a music download instead of going to the movies. What led you to your choice? What did you learn later that might have led you to a different choice?

Online Quiz
ClassZone.com

ECONOMICS IN PRACTICE

Using Scarce Resources
Suppose you are moving into your first apartment like the young woman above. You have saved $1,200 to use for this purpose. When you go shopping, you learn that these are the prices for things you had on your list of furnishings.

Item	Price ($)
Kitchen table and chairs	200
TV set	150
Dishes	45
Silverware	25
Towels	35
Couch	300
Desk & chair	175
Bed	350
Computer	400
Stereo system	300

Make Economic Choices Use these prices to decide how you will spend your budget for furnishings. Make a list of the things you will buy.

Challenge What did you have to give up to get the things you chose? Why did you decide to give those things up?

4 Assess & Reteach

Assess Discuss the questions in Reviewing Key Concepts as a whole class activity. Ask for a volunteer to sketch his or her completed cluster diagram on the board. For the Critical Thinking questions, divide the class into four groups and let each group discuss one question and then report back to the class.

Unit 1 Resource Book
- Section Quiz, p. 9

Interactive Review @ ClassZone.com
- Section Quiz

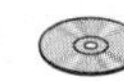

Test Generator CD-ROM
- Section Quiz

Reteach Point out that the first main heading of Section 1 is phrased as a question. Ask students to answer that question. Then model how to form a question about the material on page 5 by looking at the subheads (Principle 1, Principle 2) and relating them to the larger topic: What are two principles of scarcity? Then ask students to form questions from the remaining main headings in Section 1 and skim the text to answer them. *(What are the three economic questions? What are the factors of production?)*

Unit 1 Resource Book
- Reteaching Activity, p. 10

SECTION 1 ASSESSMENT ANSWERS

Reviewing Key Concepts

1. **a.** *wants*, p. 4; *scarcity*, p. 4
   b. *consumer*, p. 5; *producer*, p. 5
   c. *factors of production*, p. 8; *entrepreneurship*, p. 9
2. Wants are desires that can be satisfied by consuming a good or service; needs are necessary for survival. Food is a need, but you make choices about the food you eat.
3. Consumers: forces choices on what they are able to buy with their limited resources. Producers: influences which factors of production to use and in what amounts.
4. Answers will vary, but might include items from grocery store, services of teachers, public transportation, and so on.
5. Land: store occupies land; natural resources used to build stores and products. Labor: managers, sales people, delivery drivers, technicians. Capital: store, warehouses, delivery trucks. Entrepreneurship: ideas, energy, and effort that make the store a success.
6. See page 4 for an example of a completed cluster diagram. Scarcity determines what resources are available for production.

Critical Thinking

7. Students will note that this is an example of a shortage, because it is a temporary situation.
8. Answers will vary, but should show an understanding of the vision needed to succeed.
9. Answers will vary, but should show an understanding of the need to make choices.
10. Answers will vary, but should show knowledge of the factors that influence choices.

Economics in Practice

Make Economic Choices Lists will vary. Ensure that students' choices are realistic.

Challenge Answers will vary, but should demonstrate an understanding of the concept of scarcity.

1 Plan & Prepare

Section 1 Objectives

- understand why choice is at the heart of economics
- explain how incentives and utility influence people's economic choices
- consider the role of trade-offs and opportunity costs in making economic choices
- demonstrate how to do a cost-benefit analysis

2 Focus & Motivate

Connecting to Everyday Life Direct students to look at the photographs and discuss why they might be included in this section. For example, ask "What do soccer players winning a trophy have to do with economics?" *(They are representing one kind of motivation, with the trophy as an incentive.)* After reviewing all the photographs, ask students to indicate what factors influence economic choices in their lives.

Taking Notes Remind students to take notes as they read by completing a cluster diagram that helps them understand how the key concepts of the section relate to one another. They can use the Graphic Organizer at **Interactive Review @ ClassZone.com**. A sample is shown below.

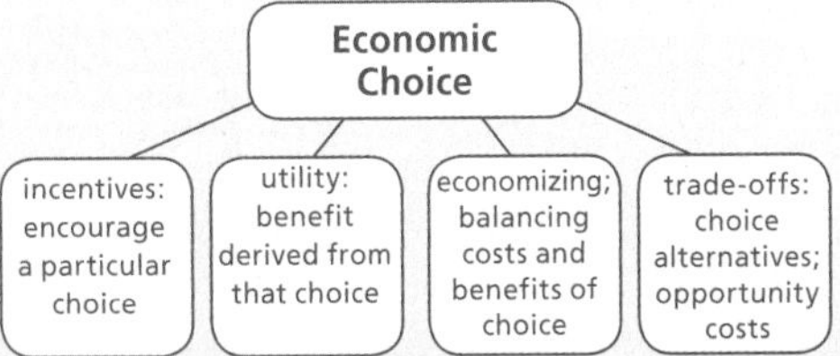

SECTION 2

Economic Choice Today: Opportunity Cost

OBJECTIVES

In Section 2, you will
- understand why choice is at the heart of economics
- explain how incentives and utility influence people's economic choices
- consider the role of trade-offs and opportunity costs in making economic choices
- demonstrate how to do a cost-benefit analysis

KEY TERMS

incentives, *p. 12*
utility, *p. 12*
economize, *p. 12*
trade-off, *p. 14*
opportunity cost, *p. 14*
cost-benefit analysis, *p. 15*
marginal cost, *p. 16*
marginal benefit, *p. 16*

TAKING NOTES

As you read Section 2, complete a cluster diagram to help you see how the key concepts relate to one another. Use the Graphic Organizer at **Interactive Review @ ClassZone.com**

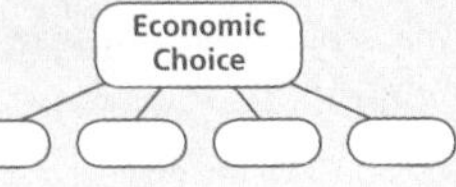

Making Choices

QUICK REFERENCE

Incentives are methods used to encourage people to take certain actions.

Utility is the benefit or satisfaction received from using a good or service.

To **economize** means to make decisions according to the best combination of costs and benefits.

KEY CONCEPTS

As you recall from Section 1, scarcity forces everyone to choose. But what shapes the economic choices that people make? One factor involves **incentives**, or benefits offered to encourage people to act in certain ways. Grades in school, wages paid to workers, and praise or recognition earned in personal and public life are all incentives. Choice is also influenced by **utility**, or the benefit or satisfaction gained from the use of a good or service. When they economize, people consider both incentives and utility. In common usage, the word *economize* means to "cut costs" or "do something cheaply." In strict economic terms, however, **economize** means to "make decisions according to what you believe is the best combination of costs and benefits."

Incentives The chance of winning a championship trophy serves as an incentive for athletes to train and play hard.

SECTION 2 PROGRAM RESOURCES

ON LEVEL

Lesson Plans
- Core, p. 2

Unit 1 Resource Book
- Reading Study Guide, pp. 11–12
- Economic Simulations, pp. 47–48
- Section Quiz, p. 19

STRUGGLING READERS

Unit 1 Resource Book
- Reading Study Guide with Additional Support, pp. 13–15
- Reteaching Activity, p. 20

ENGLISH LEARNERS

Unit 1 Resource Book
- Reading Study Guide with Additional Support (Spanish), pp. 16–18

INCLUSION

Lesson Plans
- Modified for Inclusion, p. 2

GIFTED AND TALENTED

NCEE Student Activities
- Scarcity, Opportunity Costs, and Production Possibilities Curves, pp. 1–4

TECHNOLOGY

eEdition DVD-ROM
eEdition Online
Power Presentation DVD-ROM
Economics Concepts Transparencies
- CT2 Analyzing Choices

Daily Test Practice Transparencies, TT2
ClassZone.com

YOUR ECONOMIC CHOICES

MAKING CHOICES

How will you spend time with a friend?

You and a friend have the choice of going to dinner or going to a movie. There is an incentive for choosing the movies, since dinner would surely cost more. On the other hand, your friend has offered to help you with college applications. So dining out, which allows time for conversation, has more utility to you than seeing a movie.

Dinner

Movie

FACTOR 1 Motivations for Choice

Choice powers an economy, but what powers choice? The choices people make are shaped by incentives, by expected utility, and by the desire to economize. For example, look at Your Economic Choices above. How will you decide between the two options? Like other economic decision makers, you weigh the costs against the benefits, and you make your choice purposefully. Perhaps you decide to go out to dinner. Even though you'll spend more money, you feel that the tips your friend can give you on writing your college application essay are invaluable. You've economized by choosing what represents the best mix of costs and benefits.

In making this decision, you were guided by self-interest. This does not mean that you behaved selfishly. Rather, it simply means that you looked for ways to maximize the utility you'd get from spending time with your friend.

FACTOR 2 No Free Lunch

An old saying can sum up the issue of choice in economics: "There is no such thing as a free lunch." Every choice involves costs. These costs can take the form of money, time, or some other thing you value. Let's revisit your choices. If you chose to go to dinner rather than to a movie, you gained the benefit of a satisfying, informative, and beneficial conversation with a friend. Even so, you also paid a cost—you didn't see the movie. On the other hand, if you chose to go to the movie, you gained the benefit of an entertaining evening and having more money to save or spend on something else. Once again, however, your choice involved a cost. You sacrificed the time you could have spent getting advice and guidance on the college application process from your friend.

APPLICATION Using a Decision-Making Process

A. You have enough money to buy either an MP3 player that is on sale or some fitness equipment you want. What incentives and utility would guide your decision?

See answer in Teacher's Edition. ▶

❸ Teach

Making Choices

Discuss

- What is the difference between self-interest and selfishness? *(Selfishness is a degree of self-interest usually thought to be excessive and unhealthy—putting one's self-interest ahead of other reasonable concerns. Economic behavior is often said to be governed by rational self-interest.)*

Your Economic Choices

MAKING CHOICES

How will you spend time with a friend?

Share this quote from television personality Oprah Winfrey: "It's much easier for me to make major life, multi-million dollar decisions, than it is to decide on a carpet for my front porch." Ask students: What makes some decisions easy and some more difficult? *(Decisions are more difficult when costs and benefits are roughly equal or if they are grounded more in taste or emotions.)*

Activity Ask students to create a scenario for each photo that requires the subjects to make choices that lead to the scenes pictured.

APPLICATION

Answer *Answers will vary. Most students will mention the sale price of the MP3 as an incentive and the entertainment value and the health benefits of the exercise equipment as utility.*

SMALL GROUP ACTIVITY

Playing the Economic "Ultimatum Game"

Time 15 Minutes

Task Play the economic "ultimatum game" in pairs.

Materials Needed none

Activity

- Divide students in pairs, designating one person to be Player A and the other Player B. Tell students to imagine they have been given $10. Player A has the right to make an offer about a way to split the money. If Player B accepts the offer, both players get to keep the money. If the offer is rejected, they get nothing. Give the pairs 5 minutes to play.
- Have each group report the result of their "negotiations" to the class. Tell them to relate the results to the material on pages 12 and 13.
- As a class, discuss the roles of reason and emotion in the various outcomes. Point out that if rational self-interest were the sole force behind this economic decision, Player A would be smart to offer Player B a minimum of $1, and Player B would be smart to accept it, since $1 is better than nothing.

Rubric

	Understanding of Concepts	Presentation of Information
4	excellent	clear and complete
3	good	mostly clear
2	fair	sometimes clear
1	poor	unclear

Trade-Offs and Opportunity Cost

Discuss

- What is the difference between a trade-off and an opportunity cost? *(A trade-off is a bypassed alternative; an opportunity cost is a value associated with that alternative.)* Ask students to provide examples based on Shanti and Dan. *(Possible answer: The trade-off in Shanti's case is the course she could have taken at the university. The opportunity cost is the extra credits she could have received.)*
- What trade-offs might students be weighing as they think about their life beyond high school? *(Possible answer: earning money right away vs. going on to college or vocational training; taking time off vs. actively pursuing employment or schooling)*

Economics Illustrated

Point out to students that making a choice and accepting trade-offs is like choosing the scenic route or the highway when you're on a car trip. When you take the scenic route, you get the advantage of seeing forests, mountains, and maybe even some wildlife. However, it takes much longer to get to your destination. The highway takes you directly to your destination quickly, but all you'll see along the way is concrete and other cars. This example also illustrates that the choice is not all or nothing; both routes get you to the final destination.

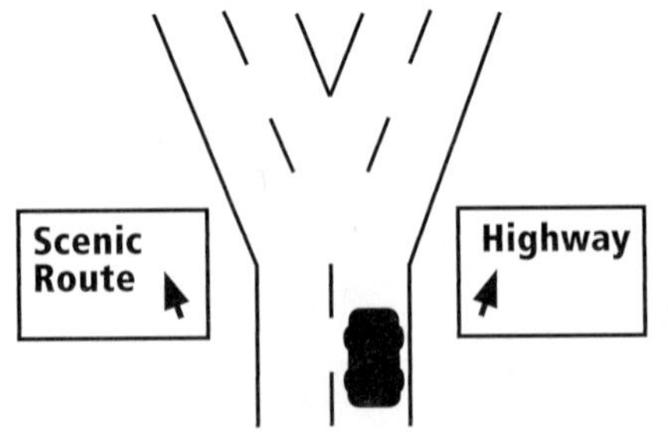

Trade-Offs and Opportunity Cost

KEY CONCEPTS

QUICK REFERENCE

A **trade-off** is the alternative people give up when they make choices.

Choices, as you have learned, always involve costs. For every choice you make, you give up something. The alternative that you give up when you make an economic choice is called a **trade-off**. Usually, trade-offs do not require all-or-nothing choices. Rather, they involve giving up some of one thing to gain more of another.

EXAMPLE 1 Making Trade-Offs

To understand how trade-offs work, let's take a look at decisions made by Shanti, who has just finished her junior year in high school. Shanti wants to go to summer school to earn some credits she can apply to college. She could take a semester-long course at a local university, or she could take an intensive six-week course at her high school. She decides on the six-week course, even though she'll earn fewer credits. However, she will have several weeks of the summer vacation to have fun and relax.

Trade-Offs All the decisions you make, including selecting school or college courses, involve choosing among alternatives.

EXAMPLE 2 Counting the Opportunity Cost

Shanti's friend Dan, who has just graduated, has decided to take off a year before going to college. He's been offered a full-time job for the whole year. However, he decides to take the job for six months and then spend time traveling.

QUICK REFERENCE

Opportunity cost is the value of something that is given up to get something else that is wanted.

Dan's choice, like all economic choices, involves an opportunity cost. The **opportunity cost** of a decision is the value of the next-best alternative, or what you give up by choosing one alternative over another. Dan decided to travel around the country and visit friends. The opportunity cost of that decision is the income he could have earned at his job. If, however, Dan had decided to work for the whole year, his opportunity cost would have been the trip around the country that he didn't take. Note that Dan's opportunity cost is not the value of all the things he might have done. Rather, it is the value of his next-best alternative, or what he gave up to get what he most wanted.

APPLICATION Applying Economic Concepts

B. Look again at Shanti's decision. What was the opportunity cost of her choice? If she had chosen the semester course, what would her opportunity cost have been?
more credits to apply to college; several weeks of fun and relaxation

DIFFERENTIATING INSTRUCTION

Struggling Readers

Find Main Ideas
Direct students to preview pages 14 and 15. Remind students of the relationship between main ideas and examples *(examples support the main idea).* Help students use the headings to identify trade-offs and opportunity costs as the main ideas. Then have students make a two-column chart to show the relationship between these ideas and the examples. Main ideas, and the way examples relate to them, should be written in complete sentences.

English Learners

Personal Dictionary: Hyphenated Words
Have students set aside a portion of a notebook or binder as a personal dictionary. They can make their first entries by locating words on pages 14–15 that are hyphenated *(trade-off, semester-long, six-week, full-time, next-best, cost-benefit, decision-making)* and then adding them to their dictionary. Point out that one use of a hyphen is to join two words that serve as a single adjective before a noun, as in *cost-benefit analysis* or *full-time work*.

Analyzing Choices

KEY CONCEPTS

Shanti and Dan did not make their choices randomly. Rather, they carefully looked at the benefits they would gain and the opportunity costs they would incur from their decisions. This practice of examining the costs and the expected benefits of a choice as an aid to decision making is called **cost-benefit analysis**. Cost-benefit analysis is one of the most useful tools for individuals, businesses, and governments when they need to evaluate the relative worth of economic choices.

QUICK REFERENCE

Cost-benefit analysis is an approach that weighs the benefits of an action against its costs.

EXAMPLE Max's Decision-Making Grid

Perhaps the simplest application of cost-benefit analysis is the decision-making grid, which shows what you get and what you give up when you make choices. Look at Max's decision-making grid in Figure 1.2 below. Max has to decide how to spend his scarce time—studying for his government class or going out with his friends. Max likes nothing better than to spend hours talking with his friends at the local juice bar. However, the F he has in the government class at the moment will not look good on his transcript. So he certainly could benefit from some extra study time.

Max knows that he has six hours available for extra study or socializing each week. He begins to build his decision-making grid by listing all the options he has for using these six hours. He then lists the benefits and opportunity costs of each of these options. After reviewing all of this information, he chooses three extra hours of study a week. He feels that the opportunity cost, three hours of time with his friends, is worth the expected benefit, a B grade.

FIGURE 1.2 Max's Decision-Making Grid

A decision-making grid helps you to see what you gain and what you lose when you make choices. Max's decision-making grid shows the costs and benefits of hours spent studying versus time spent socializing.

Choice	Benefit	Opportunity Cost
One hour of extra study	D in government class	One hour with friends
Two hours of extra study	C in government class	Two hours with friends
Three hours of extra study	B in government class	Three hours with friends
Four hours of extra study	B+ in government class	Four hours with friends
Five hours of extra study	A– in government class	Five hours with friends
Six hours of extra study	A in government class	Six hours with friends

ANALYZE TABLES

1. What is Max's opportunity cost of three extra hours of study?
2. Read the information about marginal costs on the next page. What is Max's marginal cost of moving from a grade of B+ to a grade of A–?

Analyzing Choices

Discuss

- What examples from their own lives can students think of to demonstrate a decision-making process like Max's? *(Possible answer: saving or spending their money—for every dollar saved, they are that much closer to buying what they want, but they have to give up a number of smaller things along the way)*
- What local, state, or federal government policies are generating current debate? Ask students to consider how policy makers decide among alternative solutions to problems. You may wish to tell students that one rule for policy decisions is that a change must make at least one person better off and also leave no one worse off. Ask students to discuss how realistic a goal this may be. *(Answers will vary but students may argue that there are always some negative trade-offs—encourage them to give examples.)*

Analyzing Grids: Figure 1.2

Point out that this is an example of an economic model, which students will learn more about later in this chapter. Economic models simplify the issues at hand, often by reducing the terms to only two variables (here, studying and spending time with friends), in order to see key relationships.

Answers

1. *three hours with friends*
2. *one hour with friends*

CLASS ACTIVITY

Creating a Decision-Making Grid

Time 30–45 Minutes 

Task Create an alternate decision-making grid to Max's grid

Materials Needed paper, pens or pencils

Activity

- On the board, draw a blank chart with five rows and five columns. Explain that the items in rows two to five will be the choices, such as the classes to take next semester (*Spanish, Astronomy, British Literature,* and *Improv Theater,* for example). The items that head columns two to five will be the criteria (here, these might be: *required, interesting, good teacher,* and *friends taking it.*) The first row/column should be blank.
- Discuss how the criteria are considered for each choice and then mark with a plus sign (+), minus sign (–), or 0 for neutral. Show students how to use the grid to make trade-offs.
- Direct students to make their own grids using the same pattern. When everyone is done, have students explain their grids.
- Evaluate the grids' usefulness in seeing trade-offs and opportunity costs.

Rubric

	Understanding of Concepts	Presentation of Information
4	excellent	thoughtful and complete
3	good	mostly complete
2	fair	missing a key element but a good effort
1	poor	missing several key elements

Your Economic Choices

MARGINAL BENEFITS AND COSTS

Which will you do—basketball practice or after-school job?
You may wish to have a class discussion before students begin to make their own grids to find a way to quantify the choices, as they are quantified in Max's decision-making grid on page 15. Ask for suggestions on how this might be done. *(The middle column might be amount of money earned, for example, based on an hourly wage.)*

Activity As a follow-up to their grids, ask students to write a paragraph identifying the marginal benefit and marginal cost of one of the decisions they might have made. *(Look for an understanding of the marginal cost or benefit—the value of one more unit of time or money.)*

Technomics

Cost-Benefit Analysis Tools
How does the National Aeronautics and Space Administration justify a budget request for new space programs? How does the National Institutes of Health decide whether or not to upgrade its computer system? They follow Circular # A-94, which provides guidelines from the government Office of Management and Budget on preparing a cost-benefit analysis using accepted procedures and models. In the private sector, a number of software tools are available for this purpose, most of them using a spreadsheet application to demonstrate marginal costs and benefits.

Costs and benefits change over time. So do goals and circumstances. Such changes will influence the decisions people make. For instance, Max learns that Pine Tree State, the college he wants to attend, only considers applicants with a 3.4 or better grade point average. If he needs to get a B+ or better to raise his GPA to 3.4, he might decide to spend less time with his friends and study four or five hours per week rather than three.

EXAMPLE Marginal Costs and Benefits

QUICK REFERENCE

Marginal cost is the additional cost of using one more unit of a product.

Marginal benefit is the additional satisfaction from using one more unit of a product.

How did Max arrive at his decision? To explain it, economists would look at marginal costs and marginal benefits. **Marginal cost** is the cost of using one more unit of a good or service, while **marginal benefit** refers to the benefit or satisfaction received from using one more unit of a good or service. Max's choice was to study three extra hours, which gave him a B grade at the opportunity cost of three hours with his friends. Look again at Max's decision-making grid in Figure 1.2. What would be the marginal cost of one more hour of study? As you can see, it is the loss of one more hour with his friends. The marginal benefit of that extra hour would be an improvement in grade from B to B+. Max decided that the benefit of a slight improvement in his grade was not worth the cost of one less hour with his friends.

The analysis of marginal costs and marginal benefits is central to the study of economics. It helps to explain the decisions consumers, producers, and governments make as they try to meet their unlimited wants with limited resources.

YOUR ECONOMIC CHOICES

MARGINAL BENEFITS AND COSTS

Which will you do—basketball practice or after-school job?

For every hour you practice basketball, you gain in skill and increase your chances of making the team. However, each hour you practice is an hour you could have spent working at an after-school job to save for a car or college or something else you want.

Basketball practice

Part-time job

APPLICATION Using a Decision-Making Process

C. Look at Your Economic Choices above. Construct a decision-making grid that analyzes the potential choices of attending basketball practice and working at an after-school job. Which option would you choose?
Decision grids will vary; suggest that students study Figure 1.2 on page 15 before undertaking this activity.

DIFFERENTIATING INSTRUCTION

Inclusion

Relate to Personal Experience
Have students think of examples in their own lives of how costs and benefits of a certain choice have changed over time. For example, when they were younger, if given the choice between spending and saving money they received as a birthday gift, they might have chosen to spend it. Now, as they are approaching independent living, they might see more immediate utility for saving it.

Gifted and Talented

Do a Cost-Benefit Analysis
Have students find an example of a cost-benefit analysis online and use it as a rough guide to do their own detailed (and somewhat tongue-in-cheek) analysis. Instead of considering something complex, however, have them apply the detailed "overkill" approach to a very simple economic decision, such as "Which size popcorn should I buy at the movies?" Be sure they focus on the issues at the margin.

SECTION 2 Assessment

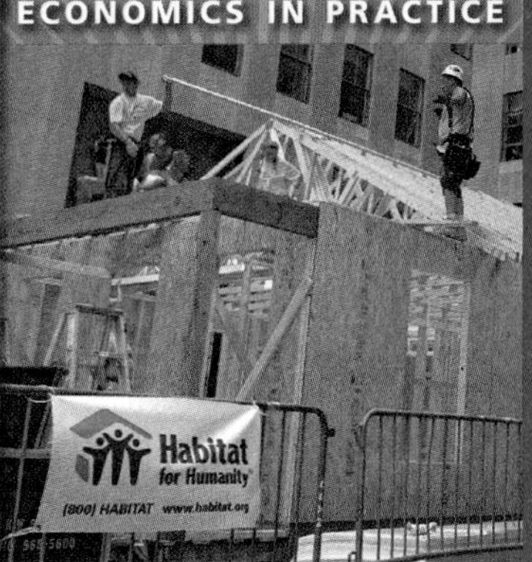

REVIEWING KEY CONCEPTS

1. Explain the relationship between the terms in each of these pairs:
   a. *incentive* *utility*
   b. *trade-off* *opportunity cost*
   c. *marginal cost* *marginal benefit*
2. Two action movies are playing at your movie-theater complex. You have a half-price coupon for one. However, you choose to see the other. How might this still be an example of economizing?
3. Think of some of the options you have for spending time after school—sports practice, hobby clubs, work, or extra study, for example. Which option would you choose? What is the opportunity cost of your choice?
4. How is a decision-making grid an example of cost-benefit analysis?
5. Use the concepts of marginal costs and marginal benefits to explain why some people might see the same movie ten times while others will watch it only once or twice.
6. **Using Your Notes** How do marginal costs and benefits relate to trade-offs? Refer to your completed cluster diagram. Use the Graphic Organizer at **Interactive Review @ ClassZone.com**

CRITICAL THINKING

7. **Applying Economic Concepts** A Web site reviewing new CDs offers you a free subscription. All you have to do is complete a brief online application. What is the opportunity cost of this "free" offer? Why do you think the offer is being made?
8. **Evaluating Economic Decisions** Explain how self-interest is part of each economic choice. Use an example from your own experience that shows how you purposely served your own self-interest in a choice you made.
9. **Conducting Marginal Cost–Marginal Benefit Analysis** You are on a limited budget and planning a four-day camping trip to a national park. Bus fare is $75 each way and the ride takes 12 hours. Plane fare is $150 each way and the ride takes an hour and a half. Conduct a cost-benefit analysis to help you choose your method of travel.
10. **Challenge** Why are all choices economic choices? Illustrate your answer with examples.

ECONOMICS IN PRACTICE

Making Choices
Some of the incentives that spur people to action are money, recognition, self-esteem, good grades, immediate benefit, future benefit, and altruism (doing good for others, such as working for Habitat for Humanity).

Consider Economic Choices Copy and complete the chart by noting the incentives that might motivate people to take the listed actions. (Several incentives might apply in some cases.)

Action	Incentive
Donate to charity.	
Get a promotion.	
Buy a friend a present.	
Attend a good college.	
Buy organic foods.	
Buy inexpensive imported goods.	

Challenge Have you ever had two or more conflicting incentives for a certain behavior? If so, how would you choose among them? If not, which of the incentives above motivates you most often?

4 Assess & Reteach

Assess Divide students into six groups to answer the Reviewing Key Concepts questions, and have each group choose one member to present the answers to the rest of the class. When the class comes together again, have one group present their answer to the first question, another group their answer to the second question, and so on. Discuss the Critical Thinking questions as a class.

Unit 1 Resource Book
- Section Quiz, p. 15

Interactive Review @ ClassZone.com
- Section Quiz

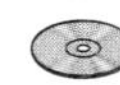

Test Generator CD-ROM
- Section Quiz

Reteach Review each main part of Section 2 with the class, focusing on tying the material to the fundamental concept of scarcity. For example, in the first part, you may want to ask: "What does making choices have to do with scarcity?" *(Because we have limited resources but unlimited wants, we always have to choose how to use the resources.)* Continue framing questions that tie the material to scarcity: "How does the idea of no free lunch relate to scarcity?" "How do trade-offs and opportunity costs relate to scarcity?" "How do marginal costs and benefits relate to scarcity?"

Unit 1 Resource Book
- Reteaching Activity, p. 16

SECTION 2 ASSESSMENT ANSWERS

Reviewing Key Concepts

1. **a.** *incentive*, p. 12; *utility*, p. 12
   b. *trade-off*, p. 14; *opportunity cost*, p. 14
   c. *marginal cost*, p. 16; *marginal benefit*, p. 16
2. The utility, or the benefit you receive, from seeing the other movie may outweigh the incentive of the half-price coupon.
3. Answers will vary, but the opportunity cost should be expressed as the value of the next best alternative to the choice made.
4. The decision-making grid evaluates the relative worth of choices by examining the costs and expected benefits of those choices.
5. For the person who sees the movie ten times, the marginal benefit (the satisfaction received from one more viewing of the movie) continues to be greater than the marginal cost (the cost of seeing the movie one more time) for several viewings.
6. See page 12 for an example of a completed cluster diagram. Marginal costs and benefits help to explain the trade-offs people make.

Critical Thinking

7. The cost is the time you might have spent doing something else of importance to you. The company sees a possible benefit—that you will continue to renew your subscription—greater than the cost of the initial free subscription.
8. Answers will vary, but should show an understanding of self-interest as a rational part of economic decision-making.
9. Answers will vary, but should show that traveling by plane is more expensive but a savings in terms of the vacation time gained.
10. Answers will vary, but should note that all choices have opportunity costs.

Economics in Practice

Consider Economic Choices Students' incentives will vary.

Challenge Answers will vary, but students who have experienced conflicting incentives might suggest that utility—the satisfaction gained from an action—might help to decide their behavior.

1 Plan & Prepare

Section 3 Objectives

- describe what a production possibilities curve is and how it is constructed
- explain what economists learn from using production possibilities curves
- analyze how production possibilities curves show economic growth

2 Focus & Motivate

Connecting to Everyday Life Ask students to discuss their extracurricular activities and to describe a typical week in their life. As students respond, note examples of days where not much is happening for the student, as well as days that seem especially full. Have students consider what would occur if all days were like their busiest. Would they be able to add more activities that interested them? Point out that sooner or later they would reach a point where there would be no more time for additional activities. Point out that businesses and economies, just like people, can reach a limit on what they can produce.

Taking Notes Remind students to take notes while they read by completing a summary chart on production possibilities. They can use the Graphic Organizer at **Interactive Review @ ClassZone.com.** A sample is shown below.

Analyzing Production Possibilities	
PPC	shows impact of scarcity
What we learn from the PPC	efficiency, underutilization, increasing opportunity costs
Shifts in the PPC	More resources, technology shifts frontier outward = economic growth

SECTION **3**

Analyzing Production Possibilities

OBJECTIVES

In Section 3, you will
- describe what a production possibilities curve is and how it is constructed
- explain what economists learn from using production possibilities curves
- analyze how production possibilities curves show economic growth

KEY TERMS

economic model, *p. 18*
production possibilities curve (PPC), *p. 18*
efficiency, *p. 20*
underutilization, *p. 20*
law of increasing opportunity costs, *p. 21*

TAKING NOTES

As you read Section 4, complete a summary chart to identify the most important points on production possibilities. Use the Graphic Organizer at **Interactive Review @ ClassZone.com**

Analyzing Production Possibilities	
PPC	shows impact of scarcity

Graphing the Possibilities

QUICK REFERENCE

An **economic model** is a simplified representation of economic forces.

The **production possibilities curve (PPC)** is a graph used by economists to show the impact of scarcity on an economy.

KEY CONCEPTS

In Section 2 you learned that all economic choices involve trade-offs. Economists have created **economic models**—simplified representations of complex economic activities, systems, or problems—to clarify trade-offs. One such model is a **production possibilities curve (PPC)**, a graph used to illustrate the impact of scarcity on an economy by showing the maximum number of goods or services that can be produced using limited resources.

Like all other economic models, the PPC is based on assumptions that simplify the economic interactions. For the PPC these assumptions are:

1. **Resources are fixed.** There is no way to increase the availability of land, labor, capital, and entrepreneurship.
2. **All resources are fully employed.** There is no waste of any of the factors of production. In other words, the economy is running at full production.
3. **Only two things can be produced.** This assumption simplifies the situation and suits the graphic format, with one variable on each axis.
4. **Technology is fixed.** There are no technological breakthroughs to improve methods of production.

Since the curve on a PPC represents the border—or frontier—between what it is possible to produce and what it is not possible to produce, this model is sometimes called a production possibilities frontier. It is a useful tool for businesses and even governments, but it works just as well with individual, small-scale economic decisions. For example, suppose you are preparing food for a soup kitchen and have the ingredients to make 12 loaves of whole wheat bread or 100 bran muffins or some combination of the two. A PPC can help you decide what to make.

SECTION 3 PROGRAM RESOURCES

ON LEVEL

Lesson Plans
- Core, p. 3

Unit 1 Resource Book
- Reading Study Guide, pp. 23–25
- Math Skills Worksheet, p. 49
- Section Quiz, p. 29

STRUGGLING READERS

Unit 1 Resource Book
- Reading Study Guide with Additional Support, pp. 23–25
- Reteaching Activity, p. 30

ENGLISH LEARNERS

Unit 1 Resource Book
- Reading Study Guide with Additional Support (Spanish), pp. 26–28

INCLUSION

Lesson Plans
- Modified for Inclusion, p. 3

GIFTED AND TALENTED

Unit 1 Resource Book

NCEE Student Activities
- Scarcity, Opportunity Cost, and Production Possibilities Curves, pp. 1–4

TECHNOLOGY

eEdition DVD-ROM

eEdition Online

Power Presentation DVD-ROM

Economics Concepts Transparencies
- CT3 Production Possibilities Table and Curve

Daily Test Practice Transparencies, TT3

ClassZone.com

Production Possibilities Curve

The production possibilities table in Figure 1.3 below shows five production possibilities for loaves of bread and bran muffins. These production possibilities run from the two extremes of all bread or all muffins through several combinations of the two products. The data in the table also can be plotted on a graph, as in Figure 1.4. The line joining the plotted points is the production possibilities curve. Each point on the curve represents the maximum number of loaves of bread that can be produced relative to the number of bran muffins that are produced.

Further, the PPC shows the opportunity cost of each choice in a visual way. Trace the curve from left to right with your finger. Notice that as you move along the curve you make fewer loaves of bread and more muffins. The opportunity cost of making more muffins is the bread that cannot be made.

Production Possibilities A production possibilities curve can show all the possible combinations for producing muffins and bread.

FIGURE 1.3 PRODUCTION POSSIBILITIES TABLE: BREAD vs. MUFFINS

	Loaves of Bread	Bran Muffins
a→	12	0
	10	35
b→	7	63
	4	84
c→	0	100

FIGURE 1.4 PRODUCTION POSSIBILITIES CURVE: BREAD vs. MUFFINS

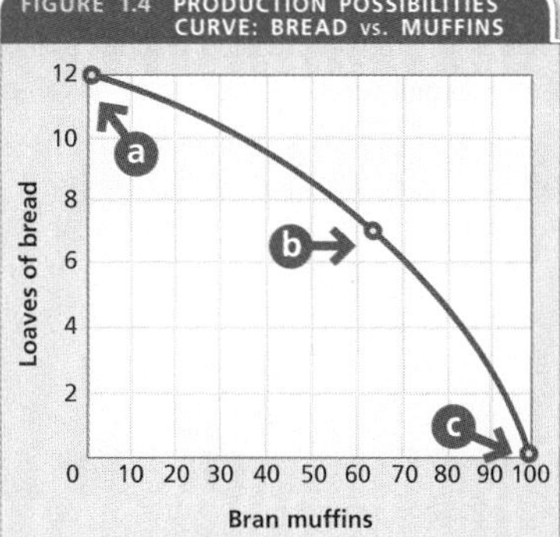

a Here you are using all the ingredients to make only bread.

b This point shows a combination of 7 loaves of bread and 63 muffins. The opportunity cost of making the 7 loaves is 37 muffins (100 – 63).

c At this point, you are making all muffins and no bread.

ANALYZE GRAPHS

1. If you decided to make ten loaves of bread, how many bran muffins could you make?
2. What is the opportunity cost of making the ten loaves of bread?

Animated Economics

Use an interactive production possibilities curve at **ClassZone.com**

APPLICATION Interpreting Graphs

A. Look at the production possibilities curve in Figure 1.4. What is the opportunity cost of increasing bread production from four loaves to seven loaves?

21 muffins (84 – 63=21)

DIFFERENTIATING INSTRUCTION

Inclusion

Use Manipulatives

Display the following information in production possibilities table:

Paper clips : rubber bands—10:0, 8:7, 6:13, 4:16, 2:18, 0:20

Place ten paper clips on a desk. Then place seven rubber bands on the desk and call on a student to remove the appropriate number of clips to meet production possibilities. Repeat the process to the end of the table, noting the opportunity cost in terms of paper clips for each new batch of rubber bands.

Gifted and Talented

Use Math Skills

Have students use the production possibilities table at the left to make a production possibilities curve. Have them label each point on the curve A-F. Then have them use the formula Slope = rise/run to find the slope between points C and D.

(Rise is the change in the value measured on the vertical axis. Run is the change in value measured on the horizontal axis. The change in value on the vertical axis between C and D is –2. The change in value on the horizontal axis is 3. –2/3= –0.666.)

3 Teach

Graphing the Possibilities

Discuss

- In what ways might the production possibilities curve be unrealistic? *(in all of the four ways that the assumptions are made: fixed resources, fully employed resources, two products only, and fixed technology)*
- How does the PPC relate to scarcity? *(Possible answer: The fixed resources highlight the fundamental problem of scarcity—that there are only so many productive resources available. As a result, you cannot make more of one thing without shifting the use of those resources from another.)*

Analyzing Tables and Graphs: Figures 1.3 and 1.4

Since this is the first graph of its kind, ask for volunteers to explain how it is constructed. You may want specifically to ask: What is the vertical axis? *(the number of loaves of bread along the vertical line)* What is the horizontal axis? *(the number of bran muffins along the horizontal line)* How is the curve plotted from the information in the table? *(The points are plotted as on a grid, first by locating the position of the value on the vertical axis and then, by moving to the right as needed until aligned with the correct value on the horizontal axis.)*

Answers

1. *35 bran muffins*
2. *65 bran muffins*

Animated Economics The production possibilities curve highlights the trade-offs in making loaves of bread or making muffins. It will help the students to see clearly the opportunity costs of each production decision. Also, it will reinforce an understanding of scarcity.

What We Learn from PPCs

Discuss

- What does a point's position in relation to the curve tell us about that level of production? *(To left of the curve, productive resources are underutilized; on the curve, productive resources are used with efficiency; right of the curve, the level of production is impossible, exceeding productive resource capacity.)*
- Why is the PPC bow-shaped? *(because each additional unit costs more to make than the last)*

Analyzing Graphs: Figure 1.5

Draw the PPC in Figure 1.5 on the board. Ask for a volunteer to come to the board. Then, have the volunteer randomly point to various spots on the graph—on the curve, inside the curve, and outside of the curve—while the class identifies whether they represent efficiency, underutilization, or impossibility. For each answer, ask for a volunteer to explain why.

Answers

1. *between 40 and 50 million guns*
2. *Possible responses: workers lack skills, factories and machinery outdated and inefficient*

Animated Economics The animation helps students read a production possibilities curve. Also, it highlights how PPCs show trade-offs involved in making economic choices.

What We Learn from PPCs

QUICK REFERENCE

Efficiency involves producing the maximum amount of goods and services possible.

Underutilization means producing fewer goods and services than possible.

KEY CONCEPTS

No economy actually operates according to the simplified assumptions underlying the PPC. However, economists use the simplified model because it spotlights concepts that work in the real world of scarce resources.

One important concept revealed in a PPC is **efficiency**, the condition in which economic resources are being used to produce the maximum amount of goods and services. Another is **underutilization**, the condition in which economic resources are not being used to their full potential. As a result, fewer goods and services are being produced than the economy is capable of making. Both of these conditions are easy to see in the PPC.

EXAMPLE Efficiency and Underutilization

Figure 1.5 shows the classic production possibilities model of guns vs. butter. In this model, "guns" is shorthand for military spending and "butter" represents consumer products. Every point along this PPC shows a different combination of military and consumer production. Regardless of the combination, each point represents efficiency, the most that can be produced with the available resources.

Any point inside the curve represents underutilization, or the inefficient use of available resources. Look again at Figure 1.5 and notice that point **3** indicates that all resources are not fully employed. The PPC shows that the economy is capable of producing either 47 million more guns (point **1** on the curve) or 30 million more pounds of butter (point

FIGURE 1.5 PPC: GUNS vs. BUTTER

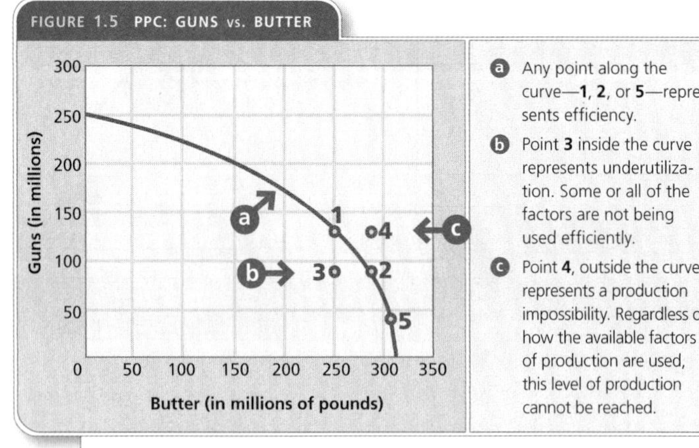

Guns (in millions)
300
250
200
150
100
50
0
50
100
150
200
250
300
350
Butter (in millions of pounds)
1
2
3
4
5
a
b
c
a Any point along the curve—1, 2, or 5—represents efficiency.
b Point 3 inside the curve represents underutilization. Some or all of the factors are not being used efficiently.
c Point 4, outside the curve, represents a production impossibility. Regardless of how the available factors of production are used, this level of production cannot be reached.

ANALYZE GRAPHS

1. What is the opportunity cost of moving butter production from **1** to **2**?
2. At **3**, factors of production are not being used efficiently. Identify a situation where this might occur.

Animated Economics

Use an interactive production possibilities curve at **ClassZone.com**

SMALL GROUP ACTIVITY

Creating a PPC

Time 30 Minutes

Task Create a PPC

Materials Needed paper and pens or pencils

Activity

- Divide the class into four or five groups.
- Tell students in each group that they are a small country that can make only two products and they must decide what to make and how many of each. Resources are fixed, technology is fixed, and all resources are fully utilized. Tell students they can be creative in their choice of products.
- Have each group create a PPC for their two products. Tell them they can make up the numbers but that the PPC has to have the characteristic slope, so they will need to manipulate the numbers. Instruct them to use the model in Figure 1.4 on page 19 as a rough guide.
- Have each group present and explain their PPC. Tell them to hold onto their PPCs for future use.

Rubric

	Understanding of Concepts	Presentation of Information
4	excellent	Clear and complete
3	good	Mostly clear
2	fair	Sometimes clear
1	poor	Unclear

2 on the curve). Any point outside the curve is impossible to meet because resources are fixed. To produce the number of guns indicated at point **4**, fewer pounds of butter would have to be made (point **1** on the curve). Similarly, to produce the amount of butter indicated at point **4**, fewer guns would have to be made (point **2** on the curve).

The shape of the PPC shows a third important economic concept. This is the **law of increasing opportunity costs**, which states that as production switches from one product to another, increasingly more resources are needed to increase the production of the second product, which causes opportunity costs to rise.

QUICK REFERENCE

The **law of increasing opportunity costs** states that as production switches from one product to another, increasing amounts of resources are needed to increase the production of the second product.

EXAMPLE Increasing Opportunity Costs

Return again to Figure 1.5. A nation makes 250 million pounds of butter (point **1** on the curve), but wants to make 280 million pounds (point **2** on the curve). The opportunity cost of making the extra 30 million pounds of butter is 37 million guns. That works out to a cost of about 1.2 guns for every pound of butter. If the nation increases its output of butter to 312 million pounds (point **5** on the curve), the opportunity cost of the change would be 63 millions guns, nearly 2 guns for every pound of butter. This increase in the opportunity cost—each additional unit costs more to make than the last—explains why the curve is bow-shaped.

Opportunity Cost In the guns vs. butter equation, if more resources are used to make military products, such as stealth bombers, there are fewer resources available for other things, such as butter and other consumer goods. The opportunity cost of making more military products is the other products that cannot be made.

The reason for the increasing costs is fairly straightforward. Making butter involves different resources than making guns. Converting from gun production to butter production is not a simple procedure. New machinery must be produced, new factories must be built, and workers must be retrained. The cost of all these actions will be fewer and fewer guns.

APPLICATION Writing about Economics

B. Write a brief paragraph explaining the concepts a PPC shows graphically.
See answer in Teacher's Edition. ▶

DIFFERENTIATING INSTRUCTION

Inclusion

Extend an Activity
Reintroduce the production possibilities table you created for the activity on page 19. Help students create a PPC for this table on a large sheet of butcher paper. Give students small post-it notes. Ask them to place the notes anywhere on the chart and explain their placement in terms of efficiency, underutilization, or impossibility. Hold onto the PPC for future use.

English Learners

Use Economic Terms in Writing
Customize students' task for the Application above. Tell them to include the following terms in their paragraph: efficiency, underutilization, inefficiency, and opportunity costs. After each word, have them write a definition in simple language. *(Possible answers: efficiency—putting everything to use; underutilization—not using some things; inefficiency (same); opportunity costs—what has to be given up to get something)*

More About . . .

Guns vs. Butter
"Guns vs. butter" was a major issue during the presidency of Lyndon B. Johnson in the 1960s. Johnson's "Great Society" program called for a "war on poverty," which required government funding of many social reforms. But an expanding war in Vietnam saw these government funds being switching from domestic programs, the so-called "butter," to defense spending, or the "guns." The opportunity cost of increasing defense production was that the social programs could not be funded.

International Economics

Guns vs. Butter in North Korea
Following World War II, North Korea came under communist control. The North Korean government made a decision to reallocate resources to strengthen its military, literally choosing guns over butter. By the late 1990s, millions of Koreans were dying of hunger because so many resources had been taken away from the production of necessities, such as food. See page 45 for more information.

APPLICATION
Answer *Answers should discuss efficiency, underutilization, and increasing opportunity costs.*

Changing Production Possibilities

Discuss

- What might cause production possibilities to change? *(Additional resources could make it possible to attain new production possibilities beyond the original frontier.)*
- What developments caused the PPC for the United States to shift outward? *(Additional land brought an abundance of natural resources; immigration added huge numbers of workers; and new technology made land, labor, and capital more efficient.)*

Analyzing Graphs: Figure 1.6

Ask the class to give examples of different factors that increase production possibilities. Tie the discussion to a specific industry, such as the auto industry *(technology, newly created materials, newly discovered resources, better trained workforce)* or farming *(fertilizers, labor-saving machinery, agribusiness methods).*

Answers

1. *a point of underutilization*
2. *Possible response: if the labor force ages or becomes less healthy, labor would not be fully efficient and production would fall*

Animated Economics This shows the impact of more resources or more efficient use of resources on production possibilities—the curve, or frontier, moves outward (to the right), signifying that the economy's total production has increased.

Changing Production Possibilities

The PPC illustrates a country's present production possibilities as if all resources are fixed. However, a country's supply of resources is likely to change over time. When additional resources become available, new production possibilities beyond the original frontier become attainable, and the PPC moves outward.

EXAMPLE A Shift in the PPC

In the late 1700s, the United States occupied a relatively narrow strip of land along the Atlantic Coast. Yet in less than a hundred years, it had expanded to the Pacific Ocean. This additional land provided the United States with an abundance of natural resources. Similarly, successive waves of immigration have added huge numbers of workers to the labor pool. Also, new technology has made the use of land, labor, and capital more efficient.

The addition of new resources or the more efficient use of resources already available meant that the United States could produce more goods and services. This is shown on the PPC as a shift of the curve outward, or to the right, as Figure 1.6 illustrates. Economists refer to this increase in the economy's total output as economic growth. You'll learn more about this concept in Chapter 12.

FIGURE 1.6 SHIFT IN THE PPC

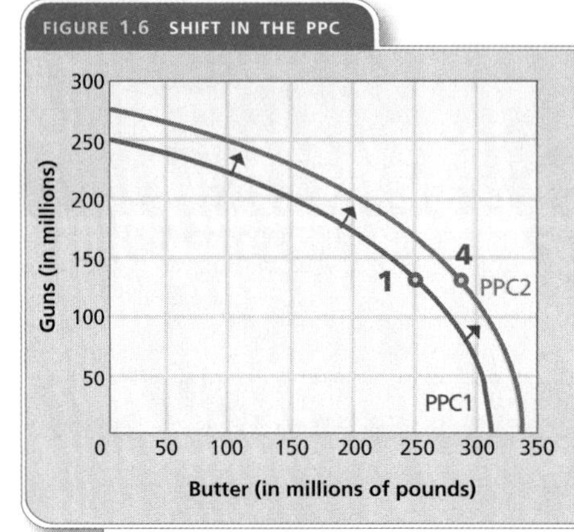

More resources or increased productivity shifts the PPC outward, or to the right, from PPC1 to PPC2. This means that the economy can produce more of both guns and butter and point **4**, which was a production impossibility in Figure 1.5 on page 20, now is located on the curve.

ANALYZE GRAPHS

1. If the curve PPC2 represents current production possibilities, what does point **1** represent?
2. What might cause the PPC to shift inward?

Animated Economics

Use an interactive production possibilities curve at **ClassZone.com**

APPLICATION Applying Economic Concepts

C. Identify three developments that would cause the PPC to move outward.
additional natural resources; increased labor resources; new technology that makes use of resources more efficient

DIFFERENTIATING INSTRUCTION

Struggling Readers

Map the Text
You may wish to have students complete the following chart to "map" the text.

Main idea: *(last line of first paragraph)*
Example: *(Growth of United States* • *More land = more resources* • *Immigrants = more workers* • *Technology = better use of land and workers)*
Graph: *(shows economic growth as a result of increased resources and greater efficiency)*

Inclusion

Extend an Activity
Introduce the PPC that you saved from the activity on page 19. Then tell students that new technology has been introduced that will allow them to produce more of both paper clips and rubber bands. Work with students to draw a new curve, labeled PPC2, that would result from this development. Call on volunteers to suggest other developments that might cause PPC to shift in this way. *(Possible responses: additional natural resources, increased labor resources, better-educated labor force)*

SECTION 3 Assessment

Online Quiz
ClassZone.com

REVIEWING KEY CONCEPTS

1. Explain how each of these terms is illustrated by the production possibilities curve.
   a. *underutilization*
   b. *efficiency*
2. On what assumptions is the PPC based? Explain how these conditions do not correspond to the real world.
3. What economic data does a PPC bring together?
4. Why do opportunity costs increase as you make more and more butter and fewer guns?
5. Based on what we learn from PPCs, what does an economy need to be able to produce more of both products on the graph?
6. **Using Your Notes** Write a one-paragraph summary of this section. Refer to your completed summary chart for the ideas to use in your summary.

Analyzing Production Possibilities	
PPC	shows impact of scarcity

Use the Graphic Organizer at **Interactive Review @ ClassZone.com**

CRITICAL THINKING

7. **Applying Economic Concepts** Explain why, in an economy that produces only fish and computers and is working at efficiency, the 500th computer made will cost more in terms of fish than the 450th computer made.
8. **Applying Economic Concepts** Suppose the owners of a car-manufacturing company are thinking of entering the motorcycle production business. How would a PPC model help them make a decision?
9. **Analyzing Cause and Effect** If new technology was introduced but there were not enough skilled workers to use it, where would the nation's production be plotted on the PPC—inside or outside the curve? Explain your answer.
10. **Challenge** During a war, a country suffers massive devastation of its industry. How would the country's PPC change from before the war to after the war? Sketch a PPC to illustrate your answer.

ECONOMICS IN PRACTICE

Creating a PPC
The following information reflects the production possibilities of an economy that makes only corn and television sets. Use the data to create a production possibilities curve.

Bushels of Corn (in thousands)	Television Sets (in thousands)
10	0
9	1
7	2
4	3
0	4

Label Points on a PPC Use the letters to locate the following points on your PPC:

A The point at which the economy makes all TVs and no corn
B A point representing efficiency
C A point representing underutilization
D A point representing an impossible level of production

Challenge Use information from your PPC to explain the law of increasing opportunity costs.

Use *SMARTGrapher* @ClassZone.com to complete this activity.

4 Assess & Reteach

Assess Have students work in pairs to complete the assessment questions. They can divide the work in any way that they choose, but both should be equally responsible for all the questions.

Unit 1 Resource Book
- Section Quiz, p. 29

Interactive Review @ ClassZone.com
- Section Quiz

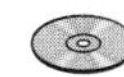

Test Generator CD-ROM
- Section Quiz

Reteach Divide students into three groups and assign each a main part of the section to review and present to the class. Instruct them to include the following in their presentations:

- A clear summary of their part of the section
- Specific examples illustrating the key concepts
- A visual aid

Evaluate the presentations on the effectiveness of each part.

Unit 1 Resource Book
- Reteaching Activity, p. 30

SMARTGrapher Students can create a production possibilities curve using **SmartGrapher @ ClassZone.com.**

SECTION 3 ASSESSMENT ANSWERS

Reviewing Key Concepts

1. **a.** *underutilization*, p. 20
   b. *efficiency*, p. 20
2. Resources are fixed and fully employed, only two things can be produced, and technology is fixed. New sources of resources are being found, new technology is always being developed, there often is inefficiency in the use of resources, and economies produce many things, not just two.
3. The maximum number of goods and services that can be produced using limited resources.
4. Making butter involves different resources than making guns. New factories and machinery must be built and workers must be trained. As a result, fewer and fewer guns will be made.
5. More resources and more efficient ways of employing resources.
6. See page 18 for an example of a completed summary chart. Summaries should outline the section's main ideas.

Critical Thinking

7. Different resources are needed to make these products. The cost of changing over to greater computer production will result in fewer and fewer fish being produced.
8. A PPC would show them the opportunity cost of switching from car production to motorcycle production.
9. inside the curve, because capital and labor resources would be used inefficiently
10. The PPC would shift to the left, showing a decrease in productivity. Sketches should reflect this shift.

Economics in Practice

Creating a PPC Have students study Figure 1.5 on page 20 before they undertake this activity.

Challenge Answers will vary, but students should note that the bow-shape of the curve shows that as production shifts from of one product to another, increasingly more resources are needed to produce the second product, which causes opportunity costs to steadily rise.

1 Plan & Prepare

Section 4 Objectives

- demonstrate how and why economists use economic models
- understand how and why economists use statistics, charts, tables, and graphs
- compare macroeconomics to microeconomics
- contrast positive economics with normative economics

2 Focus & Motivate

Connecting to Everyday Life Ask students to share how they encounter data in their daily lives. *(Possible answers: in school books, on Web sites, in newspapers and magazines, in college testing results)* Point out that the ability to interpret data in different formats is an essential skill in an increasingly technological world.

Taking Notes Remind students to take notes as they read by completing a chart noting the similarities and differences between key concepts. They can use the Graphic Organizer at **Interactive Review @ ClassZone.com.** A sample is shown below.

Concepts	Similarities	Differences
Charts & Tables vs. Graphs	Both present data in condensed form.	Charts & tables: rows and columns; Graphs: in visual form
Micro vs. Macro	Both are areas of economic study.	Micro.: individual consumer; Macro.: economy as a whole
Positive vs. Normative	Both are ways of describing and explaining economics.	Positive: as it is; Normative: as it ought to be

SECTION 4

The Economist's Toolbox

OBJECTIVES

In Section 4, you will

- demonstrate how and why economists use economic models
- understand how and why economists use statistics, charts, tables, and graphs
- compare macroeconomics to microeconomics
- contrast positive economics with normative economics

KEY TERMS

statistics, *p. 24*
microeconomics, *p. 27*
macroeconomics, *p. 27*
positive economics, *p. 29*
normative economics, *p. 29*

TAKING NOTES

As you read Section 4, complete a chart to see similarities and differences between key concepts. Use the Graphic Organizer at **Interactive Review @ ClassZone.com**

Concepts	Similarities	Differences
Charts & Tables vs. Graphs		
Micro vs. Macro		
Positive vs. Normative		

Working with Data

KEY CONCEPTS

An old joke notes that economics is everything we already know expressed in a language we don't understand. While many economists might disagree with the second part of this joke, they probably would have little argument with the first part. Economics is something that everybody engages in every day, and in that way everyone has knowledge of it. Individuals, business owners, and government officials make economic decisions all the time. Economists study these decisions and look for logical ways to explain why some nations are rich while others are poor, or why some consumers want one kind of product while others want another.

QUICK REFERENCE

Statistics are information in numerical form.

Since economists can't interview every person in every nation about economic choices, they rely on **statistics**—numerical data or information—to see patterns of behavior. To help organize and interpret the data they collect, they develop economic models. As you recall from Section 3, an economic model is a simplified representation of complex economic forces. The language of economists—these statistics and models—may sometimes be a little hard to understand. However, it is a more efficient way of explaining economic relationships and interactions than everyday language.

Using Economic Models

In science class, you may have seen a model of a lunar eclipse, which shows how, with the sun behind it, the earth casts a shadow on the moon. The model assumes certain laws of planetary orbit and simplifies the relationships among the objects in the solar system. However, these assumptions and simplifications make the process of the eclipse quite clear.

SECTION 4 PROGRAM RESOURCES

ON LEVEL

Lesson Plans

- Core, p. 4

Unit 1 Resource Book

- Reading Study Guide, pp. 31–32
- Economic Skills and Problem Solving Activity, pp, 41–42
- Section Quiz, p. 39

STRUGGLING READERS

Unit 1 Resource Book

- Reading Study Guide with Additional Support, pp. 33–35
- Reteaching Activity, p. 40

ENGLISH LEARNERS

Unit 1 Resource Book

- Reading Study Guide with Additional Support (Spanish), pp. 36–38

INCLUSION

Lesson Plans

- Modified for Inclusion, p. 4

GIFTED AND TALENTED

Unit 1 Resource Book

- Readings in Free Enterprise: The First Modern Economist, pp. 43–44
- Case Study Resources: The Real Cost of Expanding O'Hare Airport, pp. 45–46

TECHNOLOGY

eEdition DVD-ROM

eEdition Online

Power Presentation DVD-ROM

Economics Concepts Transparencies

- CT4 Revenue Bar Graph and Pie Chart

Daily Test Practice Transparencies, TT4

ClassZone.com

Economic models work in the same way. They are based on assumptions and are simplified because they focus on a limited number of variables. Economists can express their models in words, graphs, or equations. Models help economists explain why things are as they are. In some cases, models can help economists to predict future economic activity. You've already learned how economists construct and use one important economic model—the production possibilities curve—in Section 3. You'll learn about another, the circular flow model, in Chapter 2.

Using Charts and Tables

FIGURE 1.7 DEVELOPMENT ASSISTANCE

Country	Aid (in millions of U.S. Dollars)	Percentage of Total Economy
Luxembourg	236	0.83
Canada	2,599	0.27

Source: Organization for Economic Co-operation and Development, 2004 Figures

Economists study statistics in a particular way, looking for trends, connections, and other interesting relationships. They have several tools to help them with this task. Among the most common tools are charts and tables, in which data are arranged and displayed in rows and columns. (See Figure 1.7 above.) By showing numbers in relation to other numbers, charts and tables can reveal patterns in the data.

Suppose, for example, you were curious about how much money various developed countries give to help developing countries. In Figure 1.7, if you looked at one set of numbers, you would see that Luxembourg contributed $236 million, while Canada gave more than ten times that, offering nearly $2.6 billion. Your immediate interpretation of these data might be that Canada gives far more in foreign aid than Luxembourg does. But looking at other sets of numbers might suggest a different interpretation. Luxembourg may have contributed far less than Canada in actual dollar amounts. However, the foreign aid Luxembourg gave represented close to 1 percent of the value of all the goods and services the nation produced. Canada's contribution, in contrast, was about 0.3 percent of its total economy. After studying these numbers, you might conclude that in relative terms Luxembourg gives more than Canada in foreign aid.

Economics Update

Find an update on foreign aid at **ClassZone.com**

Using Graphs

When economists are interested in identifying trends in statistics, they often use graphs, or visual representations of numerical relationships. The most common type is the line graph. Line graphs are particularly useful for showing changes over time.

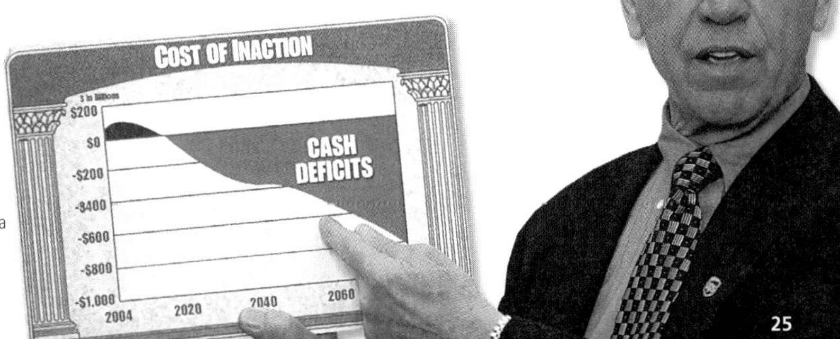

Statistics During a debate in the U.S. Senate on the future of Social Security, Senator Charles Grassley of Iowa illustrates a point using statistics in graph form.

❸ Teach

Working with Data

Discuss

- What other disciplines depend on data and numbers as their "language"? *(science, math)* Which of these disciplines is more like economics? *(probably science, since it begins with observation and collects data to test theories; math is less tied to physical phenomena)*

Analyzing Charts: Figure 1.7

Call students' attention to the source at the bottom of the chart and ask students if they have heard of that organization. If no one knows, tell them that OECD is an organization of 30 member nations, including the United States, committed to democracy and a market economy. Also mention that it is a well-known source for statistics. Point out that knowing the source of statistics is important in judging their accuracy and lack of bias. Ask students how they can learn about the sources of statistics that they encounter. *(They can do a web search or look the organization up in the library.)*

Economics Update

At **ClassZone.com,** students will see updated information on foreign aid.

SMALL GROUP ACTIVITY

Evaluating Statistics

Time 30 minutes ◑

Task Evaluate statistics by determining the mean, median, and mode

Materials Needed none

Activity

- Divide the class into three groups
- On the board, write this information on yearly charitable giving by families living on Wilcox Avenue.

  Family A: $15; Family B: $0; Family C: $50; Family D: $100; Family E: $15; Family F: $45; Family G: $5,000
- Direct one group to find the *mean* (total donations and divide by the number of families; another group to find the *median* (place numbers in value order and identify number in the middle); and *mode* (identify which number appears most often). Tell students that all of these can be considered an "average."
- Have students present their responses and compare the impression each leaves. *(mean = $746.42; median = $45; mode = $15)*

Rubric

	Understanding of Concepts	Presentation of Information
4	excellent	clearly thought out
3	good	mostly clear
2	fair	sometimes clear
1	poor	unclear

Analyzing Graphs: Figures 1.8, 1.9, and 1.10

Once again, ask students to look at the sources of information for these graphics and evaluate them. Ask students which type of graph would be best to display each of the following sets of data:

- Ethnic heritage of students at school *(pie graph)*
- Salaries of college-educated women compared to salaries of college-educated men *(bar graph)*
- State government budget *(pie graph)*
- Growth in the sale of hybrid cars since 1995 *(line graph)*

Animated Economics The variety of interactive graphs will help students appreciate the differences among the types of graphs. It also will help them gain competence at expressing information in a graphic format.

More About . . .

Bureau of Labor Statistics
The BLS is an independent agency that serves as the major fact-finding organization for the federal government. It has an outstanding website filled with fascinating statistics. One of the most-viewed offerings on that site is the *Occupational Outlook Handbook,* which predicts the professions and jobs that will be experiencing growth or decline. There is a special online version of the handbook for young people.

TYPES OF GRAPHS

FIGURE 1.8 PCs PER 100 PEOPLE IN DEVELOPING COUNTRIES

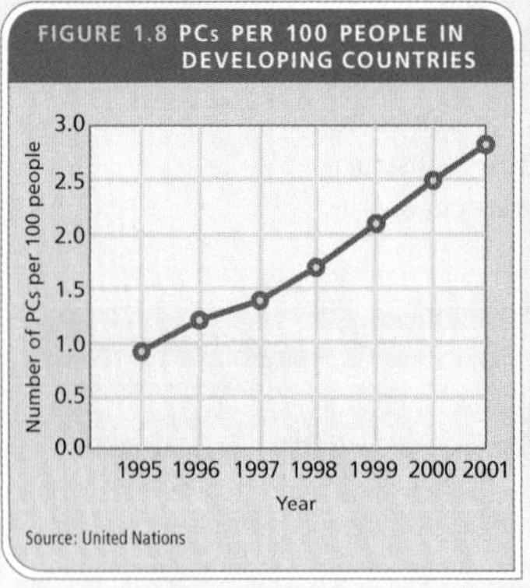

Source: United Nations

FIGURE 1.9 U.S. COMPUTER AND INTERNET ACCESS

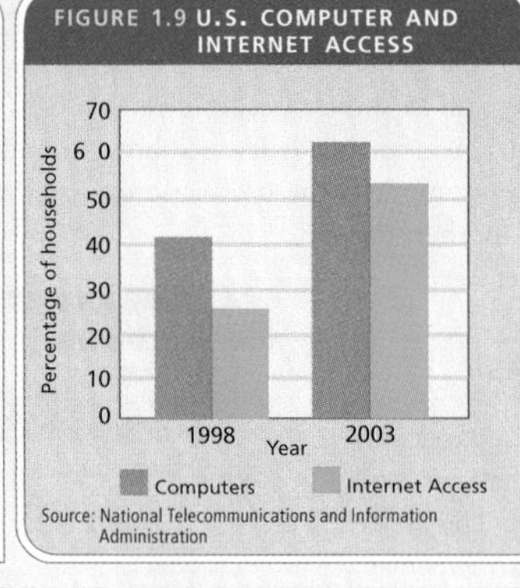

Source: National Telecommunications and Information Administration

FIGURE 1.10 INTERNET USERS BY REGION

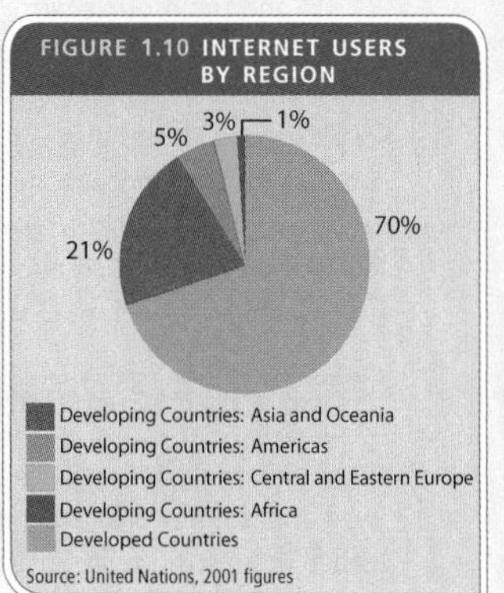

Source: United Nations, 2001 figures

ANALYZE GRAPHS

Graphs show statistics in a visual form. Line graphs (Figure 1.8) are particularly useful for showing changes over time. Bar graphs (Figure 1.9) make it easy to compare numbers or sets of numbers. Pie, or circle, graphs (Figure 1.10) show relationships among the parts of a whole.

Animated Economics

Use a variety of interactive graphs at **ClassZone.com**

All line graphs use at least two sets of numbers, or variables: one plotted along the horizontal axis, running from left to right, the other plotted along the vertical axis, running from bottom to top. On the line graph in Figure 1.8 above, the range of time from 1995 to 2001 is shown on the horizontal axis. The number of PCs (personal computers) per 100 people in developing countries is shown on the vertical axis.

The number of PCs for each year is plotted on the graph and then these points are joined to form a line. The line may slope upward, showing an upward trend, or downward, showing a downward trend. The line may be straight, keeping the same slope throughout, or it may be curved, having a varied slope. (In later chapters you'll see that where graphs are used to illustrate economic concepts, lines are referred to as curves whether they are straight or curved.) How would you describe the trend shown in Figure 1.8?

A bar graph is especially useful for comparisons. The bar graph in Figure 1.9 above shows information on the percentage of households in the United States that have access to computers and the Internet. The bars vividly illustrate that access to information technology increased dramatically in the United States between 1998 and 2003.

A pie graph, often called a pie chart or circle graph, is especially good for representing numbers in relation to a whole. Take a look at the pie graph in Figure 1.10 above. The whole circle represents all the Internet users in the world. The slices of the pie, which represent regions of the world, are drawn in proportion to the percentage of the whole they constitute.

NEED HELP?

Throughout this book, you will be asked to interpret and analyze information in graphs. If you need help with these tasks, see "Interpreting Graphs."

Skillbuilder Handbook, page R29

APPLICATION Interpreting Graphs

A. Look at the pie graph in Figure 1.10 above. Write a generalization based on information in the graph.
Answers will vary. A possible response is that the more developed a nation is, the more access to information technology it has.

DIFFERENTIATING INSTRUCTION

Inclusion

Make 3-D Graphs
Students with visual impairment may create a tactile graph with the cooperation of a sighted student or with your help. Each of the graphs on this page can be reproduced with clay and other manipulatives. For the line graph, use thinly rolled clay or string to create the vertical and horizontal axes. String can be used for the line graph itself, with thumbtacks or push-pins holding it in place at each of the points shown in the graph.

English Learners

Make Oral Presentations
Have students work in small groups to prepare oversized versions of the line graph, bar graph, and pie graph from this page. For practice in speaking English, have them each present the visual aid to the others. They should cover these points in their speech:

- why graphs are useful in economics
- what data each type of graph is good for displaying

Microeconomics and Macroeconomics

KEY CONCEPTS

For scientists, everything in the earth, air, and water—and beyond—is a source of data to be observed and studied. Yet the data often make little sense until they are seen through the lens of a microscope or telescope. Economic information, as with scientific data, takes on meaning when it is viewed through the most useful lens. Two of the lenses through which economists observe economic behavior are microeconomics and macroeconomics. **Microeconomics** is the study of the behavior of individual players in an economy, such as individuals, families, and businesses. **Macroeconomics** is the study of the behavior of the economy as a whole and involves topics such as inflation, unemployment, aggregate demand, and aggregate supply.

QUICK REFERENCE

Microeconomics is the study of individuals, families, and businesses in an economy.

Macroeconomics is the study of the economy as a whole and is concerned with large-scale economic activity.

Microeconomics

As the prefix *micro-*, meaning small, would suggest, microeconomics examines specific, individual elements in an economy. The elements include prices, costs, profits, competition, and the behavior of consumers and producers. Microeconomics can help you understand how the sandwich shop owner arrived at the price of the lunch you bought today, why the neighborhood has several sandwich shops offering the same kinds of food, and why some of these shops flourish while others fail. Microeconomics also can offer explanations for why students decide to work only on the weekends and not on school nights, why some families buy a used car rather than a new car, and why the mom-and-pop grocery store in your neighborhood closed after the superstore opened nearby.

Within the field of microeconomics there are areas of specialized concentration. Business organization, labor markets, agricultural economics, and the economics of environmental issues are among the topics that microeconomists might study. You will study the issues of microeconomics in more depth starting in Chapter 4.

Macroeconomics

Macroeconomics, as its prefix *macro-*, meaning large, would suggest, examines the economic "big picture." In other words, macroeconomics is the study of the economy as a whole. While the limited spending power of an unemployed person would be in the realm of microeconomics, the effect of widespread unemployment on the whole nation would be a macroeconomic issue. In a similar way, the rising price of coffee would interest a microeconomist, but a general rise in prices, a sign that the whole economy is experiencing inflation, would be a matter for a macroeconomist.

Microeconomics vs. Macroeconomics Changes in coffee prices might interest a microeconomist. A macroeconomist might study general changes in prices.

Microeconomics and Macroeconomics

Discuss

- Who would be concerned with a large corporation going bankrupt, a microeconomist or a macroeconomist? *(a microeconomist, since it is an individual corporation)*
- Who would be concerned with the unemployment statistics for the United States? *(a macroeconomist, since unemployment statistics are part of a bigger picture of the economy as a whole)*

More About . . .

Macroeconomics

The field of economics divided into macroeconomics and microeconomics during the worldwide economic depression in the 1930s. The prevailing economic models were not able to adequately describe the forces that led to the depression. So, economists needed new models and a new perspective. At the same time, national accounting—measuring national income and product statistics—was just coming into use. John Maynard Keynes, a British economist (see page 456), was one of the earliest and most important macroeconomists.

INDIVIDUAL ACTIVITY

Finding Graphs in Microeconomics and Macroeconomics

Time 30 minutes

Task Find graphs in this book that represent a microeconomic and a macroeconomic concept.

Materials Needed paper and pens or pencils

Activity

- Direct students to the table of contents in this book to see where Microeconomics and Macroeconomics are discussed.
- Have students find and copy two graphs (or tables, or charts), one representing a microeconomic concern, one a macroeconomic concern.
- Tell students to look for a graphic early in the chapter, which might be easier to understand than one that builds on layers of chapter concepts.
- Have students create a copy of each chart and write a two- or three-sentence explanation of why it represents either microeconomics or macroeconomics.

Rubric

	Understanding of Concepts	Presentation of Information
4	excellent	accurate
3	good	somewhat accurate
2	fair	one graphic somewhat accurate
1	poor	both graphics incorrect

Economics Essentials: Figure 1.11

Tell students that in addition to the two main branches of economics there are many sub-disciplines, and that they do not always fall neatly into either microeconomics or macroeconomics. Ask students to comment on how they would categorize these, and to give reasons. *(For all, answers will vary; look for sound reasoning.)*

- labor economics *(microeconomics, if it looks at the behavior of labor; macroeconomics if it looks at labor as part of the business sector of the national economy)*
- international economics *(microeconomics, if it looks at the behavior of consumers and producers in international trade; macroeconomics if it looks international trade in the light of government spending policies)*
- financial economics *(microeconomics, if it looks at the behavior of individual investors and spenders; macroeconomics if it looks at the effect of financial policies on a national economy)*

Analyze

Answers will vary, but should reflect a solid understanding of the two concepts.

ECONOMICS ESSENTIALS

FIGURE 1.11 The Two Branches of Economics

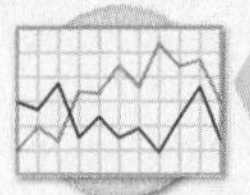

Economists Study

Macroeconomics

The study of the whole economy

Units of Study

- Economic growth
- Economic stability
- International trade

Topics of Interest

- Money, banking, finance
- Government taxing and spending policies
- Employment and unemployment
- Inflation

Microeconomics

The study of the individual consumer

Units of Study

- Consumer markets
- Business markets
- Labor markets

Topics of Interest

- Markets, prices, costs, profits, competition, government regulation
- Consumer behavior
- Business behavior

ANALYZE CHARTS

The division between microeconomics and macroeconomics is not a fixed one. Some topics fall under both areas of study. For example, a microeconomist might be interested in employment levels in the hotel industry, while a macroeconomist looks at employment levels in the economy as a whole. Identify another topic area that might be of interest to both microeconomists and macroeconomists.

While microeconomics considers the *individual* consumer, macroeconomics studies the consumer *sector,* also called the household sector. A sector is a combination of all the individual units into one larger whole. Macroeconomics also examines the business sector, and the public, or government, sector—that part of the economy that provides public goods and services.

Macroeconomists bring a national or global perspective to their work. They study the monetary system, the ups and downs of business cycles, and the impact of national tax policies on the economy. In addition, they look at such global issues as international trade and its effect on rich and poor nations. You will study macroeconomics in depth beginning in Chapter 10.

APPLICATION Categorizing Economic Information

B. Which does each of the news headlines relate to—microeconomics or macroeconomics?

1. National Unemployment Figures Rise
2. World Trade Organization Meets
3. Shipbuilder Wins Navy Contract
4. Cab Drivers on Strike!
5. Gasoline Prices Jump 25 Cents

Macroeconomics: 1, 2

Microeconomics: 3, 4, 5

DIFFERENTIATING INSTRUCTION

English Learners

Determine Meaning from Prefixes

Instruct students to add the terms *microeconomics* and *macroeconomics* to their personal dictionary. Then direct them to a dictionary to find more words with the prefixes. In a small group discussion, they should be prepared to offer at least two words for each prefix.

Gifted and Talented

Relate to Current Economic Events

Ask students to find an item in the news that has stirred debate and reflects differing viewpoints within normative economics. Examples may include the future of social security, a labor dispute between an airline and its pilots, or federal funding for education. Have students identify different normative economics stances for the issue they choose. Follow up with a small group discussion.

Positive Economics and Normative Economics

KEY CONCEPTS

Economics also can be viewed through another pair of lenses. One of those lenses is **positive economics**, a way of describing and explaining economics as it is, not as it should be. Positive economics involves verifiable facts, not value judgments. The other is **normative economics**, a way of describing and explaining what economic behavior ought to be, not what it actually is. Normative economics does involve value judgments because it seeks to make recommendations for actions.

QUICK REFERENCE

Positive economics studies economic behavior as it is.

Normative economics involves judgments of what economic behavior ought to be.

Positive Economics

Positive economics uses the scientific method to observe data, hypothesize, test, refine, and continue testing. Statements made within positive economics can be tested against real-world data and either proved (or at least strongly supported) or disproved (or at least strongly questioned). Suppose, for example, your state is debating the pros and cons of a lottery to raise money for education. In the framework of positive economics, researchers would study data from states with lotteries to see if educational spending increased after the lotteries were begun.

Normative Economics

Normative economics, in contrast, is based on value judgments. It goes beyond the facts to ask if actions are good. Since the values of people differ, so do the recommendations based on normative economics.

Consider the issue of using lottery money to fund education. Two economists might agree that the data show that state-run lotteries result in more money for schools, and that many lottery tickets are purchased by people who are poor. Their recommendations, however, might differ because they have different values. One economist might support a lottery because it increases funding for schools. The other might oppose a lottery because it places a burden on the poor.

Normative Economics Why is this statement about the North American Free Trade Agreement (NAFTA) an example of normative economics?

APPLICATION Applying Economic Concepts

C. Are the following statements examples of positive economics or normative economics?

1. Because of scarcity, everyone must make choices.
2. Americans buy too many cars and do not use mass transit enough.

1. Positive; 2. Normative

Positive Economics and Normative Economics

Discuss

- Ask students for an example of a normative macroeconomic position and a normative microeconomic position. *(Possible answers: macroeconomic—taxes should be raised to provide more social welfare programs; microeconomic—failing companies should not be helped out by governments)*

More About . . .

NAFTA

The North American Free Trade Agreement became effective in 1994 and its goal is to eliminate trade barriers among Mexico, the United States, and Canada. (Students will learn more about NAFTA in Chapter 17.) In 1992, Presidential candidate H. Ross Perot predicted that NAFTA would produce a "giant sucking sound" as jobs and investments left the United States for cheaper locations. In the early 1990s, NAFTA was the center of normative economic debates but was ultimately supported by President Bill Clinton and enacted. The loss of jobs and investments predicted by Perot has not happened.

SMALL GROUP ACTIVITY

Creating an Economic Collage

Time 30 minutes ◑

Task With a small group, create a collage from magazine and newspaper illustrations and headlines depicting one kind of economics.

Materials Needed magazines and newspapers that can be cut up; eight scissors; glue sticks or bottled glue; construction or stock paper

Activity

- Have students form four groups, corresponding to: microeconomics, macroeconomics, normative economics, and positive economics.
- Direct groups to find items in newspapers and magazines that illustrate their kind of economics. Have them use the items to create collages.
- When the collages are finished, have someone from each group present the collage, explaining each picture.

Rubric

	Understanding of Concepts	Presentation of Information
4	excellent	many good examples
3	good	several good examples
2	fair	a few good examples
1	poor	most examples do not illustrate concepts

Adam Smith

More About . . .

Adam Smith
There are many missing pieces in Smith's personal life, but the few details that are known paint a picture of a likeable, eccentric, and brilliant man. His father died some months before Smith was born. As a result, Smith developed a close relationship with his mother, who is said to have indulged him in his youth. She died only six years before Smith himself. In his adult life, Smith was known for possessing an unusually keen memory but also for talking and laughing to himself when he was alone and for seeming to be, at times, absent when in the presence of company.

More About . . .

Adam Smith's Philosophy
The influence of Adam Smith on the founders of the United States was profound. Thomas Jefferson and Alexander Hamilton were well acquainted with Smith's work, as were many of the founders of the new nation. Smith's attack on mercantilism supported the colonists' views about the right to free trade. Smith, like other Enlightenment thinkers, believed that a social system dominated by natural law would be most conducive to human happiness. To Smith, part of that natural law was the human disposition to "truck, barter, and exchange" in pursuit of self-interest.

Economics Update

ClassZone.com includes links to sites about Adam Smith. These will help students understand the role that Smith played in the development of economics.

ECONOMICS PACESETTER

Adam Smith: Founder of Modern Economics

Some 250 years ago, economics as an academic discipline did not even exist. Any discussion of economic issues usually took place in the fields of politics and philosophy. In 1776, however, Adam Smith completely changed this.

FAST FACTS

Adam Smith
Scottish political economist and moral philosopher

Born: June, 1723

Died: July 17, 1790

Accomplishment: Laying the foundation for modern economics

Other Major Work: *The Theory of Moral Sentiments* (1759)

Famous Quotation: *"It is not from the benevolence of the butcher, the brewer, or the baker, that we can expect our dinner, but from their regard to their own interest."*

Influenced:
Alexander Hamilton
Thomas Malthus
Karl Marx
Defenders of capitalism
Critics of capitalism

Economics Update
Learn more about Adam Smith at **ClassZone.com**

Seeing the Invisible

No other economist has had as much influence as Adam Smith, yet he would not have even considered himself an economist. Smith was born in Kirkcaldy, Scotland, in 1723 and studied, and later taught, literature, logic, and moral philosophy. In 1764 he traveled to France and met many European Enlightenment writers and thinkers. His discussions with them encouraged him to look at the world anew. The result was his groundbreaking work, *An Inquiry into the Nature and Causes of the Wealth of Nations,* which he published in 1776.

In *The Wealth of Nations,* Smith challenged the idea that mercantilism—a system by which the government of the homeland controlled trade with its colonies—was economically sound. Instead, he argued, a nation would be wealthier if it engaged in free trade. It was in this market where goods could be exchanged freely that Adam Smith saw a new economic relationship.

He reasoned that people behave in ways that satisfy their economic self-interest. A tailor will make clothes as long as people will buy them at a price that satisfies him. If he makes more clothes than customers wish to buy, he will cut back and make fewer until he finds the balance again. In this way, according to Smith, an "invisible hand" guides the marketplace. In such a free market, both the buyer and the seller benefit from each transaction. Smith's idea of the "invisible hand," as well as many other principles he explained in *The Wealth of Nations,* became the foundation of modern economic theory.

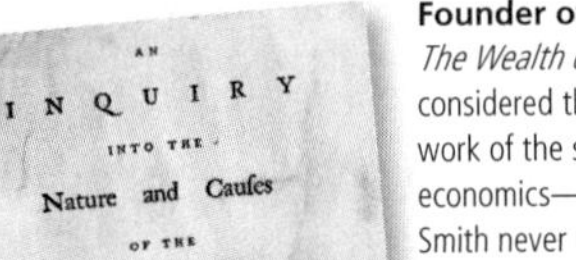

Founder of Economics
The Wealth of Nations is considered the founding work of the subject of economics—even though Smith never used the word *economics* in the book.

APPLICATION Analyzing Effects

D. What impact do you think individual self-interest has on the economy as a whole? Illustrate your answer with examples.
Answers will vary, but should suggest that individual self-interest helps to provide answers to the three basic economic questions.

30 Chapter 1

DIFFERENTIATING INSTRUCTION

Struggling Readers

Use Text Features
Tell students that throughout this book there will be biographical features about people whose ideas or actions are noteworthy in the field of economics. Every such feature will have a sidebar with Fast Facts. Ask for students to read the Fast Facts about Adam Smith aloud as a way to preview what they will be reading about in the text itself.

Inclusion

Listen and Visualize
Ask for a proficient reader to volunteer to read aloud the feature on Adam Smith. After each paragraph, ask the listeners to summarize what they heard. When the reading is complete, ask the listeners to draw a picture that represents some of the key ideas in the feature. Ask students to present their finished work to their peers, explaining why they chose the images they did.

SECTION 4 Assessment

Online Quiz
ClassZone.com

REVIEWING KEY CONCEPTS

1. Explain the differences between the terms in each of these pairs:
   a. *statistics* / *economic model*
   b. *macroeconomics* / *microeconomics*
   c. *positive economics* / *normative economics*
2. Why do economists often choose to present statistics in charts, tables, or graphs?
3. Create a simple model to explain how you decide how much time to study and how much time to unwind each evening. You may use words, charts or graphs, or equations.
4. Think of an example of a macroeconomic issue that affects an individual person, family, or business and explain its effect.
5. Explain the value of statistics and other data to positive economics and to normative economics.
6. **Using Your Notes** In what ways was Adam Smith a microeconomist? In what ways a macroeconomist? Refer to your completed comparison and contrast chart.

Concepts	Similarities	Differences
Charts & Tables vs. Graphs		
Micro vs. Macro		
Positive vs. Normative		

Use the Graphic Organizer at **Interactive Review @ ClassZone.com**

CRITICAL THINKING

7. **Making Inferences** How do you think politicians might use normative economics statements?
8. **Applying Economic Concepts** In which category does each item below belong—microeconomics or macroeconomics? Why?
   a. Studying statistics to see how well the economy is doing at creating jobs or increasing exports;
   b. Studying statistics on gasoline sales and hotel bookings to explore the impact of higher gas prices on vacation plans.
9. **Distinguishing Fact from Opinion** Consider the example of the state lottery to raise money for education. How might it be possible for two economists to see the same information and arrive at different opinions about what to do?
10. **Challenge** When you go out shopping, do you often worry that there will be a shortage of something you really want? If so, explain why you think there might be a shortage. If not, explain why there seems to be enough of everything you would want to buy.

ECONOMICS IN PRACTICE

Ford Motor Company assembly line, 1913

Using Graphs
Graphs are among the most important tools used by economists.

Create Graphs Use the following information about Model T Fords (shown above) to create two line or bar graphs.

Average price per car
1909 — $904
1911 — $811
1913 — $638
1915 — $626

Number of cars sold
1909 — 12,176
1911 — 40,400
1913 — 179,199
1915 — 355,249

Source: Model T Ford Club of America

Challenge As Henry Ford lowered the price of the Model Ts, he potentially reduced his profit—the amount of money he made—on the sale of each car. Why was that a good economic choice?

Use ***SMARTGrapher*** @ ClassZone.com to complete this activity.

4 Assess & Reteach

Assess Have students answer the first six questions in writing and then exchange papers. As you lead a class discussion of the answers, have students give their peers' responses a plus or minus sign for correctness. Discuss the critical thinking questions as a class.

Unit 1 Resource Book
- Section Quiz, p. 39

Interactive Review @ ClassZone.com
- Section Quiz

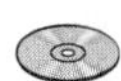
Test Generator CD-ROM
- Section Quiz

Reteach Divide the class into three groups and assign each a main part of the section to review and present to the class. Direct them to use the graphics in their part of the section as a way to anchor their review.

Unit 1 Resource Book
- Reteaching Activity, p. 40

SMARTGrapher Students can create line and bar graphs at **SmartGrapher @ ClassZone.com.**

SECTION 4 ASSESSMENT ANSWERS

Reviewing Key Concepts

1. a. *statistics*, p. 24; *economic model*, p. 25
   b. *macroeconomics*, p. 27; *microeconomics*, p. 27
   c. *positive economics*, p. 27; *normative economics*, p. 29
2. Charts, tables, and graphs clearly show the relationships among sets of statistics.
3. Models will vary, but should reflect an understanding of the characteristics of models.
4. Answers will vary. A possible response is the income tax, which affects a person's spending and saving potential.
5. Positive economics: statistics can be used to show how things work. Normative economics: statistics can be used to support or challenge recommended actions.
6. See page 24 for an example of a completed chart. Individual self-interest falls under microeconomics; application of this principle to trade is a macroeconomic approach.

Critical Thinking

7. People make their voting decisions, in large part, based on politicians' recommendations for the economy.
8. a. Macroeconomics, because the study involves the economy as a whole.
   b. Microeconomics, because the study is concerned with individual vacation plans.
9. Answers will vary, but should note that with normative economics different points of view arise on an issue.
10. Answers will vary, but most students will suggest that there will be enough of what they want because producers have gauged what consumers want.

Economics in Practice

Create Graphs Students' graphs should accurately display statistics given.

Challenge because he would sell more cars.

1 Plan & Prepare

Objectives

- Analyze multiple sources to understand the real costs of expanding O'Hare airport
- Identify normative economics in the sources
- Evaluate differing points of view on airport expansion

2 Focus & Motivate

Ask students to comment on their experience as travelers at airports. What parts of the experience went smoothly? What parts did not? After the discussion, point out that they took the perspective of a consumer using airport services. Instruct students that, as they read the sources here, they should keep their own perspective in mind but also identify the perspective of the sources.

3 Teach

Using the Sources

Encourage students to compare and contrast the different viewpoints on O'Hare expansion as they read the sources.

A. What benefits are identified in the online report? *(efficiency of airport; jobs and money pumped into local economy; larger capacity for O'Hare)* In your opinion, are those benefits convincing? Why or why not? *(Answers will vary; encourage students to back up opinions with data.)*

B. What is the point of the cartoon? *(Answers will vary, but probably will note that while noise from the trains and airplanes is accepted, the noise of protest is not.)*

C. What perspective does AReCo bring to the debate? *(They represent the concerns of people who live near the airport. They care less about efficiency and more about safety and quality-of-life issues.)*

Economics Update

Go to **Classzone.com** to find an update to this Case Study, including another article, an editable student worksheet, and an editable lesson plan.

Case Study

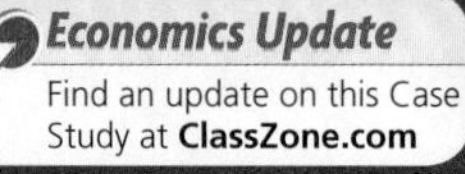

Find an update on this Case Study at **ClassZone.com**

The Real Cost of Expanding O'Hare Airport

Background Chicago's O'Hare airport is one of the busiest airports in the United States. It is a major hub for both domestic and international airlines, and its smooth running is essential if the many airlines that fly in and out of O'Hare are to remain on schedule. However, delays at O'Hare are commonplace, and this sometimes disrupts air travel throughout the United States and abroad.

Two main factors are responsible for delays at O'Hare: turbulent Midwestern weather and the layout of O'Hare's runways. Because all but one of the runways are interconnected, bad weather results in the shutting down of most of the runway system. A modernization plan to improve efficiency at O'Hare was adopted in 2005. This plan generated considerable, and often heated, discussion and debate.

What's the issue? What are the real costs involved in airport expansion? Study these sources to determine the costs tied to the expansion of O'Hare airport.

A. Online Report

This report describes the anticipated benefits of the O'Hare Modernization Plan to redesign the runway system and expand the airport.

Chicago O'Hare Airport Expansion

The modernization plan is estimated to cost $6.6 billion (in 2001 dollars), which will probably be more like $8 billion by completion. . . .

Supporters of the expansion plan say delays could be cut by 79% and that 195,000 jobs and $18 billion would be put into the local economy. In 2004 the airport played host to 69.5 million arriving, departing and connecting passengers and had total aircraft operations at nearly 929,000, an average of one landing or takeoff every 56 seconds. . . .

The airport has 178 gates on eight connected concourses and one freestanding terminal. The realignment [of the runways] and modernization program could make a great deal of difference to the efficiency of the airport. Overall, delays are expected to drop by 79%. The future airfield will be able to accommodate approximately 1.6 million aircraft operations and 76 million [passengers] per year.

Source: Airport-technology.com/projects/chicago

Thinking Economically What factors led to the development of the plan to expand O'Hare? What are the projected costs and benefits?

DIFFERENTIATING INSTRUCTION

Struggling Readers

Make a Before-and-After Chart
Have students make a two-column chart to clarify the relationship among the figures given in the online report. In the first column, they should list the figures that relate to the airport before expansion. In the second column, they should list the figures that represent the airport after expansion.

Gifted and Talented

Conduct Research
Direct students to research other areas where airport expansion is proposed. Have them gather pro- and con- positions and compare them to those offered on the O'Hare expansion. Were there any additional costs discovered in the other expansion plans? Students should share their findings by creating a visual aid that can be posted on a bulletin board.

B. Political Cartoon

Cartoonist Grizelda drew this cartoon about people protesting noise pollution at an airport.

Source: www.CartoonStock.com

Thinking Economically Which opportunity cost does this cartoon address? Explain your answer.

C. Organization Website

The Alliance of Residents Concerning O'Hare (AReCo) addresses problems related to the aviation industry. AReCo's website presents the group's findings and views regarding the expansion of O'Hare.

Area Residents Challenge Wisdom of O'Hare Expansion

AReCo cites health hazards, seeks alternatives to enlarging O'Hare.

The [aviation] industry and airport expansionists consistently try to minimize the impacts of airports and aircraft. One example of the harm that has been . . . understated by the federal government . . . [is the] underreporting [of] the amounts of deadly pollution coming from airports/aircraft.

For example, combined aircraft-related amounts of benzene [a known cause of cancer in humans] totaled 20 tons at Logan, Bradley, and Manchester airports in 1999! . . . Mega airports, such as Chicago's O'Hare, operate more aircraft annually than all of the three above-mentioned airports combined, thus emitting even more harmful and even deadly pollution in heavily urban-populated areas. . . .

In the meantime, there are intelligent steps that Chicago (and others) can take that will really modernize the metropolitan air transportation system and retain Chicago's title of "our nation's transportation hub." Such steps include placing a much stronger emphasis on [more than one type of] transportation, such as medium and high-speed rail, that would link O'Hare airport to other airports (becoming a "virtual hub") and building a new airport in a less populated peripheral area.

Source: Areco.org

Thinking Economically What alternatives does AReCo cite to O'Hare's expansion?

THINKING ECONOMICALLY Synthesizing

1. Explain the real cost of expanding O'Hare airport. Use information presented in the documents to support your answer.
2. Who are the most likely winners and losers as a result of the O'Hare expansion? Explain your answer.
3. How might supporters of expansion use a production possibilities model to strengthen their case?

Thinking Economically

Answers

A. *Factors: inefficiency and delays; costs: between $6.6 and 8 billion; benefits: greater efficiency and capacity, creation of more jobs, economic benefit to local economy*

B. *More noise is the opportunity cost of having an airport near residential areas.*

C. *high-speed rail or other innovative means of transportation; a new airport in a less populated area*

Synthesizing

1. *Cost in dollars between $6.6 and 8 billion. Opportunity costs include increased noise and air pollution and associated health hazards; creation of transportation alternatives that might prove more viable in future.*
2. *Winners: airlines and air travelers, due to increased efficiency; new "hires" due to the creation of new jobs; losers: residents of surrounding communities, due to increased air and noise pollution.*
3. *Those in favor of the expansion plan maintained that redesigning the runways would increase the number of planes able to land and take off, thereby making increased "production" possible.*

TECHNOLOGY ACTIVITY

Creating Graphs Relating to O'Hare Expansion

Time 30 Minutes ◑

Task Search the Internet for before-and-after statistics for the O'Hare expansion and then use software to create graphs to express those numbers.

Materials Needed computer with graphing software and internet access for research

Activity

- Have students work in small groups to gather as much data as they can on current operations at O'Hare, projected costs of expansion, and the improvements believed to result from expansion.
- Each group should determine the best kind of graph to represent all or some key part of their findings and use graphing software to complete it.
- When the graphs are finished, they should be printed out and shared with the rest of the class, along with an explanation of why that type of graph was chosen.

Rubric

	Understanding of Concepts	Presentation of Information
4	excellent	clear and complete
3	good	somewhat clear and complete
2	fair	acceptable
1	poor	inappropriate

Online Summary Answers

1. scarcity
2. wants
3. consumer
4. producer
5. factors of production
6. trade-off
7. opportunity cost
8. model
9. microeconomics
10. macroeconomics
11. production possibilities curve
12. underutilization

Interactive Review

Review this chapter using interactive activities at ClassZone.com

- Online Summary
- Quizzes
- Vocabulary Flip Cards
- Graphic Organizers
- Review and Study Notes

Online Summary

Complete the following activity either on your own paper or online at ClassZone.com

Choose the key concept that best completes the sentence. Not all key concepts will be used.

consumer	producer
economic model	production possibilities curve
economics	scarcity
efficiency	statistics
factors of production	trade-off
incentive	underutilization
macroeconomics	utility
microeconomics	wants
opportunity cost	

__1__ is the fundamental economic problem. It arises because human __2__ are limitless, while resources are limited. It affects what a __3__ buys and what a __4__ makes. It affects what is produced, how it is produced, and who gets what is produced. It affects how the four __5__ are put to use.

Since people cannot have everything they want, they have to make choices. Every choice, however, involves a __6__, something you have to give up to get what you want. When making an economic decision, you need to consider the __7__, the value of the thing you gave up.

Economists often use an __8__, a simplified representation of reality, to clarify concepts. Economists use such tools in __9__, the study of the economic behavior of individual persons, families, and businesses, and in __10__, the study of the economy as a whole.

One useful model, the __11__, shows the maximum amount of goods that an economy can produce. It also shows __12__, when not all resources are put to full use.

CHAPTER 1 Assessment

REVIEWING KEY CONCEPTS

Scarcity: The Basic Economic Problem (pp. 4–11)

1. In what ways does scarcity affect both consumers and producers?
2. What are the four factors of production and how do they relate to scarcity?

Economic Choice Today: Opportunity Cost (pp. 12–17)

3. What does the phrase "there's no such thing as a free lunch" mean in economic terms?
4. Why is it important to consider marginal benefits and costs when you do a cost-benefit analysis?

Analyzing Production Possibilities (pp. 18–23)

5. What are three things a PPC shows?
6. What factors could lead to economic growth?

The Economist's Toolbox (pp. 24–33)

7. What are some tools that economists use to draw meaning from large amounts of data?
8. What are the differences between microeconomics and macroeconomics?

APPLYING ECONOMIC CONCEPTS

Look at the bar graph below showing the relationship between educational level and weekly wages.

9. Describe the relationship between education and earnings for males in 1979.
10. Explain why the earnings gap between college and high school graduates might have changed between 1979 and 2004.

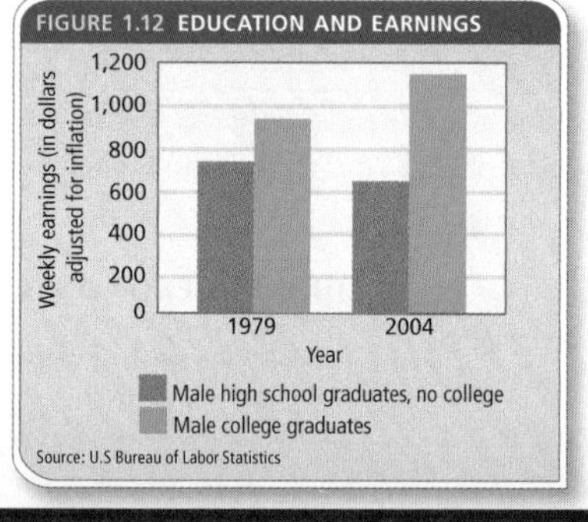

CHAPTER 1 ASSESSMENT ANSWERS

Reviewing Key Concepts

1. Scarcity limits what consumers can buy and limits producers because the resources for production are scarce.
2. The four factors are land, labor, capital, and entrepreneurship. Each is a scarce resource so their use needs to be as efficient as possible.
3. It means that everything has a cost to somebody, either in time, money, or effort.
4. The trade-offs that happen at the margin are the most revealing, since choices are rarely all-or-nothing.
5. the choices people have to make about what to produce; the trade-offs involved in their choices; and the opportunity cost of each choice
6. increased resources or improved technology
7. Charts, tables, graphs, and models help economists see numbers in relation to one another.
8. Microeconomics considers individual players in the economy, such as individual persons, families, and businesses. Macroeconomics looks at the economy as a whole.

Applying Economic Concepts

9. In 1979, male college graduates earned about $200 per week more than male high school graduates.
10. Answers will vary. One explanation would be more demand for college-educated workers and less demand for workers without a college degree.

CRITICAL THINKING

11. **Creating Graphs** Use the following information to create a bar graph showing the weekly wages for females with a high school education and those with a college education in 1979 and 2004.

    1979 High school graduates, no college, $424
    College graduates, $605

    2004 High school graduates, no college, $488
    College graduates, $860

    Source: U.S. Bureau of Labor Statistics

    Use ***SMARTGrapher*** **@ ClassZone.com** to complete this activity.

12. **Interpreting Graphs** Compare the graph you created with the one on page 34. Identify three differences between the changes over time for women and for men.
13. **Evaluating Economic Decisions** You plan to open a restaurant that specializes in meals cooked with organic products. You realize that location is very important for this kind of business. You have two options: you can rent an expensive site downtown or you can buy an inexpensive building in a quiet neighborhood. What are the benefits and the opportunity cost for each option?
14. **Conducting Cost-Benefit Analysis** You are considering taking a part-time job after school at a local veterinary surgery. Create a decision-making grid to analyze your potential choices. Include alternative jobs you might take and the costs and benefits of each. Similarly, list activities other than working that you might pursue after school. Indicate which alternative you would choose and explain your choice.
15. **Challenge** You own a small factory that makes widgets and you want to increase production, so you hire new workers. Each new worker increases productivity, but each also must be paid. When will you stop hiring new workers?

SIMULATION

Start a Business

Step 1 Team up with a partner or small group of classmates.

Step 2 With your partner or group, decide on a business you want to start. This could be anything that has a realistic chance of succeeding: computer technician, T-shirt printer, caramel-corn producer, dog walker, or anything you think may fulfill a want.

Step 3 On a chart like the one below, list the factors of production you will need to use to start and run your business.

Step 4 Develop a business plan—a way that you can use the factors of production so efficiently that you will be able to make money. Describe your business plan in a paragraph.

Step 5 Present your plan to the rest of the class. When all pairs or groups have made their presentations, hold a class vote to select the best plan.

Factors of Production	
Land	Labor
1. 2. 3.	1. 2. 3.
Capital	Entrepreneurship
1. 2. 3.	1. 2. 3.

McDougal Littell
Assessment System

Assess

Online Test Practice
- Go to **ClassZone.com** for more test practice.

Unit 1 Resource Book
- Chapter Test, Forms A, B, & C, pp. 51–62

Test Generator CD-ROM
- Chapter Test, Forms (A, B, & C), in English and Spanish

Report

Use the McDougal Littell Assessment System to score assessments and receive customized reports.

Reteach

For activities customized for individual students, use the McDougal Littell Assessment System.

SMARTGrapher For question 11, students can create a bar graph using **SmartGrapher @ ClassZone.com.**

CHAPTER 1 ASSESSMENT ANSWERS

Critical Thinking

11. Students' graphs should accurately plot the data provided.
12. Answers will vary. Possible responses: Male high school graduates made more money in 1979 than female college graduates. Male high school graduates in 2002 made less money than male high school graduates in 1979. Female college graduates in 2002 made only slightly more than males with only a high school degree in 1979.
13. Expensive site downtown: Benefit—greater customer traffic and, therefore, greater potential sales and profits; Opportunity cost—money spent on rent. Inexpensive site in quiet neighborhood: Benefit—savings on rent; Opportunity cost—lost customer traffic.
14. Decision-making grids will vary. Ensure that students study Max's decision-making grid on page 15 before they answer this question.
15. when the marginal cost of employing one more worker exceeds the marginal benefit

Simulation Rubric

	Business Plan	Presentation of Information
4	excellent	accurate, clear, and complete
3	good	mostly accurate and clear
2	fair	sometimes clear
1	poor	sketchy

Planning Guide

Resources 2Go Complete print resources all on one USB drive allow you to customize lessons.

Section Titles and Objectives	Unit 1 Resource Book and Workbooks		Assessment Resources
1 Introduction to Economic Systems pp. 38–41 • Identify the three main types of economic systems • Understand how a traditional economy operates, including its advantages and disadvantages • Analyze how modern forces are changing traditional economies	**Unit 1 Resource Book** • Reading Study Guide, pp. 63–64 • RSG with Additional Support, pp. 65–67 • RSG with Additional Support (Spanish), pp. 68–70	• Economic Simulations: Why Do People Trade?, pp. 109–110	**Unit 1 Resource Book** • Section Quiz, p. 71 • Reteaching Activity, p. 72 **Test Generator CD-ROM** **Daily Test Practice Transparencies,** TT5
2 Command Economies pp. 42–47 • Describe the main features of a command economy and explain its advantages and disadvantages • Note how socialism and communism differ • Identify modern examples of command economies	**Unit 1 Resource Book** • Reading Study Guide, pp. 73–74 • RSG with Additional Support, pp. 75–77 • RSG with Additional Support (Spanish), pp. 78–80 • Economic Skills and Problem Solving Activity, pp. 103–104	**NCEE Student Activities** • Command Economies, p. 8	**Unit 1 Resource Book** • Section Quiz, p. 81 • Reteaching Activity, p. 82 **Test Generator CD-ROM** **Daily Test Practice Transparencies,** TT6
3 Market Economies pp. 48–57 • Describe what a market is and how it works • Identify the main features of a market economy and explain its advantages and disadvantages • Analyze how the circular flow model represents economic activity in a market economy	**Unit 1 Resource Book** • Reading Study Guide, pp. 83–84 • RSG with Additional Support, pp. 85–87 • RSG with Additional Support (Spanish), pp. 88–90 • Math Skills Worksheet: Calculating Percentages, p. 111	• Readings in Free Enterprise: Capitalism: Two Views, pp. 105–106 **NCEE Student Activities** • The Circular Flow of Economic Activity, pp. 5–7	**Unit 1 Resource Book** • Section Quiz, p. 91 • Reteaching Activity, p. 92 **Test Generator CD-ROM** **Daily Test Practice Transparencies,** TT7
4 Modern Economies In a Global Age pp. 58–65 • Identify the main characteristics of a mixed economy • Understand why most modern economies are mixed economies • Explain why modern economies are becoming increasingly global	**Unit 1 Resource Book** • Reading Study Guide, pp. 93–94 • RSG with Additional Support, pp. 95–97 • RSG with Additional Support (Spanish), pp. 98–100 • Case Study Resources: Making Cars for the World; North Korea Blocks a Market Economy, pp. 107–108	**Test Practice and Review Workbook,** pp. 25–26	**Unit 1 Resource Book** • Section Quiz, p. 101 • Reteaching Activity, p. 102 • Chapter Test, (Forms A, B, & C), pp. 113–124 **Test Generator CD-ROM** **Daily Test Practice Transparencies,** TT8

Integrated Technology

No Time? To focus students on the most important content in this chapter, use Animated Economics, "The Circular Flow Model," available in Resources 2Go.

Teacher Presentation Options

Presentation Toolkit

Power Presentation DVD-ROM

- Lecture Notes
- Interactive Review
- Media Gallery
- Animated Economics
- Review Game

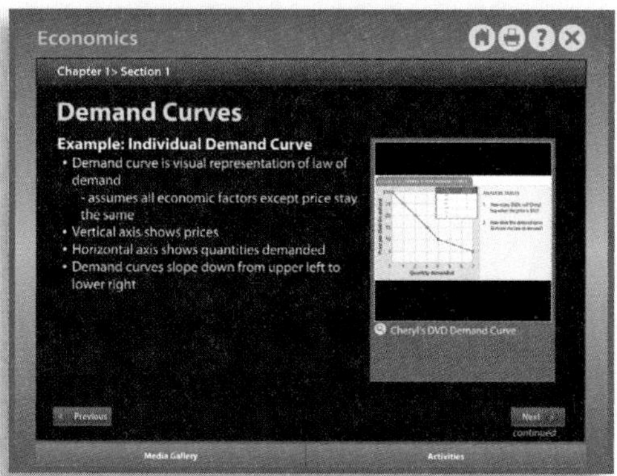

Economics Concepts Transparencies

- Traditional Economy, CT5
- Command Economies Table, CT6
- The Circular Flow Model, CT7
- Countries With Mixed Economies, CT8

Electronic Books

eEdition DVD-ROM

eEdition Online

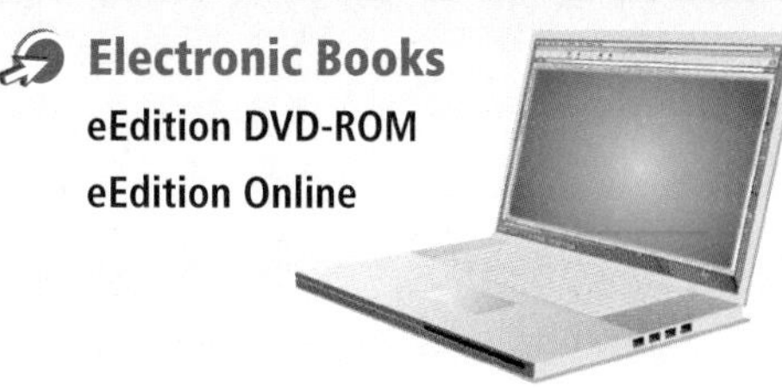

Daily Test Practice Transparencies, TT5, TT6, TT7, TT8

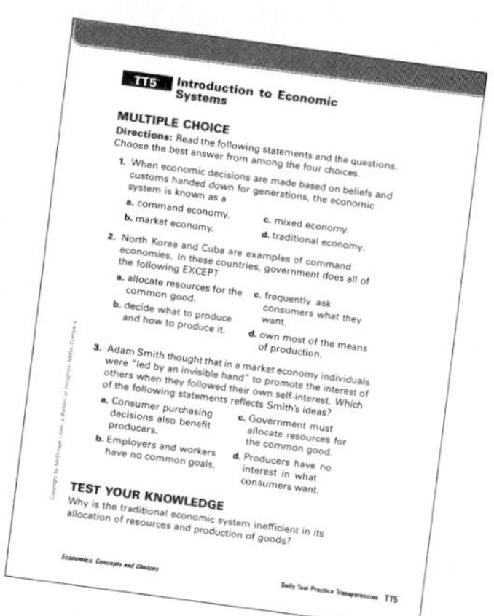

Animated Economics

- The Circular Flow Model, p. 53

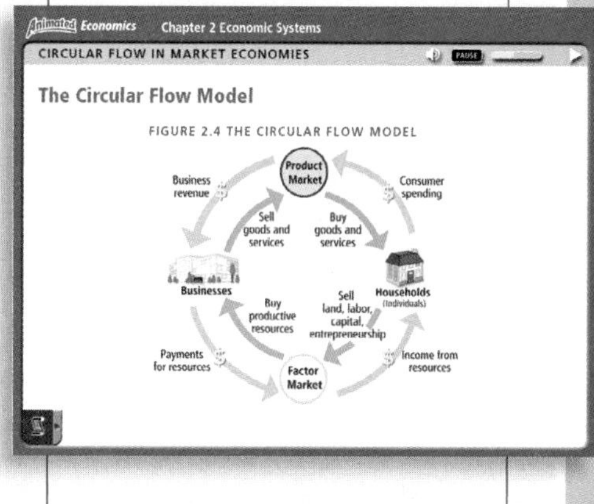

Online Activities at ClassZone.com

Economics Update

- Issues in a Market Economy, p. 39
- Karl Marx, p. 44
- Developing Market Economies in Eastern Europe, p. 54
- Global Partnerships, p. 62
- Contrasting Economies: North Korea and South Korea, p. 64

Animated Economics

- Interactive Graphics

Activity Maker

- Vocabulary Flip Cards
- Review Game

Research Center

- Graphs and Data

Interactive Review

- Online Summary
- Quizzes
- Vocabulary Flip Cards
- Graphic Organizers
- Review and Study Notes

SMARTGrapher

- Create a Graph, p. 47

Teacher-Tested Activities

Name: Sandra K. Wright

School: Adlai E. Stevenson High School

State: Illinois

Teacher-Tested Activities

At the beginning of this chapter, look for my classroom-proven idea for teaching economics concepts and thinking.

Resources for Differentiated Instruction

Struggling Readers

Teacher's Edition Activities

- Use Chronology, p. 44
- Identify Cause and Effect, p. 50
- Taking Notes on Market Economies, p. 54
- Use Text Features, p. 56
- Chart Details, p. 62

Unit 1 Resource Book

- RSG with Additional Support, pp. 65–67, 75–77, 85–87, 95–97 (A)
- Reteaching Activities, pp. 72, 82, 92, 102 (B)
- Chapter Test (Form A), pp. 113–115 (C)

ClassZone.com

- Animated Economics
- Interactive Review

Test Generator CD-ROM

- Chapter Test (Form A)
- Chapter Test (Form A), in Spanish

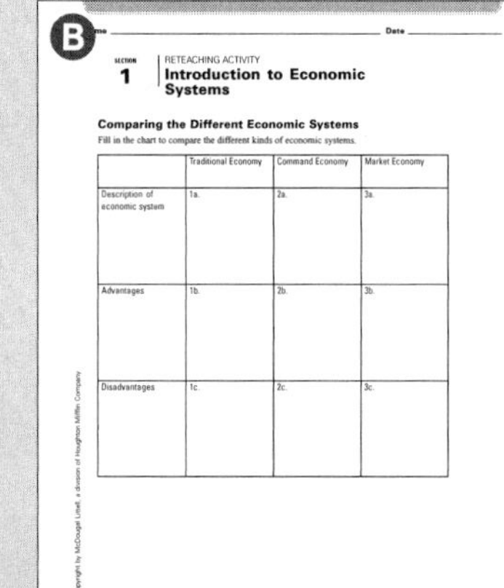

B

SECTION 1 RETEACHING ACTIVITY
Introduction to Economic Systems

Comparing the Different Economic Systems
Fill in the chart to compare the different kinds of economic systems.

	Traditional Economy	Command Economy	Market Economy
Description of economic system	1a.	2a.	3a.
Advantages	1b.	2b.	3b.
Disadvantages	1c.	2c.	3c.

Reteaching Activity 72
Unit 1 Resource Book

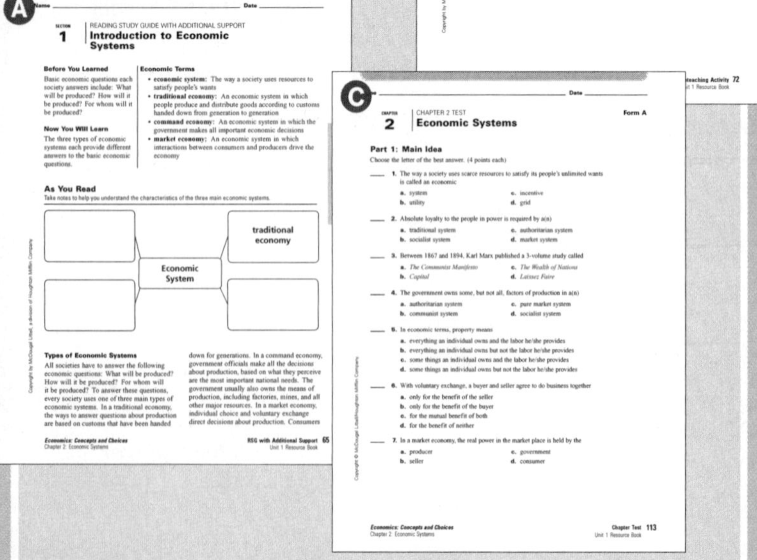

A

SECTION 1 READING STUDY GUIDE WITH ADDITIONAL SUPPORT
Introduction to Economic Systems

Before You Learned
Basic economic questions each society answers include: What will be produced? How will it be produced? For whom will it be produced?

Now You Will Learn
The three types of economic systems each provide different answers to the basic economic questions.

Economic Terms
- **economic system:** The way a society uses resources to satisfy people's wants
- **traditional economy:** An economic system in which people produce and distribute goods according to customs handed down from generation to generation
- **command economy:** An economic system in which the government makes all important economic decisions
- **market economy:** An economic system in which interactions between consumers and producers drive the economy

As You Read
Take notes to help you understand the characteristics of the three main economic systems.

Types of Economic Systems
All societies have to answer the following economic questions: What will be produced? How will it be produced? For whom will it be produced? To answer these questions, every society uses one of three main types of economic systems. In a traditional economy, the ways to answer economic questions about production are based on customs that have been handed down for generations. In a command economy, government officials make all the decisions about production, based on what they perceive are the most important national needs. The government usually also owns the means of production, including factories, mines, and all other major resources. In a market economy, individual choice and voluntary exchange direct decisions about production. Consumers

Economics: Concepts and Choices
Chapter 2 Economic Systems
RSG with Additional Support 65
Unit 1 Resource Book

C

CHAPTER 2 TEST Form A
Economic Systems

Part 1: Main Idea
Choose the letter of the best answer. (4 points each)

___ 1. The way a society uses scarce resources to satisfy its people's unlimited wants is called an economic
a. system c. incentive
b. utility d. grid

___ 2. Absolute loyalty to the people in power is required by a(n)
a. traditional system c. authoritarian system
b. socialist system d. market system

___ 3. Between 1867 and 1894, Karl Marx published a 3-volume study called
a. *The Communist Manifesto* c. *The Wealth of Nations*
b. *Capital* d. *Laissez Faire*

___ 4. The government owns some, but not all, factors of production in a(n)
a. authoritarian system c. pure market system
b. communist system d. socialist system

___ 5. In economic terms, property means
a. everything an individual owns and the labor he/she provides
b. everything an individual owns but not the labor he/she provides
c. some things an individual owns and the labor he/she provides
d. some things an individual owns but not the labor he/she provides

___ 6. With voluntary exchange, a buyer and seller agree to do business together
a. only for the benefit of the seller
b. only for the benefit of the buyer
c. for the mutual benefit of both
d. for the benefit of neither

___ 7. In a market economy, the real power in the market place is held by the
a. producer c. government
b. seller d. consumer

Economics: Concepts and Choices
Chapter 2 Economic Systems
Chapter Test 113
Unit 1 Resource Book

English Learners

Teacher's Edition Activities

- Work with Synonyms, p. 40
- Use Strategies for Unfamiliar Words, p. 46
- Develop Subject-Related Terms, p. 52
- Develop Social Studies Vocabulary, p. 60

Unit 1 Resource Book

- RSG with Additional Support (Spanish), pp. 68–70, 78–80, 88–90, 98–100 (A)

Test Generator CD-ROM

- Chapter Test (Forms A, B, & C), in Spanish (B)

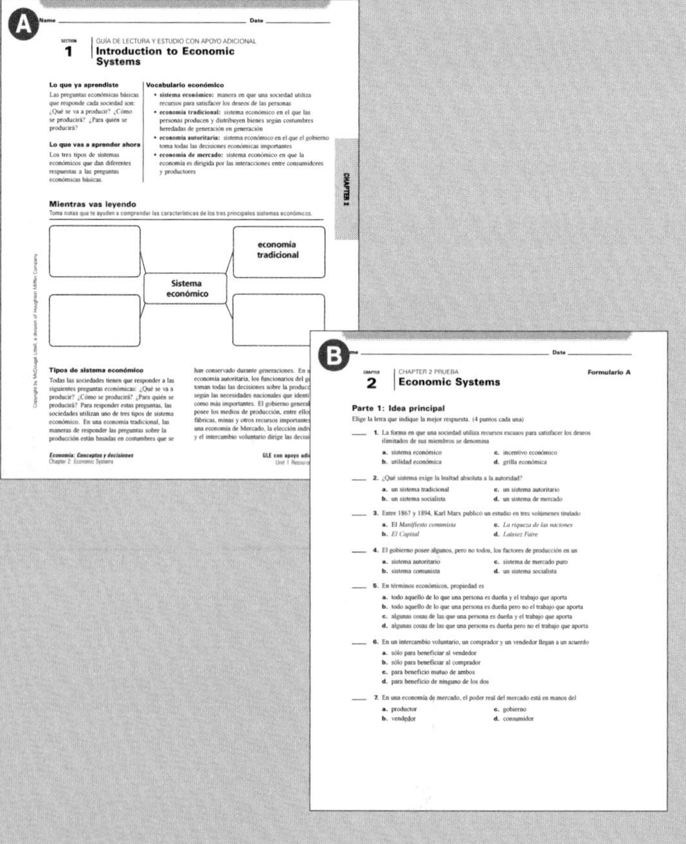

A

SECCIÓN 1 GUÍA DE LECTURA Y ESTUDIO CON APOYO ADICIONAL
Introduction to Economic Systems

Lo que ya aprendiste
Las preguntas económicas básicas que responde cada sociedad son: ¿Qué se va a producir? ¿Cómo se producirá? ¿Para quién se producirá?

Lo que vas a aprender ahora
Los tres tipos de sistemas económicos que dan diferentes respuestas a las preguntas económicas básicas.

Vocabulario económico
- **sistema económico:** manera en que una sociedad utiliza recursos para satisfacer los deseos de las personas
- **economía tradicional:** sistema económico en el que las personas producen y distribuyen bienes según costumbres heredadas de generación en generación
- **economía autoritaria:** sistema económico en el que el gobierno toma todas las decisiones económicas importantes
- **economía de mercado:** sistema económico en que la economía es dirigida por las interacciones entre consumidores y productores

Mientras vas leyendo
Toma notas que te ayuden a comprender las características de los tres principales sistemas económicos.

Tipos de sistema económico

B

CAPÍTULO 2 PRUEBA Formulario A
Economic Systems

Parte 1: Idea principal
Elige la letra que indique la mejor respuesta. (4 puntos cada una)

___ 1. La forma en que una sociedad utiliza recursos escasos para satisfacer los deseos ilimitados de sus miembros se denomina
a. sistema económico c. incentivo económico
b. utilidad económica d. grilla económica

___ 2. ¿Qué sistema exige la lealtad absoluta a la autoridad?
a. un sistema tradicional c. un sistema autoritario
b. un sistema socialista d. un sistema de mercado

___ 3. Entre 1867 y 1894, Karl Marx publicó un estudio en tres volúmenes titulado
a. *El Manifiesto comunista* c. *La riqueza de las naciones*
b. *El Capital* d. *Laissez Faire*

___ 4. El gobierno posee algunos, pero no todos, los factores de producción en un
a. sistema autoritario c. sistema de mercado puro
b. sistema comunista d. un sistema socialista

___ 5. En términos económicos, propiedad es
a. todo aquello de lo que una persona es dueña y el trabajo que aporta
b. todo aquello de lo que una persona es dueña pero no el trabajo que aporta
c. algunas cosas de las que una persona es dueña y el trabajo que aporta
d. algunas cosas de las que una persona es dueña pero no el trabajo que aporta

___ 6. En un intercambio voluntario, un comprador y un vendedor llegan a un acuerdo
a. sólo para beneficiar al vendedor
b. sólo para beneficiar al comprador
c. para beneficio mutuo de ambos
d. para beneficio de ninguno de los dos

___ 7. En una economía de mercado, el poder real del mercado está en manos del
a. productor c. gobierno
b. vendedor d. consumidor

Inclusion

Teacher's Edition Activities

- Complete Sentences, p. 40
- Use Visuals, p. 46
- Make a Chart, p. 54
- Read Aloud, p. 62
- Use Self-Monitoring, p. 64

Lesson Plans

- Modified Lessons for Inclusion, pp. 5–8 (A)

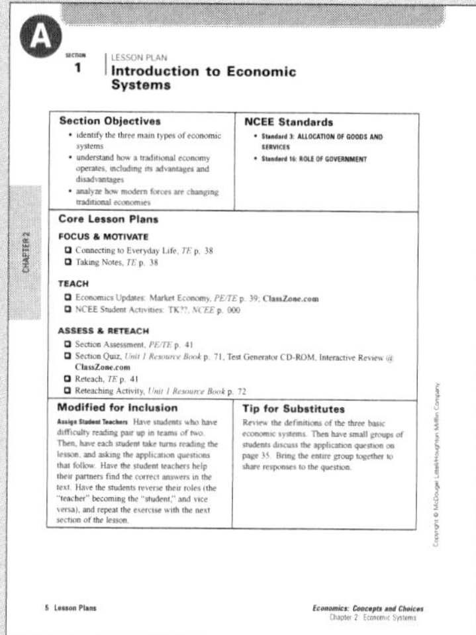

A

SECTION 1 | LESSON PLAN

Introduction to Economic Systems

CHAPTER 2

Section Objectives	NCEE Standards
• identify the three main types of economic systems • understand how a traditional economy operates, including its advantages and disadvantages • analyze how modern forces are changing traditional economies	• Standard 3: ALLOCATION OF GOODS AND SERVICES • Standard 16: ROLE OF GOVERNMENT

Core Lesson Plans

FOCUS & MOTIVATE
- ❑ Connecting to Everyday Life, *TE* p. 38
- ❑ Taking Notes, *TE* p. 38

TEACH
- ❑ Economics Updates: Market Economy, *PE/TE* p. 39; **ClassZone.com**
- ❑ NCEE Student Activities: TK??, *NCEE* p. 000

ASSESS & RETEACH
- ❑ Section Assessment, *PE/TE* p. 41
- ❑ Section Quiz, *Unit 1 Resource Book* p. 71, Test Generator CD-ROM, Interactive Review @ **ClassZone.com**
- ❑ Reteach, *TE* p. 41
- ❑ Reteaching Activity, *Unit 1 Resource Book* p. 72

Modified for Inclusion	Tip for Substitutes
Assign Student Teachers Have students who have difficulty reading pair up in teams of two. Then, have each student take turns reading the lesson, and asking the application questions that follow. Have the student teachers help their partners find the correct answers in the text. Have the students reverse their roles (the "teacher" becoming the "student," and vice versa), and repeat the exercise with the next section of the lesson.	Review the definitions of the three basic economic systems. Then have small groups of students discuss the application question on page 35. Bring the entire group together to share responses to the question.

Copyright © McDougal Littell/Houghton Mifflin Company.

5 Lesson Plans — *Economics: Concepts and Choices* Chapter 2 Economic Systems

Gifted and Talented

Teacher's Edition Activities

- Conduct Research, p. 44
- Respond to Competition, p. 50
- Create Alternate Representations, p. 52
- Revise the Passage, p. 56
- Create a Globalization Cartoon, p. 60
- Consider "What If," p. 64

Unit 1 Resource Book

- Readings in Free Enterprise: Capitalism: Two Views, pp. 105–106 (A)
- Case Study Resources: North Korea Blocks a Market Economy; Making Cars for the World, pp. 107–108 (B)

NCEE Student Activities

- The Circular Flow of Economic Activity, pp. 5–7 (C)
- Command Economies, p. 8

ClassZone.com

- Research Center

Test Generator CD-ROM

- Chapter Test (Form C)
- Chapter Test (Form C), in Spanish

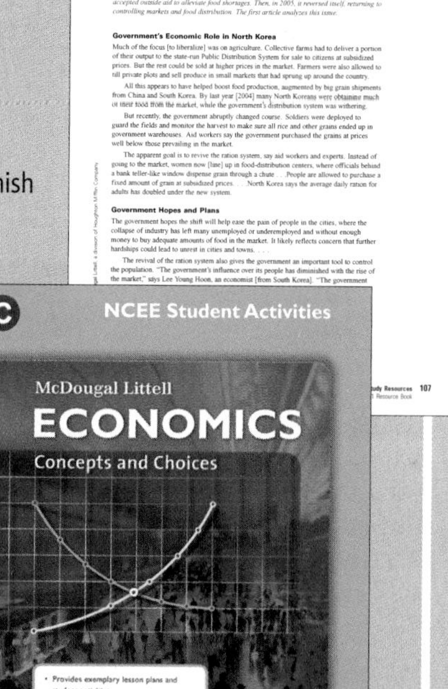

B

Date ______

CHAPTER 2 | CASE STUDY RESOURCES

Economic Systems

North Korea Blocks a Market Economy

From *The Wall Street Journal*, December 27, 2005.

In 2002, the government of North Korea loosened some of its control over markets and accepted outside aid to alleviate food shortages. Then, in 2005, it reversed itself, returning to controlling markets and food distribution. The first article analyzes this issue.

Government's Economic Role in North Korea

Much of the focus [to liberalize] was on agriculture. Collective farms had to deliver a portion of their output to the state-run Public Distribution System for sale to citizens at subsidized prices. But the rest could be sold at higher prices in the market. Farmers were also allowed to till private plots and sell produce in small markets that had sprung up around the country.

All this appears to have helped boost food production, augmented by big grain shipments from China and South Korea. By last year [2004] many North Koreans were obtaining much of their food from the market, while the government's distribution system was withering.

But recently, the government abruptly changed course. Soldiers were deployed to guard the fields and monitor the harvest to make sure all rice and other grains ended up in government warehouses. Aid workers say the government purchased the grains at prices well below those prevailing in the market.

The apparent goal is to revive the ration system, say aid workers and experts. Instead of going to the market, women now [line] up in food-distribution centers, where officials behind a bank teller-like window dispense grain through a chute . . . People are allowed to purchase a fixed amount of grain at subsidized prices. . . . North Korea says the average daily ration for adults has doubled under the new system.

Government Hopes and Plans

The government hopes the shift will help ease the pain of people in the cities, where the collapse of industry has left many unemployed or underemployed and without enough money to buy adequate amounts of food in the market. It likely reflects concern that further hardships could lead to unrest in cities and towns. . . .

The revival of the ration system also gives the government an important tool to control the population. "The government's influence over its people has diminished with the rise of the market," says Lee Young Hoon, an economist [from South Korea]. "The government

...udy Resources 107

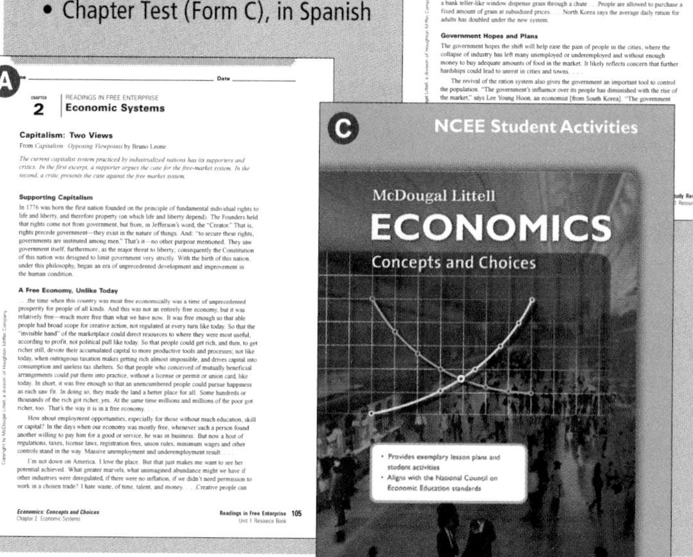

A

Date ______

CHAPTER 2 | READINGS IN FREE ENTERPRISE

Economic Systems

Capitalism: Two Views

From *Capitalism: Opposing Viewpoints* by Bruno Leone.

The current capitalist system practiced by industrialized nations has its supporters and critics. In the first excerpt, a supporter argues the case for the free-market system. In the second, a critic presents the case against the free market system.

Supporting Capitalism

In 1776 was born the first nation founded on the principle of fundamental individual rights to life and liberty, and therefore property (on which life and liberty depend). The Founders held that rights come not from government, but from, in Jefferson's word, the "Creator." That is, rights precede government—they exist in the nature of things. And: "to secure these rights, governments are instituted among men." That's it—no other purpose mentioned. They saw government itself, furthermore, as the major threat to liberty; consequently the Constitution of this nation was designed to limit government very strictly. With the birth of this nation, under this philosophy, began an era of unprecedented development and improvement in the human condition.

A Free Economy, Unlike Today

. . . the time when this country was most free economically was a time of unprecedented prosperity for people of all kinds. And this was not an entirely free economy, but it was relatively free—much more free than what we have now. It was free enough so that able people had broad scope for creative action, not regulated at every turn like today. So that the "invisible hand" of the marketplace could direct resources to where they were most useful, according to profit, not political pull like today. So that people could get rich, and then, to get richer still, devote their accumulated capital to more productive tools and processes; not like today, when outrageous taxation makes getting rich almost impossible, and drives capital into consumption and useless tax shelters. So that people who conceived of mutually beneficial arrangements could put them into practice, without a license or permit or union card, like today. In short, it was free enough so that an unencumbered people could pursue happiness as each saw fit. In doing so, they made the land a better place for all. Some hundreds or thousands of the rich got richer, yes. At the same time millions and millions of the poor got richer, too. That's the way it is in a free economy. . . .

How about employment opportunities, especially for those without much education, skill or capital? In the days when our economy was mostly free, whenever such a person found another willing to pay him for a good or service, he was in business. But now a host of regulations, taxes, license laws, registration fees, union rules, minimum wages and other controls stand in the way. Massive unemployment and underemployment result. . . .

I'm not down on America. I love the place. But that just makes me want to see her potential achieved. What greater marvels, what unimagined abundance might we have if other industries were deregulated, if there were no inflation, if we didn't need permission to work in a chosen trade? I hate waste, of time, talent, and money. . . . Creative people can

Copyright by McDougal Littell, a division of Houghton Mifflin Company.

Economics: Concepts and Choices Chapter 2 Economic Systems — Readings in Free Enterprise 105 Unit 1 Resource Book

Focus & Motivate

Objective

Explain how traditional, command, market, and mixed economies answer the three fundamental economic questions.

Why the Concept Matters

Begin by reminding students of the central concept of economics, scarcity, and the three basic questions that grow out of it: What? How? and For Whom? Then point out that many aspects of students' lives—the work they do, the wages they receive, the products they're able to buy—are determined by the way a society answers these questions.

Analyzing the Photograph

Direct students to try to draw some inferences about this farmer's daily life. *(Possible answer: perhaps lives in a simple house without much in the way of technology and has limited education; uses traditional farming methods)* Then point out to students that these are all first impressions. They should hold onto their ideas as they read the chapter to see whether they are valid and how traditional economies in general, and China specifically, relate to the discussion of economic systems and modern economic trends.

Traditional Economy

Some economic activities have changed little over time. This farmer in Guizhou Province, China, employs rice-farming methods that the Chinese have used for centuries.

36

CONTENT STANDARDS

NCEE STANDARDS

Standard 3: Allocation of Goods and Services

Students will understand that

Different methods can be used to allocate goods and services. People acting individually or collectively through government, must choose which methods to use to allocate different kinds of goods and services.

Students will be able to use this knowledge to

Evaluate different methods of allocating goods and services, by comparing the benefits and costs of each method.

Benchmarks

Students will know that

- People in all economies must address three questions: What goods and services will be produced? How will these goods and services be produced? Who will consume them? *(pages 38–40)*
- There are essential differences between a market economy, in which allocations result from individuals making decisions as buyers and sellers, and a command economy, in which resources are allocated according to central authority. *(pages 42–55)*
- National economies vary in the extent to which they rely on government directives (central planning) and signals from private markets (prices) to allocate scarce goods, services, and productive resources. *(pages 58–60)*

CHAPTER

2 Economic Systems

SECTION 1 Introduction to Economic Systems

SECTION 2 Command Economies

SECTION 3 Market Economies

SECTION 4 Modern Economies in a Global Age

CASE STUDY Contrasting Economies: North Korea and South Korea

CONCEPT REVIEW

Scarcity is the situation that exists when there are not enough resources to meet human wants.

CHAPTER 2 KEY CONCEPT

An **economic system** is the way in which a society uses its scarce resources to satisfy its people's unlimited wants.

WHY THE CONCEPT MATTERS

How does a society decide the ways to use scarce resources to meet unlimited wants? Its economic system determines what to produce, how to produce, and for whom to produce. Although every country today uses a mixture of economic systems, some mixed systems provide more economic and political freedom and create more wealth than others.

Online Highlights

More at ClassZone.com

Economics Update

Go to ECONOMICS UPDATE for chapter updates and current news on the economies of North Korea and South Korea. (See Case Study, pp. 64–65.) ▶

Animated Economics

Go to ANIMATED ECONOMICS for interactive lessons on the graphs and tables in this chapter.

Interactive Review

Go to INTERACTIVE REVIEW for concept review and activities.

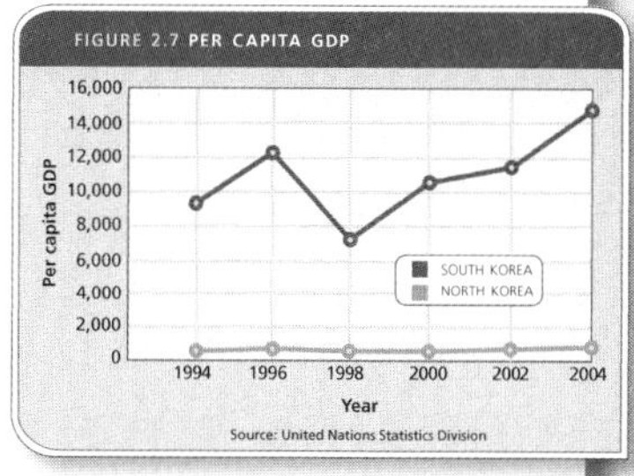

How do the economies of North Korea and South Korea compare? See the Case Study on pages 64–65.

From the Classroom

Sandra Wright, Adlai E. Stevenson H.S.

Tell students that the classroom will become an economy that produces three-color paper chains made with four-inch strips and paper airplanes with drawn-on windows and a logo on the wings. Break the students into five groups.

Command Economy

Groups must get supplies from the teacher.
Group 1 measures and marks the paper for cutting.
Group 2 cuts each strip.
Group 3 attaches strips to make three-color chains.
Group 4 folds the paper airplanes.
Group 5 draws the logos and windows.

Free Market Economy

Supplies are available from the teacher, but groups can use their own supplies. Each group decides whether to make chains or airplanes or both. Groups may trade amongst themselves. The group with the most pairs of chains and airplanes wins.

Compare the total number of chains and airplanes produced under each system. Ask who owned the factors of production and who made the decisions about what to produce and how to produce it.

Previewing Chapter Technology at ClassZone.com

Economics Update Students will find updates to information in the pupil edition on pages 39, 44, 54, 62, and 64.

Animated Economics Students will find interactive lessons related to materials on page 53.

Interactive Review Students will find additional section and chapter assessment support for materials on pages 41, 47, 57, 63, and 66.

TEACHER MEDIA FAVORITES

Books

- Buchholz, Todd G. *New Ideas from Dead Economists.* New York: Plume, 1999. Offers a readable study of the strengths and weaknesses of major economic theories.
- Heilbroner, Robert L. *The Worldly Philosophers: The Lives, Times and Ideas of the Great Economic Thinkers, 7th Edition.* New York: Touchstone, 1999. Heilbroner updates the popular overview of economic thinkers and their impact.

Videos/DVDs

- *Fundamental Economic Concepts.* 29 minutes. United Learning, 1997. Explores resource allocation, historical systems, and free market economies.
- *Economics.* 50 minutes. Bullfrog Films, 2001. Offers an alternative view of globalization through the perspective of environmentalism.

Software

- Global Economics Game CD-Rom (Windows XP) *The Global Economics Game, 2004.* Offers students an opportunity to learn about trade-offs and challenges in balancing a nation's economy.

Internet

Visit **ClassZone.com** to link to

- a variety of chapter-specific, content-reviewed sites
- updates on data and topics presented throughout the chapter sections and Case Study
- updates to the Power Presentations

1 Plan & Prepare

Section 1 Objectives

- identify the three main types of economic systems
- understand how a traditional economy operates, including its advantages and disadvantages
- analyze how modern forces are changing traditional economies

2 Focus & Motivate

Connecting to Everyday Life Ask students how important it is to feel that they have choices in their lives. Also, ask them to give examples of the choices they have available. Have them consider instances in which choice is denied and the reasons for denial. *(Possible answers include the choices of friends, activities, clothing; choices denied might include whether or not to attend school, not to vote until age 18. Reasons for the denied choices might include both the good of the society and the good of the minor person. Parallel this with the way some economies work, taking on the role of choice for individuals.)*

Taking Notes Remind students to take notes as they read by completing a cluster diagram of information on different economic systems. They can use the Graphic Organizer at **Interactive Review @ ClassZone.com.** A sample is shown below.

traditional economy: age-old customs and beliefs

Economic System

market economy: individuals and businesses

command economy: government

SECTION 1

Introduction to Economic Systems

OBJECTIVES	KEY TERMS	TAKING NOTES
In Section 1, you will • identify the three main types of economic systems • understand how a traditional economy operates, including its advantages and disadvantages • analyze how modern forces are changing traditional economies	economic system, *p. 38* traditional economy, *p. 38* command economy, *p. 39* market economy, *p. 39*	As you read Section 1, complete a cluster diagram that provides information on the different kinds of economic systems. Use the Graphic Organizer at **Interactive Review @ ClassZone.com**

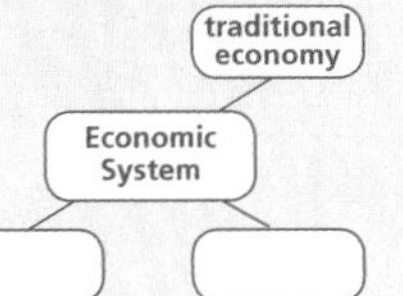

Types of Economic Systems

KEY CONCEPTS

In his book *Utopia*, 16th-century writer Thomas More describes a society without scarcity, where wants are limited and easily fulfilled. It is no accident, however, that the word *utopia* means "no place" in Greek. In the real world, scarcity is a fact of life. To address scarcity, societies must answer three questions:

- What should be produced?
- How should it be produced?
- For whom will it be produced?

The answers to these questions shape the economic system a society has. An **economic system** is the way a society uses its scarce resources to satisfy its people's unlimited wants. There are three basic types of economic systems: traditional economies, command economies, and market economies. In this chapter you will learn about these economic systems, as well as "mixed" economies that have features of more than one type.

QUICK REFERENCE

An **economic system** is the way a society uses resources to satisfy its people's wants.

A **traditional economy** is an economic system in which people produce and distribute goods according to customs handed down from generation to generation.

TYPE 1 Traditional Economy

A **traditional economy** is an economic system in which families, clans, or tribes make economic decisions based on customs and beliefs that have been handed down from generation to generation. The one goal of these societies is survival. Everyone has a set role in this task. Men often are hunters and herders. Women tend the crops and raise children. The youngest help with everyday chores while learning the skills they will need for their adult roles. There is no chance of deviating from this pattern. The good of the group always takes precedence over individual desires.

SECTION 1 PROGRAM RESOURCES

ON LEVEL

Lesson Plans
- Core, p. 5

Unit 1 Resource Book
- Reading Study Guide, pp. 63–64
- Economic Skills and Problem Solving Activity, pp. 103–104
- Economic Simulations, pp. 109–110
- Section Quiz, p.71

STRUGGLING READERS

Unit 1 Resource Book
- Reading Study Guide with Additional Support, pp. 65–67
- Reteaching Activity, p. 72

ENGLISH LEARNERS

Unit 1 Resource Book
- Reading Study Guide with Additional Support (Spanish), pp. 68–70

INCLUSION

Lesson Plans
- Modified for Inclusion, p. 5

GIFTED AND TALENTED

Unit 1 Resource Book
- Case Study Resources: North Korea Blocks a Market Economy, p. 92

TECHNOLOGY

eEdition DVD-ROM

eEdition Online

Power Presentation DVD-ROM

Economics Concepts Transparencies
- CT5 Traditional Economy

Daily Test Practice Transparencies, TT5

ClassZone.com

Traditional The Kavango people of Namibia use fishing techniques passed down from generation to generation.

Command Food was scarce and expensive in this store in the former Soviet Union, a command economy.

Market Advertisements, like these billboards in New York City, are a common sight in a market economy.

TYPE 2 Command Economy

In the second type of economic system, a **command economy**, the government decides what goods and services will be produced, how they will be produced, and how they will be distributed. In a command economy, government officials consider the resources and needs of the country and allocate those resources according to their judgment. The wants of individual consumers are rarely considered. The government also usually owns the means of production—all the resources and factories. North Korea and Cuba are current examples of command economies. Before the collapse of communism in Europe, countries such as the Soviet Union, Poland, and East Germany also were command economies.

QUICK REFERENCE

A **command economy** is an economic system in which the government makes all economic decisions.

A **market economy** is an economic system in which individual choice and voluntary exchange direct economic decisions.

TYPE 3 Market Economy

The third type of economic system, a **market economy**, is based on individual choice, not government directives. In other words, in this system consumers and producers drive the economy. Consumers are free to spend their money as they wish, to enter into business, or to sell their labor to whomever they want. Producers decide what goods or services they will offer. They make choices about how to use their limited resources to earn the most money possible.

In a market economy, then, individuals act in their own self-interest when they make economic choices. However, as they seek to serve their own interests, they benefit others. As a consumer, you choose to buy the products that best meet your wants. However, this benefits the producers who make those products, because they earn money from your purchases. As Adam Smith noted in *The Wealth of Nations* (1776), when you make economic decisions you act in your self-interest, but you are "led by an invisible hand" to promote the interests of others.

Economics Update

Find an update on issues in a market economy at **ClassZone.com**

APPLICATION Applying Economic Concepts

A. How might economic activities within a family with adults, teenagers, and young children represent aspects of traditional, command, and market economies?
See answer in Teacher's Edition. ▶

❸ Teach

Types of Economic Systems

Discuss

- How does a traditional economy answer the three economic questions? *(what—what has always been produced; how—in traditional ways; for whom—good of the group)*
- How does a command economy answer the three economic questions? *(what—the government decides; how—by government-owned means of production; for whom—the whole group)*
- How does a market economy answer the three economic questions? *(what—the goods consumers will buy are produced; how—by individually-owned enterprises; for whom—people who can afford them)*

Economics Update

At **ClassZone.com,** students will see updated information on issues in a market economy.

APPLICATION

Answer *Traditional: communal sense of everyone contributing to the good of all without exact accounting of who does what nor the expectation of profiting from one another; Command: authority of adults to make economic decisions for the family; market: payment by parents of allowance to younger children in exchange for chores—both sides benefit.*

LEVELED ACTIVITY

Understand Types of Economies

Time 30–60 minutes 

Objective Students will demonstrate the key differences among traditional, command, and market economies.

Basic

In a small group, create a poster that shows the three economic questions and how a traditional, command, and market economy answers each of those questions. Arrange the poster in any way but make sure that it contains at least one illustration for each question.

On Level

Create a two-paragraph scenario that highlights an economic decision, problem, or opportunity in a traditional, command, market, or mixed economy. Provide enough information so that classmates will be able to guess which economy is represented.

Challenge

Use an outline political map of the world. Identify through the use of color where in the world each type of economy can be found. Employ paper and coloring tools or computer graphics for this project. Accompany your map with a key that includes a definition of each type of economy.

Characteristics of Traditional Economies

Discuss

- In your opinion, what is the greatest advantage of a traditional economy? Why? *(Answers will vary, but may include the idea of strong social ties and the sense of a common good.)*
- What, if anything, do developed nations owe to developing nations as globalization reaches traditional societies? *(Answers will vary. For example, some students may think that the opportunity to expand their economy through global ties is a substantial gain for developing nations and that nothing further is owed. Others may mention that developed nations should be careful not to take advantage of workers in developing nations.)*

More About . . .

Kavango Ways of Life
Among the Kavango, about three-quarters of the land is communally owned. Each household grows what crops it needs on the land it has been given to use. Parcels of land are assigned to each adult member of the household. Livestock graze on communal lands. Farmers grow sorghum, millet, maize, beans, and pumpkins, using the methods that have been passed down through the generations. They believe that the god they worship will always provide enough rain for the next season, so they grow only enough food to last for one year. Many do not use fertilizer because growing more crops than one's neighbors often leads to accusations of *rututa,* enlisting supernatural powers.

Characteristics of Traditional Economies

KEY CONCEPTS

In the earliest times, all societies had traditional economies. Such systems serve the main purpose of traditional societies—survival—very well. The traditional economic system, however, tends to be inefficient and does not adapt to change.

TRAIT 1 Advantages and Disadvantages

The one great advantage of a traditional economy is that it so clearly answers the three economic questions. A traditional society produces what best ensures its survival. The methods of production are the same as they have always been. Systems of distribution are also determined by custom and tradition. In a traditional economy, then, there is little disagreement over economic goals and roles.

Traditional economies have several major disadvantages, too. Because they are based on ritual and custom, traditional economies resist change. Therefore, they are less productive than they might be if they adopted new approaches. Further, while traditionally defined roles eliminate conflict, they also prevent people from doing the jobs they want to do or are best suited to do. People who are in the "wrong" jobs are less productive. The lower productivity in traditional economies means that people do not acquire the material wealth that people in other societies do. As a result, people in traditional economies have a much lower standard of living.

TRAIT 2 Under Pressure to Change

Around the world, traditional economies are under pressure from the forces of change. The Kavango people of Namibia in southern Africa, for example, have lived as subsistence farmers for centuries. (Subsistence farmers grow just enough to feed their own families.) Modern telecommunications, however, have bombarded the Kavango with images of the world beyond their homeland. As a result, many young Kavango want something more than the life of subsistence farming. Thousands have left their homeland for the cities. Even the old ways of farming are beginning to change. The vast majority of the Kavango people still make a living from subsistence farming. However, a few have turned to commercial farming, where they grow crops not for their own use, but for sale.

Forces of Change The use of the cell phone has brought changes to many traditional African societies.

APPLICATION Making Inferences

B. There are no pure traditional economies today. Why do you think this is so?
Modernization and pressure from the outside world have led traditional economies to change and adopt new ways.

DIFFERENTIATING INSTRUCTION

English Learners

Work with Synonyms
Direct students to the heading structure of this lesson and ask what *trait* means. Have students think of as many synonyms as they can, or use a dictionary or thesaurus to come up with synonyms. *(quality, attribute, characteristic, property)* Have students tab a section of a spiral notebook for a collection of synonyms. Then, enter the synonyms for *trait* in that part of their notebooks.

Inclusion

Complete Sentences
Have students use the two paragraphs under the heading Trait 1 to complete the following sentences:
One great advantage is ___________.
Other advantages are that it produces what best ____________ and that there is little ________________. However, traditional economies resist _______.
They are ______ productive than if they accepted new ways. They also prevent people from ___________. As a result, people are less __________.

Online Quiz
ClassZone.com

REVIEWING KEY CONCEPTS

1. Demonstrate your understanding of the following terms by using each one in a sentence.
   a. *traditional economy* b. *command economy* c. *market economy*
2. Which is more important in a traditional economy, accumulating individual wealth or honoring tradition? Explain your answer.
3. How are economic decisions made in a command economy?
4. What drives the choices of consumers and producers in a market economy?
5. Does Adam Smith's "invisible hand" also function in traditional and command economies? Explain your answer.
6. **Using Your Notes** What do the three kinds of economic systems have in common? Refer to your completed cluster diagram.

   Use the Graphic Organizer at **Interactive Review @ ClassZone.com**

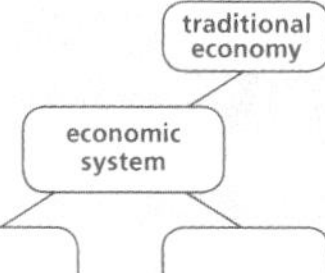

CRITICAL THINKING

7. **Drawing Conclusions** How might strongly defined economic roles and goals be both a strength and a weakness of traditional economies?
8. **Analyzing Cause and Effect** What effect might mass media have on the erosion of traditional economies in today's world?
9. **Generalizing from Economic Information** You have the following information about an economy: 1) People have little choice in the kinds of jobs they do. 2) Producers are not free to use resources as they wish. 3) People have little, if any, say in how the basic economic questions are answered. What kind of economy might this be? Explain your answer.
10. **Challenge** Most modern economies are a mixture of the three economic systems described in Section 1. Identify elements of traditional, command, and market economic systems in the American economy. (You will learn more about mixed economies in Section 4.)

ECONOMICS IN PRACTICE

Market economy in action in Mexico

Identifying Economic Systems
The three economic systems may be identified by the way they answer the basic economic questions: What to produce? How to produce? For whom to produce?

Complete a Table Copy the table below. Complete it by noting how each of the three economic systems answers the basic economic questions.

Economic System	Answers to the Basic Economic Questions
Traditional economy	
Command economy	
Market economy	

Challenge Identify modern countries that have economies that closely resemble each of the three economic systems. Explain each of your choices.

4 Assess & Reteach

Assess Have students work in pairs to answer the questions under Reviewing Key Concepts. Then, go over the answers as a class. For the Critical Thinking questions, divide the class into four groups and assign one of the questions to each group. Direct students to collaborate on a written answer and share it with the class.

Unit 1 Resource Book
- Section Quiz, p. 71

Interactive Review @ ClassZone.com
- Section Quiz

Test Generator CD-ROM
- Section Quiz

Reteach Review the characteristics of each type of economy by working through an example for each one. The Kavango can be used for the traditional economy; North Korea or Cuba for the command economy; and the United States for the market economy (even though it actually has a mixed economy). Push students to use the examples to make the points rather than simply generalizing about the different kinds of economies.

Unit 1 Resource Book
- Reteaching Activity, p. 72

SECTION 1 ASSESSMENT ANSWERS

Reviewing Key Concepts

1. a. *traditional economy*, p. 38
   b. *command economy*, p. 39
   c. *market economy*, p. 39
2. honoring tradition, because accumulating wealth could be seen as going against the good of the group as a whole
3. Government makes all economic decisions.
4. individual choice
5. No, because to act in your own self-interest requires that you have choices. In traditional and command economies people have little or no choice.
6. See page 38 for an example of a completed cluster diagram. They share the goal of dealing with the issue of scarcity.

Critical Thinking

7. Strongly defined economic roles are an advantage because they clearly state who should do what. However, they are a disadvantage because they may prevent people from doing the jobs they are best suited to.
8. Images of the outside world may tempt people in traditional economies to leave. These images may also cause traditional economies to abandon accepted ways of doing things.
9. This might be a traditional or a command economy because the noted characteristics focus on lack of individual choice, a major feature of these types of economic systems.
10. Possible responses: Traditional—family businesses that use methods passed from generation to generation; Command—government regulation of business; Market—consumers freely deciding what they will and will not buy.

Economics in Practice

Complete a Table Traditional: As they have always been answered; Command: government provides answers; Market: consumers and producers provide the answers.

Challenge Possible responses: Traditional—country, such as Namibia, where people still follow traditional way of life; Command—North Korea, Cuba; Market—United States, Great Britain.

1 Plan & Prepare

Section 2 Objectives

- describe the main features of a command economy
- note how socialism and communism differ
- identify modern examples of command economies
- explain the advantages and disadvantages of a command economy

2 Focus & Motivate

Connecting to Everyday Life Ask a volunteer to read aloud the second paragraph under the heading Government Planning. When the reading is complete, ask students to imagine that they live in a centrally planned economy. Have them suggest what everyday life might be like. *(Possible responses: they wouldn't be able to buy the consumer goods they wanted, they might not be able to get the types of jobs they wanted.)* Point out that lack of freedom is a major feature of a pure command economy.

Taking Notes Remind students to take notes as they read by completing a chart on command economies. They can use the Graphic Organizer at **Interactive Review @ ClassZone.com**. A sample is shown below.

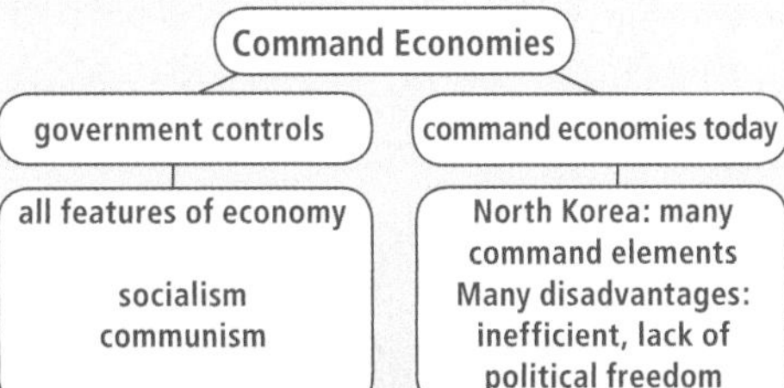

SECTION 2

Command Economies

OBJECTIVES

In Section 2, you will
- describe the main features of a command economy
- note how socialism and communism differ
- identify modern examples of command economies
- explain the advantages and disadvantages of a command economy

KEY TERMS

centrally planned economy, *p. 42*
socialism, *p. 43*
communism, *p. 43*
authoritarian, *p. 43*

TAKING NOTES

As you read Section 2, complete a hierarchy chart to categorize information about command economic systems. Use the Graphic Organizer at **Interactive Review @ ClassZone.com**

Command Economies
government controls | command economies today

Government Controls

QUICK REFERENCE

A **centrally planned economy** is a system in which central government officials make all economic decisions.

KEY CONCEPTS

In command economies, leaders decide what should be produced and how it should be produced. They also decide for whom it should be produced, in part by setting wages. By determining who earns the highest wages and who the lowest, these leaders decide who has the money to buy available products. A system in which the society's leaders, usually members of the central government, make all economic decisions is called a **centrally planned economy**.

EXAMPLE Government Planning

Think for a moment about how the federal government affects you. If you work, you have to pay taxes. If you're 18 years old and male, you have to register with the Selective Service System. State and local governments exert somewhat more control over your day-to-day life. State laws set both speed limits and the age at which people can drive. Local laws set standards for cleanliness in food stores and restaurants and for honest business practices. And state and local taxes are collected to support such services as police and fire departments and public education.

However, what if the government went further? Suppose that bureaucrats in a government office in Washington, D.C., had the power to decide which businesses could operate in your city. Further, these bureaucrats decided not only what these businesses should produce, but also how much each business should produce each month. Finally, they also decided who could have jobs and set work hours and pay scales for workers. Government controls of this type are a feature of a command, or centrally planned, economy.

SECTION 2 PROGRAM RESOURCES

ON LEVEL

Lesson Plans
- Core, p. 6

Unit 1 Resource Book
- Reading Study Guide, pp. 73–74
- Economic Skills and Problem Solving Activity, pp. 103–104
- Section Quiz, p. 81

STRUGGLING READERS

Unit 1 Resource Book
- Reading Study Guide with Additional Support, pp. 75–76
- Reteaching Activity, p. 82

ENGLISH LEARNERS

Unit 1 Resource Book
- Reading Study Guide with Additional Support (Spanish), pp. 78–80

INCLUSION

Lesson Plans
- Modified for Inclusion, p. 6

GIFTED AND TALENTED

Unit 1 Resource Book

NCEE Student Activities
- Command Economies, p. 8

TECHNOLOGY

eEdition DVD-ROM

eEdition Online

Power Presentation DVD-ROM

Economics Concepts Transparencies
- CT6 Command Economies Table

Daily Test Practice Transparencies, TT6

ClassZone.com

EXAMPLE Socialism and Communism

Modern societies that have adopted command economies have done so largely because of the influence of Karl Marx, a 19th-century German philosopher, historian, and economist. According to Marx's analysis, all of history is a struggle between classes. In his own time, the struggle was between the owners of the great industrial factories and the workers who exchanged their labor for wages. While the industrialists grew rich, the workers remained relatively poor. Marx predicted that in time the workers would overthrow this system and transfer ownership of the factories to public hands. With the means of production owned by the government, the class struggle would be resolved and all citizens would share in the wealth.

FIGURE 2.1 Comparing Economic Systems

	Communism	Socialism	Market System
Who owns resources?	Government	Government owns basic resources; the rest are privately owned	All resources privately owned
How are resources allocated?	Government planners decide how resources are used	Government planners allocate basic resources; market forces allocate privately-owned resources	Market forces allocate resources
What role does government play?	Government makes all economic decisions	Government makes decisions in the basic industries	Government's role limited—mostly to ensure market forces are free to work

ANALYZE TABLES
Government involvement varies among economic systems. How do communist systems answer the three basic economic questions?

Socialism, an economic system in which the government owns some or all of the factors of production, developed from the ideas of Marx. **Communism**, a more extreme form of socialism in which there is no private ownership of property and little or no political freedom, also grew out of Marx's thinking. Essentially, it is authoritarian socialism. An **authoritarian** system requires absolute obedience to authority. Figure 2.1 lists the major characteristics of socialism and communism.

Democratic socialism is established through the democratic political process rather than through the violent overthrow of the government. In this form of socialism, the government owns the basic industries, but other industries are privately owned. Central planners make decisions for government-owned industries. Central planners might also control other sectors—health care, for example—to ensure that everyone has access to these important services.

QUICK REFERENCE

Socialism is an economic system in which the government owns some or all of the factors of production.

Communism is an economic system in which the government owns all the factors of production and there is little or no political freedom.

Authoritarian systems require absolute obedience to those in power.

APPLICATION Comparing and Contrasting

A. How are socialism and communism similar yet different?
Both involve government control of economy. Socialism can exist in a democracy, communism is authoritarian.

3 Teach

Government Controls

Discuss

- Why is government ownership of the means of production necessary to achieve communist goals? *(to prevent individuals from making profits, which is against the Communist principle that wealth should be shared)*
- How are the goals of socialism met by allowing both government ownership and private ownership of resources? *(Government ownership of basic industries serves the same purpose as under communism, whereas private ownership fulfills the democratic principle of personal freedom.)*

Analyzing Tables: Figure 2.1

Ask students to use information in the chart to infer what the social aspect of life might be like in each type of economy. Guide the discussion by asking questions. For example: In communism, how does the relationship between the individual and the government affect society? *(Possible answer: it may create great personal frustrations in such matters as freedom of speech or religion.)*

Answer

In communist systems, government planners make all economic decisions.

LEVELED ACTIVITY

Contrast Traditional and Command Economies

Time 30 minutes ◑

Objective Students will deepen their understanding of command economies by adopting a personal viewpoint.

Basic

Work with a partner. Imagine that one of you is a teenager in a traditional farming economy; the other lives in an industrialized command economy. Write letters to each other describing a typical day.

On Level

Imagine you are a teenager transplanted from a traditional farming economy into an industrialized command economy. Write a letter to your family back home explaining some of the most startling differences you have seen.

Challenge

In which type of economy do you think you could make the fullest use of your potential, a traditional economy or a command economy? Write a personal persuasive essay putting forth your position and supporting it with personal examples.

Karl Marx

More About . . .

Karl Marx
Marx's father, Herschel, was a lawyer in the town of Trier, Germany, where Marx was born. Although he came from a long line of rabbis, Herschel converted to Lutheranism, the state religion of Prussia, to help his position. Herschel's hope was that Karl would also become a lawyer.

At his father's urging, Karl attended the University of Bonn. However, he did not focus on his studies, and his grades suffered. So, his father transferred him to a more rigorous school. His father became unhappy with that choice as well, since it is where Marx became interested in philosophy and soon developed a reputation as a radical. Marx never did settle into a profession that provided a comfortable living and throughout his life was often in debt.

More About . . .

Karl Marx's Philosophy
So much of historical importance has resulted from the work of Karl Marx that many people think he was more than an economist—that he also wrote extensively about history, political science, philosophy, and sociology. According to historian Mark Blaug, however, the facts do not bear out that assumption. While Marx penned "literally 10,000 pages on economics pure and simple," he only wrote a dozen pages on social classes, government, and history.

Economics Update

ClassZone.com includes links to sites about Karl Marx. These will help students understand the influence Marx had on command economies.

ECONOMICS PACESETTER

Karl Marx: Economic Revolutionary

Millions of lives were affected by the work of Karl Marx. Governments were toppled and new political alliances were forged on the strength of his arguments. What was it in the thousands of difficult-to-read pages he wrote that fueled revolutions?

FAST FACTS

Karl Marx
German philosopher, historian, and economist

Born: May 5, 1818

Died: March 14, 1883

Major Accomplishment: Detailed analysis of capitalism and foundation for socialist economic theory

Famous Quotation: *Workers of the world unite; you have nothing to lose but your chains.*

Influenced: Russian Revolution, 1917; Chinese Revolution, 1949

A New View of Economics

Marx was born in what is now Germany in 1818 and grew up in middle-class comfort. In college, however, he became involved in radical politics. In time, his political activism led to his exile from his homeland. He moved from country to country, eventually settling in London. During his travels, he met Friedrich Engels, the son of a factory owner. Through Engels, Marx became aware of the struggles of the working class and he undertook a deep study of economics. He concluded that the Industrial Revolution had created a system of wage slavery.

Factory owners, Marx said, looked upon labor as just another commodity that could be bought. They then used this labor to convert other productive resources into products. The factory owners made a profit by selling products at a higher price than the cost of labor and other resources. By keeping wages low, they could make ever greater profits. The whole industrial system, Marx reasoned, was based on this exploitation of workers.

To Marx, rising tension between worker and owner was an inevitable development in economic history. Over time, more and more wealth would be concentrated in fewer and fewer hands, and dissatisfied workers would revolt and create a new society without economic classes. Marx, assisted by Engels, laid out these ideas in *The Communist Manifesto* (1848). Marx discussed his economic ideas more fully in his enormous study *Das Kapital,* which was published in three volumes between 1867 and 1894.

Because of the way that communist economies worked in practice and the eventual collapse of communism in the early 1990s, Marx's theories have fallen into disfavor. Even so, few people had more impact on 20th-century economic and political thinking than Karl Marx.

Communism Marx's writings influenced revolutionary leaders such as V. I. Lenin in Russia and Mao Zedong in China.

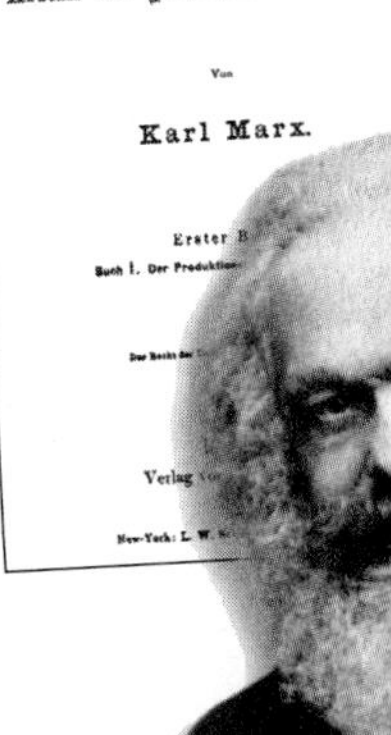

Das Kapital.

Kritik der politischen Oekonomie.

Karl Marx.

Economics Update
Learn more about Karl Marx at **ClassZone.com**

APPLICATION Drawing Conclusions

B. What did Marx think was the logical outcome of the struggle between owners and workers?
Workers would revolt and create a classless society.

DIFFERENTIATING INSTRUCTION

Gifted and Talented

Conduct Research
Direct students to research the ways in which Marx was influenced by Adam Smith. Then have them write one of the following highlighting ideas on which Smith and Marx agreed as well as areas of difference:

- a dialogue between Smith and Marx
- a letter from one to the other

Struggling Readers

Use Chronology
Understanding chronological order can help students comprehend the text. Help students recognize chronological order in this Economics Pacesetter feature. One of the most obvious is the use of dates. Ask students to find the dates and tell what happened on each. *(1818—Marx was born; 1848—*Communist Manifesto *appeared; 1867–1894—publication of* Das Kapital*; 1990s—collapse of communism)*

Command Economies Today

KEY CONCEPTS

There are no examples of pure command economies today. The forces that have brought changes to traditional economies are also transforming command economies. However, some countries—North Korea, for example—still have economies with mostly command elements.

North Korea

Once under the control of China and later Japan, Korea was split into North Korea and South Korea following World War II. North Korea came under communist control. The government controlled every economic decision. For example, it diverted many of the country's resources to the military, building up an army of more than 1 million soldiers—out of a population of about 22 million. It also developed a nuclear weapons program. However, this military buildup came at the expense of necessities. During the late 1990s and early 2000s, food was so scarce that millions of North Koreans died from hunger and malnutrition. Many North Koreans survived only because of food aid from other countries, most notably South Korea.

The failure to provide food and other important products was just one result of a flawed economic plan. For much of the 1990s, North Korea produced less and less each year, and its economy actually shrank. (See Figure 2.2 below.) In 2003, however, central planners relaxed some restrictions on private ownership and market activity. North Koreans hoped that this experiment with free markets would revive the country's ailing economy. (For more information on North Korea's economy, see the Case Study on pages 64–65.)

FIGURE 2.2 NORTH KOREA: ECONOMIC GROWTH

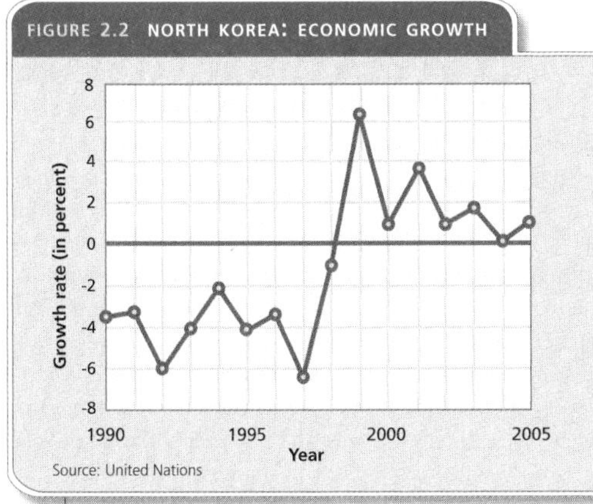

North Korea had a negative growth rate for much of the 1990s. (The red line on the graph marks 0 percent, or no growth.) The average yearly growth rate for all economies during this time period was about 3 percent.

ANALYZE GRAPHS

1. The North Korean economy began to show positive growth after 1999. To what might this development be attributed?
2. During the 1990s, some newspaper reports noted that the North Korean economy was "shrinking." How is this shown in the graph?

Command Economies Today

Discuss

- How can you explain the economic activity of Communist-controlled North Korea with a production possibilities curve? Refer students to pages 18–22. Ask for a volunteer to draw a PPC on the chalkboard demonstrating why so many starved. *(The PPC will clearly show that with fixed resources, the more money put into the military, the less there is for food.)*

Analyzing Graphs: Figure 2.2

Help students understand North Korea's negative economic growth by asking them if North Korea's economy grew from 1992 to 1994. If any students say yes, ask them to explain why. They are likely to point to the upward sloping line on the graph. Explain, however, that in all the years below the red line, the economy shrank. From 1992 to 1994 there was no economic growth but only a lower rate of economic shrinkage.

Answers

1. *Possible response: relaxing some restrictions on private ownership and market activity*
2. *Growth rate is expressed as negative numbers.*

INDIVIDUAL ACTIVITY

Researching and Reporting

Time 30–45 minutes 

Task Illuminate a famous quote by Karl Marx with historical information.

Materials Needed research sources (online or in print) and pens and paper

Activity

- Write three quotes by Karl Marx on the board. The first is the quote in the "Fast Facts" on page 44, and the others are: "The history of all hitherto existing society is the history of class struggle," (from the *Communist Manifesto*) and "The philosophers have only interpreted the world, in various ways; the point is to change it" (from *Theses on Feuerbach*).
- Instruct students to choose one of the quotes to use as the focus of their research. Their task is to find information about Karl Marx that helps explain the chosen quote and offer examples, events, ideas, and so forth.
- Tell students to write their research findings in a one-page essay.
- Invite students to read their essays to the class.

Rubric

	Understanding Ideas of Marx	Presentation of Information
4	excellent	all details support quote
3	good	most details support quote
2	fair	only a few details relate to quote
1	poor	information does not support quote

International Economics

North Korean Market Reforms?
Like many other command economies, North Korea has been trying to introduce aspects of a market economy. For example, the Kaesong Industrial Complex, a Special Economic Zone, is a cooperative project between North and South Korea. Ground-breaking took place in 2003. In the pilot phase, 15 South Korean manufacturing plants are being constructed. There are plans for 250 South Korean companies eventually to participate. However, the complex is literally fenced off from the rest of North Korea to keep capitalism from "contaminating" the rest of the nation.

More About . . .

Daily Life in North Korea
In addition to controlling economic decisions, the North Korean government tries to control social attitudes and behavior through indoctrination and harsh laws. The indoctrination takes many forms, including the requirement that workers spend several hours a day memorizing the speeches of the late Kim Il-sung, the "Eternal President" or his son, Kim Jong-Il, the "Beloved Leader." Before radios can be sold in North Korea, they are adjusted so they can receive only official state broadcasts. The punishment for straying from party ideology is harsh, including imprisonment and torture, even for such minor infractions as singing South Korean songs.

Meeting Demand (Left) In communist East Germany, government planners' decisions left this butcher with just one goose to sell. (Right) In West Germany, a market economy, store shelves were laden with consumer goods.

Impact of Command Economies

In theory, command economies have some advantages. For example, they seek to provide for everyone, even the sick and the old who are no longer productive economically. Also, leaders in a command economy can use the nation's resources to produce items that may not make money in a market economy—certain medicines, for example.

In practice, however, the disadvantages of command economies are abundantly clear. To begin with, central planners often have little understanding of local conditions. Because of this, their economic decisions are frequently misguided or wrong. Also, workers often have little motive to improve their productivity, since they know they will be paid the same wages regardless of their output. And because there is no private property, there is no motivation for workers to use resources wisely.

Centrally planned economies often set prices well below those that would be established in a market system. As a result, command economies face shortages. One scene repeated in many command economies is people standing in long lines waiting to buy goods. Such shortages often lead to creative behavior. In the former Soviet Union, for example, light bulbs were almost impossible to buy for home use. However, burned-out bulbs in factories were regularly replaced. Some people took and sold these burned-out bulbs. Why? Other people would buy them and use them to switch out with working bulbs in their factories. They then took the working bulbs to light their homes.

Perhaps the greatest failing of strict command systems is the great suffering that people living under them endured. Carrying out centrally planned economic policies requires that individual rights—even the right to life—be subordinate to the needs of the state. Millions of people died in the efforts to build huge collective farms in China and the Soviet Union. Millions more were imprisoned for exercising their political or economic rights. Estimates suggest that the deeply flawed policies of command economies are responsible for more deaths than two world wars.

APPLICATION Applying Economic Concepts

C. Why are consumer goods often in short supply in a command economy?
Command economies are interested in what is good for the nation, not in individual wants.

DIFFERENTIATING INSTRUCTION

Inclusion

Use Visuals
Call the attention of students to the photographs at the top of the page. Have students work in pairs to think of as many statements as they can about each photograph. *(Possible answers: command economy—butcher has only one goose to sell; shelves not orderly; not a great variety of products; market economy—shelves are well-stocked; diversity of products; looks like candy and other non-essentials are being sold)*

English Learners

Use Strategies for Unfamiliar Words
Students may not have encountered the word *subordinate* (in the third line of the final paragraph) before. Point out that one strategy that helps to determine the meaning of unfamiliar words involves using context. Here, the context sets up a power situation. It contrasts individual rights and the needs of the state. Through the idea that one side must predominate, the context helps explain the word *subordinate*. Have students note this strategy in their personal dictionaries.

SECTION 2 Assessment

Online Quiz
ClassZone.com

REVIEWING KEY CONCEPTS

1. Write a brief paragraph explaining the links between the following three terms.
   a. *centrally planned economy* b. *socialism* c. *communism*
2. Why do communist countries use authoritarian methods to maintain their economic and political system?
3. List and describe some advantages of centrally planned economies.
4. What are some disadvantages of centrally planned economies?
5. What is the relationship between the individual and the state in a communist nation?
6. **Using Your Notes** Write a sentence that makes a generalization about the nature of command economies. Refer to your completed hierarchy chart to complete this question.

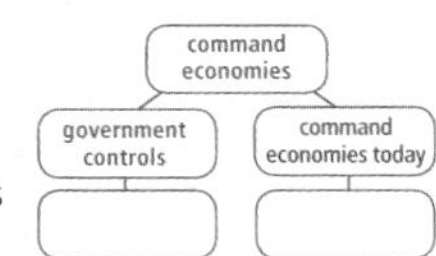

Use the Graphic Organizer at **Interactive Review @ ClassZone.com**

CRITICAL THINKING

7. **Making Inferences** Look again at the sentences about Thomas More's *Utopia* on page 38. Do you think that Karl Marx, like Thomas More, was trying to imagine a utopia in his writings? Give reasons for your answer.
8. **Explaining an Economic Concept** How do command societies address the problem of scarcity? Illustrate your answer with examples.
9. **Analyzing Cause and Effect** Read again the information about the North Korean economy on page 45. What factors caused North Korea's serious economic problems? What steps has the North Korean government taken to improve the dire economic situation?
10. **Challenge** Adam Smith used the "invisible hand" as a metaphor for the forces that balance a free market. What might be a good metaphor for the forces at work in a command economy? Explain your answer.

ECONOMICS IN PRACTICE

Celebration of communism in the Soviet Union

Using Graphs
Presenting information in a graph shows economic changes more clearly.

Create a Graph Use the following data to create a line graph.

Household Expenditures in the Soviet Union ($)	
1979	825.2 million
1981	934.7 million
1983	966.7 million
1985	1,017.1 million
1987	1,064.7 million
1989	1,152.3 million

Source: United Nations

Challenge During the 1980s, Soviet leaders introduced market elements into the economy. How might this explain the increase in household expenditures?

Use SMARTGrapher @ClassZone.com to complete this activity.

4 Assess & Reteach

Assess Have students work in pairs to answer all 10 questions in the Assessment. Go over the answers with the class, asking for volunteers to give their responses for each question.

Unit 1 Resource Book
- Section Quiz, p. 81

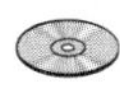

Interactive Review @ ClassZone.com
- Section Quiz

Test Generator CD-ROM
- Section Quiz

Reteach Divide students into groups of three. One person in each group will make review note cards for pages 42–43. The second will make cards for page 44. The third will be responsible for pages 45–46. When the cards are completed, have students meet in their groups. First, they should skim over each other's cards. Then, they should present the ideas they recorded on their note cards in the order in which they appear in the book.

Unit 1 Resource Book
- Reteaching Activity, p. 82

SMARTGrapher Students can create a line graph using **SmartGrapher @ ClassZone.com.**

SECTION 2 ASSESSMENT ANSWERS

Reviewing Key Concepts

1. a. *centrally planned economy*, p. 42
   b. *socialism*, p. 43
   c. *communism*, p. 43
2. People may resent lack of freedom, and to stop them from rebelling, government must threaten to or actually use force.
3. These economies, in theory, seek to provide for everyone. Also, they can use resources to make useful products that may not be profitable.
4. economic decisions frequently misguided or wrong; economic practices wasteful and unproductive; frequent shortages; great suffering endured by people
5. Individual rights are less important than those of society as a whole.
6. See page 42 for an example of a completed cluster diagram. Generalizations will vary, but probably will focus on lack of individual choice in command economies.

Critical Thinking

7. No; he believed he was describing reality not an imaginary, perfect world.
8. In theory, central planners' decisions are designed to use resources in the most efficient way; people are expected to subordinate their individual desires for the greater good of society.
9. poor economic decisions that diverted resources away from necessities to the military; experimentation with private ownership and market forces
10. Answers will vary. One possible metaphor is a vise squeezing out individual choice and other freedoms from the economy.

Economics in Practice

Create a Graph Students' graphs should accurately plot the data provided.

Challenge Answers will vary, but most students will note that with the introduction of market forces, more consumer goods probably would have been produced. Also, workers would have more opportunity to increase their wages. So, they would have had more income available to spend on these goods.

1 Plan & Prepare

Section 3 Objectives

- describe what a market is and how it works
- identify the main features of a market economy
- analyze how the circular flow model represents economic activity in a market economy
- explain the advantages and disadvantages of a market economy

2 Focus & Motivate

Connecting to Everyday Life Share with the class an experience you had selling or buying something outside of the usual retail channels—through a want ad or on eBay, for example. Without naming them, include the features of a market transaction. Ask students to offer examples of similar kinds of sales or purchases of their own. Direct students to identify the features these transactions have in common and explain that they are all key to the functioning of a market economy.

Taking Notes Remind students to take notes as they read by completing a chart on market economies. They can use the Graphic Organizer at **Interactive Review @ ClassZone.com**. A sample is shown below.

SECTION 3

Market Economies

OBJECTIVES

In Section 3, you will
- describe what a market is and how it works
- identify the main features of a market economy
- analyze how the circular flow model represents economic activity in a market economy
- explain the advantages and disadvantages of a market economy

KEY TERMS

private property rights, *p. 48*
market, *p. 48*
laissez faire, *p. 49*
capitalism, *p. 49*
voluntary exchange, *p. 49*
profit, *p. 49*
competition, *p. 49*
consumer sovereignty, *p. 50*
specialization, *p. 50*
circular flow model, *p. 52*
product market, *p. 52*
factor market, *p. 52*

TAKING NOTES

As you read Section 3, complete a chart to identify and describe the features of a market economy. Use the Graphic Organizer at **Interactive Review @ ClassZone.com**

Fundamentals of a Market Economy

QUICK REFERENCE

Private property rights are the rights of individuals and groups to own businesses and resources.

A **market** is any place where people buy and sell goods and services.

KEY CONCEPTS

Market economies have several distinct characteristics. Earlier in this chapter you read about the fundamental feature of a market economy—the fact that people's economic behavior is motivated by self-interest. Self-interested behavior is behind two other features of a market economy. One is **private property rights**, the rights of individuals and groups to own property. In economic terms, *property* means everything that an individual owns. This includes factories, offices, clothes, furniture, house, car, and other belongings; money; and even intellectual property, such as songs or ideas developed for inventions. It also includes the labor individuals provide to earn money to buy what they own.

The other feature that stems from self-interest is the **market**, any place or situation in which people buy and sell resources and goods and services. It may be the farmers' market on Saturdays in the town square, or it may be an enormous cybermarket on the Internet, such as eBay. Large or small, real or virtual, the market is where people can exchange their private property for someone else's.

Private Property Rights In a market economy, people are free to own and use private property—houses, for example.

SECTION 3 PROGRAM RESOURCES

ON LEVEL

Lesson Plans
- Core, p. 7

Unit 1 Resource Book
- Reading Study Guide, pp. 83–84
- Economic Skills and Problem Solving Activity, pp. 103–104
- Math Skills Worksheet, p. 111
- Section Quiz, p. 91

STRUGGLING READERS

Unit 1 Resource Book
- Reading Study Guide with Additional Support, pp. 85–87
- Reteaching Activity, p. 92

ENGLISH LEARNERS

Unit 1 Resource Book
- Reading Study Guide with Additional Support (Spanish), pp. 75–76

INCLUSION

Lesson Plans
- Modified for Inclusion, p. 7

GIFTED AND TALENTED

Unit 1 Resource Book
- Readings in Free Enterprise: Capitalism: Two Views, pp. 105–106

NCEE Student Activities
- The Circular Flow of Economic Activity, pp. 5–7

TECHNOLOGY

eEdition DVD-ROM

eEdition Online

Power Presentation DVD-ROM

Economics Concepts Transparencies
- CT7 The Circular Flow Model

Daily Test Practice Transparencies, TT7

ClassZone.com

FEATURE 1 Private Property and Markets

For markets to operate efficiently, private property rights need to be well defined and actively enforced by law. If you have ever bought a car, you know that an essential part of the transaction is getting possession of the title. You need proof that the person you are buying it from actually owns it and has the right to sell it. Since clear ownership is vital to any sale or exchange, private property rights are necessary to make markets work properly. If buyers could not trust that the sellers actually had the right to offer their products on the market, trade would break down. Further, suppose you are a musician but know that your songs can be downloaded for free, depriving you of your right to exchange what you own for money. In such a situation, it is doubtful that you would be motivated to record music. In protecting private property rights so that producers have motivation and consumers have trust, the government performs an important role in a market economy.

FEATURE 2 Limited Government Involvement

Sometimes the government's economic role is to stay out of the marketplace. The principle that the government should not interfere in the economy is called **laissez faire**, a French phrase meaning "leave things alone." The concept of laissez faire is often paired with **capitalism**, an economic system that is based on private ownership of the factors of production. Capitalism, the foundation of market economies, operates on the belief that, on their own, producers will create the goods and services that consumers demand. Therefore, according to laissez faire capitalism, there is no need for government involvement in the marketplace. Laissez faire capitalism is a market economy in its pure form. However, there are no pure market economies—all real-world market economies have some degree of government involvement.

QUICK REFERENCE

Laissez faire is the principle that the government should not interfere in the marketplace.

Capitalism is an economic system that is based on private ownership of the factors of production.

Voluntary exchange is a trade in which both traders believe that what they are getting is worth more than what they are giving up.

Profit is a financial gain that a seller makes from a business transaction.

Competition involves all the actions sellers, acting independently, do to get buyers to purchase their products.

FEATURE 3 Voluntary Exchange in Markets

When a buyer and seller agree to do business together, they engage in a **voluntary exchange**, a trade in which the parties involved anticipate that the benefits will outweigh the cost. Both sides in a voluntary exchange believe that what they are getting is worth more than what they are giving up. In a market economy, most trade is based on an exchange of a product for money rather than for another product.

Self-interest guides voluntary exchanges. Suppose you buy a new guitar. Even though you spend a good part of your savings, your self-interest is served because you've wanted this particular model of guitar. The seller's self-interest is likely served by **profit**, a financial gain from a business transaction. If you pay more for the guitar than the seller did, the seller earns money. In voluntary exchange, then, both sides must believe that they are gaining by trading.

FEATURE 4 Competition and Consumer Sovereignty

Market economies are also characterized by **competition**, the effort of two or more people, acting independently, to get the business of others by offering the best deal. You are able to choose today between a Macintosh and a Windows PC operating system because of the competition in the computer market. In the case of these competing systems, each has somewhat different features but mainly performs the same

3 Teach

Fundamentals of a Market Economy

Discuss

- In what ways does self-interest shape the nature of a market economy? *(in private property rights, which guarantee the owner the right to exchange the property for some other gain; in the market, where these exchanges can happen; in consumer sovereignty, since consumers will buy according to their self-interest and not according to some central plan; and in specialization, since people are free to follow their self-interest and do what they do best)*

International Economics

Laissez Faire in Hong Kong
Although there are no pure market economies in the world today, Hong Kong is often cited as modern example of a laissez-faire economy. For most of the time that it was a colony of Great Britain (from 1842 to 1997), Hong Kong was allowed to develop its economy without interference from the British government. As a result, Hong Kong developed a strong economy based on manufacturing, trade, shipping, and finance. It still has much economic autonomy even though it was returned to Chinese control in 1997.

LEVELED ACTIVITY

Relate Government and the Economy

Time 30 minutes

Objective Students will demonstrate an understanding of the relationship between economic and political freedom.

Basic

Make a two-column chart with Command Economy and Market Economy as column heads. Read Sections 2 and 3 to find information about the role of government in each type of economy. Enter findings in your chart. Use this information to write a sentence explaining the relationship between economic and political freedom.

On Level

American economist Milton Friedman wrote: "The free market is the only mechanism that has ever been discovered for achieving participatory democracy." Using information from Section 3, write a brief essay explaining how the free market can influence democracy.

Challenge

Thomas Jefferson wrote, "The democracy will cease to exist when you take away from those who are willing to work and give to those who would not." Using material in Sections 2, 3 and 4 to back up your position, write an essay evaluating Jefferson's claim.

Your Economic Choices

COMPETITION

Where will you buy your computer? What factors can you isolate to help you make a decision about where to buy your computer? (What functions you want, whether these functions are part of a standard package, how much money you have to spend, how much support services you will need, and so on.)

Activity Tell students that they have $1,500 to spend on a new computer. Have them spell out exactly why they want a computer and what level of support services they may need. Then, present these two buying options and have students prepare a presentation on which computer they would choose and why.

Computer from MainFrame (small specialty store)

- Fast processor
- 40 gig hard drive
- Standard word processor, graphics program, sound and video cards, up to two additional top-of-the-line applications of customer's choice
- 1 year on-site warranty and 15 hours of training
- Price: $1,500

Computer from Unicom (giant superstore)

- Fast processor
- 80 gig hard drive
- Standard word processor, graphics program, sound and video cards
- 90-day warranty; pay-per-incident customer support after that
- Price: $1,000

YOUR ECONOMIC CHOICES

COMPETITION

Where will you buy your computer?

You want to buy a new computer. You could buy a "standard package" from the electronics discount store. The price will be very reasonable, but you won't be able to customize the software package or the service program. Alternately, you could buy from a computer specialty store. You'll pay more, but you can choose the extras that you want and the customer support program is excellent.

Electronics discount store

Computer specialty store

functions as the other. You are free to decide which you prefer based on whatever combination of price and value appeals to you more. When you buy over-the-counter medications, you can also clearly see the competitive aspect of the market. Often next to a well-known brand-name product you will see a product with the same ingredients, similar packaging, but a different name and lower price. The producers of the lower priced item are competing for the business established by the brand-name product. If the producers of the brand-name product want to keep your business, they must lower their prices or find a way to add some other value.

That's because you, the consumer, hold the real power in the market place. **Consumer sovereignty** is the idea that because consumers are free to purchase what they want and to refuse products they do not want, they have the ultimate control over what is produced. Sovereignty means supreme authority, which is what consumers exercise as key economic decision-makers. Let's look at the over-the-counter medications again. If there were no competition, the brand-name producers could charge higher prices. It would be in their self-interest to charge as much as they possibly could. Competition, however, acts as a control on self-interested behavior, guiding the market toward a balance between higher value and lower prices. Rather than lose your business, the brand-name producers will either lower their prices or raise the value of their product. Because producers must compete for the consumer's dollar, they have to work at pleasing you, the consumer, while pleasing themselves.

QUICK REFERENCE

Consumer sovereignty is the idea that consumers have the ultimate control over what is produced because they are free to buy what they want and to reject what they don't want.

Specialization is a situation in which people concentrate their efforts in the activities that they do best.

FEATURE 5 Specialization and Markets

A market economy encourages efficient use of resources by allowing people and businesses to specialize in what they do best. **Specialization** is a situation in which people concentrate their efforts in the areas in which they have an advantage. This allows people to trade what they can most efficiently produce for goods and services

DIFFERENTIATING INSTRUCTION

Struggling Readers

Identify Cause and Effect

Help students see the cause-effect relationship of ideas in the paragraphs on this page. Show these relationships in a chart:

Cause	Effect
Lower priced competitive product appears	Brand name must lower price or raise value
Consumers have supreme authority	Producers must please consumers

Gifted and Talented

Respond to Competition

Organize students into small groups. Direct them to take on the role of product managers for a brand-name medication that is facing new competition from a lower-priced generic drug. Have them draft a proposal to increase the value or perceived value of their product in order to not lose business. Then, have them present their proposals to the other groups and discuss the relative effectiveness based on assumptions that they have made about the desires of the consumers.

ECONOMICS ESSENTIALS

FIGURE 2.3 Fundamentals of a Market Economy

Private Property Buyers and sellers are free to own and use private property.

Government Involvement Buyers and sellers must be free to operate with minimal government intervention.

Specialization Buyers and sellers are able to concentrate their efforts in areas where they have an advantage.

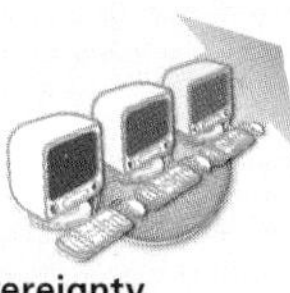

Voluntary Exchange When a buyer and seller agree to do business together, each believes that the benefits outweigh the costs.

Consumer Sovereignty Buyers can exercise their dominance over what is produced by freely deciding whether to buy or not to buy.

Competition Sellers are free to attempt to get the business of others by offering the best deal.

Profit Sellers are free to attempt to maximize their profits.

ANALYZE CHARTS

Identify a business in your community. Consider how the fundamentals of a market economy noted in the diagram are illustrated by the operations of that business. Record your ideas in a two-column table.

produced more efficiently by others. Specialization removes the need for households to be self-sufficient, and markets allow households to trade for what they need.

Suppose one adult in your house is a bank teller and another is a welder. Neither banking nor welding needs to happen within your household, but your household does need groceries. By specializing in what they do best—earning money in their jobs—in a market economy these adults are able to trade the dollars they earn for items and services others specialize in. If, however, they had to grow all the family's food themselves, they'd be less efficient than those who specialized in farming. Also, with each hour spent on growing food they would lose an hour's worth of wages from their jobs. Specialization, then, leads to higher-quality yet lower-priced products.

APPLICATION **Applying Economic Concepts**

A. Which is more important in determining the format in which recordings are offered by the music industry, new technology or consumer sovereignty? Explain.
Consumer sovereignty is more important; new technologies have been introduced, only to be forgotten when they fail to get consumer approval.

Economics Essentials: Figure 2.3

Ask students to determine which, if any, of the fundamentals shown in this graphic would also apply to a command or a traditional economy. *(specialization)* You may wish to have students create a similar graphic for command and traditional economies to show their fundamental features.

Analyze

Tables will vary. Ensure that tables include all the characteristics that are noted in the Economics Essentials chart.

Technomics

Consumer Statistics
The University of Michigan Library Documents Center has indexed a large number of online statistics and other economic information. One section is devoted to statistics and other information about consumers. It includes information from the recording industry on what types of music are popular among which age groups, for example. This section also includes information on consumer guides, consumer protection, and consumer attitudes. This data can be used as students explore the concept of consumer sovereignty.

SMALL GROUP ACTIVITY

Understanding Specialization and Efficiency

Time 30 minutes

Task Analyze specialization in various settings.

Materials Needed paper and pens or pencils

Activity

- Tell students they will be analyzing specialization in one of three different settings: a hospital emergency room, a high school, and an auto repair shop.
- Divide the class into three groups, one for each setting.
- Tell students to brainstorm a list of all of the different tasks workers do in those settings.
- From that list, choose three to use as examples to show why specialization makes the entire operation more efficient than it would be without it.
- Groups should read their list of tasks and present their conclusions to the class.

Rubric

	Understanding of Concepts	Presentation of Information
4	excellent	substantial list; well-chosen examples
3	good	good list; some well-chosen examples
2	fair	acceptable list and examples
1	poor	short list and unclear examples

Circular Flow in Market Economies

Discuss

- Why is a product market not a place? What are some examples of product markets that are not places? *(Services especially are usually not delivered in just one location; it is the exchange and not the location that qualifies it as an activity in the product market. Some examples include Internet access; heating fuel and electricity; online purchases.)*
- Give an example of a customer in the factor market and the kinds of resources that customer may need to obtain. *(Possible answers: Housing developer may need to buy land; manufacturer may need to hire workers or buy steel.)*

More About . . .

The Youth Labor Market
Employment after high school is often characterized by frequent moves from one job to another for a variety of reasons. Some feel this relatively chaotic approach to employment actually serves a beneficial purpose. For example, it gives both workers and employers a chance to know what they are really seeking. This knowledge and experience eventually will lead a worker to a job he or she finds more acceptable and will lead an employer to hire a more ideal worker. There is mounting evidence, however, to suggest that the more stable early employment is, the higher the wages earned will be throughout adulthood. For this reason, school-to-work and apprentice programs are being given careful attention.

Presentation Options

Review the characteristics of a market economy by using the following presentation options.

 **Power Presentations DVD-ROM**
Using the Display Tool, you can highlight the interactions between businesses and individuals which sets up the circular flow in a market economy.

 **Economics Concepts Transparencies**
- CT7 The Circular Flow Model

Circular Flow in Market Economies

KEY CONCEPTS

How do all these fundamental characteristics combine to allow a market economy to function? Economists have developed a model to help them answer this question. Called the **circular flow model**, it visualizes how all interactions occur in a market economy. The model represents the two key economic decision makers in a market economy—households, which are made up of individuals like you, and businesses. It also shows the two markets where households and businesses meet—that for goods and services, and that for resources. (See Figure 2.4 on the next page.)

QUICK REFERENCE

The **circular flow model** is a tool that economists use to understand how market economies operate.

The **product market** is the market where goods and services are bought and sold.

The **factor market** is the market for the factors of production—land, labor, capital, and entrepreneurship.

Product Markets

The market for goods and services is called the **product market**. This is the market you probably know best. The product market isn't a place as much as it is a set of activities. Whenever or wherever individuals purchase goods or services—at a local mall, a dentist's office, the phone company, or an online service selling concert tickets—they are doing so in the product market. The suppliers of the product market are businesses, which offer their goods or services for sale and use the money they earn from the sales to keep their businesses going.

Factor Markets

To run a business, firms must, in turn, purchase what they need from the **factor market**, the market for the factors of production—land, labor, capital, and entrepreneurship. Individuals own all the factors of production. They own some factors of production outright, such as their own labor and entrepreneurship. Others they own indirectly as stockholders in businesses. In the factor market, businesses are the customers and individuals are the producers. A restaurant buys your labor as a server, for example, to serve meals prepared by chefs whose labor they have also bought. The chefs make the meals from products bought from farmers who own the fields and farm equipment.

Circular Flow

This set of interactions between businesses and individuals is illustrated in Figure 2.4 on the next page. On the left and right of the model, you can see the two main economic decision makers, businesses and households. At the top and bottom are the two main markets, product and factor. The green arrows represent the flow of money. The blue arrows represent the flow of resources and products.

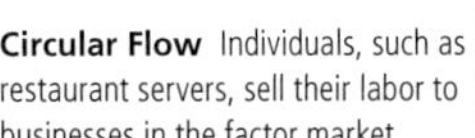

Circular Flow Individuals, such as restaurant servers, sell their labor to businesses in the factor market.

DIFFERENTIATING INSTRUCTION

Gifted and Talented

Create Alternate Representations
Ask students to think of another visual model of the interactions of the various factors and markets in an economy. A flow chart is an example. When they have finished, have them evaluate which representation better demonstrates the activity of the economy, their representation or the traditional circular flow model. Ask them to give reasons why.

English Learners

Develop Subject-Related Terms
Point out that words may have a number of meanings, depending upon the context. For example, both *product* and *factor* have a technical meaning in mathematics. Ask students what those meanings are and then encourage them to see the connections between those technical meanings and the meanings of the words as they apply to economics. *(product—what comes out after combining something or performing operations; factor—an element within something)*

FIGURE 2.4 The Circular Flow Model

Business revenue
Product Market
Consumer spending
Sell goods and services
Buy goods and services
Businesses
Households (Individuals)
Buy productive resources
Sell land, labor, capital, entrepreneurship
Payments for resources
Factor Market
Income from resources

ANALYZE CHARTS

The circular flow model is a tool for understanding the relationships among economic decision makers and various markets. Why do you think that money always flows in one direction, while resources and products always flow in the opposite direction?

Animated Economics Use an interactive circular flow model at **ClassZone.com**

Find the "Households" box at the right side of the chart. If you follow the green arrow, you see that individuals spend money in the product market to buy goods and services. From the product market, the money goes to businesses as revenue. The businesses spend this in the factor market, paying for the land, labor, capital, and entrepreneurship needed to produce goods and services. The receivers of that money are individuals who own all the factors of production. With the money they receive, individuals can make more purchases in the product market, and so the cycle continues.

If you look at the blue arrows, you can follow the route of the resources and products in the circular flow model. Once again, start with individuals. They sell their land, capital, labor, and entrepreneurship in the factor market. Follow the arrows to see that these factors of production are bought by businesses. The businesses then use these productive resources to make goods and services. The goods and services are then sold in the product market and flow to individuals who purchase them.

APPLICATION Interpreting Economic Models

B. Think of a good or a service you have recently bought. Using the circular flow model as a guide, write an explanation of the impact of your purchase on the economy.
Answers will vary but should note that money flows in one direction through the economy and resources and products in the other.

Analyzing Tables: Figure 2.4

Ask for a volunteer to describe the money path beginning with households by tracing the green arrows around the circle. *(The consumer buys something in the product market. The business selling that product takes in money, which it uses in the factor market to buy what it needs to keep producing the good or service. Factors are owned by individuals who receive payment for what the businesses buy.)*

Ask for a second volunteer to do the same task, following the blue arrows beginning with individuals. *(Individuals sell land, labor, capital, and entrepreneurship in the factor market, where they are bought by businesses to make goods and services, which are then sold in the product market, ending up back at the households.)*

Answer

because money is being exchanged for resources and products

Animated Economics The circular flow model shows the movement of resources and money through the economy. It will help students understand basic macroeconomic interactions.

INDIVIDUAL ACTIVITY

Illustrating a Circular Flow Model

Time 45 minutes

Task Create an illustrated circular flow model based on a specific product

Materials Needed poster board, cut out illustrations (photos, drawings, etc.) from magazines or websites, glue, markers or pens

Activity

- Tell students they will be creating a circular flow model based on a specific product.
- Direct them to brainstorm a list of possible products that they might be interested in following through a circular flow. Then have them choose one to research for illustrations.
- Suggest that students use a poster board and draw in the basic circular flow diagram. Leave room to paste in illustrations at each stage.
- Have students create the poster board at home and prepare to present it to the class.
- During the presentation, the student should explain each illustration on the poster.

Rubric

	Understanding of Concepts	Presentation of Information
4	excellent	accurate representation
3	good	mostly accurate representation
2	fair	poorly executed representation
1	poor	inaccurate representation

Impact of Market Economies

Discuss

- What is the appeal of a market economy in economic terms? In political terms? *(Possible answers: In economic terms—freedom to choose what to buy and to do the kind of work you are well suited to doing, to be rewarded for entrepreneurship and sound risk taking; in political terms—to have a government whose purpose is to protect individual rights and promote personal freedom)*
- What disadvantages of a market economy call for government involvement? *(Possible answers: It does not provide for public goods, such as defense or education. It does not provide for the elderly, the disabled, and others who cannot contribute economically. The only restraints on such things as mistreatment of workers and pollution are economic forces.)*

Economics Update

ClassZone.com includes links to sites with updates on emerging market economies in Eastern Europe. These provide information on the transition of Eastern Europe from command systems to market systems.

More About . . .

Attitudes During Transitions
Harvard economists Alberto Alesina and Nicola Fuchs-Schündeln studied the attitudes of people who lived through the transition from communism to a market economy in eastern Germany. They found that former East Germans were more likely than West Germans to favor government efforts to provide social services. They believe that in 20 to 40 years attitudes of East Germans will more closely resemble those of West Germans. The reseachers concluded that communism's active public sector, as well as the information citizens received through state TV and public schools that supported the government, shaped East German attitudes.

Impact of Market Economies

KEY CONCEPTS

Between the late 1940s and the early 1990s, between one-quarter and one-third of the world's population lived under command economic systems. The Soviet Union and its Eastern European neighbors, China and much of Southeast Asia, Cuba, and North Korea all had centrally planned economies. However, with the collapse of communism in the early 1990s, most of these countries have adopted some form of market economy. Also, as you read in Section 2, even those that have clung to communism and central planning have introduced market-economy measures. Why were these countries so ready to embrace the market system?

Advantages

On November 9, 1989, the Berlin Wall, a symbol of the division between the communist and democratic worlds, was finally opened. Over the next few days, hundreds of thousands of East Germans began pouring into West Germany through gates and improvised breaches in the wall. What drew these jubilant East Germans to the west? For most of them, the answer was freedom.

Economics Update
Find an update about developing market economies in Eastern Europe at **ClassZone.com**

Economic and Political Freedom Freedom is one of the chief advantages of a market economy. A market economy requires that individuals be free to make their own economic choices, since it depends on the consumer's right to buy or refuse products to determine what will be produced. Individuals are also free to develop their interests and talents in work they find satisfying, rather than being assigned to jobs.

Freedom New shopping malls, like this one in Bucharest, Romania, are a common site in many formerly communist countries.

Also, since the government does not use a heavy hand to control the economy, the political process can be much freer, with a diversity of viewpoints and open elections. Government bureaucracy is generally less cumbersome and costly in a market economy than in a command economy, since there are fewer areas of government involvement. A market economy also can be responsive to changes in conditions and accommodate those changes quickly.

Further, individuals in local communities are free to make their own economic choices without the interference of the government. These individuals' better knowledge of the resources and potential of their area leads to better economic decisions and greater productivity.

Profit The profit motive, a key feature of a market economy, insures that resources will be allocated efficiently, since inefficiencies would result in lower profits. It also serves as a reward for hard work and innovation. Knowing you can earn money

DIFFERENTIATING INSTRUCTION

Struggling Readers

Taking Notes on Market Economies
Pair students so that each pair has at least one student who is proficient in taking notes. If possible, have the students take turns reading aloud the material on pages 54–55. Have the more proficient note taker model how to take notes as the reading progresses. Instruct that student to think aloud about the process he or she uses to extract the main ideas.

Inclusion

Make a Chart
As you read aloud pages 54–55, have students complete an advantages/disadvantages chart on the market system. *(Advantages—freedom to choose; freer political process; responsive to changes; localities can determine own economic course; profit motive rewards effort and innovation; encourages competition. Disadvantages—does not provide public goods and services; cannot care for economically nonproductive; can lead to negatives, such as pollution.)*

Competition Competition among dairy companies ensures that there is a wide variety of milk and other dairy products.

if you come up with a good idea is an incentive to do so, and the more good ideas people have, the more the economy grows. The incentive to come up with good ideas is related to another advantage of a market economy: it encourages competition, letting consumers have the final say. Competition leads to higher-quality products at lower prices. It also helps to create a diverse product market.

Disadvantages

Market economies, however, have disadvantages as well. In a pure market economy, the economic good of the individual is the primary focus. A pure market economy has no mechanism for providing public goods and services, such as national defense, because it would not be profitable from a strictly economic viewpoint to do so.

Another disadvantage is that a pure market economy cannot provide security to those who, because of sickness or age, cannot be economically productive. Nor can it prevent the unequal distribution of wealth, even though that gap may be the result of unequal opportunities.

The industrial boom in the United States in the late 1800s and early 1900s illustrates the problems that can develop in a market economy with little government regulation. During this time, a few business leaders became very rich. At the same time, most of those who worked for these leaders were paid low—but increasing—wages. Further, most business leaders did little at the time to address the negative consequences of industrialization such as pollution. Issues like these led most industrialized societies to adopt some level of government involvement in the economy. The result was economic systems that mix elements of market and command economies. In Section 4, you'll learn more about such mixed economies.

APPLICATION Analyzing Causes

C. Why did many societies feel it necessary to adopt some level of government involvement in market economies?

They felt they needed to provide public goods and economic security, and to regulate economic activities.

More About . . .

The Protestant Work Ethic

The expectation that hard work will be rewarded is tightly woven into the fabric of the American experience. It is often related to the so-called Protestant work ethic that propelled some of the earliest American colonists, the Puritans, toward material gain. Puritans believed that working hard for the glory of God would keep them from the temptations of worldly pleasures. Their hard, focused work often did result in material success, which they took to be a sign that God approved of their efforts.

More About . . .

Early Industrial Pollution

During the early years of the Industrial Revolution, no one anticipated the rapid expansion of industry and the associated pollution. However, there was a mechanism in place for regulating industries that polluted—the so-called nuisance laws. Inherited from English common law, these regulations were built on the legal maxim *sic utere tuo ut alienum non laedas* ("so use your own so as not to injure others"). These laws often were applied to nuisance cases brought by people concerned with industrial pollution, and recent studies suggest many of the rulings were favorable to the plaintiffs. However, nuisance laws proved insufficient to address the magnitude of the pollution problem as industrialization spread.

SMALL GROUP ACTIVITY

Applying Advantages and Disadvantages of a Pure Market Economy

Time 30 minutes ◑

Task Consider advantages and disadvantages of a pure market economy from a specific perspective.

Materials Needed paper and pen

Activity

- Divide students into five groups and assign each group one of the following people to represent: farmer in drought-stricken area; affluent teenager; business owner; factory worker; and young child.
- Have them discuss together how a pure market economy affects them as this person, focusing on advantages and disadvantages.
- Have them draw up a list of the person's advantages and disadvantages and determine among themselves how to present the results to the class. Encourage creativity.
- After each presentation, have students reflect on ways in which the advantages and disadvantages were similar and different.

Rubric

	Understanding of Concepts	Presentation of Information
4	excellent	creative and well thought out
3	good	clear and well thought out
2	fair	somewhat clear
1	poor	confused

Comparing and Contrasting Economic Systems

1 Plan & Prepare

Objectives

- compare and contrast economic systems
- identify textual clues for comparison and contrast

2 Focus & Motivate

To focus students' attention on the content of the text, you might have them review the characteristics of command and market economies. Note their responses in a two-column chart on the board. Then encourage them to discuss the value of comparing and contrasting subjects such as economic systems.

3 Teach

Point out that comparison/contrast text may follow different kinds of patterns. One such pattern is the "whole-to-whole" organization:

- introductory paragraph that sets up comparison/contrast
- examination of one subject (whole)
- examination of second subject (whole, pointing out both similarities and differences).

Another is the "part-to-part" pattern:

- introductory paragraph that sets up comparison/contrast
- equivalent part of both subjects (similarities and differences)
- equivalent part of both subjects (similarities and differences) until all parts are covered.

For additional practice see **Skillbuilder Handbook**, page R19.

THINKING ECONOMICALLY Answers

1. *Both provide answers to the three basic economic questions. Also, modern command and market systems are mixed, and have elements of other systems.*
2. *In command systems, government planners make all decisions. In market systems, however, the individual plays the major role in answering economic questions.*
3. *Venn diagrams may differ.*

ECONOMICS SKILLBUILDER

For more information on comparing and contrasting information, see the Skillbuilder Handbook, page R19.

Comparing and Contrasting Economic Systems

Comparing means looking at the similarities and differences between two or more things. **Contrasting** means examining only the differences between them. To understand economic systems, economists compare and contrast the ways in which societies use their limited resources to meet unlimited wants.

TIPS FOR COMPARING AND CONTRASTING Look for subjects that can be compared and contrasted.

Economic Systems

An economic system is the way in which a society uses its resources to satisfy its people's needs and wants. Two common economic systems are the market system and the command system. Both systems provide answers to three basic economic questions: What to produce? How to produce? For whom to produce?

In a command economy, government economic planners decide what goods and services will be produced, how they will be produced, and for whom they will be produced. Individuals, then, have little or no influence on how economic decisions are made. In contrast, in a market economy the individual plays the major role in answering the basic economic questions. Consumers spend their money on the goods and services that satisfy them the most. In response, producers supply the goods and services that consumers want.

Few, if any, "pure" economic systems exist today. Most economic systems are "mixed." For example, market economies generally have some limited form of government control—a characteristic of command economies. Most command economic systems are likewise mixed in that they have some elements of market economies.

Comparison This passage compares two economic systems that have both similarities and differences.

Contrast To contrast, look for clue words that show how two things differ. Clue words include *however, in contrast, on the other hand,* and *unlike.*

Similarities To find similarities, look for clue words indicating that two things are alike. Clue words include *both, similarly,* and *likewise.*

THINKING ECONOMICALLY Comparing and Contrasting

1. How are market and command economic systems similar?
2. In what ways do these two economic systems differ?
3. Read the paragraphs about North Korea under the heading "Command Economies Today" on page 45. Construct a Venn diagram showing similarities and differences between the economy of North Korea and a typical market economy.

DIFFERENTIATING INSTRUCTION

Gifted and Talented

Revise the Passage
Have students use either whole-to-whole or part-to-part organization to rewrite the comparison/contrast of command and market economies. They should then exchange papers with a classmate and compare the approaches used and the relative effectiveness of the different organizational patterns.

Struggling Readers

Use Text Features
Draw students' attention to the text annotations in the left-hand margin and ask them to identify their purpose. *(to explain what is happening in the text and offer strategies for comparing and contrasting)* Help students brainstorm a list of other signal words for comparison and contrast in addition to the ones shown in the annotations. *(comparison—like, likewise, in the same or similar ways, in the same manner; contrast—conversely, on the contrary, yet, alternatively)*

SECTION 3 Assessment

REVIEWING KEY CONCEPTS

1. Explain the relationship between the terms in each of these pairs.
   a. *private property rights* *market*
   b. *laissez-faire* *capitalism*
   c. *specialization* *profit*
   d. *factor market* *product market*
2. What are the essential elements of market economies?
3. What are some advantages of market economies?
4. What are some disadvantages of market economies?
5. How does the profit motive help lead to efficient use of productive resources?
6. **Using Your Notes** Make charts for a traditional economy and a command economy and compare and contrast them with your completed market economy chart.

Use the Graphic Organizer at **Interactive Review @ ClassZone.com**

CRITICAL THINKING

7. **Analyzing Cause and Effect** Review the circular flow model on page 53. Based on the model, how do businesses benefit from the wages they pay?
8. **Creating and Interpreting Economic Models** Return to the answer you gave for Application B on page 53. Create a circular flow model to illustrate your answer.
9. **Solving Economic Problems** How do you think the disadvantages of a market economy can be minimized while its advantages continue to operate?
10. **Challenge** On August 29, 2005, Hurricane Katrina devastated regions of the Gulf Coast states of Louisiana, Mississippi, and Alabama. Most of New Orleans, for example, was flooded after the levees protecting the city broke. How would a pure market economy respond to the devastation and loss?

ECONOMICS IN PRACTICE

Employers and employee discuss salary

Understanding the Market Economy Market economies can be identified by certain fundamental characteristics. These include self-interested behavior, private property rights, voluntary exchange, profit, competition, consumer sovereignty, specialization, and a limited role for government.

Identify Features Each sentence in the chart illustrates one fundamental feature of a market economy. Complete the chart by identifying these features.

Feature	Description
	An author secures a copyright for her latest novel.
	Declining sales signal the end of production for a model of car.
	A prospective employee and a business reach an agreement on salary and benefits.
	Taking advantage of their beautiful natural environment, local planners approve development of new hotels and resorts.

Challenge Write sentences illustrating two fundamental features of market economies not illustrated in the sentences above.

4 Assess & Reteach

Assess Assign half of the class the even-numbered items and half the odd-numbered items (except for #6, which all should do). Then go over all the questions and answers as a class.

Unit 1 Resource Book
- Section Quiz, p. 91

Interactive Review @ ClassZone.com
- Section Quiz

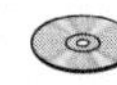

Test Generator CD-ROM
- Section Quiz

Reteach Have the class collaborate on a power presentation. Divide the class into three groups, one for each main part of Section 3. Each portion of the power presentation should include:

- clear text summaries using bulleted items
- graphics

Evaluate the presentations on the presence and effectiveness of each element.

Unit 1 Resource Book
- Reteaching Activity, p. 92

Economics in Practice

Identify Features private property rights; consumer sovereignty; voluntary exchange; limited government involvement

Challenge Sentences will vary, but should focus on the following: profit, competition, specialization.

SECTION 3 ASSESSMENT ANSWERS

Reviewing Key Concepts

1. **a.** *private property rights*, p. 48; *market*, p.48
   b. *laissez faire*, p. 49; *capitalism*, p. 49;
   c. *profit*, p. 49; *specialization*, p. 50;
   d. *factor market*, p. 52; *product market*, p. 52
2. private property rights, limited government involvement, voluntary exchange, profit, competition, specialization, consumer sovereignty
3. Answers will vary but should include such things as individual freedom, lack of government control, local decision-making, efficient allocation of resources, varied quality products at competitive prices, responsiveness to changes in conditions.
4. Answers will vary but should include such things as inability to provide for public goods and services, lack of security and no way to deal with those who are not economically productive, and difficulty dealing with negative consequences of production, such as pollution.
5. The more it costs a producer to make something, the lower the profit. The profit motive will guide producers to efficient allocation of resources in order to earn as large a profit as possible.
6. See page 48 for an example of a completed chart. Encourage students to share their chart comparisons with the rest of the class.

Critical Thinking

7. Workers spend their wages to buy the goods and services that businesses sell.
8. Models will vary. Use the rubric on page 53 to evaluate models.
9. Answers will vary. Some students might suggest government provision of public goods and limited government regulation of the economy.
10. Answers will vary. Some students might suggest that, driven by the chance to make a profit, new businesses would open to provide goods and services for the area.

Economics in Practice

See answers in side column above.

❶ Plan & Prepare

Section 4 Objectives

- identify the main characteristics of a mixed economy
- understand why most modern economies are mixed economies
- explain why modern economies are becoming increasingly global

❷ Focus & Motivate

Connecting to Everyday Life Ask students to take an inventory of all the ways in which government involvement is evident in their lives. To promote discussion, ask: How did you get to school? *(on public roads; if the student drove, then state issued the license)* Did you buy anything today? *(If so, taxes were probably paid.)* State that there is considerable economic freedom in the United States but that the economy is not a pure market economy—the government is involved in many ways.

Taking Notes Remind students to take notes as they read by completing a cluster diagram on modern economies. They can use the Graphic Organizer at **Interactive Review @ ClassZone.com**. A sample is shown below.

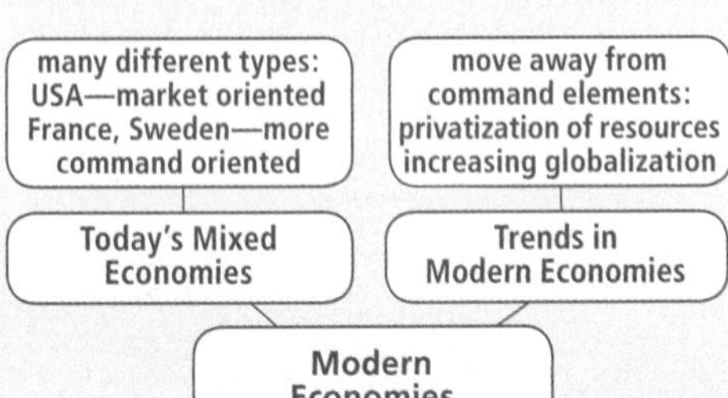

SECTION 4

Modern Economies in a Global Age

OBJECTIVES

In Section 4, you will

- identify the main characteristics of a mixed economy
- understand why most modern economies are mixed economies
- explain why modern economies are becoming increasingly global

KEY TERMS

mixed economy, *p. 58*
nationalize, *p. 61*
privatize, *p. 61*
global economy, *p. 61*

TAKING NOTES

As you read Section 4, complete a cluster diagram to record what you learn about modern economies in a global age. Use the Graphic Organizer at **Interactive Review @ ClassZone.com**

Today's Mixed Economies | Trends in Modern Economies | Modern Economies

Today's Mixed Economies

KEY CONCEPTS

QUICK REFERENCE

A **mixed economy** is an economy that has elements of traditional, command, and market systems.

Today, the **mixed economy**—an economic system that has elements of traditional, command, and market economies—is the most common type of economic system. Even the most strongly market-based modern economies have some elements of central planning. Similarly, market influences have penetrated all of today's command economies to some extent. Traditional production methods are still followed in some areas of both market and command systems. And traditional economies everywhere are experiencing greater government involvement and growing pressure from market influences.

Life in a Mixed Economy

Let's look at a farming family in the rural Midwest of the United States to see how elements of all three economic systems may be present in a mixed economy. The family has owned and operated the farm for many generations. While they use the most modern farming methods, family members still cling to some old customs. At harvest time, for example, everybody works to get in the crops. Even the youngest children have their own special tasks to do. The family's crops are sold on the market along with those of their neighbors and of farmers throughout the region. Well-maintained highways connect the farm to the various locations where the crops are sold. Two teenagers in the family attend the public high school. The oldest one works in town at a part-time job during the week, earning the minimum wage. Two grandparents who no longer work full time on the farm each receive a Social Security check every month.

SECTION 4 PROGRAM RESOURCES

ON LEVEL

Lesson Plans

- Core, p. 8

Unit 1 Resource Book

- Reading Study Guide, pp. 93–94
- Economic Simulations, pp. 109–110
- Section Quiz, p. 101

STRUGGLING READERS

Unit 1 Resource Book

- Reading Study Guide with Additional Support, pp. 95–97
- Reteaching Activity, p. 102

ENGLISH LEARNERS

Unit 1 Resource Book

- Reading Study Guide with Additional Support (Spanish), pp. 98–100

INCLUSION

Lesson Plans

- Modified for Inclusion, p. 8

GIFTED AND TALENTED

Unit 1 Resource Book

- Case Study Resources: Making Cars for the World; North Korea Blocks a Market Economy, pp. 91–92

TECHNOLOGY

eEdition DVD-ROM

eEdition Online

Power Presentation DVD-ROM

Economics Concepts Transparencies

- CT8 Countries with Mixed Economies

Daily Test Practice Transparencies, TT8

ClassZone.com

In this scenario, all three types of economic system are blended. The harvest-time customs the family follows represent the influence of a traditional economy. The command aspects of the economy are reflected in the ways that government has become involved. The well-maintained roads, the public high school, the minimum wage, and the Social Security checks are all examples of government benefits and regulations at the local, state, or national level. (You'll learn more about government involvement in the economy, including the minimum wage and Social Security, in later chapters.) The market aspects of the economy are represented in the private property rights and entrepreneurship of the family members. They own their land and have figured out the best ways to use it to make a living. Other aspects of a market economy include the competitive market in which their goods are sold, and the voluntary exchange that takes place when the family sells its crops and when one of the teenagers exchanges labor for wages.

Elements of Command One way the U.S. government intervenes in the economy is to set safety standards for automobiles and other products.

Types of Mixed Economies

Although all modern economies are mixed, they often emphasize one type of system or another. In the scenario you just read, which is based on the economy of the United States, the market economy dominates. Even though there are traditional and command elements, the driving forces of the U.S. economy are such features as private ownership and markets. So, the United States essentially has a market economic system.

Many European countries have a more even mix of market and command economies. France, for example, tried to find a "middle way" between socialism and capitalism. In the years following World War II, its economy emphasized the command system with government ownership of core industries. In the 1980s, however, many people expressed dissatisfaction with the performance of government-owned industry. As a result, the French government pulled back from its ownership role in the economy, privatizing several industries, most notably banking and insurance. Even so, it still has a controlling share of ownership in a number of industries, including energy, automobiles, transportation, communications, and defense. In addition, it provides an array of social services, including health care and education, to the French people.

Sweden, while also a mixed economy, has much greater government involvement. The Swedish government and government-related organizations own about one third of all Swedish companies. In addition, Swedish citizens receive "cradle to grave" social benefits. These include childcare for children ages 1 through 5, schooling for

3 Teach

Today's Mixed Economies

Discuss

- The photo editor for this book chose a picture of crash dummies to demonstrate a role the government plays in the economy. If you were the photo editor, what other possible subjects might you search for to represent the same idea? *(Possible answers: nutritional labels on foods; warnings on medications; people at veteran's hospital or public clinic; school classroom; police or army)*

Economics Illustrated

After students read about the levels of mixing in the economies of the United States, France, and Sweden, draw a horizontal line on the board. Label the left end of the line *Command*, the middle of the line *Mixed*, and the right end *Market*. Ask students where they think each country belongs on the line and why. *(Sweden closest to Command, France nearest Mixed, and the U.S. closest to Market; neither Sweden nor the U.S. should be at the absolute end, as each has some level of mixing.)*

Command **Mixed** **Market**

LEVELED ACTIVITY

Analyze Utopian and Dystopian Economies

Time 45–60 minutes

Objective Students will identify the elements of various types of economies in a fictional society.

Basic

Read aloud to students "Of Their Trades, and Manner of Life" and "Of Their Traffic" from Thomas More's *Utopia*. Have students work in small groups to explain in a paragraph how Utopians answer the three economic questions. They should also identify elements of traditional and command economies.

On Level

Organize students into groups and assign each group one of these Utopian/Dystopian novels: George Orwell's *1984*, Aldous Huxley's *Brave New World*, and Lois Lowry's *The Giver*. Each group should write a brief essay explaining how the economy answers the three basic economic questions.

Challenge

Divide students into groups and have each create a Utopia or Dystopia in enough detail so that it is clear how the three basic economic questions are answered. Students may wish to use Thomas More's *Utopia* or one of the books listed to the left for inspiration. Each group should describe its Utopia/Dystopia in a creative way.

Math Challenge: Figure 2.5

Calculating Percentages
Setting up the equation in a slightly different way can show the correspondence of the ratios very clearly. Since a percentage is a ratio of some value to 100, the equation can be expressed in this way:

$$\frac{\$152.4 \text{ billion}}{\$789.8 \text{ billion}} = \frac{x}{100}$$

Then the usual operations yield the result. (The billions can be dropped to reduce the fraction.) Multiply the numerator of the first fraction by 100 and then divide it by the denominator.

$$\frac{\$15240}{\$789.8} = 19.2960243$$

See page R4 of the **Math Handbook** for more on calculating percentages.

International Economics

Land and Government in Namibia
Namibia has an unequal distribution of land ownership. Most of the land is owned by white farmers, who represent only 6 percent of the population. Not wanting to destabilize the economy after the majority came into power, the government adopted a "willing seller/willing buyer" approach to getting the land back into the hands of black Namibians. Through this process, the government has the right of first refusal on properties offered for sale. If it purchases the land, it can return it to landless Namibians. The process, however, is very slow. At the rate it is progressing, it will be 40 more years before half of the black Namibian population owns land.

MATH CHALLENGE

FIGURE 2.5 Calculating Percentages

Economists often use percentages to express the level of government involvement in a country's economy.

Step 1: Read the table, which contains data on the total economy and government consumption—the value of all the goods and services government buys—for three countries.

Country	Total Economy (in billions of U.S. dollars)	Government Consumption (in billions of U.S. dollars)
Canada	789.8	152.4
Nigeria	48.8	11.4
Sweden	259.2	72.2

Source: Heritage Foundation

Step 2: Using Canada as an example, calculate government consumption as a share of the total economy.

$$\text{Share of economy consumed by government} = \frac{\text{Government consumption}}{\text{Total economy}}$$

$$\frac{\$152.4}{\$789.8} = 0.192960243$$

Step 3: Convert the answer to a percentage by multiplying by 100.

$$0.192960243 \times 100 = 19.2960243\%$$

Step 4: Round your answer to a whole number.

19.2960243 rounded to a whole number ≈ 19%

Comparing Economies To compare government consumption in the economies of two different countries, economists can calculate percentages for each country and compare the percents.

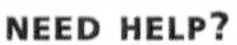

NEED HELP?

Math Handbook, "Calculating and Using Percents," page R4

children ages 6 through 16, additional years of school and college for those who choose them, health care, dental care, paid time off for raising families, and generous old-age pensions. In return, however, the Swedish pay very high tax rates, in some cases as high as 60 percent of income.

Each country has its own distinct balance of economic types. Namibia, as you read in Section 1, has a large number of people engaged in subsistence farming, following traditional production methods. Since the early 1990s, however, the Namibian government has been encouraging a more market-driven approach, including foreign investment in farming and other businesses. The country's leaders hope that these efforts will help the economy to grow and provide more economic opportunities for all Namibians.

APPLICATION Synthesizing Economic Data

A. Look at the Math Challenge above. What level of government involvement in the economy does each country shown have?
Government is more heavily involved in Sweden's economy than in the economies of Nigeria and Canada.

DIFFERENTIATING INSTRUCTION

English Learners

Develop Social Studies Vocabulary
Ask students to define *nationalize* and *privatize.* Point out the suffix *–ize,* and ask students to say what it means. *(Nouns and adjectives are changed into verbs when you add it.)* Then, have students brainstorm a list of other social studies vocabulary words that use the *–ize* suffix. *(Possible answers: civilize, tyrannize, organize, specialize, colonize, legalize, capitalize, subsidize, utilize, polarize, terrorize, socialize, stabilize, globalize)*

Gifted and Talented

Create a Globalization Cartoon
Assign students to small groups. Have them brainstorm some of the key issues associated with increasing global ties. Each group should then choose one of these issues and consider possible ways to depict it in a cartoon. They can use the cartoon on page 61 as an example. Have group members develop ways to collaborate on the creation of the cartoon. When cartoons are completed, call on group representatives to present them to the class.

Trends in Modern Economies

KEY CONCEPTS

Economies have changed, and are always changing, in response to changes in natural, social, and political conditions. In the early 1990s, for example, some Eastern European economies experienced abrupt change when their command systems broke down after the collapse of communism in the Soviet Union. Many of these economies have been making reforms to introduce more market elements. (You'll learn more about these economies in Chapter 18.)

TREND 1 Changes in Ownership

Economies in transition often go through predictable processes. Some of the most important relate to changes in ownership. After World War II, some European economies became more centrally planned. For example, the British government, to help the country more effectively recover from the war, nationalized several important industries, including coal, steel, and the railroads. To **nationalize** means to change from private ownership to government or public ownership.

More recently, many economies have moved away from command systems to market systems. In this process, government-owned industries have been privatized. To **privatize** means to change from government or public ownership to private ownership. Poland, for example, is undergoing a transition from a command to a market economy with an extensive privatization program. Since 1990, Poland has privatized a number of manufacturing, construction, trade, and service industries. The Polish government hoped that private ownership of economic resources would provide incentives for greater efficiency, which, in turn, would help the economy to grow.

QUICK REFERENCE

To **nationalize** means to change from private ownership to government or public ownership.

To **privatize** means to change from government or public ownership to private ownership.

The **global economy** refers to all the economic interactions that cross international boundaries.

TREND 2 Increasing Global Ties

One way to help privatize an industry is to open it up to foreign investors. This kind of economic tie between nations is only one example of the global economy. The **global economy** is all the economic interactions that cross international boundaries. Today, American consumers and businesses are actors in a world economy. Businesses now engage in more foreign trade than ever before, and they depend not only on the products they buy from foreign nations, but also on the foreign markets in which they sell their products.

There are several reasons for this surge in economic globalization. One reason is the opening up of the world's markets to trade. Nations have been discussing ways to open trade for many years. The outcome of these talks has been the signing of agreements that ensure that trade among nations flows as

Globalization Some people are opposed to globalization, charging that it results in the loss of national identity.

Trends in Modern Economies

Discuss

- In your opinion, are there some goods and/or services that should be publicly owned? If so, which ones? Explain. *(Answers will vary; encourage students to follow up with reasons.)*
- In what ways have your personal global ties increased in the last 10 years? *(Answers will vary but are likely to include the ease of connecting almost anywhere in the world with the Internet and also the great number of imported products that end up in everyone's household.)*

International Economics

Return to Nationalization?

In several Latin American countries, there is a growing tide of support for returning basic services, including the water supply, to government control. For example, Argentina had privatized its water supply in 1993, granting a French company the contract to provide the service. Many Argentines have complained of poor water quality and want the government to take charge. In Peru, Guatemala, Ecuador, and Panama, there have also been protests against privatized utilities. As in Argentina, these utilities have been contracted to foreign-owned companies. Some of the people in these countries complain about the quality of the service, but many are also protesting the increasing presence and influence of foreign companies.

INDIVIDUAL ACTIVITY

Understanding Global Ties

Time 60 minutes ●

Task Make a poster reflecting research on economic ties between the United States and another country.

Materials Needed poster board, markers, scissors, computer with Internet access

Activity

- Ask students to choose a country other than the United States.
- Direct students to research the kinds of economic interactions between their chosen country and the United States. They should also identify specific products and firms involved.
- Have them print out pictures and any other data, such as graphs, they find that will represent the interactions.
- Using their findings, students should design an illustrated chart showing the economic interactions between their country and the United States.
- Students should present their findings and chart to the class.

Rubric

	Understanding of Concepts	Presentation of Information
4	excellent	well-researched; creative presentation
3	good	well-researched; good presentation
2	fair	superficial research; fair presentation
1	poor	little research; poor presentation

Analyzing Charts: Figure 2.6

Direct students to study the photograph and to read the annotations carefully. Ask them what items are produced through global partnerships. *(The calculator, cell phone, shirt, and watch were produced through cooperative efforts by the United States with other countries.)*

Ask them where most of the products were manufactured and what can they infer about that area or areas of the world. *(Possible answer: Most of the products were made in Asia and Latin America, probably because they produce goods more cheaply than other places.)*

Answer

Answers will vary. Encourage students to record their responses in a chart.

Economics Update

ClassZone.com includes links to updates about global partnerships. These will help students appreciate the increasing global ties being formed today.

APPLICATION

Answer *Shared efforts lead to greater efficiency, which means lower production costs and greater profits for American businesses.*

FIGURE 2.6 **The World Student**

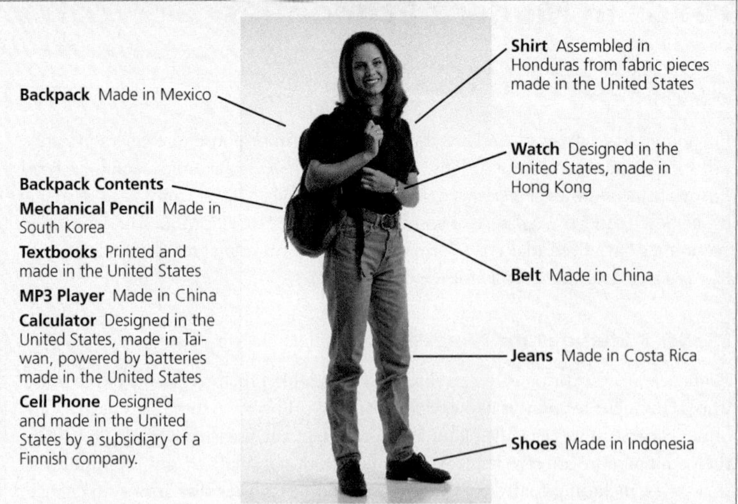

ANALYZE CHARTS

List all the things that you use in a normal day—the clothes you wear, the foods you eat, the appliances you use, and so on. Identify where each item was made—in the United States or in another country.

smoothly and freely as possible. Another reason for the growth of the global economy is the development of faster, safer, and cheaper transportation. Distribution methods have become so efficient that resources and products can be moved around the world relatively inexpensively. In addition, telephone and computer linkages have made global financial transactions quick, inexpensive, and easy.

Globalization also has been enhanced by cross-border business partnerships. For example, Ford Motor Company of the United States and Mazda Motor Corporation of Japan have long worked as partners. They design and engineer cars together, use each other's distribution systems, and share manufacturing plants. Recently, Ford and Mazda have joined with China's Changan Automotive Group to produce engines for Ford and Mazda cars. Such shared efforts lead to greater efficiency, which results in lower production costs and greater profits.

Economics Update
Find an update on global partnerships at **ClassZone.com**

Other global partnerships have grown out of the need to share the enormous costs of researching and developing new technology. For example, Hitachi of Japan has joined with two American companies, Texas Instruments Incorporated and Integrated Device Technology, to develop smaller and more powerful computer memory chips. Such joint efforts are an illustration of today's economic reality—businesses can cooperate and learn from one another even while pursuing their own interests.

APPLICATION Analyzing Effects

B. How do global business alliances benefit the U.S. economy?

◄ See Teacher's Edition for answer.

DIFFERENTIATING INSTRUCTION

Struggling Readers

Chart Details

The second and third paragraphs on this page contain a number of proper nouns, some of them foreign. They also contain information about international business alliances. Suggest that students make a three-column chart, one column labeled American Companies, one labeled Japanese Companies, and one labeled Chinese Companies. In each row, students should list the companies that have a relationship, with arrows connecting them across the columns.

Inclusion

Read Aloud

Pair a student with visual impairment with an English learner. Have the English learner read pages 61–62 aloud, taking help from the visually impaired native speaker as needed. When the reading is done, have the students ask each other questions about trends in modern economies and work together to find the answers.

SECTION 4 Assessment

Online Quiz
ClassZone.com

REVIEWING KEY CONCEPTS

1. For each of the following key terms, write a sentence that illustrates its meaning.
   a. *mixed economy*
   b. *nationalize*
   c. *privatize*
   d. *global economy*
2. What is a market-driven mixed economy? Illustrate your answer with examples.
3. In the transition from command to market economies, most economic resources are privatized. What is the expected impact of this action?
4. What forces have contributed to the growth of the global economy?
5. How are you, as an individual, affected by the global economy?
6. **Using Your Notes** Write a four-sentence summary of this section, using your completed cluster diagram as a reference.

   Today's Mixed Economies | Trends in Modern Economies | Modern Economies

   Use the Graphic Organizer at **Interactive Review @ ClassZone.com**

CRITICAL THINKING

7. **Explaining an Economic Concept** Explain, with examples, how the American economy includes elements of traditional, command, and market economic systems.
8. **Analyzing Cause and Effect** Since the fall of communism in the 1990s, countries in Eastern Europe and the former Soviet Union have abandoned command economies in favor of market economies. How do you think economic life in these countries has changed?
9. **Applying Economic Concepts** Many nations import U.S. capital and technology by purchasing equipment that U.S. businesses manufacture. Explain how this development can benefit the American people.
10. **Challenge** How do market forces operate in the global economy? Illustrate your answer with examples.

ECONOMICS IN PRACTICE

Shopping for shoes

Illustrating the Global Economy
How do you participate in the global economy? Study Figure 2.6 opposite and then complete this exercise.

Conduct a Survey Make a survey of class members to identify the "Made in" labels in their clothes, shoes, and other items they use every day. Use a chart similar to the one below to list the items and the countries in which they were produced.

Product	Where Made
Sweaters	
Shirts	
Pants or dresses	
Shoes	
Jackets	
Backpacks	

Challenge Write a short explanation of how this list illustrates the global economy.

④ Assess & Reteach

Assess Work through the first six items of the assessment as a class activity. For the Critical Thinking questions, have students work in four small groups. Each group should answer all four questions. When the class regroups, each group will have a chance to answer one of the questions.

Unit 1 Resource Book
- Section Quiz, p. 101

Interactive Review @ ClassZone.com
- Section Quiz

Test Generator CD-ROM
- Section Quiz

Reteach Divide the class into two teams. Each should develop a list of 10 questions (with answers) based on material in Section 4 in an effort to stump the other team. The teams should then take turns asking each other the questions. The team with the most correct answers wins.

Unit 1 Resource Book
- Reteaching Activity, p. 102

Economics in Practice
Conduct a Survey You might have students list countries by continent.

Challenge Answers will vary, but should note that the many countries on the list show that Americans are actors on a world economic stage.

SECTION 4 ASSESSMENT ANSWERS

Reviewing Key Concepts

1. a. *mixed economy*, p. 58
   b. *nationalize*, p. 61
   c. *privatize*, p. 61
   d. *global economy*, p. 61
2. The market element dominates the economy. In the United States, while elements of traditional and command economies are present, market elements such as private property rights and entrepreneurship predominate.
3. greater incentive to use resources efficiently, which, in turn, will help economic growth
4. opening up of the world's markets to trade; development of better transportation and communication; cross-border business partnerships
5. Answers will vary, but most students will note that the products they purchase and use come from all over the world.
6. See page 58 for an example of a completed cluster diagram. Summaries should focus on the two main points in the section: types of mixed economies and the trend toward economic globalization.

Critical Thinking

7. Answers will vary, but look for responses that identify traditional influences (family, religious, or cultural), government involvement (taxes, school), and market participation (parents' jobs, private ownership of house, and so on).
8. Answers will vary. Some students may suggest that the change from public to private ownership has led to greater economic growth.
9. Answers will vary, but should note that exports of technology will boost the American economy and that manufactured goods produced with this technology will force American companies to become more competitive.
10. Specialization, the profit motive, self-interest, and competition are some market forces at work in the global economy. Examples will vary.

Economics in Practice

See answers in side column above.

1 Plan & Prepare

Objectives

- Analyze multiple sources to understand the impact of command and market economies
- Contrast the economies of North Korea and South Korea

2 Focus & Motivate

Ask students to describe the type of atmosphere that encourages creativity. *(Most students will suggest an atmosphere where people feel free to run with their ideas.)* Then point out that although it is only one part of the difference between a command and market economy, the freedom to develop creative ideas is critical to innovation that can fuel huge economic growth, as South Korea's experience has demonstrated.

3 Teach

Using the Sources

Discuss

A. What goal was the North Korean government trying to achieve by sacrificing people in "unproductive" regions and industries? *(survival of the regime by concentrating resources on the government elite and the military)*

B. A financial crisis hit many Asian nations in 1997. It was triggered, in part, by high economic growth which led to speculation by foreign investors. Why did North Korea seem to avoid this crisis? *(Following a policy of isolationism, it had no foreign investment.)*

C. What inferences can you draw from this source about how the government supports business? *(Possible answer: The profits from Samsung are not so heavily taxed, so they can be reinvested or taken as pay by managers as reward for their initiative.)*

Economics Update

ClassZone.com includes links to sites with updated information on the economies of North and South Korea. This information will help students contrast command and market economies.

Case Study

Economics Update Find an update on this Case Study at **ClassZone.com**

Contrasting Economies: North Korea and South Korea

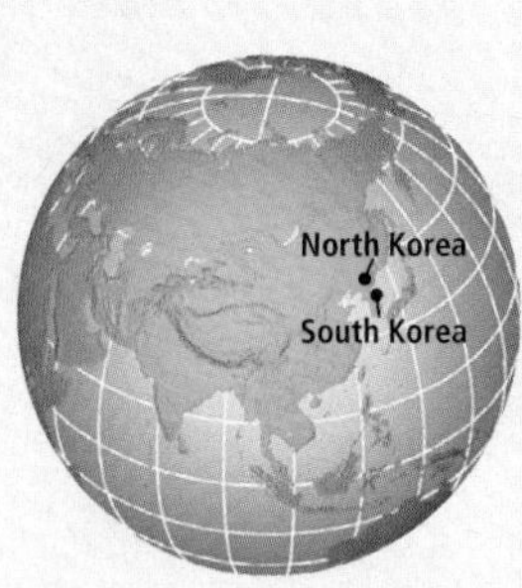

Background Korea was an independent kingdom for nearly 1,000 years. After World War II, the country was divided into two nations, North Korea and South Korea. Since then, the two countries have developed in vastly different ways. After the Korean War ended in 1953, North Korea's communist government followed an economic, political, and military policy of isolation. North Korea has a command economy, though elements of a market system are taking root.

South Korea, in contrast, is a democracy with a market economy. South Korea has achieved incredible economic growth, in part because of its *chaebols* (jeh BOLZ), huge technology conglomerates like Samsung and Hyundai that originated from a single family. Strong government support for businesses has aided the country's economic success.

What's the issue? How effective are command and market economies? Use these sources to discover how well the economies of North and South Korea function.

A. Online Article

In this article, the United States Institute of Peace (USIP) summarizes the findings of Andrew P. Natsios about the great famine in North Korea. Natsios is the author of *The Great North Korean Famine: Famine, Politics, and Foreign Policy* (2001).

North Korea Suffers Famine

Workers in "unproductive" industries die from lack of food

According to some estimates, . . . three million people died in the North Korean famine of the mid-1990s. . . .

Faced with a massive food shortage, the North Korean government "made a choice," Natsios said. Making the regime's survival its top priority, the government decided that food would go to the country's elite and its military forces. Most citizens, especially those who lived in regions or worked in industries that the government deemed "unproductive," were considered expendable. As many as three million people may have died.

Before the famine, North Korea relied on food and oil subsidies, mostly from the former Soviet Union. When that aid declined and a series of natural disasters occurred, the North Korean government cut food rations to farmers. Many people started hoarding and stealing. The system collapsed. In Natsios' view, North Koreans lost faith in the state.

Source: "The North Korean Famine." *Peace Watch Online*, June 2002

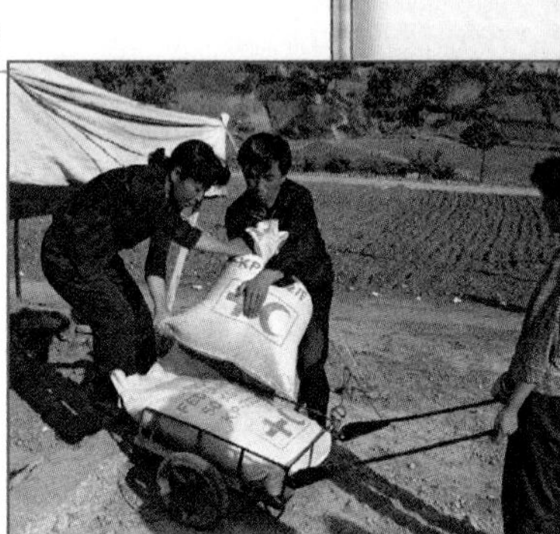

North Koreans receive contributions of rice from an international humanitarian agency.

Thinking Economically What decision described in this document is characteristic of a command economy? Explain your answer.

DIFFERENTIATING INSTRUCTION

Gifted and Talented

Consider "What If"

As the online article presents the situation, the leaders of North Korea saw only two choices. Point out the either/or fallacy in this thinking and ask students to contemplate what might have happened if North Korea had chosen a different course. Which solution would be compatible with a command economy? *(Answers will vary but may include the idea that North Korea could have redirected military resources to food production or made purchases from foreign nations.)*

Inclusion

Use Self-Monitoring

The self-contained case studies in this book provide a manageable opportunity for students to practice goal-setting and monitoring related to their IEPs. Have students develop a self-monitoring worksheet that identifies the areas they are working on, and have them note their efforts to attain their goals while completing the activities on this spread. Goals might include: asking for help when needed; following step-by-step procedures; and keeping materials organized.

B. Graph

This graph compares North Korea's and South Korea's per capita GDP—each person's share of everything produced in the economy—from 1994 to 2004.

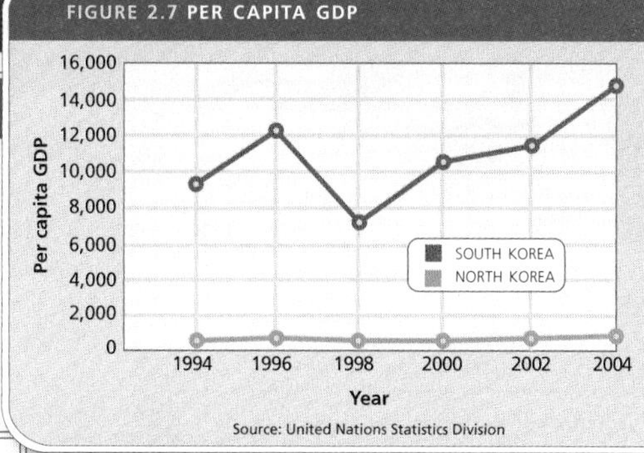

Thinking Economically What does this graph suggest about productivity in the two nations?

C. Magazine Article

This article reflects the contributions of corporations like Samsung to South Korea's growing economy.

Samsung and the "Next Great Tech Revolution"

Heading Towards a Digitized Life

Lee Jong Jin, 51, is no couch potato. But lounging in his apartment overlooking the mountains of Seoul, the international trader has little reason to leave his sofa. As he watches an interactive game show, he uses the remote to send in answers. In a corner of the 50-inch plasma screen, he can link to his online bank or control his air conditioner. Lee is one of thousands of Koreans involved in trials of Samsung Electronics' Home Network, which allows digital products to talk to each other. If Samsung has its way, millions around the world will be running their homes from the comfort of their couch within a few years.

. . . Over the last decade, [Samsung] has . . . become the most diverse and profitable consumer-electronics company on the planet. Samsung leads the global market for color televisions, VCRs, liquid crystal displays for electronic devices and digital memory devices. . . . Since 1999, revenues have doubled, and profits have risen 20 times. . . .

In the digital world all these products will finally be networked to each other . . . creating the sort of "smart" living space imagined only in science fiction. That's the idea, anyway. The change, says analyst Keith Woolcock of Westhall Capital in London, will be "the biggest event in technology for the next 10 years."

Source: "Digital Masters," *Newsweek* (International Edition), October 18, 2004

Thinking Economically What aspects of a market economy are illustrated by Samsung's financial success?

THINKING ECONOMICALLY Synthesizing

1. Based on documents A and C, in which country does the government appear to be more involved in controlling business and the economy?
2. Based on documents A and C, what can you infer about the effects of government activities on productivity in the two nations?
3. In today's global economy, is a command economy or a market economy more likely to succeed? Support your answer with information presented in the three documents.

Thinking Economically

Answers

A. *To ensure survival of the regime, the government decided that food would go to the country's elite and military. Essentially a poor decision, not based on economic reality.*

B. *Except for a dip in 1998, productivity in South Korea has markedly increased. In North Korea, however, productivity has remained stagnant.*

C. *Samsung is successful because it has set itself off from its competitors by offering a diverse line of products that employ the latest technology.*

Synthesizing

1. *The government is more controlling in North Korea. Document A states that government made major decisions about use of resources. Document C makes no mention of government involvement.*
2. *Government involvement seems to have doomed productivity in North Korea. However, productivity is thriving in South Korea, where there is little government involvement.*
3. *A market economy is more likely to succeed, as evidenced by South Korea's rapid economic growth and its success in reducing poverty. North Korea's reliance on subsidies from other nations, its failure to feed its people, and the resulting death of 3 million people suggests that decisions made in a command economy do not lead to success.*

TECHNOLOGY ACTIVITY

Creating a Web Page Comparing Technology Development

Time 60 minutes ●

Task Create a Web page comparing the development of technology in North Korea and South Korea.

Materials Needed computer with software for creating web pages and Internet access for research

Activity

- Divide students into three groups. One will create a section of the web page on technology in South Korea; one will create the section on North Korea; and the other will be responsible for illustrations and for overall site design, including a top page and all appropriate links.
- Each group should determine how to subdivide the work so that it is both fairly shared and also apportioned according to each student's strengths (that is, a good writer might be responsible for the finished text, while others with research skills might provide the data).
- When the web page is complete, arrange to view it as a class, if possible, with discussion of each part.

Rubric

	Understanding of Concepts	Presentation of Information
4	excellent	well-designed; excellent content
3	good	well-designed; good content
2	fair	fair design; some content
1	poor	careless design; little information

Online Summary Answers

1. traditional economy
2. command economy
3. socialism
4. nationalize
5. market
6. private property rights
7. competition
8. profit
9. circular flow model
10. voluntary exchange
11. mixed economy
12. global economy

Interactive Review

Review this chapter using interactive activities at **ClassZone.com**

- Online Summary
- Quizzes
- Vocabulary Flip Cards
- Graphic Organizers
- Review and Study Notes

Online Summary

Complete the following activity either on your own paper or online at **ClassZone.com**

Choose the key concept that best completes the sentence. Not all key concepts will be used.

capitalism
centrally planned economy
circular flow model
command economy
competition
factor market
global economy
laissez faire
market
market economy
mixed economy
nationalize
private property rights
privatize
product market
profit
socialism
traditional economy
voluntary exchange

In a __1__, the three basic economic questions of what to produce, how to produce, and for whom to produce are answered in the same way they have been for generations. In a __2__, in contrast, the government makes most economic decisions. Two systems in which government plays a strong role are communism and __3__. In the transition between types of economic systems, the government may __4__ industries, taking them out of private ownership.

A __5__ economy rests on private ownership, however, so __6__ guaranteed by the government are vitally important. A market economy also depends on __7__ to help produce the highest quality goods at the lowest price. Sellers are motivated by the chance to make a __8__, so they try to use their resources as efficiently as possible. The __9__ shows the flow of money as well as the flow of products and resources in the __10__ that takes place between buyers and sellers in a market economy.

The most common kind of economy today is the __11__ which blends elements from all three systems. Each modern economy is also part of the __12__, which entails all the economic interactions that cross international borders.

CHAPTER 2 Assessment

REVIEWING KEY CONCEPTS

Introduction to Economic Systems (pp. 38–41)

1. What are the three types of economic systems?
2. What are features of a traditional economy?

Command Economies (pp. 42–47)

3. What role does the government play in a command economy?
4. What are the advantages and disadvantages of a command economy?

Market Economies (pp. 48–57)

5. What are the features of a market economy?
6. What are the advantages and disadvantages of a market economy?

Modern Economies in a Global Age (pp. 58–65)

7. What are the features of a mixed economy?
8. What trends are shaping modern economies?

APPLYING ECONOMIC CONCEPTS

Look at the chart below showing statistics for four nations. Answer the following questions.

9. Which country appears to have the most productive economy?
10. Does a high percentage of GDP from agriculture make a country more or less productive? Support your answer with statistics from the chart.

FIGURE 2.8 GROWTH AND PRODUCTIVITY

Country	GDP* Growth Rate	PPP**	% of GDP from Agriculture
North Korea	1.0	1,800	30.0
Poland	3.3	12,700	2.8
Namibia	4.2	7,800	9.3
China	9.2	6,200	14.4

* Gross Domestic Product (value of everything the country produced)
** Purchasing Power Parity (shows a country's productivity relative to its population)
Source: *The CIA World Factbook, 2006*

CHAPTER 2 ASSESSMENT ANSWERS

Reviewing Key Concepts

1. traditional, command, and market
2. Economic decisions are answered by tradition; resistant to change; strong social ties; communal ownership of property.
3. It makes most, if not all, of the key economic decisions.
4. Advantages include providing for the economically nonproductive, distributing wealth more equally, and forging solidarity. Disadvantages include lack of economic and political freedom, inefficient bureaucracies, and shortages of consumer goods as a result of poor economic planning.
5. private ownership and property rights, competition, consumer sovereignty, capitalism, profit, market, voluntary exchange, specialization
6. Advantages are efficiency and productivity, economic free choice, economic growth, innovation. Disadvantages are unequal distribution of wealth and lack of a good way to provide for public goods.
7. A mixed economy has elements of traditional, command, and market economies, in different balances.
8. Transitions from command to market economies and the global economy are trends shaping modern economies.

Applying Economic Concepts

9. Poland
10. A high percentage of GDP from agriculture tends to make a country less productive, as you can see by correlating the agricultural production with the least productive countries as shown in the PPP, or by showing that countries with high PPPs have only a small percentage of their GDP from agriculture.

CRITICAL THINKING

11. **Creating Charts** Create a chart showing a continuum of countries with different types of economic systems. At the left will be the nations with the most command elements in their economic systems. On the right will be the nations with the most market elements in their economies. Use the chart below as a model.

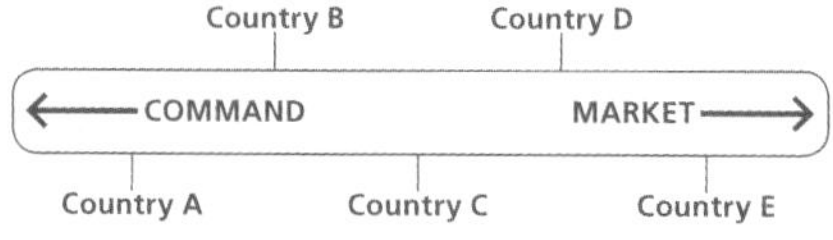

Begin with the countries listed in the chart on the previous page. Then add other countries mentioned in this chapter, such as France, Sweden, and the United States. Conduct extra research if you have difficulty placing these countries on the continuum. One useful source of information is *Economic Freedom of the World Annual Report.*

12. **Synthesizing Economic Data** Look again at Figure 2.8 on page 66. Why do you think Poland and Namibia had relatively high growth rates? In writing your answer, consider the economic changes that have taken place in these countries in recent years.
13. **Evaluating Economic Decisions** Using information in Figure 2.8, evaluate Poland's decision to privatize a number of its industries, noting whether you think it was a wise or an unwise action. Explain your evaluation.
14. **Explaining an Economic Concept** In most of the former command economies in Eastern Europe, one of the first economic changes instituted was establishing the right to own private property. Why do you think the leaders of these countries considered this feature of market economies so important?
15. **Challenge** Write a brief essay explaining how a country's political system and economic system are intertwined.

SIMULATION

Privatize Your Community's Recreation Facilities

Suppose your community felt that its administration of your park district and recreation facilities—pools, gyms, and so on—had become inefficient. As an exercise to understand the issues involved in moving from a government-owned to a privately-owned enterprise, work through the decisions you would face in privatization.

Step 1. With your whole class, divide the recreation facilities into manageable segments. One segment might be park maintenance, another might be fitness classes at the community center, and so on. Then organize pairs or small teams and assign each pair or team one of the segments.

Step 2. In your pairs or teams, discuss how to use the elements of a market economy to make your segment of the project as efficient as possible—to provide the lowest priced services at the highest possible quality.

Step 3. Draw up a plan describing the privately-owned company you think could take over your segment.

Step 4. Share your plans with the teams working on the other segments to see what other ideas came up.

Step 5. With your whole class, discuss whether privatizing services like park district facilities is a beneficial step or not. Discuss possible advantages and possible disadvantages.

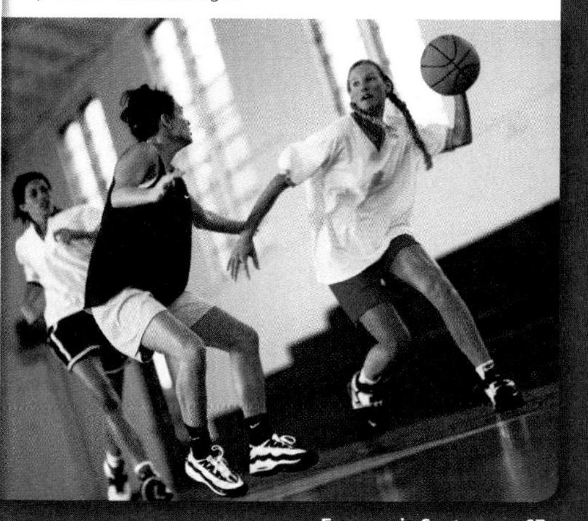

CHAPTER 2 • ASSESSMENT

McDougal Littell Assessment System

Assess

Online Test Practice
- Go to **ClassZone.com** for more test practice.

Unit 1 Resource Book
- Chapter Test, Forms A, B, & C, pp. 113–124

Test Generator CD-ROM
- Chapter Test, Forms (A, B, & C), in English and Spanish

Report

Use the McDougal Littell Assessment System to score assessments and receive customized reports.

Reteach

For activities customized for individual students, use the McDougal Littell Assessment System.

CHAPTER 2 ASSESSMENT ANSWERS

Critical Thinking

11. Placements on the continuum may vary. However, countries should be placed from left (command) to right (market): North Korea, Cuba, China, Namibia, Poland, Sweden, France, South Korea, United States.
12. Answers will vary, but should note that Poland and Namibia are undergoing a transition from a less productive economy, either a traditional one, as with Namibia, or a command economy, as with Poland.
13. Answers may vary, but some may state that Poland's growth rate suggests its privatization program was a good idea.
14. Answers will vary, but should focus on the point that private ownership tends to encourage more efficient use of economic resources and this, in turn, helps the economy to grow.
15. Answers will vary, but should note that an economy based on individual choice, such as a market economy, needs to be supported by a political system that also focuses on choice, such as democracy. Conversely, a command economy, where there is little or no individual choice, needs to be supported by an authoritarian political system.

Simulation Rubric

	Understanding of Concepts Involved	Presentation of Information
4	excellent	accurate, clear, and complete
3	good	mostly accurate and clear
2	fair	sometimes clear
1	poor	sketchy

Planning Guide

Resources 2Go Complete print resources all on one USB drive allow you to customize lessons.

Section Titles and Objectives	Unit 1 Resource Book and Workbooks		Assessment Resources
1 Advantages of the Free Enterprise System pp. 70–77 • Explain why the United States is considered to have a capitalist, or free enterprise, system • Identify the legal rights that safeguard the free enterprise system • Analyze how the profit motive and competition help to make the free enterprise system work	**Unit 1 Resource Book** • Reading Study Guide, pp. 125–126 • RSG with Additional Support, pp. 127–129 • RSG with Additional Support (Spanish), pp. 130–132 • Readings in Free Enterprise: Students Win Young Entrepreneur Prizes, pp. 157–158	• Economic Simulations: Your Own Business, pp. 161–162	**Unit 1 Resource Book** • Section Quiz, p. 133 • Reteaching Activity, p. 134 **Test Generator CD-ROM** **Daily Test Practice Transparencies,** TT9
2 How Does Free Enterprise Allocate Resources? pp. 78–83 • Explain how consumers help determine the way resources are used • Explain how producers help determine the way resources are used • Analyze a circular flow model of the U.S. economy	**Unit 1 Resource Book** • Reading Study Guide, pp. 135–136 • RSG with Additional Support, pp. 137–139 • RSG with Additional Support (Spanish), pp. 140–142 • Math Skills Worksheet: Understanding How Economists Use Negative Numbers, p. 163	**NCEE Student Activities** • Resource Allocation and the Role of Government, pp. 9–12	**Unit 1 Resource Book** • Section Quiz, p. 143 • Reteaching Activity, p. 144 **Test Generator CD-ROM** **Daily Test Practice Transparencies,** TT10
3 Government and Free Enterprise pp. 84–93 • Understand that one role of government in the U.S. economy is to address market failures • Analyze why governments provide public goods and infrastructure • Explain how governments seek to decrease negative externalities and increase positive externalities	**Unit 1 Resource Book** • Reading Study Guide, pp. 145–146 • RSG with Additional Support, pp. 147–149 • RSG with Additional Support (Spanish), pp. 150–152 • Economic Skills and and Problem Solving Activity, pp. 155–156	• Case Study Resources: Entrepreneurs and the Comeback of New York City, pp. 159–160 **Test Practice and Review Workbook,** pp. 27–28	**Unit 1 Resource Book** • Section Quiz, p. 153 • Reteaching Activity, p. 154 • Chapter Test, (Forms A, B, & C), pp. 165–176 **Test Generator CD-ROM** **Daily Test Practice Transparencies,** TT11

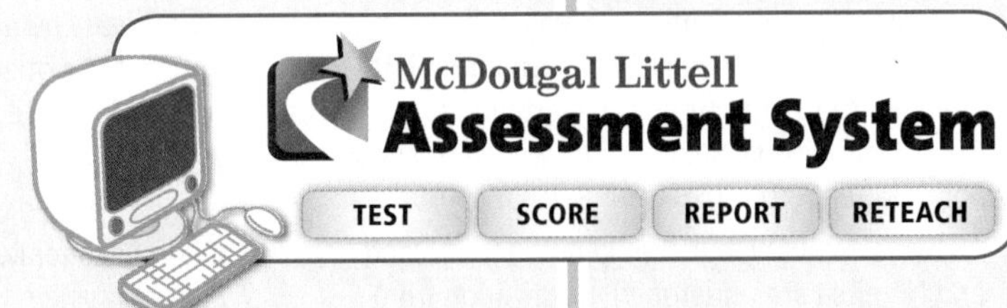

Integrated Technology

No Time? To focus students on the most important content in this chapter, use the diagram, "Free Enterprise and Legal Rights," that appears on page 74.

Teacher Presentation Options

Presentation Toolkit

Power Presentation DVD-ROM

- Lecture Notes
- Interactive Review
- Media Gallery
- Animated Economics
- Review Game

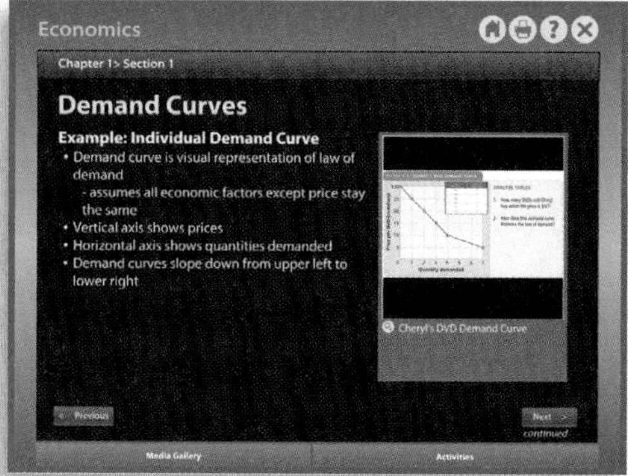

Economics Concepts Transparencies

- Legal Rights in the Free Enterprise System, CT9
- Government in the Circular Flow Model, CT10
- Government Involvement, CT11

Electronic Books

eEdition DVD-ROM

eEdition Online

Daily Test Practice Transparencies, TT9, TT10, TT11

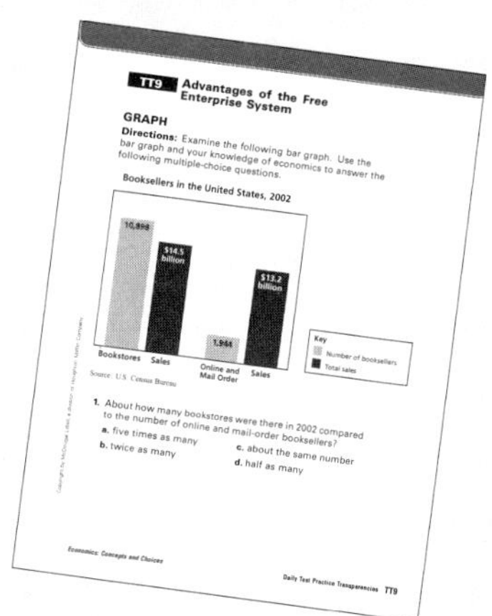

TT9 Advantages of the Free Enterprise System

GRAPH

Directions: Examine the following bar graph. Use the bar graph and your knowledge of economics to answer the following multiple-choice questions.

Booksellers in the United States, 2002

1. About how many bookstores were there in 2002 compared to the number of online and mail-order booksellers?
a. five times as many
b. twice as many
c. about the same number
d. half as many

Animated Economics

- Government in the Circular Flow Model, p. 80

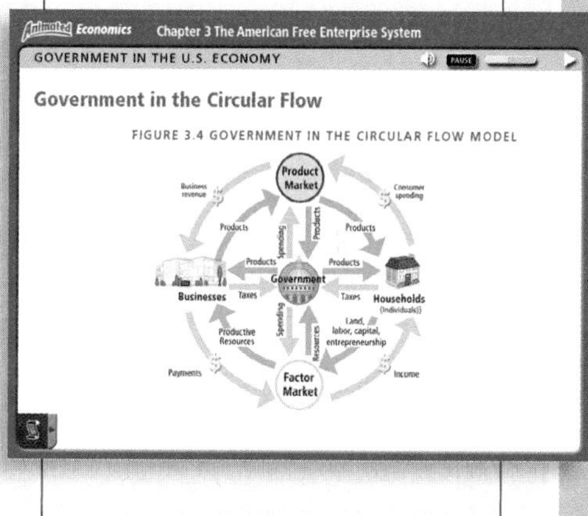

Online Activities at ClassZone.com

Economics Update

- New Business Firms and Business Firm Failures, p. 71
- Milton Friedman, p. 76
- Government Workers and Government Consumption, p. 81
- The United States: Land of Entrepreneurs, p. 92

Animated Economics

- Interactive Graphics

Activity Maker

- Vocabulary Flip Cards
- Review Game

Research Center

- Graphs and Data

Interactive Review

- Online Summary
- Quizzes
- Vocabulary Flip Cards
- Graphic Organizers
- Review and Study Notes

SMART Grapher

- Creating Graphs, p. 95

Teacher-Tested Activities

Name: Michael D. Bruce

School: William Fremd High School

State: Illinois

Teacher-Tested Activities

At the beginning of this chapter, look for my classroom-proven idea for teaching economics concepts and thinking.

Resources for Differentiated Instruction

Struggling Readers

Teacher's Edition Activities

- Create a KWL Chart, p. 72
- Use Graphics, p. 80
- Recognize Antonyms, p. 86
- Pull Out Statistics, p. 92

Unit 1 Resource Book

- RSG with Additional Support, pp. 127–129, 137–139, 147–149 (A)
- Reteaching Activities, pp. 134, 144, 154 (B)
- Chapter Test (Form A), pp. 165–168 (C)

ClassZone.com

- Animated Economics
- Interactive Review

Test Generator CD-ROM

- Chapter Test (Form A)
- Chapter Test (Form A), in Spanish

B

SECTION 1 RETEACHING ACTIVITY

Advantages of the Free Enterprise System

A. Reviewing Economic Vocabulary

B. Identifying and Evaluating Legal Rights Under Our Economic System

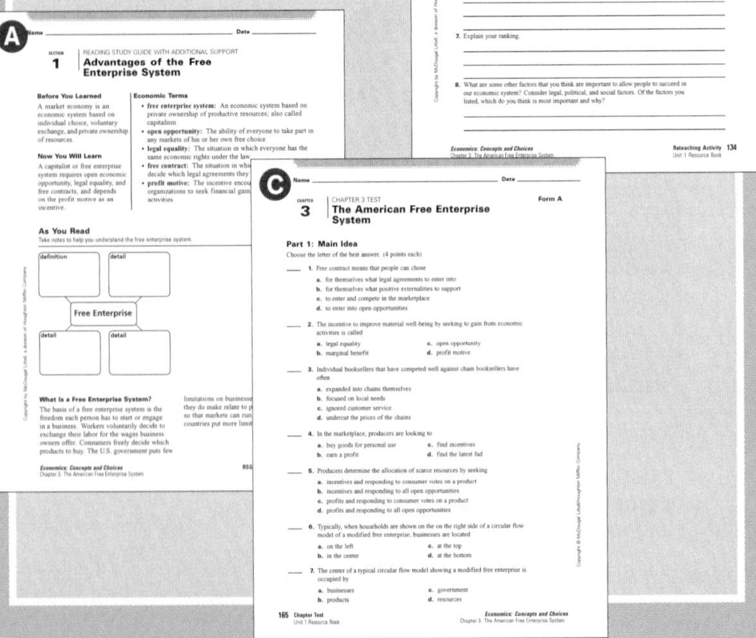

A

SECTION 1 READING STUDY GUIDE WITH ADDITIONAL SUPPORT

Advantages of the Free Enterprise System

Before You Learned

Economic Terms

Now You Will Learn

As You Read

Free Enterprise

What Is a Free Enterprise System?

C

CHAPTER 3 TEST

The American Free Enterprise System

Form A

Part 1: Main Idea

English Learners

Teacher's Edition Activities

- Share Cultural Perspectives, p. 74
- Use Spoken Language, p. 82
- Understand Idioms, p. 88

Unit 1 Resource Book

- RSG with Additional Support (Spanish), pp. 130–132, 140–142, 150–152 (A)

Test Generator CD-ROM

- Chapter Test (Forms A, B, & C), in Spanish (B)

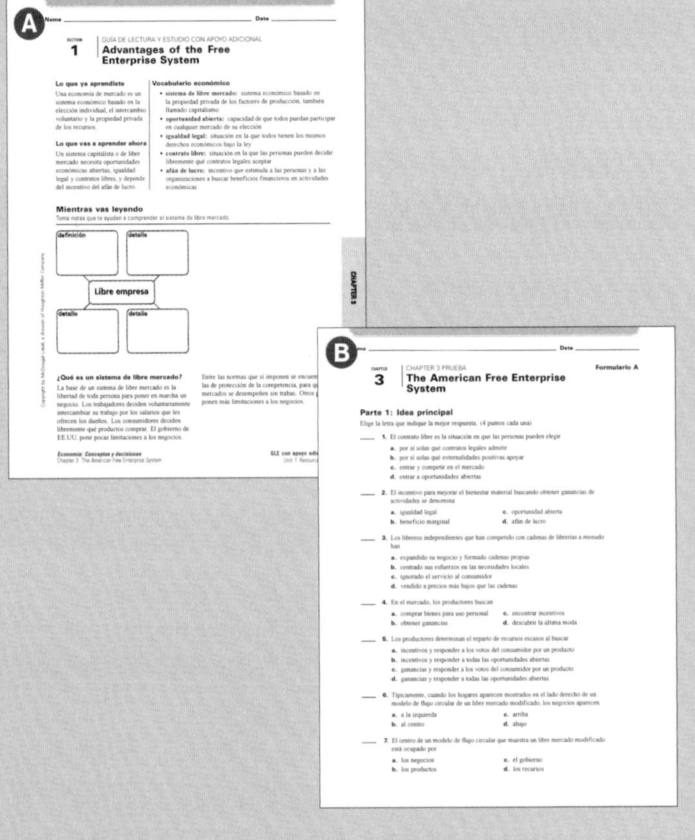

A

SECCIÓN 1 GUÍA DE LECTURA Y ESTUDIO CON APOYO ADICIONAL

Advantages of the Free Enterprise System

Lo que ya aprendiste

Vocabulario económico

Lo que vas a aprender ahora

Mientras vas leyendo

Libre empresa

¿Qué es un sistema de libre mercado?

B

CAPÍTULO 3 PRUEBA

The American Free Enterprise System

Formulario A

Parte 1: Idea principal

Inclusion

Teacher's Edition Activities

- Use Accessible Information, p. 72
- Create Alternate Presentations, p. 76
- Isolate the Parts, p. 80
- Create a Visual, p. 86
- See Economic Relationships, p. 90
- Describe Visuals, p. 92

Lesson Plans

- Modified Lessons for Inclusion, pp. 9–11 (A)

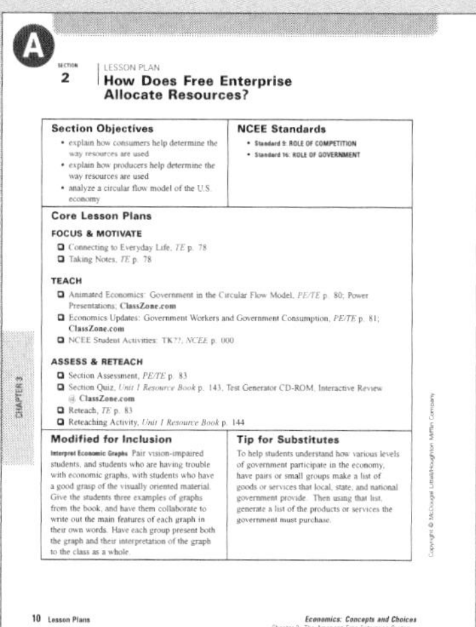
A

SECTION 2 | LESSON PLAN
How Does Free Enterprise Allocate Resources?

Section Objectives	NCEE Standards
• explain how consumers help determine the way resources are used • explain how producers help determine the way resources are used • analyze a circular flow model of the U.S. economy	• Standard 9: ROLE OF COMPETITION • Standard 16: ROLE OF GOVERNMENT

Core Lesson Plans

FOCUS & MOTIVATE

TEACH

ASSESS & RETEACH

Modified for Inclusion	Tip for Substitutes

10 Lesson Plans — *Economics: Concepts and Choices*, Chapter 3: The American Free Enterprise System

Gifted and Talented

Teacher's Edition Activities

- Identify the Economics in the Founding Documents, p. 74
- Conduct a Licensing Debate, p. 76
- Create a Line Graph, p. 82
- Research and Report, p. 88
- Create a Graph, p. 90

Unit 1 Resource Book

- Readings in Free Enterprise: Students Win Young Entrepreneur Prizes, pp. 157–158 (A)
- Case Study Resources: Entrepreneurs and the Comeback of New York City, pp. 159–160 (B)

NCEE Student Activities

- Resource Allocation; the Role of Government, pp. 9–12 (C)

ClassZone.com

- Research Center

Test Generator CD-ROM

- Chapter Test (Form C)
- Chapter Test (Form C), in Spanish

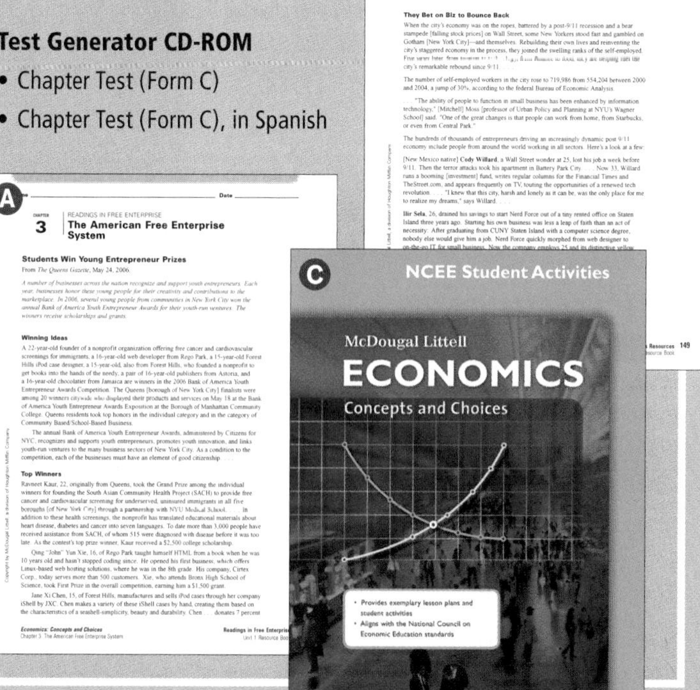
B

CHAPTER 3 | CASE STUDIES RESOURCES
The American Free Enterprise System

Entrepreneurs and the Comeback of New York City

They Bet on Biz to Bounce Back

A

CHAPTER 3 | READINGS IN FREE ENTERPRISE
The American Free Enterprise System

Students Win Young Entrepreneur Prizes

Winning Ideas

Top Winners

C

Focus & Motivate

Objective

Explain the American free enterprise system and the government's role in it.

Why the Concept Matters

Ask students what they might do during a typical week and jot their answers on the board. Their answers might include: go to school, see friends, eat, sleep, listen to music, go shopping, see a movie, take a music lesson, study, and so on. After a good list has been developed, review it and put a star by any item that relates to the free enterprise system *(listen to music, eat, go shopping, see a movie, take a music lesson, for example)* Direct students to determine what the starred items have in common. Point out that many of their daily activities relate to the free enterprise system, as well as to the larger issue of what opportunities lay ahead for them.

Analyzing the Photograph

Have students study the photograph and read the caption. Then ask them to speculate about what kind of business this couple is creating and what economic conditions might make it possible for them to start their business. Also ask them to consider why it might be appropriate to show a new business owner on a ladder. *(opportunities for climbing the economic ladder, or the "ladder of success")*

Free Enterprise

In the American free enterprise system, everyone is free to start a business like the couple shown here. Businesses will succeed or fail based on how well they respond to market forces.

CONTENT STANDARDS

NCEE STANDARDS

Standard 9: Role of Competition

Students will understand that

Competition among sellers lowers costs and prices, and encourages producers to produce more of what consumers are willing and able to buy. Competition among buyers increases prices and allocates goods and services to those people who are willing and able to pay the most for them.

Students will be able to use this knowledge to

Explain how changes in the level of competition in different markets can affect them. *(pages 73–75, 78–79)*

Standard 16: Role of Government

Students will understand that

There is an economic role for government in a market economy whenever the benefits of a government policy outweigh its costs. Governments often provide for national defense, address environmental concerns, define and protect property rights, and attempt to make markets more competitive. Most government policies also redistribute income.

Students will be able to use this knowledge to

Identify and evaluate the benefits and costs of alternative public policies, and assess who enjoys the benefits and who bears the costs. *(pages 84–90)*

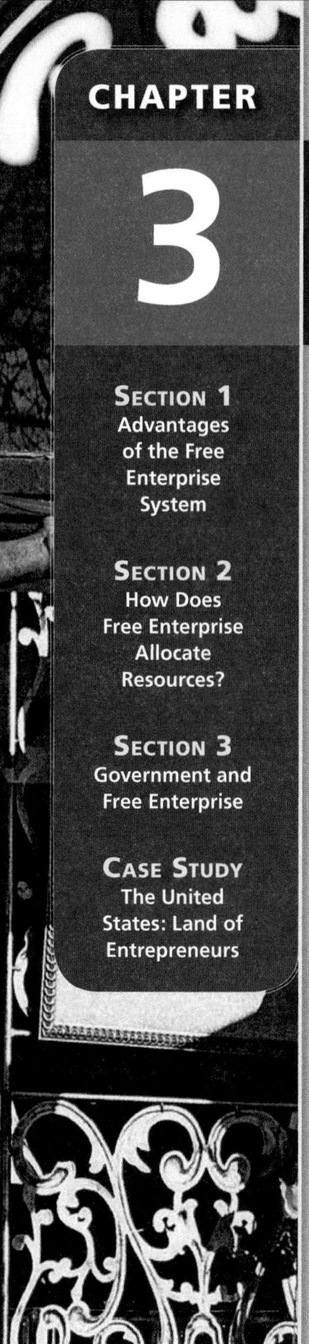

CHAPTER 3

The American Free Enterprise System

CONCEPT REVIEW

A **market economy** is an economic system based on individual choice, voluntary exchange, and the private ownership of resources.

CHAPTER 3 KEY CONCEPT

Free enterprise system is another name for capitalism, an economic system based on private ownership of productive resources. This name is sometimes used because in a capitalist system anyone is free to start a business or enterprise.

WHY THE CONCEPT MATTERS

Free enterprise is all around you, from huge suburban malls to industrial developments to neighborhood corner stores. Think about ways that the American economic system affects your day-to-day life. Consider where you shop, what you buy, where you work, and what you do there. What do you think allows this huge economic engine to run?

Online Highlights

More at ClassZone.com

Economics Update

Go to ECONOMICS UPDATE for chapter updates and current news on entrepreneurs in the United States. (See Case Study, pages 92–93).

Animated Economics

Go to ANIMATED ECONOMICS for interactive versions of diagrams in this chapter. ▶

Interactive Review

Go to INTERACTIVE REVIEW for concept review and activities.

How do households, businesses, and government interact in the economy? See Figure 3.4 in Section 2 of this chapter.

From the Classroom

Michael Bruce, William Fremd H.S.

I collect seven or eight small, random items from around the classroom. These items should not have any particular purpose known to the students. I used a crumpled up piece of paper, a broken knob from some machine, a torn piece of transparent paper, one part of a toy, and so on.

I put students into groups of three or four, gave each group one of the items, and gave them about five minutes to identify some new purpose for the item. Each group then presented their item to the class. This really showed the creativity of the students and identified some entrepreneurial talent.

An extension to this activity would be to have the group put together a brief commercial to explain the object's purpose and to convince the rest of the class that they need one.

Previewing Chapter Technology at ClassZone.com

Economics Update Students will find updates to information in the pupil edition on pages 71, 76, 81, and 92.

Animated Economics Students will find interactive lessons related to materials on page 80.

Interactive Review Students will find additional section and chapter assessment support for materials on pages 77, 83, 91, and 94.

TEACHER MEDIA FAVORITES

Books

- Friedman, Milton & Rose. *Free to Choose: A Personal Statement.* New York: Harcourt, 1990. The highly readable companion book to the PBS special that explored both the economic and social significance of the free enterprise system.
- Kuttner, Robert. *Everything for Sale: The Virtues and Limits of Markets.* New York: Alfred A. Knopf, 1997. A powerful case for mixed economies with an examination of the government's role in promoting growth and addressing inequalities.

Videos/DVDs

- *Freedom 2000.* 22 minutes. The Gus A. Stavros Center for Free Enterprise and Economic Education, 2000. Uses the idea of visitors from space to teach about the development of the free enterprise system.
- *American Enterprise Series: Government.* 29 minutes. The Gus A. Stavros Center for Free Enterprise and Economic Education, 2001. Explores the role of government in the standard of living throughout history.

Software

- *Free Enterpri$e* (Windows 95/98) Tsunami Media, 1996. Offers students an opportunity to operate a business.

Internet

Visit **ClassZone.com** to link to

- a variety of chapter-specific, content-reviewed sites
- updates on data and topics presented throughout the chapter sections and Case Study
- updates to the Power Presentations

1 Plan & Prepare

Section 1 Objectives

- explain why the United States is considered to have a capitalist, or free enterprise, system
- identify the legal rights that safeguard the free enterprise system
- analyze how the profit motive and competition help to make the free enterprise system work

2 Focus & Motivate

Connecting to Everyday Life Ask students to discuss their occupational hopes for the future. Ask them to consider their prospects for attaining their goals and to discuss what, if any, hurdles or barriers stand between them and their goals. Encourage students to draw some conclusions about their opportunities. *(Students may mention the availability of good colleges but see tuition as a hurdle; some students may mention unequal opportunities; others may argue the opportunities are there.)*

Taking Notes Remind students to take notes as they read by completing a cluster diagram on free enterprise. They can use the Graphic Organizer at **Interactive Review @ Classzone.com**. A sample is shown below.

Free Enterprise
- economic system based on private ownership of productive resources
- called free enterprise system because in it anyone is free to start a business or enterprise
- profit motive is incentive for starting a business
- key features: open opportunity, legal equality, free contract

SECTION 1

Advantages of the Free Enterprise System

OBJECTIVES

In Section 1, you will
- explain why the United States is considered to have a capitalist, or free enterprise, system
- identify the legal rights that safeguard the free enterprise system
- analyze how the profit motive and competition help to make the free enterprise system work

KEY TERMS

free enterprise system, *p. 70*
open opportunity, *p. 73*
legal equality, *p. 73*
free contract, *p. 73*
profit motive, *p. 73*

TAKING NOTES

As you read Section 1, complete a cluster diagram using information on free enterprise. Use the Graphic Organizer at **Interactive Review @ Classzone.com**

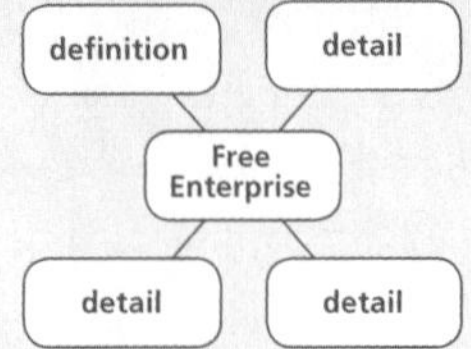

What Is a Free Enterprise System?

QUICK REFERENCE

Free enterprise system is another name for capitalism, an economic system based on private ownership of productive resources.

KEY CONCEPTS

As you recall from Chapter 2, the United States has a capitalist economic system. Capitalism is an economic system based on the private ownership of the factors of production. The central idea of capitalism is that producers are free to produce the goods and services that consumers want. Consumers are influenced by the desire to buy the goods and services that satisfy their economic wants. Producers are influenced by the desire to earn profits, the money left over after the costs have been subtracted from business revenues. A capitalist system is also known as a **free enterprise system** because anyone is free to start a business or enterprise.

EXAMPLE United States

Let's take a look at one American who took advantage of that freedom. Monica Ramirez, a makeup consultant for fashion magazines and television, noticed that very few Hispanic women purchased the cosmetics available in stores. She thought that this might present a business opportunity. So, in 2001, she created Zalia Cosmetics, a line of cosmetics specifically for

70 Chapter 3

SECTION 1 PROGRAM RESOURCES

ON LEVEL

Lesson Plans
- Core, p. 9

Unit 1 Resource Book
- Reading Study Guide, pp. 125–126
- Economics Simulation, pp. 161–162
- Section Quiz, p. 133

STRUGGLING READERS

Unit 1 Resource Book
- Reading Study Guide with Additional Support, pp. 127–129
- Reteaching Activity, p. 134

ENGLISH LEARNERS

Unit 1 Resource Book
- Reading Study Guide with Additional Support (Spanish), pp. 130–132

INCLUSION

Lesson Plans
- Modified for Inclusion, p. 9

GIFTED AND TALENTED

Unit 1 Resource Book
- Readings in Free Enterprise: Students Win Young Entrepreneur Prizes, pp. 157–158

TECHNOLOGY

eEdition DVD-ROM

eEdition Online

Power Presentation DVD-ROM

Economics Concepts Transparencies
- CT9 Legal Rights in the Free Enterprise System

Daily Test Practice Transparencies, TT9

ClassZone.com

Latinas. She put her whole savings account into starting the business. Her creativity and energy attracted attention, and she soon had backers willing to invest their money in the business.

By 2004, Zalia Cosmetics had sales outlets in the major Hispanic markets of New York, Miami, Dallas, Los Angeles, San Antonio, and Houston. Today, the business continues to grow and Ramirez is sharing her success. She donates a percentage of her profits to organizations that help and encourage Latina entrepreneurs.

As you can see in Figure 3.1 below, Zalia Cosmetics was just one of more than 585,000 new businesses started in the United States in 2001. No matter where you go in the United States, you can see similar signs of a free enterprise economy at work. If you walk through a suburban shopping mall you'll see national and regional chain stores next to small boutiques and startup shops. Sometimes you'll even see kiosks in the aisles, competing for business. Similarly, on a stroll through a city neighborhood you'll observe corner grocery stores, dry cleaners, and barber shops. At an industrial park you'll see factories that churn out an immense variety of products. In the countryside beyond the city, you'll notice farms with fields of corn or soybeans, orchards of apples or peaches, or grazing areas for livestock.

FIGURE 3.1 NEW FIRMS AND FIRM CLOSURES

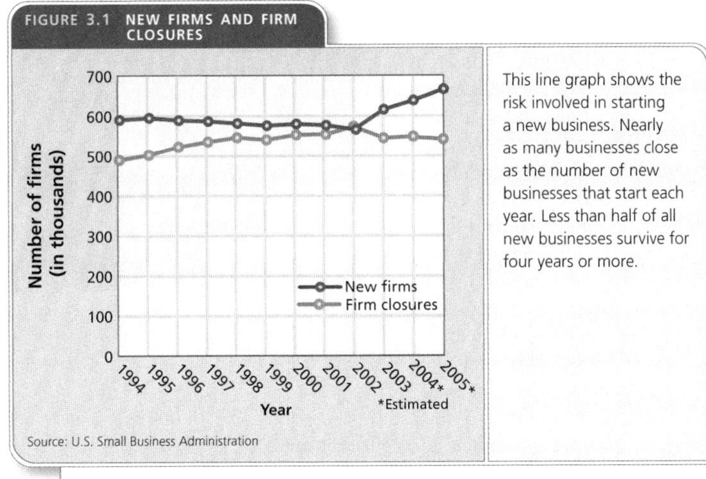

This line graph shows the risk involved in starting a new business. Nearly as many businesses close as the number of new businesses that start each year. Less than half of all new businesses survive for four years or more.

Economics Update

Find an update on new business firms and business firm closures at **ClassZone.com**

ANALYZE GRAPHS

1. What is notable about 2002 in terms of the relationship between new firms and firm closures?
2. How does this graph illustrate the fact that entrepreneurship involves risk?

What do these examples of free enterprise have in common? They are all illustrations of how individual choices are the basis of a market economy. Business owners freely make the choice to start these enterprises. Also, these owners are free to choose how they will use their scarce productive resources. The managers and workers who operate these businesses voluntarily decide to exchange their labor for the pay the owners offer. Finally, consumers make their own choices on which goods and services they will buy.

3 Teach

What Is a Free Enterprise System?

Discuss

- What aspects of free enterprise are free? *(choices of business owners to start new business; choice of how to use scarce resources; choice of workers to exchange their labor for pay; choice of consumers about what to buy)*

Analyzing Graphs: Figure 3.1

Have students summarize the trends in business creation and closure from 1994 to 2005. What period was probably the worst for starting a new business? *(From about 2000 to 2002, because nearly as many businesses closed as opened.)*

Answers

1. In 2002, more businesses closed than opened.
2. It shows that the risk of failure can be high; the number of business closures is usually close to or almost equal to the number of new businesses.

Economics Update

At **ClassZone.com**, students will see updated information on new businesses and business closures.

LEVELED ACTIVITY

Relate Government and the Economy

Time 30 minutes

Objective Students will demonstrate an understanding of the risks and rewards within the free enterprise system.

Basic

Using the example of Monica Ramirez, write a paragraph explaining what the free enterprise system is and what risks and rewards are inherent in it. Take notes on pages 70–71 and use them to write a rough draft of your paragraph. Exchange it with a classmate to get and give ideas for improvement. Then make a neat, final copy.

On Level

Use a small business in your community as an example for an essay on the risks and rewards of free enterprise. Free write about how the company got started, how it has changed, and how the owner has prospered or struggled. Use this free writing to draft your essay. Get some feedback, and then revise and edit your essay.

Challenge

Create a business plan for a new enterprise in your neighborhood. In your business plan, consider how it will be financed, how it will compete, when it can be expected to be profitable, and how many people it will need to employ. Also, indicate the possible rewards and risks, so that investors are fully informed.

More About . . .

Government Regulation of Business
There are several theories concerning government regulation of business. According to the "public interest theory," regulations protect consumers from fraudulent, inferior, and unsafe products and "fly-by-night" companies. Other theories broadly known as "public choice" theories put forward a different explanation. One suggests that government regulations actually benefit existing industries by making entry into the market by competitors more difficult. Another, called the "tollbooth" theory, says that the main beneficiaries of the regulations are politicians, who use them to "charge" businesses wanting access into the markets.

International Economics

Foreign Business in Singapore
Singapore is known for its rule of law, including guarantees to the right to own private property. This legal framework is one reason foreign investors are drawn to Singapore, for foreign and domestic investors are treated equally under the law. The Singaporean courts are also well known for upholding contracts. An exception to the openness to foreign investment is the media. All local radio and TV stations are either owned by the government or linked to it.

As you recall, government plays a relatively limited role in the American free enterprise system. The government sometimes takes actions that limit free enterprise. For the most part, however, these actions are designed to protect or encourage competition or to enforce contracts.

EXAMPLE Emerging Markets

As you read in Chapter 2, most countries today have mixed economic systems with at least some elements of free enterprise. Each economy has its own balance of tradition, free enterprise, and government involvement and its own distinctive ways in which market forces work. To illustrate this, let's look at the countries of Mexico and Singapore

In the Mexican economy, the government plays a much larger role than in the United States. The Mexican government has established many rules and regulations that make starting a new business quite difficult. As a result, an informal market that gets around these barriers has grown up. In Mexico City, for example, much of the city center is taken up with vendors' stalls, and people jam the streets to buy imported toys, clothing, shoes, CDs, and more at much lower prices than they could find at regular retail stores. Indeed, the stiff competition from street vendors has driven some of the retail stores out of business.

Competition Popular stalls on the streets of Mexico City, selling everything from candy to clothes, provide considerable competition for established stores.

The country of Singapore has a thriving free enterprise system. However, the government is so closely involved in the economy that the country is sometimes called Singapore Inc. The government establishes what benefits employers must provide to workers. It also requires all workers to put a percentage of income in the Central Provident Fund, a government savings scheme. The fund is used to pay pensions and to finance public projects, such as education, housing, and health care. Even so, the government is considered very supportive of free enterprise. Many of its policies keep business rents, taxes, and other costs low so that Singaporean companies remain competitive in the world economy.

APPLICATION Analyzing Cause and Effect

A. What steps can a government take to support free enterprise?
Answers may vary but should include such steps as protecting and encouraging competition, enforcing contracts, and keeping business costs low.

DIFFERENTIATING INSTRUCTION

Inclusion

Use Accessible Information
Because of the Americans with Disabilities Act, all governmental Web pages must be accessible for use with assistive technologies. An excellent resource for factual information on nations is the CIA's *The World Factbook,* which is updated regularly and has a text-only version that is fully compatible with assistive technologies. Ask students to use that site to find 10 economic facts about both Mexico and Singapore. They should then share those facts with the class.

Struggling Readers

Create a KWL Chart
Have students create a three-column KWL chart for reading about the free enterprise system. Students should complete the first two columns (What I **K**now, What I **W**ant to Learn) before reading pages 72 and 73. This will activate their prior knowledge and give them the proper mindset for what they are going to read. When they have finished reading, have them complete the third column (What I **L**earned). Suggest that they use this strategy often with content-area reading.

How a Free Enterprise System Works

KEY CONCEPTS

You learned in Chapter 2 that the right to private property is one of the most fundamental freedoms in a capitalist economy. With that freedom comes the right to exchange that property voluntarily. This exchange lies at the heart of a free enterprise economy. Another key freedom of this type of economy is **open opportunity**, the ability of everyone to enter and compete in the marketplace of his or her own free choice. This ensures that the market will reflect a wide range of interests and talents and will provide incentives to everyone to be efficient and productive.

Free enterprise also requires **legal equality**, a situation in which everyone has the same economic rights under the law. In other words, everyone has the same legal right to succeed or fail in the marketplace. Another important element of a market economy is the **free contract**. For voluntary exchange to work, people must be able to decide for themselves which legal agreements they want to enter into, such as business, job, or purchase commitments.

These freedoms assure that people are able to engage in free enterprise. But what motivates people to start a business? For most people, it is the **profit motive**, the incentive that encourages people and organizations to improve their material well-being by seeking to gain from economic activities. Producers, motivated by profit, seek the highest possible price for their products. Competition offsets the drive to earn profits, since it forces prices down. This helps producers find a price that is not so high that it deters buyers and not so low that it inhibits profits.

QUICK REFERENCE

Open opportunity is the ability of everyone to take part in the market by free choice.

Legal equality is a situation in which everyone has the same economic rights under the law.

A **free contract** is a situation in which people decide which legal agreements to enter into.

The **profit motive** is the force that encourages people and organizations to improve their material well being from economic activities.

EXAMPLE **Profit in Rocks**

One memorable example of how the various economic freedoms and the profit motive come together in the free enterprise system is the pet rock. Talking with friends in April 1975, advertising executive Gary Dahl joked that regular pets were too much trouble. Pet rocks, he suggested, were much easier to care for. Dahl's friends were amused by the idea. In response, he wrote a manual on pet rocks, showing how they could be house trained and taught to do tricks.

In August, Dahl began packaging his pet rocks, complete with a care manual, for sale at gift shows. Intrigued, a buyer from a major department store ordered 500. In a matter of weeks, Dahl's joke had become a national story. Articles appeared in newspapers and magazines and Dahl did several interviews on television. By the end of the year, Dahl had sold more than two tons of pet rocks and had become a millionaire. However, as 1976 began, consumers lost interest, and it quickly became obvious that the pet rock was last year's fad. Dahl decided to get out of the pet rock business, guided by the same market forces that had brought him into the business and made him rich.

Open Opportunity
Because of legal rights built into the free enterprise system, Gary Dahl was free to enter the market for pet rocks.

How a Free Enterprise System Works

Discuss

- What is the difference between open opportunity and legal equality? *(Open opportunity allows people to participate in the market of their choice in the manner in which they choose. Legal equality assures that people in each market have the same economic rights.)*
- What besides profit, if anything, might motivate a person to start a business? *(Answers will vary but some may recognize that non-profits tend to fulfill a social need and that people are motivated to create enterprises for those purposes as well.)*
- What fads like the pet rock have you seen come and go? *(Answers will vary but may include "virtual" pets, bean-stuffed small animals with cute names, and cards based on Japanese cartoon characters.)* What do these fads show about free enterprise? *(the free choice of consumers and producers)*

SMALL GROUP ACTIVITY

Understanding Consumer Choice

Time 30 minutes ◑

Task Analyze consumer wants and develop a product idea.

Materials Needed paper and pens or pencils, other materials as appropriate to each group's product

Activity

- Begin with a class discussion analyzing the pet rock phenomenon. Ask students whether they think Gary Dahl created a consumer demand for pet rocks or responded to an actual consumer want.
- After the discussion, divide the class into five groups and give each the task of using the pet rock phenomenon to develop a new fad product.
- Have students create an engaging description of their product. Students may also "prototype" their product if possible. Each group should also analyze if their product meets or creates consumers' wants.
- Have each group present their fad idea to the rest of the class.

Rubric

	Understanding Concepts	Presentation of Information
4	excellent	clever product
3	good	good product
2	fair	acceptable product
1	poor	uninspired product

Economics Essentials: Figure 3.2

To help students understand each legal right built into the free enterprise system, ask them to think of a negative example of each one. That is, what would an example be of closed opportunity, legal inequality, and forced contracts? *(Possible answers: closed opportunity—only insiders can get licenses for businesses; legal inequality—government business loans available for some start-up businesses and not others, based solely on neighborhoods; forced contract—consumers have to use only one phone company)*

Analyze

Answers may vary, but most students will note the following: open opportunity—Dahl and the various booksellers had the opportunity and ability to enter and compete in their respective markets; legal equality—Dahl and the booksellers enjoyed the same legal rights as all others in their respective market; free contract—consumers were free to buy, or not to buy, from Dahl or the booksellers.

Technomics

Business Statistics
If you are thinking of starting a business but want to stay away from risky enterprises, you can find a wealth of information on the Internet on business performance. For example, you might want to stay away from hunting and trapping, an area in which only 23.6 percent of businesses made a profit in 2002. On the other hand, the vast majority of small businesses specializing in surveying and mapping, optometry, dentistry, and charter and school bus driving showed profits. This information can be found on commercial Web sites, such as bizstats.com, which often provide some free information but reserve premium information for subscribers. Many federal government Web sites also contain vast amounts of business statistics.

ECONOMICS ESSENTIALS

FIGURE 3.2 Free Enterprise and Legal Rights

What Legal Rights Are Built into the Free Enterprise System?

Open Opportunity
Everyone should have the ability to enter and compete in any marketplace. Open participation serves as an incentive to be efficient and productive.

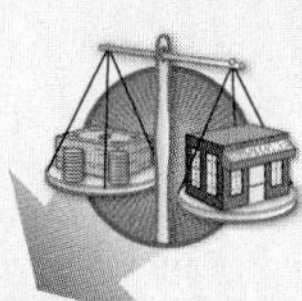

Legal Equality
Everyone should have the same economic rights under the law. In other words, the law should not give some people a better chance than others to succeed in the marketplace.

Free Contract
Everyone should have the right to decide for themselves which legal economic agreements they want to enter into. Voluntary exchange, a cornerstone of free enterprise, cannot function without freedom of contract.

ANALYZE CHARTS
The American free enterprise system is based on the idea of freedom—producers and consumers are free to pursue their economic self-interest. Certain legal rights have been established to protect and encourage this freedom. Reread the paragraphs on pet rocks on page 73 and those on books on pages 74–75. How do these examples illustrate the legal rights shown in this chart?

EXAMPLE Competition over Books

Gary Dahl did face competition from other producers who jumped into the pet rock market. Competition, however, did not drive him out of business. Rather, consumers simply stopped buying pet rocks. The market for books is somewhat different. Demand for books remains high, but booksellers have been going out of business because of new and fierce competition.

Before 1995, small chain stores and independent neighborhood booksellers dominated the book market. Around 1995, large chain stores such as Barnes & Noble Inc. and Borders Group Inc. began to compete more aggressively. Because of their huge purchasing volume, the large chain stores could buy their books at greatly discounted prices. They passed the savings on to consumers, lowering prices by anywhere from 10 percent to 40 percent. They also created a warm and welcoming atmosphere in their stores, with comfortable reading areas, cafés, and frequent readings and book signings by authors.

DIFFERENTIATING INSTRUCTION

English Learners

Share Cultural Perspectives
Encourage students from other national and cultural backgrounds to share experiences that may be fundamentally very different from those of mainstream Americans. For example, students may be from a country or region where there is little competition or economic freedom or where an idea like the pet rock would be unthinkable since there is so little disposable income. Both English speakers and English learners will benefit from the sharing of such perspectives.

Gifted and Talented

Identify the Economics in the Founding Documents
Divide students into two groups. Direct one group to review the Declaration of Independence and the other to review the U.S. Constitution, looking for the ways that the documents address economic issues and lay the foundation for a free enterprise system. Have the groups report their findings to the class.

The tactics of the large chain stores caused problems for independent booksellers. In 1991, independent booksellers accounted for more than 30 percent of all book sales in the United States. By 2005, their share of sales had fallen to less than 15 percent. And between 1995 and 2005, about 1,200 independent booksellers went out of business.

Soon, however, the large chains faced a challenge themselves: Amazon.com. The online bookseller opened for business in July, 1995 and within a few months had become an important player in the book market. Amazon's easy-to-use Web site, huge database of titles, quick and reliable delivery, and discounted prices attracted many book buyers. By the end of 2004, Amazon's sales stood at $134 million a week. Now Amazon, however, is looking over its shoulder at a new challenger. Online competitors such as Overstock.com and Buy.com have undercut Amazon's prices on hundreds of books by as much as 25 percent while matching Amazon's level of excellence in service.

Consumers have benefited from all of this competition, for they can now easily and conveniently buy books at the lowest prices. Those independent booksellers who have remained in business cannot match the lower prices offered by the large chains and online sellers. However, they can provide some things that their larger competitors cannot: personal service and a focus on local tastes or specialized subject areas. Consumers benefit from this, too. These independent booksellers who stayed in business illustrate an important aspect of free enterprise. Businesses that keep pace with changes in the market and adjust accordingly thrive. Those that do not eventually fail.

YOUR ECONOMIC CHOICES

FREE ENTERPRISE

Where will you open your restaurant?

You've decided to open a restaurant. You can lease one of two buildings. One is in a busy mall next to a highway exit. However, there are already six restaurants in that mall. The other location is in a small strip mall in a quiet neighborhood with no other restaurants nearby. Consider the chance to make profits and the level of competition, and choose.

Mall food court

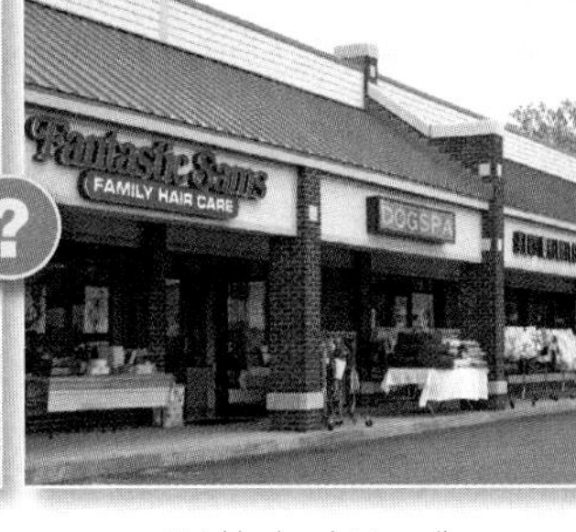

Neighborhood strip mall

APPLICATION Analyzing Cause and Effect

B. Explain the chain of cause-and-effect reactions since the mid-1990s that led to lower book prices for American consumers. See answer in Teacher's Edition. ▶

Your Economic Choices

FREE ENTERPRISE

Where will you open your restaurant?

- What are the advantages of being in the first location, the busy mall? What are the disadvantages? *(Advantages—lots of business traffic; easily accessible; probably easier to get workers because of accessibility; Disadvantages—having to share customers with competitors; very likely a higher rent)*
- What are the advantages and disadvantages of the second choice, in the small strip mall? *(Advantages—lower rent; less competition to draw customers away; disadvantages—lower volume of customer traffic)*

Activity Think of real-life examples of each of these kinds of restaurants. Analyze the advantages and disadvantages of each, then evaluate the degree to which each appears to be thriving.

APPLICATION

Answer *Large chains competed with independents, driving down prices and forcing smaller stores out of business. Amazon competed with large chains, driving prices down further. Amazon's success brought other online retailers into market, bringing even lower book prices.*

SMALL GROUP ACTIVITY

Understanding Competition

Time 45 minutes

Task Create a four-part project that explains an idea for a product to compete with an existing product.

Materials Needed paper, pens or pencils

Activity

- Pair students and direct each pair to identify a product that they both know well and then try to come up with a competing product.
- Part 1 of the project is a description of the existing product. Instruct students to list its strengths and weaknesses and the benefits it gives consumers.
- Part 2 is a description of their competing product. Direct students to note the same details about the new product as they did for the original.
- Part 3 is a brief paragraph explaining why their product will be a better value to the consumers than the original.
- Part 4 is another paragraph, this one using the example of their competing product to explain why competition is an essential part of free enterprise.

Rubric

	Understanding Competition	Presentation of Information
4	excellent	all parts well done
3	good	mostly well done
2	fair	some parts well done
1	poor	incomplete

Milton Friedman

More About . . .

Milton Friedman's Influence
George Shultz, Secretary of the Treasury under President Richard Nixon, stated that one of Friedman's greatest attributes was that he was an outstanding teacher. Through *Free to Choose,* which he co-authored with his wife Rose, Friedman brought his philosophy to millions of people around the globe. Shultz also remembered a saying about Friedman: "Everybody loves to argue with Milton, particularly when he isn't there." Friedman had a reputation as an exceptionally powerful thinker and speaker who enjoyed testing his ideas and those of others against the reality of economic experience.

APPLICATION

Answer *He would have supported the idea of the informal market for meeting people's wants, arguing that government barriers to entry into the formal market are the real problem.*

Economics Update

ClassZone.com includes links to sites about Milton Friedman. These will help students understand Friedman's devotion to free markets and influence on economic thought.

ECONOMICS PACESETTER

Milton Friedman: Promoter of Free Markets

At a glittering White House birthday celebration for Milton Friedman in 2002, President George W. Bush declared that the 90-year-old economist "has shown us that . . . in contrast to the free market's invisible hand . . . the government's invisible foot tramples on people's hopes." Economics professors are rarely guests of honor at White House galas. Why did Friedman receive such a tribute?

FAST FACTS

Milton Friedman

Born: July 31, 1912

Died: November 16, 2006

Important Publications:
Capitalism and Freedom (1962)
Free to Choose (1980)
Bright Promises, Dismal Performance: An Economist's Protest (1983)

Famous Quotation:
I am in favor of cutting taxes under any circumstances and for any excuse, for any reason, whenever it's possible.

Major Accomplishments:
Economic advisor to Presidents Richard Nixon and Ronald Reagan, and to British prime minister Margaret Thatcher

Economics Update

Find an update on Milton Friedman at **ClassZone.com**

Free to Choose

Friedman spent most of his career teaching at the University of Chicago, where he helped develop the free-market ideas now linked with what is called the "Chicago School of Economics." Central to his ideas was the belief that the market should be free to operate in all fields, even such professions as the law and medicine. Easing government restrictions in these fields—lowering licensing standards, for example—would bring more doctors and lawyers into the market. This, in turn, would bring down the cost of legal and medical services. Friedman also put forward the theory that the government's most important economic role was to control the amount of money in circulation. Without this control of the money supply, Friedman noted, the economy would experience inflation—a sustained rise in the general level of prices.

Friedman's ideas were very influential. He advised two U.S. presidents and the heads of state of several other countries on economic policy. He gained worldwide recognition in 1976 when he won the Nobel Prize for Economics. Friedman became well known outside the academic world in 1980 when *Free to Choose,* which he wrote with his wife Rose, became the year's best-selling nonfiction book in the United States.

From 1977 until his death in 2006, Friedman served as a scholar at the Hoover Institution, a conservative public-policy research center at Stanford University. In 1996, he and his wife founded the Milton and Rose D. Friedman Foundation, an organization that promotes school choice.

Economic Freedom
Personal freedom is at the center of Friedman's economic theories.

APPLICATION Making Inferences

C. How might Milton Friedman have responded to the problems associated with the informal market in Mexico?

◀See answer in Teacher's Edition.

DIFFERENTIATING INSTRUCTION

Gifted and Talented

Conduct a Licensing Debate
Friedman was known for his views on lowering licensing standards for doctors and lawyers, letting market forces help bring down prices for these services. Divide students into two teams, one taking Friedman's position and one taking the position that regulations are necessary. Direct students to research their positions carefully and prepare effective arguments. Have each side debate before the class and let the class discuss which side presented the more persuasive argument.

Inclusion

Create Alternate Presentations
Have students prepare presentations that reflect the life and professional accomplishments of Milton Friedman. Students are free to choose a medium for their presentation that is best suited to their learning: for example, an oral presentation, a visual (poster), or an enactment, such as an interviewer asking Friedman questions.

76 Chapter 3

SECTION 1 Assessment

REVIEWING KEY CONCEPTS

1. Explain the differences among the following terms.
   a. *open opportunity* **b.** *legal equality* **c.** *free contract*
2. What is the role of the profit motive in the American free enterprise system?
3. How is a free enterprise system linked to economic freedom?
4. Give examples of three different economic freedoms in a free enterprise system.
5. What force acts as a balance to the profit motive in the American free enterprise system?
6. **Using Your Notes** Write two or three paragraphs explaining how a free enterprise system works. Refer to your completed cluster diagram.
   Use the Graphic Organizer at **Interactive Review @ ClassZone.com**

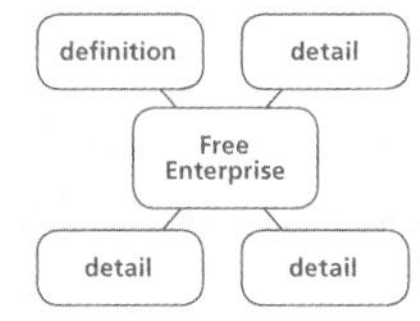

CRITICAL THINKING

7. **Applying Economic Concepts** Explain the role of competition in a free market. Illustrate your answer with examples of businesses in your local economy.
8. **Comparing and Contrasting Economic Information** Monica Ramirez and Gary Dahl both saw business opportunities and started new companies. Compare and contrast Ramirez's response to the market with that of Dahl. Use a Venn diagram to help you organize your ideas.
9. **Predicting Economic Trends** Turn back to page 74 and read again the paragraphs about competitive ideas in the bookselling market. What do you think might be the next new idea to compete with discounted books?
10. **Challenge** In a 1973 magazine interview, Milton Friedman said,

    What kind of society isn't structured on greed? The problem of social organization is how to set up an arrangement under which greed will do the least harm; capitalism is that kind of a system.

    Do you agree with Friedman that societies are structured on greed and that capitalism can reduce the harm caused by greed? Explain your answer.

Online Quiz
ClassZone.com

ECONOMICS IN PRACTICE

A new business in the United States

Analyzing Economic Information The following chart gives data about the rules and time for setting up new businesses in six countries. The rules are measured according to the number of government procedures a new business has to go through before it can begin operating. The time is the number of days it takes to complete the process of registering a new business.

Draw Conclusions What is the relationship between the rules and the time for setting up a new business?

Country	Rules (Number of Procedures)	Time (Number of Days)
Canada	2	3
Sweden	3	16
United States	5	5
Singapore	6	6
Germany	9	24
Mexico	9	58
China	13	48

Source: World Bank, 2005

Challenge Use the chart and what you know about the economies of the listed countries to write a short paragraph comparing the ease of entry into the marketplace in three countries of your choice.

77

4 Assess & Reteach

Assess Go over the questions in Reviewing Key Concepts as a class. For the Critical Thinking questions, divide the class into four groups and assign one of the questions to each group. Direct students to collaborate on a written and/or graphic answer for their question and share it with the class.

Unit 1 Resource Book
- Section Quiz, p. 133

Interactive Review @ ClassZone.com
- Section Quiz

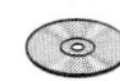

Test Generator CD-ROM
- Section Quiz

Reteach Review each main part of Section 1 with the class, focusing only on the graphics on each spread. Ask students to use them to help summarize the information in the section.

Unit 1 Resource Book
- Reteaching Activity, p. 134

Economics in Practice

Draw Conclusions The more rules, the longer time to set up.

Challenge Most answers will recognize that the more restrictive the economy generally, the harder it is for new businesses to start up; in countries with a high degree of free enterprise, the barriers to entry in the marketplace are much lower than elsewhere.

SECTION 1 ASSESSMENT ANSWERS

Reviewing Key Concepts

1. **a.** *open opportunity*, p. 73
   b. *legal equality*, p. 73
   c. *free contract*, p. 73
2. The profit motive drives people to seek financial gain by coming up with products and services that meet consumers' wants.
3. The freedoms at the heart of a free enterprise system—the right to own property and exchange it voluntarily—are the basis of economic freedom.
4. Answers will vary but may include freedom to buy what you choose, work where you want, sell what you choose, own what you choose.
5. competition
6. See page 70 for an example of a completed cluster diagram. Answers will vary, but most will note that the free enterprise system works by allowing people equal opportunity to enter the marketplace. Entrepreneurs, driven by the profit motive, seek financial gain. Competitors, free to enter the market, keep the profit motive in check by offering consumers better deals, resulting in lower prices and higher quality products.

Critical Thinking

7. Competition helps an economy operate efficiently, since competitors seek the most efficient use of their productive resources to make the highest profit. Competition benefits consumers by leading to lower prices and higher quality. Examples will vary.
8. Ramirez saw a market need and sought to fill it. Dahl created a market need with a clever idea.
9. Look for ideas that continue the trend of technology making operations more efficient.
10. Look for reasoning to back up the point of view expressed. Also look for an understanding that competition keeps greed in check.

Economics in Practice

See answers in side column above.

❶ Plan & Prepare

Section 2 Objectives

- explain how consumers help determine the way resources are used
- explain how producers help determine the way resources are used
- analyze a circular flow model of the U.S. economy

❷ Focus & Motivate

Connecting to Everyday Life Ask students what device they use to listen to music most of the time. Chances are they will overwhelmingly mention MP3 players. Point out that they, along with millions of other young people, have "voted" for MP3 players as the listening device of choice through their purchases. Ask for other examples that demonstrate the power of their dollar votes. *(Possible answers: clothing styles, popular music, foods)*

Taking Notes Remind students to take notes as they read by completing a cluster diagram on the allocation of resources. They can use the Graphic Organizer at **Interactive Review @ Classzone.com**. A sample is shown below.

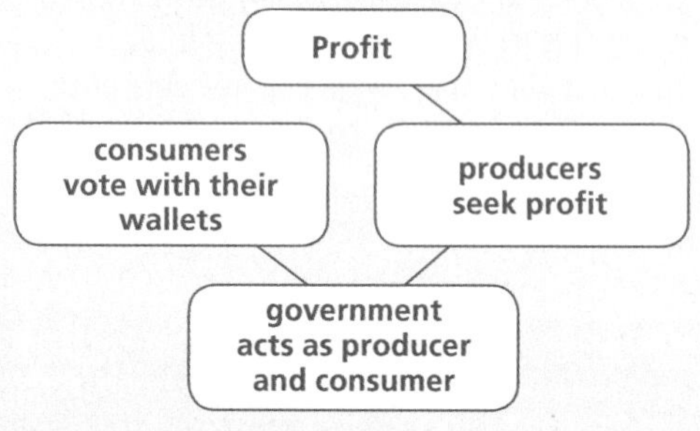

SECTION 2

How Does Free Enterprise Allocate Resources?

OBJECTIVES

In Section 2, you will

- explain how consumers help determine the way resources are used
- explain how producers help determine the way resources are used
- analyze a circular flow model of the U.S. economy

KEY TERMS

profit, *p. 78*

modified free enterprise economy, *p. 80*

TAKING NOTES

As you read Section 2, complete a cluster diagram to show how consumers, producers, and the government interact to allocate resources. Use the Graphic Organizer at **Interactive Review @ ClassZone.com**

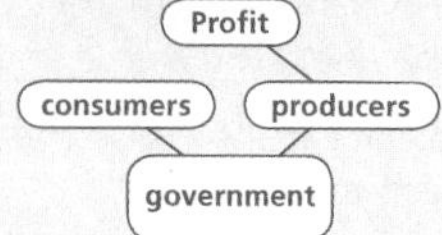

The Roles of Producers and Consumers

QUICK REFERENCE

Profit is the money left over after the costs of producing a good or service have been subtracted from the revenue gained by selling that good or service.

KEY CONCEPTS

In the marketplace, consumers buy products for their personal use from producers who make or provide goods or services. In these exchanges, consumers look to get the best deal for the money they spend. Producers, on the other hand, are looking to earn the most profit from these transactions. **Profit** is the money left over after the costs of producing a product are subtracted from the revenue gained by selling that product. Seeking opportunities to earn profits is one way producers help allocate scarce resources in the economy.

EXAMPLE Producers Seek Profit

A new neighborhood coffee shop illustrates how producers help to allocate resources. The owners of the coffee shop, motivated by the desire to earn profits, charge the highest price consumers are willing to pay. The possibilities for good profits encourage other people to open coffee shops of their own. As a result, productive resources that might have been used in some other kind of business are directed toward the coffee shops. The profit seeking of producers, then, has helped in the allocation of resources.

SECTION 2 PROGRAM RESOURCES

ON LEVEL

Lesson Plans
- Core, p. 10

Unit 1 Resource Book
- Reading Study Guide, pp. 135–136
- Economic Skills and Problem Solving Activity, pp. 155–156
- Math Skills Worksheet, p. 163
- Section Quiz, p. 143

STRUGGLING READERS

Unit 1 Resource Book
- Reading Study Guide with Additional Support, pp. 137–139
- Reteaching Activity, p. 144

ENGLISH LEARNERS

Unit 1 Resource Book
- Reading Study Guide with Additional Support (Spanish), pp. 140–142

INCLUSION

Lesson Plans
- Modified for Inclusion, p.10

GIFTED AND TALENTED

NCEE Student Activities
- Resource Allocation; The Role of Government, pp. 9–12

TECHNOLOGY

eEdition DVD-ROM

eEdition Online

Power Presentation DVD-ROM

Economics Concepts Transparencies
- CT10 Government in the Circular Flow Model

Daily Test Practice Transparencies, TT10

ClassZone.com

EXAMPLE Consumers Vote with Their Wallets

Consumers also play an important role in allocating resources in a free enterprise system. When consumers choose to buy a product, they are "voting" for their choice against competing products. These "votes" help determine what will be produced in the future, since producers, seeking opportunities to profit, try to provide what consumers want. For example, in the early 2000s, when low-carbohydrate diets were popular, consumers "voted" for low-carb and high-protein foods and against high-carb foods. (Figure 3.3 below illustrates this, showing that between 2002 and 2003 sales of typical low-carb/high-protein products increased, while sales of typical high-carb products fell.) How did food producers respond to these "votes"? They moved some of their productive resources into the low-carb market to try to meet consumer demand.

FIGURE 3.3 SALES OF SELECTED FOOD PRODUCTS

High-Carb Foods			Low-Carb/High-Protein Foods		
Product	Unit Sales, 2003 (in millions)	Percentage Change Over 2002	Product	Unit Sales, 2003 (in millions)	Percentage Change Over 2002
Instant Rice	79.1	−8.2	Frozen Meat/ Seafood	483.5	+7.7
Bulk Rice	180.2	−4.9	Meat Snacks	105.4	+7.6
Cookies	1,839.7	−5.5	Nuts	679.3	+8.8
Regular Carbonated Drinks	7,032.5	−5.9	Diet Carbonated Drinks	2,828.6	+1.0
Dry Pasta	1,227.0	−4.6	Cheese	3,424.0	+4.0
White Bread	1,606.1	−4.7	Wheat Bread	873.1	+4.0

Source: ACNielsen

ANALYZE TABLES

1. Which high-carb item showed the greatest percentage drop in sales between 2002 and 2003? Which low-carb/high-protein item showed the greatest percentage gain?
2. Consumer interest in low-carb diets began to decline after 2004. What differences might you expect to see in a similar table for 2004 and 2005?

Interest in low-carb diets peaked early in 2004, but began to fade thereafter. Once again, consumers had cast their votes in the marketplace, buying fewer low-carb and high-protein products. Producers quickly responded. By the beginning of 2005, some companies had gotten out of the low-carb market completely. Others had significantly cut back production of low-carb products. Consumer actions had caused a reallocation of productive resources.

APPLICATION Analyzing Cause and Effect

A. How would the allocation of resources have been affected if the interest in low-carb diets had continued to increase?

Producers would have shifted more resources into the low-carb market rather than moving them out.

③ Teach

The Roles of Producers and Consumers

Discuss

- How does free enterprise prevent too many coffee shops from opening up? *(At some point, the supply of coffee shops will exceed the demand. Consumers will "vote" by not spending their money at coffee shops.)*

Analyzing Tables: Figure 3.3

Ask students if they could draw this conclusion with certainty based on this table:

- Sales of such high-carbohydrate foods as rice and pasta declined in 2003, while sales of such low-carb/high-protein foods as nuts and cheese increased. *(Yes, it is a suitably limited conclusion.)*
- Sales of high-carbohydrate foods declined in 2003. *(No, only selected products are included.)*

Answers

1. *Instant rice; nuts*
2. *Percentage change in sales over previous year for low-carb foods would be smaller or in negative range; for high-carb foods, percentage change would be smaller or in positive range.*

SMALL GROUP ACTIVITY

Creating a Resources Allocation Graphic

Time 30 minutes ◑

Task Show how consumers and producers interact to allocate resources.

Materials Needed small-sized poster boards, markers, magazines or other illustration sources that can be cut up for visuals

Activity

- Review with students the example of the coffee shop on page 78 and the low-carb foods on page 79.
- Direct students to use one of these examples, or one of their own, as the basis for a graphic that shows the cause-and-effect interactions of consumers and producers in allocating resources.
- Have them draw illustrations as appropriate or use pictures cut out from magazines or other sources on a poster board.
- Invite students to present their posters to the class.

Rubric

	Use of Concepts	Presentation
4	excellent	accurate, attractive
3	good	accurate, no clear flaws
2	fair	partly accurate, some flaws
1	poor	inaccurate, flawed

Government in the U.S. Economy

Discuss

- Explain why income and spending are equal in the circular flow model. *(For every dollar spent on resources or products, someone receives a dollar in income or revenue.)*
- Is this equilibrium maintained when the government enters the picture? *(Yes. When government spends, someone receives income. When government taxes, it takes money out of the spending cycle of individuals and firms but it spends the money.)*

Analyzing Charts: Figure 3.4

Ask for three volunteers: one to explain the household portion of the circular flow, one the business portion, and one the government. Give each student a chance to talk through the cycle, beginning with spending in their portion of the economy.

Answers

Government acts as both a consumer and producer in the economy. It buys resources from individuals and products from businesses and then uses these resources and products to produce goods and services. It sells these products to individuals and businesses in return for taxes.

Animated Economics The circular flow model shows interactions of government, households, and businesses in the economy. It will help students understand the broad macroeconomic picture of how the major economic actors interact in the product and resource markets.

Presentation Options

Review how government fits into the circular flow model of market economies by using the following presentation options:

 **Power Presentations DVD-ROM**
Using the Display Tool, you can highlight the government's position as both a consumer and a producer in the circular flow model.

 **Economics Concepts Transparencies**
- CT10 Government in the Circular Flow Model

Government in the U.S. Economy

QUICK REFERENCE

A **modified free enterprise economy** is a free enterprise economic system with some government involvement.

KEY CONCEPTS

In Chapter 2 you learned that the United States economy, though based on the market system, is mixed. Government is an important element in the American economic system, but its role is relatively limited. This type of mixed economy, which includes some government protections, provisions, and regulations to adjust the free enterprise system, is sometimes called a **modified free enterprise economy**.

Modified Free Enterprise

In Figure 2.4 on page 53, you saw that the economy could be viewed as a stream of resources and products moving in a circular flow between households and businesses. Money also flows between households and businesses, facilitating this exchange of products and resources. Figure 3.4 shows how the government fits into this circular flow. It also shows how government exacts costs and dispenses benefits. Locate the two main economic decision-makers at the right and left of the chart: households (owners of resources) and businesses (makers of products). The two

FIGURE 3.4 Government in the Circular Flow Model

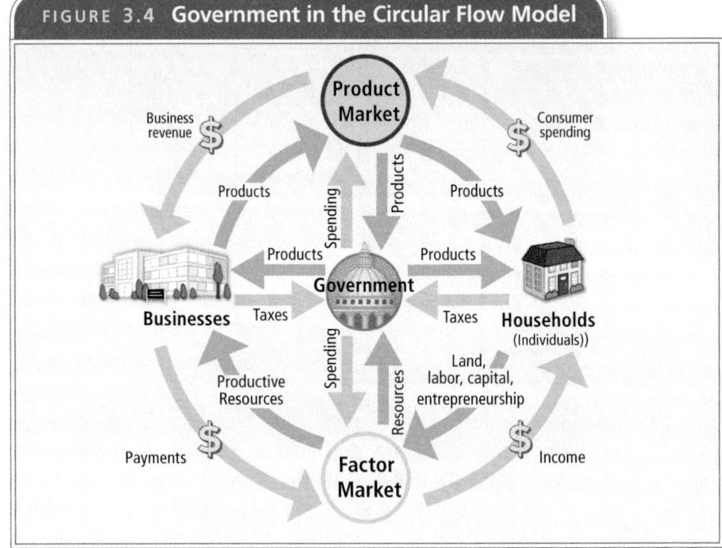

ANALYZE CHARTS
This version of the circular flow model shows the flow of resources, products, and money among households, businesses, and the government. Describe the role of government in the economy using information from this chart.

Animated Economics
Use an interactive circular flow model at **ClassZone.com**

DIFFERENTIATING INSTRUCTION

Inclusion

Isolate the Parts
To help students focus on the new element in the circular flow model, have them consider the parts separately. That is, direct them to cover the right half of the model (letting the government show) and focus first on just the government and business interactions. Then, have them cover the left side of the model, again letting the government show, and focus on the interactions between government and households.

Struggling Readers

Use Graphics
Point out to students that the text material under the heading Modified Free Enterprise is really just a verbal expression of the graphics in Figures 3.4, 3.5, and 3.6. Ask one student to read that text aloud and have the other students follow along in the graphic according to the directions in the text. Remind students that they can often use graphics to clarify text comprehension.

markets in the economy, the product market (for goods and services) and the factor market (for economic resources), are located at the top and bottom of the chart. The outer green arrows show the flow of money. The inner blue arrows show the flow of resources and products.

The government is located in the center of the chart. Like the other key actors in the circular flow, the government is both a consumer and a producer. Look at the arrows that run between government and the two markets. The government is a consumer in the resource market, spending money to buy the factors of production. It is also a consumer in the product market, spending money in exchange for products.

Now locate the arrows that run between government and households and government and business firms. Government is a producer here, providing goods and services to both households and businesses. Government collects money from households and businesses, in the form of taxes, as payment for these goods and services. It covers the costs of what it produces with this money. Government also uses this money to make purchases in the resource and product markets, and the cycle continues.

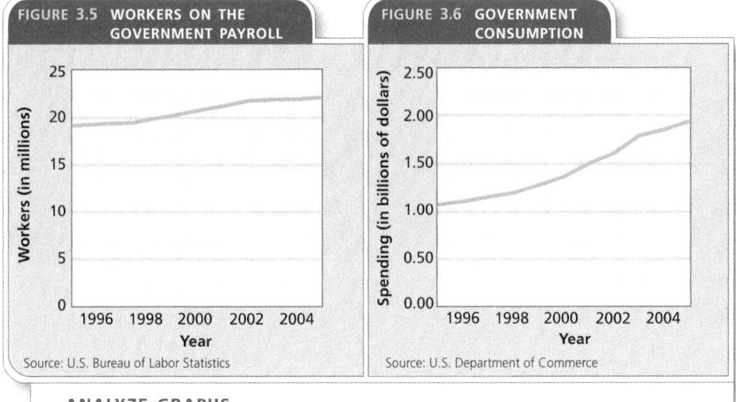

ANALYZE GRAPHS

1. About how many workers were on the government payroll in 2005?
2. Based on these two graphs, how is government's role as a consumer of products and resources changing?

Figures 3.5 and 3.6 above show that government is a major consumer of both resources and products. As you can see in Figure 3.5, all levels of government, local, state, and federal, employ almost 22 million workers. This is equal to about 16 percent of the labor force—all the labor resources available in the United States. Further, if you look at Figure 3.6 you'll see that government consumption—what all levels of government spend on goods and services—is about two trillion dollars.

Economics Update

Find an update on government workers and government consumption at **ClassZone.com**

APPLICATION Applying Economic Concepts

B The paycheck that you get for working part-time at the pet store shows what you have earned and how much is withheld for taxes. Explain how the paycheck and the taxes withheld are represented in the circular flow model.

See answer in Teacher's Edition. ▶

Analyzing Graphs: Figures 3.5 and 3.6

Point out to students that of the three levels of government, federal government employs the fewest workers—about 3 million. Local government, with a workforce of around 14 million, employs the most. In contrast, the federal government is the biggest consumer, accounting for more than 40 percent of all spending. Ask students to suggest why the federal government consumes so much. *(Most students will note that the federal government provides goods and services on a huge scale—the national highway system and national defense, for example.)*

Answers

1. *close to 22 million*
2. *The number of government employees has risen slowly, but government consumption almost doubled from 1995 to 2005.*

Economics Update

ClassZone.com includes links to updated information about the government workforce and government consumption. This information will help students recognize the scope of government involvement in the economy.

APPLICATION

Answer *Your income represents what businesses paid for labor in resource market. You may use it to buy products from businesses in the product market. Taxes go to the government in exchange for goods and services.*

SMALL GROUP ACTIVITY

Demonstrate Circular Flow

Time 30 minutes ◑
Task Devise a set of interactions to demonstrate the circular flow.
Materials Needed play money bills
Activity

- Divide the class into groups of five students. Each student will represent some key element of the circular flow model.
- Instruct students that their task is to "enact" the circular flow using the play money. They should write a script for the interactions.
- Have each group perform its enactment for the class.
- Discuss what the enactments have in common and how well they described the circular flow.

Rubric

	Understanding Concepts	Presentation of Information
4	excellent	creative, accurate
3	good	clear, accurate
2	fair	bland but accurate
1	poor	uninspired, inaccurate

Interpreting Graphs: Public Opinion Polls

1 Plan & Prepare

Objectives

- interpret graphs for information
- use features of a graph to aid comprehension

2 Focus & Motivate

American statesman Henry Clay said, "Statistics are no substitute for judgment." Ask the class what he may have meant by this statement. *(Possible answer: that you need to think about what is behind the statistics)* Remind students that statistics are often presented in graphic format. Lead the class in a discussion about why it is important to be able to interpret graphs.

3 Teach

Remind students that they are likely to be called on to make statistical graphs if they go to college or technical and trade schools or if they take certain jobs. Have them consider why they might choose to use a graph to present certain ideas rather than just to present the ideas in writing. Use the example on this page. Ask "How would a written version of this graph compare to the graphic version in terms of impact?" *(Students will probably see that the dramatic fall in consumer confidence makes a greater impact when expressed in graphic rather than written form.)*

For additional practice see **Skillbuilder Handbook**, page R29.

THINKING ECONOMICALLY Answers

1. *June or August; October*
2. *Consumer confidence dropped dramatically in the month of September and then bottomed out in October. Over the next two months, consumer confidence had a dramatic upsurge, nearly reaching its August level.*
3. *Answers will vary but probably will include other times of crises, such as the onset of war, or when the economy goes into a recession.*

ECONOMICS SKILLBUILDER

For more on interpreting graphs, see the Skillbuilder Handbook, page R29.

Interpreting Graphs: Public Opinion Polls

Public opinion polls are a useful tool for gathering information. Economists frequently use information obtained from opinion polls to measure public response to economic conditions. Polls conducted at regular intervals show changes in public opinion over a given period of time. The graph below shows the results of a poll that tracks consumer confidence. The poll, which is conducted monthly, is based on a representative sample of 5,000 households in the United States.

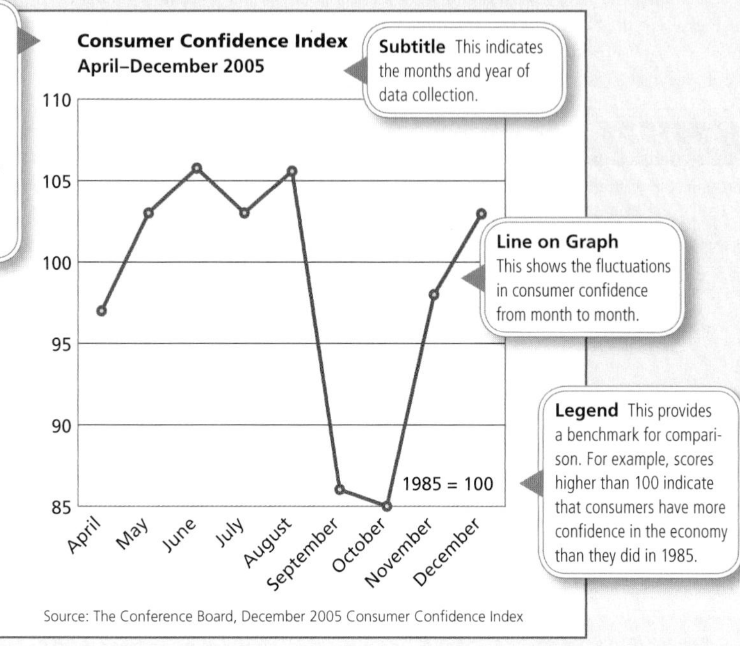
Title This indicates the type of data shown. Consumer confidence refers to the way people feel about the economy. Increasing confidence is likely to result in increased purchases of goods.
Consumer Confidence Index
April–December 2005
Subtitle This indicates the months and year of data collection.
110
105
100
95
90
85
Line on Graph This shows the fluctuations in consumer confidence from month to month.
1985 = 100
Legend This provides a benchmark for comparison. For example, scores higher than 100 indicate that consumers have more confidence in the economy than they did in 1985.
April
May
June
July
August
September
October
November
December
Source: The Conference Board, December 2005 Consumer Confidence Index

According to researchers, consumer confidence in the economy tumbled after Hurricane Katrina hit the Gulf Coast in September 2005. Falling gasoline prices and growth in the job market led to a recovery in confidence in November and December.

THINKING ECONOMICALLY Interpreting

1. During which month was consumer confidence the highest? The lowest?
2. Describe the changes in consumer confidence from August through December.
3. The devastation caused by Hurricane Katrina and resulting increase in gasoline prices led to the abrupt drop in consumer confidence shown in the graph. What other events might cause a decline in consumer confidence?

DIFFERENTIATING INSTRUCTION

English Learners

Use Spoken Language
For practice in speaking English, have students work in small groups and (1) take turns reading the page aloud; (2) read and answer the questions; and (3) reflect on and summarize what they learned about public opinion polls, graphs, and the English language.

Gifted and Talented

Create a Line Graph
Have students find their own statistics over time to use as the basis for a line graph. Direct them to include all the parts of a graph that are represented in the graph on this page. Then have them prepare a text version of the statistics, trying to make it as compelling as possible. They should then compare and contrast the effectiveness of the graphic and the written presentation.

SECTION 2 Assessment

Online Quiz
ClassZone.com

REVIEWING KEY CONCEPTS

1. Why is the U.S. economy sometimes referred to as a modified free enterprise system?
2. How does the profit motive work to allocate resources?
3. How do households and business firms interact in the product and resource markets?
4. Describe how the government interacts with the product and resource markets.
5. Study the circular flow models on pages 53 and 80. How are the two models different?
6. **Using Your Notes** Explain how producers, consumers, and the government interact to allocate resources in a free enterprise system.

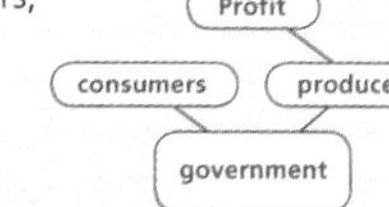

Use the Graphic Organizer at **Interactive Review @ ClassZone.com**

CRITICAL THINKING

7. **Applying Economic Concepts** Think of several examples in which consumers have voted with their dollars and driven a product from the market or into high demand. Record your ideas in a table like the one below.

Consumers Drive Product from the Market	Consumers Drive Product into High Demand

8. **Comparing and Contrasting Economic Information** Compare and contrast the role of consumers and producers in allocating resources. Which do you think has the greater power?
9. **Interpreting Economic Models** Use the circular flow chart on page 80 and what you have learned from this section to explain the ways in which government allocates resources.
10. **Challenge** What industries in today's world do you think would be wise to make changes given consumers' preferences? Give reasons for your selections.

ECONOMICS IN PRACTICE

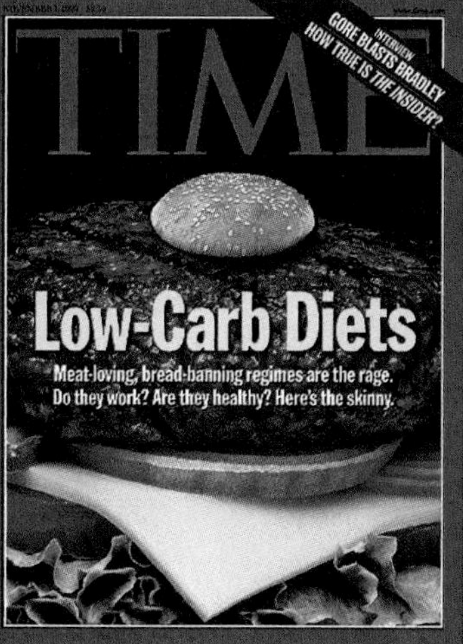

TIME
INTERVIEW
GORE BLASTS BRADLEY
HOW TRUE IS THE INSIDER?
Low-Carb Diets
Meat-loving, bread-banning regimes are the rage. Do they work? Are they healthy? Here's the skinny.

Analyzing Economic Information Look at the graph below, which shows the sales figures for a company that makes a substance that reduces carbohydrates in baked goods.

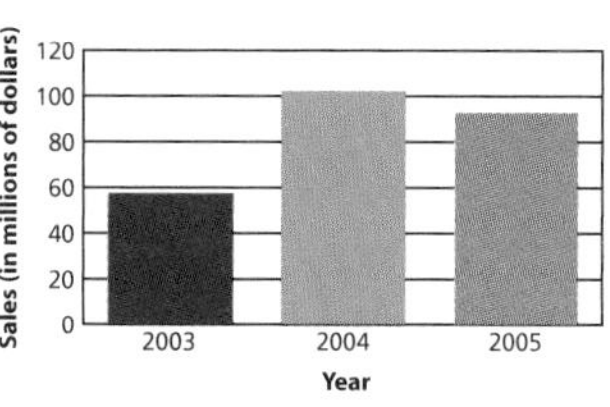

Interpret Information Write a sentence or two explaining the trend that the graph shows.

Challenge If you were the head of the company that made the substance that reduces carbohydrates in baked goods, in what direction would you move your business? How might you reallocate your resources?

4 Assess & Reteach

Assess In addition to the questions here, have each student think of a question to ask the class as you review key concepts and address the Critical Thinking questions.

Unit 1 Resource Book
- Section Quiz, p. 143

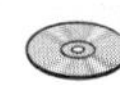
Interactive Review @ ClassZone.com
- Section Quiz

Test Generator CD-ROM
- Section Quiz

Reteach Direct students to the summary on page 94. Tell them that this Cloze method of leaving out a word for students to supply is a well-tested and effective way to help them deepen their understanding of what they have read. Divide the class into two groups. Have each student in the first group prepare a Cloze summary for pages 78-79 and each student in the other group prepare a Cloze summary for pages 80-81. Students in the first group should give their summaries to students in the second group, and vice versa. Then, each student will complete a summary on the part of the chapter on which they did not work.

Unit 1 Resource Book
- Reteaching Activity, p. 144

SECTION 2 ASSESSMENT ANSWERS

Reviewing Key Concepts

1. because it is a mixed economy that includes some government protections, provisions, and regulations to adjust the free enterprise system
2. Producers are motivated to enter those markets that offer the possibilities for highest profits, so they will use their resources accordingly.
3. Households sell their resources in the resource market to businesses for wages. With their income, households buy goods and services in the product market. With the revenue businesses receive from these sales, they buy resources.
4. The government is a consumer in both markets, buying what it needs with tax money in order to supply businesses and households with goods and services.
5. The model on page 80 builds on that on page 53, adding government to the equation of interactions among economic actors and economic markets.
6. See page 78 for an example of a completed cluster diagram. Purchases in the product market by consumers and government determine which resources are used and how these resources are used.

Critical Thinking

7. Answers will vary but should note that consumers' dollar votes determine the success or failure of products. Examples will vary.
8. Consumers have the greatest power because their dollar votes decide what will be produced and, therefore, how resources are allocated.
9. The government votes with its dollars on what will be produced. Government also allocates resources through social spending that is not driven by market considerations.
10. Answers will vary. One possible response might be that the Internet is playing an increasingly important role in the lives of consumers so industries should provide Web-based products.

Economics in Practice

Interpret Information After a dramatic rise, sales are beginning to fall.

Challenge Most answers will suggest that the owner would move resources into different products.

1 Plan & Prepare

Section 3 Objectives

- understand that one role of government in the U.S. economy is to address market failures
- analyze why governments provide public goods and infrastructure
- explain how governments seek to decrease negative externalities and increase positive externalities

2 Focus & Motivate

Connecting to Everyday Life Point out that public broadcasting is an example of the limits of market forces in allocating resources. It is rational for people to think to themselves, "If I can benefit from this and not have to pay for it, that's a good thing." Tell students that the government in a free enterprise system can help resolve such market failures.

Taking Notes Remind students to take notes as they read by completing a cluster diagram on the role of government in free enterprise. They can use the Graphic Organizer at **Interactive Review @ Classzone.com**. A sample is shown below.

providing public goods: characteristics free riders

managing externalities: who pays for negatives how positives are spread

Government

public transfer payments: providing safety net redistributing income

SECTION 3

Government and Free Enterprise

OBJECTIVES

In Section 3, you will

- understand that one role of government in the U.S. economy is to address market failures
- analyze why governments provide public goods and infrastructure
- explain how governments seek to decrease negative externalities and increase positive externalities

KEY TERMS

market failure, *p. 84*
public goods, *p. 84*
free rider, *p. 85*
infrastructure, *p. 86*
externality, *p. 87*
negative externality, *p. 87*
positive externality, *p. 87*
subsidy, *p. 88*
safety net, *p. 89*
transfer payment, *p. 89*
public transfer payment, *p. 89*

TAKING NOTES

As you read Section 3, complete a cluster diagram to show the role of government in free enterprise. Use the Graphic Organizer at **Interactive Review @ ClassZone.com**

providing public goods

Government

Providing Public Goods

KEY CONCEPTS

In the American economic system, most production decisions are made in the marketplace through the interactions of buyers and sellers. This is the free enterprise sector of our economy. Other decisions are made by different levels of government. This is the public sector of our economy. How do we decide which sector of the economy should produce a good or service? If all the costs are borne by, and all benefits go to, the buyer and seller, the free enterprise sector produces it. If people who are not part of a marketplace interaction benefit from it or pay part of the costs, there is a **market failure.** When market failures occur, the government sometimes provides the good or service. Goods and services that are provided by the government and consumed by the public as a group are **public goods.** Public goods are funded with taxes collected by the government.

QUICK REFERENCE

Market failure occurs when people who are not part of a marketplace interaction benefit from it or pay part of its costs.

Public goods are products provided by federal, state, and local governments and consumed by the public as a group.

Public Goods A city street lighting system is an example of a public good.

SECTION 3 PROGRAM RESOURCES

ON LEVEL

Lesson Plans

- Core, p. 11

Unit 1 Resource Book

- Reading Study Guide, pp. 145–146
- Economic Skills and Problem Solving Activity, pp. 155–156
- Section Quiz, p. 153

STRUGGLING READERS

Unit 1 Resource Book

- Reading Study Guide with Additional Support, pp. 147–149
- Reteaching Activity, p. 154

ENGLISH LEARNERS

Unit 1 Resource Book

- Reading Study Guide with Additional Support (Spanish), pp. 150–152

INCLUSION

Lesson Plans

- Modified for Inclusion, p. 11

GIFTED AND TALENTED

Unit 1 Resource Book

- Case Study Resources: Entrepreneurs and the Comeback of New York City, pp. 159–160

NCEE Student Activities

- Resource Allocation; The Role of the Government, pp. 9–12

TECHNOLOGY

eEdition DVD-ROM

eEdition Online

Power Presentation DVD-ROM

Economics Concepts Transparencies

- CT11 Government Involvement

Daily Test Practice Transparencies, TT11

ClassZone.com

EXAMPLE Characteristics of Public Goods

Public goods have two characteristics. First, people cannot be excluded from the benefits of the product even though they do not pay for it. Second, one person's use of the product does not reduce its usefulness to others.

Perhaps the simplest example of a public good is street lighting. When the street lighting is on, it is impossible to exclude people from using it. In addition, the benefit you receive from the safety and security street lighting provides is not diminished because others receive it too. There is simply no way for a private business to establish a realistic price for street lighting and then collect it from all users. Rather, local governments provide street lighting, paying for it with taxes.

Another example of a public good is national defense. Everyone benefits from the country being defended. Further, the security you feel knowing that there is a national defense system in place is not diminished because other people feel secure too. Given these benefits, you would readily pay for this sense of security. However, what if you discovered that your neighbors were not paying for national defense? Would you voluntarily pay then? To avoid this problem, everyone is required to pay taxes to the national government, which provides national defense.

EXAMPLE Free Riders

There is no incentive for businesses to produce public goods, because people will not voluntarily pay for them. After all, people receive the benefits of these products whether they pay for them or not. This situation is called the free-rider problem, and it is one type of market failure. A **free rider** is a person who chooses not to pay for a good or service but who benefits from it when it is provided.

QUICK REFERENCE

A **free rider** is a person who avoids paying for a good or service but who benefits from that good or service anyway.

Consider a July 4th fireworks display, which can cost $200,000 or more. If you tried to set up a business to put on such displays, you'd immediately run into problems. There is no way to charge people for watching the display, since it is visible from so many locations. Even if you were able to charge a fee to watch from a particularly good location, many people would still be able to watch it from elsewhere without paying. Those people are free riders—they receive the thrill and enjoyment of the fireworks display, but they do not share in the costs of putting it on. Because of them, there is little interest in providing fireworks displays as a business opportunity.

One way to address the free-rider problem is for government to provide certain goods and services. The city government, for example, could put on the July 4th fireworks display, using taxes to pay for it. In this way, the costs and benefits are shared throughout the community.

Free Riders Free riders will choose not to pay for fireworks displays but will still enjoy the benefits. Because of this, private companies are reluctant to provide such services.

3 Teach

Providing Public Goods

Discuss

- What are some more examples of market failures? *(industrial pollution, second-hand smoke, neighbor hiring a rock band for back yard party—could be either a free benefit or a nuisance cost to other neighbors, depending on the appeal to them of rock music)*
- Why would a lighthouse be an oft-cited example of a public good? *(Anyone can use it, and use by one ship does not detract from use by another ship.)*

Economics Illustrated

Point out to students that a market failure is like water overflowing from a glass. The glass represents a marketplace interaction, and while the water remains in the glass, only those involved in the interaction bear the costs or reap the benefits. When the water spills over the edge of the glass, however, people not involved in the interaction bear some of the costs or enjoy some of the benefits.

Normal Market Function

Market Failure

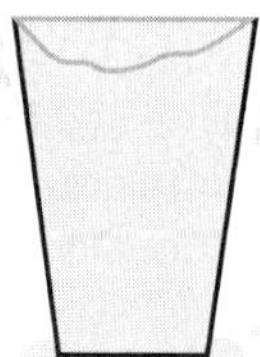

CLASS ACTIVITY

Examining Self-Interest

Time 30 minutes

Task Analyze self-interest when numerous people are involved.

Materials Needed paper, pens or pencils

Activity

- Tell the class to imagine that they are herders and share a common pasture with other herders.
- Explain the problem. For each individual farmer, the more livestock they raise and graze, the better their economic condition will be. But the more livestock that share the pasture, the sooner it will be depleted.
- Direct students to write a paragraph answering these questions: "Would you increase the number of your livestock? If so, why? If not, why not? How might the decisions of the other herders affect your own?"
- Finally, instruct students to write two sentences showing the relevance of this activity to the role of government in free enterprise.

Rubric

	Understanding of Concepts	Presentation of Information
4	excellent	clearly argued
3	good	somewhat clearly argued
2	fair	argument unclear
1	poor	off topic or not focused

More About . . .

Privatization of Public Services

Studies show that by far the most common reason given for contracting with private industry for services traditionally provided by local government is cost saving (stated about 41 percent of the time in a recent study). Other reasons include insufficient personnel support and expertise (about 33 percent) and lack of political leadership (about 31 percent). Flexibility, speedy implementation, and increased innovation were other reasons mentioned. On the other hand, desire for a higher quality service was mentioned less than 19 percent of the time.

Your Economic Choices

PUBLIC vs. PRIVATE

Will you support tax increases to improve recreational facilities?

To help make this choice, have students discuss these questions:

- What direct benefits might they receive from the presence of the water park, if any? *(use of the park)*
- What indirect benefits might they receive from the presence of the water park, if any? *(Possible answers: more part-time jobs in the community's businesses that would get a boost from tourists; possibly fewer youth problems, such as gang activity, since there would be a good outlet for energy)*
- What costs, besides the tax increase, might they incur because of the water park? *(Possible answers: more traffic congestion, money not spent on other useful projects, such as a new baseball field or more computers in the library)*

Activity If possible, bring in a property tax stub and put it on an overhead projector. Go through the itemized list discussing why each item is a public good and why it is paid for with public money. Ask students to consider whether any of these goods could be provided by private enterprise instead and discuss the pros and cons of that approach.

Another example of the free-rider problem is law enforcement. Once a policing system is established, everyone in the community is protected whether they pay for it or not. The best way to ensure that people who benefit from this protection pay a share of the costs is for government to provide the service, paying for it with taxes.

Public and Private Sectors—Shared Responsibilities

Some goods can be provided by either the public sector or the private sector. These often are toll goods—goods consumed by the public as a group, but people can be excluded from using them. For example, toll ways are open for all people to use, but those who do use them have to pay a toll. Similarly, parks are provided for the benefit of everyone, but those who want to enjoy this benefit may have to pay an entrance fee. The initial funding for toll goods is often provided by the public sector. Their day-to-day operation is often the responsibility of the private sector.

QUICK REFERENCE

The **infrastructure** consists of all the goods and services that are necessary for the functioning of society.

The private and public sectors share the responsibility for the nation's **infrastructure**, the goods and services that are necessary for the smooth functioning of society, such as highways; mass transit; power, water, and sewer systems; education and health care systems; and police and fire protection. How important is the infrastructure? Imagine, for example, what the United States would be like without its interstate highways, safe airports and seaports, and passenger and freight train systems. To begin with, the nation's economy would grind to a halt. Further, the nation would lose its ability to move troops in case of attack or to evacuate people in an emergency. A solid infrastructure, then, is essential to economic health.

YOUR ECONOMIC CHOICES

PUBLIC vs. PRIVATE

Will you support tax increases to improve recreational facilities?

The mayor wants to build a water park to attract visitors, who will spend money at your town's restaurants and stores. But what you pay in sales tax will rise by about $100 a year to cover the cost. With that money, you could buy a couple of video games. What will you choose—public wants or private wants?

Water park

Video game

APPLICATION Applying Economic Concepts

A. Identify another example in which the free rider problem makes public goods or services the best solution.

Answers will vary but could include public television or park district facilities.

86 Chapter 3

DIFFERENTIATING INSTRUCTION

Inclusion

Create a Visual

Assign students to small groups. Have each group create a visual of their choice—poster, power point presentation, Web page, collage, painting, or drawing—outlining the infrastructure of the local community. Encourage students to share ideas and responsibilities and devise a way to work together.

Struggling Readers

Recognize Antonyms

The text on page 87 contains a number of words that have a clear opposite. Students may not immediately notice the word *external* in the more challenging word *externalities.* Ask students to identify the antonym of external *(internal)* to help them lock the meaning of *externalities* in their mind. Also have students identify the antonym of negative *(positive)* to help them understand the concept of positive externalities.

Managing Externalities

KEY CONCEPTS

Another type of market failure occurs when economic transactions cause externalities. An **externality** is a side effect of a transaction that affects someone other than the producer or the buyer. A **negative externality** is an externality that is a negative effect, or cost, for people who were not involved in the original economic activity. For example, a manufacturing company discharges pollution into a nearby river. The costs of the pollution are borne by everyone who lives by the river, even if they have no connection to the manufacturing company. A **positive externality**, in contrast, is an externality that is a positive effect, or benefit, for people who were not involved in the original economic activity. Another of your neighbors, for example, plants and maintains a beautiful rose garden. All the surrounding homes benefit from the beauty.

QUICK REFERENCE

An **externality** is a side effect of a product that affects someone other than the producer or the buyer.

A **negative externality** is an externality that imposes costs on people who were not involved in the original economic activity.

A **positive externality** is an externality that creates benefits for people who were not involved in the original economic activity.

EXAMPLE Paying for Negative Externalities

One of the most commonly discussed negative externalities is industrial pollution. The owner of a factory that belches filthy smoke in the air, influenced by such

Paying for Pollution

A 1990 amendment to the Clean Air Act set a limit on the amount of sulfur dioxide that industries could release into the air. The government distributed to those industries only enough "pollution permits" to meet that limit. Instead of using their permits, some companies used cleaner production methods and sold the permits to other companies. As the price of these permits rose, more and more companies developed production methods that did not pollute.

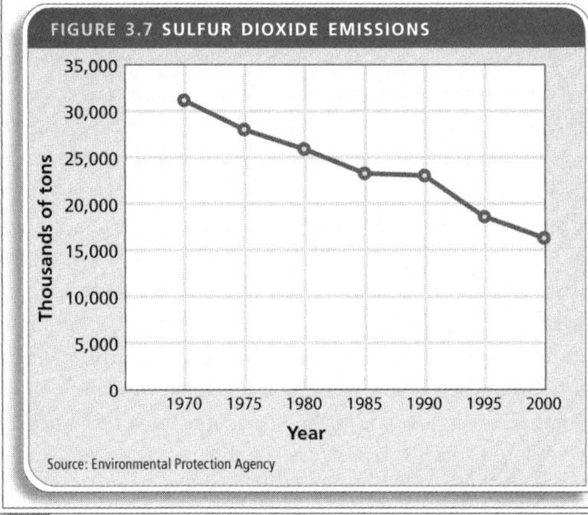

ANALYZE GRAPHS

1. How would you describe the trend in sulfur-dioxide pollution, especially since changes in government policy in 1990?
2. How did the government take a market approach to the problem of pollution?

Managing Externalities

Discuss

- Ask students to identify the economic term that would describe the effect on the rest of the class in the following example: A student in the class is unruly, and the *whole* class gets extra homework. *(negative externality, because a negative side effect affects others than those involved in the original activity)*
- What examples can you think of that show how you benefit from positive externalities in your community? *(Possible answers: Well-educated citizens usually results in the availability of good services. An addition on a neighbor's house raises their property value and yours along with it.)*

Analyzing Graphs: Figure 3.7

Some critics of the pollution permit approach argue that it is not effective. Does the information in the graph support this view? *(It appears that emissions dropped just as much before the changes in government policy. However, emissions dropped by about 7 million tons over the 20 years from 1970 to 1990 and then by 8 million tons in the much shorter 10-year period from 1990 to 2000.)*

Answers

1. *Pollution has been trending downward, with a marked reduction after 1990.*
2. *Government allowed a free market for pollution permits. As the price of these permits increased, companies developed non-polluting production methods.*

SMALL GROUP ACTIVITY

Creating a Town

Time 30 minutes

Task Develop a fictional town with at least three examples of both positive and negative externalities.

Materials Needed paper and pens

Activity

- Divide the class into small groups.
- Instruct students that their task is to create a fictional town that includes three negative and three positive externalities.
- Students should work together to draft a description of their town.
- They should also develop a draft for a town strategy to manage the externalities.
- Students should present their towns and strategies to the class.

Rubric

	Understanding of Concepts	Presentation of Information
4	excellent	creative and complete
3	good	competent and complete
2	fair	incomplete
1	poor	unclear

More About . . .

Positive Externalities

A Japanese folktale humorously demonstrates the principal of positive externalities. A poor student lives above a noodle shop and takes great delight in the smell of the noodles as they are being made. The greedy noodle maker believes the student should not enjoy those smells for free, so he takes him to court. The judge orders the student to deliver a bag of coins to even the score. When the student returns with the coins, the judge shakes the bag to jingle the coins and tells the noodle maker that the sound of the jingling money is repayment for the "stolen" smells.

More About . . .

Subsidizing Orphan Drugs

What would motivate a drug company to produce a medication for a rare disease, since very few people would need to buy it? In 1983, the Orphan Drug Act was passed to provide an incentive to pharmaceutical companies to develop medications for diseases affecting 200,000 or fewer Americans. To develop treatments for such diseases, companies are given seven years of exclusive rights to any resulting product and are often eligible for tax incentives and research grants as well.

APPLICATION

Answer *The effect of injuries to drunk drivers and others involved in crashes they cause is higher auto and medical insurance rates. Limiting drunk driving helps to manage this negative externality.*

market forces as the profit motive and competition, has little incentive in the short-term to pay the extra money required to reduce the pollution. Everyone living in the surrounding region suffers from this pollution. Not only do they bear the monetary cost of cleaning up the pollution, they suffer other costs too. They are more likely to suffer pollution-related illnesses and, therefore, face higher medical costs.

Limiting negative externalities, then, is one important role of the government in the American economy. The government taxes or fines the polluter, and in the process accomplishes two economic purposes. The money it raises through taxation and fines can offset the higher medical costs. In addition, the cost of the tax or fine to the factory owner provides an incentive to reduce pollution.

EXAMPLE Spreading Positive Externalities

Positive externalities are benefits that extend to people not involved in the original activity. For example, if a new college is built in your town, local businesses benefit from student purchases of goods and services. Workers benefit too, for as business expands to meet students' wants, more and more jobs become available. The community as a whole benefits from all the taxes collected from students. Local government is able to spend some of these funds to provide more public goods. In addition, the whole community benefits from the potential contribution a more skilled and knowledgeable population can make to the economy.

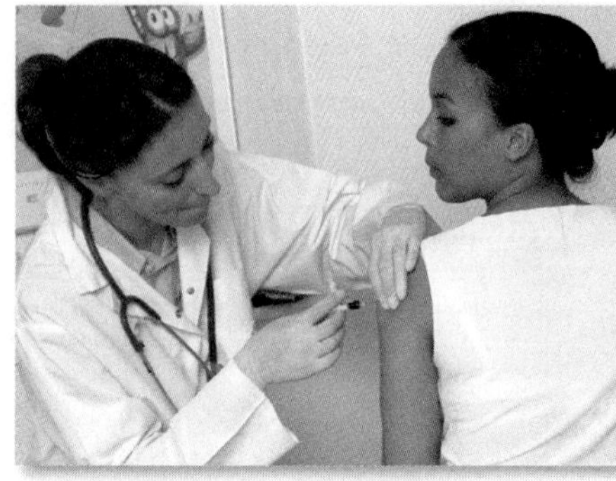

Positive Externalities The government will try to spread the benefit of a flu vaccination program—a healthier population—as widely as possible.

QUICK REFERENCE

A **subsidy** is a government payment that helps cover the cost of an economic activity that has the potential to benefit the public as a whole.

Just as government attempts to limit negative externalities, it tries to increase positive externalities. One way government does this is through subsidies. A **subsidy** is a government payment that helps cover the cost of an economic activity that is considered to be in the public interest. Since subsidies are paid for with taxes, everyone shares in their cost. Subsidies also spread the benefit of a positive externality as widely as possible. For example, the federal government might provide subsidies to drug companies to develop a new vaccine. This benefits the whole population in the long run because once the vaccine is in use there will be fewer and fewer infected people to spread the disease. Similarly, a local government might subsidize influenza shots for the community. Obviously, those people who take advantage of the free or inexpensive shots benefit because they are protected against infection. Even those people who don't get the shot still receive a benefit because they are less likely to encounter someone with the flu and therefore less likely to catch it themselves.

APPLICATION Explaining an Economic Concept

B. How might a drunk-driving law address negative externalities?

◀ See answer in Teacher's Edition.

DIFFERENTIATING INSTRUCTION

English Learners

Understand Idioms

Have students add a section to their personal dictionaries for idioms. Point out idioms on pages 88–90. For example, on page 88, the phrase *in the long run* means "over a lengthy period of time" and has nothing to do with running. Point out that the term *safety net* (page 89) refers to a net placed under certain gymnasts and tightrope walkers to catch them in case of a fall. But it is also used in economics as a metaphor for "catching" people who slip into financial trouble.

Gifted and Talented

Research and Report

Have students conduct research on Participatory Economics (often abbreviated as Parecon), an economic system proposed in the 1990s by Michael Albert and Robin Hahnel. Instruct them to write an essay explaining how Parecon would manage externalities.

Public Transfer Payments

KEY CONCEPTS

In addition to providing public goods and managing externalities, the government plays another role in the economy. One limitation of free enterprise is that people who are too old or sick to make a full economic contribution do not always have access to all economic opportunities. For these people, and others who are temporarily struggling, there is a public **safety net**, government programs designed to protect people from economic hardships.

QUICK REFERENCE

The **safety net** consists of government programs designed to protect people from economic hardship.

Transfer payments are transfers of income from one person or group to another even though the receiver does not provide anything in return.

A **public transfer payment** is a transfer payment in which the government transfers income from taxpayers to recipients who do not provide anything in return.

Redistributing Income

As many as 37 million people in the United States live below the poverty level, which was defined in 2005 as a yearly income of $9,570 for a single person, with $3,260 added for each additional household member. That is more than 12 percent of the nation's population. However, people move up and down the income ladder in the United States. Many poor families remain poor for a relatively brief time. For example, the median duration of poverty through the 1990s was between four and five months.

How does a modern society address economic issues such as poverty? One way is to encourage economic growth. Another is through **transfer payments**, transfers of income from one person or group to another even though the receiver does not provide any goods or services in return. Some transfer payments are between private individuals. When you receive cash and checks from relatives and friends for your birthday or graduation, you are receiving transfer payments. When someone dies, a transfer payment flows to his or her beneficiaries in the form of inheritance. In both cases, the receiver provides nothing in return for the payment.

A **public transfer payment** is a payment in which the government transfers income from taxpayers to recipients who do not provide anything in return. Public transfer payments, since they do not reflect exchanges within a marketplace, are not a characteristic of pure market economies. They are more characteristic of command economies, and their presence in the United States is one feature that makes the U.S. economy a mixed economy.

Most public transfer payments are in the area of social spending—spending designed to address social issues, such as poverty. Social Security benefits, for example, have significantly reduced poverty among the elderly. This program is funded by the contributions of people currently employed. They pay a social security tax to the federal government, which in turn transfers it to people who are at or past retirement age. The Social Security program also provides income for the disabled.

Public Transfer Payments

Type	2004 Expenditures (in billions of dollars)
Social Security benefits	517.8
Medicare	303.3
Medicaid	299.7
Supplemental Security Income	37.3
Unemployment compensation	37.1
Veterans' benefits	33.8
Food Stamps	25.8
Temporary Assistance for Needy Families	18.5

Source: U.S. Department of Commerce

Public Transfer Payments Social Security is the largest public transfer program.

Public Transfer Payments

Discuss

- How is a transfer payment different from other kinds of payments? *(It is not in exchange for any goods or services.)* What purpose do transfer payments serve? *(They redistribute income so that there is a safety net for those in need.)*
- If you are working, how does some of your income reach needy people? *(through taxation and social security deductions)*

International Economics

Transfer Payments in Canada
The Canadian government makes several kinds of transfer payments to the provinces. Since the provinces are responsible for administering health, education, and social welfare, the federal government makes transfer payments to the provinces to be spent in those areas. In addition, the federal government makes equalization payments to provinces that are at an economic disadvantage compared to some of the wealthier provinces, such as Ontario and Alberta. Those were the only provinces to not receive equalization payments in 2006. The provinces are allowed to spend the transfer payments as they see fit.

SMALL GROUP ACTIVITY

Studying Headlines

Time 30 minutes

Task Find, collect, and synthesize recent news stories related to transfer payments and the government's role in the economy.

Materials Needed access to news stories in newspapers, magazines, television, and online; paper or poster board, markers

Activity

- Divide the class into small groups.
- Within each group, students should decide how to divide their efforts to find current headlines about transfer payments.
- Students then should work together to prepare a visual display of the headlines that they find and be prepared to explain the story behind each.
- The groups should present their headlines to the class with a brief synthesis of the current issues.

Rubric

	Understanding of Concepts	Presentation of Information
4	excellent	creative and complete
3	good	competent and complete
2	fair	acceptable
1	poor	off topic

A Global Perspective

Social Spending in Sweden
Given the high level of worker benefits offered to Swedish employees, it may come as no surprise that about 80 percent of Sweden's workers are unionized. In contrast to many other countries, however, almost all unions in Sweden have a parallel organization made up of employers. The unions and employer organizations are completely separate from the government. There is no government-set minimum wage; instead wages are set by collective bargaining.

Answers

1. *The higher the tax levels, the more resources available for social spending.*
2. *The United States has more of a market economy, because it has a lower tax rate and lower level of social spending. This indicates that there is less government involvement in economy.*

A GLOBAL PERSPECTIVE

Social Spending in Sweden

In market economies, all economic actors—including governments—have to make choices. One economic choice governments must make involves the level of funding for social spending. Sweden's government, for example, has chosen to spend a significant amount in this area. Close to 30 percent of the country's total economy is spent on such programs as free public education through college, national health, and retirement and disability pensions. In comparison, social spending in the United States is about 15 percent of the total economy. U.S. social programs are not as comprehensive as Sweden's.

Such generosity, however, comes at a price. Sweden's workers pay hefty taxes to fund this social spending. Average Swedish workers with two children pay about 22 percent of their income in taxes. In contrast, similar American workers pay only about 9 percent.

FIGURE 3.8 SOCIAL SPENDING

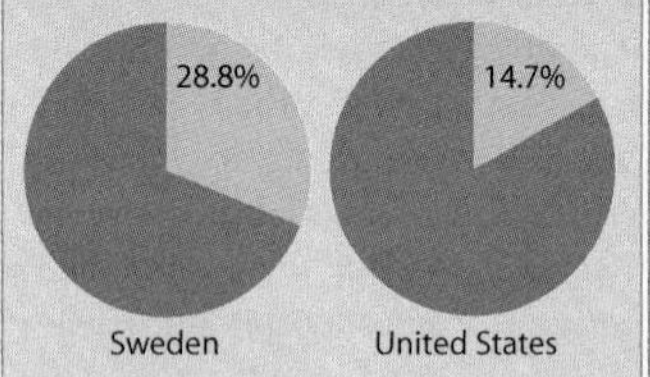

28.8%
14.7%
Sweden
United States
Percent of total economy

Source: Organization for Economic Co-operation and Development, 2001 figures

FIGURE 3.9 HOUSEHOLD TAX BURDEN

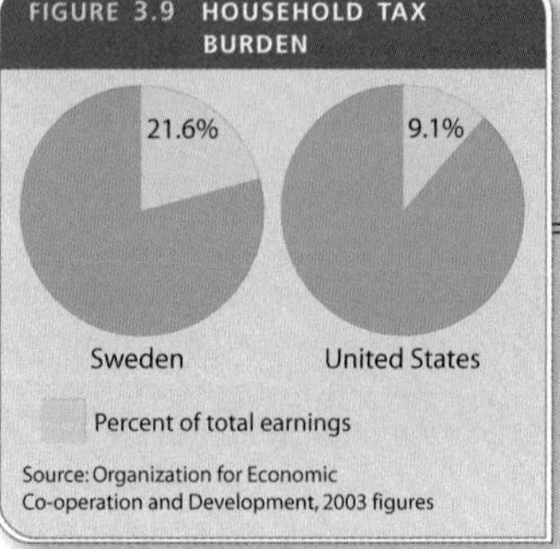

Source: Organization for Economic Co-operation and Development, 2003 figures

CONNECTING ACROSS THE GLOBE

1. **Synthesizing Economic Information** How do tax levels relate to the amount of resources devoted to social spending?
2. **Drawing Conclusions** Which country do you think has more of a market economy, Sweden or the United States? Why?

The government makes transfer payments to the very poor as well as to the aged and disabled. For many years, the program known as welfare made payments to the needy to assure their well-being. A debate developed about whether such a program fostered dependence on the government and removed incentives to break out of poverty. In response to this debate, the government introduced sweeping reforms in the mid-1990s. The new program, widely known as workfare, stressed the importance of helping welfare recipients enter or re-enter the workforce as quickly as possible. Since these reforms in 1997, 4.7 million Americans have moved from being dependent on welfare to self-sufficiency.

Public transfer payments also provide a safety net for people who lose their jobs. Unemployment compensation from a mix of federal and state money tides people over until they can find a new job. While people receive it, they must show that they are making an effort to find another job. (You will learn more about unemployment, poverty, and government social spending in later chapters.)

APPLICATION **Applying Economic Concepts**

C. What are the opportunity costs of public transfer payments?
Other programs—education, defense, infrastructure maintenance, and so on—that could have been funded with money used for these transfers.

DIFFERENTIATING INSTRUCTION

Inclusion

See Economic Relationships
To help students answer the second question in A Global Perspective, you may want to suggest that they create two pairs of bar graphs, one for Sweden and one for the United States. The first pair would show social spending and household tax burden in Sweden; the second would show the same statistics for the United States.

Gifted and Talented

Create a Graph
Have students find statistics on changes in transfer payments in the United States since 1997, when reform of the welfare system was enacted. Instruct them to make the most appropriate kind of graph to represent their findings. Encourage students to display their results.

SECTION 3 Assessment

REVIEWING KEY CONCEPTS

1. Explain the relationship between the terms in each of these pairs:
   a. *market failure* / *free rider*
   b. *negative externality* / *positive externality*
   c. *subsidy* / *positive externality*
   d. *safety net* / *public transfer payment*
2. Illustrate the two characteristics of public goods with examples.
3. How is infrastructure linked to the economy?
4. Give an example of a free rider.
5. How can government limit a negative externality? How can it spread a positive one?
6. **Using Your Notes** Explain how the government gets involved in the economy in a modified free enterprise system. Refer to your completed cluster diagram.

   providing public goods — Government

   Use the Graphic Organizer at **Interactive Review @ ClassZone.com**

CRITICAL THINKING

7. **Categorizing Economic Information** Unemployment compensation and payment of living expenses for the disabled are examples of what kind of government involvement in the American economy?
8. **Making Inferences** After several incidents of hallway disputes among students, the board of a high school decides to hire hallway guards. In economic terms, what is the school board doing? How might this decision affect other programs at the school?
9. **Evaluating Economic Decisions** As part of the welfare reform of the mid-1990s, the federal government hired 10,000 people who had been dependent on welfare in an initiative called welfare-to-work. How does this approach differ from transfer payments? What are the costs and benefits of this approach?
10. **Challenge** In 2003, Congress passed laws to encourage private charitable organizations to provide social services. They would compete for government funds to carry out community services through their own networks. Do you think this is an effective way to address social issues? Why or why not? Use economic concepts, such as markets, efficiency, and opportunity costs in developing your response.

Online Quiz
ClassZone.com

ECONOMICS IN PRACTICE

Cleaning up a toxic dump

Categorizing Economic Information Externalities are categorized according to their impact, either positive or negative.

Identify Externalities Decide whether each of the following is a positive or a negative externality and briefly explain its effect.

- A beekeeper establishes a farm next to an apple orchard and the bees move freely into the orchard.
- An airport is constructed near a residential neighborhood.
- A construction company cleans up a toxic dump near a site it is working on.
- Companies pay for programs to help employees get in shape.

Challenge Identify and explain a negative externality and a positive externality that affect you.

4 Assess & Reteach

Assess You may want to assign the even-numbered items to half the class and the odd-numbered items to the other half as homework. You can then go over all items in class, as well as cover the categorizing activity in Economics in Practice.

Unit 1 Resource Book
- Section Quiz, p. 131

Interactive Review @ ClassZone.com
- Section Quiz

Test Generator CD-ROM
- Section Quiz

Reteach Prepare a handout or transparency that has the heading structure for this section with space in between each head for notes. As you review the section, use collective note taking. That is, discuss what notes to write down under each heading that will serve as an effective summary of important points and have all students write the same notes. Model how to find main ideas and ask proficient students to do the same.

Unit 1 Resource Book
- Reteaching Activity, p.132

Economics in Practice
Identify Externalities positive: bees will pollinate trees; negative; noise pollution; positive; reduces pollution; positive: employees more productive, take fewer sick days

Challenge Answers will vary.

SECTION 3 ASSESSMENT ANSWERS

Reviewing Key Concepts

1. a. *market failure*, p. 84; *free rider*, p. 85
   b. *negative externality*, p. 87; *positive externality*, p. 87
   c. *subsidy*, p. 88; *positive externality*, p. 87
   d. *safety net*, p. 89; *public transfer payment*, p. 89
2. There is no way to make people pay for using them because they are publicly available; one person's use of them does not reduce their usefulness to others. Examples will vary.
3. it is essential to the smooth and efficient functioning of a modern economy
4. Answers will vary. One possible response is viewers of public television who do not subscribe.
5. punishing those who cause negative externality; subsidizing desired goods or services
6. See page 84 for an example of a completed cluster diagram. Government corrects market failures through public goods; supports the infrastructure; manages externalities by imposing costs on the producers of negative externalities and subsidizing positive ones; makes public transfer payments to provide a safety net.

Critical Thinking

7. public transfer payments
8. Addressing a negative externality; it may take funding away from other programs.
9. Helps people get back to work rather than making a direct payment to them. Advantages: reduces welfare budget, instills pride in new workers. Disadvantages: some people may not be able to work, or may make less working than they did on welfare.
10. Answers will vary. Some students will suggest that competition for government funds might make the provision of these services more efficient. Others will suggest that safety net services should not be subject to market forces.

Economics in Practice

See answers in side column above.

1 Plan & Prepare

Objectives

- Analyze multiple sources to deepen understanding of American free enterprise.
- Understand that running a business involves challenges and opportunities.

2 Focus & Motivate

Facilitate a discussion on the following question: Would you want to run your own business? Have students consider what type of business they would want to run—would it manufacture a product or would it provide a service? Then ask them what challenges they might face in getting their business up and running. Finally, have them suggest the benefits that owning their own business might bring. Conclude by pointing out that this case study focuses on one feature of the American economy—everyone is free to start his or her own business.

3 Teach

Using the Sources

Encourage students to examine each source to find out how and why people start their own businesses.

A. How does the launching of Fizzy Lizzy illustrate entrepreneurship? *(Marlin had a new idea and she was willing to take risks to bring it to market.)*

B. What can you infer from the chart about the role of small firms (0–9 employees) in the American economy? *(They constitute the largest number of firms in the economy.)*

C. What might be the advantages of opening a franchise? (Have students read the information about franchises on pages 248–249 before they discuss this question.) *(You can "be your own boss," but you have the backing of the larger company.)*

Economics Update

Go to **ClassZone.com** to find an update to this Case Study, including another article, an editable student worksheet, and an editable lesson plan.

Case Study

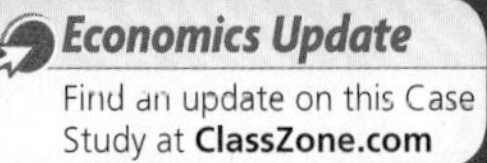
Economics Update
Find an update on this Case Study at ClassZone.com

The United States: Land of Entrepreneurs

Background The free enterprise system and the belief that everyone has the right to pursue economic success through lawful means is the backbone of American society. Many people achieve that success through working for an employer who provides a place to work, a paycheck, and other benefits. However, an increasing number of people are working for themselves, and for a variety of reasons. These reasons include a desire to market their own products, or to have more freedom.

What's the issue? What are some of the options for opening your own business? Study these sources to learn how others found their way, and the obstacles and opportunities they faced.

A. Magazine Article

This article discusses the development of Fizzy Lizzy, a new soft drink, from initial concept through launch, and introduces the entrepreneur who came up with the idea.

A Business Idea in a Bottle

Getting Fizzy Lizzy Bubbling

[Elizabeth] Marlin . . . got into the beverage business in the summer of 1996, when she set out for a long bicycle ride. . . . Not long into her trip, she realized that her favorite refreshment, which she had packed into a saddlebag—a half-gallon carton of grapefruit juice and a liter bottle of seltzer, which she'd mix together—was not only inconvenient, it was also slowing her down.

"Juice and seltzer is so simple," Marlin said. "I thought, Why can't I buy this is in a bottle?" She . . . was fixated on the idea of creating a carbonated juice, and began researching the beverage industry. She soon discovered she would need to hire a food scientist to help her. . . .

Although Marlin planned to devote her entire checking account to startup costs, that amount was nowhere near what [Abe] Bakal (consultant with 30 years' experience) was asking for R & D alone. . . . [B]ut he was so impressed by her enthusiasm that he offered to consult in return for a 20-percent stake in the business. . . .

Bakal recalled recently, ". . . one of the things I've learned in product development is that sometimes—not always, but sometimes—you can compensate with enthusiasm and commitment for money."

Source: "The Industry: Message in a Bottle," *New York Times,* June 26, 2005

Thinking Economically How did Elizabeth Marlin and Abe Bakal use their productive resources to start this enterprise?

92 Chapter 3

DIFFERENTIATING INSTRUCTION

Struggling Readers

Pull Out Statistics

The many statistics on franchises in the third source may make reading a little difficult. Have students pull out these statistics and enter them in a simple table titled "Franchise in Maryland." Suggest that they use the following as column headings: Number of Franchises; Number of Franchise Employees; Cost of Opening a Franchise; Number of Franchises Headquartered in Maryland; Examples.

Inclusion

Describe Visuals

Students with visual impairments may need a verbal description of photographs and other visuals. A good practice is to ask other students to provide these descriptions. That will also serve the purpose of heightening their observational and analytic skills and fostering collaboration.

FIGURE 3.10 BUSINESS ENTERPRISES BY EMPLOYMENT SIZE

B. Chart

These statistics show the number of self-employed entrepreneurs and their businesses relative to sizes of firms with paid employees.

Number of Employees	Number of Firms	Total Employment
No employees	770,229	0
1–9 employees	3,759,630	12,500,539
10–99 employees	1,135,443	28,516,802
100–499 employees	84,829	16,430,229
500+ employees	16,926	55,950,473
All	5,767,127	113,398,043

Source: *Statistical Abstract of the United States,* 2003 figures

Thinking Economically What is the percentage of entrepreneurial firms with no employees? What percentage of paid employees work in companies with 100 or more workers?

C. Newspaper Article

This article discusses franchises, businesses that offer entrepreneurs an option to start their own business by buying into an established company with an existing business model.

Being The Boss With Backup

The Costs and Benefits of Franchising

In Maryland, there were more than 13,000 franchises employing about 179,000 [people] in 2001, according to [a] study, which was commissioned by the International Franchise Association. More than two dozen of those franchises are headquartered in the state, including Educate Inc., with more than 1,000 Sylvan tutoring center franchises worldwide and MaggieMoos's International with 184 ice cream shops, according to the association.

Opening such a business might be just the right fit for Phil Clark, a mortgage consultant from Elkridge. The mortgage business tends to fluctuate, Clark said. A franchise would give Clark more control over his future, a prospect he finds exciting. "A franchise gives me something more stable," he said. . . .

But it comes at a price. The cost of opening a franchise can vary from $25,000 to millions of dollars.

For some, franchising can mean economic empowerment and a chance at the American dream. But buyer beware: There is no guarantee of success, and a franchise requires the same amount of commitment, sacrifice and sweat equity as any independent business. . . .

Source: "Growing Occupation: Being Your Own Boss," *Baltimore Sun,* April 21, 2006

Thinking Economically If you were to start your own business, would you buy a franchise or build a new enterprise based on your own ideas? What factors would help you in making your decision?

THINKING ECONOMICALLY Synthesizing

1. How do the legal rights built into the free enterprise system affect the businesses in A and C?
2. Which of these two businesses do you feel would provide more stability for its owner? Why?
3. Do you think entrepreneurs make up a large percentage of the work force? Why are entrepreneurs important to the economy?

Thinking Economically

Answers

A. *Marlin used her enthusiasm and money; Bakal used his experience.*

B. *13 percent; 64 percent*

C. *Answers will vary. Factors students might cite include cost of start-up, whether they are confident about going out on their own or if they would prefer the support provided by franchise, and length of time to turn a profit.*

Synthesizing

1. *Open opportunity protects the right of both Marlin and the franchisee to enter the market of their choice. Legal equality gives Marlin and the franchisee an equal chance to succeed in the market. Free contract protects Marlin's rights in her agreement with Abe Bakal. Free contract also protects the franchisee's rights in her agreements with the franchiser.*
2. *Answers will vary. Some students will suggest the franchise because of the support it provides. Others will suggest that stability depends on the commitment and effort of the business owner, not the business type.*
3. *Answers may vary. Most students will suggest that entrepreneurs do not make up a large part of the work force, citing the statistics in Document B. They also will note that even though they are small in number, entrepreneurs are key to the success of the economy because their ideas bring new products and more efficient ways of working.*

TECHNOLOGY ACTIVITY

Creating a Multimedia Presentation

Time 60 minutes ●

Task Create a multimedia presentation (screen, audio, video) on opening your own business

Materials Needed computer with software for creating power presentation and for showing video and presenting audio; computer and projection screen would be desirable for final viewing but not essential.

Activity

- Organize students into two groups. One will create a presentation on the launching of Fizzy Lizzy. The other will develop one on opening a franchise.
- Each group should determine how to subdivide the work, and one student from each group should serve as liaison with the other group. Both groups should keep in mind that their purpose is to present the challenges and opportunities of opening your own business.
- When the presentations are complete, arrange to view them as a class, if possible, with a discussion of each.

Rubric

	Understanding of Concepts	Presentation of Information
4	excellent	well-designed; solid information
3	good	well-designed; good information
2	fair	adequate design; some information
1	poor	careless

Online Summary Answers

1. free enterprise system
2. free contract
3. profit motive
4. profit
5. modified free enterprise economy
6. public goods
7. infrastructure
8. negative externality
9. positive externality
10. subsidy
11. public transfer payments

Review this chapter using interactive activities at **ClassZone.com**

- Online Summary
- Quizzes
- Vocabulary Flip Cards
- Graphic Organizers
- Review and Study Notes

Online Summary

Complete the following activity either on your own paper or online at **ClassZone.com**

Choose the key concept that best completes the sentence. Not all key concepts will be used.

capitalism	modified free enterprise economy	public goods
externality	negative externality	public transfer payments
free contract	open opportunity	safety net
free enterprise system	positive externality	subsidy
infrastructure	profit	transfer payments
legal equality	profit motive	

__1__ is another name for capitalism. Three features of this type of economy are open opportunity, legal equality, and __2__, or the right to enter into agreements of one's choice. The __3__ is a driving force in a free enterprise system, urging entrepreneurs to enter the market. The market allocates resources through the activities of both producers and consumers. Producers, seeking __4__, move their resources into the most productive areas. Consumers, through their dollar votes, help determine which products succeed and which fail.

Left on its own, however, a free market cannot address many social issues. The United States has a __5__, mixing government involvement and market forces. One role for the government is to provide __6__, such as national defense. Without a strong __7__ in place, modern economies cannot function. The government also addresses problems created by a __8__, such as the pollution from a factory that affects all those living nearby. It furthers a __9__, such as better health through vaccinations, by offering a __10__ for inoculations. The government also makes direct __11__ in the form of social security, unemployment compensation, and disability coverage.

CHAPTER 3 Assessment

REVIEWING KEY CONCEPTS

Advantages of the Free Enterprise System (pp. 70–77)

1. What is a free enterprise system?
2. What are some of the rights that must be protected for a free enterprise system to work?

How Does Free Enterprise Allocate Resources? (pp. 78–83)

3. What are the roles of consumers and producers in allocating resources?
4. What role does the government play in the economy's circular flow?

Government and Free Enterprise (pp. 84–93)

5. What problem makes public goods necessary?
6. Besides providing public goods, what two purposes can a government serve in a market economy?

APPLYING ECONOMIC CONCEPTS

Use the information in the table to answer the following questions about changes in the nation since the passage of the Clean Air Act in 1970.

Since the passage of the Clean Air Act:
• Nitrogen oxide emissions have declined by 17%
• Sulfur dioxide emissions have declined by 49%
• Lead emissions have declined by 98%
• Carbon monoxide emissions have declined by 41%
• Particulate emissions caused by combustion have declined by 82%
At the same time:
• U.S. population grew by 42%
• Overall energy consumption grew by 43%
• Total U.S. employment grew by 95%
• The number of registered vehicles grew by 111%
• The economy grew by 175%

Source: Foundation for Clean Air Progress

7. How would you use these statistics to argue that the government has effectively managed a negative externality?
8. Recently, there has been pressure to loosen clean air standards. Use economic arguments to support or oppose this proposed action.

CHAPTER 3 ASSESSMENT ANSWERS

Reviewing Key Concepts

1. It is another name for a capitalist system, an economic system that is market-driven.
2. private property, legal equality, open opportunity, free contract
3. Consumers determine what resources will be used and how they will be used by showing their purchasing preferences. Producers, driven by the profit motive, will move their resources into activities that will generate the greatest profit.
4. The government is a consumer of resources and products, using tax money from households and businesses to purchase them. It then supplies households and businesses with public goods and services, paid for with tax money.
5. They are necessary because of free riders, who would not voluntarily pay for something but who enjoy its benefits. They impede producers' incentives, so the government takes over and can charge everyone through taxes.
6. Government can manage externalities by limiting negative ones and spreading positive ones. Government also can ensure that all people have an economic safety net by making public transfer payments and other similar arrangements.

Applying Economic Concepts

7. The Clean Air Act has reduced the levels of airborne pollution yet considerable economic growth has still taken place.
8. Answers will vary. Some students might argue that clean air standards can be relaxed because market forces can be applied to the problem. Consumers can decide not to buy the products of those companies that pollute. Others may argue that government needs to maintain clean air standards; without them, polluting companies have no incentive to change their methods of production.

CRITICAL THINKING

9. **Creating Graphs** Use the statistics below to create a graph titled Businesses in the United States, 1997–2003. Use information from your graph and from Figure 3.1 on page 71 to write a generalization about businesses in the American free enterprise system.

Year	Number of Businesses (in millions)
1997	21.0
1999	21.8
2001	22.6
2003	22.7

Source: U.S. Small Business Administration

Use **SMARTGrapher @ ClassZone.com** to complete this activity.

10. **Distinguishing Fact from Opinion** Look again at the information on changes in the United States after the passage of the Clean Air Act. Which of the following statements represents a fact? Which is an opinion? Explain why.
    - Pollution has decreased since 1970.
    - Pollution has decreased as a result of the Clean Air Act.
    - The government can ease restrictions now that pollution is lower.

11. **Applying Economic Concepts** In the 1990s, efforts were made to reform the healthcare system in the United States so that much of it came under government control. Explain in terms of economic concepts you have learned in this chapter why these efforts failed.

12. **Challenge** Milton Friedman wrote,

> *Many people want the government to protect the consumer. A much more urgent problem is to protect the consumer from the government.*

Explain what you think Friedman meant by this. Illustrate your answer with examples.

SIMULATION

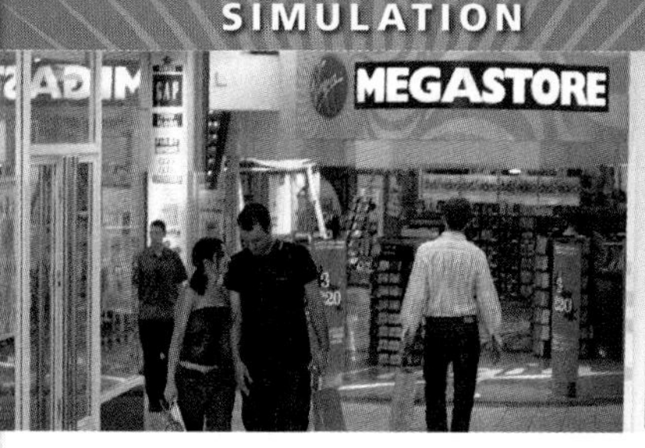

Conducting an Economic Impact Study

A manufacturing company has announced plans to open a factory in your town. The plant will consist of a manufacturing area and a warehouse area and will employ about 500 people. Production will be on a 24-hour basis, with workers working one of three 8-hour shifts. At the same time, a national megastore chain wants to open a store on the outskirts of town. The store will employ 60 people, be open 18 hours a day, and have a 200-car parking lot.

Imagine that you have been asked by local government authorities to conduct an economic impact study to identify the positive and negative externalities that the factory or megastore might create.

Step 1 Form a group with three or four classmates. Conduct research on how a factory or a megastore operates—the materials they use, the byproducts they create, and so on. Then do research to discover the impact a new factory or megastore might have on a community.

Step 2 In your group, review your findings and identify the positive and negative externalities of the factory or megastore. Record the information in a chart similar to the one below.

Externalities Created by the Factory/Megastore	
Positive	Negative

Step 3 Use your chart to write your economic impact report. Note the major externalities and suggest steps that the local government might take to limit negative externalities and to encourage positive externalities.

McDougal Littell Assessment System

Assess

Online Test Practice
- Go to **ClassZone.com** for more test practice.

Unit 1 Resource Book
- Chapter Test, Forms A, B, & C, pp. 165–176

Test Generator CD-ROM
- Chapter Test, Forms (A, B, & C), in English and Spanish

Report

Use the McDougal Littell Assessment System to score assessments and receive customized reports.

Reteach

For activities customized for individual students, use the McDougal Littell Assessment System.

CHAPTER 3 ASSESSMENT ANSWERS

Critical Thinking

9. Acceptable graphs will include all elements (title, axis labels, source line) and should accurately plot the data. Generalizations will vary but should focus on the fact that in the American economic system everyone is free to start—or close—a business if they want.

   SMARTGrapher Students can create a line or a bar graph using **SmartGrapher @ ClassZone.com.**

10. Polluting has decreased since 1970—fact, since it can be supported by data in the chart; Pollution has decreased as a result of the Clean Air Act—opinion, because while the Clean Air Act has contributed to the decrease, other factors may also have played a role; The government can ease restrictions now that pollution is lower—opinion, because nothing in the chart supports this statement.

11. Answers will vary. Some students will point out that many critics opposed the reform effort because they felt it limited free choice. Others may suggest it was defeated by pressure from insurance companies whose profits were threatened.

12. Answers will vary. Some students may focus on the idea that the more a government regulates the economy, the less efficient it is, and the consumer pays the price of this inefficiency through higher prices and lower quality products.

Simulation Rubric

	Understanding of Concepts	Presentation of Information
4	excellent	clearly argued
3	good	somewhat clearly argued
2	fair	argument unclear
1	poor	off topic or not focused

CHAPTER 4: Demand
Planning Guide

Resources 2Go Complete print resources all on one USB drive allow you to customize lessons.

Section Titles and Objectives	Unit 2 Resource Book and Workbooks		Assessment Resources
1 What Is Demand? pp. 98–105 • Define demand and outline what the law of demand says • Explain how to interpret and create demand schedules and describe the role of market research in this process • Explain how to interpret and create demand curves	**Unit 2 Resource Book** • Reading Study Guide, pp. 1–2 • RSG with Additional Support, pp. 3–5 • RSG with Additional Support (Spanish), pp. 6–8 • Economic Skills and Problem Solving Activity, pp. 31–32	• Case Study Resources: Ford Motors' Bold New Move, p. 35	**Unit 2 Resource Book** • Section Quiz, p. 9 • Reteaching Activity, p. 10 **Test Generator CD-ROM** **Daily Test Practice Transparencies,** TT12
2 What Factors Affect Demand? pp. 106–115 • Determine a change in quantity demanded • Explain the difference between change in quantity demanded and change in demand • Determine a change in demand • Analyze what factors can cause change in demand	**Unit 2 Resource Book** • Reading Study Guide, pp. 11–12 • RSG with Additional Support, pp. 13–15 • RSG with Additional Support (Spanish), pp. 16–18 • Readings in Free Enterprise: Demand for a New Source of Liquid Fuel, pp. 33–34 • Economic Simulations: How Much Can You Consume?, pp. 37–38	**NCEE Student Activities** • Movements and Shifts in Demand Curves; Consumer Surplus; Demand Elasticity, pp. 13–16	**Unit 2 Resource Book** • Section Quiz, p. 19 • Reteaching Activity, p. 20 **Test Generator CD-ROM** **Daily Test Practice Transparencies,** TT13
3 What Is Elasticity of Demand? pp. 116–125 • Define elasticity of demand • Identify the difference between elastic and inelastic demand • Define unit elasticity • Determine how total revenue is used to identify elasticity	**Unit 2 Resource Book** • Reading Study Guide, pp. 21–22 • RSG with Additional Support, pp. 23–25 • RSG with Additional Support (Spanish), pp. 26–28 • Math Skills Worksheet: Calculating Elasticity of Demand, p. 39 • Case Study Resources: Ford Motors' Bold New Move, p. 35; General Motors Misjudged Consumer Tastes, p. 36	**NCEE Student Activities** • Movements and Shifts in Demand Curves; Consumer Surplus; Demand Elasticity, pp. 13–16 **Test Practice and Review Workbook,** pp. 29–30	**Unit 2 Resource Book** • Section Quiz, p. 29 • Reteaching Activity, p. 30 • Chapter Test, (Forms A, B, & C), pp. 41–52 **Test Generator CD-ROM** **Daily Test Practice Transparencies,** TT14

Integrated Technology

No Time? To focus students on the most important content in this chapter, use Economics Concepts Transparencies, CT13, "Movement of the Demand Curve," available in Resources 2Go.

Teacher Presentation Options

Presentation Toolkit

Power Presentation DVD-ROM

- Lecture Notes
- Media Gallery
- Review Game
- Interactive Review
- Animated Economics

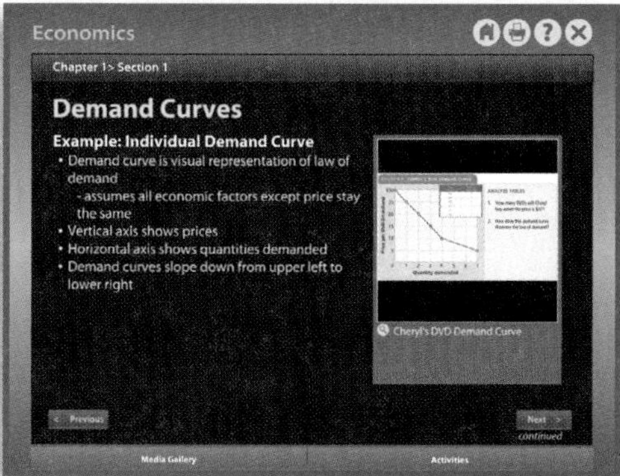

Economics Concepts Transparencies

- Shirt Market Demand Schedule, CT12
- Movement of the Demand Curve, CT13
- Estimating Elasticity, CT14

Electronic Books

eEdition DVD-ROM

eEdition Online

Daily Test Practice Transparencies, TT12, TT13, TT14

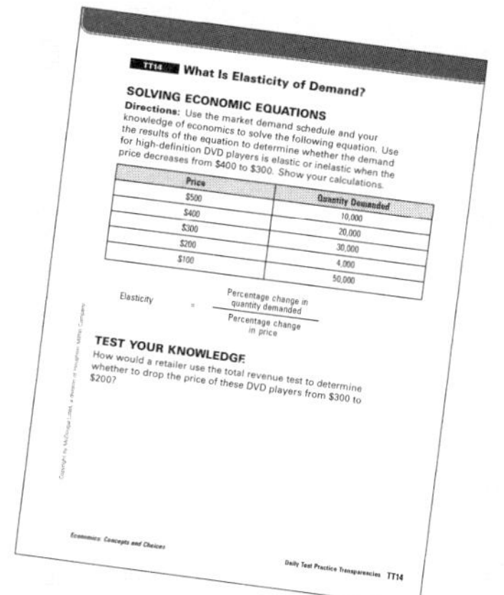

Animated Economics

- Demand Schedule, p. 100
- Demand Curve, p. 102
- Changes in Quantity Demanded, p. 108
- Change in Demand, p. 109
- Elasticity of Demand, p. 118

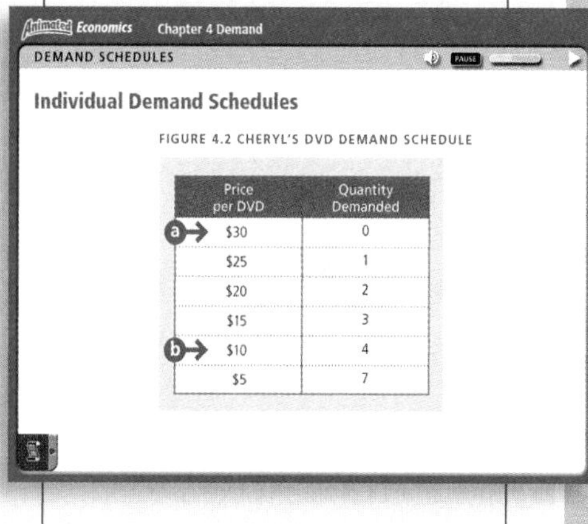

Online Activities at ClassZone.com

Economics Update

- Demand for CDs and DVDs, p. 99
- Vera Wang, p. 104
- Changing Consumer Tastes, p. 111
- Factors Affecting Elasticity, p. 119
- Fueling Automobile Demand, p. 124

Animated Economics

- Interactive Graphics

Activity Maker

- Vocabulary Flip Cards
- Review Game

Research Center

- Graphs and Data

Interactive Review

- Online Summary
- Quizzes
- Vocabulary Flip Cards
- Graphic Organizers
- Review and Study Notes

SMARTGrapher

- Create a Demand Curve, p. 103
- Create a Demand Curve, p. 105
- Create a Graph, p. 127
- Create a Demand Curve, p. 127

Teacher-Tested Activities

Name: Brother Peter Hannon

School: St. Joseph High School

State: Illinois

Teacher-Tested Activities

At the beginning of this chapter, look for my classroom-proven idea for teaching economics concepts and thinking.

Chapter 4: Demand
Resources for Differentiated Instruction

Struggling Readers

Teacher's Edition Activities

- Compare Economic Information, p. 102
- Diagram Cause and Effect, p. 104
- Contrast Key Concepts, p. 108
- Use Jigsaw Reading, p. 112
- Make a Chart, p. 118
- Create Graphic Organizers, p. 122
- Use Reciprocal Teaching, p. 124

Unit 2 Resource Book

- RSG with Additional Support, pp. 3–5, 13–15, 23–25 (A)
- Reteaching Activities, pp. 10, 20, 30 (B)
- Chapter Test (Form A), pp. 41–43 (C)

ClassZone.com

- Animated Economics
- Interactive Review

Test Generator CD-ROM

- Chapter Test (Form A)
- Chapter Test (Form A), in Spanish

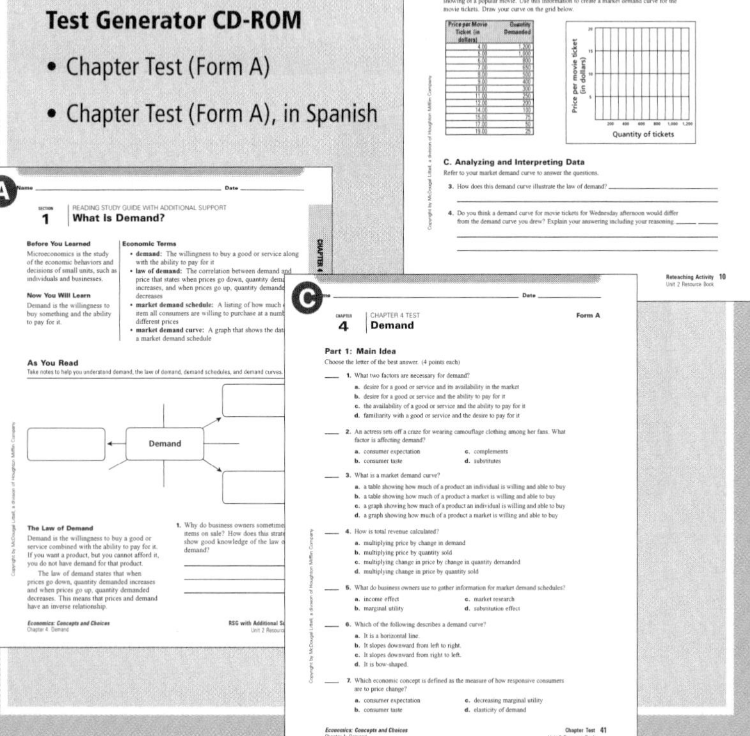

B — Section 1, Reteaching Activity: What Is Demand?

A. Explaining Economic Concepts

B. Displaying Economic Data

C. Analyzing and Interpreting Data

A — Section 1, Reading Study Guide with Additional Support: What Is Demand?

C — Chapter 4, Chapter 4 Test: Demand (Form A)

Part 1: Main Idea

English Learners

Teacher's Edition Activities

- Build Economics Vocabulary, p. 100
- Use Context Clues and Visuals, p. 104
- Understand Multiple-Meaning Words, p. 110
- Build Vocabulary, p. 114
- Create Word Search Puzzles, p. 118

Unit 2 Resource Book

- RSG with Additional Support (Spanish), pp. 6–8, 16–18, 26–28 (A)

Test Generator CD-ROM

- Chapter Test (Forms A, B, & C), in Spanish (B)

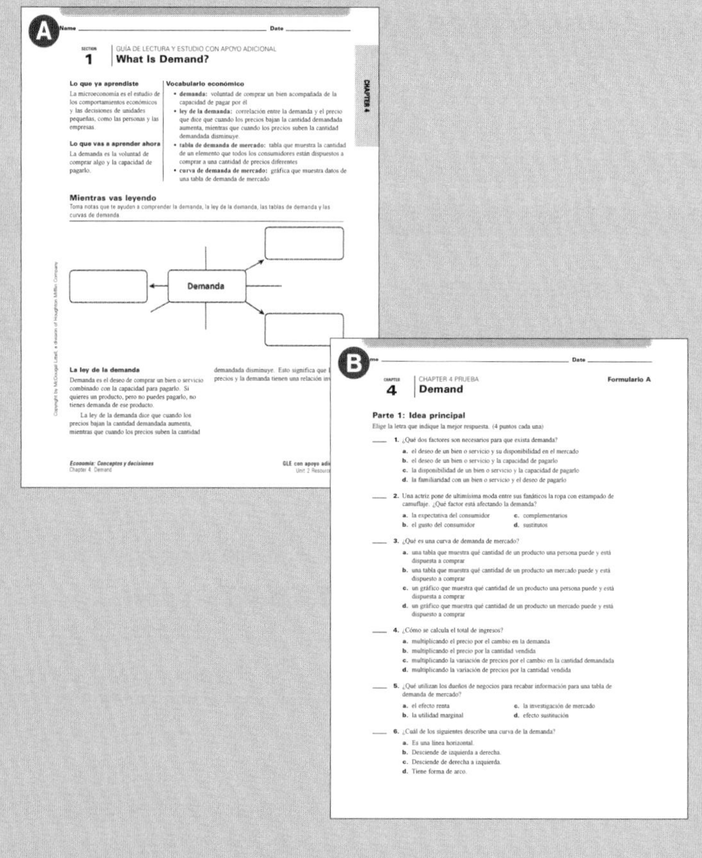

A — Sección 1, Guía de lectura y estudio con apoyo adicional: What Is Demand?

Mientras vas leyendo

B — Capítulo 4, Chapter 4 Prueba: Demand (Formulario A)

Parte 1: Idea principal

Inclusion

Teacher's Edition Activities

- Create Enlarged Demand Curves, p. 102
- Demonstrate Key Concepts, p. 108
- Use a Visual, p. 112
- Make a Graphic Organizer, p. 120
- Work in Pairs, p. 122

Lesson Plans

- Modified Lessons for Inclusion, pp. 12–14 (A)

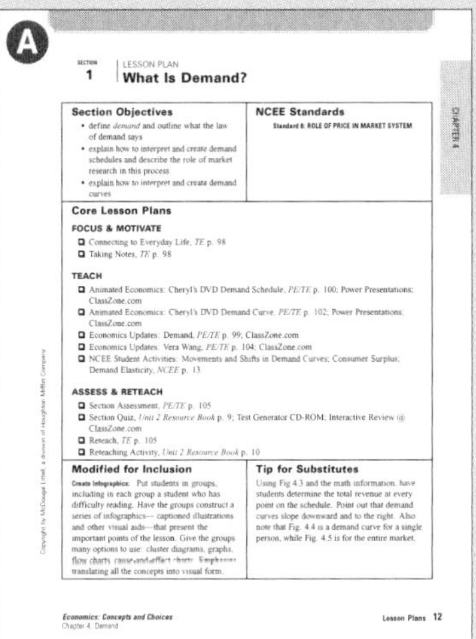
(A)

SECTION 1 | LESSON PLAN
What Is Demand?

Section Objectives	NCEE Standards
• define *demand* and outline what the law of demand says • explain how to interpret and create demand schedules and describe the role of market research in this process • explain how to interpret and create demand curves	Standard 8: ROLE OF PRICE IN MARKET SYSTEM

Core Lesson Plans

FOCUS & MOTIVATE
- Connecting to Everyday Life, *TE* p. 98
- Taking Notes, *TE* p. 98

TEACH
- Animated Economics: Cheryl's DVD Demand Schedule, *PE/TE* p. 100; Power Presentations; ClassZone.com
- Animated Economics: Cheryl's DVD Demand Curve, *PE/TE* p. 102; Power Presentations; ClassZone.com
- Economics Update: Demand, *PE/TE* p. 99; ClassZone.com
- Economics Update: Vera Wang, *PE/TE* p. 104; ClassZone.com
- NCEE Student Activities: Movements and Shifts in Demand Curves; Consumer Surplus; Demand Elasticity, *NCEE* p. 13

ASSESS & RETEACH
- Section Assessment, *PE/TE* p. 105
- Section Quiz, *Unit 2 Resource Book* p. 9; Test Generator CD-ROM; Interactive Review @ ClassZone.com
- Reteach, *TE* p. 105
- Reteaching Activity, *Unit 2 Resource Book* p. 10

Modified for Inclusion	Tip for Substitutes
Create Infographics: Put students in groups, including in each group a student who has difficulty reading. Have the groups construct a series of infographics—captioned illustrations and other visual aids—that present the important points of the lesson. Give the groups many options to use: cluster diagrams, graphs, flow charts, cause-and-effect charts. Emphasize translating all the concepts into visual form.	Using Fig 4.3 and the math information, have students determine the total revenue at every point on the schedule. Point out that demand curves slope downward and to the right. Also note that Fig. 4.4 is a demand curve for a single person, while Fig. 4.5 is for the entire market.

Economics: Concepts and Choices Chapter 4: Demand — Lesson Plans 12

Gifted and Talented

Teacher's Edition Activities

- Conduct Market Research, p. 100
- Analyze Population Shifts, p. 110
- Create a Cartoon, p. 114
- Research Gasoline Prices and Demand, p. 120
- Conduct Research, p. 124

Unit 2 Resource Book

- Readings in Free Enterprise: Demand for a New Source of Liquid Fuel, pp. 33–34 (A)
- Case Study Resources: Ford Motor's Bold New Move; General Motors Misjudged Consumer Tastes, pp. 35–36 (B)

NCEE Student Activities

- Movements and Shifts in Demand Curves; Consumer Surplus; Demand Elasticity, pp. 13–16 (C)

ClassZone.com

- Research Center

Test Generator CD-ROM

- Chapter Test (Form C)
- Chapter Test (Form C), in Spanish

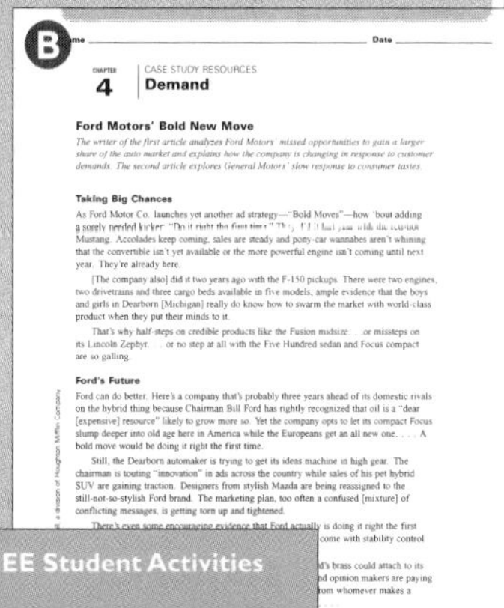
(B)

Name ________ Date ________

CHAPTER 4 | CASE STUDY RESOURCES
Demand

Ford Motors' Bold New Move

The writer of the first article analyzes Ford Motors' missed opportunities to gain a larger share of the auto market and explains how the company is changing in response to customer demands. The second article explores General Motors' slow response to consumer tastes.

Taking Big Chances

As Ford Motor Co. launches yet another ad strategy—"Bold Moves"—how 'bout adding a sorely needed kicker: "Do it right the first time." ... Mustang. Accolades keep coming, sales are steady and pony-car wannabes aren't whining that the convertible isn't yet available or the more powerful engine isn't coming until next year. They're already here.

[The company also] did it two years ago with the F-150 pickups. There were two engines, two drivetrains and three cargo beds available in five models, ample evidence that the boys and girls in Dearborn [Michigan] really do know how to swarm the market with world-class product when they put their minds to it.

That's why half-steps on credible products like the Fusion midsize. . . or missteps on its Lincoln Zephyr. . . . or no step at all with the Five Hundred sedan and Focus compact are so galling.

Ford's Future

Ford can do better. Here's a company that's probably three years ahead of its domestic rivals on the hybrid thing because Chairman Bill Ford has rightly recognized that oil is a "dear [expensive] resource" likely to grow more so. Yet the company opts to let its compact Focus slump deeper into old age here in America while the Europeans get an all new one. . . . A bold move would be doing it right the first time.

Still, the Dearborn automaker is trying to get its ideas machine in high gear. The chairman is touting "innovation" in ads across the country while sales of his pet hybrid SUV are gaining traction. Designers from stylish Mazda are being reassigned to the still-not-so-stylish Ford brand. The marketing plan, too often a confused [mixture] of conflicting messages, is getting torn up and tightened.

There's even some encouraging evidence that Ford actually is doing it right the first ... come with stability control ... d's brass could attach to its ... nd opinion makers are paying ... om whomever makes a ...

... from *The Detroit News*, May 3, 2006

Case Study Resources 35
Unit 2 Resource Book

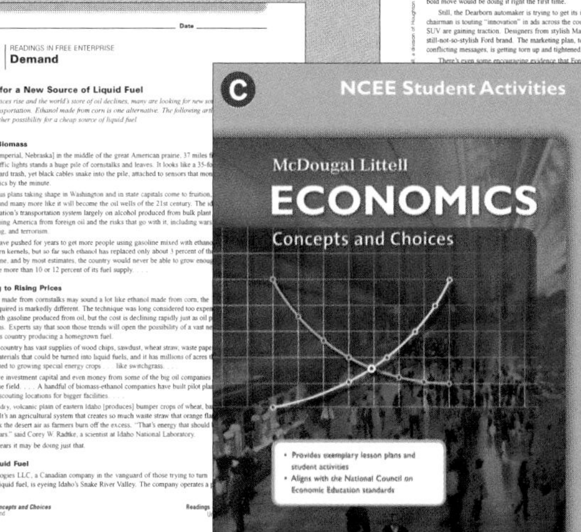
(A)

Name ________ Date ________

CHAPTER 4 | READINGS IN FREE ENTERPRISE
Demand

Demand for a New Source of Liquid Fuel

As gasoline prices rise and the world's store of oil declines, many are looking for new so... of fuel for transportation. Ethanol made from corn is one alternative. The following art... describes another possibility for a cheap source of liquid fuel.

Fuel from Biomass

Just outside [Imperial, Nebraska] in the middle of the great American prairie, 37 miles f... the nearest traffic lights stands a huge pile of cornstalks and leaves. It looks like a 35-fo... mountain of yard trash, yet black cables snake into the pile, attached to sensors that mon... its vital statistics by the minute.

If ambitious plans taking shape in Washington and in state capitals come to fruition, ... pile of stalks and many more like it will become the oil wells of the 21st century. The id... is to run the nation's transportation system largely on alcohol produced from bulk plant material, weaning America from foreign oil and the risks that go with it, including wars, global warming, and terrorism.

Farmers have pushed for years to get more people using gasoline mixed with ethano... made from corn kernels, but so far such ethanol has replaced only about 3 percent of th... nation's gasoline, and by most estimates, the country would never be able to grow enoug... corn to replace more than 10 or 12 percent of its fuel supply. . . .

Responding to Rising Prices

While ethanol made from cornstalks may sound a lot like ethanol made from corn, the technology required is markedly different. The technique was long considered too expen... to compete with gasoline produced from oil, but the cost is declining rapidly just as oil p... hit record highs. Experts say that soon those trends will open the possibility of a vast ne... industry in this country producing a homegrown fuel.

. . . [T]he country has vast supplies of wood chips, sawdust, wheat straw, waste pape... many other materials that could be turned into liquid fuels, and it has millions of acres t... could be devoted to growing special energy crops . . . like switchgrass. . . .

Speculative investment capital and even money from some of the big oil companies ... moving into the field. . . . A handful of biomass-ethanol companies have built pilot pla... and some are scouting locations for bigger facilities. . . .

The high, dry, volcanic plain of eastern Idaho [produces] bumper crops of wheat, ba... and potatoes. It's an agricultural system that creates so much waste straw that orange fla... sometimes lick the desert air as farmers burn off the excess. "That's energy that should ... going to run cars," said Corey W. Radtke, a scientist at Idaho National Laboratory.

In a few years it may be doing just that.

Making Liquid Fuel

Iogen Technologies LLC, a Canadian company in the vanguard of those trying to turn biomass into liquid fuel, is eyeing Idaho's Snake River Valley. The company operates a ...

Economics: Concepts and Choices Chapter 4: Demand — Readings ...

Focus & Motivate

Objective

Explain the law of demand and describe the factors that affect changes in demand.

Why the Concept Matters

Explain that demand is linked to the very human desire to meet wants. Ask students how much satisfaction they gain from each item they listed in the activity in the pupil's edition on p. 97. Does the level of satisfaction influence their ratings? Lead students to conclude that they are generally more willing to pay a higher price for something that is very important to them.

Analyzing the Photograph

Direct students to study the photograph and read the caption. Call on volunteers to describe what is taking place in the photograph. *(Possible answer: the sales assistant is demonstrating the various features of a particular model of computer in an attempt to persuade the customer to buy.)*

Ask students what factors the customer might consider in deciding whether or not to buy. *(Possible answers: price; whether she has enough money to make the purchase; if the computer has all the features she wants; whether she might get a better deal if she bought at a later date.)*

Conclude by pointing out that these factors all are aspects of the economic concept of demand, the subject of Chapter 4.

Microeconomics

Unit 2

Market Economies at Work

96

CONTENT STANDARDS

NCEE STANDARDS

Standard 8: Role of Price in Market System

Students will understand that
Prices send signals and provide incentives to buyers and sellers. When supply or demand changes, market prices adjust, affecting incentives.

Students will be able to use this knowledge to
Predict how prices change when the number of buyers or sellers in a market changes, and explain how the incentives facing individual buyers and sellers are affected.

Benchmarks

Students will know that

- High prices for a good or service provide incentives for buyers to purchase less of that good or service. Lower prices for a good or service provide incentives for buyers to purchase more of that good or service. *(pages 98–103)*
- An increase in the price of a good or service encourages people to look for substitutes, causing the quantity demanded to decrease, and vice versa. *(pages 98–103, 107, 112–113)*
- Demand for a product changes when there is a change in consumers' incomes or preferences, or in the prices of related goods or services, or in the number of consumers in a market. *(pages 108–113)*

CHAPTER

4

Demand

Demand
This computer store customer meets the two requirements of demand—the customer is willing to buy and is able to pay.

CONCEPT REVIEW

Microeconomics is the study of the economic behaviors and decisions of small units, such as individuals and businesses.

CHAPTER 4 KEY CONCEPT

Demand is the willingness to buy a good or service and the ability to pay for it.

WHY THE CONCEPT MATTERS

The concept of demand is demonstrated every time you buy something. List the last five goods or services that you purchased. Rate each one with a number from 1 (not important to you) to 4 (very important). Which of the goods or services would you stop buying if the price rose sharply? Describe the relationship between your ratings and your willingness to buy at a higher price.

Online Highlights

More at ClassZone.com

Economics Update
Go to ECONOMICS UPDATE for chapter updates and current news on demand in the automobile industry. (See Case Study, pages 124–125.) ▶

Animated Economics
Go to ANIMATED ECONOMICS for interactive lessons on the graphs and tables in this chapter.

Interactive Review
Go to INTERACTIVE REVIEW for concept review and activities.

What caused more people to demand hybrid cars? See the Case Study on pages 124–125.

From the Classroom
Brother Peter Hannon, St. Joseph High School

In August, when school begins and the weather is hot, I give each student in Economics class $100 in play money. Students can use the money to buy items I sell or save it for extra-credit points later in the week. I hide a cooler containing ice-cold sodas or bottled waters behind the teacher's desk. I bring one bottle out at a time and allow students to bid for cold drinks—but only one bottle at time. Of course, some students spend all of their money at the highest price; some wait, believing I have more than one bottle; and some save all their money for the extra-credit points. I found this to be a great "starter" when teaching the basic elements of the market economy and the law of supply and demand.

Previewing Chapter Technology at ClassZone.com

Economics Update Students will find updates to information in the pupil edition on pages 99, 104, 111, 119, and 124.

Animated Economics Students will find interactive lessons related to materials on pages 100, 102, 108, 109, and 118.

Interactive Review Students will find additional section and chapter assessment support for materials on pages 105, 115, 123, and 126.

TEACHER MEDIA FAVORITES

Books
- *Understanding Economics: The Content Standards in Cartoons*. Fort Atkinson, WI: Highsmith Press, 1999. Uses 20 cartoon transparencies to explore the National Council on Economic Education (NCEE) content standards. Lessons include discussion questions and activities.
- Becker, Gary S. *Accounting for Tastes*. Cambridge, MA: Harvard University Press, 1998. Nobel Prize–winning economist explores the factors that influence consumer preferences.
- Maxton, Graeme P. and John Wormald. *Time for a Model Change: Re-engineering the Global Automotive Industry.* New York: Cambridge UP, 2004. Thought-provoking ideas about changes needed in this huge industry to adapt to conditions of the 21st century.

Videos/DVDs
- *How Clothing Is Sold: Fashion Merchandising.* 20 Minutes. Learning Seed, 2003. Provides an inside look at the fashion industry, including topics such as designers and licensing and the role of the Internet.

Software
- *Virtual Economics® Version 3.0.* New York: National Council on Economic Education, 2005. Provides a complete resource library for understanding and teaching economics concepts.

Internet
Visit **ClassZone.com** to link to
- a variety of chapter-specific, content-reviewed sites
- updates on data and topics presented throughout the chapter sections and Case Study
- updates to the Power Presentations

1 Plan & Prepare

Section 1 Objectives

- define *demand* and outline what the law of demand says
- explain how to interpret and create demand schedules and describe the role of market research in this process
- explain how to interpret and create demand curves

2 Focus & Motivate

Connecting to Everyday Life Explain that this section focuses on the meaning of *demand* in economics, which involves how consumers decide what products to buy. Ask students to name some products that they buy regularly.

Taking Notes Remind students to take notes as they read by completing a cluster diagram for each key concept. They can use the Graphic Organizer at **Interactive Review @ ClassZone.com.** A sample is shown below.

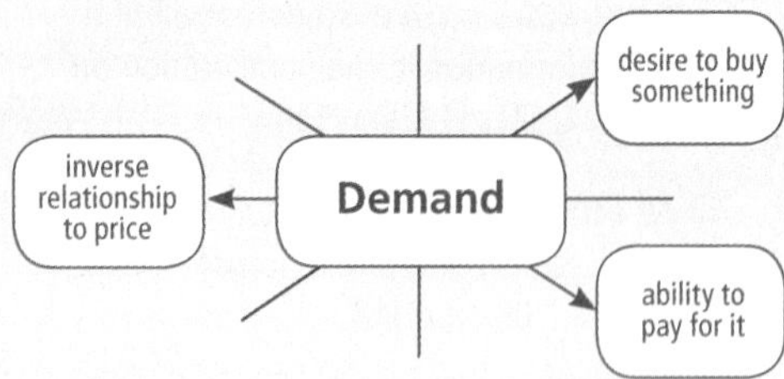

SECTION 1

What Is Demand?

OBJECTIVES

In Section 1, you will
- define *demand* and outline what the law of demand says
- explain how to interpret and create demand schedules and describe the role of market research in this process
- explain how to interpret and create demand curves

KEY TERMS

demand, *p. 98*
law of demand, *p. 99*
demand schedule, *p. 100*
market demand schedule, *p. 100*
demand curve, *p. 102*
market demand curve, *p. 102*

TAKING NOTES

As you read Section 1, complete a cluster diagram like this one for each key concept. Use the Graphic Organizer at **Interactive Review @ ClassZone.com**

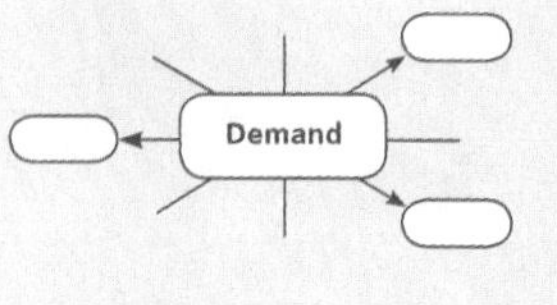

The Law of Demand

KEY CONCEPTS

In Chapter 3, you learned that the United States has a free enterprise economy. This type of economic system depends on cooperation between producers and consumers. To make a profit, producers provide products at the highest possible price. Consumers serve their own interests by purchasing the best products at the lowest possible price. The forces of supply and demand establish the price that best serves both producers and consumers. In this chapter, you'll learn about the demand side of this equation.

QUICK REFERENCE

Demand is the willingness to buy a good or service and the ability to pay for it.

Demand is the desire to have some good or service and the ability to pay for it. You may want to take a round-the-world cruise or to rent a huge apartment that overlooks the ocean. Or you may want to buy a brand-new sports car or a state-of-the-art home entertainment center. However, you may not be able to afford any of these things. Therefore, economists would say that you have no actual demand for them. Even though you want them, you don't have the money needed to buy them. Conversely, you may want the latest CDs by several of your favorite bands. And, at a price

98 Chapter 4

SECTION 1 PROGRAM RESOURCES

ON LEVEL

Lesson Plans
- Core, pp. 12

Unit 2 Resource Book
- Reading Study Guide, pp. 1–2
- Economic Skills and Problem Solving Activity, pp. 31–32
- Section Quiz, p. 9

STRUGGLING READERS

Unit 2 Resource Book
- Reading Study Guide with Additional Support, pp. 3–5
- Reteaching Activity, p. 10

ENGLISH LEARNERS

Unit 2 Resource Book
- Reading Study Guide with Additional Support (Spanish), pp. 6–8

INCLUSION

Lesson Plans
- Modified for Inclusion, p. 12

GIFTED AND TALENTED

Unit 2 Resource Book
- Case Study Resources: Ford Motors' Bold New Move, p. 35

TECHNOLOGY

eEdition DVD-ROM

eEdition Online

Power Presentation DVD-ROM

Economics Concepts Transparencies
- CT12 Shirt Market Demand Schedule

Daily Test Practice Transparencies, TT12

ClassZone.com

of between $12 and $15 each, you can afford them. Since you have both the desire for them and the ability to pay for them, you do have demand for CDs.

Price is one of the major factors that influence demand. The **law of demand** states that when the price of a good or service falls, consumers buy more of it. As the price of a good or service increases, consumers usually buy less of it. In other words, quantity demanded and price have an inverse, or opposite, relationship. This relationship is graphically illustrated in Figure 4.1 below.

QUICK REFERENCE

Law of demand states that when prices go down, quantity demanded increases. When prices go up, quantity demanded decreases.

FIGURE 4.1 LAW OF DEMAND

As **prices** fall... **quantity demanded** goes up.

As **prices** increase... **quantity demanded** goes down.

EXAMPLE Price and Demand

Let's take a look at an example of demand in action. Cheryl, a senior at Montclair High School, loves movies and enjoys collecting them on DVD. She and Malik, a friend from school, sometimes meet downtown at Montclair Video Mart to look through the DVD stacks. Rafael, the owner of the video mart, often jokes that Cheryl and Malik spend so much time at his store that he might have to give them jobs. Actually, Cheryl already has a job—stocking shelves at her neighborhood supermarket. She worked so many hours this summer that she has extra money to spend. Let's see how DVD prices at Montclair Video Mart affect her spending decisions.

Cheryl has been saving to buy the DVD boxed set of the original *Star Wars* trilogy, one of her favorite series of movies. The set costs $69.95, and Cheryl has the money to buy it this weekend. When Cheryl goes to the Montclair Video Mart, she is disappointed to learn that the *Star Wars* set is sold out and a new shipment won't arrive for a week. She decides to buy some other DVDs so that she won't go home empty-handed, but she also decides to save roughly half of her money toward a future purchase of *Star Wars*.

As she looks through the movie DVDs, she sees that most of those she wants sell for $15. How many will she buy at that price? Let's say she decides to buy three and keep the rest of her money for the *Star Wars* trilogy. But what if each of the DVDs she wants costs just $5? Cheryl might decide that the price is such a good deal that she can buy seven. As you can see, the law of demand is more than just an economic concept. It's also a description of how consumers behave.

Economics Update

Find an update on the demand for CDs and DVDs at **ClassZone.com**

APPLICATION Applying Economic Concepts

A. You have $50 and want to buy some CDs. If prices of CDs rose from $5 each to $10, how would your quantity demanded of CDs change?

Quantity demanded would decrease from ten to five.

3 Teach

The Law of Demand

Discuss

- Why do economists include ability to pay in their definition of demand? *(because producers want to sell goods and services and only people who can pay for them are possible consumers)*
- Why do price and demand have an inverse relationship? *(because consumers have a limited amount of money and will usually buy less of something if the price goes up)*

Economics Illustrated

To better understand the law of demand, you might think of it as a seesaw, with one end labeled "Prices" and the other labeled "Quantity Demanded." As the "Prices" end rises, the "Quantity Demanded" end goes down, and as the "Prices" end falls, the "Quantity Demanded" end goes up.

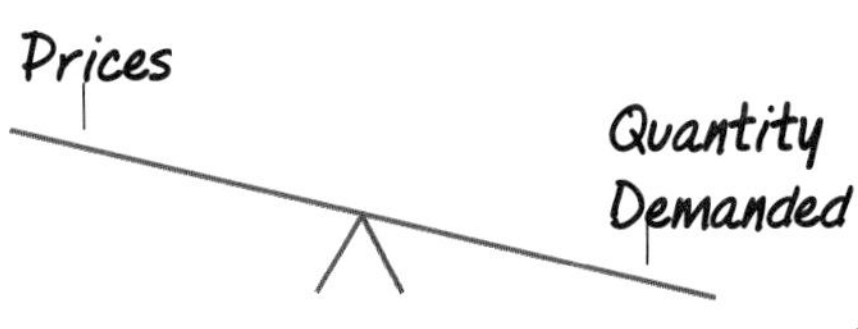

Economics Update

At **ClassZone.com,** students will see updated information on the demand for CDs and DVDs.

LEVELED ACTIVITY

Developing New Product Ideas

Time 30 minutes

Objective Students will demonstrate an understanding of the factors that affect demand and price elasticity of demand for a new product. (Elasticity is discussed in Section 3.)

Basic	On Level	Challenge
Set prices for the product and create a demand schedule and demand curve for it. Illustrate external factors other than price that might affect the demand for the product in a graphic organizer such as Figure 4.12 on p. 113. Estimate whether demand is elastic or inelastic by using the guidelines in Figure 4.15 on p. 120.	Set prices for the product and create a market demand curve for it. Describe external factors other than price that might affect the demand for the product. Choose one factor and illustrate an increase or decrease in demand by showing a shift in the demand curve. Determine elasticity of demand.	Set prices for the product and create a market demand curve for it. Illustrate both an increase and a decrease in demand caused by factors other than price by showing shifts in the demand curve. Determine elasticity of demand using the calculations on p.121. Write a new product proposal that analyzes potential demand.

Demand Schedules

Discuss

- What is the difference between a demand schedule and a market demand schedule? *(A demand schedule shows the relationship between demand and price for an individual consumer and a market demand schedule shows this relationship for all consumers in a particular market.)*
- Why do markets behave the same way as individual consumers? *(because markets are made up of individual consumers and the group behavior reflects individual behavior)*

Analyzing Tables: Figure 4.2

Point out the convention that is used in creating demand schedules, with the highest price at the top of the first column and the lowest at the bottom. The quantity demanded shown in the second column starts with the lowest and increases as the price drops. Refer to Figure 4.1 and ask students in which direction the arrow would point for each column of the demand schedule. *(Answers: down for the first column and up for the second)*

Answers

1. *three*
2. *The quantities demanded show the increase in Cheryl's demand as the price decreases.*

Animated Economics Animation and audio highlight how many DVDs Cheryl will buy at various prices. This will help students understand the relationship between price and quantity demanded.

Demand Schedules

QUICK REFERENCE

Demand schedule is a listing of how much of an item an individual is willing to purchase at each price.

Market demand schedule is a listing of how much of an item all consumers are willing to purchase at each price.

KEY CONCEPTS

A **demand schedule** is a table that shows how much of a good or service an individual consumer is willing and able to purchase at each price in a market. In other words, a demand schedule shows the law of demand in chart form. A **market demand schedule** shows how much of a good or service all consumers are willing and able to buy at each price in a market.

EXAMPLE Individual Demand Schedule

A demand schedule is a two-column table that follows a predictable format. The left-hand column of the table lists various prices of a good or service. The right-hand column shows the quantity demanded of the good or service at each price.

Cheryl's demand for DVDs can be expressed in a demand schedule. Let's take a look at the price list in Figure 4.2 below. How many DVDs will Cheryl buy if they cost $20 each? How many will she buy when the price stands at $10? Your answers to these questions show one thing very clearly. Cheryl's demand for DVDs depends on their price.

FIGURE 4.2 CHERYL'S DVD DEMAND SCHEDULE

	Price per DVD ($)	Quantity Demanded
a →	30	0
	25	1
	20	2
	15	3
b →	10	4
	$5	7

ⓐ At the top price of $30, Cheryl is not willing to buy any DVDs.

ⓑ At $10, she will buy four DVDs.

Notice that when the price falls, the number of DVDs Cheryl will buy rises. When the price rises, the number she will buy falls. So quantity demanded and price have an inverse, or opposite, relationship.

ANALYZE TABLES

1. How many DVDs will Cheryl be likely to buy if the price is $15?
2. What is the relationship between Cheryl's demand for DVDs and various quantities demanded shown on this table?

Animated Economics Use an interactive demand schedule at **ClassZone.com**

Price and Demand Storeowners often offer products at sale prices to encourage consumers to make more purchases.

DIFFERENTIATING INSTRUCTION

English Learners

Build Economics Vocabulary

Help students understand how economics terms are different from, yet related to, everyday meanings of words.

- Have students use a dictionary and the definitions in the textbook to create a two-column chart of the following words with an everyday meaning and the economics meaning: *demand, law, market, schedule, table.*
- Encourage students to add other words, such as *curve* and *elastic,* to their charts as they continue reading.

Gifted and Talented

Conduct Market Research

Organize students into small groups and have each group design a questionnaire that Rafael might have used to survey his customers about how many DVDs they would buy at different prices. Direct groups to exchange and then complete questionnaires. Have students work as a class to tabulate the questionnaire responses and to use the results to create a market demand schedule. Invite them to compare their results with Figure 4.3 and discuss similarities and differences.

EXAMPLE Market Demand Schedule

The demand schedule in Figure 4.2 shows how many DVDs an individual, Cheryl, is willing and able to buy at each price in the market. The schedule also shows that the quantity of DVDs that Cheryl demands rises and falls in response to changes in price. Sometimes, however, an individual demand schedule does not give business owners enough information. For example, Rafael, who owns Montclair Video Mart, needs information about more than just one consumer before he can price his merchandise to gain the maximum number of sales. He needs a market demand schedule, which shows the quantity demanded by all the people in a particular market who are willing and able to buy DVDs.

Take a look at the DVD market demand schedule below. Notice that it's similar to the individual demand schedule except that the quantities demanded are much larger. It also shows that, like individual demand, market demand depends on price.

FIGURE 4.3 DVD MARKET DEMAND SCHEDULE

	Price per DVD ($)	Quantity Demanded
a →	30	50
	25	75
	20	100
b →	15	125
	10	175
c →	5	300

(a) At the top price of $30, Rafael's customers will buy 50 DVDs.

(b) At the middle price of $15, the quantity demanded of DVDs is 125.

(c) At the low price of $5, the quantity demanded rises to 300.

So, markets behave in the same way as individual consumers. As prices fall, the quantity demanded of DVDs rises. As prices rise, the quantity demanded falls.

ANALYZE TABLES

1. How does the quantity demanded of DVDs change when the price drops from $25 to $10?
2. How does this market demand schedule illustrate the law of demand?

CONNECT TO MATH

How would a merchant use this schedule to decide on a price? First, the merchant would calculate the total revenue at each price. To figure out total revenue, multiply the price per DVD by the quantity demanded.

$30.00	Price
× 50	× Quantity
$1,500.00	Total Revenue

How did Rafael create a market demand schedule? First, he surveyed his customers, asking them how many DVDs they would buy at different prices. Next, he reviewed his sales figures to see how many DVDs he sold at each price. Techniques such as these for investigating a specific market are called market research. Market research involves the gathering and evaluating of information about customer preferences. (You'll learn more about market research in Chapter 7.) By tabulating the results of his market research, Rafael created his market demand schedule.

APPLICATION Applying Economic Concepts

B. Imagine that you have discovered a restaurant that makes the best pizza you have ever tasted. Create a demand schedule showing how many pizzas a month you would buy at the prices of $25, $20, $15, $10, and $5.

Student demand schedules should list the prices in descending order in the first column and reflect the law of demand by showing an increase in the quantity demanded in the second column as the price decreases.

Analyzing Tables: Figure 4.3

Ask students how this table differs from that in Figure 4.2 and why. *(The quantities demanded are much larger because they reflect all consumers in the market.)*

Invite volunteers to calculate the total revenue at each price to discover at which price total revenue will be the highest. *(Total revenues are $1,500, $1,875, $2,000, $1,875, $1,750, $1,500. Total revenue will be the highest at the price of $20.)*

Answers

1. *It increases from 75 to 175.*
2. *It shows that as prices rise quantity demanded goes down and as prices fall quantity demanded goes up.*

More About . . .

Pirating DVDs

The Motion Picture Association of America estimates that the U.S. film industry loses more than $3.5 billion per year from the illegal sale of counterfeit copies of films. Consumers buy the counterfeit copies on the street or over the Internet for a substantially lower price, sometimes before a film has even reached theaters. The problem is worldwide and DVD technology has caused it to increase dramatically. The number of counterfeit films in all formats seized by law enforcement officials jumped by more than 500 percent between 1997 and 2002.

SMALL GROUP ACTIVITY

Illustrating the Law of Demand

Time 30 minutes

Task Create a demand schedule and a market demand schedule for a common product.

Materials Needed two blank two-column charts (1 per student and 1 per group), pen or pencils

Activity

- Organize students into small groups and ask each group to determine a product for which all the members of the group have a demand. Then have groups set five different prices for their selected product.
- Direct each student in the group to create a demand schedule that shows how many of the products he or she would buy in a month at the different prices.
- Instruct group members to combine the information in their demand schedules to create a market demand schedule.
- Invite volunteers to share their market demand schedules with the class and state how these schedules reflect the law of demand.

Rubric

	Understanding Concepts	Presentation of Information
4	excellent	clear and complete
3	good	mostly clear
2	fair	sometimes clear
1	poor	sketchy

Demand Curves

Discuss

- How is a demand curve related to a demand schedule? *(A demand curve is the representation on a line graph of the information in a demand schedule.)*
- What do the points on the demand curve represent? *(They reflect the quantity demanded at each price.)*

Presentation Options

Review the relationship between demand schedules and curves by using the following presentation options.

 **Power Presentations DVD-ROM** Project the animated demand curve. Using the Display Tool, you can highlight the major features of the demand curve and schedule.

Animated Economics An interactive demand curve at **ClassZone.com** shows how a demand curve is constructed from a demand schedule.

 **Economics Concepts Transparencies**
- CT12 Shirt Market Demand Schedule

Demand Curves

QUICK REFERENCE

Demand curve graphically shows the data from a demand schedule.

Market demand curve graphically shows the data from a market demand schedule.

KEY CONCEPTS

A **demand curve** is a graph that shows how much of a good or service an individual will buy at each price. In other words, it displays the data from an individual demand schedule. Creating a demand curve simply involves transferring data from one format, a table, to another format, a graph.

A **market demand curve** shows the data found in the market demand schedule. In other words, it shows the quantity that all consumers, or the market as a whole, are willing and able to buy at each price. A market demand curve shows the sum of the information on the individual demand curves of all consumers in a market.

EXAMPLE Individual Demand Curve

Study the demand curve (Figure 4.4 below) created from Cheryl's demand schedule. How many DVDs will Cheryl buy at the price of $15? How will Cheryl's quantity demanded change if the price rises by $5 or falls by $5? Find the answers to these questions by running your finger along the curve. As you can see, the demand curve is a visual representation of the law of demand. When prices go up, the quantity demanded goes down; when prices go down, the quantity demanded goes up.

You should note that this demand curve and the schedule on which it is based were created using the assumption that all other economic factors except price remain the same. You'll learn more about these factors and how they affect demand in Section 2.

CONNECT TO MATH

One common mistake people make is to look at the downward-sloping graph and think it means that quantity demanded is decreasing. However, if you move your finger downward and to the right on the demand curve, you'll notice that the quantity demanded is increasing.

FIGURE 4.4 CHERYL'S DVD DEMAND CURVE

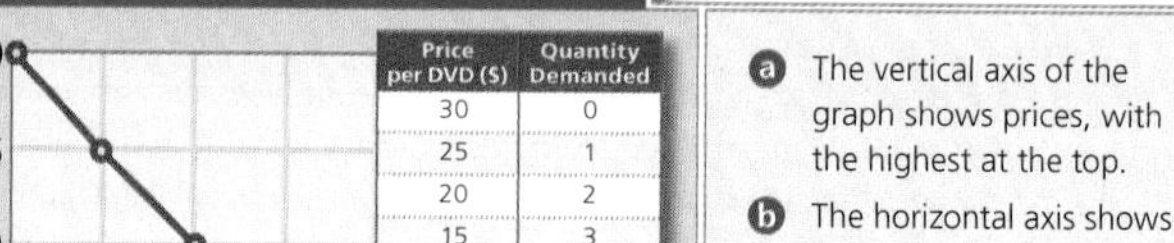

Price per DVD ($)	Quantity Demanded
30	0
25	1
20	2
15	3
10	4
5	7

ⓐ The vertical axis of the graph shows prices, with the highest at the top.

ⓑ The horizontal axis shows quantities demanded, with the lowest on the far left.

ⓒ Notice that **demand curves** slope downward from upper left to lower right.

ANALYZE GRAPHS

1. How many DVDs will Cheryl buy when the price is $10?
2. How does this demand curve illustrate the law of demand?

Animated Economics

Use an interactive demand curve at **ClassZone.com**

DIFFERENTIATING INSTRUCTION

Struggling Readers

Compare Economic Information
Help students understand that the law of demand has been expressed in four different forms in the section. It has been stated in words on page 99, shown in a diagram in Figure 4.1, and presented through examples in demand schedules (Figures 4.2 and 4.3) and demand curves (Figures 4.4 and 4.5). Have students study the figures and reread the appropriate text material to see how the figures help them understand the text.

Inclusion

Create Enlarged Demand Curves
Help students create enlarged versions of Figures 4.4 and 4.5 on poster-sized pieces of graph paper. If students have difficulty reading the values on the demand schedules on which the curves are based, read the values aloud as students set up the axes of the graphs and plot the points. Students might also create enlarged demand curves using string and pushpins to plot the points on a bulletin board.

EXAMPLE Market Demand Curve

Like Cheryl's individual demand curve, the market demand curve for Montclair Video Mart shows the quantity demanded at different prices. In other words, the graph shows the quantity of DVDs that all consumers, or the market as a whole, are willing and able to buy at each price. Despite this difference, the market demand curve for Montclair Video Mart (Figure 4.5) is constructed in the same way as Cheryl's individual demand curve. As in Figure 4.4, the vertical axis displays prices and the horizontal axis displays quantities demanded.

FIGURE 4.5 DVD MARKET DEMAND CURVE

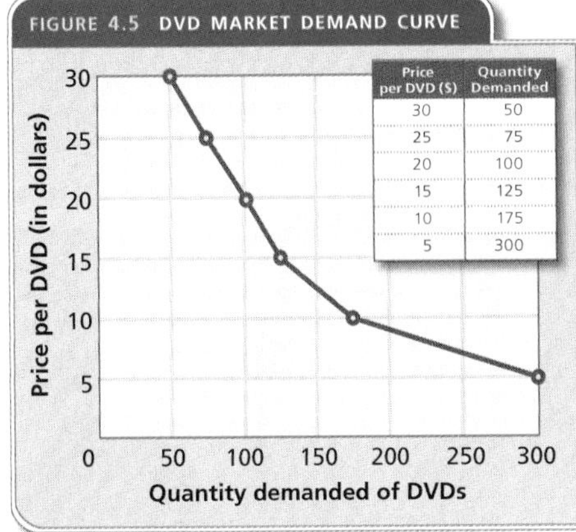

Price per DVD ($)	Quantity Demanded
30	50
25	75
20	100
15	125
10	175
5	300

Notice that **market demand curves** slope downward from upper left to lower right, just as individual demand curves do.

The main difference between the two types of demand curves is that the quantities demanded at each price are much larger on a market demand curve. This is because the curve represents a group of consumers (a market), not just one consumer.

ANALYZE GRAPHS

1. At which price will Montclair Video Mart sell 175 DVDs?
2. Cheryl was unwilling to buy any DVDs at $30. Montclair Video Mart can sell 50 DVDs at that price. How do you explain the difference?

NEED HELP?

Throughout this chapter, you will be asked to create and to analyze demand curves. If you need help with those activities, see "Interpreting Graphs."

Skillbuilder Handbook, page R29

Look at Figure 4.5 above one more time. What is the quantity demanded at the price of $15? How will quantity demanded change if the price increases by $5 or drops by $5? Once again, find the answers to these questions by running your finger along the curve. As you can see, the market demand curve—just like the individual demand curve—vividly illustrates the inverse relationship between price and quantity demanded. If price goes down, the quantity demanded goes up. And if price goes up, the quantity demanded goes down. Also, like the individual demand curve, the market demand curve is constructed on the assumption that all other economic factors remain constant—only the price of DVDs changes.

SMARTGrapher Create a demand curve at **ClassZone.com**

APPLICATION Applying Economic Concepts

C. Look back at the demand schedule for pizzas you created for Application B on page 101. Use it to create a demand curve.

Students' demand curves should slope downward from upper left to lower right.

Analyzing Graphs: Figures 4.4 and 4.5

Make sure students understand that the demand schedules shown with the demand curves are the same ones shown in Figures 4.2 and 4.3. Ask why the vertical axes of the two graphs are the same but the horizontal axes are different. *(Possible answer: In both cases the vertical axis reflects the prices of DVDs but the horizontal axis in one reflects the quantity demanded by an individual and in the other the quantity demanded by all the consumers in the market.)*

Answers

Figure 4.4

1. *four*
2. *The curve is downward sloping from upper left to lower right, showing that as prices fall quantity demanded increases.*

Figure 4.5

1. *$10*
2. *Cheryl is just one consumer. Montclair Video serves a market made up of many consumers. Some consumers have greater demand for DVDs than Cheryl.*

Animated Economics The demand curve shows how the law of demand can be shown on a graph. It will help students understand how the quantity demanded decreases as price increases.

INDIVIDUAL ACTIVITY

Illustrating the Law of Demand

Time 30 minutes

Task Create a personal expression of the law of demand.

Materials Needed paper and markers, pens, or colored pencils

Activity

- Invite students to illustrate the law of demand in a visual (e.g., cartoon, poster, bar graph) or verbal (e.g., poem, rap, story) way that is different from those used in the textbook.
- Explain that their illustration might be a general expression of the law (see Fig. 4.1) or might reflect the information in a particular demand schedule for DVDs, pizza, or some other product.
- Bar graph hint: Each bar represents a price (increase from left to right) and the height matches the quantity demanded.
- Allow students to share their creations in small groups.

Rubric

	Understanding Concepts	Presentation of Information
4	excellent	clear, complete, creative
3	good	mostly clear, somewhat creative
2	fair	sometimes clear, some creativity
1	poor	sketchy, unoriginal

Vera Wang

More About . . .

Vera Wang

Vera Wang grew up in a wealthy Chinese-American family in New York City and studied theater and art history in college. Later, she attended the University of Paris-Sorbonne, one of the most prestigious universities in Europe.

Wang learned about the fashion industry by working as an editor at *Vogue* magazine and as a designer for Ralph Lauren before opening her own business. Until her late teens, Wang was a competitive ice skater. Her sporting and work interests came together when she designed costumes for Olympic skaters Nancy Kerrigan and Michelle Kwan.

More About . . .

Vera Wang Ltd.

Since its establishment in 1990, Vera Wang Ltd. has grown well beyond the bridal industry. The variety of products that carry the Vera Wang brand show that she is focusing on the total lifestyle of the affluent, sophisticated women who were the initial target for her wedding gowns. The company employs about 200 people directly and most of the bridal gowns are made in the United States.

As she has expanded into other product categories, such as footwear and eyewear, Wang has teamed up with partners around the world who help to bring her design vision to life. Her products are sold in her own salon in New York City as well as in major department stores and exclusive boutiques.

Economics Update

ClassZone.com includes a link to Vera Wang's company. Students can review how Wang is responding to changes in consumer demand.

ECONOMICS PACESETTER

Vera Wang: Designer in Demand

FAST FACTS

Vera Wang

Title: Chairman and CEO of Vera Wang Ltd.

Born: June 27, 1949, New York, New York

Major Accomplishment: Designer of high-fashion wedding gowns

Other Products: Clothing, perfume, eyewear, shoes, jewelry, home fashions

Books: *Vera Wang on Weddings* (2001)

Price Range for Vera Wang Wedding Gowns: about $2,000 to $20,000

In this section, you've learned about the law of demand. You've also seen demand in action in some hypothetical situations. The story of fashion designer Vera Wang, however, provides a real-world example of demand at work.

When they married, Mariah Carey, Jennifer Lopez, and several other stars turned to Wang for their wedding dresses. What explains the demand for this one woman's gowns?

Responding to Demand

Vera Wang had worked in the fashion industry for more than 15 years by the time she started planning her own wedding in 1989. So she was frustrated when she couldn't find the type of sophisticated bridal gown she wanted. She knew that many modern brides were savvy career women who preferred designer clothing. Yet, no one was making wedding dresses for those women.

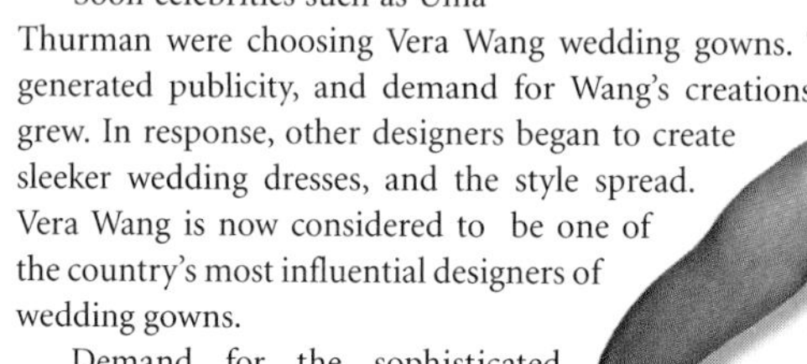

Changing Styles Vera Wang wanted to change traditional wedding dress styles that, she thought, made brides look "like the bride on top of a cake, very decorated."

The next year, Wang decided to fill that unmet demand. She created her own line of gowns featuring elegant sleeveless styles rather than the hooped skirts, puffed sleeves, and lace flounces that had dominated wedding-dress designs before.

Soon celebrities such as Uma Thurman were choosing Vera Wang wedding gowns. This generated publicity, and demand for Wang's creations grew. In response, other designers began to create sleeker wedding dresses, and the style spread. Vera Wang is now considered to be one of the country's most influential designers of wedding gowns.

Demand for the sophisticated Wang style has spread beyond weddings. In recent years, Wang has expanded her product line to include ready-to-wear dresses, perfume, accessories, and home fashions.

Economics Update

Find the latest on Vera Wang's business at **ClassZone.com**

APPLICATION Analyzing Cause and Effect

D. In what ways did Vera Wang respond to consumer demand? In what ways did she generate consumer demand?

Responded to unmet demand for more fashionable, sophisticated wedding dresses. Created demand by expanding into other product categories.

DIFFERENTIATING INSTRUCTION

English Learners

Use Context Clues and Visuals

Encourage students to use visuals to help them preview what this feature is about. They may use the visuals along with context clues to figure out the meaning of words such as stars (the word *celebrity* and people's names) and *bridal gown* (or *wedding dress*). Invite students to summarize the article in their own words.

Struggling Readers

Diagram Cause and Effect

Help students create a cause-and-effect chain to show how Vera Wang went from her experience with her own wedding to becoming a designer of wedding gowns, influencing the whole market for wedding gowns, and then designing other products for women who had similar tastes to hers. Invite students to use the diagram to describe the factors that affect demand.

SECTION 1 Assessment

Online Quiz
ClassZone.com

REVIEWING KEY CONCEPTS

1. Explain the differences between the terms in each of these pairs:
   a. *demand* / *law of demand*
   b. *demand schedule* / *demand curve*
   c. *market demand schedule* / *market demand curve*
2. Look at Figure 4.1 on page 99. Write a caption for the figure that explains the law of demand.
3. Review the information on Vera Wang on the opposite page. Why is it unlikely that most brides will have demand for an original Vera Wang gown?
4. How might an owner of a bookstore put together a market demand schedule for his or her store?
5. Why does the demand curve slope downward?
6. **Using Your Notes** How are price and quantity demanded related? Refer to your completed cluster diagram.

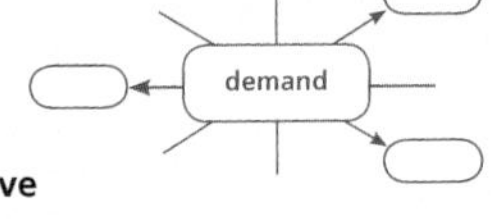

Use the Graphic Organizer at **Interactive Review @ ClassZone.com**

CRITICAL THINKING

7. **Drawing Conclusions** List three products that you are familiar with and the approximate price of each. Which of the products, if any, do you have a demand for? Consider the two requirements of demand as you answer this question.
8. **Making Inferences** Why might Rafael's market demand schedule and curve not be an accurate reflection of the actual market? To answer this question, consider the assumption that was made when the schedule and curve were created.
9. **Applying Economic Concepts** Return to the demand schedule for pizzas you created for Application B on page 101. Assume that your class is the market for pizzas. Tabulate these individual demand schedules to create a market demand schedule. Then use that schedule to draw a market demand curve.
10. **Challenge** Does quantity demanded always fall if the price rises? List several goods or services that you think would remain in demand even if the price rose sharply. Why does demand for those items change very little? (You will learn more about this topic in Section 3.)

ECONOMICS IN PRACTICE

Making a Market Demand Curve
Suppose that you own a store that sells athletic shoes. You survey your customers and analyze your sales data to see how many pairs of shoes you can expect to sell at various prices. Your research enables you to make the following market demand schedule.

Price per Pair of Shoes ($)	Quantity Demanded
175	0
150	10
125	20
100	40
75	70
50	110

Create a Demand Curve Use this market demand schedule to create a market demand curve.

Challenge Write a caption for your market demand curve explaining what it shows.

Use *SMARTGrapher* @ClassZone.com to complete this activity.

4 Assess & Reteach

Assess Have students work in pairs on the questions and note the location of the answers. Discuss Critical Thinking questions as a class.

Unit 2 Resource Book
- Section Quiz, p. 9

Interactive Review @ ClassZone.com
- Section Quiz

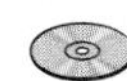

Test Generator CD-ROM
- Section Quiz

Reteach Divide students into five groups. Assign each group one of the figures in the section. Have each group decide how to reteach the key concept illustrated in their figure to the rest of the class.

Unit 2 Resource Book
- Reteaching Activity, p. 10

SMARTGrapher Students can create a demand curve using **SmartGrapher @ ClassZone.com.**

SECTION 1 ASSESSMENT ANSWERS

Reviewing Key Concepts

1. a. *demand*, p. 98; *law of demand*, p. 99
   b. *demand schedule*, p. 100; *demand curve*, p. 102
   c. *market demand schedule*, p. 100; *market demand curve*, p. 102
2. Captions will vary. A typical caption might be: As the price of DVDs rises, people will buy fewer of them. As the price falls, they will buy more.
3. Wang's gowns are too expensive for most brides.
4. by using market research techniques, such as customer surveys and reviews of sales figures
5. The intersection of the highest price and the lowest quantity demanded is at the upper left, and the intersection of the greatest quantity demanded and the lowest price is at the lower right.
6. See page 98 for an example of a completed cluster diagram. They are inversely related.

Critical Thinking

7. Answers will vary. Students have demand for the products they want to buy and can afford.
8. Students should conclude that there might be factors other than price that will affect demand.
9. Have students work as a class to tabulate the individual demand schedules into a market demand schedule. Encourage them to study the market demand curve in Fig. 4.5 before they create their market demand curves.
10. Quantity demanded does not necessarily fall if the price rises. Examples might include gasoline and some types of prescription drugs. These products are considered necessities so demand for them would change little.

Economics in Practice

Create a Demand Curve Encourage students to view examples of demand curves in the section before they construct their market demand curve.

Challenge Captions may vary, but should note that the curve shows that price and quantity demanded are inversely related as it slopes downward from upper left to lower right.

1 Plan & Prepare

Section 2 Objectives

- determine a change in quantity demanded
- explain the difference between change in quantity demanded and change in demand
- determine a change in demand
- analyze what factors can cause change in demand

2 Focus & Motivate

Connecting to Everyday Life Explain that this section focuses on changes in the marketplace that affect demand. Ask students to brainstorm examples of times when something other than price affected their decisions to buy.

Taking Notes Remind students to take notes as they read by completing the chart. They can use the Graphic Organizer at **Interactive Review @ ClassZone.com**. A sample is shown below.

Factor That Changes Demand	Reason Why Demand Changes
income	people have more or less to spend
market size	number of potential buyers changes
consumer tastes	popularity increases demand
consumer expectations	possible future prices affect present buying
substitutes	some products are interchangeable
complements	some products are used together

SECTION 2

What Factors Affect Demand?

OBJECTIVES

In Section 2, you will
- determine a change in quantity demanded
- explain the difference between change in quantity demanded and change in demand
- determine a change in demand
- analyze what factors can cause change in demand

KEY TERMS

law of diminishing marginal utility, *p. 106*
income effect, *p. 107*
substitution effect, *p. 107*
change in quantity demanded, *p. 108*
change in demand, *p. 109*
normal goods, *p. 110*
inferior goods, *p. 110*
substitutes, *p. 112*
complements, *p. 112*

TAKING NOTES

As you read Section 2, complete a chart that shows each factor that causes change in demand. Use the Graphic Organizer at **Interactive Review @ ClassZone.com**

Factor That Changes Demand	Reason Why Demand Changes

More About Demand Curves

KEY CONCEPTS

The demand schedules and demand curves that you studied in Section 1 were created using the assumption that all other economic factors except the price of DVDs would remain the same. If all other factors remain the same, then the only thing that influences how many DVDs consumers will buy is the price of those DVDs. The demand curve graphically displays that pattern.

Now think about the shape of demand curves. Why do they slope downward? The reason is the **law of diminishing marginal utility**, which states that the marginal benefit from using each additional unit of a good or service during a given time period tends to decline as each is used. Recall that utility is the satisfaction gained from the use of a good or service. Suppose it is a hot day, and you have just gulped down a glass of lemonade. Would you gain the same benefit from drinking a second glass? How about a third? In all likelihood, you'd find the second glass less satisfying than the first, and the third glass less satisfying than the second.

QUICK REFERENCE

Law of diminishing marginal utility states that the marginal benefit of using each additional unit of a product during a given period will decline.

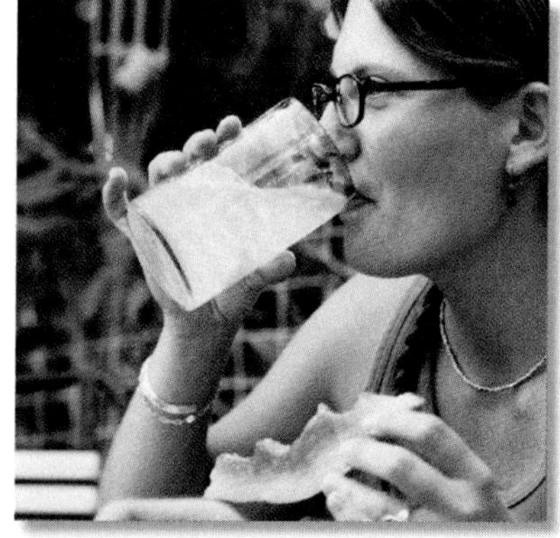

Because consumers receive less satisfaction from each new glass of lemonade they drink, they don't want to pay as much for additional purchases. So, they will buy

SECTION 2 PROGRAM RESOURCES

ON LEVEL

Lesson Plans
- Core, p. 13

Unit 2 Resource Book
- Reading Study Guide, pp. 11–12
- Economic Simulations, pp. 37–38
- Section Quiz, p. 19

STRUGGLING READERS

Unit 2 Resource Book
- Reading Study Guide with Additional Support, pp. 13–15
- Reteaching Activity, p. 20

ENGLISH LEARNERS

Unit 2 Resource Book
- Reading Study Guide with Additional Support (Spanish), pp. 16–18

INCLUSION

Lesson Plans
- Modified for Inclusion, p. 13

GIFTED AND TALENTED

Unit 2 Resource Book
- Readings in Free Enterprise: Demand for a New Source of Liquid Fuel, pp. 33–34

NCEE Student Activities
- Movements and Shifts in Demand Curves; Consumer Surplus; Demand Elasticity, pp. 13–16

TECHNOLOGY

eEdition DVD-ROM

eEdition Online

Power Presentation DVD-ROM

Economics Concepts Transparencies
- CT13 Movement of the Demand Curve

Daily Test Practice Transparencies, TT13

ClassZone.com

two glasses only if the lemonade is offered at a lower price, and they will buy three only if the price is even lower still. This pattern of behavior, which holds true for most consumer goods and services, creates the downward slope of the demand curve. For another example, see Figure 4.6 below, which displays the demand that a young man named Kent has for video games.

FIGURE 4.6 DIMINISHING MARGINAL UTILITY

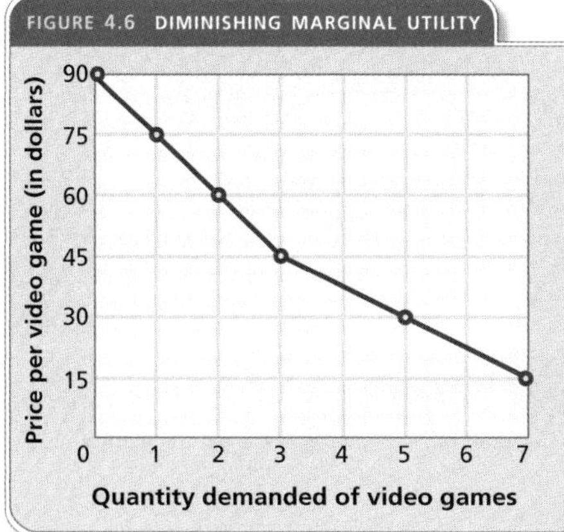

This graph displays the demand for video games by a high school senior named Kent.

The demand curve slopes downward because of the **law of diminishing marginal utility**, which states that the marginal benefit of using each additional unit of a product during a given period will decline. Because of that declining satisfaction, Kent will buy additional games only at lower prices.

ANALYZE GRAPHS

How many video games is Kent willing to buy at a price of $45? How does the law of diminishing marginal utility explain his refusal to buy more games at that price?

Why do consumers demand more goods and services at lower prices and fewer at higher prices? Economists have identified two patterns of behavior as causes: the income effect and the substitution effect.

The **income effect** is the term used for a change in the amount of a product that a consumer will buy because the purchasing power of his or her income changes—even though the income itself does not change. For example, you can buy more paperback books if they are priced at $7 than if they are priced at $15. If you buy a $7 book, you will feel $8 "richer" than if you buy a $15 book, so you are more likely to buy another book. The income effect also influences behavior when prices rise. You will feel $8 "poorer" if you buy a $15 book instead of a $7 one, so you will buy fewer books overall.

The **substitution effect** is the pattern of behavior that occurs when consumers react to a change in the price of a good or service by buying a substitute product—one whose price has not changed and that offers a better relative value. For example, if the price of paperback books climbs above $10, consumers might decide to buy fewer books and choose instead to buy $4 magazines.

QUICK REFERENCE

Income effect is the change in the amount that consumers will buy because the purchasing power of their income changes.

Substitution effect is a change in the amount that consumers will buy because they buy substitute goods instead.

APPLICATION Drawing Conclusions

A. Malik goes to the mall to buy a $40 pair of blue jeans and discovers that they are on sale for $25. If Malik buys two pairs, is this an example of the income effect or the substitution effect? Explain your answer.

income effect, because the lower price increased purchasing power of Malik's income

3 Teach

More About Demand Curves

Discuss

- Why might a restaurant owner offer soft drink refills for half the cost of the original drink? *(because consumers will generally only buy more of a certain item in a given period of time if the price decreases)*
- What do the income effect and the substitution effect have in common? *(They both explain why people tend to buy more goods and services at lower prices and fewer at higher prices.)*

Analyzing Graphs: Figure 4.6

Explain that any demand curve may be used to illustrate the law of diminishing marginal utility. Ask students why Kent's satisfaction with each video game he buys during a certain period declines. *(The first game satisfied many of his wants connected with video games, but subsequent games are not as exciting and interesting because his demand has already been partially met.)* What are the implications of this declining satisfaction? *(Kent will only buy more games at lower prices.)*

Answer

Three; Because his satisfaction decreases with each new video game he buys, he does not want to spend so much money to acquire more.

LEVELED ACTIVITY

Analyzing the Income and Substitution Effects

Time 20 minutes

Objective Students will demonstrate an understanding of the income and substitution effects.

Basic

Have each student write an example of the income or substitution effect on a sheet of paper. Invite volunteers to take turns sharing their examples, and ask the rest of the class to say "income" or "substitution" to indicate which effect the example shows. Ask volunteers to explain why each example is one or the other.

On Level

Divide the class into two groups and have each group write examples of the income or substitution effect on a sheet of paper. Invite volunteers from one group to take turns sharing their examples, and ask members of the other group to say "income" or "substitution" to indicate which effect the example shows. Ask a volunteer to explain why it is one or the other.

Challenge

Divide class into pairs and have each pair write several examples of the income or substitution effect on a sheet of paper. Each pair will take turns sharing their examples, and the other pairs will say "income" or "substitution" to indicate which effect the example shows. Each member of the pair should take turns explaining why it is one or the other.

Change in Quantity Demanded

Discuss

- How is change in quantity demanded related to the law of demand? *(The law of demand states that change in quantity demanded has an inverse relationship to price.)*
- How do points on a demand curve reflect change in quantity demanded? *(Each point on the demand curve reflects the quantity demanded at a particular price. Movement from one point to another shows the change.)*

Analyzing Graphs: Figure 4.7

Explain that when price is the only variable it is quantity demanded that changes, not demand. Restate the concept as change in the amount of a good or service that will be brought as price goes up or down. Direct students to look at the horizontal axis to remember that an increase in quantity demanded will move to the right and a decrease will move to the left along the demand curve.

Answers

1. *Quantity demanded changes from 2 to 4, so the change in quantity demanded is 2.*
2. *to the left*

Animated Economics This demand curve demonstrates changes in quantity demanded. It will help students understand that changes in quantity demanded are shown by movement to the right or to left *along* the curve.

Change in Quantity Demanded

QUICK REFERENCE

Change in quantity demanded is an increase or decrease in the amount demanded because of change in price.

KEY CONCEPTS

Remember that each demand curve represents a specific market situation in which price is the only variable. A change in the amount of a product that consumers will buy because of a change in price is called a **change in quantity demanded**. Each change in quantity demanded is shown by a new point on the demand curve. A change in quantity demanded does not shift the demand curve itself.

EXAMPLE Changes Along a Demand Curve

Let's look again at Cheryl's demand curve for DVDs (Figure 4.7 below). Note the quantities demanded at each price. Notice that as quantity demanded changes, the change is shown by the direction of the movement right or left along the demand curve.

FIGURE 4.7 CHANGE IN QUANTITY DEMANDED

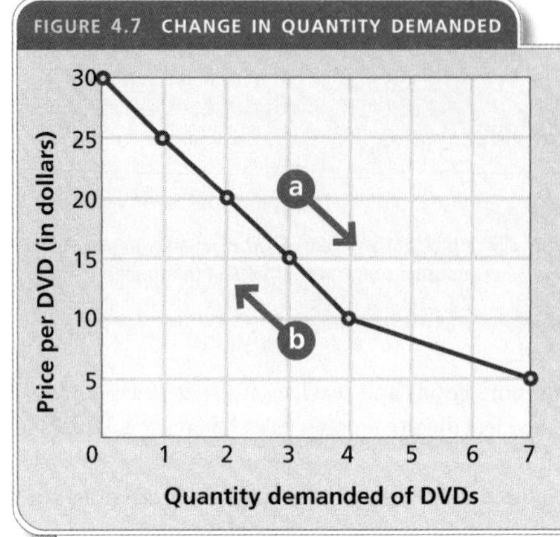

A **change in quantity demanded** doesn't shift the demand curve. The change refers to movement along the curve itself. Each point on the curve represents a new quantity demanded.

ⓐ As you move to the right along the curve, the quantity demanded increases.

ⓑ As you move to the left, the quantity demanded decreases.

ANALYZE GRAPHS

1. What is the change in quantity demanded when the price drops from $20 to $10?
2. What is the direction of the movement along the demand curve when the quantity decreases?

Animated Economics

Use an interactive demand curve to see changes in quantity demanded at **ClassZone.com**

Figure 4.7 shows change in quantity demanded for one person. A market demand curve provides similar information for an entire market. However, market demand curves have larger quantities demanded and larger changes to quantity demanded because they combine data from all individual demand curves in the market.

APPLICATION Applying Economic Concepts

B. Why do increases or decreases in quantity demanded not shift the position of the demand curve?
because change in quantity demanded refers to the movement from one point to another along a demand curve

108 Chapter 4

DIFFERENTIATING INSTRUCTION

Struggling Readers

Contrast Key Concepts

Have pairs of students create two-column charts in which they contrast Change in Quantity Demanded with Change in Demand. Suggest that they start their charts by restating the quick reference definition in their own words. Then have them list differences that they learn by reading the material and studying the graphs on pages 108 and 109.

Inclusion

Demonstrate Key Concepts

Set up six chairs in a line to approximate the shape of the original demand curve in Fig. 4.7. Tape a piece of paper to each one, stating the price and quantity demanded. Invite students to move from chair to chair to demonstrate changes in quantity demanded. Then change the quantity demanded at each price, and ask students to move the chairs to the right or left to form new curves that show changes in demand.

Change in Demand

KEY CONCEPTS

Consider what might happen if you lose your job. If you aren't earning money, you aren't likely to buy many CDs or movie tickets or magazines—no matter how low the price. Similarly, when national unemployment rises, people who are out of work are more likely to spend their limited funds on food and housing than on entertainment. Fewer people would be buying DVDs at every price, so market demand would drop.

This is an example of a **change in demand**, which occurs when a change in the marketplace such as high unemployment prompts consumers to buy different amounts of a good or service at every price. Change in demand is also called a shift in demand because it actually shifts the position of the demand curve.

QUICK REFERENCE

Change in demand occurs when something prompts consumers to buy different amounts at every price.

FIGURES 4.8 AND 4.9 CHANGE IN DEMAND

FIGURE 4.8 **DECREASE IN DEMAND**

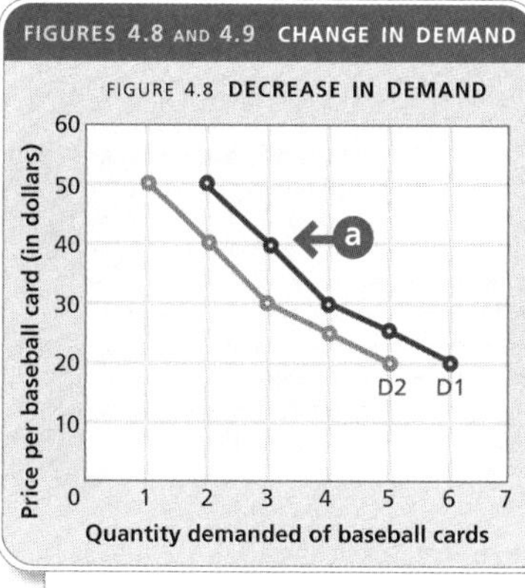

FIGURE 4.9 **INCREASE IN DEMAND**

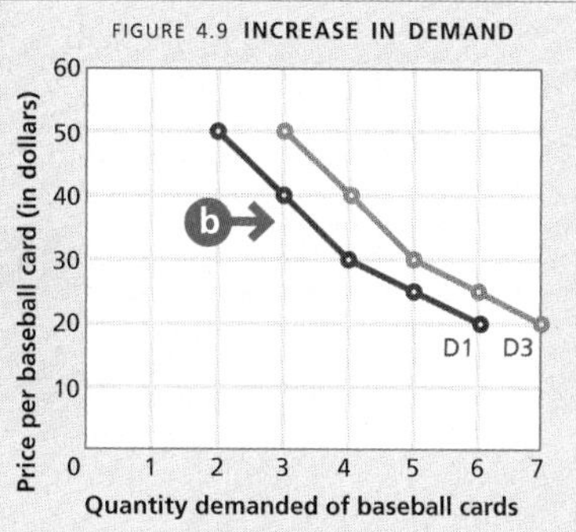

When a **change in demand** occurs, the demand curve shifts.

ⓐ As Figure 4.8 shows, a shift to the left (D2) indicates a decrease in demand.

ⓑ As Figure 4.9 shows, a shift to the right (D3) indicates an increase in demand.

ANALYZE GRAPHS

1. In Figure 4.8, how has demand for baseball cards changed at each of these prices: $20, $30, and $40?
2. In Figure 4.9, how has demand for baseball cards changed at each of these prices: $30, $40, and $50?

Animated Economics

Use an interactive version of shifting demand curves at **ClassZone.com**

Six factors can cause a change in demand: income, market size, consumer tastes, consumer expectations, substitute goods, and complementary goods. An explanation of each one follows.

FACTOR 1 Income

If a consumer's income changes, either higher or lower, that person's ability to buy goods and services also changes. For example, Tyler works at a garden center. He uses his earnings to buy baseball cards for his collection. In the fall, people garden less and buy fewer gardening products, so Tyler works fewer hours. His smaller paycheck means that he has less money to spend, so he demands fewer baseball cards at every price. Figure 4.8 shows this change. The entire demand curve shifts to the left.

Analyzing Graphs: Figures 4.8 and 4.9

Shifts in demand occur when something besides price affects consumers' willingness or ability to buy. Explain that a shift in demand means an increase in quantity demanded at every price and a decrease in demand means a decrease in quantity demanded at every price.

Answers

1. *–1 (from 6 to 5), –1 (4 to 3), –1 (3 to 2)*
2. *+1 (from 4 to 5), +1 (3 to 4), +1 (2 to 3)*

Animated Economics These graphs demonstrate changes in demand. They will help students understand that a decrease in demand shifts the curve to the left and an increase in demand shifts the curve to the right.

More About . . .

Advertising's Effect On Demand

Advertising is designed to change the tastes and preferences of consumers and, thus, cause a change in demand. Companies spend millions of dollars of their profits generating awareness for their products. By outspending their competitors in the various media, they hope to get the biggest market share of their product category.

Companies accomplish this by following a basic formula: the percentage change in demand divided by the percentage change in advertising expenditures measures how much changes in advertising expenditures affect consumer purchases.

INDIVIDUAL ACTIVITY

Illustrating Change in Income, Demand

Time 30 Minutes ◑

Task Illustrate examples of how change in income changes demand.

Materials Needed paper and markers, pens or colored pencils

Activity

- Encourage students to think about different times in their lives and what their income was then. Income might come from an allowance, gifts, or a job after school or during the summer. Ask them to think about how their income might change after high school.
- Have students illustrate how these changes in income affected their demand (specific income need not be shown). Remind them to think about how much money they had to spend and what they wanted to spend it on. Students may create posters, time lines, or other graphic organizers.
- Allow students to share their work with a partner and discuss how their demand was affected by their changes in income as well as other factors, such as age or interests.

Rubric

	Understanding Concepts	Presentation of Information
4	excellent	clear and complete
3	good	mostly clear
2	fair	sometimes clear
1	poor	sketchy

Your Economic Choices

NORMAL GOODS AND INFERIOR GOODS

If your income rises, which car will you choose?

- Two to three times as many used cars are sold each year compared with new cars. What can you infer from this statistic? *(Most people cannot afford new cars and believe used cars are a better value.)*
- What are some of the pros and cons of buying a new car vs. buying a used car? *(New cars cost more but come with warranties so buyers are not likely to have to pay for repairs for a long time. Used cars cost less, but there is a greater risk that a used car will require repairs sooner.)*

Activity Have students work in pairs or small groups to research articles about the benefits of buying a new car or a used car. Articles are available on the Internet or in the library. Invite volunteers to share the results of their research. Take an informal poll to see how many students would choose a new car and how many would choose a used car.

Technomics

Tracking Population Shifts
Most of the information about changing market size in the United States is based on the U.S. Census. A complete census is taken every ten years, and an economic census that tracks American business is published every five years. Census data is available free on the Internet at www.census.gov.

Many organizations analyze the data to create reports that are aimed at marketers in publications such as *Advertising Age's American Demographics* or in customized reports that are produced for specific industries. Marketers track such information to determine their market share and decide where to locate new stores or introduce new products.

Suppose, however, that Tyler is promoted to supervisor and receives a raise of $2 an hour. Now he has more money to spend, so his demand for baseball cards increases and his demand curve shifts to the right—as shown in Figure 4.9 on page 109.

QUICK REFERENCE

Normal goods are goods that consumers demand more of when their incomes rise.

Inferior goods are goods that consumers demand less of when their incomes rise.

As you might guess, changes in income also affect market demand curves. When the incomes of most consumers in a market rise or fall, the total demand in that market also usually rises or falls. The market demand curve then shifts to the right or to the left.

Increased income usually increases demand, but in some cases, it causes demand to fall. **Normal goods** are goods that consumers demand more of when their incomes rise. **Inferior goods** are goods that consumers demand less of when their incomes rise. Before his raise, Tyler shopped at discount stores for jeans and T-shirts. Now that he earns more, Tyler can afford to spend more on his wardrobe. As a result, he demands less discounted clothing and buys more name-brand jeans and tees. Discounted clothing is considered an inferior good. Other products that might be considered inferior goods are used books and generic food products.

YOUR ECONOMIC CHOICES

NORMAL GOODS AND INFERIOR GOODS

If your income rises, which car will you choose?

Most people prefer to buy a new car if they can afford it. Used cars are an example of inferior goods—demand for them drops when incomes rise because people prefer new-car quality to getting a bargain.

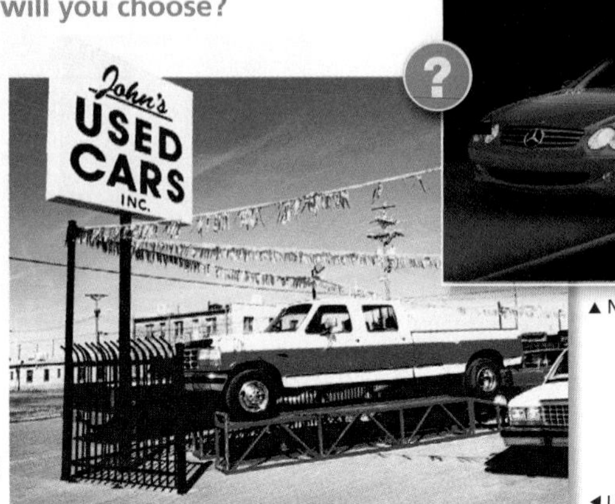

▲ New car

◀ Used truck

FACTOR 2 Market Size

If the number of consumers increases or decreases, the market size also changes. Such a change usually has a corresponding effect on demand. Suppose that the town of Montclair is on the ocean. Each summer, thousands of tourists rent beachfront cottages there. As a result, the size of the population and the market grows. So what do you think happens to the market demand curve for pizza in Montclair in the summer? Check the two graphs at the top of the next page.

Population shifts have often changed the size of markets. For example, in the last 30 years, the Northeast region of the United States lost population as many people moved to the South or the West. The causes of the population shift included the search for a better climate, high-tech jobs, or a less congested area.

DIFFERENTIATING INSTRUCTION

English Learners

Understand Multiple-Meaning Words
Explain that in economics *inferior goods* are those that people buy more of when their incomes are lower. One meaning of *inferior* is lower. Inferior goods have a lower price but are not necessarily of lower quality. Items such as store-brand medications and food are often just as good as name-brand items. *Normal goods* are those that people buy more of when their incomes are higher. A synonym might be *standard.*

Gifted and Talented

Analyze Population Shifts
Have students analyze population changes in their state or region by comparing U.S. Census data from 1990 and 2000. Remind students that this information may be found at www.census.gov. Encourage them to track changes in the size of subgroups based on age, gender, or ethnicity. Ask them to infer how these population changes might affect demand for various kinds of goods. Allow students to present their findings in oral reports to the class.

FIGURES 4.10 AND 4.11 IMPACT OF CHANGES IN MARKET SIZE

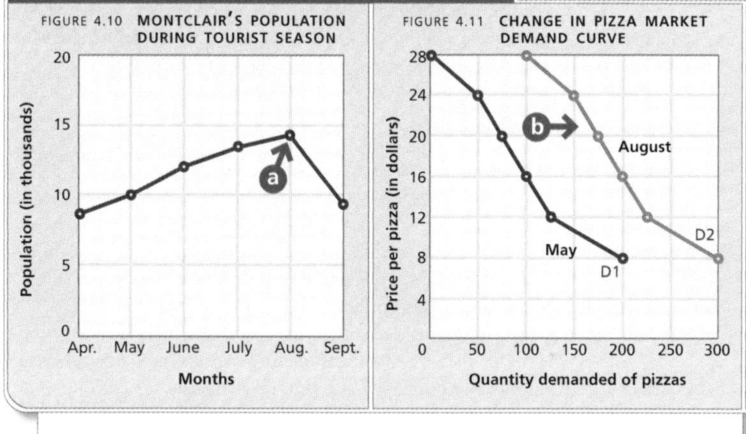

FIGURE 4.10 **MONTCLAIR'S POPULATION DURING TOURIST SEASON**

FIGURE 4.11 **CHANGE IN PIZZA MARKET DEMAND CURVE**

When a change in market size occurs, it often causes a change in demand.

ⓐ Figure 4.10 shows how the population of Montclair changed during the last tourist season. Notice which month had the highest population.

ⓑ Notice that the market demand curve (D2) shifts to the right between May and August.

ANALYZE GRAPHS

1. During what month was the population of Montclair at its highest? What happened to the demand for pizzas during that month? Explain.
2. What would you expect to happen to the market demand curve in September? Explain.

One economic result of the migration is that the overall market size of the Northeast has shrunk, while the market size of the South and the West has grown. This change in market size has altered the demand for many products, from essentials such as homes, clothing, and food to nonessentials such as movie tickets. Demand for most items will grow in booming regions and decrease in regions that are shrinking.

FACTOR 3 Consumer Tastes

Because of changing consumer tastes, today's hot trends often become tomorrow's castoffs. When a good or service enjoys high popularity, consumers demand more of it at every price. When a product loses popularity, consumers demand less of it.

Advertising has a strong influence on consumer tastes. Sellers advertise to create demand for the product. For example, some people stop wearing perfectly good pants that still fit because advertising convinces them that the style is no longer popular and that a new style is better.

Think about your own closet. Doesn't it contain some item of clothing that you just had to have a year ago, but would never pay money for now? You've just identified an instance of consumer taste changing demand. Consumer tastes also affect demand for other products besides clothing. When was the last time you saw someone buying a telephone that had to be attached to the wall by a cord?

Economics Update

Find an update on changing consumer tastes at **ClassZone.com**

FACTOR 4 Consumer Expectations

Your expectations for the future can affect your buying habits today. If you think the price of a good or service will change, that expectation can determine whether you buy it now or wait until later.

Analyzing Graphs: Figures 4.10 and 4.11

Explain that the two graphs show how a change in seasonal market size affects demand for pizzas. The two graphs track completely different data; combining the information from both graphs allows you to draw conclusions about how change in market size affects demand. Ask students to describe what each of the graphs tracks and how they are related. *(Fig. 4.10 tracks population growth during the tourist season; Fig. 4.11 shows that with this increased population there is increased demand for pizza.)*

Answers

1. *August; It increased because more people demanded more pizza at every price.*
2. *It will move to about where the curve was in May, because the population in September is about the same as in May.*

Economics Update

At **ClassZone.com,** students will see updated information on changing consumer tastes.

SMALL GROUP ACTIVITY

Analyzing How Advertising Influences Consumer Tastes

Time 30 minutes ◑

Task Create a chart and discuss personal experiences with advertising.

Materials Needed poster board and markers, pens or pencils

Activity

- Group students and direct them to recall advertising messages that they have seen or heard in the previous day or week.
- Encourage groups to make a chart about the ads, listing the product, the medium (e.g., radio, television, billboard, newspaper, magazine, the Internet, or the mail), and the way the ad sought to create demand. Ask students to discuss which ads were most effective and why.
- Allow each group to present its chart to the class and share any conclusions about the role of advertising in influencing consumer taste.

Rubric

	Understanding of Concepts	Presentation of Information
4	excellent	clear and complete
3	good	mostly clear
2	fair	sometimes clear
1	poor	sketchy

More About . . .

Substitutes—Alternative Fuels
In the short term, it is difficult for consumers to find a substitute for gasoline when driving their cars. However, a variety of alternative fuels are being developed for certain kinds of newer vehicles. Some alternative fuels include biodiesel, made from soybean oil and cooking grease; ethanol, made from corn; and various forms of natural gas and propane.

Hybrid electric vehicles (see Case Study, page 125) are powered by a combination of gasoline and a rechargeable electric battery. Rising prices of oil and natural gas are also increasing demand for renewable energy sources to generate electricity, including solar and wind power.

Your Economic Choices

SUBSTITUTE SERVICES

How would you decide whether to take a cab or a bus?

- Most people who ride public transportation use it for commuting to work or school. Why? *(Schedules and routes are probably geared to commuters, so it is most convenient for these purposes.)*
- Why does it make more sense for a group of people to use a taxicab than for a single person? *(Cab fares are based on distance; there is not an individual fare for each passenger. So, a number of people can share the cost.)*

Activity Invite students to share their experiences using these forms of transportation, describing the pros and cons of each. Encourage students to study a local transit system map and schedule and to discuss what places they could easily reach with public transportation.

Let's look at one example of how consumer expectations shape demand. Automobiles usually go on sale at the end of summer because dealers want to get rid of this year's models before the new models arrive. Would you expect demand for new cars to be higher in May, before the sales, or in August, during the sales? It is higher in August because consumers expect the sales and often choose to wait for them.

FACTOR 5 Substitute Goods

QUICK REFERENCE

Substitutes are goods and services that can be used in place of each other.

Goods and services that can be used in place of other goods and services to satisfy consumer wants are called **substitutes.** Because the products are interchangeable, if the price of a substitute drops, people will choose to buy it instead of the original item. Demand for the substitute will increase while demand for the original item decreases. People may also turn to substitutes if the price for the original item becomes too high. Again, demand for the substitute rises while demand for the original item drops.

Substitutes can be used in place of each other. For example, when gasoline prices are high, some people decide to commute to school by bus or train. When gasoline prices are low, a higher number of people choose to drive instead of to take public transportation. As you can see from that example, when the price of one good rises, demand for it will drop while demand for its substitute will rise.

YOUR ECONOMIC CHOICES

SUBSTITUTE SERVICES

How would you decide whether to take a cab or a bus?

Taxis have certain advantages; they will take you to a specific place at a specific time. But if taxi fares rise, you might give up the convenience and go by bus instead.

Taxi

City bus

FACTOR 6 Complementary Goods

QUICK REFERENCE

Complements are goods that are used together, so a rise in demand for one increases the demand for the other.

When the use of one product increases the use of another product, the two products are called **complements.** An increase in the demand for one will cause an increase in the demand for the other. Likewise, a decrease in demand for one will cause a decrease in demand for the other.

In contrast to substitutes, complements are goods or services that work in tandem with each other. An increase in demand for one will cause an increase in demand for the other. One example is CDs and CD players. Consumers who bought CD players

DIFFERENTIATING INSTRUCTION

Struggling Readers

Use Jigsaw Reading
Divide students into home groups of six and assign each student in a group a number that corresponds to one of the factors that cause a change in demand. Have the students regroup, with all those studying a particular factor grouped together. Tell students that they should read and discuss the information about their assigned factor, so that they can return to their home groups and share what they have learned.

Inclusion

Use a Visual
Explain that Figure 4.12 summarizes the information on the six factors that affect demand. Pair students who have difficulty reading with a more proficient reader. Have the more proficient reader read aloud the full text material that applies to each factor. Have the less proficient reader point to the part of the diagram that applies to that factor and explain how the visual illustrates the factor.

ECONOMICS ESSENTIALS

FIGURE 4.12 Factors That Cause a Change in Demand

Income Increased income means consumers can buy more. Decreased income means consumers can buy less.

Complements When the use of one product increases the use of another product, the two are called complements.

Market Size A growing market usually increases demand. A shrinking market usually decreases demand.

What Causes a Change in Demand?

Substitutes Substitutes are goods and services that can be used instead of other goods and services, causing a change in demand.

Consumer Tastes The popularity of a good or service has a strong effect on the demand for it, and in today's marketplace, popularity can change quickly.

Consumer Expectations What you expect prices to do in the future can influence your buying habits today.

ANALYZE CHARTS

Choose a product used by most consumers, and create a hypothetical demand curve showing demand for that product in a town of 1,000 people. Label it A. On the same graph, add a demand curve showing demand if the population drops to 700. Label it B. Which factor on the chart does the shift in the demand curve represent?

also demanded CDs to play on them. And, as CDs became more popular, demand for CD players grew until they began to appear in places they had never been before, such as in the family minivan.

Therefore, with complements, if the price of one product changes, demand for both products will change in exactly the same way. If the price for one product rises, demand for both will drop. Conversely, if the price for one product drops, demand for both will rise.

APPLICATION Categorizing Information

C. Choose one of the following products: soda, hamburgers, pencils, or tennis rackets. On your own paper, list as many substitutes and complements for the product as you can. Compare your lists with those of a classmate.

Answers will vary. Sample Answer: soda: substitutes—juice, water, sports drinks, milk, lemonade; complements—potato chips, pretzels, tortilla chips

Economic Essentials: Figure 4.12

Encourage students to visualize the infographic to help them remember the six factors and how each one affects demand.

- How does an advertisement that shows people dunking a certain brand of cookies in milk reflect two of the factors? *(It is trying to influence consumer taste and also shows the complements of cookies and milk.)*
- Seasonal clothing, such as bathing suits or winter coats, often goes on sale at the end of the season. How might consumers take advantage of this knowledge? What other factor might cause some consumers to buy at the higher price at the beginning of a season? *(Possible answers: Consumers could buy clothing at the end of the season to use the following year. Consumers might prefer to have the current season fashion rather than get the lower price.)*

Analyze

Change in market size causes a decrease in demand. (The graph should resemble Figure 4.8, with the curve on the left labeled B and the curve on the right labeled A.)

LEVELED ACTIVITY

Understanding Factors Affecting Market Demand

Time 30 minutes

Objective Students will demonstrate an understanding of the factors that affect market demand for designer jeans.

Basic

Assign groups of students two of the factors to consider. Make sure all six factors are assigned. Groups will brainstorm scenarios that show how their assigned factors affect the demand for designer jeans. Groups will share their ideas in a visual form such as a poster, cartoon, or diagram.

On Level

Assign groups of students three of the factors to consider. Make sure all six factors are assigned. Groups will brainstorm scenarios that show how their assigned factors affect the demand for designer jeans. Groups will share their ideas in oral presentations.

Challenge

Students will work individually or in groups to develop scenarios that show how each of the six factors affect the demand for designer jeans. Students will share their ideas in a report written as a jeans marketer. The report should include ideas for how the marketer will try to deal with each of the scenarios.

Analyzing Political Cartoons

1 Plan & Prepare

Objectives

- Analyze the techniques used in political cartoons.
- Interpret the meaning of a political cartoon about demand.

2 Focus & Motivate

Explain that students need to put together information from words and visuals to understand the point that a cartoonist is trying to make. Have students consider these questions as they study the cartoon.

3 Teach

Encourage students to look at the cartoon as a whole to get an idea of its subject matter before they read the boxes, describing the techniques used. Explain that stereotypes are based on common beliefs that are not fully accurate. Cartoonists use them because they communicate ideas simply and quickly.

For additional practice see **Skillbuilder Handbook**, page R26.

THINKING ECONOMICALLY
Answers

1. *that the driver thinks gas prices are too high; it might also mean that the driver, after seeing the high gas prices, thinks that his car is "too high," or too big*
2. *automobiles and gasoline; they are complementary because they are used together*
3. *Possible Answer: This cartoon relates to demand because increased demand for large cars increases demand for gasoline. Similarly, a fall in demand for gasoline because of rising prices will be accompanied by a fall in demand for large cars.*

ECONOMICS SKILLBUILDER

For more on analyzing political cartoons, see the Skillbuilder Handbook, page R26.

Analyzing Political Cartoons

Political cartoons often deal with economic themes. Because of this, you will find that the skill of interpreting political cartoons helps you to understand the economic issues on people's minds.

TECHNIQUES USED IN POLITICAL CARTOONS Political cartoonists use many techniques to deliver their message. The techniques used in this cartoon include:

Exaggeration The cartoonist has shown the automobile as towering over humans to make the point that some Americans drive big cars that are gas-guzzlers.

Source: © *The Economist*

Labels Cartoonists use written words to identify people, groups, or events. Notice the sign on the gas pump referring to OPEC (Organization of Petroleum Exporting Countries) and the license plate on the car.

Stereotyping Here a stereotype image of a man in Arab robes stands for OPEC, even though not all OPEC countries are in the Middle East.

Other techniques that political cartoonists use include **caricature**, or creating a portrait that distorts a person's features; **symbolism**, using an object or idea to stand for something else; and **satire**, attacking error or foolishness by ridiculing it.

THINKING ECONOMICALLY Analyzing

1. What does the phrase "Too high!!" mean?
2. What complementary goods are shown in this cartoon? Why are they complementary?
3. How does this cartoon relate to demand? Consider the effect of rising prices, especially rising prices for complementary goods.

DIFFERENTIATING INSTRUCTION

English Learners

Build Vocabulary

Encourage students to use visual clues in the cartoon to understand the words *towering* and *gas-guzzlers* in the annotation on Exaggeration. If they are unfamiliar with the word *tower* explain that it is a tall structure and ask how it relates to the car. Explain that the verb *guzzle* is usually used to refer to someone who drinks a lot quickly. What does it mean in relation to the car?

Gifted and Talented

Create a Cartoon

Point out to students that rising gasoline prices have made hybrid cars more attractive to many consumers. Suggest that students read Document C on page 125 of this chapter's Case Study. Then ask them to create a cartoon that illustrates the connection between rising gas prices and the growth of demand for hybrids. Encourage them to use the techniques discussed in this Skillbuilder—exaggeration, labeling, and stereotyping. Call on volunteers to display and discuss their completed cartoons.

SECTION 2 Assessment

REVIEWING KEY CONCEPTS

1. Explain the differences between the terms in each of the pairs below:
   a. *change in quantity demanded* *change in demand*
   b. *income effect* *substitution effect*
   c. *normal goods* *inferior goods*
   d. *substitutes* *complements*
2. What feature of demand curves is explained by the law of diminishing marginal utility?
3. How does the income effect influence consumer behavior when prices rise?
4. Why might an increase in income result in a decrease in demand?
5. What else besides migration might account for a change in market size?
6. **Using Your Notes** Why does a change in market size affect demand? Refer to your completed chart.

   Use the Graphic Organizer at **Interactive Review @ ClassZone.com**

Factor That Changes Demand	Reason Why Demand Changes

CRITICAL THINKING

7. **Analyzing Causes** A new version of the computer game Big-Hit Football just came out. Malik buys it now because it has improvements over the current version, which he is bored with. Cheryl decides to wait to see if the price drops. Which of the factors shown in the chart on page 113 affected their decisions?
8. **Applying Economic Concepts** The U.S. government has used many strategies to reduce smoking. It banned television ads for cigarettes, ran public service messages about the health risks of smoking, and imposed taxes on cigarettes. Which factors that affect demand was the government trying to influence?
9. **Analyzing Effects** Take out the market demand curve for athletic shoes that you created on page 105. Add a new curve showing how demand would be changed if the most popular basketball player in the NBA endorses a brand of shoes that your store does not sell. Share your graph with a classmate and explain your reasoning.
10. **Challenge** Do you think changes in consumer taste are most often initiated by the consumers themselves or by manufacturers and advertisers? Explain your answer, using real-life examples.

ECONOMICS IN PRACTICE

Explaining Changes in Demand Think about different types of bicycles: road bikes, mountain bikes, hybrid bikes. What factors affect demand for bicycles?

Identify Factors Affecting Demand The table below lists examples of a change in demand in the market for bicycles. For each example, identify which factor that affects demand is involved.

Example of Change in Demand	Factor That Affected Demand
Electric scooter sales rise, and bike sales fall.	
The cost of aluminum alloy bike frames is about to rise; consum–ers buy bikes now.	
Using a folding bicycle becomes a fad among commuters. Sales of this type of bike boom.	
The U.S. birth rate declined for 10 years in a row, eventually causing a drop in sales of children's bikes.	

Challenge Identify the two factors affecting demand that do not appear on this table. Provide examples of how these factors might affect demand for bicycles.

CHAPTER 4 • SECTION 3

1 Plan & Prepa…

Section 3 obj…

• define e…

• ide…

• …

Test…

• Sec…

Reteach Invite volunteers to name the six factors that affect demand and to give examples of each one. Encourage all students to take notes as the information is reviewed.

Unit 2 Resource Book
- Reteaching Activity, p. 20

Economics in Practice

Identify Factors Affecting Demand *Row 1: substitute; Row 2: consumer expectations; Row 3: consumer taste; Row 4: market size*

Challenge *complements: more people buy bicycles, so they also buy bicycle helmets because they want to ride safely; income: a factory closes down, leading to decreased income and fewer bicycles sold.*

SECTION 2 ASSESSMENT ANSWERS

Reviewing Key Concepts

1. a. *change in quantity demanded*, p. 108; *change in demand*, p. 109
   b. *income effect*, p. 107; *substitution effect*, p. 107
   c. *normal goods*, p. 110; *inferior goods*, p. 110
   d. *substitute*, p. 112; *complement*, p. 112
2. the downward slope
3. Consumers tend to buy fewer of the good or service whose price has risen.
4. Generally, a rise in income leads to a fall in demand for inferior goods.
5. change in birth rate or death rate
6. See page 106 for an example of a completed chart. It increases or decreases the number of consumers who will be willing and able to buy a good or service.

Critical Thinking

7. Malik—consumer taste; Cheryl—consumer expectations
8. The government was trying to influence consumer taste and consumer expectations (higher taxes will mean higher prices in the future).
9. The demand curve would shift to the left because consumer taste had changed.
10. Accept all reasonable answers that are supported with appropriate evidence. Students who believe that consumers play the biggest role may say that producers are simply giving people what they want; students who say that manufacturers and advertisers play the biggest role may say that advertising is the primary force in changing consumer taste.

Economics in Practice

See answers in side column above.

...re

...ectives

- ...sticity of demand
- ...ntify the difference between elastic and inelastic demand
- define unit elastic
- determine how total revenue is used to identify elasticity

2 Focus & Motivate

Connecting to Everyday Life Explain that this section focuses on how consumer demand for certain products responds to changes in price. Ask students to give examples of things that they buy regularly and say how important a price increase would be in deciding whether they would still buy the product.

Taking Notes Remind students to take notes as they read by completing the cluster diagram. They can use the Graphic Organizer at **Interactive Review @ ClassZone.com**. A sample is shown below.

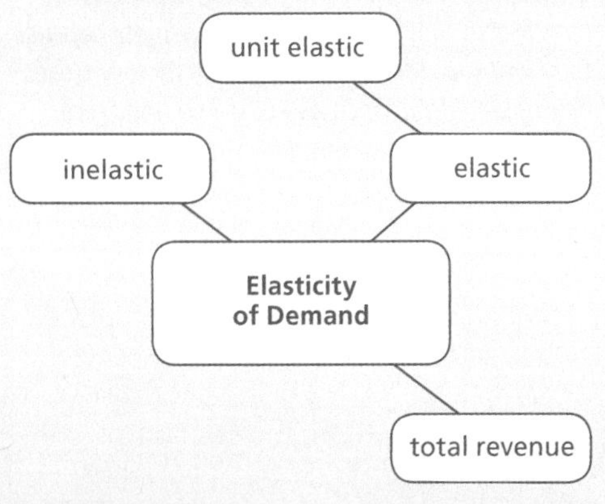

SECTION 3

What Is Elasticity of Demand?

OBJECTIVES

In Section 3, you will
- define *elasticity of demand*
- identify the difference between elastic and inelastic demand
- define *unit elastic*
- determine how total revenue is used to identify elasticity

KEY TERMS

elasticity of demand, *p. 117*
elastic, *p. 117*
inelastic, *p. 117*
unit elastic, *p. 118*
total revenue, *p. 122*
total revenue test, *p. 122*

TAKING NOTES

As you read Section 3, complete a cluster diagram using the key concepts and other terms. Use the Graphic Organizer at **Interactive Review @ ClassZone.com**

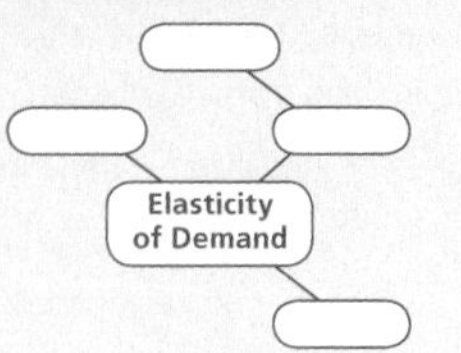

Elasticity of Demand

KEY CONCEPTS

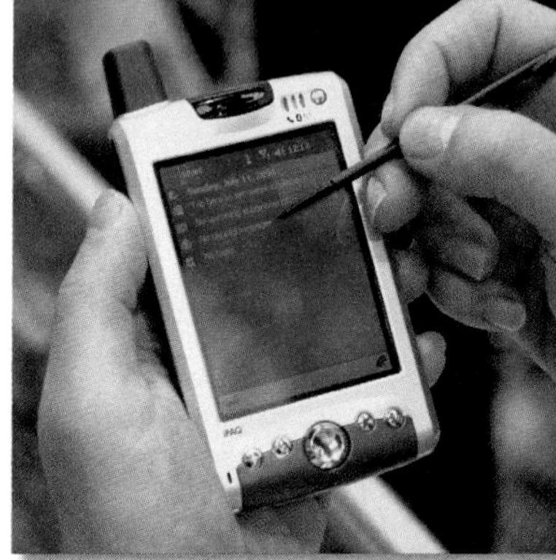

You have learned that there are many factors that influence the demand for a product. However, those factors alone are not the only influences on the sales of goods and services. How does the owner of an electronics store know how to price his or her goods so that the entire inventory of PDAs, or personal digital assistants, are sold?

Store owners know that consumers are responsive to changes in price. Let's examine the relationship between price and demand, and how it affects consumers' buying habits.

Consumer demand is not limitless. It is highly dependent on price. But as you know, demand is seldom fixed. As a result, price is also seldom fixed. Generally, people assume that if prices rise consumers will buy less, and if prices drop consumers will buy more. However, this isn't always the case. The relationship between price and demand is somewhat more complicated than you might think. Change in consumer buying habits is also related to the type of good or service being produced and how important the good or service is to the consumer. The marketplace certainly is very sensitive to changes in price—but not all increases in price will result in a decrease in demand.

SECTION 3 PROGRAM RESOURCES

ON LEVEL

Lesson Plans
- Core, p. 14

Unit 2 Resource Book
- Reading Study Guide, pp. 21–22
- Math Skills Worksheet, p. 39
- Section 3 Quiz, p. 29

STRUGGLING READERS

Unit 2 Resource Book
- Reading Study Guide with Additional Support, pp. 23–25
- Reteaching Activity, p. 30

ENGLISH LEARNERS

Unit 2 Resource Book
- Reading Study Guide with Additional Support (Spanish), pp. 26–28

INCLUSION

Lesson Plans
- Modified for Inclusion, p. 14

GIFTED AND TALENTED

Unit 2 Resource Book
- Case Study Resources: Ford Motors' Bold New Move, p. 35; General Motors Misjudged Consumer Tastes, p. 36

NCEE Student Activities
- Movements and Shifts in Demand Curves; Consumer Surplus; Demand Elasticity, pp. 13–16

TECHNOLOGY

eEdition DVD-ROM

eEdition Online

Power Presentation DVD-ROM

Economics Concepts Transparencies
- CT14 Estimating Elasticity

Daily Test Practice Transparencies, TT14

ClassZone.com

Economists use the term **elasticity of demand** to describe how responsive consumers are to price changes in the marketplace. Economists describe demand as being either elastic or inelastic. Demand is **elastic** when a change in price, either up or down, leads to a relatively larger change in the quantity demanded. The more responsive to change the market is, the more likely the demand is elastic. On the other hand, demand is **inelastic** when a change in price leads to a relatively smaller change in the quantity demanded. For this reason, elastic goods and services are often said to be price sensitive. So, in the case of inelastic demand, changes in price have little impact on the quantity demanded.

Another way to think about elasticity is to imagine that a rubber band represents quantity demanded. When the quantity demanded increases by a marked amount, the demand is elastic and the rubber band stretches. If the quantity demanded barely changes, demand is inelastic and the rubber band stretches very little.

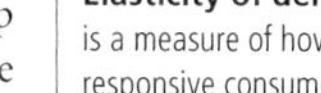

QUICK REFERENCE

Elasticity of demand is a measure of how responsive consumers are to price changes.

Demand is **elastic** if quantity demanded changes significantly as price changes.

Demand is **inelastic** if quantity demanded changes little as price changes.

EXAMPLE Elasticity of Demand for Goods and Services

Let's look at an example of elastic demand. Suppose that a certain brand of PDAs goes on sale. If the price of that brand goes down 20 percent, and the quantity demanded goes up 30 percent, then demand is elastic. The percentage change in quantity demanded is greater than the percentage change in price. Goods that have a large number of substitutes fall into the elastic category, since if the prices change, consumers can choose other products.

Now think about a completely different type of good—the medicine insulin. Many diabetics require daily insulin injections to regulate their blood sugar levels. Even if the price of insulin were to rise sharply, diabetics would still need the same amount of insulin as they did before. If the price were to drop, they would not need any more insulin than their required dosage. As a result, the demand for insulin is inelastic because the quantity demanded remains relatively constant.

YOUR ECONOMIC CHOICES

NECESSITY OR CHOICE

Which of these services could you give up?

Most people consider getting a cavity filled to be a necessity. Having your teeth whitened is a service that can be postponed or eliminated without harm. As a result, the demand for whitening is more elastic than the demand for fillings.

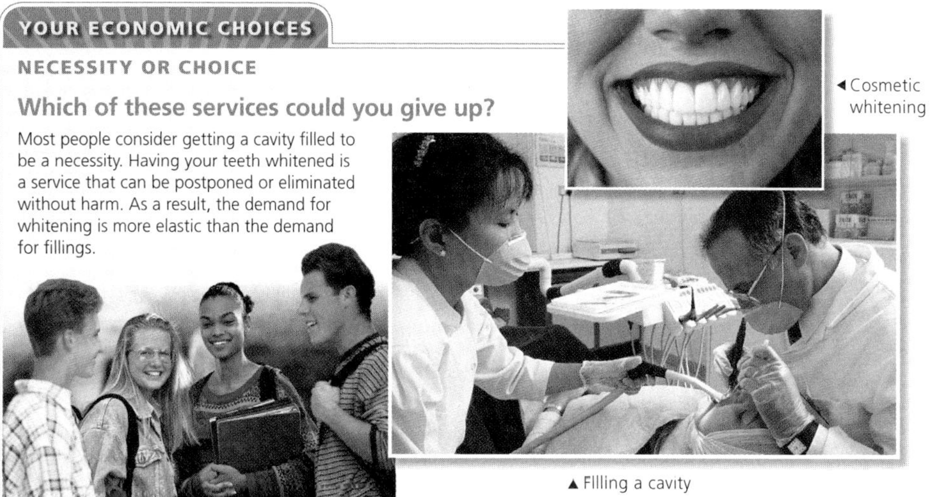

◄ Cosmetic whitening

▲ Filling a cavity

3 Teach

Elasticity of Demand

Discuss

- How is consumer choice related to elasticity of demand? *(When consumers have many choices for a particular type of product, demand will be elastic. When there are few choices, demand will be inelastic.)*
- Why is the demand for aspirin elastic while the demand for insulin is inelastic? *(There are many different brands of aspirin, and there are also other pain relievers available as substitutes. There is no good substitute available for insulin, and many diabetics depend on it to stay alive.)*

Your Economic Choices

NECESSITY OR CHOICE

Which of these services could you give up?

- Why do most people consider it a necessity to get a cavity filled? (*because not taking care of the cavity can lead to greater problems in the future, such as needing to have a tooth pulled)*
- What are some substitutes for cosmetic whitening by a dentist? *(Students may mention toothpastes that claim to whiten teeth and whitening strips and other similar products sold in stores.)*

Activity Have students work in pairs or small groups to research prices that various dentists charge for these two services (either online or through checking local dentists) and present their findings in brief oral reports.

CLASS ACTIVITY

Demonstrating Elastic and Inelastic Demand

Time 20 minutes

Objective Demonstrate an understanding of elastic and inelastic demand.

Materials Needed materials with varying degrees of elasticity, such as rubber bands, balloons, elastic bandages, bungee cords, foam balls, and stretch toys

Activity

- Work with the class to brainstorm examples of items with various amounts of stretch and record ideas on the board.
- Place the items in a large box. Group students and direct each group to select an item from the box without looking.
- Invite group members to discuss how they can use the item to demonstrate the concepts of elastic and inelastic demand.
- Allow each group to present its demonstration to the class, with an explanation of how price and quantity demanded are related and an example of a good or service that fits their example.

Rubric

	Understanding Concepts	Presentation of Information
4	excellent	clear and complete
3	good	mostly clear
2	fair	sometimes clear
1	poor	sketchy

Analyzing Graphs: Figures 4.13 and 4.14

Invite students to imagine walking up the slopes shown by the curves to understand that the inelastic curve is steeper (and would be harder to climb). They might use this analogy to remember that it is harder to increase demand for something like fillings by lowering the price. Ask students why the demand curves that they have seen earlier in the chapter looked more like Fig. 4.13 than Fig. 4.14. *(because they were for products with elastic demand such as DVDs, pizza, and baseball cards)*

Answers

1. *Quantity demanded increases from 2000 to 6000.*
2. *There are about 15 more fillings at the lowest price (an increase from about 20 to about 35).*

Animated Economics These graphs show demand curves for products that have elastic and inelastic demand. They will help students understand how quantity demanded varies with price based on elasticity of demand.

More About . . .

Unit Elasticity

Economists use the term unit elastic to describe the point on a straight line demand curve between elastic and inelastic demand—in other words, where a percentage change in price results in exactly the same percentage change in quantity demanded. At that point the ratio is 1 to 1, or unity. Another good way to look at it is to note that if demand were unit elastic, total revenue (which is discussed on page 122) would not change if price was increased or decreased.

Over time the elasticity of demand for a particular product may change. If more substitutes for a product become available, the demand may become more elastic. For example, the cost of cell phones and their service has become more elastic as more providers enter the market. On the other hand, in the case of prescription drugs, if a product is withdrawn from the market and there are fewer choices for the consumer, the demand may become inelastic.

The data for elastic demand and the data for inelastic demand produce demand curves that look very different from each other. Compare Figure 4.13 and Figure 4.14 below. Notice that the inelastic demand curve has a steeper slope than the elastic demand curve does. The reason for this difference is that the changes along the vertical axis (the price) are proportionally greater than the changes along the horizontal axis (the quantity demanded).

FIGURE 4.13 ELASTIC DEMAND CURVE

FIGURE 4.14 INELASTIC DEMAND CURVE

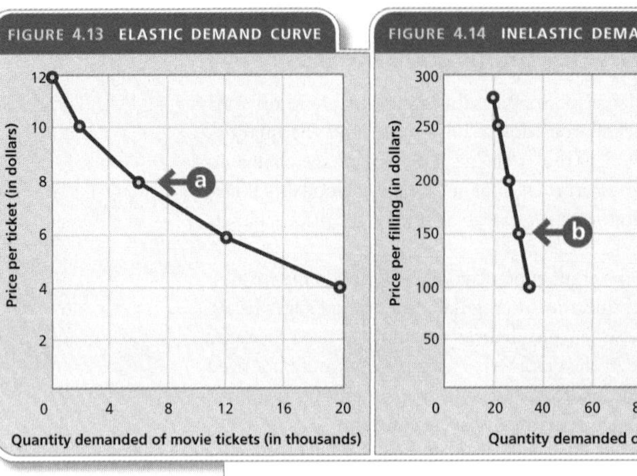

ⓐ In Figure 4.13, elastic demand curves have gradual slopes. They are more horizontal than vertical because of the greater changes in quantity demanded.

ⓑ In Figure 4.14, inelastic demand curves have steep slopes. They are more vertical than horizontal because quantity demanded changes very little.

ANALYZE GRAPHS

1. In Figure 4.13, what happens to the quantity demanded when price drops from $10 to $8?
2. In Figure 4.14, what is the difference in quantity demanded between the most expensive and least expensive filling?

Animated Economics

Use elastic and inelastic demand curves at **ClassZone.com**

QUICK REFERENCE

Demand is **unit elastic** when the percentage change in price and quantity demanded are the same.

Demand is said to be **unit elastic** when the percentage change in price and quantity demanded are the same. In other words, a 10 percent increase in price would cause exactly a 10 percent drop in quantity demanded, while the reverse would be true.

No good or service is ever really unit elastic. Instead, unit elasticity is simply the dividing point between elastic and inelastic demand. It is a useful concept for figuring out whether demand is elastic or inelastic.

APPLICATION Drawing Conclusions

A. Decide how elastic demand is for the following item. Explain your reasoning.

When a grocery store sells soup at $1.09 per can, it sells 1,500 cans per week. When it dropped the price to $0.75, it sold an additional 1,000 cans.

elastic, because price decreased by 31 percent while quantity demanded increased by 67 percent

DIFFERENTIATING INSTRUCTION

Struggling Readers

Make a Chart

Have students keep track of examples of goods and services that have elastic demand and those that have inelastic demand by entering them in a chart while they read. In the third column of the chart, direct students to note the reason why the demand is elastic or inelastic. Allow students to compare their charts with a partner and to discuss conclusions about what kinds of goods tend to have elastic or inelastic demand.

English Learners

Create Word Search Puzzles

Divide students into groups of three, and direct each group to create a Word Search puzzle for these terms: *elastic, inelastic,* or *unit elastic.* As an aid to writing clues for the puzzle, remind students that the prefix *in* means "not," while the word *unit* means "one." Have groups exchange and complete the Word Search puzzles.

What Determines Elasticity?

KEY CONCEPTS

Just as there are factors that cause a change in demand, there are also factors that affect the elasticity of demand. The factors that affect elasticity include the availability of substitute goods or services, the proportion of income that is spent on the good or service, and whether the good or service is a necessity or a luxury.

FACTOR 1 Substitute Goods or Services

Generally speaking, if there is no substitute for a good or service, demand for it tends to be inelastic. Think back to the consumers who need insulin to regulate their blood sugar levels. No substitute exists for insulin, so consumers' demand is inelastic even when the price goes up. If many substitutes are available, however, demand tends to be elastic. For example, if the price shoots up for beef, consumers can eat chicken, pork, or fish. In this case, demand is elastic.

Economics Update

Find an update on factors affecting elasticity at **ClassZone.com**

FACTOR 2 Proportion of Income

The percentage of your income that you spend on a good or service is another factor that affects elasticity. Suppose that photography is your hobby, and you spend about 10 percent of your income on a digital camera, memory cards, software programs, and lenses. If the price for any of these rises even slightly, your demand will likely fall because you just don't have any more money to spend on your hobby. Your demand is elastic. At the same time, demand for products that cost little of your income tends to be inelastic. For example, if the cost of pencils or ballpoint pens rose, would you buy fewer pencils and pens? Probably not. You spend so little on these items that you could easily pay the increase.

YOUR ECONOMIC CHOICES

PROPORTION OF INCOME

How much would you invest in a hobby?

This amateur photographer spends about 10 percent of her income to pay for her digital camera and supplies. If the costs of taking photographs rise sharply, she won't be able to increase her demand by an equal amount because she won't have enough money to pay for the additional expenses.

3 Teach

What Determines Elasticity

Discuss

- Why do substitutes affect both demand and elasticity of demand? *(because in both cases substitutes offer consumers a choice, if the price of a particular good rises, to switch to something else that meets the same wants at a better price)*

Economics Update

At **ClassZone.com**, students will see updated information on factors affecting elasticity.

Your Economic Choices

PROPORTION OF INCOME

How much would you invest in a hobby?

How could the photographer get more money for her hobby without increasing the proportion of her income she spends on it? *(If she increases her income, she would have more money to spend.)*

Activity Have students work in small groups to brainstorm ideas for ways to make the photographer's budget for her hobby stretch, for example, lookinq for used equipment or sharing equipment. Invite groups to share their ideas with the class and discuss the role of substitutes.

INDIVIDUAL ACTIVITY

Illustrating How Proportion of Income Affects Elasticity

Time 30 Minutes ◑

Task Create a pie graph to show proportion of income spent on different categories.

Materials Needed paper and markers, pens or colored pencils

Activity

- Ask students to try to estimate the amount of their monthly income that they spend on different categories, such as food, clothing, transportation, entertainment, personal care, hobbies, and other miscellaneous items.
- Have students calculate the percent of the whole that they spend on each category and create a pie graph that shows how their income is spent. Remind students that their percentages must add up to 100.
- Refer students who need help to Math Handbook, pages R3 and R10.
- Allow students to share their pie graphs with a partner and discuss which categories have the greatest elasticity of demand and why.

Rubric

	Understanding Concepts	Presentation of Information
4	excellent	clear and complete
3	good	mostly clear
2	fair	sometimes clear
1	poor	sketchy

Analyzing Tables: Figure 4.15

Point out that the table graphically demonstrates how the three factors that affect elasticity are applied to different product categories. What do ice cream and braces have in common that makes demand for both elastic? *(They are both luxuries.)*

Answer

Possible response: Products that have inelastic demand tend to be ones that are necessities with no good substitutes and that consume a small proportion of income.

More About . . .

Inelastic Demand for Gasoline

The lack of good substitutes for gasoline makes it difficult for consumers to respond quickly to changes in gas prices. From 1984 to 2004, gasoline prices were relatively stable and overall demand for gasoline increased. In spite of price increases of 20 percent or more between 2004 and 2005, overall demand declined only slightly.

From 1994 to 2004, average annual gasoline usage was steady at about 10 gallons per vehicle per week. Therefore the average driver was spending less than $5 more a week, a relatively small proportion of income for most consumers. Individual drivers with lower incomes or who drive more miles or have less fuel-efficient cars will be affected more.

If the level of your income increases, you are likely to increase your demand for some goods or services. Suppose you ordinarily see one movie per month. If your income increases, you may choose to attend the movies several times a month.

FACTOR 3 Necessities Versus Luxuries

A necessity is something you must have, such as food or water. Demand for necessities tends to be inelastic. Even if the price rises, consumers will pay whatever they can afford for necessary goods and services.

But that doesn't mean that consumers will buy the same quantities no matter what the price. If the price of a necessity such as milk rises too much, consumers may choose to buy a substitute, such as a cheaper brand of milk or powdered milk. The quantity demanded of milk will change as the law of demand predicts; however, the change in quantity demanded is smaller than the change in price, so demand is inelastic.

In contrast, a luxury is something that you desire but that is not essential to your life, such as a plasma television. The demand for luxuries tends to be elastic. Consumers will think twice about paying a higher price for something they don't truly need. The change in quantity demanded is much greater than the change in price.

FIGURE 4.15 Estimating Elasticity

By examining the three factors that affect elasticity, you can often estimate whether demand for a certain good or service will be elastic or inelastic.

Factors that affect elasticity	Table Salt	Ice Cream	Sports Car	Gasoline	Insulin	Braces on Teeth
Are there good substitutes? yes = elastic; no = inelastic	no	yes	yes	no	no	no
What proportion of income does it use? large = elastic; small = inelastic	small	small	large	small	small	large
Is it a necessity or a luxury? luxury = elastic; necessity = inelastic	necessity	luxury	luxury	necessity	necessity	luxury
Conclusion	inelastic	elastic	elastic	inelastic	inelastic	elastic

ANALYZE TABLES

What patterns can you see in the factors that affect elasticity? Write a sentence summarizing your answer.

APPLICATION Evaluating

B. Create a chart like the one above for the following products: mountain bikes, airplane tickets, and home heating oil. Determine if the products are elastic or inelastic.

mountain bikes—elastic; airplane tickets—answer will depend on whether the tickets are a necessity or luxury; home heating oil—inelastic

DIFFERENTIATING INSTRUCTION

Inclusion

Make a Graphic Organizer

Have students work in pairs to create a graphic organizer to show the three factors that affect elasticity. Encourage students to use Fig. 4.12 on page 113 as a model. Have them include a sketch along with a sentence to describe how each of the three factors determines whether demand for a good or service is elastic or inelastic. Review student work and clarify understanding as needed.

Gifted and Talented

Research Gasoline Prices and Demand

Have students conduct research on the Internet or in their community to find out the latest trends in gasoline prices and demand. Encourage students to create a demand curve for gasoline at various prices and present their findings on the current elasticity of demand for gasoline in the form of a handout to other members of the class.

Calculating Elasticity of Demand

KEY CONCEPTS

Businesses find it useful to figure the elasticity of demand because it helps them to decide whether to make price cuts. If demand for a good or service is elastic, price cuts might help the business earn more. If demand is inelastic, price cuts won't help.

To determine elasticity, economists look at whether the percentage change in quantity demanded is greater than the percentage change in price. To calculate that relationship, economists use mathematical formulas. One such set of formulas is shown below. Another way to determine elasticity is shown on page 122.

MATH CHALLENGE

FIGURE 4.16 Calculating the Elasticity of Demand

Step 1: Calculate percentage change in quantity demanded. (If the final result is a negative number, treat it as positive.)

$$\frac{\text{Original quantity} - \text{New quantity}}{\text{Original quantity}} \times 100 = \text{Percentage change in quantity demanded}$$

Example Calculations

$$\frac{2{,}000 - 6{,}000}{2000} \times 100 = 200\%$$

Step 2: Calculate percentage change in price. (If the final result is a negative number, treat it as positive.)

$$\frac{\text{Original price} - \text{New price}}{\text{Original price}} \times 100 = \text{Percentage change in price}$$

$$\frac{10 - 8}{10} \times 100 = 20\%$$

Step 3: Calculate elasticity.

$$\frac{\text{Percentage change in quantity demanded}}{\text{Percentage change in price}} = \text{Elasticity}$$

$$\frac{200\%}{20\%} = 10$$

Step 4: After doing your calculations, if the final number is greater than 1, demand is elastic. If the final number is less than 1, demand is inelastic.

Advanced Calculations Economists use a more complex version of these formulas. In Step 1, instead of dividing the change in quantity demanded by the original quantity demanded, they divide it by the average of the original and new quantities. In Step 2, they divide change in price by an average of the original price and new price.

NEED HELP?

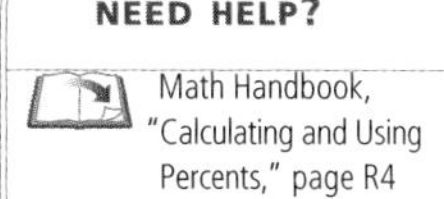

Math Handbook, "Calculating and Using Percents," page R4

APPLICATION Applying Economic Concepts

C. Choose two points on the demand curve shown in Figure 4.13 and determine the price and quantity demanded for each point. Then use that data to calculate elasticity of demand. Students may choose any two points (except $12 and 0 because you cannot divide by 0) to calculate elasticity. Demand is elastic throughout the points on the curve.

Calculating Elasticity of Demand

Discuss

- Why do economists compare percentages of change rather than change in units to calculate elasticity? *(because comparing percentages is a better way to know whether the increase in demand is enough to offset the decrease in price)*

Math Challenge: Figure 4.16

Calculating the Elasticity of Demand This example is related to the question asked in Analyzing Fig. 4.13; it calculates elasticity of demand for movie tickets when the price decreases from $10 to $8 and quantity increases by 4,000. The change in quantity demanded is always a negative number when moving to the right on the demand curve because of the downward slope of the curve. It is important to start with the original quantity and price because that is the base, used as the denominator in each equation. Step 4 refers to 1 as the dividing point between elastic and inelastic demand, i.e. unit elasticity.

Advanced Calculations Determine the average by adding the original and new quantities (or prices) and dividing by 2, in this case 4,000 and 9. Elasticity would be 100 percent divided by 22 percent or 4.5.

SMALL GROUP ACTIVITY

Understanding the Factors That Influence Elasticity

Time 30 minutes ◑

Task Create a shopping cart full of items that exhibit different degrees of elasticity.

Materials Needed paper and markers, pens or pencils

Activity

- Group students and ask them to brainstorm a list of about 20 items that an average family buys at the supermarket regularly.
- Direct students to include items with inelastic demand, such as table salt, matches, and toothpicks; items with clearly elastic demand, such as ice cream, snack foods, and soft drinks; and items that fall in between, such as staple items like bread, milk, and toilet paper. For the latter category, ask them to think about how elasticity for a type of item might be different from elasticity for a particular brand.
- Have students show the items in their shopping cart along with information about their elasticity in a graphic organizer to share with the class.

Rubric

	Understanding Concepts	Presentation of Information
4	excellent	clear and complete
3	good	mostly clear
2	fair	sometimes clear
1	poor	sketchy

Total Revenue Test

Discuss

- How does the total revenue test measure elasticity? *(If total revenue increases when price is decreased, then demand is elastic; if revenue decreases, then demand is inelastic.)*
- How does the total revenue test help business owners decide whether to lower prices? *(It allows them to see whether the increased quantity sold makes up for the lower amount of revenue from each item.)*

More About . . .

Total Revenue Test
The mathematics involved in the total revenue test is simpler than using percentage change to calculate elasticity. Economists use the percentage change method to compare the way consumers respond to price changes in different items. Business owners are concerned about revenue and profits so the total revenue test is more important to them than an abstract measure of elasticity.

Analyzing Tables: Figure 4.17

This table uses the data from the demand curve in Fig. 4.13, except that it has changed the quantity demanded at $12 from 0 to 1,000. The first two columns are a demand schedule. Ask students how much the quantity demanded would have to be at a price of $2 to exceed the revenue from $4 tickets. *(more than 40,000)* Is demand at $2 likely to be elastic or inelastic? *(inelastic because it is unlikely quantity would more than double, based on the pattern shown in the table)*

Answer

Demand is elastic because total revenue has increased.

Total Revenue Test

QUICK REFERENCE

Total revenue is a company's income from selling its products.

Total revenue test is a method of measuring elasticity by comparing total revenues.

KEY CONCEPTS

Businesses need to know about elasticity of demand because it influences the amount of revenue they will earn. Economists measure elasticity of demand by calculating a seller's **total revenue**, the amount of money a company receives for selling its products. Total revenue is calculated using the following formula, in which P is the price and Q is the quantity sold: **TOTAL REVENUE = P × Q.**

You can measure elasticity by comparing the total revenue a business would receive when offering its product at various prices. This method is the **total revenue test.**

If total revenue increases after the price of a product drops, then demand for that product is considered elastic. Why? Because even though the seller makes less on each unit sold, the quantity demanded has increased enough to make up for the lower price. For example, if a hot dog stand sells 100 hot dogs for $2.50 each, the total revenue is $250 for the day. However, if the price of hot dogs drops to $2.00 each and 150 are sold, the total revenue for the day will be $300. The demand is elastic.

But if the total revenue decreases after the price is lowered, demand is considered inelastic. If the hot dog stand lowers its price to $1.00 each and sells 200 hot dogs, it makes $200 in total revenue. Clearly, the price reduction has caused only a modest increase in quantities sold, which is not enough to compensate for lower revenues.

EXAMPLE Revenue Table

Let's look at an example of demand for movie tickets. In Figure 4.17, you can see how total revenues show whether demand is elastic or inelastic.

FIGURE 4.17 MOVIE TICKET REVENUE TABLE

	Price of a Movie Ticket ($)	Quantity Demanded per Month	Total Revenue ($)
	12	1,000	12,000
a →	10	2,000	20,000
b →	8	6,000	48,000
	6	12,000	72,000
	4	20,000	80,000

a At $10 a ticket, the quantity demanded is 2,000. Total revenue is $20,000.

b When the price drops to $8, the quantity demanded rises to 6,000. Total revenue rises to $48,000. So, demand is elastic.

ANALYZE TABLES
When the price range changes from $8 to $6, is demand elastic or inelastic? Explain.

APPLICATION Creating Tables

D. Use the information from Figure 4.14 to estimate prices to make a total revenue table. Estimated prices and quantities demanded are: $180/20, $160/23; $120/25; $80/30, $40/33. Total revenue figures should reflect the inelastic demand for fillings.

DIFFERENTIATING INSTRUCTION

Struggling Readers

Create Graphic Organizers
Have students create a total revenue table like Fig. 4.17 to help them understand the example of the hot dog stand and how demand is elastic between $2.50 and $2.00 but inelastic between $2.00 and $1.00. Encourage students to use the first two columns of the table to create a demand curve for the hot dogs at the three prices. Point out the steep slope of the curve that shows demand is inelastic below $2.00.

Inclusion

Work in Pairs
Allow pairs of students to work together on Application D. Remind students to use the axes of the graph to estimate the prices and quantities demanded since many of the points on the curve do not fall exactly on the intersection of numbers shown. Encourage students to write the formula P x Q = TR at the top of their table to help them calculate the total revenue.

Online Quiz
ClassZone.com

SECTION 3 Assessment

REVIEWING KEY CONCEPTS

1. Use each of the terms below in a sentence that gives an example of the term:
   a. *elastic* **b.** *inelastic* **c.** *total revenue*
2. How is total revenue related to elasticity of demand?
3. Why are elastic goods and services said to be price sensitive?
4. What are the factors that affect elasticity of demand and how does each affect elasticity?
5. Analyze the factors that determine elasticity to explain why utilities companies never offer sale prices on their services.
6. **Using Your Notes** How does the concept of unit elasticity relate to the concepts of elasticity and inelasticity? Refer to your completed cluster diagram.

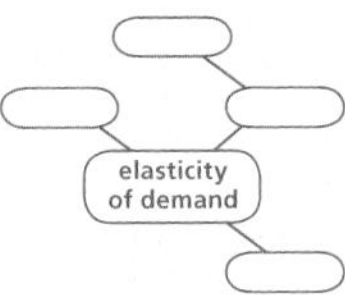

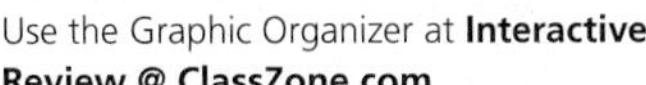
Use the Graphic Organizer at **Interactive Review @ ClassZone.com**

CRITICAL THINKING

7. **Analyzing Causes** In early 2004, news articles reported that prescription drug prices were rising almost three times faster than the prices of other products. Identify the factors that explain why the drug companies were able to raise prices so sharply.
8. **Analyzing Data** In June, Snead's Snack Bar sold 1,000 fruit smoothies at a price of $2.50 each. In July, they sold 1,300 fruit smoothies at a price of $2.00. Is the demand for fruit smoothies elastic or inelastic? Use the formula on page 121 to decide. Show the math calculations to support your answer.
9. **Applying Economic Concepts** Suppose the company that runs concession stands at a local sports arena wants to increase revenue on sales of soft drinks. The manager believes the only solution is to charge higher prices. As a business consultant, what advice would you give the manager? Use economic thinking to support your answer.
10. **Challenge** You learned in this section that no product ever has demand that is unit elastic. What possible reasons can you give for that? Draw on what you know about utility, demand, and elasticity as you formulate your answer.

ECONOMICS IN PRACTICE

Calculating Elasticity
Determine the elasticity of bottled water by calculating elasticity and using the revenue table below. Use the information on pages 121 and 122 to help you.

Number of Bottles Sold	Price ($)
35	2.00
75	1.50
100	1.25
120	1.00

Write a Summary After you have determined whether bottled water is elastic or inelastic, think about what factors affect the demand for bottled water. Write a summary of your conclusions explaining whether demand is elastic or inelastic and why, and what factors affect the elasticity of water.

Challenge What effect might the introduction of a new energy drink have on the demand for bottled water? Use economic thinking to support your answer.

4 Assess & Reteach

Assess Have students answer the questions in pairs. First, one student answers the question orally and the other writes down the answer. Then they switch and continue taking turns until all the questions are answered.

Unit 2 Resource Book
- Section Quiz, p. 29

Interactive Review @ ClassZone.com
- Section Quiz

Test Generator CD-ROM
- Section Quiz

Reteach Divide students into four groups. Each group is responsible for preparing a set of notes about material under one of the main headings of the section. Then have students move into new groups, each having representatives from the original groups. Each student is responsible for teaching the information he or she originally worked on.

Unit 2 Resource Book
- Reteaching Activity, p. 30

SECTION 3 ASSESSMENT ANSWERS

Reviewing Key Concepts

1. **a.** *elastic*, p. 117
   b. *inelastic*, p. 117
   c. *total revenue*, p. 122
2. If total revenue increases when price decreases, then demand is elastic.
3. Changes in price for such goods lead to a relatively larger change in quantity demanded.
4. The factors that affect elasticity are: substitutes, proportion of income, and necessities versus luxuries. The greater number of substitute goods, the greater proportion of income used to purchase the product, and the more a good or service is considered a luxury the more elastic the demand is.
5. There are few or no substitutes for the necessary services offered by utilities companies.
6. See page 116 for an example of a completed chart. Unit elastic is the dividing point between elastic and inelastic demand.

Critical Thinking

7. Prescription drugs are often necessities with few good substitutes, so demand is inelastic.
8. 1.2; Demand is elastic.
9. By lowering prices, you may be able to increase quantity demanded and also increase revenue. Consumers may not have good substitutes at the sports arena and so might be less sensitive to price changes than they would be in a store.
10. Unit elastic is a concept that requires the percentage changes in price and quantity demanded to be exactly the same. Based on the law of marginal utility, the percentage change in quantity demanded gets smaller over time while the percentage change in price gets larger and demand becomes inelastic.

Economics in Practice

Write a Summary Summaries may vary, but should note that demand is elastic at $1.25 and above, and inelastic at $1.00. Reasons should include substitutes, small proportion of income, and luxury.

Challenge Because the energy drink is a substitute for bottled water the demand for bottled water may go down.

❶ Plan & Prepare

Objectives

- Analyze multiple sources to understand factors that affect demand for automobiles.
- Compare and contrast different factors that affect demand for automobiles.

❷ Focus & Motivate

Ask students what things they consider to help them choose among different brands of products that they buy regularly. Explain that this case study focuses on factors that influence the kinds of vehicles that people buy.

❸ Teach

Using the Sources

Encourage students to compare and contrast the different factors that influence demand for automobiles as they read the sources.

A. Why is free car insurance an incentive for college graduates and first-time buyers? *(Possible answer: It helps them afford a new car by taking care of a big related expense.)*

B. Why does the car dealer say that the gas station is bad for business? *(High gas prices might discourage people from buying SUVs, which use a lot of gas.)*

C. How are auto manufacturers "helping Americans have their cake and eat it too"? *(Americans like SUVs and now they are able to buy hybrid SUVs that are more fuel efficient.)*

Economics Update

Go to **ClassZone.com** to find an update to this Case Study, including another article, an editable student worksheet, and an editable lesson plan.

Case Study

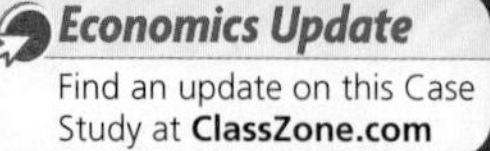

Find an update on this Case Study at **ClassZone.com**

Fueling Automobile Demand

Background Automobiles make up a huge portion of the American economy. In recent years the demand for automobiles and all the services connected with them has accounted for approximately one-fifth of all retail sales. Over the past decade, the total number of automobiles, including light trucks and SUVs (Sport Utility Vehicles), sold has been over 16 million units.

Car dealers are constantly looking for ways to sustain and increase demand for their product. Paul Taylor, chief economist of the National Automobile Dealers Association, observed, "The key to sales of 16.9 million will be the continued strong economy and sustained incentives." Incentives are awards designed to lure potential buyers into an automobile showroom and encourage sales. Manufacturers have tried everything from giving away mountain bikes to zero percent financing.

What's the issue? How does demand affect your selection of a vehicle? Study these sources to discover how the law of demand and the factors that affect demand shape the market.

A. Online Article

Most car dealers offer some sort of incentive. This article discusses Volkswagen's new approach in dealer incentives to car buyers.

Volkswagen Tries 12 Months of Free Car Insurance to Lure Buyers

To fight slumping sales, Volkswagen introduces a new incentive to attract buyers.

The German automaker [Volkswagen]. . . will test the program by offering 12 months of free insurance to people with valid driver's licenses who buy or lease new Golfs, Beetle coupes and Beetle convertibles. . . .

"I think it will be a lure for college graduates and first-time buyers," said Harry Nesbitt, sales manager. . . . "It's a way to get people in the dealership without sounding like everyone else. . . ."

General Motors Corp., the world's largest automaker, has also been varying its ways of luring buyers this year. Its offers have included overnight test drives, 72-hour sales and a program tied to the U.S. federal interest rate increase that allowed buyers to lock in an interest rate this year on a car or truck purchase five years in the future.

The Volkswagen program would be the first insurance giveaway by an automaker.

Source: Bloomberg.com

Thinking Economically Do incentives described in this document change the demand for automobiles or the quantity demanded? Explain your answer.

DIFFERENTIATING INSTRUCTION

Struggling Readers

Use Reciprocal Teaching

Have pairs of students take turns reading paragraphs out loud and asking their partners to summarize what they have just heard. Students who are reading may also ask their partners questions about what they've read. Have students discuss all the Thinking Economically questions together and agree on answers.

Gifted and Talented

Conduct Research

Interested students might like to conduct research on the kinds of incentives automobile dealers in their community use to sell cars. Sources of information include articles in the local newspaper's business section and advertisements in the print and electronic media. Students also might conduct interviews with automobile dealers. Encourage students to present their findings in a written report on the impact of incentives on auto sales.

B. Political Cartoon

Brian Duffy, a cartoonist with the *Des Moines Register*, drew this cartoon about the rising price of gasoline.

Thinking Economically Which of the factors that cause a change in demand does this cartoon address? Explain your answer.

C. Online Report

An auto-buying service linking buyers and sellers examines demand for hybrid automobiles. Hybrid cars get power from a combination of batteries and a gas-powered engine.

The Year of the Hybrid

Stellar Fuel Efficiency, Low Emissions, and More Power

Why do we think 2005 will be The Year of the Hybrid? We can sum it up in two words: Power and SUV. There's something reassuring about how auto manufacturers are helping Americans have their cake and eat it too by offering up more fuel-efficient SUVs. Let's face it, America's love affair with the SUV shows no sign of waning. Yet . . . we can't live in denial that the SUV has a fat appetite for gasoline. And then there's the power argument. Despite the crowd pleasing fuel efficiency standards offered by hybrids, there was still the complaint that they lacked juice, or horsepower. . . . 2005's hybrids will appeal to those of us . . . who absolutely demand a lot of horsepower. As if overcompensating for being picked on when they were little, 2005's hybrids are coming out with more horsepower than their gas-only counterparts.

Though hybrids tend to be more expensive than their gas- or diesel-only powered cousins, the savings in fuel (and sometimes in taxes) can more than offset this difference in the long run.

Source: Invoicedealers.com

Thinking Economically Which of the factors affecting demand is evident in this article? Use evidence from the article to support your answer.

THINKING ECONOMICALLY Synthesizing

1. How would the demand for automobiles be affected by information presented in each of these documents? Support your answer with examples from the documents.
2. Identify and discuss the factors that affect elasticity of demand illustrated in these documents.
3. Explain how Documents B and C illustrate a cause and effect relationship in the demand for SUVs. Use evidence from these documents to support your answer.

Thinking Economically

Answers

A. *Since these incentives do not change the price of the car, they change the demand, not the quantity demanded.*

B. *It shows consumer taste for SUVs and the complements of cars and gasoline. If consumers expect gasoline prices to keep rising, they may not buy as many SUVs.*

C. *This article describes consumer taste for SUVs and shows how new hybrid SUVs may be a substitute for traditional SUVs.*

Synthesizing

1. *Documents A and C—demand may increase as incentives and hybrid SUVs persuade buyers to purchase new vehicles. Document B—demand for SUVs might go down; higher prices of gasoline might make people buy more fuel-efficient substitutes.*
2. *Demand for automobiles is elastic. There are many different brands (substitutes) so manufacturers use incentives to increase demand. A large proportion of income is used to buy a car and high gas prices add to the proportion used for transportation. Hybrids can be substitutes for regular SUVs.*
3. *Document B—high gas prices may cause demand for SUVs to decline. Document C —hybrid SUVs that are more fuel efficient may cause demand to increase.*

TECHNOLOGY ACTIVITY

Researching Trends in Gasoline Prices and SUV Sales

Time 30 minutes ◑

Task Use the Internet to research recent trends in gasoline prices and sales of SUVs and hybrids and prepare a written report.

Materials Needed a computer with Internet access, word processing software, optional graphing software

Activity

- Organize students into groups. Have groups research one of these trends: gasoline prices, sales of SUVs, sales of hybrids.
- Have each group prepare a report of its findings and encourage students to include visuals in their presentations. Direct them to draw conclusions about influences on demand or elasticity.
- Have groups share reports with the class. Discuss how these trends are related.

Rubric

	Understanding Concepts	Presentation of Information
4	excellent	clear, complete
3	good	mostly clear
2	fair	sometimes clear
1	poor	sketchy

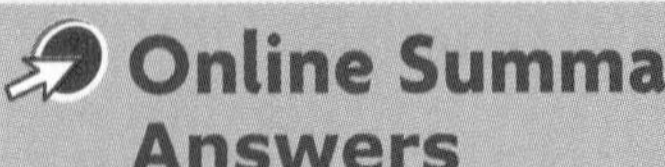

Online Summary Answers

1. demand
2. law of demand
3. demand schedule
4. demand curve
5. market demand schedule
6. market demand curve
7. change in quantity demanded
8. change in demand
9. substitutes
10. elasticity of demand
11. elastic
12. inelastic
13. unit elastic
14. total revenue

Interactive Review

Review this chapter using interactive activities at ClassZone.com

- Online Summary
- Quizzes
- Vocabulary Flip Cards
- Graphic Organizers
- Review and Study Notes

Online Summary

Complete the following activity either on your own paper or online at **ClassZone.com**

Choose the key concept that best completes the sentence. Not all key concepts will be used.

change in demand	law of demand
change in quantity demanded	market demand curve
demand	market demand schedule
demand curve	normal goods
demand schedule	substitutes
elastic	substitution effect
elasticity of demand	total revenue
income effect	total revenue test
inelastic	unit elastic
inferior goods	

__1__ is the desire for a product and the ability to pay for it. According to the __2__, when price decreases, demand rises, and when price increases, demand falls.

Demand can be displayed in a table called a __3__ or on a graph called a __4__. A __5__ is a table that shows how much demand all consumers in a market have. When that same information is displayed on a graph, it is called a __6__.

The different points on a demand curve show a __7__. A __8__ occurs when consumers are willing to buy different amounts of a product at every price. The six factors that change demand are income, market size, consumer expectations, consumer taste, complement, and __9__.

The term __10__ describes how responsive consumers are to price changes. Demand that changes significantly when prices change is __11__. Demand that doesn't change significantly when prices change is __12__. The dividing line between the two is where demand is __13__.

__14__ is calculated by multiplying price by quantity sold.

CHAPTER 4 Assessment

REVIEWING KEY CONCEPTS

What Is Demand? (pp. 98–105)

1. What two things are necessary for a consumer to have demand for a good or service?
2. What do economists mean when they say that quantity demanded and price have an inverse relationship?

What Factors Affect Demand? (pp. 106–115)

3. What is the difference between change in quantity demanded and change in demand?
4. How do consumer expectations affect demand?

What Is Elasticity of Demand? (pp. 116–125)

5. Explain the difference between elastic and inelastic demand.
6. What are two methods for calculating elasticity of demand?

APPLYING ECONOMIC CONCEPTS

Look at the graph below showing personal spending for two types of products: computers and stationery.

7. What is the general trend of how spending for each of these product types has changed? Are the two trends alike or different?
8. In what way might these products be complements? In what way might they be substitutes?

FIGURE 4.18 PERSONAL SPENDING ON COMPUTERS AND STATIONERY

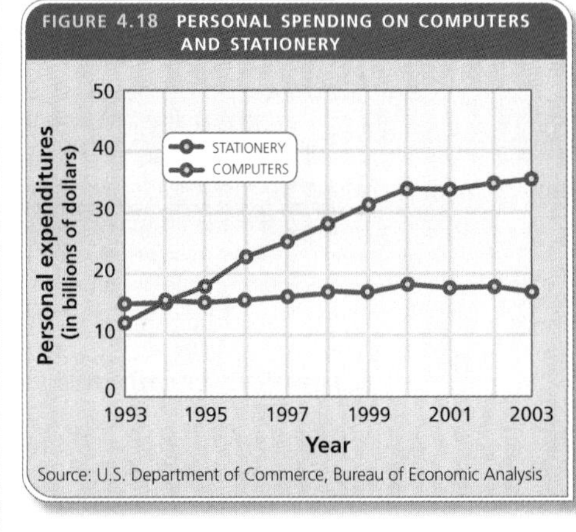

Source: U.S. Department of Commerce, Bureau of Economic Analysis

CHAPTER 4 ASSESSMENT ANSWERS

Reviewing Key Concepts

1. the desire to buy a good or service and the ability to pay for it
2. Price and quantity demanded have an opposite relationship; as price goes down, quantity demanded goes up.
3. A change in quantity demanded is an increase or decrease in the amount demanded because of a change in price. A change in demand occurs when a change in the marketplace prompts consumers to buy different amounts of goods or services at every price.
4. Expectations about the future can prompt a consumer to buy sooner or perhaps later based on anticipated price changes.
5. Elastic demand is price sensitive; inelastic demand is not as strongly affected by price changes.
6. One method is to calculate the relationship between the percentage change in quantity demanded and the percentage change in price. The second is to use a total revenue table.

Applying Economic Concepts

7. Spending for stationery has changed little in ten years; spending for computers has increased significantly. The trends are different.
8. Using a computer may involve the use of paper to print documents, making paper a complement. Using a computer may eliminate the need for paper copies of documents and thus is a substitute for paper.

CRITICAL THINKING

9. **Creating Graphs** A tornado destroys a town. Think of three goods for which demand will rise in the weeks after the storm and three goods for which demand will fall. For each good, create a graph with two demand curves: curve A representing demand before the storm and curve B representing demand after the storm. Under each graph, write a caption explaining the change in demand.

   Use **SMARTGrapher @ ClassZone.com** to complete this activity.

10. **Identifying Causes** A certain stuffed toy is popular during the holiday season, but sells for half the listed price after the holidays. Which factor in change in demand is at work here? Explain.

11. **Identifying Causes** In the last few decades, demand for ketchup has dropped in the United States, while demand for salsa has risen. Which factors that affect demand account for this?

12. **Using Economic Concepts** Airlines give discounts to travelers who book in advance and stay over a weekend. Travelers who book at the last minute and do not stay over a weekend usually pay full-price. How does the concept of elasticity explain the difference between the two groups' demand for tickets and the airlines' pricing decisions?

13. **Challenge** Suppose that you read the following article in the newspaper:

    Meteorologists announced today that this has been the warmest winter in 57 years. The unusual weather has affected local businesses. According to Pasha Dubrinski, owner of Pasha's Outerwear, sales of winter parkas are 17 percent lower than last year. Dubrinski said, "Instead of buying down-filled parkas, people have been buying substitute items such as leather coats."

    Across town, Michael Ellis, owner of Home Hardware, said that his sales of snow blowers are also down. "Next week, I will cut the price. That will increase demand."

    Are these two storeowners correct in the way they use economic terms? Explain your answer.

SIMULATION

Equip Your Team

Step 1 Choose a partner. Imagine you are equipment managers for your school's baseball team. You must equip the nine starters with a budget of $5,000. The equipment supplier sends you the list of prices shown in column A of the table below. Create a list telling how many of each item you will buy.

SPORTING GOODS PRICES

Item	Prices (in dollars) A	B	C
Bat	130	170	200
Baseball	2	3	4
Glove or Mitt	80	130	160
Catcher's Mask	80	90	100
Full Uniform	65	100	135
Jersey Only	30	60	90
Cleats	25	60	90
Sunglasses	20	30	40
Team Jacket	50	75	100

Step 2 When you call in the order, you learn that a big sporting goods factory has burned. Prices have risen to those shown in column B. You must redo your order using the new prices but the same budget.

Step 3 The economy is hit with sudden and severe price hikes. Redo your order using the prices in column C.

Step 4 Share your three purchasing lists with the class. As a class, use the collected data to create a market demand curve for each item.

Step 5 Use the collected data to calculate elasticity for each item. (You may use either method explained in this chapter.) Then as a class discuss your results. What factors influenced elasticity?

Use **SMARTGrapher @ ClassZone.com** to complete this activity.

McDougal Littell
Assessment System

Assess

Online Test Practice
- Go to **ClassZone.com** for more test practice.

Unit 2 Resource Book
- Chapter Test, Forms A, B, C, pp. 41–52

Test Generator CD-ROM
- Chapter Test, Forms (A, B, & C), in English and Spanish

Report

Use the McDougal Littell Assessment System to score assessments and receive customized reports.

Reteach

For activities customized for individual students, use the McDougal Littell Assessment System.

SMARTGrapher Students can create demand curves using **SmartGrapher @ ClassZone.com.**

CHAPTER 4 ASSESSMENT ANSWERS

Critical Thinking

9. Demand will increase for goods such as building supplies (wood, nails, hammers, saws, and so on); demand will decrease for luxuries such as movie tickets, restaurant meals, and DVD rentals. For graphs showing increase in demand, curve B should shift to the right of curve A. For graphs showing decrease in demand, curve B should shift to the left.

   SMARTGrapher Students can create demand curves using **SmartGrapher @ ClassZone.com.**

10. Consumer tastes drive the purchase of the toy during the holiday season. When the holiday season is over the demand for the toy is less and the seller reduces the price.

11. The population demanding salsa has increased because of increased Hispanic immigration and changes in consumer tastes.

12. People booking at the last minute may have little flexibility if they wish to fly. Demand is inelastic. Those booking in advance can wait to find the best deals on tickets. Demand is elastic.

13. Substitutes are generally goods that are interchangeable. People are not buying leather jackets because they are cheaper but because they are not as warm. Cutting the price of snow blowers will not increase demand because there is no need for the product.

Simulation Rubric

	Understanding Concepts	Presentation of Information
4	excellent	accurate, clear, complete
3	good	mostly accurate, clear
2	fair	sometimes clear
1	poor	sketchy

Chapter 5: Supply
Planning Guide

Resources 2Go Complete print resources all on one USB drive allow you to customize lessons.

Section Titles and Objectives	Unit 2 Resource Book and Workbooks		Assessment Resources
1 What Is Supply? pp. 130–137 • Define supply and outline what the law of supply says • Explain how to create and interpret supply schedules • Explain how to create and interpret supply curves	**Unit 2 Resource Book** • Reading Study Guide, pp. 53–54 • RSG with Additional Support, pp. 55–57 • RSG with Additional Support (Spanish), pp. 58–60 • Readings in Free Enterprise: Is It Demand?, p. 95	• Economic Skills and Problem Solving Activity, pp. 93–94	**Unit 2 Resource Book** • Section Quiz, p. 61 • Reteaching Activity, p. 62 **Test Generator CD-ROM** **Daily Test Practice Transparencies,** TT15
2 What Are the Costs of Production? pp. 138–145 • Analyze how businesses calculate the right number of workers to hire • Determine how businesses calculate production costs • Explain how businesses use those calculations to determine the most profitable output	**Unit 2 Resource Book** • Reading Study Guide, pp. 63–64 • RSG with Additional Support, pp. 65–67 • RSG with Additional Support (Spanish), pp. 68–70 • Economic Skills and Problem Solving Activity, pp. 93–94	**NCEE Student Activities** • Costs of Production, pp. 17–20	**Unit 2 Resource Book** • Section Quiz, p. 71 • Reteaching Activity, p. 72 **Test Generator CD-ROM** **Daily Test Practice Transparencies,** TT16
3 What Factors Affect Supply? pp. 146–153 • Explain the difference between change in quantity supplied and change in supply • Understand how to determine a change in supply • Identify the factors that can cause a change in supply	**Unit 2 Resource Book** • Reading Study Guide, pp. 73–74 • RSG with Additional Support, pp. 75–77 • RSG with Additional Support (Spanish), pp. 78–80 • Readings in Free Enterprise: Is It Demand?, p. 95; Is It Supply?, p. 96	• Economic Simulations: Reasons for Changes in Supply, pp. 99–100	**Unit 2 Resource Book** • Section Quiz, p. 81 • Reteaching Activity, p. 82 **Test Generator CD-ROM** **Daily Test Practice Transparencies,** TT17
4 What Is Elasticity of Supply? pp. 154–159 • Define the term elasticity of supply • Explain the difference between elastic and inelastic supply • Identify the factors that affect elasticity of supply	**Unit 2 Resource Book** • Reading Study Guide, pp. 83–84 • RSG with Additional Support, pp. 85–87 • RSG with Additional Support (Spanish), pp. 88–90 • Math Skills Worksheet: Calculating Elasticity of Supply, p. 101 • Case Study Resources: Penelope, Archie, and REMI, p. 97; Personal Robots, p. 98	**Test Practice and Review Workbook,** pp. 31–32	**Unit 2 Resource Book** • Section Quiz, p. 91 • Reteaching Activity, p. 92 • Chapter Test, (Forms A, B, & C), pp. 103–114 **Test Generator CD-ROM** **Daily Test Practice Transparencies,** TT18

Integrated Technology

No Time? To focus students on the most important content in this chapter, use Animated Economics, "Changes in Quantity Supplied," available in Resources 2Go.

Teacher Presentation Options

Presentation Toolkit

Power Presentation DVD-ROM

- Lecture Notes
- Interactive Review
- Media Gallery
- Animated Economics
- Review Game

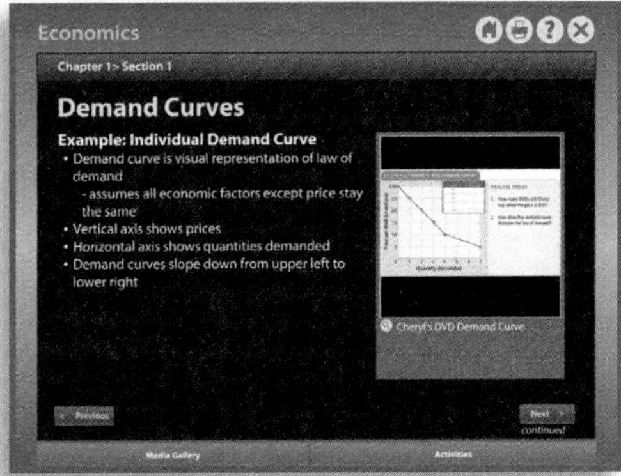

Economics Concepts Transparencies

- Petroleum Market Supply, CT15
- Productions Costs and Revenues Schedule for Manufacturing Footballs, CT16
- Factors Influencing Changes in Supply, CT17
- Limit on Changing Production, CT18

Electronic Books

eEdition DVD-ROM

eEdition Online

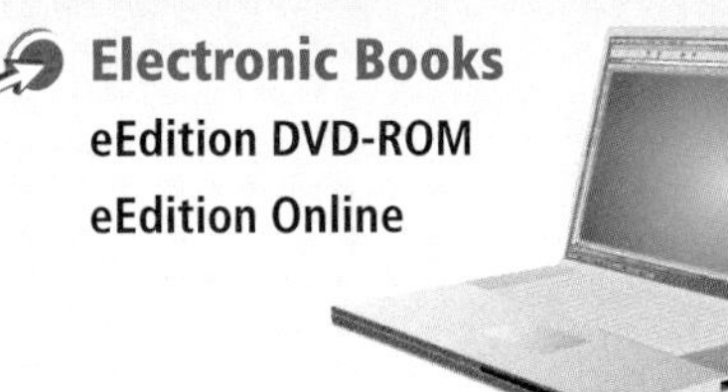

Daily Test Practice Transparencies, TT15, TT16, TT17, TT18

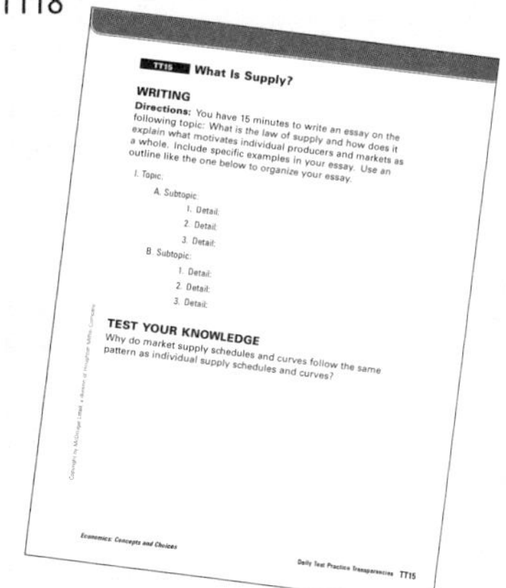

TT15 What Is Supply?

WRITING

Directions: You have 15 minutes to write an essay on the following topic: What is the law of supply and how does it explain what motivates individual producers and markets as a whole. Include specific examples in your essay. Use an outline like the one below to organize your essay.

I. Topic
A. Subtopic
1. Detail
2. Detail
3. Detail
B. Subtopic
1. Detail
2. Detail
3. Detail

TEST YOUR KNOWLEDGE

Why do market supply schedules and curves follow the same pattern as individual supply schedules and curves?

Economics: Concepts and Choices

Daily Test Practice Transparencies TT15

Animated Economics

- Supply Schedules, p. 132
- Supply Curves, p. 134
- Changes in Quantity Supplied, p. 147
- Interactive Version of Shifting Supply Curves, p. 148
- Elastic and Inelastic Supply Curves, p. 155

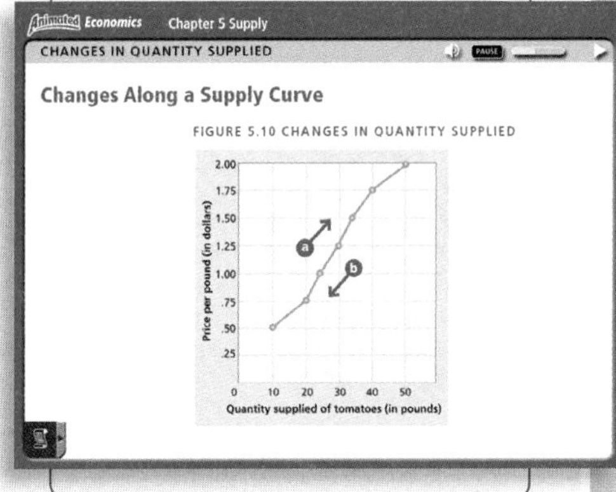

Online Activities at ClassZone.com

Economics Update

- Farmers' Markets, p. 131
- Robert Johnson, p. 152
- Robots—Technology Increases Supply, p. 158

Animated Economics

- Interactive Graphics

Activity Maker

- Vocabulary Flip Cards
- Review Game

Research Center

- Graphs and Data

Interactive Review

- Online Summary
- Quizzes
- Vocabulary Flip Cards
- Graphic Organizers
- Review and Study Notes

SMARTGrapher

- Create a Supply Curve, p. 136
- Create a Supply Curve, p. 137
- Create a Supply Curve, p. 157
- Create a Market Supply Curve, p. 161

Teacher-Tested Activities

Name: Joanne Benjamin (ret.)

School: Los Gatos High School

State: California

Teacher-Tested Activities

At the beginning of this chapter, look for my classroom-proven idea for teaching economics concepts and thinking.

Resources for Differentiated Instruction

Struggling Readers

Teacher's Edition Activities

- Review Key Concepts, p. 132
- Summarize Information, p. 134
- Read a Chart, p. 140
- Identify Main Ideas, p. 148
- Make a Chart, p. 156
- Skim for Text Features, p. 158

Unit 2 Resource Book

- Reading Study Guide with Additional Support, pp. 55–57, 65–67, 75–77, 85–87 (A)
- Reteaching Activities, pp. 62, 72, 82, 92 (B)
- Chapter Test (Form A), pp. 103–106 (C)

ClassZone.com

- Animated Economics
- Interactive Review

Test Generator CD-ROM

- Chapter Test (Form A)
- Chapter Test (Form A), in Spanish

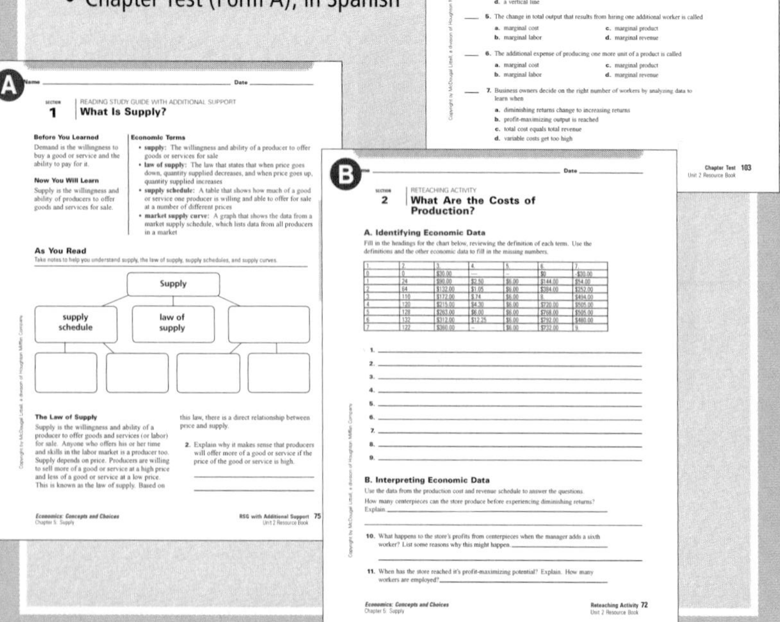

English Learners

Teacher's Edition Activities

- Compare and Contrast, p. 132
- Use Synonyms and Antonyms, p. 136
- Build Economics Vocabulary, p. 140
- Understand Cause and Effect, p. 148
- Create a Time Line, p. 152
- Use Suffixes to Understand, p. 158

Unit 2 Resource Book

- RSG with Additional Support (Spanish), pp. 58–60, 68–70, 78–80, 88–90 (A)

Test Generator CD-ROM

- Chapter Test (Forms A, B, & C), in Spanish (B)

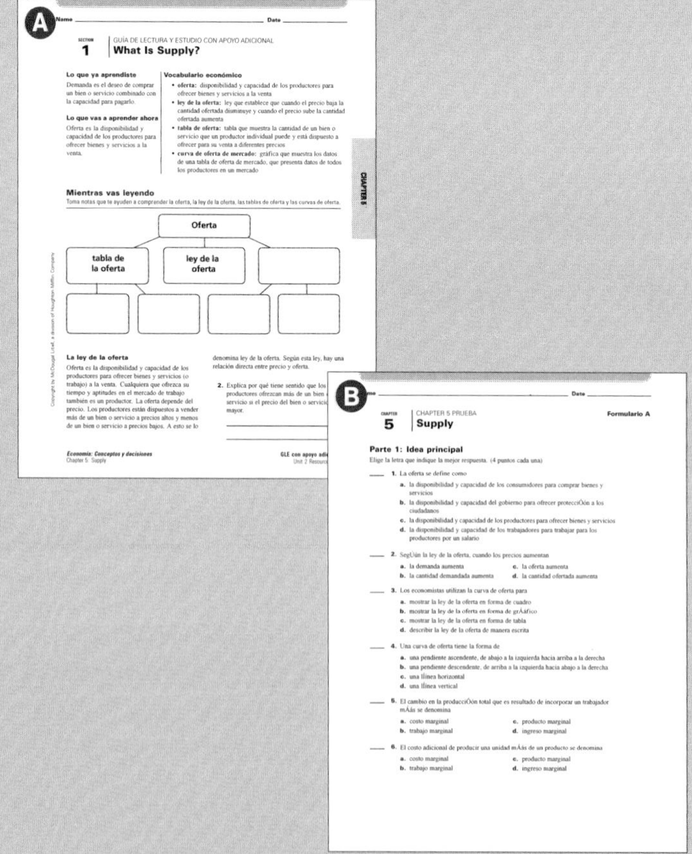

Inclusion

Teacher's Edition Activities

- Enlarge Graphs, p. 134
- Create a Master Chart, p. 142
- Diagram a Source, p. 144
- Use the Visual, p. 150
- Listen to the Section, p. 156

Lesson Plans

- Modified Lessons for Inclusion, pp. 15–18 Ⓐ

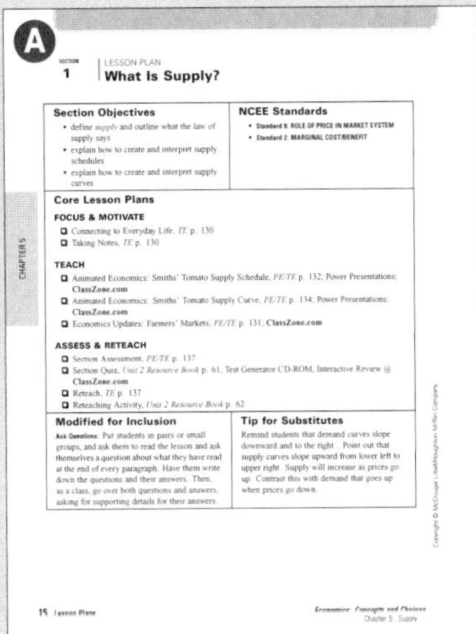

A

SECTION 1 | LESSON PLAN
What Is Supply?

Section Objectives	**NCEE Standards**
• define *supply* and outline what the law of supply says • explain how to create and interpret supply schedules • explain how to create and interpret supply curves	• Standard 8: ROLE OF PRICE IN MARKET SYSTEM • Standard 2: MARGINAL COST/BENEFIT

Core Lesson Plans

FOCUS & MOTIVATE

- ☐ Connecting to Everyday Life, *TE* p. 130
- ☐ Taking Notes, *TE* p. 130

TEACH

- ☐ Animated Economics: Smiths' Tomato Supply Schedule, *PE/TE* p. 132; Power Presentations: **ClassZone.com**
- ☐ Animated Economics: Smiths' Tomato Supply Curve, *PE/TE* p. 134; Power Presentations: **ClassZone.com**
- ☐ Economics Updates: Farmers' Markets, *PE/TE* p. 131; **ClassZone.com**

ASSESS & RETEACH

- ☐ Section Assessment, *PE/TE* p. 137
- ☐ Section Quiz, *Unit 2 Resource Book* p. 61, Test Generator CD-ROM, Interactive Review @ **ClassZone.com**
- ☐ Reteach, *TE* p. 137
- ☐ Reteaching Activity, *Unit 2 Resource Book* p. 62

Modified for Inclusion	**Tip for Substitutes**
Ask Questions: Put students in pairs or small groups, and ask them to read the lesson and ask themselves a question about what they have read at the end of every paragraph. Have them write down the questions and their answers. Then, as a class, go over both questions and answers, asking for supporting details for their answers.	Remind students that demand curves slope downward and to the right. Point out that supply curves slope upward from lower left to upper right. Supply will increase as prices go up. Contrast this with demand that goes up when prices go down.

CHAPTER 5

Copyright © McDougal Littell/Houghton Mifflin Company

15 Lesson Plans — *Economics: Concepts and Choices* Chapter 5: Supply

Gifted and Talented

Teacher's Edition Activities

- Conduct Research, p. 136
- Perform a Marginal Analysis, p. 142
- Use Internet Sources, p. 144
- Write a Mini-Case Study, p. 150
- Research Other Suppliers, p. 152

Unit 2 Resource Book

- Readings in Free Enterprise: Is It Demand? Is It Supply?, pp. 95–96 
- Case Study Resources: Penelope, Archie, and REMI; Personal Roots, pp. 97–98 Ⓑ

NCEE Student Activities

- Costs of Production, p. 17–20 Ⓒ

ClassZone.com

- Research Center

Test Generator CD-ROM

- Chapter Test (Form C)
- Chapter Test (Form C), in Spanish

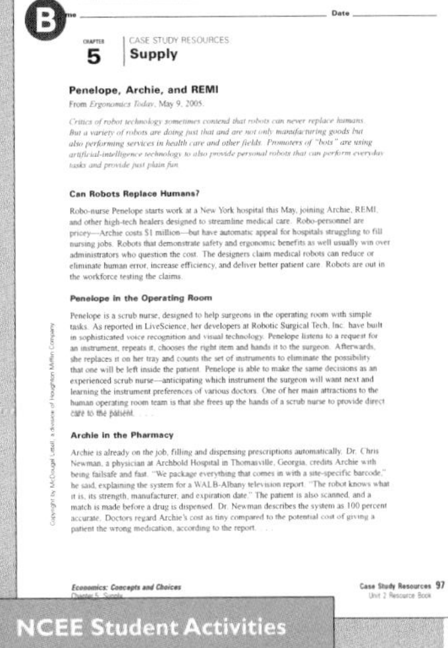

B

Name ______ Date ______

CHAPTER 5 | CASE STUDY RESOURCES
Supply

Penelope, Archie, and REMI

From *Ergonomics Today*, May 9, 2005.

Critics of robot technology sometimes contend that robots can never replace humans. But a variety of robots are doing just that and are not only manufacturing goods but also performing services in health care and other fields. Promoters of "bots" are using artificial-intelligence technology to also provide personal robots that can perform everyday tasks and provide just plain fun.

Can Robots Replace Humans?

Robo-nurse Penelope starts work at a New York hospital this May, joining Archie, REMI, and other high-tech healers designed to streamline medical care. Robo-personnel are pricey—Archie costs $1 million—but have automatic appeal for hospitals struggling to fill nursing jobs. Robots that demonstrate safety and ergonomic benefits as well usually win over administrators who question the cost. The designers claim medical robots can reduce or eliminate human error, increase efficiency, and deliver better patient care. Robots are out in the workforce testing the claims.

Penelope in the Operating Room

Penelope is a scrub nurse, designed to help surgeons in the operating room with simple tasks. As reported in LiveScience, her developers at Robotic Surgical Tech, Inc. have built in sophisticated voice recognition and visual technology. Penelope listens to a request for an instrument, repeats it, chooses the right item and hands it to the surgeon. Afterwards, she replaces it on her tray and counts the set of instruments to eliminate the possibility that one will be left inside the patient. Penelope is able to make the same decisions as an experienced scrub nurse—anticipating which instrument the surgeon will want next and learning the instrument preferences of various doctors. One of her main attractions to the human operating room team is that she frees up the hands of a scrub nurse to provide direct care to the patient. . . .

Archie in the Pharmacy

Archie is already on the job, filling and dispensing prescriptions automatically. Dr. Chris Newman, a physician at Archbold Hospital in Thomasville, Georgia, credits Archie with being failsafe and fast. "We package everything that comes in with a site-specific barcode," he said, explaining the system for a WALB-Albany television report. "The robot knows what it is, its strength, manufacturer, and expiration date." The patient is also scanned, and a match is made before a drug is dispensed. Dr. Newman describes the system as 100 percent accurate. Doctors regard Archie's cost as tiny compared to the potential cost of giving a patient the wrong medication, according to the report. . . .

Copyright by McDougal Littell, a division of Houghton Mifflin Company

Economics: Concepts and Choices Chapter 5: Supply — Case Study Resources 97 Unit 2 Resource Book

A

Name ______ Date ______

CHAPTER 5 | READINGS IN FREE ENTERPRISE
Supply

Is It Demand?

Economists often debate what causes increases in prices. The following article provides one explanation for the increase in gas prices in 2006.

Demand Shock

With the partial shutdown of Prudhoe Bay [in Alaska] last week, motorists who have felt the pain at the pump [of $3 per gallon gas] had more to moan about as the simple dynamics of supply and demand kept the prices hovering at a level that seemed unfathomable a few years ago. . . .

The latest target of drivers' venom is BP PLC [British Petroleum Public Limited Company], which admitted it failed to properly test and maintain pipes that became corroded and leaked twice this year near the edge of the Arctic Ocean.

While the loss of about 200,000 barrels of Alaskan crude a day will contribute to the high price of gasoline, $3-per-gallon gas is likely to become the norm until the desire for it declines.

"The real story here is this is demand price shock, not a supply shock," said Severin Borenstein, director of the University of California Energy Institute. "$3 a gallon is not much of a story anymore. People don't like it, but they adjust and go on with their lives". . . .

The last time the market was normal was in January 2003, Borenstein said. That was before the U.S. invasion of Iraq. The economy was still lukewarm and the price of a barrel of oil was in the $20s and forecast to stay that way for another 20 years. The Iraq invasion led to a huge cutback in production there, eventually taking a million barrels a day off the market. At the same time, the U.S. and world economies improved and demand for oil increased.

In June 2004, drivers got the first bitter taste of $2-a-gallon gas, according to the Energy Information Administration. . . .It then dropped below $1.80 a gallon before starting a mostly steady climb to a record high of nearly $3.07 in September, pushed up by hurricanes Katrina and Rita that knocked out oil wells and refineries in the Gulf of Mexico.

"Whenever there is a disruption, whether political unrest in Nigeria or worries about what will happen in Iran or the hurricanes in the Gulf of Mexico last year, if you lose supply in one of these places it's hard to find," said Ron Planting, an economist with the American Petroleum Institute. . . .

With the slight hike in prices last week many motorists were shaking their fists at BP, which like other oil companies reported record profit as the price of gas skyrocketed. But Borenstein said the laws of the market, not the oil companies, are to blame. "People seem to think this is shocking and outrageous," he said. "Gas costs a lot and anyone who has it is going to make more money. It's like asking someone in San Francisco to sell a home below market price because they're already making a lot of money."

From the Durham, N.C. *Herald Sun*, August 14, 2006.

Copyright by McDougal Littell, a division of Houghton Mifflin Company

Economics: Concepts and Choices Chapter 5: Supply — Readings in Free Enterpris[e] Unit 2 Resource Bo[ok]

Focus & Motivate

Objective

Explain the law of supply and describe the factors that affect changes in supply.

Why the Concept Matters

Explain that most people are both consumers and producers. Encourage students to consider both financial and intangible costs and rewards for the things that they listed in the activity in the pupil edition on p. 129. Lead students to conclude that greater rewards give them an incentive to produce more and higher costs are an incentive to produce less.

Analyzing the Photograph

Direct students to study the photograph and read the caption. Discuss with the class what factors, other than wages paid, might play into how workers affect production. *(Possible answers: level of skill or precision that each worker has; absenteeism; theft; being highly motivated)*

Now ask students to consider how the other factors mentioned in the caption might affect production. *(Possible answers: If the cost of raw materials went up, then production might slow down. If access to a raw material was cut off, production might stop. If management decided to add employees, production might increase.)*

Conclude by telling students that most anything they mention is ultimately tied into price, and price is the driver of supply.

Supply
The cost of raw materials, the wages paid to workers, and the production decisions made by managers all affect the supply of televisions.

128

CONTENT STANDARDS

NCEE STANDARDS

Standard 8: Role of Price in Market Systems

Students will understand that
Prices send signals and provide incentives to buyers and sellers. When supply or demand changes, market prices adjust, affecting incentives.

Students will be able to use this knowledge to
Predict how prices change when the number of buyers or sellers in a market changes, and explain how the incentives facing individual buyers and sellers are affected.

Benchmarks

Students will know that

- High prices for a good or service provide incentives for . . . producers to make or sell more of it. Lower prices for a good or service provide incentives for . . . producers to make or sell less of it. *(pages 131–136)*
- Supply of a product changes when there are changes in either the prices of the productive resources used to make the good or service, the technology used to make the good or service, the profit opportunities available to producers by selling other goods or services, or the number of sellers in a market. *(pages 146–151)*

CHAPTER

5 Supply

CONCEPT REVIEW

Demand is the willingness to buy a good or service and the ability to pay for it.

CHAPTER 5 KEY CONCEPT

Supply is the willingness and ability of producers to offer goods and services for sale.

WHY THE CONCEPT MATTERS

You may not think of yourself as a producer, but you are. You offer your labor when you do chores around the house or work at a part-time job. If you have a car, you sometimes provide transportation for your friends. Also, if you belong to a sports or academic team, you supply your skills and knowledge. List five things that you supply. Then list the costs you incur and the rewards you receive for supplying them. How would your willingness and ability to supply these things be affected if these costs and rewards changed?

Online Highlights

More at ClassZone.com

Go to ECONOMICS UPDATE for chapter updates and current news on the use of robots in industry. (See Case Study, pp. 158–159.) ▶

Animated Economics

Go to ANIMATED ECONOMICS for interactive lessons on the graphs and tables in this chapter.

Interactive Review

Go to INTERACTIVE REVIEW for concept review and activities.

How does the use of robots affect the supply of goods and services? See the Case Study on pages 158–159.

From the Classroom

Joanne Benjamin, Los Gato

What Is Supply?

Remind students that supply in econom refers to people or businesses willing and to supply a good or service. The profit incent is important in determining whether they are willing and able.

Tell students you are issuing an exclusive contract to sell soda on campus during lunch. The wholesale price for soda is $0.25 per can. Ask students to raise their hands if they are willing to become the campus supplier if they have to sell the soda for $0.25 per can (retail) and record the number of students on the board. What if the retail price were $0.35 per can? Continue to ask, in increments of $0.10, if they would be willing to supply soda, and record the number each time. Then place the recorded numbers into a supply schedule and graph the supply curve for the class. Conclude by discussing the relationship between quantity supplied and price.

Previewing Chapter Technology at ClassZone.com

Economics Update Students will find references to online articles or statistics that update information in the pupil edition on pages 131, 152, and 158.

Animated Economics Students will find interactive supply schedules, supply curves, production costs schedules, and elasticity examples related to materials on pages 132, 134, 147, 148, and 155.

Interactive Review Students will find additional section and chapter assessment support for materials on pages 137, 145, 153, 157, 160.

TEACHER MEDIA FAVORITES

Books

- Cortada, James W. *The Digital Hand: Volume I: How Computers Changed the Work of American Manufacturing, Transportation, and Retail Industries.* New York: Oxford UP, 2004. Broad survey of how computer technology changed the American economy.
- Oliver, Lianabel. *The Cost Management Toolbox: A Manager's Guide to Controlling Costs and Boosting Profits.* New York: American Management Association, 2000. Real-life examples show how manufacturers and service providers use information about costs to improve their businesses' profitability.
- Thro, Ellen. *Robotics: Intelligent Machines for the New Century.* New York: Facts on File, 2003. Relates the complex subject of robotics to practical applications in an interesting manner.

Videos/DVDs

- *The Invisible Hand: Economics in Daily Life.* 22 Minutes. Learning Seed, 2004. Explores economic concepts used everyday, including cost, supply and demand, prices, and profits and losses.
- *The Firm/Supply & Demand.* Two 30-minute programs. Economics USA, 1985. Part of the Annenberg/CPB Collection. Uses a TV news format to analyze topics of importance to understanding the U.S. economy.

Software

- *Virtual Economics® Version 3.0.* New York: National Council on Economic Education, 2005. Provides a complete resource library for understanding and teaching basic economics concepts.

Internet

Visit **ClassZone.com** to link to

- a variety of chapter-specific, content-reviewed sites
- updates on data and topics presented throughout the chapter sections and Case Study
- updates to the Power Presentations

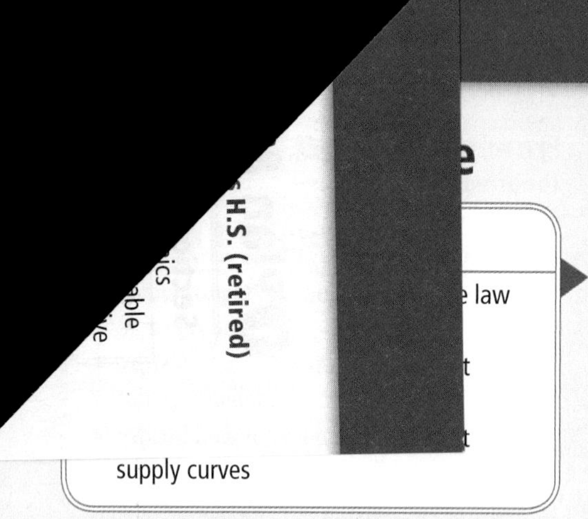

❷ Focus & Motivate

Connecting to Everyday Life Explain that this section focuses on the meaning of *supply* in economics, which concerns the ways producers decide what goods or services to sell. Ask students to name different types of businesses that provide some products that they use regularly.

Taking Notes Remind students to take notes as they read by completing a cluster diagram. They can use the Graphic Organizer at **Interactive Review @ ClassZone.com**. A sample is shown below.

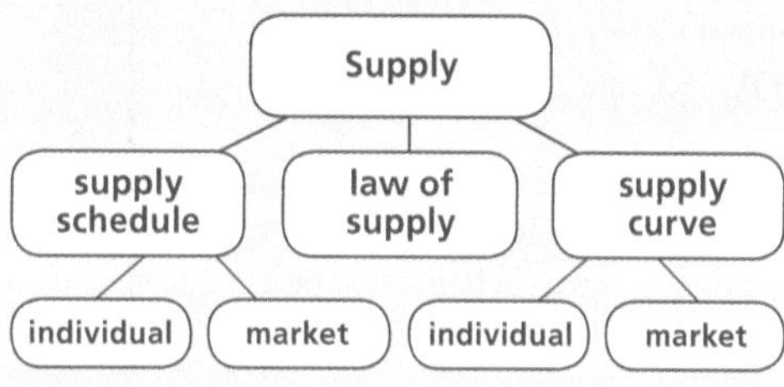

SECTION 1

What Is Supply?

OBJECTIVES

In Section 1, you will
- define *supply* and outline what the law of supply says
- explain how to create and interpret supply schedules
- explain how to create and interpret supply curves

KEY TERMS

supply, *p. 130*
law of supply, *p. 131*
supply schedule, *p. 132*
market supply schedule, *p. 132*
supply curve, *p. 134*
market supply curve, *p. 134*

TAKING NOTES

As you read Section 1, complete a cluster diagram like the one shown using the key concepts and other helpful words and phrases. Use the Graphic Organizer at **Interactive Review @ ClassZone.com**

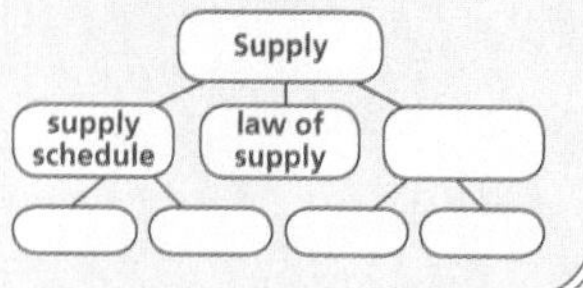

The Law of Supply

KEY CONCEPTS

In Chapter 4, you learned about the demand side of market interactions and how consumers serve their interests by purchasing the best products at the lowest possible price. You also discovered that there are other factors that change demand at every price. Demand, however, is only one side of the market equation. In this chapter, you will learn about the supply side of the equation in order to understand why producers want to provide products at the highest possible price.

QUICK REFERENCE

Supply is the desire and ability to produce and sell a product.

Supply refers to the willingness and ability of producers to offer goods and services for sale. Anyone who provides goods or services is a producer. Manufacturers who make anything from nutrition bars to automobiles are producers. So, too, are farmers who grow crops, retailers who sell products, and utility companies, airlines, or pet sitters who provide services.

The two key words in the definition of supply are *willingness* and *ability*. For example, the Smith family grows various fruits and vegetables on their small farm. They sell their produce at a local farmers' market. If the prices at the market are too low, the Smiths may not be willing to take on the expense of growing and

Supplying a Service Service providers, such as utility companies, are producers too.

SECTION 1 PROGRAM RESOURCES

ON LEVEL

Lesson Plans
- Core, p. 15

Unit 2 Resource Book
- Reading Study Guide, pp. 53–54
- Economic Skills and Problem Solving Activity, pp. 93–94
- Section Quiz, p. 61

STRUGGLING READERS

Unit 2 Resource Book
- Reading Study Guide with Additional Support, pp. 55–57
- Reteaching Activity, p. 62

ENGLISH LEARNERS

Unit 2 Resource Book
- Reading Study Guide with Additional Support (Spanish), pp. 58–60

INCLUSION

Lesson Plans
- Modified for Inclusion, p. 15

GIFTED AND TALENTED

Unit 2 Resource Book
- Readings in Free Enterprise: Is It Demand?, p. 95; Is It Supply?, p. 96

TECHNOLOGY

eEdition DVD-ROM

eEdition Online

Power Presentation DVD-ROM

Economics Concepts Transparencies
- CT15 Petroleum Market Supply Schedule and Supply Curve

Daily Test Practice Transparencies, TT15

ClassZone.com

transporting their produce. Also, if the weather is bad and the Smiths' crops of fruits and vegetables are ruined, they will not be able to supply anything for the market. In other words, they will not offer produce for sale if they do not have both the willingness and the ability to do so.

As is true with demand, price is a major factor that influences supply. The **law of supply** states that producers are willing to sell more of a good or service at a higher price than they are at a lower price. Producers want to earn a profit, so when the price of a good or service rises they are willing to supply more of it. When the price falls, they want to supply less of it. In other words, price and quantity supplied have a direct relationship. This relationship is illustrated in Figure 5.1.

QUICK REFERENCE

The **law of supply** states that when prices decrease, quantity supplied decreases, and when prices increase, quantity supplied increases.

FIGURE 5.1 LAW OF SUPPLY

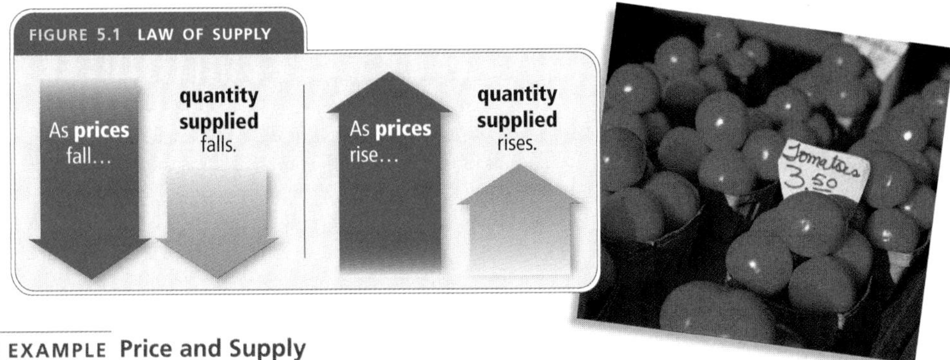

EXAMPLE Price and Supply

Let's take a closer look at how price and quantity supplied are related by returning to the Smiths and their produce business. The Smiths travel to the Montclair Farmers' Market every Wednesday and Saturday to sell a variety of fruits and vegetables—blueberries, peaches, nectarines, sweet corn, peppers, and cucumbers. However, their specialty crop is the tomato. How should the Smiths decide on the quantity of tomatoes to supply to the farmers' market? The price they can get for their crop is a major consideration.

The Smiths know that the standard price for tomatoes is $1 per pound. What quantity of tomatoes will the Smiths offer for sale at that price? They decide that they are willing to offer 24 pounds. What if the price of tomatoes doubled to $2 per pound? The Smiths might decide that the price is so attractive that they are willing to offer 50 pounds of tomatoes for sale on the market. In contrast, if the price fell to 50 cents, the Smiths might decide to supply only 10 pounds. Furthermore, at prices under 50 cents per pound, they may not be willing to supply any tomatoes. Look again at the definition of the law of supply. As you can see, it provides a concise description of how producers behave.

Economics Update

Find an update on farmers' markets at **ClassZone.com**

APPLICATION Analyzing Effects

A. You sell peppers at the Montclair Farmers' Market. If the price of peppers increased from 40 cents to 60 cents each, how would your quantity supplied of peppers change? How would your quantity supplied change if the price decreased to 25 cents? Quantity supplied would increase. Quantity supplied would decrease.

3 Teach

The Law of Supply

Discuss

- Why do price and supply have a direct relationship? *(because producers will supply more of something if they can make more money by selling at a higher price)*
- Why do producers and consumers have different attitudes toward price? *(because producers want to make money by charging higher prices while consumers want to save money by paying lower prices)*

More About . . .

Farmers' Markets

Farmers' markets have become increasingly popular since the mid-1990s. The U.S. Department of Agriculture estimates that there were about 3,100 across the country in 2002. These markets provide a way for farmers to receive a greater part of the revenue for their produce because they are selling at retail rather than wholesale. Many smaller farmers find it difficult to get their produce into supermarkets.

These farmers recognize that they can often charge higher prices at farmers' markets because the produce there is generally fresher and, therefore, of higher quality than at supermarkets.

Economics Update

At **ClassZone.com**, students will see updated information on farmers' markets.

LEVELED ACTIVITY

Pricing Produce for the Farmers' Market

Time 30 minutes

Objective Students will demonstrate an understanding of the law of supply as it relates to produce at a farmers' market.

Basic

Choose two additional fruits or vegetables from those listed in the text on page 131. Set prices for each one and create supply schedules and supply curves for them. Compare the prices of these products to the prices of tomatoes. Then, decide which product you would want to take more of to the market, based on the law of supply.

On Level

Choose three additional fruits or vegetables from those listed in the text on page 131. Set prices for each one and create market supply curves for them. Compare these market supply curves to the market supply curve for tomatoes. Rank the four products in their order of popularity among farmers, based on their prices.

Challenge

As the manager of the market, set prices for six products listed in the text on page 131 and create market supply curves for them. Write a report summarizing the produce available and the prices of each type. Include ideas for ways farmers might get better prices for the produce they offer at the market.

Supply Schedules

Discuss

- Why do the farmers want to sell more tomatoes at $2 per pound than at $1 per pound? *(because the farmers follow the law of supply and prefer to sell more at higher prices)*
- What is the relationship between a market supply schedule and an individual supply schedule? *(A market supply schedule reflects the sum of all the individual supply schedules in a market.)*

Analyzing Tables: Figure 5.2

Point out that supply schedules are created in a similar way to demand schedules, with the highest price at the top of the first column and the lowest at the bottom. The quantity supplied, shown in the second column, also starts with the highest and decreases as the price drops. Refer back to Figure 5.1 and ask students in which direction the arrow would point for each column of the supply schedule. *(Answer: down for both columns)*

Answer

1. *40*
2. *The right-hand column shows quantity supplied rather than quantity demanded. It also shows that price and quantity supplied have a direct relationship, while a demand schedule shows that price and quantity demanded have an inverse relationship.*

Animated Economics The supply schedule highlights how many tomatoes the Smiths will sell at various prices. It will help students understand the relationship between price and quantity supplied.

Supply Schedules

QUICK REFERENCE

A **supply schedule** lists how much of a good or service an individual producer is willing and able to offer for sale at each price.

A **market supply schedule** lists how much of a good or service all producers in a market are willing and able to offer for sale at each price.

KEY CONCEPTS

A **supply schedule** is a table that shows how much of a good or service an individual producer is willing and able to offer for sale at each price in a market. In other words, a supply schedule shows the law of supply in table form. A **market supply schedule** is a table that shows how much of a good or service all producers in a market are willing and able to offer for sale at each price.

EXAMPLE Individual Supply Schedule

A supply schedule is a two-column table that is similar in format to a demand schedule. The left-hand column of the table lists various prices of a good or service, and the right-hand column shows the quantity supplied at each price.

The Smiths' supply of tomatoes can be expressed in a supply schedule (Figure 5.2). How many pounds of tomatoes are the Smiths willing to sell when the price is $1.25 per pound? What if the price is $0.50 per pound? Or $2.00 per pound? Your answers to these questions show that the Smiths' quantity supplied of tomatoes depends on the price.

FIGURE 5.2 THE SMITHS' TOMATO SUPPLY SCHEDULE

	Price per Pound ($)	Quantity Supplied (in pounds)
a →	2.00	50
	1.75	40
	1.50	34
	1.25	30
	1.00	24
	0.75	20
b →	0.50	10

a At the top price of $2.00, the Smiths are willing to sell 50 pounds of tomatoes.

b At $0.50, the Smiths are willing to provide only 10 pounds of tomatoes for sale.

Notice that when the price falls, the quantity of tomatoes that the Smiths are willing to sell also falls. When the price rises, the quantity they are willing to sell rises. So quantity supplied and price have a direct relationship.

ANALYZE TABLES

1. How many pounds of tomatoes will the Smiths offer for sale if the price is $1.75?
2. How is this supply schedule different from a demand schedule for tomatoes?

Animated Economics Use an interactive supply schedule at **ClassZone.com**

DIFFERENTIATING INSTRUCTION

Struggling Readers

Review Key Concepts

Explain that key concepts in Sections 1, 3, and 4 of this chapter are parallel to many concepts relating to demand in Chapter 4. Help students review these concepts by inviting volunteers to explain what they know about the law of demand, demand schedules, and demand curves. Write student information on the board for them to refer to as they read. Repeat the process for each section. Invite students to refer back to definitions and figures in Chapter 4 as needed.

English Learners

Compare and Contrast

Point out that the words *similar, both,* and *like* often signal a comparison; the words *different, but,* and *except* signal a contrast.

- Have students note places where these words appear. This will help them understand when to compare and contrast key concepts throughout the chapter.
- Help students formulate one compare and one contrast statement about supply schedules and market supply schedules. Tell them to use these models to answer question 2 under Figure 5.2.

EXAMPLE **Market Supply Schedule**

The supply schedule in Figure 5.2 shows how many pounds of tomatoes an individual producer, the Smith family, is willing and able to offer for sale at each price in the market. The schedule also shows that, in response to changes in price, the Smiths will supply a greater or lesser number of tomatoes. However, sometimes an individual supply schedule does not provide a complete picture of the quantity of a good or service that is being supplied in a given market. For example, several fruit and vegetable stands at the Montclair Farmers' Market sell tomatoes. If you want to know the quantity of tomatoes available for sale at different prices at the entire farmers' market, you need a market supply schedule. This shows the quantity supplied by all of the producers who are willing and able to sell tomatoes.

Take a look at the market supply schedule for tomatoes in Figure 5.3. Notice that it is similar to the Smiths' supply schedule, except that the quantities supplied are much larger. It also shows that, as with individual quantity supplied, market quantity supplied depends on price.

FIGURE 5.3 TOMATO MARKET SUPPLY SCHEDULE

	Price per Pound ($)	Quantity Supplied (in pounds)
a →	2.00	350
	1.75	300
	1.50	250
b →	1.25	200
	1.00	150
	0.75	100
c →	0.50	50

ⓐ At the top price of $2.00, the fruit and vegetable stands will offer 350 pounds of tomatoes for sale.

ⓑ At $1.25, the quantity supplied of tomatoes is 200 pounds.

ⓒ At the low price of $0.50, the quantity supplied falls to 50 pounds.

So, markets behave in the same way as individual suppliers. As prices decrease, the quantity supplied of tomatoes decreases. As prices increase, the quantity supplied increases.

ANALYZE TABLES

1. How does the quantity supplied of tomatoes change when the price rises from $0.75 a pound to $1.75 a pound?
2. How does this market supply schedule illustrate the law of supply?

In Chapter 4, you learned that Rafael, the owner of Montclair Video Mart, used market research to create a market demand schedule. Market research can also be used to create a market supply schedule. Producers in some markets are able to use research conducted by the government or by trade organizations to learn the prices and quantity supplied by all the producers in a given market.

APPLICATION **Applying Economic Concepts**

B Imagine that you own a health food store that sells several brands of nutrition bars. Create a supply schedule showing how many bars you would be willing to sell each month at prices of $5, $4, $3, $2, and $1.

Supply schedules should reflect the law of supply by showing higher quantities supplied at higher prices than at lower prices.

Analyzing Tables: Figure 5.3

Ask students how and why this table and Figure 5.2 are similar and different. *(similarity: both show the same prices in the first column because both are about the prices of tomatoes used by individual producers; difference: the quantities supplied are much larger because they reflect all producers in the market)*

Answer

1. *It increases from 100 to 300.*
2. *It shows that as prices rise, quantity supplied increases; as prices fall, quantity supplied decreases.*

Technomics

Market Research Sources
The website KnowThis.com is the WWW–Virtual Library site dedicated to market research. The Web page entitled "Demographics, Economic and Business Statistics" contains descriptions of and links to a variety of federal government websites that provide information about domestic and international business. Much of the information is free, but some sites, such as STAT-USA, charge for their reports. KnowThis.com also contains links to company and industry information, research report sources, and free articles and tutorials about marketing.

SMALL GROUP ACTIVITY

Creating Supply and Market Supply Schedules

Time 30 minutes ◑

Task Create a supply schedule and a market supply schedule for a common product.

Materials Needed two blank two-column charts (one per student and one per group), pens or pencils

Activity

- Organize students into small groups. Ask each group to determine a product that all members of the group would like to sell to raise money for a class trip. Then have groups set five different prices for their selected product.
- Direct each student in the group to create a supply schedule that shows how many of the products he or she would sell in a month at the different prices.
- Instruct group members to combine the information in their supply schedules to create a market supply schedule.
- Invite volunteers to share their market supply schedules with the class and state how they reflect the law of supply.

Rubric

	Understanding Supply and Market Supply Schedules	Presentation of Information
4	excellent	clear; complete
3	good	mostly clear
2	fair	sometimes clear
1	poor	sketchy

Supply Curves

Discuss

- How is a supply curve related to a supply schedule? *(A supply curve is the representation on a line graph of the information in a supply schedule.)*
- What do the points on the supply curve represent? *(They reflect the quantity supplied at each price.)*

Presentation Options

Review supply curves by using the following presentation options:

 **Power Presentations DVD-ROM**
Using the Display Tool, you can learn about how producers price goods and services in the market by highlighting data from a market supply schedule.

 **Economics Concepts Transparencies**
- CT15 Petroleum Market Supply Schedule and Supply Curve

Supply Curves

QUICK REFERENCE

A **supply curve** shows the data from a supply schedule in graph form.

A **market supply curve** shows the data from a market supply schedule in graph form.

KEY CONCEPTS

A **supply curve** is a graph that shows how much of a good or service an individual producer is willing and able to offer for sale at each price. To create a supply curve, transfer the data from a supply schedule to a graph. A **market supply curve** shows the data from the market supply schedule. In other words, it shows how much of a good or service all of the producers in a market are willing and able to offer for sale at each price.

EXAMPLE Individual Supply Curve

Study the supply curve (Figure 5.4) created from the Smiths' supply schedule. How many pounds of tomatoes will the Smiths supply at $1.50 per pound? How will the Smiths' quantity supplied change if the price increases or decreases by 25 cents? Find the answers to these questions by running your finger along the curve. As you can see, the supply curve is a graphic representation of the law of supply. When the price increases, the quantity supplied increases; when the price decreases, the quantity supplied decreases. Note that the supply curve in Figure 5.4, and the schedule on which it is based, were created using the assumption that all other economic factors except price remain the same. You'll learn more about these other factors in Section 3.

FIGURE 5.4 THE SMITHS' TOMATO SUPPLY CURVE

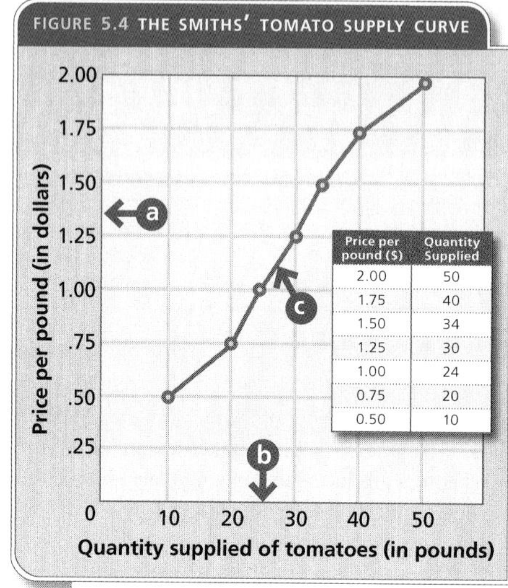

Price per pound ($)	Quantity Supplied
2.00	50
1.75	40
1.50	34
1.25	30
1.00	24
0.75	20
0.50	10

Notice that **supply curves** always slope upward from lower left to upper right.

- **a** The vertical axis of the graph shows prices, with the highest at the top.
- **b** The horizontal axis shows quantities supplied, with the lowest on the far left.
- **c** The specific quantities supplied at specific prices listed on the supply schedule are plotted as points on the graph and connected to create the supply curve.

ANALYZE GRAPHS

1. How many pounds of tomatoes will the Smiths offer for sale when the price is $1.50?
2. How does this supply curve illustrate the law of supply?

Animated Economics
Use an interactive supply curve at **ClassZone.com**

DIFFERENTIATING INSTRUCTION

Struggling Readers

Summarize Information
Have students work in pairs to summarize what they have learned about supply by filling in a graphic organizer like the one shown below.

Law of Supply	Supply Schedules	Supply Curves

Inclusion

Enlarge Graphs
Students who have visual impairments may benefit from enlarged versions of Figures 5.4 and 5.5. These are available online on the eEdition of the pupil edition at **ClassZone.com**.

EXAMPLE Market Supply Curve

Like the Smiths' individual supply curve, the market supply curve for all the stands that sell tomatoes at the Montclair Farmers' Market shows the quantity supplied at different prices. In other words, the graph shows the quantity of tomatoes that all of the producers, or the market as a whole, are willing and able to offer for sale at each price. The market supply curve (Figure 5.5) differs in scope from the Smiths' individual supply curve, but it is constructed in the same way. As in Figure 5.4, the vertical axis displays prices and the horizontal axis displays quantities supplied.

FIGURE 5.5 TOMATO MARKET SUPPLY CURVE

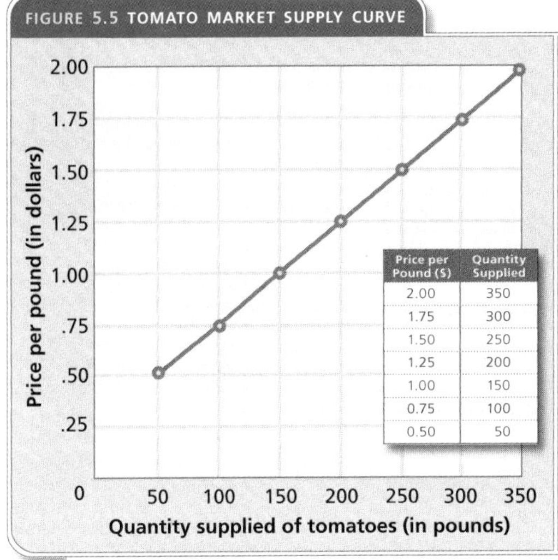

Notice that **market supply curves** slope upward from lower left to upper right, just as individual supply curves do.

The main difference between the two types of curves is that the quantities supplied at each price are much larger on a market supply curve. This is because the curve represents a group of producers (a market), not just one producer.

ANALYZE GRAPHS

1. At which price will all the fruit and vegetable stands want to sell 200 pounds of tomatoes?
2. How is the slope of this supply curve different from the slope of a market demand curve?

Look at Figure 5.5 one more time. What is the quantity supplied at $1.50? How will quantity supplied change if the price increases by 25 cents or decreases by 25 cents? Once again, find the answers to these questions by running your finger along the curve. As you can see, the market supply curve, just like the individual supply curve, vividly illustrates the direct relationship between price and quantity supplied. If the price of tomatoes increases among all of the suppliers at the farmers' market, then the quantity supplied of tomatoes also increases. And, conversely, if the price decreases, then the quantity supplied decreases as well. As with the individual supply curve, the market supply curve is constructed on the assumption that all other economic factors remain constant—only the price per pound of tomatoes changes.

Analyzing Graphs: Figures 5.4 and 5.5

Make sure students understand that the supply schedules shown with the supply curves are the same ones shown in Figures 5.2 and 5.3. Direct them to note where the values from the supply schedules are placed on the axes of the graphs. Point out that values on each axis increase from zero in the lower left corner. Ask why the vertical axes of the two graphs are the same but the horizontal axes are different. *(In both cases, the vertical axis reflects the prices of tomatoes. However, the horizontal axis in 5.4 reflects the quantity supplied by an individual supplier, while the horizontal axis in 5.5 reflects the quantity supplied by all the suppliers in the market.)*

Answers

Figure 5.4

1. *34*
2. *It shows that the quantity supplied increases in direct relationship to increases in price.*

Figure 5.5

1. *$1.25*
2. *The supply curve slopes upward from lower left to upper right, while the demand curve slopes downward from upper left to lower right.*

Animated Economics The supply curve shows how the law of supply can be shown on a graph. It will help students understand how the quantity supplied increases as price increases.

INDIVIDUAL ACTIVITY

Illustrating Supply Curves

Time 30 minutes

Task Create a graphic to show the relationship of a supply curve to a market supply curve.

Materials Needed paper and markers, pens, or colored pencils

Activity

- Invite students to develop a visual to show how a supply curve is related to a market supply curve. Use Figures 5.4 and 5.5 as the basis of information to illustrate.
- Some possible visuals include two lines on a single graph, multiple supply curves that add up to the market supply curve, a bar graph, an illustration, or a collage.
- Bar graph hint: Prices increase from left to right on the horizontal axis and quantity is shown on the vertical axis. Students may use a single bar at each price divided into segments or two bars to show the Smiths' supply compared to the market supply.
- Allow students to share their visuals in small groups.

Rubric

	Understanding Supply and Market Supply Curves	Presentation of Information
4	excellent	clear; complete
3	good	mostly clear
2	fair	sometimes clear
1	poor	sketchy

A Global Perspective

Answers

1. *As the price (average salary) has increased, the quantity supplied of foreign players has also increased.*
2. *If price (average salary) decreases, quantity supplied will also decrease. Fewer foreign players might cause a decrease in the number of foreign fans and therefore a decrease in merchandise sold overseas.*

More About . . .

The Slope of Supply Curves
Producers construct supply curves based on their long-term marginal costs of production, which are the costs to produce each additional product and deliver it to market. Marginal cost is explained in Section 2. Because these costs increase as the quantity supplied increases, producers are only willing to produce more if prices are higher to offset their increased costs.

While most supply curves slope upward, there are a few exceptions. One is the supply curve for labor. If the price (wage) gets extremely high, for example $1 million per hour, the quantity of labor supplied actually decreases, since the worker does not need to work long to earn a large sum.

A GLOBAL PERSPECTIVE

The NBA Goes International

Until recently, nearly all of the National Basketball Association's (NBA) players were U.S-born. Before 1984, there were only 12 foreign-born players in the league, but that has changed. Opening day rosters in the 2005–06 season listed 82 international players, and they hailed from all over the world—from Spain and Slovenia in Europe to Senegal and the Sudan in Africa. Why has the supply of international players risen so dramatically? The average annual salary of an NBA player, which has risen from about $2 million in 1997 to over $4 million in 2006, is a likely explanation.

The international players are not the only group reaping monetary rewards. With people in China watching Yao Ming (at right), and French fans following Tony Parker, the NBA's overseas merchandise sales have increased rapidly. In 2004, the NBA sold an estimated $600 million in merchandise outside of the United States—about 20 percent of its overall merchandise sales.

FIGURE 5.6 INTERNATIONAL PLAYERS IN THE NBA

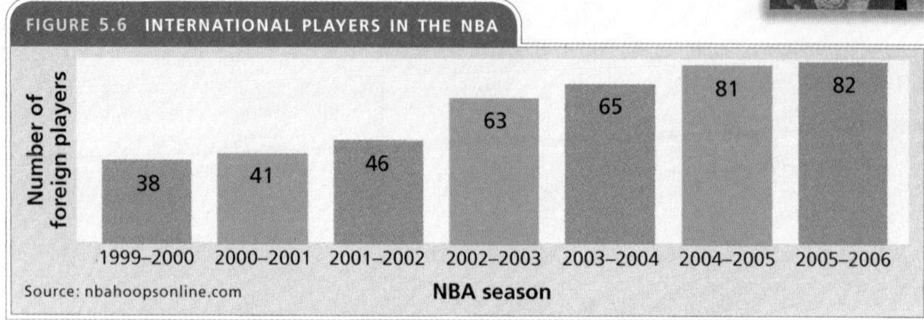

CONNECTING ACROSS THE GLOBE

1. **Synthesizing Economic Information** How do price and quantity supplied relate to salaries and labor in the NBA?
2. **Drawing Conclusions** What effect might a large drop in NBA salaries have on international sales of NBA merchandise?

Supply curves for all producers follow the law of supply. Whether the producers are manufacturers, farmers, retailers, or service providers, they are willing to supply more goods and services at higher prices, even though it costs more to produce more. A farmer, for example, spends more on seeds and fertilizer to grow more soybeans. Why are farmers and other producers willing to spend more when prices are higher? The answer is that higher prices signal the potential for higher profits, and the desire to increase profits drives decision making in the market. You will learn more about the costs of production and about maximizing profits in Section 2.

SMARTGrapher Create a supply curve at **ClassZone.com**

APPLICATION **Applying Economic Concepts**

C. Look back at the supply schedule for nutrition bars you created for Application B on page 133. Use it to create a supply curve.
Supply curves should accurately reflect data on the supply schedule and slope upward from lower left to upper right.

DIFFERENTIATING INSTRUCTION

English Learners

Use Synonyms and Antonyms
Explain that synonyms are words with similar meanings and antonyms are words with opposite meanings. Point out that the words *consumers* and *buyers* are synonyms for *demanders,* although the latter is not commonly used. *Producers* and *sellers* are synonyms for *suppliers. Producers* and *consumers* and *sellers* and *buyers* are pairs of antonyms. Encourage students to find other words used in the text as synonyms for producers. *(manufacturers, farmers, retailers, service providers)*

Gifted and Talented

Conduct Research
Have interested students use the Internet or library resources to research the growing numbers of foreign players in the National Basketball Association (NBA). Students may compare and contrast the information they find with that included in the Global Perspectives and related links. Encourage students to submit their findings in a written report that discusses the present and future economic benefits to the NBA of the increasing supply of foreign players.

SECTION 1 Assessment

Online Quiz
ClassZone.com

REVIEWING KEY CONCEPTS

1. Explain the differences between the terms in each of these pairs:
   a. *supply* / *law of supply*
   b. *supply schedule* / *supply curve*
   c. *market supply schedule* / *market supply curve*
2. Why does a supply curve slope upward?
3. What do the points on a market supply curve represent?
4. If the price of a video game increased, what would the law of supply predict about the quantity supplied of the game?
5. How is the law of supply similar to the law of demand? How is it different?
6. **Using Your Notes** How is a supply schedule different from a market supply schedule? Refer to your completed cluster diagram. Use the Graphic Organizer at **Interactive Review @ ClassZone.com**

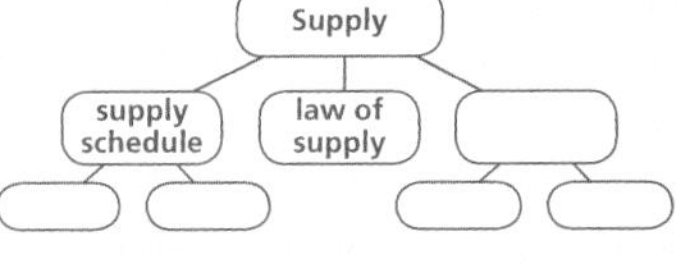

CRITICAL THINKING

7. **Explaining an Economic Concept** Focus on one item you buy regularly for which the price has changed. How did this shift in price influence supply?
8. **Making Inferences** The market supply schedule on page 133 shows that the quantity supplied of tomatoes priced at 50 cents per pound was 50 pounds. However, market research of customers at the farmers' market showed that the market demand at that price was 250 pounds of tomatoes. How do you explain the difference?
9. **Applying Economic Concepts** Return to the supply schedule for nutrition bars you created for Application B on page 133. Assume that the class represents all the sellers of nutrition bars in the market. Tabulate these individual supply schedules to create a market supply schedule. Then use that schedule to draw a market supply curve.
10. **Challenge** Why might producers not always be able to sell their products at the higher prices they prefer? Think about the laws of demand and supply and the different attitudes that consumers and producers have toward price. How might the market resolve this difference? (You will learn more about this in Chapter 6.)

ECONOMICS IN PRACTICE

Making a Market Supply Curve
Suppose that you are the head of the sporting goods dealers' association in your city. You survey all the stores that sell skis and determine how many pairs of skis they are willing to sell at various prices. Your research enables you to make the following market supply schedule.

Price per Pair ($)	Quantity Supplied
500	600
425	450
350	325
275	225
200	150
125	100

Create a Supply Curve Use this market supply schedule to draw a market supply curve. Be sure to label each axis of your graph.

Challenge Write a caption for your supply curve explaining what it shows.

Use ***SMARTGrapher*** @ ClassZone.com to complete this activity.

4 Assess & Reteach

Assess Review the Key Concepts questions with the class. Allow students to work in small groups on the Critical Thinking questions and discuss the answers as a class.

Unit 2 Resource Book
- Section Quiz, p. 61

Interactive Review @ ClassZone.com
- Section Quiz

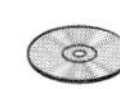

Test Generator CD-ROM
- Section Quiz

Reteach Divide students into three groups. Have each group review the material under one of the section's main headings and decide how to reteach that material to the rest of the class.

Unit 2 Resource Book
- Reteaching Activity, p. 62

Economics in Practice

Create a Supply Curve Students' market supply curves should accurately reflect the data on the market supply schedule, with prices on the vertical axis and quantities supplied on the horizontal axis, and should slope upward to reflect the law of supply.

Challenge Students' captions should apply the law of supply to the scenario.

SMARTGrapher Students can create a supply curve using **SmartGrapher @ ClassZone.com.**

SECTION 1 ASSESSMENT ANSWERS

Reviewing Key Concepts

1. a. *supply*, p. 130; *law of supply*, p. 131
   b. *supply schedule*, p. 132; *supply curve*, p. 134
   c. *market supply schedule*, p. 132; *market supply curve*, p. 134
2. because price and quantity supplied have a direct relationship
3. Each point represents the quantity supplied by all producers in a market at a given price.
4. The manufacturer would be willing to supply more games to the market.
5. Both show that quantity supplied is affected by price. The law of supply shows a direct relationship, while the law of demand shows an inverse relationship.
6. See page 130 for an example of a completed diagram. A supply schedule shows the quantity supplied by an individual producer at different prices; a market supply schedule shows the quantity supplied by all the producers in a given market.

Critical Thinking

7. Students should say that if the price increased, then quantity supplied increased, and if price decreased, then quantity supplied decreased.
8. The law of demand states that quantity demanded increases as prices decrease. That is why quantity demanded was larger than quantity supplied (which decreases when prices decrease).
9. Quantities supplied on the market supply schedule should reflect the sum of all the individual supply schedules. The market supply curve should accurately reflect the data on the market supply schedule and slope upward from lower left to upper right.
10. Students may say there may be little or no consumer demand at higher prices. They may suggest that the market will find a median price that satisfies consumers and producers.

Economics in Practice
See answers in side column above.

1 Plan & Prepare

Section 2 Objectives

- analyze how businesses calculate the right number of workers to hire
- determine how businesses calculate production costs
- explain how businesses use those calculations to determine the most profitable output

2 Focus & Motivate

Connecting to Everyday Life Explain that this section focuses on the costs that producers incur in bringing goods and services to market. Ask students to suggest some of the costs that their school might have in providing education to students.

Taking Notes Remind students to take notes as they read by completing a hierarchy diagram. They can use the Graphic Organizer at **Interactive Review @ ClassZone.com**. A sample is shown below.

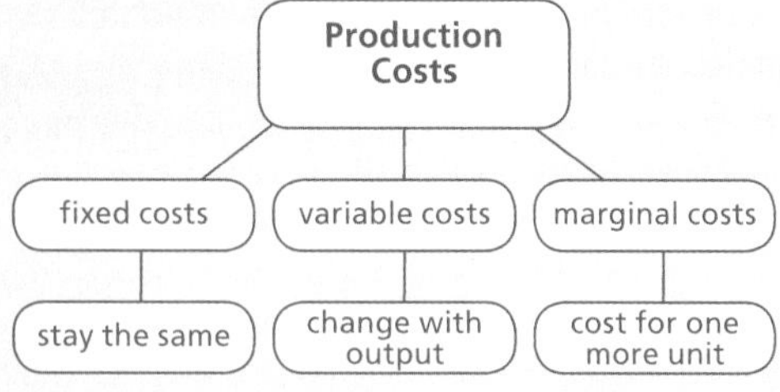

SECTION 2

What Are the Costs of Production?

OBJECTIVES	KEY TERMS	TAKING NOTES
In Section 2, you will • analyze how businesses calculate the right number of workers to hire • determine how businesses calculate production costs • explain how businesses use those calculations to determine the most profitable output	marginal product, *p. 138* specialization, *p. 138* increasing returns, *p. 139* diminishing returns, *p. 139* fixed cost, *p. 140* variable cost, *p. 140* total cost, *p. 140* marginal cost, *p. 140* marginal revenue, *p. 142* total revenue, *p. 142* profit-maximizing output, *p. 143*	As you read Section 2, complete a hierarchy diagram like this one to track main ideas and supporting details. Use the Graphic Organizer at **Interactive Review @ ClassZone.com**

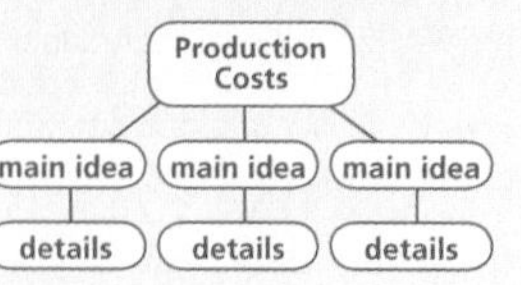

Labor Affects Production

KEY CONCEPTS

Let's look at an individual producer and the costs involved in supplying goods to the market. Janine owns a small factory that produces custom blue jeans. The factory has three sewing machines, and when there are three workers, one day's product is 12 pairs of jeans. She wonders how hiring one more worker will affect production. The change in total product that results from hiring one more worker is called the **marginal product**. With four workers, the factory produces 19 pairs of jeans a day, so the new employee's marginal product is 7 pairs of jeans. With a fifth worker, output jumps from 19 to 29—a marginal product of 10. Why did marginal product increase?

QUICK REFERENCE

Marginal product is the change in total output brought about by adding one more worker.

Specialization is having a worker focus on a particular aspect of production.

Each of Janine's original three workers had a sewing machine to operate, but they also had to cut cloth, package the finished jeans, and keep the shop clean. So, Janine's employees only spent half of their time sewing. The fourth employee helped with the other tasks, so marginal product increased. But the sewing machines were often still idle. The fifth worker allowed labor to be divided even more efficiently, which caused marginal product to increase markedly. Having each worker focus on a particular facet of production is called **specialization**. But does hiring more workers always cause marginal product to increase?

SECTION 2 PROGRAM RESOURCES

ON LEVEL

Lesson Plans
- Core, p. 16

Unit 2 Resource Book
- Reading Study Guide, pp. 63–64
- Economic Skills and Problem Solving Activity, pp. 93–94
- Section Quiz, p. 71

STRUGGLING READERS

Unit 2 Resource Book
- Reading Study Guide with Additional Support, pp. 65–67
- Reteaching Activity, p. 72

ENGLISH LEARNERS

Unit 2 Resource Book
- Reading Study Guide with Additional Support (Spanish), pp. 68–70

INCLUSION

Lesson Plans
- Modified for Inclusion, p. 16

GIFTED AND TALENTED

Unit 2 Resource Book

NCEE Student Activities
- Costs of Production, pp. 17–20

TECHNOLOGY

eEdition DVD-ROM

eEdition Online

Power Presentation DVD-ROM

Economics Concepts Transparencies
- CT16 Production Costs and Revenues Schedule for Manufacturing Footballs

Daily Test Practice Transparencies, TT16

ClassZone.com

EXAMPLE Marginal Product Schedule

A marginal product schedule shows the relationship between labor and marginal product. As you can see from Janine's marginal product schedule (Figure 5.7), one or two workers produced very little. But marginal product was still slightly larger with each added worker. Then with between three and six workers, the benefits of specialization become increasingly apparent. With up to six employees, Janine's operation experiences **increasing returns**, meaning each new worker adds more to total output than the last, as shown by the marginal product.

QUICK REFERENCE

Increasing returns occur when hiring new workers causes marginal product to increase.

FIGURE 5.7 JANINE'S MARGINAL PRODUCT SCHEDULE

Number of Workers	Total Product	Marginal Product
0	0	0
1	3	3
2	7	4
3	12	5
4	19	7
5	29	10
6	42	13
7	53	11
8	61	8
9	66	5
10	67	1
11	65	–2

(a) Four workers can produce 19 pairs of jeans. **Specialization** causes a healthy increase in **marginal product.**

(b) With seven workers, total product still increases, but marginal product begins to decrease.

(c) With eleven workers, total product decreases, and the marginal product is a negative number.

ANALYZE TABLES

1. At what number of workers is total product highest?
2. On the basis of this table, does it make sense for Janine to hire more than six workers? Explain your answer.

Figure 5.7 shows that increasing returns stop with the seventh worker. This is also related to specialization. Workers seven, eight, nine, and ten can still add to productivity, but their work overlaps with that of the first six workers. With between seven and ten employees, Janine's operation experiences **diminishing returns**, as each new worker causes total output to grow but at a decreasing rate. With eleven workers, total output actually decreases, and Janine experiences negative returns. This may happen as employees become crowded and operations become disorganized. It is rare, however, for a business to hire so many workers that it has negative returns.

QUICK REFERENCE

Diminishing returns occur when hiring new workers causes marginal product to decrease.

APPLICATION Drawing Conclusions

A. Why do Janine's increasing returns peak with six employees?
because there are are six tasks involved in production in her factory, so each worker has one specialized task

3 Teach

Labor Affects Production

Discuss

- What are some different problems a business might face if it has too few or too many workers? *(too few: resources are not used to full capacity, cannot produce as much as it wants; too many: workers get in each other's way, not enough work to keep all workers busy)*
- How are the stages of production related to total and marginal product? *(Increasing returns: marginal and total product both increase; diminishing returns: total product increases but marginal product decreases; negative returns: total output decreases because marginal product is a negative number)*

Analyzing Tables: Figure 5.7

Point out that marginal product is determined by looking at the increase in total product from one row to the next. For example, when the second worker is hired, total product increases from 3 to 7, so marginal product is 4. Suggest that students cover the Marginal Product column and calculate the marginal product by looking just at the total product column.

Answers

1. *10*
2. *Not on the basis of this table because of diminishing returns after six workers. However, the table does not account for profit level, which ultimately shows how many workers to hire.*

LEVELED ACTIVITY

Staffing and Running a Profitable Car Wash

Time 45 minutes

Objective Students will demonstrate an understanding of the stages of production, production costs, and profits for a car wash. (These concepts are covered in Section 2.)

Basic

Illustrate the three stages of production and describe how they relate to the number of workers you would hire. Give examples of fixed and variable costs and state how they relate to total costs. Describe what marginal cost means for a car wash. Write a sentence describing how you would determine profits.

On Level

Create a marginal product schedule like Figure 5.7. Identify the three stages of production. Illustrate the different types of costs related to the car wash business. Set the price of a car wash and calculate total revenue for each product level. Describe what you would need to know to maximize profit.

Challenge

Create a spreadsheet showing marginal product, production costs, and revenues modeled on Figures 5.7, 5.8, and 5.9. Identify profit-maximizing output. Write a business plan that provides detail on your different categories of costs. Suggest ways to increase profits by cutting costs or raising revenue.

Production Costs

Discuss

- Does change in the number of workers affect fixed costs or variable costs? Why? *(variable, because the number of workers, and therefore the total wages paid, varies with the amount of output)*
- How do changes in variable costs relate to the slope of the supply curve? *(Since variable costs increase as quantity supplied increases, a producer will only supply more product if he or she can charge higher prices to cover the costs.)*

More About . . .

Comparative Labor Costs
The U.S. Bureau of Labor Statistics (BLS) regularly measures labor costs in 31 foreign economies. In 2004, the average hourly labor compensation (wages and benefits) for manufacturing workers in these economies was 78 percent of that for U.S. workers. Those closest to U.S. rates were in Europe, Canada, and Japan.

Other Asian economies, including Hong Kong, South Korea, Singapore, and Taiwan, were far below the U.S. rate— about $6 compared to $23. Mexico was the lowest of the economies studied—about $3. An independent consultant found that the average hourly compensation for manufacturing workers in mainland China was only 57 cents in 2002.

Production Costs

QUICK REFERENCE

Fixed costs are those that business owners incur no matter how much they produce.

Variable costs depend on the level of production output.

Total cost is the sum of fixed and variable costs.

Marginal cost is the extra cost of producing one more unit.

KEY CONCEPTS

The goal of every business is to earn as much profit as possible. Profit is the money that businesses get from selling their products, once the money it costs to make those products has been subtracted. Businesses have different kinds of costs. **Fixed costs** are expenses that the owners of a business must incur whether they produce nothing, a little, or a lot. **Variable costs** are business costs that vary as the level of production output changes. Businesses find the **total cost** of production by adding fixed and variable costs together. Finally, businesses are interested in knowing their **marginal cost**, or the additional cost of producing one more unit of their product.

EXAMPLE Fixed and Variable Costs

Janine's fixed costs include the mortgage on her factory, her insurance, and the utilities that are on even when the factory is closed at night and on weekends. These costs are the same whether she is producing no jeans, 3 pairs, or 42 pairs of jeans per day. She must also pay the salaries of managers who keep the company running but are not involved directly in production.

Wages are one of Janine's chief variable costs. As she hires additional workers to increase the level of production, her costs for wages increase. She also incurs additional costs for more fabric, thread, zippers, and buttons as well as increased electricity costs to run the machines and light the factory. Shipping her jeans to customers is another variable cost. The more pairs of jeans that Janine's factory produces, the more her variable costs increase. Conversely, if she decides to cut back the hours or the number of workers, or if she closes the factory for a week's vacation, her variable costs decrease.

To determine the total cost to produce a certain number of pairs of jeans, Janine can add her fixed and variable costs. And by figuring out her marginal cost, she can determine what it costs to produce each additional pair of jeans.

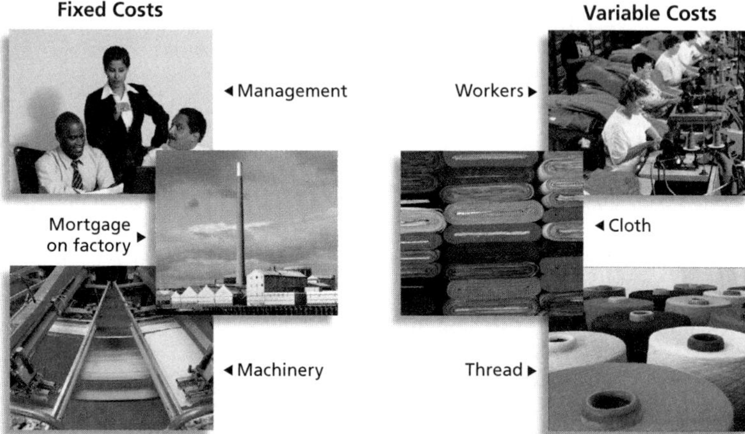

DIFFERENTIATING INSTRUCTION

Struggling Readers

Read a Chart
Suggest that students use a ruler or a piece of paper to help them focus when reading text that refers to specific parts of a complex table. They can use the ruler or paper to guide them as they read across a row or to block out other information as they focus on a single column. Encourage students to use this strategy whenever they come across a complex table. Also, they might want to write an equation at the top of Figure 5.8 to show the relation between columns 3, 4, and 5 (F + V = T).

English Learners

Build Economics Vocabulary
Help students understand the meaning of compound nouns that include *cost*. Relate the everyday meanings of *fixed*, *variable*, and *marginal* to their economic meanings when combined with *cost.*

- Have students make index cards with the word's everyday meaning on one side and the related economics term on the other. For example, *fixed* means "stays the same," *fixed costs* are those that do not change with amount of production.

EXAMPLE Production Costs Schedule

By looking at Figure 5.8, we can see Janine's costs and how they change as her quantity of jeans produced changes. Remember that her total product increased through the addition of the tenth worker and declined after the eleventh worker was added. The change in the number of workers is a major factor in the increase in variable costs at each quantity. You'll notice that the fixed costs remain the same no matter what the total product amounts to.

FIGURE 5.8 JANINE'S PRODUCTION COSTS SCHEDULE

Number of Workers	Total Product	(a) Fixed Costs ($)	(a) Variable Cost ($)	Total Cost ($)	Marginal Cost ($)
0	0	40	0	40	—
1	3	40	30 (b)→	70	10
2	7	40	62	102	8
3	12	40	97	137	7
4	19	40	132	172	5
5	29	40	172	212	4
6	42	40	211	251	3
7	53	40	277	317	6
8	61	40	373	413	12
9	66	40	473	513	20
10	67	40	503	543	30
11	65	40	539	579	—

(a) **Fixed costs** remain constant, while **variable costs** change at each quantity.

(b) Calculate **total costs** by adding together fixed costs and variable costs.

ANALYZE TABLES

1. How do the variable costs change when the total product increases from 7 pairs to 12 pairs?
2. When Janine has no workers, why are her fixed and total costs the same?

CONNECT TO MATH

To determine marginal cost, divide the change in total cost by the change in total product.

1. In Figure 5.8, total cost with four workers is $172; with three workers it is $137. 172−137=35
2. Total product with four workers is 19; with three workers it is 12. 19−12=7
3. Marginal cost in this case is figured by dividing 35 by 7. 35÷7=5

Marginal cost is determined by dividing change in total cost by change in total product. Notice in Figure 5.8 that marginal cost declines at first and then increases. The initial decline occurs because of increasing worker efficiency due to specialization. After that the marginal cost increases because of diminishing returns.

Janine now knows when her returns are increasing or diminishing and what it costs her to produce each additional pair of jeans. Her next step is to figure out her revenue, the money she makes from selling jeans, at each level of production.

APPLICATION Analyzing and Interpreting Data

B. Why does it cost Janine more to produce 65 pairs of jeans with 11 workers than to produce 66 pairs of jeans with 9 workers?

because her variable costs are higher by paying 11 workers instead of 9

Analyzing Tables: Figure 5.8

Point out that marginal cost decreases throughout the stage of increasing returns. A major reason for this decrease is that the fixed costs are spread across a greater number of units so each one costs less to make. Production resources are being used more efficiently. After this point, marginal costs rise due to diminishing returns. Remind students that the change in total product is the same thing as marginal product. Therefore, the formula might be restated as marginal cost = change in total cost/marginal product.

Answers

1. *They increase from $62 to $97.*
2. *Since there are no workers and total product is zero, there are no variable costs. As a result, Janine's fixed costs are her total costs.*

SMALL GROUP ACTIVITY

Brainstorming Fixed and Variable Costs

Time 20 minutes

Task Develop lists of fixed and variable costs for different types of producers.

Materials Needed one blank two-column chart per group, pens or pencils

Activity

- Organize students into four groups, each one representing a different type of producer: manufacturer, farmer, retailer, or service provider.
- Direct each group to determine a specific good or service that it will produce.
- Then instruct group members to discuss what kinds of fixed and variable costs their producer would incur. Tell them to list as many different costs as possible in their charts, with fixed costs in the first column and variable costs in the second.
- Invite groups to share their lists with the class. Discuss the similarities and differences in the kinds of cost each producer incurs.

Rubric

	Understanding Fixed and Variable Costs	Presentation of Information
4	excellent	clear and complete
3	good	mostly clear
2	fair	sometimes clear
1	poor	sketchy

Earning the Highest Profit

Discuss

- What are the costs and benefits that Janine is comparing when she performs a marginal analysis of her business? *(the variable costs involved in hiring an additional worker and producing more jeans and the increased revenue she receives from selling more jeans)*
- Why is it important for a producer to compare marginal revenue to marginal cost at each level of production? *(because as long as marginal revenue exceeds marginal cost it is profitable to keep producing additional product; when they are equal the point of maximum profit has been reached)*

More About . . .

Marginal Analysis

Marginal analysis is sometimes called cost/benefit analysis. As used by economists, *marginal* refers to the costs or benefits that are extra or due to a change. Economists and business owners are not the only ones who use this kind of analysis when making decisions. Ordinary people also use this kind of thinking, although not always in a quantitative way. Weighing the pros and cons or the trade-offs involved in a decision is a form of marginal analysis.

Earning the Highest Profit

QUICK REFERENCE

Marginal revenue is the money made from the sale of each additional unit of output.

Total revenue is a company's income from selling its products.

KEY CONCEPTS

Before a business can decide how much to produce in order to earn as much profit as possible, it must figure its marginal revenue and total revenue. **Marginal revenue** is the added revenue per unit of output, or the money made from each additional unit sold. In other words, marginal revenue is the price. If, for example, baseball hats were priced at $5 each, the money earned from each additional hat sold would be $5. **Total revenue** is the income a business receives from selling a product. It can be expressed by the formula **Total Revenue = P × Q**, where *P* is the price of the product and *Q* is the quantity purchased at that price. (Recall that you used this same formula to calculate total revenue on page 101.)

EXAMPLE Production Costs and Revenues Schedule

You have seen how Janine explored the relationship between labor and marginal product. You have also seen what it cost her to produce various quantities of jeans. Next, you will learn how she calculates her revenue and her profits.

Look at Figure 5.9, which shows Janine's costs, revenues, and profit for various levels of total product. Janine calculates her total revenue by multiplying the marginal revenue—$20 per pair of jeans—by the total product. Then she can determine her profit by subtracting her total costs from her total revenue. Remember that Janine is trying to decide how many workers she should hire and how many pairs of jeans she should produce in order to make the most profit. To make these decisions, she needs to perform a marginal analysis, which is a comparison of the added costs and benefits of an economic action. In other words, she needs to look at the costs and benefits of adding each additional worker and producing additional pairs of jeans.

Using Figure 5.9, Janine can see that when she has no employees, and therefore does not produce any jeans, she loses money because she still incurs fixed costs. If she hires one worker who produces three pairs of jeans, her costs are $70, but she only collects $60 in total revenue. Therefore, she still doesn't earn a profit. When she hires a second worker and together the two workers produce seven pairs of jeans, costs are $102 and revenues are $140, so she earns a very small profit of $38. Janine has finally passed the break-even point, the point at which enough revenue is being generated to cover expenses. At the break-even point, total costs and total revenue are exactly equal.

Like all business owners, Janine wants to do a lot better than break even. She wants to earn as much profit as possible. She can see that as she adds additional workers and produces more jeans, her profits increase.

DIFFERENTIATING INSTRUCTION

Inclusion

Create a Master Chart

Have students of varying abilities work in groups to create a large chart combining the information in Figures 5.7, 5.8, and 5.9. Divide students into three groups, each group copying information from one of the figures onto poster-sized graph paper. Have students combine the charts. Some columns repeat in each figure, so the master chart should have 10 columns. Encourage students to use the chart to discuss the relationship between workers, product, costs, and revenues.

Gifted and Talented

Perform a Marginal Analysis

Invite students to consider how the concepts of marginal analysis and diminishing returns might be applied to the amount of studying they do. Ask them to think about the number of hours they spend studying each week and consider the costs and benefits of additional hours of study. What will they give up (opportunity cost) by studying more? What will they gain? Would they reach a point of diminishing or even negative returns? Allow students to share their analysis in small groups.

FIGURE 5.9 JANINE'S PRODUCTION COSTS AND REVENUES SCHEDULE

Number of Workers	Total Product	Total Cost ($)	Marginal Cost ($)	Marginal Revenue ($)	(a) Total Revenue ($)	(b) Profit ($)
0	0	40	—	—	0	−40
1	3	70	10	20	60	−10
2	7	102	8	20	140 (c)	38
3	12	137	7	20	240	103
4	19	172	5	20	380	208
5	29	212	4	20	580	368
6	42	251	3	20	840	589
7	53	317	6	20	1,060	743
8	61	413	12	20	1,220	807
9	66	513	20 (d)	20	1,320	807
10	67	543	30	20	1,340	797
11	65	579	—	20	1,300	721

(a) Total revenue = marginal revenue (price) x total product.

(b) Profit = total revenue − total cost.

(c) When **total revenue** first exceeds total cost, a producer has passed the break-even point.

(d) At profit-maximizing output, marginal cost = marginal revenue.

ANALYZE TABLES

1. How does Janine calculate her total revenue and profits when she produces 42 pairs of jeans?
2. What happens to Janine's profits when she increases production from 66 to 67 pairs of jeans? Why does this happen?

When you look at Figure 5.9 again, you can see that Janine's profits continue to rise as she adds workers—up to and including the ninth worker—and produces more jeans. Why does this happen? Recall that during the stage of diminishing returns (see Figure 5.7 on page 139), total production continues to rise, but it rises more slowly. Although Janine is getting less production from each additional worker, marginal revenue is still greater than marginal cost, so Janine hires more workers, produces more, and increases profits.

When Janine's factory has nine workers producing 66 pairs of jeans, it has reached the level of production where it realizes the greatest amount of profit. This is called **profit-maximizing output**. This level of output is reached when the marginal cost and the marginal revenue are equal (here, both at $20). After that point, profits begin to decline. When Janine adds a tenth worker, the marginal product of one pair of jeans increases total revenue, but the increase in marginal cost is greater than the increase in marginal revenue. Since the goal of every business is to maximize profit, having a tenth employee runs counter to Janine's best interests.

QUICK REFERENCE

Profit-maximizing output is the level of production at which a business realizes the greatest amount of profit.

APPLICATION Analyzing and Interpreting Data

C. If the price of jeans increased to $22 per pair, how would it affect Janine's total revenue and profit? Total revenue would increase because total revenue is price multiplied by total product. Profit would also increase because total revenue would increase while costs remained unchanged.

Analyzing Tables: Figure 5.9

Point to the specific columns involved as you read each of the callouts. Encourage students to cover the Total Revenue column and perform the calculations suggested by callout "a." Then have them follow a similar process to determine profit, based on callout "b."

Answers

1. *42 x $20 (marginal revenue) = $840 total revenue; $840 – $251 (total cost) = $589 profit*
2. *Profits decline from $807 to $797 because marginal cost exceeds marginal revenue by $10.*

More About . . .

Law of Diminishing Returns

The law of diminishing returns states that when variable resources (such as labor) are added to fixed resources (such as a farmer's land, a factory's equipment, or the hours in a day) the output will increase up to a point and then begin to decline. This law applies to business production and also to personal decisions about how to spend our productive time. We can work, or study, or garden for more hours each week and will gain additional benefits up to a point, the point of diminishing returns.

CLASS ACTIVITY

Role-Playing Key Concepts

Time 60 minutes ●

Task Create and perform a skit to illustrate the costs of production in the jeans factory.

Materials Needed poster board, markers, and optional props

Activity

- Have students use the information in the section to create and perform a skit based on the key concepts as they relate to Janine's factory.
- Some students may be assigned to write the script, others may make simple graphics or props to illustrate concepts, and others may play the roles of Janine and her workers. One student may take the role of an economist who helps Janine make decisions about her factory.
- Suggest that students use the three main headings to create three scenes to portray the different stages of Janine's decision making.
- Allow students to perform the skit and discuss the concepts as a class.

Rubric

	Understanding of Costs of Production	Presentation of Information
4	excellent	clear and creative
3	good	mostly clear
2	fair	sometimes clear
1	poor	sketchy

Evaluating Sources

1 Plan & Prepare

Objectives

- Analyze techniques used in reading source material.
- Evaluate the sources used in a passage about supply.

2 Focus & Motivate

Explain that students need to closely examine source materials before accepting them as credible. Information from the Internet, in particular, should be carefully considered, since anyone who can build a Web site can post information. When evaluating sources on the Internet, most *.gov* and many *.edu* sites are quite reliable. However, professors or students post undergraduate student essays—unreliable sources—on some *.edu* Web pages.

3 Teach

Encourage students to read the passage through once before going over it again and reading the boxes. Explain that words like *first* and *another* often signal that key points in the source are about to be raised. Also explain that this piece comes from a .org site. These are often credible, but they cannot be accepted as such across the board.

For additional practice see **Skillbuilder Handbook**, page R28.

THINKING ECONOMICALLY Answers

1. *the level of demand, shipping capacity and cost*
2. *Possible answer: As long as the world economy remains strong and the level of shipping remains constant, cement will continue to be in short supply in the United States.*
3. *developers and builders, because they need this type of information to acquire funding for projects and to make long-range plans*

ECONOMICS SKILLBUILDER

For more on evaluating sources, see the Skillbuilder Handbook, page R28.

Evaluating Sources

There are many sources of economic information, including news articles, reports, books, and electronic media. Knowing how to interpret sources is how we gain economic information.

TECHNIQUES FOR READING SOURCE MATERIAL The following passage appeared on the Web site of the Portland Cement Association. The passage is a source of information about the supply of cement in the United States in 2004. To interpret this source of information, use the following strategies.

Identify the subject of the passage. Then ask yourself what, if any, economic concept is involved. This passage is about cement. The economic concept discussed is supply.

Cement Supply Falls Short

Several factors have converged to create tight supplies of cement, the key ingredient in concrete, which is used in nearly every type of construction.

First, strong construction markets have increased demand. The flare in demand arrived on the heels of an unusually active winter for construction, traditionally a down period when plants can stockpile cement in anticipation of the spring construction surge. Instead, there was no letup in demand during the 2003/04 winter and little opportunity to prepare a strong inventory for spring when construction activity traditionally increases.

Another factor is freight—limited availability of transport ships and escalating shipping rates. According to figures from the U.S. Geological Survey, 2003 U.S. portland cement consumption was 107.5 million metric tons. Of that total, 23.2 million tons or 21.6 percent was imported cement.

Since the beginning of the spring 2004, shipping rates have skyrocketed and availability of ships is limited. The booming Asian economies are straining worldwide cement capacity and shipping availability.

Source: www.cement.org

Identify economic factors that are relevant to the discussion. The cement shortage is explained in part by an increase in market demand and by the rising cost and limited availability of ships to carry imported cement.

Evaluate the passage's credibility. Do you think the source of the passage is reliable? Are other cited sources reliable? Information from this association and the U.S. Geological Survey is likely to be reliable.

THINKING ECONOMICALLY Interpreting

1. According to the passage, what variables affect the supply of concrete in the United States?
2. Do you think cement will continue to be in short supply in the United States? Explain your answer using information from the passage.
3. Who do you think is most likely to benefit from the information provided in the passage? Why?

DIFFERENTIATING INSTRUCTION

Inclusion

Diagram a Source

Help students evaluate a source by making a transparency out of a sample source article of your choosing. As in the Skillbuilder article, highlight important economic concepts and factors that might be relevant to a further discussion of the topic. Ask students for suggestions for explanatory notes to put in the margins. Discuss the source of the article, and any that are cited in the piece, and come to some conclusions about whether the source is credible.

Gifted and Talented

Use Internet Sources

Choose a research topic for students to investigate on the Internet. There should be a lot of varied information available on the topic. Ask students to find three sources on the topic that they consider to be credible, and three sources that they consider to be questionable. As a group, discuss why students have categorized their sources as they have. Try to come to some conclusions about what categories of Web sites are more credible than others.

SECTION 2 Assessment

REVIEWING KEY CONCEPTS

1. Explain the differences between the terms in each of these groups:
   a. *marginal product* / *profit-maximizing output*
   b. *increasing returns* / *diminishing returns*
   c. *fixed cost* / *variable cost*
2. Why does the marginal cost in Janine's factory decrease as marginal product increases?
3. Explain why marginal revenue and price are the same in Figure 5.9 on page 143.
4. What changes for a company when it reaches the break-even point?
5. How does a business use marginal analysis to decide how many workers to employ?
6. **Using Your Notes** How does a business calculate its total costs? Refer to your completed hierarchy diagram. Use the Graphic Organizer at **Interactive Review @ ClassZone.com**

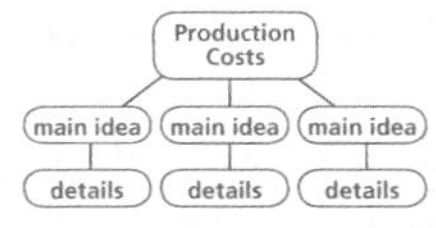

CRITICAL THINKING

7. **Categorizing Economic Information** Categorize the following costs incurred by a bookstore owner as fixed or variable: accountant, electricity for extra holiday hours, wages, clerks' insurance, manager's salary, purchase of books, rent, telephone.
8. **Applying Economic Concepts** Suppose that you own a video store that has total costs of $3,600 per month. If you charge $12 for each DVD you sell, how many do you need to sell each month in order to break even? Explain how you arrived at your answer.
9. **Applying Economic Concepts** The owner of a factory that produces soccer balls determines that his marginal product is at its peak when he has 100 employees. He determines that his marginal cost and marginal revenue are equal when he has 150 employees. What number of employees should he hire in order to maximize his profits? Explain the reason for your answer.
10. **Challenge** Many companies choose to manufacture their products in countries where workers are paid lower wages than in the United States. Which variable costs decrease and which ones increase as a result of this decision? Why do companies make this choice? Consider what you know about the relationship of costs to profits as you formulate your answer.

ECONOMICS IN PRACTICE

Calculating Costs and Revenues
Suppose you are a manufacturer of video games. You have analyzed your costs of production to create the following table.

Total Product	Fixed Cost ($)	Variable Cost ($)
0	500	0
25	500	800
50	500	1,200
100	500	1,800
175	500	2,550
275	500	3,350
350	500	4,250
400	500	5,750

Calculate Costs Copy the information in the table on your own paper and add two columns: Total Costs and Marginal Costs. Use the information given to calculate the values and fill in those two columns.

Challenge You sell the video games for $40 each. Add columns for Marginal Revenue, Total Revenue, and Profit to your chart and calculate the values for each quantity of total product.

4 Assess & Reteach

Assess Have students work individually on the questions and then check their answers for the Reviewing Key Concepts section in the textbook. Allow students to share their answers to Critical Thinking questions with a partner.

Unit 2 Resource Book
- Section Quiz, p. 71

Interactive Review @ ClassZone.com
- Section Quiz

Test Generator CD-ROM
- Section Quiz

Reteach Write the key terms on the board. Read Quick Reference definitions and ask volunteers to identify the key term. Encourage students to provide additional information they know about each term.

Unit 2 Resource Book
- Reteaching Acivity, p. 72

Economics in Practice

Calculate Costs Total Costs column (top to bottom, in $): 500; 1,300; 1,700; 2,300; 3,050; 3,850; 4,750; 6,250; 7,250; 7,750. Marginal Costs column (top to bottom, in $): 0; 32; 16; 12; 10; 8; 12; 30; 40; 50.

Challenge Marginal Revenue column (top to bottom, in $): 0, 40 (x9). Total Revenue column (top to bottom, in $): 0; 1,000; 2,000; 4,000; 7,000; 11,000; 14,000; 16,000; 17,000; 17,400. Profit column (top to bottom, in $): –500; –300; 300; 1,700; 3,950; 7,150; 9,250; 9,750; 9,750; 9,650.

SECTION 2 ASSESSMENT ANSWERS

Reviewing Key Concepts

1. a. *marginal product*, p. 138; *profit-maximizing output*, p. 143
   b. *increasing returns*, p. 139; *diminishing returns*, p. 139
   c. *fixed cost*, p. 140; *variable cost*, p. 140
2. because efficiency increases, up to a point
3. Here, for every additional pair of jeans sold, another $20 is earned. So, each additional pair represents one unit of product at the margin.
4. The company's total revenue has become as large as (or larger than) its total costs.
5. Marginal analysis is used to help determine profit-maximizing output. The number of employees at this level of output is the number to employ.
6. See page 138 for an example of a completed diagram. Total costs are determined by adding together fixed costs and variable costs.

Critical Thinking

7. fixed costs: accountant, insurance, manager's salary, rent, telephone; variable costs: electricity for extended holiday hours, wages, purchase of books
8. 300; at the break-even point, total revenue equals total costs, in this case $3,600. If he earns $12 of revenue on each DVD, he divides $3,600 by that to get 300.
9. He would hire 150 because profit-maximizing output occurs when marginal cost equals marginal revenue. Businesses make decisions on the basis on profit.
10. Possible answer: Costs for workers' wages would decrease while shipping costs would increase. Companies make this decision because they want to reduce their total costs in order to increase profits.

Economics in Practice
See answers in side column above.

1 Plan & Prepare

Section 3 Objectives

- explain the difference between change in quantity supplied and change in supply
- understand how to determine a change in supply
- identify the factors that can cause a change in supply

2 Focus & Motivate

Connecting to Everyday Life Explain that this section focuses on changes in the marketplace that affect supply. Invite students to suggest instances when something other than the reward they hope to receive might influence their willingness or ability to supply their time or a good or a service.

Taking Notes Remind students to take notes as they read by completing a chart. They can use the Graphic Organizer at **Interactive Review @ ClassZone.com**. A sample is shown below.

Factor That Changes Supply	Reason Why Supply Changes
input costs	supplier's costs increase
labor productivity	increased productivity decreases costs
technology	better technology improves production
government actions	government action can help or hinder production
producer expectations	future prices affect production
number of producers	more producers = more product

SECTION 3

What Factors Affect Supply?

OBJECTIVES

In Section 3, you will
- explain the difference between change in quantity supplied and change in supply
- understand how to determine a change in supply
- identify the factors that can cause a change in supply

KEY TERMS

change in quantity supplied, *p. 146*
change in supply, *p. 148*
input costs, *p. 148*
labor productivity, *p. 149*
technology, *p. 149*
excise tax, *p. 149*
regulation, *p. 150*

TAKING NOTES

As you read Section 3, complete a chart like this one showing each factor that causes change in supply. Use the Graphic Organizer at **Interactive Review @ ClassZone.com**

Factor That Changes Supply	Reason Why Supply Changes

Changes in Quantity Supplied

KEY CONCEPTS

The supply schedules and supply curves that you studied in Section 1 were created using the assumption that all other economic factors except the price of tomatoes would remain the same. If all other factors remain the same, then the only thing that influences how many tomatoes producers will offer for sale is the price of those tomatoes. The supply curve shows that pattern.

In Chapter 4, you learned the difference between change in demand and change in quantity demanded. Change in quantity demanded is shown by the points along an existing demand curve, while change in demand actually shifts the demand curve itself. Similarly, the different points on a supply curve show change in quantity supplied. **Change in quantity supplied** is an increase or decrease in the amount of a good or service that producers are willing to sell because of a change in price.

QUICK REFERENCE

Change in quantity supplied is a rise or fall in the amount producers offer for sale because of a change in price.

A change in the price of bicycles. . .

. . . causes a change in the quantity supplied.

SECTION 3 PROGRAM RESOURCES

ON LEVEL

Lesson Plans
- Core, p. 17

Unit 2 Resource Book
- Reading Study Guide, pp. 73–74
- Economic Simulations, pp. 99–100
- Section Quiz, p. 81

STRUGGLING READERS

Unit 2 Resource Book
- Reading Study Guide with Additional Support, pp. 75–77
- Reteaching Activity, p. 82

ENGLISH LEARNERS

Unit 2 Resource Book
- Reading Study Guide with Additional Support (Spanish), pp. 78–80

INCLUSION

Lesson Plans
- Modified for Inclusion, p. 17

GIFTED AND TALENTED

Unit 2 Resource Book
- Readings in Free Enterprise: Is It Demand?, p. 95; Is It Supply?, p. 96

TECHNOLOGY

eEdition DVD-ROM

eEdition Online

Power Presentation DVD-ROM

Economics Concepts Transparencies
- CT17 Factors Influencing Changes in Supply

Daily Test Practice Transparencies, TT17

ClassZone.com

EXAMPLE Changes Along a Supply Curve

Each new point on the supply curve shows a change in quantity supplied. A change in quantity supplied does not shift the supply curve itself. Let's look again at the Smiths' supply curve for tomatoes (Figure 5.10). Note the quantities supplied at each price. Notice that as quantity supplied changes, the change is shown by the direction of movement, right or left, along the supply curve. A movement to the right indicates an increase in both price and quantity supplied. A movement to the left shows a decrease in both price and quantity supplied.

FIGURE 5.10 CHANGES IN QUANTITY SUPPLIED

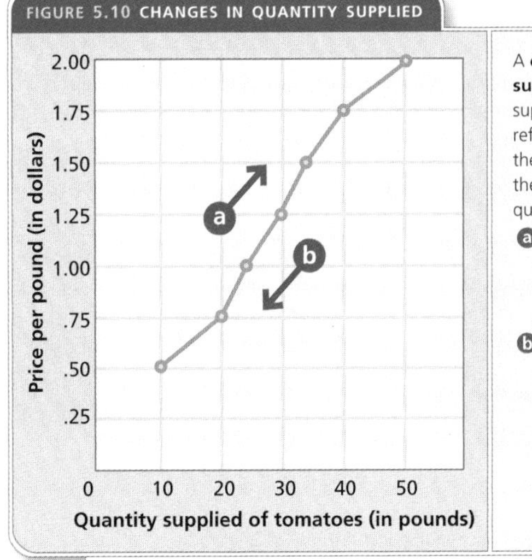

A **change in quantity supplied** doesn't shift the supply curve. The change refers to movement along the curve itself. Each point on the curve represents a new quantity supplied.

ⓐ As you move to the right along the curve, the quantity supplied increases.

ⓑ As you move to the left along the curve, the quantity supplied decreases.

ANALYZE GRAPHS

1. What is the change in quantity supplied when price increases from $0.75 to $1.50?
2. What is the change in price when quantity supplied changes from 50 to 24 pounds?

Animated Economics Use an interactive supply curve to see changes in quantity supplied at **ClassZone.com**

Just as Figure 5.10 shows change in quantity supplied by one individual, a market supply curve shows similar information for an entire market. However, market supply curves have larger quantities supplied, and therefore larger changes to quantity supplied, because they combine the data from all the individual supply curves in the market. For example, when the price increases from $0.75 to $1.75 on the market supply curve (Figure 5.5), the quantity supplied increases from 100 pounds to 300. Compare this with the change in quantity supplied at those prices in Figure 5.10.

APPLICATION Applying Economic Concepts

A. Changes in quantity supplied do not shift the position of the supply curve. Why? because the changes in quantity supplied refer to the movement from point to point along the supply curve, which shows different quantities offered for sale at different prices

❸ Teach

Changes in Quantity Supplied

Discuss

- How is change in quantity supplied related to the law of supply? *(The law of supply states that change in quantity supplied has a direct relationship to price.)*
- How do points on a supply curve reflect change in quantity supplied? *(Each point on the supply curve reflects the quantity supplied at a particular price. Movement from one point to another shows the change.)*

Analyzing Graphs: Figure 5.10

Remind students that the Smith's supply curve in Figure 5.10 is based on the assumption that everything besides price remains constant. This is the same supply curve shown in Fig. 5.4.

Answers

1. *It increases from 20 to 34.*
2. *It changes from $2 to $1.*

Animated Economics Animation and audio highlight how the quantity of tomatoes supplied by the Smiths varies with price. It will help students understand changes in quantity supplied.

LEVELED ACTIVITY

Analyzing Changes in Supply

Time 30 Minutes ◑

Objective Students will demonstrate an understanding of the factors that affect the supply of electric scooters. (The factors that cause a change in supply are covered in Section 3.)

Basic

Assign groups of students two factors to consider, making sure all six factors are assigned. Groups should brainstorm scenarios that show how their assigned factors might affect the supply of electric scooters. Then, students create a visual such as a diagram, poster, or cartoon to share their ideas with the class.

On Level

Assign groups of students three factors to consider, making sure all six factors are assigned. Groups may be assigned variations of certain factors. Groups should brainstorm scenarios that show how their assigned factors might affect the supply of electric scooters. Students then share their ideas in oral presentations.

Challenge

Students work individually or in groups to develop scenarios that show how all six factors affect the supply of electric scooters. Students then share their ideas in a news report about changes in the electric scooter market. The report should reflect the understanding that different factors may have various effects.

Changes in Supply

Discuss

- How do input costs affect supply? *(Increased input costs cause supply to decrease; decreased input costs cause supply to increase.)*
- What shifts when there is a change in supply? Why? *(The position of the supply curve shifts to the left or right to show a decrease or increase in quantity supplied at every price.)*

Analyzing Graphs: Figures 5.11 and 5.12

Figure 5.11 shows what happens when the price of peanuts increases. Figure 5.12 shows what happens to Anna's supply when the price of peanuts decreases. Ask students why input costs have an inverse relationship to supply. *(When input costs go up, producers cannot afford to make as much product and supply decreases, and vice versa.)*

Answers

1. *It has decreased by 15 bars.*
2. *It has increased by 15 bars.*

Animated Economics Animation and audio show what happens to Anna's supply of nutrition bars when her production costs increase and decrease. They will help students understand that changes in supply cause the supply curve to shift.

Changes in Supply

QUICK REFERENCE

Change in supply occurs when a change in the marketplace prompts producers to sell different amounts at every price.

KEY CONCEPTS

Consider what might happen if the workers at an automobile factory negotiate a large wage increase so that it's more expensive to produce each automobile. As the firm's costs increase, it is less willing and able to offer as many automobiles for sale. Any action such as this, which changes the costs of production, will change supply. **Change in supply** occurs when something prompts producers to offer different amounts for sale at every price. When production costs increase, supply decreases; when production costs decrease, supply increases.

Just like change in demand, change in supply actually shifts the supply curve. Six factors cause a change in supply: input costs, labor productivity, technology, government actions, producer expectations, and number of producers.

FACTOR 1 Input Costs

QUICK REFERENCE

Input costs are the price of the resources used to make products.

Input costs are a major factor that affects production costs and, therefore, supply. **Input costs** are the price of the resources needed to produce a good or service. For example, Anna makes nutrition bars that contain peanuts. If the price of peanuts increases, Anna's costs increase. She cannot afford to produce as many nutrition bars, and her supply curve shifts to the left (Figure 5.11). When the price of peanuts decreases, her costs decrease. She is willing and able to increase the quantity she can supply at every price, and the curve shifts to the right (Figure 5.12).

FIGURES 5.11 AND 5.12 SHIFTS IN SUPPLY

FIGURE 5.11 DECREASE IN SUPPLY

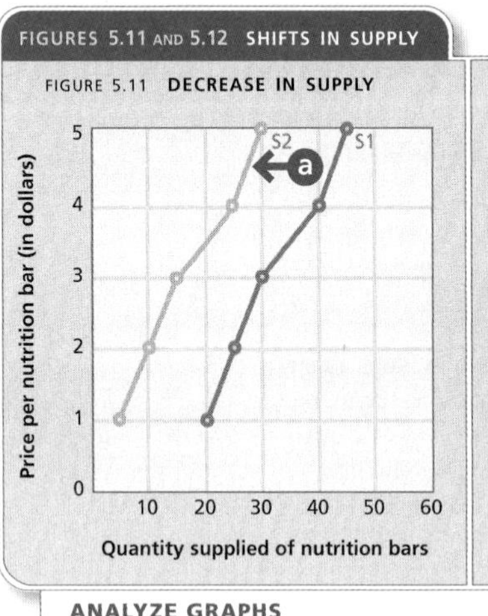

FIGURE 5.12 INCREASE IN SUPPLY

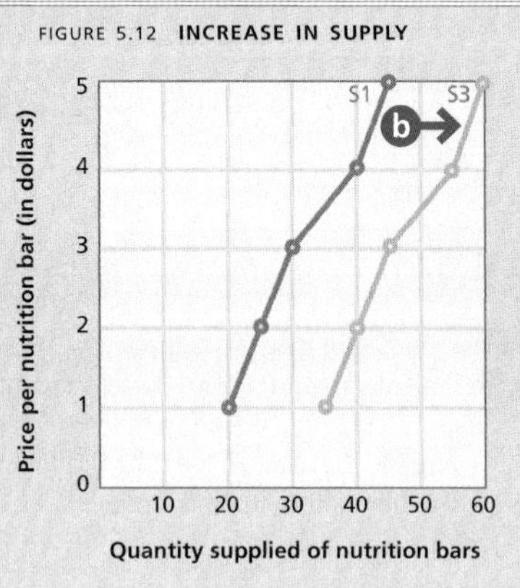

When a **change in supply** occurs, the supply curve shifts.

ⓐ As Figure 5.11 shows, a shift to the left (S2) indicates a decrease in supply.

ⓑ As Figure 5.12 shows, a shift to the right (S3) indicates an increase in supply.

ANALYZE GRAPHS

1. In Figure 5.11, how has the supply of nutrition bars changed at every price?
2. In Figure 5.12, how has the supply of nutrition bars changed at every price?

Animated Economics

Use an interactive version of shifting supply curves at **ClassZone.com**

DIFFERENTIATING INSTRUCTION

Struggling Readers

Identify Main Ideas

Have students work in pairs to read the material on the six factors that affect supply. Encourage them to pause after each paragraph and state the main idea contained in the paragraph. Remind them to use topic sentences and other clues to identify main ideas. Then have them discuss each factor and agree on a main idea statement about that factor. Invite them to record their statements in a chart that lists the factor in the first column and the main idea in the second.

English Learners

Understand Cause and Effect

Explain that the six factors are causes and that the effects are the changes in supply shown by shifts in the supply curve. Point out that under each heading there may be several causes and effects described.

- Have partners read the material and create a chart that lists causes in the left column and effects in the right column.
- Encourage students to use their charts to make cause and effect statements, for example, "The effect of higher productivity is increased supply."

FACTOR 2 Labor Productivity

Labor productivity is the amount of goods and services that a person can produce in a given time. Increasing productivity decreases the costs of production and therefore increases supply. For example, a specialized division of labor can allow a producer to make more goods at a lower cost, as was the case at Janine's factory in Section 2. Her marginal costs decreased when there were six workers, each of whom had a separate job to do.

Better-trained and more-skilled workers can usually produce more goods in less time, and therefore at lower costs, than less-educated or less-skilled workers. For example, a business that provides word-processing services can produce more documents if its employees type quickly and have a lot of experience working with word-processing software.

QUICK REFERENCE

Labor productivity is the amount of goods and services that a person can produce in a given time.

Technology entails applying scientific methods and innovations to production.

FACTOR 3 Technology

One way that businesses improve their productivity and increase supply is through the use of technology. **Technology** involves the application of scientific methods and discoveries to the production process, resulting in new products or new manufacturing techniques. Influenced by the profit motive, manufacturers have, throughout history, used technology to make goods more efficiently. Increased automation, including the use of industrial robots, has led to increased supplies of automobiles, computers, and many other products. (See the Case Study on pages 158–159.)

Improved technology helps farmers produce more food per acre. It also allows oil refiners to get more gasoline out of every barrel of crude oil and helps to get that gasoline to gas stations more quickly and more safely. In addition, technological innovations, such as the personal computer, enable workers to be more productive. This, in turn, helps businesses to increase the supply of their services, such as processing insurance claims or selling airline tickets.

The Typewriter's End The move from typewriter to computer shows how technology helps to boost productivity.

FACTOR 4 Government Action

Government actions can also affect the costs of production, both positively and negatively. An **excise tax** is a tax on the production or sale of a specific good or service. Excise taxes are often placed on items such as alcohol and tobacco—things whose consumption the government is interested in discouraging. The taxes increase producers' costs and, therefore, decrease the supply of these items.

Taxes tend to decrease supply; subsidies have the opposite effect. You learned in Chapter 3 that a subsidy is a government payment that partially covers the cost of an economic activity. The subsidy's purpose is to encourage or protect that activity. Most forms of energy production in the United States receive some form of subsidy. For example, subsidies helped to double the supply of ethanol, a gasoline substitute made from corn, between 2000 and 2004.

QUICK REFERENCE

An **excise tax** is a tax on the making or selling of certain goods or services.

More About . . .

Productivity

Productivity is a measure of how efficiently a producer uses resources. The most widely used measure of productivity is labor productivity. The U.S. Bureau of Labor Statistics (BLS) measures productivity as a ratio of goods and services produced to the hours of labor required to produce them.

In the United States, labor costs account for more than 60 percent of the value of non-farm goods and services produced. BLS productivity statistics are based on the U.S. business sector, which accounts for about 78 percent of total U.S. gross domestic product.

International Economics

Gasoline Excise Taxes

U.S. gasoline prices are actually among the lowest in the world. The main reason for the difference is not the price of the gasoline itself but the higher excise taxes in most other countries. In North America, the U.S. excise tax per gallon in 2005 was 18.4 cents compared to 37 cents in Canada. Mexico has no excise tax but has a higher sales tax than its neighbors.

European countries, as well as Japan, Korea, and Australia all have much higher excise taxes, ranging from $1.12 per gallon in Australia to $3.90 per gallon in Turkey.

INDIVIDUAL ACTIVITY

Graphing Changes in Supply

Time 30 Minutes

Task Create supply curves to show the effects of labor productivity, technology, or government action on supply.

Materials Needed graph paper and pencils or graphing software

Activity

- Assign students one of the factors discussed on pages 148–150 (or allow students to select one) and have them apply it to the supply of a particular good or service of their choosing.
- Direct each student to draw a market supply curve for the chosen good or service. Then tell them to add a second supply curve, showing the effect of the specific factor on supply.
- Ask students to write a caption that describes what each of their graphs shows.
- Invite volunteers to share their graphs and captions with the class. Discuss generalizations about how these factors affect supply.

Rubric

	Understanding of How Factors Affect Supply	Presentation of Information
4	excellent	accurate and clear
3	good	mostly accurate
2	fair	somewhat accurate
1	poor	many errors

Discuss

- Quantity supplied can increase or decrease depending on whether the number of producers increases or decreases. Can regulation affect the quantity supplied in both ways too? *(As in the example given, a worker safety regulation can increase costs and reduce supply or save money and increase supply.)*

Analyzing Graphs: Figure 5.13

Instruct students to compare the number of ice cream cones supplied at each price when there was only one supplier in the market and after three more suppliers entered the market. Ask students which curve represents the best situation for consumers and why. *(curve "b," because there are more ice cream cones available at all prices, including lower prices)* Have them indicate where the supply curve would be if only two more suppliers had entered the market. *(between the two curves shown on the graph)*

Answers

1. *50*
2. *The supply curve shifts to the right, showing that as more suppliers enter the market the supply of ice cream cones at every price increases.*

QUICK REFERENCE

Regulation is a set of rules or laws designed to control business behavior.

Government **regulation**, the act of controlling business behavior through a set of rules or laws, can also affect supply. Banning a certain pesticide might decrease the supply of the crops that depend on the pesticide. Worker safety regulations might decrease supply by increasing a business's production costs or increase supply by reducing the amount of labor lost to on-the-job injuries.

FACTOR 5 Producer Expectations

If producers expect the price of their product to rise or fall in the future, it may affect how much of that product they are willing and able to supply in the present. Different kinds of producers may react to future price changes differently. For example, if a farmer expects the price of corn to be higher in the future, he or she may store some of the current crop, thereby decreasing supply. A manufacturer who believes the price of his or her product will rise may run the factory for an extra shift or invest in more equipment to increase supply.

FACTOR 6 Number of Producers

When one company develops a successful new idea, whether it's designer wedding gowns, the latest generation of cell phones, or fast-food sushi, other producers soon enter the market and increase the supply of the good or service. When this happens, the supply curve shifts to the right, as you can see in Figure 5.13.

FIGURE 5.13 NUMBER OF PRODUCERS

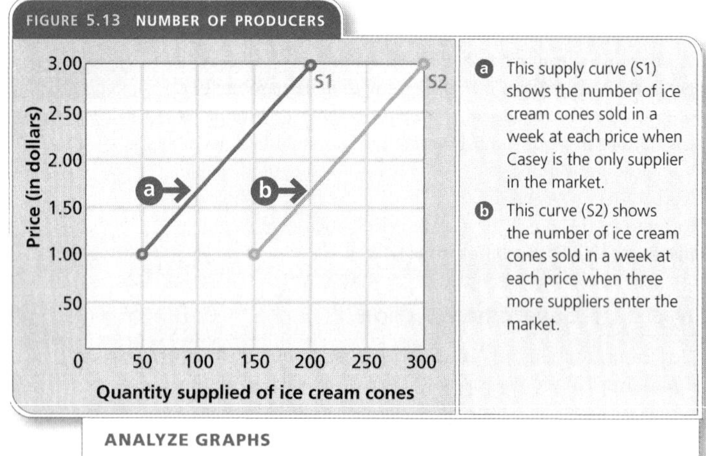

3.00
2.50
2.00
1.50
1.00
.50
0
Price (in dollars)
50
100
150
200
250
300
Quantity supplied of ice cream cones
S1
S2
a
b
a This supply curve (S1) shows the number of ice cream cones sold in a week at each price when Casey is the only supplier in the market.
b This curve (S2) shows the number of ice cream cones sold in a week at each price when three more suppliers enter the market.

ANALYZE GRAPHS

1. About how many ice cream cones were sold at $1.00 when Casey was the only producer in the market?
2. How do these two curves show the effect of the number of producers on the supply of ice cream cones in the market?

An increase in the number of producers means increased competition, which may eventually drive less-efficient producers out of the market, decreasing supply. (You'll learn more about competition in Chapter 7.) Competition has a major impact on supply, as producers enter and leave the market constantly.

DIFFERENTIATING INSTRUCTION

Inclusion

Use the Visual

Explain that Figure 5.14 summarizes the six factors that affect supply. Describe each visual in turn and read the heading of the accompanying caption. Invite volunteers to say in their own words how that visual illustrates the particular factor. Encourage other students to contribute additional information that they may know about how each factor affects supply.

Gifted and Talented

Write a Mini-Case Study

Invite students to present an actual example of how the number of producers affected the supply of a particular good or service. Students may choose an example from their experience, such as a change in the number of restaurants or music stores in their community. Or they may research an example of a particular type of product or industry, such as the increased number of suppliers of new technology products. Have each student write a mini-case study of the example to share in a small group.

ECONOMICS ESSENTIALS

FIGURE 5.14 Factors That Cause a Change in Supply

Input Costs Input costs, the collective price of the resources that go into producing a good or service, affect supply directly.

Labor Productivity Better-trained or more-skilled workers are usually more productive. Increased productivity decreases costs and increases supply.

Number of Producers A successful new product or service always brings out competitors who initially raise overall supply.

Producer Expectations The amount of product producers are willing and able to supply may be influenced by whether they believe prices will go up or down.

Technology By applying scientific advances to the production process, producers have learned to generate their goods and services more efficiently.

Government Action Government actions, such as taxes or subsidies, can have a positive or a negative effect on production costs.

ANALYZE CHARTS

A newspaper article states that the supply of snowboards has risen dramatically over the past six months. Choose four of the six factors that cause a change in supply and explain how each might have resulted in the recent influx of snowboards.

Figure 5.13 shows what happens to the supply of ice cream cones in a neighborhood as more producers enter the market. When Casey opened his ice cream store it was the only one in the area. It was an instant success. Within six months, three competing stores had opened in the neighborhood, and the supply of ice cream cones increased at all price levels. A year later, though, this intense competition forced one of the producers to leave the market.

APPLICATION **Applying Economic Concepts**

B. Choose an item of food or clothing that you buy regularly. List as many input costs as you can that might affect the supply of that product. Compare your list with a classmate's and see if you can add to each other's lists. Students should list input costs such as raw materials, labor, power, and equipment involved in production. The best answers will take the process of production back as far as possible.

Economics Essentials: Figure 5.14

Encourage students to visualize the infographic to help them remember the six factors and how each one affects supply.

- Market research tells J.B. Electronics that their headphones are going to be hot sellers this holiday season. Explain which of the six factors this is related to *(producer expectations)* and whether supply will increase or decrease. *(Supply will increase because an increase in demand means an increase in price. When price goes up, producers want to supply more.)*
- Monster Truck Motors is using a new robot to help assemble its trucks. To its disappointment, Monster Trucks has found that the robot itself in is need of repair almost daily. How will this new technology affect supply? *(Although most technology that's applied to production increases supply, in this case, supply will likely decrease because the machinery keeps breaking.)*

Analyze

(Possible answers: The cost of the fiberglass used to make snowboards has decreased; the workers making snowboards are now better trained; a new machine to produce the snowboard's bindings has sped production; a large sporting goods company has joined the snowboard market.)

CLASS ACTIVITY

Identifying Factors that Affect Supply

Time 30 Minutes ◑

Task Create and play a card game on the factors that affect supply.

Materials Needed index cards and markers, pens, or pencils

Activity

- Have each student write an example of a factor that affects supply on one side of an index card and the type of factor on the other side. Direct each student to make three cards.
- Shuffle the cards into a deck so that different sides of the cards face up.
- Divide students into teams that take turns picking a card and either identify the factor based on the example, or give an example if the factor side is showing.
- If a student answers incorrectly, a member of the other team may answer.
- When students answer correctly, their team keeps the card. The team with the most cards wins.

Rubric

	Identify Factors that Affect Supply	Presentation of Information
4	excellent	clear and accurate
3	good	mostly accurate
2	fair	somewhat accurate
1	poor	inaccurate

Robert Johnson

More About . . .

Robert Johnson
Born in Mississippi, Robert Johnson grew up in Freeport, Illinois. He was the only one of 10 siblings to attend college and received a bachelor's degree from the University of Illinois and a master's degree in international affairs from Princeton.

He considered careers in teaching and the foreign service, but his experience at the cable TV trade association exposed him to business leaders. He then began thinking of starting a business. His connections from the trade association job led to BET. After selling BET to Viacom, Johnson founded RLJ Companies, which invests in a variety of business ventures. He also owns NBA and WNBA teams in North Carolina.

More About . . .

Black Entertainment Television
BET became profitable after five years, largely due to Robert Johnson's decision to keep his programming costs as low as possible. The network mainly offered music videos and reruns of sitcoms to appeal to its 18-to-34-year-old target audience. Although many criticized his decisions, the audience for the programs grew.

BET was the first company controlled by African Americans to trade on the New York Stock Exchange (1991–1998). Growth during the 1990s came from extending the brand into other media. The sale to Viacom and increased competition prompted BET to begin investing more in programming.

Economics Update

ClassZone.com includes links to sites about Robert Johnson. It will help students understand how BET increased the supply of African-American entertainment.

ECONOMICS PACESETTER

Robert Johnson: Supplying African-American Entertainment

In this section, you've learned about the factors that influence supply. You've also seen some examples of how these factors work. The story of media entrepreneur Robert Johnson provides a real-world example of how the entrance of a new supplier can affect a market.

FAST FACTS

Robert Johnson

Title: Chairman of BET Holdings II, Inc., retired

Born: April 8, 1946, Hickory, Mississippi

Major Accomplishment: BET is the leading supplier of cable TV programming aimed at African Americans.

Other Enterprises: Digital music networks, publishing, events production, BET.com Web portal, NBA team Charlotte Bobcats, and WNBA Charlotte Sting

Honors: Broadcasting and Cable Magazine Hall of Fame Award, NAACP Image Award

EXAMPLE Expanding the Number of Producers

In the late 1970s, Robert Johnson was working as a Washington lobbyist for the National Cable Television Association. He recognized that current suppliers in the cable TV industry were ignoring a substantial market—African Americans. To fill this void, Johnson conceived the idea for Black Entertainment Television (BET), the first cable channel owned by and focused on African Americans.

To launch his dream, Johnson took out a $15,000 bank loan. He also persuaded a major investor to put up $500,000. Next, he secured space on a cable TV satellite for his new channel. BET's first program appeared on January 8, 1980. The company grew from offering two hours of programming a week to round-the-clock programming on five separate channels. Cable operators in the United States, Canada, and the Caribbean saw the value of this kind of targeted programming, and began to buy BET's shows.

A Vast Reach BET supplies programming to more than 80 million households in Canada, the United States, and the Caribbean.

At first, BET targeted young viewers with programs similar to those on MTV. As the cable TV industry grew and became more profitable, Johnson invested in more diverse programming. Of this transition he explained, "Now we're a music video channel with a public affairs footprint. . . ." BET could "play music, but also . . . cover issues that are of concern to African Americans." BET.com, the number one Internet portal for African Americans, soon followed.

In 2001, Johnson sold BET to the giant media company Viacom International Inc. for $3 billion and became the nation's first black billionaire. After the sale, Johnson stayed on at BET and continued to run the company for five more years. His success demonstrated that there was a strong market for African-American entertainment. As a result, many suppliers—some with no traditional ties to the African-American community—now offer the kind of programming Johnson pioneered.

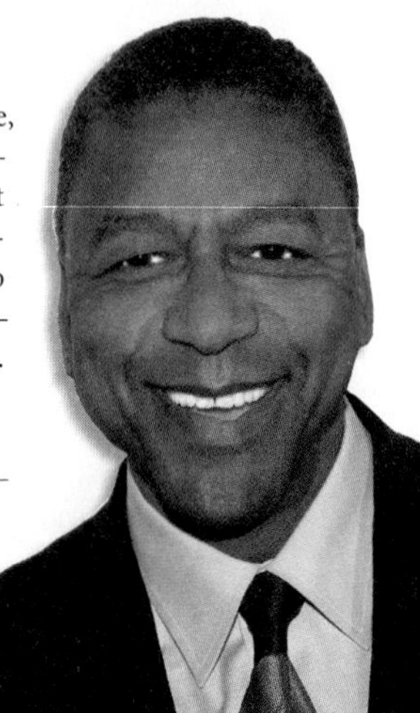

Economics Update

Find an update on Robert Johnson at **ClassZone.com**

APPLICATION Making Inferences

C. What effects might BET's success have on the supply of African-American programming? The success of BET will cause an increase in African-American programming as competitors enter the market.

DIFFERENTIATING INSTRUCTION

English Learners

Create a Time Line
Help students sequence events in this biography by having them work in pairs to create a time line. Remind them that some dates are stated explicitly and others must be inferred from phrases such as "for five more years." Encourage students to notice sequencing words such as *first, next,* and *then.* They may want to enter information about events not specifically dated but that occur between two dated events. Invite them to use their time lines to summarize the piece in their own words.

Gifted and Talented

Research Other Suppliers
Invite students to do research on other suppliers of television programming targeted to African Americans. They may focus on another network that competes with BET, such as TV One. Students may wish to study other suppliers, such as Oprah Winfrey, who offer programming through broader TV networks. Encourage students to find out about ownership, target audience, types of programming, and economic success. Invite students to present their research in a panel discussion.

SECTION 3 Assessment

Online Quiz
ClassZone.com

REVIEWING KEY CONCEPTS

1. Explain the differences between the terms in each of these pairs:
   a. *change in quantity supplied* / *change in supply*
   b. *input costs* / *technology*
   c. *excise tax* / *regulation*
2. What else besides raw materials would be included in input costs?
3. Why might an increase in oil prices lead to a decrease in the supply of fruits and vegetables in your local supermarket?
4. Why do excise taxes and subsidies affect supply differently?
5. Does expectation of a change in price affect supply? Illustrate your answer with examples.
6. **Using Your Notes** How does a change in number of producers affect supply? Refer to your completed chart.

   Use the Graphic Organizer at **Interactive Review @ ClassZone.com**

Factor That Changes Supply	Reason Why Supply Changes

CRITICAL THINKING

7. **Applying Economic Concepts** How do each of these examples of government actions affect the supply of gasoline?
   a. In 2005, the government continued support for ethanol, a gasoline substitute.
   b. The state of California requires a special blend of gasoline that meets stricter environmental standards than other regions in the country.
   c. Many states use gasoline taxes to help fund highway construction and maintenance.
8. **Making Inferences** Why do you think governments want to influence the supply of alcohol and tobacco products by imposing excise taxes?
9. **Analyzing Effects** Take out the market supply curve for skis that you created on page 137. Add new curves showing how supply would be changed in each of the following cases. Share your graph with a classmate and explain your reasoning.
   a. The price of titanium, used in skis, declines dramatically.
   b. A large manufacturer decides to stop producing skis.
10. **Challenge** How does an increased number of producers affect the prices of goods in a market? What is the reason for this effect? Think about what you know about demand and supply and review Figure 5.12 as you formulate your answer.

ECONOMICS IN PRACTICE

Explaining Changes in Supply
Suppose that you are a manufacturer of personal digital music players (PDMPs). What factors affect supply for PDMPs? The chart below lists examples of a change in supply in the market for PDMPs. For each example, identify which factor that affects supply is involved and state whether supply increases or decreases.

Example of Change That Affects Supply	Factor and How It Affected Supply
You give each worker in your factory a specialized job.	
Price of computer chips used in PDMPs rises.	
New machinery speeds up the manufacturing process.	
Your success prompts three new companies to start producing PDMPs.	
A new law requires producers to recycle the wastewater from their factories.	

Challenge Identify which of the six factors that affect supply does not appear on this chart. What would be an example of how that factor might affect the market for PDMPs?

④ Assess & Reteach

Assess Have students review the questions individually and then quiz each other in pairs.

Unit 2 Resource Book
- Section Quiz, p. 81

Interactive Review @ ClassZone.com
- Section Quiz

Test Generator CD-ROM
- Section Quiz

Reteach Use the headings and subheadings from the section to create an outline on the board. Leave space under each heading and invite volunteers to provide facts that can be added under each one to fill in the outline.

Unit 2 Resource Book
- Reteaching Activity, p. 82

Economics in Practice

Row 1: Labor productivity, supply increases

Row 2: Input costs, supply decreases

Row 3: Technology, supply increases

Row 4: Number of producers, supply increases

Row 5: Government regulation, supply decreases

Challenge Producer expectations. Possible example, you think prices will rise during the holiday shopping season so you gear up production to increase supply or decrease current supply by holding product back to sell when the price is higher.

SECTION 3 ASSESSMENT ANSWERS

Reviewing Key Concepts

1. a. *change in quantity supplied*, p. 146; *change in supply*, p. 148
   b. *input costs*, p. 148; *technology*, p. 149
   c. *excise tax*, p. 149; *regulation*, p. 150
2. the costs of labor, power, and machinery
3. An increase in oil prices would translate to an increase in shipping costs—another input cost.
4. Excise taxes increase producer costs and therefore decrease supply, while subsidies decrease producer costs and increase supply.
5. Yes. Examples should show that the expectation of an increase in price causes an increase in supply, while expectation of a decrease in price causes a decrease in supply.
6. See page 146 for an example of a completed graphic. More producers increases supply, fewer producers decreases supply.

Critical Thinking

7. a. Change in government regulations causes short-term decrease in supply. Subsidy of ethanol may increase supply but higher costs could tend to decrease supply.
   b. Government regulation decreases the supply of gasoline that residents of California can use.
   c. Excise taxes increase producer prices and decrease the supply of gasoline.
8. Excise taxes increase producers' costs and therefore the prices of alcohol and tobacco products. The government hopes that higher prices may discourage some consumers from buying the products.
9. a. Curve shifts to the right because decrease in input costs increases supply.
   b. Curve shifts to the left because decrease in the number of producers decreases supply.
10. More producers increases supply and competition. With more competition, prices go down because more goods are available at every price, including lower prices, as supply increases. Consumer demand has more chance of being satisfied at lower prices when there are more suppliers in a market.

Economics in Practice

See answers in side column above.

1 Plan & Prepare

Section 4 Objectives

- define the term *elasticity of supply*
- explain the difference between elastic and inelastic supply
- identify the factors that affect elasticity of supply

2 Focus & Motivate

Connecting to Everyday Life Explain that this section focuses on how responsive producers are to changes in price. Have students brainstorm reasons why businesses might not be able to respond quickly to such changes.

Taking Notes Remind students to take notes as they read by completing a cluster diagram. They can use the Graphic Organizer at **Interactive Review @ ClassZone.com**. A sample is shown below.

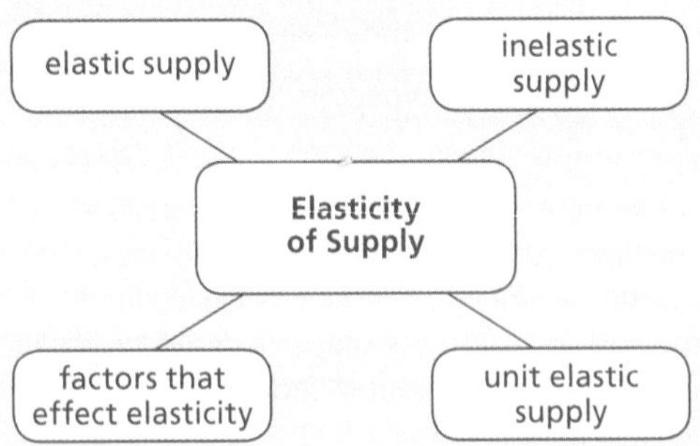

SECTION 4

What Is Elasticity of Supply?

OBJECTIVES

In Section 4, you will

- define the term *elasticity of supply*
- explain the difference between elastic and inelastic supply
- identify the factors that affect elasticity of supply

KEY TERMS

elasticity of supply, *p. 154*

TAKING NOTES

As you read Section 4, complete a cluster diagram like the one shown. Use the Graphic Organizer at **Interactive Review @ ClassZone.com**

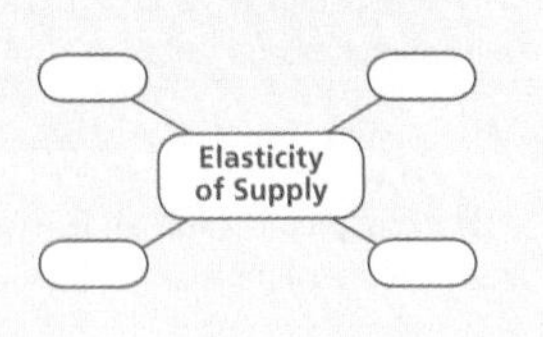

Elasticity of Supply

KEY CONCEPTS

According to the law of supply, as price increases so will the supply of a good or service. When Toyota Motor Corporation introduced its Prius hybrid in 2000, it was surprised by the automobile's instant popularity. Consumers were willing to pay more than the manufacturer's suggested price. Yet Toyota was not able to increase supply at the same pace that consumer demand and prices rose. Even five years later, Toyota could not meet rising demand. This inability to effectively respond to and meet increased demand suggests that the supply of the Prius was inelastic.

QUICK REFERENCE

Elasticity of supply is a measure of how responsive producers are to price changes in the marketplace.

In Chapter 4, you learned that elasticity of demand measures how responsive consumers are to price changes. In a similar way, **elasticity of supply** is also a measure of how responsive producers are to price changes.

If a change in price leads to a relatively larger change in quantity supplied, supply is said to be elastic. In other words, supply is elastic if a 10 percent increase in price causes a greater than 10 percent increase in quantity supplied. If a change in price leads to a relatively smaller change in quantity supplied, supply is said to be inelastic. If the price and the quantity supplied change by exactly the same percentage, supply is unit elastic.

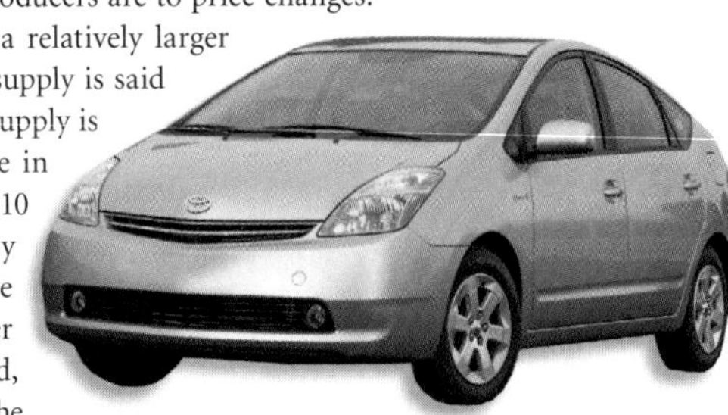

Inelastic Supply The supply of expensive and complicated items, such as this Prius hybrid, is often inelastic.

SECTION 4 PROGRAM RESOURCES

ON LEVEL

Lesson Plans

- Core, p. 18

Unit 2 Resource Book

- Reading Study Guide, pp. 83–84
- Math Skills Worksheet, p. 101
- Section Quiz, p. 91

STRUGGLING READERS

Unit 2 Resource Book

- Reading Study Guide with Additional Support, pp. 85–87
- Reteaching Activity, p. 92

ENGLISH LEARNERS

Unit 2 Resource Book

- Reading Study Guide with Additional Support (Spanish), pp. 88–90

INCLUSION

Lesson Plans

- Modified for Inclusion, p. 18

GIFTED AND TALENTED

Unit 2 Resource Book

- Case Study Resources: Penelope, Archie, and REMI, p. 97; Personal Roots, p. 98

TECHNOLOGY

eEdition DVD-ROM

eEdition Online

Power Presentation DVD-ROM

Economics Concepts Transparencies

- CT18 Limit on Changing Production to Respond to a Price Change

Daily Test Practice Transparencies, TT18

ClassZone.com

EXAMPLE Elastic Supply

Let's look at an example of elastic supply. Figure 5.15 illustrates how the quantity supplied of a new style of leather boots was elastic. As the boots gained in popularity, a shortage developed. The boot makers raised the price of the boots from $60 to $150 dollars, and the quantity supplied more than kept up, escalating from 10,000 to 50,000 pairs. The producer was able to rapidly increase the quantity supplied because, unlike car manufacturing for instance, the raw materials needed to make boots are neither particularly expensive nor hard to come by. The actual manufacturing process is also, relatively speaking, fairly uncomplicated and easy to increase.

EXAMPLE Inelastic Supply

In Chapter 4, you learned that demand for gasoline was inelastic. The supply of gasoline is also inelastic. Although gasoline prices rose 20 to 30 percent between 2004 and 2005, producers were not able to increase supply by the same amount because of the limited supply of crude oil and refining capacity.

Figure 5.16 shows how the supply of olive oil is also inelastic. When the price of olive oil rose by a factor of four, supply could not keep pace, as the oil comes from the previous season's olives and is exported from the Mediterranean region.

FIGURE 5.15 ELASTIC SUPPLY CURVE

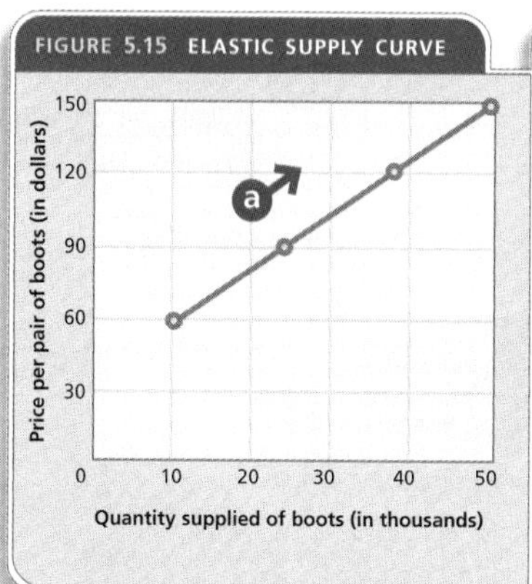

FIGURE 5.16 INELASTIC SUPPLY CURVE

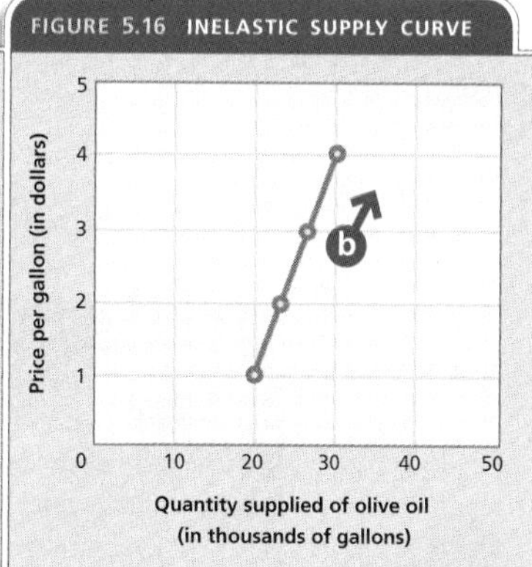

ⓐ The curve in Figure 5.15 slopes gradually. It slopes more horizontally than vertically because of greater changes in quantity supplied.

ⓑ The curve in Figure 5.16 slopes steeply. It slopes more vertically than horizontally because of lesser changes in quantity supplied.

ANALYZE GRAPHS

1. If the price of leather rose dramatically for the boots in Figure 5.15, how might this affect elasticity of supply?
2. In the United States, would the supply of corn oil be more elastic than the supply of olive oil? Why or why not?

Animated Economics Use elastic and inelastic supply curves at **ClassZone.com**

APPLICATION Drawing Conclusions

A. A bakery produces 200 muffins per week that sell for $1.50 each. When the price increases to $2.00, it produces 300 muffins per week. Is supply elastic or inelastic? Explain your answer.

Supply is elastic because quantity supplied increases by 50 percent with a price increase of 33 percent.

❸ Teach

Elasticity of Supply

Discuss

- How is elasticity related to the law of supply? *(Elasticity measures whether change in quantity supplied is proportional to change in price.)*
- How do the examples given in the text demonstrate the difference between elastic and inelastic supply? *(Boots had elastic supply; the change in quantity supplied was greater than the change in price. The Toyota Prius, gasoline, and olive oil had inelastic supply; the change in quantity supplied did not increase as much as change in price.)*

Analyzing Graphs: Figures 5.15 and 5.16

Ask students to look at Figures 5.11 and 5.12 on p. 148 of the pupil edition. Is the supply of nutrition bars elastic or inelastic? *(inelastic because the price increased by 5 times but the supply increased by 2.25 times)*

Answers

1. *It would be less elastic; higher input costs reduce supply.*
2. *Yes, corn is plentiful and inexpensive in the United States.*

Animated Economics These supply curves highlight the difference between elastic and inelastic supply. They will help students understand elasticity of supply.

LEVELED ACTIVITY

Developing New Business Ideas

Time 40 Minutes

Objective Students will demonstrate an understanding of the law of supply, the costs of production, the factors that affect supply, and the elasticity of supply for a new business.

Basic

Determine the type of business. List some costs of production and set prices for the product. Develop a supply schedule and a supply curve for it. In a graphic organizer, show factors other than price that affect supply. State what factors determine elasticity of supply.

On Level

Determine the type of business. Outline costs of production and set prices for the product. Develop a supply curve for it. Describe factors other than price that might affect supply. Illustrate one change in supply by showing a shift in the supply curve. Determine elasticity of supply over a month and a year.

Challenge

Determine the type of business. Analyze costs of production and set prices for the product. Develop a market supply curve and illustrate both an increase and decrease in supply by showing shifts in the supply curve. Recommend ways to respond to a price change that reflect an analysis of elasticity of supply.

What Affects Elasticity of Supply?

Discuss

- Why is supply more elastic over a year than over a month? *(because the amount of time a supplier has to respond to price changes is the main factor that determines elasticity)*
- Why are service industries more likely to have elastic supply than manufacturing businesses? *(because service businesses generally require less capital and difficult-to-obtain resources than those in the manufacturing sector)*

Your Economic Choices

ELASTICITY OF SUPPLY

Which supply of cupcakes is more elastic?

- Why is the level of elasticity of supply an issue in this scenario? *(If you need to order a week ahead of time, and you don't know how many fans will attend the game a week ahead of time, it's possible that you'll order too many cupcakes and not be able to sell them.)*
- What are other possible pros and cons of getting the cupcakes from either supplier? *(bakery pros: quality will be consistent, quantity is guaranteed; bakery cons: have to pay for the cupcakes, so charity gets less money; volunteer pros: free cupcakes; there will be a variety; volunteer cons: quality is a question mark, can't count on quantity, food safety not regulated as in a professional setting)*

Activity Ask students to consider the bakery business itself in relation to the factors that affect elasticity of supply listed on this page. Using these criteria, are bakery goods elastic or inelastic? *(A bakery does not require highly skilled labor or difficult-to-obtain resources. Also, although starting a bakery from the beginning is very capital intensive, upping the production from an existing bakery would only require another shift or a few more workers. So, the supply of bakery goods is most likely elastic.)*

What Affects Elasticity of Supply?

KEY CONCEPTS

Just as there are factors that cause a change in supply, there are also factors that affect the elasticity of supply. There are far fewer of these factors than for elasticity of demand. The ease of changing production to respond to price change is the main factor in determining elasticity of supply. Given enough time, the elasticity of supply increases for most goods and services. Supply will be more elastic over a year or several years than it will be if the time frame to respond is a day, a week, or a month.

Industries that are able to respond quickly to changes in price by either increasing or decreasing production are those that don't require a lot of capital, skilled labor, or difficult-to-obtain resources. For example, the quantity supplied of dog-walking services can increase rapidly with the addition of more people to walk dogs. A small business that sells crafts made from recycled materials would be able to respond quickly to changes in the price of its various products by applying its resources to increase the supply of its higher priced items.

For other industries, it takes a great deal of time to shift the resources of production to respond to price changes. Automakers and oil refiners are examples of industries that rely on large capital outlays or difficult-to-obtain resources. It might take such suppliers a considerable amount of time to respond to price changes.

YOUR ECONOMIC CHOICES

ELASTICITY OF SUPPLY

Which supply of cupcakes is more elastic?

You're planning to sell cupcakes at your school's football game to raise funds for a charitable cause, but it's hard to say in advance how many fans will attend the game. You can place an order with a bakery (which you need to do a week early) or have volunteers do the baking the night before the game. Which supply of cupcakes is more elastic? Why?

APPLICATION Applying Economic Concepts

B. Is the elasticity of a farmer's crop of sweet corn greater at the beginning of the growing season or in the middle of the growing season? Why?
at the beginning of the growing season, because the farmer has more options to use resources such as the number of plants or type of fertilizer to increase the size of the crop

DIFFERENTIATING INSTRUCTION

Struggling Readers

Make a Chart
Have students take notes about examples of goods and services that have elastic supply and those that have inelastic supply by filling in a two-column chart as they read. Encourage students to discuss their charts with a partner and to draw conclusions about what kinds of businesses tend to have elastic or inelastic supply and the reasons why.

Inclusion

Listen to the Section
Have students who are visually impaired work with partners who are not. Ask the unimpaired students to read the section aloud to their partners. Encourage them to describe the graphs and visuals. The readers should stop to ask all Application and Analyze Graph questions, and the team should work together to determine the answers.

Online Quiz
ClassZone.com

REVIEWING KEY CONCEPTS

1. Use each of the following three terms in a sentence that gives an example of the term as it relates to supply:
   a. *elastic* b. *inelastic* c. *elasticity of supply*
2. How is elasticity of supply similar to elasticity of demand? How is it different?
3. Is the supply of genuine antique furniture elastic or inelastic? Why?
4. What is the difference between industries that have elastic supply and those that have inelastic supply?
5. What is the main factor that affects elasticity of supply and how does it affect elasticity?
6. **Using Your Notes** How is time related to elasticity of supply? Refer to your completed cluster diagram. Use the Graphic Organizer at **Interactive Review @ ClassZone.com**

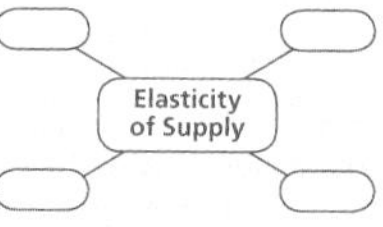

CRITICAL THINKING

7. **Analyzing Causes** Between 1997 and 2002, many gold producers cut their budgets for exploring for new sources in order to stay profitable when the price of gold was less than $350 per ounce. When the price rose above $400 per ounce in 2004, gold producers were not able to respond quickly to the increase. Use what you know about elasticity of supply to explain this cause-and-effect relationship.
8. **Analyzing Data** In May, Montclair Electronics sold 100 portable DVD players at $150 each. High consumer demand at the start of the summer travel season increased the price to $180. In June, the store sold 115 DVD players at the higher price. Is the supply of DVD players elastic or inelastic? Show your math calculations to support your answer.
9. **Applying Economic Concepts** Analyze the factors that determine elasticity of supply to explain why it is difficult for orange growers to respond quickly to changes in the price of orange juice.
10. **Challenge** Prices are up 8 percent at the local juice shop. Its raw materials are inexpensive and easy to find, and the labor is unskilled. Should the shop be able to raise quantity supplied more than 8 percent? Why?

ECONOMICS IN PRACTICE

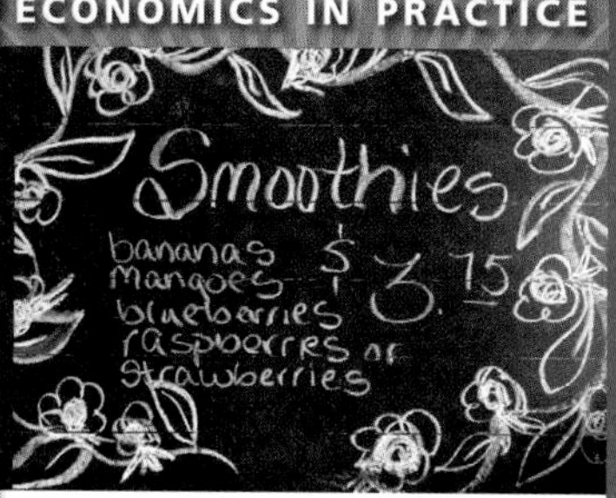

Smoothies
bananas
mangoes
blueberries
raspberries or
strawberries
$3.15

Calculating Elasticity
The growing market for bottled yogurt smoothies is shown in the supply schedule below. Use the information in the table to determine whether the quantity supplied is growing proportionately more than increases in price. Would you expect supply for yogurt smoothies to be elastic or inelastic over a period of six months?

Price ($)	Quantity Supplied of Smoothies
2.00	600
1.75	450
1.50	300
1.25	200

Create a Supply Curve Use the information in the supply schedule to create a supply curve for yogurt smoothies. What does the slope of this curve indicate about elasticity of supply for yogurt smoothies?

Challenge Adapt the information in the Math Challenge on page 121 to calculate the elasticity of supply using the data in the supply schedule above. Substitute quantity supplied for quantity demanded in the formula.

Use **SMARTGrapher @ ClassZone.com** to complete this activity.

4 Assess & Reteach

Assess Have students outline the ideas they would include in answers to the Critical Thinking questions. Then discuss possible responses as a class.

Unit 2 Resource Book
- Section Quiz, p. 91

Interactive Review @ ClassZone.com
- Section Quiz

Test Generator CD-ROM
- Section Quiz

Reteach Have students work on their own to complete the Reading Study Guide for this section. Discuss their responses as a class.

Unit 2 Resource Book
- Reteaching Activity, p. 92

Economics in Practice

Create a Supply Curve Supply curves should accurately graph the values on the supply schedule and show a gradual slope, indicating elasticity.

Challenge Student calculations should show elasticity at every price range on the table, with elasticity of 2.4, 3.1, and 2.5 from top to bottom.

SMARTGrapher Students can create a supply curve using **SmartGrapher @ ClassZone.com.**

SECTION 4 ASSESSMENT ANSWERS

Reviewing Key Concepts

1. a. *elastic*, p. 154
   b. *inelastic*, p. 154
   c. *elasticity of supply*, p. 154
2. Both measure responsiveness of the market to price changes. Elasticity of supply relates to producers; elasticity of demand relates to consumers.
3. Inelastic—there is only so much and more cannot be "produced" to meet increased demand.
4. Industries that have elastic supply do not require lots of capital, skilled labor, or rare resources; those with inelastic supply are the opposite.
5. The ease with which a producer can change production to respond to price changes is the main factor that affects supply. Producers that can respond more easily and quickly will have more elastic supply than producers who have a difficult time responding to price changes.
6. See page 154 for an example of a completed diagram. The more time a producer has to respond to a price change the more elastic the supply of a good or service will be.

Critical Thinking

7. Increasing gold supply is difficult and time consuming. Exploration is the first step in changing production to increase supply. By not investing in exploration, producers were not able to increase supply when the prices rose.
8. Supply is inelastic, 15 percent increase in quantity supplied/ 20 percent increase in price.
9. Orange production cannot be immediately increased in response to short-term increases in demand. Even importing oranges from a different part of the world would take some time and limit the level of elasticity of orange juice production.
10. yes, because more raw materials and labor are inexpensive and plentiful and the production process is uncomplicated

Economics in Practice

See answers in side column above.

1 Plan & Prepare

Objectives

- Analyze the effect of robot technology on supply and productivity.
- Describe some applications of robot technology

2 Focus & Motivate

Connecting to Everyday Life Ask students to think of examples of robots from books, movies, or television shows. Lead a brief discussion of the kinds of activities those robots perform. Relate the discussion to specialization and productivity: What can robots do better than humans, and vice versa?

3 Teach

Using the Sources

Direct students to note the sources of all three exhibits. Encourage them to make a practice of examining the sources in order to assess the objectivity or bias that might be present.

A. What practical goals is Toyota trying to achieve through the use of robots on increasingly complex tasks? *(to compensate for the expected shortage of workers resulting from the low birth rate and to keep production costs in Japan as low as they are in China)*

B. What point is the cartoon making about what people can do that robots cannot? *(that robots eliminate some of the labor issues that often arise in manufacturing)*

C. What effect would the use of cake-decorating robots have on the bakery's employment practices during busy holidays? *(They will no longer have to scramble to fill spots and train new employees.)*

Economics Update

Go to **ClassZone.com** to find an update to this Case Study, including another article, an editable student worksheet, and an editable lesson plan.

Case Study

Find an update on this Case Study at **ClassZone.com**

Robots—Technology Increases Supply

Background The increasing sophistication of technology continues to have a profound impact on the production and supply of manufactured goods. Robots—machines that can be programmed to perform a variety of tasks—are a prime example of technology's effect on industry.

Today, industrial robots perform a wide variety of functions. Although robots do everything from packaging pharmaceuticals to dispensing genetic material in biotechnical laboratories, half of all industrial robots are used to make automobiles. Robots are ideal for lifting heavy objects and for performing repetitive activities that humans find boring. Lately, though, robots are being used more for tasks that require refined skills.

What's the issue? How does technology increase supply? Study these sources to discover how robots can increase productivity.

A. Online Article

Japan's low birthrate is likely to result in a shortage of workers. This article discusses how Toyota plans to use robots to solve this problem.

Toyota to Use "Super" Robots

As the Japanese labor pool declines, Toyota turns to robots.

Toyota is deploying at all 12 of its domestic plants robots capable of performing several simultaneous operations. It aims to be the first automaker to introduce robots that, in addition to machine work and engine assembly, perform the finishing touches on the assembly line. . . .

In the automobile industry robots mainly perform relatively dangerous tasks such as welding and coating, while, in order to preserve quality, human workers accomplish such complicated final processes as attaching interior trim.

But Toyota plans to introduce robots to final assembly processes after establishing the necessary control technology and safeguards, and developing parts easily assembled by android [robotic] hands.

Even this super robot will not result in the total replacement of man by machine; rather it will reinforce the strengths of the production line and compensate for manpower shortages in a truly Toyota-style production innovation.

The company plans to use robots to keep production costs at the level of those in China. . . . Toyota presently uses between 3,000 and 4,000 standard robots. It expects a total of 1,000 super robots to join them.

Source: japaninc.net

Thinking Economically Will the use of robots as described in this article affect the supply of Toyota automobiles? Explain your answer.

DIFFERENTIATING INSTRUCTION

Struggling Readers

Skim for Text Features

Direct students to skim Source C. Point out the use of the words *Problem:*, *Solution:*, and *Benefits:*. Explain that some informational texts use this approach to highlight the parts of the text. Suggest that students use this text feature when taking notes to represent the main ideas. Model for them how notes might look. *(Problem: handling big holiday demand as cheaply as possible; Solution: use of robots and various positioning tools; Benefits: higher production, consistent quality, lower training costs.)*

English Learners

Use Suffixes to Understand

Write the word *robot* and its definition on the board. Beneath *robot* write the word *robotic*. Ask students for a definition. *(having the characteristics of a robot)* Next ask students what part of speech each word is. (robot=*noun;* robotic=*adjective*) Point out that the suffix *–ic* often serves the purpose of changing a noun to an adjective.

Have students copy the words *artist* and *symbol* and find and write their definitions. Then have them write the adjective forms ending in *–ic* and each definition.

B. Political Cartoon

John Morris drew this cartoon about the use of robots in manufacturing. *Parity* means "equality." In the cartoon, *parity* refers to equal pay and benefits.

"The robots have gone on strike - they want parity with the robots at Ford."

Source: www.CartoonStock.com

Thinking Economically How are the robots in the cartoon affecting productivity?

C. Industry Report

Epson, a maker of industrial robots, presents a case study involving the use of robots in a bakery.

Robots Decorate Cakes

English bakery turns to robots during peak seasons.

Problem: A large English commercial bakery decorates cakes with written messages iced on the top—a task generally undertaken by skilled staff. . . .

During seasonal holiday periods consumer demand for these decorated cakes increases fourfold. Training of additional staff to cope with the expanded demand . . . takes a significant period of time and so volume planning is critical.

Solution: System Devices, the EPSON Robots agent for the [United Kingdom], worked with Integrated Dispensing Systems to design and build a robotic cake decorating cell that . . . used an EPSON SCARA robot. . . .

Cakes are fed to the EPSON robot via a conveyor. A simple optical positioning system ensures that the cakes are presented to the robot in a consistent position.

A CAD [computer-aided design] file of the decoration shape is downloaded to the robot. Because individual cake heights may vary, a laser range finder tells the robot the height of each cake as it enters the work cell. The robot moves over the top of the cake and writes the decorative inscription. . . .

Benefits: Ability to boost production during peak seasonal demand periods; consistently high product quality due to reduced variability on decorations; reduced . . . training costs.

Source: www.robots.epson.com

Thinking Economically In this report, how does the use of robots help the supplier respond to a seasonal change in demand? Would this robotic solution help a department store facing a holiday staffing shortage? Why or why not?

THINKING ECONOMICALLY Synthesizing

1. Which of the six factors that can cause a change in supply is highlighted in the three documents? Does this factor generally increase or decrease supply?
2. Which document, B or C, addresses the issue of elasticity? Explain.
3. In which article, A or C, are the robots an example of variable costs? Why?

CHAPTER 5 • ASSESSMENT

Online Summ... Answers

1. supply
2. law of s...
3. s...

...ued
... mechanical as
th... ...y.

Synthesizing

1. *technology; increases supply*
2. *Document C. addresses elasticity, since it shows how robots allowed the baker to quickly increase supply.*
3. *C., because they're brought in to help only during one time of year when they're needed*

TECHNOLOGY ACTIVITY

Researching Industrial Robots

Time 45 minutes 

Task Find examples of robots used to increase supply.

Materials Needed a computer with Internet access, software for making a slideshow

Activity

- Divide students into three or four groups. Direct them to choose an industry they find interesting. They should then research that industry, focusing on how, if at all, robots are used in it.
- Have students collect representative photographs and other graphics by saving them onto a disc.
- Direct each group to compile their photographs and other graphics into a slideshow and prepare a narration script to accompany it. The narration should include the company name, what part of the industry the company represents, and how it uses robots to increase supply.
- Ask each group to present its slideshow to the rest of the class. Group members can take turns reading the narration.

Rubric

	Understanding of Robots and Supply	Presentation of Information
4	excellent	clear and complete
3	good	mostly clear
2	fair	sometimes clear
1	poor	sketchy

...ary

...supply
...pply schedule
4. supply curve
5. marginal product
6. total product
7. diminishing returns
8. fixed costs
9. marginal cost
10. marginal revenue
11. profit-maximizing output
12. change in supply
13. labor productivity
14. elasticity of supply
15. change in quantity supplied

Interactive Review

Review this chapter using interactive activities at **ClassZone.com**

- Online Summary
- Quizzes
- Vocabulary Flip Cards
- Graphic Organizers
- Review and Study Notes

Online Summary

Complete the following activity either on your own paper or online at **ClassZone.com**

Choose the key concept that best completes the sentence. Not all key concepts will be used.

break-even point	marginal product
change in quantity supplied	marginal revenue
change in supply	productivity
diminishing returns	profit-maximizing output
elasticity of supply	supply
fixed cost	supply curve
increasing returns	supply schedule
input costs	total product
law of supply	total revenue
marginal cost	variable cost

__1__ is the quantity of a product that producers are willing and able to offer for sale. According to the __2__, when price increases, quantity supplied increases, and when price decreases, quantity supplied decreases. Quantity supplied can be displayed on a chart called a __3__ or on a graph called a __4__.

__5__ is the change in __6__ caused by hiring one additional worker. When marginal product begins to decrease, production is in the stage of __7__.

Total cost is the sum of __8__ and variable costs. __9__ is the additional cost of producing one more unit. When marginal cost equals __10__, a company has reached __11__.

A __12__ occurs when producers are willing to sell different amounts of a product at every price. The six factors that change supply are input costs, __13__, technology, government action, producer expectations, and number of producers.

The term __14__ describes how responsive producers are to price changes. It is measured by comparing __15__ to change in price.

CHAPTER 5 Assessment

REVIEWING KEY CONCEPTS

What Is Supply? (pp. 130–137)

1. What two requirements of supply must someone meet to be considered a producer?
2. What does it mean to say that quantity supplied and price have a direct relationship?

What Are the Costs of Production? (pp. 138–145)

3. How does marginal product change during the three stages of production?
4. What is the relationship of total costs to profit?

What Factors Affect Supply? (pp. 146–153)

5. What is the difference between change in quantity supplied and change in supply?
6. How do input costs affect supply?

What Is Elasticity of Supply? (pp. 154–159)

7. How are elastic and inelastic supply different?
8. How might you calculate elasticity of supply?

APPLYING ECONOMIC CONCEPTS

Look at the graph below showing price changes for two commodities: crude oil and gasoline.

9. How is the price of gasoline related to the price of crude oil?
10. What factor that affects the supply of gasoline is shown in this graph? How does this factor affect the supply of gasoline?

FIGURE 5.17 U.S. PRICES OF CRUDE OIL AND GASOLINE

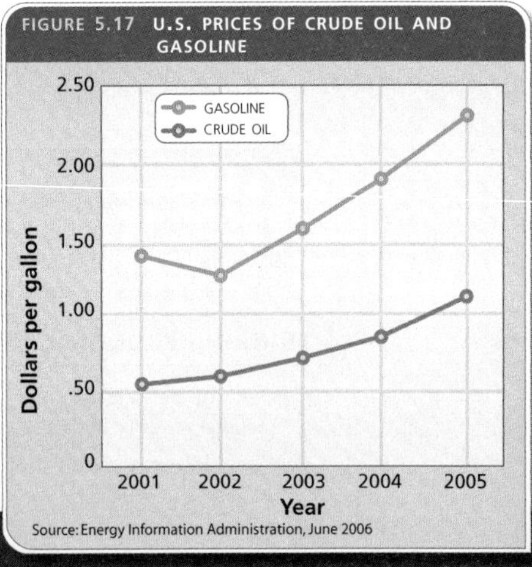

Source: Energy Information Administration, June 2006

CHAPTER 5 ASSESSMENT ANSWERS

Reviewing Key Concepts

1. To be considered producers, people must be willing and able to supply products.
2. Quantity supplied and price change in the same direction, when one increases or decreases so does the other.
3. During the stage of increasing returns, marginal product increases, during the stage of diminishing returns, marginal product decreases, and during the stage of negative returns, marginal product is a negative number.
4. Profit is total revenue minus total cost.
5. Change in quantity supplied is a movement from one point to another along a supply curve. Change in supply is a shift in the supply curve when something prompts producers to offer more or less of their product at every price.
6. When input costs increase, supply decreases, and when input costs decrease, supply increases.
7. Elastic supply means that change in quantity supplied is proportionately greater than change in price. Inelastic supply means that change in quantity supplied is proportionately less than change in price.
8. Divide percent change in quantity supplied by percent change in price. (See Math Challenge on page 121; substitute *quantity supplied* for *quantity demanded* in the formula.)

Applying Economic Concepts

9. The price of gasoline is higher than the price of crude oil and trends in the same direction.
10. Crude oil is a raw material used in making gasoline, so the cost of crude oil is one of gasoline's input costs. When the price of crude oil rises, the supply of gasoline declines.

Critical Thinking

11. Break-even occurs when total product is 400; profit-maximizing output is 700 backpacks.
12. Supply of soft drinks will decrease and supply of the other beverages will increase as a result of this government action.
13. Demand for sports cars is elastic because they are expensive luxuries with many substitutes.

CRITICAL THINKING

11. Analyzing Data Suppose that you own a factory producing backpacks that sell for $20 each. Use the information in this table to calculate marginal cost, total revenue, and profit at each level of output. Identify the break-even point and profit-maximizing output.

BACKPACK PRODUCTION COSTS

Production Costs	
Total Product	Total Cost ($)
100	3,500
200	5,300
300	7,000
400	8,000
500	8,800
600	9,800
700	11,800
800	14,300
900	17,000

12. Analyzing Effects A city puts a new rule into effect about the kinds of beverages that may be sold in schools. Sugary sodas must be replaced by bottled water, fruit juices, and sports drinks. How will this decision affect the supply of each category of beverage at the schools? What factor that affects supply is demonstrated in this situation?

13. Drawing Conclusions Both demand and supply for gasoline are inelastic. Would the elasticity of supply and demand be the same for sports cars? Why or why not?

14. Challenge When a string of hurricanes hit Florida, preparation for and cleanup from the storms increased demand for plywood. Yet prices rose only slightly, partly because large chains shipped plywood from stores around the country in anticipation of the increased demand. How does this story illustrate the law of supply and elasticity of supply?

SIMULATION

How Much Are You Willing to Supply?

Choose a partner. Imagine that the two of you run a software company. Your best-selling product is a program that helps businesses manage their inventory. Next year you will produce 20,000 units. The following partial supply schedule shows the prices at which you will likely sell your product during that period.

SOFTWARE SUPPLY SCHEDULE

Price ($)	Quantity Supplied
70	7,500
65	
60	
55	
50	1,000

Step 1 Copy the schedule onto a sheet of paper and fill in the missing amounts in the Quantity Supplied column. Be sure that the amounts you choose adhere to the law of supply.

Step 2 Draw a supply curve to illustrate your schedule. Be sure to label each axis of your curve.

Step 3 Get together with three other groups. These are your competitors. Bring all of your individual supply schedules together to make a market supply schedule. Then convert the market supply schedule into a market supply curve.

Step 4 You and your competitors find out that several other companies are getting ready to introduce similar inventory-control software. On your market supply curve, show how this development causes a shift in supply.

Step 5 Although writing your program was difficult, now that it is written, it is relatively quick and easy to produce copies for sale. Is the supply of your product elastic or inelastic? Why?

Use **SMARTGrapher @ ClassZone.com** to complete this activity.

CHAPTER 5 • ASSESSMENT

McDougal Littell **Assessment System**

Assess

Online Test Practice
- Go to **ClassZone.com** for more test practice.

Unit 2 Resource Book
- Chapter Test, Forms A, B, C, pp. 103–114

Test Generator CD-ROM
- Chapter Test, Forms (A, B, & C), in English and Spanish

Report

Use the McDougal Littell Assessment System to score assessments and receive customized reports.

Reteach

For activities customized for individual students, use the McDougal Littell Assessment System.

SMARTGrapher Students can create a market supply curve using **SmartGrapher @ ClassZone.com.**

CHAPTER 5 ASSESSMENT ANSWERS

Supply is inelastic because producing sports cars requires a lot of capital, skilled labor, and hard-to-obtain materials and requires a lot of time to increase quantity supplied.

14. The story shows that producers will increase quantity supplied when they expect demand to increase. Expectations of higher prices in Florida caused the producer to shift supply from other areas. Supply for plywood tends to be inelastic in the short term with regard to production, but the story showed that supply was more elastic with regard to distribution. This allowed the producer to shift quantity supplied from one place to another fairly quickly.

SIMULATION

Step 2: Be sure that the amounts that students fill in follow the law of supply. So as price rises, quantity supplied should also rise. No price above $50 should have a quantity supplied below $1,000, and no price below $70 should have a quantity supplied higher than 7,500.

Step 4: Since the number of producers is increasing, the overall supply will also increase. Their supply curve should shift to the right.

Step 5: Answer: The supply is elastic since it is quick and easy to make many more of the finished product. The fact that the initial product-development process was difficult has no bearing on the product's ultimate elasticity of supply.

Simulation Rubric

	Understanding of Concepts Involved	Presentation of Information
4	excellent	accurate, clear, and complete
3	good	mostly accurate and clear
2	fair	sometimes clear
1	poor	sketchy

Planning Guide

Resources 2Go Complete print resources all on one USB drive allow you to customize lessons.

Section Titles and Objectives	Unit 2 Resource Book and Workbooks		Assessment Resources
1 Seeking Equilibrium: Supply and Demand pp. 164–173 • Explore market equilibrium and see how it is reached • Explain how supply and demand interact to determine equilibrium price • Analyze what causes surplus, shortage, and disequilibrium • Identify how changes to demand and supply affect the equilibrium price	**Unit 2 Resource Book** • Reading Study Guide, pp. 115–116 • RSG with Additional Support, pp. 117–119 • RSG with Additional Support (Spanish), pp. 120–122 • Economic Simulations: Price and Your Choice, pp. 151–152	**NCEE Student Activities** • Equilibrium Prices and Quantities, pp. 21–24	**Unit 2 Resource Book** • Section Quiz, p. 123 • Reteaching Activity, p. 124 **Test Generator CD-ROM** **Daily Test Practice Transparencies,** TT19
2 Prices as Signals and Incentives pp. 174–179 • Analyze how the price system works • Explain how prices provide information about markets • Describe how prices act as incentives to producers	**Unit 2 Resource Book** • Reading Study Guide, pp. 125–126 • RSG with Additional Support, pp. 127–129 • RSG with Additional Support (Spanish), pp. 130–132 • Economic Skills and Problem Solving Activity, pp. 145–146	• Readings in Free Enterprise: Who Is to Blame for the Real Estate Bubble?, pp. 147–148	**Unit 2 Resource Book** • Section Quiz, p. 133 • Reteaching Activity, p. 134 **Test Generator CD-ROM** **Daily Test Practice Transparencies,** TT20
3 Intervention in the Price System pp. 180–187 • Explain how government uses price ceilings to keep prices from rising too high • Describe how government uses price floors to keep prices from going too low • Discuss how government uses rationing to allocate scarce resources and goods	**Unit 2 Resource Book** • Reading Study Guide, pp. 135–136 • RSG with Additional Support, pp. 137–139 • RSG with Additional Support (Spanish), pp. 140–142 • Math Skills Worksheet: Calculating the Government Costs of Price Support, p. 153	• Case Study Resources: Outside the Box Office, pp. 149–150 **Test Practice and Review Workbook,** pp. 33–34	**Unit 2 Resource Book** • Section Quiz, p. 143 • Reteaching Activity, p. 144 • Chapter Test, (Forms A, B, & C), pp. 155–166 **Test Generator CD-ROM** **Daily Test Practice Transparencies,** TT21

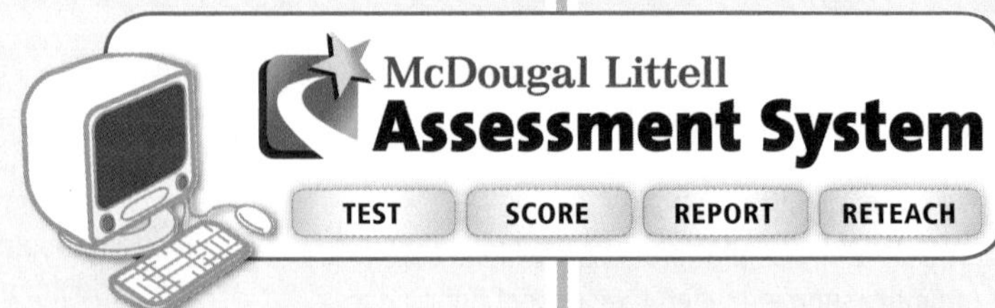

Integrated Technology

No Time? To focus students on the most important content in this chapter, use Economics Concepts Transparencies, CT19, "Surplus, Shortage, and Equilibrium," available in Resources 2Go.

Teacher Presentation Options

Presentation Toolkit

Power Presentation DVD-ROM

- Lecture Notes
- Interactive Review
- Media Gallery
- Animated Economics
- Review Game

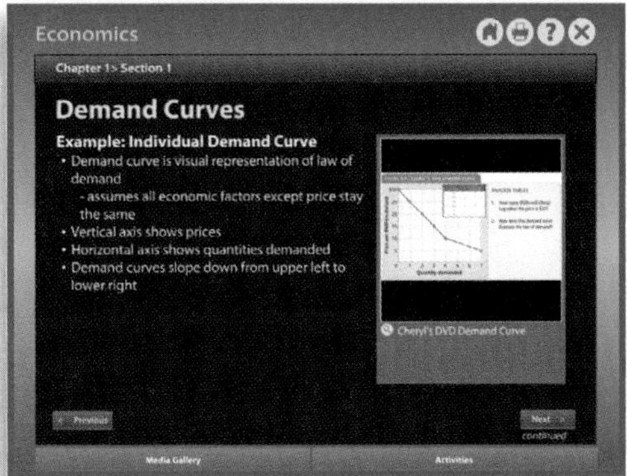

Economics Concepts Transparencies

- Surplus, Shortage, and Equilibrium, CT19
- Market Signals, CT20
- Supply and Demand Graph, CT21

Electronic Books

eEdition DVD-ROM

eEdition Online

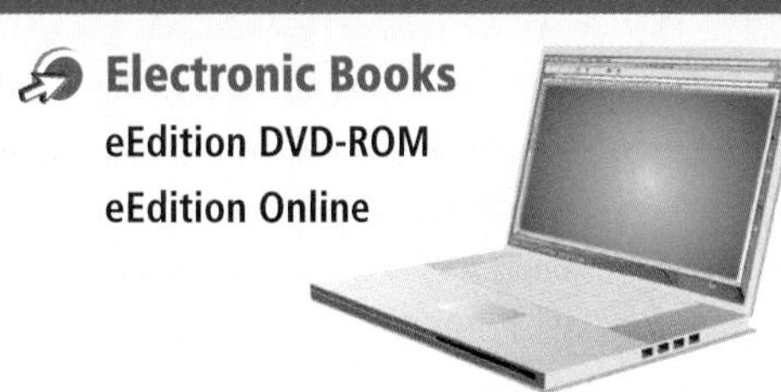

Daily Test Practice Transparencies, TT19, TT20, TT21

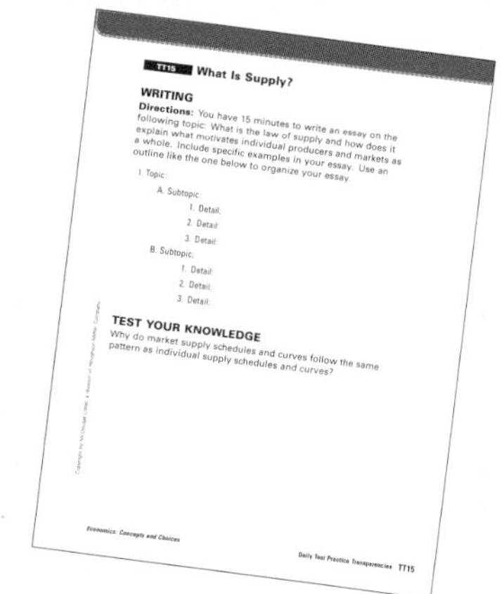

Animated Economics

- Interactive Market Demand and Supply Schedule and Curve, p. 165
- Interactive Market Demand and Supply Curve, p. 169

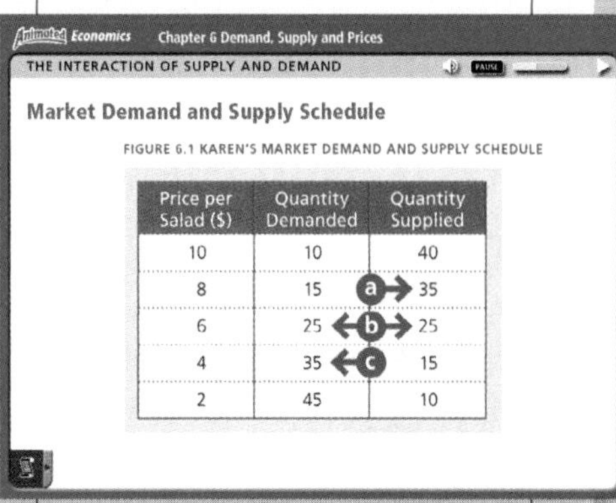

Price per Salad ($)	Quantity Demanded	Quantity Supplied
10	10	40
8	15	35
6	25	25
4	35	15
2	45	10

Online Activities at ClassZone.com

Economics Update

- Market Equilibrium, p. 165
- Michael Dell, p. 178
- Minimum Wage, p. 182
- Prices for Concert Tickets, p. 186

Animated Economics

- Interactive Graphics

Activity Maker

- Vocabulary Flip Cards
- Review Game

Research Center

- Graphs and Data

Interactive Review

- Online Summary
- Quizzes
- Vocabulary Flip Cards
- Graphic Organizers
- Review and Study Notes

SMARTGrapher

- Create a Demand and Supply Curve, p. 168
- Create Demand and Supply Curves, p. 189
- Create a Demand and Supply Curve, p. 189

Teacher-Tested Activities

Name: Lisa Herman-Ellison

School: Kokomo High School

State: Indiana

Teacher-Tested Activities

At the beginning of this chapter, look for my classroom-proven idea for teaching economics concepts and thinking.

Chapter 6: Demand, Supply, and Prices
Resources for Differentiated Instruction

Struggling Readers

Teacher's Edition Activities

- Sequence Events, p. 168
- Diagram Cause and Effect, p. 170
- Illustrate the Biography, p. 178
- Compare and Contrast, p. 184

Unit 2 Resource Book

- RSG with Additional Support, pp. 117–119, 127–129, 137–139 (A)
- Reteaching Activities, pp. 124, 134, 144 (B)
- Chapter Test (Form A), pp. 155–158 (C)

ClassZone.com

- Animated Economics
- Interactive Review

Test Generator CD-ROM

- Chapter Test (Form A)
- Chapter Test (Form A), in Spanish

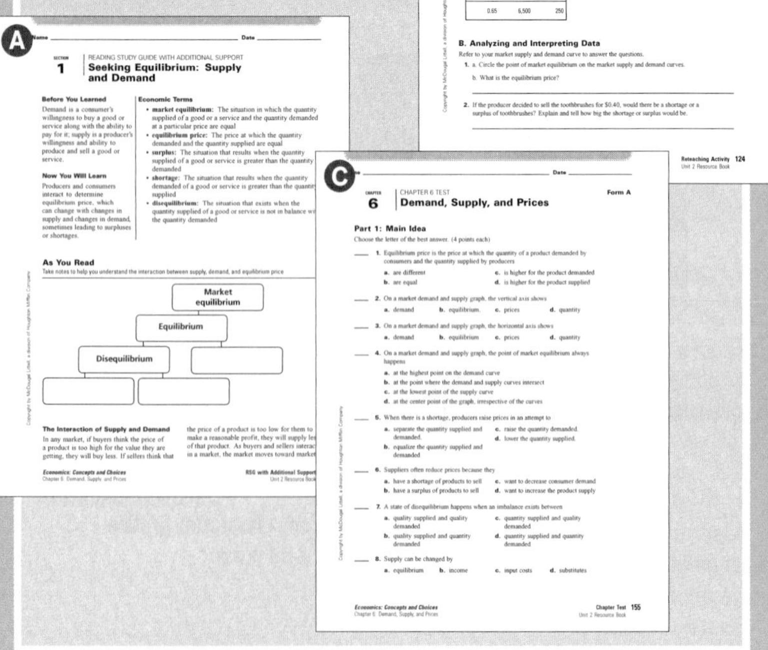

B — Section 1 Reteaching Activity: Seeking Equilibrium: Supply and Demand

A — Section 1 Reading Study Guide with Additional Support: Seeking Equilibrium: Supply and Demand

C — Chapter 6 Test: Demand, Supply, and Prices — Form A

English Learners

Teacher's Edition Activities

- Use Word Parts, p. 166
- Use Spoken Language, p. 172
- Create Word Webs, p. 176
- Build Economics Vocabulary, p. 182
- Understand Colloquial English, p. 186

Unit 2 Resource Book

- RSG with Additional Support (Spanish), pp. 120–122, 130–132, 140–142 (A)

Test Generator CD-ROM

- Chapter Test (Forms A, B, & C), in Spanish (B)

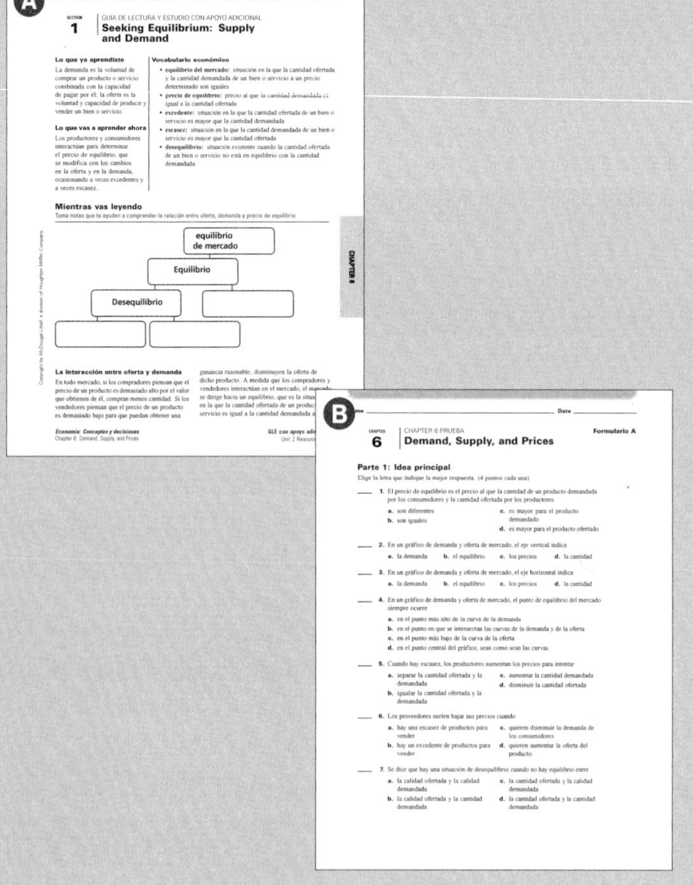

A — Sección 1 Guía de lectura y estudio con apoyo adicional: Seeking Equilibrium: Supply and Demand

B — Chapter 6 Prueba: Demand, Supply, and Prices — Formulario A

Inclusion

Teacher's Edition Activities

- Use Transparencies, p. 166
- Use the Visuals, p. 170
- Support Class Discussion, p. 182
- Use the Audio DVD, p. 186

Lesson Plans

- Modified Lessons for Inclusion, pp. 19–21 (A)

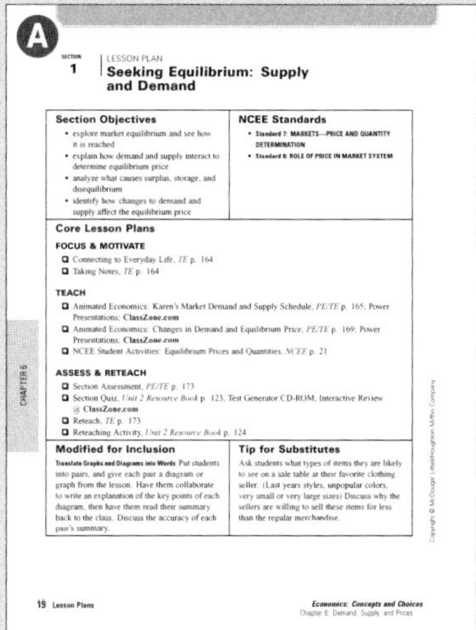

A

SECTION 1 | LESSON PLAN

Seeking Equilibrium: Supply and Demand

Section Objectives	NCEE Standards
• explore market equilibrium and see how it is reached • explain how demand and supply interact to determine equilibrium price • analyze what causes surplus, storage, and disequilibrium • identify how changes to demand and supply affect the equilibrium price	• Standard 7: MARKETS—PRICE AND QUANTITY DETERMINATION • Standard 8: ROLE OF PRICE IN MARKET SYSTEM

Core Lesson Plans

FOCUS & MOTIVATE

- ❑ Connecting to Everyday Life, *TE* p. 164
- ❑ Taking Notes, *TE* p. 164

TEACH

- ❑ Animated Economics: Karen's Market Demand and Supply Schedule, *PE/TE* p. 165; Power Presentations: **ClassZone.com**
- ❑ Animated Economics: Changes in Demand and Equilibrium Price, *PE/TE* p. 169; Power Presentations: **ClassZone.com**
- ❑ NCEE Student Activities: Equilibrium Prices and Quantities, *NCEE* p. 21

ASSESS & RETEACH

- ❑ Section Assessment, *PE/TE* p. 173
- ❑ Section Quiz, *Unit 2 Resource Book* p. 123, Test Generator CD-ROM, Interactive Review @ **ClassZone.com**
- ❑ Reteach, *TE* p. 173
- ❑ Reteaching Activity, *Unit 2 Resource Book* p. 124

Modified for Inclusion	Tip for Substitutes
Translate Graphs and Diagrams into Words Put students into pairs, and give each pair a diagram or graph from the lesson. Have them collaborate to write an explanation of the key points of each diagram, then have them read their summary back to the class. Discuss the accuracy of each pair's summary.	Ask students what types of items they are likely to see on a sale table at their favorite clothing seller. (Last years styles, unpopular colors, very small or very large sizes) Discuss why the sellers are willing to sell these items for less than the regular merchandise.

CHAPTER 6

19 Lesson Plans

Economics: Concepts and Choices
Chapter 6: Demand, Supply, and Prices

Gifted and Talented

Teacher's Edition Activities

- Research Surplus and Shortage, p. 168
- Graph Shifting Supply, p. 172
- Compare Product Prices, p. 176
- Create a Buying Guide, p. 178
- Hold a Panel Discussion, p. 184

Unit 2 Resource Book

- Readings in Free Enterprise: Who Is to Blame for the Real Estate Bubble?, pp. 147–148 (A)
- Case Study Resources: Outside the Box Office, pp. 149–150 (B)

NCEE Student Activities

- Equilibrium Prices and Quantities, pp. 21–24 (C)

ClassZone.com

- Research Center

Test Generator CD-ROM

- Chapter Test (Form C)
- Chapter Test (Form C), in Spanish

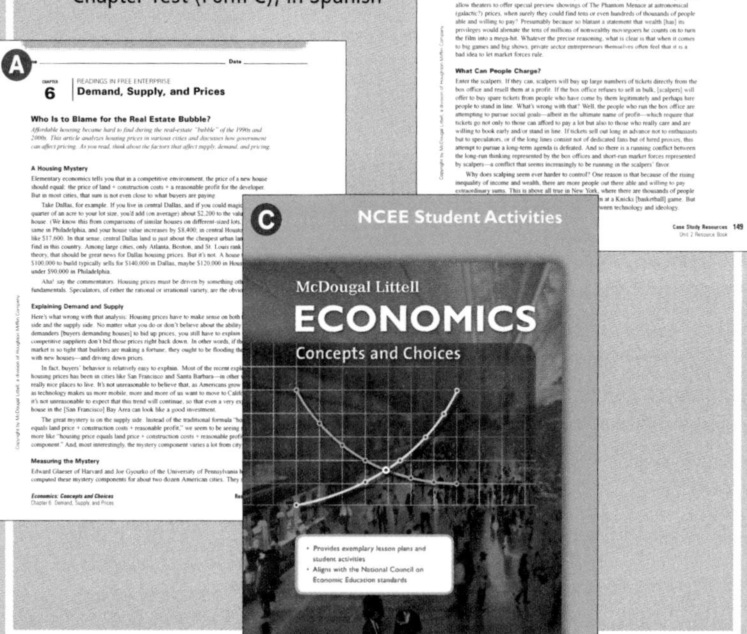

B
CHAPTER 6 | CASE STUDY RESOURCES
Demand, Supply, and Prices
Outside the Box Office
What Would You Pay?
What Can People Charge?
Case Study Resources 149
A
CHAPTER 6 | READINGS IN FREE ENTERPRISE
Demand, Supply, and Prices
Who Is to Blame for the Real Estate Bubble?
A Housing Mystery
Explaining Demand and Supply
Measuring the Mystery
C
NCEE Student Activities
McDougal Littell
ECONOMICS
Concepts and Choices

Focus & Motivate

Objective

Describe how demand and supply interact in the market to determine prices.

Why the Concept Matters

Explain that buyers and sellers do not always interact directly, as in the bargaining described on page 163. However, in all markets, producers offer goods for sale, and consumers decide whether or not to buy them. It is these individual decisions by many buyers and sellers that combine to determine market prices.

Analyzing the Photograph

Have students study the photograph and read the caption. Invite volunteers to describe what the photograph tells them about consumer taste and how this might relate to price considerations. *(Possible answer: The women are smiling, so they probably like the sweaters. Liking them is the first step to buying, but the price will have to be right.)*

Ask students what they can infer from the photograph about factors producers consider when setting the price of the sweaters. *(Possible answer: the costs of making, shipping, and selling them, and a high enough price to allow a profit for manufacturer and retailer)* Explain that Chapter 6 explores the factors that affect demand and supply and how they work together in the market to determine prices.

How are prices set?

Prices greatly influence consumers' buying decisions. A reduced price on this sweater may act as an incentive for these young women to make a purchase.

162

CONTENT STANDARDS

NCEE STANDARDS

Standard 7: Markets—Price and Quantity Determination

Students will understand that

Markets exist when buyers and sellers interact. This interaction determines market prices and thereby allocates scarce goods and services.

Students will be able to use this knowledge to

Identify markets in which they have participated as a buyer and as a seller and describe how the interaction of all buyers and sellers influences prices. *(pages 164–168)*

Standard 8: Role of Price in a Market System

Students will understand that

Prices send signals and provide incentives to buyers and sellers. When supply or demand changes, market prices adjust, affecting incentives.

Students will be able to use this knowledge to

Predict how prices change when the number of buyers or sellers in a market changes, and explain how the incentives facing individual buyers and sellers are affected. *(pages 169–171, 176–177, 180–184)*

CHAPTER

Demand, Supply, and Prices

CONCEPT REVIEW

Demand is the willingness to buy a good or a service and the ability to pay for it.
Supply is the willingness and ability to produce and sell a product.

CHAPTER 6 KEY CONCEPT

The **equilibrium price** is the price at which quantity demanded and quantity supplied are the same.

WHY THE CONCEPT MATTERS

You've been looking for a vintage concert T-shirt to buy. You see the shirt you want offered on an Internet site, but the price is too high. After exchanging several e-mails, you and the seller set a price. It's higher than you wanted to pay and lower than the seller wanted to receive, but it's acceptable to you both. In a market economy, the forces of demand and supply act in much the same way. They work together to set a price that buyers and sellers find acceptable.

Online Highlights

More at ClassZone.com

Economics Update
Go to ECONOMICS UPDATE for chapter updates and current news on ticketing companies' pricing practices. (See Case Study, pp. 186–187.) ▶

Animated Economics
Go to ANIMATED ECONOMICS for interactive lessons on the graphs and tables in this chapter.

Interactive Review
Go to INTERACTIVE REVIEW for concept review and activities.

Why have some rock bands questioned the pricing practices of certain ticketing companies? See the Case Study on pages 186–187.

From the Classroom
Lisa Herman-Ellison, Kokomo High School

Supply and Demand in the News
Have students work in pairs. Give each pair a section of a local newspaper. Use several different days and sections to avoid duplication.

Ask students to look for supply and demand issues in each story. Have students summarize how supply and demand play a part in the story, explain which curve moved and why, and illustrate what happened with a graph. To conclude the exercise, ask each pair to explain their best story. Story summaries and graphs can be used for bulletin board displays.

This exercise helps students understand that economics is more than theory. As a result, it becomes easier for them to recognize economic principles in action.

Previewing Chapter Technology at ClassZone.com

Economics Update Students will find references to online articles or statistics that update information in the pupil edition on pages 165, 178, 182, and 186.

Animated Economics Students will find interactive lessons related to materials on pages 165 and 169.

Interactive Review Students will find additional section and chapter assessment support for materials on pages 173, 179, 185, and 188.

TEACHER MEDIA FAVORITES

Books

- Holzner, Steven. *How Dell Does It.* New York: McGraw-Hill, 2005. Computer industry analyst explores the business principles that led to the success of Dell Inc.
- Keating, W. Dennis, Michael B. Teitz, and Andrejs Skaburskis, eds. *Rent Control: Regulation and the Rental Housing Market.* New Brunswick, NJ: Center for Urban Policy Research, 1998. Essays detailing the history, economics, and politics of rent control.
- Kusek, David, and Gerd Leonhard. *The Future of Music: Manifesto for the Digital Music Revolution.* Boston: Berklee Press Publications, 2005. Provocative look at how technology is changing the distribution and pricing of music.
- Quart, Alissa. *Branded: The Buying and Selling of Teenagers.* Cambridge, MA: Basic Books, 2004. Journalist details how corporate marketers take advantage of teens' desire to create a strong self-image.

Videos/DVDs

- *Economics: A Framework for Teaching the Basic Concepts: Microeconomic Concepts.* 28 Minutes. United Learning, 1997. Shows how the market sets prices and allocates resources to production of specific kinds and quantities of products.

Software

- *Virtual Economics® Version 3.0.* New York: National Council on Economic Education, 2005. A complete resource library for teaching basic economics concepts.

Internet

Visit **ClassZone.com** to link to

- a variety of chapter-specific, content-reviewed sites
- updates on data and topics presented throughout the chapter sections and Case Study
- updates to the Power Presentations

1 Plan & Prepare

Section 1 Objectives

- explore market equilibrium and see how it is reached
- explain how demand and supply interact to determine equilibrium price
- analyze what causes surplus, shortage, and disequilibrium
- identify how changes to demand and supply affect the equilibrium price

2 Focus & Motivate

Connecting to Everyday Life Explain that this section focuses on the ways that supply and demand interact in the marketplace to determine prices. Ask students to describe different kinds of markets where producers and consumers interact.

Taking Notes Remind students to take notes as they read by completing a cluster diagram for each key concept. They can use the Graphic Organizer at **Interactive Review @ ClassZone.com.** A sample is shown below.

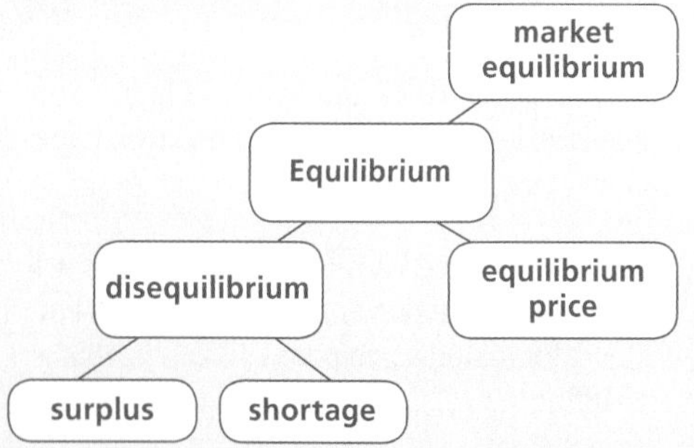

SECTION 1

Seeking Equilibrium: Demand and Supply

OBJECTIVES

In Section 1, you will
- explore market equilibrium and see how it is reached
- explain how demand and supply interact to determine equilibrium price
- analyze what causes surplus, shortage, and disequilibrium
- identify how changes to demand and supply affect the equilibrium price

KEY TERMS

market equilibrium, *p. 164*
equilibrium price, *p. 164*
surplus, *p. 167*
shortage, *p. 167*
disequilibrium, *p. 169*

TAKING NOTES

As you read Section 1, complete a cluster diagram like the one shown using the key concepts and other helpful words and phrases. Use the Graphic Organizer at **Interactive Review @ ClassZone.com**

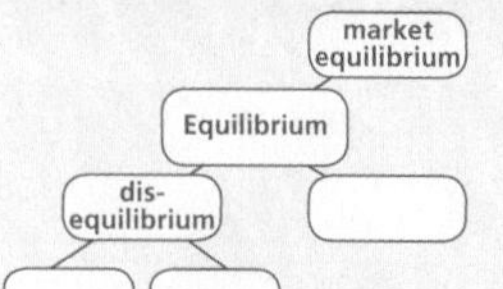

The Interaction of Demand and Supply

QUICK REFERENCE

Market equilibrium occurs when the quantity demanded and the quantity supplied at a particular price are equal.

Equilibrium price is the price at which the quantity demanded and the quantity supplied are equal.

KEY CONCEPTS

In Chapters 4 and 5, you learned about how demand and supply work in the market. Recall that a market is any place or situation in which people buy and sell goods and services. Since the market is the place where buyers and sellers come together, it is also the place where demand and supply interact.

As buyers and sellers interact, the market moves toward **market equilibrium**, a situation in which the quantity demanded of a good or service at a particular price is equal to the quantity supplied at that price. **Equilibrium price** is the price at which the quantity of a product demanded by consumers and the quantity supplied by producers are equal.

EXAMPLE Market Demand and Supply Schedule

Let's look at an example of how this concept works in a particular market. Karen runs a sandwich shop near an office park. Recently, she decided to offer a new product at lunchtime—prepared salads. On the first day, she makes up 40 salads and offers them at $10 each. She is disappointed when she sells only 10 and has to throw the rest away. The next day she is more cautious. She lowers

SECTION 1 PROGRAM RESOURCES

ON LEVEL

Lesson Plans
- Core, p. 19

Unit 2 Resource Book
- Reading Study Guide, pp. 115–116
- Economic Simulations, pp. 151–152
- Section Quiz, p. 123

STRUGGLING READERS

Unit 2 Resource Book
- Reading Study Guide with Additional Support, pp. 117–119
- Reteaching Activity, p. 124

ENGLISH LEARNERS

Unit 2 Resource Book
- Reading Study Guide with Additional Support (Spanish), pp. 120–122

INCLUSION

Lesson Plans
- Modified for Inclusion, p. 19

GIFTED AND TALENTED

NCEE Student Activities
- Equilibrium Prices and Quantities, pp. 21–24

TECHNOLOGY

eEdition DVD-ROM

eEdition Online

Power Presentation DVD-ROM

Economics Concepts Transparencies
- CT19 Surplus, Shortage, and Equilibrium

Daily Test Practice Transparencies, TT19

ClassZone.com

the price to $4 each and makes only 15 salads. She discovers that 35 customers wanted her salads at the lower price. How can Karen find the right price?

Over the course of a week, Karen experiments with different combinations of price and quantity of salads supplied until she discovers market equilibrium at $6 per salad. At that price, she is willing to offer 25 salads for sale, and she sells all of them. When she has either too many or too few salads, she is motivated to change her price. Market equilibrium is the point at which quantity demanded and quantity supplied are in balance.

FIGURE 6.1 KAREN'S MARKET DEMAND AND SUPPLY SCHEDULE

Price per Salad ($)	Quantity Demanded	Quantity Supplied
10	10	40
8	15 (a) →	35
6	25 ← (b) →	25
4	35 ← (c)	15
2	40	10

(a) At prices above $6, quantity supplied exceeds quantity demanded.

(b) At the price of $6, the quantity demanded and the quantity supplied are equal.

(c) At prices below $6, the quantity demanded exceeds the quantity supplied.

Only at the **equilibrium price** of $6 are the quantity demanded and the quantity supplied equal.

ANALYZE TABLES

1. What is the difference between quantity supplied and quantity demanded when the price is $10? What is the difference when the price is $2?
2. How does this market demand and supply schedule illustrate the laws of demand and supply?

Animated **Economics**

Use an interactive market demand and supply schedule and curve at **ClassZone.com**

Look at Figure 6.1 to see the information that Karen gathered from her first week selling prepared salads. This table is a combined market demand and supply schedule that shows the quantities of salads supplied and demanded at various prices. Notice that quantity demanded and quantity supplied are different at every line of the schedule except one. That line represents market equilibrium and shows the equilibrium price of $6. When Karen offers salads at prices above $6, she produces more salads than she can sell and has to throw some away. When she offers salads at prices below $6, there is unmet demand because people want more salads than Karen is willing to offer at those prices.

Karen's experience shows how the laws of demand and supply interact in the market. She wants to offer more salads at higher prices than at lower prices because she wants to earn more profit. Her costs would make it impossible to earn much, if any, profit if she were to sell the number of salads that the office workers would like to buy at the lower prices. In a similar way, while the office workers may like the idea of fresh salads for lunch, they are not willing to buy the quantity of salads that Karen wants to sell at higher prices.

Economics Update

Find an update on market equilibrium at **ClassZone.com**

CHAPTER 6 • SECTION 1

3 Teach

The Interaction of Demand and Supply

Discuss

- Why is Karen motivated to change her price when she makes too many or too few salads? *(because she has not found the price where quantity supplied and demanded are equal)*

Analyzing Tables: Figure 6.1

Encourage students to read the table two columns at a time (1st and 2nd and 1st and 3rd) to emphasize that this is a combination of a supply schedule and a demand schedule. Have them read each row to compare quantity supplied and demanded.

Answers

1. *at $10, +30; at $2, −30*
2. *It shows that consumers are willing to buy more goods at lower prices, while producers are willing to offer more goods at higher prices.*

Animated **Economics** The supply schedule highlights how many salads are supplied and demanded at each price. It will help students understand market equilibrium and equilibrium price.

Economics Update

At **ClassZone.com,** students will see updated information on market equilibrium.

LEVELED ACTIVITY

Analyzing News Stories

Time 45 Minutes

Objective Students will describe how changes in supply and demand affect equilibrium price in real-world situations shown in news articles. (These concepts are covered in Section 1.)

Basic

Use Internet or library resources to find a news story that is an example of a change in supply or a change in demand in a particular market. Web sites operated by newspapers or television news networks are good resources. Write a brief summary of the story. Indicate how the change affects the equilibrium price.

On Level

Use Internet or library resources to find two news stories. One story should show a change in supply in particular markets and the other a change in demand. Create supply and demand curves to illustrate the stories and show how the curves shift. Write captions that explain how the changes affected price.

Challenge

Use Internet or library resources to find several news stories to illustrate changes in supply and demand in various markets. Use the results of your research to create a script for a TV news program on how supply and demand interact in the market to set prices. Create visuals to include in your program.

Discuss

- Why does Karen want to sell more salads at $6 per salad than at $2 per salad? *(because she follows the law of supply and prefers to sell more at higher prices)*
- What is the relationship between a market supply schedule and an individual supply schedule? *(A market supply schedule reflects the sum of all the individual supply schedules in a market.)*

Analyzing Graphs: Figure 6.2

Invite students to look at each curve individually and identify the supply curve and the demand curve. Have them check that the values on the curves match the values in Figure 6.1. Ask them why it is easier to identify equilibrium price on a graph than on a table. *(Possible answer: because the point where the curves intersect is easier to see than finding the correct row on a table)*

Answers

1. *35, 15*
2. *It shows that at the price of $6, where the two curves intersect, the quantity supplied and the quantity demanded are the same (25 salads).*

Economics Illustrated

To better understand the concept of market equilibrium, picture it as a pair of scales, with quantity supplied on one side and quantity demanded on the other. The scales are balanced when the two quantities are equal, that is, at equilibrium price. If either side is greater than the other the scales will not be in balance.

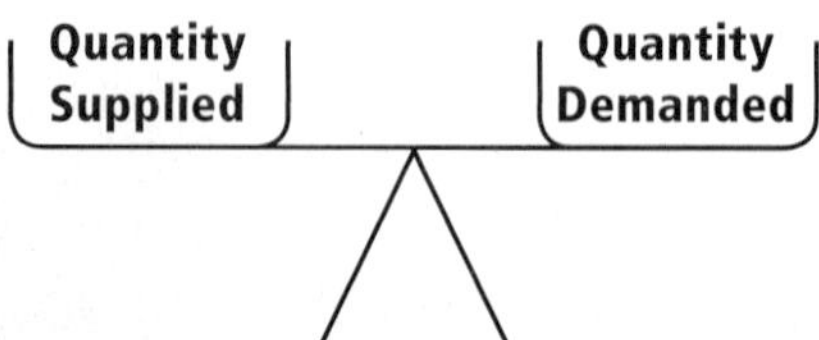

EXAMPLE Market Demand and Supply Curve

Just as it is possible to convert a market demand schedule to a market demand curve or a market supply schedule to a market supply curve, it is possible to graph a combined market demand and supply schedule.

Figure 6.2 portrays Karen's market demand and supply schedule on a combined graph. On the graph, the vertical axis shows the various prices at which salads are offered for sale and bought. The horizontal axis shows the quantity of salads, whether it is the quantity demanded or the quantity supplied. The demand curve (D) is plotted using the prices and the quantities demanded (Figure 6.1, columns 1 and 2). The supply curve (S) is plotted using the prices and the quantities supplied from the combined schedule (Figure 6.1, columns 1 and 3). You can read each individual curve the same way that you did in Chapters 4 and 5, when demand and supply were shown on separate graphs. Each point on the demand curve shows the intersection of price and quantity demanded. Each point on the supply curve shows the intersection of price and quantity supplied.

FIGURE 6.2 MARKET DEMAND AND SUPPLY CURVES

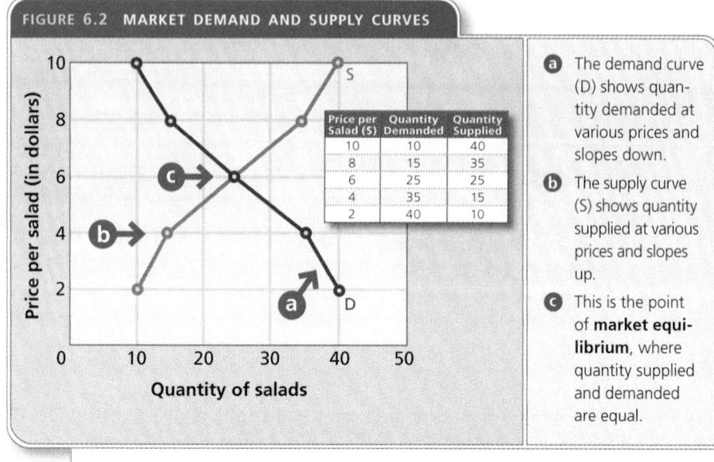

Price per Salad ($)	Quantity Demanded	Quantity Supplied
10	10	40
8	15	35
6	25	25
4	35	15
2	40	10

ⓐ The demand curve (D) shows quantity demanded at various prices and slopes down.

ⓑ The supply curve (S) shows quantity supplied at various prices and slopes up.

ⓒ This is the point of **market equilibrium**, where quantity supplied and demanded are equal.

ANALYZE GRAPHS

1. What is the quantity supplied at $8? What is the quantity demanded at $8?
2. How do these market demand and supply curves illustrate the concept of equilibrium price?

Look at Figure 6.2 again and notice that the two curves intersect at only one point; this is the point of market equilibrium. It occurs when quantity demanded and quantity supplied are the same—25 salads at $6. Showing the two curves together allows you to see the interaction of demand and supply graphically.

APPLICATION Applying Economic Concepts

A. Create a combined market demand and supply schedule for pizza at prices of $25, $20, $15, $10, and $5, where $10 is the price at which there is equilibrium.
The schedule should reflect the laws of demand and supply with an equal quantity supplied and demanded at one price—$10.

DIFFERENTIATING INSTRUCTION

English Learners

Use Word Parts

Explain that the words *equilibrium* and *equal* come from the same root, meaning "even" or "balanced." Remind them that an equal sign (=) in an equation means the two sides have the same value or are balanced. Refer to the Economics Illustrated feature and ask them what two things are equal at market equilibrium *(quantity supplied and quantity demanded)*. Invite volunteers to define *equilibrium price* in their own words.

Inclusion

Use Transparencies

To help students understand how Figure 6.2 was created, re-create the demand and supply curves on separate overhead transparencies. Make sure that you use the same scale on both. Display each one individually and have students identify the demand curve and the supply curve. Then place the two transparencies together to show how the curves intersect. Invite volunteers to describe how the new graph illustrates the concepts of market equilibrium and equilibrium price.

Reaching the Equilibrium Price

KEY CONCEPTS

It's clear from the example of Karen's salads that markets don't arrive at equilibrium price instantly; they often require a process of trial and error. The market may experience a **surplus**, which is the result of quantity supplied being greater than quantity demanded, usually because prices are too high. Or a **shortage** may occur, the result of quantity demanded being greater than quantity supplied, usually because prices are too low.

QUICK REFERENCE

Surplus is the result of quantity supplied being greater than quantity demanded.

Shortage is the result of quantity demanded being greater than quantity supplied.

EXAMPLE Surplus, Shortage, and Equilibrium

In Figure 6.3, we can see how Karen's experience demonstrates the concepts of surplus and shortage. It also shows that equilibrium occurs when there is neither a surplus nor a shortage, because quantity demanded and quantity supplied are equal.

FIGURE 6.3 SURPLUS, SHORTAGE, AND EQUILIBRIUM

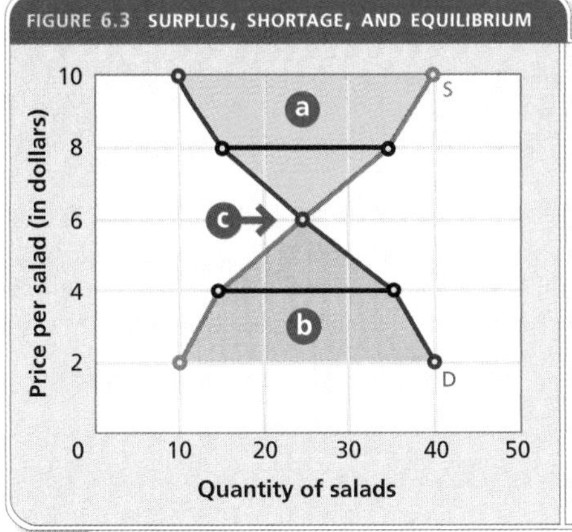

ⓐ When the price is above $6, quantity supplied exceeds quantity demanded, and there is a **surplus** (shaded in orange).

ⓑ When the price is below $6, quantity demanded exceeds quantity supplied, and there is a **shortage** (shaded in blue).

ⓒ At the equilibrium price, there is neither a surplus nor a shortage.

ANALYZE GRAPHS

1. Is there a surplus or a shortage when the price is $10? How big is that surplus or shortage? How great is the surplus or shortage when the price is $2?
2. What does this graph illustrate about surplus, shortage, and equilibrium price?

In Figure 6.3, there is a surplus in the area shaded orange. As Karen discovered when she tried to sell salads at prices above $6, she had too many and had to throw some away. The amount of surplus is measured by the horizontal distance between the two curves at each price. For example, at the price of $8, the distance shown by the black line between 15 and 35 shows a surplus of 20 salads.

When there is a surplus, prices tend to fall until the surplus is sold and equilibrium is reached. Producers might also choose to cut back their production to a quantity that is more in line with what consumers demand at the higher prices.

Reaching the Equilibrium Price

Discuss

- Why does a surplus suggest that prices were too high? *(because consumers were not willing to buy the quantity supplied at those prices)*
- How do producers respond to a shortage? *(They can raise prices or increase quantity supplied.)*

Analyzing Graphs: Figure 6.3

Point out that surplus is shown in the area above equilibrium price and that surplus might be defined as quantity supplied being more than or above the amount demanded. Ask students to use a similar process to relate the definition of shortage to its location on the graph. *(Possible answer: Shortage is shown in the area below equilibrium price. Shortage can be defined as quantity supplied being less than or below the quantity demanded.)*

Answers

1. *at $10: surplus of 30 salads; at $2: shortage of 30 salads*
2. *It shows that equilibrium price is the only price at which there is neither a shortage nor a surplus.*

SMALL GROUP ACTIVITY

Graphing Market Demand and Supply

Time 20 Minutes

Task Create a market demand and supply curve for a common product.

Materials Needed blank graph paper (one per student and one per group) and pencils

Activity

- Have students work in pairs and ask partners to choose a product that both buy regularly. Direct pairs to set five different prices for their product.
- Assign one student in each pair to represent consumers and draw a demand curve for the chosen product. The other student represents producers and draws a supply curve.
- Instruct pairs to combine their curves on a market demand and supply graph and to label equilibrium price, surplus, and shortage.
- Invite volunteers to share their graphs with the class and discuss how they show the interaction of demand and supply in the market to determine equilibrium price.

Rubric

	Understanding of How Supply and Demand Interact	Presentation of Information
4	excellent	clear and accurate
3	good	mostly accurate
2	fair	at times accurate
1	poor	sketchy

Presentation Options

Review the concepts of surplus and shortage by using the following presentation options:

Power Presentations DVD-ROM
Using the Display Tool, you can highlight the balance between surplus and shortage in moving to equilibrium.

Economics Concepts Transparencies
- CT19 Surplus, Shortage, and Equilibrium

International Economics

Toy Manufacturing
Due to lower labor costs, most toys are now manufactured in China, Hong Kong, or Macau, even though about 70 percent of the toy market is in the United States and Europe. The International Council of Toy Industries started a program to certify toy factories that comply with fair labor practices. However, an independent report in 2005 cautioned that toy companies' emphasis on lower prices and quicker delivery times may conflict with these standards.

The blue area in Figure 6.3 represents where there is a shortage. When Karen decided to charge less than $6, she had too few salads and lots of unhappy customers who weren't able to get the salads they wanted. As with the surplus, the amount of shortage is measured by the horizontal distance between the two curves at each price. For example, at the price of $4, the distance shown by the black line between 15 and 35 salads shows a shortage of 20 salads.

When there is a shortage, producers raise prices in an attempt to balance quantity supplied and quantity demanded. Producers may also try to increase quantity supplied to meet the quantities demanded at the lower prices.

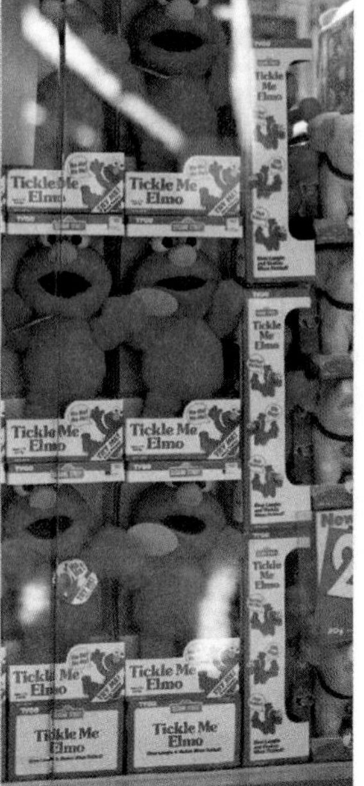

Holiday Shortages
Consumer tastes often cause spikes in demand for certain items during the holidays.

EXAMPLE Holiday Toys

The concepts of surplus and shortage and the move to equilibrium are active in many markets at different times. Perhaps they are most visible in the market for toys during the holiday shopping season. Toys are often fads, and children's tastes change rapidly. It is difficult for marketers to know how much to supply and at what price to best meet the quantities demanded by consumers. Sometimes they overestimate a toy's popularity and end up with a surplus. If they underestimate popularity, they are faced with a shortage.

In 1996, for example, Tyco Toys Inc. introduced Tickle Me Elmo. The toy included a microchip that made the toy laugh when it was touched. Tyco expected the toy to be popular and ordered about 500,000 for the holiday season. It was priced around $30.

Sales started slowly, and stores thought they might have a surplus. But after several popular television personalities promoted it, Tickle Me Elmo became the hottest toy of that holiday season, and a shortage developed. Even when prices increased markedly, buyers were undeterred. They continued to purchase the toys until they were all gone.

Tyco tried to increase its supply, but the factories that made Tickle Me Elmo were located in Asia, and the shortage persisted throughout the holiday season. By spring, the quantity supplied had doubled. By then, however, the height of the fad was over. Initially, stores tried to sell the toys at the same high prices charged during the holiday season. But consumers were reluctant to buy, and a surplus resulted. Eventually, the market reached equilibrium at a price of about $25.

When you see suppliers reducing prices, it is often because they have a surplus of products to sell. Consider, for example, what happens to the prices of clothing items that are out of season or no longer in fashion. On the other hand, if an item becomes particularly popular or is in short supply for some other reason, suppliers will raise prices. The market does not always reach equilibrium quickly, but it is always moving toward equilibrium.

SMARTGrapher
Create a demand and supply curve at **ClassZone.com**

APPLICATION Applying Economic Concepts

B. Look back at the market demand and supply schedule you created for Application A on p. 166. Use it to create a graph showing the interaction of demand and supply and mark it to show surplus, shortage, and equilibrium. Curves should accurately reflect data on the schedule, the area above the intersection at equilibrium price should be marked surplus. The area below equilibrium should be marked shortage.

DIFFERENTIATING INSTRUCTION

Struggling Readers

Sequence Events
Help students create a flow chart to sequence the events in the Tickle Me Elmo example. Have them mark the points where there was a surplus or a shortage and note what happened to the price as a result. Invite volunteers to use the flow chart to describe how demand and supply interact in the market as it moves toward equilibrium.

Gifted and Talented

Research Surplus and Shortage
Invite students to think of other examples of producers raising or lowering prices as a result of shortage or surplus. Some possible examples include surplus autos at the end of a model year or shortages of certain fruits or vegetables after bad weather. Have them choose one example and use the Internet or library resources to find out more information about it. Allow students to share the results of their research in brief oral reports to the class.

Equilibrium Price in Real Life

KEY CONCEPTS

In theory, the relationship between demand and supply in the market seems straightforward. The real world, however, is more complex. In earlier chapters, you learned that there are several factors that can cause demand and supply to change. When there is an imbalance between quantity demanded and quantity supplied, a state of **disequilibrium** exists, and the process of finding equilibrium starts over again.

QUICK REFERENCE

Disequilibrium occurs when quantity demanded and quantity supplied are not in balance.

EXAMPLE Change in Demand and Equilibrium Price

Let's take a look at how the market moves from disequilibrium by considering the effect of changes in demand on the equilibrium price for athletic shoes. Recall that a change in demand occurs when one of six factors—income, consumer taste, consumer expectations, market size, substitutes, and complements—prompts consumers to change the quantity demanded at every price.

In Figures 6.4 and 6.5, the intersection of the demand curve (D1) and the supply curves (S) shows an equilibrium price of $75, with quantity demanded and supplied of 3,000 pairs of shoes. When a change in consumer taste causes a decrease in demand for athletic shoes at every price, the demand curve shifts to the left, as shown in Figure 6.4. Notice that this new demand curve (D2) intersects the supply curve at a lower price, around $65. This becomes the new equilibrium price. At this

FIGURES 6.4 AND 6.5 CHANGES IN DEMAND AND EQUILIBRIUM PRICE

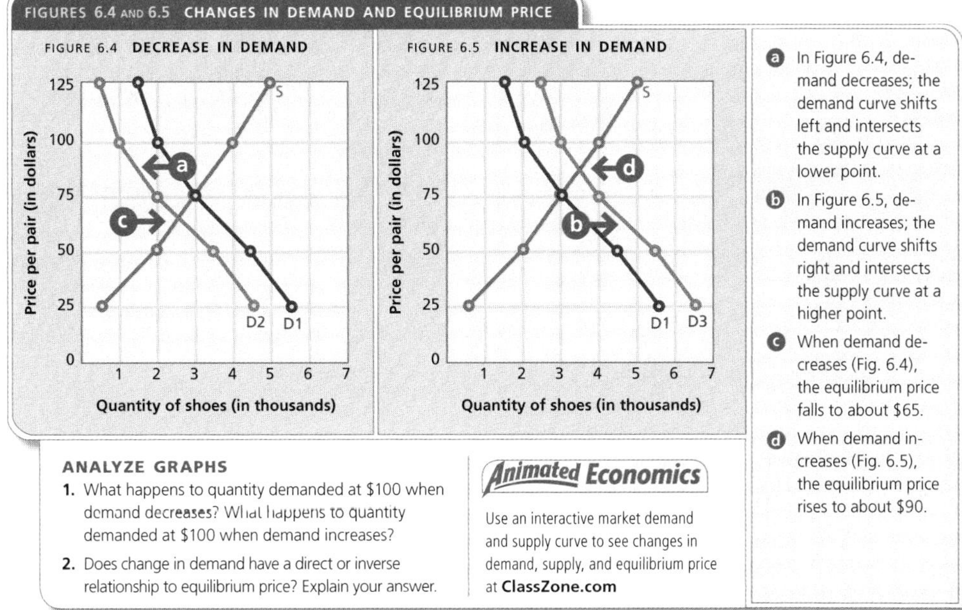

a In Figure 6.4, demand decreases; the demand curve shifts left and intersects the supply curve at a lower point.

b In Figure 6.5, demand increases; the demand curve shifts right and intersects the supply curve at a higher point.

c When demand decreases (Fig. 6.4), the equilibrium price falls to about $65.

d When demand increases (Fig. 6.5), the equilibrium price rises to about $90.

ANALYZE GRAPHS

1. What happens to quantity demanded at $100 when demand decreases? What happens to quantity demanded at $100 when demand increases?
2. Does change in demand have a direct or inverse relationship to equilibrium price? Explain your answer.

Animated Economics

Use an interactive market demand and supply curve to see changes in demand, supply, and equilibrium price at **ClassZone.com**

Equilibrium Price in Real Life

Discuss

- Why is it difficult for markets to maintain equilibrium? *(because many factors can cause demand or supply to change and create disequilibrium)*
- Would an increase in the number of shoe manufacturers cause equilibrium price to rise or fall? Why? *(fall, because more producers increases supply)*

Analyzing Graphs: Figures 6.4 and 6.5

Point out that these graphs assume that the supply curve remains constant. Ask them how the slope of the supply curve relates to the change in price. *(It slopes up. So, an intersection further to the left means price decreases and an intersection further to the right means price increases.)*

Answers

1. *It decreases from 2,000 to 1,000. It increases from 2,000 to 3,000.*
2. *It has a direct relationship. When demand decreases, equilibrium price falls; when demand increases, equilibrium price rises.*

Animated Economics These graphs show how changes in demand for shoes result in changes in price. They will help students understand the relationship between changes in demand and equilibrium price.

INDIVIDUAL ACTIVITY

Illustrating the Life of a Fad

Time 30 minutes ◑

Task Create a visual or verbal representation of the concepts of surplus and shortage as they relate to fads.

Materials Needed paper and markers, pens, or colored pencils

Activity

- Define a fad as a fashion that is popular for a short period of time. Invite students to think of examples of fads in clothing, food, music, toys, or other categories.
- Have each student choose one example and think about the life cycle of the fad, using the Tickle Me Elmo example as a model.
- Encourage them to create a visual (poster, collage, or cartoon) or verbal representation (story, poem, rap, song) of that fad that shows an understanding of surplus and shortage and how they relate to price.
- Allow students to share their creations in small groups.

Rubric

	Understanding Surplus and Shortage	Presentation of Information
4	excellent	clear, very creative
3	good	clear, creative
2	fair	at times clear, creative
1	poor	sketchy; unoriginal

Analyzing Graphs: Figures 6.6 and 6.7

Point out that the red curve and the green curve in these graphs are the same as the ones in Figures 6.4 and 6.5. Ask students what is different in these graphs compared to the earlier ones. *(The supply curve shifts, while the demand curve remains constant.)* How does the slope of the demand curve relate to the change in price? *(It slopes down. So, an intersection further to the left means price increases and an intersection further to the right means price decreases.)*

Answers

1. *It decreases from 4,000 to 3,000. It increases from 4,000 to 6,000.*
2. *They show that when supply decreases, equilibrium price rises, and when supply increases, the equilibrium price falls.*

new, lower equilibrium price, the quantity demanded decreases to 2,500 pairs of shoes. In other words, when consumers demand fewer goods and services at every price, the equilibrium price will fall and suppliers will sell fewer units—even though the price is lower.

Suppose that an increase in the number of young adults causes demand for athletic shoes to increase. When there is an increase in demand, the demand curve shifts to the right, as shown in Figure 6.5. Notice that the new demand curve (D3) intersects the supply curve at a higher price, around $90. As the equilibrium price increases to this higher level, the quantity demanded also increases to 3,500 pairs of shoes. When consumers demand more goods and services at every price, equilibrium price will rise and suppliers will sell more, even at higher prices.

EXAMPLE Change in Supply and Equilibrium Price

Now let's consider how changes in supply might affect equilibrium price. Recall that a change in supply occurs when something in the market prompts producers to offer different amounts for sale at every price. Remember from Chapter 5 that the six factors that can change supply are input costs, productivity, technology, government action, producer expectations, and number of producers.

In Figures 6.6 and 6.7, the intersection of the supply curve (S1) and the demand curve (D) shows an equilibrium price of $75, with quantity supplied and demanded of 3,000 pairs of shoes. If the price of the raw materials needed to produce athletic shoes increases, the result is a decrease in supply of these shoes at every price.

FIGURES 6.6 AND 6.7 CHANGES IN SUPPLY AND EQUILIBRIUM PRICE

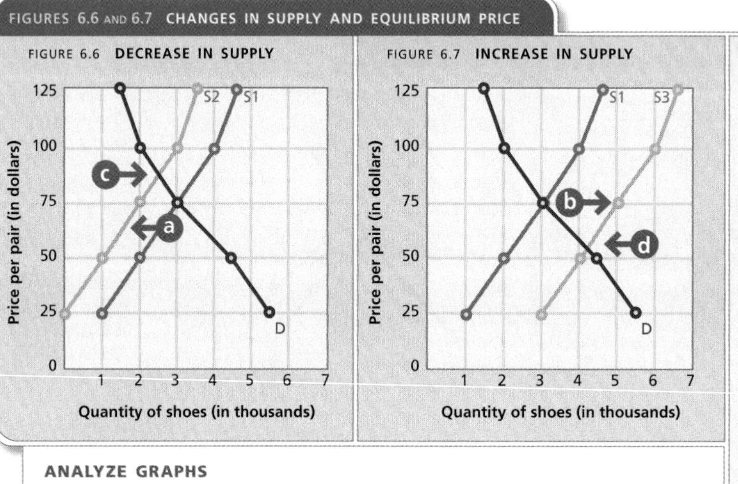

a In Figure 6.6, supply decreases; the supply curve shifts left and intersects the demand curve at a higher point.

b In Figure 6.7, supply increases; the supply curve shifts right and intersects the demand curve at a lower point.

c When supply decreases (Fig. 6.6) the equilibrium price rises to about $90.

d When supply increases (Fig. 6.7) the equilibrium price falls to about $55.

ANALYZE GRAPHS

1. What happens to quantity supplied at $100 when supply decreases? What happens to quantity supplied at $100 when supply increases?
2. How do these graphs illustrate the relationship between change in supply and change in equilibrium price?

DIFFERENTIATING INSTRUCTION

Struggling Readers

Diagram Cause and Effect

Model how to create a cause-and-effect chain for the first example of change in demand described on page 169. Point out that the final effect is the decrease in the equilibrium price.

- Have students work in pairs to create similar chains for the other examples as they read pages 170–171.
- Ask volunteers to describe how their diagrams relate to the graphs and to notice which causes have similar results (summarized in Figure 6.8).

Inclusion

Use the Visuals

Allow students to work in pairs to match the arrows in Figure 6.8 with the related graphs. *(Figures 6.4 and 6.7 show equilibrium price falling; 6.5 and 6.6, rising.)*

- Ask volunteers to take turns reading the paragraphs on pages 169–171 that relate to each graph while other students compare what they are hearing to the information shown on the graph.
- Check students' understanding by asking what happens to equilibrium price when each type of change occurs.

In this situation, the supply curve shifts to the left, as shown in Figure 6.6. Notice that the new supply curve (S2) intersects the demand curve at a higher price, around $90. This is the new equilibrium price. Because of this increase in price, the quantity demanded at equilibrium decreases to 2,500 pairs of shoes. In other words, when there are fewer goods and services available at every price, equilibrium price will rise.

When new technology allows the manufacturer to produce shoes more efficiently, supply increases, and the supply curve shifts to the right, as shown in Figure 6.7. Notice that the new supply curve (S3) intersects the demand curve at a lower price, about $55. This is the new equilibrium price. Because of this decrease in price, the quantity demanded at equilibrium increases to about 4,100 pairs of shoes. In other words, when there are more goods and services available at every price, equilibrium price will fall.

Technology Both supply and equilibrium price are affected when technology improves the manufacturing process.

Look at Figures 6.4, 6.5, 6.6, and 6.7 once more and notice which situations cause equilibrium price to fall and which cause equilibrium price to rise. The relationships between changes in demand or supply and changes in equilibrium price are illustrated in Figure 6.8. Equilibrium price falls when there is a decrease in demand or an increase in supply. Equilibrium price rises when there is an increase in demand or a decrease in supply. In other words, when consumers want less or producers supply more, prices will fall. When consumers want more or producers supply less, prices will rise.

FIGURE 6.8 EQUILIBRIUM PRICE AND CHANGES IN DEMAND AND SUPPLY

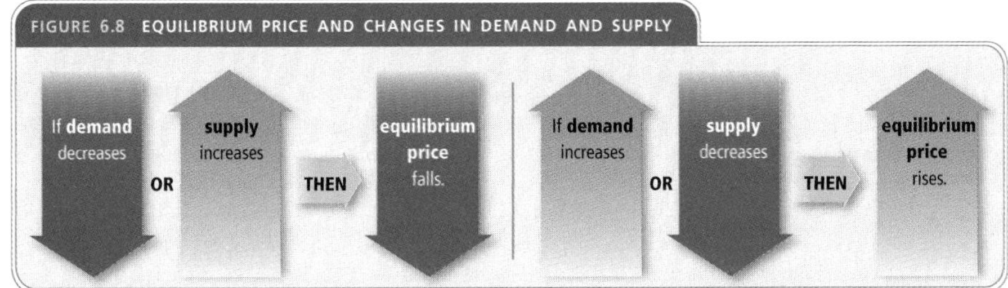
If **demand** decreases
OR
supply increases
THEN
equilibrium price falls.
If **demand** increases
OR
supply decreases
THEN
equilibrium price rises.

APPLICATION Analyzing Effects

C. If one of the three pizza parlors in your neighborhood closes, what will happen to the supply of pizza? How will that affect the equilibrium price of pizza? It will decrease the supply of pizza and cause the equilibrium price to rise.

More About . . .

The Athletic Shoe Market
Athletic footwear sales accounted for more than one-third of the $42 billion U.S. footwear market in 2005. About 9 percent of the dollar volume of athletic footwear was sold through discount stores, and about 70 percent of the pairs sold overall cost less than $45 per pair. These figures include both adult and children's shoes.

About 98 percent of the footwear sold in the United States is manufactured overseas, mostly in China. Most athletic shoe manufacturers target the teen market because teens often buy multiple pairs of shoes to express their personal style.

SMALL GROUP ACTIVITY

Describing Changes in Equilibrium Price

Time 30 minutes ◑

Task Create market supply and demand curves to illustrate factors that affect equilibrium price in the laptop computer market.

Materials Needed blank graph paper (one for each factor assigned per group) and pencils or graphing software

Activity

- Organize students into small groups and assign each group one or more of the factors that affect demand or supply.
- Direct groups to create demand and supply curves for the laptop market and then show how a curve shifts based on the assigned factors.
- Instruct students to write a caption for each graph describing the change and what happens to equilibrium price as a result.
- Allow each group to present its graphs to the class and draw conclusions about changes in supply and demand and equilibrium price.

Rubric

	Understanding of Equilibrium Price	Presentation of Information
4	excellent	clear and complete
3	good	mostly clear
2	fair	sometimes clear
1	poor	sketchy

Interpreting Graphs: Shifting Curves

1 Plan & Prepare

Objectives

- Interpret graphs for information.
- Use features of a graph to aid comprehension.

2 Focus & Motivate

Remind students that equilibrium price can increase or decrease due to a change in supply or a change in demand. Ask which change in demand, an increase or a decrease, results in a lower equilibrium price. *(decrease in demand)* Tell students that being an entrepreneur and running one's own business is how the founders of Microsoft, Dell, Nike, and most other successful companies got started. In order to be successful when running one's own business, it's important to be able to chart the equilibrium price of your product in the marketplace.

3 Teach

Tell students to recall the law of supply. Producers want to supply more of their product for sale at higher prices. As we can see, the competitor entered the market when equilibrium price was about $3.75 per sandwich. However, by increasing quantity supplied at every price, the new supplier is causing equilibrium price to fall.

For additional practice see **Skillbuilder Handbook**, page R29.

THINKING ECONOMICALLY Answers

1. *about $3.75 pre-shift and about $2.35 post-shift; no; If demand also shifts, equilibrium price could stay the same or increase.*
2. *Equilibrium price will decrease because the demand curve will shift to the left and intersect the supply at a lower point.*
3. *They have both shifted to the right of curves SI and D. Their positions show that supply has increased but demand has increased even more. So, equilibrium price has risen from about $3.75 to $4.00.*

ECONOMICS SKILLBUILDER

For more on interpreting graphs, see the Skillbuilder Handbook, page R29.

Interpreting Graphs: Shifting Curves

Graphs show statistical information in a visual manner. A graph that shows a shifting curve should immediately alert the reader to one of the following: a change in quantity demanded at every price, or a change in quantity supplied at every price. In Figure 6.9, a change in the number of producers has caused an increase in supply at every price. The sandwich shop across the street from Forest View High School now has a competitor.

TECHNIQUES FOR ANALYZING SHIFTING CURVES Use the following strategies, along with what you learned throughout Section 1, to analyze the graph.

Use the title to identify the main idea of the graph. If supply has shifted, then we know that quantity supplied at every price has either increased or decreased.

Use the annotations to find key elements of the graph. Annotation ⓐ shows the equilibrium price where curve S1 meets curve D.

FIGURE 6.9 SHIFT IN SUPPLY OF SANDWICHES

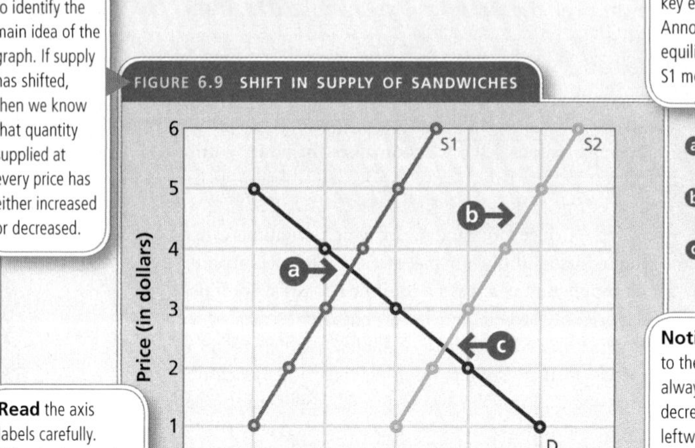

ⓐ This is the initial equilibrium price.
ⓑ Curve shifts to the right.
ⓒ This is the new equilibrium price.

Read the axis labels carefully. When both quantity supplied and demanded are present, look for an intersection to find equilibrium price.

Notice that ⓑ shows a shift to the right. An increase in supply always shows a rightward shift; a decrease in supply always causes a leftward shift.

Notice the new equilibrium price, ⓒ. An increase in supply results in a lower equilibrium price.

THINKING ECONOMICALLY Analyzing

1. What are the pre-shift and post-shift equilibrium prices for a sandwich? Will an increase in quantity supplied at every price always result in a lower equilibrium price? Why?
2. Imagine that instead of an increase in supply, there is a decrease in demand. How will the equilibrium price change? Why?
3. On a separate sheet of paper, sketch intersecting quantity supplied and demanded curves with an equilibrium price of $4 at 80 sandwiches. How have the curves shifted from those that appear in Figure 6.9?

DIFFERENTIATING INSTRUCTION

English Learners

Use Spoken Language

For practice in speaking English, have students work in small groups to (1) take turns reading the page aloud; (2) read and answer the questions; and (3) reflect on and summarize what they learned about how to interpret shifting curves.

Gifted and Talented

Graph Shifting Supply

Create a scenario whereby four of the factors that cause a shift in supply come into play. Create five market demand and supply schedules to show the initial situation and changes over time. Have students create an initial demand and supply graph and show the first shift. Then have them create a new graph with the values from the first shift as the baseline curve, and the values from the next schedule reflecting a shift, and so on. Discuss curve movement and equilibrium price for each graph.

SECTION 1 Assessment

Online Quiz
ClassZone.com

REVIEWING KEY CONCEPTS

1. Explain the differences between the terms in each of these pairs:
   a. *market equilibrium* *disequilibrium*
   b. *surplus* *shortage*
2. How are surplus and shortage related to equilibrium price?
3. Why is equilibrium price represented by the intersection of the supply and demand curves in a particular market?
4. Why do changes in demand or supply cause disequilibrium?
5. Why is the market always moving toward equilibrium?
6. **Using Your Notes** How is equilibrium price related to market equilibrium? Refer to your completed cluster diagram.

   Use the Graphic Organizer at **Interactive Review @ ClassZone.com**

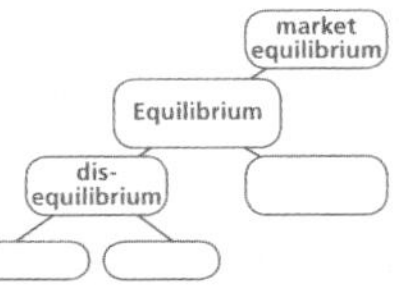

CRITICAL THINKING

7. **Analyzing Data** Look at Figures 6.4, 6.5, 6.6, and 6.7 again. What happens to surplus and shortage as equilibrium price changes in each graph? What general conclusions can you draw from this information?
8. **Analyzing Causes** Suppose that the federal government decides to increase the excise tax on cellular phone services by 0.1 percent. Why will this action cause the equilibrium price of cellular phone services to rise?
9. **Applying Economic Concepts** Between 2003 and 2005, there was huge growth in the market for premium blue jeans priced at $200 or more per pair. The growth was largely fueled by popular magazines showing celebrities wearing certain brands. Then, in the summer of 2005, major department stores started cutting prices on the jeans; they were also found on Web sites that offer jeans at discount prices. Use the economic concepts that you learned in this section to describe what is happening in this market.
10. **Challenge** Study Figures 6.4, 6.5, 6.6, and 6.7 again. What would happen if a change in consumer taste caused an increase in demand for athletic shoes and more suppliers entered the market at the same time? Assume that the increases in demand and in supply are proportionately the same. How would this result be different if each of these changes happened separately?

ECONOMICS IN PRACTICE

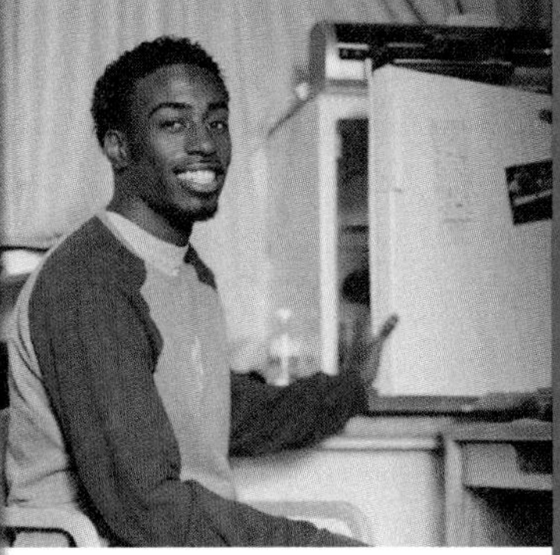

Finding Equilibrium Price
Suppose that you are a manufacturer of a new mini refrigerator for college dorm rooms. You expect your product to be popular because of its compact size and high tech design. After a few weeks in the market you are able to develop the following market demand and supply schedule.

Price per Refrigerator ($)	Quantity Demanded	Quantity Supplied
225	500	6,000
200	1,000	4,500
175	1,500	3,500
150	2,500	2,500
125	4,000	1,500

Create a Demand and Supply Curve Use this market demand and supply schedule to create a market demand and supply curve and determine the equilibrium price.

Challenge Calculate surplus or shortage at every price and suggest ways the manufacturer could try to eliminate the surplus and raise the equilibrium price.

4 Assess & Reteach

Assess Divide students into three groups. Assign each group two of the Reviewing Key Concepts questions and one of the Critical Thinking questions to answer. Allow each group to present its answers to the class.

Unit 2 Resource Book
- Section Quiz, p. 123

Interactive Review @ ClassZone.com
- Section Quiz

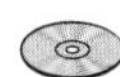

Test Generator CD-ROM
- Section Quiz

Reteach Review each of the figures shown in the section. Invite volunteers to state in their own words what the main idea of the figure is.

Unit 2 Resource Book
- Reteaching Activity, p. 124

Economics in Practice
Create a Demand and Supply Curve The curve should accurately reflect the data on the table and show an equilibrium price of $150 with a quantity at that price of 2,500.

Challenge Surplus: $225—5,500; $200—3,500; $175—2,000; Shortage: $125—2,500. Ordinarily a supplier might reduce prices to reduce surplus. If the supplier wants to raise the equilibrium price he or she must try to increase demand (perhaps through advertising to influence consumer taste) or decrease supply.

SECTION 1 ASSESSMENT ANSWERS

Reviewing Key Concepts

1. a. *market equilibrium*, p. 164; *disequilibrium*, p. 169
   b. *surplus*, p. 167; *shortage*, p. 167
2. At any price above equilibrium price there is a surplus, and at any price below equilibrium price there is a shortage.
3. because the point of intersection is where the quantity demanded and supplied at that price are equal, making that price the equilibrium price
4. Changes in supply or demand cause changes in the quantities supplied or demanded at every price. Therefore the quantities will no longer be equal at the original equilibrium price.
5. because a surplus or a shortage motivates producers to adjust prices until quantity supplied and quantity demanded are the same
6. See page 164 for an example of a completed graphic. Equilibrium price is the price at which market equilibrium occurs, as when quantity supplied and quantity demanded are equal.

Critical Thinking

7. When equilibrium price rises, as when demand increases (6.5) or supply decreases (6.6), surplus decreases and shortage increases. When equilibrium price falls, as when demand decreases (6.4) or supply increases (6.7), surplus increases and shortage decreases.
8. Imposition of a larger excise tax will cause supply to decrease and therefore cause equilibrium price to rise.
9. Early on, the jeans the celebrities wore were in short supply, so the equilibrium price stayed high. But when more and more department stores and then finally discount Web sites joined the market, supply increased to the point that the equilibrium price was pushed down.
10. If demand and supply increase in proportion to one another, then both curves shift the same amount and equilibrium price remains the same. If they happened separately, there would be a price rise and then a price fall (or vice versa), but the end result would be the same.

Economics in Practice

See answers in side column above.

1 Plan & Prepare

Section 2 Objectives

- analyze how the price system works
- explain how prices provide information about markets
- describe how prices act as incentives to producers

2 Focus & Motivate

Connecting to Everyday Life Explain that this section focuses on the ways that prices provide information and motivation to consumers and producers. Invite students to list some ways prices communicate to them as consumers.

Taking Notes Remind students to take notes as they read by completing a chart. They can use the Graphic Organizer at **Interactive Review @ ClassZone.com.** A sample is shown below.

	Producers	Consumers
Competitive pricing	lower prices to take market share from competitors; maintain profitability by selling more units	get lower prices
Incentive	Rising prices: an incentive to enter a market; falling prices: an incentive to leave a market	low prices, incentive to buy; high prices, incentive to find substitutes

SECTION 2

Prices as Signals and Incentives

OBJECTIVES

In Section 2, you will

- analyze how the price system works
- explain how prices provide information about markets
- describe how prices act as incentives to producers

KEY TERMS

competitive pricing, *p. 174*
incentive, *p. 176*

TAKING NOTES

As you read Section 2, complete a chart like the one shown to keep track of how each key concept affects producers and consumers. Use the Graphic Organizer at **Interactive Review @ ClassZone.com**

	Producers	Consumers
Competitive pricing		
Incentive		

How the Price System Works

QUICK REFERENCE

Competitive pricing occurs when producers sell products at lower prices to lure customers away from rival producers, while still making a profit.

KEY CONCEPTS

To better understand how price works in the market, let's look at how one kind of change in supply affects the equilibrium price. More producers in a market increases supply, which leads to increased competition and a lower equilibrium price. **Competitive pricing** occurs when producers sell goods and services at prices that best balance the twin desires of making the highest profit and luring customers away from rival producers. By entering a market at a lower price, a new supplier can add to its customer base while it maintains overall profits by selling more units.

EXAMPLE Competitive Pricing

Let's look at an example of competitive pricing. As winter approaches, Elm Street Hardware prices its snow shovels at $20. But Uptown Automotive sees an opportunity to take some customers (mostly for tools, which both stores sell) from Elm Street. Uptown enters the snow shovel market, raising the overall supply. It also prices the shovels at $13. Uptown has a lower profit margin per shovel, but hopes to sell hundreds of them in order to maintain overall profit. Elm Street can choose to lower its prices as well or risk losing customers.

SECTION 2 PROGRAM RESOURCES

ON LEVEL

Lesson Plans
- Core, p. 20

Unit 2 Resource Book
- Reading Study Guide, pp. 125–126
- Economic Skills and Problem Solving Activity, pp. 145–146
- Section Quiz, p. 133

STRUGGLING READERS

Unit 2 Resource Book
- Reading Study Guide with Additional Support, pp. 127–129
- Reteaching Activity, p. 134

ENGLISH LEARNERS

Unit 2 Resource Book
- Reading Study Guide with Additional Support (Spanish), pp. 130–132

INCLUSION

Lesson Plans
- Modified for Inclusion, p. 20

GIFTED AND TALENTED

Unit 2 Resource Book
- Readings in Free Enterprise: Who Is to Blame for the Real Estate Bubble?, pp. 147–148

TECHNOLOGY

eEdition DVD-ROM

eEdition Online

Power Presentation DVD-ROM

Economics Concepts Transparencies
- CT20 Market Signals

Daily Test Practice Transparencies, TT20

ClassZone.com

EXAMPLE Characteristics of the Price System

In a market economy, the price system has four characteristics.

1. **It is neutral.** Prices do not favor either the producer or consumer because both make choices that help to determine the equilibrium price. The free interactions of consumers (who favor lower prices) and producers (who favor higher prices) determines the equilibrium price in the market.
2. **It is market driven.** Market forces, not central planning, determine prices, so the system has no oversight or administration costs. In other words, the price system runs itself.
3. **It is flexible.** When market conditions change, prices are able to change quickly in response. Surpluses and shortages motivate producers to change prices to reach equilibrium.
4. **It is efficient.** Prices will adjust until the maximum number of goods and services are sold. Producers choose to use their resources to produce certain goods and services based on the profit they can make by doing so.

ECONOMICS ESSENTIALS

FIGURE 6.10 Characteristics of the Price System in a Market Economy

Neutral Both the producer and the consumer make choices that determine the equilibrium price.

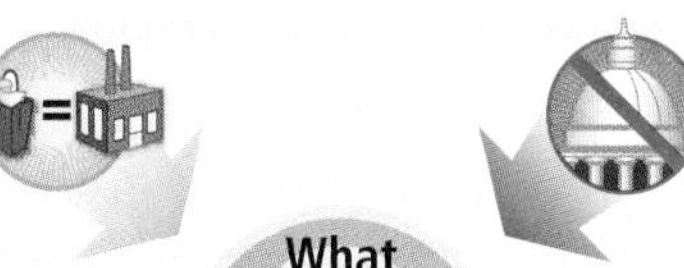

Market Driven Market forces, not government policy, determine prices. In effect, the system runs itself.

What Are the Characteristics of the Price System?

Efficient Resources are allocated efficiently since prices adjust until the maximum number of goods and services are sold.

Flexible When market conditions change, so do prices.

ANALYZE CHARTS

Choose two of the characteristics of the price system shown in the chart and explain how each is illustrated through the example of competitive pricing.

APPLICATION Analyzing and Interpreting Data

A. If Karen sold 25 salads at $6 each, how many would she need to sell at $5.50 to make at least the same amount of total revenue? She would need to sell 28 salads to make $154; her previous total revenue was $150.

❸ Teach

How the Price System Works

Discuss

- To what state are the characteristics of the price system always pushing prices? *(equilibrium)*
- How does the flexibility of the price system help the market move toward equilibrium? *(Possible answer: The market responds to surplus or shortage by quickly adjusting prices to reach a new equilibrium.)*

Economics Essentials: Figure 6.10

Explain that the diagram of the characteristics of the price system follows the order in the text by starting at the top-left corner and moving clockwise.

- What kinds of choices do consumers and producers make to help determine equilibrium price? *(Possible answer: Consumers choose which products to buy and at what prices; producers decide what to offer for sale, the quantity, and what prices to charge.)*

Analyze

Possible answers: neutral—producers choose to lower prices, and consumers decide who to buy from; market driven—producers, not the government, decide to lower prices.

LEVELED ACTIVITY

Introducing a New Technology Product

Time 30 Minutes

Objective Students will demonstrate an understanding of the ways the price system provides information and motivation for producers and consumers of a new technology product.

Basic

Choose a new technology product that you plan to introduce to the market. List the four characteristics of the price system and give an example of how each one applies to the product. Explain how prices will act as signals and incentives in different ways for you as a producer and for your customers.

On Level

Illustrate the life cycle of a new technology product in the market, showing the different characteristics of the price system at work. Describe how prices will act as signals and incentives at different stages of the cycle. Explain the different effects that prices have on producers and customers.

Challenge

Outline a multi-year business plan for a new technology product that you will introduce to the market. Indicate how you expect market interactions to affect prices over time. Describe how prices helped you determine to enter the market and how they might affect decisions about allocating your business resources.

Prices Motivate Producers and Consumers

Discuss

- How do shortage and surplus send signals to producers? *(A shortage signals rising prices and a time for producers to enter the market. A surplus signals falling prices and a time to exit the market.)*
- How is the saying "you get what you pay for" related to prices as signals to consumers? *(Possible answer: It suggests that a higher price sends a signal that the product is of better quality than a lower-priced product.)*

More About . . .

Changes in the Music Industry
Music CD sales continued to decline in 2005 but still accounted for 95 percent of all music sales. CD sales among teens increased by 5 percent but declined among young adults and especially among adults age 25 and over.

Meanwhile, digital music sales grew by 150 percent. More consumers chose to pay for legal music downloads but many still copied songs from CDs or used peer-to-peer file sharing. While the standard price for legal downloads was 99 cents per song, record companies wanted more flexibility to vary pricing based on consumer demand.

Prices Motivate Producers and Consumers

QUICK REFERENCE

An **incentive** encourages people to act in certain ways.

KEY CONCEPTS

The laws of demand and supply show that consumers and producers have different attitudes toward price. Consumers want to buy at low prices; producers want to sell at high prices. Therefore, prices motivate consumers and producers in different ways. You learned in Chapter 1 that an **incentive** is a way to encourage people to take a certain action. Here, you'll learn that in the price system, incentives encourage producers and consumers to act in certain ways consistent with their best interests.

EXAMPLE Prices and Producers

For producers, the price system has two great advantages: it provides both information and motivation. Prices provide information by acting as signals to producers about whether it is a good time to enter or leave a particular market. Rising prices and the expectation of profits motivate producers to enter a market. Falling prices and the possibility of losses motivate them to leave a market.

A shortage in a market is a signal that consumer demand is not being met by existing suppliers. Recall that a shortage often occurs because prices are too low relative to the quantities demanded by consumers. Producers will view the shortage as a signal that there is an opportunity to raise prices. Higher prices act as an incentive for producers to enter a market. In other words, the prospect of selling goods at higher prices encourages producers to offer products for that market.

As more producers are motivated by high prices to enter a market, quantity supplied increases. When prices are too high relative to consumer demand, a surplus occurs. Producers can respond to a surplus either by reducing prices, or by reducing production to bring it in line with the quantity demanded at a particular price. Either way, falling prices signal that it is a good time for producers to leave the market. Sometimes, less efficient producers leave a market completely, as increased competition and lower prices drive them out of business. More often, producers shift their business to focus on opportunities in markets with higher potential profits.

FIGURE 6.11 CD PRICES AND PRODUCERS

1. Competition from DVDs and video games causes a slump in CD sales–a surplus in CDs.

CD prices decrease

2. Some CD makers switch production to DVDs, video games; fewer CDs are produced–a shortage of CDs.

CD prices increase

3. Discount chains begin to sell CDs, often below cost, to attract customers; competitive pricing of CDs.

CD prices decrease

4. Many small record stores go out of business or devote less shelf space to CDs, more to DVDs and video games.

DIFFERENTIATING INSTRUCTION

English Learners

Create Word Webs
Help students understand the different roles of prices by having them create two word webs, one for *signals* and one for *incentives.* Point out that *information* goes with *signals* while *motivation* goes with *incentives.* These synonyms provide clues to tell which concepts belong together. Allow students to work in pairs to create their word webs from the information on pages 176–177. Instruct them to take turns explaining how their words relate to either *signals* or *incentives.*

Gifted and Talented

Compare Product Prices
Encourage students to compare prices among different brands in categories such as foods or clothing. They might survey merchandise at a local store or use Internet resources for comparison pricing. Invite students to summarize their findings in charts and share conclusions about the ways brand marketers try to overcome consumer preference for low prices. Suggest they draw on their own experiences to decide whether brand identity justifies higher prices.

Competitive pricing in the market often informs the choices made by producers. When a market is growing, and when there is unmet demand, a producer may decide to enter the market with a price that is lower than its competitor's. The new producer can still, however, earn a profit by selling more units at the lower price. So, while prices are the signals that are visible in the market, it is the expectation of profits or the possibility of losses that motivates producers to enter or leave a market.

EXAMPLE Prices and Consumers

Prices also act as signals and incentives for consumers. Surpluses that lead to lower prices tell consumers that it is a good time to buy a particular good or service. Producers often send this signal to consumers through advertising and store displays that draw consumers to certain products. Producers may also suggest that the low prices won't last, encouraging consumers to buy sooner rather than later.

High prices generally discourage consumers from buying a particular product and may signal that it is time for them to switch to a substitute that is available at a lower price. A high price may signal that a particular product is in short supply or has a higher status. Brand marketers rely on the consumer perception that a certain logo is worth a higher price.

Recall what you learned about normal and inferior goods in Chapter 4. Most consumers prefer to buy normal goods at the best possible price. They will buy inferior goods only when they cannot afford something better. While price is a powerful incentive to consumers, the other factors that affect demand also influence consumers' buying habits.

YOUR ECONOMIC CHOICES

PRICES AND CONSUMERS

How Does Price Affect Your Decision?

A new digital video camera with state-of-the-art features costs $500, but you've saved only $250. You can either buy a less expensive substitute with the money you have now, or you can save up to buy the advanced camera later. If other consumers also choose to wait to buy the new camera, a surplus may develop, and the price may decrease.

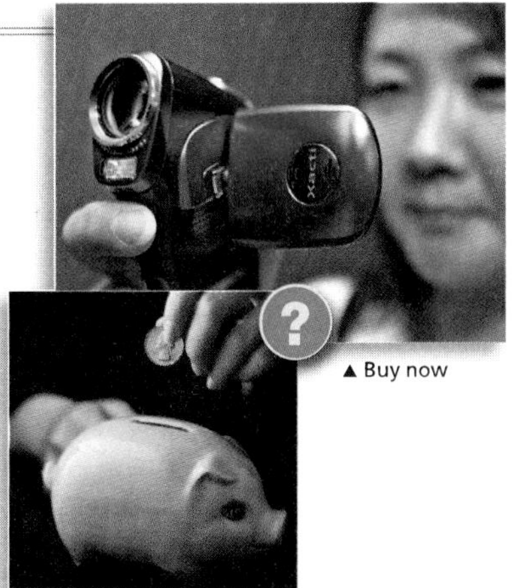

▲ Buy now

▲ Save for later

APPLICATION Making Inferences

B. A cup of gourmet coffee commands a higher price than a regular coffee. How will this fact influence the take-out coffee market? More producers will offer the higher-priced beverages and the quantity supplied will increase.

Your Economic Choices

PRICES AND CONSUMERS

How does price affect your decision?

- People who want to own the latest technology products are called "early adopters." Why is it more likely they will pay a higher price than people who wait until a technology is more established? *(Possible answer: because a new technology may be in short supply and prices will be highest when there are fewer suppliers)*
- How do these choices show that price is only one influence on consumer demand? *(Possible answer: They suggest some consumers will pay a higher price to get what they want.)*

Activity Divide students into three groups based on which option they would choose—buy at a high price, buy a less expensive substitute, or save to buy later. Invite members of each group to discuss the reasons for their choice. Ask for a volunteer from each group to summarize the group's discussion then discuss as a class.

CLASS ACTIVITY

Creating a Multimedia Presentation

Time 45 Minutes

Task Gather examples of promotional materials focused on price and create a multimedia presentation.

Materials Needed newspapers, magazines, computer with Internet access, poster board

Activity

- Have students find examples of advertisements and store displays that use prices as signals and incentives for consumers.
- Some students may focus on print media while others might take photos of store displays or billboards. Others might record radio or TV commercials or print out examples of price promotions from web pages.
- Direct students to work together to combine their examples into a coherent multimedia presentation about prices and consumers.
- Encourage them to draw conclusions about which markets use price promotions most frequently and most effectively.

Rubric

	Understanding Prices, Consumers	Presentation of Information
4	excellent	clear; creative
3	good	often clear, creative
2	fair	at times clear, creative
1	poor	sketchy

Michael Dell

More About . . .

Michael Dell

Michael Dell showed impatience with traditional schooling along with entrepreneurial tendencies from an early age. He tried to get a high school equivalency diploma when he was only 8 years old and ran a mail-order business for stamp traders when he was 12. By the time Dell was 16, he was selling newspaper subscriptions through telephone and direct-mail marketing, techniques he would later use to sell computers.

Dell entered the University of Texas at Austin as a biology major who planned to become a doctor. He later said that a career as a doctor is "not nearly as exciting a business, and the failure rate is much higher."

More About . . .

Dell Inc.

Michael Dell began his company with an initial investment of $1,000. At the end of its fiscal year 2006, the company's revenues were almost $56 billion, and it had an 18.2 percent share of PC shipments worldwide.

Most of Dell Inc.'s business still comes from PCs and notebook computers, along with servers and digital storage products for large organizations. The consumer electronics market receded in importance for the company as much of its marketing strategy in 2006 focused on rapidly growing computer markets, such as China, India, and Latin America.

APPLICATION

Answer *Dell's incentive was to gain market share and earn greater revenues, and thereby, greater profits. Clearly, this strategy was successful.*

Economics Update

ClassZone.com includes links to sites about Michael Dell. Students can review how Dell Inc. is responding to its competition.

ECONOMICS PACESETTER

Michael Dell: Using Price to Beat the Competition

High-tech entrepreneur Michael Dell saw an opportunity to use competitive pricing to take business away from much larger companies. By 2005, IBM Corporation, Compaq Computer Corporation, and others had either left the PC market or were facing major problems. How did Dell thrive as its competitors struggled?

FAST FACTS

Michael S. Dell

Title: Chairman of Dell Inc.

Born: February 23, 1965, Houston, Texas

Major Accomplishment: Pioneered the direct sale of personal computers to consumers

Key Product Lines: Desktop PCs, notebook computers, workstation systems, servers, printers, flat-screen TVs, PDAs

Honors: Youngest CEO of a Fortune 500 company (1992), America's Most Admired Company (2005)

Personal Fortune: $16 billion (2005)

Employees: 65,200 (2006)

Lowering Costs to Reduce Prices

Michael Dell began assembling and selling computers as a freshman in college. He became so successful that he quit college in 1984 to focus on his business. He had sales worth $6 million in his first year.

Dell's success was largely due to his approach to marketing and production. He bypassed computer retailers and sold over the telephone directly to knowledgeable computer users in business and government. Each computer was built to customer requirements and assembled after it was ordered. In this way, Dell lowered his costs significantly and became the low-price leader in the market. The company's sales grew from $69.5 million in 1986 to almost $258 million in 1989.

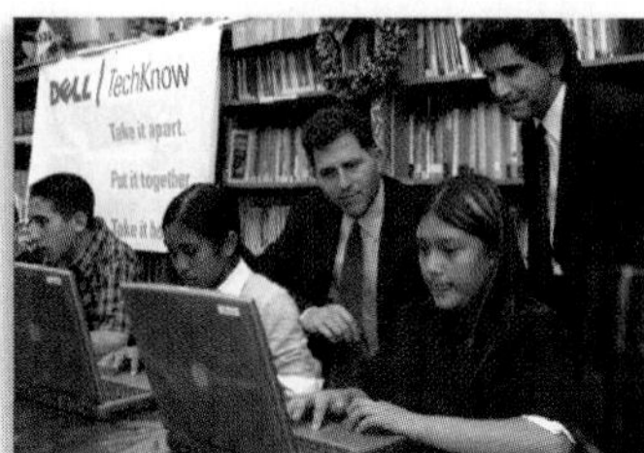

In Dell's TechKnow program, students learn to assemble and upgrade a computer, which they can then keep.

Dell was also a pioneer in recognizing the potential for sales via the Internet. This strategy allowed the company to maintain close contact with its customers and to adjust its prices frequently, up and down, as market conditions dictated. Competitors who sold only in retail stores found it hard to compete on price because their costs were much higher. By 2005, Dell was the world's leading supplier of PCs, with annual sales of almost $50 billion.

Now Dell is using his experience to make waves in the consumer electronics (flat-panel TVs, MP3 players, and the like) market. He sees the line between these two markets eventually fading. "The whole new ballgame is these worlds [computing and consumer electronics] converging," Dell believes, "and that's a world we're comfortable in."

Economics Update

Find an update on Michael Dell at **ClassZone.com**

APPLICATION Drawing Conclusions

C. What incentive did Michael Dell have to sell computers at lower prices than his competitors?

◄ See answer in Teacher's Edition.

178 Chapter 6

DIFFERENTIATING INSTRUCTION

Struggling Readers

Illustrate the Biography

Help students understand the main ideas in the story of Dell Inc. by modeling how to sketch the most important information in each paragraph. Explain that artistic talent is less important than focusing on a simple visual that can remind them of the main point of the paragraph. Invite a volunteer to suggest a caption for your visual. Encourage students to create sketches and captions for the remaining paragraphs and then share their work with a partner.

Gifted and Talented

Create a Buying Guide

Invite students to gather information about competitive prices for desktop and laptop computers by researching online and at local retailers. Point out that computers are sold in many different markets, including large office supply and computer electronics stores, discount stores, local computer retailers that assemble computers from standard components, as well as from companies like Dell. Have students present their research in the form of a buying guide for their classmates.

SECTION 2 Assessment

REVIEWING KEY CONCEPTS

1. Use each of the two terms below in a sentence that illustrates the meaning of the term:
   a. *competitive pricing* b. *incentive*
2. Explain the four characteristics of the price system.
3. Why is the price system an efficient way to allocate resources?
4. How do prices serve as signals and incentives to producers to enter a particular market? to leave a certain market?
5. How does the story of Dell Inc. demonstrate the effects of competitive pricing?
6. **Using Your Notes** How does competitive pricing affect consumers? Refer to your completed chart. Use the Graphic Organizer at **Interactive Review @ ClassZone.com**

	Producers	Consumers
Competitive pricing		
Incentive		

CRITICAL THINKING

7. **Making Inferences** A local supermarket decides to sell a premium brand of meats and cheeses in its deli department. This brand is priced about $2 more per pound than the store brand. About 80 percent of the space in the deli display cases is devoted to the premium brand and 20 percent to the store brand.
   a. How did price serve as an incentive to the supermarket?
   b. What kind of signals is the supermarket sending to its customers with this pricing strategy?
8. **Applying Economic Concepts** A candy company whose products sold in supermarkets for about $3 a bag decided to enter the growing gourmet chocolate market. It purchased two small companies that made premium chocolates that sold for much higher prices. How does this story reveal the way the price system works as an incentive for producers while allocating resources efficiently?
9. **Challenge** A large discount store has built its reputation on offering consumers low prices. However, its customers come from many different income levels. Recently, the store began offering higher priced jewelry and consumer electronics products. What signal might this send to producers of other premium products who have never sold in discount stores before?

ECONOMICS IN PRACTICE

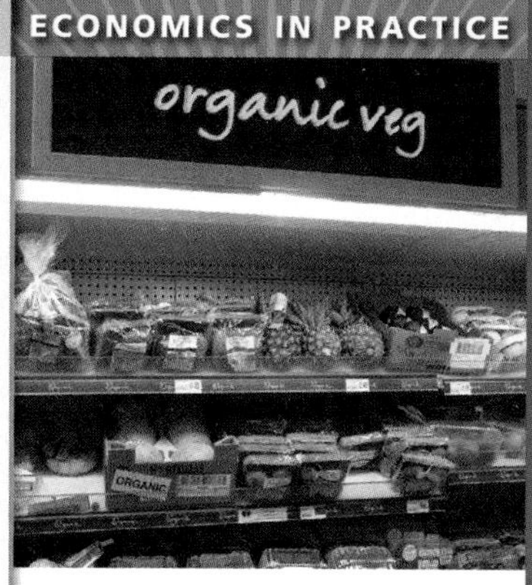

Using Prices as Incentives As you've learned in Section 2, prices motivate producers to act in certain ways. What actions do producers take in response to rising prices? How about falling prices?

Identify Price Incentives Consider each situation that follows. Decide whether the scenario described is associated with rising prices or with falling prices.

- A farmer switches to organic methods when a report says organic foods are healthier.
- To maintain market share, a car wash adjusts its prices to meet a competitor's.
- After a hot, dry spring, a landscaper decides to get out of the business.
- A retailer decides to begin selling this holiday season's must-have toy.

Challenge Which of the above situations descibes a case of competitive pricing? What might happen to the producer if it did not take the action described?

4 Assess & Reteach

Assess Have students review the questions individually. Then ask for volunteers to facilitate a class discussion on each question and to record answers on the board.

Unit 2 Resource Book
- Section Quiz, p. 133

Interactive Review @ ClassZone.com
- Section Quiz

Test Generator CD-ROM
- Section Quiz

Reteach Turn each of the main headings in the section into a question. Ask a volunteer to state one thing she or he knows about the question. Invite students to continue adding to the information until there is no more to be said on that question. Repeat the process with each question.

Unit 2 Resource Book
- Reteaching Activity, p. 134

SECTION 2 ASSESSMENT ANSWERS

Reviewing Key Concepts

1. **a.** *competitive pricing*, p. 174
   b. *incentive*, p. 176
2. It favors producers and consumers equally; it runs itself; it is flexible in responding to changes in the market; it allocates resources efficiently.
3. Decisions about what and how much to produce are based on what consumers have demand for and the prices at which producers can make money.
4. Rising prices provide the incentive to enter a market by signaling the possibility of increasing revenue and, therefore, profits. Falling prices provide the incentive to leave a market, as they signal the possibility of decreasing revenue and, therefore, profits.
5. It showed that when a strong competitor offers similar products for lower prices other producers must also lower their prices. Less efficient companies were driven from the market.
6. See page 174 for an example of a completed diagram. It provides consumers with lower prices.

Critical Thinking

7. **a.** Higher price of the premium brand was an incentive for the supermarket to begin offering more of those products for sale.
   b. The supermarket wants to encourage customers to buy the higher priced products but still offers the lower priced products so it won't lose those sales.
8. The incentive to sell high-priced chocolates caused this producer to allocate its resources toward the purchase of two small companies that make high-end chocolates.
9. These manufacturers would see signals that there might be opportunities for them to sell through the discount store market and still make a profit.

Economics in Practice

Identify Price Incentives rising prices; falling prices; falling prices; rising prices

Challenge the carwash example; it might lose market share to the competitor

1 Plan & Prepare

Section 3 Objectives

- explain how government uses price ceilings to keep prices from rising too high
- describe how government uses price floors to keep prices from going too low
- discuss how government uses rationing to allocate scarce resources and goods

2 Focus & Motivate

Connecting to Everyday Life Explain that this section focuses on instances when something besides market forces determines price. Ask students for suggestions of how you might distribute ten bottles of juice among class members other than by seeing who would pay the highest price for them.

Taking Notes Remind students to take notes as they read by completing a hierarchy diagram. The can use the Graphic Organizer at **Interactive Review @ ClassZone.com**. A sample is shown below.

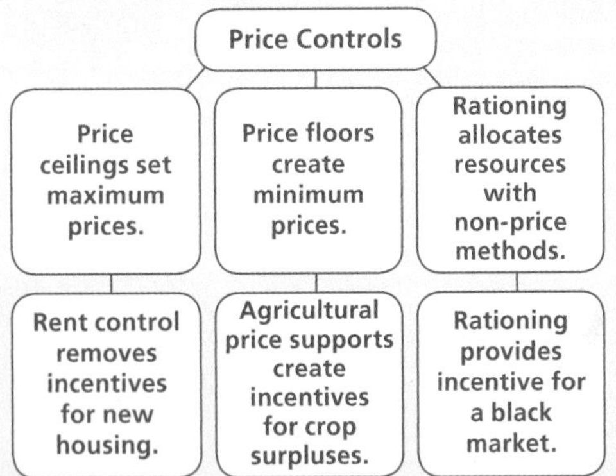

SECTION 3

Intervention in the Price System

OBJECTIVES

In Section 3, you will
- explain how government uses price ceilings to keep prices from rising too high
- describe how government uses price floors to keep prices from going too low
- discuss how government uses rationing to allocate scarce resources and goods

KEY TERMS

price ceiling, *p. 180*
price floor, *p. 182*
minimum wage, *p. 182*
rationing, *p. 183*
black market, *p. 183*

TAKING NOTES

As you read Section 3, complete a hierarchy diagram like this one to track main ideas and supporting details. Use the Graphic Organizer at **Interactive Review @ ClassZone.com**

Price Controls
main idea | main idea | main idea
details | details | details

Imposing Price Ceilings

QUICK REFERENCE

A **price ceiling** is the legal maximum price that sellers may charge for a product.

KEY CONCEPTS

You've seen how prices adjust to changes in demand and supply as the market constantly strives for equilibrium. Sometimes, however, people think it is a good idea to interfere with the free market mechanism in order to keep the price of a good or service from going too high. An established maximum price that sellers may charge for a good or service is called a **price ceiling**. The price ceiling is set below the equilibrium price, so a shortage will result.

EXAMPLE Football Tickets and Price Ceilings

Let's look at an example of a price ceiling in ticket prices for college football. The Trenton University Tigers are a winning team with many loyal fans. The university prints 30,000 tickets for every game and sells them for $15 each. At that price, 60,000 fans want to buy the tickets, so there is a shortage of 30,000 tickets for every game.

The university could resolve the shortage by letting the price rise until quantity demanded and quantity supplied are equal. When this solution is proposed, the university president says she would rather keep the tickets affordable for students. Indeed many students get tickets for $15. On game day, however, ticket scalpers stand outside the stadium and sell some tickets for $50 or more.

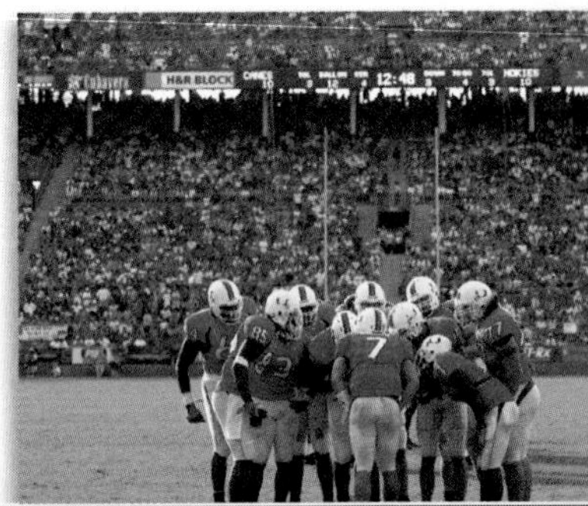

SECTION 3 PROGRAM RESOURCES

ON LEVEL

Lesson Plans
- Core, p. 21

Unit 2 Resource Book
- Reading Study Guide, pp. 135–136
- Math Skills Worksheet, p. 153
- Section Quiz, p. 143

STRUGGLING READERS

Unit 2 Resource Book
- Reading Study Guide with Additional Support, pp. 137–139
- Reteaching Activity, p. 144

ENGLISH LEARNERS

Unit 2 Resource Book
- Reading Study Guide with Additional Support (Spanish), pp. 140–142

INCLUSION

Lesson Plans
- Modified for Inclusion, p. 21

GIFTED AND TALENTED

Unit 2 Resource Book
- Case Study Resources: Outside the Box Office, pp. 149–150

TECHNOLOGY

eEdition DVD-ROM

eEdition Online

Power Presentation DVD-ROM

Economics Concepts Transparencies
- CT21 Supply and Demand Graph

Daily Test Practice Transparencies, TT21

ClassZone.com

EXAMPLE Rent Control as a Price Ceiling

In the past, many cities passed rent control laws in an effort to keep housing affordable for lower-income families. These laws control when rents can be raised and by how much, no matter what is going on in the market. Of course, the people who live in rent-controlled housing appreciate the lower price in the short term.

But rent control can have unexpected consequences. Without the possibility of raising rents to match the market, there is no incentive to increase the supply of rental housing, and a shortage soon develops. In addition, landlords are reluctant to increase their costs by investing money in property maintenance, so housing conditions often deteriorate. By 2005, rent control was becoming far less common as most cities realized it made housing shortages worse in the long run.

Santa Monica, California, is an example of a city that had strict rent control laws. In the late 1990s, state legislators passed a law that changed the way local communities could regulate rental housing. As a result, property owners in Santa Monica could let the market determine the initial rent when a new tenant moved in, although the city's rent control board still regulated yearly rent increases thereafter. Figure 6.12 illustrates what happened to rents when the new law fully took effect. Rents increased by 40 to 85 percent, showing that the apartments had been priced artificially low. The increases reflect the shortage that rent control had created.

FIGURE 6.12 RENT CONTROL IN SANTA MONICA

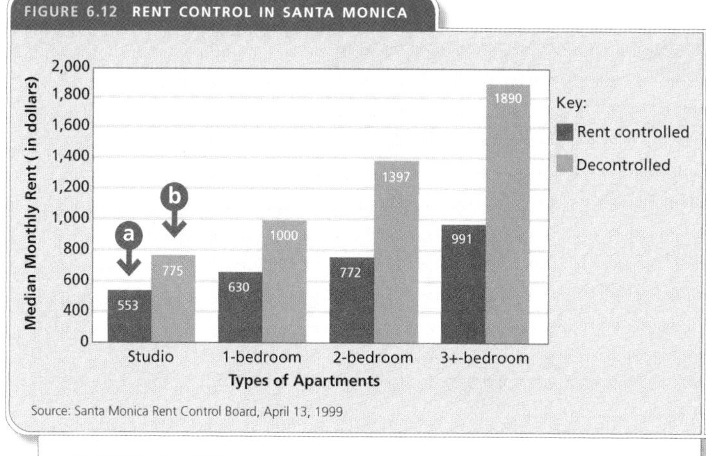

Source: Santa Monica Rent Control Board, April 13, 1999

ⓐ The red bars show the median rent for each type of apartment when rent control was in effect.

ⓑ The blue bars show the median rent for each type of apartment when the new law allowed the market to set the rent for new tenants.

The graph shows that rent control had kept the rate lower than what the market would bear.

ANALYZE GRAPHS

1. What happened to the rent for one-bedroom apartments when the new law ended rent control?
2. Who would be more in favor of the changes that happened in the rental market in Santa Monica, landlords or tenants? Why?

APPLICATION Applying Economic Concepts

A. Create a demand and supply graph for Trenton University football tickets showing how the price ceiling of $15 is below the equilibrium price. Curves should intersect at a price above $15 with a quantity supplied and demanded at that price of 30,000—the number of tickets available.

❸ Teach

Imposing Price Ceilings

Discuss

- Why is a price ceiling set below equilibrium price rather than above it? *(because the intent is to keep the price from rising too high when equilibrium is considered too high)*
- What negative incentives does rent control pricing give to producers and consumers? *(It discourages landlords from increasing supply or maintaining existing housing and discourages consumers from moving.)*

Analyzing Graphs: Figure 6.12

Explain that median rent means that half the apartments of each type were priced below that amount and half were priced above it. Ask students how the graph illustrates the disequilibrium in the Santa Monica rental housing market. *(Possible answer: It shows that there was a shortage of affordable housing since demand exceeded supply, causing prices to rise.)*

Answers

1. *It rose from $630 to $1,000.*
2. *landlords, because they could now command higher prices and make more money on renting apartments*

LEVELED ACTIVITY

Analyzing Intervention in the Price System

Time 30 Minutes ◑

Objective Students will demonstrate an understanding of the effects of intervention in the price system.

Basic

Create an infographic that illustrates the three kinds of intervention in the price system based on the examples on pages 180–183. Include information on the motivation for each one, as well as the intended and unintended consequences. Describe how each one relates to the concepts of surplus and shortage.

On Level

Use the information in Figure 6.12 to create a hypothetical market supply and demand curve for apartments in Santa Monica. Show where the price ceiling or price floor would be set and indicate whether it would create a surplus or a shortage in each example.

Challenge

Imagine that your community is proposing to institute rent control or increase the minimum wage. Research arguments for and against one of these scenarios. Write an editorial stating your position on the issue using the results of your research and the economic concepts in this section to support your argument.

Setting Price Floors

Discuss

- Why is a price floor set above equilibrium price rather than below it? *(because the intent is to keep the price from falling too low when equilibrium is considered too low)*
- Why might the minimum wage decrease the supply of low-wage jobs? *(Possible answer: because higher wages would increase the costs of employers and might discourage them from hiring new workers)*

Analyzing Graphs: Figure 6.13

Be sure that students understand the explanations of annos «b» and «c.» Ask students what the length of black dotted line that falls between the demand and supply curves represents? *(a surplus of labor)* What does the corresponding length of blue dotted line represent? *(a shortage of labor)*

Answers

1. *higher costs for employers, fewer jobs for workers; higher wages for workers*
2. *no, because it is below equilibrium price and provides neither an adequate number of workers for employers nor adequate wages for workers*

At **ClassZone.com,** students will find updated information on the minimum wage.

Setting Price Floors

QUICK REFERENCE

A **price floor** is a legal minimum price that buyers must pay for a product.

The **minimum wage** is a legal minimum amount that an employer must pay for one hour of work.

Economics Update

Find an update on the minimum wage at **ClassZone.com**

KEY CONCEPTS

Sometimes the government decides to intervene in the price system to increase income to certain producers. A **price floor** is an established minimum price that buyers must pay for a good or service. For example, the government has used various programs designed to provide price floors under corn, milk, and other agricultural products. The goal of these price floors is to encourage farmers to produce an abundant supply of food.

EXAMPLE Minimum Wage as a Price Floor

One well-known example of a price floor is a minimum wage. A **minimum wage** is the minimum legal price that an employer may pay a worker for one hour of work. The United States government established its first minimum wage in 1938. The 1930s were a period of low wages, and the government hoped to increase the income of workers. If the minimum wage is set above the equilibrium price for certain jobs in a market, employers may decide that paying the higher wages is not profitable. As a result, they may choose to employ fewer workers, and unemployment will increase. If the minimum wage is set below the equilibrium price, then it will have no effect.

FIGURE 6.13 MINIMUM WAGE AS A PRICE FLOOR

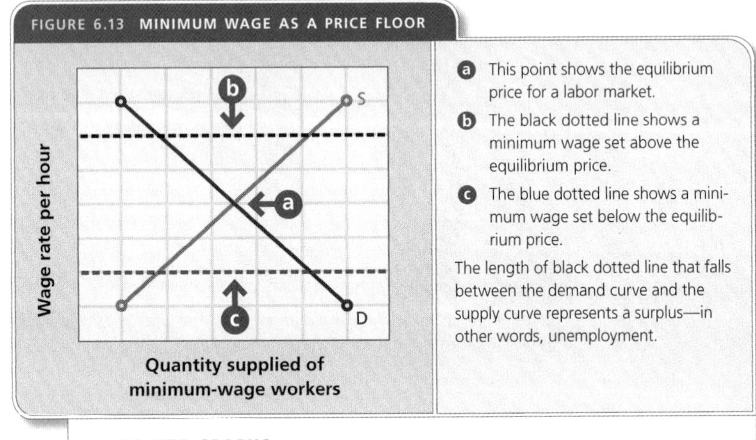

ⓐ This point shows the equilibrium price for a labor market.

ⓑ The black dotted line shows a minimum wage set above the equilibrium price.

ⓒ The blue dotted line shows a minimum wage set below the equilibrium price.

The length of black dotted line that falls between the demand curve and the supply curve represents a surplus—in other words, unemployment.

ANALYZE GRAPHS

1. Assume the minimum wage is set at the dotted black line. What are the costs and benefits of increasing it?
2. Is the minimum wage set at the dotted blue line an effective price floor? Why?

APPLICATION Analyzing Effects

B. Suppose that the Trenton University Tigers were so bad that only 10,000 people want to buy tickets for $15. What effect would keeping $15 as a price floor have?
It would result in a surplus of 20,000 unsold tickets for each game.

DIFFERENTIATING INSTRUCTION

English Learners

Build Economics Vocabulary

Help students understand the difference between *price floor* and *price ceiling* by building on their understanding of the everyday meanings of *floor* and *ceiling.* Invite volunteers to define each term as it relates to a room. *(The floor is the bottom boundary of the room; the ceiling is the top.)* Then ask them to state in their own words what a price floor and a price ceiling are. *(A price floor is the bottom price for something; a price ceiling is the top.)*

Inclusion

Support Class Discussion

Help visual learners, including those with hearing impairments, to participate more fully in class discussions by writing discussion questions on the board. Being able to read the questions helps some students to understand the questions better and to stay focused on the question. It also provides time to think about how to respond. You may also want to write key words and phrases on the board during the discussion to help students follow the main ideas.

Rationing Resources and Products

KEY CONCEPTS

The market uses prices to allocate goods and services. Sometimes in periods of national emergency, such as in wartime, the government decides to use another way to distribute scarce products or resources. **Rationing** is a system in which the government allocates goods and services using factors other than price.

The goods might be rationed on a first-come, first-served basis or on the basis of a lottery. Generally, a system is set up that uses coupons allowing each person a certain amount of a particular item. Or the government may decree that certain resources be used to produce certain goods. When such a system is used, some people try to skirt the rules to get the goods and services they want, creating what is known as a black market. In a **black market**, goods and services are illegally bought and sold in violation of price controls or rationing.

QUICK REFERENCE

Rationing is a government system for allocating goods and services using criteria other than price.

The **black market** involves illegal buying or selling in violation of price controls or rationing.

EXAMPLE Rationing Resources

During World War II, the United States government empowered the Office of Price Administration, which was established in 1941, to ration scarce goods. The hope was that these goods would be distributed to everyone, not just those who could afford the higher market prices born of shortages. It also allocated resources in ways that favored the war effort rather than the consumer market. Figure 6.14 shows some of the goods that were rationed. Rationing also led consumers to look for substitutes. Margarine, a butter substitute, was purchased in huge quantities during the war.

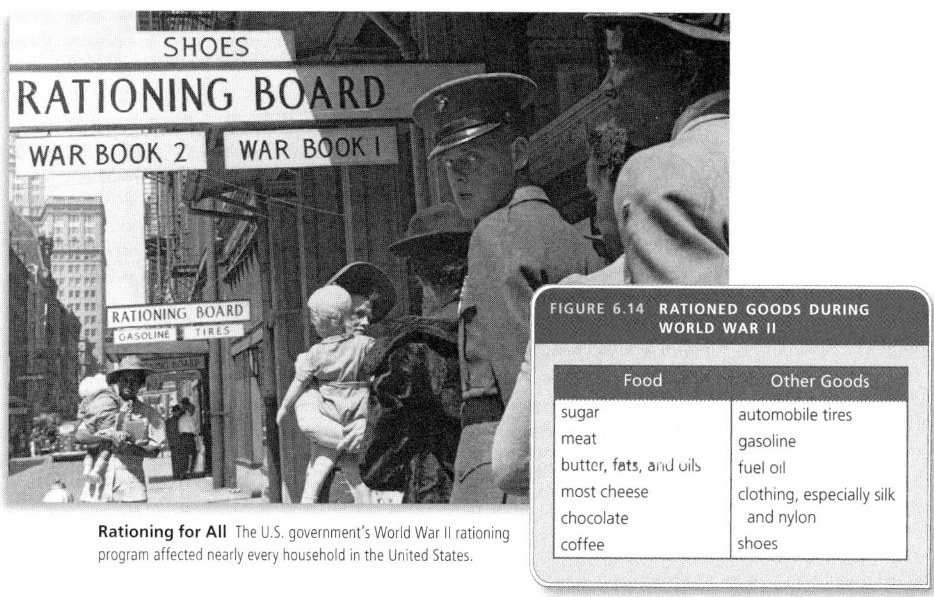

Rationing for All The U.S. government's World War II rationing program affected nearly every household in the United States.

FIGURE 6.14 RATIONED GOODS DURING WORLD WAR II

Food	Other Goods
sugar	automobile tires
meat	gasoline
butter, fats, and oils	fuel oil
most cheese	clothing, especially silk and nylon
chocolate	
coffee	shoes

Rationing Resources and Products

Discuss

- How is rationing different from the market in the way it allocates goods and services? *(The market allocates goods and services based on price. Rationing uses other criteria.)*
- During World War II, the U.S. government mandated that automobile factories stop making cars and start making tanks and planes. Why would the government use this form of rationing? *(Possible answer: because it wanted scarce resources to be used to support the war rather than being used for civilian purposes)*

More About . . .

The Office of Price Administration
President Franklin Roosevelt established the Office of Price Administration and Civilian Supply (OPA) in April 1941, before the United States had officially entered World War II. Rationing started early in 1942, with automobile tires. Eventually, price ceilings were placed on about eight million different items. The OPA set up a large bureaucracy in local communities to administer the price control system.

About 500 communities in areas with a large amount of defense-related rental housing instituted rent controls. Price controls on most goods were lifted in November 1946, but controls on sugar, rice, and rent remained. The OPA ceased operations in June 1947.

INDIVIDUAL ACTIVITY

Reflecting on Life Under Rationing

Time 30 Minutes ◑

Task Write or record thoughts on the effects of rationing.

Materials Needed paper and pens, computer with word processing software, or tape recorder (optional)

Activity

- Have students review the descriptions of rationing on pages 183–184 and imagine what it would be like to live under those conditions.
- Direct students to write a journal entry or letter describing the effects of rationing on their lives. They may write from the point of view of a consumer, a producer, or a government official. Encourage them to include economic concepts in their writing.
- Allow students who have difficulty writing to use word processing software or a tape recorder to express their thoughts.
- Invite volunteers to share their descriptions with the class.

Rubric

	Understanding of Rationing	Presentation of Information
4	excellent	clear, creative
3	good	mostly clear, creative
2	fair	at times clear, creative
1	poor	sketchy

International Economics

Food Shortages in North Korea

The government of North Korea re-instituted its food rationing system in October 2005. It asked outside relief agencies to switch from giving emergency food to helping with projects that would allow the country to become self-sufficient in food production. However, a February 2006 report by the United Nations' World Food Programme (WFP) indicated that the rationing system was uneven in its success. People in cities and regions with less food production still faced shortages.

The WFP approved a two-year transition program to provide food for almost two million people. In addition, significant food assistance continued to come from South Korea and China.

Rationing in China
Shortages of tofu, a staple of the Chinese diet, led to rationing in 1989.

North Korea maintained a strict rationing system between 1946 and 2002. Most importantly, staple foods—meat, rice, and cabbage—were strictly rationed. However, the system was plagued by inefficiency and corruption. The amount of your ration was generally determined by who you knew, where you lived, and what your occupation was. Government officials in the largest cities often received more than their allotment, while the majority of people got by with less (or received less-nutritious substitutes). Some families had meat or fish only a few times a year.

Between 1996 and 2000, widespread famine in North Korea made the situation desperate. Ration coupons were still distributed, but in most cases, the rations were not. As many as a million people died due to the famine. In response, people established unofficial markets where they traded handicrafts for food. In 2002, the government officially legalized these market activities, and prices rose sharply. Wages also increased. Skeptical of markets, however, the leaders of North Korea were, in 2005, considering a return to the rationing system that failed them in the past.

EXAMPLE Black Markets—An Unplanned Result of Rationing

When rationing is imposed, black markets often come into existence. During World War II, black markets in meat, sugar, and gasoline developed in the United States. Some people found ways, including the use of stolen or counterfeit ration coupons, to secure more of these scarce goods.

During the height of North Korea's rationing system, free trade in grain was expressly forbidden, and most other markets were severely restricted. Prices were very high at the markets that did exist. In 1985, it cost half of the average monthly salary of a typical North Korean to buy a chicken on the black market. Even after the government began allowing some market activities in 2002, the black market flourished because many forms of private property, including homes and cars, were still illegal. Some people started smuggling clothes, televisions, and other goods from China to sell in North Korea. (You'll read more about the black market in the discussion of the underground economy in Chapter 12.)

APPLICATION Making Inferences

C. How does the example of rationing during World War II show that the price system is a more efficient way to allocate resources?
The fact that a government bureaucracy was needed to manage the rationing system shows that rationing is much less efficient than the price system, which runs itself.

DIFFERENTIATING INSTRUCTION

Struggling Readers

Compare and Contrast

Allow students to work in pairs to compare the examples of rationing during World War II and in North Korea. Encourage them to use a two-column chart to take notes on the examples. Direct them to list facts about World War II in the first column and about North Korea in the second. Invite students to use the information in their charts to take part in a class discussion comparing and contrasting the use of rationing in these two situations.

Gifted and Talented

Hold a Panel Discussion

Invite students to use Internet or library resources to gather additional information about rationing. They may focus on World War II (perhaps other nations, such as Great Britain), North Korea, or historical examples in other command economies, such as the Soviet Union, China, Romania, or Cuba. Have students serve as experts on their topic and hold a panel discussion on the effectiveness of rationing as a way to allocate resources compared to a market economy's use of the price system.

SECTION 3 Assessment

REVIEWING KEY CONCEPTS

1. Explain the relationship between the terms in each of these pairs.
   a. *price floor* *minimum wage*
   b. *rationing* *black market*
2. What is the difference between a price floor and a price ceiling?
3. What kind of surplus might be created by the minimum wage?
4. How does the existence of the black market work against the intended purpose of rationing?
5. Aside from turning to the black market, how do consumers make up for goods that are rationed?
6. **Using Your Notes** What is the usual result of a price ceiling? Refer to your completed diagram. Use the Graphic Organizer at **Interactive Review @ ClassZone.com**

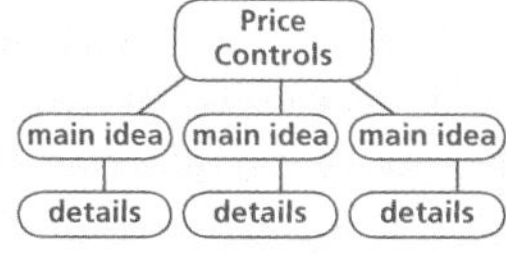

CRITICAL THINKING

7. **Analyzing Causes** Opponents of rent control cite comparisons of cities that regulate rents with cities that do not. Their evidence shows that there is more moderately priced housing available in cities that let the market set the rates for rent. What would account for the differences in availability?
8. **Making Inferences** The percentage of workers who were paid the minimum wage or less decreased from 6.5 percent in 1988 to 3 percent in 2002 to 2.7 percent in 2004. What does this trend tell you about the relationship of the minimum wage to the equilibrium wage for those kinds of work?
9. **Applying Economic Concepts** In the wake of sharply rising gasoline prices in the summer of 2005, several states considered putting a ceiling on the wholesale price of gasoline. What would be the likely result of such a price control? Would it be an effective strategy for lowering gas prices?
10. **Challenge** Many states have laws against so-called price gouging. These laws make it illegal to sell goods and services at levels significantly above established market prices following a natural disaster. What economic argument might be used against such laws?

ECONOMICS IN PRACTICE

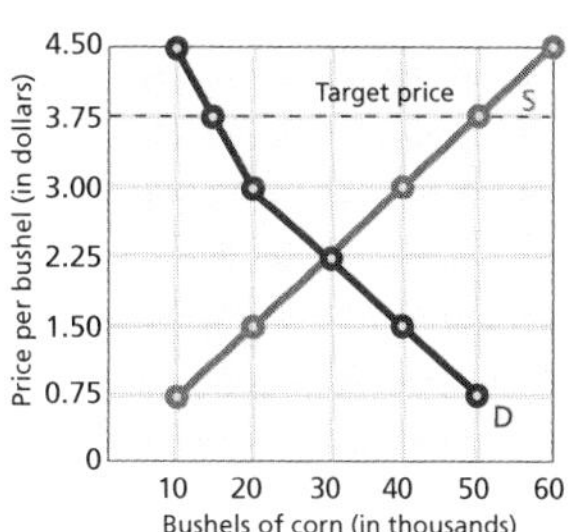

Understanding Price Floors
In agriculture, price floors are known as price supports. The government sets a target price for each crop, and if the market price is below that target, it will pay farmers the difference. Suppose that you are a farmer with 400 acres planted in corn. The following graph shows the supply and demand for your crop.

Price per bushel (in dollars): 0, 0.75, 1.50, 2.25, 3.00, 3.75, 4.50
Bushels of corn (in thousands): 10, 20, 30, 40, 50, 60
Target price
S
D

Calculate the Effect of the Price Support How many bushels of corn will you sell at the equilibrium price? How much revenue will you make? How many bushels do you want to sell at the target price? How many bushels are consumers willing to buy at that price? What is the difference? How much will the government have to pay you for that surplus?

Challenge What changes in supply or demand would move the market equilibrium price closer to the target price?

4 Assess & Reteach

Assess Have students work in pairs and take turns quizzing each other on the Reviewing Key Concepts questions. Encourage partners to discuss the Critical Thinking questions together and agree on an answer.

Unit 2 Resource Book
- Section Quiz, p. 143

Interactive Review @ ClassZone.com
- Section Quiz

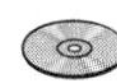

Test Generator CD-ROM
- Section Quiz

Reteach Divide students into groups of three. Assign one of the three main headings in the section to a student in each group. Have students employ the hierarchy diagrams they used to take notes to help them write a short paragraph summarizing their assigned topic. Have students share their paragraphs in their groups.

Unit 2 Resource Book
- Reteaching Activity, p. 144

Economics in Practice
Calculate the Effect of the Price Support at equilibrium price, 30,000 bushels; $67,500 in revenue; 50,000 bushels; 15,000 bushels; difference of 35,000 bushels; $131,250

Challenge If supply decreased or demand increased, the equilibrium price would rise closer to the target price.

SECTION 3 ASSESSMENT ANSWERS

Reviewing Key Concepts

1. a. *price floor*, p. 182; *minimum wage*, p. 182
   b. *rationing*, p. 183; *black market*, p. 183
2. A price floor is the minimum price that buyers may pay for a product; a price ceiling is a maximum price that may be charged for a product.
3. There might be more workers willing to work for the minimum wage than there are jobs that employers are willing to offer at the wage above equilibrium.
4. Rationing attempts to allocate scarce resources fairly to everyone, regardless of their ability to pay. The black market undermines this by allowing those who can pay higher prices to get more of the rationed goods.
5. They look for substitutes for the rationed goods.
6. See page 180 for an example of a completed diagram. Price ceilings create shortages by keeping prices below the equilibrium price.

Critical Thinking

7. Left alone, the market would seek to fill unmet demand by increasing the amount of moderately priced housing. Rent control removes incentives to increase supply and leads to a shortage.
8. The minimum wage is getting close to the equilibrium as there are fewer workers actually working at or below that minimum.
9. Price controls are likely to reduce supply and make it harder for people to get the gasoline they need. The shortage will actually cause prices to rise in the long term.
10. Economists argue that if prices increase after a disaster, more producers will be drawn to the market, causing prices to come down again quickly. If price ceilings are set, shortages will result and people will not have access to all the goods and services they need. Prices will stay high longer as producers will not be drawn to the market.

Economics in Practice

See answers in side column above.

1 Plan & Prepare

Objectives

- Analyze multiple sources to understand factors that affect supply and demand for concert tickets.
- Explain the relationship of supply, demand, and price of concert tickets.

2 Focus & Motivate

Connecting to Everyday Life Explain that this Case Study focuses on factors that affect the price of concert tickets. Have students brainstorm ideas about influences on ticket prices based on their experiences.

3 Teach

Using the Sources

Encourage students to read each source and look for the factors that affect supply, demand, and price of concert tickets.

More About . . .

TicketMaster
TicketMaster sells tickets to music, sports, arts, and theater events worldwide, through retail outlets, telephone, and the Internet. In 2005, it sold 119 million tickets with a value of $6 billion. Sales for the top 100 concert tours in 2005 was about 36.1 million tickets. That year, overall gross sales for the top 100 North American shows came to $3.1 billion.

TicketMaster has exclusive contracts to print and distribute tickets for about 88 percent of the top arenas and amphitheaters in the United States, as well as about 70 percent of the top theaters.

Economics Update

Go to **ClassZone.com** to find an update to this Case Study, including another article, an editable student worksheet, and an editable lesson plan.

Case Study

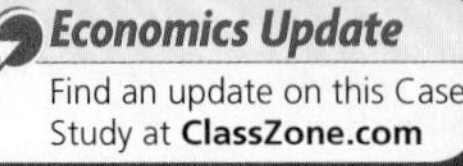
Economics Update
Find an update on this Case Study at ClassZone.com

Prices for Concert Tickets

Background Americans spend billions of dollars on concert tickets yearly—an estimated $3 billion in 2005. With ticket prices for the most popular acts averaging more than $50, most younger or less affluent fans can no longer afford to attend many live concerts. And yet, remarkably, forecasters believe that concert ticket prices have yet to peak.

Ticket prices reflect a number of costs. Performers must cover expenses such as travel, costumes, instruments, and equipment before they reap a profit. Venues, or places where concerts are held, also seek to make a profit, as do ticket distributors. However, in the United States, the sale of concert tickets, along with most other goods and services, is driven by three basic elements of a market economy—demand, supply, and pricing.

What's the issue? How do demand, supply, and pricing affect the concert ticket market? Study these sources to discover the factors that affect demand and supply, and their impact on the price of concert tickets.

A. Congressional Transcript

Pearl Jam believed that TicketMaster Corporation, their ticket distributor, was setting too high a price on the band's concert tickets. This statement, submitted to Congress along with oral testimony on June 30, 1994, explains Pearl Jam's stance.

Pearl Jam Tries to Place Ceiling on Ticket Prices

To keep ticket prices affordable, Pearl Jam appeals to Congress.

Many of Pearl Jam's most loyal fans are teenagers who do not have the money to pay the $50 or more that is often charged today for tickets to a popular concert. Although, given our popularity, we could undoubtedly continue to sell out our concerts with ticket prices at that premium level, we have made a conscious decision that we do not want to put the price of our concerts out of the reach of many of our fans. . . .

For these reasons, we have attempted to keep the ticket prices to our concerts to a maximum of $18. . . . Even where a service charge is imposed, our goal is . . . that no one will pay more than $20 to see a Pearl Jam concert.

Our efforts to try to keep prices . . . to this low level and to limit the possibility of excessive service charge mark-ups have put us at odds with TicketMaster . . . a nationwide computerized ticket distribution service that has a virtual monopoly on the distribution of tickets to concerts in this country.

Thinking Economically How would placing a ceiling on the price of Pearl Jam concert tickets have affected demand and supply? Explain your answer based on the information in the document.

DIFFERENTIATING INSTRUCTION

English Learners

Understand Colloquial English
Explain that document C contains examples of figurative language that is not meant to be understood literally—"the sky's the limit" and "fed up."

- Pair English learners with native English speakers. Have them take turns reading a paragraph aloud. Encourage the native speaker to help the English learner use context clues to figure out the meaning of any confusing language.
- Invite volunteers to summarize document C in their own words.

Inclusion

Use the Audio DVD
Allow students who learn better through listening to use the Audio DVD of the Case Study to improve their comprehension.

- Encourage students to read along as they listen and to pause the recording at the end of each article to summarize what they've heard in their own words.
- Have students discuss the Thinking Economically questions in small groups.

B. Academic Study

Marie Connolly and Alan Krueger, of Princeton University, compiled these data on concert ticket prices for their study "Rockonomics: The Economics of Popular Music."

FIGURE 6.15 CONCERT TICKET PRICES

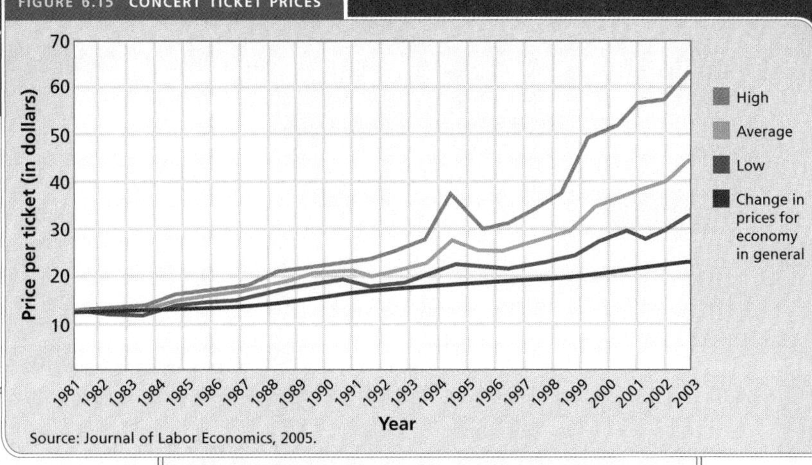

Source: Journal of Labor Economics, 2005.

Thinking Economically In what three years was the high price per ticket about the same as the low price in 2003?

C. Online Newspaper Article

TicketMaster hoped to increase profits by auctioning tickets online. This article discusses the program's potential effect on ticket prices.

TicketMaster Plans to Launch Ticket Auction

The sky's the limit, as bidders compete for the best seats in the house.

Fed up with watching ticket scalpers and brokers rake in the huge bucks for prime seats at their venues, TicketMaster plans to debut an online auction program for choice seats to selected concerts and sports events later this year.

The move may drive up the price of front row seats when they start going to the highest bidder, but some analysts say the impact would likely be minimal. . . .

Princeton University economics professor Alan B. Krueger . . . called the open auction a "positive development."

"For the top artists, tickets are still sold below what the market would bear, even though prices have shot up over the last six years," Krueger told POLLSTAR. "This is especially the case for the best seats in the most expensive cities.

"If the auction is widely used, I suspect price variability will increase; we will see greater dispersion in prices across artists, across cities and seats for the same artist." . . .

Source: Pollstar.com

Thinking Economically How might TicketMaster's online auction program lead to market equilibrium for the best tickets?

THINKING ECONOMICALLY Synthesizing

1. Do you think TicketMaster's plan in document C would help or harm Pearl Jam's wish "that no one will pay more than $20" to see them (document A)? Explain your answer.
2. What do you think happened to quantity supplied of tickets over the span of the graph in document B? Why?
3. In what year in Figure 6.15 did the high price for concert tickets hit $50—the high price that Pearl Jam speaks of in document A? What year was it $20—the desired price they mention?

More About . . .

Ticket Resellers

Reselling tickets for a profit is known as ticket scalping and it is illegal in ten states. Ticket brokers who sell over the Internet have moved most ticket reselling away from the venues themselves.

StubHub is not a broker but an online market that brings buyers and sellers together. Many of these sellers are season-ticket holders who are not able to attend all games. Tickets are also resold through online auction sites such as eBay.

Thinking Economically

Answers

A. *Supply would remain the same; there's nothing about doing more concerts. They say they are popular enough to sell out without the ceiling, so a ceiling would likely cause demand to increase greatly. This would cause a shortage.*

B. *1994, 1995, and 1997*

C. *The characteristics of the price system, as discussed on p. 175, will move the price to equilibrium.*

Synthesizing

1. *It would harm this goal, as an auction is effectively the opposite of a price ceiling; a ceiling limits while an auction allows the price system to act freely.*
2. *The quantity supplied of tickets increased; the law of supply says that when prices increase quantity supplied increases.*
3. *1999; 1988*

TECHNOLOGY ACTIVITY

Comparing Ticket Prices

Time 45 Minutes 

Task Use the Internet to research concert ticket prices through different sellers and prepare a spreadsheet.

Materials Needed a computer with Internet access, spreadsheet software

Activity:

- Organize students into groups. Have groups research ticket prices for three upcoming concerts. Encourage students to search multiple types of sellers, such as those mentioned in the Case Study. Tell them to include service charges or shipping costs that are added to the ticket price.
- Have each group summarize the results of its research in a spreadsheet. Direct them to draw conclusions about factors that affect demand, supply, and price.
- Invite groups to share their spreadsheets with the class. Discuss the pros and cons of dealing with each type of seller.

Rubric

	Understanding of the Price System	Presentation of Information
4	excellent	clear and complete
3	good	mostly clear
2	fair	sometimes clear
1	poor	sketchy

 Online Summary Answers

1. market equilibrium
2. equilibrium price
3. surplus
4. shortage
5. competitive pricing
6. incentives
7. price ceiling
8. price floor
9. rationing
10. black market

Online Review

Review this chapter using interactive activities at **ClassZone.com**

- Online Summary
- Graphic Organizers
- Quizzes
- Review and Study Notes
- Vocabulary Flip Cards

Online Summary

Complete the following activity either on your own paper or online at **ClassZone.com**

Choose the key concept that best completes the sentence. Not all key concepts will be used.

black market	minimum wage
competitive pricing	price ceiling
disequilibrium	price floor
equilibrium price	rationing
incentive	shortage
market equilibrium	surplus

__1__ is a situation that occurs when quantity demanded and quantity supplied at a particular price are equal. The price at which that situation occurs is the __2__. If quantity supplied is greater than quantity demanded, a __3__ occurs. If quantity demanded exceeds quantity supplied, then a __4__ occurs.

When a producer enters a market at a lower price (hoping to increase its customer base while maintaining profits by selling more units), it is engaging in __5__. Rising prices are __6__ that draws producers into markets.

Sometimes government intervenes in the price system. A __7__ is the legal maximum that producers may charge for certain goods or services. A __8__ is the legal minimum amount that may be paid for a particular good or service.

When certain goods or resources are scarce, the government may institute a system of __9__, using some criteria besides price to allocate resources. An unplanned consequence of this action by the government is the development of a __10__, where goods are bought and sold illegally.

CHAPTER 6 Assessment

REVIEWING KEY CONCEPTS

Seeking Equilibrium: Demand and Supply (pp. 164–173)

1. How does the concept of market equilibrium reflect the interaction of producers and consumers in a market?
2. Why are surpluses and shortages examples of disequilibrium?

Prices as Signals and Incentives (pp. 174–179)

3. How are producers and consumers equally involved in the price system?
4. When do prices serve as signals and incentives for producers to enter a market?

Intervention in the Price System (pp. 180–187)

5. What is the usual result of a price floor?
6. What motivates producers and consumers in the black market?

APPLYING ECONOMIC CONCEPTS

Look at the table below showing prices and sales figures for VCRs between 1998 and 2003.

7. Why did dollar sales increase between 1998 and 1999?
8. What is the trend in the average unit price of VCRs between 1998 and 2003? What does this trend signal?

FIGURE 6.16 VCR SALES TO DEALERS

	Unit Sales (in thousands)	Sales (in millions $)	Average Unit Price ($)
1998	18,113	2,049	113
1999	22,809	2,333	102
2000	23,072	1,869	81
2001	14,910	1,058	71
2002	13,538	826	61
2003*	11,916	727	61

* projected
Source: *Consumer Electronics Association Market Research*, January, 2003

CHAPTER 6 ASSESSMENT ANSWERS

Reviewing Key Concepts

1. It shows that interactions of producers and consumers drive the price to a point where quantity supplied and quantity demanded are equal.
2. Each is an example of a situation when quantity supplied and quantity demanded are unequal.
3. Neither producers nor consumers alone can determine the price. It is the interaction of supply and demand that determines price.
4. When prices are rising they send a signal to producers to enter a market. Higher prices are an incentive to producers because they can increase revenue, and possibly profits, at higher prices.
5. a surplus
6. Producers want to make money by selling rationed goods at higher prices. Consumers want to get a greater quantity of a scarce good even if they have to pay a higher price.

Applying Economic Concepts

7. because the number of units sold increased enough to offset the decline in the average price of a VCR
8. Prices are falling, which signals that it is time to leave the market.

Critical Thinking

9. Curves should follow the laws of supply and demand and show an equilibrium price. Scenarios should reflect an increase in demand and equilibrium price, a decrease in demand and equilibrium price, and a decrease in supply and an increase in equilibrium price.
10. The entrance of a new supplier into the market will increase supply and therefore cause equilibrium price to fall.

CRITICAL THINKING

9. **Creating Graphs** Suppose that you are the owner of a toy store. Create demand and supply curves for three products that you expect will sell well during the upcoming holiday shopping season. Then consider the following scenarios: one product becomes much more popular than you expected, one is much less popular than you expected, and the third loses half of its production capacity when a factory is leveled by an earthquake. Draw an additional curve on each of your graphs to show the change in demand or supply represented by these scenarios. Under each graph write a caption explaining the change shown and the effect on the equilibrium price.

   Use ***SMARTGrapher*** **@ ClassZone.com** to complete this activity.

10. **Analyzing Effects** Consumer concerns about nutrition and obesity contribute to a decrease in white bread sales and an increase in sales of whole wheat bread. This change in consumer taste prompts a major manufacturer known for its white bread to enter the market with a whole wheat bread product. What effect will this action have on the supply and equilibrium price of whole wheat bread?

11. **Using Economic Concepts** In 2004, the price of U.S. butter imports increased by more than 30 percent compared to the previous year. In 2003, Canada and New Zealand together supplied more than 80 percent of the butter imported into the United States. In 2004, their combined market share decreased to about 67 percent. What happened in the market to cause this change? How did price serve as a signal and incentive to producers?

12. **Analyzing Effects** How would U.S. government price supports for U.S.-made tennis rackets affect producers and consumers?

13. **Challenge** How would elasticity of demand help producers decide whether competitive pricing is a good strategy for their businesses?

SIMULATION

Find the Best Price

Step 1 Form a group with five other students. Imagine that together you are the market for jeans. Three are buyers and three are sellers, according to the following table. Your goal is to bargain with one another for a pair of jeans. Buyers try to get the lowest price possible, without going above their maximum, and sellers try to get the highest price possible, without going below their minimum.

SIX-PERSON JEANS MARKET

		Price ($)	
Buyers	A	20	**Maximum** price you are willing to pay for a pair of jeans
	B	30	
	C	40	
Sellers	D	15	**Minimum** price you are willing to sell a pair of jeans for
	E	25	
	F	35	

Step 2 Choose a letter to determine your role. On a piece of paper write your letter and name, identify yourself as a buyer or seller, and show the dollar amount from the table.

Step 3 Keep track of each proposed transaction in order on a sheet of paper. Recall what you know about demand, supply, and competitive pricing as you bargain to see who will buy and sell jeans and at what price. Bargaining ends when you reach equilibrium. What is quantity and price at equilibrium?

Step 4 Use the information on the chart to create a demand and supply curve for this market. Does the curve reflect your group's bargaining experience?

Step 5 As a class, discuss what you learned from this exercise about how markets reach equilibrium.

Use ***SMARTGrapher*** **@ ClassZone.com** to complete this activity.

McDougal Littell Assessment System

Assess

Online Test Practice
- Go to **ClassZone.com** for more test practice.

Unit 2 Resource Book
- Chapter Test, Forms A, B, & C, pp. 155–166

Test Generator CD-ROM
- Chapter Test, Forms (A, B, & C), in English and Spanish

Report

Use the McDougal Littell Assessment System to score assessments and receive customized reports.

Reteach

For activities customized for individual students, use the McDougal Littell Assessment System.

SMARTGrapher In question 9 and in the Simulation, students can create graphs using **SmartGrapher @ ClassZone.com**.

CHAPTER 6 ASSESSMENT ANSWERS

11. Canada and New Zealand lost market share as new competitors entered the market drawn by the increase in prices.

12. Price supports above the market equilibrium would provide producers with extra income and cause consumers to have to pay higher prices for tennis rackets.

13. Goods or services that are highly elastic are more price sensitive, so competitive pricing makes sense for them. For products that have inelastic demand, changes in price will make little difference in overall demand. Competitive pricing could allow one company to take market share from another but there is little opportunity to make up profits with volume in such markets.

Simulation Rubric

4	Demonstrates thorough understanding of supply, demand, and pricing; market reaches equilibrium
3	Demonstrates good understanding of supply and demand; market reaches equilibrium
2	Matches buyers and sellers with no bargaining or equilibrium achieved
1	Unable to match buyers and sellers accurately

Planning Guide

Resources 2Go Complete print resources all on one USB drive allow you to customize lessons.

Section Titles and Objectives	Unit 2 Resource Book and Workbooks	Assessment Resources
1 What Is Perfect Competition? pp. 192–197 • Learn that perfect competition is the ideal by which economics measures all market structures • Explain the characteristics of perfect competition and why it doesn't exist in the real world • Analyze examples of markets that come close to perfect competition	**Unit 2 Resource Book** • Reading Study Guide, pp. 167–168 • RSG with Additional Support, pp. 169–171 • RSG with Additional Support (Spanish), pp. 172–174 • Math Skills Worksheet: Constructing and Analyzing Data from Line Graphs, p. 215 • Case Study Resources: Innovation Continues to Drive Competition, pp. 211–212	**Unit 2 Resource Book** • Section Quiz, p. 175 • Reteaching Activity, p. 176 **Test Generator CD-ROM** **Daily Test Practice Transparencies,** TT22
2 The Impact of Monopoly pp. 198–205 • Describe the characteristics of a monopoly • Analyze four different types of monopolies and discuss how they come about • Explain how a monopoly sets its prices and production goals	**Unit 2 Resource Book** • Reading Study Guide, pp. 177–178 • RSG with Additional Support, pp. 179–181 • RSG with Additional Support (Spanish), pp. 182–184 • Readings in Free Enterprise: Will Deregulation Ultimately Lead to Big Box Banks?, pp. 209–210 • Economic Simulations: Monopoly and Competition, pp. 213–214	**Unit 2 Resource Book** • Section Quiz, p. 185 • Reteaching Activity, p. 186 **Test Generator CD-ROM** **Daily Test Practice Transparencies,** TT23
3 Other Market Structures pp. 206–213 • Learn that monopolistic competition and oligopoly are market structures that fall between perfect competition and monopoly • Identify the characteristics of monopolistic competition • Describe the characteristics of oligopoly	**Unit 2 Resource Book** • Reading Study Guide, pp. 187–188 • RSG with Additional Support, pp. 189–191 • RSG with Additional Support (Spanish), pp. 192–194 • Economic Skills and Problem Solving Activity, pp. 207–208	**Unit 2 Resource Book** • Section Quiz, p. 195 • Reteaching Activity, p. 196 **Test Generator CD-ROM** **Daily Test Practice Transparencies,** TT24
4 Regulation and Deregulation Today pp. 214–221 • Explain how government acts to prevent the formation of monopolies • Describe how government acts to protect consumers • Discuss why some industries have been deregulated and the results of that deregulation	**Unit 2 Resource Book** • Reading Study Guide, pp. 197–198 • RSG with Additional Support, pp. 199–201 • RSG with Additional Support (Spanish), pp. 202–204 • Economic Simulations: Monopoly and Competition, pp. 213–214 • Readings in Free Enterprise: Will Deregulation Ultimately Lead to Big Box Banks?, pp. 209–210 • Case Study Resources: Innovation Continues to Drive Competition, pp. 211–212 **NCEE Student Activities** • Regulation and Deregulation, pp. 25–28 **Test Practice and Review Workbook,** pp. 35–36	**Unit 2 Resource Book** • Section Quiz, p. 205 • Reteaching Activity, p. 206 • Chapter Test, (Forms A, B, & C), pp. 217–228 **Test Generator CD-ROM** **Daily Test Practice Transparencies,** TT25

Integrated Technology

No Time? To focus students on the most important content in this chapter, use the table "Comparing Market Structures" that appears on page 211.

Teacher Presentation Options

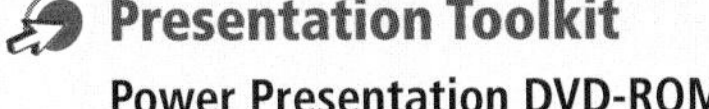

Presentation Toolkit

Power Presentation DVD-ROM

- Lecture Notes
- Interactive Review
- Media Gallery
- Animated Economics
- Review Game

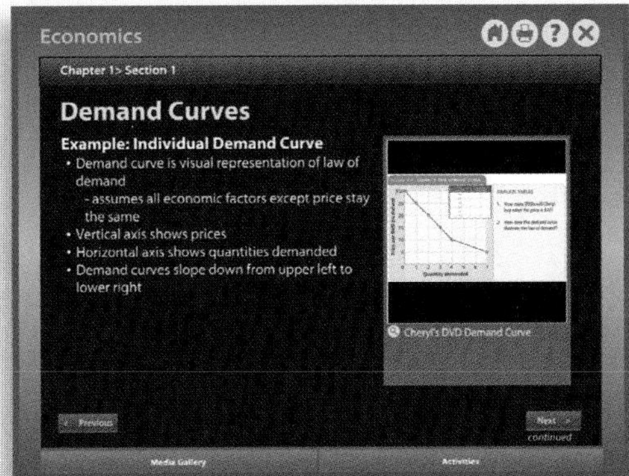

Economics Concepts Transparencies

- Characteristics of Perfect Competition, CT22
- Characteristics of a Monopoly, CT23
- How Monopolistic Competition and Oligopoly Differ, CT24
- A Brief History of Standard Oil Company, CT25

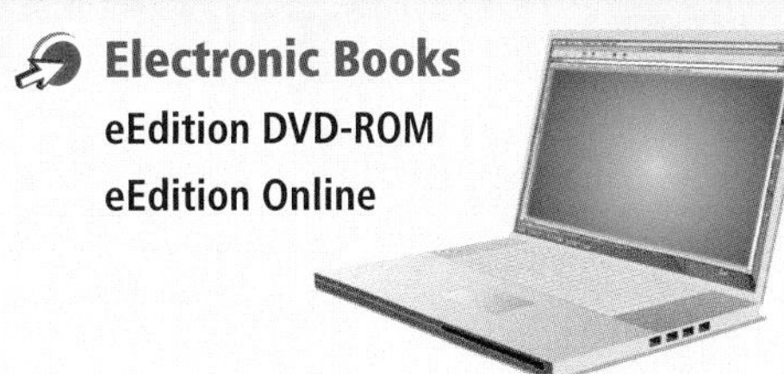

Electronic Books

eEdition DVD-ROM

eEdition Online

Daily Test Practice Transparencies, TT22, TT23, TT24, TT25

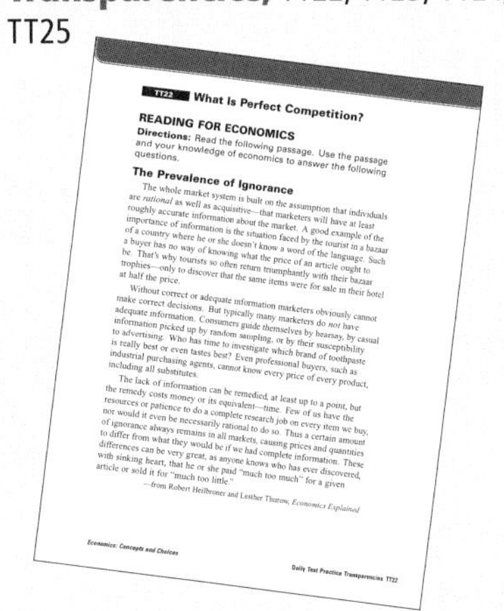

TT22 What is Perfect Competition?

READING FOR ECONOMICS

Directions: Read the following passage. Use the passage and your knowledge of economics to answer the following questions.

The Prevalence of Ignorance

The whole market system is built on the assumption that individuals are *rational* as well as acquisitive—that marketers will have at least roughly accurate information about the market. A good example of the importance of information is the situation faced by the tourist in a bazaar of a country where he or she doesn't know a word of the language. Such a buyer has no way of knowing what the price of an article ought to be. That's why tourists so often return triumphantly with their bazaar trophies—only to discover that the same items were for sale in their hotel at half the price.

Without correct or adequate information marketers obviously cannot make correct decisions. But typically many marketers do *not* have adequate information. Consumers guide themselves by hearsay, by casual information picked up by random sampling, or by their susceptibility to advertising. Who has time to investigate which brand of toothpaste is really best or even tastes best? Even professional buyers, such as industrial purchasing agents, cannot know every price of every product, including all substitutes.

The lack of information can be remedied, at least up to a point, but the remedy costs money or its equivalent—time. Few of us have the resources or patience to do a complete research job on every item we buy, nor would it even be necessarily rational to do so. Thus a certain amount of ignorance always remains in all markets, causing prices and quantities to differ from what they would be if we had complete information. These differences can be very great, as anyone knows who has ever discovered, with sinking heart, that he or she paid "much too much" for a given article or sold it for "much too little."

—from Robert Heilbroner and Lester Thurow, *Economics Explained*

Economics: Concepts and Choices

Daily Test Practice Transparencies TT22

SMART Grapher

- Creating a Line Graph, p. 196

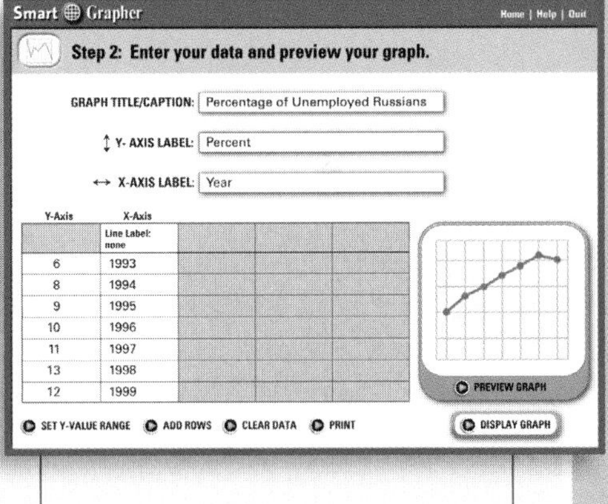

Online Activities at ClassZone.com

Economics Update

- Perfect Competition, p. 193
- Monopolies, p. 203
- Monopolistic Competition, p. 207
- Oligopolies, p. 210
- Joan Robinson, p. 212
- Unfair Business Practices, p. 216
- Competition in Gadgets and Gizmos, p. 220

Activity Maker

- Vocabulary Flip Cards
- Review Game

Research Center

- Graphs and Data

Interactive Review

- Online Summary
- Quizzes
- Vocabulary Flip Cards
- Graphic Organizers
- Review and Study Notes

SMART Grapher

- Create a Graph, p. 196

Teacher-Tested Activities

Name: Bill Smiley (ret.)

School: Leigh High School

State: California

Teacher-Tested Activities

At the beginning of this chapter, look for my classroom-proven idea for teaching economics concepts and thinking.

Chapter 7: Market Structures

Resources for Differentiated Instruction

Struggling Readers

Teacher's Edition Activities

- Work in Pairs, p. 196
- Create a Chart, p. 200
- Compare and Contrast, p. 208
- Review Prior Knowledge, p. 212
- Understand Cause and Effect, p. 218
- Use Jigsaw Reading, p. 220

Unit 2 Resource Book

- RSG with Additional Support, pp. 169–171, 179–181, 189–191, 199–201 (A)
- Reteaching Activities, pp. 176, 186, 196, 206 (B)
- Chapter Test (Form A), pp. 217–220 (C)

ClassZone.com

- Animated Economics
- Interactive Review

Test Generator CD-ROM

- Chapter Test (Form A)
- Chapter Test (Form A), in Spanish

B

SECTION 1 | RETEACHING ACTIVITY

What Is Perfect Competition?

A. Finding Main Ideas

Complete each sentence with the most appropriate term.

B. Making Inferences

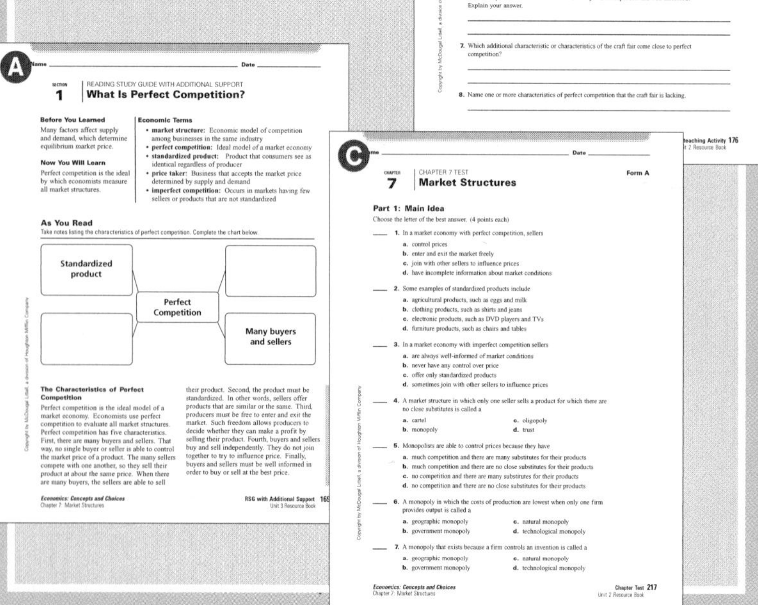

A

SECTION 1 | READING STUDY GUIDE WITH ADDITIONAL SUPPORT

What Is Perfect Competition?

C

CHAPTER 7 | CHAPTER 7 TEST

Market Structures

Form A

Part 1: Main Idea

English Learners

Teacher's Edition Activities

- Create a Word Web, p. 194
- Make Vocabulary Cards, p. 202
- Build Complex Words, p. 208
- Analyze Word Parts, p. 212
- Understand Compound Nouns, p. 216
- Analyze Hyphenated Words, p. 220

Unit 2 Resource Book

- RSG with Additional Support (Spanish), pp. 172–174, 182–184, 192–194, 202–204 (A)

Test Generator CD-ROM

- Chapter Test (Forms A, B, & C), in Spanish (B)

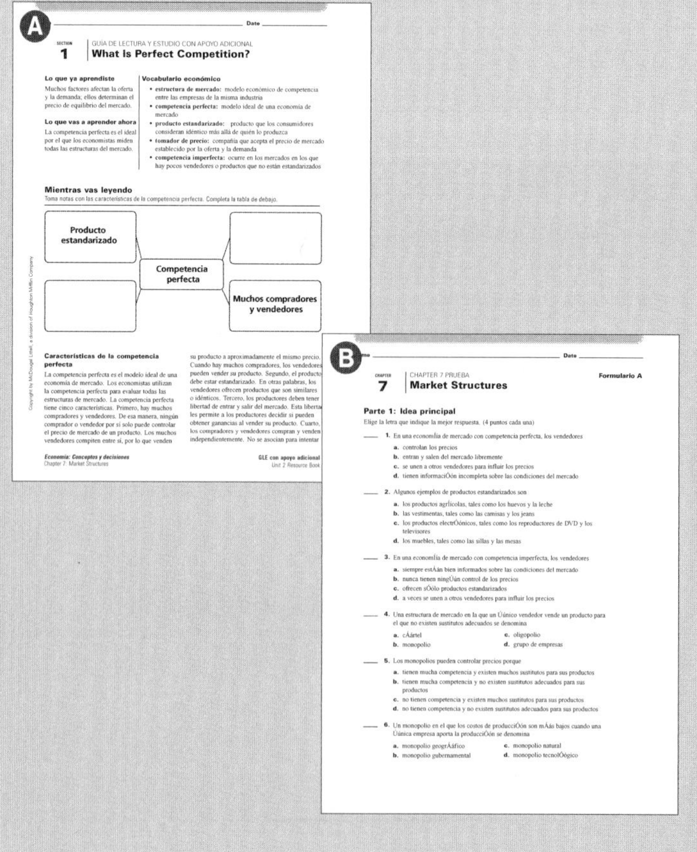

A

SECTION 1 | GUÍA DE LECTURA Y ESTUDIO CON APOYO ADICIONAL

What Is Perfect Competition?

B

CHAPTER 7 | CHAPTER 7 PRUEBA

Market Structures

Formulario A

Parte 1: Idea principal

Inclusion

Teacher's Edition Activities

- Describe the Visual, p. 194
- Listen and Summarize, p. 200
- Enlarge the Visual, p. 204
- Draw a Competitive Continuum, p. 210
- Discuss in a Circle, p. 216

Lesson Plans

- Modified Lessons for Inclusion, pp. 22–25 (A)

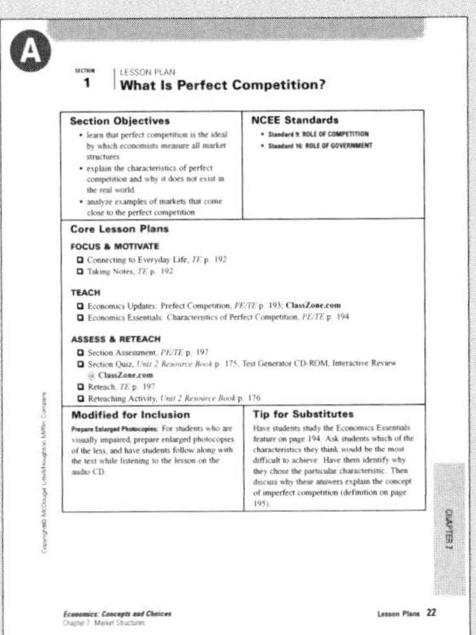
SECTION 1 LESSON PLAN
What Is Perfect Competition?

Section Objectives | NCEE Standards

Core Lesson Plans

Modified for Inclusion | Tip for Substitutes

Gifted and Talented

Teacher's Edition Activities

- Create an Expanded Model, p. 196
- Research Patents for Technology Products, p. 202
- Compare Drug Prices, p. 204
- Investigate Market Concentration, p. 210
- Debate Airline Deregulation, p. 218

Unit 2 Resource Book

- Readings in Free Enterprise: Will Deregulation Ultimately Lead to Big Box Banks?, pp. 209–210 (A)
- Case Study Resources: Innovation Continues to Drive Competition, pp. 211–212 (B)

NCEE Student Activities

- Regulation and Deregulation, pp. 25–28 (C)

ClassZone.com

- Research Center

Test Generator CD-ROM

- Chapter Test (Form C)
- Chapter Test (Form C), in Spanish

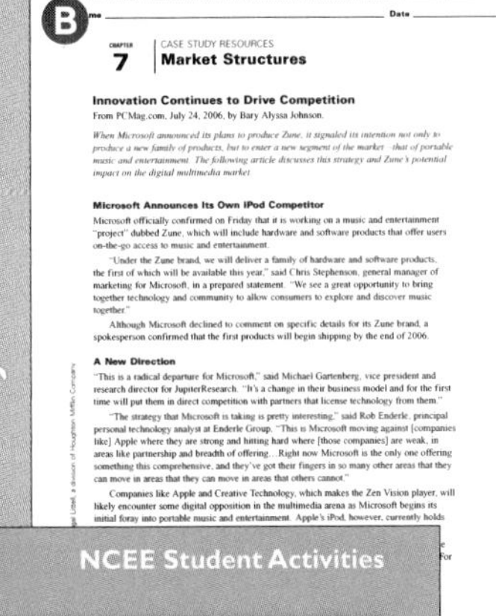
CHAPTER 7 CASE STUDY RESOURCES
Market Structures

Innovation Continues to Drive Competition

Microsoft Announces Its Own iPod Competitor

A New Direction

Focus & Motivate

Objective

Explain how economists use market structures to examine the competitiveness of an industry.

Why the Concept Matters

Explain that competition not only helps keep prices lower, it also leads to innovation and better allocation of resources. Looking for ways to attract customers often leads businesses to improve their products and processes and to find new ways of doing things.

Analyzing the Photograph

Have students study the photograph and read the caption. Invite volunteers to describe how the photograph shows sellers trying to make their products stand out from the competition. *(Possible answers: variety of foods offered in the food court; different brands; signage that communicates distinct styles for different stores)*

Ask students what they can infer from the photograph about why malls attract so many buyers and sellers. *(Possible answer: Buyers like having many sellers to choose from in one location; sellers like being in a location that attracts large numbers of buyers.)*

Explain that markets in which there are large numbers of buyers and sellers, and products that are similar but not identical exhibit the characteristics of monopolistic competition. Chapter 7 examines this type of market structure and many others.

Market Structures

In markets where businesses offer similar products, sellers compete by trying to make their products stand out from the competition.

CONTENT STANDARDS

NCEE STANDARDS

Standard 9: Role of Competition

Students will understand that

Competition among sellers lowers costs and prices, and encourages producers to produce more of what consumers are willing and able to buy. Competition among buyers increases prices and allocates goods and services to those people who are willing and able to pay the most for them.

Students will be able to use this knowledge to

Explain how changes in the level of competition in different markets can affect them. *(pages 192–195, 198–204, 206–211)*

Standard 16: Role of Government

Students will understand that

There is an economic role for government in a market economy whenever the benefits of a government policy outweigh its costs. Governments often address environmental concerns, define and protect property rights, and attempt to make markets more competitive.

Students will be able to use this knowledge to

Identify and evaluate the benefits and costs of alternative public policies, and assess who enjoys the benefits and who bears the costs. *(pages 214–218)*

CHAPTER

7

Market Structures

CONCEPT REVIEW

Competition involves all the actions that sellers, acting independently, take to get buyers to purchase their products.

CHAPTER 7 KEY CONCEPT

A **market structure** is an economic model that helps economists examine the nature and degree of competition among businesses in the same industry.

WHY THE CONCEPT MATTERS

On trips to the mall, you've probably noticed something about the prices of products you're looking to buy. If there are several different brands of the same kind of product, prices tend to be lower. If there's just one brand, however, prices tend to be higher. The level of competition in a market has a major impact on the prices of products. The more sellers compete for your dollars, the more competitive prices will be.

Online Highlights

More at ClassZone.com

Economics Update
Go to ECONOMICS UPDATE for chapter updates and current news on competition in the cellular telephone industry. (See Case Study, pp. 220–221.) ▶

SMARTGrapher
Go to SMART GRAPHER to complete graphing activities in this chapter.

Interactive Review
Go to INTERACTIVE REVIEW for concept review and activities.

How do cellular phone makers compete for your business? See the Case Study on pages 220–221.

From the Classroom

Bill Smiley, Leigh High School (retired)

The Power of Advertising

The following exercise helps students understand how advertising affects the way we all think, buy, and live. It will help them understand that a key purpose of advertising is product differentiation.

Divide students into creative ad teams and ask each team to produce a television ad, a radio commercial, or a print ad for a product of their choice. TV ads should contain an opening that makes a lasting impression and a script that leaves an indelible memory of the product. Radio commercials should contain a slogan or jingle for the product and background music or other sound effects. Print ads should contain artistic drawings or cut-outs from magazines that both illustrate the product and capture attention. Have each group share its creation with the rest of the class, and discuss how the advertisements help make each product seem distinct from competing products.

Previewing Chapter Technology at ClassZone.com

Economics Update Students will find updates to information in the pupil edition on pages 193, 203, 207, 210, 212, 216, and 220.

Interactive Review Students will find additional section and chapter assessment support for materials on pages 197, 205, 213, 219, and 222.

TEACHER MEDIA FAVORITES

Books

- Brobeck, Stephen, et al., eds. *Encyclopedia of the Consumer Movement.* Santa Barbara, CA: ABC-Clio, 1997. A comprehensive overview of the consumer protection movement.
- Brock, James, and Walter Adams eds. *Structure of American Industry.* 11th ed. Upper Saddle River, NJ: Pearson, 2005. Real world market structures shown via 12 current case studies.
- Jaffe, Adam, and Josh Lerner. *Innovation and Its Discontents: How Our Broken Patent System Is Endangering Innovation and Progress, and What to Do About It.* Princeton, NJ: Princeton UP, 2004. A clear, compelling look at how the current patent system hinders economic growth.
- Kwoka, John E., and Lawrence J White, eds. *The Antitrust Revolution: Economics, Competition, and Policy.* 4th ed. New York: Oxford UP, 2003. Explores anticompetitive practices involved in recent antitrust cases and mergers.

Videos/DVDs

- *Perfect Competition & Inelastic Demand/Economic Efficiency.* Two 30-minute programs. Economics USA, 2003. Uses TV news format to explore market structures and related topics and make them relevant to students' lives.

Software

- *Virtual Economics® Version 3.0.* New York: National Council on Economic Education, 2005. Provides a complete resource library for understanding and teaching basic economics concepts.

Internet

Visit **ClassZone.com** to link to

- a variety of chapter-specific, content-reviewed sites
- updates on data and topics presented throughout the chapter sections and Case Study
- updates to the Power Presentations

1 Plan & Prepare

Section 1 Objectives

- learn that perfect competition is the ideal by which economists measure all market structures
- explain the characteristics of perfect competition and why it does not exist in the real world
- analyze examples of markets that come close to perfect competition

2 Focus & Motivate

Connecting to Everyday Life Explain that this section focuses on the way the most competitive kind of market would be structured. Encourage students to consider whether producers or consumers would prefer to have a highly competitive market.

Taking Notes Remind students to take notes as they read by completing a cluster diagram. They can use the Graphic Organizer at **Interactive Review @ ClassZone.com**. A sample is shown below.

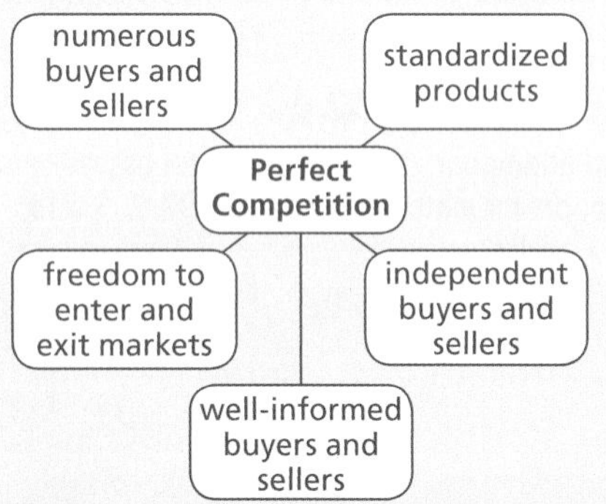

SECTION 1

What Is Perfect Competition?

OBJECTIVES

In Section 1, you will
- learn that perfect competition is the ideal by which economists measure all market structures
- explain the characteristics of perfect competition and why it does not exist in the real world
- analyze examples of markets that come close to perfect competition

KEY TERMS

market structure, *p. 192*
perfect competition, *p. 192*
standardized product, *p. 192*
price taker, *p. 193*
imperfect competition, *p. 195*

TAKING NOTES

As you read Section 1, complete a cluster diagram to identify the major characteristics of perfect competition. Use the Graphic Organizer at **Interactive Review @ ClassZone.com**

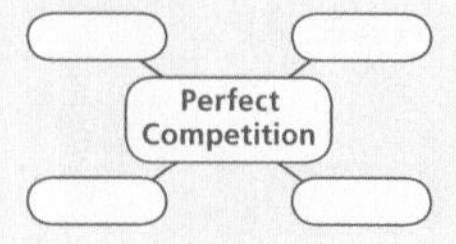

The Characteristics of Perfect Competition

QUICK REFERENCE

A **market structure** is an economic model of competition among businesses in the same industry.

Perfect competition is the ideal model of a market economy.

A **standardized product** is one that consumers see as identical regardless of producer.

KEY CONCEPTS

When you buy new clothes, you probably shop around for the best deal. But when you buy milk, you know that a gallon will be about the same price no matter where you shop. The market for clothes has a different level of competition than the market for milk. Economists classify markets based on how competitive they are. A **market structure** is an economic model that allows economists to examine competition among businesses in the same industry.

Perfect competition is the ideal model of a market economy. It is useful as a model, but real markets are never perfect. Economists assess how competitive a market is by determining where it falls short of perfect competition. Perfect competition has five characteristics.

1. **Numerous buyers and sellers.** No one seller or buyer has control over price.
2. **Standardized product.** Sellers offer a **standardized product**—a product that consumers consider identical in all essential features to other products in the same market.
3. **Freedom to enter and exit markets.** Buyers and sellers are free to enter and exit the market. No government regulations or other restrictions prevent a business or customer from participating in the market. Nor is a business or customer required to participate in the market.
4. **Independent buyers and sellers.** Buyers cannot join other buyers and sellers cannot join other sellers to influence prices.

SECTION 1 PROGRAM RESOURCES

ON LEVEL

Lesson Plans
- Core, p. 22

Unit 2 Resource Book
- Reading Study Guide, pp. 167–168
- Math Skills Worksheet, p. 215
- Section Quiz, p. 175

STRUGGLING READERS

Unit 2 Resource Book
- Reading Study Guide with Additional Support, pp. 169–171
- Reteaching Activity, p. 176

ENGLISH LEARNERS

Unit 2 Resource Book
- Reading Study Guide with Additional Support (Spanish), pp. 172–174

INCLUSION

Lesson Plans
- Modified for Inclusion, p. 22

GIFTED AND TALENTED

Unit 2 Resource Book
- Case Study Resources: Innovation Continues to Drive Competition, pp. 183–184

TECHNOLOGY

eEdition DVD-ROM
eEdition Online
Power Presentation DVD-ROM
Economics Concepts Transparencies
- CT22 Characteristics of Perfect Competition

Daily Test Practice Transparencies, TT22
ClassZone.com

5. **Well-informed buyers and sellers.** Both buyers and sellers are well-informed about market conditions. Buyers can do comparison shopping, and sellers can learn what their competitors are charging.

When these five conditions are met, sellers become price takers. A **price taker** is a business that cannot set the prices for its products but, instead, accepts the market price set by the interaction of supply and demand. Only efficient producers make enough money to serve perfectly competitive markets.

QUICK REFERENCE

A **price taker** is a business that accepts the market price determined by supply and demand.

CHARACTERISTIC 1 Many Buyers and Sellers

A large number of buyers and sellers is necessary for perfect competition so that no one buyer or seller has the power to control the price in the market. When there are many sellers, buyers can choose to buy from a different producer if one tries to raise prices above the market level. But because there are many buyers, sellers are able to sell their products at the market price.

Let's consider the Smith family, whom you met in Chapter 5. The Smiths grow raspberries in the summer to sell at the Montclair Farmers' Market. Because many farmers grow and sell raspberries at the same market, all of the farmers charge about the same price. If one farmer tries to charge more than the market price for raspberries, consumers will buy from the other farmers. Because there are many buyers—in other words, sufficient demand—the Smiths and other producers know that they can sell their product at the market price. Lack of demand will not cause them to lower their prices.

Perfect Competition Farmers' markets exhibit many of the characteristics of perfect competition.

CHARACTERISTIC 2 Standardized Product

In perfect competition, consumers consider one producer's product essentially the same as the product offered by another. The products are perfect substitutes. Agricultural products such as wheat, eggs, and milk, as well as other basic commodities such as notebook paper or gold generally meet this criterion.

Considering the Montclair Farmers' Market, while no two pints of raspberries are exactly alike, they are similar enough that consumers will choose to buy from any producer that offers raspberries at the market price. Price becomes the only basis for a consumer to choose one producer over another.

CHARACTERISTIC 3 Freedom to Enter and Exit Markets

In a perfectly competitive market, producers are able to enter the market when it is profitable and to exit when it becomes unprofitable. They can do this because the investment that a producer makes to enter a market is relatively low. Market forces alone encourage producers to freely enter or leave a given market.

The Smiths and other farmers consider the market price for raspberries when planning their crops. If they believe they can make a profit at that price, they grow raspberries. If not, they try some other crop.

Economics Update

Find an update about perfect competition at **ClassZone.com**

3 Teach

The Characteristics of Perfect Competition

Discuss

- How is the market price in a perfectly competitive market related to the equilibrium price? *(They are the same thing.)*
- Why is perfect competition considered the ideal model of a market economy? *(because only the market forces of supply and demand determine production and prices)*
- Why are well-informed buyers and sellers important for perfect competition? *(Possible answer: Without enough information, consumers might pay more than they should or producers might make less profit than they could.)*

Economics Update

At **ClassZone.com,** students will see updated information on perfect competition.

LEVELED ACTIVITY

Comparing Market Structures

Time 30 Minutes

Objective Students will compare perfect competition to other market structures. (Information on other market structures is covered in Sections 2 and 3.)

Basic

Create a graphic organizer that includes the following: the five characteristics of perfect competition; an indication of how monopoly, monopolistic competition, and oligopoly lack one or more of these characteristics; and an example of each market structure. Explain what market structures measure.

On Level

Choose a market that is close to perfect competition. Describe how the five characteristics of perfect competition apply to that market. Then, illustrate how that market would be different under each of the other three market structures. Give specific examples of how the market would change.

Challenge

Analyze the pros and cons of each market structure for producers and consumers. Write a recommendation for the way the market economy should be structured for the greatest benefit for society as a whole. Support your recommendation with specific examples based on your analysis of the pros and cons.

Economics Essentials: Figure 7.1

Explain that the diagram in Figure 7.1 uses visuals and brief captions to summarize the five characteristics of perfect competition.

- What motivates producers to enter or exit a perfectly competitive market? *(whether they can make a profit in the market)*
- Why does the diagram show a person using a computer to represent well-informed buyers and sellers? *(because the Internet helps people learn about products and compare prices)*

Analyze

Answers will vary. Students should follow the model shown and demonstrate an understanding of how the five characteristics apply to a raspberry farmer at the Farmers' Market.

More About . . .

Information Asymmetry

Economists use the term *information asymmetry* or *asymmetrical information* to describe a situation in which buyers or sellers have unequal information about a market transaction. Generally, sellers have more information about a product than buyers. Some common examples are sellers of used cars, real estate, stocks, and life insurance.

The Internet now offers buyers an easier way to gain information about products. This new source of information puts buyers and sellers on a more equal footing and makes markets more competitive.

ECONOMICS ESSENTIALS

FIGURE 7.1 Characteristics of Perfect Competition

Many Buyers and Sellers A large number of buyers and sellers ensures that no one controls prices.

Standardized Products All products are essentially the same.

What Are the Characteristics of Perfect Competition?

Well-informed Buyers and Sellers Both buyers and sellers know the market prices and other conditions.

Freedom to Enter and Exit Markets Producers can enter or exit the market with no interference.

Independent Buyers and Sellers Buyers and sellers do not band together to influence prices.

ANALYZE CHARTS

Imagine that you own a farm and that you have decided to sell raspberries at the Montclair Farmers' Market. Construct your own diagram to show how the five characteristics of perfect competition will apply to your enterprise.

CHARACTERISTIC 4 Independent Buyers and Sellers

In a perfectly competitive market, neither buyers nor sellers join together to influence price. When buyers and sellers act independently, the interaction of supply and demand sets the equilibrium price. Independent action ensures that the market will remain competitive. At the Montclair Farmers' Market, the farmers do not band together to raise prices, nor do the consumers organize to negotiate lower prices.

CHARACTERISTIC 5 Well-informed Buyers and Sellers

Buyers and sellers in a perfectly competitive market have enough information to make good deals. Buyers can compare prices among different sellers, and sellers know what their competitors are charging and what price consumers are willing to pay. Buyers and sellers at the Montclair Farmers' Market make informed choices about whether to buy or sell raspberries in that market. With all five characteristics met, the Smiths accept the market price for raspberries. All raspberry producers become price takers.

APPLICATION Making Inferences

A. Can you think of another market that comes close to perfect competition? Which of the characteristics does it lack?
Examples include wholesale agricultural markets, standardized products sold on eBay, streets with many different gas stations.

DIFFERENTIATING INSTRUCTION

English Learners

Create a Word Web

Explain that this section contains words related to *compete*, which is a verb.

- Invite them to create a word web with *compete* in the center and to add related words as they read pages 192–195.
- Allow students to use a dictionary to identify the correct parts of speech and to discover meanings for *competition, competitive,* and *competitor.*
- Check understanding by writing fill-in-the-blank sentences on the board and asking students to use the correct form.

Inclusion

Describe the Visual

Help students to understand the characteristics of perfect competition by using the Economics Essentials graphic.

- Describe the visual and read the related caption for each characteristic.
- Then, call on volunteers to state their understanding of each characteristic in their own words.
- Repeat this process with the Economics Essentials graphic related to monopoly in Section 2.

Competition in the Real World

KEY CONCEPTS

In the real world, there are no perfectly competitive markets because real markets do not have all of the characteristics of perfect competition. Market structures that lack one of the conditions needed for perfect competition are examples of **imperfect competition**. (You'll learn more about imperfect competition in Sections 2 and 3.) However, there are some markets—the wholesale markets for farm products such as corn and beef, for example—that come close to perfect competition.

QUICK REFERENCE

Imperfect competition occurs in markets that have few sellers or products that are not standardized.

EXAMPLE 1 Corn

In the United States, there are thousands of farmers who grow corn, and each one contributes only a small percentage of the total crop. Therefore, no one farmer can control the price of corn, and all farmers accept the market price. Individual farmers decide only how much corn to produce to offer for sale at that price. At the same time, there are a large number of buyers, and the price on the wholesale market is easy to determine. Corn is a fairly standardized product, and buyers usually have no reason to prefer one farmer's corn to another's. Buyers will not pay more than the market price.

In reality, there are several reasons that imperfect competition occurs in the corn market. For one thing, the U.S. government pays subsidies to corn farmers to protect them from low corn prices. In addition, sometimes corn farmers band together to try to influence the price of corn in their favor, and corn buyers sometimes pursue the same strategy. Subsidies, group action, and other deviations from perfect competition interfere with the market forces of supply and demand.

Close to Perfect Competition
Wholesale markets for agricultural products, such as corn, come close to perfect competition.

EXAMPLE 2 Beef

The wholesale market for raw beef is another that comes close to perfect competition. There are many cattle producers, and there is little variation in a particular cut of beef from one producer to the next. Because the beef is so similar, the wholesale buyer's primary concern will be price. Both buyers and sellers can easily determine the market price, and producers sell all their beef at that price. Cattle sellers can adjust only their production to reflect the market price.

As in the corn market, there are several reasons that imperfect competition occurs in the beef market. Cattle ranchers, like corn farmers, may try to join together to influence the price of beef in their favor. In addition, many beef producers try to persuade buyers that there are significant differences in their products that warrant higher prices. For example, cattle that eat corn supposedly produce better tasting beef.

APPLICATION Drawing Conclusions

B. Why is the market for corn closer to perfect competition than the market for corn flakes?
Corn is a standardized product. Corn flakes are a differentiated product. Price will be the primary concern for corn consumers, but quality and other concerns may influence the corn flake consumer.

Competition in the Real World

Discuss

- Why are corn farmers and cattle ranchers price takers? *(because there are so many of them that no individual producer can influence the price)*
- Why would corn growers and cattle ranchers want to increase demand for their product? *(Possible answer: Since they cannot control the price, the only way they can increase their revenue is to increase the amount that they sell.)*

International Economics

The World Beef Market

Animal diseases such as bovine spongiform encephalopathy (BSE), commonly known as Mad Cow disease, and foot and mouth disease (FMD) have caused shortages in the world beef market. U.S. beef was banned from many markets after outbreaks of BSE in 2003, and the United States dropped from second to ninth place among beef exporters.

Japan had been the major importer of U.S. beef. It switched to beef from Australia and New Zealand. Brazil and Argentina were expected to export 35 percent of the world's beef in 2006. But outbreaks of FMD in Brazil and an export ban in Argentina limited their ability to meet demand. Consequently, supply shortages kept beef prices high.

SMALL GROUP ACTIVITY

Researching Agricultural Markets

Time 45 Minutes

Task Gather information on agricultural markets and present findings in oral reports.

Materials Needed computer with Internet access

Activity

- Organize students into groups. Assign each group to research information on the markets for corn, beef, or other U.S. agricultural products.
- Topics might include prices, number and location of producers, production and consumption statistics, and domestic vs. export markets. A good research starting place is the Web site of the U.S. Department of Agriculture's Economic Research Service.
- Allow groups to present their findings in oral reports to the class. Discuss how these markets come close to perfect competition and how they do not match the market structure completely.

Rubric

	Understanding of Perfect Competition	Presentation of Information
4	excellent	clear and complete
3	good	mostly accurate
2	fair	sometimes clear
1	poor	sketchy

Creating and Interpreting Economic Models

1 Plan & Prepare

Objectives

- Analyze the ways a graph can communicate information visually.
- Make inferences from an economic model of baseball production.

2 Focus & Motivate

Analyze Advise students to examine the table to see which columns provide the information that they need to create their graph. Have students consider these questions as they work on their graph.

- How does the graph show the stages of production? *(It shows that marginal costs first decline then increase until they lead to negative returns.)*
- How is marginal revenue related to price per unit in a perfectly competitive market? *(They are the same.)*

3 Teach

- Point out that most economic models are mathematical. Economists create equations that describe economic processes. A graph is just a visual depiction of an economic model.
- Invite students to recall what they learned about profit maximizing output to help them interpret the model.

For additional practice see **Skillbuilder Handbook**, page R16.

THINKING ECONOMICALLY
Answers

1. *nine*
2. *The demand curve is a straight line from 1, $1.00 through 11, $1.00. It coincides with the marginal revenue curve.*
3. *The price of a baseball remains the same regardless of quantity demanded. A business in a perfectly competitive market has no power to charge more for its products than competing businesses. All sellers become price takers by accepting the market price for a baseball ($1.00).*

ECONOMICS SKILLBUILDER

For more information on creating and interpreting economic models, see the Skillbuilder Handbook, page R16.

Creating and Interpreting Economic Models

Economic models help solve problems by focusing on a limited set of variables. A production costs and revenue schedule, which you learned about in Chapter 5, is a model that helps businesses decide how much to produce. Creating a graph as part of the model paints a picture of the data that makes it easier to understand.

In this example, imagine you own a business that produces baseballs in a perfectly competitive market. The market price of a baseball is $1, but your costs vary depending on how many you produce. Follow the instructions to create a graph that will help you visualize the way a perfectly competitive market works.

CREATING AN ECONOMIC MODEL OF BASEBALL PRODUCTION

1. Copy the graph below onto your own paper, or use ***SMARTGrapher* @ ClassZone.com**.
2. Using data from the table below, plot the curve showing the marginal costs of producing different numbers of baseballs. Label the curve "MC."
3. Using data from the table below, plot the curve showing the marginal revenue of producing different numbers of baseballs. Label the curve "MR."

BASEBALL PRODUCTION COSTS AND REVENUES SCHEDULE

Total Produced	Total Revenue (in dollars)	Total Cost (in dollars)	Total Profit (in dollars)	Marginal Revenue (in dollars)	Marginal Cost (in dollars)
0	0.00	1.00	–1.00	—	—
1	1.00	2.00	–1.00	1.00	1.00
2	2.00	2.80	–0.80	1.00	0.80
3	3.00	3.50	–0.50	1.00	0.70
4	4.00	4.00	0.00	1.00	0.50
5	5.00	4.50	0.50	1.00	0.50
6	6.00	5.20	0.80	1.00	0.70
7	7.00	6.00	1.00	1.00	0.80
8	8.00	6.86	1.14	1.00	0.86
9	9.00	7.86	1.14	1.00	1.00
10	10.00	9.36	0.64	1.00	1.50
11	11.00	11.50	–0.50	1.00	2.14

BASEBALL PRODUCTION

THINKING ECONOMICALLY Analyzing

1. How many baseballs should you produce each day to maximize profits?
2. Using the same graph, plot the demand curve for this perfectly competitive market. Remember that the market price will not change no matter how many baseballs are demanded.
3. How does the graph help explain the term "price takers"?

DIFFERENTIATING INSTRUCTION

Struggling Readers

Work in Pairs

Allow students to work with a partner to create the graph and interpret the data.

- Have them follow the directions step-by-step to create the graph.
- Ask them to identify the table column related to the horizontal axis of the graph. *(total produced)*
- Suggest that one read the values from the appropriate columns while the other plots the values on the graph.
- Direct the pairs to discuss and answer the Thinking Economically questions.

Gifted and Talented

Create an Expanded Model

Invite students to create a new graph that shows total profit for each level of production, in addition to marginal revenue and marginal cost. Suggest that students use different colors to distinguish the three curves and to include a key.

- Allow volunteers to explain to the class how their graph needed to be changed to include the additional data.
- Ask students to develop questions that can be answered by the new graph and ask classmates to answer them.

SECTION 1 Assessment

REVIEWING KEY CONCEPTS

1. Explain the differences between the terms in each of these pairs:
   a. *market*
   market structure
   b. *perfect competition*
   imperfect competition
2. Why are sellers in a perfectly competitive market known as *price takers*?
3. Why is it necessary to have standardized products in order to have perfect competition?
4. Why is independent action of buyers and sellers important to achieving perfect competition?
5. How is imperfect competition different from perfect competition?
6. **Using Your Notes** What are the five characteristics of perfect competition? Refer to your completed cluster diagram.

Use the Graphic Organizer at **Interactive Review @ ClassZone.com**

CRITICAL THINKING

7. **Drawing Conclusions** Suppose that you went to a farmers' market and found several different farmers selling cucumbers. Would you be likely to find a wide range of prices for cucumbers? Why or why not?
8. **Analyzing Effects** What would happen to a wheat farmer who tried to sell his wheat for $2.50 per bushel if the market price were $2.00 per bushel? Why?
9. **Making Inferences** Why are brand-name products not found in a perfectly competitive market? You will learn more about this topic in Section 3 of this chapter.
10. **Challenge** At an auction, sellers show their goods before an audience of buyers. The goods for sale may be similar to each other, as in an auction of used cars, or they may be one-of-a-kind, as in an art auction. Buyers usually have an opportunity to inspect items prior to the auction. During the auction, buyers bid against one another to see who is willing to pay the highest price. In what ways is an auction similar to a perfectly competitive market? In what ways is it different?

Online Quiz
ClassZone.com

ECONOMICS IN PRACTICE

How competitive is the market for snowboards?

Identifying Perfect Competition Perfectly competitive markets can be identified by specific characteristics. The chart below lists these characteristics.

Characteristics of Perfect Competition	Markets				
	Applesauce	Snowboards	Hairbrushes	Computer games	Paper clips
Many buyers and sellers					
Standardized product					
Freedom to enter and leave the market					
Independent action					
Well-informed buyers and sellers					

Complete a Chart Five different markets are shown in the chart. On your own paper, complete the chart by marking which of the characteristics each market has.

Challenge Choose one market from the chart and explain what would need to be done to make it perfectly competitive.

4 Assess & Reteach

Assess Assign small groups to answer one of the assessment questions. Have them write their responses on the board. Review the answers as a class.

Unit 2 Resource Book
- Section Quiz, p. 175

Interactive Review @ ClassZone.com
- Section Quiz

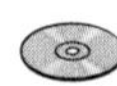
Test Generator CD-ROM
- Section Quiz

Reteach Invite volunteers to name the five characteristics of perfect competition and to say how each one makes a market competitive. Encourage all students to take notes as the information is reviewed.

Unit 2 Resource Book
- Reteaching Activity, p. 176

Economics in Practice
Complete a Chart
Many buyers & sellers: all
Standardized product: applesauce, paper clips
Freedom to enter & leave the market: none (The existing producers dominate the markets, making them difficult to enter.)
Independent action: all except computer games (which are tied to specific platforms)
Well-informed buyers & sellers: all

Challenge Look for answers that not only list the missing characteristics but explain the details of how the specific market would adapt the missing characteristics.

SECTION 1 ASSESSMENT ANSWERS

Reviewing Key Concepts

1. a. *market*, p. 48; *market structure*, p. 192
   b. *perfect competition*, p. 192; *imperfect competition*, p. 195
2. because no one seller can control the price but must accept the market price as determined by the forces of supply and demand
3. because differentiated products would allow competition on a basis other than price
4. If buyers or sellers banded together they could interfere with the interaction of supply and demand determining prices.
5. Imperfect competition lacks one or more of the characteristics of perfect competition.
6. See page 192 for an example of a completed diagram. The five characteristics are many buyers and sellers; standardized product; freedom to enter or exit the market; independent action of buyers and sellers; well-informed buyers and sellers.

Critical Thinking

7. There would be little price variation on cucumbers because the multiple sellers of these standardized products would have to accept the market price. Consumers could easily compare prices and would choose the lowest price if vendors offered different prices.
8. The farmer would not be able to sell his wheat above the market price. The market for wheat is close to being perfectly competitive.
9. Brand names allow companies to compete on characteristics other than price. In perfect competition, price is the only basis for competition.
10. Similar: many buyers; sellers are price takers (accept the winning bid); free to enter and exit the market; independent buyers and sellers. Different: only one seller for each unique product; non-standard products; buyers may not know enough to determine a good price

Economics in Practice
See answers in side column above.

❶ Plan & Prepare

Section 2 Objectives

- describe the characteristics of a monopoly
- analyze four different types of monopolies and discuss how they come about
- explain how a monopoly sets its prices and production goals

❷ Focus & Motivate

Connecting to Everyday Life Explain that this section focuses on the least competitive market structure, known as monopoly. Invite students to list situations when they have had no close substitutes for a good or service that they wanted to buy.

Taking Notes Remind students to take notes as they read by completing a chart. They can use the Graphic Organizer at **Interactive Review @ ClassZone.com**. A sample is shown below.

	One Seller	Restricted Market	Control of Prices
Natural Monopoly	Costs are most efficient with one supplier	Economies of scale limit number of firms	Prices subject to government regulation
Government Monopoly	Government runs the business or licenses one supplier	Market entry limited by government control or regulation	Prices determined by government regulation
Technological Monopoly	Results from ownership of an invention or technology	Patents serve as barriers to entry	Charges higher prices while the monopoly lasts
Geographic Monopoly	No competition in the local area	Location or size of market limits number of suppliers	Charges higher prices due to lack of competition

SECTION 2

The Impact of Monopoly

OBJECTIVES

In Section 2, you will
- describe the characteristics of a monopoly
- analyze four different types of monopolies and discuss how they come about
- explain how a monopoly sets its prices and production goals

KEY TERMS

monopoly, *p. 198*
cartel, *p. 198*
price maker, *p. 198*
barrier to entry, *p. 198*
natural monopoly, *p. 201*
government monopoly, *p. 201*
technological monopoly, *p. 201*
geographic monopoly, *p. 201*
economies of scale, *p. 201*
patent, *p. 202*

TAKING NOTES

As you read Section 2, complete a chart to show how different types of monopolies exhibit the characteristics of monopoly. Use the Graphic Organizer at **Interactive Review @ ClassZone.com**

	One Seller	Restricted Market	Control of Prices
Natural Monopoly			
Government Monopoly			
Technological Monopoly			
Geographic Monopoly			

Characteristics of a Monopoly

QUICK REFERENCE

Monopoly occurs when there is only one seller of a product that has no close substitutes.

A **cartel** is a group that acts together to set prices and limit output.

A **price maker** is a firm that does not have to consider competitors when setting the prices of its products.

A **barrier to entry** makes it hard for a new business to enter a market.

KEY CONCEPTS

Perfect competition is the most competitive market structure. The least competitive is **monopoly**, a market structure in which only one seller sells a product for which there are no close substitutes. The term *monopoly* may be used for either the market structure or the monopolistic business. Pure monopolies are as rare as perfect competition, but some businesses come close. For example, a **cartel** is a formal organization of sellers or producers that agree to act together to set prices and limit output. In this way, a cartel may function as a monopoly.

Because a monopoly is the only seller of a product with no close substitutes, it becomes a **price maker**, a business that does not have to consider competitors when setting its prices. Consumers either accept the seller's price or choose not to buy the product. Other firms may want to enter the market, but they often face a **barrier to entry**—something that hinders a business from entering a market. Large size, government regulations, or special resources or technology are all barriers to entry.

Let's take a closer look at the three characteristics of monopoly through the De Beers cartel, which held a virtual monopoly on the diamond market for most of the 20th century. At one time it controlled as much as 80 percent of the market in uncut diamonds. De Beers used its monopoly power to control the price of diamonds and created barriers to entry that kept other firms from competing.

198 Chapter 7

SECTION 2 PROGRAM RESOURCES

ON LEVEL

Lesson Plans
- Core, p. 23

Unit 2 Resource Book
- Reading Study Guide, pp. 177–178
- Economic Simulations, pp. 213–214
- Section Quiz, p. 185

STRUGGLING READERS

Unit 2 Resource Book
- Reading Study Guide with Additional Support, pp. 179–181
- Reteaching Activity, p. 186

ENGLISH LEARNERS

Unit 2 Resource Book
- Reading Study Guide with Additional Support (Spanish), pp. 182–184

INCLUSION

Lesson Plans
- Modified for Inclusion, p. 23

GIFTED AND TALENTED

Unit 2 Resource Book
- Readings in Free Enterprise: Will Deregulation Ultimately Lead to Big Box Banks?, pp. 209–210

TECHNOLOGY

eEdition DVD-ROM

eEdition Online

Power Presentation DVD-ROM

Economics Concepts Transparencies
- CT23 Characteristics of a Monopoly

Daily Test Practice Transparencies, TT23

ClassZone.com

ECONOMICS ESSENTIALS

FIGURE 7.2 Characteristics of a Monopoly

What Are the Characteristics of a Monopoly?

Only One Seller
A single business controls the supply of a product that has no close substitutes.

Control of Prices
Monopolies act as price makers because they sell products that have no close substitutes and they face no competition.

Restricted, Regulated Market
Government regulations or other barriers to entry keep other firms out of the market.

ANALYZE CHARTS
Imagine that you are a business person with unlimited funds. Could you gain a monopoly over the market for housing in your neighborhood? Using the chart, explain the steps you would need to take. How might your neighborhood change if one person controlled property prices?

CHARACTERISTIC 1 Only One Seller

In a monopoly, a single business is identified with the industry because it controls the supply of a product that has no close substitutes. For example, De Beers once produced more than half of the world's diamond supply and bought up diamonds from smaller producers to resell. In this way, it controlled the market.

CHARACTERISTIC 2 A Restricted, Regulated Market

In some cases, government regulations allow a single firm to control a market, such as a local electric utility. In the case of De Beers, the company worked with the South African government to ensure that any new diamond mines were required to sell their diamonds through De Beers. The company also restricted access to the market for raw diamonds for producers outside of South Africa. By controlling the supply of diamonds, De Beers made it difficult for other producers to make a profit.

CHARACTERISTIC 3 Control of Prices

Monopolists can control prices because there are no close substitutes for their product and they have no competition. When economic downturns reduced demand for diamonds, De Beers created artificial shortages by withholding diamonds from the market. The reduced supply allowed the cartel to continue charging a higher price.

APPLICATION Analyzing Effects

A. What effect did the De Beers diamond monopoly have on the price of diamonds?
Prices were higher than if there had been a competitive market.

3 Teach

Characteristics of a Monopoly

Discuss

- How is the concept of elasticity of demand related to monopolists as price makers? *(Because there are no close substitutes for the product, the demand will tend to be inelastic or not price sensitive.)*
- Which characteristic of perfect competition is affected by barriers to entry? *(freedom to enter and leave a market)*

Economics Essentials: Figure 7.2

Explain that the diagram in Figure 7.2 shows the characteristics of monopoly visually to make them easier to remember.

- What does the visual of the single seller suggest about the economic benefits of being a monopolist? *(Being able to control supply makes a monopolist rich.)*
- What analogy does the diagram use to convey that a monopoly controls prices? *(A monopolist acts like someone controlling the strings on a puppet.)*

Analyze

Answers will vary. Example: a student might try to buy all the houses by offering homeowners large sums. Then, they could control the prices of homes in the neighborhood. With this power, they could keep prices high or could tear down houses and build a shopping center.

LEVELED ACTIVITY

Investigating Professional Sports Monopolies

Time 30 Minutes

Objective Students will demonstrate an understanding of how the characteristics of monopoly apply to professional sports leagues. (Challenge uses antitrust information from Section 4.)

Basic

Choose one of the four major U.S. professional sports leagues: baseball, basketball, football, or hockey. Create a map showing where teams are located. Write a caption for your map describing why the teams have a monopoly and what that monopoly allows the teams to do.

On Level

Choose one of the four major U.S. professional sports leagues. Find a city with one team and another city with two teams in the same general region. Create a chart comparing ticket prices for the teams. Write a caption stating how monopoly limits competition and affects prices.

Challenge

Choose one of the four major U.S. professional sports leagues. Research how the league limits competition, through such policies as where to locate new franchises. Include information on how the government supports these practices and why. Present your findings in a written or oral report.

A Global Perspective

OPEC: Controlling the Oil Pipelines
The U.S. Energy Information Administration (EIA) projected world oil demand for 2007 at 87 million barrels per day (Mbbl/d) with supply at 87.1 Mbbl/d. A trend of strong demand growth in Asia was expected to continue. Because there was so little excess supply and because OPEC countries were already producing at near capacity levels, OPEC had less ability to influence prices on world markets.

From 2000 to 2005, OPEC attempted to keep the average price of its crude oil between $22 and $28 per barrel by adjusting supply. The price averaged about $36 in 2004 and $51 in 2005. In January 2005, OPEC decided that its previous price range was unrealistic.

Answers

1. *It tries to control price by controlling supply.*
2. *As more substitutes for oil become available, OPEC will exert less monopolistic power.*

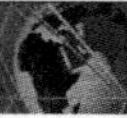

A GLOBAL PERSPECTIVE

OPEC: Controlling the Oil Pipelines

The Organization of the Petroleum Exporting Countries (OPEC) does not have a monopoly on oil reserves or oil production. However, the 11 member nations of the cartel possess more than two-thirds of the world's oil reserves and produce about two-fifths of the world's oil supply. By regulating the amount of oil that flows through its pipelines, OPEC exerts control over the market price for oil.

Market forces often counteract OPEC's supply adjustments. For example, in the early 1980s demand for oil fell as consumers and businesses implemented strategies to reduce energy use. Despite OPEC's efforts to reduce supply and stabilize the price, crude oil prices fell through most of the 1980s. Another factor that limits OPEC's control over oil prices is member unity. Members sometimes choose not to follow OPEC moves to reduce oil output—because that would reduce their revenues. Despite these limitations, OPEC continues to play a major role in the world market for petroleum.

FIGURE 7.3 OPEC MEMBERS

Country	Joined OPEC	Location
Algeria	1969	Africa
Indonesia	1962	Asia
Iran	1960	Middle East
Iraq	1960	Middle East
Kuwait	1960	Middle East
Libya	1962	Africa
Nigeria	1971	Africa
Qatar	1961	Middle East
Saudi Arabia	1960	Middle East
United Arab Emirates	1967	Middle East
Venezuela	1960	South America

Source: OPEC

FIGURE 7.4 OPEC Member Nations

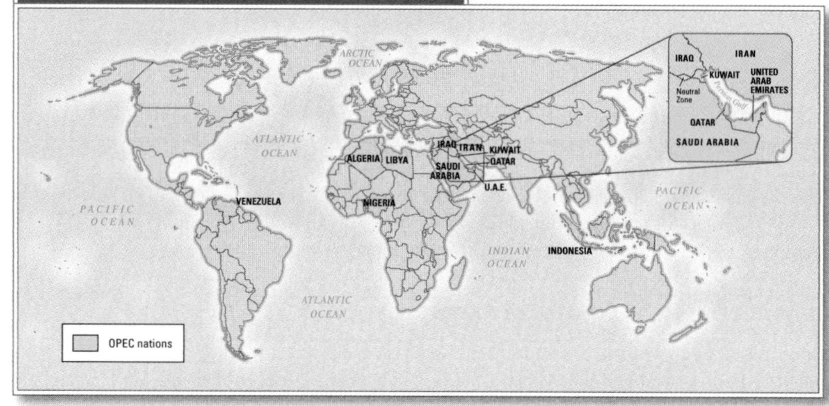

CONNECTING ACROSS THE GLOBE

1. **Applying Economic Concepts** In what ways does OPEC act like a monopoly?
2. **Making Inferences** What will happen to OPEC's monopolistic power as the world discovers new sources of energy? Explain your answer.

DIFFERENTIATING INSTRUCTION

Struggling Readers

Create a Chart
Help students understand the different types of monopolies by having them take notes in a two-column chart as they read pages 201–203.

- Instruct them to list the four types of monopolies in the first column and examples of each in column two. Allow students to share their charts with a partner.
- Encourage students to use their charts as they discuss the similarities and differences in the types of monopolies.

Inclusion

Listen and Summarize
Pair students who have visual impairments with those who do not. The students without impairments may read the section aloud to their partner. Encourage students with vision impairments to orally summarize what they have heard after each subhead. Ask partners to work together to determine the answer to each Application question.

Types of Monopolies

KEY CONCEPTS

There are several reasons why monopolies exist, and not all monopolies are harmful to consumers. A **natural monopoly** is a market situation in which the costs of production are lowest when only one firm provides output. A **government monopoly** is a monopoly that exists because the government either owns and runs the business or authorizes only one producer. A **technological monopoly** is a monopoly that exists because the firm controls a manufacturing method, an invention, or a type of technology. A **geographic monopoly** is a monopoly that exists because there are no other producers or sellers within a certain region.

QUICK REFERENCE

A **natural monopoly** occurs when the costs of production are lowest with only one producer.

A **government monopoly** exists when the government either owns and runs the business or authorizes only one producer.

A **technological monopoly** occurs when a firm controls a manufacturing method, invention, or type of technology.

A **geographic monopoly** exists when there are no other producers within a certain region.

Economies of scale occur when the average cost of production falls as the producer grows larger.

EXAMPLE 1 Natural Monopoly: A Water Company

In some markets, it would be inefficient to have more than one company competing for consumers' business. Most public utilities fall into this category. Let's look at the water company in your community as an example. It pumps the water from its source through a complex network of pipes to all the homes, businesses, and public facilities in the community. It also monitors water quality for safety and removes and treats wastewater so that it may be recycled.

It would be a waste of community resources to have several companies developing separate, complex systems in order to compete for business. A single supplier is most efficient due to **economies of scale**, a situation in which the average cost of production falls as the producer grows larger. The more customers the water company serves, the more efficient its operation becomes, as its high fixed costs are spread out over a large number of buyers. These economies of scale result in government support for natural monopolies. While supporting natural monopolies, the government also regulates them to ensure that they do not charge excessively high prices for their services.

Natural Monopolies Most public utilities require complex systems, such as this water treatment facility.

EXAMPLE 2 Government Monopoly: The Postal Service

Government-run businesses provide goods and services that either could not be provided by private firms or that are not attractive to them because of insufficient profit opportunities. One of the oldest government monopolies in the United States is the U.S. Postal Service, which has the exclusive right to deliver first-class mail. Originally, only the government could provide this service in an efficient and cost-effective manner. However, new services and new technologies have been chipping away at this monopoly. Private delivery companies offer services that compete with the U.S. Postal Service. Many people now send information by fax, e-mail, and text messages. In addition, many pay their bills online.

Types of Monopolies

Discuss

- Compare a natural monopoly to a geographic monopoly. *(Both are the only producer of a product in a region, but natural monopoly arises due to economies of scale while geographic monopoly usually results from small market size or isolated location.)*
- How does new technology limit many kinds of monopolies? *(Possible answer: It gives consumers substitute ways to achieve the same result, such as sending mail, taking pictures, or shopping.)*

More About . . .

Natural Monopolies

Natural monopolies exist because the monopolist has higher fixed costs and lower marginal costs than in most industries. For most firms, marginal costs decline for a time but then increase, causing average total costs to increase as well. If a firm's average total costs are still declining at the point where costs intersect with demand, it is a natural monopoly.

Some economists argue that such monopolies are only possible in theory and depend on government regulation to limit competition. For example, deregulation of some aspects of the electricity and telephone industries have shown that a single provider was not the most efficient way to deliver such service.

CLASS ACTIVITY

Creating a Bulletin Board Display

Time 90 Minutes ●◑

Task Gather information on local utilities and create a bulletin board display.

Materials Needed paper, markers, computer with Internet access

Activity

- Assign students to work alone or in small groups to gather information about public utilities in your community, such as those that provide water, electricity, or natural gas.
- Internet and library resources might be combined with material directly from the utilities or interviews with key personnel. Have some students focus on the role of the public utilities commission or other regulatory bodies.
- Direct students to combine their information to create a coherent bulletin board display.
- Discuss as a class how utilities show the characteristics of a natural monopoly.

Rubric

	Understanding of Natural Monopoly	Presentation of Information
4	excellent	clear and creative
3	good	accurate summary
2	fair	only partly clear
1	poor	sketchy

Your Economic Choices

GOVERNMENT MONOPOLY

Which mail service will you choose?

- What are the costs and benefits of using each type of mail service? *(Possible answers: Regular mail costs stationery and stamps but is more personal. E-mail requires a computer, Internet access, and e-mail service. If you have these, e-mail is faster and more convenient.)*
- Marshall McLuhan said, "The medium is the message." What is the difference in the message sent by a hand-written thank-you note compared to an e-mail? *(Possible answer: A hand-written note says that the writer cared enough to send a personal message. An e-mail says the writer is comfortable with new technology and likes to communicate quickly.)*

Activity Have students brainstorm examples of times when regular mail is the best choice and times when e-mail is the best choice. List student information in a two-column chart on the board. Invite volunteers to generalize when each type of mail service is most appropriate.

More About . . .

Patents

The United States Patent and Trademark Office (USPTO) grants new patents for almost everything that humans can create and for the processes that may be used to make them. Software patents, including patents for Internet business methods, are now the most common type of patents. In 2004, the USPTO received almost 400,000 patent applications.

Critics claim that it is too easy to get patents, with an estimated 85 percent of applications being approved. Suggested reforms include shortening the patent's term and narrowing the definition of what can be patented.

YOUR ECONOMIC CHOICES

GOVERNMENT MONOPOLY

Which mail service will you choose?

If you need to send thank-you notes, you could send them by regular mail, which is a government monopoly. Or you could send electronic thank-you notes by computer.

▲ E-mail message

▲ Handwritten note

EXAMPLE 3 Technological Monopoly: Polaroid

In 1947, Edwin Land, the founder of the Polaroid Corporation, invented the first instant camera. Land's camera used a special type of film that allowed each picture to develop automatically in about a minute. Through a series of patents, Polaroid created a monopoly in the instant photography market.

A **patent** is a legal registration of an invention or a process that gives the inventor the exclusive property rights to that invention or process for a certain number of years. The government supports technological monopolies through the issuing of patents. Through patents, businesses are able to recover the costs that were involved in developing the invention or technology.

QUICK REFERENCE

A **patent** gives an inventor the exclusive property rights to that invention or process for a certain number of years.

Polaroid's control of instant photography technology through its patents was a barrier to entry for other firms. In 1985, Polaroid won a lawsuit against Eastman Kodak Company for patent infringement. The court ruled that Kodak's instant camera and film had violated Polaroid's property rights, which were protected by several patents. The lawsuit effectively blocked Kodak from the instant photography market.

Technological monopolies last only as long as the patent—generally 20 years—or until a new technology creates close substitutes. The rise of easier-to-use 35mm cameras, one-hour photo processing, and digital cameras all contributed to a steep decline in Polaroid's business. While the company remains the leading seller of instant cameras and film, the technology has become a minor segment of the consumer photography market.

Technological Monopoly Polaroid instant cameras use patented technology.

DIFFERENTIATING INSTRUCTION

English Learners

Make Vocabulary Cards

Help students understand the four types of monopolies.

- Have pairs write the modifier, such as *natural,* along with its everyday definition on one side of an index card and the compound noun, with its economics definition, on the other. Suggest they add an example to help remember the definition.
- Have them quiz each other on definitions. One might read an example and ask the other to name the type.

Gifted and Talented

Research Patents for Technology Products

Invite students to choose a technology product that they use regularly, such as a cell phone, MP3 player, or computer. Have them use Internet resources to find out information about some of the patents related to that product. Encourage students to discover whether the patent provided a competitive advantage to the manufacturer. Allow students to present their findings in brief oral reports to the class.

EXAMPLE 4 Geographic Monopoly: Professional Sports

One type of geographic monopoly in the United States is the professional sports team. The major sports leagues require that teams be associated with a city or region and limit the number of teams in each league. In other words, the leagues create a restricted market for professional sports. Most cities and towns are not directly represented by a team, so many teams draw their fans from a large surrounding geographic region. Because of their geographic monopolies, the owners of these teams are able to charge higher prices for tickets to games than if they faced competition. They also have a ready market for sports apparel and other merchandise featuring the team logo and colors.

Geographic Monopolies The Boston Red Sox is the only baseball team in New England, so it draws fans from across the six-state region.

Another type of geographic monopoly is created by physical isolation. For example, Joe operates the only gas station at an interstate exit in the middle of a desert. The next station in either direction is more than 50 miles away. Joe has a geographic monopoly because he is the only supplier of a product with no close substitutes. Drivers on the interstate in that area depend on Joe's gas and have no other choice of supplier. They can either buy gas from Joe or risk running out of gas before they reach the next station. Because of his geographic location as the single supplier of a product that has no close substitutes, Joe is able to control the price that he charges—and gas at Joe's is always very expensive.

Economics Update

Find an update on monopolies at **ClassZone.com**

Isolated locations or small communities may have other examples of geographic monopolies if the market is too small to support two similar businesses. Geographic monopolies have become less common in the United States. Cars allow people to travel greater distances to shop, and catalog marketers and Internet businesses, combined with efficient delivery companies, offer consumers more alternatives to shopping at local stores.

APPLICATION Drawing Conclusions

B. Which type of monopoly do you think is least harmful to consumers? Why?

Natural monopolies, because economies of scale allow one firm to deliver the service efficiently and government regulation keeps prices from going too high.

More About . . .

Professional Sports Monopolies

The structure of major U.S. professional sports leagues allows them to exert monopoly power that results in higher ticket prices. In basketball and hockey, only the New York and Los Angeles markets have more than one team. Football has three such markets and baseball has five. Because the leagues' policies restrict the market, teams have a great deal of economic power in the cities where they are located.

The Supreme Court ruled in 1922 that major league baseball was exempt from antitrust regulations. While there have been some changes since then, the industry still enjoys a high level of government support for its business practices.

Economics Update

At **ClassZone.com,** students will see updated information about monopolies.

INDIVIDUAL ACTIVITY

Creating Visual Summaries

Time 20 Minutes

Task Summarize the four types of monopolies in a visual form.

Materials Needed paper and markers, photographs from magazines, newspapers, or the Internet

Activity

- Have students review the information on the four types of monopolies on pages 201–203, making notes on how they come about and examples of each.
- Direct students to create a summary of the material in a visual form, such as a diagram, poster, or collage.
- Encourage students to share their work in small groups and discuss how each type represents the characteristics of a monopoly.
- Invite groups to share the conclusions of their discussion with the class.

Rubric

	Understanding of Types of Monopolies	Presentation of Information
4	excellent	clear and creative
3	good	accurate summary
2	fair	only partly clear
1	poor	sketchy

Profit Maximization by Monopolies

Discuss

- How do supply and demand affect the price that a monopolist can charge? *(The monopolist supplies less than the quantity demanded at equilibrium price in order to create a shortage and charge a higher price.)*
- How do patents help drug manufacturers maximize their profits? *(The patent allows them to sell the product without competition for a period of years, so that they can charge higher prices and make greater profits.)*

More About . . .

Pharmaceutical Industry Profits
According to a 2003 study by the Public Citizen's Congress Watch, median profits for the 10 drug companies listed on the Fortune 500 in 2002 were 17 percent of revenues. The median profit for all Fortune 500 companies that year was about 3 percent. This situation was not new, as drug industry profits had been two to four times higher than the Fortune 500 median since the 1970s.

The study also showed that prescription drug prices grew at a rate well above inflation and that drug companies raised prices often during the life of their patents.

Profit Maximization by Monopolies

KEY CONCEPTS

Although a monopoly firm is the only supplier in its market, the firm cannot charge any price it wishes. A monopolist still faces a downward-sloping demand curve. In other words, the monopoly will sell more at lower prices than at higher prices. The monopolist controls price by controlling supply. A monopoly produces less of a product than would be supplied in a competitive market, thereby artificially raising the equilibrium price.

It's difficult to study this process in the real world because most countries have laws to prevent monopolies. We have to look at small instances in which a company has a monopoly over one particular specialized product. Such a limited monopoly lasts only for the life of the patent or until a competitor develops a similar product.

EXAMPLE Drug Manufacturer

Pharmaceutical manufacturers offer an example of how companies with limited monopolies try to maximize their profits. On average, drug patents last for about 11 years in the United States. Drug companies try to maximize their profits during that period because when the patent expires they face competition from other manufacturers who begin marketing generic versions of the drug. A generic drug contains the same ingredients and acts in the same way as the patented drug, but it is sold at much lower prices.

"NOW HERE'S MY IDEA... WE COME UP WITH A REALLY HIGH-PRICED DRUG TO TREAT DRUG SIDE EFFECTS..."

As an example, consider the Schering-Plough company and its antihistamine Claritin. The drug was originally approved for use as a prescription medication in the United States in 1993, although it had been patented earlier. Unlike many other such drugs, Claritin did not make users drowsy. This advantage, combined with a strong marketing campaign, led Claritin to become a top seller, making as much as $3 billion in annual worldwide sales.

When the patent on Claritin expired in 2002, numerous generic equivalents entered the market. In response, Schering-Plough lowered Claritin's price and gained approval for a nonprescription form of the drug. But sales of Claritin fell to about $1 billion as consumers switched to less costly generic equivalents.

APPLICATION Applying Economic Concepts

C. Using the three characteristics of monopoly, explain what happened to the market for Claritin when its patent expired. Many other suppliers entered the market with drugs that were close substitutes for Claritin. Without the patent, access to the market was no longer restricted. Schering-Plough lost its ability to control the price.

204 Chapter 7

DIFFERENTIATING INSTRUCTION

Inclusion

Enlarge the Visual
Students with visual impairments may benefit from using an enlarged version of the cartoon on page 204. You might use the version from the eEdition available online at **ClassZone.com** or make enlarged photocopies to distribute to students. Have students work in pairs to describe what the cartoon shows and how it is related to the topic of profit maximization by monopolies.

Gifted and Talented

Compare Drug Prices
Invite students to compare prices for one category of medication (for example, cholesterol-lowering drugs).

- Have students use the Internet to find three drugs in their category and to research prices of patented and generic variations of each. Have them record their findings in a chart.
- Allow students to share their charts with the class and to lead a discussion about how drug manufacturers' technological monopolies affect prices and profits.

SECTION 2 Assessment

REVIEWING KEY CONCEPTS

1. Explain the differences between the terms in each of these pairs:
   a. *monopoly* / *cartel*
   b. *natural monopoly* / *geographic monopoly*
   c. *technological monopoly* / *government monopoly*
2. What is the relationship between economies of scale and a natural monopoly?
3. How does a patent awarded to one company act as a barrier to entry to another company wishing to enter the same market?
4. Why is a monopolist a price maker rather than a price taker?
5. Why do technological monopolies exist only for a limited time?
6. **Using Your Notes** Why is a geographic monopoly able to control the price of its product? Refer to your completed chart.

   Use the Graphic Organizer at **Interactive Review @ ClassZone.com**

	One Seller	Restricted Market	Control of Prices
Natural Monopoly			
Government Monopoly			
Technological Monopoly			
Geographic Monopoly			

CRITICAL THINKING

7. **Analyzing Causes and Effects** Companies that produce generic drugs are not required to repeat the clinical tests that the original manufacturer of the drug is required to run before the drug receives its patent. How does this fact affect the prices of generic drugs and why?
8. **Analyzing Effects** A powerful monopoly is broken up into several smaller, competing companies. What are the costs and benefits for the general public?
9. **Drawing Conclusions** In 2003, 95 percent of the households in America had access to only one cable TV company in their area. What kind of monopoly did cable TV companies have? Explain your answer.
10. **Challenge** Among the drugs to fight high cholesterol, the most effective are known as statins. The drugs are similar, but each is different enough to have its own patent. In 2005, there were seven such drugs on the market. In 2006, the patents ended for two of the drugs. What effect did this have on the entire category of statin drugs, including those whose patents were still in effect through 2006? Explain why this might be the case.

ECONOMICS IN PRACTICE

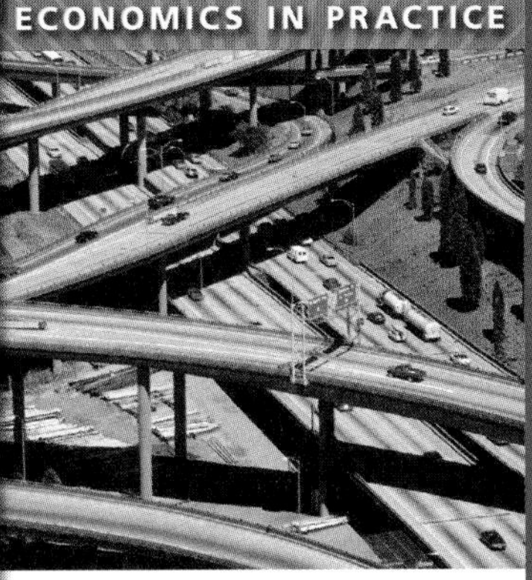

Identifying Types of Monopolies
You learned in this section that there are four types of monopolies: natural, government, technological, and geographical.

What Type? The table below lists examples of several monopolies. For each example, identify the type of monopoly. Some types have more than one example.

Example of Monopoly	Type of Monopoly
U.S. interstate highway system	
Electric utility company	
The only bank in a small town	
The company that received a patent for the Frisbee	
A city's public transportation system	
Natural gas company	

Challenge In which type of monopoly is the government least likely to be involved? Give reasons for your answer.

4 Assess & Reteach

Assess Divide the class into teams and hold a quiz show to answer the assessment questions. Award teams one point for each correct answer to the first six questions and two points for each correct answer for questions 7–10.

Unit 2 Resource Book
- Section Quiz, p. 185

Interactive Review @ ClassZone.com
- Section Quiz

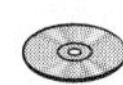

Test Generator CD-ROM
- Section Quiz

Reteach Allow students a brief time to review the section. Then, ask them to close their texts. Ask students to take turns identifying one fact that they remember from the section. When students have no more information to contribute, have them return to their texts to fill in any blanks or to verify details.

Unit 2 Resource Book
- Reteaching Activity, p. 186

Economics in Practice

What Type? government; natural; geographic; technological; government; natural

Challenge The government is least likely to be involved in a geographic monopoly, because it results from lack of competition in a region. In natural monopolies, government regulates prices; in government monopolies, government runs the business or licenses one supplier; in technological monopolies, government issues patents, which are the basis for most technological monopolies.

SECTION 2 ASSESSMENT ANSWERS

Reviewing Key Concepts

1. a. *monopoly*, p. 198; *cartel*, p. 198
   b. *natural monopoly*, p. 201; *geographic monopoly*, p. 201
   c. *technological monopoly*, p. 201; *government monopolies*, p. 201
2. Natural monopolies arise because economies of scale make it most efficient for a single company to provide a particular service.
3. A patent gives one company exclusive property rights over an invention or technology and keeps other companies from entering that market.
4. A monopolist is a price maker because the company has no competition and controls the price in the market by controlling supply.
5. because patents expire or a competing technology comes along
6. See p. 198 for an example of a completed chart. Geographic monopolies control the price of their product because there are no competitors for the product in their region.

Critical Thinking

7. Generic drug companies can charge lower prices because they do not pay the high costs of running clinical tests for new drugs.
8. Costs: tax dollars to pay the government lawyers and regulators who break up the monopoly; possible interruptions in service or supply during the transition period
   Benefits: competition should lead to lower prices and better service
9. Cable TV companies are geographic monopolies because there is generally only one cable company in a region.
10. When generic equivalents became available for some statin drugs, the prices of all statins fell because the supply of statin drugs increased when generic competitors entered the market.

Economics in Practice

See answers in side column above.

1 Plan & Prepare

Section 3 Objectives

- learn that monopolistic competition and oligopoly are market structures that fall between perfect competition and monopoly
- identify the characteristics of monopolistic competition
- describe the characteristics of oligopoly

2 Focus & Motivate

Connecting to Everyday Life Explain that this section focuses on the two market structures that are most common in the real world, monopolistic competition and oligopoly. Invite students to describe some ways that sellers compete for their business other than by offering low prices.

Taking Notes Remind students to take notes as they read by completing a compare and contrast chart on monopolistic competition and oligopoly. They can use the Graphic Organizer at **Interactive Review @ ClassZone.com**. A sample is shown below.

Monopolistic Competition	Oligopoly
Many sellers and many buyers	Few sellers and many buyers
Similar but differentiated products	standardized or differentiated products
limited control of prices	more control of prices
freedom to enter or exit market	little freedom to enter or exit market

SECTION 3

Other Market Structures

OBJECTIVES

In Section 3, you will

- learn that monopolistic competition and oligopoly are market structures that fall between perfect competition and monopoly
- identify the characteristics of monopolistic competition
- describe the characteristics of oligopoly

KEY TERMS

monopolistic competition, *p. 206*
product differentiation, *p. 206*
nonprice competition, *p. 207*
focus group, *p. 208*
oligopoly, *p. 209*
market share, *p. 209*
start-up costs, *p. 209*

TAKING NOTES

As you read Section 3, complete a chart to compare and contrast monopolistic competition and oligopoly. Use the Graphic Organizer at **Interactive Review @ ClassZone.com**

Monopolistic Competition	Oligopoly

Characteristics of Monopolistic Competition

QUICK REFERENCE

Monopolistic competition occurs when many sellers offer similar, but not standardized, products.

Product differentiation is the effort to distinguish a product from similar products.

KEY CONCEPTS

Most markets in the real world fall somewhere between the models of perfect competition and monopoly. One of the most common market structures is **monopolistic competition,** in which many sellers offer similar, but not standardized, products. The market for T-shirts printed with images or slogans is one example. The market is competitive because there are many buyers (you, your friends, and many other buyers) and many sellers (stores at the mall, online merchants, sports teams, and many other sellers). The market is monopolistic because each seller has influence over a small segment of the market with products that are not exactly like those of their competitors. Someone looking for a pink T-shirt with fuzzy kittens would not accept a black monster-truck rally T-shirt as a close substitute.

Product differentiation and nonprice competition are the distinguishing features of monopolistic competition. **Product differentiation** is the attempt to distinguish a product from similar products. Sometimes, the effort focuses on substantial differences between products, such as vehicle gas mileage ratings.

SECTION 3 PROGRAM RESOURCES

ON LEVEL

Lesson Plans

- Core, p. 24

Unit 2 Resource Book

- Reading Study Guide, pp. 187–188
- Economic Skills and Problem Solving Activity, pp. 207–208
- Section Quiz, p. 195

STRUGGLING READERS

Unit 2 Resource Book

- Reading Study Guide with Additional Support, pp. 189–191
- Reteaching Activity, p. 196

ENGLISH LEARNERS

Unit 2 Resource Book

- Reading Study Guide with Additional Support (Spanish), pp. 192–194

INCLUSION

Lesson Plans

- Modified for Inclusion, p. 24

GIFTED AND TALENTED

Unit 2 Resource Book

- Case Study Resources: Innovation Continues to Drive Competition, pp. 211–212

TECHNOLOGY

eEdition DVD-ROM

eEdition Online

Power Presentation DVD-ROM

Economics Concepts Transparencies

- CT24 How Monopolistic Competition and Oligopoly Differ

Daily Test Practice Transparencies, TT24

ClassZone.com

But companies also try to differentiate their products when there are few real differences between products. For example, a battery company might spend millions of dollars on advertising to convince consumers that their batteries last longer than other batteries—even though the real difference in longevity may be minimal.

Another way companies in monopolistic competitive markets try to gain business is through nonprice competition. **Nonprice competition** means using factors other than low price—such as style, service, advertising, or giveaways—to try to convince customers to buy one product rather than another. If you've ever decided to eat at a particular fast food restaurant just to get the cool gizmo it's giving away, you have participated in nonprice competition.

QUICK REFERENCE

Nonprice competition occurs when producers use factors other than low price to try to convince customers to buy their products.

Monopolistic competition has four major characteristics: many buyers for many sellers, similar but differentiated products, limited lasting control over prices, and freedom to enter or exit the market. Let's take a closer look at each of these characteristics by focusing on the market for hamburgers.

CHARACTERISTIC 1 Many Sellers and Many Buyers

In monopolistic competition there are many sellers and many buyers. The number of sellers is usually smaller than in a perfectly competitive market but sufficient to allow meaningful competition. Sellers act independently in choosing what kind of product to produce, how much to produce, and what price to charge.

When you want a hamburger, you have many different restaurants from which to choose. The number of restaurants assures that you have a variety of kinds of hamburgers to choose from and that prices will be competitive. No single seller has a large enough share of the market to significantly control supply or price.

However, there are probably a few restaurants that make burgers you really like and others with burgers you really don't like. The restaurants that make your favorite burgers have a sort of monopoly on your business.

Economics Update

Find an update about monopolistic competition at **ClassZone.com**

CHARACTERISTIC 2 Similar but Differentiated Products

Sellers in monopolistic competition gain their limited monopoly-like power by making a distinctive product or by convincing consumers that their product is different from the competition. Hamburger restaurants might advertise the quality of their ingredients or the way they cook the burger. They might also use distinctive packaging or some special service—a money-back guarantee if the customer is not satisfied with the meal, for example. One key method of product differentiation is the use of brand names, which

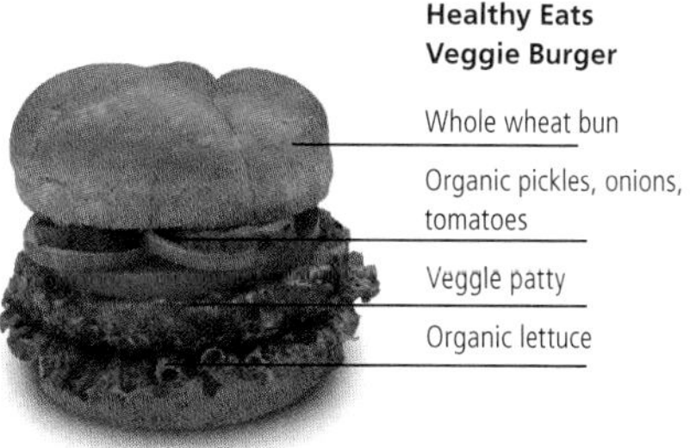

3 Teach

Characteristics of Monopolistic Competition

Discuss

- Why does increased competition give companies an incentive to improve their products? *(Possible answer: Suppliers can only control price and be successful in monopolistic competition when they have something better to offer consumers.)*

Presentation Options

Review the characteristics of monopolistic competition by using the following presentation options:

Power Presentations DVD-ROM
Using the Display Tool, you can highlight the major features of monopolistic competition.

Economics Concepts Transparencies
- CT24 How Monopolistic Competition and Oligopoly Differ

Economics Update

At **ClassZone.com,** students will see updated information on monopolistic competition.

LEVELED ACTIVITY

Exploring Monopolistic Competition

Time 45 Minutes 

Objective Students will demonstrate an understanding of how different businesses exhibit the characteristics of monopolistic competition.

Basic

Choose a category of business in your community such as restaurants, clothing stores, or hair salons. Study the yellow pages to discover how many sellers are in that category. Explain how these businesses show the characteristics of monopolistic competition. Present your information in a graphic organizer.

On Level

Choose a type of small business you would like to start. Study the yellow pages or local media to see what the competition is like. Decide how you would differentiate your business from similar businesses in your market. Create a brochure describing your business and what makes it different from others.

Challenge

Choose a category of business in your community that contains locally-owned firms as well as large chains. Analyze how these businesses compete. Consider the benefits to consumers of each type of business. Prepare an oral report on how well this category exhibits the characteristics of monopolistic competition.

More About . . .

Small Businesses

U.S. Census data show that there were 23.3 million businesses in 2002. Of these, 17.6 million had no employees—they were one-person businesses. Only 17,000 of the 5.7 million firms with employees had more than 500 employees. Therefore, 99.9 percent of all businesses were relatively small.

The Small Business Administration estimated that in 2005 there were about 671,800 new firms with employees and about 544,800 business closures. About two-thirds of new businesses last for at least two years, and over two-fifths last for at least four years.

encourage consumer loyalty by associating certain desirable qualities with a particular brand of hamburger. Producers use advertising to inform consumers about product differences and to persuade them to choose their offering.

How do hamburger restaurants decide how to differentiate their products? They conduct market research, the gathering and evaluation of information about consumer preferences for goods and services. For local restaurants, market research may be limited to listening to their customers' praise or complaints and paying attention to what competing restaurants offer.

QUICK REFERENCE

A **focus group** is a moderated discussion with small groups of consumers.

The large chain restaurants can afford to use more sophisticated research techniques to gain information about consumers' lifestyles and product preferences. One technique is the **focus group**—a moderated discussion with small groups of consumers. Another market research technique is the survey, in which a large number of consumers are polled, one by one, on their opinions. The results of market research help the restaurants differentiate their hamburgers and attract more customers.

CHARACTERISTIC 3 Limited Control of Prices

Product differentiation gives producers limited control of price. Hamburger restaurants charge different prices for their product depending on how they want to appeal to customers. The price of some hamburgers is set as low as possible to appeal to parents of younger eaters or to those on tight budgets. Prices for name-brand hamburgers or burgers with better quality ingredients may be set slightly higher. If consumers perceive that the differences are important enough, they will pay the extra price to get the hamburger they want.

Yet producers in monopolistic competition also know that there are many close substitutes for their product. They understand the factors that affect demand and recognize that consumers will switch to a substitute if the price goes too high.

CHARACTERISTIC 4 Freedom to Enter or Exit Market

There are generally no huge barriers to entry in monopolistically competitive markets. It does not require a large amount of capital for someone to open a hamburger stand, for example. When firms earn a profit in the hamburger market, other firms will enter and increase competition. Increased competition forces firms to continue to find ways to differentiate their products. The competition can be especially intense for small businesses facing much larger competitors.

Some firms will not be able to compete and will start to take losses. This is the signal that it is time for those firms to exit the market. Leaving the restaurant market is relatively easy. The owners sell off the cooking equipment, tables, and other supplies at a discount. If their finances are solid, they may then look for another market where profits might be made.

Ease of Entry and Exit
In monopolistic competition, sellers may enter and exit the market freely.

APPLICATION Applying Economic Concepts

A. Think about an item of clothing that you purchased recently. How did the seller differentiate the product? List several ways, then compare lists with a classmate.
Student lists should include things such as physical characteristics, brand, store where the item was purchased, and advertising campaigns.

DIFFERENTIATING INSTRUCTION

Struggling Readers

Compare and Contrast

Help students understand monopolistic competition by comparing it to monopoly and perfect competition.

- Have pairs of students create Venn diagrams to show the similarities and differences of monopolistic competition and the other two market structures.
- Invite volunteers to share one of their diagrams with the class. Discuss what characteristics monopolistic competition shares with each of the other market structures and what makes it different.

English Learners

Build Complex Words

Have students create verbal building blocks to help them understand complex words.

- Tell pairs to write these word parts on index cards: *mono-, oligo-, -poly, -ies, -ist,- ic, -ally*.
- Invite pairs to build different words by putting the parts together. Point out that an *i* replaces the *y* at the end of *–poly* when forming new words.
- Ask students to make a list of the words they formed. Call on volunteers to use the words in a sentence.

Characteristics of an Oligopoly

KEY CONCEPTS

Oligopoly (OL-ih-GOP-ah-lee), a market structure in which only a few sellers offer a similar product, is less competitive than monopolistic competition. In an oligopoly, a few large firms have a large **market share**—percent of total sales in a market—and dominate the market. For example, if you want to see a movie in a theater, chances are the movie will have been made by one of just a few major studios. What's more, the theater you go to is probably part of one of just a few major theater chains. Both the market for film production and the market for movie theaters are oligopolies.

There are few firms in an oligopoly because of high **start-up costs**—the expenses that a new business must pay to enter a market and begin selling to consumers. Making a movie can be expensive, especially if you want to make one that can compete with what the major studios produce. And getting it into theaters across the country requires a huge network of promoters and distributors—and even more money.

An oligopoly has four major characteristics. There are few sellers but many buyers. In industrial markets, sellers offer standardized products, but in consumer markets, they offer differentiated products. The few sellers have more power to control prices than in monopolistic competition, but to enter or exit the market is difficult.

QUICK REFERENCE

Oligopoly is a market structure in which only a few sellers offer a similar product.

Market share is a company's percent of total sales in a market.

Start-up costs are the expenses that a new business faces when it enters a market.

CHARACTERISTIC 1 Few Sellers and Many Buyers

In an oligopoly, a few firms dominate an entire market. There is not a single supplier as in a monopoly, but there are fewer firms than in monopolistic competition. These few firms produce a large part of the total product in the market. Economists consider an industry to be an oligopoly if the four largest firms control at least 40 percent of the market. About half of the manufacturing industries in the United States are oligopolistic.

The breakfast cereal industry in the United States is dominated by four large firms that control about 80 percent of the market. Your favorite cereal is probably made by one of the big four manufacturers. Although they offer many varieties of cereals, there is less competition than there would be if each variety were produced by a different, smaller manufacturer.

The Breakfast Cereal Industry
Just a few large companies produce the majority of breakfast cereals available.

CHARACTERISTIC 2 Standardized or Differentiated Products

Depending on the market, an oligopolist may sell either standardized or differentiated products. Many industrial products are standardized, and a few large firms control these markets. Examples include the markets for steel, aluminum, and flat glass. When products are standardized, firms may try to differentiate themselves based on brand name, service, or location.

Breakfast cereals, soft drinks, and many other consumer goods are examples of differentiated products sold by oligopolies. Oligopolists market differentiated prod-

Characteristics of an Oligopoly

Discuss

- Is the number of brands in a product category a good indication of how competitive that market is? Why or why not? *(no, because a single company might produce products under several different brands)*
- What are some barriers to entry that exist in an oligopoly? *(Possible response: high start-up costs, established brands, large advertising budgets, or other marketing resources)*

Technomics

Industry Concentration Data
Information on the concentration of output in different industries is part of the U.S. Census Bureau's Economic Census, which is conducted every five years (years ending in 2 and 7). Links to information from the three most recent censuses is available online.

Concentration data is provided for 17 different industries, based on the North American Industry Classification System. Reports show the percentage of output from the largest 4, 8, 20, and 50 companies in each category.

SMALL GROUP ACTIVITY

Studying an Oligopoly

Time 60 Minutes ●

Task Gather information on a major breakfast cereal company and prepare an oral report with visuals.

Materials Needed paper, markers, computer with Internet access

Activity

- Divide students into four groups and assign each group one of the four major breakfast cereal companies to research: Kellogg's, General-Mills, Post, or Quaker.
- Ask students to find information about their company's market share, major brands, and ways it tries to differentiate its products.
- Encourage students to go beyond company Web sites to include information from encyclopedias, trade magazines, or other news sources.
- Allow each group to give an oral report on its company. Discuss how oligopoly limits competition and affects consumers.

Rubric

	Understanding of Oligopoly	Presentation of Information
4	excellent	clear and complete
3	good	accurate
2	fair	sometimes clear
1	poor	sketchy

At **ClassZone.com,** students will see updated information about oligopolies.

More About . . .

The Breakfast Cereal Industry
Americans buy over 2.5 billion packages of breakfast cereal each year. That adds up to about 10 pounds of breakfast cereal per person each year. The breakfast cereal industry sold almost $9 billion worth of cereal in 2005.

However, sales of breakfast cereals declined by about 7 percent from 2000 to 2005. Analysts pointed to the shift to low-carbohydrate diets as an explanation for the decline. In response, the industry created more cereals with low or medium sugar content.

Another trend over the same period was that sales of hot cereals increased as sales of cold cereals fell. Manufacturers followed the trend, creating a wider variety of hot cereals.

ucts using marketing strategies similar to those used in monopolistic competition. They use surveys, focus groups, and other market research techniques to find out what you like. The companies then create brand-name products that can be marketed across the country or around the world.

CHARACTERISTIC 3 More Control of Prices

Economics Update
Find an update about oligopolies at **ClassZone.com**

Because there are few sellers in an oligopoly, each one has more control over product price than in a monopolistically competitive market. For example, each breakfast cereal manufacturer has a large enough share of the market that decisions it makes about supply and price affect the market as a whole. Because of this, a seller in an oligopoly is not as independent as a seller in monopolistic competition. A decision made by one seller may cause the other sellers to respond in some way.

For example, if one of the leading breakfast cereal manufacturers lowers its prices, the other manufacturers will probably also lower prices rather than lose customers to the competition. Therefore, no firm is likely to gain market share based on price, and all risk losing profits. But if one manufacturer decides to raise prices, the others may not follow suit, in order to take customers and gain market share. Consequently, firms in an oligopoly try to anticipate how their competitors will respond to their actions before they make decisions on price, output, or marketing.

CHARACTERISTIC 4 Little Freedom to Enter or Exit Market

Start-up costs for a new company in an oligopolistic market can be extremely high. Entering the breakfast cereal industry on a small scale is not very expensive—but the profits are low too. The factories, warehouses, and other infrastructure needed to compete against the major manufacturers require large amounts of funds. In addition, existing manufacturers may hold patents that act as further barriers to entry.

Firms in an oligopoly have established brands and plentiful resources that make it difficult for new firms to enter the market successfully. For example, breakfast cereal manufacturers have agreements with grocery stores that guarantee them the best shelf space. Existing manufacturers also have economies of scale that help them to keep their expenses low. Smaller firms, with smaller operations, lack the economies of scale.

High Start-up Costs
New firms may not have the funds to construct large factories.

However, all of the investments by firms in an oligopoly make it difficult for them to exit the market. When a major breakfast cereal manufacturer begins losing money, its operations are too vast and complex to sell and reinvest easily, as a small business might. It must trim its operations and work to stimulate demand for its product.

APPLICATION Categorizing Information

B. Which of these products produced by oligopolies are standardized and which are differentiated: automobiles, cement, copper, sporting goods, tires?
Standardized: cement, copper; differentiated: automobiles, sporting goods, tires.

DIFFERENTIATING INSTRUCTION

Inclusion

Draw a Competitive Continuum
Help students create a continuum to show how the four market structures have different degrees of competition.

- Draw a line on the board. Label one end "least competitive" and the other "most competitive."
- Have a volunteer write the four market structures along the line in order of competitiveness.
- Discuss with the class why each successive market structure is more competitive than the one before.

Gifted and Talented

Investigate Market Concentration
Invite students to use the latest Economic Census to investigate concentration data in a particular industry category. (Data is available at the Census Bureau's Web site.)

- Encourage students to create charts that identify segments of the industry that reflect oligopoly and others that reflect monopolistic competition.
- Allow students to choose one industry segment that exemplifies oligopoly and to find out more about the companies that dominate that market.

Comparing Market Structures

KEY CONCEPTS

Each of the four market structures has different benefits and problems. And each type creates a different balance of power—namely, the power to influence prices—between producers and consumers.

Consumers get the most value in markets that approach perfect competition. No actual markets are perfectly competitive, but in those that come close, prices are set primarily by supply and demand. However, such markets usually deal in a standardized product, so consumers have little choice other than the best price.

In monopolistic competition, consumers continue to benefit from companies competing for their business. But businesses gain some control over prices, so they are more likely to earn a profit. Opening a business in such a market is usually relatively affordable, which is another benefit for businesses.

In markets dominated by oligopolies, consumer choices may be more limited than in more competitive markets. Businesses in such markets gain more control of price, making it easier for them to make a profit. However, the cost of doing business in such a market is high.

A market ruled by a monopoly is very favorable for the business that holds the monopoly. It faces little or no competition from other companies. And monopoly gives consumers the least influence over prices. They decide only whether they are willing to buy the product at the price set by the monopolist.

FIGURE 7.5 Comparing Market Structures

	Number of Sellers	Type of Product	Sellers' Control over Prices	Barriers to Enter or Exit Market
Perfect Competition	Many	Standardized	None	Few
Monopolistic Competition	Many	Similar but differentiated	Limited	Few
Oligopoly	Few	Standardized for industry; differentiated for consumers	Some	Many
Monopoly	One	Standardized, but no close substitutes	Significant	Very many—market restricted or regulated

ANALYZE CHARTS

1. If you were starting a business, which market structures would make it easiest for you to enter the market?
2. Which market structures offer the highest potential profits? Why?

APPLICATION Drawing Conclusions

C. What difference does it make to consumers whether a market is ruled by monopolistic competition or by an oligopoly?
Monopolistic competition—wider variety of product choices and more control over prices. Oligopoly—more limited product choices and higher prices.

3 Teach

Comparing Market Structures

Discuss

- What is the main drawback for consumers in a market that approaches perfect competition? *(Consumers have less choice because products are standardized.)*
- Which market structure seems to offer the best balance of benefits to producers and consumers? *(Possible answer: monopolistic competition, because it allows producers to make more profit while giving consumers the benefits of competition and choice)*

Analyze Charts Figure 7.5

Point out that the table starts with the most competitive market structure, *perfect competition*, and ends with the least competitive, *monopoly*. Ask students to look at the table and explain why perfect competition provides consumers with the best prices. *(because prices are set purely by supply and demand)*

Answers

1. *perfect competition and monopolistic competition, because they have the lowest barriers to entry*
2. *oligopoly and monopoly, because they have the most control over prices*

CLASS ACTIVITY

Modeling Market Structures

Time 20 Minutes

Task Create living models of the four market structures and discuss their characteristics.

Activity

- Divide the class into two groups. One group represents buyers and one represents sellers. Invite volunteers from each group to describe the characteristics of perfect competition that apply to their group.
- Ask each group how their characteristics would change under monopolistic competition.
- Allow students to regroup themselves to show oligopoly and then monopoly. Discuss the characteristics of each.
- Make sure students understand the benefits and problems of each market structure as they affect buyers and sellers. Also, have them consider what would happen if there were only a few buyers in each market structure.

Rubric

	Understanding of Market Structures	Presentation of Information
4	excellent	clear and complete
3	good	accurate
2	fair	sometimes clear
1	poor	sketchy

Joan Robinson

More About . . .

Joan Robinson

Joan Maurice was born in Surrey, England, and studied economics at Girton College at Cambridge University. After graduation in 1925, she married the economist Austin Robinson and spent three years with him in India.

Joan Robinson spent her career as an academic economist at Cambridge University, 1928–1971. She did not become a full professor until 1965, probably because of her gender. Many expected her to win the Nobel Prize in 1975, but she was passed over for the honor, possibly because she was too vocal in her support for the Chinese Cultural Revolution. In 1979, she became the first woman fellow at Kings College, Cambridge.

More About . . .

Joan Robinson's Ideas

Throughout her career, Joan Robinson wrote on many different topics. Her book *The Economics of Imperfect Competition* launched what was called the monopolistic competition revolution. Yet she quickly moved on to other areas. She was part of a group of young economists at Cambridge that focused on the ideas in John Maynard Keynes's 1936 book *The General Theory* (see page 456). Robinson wrote a number of works that helped clarify Keynes's ideas. She was also one of the first to seriously study Marx's economic theories. Many consider her 1956 book *The Accumulation of Capital* to be her most important. She continued to publish until she died.

Economics Update

At **ClassZone.com,** students will see an article about Joan Robinson.

ECONOMICS PACESETTER

Joan Robinson: Challenging Established Ideas

In this section, you learned about monopolistic competition and oligopoly. British economist Joan Robinson was one of the first to write about these market structures. As strange as it may seem to us now, most economists before 1930 described market competition only in terms of the extremes of perfect competition and monopoly.

FAST FACTS

Joan Robinson

Career: Economics professor, Cambridge University

Born: October 31, 1903

Died: August 5, 1983

Major Accomplishment: Developed theory of imperfect competition

Books: *The Economics of Imperfect Competition* (1933), *The Accumulation of Capital* (1956), *Economic Philosophy* (1963), *Introduction to Modern Economics* (1973)

Famous Quotation: *"It is the business of economists, not to tell us what to do, but show why what we are doing anyway is in accord with proper principles."*

Explaining Real-World Competition

In 1933, Joan Robinson challenged the prevailing ideas about competition. Her first major book, *The Economics of Imperfect Competition,* described market structures that existed between monopoly and perfect competition. Robinson's work appeared shortly after Harvard economist Edward Chamberlin published his book *Theory of Monopolistic Competition.* The two economists had developed their ideas independently.

Robinson and Chamberlin described the type of competition that exists among firms with differentiated products. Such firms gain more control over the price of their product, but their control is limited by the amount of competition. They also described the nature of oligopoly and of monopsony, a market structure in which there are many sellers but only one large buyer.

Robinson continued to contribute important ideas throughout her long career in economics. Her theory of imperfect competition remains a key element of the field of microeconomics today. Economists recognized that Robinson's theory more accurately reflected modern market economies in which firms compete through product differentiation and advertising and in which many industries are controlled by oligopolies.

Joan Robinson developed the theory of imperfect competition.

Economics Update

Learn more about Joan Robinson at **ClassZone.com**

APPLICATION Making Inferences

D. Why do you think Joan Robinson chose the term *imperfect competition* to describe the nature of most real-world markets?
She wanted to emphasize that competition in the real world did not match the model of perfect competition.

212 Chapter 7

DIFFERENTIATING INSTRUCTION

Struggling Readers

Review Prior Knowledge

Help students understand how Joan Robinson's ideas changed economics.

- Write *monopoly* and *perfect competition* on the board. Ask volunteers to define them. Explain that this is how economists used to understand markets.
- Then write *imperfect competition, monopolistic competition, oligopoly,* and *product differentiation* on the board. Ask students to explain each and describe how they are related. Explain that Robinson introduced these concepts.

English Learners

Analyze Word Parts

Help students analyze word parts to compare the meanings of *monopoly* and *monopsony.*

- Write *monopoly* on the board. Invite a volunteer to give the meaning.
- Then write *monopsony.* Ask a volunteer to circle the part of the word that is the same in each (*mono*) and say what she or he thinks it means (*one*).
- Direct students to find the word *monopsony* on page 212 and see how its meaning contrasts to *monopoly.*

SECTION 3 Assessment

Online Quiz
ClassZone.com

REVIEWING KEY CONCEPTS

1. Explain the relationship between the terms in each of these pairs:
   a. *product differentiation* / *nonprice competition*
   b. *focus group* / *market share*
   c. *oligopoly* / *start-up costs*
2. How is monopolistic competition similar to perfect competition and how is it similar to monopoly?
3. Describe some of the techniques sellers use to differentiate their products.
4. Why are standardized products sometimes found in oligopoly but not in monopolistic competition?
5. Is it easier for a new firm to enter the market under monopolistic competition or oligopoly? Why?
6. **Using Your Notes** How does the number of sellers compare in monopolistic competition and oligopoly? Refer to your completed chart.

Monopolistic Competition	Oligopoly

Use the Graphic Organizer at **Interactive Review @ ClassZone.com**

CRITICAL THINKING

7. **Contrasting Economic Information** What makes the market for wheat different from the markets for products made from wheat, such as bread, cereal, and pasta?
8. **Applying Economic Concepts** In 2005, a major U.S. automaker announced a new discount plan for its cars for the month of June. It offered consumers the same price that its employees paid for new cars. When the automaker announced in early July that it was extending the plan for another month, the other two major U.S. automakers announced similar plans. What market structure is exhibited in this story and what specific characteristics of that market structure does it demonstrate?
9. **Analyzing Effects** Blue jeans are produced under monopolistic competition, so their prices are higher than if they were produced under perfect competition. Do the positive effects for consumers of blue jeans justify the higher prices? Why or why not?
10. **Challenge** Why do manufacturers of athletic shoes spend money to sign up professional athletes to wear and promote their shoes rather than differentiating their products strictly on the basis of physical characteristics such as design and comfort?

ECONOMICS IN PRACTICE

Perfect competition or monopoly?

The Impact of Market Structure Each of the four market structures carries different consequences for businesses and consumers. Imagine what would happen if there were only one type of market structure. Use Figure 7.5 on page 211 as a guide as you do this exercise.

a. What would your town look like if every market was perfectly competitive? What would happen to your consumer choices?
b. What would happen if every market was ruled by monopolistic competition?
c. What would the town look like if oligopolies controlled every market?
d. What if every market in your town was ruled by a monopoly? How could you tell the difference between situation A and D?

Challenge Now think about what your town actually looks like. What types of market structures are most prevalent? Are you satisfied with the mix of market structures, or do you think some markets would be better served by different structures?

4 Assess & Reteach

Assess Have students write out their answers for questions 2–9. Then have them exchange papers and correct each other's work.

Unit 2 Resource Book
- Section Quiz, p. 195

Interactive Review @ ClassZone.com
- Section Quiz

Test Generator CD-ROM
- Section Quiz

Reteach Call on volunteers to use the information in Figure 7.5 to describe each of the four market structures. Invite other class members to contribute additional information.

Unit 2 Resource Book
- Reteaching Activity, p. 196

Economics in Practice

a. many suppliers for every product; all products generic and the same price

b. many suppliers for every product; wide variety of products; no two stores would be the same; prices would be competitive

c. nothing but chain stores; a variety of products; prices would be higher

d. only one supplier for every product or service; prices much higher; all of the products the same, as in situation A, but fewer sellers and higher prices.

Challenge In most towns, oligopolies are the dominant market structure. Answers will vary to the opinion questions.

SECTION 3 ASSESSMENT ANSWERS

Reviewing Key Concepts

1. a. *product differentiation*, p. 206; *nonprice competition*, p. 207
   b. *focus group*, p. 208; *market share*, p. 209
   c. *oligopoly*, p. 209; *start-up costs*, p. 209
2. In perfect competition and monopolistic competition, there are many buyers and sellers and freedom to enter or exit the market. In perfect competition and monopoly, sellers have control over the price of their particular product, although competition limits that control.
3. advertising, packaging, services, guarantees, brand names
4. In industrial oligopolies, sellers compete on service or other non-product related grounds.
5. monopolistic competition, because there are usually high start-up costs or other barriers to entry in an oligopoly
6. See page 206 for an example of a completed chart. There are many sellers in monopolistic competition and few sellers in an oligopoly.

Critical Thinking

7. In the wheat market, there is no product differentiation and producers are price takers. The markets for bread, cereal, and pasta have product differentiation, and producers have some control over price.
8. The three automakers represent an oligopoly. Their actions show how when one firm changes prices, others choose to follow its lead rather than risk losing market share based on price.
9. Possible answers: Yes, because different people have different tastes in jeans, so it is better to have more choices. No, the differences between jeans do not justify the higher prices.
10. Possible answer: Using celebrities associates the athlete's particular style or personality with the shoes. Many consumers are more likely to buy a shoe because of an endorsement than because of physical characteristics.

Economics in Practice

See answers in side column above.

1 Plan & Prepare

Section 4 Objectives

- explain how government acts to prevent monopolies
- analyze the effects of anti-competitive business practices
- describe how government acts to protect consumers
- discuss why some industries have been deregulated and the results of that deregulation

2 Focus & Motivate

Connecting to Everyday Life Explain that this section focuses on how the government helps to promote competition and to protect consumers. Encourage students to brainstorm examples from their own experience of ways the government protects consumers.

Taking Notes Remind students to take notes as they read by completing a hierarchy diagram. They can use the Graphic Organizer at **Interactive Review @ ClassZone.com**. A sample is shown below.

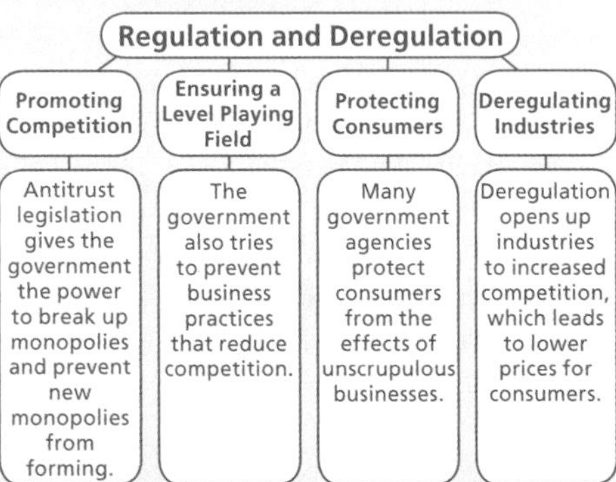

Regulation and Deregulation
Promoting Competition
Ensuring a Level Playing Field
Protecting Consumers
Deregulating Industries
Antitrust legislation gives the government the power to break up monopolies and prevent new monopolies from forming.
The government also tries to prevent business practices that reduce competition.
Many government agencies protect consumers from the effects of unscrupulous businesses.
Deregulation opens up industries to increased competition, which leads to lower prices for consumers.

SECTION 4

Regulation and Deregulation Today

OBJECTIVES

In Section 4, you will

- explain how government acts to prevent monopolies
- analyze the effects of anti-competitive business practices
- describe how government acts to protect consumers
- discuss why some industries have been deregulated and the results of that deregulation

KEY TERMS

regulation, *p. 214*
antitrust legislation, *p. 214*
trust, *p. 214*
merger, *p. 214*
price fixing, *p. 216*
market allocation, *p. 216*
predatory pricing, *p. 216*
cease and desist order, *p. 217*
public disclosure, *p. 217*
deregulation, *p. 218*

TAKING NOTES

As you read Section 4, complete a hierarchy diagram to track main ideas and supporting details. Use the Graphic Organizer at **Interactive Review@ ClassZone.com**

Regulation and Deregulation
Promoting Competition
details

Promoting Competition

QUICK REFERENCE

Regulation is a set of rules or laws designed to control business behavior.

Antitrust legislation defines monopolies and gives government the power to control them.

A **trust** is a group of firms combined in order to reduce competition in an industry.

A **merger** is the joining of two firms to form a single firm.

KEY CONCEPTS

The forces of the marketplace generally keep businesses competitive with one another and attentive to consumer welfare. But sometimes the government uses **regulation**—controlling business behavior through a set of rules or laws—to promote competition and protect consumers. The most important laws that promote competition are collectively called **antitrust legislation**, laws that define monopolies and give government the power to control them and break them up. A **trust** is a group of firms combined for the purpose of reducing competition in an industry. (A trust is similar to a cartel, which you learned about in Section 2.) To keep trusts from forming, the government regulates business mergers. A **merger** is when one company combines with or purchases another to form a single firm.

Standard Oil Company This cartoon dramatizes how Standard Oil controlled the oil industry.

Origins of Antitrust Legislation

During the late 1800s, a few large trusts, such as Standard Oil, dominated the oil, steel, and railroad industries in the United States. The U.S. government became concerned that these combinations would use their power to control prices and output. As a result, in 1890, the government passed the Sherman

SECTION 4 PROGRAM RESOURCES

ON LEVEL

Lesson Plans
- Core, p. 25

Unit 2 Resource Book
- Reading Study Guide, pp. 197–198
- Economic Simulations, pp. 213–214
- Section Quiz, p. 205

STRUGGLING READERS

Unit 2 Resource Book
- Reading Study Guide with Additional Support, pp. 199–201
- Reteaching Activity, p. 206

ENGLISH LEARNERS

Unit 2 Resource Book
- Reading Study Guide with Additional Support (Spanish), pp. 202–204

INCLUSION

Lesson Plans
- Modified for Inclusion, p. 25

GIFTED AND TALENTED

Unit 2 Resource Book
- Readings in Free Enterprise: Will Deregulation Ultimately Lead to Big Box Banks?, pp. 209–210
- Case Study Resources: Innovation Continues to Drive Competition, pp. 211–212

NCEE Student Activities
- Regulation and Deregulation, pp. 25–28

TECHNOLOGY

eEdition DVD-ROM

eEdition Online

Power Presentation DVD-ROM

Economics Concepts Transparencies
- CT25 A Brief History of Standard Oil Company

Daily Test Practice Transparencies, TT25

ClassZone.com

Antitrust Act. This gave government the power to control monopolies and to regulate business practices that might reduce competition. Over time, other laws strengthened the government's ability to regulate business and to encourage competition.

To understand why government officials pushed for antitrust laws, consider one of the trusts that developed in the late 1800s—the Standard Oil Company. By merging with other companies and eliminating competitors, Standard Oil gained control of about 90 percent of the U.S. oil industry. Such a huge holding, government officials contended, gave Standard Oil the ability to set production levels and prices. In 1911, the U.S. government won a court case under the Sherman Antitrust Act that required the breakup of the trust. In order to increase competition, Standard Oil was forced to relinquish control of 33 companies that had once been part of the trust.

Antitrust Legislation Today

At various times, the U.S. government has used antitrust legislation to break up large companies that attempt to maintain their market power through restraint of competition. The government might allow a large dominant firm to remain intact because it is the most efficient producer. Or it might order that the company change its business practices to allow other firms to compete more easily.

The responsibility for enforcing antitrust legislation is shared by the Federal Trade Commission (FTC) and the Department of Justice. A major focus of their work is the assessment of mergers. The government tends to support mergers that might benefit consumers. For example, larger firms are often able to operate more efficiently, and lower operating costs may lead to lower prices for consumers. On the other hand, the government tends to block mergers that lead to greater market concentration in the hands of a few firms. A merger that makes it more difficult for new firms to enter a market will also be looked upon with concern.

To evaluate a potential merger, the government looks at how a particular market is defined. A company that is proposing a merger would try to define its market as broadly as possible, in order to make its control of the market seem smaller. For example, a soft drink producer might claim that its market competition includes all beverages, such as water, tea, coffee, and juice.

To determine whether the merger will increase the concentration in the market and decrease competition, the government considers the market share of the firms before and after the proposed merger. Government regulators also look at whether the merger allows a firm to eliminate possible competitors. If this analysis shows that a merger will reduce competition and more than likely lead to higher prices for consumers, the regulators will deny the companies' effort to merge.

The Federal Trade Commission (FTC)
In 2004, Deborah Platt Majoras became head of the FTC, an agency that enforces antitrust laws.

APPLICATION Drawing Conclusions

A. Which of these mergers would the government be more likely to approve and why: two airlines that serve different cities or two banks in a small town?
Two airlines—no direct competition, therefore unlikely to increase prices for consumers. Bank merger would decrease competition in the town.

3 Teach

Promoting Competition

Discuss

- Why did the government pass the Sherman Antitrust Act? *(because it was concerned that trusts controlled such a large part of their market that they could control output and prices)*
- Which kinds of mergers will the government tend to support and which will it oppose? *(support: mergers that lead to economies of scale and lower prices; oppose: mergers that decrease competition)*

International Economics

Competition Law
Most other countries use the term *competition law* rather than *antitrust law*. Prior to World War II, Norway was the only European country that had such a law, and most countries actually supported cartels. The European Union now enforces competition law among its members. Japan enacted such reforms in the mid-1990s.

In 2001, 14 antitrust agencies throughout the world established the International Competition Network (ICN). The purpose of this organization is to promote a more consistent antitrust policy in the context of a global economy. The ICN enables antitrust agencies from many countries to share information and best practices.

LEVELED ACTIVITY

Reporting on Government Agencies

Time 45 Minutes

Objective Students will demonstrate an understanding of how government action promotes competition and protects consumers.

Basic

Use the information on pages 214–218 to create a time line showing how the government's role in promoting competition and protecting consumers has evolved over time. Use the time line to present an oral report summarizing the government's efforts. Explain how these efforts benefit consumers.

On Level

Choose one of the agencies listed in Figure 7.6 on page 217. Use Internet or library resources to find out more about the agency, including its purpose, structure, and examples of some of its recent actions. Evaluate the agency's role in protecting consumers. Write a short report on the agency to share with the class.

Challenge

Research a recent antitrust case or example of a major merger reviewed by the Department of Justice and the Federal Trade Commission. Summarize the important issues involved and describe the outcome. Prepare a news report that includes analysis of how the government's decision affects producers and consumers.

Ensuring a Level Playing Field

Discuss

- Why does the government care whether businesses work together to set prices? *(Price fixing hurts consumers, who pay more than they otherwise would.)*
- What is the main difference between the FTC and the other government agencies that protect consumers? *(The FTC focuses on promoting competition and preventing unfair business practices in general; the other agencies regulate one or more industries.)*

More About . . .

Predatory Pricing

The FTC has not won a case against a company for predatory pricing since 1993. At that time, the Supreme Court ruled that plaintiffs must show that the pricing affects competition in the whole market and that prices are below costs.

The purpose of antitrust laws is to protect consumers, and consumers generally benefit from extremely competitive pricing. Furthermore, critics argue that it is irrational for a company to cut prices so that it loses money in the short term. They cite a high risk that the firm will not be able to recoup those losses even in the long run because new competitors have an incentive to enter the market.

Economics Update

At **ClassZone.com,** students will see updated information about unfair business practices.

Ensuring a Level Playing Field

KEY CONCEPTS

In addition to evaluating mergers, the government also tries to make sure that businesses do not engage in practices that would reduce competition. As you have learned, competition enables the market economy to work effectively. When businesses take steps that counteract the effects of competition, prices go up and supplies go down. In the United States, laws prohibit most of these practices. The FTC and the Department of Justice enforce these laws.

Prohibiting Unfair Business Practices

QUICK REFERENCE

Price fixing occurs when businesses agree to set prices for competing products.

Market allocation occurs when competing businesses divide a market amongst themselves.

Predatory pricing occurs when businesses set prices below cost for a time to drive competitors out of a market.

Businesses that seek to counteract market forces can use a variety of methods. One is **price fixing**, which occurs when businesses work together to set the prices of competing products. A related technique is when competing businesses agree to restrict their output, thereby driving up prices.

For example, in the mid-1990s the five major recorded music distributors began enforcing a "minimum advertised price" for compact discs sold in the United States. As a result, CD prices remained artificially high. The FTC estimated that consumers paid about $480 million more for CDs than they would have if prices had been established by market forces. In 2000 the FTC reached an agreement with the distributors to end this anticompetitive practice.

Another way businesses seek to avoid competition is by **market allocation**, which occurs when competing businesses negotiate to divide up a market. By staying out of each other's territory, the businesses develop limited monopoly power in their own territory, allowing them to charge higher prices.

For example, in the early 1990s agribusiness conglomerate Archer Daniels Midland (ADM) conspired with companies in Japan and Korea to divide the worldwide market for lysine, an additive used in livestock feeds. Around the same time, ADM also conspired with European companies to divide the worldwide market for citric acid, an additive used in soft drinks, canned foods, and other consumer products. Both of these illicit agreements also included price fixing. In 1996, the Department of Justice charged ADM with antitrust violations in both the lysine and citric acid markets. ADM pleaded guilty and paid a $100 million fine.

Economics Update

Find an update about unfair business practices at **ClassZone.com**

Occasionally, businesses use anticompetitive methods to drive other firms out of a market. One technique used by cartels or large producers is **predatory pricing**, setting prices below cost so that smaller producers cannot afford to participate in a market. Predatory pricing can be difficult to distinguish from competitive pricing. Larger businesses are usually able to offer lower prices because they have economies of scale unavailable to smaller firms.

APPLICATION Applying Economic Concepts

B. If you owned an ice cream store, could you negotiate with other ice cream store owners to set a standard price for a scoop of ice cream? Why or why not?
No, you could not. This would be price fixing, and it would reduce competition and result in higher prices for consumers.

DIFFERENTIATING INSTRUCTION

English Learners

Understand Compound Nouns

Help students use their knowledge of everyday meanings to learn definitions of compound nouns on page 216.

- Have pairs create vocabulary lists by writing the meaning of each part of a compound noun, then put the parts together to come up with a definition. Allow students to use a dictionary.
- Have students compare their definitions with those in the text. Invite volunteers to share how everyday meanings help them understand economic meanings.

Inclusion

Discuss in a Circle

Arrange students in a circle during class discussions so students see each speaker's face. This will help students with hearing impairments follow the discussion. It will also help all students to stay focused. Establish that only one student speaks at a time and encourage all to speak clearly and distinctly. Ask a volunteer to take notes of important points and to share them with students who may have trouble following the verbal exchanges.

Protecting Consumers

KEY CONCEPTS

When the government becomes aware that a firm is engaged in behavior that is unfair to competitors or consumers, it may issue a **cease and desist order**, a ruling that requires a firm to stop an unfair business practice. The government also enforces a policy of **public disclosure**, which requires businesses to reveal product information to consumers. This protects consumers and promotes competition by giving consumers the information they need to make informed buying decisions.

QUICK REFERENCE

A **cease and desist order** requires a firm to stop an unfair business practice.

Public disclosure is a policy that requires businesses to reveal product information.

Consumer Protection Agencies

Besides enforcing laws that ensure competitive markets, the government protects consumers by regulating other aspects of business. Figure 7.6 shows some of the most important federal agencies that protect consumers. The Federal Trade Commission has primary responsibility for promoting competition and preventing unfair business practices. The Federal Communications Commission and Securities and Exchange Commission regulate specific industries. The Food and Drug Administration, Environmental Protection Agency, and Consumer Product Safety Commission protect consumers by regulating multiple industries to ensure the safety and quality of specific products and to protect consumer health.

FIGURE 7.6 Federal Consumer Protection Agencies

Agency	Created	Purpose
Food and Drug Administration (FDA)	1906	Protects consumers from unsafe foods, drugs, or cosmetics; requires truth in labeling of these products
Federal Trade Commission (FTC)	1914	Enforces antitrust laws and monitors unfair business practices, including deceptive advertising
Federal Communications Commission (FCC)	1934	Regulates the communications industry, including radio, television, cable, and telephone services
Securities and Exchange Commission (SEC)	1934	Regulates the market for stocks and bonds to protect investors
Environmental Protection Agency (EPA)	1970	Protects human health by enforcing environmental laws regarding pollution and hazardous materials
Consumer Product Safety Commission (CPSC)	1972	Sets safety standards for thousands of types of consumer products; issues recalls for unsafe products

ANALYZE TABLES

1. What's the difference between the FTC and the SEC?
2. Pick one agency, note the year it was created, and explain what might have led to its creation.

APPLICATION Making Inferences

C. Why do you think the government has decided to set up agencies to protect consumers from unsafe products?

Producers who are motivated by making profit may not always be concerned about making sure their products are safe.

Analyzing Tables: Figure 7.6

Point out that the table shows only the most important consumer protection agencies. Have students note when the first such agency, the Food and Drug Administration, was established and what areas of life it protected. *(1906; protection against unsafe foods, drugs, or cosmetics)* Ask students to name other areas of life that have come under protection during the last century. *(business practices, communications, stock market, environment, consumer products)*

Answers

1. *The FTC oversees all business, while the SEC regulates one specific industry.*
2. *Example: The Federal Trade Commission, created in 1914, might have been created as a reaction to the Standard Oil Company trust that was broken to increase competition.*

More About . . .

Food and Drug Administration

In 1906, Upton Sinclair's book about the meatpacking industry, *The Jungle*, helped lead to the passage of the Pure Food and Drug Act. The Bureau of Chemistry was responsible for enforcing the legislation. In 1930, it became the FDA.

The FDA monitors the safety of products that make up one-fourth of U.S. consumer spending. The agency inspects factories, conducts scientific product testing, and monitors new products.

INDIVIDUAL ACTIVITY

Analyzing Nutrition Facts Labels

Time 45 Minutes

Task Study information on food labels and prepare a written report.

Materials Needed food labels, paper and pens, computer with Internet access

Activity

- Ask students to study nutrition facts labels on at least two foods they eat regularly. They might compare varieties of foods from the same category, such as different types of cereal or juice. Or they might compare products that represent a choice, such as tortilla chips vs. potato chips.
- Direct students to use the FDA Web site or other sources to help them interpret the labels.
- Have students write one-page reports on what they learned from this experience.
- Invite volunteers to share their reports with the class. Discuss how government regulations help to protect consumers.

Rubric

	Understanding of Food Labels	Presentation of Information
4	excellent	clear and complete
3	good	accurate
2	fair	sometimes clear
1	poor	sketchy

Deregulating Industries

Discuss

- Why did the government keep safety regulations in place when it deregulated the airlines? *(to make sure that airlines did not sacrifice safety in an attempt to cut costs and be more competitive)*
- How did deregulation provide an incentive for new airlines to enter the market? *(New airlines saw that they would have an opportunity to make a profit once deregulation lifted rules that limited competition.)*

More About . . .

Deregulation
Beginning in the 1970s, the government saw that many regulated industries were operating inefficiently and were not natural monopolies but industries that could become competitive. In addition to airlines, other deregulated industries include railroads, trucking, financial services, natural gas, television, and telecommunications.

Most studies show that deregulation led to lower costs, lower prices, increased output, and greater efficiency. However, deregulation of the electricity industry was less successful, as exemplified by the fate of California. In 2001, just three years after deregulating the industry, electricity prices skyrocketed as generating capacity failed to keep up with demand.

Deregulating Industries

QUICK REFERENCE

Deregulation reduces or removes government control of business.

KEY CONCEPTS

Much government regulation in the 20th century focused on controlling industries that provided important public services. For example, in the 1930s, in response to bank closings and other problems during the Great Depression, the U.S. Congress passed many laws for oversight of the financial services industry. In the 1970s, a trend toward deregulation began. **Deregulation** involves actions taken to reduce or to remove government oversight and control of business.

Deregulation has benefits and drawbacks. Deregulation generally results in lower prices for consumers because the markets become more competitive. Firms in industries with regulated prices have little or no incentive to reduce costs. But deregulation may lead to fewer protections for consumers.

Deregulating the Airlines

The Airline Deregulation Act of 1978 removed all government control of airline routes and rates. Only safety regulations remained in place. Prior to 1978, there was limited competition, and airlines differentiated based on service rather than price.

As a result of deregulation, the industry expanded as many new carriers entered the market. Increased competition led to greater efficiency. Economists estimate that prices fell by 10 to 18 percent, falling most sharply on heavily traveled routes where there was the greatest amount of competition. More people than ever before, lured by lower prices, chose to travel by plane.

However, the quality of service declined as airlines cut back on food and other in-flight amenities to reduce costs. In addition, many travelers encountered crowded airports as a result of the increase in air travel. It took time for local governments to expand facilities to accommodate the increase in traffic.

The financial pressures led to a large number of bankruptcies among the airline companies. Airline employees faced increased layoffs, lower wages, and loss of pensions.

APPLICATION Analyzing Causes

C. Why did deregulation of the airline industry lead to lower prices for many consumers? Deregulation allowed increased competition that led to lower prices.

218 Chapter 7

DIFFERENTIATING INSTRUCTION

Struggling Readers

Understand Cause and Effect
Help students understand cause and effect in deregulation of the airlines.

- Explain that before 1978, the government controlled which airlines could fly between different cities and what they could charge. This situation led to deregulation.
- Then, have students find the effects of deregulation described in the text. Lead them to conclude that deregulation increased competition, which led to many effects on airlines and consumers.

Gifted and Talented

Debate Airline Deregulation
Ask students to use the Internet and the library to learn more about deregulation's effects on the airline industry.

- Have students form teams to develop arguments for or against deregulation as a whole or certain aspects of it.
- Allow the teams to stage an informal debate for the class on the effects of deregulation based on their research.
- Engage the class in a discussion on which arguments were most persuasive and why.

SECTION 4 Assessment

Online Quiz
ClassZone.com

REVIEWING KEY CONCEPTS

1. Explain the differences between the terms in each of these pairs:
   a. *trust* / *merger*
   b. *price fixing* / *predatory pricing*
   c. *regulation* / *deregulation*
2. What is the main purpose of antitrust legislation?
3. How does market allocation lead to reduced competition?
4. When would the government issue a cease and desist order?
5. How do public disclosure requirements protect consumers?
6. **Using Your Notes** Why is it important for the government to evaluate and approve mergers? Refer to your completed hierarchy diagram.

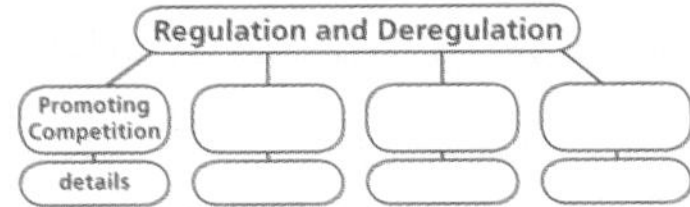

Use the Graphic Organizer at **Interactive Review @ ClassZone.com**

CRITICAL THINKING

7. **Analyzing Causes and Effects** In 2005, the FTC approved the merger of The Gillette Company with Procter & Gamble. Experts who reviewed the merger said it made sense that it was approved because the two companies had few products in the same market categories. In order to satisfy the government, the companies had to sell only two of their brands to other companies. What factors that affect mergers are illustrated in this story?
8. **Applying Economic Concepts** In the early 2000s, a new form of marketing emerged called word-of-mouth marketing or buzz marketing. Companies hired ordinary people to talk about the benefits of their products to others. Marketing industry lawyers warned their clients that it was important that the hired spokespeople reveal that they were paid for their endorsements. What are the lawyers concerned about? Use the concepts from this section to formulate your answer.
9. **Challenge** The Telecommunications Act of 1996 included provisions to deregulate the cable television industry. In 2003, consumer organizations complained that cable rates had increased by 45 percent since the law was passed. Only 5 percent of American homes had a choice of more than one cable provider in 2003. Those homes paid about 17 percent less than those with no choice of cable provider. How effective had deregulation been in the cable industry by 2003? Cite evidence to support your answer.

ECONOMICS IN PRACTICE

Identifying Regulatory Agencies Several federal agencies provide protection for consumers. Many of them are listed in Figure 7.6 on page 217. Decide which agency or agencies from Figure 7.6 would best protect consumers in each of the situations below.

a. Children's necklaces sold over the Internet are found to contain high levels of lead. Consumers are concerned about the chance of lead poisoning.
b. Advertising for a skin cream claims that it will eliminate acne problems. Consumers find that the product does not live up to its claim and in fact seems to irritate people's faces and cause rashes.
c. Some apple farmers use a pesticide on their trees that causes illness. More and more of the pesticide has been found in groundwater supplies.

Challenge Find out about a government regulatory agency not listed in Figure 7.6. Discuss the agency's purpose with your class.

4 Assess & Reteach

Assess Allow students to choose two questions to answer. Make sure all questions are covered. Call on volunteers to present their answers to the class. Clarify understanding as needed.

Unit 2 Resource Book
- Section Quiz, p. 205

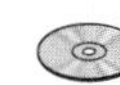

Interactive Review @ ClassZone.com
- Section Quiz

Test Generator CD-ROM
- Section Quiz

Reteach Invite volunteers to use their hierarchy diagrams to present the main ideas and details of each of the main topics of the section.

Unit 2 Resource Book
- Reteaching Activity, p. 206

Economics in Practice

a. The Consumer Products Safety Commission (CPSC) would recall these dangerous products from the market.
b. The Food and Drug Administration (FDA) would be concerned about the ingredients in the skin cream that caused rashes and would monitor the product labeling. The Federal Trade Commission (FTC) would ask the manufacturer to cease and desist from its deceptive advertising.
c. The FDA would investigate the effects on consumer health. The Environmental Protection Agency (EPA) would investigate the pollution of the groundwater supplies.

SECTION 4 ASSESSMENT ANSWERS

Reviewing Key Concepts

1. a. *trust*, p. 214; *merger*, p. 214
   b. *price fixing*, p. 216; *predatory pricing*, p. 216
   c. *regulation*, p. 214; *deregulation*, p. 218
2. to regulate monopolies and prevent monopolies from forming in the future
3. firms agree not to compete with one another in certain markets
4. when it wants a firm to stop using an unfair business practice
5. by providing product information that is necessary for consumers to make informed purchasing decisions or to alert them to safety concerns or unfair business practices
6. See p. 214 for a sample of a completed diagram. It is important to see how the merger will affect competition in a particular market.

Critical Thinking

7. The FTC will approve mergers that don't decrease competition or lead to greater concentration in particular markets. The FTC ordered the company to sell some brands to make sure this didn't happen in those markets.
8. The lawyers were concerned about public disclosure and whether it is deceptive to consumers to let them think that a particular spokesperson is just promoting the product because of personal belief rather than because of being paid for the endorsement.
9. Deregulation has not been very successful in the cable television industry because for most American homes there is only one cable company to choose. That company has monopoly power in setting prices. Greater competition would lead to lower prices.

Economics in Practice

See answers in side column above.

1 Plan & Prepare

Objectives

- Explain why product differentiation is so important to cell phone producers.
- Describe how cell phone producers use product differentiation to compete for business.

2 Focus & Motivate

Connecting to Everyday Life Have students discuss what factors are most important to them when deciding to buy a cell phone. Explain that this case study focuses on ways that cell phone makers differentiate their products in a highly competitive market.

3 Teach

Using the Sources

Encourage students to examine each source to find out how and why cell phone makers use product differentiation.

A. Why does Nokia think that mobile TV will be easier to sell than other cell phone features? *(because it is an idea that people easily understand)*

B. What analogy does the cartoon use to make its point about cell phone features? *(It compares cell phones to a type of pocketknife that includes many other gadgets, such as scissors.)*

C. Why does the second article conclude that, "Only the sharpest players will survive"? *(Possible answer: Companies must figure out how to provide products with the most desirable features at lower prices.)*

Economics Update

Go to **ClassZone.com** to find an update to this Case Study, including another article, an editable student worksheet, and an editable lesson plan.

Case Study

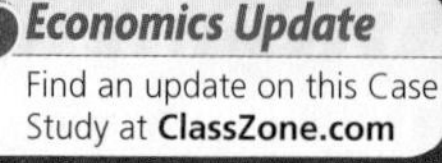

Find an update on this Case Study at **ClassZone.com**

Competition in Gadgets and Gizmos

Background Cellular phones are a highly successful telecommunications product. Since they first appeared on the market in the 1980s, cell phone sales have grown steadily. Now, billions of people around the world own cell phones.

As the global market becomes saturated with cell phones, sales growth will slow. To counteract this, cell phone producers rely on product differentiation to increase sales. New gadgets and gizmos aim to make the cell phone both irresistible and indispensable. A director of business development at one cell phone maker summed up his strategy this way: "We are trying to drive the cell phone in[to] every aspect of your life."

What's the issue? What affects your selection of a cell phone? Study these sources to discover how producers use product differentiation to compete for your business.

A. Magazine Article

Nokia Corporation, a maker of phone handsets, developed several add-ons to boost sales. This article describes one of Nokia's plans.

Nokia Hopes to Attract Consumers with Mobile-TV

Web-browsing, picture-messaging, videos, and now TV

Nokia, the world's largest handset-maker, has just released the results of a mobile-TV trial in Helsinki which found that 41% of participants were willing to pay for the service, and thought a monthly fee of €10 [€ is the European Union currency, the euro] ($12.50) was reasonable.

As revenue from voice calls has stopped growing in developed markets, the industry has been searching for new avenues for growth. In recent years, it has championed mobile web-browsing, picture-messaging and video-telephony. . . . But . . . consumers have not taken to these things in large numbers. . . .

Ah, but mobile TV is different from all those other services . . . because there is no need to educate the consumer. "Everyone gets it if you say 'mobile TV'," says Richard Sharp of Nokia.

Source: "Anyone for Telly?" *The Economist*, September 10, 2005

Thinking Economically What caused Nokia to develop mobile-TV? Explain, using evidence from the article.

DIFFERENTIATING INSTRUCTION

Struggling Readers

Use Jigsaw Reading

Divide students into groups of three and ask each to study one of the documents.

- Regroup the students based on the material they were assigned. Have them read and discuss the material and decide how to present it to other groups.
- Allow students to return to the original groups and ask them to take turns summarizing the material they studied.
- Have these groups discuss all Thinking Economically questions and agree on answers.

English Learners

Analyze Hyphenated Words

Point out the hyphenated words in document A. The hyphen signals that two words should be understood as one.

- Suggest that students reverse the order of the words to understand the meaning more easily. For example, *Web-browsing* refers to browsing the Web. Have students apply this strategy to *picture-messaging* and *handset-maker.*
- Ask students to guess what *video-telephony* means by combining the meaning of each part *(picture phones).*

B. Cartoon

This cartoon makes light of the dozens of features packed into most cellular phones.

Swiss Army Phone

Source: www.CartoonStock.com

Thinking Economically Why do cellular phone makers include so many features in their phones?

C. Online Press Release

Gartner, Inc. provides research and analysis on the information technology industry. This press release presents its projections on mobile phone sales.

Gartner Says Mobile Phone Sales Will Exceed One Billion in 2009

Sales will increase, but so will competition.

Gartner estimates there will be 2.6 billion mobile phones in use by the end of 2009. . . . "The sales volume cannot be attributed to one region in particular. It's a truly global phenomenon," said Carolina Milanesi, principal analyst at Gartner for mobile terminals. "In mature markets like Europe and North America, subscribers are still buying replacement phones. In emerging markets like Brazil and India, new customers are signing up for mobile services at an even faster rate." . . .

Despite spectacular growth on all fronts, not everything is rosy. [Ben] Wood, research vice president for mobile terminals at Gartner, cautioned that "Sales numbers are impressive, but the big names in this industry will have to deliver value as well as volume. We expect the average wholesale price of a mobile phone will decline from US$174 in 2004 to US$161 in 2009. At the same time, phones will keep getting more complex and become ever-more packed with features. Only the sharpest players will survive."

Source: www.gartner.com

Thinking Economically Are manufacturers more likely to offer differentiated products in new markets or in those already established? Explain your answer.

THINKING ECONOMICALLY Synthesizing

1. Compare the product described in document A and the one illustrated in B. Are cell phones likely to become more or less complex? Explain why or why not.
2. Which of the four market structures best fits the market for cellular phones? Use evidence from documents A and C to explain your answer.
3. In documents A and C, compare the role that market research plays in the development of new products. Use evidence from the documents.

International Economics

Cell Phones in Developing Countries
Cell phones have fostered economic growth in developing countries. In Bangladesh, a bank set up a nonprofit phone company and provided small loans to rural entrepreneurs, mostly women, who sold low-cost phone service to other villagers. The model has since been used in Africa.

The entrepreneurs make a profit, and villagers have a way to find jobs, check prices of farm products, and access the Internet. Mobile phone makers developed low-cost phones with features these customers need, such as long battery life.

Thinking Economically

Answers

A. *Nokia looked for new ways to increase revenue. They picked mobile TV because consumers understand the concept.*

B. *to better compete in a crowded market*

C. *established markets, because there is more competition*

Synthesizing

1. *more, because competition will cause continued innovation*
2. *oligopoly: few sellers, differentiated products, high barriers to entry*
3. *In A, research showed that consumers were willing to pay for the product and how much. In C, forecasting the future growth of the industry helps companies know how to plan.*

TECHNOLOGY ACTIVITY

Promoting Cell Phones

Time 45 Minutes 

Task Brainstorm ideas for a cell phone with many features and design a Web page to promote it.

Materials Needed a computer with Internet access, graphics software

Activity:

- Have student groups brainstorm ideas for a cell phone they would like to sell to young adults.
- Encourage students to consider features they would include to differentiate their product from competitors.
- Have each group design a Web page for its product that includes visuals, product description, and price.
- Invite groups to view one another's Web page. Ask each student to choose the phone that she or he would be most likely to buy and give the reasons why.

Rubric

	Understanding of Product Differentiation	Presentation of Information
4	excellent	clear and creative
3	good	clear
2	fair	partly clear
1	poor	sketchy

Online Summary Answers

1. Market structure
2. perfect competition
3. monopoly
4. natural monopoly
5. economies of scale
6. cartel
7. barrier to entry
8. monopolistic competition
9. nonprice competition
10. oligopoly
11. start-up costs
12. price fixing
13. Antitrust legislation

Interactive Review

Review this chapter using interactive activities at **ClassZone.com**

- Online Summary
- Quizzes
- Vocabulary Flip Cards
- Graphic Organizers
- Review and Study Notes

Online Summary

Complete the following activity either on your own paper or online at **ClassZone.com**

Choose the key concept that best completes the sentence. Not all key concepts will be used.

antitrust legislation	monopoly
barrier to entry	natural monopoly
cartel	nonprice competition
cease and desist order	oligopoly
deregulation	patent
economies of scale	perfect competition
geographic monopoly	price fixing
market structure	price taker
merger	standardized product
monopolistic competition	start-up costs

__1__ is an economic model of the nature and degree of competition among businesses in the same industry. In __2__ there are many buyers and sellers of standardized products.

In a __3__ there is a single seller of a product with no close substitutes. The local water company is an example of a __4__ because __5__ make it most efficient for a single company to provide the service.

A __6__ is a group of sellers that acts together to set prices and limit output. A __7__ is anything that makes it difficult for a business to enter a market.

In __8__ there are many buyers and sellers of similar but differentiated products. In such a market the sellers engage in __9__.

In __10__ there are only a few sellers for many buyers. It is hard for new firms to enter such a market due to high __11__. Sellers in such a market engage in __12__ when they all agree to charge the same price for their products.

__13__ gives the government the power to control monopolies and to promote competition.

222 Chapter 7

CHAPTER 7 Assessment

REVIEWING KEY CONCEPTS

What Is Perfect Competition? (pp. 192–197)

1. What determines the difference between one market structure and another?
2. Why is perfect competition not found in real markets?

The Impact of Monopoly (pp. 198–205)

3. How does a monopoly control the price of its product?
4. Name three ways in which a monopoly differs from perfect competition.

Other Market Structures (pp. 206–213)

5. Why is product differentiation necessary for monopolistic competition?
6. Why are firms in an oligopoly less independent in setting prices than firms in monopolistic competition?

Regulation and Deregulation Today (pp. 214–221)

7. What factors does the government consider in deciding whether to approve a merger?
8. Why do economists generally favor deregulation of most industries?

APPLYING ECONOMIC CONCEPTS

Look at the table below showing retail sales.

9. Which retail market is the least concentrated? Which market is most concentrated?
10. Which markets are closer to monopolistic competition and which are closer to oligopoly?

FIGURE 7.7 SALES CONCENTRATION IN RETAIL TRADE

Retail Market	Percent of Total Sales by the Four Largest Firms
Furniture	8
Clothing	29
Supermarkets	33
Music	58
Athletic footwear	71
Books	77
Discount department stores	95

Source: U.S. Census Bureau, 2002 data

CHAPTER 7 ASSESSMENT ANSWERS

Reviewing Key Concepts

1. the level of competition
2. because real markets lack one or more of the characteristics of perfect competition (usually by having few sellers or nonstandardized products)
3. by limiting supply
4. number of sellers (one vs. several); sellers' control over prices (none vs. significant); barriers to market entry (restricted vs. free)
5. because product differentiation gives a firm limited control over price (otherwise it would be just like perfect competition)
6. because there are so few firms and each one has a large enough market share that its actions affect all other firms in the oligopoly
7. whether the merger will decrease competition or make it harder for new firms to enter the market
8. because deregulation fosters efficiency and increases competition, which causes companies to differentiate and results in lower prices for consumers

Applying Economic Concepts

9. least: furniture; most: discount department stores
10. monopolistic competition: furniture, clothing, supermarkets; oligopoly: music, athletic footwear, books, discount department stores

Critical Thinking

11. **a.** monopolistic aspect because of the exclusive marketing

    b. Prices will be higher than if the CDs were available in other stores because the retailers know that consumers have no options if they want those particular CDs.

CRITICAL THINKING

11. Applying Economic Concepts In 2004, a new trend started in the marketing of music CDs. A variety of retailers, from coffee shop and restaurant chains to large discount stores, began negotiating marketing deals that allowed them to sell a particular recording artist's CDs exclusively for a period of time.

- **a.** What part of monopolistic competition does this trend reinforce: the monopolistic aspect or the competition aspect?
- **b.** How is this trend likely to affect prices for these CDs? Give reasons why.

12. Analyzing Causes and Effects After deregulation of the airline industry, many of the largest U.S. airlines struggled financially. These airlines then increased their business in the international market in order to boost their profits. What effect of deregulation caused the airlines to make this move?

13. Making Inferences The company that invented the first xerographic photocopier initially enjoyed 70 percent profit margins and a 95 percent market share. Several years later a Japanese camera company invented another way to make photocopiers. Over time, the original company's market share fell to 13 percent. What specific kind of market structure is illustrated by this example? When a company invents a new product or process, what concerns might they have, if they studied this example?

14. Drawing Conclusions An herbal supplement company claimed that its product would cure serious diseases and promote weight loss. In 2005, the Federal Trade Commission (FTC) required the company to stop making those claims. Why did the FTC rather than the Food and Drug Administration (FDA) handle this case?

15. Challenge Why might a local electric company be in favor of regulations that would allow it to remain a natural monopoly? Why might it oppose regulations that would require monitoring the pollution from its generating plants?

SIMULATION

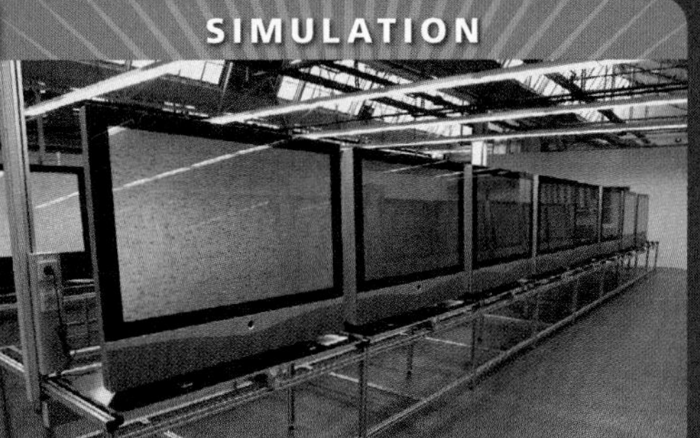

Compete for Buyers

Step 1. Choose a partner. Imagine that together you run a company that produces flat-screen televisions under monopolistic competition. Use the criteria in this table to decide how to differentiate your product.

Product and Marketing Considerations
• Physical characteristics
• Where it will be sold
• Packaging or labeling
• Service
• Advertising and promotion
• Price (from $500 to $1,500)

Step 2. Create a poster that outlines your product and marketing decisions. Include a sketch of one of your televisions along with the price.

Step 3. Display all the posters in the classroom. Allow all students to buy a television from the company of their choice. Tally the results and see how many buyers each company attracted.

Step 4. Merge with two or three other companies to form a larger company. There should now be only three or four producers. Discuss how this new situation might affect your marketing decisions.

Step 5. As a class, discuss what would happen if the three or four firms became a cartel and acted like a monopoly.

Challenge Which of these scenarios would you prefer as a producer? Which would you prefer as a consumer?

McDougal Littell Assessment System

Assess

Online Test Practice
- Go to **ClassZone.com** for more test practice.

Unit 2 Resource Book
- Chapter Test, Forms A, B, & C, pp. 217–228

Test Generator CD-ROM
- Chapter Test, Forms (A, B, & C), in English and Spanish

Report

Use the McDougal Littell Assessment System to score assessments and receive customized reports.

Reteach

For activities customized for individual students, use the McDougal Littell Assessment System.

CHAPTER 7 ASSESSMENT ANSWERS

12. Increased price competition made domestic flights less profitable, causing the airlines to look for markets where there was less price competition.

13. Technological monopoly. Companies with new products or processes might be concerned about maintaining their market share when their patent expires or competitors develop a substitute technology.

14. The case involved deceptive trade practices rather than a question of product safety.

15. The first kind of regulation protects the company from competition. The second kind imposes additional costs on the company, which it may not be able to pass on to consumers.

Simulation Rubric

	Understanding of Concepts Involved	Presentation of Information
4	excellent	accurate, clear, and complete
3	good	mostly accurate and clear
2	fair	sometimes clear
1	poor	sketchy

CHAPTER 8: Types of Business Organizations
Planning Guide

Resources 2Go Complete print resources all on one USB drive allow you to customize lessons.

Section Titles and Objectives	Unit 3 Resource Book and Workbooks		Assessment Resources
1 Sole Proprietorships pp. 226–231 • Identify the characteristics of sole proprietorships • Explain how sole proprietorships are set up • Compare the economic advantages and economic disadvantages of sole proprietorships	**Unit 3 Resource Book** • Reading Study Guide, pp. 1–2 • RSG with Additional Support, pp. 3–5 • RSG with Additional Support (Spanish), pp. 6–8 • Economic Simulations: To Merge or Not to Merge, pp. 47–48	• Case Study Resources: The Evolution of Levi Strauss & Co.—A Matter of Values, pp. 45–46	**Unit 3 Resource Book** • Section Quiz, p. 9 • Reteaching Activity, p. 10 **Test Generator CD-ROM** **Daily Test Practice Transparencies,** TT26
2 Forms of Partnerships pp. 232–237 • Identify the characteristics and types of partnerships • Compare the economic advantages and disadvantages of partnerships	**Unit 3 Resource Book** • Reading Study Guide, pp. 11–12 • RSG with Additional Support, pp. 13–15 • RSG with Additional Support (Spanish), pp. 16–18	• Math Skills Worksheet: Comparing Data from Different Years, p. 49 • Case Study Resources: The Evolution of Levi Strauss & Co.—A Matter of Values, pp. 45–46	**Unit 3 Resource Book** • Section Quiz, p. 19 • Reteaching Activity, p. 20 **Test Generator CD-ROM** **Daily Test Practice Transparencies,** TT27
3 Corporations, Mergers, and Multinationals pp. 238–247 • Identify the characteristics of corporations • Compare the advantages and disadvantages of corporations • Describe how corporations consolidate to form larger business combinations • Explain the role of multinational corporations in the world economy	**Unit 3 Resource Book** • Reading Study Guide, pp. 21–22 • RSG with Additional Support, pp. 23–25 • RSG with Additional Support (Spanish), pp. 26–28 • Economic Simulations: To Merge or Not to Merge, pp. 47–48	• Case Study Resources: The Evolution of Levi Strauss & Co.—A Matter of Values, pp. 45–46 **NCEE Student Activities** • Researching Companies, pp. 29–32	**Unit 3 Resource Book** • Section Quiz, p. 29 • Reteaching Activity, p. 30 **Test Generator CD-ROM** **Daily Test Practice Transparencies,** TT28
4 Franchises, Co-ops, and Nonprofits pp. 248–253 • Explain how franchises function • Identify the characteristics and purpose of cooperatives • Describe the types and purpose of nonprofit organizations	**Unit 3 Resource Book** • Reading Study Guide, pp. 31–32 • RSG with Additional Support, pp. 33–35 • RSG with Additional Support (Spanish), pp. 36–38 • Readings in Free Enterprise: Organic Valley Family of Farms, pp. 43–44 • Case Study Resources: The Evolution of Levi Strauss & Co.—A Matter of Values, pp. 45–46	**Test Practice and Review Workbook,** pp. 37–38	**Unit 3 Resource Book** • Section Quiz, p. 39 • Reteaching Activity, p. 40 • Chapter Test, (Forms A, B, & C), pp. 51–62 **Test Generator CD-ROM** **Daily Test Practice Transparencies,** TT29

Integrated Technology

No Time? To focus students on the most important content in this chapter, use Animated Economics, "Interactive Merger Chart," available in Resources 2Go.

Teacher Presentation Options

Presentation Toolkit

Power Presentation DVD-ROM

- Lecture Notes
- Interactive Review
- Media Gallery
- Animated Economics
- Review Game

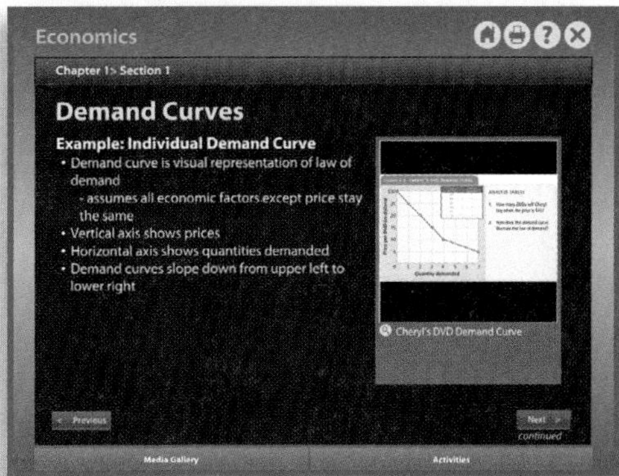

Economics Concepts Transparencies

- Advantages and Disadvantages of Running a Sole Proprietorship, CT26
- Which Type of Partnership is Right for You? CT27
- Corporation Organizational Chart, CT28
- Franchises, CT29

Electronic Books

eEdition DVD-ROM

eEdition Online

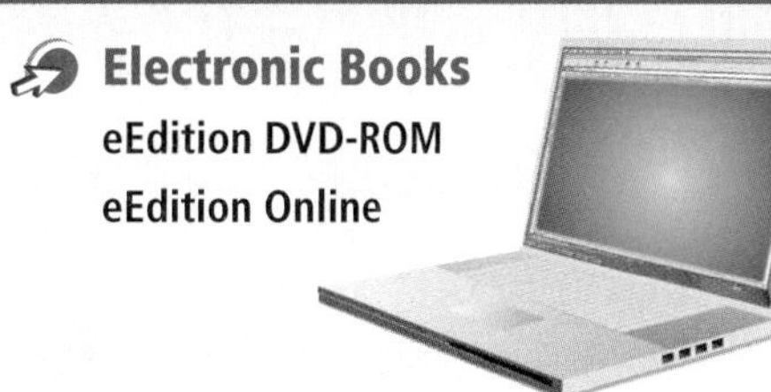

Daily Test Practice Transparencies, TT26, TT27, TT28, TT29

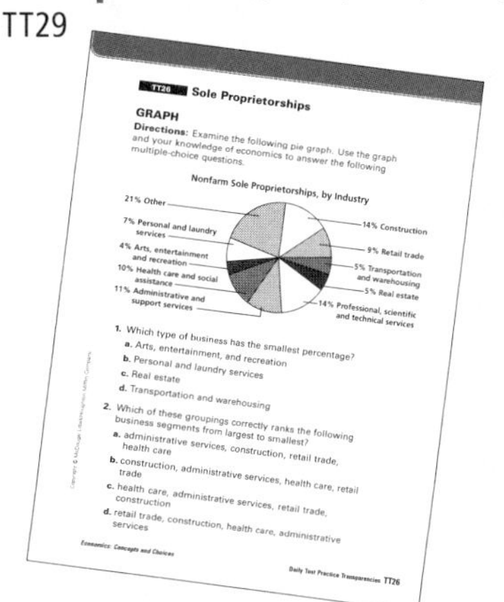

TT26 Sole Proprietorships

GRAPH

Directions: Examine the following pie graph. Use the graph and your knowledge of economics to answer the following multiple-choice questions.

Nonfarm Sole Proprietorships, by Industry

1. Which type of business has the smallest percentage?
   a. Arts, entertainment, and recreation
   b. Personal and laundry services
   c. Real estate
   d. Transportation and warehousing
2. Which of these groupings correctly ranks the following business segments from largest to smallest?
   a. administrative services, construction, retail trade, health care
   b. construction, administrative services, health care, retail trade
   c. health care, administrative services, retail trade, construction
   d. retail trade, construction, health care, administrative services

Economics: Concepts and Choices

Daily Test Practice Transparencies TT26

Animated Economics

- Interactive Merger Chart, p. 243

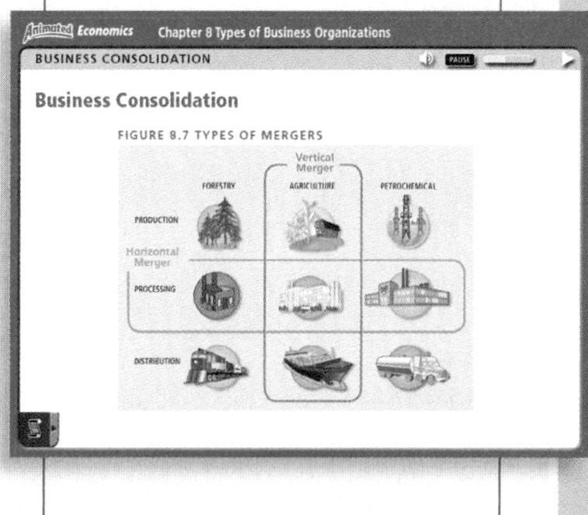

Online Activities at ClassZone.com

Economics Update

- Sole Proprietorships, p. 227
- Mary Kay, Inc. p. 230
- Partnerships, p. 234
- Corporations, p. 240
- Bill Gates and Microsoft, p. 246
- Apple: The Evolution of One Company, p. 252

Animated Economics

- Interactive Graphics

Activity Maker

- Vocabulary Flip Cards
- Review Game

Research Center

- Graphs and Data

Interactive Review

- Online Summary
- Quizzes
- Vocabulary Flip Cards
- Graphic Organizers
- Review and Study Notes

Teacher-Tested Activities

Name: Steve Lueck

School: Park Hill South High School

State: Missouri

Teacher-Tested Activities

At the beginning of this chapter, look for my classroom-proven idea for teaching economics concepts and thinking.

Resources for Differentiated Instruction

Struggling Readers

Teacher's Edition Activities

- Make a Chart, p. 228
- Make a Chart, Part 2, p. 234
- The Power of One, p. 240
- Map the Text, p. 244
- Understand Quotes, p. 246

Unit 3 Resource Book

- RSG With Additional Support, pp. 3–5, 13–15, 23–25, 33–35 Ⓐ
- Reteaching Activities, pp. 10, 20, 30, 40 Ⓑ
- Chapter Test (Form A), pp. 51–54 Ⓒ

ClassZone.com

- Animated Economics
- Interactive Review

Test Generator CD-ROM

- Chapter Test (Form A)
- Chapter Test (Form A), in Spanish

Ⓑ SECTION 1 RETEACHING ACTIVITY
Sole Proprietorships

Explaining Economic Concepts
The following questions deal with sole proprietorships. Answer them in the space provided.

1. What is a sole proprietorship?
2. How do sole proprietorships earn a profit?
3. What does setting up a sole proprietorship involve?
4. What are the advantages of a sole proprietorship?
5. How might unlimited liability affect a sole proprietor if the business fails?
6. What are the other limitations of a sole proprietorship?

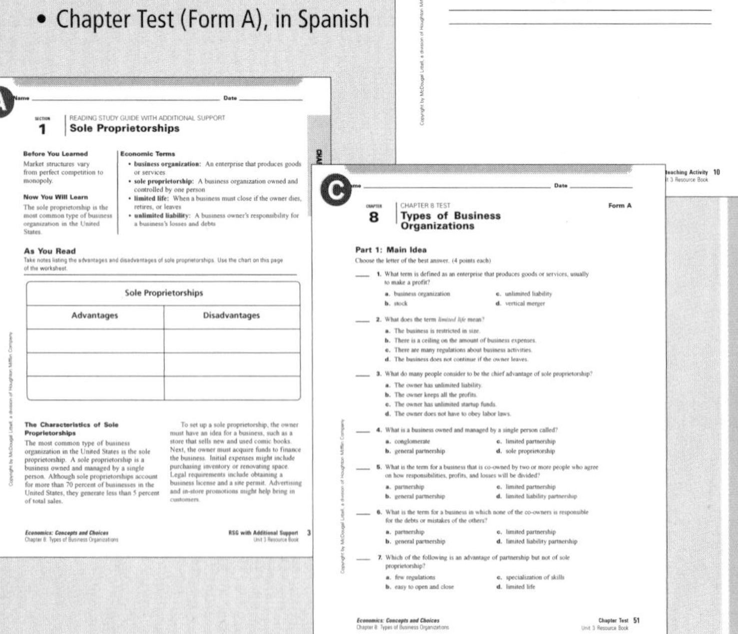

Ⓐ SECTION 1 READING STUDY GUIDE WITH ADDITIONAL SUPPORT
Sole Proprietorships

Before You Learned Market structures vary from perfect competition to monopoly.

Now You Will Learn The sole proprietorship is the most common type of business organization in the United States.

Economic Terms
- **business organization:** An enterprise that produces goods or services
- **sole proprietorship:** A business organization owned and controlled by one person
- **limited life:** When a business must close if the owner dies, retires, or leaves
- **unlimited liability:** A business owner's responsibility for a business's losses and debts

As You Read
Take notes listing the advantages and disadvantages of sole proprietorships. Use the chart on this page of the worksheet.

Sole Proprietorships	
Advantages	Disadvantages

The Characteristics of Sole Proprietorships

Ⓒ CHAPTER 8 TEST Form A
Types of Business Organizations

Part 1: Main Idea
Choose the letter of the best answer. (4 points each)

1. What term is defined as an enterprise that produces goods or services, usually to make a profit?
a. business organization c. unlimited liability
b. stock d. vertical merger
2. What does the term *limited life* mean?
a. The business is restricted in size.
b. There is a ceiling on the amount of business expenses.
c. There are many regulations about business activities.
d. The business does not continue if the owner leaves.
3. What do many people consider to be the chief advantage of sole proprietorship?
a. The owner has unlimited liability.
b. The owner keeps all the profits.
c. The owner has unlimited startup funds.
d. The owner does not have to obey labor laws.
4. What is a business owned and managed by a single person called?
a. conglomerate c. limited partnership
b. general partnership d. sole proprietorship
5. What is the term for a business that is co-owned by two or more people who agree on how responsibilities, profits, and losses will be divided?
a. partnership c. limited partnership
b. general partnership d. limited liability partnership
6. What is the term for a business in which none of the co-owners is responsible for the debts or mistakes of the others?
a. partnership c. limited partnership
b. general partnership d. limited liability partnership
7. Which of the following is an advantage of partnership but not of sole proprietorship?
a. few regulations c. specialization of skills
b. easy to open and close d. limited life

English Learners

Teacher's Edition Activities

- Use Oral Language, p. 230
- Analyze Words, p. 234
- Read the News, p. 242
- Understand Suffixes, p. 250
- Interpret the Time Line, p. 252

Unit 3 Resource Book

- RSG with Additional Support (Spanish), pp. 6–8, 16–18, 26–28, 36–38 Ⓐ

Test Generator CD-ROM

- Chapter Test (Forms A, B, & C), in Spanish Ⓑ

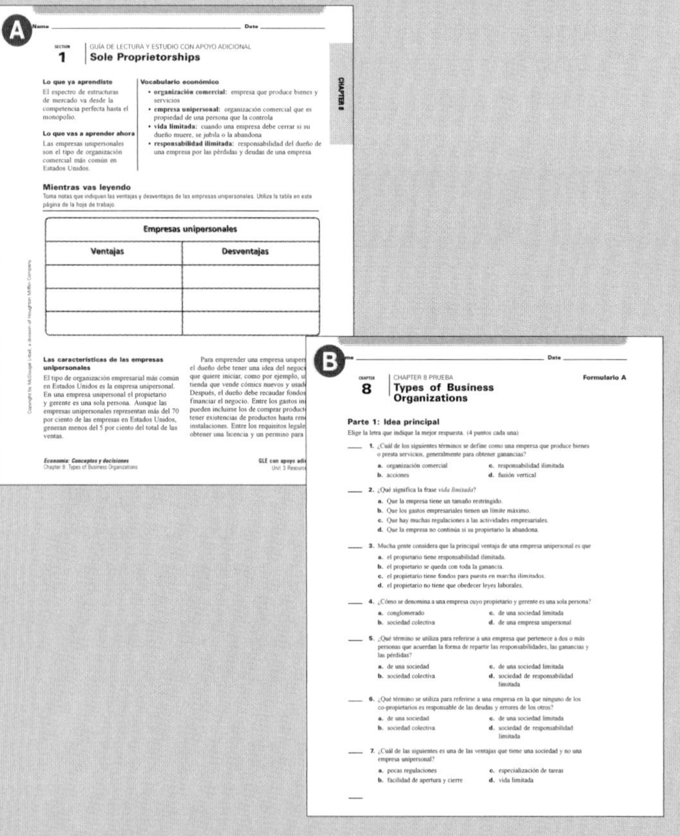

Ⓐ SECTION 1 GUÍA DE LECTURA Y ESTUDIO CON APOYO ADICIONAL
Sole Proprietorships

Lo que ya aprendiste El espectro de estructuras de mercado va desde la competencia perfecta hasta el monopolio.

Lo que vas a aprender ahora Las empresas unipersonales son el tipo de organización comercial más común en Estados Unidos.

Vocabulario económico
- **organización comercial:** empresa que produce bienes y servicios
- **empresa unipersonal:** organización comercial que es propiedad de una persona que la controla
- **vida limitada:** cuando una empresa debe cerrar si su dueño muere, se jubila o la abandona
- **responsabilidad ilimitada:** responsabilidad del dueño de una empresa por las pérdidas y deudas de una empresa

Mientras vas leyendo

Empresas unipersonales	
Ventajas	Desventajas

Las características de las empresas unipersonales

Ⓑ CHAPTER 8 PRUEBA Formulario A
Types of Business Organizations

Parte 1: Idea principal
Elige la letra que indique la mejor respuesta. (4 puntos cada una)

1. ¿Cuál de los siguientes términos se define como una empresa que produce bienes o presta servicios, generalmente para obtener ganancias?
a. organización comercial c. responsabilidad ilimitada
b. acciones d. fusión vertical
2. ¿Qué significa la frase *vida limitada*?
3. Mucha gente considera que la principal ventaja de una empresa unipersonal es que
4. ¿Cómo se denomina a una empresa cuyo propietario y gerente es una sola persona?
a. conglomerado c. de una sociedad limitada
b. sociedad colectiva d. de una empresa unipersonal
5. ¿Qué término se utiliza para referirse a una empresa que pertenece a dos o más personas que acuerdan la forma de repartir las responsabilidades, las ganancias y las pérdidas?
6. ¿Qué término se utiliza para referirse a una empresa en la que ninguno de los co-propietarios es responsable de las deudas y errores de los otros?
7. ¿Cuál de las siguientes es una de las ventajas que tiene una sociedad y no una empresa unipersonal?

Inclusion

Teacher's Edition Activities

- Make an Illustrated Timeline, p. 230
- Highlight Text, p. 236
- "Listen" to Graphics, p. 240
- Make a Collage, p. 244

Lesson Plans

- Modified Lessons for Inclusion, pp. 26–29 (A)

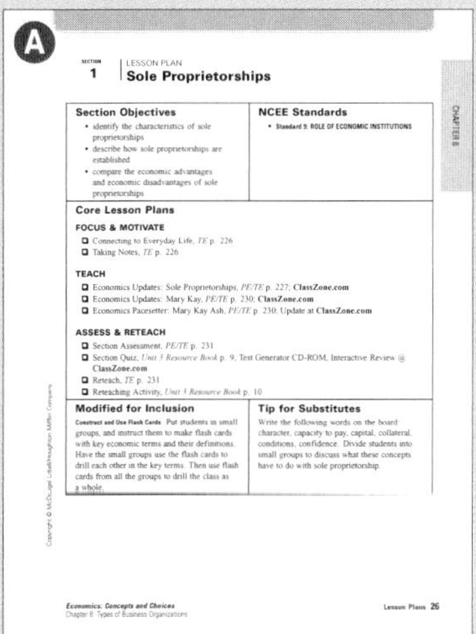

(A)

SECTION 1 | LESSON PLAN
Sole Proprietorships

Section Objectives
- identify the characteristics of sole proprietorships
- describe how sole proprietorships are established
- compare the economic advantages and economic disadvantages of sole proprietorships

NCEE Standards
- Standard 9: ROLE OF ECONOMIC INSTITUTIONS

CHAPTER 8

Core Lesson Plans

FOCUS & MOTIVATE
- ❑ Connecting to Everyday Life, *TE* p. 226
- ❑ Taking Notes, *TE* p. 226

TEACH
- ❑ Economics Updates: Sole Proprietorships, *PE/TE* p. 227; **ClassZone.com**
- ❑ Economics Updates: Mary Kay, *PE/TE* p. 230; **ClassZone.com**
- ❑ Economics Pacesetter: Mary Kay Ash, *PE/TE* p. 230; Update at **ClassZone.com**

ASSESS & RETEACH
- ❑ Section Assessment, *PE/TE* p. 231
- ❑ Section Quiz, *Unit 3 Resource Book* p. 9, Test Generator CD-ROM, Interactive Review @ **ClassZone.com**
- ❑ Reteach, *TE* p. 231
- ❑ Reteaching Activity, *Unit 3 Resource Book* p. 10

Modified for Inclusion
Construct and Use Flash Cards Put students in small groups, and instruct them to make flash cards with key economic terms and their definitions. Have the small groups use the flash cards to drill each other in the key terms. Then use flash cards from all the groups to drill the class as a whole.

Tip for Substitutes
Write the following words on the board: character, capacity to pay, capital, collateral, conditions, confidence. Divide students into small groups to discuss what these concepts have to do with sole proprietorship.

Copyright © McDougal Littell/Houghton Mifflin Company

Economics: Concepts and Choices
Chapter 8 Types of Business Organizations
Lesson Plans 26

Gifted and Talented

Teacher's Edition Activities

- Interview a Proprietor, p. 228
- Form Supported Opinions, p. 236
- Research and Debate, p. 242
- Read and Discuss, p. 246
- Analyze Franchising, p. 250
- Extend the Time Line, p. 252

Unit 3 Resource Book

- Readings in Free Enterprise: Organic Valley Family of Farms, pp. 43–44 (A)
- Case Study Resources: The Evolution of Levi Strauss & Co.— A Matter of Values, pp. 45–46 (B)

NCEE Student Activities

- Researching Companies, pp. 29–32 (C)

ClassZone.com

- Research Center

Test Generator CD-ROM

- Chapter Test (Form C)
- Chapter Test (Form C), in Spanish

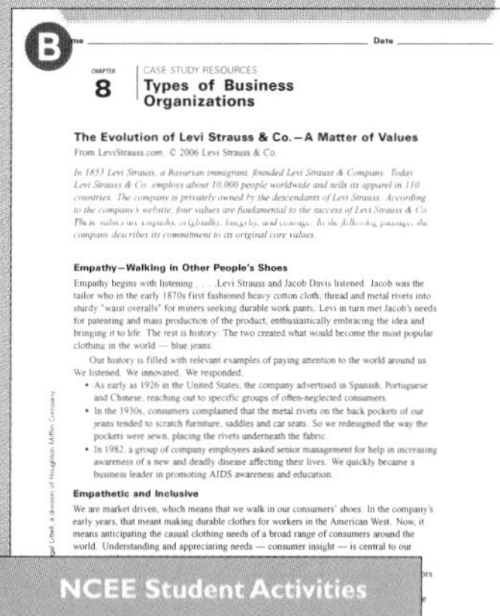

(B)

Name ______ Date ______

CHAPTER 8 | CASE STUDY RESOURCES
Types of Business Organizations

The Evolution of Levi Strauss & Co.—A Matter of Values
From LeviStrauss.com. © 2006 Levi Strauss & Co.

In 1853 Levi Strauss, a Bavarian immigrant, founded Levi Strauss & Company. Today Levi Strauss & Co. employs about 10,000 people worldwide and sells its apparel in 110 countries. The company is privately owned by the descendants of Levi Strauss. According to the company's website, four values are fundamental to the success of Levi Strauss & Co. These values are empathy, originality, integrity, and courage. In the following passage, the company describes its commitment to its original core values.

Empathy—Walking in Other People's Shoes
Empathy begins with listening . . . . Levi Strauss and Jacob Davis listened. Jacob was the tailor who in the early 1870s first fashioned heavy cotton cloth, thread and metal rivets into sturdy "waist overalls" for miners seeking durable work pants. Levi in turn met Jacob's needs for patenting and mass production of the product, enthusiastically embracing the idea and bringing it to life. The rest is history: The two created what would become the most popular clothing in the world — blue jeans.

Our history is filled with relevant examples of paying attention to the world around us. We listened. We innovated. We responded.

- As early as 1926 in the United States, the company advertised in Spanish, Portuguese and Chinese, reaching out to specific groups of often-neglected consumers.
- In the 1930s, consumers complained that the metal rivets on the back pockets of our jeans tended to scratch furniture, saddles and car seats. So we redesigned the way the pockets were sewn, placing the rivets underneath the fabric.
- In 1982, a group of company employees asked senior management for help in increasing awareness of a new and deadly disease affecting their lives. We quickly became a business leader in promoting AIDS awareness and education.

Empathetic and Inclusive
We are market driven, which means that we walk in our consumers' shoes. In the company's early years, that meant making durable clothes for workers in the American West. Now, it means anticipating the casual clothing needs of a broad range of consumers around the world. Understanding and appreciating needs — consumer insight — is central to our

Study Resources 45
Unit 3 Resource Book

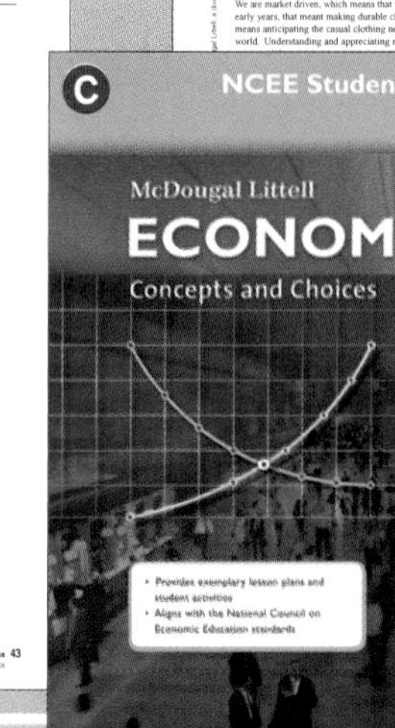

(A)

Name ______ Date ______

CHAPTER 8 | READINGS IN FREE ENTERPRISE
Types of Business Organizations

Organic Valley Family of Farms
Organic Valley Family of Farms™ is the largest cooperative of organic farmers in the United States. Its mission is to "keep small and mid-sized farmers farming." Organic Valley products are sold in supermarkets, natural foods stores, and food cooperatives across the country. Home Grown Wisconsin is another cooperative of organic food producers. It has a Community Supported Agriculture program (CSA), which serves restaurants on a subscription basis. For a set amount, usually paid in advance, subscribers receive weekly produce straight from the farm. As you read the following information from the organizations' websites, consider the similarities and differences between Organic Valley Family of Farms™ and Home Grown Wisconsin.

Organic Valley Cooperative Structure
Organic Valley Family of Farms™ is the largest organic farmer-owned cooperative in North America. . . . Being a cooperative means that the farm families that produce Organic Valley™'s brown eggs and dairy products, as well as certified organic meat products, are the direct owners of the business. From the time we began, with only seven Wisconsin farmers, to the present with over [800] farmer members in [24] states, our farmers have been directly involved in every decision we make. Over the years, we've learned a lot about how to organize, govern, and make decisions for ourselves. . . .

Each year we elect a hard-working board of directors, as well as having representatives meet monthly in each region. We publish a quarterly newsletter to keep all our members informed. Each farm family that seeks membership makes a serious investment in having a voice in their own future. . . .

Why is Being a Cooperative Important to Us? The support and resources of being part of a big extended family come in mighty handy in the agricultural world, where large corporations have taken over 600,000 family farms since 1960. As the sole owners, we make all the important decisions for our company. That gives us independence, and stability for our families and our way of life. We decide what new products to introduce [and] how to allocate our profits. . . .

More of Your Dollar Returns to Our Family Farms When you buy Organic Valley Family of Farms™ products, more of your dollar goes directly back to the farming families. We are involved in every step of the process of bringing our products to market. We approve the plants, the quality and flavor of our products, the packaging, the freighting—every aspect from the moment our products leave the farm until they appear on your grocer's shelves.

Why does a cooperative of small family farms make a difference to you? Your purchase of Organic Valley's products helps support sustainable family farms, which might not otherwise be able to continue farming. Also, you can be assured that not only are you purchasing the finest organic products available, but of our commitment to humane animal treatment, and the stewardship of our environment. We strive to safeguard our critically important natural resources—soil, air, and water—and to protect and preserve biodiversity.

From OrganicValley.com

Copyright by McDougal Littell, a division of Houghton Mifflin Company

Economics: Concepts and Choices
Chapter 8 Types of Business Organizations
Readings in Free Enterprise 43
Unit 3 Resource Book

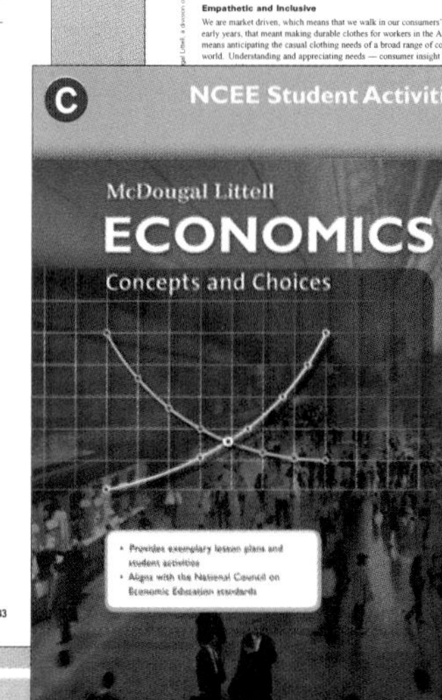

Focus & Motivate

Objective

Explain types of business structures and the advantages and disadvantages of each.

Why the Concept Matters

Point out that as students enter the world of work, they interact with businesses in a whole new way. Explain that they are no longer just consumers but also producers, or at least the employees of producers. Knowing the organization of the businesses they work for—and knowing what possibilities they may explore if they want to start their own business—will help them to understand the kinds of benefits they can expect to gain in various capacities in the workforce.

Analyzing the Photograph

Ask a student to describe the photograph in some detail and to read the caption. Then discuss the following questions:

- Does this look like a store that you have visited? If so, in what ways? *(Answers will vary. However, most students will have experienced a small shop and can relate to the idea of a physically small space, relatively few employees, and personal service.)*
- What kind of business structure might this florist have? *(Possible answers: single owner; part of large chain; a concession within another business, such as in a hospital)*

Point out that in this chapter students will learn about a number of different business structures, including those mentioned in the discussion.

Microeconomics

Unit 3

Partners in the American Economy

Types of Businesses
Businesses are organized in different ways. The organization that suits a small business, such as this florist, may not be appropriate for a large manufacturer.

224

CONTENT STANDARDS

NCEE STANDARDS

Standard 10: Role of Economic Institutions

Students will understand that
Institutions evolve in market economies to help individuals and groups accomplish their goals. Banks, labor unions, corporations, legal systems, and not-for-profit organizations are examples of important institutions. A different kind of institution—clearly defined and enforced property rights—is essential to a market economy.

Students will be able to use this knowledge to
Describe the roles of various economic systems.

Benchmarks

Students will know that
Incorporation allows firms to accumulate sufficient financial capital to make large-scale investments and achieve economies of scale. Incorporation also reduces the risk to investors by limiting stockholders' liability to their share of ownership of the corporation. *(pages 238–247)*

Not-for-profit organizations are established primarily for religious, health, educational, civic, or social purposes, and many are exempt from certain taxes. *(page 250)*

CHAPTER

8

Types of Business Organizations

CONCEPT REVIEW

A **producer** is a maker of goods or provider of services.

CHAPTER 8 KEY CONCEPT

Most of the producers in a market economy are **business organizations,** commercial or industrial enterprises and the people who work in them. The purpose of most business organizations is to earn a profit.

WHY THE CONCEPT MATTERS

Do you have a part-time job after school or on weekends? Perhaps you work behind the counter at the local flower shop or as a server at the juice bar downtown. Or perhaps you work as a stocker at one of the large clothing stores at the shopping mall. These businesses are of varying sizes and are organized differently. The American free enterprise system allows producers to choose the kind of business organization that best suits their purpose.

Online Highlights

More at ClassZone.com

Economics Update

Go to ECONOMICS UPDATE for chapter updates and current news on Apple Inc. (See Case Study, pp. 252–253.)

Animated Economics

Go to ANIMATED ECONOMICS for interactive lessons on the graphs and tables in this chapter.

Interactive Review

Go to INTERACTIVE REVIEW for concept review and activities.

How did Apple Inc., which began in a garage, grow into a major multinational corporation? See the Case Study on pages 252–253.

From the Classroom

Steve Lueck, Park Hill South High School

Business Research Project

Have students research how to start their own business or learn about a business that already exists. They should provide at least one paragraph of explanation for each of the following items:

1 Business name and function
2. Type of business organization, with advantages and disadvantages
3. Target market for the product or service
4. Competing businesses
5. Essential equipment, machinery, and materials; cost
6. Job descriptions for each type of worker needed and number of workers at each position; salaries
7. Location of business; cost of rent or real estate
8. Taxes collected, taxes paid
9. Licenses and permits needed; cost
10. Types of insurance needed and reason needed; cost
11. Expected revenues and expenses
12. Total cost of starting the business and the source of start-up money

Previewing Chapter Technology at ClassZone.com

Economics Update Students will find updates to information in the pupil edition on pages 227, 230, 234, 240, 246, and 252.

Animated Economics Students will find an interactive lesson related to material on page 243.

Interactive Review Students will find additional section and chapter assessment support for materials on pages 231, 237, 247, 251, and 254.

TEACHER MEDIA FAVORITES

Books

- Jensen, Michael C. *Foundations of Organizational Strategy.* Cambridge, MA: Harvard UP, 2001. Uses rigorous economic analysis to shed light on the firm and the individuals within it—owners, partners, and employees.
- Ash, Mary Kay. *Mary Kay: You Can Have it All: Lifetime Wisdom from America's Foremost Woman Entrepreneur.* Rocklin, CA: Prima Lifestyles Publishing, Inc., 1995. An inspirational book to motivate women to achieve success in business.
- Wallace, James, and Jim Erickson. *Hard Drive: Bill Gates and the Making of the Microsoft Empire.* New York: HarperCollins, 1993. A highly readable book about the drive of the world's richest entrepreneur.

Videos/DVDs

- *Economics U$A: The Firm/Supply & Demand.* Two 30-minute programs from the Annenberg/CPB Collection, 2002. Uses a fast-paced TV news format to examine issues in the American economy.
- *Economics at Work: Market Street.* 15 minutes. Agency for Instructional Technology / Zenger Media, 2003. Explores economic concepts through scenarios with teenagers.

Software

- *Hot Shot Business.* Disney Online and Kauffman Foundation. This simulation presents students with an opportunity to make choices that business owners must face. Geared more toward middle school students.

Internet

Visit **ClassZone.com** to link to

- a variety of chapter-specific, content-reviewed sites
- updates on data and topics presented throughout the chapter sections and Case Study
- updates to the Power Presentation

1 Plan & Prepare

Section 1 Objectives

- identify the characteristics of sole proprietorships
- describe how sole proprietorships are established
- compare the economic advantages and economic disadvantages of sole proprietorships

2 Focus & Motivate

Connecting to Everyday Life Preview the characteristics of entrepreneurs by asking students to discuss the questions in the first paragraph of page 230. Spend enough time gathering answers that students clearly understand the meaning of the question and its relevance to starting a business. For example, ask students to give an example from their own experience to the question "Can you live with uncertainty?" Then ask them to explain why that quality might be necessary for a business owner.

Taking Notes Remind students to take notes as they read by completing a two-column chart showing the advantages and disadvantages of sole proprietorships. They can use the Graphic Organizer at **Interactive Review @ ClassZone.com**. A sample is shown below.

Sole Proprietorships	
Advantages	**Disadvantages**
easy to open or close	limited funds
few regulations	limited life
freedom and control	unlimited liability
owner keeps profits	

SECTION 1

Sole Proprietorships

OBJECTIVES

In Section 1, you will
- identify the characteristics of sole proprietorships
- describe how sole proprietorships are established
- compare the economic advantages and economic disadvantages of sole proprietorships

KEY TERMS

business organization, *p. 226*
sole proprietorship, *p. 226*
limited life, *p. 228*
unlimited liability, *p. 228*

TAKING NOTES

As you read Section 1, complete a chart showing the advantages and disadvantages of sole proprietorships. Use the Graphic Organizer at **Interactive Review @ ClassZone.com**

Sole Proprietorships	
Advantages	Disadvantages

The Characteristics of Sole Proprietorships

KEY CONCEPTS

Every business begins with a person who has an idea about how to earn money and the drive to follow through on the idea and to create a business organization. A **business organization** is an enterprise that produces goods or provides services. Most of the goods and services available in a market economy come from business organizations.

QUICK REFERENCE

A **business organization** is an enterprise that produces goods or provides services, usually in order to make a profit.

A **sole proprietorship** is a business organization owned and controlled by one person.

The purpose of most business organizations is to earn a profit. They achieve this purpose by producing the goods and services that best meet consumers' wants and needs. In the course of meeting consumer demand, business organizations provide jobs and income that can be used for spending and saving. Business organizations also pay taxes that help finance government services.

The most common type of business organization in the United States is the **sole proprietorship**, a business owned and managed by a single person. Sole proprietorships include everything from mom-and-pop grocery stores to barbershops to computer repair businesses. They account for more than 70 percent of all businesses in the United States. However, they generate less than 5 percent of all sales by American businesses.

Sole Proprietorships Beauty salons are frequently operated by one owner.

226 Chapter 8

SECTION 1 PROGRAM RESOURCES

ON LEVEL

Lesson Plans
- Core, p. 26

Unit 3 Resource Book
- Reading Study Guide, pp. 1–2
- Economic Simulations, pp. 47–48
- Section Quiz, p. 9

STRUGGLING READERS

Unit 3 Resource Book
- Reading Study Guide with Additional Support, pp. 3–5
- Reteaching Activity, p. 10

ENGLISH LEARNERS

Unit 3 Resource Book
- Reading Study Guide with Additional Support (Spanish), pp. 6–8

INCLUSION

Lesson Plans
- Modified for Inclusion, p. 26

GIFTED AND TALENTED

Unit 3 Resource Book
- Case Study Resources: The Evolution of Levi Strauss & Co.—A Matter of Values, pp. 45–46

TECHNOLOGY

eEdition DVD-ROM
eEdition Online
Power Presentation DVD-ROM
Economics Concepts Transparencies
- CT26 Advantages and Disadvantages of Running a Bicycle Repair Shop as a Sole Proprietorship

Daily Test Practice Transparencies, TT26
ClassZone.com

EXAMPLE Bart's Cosmic Comics

To understand how sole proprietorships are set up and run, let's look at the example of Bart's Cosmic Comics. Bart started collecting comic books in grade school. Over the years, he amassed a huge collection of comics as well as other related items—lunch boxes, action figures, and so on. At the same time, he learned a lot about the comic book business. So, few of his friends expressed surprise when Bart announced that he wanted to open a business selling comic books and related merchandise.

Raising Funds Bart needed money to rent and renovate the space he found downtown and to buy new and used comics to stock the store. A hefty withdrawal from his savings account got him started, but he needed to borrow to get the job finished. He tried to get a loan from a local bank. However, because he was not yet an established business owner, bank officers were reluctant to approve the loan. Finally, he turned to his family and friends, who together lent him $15,000.

Preparing to Open After raising the necessary funds, Bart completed the few legal steps required to open his business. These included obtaining a business license and a site permit, a document stating that the local government allowed him to use the space he was renting for business. He also registered the name he had chosen for his business—Bart's Cosmic Comics.

Initial Difficulties At first, business was slow. Bart worried that the store would fail and he would be stuck with no income and no way to repay the loans. He thought the safest course of action might be to hang on to what cash he had so he could keep the store open for as long as possible. After much consideration, however, he decided to take another risk, spending $1,000 on advertisements in local newspapers. He also ran several in-store promotions. His business began to take off.

Find an update on sole proprietorships at **ClassZone.com**

Success Within 18 months, Bart had paid back his loans and was earning a profit. Shortly after, he decided to expand his inventory to include T-shirts and posters and to hire an assistant to help run the store. This time when he asked the bank for a loan to pay for the expansion, bank officers were ready to approve the financing. Bart's success indicated that giving him a loan would be a good business decision.

APPLICATION Applying Economic Concepts

A. Identify two or three examples of businesses you might want to establish as sole proprietorships.

Answers will vary. Look for reasonable enterprises that involve sole owners, such as lawn care, computer consulting, dog walking, and dressmaking.

3 Teach

The Characteristics of Sole Proprietorships

Discuss

- What might motivate someone to start a business rather than work for someone else? *(chances of making more money and being one's own boss)*
- What might keep a person from starting a business? *(start up costs, wrong personality type, fear of risk)*

More About . . .

Incubators

Business incubators are organizations that help start-up businesses get off the ground. They can be sponsored by universities, corporations, communities, or economic development groups. Their goals depend, in part, upon their sponsorship. Generally, their purpose is to provide discounted rent, as well as discounted or even free business and legal support for promising start-ups.

After the dot-com bubble burst in the 1990s, many incubators dissolved. But incubators made a comeback in the early 2000s.

Economics Update

Go to **ClassZone.com** to find updated information on sole proprietorships.

LEVELED ACTIVITY

Analyzing News Stories

Time 30 Minutes 

Objective Students will demonstrate an understanding of the advantages and disadvantages of various business structures. (These various business structures are covered throughout Chapter 8.)

Basic

Considering your personal strengths, which of the following choices appeals to you the most?
- being in business for yourself
- working for someone else in a for-profit enterprise; in a nonprofit enterprise

Refer to advantages and disadvantages of each, answering the question in a few paragraphs.

On Level

Considering your personal strengths, which of the following choices appeals to you the most?
- starting a sole proprietorship; a partnership
- working for a corporation; for a nonprofit
- starting a nonprofit organization

Refer to advantages and disadvantages of each, answering the question in a short essay.

Challenge

Considering your personal strengths, skills, knowledge, and interests, what kind of business might you start? Which of the business structures would best suit your personal traits, as well as your business idea? Explain your answer in an essay. Refer to the advantages and disadvantages of each business structure as you develop your essay.

Sole Proprietorships: Advantages and Disadvantages

Discuss

- Given the disadvantages, why do you think so many people choose to start a sole proprietorship? *(Possible answer: They believe that the advantages—ease of start-up, freedom and control, relatively few regulations, and the right to all profits—outweigh the disadvantages—difficulty in raising funds and the attendant problems, limited life, and unlimited liability.)*
- What regulations must a sole proprietor follow? *(zoning laws, labor laws, laws governing the opening or closing of a business, tax laws)* Why would a government want to limit the number of regulations for a new business? *(to encourage more people to start one in the formal market, as opposed to the informal market, in order to broaden the tax base and help grow the economy)*

Technomics

Small Business Administration
The federal government's Small Business Administration maintains a comprehensive Web site for people starting up and managing a small business. Some of the many resources available online are:

- planning guides
- links to mentoring programs
- downloadable government forms
- funding resources
- library of articles and data

Presentation Options

Review the characteristics of sole proprietorships by using the following presentation options:

 **Power Presentations DVD-ROM**
Using the Display Tool, you can highlight advantages and disadvantages of sole proprietorships.

 **Economics Concepts Transparencies**

- CT26 Advantages and Disadvantages of Running a Bicycle Repair Shop as a Sole Proprietorship

Sole Proprietorships: Advantages and Disadvantages

QUICK REFERENCE

Limited life is a situation where a business closes if the owner dies, retires, or leaves for some other reason.

Unlimited liability means that a business owner is responsible for all the business's losses and debts.

KEY CONCEPTS

The sole proprietorship has certain advantages and disadvantages that set it apart from other kinds of business structures. For example, sole proprietorships are not governed by as many regulations as other types of businesses. Also, sole proprietorships have **limited life**, a situation in which a business ceases to exist if the owner dies, retires, or leaves the business for some other reason. Finally, sole proprietors have **unlimited liability**, a situation in which a business owner is responsible for all the losses, debts, and other claims against the business.

ADVANTAGES Sole Proprietorships

There is a reason that sole proprietorships are by far the most common type of business structure: they have several significant advantages.

Easy to Open or Close Bart's start-up requirements were typical: funding, a license, a site permit, and a legally registered name. If Bart wanted to get out of the business, he would find that process easy as well. As long as he has settled all his bills, Bart may close the business when he sees fit.

Few Regulations Compared with other business organizations, sole proprietorships are lightly regulated. Bart, for example, must locate his store in an area zoned, or officially set aside, for businesses. He also must treat his employees according to various labor laws.

Freedom and Control Bart makes all the decisions and does so quickly without having to check with partners or boards of directors. Having complete control and seeing his ideas come to life gives Bart, like many other sole proprietors, a strong sense of personal satisfaction. In other words, he enjoys being his own boss.

Owner Keeps Profits Bart also enjoys the chief economic advantage of the sole proprietorship. Since he is the sole owner of the business, he gets to keep all the profits the business earns.

Sole Proprietors Are Fully Responsible The owner bears full responsibility for running the business but also keeps all of the profits.

DIFFERENTIATING INSTRUCTION

Struggling Readers

Make a Chart
Have students make a chart of the advantages and disadvantages of a sole proprietorship. They should use the subheads from the text (for example, Easy to Open or Close, Few Regulations) under the appropriate column and write a one-sentence statement to accompany each subhead. Direct students to hold onto their charts for future use.

Gifted and Talented

Interview a Proprietor
Have pairs of students work together to identify a sole proprietorship in the community and arrange an interview with the owner. They should go prepared with a list of questions related to how the proprietor got started, as well as to the advantages and disadvantages of that form of business. Students should bring along a tape recorder and ask permission to record when they arrive. Then, they should transcribe the interview and share it with the class.

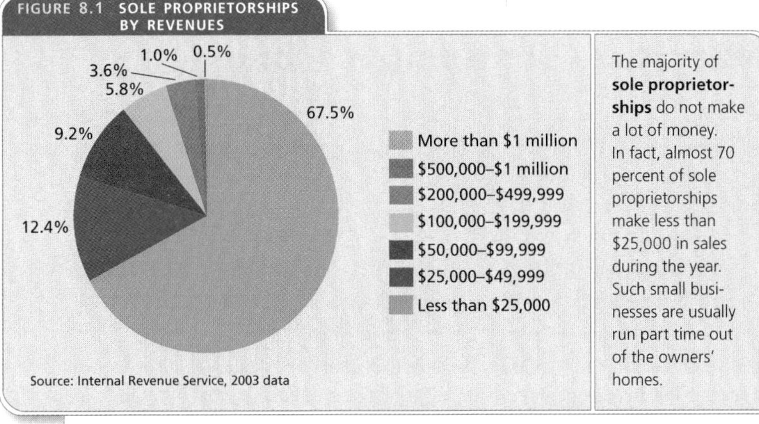

The majority of **sole proprietorships** do not make a lot of money. In fact, almost 70 percent of sole proprietorships make less than $25,000 in sales during the year. Such small businesses are usually run part time out of the owners' homes.

ANALYZE GRAPHS

1. About what percentage of sole proprietorships make less than $50,000 in annual sales?
2. Make a generalization about sole proprietorships based on information in the graph.

DISADVANTAGES Sole Proprietorships

Bart's story hints at some of the disadvantages of sole proprietorships as well.

Limited Funds Especially at start-up, Bart had very limited funds. This disadvantage is one of the key reasons that sole proprietorships are far more likely to fail than other types of business organizations. Until he had established his business, Bart had trouble securing a bank loan. Without monetary reserves to fall back on, he found it a struggle to stay in business. Even when the business became successful, Bart felt that the lack of funds hurt him. He worried that he would not be able to attract and keep good workers because his limited funds meant he could not pay competitive wages or offer benefits such as health insurance.

Limited Life Bart found that some of the advantages of the sole proprietorship may also prove to be disadvantages. He appreciated the ease with which you can set up or close a sole proprietorship. However, this means that sole proprietorships have limited life. If he leaves the business, Bart's Cosmic Comics ceases to exist.

Unlimited Liability Bart enjoys having total responsibility for running the business, even though that means that he works long hours. Having total responsibility for the business produces perhaps the greatest disadvantage of a sole proprietorship—unlimited liability. Bart is legally responsible for all the financial aspects of the business. If Bart's Cosmic Comics fails, he must still pay all its debts, even without income from the business. If necessary, he may have to sell property and use his personal savings to pay off debts. Sole proprietors, then, may lose their homes, cars, or personal savings if their businesses fail.

APPLICATION Analyzing Cause and Effect

B. Why do you think that sole proprietorships are the most common form of business organization in the United States?
Ease of start-up, full control, relative freedom from regulation, ability to leave the business at any time, all profits to sole proprietor.

Analyzing Graphs: Figure 8.1

Explain that there are about 20 million non-farm sole proprietorships in the U.S., according to tax returns. Given that information and the information on the graph, ask students how many sole proprietors make more than $1 million a year? *(20 million x 0.5%=10,000)* How many make less than $100,000? *(9.2% + 12.4% + 67.5% = 89.1%. 20 million x 89.1%=17,820,000)*

Answers

1. *about 80%*
2. *Possible answer: Most sole proprietorships make less than $25,000 a year, and very few make their owners rich.*

More About . . .

Health Care: Another Disadvantage
One of the most vexing problems with self-employment is the cost of health care. Self-employed workers not only have to pay for their health insurance premiums, they also have to pay a self-employment tax on those premiums. They can deduct the cost of those premiums from their income tax liability, but not from their self-employment tax liability.

SMALL GROUP ACTIVITY

Evaluating Risk and Reward

Time 30 Minutes ◑

Task Evaluate the risks and rewards of a potential new business.

Materials Needed paper and pens

Activity

- Have pairs develop a one-page or less description of a business idea and a loan request. Their request should include the reason for the loan and the potential reward of the endeavor.
- Then, let one of the pair be the banker whose job it is to approve or deny a loan and the other be a sole proprietor seeking a loan. The proprietor should present the case orally as well as in writing.
- Have the banker respond orally to the proprietor, approving or disapproving, and giving reasons.
- Have each pair present their ideas and outcomes to the class.

Rubric

	Understanding of Risk and Reward	Presentation of Information
4	excellent	clear and complete
3	good	mostly clear
2	fair	sometimes clear
1	poor	unclear

Mary Kay Ash

More About . . .

Mary Kay Ash

After she left World Gifts in disappointment, Mary Kay Ash set herself the task of writing a book to help women succeed in a business world where men held most positions of authority. As she planned her book, she made two lists. One list was about favorable factors for women that she came across in her business experience. The other was about problem areas for women.

As she looked at those lists, Ash realized that instead of a book outline she had a business plan for a new company. Mary Kay Cosmetics, whose motto is "to enrich women's lives," came into being that same year.

More About . . .

Mary Kay Cosmetics

Ash had her company form a Corporate Heritage Department. Its purpose was to make sure that the traditions that made Ash so effective would not be forgotten when she was no longer around to attend to them.

The traditions included such personal touches as sending a birthday card to each saleswoman and maintaining a care list of beauty consultants who were experiencing personal problems. The consultants would receive a phone call from senior management—often Mary Kay herself—offering support and encouragement. Ash had several secretaries just to handle the personal exchanges she had with her beauty consultants and others with whom she did business.

Economics Update

At **ClassZone.com,** students will find updated information on Mary Kay Inc.

ECONOMICS PACESETTER

Mary Kay Ash: Going It Alone

FAST FACTS

Mary Kay Ash

Title: Founder of Mary Kay Inc.

Born: May 12, 1918

Died: November 22, 2001

Major Accomplishment: Creating Mary Kay Inc., a company that offers women unique rewards for business success

Sales Milestones:
1965—$800 thousand
1991—$500 million
2005—$2 billion

Mary Kay Career Cars: Sales people who have qualified for a pink Cadillac or other Mary Kay career car: more than 100,000

Famous Quotation: *"If you think you can, you can. And if you think you can't, you're right."*

Economics Update

Find an update on Mary Kay Inc. at **ClassZone.com**

Do you have what it takes to "go it alone" as an entrepreneur? See how many of these questions you can answer with a "yes."

- Are you willing to take risks?
- Can you live with uncertainty?
- Are you self-confident?
- Are you self-directed, able to set and reach goals for yourself?
- Are you optimistic, energetic, and action-oriented?

Like other entrepreneurs, Mary Kay Ash had all of these qualities. She used them to turn $5,000 in personal savings into Mary Kay Inc., a business that now sells billions of dollars of cosmetics and other merchandise every year.

Building a Business

While raising three children on her own, Ash built a very successful career in direct sales. In 1963, however, Ash suffered a blow when she lost out on a promotion that was given instead to a man she had trained. Feeling she had been treated unfairly, Ash resolved to create an enterprise that would reward women for their hard work. Later that year, she started a cosmetics company with her son Richard and nine sales people—whom Ash referred to as "beauty consultants." In 1964, sales exceeded $198,000. By the end of 1965, sales had skyrocketed to more than $800,000.

Since its founding, Mary Kay® products have been sold at in-home parties rather than in stores. Mary Kay has always had distinctive programs for recognizing women who reached certain goals. Pink Cadillacs, diamond-studded jewelry, luxury vacations, and other incentives spur the sales representatives to greater and greater efforts.

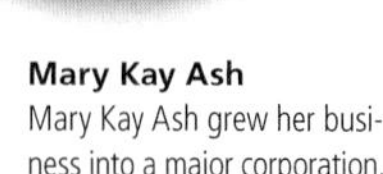

Mary Kay Ash
Mary Kay Ash grew her business into a major corporation.

In 1987, Ash assumed the title of chairman emeritus, though she remained active in the company until her death in 2001. Her company and its culture continued to flourish. In 2005, over 1.6 million Mary Kay beauty consultants operated in more than 30 countries worldwide. As the company expanded globally, China became Mary Kay's largest market outside the United States.

APPLICATION Making Inferences

C. Why do you think Mary Kay Ash proved so successful in her cosmetics venture?
Answers will vary but should focus on her entrepreneurial skills and her innovation in sales techniques and incentives.

DIFFERENTIATING INSTRUCTION

English Learners

Use Oral Language

Pair an English learner with an English speaker. They should take turns reading the Economics Pacesetter aloud to promote fluency and comprehension. Encourage the English learner to ask about unfamiliar words or expressions and the English speaker to explain these and give more examples. Also, have the pair discuss the Application question.

Inclusion

Make an Illustrated Timeline

Direct students to make an illustrated timeline of the events covered in the Economics Pacesetter feature in order to help them sequence events. Tell them to use the Fast Facts sidebar information as well. They may use their own drawings or visuals from Internet or library sources.

SECTION 1 Assessment

REVIEWING KEY CONCEPTS

1. Explain the relationship between the terms in each of these pairs:
   a. *business organization* *sole proprietorship*
   b. *limited life* *unlimited liability*
2. What are the main advantages of a sole proprietorship?
3. What are the main disadvantages of a sole proprietorship?
4. Who gets the profits from a sole proprietorship? Who has to pay all the debts?
5. What steps do new sole proprietorships usually need to take before they can open?
6. **Using Your Notes** Select one of the businesses you identified in Application A on page 227. If you were starting that business, do you think the advantages of a sole proprietorship would outweigh the disadvantages or vice versa? Why? Refer to your completed chart as you formulate your answer. Use the Graphic Organizer at **Interactive Review @ ClassZone.com**

Sole Proprietorships	
Advantages	Disadvantages

CRITICAL THINKING

7. **Evaluating Economic Decisions** Suppose Cosmic Comics becomes very successful, and Bart decides to try opening a second store. What issues should Bart consider? What challenges will he face?
8. **Making Inferences and Drawing Conclusions** In what ways might limited life be considered an advantage for sole proprietors?
9. **Applying Economic Concepts** Explain how a sole proprietorship rests on the principles of free enterprise.
10. **Writing About Economics** Write a brief paragraph explaining what Bart might learn from Mary Kay Ash.
11. **Challenge** How many "yes" answers did you provide to the questions at the top of page 230? If you had one or more "no" answers, explain how you would change a sole proprietorship in order to suit your skills and abilities. If you answered "yes" to all of the questions, explain what you would like about running your own business.

ECONOMICS IN PRACTICE

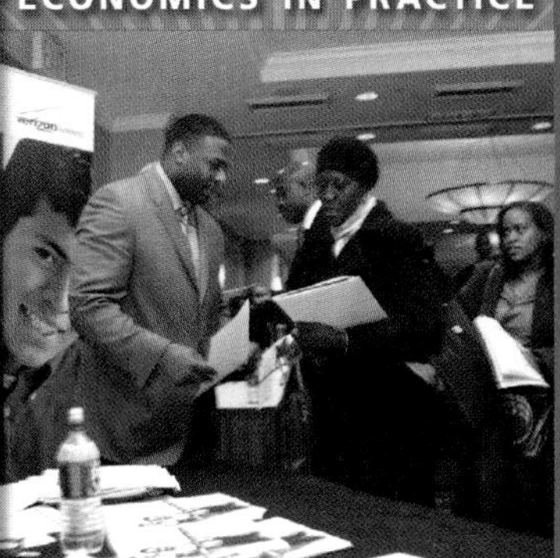
Business fairs promote new opportunities.

Starting Your Own Business
Each year, thousands of Americans start businesses as sole proprietorships.

Write a Business Plan Choose a business that you might like to start as a sole proprietorship. Use the following questions to develop a plan that shows how the business will make a profit.

- How much money will it take to start the business? Detail each expense.
- How much money will it take to run the business each month? Detail each expense.
- Who will the customers be and how will you attract them?
- Once the business is established, how much will it earn each month? Detail each source of income.
- How much profit will you earn?

Challenge What challenges do you think you would face in making this business a success? Write a paragraph explaining how you would address these challenges.

4 Assess & Reteach

Assess Discuss the questions in Reviewing Key Concepts as a class. For question 6, ask for volunteers to share their conclusions and encourage a brief discussion about each. You may wish to give students a choice between questions 9 and 11 as the basis for an extended essay.

Unit 3 Resource Book
- Section Quiz, p. 9

Interactive Review @ ClassZone.com
- Section Quiz

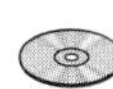
Test Generator CD-ROM
- Section Quiz

Reteach Have students analyze the business plan they develop for Economics in Practice or the ideas for a sole proprietorship they had for the Application question on page 227. Ask them to write two or three sentences under each heading to describe their chosen business:

Setting Up
Raising Funds
Preparing to Open
Initial Difficulties
Success

Advantages
Easy to Open or Close
Few Regulations
Freedom and Control
Owner Keeps Profits

Disadvantages
Limited Funds
Limited Life
Unlimited Liability

Unit 3 Resource Book
- Reteaching Activity, p. 10

SECTION 1 ASSESSMENT ANSWERS

Reviewing Key Concepts

1. a. *business organization*, p. 226; *sole proprietorship*, p. 226
   b. *limited life*, p. 228; *unlimited liability*, p. 228
2. ease of start-up, few regulations, full control, all profits to sole proprietor
3. limited funds, limited life, unlimited liability
4. the owner
5. Businesses usually need to get a business license, site permit, and legal name.
6. See page 226 for an example of a completed diagram. Answers will vary, but look for an understanding of the basic concepts.

Critical Thinking

7. Answers will vary but may include funding, location, advertising, finding a reliable manager.
8. Limited life reflects the ease of exit from the business; a business with unlimited life must create a succession plan.
9. If sole proprietors provide what customers want at a fair price, they will succeed; if not, they will fold. They have economic as well as legal equality, and they operate from a base of private property.
10. Answers will vary. Look for an understanding of lessons for entrepreneurs, such as rewarding employees to motivate them.
11. Answers will vary. Students who answered 'no' to some questions should explain how they might adapt their business to suit their needs. Those who answered 'yes' to all questions should spell out what they like about the idea of running their own business.

Economics in Practice

Answers will vary, but look for an explanation of why the particular business was chosen and the challenges the student might face in starting such a business.

1 Plan & Prepare

Section 2 Objectives

- identify the characteristics and types of partnerships
- compare the economic advantages and disadvantages of partnerships

2 Focus & Motivate

Connecting to Everyday Life Facilitate a brief discussion with students about the value of partnerships. Ask them to offer examples of how they have worked with a partner in their own experience. *(Possible answers: musical partnership, game partnership, school projects, swimming "with a buddy", and so on)* From these specifics, have students generalize about what partnerships offer. *(Answers will vary, but try to elicit the idea that each partner brings different strengths and complements the other.)* Explain that business partnerships have some of the same advantages.

Taking Notes Remind students to take notes as they read by completing a comparison and contrast chart to show similarities and differences between partnerships and sole proprietorships. They can use the Graphic Organizer at **Interactive Review @ ClassZone.com**. A sample is shown below.

Sole Proprietorships	Partnerships
one owner	two or more owners
easy to open	easy to open
few regulations	few regulations
freedom and control	joint decision making
limited funds	access to resources
limited life	limited life
unlimited liability	unlimited liability in most cases

SECTION 2

Forms of Partnerships

OBJECTIVES

In Section 2, you will
- identify the characteristics and types of partnerships
- compare the economic advantages and disadvantages of partnerships

KEY TERMS

partnership, *p. 232*
general partnership, *p. 233*
limited partnership, *p. 233*
limited liability partnership, *p. 233*

TAKING NOTES

As you read Section 2, complete a comparison and contrast chart to show similarities and differences between partnerships and sole proprietorships. Use the Graphic Organizer at **Interactive Review @ ClassZone.com**

Sole Proprietorships	Partnerships
One owner	Two or more owners

The Characteristics of Partnerships

KEY CONCEPTS

In Section 1, you read how Bart set up his business as a sole proprietorship. His sister, Mary, who is a whiz at bookkeeping, began helping him with the accounting tasks. As her role in the business expanded, Bart proposed that they join forces in a partnership. A **partnership** is a business co-owned by two or more people, or "partners," who agree on how responsibilities, profits, and losses will be divided. Bart lacks the bookkeeping skills his sister has, and the extra funds she brings could help Cosmic Comics to grow. Forming a partnership might be a good business decision.

QUICK REFERENCE

A **partnership** is a business co-owned by two or more partners who agree on how responsibilities, profits, and losses of that business are divided.

Partnerships are found in all kinds of businesses, from construction companies to real estate groups. However, they are especially widespread in the areas of professional and financial services—law firms, accounting firms, doctors' offices, and investment companies. There are several different types of partnerships—general partnerships, limited partnerships, and limited liability partnerships—but they are all run in the same general way.

SECTION 2 PROGRAM RESOURCES

ON LEVEL

Lesson Plans
- Core, p. 27

Unit 3 Resource Book
- Reading Study Guide, pp. 11–12
- Math Skills Worksheet, pp. 33–34
- Section Quiz, p. 19

STRUGGLING READERS

Unit 3 Resource Book
- Reading Study Guide with Additional Support, pp. 13–15
- Reteaching Activity, p. 20

ENGLISH LEARNERS

Unit 3 Resource Book
- Reading Study Guide with Additional Support, (Spanish), pp. 16–18

INCLUSION

Lesson Plans
- Modified for Inclusion, p. 27

GIFTED AND TALENTED

Unit 3 Resource Book
- Case Study Resources: The Evolution of Levi Strauss & Co.—A Matter of Values, pp. 45–46

TECHNOLOGY

eEdition DVD-ROM

eEdition Online

Power Presentation DVD-ROM

Economics Concepts Transparencies
- CT27 Which Type of Partnership Is Right for You?

Daily Test Practice Transparencies, TT27

ClassZone.com

TYPE 1 General Partnerships

The most common type of partnership is the **general partnership**, a partnership in which partners share responsibility for managing the business and each one is liable for all business debts and losses. As in a sole proprietorship, that liability could put personal savings at risk. The trade-off for sharing the risky side of the business enterprise is sharing the rewards as well. Partners share responsibility, liability, and profits equally, unless there is a partnership agreement that specifies otherwise. This type of partnership is found in almost all areas of business.

TYPE 2 Limited Partnerships

In a general partnership, each partner is personally liable for the debts of the business, even if another partner caused the debt. There is a way, however, to limit one's liability in this kind of business organization. This is through a **limited partnership**, a partnership in which at least one partner is not involved in the day-to-day running of business and is liable only for the funds he or she has invested.

All limited partnerships must have at least one general partner who runs the business and is liable for all debts, but there can be any number of limited partners. Limited partners act as part owners of the business, and they share in the profits. This form of partnership allows the general partner or partners to raise funds to run the business through the limited partners.

QUICK REFERENCE

In a **general partnership** partners share management of the business and each one is liable for all business debts and losses.

A **limited partnership** is one in which at least one partner is not involved in the day-to-day running of business and is liable only for the funds he or she has invested.

In a **limited liability partnership** (LLP), all partners are limited partners and not responsible for the debts and other liabilities of other partners.

TYPE 3 Limited Liability Partnerships

Another kind of partnership is the **limited liability partnership** (LLP), a partnership in which all partners are limited partners and not responsible for the debts and other liabilities of other partners. If one partner makes a mistake that ends up costing the business a lot of money, the other partners cannot be held liable. In LLPs, partners' personal savings are not at risk unless the debts arise from their own mistakes.

Not all businesses can register as LLPs. Those that can include medical partnerships, law firms, and accounting firms. These are businesses in which malpractice—improper, negligent, or unprincipled behavior—can be an issue. LLPs are a fairly new form of business organization, and the laws governing them vary from state to state.

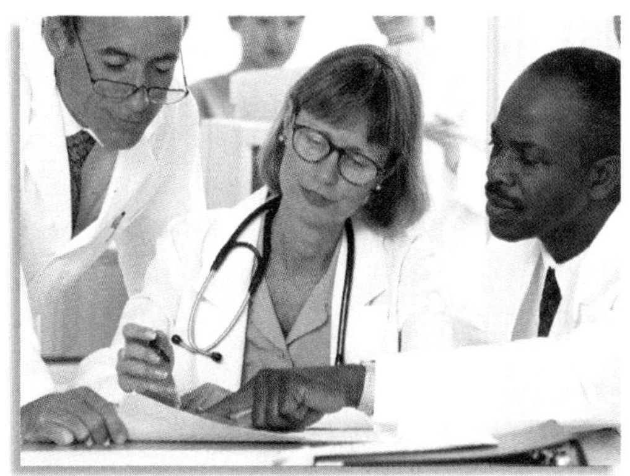

Partnerships Doctors' offices are often run as limited liability partnerships.

APPLICATION Comparing and Contrasting Economic Information

A. What are the differences in liability that distinguish general partnerships, limited partnerships, and limited liability partnerships? General partnerships—each partner fully liable; limited partnerships—at least one general partner liable for entire business; limited liability partnerships—all limited partners, not responsible for others' actions or debts.

3 Teach

The Characteristics of Partnerships

Discuss

- In what way is a general partnership different from a sole proprietorship? In what ways are they similar? *(different—two or more people rather than just one; similar—unlimited personal liability for each person; limited life)*
- Based on the information on this page, what do you think the term *silent partner* may mean when used in a business setting? *(a partner who does not participate in the day-to-day management of the company and is liable only for the funds he or she has invested)*

More About . . .

Limiting Liability

In addition to choosing the most appropriate structure, people wishing to limit liability for their business venture may want to incorporate in a state other than their own. The laws of the state in which the business is formed are the ones that govern the affairs of the business, even if all the day-to-day business operations are conducted in another state. Delaware and Nevada are especially popular states in which to incorporate because they offer greater liability protection for some business owners.

SMALL GROUP ACTIVITY

Creating Partnerships

Time 30 Minutes

Task Draft an agreement to form a particular kind of partnership.

Materials Needed paper and pen

Activity

- Divide students into three groups. One will form a general partnership; the second will form a limited partnership; and the third will form a limited liability partnership.
- Direct students in each group to agree on a focus for their business.
- Have each group draw up a draft agreement explaining the amount of each person's investment (can be arbitrary); each person's role, if any, in the day-to-day operations; and each person's liability.
- Ask each group to present its plan orally to the class. Encourage discussion after each presentation.

Rubric

	Understanding of Risk and Reward	Presentation of Information
4	excellent	accurate
3	good	mostly accurate
2	fair	sometimes inaccurate
1	poor	mostly inaccurate

Partnerships: Advantages and Disadvantages

Discuss

- What might happen, both good and bad, when a partnership ends? *(If both partners agree and all bills are settled, the dissolution of the partnership can be very clean and simple. However, if the partnership ends because of financial problems, at least one and possibly all of the partners will assume liability for the partnership's debts.)*
- A partnership calls for joint decision making, although this can lead to conflict between partners. What are some ways to limit the potential for conflict? *(limited partnership; give one partner a controlling stake in the firm)*

Analyzing Graphs: Figure 8.2

Refer students back to Figure 8.1 on page 229. Ask them to look carefully at the wedges of the pie as they move above the "Less than $25,000" category and to generalize about the trend. *(Each wedge gets progressively thinner, meaning that fewer people achieve the income level as the income level rises.)* Now ask students to look at Figure 8.2 for the same information and generalize the pattern. *(In each , most businesses are small. However, partnerships are more evenly divided among the revenue groups than are sole proprietorships.)* Ask students to suggest explanations for this. *(Possible answer: Income that is sufficient incentive for one person to stay in business may not be enough for members of a partnership.)*

Answers

1. *29.2%*
2. *The potential for higher revenues is increased by the greater human capital and greater access to funds.*

At **ClassZone.com,** students will find updated information on partnerships.

Partnerships: Advantages and Disadvantages

KEY CONCEPTS

Some of the economic advantages of partnerships are similar to those of sole proprietorships. Like sole proprietorships, partnerships are easy to set up and dissolve and have few government regulations. Compared with sole proprietorships, however, partners have greater access to funds. Also, possibilities exist for specialization among partners, which can promote efficiency.

The disadvantages of partnerships are similar to the disadvantages of sole proprietorships. Like the sole proprietor, at least one of the partners, except in LLPs, faces unlimited liability. Partnerships, too, have limited life. However, partnerships have at least one disadvantage that sole proprietorships avoid. Disagreements among partners can lead to serious problems in running the business.

ADVANTAGES Partnerships

Bart and Mary realized that if they formed a partnership they would benefit from some of the same advantages that sole proprietorships have, plus some important additional advantages.

Easy to Open and Close Partnerships, like sole proprietorships, are easy to start up and dissolve. Ending the partnership would be equally straightforward for Bart and

Economics Update

Find an update on partnerships at **ClassZone.com**

FIGURE 8.2 PARTNERSHIPS BY REVENUES

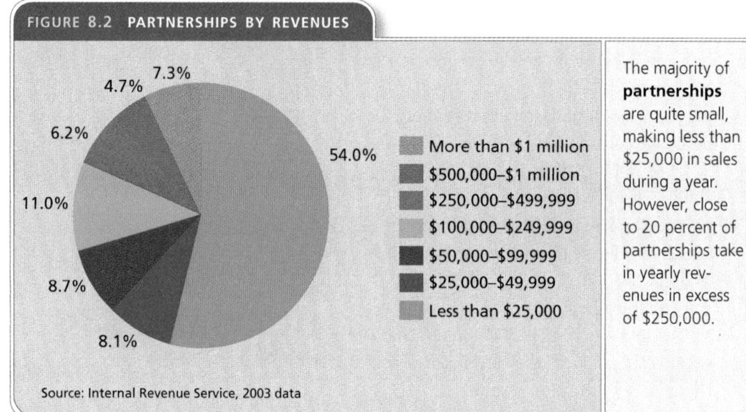

The majority of **partnerships** are quite small, making less than $25,000 in sales during a year. However, close to 20 percent of partnerships take in yearly revenues in excess of $250,000.

ANALYZE GRAPHS

1. What percentage of partnerships made more than $100,000 in sales?
2. Some 7 percent of partnerships took in more than $1 million in revenues, compared to just 0.5 percent of sole proprietorships. Why do you think partnerships generate more revenues than sole proprietorships?

DIFFERENTIATING INSTRUCTION

English Learners

Analyze Words

Ask students to explain how the prefix *dis-* affects the meaning of the word *disadvantages.* Point out that *dis-* is one of a number of negative prefixes. Direct students to the last paragraph of page 233 for other negative prefixes (*mal*practice, *im*proper, *un*principled). Suggest that students make a chart in their personal dictionaries with the following column headings to keep track of words they find with negative prefixes.

dis-	mal-	un-	im-	in-	ir-

Struggling Readers

Make a Chart, Part 2

Have students review the chart that they made in Section 1 of the advantages and disadvantages of a sole proprietorship. Now, they should make another chart of the same type for the advantages and disadvantages of partnerships. Once again, instruct students to hold onto the new chart for future use.

his sister. As long as they have settled all their bills, Bart and Mary may dissolve the partnership when they see fit.

Few Regulations Bart and Mary would not be burdened with a host of government regulations. They would enter into a legal agreement spelling out their rights and responsibilities as partners. Partners are covered under the Uniform Partnership Act (UPA), a law, adopted by most states, that lays out basic partnership rules.

Access to Resources Mary would bring additional funds to Cosmic Comics. In addition, partnerships generally make it easier to get bank loans for business purposes. A greater pool of funds also makes it easier for partnerships to attract and keep workers.

Joint Decision Making In most partnerships, partners share in the making of business decisions. This may result in better decisions, for each partner brings his or her own particular perspective to the process. The exception is limited partnerships, in which the limited partner does not participate in running the business.

Specialization Also, each partner may bring specific skills to the business. For example, Bart brings knowledge of comic books, while Mary, who studied business accounting in college, brings skills in bookkeeping and finance. Having partners focus on their special skills promotes efficiency.

Joint Decision Making Partners benefit by making decisions together. But sometimes disagreements can interfere with running the business.

DISADVANTAGES Partnerships

Bart and Mary also considered the disadvantages of partnerships.

Unlimited Liability The biggest disadvantage of most partnerships is the same as that of sole proprietorships: unlimited liability. Both Bart and Mary are personally responsible for the full extent of the partnership's debts and other liabilities. So they risk having to use their personal savings, and even having to sell their property, to cover their business debts.

Potential for Conflict As partners, they may encounter a new disadvantage as well. Having more than one decision maker can often lead to better decisions. However, it can also detract from efficiency if there are many partners and each decision requires the approval of all. Further, disagreements among partners can become so severe that they lead to the closing of the business.

Limited Life Like sole proprietorships, partnerships have limited life. When a partner dies, retires, or leaves for some other reason, or if new partners are added, the business as it was originally formed ceases to exist legally. A new partnership arrangement must be established if the enterprise is to continue.

APPLICATION Applying Economic Concepts

B. Consider the businesses you identified in Application A on page 227 of Section 1. Would these businesses work as partnerships? Why or why not?
Answers will vary but should involve a discussion of the advantages and disadvantages of partnerships.

More About . . .

Effective Business Partnerships
Darrell Zahorsky, in About.com's *Small Business Information Guide* recommends the following for effective business partnerships:

- shared vision
- clearly defined business roles
- slightly unequal sharing, with one partner having 51% ownership as opposed to 49% by the other owner (This avoids deadlocks in decision making.)
- monthly meetings of the partners
- a formal partnership agreement

More About . . .

The Veil of Liability
While the law allows business owners to protect personal assets, and in some cases even business assets, attempts to avoid all risk and exposure are routinely challenged by creditors. Businesses have to follow stringent rules for investment levels and must maintain proper documentation. Failure to do so can result in a lawsuit that "pierces the veil of liability."

INDIVIDUAL ACTIVITY

Advertising for a Business Partner

Time 30 Minutes ◑

Task Create a want ad to attract one or more partners to a business venture.

Materials Needed paper and pen

Activity

- Direct students to think of a business that they might start and choose one of the partnership forms as their business structure.
- Have students create a want ad for a magazine that reaches potential partners and investors.
- The want ad should focus on the advantages of the partnership but also disclose the disadvantages.
- Publish the want ads in a class magazine.

Rubric

	Understanding of Advantages and Disadvantages of Partnerships	Presentation of Information
4	excellent	clear and complete
3	good	mostly clear
2	fair	sometimes clear
1	poor	unclear

Distinguishing Fact from Opinion

1 Plan & Prepare

Objectives

- distinguish fact from opinion
- recognize words that signal an opinion or judgment

2 Focus & Motivate

One of the most famous business partnerships in recent times is that between Ben Cohen and Jerry Greenfield, founders of Ben & Jerry's, which is known for its premium ice cream and social responsibility. Ask students to tell what they know about the company. Then discuss the differences between these two statements: (1) Ben & Jerry's donates 7.5 percent of pre-tax profits to nonprofit organizations. (2) More companies should follow Ben & Jerry's model of social responsibility. *(The first can be proved true; the second is a judgment open to disagreement.)*

3 Teach

Ask a student to read the passage aloud. Ask another student to read the callouts. Point out that sometimes the difference between fact and opinion is somewhat harder to determine, with no obvious signal words. For example, read the following sentence and ask students whether it states a fact or an opinion. "The years 2002 and 2003 were bad for small businesses." *(This is an opinion, since it expresses a judgment even though the facts seem to support it.)* Next ask students to revise that sentence so that it does express a fact. *(Possible answer: In 2002 and 2003, more firms went out of business than were started.)*

For additional practice see **Skillbuilder Handbook**, page R27.

THINKING ECONOMICALLY Answers

1. The number of new firms created seems to support the assertion in the first sentence.

2. Answers will vary. Possible answers: *Fact—Although the number of firm closures increased from 2001 to 2002, the number of bankruptcies decreased; Opinion—The year 2000 was a better year for small businesses than 2001.*

ECONOMICS SKILLBUILDER

For more information on distinguishing fact from opinion, see the Skillbuilder Handbook, page R27.

Distinguishing Fact from Opinion

Facts are events, dates, statistics, and statements that can be proved to be true. Facts can be checked for accuracy. Economists use facts to develop **opinions**, which may be expressed as judgments, beliefs, or theories. By learning to distinguish between facts and opinions, you will be able to think critically about the economic theories, interpretations, and conclusions of others.

TIPS FOR ANALYZING TEXT Use the following guidelines to analyze economic information in written works:

FIGURE 8.3 **STARTS AND CLOSURES OF SMALL EMPLOYER FIRMS**

	2000	2001	2002	2003	2004
New Firms	574,300	585,140	569,750	553,500	580,990
Firm Closures	542,831	553,291	586,890	572,300	576,200
Bankruptcies	35,472	40,099	38,540	35,037	34,317

Sources: U.S. Bureau of the Census; Administrative Office of the U.S. Courts; U.S. Department of Labor, Employment and Training Administration.

Facts used by economists are often in the form of statistics, like the ones in this table.

Many Americans have faith that their ideas will bring them wealth or at least a comfortable living. According to the U.S. government, Americans created more than half a million small firms, or businesses, in the United States each year from 2000 to 2005. While prospective entrepreneurs may interpret these figures as a small business bonanza, overall closures of small businesses also exceeded the half-million mark each year during the same period. And in 2002 and 2003, more small firms closed their doors than opened them, suggesting that market conditions for those two years were particularly unfavorable for the prolonged success of small businesses. Yet bankruptcies among small firms declined in 2002 and 2003. Although such data are likely to be of interest to prospective entrepreneurs, it is limited in nature. Anyone planning to start a business venture would be wise to conduct more extensive research.

Opinions. Look for words, such as *suggest, suggesting, belief,* and *believe,* which often express assertions, claims, and hypotheses.

Facts include economic data that can be proved. The writer bases this statement on verifiable facts from the table.

Judgments, another form of opinion, often use descriptive words such as *wise, foolish, sensible,* and *fortunate,* which have an emotional quality.

THINKING ECONOMICALLY Distinguishing Fact from Opinion

1. What facts, if any, does the author use to support the first sentence in the paragraph?
2. Using information from the table and article, write one statement of fact and one statement of opinion. As a class, share your statements and discuss.

DIFFERENTIATING INSTRUCTION

Inclusion

Highlight Text

For hands-on learning, make photocopies of page 236 for students and distribute them before discussing the Economics Skillbuilder lesson. Encourage students to use highlighters to mark important information in the text, especially words that signal opinions and judgments.

Gifted and Talented

Form Supported Opinions

Use the statistics provided in the Economics Skillbuilder to come up with three factual and three well-supported opinions. A few examples: Fact—There were fewer bankruptcies in 2002 than in 2001. Opinion—Since the number of bankruptcies has declined overall from 2000 to 2004 but the number of closures has increased, there may be a growing number of closures based on personal choice rather than on a pressing financial situation.

SECTION 2 Assessment

Online Quiz
ClassZone.com

REVIEWING KEY CONCEPTS

1. Explain the relationship between the terms in each of these pairs:
   a. *partnership* / *general partnership*
   b. *limited partnership* / *limited liability partnership*
2. What are the main advantages of a partnership?
3. What are the main disadvantages of a partnership?
4. In what ways do the increased resources of a partnership help a business?
5. What determines how partners will divide responsibilities, profits, and debts?
6. **Using Your Notes** Which type of partnership is most like a sole proprietorship? Explain your answer with specific characteristics. Refer to your completed chart.

Sole Proprietorships	Partnerships
One owner	Two or more owners

Use the Graphic Organizer at **Interactive Review @ ClassZone.com**

CRITICAL THINKING

7. **Applying Economic Concepts** If you were looking to start a business as a partnership, what traits would you look for in potential partners? Draw up a list of five traits and give a brief explanation for each. Be sure to take the advantages and disadvantages of partnerships into consideration.
8. **Comparing and Contrasting Economic Information** Briefly explore the differences in potential for job satisfaction between sole proprietorships and partnerships. One size does not fit all—try to determine which of these two business organizations would suit you best.
9. **Writing About Economics** American business leader John D. Rockefeller said, "A friendship founded on business is a good deal better than a business founded on friendship." What do you think he had in mind? Write a brief paragraph agreeing or disagreeing, with reference to partnerships.
10. **Challenge** Do you think that major retail or manufacturing businesses would work as partnerships? Why or why not?

ECONOMICS IN PRACTICE

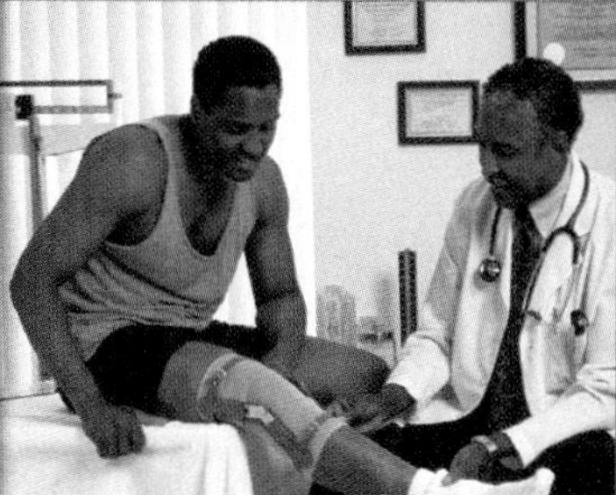

Types of Partnerships
The different types of partnerships suit different types of businesses.

Identify Partnerships Identify the type of partnership represented in each description.

1. Doctors choose this type of partnership because it protects them from malpractice suits brought against other partners.
2. The only role that George plays in the partnership is to collect profits or bear losses based on the amount of funds he contributed.
3. Stephen and Mike start a consulting service to help businesses manage their trademarks and patents. They are the only partners, sharing equally in the work, profits, and losses.
4. Rosa and Serena carefully review expansion plans after new partners provide extra funds. However, they know that they remain fully liable if their decisions are not sound.

Challenge Write a description of three different business partnerships without naming them. Exchange your descriptions with a classmate and identify each other's partnerships.

④ Assess & Reteach

Assess You may wish to assign the questions in Reviewing Key Concepts as an individual written review. For the Critical Thinking questions, divide the class into four groups, one for each question. Then direct students within the group to collaborate on providing a response. Go over the Economics in Practice activity as a class.

Unit 3 Resource Book
- Section Quiz, p. 19

Interactive Review @ ClassZone.com
- Section Quiz

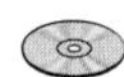
Test Generator CD-ROM
- Section Quiz

Reteach Make a transparency or use the board to display the following chart, and have the class complete it together. Ask students to explain whether the trait is present in each of the business organizations and, if so, how.

	Sole Prop.	General Partner	Limited Partner	LLP
owner operates business				
limited life				
unlimited liability				
limited funds				
ease of start-up and closure				

Unit 3 Resource Book
- Reteaching Activity, p. 20

SECTION 2 ASSESSMENT ANSWERS

Reviewing Key Concepts

1. a. *partnership*, p. 232; *general partnership*, p. 233
   b. *limited partnership*, p. 233; *limited liability partnership*, p. 233
2. ease of start-up, few regulations, access to resources, shared decision making, specialization
3. limited life, potential for disagreements among partners, liability issues depending on type of partnership
4. They help them to secure loans and to attract and keep good workers.
5. either a legal agreement among the parties or the Uniform Partnership Act
6. See page 232 for an example of a completed diagram. Answers will vary. General partnerships are like sole proprietorships because of the full involvement of the owners, the unlimited liability, and the limited life. A limited partnership is like a sole proprietorship because there can be just one general partner making all the decisions and with full liability. The LLP is like the sole proprietorship because each partner has full responsibility for his or her errors.

Critical Thinking

7. Answers will vary but may include the following traits: a specialty that complements the other partners; an established base of customers; an easy-to-get-along-with personality; funds to invest in the business.
8. Answers will vary but should reflect an understanding of sole proprietorships or partnerships.
9. Answers will vary but look for a position agreeing or disagreeing and for examples and reasons to back it up.
10. The unlimited liability would make it risky to run such a large enterprise. Also, a partnership might not be able to raise enough money.

Economics in Practice

Identify Partnerships

1. limited liability partnership
2. limited partnership
3. general partnership
4. limited partnership

Challenge Student writings should clearly describe each type of partnership.

Types of Business Organizations 237

1 Plan & Prepare

Section 3 Objectives

- identify the characteristics of corporations
- compare the advantages and disadvantages of corporations
- describe how corporations consolidate to form larger business combinations
- explain the role of multinational corporations in the world economy

2 Focus & Motivate

Connecting to Everyday Life Open a discussion on the popular view of corporations. Ask students to give examples of how corporations are portrayed in movies and on television or in popular novels. *(Generally, negative views come across. Films such as* Titanic *and* The Insider *show corporate greed endangering lives.)* Next, ask students to think of how they interact with corporations every day. Ask students to speculate about why corporations, which are such an integral part of American culture, may be cast as the "bad guy" in the popular media.

Taking Notes Remind students to take notes as they read by completing a cluster diagram for information about corporations. They can use the Graphic Organizer at **Interactive Review @ ClassZone.com**.

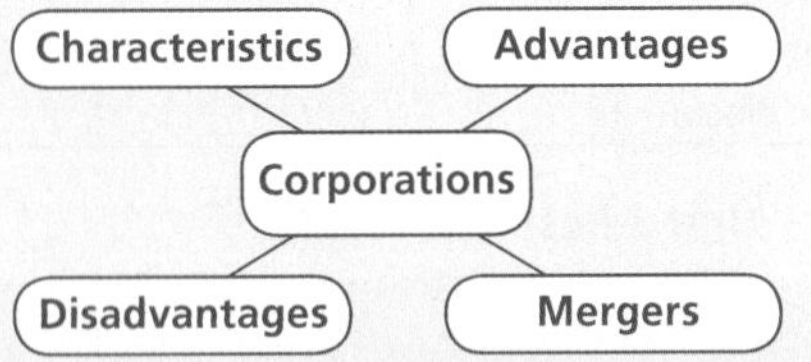

SECTION 3

Corporations, Mergers, and Multinationals

OBJECTIVES

In Section 3, you will
- identify the characteristics of corporations
- compare the advantages and disadvantages of corporations
- describe how corporations consolidate to form larger business combinations
- explain the role of multinational corporations in the world economy

KEY TERMS

corporation, *p. 238*
stock, *p. 238*
dividend, *p. 238*
public company, *p. 238*
private company, *p. 238*
bond, *p. 240*
limited liability, *p. 240*
unlimited life, *p. 240*
horizontal merger, *p. 243*
vertical merger, *p. 243*
conglomerate, *p. 243*
multinational corporation, *p. 243*

TAKING NOTES

As you read Section 3, complete a cluster diagram that categorizes information about corporations. Use the Graphic Organizer at **Interactive Review @ ClassZone.com**

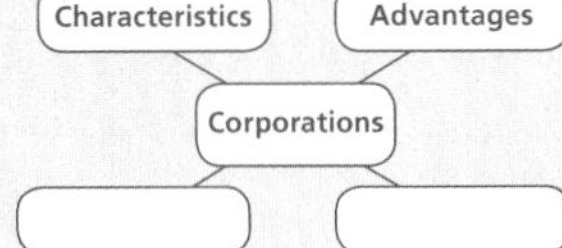

Characteristics of Corporations

QUICK REFERENCE

A **corporation** is a business owned by stockholders, who own the rights to the company's profits but face limited liability for the company's debts and losses.

Stock is a share of ownership in a corporation.

A **dividend** is part of a corporation's profit that is paid out to stockholders.

A **public company** issues stock that can be publicly traded.

A **private company** controls who can buy or sell its stock.

KEY CONCEPTS

Corporations are the third main kind of business organization. A **corporation** is a business owned by individuals, called shareholders or stockholders. The shareholders own the rights to the company's profits, but they face limited liability for the company's debts and losses. These individuals acquire ownership rights through the purchase of **stock**, or shares of ownership in the corporation.

For example, suppose a large company sells a million shares in the form of stock. If you bought 10,000 shares, you would own 1 percent of the company. If the company runs into trouble, you would not be responsible for any of its debt. Your only risk is that the value of your stock might decline. If the company does well and earns a profit, you might receive a payment called a **dividend**, part of the profit that the company pays out to stockholders.

A corporation that issues stock that can be freely bought and sold is called a **public company**. One that retains control over who can buy or sell the stock is called a **private company**. Corporations make up about 20 percent of the number of businesses in the United States, but they produce most of the country's goods and services and employ the majority of American workers.

EXAMPLE F & S Publishing, Inc.

To better understand how corporations operate, let's look at F & S Publishing, Inc., a successful publishing business. Frank and Shirley, the founders, decided to turn their business into a corporation because they wished to avoid unlimited liability. A corporation, unlike a partnership or sole proprietorship, is a formal, legal entity separate from the individuals who own and run it. The financial liabilities of F & S

SECTION 3 PROGRAM RESOURCES

ON LEVEL

Lesson Plans
- Core, p. 28

Unit 3 Resource Book
- Reading Study Guide, pp. 21–22
- Economic Simulations, pp. 47–48
- Section Quiz, p. 29

STRUGGLING READERS

Unit 3 Resource Book
- Reading Study Guide with Additional Support, pp. 23–25
- Reteaching Activity, p. 30

ENGLISH LEARNERS

Unit 3 Resource Book
- Reading Study Guide with Additional Support (Spanish), pp. 26–28

INCLUSION

Lesson Plans
- Modified for Inclusion, p. 28

GIFTED AND TALENTED

Unit 3 Resource Book
- Case Study Resources: The Evolution of Levi Strauss & Co.—A Matter of Values, pp. 45–46

NCEE Student Activities
- Researching Companies, pp. 29–32

TECHNOLOGY

eEdition DVD-ROM

eEdition Online

Power Presentation DVD-ROM

Economics Concepts Transparencies
- CT28 Corporation Organizational Chart

Daily Test Practice Transparencies, TT28

ClassZone.com

FIGURE 8.4 CORPORATE STRUCTURE

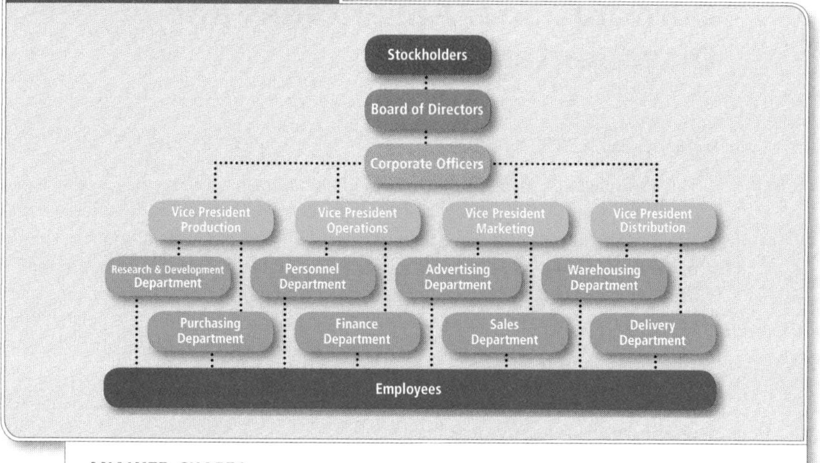

ANALYZE CHARTS
This chart shows the organization of a typical corporation. Smaller corporations may only have stockholders, corporate officers, and employees. Larger corporations may be much more complex. Imagine you own a company that makes a product you like. Draw an organization chart for your corporation.

Publishing, Inc., are separate from the personal financial liabilities of Frank, Shirley, and other F & S stockholders. If the business fails, only the assets of F & S itself—the office building, equipment, and company bank accounts—are at risk.

Setting up a corporation involves more work and expense than establishing a sole proprietorship or partnership. Frank and Shirley hired a law firm to draw up and file papers requesting permission from the state government to incorporate. The state government agreed to the request and issued a corporate charter. This document named F & S Publishing, Inc., as the business, stated its address and purpose, and specified how much stock Frank and Shirley could sell.

F & S Publishing, Inc., is organized like the majority of corporations. Stockholders—the owners of the corporation—elect a board of directors. The board hires corporate officers, such as the president and the vice-presidents in charge of sales, production, finance, and so on. These officers are responsible for the smooth running of the corporation. In most corporations, the stockholders and the board of directors are not involved in the day-to-day running of the business. F & S Publishing, Inc., however, is a small company, and Frank and Shirley became members of the board of directors as well as managers.

Frank and Shirley decided to make their business a public company. They bought enough of the stock themselves so that they would each have a seat on the board of directors. They sold the rest of the stock to raise money to expand the business.

APPLICATION Applying Economic Concepts

A. Frank and Shirley were worried about unlimited liability. How did incorporating protect them from this problem? A corporation is a legal entity separate from its owners and managers, so the liabilities of a corporation are separate from those of its owners and managers.

3 Teach

Characteristics of Corporations

Discuss

- What is the difference between a public company and a private company? *(public—stock can be freely bought and sold by anyone; private—corporation controls who can buy and sell stock)*
- Why could Frank and Shirley not find the protection from unlimited liability they wanted in a limited liability partnership? *(They would still be liable for any debts incurred through their own errors. Under a corporate structure, only the corporation would be liable.)*

Analyzing Charts: Figure 8.4

A corporation is a business organization defined by legalities and formalities. To establish a clear chain of command, a corporate structure is formed. A chart such as this one shows a hierarchy of power in the corporation. The stockholders appear at the top because they are the owners of the company. Positions across the same row are considered of equal significance.

Answer

Students should follow the model shown and demonstrate an understanding of how an organization chart should be established for a company of their choosing.

SMALL GROUP ACTIVITY

Tracking Stock Prices

Time 45 minutes over five days

Task Choose a stock and track its performance in the stock market for a week.

Materials Needed financial section of a newspaper for five consecutive days

Activity

- Organize the class into groups. Direct each group to choose a stock and calculate how many shares they could buy with $1,000.
- Have each group record the number of shares they purchased and the total investment. Since they purchase whole shares, the total investment for most groups will be slightly less than $1,000.
- Within each group, have a different student take responsibility for finding and reporting on the change in the stock price each day for a week.
- Instruct each group to record their stock's performance in a line graph and to calculate how much they made or lost.
- Have each group share their stock's performance with the class.

Rubric

	Understanding of Stock Purchases	Presentation of Information
4	excellent	clear and complete
3	good	mostly clear
2	fair	sometimes clear
1	poor	unclear

Corporations: Advantages and Disadvantages

Discuss

- How might the advantages of corporations help explain why more corporations than other kinds of businesses take in $1 million or more a year? *(They can raise more funding, which supports more products; they have professional managers who are usually experienced.)*
- Which disadvantage of corporations might be the most significant? Explain. *(Possible answers: heavy regulation because meeting the regulations, which often involves hiring lawyers and/or accountants, is time consuming and expensive)*

Analyzing Graphs: Figure 8.5

Have students compare Figures 8.5, 8.1, and 8.2. Ask them which type of business structure has the most even distribution of income levels. *(corporations)* Ask students to speculate why this might be so and give reasons for their answers. *(Possible answer: no matter what the size of their business, people are eager to take advantage of the benefits of incorporation.)*

Answers

1. *43.0%*
2. *corporations, with 18.2%*

Economics Update

At **ClassZone.com,** students will find updated information on corporations.

Corporations: Advantages and Disadvantages

QUICK REFERENCE

A **bond** is a contract issued by a corporation that promises to repay borrowed money, plus interest, on a fixed schedule.

Limited liability means that a business owner's liability for debts and losses of the business is limited.

Unlimited life means that a corporation continues to exist even after an owner dies, leaves the business, or transfers his or her ownership.

KEY CONCEPTS

The advantages of corporations often address the major disadvantages of sole proprietorships and partnerships. For example, corporations are more effective than either of the other business structures at raising large amounts of money. The key methods of raising money are the sale of stock and the issuing of bonds. A **bond** is a contract the corporation issues that promises to repay borrowed money, plus interest, on a fixed schedule. Also, unlike sole proprietorships and most partnerships, corporations provide their owners with **limited liability**, which means that the business owner's liability for business debts and losses is limited. Further, corporations have **unlimited life**—they continue to exist even after a change in ownership. Sole proprietorships and partnerships do not.

Most of the disadvantages of corporations are related to their size and organizational complexity. Corporations are costly and time-consuming to start up; they are governed by many more rules and regulations; and, because of the organizational structure, the owners may have little control over business decisions. Despite these drawbacks, corporations can be efficient and productive business organizations.

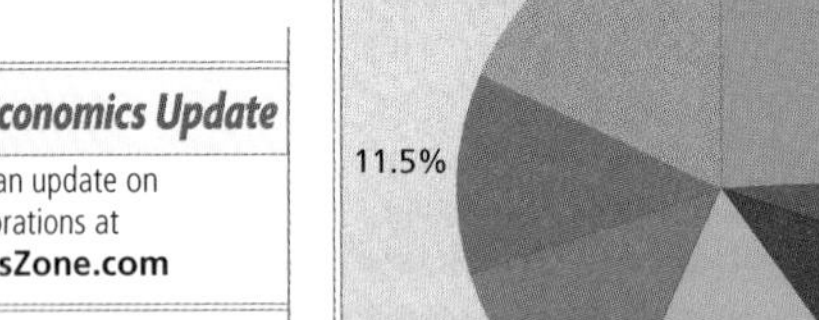

Economics Update
Find an update on corporations at **ClassZone.com**

FIGURE 8.5 CORPORATIONS BY REVENUES

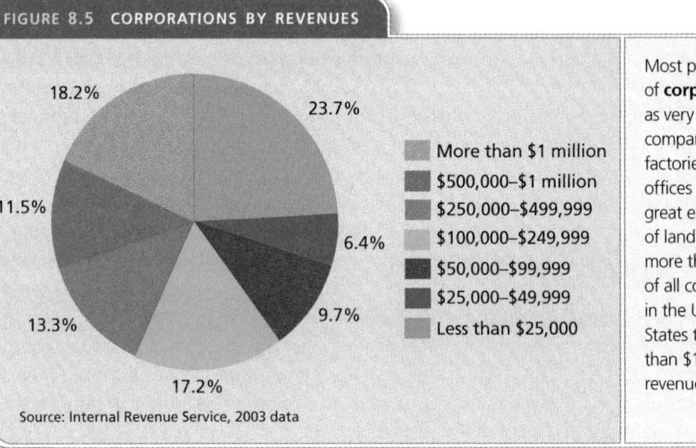

Source: Internal Revenue Service, 2003 data

Most people think of **corporations** as very large companies with factories and offices that occupy great expanses of land. Actually, more than a third of all corporations in the United States take in less than $100,000 in revenues each year.

ANALYZE GRAPHS

1. What percentage of corporations made more than $250,000 in sales?
2. Compare Figure 8.5 with Figure 8.1 on p. 229 and Figure 8.2 on p. 234. According to the graphs, which type of business has the highest percentage of firms that earn over $1 million in revenues each year?

DIFFERENTIATING INSTRUCTION

Struggling Readers

The Power of One

Help students understand that the material on page 240 is general information, a summary of the key concepts for this part of Section 3. The material on pages 241–242, in contrast, is an extended example showing the general information applied to a specific case. Point out that this "power of one" example to illustrate more general points is very common in explanatory writing. The specific information about Frank and Shirley is for the purpose of understanding the general information.

Inclusion

"Listen" to Graphics

Pair students who have visual impairments with non-impaired students. Ask the non-impaired students to read the information from all three graphs (Figures 8.1, 8.2, and 8.5). But instruct them to read the information from the three graphs category by category to show comparisons. For example, "23.7 percent of corporations earn under $25,000 a year, while 67.5 percent of sole proprietorships and 54 percent of partnerships earn that amount."

ADVANTAGES Corporations

Frank and Shirley had operated F & S as a partnership for several years. They decided to incorporate to gain the advantages of the corporate business structure.

Access to Resources Frank and Shirley have ideas to expand their business, but implementing the ideas may require more money than profits from the business will provide. As a corporation, they have better opportunities for obtaining additional money. Besides borrowing from banks, F & S can raise money by selling more stock or by issuing bonds. This greater access to funds leads to greater potential for growth.

"Our investors' enthusiasm was gratifying... first time I've ever seen a mosh pit at a stockholders' meeting!"

Source: www.CartoonStock.com

Professional Managers Frank and Shirley are involved in the running of F & S Publishing, Inc. Frank serves as chief executive officer (CEO), while Shirley is chief operations officer (COO). However, they decided to hire managers with strong backgrounds in finance and sales as company treasurer and vice-president for sales. Having professionals in charge of financial and sales matters will probably lead to higher profits.

Limited Liability Because of limited liability, F & S Publishing, Inc., alone is liable for any debts or losses it incurs. Frank, Shirley, and F & S stockholders are liable only for the money they paid for their stock. The board of directors and officers of the corporation, too, are protected from liability.

Unlimited Life If any of the owners—the stockholders—of F & S dies or decides to end his or her relationship with the company, the business would continue to operate as before. This even applies to Frank and Shirley. If either or both of them move on to another business, F & S Publishing, Inc., can continue without them for as long as it is a viable business.

DISADVANTAGES Corporations

Frank and Shirley discovered some of the disadvantages to incorporating when they first began the process. They learned about other disadvantages of corporations as they ran their business.

Start-Up Cost and Effort When they first started, Frank and Shirley set up their business as a partnership. Compared to setting up the partnership, Frank and Shirley found the process of setting up a corporation more time-consuming, difficult, and expensive. The paperwork they had to prepare and file with the state government was extensive, and they had to hire a law firm to help with this task.

Heavy Regulation As a public company, F & S Publishing, Inc., must prepare annual reports for the Securities and Exchange Commission (SEC), the government agency

More About . . .

Corporate "Personhood"

The reason corporations protect owners from liability is a concept known as a legal fiction, something assumed by the courts to be true even if it is not. The legal fiction regarding corporations is that they are "persons." The personhood concept arose because corporations claimed they could not be sued, since they were not persons. However, that left those who were harmed by a corporation no legal recourse.

So, in the 1886 case *Santa Clara County* v. *Southern Pacific Railroad Company*, the courts devised the legal fiction of personhood for corporations, allowing them to be sued.

International Economics

Kasky* v. *Nike

Corporate personhood was an issue in a 2003 court case, *Kasky* v. *Nike*. This case concerned Nike's overseas labor practices, especially in Vietnam. Spot audits had revealed violations of labor codes. However, Nike issued statements denying poor working conditions.

In light of Nike's denials, labor activist Marc Kasky sued Nike for false advertising. Nike defended its right to say what it wanted under the free speech protection granted to "real" persons. Courts at various levels went back and forth on the decision, and the case was eventually settled, with Nike agreeing to pay $1.5 million to the Fair Labor Association.

SMALL GROUP ACTIVITY

Drawing Corporate Cartoons

Time 30 minutes ◑

Task Create cartoons about corporate subjects.

Materials Needed paper and pens or pencils

Activity

- Lead a discussion with the class of the corporate cartoon found on page 241.
- Organize students into pairs.
- Direct students to use the cartoon as an inspiration to create their own cartoon involving a corporate situation.
- The finished cartoon should show some aspect of an advantage or disadvantage of corporations.
- Display the finished cartoons to the class and discuss the advantages and disadvantages each illustrates.

Rubric

	Understanding of Corporate Advantages and Disadvantages	Presentation of Information
4	excellent	clear and creative
3	good	clear message
2	fair	partly clear
1	poor	off topic or unclear

Analyzing Tables: Figure 8.6

Ask the class to discuss what possibilities there are for entrepreneurs who prefer partnerships over corporations but who wish to avoid unlimited liability. *(limited partnerships, in which at least one partner is not involved in the day-to-day running of a business and is liable only for the funds he or she has invested; or limited liability partnerships, in which all partners are limited partners and not responsible for the debts of the other partners)*

Answers

Answers will vary. Students should demonstrate an understanding of the type of organization their chosen business represents. They should be fully aware of advantages and disadvantages that are presented and be able to discuss and justify their choice in view of these issues.

More About . . .

Double Taxation

In 2003, a bill that reduces the penalty of double taxation on dividends for people in a low income bracket was enacted into law by Congress. Under this law, most dividend recipients are taxed at the rate of 15 percent. However, people in low income brackets are taxed at the rate of 5 percent through 2007 and will not be taxed at all beginning in 2008. These provisions of the law expire in 2011.

FIGURE 8.6 **Business Organizations: Advantages and Disadvantages**

Type of Organization	Advantages	Disadvantages
Sole Proprietorship	• Easy to start up, close down • Sole proprietor has satisfaction of running business his or her own way • Few regulations • Sole proprietor keeps all the profits	• Limited funds • Limited life • Unlimited liability
Partnership	• Easy to start up, close down • Few regulations • Greater access to funds • Partners share in decision making • Partners may bring complementary skills to the business	• Unlimited liability • Shared decision making may create conflict among partners • Limited life
Corporation	• Greatest access to funds • Business run by professionals • Limited liability • Unlimited life	• Difficult to start up • More regulations • Double taxation • Owners may have less control of running the business

ANALYZE TABLES

All three forms of business organizations have distinct advantages and disadvantages. If you were starting a business, which form of business organization would you choose? Why?

that oversees the sale of stocks. It also has to prepare and issue quarterly financial reports for stockholders. Further, the company must hold yearly meetings for its stockholders. All of these regulations help ensure that corporations are run for the benefit of the shareholders. Private companies are subject to fewer regulations related to their ownership.

Double Taxation Frank and Shirley experience an effect known as double taxation. As officers of the company, they are well aware of the taxes on profits that the corporation must pay. As stockholders, they know that their dividend income, paid out of the company profits, is also taxed. Some small corporations qualify for S corporation status, a tax status which avoids double taxation.

Loss of Control Frank and Shirley, as founders, owners, and directors, expect to have a major voice in deciding the direction that F & S Publishing, Inc., will take. However, they experienced some loss of control when the rest of the board of directors voted against them and brought in a new sales manager.

APPLICATION Evaluating Economic Decisions

B. F & S was successful as a partnership. What will Frank and Shirley gain by making their company a corporation?

They will have even greater access to funds to grow the company; they will benefit from having professional managers to run the business; Frank and Shirley will no longer be personally liable for the company's debts.

DIFFERENTIATING INSTRUCTION

English Learners

Read the News

Direct English learners to the first paragraph on page 243, which discusses business consolidations. Ask them to find an example of a current news story about a business consolidation and to print out the article, if it is online, or to bring in the article, if it is from a newspaper or magazine. Have the students read the article aloud to the rest of the class or in a small group.

Gifted and Talented

Research and Debate

Have students research the 2003 case of *Kasky* v. *Nike.* (See the More About… on page 241.) Instruct them to focus their research on two points—the arguments on both sides and the conflicting rulings the various courts handed down on the case. Then, have students take sides. Ask them to debate the issue as if they were offering arguments before the U.S. Supreme Court.

Business Consolidation

KEY CONCEPTS

You've probably seen news stories about them—business consolidations that merge, or combine, several large companies into one mega-company. These consolidations take place for several possible reasons. These include increasing efficiency, gaining a new identity as a business or losing an old one, keeping rivals out of the marketplace, and diversifying the product line.

There are two main kinds of mergers (see Figure 8.7). A **horizontal merger** describes the joining of companies that offer the same or similar products or services. A **vertical merger** describes the combining of companies involved in different steps of production or marketing of a product or service. An alternative to the two main types is a **conglomerate**, which results from a merger of companies that produce unrelated goods or services. Through growth, consolidations, and other means, an enterprise can grow so big that it becomes a **multinational corporation**, a large corporation with branches in several countries.

QUICK REFERENCE

A **horizontal merger** is the combining of two or more companies that produce the same product or similar products.

A **vertical merger** is the combining of companies involved in different steps of producing or marketing a product.

A **conglomerate** is a business composed of several companies, each one producing unrelated goods or services.

A **multinational corporation** is a large corporation with branches in several countries.

FIGURE 8.7 TYPES OF MERGERS

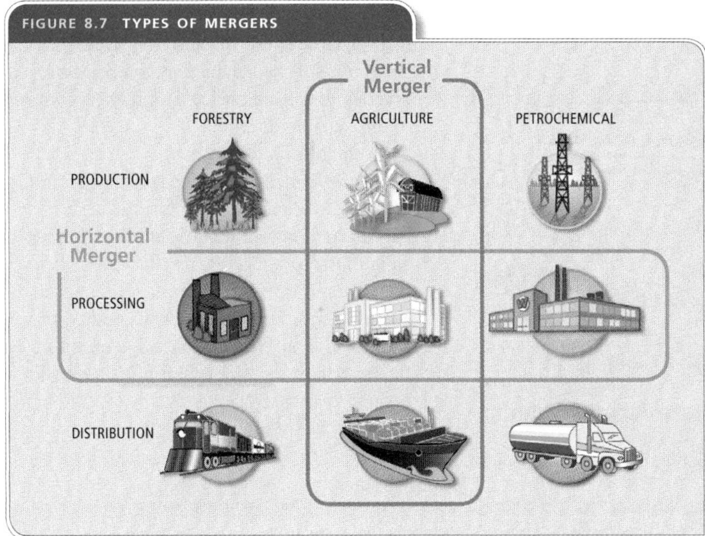

ANALYZE CHARTS

What kind of mergers took place in each of the following situations?

1. In 1999, Ford Motor Co. purchased Swedish-based car manufacturer Volvo.
2. In 1989, Japanese electronics giant Sony purchased Columbia Pictures Entertainment.

Animated Economics

Use an interactive merger chart at **ClassZone.com**

Business Consolidation

Discuss

- What effect, if any, might the trend of more and more mergers and consolidations have on small business owners? *(Answers will vary. Some students might suggest that with the greater resources of the corporate giants smaller businesses will have a harder time staying competitive.)*
- What products come to mind when you think of the giant corporation Sony? *(Possible answers: consumer electronics, movies)* Point out that Sony, as a conglomerate, also has divisions for life insurance, international finance, record labels, and many more products and services.

Analyzing Charts: Figure 8.7

The chart on the types of mergers will help students understand the differences between horizontal and vertical mergers.

Answers

1. *horizontal merger*
2. *vertical merger*

SMALL GROUP ACTIVITY

Reporting Business "News"

Time 30 minutes ◑

Task Create a press release about a fictional business consolidation.

Materials Needed paper and pens or pencils

Activity

- Divide the class into four groups based on the four kinds of business consolidations that are presented as key terms on page 243.
- Instruct students to use F & S Publishing, Inc., as one of the corporations involved.
- Have each group develop and draft a press release announcing the details of a horizontal merger, vertical merger, or consolidation as part of a conglomerate.
- Direct each group to prepare a visual to accompany the press release, showing the structure of the new business.

Rubric

	Understanding of Business Consolidations	Presentation of Information
4	excellent	clear and creative
3	good	accurate
2	fair	partly clear
1	poor	sketchy

More About . . .

The Adidas-Reebok Merger
The major retailers of sporting goods, such as The Sports Authority and Dick's Sporting Goods, were optimistic about the Adidas-Reebok merger. For the retailers, that meant dealing with only one supplier's accounting and distribution units instead of two.

However, at the time of the merger, Adidas planned to keep all of its offices open to avoid major layoffs. So, it was possible that the cost savings might not reach consumers for some time, if at all.

International Economics

Global Google
Google must obey the laws of each nation in which it does business. In France and Germany, for example, it is illegal to deny that there was a Holocaust, in which six million Jews and others were killed by Germany's Nazi government, as well as to use words associated with racial hatred. So, in those countries, Google blocks key words that could lead to Web sites with those illegal ideas and terms.

In China, Google follows the orders of the Communist government and blocks the words *democracy, human rights,* and *Taiwan independence.*

Economics Illustrated

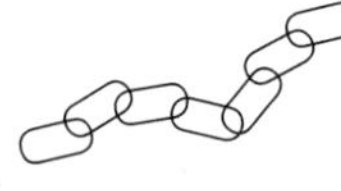

A vertical merger can be represented by a drawing of a flower: each part of the flower is different, but they are all related because each part depends on the other parts. A horizontal merger is more like a chain: each link is similar.

Mergers

An example of a horizontal merger is the one between Reebok and Adidas in 2005. At the time, they were the second- and third-biggest makers of sports shoes. The subtitle of an article about the merger summed up the potential benefits of all mergers: "Adidas-Reebok merger could trim costs for companies and maybe even some dollars for consumers." The two companies planned to cut production and distribution costs by combining their operations. This, they hoped, would improve their ability to compete against the largest sport-shoe maker, Nike. More efficient production usually leads to lower prices, which would draw consumers away from Nike.

An example of a vertical merger took place in the late 1990s during a period when the oil and gas industry was undergoing major consolidations. Shell Oil, which owned more refineries, joined with Texaco, which owned more gas stations. This type of merger is vertical, since companies involved in different steps of production (refining) or distribution (getting gasoline to customers) combined.

Conglomerates

Another kind of business consolidation, the conglomerate, is formed when two or more companies in different industries come together. In theory, the advantage of this form of consolidation is that, with diversified businesses, the parent company is protected from isolated economic pressures, such as changing demand for a specific product. In practice, it can be difficult to manage companies in unrelated industries.

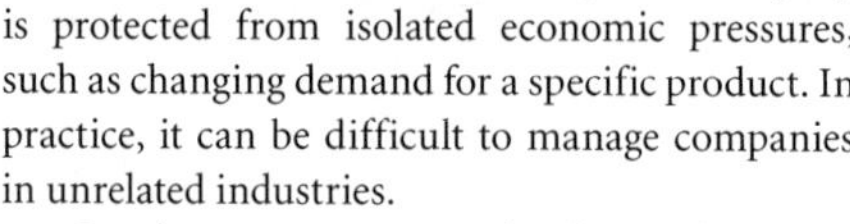

"I've come up with our new logo, JB."
Source: www.CartoonStock.com

Conglomerates were popular during the 1960s. One conglomerate of the 1960s was Gulf and Western, which included companies in such diverse fields as communications, clothing, mining, and agricultural products. As with many other conglomerates formed in the 1960s, however, Gulf and Western did not produce the desired financial gains. Gulf and Western sold all its companies but the entertainment and publishing endeavors and became known as Viacom.

Multinational Corporations

When you use Google to do an Internet search, you are using the services of a multinational corporation, a large corporation with branches in several countries. Google's headquarters are in Mountain View, California, but it has branch offices in many other countries. Coca-Cola, McDonald's, Nike, and Sony are all examples of multinational, or transnational, corporations.

Multinational corporations like Google are a major force in globalization, commerce conducted without regard to national boundaries. Multinational corporations have many beneficial effects. They provide new jobs, goods, and services around the world and spread technological advances. When such companies open businesses in poorer countries, the jobs and the tax revenues help raise the standard of living.

DIFFERENTIATING INSTRUCTION

Struggling Readers

Map the Text
Help students to understand what is involved in each type of business consolidation. Have them read the three sections on pages 244–245 and complete the following text map for each:

Subject:

Main Idea:

Example:

Inclusion

Make a Collage
Make the organization chart of General Electric come alive for students by directing them to make a collage with at least one illustration representing each of the business units. Pictures from magazines or the Internet can serve as the illustrations, or students may draw the pictures. As an alternative, students can make a collage showing both the benefits and drawbacks of multinational corporations.

A GLOBAL PERSPECTIVE

General Electric: Multinational Corporation

The operations of General Electric (GE), one of the world's largest multinational corporations, span the globe. While its headquarters is located in the United States, GE has manufacturing and production centers located in countries far and near. To supply these centers, GE purchases raw materials from all over the world. Further, the corporation has sales centers on six of the seven continents.

GE is both a multinational and a conglomerate, offering a wide range of services and products. The diagram below offers a view of GE's six major businesses and the units that make up these businesses. GE owns many companies that you know. For example, GE owns 80 percent of NBC Universal, which is made up of the NBC television network, Universal Pictures, and many related businesses. GE's Consumer and Industrial unit manufactures such common products as refrigerators, ovens, and light bulbs. But many of GE's businesses are less well-known because they provide services and products for businesses and governments.

FIGURE 8.8 GENERAL ELECTRIC

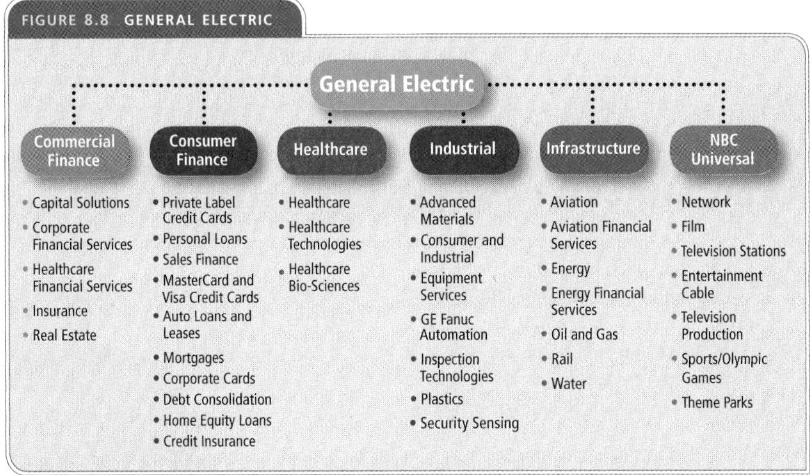

CONNECTING ACROSS THE GLOBE

1. **Applying Economic Information** What characteristics of General Electric define it as "multinational"?
2. **Analyzing Charts** General Electric operates in a wide range of industries. Name some industries in which it does not participate. Make sure to check your answer against the chart.

However, multinational corporations can also create problems. Some build factories that emit harmful waste products in countries with lax government regulation. Others operate factories where workers toil for long hours in unsafe working conditions. You will learn more about the impact of multinationals on the world economy in Chapter 17.

APPLICATION Applying Economic Concepts

C. Make up an imaginary conglomerate based on three real companies.
Answers will vary, but companies should all be in different industries.

A Global Perspective

General Electric: Multinational Corporation

In spring of 2005, GE announced a new initiative that it hoped would demonstrate its commitment to global responsibility. Named "Ecomagination," this initiative calls for doubling GE's investment in research in such "green" energy sources as wind-power and more efficient train and airplane performance. GE also pledged to reduce greenhouse gas emissions from its factories by 1 percent by the year 2012.

Answers

1. *It is headquartered in the United States, but it manufactures goods, purchases raw materials, and sells products all over the world.*
2. *Anwers will vary. Possible answers: agriculture, clothing, restaurants*

Analyzing Charts: Figure 8.8

Ask students to identify products they use that are produced by a unit of General Electric. *(Students might identify credit cards, health care, energy, television, etc.)* What does this indicate about the influence of a large corporation? *(Students might focus on the wide variety of products and services offered by GE, or on how the different units work together.)*

INDIVIDUAL ACTIVITY

Mapping Multinationals

Time 30 Minutes ◑

Task Locate the international locations of a multinational corporation.

Materials Needed world outline maps, colored pencils

Activity

- Instruct students to select one of the multinational corporations mentioned on page 244.
- Direct them to research the international locations of their chosen corporation and indicate the sites on the world outline map.
- Have students display their completed maps.
- Engage students in a discussion on what parts of the world seem to have many international business ties.

Rubric

	Understanding of Multinationals	Presentation of Information
4	excellent	creative and complete map
3	good	neat and complete map
2	fair	acceptable map
1	poor	sketchy

Bill Gates

More About . . .

Bill Gates
Bill Gates's fascination with computers began not long after he enrolled at Lakeside, an exclusive private high school in Washington, in the late 1960s. Gates, Paul Allen (who would help him found Microsoft), and other friends would stay in the school's computer room day and night, learning all they could about these early computers and writing computer programs.

They spent so much time with the computers that they skipped classes and turned in late homework. But Gates became a computer "whiz." He was asked to program the school's class schedules. Much later, Gates said that he mischievously "added a few instructions [to the program] and found myself nearly the only guy in a class full of girls."

More About . . .

Microsoft
When hiring people for jobs at Microsoft, Gates preferred a natural and analytical problem-solver to someone with lots of experience. He liked the idea of working with a "raw" brain. Gates also met two or three times a day with production teams working on a myriad of projects and listened to employee ideas.

The work culture at Microsoft includes a number of "think tanks" in which employees are encouraged to take part. For example, in the Greenhouse, entrepreneurial employees can nurture their own innovative ideas.

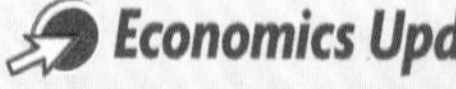

ClassZone.com includes links to sites about Bill Gates and Microsoft. Students can review how Gates's personality has driven Microsoft.

ECONOMICS PACESETTER

Bill Gates: Entrepreneur and Corporate Leader

A reporter once asked multibillionaire Bill Gates, founder of Microsoft Corporation, if he thought there was a larger meaning in the universe. Gates joked, "It's possible ... that the universe exists only for me. If so, it's sure going well for me, I must admit." From a small beginning, Bill Gates created the world's largest software company. Microsoft employs more than 60,000 people in more than 100 countries.

FAST FACTS

Bill Gates

Title: Chairman, Microsoft Corporation

Born: October 28, 1955, Seattle, Washington

Major Accomplishments: Cofounder, Microsoft, 1975; *Time Magazine's* Person of the Year, 2005 (for his charitable work)

Books: *The Road Ahead* (1995); *Business @ the Speed of Thought* (1999)

Estimated Personal Fortune: $46.5 billion in 2005 (ranked #1 in the world)

Famous Quotation: *"I have always loved the competitive forces in this business. That's what keeps my job one of the most interesting in the world."*

Microsoft Corporation

Gates was always fascinated with computers and software. He developed software for his high school to schedule classes and for his hometown of Seattle to monitor traffic. At Harvard, he and his friend Paul Allen developed the BASIC language for personal computers. In 1975, during his third year, Gates left college to form a business with Allen to supply BASIC programming for an early brand of personal computers. Gates and Allen called their company Micro-soft (later changed to Microsoft). "I think my most important work was the early work," Gates said in 2005, "conceiving of the idea of the PC and how important that would be, and the role software would play. . . . "

Microsoft incorporated in 1981. When it struck a deal to provide the operating system for IBM personal computers, it secured its dominance. Microsoft became an international corporation in 1985, when it opened a production facility in Dublin, Ireland. That same year, it released what would become the world's most popular operating system, Microsoft Windows. Initially, Microsoft focused on corporate computing. With the release of Windows 95, however, it turned to the consumer market.

Bill Gates Bill Gates cofounded Microsoft in 1975. It became one of the world's most successful corporations.

Gates led Microsoft as it continued to dominate the computer industry. In 1994, Gates established a foundation for charitable giving that quickly became the largest charitable foundation in the world. The foundation focuses on global health and education. In 2006, Gates began shifting away from the day-to-day responsibilities of running Microsoft and toward running the foundation.

Economics Update
Find an update on Bill Gates and Microsoft at **ClassZone.com**

APPLICATION Categorizing Economic Information

D. Create a timeline showing the development of Microsoft from its founding to its status as a major multinational corporation.
Timelines will vary, but should include the major facts noted in this Economics Pacesetter feature.

246 Chapter 8

DIFFERENTIATING INSTRUCTION

Struggling Readers

Understand Quotes
Direct students to the three quotations by Bill Gates on this page—in Fast Facts, the introductory text paragraph, and the second text paragraph. Ask someone to read each quote aloud. Then discuss what these quotes add to their understanding of Gates. Point out that quotations are often used in biographical sketches to give a flavor of an individual's personality and also to let a specific expression stand for a larger characteristic.

Gifted and Talented

Read and Discuss
Have students select one of the books that Bill Gates has written and participate in a book discussion group as they read it. Arrange for the group to meet twice a week. For each meeting, a different student should be in charge of leading the discussion. Also, at the meeting, the group should decide how many pages should be read for the next meeting.

SECTION 3 Assessment

Online Quiz ClassZone.com

REVIEWING KEY CONCEPTS

1. Explain the relationship between the terms in each of these groups.
   a. *stock* *bond*   b. *public company* *private company*   c. *merger* *conglomerate*
2. What are the main advantages of a corporation?
3. What are the main disadvantages of a corporation?
4. How do corporations raise money?
5. What is a multinational corporation?
6. **Using Your Notes** What is the difference between a vertical merger and a horizontal merger? Refer to your completed cluster diagram.

   Use the Graphic Organizer at **Interactive Review @ ClassZone.com**

Characteristics — Advantages — Corporations

CRITICAL THINKING

7. **Analyzing Cause and Effect** Review the table below. If the two largest bottled water manufacturers consolidated in a horizontal merger, what might the effect be on competition?

Company	Annual Sales (in millions of dollars)	Percent of Market
Nature's Springs	1,000	25
Well Water, Inc.	600	15
Best Taste	400	10
Empyrean Isles	400	10
No-Tap Water	200	5

8. **Writing About Economics** In what ways might a vertical merger in the oil industry influence gas prices?
9. **Explaining an Economic Concept** What are the benefits of combining several companies to form a conglomerate? Name an example of a conglomerate.
10. **Challenge** So far in this chapter, you have learned about business enterprises that seek profits. In Section 4, you will learn about nonprofit organizations. How do you think the structure of such organizations might differ from the structure of profit-seeking organizations?

ECONOMICS IN PRACTICE

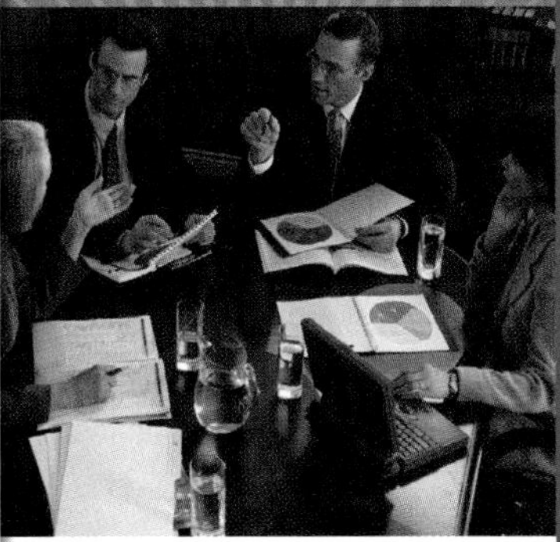

Analyzing Data
When companies decide to merge, they must carefully evaluate how to combine their operations.

Will This Merger Work? Leviathan Motion Pictures wants to purchase Pipsqueak Computer Games.

	Leviathan	Pipsqueak
Head of Company	Ivana Getrich, age 60	Bob L. Head, age 30
Board of Directors	15 business executives	Bob and a couple of his buddies
Publicly Owned Shares	200,000,000	250,000
Market Capitalization	$5,000,000,000	$250,000,000
2008 Sales	$1,000,000,000	$10,000,000
Production Studios	4 in California, 1 in New York	1 in Austin
Employees	15,000 worldwide	150 in Austin

Review the table and imagine what would happen if the companies merge. Write a paragraph describing the challenges and the benefits.

Challenge If you were Bob, would you retire after selling Pipsqueak, or would you want to continue running the company? Explain your answer.

Types of Business Organizations 247

4 Assess & Reteach

Assess Go through the Reviewing Key Concepts and Critical Thinking questions as a class. For Economics in Practice, divide the class into groups and let each group report its conclusions to the rest of the class.

Unit 3 Resource Book
- Section Quiz, p. 29

Interactive Review @ ClassZone.com
- Section Quiz

Test Generator CD-ROM
- Section Quiz

Reteach Review Section 3 by focusing on the graphics. Call on students to use them to summarize the key information on corporations on each spread of the text.

Unit 3 Resource Book
- Reteaching Activity, p. 30

SECTION 3 ASSESSMENT ANSWERS

Reviewing Key Concepts

1. a. *stock*, p. 238; *bond*, p. 240
   b. *public company*, p. 238; *private company*, p. 238
   c. *merger*, p.243; *conglomerate*, p. 243
2. limited liability for the owners, the ability to raise funds, unlimited life, ability to hire expert managers and decision makers
3. cost and complexity of start-up, heavy regulation, double taxation, loss of control for the owners
4. by selling stocks and issuing bonds
5. a corporation with locations in more than one country
6. See page 238 for an example of a completed diagram. A horizontal merger results in a larger company that does essentially the same thing as the smaller companies; a vertical merger combines the specialties of the component companies.

Critical Thinking

7. The effect might be to dampen competition, since the strongest rivals would now control 40 percent of the market, or four times as much as the next largest company.
8. A vertical merger might result in lower prices if the cost savings from combining production, processing, and distribution were passed on to consumers.
9. protection from the financial hardships that any one industry might experience; examples: GE, Viacom, Sony
10. Answers will vary but some may recognize that they, too, need a business structure to pay employees and keep their operation running.

Economics in Practice

Will This Merger Work? Answers will vary, but might include culture conflicts, Ivana trying to drive out Bob, or movies related to the computer games.

Challenge Answers will vary.

1 Plan & Prepare

Section 4 Objectives

- explain how franchises function
- identify the characteristics and purpose of cooperatives
- describe the types and purposes of nonprofit organizations

2 Focus & Motivate

Connecting to Everyday Life Read the following scenario aloud: A student gets a haircut at Supercuts, then picks up some nachos at Taco Bell. Next, he stops at Mail Boxes, Etc. to mail a package to his brother in college. Ask students what these businesses have in common. Ask students who owns each business. Explain that they are "independently owned and operated" franchises, the subject of part of this section.

Taking Notes Remind students to take notes as they read by completing a summary chart on these organizations. They can use the Graphic Organizer at **Interactive Review @ ClassZone.com**. A sample is shown below.

Franchises	Co-ops	Nonprofits
advantages: training, advertising	consumer	charitable
disadvantages: risk, loss of control	service	professional
	producer	

SECTION 4

Franchises, Co-ops, and Nonprofits

OBJECTIVES

In Section 4, you will
- explain how franchises function
- identify the characteristics and purpose of cooperatives
- describe the types and purposes of nonprofit organizations

KEY TERMS

franchise, *p. 248*
franchisee, *p. 248*
cooperative, *p. 250*
nonprofit organization, *p. 250*

TAKING NOTES

As you read Section 4, complete a summary chart with information on specialized organizations. Use the Graphic Organizer at **Interactive Review @ ClassZone.com**

Franchises	Co-ops	Nonprofits

Franchises

QUICK REFERENCE

A **franchise** is a business that licenses the right to sell its products in a particular area.

A **franchisee** is a semi-independent business that buys the right to run a franchise.

KEY CONCEPTS

A **franchise** is a business made up of semi-independent businesses that all offer the same products or services. Each **franchisee**, as the individual businesses are known, pays a fee to the parent company in return for the right to sell the company's products or services in a particular area. Fast-food restaurants are the most common franchised business. However, this kind of business organization is also found in many other industries, including hotels, rental cars, and car service.

EXAMPLE An Almost Independent Business

The Mango Grove Juice and Nut Bar in the city center provides an illustration of how a franchise works. Tim, who runs the Mango Grove, had worked as assistant manager at a local restaurant for several years. He really wanted to run his own business, but he didn't think he had the experience or the funds to go it alone. On trips to other cities, he had been impressed by the popularity of the Mango Grove Juice and Nut Bar, an organic juice and sandwich restaurant. So he looked into becoming a franchisee of that business in his home city.

FIGURE 8.9 World's Leading Franchises

Corporation	Franchisees
1. McDonald's	30,300
2. Yum! Brands (KFC, Taco Bell, etc.)	29,300
3. 7-Eleven	28,200
4. Cendent (Howard Johnson, Avis, etc.)	24,600
5. Subway	21,000

Source: International Franchise Association, 2004 data

SECTION 4 PROGRAM RESOURCES

ON LEVEL

Lesson Plans
- Core, p. 29

Unit 3 Resource Book
- Reading Study Guide, pp. 31–32
- Economic Skills and Problem Solving Activity, pp. 41–42
- Section Quiz, p. 39

STRUGGLING READERS

Unit 3 Resource Book
- Reading Study Guide with Additional Support, pp. 33–35
- Reteaching Activity, p. 40

ENGLISH LEARNERS

Unit 3 Resource Book
- Reading Study Guide with Additional Support (Spanish), pp. 36–38

INCLUSION

Lesson Plans
- Modified for Inclusion, p. 29

GIFTED AND TALENTED

Unit 3 Resource Book
- Readings in Free Enterprise: Organic Valley Family of Farms, pp. 43–44
- Case Study Resources: The Evolution of Levi Strauss & Co.—A Matter of Values, pp. 45–46

TECHNOLOGY

eEdition DVD-ROM
eEdition Online
Power Presentation DVD-ROM
Economics Concepts Transparencies
- CT29 Franchises

Daily Test Practice Transparencies, TT29
ClassZone.com

YOUR ECONOMIC CHOICES

FRANCHISES

Which franchise would you like to run?

Hundreds of different businesses operate as franchises. Fast-food restaurants and coffee bars are among the most common. Which type of franchise would you like to run? Why?

?

ADVANTAGES Franchises

Becoming a franchisee of Mango Grove Juice and Nut Bar appealed to Tim for several reasons. First, he would have a level of independence he did not have in his job at the restaurant. Second, the franchiser, Mango Grove Fruit and Nut Bar, would provide good training in running the business, since his success affected their own. They would also provide proven products—their famous mango smoothie mixes and nut bread for sandwiches—as well as other materials, such as the décor common to all the Mango Grove juice bars, at a relatively low cost. Further, the franchiser would pay for national or regional advertising that would bring in customers.

DISADVANTAGES Franchises

Tim also thought through the disadvantages. He would have to invest most of the money he had saved, with no assurance of success in the business. He would also have to share some of the profits with the franchiser. Further, he would not have control over some aspects of the business. For example, he would have to meet the franchiser's operating rules, such as buying materials only from the franchiser and limiting the products he offered to those from the franchiser.

After considerable thought, Tim decided to apply to become a franchisee. He was accepted, and before long his business became a success. In time, a number of other Mango Grove bars opened in other parts of the city. Since both the franchiser and franchisees had the same incentive—financial reward if the business was successful—they worked well together to make the juice bars succeed.

APPLICATION Evaluating Economic Decisions

A. What advantage does the franchiser have over a business that owns and operates all of its own shops?
Franchiser saves the costs of running each shop; it also may encourage higher sales by giving the franchisee high motivation to succeed.

3 Teach

Franchises

Discuss

- What are the differences between franchises and other kinds of companies? *(Franchises are businesses in which the owner pays a parent company for the right to sell its product, whereas other companies sell their products themselves.)*
- Why is it in the parent company's best interest to provide good support for its franchisees? *(The better the support, the more products the franchisee will sell, and the more franchisees the company will attract.)*

Your Economic Choices

FRANCHISES

Which franchise would you like to run?
Point out that a good personal fit is necessary for a franchise to succeed. Ask students what factors may enter into such a fit. *(Possible answers: interest in the product, interest in a particular community, the kinds of work required from the franchise)*

Activity Have students pick a specific franchise in your area. Ask them to write a paragraph about what they would find advantageous about being an owner/operator of that franchise and what they would regard as a disadvantage. Be sure they give reasons for their choices.

SMALL GROUP ACTIVITY

Developing a Nonprofit Organization

Time 30 Minutes ◑

Task Identify a community need for a nonprofit organization.

Materials Needed paper and pens

Activity

- Organize groups of two to four students and ask each group to think about the nonprofits that currently exist in their community. These might include such organizations as the YMCA and Meals on Wheels.
- Instruct students to think of problem areas in their community and possible nonprofit organizations that might help improve those problems.
- Direct each group to pick one of their ideas and to write a one-page proposal for their nonprofit.
- Invite volunteers to share their proposals with the class.

Rubric

	Understanding of Nonprofits	Presentation of Information
4	excellent	clear and complete
3	good	accurate
2	fair	partly clear
1	poor	unclear

Cooperatives and Nonprofits

Discuss

- How does the purpose of a cooperative differ from that of a professional organization? *(A cooperative provides a financial benefit to its members; a professional organization serves its members' common interests.)*
- What are some examples of local nonprofits? *(Answers will vary.)* National nonprofits? *(Sierra Club; American Cancer Society; Parent-Teacher Association; Boy and Girl Scouts)* International nonprofits? *(Red Cross; Oxfam; Greenpeace; Amnesty International; Doctors without Borders)*

More About . . .

The Profit-Nonprofit Connection
Steve and Wai Ling Eng, husband and wife, are owner/operators of several McDonald's franchises in the San Francisco area. They have been McDonald's franchisees since 1990. They have used their success in business to help others through nonprofit agencies.

Steve Eng, for example, plays a key role in the Asian McDonald's Operators Association. Wai Ling helped to create a nonprofit organization, the Asian and Pacific Islander American Scholarship Fund (APIASF), to promote education among Asian and Pacific Islander Americans. McDonald's is one of the sponsors of this nonprofit.

Cooperatives and Nonprofits

KEY CONCEPTS

The primary purpose of most businesses is to earn money for the owners—in other words, to make a profit. But not all businesses exist solely to make a profit. A **cooperative** is a type of business operated for the shared benefit of the owners, who are also its customers. A **nonprofit organization** is an institution that acts like a business organization, but its purpose is usually to benefit society, not to make a profit.

QUICK REFERENCE

A **cooperative** is a business operated for the shared benefit of the owners, who also are its customers.

A **nonprofit organization** is a business that aims to benefit society, not to make a profit.

A Business Organization for Its Members

When people who need the same goods or services band together and act as a business, they can offer low prices by reducing or eliminating profit. Such organizations are called cooperatives, or co-ops. There are three basic types of cooperatives: consumer, service, and producer.

Consumer Consumer, or purchasing, co-ops can be small organizations, like an organic food cooperative, or they can be giant warehouse clubs. Consumer co-ops require some kind of membership payment, either in the form of labor (keeping the books or packaging orders) or monetary fees. They keep prices low by purchasing goods in large volumes at a discount price.

Service Service co-ops are business organizations, such as credit unions, that offer their members a service. Employers often form service cooperatives to reduce the cost of buying health insurance for their employees.

Producer Producer cooperatives are mainly owned and operated by the producers of agricultural products. They join together to ensure cheaper, more efficient processing or better marketing of their products.

A Purpose Other Than Profit

There are several different types of nonprofits. Some, like the American Red Cross, have the purpose of benefiting society. They provide their goods or services for free or for a minimal fee. Other nonprofits, like the American Bar Association, are professional organizations. Such organizations exist to promote the common interests of their members. Business associations, trade associations, labor unions, and museums are all examples of organizations pursuing goals other than profits.

The structure of a nonprofit resembles that of a corporation. A nonprofit must receive a government charter, for example, and has unlimited life. Unlike a corporation, however, many nonprofit organizations are not required to pay taxes because they do not generate profits and they serve society. Nonprofits raise most of their money from donations, grants, or membership fees. Some nonprofits sell products or services, but only as a way of raising funds to support their mission.

APPLICATION Making Inferences

B. The National Association of Home Builders promotes the interests of construction companies. Habitat for Humanity builds homes for the disadvantaged. Which of these nonprofits is the government more likely to excuse from paying taxes? Why?
Habitat for Humanity, because it serves society

DIFFERENTIATING INSTRUCTION

English Learners

Understand Suffixes
Point out the words *franchise* and *franchisee*. Discuss their relationship and the meaning of the suffix *–ee (one that receives or benefits from a specified action)*. To help students understand words such as these, instruct them to keep a list of such words in their personal dictionaries. Ask students to give the meaning of the following, and their relationship to the original verb: retiree, trainee, employee, and trustee.

Gifted and Talented

Analyze Franchising
Have students select two or three different types of franchises to research. They should focus on the franchises' products and their franchisees. Then direct the students to write a few paragraphs about these franchises, explaining the differences between the customer base of the franchising company and the customer base of the individual franchisees.

SECTION 4 Assessment

Online Quiz ClassZone.com

REVIEWING KEY CONCEPTS

1. Give an example of each of the following terms.
   a. *franchise* b. *cooperative* c. *nonprofit organization*
2. What are the main advantages of a franchise?
3. What are the main disadvantages of a franchise?
4. How do consumer and service cooperatives save their members money?
5. What are some purposes of nonprofit organizations?
6. **Using Your Notes** What are the chief distinctions among franchises, cooperatives, and nonprofits? Refer to your completed summary chart.

Franchises	Co-ops	Nonprofits

Use the Graphic Organizer at **Interactive Review @ ClassZone.com**

CRITICAL THINKING

7. **Explaining an Economic Concept** Explain how franchisees share the risk of the business venture with the franchiser.
8. **Making Inferences and Drawing Conclusions** How do nonprofits get the money needed to pay the people who work for them and to provide services?
9. **Evaluating Economic Decisions** You're shopping for a new camera. You could buy it from a specialty camera store that offers expert advice or from a discount retail store that carries hundreds of other products. Or you could join a camera club that offers a buying cooperative. What are the advantages and disadvantages of each option?
10. **Challenge** Helping society can be big business. The largest nonprofits generate annual revenues in the billions of dollars. Even small nonprofit organizations can make as much money as many for-profit businesses. Nonprofits employ professional managers, accountants, and marketers, just as any other business would. Should the chief executive officer (CEO) of a nonprofit with $500 million in annual revenue be paid the same salary as the CEO of a for-profit company with the same amount of revenue? Explain your answer.

ECONOMICS IN PRACTICE

Identifying Business Organizations Franchises, co-ops, and nonprofits have distinctive features.

What Kind of Organization? Review the following descriptions of business organizations. Decide what kind of business organization fits each description. Remember that there are three different types of cooperatives.

- Several companies in your city join together to get a better deal on the health insurance they offer to their workers.
- Dan pays a fee for the right to sell Soft Freeze ice cream. Soft Freeze provides all the equipment Dan needs.
- Rachel and Serafina join an association that offers relatively cheap organic products. In return, they pay a small monthly membership fee.
- The Portswood Road Church Club provides a free food service for the poor of the neighborhood.

Challenge Imagine a cooperative you and your friends might form. Describe how it would operate and how it would save you money.

4 Assess & Reteach

Assess Assign the Reviewing Key Concepts questions and Economics in Practice as homework. You can go over the Critical Thinking questions in a class discussion.

Unit 3 Resource Book
- Section Quiz, p. 39

Interactive Review @ ClassZone.com
- Section Quiz

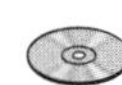

Test Generator CD-ROM
- Section Quiz

Reteach Divide the class into five groups. Assign each group one of the following topics to summarize and review for the class:

- Key Concepts of Franchises
- Advantages of Franchises
- Disadvantages of Franchises
- Cooperatives
- Nonprofits

Encourage students to be creative in their presentations—enactments, visuals, technology—in order to engage the class.

Unit 3 Resource Book
- Reteaching Activity, p. 40

SECTION 4 ASSESSMENT ANSWERS

Reviewing Key Concepts

1. a. *franchise*, p. 248
   b. *cooperative*, p. 250
   c. *nonprofit organization*, p. 250
2. relative independence, training, product consistency, support from franchisee, name recognition
3. cost of initial investment, share of profits to franchiser, can't expand product line
4. They reduce prices by eliminating profit from the cost of products or services.
5. serving the community or serving a community of professionals
6. See page 248 for an example of a completed diagram. Franchises are for-profit businesses; cooperatives are businesses owned by the members, who are also the customers; nonprofits do not seek profit but instead serve society.

Critical Thinking

7. The franchiser provides training, proven products, and advertising; the franchisee is responsible for making the business work in a particular location.
8. donations, government grants, fundraising, corporate grants, membership fees
9. specialty store: best products and customer service, higher prices; discount store: best prices, sketchy customer service; camera club: good price, good advice, no warrantee support
10. Possible answers: yes, because the two CEOs oversee the same amount of revenues, so they should be paid the same; no, because the nonprofit CEO should make less because the money should go to serve the organization's cause

Economics in Practice

What Kind of Organization?
1. producer co-op
2. franchise
3. consumer co-op
4. nonprofit

Challenge Answers will vary but should reflect an understanding of the elements of whichever type of co-op is chosen.

1 Plan & Prepare

Objectives

- Analyze multiple sources to deepen understanding of a topic.
- Understand the evolution of an idea into a successful corporation.

2 Focus & Motivate

Ask students to give a brief history of the computers that they have used during their schooling. Chances are most of them will have used some Apple products. Also, inquire if students use the same computers at home. If so, why? If not, why not? Point out that answers to these questions will help to explain the path an idea must follow to become a successful product.

3 Teach

Using the Sources

Discuss

A. What is the focus of the first paragraph? *(the development and reliability of the product itself)* What is the focus of the second paragraph? *(the passionate belief that drove the young men)* What is the focus of the third paragraph? *(how they raised money to start their business)* Which of these focus points was most important in the eventual success of the business? Explain. *(Answers will probably vary between the first and second; look for good explanations.)*

B. As a source, how does an interview differ from an article such as the online biography? *(represents one viewpoint; may be based on memory rather than fresh research; language is often more conversational and colorful)*

C. How might a time line be an unreliable source for a complete picture of a subject? *(By its nature, a time line is selective, and the events included may not be fully representative.)*

Economics Update

At **ClassZone.com,** students will find links to updated information on the evolution of Apple Inc.

Case Study

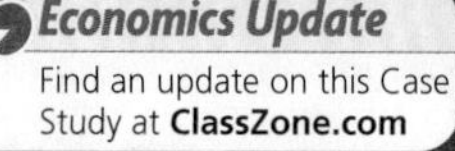

Find an update on this Case Study at **ClassZone.com**

Apple: The Evolution of One Company

Background Steve Jobs and Steve Wozniak joined forces when they were students. Together, they created a personal computer, named it Apple, and in 1976 started a company with the same name. In the years that followed, their company attained worldwide prominence. While the success story of Jobs and Wozniak often sounds like a fairy tale, the evolution of the company was not without its ups and downs. But by 2005, Apple had annual revenues of nearly $14 billion.

What's the issue? How does a company evolve from an idea into a billion-dollar enterprise? Study these sources to discover the factors behind the success of Apple Inc.

A. Online Biography

This article describes how two young men with an interest in computers created the basis for Apple Inc.

Two American Entrepreneurs Start Out in a Garage

Young inventors build their first of many computers.

When the two first met, Wozniak (born 1950) was 18, Jobs (born 1955) only 13. The pair put their electronics and inventing talents to work making unusual devices, and a few years later purchased a $25 microprocessor with the intention of building a computer. Although this first computer was crude and came without memory, a power supply or even a keyboard, it was very reliable. Jobs and Wozniak decided on a name that would convey the simplicity of the product's design and use: the Apple.

Jobs had a passionate belief in bringing computer technology to everyone. So in 1976, Jobs and Wozniak started a company to build and distribute their invention. In true American-dream fashion, their company began in a garage.

To finance their venture, Jobs sold his Volkswagen van and Wozniak sold his programmable calculator to raise $1,300. Weeks later, Jobs secured the company's first sale: 50 Apple I computers at [the retail price of] $666 each.

Source: Inventor of the Week Archive, MIT

Steve Wozniak (left) and Steve Jobs (right) founded Apple Computer in 1976.

Thinking Economically According to the document, why were Jobs and Wozniak able to succeed in starting their own company?

DIFFERENTIATING INSTRUCTION

English Learners

Interpret the Time Line

The callout next to the time line says it shows both highlights and challenges that Apple has experienced. Go through each item on the time line, which is written in very condensed language, and ask students to determine whether it represents a highlight or a challenge. Have them give reasons for their answers.

Gifted and Talented

Extend the Time Line

Have students continue with the time line as if they were writing from the vantage point of the year 2030. Direct them to include events that relate to those already on the time line but that show an evolution of ideas and issues over time. Have the students present and discuss their time lines in class.

B. Interview

In this interview, Evelyn Richards, who covered computers for *Mercury News* in the 1980s, describes Apple's innovative approach to introducing Macintosh, the company's new personal computer.

1984–Apple Launches Macintosh

Marketing plays key role in product's success.

They [Apple] were really more attuned to magazines much more than other tech companies, because magazines can reach a mass market. . . . Steve Jobs got on the cover of *Time* right around then.

The press kit was all really well-packaged. There was the press release for the non-techie people that just talked about how wonderful Macintosh was and how it was going to change the world. Then there were techier press releases, where they talked about the RAM, or the keyboard, or other things. . . .

It was really easily digestible, and easy to use by the press. Lots of great photos, professionally done. Now all that is standard.

Source: **Stanford Library; Interview with Evelyn Richards, 22 June 2000**

Thinking Economically How did Apple's marketing of Macintosh contribute to its success?

C. Timeline

This timeline shows some of the highlights and challenges that Apple Inc. has experienced.

Highlights in Apple Company History

1976–Jobs and Wozniak incorporate Apple Computer
1977–Apple II computer, the first PC with color graphics, introduced
1980–Apple becomes public company, offering 4.6 million shares for sale
1984–Commercial during Super Bowl XVIII introduces the first Macintosh
1985–Both Jobs and Wozniak leave Apple
1988–Apple sues Microsoft when Windows begins using features similar to those developed by Apple
1989–First portable Macintosh introduced
1993–Debut of Newton, an early personal digital assistant
1995–Apple loses its case against Microsoft
1997–Jobs returns to Apple as chief executive officer
1998–Newton discontinued
2001–Portable digital music player iPod introduced
2003–Safari browser introduced; iTunes Music Store debuts
2006–Apple computers begin using Intel Core Duo processors

Sources: **Macworld March 30, 2006; Apple Inc.**

Thinking Economically How might Apple's history have been different if it had become a partnership instead of a corporation? Explain your answer.

THINKING ECONOMICALLY Synthesizing

1. Based on information in the documents, how would you describe the evolution of Apple Inc.?
2. How did Apple's advertising and marketing affect its success or failure? Use examples from the documents in your answer.
3. What single overriding concern has defined the evolution of Apple and determined its success? Use information from the documents to support your answer.

More About . . .

Apple's Beliefs
The first source mentions the passionate belief of Jobs and Wozniak. That passion often carried over to Apple employees and users. Some became known as Apple Evangelists because they sought to convert PC users to the Apple platform. Guy Kawasaki, the best-known Apple evangelist, is sometimes called the father of evangelism marketing.

Thinking Economically

Answers

A. *electronic and inventing talents, product simplicity, passionate belief*

B. *Apple tailored different messages to fit each interested audience.*

C. *The business might have been smaller due to less funding; Jobs and Wozniak might have continued running the business; different products might have been invented.*

Synthesizing

1. *Apple evolved from a small investment and the human capital of Jobs and Wozniak into a large corporation.*
2. *Jobs and Wozniak picked a name that would "convey the simplicity of the product's design and use" (A); press releases for different audiences helped to broaden appeal (B); Super Bowl advertisement reached millions (C).*
3. *bringing computer technology to everyone*

TECHNOLOGY ACTIVITY

Creating a Web Page

Time 60 Minutes 

Task Create a Web page evangelizing for either the Mac or the PC platform

Materials Needed computer with Internet access and software for creating Web pages; projector desirable for final viewing but not essential

Activity

- Divide students into two groups. One will create a Web page that evangelizes for the PC platform; the other for the Mac platform.
- Each group should determine how to subdivide the work, keeping in mind the strengths of each group member.
- Encourage students to use imagery in their Web pages, as Apple did during the 1980s when it portrayed the "enemy" PC as Big Brother with drones mindlessly following along until one bold user breaks free.

Rubric

	Understanding of Platform Marketing	Presentation of Information
4	excellent	clever and well-designed
3	good	communicative
2	fair	close to the target
1	poor	sloppy

Online Summary Answers

1. sole proprietorship
2. unlimited liability
3. general partnership
4. limited partnership
5. limited liability partnership
6. corporation
7. stock
8. unlimited life
9. merger
10. horizontal merger
11. multinational corporation
12. franchise
13. cooperative
14. nonprofit organization

Interactive Review

Review this chapter using interactive activities at ClassZone.com

- Online Summary
- Quizzes
- Vocabulary Flip Cards
- Graphic Organizers
- Review and Study Notes

Online Summary

Complete the following activity either on your own paper or online at **ClassZone.com**

Choose the key concept that best completes the sentence. Not all key concepts will be used.

bond	limited partnership
conglomerate	merger
cooperative	multinational corporation
corporation	nonprofit organization
dividend	partnership
franchise	regulation
general partnership	sole proprietorship
horizontal merger	stock
limited liability	unlimited liability
limited liability partnership	unlimited life
limited life	vertical merger

In a __1__, the business is owned and managed by a single person. One key drawback of this is that the owner has __2__, putting even personal savings at risk. A __3__ is a business structure in which two or more owners share the management of the business, profits, and full liability. The __4__ and __5__ provide ways for some partners to risk only the amount of their investment.

A __6__ is a business that can raise money by selling __7__ and allows for limited liability of its owners and __8__ of the enterprise. Two or more businesses can consolidate through a __9__. If they provide the same kinds of goods or services, their consolidation is known as a __10__. When a business has branches in other countries, it is known as a __11__.

If someone pays for the right to sell a company's goods or services in a certain area, that person is operating a __12__. A business whose owners are also its customers is known as a __13__. A __14__ is structured like a business but pursues goals other than profits.

CHAPTER 8 Assessment

REVIEWING KEY CONCEPTS

Sole Proprietorships (pp. 226–231)

1. What are the advantages of a sole proprietorship?
2. What are the disadvantages?

Forms of Partnerships (pp. 232–237)

3. What are three different kinds of partnerships, and how do they differ?
4. What are the advantages and disadvantages of a partnership?

Corporations, Mergers, and Multinationals (pp. 238–247)

5. What are the advantages and disadvantages of a corporation?
6. In what three ways can companies consolidate?

Franchises, Co-ops, and Nonprofits (pp. 248–253)

7. How is a franchise "an almost independent" business?
8. What is the difference between a cooperative and a nonprofit organization?

APPLYING ECONOMIC CONCEPTS

9. What might be the outcome of raising the fees and requiring more paperwork in order to start a corporation? What would happen if fees were lowered and the application process was simplified?
10. Do you think the number of multinationals will continue to increase? Give reasons for your answer.
11. As you have read, sometimes merged companies are not more efficient than they were separately. In some cases, the chief executive officers (CEOs) who arranged the deal make an enormous amount of money from the merger even though the deal itself does not improve profits. What incentives might a board of directors offer to CEOs to make sure they make deals that pay off in profits?

CHAPTER 8 ASSESSMENT ANSWERS

Reviewing Key Concepts

1. ease of start-up, full control, relative freedom from regulation, ability to leave the business at any time, all profits to sole proprietor
2. limited life, unlimited liability, risk of inefficiency because of lack of specialization, lack of access to financial resources, and difficulty attracting good workers
3. In a general partnership, both partners are liable for the debts of the partnership and both are actively involved in the day-to-day business. In a limited partnership, at least one general partner assumes all liabilities and makes the business decisions; the limited partners contribute only money and are liable only for the amount of capital they invest. Limited liability partnerships protect each partner from liability for the mistakes or negligence of other partners.
4. advantages: ease of start-up, relative freedom from regulation, ability to leave the business at any time, potential for specialization, shared decision-making, increased access to financial resources, easier to attract and keep good workers; disadvantages: limited life, risk of inefficiency, potential for disagreements among partners, liability issues depending on type of partnership
5. advantages: access to financial resources, professional managers, limited liability, unlimited life; disadvantages: start up cost and effort, heavy regulation, double taxation, loss of control by owners
6. vertical merger, horizontal merger, conglomerate
7. A franchisee is an independently owned enterprise, but it pays for the right to sell the franchise's products.
8. A cooperative exists to help its members, who are also the customers, save money. A nonprofit's purpose is to provide social services or to fulfill another goal besides profit-seeking.

CRITICAL THINKING

Use the following graph showing the number of mergers in the years from 1970 to 2000 to answer questions 12–14.

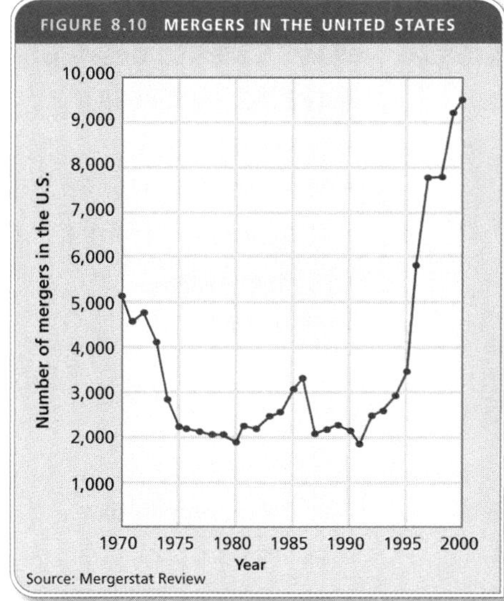

12. **Analyzing Graphs** Which of the following can you determine from the information about mergers in the graph?
    a. how many companies merged in any given year from 1970 to 2000
    b. how many more mergers took place in 2000 than in 1990
    c. how long each of the new companies lasted after the merger
13. **Predicting Economic Trends** Which decade saw the greatest increase in the number of mergers? What probably happened after that decade?
14. **Challenge** The number of mergers can reflect the economic times, which in turn are often affected by national and world events. What events may have contributed to tighter economic times—and therefore a decrease in mergers—in the 1970s?

SIMULATION

Design a New Business Structure

Each business structure you have read about in this chapter has both advantages and disadvantages. Follow the steps below to design a new business structure that attempts to avoid the worst disadvantages and to capitalize on the most important advantages of the other structures. You can imagine changing laws to accommodate your new structure, but try to make sure your creation makes economic sense.

Step 1. Break into small groups. In your group, draw up a list of advantages and disadvantages of all the business structures. The table on page 242 will help you begin the list.

Step 2. Discuss how the advantages and disadvantages would affect the ability of a business to earn a profit. Choose the three advantages and three disadvantages that your group feels have the most impact.

Step 3. Brainstorm possible ways to avoid the disadvantages and make the most of the advantages. Remember that in brainstorming any idea is allowed, no matter how crazy or simple it might sound.

Step 4. Sort through your brainstorming ideas. Use them to develop a new "ideal" business structure.

Step 5. Share your business structure with the rest of the class, and compare your efforts to those of your classmates.

Assess

Online Test Practice
- Go to **ClassZone.com** for more test practice.

Unit 3 Resource Book
- Chapter Test, Forms A, B, & C, pp. 51–62

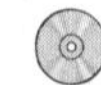

Test Generator CD-ROM
- Chapter Test, Forms (A, B, & C), in English and Spanish

Report

Use the McDougal Littell Assessment System to score assessments and receive customized reports.

Reteach

For activities customized for individual students, use the McDougal Littell Assessment System.

CHAPTER 8 ASSESSMENT ANSWERS

Applying Economic Concepts

9. Higher fees and more paperwork would discourage people from going into business and might result in corruption as people try to bypass procedures. Lower fees and simplified applications would lead to more new businesses and less corruption.
10. Answers will vary. Yes–successful businesses will expand to serve other countries, globalization; no–existing multinationals will grow larger instead of new companies becoming multinational, threat of terrorism.
11. Make the CEO's pay dependent on company performance after the merger; grant shares of stock and stock options, but only redeemable a period of time after the merger.

Critical Thinking

12. **a.** cannot be determined because the graph shows number of mergers, not number of companies involved
    b. can be determined by comparing the data for 2000 to that for 1990
    c. cannot be determined because the graph does not show that information
13. The 1990s had the greatest increase in merger activity. Answers will vary but should show sound reasoning.
14. inflation, oil embargo, end of American involvement in the Vietnam War, Watergate scandal

Simulation Rubric

	Understanding of Concepts Involved	Presentation of Information
4	excellent	accurate, clear, and complete
3	good	mostly accurate and clear
2	fair	sometimes clear
1	poor	sketchy

Planning Guide

Resources 2Go Complete print resources all on one USB drive allow you to customize lessons.

Section Titles and Objectives	Unit 3 Resource Book and Workbooks		Assessment Resources
1 How Are Wages Determined? pp. 258–265 • Identify what wages are • Describe how the interaction of supply and demand determines wages • Explain why wage rates differ	**Unit 3 Resource Book** • Reading Study Guide, pp. 63–64 • RSG with Additional Support, pp. 65–67 • RSG with Additional Support (Spanish), pp. 68–70 • Math Skills Worksheet: Calculating Hourly Wages, p. 101	**NCEE Student Activities** • Productivity, pp. 33–36	**Unit 3 Resource Book** • Section Quiz, p. 71 • Reteaching Activity, p. 72 **Test Generator CD-ROM** **Daily Test Practice Transparencies,** TT30
2 Trends in Today's Labor Market pp. 266–273 • Identify the changes that have taken place in the labor force • Explain how occupations have changed • Explain how the way people work has changed	**Unit 3 Resource Book** • Reading Study Guide, pp. 73–74 • RSG with Additional Support, pp. 75–77 • RSG with Additional Support (Spanish), pp. 78–80 • Case Study Resources: A Changing Work Life, pp. 97–98	• Economic Simulations: Human Capital and Productivity, pp. 99–100	**Unit 3 Resource Book** • Section Quiz, p. 81 • Reteaching Activity, p. 82 **Test Generator CD-ROM** **Daily Test Practice Transparencies,** TT31
3 Organized Labor in the United States pp. 274–283 • Describe how the labor movement developed in the United States • Discuss why organized labor has declined in the United States • Explain how labor unions affect wage rates and employment	**Unit 3 Resource Book** • Reading Study Guide, pp. 83–84 • RSG with Additional Support, pp. 85–87 • RSG with Additional Support (Spanish), pp. 88–90 • Readings in Free Enterprise: A Closer Look Inside Labor's Fastest-Growing Union, pp. 95–96	• Case Study Resources: A Changing Work Life, pp. 97–98 **Test Practice and Review Workbook,** pp. 39–40	**Unit 3 Resource Book** • Section Quiz, p. 91 • Reteaching Activity, p. 92 • Chapter Test, (Forms A, B, & C), pp. 103–114 **Test Generator CD-ROM** **Daily Test Practice Transparencies,** TT32

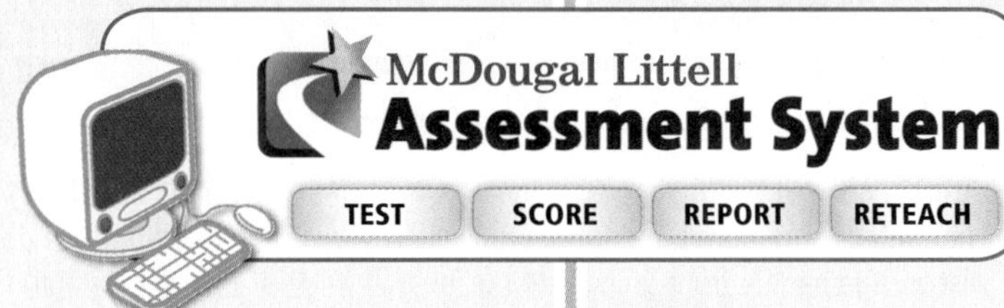

Integrated Technology

No Time? To focus students on the most important content in this chapter, use Economics Concepts Transparencies, CT31, "Trends in the Labor Market," available in Resources 2Go.

Teacher Presentation Options

Presentation Toolkit

Power Presentation DVD-ROM

- Lecture Notes
- Interactive Review
- Media Gallery
- Animated Economics
- Review Game

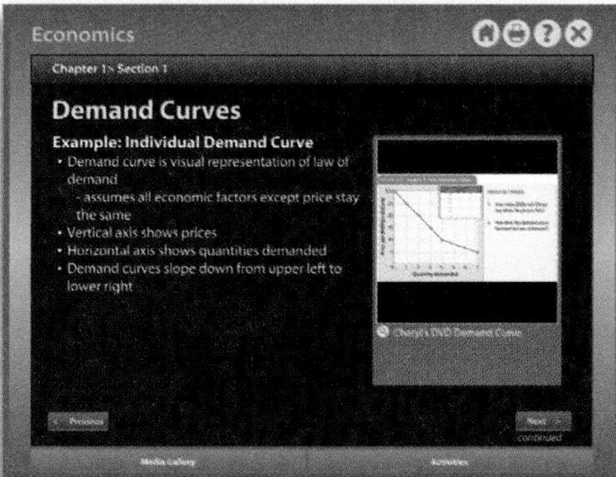

Economics Concepts Transparencies

- Tire Factory—Wages and Workers, CT30
- Trends in the Labor Market, CT31
- Labor Movement Timeline, CT32

Electronic Books

eEdition DVD-ROM

eEdition Online

Daily Test Practice Transparencies, TT30, TT31, TT32

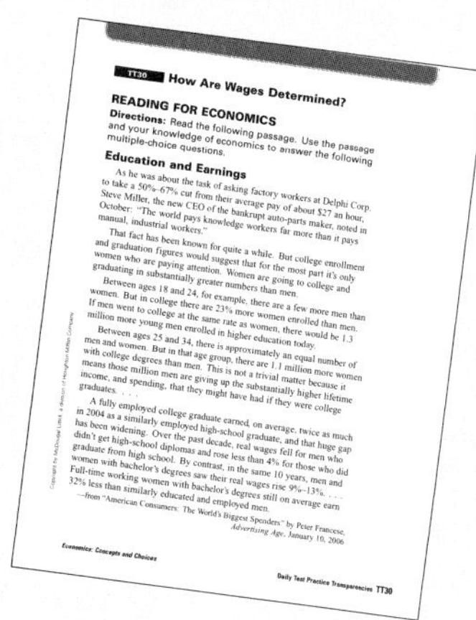

TT30 How Are Wages Determined?

READING FOR ECONOMICS

Directions: Read the following passage. Use the passage and your knowledge of economics to answer the following multiple-choice questions.

Education and Earnings

As he was about the task of asking factory workers at Delphi Corp. to take a 50%–67% cut from their average pay of about $27 an hour, Steve Miller, the new CEO of the bankrupt auto-parts maker, noted in October: "The world pays knowledge workers far more than it pays manual, industrial workers."

That fact has been known for quite a while. But college enrollment and graduation figures would suggest that for the most part it's only women who are paying attention. Women are going to college and graduating in substantially greater numbers than men.

Between ages 18 and 24, for example, there are a few more men than women. But in college there are 23% more women enrolled than men. If men went to college at the same rate as women, there would be 1.3 million more young men enrolled in higher education today.

Between ages 25 and 34, there is approximately an equal number of men and women. But in that age group, there are 1.1 million more women with college degrees than men. This is not a trivial matter because it means those million men are giving up the substantially higher lifetime income, and spending, that they might have had if they were college graduates. . . .

A fully employed college graduate earned, on average, twice as much in 2004 as a similarly employed high-school graduate, and that huge gap has been widening. Over the past decade, real wages fell for men who didn't get high-school diplomas and rose less than 4% for those who did graduate from high school. By contrast, in the same 10 years, men and women with bachelor's degrees saw their real wages rise 9%–13%. . . . Full-time working women with bachelor's degrees still on average earn 32% less than similarly educated and employed men.

—from "American Consumers: The World's Biggest Spenders" by Peter Francese, *Advertising Age*, January 10, 2006

Economics: Concepts and Choices

Daily Test Practice Transparencies TT30

Animated Economics

- Demand and Supply Curves for Labor, p. 259

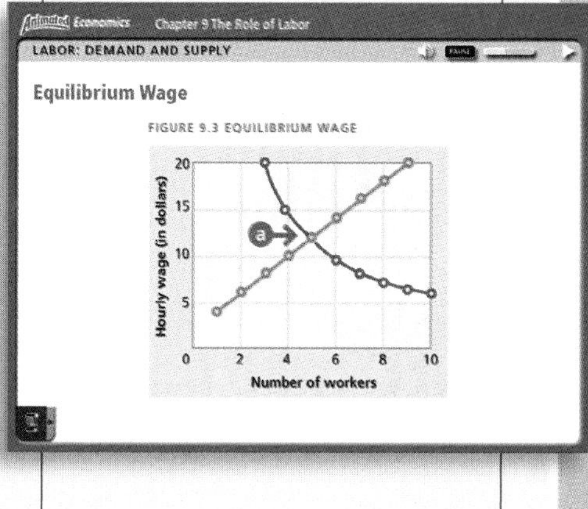

Online Activities at ClassZone.com

Economics Update

- Demand and Supply of Labor, p. 259
- Gary Becker, p. 264
- U.S. Work Force, p. 267
- Labor Unions, p. 278
- Managing Change in Your Work Life, p. 282

Animated Economics

- Interactive Graphics

Activity Maker

- Vocabulary Flip Cards
- Review Game

Research Center

- Graphs and Data

Interactive Review

- Online Summary
- Quizzes
- Vocabulary Flip Cards
- Graphic Organizers
- Review and Study Notes

SMARTGrapher

- Graphing Equilibrium Wages, p. 265
- Create a Bar Graph, p. 285

Teacher-Tested Activities

Name: Tim O'Driscoll (ret.)

School: Arrowhead High School

State: Wisconsin

Teacher-Tested Activities

At the beginning of this chapter, look for my classroom-proven idea for teaching economics concepts and thinking.

Chapter 9: The Role of Labor
Resources for Differentiated Instruction

Struggling Readers

Teacher's Edition Activities
- Analyze Cause and Effect, p. 260
- Recall What You Read, p. 268
- Read in Order, p. 272
- Listen for Information, p. 278
- Use the Callouts, p. 282

Unit 3 Resource Book
- RSG with Additional Support, pp. 65–67, 75–77, 85–87 (A)
- Reteaching Activities, pp. 72, 82, 92 (B)
- Chapter Test (Form A), pp. 103–106 (C)

ClassZone.com
- Animated Economics
- Interactive Review

Test Generator CD-ROM
- Chapter Test (Form A)
- Chapter Test (Form A), in Spanish

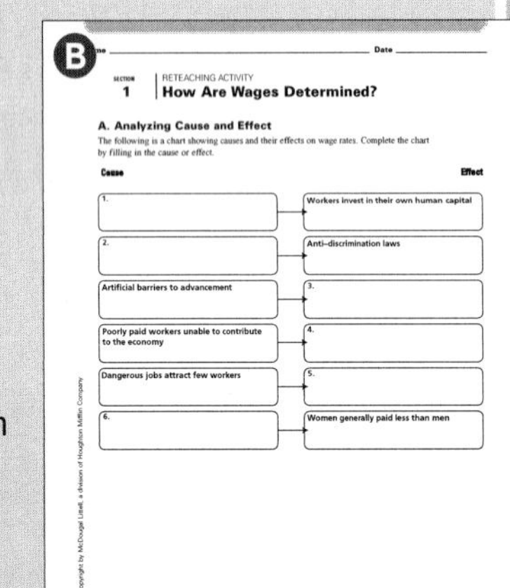
(B)
Name ______ Date ______

SECTION 1 | RETEACHING ACTIVITY
How Are Wages Determined?

A. Analyzing Cause and Effect
The following is a chart showing causes and their effects on wage rates. Complete the chart by filling in the cause or effect.

Cause	Effect
1.	Workers invest in their own human capital
2.	Anti-discrimination laws
Artificial barriers to advancement	3.
Poorly paid workers unable to contribute to the economy	4.
Dangerous jobs attract few workers	5.
6.	Women generally paid less than men

Copyright by McDougal Littell, a division of Houghton Mifflin Company

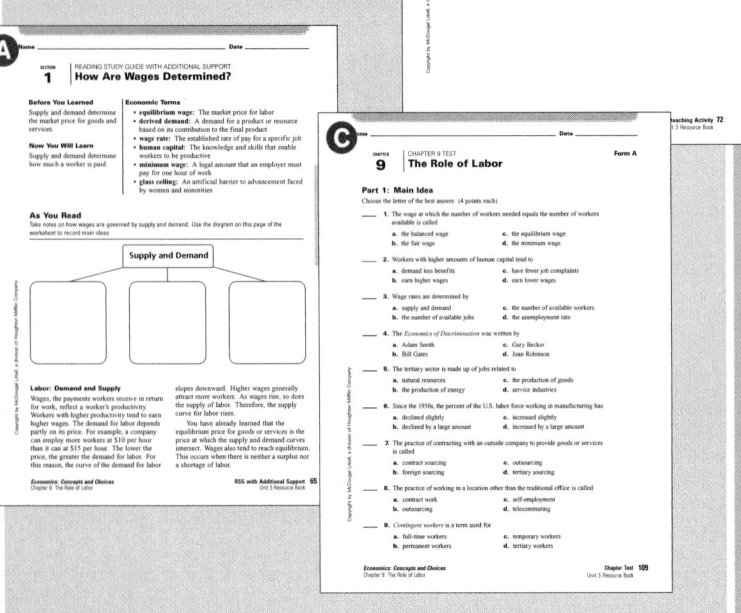
(A)
Name ______ Date ______

SECTION 1 | READING STUDY GUIDE WITH ADDITIONAL SUPPORT
How Are Wages Determined?

Before You Learned
Supply and demand determine the market price for goods and services.

Now You Will Learn
Supply and demand determine how much a worker is paid.

Economic Terms
- **equilibrium wage:** The market price for labor
- **derived demand:** A demand for a product or resource based on its contribution to the final product
- **wage rate:** The established rate of pay for a specific job
- **human capital:** The knowledge and skills that enable workers to be productive
- **minimum wage:** A legal amount that an employer must pay for one hour of work
- **glass ceiling:** An artificial barrier to advancement faced by women and minorities

As You Read
Take notes on how wages are governed by supply and demand. Use the diagram on this page of the worksheet to record main ideas

Supply and Demand

Labor: Demand and Supply
Wages, the payments workers receive in return for work, reflect a worker's productivity. Workers with higher productivity tend to earn higher wages. The demand for labor depends partly on its price. For example, a company can employ more workers at $10 per hour than it can at $15 per hour. The lower the price, the greater the demand for labor. For this reason, the curve of the demand for labor slopes downward. Higher wages generally attract more workers. As wages rise, so does the supply of labor. Therefore, the supply curve for labor rises.

You have already learned that the equilibrium price for goods or services is the price at which the supply and demand curves intersect. Wages also tend to reach equilibrium. This occurs when there is neither a surplus nor a shortage of labor.

Economics: Concepts and Choices Chapter 9: The Role of Labor — RSG with Additional Support 65, Unit 3 Resource Book

Copyright by McDougal Littell, a division of Houghton Mifflin Company

(C)
Name ______ Date ______

CHAPTER 9 | CHAPTER 9 TEST — Form A
The Role of Labor

Part 1: Main Idea
Choose the letter of the best answer. (4 points each)

____ 1. The wage at which the number of workers needed equals the number of workers available is called
a. the balanced wage c. the equilibrium wage
b. the fair wage d. the minimum wage

____ 2. Workers with higher amounts of human capital tend to
a. demand less benefits c. have fewer job complaints
b. earn higher wages d. earn lower wages

____ 3. Wage rates are determined by
a. supply and demand c. the number of available workers
b. the number of available jobs d. the unemployment rate

____ 4. The *Economics of Discrimination* was written by
a. Adam Smith c. Gary Becker
b. Bill Gates d. Joan Robinson

____ 5. The tertiary sector is made up of jobs related to
a. natural resources c. the production of goods
b. the production of energy d. service industries

____ 6. Since the 1950s, the percent of the U.S. labor force working in manufacturing has
a. declined slightly c. increased slightly
b. declined by a large amount d. increased by a large amount

____ 7. The practice of contracting with an outside company to provide goods or services is called
a. contract sourcing c. outsourcing
b. foreign sourcing d. tertiary sourcing

____ 8. The practice of working in a location other than the traditional office is called
a. contract work c. self-employment
b. outsourcing d. telecommuting

____ 9. *Contingent workers* is a term used for
a. full-time workers c. temporary workers
b. permanent workers d. tertiary workers

Economics: Concepts and Choices Chapter 9: The Role of Labor — Chapter Test 109, Unit 3 Resource Book

Copyright by McDougal Littell, a division of Houghton Mifflin Company

English Learners

Teacher's Edition Activities
- Understand Language Rights, p. 262
- Recognize Coined Words, p. 268
- Understand Multiple Meanings, p. 272
- Understand Acronyms, p. 276
- Recognize Idioms, p. 280

Unit 3 Resource Book
- RSG with Additional Support (Spanish), pp. 68–70, 78–80, 88–90 (A)

Test Generator CD-ROM
- Chapter Test (Forms A, B, & C), in Spanish (B)

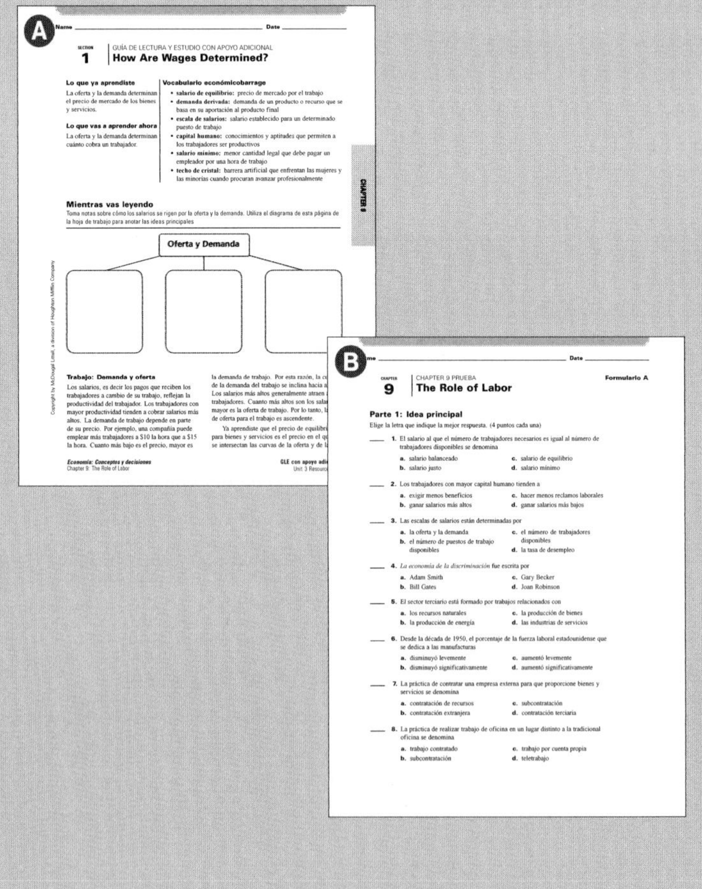
(A)
Name ______ Date ______

SECTION 1 | GUÍA DE LECTURA Y ESTUDIO CON APOYO ADICIONAL
How Are Wages Determined?

Lo que ya aprendiste
La oferta y la demanda determinan el precio de mercado de los bienes y servicios.

Lo que vas a aprender ahora
La oferta y la demanda determinan cuánto cobra un trabajador.

Vocabulario económicobarrage
- **salario de equilibrio:** precio de mercado por el trabajo
- **demanda derivada:** demanda de un producto o recurso que se basa en su aportación al producto final
- **escala de salarios:** salario establecido para un determinado puesto de trabajo
- **capital humano:** conocimientos y aptitudes que permiten a los trabajadores ser productivos
- **salario mínimo:** menor cantidad legal que debe pagar un empleador por una hora de trabajo
- **techo de cristal:** barrera artificial que enfrentan las mujeres y las minorías cuando procuran avanzar profesionalmente

CHAPTER 9

Mientras vas leyendo
Toma notas sobre cómo los salarios se rigen por la oferta y la demanda. Utiliza el diagrama de esta página de la hoja de trabajo para anotar las ideas principales

Oferta y Demanda

Trabajo: Demanda y oferta
Los salarios, es decir los pagos que reciben los trabajadores a cambio de su trabajo, reflejan la productividad del trabajador. Los trabajadores con mayor productividad tienden a cobrar salarios más altos. La demanda de trabajo depende en parte de su precio. Por ejemplo, una compañía puede emplear más trabajadores a $10 la hora que a $15 la hora. Cuanto más bajo es el precio, mayor es la demanda de trabajo. Por esta razón, la cu… de la demanda del trabajo se inclina hacia a… Los salarios más altos generalmente atraen … trabajadores. Cuanto más altos son los sala… mayor es la oferta de trabajo. Por lo tanto, l… de oferta para el trabajo es ascendente.

Ya aprendiste que el precio de equilibri… para bienes y servicios es el precio en el qu… se intersectan las curvas de la oferta y de l…

Economía: Conceptos y decisiones Chapter 9: The Role of Labor — GLE con apoyo adi… Unit 3 Resourc…

Copyright by McDougal Littell, a division of Houghton Mifflin Company

(B)
Name ______ Date ______

CHAPTER 9 | CHAPTER 9 PRUEBA — Formulario A
The Role of Labor

Parte 1: Idea principal
Elige la letra que indique la mejor respuesta. (4 puntos cada una)

____ 1. El salario al que el número de trabajadores necesarios es igual al número de trabajadores disponibles se denomina
a. salario balanceado c. salario de equilibrio
b. salario justo d. salario mínimo

____ 2. Los trabajadores con mayor capital humano tienden a
a. exigir menos beneficios c. hacer menos reclamos laborales
b. ganar salarios más altos d. ganar salarios más bajos

____ 3. Las escalas de salarios están determinadas por
a. la oferta y la demanda c. el número de trabajadores disponibles
b. el número de puestos de trabajo disponibles d. la tasa de desempleo

____ 4. *La economía de la discriminación* fue escrita por
a. Adam Smith c. Gary Becker
b. Bill Gates d. Joan Robinson

____ 5. El sector terciario está formado por trabajos relacionados con
a. los recursos naturales c. la producción de bienes
b. la producción de energía d. las industrias de servicios

____ 6. Desde la década de 1950, el porcentaje de la fuerza laboral estadounidense que se dedica a las manufacturas
a. disminuyó levemente c. aumentó levemente
b. disminuyó significativamente d. aumentó significativamente

____ 7. La práctica de contratar una empresa externa para que proporcione bienes y servicios se denomina
a. contratación de recursos c. subcontratación
b. contratación extranjera d. contratación terciaria

____ 8. La práctica de realizar trabajo de oficina en un lugar distinto a la tradicional oficina se denomina
a. trabajo contratado c. trabajo por cuenta propia
b. subcontratación d. teletrabajo

Inclusion

Teacher's Edition Activities

- Understand Employment Rights, p. 262
- Create a Poster, p. 264
- Evaluate Strengths and Challenges, p. 270
- Listen for Information, p. 278
- Read Visual Sources, p. 282

Lesson Plans

- Modified Lessons for Inclusion, pp. 30–32 (A)

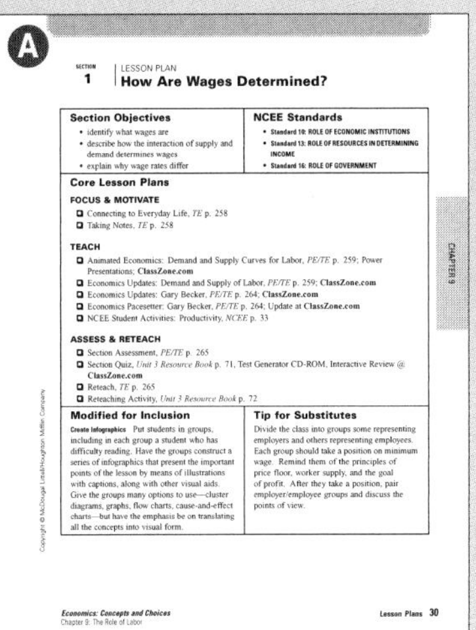

A

SECTION 1 | LESSON PLAN
How Are Wages Determined?

Section Objectives	NCEE Standards
• identify what wages are • describe how the interaction of supply and demand determines wages • explain why wage rates differ	• Standard 10: ROLE OF ECONOMIC INSTITUTIONS • Standard 13: ROLE OF RESOURCES IN DETERMINING INCOME • Standard 16: ROLE OF GOVERNMENT

Core Lesson Plans

FOCUS & MOTIVATE
- Connecting to Everyday Life, *TE* p. 258
- Taking Notes, *TE* p. 258

TEACH
- Animated Economics: Demand and Supply Curves for Labor, *PE/TE* p. 259; Power Presentations; **ClassZone.com**
- Economics Updates: Demand and Supply of Labor, *PE/TE* p. 259; **ClassZone.com**
- Economics Updates: Gary Becker, *PE/TE* p. 264; **ClassZone.com**
- Economics Pacesetter: Gary Becker, *PE/TE* p. 264; Update at **ClassZone.com**
- NCEE Student Activities: Productivity, *NCEE* p. 33

ASSESS & RETEACH
- Section Assessment, *PE/TE* p. 265
- Section Quiz, *Unit 3 Resource Book* p. 71, Test Generator CD-ROM, Interactive Review @ **ClassZone.com**
- Reteach, *TE* p. 265
- Reteaching Activity, *Unit 3 Resource Book* p. 72

Modified for Inclusion	Tip for Substitutes
Create Infographics Put students in groups, including in each group a student who has difficulty reading. Have the groups construct a series of infographics that present the important points of the lesson by means of illustrations with captions, along with other visual aids. Give the groups many options to use—cluster diagrams, graphs, flow charts, cause-and-effect charts—but have the emphasis be on translating all the concepts into visual form.	Divide the class into groups some representing employers and others representing employees. Each group should take a position on minimum wage. Remind them of the principles of price floor, worker supply, and the goal of profit. After they take a position, pair employer/employee groups and discuss the points of view.

CHAPTER 9

Copyright © McDougal Littell/Houghton Mifflin Company

Economics: Concepts and Choices
Chapter 9: The Role of Labor
Lesson Plans 30

Gifted and Talented

Teacher's Edition Activities

- Research and Write, p. 260
- Apply Economic Thinking, p. 264
- Look Backwards, p. 270
- Make a World Labor Events Time Line, p. 276
- Create a Graph, p. 280

Unit 3 Resource Book

- Readings in Free Enterprise: A Closer Look Inside Labor's Fastest-Growing Union, pp. 95–96 (A)
- Case Study Resources: A Changing Work Life, pp. 97–98 (B)

NCEE Student Activities

- Productivity, pp. 33–36 (C)

ClassZone.com

- Research Center

Test Generator CD-ROM

- Chapter Test (Form C)
- Chapter Test (Form C), in Spanish

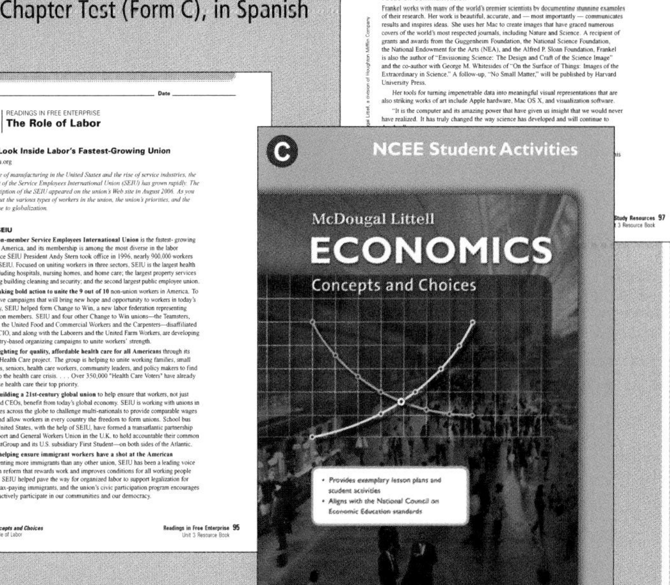

B

Name ______ Date ______

CHAPTER 9 | CASE STUDY RESOURCES
The Role of Labor

A Changing Work Life
by Tim McIntire

The following article about science photographer Felice Frankel appeared on Apple's Web site in 2006. In addition to describing Frankel's work and her use of Apple products, the article provides insight into how change has affected Frankel's work life.

Felice Frankel: Scientific Discovery Through Visualization

As one of the world's leading science photographers, Felice Frankel combines a scholar's knowledge of science, a photographer's skill for visualization, and a designer's intuitive sense of aesthetics [artistic beauty].

She started out as a biologist and lab technician. She later became a landscape and architectural photographer, earned a fellowship in design at Harvard University, and went on to work at the Massachusetts Institute of Technology as an artist in residence, eventually becoming a research scientist in the School of Science. In July, she became Senior Research Fellow at Harvard, as part of the new Initiative in Innovative Computing, while maintaining a part-time office at MIT's Center for Materials Science and Engineering as a research scientist.

Focus on Communication

Frankel works with many of the world's premier scientists by documenting stunning examples of their research. Her work is beautiful, accurate, and — most importantly — communicates results and inspires ideas. She uses her Mac to create images that have graced numerous covers of the world's most respected journals, including Nature and Science. A recipient of grants and awards from the Guggenheim Foundation, the National Science Foundation, the National Endowment for the Arts (NEA), and the Alfred P. Sloan Foundation, Frankel is also the author of "Envisioning Science: The Design and Craft of the Science Image" and the co-author with George M. Whitesides of "On the Surface of Things: Images of the Extraordinary in Science." A follow-up, "No Small Matter," will be published by Harvard University Press.

Her tools for turning impenetrable data into meaningful visual representations that are also striking works of art include Apple hardware, Mac OS X, and visualization software.

"It is the computer and its amazing power that have given us insight that we would never have realized. It has truly changed the way science has developed and will continue to

Study Resources 97
3 Resource Book

A

Name ______ Date ______

CHAPTER 9 | READINGS IN FREE ENTERPRISE
The Role of Labor

A Closer Look Inside Labor's Fastest-Growing Union
From www.seiu.org

With the decline of manufacturing in the United States and the rise of service industries, the size and impact of the Service Employees International Union (SEIU) has grown rapidly. The following description of the SEIU appeared on the union's Web site in August 2006. As you read, think about the various types of workers in the union, the union's priorities, and the union's response to globalization.

Growth of SEIU

•**The 1.8 million-member Service Employees International Union** is the fastest- growing union in North America, and its membership is among the most diverse in the labor movement. Since SEIU President Andy Stern took office in 1996, nearly 900,000 workers have united in SEIU. Focused on uniting workers in three sectors, SEIU is the largest health care union, including hospitals, nursing homes, and home care; the largest property services union, including building cleaning and security; and the second largest public employee union.

•**SEIU is taking bold action to unite the 9 out of 10** non-union workers in America. To launch innovative campaigns that will bring new hope and opportunity to workers in today's global economy, SEIU helped form Change to Win, a new labor federation representing nearly six million members. SEIU and four other Change to Win unions—the Teamsters, UNITE HERE, the United Food and Commercial Workers and the Carpenters—disaffiliated from the AFL-CIO, and along with the Laborers and the United Farm Workers, are developing strategic, industry-based organizing campaigns to unite workers' strength.

•**SEIU is fighting for quality, affordable health care for all Americans** through its Americans for Health Care project. The group is helping to unite working families, small business owners, seniors, health care workers, community leaders, and policy makers to find real solutions to the health care crisis. . . . Over 350,000 "Health Care Voters" have already pledged to make health care their top priority.

•**SEIU is building a 21st-century global union** to help ensure that workers, not just corporations and CEOs, benefit from today's global economy. SEIU is working with unions in similar industries across the globe to challenge multi-nationals to provide comparable wages and benefits, and allow workers in every country the freedom to form unions. School bus drivers in the United States, with the help of SEIU, have formed a transatlantic partnership with the Transport and General Workers Union in the U.K. to hold accountable their common employer—FirstGroup and its U.S. subsidiary First Student—on both sides of the Atlantic.

• **SEIU is helping ensure immigrant workers have a shot at the American dream.** Representing more immigrants than any other union, SEIU has been a leading voice for immigration reform that rewards work and improves conditions for all working people in this country. SEIU helped pave the way for organized labor to support legalization for hard-working, tax-paying immigrants, and the union's civic participation program encourages immigrants to actively participate in our communities and our democracy.

Copyright by McDougal Littell, a division of Houghton Mifflin Company

Economics: Concepts and Choices
Chapter 9: The Role of Labor
Readings in Free Enterprise 95
Unit 3 Resource Book

Focus & Motivate

Objective

Explain the role of labor in the economy in the past, present, and future.

Why the Concept Matters

Point out that each year 100 million new workers join the global workforce. In order to find their way successfully to their most advantageous careers, students need to understand how to enhance the value of their labor and to distinguish themselves from other workers. This understanding requires knowing the broad picture of the labor market in order to determine their prospects.

Analyzing the Photograph

The photograph on this page shows workers in a modern office building.

- What does the office layout tell you about the environment in which the employees work? *(The office is arranged to allow employees to work individually at separate work stations or jointly at a conference table.)*
- What kind of work are the people doing? *(One person seems to be studying a report; three people are involved in a conference; and two others are engaged in a more casual conversation at an individual work station.)*
- What appears to be the work atmosphere in the office? *(The people appear to be engaged in their duties, whether working individually or together as a team, in a pleasant yet work-conducive atmosphere.)*

The Role of Labor
The service sector makes up the largest part of the U.S. economy. More people work in offices than ever before.

256

CONTENT STANDARDS

NCEE STANDARDS

Standard 10: Role of Economic Institutions
Students will understand that
Institutions in market economies help individuals and groups accomplish their goals. Banks, labor unions, corporations, and legal systems are examples of important institutions. A different kind of institution, clearly defined and enforced property rights, is essential to a market economy.

Students will be able to use this knowledge to
Understand that many institutions work to promote the goals of certain interest groups. *(pages 274, 280)*

Standard 13: Role of Resources in Determining Income
Students will understand that
Income for most people is determined by the market value of the productive resources they sell. What workers earn depends, primarily, on the market value of what they produce and how productive they are.

Students will be able to use this knowledge to
Predict future earnings based on their current plans for education, training, and career options. *(pages 258–264)*

Standard 16: Role of Government
Students will understand that
There is an economic role for government in a market economy whenever the benefits of a government policy outweigh its costs. Governments often address environmental concerns, define and protect property rights, and attempt to make markets more competitive.

Students will be able to use this knowledge to
Identify and evaluate the benefits and costs of alternative public policies, and assess who enjoys the benefits and who bears the costs. *(pages 263, 276, 279)*

CHAPTER

9

The Role of Labor

CONCEPT REVIEW

Labor productivity is the value of the goods or services a worker can produce in a set amount of time.

CHAPTER 9 KEY CONCEPT

Labor, the human effort used to produce goods and services, is subject to the same forces of demand and supply that govern the rest of the economy.

WHY THE CONCEPT MATTERS

The value of your labor depends on the demand for what you do and the supply of other people able to do the same thing. It's up to you to figure out what you do best and to distinguish yourself from other workers. Maybe what you really want to do will require special training or years of experience. Think of your dream job, and write a plan for how you will get that job. Evaluate the demand for the job and the supply of people capable of performing it.

Online Highlights

More at ClassZone.com

Economics Update

Go to ECONOMICS UPDATE for chapter updates and current news on managing change in your worklife. (See Case Study, pp. 282–283.) ▶

Animated Economics

Go to ANIMATED ECONOMICS for interactive lessons on the graphs and tables in this chapter.

Interactive Review

Go to INTERACTIVE REVIEW for concept review and activities.

The world of work is changing. Will you be able to keep pace? See the Case Study on pages 282–283.

From the Classroom

Tim O'Driscoll, Arrowhead H.S. (retired)

Students have a difficult time understanding how people in diverse occupations earn such different incomes. Is there a direct link between the amount of income that one receives and the societal good that the worker provides? Why do some people earn more than others?

U.S. median household income for 2005: $43,389

Celebrities' incomes for 2005:
Oprah Winfrey, $163 million; Tiger Woods, $77 million; Julia Roberts, $24 million; Kobe Bryant, $22 million ; Derek Jeter, $18 million

Put students into small groups and ask them to list five factors that determine the amount of an individual's annual salary. (*Possible answers: supply and demand; level of human capital—education, skills, experience; skills in a high demand/low supply occupation more valuable than skills in a high supply/low demand field; unique artistic talent or athletic ability [high demand / low supply]; technology allows celebrities to deliver their services to millions)*

Previewing Chapter Technology at ClassZone.com

Economics Update Students will find updates to information in the pupil edition on pages 259, 264, 267, 278, and 282.

Animated Economics Students will find interactive lessons related to materials on page 259.

Interactive Review Students will find additional section and chapter assessment support for materials on pages 265, 273, 281, and 284.

TEACHER MEDIA FAVORITES

Books

- Dychtwald, Ken, Tamara J. Erickson, and Robert Morison. *Workforce Crisis: How to Beat the Coming Shortage of Skills and Talent.* Cambridge, MA: Harvard Business School Press, 2006. Goes beyond the impact of the retirement of baby boomers and lays out suggestions for creating an engaged and diverse workforce in all age brackets.
- Uchitelle, Louis. *The Disposable American: Layoffs and Their Consequences.* New York: Knopf, 2006. A veteran *New York Times* business reporter explores the far-reaching effects of layoffs made to improve the short-term bottom line.
- Beik, Millie. *Labor Relations.* Westport, CT: Greenwood Press, 2005. Part of the *Major Issues in American History* series, this book presents a survey of labor history through 11 watershed events.

Videos/DVDs

- *Bread and Roses.* 110 minutes. Directed by Ken Loach. The story of the organizing efforts of janitors and other low-skilled workers in California.
- *How People Are Paid.* 19 minutes. The Learning Seed. Explores real-world issues of paychecks and benefits.

Internet

Visit **ClassZone.com** to link to

- a variety of chapter-specific, content-reviewed sites
- updates on data and topics presented throughout the chapter sections and Case Study
- updates to the Power Presentation

1 Plan & Prepare

Section 1 Objectives

- identify what wages are
- describe how the interaction of supply and demand determines wages
- explain why wage rates differ

2 Focus & Motivate

Connecting to Everyday Life Direct students to the graph on page 261 that shows Median Earnings by Education. Ask students to discuss how learning about wages will have an impact on their lives. (Students will no doubt recognize that the choices they make now in regard to training or education will have a direct impact on future wages. The more they know about wages, the better informed their choices will be.)

Taking Notes Remind students to take notes as they read using a cluster diagram to record what they learn about wages. They can use the Graphic Organizer at **Interactive Review @ ClassZone.com**. A sample is shown below.

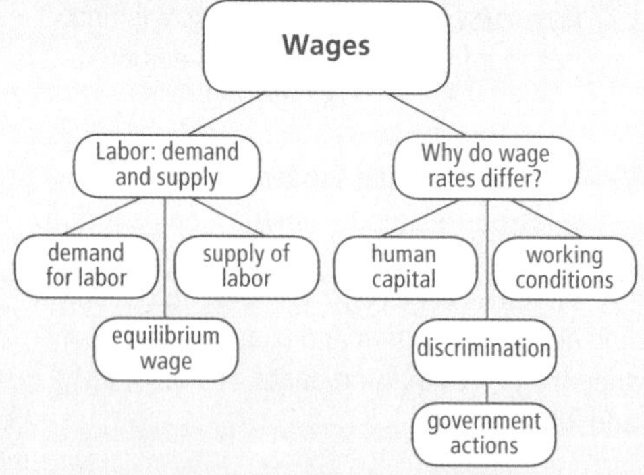

SECTION 1

How Are Wages Determined?

OBJECTIVES

In Section 1, you will
- identify what wages are
- describe how the interaction of supply and demand determines wages
- explain why wage rates differ

KEY TERMS

wages, *p. 258*
equilibrium wage, *p. 258*
derived demand, *p. 259*
wage rate, *p. 261*
human capital, *p. 261*
glass ceiling, *p. 262*
minimum wage, *p. 262*

TAKING NOTES

As you read Section 1, complete a cluster diagram like the one below to record what you learn about wages. Use the Graphic Organizer at **Interactive Review @ ClassZone.com**

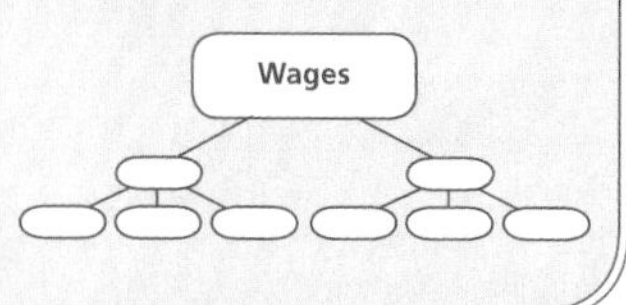

Labor: Demand and Supply

QUICK REFERENCE

Wages are payments received in return for work.

Equilibrium wage is the wage at which the quantity of workers demanded equals the quantity of workers supplied; the market price for labor.

KEY CONCEPTS

Have you ever wondered why working at a fast food restaurant pays so little? This section will help answer that question. In Chapter 1 you learned about the four factors of production: land, labor, capital, and entrepreneurship. Each of those has a price that must be figured into production costs. The price of labor is **wages**, the payments workers receive in return for work.

Wages, just like the other factors of production, are governed by the forces of supply and demand. The interaction of these two economic forces produces an equilibrium, or balance. An **equilibrium wage** is the wage at which the number of workers needed equals the number of workers available. In other words, an equilibrium wage produces neither a surplus nor a shortage of workers. Let's look at demand and supply separately and see how they affect wages at fast food restaurants.

Demand for Labor

In a competitive labor market, wages reflect a worker's labor productivity—the value of the goods or services a worker produces in a set amount of time. A business hires workers to help it produce goods or provide

SECTION 1 PROGRAM RESOURCES

ON LEVEL

Lesson Plans
- Core, p. 30

Unit 3 Resource Book
- Reading Study Guide, pp. 63–64
- Math Skills Worksheet, p. 101
- Section Quiz, p. 71

STRUGGLING READERS

Unit 3 Resource Book
- Reading Study Guide with Additional Support, pp. 65–67
- Reteaching Activity, p. 72

ENGLISH LEARNERS

Unit 3 Resource Book
- Reading Study Guide with Additional Support (Spanish), pp. 68–70

INCLUSION

Lesson Plans
- Modified for Inclusion, p. 30

GIFTED AND TALENTED

NCEE Student Activities
- Productivity, pp. 33–36

TECHNOLOGY

eEdition DVD-ROM

eEdition Online

Power Presentation DVD-ROM

Economics Concepts Transparencies
- CT30 Tire Factory—Wages and Workers

Daily Test Practice Transparencies, TT30

ClassZone.com

services. A producer's demand for labor is therefore a **derived demand**, a demand for a product or resource because of its contribution to the final product.

Workers with higher productivity tend to earn higher wages. In one hour, a fast food chef might be able to produce $50 worth of food that customers want. An attorney, by contrast, might be able to provide services worth $300 in the same hour's time. Employers, then, are willing to pay attorneys higher wages than fast food chefs.

The demand for labor depends in part on its price. As with anything else, when the price goes down, the quantity demanded goes up; and when the price goes up, the quantity demanded goes down. For example, suppose that fast food chefs are paid $12 per hour. If the wage should fall to $10 per hour, many restaurants would hire additional chefs. On the other hand, if the wage rose to $14 per hour, some restaurants would stop hiring and others would have to lay off some chefs. This is illustrated in Figure 9.1. The demand curve for labor, then, is a downward slope—the lower the price of labor, the greater the quantity of labor employers would demand.

QUICK REFERENCE

Derived demand is a demand for a product or resource based on its contribution to the final product.

FIGURES 9.1 AND 9.2 DEMAND AND SUPPLY CURVES FOR LABOR

FIGURE 9.1 **DEMAND CURVE**

Hourly wage (in dollars): 0, 5, 10, 15, 20
Number of workers: 0, 2, 4, 6, 8, 10
a

FIGURE 9.2 **SUPPLY CURVE**

Hourly wage (in dollars): 0, 5, 10, 15, 20
Number of workers: 0, 2, 4, 6, 8, 10
b

These graphs show demand and supply curves for fast food chefs.

(a) The restaurant is willing to hire more chefs if the hourly wage is lower.

(b) As the wage increases, so does the number of workers willing to work as fast food chefs.

ANALYZE GRAPHS

1. How many fast food chefs would the restaurant hire at the wage $10 per hour?
2. How many workers would be willing to be fast food chefs at the wage of $10 per hour?
3. What would happen if the restaurant tried to hire chefs at $10 per hour?

Animated Economics

Use interactive demand and supply curves for labor at **ClassZone.com**

Supply of Labor

Now let's consider the situation from the worker's point of view, to see how the supply of labor works. Suppose a new fast food restaurant opens and wants to hire chefs. If it puts an ad in the newspaper for chefs who would be paid $10 per hour, fewer people will respond—and probably none of the chefs currently employed at $12 per hour. Workers who are earning less than $10 per hour in some other kind of job might leave their jobs and become fast food chefs because the wages are higher than their current wages.

Economics Update

Find an update on demand and supply of labor at **ClassZone.com**

3 Teach

Labor: Demand and Supply

Discuss

- What would happen to nurses' wages if there were fewer nurses than positions that needed filling? Why? *(Wages would go up because demand would exceed the supply.)*

Analyze Graphs: Figures 9.1 and 9.2

When a person's wages rise dramatically, he or she will sometimes work fewer hours in order to enjoy more leisure time. This is a "backward bending" supply curve of labor. Work with students to plot a graph that shows this.

Answers

1. *6*

2. *4*

3. *a shortage of two chefs*

Animated Economics Animation and audio highlight labor demand and supply curves. Working with the animated graphs will help students see the interactions between labor demand and supply and their relation to equilibrium wage.

Economics Update

At **ClassZone.com,** students will see updated information on demand and supply of labor.

LEVELED ACTIVITY

Analyzing Wage Factors

Time 30 Minutes

Objective Students will analyze a job on the basis of supply and demand, human capital, working conditions, discrimination, and government actions. (These concepts are covered in Section 1.)

Basic

Choose a job that you know something about. Give one-sentence answers to the following:

- How much human capital is required?
- How would you rate working conditions?
- Is the job likely to be affected by discriminatory practices?
- Is this job affected by government actions?

On Level

Choose two very different jobs. Write a comparison/contrast of them based on the following attributes:

- level of human capital required
- working conditions
- discriminatory practices
- effect, if any, of government actions

Challenge

Consider three possible careers. Evaluate each on the basis of the factors affecting wages: level of human capital, working conditions, discriminatory practices, and the effect of government actions. Express your evaluation in an essay, and conclude with a preferred career choice based on the results of your evaluation.

Technomics

Occupational Employment and Wage Estimates
Students may be interested to know they can check out estimated wages for the fields they are considering as professions. This information is found on the Web site of the U.S. Department of Labor, Bureau of Labor Statistics.

Analyzing Graphs: Figure 9.3

Remind students of the idea of marginal benefit. Then, introduce the concept of marginal revenue product, the extra revenue produced with each additional unit of labor, or price times the marginal product of each worker. As long as the extra revenue does not exceed the wages, businesses will continue to hire more workers. Ask students to give an example to explain this concept. *(Possible answer: Each time Joe's restaurant hires an additional server, its profits go up. Eventually, say with the 10th server, the wages begin to exceed the marginal revenue product, and profits go down.)*

Answers

1. *4*
2. *6*
3. *a surplus of two workers*

But suppose the new restaurant offers fast food chefs $15 per hour. Any worker earning less than that will be interested—including experienced chefs currently employed at $12 per hour. More workers will be willing to work at higher wages than at lower wages. For this reason, the supply curve for labor is upward sloping, as illustrated in Figure 9.2 on page 259.

Equilibrium Wage

You learned in Chapter 6 that the equilibrium price for goods or services is the price at which there is neither a surplus nor a shortage—in other words, the point at which the supply curve and the demand curve intersect. Since wages are the price of labor, they too gravitate toward equilibrium.

For example, fast food restaurants might offer higher wages to attract chefs. Given the upward-sloping supply curve, before long there would be more people wanting to be chefs than there are jobs, resulting in a labor surplus. With so many chefs to choose from, restaurants could lower the wage and still attract workers. If they offered a wage that was too low, however, people would have less incentive to work as fast food chefs. A shortage would eventually result, so restaurants would need to raise the wages to attract more. The downward and upward forces push until an equilibrium wage is reached, as illustrated in Figure 9.3.

FIGURE 9.3 EQUILIBRIUM WAGE

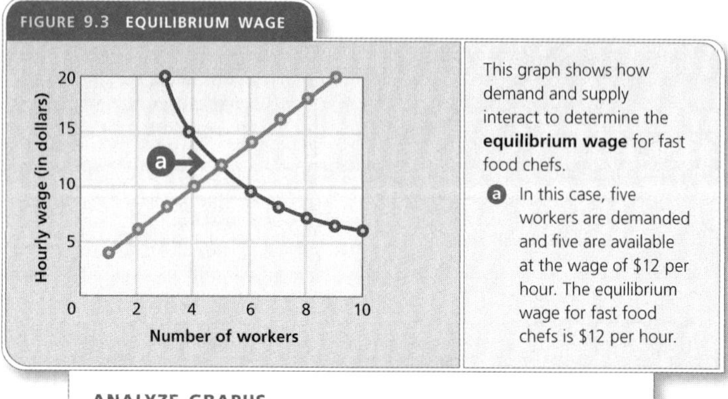

This graph shows how demand and supply interact to determine the **equilibrium wage** for fast food chefs.

ⓐ In this case, five workers are demanded and five are available at the wage of $12 per hour. The equilibrium wage for fast food chefs is $12 per hour.

ANALYZE GRAPHS

1. How many fast food chefs would the restaurant hire at the wage of $15 per hour?
2. How many workers would be willing to be fast food chefs if the wage rose to $15 per hour?
3. What would result if the wage rose to $15 per hour?

APPLICATION Applying Economic Concepts

A. Suppose that a new high school opens next to a popular fast food restaurant. Explain what will happen to the derived demand for chefs at the restaurant.

The restaurant will need more chefs to make food for its new customers. Therefore, its derived demand for chefs will increase

260 Chapter 9

DIFFERENTIATING INSTRUCTION

Struggling Readers

Analyze Cause and Effect
Have students analyze the cause-and-effect chain in paragraph two under the heading Equilibrium Wage. You may want to suggest that they represent the cause-and-effect chain this way:

Cause → Effect
Higher wages → more chefs
↓
Cause → Effect
more chefs → surplus workers
↓
Cause and so on

Gifted and Talented

Research and Write
Have students research the law of diminishing returns. Then, instruct them to develop and write an example that explains the law in operation and why employers will not want to hire workers past the point where the worker's wage equals the worker's marginal revenue product.

Why Do Wage Rates Differ?

KEY CONCEPTS

Different jobs have different **wage rates**, the rates of pay for specific jobs or work performed. Wage rates are determined by supply and demand, which in turn are influenced by four key factors: (1) **human capital**, which is the knowledge and skills that enable workers to be productive, (2) working conditions, (3) discrimination in the workplace, and (4) government actions.

QUICK REFERENCE

Wage rate is the established rate of pay for a specific job or work performed.

Human capital is the knowledge and skills that enable workers to be productive.

FACTOR 1 Human Capital

Economists group workers according to the amount of human capital they have. *Unskilled workers*, such as house cleaners and sanitation workers, have a low level of human capital. *Semiskilled workers*—construction and clerical workers, for example—have received some training, so their human capital is higher. *Skilled workers*, such as plumbers and electricians, have made a significant investment in human capital in the form of specialized training. *Professional workers*—doctors, lawyers, and others with intensive specialized training—have the highest human capital.

The demand for skilled and professional workers is high, but the supply of these workers is relatively low. For this reason and because training increases their productivity, highly skilled workers tend to receive higher wages. The prospect of higher wages leads many people to invest in their human capital and enroll in vocational school, specialist training programs, and higher education.

FIGURE 9.4 AND 9.5 **U.S. LABOR FORCE BY EDUCATION**

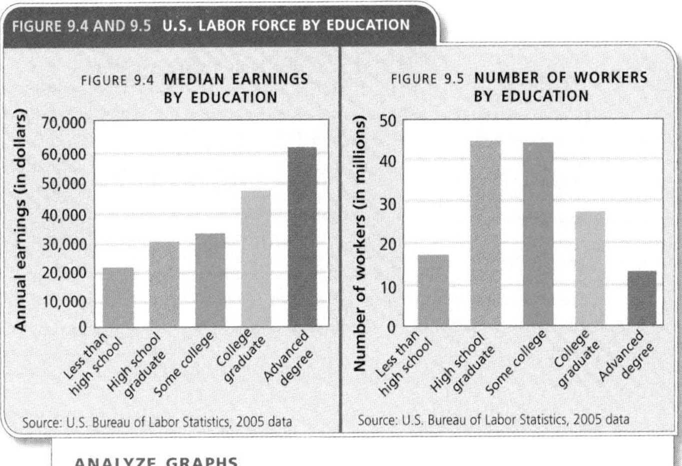

ANALYZE GRAPHS

1. In terms of average annual salary, about how much is graduating from high school worth?
2. There are almost as few people without a high school diploma as with an advanced degree. Why doesn't the reduced supply make their salaries as high as the salaries for people with an advanced degree?

Why Do Wage Rates Differ?

Discuss

- If higher education leads to higher wages, why don't more people get advanced degrees? *(Possible answers: can't afford it; grades not good enough; must work to support a family)*
- Of the four factors that influence wage rates, workers have the most control over which? *(Human capital and working conditions. But remind students of the previous question. For example, in a coal-mining town many people face severe limitations in selecting their jobs.)*

Analyze Graphs: Figures 9.4 and 9.5

Calculate costs versus benefits of a college education. Compute how many years it would take to break even with someone who started working after graduating from high school. Assume that each makes the median annual income ($30,000 and $48,000) and that a college education costs $82,800 in student loans and interest ($8,280 per year for 10 years). About 15 years after high school graduation, the college grad would break even with the high school grad. By the end of their work lives (50 years after high school graduation), the college grad would have earned over $600,000 more.

Answers

1. *about $10,000*
2. *Demand is higher for people with an advanced degree because they have a much higher level of human capital.*

SMALL GROUP ACTIVITY

Analyzing Want Ads

Time 30 Minutes ◑

Task Analyze the want ads for evidence of factors influencing wage rates.

Materials Needed paper, pens, four pages or sections of want ads for jobs

Activity

- Have students work in small groups. Together, they should look over their section of the job listings.
- Instruct them to note whether there are references to any factors that influence wages: human capital, working conditions, discrimination, or government actions.
- Direct each group to choose a want ad to present to class, being prepared to indicate how the ad shows one or more of the factors determining wages.
- Engage students in a discussion to tie the ideas together after the presentations.

Rubric

	Understanding of Why Wages Differ	Presentation of Information
4	excellent	clear and complete
3	good	mostly clear
2	fair	sometimes clear
1	poor	unclear

More About . . .

Working Conditions
According to the Bureau of Labor Statistics, timber cutters, fishers, pilots and navigators, roofers, and electrical power installers are among the top ten most dangerous occupations, based on the fatality rate. However, highway collisions account for the most fatalities each year (1,372 in 2002), with workplace violence accounting for the second highest number of fatalities (840 in 2002). The most dangerous industry overall, according to the BLS, is mining.

More About . . .

Equal Opportunity
The Equal Employment Opportunity Commission (EEOC) exists to protect workers from discrimination. Specifically, most workers are guaranteed the right to

- work free of discrimination because of their race, color, religion, sex (including pregnancy), national origin, disability, or age
- work free of harassment
- complain about job discrimination without punishment
- request workplace changes for their religion or disability
- keep medical information private

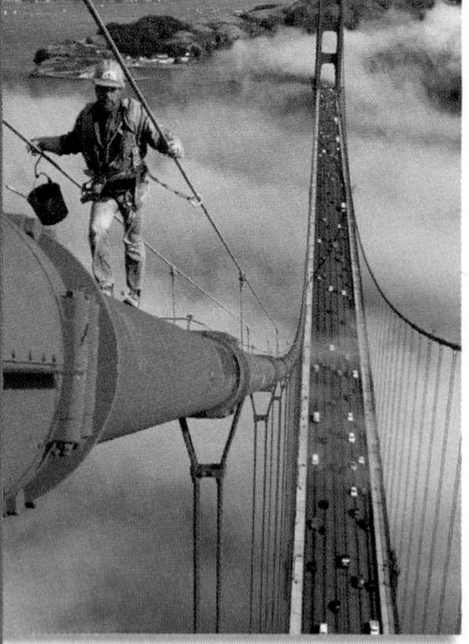

Working Conditions
Painters who work at high altitudes receive higher wages.

FACTOR 2 Working Conditions

"It's a tough job, but someone has to do it." That statement is often used humorously by people who have dream jobs, such as vacation planners who get to go on fabulous trips as "research" or taste testers who sample chocolate or other goodies. However, some jobs really are tougher than others. Some jobs, such as washing windows on a skyscraper, are very dangerous. Other jobs can be very unpleasant, such as collecting garbage. Higher wages are often paid to workers in dangerous and unpleasant occupations in order to attract qualified people to those jobs.

While the disadvantages of some jobs may be offset by higher wages, the advantages of other jobs may make up for low wages. These advantages vary widely, depending on the worker. For example, a student who loves movies might take a job as a clerk at a video store. Although the pay is low, the student might get to borrow movies free of charge. Someone tired of a long commute in rush hour traffic might welcome a lower-paying job that is only minutes away from home.

FACTOR 3 Discrimination

Another factor affecting differences in wage rates is discrimination. Wage discrimination may be based on race, ethnicity, gender, or other factors. For example, the average pay of women tends to be lower than that of men doing the same job. Racial prejudices sometimes lead to discrimination in wages. A prejudiced employer might be unwilling to hire a minority candidate except at a lower wage.

However, employers who discriminate may actually lose money. By eliminating qualified candidates because of their gender, ethnic group, or other trait irrelevant to performance, employers may miss out on the best worker for the job.

Wage differences may also result from occupational segregation. Some low-paying jobs have been viewed as the "realm" of women or certain racial or ethnic groups. Occupational segregation becomes a vicious cycle: groups can become trapped in these jobs, unable to earn enough to invest in human capital that could move them upward. In the United States, the federal government has tried to break this cycle by passing such antidiscrimination laws as the Equal Pay Act (1963) and the Civil Rights Act (1964).

Artificial barriers to advancement may also limit the wages of women and minorities. They may have the skills and experience necessary to advance, but find that they are never promoted. The term **glass ceiling** describes these unseen barriers to advancement.

QUICK REFERENCE

Glass ceiling is an artificial barrier to advancement faced by women and minorities.

The **minimum wage** is the legal minimum amount that an employer must pay for one hour of work.

FACTOR 4 Government Actions

In a pure market economy, wages would be set strictly by economic forces. However, in many countries, including the United States, the government steps in when market forces produce results that people disagree with. The **minimum wage**, the lowest wage legally allowed for one hour of work, is one example. As you read in Chapter 6, the minimum wage acts as a price floor designed to boost wages for low-income workers. The forces of supply and demand might set the equilibrium wage

DIFFERENTIATING INSTRUCTION

English Learners

Understand Language Rights
Language discrimination is one of the topics frequently addressed in the government's effort to assure equal employment opportunity and freedom from discrimination. Have students research and write about one of the following subtopics:

- English tests for employment
- English-speaking-only rules in the workplace
- how to file a discrimination complaint

Inclusion

Understand Employment Rights
Direct students to research Title I of the Americans with Disabilities Act. This act covers workplace rights for workers with disabilities. Have students present their research to the rest of the class in a manner suited to their learning style.

MATH CHALLENGE

FIGURE 9.6 Calculating Annual Wages

Suppose you are offered two jobs, one that pays $12.50 per hour or another that pays $30,000 per year. In both jobs, you will work 40 hours per week and get two weeks off per year. Assuming both offer the same benefits, which job pays better?

You could either figure out how much you would make in a year at the hourly job or you could convert the annual salary into an hourly wage. In this exercise, we will calculate how much a wage of $12.50 per hour pays for a year's worth of work.

Step 1: Multiply to determine the number of hours worked per year. Assume the job includes two weeks of unpaid vacation.

Hours per week	×	Weeks per year	=	Total hours per year	Example Calculations: 40	×	50	=	2,000

Step 2: Then, multiply to find the amount of pay annually.

Total hours per year	×	Hourly wage	=	Annual wages	2,000	×	$12.50	=	$25,000

The job that pays a salary of $30,000 per year pays better than the one that pays a wage of $12.50 per hour.

Comparing Earnings Use the calculations to determine the annual wages of a job that pays $15 per hour for 40 hours per week. What about one that pays $20 per hour but only offers 20 hours of work each week? What other factors do you need to consider when comparing pay between jobs?

for certain jobs so low that no one could reasonably make a living at these jobs. The minimum wage attempts to help the people who hold these jobs to make ends meet. However, businesses point out that they might hire more workers if they were allowed to pay a lower wage.

The first national minimum wage law in the United States was passed in 1933 during the Great Depression. In part, it was intended to raise wages so that workers could consume products and help the economy recover. In 1938, the minimum wage became part of the Fair Labor Standards Act, which included other protections for workers. The U.S. Congress has increased the minimum wage several times, but the increases have not kept up with the general rise in prices. In response, some state and local governments have passed their own laws requiring minimum wages higher than the federal standard.

APPLICATION **Applying Economic Concepts**

B. Explain how each of the four factors influences wages at fast food restaurants.
Such work requires little human capital; working conditions are unpleasant, but not dangerous; discrimination may be a factor; the government requires that employers pay at least the minimum wage.

Math Challenge: Figure 9.6

Calculating Annual Wages
In 2005, benefits accounted for nearly 30 percent of the employer's costs for each worker. Ask students to consider the question posed at the end of the Math Challenge with an additional variable: the full-time job paying $15 an hour comes with benefits worth an additional 30 percent. The part-time job has benefits worth only an additional 10 percent.

What are the annual wages for each, including benefits? *($15 x 0.30 = $4.50. $4.50 + $15.00 = $19.50. 19.50 x 2000 = $39,000. $20 x 0.10 = $2. $20 + $2 = $22. $22 x 1000 = $22,000.)* The part-time worker needs to pay more to get benefits as good as what the full-time has. When that 20 percent is deducted, the part-time wages fall to $18,000 per year.

More About . . .

The Living Wage
In more than 60 municipalities around the nation, lawmakers have established wage floors higher than the federal minimum wage. These "living wage" laws try to ensure that workers receive wages high enough to keep themselves and their families out of poverty.

Opponents of such laws argue that the higher the minimum wage is set, the fewer jobs there will be. However, studies of the living wage have shown that the slight job losses are easily outweighed by the reduction in family poverty.

INDIVIDUAL ACTIVITY

Using Economic Models

Time 30 Minutes

Task Create a graph that illustrates the effects of a minimum wage.

Materials Needed this text, paper, and pens

Activity

- Instruct students to identify the graph in this section that could be used to show the effect of the minimum wage on the number of workers employed (Figure 9.3).
- Have them draw a graph showing supply and demand creating an equilibrium wage for an unspecified, but low-paying position. Then have them draw a new demand curve graph that shows what happens when the minimum wage is set above the equilibrium wage.
- Instruct students to decide whether or not the graph makes a convincing argument against a minimum wage. Ask them to explain their reasoning in a written composition accompanying the graph.

Rubric

	Understanding of Use and Limits of Economic Models	Understanding of Law of Demand
4	excellent	clear and complete
3	good	mostly clear
2	fair	sometimes clear
1	poor	unclear

Gary Becker

More About . . .

Gary Becker's Family

Both of Gary Becker's parents left school after 8th grade. His father left his school in Montreal because he wanted to start early to earn money. He ended up owning a small business in Pennsylvania, where Becker grew up. His mother left school at a young age because, at that time, girls were not expected to get much education.

While Becker's parents did not invest in their own human capital, at least in terms of formal education, they fostered an environment with much reading and lively discussions, investing in the human capital of their children. Of course, one child went on to win the Nobel Prize and is best known for his focus on human capital.

More About . . .

Becker's Ideas

Gary Becker, paraphrasing George Bernard Shaw, has said that economics "is the art of making the most of life." By this, he meant that people act rationally to maximize utility or wealth no matter what realm of life in which they operate.

Becker also sees families as "small factories" in which such goods as meals, entertainment, and a place to live are "produced." Using this model, he has analyzed the economic motives behind such family issues as women entering the workforce, divorce, and fertility.

ClassZone.com includes links to information on Gary Becker.

ECONOMICS PACESETTER

Gary Becker: The Importance of Human Capital

FAST FACTS

Gary Becker

Born: December 2, 1930 Pottsville, Pennsylvania

Major Accomplishment: Extending an economic way of thinking into other areas of life and using economics to explain social behavior

Inspiration for Ideas About Economics and Crime: When he arrived late one day at Columbia University in New York, Becker decided to save time by parking illegally, even though he knew he might get caught and fined. This led him to wonder if people committing other crimes considered the consequences of their decisions rationally.

Famous Quotation: *"No discussion of human capital can omit the influence of families on the knowledge, skills, values, and habits of their children."*

Economics Update

Find an update on Gary Becker at **ClassZone.com**

"I believe an economist should . . . express concepts in simple language and show how to deal with important problems in a fairly simple way." With those words, Nobel laureate economist Gary Becker aptly described his own approach. He proposed that the general economic principle of rational choice could be applied to the decisions people make in all spheres of life. Becker extended an economic way of thinking into new areas, including crime and punishment, households and family relations, and human competence.

Investing in Yourself

When Gary Becker graduated from high school, he was torn between following a career in mathematics and doing something to help solve social problems. He studied economics at Princeton University and the University of Chicago, and he went on to teach at Chicago and at Columbia University. In 1957, Becker published *The Economics of Discrimination*, which examined the "effects of prejudice on the earnings, employment, and occupations of minorities." However, most economists did not pay much attention, feeling that such a study belonged in the fields of sociology or psychology. Today, though, Becker's approach is widely appreciated and has led economists to explore new areas.

Becker is best known for his contributions to the idea of human capital and for formulating the economic theory that explains differences in wages in terms of investments in human capital. To Becker, human capital is more than education and training: it is all the investments people make in themselves to improve their output, including the development of good work habits and receiving good medical treatment. The more abundant the capital, the more productive the labor. Becker helped to quantify the importance of education and on-the-job training and, by doing so, broadened the reach of economics.

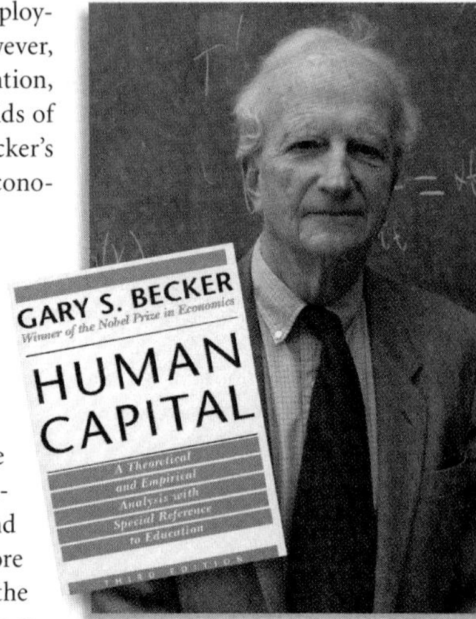

Gary Becker won the Nobel Prize for Economics in 1992 and the National Medal of Science in 2000.

APPLICATION Conducting Cost-Benefit Analysis

C. Becker debated with himself about whether to park illegally, weighing the possible costs against the advantages. Explain a decision you made using cost-benefit analysis. Is that always the best way to make a decision? Why or why not?

Answers will vary but may include whether to complete all of a homework assignment or to call in sick for a job. It is not always the best way to decide because sometimes the right thing to do is not the same as the expedient thing.

DIFFERENTIATING INSTRUCTION

Inclusion

Create a Poster

Organize students into pairs and have them take turns reading the feature on Gary Becker aloud. Then, instruct students to work together to design a poster that highlights what they have learned about Becker and his contributions to economics.

Gifted and Talented

Apply Economic Thinking

Have students choose a realm of activity not usually associated with economics (how they choose and develop friendships, for example) and apply the economic principal of rational maximizing of utility or wealth that Becker used as a foundation for his analyses. Have students report on their application in a brief essay.

SECTION 1 Assessment

Online Quiz ClassZone.com

REVIEWING KEY CONCEPTS

1. Explain the relationship between the terms in each of these pairs.
   a. *wages* / *derived demand*
   b. *equilibrium wage* / *minimum wage*
   c. *wage rate* / *human capital*
2. What market forces influence wages?
3. What nonmarket forces influence wages?
4. Why are education and training considered a kind of capital?
5. Why would a star athlete receive wages so much higher than an insurance sales representative?
6. **Using Your Notes** Suppose you are the owner of a video store. Explain how you would decide what to pay your workers, making reference to the terms in your completed cluster diagram.

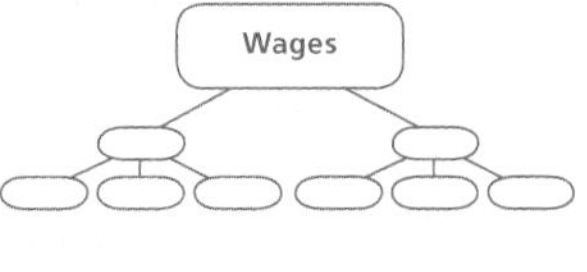

Use the Graphic Organizer at **Interactive Review @ ClassZone.com**

CRITICAL THINKING

7. **Analyzing Cause and Effect** If the equilibrium wage for bowling alley managers is $16 per hour, why would a wage of $20 per hour result in a labor surplus? Why would a wage of $12 per hour lead to a labor shortage?
8. **Solving Economic Problems** What economic problem does the minimum wage try to address?
9. **Applying Economic Concepts** Explain why working conditions can either justify higher wages or make up for lower wages.
10. **Making Inferences and Drawing Conclusions** Despite efforts to close the wage gap between men and women, the gap has actually been widening. Using what you have learned in this section, write a paragraph discussing what could be done to close the gap.
11. **Challenge** Gary Becker said that economics "is easy in the sense that there are only a few principles that really guide most economic analysis." Identify the basic principles behind how wages operate.

ECONOMICS IN PRACTICE

Graphing Equilibrium Wages Read each job description below. Then make a graph showing a hypothetical equilibrium wage for each job using the same values for both axes in each graph.

Job Description #1	Job Description #2
Structural metal worker for high-rise construction project. Must have at least 2 years of experience.	Filing clerk, small accounting office. No experience necessary, but must have a high school diploma or GED.

Apply Economic Concepts Using the economic knowledge you gained in this section, briefly explain why each graph appears as it does.

Challenge In many dangerous industries, including mining, safety laws establish standards that protect workers. Explain what effect these laws might have on wages.

Use **SMARTGrapher @ ClassZone.com** to complete this activity.

4 Assess & Reteach

Assess Discuss as a class the questions in Reviewing Key Concepts. For question 6, ask for a few volunteers to share their graphic organizers and their answer to the question about what to pay workers in the video store. You may wish to give students a choice between questions 10 and 11 as the basis for an extended essay.

Unit 3 Resource Book
- Section Quiz, p. 71

Interactive Review @ ClassZone.com
- Section Quiz

Test Generator CD-ROM
- Section Quiz

Reteach Divide students into three groups. Each group will prepare a segment for an educational TV show about one of the concepts in the chapter—Labor: Demand and Supply; Why Do Wage Rates Differ?; or Gary Becker. The first two segments should feature an anchor and several associates who handle graphs and other supporting materials. The third segment should be an interview with Gary Becker. Have the groups present their segments to the class.

Unit 3 Resource Book
- Reteaching Activity, p. 72

SMARTGrapher Students can create a equilibrium wage graph using **SmartGrapher @ ClassZone.com**.

SECTION 1 ASSESSMENT ANSWERS

Reviewing Key Concepts

1. **a.** *wages*, p. 258; *derived demand*, p. 259
   b. *equilibrium wage*, p. 258; *minimum wage*, p. 262
   c. *wage rate*, p. 261; *human capital*, p. 261
2. supply and demand
3. minimum wage laws, discrimination
4. because they are used by workers to produce goods or services, similar to the way physical capital is used
5. supply and demand—far fewer star athletes than insurance sales representatives
6. See page 258 for an example of a completed diagram. Answers will vary, but look for references to the key factors in this section: supply and demand; wage rate; working conditions; level of human capital needed, and so on.

Critical Thinking

7. The higher wage would attract more workers—a surplus. A lower wage would attract fewer job seekers—a shortage.
8. The minimum wage tries to prevent poverty by providing the lowest-paid workers with a wage that allows them to support themselves and their families.
9. Higher wages are needed to attract and keep people in dangerous or unpleasant jobs; low wages can be acceptable when other aspects of the job—convenience, lack of pressure, hours, training and experience it offers, and so on—are favorable to the employee.
10. Answers should include references to the chapter's key concepts. Some students may suggest just letting market forces solve the problem.
11. Supply and demand are the basic principles at work in wages.

Economics in Practice

Apply Economic Concepts The graph Job Description 1 will show a higher equilibrium wage and fewer qualified workers than the graph for Job Description 2.

Challenge Safety laws might result in lower wages because they improve working conditions.

❶ Plan & Prepare

Section 2 Objectives

- identify the changes that have taken place in the labor force
- explain how occupations have changed
- explain how the way people work has changed

❷ Focus & Motivate

Connecting to Everyday Life Lead a discussion about the kinds of jobs students want to have. Ask them to discuss their expectations about future employment, including the use of computers. Ask students about their expectations regarding coworkers in terms of gender, race, ethnic origin, first language, and disabilities. Continue until the contributions paint a representative picture of the U.S. labor force *(high use of technology; possibly telecommuting; gender, racial, and cultural diversity; inclusion)*

Taking Notes Remind students to take notes as they read by completing a hierarchy chart on trends in the labor market. They can use the Graphic Organizer at **Interactive Review @ ClassZone.com**. A sample is shown below.

SECTION 2

Trends in Today's Labor Market

OBJECTIVES

In Section 2, you will
- identify the changes that have taken place in the labor force
- explain how occupations have changed
- explain how the way people work has changed

KEY TERMS

civilian labor force, *p. 266*
outsourcing, *p. 269*
insourcing, *p. 269*
telecommuting, *p. 270*
contingent employment, *p. 270*
independent contractor, *p. 270*

TAKING NOTES

As you read Section 2, complete a hierarchy chart like the one below. In each box write the main ideas. Use the Graphic Organizer at **Interactive Review @ ClassZone.com**

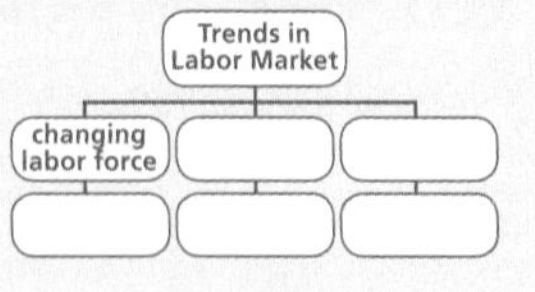

A Changing Labor Force

KEY CONCEPTS

The labor market in the United States has changed dramatically since the 1950s, and it continues to change. For example, in the 1950s, many companies hired workers with the expectation that they would stay with the company for most of their working lives. After a lifetime of service, workers could count on company pension plans to help fund their retirement. Today, few workers stay with the same company their entire career, and workers take more responsibility for funding their retirement.

Those are only some of the profound changes that affect the **civilian labor force**, people who are 16 or older who are employed or actively looking for and available to do work. The civilian labor force excludes people in the military, in prison, or in other institutions. In 2005, about 150 million Americans made up the civilian labor force. That figure was up from 126 million workers in 1990 and is expected to rise to almost 165 million workers by 2020.

QUICK REFERENCE

The **civilian labor force** is made up of people age 16 or older who are employed or actively looking for and available to do work.

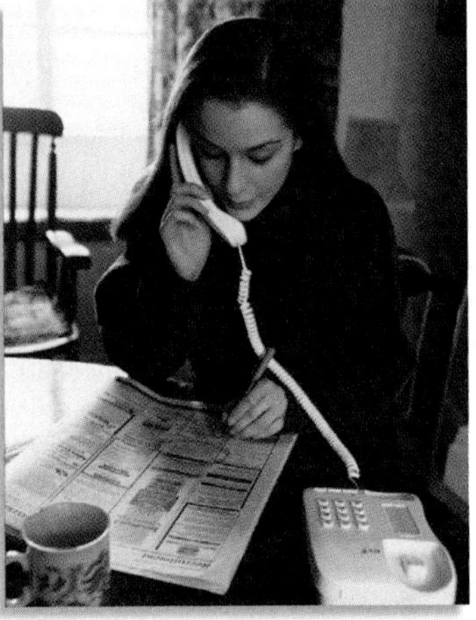

Labor Force
The civilian labor force is composed of people age 16 or older who are working or looking for work.

SECTION 2 PROGRAM RESOURCES

ON LEVEL

Lesson Plans
- Core, p. 31

Unit 3 Resource Book
- Reading Study Guide, pp. 63–64
- Economic Simulations, pp. 99–100
- Section Quiz, p. 81

STRUGGLING READERS

Unit 3 Resource Book
- Reading Study Guide with Additional Support, pp. 75–77
- Reteaching Activity, p. 82

ENGLISH LEARNERS

Unit 3 Resource Book
- Reading Study Guide with Additional Support (Spanish), pp. 78–80

INCLUSION

Lesson Plans
- Modified for Inclusion, p. 31

GIFTED AND TALENTED

Unit 3 Resource Book
- Case Study Resources: A Changing Work Life, pp. 97–98

TECHNOLOGY

eEdition DVD-ROM

eEdition Online

Power Presentation DVD-ROM

Economics Concepts Transparencies
- CT31 Trends in the Labor Market

Daily Test Practice Transparencies, TT31

ClassZone.com

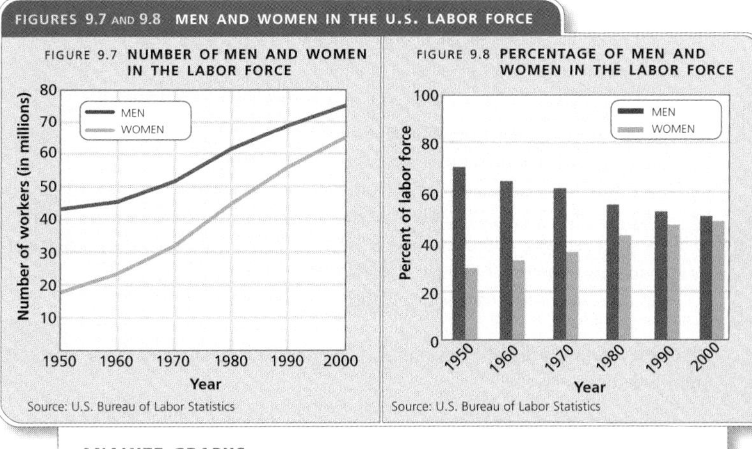

ANALYZE GRAPHS

1. About how many more men were in the labor force than women in 1950? in 2000?
2. What percentage of the labor force did women account for in 1950? in 2000?

Changes in the U.S. Labor Force

To understand some of the changes in the U.S. labor force, consider these two scenes. In the first scene, the year is 1955. A young woman pulls into a gas station, and the attendant fills up her car with gas. Then she picks up her children at school and heads home to get dinner ready in time for her husband's arrival from work. The second scene is set in today's world. A young mother pulls into a gas station, swipes her credit card, and fills up her tank. Her business meeting ran long, and she is late getting to the daycare center. Her husband will pick up dinner for the family on his way home from work.

One obvious change these scenes demonstrate is the addition of many more women to the work force. As shown in Figures 9.7 and 9.8, women have been a significant factor in the growth of the labor market in the United States. Since the 1950s, the kinds of jobs open to women have expanded. As job opportunities have improved, wages for women have risen, and many more women have been drawn into the work force.

Economics Update
Find an update on the U.S. work force at ClassZone.com

The U.S. work force has also become better educated. About 30 percent of people in the labor force have a college degree, and an additional 30 percent of workers have some college credits. In a work force with such a high degree of human capital, productivity and wages are also high compared with many other nations.

APPLICATION Evaluating Economic Decisions

A. Explain how rising opportunity costs have led more women into the workplace.
As wages for women increased, the opportunity cost of staying at home versus working also increased and, for many, staying at home became too costly.

3 Teach

A Changing Labor Force

Discuss

- What may account for some of the changes in the labor force? *(Possible answers: work ethic focused on individual gain; increased population; later retirement age; women's participation in the World War II effort; greater access to higher education)*
- What social changes may be related to the changes in the labor force? *(Possible answers: more frequent relocations; more children in day care; more disposable income for two-income families; healthier population)*

Analyze Graphs: Figures 9.7 and 9.8

Have students check the consistency of the graphs. Use the number of men and women shown in 9.7 to calculate the percentages shown in 9.8. Point out that students will need to estimate, since the graphs do not show exact numbers.

Answers

1. *1950–about 25 million; 2000–about 10 million*
2. *1950–about 30 percent; 2000–about 47 percent*

Economics Update

At **ClassZone.com,** students will see updated information on changes in the U.S. work force.

SMALL GROUP ACTIVITY

Creating Labor Force Scenarios

Time 60 Minutes 

Task Create two scenarios from different eras showing changes in the labor force.

Materials Needed paper and pens

Activity

- Direct student groups of three or four to the example of the young working mother on page 267. Tell them that their task is to create a different set of "then" and "now" scenes representing changes in the labor force.
- Instruct students to write a short script for each scene and use a narrator, if necessary, to set the scene. Props would be a plus!
- Have each group act out their scenes for the class.
- Encourage discussion after each presentation to understand the significance of the changes.

Rubric

	Understanding of Change in Labor Force	Presentation of Information
4	excellent	accurate, creative
3	good	accurate
2	fair	some key points
1	poor	shows little understanding

Changing Occupations

Discuss

- What possible relationship might there be between the growth in service sector jobs and the spread of technology? *(Possible answers: Technology takes over some of the jobs in the primary and secondary sectors; as technology develops, there is a greater need for education and training to use it to its fullest advantage.)*
- What effect do you think the creation of jobs in foreign nations through American outsourcing has had on the people of those foreign nations? *(Possible answers: better wages than they had before; opportunity to learn new skills; exposure to American culture and people; maybe pollution, depending on the outsourced activity)*

Analyze Graphs: Figures 9.9 and 9.10

Ask students what the two graphs show about the increase in numbers in the labor force. *(They do not show anything about specific numbers. They do reflect sector trends and percentage increases and decreases in sectors.)*

Answers

1. *The tertiary sector expanded from 53 to 79 percent, an increase of 26 percentage points. Alternatively, it grew by about 50 percent of its size in 1950.*
2. *1950–47 percent; 2000–21 percent*

Changing Occupations

KEY CONCEPTS

Economists group occupations into three economic sectors. The *primary sector* is made up of jobs related directly to natural resources, such as farming, forestry, fishing, and mining. Jobs in the *secondary sector* are related to the production of goods, including the materials and energy needed to produce them. Examples include welders, truck drivers, and construction workers. The *tertiary sector* is made up of service-related jobs in such industries as banking, insurance, retail, education, and communications. As you can see in Figures 9.9 and 9.10, U.S. manufacturing jobs have declined since the 1950s, while service-sector jobs have increased dramatically. All of the ten fastest-growing occupations are service related, most of them in the area of medical services.

FIGURES 9.9 AND 9.10 EMPLOYMENT IN THE UNITED STATES BY ECONOMIC SECTOR

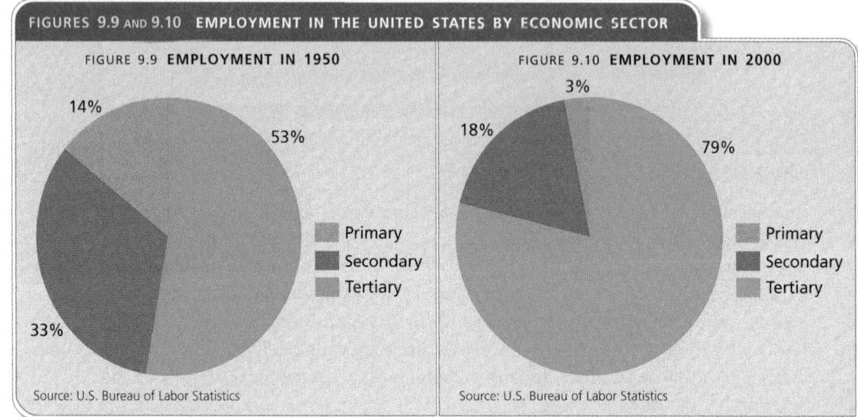

ANALYZE GRAPHS

1. Which sector grew the most from 1950 to 2000? By how much did it grow?
2. How much of the civilian labor force was employed in the combined primary and secondary sectors in 1950? How much in 2000?

Technology and Change

Think back for a moment to the young mother at the gas station. In the years between 1955 and today, the job of gas station attendant has been mainly replaced by the computerized, credit-card operated gasoline pump. In the same way, ATMs have greatly affected the occupation of bank teller. Technological changes have eliminated or redefined many other jobs in all three sectors.

The personal computer and the Internet have drastically changed the way on-the-job information is stored, transferred, and used. About half of all American workers use a computer on the job. As a result, those occupations that support the

DIFFERENTIATING INSTRUCTION

Struggling Readers

Recall What You Read

Point out that the material under the heading Technology and Change asks readers to think back to what they read in the previous section about the young working mother. Model for students how you would skim the previously read text looking for such key words as *mother* and *business meeting* to remind yourself of what you read.

English Learners

Recognize Coined Words

Tell students that *outsourcing* and *insourcing* are coined words, recently made-up words. Related to these words is *homesourcing*, used most often in relation to call-center representatives who do their work from home. Other coined words that students are likely to find in business-related texts are *downsizing* and all its variations (*upsizing, rightsizing, timesizing).* Suggest that students make a note of these in their personal dictionaries as they come across them in their reading.

1950s gas station

2000s gas station

use of computers—software engineers and network and data communications analysts, for example—have been among the fastest growing in the United States.

More than 80 percent of managers and professionals use a computer at work. However, even in less skilled jobs, more and more workers are using computers. About 20 percent of machine operators, laborers, and farmers use a computer on the job. Basic computer skills have become necessary for many different types of jobs.

Globalization and Jobs

Today's labor market is global. Technology allows companies to employ people not just all over the country, but all over the world. Many companies have sought to cut their costs by **outsourcing**, the practice of contracting with an outside company to provide goods or services.

Most outsourcing by U.S. companies goes to other U.S. companies. For example, many American businesses hire other American firms to handle their accounting. However, the term outsourcing has become connected with the practice of moving jobs from the United States to foreign countries where wages are lower. As this happens more frequently, it would seem that their American operations would lose jobs. But many companies actually add more jobs in the United States than they outsource abroad, just in different parts of their businesses. In 2004, IBM decided to send about 3,000 jobs overseas. But at the same time, it created about 4,500 jobs in the United States.

The American economy has also benefited from **insourcing**, the practice of foreign companies establishing operations in, and therefore bringing jobs to, the United States. Both outsourcing and insourcing are tied to the trends toward more service-related jobs and more technology-related work.

QUICK REFERENCE

Outsourcing is the practice of contracting with an outside company, often in a foreign country, to provide goods or services.

Insourcing is the practice of foreign companies establishing operations in, and therefore bringing jobs to, the United States.

APPLICATION Predicting Economic Trends

B. Think of an example of an occupation that is likely to be eliminated or substantially redefined as a result of technology. Answers will vary. One example is printing and many related occupations, since more people get information electronically.

More About . . .

Outsourcing Trends

Many of the world's biggest companies use outsourcing for day-to-day business processes. This is known as BPO, business process outsourcing. Such functions as accounting, human resources, and information technology, when outsourced, can help a company shave 10 to 40 percent off their operating costs and free managers to focus on keeping profits strong.

BP America, American Express, J.P. Morgan, and Lockheed Martin, all giant corporations, use BPO to a high degree. Even smaller companies, however, outsource some of their functions to save money.

More About . . .

Insourcing and Job Creation

Most of the jobs held by Americans in foreign-owned companies are in pre-existing businesses that were acquired by foreign interests, such as Daimler's purchase of Chrysler. According to an analysis of U.S. Department of Commerce data by the Economic Policy Institute, only 6.2 percent of job growth came from newly established foreign-owned companies.

Other experts assert that the number of jobs is not as much the issue as the kinds of jobs. Many feel that while the U.S. is trading away lower-end jobs, it is gaining jobs in technology-driven fields.

SMALL GROUP ACTIVITY

Predicting Future Jobs

Time 30 Minutes

Task Follow today's workplace trends to imagine future changes.

Materials Needed paper and pens

Activity

- Divide students into three groups.
- Direct the first group to think of five jobs that might disappear in 25 years; the next group, five jobs that will still be needed; and the last group, five newly created jobs.
- Make sure each group discusses the reasons for their choices and appoints a spokesperson for the group.
- Have each spokesperson present the group's ideas and follow with a class discussion.

Rubric

	Understanding of Changing Occupations	Presentation of Information
4	excellent	clear and complete
3	good	mostly clear
2	fair	sometimes clear
1	poor	unclear

Changes in the Way People Work

Discuss

- Ask students if they know anyone who works from home. If they do, ask them what they might know about that person's work life, and why he or she has chosen to work from home? If no one knows anyone who works from home, offer an example from your own experience or tell students to imagine what a typical day for an at-home worker might be like. *(Answers will vary but will probably stress the freedom from imposed schedule and a focus on output rather than time spent.)*
- What other factors besides the rapidly changing nature of jobs might explain why people move on to other careers more often now than they did in the past? *(Possible answers: a culture that values personal fulfillment; stages in a working person's life that include time out for family care, which may make a fresh perspective possible)*

Your Economic Choices

TELECOMMUTING

Where would you want to work?
To decide where you would be most comfortable working, analyze your personality. Are you a self-starter? Are you organized? Do you like to be alone or do you prefer being with others? Could you maintain a balance between personal and professional life without each having its own location? Do you prefer to be given tasks to do or to generate tasks yourself?

Activity Devise a checklist of personality traits that the work-at-home employee or entrepreneur might need to succeed. Give each trait a weighted number from 1–5 (1 indicating the trait is weak or non-existent in you; 5 indicating it is strong). Rate yourself and total your points, and then compare answers with your classmates.

Changes in the Way People Work

QUICK REFERENCE

Telecommuting means performing office work in a location other than the traditional office.

Contingent employment refers to temporary or part-time work.

An **independent contractor** is someone who sells their services on a contract basis.

KEY CONCEPTS

The way people work has been transformed by technology. In the past, many workers needed to physically commute to and from an office in order to accomplish their work. The Internet and laptop computers have allowed some of these workers to engage in **telecommuting**, the practice of doing office work in a location other than the traditional office.

But the job market has also changed. In the past, companies offered most workers permanent positions. Today, companies offer fewer permanent positions and more **contingent employment**, work that is temporary or part-time. Similarly, more people work as **independent contractors**, selling their services to businesses on a contract basis. People used to enter a field and stay in more or less the same line of work for most of their work life. Now, most people will change careers several times as the world of work continues to evolve.

Working at the Office from Home

Many telecommuters enjoy the reduced stress, flexibility in work time, and increased free time they have by avoiding a commute to work. Employers benefit from an expanded labor pool, increased productivity, and lower real estate costs. Society benefits, too, from fewer drivers on crowded freeways and lower pollution.

However, there are also costs. People who work at home may feel that their work too often spills over into their personal time. Some miss the social life of the office and the chance to network. Some at-home workers also fear that on-site workers might be more likely to get promoted. Still, experts estimate that the number of telecommuting workers grew by about 20 percent each year from 2000 to 2005.

YOUR ECONOMIC CHOICES

TELECOMMUTING

Where would you want to work?

Technology allows people to work in many different places. Alternative work places have different benefits—and drawbacks—than the traditional office.

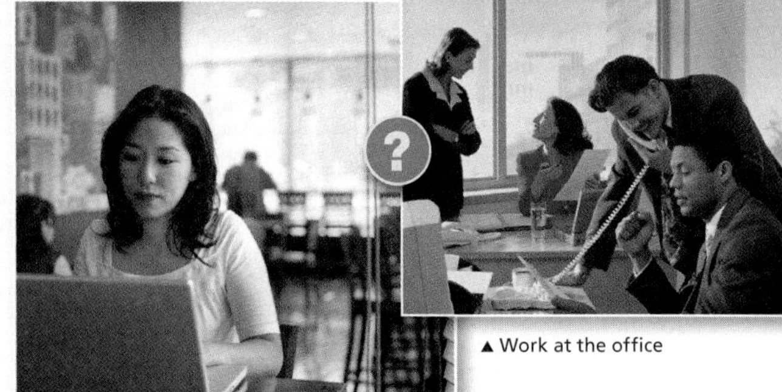

▲ Work at the coffee shop

▲ Work at the office

DIFFERENTIATING INSTRUCTION

Inclusion

Evaluate Strengths and Challenges
Instruct students to make a two-column chart to evaluate their strengths as potential workers and the challenges they might face either in a traditional workplace or working at home. Be sure to point out that most employers are required to make reasonable accommodations. Then have students write a paragraph or make a brief oral presentation to peers about which setting, home or office, might be more suitable for them.

Gifted and Talented

Look Backwards
Ask students to imagine that they are at their own retirement party and are looking back over their working life. Direct them to write the chronology of the jobs they have had and why they made changes, if they did make changes. Encourage students to base their "reflections" on their genuine interests and the ideas they have now about where their career may take them.

Alternatives to Permanent Employment

Through much of the 1900s, U.S. companies would hire workers for permanent, full-time jobs. Employees would work 40 hours per week in exchange for both wages and benefits. In the 1990s, companies began to hire fewer full-time employees and more contingent employees and contract workers. Contingent workers, sometimes called temps, make up over 5 percent of the total work force. Independent contractors make up over 7 percent of the work force.

Hiring contingent employees and contract workers makes it easier for businesses to adjust their work force to suit production demands. Discharging temporary workers is easier and less costly than discharging permanent employees. Since most temporary workers do not receive benefits, labor costs are also lower.

Most contingent workers would prefer to have the steady income and benefits that come with permanent, full-time employment. But many independent contractors prefer the flexibility of being their own boss to working in a permanent position. They are willing to take the risk of not having enough work to support themselves, and they find alternative ways to pay for health insurance and retirement. Businesses sometimes offer permanent positions to contingent and contract workers who have done a good job.

Changing Careers More Often

As technology has advanced, jobs have changed, too. Much of the work done today in the United States and other advanced countries did not exist 100 years ago. Some of the work did not exist even ten years ago. With every new technology, new types of jobs are created. But as technology advances, many older professions become less in demand or even obsolete. To fill the new jobs, workers must learn and adapt to the new technologies. Someone who started out as a radio repair technician might need to learn how to work with cellular phone technology.

In a similar way, the economy changes more quickly than it did in the past. Companies have become more flexible, changing their business plans constantly to maximize profits. Globalization allows companies to move jobs across national boundaries. As the economy changes, workers must change and adapt. The technician who adapted to cellular phone technology might need to change yet again in a few years.

Changing Careers
As the demand for healthcare workers increases, some people will change careers to fill these jobs.

APPLICATION Analyzing Cause and Effect

C. A 2003 report concluded that telecommuters can save their employers $5,000 a year. Explain how that savings may come about.
Increased productivity and lower real estate costs.

More About . . .

Contingent Workers
According to government statistics, contingent workers are

- twice as likely as noncontingent workers to be under age 25
- less likely to be white than noncontingent workers
- more likely to have less than a high school diploma

Of the various types of contingent workers:

- independent contractors were more likely to be older, male, and white
- temporary help agency workers were more likely to be young, female, and black, Hispanic, or Latino

Economics Illustrated

To illustrate the way telecommuting works, use two clock faces to document when your class studies economics. Color in a wedge representing the time that the class meets "at the office." Take a survey to find out when the students do their homework for this class. Use a different color to mark when students are "telecommuting."

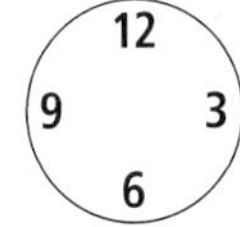

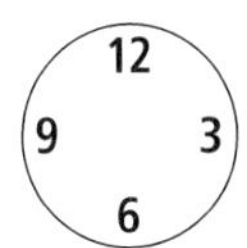

SMALL GROUP ACTIVITY

Creating Job Descriptions

Time 30 Minutes ◑

Task Describe the kind of tasks and workers associated with different kinds of employment.

Materials Needed paper and pens

Activity

- Divide students into three groups. Direct the first to write a job description for a full-time at-home employee; the second, a part-time contract worker; and the third, a part-time worker supplied by a temporary employment agency.
- Instruct students to have a specific job in mind but to be sure that it is representative of that kind of employment.
- Have them include details of both the job and the qualities needed to be a successful worker.
- Have each group present their job description to the class.

Rubric

	Understanding of Kinds of Employment	Presentation of Information
4	excellent	clear and complete
3	good	mostly clear
2	fair	sometimes clear
1	poor	unclear

Drawing Conclusions from Graphs

1 Plan & Prepare

Objectives

- Analyze a source of information.
- Read each part of a bar graph and then put it together to draw conclusions.

2 Focus & Motivate

In July 2005, the Food and Drug Administration warned several pharmaceutical companies to stop producing misleading graphs. Facilitate a discussion with students about ways they might look to graphs to make important buying decisions. *(Possible answers: to check crash tests when buying a car; to compare nutrition information)* Point out that the way graphs are constructed might lead to misrepresentation. It is essential to analyze each part of a graph in order to draw accurate conclusions.

3 Teach

Focus the students' attention on what can and cannot be concluded from these two graphs. Point out that these are projections, and ask when these figures could be verified. *(in 2015 or later, when data for 2004–2014 is available)*

For additional practice see **Skillbuilder Handbook**, page R29.

THINKING ECONOMICALLY Answers

1. *9.11 uses number of jobs added; 9.12 uses the percent change in the number of jobs*
2. *An argument could be made for either graph. 9.11 shows the fastest growth in terms of the number of people who will be hired. 9.12 shows the fastest growth compared to the number of people employed in those occupations in 2004.*
3. *9.11 Fastest Growing Occupations by Number of Jobs Added*

   9.12 Fastest Growing Occupations by Percentage Change in Number of Jobs
4. *The jobs with the highest percentage change in number of jobs are likely to have higher than average wages, because there will be fewer qualified people to fill those jobs.*

ECONOMICS SKILLBUILDER

For more on interpreting graphs, see the Skillbuilder Handbook, page R29.

Drawing Conclusions from Graphs

Drawing conclusions means analyzing a source of information and forming an opinion. You have already had some practice analyzing line and pie graphs in Chapters 6 and 8. These graphs are bar graphs.

PRACTICING THE SKILL Begin by using the following strategies to analyze the graphs. They are similar to the strategies you used in Chapter 6 to analyze a line graph. Your analysis will enable you to draw conclusions about the information shown on the graphs.

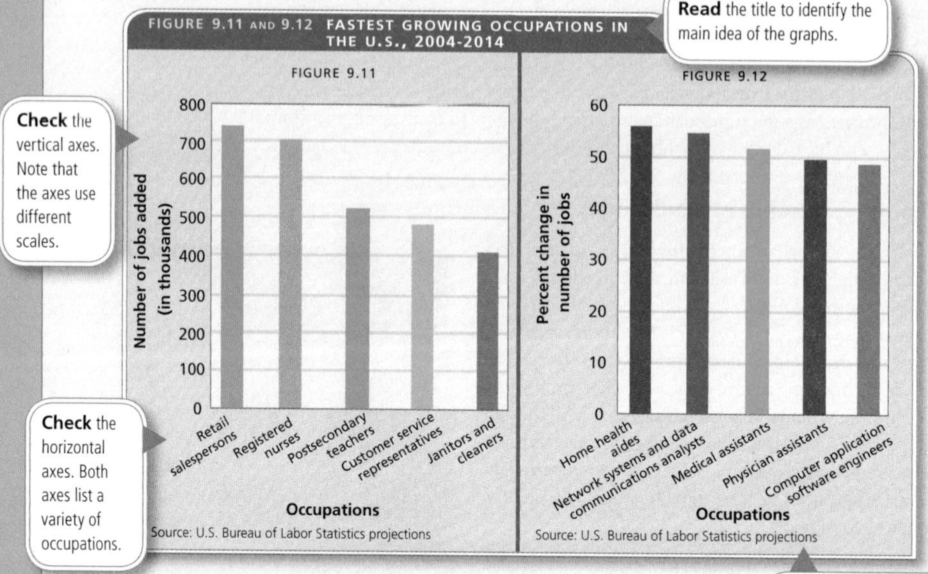

NOW PUT IT ALL TOGETHER Both graphs claim to present the same information. Compare the two graphs, and consider their differences.

THINKING ECONOMICALLY Drawing Conclusions

1. What is the main difference between the two graphs?
2. Which graph really shows the fastest growing occupations? Explain your answer.
3. What would be a better title for each graph?
4. Which of these jobs are most likely to have higher than average wages? Why?

DIFFERENTIATING INSTRUCTION

Struggling Readers

Read in Order

Students coming upon an annotated graphic such as the one above may not know where to begin reading. Explain that no matter which annotation they read first, they can usually piece the instruction together. Point out that one strategy for reading in the most effective order is to skim the item to figure out its general plan. In this case, the general plan is to explain strategies for interpreting a graph. So, it is logical to begin with the title, which orients the reader to the task at hand.

English Learners

Understand Multiple Meanings

Point out to students that many words have multiple meanings. The word *drawing* in the title of this Skillbuilder is one such example. Refer students to a dictionary and tell them to identify at least five other meanings for this word. Direct them to write a sentence using the word in each of the meanings that they have chosen. Then, have them share the sentences with a partner.

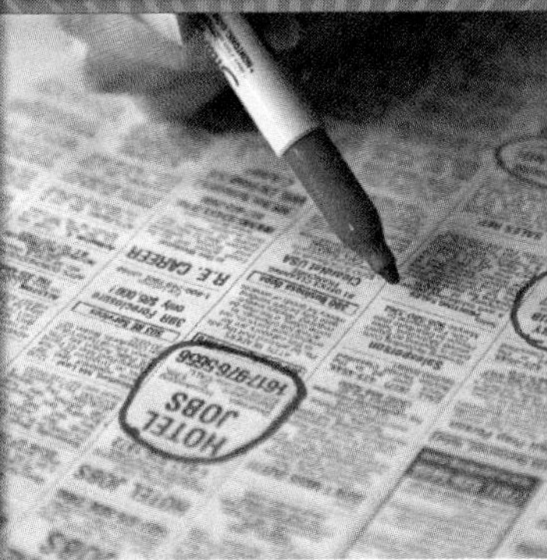

SECTION 2 Assessment

REVIEWING KEY CONCEPTS

1. Explain the differences between the terms in each of these pairs.
   a. *outsourcing* *insourcing*
   b. *contingent employment* *independent contractor*
2. Name three of the fastest growing occupations. What do they have in common?
3. What are the economic reasons that explain why so many women joined the labor force in the late 1900s?
4. Name two ways technology has altered the U.S. labor market.
5. For an employee, what are the advantages and disadvantages of telecommuting?
6. **Using Your Notes** Write a paragraph explaining how you can use the information in this section to prepare for your future career. Refer to your completed hierarchy chart to help you anticipate the employment trends you will be facing.

Use the Graphic Organizer at **Interactive Review @ ClassZone.com**

CRITICAL THINKING

7. **Making Inferences and Drawing Conclusions** Given the trends in the labor market, do you think today's employees will need to be more independent than the last generation's or less independent? Why?
8. **Analyzing Cause and Effect** Explain how changing technologies have led to workers changing careers more often.
9. **Evaluating Economic Decisions** The United States has shifted to an economy driven by service industries. The primary sector, which deals in natural resources, and the secondary sector, which produces goods, are both shrinking. Do you think the shift toward a service economy is helping American workers or hurting them? Give reasons for your answer.
10. **Challenge** Adam Smith explained that countries maximize their wealth when they concentrate on producing the goods that they produce most efficiently and rely on international trade for goods they don't produce efficiently. Explain how outsourcing is an example of this concept.

ECONOMICS IN PRACTICE

Examining Labor Market Trends
Make a copy of the table below. On your copy, list the reasons for the trend toward contingent labor in the left column. In the right column, describe its impact on the labor force.

Move to Contingent Labor	
Why?	Impact on Labor Force

Analyze Cause and Effect
In what ways have women in the work force influenced the growth of contingent labor? In what ways has the growth of contingent labor influenced women?

Challenge What personal issues might lead a worker to seek part-time employment?

4 Assess & Reteach

Assess Discuss questions 1–5 in Reviewing Key Concepts as a class. You may wish to give them a choice of one of the Critical Thinking questions to use as a prompt for an extended written composition. For the Economics in Practice, divide the class in two groups and have each group handle one column of the chart.

Unit 3 Resource Book
- Section Quiz, p. 81

Interactive Review @ ClassZone.com
- Section Quiz

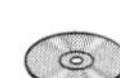

Test Generator CD-ROM
- Section Quiz

Reteach Select a student who has filled out the graphic organizer very well. Have the student prepare a transparency of the organizer, then use it to lead the class in a review of the section.

Unit 3 Resource Book
- Reteaching Activity, p. 82

Economics in Practice
Analyze Cause and Effect Women fill the majority of part-time positions. Their entry into the work force led to an increase in part-time work. At the same time, companies looked to reduce costs and to streamline in-house employees. The availability of part-time work leads women, especially second wage-earners, to return to the work force after having children or at other times.

Challenge Sample answers: birth of a child, care for aging parents, illness of a spouse or child, burnout at a full-time job, desire to pursue education

SECTION 2 ASSESSMENT ANSWERS

Reviewing Key Concepts

1. **a.** *outsourcing*, p. 269; *insourcing*, p. 269
   b. *contingent employment*, p. 270; *independent contractor*, p. 270
2. Answers will vary. Sample answer: registered nurse, home health aide, medical assistant; they're all in health care.
3. Types of jobs open to women have expanded; wages for women have risen; fewer men earn enough to allow wives to stay at home.
4. eliminated jobs; changed jobs; allowed for telecommuting
5. advantages—no commute (so more free time), flexibility, low stress
   disadvantages—lack of social contact with peers; lack of networking opportunities; fears that only in-house people may be promoted
6. See page 266 for an example of a completed diagram. Answers will vary, but should demonstrate an understanding of such trends as computers on the job, telecommuting, part-time or contingent work, wage discrimination, and so on.

Critical Thinking

7. Answers will vary; look for good supporting ideas and references to chapter concepts. Many students may lean toward "more independent" because of the trend toward telecommuting.
8. As new technologies replace old technologies, people who had been employed working with the old technologies need to find new work. Each new technology requires a new set of experts.
9. Answers will vary. Possible answer: hurting the economy because service jobs pay less
10. Outsourcing allows a company to focus its resources on its core business. By shifting non-core jobs to other companies that can do them more efficiently, a company frees up resources that can be used to expand the business.

Economics in Practice
See answers in side column above.

1 Plan & Prepare

Section 3 Objectives

- describe how the labor movement developed in the United States
- discuss why organized labor has declined in the United States
- explain how labor unions affect wage rates and employment

2 Focus & Motivate

Connecting to Everyday Life Read the following quote by Margaret Mead: "Never doubt that a small group of thoughtful, committed people can change the world. Indeed, it is the only thing that ever has." Ask students to think of examples in their own experience when committed people working together have made a difference, and have them compare the efforts to those of individuals.

Taking Notes Remind students to take notes as they read by completing a summary chart of the section. They can use the Graphic Organizer at **Interactive Review @ ClassZone.com**. A sample is shown below.

Topic	Main Ideas	Related Facts
Labor movement's rise to power	devlop new model; gain power	support pro-union candidates; legal reforms
Labor movement's steady decline	lose reputation; labor force change; laws change	featherbedding, organized crime; shift to service jobs; right to work laws
Union negotiating methods	collective bargaining	mediation; binding arbitration

SECTION 3

Organized Labor in the United States

OBJECTIVES

In Section 3, you will

- describe how the labor movement developed in the United States
- discuss why organized labor has declined in the United States
- explain how labor unions affect wage rates and employment

KEY TERMS

labor union, *p. 274*
strike, *p. 274*
closed shop, *p. 279*
union shop, *p. 279*
right-to-work law, *p. 279*
collective bargaining, *p. 280*
binding arbitration, *p. 280*

TAKING NOTES

As you read Section 3, complete a summary chart like the one below. In each box, write the main ideas for each topic. Use the Graphic Organizer at **Interactive Review @ ClassZone.com**

Topic	Main Ideas	Related Facts
Labor movement's rise to power		

The Labor Movement's Rise to Power

KEY CONCEPTS

Organized labor helped to shape the modern workplace. Most of the benefits that workers in the United States take for granted today did not exist 200 years ago. The eight-hour workday, the five-day work week, vacations, even sick leave—none of these basic amenities would have existed without the efforts of organized labor.

In the industries of the 1800s, workers put in long hours—often 60 hours per week or more—for low pay. Factory laborers often worked in dangerous conditions. Individual workers had little power to demand improvements from a business owner. If a worker complained too much, they would be fired. Workers in industrialized nations around the world faced similar problems, but this section will focus on the labor movement in the United States.

QUICK REFERENCE

A **labor union** is an organization of workers that seeks to improve wages, working conditions, fringe benefits, job security, and other work-related matters for its members.

A **strike** is a work stoppage used to convince an employer to meet union demands.

To improve their bargaining power, factory workers in the 1800s began to join together and act as a group. A **labor union** is an organization of workers who collectively seek to improve wages, working conditions, benefits, job security, and other work-related matters. Unions attempted to negotiate with businesses to achieve their goals, but businesses often resisted. As unions sought ways to gain negotiating power, they turned to the **strike**, or work stoppage. The threat of shutting down production demonstrated the power of organized labor.

Different types of unions addressed different needs. Some workers joined a craft union, a union of workers with similar skills who work in different industries for different employers. Examples include typesetters or, more recently, electricians. Others joined an industrial union, a union for workers with different skills who work in the same industry. For example, workers in the textile industry formed some of the earliest industrial unions.

SECTION 3 PROGRAM RESOURCES

ON LEVEL

Lesson Plans

- Core, p. 32

Unit 3 Resource Book

- Reading Study Guide, pp. 83–84
- Economic Skills and Problem Solving Activity, pp. 93–94
- Section Quiz, p. 91

STRUGGLING READERS

Unit 3 Resource Book

- Reading Study Guide with Additional Support, pp. 85–87
- Reteaching Activity, p. 92

ENGLISH LEARNERS

Unit 3 Resource Book

- Reading Study Guide with Additional Support (Spanish), pp. 88–90

INCLUSION

Lesson Plans

- Modified for Inclusion, p. 32

GIFTED AND TALENTED

Unit 3 Resource Book

- Readings in Free Enterprise: A Closer Look Inside Labor's Fastest-Growing Union, pp. 95–96

TECHNOLOGY

eEdition DVD-ROM

eEdition Online

Power Presentation DVD-ROM

Economics Concepts Transparencies

- CT32 Labor Movement Timeline

Daily Test Practice Transparencies, TT32

ClassZone.com

Early Developments

Local craft unions were the main kind of worker association during the early years of the United States. By the 1830s, local unions began joining together into federations to advance their common cause. The first national federation was the National Trades Union (NTU), founded in 1834. A financial crisis that gripped the country in 1837 brought an end to the NTU and temporarily subdued union activity.

In 1869, organized labor took a huge step forward when Uriah Stephens founded the Knights of Labor. Unlike other unions, it organized workers by industry, not by trade or skill level. The Knights of Labor became a nationwide union and adopted political goals including an eight-hour workday for all workers and the end of child labor. Its membership grew quickly, especially after the union helped workers win concessions from the big railroad companies in the 1880s.

During the explosion of industrialism in the late 1800s, employers strongly resisted the efforts of workers to organize, and many labor protests turned violent.

- In 1886, one person was killed and several others were seriously wounded when police attacked workers protesting for an eight-hour workday outside the McCormick Harvester Company in Chicago. The next day, people gathered at Haymarket Square to protest the deaths, and police troops arrived to disperse the crowd. Someone threw a bomb into the police, killing seven officers, and the riot that followed left dozens of other people dead and hundreds injured.
- In 1892, ten workers were killed in a strike against Carnegie Steel in Homestead, Pennsylvania, and the union was broken up.
- In 1894, a strike in Illinois against the Pullman Palace Car Company won the support of railway workers across the country, who collectively brought the nation's railroads to a halt. The dispute turned violent when National Guard troops were brought in to keep the nation's railroads running. A federal court ruled that the American Railway Union could not interfere with the trains, and the strike was broken.

A New Model for Unions

The violence associated with organized labor, as well as its often controversial political agenda, led to a decline in union membership. But Samuel Gompers offered a different model for union organization. In 1886, he founded the American Federation of Labor (AFL), an organization of craft unions that focused on the interests of skilled labor. The AFL continued to seek improvements in wages, benefits, and working conditions, but it focused on achieving these goals through the economic power of workers, instead of through legislation. By the early 1900s, the AFL had a membership of about 1.7 million workers. Legal action against organized labor forced Gompers to modify his stance against political activity, and the AFL began supporting pro-union candidates.

The International Ladies' Garment Workers Union was founded in 1900. The union gained strength following successful strikes in 1909 and 1910. Perhaps the most famous

Union Organizing
A union rally takes place at a shipyard in 1943.

3 Teach

The Labor Movement's Rise to Power

Discuss

- What were the differences in the way the Knights of Labor and the American Federation of Labor approached organizing? *(The Knights of Labor organized workers by industry, not by trade, and got involved in politics; the AFL focused on skilled workers and craft unions and stayed out of politics.)*

More About . . .

Early Mill Workers
The first all-female strike took place in 1828, when hundreds of girls and women who worked in a textile mill in Dover, New Hampshire, walked off their jobs. They were protesting a wage cut and such rules as large fines for being tardy and no talking on the job. Under threats that the company would just hire new workers, they returned to their jobs with no concessions gained.

In 1836, female mill workers in Lowell, Massachusetts, took to the streets to protest a wage cut. They chanted: "Oh isn't it a pity, such a pretty girl as I/Should be sent into a factory to pine away and die."

LEVELED ACTIVITY

Tracing Labor History

Time 30 Minutes

Objective Students will summarize the labor movement's rise to power and recent decline.

Basic

Write a 10-sentence summary of the rise and decline of unions, answering these questions:

- What did the Knights of Labor accomplish?
- What are three examples of labor violence?
- Why did the government boost unions?
- What led to the decline of unions?

On Level

Write an essay on the rise and decline of the U.S. labor movement, covering the following:

- kinds of unions and why they were begun
- the history of labor violence
- role of government in labor matters
- changes in labor following World War II

Challenge

Write an essay tracing the rise and decline of the labor movement in the United States. Use what you know about the present state of labor unions and trends in jobs and the economy. Include in your essay a prediction about the role of the labor movement in the economy of the future.

Discuss

- How did the government strengthen unions during the depression? *(As part of New Deal legislation, workers gained the right to form and join unions, to use strikes, and to earn a minimum wage and overtime pay.)*

More About . . .

The Fair Labor Standards Act
In 2005, the Act was once again in the news, as a revision that affected about 100,000 workers became law. That revision centered on which employees are entitled to overtime and which are considered exempt. In the past, employees who met certain tests (receive salaries rather than hourly wages, perform managerial tasks, and so on) were exempt from the overtime provision.

After the 2005 change, computer programmers and outside sales representatives were also exempted. Employers welcomed the change, which determined overtime eligibility and saved them money. Many of these workers now often work over 40 hours a week with no additional compensation.

More About . . .

The UAW Sit-Down Strike in Flint
On Dec. 30, 1936, United Auto Workers members began a sit-down strike that lasted 44 days. Workers at the Flint, Michigan, plant of General Motors occupied the plant and refused to work until management recognized the rights of their union.

Union leader John L. Lewis refused to end the strike even after police-worker violence and the calling out of the Michigan National Guard. Governor Frank Murphy stepped in as mediator, and General Motors agreed to recognize the UAW as the workers' sole bargaining agent. The strike ended on Feb. 11, 1937.

FIGURE 9.13 **History of the American Labor Movement**

1825
1850
1875
1900
1834 National Trades Union formed.
1869 ◀ Uriah Stephens founds the Knights of Labor.
1886 ◀ Protest in Chicago, advertised by this flyer, turns into the Haymarket Riot.
1886 American Federation of Labor (AFL) founded by Samuel Gompers.
1893 ▼ Eugene V. Debs founds the American Railway Union.
1894 Labor Day becomes a national holiday.
1900 ▲ International Ladies' Garment Workers' Union founded.

woman to participate in the U.S. labor movement was Mary Harris Jones, known as Mother Jones. In 1903, she led 80 children, many of whom had been injured while working, on a march to the home of President Theodore Roosevelt. The march helped to emphasize the need for child labor laws.

Unions Gain Power

During the Great Depression of the 1930s, union membership in the United States declined as millions of people lost their jobs. Yet unions gained power through laws passed as part of the New Deal, a series of reforms that attempted to revive the country's economy.

- The Norris-LaGuardia Act (1932) outlawed the practice of hiring only workers who agreed not to join a union. It also required employers to allow workers to organize without interference from their employer.
- The National Labor Relations Act (1935), also known as the Wagner Act, protected the rights of workers in the private sector to form unions and to use strikes and other job actions.
- The Fair Labor Standards Act (1938) set a minimum wage, required extra pay for overtime work, and made most child labor illegal.

During this period, the Congress of Industrial Organizations (CIO) organized unions for industrial workers. Originally part of the AFL, which favored skilled workers in craft unions, the CIO broke away in 1938. The two organizations came together again in 1955 as the AFL-CIO.

The AFL succeeded in organizing the United Auto Workers (UAW) union in 1935. After a tense sit-down strike in Flint, Michigan, in 1937, General Motors

DIFFERENTIATING INSTRUCTION

English Learners

Understand Acronyms
Have students create a section in their personal dictionary for acronyms associated with the social sciences. You may wish to point out that the Fair Labor Standards Act is often just referred to as the FLSA. Explain, however, that in formal writing each acronym will first be identified by its full name before the abbreviated form is used.

Gifted and Talented

Make a World Labor Events Time Line
Direct students to research important labor leaders and labor-related events from other parts of the world. Then, instruct them to create a world labor events time line. Explain that the time line should cover the same years that are shown in the time line above and include at least 10 items.

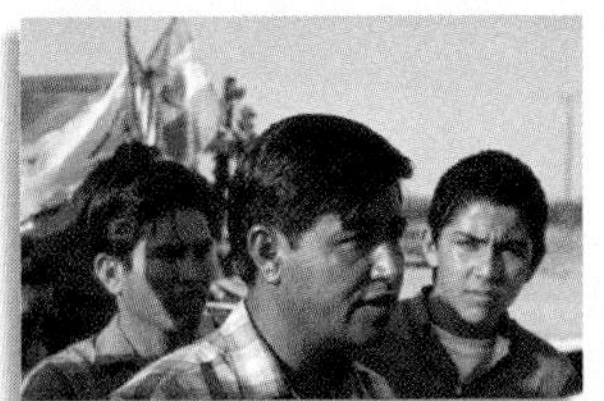

1962
◀ Cesar Chavez founds National Farm Workers Association (NFWA), which later becomes United Farm Workers.

2005
Service Employees International Union breaks away from AFL-CIO.

1925 | 1950 | 1975 | 2000

1935
Congress passes the National Labor Relations Act, also called the Wagner Act.

1935
United Auto Workers organized.

1959
Congress passes Landrum-Griffin Act.

1981
▶ Air traffic controllers' strike is unsuccessful.

became the first automaker to recognize the union. Chrysler and Ford soon followed. In the 1940s, Walter Philip Reuther, as president of the UAW, helped auto workers become some of the nation's highest paid industrial workers. Also in the 1940s, John L. Lewis, the tough-talking, cigar-smoking leader of the CIO, brought his own United Mine Workers back from near failure and waged a fierce and successful fight to organize the nation's steelworkers.

Backlash Against Unions Following World War II

The end of World War II ushered in a period of anti-union legislation. In 1947, over the veto of President Harry S. Truman, the Taft-Hartley Act was passed. It amended the Wagner Act and limited union activities, increasing the government's power to intervene if a strike might threaten national security.

America's fear of Communism, the political and economic system of the Soviet Union, led to further restrictions on unions. The Landrum-Griffin Act (1959) forbade communists from holding union offices and required tighter financial and electoral accounting. George Meany, president of the AFL-CIO from 1955 to 1979, was a strong anti-communist and worked to get rid of unions that he considered sympathetic to communist ideas.

APPLICATION Comparing and Contrasting Economic Information

A. What motivated workers in the 1800s to form unions? Why did they continue to form unions in the early- to mid-1900s?
The inability of individual workers to improve working conditions led workers to form unions. In the 1900s, workers sought continued improvements in working conditions, as well as better wages and benefits.

More About . . .

The Landrum-Griffin Act
Changes made to the Landrum-Griffin Act in 1984 further limited who could hold a union office by outlining ways for officials to be debarred. These changes targeted people who had been convicted of racketeering and other related crimes. The goal of this change was to establish a mechanism for ridding unions of corruption.

Many unionists objected to the changes for two main reasons: (1) the changes gave the government control over what should be in the control of the union members; and (2) they did not require similar removal from employment for members of a company's management.

International Economics

AFL's Free Trade Union Committee
The fight against communism in unions was waged not only in the United States but also abroad. A committee of the AFL, the Free Trade Union Committee, led by Irving Brown and secretly supported by the CIA, worked to undermine the power of the World Federation of Trade Unions. The WFTU had been founded in 1945 by 56 nations and included Communists.

George Meany believed that the WFTU wanted "to secure world political power for the Communists in a postwar world." Through bribery and other clandestine means, and using money in the Marshall Plan, Brown established a rival organization, the International Confederation of Free Trade Unions, in 1949.

SMALL GROUP ACTIVITY

Developing a Time Line

Time 45 Minutes

Task Expand and illustrate an existing time line.

Materials Needed four poster boards or eight large sheets of construction paper, Internet access with printing capabilities, scissors, glue, markers

Activity

- Tell students that they will be expanding the time line on pages 276–277 and illustrating key events. Have them work in four groups, with each group being responsible for one 50-year period.
- Direct each group to make a basic time line by copying the one in the book. Instruct them to add at least five new items of labor history, as well as two items of general history. Use internet resources or their own drawings to illustrate.
- The time lines should be presented to the class. Each segment will be added to the previous one for a completed time line that can remain on display in the classroom.

Rubric

	Understanding of Labor History	Presentation of Information
4	excellent	informative, attractive
3	good	detailed, neat
2	fair	some detail, neat
1	poor	uninformative, sloppy

The Labor Movement's Steady Decline

Discuss

- Which of the reasons for the decline in union membership offered here seems to be the most influential? Why? *(Answers will vary, but be sure students offer some reasoning for their answers.)*
- Do you think unions have outlived their usefulness? If so, why? If not, what issues may become part of their future agenda? *(Answers will vary. Possible answers: unions were so successful at raising the quality of workers' lives that they are no longer needed; manufacturing jobs lend themselves to unions more than service jobs, since factory work often involves difficult working conditions; unions will always be needed wherever businesses make use of low-skilled workers; future union goals could include more focused efforts to unionize contingent and other part-time workers.)*

Analyze Graphs: Figure 9.14

Ask students: What was the greatest five-year period of growth for unions since 1930? *(from 1935 to 1940)* Why was there such a steep decline after 1945? *(war production factories closed)* Discuss with students the historical context of these time periods. Union growth peaked after the Wagner Act was passed in 1935. This act gave employees the right of self-organization, to form, join, or assist labor organizations, and to bargain collectively. Union influence declined following World War II, when returning soldiers in search of jobs added to labor unrest. The government stepped in, enacting laws to adjust the balance that had tilted in labor's favor.

Answers

1. *1945; about 35 percent*
2. *1933; about 11 percent*

At **ClassZone.com,** students will see updated information on labor unions.

The Labor Movement's Steady Decline

KEY CONCEPTS

For 30 years following World War II, labor unions represented about 30 percent of the U.S. work force. Since the mid-1970s, membership in unions has declined steadily, falling to about 12.5 percent in 2005. The decline in unions can be traced to three causes: unions' tarnished reputations, changes in the labor force, and laws restricting union influence.

Loss of Reputation and Labor Force Changes

In the late 1900s, labor unions began to lose their luster in the eyes of many Americans. Prolonged strikes both disrupted the public and placed a burden on the striking families. Some unions began requiring companies to employ more workers than necessary, a tactic known as featherbedding. Featherbedding, especially in the railroad industry, raised criticisms of wastefulness. Investigators discovered that a few labor unions had ties to organized crime, which reflected badly on all unions.

Economics Update
Find an update on labor unions at **ClassZone.com**

The changing nature of the U.S. work force also led to reduced union membership. Union membership was traditionally rooted in manufacturing industries. But the number of manufacturing jobs in the United States fell sharply in the second half of the 20th century as the economy shifted toward service industries. The increase in the number of contingent and contract workers also led to lower union membership because such workers are less likely to pursue union representation.

As manufacturing declined, unions shifted their organizing efforts toward service workers. The American Federation of State, County, and Municipal Employees

FIGURE 9.14 UNION MEMBERSHIP IN THE UNITED STATES

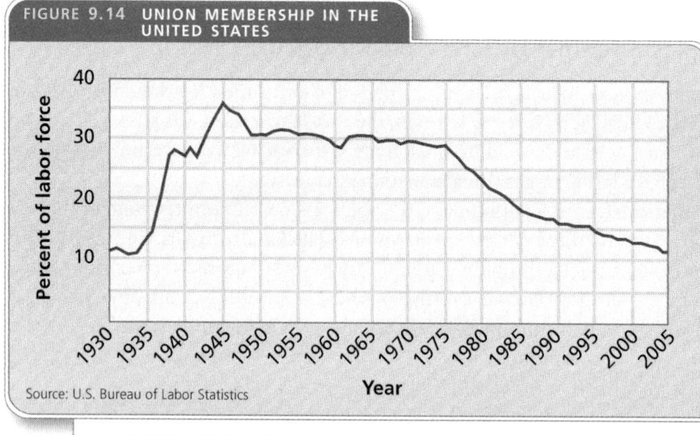

ANALYZE GRAPHS

1. During this time period, when was union membership highest? What percent of the labor force belonged to a union that year?
2. Which year was union membership lowest, and what percent of the labor force belonged to a union then?

DIFFERENTIATING INSTRUCTION

Inclusion

Listen for Information
Ask for three volunteers to read aloud pages 278–279. One should read the introductory paragraph. The others should each read the material under one of the headings (Loss of Reputation and Labor Force Changes; Right-to-Work Laws). Direct students to listen carefully. Point out that the introductory paragraph mentions what will be covered. The other sections follow through on that coverage. After reading, have students ask each other questions about what they have heard.

Struggling Readers

Listen for Information
You can use the activity suggested for inclusion students for the struggling readers in your class, as well. You may wish to follow up the reading by distributing copies of pages 278–279 and pointing out ways to highlight text. For example, in the first paragraph, "three causes" and all the words that follow that might be highlighted. Then model how you might highlight other parts of the text to keep your reading focused on those three main causes.

had about 1.4 million members in 2005. The Service Employees International Union (SEIU), which organizes such service workers as caregivers and janitors, had a membership of 1.8 million in 2005. The SEIU was the largest union in the AFL-CIO, but in 2005 it left the group. Several other smaller unions also left the AFL-CIO and joined SEIU to form a new coalition with different priorities.

Right-to-Work Laws

Another factor in the steady decline of union membership in the United States is legislation that tries to limit union influence. Unions had developed the **closed shop**, a business required to hire only union members. The closed shop was intended to maintain union standards for workers who only work at a business briefly, such as musicians or restaurant employees. Unions also developed the **union shop**, a business where workers are required to join a union within a set time period after being hired. Union shops allowed businesses to hire nonunion workers without diluting the strength of the union.

The Taft-Hartley Act outlawed the closed shop and weakened possibilities for a union shop. It also gave states the power to make it illegal to require workers to join unions. Such laws became known as **right-to-work laws**, a name meant to emphasize that workers are free not to join a union. However, the effect of right-to-work laws and similar legislation is to weaken unions and to help businesses operate without unions. Most right-to-work states are in the Southeast and the central West, and union membership in these areas is low.

QUICK REFERENCE

A **closed shop** is a business where an employer can hire only union members.

A **union shop** is a business where workers are required to join a union within a set time period after being hired.

Right-to-work laws make it illegal to require workers to join unions.

FIGURE 9.15 **RIGHT-TO-WORK STATES MAP**

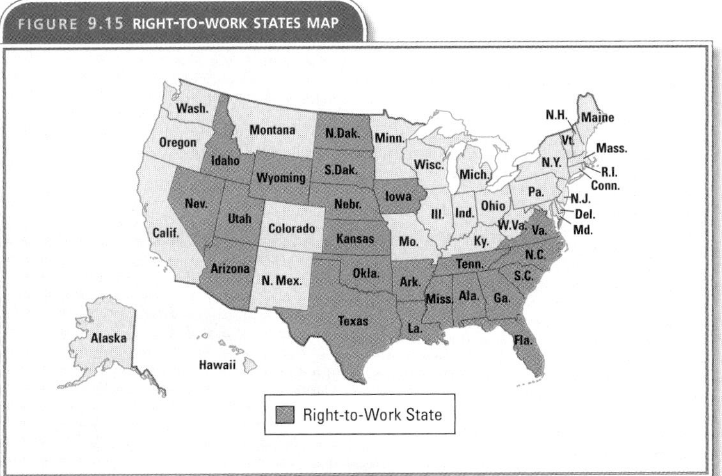

APPLICATION Predicting Economic Trends

B. Consider the trends in today's labor force that you learned about in Section 2. As more service industries unionize, is union membership, as a percent of the labor force, likely to return to the levels of the mid-1900s? Why or why not?

Union membership could grow as large, considering how much of the labor force works in service industries. Or it could fail to grow as large, considering the trends toward temporary employment and frequent career changes.

More About . . .

New Efforts in Union Organizing
Since the 1980s, there have been many attempts to bolster union membership. For example, the United Auto Workers has looked to service industries and has been organizing "academic student employees," such as graduate teaching assistants and tutors. In Michigan, the UAW also represents writers, graphic artists, and public employees.

Analyze Maps: Figure 9.15

What patterns of economic development may partially explain why the states with right-to-work laws are clustered as they are? *(States that are more agricultural and that do not have a long history of unionization tend to enact right-to-work laws.)*

INDIVIDUAL ACTIVITY

Comparing Maps

Time 15 Minutes

Task Compare a recent election map with the map showing right-to-work states.

Materials Needed copies of a recent election map (or one prepared for use with an overhead projector), paper, pens

Activity

- Pass out or display the recent election map, preferably one from a recent presidential election, that shows through color coding which states voted Republican and which Democratic.
- Direct students to compare the two maps, looking especially for overlapping clusters.
- Direct each student to write a brief, concise paragraph explaining what relation, if any, they can draw between a state's political leaning and its attitude toward labor laws.
- Ask for a few volunteers to share their finished comparison and conclusions, and allow time for a brief discussion.

Rubric

	Understanding of Labor and Politics	Presentation of Information
4	excellent	accurate, insightful
3	good	accurate
2	fair	generally accurate
1	poor	inaccurate and/or incomplete

Union Negotiating Methods

Discuss

- What are some of the issues that might be negotiated in collective bargaining? *(Answers will vary, but continue the discussion until the following are included: wages, benefits, working conditions, grievance procedures, and pensions.)*
- What might economist Milton Friedman think about labor unions? Why? *(He would probably argue that since they interfere with free market forces, they are not useful and are likely to be harmful.)*

More About . . .

Negotiating Strategies
Some negotiators are turning away from adversarial techniques. Instead they are trying "interest-based" negotiations, approaching the differences with mutual problem-solving. In 1998, for example, health-care managers in the Minneapolis area used problem-solving to effectively negotiate an agreement with the area's nurses.

Presentation Options

Review the methods by which organized labor is able to improve working conditions for its union members by using the following presentation options:

 **Power Presentations DVD-ROM**
Using the Display Tool, you can highlight negotiating methods unions use in collective bargaining.

 **Economics Concepts Transparencies**
- CT32 Labor Movement Time Line

Union Negotiating Methods

QUICK REFERENCE

Collective bargaining is the way businesses and unions negotiate wages and working conditions.

KEY CONCEPTS

Despite the decline in membership, organized labor still wields power in the American economy. Unions continue to use **collective bargaining**, the process of negotiation between businesses and their organized employees to establish wages and to improve working conditions. Since it represents many employees together, a union can arrive at a better deal for workers than if each employee bargained with the employer separately. As a result, unionized companies tend to pay higher wages than companies without unions.

Collective Bargaining

In the 1930s and 1940s, unions negotiated for higher wages, better working conditions, and fair grievance procedures for workers who felt that they had been treated unjustly. As these demands were increasingly met, unions negotiated for job security and such fringe benefits as health insurance. Benefits and job security are important issues in today's negotiations as well, but in many cases today's workers are not pressing for higher wages. Instead they are trying to hold the line against pay cuts and reductions in benefits, including pensions.

Unions have the threat of a strike to provide a motivation for management to come to terms, but strikes occur much less frequently than in the past. Large-scale work stoppages in the United States occurred hundreds of times a year before the 1980s but dropped to about 20 per year by the 2000s. This is partly a result of the decline in union membership, but it also reflects the willingness of management to use replacement workers or to close a plant permanently.

The vast majority of union contracts are settled without such action. However, some negotiations require additional interventions if the two sides cannot agree. First, a mediator may be brought in to help the sides come to terms. If that fails, the dispute may be settled by **binding arbitration**—a decision by a neutral third party that each side agrees ahead of time to accept. For industries related to public safety, the government might issue an injunction to force workers back to work after a stoppage, or to stop protest activities that may interfere with public safety.

QUICK REFERENCE

Binding arbitration is a process in which an impartial third party resolves disputes between management and unions.

Collective Bargaining
Union leaders meet with business management to negotiate the details of union contracts.

APPLICATION Analyzing Cause and Effect

C. Explain why high wages and high employment do not necessarily go hand in hand.
The higher the cost of labor, the fewer workers management will hire.

DIFFERENTIATING INSTRUCTION

English Learners

Recognize Idioms
This page contains the idioms "fringe benefits" and "hold the line." Tell students that fringe is literally a decorative border. Thus, fringe benefits are "extras" that employers offer in addition to wages. Point out that "hold the line" means to hold a position securely, as an army might against attack. Students may confuse this with the phrase used while on a phone: "hold the line while I get a pencil. . . ." Tell students to keep track of idioms and their meanings in their personal dictionaries.

Gifted and Talented

Create a Graph
Direct students to create a graph showing the effect of unions on wages and referring to the equilibrium wage. Have them suppose, for example, that a construction union has negotiated a wage of $20 when the equilibrium wage is $15. Instruct them to show how this will affect the supply curve. Then, encourage them to discuss the next logical stages, starting with the premise that employers will hire fewer workers.

SECTION 3 Assessment

Online Quiz
ClassZone.com

REVIEWING KEY CONCEPTS

1. Explain the differences between the terms in each of these pairs.
   a. *closed shop* / *union shop*
   b. *strike* / *collective bargaining*
2. Why was the formation of the Knights of Labor a key event for organized labor in the United States?
3. Name two laws that supported labor's rights and two laws that restricted them.
4. Opponents of right-to-work laws sometimes call them "work-for-less" laws. Why do you think they use that name?
5. Why would a business care if its workers went on strike?
6. **Using Your Notes** Write a paragraph explaining why unions grew in the 1800s and the first half of the 1900s. Refer to your completed summary chart to help you develop your argument with strong supporting detail.

Topic	Main Ideas	Related Facts
Labor movement's rise to power		

Use the Graphic Organizer at **Interactive Review @ ClassZone.com**

CRITICAL THINKING

7. **Analyzing Cause and Effect** What effect might outsourcing have on union membership?
8. **Evaluating Economic Decisions** In 1981, a group of air traffic controllers, employees of the Federal Aviation Administration, went on strike. They wanted to reduce their workweek to 32 hours instead of the usual 40 because of the high stress of their jobs. President Ronald Reagan broke the strike and disbanded the union of air traffic controllers, claiming that they were striking illegally. About 100 strikers were arrested, and all of them were banned for life from jobs in air traffic control. Did Reagan do the right thing by firing the striking workers? Explain your answer.
9. **Challenge** The firing of the air traffic controllers and the breaking of their union was one of the key events for labor in the United States. What trends in organized labor are evident in that event?

ECONOMICS IN PRACTICE

Automated factories reduced the need for assembly line workers.

Analyzing Economic Data
Look at Figure 9.14 on page 278, which shows changes in union membership in the United States.

Analyze Union Membership
Compare the upward and downward movements of the graph to the events going on in the United States and world.

1930s—The Great Depression
1940s—World War II; postwar recovery
1950s—Korean War; economy thrives
1960s—Civil Rights movement; Vietnam War; steady economy
1970s—End of Vietnam War; oil embargo; inflation
1980s—Recession and recovery
1990s—Fall of Communism in Europe and Russia; Internet boom
2000s—September 11; Iraq War; recession and recovery

Challenge Does there seem to be a relationship between how well the economy is doing and union membership? Explain.

4 Assess & Reteach

Assess Assign the first five Key Concept questions to students in pairs, and have them give their answers to the class. Discuss the Critical Thinking questions as a class. Have students return to their pairs to work on the activity in Economics in Practice.

Unit 3 Resource Book
- Section Quiz, p. 91

Interactive Review @ ClassZone.com
- Section Quiz

Test Generator CD-ROM
- Section Quiz

Reteach Use the time line on pages 276–277 and any other time lines students have created to review the history of the labor movement.

Unit 3 Resource Book
- Reteaching Activity, p. 92

Economics in Practice

Analyze Union Membership Union membership leapt in the late 1930s as millions worked in factories. It jumped again as factories made supplies for WW II. After WW II, membership fell as people returned to other work. Membership held steady through the 1950s and 1960s. It began to drop in the 1970s as inflation led to unemployment. Membership continued to fall in the recession of the early 1980s and the anti-union Reagan and Bush administrations. The decline continued through the 1990s and 2000s as jobs continued to shift away from manufacturing and toward services.

Challenge Answers will vary regarding cause and effect; look for well-supported positions.

SECTION 3 ASSESSMENT ANSWERS

Reviewing Key Concepts

1. a. *closed shop*, p. 279; *union shop*, p. 279
   b. *strike*, p. 274; *collective bargaining*, p. 280
2. It was the first union organized by industry. It became a powerful nationwide union.
3. supported: Norris-LaGuardia Act (1932), National Labor Relations Act, also known as the Wagner Act (1935), Fair Labor Standards Act (1938); restricted: Taft-Hartley Act (1947), Landrum-Griffin Act (1959), right-to-work laws
4. because non-union jobs usually pay less than equivalent union jobs
5. Strikes interfere with a business producing goods or providing services, and thereby reduce profits.
6. See page 274 for an example of a completed diagram. Possible answers: grew because workers were being treated unfairly and even attacked and killed for standing up for their rights; grew because industrial workers were a large and growing part of the workforce

Critical Thinking

7. It would be likely to reduce union membership as jobs themselves are reduced, especially in manufacturing.
8. Answers will vary. Possible answers: Yes, Reagan did the right thing because the strike was disrupting air travel. Workers in important jobs like air traffic control should not have the right to strike. No, Reagan did not do the right thing because all workers should have the right to strike for better working conditions. Reagan went too far in banning the workers for life from jobs in air traffic control.
9. the shift toward services, the weakening of the unions generally, the threat of management to hire replacement workers

Economics in Practice

See answers in side column above.

1 Plan & Prepare

Objectives

- Analyze multiple sources to deepen understanding of changes in work life.
- Understand the global changes that affect many industries today.

2 Focus & Motivate

Ask students how they have coped with changes in their lives. What was the transition like from middle school to high school? How did they have to adjust their study behavior, for example, and how did they change in the process? Also, ask what changes they think they'll face when they move on to a job or college. How will they deal with these changes? Point out that change is a lifelong challenge.

3 Teach

Using the Sources

Discuss

A. What does the title of the article mean? *(It is a play on the geological term "continental drift" and calls attention to the movement [drift] of some young Western workers to the Indian subcontinent.)* What benefits do the workers get from their move? *(interesting life experience living in a foreign culture, continued work experience)*

B. What technique does the cartoon use to make its point? *(Answers will vary, but chief among the techniques of this and most other cartoons is exaggeration—taking a somewhat reasonable idea to its extreme and often laughable outer limits.)*

C. What role do quotations play in this source? *(They repeat the general points already made, but this time they come from a real person who is involved.)* Read the article without the quotes. Then ask students what, if anything, is missing without the quotes. *(Answers will vary, but most students will probably agree that without the connection to real people's lives and concerns, the story loses much of its appeal.)*

Economics Update

Go to **ClassZone.com** to find an update to this Case Study, including another article, an editable student worksheet, and an editable lesson plan.

Case Study

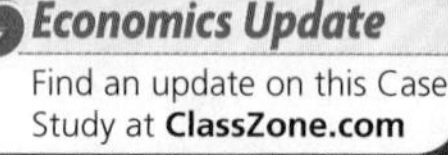

Economics Update

Find an update on this Case Study at **ClassZone.com**

Managing Change in Your Work Life

Background The United States economy has shifted from manufacturing to service and knowledge-based industries. New technologies offer increasingly sophisticated tools. Telecommuting provides businesses the option of having employees work effectively from outside the office.

Globalization has revolutionized the way companies do business. Companies are no longer tied to a specific location. Instead, they establish offices around the globe. The outsourcing and insourcing of jobs result both in benefits and challenges. The dynamics of the workplace are defined by a single factor—change.

What's the issue? How will you respond to the changing dynamics of the work environment? Study these sources to discover how change affects the type of work we do, as well as where and how we do it.

A. Online Magazine Article

Call centers in India help businesses reduce costs because local wages are low. But some Westerners accept the low wages for a chance to live in India.

Subcontinental Drift

More Westerners are beefing up their resumés with a stint in India

After a year answering phones for Swiss International Air Lines Ltd. in a Geneva call center, Myriam Vock was eager to see something of the world. So she packed her bags and hopped a plane to India. Two and a half years later she's still there, sharing a five-bedroom apartment in an upscale New Delhi suburb with four other foreigners.

And how does she pay the bills? She works in a call center, getting paid a fraction of what she did back home. "I'm not earning much, but there is enough to live well and travel," says Vock, 21. . . . "I don't pay taxes here, and life is so much cheaper," she says.

Worried about your job fleeing to India? One strategy is to chase it—an option a growing number of twentysomething Westerners are choosing. Sure, the trend will never make up for the thousands of positions lost back home, but for adventurous young people, a spell in a call center in Bangalore or Bombay can help defray the costs of a grand tour of the subcontinent and beyond.

Source: **BusinessWeek.com, January 16, 2006**

Call centers in India serve customers of companies all over the world.

Thinking Economically Explain Myriam's decision to work in a call center in India using cost-benefit analysis.

DIFFERENTIATING INSTRUCTION

Struggling Readers

Use the Callouts

Instruct the students to read the callouts for Sources A, B, and C both before and after reading the source itself. Point out to them that in instructional material features such as these, callouts can help readers make sense of text that is outside of the main narrative of the book.

Inclusion

Read Visual Sources

The photograph on page 282 is another source that some students may relate to more easily than the written sources. Model for students how to "read" a photograph in order to get the most information from it. The following questions may help:

- What is the main subject?
- From what perspective was it taken?
- Where and when was the photo taken?
- What can you infer about any one or all of the people in the photograph?

B. Business Cartoon

Canadian cartoonist Andrew Toos drew this cartoon about working in an increasingly technological society.

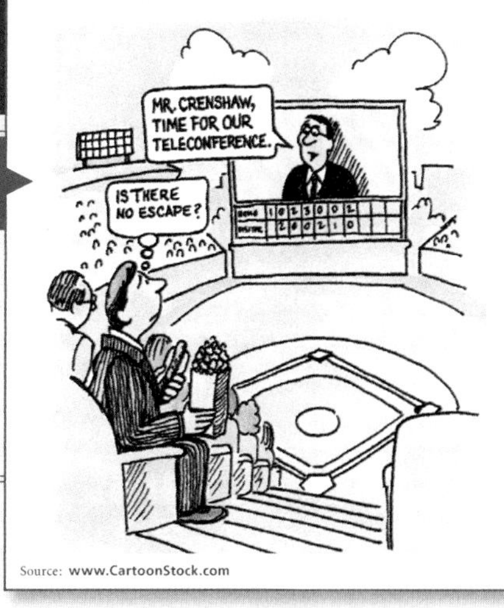

Source: www.CartoonStock.com

Thinking Economically What does the cartoon suggest about new technological developments in the world of work? Explain your answer.

C. Online Newspaper Article

Many worry that outsourcing may reduce the number of jobs in the United States. This article presents a different perspective.

Outsourcing Benefits Permac Employees

Permac creates a win-win situation.

Permac Industries in Burnsville [Minnesota] fashions parts ranging from rings that tie parachutes to small planes to parts for soda fountain machines and construction trucks. President and CEO Darlene Miller plans to send some work to China, but she said it's to the benefit of her 27 Minnesota employees.

"No one here will lose a job. We're not planning to let anybody go—in fact, we're hiring," she said.

Miller is investing in a $700,000 piece of equipment to give workers in Burnsville better tools for specialized work that demands higher skills than the work she plans to send to China. A side benefit for the company's Burnsville workers is that the work going to China will reduce the need for what at times has seemed relentless overtime.

"The simple parts eat up a lot of machine time," said John Keith, a Permac team leader. "If we farm that out we have time to look at getting new business, more complicated business."

Source: www.startribune.com, September 5, 2004

Thinking Economically How will Permac employees benefit from outsourcing? Identify others who also will benefit and explain why.

THINKING ECONOMICALLY Synthesizing

1. What skills are you likely to need in order to manage change successfully in your work life? Support your answer with examples from the documents.
2. In documents A and B, are the types of change similar or different? Are their effects on workers positive or negative? Explain your answer.
3. Compare the opportunities afforded by change in documents A and C. How are they similar? How are they different?

More About . . .

Students Shaping the Work Force

In 2004, Microsoft Corporation began inviting talented college students from around the globe to help them envision the workplace of the future. Microsoft calls the group the Office Information Worker Board of the Future. Microsoft hopes to use ideas from the group to shape the technology products of the future. The students are given complete control over the conclusions they draw and the recommendations they make.

Thinking Economically

Answers

A. *For the same amount of work, she gets less in wages but gets to see India.*

B. *There may be a downside to telecommuting and advanced technology.*

C. *Permac employees learn new skills and work less overtime. The Chinese get new jobs, and Permac gains new capabilities.*

Synthesizing

1. *Possible answers: communication skills, as in the call center of A and teleconferencing in B; adaptability to change, as in moving to a new country in A and learning new skills in C*
2. *Similar: working in new environments Different: A represents a sense of freedom, while B represents a lack of it.*
3. *Similar: Both concern new job opportunities. Different: C shows how firms can retain highly skilled jobs by outsourcing less skilled jobs, while case A concerns jobs that have been outsourced.*

TECHNOLOGY ACTIVITY

Creating a Power Presentation

Time 60 Minutes ●

Task Create a Power Presentation describing the workplace of the future.

Materials Needed a computer with software for creating slides, projector for final viewing desirable but not essential

Activity

- Divide students into three groups. Each will create a power presentation showing a workplace of the future. Students should choose a real company and project what it will be like in 25 years.
- Students should create the presentation as if they were workers 25 years from now reporting on their company.
- Each group should subdivide the work, keeping in mind the strengths of each member.
- Encourage students to draw on known trends, as well as their own intuition and experiences.

Rubric

	Understanding of Workplace Change	Presentation of Information
4	excellent	clever and well-designed
3	good	interesting and clear
2	fair	somewhat interesting and adequately clear
1	poor	lacks reflection, sloppy

Online Summary Answers

1. Wages
2. derived demand
3. equilibrium wage
4. human capital
5. minimum wage
6. civilian labor force
7. glass ceiling
8. telecommuting
9. contingent employment
10. outsourcing
11. insourcing
12. labor union
13. collective bargaining
14. strike

Interactive Review

Review this chapter using interactive activities at ClassZone.com
- Online Summary
- Quizzes
- Vocabulary Flip Cards
- Graphic Organizers
- Review and Study Notes

Online Summary

Complete the following activity either on your own paper or online at ClassZone.com

Choose the key concept that best completes the sentence. Not all key concepts will be used.

civilian labor force
closed shop
collective bargaining
contingent employment
craft union
derived demand
equilibrium wage
glass ceiling
human capital
industrial union
insourcing
labor union
minimum wage
outsourcing
productivity
right-to-work law
strike
telecommuting
union shop
wages

__1__ are the cost of labor. The demand for labor is a __2__, growing out of the demand for the goods or services workers can produce. The forces of supply and demand determine the __3__, at which there is neither a surplus nor a shortage of workers. Wages are directly correlated to a worker's __4__. Workers with the lowest level often earn only the __5__.

Since the 1950s, many women have entered the __6__. They are sometimes limited by the __7__, which keeps them from reaching the highest levels of management. Other trends in the labor market include __8__, working away from a central office, and __9__, working part-time or temporary jobs. U.S. firms sometimes use __10__ to hire workers in other countries. When foreign companies open plants in the United States, it is called __11__.

Changes in the work force have reduced the number of workers who belong to a __12__. Such organizations press for higher pay and better working conditions through __13__. If talks fail, union workers might __14__, putting pressure on employers to meet their demands.

CHAPTER 9 Assessment

REVIEWING KEY CONCEPTS

How Are Wages Determined? (pp. 258–265)

1. What forces determine the equilibrium wage?
2. What four factors contribute to differences in wages?

Trends in Today's Labor Market (pp. 266–273)

3. How has the labor market in the United States changed since the 1950s?
4. Name two new developments in the way Americans work.

Organized Labor in the United States (pp. 274–283)

5. Name an important U.S. labor leader and describe what he or she contributed to the labor movement.
6. What are some of the reasons membership in unions has declined since the 1950s?

APPLYING ECONOMIC CONCEPTS

The table below shows the median weekly earnings of full-time wage and salary workers by union affiliation and selected characteristics.

FIGURE 9.16 UNION AND NONUNION WAGES

Median Weekly Earnings of Full-Time Workers in the United States (in dollars)

Race or Ethnicity	Union		Nonunion	
	Men	Women	Men	Women
African-American	689	632	523	478
Asian	819	789	827	643
Hispanic	713	609	473	414
White	884	749	714	576

Source: U.S. Bureau of Labor Statistics, 2005 data

7. What is the only group for which union affiliation does not yield higher pay?
8. Calculate the percentage difference between each group's union and nonunion wages. Which group gains the most in wages from union membership?

CHAPTER 9 ASSESSMENT ANSWERS

Reviewing Key Concepts

1. supply and demand
2. human capital, working conditions, discrimination, government action
3. many more women in the labor force; more contingent workers; fewer union members
4. Technology has eliminated or redefined many jobs and how people do their jobs, including via telecommuting; jobs shifted dramatically away from manufacturing and toward services.
5. Uriah Stephens – founded Knights of Labor
   Samuel Gompers – founded American Federation of Labor (AFL)
   Eugene V. Debs – founded American Railway Union
   Mary Harris Jones (Mother Jones) – led children's march
   Walter Philip Reuther – president of United Auto Workers
   John L. Lewis – led United Mine Workers and Congress of Industrial Organizations (CIO)
   George Meany – president of AFL-CIO
   Cesar Chavez – founded National Farm Workers Association
6. laws limiting union activities, including the "right-to-work" laws; the shift from manufacturing to services; labor's loss of reputation; more temporary employees, fewer full-time employees

Applying Economic Concepts

7. Asian men
8. African-American men who are not unionized earn about 76 percent of the pay of their union counterparts.
   African-American women who are not unionized earn about 76 percent of the pay of their union counterparts.
   Asian men who are not unionized earn about 101 percent of the pay of their union counterparts.
   Asian women who are not unionized earn about 81 percent of the pay of their union counterparts.
   Hispanic men who are not unionized earn about 66 percent of the pay of their union

CRITICAL THINKING

9. **Creating Graphs** Create a bar graph using the following information about alternative work arrangements in the United States. Include an appropriate title and a source line showing that the data, which are for 2005, come from the Bureau of Labor Statistics.

   Independent contractors (Self-employed workers, such as independent sales consultants or freelance writers): 10.3 million

   On-call workers (Workers called as needed, sometimes working several days or weeks in a row, such as substitute teachers): 2.5 million

   Temporary workers (Workers paid by the hour, such as file clerks, hired through a temporary employment agency): 1.2 million

   Contract workers (Workers paid a salary, such as training specialists, provided by contract firms and hired for a limited contract): 0.8 million

   Use ***SMARTGrapher*** **@ ClassZone.com** to complete this activity.

10. **Synthesizing Economic Data** Explain the differences in median weekly earnings in Figure 9.16 in terms of this chapter's key concepts.

11. **Explaining an Economic Concept** Have you ever been paid to work? If so, explain how the rate you were paid was determined. If not, think of someone you know who has earned money and explain how that person's wages were determined.

12. **Applying Economic Concepts** Think back to a time when you negotiated with someone in a position of authority for something you strongly wanted. Briefly describe the tactics you used and look for similarities or differences between those and the tactics unions use with employers.

13. **Challenge** In 2003, the Fair Labor Standards Act was amended to clarify who was entitled to overtime pay. At the center of the issue were computer programmers, who lost entitlement to overtime if their regular pay is $65,000 per year or more. What impact might this have had on the workers and the economy?

SIMULATION

Collective Bargaining

It's time to renegotiate the union contract at the Acme auto parts factory in Springfield. Read these descriptions of the two sides, then follow the instructions to experience what union negotiations are like.

Union workers currently earn $25 per hour, plus overtime pay if they have to work more than 35 hours per week. Benefits include health-care insurance paid for by the company, plus vision and dental coverage, also funded by the company. The workers' pension fund is handled through the union.

The Acme company is a conglomerate based in the United States. Its auto parts business has been struggling to make a profit, so it is considering outsourcing the work to a factory in China. It would then like to turn the Springfield factory into a computer manufacturing facility.

Step 1 Divide the class evenly into union members and the Acme management team.

Step 2 Separately and privately, each group discusses its objectives and negotiating strategies. Try to keep the conversation quiet so that the other side does not gain an advantage by learning your bargaining points.

Step 3 Each group chooses three representatives to conduct the negotiations.

Step 4 The representatives from both sides meet and negotiate the new contract. The rest of the two groups may listen to the negotiations, but they may not participate. If the two sides still disagree on an issue after several minutes of negotiations, put that issue aside for the moment. Keep a list showing the status of each issue.

Step 5 If time permits, repeat steps 2–4 to address the unresolved issues.

Discuss what happened. Did one side have more bargaining power? How did the two sides resolve their differences? Why were some issues more difficult to resolve than others?

McDougal Littell Assessment System

Assess

Online Test Practice
- Go to **ClassZone.com** for more test practice.

Unit 3 Resource Book
- Chapter Test, Forms A, B, & C, pp. 103–114

Test Generator CD-ROM
- Chapter Test, Forms (A, B, & C), in English and Spanish

Report

Use the McDougal Littell Assessment System to score assessments and receive customized reports.

Reteach

For activities customized for individual students, use the McDougal Littell Assessment System.

CHAPTER 9 ASSESSMENT ANSWERS

counterparts. (They stand to gain the most.) Hispanic women who are not unionized earn about 68 percent of the pay of their union counterparts.
White men who are not unionized earn about 81 percent of the pay of their union counterparts. White women who are not unionized earn about 77 percent of the pay of their union counterparts.

9. Look for a bar graph accurately representing the number of each kind of worker.
10. The breakdown shows the effect of unionization on wages. The table implies a wage gap between men and women and discrimination affecting the earnings of African American and Hispanic workers. However, it does not contain sufficient information to support these conclusions. It would need to show differences in wages for people with the same jobs and the same level of skills and experience.
11. Answers will vary but look for an understanding of supply and demand, human capital, and other key concepts.
12. Answers will vary.
13. Answers will vary but may emphasize the economic importance of the computer industry. The impact on the workers is that they may have little choice but to put in long hours with no expectation of overtime. The impact on the economy may be higher profits for companies that use many computer programmers.

Simulation Rubric

	Understanding of Concepts Involved	Presentation of Information
4	excellent	accurate, clear, and complete
3	good	mostly accurate and clear
2	fair	sometimes clear
1	poor	sketchy

Planning Guide

Resources 2Go Complete print resources all on one USB drive allow you to customize lessons.

Section Titles and Objectives	Unit 4 Resource Book and Workbooks		Assessment Resources
1 Money: Its Functions and Properties pp. 288–295 • Outline the functions that money performs and the characteristics that money possesses • Explain why the different types of money have value • Describe how the money supply in the United States is measured	**Unit 4 Resource Book** • Reading Study Guide, pp. 1–2 • RSG with Additional Support, pp. 3–5 • RSG with Additional Support (Spanish), pp. 6–8 • Math Skills Worksheet: Constructing and Analyzing Data from a Circle Graph, p. 39	**NCEE Student Activities** • Exchange Rates: Money Around the World, pp. 37–40	**Unit 4 Resource Book** • Section Quiz, p. 9 • Reteaching Activity, p. 10 **Test Generator CD-ROM** **Daily Test Practice Transparencies,** TT33
2 The Development of U.S. Banking pp. 296–303 • Describe how banking developed in the United States • Identify the banking institutions that operate in the United States	**Unit 4 Resource Book** • Reading Study Guide, pp. 11–12 • RSG with Additional Support, pp. 13–15 • RSG with Additional Support (Spanish), pp. 16–18 • Economic Simulations, p. 37	• Readings in Free Enterprise: Both Post Office and Bank?, pp. 33–34	**Unit 4 Resource Book** • Section Quiz, p. 19 • Reteaching Activity, p. 20 **Test Generator CD-ROM** **Daily Test Practice Transparencies,** TT34
3 Innovations in Modern Banking pp. 304–313 • Describe the services that banks provide • Discuss the changes that deregulation has brought to banking • Explain how technology has changed banking in the United States	**Unit 4 Resource Book** • Reading Study Guide, pp. 21–22 • RSG with Additional Support, pp. 23–25 • RSG with Additional Support (Spanish), pp. 26–28 • Economic Skills and Problem Solving Activity, pp. 31–32 • Case Study Resources: New Math for College Costs, pp. 35–36	**Test Practice and Review Workbook,** pp. 41–42	**Unit 4 Resource Book** • Section Quiz, p. 29 • Reteaching Activity, p. 30 • Chapter Test, (Forms A, B, & C), pp. 41–52 **Test Generator CD-ROM** **Daily Test Practice Transparencies,** TT35

Integrated Technology

No Time? To focus students on the most important content in this chapter, use the Economics Essentials diagram, "Functions of Money," that appears on page 289.

Teacher Presentation Options

Presentation Toolkit

Power Presentation DVD-ROM

- Lecture Notes
- Interactive Review
- Media Gallery
- Animated Economics
- Review Game

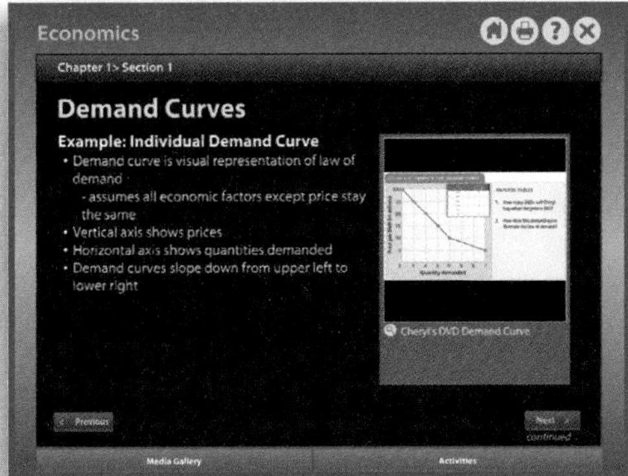

Economics Concepts Transparencies

- Function of Money, CT33
- History of Banking Timeline, CT34
- Federal Reserve Requirement, CT35

Electronic Books

eEdition DVD-ROM

eEdition Online

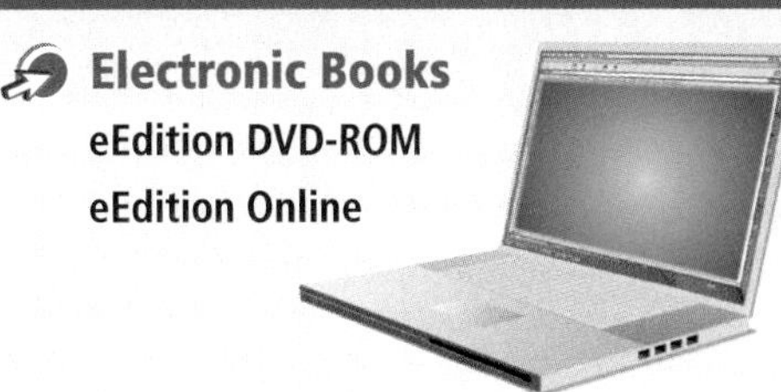

Daily Test Practice Transparencies, TT33, TT34, TT35

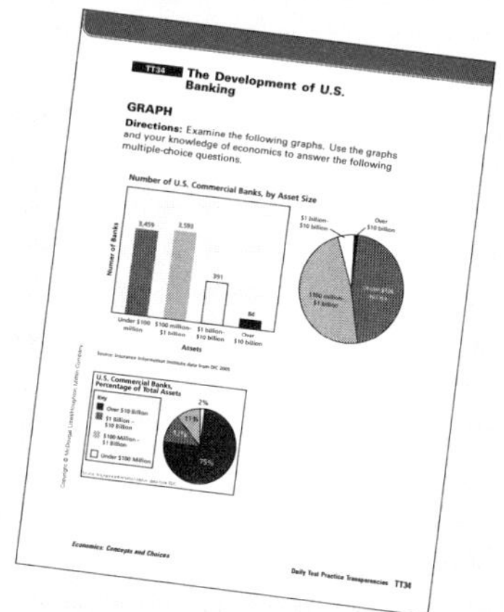

Animated Economics

- Fractional Reserve Banking, p. 305

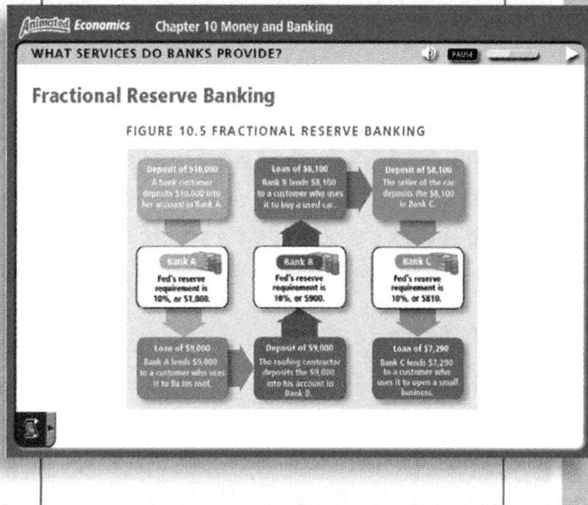

Online Activities at ClassZone.com

Economics Update

- The Functions of Money, p. 289
- Money Supply, p. 294
- Alexander Hamilton, p. 297
- U.S. Financial Institutions, p. 301
- Case Study: Student Loans, p. 312

Animated Economics

- Interactive Graphics

Activity Maker

- Vocabulary Flip Cards
- Review Game

Research Center

- Graphs and Data

Interactive Review

- Online Summary
- Quizzes
- Vocabulary Flip Cards
- Graphic Organizers
- Review and Study Notes

SMARTGrapher

- Create Pie Graphs, p. 303
- Create Line Graphs, p. 303

Teacher-Tested Activities

Name: Lisa Herman-Ellison

School: Kokomo High School

State: Indiana

Teacher-Tested Activities

At the beginning of this chapter, look for my classroom-proven idea for teaching economics concepts and thinking.

Resources for Differentiated Instruction

Struggling Readers

Teacher's Edition Activities

- Create Graphic Organizers, p. 290
- Diagram Cause and Effect, p. 300
- Compare and Contrast, p. 302
- Access Prior Knowledge, p. 306
- List Pros and Cons, p. 310

Unit 4 Resource Book

- RSG with Additional Support, pp. 3–5, 13–15, 23–25 (A)
- Reteaching Activities, pp. 10, 20, 30 (B)
- Chapter Test (Form A), pp. 41–44 (C)

ClassZone.com

- Animated Economics
- Interactive Review

Test Generator CD-ROM

- Chapter Test (Form A)
- Chapter Test (Form A), in Spanish

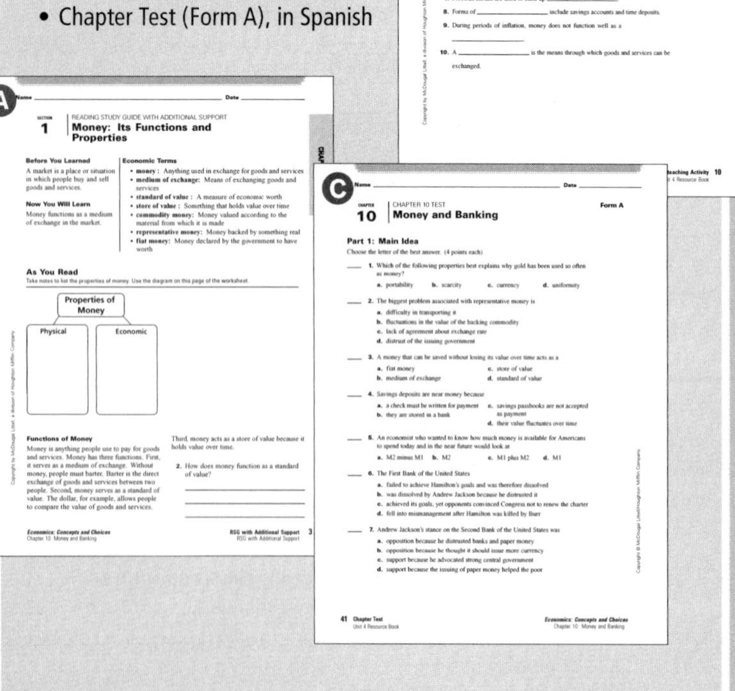

B — SECTION 1 RETEACHING ACTIVITY
Money: Its Functions and Properties

A — SECTION 1 READING STUDY GUIDE WITH ADDITIONAL SUPPORT
Money: Its Functions and Properties

C — CHAPTER 10 TEST
Money and Banking — Form A

Part 1: Main Idea

English Learners

Teacher's Edition Activities

- Analyze Word Forms, p. 290
- Understand Compound Nouns, p. 294
- Create a Cluster Diagram, p. 300
- Distinguish Between Similar Words, p. 308
- Study Multiple-Meaning Words, p. 310

Unit 4 Resource Book

- RSG with Additional Support (Spanish), pp. 6–8, 16–18, 26–28 (A)

Test Generator CD-ROM

- Chapter Test (Forms A, B, & C), in Spanish (B)

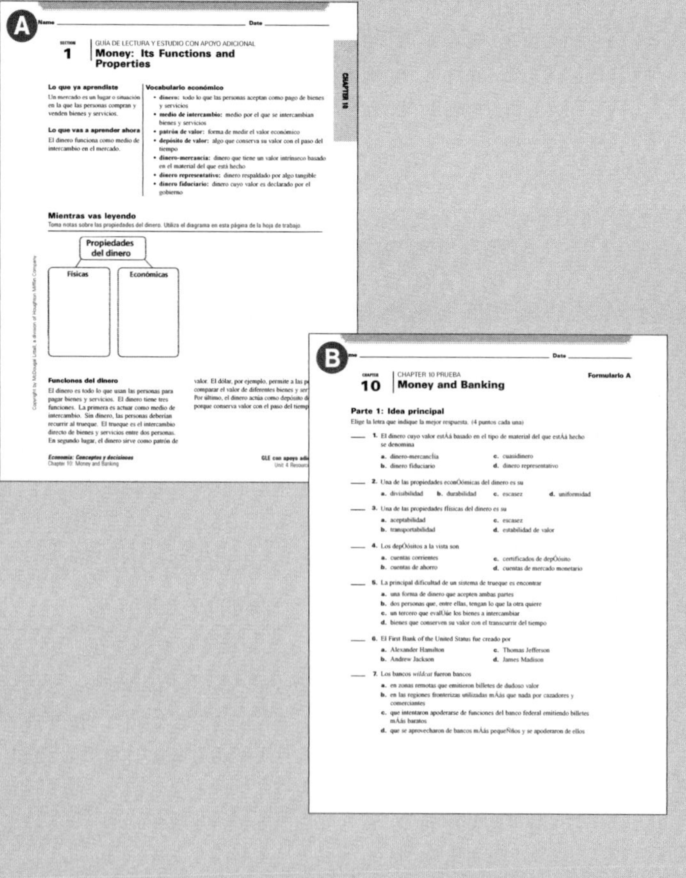

A — SECTION 1 GUÍA DE LECTURA Y ESTUDIO CON APOYO ADICIONAL
Money: Its Functions and Properties

B — CHAPTER 10 PRUEBA
Money and Banking — Formulario A

Parte 1: Idea principal

Inclusion

Teacher's Edition Activities

- Use a Map, p. 292
- Compare Different Forms of Information, p. 294
- Follow the Time Line, p. 298
- Create Electronic Banking Cards, p. 308
- Understand Data, p. 312

Lesson Plans

- Modified Lessons for Inclusion, pp. 33, 34, 35 (A)

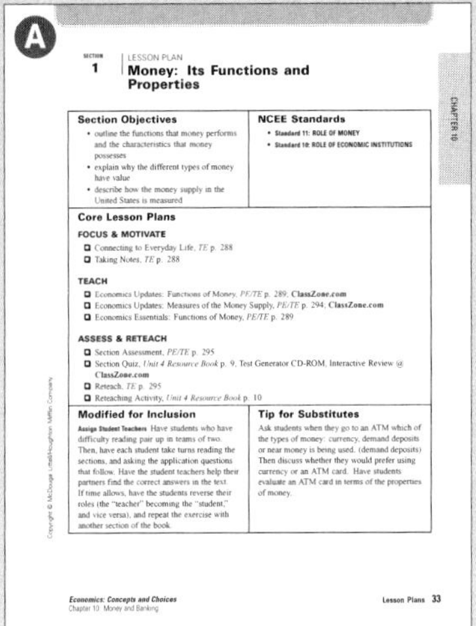
A

SECTION 1 | LESSON PLAN
Money: Its Functions and Properties

Section Objectives	NCEE Standards
• outline the functions that money performs and the characteristics that money possesses • explain why the different types of money have value • describe how the money supply in the United States is measured	• Standard 11: ROLE OF MONEY • Standard 10: ROLE OF ECONOMIC INSTITUTIONS

Core Lesson Plans

FOCUS & MOTIVATE
- Connecting to Everyday Life, TE p. 288
- Taking Notes, TE p. 288

TEACH
- Economics Update: Functions of Money, PE/TE p. 289, ClassZone.com
- Economics Update: Measures of the Money Supply, PE/TE p. 294, ClassZone.com
- Economics Essentials: Functions of Money, PE/TE p. 289

ASSESS & RETEACH
- Section Assessment, PE/TE p. 295
- Section Quiz, Unit 4 Resource Book p. 9; Test Generator CD-ROM; Interactive Review @ ClassZone.com
- Reteach, TE p. 295
- Reteaching Activity, Unit 4 Resource Book p. 10

Modified for Inclusion	Tip for Substitutes
Assign Student Teachers Have students who have difficulty reading pair up in teams of two. Then, have each student take turns reading the sections, and asking the application questions that follow. Have the student teachers help their partners find the correct answers in the text. If time allows, have the students reverse their roles (the "teacher" becoming the "student," and vice versa), and repeat the exercise with another section of the book.	Ask students when they go to an ATM which of the types of money: currency, demand deposits or near money is being used. (demand deposits) Then discuss whether they would prefer using currency or an ATM card. Have students evaluate an ATM card in terms of the properties of money.

Economics: Concepts and Choices Chapter 10 Money and Banking — Lesson Plans 33

Gifted and Talented

Teacher's Edition Activities

- Research the Euro, p. 292
- Debate the Gold Standard, p. 298
- Use the Statistical Abstract, p. 302
- Evaluate Deregulation, p. 306
- Create Fact Sheets, p. 312

Unit 4 Resource Book

- Readings in Free Enterprise: Both Post Office and Bank?, pp. 33–34 (A)
- Case Study Resources: New Math for College Costs, pp. 35–36 (B)

NCEE Student Activities

- Exchange Rates: Money Around the World, pp. 37–40 (C)

ClassZone.com

- Research Center

Test Generator CD-ROM

- Chapter Test (Form C)
- Chapter Test (Form C), in Spanish

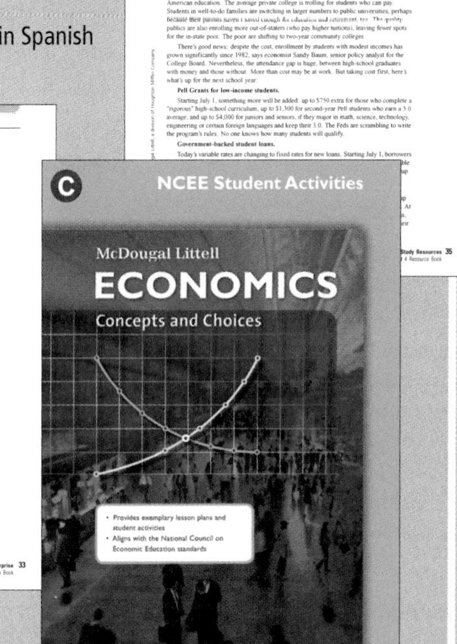

Focus & Motivate

Objective

Describe how money and banking help the market economy work more efficiently.

Why the Concept Matters

Encourage students to share their thoughts about making the transactions described on page 287 without money. Lead them to conclude that money is vital to an efficient economic system. Explain that banks allow money to circulate throughout the economy in a smooth and productive way.

Analyzing the Photograph

Have students study the photograph and read the caption. Invite volunteers to describe how the visuals show the relationship between money and the government. *(Possible answers: Money shows pictures of early government leaders—Benjamin Franklin, George Washington, Abraham Lincoln, and Alexander Hamilton—and a picture of the U.S. Treasury building; the words* United States of America *and* Federal Reserve *suggest that the money is issued by the government.)*

Give students some sense of the properties and functions of effective moneys and ask them if and how they think U.S. currency performs them. *(Possible answers: Everyone accepts it and knows what it is worth; it is portable, uniform, and stable.)*

Explain that Chapter 10 will describe why money issued by the government has value and how banks play an essential role in allowing money to be used for the benefit of individuals and the economy as a whole.

Macroeconomics

Unit 4 Money, Banking, and Finance

What constitutes money?

Money isn't born, it's made. Each society decides what it will accept as money, but effective moneys all share certain attributes and perform certain functions.

CONTENT STANDARDS

NCEE STANDARDS

Standard 11: Role of Money

Students will understand that

Money makes it easier to trade, borrow, save, invest, and compare the value of goods and services.

Students will be able to use this knowledge to

Explain how their lives would be more difficult in a world with no money, or in a world where money sharply lost its value. *(pages 288–294)*

Standard 10: Role of Economic Institutions

Students will understand that

Institutions evolve in market economies to help individuals and groups accomplish their goals. Banks . . . are an example of an important institution.

Students will be able to use this knowledge to

Describe the roles of various economic institutions. *(pages 296–302, 304–310)*

CHAPTER 10

Money and Banking

CONCEPT REVIEW

Macroeconomics is the study of the behavior of the economy as a whole and how major economic sectors, such as industry and government, interact.

CHAPTER 10 KEY CONCEPT

Money provides a low-cost method of trading one good or service for another. It makes the system of voluntary exchange efficient.

WHY THE CONCEPT MATTERS

What were the last three economic transactions you completed using money? Perhaps you put four quarters in the fare machine on the bus to school or bought a slice of pizza and a drink in the cafeteria at lunch. Or maybe you caught an early movie after school yesterday. To gauge the importance of money to the economy, imagine trying to make such transactions without the familiar paper bills and coins.

Online Highlights

More at ClassZone.com

Economics Update
Go to ECONOMICS UPDATE for chapter updates and current news on student loans. (See Case Study, pp. 312–313.) ▶

Animated Economics
Go to ANIMATED ECONOMICS for interactive lessons on the graphs and tables in this chapter.

Interactive Review
Go to INTERACTIVE REVIEW for concept review and activities.

Source: www.CartoonStock.com

How important are student loans in the U.S. higher education system? See the Case Study on pages 312–313.

CHAPTER 10

From the Classroom

Lisa Herman-Ellison, Kokomo High School

Money That Works

Get four envelopes and place one item in each: a paper clip, a piece of candy, a scrap of paper, and a penny. Explain to the students that money is anything acceptable as a medium of exchange. Explain the different roles money plays and the difference between commodity and fiat money. Give students the envelopes to open and ask them which item is money (the penny, in our system). Then tell students that the price of an "A" for this Economics course is one paper clip. Did the paper clip become money? Why? Which items are commodity and fiat money? Why wouldn't the other items work as money in our system?

Previewing Chapter Technology at ClassZone.com

Economics Update Students will find updates to information in the pupil edition on pages 289, 294, 297, 301, and 312.

Animated Economics Students will find an interactive lesson related to the material on page 305.

Interactive Review Students will find additional section and chapter assessment support for materials on pages 295, 303, 311, and 314.

TEACHER MEDIA FAVORITES

Books

- Allen, Larry. *Encyclopedia of Money.* New York: Checkmark Books, 2001. More than 350 entries on money and monetary systems around the world.
- Chernow, Ron. *Alexander Hamilton.* New York: Penguin, 2004. In-depth analysis of Hamilton's achievements.
- Cortada, James W. *The Digital Hand. Volume II: How Computers Changed the Work of American Financial, Telecommunications, Media, and Entertainment Industries.* New York: Oxford UP, 2006. Examines how computer and telecommunications technology changed the economy.
- Mayer, Martin. *The Bankers: The Next Generation.* New York: Truman Talley Books, 1997. A look at the nature of money and recent changes to the banking system.

Videos/DVDs

- *The History of Money.* 55 Minutes. FFI: Films for Humanities and Sciences, 1997. Examines innovations in money over 5,000 years and explores their effects.
- *Banks: A User's Guide.* 25 minutes. Learning Seed. Covers the basics and trends in electronic banking.

Software

- *Virtual Economics® Version 3.0.* New York: National Council on Economic Education, 2005. A resource library for understanding and teaching economics concepts.

Internet

Visit **ClassZone.com** to link to

- a variety of chapter-specific, content-reviewed sites
- updates on data and topics presented throughout the chapter sections and the Case Study
- updates to the Power Presentations

1 Plan & Prepare

Section 1 Objectives

- outline the functions that money performs and the characteristics that money possesses
- explain why the different types of money have value
- describe how the money supply in the United States is measured

2 Focus & Motivate

Connecting to Everyday Life Explain that this section focuses on the role of money in the economy. Invite students to describe examples of trades they have made that did not use money. Encourage them to talk about the pros and cons of this kind of exchange.

Taking Notes Remind students to take notes as they read by completing a cluster diagram. They can use the Graphic Organizer at **Interactive Review @ClassZone.com**. A sample is shown below.

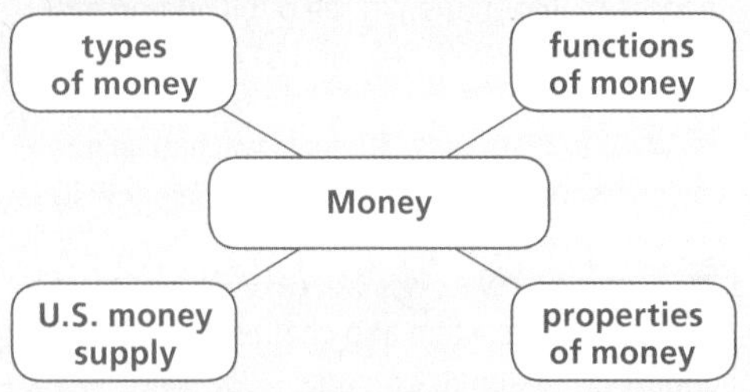

SECTION 1

Money: Its Functions and Properties

OBJECTIVES

In Section 1, you will

- outline the functions that money performs and the characteristics that money possesses
- explain why the different types of money have value
- describe how the money supply in the United States is measured

KEY TERMS

money, *p. 288*
medium of exchange, *p. 288*
barter, *p. 288*
standard of value, *p. 289*
store of value, *p. 289*
commodity money, *p. 291*
representative money, *p. 291*
fiat money, *p. 291*
currency, *p. 293*
demand deposits, *p. 293*
near money, *p. 293*

TAKING NOTES

As you read Section 1, complete a cluster diagram summarizing key information about money. Use the Graphic Organizer at **Interactive Review @ ClassZone.com**

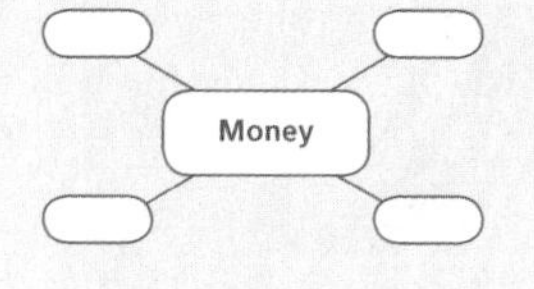

Functions of Money

QUICK REFERENCE

Money is anything that people will accept in exchange for goods and services.

A **medium of exchange** is a means through which goods and services can be exchanged.

Barter is the exchange of goods and services without using money.

KEY CONCEPTS

What do the following things have in common: cattle, corn, rice, salt, copper, gold, silver, seashells, stones, and whale teeth? At different times and in different places, they have all been used as money. In fact, **money** is anything that people will accept as payment for goods and services. Whatever it is that people choose to use as money, it should perform three important functions.

FUNCTION 1 Medium of Exchange

Money must serve as a **medium of exchange**, or the means through which goods and services can be exchanged. Without money, economic transactions must be made through **barter**—exchanging goods and services for other goods and services. Barter is cumbersome and inefficient because two people who want to barter must at the same time want what the other has to offer. For example, suppose you want to trade two T-shirts for a pair of jeans. One classmate might have the jeans but not want your shirts; another might want your shirts but not have jeans to trade. It is much easier for you to buy a pair of jeans by giving money to the seller who, in turn, can use it to buy something else. Money allows for the precise and flexible pricing of goods and services, making any economic transaction convenient.

A World of Money Currencies come in a wide variety of colors and sizes. This is a collage of the currencies of South America.

SECTION 1 PROGRAM RESOURCES

ON LEVEL

Lesson Plans

- Core, p. 33

Unit 4 Resource Book

- Reading Study Guide, pp. 1–2
- Economic Skills and Problem Solving Activity, pp. 31–32
- Math Skills Worksheet, p. 39
- Section Quiz, p. 9

STRUGGLING READERS

Unit 4 Resource Book

- Reading Study Guide with Additional Support, pp. 3–5
- Reteaching Activity, p. 10

ENGLISH LEARNERS

Unit 4 Resource Book

- Reading Study Guide with Additional Support (Spanish), pp. 6–8

INCLUSION

Lesson Plans

- Modified for Inclusion, p. 33

GIFTED AND TALENTED

NCEE Student Activities

- Exchange Rates: Money Around the World, pp. 37–40

TECHNOLOGY

eEdition DVD-ROM

eEdition Online

Power Presentation DVD-ROM

Economics Concepts Transparencies

- CT33 Function of Money

Daily Test Practice Transparencies, TT33

ClassZone.com

FUNCTION 2 Standard of Value

Money also serves as a **standard of value**, the yardstick of economic worth in the exchange process. It allows people to measure the relative costs of goods and services. A $20 T-shirt is worth two $10 phone cards, four $5 burritos, or twenty $1 bus rides. The basic monetary unit in the United States is the dollar, which serves as the standard by which the economic worth of all goods and services can be expressed and measured.

FUNCTION 3 Store of Value

Finally, money acts as a **store of value**, that is, something that holds its value over time. People, therefore, do not need to spend all their money at once or in one place; they can put it aside for later use. They know that it will be accepted wherever and whenever it is presented to purchase goods and services.

One situation where money does not function well as a store of value is when the economy experiences significant inflation—a sustained rise in the general level of prices. For example, in Argentina in the first half of 2002, prices rose by about 70 percent. Basic goods that cost 150 pesos in January cost 255 pesos in June. In other words, in that time period, Argentina's money lost over two-thirds of its purchasing power. You'll learn more about inflation in Chapter 13.

QUICK REFERENCE

A **standard of value** determines the economic worth in the exchange process.

A **store of value** is something that holds its value over time.

Economics Update

Find an update on the functions of money at **ClassZone.com**

ECONOMICS ESSENTIALS

FIGURE 10.1 Functions of Money

What Functions Does Money Perform?

Standard of Value Money provides both a way to express and measure the relative costs of goods and services and a way to compare the worths of different goods and services.

Medium of Exchange Money provides a flexible, precise, and convenient way to exchange goods and services.

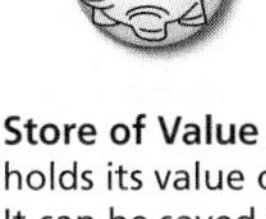

Store of Value Money holds its value over time. It can be saved for later use because it can be exchanged at any time for goods and services.

ANALYZE CHARTS

You've read that salt was used as money in the past. How effectively do you think salt would function as money? Use the three functions of money in the chart to frame your answer.

APPLICATION Applying Economic Concepts

A. How does money help to make clear the opportunity cost of an economic decision?
As a standard of value, money allows people to compare the costs of choices and to determine opportunity cost.

3 Teach

Functions of Money

Discuss

- Why are economic transactions less expensive with money than with barter? *(Possible answer: Money saves people time since it's easier for buyers to get what they want and for sellers to find buyers.)*
- What function of money helps you figure out how many hours you have to work to buy a new DVD? *(standard of value, because you can compare the amount of money you earn per hour with the amount the DVD costs)*

Economics Update

At **ClassZone.com** students will see updated information on the functions of money.

Economics Essentials: Figure 10.1

Ask students: How does money as a standard of value help you when you go shopping? *(It allows you to compare prices of different items or brands and helps you decide what you want to buy.)*

Analyze

Answers will vary. Students may say that salt is not very convenient or precise as a medium of exchange, that it may not hold its value well over time, and that it would be difficult to use as a standard of value.

LEVELED ACTIVITY

Evaluating the Importance of Money and Banking

Time 60 Minutes ●

Objective Students will demonstrate an understanding of the ways money and banking help the economy work more efficiently. (Information on banking is covered in Sections 2 and 3.)

Basic

Keep track of the times you or your family use money or the banking system during a week. Note the purpose of each transaction and how it affected your life. Use the data to write a paragraph drawing conclusions about the role of money and banking in the economy. Use key concepts from the chapter.

On Level

Choose an example of an economic transaction. Write a brief essay showing how the transaction would be different in a barter system, a cash-only system, a system with cash and checks, and in today's world of electronic banking. Draw conclusions about how changes in money and banking affect the economy.

Challenge

Create an economic model to show the roles and relationship of money and banking in a market economy. Consider the different kinds of money in the United States and how each is used. Think about how banks create money and help it circulate. Incorporate ideas from your own experience and from the chapter.

Properties of Money

Discuss

- Why does divisibility allow for precise pricing? *(It allows sellers to set any price for which they can make change.)*
- How is the physical property of uniformity related to the economic property of acceptability? *(Money must have special uniform characteristics so that people recognize it as an acceptable medium of exchange.)*

Presentation Options

Review the properties of money by using the following presentation options:

 **Power Presentations DVD-ROM**
Using the display tool, you can review the physical and economic properties of useful money.

 **Economics Concepts Transparencies**
- CT33 Functions of Money

APPLICATION
Answer *It is a medium of exchange because you can trade U.S. dollars for goods and services. It is a standard of value because you can use dollars to measure the relative costs of goods and services. It is a store of value because dollars hold their value over time.*

Properties of Money

KEY CONCEPTS

To perform the three functions of money, an item must possess certain physical and economic properties. Physical properties of money are the characteristics of the item itself. Economic properties are linked to the role that money plays in the market.

PROPERTY 1 Physical

The following are physical properties of useful money:

Durability Money should be durable, or sturdy, enough to last throughout many transactions. Something that falls apart when several people handle it or that spoils easily would not be a good item to use as money.

Portability Money needs to be small, light, and easy to carry. It's easy to see why paper bills are preferable to cattle as money.

Divisibility Money should also be divisible so that change can be made. For example, the dollar can be divided an endless number of ways using different combinations of pennies, nickels, dimes, or quarters. Divisibility also allows flexible pricing.

Uniformity Lastly, money must be uniform, having features and markings that make it recognizable. Coins that are used as money look different from other flat metal disks. Paper money is a consistent size and uses special symbols and printing techniques. All money that represents a certain amount in a given country has distinctive characteristics that help identify its value. These distinctive markings also make it more difficult to counterfeit.

Chinese Coins
Bronze, spade-shaped coins, 8th–7th century B.C.

PROPERTY 2 Economic

Useful money must also have the following economic properties:

Stability of Value Money's purchasing power, or value, should be relatively stable. In other words, the amount of goods and services that you can buy with a certain amount of money should not change quickly. Rapid changes in purchasing power would mean that money would not successfully serve as a store of value.

Scarcity Money must be scarce to have any value. As you recall from Chapter 7, when the supply of a product outstrips demand, there is a surplus and prices for that product fall. Similarly, when the supply of money outstrips demand, money loses value, or purchasing power.

Acceptability People who use the money must agree that it is acceptable—that it is a valid medium of exchange. In other words, they will accept money in payment for goods and services because others will also accept it as payment.

APPLICATION Applying Economic Concepts

B. Describe how U.S. dollars serve each of the three functions of money.
◄ See Teacher's Edition for answer.

DIFFERENTIATING INSTRUCTION

Struggling Readers

Create Graphic Organizers
Help students understand the properties and types of money by having them create Economics Essentials graphic organizers.

- Organize students into three groups. Have one group each work on the physical and economic properties, and one work on the three types of money.
- Direct students to use Figure 10.1 on page 289 as a model. Have them use a combination of visuals and captions to create their graphic organizers.

English Learners

Analyze Word Forms
Explain that money's properties are expressed as nouns formed by combining an adjective, such as *durable,* with the suffix *-ity,* meaning "quality." For example, *durability* means "the quality of being durable."

- Have a volunteer state how *durable* changes to become *durability. (Change* le *to* il *and add suffix.)*
- Direct partners to use the adjective and noun forms of each physical and economic property in sentences.

Types of Money

KEY CONCEPTS

In the discussion of the functions and properties of money, one theme recurs—value. Money draws its value from three possible sources. **Commodity money** derives its value from the type of material from which it is composed. **Representative money** is paper money backed by something tangible—such as silver or gold—that gives it value. **Fiat money** has no tangible backing, but it is declared by the government that issues it, and accepted by citizens who use it, to have worth.

QUICK REFERENCE

Commodity money has intrinsic value based on the material from which it is made.

Representative money is backed by something tangible.

Fiat money is declared by the government and accepted by citizens to have worth.

TYPE 1 Commodity Money

Commodity money is something that has value for what it is. Items used as commodity money have value in and of themselves, apart from their value as money. Over the course of history, for example, gold, silver, precious stones, salt, olive oil, and rice have all been valued enough for their scarcity or for their usefulness to be used as money.

However, the most common form of commodity money throughout history has been coins made from precious metals. Such coins contain enough of the precious metal that if each was melted down it would be worth at least its face value. One problem with commodity money is that if the item becomes too valuable, people will hoard it rather than circulate it, hoping it will become more valuable in the future. Commodity money is rarely used today.

Commodity Money Until recently, cattle was an important medium of exchange for the Masai people of East Africa.

TYPE 2 Representative Money

Representative money is paper money that can be exchanged for something else of value. The earliest forms of representative money were seen in the Middle Ages, when merchants, goldsmiths, and moneylenders began issuing receipts that promised to pay a certain amount of gold or silver. This came about because it was not always convenient or safe to transport large quantities of those precious metals from place to place for the purpose of trading. These practices signal the beginning of the widespread modern use of paper money.

Eventually, governments got involved with representative money by regulating how much metal needed to be stored to back up the paper money. One problem with representative money is that its value fluctuates with the supply and price of gold or silver, which can cause problems of inflation or deflation—a sustained rise or fall, respectively, in the general level of prices.

Types of Money

Discuss

- Why did representative money become more common than commodity money? *(because paper money was safer and more convenient to transport than coins or other commodities)*
- What is the difference between representative money and fiat money? *(Representative money is backed by and can be exchanged for something of value. Fiat money is backed only by the government that issues it and cannot be exchanged for anything else of value.)*

More About . . .

The Value of Pennies

Since 1982, pennies have been made mostly from zinc because copper had become too valuable. From 2003 to 2006, the price of zinc tripled, so that the value of the metal in a penny was 0.8 cents. The U.S. Mint spent about 0.6 cents in addition to the price of the metal to make each penny, so it was losing 0.4 cents on each of the 9 billion pennies it produced annually.

Many Americans do stockpile pennies, but the motivation usually is the inconvenience of carrying them around rather than the value of the metal. That could change if the price of zinc continued to rise.

INDIVIDUAL ACTIVITY

Studying Foreign Money

Time 45 Minutes

Task Gather information on money used in a foreign country and create an informational poster.

Materials Needed computer with Internet access and/or library resources, poster board, markers

Activity

- Allow students to choose a particular country and use the Internet or library resources to research the type of money used in that country.
- Encourage students to see if the type of money has changed over time and to find photographs or illustrations of the different denominations of money.
- Direct students to create posters showing the type of money and describing how it exhibits all the properties of money.
- Display the posters in the classroom. Discuss the similarities and differences among the different moneys.

Rubric

	Understanding of Properties & Types of Money	Presentation of Information
4	excellent	clear and complete
3	good	mostly clear
2	fair	sometimes clear
1	poor	sketchy

A Global Perspective

The Euro as a Common Currency
Before the euro currency was introduced in 2002, most EU countries had a three-year transition period during which prices were shown both in the euro and in the country's existing currency. Three EU countries—the United Kingdom (UK), Denmark, and Sweden—chose not to adopt the euro. Government leaders in those countries were often in favor of adopting the euro, but public opinion was against it.

The countries were concerned about losing their financial independence to the European Central Bank. For example, some in the UK feared that losing the country's ability to set its own interest rates would hurt their economy.

Answers

1. *Possible answer: It will facilitate trade, encourage tourism, make it easier for people to compare prices of goods from different countries, and bring the countries economically closer together.*
2. *because it is the official currency of the EU and its supply is controlled by the European Central Bank*

A GLOBAL PERSPECTIVE

The Euro as a Common Currency

On January 1, 2002, a new currency—the euro—was put into full use in 12 European countries, each a member of the European Union (EU). The symbol for the euro is €. Each country that adopted the euro gave up its own national currency

The EU seeks the economic and political integration of Europe, and the euro is a key step toward this goal. The common currency makes trade among member nations easier and cheaper. As the EU expands, new members must meet specific economic standards before they can adopt the euro. Several small European countries that are not members of the EU have also begun using the euro.

Like all modern currencies, the euro is categorized as fiat money. Its value is derived from public confidence in the EU. Control of the supply of euros is maintained by the European Central Bank, located in Frankfurt, Germany. Each member nation of the EU has a seat on the Central Bank's decision-making board.

EU Members That Adopted the Euro in 2002

- Austria
- Belgium
- Finland
- France
- Germany
- Greece
- Ireland
- Italy
- Luxembourg
- Netherlands
- Portugal
- Spain

CONNECTING ACROSS THE GLOBE

1. **Making Inferences** How do you think having a common currency might benefit the EU?
2. **Recognizing Effects** Why does the euro have value as currency?

TYPE 3 Fiat Money

Unlike representative money, fiat money has value only because the government has issued a fiat, or order, saying that this is the case. The value of the U.S. dollar was linked to the value of gold until 1971. Since then, a $10 bill can no longer be exchanged for gold; it can only be converted into other combinations of U.S. currency that also equal $10.

In fiat money, coins contain only a token amount of precious metal that is worth far less than the face value of those coins. Paper money has no intrinsic value, and people cannot exchange it for a certain amount of gold or silver. Fiat money has value because the government says it can be used as money and because people accept that it will fulfill all the functions of money.

Dollar bills in the United States carry the statement "This note is legal tender for all debts, public and private." This statement assures people that sellers will accept such money from buyers as payment for goods or services and lenders will accept it as payment for debts. A crucial role of the government in maintaining the value of fiat money is controlling its supply—in other words, maintaining its scarcity.

APPLICATION Analyzing Cause and Effect

C. Which type of money's value would be most affected by political instability? Why?
fiat money, because the value of such money depends on confidence in the government that issues the money

DIFFERENTIATING INSTRUCTION

Inclusion

Use a Map
Help students visualize the importance of the euro by encouraging them to use a map to locate countries that use the euro.

- Direct them to locate the UK, Denmark, and Sweden. Explain that these EU members do not use the euro.
- Suggest that they locate countries recently admitted to the EU that plan to adopt the euro. *(Possible countries: Lithuania, Estonia, Slovenia)*

Gifted and Talented

Research the Euro
Have students explore issues related to the adoption of the euro as a common currency. Possible topics include the terms of the Maastricht Treaty of 1991 relating to members' financial requirements, the role of the European Central Bank, arguments for and against the euro in the countries that have yet to adopt it, and reactions of consumers and producers to the euro in the countries using it. Allow students to present their research as a news program for the class.

Money in the United States

KEY CONCEPTS

In this section so far, you have learned what has been used as money, what functions money performs, what properties it possesses, and why money has value. But what serves as money in the United States today? In its narrowest sense, money consists of what can be used immediately for transactions—currency, demand deposits, and other checkable deposits. **Currency** is paper money and coins. Checking accounts are called **demand deposits** because funds in checking accounts can be converted into currency "on demand."

There are other monetary instruments that are almost, but not exactly, like money. Known as **near money**, it includes savings accounts and other similar time deposits that cannot be used as a medium of exchange but can be converted into cash relatively easily.

QUICK REFERENCE

Currency is paper money and coins.

Demand deposits are checking accounts.

Near money is savings accounts and time deposits that can be converted into cash relatively easily.

Money in the Narrowest Sense

In the narrowest sense, money is what can be immediately used for transactions. This definition of money sometimes uses the term *transactions money*. Most of the money that you and your friends and family spend is transactions money. About half of such money is currency, both paper money and coins, that is used by individuals and businesses.

Most demand deposits are noninterest-bearing checking accounts that can be converted into currency simply by writing a check. Traveler's checks, which are drafts that can be purchased in a number of money amounts and redeemed in many parts of the world, represent a small share of overall demand deposits. Other checkable deposits include negotiable order of withdrawal (NOW) accounts, which are interest-bearing savings accounts against which drafts may be written.

Are Savings Accounts Money?

Near money, such as savings accounts and other interest-bearing accounts, cannot be used directly to make transactions. Your local sporting goods store will not accept a savings passbook as payment for a new basketball or for your tennis racket to be restrung. But money in a savings account can be easily transferred into a checking account or removed directly from an automatic teller machine and put toward a desired good or service.

Near money takes many forms in addition to traditional savings accounts. Time deposits are funds that people place in a financial institution for a specific period of time in return for a higher interest rate. These deposits are often placed in certificates of deposit (CDs). Money market accounts place restrictions on the number of transactions you can make in a month and require you to maintain a certain balance in the account (as low as $500 but often substantially more) in order to receive a higher rate of interest.

Near Money A savings account contains money but is not, strictly, money.

Money in the United States

Discuss

- How are currency and demand deposits similar? *(Both can be used as a medium of exchange.)*
- How is near money converted to transactions money? *(by withdrawing the money from a savings account, CD, or money market account as cash or a check)*

SMALL GROUP ACTIVITY

Comparing Forms of Money

Time 30 minutes

Task Gather information on different forms of money and present findings in oral reports.

Materials Needed computer with Internet access or information from financial institutions

Activity

- Organize students into two groups. One group will research transactions money and the other will research near money.
- Divide the two large groups into smaller subgroups to gather information on the different examples of each kind of money described on page 293.
- Encourage related subgroups to discuss their findings together to note the similarities and differences among the different varieties of money in their category.
- Allow groups to present their research results in oral reports to the class. Invite volunteers to summarize the characteristics of transactions money and near money.

Rubric

	Understanding of Forms of Money	Presentation of Information
4	excellent	clear and complete
3	good	mostly clear
2	fair	sometimes clear
1	poor	sketchy

Economics Update

At **ClassZone.com** students will see updated information on measures of the money supply.

Analyzing Tables and Graphs: Figure 10.2

Explain that the Federal Reserve, the central bank of the United States, tracks the nation's money supply and releases information on the amount of each type of money every week. Ask students how the pie graphs are constructed from the related tables. *(The amount of each component is divided by the total to determine the percentages. For example, $723.8/1,368.9 = 52.9 %.)*

Invite volunteers to subdivide the M1 percentage in the second pie graph into the percentages for demand deposits and other checkable deposits by dividing the amount of each by the total of M2. *(demand deposits, 4.9%; other checkable deposits, 4.7%; total of 20.4% is slightly off because of rounding)*

Answers

1. *$5,311.6 billion, which is the total minus the amount of MI*
2. *10.8%*

How Much Money?

How much money is in supply in the United States? Economists use various instruments to measure the money supply, but the most often cited are M1 and M2. M1 is the narrowest measure of the money supply, consisting of currency, demand deposits, and other checkable deposits. It is synonymous with transactions money. The elements of M1 are referred to as liquid assets, which means that they are or can easily become currency.

M2 is a broader measure of the money supply, consisting of M1 plus various kinds of near money. M2 includes savings accounts, other small-denomination time deposits (CDs of less than $100,000), and money market mutual funds. You will learn about these financial instruments in Chapter 11.

Figure 10.2 shows the amounts of the different forms of money that make up M1 and M2. You can see that M1 is almost evenly split between currency and checkable deposits. Notice that more of M2 comes from savings than from M1. You will learn the importance of the money supply in the economy and how the government manages it in Chapter 16.

Economics Update

Find an update on measures of the money supply at **ClassZone.com**

FIGURE 10.2 COMPONENTS OF THE U.S. MONEY SUPPLY

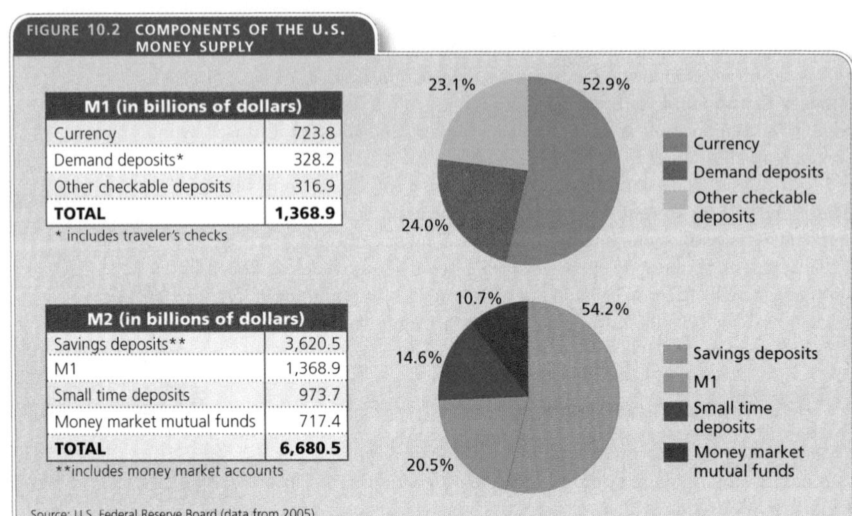

M1 (in billions of dollars)	
Currency	723.8
Demand deposits*	328.2
Other checkable deposits	316.9
TOTAL	**1,368.9**

* includes traveler's checks

M2 (in billions of dollars)	
Savings deposits**	3,620.5
M1	1,368.9
Small time deposits	973.7
Money market mutual funds	717.4
TOTAL	**6,680.5**

**includes money market accounts

Source: U.S. Federal Reserve Board (data from 2005)

ANALYZE TABLES

1. What amount of M2 does not come from currency and checkable deposits?
2. If currency is 52.9 percent of M1, and M1 is 20.5 percent of M2, what percentage of M2 is currency?

APPLICATION Applying Economic Concepts

D. Classify each of the following as M1 and M2: **a.** dollar bill; **b.** savings account; **c.** money market account; **d.** traveler's check; **e.** $50,000 CD.

a. M1; **b.** M2; **c.** M2; **d.** M1; **e.** M2.

DIFFERENTIATING INSTRUCTION

English Learners

Understand Compound Nouns

Have partners list the compound nouns (combinations of adjective and noun) on pages 293–294. Direct them to group similar terms (such as *demand deposits, checkable deposits,* and *time deposits.*)

- Ask volunteers to explain how grouping the terms helps them learn meanings.
- Invite students to use context clues to find the meaning of each term. Allow them to use a dictionary, if necessary.
- Ask them to use the terms in sentences.

Inclusion

Compare Different Forms of Information

Help students understand the differences between the two measures of the money supply by comparing text descriptions with the data in Figure 10.2.

- Have volunteers read each paragraph on pages 293–294 aloud. At the end of each paragraph, ask students to identify which part of Figure 10.2 text is discussing. Direct them to look for key words used in both places that link the two forms of information.

SECTION 1 Assessment

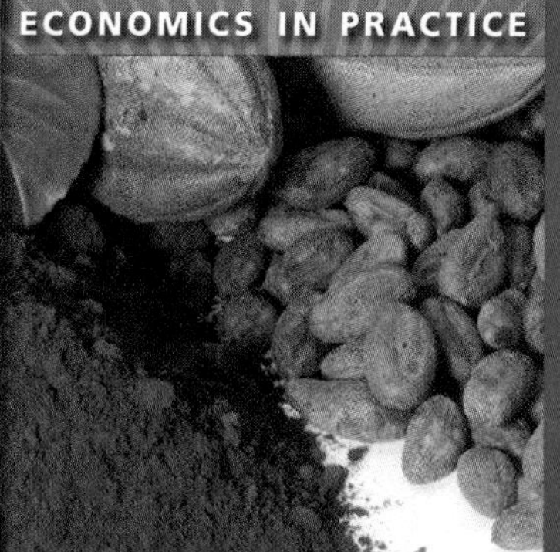

REVIEWING KEY CONCEPTS

1. Explain the difference between the terms in each of these pairs.
   a. *standard of value* / *store of value*
   b. *commodity money* / *representative money*
   c. *demand deposits* / *near money*
2. Why are economic transactions easier with money than with barter?
3. Why is it important that money be divisible?
4. Why are checking accounts called demand deposits?
5. What aspect of fiat money allows it to have more stability than representative money?
6. **Using Your Notes** How are the economic properties of money related to its functions? Refer to your completed cluster diagram.

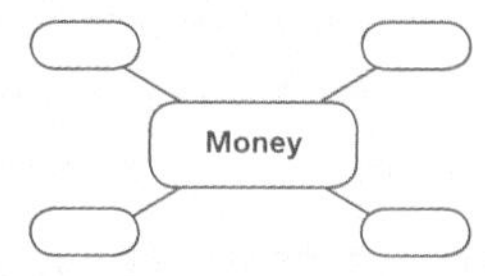

Use the Graphic Organizer at **Interactive Review @ ClassZone.com**

CRITICAL THINKING

7. **Categorizing Economic Information** Which of these forms of money are included in M1:
   - checking accounts
   - coins
   - money market accounts
   - paper money
   - savings accounts
   - time deposits
   - traveler's checks
   - NOW accounts
8. **Making Inferences** The U.S. government has tried to get people to use dollar coins rather than dollar bills. Most consumers prefer to use dollar bills. Which physical properties of money are involved in these different preferences?
9. **Applying Economic Concepts** Maria's parents told her that for the ten years prior to her high school graduation, they saved $200 per month for her college education—$24,000 (plus interest). Which function of money does this example best illustrate? Why?
10. **Challenge** Why is there more near money than transactions money in the U.S. money supply?

ECONOMICS IN PRACTICE

Evaluating Economic Decisions
In the past, indigenous people of Central and South America used cacao beans (the source of chocolate) as currency.

Evaluate Money In Section 1, you learned that money should function as a medium of exchange, a standard of value, and a store of value. Use what you've learned about these functions to evaluate how useful cacao beans might be as money today. Show your answer by filling in the table below.

Function	Possible Problems
Medium of exchange	
Standard of value	
Store of value	

Challenge How well do cacao beans exhibit each of the physical and economic properties of money?

4 Assess & Reteach

Assess Have students review the questions individually and jot down notes to help them answer each one. Then call on volunteers to answer the questions orally. Invite other students to add additional information, if desired.

Unit 4 Resource Book
- Section Quiz, p. 9

Interactive Review @ ClassZone.com
- Section Quiz

Test Generator CD-ROM
- Section Quiz

Reteach Organize students into four groups. Assign each group one of the main headings in the section in the form of a question. Have groups discuss their question and agree on an answer. Allow each group to present its question and answer to the class.

Unit 4 Resource Book
- Reteaching Activity, p. 10

Economics in Practice

Evaluate Money Possible problems: Medium of exchange—could be cumbersome or unacceptable; Standard of value—unclear what the beans are worth or how to measure them against other items; Store of value—not durable enough to retain value over time.

Challenge Physical: not as durable as coins; light but cumbersome; not divisible; lack uniformity (different sizes, shades, weights). Economic: unstable due to fluctuating supply; scarce until more are grown; not universally acceptable.

SECTION 1 ASSESSMENT ANSWERS

Reviewing Key Concepts

1. **a.** *standard of value*, p. 289; *store of value*, p. 289
   b. *commodity money*, p. 291; *representative money*, p. 291
   c. *demand deposits*, p. 293; *near money*, p. 293
2. With money as a medium of exchange, it is not necessary that buyers and sellers find someone who wants to trade for what they have to offer.
3. so that change can be made and so that prices can be flexible
4. because the owner of the checking account can use checks to convert the funds in the account into currency on demand
5. Fiat money is not dependent on the supply of a commodity to remain stable. The government controls the supply of fiat money to maintain stability.
6. See page 288 for an example of a completed diagram. Stability refers to the store of value and it is scarcity that allows money to have value. Acceptability is related to people using money as a medium of exchange.

Critical Thinking

7. checking accounts, coins, paper money, travelers' checks
8. The government prefers coins' durability; consumers prefer dollar bills' portability.
9. store of value because the money (plus interest) was there for Maria after 10 years
10. because people prefer to keep their money where it can earn interest and then convert it to transactions money when they need it

Economics in Practice

See answers in side column above.

1 Plan & Prepare

Section 2 Objectives

- describe how banking developed in the United States
- identify the banking institutions that operate in the United States

2 Focus & Motivate

Connecting to Everyday Life Explain that this section focuses on the development of the U.S. banking system. Encourage students to suggest some of the benefits that banks provide based on their personal experiences.

Taking Notes Remind students to take notes as they read by completing a chart. They can use the Graphic Organizer at **Interactive Review @ClassZone.com**. A sample is shown below.

Development of U.S. Banking

Origins	19th Century	20th Century
First bank of the United States, 1791–1811 privately owned national bank helped control currency opposed by Antifederalists	Second bank of the United States, 1816–1836 wildcat banking—state banks, little regulation, multiple currencies 1860s—greenbacks, system of national banks, currency backed by U.S. bonds 1900—gold standard	Federal reserve system (1913), true central bank, national currency tight regulation begins during Great Depression, FDIC protects depositors deregulation contributes to S&L crisis in 1980

SECTION 2

The Development of U.S. Banking

OBJECTIVES

In Section 2, you will
- describe how banking developed in the United States
- identify the banking institutions that operate in the United States

KEY TERMS

state bank, *p. 296*
national bank, *p. 299*
gold standard, *p. 299*

TAKING NOTES

As you read Section 2, complete a chart using the key concepts and other helpful words and phrases. Use the Graphic Organizer at **Interactive Review @ ClassZone.com**

Development of U.S. Banking		
Origins	19th Century	20th Century

The Origins of Banking

KEY CONCEPTS

Modern banking arose in Italy in the late Middle Ages. Italian merchants stored money or valuables for wealthy people and issued receipts that promised to return the property on demand. They realized that they did not have to hold all the deposits, since all depositors did not reclaim their property at the same time, but could lend some of the deposits and earn interest on those loans. This was the beginning of fractional reserve banking (see Section 3), the practice of holding only a fraction of the money deposited in a bank and lending the rest.

Early "Bankers" The Italian word *banco,* means "bench." From benches in the street, Italian merchants used some practices that are part of banking today.

In colonial America, many merchants followed the same practice. However, these banks were far from secure. If a merchant's business failed, depositors lost all of their savings. After the Revolutionary War, many **state banks**—banks chartered, or licensed, by state governments—were established. Some of these banks, however, followed practices that tended to create instability and disorder. Many issued their own currency that was not linked to reserves of gold or silver held by the bank.

QUICK REFERENCE

A **state bank** is a bank chartered by a state government.

SECTION 2 PROGRAM RESOURCES

ON LEVEL

Lesson Plans
- Core, pp. 34

Unit 4 Resource Book
- Reading Study Guide, pp. 11–12
- Economic Skills and Problem Solving Activity, pp. 31–32
- Section Quiz, p. 19

STRUGGLING READERS

Unit 4 Resource Book
- Reading Study Guide with Additional Support, pp. 13–15
- Reteaching Activity, p. 20

ENGLISH LEARNERS

Unit 4 Resource Book
- Reading Study Guide with Additional Support (Spanish), pp. 16–18

INCLUSION

Lesson Plans
- Modified for Inclusion, pp. 34

GIFTED AND TALENTED

Unit 4 Resource Book
- Readings in Free Enterprise: Both Post Office and Bank? pp. 33–34

TECHNOLOGY

eEdition DVD-ROM

eEdition Online

Power Presentation DVD-ROM

Economics Concepts Transparencies
- CT34 History of Banking Timeline

Daily Test Practice Transparencies, TT34

ClassZone.com

ECONOMICS PACESETTER

Alexander Hamilton: Shaping a Banking System

Imagine what it would be like if every bank issued its own currency. How would buyers know if sellers would accept their money? How would sellers know if the money they received was worth anything? That was the confusing situation that Alexander Hamilton faced when he became Secretary of the Treasury in 1789. He immediately set to work to bring stability to U. S. banking.

The First Bank of the United States

Hamilton was a leading Federalist who believed in a strong central government. He proposed chartering a privately owned national bank to put the government on a sound financial footing. This bank would issue a national currency and help control the money supply by refusing to accept currency from state banks that was not backed by gold or silver. It also would lend money to the federal government, state banks, and businesses.

The Constitution did not specifically authorize Congress to charter a national bank. The Antifederalists, led by Thomas Jefferson and James Madison, interpreted the Constitution strictly and feared putting too much power in the hands of the central government. Hamilton argued that the Constitution implied that the federal government had the authority to create a national bank to carry out its duty to regulate the currency.

Hamilton won the fight, and the First Bank of the United States was chartered in 1791. Over time, it achieved the financial goals that Hamilton had set. However, opponents argued that the bank's policies restrained economic growth, and Congress refused to renew the charter in 1811.

The fact that Hamilton was the architect of the bank was always a strike against it, as he had made many enemies during his career. (One, Aaron Burr, killed him in a duel.) Maybe Hamilton was right when he said, "Men often oppose a thing merely because they have had no agency in planning it, or because it may have been planned by those whom they dislike."

Alexander Hamilton (above) and the First Bank of the United States (right)

FAST FACTS

Alexander Hamilton

Position: First Secretary of the Treasury (1789–1795)

Born: January 11, 1755 in Nevis, British West Indies

Died: July 12, 1804

Writings: *The Federalist Papers* (1787), with James Madison and John Jay; *Report on a National Bank* (1790)

Major Accomplishment: Strengthened the national government and established the First Bank of the United States

Hamilton's Visible Legacy: Portrait on the $10 bill

Economics Update

Learn more about Alexander Hamilton at **ClassZone.com**

APPLICATION Making Inferences

A. How did the First National Bank force state banks to become more stable?
by requiring that they back their paper money with gold and silver coin

3 Teach

The Origins of Banking

Discuss

- How did Italian merchants begin the practice of fractional reserve banking? *(They lent money that was deposited with them because not all deposits were reclaimed at once.)*
- Why was currency that was not backed by gold or silver a cause of financial instability? *(There was nothing to give the money value.)*

Alexander Hamilton

More About . . .

The First Bank of the United States
Hamilton modeled the First Bank on the Bank of England. The bank was headquartered in Philadelphia, with branches in eight cities. It was set up with capital of $10 million.

The bank was run in a conservative fashion and met the government's needs for depositing funds, collecting taxes, paying bills, and borrowing money.

Economics Update

At **ClassZone.com** students will find additional information about Alexander Hamilton.

INDIVIDUAL ACTIVITY

Researching Banking History

Time 45 Minutes 

Task Research some aspect of early banking history and write a report.

Materials Needed computer with Internet access or library resources, paper and pen

Activity

- Allow students to choose a topic related to the events in banking history mentioned on pages 296–297. Some possible topics include early Italian banking, banking in colonial America, early state banks, and supporters or opponents of the First Bank.
- Direct students to use the Internet or library resources to research their topic. Remind them to keep a list of their sources and include it at the end of the report.
- Have students write a one- or two-page report on their topic.
- Invite volunteers to share their reports with the class. Discuss some common problems that banks face.

Rubric

	Understanding of Origins of Banking	Presentation of Information
4	excellent	clear and complete
3	good	mostly clear
2	fair	sometimes clear
1	poor	sketchy

19th-Century Developments

Discuss

- Why did the need for a national bank become more urgent in times of war? *(Possible answer: because the central government needed a way to raise money to finance the war and to have more control over the economy as a whole)*
- How did the National Banking Act of 1863 try to address some of the earlier criticism of the National Bank? *(It created a system of banks chartered and regulated by the federal government, instead of a single national bank that could be seen as too powerful.)*

More About . . .

The Second Bank of the United States

The Second Bank was similar in structure to the First Bank, but had capital of $35 million. While the First Bank had always been well-run and financially successful, the Second Bank was not strong in its first seven years, and many people were hostile to it.

After Nicholas Biddle became president of the bank in 1823, he turned it into a strong central bank with 29 branches. Although Biddle was a very competent banker, he was arrogant and used the bank to further his political goals and to increase his power in Philadelphia. Biddle's actions caused the bank to develop many enemies. They included President Jackson, New York Democrats, and other bankers.

FIGURE 10.3 **Major Developments in American Banking**

1816 ◂ Congress charters Second Bank of the United States.

1863 ◂ Congress creates national banks and currency.

1775 | 1800 | 1825 | 1850 | 1875

1791 Congress charters First Bank of the United States.

1837–1865 Wildcat banking leads to unstable currency. ▸

19th-Century Developments

KEY CONCEPTS

Without a central bank, the government had difficulty financing the War of 1812 against Britain. Furthermore, state banks soon returned to the unrestrained issuing of currency that was not linked to reserves of gold or silver held by the banks. The resulting increase in the money supply led to inflation during the war.

The Second Bank of the United States

Congress finally agreed to charter the Second Bank of the United States in 1816. The new bank had greater financial resources than the First Bank and succeeded in making the money supply more stable. Opponents continued to see the central bank as too powerful and too closely aligned with the wealthy. President Andrew Jackson was an outspoken critic who mistrusted banks and paper money He vetoed the renewal of its charter in 1832.

Wildcat Banking

After the Second Bank's charter lapsed in 1836, there was no federal oversight of the banking industry. During this period, all banks were state banks, each of which issued its own paper currency, called bank notes. States passed free banking laws that allowed individuals or groups that met its requirements to open banks.

Jackson and the Second Bank This 1828 cartoon lampoons Jackson's battle against the bank.

DIFFERENTIATING INSTRUCTION

Inclusion

Follow the Time Line

Have students use the time line to focus on events in the development of U.S. banking. Explain that the time line provides a visual summary of key topics in Sections 2 and 3.

- Make photocopies of the time line. Invite students to add other dates that they find in the text. Help them look for cause-and-effect relationships.
- At the end of each section, call on volunteers to use their time lines to summarize the significance of events.

Gifted and Talented

Debate the Gold Standard

Explain that the decision to adopt the gold standard in 1900 was controversial. Invite students to research the topic to find out who supported and opposed it and what their arguments were. Suggest that they look into the 1896 presidential campaign. Have students form two teams and informally debate the gold standard. Allow the class to vote on whether they are "for" or "against" based on the arguments. Discuss how the gold standard helped create stability in the banking system.

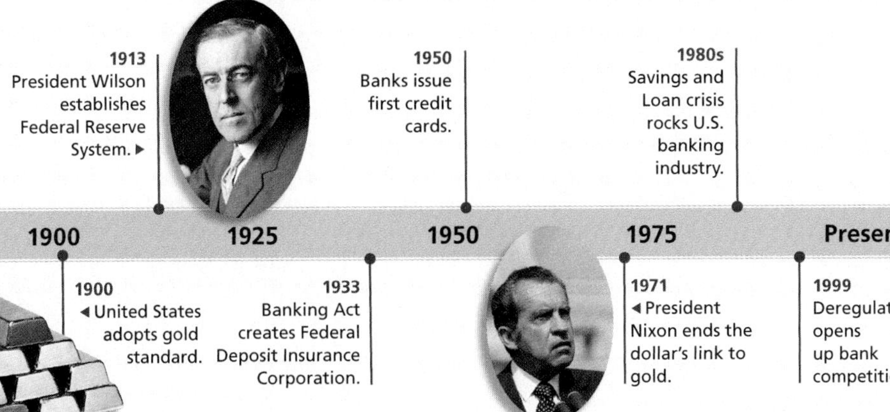
1913
President Wilson establishes Federal Reserve System. ▶
1950
Banks issue first credit cards.
1980s
Savings and Loan crisis rocks U.S. banking industry.
1900
1925
1950
1975
Present
1900
◀ United States adopts gold standard.
1933
Banking Act creates Federal Deposit Insurance Corporation.
1971
◀ President Nixon ends the dollar's link to gold.
1999
Deregulation opens up bank competition.

Some of these banks were located in remote areas to discourage people from redeeming their bank notes, which were often worth less outside the region where they had been issued. It was this practice, along with the questionable quality of many bank notes that resulted in the term *wildcat bank*. In addition, such banks were susceptible to bank runs when depositors demanded gold or silver for their currency. Since the banks often did not have sufficient reserves of these precious metals, financial panics and economic instability were common results.

The Struggle for Stability

During the Civil War, it was particularly difficult for the government to finance its operations without a national currency and a federal bank. The government's first solution to this problem was to issue a new currency backed by government bonds. These U.S. bank notes, called greenbacks, were printed with green ink.

In 1863, Congress passed the National Banking Act, which led to the creation of a system of **national banks**, banks chartered by the national government. The act provided for a national currency backed by U.S. Treasury bonds and regulated the minimum amount of capital required for national banks as well as the amount of reserves necessary to back the currency. Congress taxed state bank notes issued after 1865, effectively eliminating these notes from circulation.

In 1900, the government officially adopted the **gold standard**, a system in which the basic monetary unit—for example, one dollar—is equal to a set amount of gold. The national currency and gold standard helped to bring some stability to the banking system. Money was now uniform throughout the country, backed by something of intrinsic value, and limited by the supply of gold.

QUICK REFERENCE

National banks are banks chartered by the national government.

The **gold standard** is a system that backs the basic monetary unit with a set amount of gold.

APPLICATION Analyzing Effects

B. How did the National Banking Act of 1863 attempt to eliminate the problems caused by wildcat banking?

It set strict standards for national banks and provided for a national currency backed by government bonds to replace the state bank notes.

More About . . .

Greenbacks

Greenbacks are also referred to as "legal tenders" or "demand notes" and were the first fiat money issued by the U.S. government. They are also known as U.S. notes to distinguish them from Federal Reserve notes that make up most U.S. currency in circulation today.

Greenbacks were issued in denominations ranging from $1 to $1,000. During the Civil War their value depreciated rapidly; $1 in gold soon bought $2.85 worth of greenbacks. In 1878, Congress set a limit of about $300 million in greenbacks in circulation. None have been placed in circulation since 1971, although they are still legal tender and are redeemable at face value. They may be worth more than that to collectors.

CLASS ACTIVITY

Role-Playing Wildcat Banking

Time 45 Minutes 

Task Role-play scenarios that reflect the problems of wildcat banking.

Materials Needed paper (different colors optional) and markers

Activity

- Organize students into three groups representing bankers, businesses, and consumers. Invite each group to discuss the ways banking practices in the era of wildcat banking affected them.
- Have each banker create currency using different colored paper or a design with the name of the bank on it. Suggest that they also list some rules for customers.
- Ask students to role-play scenarios showing how banks caused difficulties for businesses and consumers, such as problems with acceptability, redemption (decline in value of bank notes), and bank runs.
- Discuss how the role-plays showed the problems with wildcat banking.

Rubric

	Wildcat Banking	Presentation of Information
4	excellent	clear; creative
3	good	mostly clear and creative
2	fair	sometimes clear and creative
1	poor	sketchy

20th-Century Developments

Discuss

- Why was the system of national banks unable to create economic stability? *(because the system had no central decision-making authority and was unable to regulate the money supply)*
- What were the causes of the failures of financial institutions during the Great Depression and the S&L crisis? *(Banks failed during the depression due to bank runs by depositors; S&Ls failed due to risky lending practices.)*

More About . . .

The Savings & Loan Crisis
Deregulation of the S&Ls in the 1980s occurred against the backdrop of high interest rates and a booming real estate market. These factors combined to give the S&Ls an incentive to offer higher rates to attract depositors. At the same time, they made riskier nonresidential and commercial loans for which they could charge higher interest.

The S&Ls also began to issue credit cards. These practices made them competitive with commercial banks. But the S&Ls were not supervised as closely as the banks. In the aftermath of the crisis, S&Ls became more tightly integrated into the banking system with similar levels of supervision and FDIC insurance.

20th-Century Developments

KEY CONCEPTS

The system of national banks and a national currency linked to the gold standard initially brought stability to U.S. banking. Yet the economy still experienced periods of inflation and recession and financial panics. This economic instability was largely due to the lack of a central decision-making institution that could manage the money supply in a flexible way to meet the economy's changing needs.

A New Central Bank

In 1913, Congress passed the Federal Reserve Act, which established the Federal Reserve System (commonly known as the Fed)—a true central bank. It consists of 12 regional banks with a central decision-making board. The Fed provides financial services to the federal government, makes loans to banks that serve the public, issues Federal Reserve notes as the national currency, and regulates the money supply to ensure that money retains its purchasing power. You'll learn more about the structure and functions of the Federal Reserve in Chapter 16.

The Great Depression and the New Deal

At the start of the Great Depression in 1929, many banks failed due to bank runs, as consumers panicked and withdrew all of their money. When the banks failed, many more depositors lost their money. Part of President Franklin Roosevelt's New Deal program was the Banking Act of 1933, which instituted reforms such as regulating interest rates that banks could pay and prohibiting banks from selling stocks. The Federal Deposit Insurance Corporation (FDIC) provided federal insurance so that if a bank failed, people would no longer lose their money. This legislation set the tone for almost 50 years by increasing the regulation of banking in the United States.

Deregulation and the S&L Crisis

In 1980 and 1982, Congress passed laws that lifted government limits on savings interest rates. This allowed savings and loans associations (S&Ls) to operate much like commercial banks. Deregulation encouraged the S&Ls to take more risks in the types of loans they made. As a result, many S&Ls failed and lost their depositors' money. Congress agreed to fund the S&L industry's restructuring in order to protect consumers, which cost taxpayers hundreds of billions of dollars.

The S&L Crisis Depositors camp out to withdraw their money in May 1985.

APPLICATION Comparing and Contrasting

C. How are the First Bank of the United States and the Federal Reserve different?
First Bank—single bank with no direct control of state banks and their currency; Federal Reserve—system of regional banks, which issues the only legal currency

DIFFERENTIATING INSTRUCTION

Struggling Readers

Diagram Cause and Effect
Help students understand cause-and-effect relationships in 20th-century U.S. banking.

- Model the creation of a cause-and-effect chain based on the Key Concepts paragraph. Explain that the words *due to* signal a cause, which may have both short-term and long-term effects.
- Organize students into three groups. Have each create a similar diagram for one of the developments on page 300.
- Allow each group to explain its diagram.

English Learners

Create a Cluster Diagram
Help students understand the relationship between the term *bank* and the types of financial institutions described on pages 301–302. Create a cluster diagram on the board with *bank* in the center. Have students suggest terms from the Key Concepts paragraphs. Clarify which are synonyms for *bank (financial institution, commercial bank, savings and loan institution, credit union)* and which provide information about bank services *(deposits, loans).*

Financial Institutions in the United States

KEY CONCEPTS

The term *bank* is used to refer to almost any kind of financial institution that takes in deposits and makes loans, helping individuals, businesses, and governments to manage their money. In the end, though, the goal of a bank is to earn a profit.

All financial institutions receive a charter from the government, either state or federal. Government regulations set the amount of money the owners of a bank must invest in it, the size of the reserves a bank must hold, and the ways that loans may be made. The term may refer to commercial banks, savings and loan associations, or credit unions.

Economics Update
Find an update on U.S. financial institutions at **ClassZone.com**

In the past, these institutions provided very different and distinct services. Today, however, because of the deregulation of banking, these distinctions are much less apparent. The distinctive characteristics of each type of financial institution are described in more detail below. Figure 10.4 on page 302 compares the three types of banks based on numbers of institutions and total assets.

TYPE 1 Commercial Banks

Privately owned commercial banks are the oldest form of banking and are the financial institutions most commonly thought of as banks. As their name implies, commercial banks were initially established to provide loans to businesses. Now they provide a wide range of services, including checking and savings accounts, loans, investment assistance, and credit cards to both businesses and individual consumers. You will learn more about these services in Section 3.

In 2003, there were about 2,000 national commercial banks and about 5,800 state-chartered banks insured by the FDIC. All national commercial banks belong to the Federal Reserve System, but only about 16 percent of state-chartered banks choose to join the Fed. About 1,500 of these commercial banks are large ones with assets of $300 million dollars or more. In 2005, the seven largest banks in the United States held 50 percent of the total assets controlled by all these large banks.

TYPE 2 Savings Institutions

Savings and loan associations (S&Ls) began in the United States in the 1830s. They were originally chartered by individual states as mutual societies for two purposes—to take savings deposits and provide home mortgage loans. In other words, groups of people pooled their savings in a safe place to earn interest and have a source of financing for families who wanted to buy homes.

The S&Ls continue to fulfill these purposes, but they now also offer many of the services provided by commercial banks. Since 1933, the federal government may also charter S&Ls, and since 1982, many federally chartered S&Ls have chosen to call themselves savings banks. Many savings institutions are now financed through the sale of stock, just as commercial banks are.

Financial Institutions in the United States

Discuss

- Why are the three kinds of financial institutions more similar now than in the past? *(because deregulation allows them all to offer basically the same services)*
- What was different about the original purpose of commercial banks and savings and loan associations? *(Commercial banks were set up to make loans to businesses. S&Ls were set up to help individuals save and buy homes.)*
- What are two ways that credit unions are different from other financial institutions? *(They have membership requirements, and they are nonprofit organizations.)*

At **ClassZone.com** students will find additional information about U.S. financial institutions.

SMALL GROUP ACTIVITY

Exploring Local Financial Institutions

Time 45 Minutes 

Task Gather information on local financial institutions and hold a panel discussion.

Materials Needed computer with Internet access or information from financial institutions

Activity

- Organize students into three groups to research the three types of financial institution.
- Direct groups to use the yellow pages of the phone book to estimate the number of each type in your community.
- Encourage each group to study one or two representative institutions in more depth by using the Internet or visiting the institutions to gather information about their history, size, and services.
- Have groups organize their information and choose one or two representatives to speak as "experts" on a panel about the different kinds of financial institutions.

Rubric

	Understanding of Financial Institutions	Presentation of Information
4	excellent	clear and complete
3	good	mostly clear
2	fair	sometimes clear
1	poor	sketchy

Technomics

Statistical Abstract of the United States
The U.S. Census Bureau publishes the *Statistical Abstract of the United States* once per year (a recent exception being a combined 2004–2005 edition). These publications, dating back to 1878, are available online at www.census.gov. Files are available for downloading and may be saved for offline viewing.

Section 25 of the *Statistical Abstract* covers many aspects of banking, finance, and insurance. Each edition provides both current and recent historical data, with specific sources cited for each table. The introduction to the section also points to additional sources of information.

Analyzing Graphs: Figure 10.4

Direct students to read the key to make sure they understand that one bar in each pair represents the number of institutions and the other represents the financial assets of those institutions. Financial assets include things such as cash, loans, property, and securities (stocks and bonds). Ask students what conclusion they can draw about the average size of credit unions compared to other types of institutions. *(Most credit unions are small compared to banks and savings institutions.)*

Answers

1. *credit unions; they're affiliated with thousands of workplaces and organizations nationwide*
2. *The assets in savings institutions are about 20 percent of the assets in commercial banks.*

In 2003, there were about 800 federally chartered savings institutions and 600 state-chartered institutions. These institutions are now insured under a specific fund of the FDIC as part of the reforms that followed the S&L crisis of the 1980s.

TYPE 3 Credit Unions

Credit unions are cooperative savings and lending institutions, rather like the early S&Ls. They offer services similar to commercial banks and S&Ls, including savings and checking accounts, but specialize in mortgages and auto loans.

The first credit union in the United States was chartered in 1909. The Federal Credit Union Act of 1934 created a system of federally chartered credit unions. In 2003, there were about 5,800 federally chartered credit unions and about 3,600 chartered by the states. Most credit unions have deposit insurance through the National Credit Union Association (NCUA), similar to the FDIC.

The major difference between credit unions and other financial institutions is that credit unions have membership requirements. To become a member, a person must work for a particular company, belong to a particular organization, or be part of a particular community affiliated with the credit union. Credit unions are cooperatives—nonprofit organizations owned by and operated for members, who numbered more than 80 million nationwide in 2003.

FIGURE 10.4 BANKING INSTITUTIONS IN THE UNITED STATES

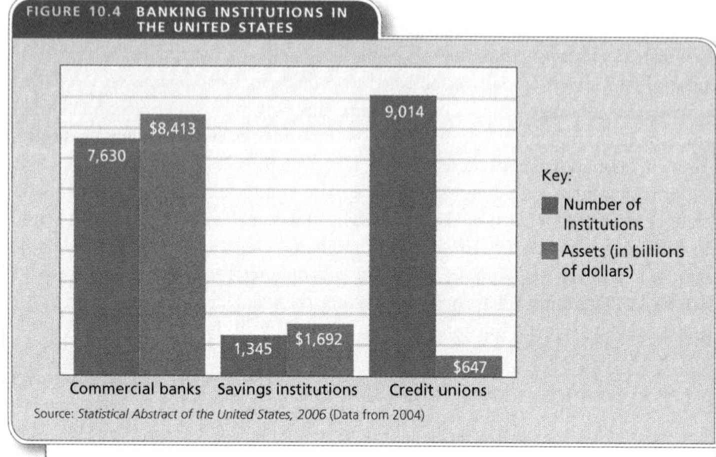

Source: *Statistical Abstract of the United States, 2006* (Data from 2004)

ANALYZE CHARTS

1. Which type of bank has the largest number of institutions? Why?
2. How do the assets held in savings institutions compare to the assets held in commercial banks?

APPLICATION Analyzing and Interpreting Data

D. Which type of bank described above has the largest percentage of its institutions chartered by the federal government? Why might this situation have developed?
Credit unions, 61 percent. Credit unions had a shorter history of being chartered by states before the Federal Credit Union Act passed in 1934.

DIFFERENTIATING INSTRUCTION

Struggling Readers

Compare and Contrast
Help students understand similarities and differences among the different types of financial institutions by working with them to create a three-way Venn diagram on the board. Ask volunteers to read Key Concepts paragraphs and the description of each type of institution aloud. Point out that the differences among institutions may be from the past. Have students suggest where to place the characteristics and give reasons for their choices. Call on volunteers to summarize the diagram.

Gifted and Talented

Use the Statistical Abstract
Direct students to the online version of the *Statistical Abstract of the United States* at www.census.gov to find additional data about the three types of financial institutions. They might focus on the amount of assets, the number of branch offices, or a breakdown of institutions by state. Encourage students to create graphs from the data they research. Allow volunteers to present their graphs to the class and explain what additional insights they gained about U.S. financial institutions.

SECTION 2 Assessment

Online Quiz
ClassZone.com

REVIEWING KEY CONCEPTS

1. Use each of the three terms below in a sentence that illustrates the meaning of the term.
   a. *state bank* **b.** *national bank* **c.** *gold standard*
2. Explain the relationship between the gold standard and the concept of representative money.
3. How does the Federal Reserve System serve as a central bank?
4. What is the difference between a national bank and a state bank?
5. How did the FDIC make fractional reserve banking less risky for consumers?
6. **Using Your Notes** What role did state banks play in the era of wildcat banking? Refer to your completed chart.

Development of U.S. Banking		
Origins	19th Century	20th Century

Use the Graphic Organizer at **Interactive Review @ ClassZone.com**

CRITICAL THINKING

7. **Creating Graphs** Use the information in Figure 10.4 to create two pie graphs, one showing the percentage that each type of bank contributes to the total number of financial institutions and another showing the percentage that each type of bank contributes to total bank assets. State one conclusion that you can draw from the two graphs.
   Use ***SMARTGrapher*** **@ ClassZone.com** to complete this activity.
8. **Synthesizing Economic Information** On the basis of what you learned about the history of U.S. banking in the 19th and 20th centuries, were Alexander Hamilton's ideas about the need for a central bank and a national currency shown to be mostly accurate? Cite specific examples to support your answer.
9. **Applying Economic Concepts** Suppose that Mariel deposits $100 in her local bank. If the Fed's reserve requirement is 15 percent, how much can the bank loan out on the basis of Mariel's deposit? What concept does this scenario illustrate?
10. **Challenge** How do banks facilitate saving and borrowing in the same way that money facilitates buying and selling?

ECONOMICS IN PRACTICE

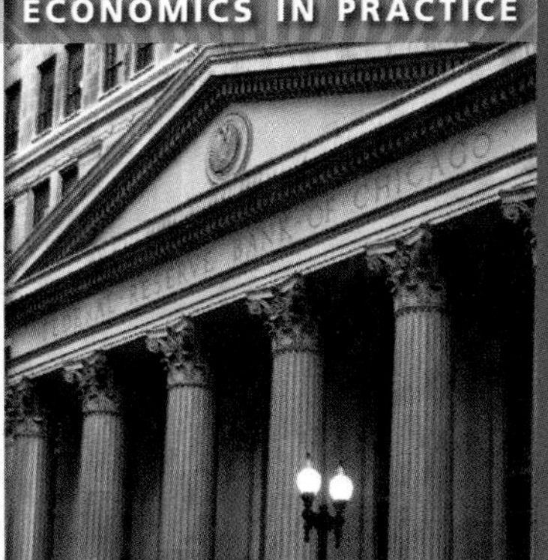

Constructing Graphs
Consider what you have learned about different types of financial institutions. The table below shows how the numbers of commercial banks and savings institutions have changed over time.

Year	Commercial Banks	Savings Institutions
1985	14,417	3,626
1990	12,347	2,815
1995	9,942	2,030
2000	8,315	1,589
2004	7,630	1,345

Create Line Graphs Use the information in the table to create two line graphs that show the changes in the numbers of each type of bank.

Use ***SMARTGrapher*** **@ ClassZone.com** to complete this activity.

Challenge On the basis of this information, what trends can you identify? Which type of financial institution experienced a greater percentage loss from 1985 to 2004?

4 Assess & Reteach

Assess Have pairs of students use the Section Assessment to quiz each other, taking turns answering the questions.

Unit 4 Resource Book
- Section Quiz, p. 19

Interactive Review @ ClassZone.com
- Section Quiz

Test Generator CD-ROM
- Section Quiz

Reteach Write each event from the time line on pages 298–299 on a slip of paper. (Skip the four events that will be covered in Section 3.) Call on nine volunteers to choose one of the slips of paper. Have these students arrange themselves into a living time line and explain the significance of their event to the development of U.S. banking.

Unit 4 Resource Book
- Reteaching Activity, p. 20

SMARTGrapher Students can create graphs for question 7 and the Economics in Practice using **SmartGrapher @ ClassZone.com.**

SECTION 2 ASSESSMENT ANSWERS

Reviewing Key Concepts

1. **a.** *state bank*, p. 296
   b. *national bank*, p. 299
   c. *gold standard*, p. 299
2. When a currency is on the gold standard it is the value of the gold that backs the value of the representative money.
3. It regulates the activities of U.S. banks and issues a national currency. It also serves as the main bank for the federal government.
4. A national bank is chartered by the federal government; state banks are chartered by state governments.
5. The FDIC ensures that if a bank fails, depositors will not lose all of their money.
6. See page 296 for an example of a completed diagram. The era of wildcat banking was characterized by large numbers of loosely regulated state banks, each of which issued its own currrency.

Critical Thinking

7. Pie graphs: financial institutions—commercial banks 42%, savings institutions 8%, credit unions 50%; assets—banks 78%, savings 16%, credit unions 6%. Possible conclusion: commercial banks are less than 50% of the institutions but control about 80%of assets.
8. Possible answers: He was right because without a national bank the government had difficulty raising money; lack of a national currrency led to instability (wildcat era).
9. $85; fractional reserve banking
10. Without banks it would be difficult for savers/borrowers to come together, just as money makes it easier for buyers and sellers to come together.

Economics in Practice

Create Line Graphs Line graphs should accurately reflect the data shown on the table, showing a steady decline of both kinds of institutions over the period.

Challenge The number of banks is decreasing. Savings institutions decreased by 63%, while commercial banks decreased by 47%.

1 Plan & Prepare

Section 3 Objectives

- describe the services that banks provide
- discuss the changes that deregulation has brought to banking
- explain how technology has changed banking in the United States

2 Focus & Motivate

Connecting to Everyday Life Explain that this section focuses on recent changes in banking. Invite students to predict some ways that computer technology will further change the banking industry.

Taking Notes Remind students to take notes as they read by completing a hierarchy diagram. They can use the Graphic Organizer at **Interactive Review @ ClassZone.com**. A sample is shown below.

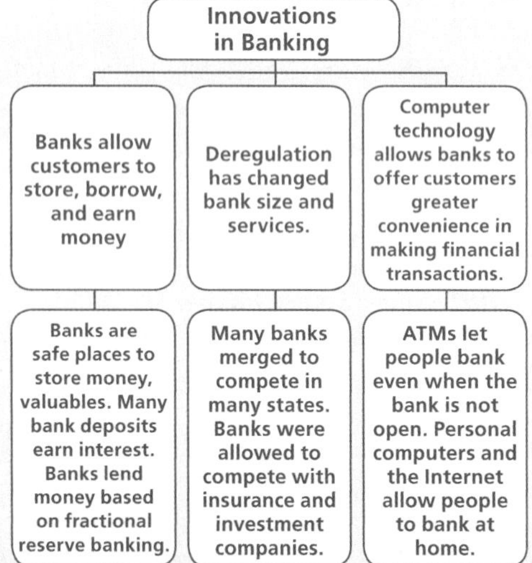

SECTION 3

Innovations in Modern Banking

OBJECTIVES

In Section 3, you will
- describe the services that banks provide
- discuss the changes that deregulation has brought to banking
- explain how technology has changed banking in the United States

KEY TERMS

automated teller machine, *p. 308*
debit card, *p. 308*
stored-value card, *p. 308*

TAKING NOTES

As you read Section 3, complete a hierarchy diagram to track main ideas and supporting details. Use the Graphic Organizer at **Interactive Review @ ClassZone.com**

Innovations in Banking
main idea | main idea | main idea
details | details | details

What Services Do Banks Provide?

KEY CONCEPTS

Banks offer a number of services that allow them to act like "money stores." In other words, just as stores are places where goods are bought and sold, banks are places where money can be bought (borrowed) and sold (lent). By using these services, customers are able to do three things—store money, earn money, and borrow money. Banks are businesses that earn money by charging interest or fees on these services.

SERVICE 1 Customers Can Store Money

As you read in Section 2, banks began as safe places to store money and other valuables. They still serve the same purpose today. Customers deposit money in the bank, and the bank stores currency in vaults and is also insured against theft and other loss. Customers' bank accounts are also insured in case the bank fails. Banks are also a safe place to store important papers and valuables—through the use of safe deposit boxes.

SERVICE 2 Customers Can Earn Money

When customers deposit their money in bank accounts, they can earn money on their deposits. Savings accounts and some checking accounts pay some level of interest. Banks offer other accounts, such as money market accounts and certificates of deposits (CDs), that pay a higher rate of interest. You will learn more about saving and investing in Chapter 11 and in Consumer and Personal Finance, which begins on page 574.

SECTION 3 PROGRAM RESOURCES

ON LEVEL

Lesson Plans
- Core, p. 35

Unit 4 Resource Book
- Reading Study Guide, pp. 21–22
- Economic Skills and Problem Solving Activity, pp. 31–32
- Section Quiz, p. 29

STRUGGLING READERS

Unit 4 Resource Book
- Reading Study Guide with Additional Support, pp. 23–25
- Reteaching Activity, p. 30

ENGLISH LEARNERS

Unit 4 Resource Book
- Reading Study Guide with Additional Support (Spanish), pp. 26–28

INCLUSION

Lesson Plans
- Modified for Inclusion, p. 35

GIFTED AND TALENTED

Unit 4 Resource Book
- Case Study Resources: New Math for College Costs, pp. 35–36

TECHNOLOGY

eEdition DVD-ROM

eEdition Online

Power Presentation DVD-ROM

Economics Concepts Transparencies
- CT35 Fed Reserve Requirement

Daily Test Practice Transparencies, TT35

ClassZone.com

SERVICE 3 Customers Can Borrow Money

Banks also allow customers to borrow money through the practice of fractional reserve banking. (See Figure 10.5.) The percent of deposits that banks must keep in reserve is set by the Fed.

Banks provide customers, each of whom must be approved by the bank, with different loans for different circumstances. One common loan is a mortgage. A mortgage loan allows a buyer to purchase a real estate property, such as a house, without paying the entire value of the property up front. The lender and the borrower agree on a time period for the loan (often up to 30 years) and an interest rate to be paid to the lender. From this, a monthly mortgage payment amount is settled. In this arrangement, the real estate property acts as collateral. So if the borrower defaults on the loan (stops making the payments), the lender takes control of the property. It can then be sold by the bank to cover the balance of the mortgage.

It may not seem so, but a purchase made on a credit card is a loan too. Credit cards are issued by banks to users who are, in effect, borrowers. When you use a credit card to buy a new skateboard or a tank of gasoline, the issuing bank pays the seller and lends you the money. When you pay the bank back, you're repaying a loan. And if you don't pay it back within a month, you'll owe the bank extra in interest.

FIGURE 10.5 Fractional Reserve Banking

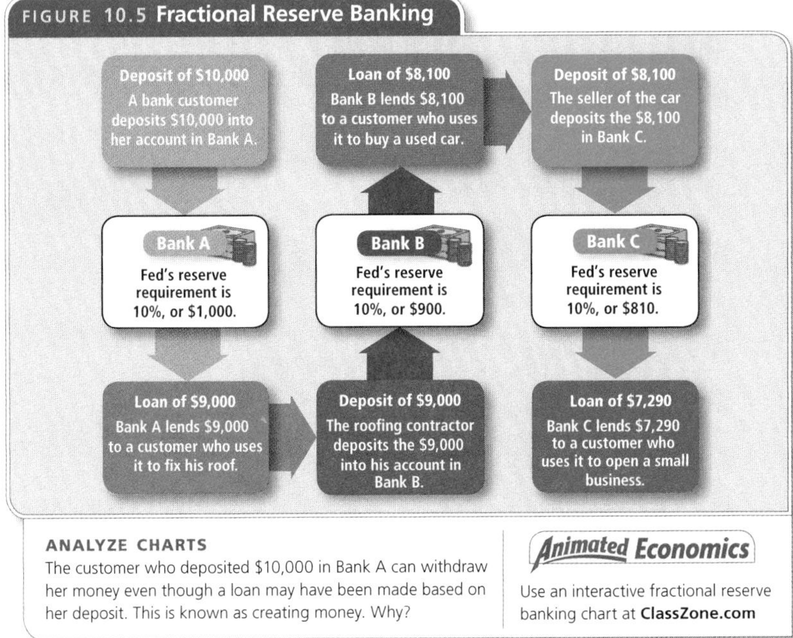

ANALYZE CHARTS
The customer who deposited $10,000 in Bank A can withdraw her money even though a loan may have been made based on her deposit. This is known as creating money. Why?

Animated Economics
Use an interactive fractional reserve banking chart at **ClassZone.com**

APPLICATION Applying Economic Concepts

A. Explain the ways in which bank transactions are beneficial to customers and banks.
Customers: safe place for money and other valuables; can earn interest; can obtain needed loans. Banks: can earn money by making loans and charging interest.

3 Teach

What Services Do Banks Provide?

Discuss

- Why do banks pay interest on some bank accounts? *(Possible answer: to encourage people to deposit money in the bank, so the bank can make loans at a higher rate of interest)*
- What do a mortgage and a credit card have in common? *(Both are loans from a bank.)*

Analyzing Charts: Figure 10.5

On the board, continue the fractional reserve banking scenario through Bank D, Bank E, and Bank F. Round any numbers that are not whole dollars. *(Bank D: $7,290 deposit, $729 reserve, $6,561 loan; Bank E: $6,561 deposit, $656 reserve, $5,905 loan; Bank F: $5,905 deposit, $591 reserve, $5,314 loan)*

Answer

Because of her deposit the bank was eligible to make a loan. The depositor has her money and the person who receives the loan also now has money. The loan recipient's money was, in effect, created by the initial $10,000 deposit.

Animated Economics Animation and audio highlight how fractional reserve banking works. It will help students understand how a savings deposit creates money.

SMALL GROUP ACTIVITY

Researching Banking Services

Time 45 Minutes 

Task Research a category of banking services and create a classroom display.

Materials Needed computer with Internet access or information from financial institutions, paper and markers

Activity

- Organize students into three groups to research the three categories of banking services.
- One group might research bank security measures, deposit insurance, and safe deposit boxes. Other groups might research different kinds of interest-bearing accounts or loans.
- Encourage students to use Internet resources or visit local banks to gather information. Have them find out how banks make money on these services.
- Allow groups to create classroom displays of the information they find and present their findings to the class.

Rubric

	Understanding of Banking Services	Presentation of Information
4	excellent	clear and complete
3	good	mostly clear
2	fair	sometimes clear
1	poor	sketchy

Banking Deregulation

Discuss

- Why has the pace of mergers slowed down since 1998? *(Possible answer: because there are now fewer banks left to merge due to earlier mergers)*
- What is the presumed benefit to consumers of financial "supermarkets?" *(Such organizations would make it easier for consumers to get all their financial services in one place.)*

Analyzing Charts: Figure 10.6

Explain that mergers usually happen over a period of time, with banks being acquired one by one. This chart summarizes how several large banking organizations emerged from a series of mergers. Many of the banks shown in the left-hand column may have resulted from earlier mergers. Point out that when banks merge, the acquired banks usually take on the name of the acquiring bank. Have students find bank names that suggest the region where the banks were located. *(Bank Boston, Chase Manhattan, First Chicago)*

Answers

Possible answer: Target banks may want to benefit from a larger bank's resources, such as a well-known name, a better computer system, or more capital.

Banking Deregulation

KEY CONCEPTS

Prior to the 1980s, government tightly regulated the amount of interest that banks could pay on deposits and could charge on loans. Regulations also prevented banks from operating in more than one state. Several states also had limitations on the number of branches that a bank could have within a state. Deregulation in the 1980s and 1990s ended these restrictions and brought major changes to what we think of as banks and how they operate.

Bank Mergers

The end of restrictions on interstate banking led to a large number of mergers, as larger banks acquired smaller ones and smaller ones joined together to be able to enter different geographic markets. The number of mergers has steadily declined since 1998, when there were almost 500, to less than 200 in 2003. Yet as Figure 10.6 shows, mergers that created very large banking organizations continued. In 2004,

FIGURE 10.6 Major Bank Mergers

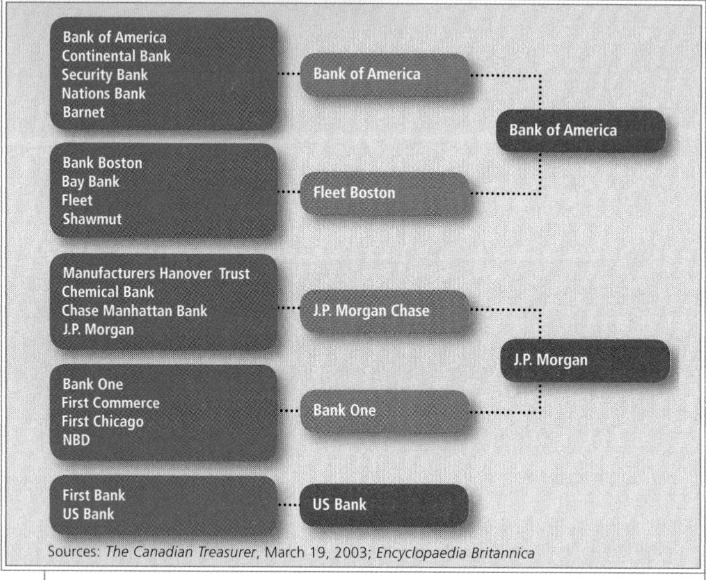

Sources: *The Canadian Treasurer*, March 19, 2003; *Encyclopaedia Britannica*

ANALYZE CHARTS

In most of the mergers shown here, the acquiring banks hoped to increase their customer base by gaining offices in regions where they had no presence. What reasons might target banks (the banks acquired) have for entering into a merger?

306 Chapter 10

DIFFERENTIATING INSTRUCTION

Struggling Readers

Access Prior Knowledge

Have students recall what they learned about deregulation, mergers, and competition in Chapter 7. Call on volunteers to define these terms and write the definitions on the board. Discuss governmental bodies that are involved in evaluating mergers *(the Federal Trade Commission and the Department of Justice)* and in passing laws that regulate businesses *(Congress).* Ask students to look on page 307 for some benefits and problems that have resulted from banking deregulation.

Gifted and Talented

Evaluate Deregulation

Invite students to use Internet or library resources to research an aspect of bank deregulation. They might choose specific bank mergers—perhaps ones that affected their community—and evaluate the effects on consumers, employees, and communities. Or they might choose to research how financial services companies are competing after the Financial Services Act of 1999. Have students present their findings and draw conclusions about them in written reports.

Bank of America Investment Services Inc. and J. P. Morgan Chase & Co. became two of the largest banks in the United States, with assets of around $1 trillion each. In contrast, some 95 percent of commercial banks have assets of $1 billion or less.

One benefit from the mergers has been increased competition that has kept interest rates low and resulted in more consumer services. There has also been an increase in the number of bank branches, even while the number of banks has declined. Larger banks and more branches offer customers greater availability of services. Many banks also cite economies of scale made possible by the mergers, as banks are able to spread their costs, especially for new technology, over more customers. However, some see potential problems associated with mergers. Although competition between these merged banks has heated up, there are increasingly fewer banks to choose from. Further, it is feared that larger banks may show less interest in small customers and local community issues. If this is the case, consumers will choose a bank that provides them with what they want, and the large banks will either respond or lose customers.

Banking Services

The Financial Services Act of 1999 lifted the last restrictions from the Banking Act of 1933 that had prevented banks, insurance companies, and investment companies from selling the same products and competing with one another. This change allowed banks to sell stocks, bonds, and insurance. At the same time, some investment companies and insurance companies began offering traditional banking services.

The change in banking services was based on the idea that consumers would prefer to have a single source for all their financial services needs—something that might function as a kind of "financial supermarket." However, banks have not always been able to effectively realize the benefits they had envisioned from offering this array of services. While banks establish relationships with customers through deposit accounts and loans for homes and autos, they have not been as successful in selling insurance or in helping customers to buy and sell stocks and bonds. Most bank customers continue to look to traditional insurance companies for their insurance needs and investment brokers and mutual fund companies to meet investment desires.

Financial Freedom President Clinton signs the bill that eliminated restrictions in place since 1933.

▲ Roosevelt and the Banking Act of 1933

▲ Clinton and the Financial Services Act of 1999

APPLICATION Analyzing Effects

B. How did deregulation change the ways that banks competed?

Banks were able to operate in any state, they could compete nationwide, and they could also offer stocks, bonds, and insurance to compete with investment companies and insurance companies.

International Economics

European Bank Mergers

Bank mergers in European countries are not unusual. However, mergers across European borders were far less common because of different banking regulations and resistance to foreign ownership of banks in some countries. These difficulties led many European banks to look outside the region, particularly to the United States, for acquisition targets.

From 1985 to 1998, U.S. banks were three times as likely to be the targets rather than the acquirers in cross-border bank mergers. During 2001–2002, another wave of U.S. acquisitions by European banks occurred. In 2005, the European Commission announced that it would change banking laws to make cross-border mergers in Europe easier.

INDIVIDUAL ACTIVITY

Conducting an Interview about Banking Changes

Time 45 Minutes

Task Interview someone about changes in banking and write a summary.

Materials Needed paper and pen

Activity

- Invite students to interview a parent, grandparent, or other relative or friend who can comment on changes they have seen in banking during their lifetime. Encourage students to probe for changes in bank organizations, services, or technology.
- Ask students to write brief summaries of their interviews. Encourage them to put the personal experiences of the person they interviewed in the context of changes caused by deregulation or technology.
- Invite volunteers to share their interview summaries with the class. Discuss the causes of changes to the banking industry and the positive and negative effects of these changes as a class.

Rubric

	Understanding of Changes in Banking	Presentation of Information
4	excellent	clear and complete
3	good	mostly clear
2	fair	sometimes clear
1	poor	sketchy

Technology and Banking

Discuss

- How do ATMs allow banks to operate more efficiently? *(With the use of ATMs, banks need fewer tellers and full branches and can process transactions less expensively.)*
- What do customers like about online banking? *(It allows them to bank from their computer whenever it is most convenient for them and saves the costs of writing and mailing checks.)*

More About . . .

ATM Fees

According to a 2006 Bankrate.com survey, 98 percent of the largest banks in the 25 largest markets charge fees to noncustomers who use their ATMs. The average fee is $1.60 per transaction. Of those same banks, 81 percent charge their customers a fee if they use an ATM owned by another bank. Bankrate estimated 2006 ATM fees at $4.2 billion.

Credit unions and some smaller banks with few ATM locations belong to alliances of ATMs that allow their customers to avoid paying fees. About 60 percent of the ATM machines in the United States are owned by independent service operators rather than by banks. These ATMs charge fees for all users.

Technology and Banking

QUICK REFERENCE

An **automated teller machine** (ATM) is an electronic device that allows bank customers to make transactions without seeing a bank officer.

A **debit card** can be used like an ATM card or like a check.

A **stored-value card** represents money that the holder has on deposit with the issuer.

KEY CONCEPTS

Deregulation is not the only thing that has changed the nature of banking. Technology—particularly computer technology—has changed the way customers use banks, producing a system generally referred to as electronic banking. For example, banks have begun using **automated teller machines** (ATMs), electronic devices that allow bank customers to make deposits, withdrawals, and transfers and check their account balances at any time without seeing a bank officer. Other innovations include **debit cards**, cards that can be used like an ATM card to withdraw cash or like a check to make purchases, and **stored-value cards**—cards that represent money that the holder has on deposit with the issuer, such as a department store. These cards give customers the ability to use the money in their accounts in more convenient ways. (You'll learn more about ATM and debit cards in Consumer and Personal Finance.)

Automated Teller Machines

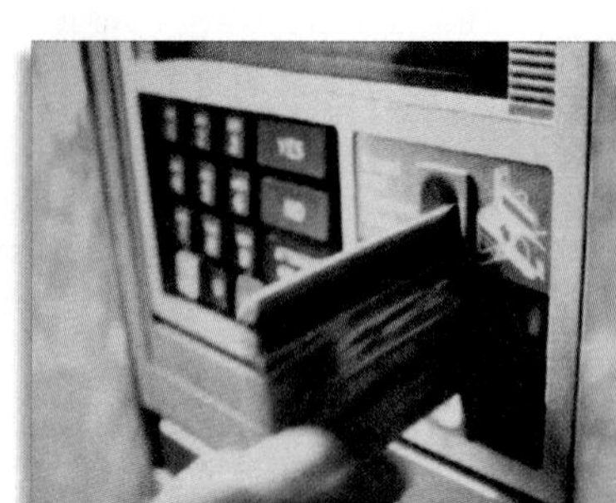

ATM Boom Between 1998 and 2003, the number of ATMs in the United States nearly doubled, from 187,00 to 371,000. By 2007, there were over 1.5 million ATMs worldwide.

Between school, sports practice, and a part-time job, you might find it difficult to get to the bank while it is open to deposit your paycheck and to withdraw spending money. The ATM solves that problem. ATMs are the oldest and most familiar of the developments in electronic banking. They began to be used widely in the 1970s and are now located not just at banks but also at retail stores, workplaces, airports, and entertainment venues, such as movie theaters and sports stadiums.

ATMs are basically data terminals that are linked to a central computer that is in turn linked to individual banks' computers. The bank provides you with a plastic ATM card with a magnetic strip on the back that contains your account information. You insert your card into the ATM, enter your personal identification number (PIN), and follow the instructions on the screen. You may check your account balance, make deposits, withdraw cash, transfer money between accounts, and make loan payments through the ATM.

All ATM networks are connected so that consumers can use their ATM cards at any machine, no matter what bank owns it. Some banks charge fees for ATM use, especially to consumers who do not have an account at the bank that owns the particular ATM. ATMs allow people to bank even when the bank is closed and to avoid waiting in line for simple transactions. Many drive-through ATMs allow customers to bank from their cars. ATMs save banks money because it is much less expensive to process ATM transactions than transactions that involve a teller. They also allow banks to provide services at more locations without constructing complete bank branch offices.

DIFFERENTIATING INSTRUCTION

English Learners

Distinguish Between Similar Words

Make sure that students understand the difference between *debit* and *debt.* Both come from the same root but are used in slightly different ways. A debit is a subtraction from an account balance. When a debit card is used for a purchase, the amount is subtracted immediately from a bank account. A debt is also something that is owed but generally is paid back in the future. Credit card purchases build up debt because credit cards are like loans.

Inclusion

Create Electronic Banking Cards

Kinesthetic learners may benefit from handling different forms of electronic banking cards. Invite students to show cards they have or find photos on the Internet or from local bank or retailer brochures. Have students work in pairs to create examples of different kinds of cards (ATM, debit, credit, stored-value), using index cards and markers. Call on volunteers to hold up one card and describe how it is used. Discuss the similarities and differences in the various cards.

Debit Cards

Debit cards are similar to ATM cards but offer additional benefits. Like ATM cards, debit cards can be used to withdraw cash and make other transactions at ATM machines. Debit cards are sometimes called check cards because they are linked to bank accounts and can be used like checks to make purchases at many retail outlets. Retailers often prefer debit cards because they avoid the problem of people writing checks with insufficient funds in their accounts.

Debit cards often look like credit cards, and they are similar in that they can be used to make purchases at stores. An important difference is that credit card purchases involve getting a loan. Your money stays in your account until you pay your credit card bill. With a debit card you make an immediate payment, since the price of your purchase is deducted from the account that is linked to your card. Therefore, it is important to keep track of debit card purchases along with checks so that you know how much money is available in your account at any given time.

Because of the way debit cards work, they are often seen as safer ways to manage your money than with credit cards. With credit cards, if you do not pay your balance in full each month, you pay interest on the outstanding balance and can build up considerable debt. With debit cards, you can only spend money that you actually have in a bank account.

YOUR ECONOMIC CHOICES

CREDIT CARD VS. DEBIT CARD

Which one should you use?

You have $250 in your checking account, and you don't get your next paycheck for a week. You want to buy a $75 birthday gift for a friend, and you have to pay $225 for a car repair. With your classmates, talk through each of the ways to handle the situation to find out what works best.

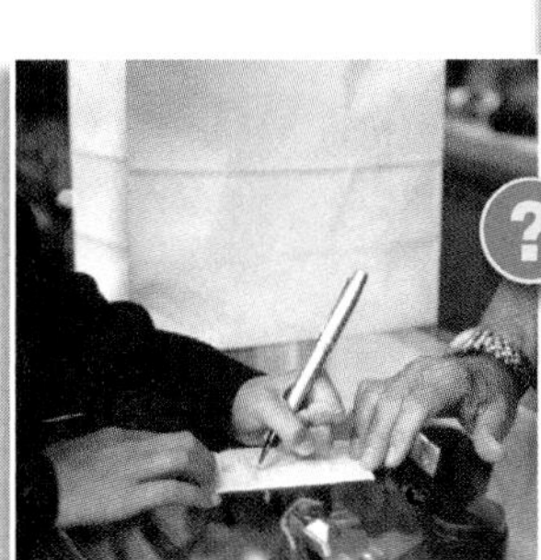

Signing for a credit card

Entering a PIN for a debit card

Stored-Value Cards

Stored-value cards, which represent money that the holder has on deposit with the card issuer, give consumers another convenient way to use electronic banking. These cards are sometimes called prepaid cards because customers have paid a certain amount of money for the card and can then use it to make payments for various goods and services. Some examples of stored-value cards include transit fare cards, gift cards from retail stores, and telephone cards. Consumers benefit from using transit fare cards and telephone cards because they do not have to worry about having the exact change needed each time they ride the bus or use a pay phone.

More About . . .

Online and Offline Debit Cards
There are two slightly different ways to use debit cards. Online transactions require the customer to enter a Personal Identification Number (PIN) at the point of sale. With these transactions, the amount is deducted immediately from your bank account. With offline transactions, the customer signs a receipt rather than entering a PIN. These transactions look more like credit card transactions. The money is usually deducted from your account two or three days later.

Many banks charge customers a transaction fee when they use their PIN to encourage them to opt for the offline transaction. Banks charge merchants higher fees for these transactions.

Your Economic Choices

CREDIT CARD VS. DEBIT CARD

Which one should you use?

- What are the possible problems with using each kind of card? *(credit card—you can build up debt and have to pay interest; debit card—you might overdraw your checking account.)*

Activity Have students use Internet resources to learn more about the benefits and drawbacks of using each kind of card. Have students present the results of their research orally. Discuss how to use each kind of card responsibly.

CLASS ACTIVITY

Creating a Banking Technology Mural

Time 45 Minutes 

Task Create a mural depicting how computer technology has changed banking.

Materials Needed large sheets of paper, markers or poster paints, computer with Internet access (optional)

Activity

- Explain the task and suggest that students split the mural into four sections based on the headings on pages 308–310.
- Have students meet in small groups to brainstorm ideas for visuals for their section. Encourage them to review the textbook for ideas. Allow students to use Internet resources to gather visual references, if desired.
- Direct students to sketch their ideas, with emphasis on cause-and-effect relationships. Then have each group complete its section of the mural.
- Discuss generalizations about how technology has changed the nature of banking.

Rubric

	Technology and Banking	Presentation of Information
4	excellent	clear, creative
3	good	mostly clear and creative
2	fair	sometimes clear, creative elements
1	poor	sketchy

International Economics

Worldwide Smart Card Usage
Stored-value cards are often called smart cards because they use embedded computer chips. Europe accounted for 68 percent of smart card usage in 2005. Cards were also more popular in Asia and South America than in North America. However, it is estimated that by 2010, Europe, Asia, and the United States will each use about one-third of all smart cards.

One of the most successful smart cards is Hong Kong's Octopus card. Introduced as a transit fare card in 1997, it is now also used for payments at many stores, restaurants, payphones, parking meters, and government recreation facilities. Similar systems are planned for the Netherlands and for parts of mainland China.

In 2004, there were more than 2,000 different stored-value card programs in the United States with about 20 million users. The number of users was expected to be 49 million by 2008. The $42 billion in transactions in 2003 was expected to grow to more than $72 billion by 2006.

Multipurpose stored-value cards—cards that can be used like debit cards—are becoming more popular. This type of card may take the place of a checking account, especially for people who have not traditionally used banks. While stored-value cards are a convenient way for people to make purchases and pay bills, consumers need to evaluate the fees involved in using such cards to determine whether they are less expensive than having a checking account or using a check-cashing service. In addition, the money paid into such cards is not always covered by FDIC insurance to protect customer deposits in case of a bank's failure.

Electronic Banking

Electronic banking allows customers who have set up accounts with a bank to perform practically every transaction without setting foot in a bank. Indeed, some banks are virtual banks with no physical buildings at all. Through the use of the Internet, customers can arrange for direct deposit of their paychecks, transfer funds from account to account, and pay their bills.

Most bank Web sites allow customers to review the most recent transactions on their accounts, view images of canceled checks, and download or print their periodic statements. Through electronic fund transfers, consumers can pay a credit card bill at one bank with funds from a checking account at another bank. Recurring bills, such as mortgage payments, may be paid automatically from a customer's checking account each month or through their bank's bill paying service.

However, electronic banking presents several challenges. Information security and identity theft are related, high-profile issues for the industry. Electronic banking allows banks to amass large amounts of information about their customers. Banks contend that this allows them to provide customers with better service. New laws require that banks make customers aware of privacy policies and offer them the opportunity to decide what information may be shared with others. Consumer concerns have led banks to developing increasingly sophisticated information security systems. (For information on identity theft, see Consumer and Personal Finance, which begins on p. 574.)

Online Convenience Online bill paying cuts time and expense by eliminating the need to mail checks.

APPLICATION Contrasting Economic Information

C. How are debit cards different from most stored-value cards? Debit cards can be used to withdraw money from ATMs and make purchases in stores. Most stored-value cards may only be used for a specific purpose, such as transit fares, phone calls, or purchases at a specific store.

DIFFERENTIATING INSTRUCTION

Struggling Readers

List Pros and Cons
Help students understand the benefits and challenges of new banking technologies. Suggest they take notes using a two-column pros-and-cons chart for each technology described on pages 308–310. Explain that pros are positive attributes and cons are negative attributes. Encourage them to look for clue words, such as *benefits, promises, problems,* and *challenges,* to help focus on the pros and cons. Invite students to use their notes to contribute to a class discussion on banking changes.

English Learners

Study Multiple-Meaning Words
Explain that certain words on page 310 have multiple meanings, for example *change* and *virtual*. Encourage students to use context clues to figure out their meanings. Point out that the phrase *exact change* signals that the word *change* refers to money, often in the form of coins. The phrase *virtual banks,* in the context of electronic banking, refers to banks that are only online. Virtual often refers to things created by a computer that are similar to physical objects or activities.

SECTION 3 Assessment

REVIEWING KEY CONCEPTS

1. How are these three terms related? How are they different?
   a. *automated teller machine* b. *debit card* c. *stored-value card*
2. What are two reasons that people deposit money in banks?
3. It is said that fractional reserve banking allows banks to create money? What is meant by this?
4. How did deregulation lead to a decrease in the number of banks between 1980 and the present?
5. How are debit cards related to automated teller machines?
6. **Using Your Notes** How does computer technology support home banking? Refer to your completed hierarchy diagram.

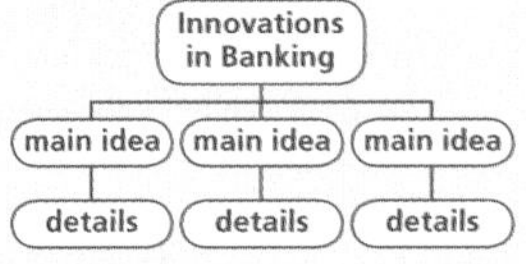

Use the Graphic Organizer at **Interactive Review @ ClassZone.com**

CRITICAL THINKING

7. **Analyzing Data** Over the course of one year, Hometown Bank paid Mary Lee 3 percent interest on a $1,000 deposit and charged Owen's Bakery 8 percent interest on a $900 loan. How much net income did Hometown bank make? Show your calculations.
8. **Applying Economic Concepts** Suppose that Liz inherits $2,000 from her grandmother and deposits it into her college savings account at Hamilton Savings Bank. Assume that the reserve requirement is 20 percent. Create a chart showing five successive loans that could be made from this initial deposit.
9. **Making Inferences** Some parents think that allowing teenagers to use a debit card prepares them for using a credit card. What are the possible reasons behind this thinking? Do you think this reasoning is sound? Why or why not?
10. **Challenge** Look again at Figure 10.5, Fractional Reserve Banking, on page 305. Suppose that when Bank A made the $9,000 loan to the man with the leaky roof, it turned out the job cost only $7,000. The contractor deposited that money into Bank B. How much could Bank B then lend to the used-car buyer? If she bought a car for that amount, and the seller of the car deposited the money in Bank C, what size small-business loan could Bank C then turn around and make?

ECONOMICS IN PRACTICE

Starting a Bank
Think about what you have learned about the services that banks provide and how banks make money. Imagine that you are starting a bank for the other members of the class. Consider the following questions:

- What services would you provide? Why?
- How would your bank make a profit?
- What challenges might you face in making your bank profitable?

Write a Proposal Answer the above questions in a one-page proposal outlining what your bank would be like. Share your proposal with a classmate.

Challenge Include a section in your proposal about what you would do to make your bank more attractive to customers than the other banks run by your classmates.

4 Assess & Reteach

Assess Have students answer the Reviewing Key Concepts questions individually and check their answers in the textbook. Discuss the Critical Thinking questions as a class.

Unit 4 Resource Book
- Section Quiz, p. 29

Interactive Review @ ClassZone.com
- Section Quiz

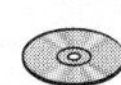

Test Generator CD-ROM
- Section Quiz

Reteach Call on volunteers to use the figures and photographs throughout the section to explain the main ideas related to banking services and innovations. Invite other students to contribute additional information.

Unit 4 Resource Book
- Reteaching Activity, p. 30

Economics in Practice

Write a Proposal Student proposals should
- include services that allow customers to store money, earn money, and borrow money, and may include insurance and investment services
- state that banks make profits by charging more in loan interest and fees than they pay out in interest on deposits and other costs
- show an understanding that bankers face risks in collecting money from borrowers

Challenge Possible answers: offering better interest rates on deposits or loans, charging lower fees, offering better customer service

SECTION 3 ASSESSMENT ANSWERS

Reviewing Key Concepts

1. a. *automated teller machine*, p. 308
   b. *debit card*, p. 308
   c. *stored-value card*, p. 308
2. for safety and to earn interest
3. Each loan made is considered to be money created. If you deposit money in an account and a loan is made on the basis of reserve on that deposit, you can still go back a week later and withdraw your money.
4. Deregulation encouraged bank mergers as banks combined to be able to enter different states.
5. Debit cards can be used like ATM cards to make transactions at automated teller machines.
6. See page 304 for an example of a completed diagram. With personal computers and the Internet, consumers can access their bank accounts at home and make needed transactions online.

Critical Thinking

7. .03 × $1,000 = $30 paid out; .08 × $900 = $72 received. Bank net income is $72 – $30 = $42
8. For each loan, (D) stands for deposit, (R) for reserve, and (L) for loan.
   Loan 1: (D)=$2,000, (R)=$400, (L)=$1,600
   Loan 2: (D)=$1,600, (R)=$320, (L)=$1,280
   Loan 3: (D)=$1,280, (R)=$256, (L)=$1,024
   Loan 4: (D)=$1,024, (R)=$204.80, (L)=$819.20
   Loan 5: (D)=$819.20, (R)=$163.84, (L)=$655.36
9. Possible answer: This is sound reasoning because using a debit card teaches one to spend only what one has. This may teach young people not to get into credit card debt.
10. It could only lend $6,300 to the car buyer. Bank C could only lend $5,670 for the small business.

Economics in Practice

See answers in side column above.

1 Plan & Prepare

Objectives

- Explain how student loans are different from other loans.
- Describe programs that provide loans for college students.

2 Focus & Motivate

Explain that this Case Study explores some of the programs that provide student loans. Ask students to suggest reasons why they might borrow money to pay for college.

3 Teach

Using the Sources

Encourage students to examine each source to understand the importance of college loans and who provides them.

A. How is the article related to the Figure 10.7 *(Together they paint a daunting picture of the task of paying for college in the future. Prices are going up and so are loan rates.)*

B. Why might students take a loan officer to meet with college officials? *(Possible answer: so they can have someone with them who is going to help them arrange to pay for college)*

C. What is the major problem associated with loan repayment after college graduation? *(Some graduates have unmanageable levels of debt from their student loans and default.)*

Economics Update

Go to **ClassZone.com** to find an update to this Case Study, including another article, an editable student worksheet, and an editable lesson plan.

Case Study

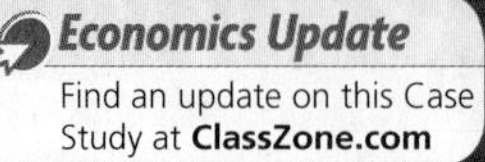
Economics Update
Find an update on this Case Study at ClassZone.com

Student Loans

Background In the United States, the cost of higher education may still be affordable to some, but it certainly is not cheap. Because of rising costs, more and more students (and their parents) borrow money to finance at least part of their college education. According to the U.S. Department of Education, about 10 million students take out Stafford loans each year, while about 800,000 parents take out PLUS loans.

Although banks, S&Ls, and credit unions are the primary lenders of money in the United States, this is not the case for student loans. Students and parents have the option of borrowing wherever they choose, but federally guaranteed loans are their main source of funding.

What's the issue? What is the current situation with student loans? What are the future ramifications of the increasing cost of paying for college? Study these sources to learn about student loans.

A. Online News Story

This story explains a change in the way the government figures the interest rate on student loans.

Congress Cuts Funding for Student Loans

Graduates face higher interest payments, fewer options.

Congress yesterday cut funding for federal student-loan programs, a move that is expected to increase the debt burden for many future college graduates and their families. . . .

To help limit spending, Congress raised interest rates on the popular Stafford loans to a fixed 6.8%, even if commercial rates are lower. . . .

The changes come at a time when families have been struggling with skyrocketing tuition bills. After adjusting for inflation, private-college tuition and fees have increased 37% over the past decade, while public tuition has risen 54%. Today, most college students borrow money to pay for college. . . .

The interest rate on a Stafford loan is variable and reset annually, depending on a formula that looks at prevailing market interest rates. Today, that rate is as low as 4.7%. . . .

Under the new legislation, the interest rate changes to a fixed rate of 6.8% starting July 1, 2006. . . .

Source: WSJClassroom.com, Anne Marie Chaker, December 22, 2005

FIGURE 10.7 AVERAGE COST OF TUITION, ROOM, AND BOARD AT A FOUR-YEAR INSTITUTION

Cost (in dollars, not adjusted for inflation)
16,000
14,000
12,000
10,000
8,000
6,000
4,000
2,000
1989–1990
1991–1992
1993–1994
1995–1996
1997–1998
1999–2000
2001–2002
2003–2004
School Year

Source: National Center for Education Statistics

Thinking Economically If interest rates hit 10 percent, would the new fixed rate established by Congress still harm student borrowers? Why or why not?

DIFFERENTIATING INSTRUCTION

Inclusion

Understand Data

Help students understand the study's data.

- Ask students if the Background information is reinforced by the data in Figure 10.7. *(The figure shows that, indeed, the cost of a college education is rising. It's likely that the more expensive tuition costs get, the more students and parents are going to have to borrow.)*
- Help students calculate the percentage rise in tuition costs per year. For example: \$12,922 – \$12,352 = \$570. \$570/\$12,352 = +4.6%.

Gifted and Talented

Create Fact Sheets

Invite students to research trends in financial aid and the relative importance of loans compared to other types of aid. Students may use Internet resources or materials on student aid from the library or the guidance office. Encourage students to summarize their research in fact sheets that may include charts or graphs. Allow students to share their fact sheets with the class and lead a discussion on how these trends affect students preparing for college or other schooling after high school.

B. Cartoon

Ralph Hagen drew this cartoon about student loans as a factor in higher education.

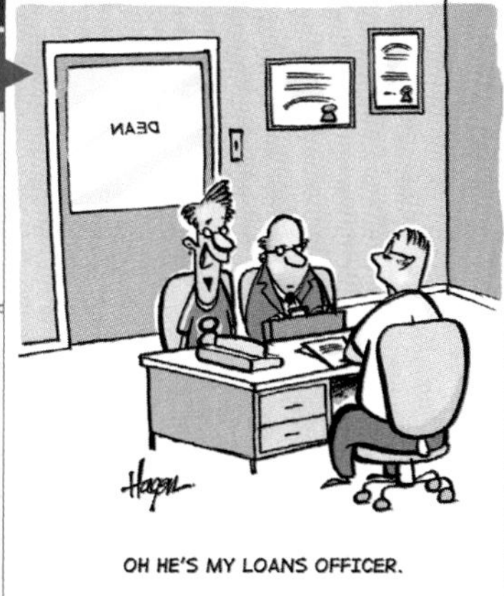

OH HE'S MY LOANS OFFICER.

Source: www.CartoonStock.com

Thinking Economically What does the cartoon suggest about student reliance on college loans? Explain your answer.

C. Newspaper Article

This article discusses the problems associated with debt and loan repayment after college graduation.

It's Payback Time

More student loans increase debt pressure on graduates.

Student loans are two-edged: the more money a student can borrow, the more schooling falls within reach. But of course, the more debt a student has, the more painful repayment becomes. . . .

"More students will be required to take out more money from the federal government and from private lenders," says Jasmine L. Harris, legislative director at the United States Student Association, a student advocacy group in Washington. Over time, she continues, "It's a great formula for unmanageable levels of debt and hence higher default rates.". . .

The consequences of defaulting, too, are worse than they have been in years past.

A provision of a law that took effect last year, for example, makes it next to impossible to discharge private student loans in personal bankruptcy proceedings (federal loans were already barred). . . .

[Theresa] Shaw of the Education Department advises that a struggling borrower should try to make a payment of any kind, however small, to avoid default.

Source: The *New York Times*, April 23, 2006

Thinking Economically Explain in your own words why you think the article calls student loans "two-edged."

THINKING ECONOMICALLY Synthesizing

1. Compare the financial news presented in documents A and C. What bearing do you think the information in document A might have on what you learned from document C?
2. Document B humorously points to the prominence of student loans in U.S. higher education. Specifically, what parts of documents A and C support this view?
3. In document A, what does the federal government seem to be saying about who should pay for a college education? With this in mind, what does Figure 10.7 mean for students and parents?

Thinking Economically

Answers

A. *It would help borrowers because the rate is now fixed at a rate below 10 percent.*

B. *The cartoon suggests that student reliance on college loans is vital, since the student has decided to bring his loans officer into a meeting with the dean.*

C. *Student loans may be the only thing that allows certain students to go to college, but these loans also give the students dangerous levels of debt.*

Synthesizing

1. *Document C says that students have too much debt from student loans. Document A says that the debt load for parents and students is getting worse.*
2. *Document A says that most students must borrow to pay for college, while document C says that "more students will be required to take out more money. . . ."*
3. *The government seems to be saying that, to a greater degree, students and their families, rather than the government, should pay. Figure 10.7 means more loans and higher costs.*

TECHNOLOGY ACTIVITY

Researching Sources of Student Loans

Time 45 Minutes 

Task Gather information on providers of student loans and create a Power Presentation.

Materials Needed a computer with Internet access, presentation software

Activity:

- Organize students into groups. Have groups use the Internet to research different sources of student loans, including federal programs for students and parents, private lenders, and if applicable, state loan programs.
- Have each group gather information on the types of loans offered, general terms, interest rates, and fees. Direct students to prepare a Power Presentation on their topic.
- Invite groups to give their presentations to the class. Discuss the options available to families to borrow for college.

Rubric

	Understanding of Student Loans	Presentation of Information
4	excellent	clear and complete
3	good	mostly clear
2	fair	sometimes clear
1	poor	sketchy

Online Summary Answers

1. Money
2. medium of exchange
3. standard of value
4. store of value
5. commodity money
6. fiat money
7. M1
8. currency
9. demand deposits
10. near money
11. Fractional reserve banking
12. national bank
13. automated teller machine
14. debit card

Interactive Review

Review this chapter using interactive activities at **ClassZone.com**

- Online Summary
- Quizzes
- Vocabulary Flip Cards
- Graphic Organizers
- Review and Study Notes

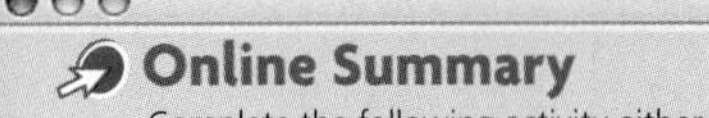

Online Summary

Complete the following activity either on your own paper or online at **ClassZone.com**

Choose the key concept that best completes the sentence. Not all key concepts will be used.

automated teller machine	M2
barter	medium of exchange
commodity money	money
currency	national bank
debit card	near money
demand deposits	representative money
fiat money	standard of value
fractional reserve banking	state bank
gold standard	store of value
M1	stored-value card

__1__ is anything that people will accept as payment for goods and services. Money makes trade easier by serving as a __2__. As a __3__, money allows people to compare the prices of goods and services. Money must be a __4__, or something that holds its value over time.

Gold coins and salt are both examples of __5__. Most money in the world today is __6__, which has no tangible value but is declared by the government to have worth.

__7__ consists of __8__, which includes paper money and coins and __9__, which is another name for checking accounts. Savings accounts and time deposits are called __10__ because they can be converted into cash easily.

__11__ allows banks to hold only part of their deposits and make loans based on the rest. The Federal Reserve Bank is the central __12__ in the nation.

The __13__ is the oldest form of electronic banking. A __14__ can be used like an ATM card or like a check.

CHAPTER 10 Assessment

REVIEWING KEY CONCEPTS

Money: Its Functions and Properties (pp. 288–295)

1. What three functions does money serve in the economy?
2. Why do economists make a distinction between M1 and M2?

The Development of U.S. Banking (pp. 296–303)

3. Why does fractional reserve banking leave banks vulnerable to failure if too many consumers demand their money at the same time?
4. How is the Federal Reserve System different from the system of national banks created in the 1860s?

Innovations in Modern Banking (pp. 304–313)

5. How did the automated teller machine change the nature of banking?
6. Which type of stored-value card is most like a debit card?

APPLYING ECONOMIC CONCEPTS

Look at the table below showing changes in use of electronic payments between 1995 and 2001.

7. Which type of electronic banking increased the most among all households between 1995 and 2001?
8. How did education generally affect the use of electronic payments?

FIGURE 10.8 PERCENTAGE OF HOUSEHOLDS USING ELECTRONIC BANKING

Education of head of household	ATM		Debit card		Automatic bill paying	
	1995	2001	1995	2001	1995	2001
All households	61.2	69.8	17.6	47.0	21.8	40.3
No college degree	52.8	63.7	14.3	42.3	18.2	33.7
College degree	80.1	81.6	25.2	56.2	30.1	53.2

Source: *Statistical Abstract of the United States, 2006*

CHAPTER 10 ASSESSMENT ANSWERS

Reviewing Key Concepts

1. It serves as a medium of exchange, a standard of value, and a store of value.
2. to distinguish between the money that is immediately available for transactions and that which cannot be used for transactions directly but can be converted to cash
3. because banks make loans based on only a part of their reserves, on the assumption that not all customers will demand their deposits at the same time
4. The Fed has central decision making authority that is able to regulate banks and the money supply, while the earlier national banks had national charters but no central authority.
5. It allowed customers to access their accounts at any time and in more places without constructing full branches. It cut down on the number of in-person transactions.
6. a multipurpose card that can be used for a variety of transactions rather than being limited to just one kind of transaction such as transit fares or phone calls

Applying Economic Concepts

7. debit cards, from 17.6 percent to 47 percent
8. Household heads who had college degrees were most likely to use electronic payments.

Critical Thinking

9. The amount of money in M1 would decrease by about 10 percent and the amount in M2 would increase by the same amount.
10. The problems of the 19th century are avoided because now the Federal Reserve mandates a national currency and requires banks to maintain certain reserve levels, limiting state banks' autonomy.
11. **a.** Tara; her gift card limits her to one store.
    b. Charlotte, because her money stays in her checking account until she pays her credit card bill. With an ATM card or a debit card, funds are withdrawn immediately.

CRITICAL THINKING

9. **Analyzing Effects** Suppose that the government changes the tax policy so that people pay lower taxes if they save more money. The benefits are significant enough that people shift about 10 percent of their money from their checking accounts into certificates of deposit. How would this change affect the amount of money in M1 and M2?

10. **Drawing Conclusions** Today, there are about three times as many state chartered commercial banks as there are nationally chartered commercial banks. How does the current U.S. economy avoid the kinds of problems caused by state banks in the 19th century?

11. **Applying Economic Concepts** One Saturday, four friends go shopping at the local mall. Catherine uses her ATM card to withdraw some cash. Tara has a gift card that she received for her birthday. It is worth $50 at her favorite clothing store. Charlotte uses a credit card, and Alyssa pays with a debit card.
    a. Which of the shoppers has a stored-value card? Why does she have less flexibility in her shopping than the other shoppers?
    b. If Catherine, Charlotte, and Alyssa each spend $50, which one has not reduced the amount of money in her checking account at the end of the day? Why?
    c. Which shopper may end up paying more than face value for her purchases?

12. **Analyzing Causes** What are the different motives behind these two mergers: a stock brokerage firm buys a bank; a California bank buys a Florida bank?

13. **Challenge** Why are credit cards and debit cards not considered to be money?

SIMULATION

Promote Electronic Banking

Step 1 Choose a partner. Imagine that you work for a bank in the late 1990s. Your bank intends to be a pioneer in Internet banking and asks you to design its first Web page. Your boss gives you the following criteria for the Web page:

- Allow existing customers to access account balances and transfer funds between accounts.
- Promote traditional bank products, including checking, savings, CDs, credit cards, mortgages, and auto loans.
- Allow customers to find the most convenient branch or ATM location.

Step 2 Sketch out a design for the Web page to meet your boss's criteria, showing appropriate links.

Step 3 Two years later, deregulation has led to significant changes in the banking industry. In addition, more consumers are interested in Internet banking. Your boss asks you to redesign the Web page with these additional criteria:

- Allow customers to pay bills, apply for loans, buy stocks, and shop for insurance through the bank's Web site.
- Allow customers to view transactions on all their accounts, including credit and debit card transactions, and receive statements and other bank communications electronically.
- Reassure customers that online banking is secure and that their privacy will be protected.

Step 4 Sketch out a new Web page that shows the complete range of services the bank now offers and that meets all six criteria.

Step 5 Share your Web page designs with another pair of students and discuss what aspects would be most important and effective for you as a customer.

McDougal Littell Assessment System

Assess

Online Test Practice
- Go to **ClassZone.com** for more test practice.

Unit 1 Resource Book
- Chapter Test, Forms A, B, & C, pp. 41–52

Test Generator CD-ROM
- Chapter Test, Forms (A, B, & C), in English and Spanish

Report

Use the McDougal Littell Assessment System to score assessments and receive customized reports.

Reteach

For activities customized for individual students, use the McDougal Littell Assessment System.

CHAPTER 10 ASSESSMENT ANSWERS

c. Charlotte, because she uses a credit card to make purchases. If she doesn't pay the full amount due to her credit card company right away, she'll end up paying interest.

12. A stock brokerage firm buys a bank in order to offer a wider range of products and compete with banks; a California bank buys a Florida bank in order to compete in an expanded geographic area.

13. A credit card is like a loan; money is used when the loan is repaid. A debit card is linked to a checkable deposit or a savings account. The funds in the account are the money; the card is just a convenient way of accessing it.

Simulation Rubric: Steps 1–2

4	Content is organized and complete; design is creative and structured.
3	Content mostly organized, complete; design often creative, structured
2	Content somewhat organized, complete; design sometimes creative
1	Content is disorganized and incomplete; design lacks creativity and structure.

Steps 3–4

4	Meets all new criteria; maintains excellent design
3	Meets most new criteria; maintains good design
2	Meets some new criteria; design somewhat cluttered
1	Meets few new criteria; design has major flaws

CHAPTER 11: Financial Markets
Planning Guide

Resources 2Go Complete print resources all on one USB drive allow you to customize lessons.

Section Titles and Objectives	Unit 4 Resource Book and Workbooks		Assessment Resources
1 Savings and Investment pp. 318–323 • Identify what constitutes the financial system • Describe the various financial intermediaries • Explain how economists categorize the various markets where financial assets are sold	**Unit 4 Resource Book** • Reading Study Guide, pp. 53–54 • RSG with Additional Support, pp. 55–57 • RSG with Additional Support (Spanish), pp. 58–60	• Math Skills: Calculating Simple & Compound Interest, p. 101 • Readings in Free Enterprise: Saving Too Little or Too Much?, pp. 95–96	**Unit 4 Resource Book** • Section Quiz, p. 61 • Reteaching Activity, p. 62 **Test Generator CD-ROM** **Daily Test Practice Transparencies,** TT36
2 Investing in a Market Economy pp. 324–329 • Discuss the issues that should be considered when making investment decisions • Explain how risk and return are related	**Unit 4 Resource Book** • Reading Study Guide, pp. 63–64 • RSG with Additional Support, pp. 65–67 • RSG with Additional Support, (Spanish), pp. 68–70	• Economic Simulations: Wall Street Reacts, pp. 99–100	**Unit 4 Resource Book** • Section Quiz, p. 71 • Reteaching Activity, p. 72 **Test Generator CD-ROM** **Daily Test Practice Transparencies,** TT37
3 Buying and Selling Stocks pp. 330–337 • Discuss why people buy stocks • Describe how stocks are traded • Explain how the performance of stocks is measured	**Unit 4 Resource Book** • Reading Study Guide, pp. 73–74 • RSG with Additional Support, pp. 75–77 • RSG with Additional Support, (Spanish), pp. 78–80 • Economic Simulations: Wall Street Reacts, pp. 99–100	**Test Practice and Review Workbook,** pp. 43–44	**Unit 4 Resource Book** • Section Quiz, p. 81 • Reteaching Activity, p. 82 **Test Generator CD-ROM** **Daily Test Practice Transparencies,** TT38
4 Bonds and Other Financial Instruments pp. 338–345 • Discuss why people buy bonds • Describe the different kinds of bonds • Explain the factors that affect bond trading • Outline investment options other than stocks and bonds	**Unit 4 Resource Book** • Reading Study Guide, pp. 83–84 • RSG with Additional Support, pp. 85–87 • RSG with Additional Support (Spanish), pp. 88–90 • Case Study Resources: Dot-coms' Song and Dance No Longer Entertains Investors, pp. 97–98	**NCEE Student Activities** • Reading the Financial Pages, pp. 41–44 **Test Practice and Review Workbook,** pp. 43–44	**Unit 4 Resource Book** • Section Quiz, p. 91 • Reteaching Activity, p. 92 • Chapter Test, (Forms A, B, & C), pp. 103–114 **Test Generator CD-ROM** **Daily Test Practice Transparencies,** TT39

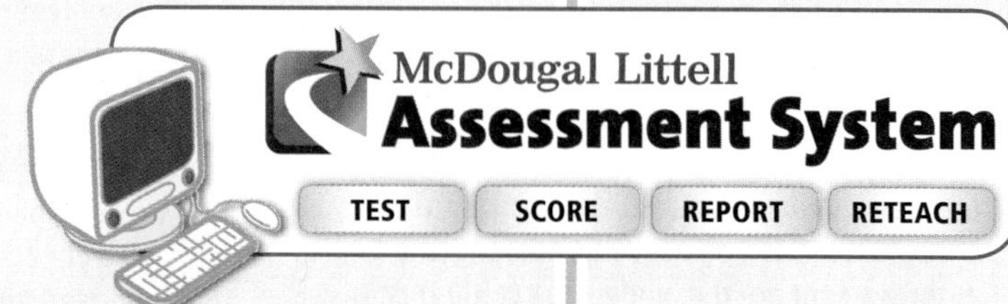

Integrated Technology

No Time? To focus students on the most important content in this chapter, use the Economics Essentials diagram, "The Financial System," that appears on page 319.

Teacher Presentation Options

Presentation Toolkit

Power Presentation DVD-ROM

- Lecture Notes
- Interactive Review
- Media Gallery
- Animated Economics
- Review Game

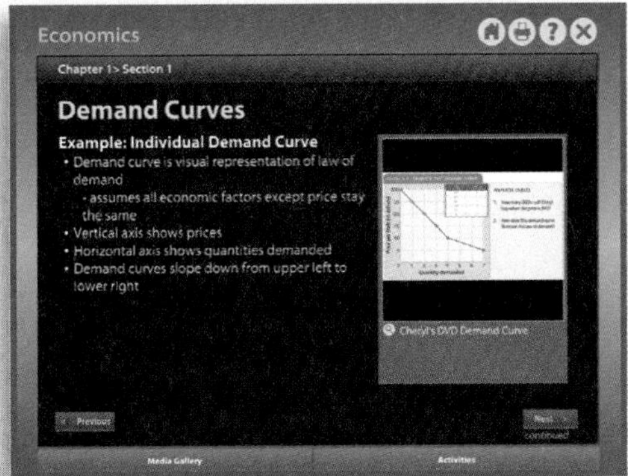

Economics Concepts Transparencies

- Financial Institutions, CT36
- Investment 1990 to 2005, CT37
- Performance of Leading Stocks, CT38
- Types of Bonds, CT39

Electronic Books

eEdition DVD-ROM

eEdition Online

Daily Test Practice

Transparencies, TT36, TT37, TT38, TT39

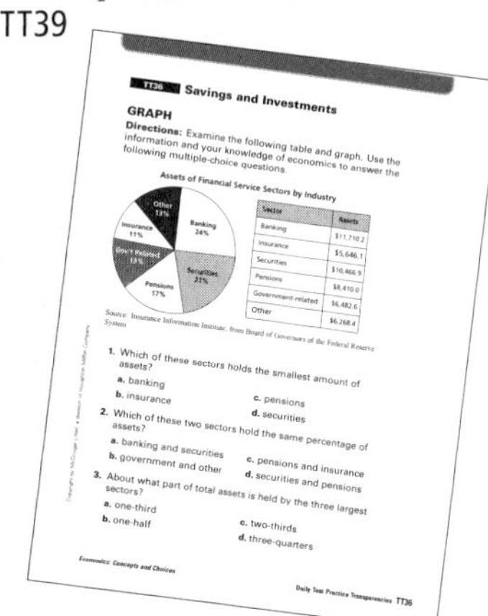

SMARTGrapher

- Create Pie Graphs, p. 347

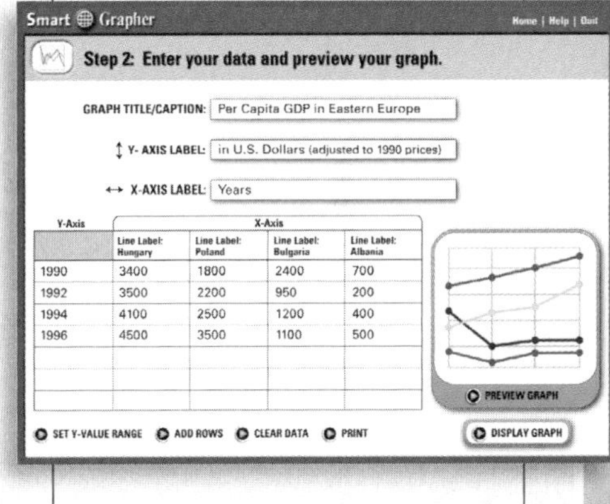

Online Activities at ClassZone.com

Economics Update

- Saving, p. 318
- Investing, p. 325
- Mellody Hobson, p. 326
- Stocks in the Dow Jones Industrial Average, p. 334
- Case Study: The Rise and Fall of Dot-Coms, p. 344

Activity Maker

- Vocabulary Flip Cards
- Review Game

Research Center

- Graphs and Data

Interactive Review

- Online Summary
- Quizzes
- Vocabulary Flip Cards
- Graphic Organizers
- Review and Study Notes

SMARTGrapher

- Create Pie Graphs, p. 347

Teacher-Tested Activities

Name: Douglas Young

School: Croton-Harmon High School

State: New York

Teacher-Tested Activities

At the beginning of this chapter, look for my classroom-proven idea for teaching economics concepts and thinking.

Resources for Differentiated Instruction

Struggling Readers

Teacher's Edition Activities

- Compare and Contrast, p. 320
- Annotate the Graph, p. 328
- Use Jigsaw Reading, p. 332
- Compare Economic Information, p. 334
- Work in Pairs, p. 342

Unit 4 Resource Book

- RSG with Additional Support, pp. 55–57, 65–67, 75–77, 85–87 (A)
- Reteaching Activities, pp. 62, 72, 82, 92 (B)
- Chapter Test (Form A), pp. 103–106 (C)

ClassZone.com

- Animated Economics
- Interactive Review

Test Generator CD-ROM

- Chapter Test (Form A)
- Chapter Test (Form A), in Spanish

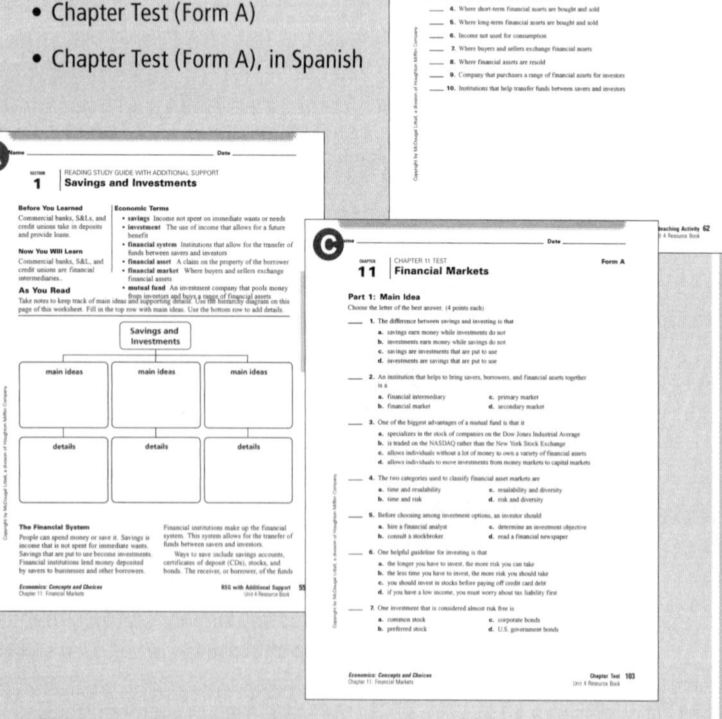

(B) Name ______ Date ______

SECTION 1 | RETEACHING ACTIVITY **Savings and Investments**

A. Explaining Economic Concepts
Write the letter of the term before the description that best explains it.

a. savings
b. investment
c. financial system
d. financial asset
e. financial market
f. financial intermediary
g. mutual fund
h. capital market
i. money market
j. secondary market

____ 1. A financial institution that reinvests funds collected from savers
____ 2. The use of income that allows for a future benefit
____ 3. A claim on the property of the borrower
____ 4. Where short-term financial assets are bought and sold
____ 5. Where long-term financial assets are bought and sold
____ 6. Income not used for consumption
____ 7. Where buyers and sellers exchange financial assets
____ 8. Where financial assets are resold
____ 9. Company that purchases a range of financial assets for investors
____ 10. Institutions that help transfer funds between savers and investors

Reteaching Activity 62
Unit 4 Resource Book

(A) Name ______ Date ______

SECTION 1 | READING STUDY GUIDE WITH ADDITIONAL SUPPORT **Savings and Investments**

Before You Learned
Commercial banks, S&Ls, and credit unions take in deposits and provide loans.

Now You Will Learn
Commercial banks, S&L, and credit unions are financial intermediaries.

Economic Terms
- **savings** Income not spent on immediate wants or needs
- **investment** The use of income that allows for a future benefit
- **financial system** Institutions that allow for the transfer of funds between savers and investors
- **financial asset** A claim on the property of the borrower
- **financial market** Where buyers and sellers exchange financial assets
- **mutual fund** An investment company that pools money from investors and buys a range of financial assets

As You Read
Take notes to keep track of main ideas and supporting details. Use the hierarchy diagram on this page of this worksheet. Fill in the top row with main ideas. Use the bottom row to add details.

Savings and Investments
main ideas | main ideas | main ideas
details | details | details

The Financial System
People can spend money or save it. Savings is income that is not spent for immediate wants. Savings that are put to use become investments. Financial institutions lend money deposited by savers to businesses and other borrowers.

Financial institutions make up the financial system. This system allows for the transfer of funds between savers and investors.

Ways to save include savings accounts, certificates of deposit (CDs), stocks, and bonds. The receiver, or borrower, of the funds

Economics: Concepts and Choices Chapter 11 Financial Markets
RSG with Additional Support 55
Unit 4 Resource Book

(C) Name ______ Date ______

CHAPTER 11 | CHAPTER 11 TEST **Financial Markets** Form A

Part 1: Main Idea
Choose the letter of the best answer. (4 points each)

____ 1. The difference between savings and investing is that
a. savings earn money while investments do not
b. investments earn money while savings do not
c. savings are investments that are put to use
d. investments are savings that are put to use

____ 2. An institution that helps to bring savers, borrowers, and financial assets together is a
a. financial intermediary c. primary market
b. financial market d. secondary market

____ 3. One of the biggest advantages of a mutual fund is that it
a. specializes in the stock of companies on the Dow Jones Industrial Average
b. is traded on the NASDAQ rather than the New York Stock Exchange
c. allows individuals without a lot of money to own a variety of financial assets
d. allows individuals to move investments from money markets to capital markets

____ 4. The two categories used to classify financial asset markets are
a. time and availability c. availability and diversity
b. time and risk d. risk and diversity

____ 5. Before choosing among investment options, an investor should
a. hire a financial analyst c. determine an investment objective
b. consult a stockbroker d. read a financial newspaper

____ 6. One helpful guideline for investing is that
a. the longer you have to invest, the more risk you can take
b. the less time you have to invest, the more risk you should take
c. you should invest in stocks before paying off credit card debt
d. if you have a low income, you must worry about tax liability first

____ 7. One investment that is considered almost risk free is
a. common stock c. corporate bonds
b. preferred stock d. U.S. government bonds

Economics: Concepts and Choices Chapter 11 Financial Markets
Chapter Test 103
Unit 4 Resource Book

English Learners

Teacher's Edition Activities

- Create Word Webs, p. 320
- Build Background Knowledge, p. 326
- Understand Abbreviations, p. 332
- Create Word Squares, p. 334
- Understand Word Derivation, p. 344

Unit 4 Resource Book

- RSG with Additional Support (Spanish), 58–60, 68–70, 78–80, 88–90 (A)

Test Generator CD-ROM

- Chapter Test (Forms A, B, & C), in Spanish (B)

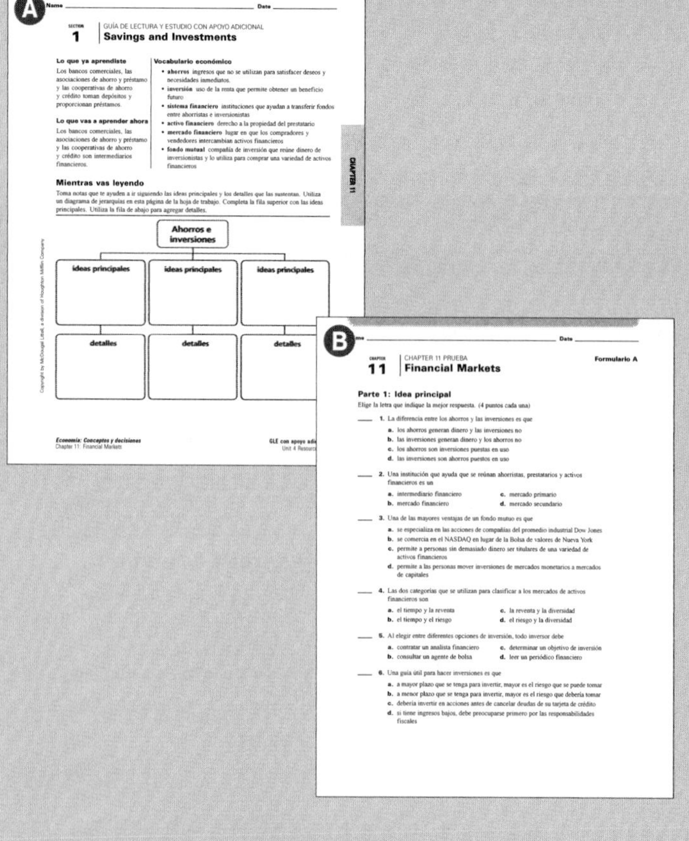

(A) Name ______ Date ______

SECTION 1 | GUÍA DE LECTURA Y ESTUDIO CON APOYO ADICIONAL **Savings and Investments**

Lo que ya aprendiste
Los bancos comerciales, las asociaciones de ahorro y préstamo y las cooperativas de ahorro y crédito toman depósitos y proporcionan préstamos.

Lo que vas a aprender ahora
Los bancos comerciales, las asociaciones de ahorro y préstamo y las cooperativas de ahorro y crédito son intermediarios financieros.

Vocabulario económico
- **ahorros** ingresos que no se utilizan para satisfacer deseos y necesidades inmediatos
- **inversión** uso de la renta que permite obtener un beneficio futuro
- **sistema financiero** instituciones que ayudan a transferir fondos entre ahorristas e inversionistas
- **activo financiero** derecho a la propiedad del prestatario
- **mercado financiero** lugar en que los compradores y vendedores intercambian activos financieros
- **fondo mutual** compañía de inversión que reúne dinero de inversionistas y lo utiliza para comprar una variedad de activos financieros

Mientras vas leyendo
Toma notas que te ayuden a ir siguiendo las ideas principales y los detalles que las sustentan. Utiliza un diagrama de jerarquías en esta página de la hoja de trabajo. Completa la fila superior con las ideas principales. Utiliza la fila de abajo para agregar detalles.

Ahorros e inversiones
ideas principales | ideas principales | ideas principales
detalles | detalles | detalles

CHAPTER 11

Economía: Conceptos y decisiones Chapter 11 Financial Markets
GLE con apoyo adicional
Unit 4 Resource Book

(B) Name ______ Date ______

CHAPTER 11 | CHAPTER 11 PRUEBA **Financial Markets** Formulario A

Parte 1: Idea principal
Elige la letra que indique la mejor respuesta. (4 puntos cada una)

____ 1. La diferencia entre los ahorros y las inversiones es que
a. los ahorros generan dinero y las inversiones no
b. las inversiones generan dinero y los ahorros no
c. los ahorros son inversiones puestas en uso
d. las inversiones son ahorros puestos en uso

____ 2. Una institución que ayuda que se reúnan ahorristas, prestatarios y activos financieros es un
a. intermediario financiero c. mercado primario
b. mercado financiero d. mercado secundario

____ 3. Una de las mayores ventajas de un fondo mutuo es que
a. se especializa en las acciones de compañías del promedio industrial Dow Jones
b. se comercia en el NASDAQ en lugar de la Bolsa de valores de Nueva York
c. permite a personas sin demasiado dinero ser titulares de una variedad de activos financieros
d. permite a las personas mover inversiones de mercados monetarios a mercados de capitales

____ 4. Las dos categorías que se utilizan para clasificar a los mercados de activos financieros son
a. el tiempo y la reventa c. la reventa y la diversidad
b. el tiempo y el riesgo d. el riesgo y la diversidad

____ 5. Al elegir entre diferentes opciones de inversión, todo inversor debe
a. contratar un analista financiero c. determinar un objetivo de inversión
b. consultar un agente de bolsa d. leer un periódico financiero

____ 6. Una guía útil para hacer inversiones es que
a. a mayor plazo que se tenga para invertir, mayor es el riesgo que se puede tomar
b. a menor plazo que se tenga para invertir, mayor es el riesgo que debería tomar
c. debería invertir en acciones antes de cancelar deudas de su tarjeta de crédito
d. si tiene ingresos bajos, debe preocuparse primero por las responsabilidades fiscales

Inclusion

Teacher's Edition Activities

- Describe Financial Markets, p. 322
- Create a Pie Chart, p. 328
- Explain the Chart, p. 336
- Create a Risk Continuum, p. 340
- Enlarge the Graph, p. 342

Lesson Plans

- Modified Lessons for Inclusion, pp. 36–39 **A**

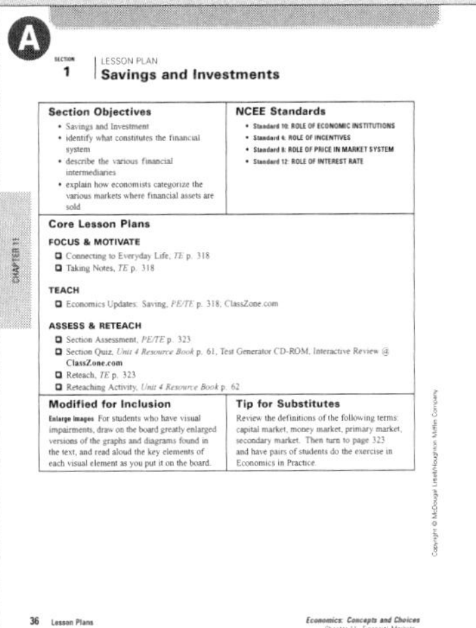
A

SECTION 1 | LESSON PLAN
Savings and Investments

Section Objectives	NCEE Standards
• Savings and Investment • identify what constitutes the financial system • describe the various financial intermediaries • explain how economists categorize the various markets where financial assets are sold	• Standard 10: ROLE OF ECONOMIC INSTITUTIONS • Standard 4: ROLE OF INCENTIVES • Standard 8: ROLE OF PRICE IN MARKET SYSTEM • Standard 12: ROLE OF INTEREST RATE

Core Lesson Plans

FOCUS & MOTIVATE
- ☐ Connecting to Everyday Life, *TE* p. 318
- ☐ Taking Notes, *TE* p. 318

TEACH
- ☐ Economics Updates: Saving, *PE/TE* p. 318; ClassZone.com

ASSESS & RETEACH
- ☐ Section Assessment, *PE/TE* p. 323
- ☐ Section Quiz, *Unit 4 Resource Book* p. 61, Test Generator CD-ROM, Interactive Review @ **ClassZone.com**
- ☐ Reteach, *TE* p. 323
- ☐ Reteaching Activity, *Unit 4 Resource Book* p. 62

Modified for Inclusion	Tip for Substitutes
Enlarge Images For students who have visual impairments, draw on the board greatly enlarged versions of the graphs and diagrams found in the text, and read aloud the key elements of each visual element as you put it on the board.	Review the definitions of the following terms: capital market, money market, primary market, secondary market. Then turn to page 323 and have pairs of students do the exercise in Economics in Practice.

CHAPTER 11

Copyright © McDougal Littell/Houghton Mifflin Company

36 Lesson Plans — *Economics: Concepts and Choices* Chapter 11 Financial Markets

Gifted and Talented

Teacher's Edition Activities

- Research Savings Bonds, p. 322
- Write a Proposal, p. 326
- Investigate Global Stock Indexes, p. 336
- Hold a Panel Discussion, p. 340
- Analyze Venture Capitalists, p. 344

Unit 4 Resource Book

- Readings in Free Enterprise: Saving Too Little or Too Much?, pp. 95–96 **B**
- Case Study Resources: Dot-coms' Song and Dance No Longer Entertains Investors, pp. 97–98 **B**

NCEE Student Activities

- Reading the Financial Pages, pp. 41–44 **C**

ClassZone.com

- Research Center

Test Generator CD-ROM

- Chapter Test (Form C)
- Chapter Test (Form C), in Spanish

B

Name ______ Date ______

CHAPTER 11 | CASE STUDY RESOURCES
Financial Markets

Dot-coms' Song and Dance No Longer Entertains Investors

Financial markets columnist Matt Krantz takes a look at the difficulty of finding investors for dot-com stocks several years after the dot-com boom and crash. Instead of selling their stock on the public stock market, many smaller dot-com companies are now selling to Internet industry giants.

Blogs. 99-cent music downloads. Podcasts. Phoning home via the Internet. Online social networking. It's the golden age of the Internet.

But you wouldn't know it if you've just been watching Internet stocks. Outside of Google and a few other choice names, it's hard to find an Internet company that gets investors' juices flowing -- let alone gets them to pull out their wallets. From a technological standpoint, the Internet has lived up to and even surpassed its wildest expectations. But investment-wise, the recent results have been a disappointment at best.

That's completely opposite from six years ago, when dot-com stocks were exciting, but the companies themselves were largely duds. Today's environment says as much about the Internet itself as about the harsh lessons investors have learned. In 2000, investors were willing to buy an Internet stock on the hopes the company, some day, might have a breakthrough product -- or any product at all -- and make money. That was before the bubble popped. Now investors need to see real products, real cash flow and real earnings before they'll make a move. Internet stocks have become the ultimate "show me" plays.

"Something has changed (with Internet investing)," says Ryan Jacob, portfolio manager of the Jacob Internet fund. "You don't have the craziness of a wild IPO [initial public offering] market."

In many ways, this is a healthy change and somewhat of a return to normal in that companies must show their worth before they can hit up the public for cash to expand. After all, it was the freewheeling IPO craze that sparked one of the biggest speculative bubbles in financial history.

Still, it's clear that even though the Internet as a tool is such a key part of our everyday lives, the Internet as an investment is not....

Some Internet companies have resorted to formerly unthinkable lengths to attract investors. Internet access provider United Online even starting paying a dividend, something more associated with slow-growing electric utilities.

...Study Resources 97

A

Name ______ Date ______

CHAPTER 11 | READINGS IN FREE ENTERPRISE
Financial Markets

Saving Too Little or Too Much?

Workers in the United States may not save enough of their income, but the rest of the world may be saving too much. These two articles examine these seemingly contradictory ideas.

End of the Bubble Ballouts

For a quarter-century, Americans' spending binge has been fueled by a declining savings rate and increased borrowing. The savings rate of American consumers has fallen from 12% in the early 1980s to –1.7% today. . . . This means that, on average, consumer spending has risen about a half percentage point more than disposable, or after-tax, income per year for a quarter-century.

The fact that Americans are saving less and less of their after-tax income is only half the profligate consumer story. If someone borrows to buy a car, his savings rate declines because his outlays go up but his disposable income doesn't. So the downward march in the personal savings rate is closely linked to the upward march in total consumer debt (mortgage, credit card, auto, etc.) in relation to disposable income.

Robust consumer spending was fueled first by the soaring stock market of the 1990s and, more recently, by the housing bubble, as house prices departed from their normal close link to the Consumer Price Index and subsequently racked up huge appreciation for homeowners, who continued to save less and spend more. Thanks to accommodative lenders eager to provide refinancings and home equity loans, Americans extracted $719 billion in cash from their houses last year after a $633 billion withdrawal in 2004, according to the Federal Reserve.

When the Bubble Bursts

But the housing bubble is deflating rapidly. . . . A bursting of the bubble would force many homeowners to curb their outlays in order to close the gaps between their income and spending growth. That would surely precipitate a major recession that would become global, given the dependence of most foreign countries on U.S. consumers to buy the excess goods and services for which they have no other markets. . . .

With soaring stock portfolios now ancient history and leaping house prices about to [come to an end], no other sources, such as inheritance or pension fund withdrawals, are likely to fill the gap between robust consumer spending and weak income growth. Consumer retrenchment and the saving spree I've been expecting may finally be about to commence. And the effects on consumer behavior, especially on borrowing and discretionary spending, will be broad and deep.

Source: A. Gary Shilling, *INSIGHT*, August 2006

The Global Savings Glut

We are all taught that saving is good—indeed, Americans are often chided for spending too much and saving too little. But what if the problem of today's global economy is that people elsewhere—in Europe, Asia and Latin America—are saving too much and spending too little?

Copyright © McDougal Littell, a division of Houghton Mifflin Company

Economics: Concepts and Choices Chapter 11 Financial Markets — Readings in Free Enterprise 95 Unit 4 Resource Book

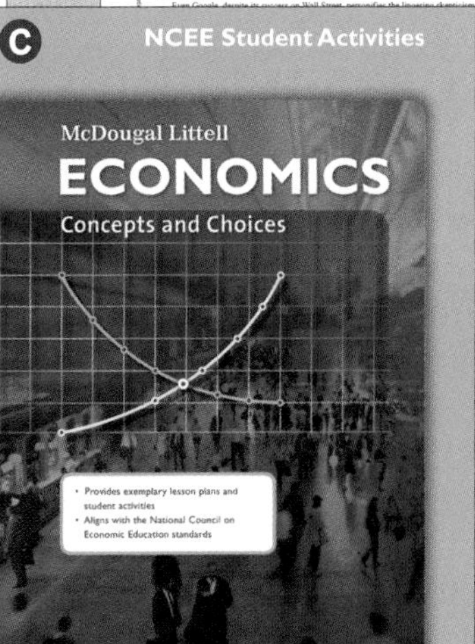

CHAPTER 11

Focus & Motivate

Objective

Explain how the financial system helps transfer funds between savers and investors.

Why the Concept Matters

Invite students to suggest reasons why they save money. Ask them to think about what the financial institutions that hold their savings might do with the money. Explain that their savings are put to work when the money is borrowed and invested by businesses and the government. Lead them to recognize that they are not the only ones to benefit from their savings.

Analyzing the Photograph

Have students study the photograph and read the caption. Invite volunteers to describe what the photograph shows. *(Possible responses: information on different parts of the economy, for example finance, banking, telecommunication, and computers, and changes in stock prices shown in percentages and numbers)*

Ask students what the photograph and caption suggest about the nature of the stock market. *(Possible response: Buyers and sellers keep careful track of changes in stock and bond prices, which may rise or fall based on the interaction of supply and demand.)* Explain that Chapter 11 will describe how investors use a number of financial markets to buy and sell various financial assets in order to make profits.

Stock Market

The stock market, which consists of institutions such as the NASDAQ, is where stocks and bonds are traded.

316

CONTENT STANDARDS

NCEE STANDARDS

STANDARD 10: ROLE OF ECONOMIC INSTITUTIONS

Students will understand that

Institutions evolve in market economies to help individuals and groups accomplish their goals. Banks . . . [and] corporations . . . are examples of important institutions.

Students will be able to use this knowledge to

Describe the roles of various economic institutions.

Benchmarks

Students will know that

- Banks are institutions where people save money and earn interest, and where other people borrow money and pay interest. *(pages 320, 341)*
- Saving is the part of income not spent on taxes or consumption. *(pages 318, 324–325)*
- Banks and other financial institutions channel funds from savers to borrowers and investors. *(pages 318–322, 330–336, 338–341)*

CHAPTER

11

Financial Markets

CONCEPT REVIEW

Voluntary exchange is a trade in which both parties involved believe that what they are getting is worth more than what they are giving up.

CHAPTER 11 KEY CONCEPT

The **financial system** consists of institutions, such as banks, insurance markets, bond markets, and stock markets, that help transfer funds between savers and investors.

WHY THE CONCEPT MATTERS

Do you have a savings account? If so, you play a very important role in our economy. Your savings—what you gave up to get those assets—will be borrowed and invested by businesses and the government to build factories, offices, roads, and so on. The jobs and new products and services created by these investments, in turn, further help to fuel the nation's economy.

Online Highlights

More at ClassZone.com

Economics Update

Go to ECONOMICS UPDATE for chapter updates and current news on investing in Internet companies. (See Case Study, pp. 344–345.)

SMART Grapher

Go to SMART GRAPHER to complete graphing activities in this chapter.

Interactive Review

Go to INTERACTIVE REVIEW for concept review and activities.

"The good news is we've financed another dot.com for no fathomable reason."

Source: www.CartoonStock.com

Why did the dot com companies experience such a rapid rise and fall? See the Case Study on pages 344–345.

From the Classroom

Doug Young, Croton-Harmon High School

The Virtual Stock Exchange

To acquaint students with the basics of investing in the stock market, I have students use the free Internet site www.virtualstockexchange.com. Each student starts with $10,000. They must invest in at least two stocks, and they must make at least two trades during the course of the simulation. The simulation can last as little as one month or as long as the entire school year. At the end, students submit a report that contains a detailed history of their transactions (available through the Virtual Stock Exchange Web site), articles about the companies whose stocks they picked, and an essay explaining what they learned. Anyone whose total portfolio gains more than 10 percent after commissions receives a 5-point bonus. I remind students that "bulls buy, bears sell, chickens are afraid, and pigs get slaughtered."

Previewing Chapter Technology at ClassZone.com

Economics Update Students will find references to online articles or statistics that update information in the pupil edition on pages 318, 325, 326, 334, and 344.

Interactive Review Students will find additional section and chapter assessment support for materials on pages 323, 329, 337, 343, and 346.

TEACHER MEDIA FAVORITES

Books

- Abramson, Bruce. *Digital Phoenix: Why the Information Economy Collapsed and How It Will Rise Again*. Cambridge, MA: MIT Press, 2005. Economics behind the dot-com bubble and the future of the new economy.
- Loviscek, Anthony L., and Randy I. Anderson. *Investing Made Simple: Revised and Updated*. New York: Made Simple, 2004. Varied topics from investment objectives and choices to portfolio management.
- Roberts, Richard. *Wall Street: The Markets, Mechanisms and Players*. New York: Bloomberg, 2003. From the *Economist* series, a guide to the history, workings, and importance of the U.S. financial services industry.
- Stross, Randall E. *eBoys: The First Inside Account of Venture Capitalists at Work*. New York: Crown Business, 2000. Profile of the firm that backed eBay, Priceline.com, and Webvan.

Videos/DVDs

- *A Penny Saved: How to Grow Money.* 21 Minutes. Learning Seed, 2000. Explains simple and compound interest and different investment options.
- *Stock Market Basics: Learning Without Losing.* 24 Minutes. Learning Seed, 2004. Explores dividends, risk, and volatility. Describes how to invest in stocks, bonds, and mutual funds.

Software

- *Virtual Economics® Version 3.0*. New York: National Council on Economic Education, 2005. Complete resource library for understanding and teaching basic economics concepts.

Internet

Visit **ClassZone.com** to link to

- a variety of chapter-specific, content-reviewed sites
- updates on data and topics presented throughout the chapter sections and the Case Study
- updates to the Power Presentations

1 Plan & Prepare

Section 1 Objectives

- identify what constitutes the financial system
- describe the various financial intermediaries
- explain how economists categorize the various markets where financial assets are sold

2 Focus & Motivate

Connecting to Everyday Life Explain that this section focuses on how financial institutions transfer money from savers to borrowers and investors. Encourage students to review what they have learned about how banks use savings deposits to make loans.

Taking Notes Remind students to take notes as they read by completing a hierarchy diagram. They can use the Graphic Organizer at **Interactive Review @ ClassZone.com**. A sample is shown below.

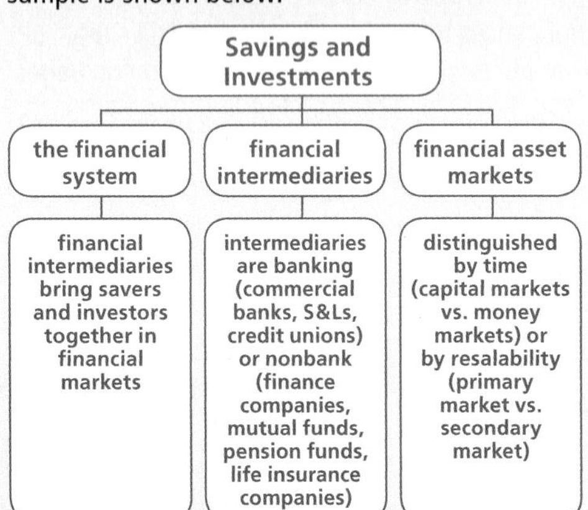
Savings and Investments
the financial system
financial intermediaries
financial asset markets
financial intermediaries bring savers and investors together in financial markets
intermediaries are banking (commercial banks, S&Ls, credit unions) or nonbank (finance companies, mutual funds, pension funds, life insurance companies)
distinguished by time (capital markets vs. money markets) or by resalability (primary market vs. secondary market)

SECTION 1

Savings and Investment

OBJECTIVES

In Section 1, you will
- identify what constitutes the financial system
- describe the various financial intermediaries
- explain how economists categorize the various markets where financial assets are sold

KEY TERMS

savings, *p. 318*
investment, *p. 318*
financial system, *p. 318*
financial asset, *p. 319*
financial market, *p. 319*
financial intermediary, *p. 319*
mutual fund, *p. 320*
capital market, *p. 322*
money market, *p. 322*
primary market, *p. 322*
secondary market, *p. 322*

TAKING NOTES

As you read Section 1, complete a hierarchy diagram to track main ideas and supporting details. Use the Graphic Organizer at **Interactive Review @ ClassZone.com**

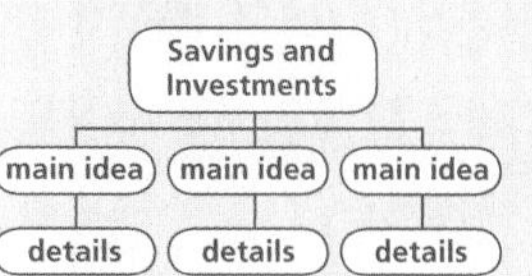
Savings and Investments
main idea
main idea
main idea
details
details
details

The Financial System

QUICK REFERENCE

Savings is income not used for consumption.

Investment is the use of income today that allows for a future benefit.

The **financial system** is all the institutions that help transfer funds between savers and investors.

KEY CONCEPTS

There are two things you can do with your money—spend it or save it. **Savings** is income not used for consumption, in other words not spent on immediate wants. Savings that are put to use are investments. In general, **investment** is the use of income today in a way that allows for a future benefit. More specifically, *economic investment* refers to money lent to businesses—to finance the construction of a new factory, for example. *Personal investment* refers to the act of individuals putting their savings into financial assets, such as CDs, stocks, bonds, or mutual funds.

Consider what happens when you put money in a savings account. Through this act, you benefit—your savings account earns interest—but others do too. By saving, you make funds available for the bank to lend. Borrowers use these funds for many purposes, such as investing in new businesses or in new equipment for established businesses. The **financial system**, which consists of institutions such as banks, insurance markets, bond markets, and stock markets, allows for this transfer of funds between savers and investors.

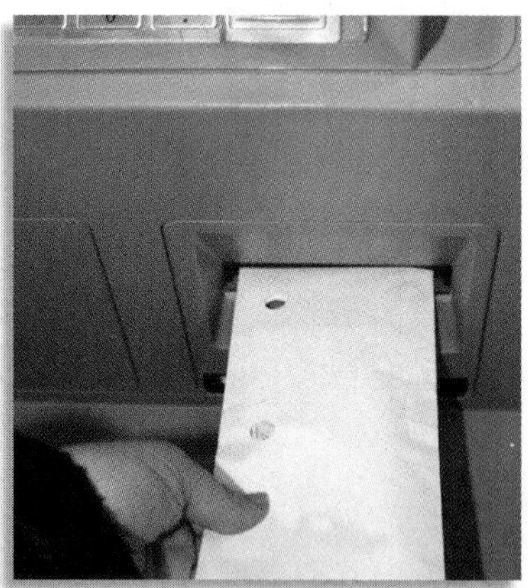

ATM Deposits Using an ATM to make deposits makes saving easy and convenient.

Economics Update

Find an update on saving at **ClassZone.com**

SECTION 1 PROGRAM RESOURCES

ON LEVEL

Lesson Plans
- Core, p. 36

Unit 4 Resource Book
- Reading Study Guide, pp. 53–54
- Math Skills Worksheet, p. 101
- Section Quiz, p. 61

STRUGGLING READERS

Unit 4 Resource Book
- Reading Study Guide with Additional Support, pp. 55–57
- Reteaching Activity, p. 62

ENGLISH LEARNERS

Unit 4 Resource Book
- Reading Study Guide with Additional Support (Spanish), pp. 58–60

INCLUSION

Lesson Plans
- Modified for Inclusion, p. 36

GIFTED AND TALENTED

Unit 4 Resource Book
- Readings in Free Enterprise: Saving Too Much or Too Little, pp. 95–96

TECHNOLOGY

eEdition DVD-ROM

eEdition Online

Power Presentation DVD-ROM

Economics Concepts Transparencies
- CT36 Financial Institutions

Daily Test Practice Transparencies, TT36

ClassZone.com

FIGURE 11.1 **The Financial System**

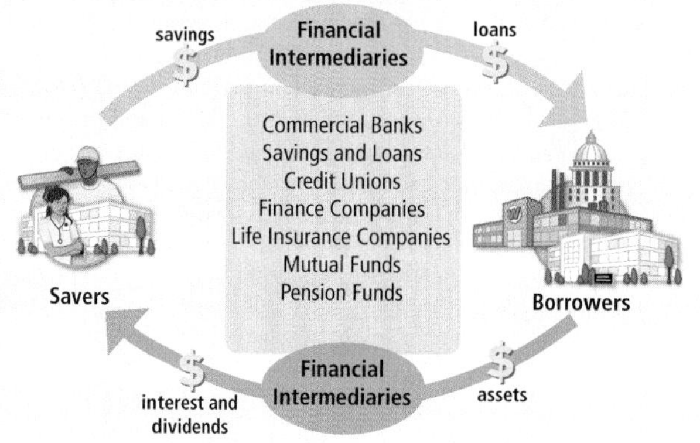

savings

Financial Intermediaries

loans

Commercial Banks
Savings and Loans
Credit Unions
Finance Companies
Life Insurance Companies
Mutual Funds
Pension Funds

Savers

Borrowers

Financial Intermediaries

interest and dividends

assets

ANALYZE CHARTS

1. What do savers get in exchange for the funds they deposit with financial intermediaries?
2. Why do you think that financial intermediaries perform their vital function? Think back to Chapter 10 if you need help.

Bringing Savings and Investment Together

Individuals and businesses can save surplus funds in many ways, including savings accounts at commercial banks or S&Ls, certificates of deposit (CDs), corporate or government bonds, and stocks. The agent receiving these funds is a borrower, who issues savers written confirmation of the transaction. This written confirmation is called a **financial asset**, or a claim on the property of the borrower.

Sometimes savers and borrowers come together directly in a **financial market**, a situation in which buyers and sellers exchange particular types of financial assets. For example, an individual or business might buy corporate bonds or shares of stock. More often, however, financial intermediaries bring savers, borrowers, and financial assets together. A **financial intermediary** is a financial institution that collects funds from savers and then invests these funds in loans and other financial assets. Figure 11.1 shows how funds flow from savers to investors through the financial markets and financial intermediaries that make up the financial system.

QUICK REFERENCE

A **financial asset** is a claim on the property of the borrower.

A **financial market** is where buyers and sellers exchange financial assets.

A **financial intermediary** is an institution that collects funds from savers and invests the funds in financial assets.

APPLICATION Applying Economic Concepts

A. Look again at the example opposite of a person depositing money into a savings account. How is this an example of Adam Smith's "invisible hand"?
Your self-interested action of earning interest helps to channel savings into real investment, thus benefiting the bank and investors, businesses, workers, and consumers.

3 Teach

The Financial System

Discuss

- What is the difference between economic investment and personal investment? *(Economic investment involves lending money to businesses. Personal investment involves putting money in financial assets in order to make money.)*
- How is a financial market different from a financial intermediary? *(Financial markets allow direct exchange of financial assets between buyers and sellers. A financial intermediary transfers funds between savers and borrowers or investors, without direct interaction.)*

Economics Update

At **ClassZone.com** students will see updated information on saving.

Analyze Charts: Figure 11.1

Explain that the diagram summarizes how various financial intermediaries bring savers and borrowers together.

Answers

1. *assets, interest, and dividends*
2. *They perform their function to earn a profit.*

LEVELED ACTIVITY

Educating New Investors

Time 45 Minutes

Objective Students will demonstrate an understanding of how the financial system helps investors achieve their investment objectives. (Draws on material from all four sections.)

Basic

Create a poster to educate personal investors on how the financial system helps them buy and sell financial assets. Include illustrations of some common investment objectives and show specific types of financial assets that are most appropriate to different types of objectives. Explain why diversification is important.

On Level

Create a brochure explaining the basics of savings and investment to young adults. Show a step-by-step process that includes setting investment objectives, analyzing risk and return, and choosing among financial assets to achieve diversification. Explain the role of the financial system in the process.

Challenge

Start with Figure 11.1 as a visual on the home page of an educational Web site on investing. Expand on the diagram by creating copy for linked pages to provide more detail on the role of the financial system, reasons for investing, and types of financial assets appropriate for achieving different objectives.

Financial Intermediaries

Discuss

- What do all banking financial intermediaries have in common? *(They all take deposits and make loans.)*
- What benefits do mutual funds offer to individual investors? *(They make it easier for investors to own a wide variety of financial assets without having to make frequent investment decisions.)*

More About . . .

Mutual Funds
Mutual funds have become popular with both individual investors and large institutional investors, such as pension funds. There are about 8,000 funds available to U.S. investors. Funds offer different types of financial assets to allow investors to meet a variety of objectives.

Most funds allow investors to automatically reinvest dividends in additional shares. Investors realize capital gains if the net asset value (NAV) of the fund's shares increases. The NAV is calculated by dividing the total value of all holdings by the number of shares in the fund. The NAV is reported daily after stock markets close.

Financial Intermediaries

KEY CONCEPTS

Financial intermediaries bring savers and investors together. In Chapter 10, you learned about one group of financial intermediaries—commercial banks, S&Ls, and credit unions. These financial institutions take in deposits from savers and provide loans to individuals and businesses. Many offer other financial assets as well.

Other common financial intermediaries include finance companies, which make small loans; pension funds, which invest money for groups of workers; and life insurance companies, which invest funds collected from policyholders. A **mutual fund** is a pool of money managed by an investment company that gathers money from individual investors and purchases a range of financial assets. Investors own shares of the entire fund based on the amount of their investment. These institutions gather their money in different ways and provide many different financial assets to a variety of investors.

QUICK REFERENCE

A **mutual fund** is an investment company that gathers money from individual investors and purchases a range of financial assets.

EXAMPLE Banking Financial Intermediaries

This group of financial intermediaries includes commercial banks, S&Ls, and credit unions. All of these institutions provide checking and savings accounts. Depositors earn interest on their savings deposits and some checking deposits. Most also offer CDs and money market deposit accounts that pay slightly higher rates of interest. (Figure 11.2 explains how savers earn money from interest.) The federal government insures deposits, including CDs and money market accounts, up to $100,000 per depositor in any given bank.

These institutions lend a portion of their deposits to borrowers. Banks charge borrowers a higher rate of interest than they pay to savers and hope to earn a profit. The loans are financial assets to the bank. If a borrower does not pay back the loan on time, the bank may repossess the property, such as a home or a car.

Deregulation has allowed banks to offer other financial assets, such as money market mutual funds, stocks, bonds, and insurance. The federal government does not insure funds invested in these financial assets.

The New York Stock Exchange Stocks are an important element of the assets that make up a mutual fund.

EXAMPLE Nonbank Financial Intermediaries

This group of financial intermediaries includes finance companies, mutual funds, pension funds, and life insurance companies. Finance companies make loans to households and small businesses. Generally, the loans are under $2,000 and are paid back in monthly installments, including interest, over a few years.

A mutual fund pools money from many personal investors. In return, each investor receives shares in a fund that is made up of a large number and variety of stocks, bonds, or other financial assets. Mutual funds make it easier and more affordable for individual investors to own a wide variety of financial assets. Once investors purchase shares of a fund, they allow its managers to make investment decisions.

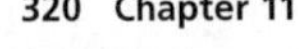

DIFFERENTIATING INSTRUCTION

Struggling Readers

Compare and Contrast
Encourage students to take notes on banking and nonbanking financial intermediaries in a two-column chart. Students should list the types of institutions in each group and the types of financial services that they provide. Call on volunteers to use their charts to describe some of the similarities and differences among institutions in each broad category and between the two categories. Summarize how financial intermediaries bring savers and investors together.

English Learners

Create Word Webs
Help students use word webs to understand different forms of several key verbs in this section, including *save, invest, deposit, lend, borrow.*

- Model a word web with *invest* in the center and *investment, investing,* and *investor* around it. Explain the different uses of each and encourage students to find examples used in sentences.
- Point out that some words signifying an actor are formed by adding *-er* or *-or* to the end of the verb.

Pension funds allow employees to save money for retirement and sometimes include contributions from employers. The pension fund then invests these pooled contributions in various financial assets that will increase in value and provide workers with more money when they retire.

Life insurance companies allow individuals to accumulate savings by building cash values and protect against losses from death or disability. Just as banks lend some of their deposits, insurance companies lend or invest some of the income earned from policyholders in a variety of financial assets.

MATH CHALLENGE

FIGURE 11.2 Calculating Interest

Banks pay savers interest in order to use their money. A saver's initial deposit is called the principal. Simple interest is the interest paid on the principal alone. Compound interest is paid on the principal plus any earned interest. The following steps show how an annual rate of 5 percent interest is paid on the principal ($1,000) over three years.

Year 1 Simple interest is calculated using the following formula:

Principal	×	Interest rate	=	Interest earned	$1,000	×	.05	=	$50.00

Year 2 The amount in this account is now $1,050.00. Compound interest, which is paid on the principal plus the earned interest, is calculated as follows:

(Principal + Year 1 interest)	×	Interest rate	=	Interest earned	($1,000.00 + $50.00)	×	.05	=	$52.50

Year 3 There is now $1,102.50 in the account. Interest continues to compound.

(Principal + Year 1 interest + Year 2 interest)	×	Interest rate	=	Interest earned	($1,000.00 + $50.00 + 52.50)	×	.05	=	$55.13

After three years, the total in the account is $1,157.63.

Using a Formula Instead of using the multiple steps shown above, you can calculate the total value of an account using the following formula (wherein P=principal, r=interest rate, and t=number of years):

$P(1+r)^t$	=	total value	$1,000.00(1+.05)^3$	=	$1,157.63

NEED HELP?

Math Handbook, "Calculating Compound Interest," page R6

APPLICATION Comparing and Contrasting

B. How is a pension fund like a savings account? How is it different? Both allow individuals to save money. Savings account—funds insured; depositor earns interest, can withdraw money at any time. Pension fund—not insured; depositor earns money from investments made by fund, must use money for retirement.

Math Challenge: Figure 11.2

Calculating Interest

Explain that the first formula is the formula for simple interest. If a depositor takes interest out of the account at the end of each year, the amount of interest at the end of three years would be 3 × $50 or $150. Remind students that the *3* in the formula for compound interest indicates that the amount in the parentheses is multiplied by itself three times.

Students will need calculators with an exponent key or may use online calculators. The formula for compound interest shown here assumes that interest is compounded once per year. Interest actually may be compounded more frequently. The more frequent the compounding, the greater the interest earned.

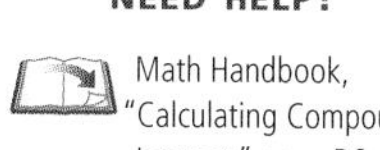

Math Handbook

Calculating Compound Interest, p. R6

SMALL GROUP ACTIVITY

Researching Nonbank Financial Intermediaries

Time 45 Minutes 

Task Gather information on different kinds of financial intermediaries and present findings in oral reports.

Materials Needed computer with Internet access or library resources

Activity

- Organize students into four groups. Assign each group to research one of the types of nonbank financial intermediaries described on pages 320–321.
- Direct students to gather information about the institutions, their customers, and the financial services they provide.
- Encourage them to give specific examples of the particular type of institution that may be relevant to members of your community.
- Allow groups to present their findings in oral reports. Discuss how these institutions contribute to the flow of funds between savers and investors.

Rubric

	Understanding of Financial Intermediaries	Presentation of Information
4	excellent	clear and complete
3	good	mostly clear
2	fair	sometimes clear
1	poor	sketchy

Financial Asset Markets

Discuss

- What kinds of projects are financed through the capital market? *(those that require large amounts of money, such as buying homes, building or refurbishing factories, and building roads or government facilities)*
- How do secondary markets give investors liquidity? *(They allow investors to resell their financial assets at any time for cash.)*

More About . . .

Savings Bonds

Savings bonds are specifically targeted to individual investors and are the only type of federal government security that is not traded on the secondary market. More than 50 million people have invested $200 billion in savings bonds over the years.

Small denomination bonds were first issued in the 1930s, and Series E bonds were a major source of funding for World War II. Now, however, savings bonds account for less than 3 percent of the public debt. The Treasury Department plans to eliminate paper bonds completely at a future date. Savings bonds have been sold electronically since 2002, and about one-quarter of savings bonds are now purchased online.

Financial Asset Markets

QUICK REFERENCE

The **capital market** is where long-term financial assets are bought and sold.

The **money market** is where short-term financial assets are bought and sold.

The **primary market** is for buying financial assets directly from the issuer.

The **secondary market** is where financial assets are resold.

KEY CONCEPTS

The different financial assets discussed in this section are bought and sold on various financial markets. Economists tend to categorize these markets based on two factors—time (how long the loan is for) and whether the financial assets can be resold. Based on time, economists distinguish between the **capital market**, the market for buying and selling long-term financial assets, and the **money market**, the market for buying and selling short-term financial assets. In regard to resalability, economists distinguish between the **primary market**, which is the market for buying newly created financial assets directly from the issuing entity, and the **secondary market**, which is the market where financial assets are resold.

FACTOR 1 Time

There are two time-sensitive markets. Capital markets are markets where assets are held for longer than a year. Some examples of assets sold on the capital market include certain kinds of securities, namely stocks and bonds, mortgages, and long-term CDs. Because these loans are for longer periods of time, the money may be invested in projects that require large amounts of capital, such as buying homes, building new factories, retooling established factories, or financing government projects.

Money markets are markets where loans are made for less than a year. Examples of assets traded in these markets include short-term CDs that depositors can redeem in a few months and Treasury bills, which allow the U.S. government to borrow money for short periods of time.

Return on Investment Time is an important factor in the level of return for many investments.

FACTOR 2 Resalability

There also are two kinds of markets based on whether the financial assets can be resold. Primary markets are markets for financial assets that can be redeemed only by the original buyer. Examples include savings bonds and small denomination CDs. The term *primary market* also refers to the market where the first issue of a stock is sold to the public through investment bankers.

Secondary markets are resale markets for financial assets. These markets offer liquidity to personal investors. So, investors are able to turn their assets into cash relatively quickly. Stocks and bonds, which you'll learn more about later in this chapter, are two of the most prominent financial assets sold on the secondary market.

APPLICATION Analyzing Effects

C. Why are stocks and bonds part of the capital market and the secondary market?
Because they are long-term investments, they are part of the capital market, and yet they can be resold on the secondary market at almost any time.

DIFFERENTIATING INSTRUCTION

Inclusion

Describe Financial Markets

Help students understand the four categories of financial markets. Organize students into groups; one for each market on p. 322.

- Have students write the name, definition, characteristics, and examples of their market on a sheet of newsprint.
- Allow each group to present its information.
- Point out that financial assets may be listed on more than one sheet because markets are categorized in two ways, based on time and resalability.

Gifted and Talented

Research Savings Bonds

Invite students to research additional information on savings bonds. They may use online resources to learn about different types of savings bonds and about why bonds are attractive to investors. Encourage students to create a brochure that promotes savings bonds and their benefits to individual investors. Have them include information on how bonds may be purchased. Allow students to share their brochures with the class.

SECTION 1 Assessment

Online Quiz
ClassZone.com

REVIEWING KEY CONCEPTS

1. Explain the difference between the terms in each of these pairs.
   a. *savings* / *investment*
   b. *capital market* / *money market*
   c. *primary market* / *secondary market*
2. What is the purpose of the financial system?
3. Why do banks receive financial assets when they make loans?
4. How does a mutual fund serve as a financial intermediary?
5. What determines whether a loan is part of the capital market or the money market?
6. **Using Your Notes** What is the relationship between financial intermediaries and the financial system? Refer to your completed hierarchy diagram.

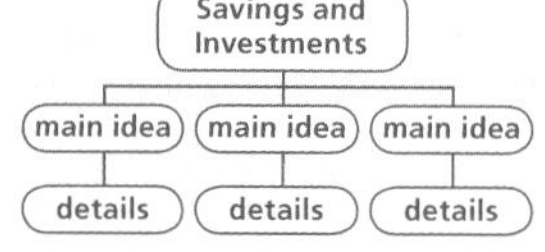

Use the Graphic Organizer at **Interactive Review @ ClassZone.com**

CRITICAL THINKING

7. **Categorizing Information** Which of the following are banking financial intermediaries and which are nonbanking financial intermediaries?
   - Consumer Finance Company
   - Family Life Insurance Company
   - First National Bank
   - Home Savings and Loan
   - Investors' Mutual Fund
   - Employee Credit Union
   - Employee Pension Fund
8. **Making Inferences** A local bank offers savings accounts that have no minimum balance requirement and pay 3 percent interest per year. Account holders can withdraw any amount of money from their accounts at any time. The bank also offers money market accounts that require a $500 minimum balance and pay 4 percent interest each year. Account holders are allowed two withdrawals per month, but each must be for at least $100. Why does the money market account pay a higher interest rate?
9. **Applying Economic Concepts** Suppose that you deposit $100 into your savings account, which earns 3 percent interest per year. Use what you've learned about calculating interest to determine how much money you'll have in your account at the end of one year and at the end of six years.
10. **Challenge** Why might a decrease in household savings have an adverse effect on small businesses in a local community?

ECONOMICS IN PRACTICE

Stock certificates

Identifying Markets
Consider how economists categorize financial markets. Copy the table shown below. Review the bulleted list of financial assets and place each one in the correct location(s) in the table. Assets may be placed in more than one category.

- 15-year mortgage
- 6-month CD for $1,000
- 2-year CD for $25,000
- 5-year corporate bond
- 10-year savings bond
- Shares of stock
- 26-week Treasury bill
- 30-year Treasury bond

Capital Market	Money Market
Primary Market	**Secondary Market**

Challenge Why do savings bonds and small certificates of deposit have less liquidity than shares of stock?

④ Assess & Reteach

Assess Have all students work on the assessment questions. Ask volunteers to share their responses with the class. Discuss answers and assess individual student's understanding of the concepts and details.

Unit 4 Resource Book
- Section Quiz, p. 61

Interactive Review @ ClassZone.com
- Section Quiz

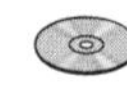

Test Generator CD-ROM
- Section Quiz

Reteach Organize the class into small groups. Write the key terms on the board. Have each group work together to write sentences containing the key terms. Then have the groups share and discuss their responses.

Unit 4 Resource Book
- Reteaching Activity, p. 62

SECTION 1 ASSESSMENT ANSWERS

Reviewing Key Concepts

1. **a.** *savings*, p. 318; *investment*, p. 318
   b. *capital market*, p. 322; *money market*, p. 322
   c. *primary market*, p. 322; *secondary market*, p. 322
2. to transfer funds between savers and investors
3. The loan gives the bank a claim on the property of the borrower, which is a financial asset.
4. A mutual fund gathers savings from many savers and invests it in a variety of financial assets.
5. Loans that are for more than a year are part of the capital market; loans made for less than a year are part of the money market.
6. See page 318 for an example of a completed diagram. Financial intermediaries are the institutions that make up the financial system and transfer funds between savers and investors.

Critical Thinking

7. banking: First National Bank, Home Savings and Loan, Employee Credit Union; nonbanking: Consumer Finance Company, Family Life Insurance Company, Employee Pension Fund
8. Because the money market account has restrictions that give the bank use of more money for longer periods of time, the bank is willing to pay more interest.
9. one year: $103; six years: $119.41
10. When households save less, banks and other financial institutions cannot lend as much to borrowers, such as small businesses.

Economics in Practice

Capital Market: 15-year mortgage; 2-year CD for $25,000; 5-year corporate bond; 10-year savings bond; Shares of stock; 30-year Treasury bond
Money Market: 6-month CD for $1,000; 26-week Treasury bill
Primary Market: 6-month CD for $1,000; 10-year savings bond
Secondary Market: 15-year mortgage; 2-year CD for $25,000; 5-year corporate bond; Shares of stock; 30-year Treasury bond

Challenge because they cannot be resold and require the holder to keep the investment for a specific period of time

1 Plan & Prepare

Section 2 Objectives

- discuss the issues that should be considered when making investment decisions
- explain how risk and return are related

2 Focus & Motivate

Connecting to Everyday Life Explain that this section focuses on the issues to consider when investing. Invite students to suggest reasons for investing for the future.

Taking Notes Remind students to take notes as they read by completing a chart. They can use the Graphic Organizer at **Interactive Review @ ClassZone.com**. A sample is shown below.

Investing in a Market Economy	
objectives	risk vs. return
Time and income play the largest roles in determining the best investments.	There is a direct relationship between risk and return. The greater the risk, the greater the potential return. Investors diversify their portfolios to limit risk and maximize return.

SECTION 2

Investing in a Market Economy

OBJECTIVES

In Section 2, you will
- discuss the issues that should be considered when making investment decisions
- explain how risk and return are related

KEY TERMS

investment objective, *p. 324*
risk, *p. 327*
return, *p. 327*
diversification, *p. 327*

TAKING NOTES

As you read Section 2, complete a chart like the one shown using the key concepts and other helpful words and phrases. Use the Graphic Organizer at **Interactive Review @ ClassZone.com**

Investing in a Market Economy	
objectives	risk vs. return

Why Are You Investing?

KEY CONCEPTS

In Section 1, you saw that there are two types of investing: personal and economic. Note that for the remainder of the chapter, we'll be using all forms of the word *invest* as a quick way to refer to personal investing—which is, in effect, saving.

You've now learned that there are a number of assets you can own. But how do you determine which is, or are, right for you? The first thing that you might do is to decide why you are investing. This reason is your **investment objective**, a financial goal that an investor uses to determine if an investment is appropriate. Some possible financial goals are saving money for retirement, for a down payment on a house or an automobile, for college tuition, or for a vacation. Your goal helps you to determine the right investments.

QUICK REFERENCE

An **investment objective** is a financial goal used to determine if an investment is appropriate.

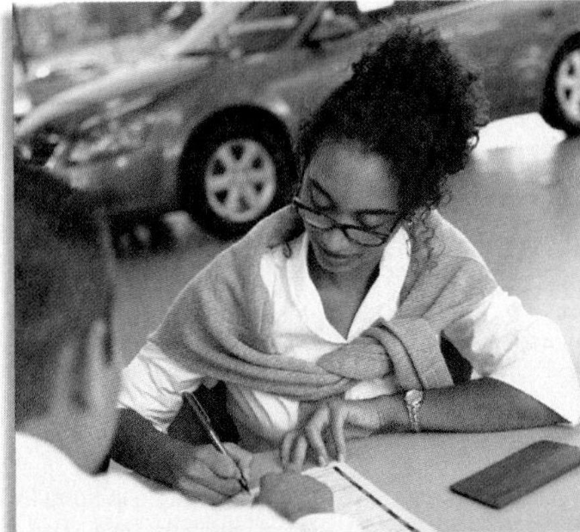

Savings Goals Saving for a car down payment suggests certain kinds of longer-term investments.

Investment Objectives

Two issues play a major role in determining which investments work best to achieve different investment objectives. The first issue is time. For example, is this a short-term financial goal, such as saving for a vacation, or a long-term financial goal, such as saving for

SECTION 2 PROGRAM RESOURCES

ON LEVEL

Lesson Plans
- Core, p. 37

Unit 4 Resource Book
- Reading Study Guide, pp. 63–64
- Economic Skills and Problem Solving Activity, pp. 93–94
- Economic Simulations, 99–100
- Section Quiz, p. 71

STRUGGLING READERS

Unit 4 Resource Book
- Reading Study Guide with Additional Support, pp. 65–67
- Reteaching Activity, p. 72

ENGLISH LEARNERS

Unit 4 Resource Book
- Reading Study Guide with Additional Support (Spanish), pp. 68–70

INCLUSION

Lesson Plans
- Modified for Inclusion, p. 37

GIFTED AND TALENTED

Unit 4 Resource Book
- Case Study Resources: Dot-Coms' Song and Dance No Longer Entertains Investors, pp. 97–98

TECHNOLOGY

eEdition DVD-ROM

eEdition Online

Power Presentation DVD-ROM

Economics Concepts Transparencies
- CT37 Investment Risk and Return, 1990 to 2005

Daily Test Practice Transparencies, TT37

ClassZone.com

YOUR ECONOMIC CHOICES

INVESTMENT OBJECTIVES

What reasons do you have for investing?

Do you have any investment objectives? Maybe you have a short-term objective, such as saving money to go on spring break. Or your objective is more long term, such as saving for college. What kinds of investments might be appropriate for your objective?

Saving for vacation

Saving for college

retirement? The amount of time you have to build your savings influences the kinds of investments that would be most appropriate.

The second issue is income. How much money do you have available to save after meeting current expenses? The answer to this question is influenced by a series of other questions: Will your income change in the future? Is there money available for emergencies? To respond to all these questions, having a savings plan that is realistic and that is flexible enough to adjust to changing circumstances can be a big help.

Other important questions are: Do you have any outstanding debts? Are you paying taxes on time? Paying off debts is an important first step to investing. Generally, the interest you pay on debts, such as credit card balances, is higher than what you can earn through most investments. Tax considerations are most important for investors with higher incomes who are subject to higher tax rates.

Different types of investments are suitable to various investment objectives. For example, savings for emergencies should be in highly liquid investments, such as savings accounts or money market accounts. With these investments, the risk of loss is low and money can be withdrawn at any time. Saving for a vacation would also require investments that are short-term and liquid. Investors who are saving for longer-term goals may be less concerned with immediate liquidity and may want to invest in stocks that increase in value over a longer period of time. CDs that commit funds for a certain length of time may be chosen to coincide with the timing of certain savings goals, such as making a major purchase or starting college. Many bonds offered by state and local governments offer tax-free earnings.

Economics Update

Find an update on investing at **ClassZone.com**

APPLICATION Drawing Conclusions

A. Would a CD be a more appropriate way to save for a down payment on a car or for emergencies? Why? A CD that fits with the timing of when you want to buy a car is appropriate to save for a down payment. CDs are not good for emergencies because money must be committed for a certain period of time.

❸ Teach

Why Are You Investing?

Discuss

- Why is it important to pay off debts before investing? *(because the interest on debts usually exceeds the amount you can earn from most investments)*

Your Economic Choices

INVESTMENT OBJECTIVES

What reasons do you have for investing?

- How does having an investment objective like going on a trip help someone save? *(Possible answer: It is easier to save toward a specific goal because a future reward gives you an incentive not to spend all of your money now.)*

Activity Have students work individually to research the cost of something they would like to buy or do in the next year or two. Ask them to think about how they would save money to pay for it. Allow students to share their ideas in small groups.

 **Economics Update**

At **ClassZone.com**, students will see updated information on investing.

INDIVIDUAL ACTIVITY

Outlining an Investment Plan

Time 20 Minutes 

Task Think about short-term and long-term investment objectives and outline the steps to achieve them.

Materials Needed paper and pens

Activity

- Have students consider financial goals for the next year or two, for five years in the future, and for later in their life.
- Encourage them to use the questions on page 325 to help them think about what they need to do to achieve those goals.
- Direct students to outline an investment plan that is realistic for them, including some ideas for the types of investments that would be most appropriate for reaching each objective.
- Invite volunteers to share with the class some insights that they learned from this activity.

Rubric

	Understanding of Investment Objectives	Presentation of Information
4	excellent	clear and complete
3	good	mostly clear
2	fair	sometimes clear
1	poor	sketchy

Mellody Hobson

More About . . .

Mellody Hobson

Mellody Hobson grew up in Chicago, the youngest of six children. She graduated from Princeton University with a bachelor's degree from the Woodrow Wilson School of International Relations and Public Policy.

Hobson cites her educational experience, which taught her how to solve problems on a large scale, as providing her with valuable skills to apply to the problems she faces in business. For her leadership and community-outreach work, Hobson has been honored by a number of publications and organizations as an important global leader for the future.

More About . . .

Ariel Capital Management

John Rogers founded Ariel Capital Management in 1983 with an investment philosophy based on patience. The firm looks for capital growth over time by investing in companies that are well run but are undervalued or ignored by the market as a whole. Traditionally, the company focused on small to mid-sized U.S. companies, but it has recently added larger-company stocks.

Ariel manages separate accounts for institutional investors, such as retirement funds, unions, and nonprofit organizations. In addition, the firm offers three mutual funds to individual investors.

APPLICATION

Answer *Her goal is for people of all races and economic backgrounds to benefit from investing. For that to happen, investing has to become a topic that's spoken of like any other everyday topic—at the dinner table.*

At **ClassZone.com,** students will see an article about Mellody Hobson.

ECONOMICS PACESETTER

Mellody Hobson: Investing in the Future

FAST FACTS

Mellody Hobson

Title: President of Ariel Capital Management, LLC

Born: April 3, 1969, Chicago, Illinois

Major Accomplishment: Educates millions of people about the benefits of investing.

Ariel's Assets Under Management: $21.3 billion (2005)

Other Roles: Financial contributor to *Good Morning America* on ABC

Board Member: Chicago Public Library, the Field Museum, the Chicago Public Education Fund, and the Sundance Institute

Director: DreamWorks Animation SKG, Inc., the Estée Lauder Companies Inc., and Starbucks Corporation

Find an update on Mellody Hobson at **ClassZone.com**

What do the Chicago Bulls, hip-hop stars, and inner-city elementary school students have in common? All are part of Mellody Hobson's efforts to get investment "discussed around every dinner table." Hobson believes that many people lack the necessary knowledge to determine their investment objectives and manage their money to create wealth. How is she trying to change this situation?

Creating Educated Investors

Mellody Hobson discovered her career in investing as a college intern. When she got her degree in 1991, Hobson landed a position in the marketing department at Ariel Capital Management LLC. In 2000, she became the president of the company, making her the most powerful African-American woman in the mutual-fund industry. As president of Ariel, Hobson runs an operation with over $21 billion in assets.

Ariel was the first minority-owned mutual fund company in the country and pioneered programs to teach inner-city schoolchildren about investing. Hobson's passion for investment education led her to give presentations in locations from PTA meetings to union halls. She developed the first ongoing study of investing by African Americans and looked for ways to increase their participation in the stock market. "The stock market represents a major source of wealth creation in this country," Hobson has stated, "but . . . African Americans have been largely left out." Ariel's marketing efforts to the black community included cosponsoring events with the Chicago Bulls and creating a stock-picking contest involving well-known hip hop stars.

Mellody Hobson

When Hobson became the financial contributor to the *Good Morning America* television program in 2000, she was able to reach millions of people with easy-to-understand information about economic matters. Hobson believes that more knowledge about the benefits of investing in stocks and greater diversity in the investment industry will help bring the benefits of investing to people of all racial and economic backgrounds.

APPLICATION Making Inferences

B. Why might Mellody Hobson think it is important for families to talk about investing at the dinner table? ◀ See Teacher's Edition for answer.

DIFFERENTIATING INSTRUCTION

English Learners

Build Background Knowledge

Help students understand unfamiliar terms.

- Explain that the term *inner-city* means an older, central, often run-down part of a city. Low-income families often live in the inner city.
- *PTA meetings* refers to meetings of the Parent Teacher Association, a volunteer group working to support the school.
- A college intern is a student who works for a company during the summer or part-time during the school year.

Gifted and Talented

Write a Proposal

Encourage students to use the Ariel Capital Management Web site and other Internet resources to find out more about Ariel's education and marketing outreach programs. The Ariel site also has information about the annual survey of African-American investors. Invite students to use this information to develop proposals for educational or marketing projects aimed at helping nontraditional investors achieve their goals. Have students share and discuss their proposals with the class.

Risk and Return

KEY CONCEPTS

Once investors have decided their financial objectives, there are two other related issues they might consider—risk and return. **Risk** is the possibility for loss on an investment, and **return** is the profit or loss made on an investment.

While savings deposits in banks are insured against loss, most investments carry some possibility of losing part of the money invested. Return may refer to the interest paid on a savings account or CD or the increase in value of a stock over time. Most investors try to balance risk and return through **diversification**, the practice of distributing investments among different financial assets to maximize return and limit risk.

QUICK REFERENCE

Risk is the possibility for loss on an investment.

Return is profit or loss made on an investment.

Diversification is the practice of distributing investments among different financial assets.

What Kind of Risk Are You Willing to Take?

When most investors think about risk, they think about the possibility of losing some of their initial investment, often referred to as their principal. Even if they don't earn a lot of money on the investment, they want to get back at least what they put in. Investments that guarantee no loss of principal include insured savings deposits and CDs. Bonds that are backed by the U.S. government are also considered to be almost risk-free because it is highly unlikely that the government would not pay back its loans. Almost all other investments carry some risk.

One of the biggest risks investors face, even with safe investments like those described above, is loss of the purchasing power of the money invested due to inflation. (Remember that inflation is a general rise in the level of prices.) That is why many financial advisers warn against investing everything in safe investments that pay a guaranteed rate of interest that may not keep up with inflation.

Other investments, such as stocks and corporate bonds, carry a higher degree of risk because the return depends on how profitable the company is. Investors who purchase stock with the expectation that it will appreciate in value over time may lose some of their money if the company runs into problems or other economic factors affect the value of the stock. In that case, investors may find that they cannot sell the stock for as much as they paid for it, and they suffer a loss. Investors in corporate bonds face similar risks, although bonds are considered less risky than stocks because creditors such as bondholders are paid off before stockholders if a company has financial problems.

FIGURE 11.3 THE RELATIONSHIP OF RISK AND RETURN

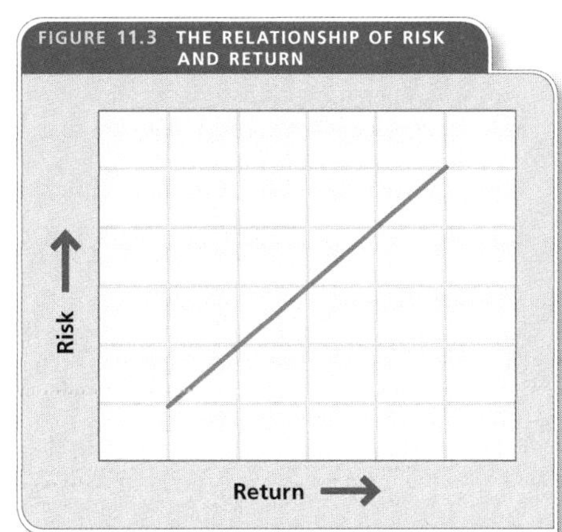

Risk and Return
Risk and return have a direct relationship—the higher the risk of the investment, the greater the possible return.

Risk and Return

Discuss

- What kind of risk is involved in putting money in a bank savings account? *(the risk that the money will lose its purchasing power if the amount of interest does not equal or exceed the rate of inflation)*
- Why are long-term investors generally more tolerant of risk than short-term investors? *(because investing for the long-term gives them time to recoup short-term losses in a bad year)*

More About . . .

Inflation Risk
Inflation always reduces the value of return on an investment, even when it does not wipe it out entirely. Even a low annual inflation rate of 2 percent turns a 6 percent nominal interest rate into a 4 percent real return. Therefore, no investment is entirely risk free. Investors must balance inflation risk with investment risk.

Stocks generally carry a greater investment risk but little inflation risk because a company's revenues and profits tend to keep up with inflation. Safer investments such as CDs and government bonds offer lower returns. So, they are the kinds of investments most susceptible to inflation risk.

INDIVIDUAL ACTIVITY

Illustrating Risk and Return

Time 20 Minutes

Task Create a visual or verbal expression of the relationship of risk and return.

Materials Needed paper and pens or markers

Activity

- Invite students to reflect on what they have learned about the relationship of risk and return. Encourage them to think of ways that this principle might be reflected in areas beyond investing.
- Suggest that they might think about putting a lot of effort into a project for which there is no guaranteed reward but which might offer great satisfaction.
- Invite them to illustrate the relationship of risk and return through a visual, such as a poster, a collage, or a model, or through a story, a poem, or a song. They might use an analogy but should also relate their example to investing.
- Allow students to share their work in small groups.

Rubric

	Understanding of Risk and Return	Presentation of Information
4	excellent	clear, complete, and creative
3	good	mostly clear and somewhat creative
2	fair	sometimes clear, with some creative elements
1	poor	sketchy and unoriginal

Your Economic Choices

RISK AND RETURN

How can you balance risk and return?

- Why is it important to acknowledge that an investment involves the potential for both high return and loss? *(Possible answer: in order to be realistic about whether the possible losses are something you can accept)*
- Why is it easy to lose sight of the possible loss that can come from inflation? *(Possible answer: because the amount of money you have does not decline, and you do not realize how inflation has affected your investment until you go to spend your money)*

Activity Have students work in small groups to develop short questionnaires that they might use to assess their tolerance for risk when it comes to investment. Allow groups to trade questionnaires and have each student fill one out. Discuss what they learned about the level of risk they can tolerate when making investment decisions.

Economics Illustrated

To better understand diversification consider the old saying, "Don't put all your eggs in one basket." When your eggs (investments) are in several baskets (types of financial assets) you are protected from losing all of them if one basket breaks.

stocks

bonds

CDs

YOUR ECONOMIC CHOICES

RISK AND RETURN

How can you balance risk and return?

When you consider what financial assets further your investment objective, you must address both risk and return. A high-risk investment may bring large returns, but can you absorb the potential losses? A low-risk investment may provide a steady return, but because of inflation you may be losing money. How would you decide which type of investment to make?

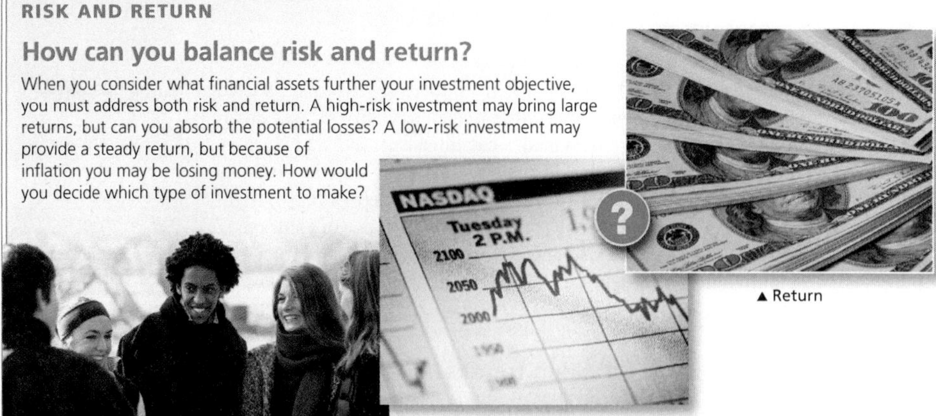

▲ Return

▲ Risk

What Kind of Return Do You Want?

When making investment decisions, investors estimate what kind of return they expect to earn. The safest investments, such as Treasury bills, interest-bearing savings accounts, and shorter-term CDs, generally offer the lowest return in the form of fixed rates of interest. The returns on stocks and bonds are not guaranteed and may vary considerably at different times, depending on how the company you invest in performs and the state of the economy as a whole. Generally, stocks provide a higher return over time than do other investments.

As Figure 11.3 on page 327 shows, risk and return are directly related—the greater the possible return, the higher the risk that the investment will lose value. Investors always want the highest return possible, but they must balance that desire with a realistic understanding about the level of risk they can tolerate. The factors of time and income come into play here. People who are investing for retirement over a period of 20 to 30 years may be willing to take more risk by investing in stocks because their investments are likely to increase over that period, even though they might have losses in some years. People with less time and less income to invest might not be willing to risk possible losses.

Diversification is the most common way for investors to maximize their returns and limit their risks. For example, you might put 70 percent of your investments for retirement in a variety of stocks, 20 percent in bonds, and 10 percent in CDs. By spreading out your money in a variety of assets, you have a better chance of offsetting losses from one investment with gains from another. Mutual funds, which invest in a large number of stocks or bonds, help small investors diversify their investments.

APPLICATION Drawing Conclusions

C. Is it possible to have a low-risk, high-return investment? Why or why not?
Because risk and return have a direct relationship, this type of investment is not possible. Investors accept a lower return for the safety of less risk.

DIFFERENTIATING INSTRUCTION

Struggling Readers

Annotate the Graph
Have students copy Figure 11.3 on their own paper. Then, encourage them to annotate the graph with additional information and examples from their reading of the material on pages 327–328. Students may work individually or in pairs. This activity will help students understand the practical implications of understanding the relationship of risk and return. Invite volunteers to use their annotated graphs to summarize the relationship between risk and return in investing. Clarify understanding as needed.

Inclusion

Create a Pie Chart
Allow students to work with a partner to create a pie chart from the example of diversification in the last paragraph on page 328. Direct them to label the type of financial asset and the percentage of each. Have them write a caption that states how the pie chart illustrates the concept of diversification. Invite volunteers to state in their own words why diversification is important to investors.

SECTION 2 Assessment

REVIEWING KEY CONCEPTS

1. Use each of the three terms below in a sentence that illustrates the meaning of the term:
   a. *investment objective* **b.** *return* **c.** *diversification*
2. What is the relationship between risk and return?
3. How would the risk of investing in a single stock compare with the risk of investing in a mutual fund? Why?
4. How is diversification related to risk and return?
5. How are risk and return related to investment objectives?
6. **Using Your Notes** How do time and income influence investment objectives? Refer to your completed chart.

Investing in a Market Economy	
objectives	risk vs. return

Use the Graphic Organizer at **Interactive Review @ ClassZone.com**

CRITICAL THINKING

7. **Comparing and Contrasting** Matthew's parents started saving for his college education when he was born. When Matthew turned 16, he got a part-time job and saved part of his earnings for his college expenses. Compare and contrast the investment objectives of Matthew and his parents and describe the factors that influenced their investment decisions.
8. **Drawing Conclusions** Ryan owns shares in a single mutual fund that includes stocks and bonds. Maggie invests her money in Treasury bonds, state bonds, and corporate bonds. Joshua invests in shares of stock in five different high-tech companies. Which of these investors best understands the concept of diversification? Give reasons for your answer.
9. **Applying Economic Concepts** Inez bought 100 shares of a mutual fund for $10 each and sold them five years later for $15 each. Ethan put $1,000 in a 5-year CD and received a total of $235 in interest. Which investment provided the better return? How does this illustrate the relationship between risk and return?
10. **Challenge** Stocks that are sold on the secondary market and savings accounts both provide liquidity. For each of these investments, what kinds of risks does this liquidity entail?

Online Quiz
ClassZone.com

ECONOMICS IN PRACTICE

Evaluating Investments
Consider what you have learned about risk and return as they relate to various investments, then study the table below and evaluate each investment.

Identify Risk and Return Place a check mark in the appropriate columns for each investment.

Investment	Risk		Return	
	Low	High	Low	High
$1,000 CD				
100 shares of a mutual fund				
100 shares of stock				
Corporate bond				
Government bond				
Regular savings account				

Challenge Rank the investments in order from the lowest risk to the highest risk and from the lowest return to the highest return. Make a generalization about risk and return based on your rankings.

4 Assess & Reteach

Assess Divide the class into three groups. Assign each group two Reviewing Key Concepts questions and one Critical Thinking question to answer. Have groups present their answers to the class. Clarify understanding as needed. Invite volunteers to answer the Challenge question.

Unit 4 Resource Book
- Section Quiz, p. 71

Interactive Review @ ClassZone.com
- Section Quiz

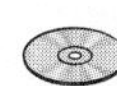

Test Generator CD-ROM
- Section Quiz

Reteach Have each student write a True or False question related to the content of the section. Write students' questions on the board and answer them as a class. Challenge students to make the false statements true by changing a word or phrase.

Unit 4 Resource Book
- Reteaching Activity, p. 72

Economics in Practice
Identify Risk and Return $1,000 CD: risk and return, low; 100 shares of a mutual fund: risk and return, high; 100 shares of stock: risk and return, high; Corporate bonds: risk and return, high; Government bonds: risk and return, low; Regular savings account: risk and return, low

Challenge Ranking: savings account, CD, government bond, corporate bond, mutual fund shares, shares of stock; possible generalization: The lowest risk brings the smallest return.

SECTION 2 ASSESSMENT ANSWERS

Reviewing Key Concepts
1. **a.** *investment objective*, p. 324
   b. *return*, p. 327
   c. *diversification*, p. 327
2. They have a direct relationship—the higher the risk, the higher the potential return.
3. Investing in a single stock is more risky than investing in a mutual fund because there is no diversification in owning a single stock.
4. Diversification helps investors to limit risk and maximize return.
5. Shorter-term objectives generally focus on lower risk investments than do longer-term objectives.
6. See page 324 for an example of a completed diagram. Short-term investment objectives lead to safe, liquid investments, while long-term investment objectives may allow more risk and potential for growth over time. The amount of income available for savings may vary over time and may be affected by more immediate needs.

Critical Thinking
7. Both Matthew and his parents have the same objective, saving for college. However, for his parents the objective is a long-term one. The longer time and their greater income may allow them to choose higher risk investments. Matthew's shorter time frame and smaller income may lead him to a safer investment.
8. Ryan, because he owns a greater number and variety of investment vehicles through the mutual fund than either of the other two
9. Inez earned a 50 percent return on her investment compared to Ethan's 23.5 percent. Inez's higher risk investment provided a higher return, although that return was not guaranteed as Ethan's return was.
10. Stocks sold on the secondary market may decline in value, and if the shareholder needs to sell the stock at that time, he or she will lose some of the money invested. Savings accounts face the risk of losing value to inflation because they pay a low rate of return.

Economics in Practice
See answers in side column above.

❶ Plan & Prepare

Section 3 Objectives

- discuss why people buy stocks
- describe how stocks are traded
- explain how the performance of stocks is measured

❷ Focus & Motivate

Connecting to Everyday Life Explain that this section focuses on the markets for buying and selling stocks. Invite students to review what they know about markets and to suggest some ways that the stock market is likely to be similar to other markets.

Taking Notes Remind students to take notes as they read by completing a cluster diagram. They can use the Graphic Organizer at **Interactive Review @ ClassZone.com**. A sample is shown below.

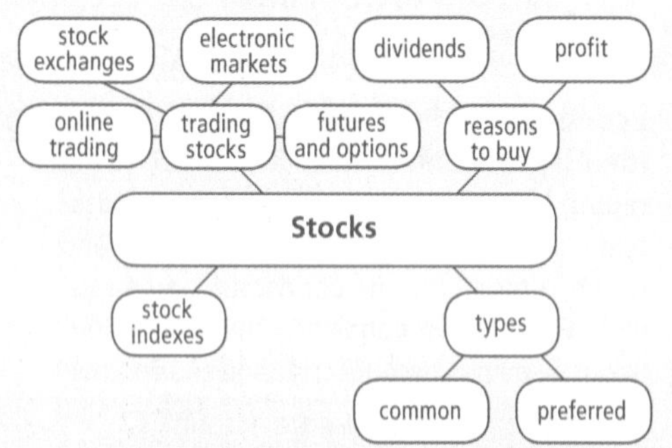

SECTION 3

Buying and Selling Stocks

OBJECTIVES	KEY TERMS	TAKING NOTES
In Section 3, you will • discuss why people buy stocks • describe how stocks are traded • explain how the performance of stocks is measured	stock exchange, *p. 330* capital gain, *p. 330* common stock, *p. 331* preferred stock, *p. 331* stockbroker, *p. 332* future, *p. 333* option, *p. 333* stock index, *p. 334* bull market, *p. 335* bear market, *p. 335*	As you read Section 3, complete a cluster diagram using the key concepts and other helpful words and phrases. Use the Graphic Organizer at **Interactive Review @ ClassZone.com** 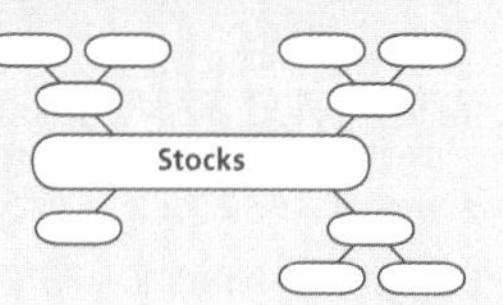

The Stock Market

KEY CONCEPTS

Recall that in Chapter 8 you learned that corporations raise money through stock and bond issues. You will learn more about the sale—and resale—of stocks in this section. When a company first issues stock, it is sold to investment bankers in the primary market. Known as an initial public offering, or IPO, this is the stock sale that raises money for the corporation.

However, most stock is then resold to investors through a **stock exchange**, a secondary market where securities (stocks and bonds) are bought and sold. Most people buy stocks as a financial investment, with the expectation that the stock price will rise and that they can resell the stock for a profit. Gains made from the sale of securities are called **capital gains**.

QUICK REFERENCE

A **stock exchange** is a market where securities are bought and sold.

Capital gain is profit made from the sale of securities.

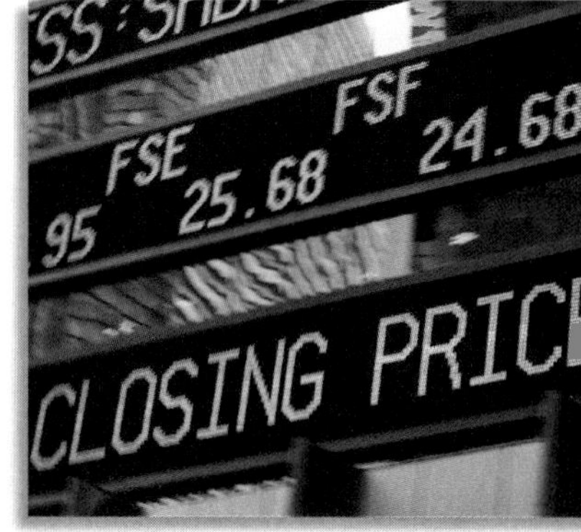

Why Buy Stock?

Investors buy stock for two reasons. The first is to earn dividend payments, which are a share of the corporation's profits that are paid back to the corporation's stockholders. The second reason is to earn capital gains by selling the stock at a price greater than the purchase price. If stock is sold below the buying price, the seller makes a capital loss. Investors who want to earn income

SECTION 3 PROGRAM RESOURCES

ON LEVEL

Lesson Plans
- Core, p. 38

Unit 4 Resource Book
- Reading Study Guide, pp. 73–74
- Economic Simulations, pp. 99–100
- Section Quiz, p. 81

STRUGGLING READERS

Unit 4 Resource Book
- Reading Study Guide with Additional Support, pp. 75–77
- Reteaching Activity, p. 82

ENGLISH LEARNERS

Unit 4 Resource Book
- Reading Study Guide with Additional Support (Spanish), pp. 78–80

INCLUSION

Lesson Plans
- Modified for Inclusion, p. 38

GIFTED AND TALENTED

Unit 4 Resource Book
- Case Study Resources: Dot-Com's Song and Dance No Longer Entertains Investors, pp. 97–98

TECHNOLOGY

eEdition DVD-ROM

eEdition Online

Power Presentation DVD-ROM

Economics Concepts Transparencies
- CT38 Performance of Leading Stocks

Daily Test Practice Transparencies, TT38

ClassZone.com

from their investment will be most interested in dividends. Those who want to see their investment grow over time will be most interested in potential for capital gain.

As you learned in the previous section, investing in stocks carries a higher risk than most other investments but provides the opportunity for higher returns over time. Corporations are not required to pay dividends, so an investor has no guarantee that they will earn income from stocks. Similarly, there is no guarantee that the stock price will be higher when the investor wants to sell the stock.

"IN LIEU OF A DIVIDEND, YOU'LL BE E-MAILED A 'STOCK TIP DU JOUR'."

Source: www.CartoonStock.com

No Guarantees Dividend payments are a possibility, not a certainty; stocks come with risk.

Types of Stock

There are essentially two types of stock—common stock and preferred stock. **Common stock** is share of ownership in a corporation, giving holders voting rights and a share of profits. **Preferred stock** is share of ownership in a corporation giving holders a share of profits (paid before common stockholders) but no voting rights. Most people who buy stock choose to buy common stock.

Figure 11.4 shows the similarities and differences between the two types of stock. Notice that both types of stock give a share of ownership in the corporation that entitles a shareholder to receive dividends. The difference is that holders of preferred stock receive guaranteed dividends and will be paid before common stockholders if the company is liquidated. As a tradeoff for this preference, holders of preferred stock generally have no voting rights in the corporation, and their dividends do not increase if the company's stock increases in value. Each holder of common stock generally gets one vote per share owned to elect the board of directors, which makes important decisions about how the company conducts business.

QUICK REFERENCE

Common stock gives shareholders voting rights and a share of profits.

Preferred stock gives shareholders a share of profits but, in general, no voting rights.

FIGURE 11.4 Common Stock and Preferred Stock

Characteristic	Preferred Stock	Common Stock
Share of ownership	Yes	Yes
Eligible for dividends	Yes	Yes
Guaranteed dividends	Yes	No
Voting rights	No	Yes

ANALYZE CHARTS

1. What preference do holders of preferred stock have?
2. What do holders of common stock have that holders of preferred stock do not have?

APPLICATION Drawing Conclusions

A. What kind of stock do you think investors who wanted a steady income from their investment would buy? Why?

preferred stock, because it is more focused on a steady stream of return through dividends

3 Teach

The Stock Market

Discuss

- What is the difference between dividends and capital gains? *(Dividends are a way that companies share their profits with investors. Capital gains are profits that investors make from selling stock that has increased in value.)*
- Why are stocks riskier than other types of investments? *(because there is no guarantee that the company will pay dividends or that the stock's price will be higher when the investor wants to sell it)*

Analyzing Charts: Figure 11.4

Explain that this chart summarizes the similarities and differences between common stock and preferred stock. Ask students what the two types of stocks have in common. *(They both give a share of ownership in a company and make the shareholder eligible for dividends.)*

Answers

1. *They receive guaranteed dividends.*
2. *voting rights*

SMALL GROUP ACTIVITY

Expanding Key Concepts

Time 30 Minutes

Task Gather information on key concepts related to stocks, and share the information in oral reports.

Materials Needed computer with Internet access

Activity

- Organize students into small groups to research concepts introduced on this spread.
- Possible topics are: (1) the primary market for stocks—role of investment bankers and initial public offerings (IPOs), (2) dividends—when they are paid, what kind of investors look for them, (3) capital gains—how they are earned and taxed, (4) preferred stock—how investors benefit and any drawbacks, and (5) common stock—how are voting rights exercised.
- Encourage students to use the Internet or library resources and to take notes on their topic.
- Allow each group to present its findings in an oral report.

Rubric

	Understanding of Key Concepts	Presentation of Information
4	excellent	clear and complete
3	good	mostly clear
2	fair	sometimes clear
1	poor	sketchy

Trading Stock

Discuss

- How does the stock market follow the laws of supply and demand? *(Buyers will buy more stock at lower prices, and sellers will sell more stock at higher prices.)*
- What is the difference between a future and an option? *(A future contract requires the investor to buy or sell the stock on a specific date for a specific price. An option contract gives the investor a choice about whether to buy or sell the stock at the specified date and price.)*

More About . . .

The New York Stock Exchange

The NYSE is also referred to as the Big Board, and its origins date back to 1792. Although NASDAQ trades more shares, the dollar volume on the NYSE is still the largest in the world. The capitalization of companies listed on the NYSE was about $15 trillion in 2006. About one-third of that amount was in non-U.S. companies.

When the NYSE merged with Archipelago Holdings, it formed the NYSE Group as a for-profit corporation whose stock is traded on the NYSE. The owners of NYSE trading licenses at the time of the merger received payment in cash and shares of NYSE Group. The 1,366 licenses are now sold for an annual licensing fee.

Trading Stock

KEY CONCEPTS

Most people who invest in stock do so with the hope of earning capital gains when they sell it. Like anything else sold in a free market, stock prices are determined by demand and supply. Some factors that affect stock prices include company profits or losses, technological advances that may affect a company's business or a whole industry, and the overall state of the economy. When investors perceive that a company's value is likely to increase, the demand for the stock will increase and its price will rise. As the price rises, more people will want to sell the stock for a profit.

Few companies sell stock directly to investors. When investors want to buy or sell stock, they use a **stockbroker**, an agent who, for a commission, buys and sells securities for customers. Stockbrokers, sometimes just called brokers, generally work for brokerage firms. Investors may interact with brokers in person, by phone, or online. The broker's primary job is to carry out the investor's instructions to make trades. Some brokers also provide investment advice. Brokers buy and sell stocks for their customers on a variety of stock exchanges.

QUICK REFERENCE

A **stockbroker** buys and sells securities for customers.

Controlled Chaos Don't be fooled by the seeming disorder of the exchange floor. It is a secure and organized trading system.

Organized Stock Exchanges

The New York Stock Exchange (NYSE) is the oldest and largest of the organized stock exchanges in the United States. It is located on Wall Street in New York City, and the street name has become synonymous with the U.S. stock market. Almost 1.5 billion shares of about 2,800 of the largest and most successful U.S. companies are traded on the NYSE each day. Brokerage firms pay for the privilege of being one of the 1,336 members of the exchange.

Traditionally, trading on the NYSE was in an organized auction format. Each stock had a specified location or trading post on the floor of the exchange. A specialist representing that stock ran the auction that matched buyers and sellers through open bidding to determine the price of shares. Prices for a stock often varied from minute to minute as the auction process continued throughout the day.

Changes in technology have brought changes to the NYSE. Since 1996, floor traders have used small hand-held computers to execute many trades, and more than half of the orders to buy and sell are now sent electronically. In 2006, the NYSE merged with Archipelago Exchange, an electronic trading company. This allowed the NYSE not only to speed up its transactions, but also to trade stocks normally traded in electronic markets.

The smaller American Stock Exchange (AMEX) is also located in New York City. Trading at the AMEX is structured in a similar way to the NYSE, although AMEX-traded companies are generally smaller than those listed on the NYSE. In 2006, AMEX introduced new practices that combined the benefits of floor trading and electronic trading.

DIFFERENTIATING INSTRUCTION

Struggling Readers

Use Jigsaw Reading

Review the Key Concepts paragraphs. Then, organize students into home groups of four. Assign one person in each group to one of the subheadings on pages 332–333. Have students form new groups based on their subhead. Instruct them to read and discuss the material. They may want to take notes to refer to when they return to their home groups. After students reassemble in their home groups, allow each student a few minutes to explain the material studied to the others.

English Learners

Understand Abbreviations

Help students understand the meaning and pronunciation of abbreviations associated with trading stocks.

- Explain that these abbreviations are formed from the first letters or syllables of a phrase. Some are pronounced letter by letter, such as NYSE, OTC, and ECN.
- Acronyms are pronounced as a word, for example NASDAQ (NAZ-dak).
- Apply this process to the names of stock indexes on page 334. DAX and FTSE (FOOT-see) are acronyms.

Electronic Markets

The term *over-the-counter* (OTC) is used to describe the market for stocks that are not traded on the NYSE or AMEX. In 1970, the National Association of Securities Dealers (NASD) introduced a centralized computer system that allows OTC traders around the country to make trades at the best prices possible.

This automated quotation system is known as NASDAQ. In 2005, NASDAQ was the second-largest stock exchange in the world in number of companies listed (about 3,200) and number of shares traded daily. The companies listed on NASDAQ cover many sectors of the U.S. economy, although the majority are involved in technology. The NASD also regulates the OTC Bulletin Board as an electronic market for trading shares in companies that are too small to be traded on NASDAQ.

FIGURE 11.5 SOME NASDAQ STOCKS

Apple Inc.	Peets Coffee & Tea
Dell Inc.	Priceline.com
Fujifilm Corporation	Sirius Satellite Radio
Google	Sun Microsystems Inc.
Intel Corporation	United Stationers Inc.

Futures and Options Markets

Most investors do not trade futures and options because they are complicated and high-risk investments that involve trying to predict the future. A **future** is a contract to buy or sell a stock on a specified future date at a preset price. An investor who wants to buy in the future wants to lock in a low price. An investor who wants to sell in the future wants to lock in a high price.

An **option** is a contract giving the investor the right, but not the obligation, to buy or sell stock at a future date at a preset price. As you can see, the difference between a future and an option is that a futures contract requires the investor to buy or sell, while an option contract offers the possibility of buying or selling but does not require it. In options trading, an investor pays a small fraction of a stock's current price for an option to buy or sell the stock at a better price in the future.

QUICK REFERENCE

A **future** is a contract to buy or sell a stock on a specific future date at a preset price.

An **option** gives an investor the right to buy or sell stock at a future date at a preset price.

Recent Developments

In the late 1990s, new stock market regulations and advances in computer technology changed the way that stocks were traded. Stocks listed on any exchange are now available to any trading firm. The growth of electronic communications networks (ECNs) increased electronic stock trading, especially on the NASDAQ market. Trades now take place 24 hours a day, not just when the stock exchanges are open.

Many individual investors have access to the Internet and have become more knowledgeable about investing. They wanted ways to trade stocks without relying on traditional stockbrokers. The result has been huge growth in online brokerage companies. Investors now have the ability to make trades at any time and generally pay lower commissions than those charged by traditional brokers. Computer technology matches buyers and sellers automatically, providing rapid trades at the best possible prices.

APPLICATION Drawing Conclusions

B. How is NASDAQ similar to the NYSE? How are they different?

Both are stock exchanges. The stocks traded and the ways they are traded are different on the two exchanges.

Presentation Options

Review some of the elements of trading stock by using the following presentation options:

Power Presentations DVD-ROM
Using the Display Tool, you can highlight the major features of investing in the stock market.

Economics Concepts Transparencies
- CT38 Performance of Leading Stocks

Technomics

Securities and Exchange Commission
The Securities and Exchange Commission (SEC) is the federal regulatory body with oversight of all securities trading in the United States. The commission's Web site has a wealth of information for investors, including online publications on a wide variety of topics.

Publications cover subjects such as different financial assets, financial intermediaries, brokers, stock exchanges, and online investing. There is also a special section for teachers and students.

SMALL GROUP ACTIVITY

Researching Stock Trading

Time 45 Minutes 

Task Research different ways that stocks are traded and create a news program segment.

Materials Needed computer with Internet access

Activity
- Organize students into groups to research different ways that stocks are traded. They should research the NYSE, AMEX, and NASDAQ markets and also brokerage companies, ECNs, and futures and options markets.
- Information may be found on individual market Web sites or in other online resources, such as encyclopedias or the government Web site of the Securities and Exchange Commission.
- Encourage each group to prepare a three- to five-minute segment for a news program on stock trading.
- Discuss as a class how stock trading has changed over time.

Rubric

	Understanding of Stock Trading	Presentation of Information
4	excellent	clear and complete
3	good	mostly clear
2	fair	sometimes clear
1	poor	sketchy

Measuring How Stocks Perform

Discuss

- What do all stock indexes have in common? *(They measure the change in price of a particular group of stocks.)*
- Why are the stocks on the DJIA called "blue chip" stocks? *(Possible answer: because they represent the most successful and important companies on the market)*

Economics Update

At **ClassZone.com,** students will see updated information on stocks in the Dow Jones Industrial Average.

Analyzing Graphs and Tables: Figures 11.6 and 11.7

Explain that Figure 11.6 is based on the year-end closing average of the DJIA and therefore reflects overall trends rather than the ups and downs that the market might experience from day to day. Ask them to compare the trends during the periods 1985–1995 and 1995–2005. *(1985–1995, the Dow went up gradually; 1995–2005, the Dow rose sharply for about 5 years, declined for awhile, but then recovered and was still much higher than it was in 1995)* Point out that Figure 11.7 is based on the percentage of change from the previous year rather than the closing average.

Answers

1. *The volume of shares traded and the DJIA seem to have a direct relationship.*
2. *1954, 5th best; 1937, 5th worst*

Measuring How Stocks Perform

KEY CONCEPTS

QUICK REFERENCE

A **stock index** measures and reports the change in prices of a set of stocks.

About half of all U.S. households now own stocks, and the stock market's performance is followed closely on the nightly news, not just in specialized business media. Perhaps you have heard a statement like this one: "Wall Street responded positively to the latest employment figures, with the Dow making robust gains for the first time in several weeks." The Dow is a **stock index**, an instrument used to measure and report the change in prices of a set of stocks. Stock indexes measure the performance—whether gaining or declining in value—of many individual stocks and the stock market as a whole.

Stock Indexes

Economics Update

Find an update on stocks in the Dow Jones Industrial Average at **ClassZone.com**

Stock indexes provide a snapshot of how the stock market is performing. The Dow—short for the Dow Jones Industrial Average (DJIA)—is the most well known. (For help reading Figure 11.6, turn to the Skillbuilder on page 342.) Other U.S. indexes often cited include the Standard & Poor's 500 (S&P 500) and the NASDAQ Composite. Global stock indexes include the Hang Seng Index (Hong Kong), the DAX (Germany), the Nikkei 225 (Japan), and the FTSE 100 (Britain). Each index measures the performance of a different group of stocks.

FIGURE 11.6 DOW JONES INDUSTRIAL AVERAGE, 1929–2006

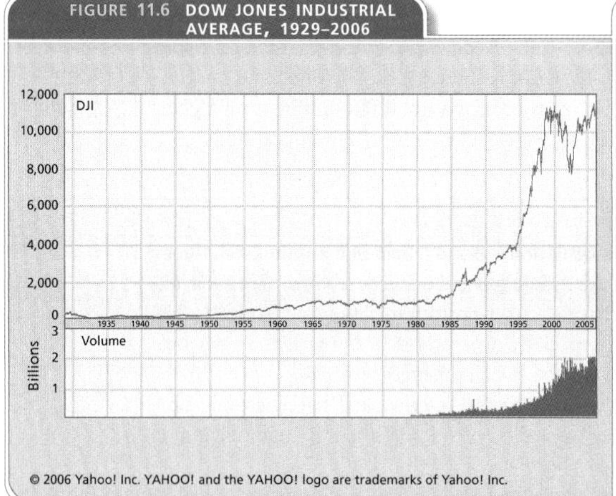

© 2006 Yahoo! Inc. YAHOO! and the YAHOO! logo are trademarks of Yahoo! Inc.

FIGURE 11.7 THE DOW'S BEST AND WORST YEARS

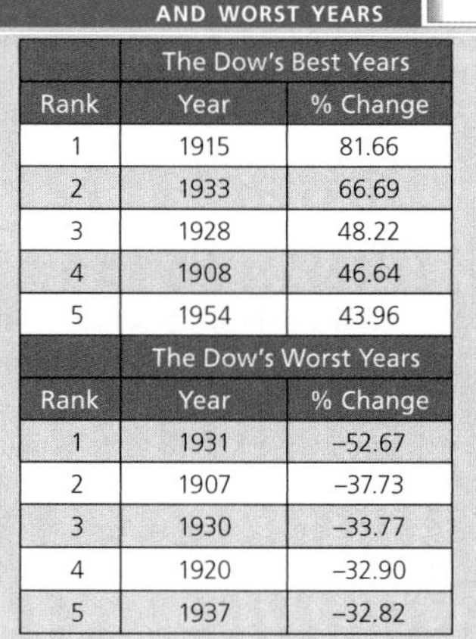

The Dow's Best Years		
Rank	Year	% Change
1	1915	81.66
2	1933	66.69
3	1928	48.22
4	1908	46.64
5	1954	43.96
The Dow's Worst Years		
Rank	Year	% Change
1	1931	–52.67
2	1907	–37.73
3	1930	–33.77
4	1920	–32.90
5	1937	–32.82

ANALYZE CHARTS

1. Does Figure 11.6 suggest a relationship between the level of the DJIA (above) and the volume of shares traded (below)? Explain.
2. What were the most recent best and worst years for the Dow?

DIFFERENTIATING INSTRUCTION

Struggling Readers

Compare Economic Information

Direct students to Figures 11.6 and 11.7, as they read "Tracking the Dow." Comparing the closings described there with those shown in Figure 11.7 will help them see how rapidly stock prices rose between 1985 and 2000. They can also see how the end of the 1990s bull market was not as drastic as the bear market after the 1929 crash. Encourage students to see how Figure 11.7 shows the effects of the 1929 crash. *(1930 and 1931 were two of the Dow's three worst years.)*

English Learners

Create Word Squares

Explain that *bull market* and *bear market* have been used for hundreds of years, although most people no longer know where the terms came from. Have pairs work to create word squares for each term to help them remember the difference between them. Invite students to form literal translations of the phrases in their first language, and to include similar phrases, if they exist, that may not be exact translations. Have volunteers share their word squares with the class.

FIGURE 11.8 THE 30 STOCKS IN THE DJIA

Alcoa Inc.	Exxon Mobil Corp.	McDonald's Corp.
Altria Group, Inc.	General Electric Co.	Merck & Co.
American Express Co.	General Motors Corp.	Microsoft Corp.
American International Group Inc.	Hewlett-Packard Co.	3M
AT&T Inc.	Home Depot Inc.	Pfizer Inc.
Boeing Co.	Honeywell International Inc.	Procter & Gamble Co.
Caterpillar Inc.	Intel Corp.	United Technologies Corp.
Citigroup Inc.	International Business Machines Corp.	Verizon Communications Inc.
Coca-Cola Co.	J.P. Morgan & Co.	Wal-Mart Stores Inc.
Dupont Co.	Johnson & Johnson	Walt Disney Co

The Dow Jones Company, publisher of the *Wall Street Journal* newspaper, first published the DJIA in 1896. The index included the stocks of 12 companies that reflected the economy of the time, which was focused heavily on agriculture and mining. Since 1928, the Dow has included 30 companies. General Electric is the only one of the original companies that is on the current index. As the U.S. economy has changed from agriculture to industry to services, the companies in the index have changed to reflect the most successful companies in the most important sectors of the economy. These stocks are often referred to as blue chip stocks.

The DJIA is a price index, in other words it measures changes in the prices at which the stocks on the index are traded. The original DJIA was the actual average of the prices of the 12 stocks. Now the average is weighted so that higher-priced stocks have more influence on the average than lower-priced stocks. The number that is quoted is not a price but an average measured in points not dollars.

QUICK REFERENCE

A **bull market** occurs when stock market prices rise steadily over time.

A **bear market** occurs when stock market prices decline steadily over time.

Tracking the Dow

Changes in the Dow reflect trends in stock market prices. The terms *bull market* and *bear market* are commonly used to describe these trends. A **bull market** is a situation where stock market prices rise steadily over a relatively long period of time. A **bear market** is a situation where stock market prices decline steadily over a relatively long period of time. Those who follow the stock market track the Dow and other indexes to determine if the market is trending toward bull or bear.

The first DJIA measure was 40.94. In 1972, it reached 1,000 for the first time, and in May 1999, it topped 11,000. When the Dow hit its all-time high of 11,722.98 on January 14, 2000, it marked the end of the longest bull market in history. During the 1990s the Dow had climbed from 2,800 to its peak. Most bull markets last two to three years.

A well-known bear market followed the Stock Market Crash of 1929. During the 1920s, the Dow had risen from 60 to a high of 381.17 in early September of 1929. In the month after October 29, 1929, it fell to a low of just under 199. The next time it achieved a closing price of 400 was December 29, 1954.

'Better order in more porridge'

Source: www.CartoonStock.com

International Economics

Global Stock Indexes

Many major global stock indexes reflect the largest stock market in individual countries. The Hang Seng Index tracks the 33 largest companies on the Hong Kong Stock Exchange. The DAX (abbreviation from *Deutscher Aktienindex*) is similar to the DJIA and tracks 30 blue-chip stocks on the Frankfurt Stock Exchange.

The FTSE (from Financial Times Stock Exchange) tracks the 100 largest companies on the London Stock Exchange. The Nikkei 225 tracks the most important companies on the Tokyo Stock Exchange. The leading Canadian index is the S&P/TSX Composite, which tracks about 200 companies on the Toronto Stock Exchange.

CLASS ACTIVITY

Exploring the Stocks on the Dow

Time 45 Minutes

Task Gather information on stocks that make up the DJIA, prepare fact sheets, and discuss.

Materials Needed computer with Internet access, paper and pen

Activity

- Depending on the size of the class, assign students to research one or more companies listed in Figure 11.8.
- Discuss with students the type of information to be gathered on each company, such as stock symbol, previous closing price, 52-week high and low prices, market capitalization ($ billion), market sector, industry, and brief business summary. Consider creating a fact sheet template for students to fill in.
- Allow students to present their information to the class. Discuss how well the DJIA reflects the U.S. economy.

Rubric

	Understanding of the DJIA Stocks	Presentation of Information
4	excellent	clear and complete
3	good	mostly clear
2	fair	sometimes clear
1	poor	sketchy

A Global Perspective

Investing Money Overseas

Foreign stocks are traded on the NYSE, AMEX, and NASDAQ in the form of American Depositary Receipts (ADRs). The ADRs represent shares of foreign stock that have been purchased by U.S. banks. The banks then trade the ADRs on U.S. markets. This practice allows U.S. investors to trade in foreign stock in U.S. dollars.

Companies that offer ADRs on the major markets must register with the SEC. Many U.S. investors choose to invest in mutual funds that invest in foreign stocks. International funds invest only in non-U.S. companies, while global funds may include some U.S. companies. Some funds focus on certain regions or countries.

Answers

1. *yes, because the global market is increasingly important and electronic trading makes it easier to access overseas stock markets*
2. *the Bombay Stock Exchange and the Cairo and Alexandria Stock Exchange; the New York Stock Exchange*

A GLOBAL PERSPECTIVE

Investing Money Overseas

In an increasingly international economy, the NYSE is no longer the "only game in town" for U.S. investors. There are over 20 major stock markets overseas. With U.S. stocks representing only about half of the total value of global markets, international investing has become an important option for Americans.

Investing money overseas offers both advantages and risks. For example, an investment in an emerging country—one with an economy that is rapidly growing—offers the prospect of a greater and more rapid return. Such an investment also may involve greater risk, for political instability in an emerging country can drive stock prices down in a hurry. However, many investors view increased diversification as the primary advantage of investing overseas.

FIGURE 11.9 Leading World Stock Markets

Market	Number of Companies Listed	Value of Stocks (in billions of US dollars)	Main Index
New York Stock Exchange (United States)	2,278	15,138	Dow Jones Industrial Average
Tokyo Stock Exchange (Japan)	2,392	4,550	Nikkei 225
London Stock Exchange (United Kingdom)	3,231	3,718	FTSE 100
Bombay Stock Exchange (India)	4,786	801	Sensex
Sao Paulo Stock Exchange (Brazil)	347	660	Ibovespa
Cairo and Alexandria Stock Exchanges (Egypt)	618	88	CASE 30

Source: World Federation of Exchanges, November 2006 data

CONNECTING ACROSS THE GLOBE

1. **Synthesizing Economic Information** Do you think it likely that U.S. investment in overseas stock markets will become increasingly common? Explain your answer.
2. **Drawing Conclusions** Compare the total value of stocks to the number of companies listed. Which two exchanges have the least expensive stocks, on average? Which exchange has the most expensive stocks?

Many factors affect the Dow's performance. Among these are the market's previous close, actions by the Federal Reserve that affect interest rates or the money supply, the performance of foreign indexes, and the trade balance between imports and exports.

APPLICATION Drawing Conclusions

C. Why have the stocks on DJIA changed over time?
to reflect changes in the American economy

DIFFERENTIATING INSTRUCTION

Inclusion

Explain the Table

Help students to understand Figure 11.9 by explaining that it presents a snapshot of the markets from November 2006. The number of companies listed and the total value of stocks change from day to day. Use the table to help students understand the information presented on pages 332–336.

Gifted and Talented

Investigate Global Stock Indexes

Invite students to use the Internet to research global stock indexes, such as those mentioned on this page or others they may discover. Encourage them to find out how the index is related to the country's stock market. They may also research global indexes that track one or more countries or regions and that are compiled by U.S. companies, such as the NYSE Group, Standard & Poor's (S&P), and Dow Jones & Company. Allow students to present their findings in oral reports.

SECTION 3 Assessment

Online Quiz ClassZone.com

REVIEWING KEY CONCEPTS

1. Explain the relationship between the terms in each of these pairs:
   - **a.** *stock exchange* / *stockbroker*
   - **b.** *future* / *option*
   - **c.** *bear market* / *bull market*
2. Are owners of common stock generally more interested in dividends or capital gains? Why?
3. Why do most people who buy stock choose common stock over preferred stock?
4. What is the difference between a bear market and a bull market?
5. How has the growth of individual online trading affected stockbrokers?
6. **Using Your Notes** What are the four different ways that stocks are traded? Refer to your completed cluster diagram.

Use the Graphic Organizer at **Interactive Review @ ClassZone.com**

CRITICAL THINKING

7. **Applying Economic Concepts** Rachel paid $10 per share for 100 shares of common stock in her favorite clothing store.
   - **a.** If she receives 10 cents per share in dividends each year, about how many years would it take her to earn $100 on her investment?
   - **b.** If the share price increases to $11 in two years and she chooses to sell the stock, how much capital gain would she make?
8. **Analyzing and Interpreting Data** Rearrange the data in Figure 11.7 into one table in chronological order. Use a plus sign to indicate a best year and a minus sign to indicate a worst year.
   - **a.** What relationship, if any, do you see between best years and worst years?
   - **b.** What does the data reveal about the stock market in the 1930s?
9. **Challenge** The Standard and Poor's 500 (S&P 500) is an index composed of 500 stocks, while the Dow Jones Industrial Average is composed of 30 stocks. Many analysts feel the S&P 500 is a better representation of the U.S. stock market. Do you agree? Why?

ECONOMICS IN PRACTICE

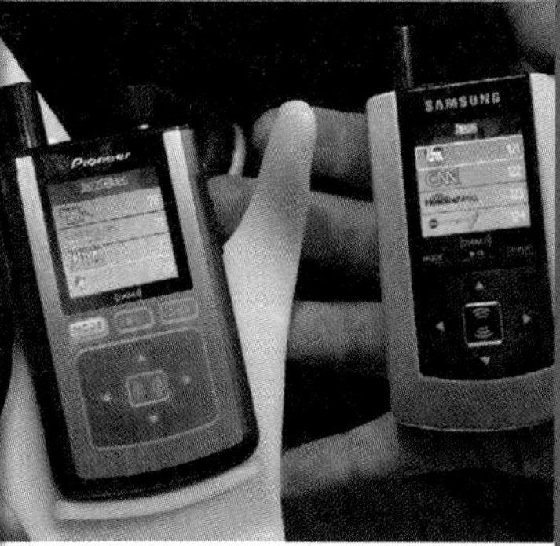

Analyzing Demand for Stock The graph below shows the combined market demand and supply curve for the stock of a company that makes mp3 players.

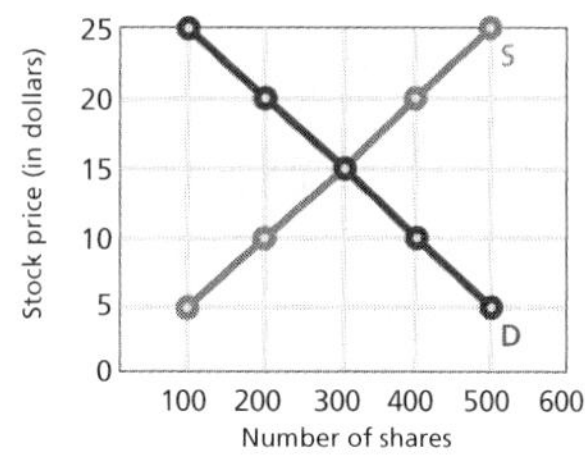

Draw New Demand Curves Copy the graph above on your own paper and draw new demand curves to reflect each of the following scenarios:

- **a.** A competitor announces a technological breakthrough that will dramatically cut its production costs.
- **b.** The company announces a new product that offers features that consumers have been asking for.

Challenge How does the change in demand in each scenario affect the price of the stock?

4 Assess & Reteach

Assess Allow students to work in pairs on the questions and take turns quizzing each other. Discuss the Critical Thinking questions as a class.

Unit 4 Resource Book
- Section Quiz, p. 81

Interactive Review @ ClassZone.com
- Section Quiz

Test Generator CD-ROM
- Section Quiz

Reteach Call on volunteers to use the photographs and figures in the section to explain the main ideas and details about buying and selling stocks.

Unit 4 Resource Book
- Reteaching Activity, p. 82

SMARTGrapher Students can create demand curves using **SmartGrapher @ ClassZone.com**.

SECTION 3 ASSESSMENT ANSWERS

Reviewing Key Concepts

1. **a.** *stock exchange*, p. 330; *stockbroker*, p. 332
   b. *future*, p. 333; *option*, p. 333
   c. *bear market*, p. 335; *bull market*, p. 335
2. capital gains, because they have no guarantee that they will receive dividends
3. because they want the possibility of capital gains and want to have voting rights in the company
4. In a bear market, prices decrease over a period of time; in a bull market, prices increase over time.
5. It has generally decreased the amount of commission that brokers earn because the investors are doing more of the work themselves.
6. See page 330 for an example of a completed diagram. Stocks are traded on listed exchanges that combine floor trading and computer trading, on the over-the-counter market using a centralized computer system, on the futures and options market, and through individual online trading.

Critical Thinking

7. **a.** She earns about $10 per year (even with dividend reinvestment) and would take about 10 years to earn $100 in dividends.
   b. She would earn $1 per share or $100 in two years.
8. **a.** The market goes in cycles, best years often followed worst years and vice versa.
   b. Increase in 1933 did not offset the declines in the other years in the decade, which included three of the worst years in the top five.
9. yes, because the S&P 500 includes many more companies than the DJIA, which only includes 30 of the largest and generally most successful companies

Economics in Practice

Draw New Demand Curves

a. demand increases, curve shifts to the right

b. demand increases, curve shifts to the right

Challenge When demand increases the stock price increases.

❶ Plan & Prepare

Section 4 Objectives

- discuss why people buy bonds
- describe the different kinds of bonds
- explain the factors that affect bond trading
- outline investment options other than stocks and bonds

❷ Focus & Motivate

Connecting to Everyday Life Explain that this section focuses on bonds and other investment options. Invite students to discuss why investors might want to loan money to corporations and governments.

Taking Notes Remind students to take notes as they read by completing a chart. A sample is shown below.

Bonds	Other Financial Instruments
• issuer pays bondholder par value at maturity • pay interest (coupon rate) and may be resold • issued by governments or corporations • usually less risky than stocks • consider yield, price, interest rates, risk when investing • Moody's and Standard & Poor's rate bonds based on level of risk	• CDs and MMMFs are both low risk and pay interest, generally not resold • CDs = time deposits, penalty for early withdrawal • higher interest for longer maturity or higher denomination • MMMFs invest in short term government bills, CDs, corporate bonds • not insured but regulated, little risk

SECTION 4

Bonds and Other Financial Instruments

OBJECTIVES

In Section 4, you will
- discuss why people buy bonds
- describe the different kinds of bonds
- explain the factors that affect bond trading
- outline investment options other than stocks and bonds

KEY TERMS

par value, *p. 338*
maturity, *p. 338*
coupon rate, *p. 338*
yield, *p. 338*
junk bond, *p. 339*

TAKING NOTES

As you read Section 4, summarize what you learn by completing a chart using the key concepts and other helpful words and phrases. Use the Graphic Organizer at **Interactive Review @ ClassZone.com**

Bonds	Other Financial Instruments

Why Buy Bonds?

QUICK REFERENCE

Par value is the amount a bond issuer must pay the buyer at maturity.

Maturity is the date when a bond is due to be repaid.

The **coupon rate** is the interest rate a bondholder receives every year until maturity.

Yield is the annual rate of return on a bond.

KEY CONCEPTS

You learned in Chapter 8 that a bond is a contract issued by a corporation promising to repay borrowed money, plus interest, on a fixed schedule. Governments also issue bonds. The amount that the bond issuer promises to pay the buyer at maturity is its **par value. Maturity** is the date when the bond is due to be repaid. The **coupon rate** is the interest rate a bondholder receives every year until a bond matures.

There are two reasons to invest in bonds—the interest paid on bonds and the gains made by selling bonds. Most people buy bonds for the interest. Generally, bonds are considered less risky than stocks because bondholders are paid before stockholders. It is important to determine the **yield**—the annual rate of return—for a bond when deciding to buy and sell bonds. If a bond is sold at par value, the yield is the same as the coupon rate. If a bond is sold for less than par value, the yield will be higher than the coupon rate. On the other hand, if demand is strong and the price of a bond is higher than the par value, the yield will be lower than the coupon rate.

Generally speaking, bonds with longer maturity dates have higher yields than those with shorter dates. This is because there is more uncertainty and risk involved with repayment dates that are farther in the future.

Types of Bonds

Investors may choose to invest in many different kinds of bonds. The yields and risks associated with these bonds vary considerably. As is the case with stocks, the higher the risk the greater the potential yield of a bond. Figure 11.10 shows the yields for different types of bonds. Bonds are classified based on who issues the bonds.

SECTION 4 PROGRAM RESOURCES

ON LEVEL

Lesson Plans
- Core, p. 39

Unit 4 Resource Book
- Reading Study Guide, pp. 83–84
- Economic Skills and Problem Solving Activity, pp. 93–94
- Section Quiz, p. 91

STRUGGLING READERS

Unit 4 Resource Book
- Reading Study Guide with Additional Support, pp. 85–87
- Reteaching Activity, p. 92

ENGLISH LEARNERS

Unit 4 Resource Book
- Reading Study Guide with Additional Support (Spanish), pp. 88–90

INCLUSION

Lesson Plans
- Modified for Inclusion, p. 39

GIFTED AND TALENTED

Unit 4 Resource Book
- Case Study Resources: Dot-Com's Song and Dance No Longer Entertains Investors, pp. 97–98

NCEE Student Activities
- Reading the Financial Pages, pp. 41–44

TECHNOLOGY

eEdition DVD-ROM

eEdition Online

Power Presentation DVD-ROM

Economics Concepts Transparencies
- CT39 Types of Bonds

Daily Test Practice Transparencies, TT39

ClassZone.com

FIGURE 11.10 AVERAGE BOND YIELDS

Source: *Statistical Abstract of the United States*

ANALYZE GRAPHS

1. Which type of bond had the lowest average yield in most years?
2. Which type of bond carries the highest risk? How do you know?

Corporate bonds help businesses expand.

Treasury bonds help keep the federal government operating.

Municipal bonds make state and local projects possible.

The U.S. government issues securities called Treasury bonds, notes, or bills. The different terms denote loans with different maturity dates, with Treasury bonds having the longest maturity (more than ten years) and Treasury bills having the shortest (one year or less). The money borrowed through the sale of these securities helps keep the government running. Because they are backed by the "full faith and credit" of the federal government, these securities are considered to be virtually risk free. Governments all over the world issue bonds for the same reasons as the U.S. government. The risk level of international bonds depends on the financial strength of the particular government.

Bonds issued by state and local governments are called municipal bonds. Funds raised by these bonds finance government projects such as construction of roads, bridges, schools, and other public facilities. The interest earned on many municipal bonds is not subject to federal income tax. Generally, municipal bonds are considered low-risk investments. A major reason for this is that state and local governments collect taxes, so it is assumed that they'll be able to make interest payments and repay the buyer upon maturity. However, there have been instances of governments being unable to repay bondholders the full amount of their loans.

One way that companies finance expansion is by issuing corporate bonds. These bonds generally pay a higher coupon rate than government bonds because the risk is higher. One kind of corporate bond, a **junk bond**, is considered high risk but has the potential for high yields. The risk involved with investing in junk bonds is similar to that of investing in stocks.

QUICK REFERENCE

Junk bonds are high-risk, high-yield corporate bonds.

❸ Teach

Why Buy Bonds?

Discuss

- How do the reasons that people buy bonds compare to the reasons that they buy stocks? *(People generally buy bonds for the interest income, while people generally buy stocks for capital gains.)*
- How are bond yields and prices related? *(They have an inverse relationship. When prices rise, interest rates and thus yield will fall, and vice versa.)*

Analyzing Graphs: Figure 11.10

Direct students to read the key, so that they understand what each line on the graph represents. Ask them to use the information on the graph to identify the yield for particular types of bonds in different years.

Answers

1. *Treasury bonds were lowest most often.*
2. *corporate bonds, because they offer the highest yield—a sign of higher risk*

CLASS ACTIVITY

Creating a Classroom Display on Bonds

Time 45 Minutes

Task Gather information on local municipal bond projects and create a classroom display.

Materials Needed computer with Internet access, poster board and markers

Activity

- Discuss with the class the kinds of projects funded by municipal bonds, as described on page 339.
- Invite students to use the Internet to find out about local projects funded by bonds.
- Suggest that students use the name of your city, county, or state and the words *bond issues* as search terms.
- Then, allow students to research a particular project or projects, perhaps through interviews with government officials. Some may research the project, while others research the bond sale details.
- Have students create a classroom display based on their research.

Rubric

	Understanding of Municipal Bonds	Presentation of Information
4	excellent	clear and complete
3	good	mostly clear
2	fair	sometimes clear
1	poor	sketchy

More About . . .

Bond Rating Organizations
Moody's Investors Service and Standard & Poor's are the two largest institutional credit rating agencies in the United States. They are the top two of the five Nationally Recognized Statistical Rating Organizations (NSRSO) designated by the SEC. Ratings by a NSRSO are used to determine whether bonds held by a bank, mutual fund, or insurance company meet government regulations.

In the 1970s, the ratings agencies began charging bond issuers for ratings. Corporations may pay as much as $300,000 for a credit rating. Schools and cities pay much lower fees. Some critics claim that the credit rating companies have too much power and too little regulation.

Analyzing Tables: Figure 11.11

Explain that the bond ratings shown in the table are like grades that are given by the rating agencies. They reflect the credit rater's assessment of the financial health of the bond issuer. The Moody's system uses the same letter ratings that credit rating systems used in the late 1800s. Although the designations are slightly different, the ratings are generally comparable.

Answers

1. *Moody's, Baa; Standard & Poor's, BBB*
2. *because they have a higher risk that the bond issuer will default*

Buying Bonds

Investors need to determine their reason for buying bonds in order to purchase the right type of bond. Most investors purchase bonds because they want the guaranteed interest income. Yield will be most important to those investors. Coupon rate and price relative to the par value will determine the yield. Investors who want to sell bonds before they reach maturity study the bond market to see if they can sell their investment at a profit.

Market interest rates are another important consideration for bond investors. There is an inverse relationship between the price of existing bonds and interest rates. For example, as interest rates rise, the price of existing bonds falls because bonds that were issued with a lower interest rate will be less in demand. Conversely, if interest rates fall, the price of existing bonds rises because there will be more demand for those bonds issued at a higher interest rate.

The main risk that bond buyers face is that the issuer will default, or be unable to repay the borrowed money at maturity. Therefore, the level of risk is directly tied to the financial strength of the bond issuer. When governments or corporations want to issue bonds, they pay a credit-rating company to evaluate how likely it is that they will repay the loans. In this way, investors have a standard by which to judge the risk of the bonds. The two most well-known systems of bond ratings are those established by Standard & Poor's and Moody's. These companies use a system of letters to designate the relative credit risk of bonds. Bonds are rated from the lowest risk of U.S. Treasury securities (Aaa or AAA) to the higher risks associated with junk bonds. (See Figure 11.11.)

FIGURE 11.11 Bond Ratings

Bond Rating		Grade	Risk
Moody's	Standard & Poor's		
Aaa	AAA	Investment	Lowest risk
Aa	AA	Investment	Low risk
A	A	Investment	Low risk
Baa	BBB	Investment	Medium risk
Ba, B	BB, B	Junk	High risk
Caa/Ca	CCC/CC/C	Junk	Highest risk
C	D	Junk	In default

ANALYZE TABLES
1. What are the lowest-rated investment grade bonds in each system?
2. Why do junk bonds have lower ratings than investment grade bonds?

APPLICATION Drawing Conclusions

A. Why is bond yield not always the same as the coupon rate?
because bonds are not always sold for par value

DIFFERENTIATING INSTRUCTION

Inclusion

Create a Risk Continuum
Help students understand that Figure 11.11 shows that bond rating systems indicate a range of risks. Create a risk continuum on the board using a horizontal line. Show the lowest risk on the left (Aaa/AAA) and the highest risk on the right (C/D). Write Moody's ratings above the line and Standard & Poor's below. Have a volunteer show where the line would be marked to separate investment grade and junk bonds. Make sure students understand that the highest grades indicate lowest risk.

Gifted and Talented

Hold a Panel Discussion
Invite students to use Internet resources to research more information about how the bond rating agencies work. They might investigate the kinds of information used to determine a bond rating, how companies work with bond issuers, or the role that rating agencies play in the issuance of corporate or municipal bonds. Some might wish to find news stories about how changes in ratings have affected particular bond issuers. Allow students to hold a panel discussion on the topic.

Other Financial Instruments

KEY CONCEPTS

Investors have investment options other than bonds and stocks. The most common of these are certificates of deposit (CDs) and money market mutual funds. Both of these investments have very low risk and provide income in the form of interest. Individual investors do not generally sell these financial instruments for profit.

Certificates of Deposit

As you learned earlier, CDs are a form of time deposit offered primarily by banks, savings and loans, and credit unions. Like bonds, CDs have a maturity date (usually 6 months to 5 years), when the investor receives the principal back with interest.

The issuer of the CD pays the investor a rate of either fixed or variable interest during the period that the CD is held. Usually the interest is reinvested in the CD so that the investor enjoys the benefits of compound interest. In general, CDs with longer maturity dates pay higher rates of interest. For example, a 6-month CD might pay 3.4 percent interest while a 5-year CD might pay 4.4 percent.

The federal government insures funds deposited in CDs at most banks and credit unions up to $100,000 per depositor in any given institution. The main risk that investors in CDs face is the loss of interest or possibly some principal if funds are withdrawn before the maturity date. In addition, investors might face interest-rate risk if rates rise and funds are locked in for a length of time at a lower rate.

Money Market Mutual Funds

Recall from Section 1 that the money market involves financial assets with maturities of one year or less. Also, remember that mutual funds allow investors to buy shares that represent an investment in all the financial assets held by the fund. Money market mutual funds (MMMF) allow investors to own a variety of short-term financial assets, such as Treasury bills, municipal bonds, large-denomination CDs, and corporate bonds.

These mutual funds give investors a higher yield than bank savings accounts, but provide a similar level of liquidity. Investors can redeem their shares by check, by phone, or by electronic transfer to a separate checking account.

Although the federal government does not insure MMMFs, the funds are tightly regulated, and these investments are considered to be quite safe with regard to loss of principal. There is less interest-rate risk than with CDs because the money is not committed for a specified length of time. The yield of the MMMF varies based on the yield of the assets in the fund.

"'Oh, no,' said Goldilocks, 'don't tell me that the return on invested capital is only *three* percent—less than you can earn on a money-market account!'"

Source: www.CartoonStock.com

APPLICATION Making Inferences

B. Why do longer-term CDs pay higher interest rates than shorter-term CDs?

because the issuer has use of the investor's money for a longer period of time, when it can be used to support loans

Other Financial Instruments

Discuss

- Are CDs and money market mutual funds more like stocks or like bonds? Why? *(Possible answer: bonds, since investors usually buy them for the lower risk and likely income, not for capital gains)*
- Compare how the yield is determined for CDs and money market mutual funds. *(CD—based on the rate of interest, compounded for the term of the CD; MMMF—depends on the yield of the assets held by the fund)*

More About . . .

Money Market Mutual Funds

The first money market mutual fund (MMMF) was offered in 1972. In 2006, there were about 900 funds available. MMMFs account for about 11 percent of all mutual funds, but hold about 22 percent of the total assets, more than $2 trillion. Individual investors hold about three-quarters of the assets, and institutional investors hold the balance. Both kinds of investors use the funds as a safe place to put cash.

Institutional investors are more likely to invest in MMMFs than in other kinds of mutual funds. MMMFs are different from money market deposit accounts offered by banks and thrifts. MMMFs are offered by licensed investment companies and are not insured.

SMALL GROUP ACTIVITY

Researching Other Financial Instruments

Time 30 Minutes ◑

Task Gather information on CDs or MMMFs and present findings in graphic organizers.

Materials Needed computer with Internet access, paper and pens or markers

Activity

- Organize students into groups. Assign each group to research information on CDs or MMMFs.
- Topics on CDs might include institutions that offer CDs, current rates and terms, penalties for early withdrawal.
- Topics on MMMFs might include types of funds available, who offers the funds, kinds of assets held in different types of funds, fees associated with MMMFs, current yields. BankRate.com provides comparative rate information on a variety of financial assets.
- Have groups organize their findings into graphic organizers to share with their classmates. Discuss why investors might choose these options.

Rubric

	Understanding of Investment Options	Presentation of Information
4	excellent	clear and complete
3	good	mostly clear
2	fair	sometimes clear
1	poor	sketchy

Interpreting Graphs: Online Financial Information

1 Plan & Prepare

Objectives

- Analyze financial information about stocks available from online sources.
- Draw conclusions from online financial information about a particular company.

2 Focus & Motivate

Advise students to examine the graph to see how it might be used to help investors learn about a company's stock. Have students consider these questions as they review the information.

- Why might investors want to see price and volume information for a 12-month period? *(so they can see trends in the way the stock is trading)*
- How does this graph reflect the risk involved in investing in stocks? *(It shows that prices may rise and fall rather sharply. So, investors may lose money or realize a gain depending on when they buy and sell the stock.)*

3 Teach

- Point out that a main feature of online information is that it is updated frequently. It is important to note how recent the information is. Suggest that students check the current 12-month trend for Microsoft stock and compare it with the graph in the text.
- Invite students to recall what they know about supply, demand, and price to evaluate when it would have been the best time to buy or sell the stock.

For additional practice see **Skillbuilder Handbook**, page R29.

THINKING ECONOMICALLY
Answers

1. *at the end of May/beginning of June, since that was when the price was lowest*
2. *The price per share at the beginning of June was about $33, while at its peak in January, the price was about $88.*
3. *Yes; when prices are high, many shareholders want to sell, and when prices are low many investors want to buy.*

ECONOMICS SKILLBUILDER

For more information on interpreting graphs, see the Skillbuilder Handbook, page R29.

Interpreting Graphs: Online Financial Information

Evaluating means to make a judgment about information. Investors make judgments about stocks based on their analysis of financial information. Many use the Internet as a resource for acquiring minute-to-minute information about stock market trading. The graphs on this page provide information about Apple Computer Inc., a stock traded on the NASDAQ. These graphs, which are updated online throughout trading, offer an example of the type of online information investors use to evaluate stocks.

TIPS FOR EVALUATING ONLINE INFORMATION Use the following guidelines to evaluate economic information online:

Read the title to identify the company for which stock information is shown. Here it is Apple Computer (AAPL), traded on the NASDAQ (Q).

Read the vertical axis. This graph has two parts. The upper part shows the stock's price; the lower part shows the volume of shares traded.

Look for other information This statement shows the lag time for information—15 minutes in this case.

Read the horizontal axis. This graph shows stock prices and volume traded from May 2005 through April 2006.

Apple Computer (AAPL-Q) — as of 19-Apr-06

US Dollars: 90.00, 80.00, 70.00, 60.00, 50.00, 40.00

Volume (mil): 50, 0

May05 Jun Jul Aug Sep Oct Nov Dec Jan06 Feb Mar Apr

Quotes delayed 15 minutes except NYSE and Amex which are 20 minutes.

Source: TheGlobeandMail.com

THINKING ECONOMICALLY Evaluating

1. As an investor, which month would have been best for you to acquire Apple stock? Why?
2. How does the price per share at the beginning of June 2005 compare with the price in mid-January 2006? Use information from the graph in your answer.
3. From January through April of 2006, the price of Apple shares fluctuated greatly. Volume of trading was also very heavy. Are these two facts related? Why?

DIFFERENTIATING INSTRUCTION

Struggling Readers

Work in Pairs

Have students work with a partner to evaluate information in this graph.

- Encourage partners to take turns reading paragraphs and callouts aloud and then restate them in their own words.
- To give students more practice, invite them to look up similar recent financial information for another company.
- Have students discuss the Thinking Economically questions with their partners and agree on an answer. Call on volunteers to share their answers.

Inclusion

Enlarge the Graph

Students with visual impairments may benefit from working with an enlarged version of the graph, available in the eEdition at **ClassZone.com**. Allow these students to work with a partner without visual impairments who might describe the graph and help clarify information. Encourage partners to discuss the Thinking Economically questions together and agree on an answer.

342 Chapter 11

SECTION 4 Assessment

REVIEWING KEY CONCEPTS

1. Use each of the three terms below in a sentence that illustrates the meaning of the term:
   a. *coupon rate* b. *maturity* c. *yield*
2. What does par value represent to the issuer of a bond?
3. What is the relationship between par value and maturity?
4. When does yield equal the coupon rate?
5. Why do junk bonds offer a higher yield than other types of bonds?
6. **Using Your Notes** Compare the risk of investing in a CD with the risk of investing in a money market mutual fund. Refer to your completed chart.

Bonds	Other Financial Instruments

Use the Graphic Organizer at **Interactive Review @ ClassZone.com**

CRITICAL THINKING

7. **Comparing and Contrasting** Dmitri bought a $1,000 bond at par value with a coupon rate of 5 percent. He determines the yield by dividing the amount of interest he earns by the price.
   a. How much interest would he earn in the first year and what would be the yield?
   b. How much interest would he earn in the first year and what would be the yield if he had paid $950 for the bond? What would be the interest and yield if he paid $1,050?
8. **Making Inferences** In 2003, Molly bought a 10-year Treasury note for $1,000. The market interest rate was 3.5 percent. In 2005, Molly wanted to sell the note to pay for college expenses. Interest rates had risen to 4.5 percent. How would the change in interest rates affect the price that Molly was likely to receive for her note? Give reasons for your answer.
9. **Applying Economic Concepts** Julie has accumulated $1,000 in a bank savings account, which pays 2.7 percent interest. She investigates several options and finds that she can invest her money in a 1-year Treasury note paying 4.4 percent interest, a 1-year CD paying 3.9 percent interest, or a money market mutual fund with an average yield of 3.7 percent. What are the pros and cons of each of these investment options?
10. **Challenge** How would a lower bond rating by Moody's or Standard & Poor's affect the coupon rate that a corporation has to offer when it issues its bonds? Give reasons for your answer.

Online Quiz ClassZone.com

ECONOMICS IN PRACTICE

Making Investment Decisions
Suppose that you have been advised to invest in bonds. Recall what you have learned about the factors to consider when buying and selling bonds and then complete the following activities.

Ask Investment Questions Fill in the chart by developing a series of questions you might ask to help you decide which type of bond to buy.

Categories of Questions to Ask About Bonds	My Questions
Investment objectives	
Tolerance for risk	
Desired return	
Resalability of bonds	

Challenge How might you apply the concept of diversification to a portfolio of bond investments?

4 Assess & Reteach

Assess Assign small groups one of the assessment questions to answer. Have them write their responses on the board. Review the answers as a class.

Unit 4 Resource Book
- Section Quiz, p. 91

Interactive Review @ ClassZone.com
- Section Quiz

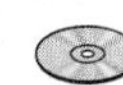

Test Generator CD-ROM
- Section Quiz

Reteach Organize students into four groups. Assign each to study one of the subheads in the section and present a summary to the rest of the class. Encourage all students to take notes as the information is reviewed.

Unit 4 Resource Book
- Reteaching Activity, p. 92

Economics in Practice

Ask Investment Questions Possible questions: Investment objectives—Am I more interested in earning interest or making a profit through resale?; Tolerance for risk—Who is issuing the bond? What is the bond issuer's rating?; Desired return—How is the price related to par value? What is the coupon rate? What is the yield?; Resalability of bonds—How will changes in interest rates affect possible resale price?

Challenge by including different types of bonds in the portfolio and by having bonds with different maturity dates

SECTION 4 ASSESSMENT ANSWERS

Reviewing Key Concepts

1. a. *coupon rate*, p. 338
   b. *maturity*, p. 338
   c. *yield*, p. 338
2. the amount of money that is being borrowed and must be repaid
3. At maturity the bond issuer must pay the par value of the bond to the bondholder.
4. when the price of the bond is equal to the par value
5. because they have a higher risk that the issuer will default
6. See page 338 for an example of a completed diagram. CDs are insured so there is no risk of losing the principal if held to maturity. There is a risk of losing interest or principal if the CD is redeemed early. Money market mutual funds are not insured but there is little risk since they are highly regulated. The yield is not guaranteed but fluctuates with the yield of the assets in the fund.

Critical Thinking

7. a. $50 interest, 5 percent yield
   b. The amount of interest remains the same whatever the price; $950 = 5.3 percent yield; $1050 = 4.8 percent yield
8. The price will be lower because there is an inverse relationship between interest rates and the price of existing bonds.
9. All pay more interest than the savings account. 1-year Treasury note = highest rate of interest, resale price before maturity depends on change in market interest rates; 1-year CD = 2nd highest rate of interest but penalty for early withdrawal (liquidity); MMMF = lower interest rate than the other two but greater liquidity.
10. A lower bond rating means higher risk, therefore the corporation will have to offer a higher coupon rate (higher potential yield) to attract investors. A lower bond rating means it costs a corporation more to borrow money.

Economics in Practice

See answers in side column above.

1 Plan & Prepare

Objectives

- Analyze factors that affect stock prices.
- Describe the causes and effects of the dot-com bubble.

2 Focus & Motivate

Invite students to describe some Internet businesses that they use regularly. Explain that this Case Study explores the rise and fall of Internet-based businesses in the late 1990s.

3 Teach

Using the Sources

Encourage students to examine each source to understand some factors that caused the value of dot-coms to change rapidly.

A. Why was Kozmo's business model criticized? *(because it offered an expensive business service without charging for it)*

B. How does the cartoonist portray investors' attitudes toward dot-coms? *(Possible answer: Investors' opinions were positive but not based on solid evidence.)*

C. Based on this news story, why was advertising important to dot-coms? *(They were trying to create awareness and bring customers to their Web sites.)*

Economics Update

Go to **ClassZone.com** to find an update to this Case Study, including another article, an editable student worksheet, and an editable lesson plan.

Case Study

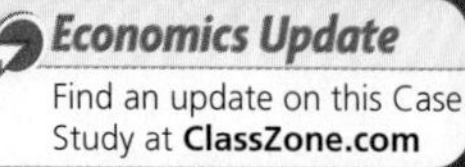

Economics Update Find an update on this Case Study at **ClassZone.com**

The Rise and Fall of Dot-Coms

Background The availability of products and services on the Internet is old news. But when the Internet first emerged, it provided a unique and exciting tool for almost instant access to potential buyers worldwide. Young people in particular were quick to grasp the possibilities of the electronic marketplace. As a result, many new companies, known as dot-coms, quickly appeared on the Internet.

Like the stock of many companies based on new technologies, the value of dot-com stocks rose quickly. Investors, attracted by the initial success of dot-coms and spurred on by low interest rates in the late 1990s, were quick to join the dot-com boom. The boom, however, proved to be a financial bubble. In 2000 and 2001, the bubble burst as dot-com stocks fell dramatically. Many dot-coms went out of business, and their investors sustained heavy financial losses.

What's the issue? Why did so many dot-com companies fail? Study these sources to discover what investors learned when the dot-com bubble burst.

A. Online Encyclopedia Article

Many young entrepreneurs jumped into the dot-com market, often with disastrous results. This article describes one such venture.

Kozmo.com Offered New Yorkers Free, One-Hour Delivery

Despite millions in capital investment, Kozmo.com's choices led to failure.

Kozmo.com was a venture-capital-driven online company that promised free one-hour delivery of anything from DVDs to Starbucks coffee. It was founded by young investment bankers Joseph Park and Yong Kang in March 1998 in New York City. The company is often referred to as an example of the dot-com excess.

Kozmo promoted an incredible business model; it promised to deliver small goods free of charge. The company raised about $280 million, including $60 million from Amazon.com. The business model was heavily criticized by business analysts, who pointed out that one-hour point-to-point delivery of small objects is extremely expensive and there was no way Kozmo could make a profit as long as it refused to charge delivery fees. Not surprisingly, the company failed soon after the collapse of the dot-com bubble, laying off its staff of 1,100 employees and shutting down in April 2001.

Source: **Wikipedia.org**

Thinking Economically Why do you think Park and Kang were so successful in raising capital to fund their business venture?

DIFFERENTIATING INSTRUCTION

English Learners

Understand Word Derivation

Help students understand the derivation of *dot-com*. This word developed because many Internet-based companies added the ending of their Internet address—*.com*—to their company name. Point out that *dot* refers to the period. The ending *com* was used for commercial websites. Have students find dot-com names in the documents. *(Kozmo.com, Amazon.com, whatchamacalit.com)* Explain that the latter is fictitious, suggesting any company, and is slang for "what you may call it."

Gifted and Talented

Analyze Venture Capitalists

Explain that many dot-coms came out of the technology culture of areas like Silicon Valley in California. Invite students to research the role of venture capital firms in the rise and fall of these companies. Students may use Internet or library sources to find out how venture capital firms are structured, why they invested in Internet start-ups, and how they contributed to and were affected by the dot-com bubble. Have students present their findings in written reports.

B. Cartoon

Cartoonist Andrew Toos drew this commentary about the dot-com bubble.

"The good news is we've financed another dot.com for no fathomable reason."

Source: www.CartoonStock.com

Thinking Economically What comment does the cartoon make about investing in the dot-com financial market?

C. Online News Story

Early dot-coms typically spent huge amounts of money on advertising. This article compares purchases of advertising during the 2000 Super Bowl telecast to Napoleon's 1815 defeat at Waterloo.

The Bubble Bowl

Expensive advertising failed to market dot-com products.

It was just five years ago, although it seems like a different age entirely. It was a time of singing-sock-puppets, 21-year-old chief executives, gravity-defiant stock prices, revolutionary technologies and half-baked business plans.

And in this atmosphere, during the final, halcyon days of the Internet boom, the St. Louis Rams played the Tennessee Titans in Super Bowl XXXIV, a moment that will be forever remembered as the dot-com bubble's Waterloo.

Football fans got a heavy dose of the fever that day: More than a dozen internet companies spent an average of $2.2 million for 30-second spots, amounting to more than $40 million of stockholder cash and not-so-hard-won venture capital.

These startups hoped that Super Bowl exposure would sear their web address into the minds of consumers. But most viewers were left with only vague memories of chimpanzees dancing to "La Cucaracha" to promote whatchamacalit.com... while the businesses themselves were left with empty wallets.

Today, most of these Internet pioneers are dead and gone, forgotten as the score of the game (St. Louis 23, Tennessee 16).

Source: "The Bubble Bowl," by David M. Ewalt. Forbes.com, January 27, 2005

Thinking Economically Why do you think the author compares the dot-com Super Bowl advertising to Waterloo, a major military defeat?

THINKING ECONOMICALLY Synthesizing

1. During the dot-com bubble, do you think it was relatively easy or difficult for Internet start-up companies to raise capital? Explain your answer, using information from the documents.
2. Why do you think so many dot-coms failed? Use evidence from the documents in your answer.
3. What lessons might investors learn from the information presented in documents A and C?

Thinking Economically

Answers

A. *There was a wave of enthusiasm for dot-coms and Park and Kang clearly had connections in the investment banking world.*

B. *that there was lots of money being thrown at these companies, but there was little reasonable foundation for the investments*

C. *Just as with Napoleon's Waterloo, this was a kind of last hurrah for many of these companies. They were soon in shambles like a defeated army.*

Synthesizing

1. *easy; Kozmo raised $280 million with almost no business plan; the cartoon makes light of funding given for no reason; small companies lavished money on expensive Super Bowl ads*
2. *They seemed to operate outside of normal business ideas of profitability and considered planning.*
3. *Don't get caught up in fad investments; do lots of research and make sure what you're investing in is sound.*

TECHNOLOGY ACTIVITY

Researching Dot-Com Successes and Failures

Time 45 Minutes

Task Gather information on dot-coms and create a multimedia presentation.

Materials Needed a computer with Internet access, presentation software (optional)

Activity

- Organize students into groups. Have each group use the Internet to research a dot-com. Include successes, such as Yahoo!, Amazon.com, and eBay, as well as failures, such as Pets.com, Webvan, and eToys.
- Direct groups to gather information on their company's business and how it was financed. Encourage them to find information on how the stock price varied over time.
- Have groups collaborate on a multimedia presentation on the dot-com bubble, using the examples they have researched to illustrate what happened to the stock market between 1997 and 2001. Discuss why some companies succeeded while others failed.

Rubric

	Understanding of Dot-Coms	Presentation of Information
4	excellent	clear and complete
3	good	mostly clear
2	fair	sometimes clear
1	poor	sketchy

Online Summary Answers

1. Savings
2. Investment
3. financial asset
4. financial intermediary
5. money market
6. secondary market
7. investment objective
8. return
9. risk
10. diversification
11. Capital gain
12. Common stock
13. stock index
14. Coupon rate
15. par value

Interactive Review

Review this chapter using interactive activities at **ClassZone.com**

- Online Summary
- Quizzes
- Vocabulary Flip Cards
- Graphic Organizers
- Review and Study Notes

Online Summary

Complete the following activity either on your own paper or online at **ClassZone.com**

Choose the key concept that best completes the sentence. Not all key concepts will be used.

capital gain	money market
capital market	par value
common stock	preferred stock
coupon rate	primary market
diversification	return
financial asset	risk
financial intermediary	savings
investment	secondary market
investment objective	stock index
maturity	yield

__1__ is income not used for consumption. __2__ is the use of income today that allows for greater production in the future.

A __3__ is a claim on the property of a borrower. A __4__ collects funds from savers and invests the funds in loans and other financial assets. Examples include banks and mutual funds. The __5__ is the market for buying and selling short-term financial assets. The __6__ is the market where financial assets are resold.

The two issues that play a major role in setting an __7__ are time and income. Investors try to maximize __8__ and limit __9__ through __10__, the practice of distributing investments among different financial assets.

__11__ is profit made from the sale of securities. __12__ is share of ownership in a corporation that gives holders voting rights and a share of the profit. The Dow Jones Industrial Average is a __13__ that measures the performance of a group of 30 stocks. __14__ is the interest rate paid on a bond. The __15__ is the amount that a bond issuer promises to pay the buyer at maturity.

CHAPTER 11 Assessment

REVIEWING KEY CONCEPTS

Savings and Investment (pp. 318–323)

1. How are savings and investment related?
2. What is the role of financial intermediaries in the circular flow of the financial system?

Investing in a Market Economy (pp. 324–329)

3. Why do investors need to determine their investment objective before they invest?
4. Explain the relationship between risk and return.

Buying and Selling Stocks (pp. 330–337)

5. How do people earn money by investing in stocks?
6. How does the Dow Jones Industrial Average reveal trends in the stock market?

Bonds and Other Financial Instruments (pp. 338–345)

7. What are the two reasons people buy bonds?
8. How are interest rates and bond prices related?

APPLYING ECONOMIC CONCEPTS

Look at the graph below showing savings as a percentage of after-tax income in various countries.

9. Which country has the lowest rate of savings?
10. What is the overall trend from 1980 to 2000?

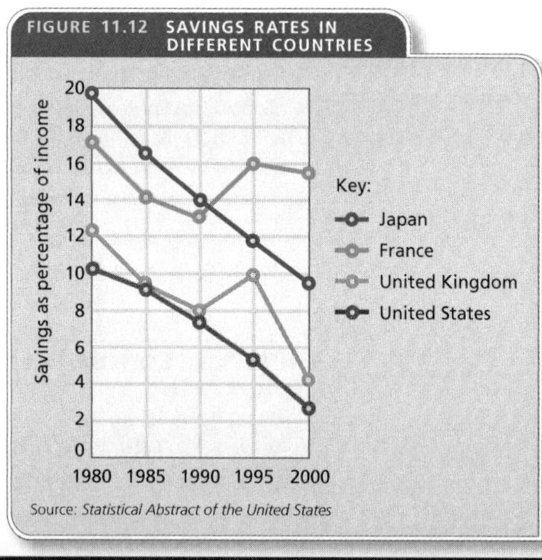

FIGURE 11.12 SAVINGS RATES IN DIFFERENT COUNTRIES

Source: *Statistical Abstract of the United States*

CHAPTER 11 ASSESSMENT ANSWERS

1. Investments are made from savings, money that is not spent on current consumption.
2. Financial intermediaries accept money from households and businesses in the form of savings and investment. They return money to investors in the form of interest and profits. They loan money to businesses and individuals.
3. because knowing their investment objective allows investors to determine what investments are most appropriate for them
4. As risk increases so does potential return.
5. by receiving dividends or by selling stock for capital gain
6. It tracks the price changes of a group of stocks that reflect the overall market. If the DJIA trends up for a long period it's a bull market. If it trends down, it's a bear market.
7. to receive interest and to make a profit by selling the bonds
8. There is an inverse relationship, as interest rates rise the price of existing bonds falls and as rates fall, prices rise.

Applying Economic Concepts

9. the United States
10. The ratio of savings has generally declined over the period.

Critical Thinking

11. a. Stock prices for these companies would probably increase because there is increased demand when there is a potential for investors to make more money as the companies become more successful.
    b. Stock prices would probably decline because the long-term potential for newspapers to remain profitable is declining and demand for the stock would decrease.

CRITICAL THINKING

11. **Analyzing Causes and Effects** In 2005, many leading advertisers announced plans to increase use of online advertising and to decrease the amount of advertising dollars spent in traditional print media, such as newspapers. In addition, newspaper circulation figures declined steadily as more people read news on the Internet.
    a. How was this situation likely to affect the stock prices of online search-engine companies that featured banner ads and sponsored links on their Web pages?
    b. How would it affect the stock prices of newspapers? Explain your answers.
12. **Comparing and Contrasting** What are the similarities and differences between stock dividends, a bond coupon rate, and interest on a CD?
13. **Drawing Conclusions** Alex, Kate, and Rashid all invested money in a software company. Alex bought a corporate bond, Kate bought shares of common stock, and Rashid bought shares of preferred stock. Which of these investors would be least at risk of losing money if the company became unprofitable?
14. **Making Inferences** Suppose that you heard the following statement on the financial news: "Bonds fell as the yield on 10-year Treasury notes rose to 4.56 percent, the highest in two years." What does "bonds fell" mean and how is it related to the increase in yield?
15. **Challenge** Steve purchases an option contract to buy 100 shares of stock in a big high-tech company for $50 per share in six months. The stock is currently selling for $40 per share. Steve pays $5 per share for the option contract. If the share price rises to $60, Steve exercises his option to buy the shares at $50 and then resells the stock on the market for $60 per share. How much profit does Steve make per share? If the price never rises to $50 before the option expires, how much money does Steve lose?

SIMULATION

Advise Your Clients

Choose a partner. Imagine that you are financial planners whose job is to help clients meet their investment objectives and use diversification to maximize return and limit risk.

Step 1 Make a list of several possible financial instruments that you might recommend and rate them for risk and return.

Step 2 Review each client's objectives and risk tolerance to consider what investments to recommend.

a. Carlos and Juanita Diaz want to invest for their two young children's college education. They would like a return of 7 to 10 percent a year and have a moderate tolerance for risk.

b. Patrick Hurd is 30 years old and wants to begin saving for his retirement. He wants the highest return possible and is willing to take risks.

c. Alison Leveridge has recently retired. She wants to invest the money from her pension fund so that she can have a guaranteed amount of income and little risk of losing her capital.

Step 3 Decide what percentage of each client's money to invest in different types of financial instruments. Create pie graphs to show your recommendations for each client.

Step 4 Present your recommendations to another pair of students. Discuss the choices that each of you made.

Step 5 As a class, discuss how changes in your clients' financial circumstances or changes in the stock market might affect your recommendations.

Use ***SMARTGrapher*** **@ ClassZone.com** to complete this activity.

McDougal Littell
Assessment System

Assess

Online Test Practice
- Go to **ClassZone.com** for more test practice.

Unit 1 Resource Book
- Chapter Test, Forms A, B, & C, pp. 103–114

Test Generator CD-ROM
- Chapter Test, Forms (A, B, & C), in English and Spanish

Report

Use the McDougal Littell Assessment System to score assessments and receive customized reports.

Reteach

For activities customized for individual students, use the McDougal Littell Assessment System.

SMARTGrapher Students can create a pie graph using **SmartGrapher @ ClassZone.com**.

CHAPTER 11 ASSESSMENT ANSWERS

12. They are all ways that investors earn income. Companies are not required to pay dividends, and they will only be paid if a company is profitable. Issuers of bonds and CDs are required to pay interest. The amount of interest depends on a variety of factors, including risk and maturity date.
13. Alex, because bond holders get paid before stockholders
14. Bond prices fell as the yield increased because there is an inverse relationship between bond prices and interest rates. Yield increases when interest rates increase.
15. Steve would make $5 profit per share because he had to cover the $5 per share he paid for the option contract. If Steve never exercises the option he loses $5 per share or $500 total.

Simulation Rubric: Steps 1–3

	Investment Lists	Recommendations
4	many options, for risk and return	excellent decisions
3	several options	good decisions
2	basic options	some understanding
1	limited options	little understanding

Steps 4–5

	Presentation	Class Discussion
4	able to defend decisions	excellent understanding
3	mostly able to defend decisions	good understanding
2	limited ability to defend decisions	incomplete understanding
1	unable to defend decisions	very little understanding

Planning Guide

Resources 2Go Complete print resources all on one USB drive allow you to customize lessons.

Section Titles and Objectives	Unit 5 Resource Book and Workbooks		Assessment Resources
1 Gross Domestic Product and Other Indicators pp. 350–357 • Define GDP and describe how it is measured • Explain how GDP has certain limitations • Identify other national income accounting measures	**Unit 5 Resource Book** • Reading Study Guide, pp. 1–2 • RSG with Additional Support, pp. 3–5 • RSG with Additional Support (Spanish), pp. 6–8 • Math Skills Worksheet: Analyzing Components of the Gross Domestic Product, p. 39	**NCEE Student Activities** • Economic Indicators and Measurements, pp. 45–48	**Unit 5 Resource Book** • Section Quiz, p. 9 • Reteaching Activity, p. 10 **Test Generator CD-ROM** **Daily Test Practice Transparencies,** TT40
2 Business Cycles pp. 358–367 • Describe the phases of the business cycle • Discuss aggregate demand and aggregate supply • Identify the causes of the changes in the business cycle • Explain how economists predict business cycle changes • Outline major business cycles in U.S. history	**Unit 5 Resource Book** • Reading Study Guide, pp. 11–12 • RSG with Additional Support, pp. 13–15 • RSG with Additional Support (Spanish), pp. 16–18 • Economic Skills and Problem Solving Activity, p. 31–32 • Case Study Resources: Cheer Up, pp. 35–36	**NCEE Student Activities** • Economic Indicators and Measurements, pp. 45–48	**Unit 5 Resource Book** • Section Quiz, p. 19 • Reteaching Activity, p. 20 **Test Generator CD-ROM** **Daily Test Practice Transparencies,** TT41
3 Stimulating Economic Growth pp. 368–377 • Explain how economists measure growth • Analyze the causes of economic growth • Discuss how productivity and economic growth are related	**Unit 5 Resource Book** • Reading Study Guide, pp. 21–22 • RSG with Additional Support, pp. 23–25 • RSG with Additional Support (Spanish), pp. 26–28 • Economic Simulations: Achieving Macroeconomic Goals, pp. 37–38 • Readings in Free Enterprise: The Imagination Economy, pp. 33–34 • Case Study Resources: Cheer Up, pp. 35–36	**Test Practice and Review Workbook,** pp. 45–46	**Unit 5 Resource Book** • Section Quiz, p. 29 • Reteaching Activity, p. 30 • Chapter Test, (Forms A, B, & C), pp. 41–52 **Test Generator CD-ROM** **Daily Test Practice Transparencies,** TT42

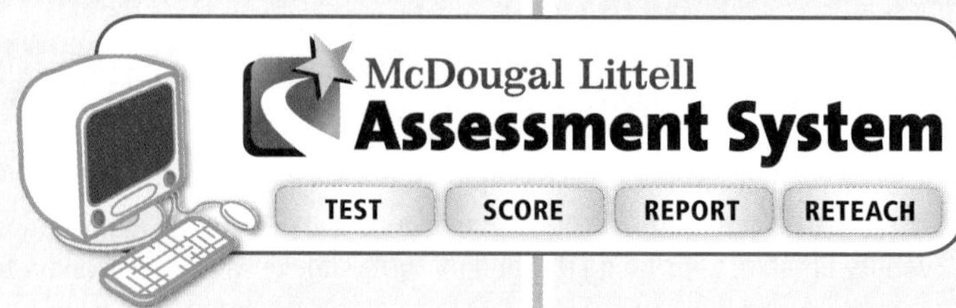

Integrated Technology

No Time? To focus students on the most important content in this chapter, use Animated Economics, "Aggregate Supply and Demand," available in Resources 2Go.

Teacher Presentation Options

Presentation Toolkit

Power Presentation DVD-ROM

- Lecture Notes
- Media Gallery
- Review Game
- Interactive Review
- Animated Economics

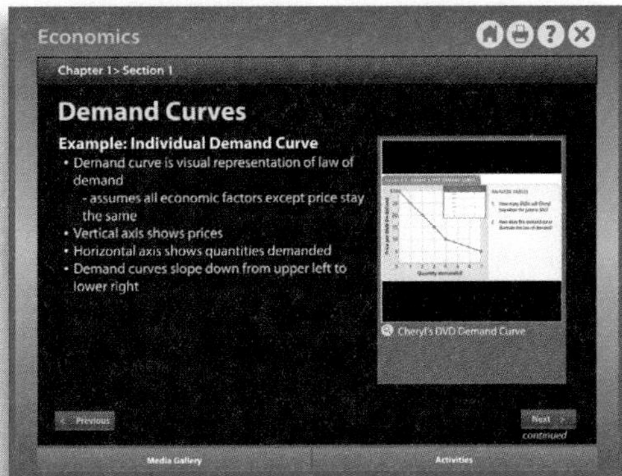

Economics Concepts Transparencies

- Gauging Economic Performance, CT40
- Economic Indicators that Predict Stages of a Business Cycle, CT41
- GDP of World's Leading Economies, CT42

Electronic Books

eEdition DVD-ROM

eEdition Online

Daily Test Practice Transparencies, TT40, TT41, TT42

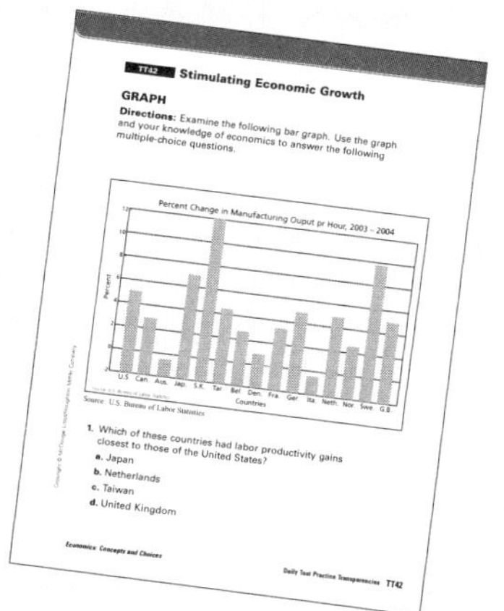

Animated Economics

- Aggregate Demand and Supply, p. 360

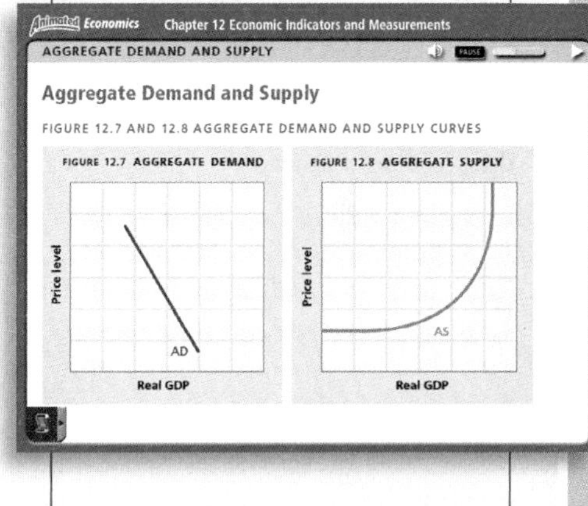

Online Activities at ClassZone.com

Economics Update

- U.S. GDP, p. 351
- Factors Affecting the Business Cycle, p. 362
- U.S. Real GDP Per Capita, p. 369
- Thomas Robert Malthus, p. 374
- Poland: Economic Freedom and Economic Growth, p. 376

Animated Economics

- Interactive Graphics

Activity Maker

- Vocabulary Flip Cards
- Review Game

Research Center

- Graphs and Data

- Online Summary
- Quizzes
- Vocabulary Flip Cards
- Graphic Organizers
- Review and Study Notes

SMARTGrapher

- Draw Aggregate Demand and Aggregate Supply Curves, p. 367
- Create a Line Graph, p. 379

Teacher-Tested Activities

Name: Douglas Young

School: Croton-Harmon High School

State: New York

Teacher-Tested Activities

At the beginning of this chapter, look for my classroom-proven idea for teaching economics concepts and thinking.

Resources for Differentiated Instruction

Struggling Readers

Teacher's Edition Activities

- Recognze Signal Words, p. 352
- Recognize Text Patterns p. 356
- Use Text and Graphics Together, p. 360
- Use Typography to Understand, p. 364
- Create a Visual, p. 366
- Use Questions to Understand, p. 372
- 2004 Economic Data for Poland, p. 376

Unit 5 Resource Book

- RSG with Additional Support, pp. 3–5, 13–15, 23–25 (A)
- Reteaching Activities, pp. 10, 20, 30 (B)
- Chapter Test (Form A), pp. 41–44 (C)

ClassZone.com

- Animated Economics
- Interactive Review

Test Generator CD-ROM

- Chapter Test (Form A)
- Chapter Test (Form A), in Spanish

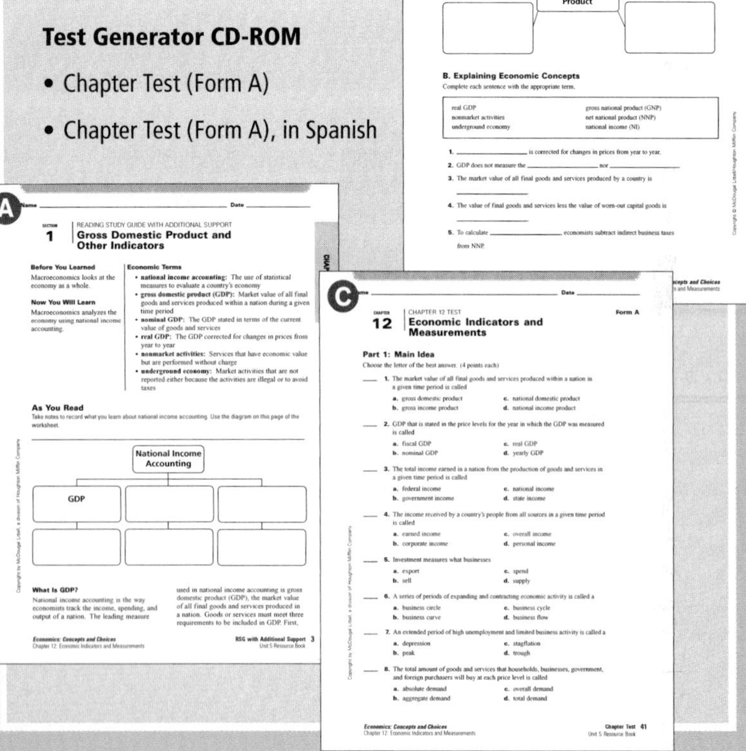

English Learners

Teacher's Edition Activities

- Understand Root Words, p. 352
- Understand Metaphorical Language, p. 362
- Isolate New Words, p. 370
- Learn Word Families, p. 374

Unit 5 Resource Book

- RSG with Additional Support (Spanish), pp. 6–8, 16–18, 26–28 (A)

Test Generator CD-ROM

- Chapter Test (Forms A, B, & C), in Spanish (B)

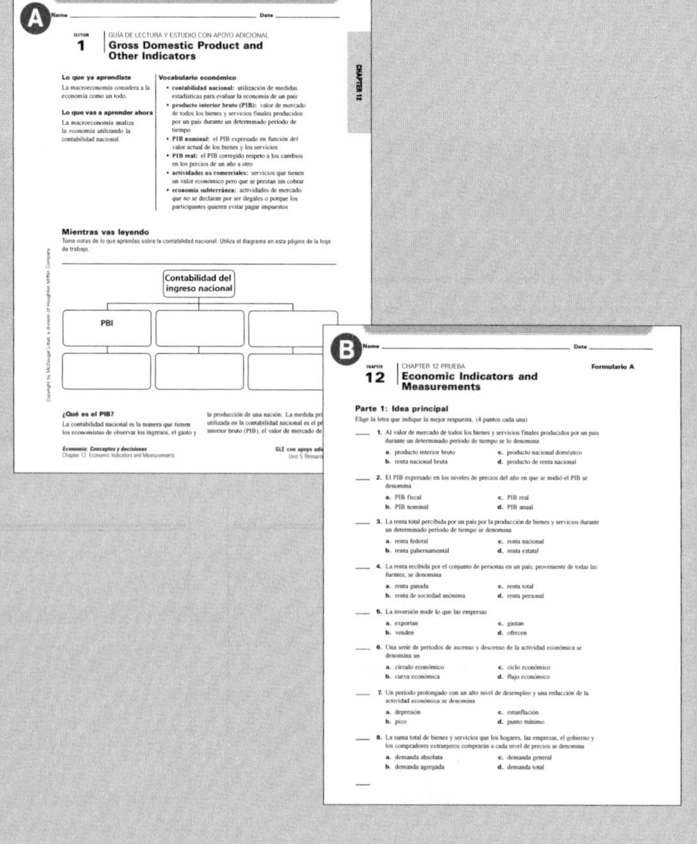

Inclusion

Teacher's Edition Activities

- Create a Visual, p. 354
- Work in Pairs, p. 360
- Research the WPA, p. 364
- Draw a Graph, p. 372
- Use Government Sources, p. 376

Lesson Plans

- Modified Lessons for Inclusion, pp. 40–42 (A)

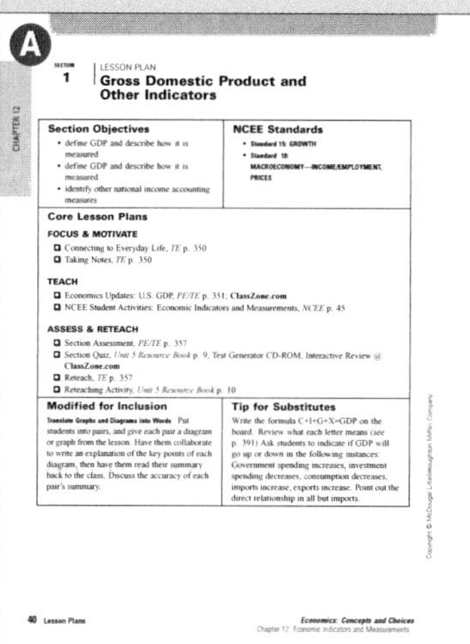

SECTION 1 | LESSON PLAN
Gross Domestic Product and Other Indicators

CHAPTER 12

Section Objectives	NCEE Standards
• define GDP and describe how it is measured • define GDP and describe how it is measured • identify other national income accounting measures	• Standard 15: GROWTH • Standard 18: MACROECONOMY—INCOME/EMPLOYMENT, PRICES

Core Lesson Plans

FOCUS & MOTIVATE
- ☐ Connecting to Everyday Life, *TE* p. 350
- ☐ Taking Notes, *TE* p. 350

TEACH
- ☐ Economics Updates: U.S. GDP, *PE/TE* p. 351; **ClassZone.com**
- ☐ NCEE Student Activities: Economic Indicators and Measurements, *NCEE* p. 45

ASSESS & RETEACH
- ☐ Section Assessment, *PE/TE* p. 357
- ☐ Section Quiz, *Unit 5 Resource Book* p. 9, Test Generator CD-ROM, Interactive Review @ **ClassZone.com**
- ☐ Reteach, *TE* p. 357
- ☐ Reteaching Activity, *Unit 5 Resource Book* p. 10

Modified for Inclusion	Tip for Substitutes
Translate Graphs and Diagrams into Words Put students into pairs, and give each pair a diagram or graph from the lesson. Have them collaborate to write an explanation of the key points of each diagram, then have them read their summary back to the class. Discuss the accuracy of each pair's summary.	Write the formula C+I+G+X=GDP on the board. Review what each letter means (see p. 391) Ask students to indicate if GDP will go up or down in the following instances: Government spending increases, investment spending decreases, consumption decreases, imports increase, exports increase. Point out the direct relationship in all but imports.

Copyright © McDougal Littell/Houghton Mifflin Company

40 Lesson Plans — *Economics: Concepts and Choices* Chapter 12: Economic Indicators and Measurements

Gifted and Talented

Teacher's Edition Activities

- Research and Report, p. 354
- Make Alternate Presentation, p. 356
- Investigate Interest Rates, p. 362
- Analyze a Motion Picture, p. 366
- Examine the "Resource Curse," p. 370
- Research Population Control, p. 374

Unit 5 Resource Book

- Readings in Free Enterprise: The Imagination Economy, pp. 33–34 (A)
- Case Study Resources: Cheer Up, pp. 35–36 (B)

NCEE Student Activities

- Economic Indicators and Measurements, pp. 45–48 (C)

ClassZone.com

- Research Center

Test Generator CD-ROM

- Chapter Test (Form C)
- Chapter Test (Form C), in Spanish

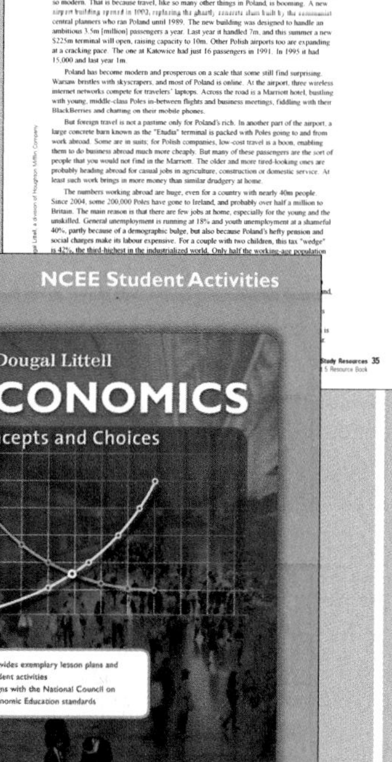

Date

CHAPTER 12 | CASE STUDY RESOURCES
Economic Indicators and Measurements

"Cheer Up"

Poland's economy is marching forward despite problems with a giant bureaucracy and enormous taxes. Many Poles work abroad, and unemployment numbers are huge, but this democratic nation's entry into the European Union (EU) has allowed trade expansion, which has helped businesses.

WARSAW airport immediately strikes the visitor as oddly cramped for something that seems so modern. That is because travel, like so many other things in Poland, is booming. A new airport building opened in 1992, replacing the ghastly concrete slum built by the communist central planners who ran Poland until 1989. The new building was designed to handle an ambitious 3.5m [million] passengers a year. Last year it handled 7m, and this summer a new $225m terminal will open, raising capacity to 10m. Other Polish airports too are expanding at a cracking pace. The one at Katowice had just 16 passengers in 1991. In 1995 it had 15,000 and last year 1m.

Poland has become modern and prosperous on a scale that some still find surprising. Warsaw bristles with skyscrapers, and most of Poland is online. At the airport, three wireless internet networks compete for travelers' laptops. Across the road is a Marriott hotel, bustling with young, middle-class Poles in-between flights and business meetings, fiddling with their BlackBerries and chatting on their mobile phones.

But foreign travel is not a pastime only for Poland's rich. In another part of the airport, a large concrete barn known as the "Etudia" terminal is packed with Poles going to and from work abroad. Some are in suits; for Polish companies, low-cost travel is a boon, enabling them to do business abroad much more cheaply. But many of these passengers are the sort of people that you would not find in the Marriott. The older and more tired-looking ones are probably heading abroad for casual jobs in agriculture, construction or domestic service. At least such work brings in more money than similar drudgery at home.

The numbers working abroad are huge, even for a country with nearly 40m people. Since 2004, some 200,000 Poles have gone to Ireland, and probably over half a million to Britain. The main reason is that there are few jobs at home, especially for the young and the unskilled. General unemployment is running at 18% and youth unemployment at a shameful 40%, partly because of a demographic bulge, but also because Poland's hefty pension and social charges make its labour expensive. For a couple with two children, this tax "wedge" is 42%, the third-highest in the industrialized world. Only half the working-age population

Study Resources 35

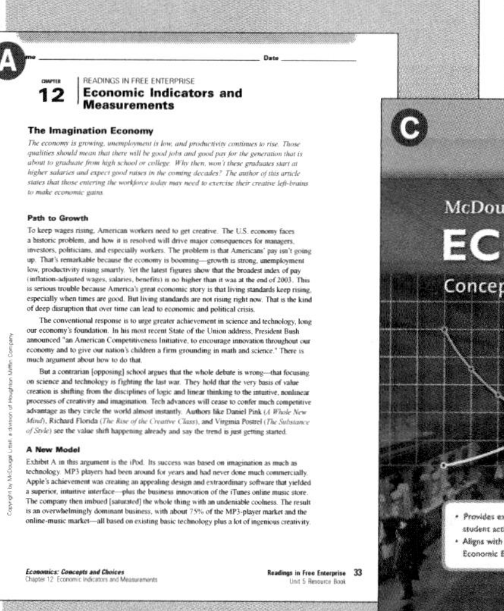

Date

CHAPTER 12 | READINGS IN FREE ENTERPRISE
Economic Indicators and Measurements

The Imagination Economy

The economy is growing, unemployment is low, and productivity continues to rise. Those qualities should mean that there will be good jobs and good pay for the generation that is about to graduate from high school or college. Why then, won't these graduates start at higher salaries and expect good raises in the coming decades? The author of this article states that those entering the workforce today may need to exercise their creative left-brains to make economic gains.

Path to Growth

To keep wages rising, American workers need to get creative. The U.S. economy faces a historic problem, and how it is resolved will drive major consequences for managers, investors, politicians, and especially workers. The problem is that Americans' pay isn't going up. That's remarkable because the economy is booming—growth is strong, unemployment low, productivity rising smartly. Yet the latest figures show that the broadest index of pay (inflation-adjusted wages, salaries, benefits) is no higher than it was at the end of 2003. This is serious trouble because America's great economic story is that living standards keep rising, especially when times are good. But living standards are not rising right now. That is the kind of deep disruption that over time can lead to economic and political crisis.

The conventional response is to urge greater achievement in science and technology, long our economy's foundation. In his most recent State of the Union address, President Bush announced "an American Competitiveness Initiative, to encourage innovation throughout our economy and to give our nation's children a firm grounding in math and science." There is much argument about how to do that.

But a contrarian [opposing] school argues that the whole debate is wrong—that focusing on science and technology is fighting the last war. They hold that the very basis of value creation is shifting from the disciplines of logic and linear thinking to the intuitive, nonlinear processes of creativity and imagination. Tech advances will cease to confer much competitive advantage as they circle the world almost instantly. Authors like Daniel Pink (*A Whole New Mind*), Richard Florida (*The Rise of the Creative Class*), and Virginia Postrel (*The Substance of Style*) see the value shift happening already and say the trend is just getting started.

A New Model

Exhibit A in this argument is the iPod. Its success was based on imagination as much as technology. MP3 players had been around for years and had never done much commercially. Apple's achievement was creating an appealing design and extraordinary software that yielded a superior, intuitive interface—plus the business innovation of the iTunes online music store. The company then imbued [saturated] the whole thing with an undeniable coolness. The result is an overwhelmingly dominant business, with about 75% of the MP3-player market and the online-music market—all based on existing basic technology plus a lot of ingenious creativity.

Copyright by McDougal Littell, a division of Houghton Mifflin Company

Economics: Concepts and Choices Chapter 12: Economic Indicators and Measurements — Readings in Free Enterprise 33 Unit 5 Resource Book

Focus & Motivate

Objective

Explain national income accounting and patterns of growth and contraction in the economy.

Why the Concept Matters

Start a discussion about the Information Age. Ask students what they think that term means. Many will probably tie it to the spread of the Internet and other technology that allows information sharing so easily. Then, ask them how being in the Information Age affects economic decision making. Point out that in the Information Age, there is no reason why every person cannot make the best possible economic decisions for himself or herself. Understanding the state of the national economy is one key part of sound decision making.

Analyzing the Photograph

Direct students to study the photograph and read the caption. Call on volunteers to describe what is taking place in the photograph. *(Possible answer: An investor is looking at the financial section of a newspaper to see how her stocks are performing.)* Point out that in this chapter students will learn about statistical measures that are used to determine how the national economy is performing and how this information affects individual and collective economic decisions.

Macroeconomics

Unit 5

Measuring and Monitoring Economic Performance

Measuring the Economy Millions of workers and businesses participate in the U.S. economy. Measuring the country's economy requires special economic tools.

348

CONTENT STANDARDS

NCEE STANDARDS

Standard 15: Growth

Students will understand that

Investment in factories, machinery, new technology, and in the health, education, and training of people can raise future standards of living.

Students will be able to use this knowledge to

Predict the consequences of investment decisions made by individuals, businesses, and governments. *(pages 350–373)*

Standard 18: Macroeconomy—Income/Employment, Prices

Students will understand that

A nation's overall levels of income, employment, and prices are determined by the interaction of spending and production decisions made by all households, firms, government agencies, and others in the economy.

Students will be able to use this knowledge to

Interpret media reports about current economic conditions and explain how these conditions can influence decisions made by consumers, producers, and government policy makers. *(pages 350–373)*

CHAPTER

12

Section 1
Gross Domestic Product and Other Indicators

Section 2
Business Cycles

Section 3
Stimulating Economic Growth

Case Study
Poland: Economic Freedom and Economic Growth

Economic Indicators and Measurements

CONCEPT REVIEW

Macroeconomics is the study of the economy as a whole and how major sectors of the economy interact.

CHAPTER 12 KEY CONCEPT

National income accounting uses statistical measures of income, spending, and output to help people understand what is happening to a country's economy.

WHY THE CONCEPT MATTERS

Your economic decisions—combined with those of millions of other people—determine the fate of the nation's economy. Can you afford to buy a new car? Is now a good time to change jobs? Should you take a risk in the stock market or keep your money safe in the bank? Understanding what is happening to the country's economy will help you make better economic decisions.

Online Highlights

More at ClassZone.com

Economics Update

Go to **ECONOMICS UPDATE** for chapter updates and current news on the economy of Poland. (See Case Study, pp. 376–377.) ▶

Animated Economics

Go to **ANIMATED ECONOMICS** for interactive lessons on the graphs and tables in this chapter.

Interactive Review

Go to **INTERACTIVE REVIEW** for concept review and activities.

How has free enterprise transformed Poland's economy? See the Case Study on pages 376–377.

CHAPTER 12

From the Classroom

Doug Young, Croton-Harmon High School

Measuring the Nation's Economy

This assignment looks at the many statistics which are used in making economic policy for the nation. Each student becomes responsible for one of the economic indicators used to assess the state of the economy. Students should share their research with the class using presentation software with no more than four slides. The slides must include (1) the indicator and definition, (2) a graph showing changes in the indicator with an explanation of the implication for the economy, and (3) how this indicator might either reflect the current economic situation or have an impact on the economy in the near future.

Indicators

Civilian Labor Force, Employees on Nonfarm, Payrolls, Unemployment, Manufacturing Trade, Inventories, Capacity Utilization (Productivity), Durable Goods, Advanced Retail Sales, Corporate, Profits, Producer Price Index, Prices Received by Farmers, Crude Oil Prices, Housing Starts, Household Wealth, Household Income, Per Capita Income, Disposable Personal Income, Personal Savings Rate, Personal Consumption Exp., Consumer Price Index, Poverty Rate

Previewing Chapter Technology at ClassZone.com

Economics Update Students will find updates to information in the pupil edition on pages 351, 362, 369, 374, and 376.

Animated Economics Students will find interactive lessons related to material on page 360.

Interactive Review Students will find additional section and chapter assessment support for materials on pages 357, 367, 375, and 378.

TEACHER MEDIA FAVORITES

Books

- Tvede, Lars. *Business Cycles: From John Law to the Internet Crash, 2nd Edition.* London: Routledge–Taylor and Francis Group, 2001. Engaging look at the history of business cycle theories.
- Friedman, Benjamin M. *The Moral Consequences of Economic Growth.* New York: Knopf, 2005. Renowned Harvard economist argues that economic growth is vital for the creation of a liberal, open society.
- Kyvig, David E. *Daily Life in the United States, 1920–1940: How Americans Lived During the Roaring Twenties and the Great Depression.* Chicago: Ivan R. Dee, 2004. An award-winning historian details daily life during the 1920s and 1930s.

Videos/DVDs

- *The Operation of an Economy.* 21 minutes. Clearvue/eav, 2001. Part of the "Introduction to Economics" series, this video explores such topics as equilibrium and disequilibrium and the paradox of thrift.
- *The Prime-Time World of Macroeconomics.* 135 minutes. Cerebellum, 1995. Part of the "World of Economics: The Standard Deviants" series, this video addresses economic measurement and other topics.
- *Macroeconomics Concepts.* Approx. 28 minutes. United Learning, 1997. Part of the "Economics: A Framework for Teaching the Basic Concepts" series, this video covers such topics as aggregates, GDP, unemployment, and inflation.
- *U.S. Economic Growth/Boom & Busts.* 30 minutes. Annenberg/CPB Collection, updated 2002. These videos are part of the "Economics U$A" series.

Software

- *WinEcon Macroeconomics Student Edition*, WinEcon Consortium, 6.1. Advanced program with interactive graphics, self-assessment tools, and other activities.

Internet

Visit **ClassZone.com** to link to

- a variety of chapter-specific, content-reviewed sites
- updates on data and topics presented throughout the chapter sections and Case Study
- updates to the Power Presentations

❶ Plan & Prepare

Section 1 Objectives

- define GDP and describe how it is measured
- explain how GDP has certain limitations
- identify other national income accounting measures

❷ Focus & Motivate

Connecting to Everyday Life Ask how many students are planning to work during the summer. Also inquire how many students are hoping to get or have already received a student loan for college. Point out that the availability of jobs and loans depends, in part, on the state of the economy. While macroeconomic ideas may seem distant to students, the state of the economy affects individuals profoundly. Keeping track of the economy is a vital task.

Taking Notes Remind students to take notes as they read by completing a hierarchy chart. They can use the Graphic Organizer at **Interactive Review @ ClassZone.com**. A sample is shown below.

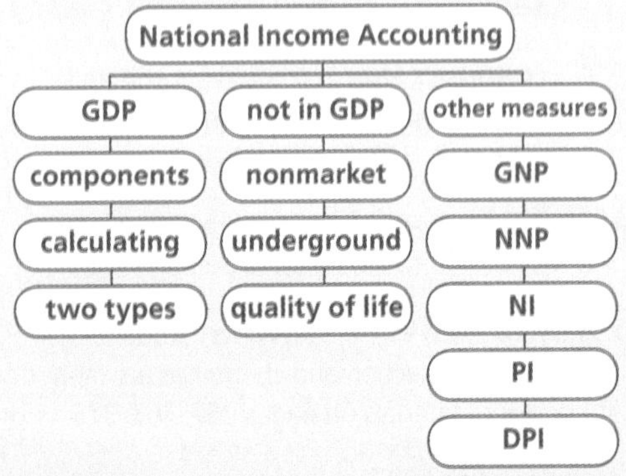

SECTION 1

Gross Domestic Product and Other Indicators

OBJECTIVES

In Section 1, you will
- define GDP and describe how it is measured
- explain how GDP has certain limitations
- identify other national income accounting measures

KEY TERMS

national income accounting, *p. 350*
gross domestic product (GDP), *p. 350*
nominal GDP, *p. 352*
real GDP, *p. 352*
nonmarket activities, *p. 354*
underground economy, *p. 354*
gross national product (GNP), *p. 355*
net national product (NNP), *p. 355*
national income (NI), *p. 355*
personal income (PI), *p. 355*
disposable personal income (DPI), *p. 355*

TAKING NOTES

As you read Section 1, complete a hierarchy chart like the one below to record what you learn about national income accounting. Use the Graphic Organizer at **Interactive Review @ ClassZone.com**

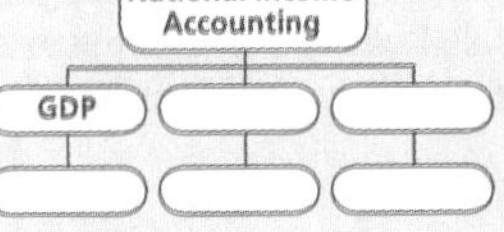

What Is GDP?

KEY CONCEPTS

QUICK REFERENCE

National income accounting is a way of evaluating a country's economy using statistical measures of its income, spending, and output.

Gross domestic product (GDP) is the market value of all final goods and services produced within a nation in a given time period.

As you have read, microeconomics and macroeconomics look at the economy through different lenses. While microeconomics examines the actions of individuals and single markets, macroeconomics examines the economy as a whole. Macroeconomists analyze the economy using **national income accounting**, statistical measures that track the income, spending, and output of a nation. The most important of those measures is **gross domestic product (GDP)**, the market value of all final goods and services produced within a nation in a given time period.

The Components of GDP

To be included in GDP, a good or service has to fulfill three requirements. First, it has to be final rather than intermediate. For example, the fabric used to make a shirt is an intermediate good; the shirt itself is a final good. Second, the good or service must be produced during the time period, regardless of when it is sold. For example, cars made this year but sold next year would be counted in this year's GDP. Finally, the good or service must be produced within the nation's borders. Products made in foreign countries by U.S. companies are not included in the U.S. GDP.

Products Included in GDP
Cars made in the United States are an example of goods counted toward U.S. gross domestic product (GDP).

SECTION 1 PROGRAM RESOURCES

ON LEVEL

Lesson Plans
- Core, p. 40

Unit 5 Resource Book
- Reading Study Guide, pp. 1–2
- Math Skills Worksheet, p. 39
- Section Quiz, p. 9

STRUGGLING READERS

Unit 5 Resource Book
- Reading Study Guide with Additional Support, pp. 3–5
- Reteaching Activity, p. 10

ENGLISH LEARNERS

Unit 5 Resource Book
- Reading Study Guide with Additional Support (Spanish), pp. 6–8

INCLUSION

Lesson Plans
- Modified for Inclusion, p. 40

GIFTED AND TALENTED

NCEE Student Activities
- Economic Indicators and Measurements, pp. 45–48

TECHNOLOGY

eEdition DVD-ROM

eEdition Online

Power Presentation DVD-ROM

Economics Concepts Transparencies
- CT40 Gauging Economic Performance

Daily Test Practice Transparencies, TT40

ClassZone.com

Calculating GDP

Although there are several different ways to calculate GDP, economists often use the expenditures approach. With this method, they group national spending on final goods and services according to the four sectors of the economy: spending by households, or consumption; spending by businesses, or investment; government spending; and total exports minus total imports, or net exports. Economists identify consumption with the letter *C*; investment with the letter *I*; government spending with the letter *G*; and net exports with the letter *X*. To calculate GDP, economists add the expenditures from all sectors together: C+I+G+X=GDP.

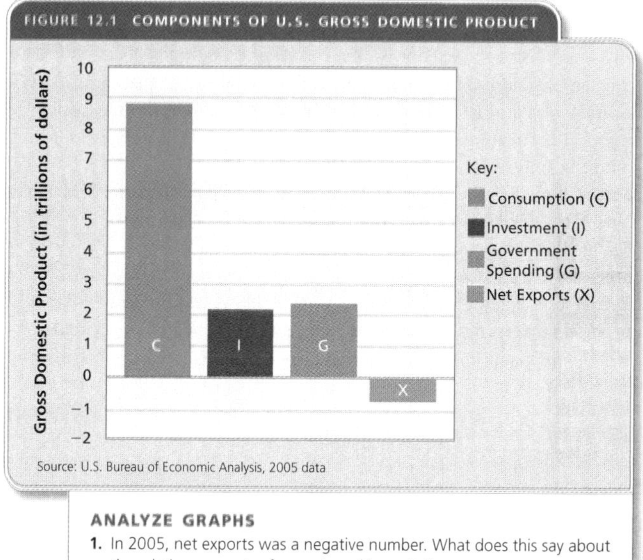

ANALYZE GRAPHS

1. In 2005, net exports was a negative number. What does this say about the relative amounts of exports and imports?
2. Did households, businesses, or the government contribute the most to U.S. GDP in 2005?

Economics Update

Find an update on the U.S. GDP at **ClassZone.com**

Consumption includes all spending by households on durable goods, nondurable goods, and services. You drive to the movies in a durable good (an item that does not wear out quickly). You purchase a service when you pay for the movie (since you are not buying to own something). And you obtain a nondurable good (a good that is used up relatively soon after purchase) when you buy popcorn.

Investment, which measures what businesses spend, has two categories. One is fixed investment, which includes new construction and purchases of such capital goods as equipment, machinery, and tools. The other is inventory investment. This category, also called unconsumed output, is made up of the unsold goods that businesses keep on hand.

Government spending includes all the expenditures of federal, state, and local governments on goods and services. Examples include spending for defense, highways,

3 Teach

What Is GDP?

Discuss

- Why not just add the amounts that everyone spends in the national economy to find GDP, with the expenditures approach? *(There would be items represented more than once, as in the case of transfer payments made by the government and then spent by the recipients.)*
- Where do economists get the numbers to do the calculations for GDP? *(government records, especially tax forms)*

Analyze Graphs: Figure 12.1

Ask students to look at the graph to see the four components that make up the GDP. Have them use the formula C + I + G + X = GDP to obtain the approximate Gross Domestic Product shown on the graph. *(9 + 2 + 2 + [–1] = 12 trillion dollars)*

Answers

1. *The U.S. imported much more than it exported in 2005.*
2. *households*

Economics Update

At **ClassZone.com** students will see updates on the U.S. GDP.

LEVELED ACTIVITY

Understanding Business Cycles

Time 30 Minutes

Objective Students will demonstrate an understanding of the business cycles and their social impact. Concepts for this activity are covered in Sections 1 and 2 of this chapter.

Basic

Write two paragraphs. One should be a description of a recession; the other, an expansion. Cover the impact of these phases of the business cycle on:

- businesses
- workers
- consumers
- government programs

On Level

Create a story in which you show the impact of either an economic recession or an expansion on two fictional characters from different generations. For each character, show how the phase of the business cycle affects educational or job opportunities, level of material comfort, and general quality of life.

Challenge

Make a time line of the business cycles in the United States since the year 1900. Add events to the time line from social and cultural history, such as civil rights, the arts, motion pictures, politics, the media, and so on.

Technomics

Updated GDP Figures
The Bureau of Economic Analysis, which is part of the Department of Commerce, publishes quarterly news releases that include changes in the GDP at their Web site. It also has a Web page devoted entirely to the GDP.

Analyze Graphs: Figure 12.2

Ask students if they have heard older adults complain about how much more expensive things are now than when they were young. A soda is still basically the same as it was 50 years ago, but it costs much more now. If economists did not take such price increases into account, the only measure would be nominal GDP, and economic growth would be exaggerated, as demonstrated by the graph.

Answers

1. *by about $4 trillion or about two-thirds*
2. *by about $3 trillion or about three-sevenths*
3. *Since real GDP is stated in terms of what the dollar was worth in 2000, real and nominal GDP are the same for 2000.*

and public education. However, government spending on transfer payments, such as social security and unemployment benefits, is not included. These payments allow the recipients to buy goods and services, and these are counted as consumption.

Net exports, the final component of GDP, represents foreign trade. This component takes into account the goods and services produced in the United States but sold in foreign countries—in other words, exports. However, U.S. consumers and businesses also buy, or import, goods made in foreign countries. Cars, car parts, and crude oil are the largest imports in dollar value. The GDP counts only net exports—the value of U.S. exports minus the value of U.S. imports.

Two Types of GDP

QUICK REFERENCE

Nominal GDP states GDP in terms of the current value of goods and services.

Real GDP states GDP corrected for changes in prices from year to year.

Economists use GDP to gauge how well a country's economy is doing. When GDP is growing, an economy creates more jobs and more business opportunities. When GDP declines, jobs and more business opportunities become less plentiful. To get a clearer picture of a country's economic health, economists calculate two forms of GDP—nominal and real.

The most basic form is **nominal GDP**, which is stated in the price levels for the year in which the GDP was measured. If prices never changed, nominal GDP would be sufficient. But prices tend to increase over time. In Figure 12.2, find the line that represents nominal GDP. If you estimate the difference from 1990 to 2005, the nominal GDP of the United States about doubled. However, during this time prices went up, adding dollars to GDP without adding value to the nation's output.

To factor out rising prices, economists use **real GDP**, which is nominal GDP adjusted for changes in prices. Real GDP is an estimate of the GDP if prices were to

FIGURE 12.2 U.S. NOMINAL AND REAL GROSS DOMESTIC PRODUCT

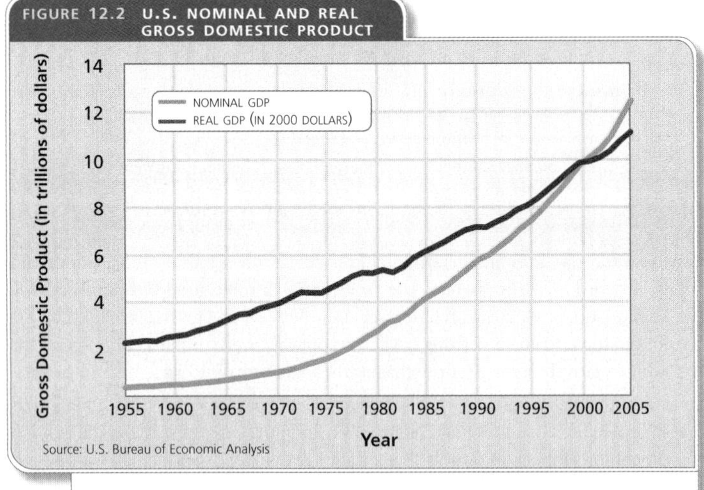

Source: U.S. Bureau of Economic Analysis

ANALYZE GRAPHS

1. About how much did nominal GDP increase from 1990 to 2000?
2. About how much did real GDP increase over the same period?
3. Why do the two lines cross at the year 2000?

DIFFERENTIATING INSTRUCTION

Struggling Readers

Recognize Signal Words
Direct students to the first paragraph on page 352 and the third paragraph on page 355. Have them follow along as you read the sentence on each page that contains the phrase *in other words*. Point out to students that these words signal to readers that an explanation is to follow. So, if struggling readers did not understand something, they will be getting an additional explanation of the concept. Mention other phrases containing signal words, such as *that is*.

English Learners

Understand Root Words
Direct students to the word *nominal* and have them look up its derivation (from the Latin word meaning "name"). Perhaps they may be familiar with the word in relation to nouns, which also are naming words. Ask them if they are aware of other meanings. Some might know that it also means "small amount." *(nominal fee)* Help students understand its reference to one type of GDP. *(*Nominal *means "at face value," or "by name.")*

MATH CHALLENGE

FIGURE 12.3 Understanding Nominal and Real GDP

To better understand nominal and real GDP, imagine a country that produces only one good: TVs. If you know the price of TVs and the number produced, you can calculate that country's nominal and real GDP. Use the table to find the data for these calculations.

	2004	2005	2006
TVs Produced	500	600	600
TV Price	$100	$100	$120
Nominal GDP	$50,000	$60,000	$72,000
Real GDP, base: 2004	$50,000	$60,000	$60,000

Step 1: Calculate nominal GDP for 2004. Nominal GDP is the product of the number of TVs produced and the price of TVs that year.

Number produced × Price in that year = Nominal GDP   500 × $100 = $50,000

The table shows that nominal GDP grew each year. If you judged only by nominal GDP, the economy of this country would seem to be growing.

Step 2: Analyze the nominal GDP figures. Why did nominal GDP increase from 2004 to 2005? The number of TVs produced increased. Why did nominal GDP increase from 2005 to 2006? The price of TVs increased.

The output of the country's economy grew from 2004 to 2005, but it stayed the same from 2005 to 2006, despite the increase in prices. Calculating real GDP produces a better estimate of how much a country's economy is growing.

Step 3: Calculate real GDP for 2006. Real GDP is the product of the number of TVs produced in the current year and the price of TVs in the base year. In this case, use 2004 as the base year.

Number produced × Price in the base year = Real GDP   600 × $100 = $60,000

Since 2004 is the base year, nominal and real GDP are the same for 2004. Real GDP allows you to compare the output of the country's economy in different years.

remain constant from year to year. To find real GDP, economists compare nominal GDP to a base year. Look again at Figure 12.2, which uses 2000 as a base year. Since real GDP eliminates price differences, the line for real GDP rises more gradually than the line for nominal GDP. Real GDP provides a more accurate measure of economic performance.

APPLICATION Applying Economic Concepts

A. If output remained the same, how would a year of falling prices affect nominal GDP? How would it affect real GDP?
Nominal GDP would fall compared with earlier years. Real GDP would not change.

Math Challenge: Figure 12.3

For more practice, work through the following additional example with students. Give them only the first two rows. Then, help them calculate the third and fourth. They should assume that MP3 players are the country's only product.

	2004	2005	2006
MP3 players produced	200	200	225
Price	$75	$100	$100
Nominal GDP	*($15,000)*	*($20,000)*	*($22,500)*
Real GDP, base: 2004	*($15,000)*	*($15,000)*	*($16,875)*

More About . . .

Base Years and the GDP
The farther away from the base year you go, the less accurate the correction for price increases becomes. This is because to compare years requires estimating relative production costs. For example, the cost of making MP3 players is X and the cost of making portable cassette tape players is Y. Over time, production costs for MP3 players will fall, while production costs for the older, less popular technology will rise. More producers will make MP3 players, but this differential may not be reflected in real GDP farther away from the base year.

SMALL GROUP ACTIVITY

Using GDP Data

Time 30 Minutes

Task Understand how people in various sectors of the economy use GDP data.

Materials Needed paper and pens

Activity

- Divide students into four groups: consumers, business leaders, workers, and government policymakers.
- Have each group discuss among themselves how they are affected by increases in real GDP and by decreases.
- Each group should then devise an original way to present the substance of their discussion to the rest of the class.
- Have the groups make their presentation, following each with a brief class discussion.

Rubric

	Understanding of the Importance of GDP	Presentation of Information
4	excellent	clear and accurate
3	good	mostly accurate
2	fair	somewhat accurate
1	poor	sketchy

What GDP Does Not Measure

Discuss

- What would the GDP of an economy that uses barter as the basis for much of its economic activity look like? *(Although barter is an economic activity, it does not involve money, so it is not measured by GDP. Compared to other nations, the GDP would be smaller.)*
- What, if anything, does GDP tell us about the well-being of a nation's people? *(It is strictly a measurement of economic output, not standard of living. However, nations with a high GDP tend to have a high standard of living as well.)*

More About . . .

The Genuine Progress Indicator (GPI)
Even as a strictly economic measure, GDP may tell an incomplete story. For example, it focuses only on production and consumption—the greater those, the higher the GDP. It does not include a value for conservation of resources. Further, environmental disasters, such as oil spills, may actually increase GDP, since cleanup services are reflected in production figures.

For these and other reasons, some economists favor different measures, including the Genuine Progress Indicator (GPI). The GPI factors in the costs behind consumption and production in the form of pollution or depletion of resources. These costs are subtracted from GDP, just as costs are subtracted from gross profits to identify net profits.

What GDP Does Not Measure

QUICK REFERENCE

Nonmarket activities are services that have potential economic value but are performed without charge.

Underground economy describes market activities that go unreported because they are illegal or because those involved want to avoid taxation.

KEY CONCEPTS

Although GDP provides an important estimate of how well the economy is performing, it does not measure all output. It does not measure **nonmarket activities**, such as home childcare or performing one's own home repairs. GDP also does not measure output from the **underground economy**, market activities that go unreported because they are illegal or because those involved want to avoid taxation. Further, GDP does not measure "quality of life" issues related to economic output.

Nonmarket Activities

Some productive activities do not take place in economic markets. For example, there is no effective way to measure the output of plumbers who install or repair plumbing systems in their own homes or people who do volunteer work for schools or hospitals. By far the biggest nonmarket activity, also left out of GDP, consists of the many services—cooking, cleaning, childcare—provided by homemakers.

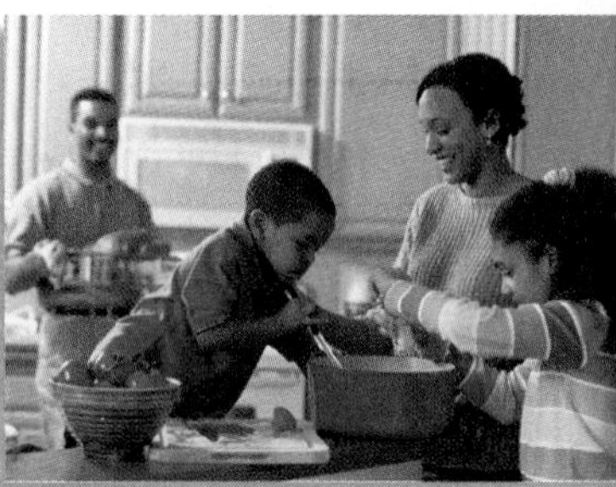

Nonmarket Activities Housework is an example of a productive activity not measured by GDP.

Underground Economy

Also missing from GDP is the underground sector of the economy. Some activities are kept underground because they are illegal—drug dealing, smuggling, gambling, and selling stolen goods, for example. When goods are rationed or otherwise restricted, illegal trading occurs on what is called the black market. Other underground activities are themselves legal, but the way the payment is handled is not. For example, a plumber who does repairs for a neighbor might receive payment in cash and not declare it as taxable income. Estimates suggest that the underground economy would make up 8 to 10 percent of the U.S. GDP.

Quality of Life

Countries with high GDPs have high living standards. But GDP does not show how the goods and services are distributed. The United States has the largest GDP of any country, but more than 10 percent of its people still live in poverty. GDP also does not express what products are being built and services offered: for example, are there more jails being built than schools?

APPLICATION Explaining an Economic Concept

B. If you get paid in cash to baby-sit, mow lawns, or do other chores for neighbors, are you part of the underground economy? Why or why not?
yes, if you are required to file taxes and you do not report the income to the IRS
no, if you do report taxable income.

DIFFERENTIATING INSTRUCTION

Inclusion

Create a Visual
Instruct students who have visual strengths and writing and reading challenges to create a visual with illustrations showing what is included in GDP and what is not. Suggest that they design their visual to clearly show that some things are included while others are not, and to use old magazines or online pictures for their illustrations.

Gifted and Talented

Research and Report
Direct students to research another economic measure, proposed in 1972 by the king of Bhutan, called Gross National Happiness (GNH). Have students explore this topic by attempting to determine the relation between happiness and the economy, especially in classical liberal economic theory. They should present their findings in a written report or other type of presentation.

Other Economic Performance Measures

KEY CONCEPTS

GDP is not the only measure that economists use to gauge economic performance. Several other measures are derived by making adjustments to GDP.

- **Gross national product (GNP)** is the market value of all final goods and services a country produces in a given time period. GNP equals GDP plus the income from goods and services produced by U.S. companies and citizens in foreign countries but minus the income foreign companies and citizens earn here.
- **Net national product (NNP)** is GNP minus depreciation of capital stock—in other words, the value of final goods and services less the value of capital goods that became worn out during the time period.
- **National income (NI)** is the total income earned in a nation from the production of goods and services in a given time period. It is calculated by subtracting indirect business taxes, such as property and sales taxes, from NNP.
- **Personal income (PI)** is the income received by a country's people from all sources in a given time period. It can be calculated from NI by subtracting social security taxes, corporate profit taxes, and corporate profits not paid to stockholders and by adding social security, unemployment, and welfare payments.
- **Disposable personal income (DPI)** is personal income minus personal income taxes. It shows how much money is actually available for consumer spending.

QUICK REFERENCE

Gross national product (GNP) is the market value of all final goods and services produced by a country.

Net national product (NNP) is the value of final goods and services less the value of capital goods that have become worn out.

National income (NI) is the total income earned in a nation from the production of goods and services.

Personal income (PI) is the income received by a country's people from all sources.

Disposable personal income (DPI) is personal income minus taxes.

FIGURE 12.4 **National Income Accounting**

GDP + income earned abroad by U.S. businesses and citizens
− income earned in U.S. by foreign businesses and citizens
= GNP − depreciation of capital stock
= NNP − indirect business taxes
= NI − income earned but not received
+ income received but not earned
= PI − personal taxes
= DPI

ANALYZE CHARTS

What three figures do you need in order to calculate personal income (PI)?

APPLICATION **Making Inferences**

C. Under what circumstances might a country's GNP be greater than its GDP?
if the country's businesses and citizens earn more abroad than foreign businesses and citizens earn in the country

Other Economic Performance Measures

Discuss

- What is the difference between GDP and GNP? *(GNP measures income rather than spending, including income received for goods and services produced outside of the United States.)* The U.S. focused on GNP until 1991. One reason for the switch was that GDP data is available more quickly than GNP data and that other nations use GDP.
- Which is most relevant to you of all the measurements listed on this page? *(Answers will vary, but probably most students would say Disposable Personal Income because that is money that is available to them.)*

Analyze Charts: Figure 12.4

Point out to students that five steps are necessary to move from GDP to DPI in the National Income Accounting chart. *(GDP to GNP to NNP to NI to PI to DPI)* Ask students at what component levels taxation enters the computations. *(NNP [indirect business taxes] and PI [personal taxes])*

Answer

National Income (NI), income earned but not received, income received but not earned

SMALL GROUP ACTIVITY

Estimating Nonmarket Values

Time 30 minutes

Task Understand how economic value might be assigned to homemaking activities.

Materials Needed paper and pens

Activity

- Invite a volunteer to read aloud the paragraph under the heading Nonmarket Activities on page 354.
- Divide students into four groups.
- Direct each group to attempt to determine a dollar value for one adult's full-time homemaking activities for one year.
- Instruct them take notes about the process they use to arrive at that figure.
- Ask each group to present its ideas to the class and to follow each presentation with a brief class discussion.

Rubric

	Understanding Importance of Nonmarket Activities	Presentation of Information
4	excellent	creative and thorough
3	good	clear and complete
2	fair	mostly clear
1	poor	sketchy

Synthesizing Economic Data

1 Plan & Prepare

Objectives

- synthesize economic data by finding relationships and making generalizations
- interpret a table

2 Focus & Motivate

Invite students who are going to college to explain how they made their choice of which college to attend. Point out that a good decision requires synthesizing—taking separate bits of information and putting them together to form an opinion. Students probably combined information they learned from a variety of sources: surveys and rankings of colleges, personal visits, anecdotal evidence from alumni, and so on. Synthesizing disparate pieces of information into a meaningful whole is the process behind most important life decisions.

3 Teach

Point out that sometimes the data that stands out as clearly different from other data can provide the most interesting insights. In this chart, for example, the figures in all columns show a steady rising pattern, except for the column showing Net Export Expenditures. Ask students to determine whether or not there is a pattern in those figures. *(There is a general but not steady movement downwards, although the increments are unpredictable.)* Ask students what they might do next if they wanted to understand the variation in Net Exports. *(Answers will vary but should involve looking for more data, either economic data or historical circumstances, that might explain the changes.)*

For additional practice see **Skillbuilder Handbook**, page R23.

THINKING ECONOMICALLY Answers

1. *Nominal GDP increases every five years. The economy seems to be growing, but real GDP numbers are needed to be sure.*
2. *Consumption*
3. *Consumption grew in relation to Investment and Government. In 1980, 1985, and 1990, I + G was much more than half of C. In 1995, 2000, and 2005, I + G was close to half of C.*

ECONOMICS SKILLBUILDER

For more on synthesizing economic data, see the Skillbuilder Handbook, page R23.

Synthesizing Economic Data

Synthesizing is a skill used by economists to interpret economic trends. Synthesizing involves interpreting various data to form an overview of economic performance. A synthesis is often stated as a broad summary statement.

PRACTICING THE SKILL National income accounting involves the collection and analysis of data on key economic variables. Economists synthesize the data to arrive at an overview of national economic performance. The table below presents data for variables used to determine gross domestic product (GDP), a key factor in national income accounting.

Read the title to learn the main idea of the table. This table shows the components of U.S. GDP for selected years.

Read the column heads carefully. The four types of expenditures are used to determine GDP.

Determine how the types of data relate to one another. For 1990, calculating the sum of the four expenditures yields $5,803 billion, the nominal GDP for 1990.

FIGURE 12.5 COMPONENTS OF U.S. GDP (IN BILLIONS OF DOLLARS)

Year	Consumption Expenditure	Investment Expenditure	Government Expenditure	Net Export Expenditure	Nominal GDP
1980	1,757	479	566	−13	2,789
1985	2,720	736	879	−115	4,220
1990	3,840	861	1,180	−78	5,803
1995	4,976	1,144	1,369	−91	7,398
2000	6,739	1,736	1,722	−380	9,817
2005	8,746	2,105	2,363	−727	12,487

Source: U.S. Bureau of Economic Analysis

Check the source of the data to evaluate its reliability.

Look for patterns in the data. For example, notice that net exports have been negative.

THINKING ECONOMICALLY Synthesizing

1. What trend can be seen in U.S. nominal GDP? What can you tell from this about the growth of the U.S. economy? Do you need more information?
2. Which expenditure accounts for most of GDP?
3. Does the proportion of this expenditure to the other two positive expenditures remain about the same in the six years shown here? Briefly explain how you estimated this.

DIFFERENTIATING INSTRUCTION

Struggling Readers

Recognize Text Patterns

Have students note that each Skillbuilder uses the same basic pattern. It begins with a definition of the skill involved and an explanation of how it is used in economics. The feature continues with a practical application of the skill, using economics-related material. Most Skillbuilders also contain words in boldface that stress important elements in practicing the skill. Remind students that knowing the patterns of text features can help them understand what they read.

Gifted and Talented

Make Alternate Presentation

Invite the students to use the data in the table to make a color-coded line graph of each variable, with the time span across the x-axis. Ask them to share their graphs with the rest of the class and to explain the difference between the way the table presents the data and the way their graph does.

SECTION 1 Assessment

REVIEWING KEY CONCEPTS

1. Explain the relationship between the terms in each of these pairs.
   a. *nominal GDP* / *real GDP*   **b.** *gross national product* / *net national product*   **c.** *personal income* / *disposable personal income*
2. What are the four components of GDP?
3. What is an example of a durable good? a nondurable good?
4. Name two economic activities that GDP does not measure.
5. Why are transfer payments not included as a government expenditure when calculating GDP?
6. **Using Your Notes** Write a brief summary of the methods used to calculate national income and the purposes of each accounting method. Refer to your completed hierarchy chart.

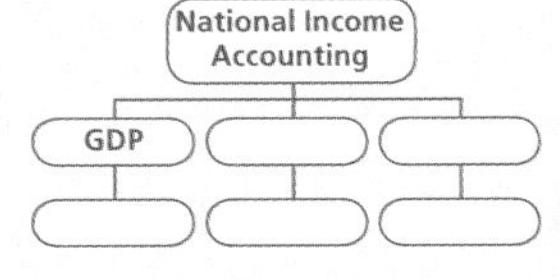

Use the Graphic Organizer at **Interactive Review @ ClassZone.com**

CRITICAL THINKING

7. **Drawing Conclusions** List some things that have become more expensive during your lifetime. Explain how a rise in price level affects nominal GDP and real GDP.
8. **Making Inferences** If consumption is especially high compared with other years, what might you generalize about the health of the economy?
9. **Explaining an Economic Concept** What is the underground economy? What impact does it have on a nation's GDP?
10. **Drawing Conclusions** Imagine that a new country is discovered on an island in the middle of the Pacific Ocean. The country's people have never left the island, and no foreigners have ever been there. What would the relationship be between the country's GDP and its GNP? Why?
11. **Challenge** How would the following affect GDP?
    a. Government transfer payments increase.
    b. Student sells used CD to record store.
    c. Car owner pays auto repair shop $500 to fix his car.

Online Quiz
ClassZone.com

ECONOMICS IN PRACTICE

Identifying Intermediate and Final Goods
Look at the following list of goods and who purchased them.

Goods	Purchaser
copier paper	accounting firm
refrigerator	home consumer
stainless steel	manufacturer
eggs	home consumer
eggs	factory that makes frozen baked goods
battery	car owner
paint	furniture maker

Categorize Economic Information Decide whether each good is an intermediate good or a final good.

Challenge Why is it important to make a distinction in national income accounting between intermediate and final goods?

357

4 Assess & Reteach

Assess Assign the first six questions as written work and use the Critical Thinking questions and Economics in Practice as starters for class discussions. Ask students to think of more examples to categorize as intermediate and final goods.

Unit 5 Resource Book
- Section Quiz, p. 9

Interactive Review @ ClassZone.com
- Section Quiz

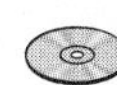

Test Generator CD-ROM
- Section Quiz

Reteach Divide students into three groups, one for each main part of Section 1. Have the students work together to come up with "talking points" for their part. These would be bulleted lists with brief notes that students can use to present their part of Section 1 to the class as a review. After the presentations, make copies of the talking points for each student in the class.

Unit 5 Resource Book
- Reteaching Activity, p. 10

Economics in Practice
Categorizing Economic Information copier paper—final; refrigerator—final; stainless steel—intermediate; eggs to consumer—final; eggs to factory—intermediate; battery—final; paint—intermediate

Challenge so they don't get counted more than once

SECTION 1 ASSESSMENT ANSWERS

Reviewing Key Concepts

1. **a.** *nominal GDP*, p. 352; *real GDP*, p. 352
   b. *gross national product*, p. 355; *net national product*, p. 355
   c. *personal income*, p. 355; *disposable personal income*, p. 355
2. consumption, investment, government spending, net exports
3. sample answers: durable good—car; nondurable good—coat
4. Answers will vary but should include examples of nonmarket or underground activities.
5. because they are counted in the consumer sector, since people spend the money received through transfer payments on living expenses
6. See page 350 for an example of a completed diagram. Answers should include a thumbnail description of GDP plus summaries similar to those on p. 355 for the other national income accounting methods.

Critical Thinking

7. Examples will vary. A rise in price will increase nominal GDP but not real GDP.
8. High consumption indicates that the economy is healthy.
9. The underground economy includes illegal activities and unreported income. It is not counted as part of GDP.
10. They would be the same, since the only difference is the balance of trade, and there would be no trade.
11. **a.** no effect (Transfer payments do not count toward GDP, but recipients' use of payments would eventually add to consumption.)
    b. no effect
    c. add $500 to GDP

Economics in Practice
See answers in side column above.

1 Plan & Prepare

Section 2 Objectives

- describe the phases of the business cycle
- discuss aggregate demand and aggregate supply
- identify the causes of the changes in the business cycle
- explain how economists predict business cycle changes
- outline major business cycles in U.S. history

2 Focus & Motivate

Connecting to Everyday Life Bring in news items that relate to business decisions, changes in interest rates, consumer expectations, natural disasters, or political unrest, all of which can affect the business cycle. Ask students to discuss how each item might affect the economy, previewing the notion of the business cycle.

Taking Notes Remind students to take notes as they read by completing a cluster diagram for each key concept. They can use the Graphic Organizer at **Interactive Review @ ClassZone.com**. A sample is shown below.

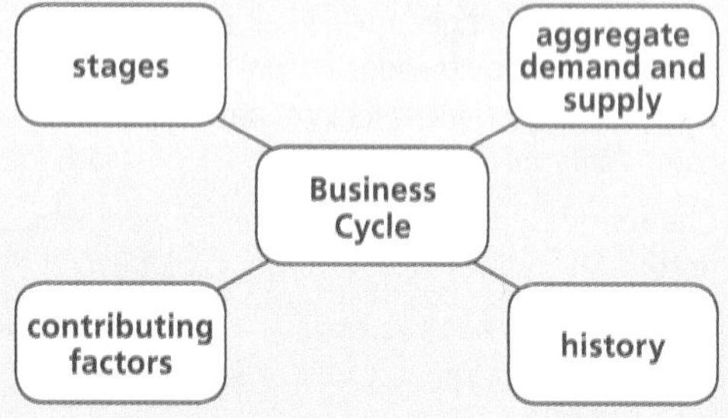

SECTION 2

Business Cycles

OBJECTIVES

In Section 2, you will

- describe the phases of the business cycle
- discuss aggregate demand and aggregate supply
- identify the causes of the changes in the business cycle
- explain how economists predict business cycle changes
- outline major business cycles in U.S. history

KEY TERMS

business cycle, *p. 358*
economic growth, *p. 358*
recession, *p. 359*
depression, *p. 359*
stagflation, *p. 359*
aggregate demand, *p. 360*
aggregate supply, *p. 360*
macroeconomic equilibrium, *p. 361*
leading indicators, *p. 364*
coincident indicators, *p. 364*
lagging indicators, *p. 364*

TAKING NOTES

As you read Section 2, complete a cluster diagram like the one below to record what you learn about business cycles. Use the Graphic Organizer at **Interactive Review @ ClassZone.com**

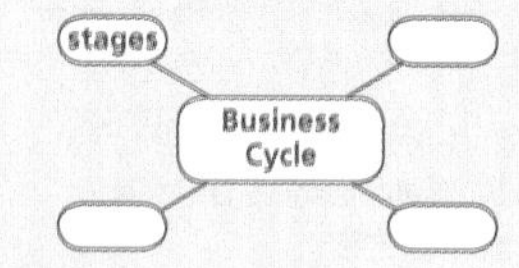

What Is the Business Cycle?

QUICK REFERENCE

The **business cycle** is the series of growing and shrinking periods of economic activity, measured by increases or decreases in real GDP.

Economic growth is the increase in a nation's real GDP over a period of time.

KEY CONCEPTS

Economic changes often follow a broad pattern. During the 1990s, the U.S. economy expanded. In 2001, the economy slowed down. It then returned to a period of growth. Such changes are an example of the **business cycle**, a series of periods of expanding and contracting economic activity. The business cycle is measured by increases or decreases in real GDP. The cycle has four distinct stages: expansion, peak, contraction, and trough.

STAGE 1 Expansion

In the expansion phase, real GDP grows from a low point, or trough, as you can see in the graph in Figure 12.6. The expansion is a period of **economic growth**, an increase in a nation's real gross domestic product (GDP). During an expansion, jobs are relatively easy to find, so unemployment goes down. More and more resources are needed to keep up with spending demand. As resources become more scarce, their prices rise. The length of each phase may vary both within a cycle and from cycle to cycle. The longest expansion in U.S. history took place over the course of ten years from 1991 to 2001.

Business Cycles Workers and businesses ride the ups and downs of the economy.

358 Chapter 12

SECTION 2 PROGRAM RESOURCES

ON LEVEL

Lesson Plans
- Core, p. 41

Unit 5 Resource Book
- Reading Study Guide, pp. 11–12
- Economic Skills and Problem Solving Activity, pp. 31–32
- Section Quiz, p. 19

STRUGGLING READERS

Unit 5 Resource Book
- Reading Study Guide with Additional Support, pp. 13–15
- Reteaching Activity, p. 20

ENGLISH LEARNERS

Unit 5 Resource Book
- Reading Study Guide with Additional Support (Spanish), pp. 16–18

INCLUSION

Lesson Plans
- Modified for Inclusion, p. 41

GIFTED AND TALENTED

Unit 5 Resource Book
- Case Study Resources: Cheer Up, pp. 35–36

NCEE Student Activities
- Economic Indicators and Measurements, pp. 45–48

TECHNOLOGY

eEdition DVD-ROM

eEdition Online

Power Presentation DVD-ROM

Economics Concepts Transparencies
- CT41 Economic Indicators That Predict Stages of a Business Cycle

Daily Test Practice Transparencies, TT41

ClassZone.com

FIGURE 12.6 THE BUSINESS CYCLE

ⓐ In the expansion phase, real GDP grows rapidly.

ⓑ The peak is where real GDP reaches its highest point in the cycle.

ⓒ In the contraction phase, real GDP declines.

ⓓ The trough marks the end of the contraction.

ANALYZE CHARTS

1. What stage occurred before point A?
2. What stage will occur after point D?
3. How might the business cycle curve change if nominal GDP was used instead of real GDP?

STAGE 2 Peak

The point at which real GDP is the highest represents the peak of the business cycle. As prices rise and resources tighten, businesses become less profitable. From that point on, real GDP declines as businesses curtail production.

STAGE 3 Contraction

The contraction phase begins after the peak. As producers cut back, resources become less scarce and prices tend to stabilize or fall. Unemployment rises because employers produce less. Sometimes the contraction phase becomes a **recession**, a contraction lasting two or more quarters (six months or more). On rare occasions, as in the 1930s, a contraction turns into a **depression**, an extended period of high unemployment and limited business activity. While prices usually remain about the same or go down during the contraction phase, sometimes they go up. These are periods of **stagflation**—stagnation in business activity and inflation of prices.

QUICK REFERENCE

Recession is a prolonged economic contraction lasting two or more quarters (six months or more).

Depression is an extended period of high unemployment and reduced business activity.

Stagflation describes periods during which prices rise at the same time that there is a slowdown in business activity.

STAGE 4 Trough

The final phase of the business cycle is the trough, the point at which real GDP and employment stop declining. A business cycle is complete when it has gone through all four phases, from trough to trough or from peak to peak.

APPLICATION Explaining an Economic Concept

A. In terms of the business cycle, what is unusual about stagflation? Usually prices fall or remain stable during a slowdown in business activity.

❸ Teach

What Is the Business Cycle?

Discuss

- Are business cycles inevitable? *(According to the traditional explanation, yes. However, the work of recent Nobel Prize winners Finn E. Kydland and Edward C. Prescott suggests that real GDP climbs generally upward but has periodic deviations from its path due to outside forces. This theory is just one example of many ongoing debates in economics and the different ways data can be interpreted.)*
- Where in the business cycle is the economy today? *(Answers will depend on the economy, but look for explanations that show an understanding of the four phases.)*

Analyze Charts: Figure 12.6

Ask students to explain what each point on the curve in Figure 12.6 represents. Then give students these statistics on a nation's changing GDP: 1st quarter +2.8 percent; 2nd quarter +1.0 percent; 3rd quarter –1.6 percent; 4th quarter –3.9 percent.

Chart these figures on a rough diagram, and ask what phase of the business cycle the 3rd quarter represents. *(contraction)*

Answers

1. *trough*
2. *expansion*
3. *It would have a steeper slope because price increases would make it rise faster.*

INDIVIDUAL ACTIVITY

Creating an Economic Cartoon

Time 30 minutes ◑

Task Express some aspect of the business cycle in an original and visual way.

Materials Needed paper and pens, markers

Activity

- Introduce the concept of an economic bubble—a market condition in which the price of an asset rises far higher than its fundamental value.
- Discuss the dot-com bubble and its role in bringing about the end of the long economic expansion of 1991–2001.
- Discuss the bubble in housing prices and its effect on the economy.
- Discuss the bubble in the market for tulip bulbs in Holland in the 1600s, when people spent fortunes on rare bulbs. When the market crashed, it led to an economic depression.
- Have students create an original cartoon that illustrates a bubble and its effects on the economy.
- Display and discuss the finished works.

Rubric

	Understanding of the Business Cycle	Presentation of Information
4	excellent	original with clear economic point
3	good	clear and appropriate
2	fair	rough presentation but clear ideas
1	poor	rough drawing with unclear point

Aggregate Demand and Supply

Discuss

- How would you compare microeconomic and macroeconomic supply and demand curves? *(An aggregate demand curve, like the demand curve in microeconomics, slopes downward; aggregate supply, however, has an almost horizontal curve when GDP is low and almost vertical curve when it is high.)*
- How do shifts in the aggregate supply and demand curves explain business cycles? *(An increase in aggregate demand shifts the curve to the right, signaling that demand is greater at all price levels. The equilibrium point rises as well, showing an economic expansion. The same process happens in reverse when demand decreases.)*

Analyze Graphs: Figures 12.7 and 12.8

Ask students to explain why the aggregate supply curve becomes almost vertical. *(In times of inflation, prices rise without contributing to real GDP.)* Tell them that another way to think of this is to recognize that when an economy reaches its full capacity, even price increases cannot cause GDP to rise in the short run.

Answers

1. *quantity; price*
2. *because real GDP measures the aggregate production of an economy and price level measures the aggregate change in prices*

Animated Economics Animation and audio highlight aggregate supply and aggregate demand curves. Working with the animated graphs will help students see the interactions between aggregate supply and demand and their relation to real GDP and expansion or contraction.

Aggregate Demand and Supply

KEY CONCEPTS

One way to understand business cycles is through the concepts of demand and supply. In this case the concepts apply not to a single product or business but to the economy as a whole.

QUICK REFERENCE

Aggregate demand is the sum of all the demand in the economy.

Aggregate supply is the sum of all the supply in the economy.

Aggregate Demand

Aggregate demand is the total amount of goods and services that households, businesses, government, and foreign purchasers will buy at each and every price level. In Figure 12.7, the vertical axis, labeled "Price level," shows the average price of all goods and services. The horizontal axis, labeled "Real GDP," shows the economy's total output. The aggregate demand curve (AD) is downward sloping. As the price level decreases the purchasing power of money increases.

Aggregate Supply

Aggregate supply is the total amount of goods and services that producers will provide at each and every price level. Note that in Figure 12.8 the aggregate supply curve (AS) does not look like the supply curves in Chapter 5. The aggregate supply curve is almost horizontal when real GDP is low—during times of recession or depression—because businesses try not to raise their prices when the economy is weak. The middle part of the aggregate supply curve slopes upward, with prices increasing as real GDP increases. But during times of high inflation, prices rise without contributing to real GDP, and the aggregate supply curve becomes almost vertical.

FIGURES 12.7 AND 12.8 AGGREGATE DEMAND AND SUPPLY CURVES

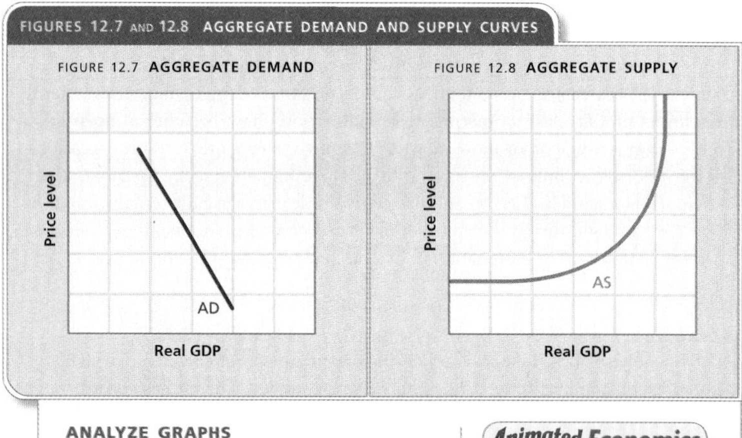

ANALYZE GRAPHS

1. What does a normal demand or supply graph use as an x-axis? What does it use as a y-axis?
2. Why are the x and y axes different for the aggregate demand and supply graphs?

Animated Economics Use an interactive aggregate demand and aggregate supply graph at **ClassZone.com**

DIFFERENTIATING INSTRUCTION

Struggling Readers

Use Text and Graphics Together

Point out that virtually all the text on pages 360–361 relates to the graphs. The text explains the graphs, and the graphs demonstrate the concepts in the text. Model for students how to integrate reading both. Do a "think aloud" as you read through the Aggregate Demand text. Articulate your thought process as you reach the text reference to Figure 12.7 and then look at the graphic. Point out that simply reading the text is unlikely to result in complete understanding.

Inclusion

Work in Pairs

Pair students to work together online to create animated versions of the graphs on these pages. (See above.) Have them identify each part of the graph (what the x-axis represents, the y-axis, and so on) and then describe what they see in the animations when they manipulate the graphs.

Macroeconomic Equilibrium

When the quantity of aggregate demand equals the quantity of aggregate supply, the economy reaches **macroeconomic equilibrium**. Figures 12.9 and 12.10 illustrate a variety of different possibilities, but let's consider one particular example shown in Figure 12.9. Macroeconomic equilibrium occurs where the aggregate demand curve (AD1) intersects the aggregate supply curve (AS). P1 indicates the equilibrium price level, and Q1 shows the equilibrium level of real GDP.

Think about business cycles. An increase in aggregate demand shifts the aggregate demand curve to the right (AD2). Aggregate demand becomes greater at all price levels, and equilibrium real GDP rises (Q2), marking an expansion phase. If aggregate demand were to decrease, the aggregate demand curve would shift to the left (AD3). This would result in a lower equilibrium real GDP (Q3)—in other words, an economic contraction.

Shifts in aggregate supply affect real GDP in a similar way, as you can see in Figure 12.10. An increase in aggregate supply shifts the aggregate supply curve to the right (AS2). As aggregate supply increases, the price level goes down (P2) and equilibrium real GDP rises (Q2), marking an expansion phase. If aggregate supply were to decrease, the aggregate supply curve would shift to the left (AS3). The result would be a higher price level (P3) and lower equilibrium real GDP (Q3)—in other words, stagflation.

QUICK REFERENCE

Macroeconomic equilibrium is the point where the quantity of aggregate demand equals the quantity of aggregate supply.

FIGURES 12.9 AND 12.10 CHANGES IN AGGREGATE DEMAND AND SUPPLY

FIGURE 12.9 **CHANGE IN AGGREGATE DEMAND**

FIGURE 12.10 **CHANGE IN AGGREGATE SUPPLY**

ANALYZE GRAPHS

1. As aggregate demand decreases, what happens to price level and real GDP?
2. As aggregate supply decreases, what happens to price level and real GDP?

APPLICATION Analyzing Cause and Effect

B. Assuming aggregate demand remains the same, why does the price level go up when aggregate supply decreases?

The same amount of demand chasing fewer goods results in higher prices.

More About . . .

Equilibrium Prices

The assumption underlying the conventional idea of equilibrium prices is that agents act according to rational self-interest and look for ways to maximize utility. With this reasoning, all equilibrium prices are optimal and agents in the economy are assumed to have full knowledge of the situation.

Another approach is to assume that prices reflect *disequilibrium*. In this view, economic actors always have insufficient or imperfect information, and prices reflect that. Economic actors use prices as a way to gain information and recognize economic opportunities.

Analyze Graphs: Figures 12.9 and 12.10

Use the graphs to show various phases of the business cycle. Ask for volunteers to explain, using the graphs, what is happening to the economy at points Q2 and Q3. *(Q2—expansion; Q3—contraction)*

Answers

1. *both price level and real GDP go down*
2. *price level goes up, real GDP goes down*

SMALL GROUP ACTIVITY

Influencing Aggregate Demand and Supply

Time 30 Minutes

Task Understand the role of individual behavior on aggregate supply and demand.

Materials Needed none

Activity

- Instruct groups to think of an economic activity they might undertake. Examples might be accepting a new job, quitting a job, starting a savings account, buying a car, and so on.
- Have each group discuss the effect that activity would have on aggregate demand or aggregate supply.
- Direct the students in each group to work out a way to present their activity and its effect on aggregate supply and demand to the class. Each member of the group should take part in the presentation.
- Engage the class in a discussion about the ways in which individual behaviors affect the aggregate.

Rubric

	Understanding Impact of Behavior	Presentation of Information
4	excellent	polished, clear, and complete
3	good	clear and complete
2	fair	rough presentation but clear ideas
1	poor	rough and unclear presentation

Why Do Business Cycles Occur?

Discuss

- What factors cause changes in the business cycle? *(decisions by businesses, interest rate changes, consumer expectations, external shocks to the economy)*
- Does any one of the four factors generally have a more far-reaching effect on the business cycle than the others? *(Answers will vary, but should show understanding of the factors and of the prerequisites necessary to cause a ripple effect throughout the economy.)*

Economics Update

At **ClassZone.com,** students will see updated information on factors affecting the business cycle.

International Economics

Global Business Cycles
A number of studies have looked at whether or not business cycles are synchronous internationally. One thorough study found that the degree of symmetry in international business cycles has changed. In recent years there is more similarity than there had been in the past.

This similarity may be a reflection of the increasingly global nature of economic dealings. Nations within a bloc, such as those in the European Union, have long had similar business cycles.

Why Do Business Cycles Occur?

KEY CONCEPTS

You have seen that shifts in aggregate demand and aggregate supply indicate changes in the business cycle. But what causes these shifts? Four factors are especially important: (1) decisions made by businesses, (2) changes in interest rates, (3) the expectations of consumers, and (4) external shocks to the economy. These factors involve the "ripple effect," the cause-and-effect interactions that ripple through the economy.

FACTOR 1 Business Decisions

When businesses decide to decrease or increase production, their decisions can have far-reaching effects. If enough businesses make similar decisions, it can lead to a change in the business cycle.

Economics Update
Find an update on factors affecting the business cycle at **ClassZone.com**

Demand slump Consider the ripple effect of a decision by businesses in the recording industry. In response to a slump in demand, the producers decide to reduce production of compact discs. First, they reduce the number of hours worked at their compact disc manufacturing facilities. Some workers get laid off, others work shorter hours. In a related move, the recording businesses cut back on their investment in new CD manufacturing equipment. That decision will lead to a decrease in the demand for machinery, which puts producers of the machinery in the same situation that the recording businesses were in. The machinery businesses will also cut back on production and lay off workers. The recording industry businesses also decide to reduce the number of new recordings they commission, thereby reducing the income of musicians, recording engineers, record promoters, and other associated workers. All of the workers that are now unemployed or working less must cut back on their purchases.

The single decision by the recording industry businesses had numerous consequences. By itself, it might not be enough to change the business cycle for the entire country. But if enough businesses make similar decisions, a contraction in the business cycle might result.

New technology Alternatively, business decisions can also increase aggregate supply and fuel an expansion. For example, suppose computer chip manufacturers adopt a new technology that greatly reduces production costs. Those manufacturers become more productive—the supply of their products increases and the cost of their products goes down. Businesses that make products that use computer chips can make their products more cheaply. Other businesses may now be able to make new products with the more readily available computer chips. All of these businesses hire more workers to handle the increased production. The aggregate supply increases, and the economy experiences an expansion.

DIFFERENTIATING INSTRUCTION

English Learners

Understand Metaphorical Language
Point out that on these pages there are several instances of language used to create a metaphor. These include "shocks" to the economy and "the ripple effect" (first paragraph) and "fuel" used as a verb (fifth paragraph, first sentence). Discuss both the literal and figurative uses of these words. Have students create a section of their personal dictionary to note words that evoke strong images.

Gifted and Talented

Investigate Interest Rates
Invite students to research the current interest rates, the direction in which most economic analysts believe they are heading, and the impact on the economy if the predicted changes come to pass. Have students create a fictional family and demonstrate these effects through a written narrative revealing the family's economic behavior.

FACTOR 2 Changes in Interest Rates

Another event that has a ripple effect in the economy and causes shifts in aggregate demand and supply is a change in interest rates. Rising interest rates, for example, make it more costly for consumers to borrow money to make purchases—from televisions to cars to houses. This decreased purchasing power lowers the level of aggregate demand and promotes a contraction in the economy. When interest rates fall, the opposite happens. Aggregate demand rises, promoting an expansion.

Consider what may happen to businesses when interest rates rise. With the higher cost of borrowing money, businesses may cut back on their investment in capital goods. As you saw earlier, such a cutback would lead to less business activity for the producers of capital goods. As the aggregate supply decreases, a contraction in the economy is likely. But falling interest rates would lead to an increase in aggregate supply and an economic expansion.

Higher or lower interest rates also affect the housing market. When interest rates are low, people are inclined to purchase housing rather than rent, so housing sales and all related economic activities increase, contributing to an economic expansion. When interest rates rise, the high cost of loans limits mortgage eligibility, so more people rent. Housing sales slow down, contributing to an economic contraction.

FACTOR 3 Consumer Expectations

Every month, 5,000 households are surveyed to find out how people are feeling about the economy, and the results are published in the Consumer Confidence Survey report. Why? The way consumers are feeling about prices, business activity, and job prospects influences their economic choices, and their choices can bring about changes in aggregate demand. For example, when consumers are confident about the future and believe that they are economically secure, they tend to consume more, driving up aggregate demand and encouraging an economic expansion.

FACTOR 4 External Issues

A nation's economy can also be strongly influenced by issues and events beyond its control or outside of its borders. Examples include such natural disasters as Hurricanes Katrina and Rita, which struck the Gulf Coast in the summer of 2005. The hurricanes damaged oil refineries, oil wells, and offshore oil platforms. The effects of Katrina and Rita, combined with conflicts in other oil-producing countries, led to higher oil prices and slowed down the growth of the U.S. economy.

The oil embargo of 1973 is another example. The Organization of the Petroleum Exporting Countries (OPEC) reduced the amount of oil supplied to Western nations that had supported Israel in the Yom Kippur and October wars. The price of oil rose by 400 percent. The higher prices raised production costs and resulted in an economic contraction in the United States.

External Issues
Natural disasters can affect the economy. Hurricane Katrina washed this oil-drilling platform into this bridge.

APPLICATION Analyzing Cause and Effect

C. Describe the ripple effect of a natural disaster like Hurricane Katrina on the economy.
The disaster might wipe out resources and hurt consumer confidence, which could lead to a contraction. But cleaning up after the disaster might drive up demand for construction materials and construction workers.

More About . . .

Consumer Internet Barometer
The same group that coordinates the Consumer Confidence Survey also monitors what it calls the Consumer Internet Barometer. Its purpose is to track how consumers use the Internet and feel about it, with an eye to predicting trends that may affect marketing strategies and business opportunities.

The Consumer Internet Barometer is published quarterly. In a press release in 2006, the CIB revealed that increasing numbers of consumers were filing their taxes online, and they were doing so because of do-it-yourself tax software programs. To gather information such as this, the researchers survey approximately 10,000 households.

SMALL GROUP ACTIVITY

Graphing Changes in Aggregate Supply and Demand

Time 30 minutes

Task Express in graphs the impact of various economic factors on the course of business cycles.

Materials Needed paper and pens

Activity

- Divide students into four groups, one for each factor named on pages 362–363.
- Review the graphs on pages 360–361 with the students.
- Instruct each group to develop a possible scenario within its topic (business decisions, changes in interest rates, consumer expectations, and external issues) and to write a description of that scenario.
- Have each group make a graph showing how the change in their scenario would shift the supply or demand curves and affect GDP.

Rubric

	Understanding of Why Business Cycles Occur	Presentation of Information
4	excellent	clear and accurate
3	good	mostly accurate
2	fair	good effort, but inaccurate
1	poor	little or no effort

Predicting Business Cycles

Discuss

- Why do you think the government goes to so much trouble to collect economic information? *(Answers will vary, but help students articulate how this information can be used to make economic decisions by consumers, producers, and government policymakers.)*
- Specifically, how might consumers use this information? *(If consumers anticipate an expansion in the economy, they are more likely to spend money, feeling relatively secure in the prospects of getting and keeping a job. If they anticipate a contraction, they are less likely to take on new debt for expensive items.)*

Analyze Graphs: Figure 12.11

A group called The Conference Board is responsible for generating the indexes of leading, coincident, and lagging economic indicators. In 1996, the U.S. government transferred responsibility for the three indexes to the group, which was founded in 1916. The Conference Board produces the indexes monthly, but the government produces GDP figures quarterly. Hence, the graph shows monthly changes in LEI, but quarterly changes in GDP.

Answers

1. *LEI down 2000 Q2–2001 QI, prior to the recession; LEI generally up all other quarters, prior to upward trend in GDP*
2. *No—it is difficult to predict what will happen to the economy.*

Predicting Business Cycles

QUICK REFERENCE

Leading indicators are measures of economic performance that usually change *before* real GDP changes.

Coincident indicators are measures of economic performance that usually change *at the same time as* real GDP changes.

Lagging indicators are measures of economic performance that usually change *after* real GDP changes.

KEY CONCEPTS

Economists try to predict changes in the business cycle to help businesses and the government make informed economic choices. They base their predictions on sets of economic indicators.

- **Leading indicators** are measures of economic performance that usually change six to nine months *before* real GDP changes. Examples include new building permits, orders for capital goods and consumer goods, consumer expectations, average manufacturing workweek, stock prices, and the money supply. Economists look for trends in these indicators that last several months before they predict a change.
- **Coincident indicators** are measures of economic performance that usually change *at the same time as* real GDP changes. These indicators include such items as employment, sales volume, and personal income.
- **Lagging indicators** are measures of economic performance that usually change *after* real GDP changes. Such indicators are useful for confirming the end of an expansion or contraction in the business cycle. They include length of unemployment and the ratio of consumer credit to personal income.

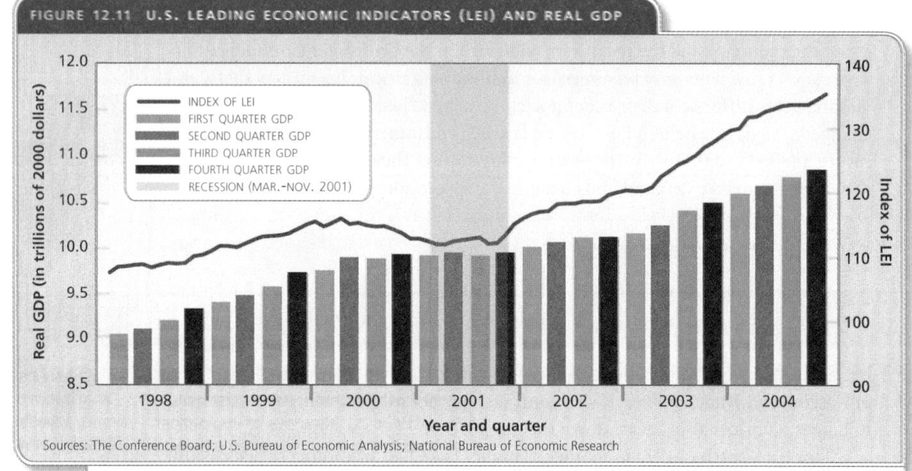

FIGURE 12.11 U.S. LEADING ECONOMIC INDICATORS (LEI) AND REAL GDP

Sources: The Conference Board; U.S. Bureau of Economic Analysis; National Bureau of Economic Research

ANALYZE GRAPHS

1. Find a period of at least four quarters in which the index of leading economic indicators accurately predicted a change in real gross domestic product.
2. Do changes in the real gross domestic product always echo changes in the index of leading economic indicators? What does this say about predicting changes in the nation's economy?

APPLICATION Using a Decision-Making Process

D. If you were the manager of an electronics store, how might you use the news that leading indicators suggest a contraction in the economy in six months?

Answers will vary but look for an understanding of the need to respond to expectations of lower demand, such as lowering buying, considering layoffs, and so on.

DIFFERENTIATING INSTRUCTION

Struggling Readers

Use Typography to Understand

Ask students the three ways that key points are indicated on the top half of this page. *(bullet points, boldface, and quick reference terms)* Model for students how you use those typographical features. *(You might say, "When I see a bulleted list, I know the items will be related and parallel, and I look for repeated words, in this case* indicators. *When I see a boldface term, I know it is important, in this case a vocabulary term," and so on.)*

Inclusion

Research the WPA

Instruct students to research the arts during the Great Depression. Include those produced under the Works Project Administration and those produced independently. Have students prepare a presentation for the rest of the class in a form best suited to their strengths in learning and expression.

Business Cycles in U.S. History

KEY CONCEPTS

The agency that tracks economic indicators and business cycles in the United States is the National Bureau of Economic Research (NBER). It measures contractions from peak to trough and expansions from trough to peak. NBER identified about 20 extended contractions, or recessions, in the American economy in the 20th century. The worst of these by far was the Great Depression.

The Great Depression Millions of Americans were thrown into poverty during the 1930s. These people received soup from a charity kitchen.

The Great Depression

"Back in those dark depression days," President Ronald Reagan once recalled, "I saw my father on a Christmas Eve open what he thought was a Christmas greeting from his boss. Instead, it was the blue slip telling him he no longer had a job. The memory of him sitting there holding that slip of paper and then saying in a half whisper, 'That's quite a Christmas present' –it will stay with me as long as I live." Millions of people who lived through the Great Depression were haunted by such memories. For more than a decade, beginning with the stock market crash in 1929, the United States and much of the world suffered a terrible economic contraction. Not until the United States entered World War II in 1941 did the American economy begin a full recovery.

Between the years 1929 and 1933, when the depression was at its worst, U.S. real GDP declined by about a third. Sales in some big businesses, including General Motors Corporation, declined by as much as 50 percent. In the resulting cutbacks, millions of workers lost their jobs. The unemployment rate skyrocketed from 1929 to 1933, leaving one in four American workers jobless. Businesses failed at a higher than usual rate, and banks failed at a tremendously high rate. The number of bank closings, either temporary or permanent, soared from 659 in 1929 to 4,000 in 1933.

In this cartoon, Franklin D. Roosevelt is surrounded by children representing programs created as part of the New Deal.

The New Deal

President Herbert Hoover, who had been elected in 1928, was not able to bring about a recovery. Franklin D. Roosevelt, accepting the nomination to run for president against Hoover in 1932, promised Americans "a new deal," and the programs he enacted after winning the election came to be known by that name. Roosevelt's New Deal programs focused on federal spending to help the economy revive. Through a number of government agencies created just for this purpose, the American economy came under closer government regulation and many Americans were put back to work—employed by the federal government itself. Spending by the federal government rose from about 3 percent of GDP in the 1920s to about 10 percent in the mid-1930s.

Business Cycles in U.S. History

Discuss

- What caused the Great Depression? *(Point out that economists still debate this topic. Many economists hold that the Federal Reserve Board mishandled the money supply. Others point to excess production capacity that was not matched by the income to consume it. Still others believe "structural" problems in the economy—overinvestment, for example—were behind the economic downturn.)*
- What brought the Great Depression to an end? *(New Deal legislation and the wartime production when the United States entered World War II)*

International Economics

Impact of the Great Depression
The Great Depression started in the United States, but it affected nearly every country in the world. Argentina, Australia, Brazil, Canada, France, Japan, South Africa, and the United Kingdom all suffered during the Depression. Many countries were not hit as hard as the United States, but most suffered large declines in production and increases in unemployment.

In Germany, the Depression made a bad political situation worse. Adolph Hitler gained supporters by accusing the government of failing to address the country's economic problems.

INDIVIDUAL ACTIVITY

Relating Personal Experience

Time 30 minutes (for presentation) ◑

Task Appreciate the human face of the Great Depression.

Materials Needed paper and pens, computer with Internet access

Activity

- Ask a student volunteer to read aloud Ronald Reagan's personal memory of the Depression above.
- Direct students to interview family members or neighbors to capture a personal experience from those times.
- Students should take notes or use a recording device when hearing the story and be prepared to share it in an engaging way with the class.
- If students do not have a relative or neighbor with a personal memory, they can find such an experience online to share with the class.
- Tell students that their presentation must include at least two details that reveal economic conditions and two details that show their effect on people.

Rubric

	Understanding of the Great Depression	Presentation of Information
4	excellent	4 or more engaging details
3	good	3 or 4 interesting details
2	fair	2 or 3 details
1	poor	1 detail or less

Analyze Graphs: Figure 12.12

Ask students what general statement can be made about the U.S. economy during the past 80 years, based on the data in Figure 12.12. *(that the U.S. economy has continued to expand despite brief periods of economic contraction)* How do business cycles appear on the graph? *(marked by recession periods, either from end to end [troughs] of a period or from start to start [peaks])*

Answers

1. *12 (including the Great Depression)*
2. *Three cycles on this graph appear roughly equal: 1960-1970, 1981-1991, 1991-2001. In reality, the 1991-2001 cycle lasted the longest (128 months).*

More About . . .

Economic Impact of 9/11 Attacks
The terrorist attacks affected the U.S. economy in a number of ways.

Short-term:

- about a 30 percent reduction of office space in lower Manhattan
- destruction, rescue, and cleanup costs of more than $27 billion
- immediately lowered GDP estimate, which, in turn, affected consumer confidence

Medium-term:

- industries most affected—insurance, airlines, tourism and travel, shipping, and defense and security

Long-term:

- higher operating costs
- shift of resources from private to military production
- complicated globalization efforts

Economists debate whether the New Deal programs led to sustained economic growth. But when the United States entered World War II in 1941, spending on the war effort also helped the economy to recover. Unemployment plunged to 1.2 percent by 1944.

Business Cycles Since the Great Depression

According to NBER, there have been about a dozen economic contractions and expansions in the U.S. economy since the Great Depression. The recessions have been less severe and have occurred less often than those before the 1930s. However, the contraction of the mid-1970s was an especially difficult time, triggered in part by the Oil Embargo of 1973. The unemployment rate rose from an average of 5.4 percent in the first half of the decade to an average of 7.4 percent from 1975 to 1979. At the same time, prices also rose, creating stagflation.

FIGURE 12.12 U.S. BUSINESS CYCLES

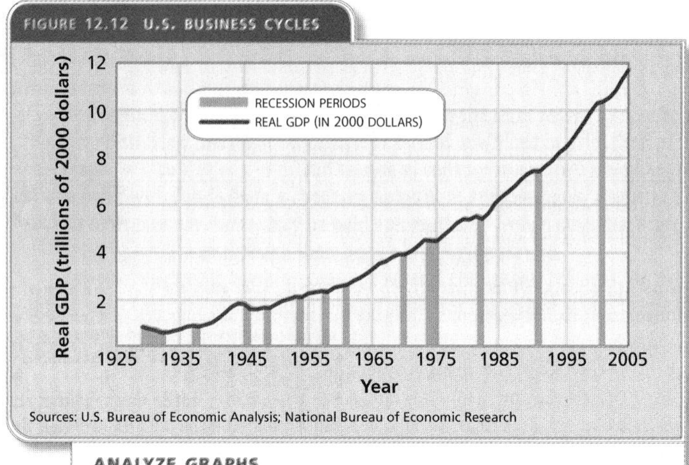

Sources: U.S. Bureau of Economic Analysis; National Bureau of Economic Research

ANALYZE GRAPHS

1. According to the graph, how many recessions occurred from 1929 to 2005?
2. About how long was the longest business cycle shown on this graph?

The 1990s, in contrast, saw strong economic expansion, fueled in part by the explosive growth of information technology. The economy experienced a brief recession in the early 2000s, which was extended slightly by the terrorist attacks on September 11, 2001. Through 2005, the U.S. economy continued to expand, although not at the heated pace of the 1990s.

APPLICATION Making Inferences and Drawing Conclusions

E. One industry that flourished during the Great Depression was the movie industry. Comedies were especially popular, and stories often portrayed the lives of the wealthy. Why do you think the movie industry fared so well? It provided escape from the troubles of depression life. The film industry tailored its products to the fantasies of people down on their luck, portraying lavish lifestyles and extraordinary spectacles. Adding sound to the moving pictures increased interest in movies.

DIFFERENTIATING INSTRUCTION

Struggling Readers

Create a Visual
Have students represent the textual information at the top of the page in another format. This may be a time line, or if resources are available, an illustrated time line. As an inverse activity, have students translate Figure 12.12 into a textual passage.

Gifted and Talented

Analyze a Motion Picture
Have students choose a Depression-era film to watch and then to present a review of it to the class. Include video clips, if possible. Show how the film addressed themes related to the Depression and expressed social attitudes of the time.

SECTION 2 Assessment

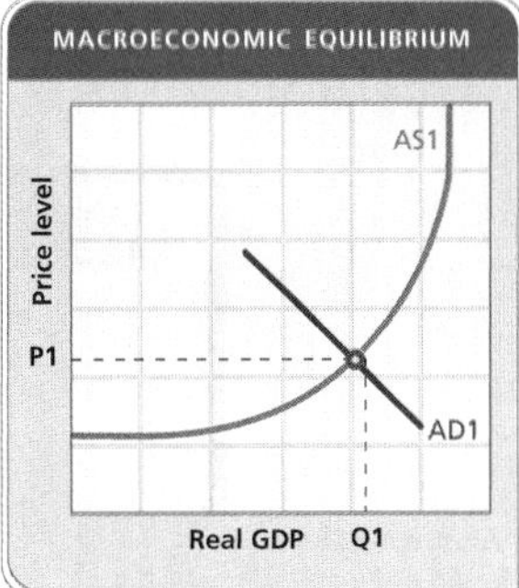

REVIEWING KEY CONCEPTS

1. Explain the relationship between the terms in each of these pairs.
   a. *contraction* *expansion*
   b. *aggregate demand* *aggregate supply*
   c. *leading indicators* *lagging indicators*
2. Between which two points of the business cycle is a contraction measured?
3. What is the difference between *demand* and *aggregate demand*?
4. Name four factors that can trigger changes in the business cycle.
5. Name three coincident indicators of the Great Depression.
6. **Using Your Notes** Write a brief statement of your expectations for the economy from the point of view of the consumer. Use your completed cluster diagram and make references to what you have learned about the business cycle.

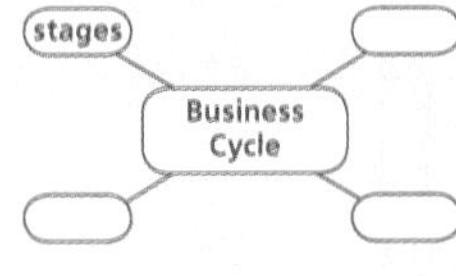

Use the Graphic Organizer at **Interactive Review @ ClassZone.com**

CRITICAL THINKING

7. **Comparing and Contrasting Economic Information** What were the similarities and differences between the Great Depression and the recession in the 1970s?
8. **Solving Economic Problems** Did President Roosevelt's New Deal focus on generating aggregate demand, or was its main focus on increasing aggregate supply? Explain.
9. **Analyzing Cause and Effect** Are the components that are considered leading economic indicators causes or effects of changes in the business cycle?
10. **Challenge** In the 1990s many people speculated that the economy had been transformed by new technologies. Paul A. Volcker, former chairman of the U.S. Federal Reserve Bank, described it this way: "The speed of communication, the speed of information transfer, the cheapness of communication, the ease of moving things around the world are a difference in kind as well as degree." Do you think that business cycles are inevitable? Can they ever be eliminated entirely? Explain your answer.

ECONOMICS IN PRACTICE

MACROECONOMIC EQUILIBRIUM

Price level / Real GDP	
Curves	AS1, AD1
Equilibrium	P1, Q1

Interpreting Graphs
The graph shows an economy at its macroeconomic equilibrium, where the aggregate demand curve (AD1) intersects the aggregate supply curve (AS1). P1 indicates the equilibrium price level, and Q1 shows the equilibrium level of real GDP.

Draw Aggregate Demand and Aggregate Supply Curves
Read the following scenarios. Copy the graph onto your own paper, then graph the changes that would occur in the Scenario 1 in blue. Graph the changes that would occur in the Scenario 2 in red.

Scenario 1: In a booming economy, interest rates begin to rise. Manufacturers and other producers, wary of borrowing money at higher rates, begin to cut back on production.

Scenario 2: Consumer confidence is high. Most people are optimistic about their job prospects and security, and they are willing to spend money on luxuries.

Challenge As a consumer, how might your confidence be affected in Scenario 1?

Use **SMARTGrapher @ ClassZone.com** to complete this activity.

367

4 Assess & Reteach

Assess Discuss the first five questions as a class. Direct students to choose one of the Critical Thinking questions as a basis for formal writing. Have at least one student per question read his or her paper to the class.

Unit 5 Resource Book
- Section Quiz, p. 19

Interactive Review @ ClassZone.com
- Section Quiz

Test Generator CD-ROM
- Section Quiz

Reteach Call on students to use the graphs and other visuals to review the main points in Section 2. After each student completes the explanation, he or she should ask the class for questions, or if there are none, should pose questions for the class to answer.

Unit 5 Resource Book
- Reteaching Activity, p. 20

Economics in Practice
Drawing Aggregate Supply and Aggregate Demand Curves In Scenario 1, the aggregate supply curve shifts to the left, and real GDP declines. In Scenario 2, the aggregate demand curve shifts to the right, and real GDP increases.

Challenge You, too, would be wary of making a lot of purchases, especially those that involved credit. Your confidence would tend to be lower as jobs became harder to find.

SECTION 2 ASSESSMENT ANSWERS

Reviewing Key Concepts
1. a. *expansion*, p. 358; *contraction*, p. 359
   b. *aggregate demand*, p. 360; *aggregate supply*, p. 360
   c. *leading indicators*, p. 364; *lagging indicators*, p. 364
2. peak to trough
3. Demand refers to a single product or industry; aggregate demand refers to the sum of all the demand in an economy.
4. business decisions, interest rates, consumer expectations, external issues
5. Answers will vary but should include high unemployment, declining GDP (sales volume), declining personal income.
6. See page 358 for an example of a completed diagram. Answers will vary, but look for an understanding of the variables in the economy that affect consumer confidence, such as interest rates, employment, economic growth.

Critical Thinking
7. Both were economic contractions. The Depression lasted longer and was much more severe. In the 1970s, prices rose, but they fell during the Great Depression.
8. The New Deal focused on demand, by putting more money into the hands of consumers through government programs.
9. They are effects, but as all effects in an economy, they can have a ripple effect.
10. Answers will vary but are likely to focus on forces of change: increased demand will result in increased supply; in time, the factors of production will become scarcer and prices will rise; with rising prices producers will cut back. Look for an understanding of key economic concepts.

Economics in Practice
See answers in side column above.

1 Plan & Prepare

Section 3 Objectives

- explain how economists measure growth
- analyze the causes of economic growth
- discuss how productivity and economic growth are related

2 Focus & Motivate

Connecting to Everyday Life Give students the following scenario: A person in 1950 decides to put $1,000 in a lock box each year. Is that person wealthier in 2000 than before the savings program? As students attempt to answer this question, identify how they are defining wealth and note these on the board. *(cash on hand, purchasing power, opportunity costs, and so on)* At the end of the discussion, point out that it is impossible to answer the question with the limited information provided. All that can be safely said is that the person has $50,000 cash in the box.

Taking Notes Remind students to take notes as they read by completing a summary chart. They can use the Graphic Organizer at **Interactive Review @ ClassZone.com**. A sample is shown below.

What Is Economic Growth?	What Determines Economic Growth?	Productivity and Economic Growth
historic ideas of growth	natural resources	multifactor productivity
best measured by real GDP	human resources	improving productivity
real GDP per capita	capital	productivity and growth
	technology and innovation	

SECTION 3

Stimulating Economic Growth

OBJECTIVES

In Section 3, you will
- explain how economists measure growth
- analyze the causes of economic growth
- discuss how productivity and economic growth are related

KEY TERMS

real GDP per capita, *p. 369*
labor input, *p. 371*
capital deepening, *p. 371*
productivity, *p. 372*
multifactor productivity, *p. 372*

TAKING NOTES

As you read Section 3, complete a summary chart like the one below to record what you learn about economic growth. Use the Graphic Organizer at **Interactive Review @ ClassZone.com**

What Is Economic Growth?		

What Is Economic Growth?

KEY CONCEPTS

In Section 2 you learned about the business cycle, the pattern of expansion and contraction in a nation's economy. In this section you will learn more about economic growth, as measured by changes in real gross domestic product (GDP).

Gauging Economic Growth

Before Adam Smith (whom you learned about in Chapter 1, Section 4), many people believed that population growth and higher taxation were the secrets to economic growth. The theory held that more people paying more taxes was the best way to fill a nation's treasury. Another view, called mercantilism, argued that increased national wealth came through exporting more goods than a country imports. In this way, the country would gain gold or silver currency from other countries.

Adam Smith, however, saw that the real "wealth of nations" lay in their productive capacities. Taxes could be so high that they limit the amount of funds available for business investment and consumer spending, thereby reducing economic growth. In Smith's view, foreign trade allows a country to focus its resources on what it does best. The more efficiently a nation uses its resources, the more productive it will be and the larger its economy will grow. Smith's views proved to be accurate, and they serve as the basis for modern economics.

The best measure of economic growth is not simply the amount of money a nation has or how much its population increases, but rather the increase in its real GDP. The rate at which real GDP changes is a good indicator of how well a country's resources are being utilized.

SECTION 3 PROGRAM RESOURCES

ON LEVEL

Lesson Plans
- Core, p. 42

Unit 5 Resource Book
- Reading Study Guide, pp. 21–22
- Economic Simulations, pp. 37–38
- Section Quiz, p. 29

STRUGGLING READERS

Unit 5 Resource Book
- Reading Study Guide with Additional Support, pp. 23–25
- Reteaching Activity, p. 30

ENGLISH LEARNERS

Unit 5 Resource Book
- Reading Study Guide with Additional Support (Spanish), pp. 26–28

INCLUSION

Lesson Plans
- Modified for Inclusion, p. 42

GIFTED AND TALENTED

Unit 5 Resource Book
- Readings in Free Enterprise: The Imagination Economy, pp. 33–34
- Case Study Resources: Cheer Up, pp. 35–36

TECHNOLOGY

eEdition DVD-ROM

eEdition Online

Power Presentation DVD-ROM

Economics Concepts Transparencies
- CT42 GDP of World's Leading Economies

Daily Test Practice Transparencies, TT42

ClassZone.com

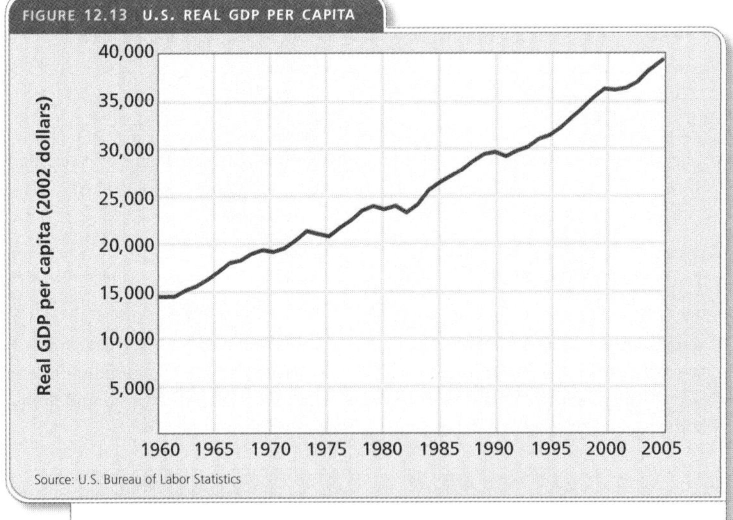

ANALYZE GRAPHS

1. About how much was real GDP per capita in 1990?
2. About how many years did it take for real GDP per capita to double from its level in 1960?

Economics Update

Find an update on U.S. real GDP per capita at **ClassZone.com**

Population and Economic Growth

Population growth influences economic growth. A country's real GDP might be growing, but if its population is growing at an even faster rate, the increase in real GDP might simply reflect more workers contributing to the economy. Think of a potluck dinner. If each person brings one dish, the amount of food per person will be the same whether you invite 10 people or 100.

To get a clearer picture of economic growth, economists use a measure called **real GDP per capita**, which is real GDP divided by total population. Real GDP per capita reflects each person's share of real GDP. In terms of the potluck dinner, if each person brings more than one dish to the next potluck, the amount of food per person will have increased.

Real GDP per capita is the usual measure of a nation's standard of living. Nations with higher real GDP per capita tend to have populations that are better educated and healthier. However, real GDP per capita does not mean that each person gets that amount of money. Some people will get more, others less. It also does not measure quality of life. For example, people might have to work longer hours to achieve higher rates of economic growth, leaving them with less leisure time.

QUICK REFERENCE

Real GDP per capita is real GDP divided by total population.

APPLICATION Explaining an Economic Concept

A. Why does a nation's real GDP have to increase at a faster rate than its population for significant economic growth to take place? If they increased at the same pace, the real GDP per capita would be unchanged. If population increased at a faster rate than real GDP, the growth might be accounted for through the population increase rather than increased economic growth.

3 Teach

What Is Economic Growth?

Discuss

- What is the relationship between economic growth and population growth? *(Population growth can help to increase GDP. But for real economic growth, the economy must grow at a faster rate than the increase in population.)*
- How does per capita GDP provide a relatively accurate picture of economic growth? *(It factors out the possibility that GDP grew simply because of population growth.)*

Analyze Graphs: Figure 12.13

If there were about 200 million people in the U.S. in 1970, about how much was the U.S. GDP in 1970 (in 2002 dollars)? *(200 million X $19,000 = $3.8 trillion)* Does the graph show that the average person made about $15,000 in 1960 and about $39,000 in 2005? *(No, it only shows GDP, adjusted for inflation, divided by population.)*

Answers

1. *almost $30,000*
2. *about 30 years*

Economics Update

At **ClassZone.com**, students will see an update on U.S. real GDP per capita.

SMALL GROUP ACTIVITY

Interpreting GDP Data

Time 15 Minutes 

Task Identify what is revealed and not revealed by various measures of GDP.

Materials Needed paper and pens

Activity

- Organize students into two groups.
- Have one group brainstorm relevant and accurate inferences from GDP figures; that is, they will identify what GDP tells about a nation.
- Instruct them also to develop a list of inferences that cannot reasonably be drawn from GDP data. Each list should have at least 5 items.
- Direct the second group to do the same activity, but use GDP per capita as the baseline data.
- Ask each group to present their lists to the class.

Rubric

	Understanding of GDP	Presentation of Information
4	excellent	more than 10 items, all reasonable
3	good	10 items, most reasonable
2	fair	7–9 items, many reasonable
1	poor	fewer than 8 items, most unreasonable

What Determines Economic Growth?

Discuss

- Ask students if they agree with some economists that human capital is the most important element in economic growth. Have them explain their answers. *(Answers will vary, but look for an understanding that the other factors are useless without human skill and knowledge to make the most of them. For example, advanced technology is worthless without the knowledge of how to use it.)*
- What is another example of capital deepening? *(Possible answer: A firm makes laptops and wireless networks available to its employees, so they can work away from their desks.)*

A Global Perspective

Do Natural Resources Guarantee Wealth?

Nigeria's gas reserves are as impressive as its oil reserves, and they rank fifth largest in the world. However, energy companies have not been prospecting for the reserves despite the great potential for wealth they hold. The reason, according to Nigerian Senator Jonathan Zwingina, is that there is no legal framework for the gas sector as there is for the oil sector. So international investors are wary.

It has been suggested that a gas regulatory commission and other clearly defined mechanisms would attract the international investment needed for Nigeria to benefit from its gas reserves.

Answers

1. *While they can be an important factor, lack of resources can be overcome by human capital and strong economic institutions.*
2. *Possible answers: Decreased production would help Nigeria by making the process more competitive, leading to higher equilibrium; it would hurt Japan by increasing the amount the country pays for imported oil. Increased production might lower prices and could also hinder Nigeria by continuing the country's reliance on selling natural resources; it would help Japan by reducing its dependence on foreign oil.*

What Determines Economic Growth?

KEY CONCEPTS

What drives economic growth? Why are some nations growing at a faster pace than others? Four key factors influence the rate of economic growth—natural resources, human resources, capital, and technology and innovation.

FACTOR 1 Natural Resources

One factor in economic growth is access to natural resources, especially arable land, water, forests, oil, and mineral resources. However, some countries, such as Japan, have very limited natural resources, yet their economies have grown rapidly. Others, such as India, which has the fourth-largest reserve of coal in the world and arable land covering more than half its territory, have developed more slowly.

A GLOBAL PERSPECTIVE

Do Natural Resources Guarantee Wealth?

Not necessarily. In fact, countries with abundant natural resources generally do not perform as well economically as countries with fewer natural resources—a phenomenon economists refer to as "the resource curse." In Nigeria, for example, although oil is plentiful, personal income is low. GDP per capita is about $1,400 (in U.S. dollars). Poverty is widespread, with an estimated 60 percent of Nigeria's population below the poverty line—and Nigeria has the largest population of any African country.

At the other end of the spectrum is Japan. Although the country has few natural resources, the strength of Japan's economy is second only to that of the United States. GDP per capita is about $30,000 (in U.S. dollars). What Nigeria lacks, but Japan has, are the basic structures of a free market economy—private ownership, the profit motive, an effective government, and economic competition. These economic institutions are more important than natural resources for generating economic growth. Japan, with few natural resources, achieved economic success by developing alternative sources of wealth—industry and foreign trade.

FIGURE 12.14 OIL PRODUCTION AND CONSUMPTION

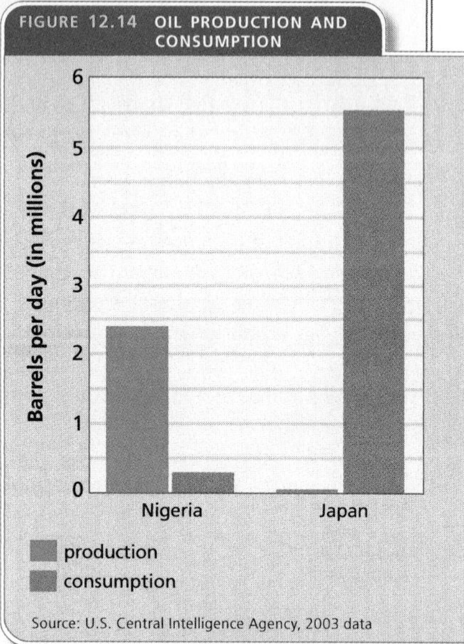

Source: U.S. Central Intelligence Agency, 2003 data

CONNECTING ACROSS THE GLOBE

1. **Synthesizing Economic Information** What role do natural resources play in a country's economic strength? Explain your answer.
2. **Drawing Conclusions** Figure 12.14 illustrates oil production and consumption in Nigeria and Japan. What would happen to each country's economy if it produced less oil? What if each produced more?

DIFFERENTIATING INSTRUCTION

English Learners

Isolate New Words

Students should now be well aware of the quick reference tabs in the margins that offer definitions of the vocabulary words. Point out that in many less "considerate" texts, there will be no such feature. However, students may create their own version of the feature by using sticky notes in the margins and jotting down definitions of unfamiliar words.

Gifted and Talented

Examine the "Resource Curse"

Invite students to research the phrase *resource curse* and develop a presentation for the rest of the class. Instruct students to include an explanation of what it means and also to apply it to another nation that may have a resource curse.

FACTOR 2 Human Resources

Another key factor in economic growth is the labor force. Economists measure this partly through **labor input**—the size of the labor force multiplied by the length of the workweek. The steady declines in the length of the workweek in most countries since the early 1900s have been more than made up for by the growth in the population, so labor input has grown. Perhaps even more important than the raw numbers, however, is the level of human capital—the skills and knowledge—that the labor force brings to its tasks. Some economists believe that human capital is the single most important component in economic growth.

QUICK REFERENCE

Labor input is the size of the labor force multiplied by the length of the workweek.

FACTOR 3 Capital

You learned in Chapter 1 that natural resources, labor, and capital come together through the creativity of an entrepreneur to produce goods and services. Capital is critical to this process and to economic growth. More and better capital goods increase output: the more machines a factory has and the better designed they are, the more goods the factory can churn out. Multiply this by the number of factories across a nation and the increased output equals higher GDP.

The economy also grows when more capital is available per worker. An increase in the capital to labor ratio is called **capital deepening**. In other words, workers are provided with more and better equipment to work with. The Industrial Revolution is a prime example of capital deepening. Sewing machines, for example, allowed clothing manufacturers to make more clothing per worker than if the workers had been sewing by hand.

QUICK REFERENCE

Capital deepening is an increase in the ratio of capital to labor.

FACTOR 4 Technology and Innovation

Technology and innovation are also important factors in economic growth. These factors promote the efficient use of other resources, which in turn leads to increased output. Some of the key technological developments that have contributed to economic growth include steam power, electricity, and the automobile.

Innovations can also increase economic growth. Something as simple as adjusting an order form can contribute to economic growth by reducing the amount of time needed to complete a task. Other innovations might improve customer service or reduce the amount of material needed to create a product.

Information technology has had a strong impact on economic growth. Technological advances in producing the information technology itself have led to a dramatic decline in prices. With lower prices for technology, firms are engaging in capital deepening without having to spend more money.

Technology and Innovation
Technological advancements have increased economic growth.

APPLICATION Writing About Economics

B. Using the four factors, explain how developing countries like Nigeria might improve their economic growth.

Answers will vary, but look for an understanding of the four factors.

Economics Illustrated

To illustrate the change in labor input, draw two squares, one somewhat larger than the other. Divide the smaller square into four equal squares and the larger square into nine equal squares. The smaller square represents total labor input from the 1800s, and its component squares represent fewer workers working longer hours. The larger square represents total labor input from more recent times. Each worker works fewer hours, but the number of workers results in more total labor.

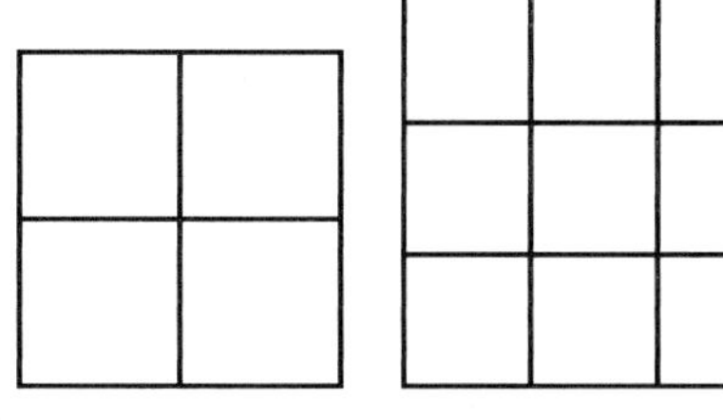

SMALL GROUP ACTIVITY

Evaluating Factors of Economic Growth

Time 30 Minutes

Task Plan for economic development when limited to only three of the four factors that influence economic growth.

Materials Needed paper and pens

Activity

- Organize students into small groups.
- Tell them that they are leaders of a developing nation's economy, and that the nation has only three of the four factors of economic growth discussed on pages 370–371.
- Instruct students to discuss the relative importance of each factor. Have them then select three factors, having clear reasons for their choices.
- Each group should then draw up an economic development plan for their nation explaining how they would use these factors to promote growth.
- Ask students to present their plans to the class.

Rubric

	Understanding of Economic Growth Factors	Presentation of Information
4	excellent	clever, clear, and complete
3	good	clear and complete
2	fair	somewhat clear and mostly complete
1	poor	unclear, sketchy

Productivity and Economic Growth

Discuss

- Could the buyout of a neighborhood restaurant by a chain restaurant be considered productive? *(yes, if the chain generates more profits)* Besides higher productivity, what else might change? *(profits go to corporation instead of local owner)*
- On average, worker productivity declines after age 50. Suppose that the average retirement age rises from 62 to 67. What might happen to real GDP? *(Real GDP might not be affected. Labor productivity would be slightly lower, but there would be more total workers.)*

More About . . .

Productivity Trends

The increase in American productivity has been dramatic. In the 1870s, an individual had to work 1,800 hours to earn enough money to supply a household's food for a year. In the 2000s, only 260 hours of labor were needed to accomplish that goal. Over roughly the same time period, the typical work year has contracted from 3,100 to 1,730 hours, but real GDP per capita has increased about 15 times.

More About . . .

Multifactor Productivity

Economists have looked to three sources for the growth of the mid-1990s to the early 2000s. They are capital deepening, human capital, and multifactor productivity (MFP). MFP is productivity that cannot be explained by the other two sources. Examples include improved management techniques, such as just-in-time inventory management (inventory is only restocked when it is clear that the supply is low).

From 1996 to 2001, the roughly 2 percent increase in productivity could be attributed to equal amounts of capital deepening and higher MFP. But from 2002 to 2004, after the dot-com bubble burst, MFP accounted for nearly all of the 4 percent productivity increase.

Productivity and Economic Growth

KEY CONCEPTS

QUICK REFERENCE

Productivity is the ratio of the amount of output produced to the amount of input.

Productivity refers to the amount of output produced from a set amount of inputs. When the same amount of inputs produces more output, productivity has increased. In Chapter 9, you learned about labor productivity—the amount of goods or services produced by a worker in an hour. But the broader sense of productivity includes the productivity of both labor and capital.

For example, imagine that you begin building bookshelves. The inputs would include your labor plus capital, in the form of the workshop, hammers, glue, and other supplies. At first, it may take you a week to complete one bookshelf. In the process, you may waste materials as you make mistakes, and you may find that some of your tools are not ideal for the task. But after you have built several bookshelves and acquired the right tools for the job, your productivity increases. Using the same amount of input, you might now be able to produce two bookshelves per week.

This section concerns the productivity of a country's entire economy. As a country becomes more productive, its economy is likely to grow.

How Is Productivity Measured?

QUICK REFERENCE

Multifactor productivity is the ratio between the amount of output produced by an industry or business sector and the amount of inputs used.

To measure the productivity of a single business, you would compare the inputs to the outputs. Using the bookshelf example, you would compare the amount of capital and number of hours worked to the number of bookshelves produced. But how can we measure the productivity of a nation's economy, which is made up of millions of different people and businesses? Economists use a measurement called **multifactor productivity**, the ratio between an industry's economic output and its labor and capital inputs. By collecting multifactor productivity data on a country's major industries and business sectors, economists can estimate the productivity of the entire economy.

What Contributes to Productivity?

Several factors contribute to changes in productivity.

Quality of Labor A better educated, healthier workforce tends to be more productive. Using the bookshelf example, if you were to take classes in woodworking, your enhanced knowledge would enable you to produce more and better shelves. In general, the more educated the workforce, the more productive it is. As for health, people are usually more productive when they feel well than when they feel sluggish or ill.

Technological Innovation Historically, as during the Industrial Revolution, new machines and technologies helped countries produce more output from the same amount of inputs. In recent times, the desktop computer and computer technology generally have generated productivity gains.

Energy Costs Gas, electricity, and other fuels power the technologies that increase productivity. When energy costs rise, those tools become more expensive to use and productivity declines. By the same token, when energy costs fall, using advanced tools becomes less expensive and productivity rises.

DIFFERENTIATING INSTRUCTION

Struggling Readers

Use Questions to Understand

Point out that the headings on pages 372–373 are questions. Keeping questions in mind as you read is an effective comprehension strategy. Explain that even when a heading is not a question, readers can form one. Model this process with the headings on pages 368–369. "Gauging Economic Growth" can be "How do you gauge economic growth?" Ask students to rephrase "Population and Economic Growth." Model how readers mentally answer the questions as they read.

Inclusion

Draw a Graph

Direct students to copy the graph in Figure 12.13 on a separate piece of paper, leaving room to add the graph in Figure 12.15 next to it. After students have copied both graphs, they will more easily be able to see the relationship between growth and productivity. Have students summarize that relationship in a sentence. *(Multifactor productivity and growth in real GDP per capita seem to be related because they follow the same pattern.)*

Financial Markets The easier it is for funds to flow to where they are needed, the more productive the economy becomes. Banks, stock markets, and similar institutions allow a country's funds to be put to their best use. When such institutions do not exist or when they do not function efficiently, productivity is reduced.

FIGURE 12.15 U.S. PRIVATE BUSINESS MULTIFACTOR PRODUCTIVITY

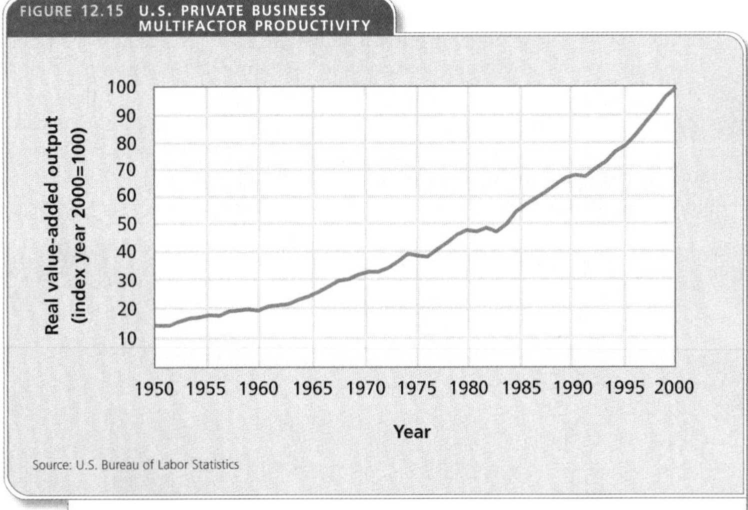

Source: U.S. Bureau of Labor Statistics

ANALYZE GRAPHS

1. What happened to productivity in the three years after the 1973 oil embargo? Why?
2. Compare this graph with Figure 12.13 on page 369, which shows real per capita GDP. How closely is economic growth related to productivity?

How Are Productivity and Growth Related?

Economic growth is a measure of change in production. It does not consider how much effort or how many resources it took to produce that quantity of production. Productivity, on the other hand, is a measure of efficiency. It reflects the amount of effort and resources it took to produce a certain quantity.

A country could experience economic growth—as measured by real GDP—without increasing its productivity. Such growth would be tied to an increase in the quantity of natural resources, labor, capital, or technology. If the productivity of a country increases, its real GDP can grow without increasing the quantity of inputs.

As shown in Figure 12.15, productivity in the United States grew at a steady pace from 1950 to 2000. Among other things, a better educated labor force and advances in information technology contributed to the increase. The dips in the graph represent productivity setbacks, such as tighter financial markets during recessions.

APPLICATION Drawing Conclusions

C. Some countries have limited natural resources but high economic growth. Does this prove that worldwide economic growth is unlimited by natural resources? Why or why not? No, it does not. Countries with limited natural resources depend on the natural resources of other countries. If the entire world runs out of a resource, there's not another supply somewhere else.

Presentation Options

Review the relationship between productivity and economic growth by using the following presentation options.

Power Presentations DVD-ROM
Using the Display Tool, trace the changes in U.S. business productivity from 1950 to 2000.

Economics Concepts Transparencies

- CT42 GDP of World's Leading Economies

Analyze Graphs: Figure 12.15

Help students understand the relationship between lower productivity and higher energy prices. Pose this question: if a company has to spend more money to fuel its operations, how does that affect its ability to invest in other aspects of the business? *(It leaves less available for other productive developments.)*

Answers

1. *Productivity declined because of increased energy costs.*
2. *Very closely—the graphs are very similar.*

SMALL GROUP ACTIVITY

Managing Economic Growth

Time 30 minutes ◑

Task Decide whether it would be more productive to continue using fossil fuels or to shift to renewable sources of energy such as wind and solar power.

Materials Needed paper and pens

Activity

- Organize students into small groups.
- Direct students to use the factors that contribute to productivity to analyze the options and to estimate the relative costs of each.
- Have each group come up with a proposed solution and present it to the class.
- The presentations should address not only why their plan is good but why the other choice is less good.
- Encourage debate after each presentation.

Rubric

	Understanding of Economic Growth Choices	Presentation of Information
4	excellent	creative, well-developed presentation
3	good	clear and complete
2	fair	mostly clear and complete
1	poor	unclear and incomplete

Thomas Robert Malthus

More About . . .

Thomas Robert Malthus
Malthus was the sixth of eight children born to Daniel and Henrietta Malthus. His father was an acquaintance of the philosophers David Hume and Jean-Jacques Rousseau. Both visited the Malthus home when Robert (who was never called Thomas) was a child.

The Malthus home was always filled with lively discussions, and young Robert was an active participant. Years later, after one such intellectual debate with his father on the "perfectibility of society," Malthus decided to set down his arguments and observations on paper. With the encouragement of his father, Malthus published his ideas in *An Essay on the Principle of Population* in 1798.

More About . . .

Malthus's Influence
Charles Darwin was much influenced by the writings of Thomas Robert Malthus. In his 1876 autobiography, Darwin wrote:

In October 1838, that is, fifteen months after I had begun my systematic inquiry, I happened to read for amusement Malthus on Population, *and being well prepared to appreciate the struggle for existence which everywhere goes on from long-continued observation of the habits of animals and plants, it at once struck me that under these circumstances favourable variations would tend to be preserved, and unfavourable ones to be destroyed. The results of this would be the formation of a new species. Here, then I had at last got a theory by which to work.*

Economics Update

ClassZone.com includes links to sites about Thomas Robert Malthus and his ideas. These links will help students appreciate the context in which Malthus worked and his contribution to modern economics.

ECONOMICS PACESETTER

Thomas Robert Malthus: The Population Problem

FAST FACTS

Thomas Robert Malthus

Career: British economist

Born: February 17, 1766

Died: December 23, 1834

Major Accomplishment: Calling attention to the issue of population growth

Major Work: *Essay on the Principle of Population* (1798, revised 1803)

Famous Quotation: *"Population, when unchecked, increases in geometrical ratio. Subsistence increases only in an arithmetical ratio."*

Influenced: David Ricardo, Charles Darwin

In the late 1700s, many European thinkers and writers predicted a future of peace and harmony in which poverty and hunger would be eliminated. Discussing humanity's future with his father led Thomas Robert Malthus to question whether the prevailing view was perhaps too rosy. Malthus saw a problem that others had overlooked, namely, that the world's population seemed likely to outgrow the available supply of food. He published his ideas in 1798 in "An Essay on the Principle of Population as It Affects the Future Improvement of Society."

A Natural Limit to Economic Growth?

Thomas Robert Malthus
Malthus predicted a population explosion that would result in poverty and famine.

Malthus's essay argued that human population would increase geometrically—that is, it would double—every 25 years. Malthus also estimated that food production would only increase arithmetically—that is, by the same amount each time—over that time period. Figure 12.16 uses hypothetical numbers to illustrate the problem. As time went on, agriculture would produce less food per person, and millions would be thrown into poverty and starvation.

"An Essay on the Principle of Population" caused a tremendous backlash. People could not accept that the rosy future they had imagined might not come to pass. Malthus and his essay were widely attacked and criticized—but no one could ignore his argument.

Malthus's estimates turned out to be flawed. Human population increased at a slower pace than he predicted. World population was about 1 billion in 1800, but it took until 1930 to reach 2 billion. Agricultural productivity rose dramatically with the introduction of mechanized farming and advances in fertilization and pest control. Although world population accelerated around 1950, reaching about 6.5 billion by 2005, agricultural production kept pace with the growing population.

Economics Update
Find an update on Thomas Robert Malthus at **ClassZone.com**

FIGURE 12.16 MALTHUS'S POPULATION PROBLEM

Elapsed Years	Bushels of Wheat (in millions)	Population (in millions)	Bushels per Person
0	10	10	1.00
25	20	20	1.00
50	30	40	0.75
75	40	80	0.50
100	50	160	0.31

APPLICATION Applying Economic Concepts

D. How is Malthus's population problem an example of the problem of scarcity?
Answers may vary, but as time goes on, food becomes more scarce and economic decisions would need to be made.

374 Chapter 12

DIFFERENTIATING INSTRUCTION

English Learners

Learn Word Families
The word *population,* discussed in this section, is just one of many words associated with people. Have students use a thesaurus or other research source to find at least five more words in this family. *(Possible answers: people, populace, populated, popular, unpopular)*

Gifted and Talented

Research Population Control
Direct students to research population control efforts, especially in China and India. Instruct them to pay special attention to China's one-child policy, its effect on that country's social structure and economy, and whether it achieved its purpose. Ask them to compare China's approach with India's efforts. If more workers lead to an increase in GDP, why do these countries want to limit population growth?

SECTION 3 Assessment

REVIEWING KEY CONCEPTS

1. Explain the differences between the terms in each of these pairs.
   a. *economic growth* / *real GDP per capita*
   b. *capital deepening* / *labor input*
2. Name the key measurement of economic growth.
3. What four factors drive economic growth?
4. How are productivity and growth related?
5. Briefly explain the problem Malthus identified.
6. **Using Your Notes** Write a persuasive paragraph arguing one side or the other of economic growth possibilities. Refer to your completed summary chart.

What Is Economic Growth?		

Use the Graphic Organizer at **Interactive Review @ ClassZone.com**

CRITICAL THINKING

7. **Solving Economic Problems** In 2000, the world's population was about 6 billion, and about 800 million of those people did not have enough to eat. By 2050, the world's population is expected to grow to about 9 billion. What steps should we take now to avoid having more than 1 billion people without enough to eat by 2050? Employ the ideas you learned about in this section in formulating your solution.
8. **Explaining an Economic Concept** Why is real GDP per capita a useful measure? Why couldn't real GDP or GDP per capita be used for the same purpose?
9. **Analyzing Cause and Effect** Globalization opens international boundaries to companies, creating markets that stretch around the world. What role might global competition play in the development of innovations?
10. **Challenge** Going to school is your job. Your product is increasing your knowledge, and your grades are the main measure of this. Increasing your productivity would result in better grades—and more free time. Adapt the factors that contribute to economic productivity to explain how you might increase your productivity as a student.

Online Quiz
ClassZone.com

ECONOMICS IN PRACTICE

A busy factory is one route to economic growth.

Stimulating Economic Growth
Government policies affect economic growth. Some policies have immediate effects that last for a short time. Other policies take longer to show results but have lasting impact.

Create a Healthy Economy
Reflecting on what you learned in this section, consider the following possible government actions.

- open a protected wilderness area for coal mining
- increase funding for scholarships for low-income students
- provide tax breaks for companies purchasing new equipment
- strengthen laws protecting the rights of inventors

Explain how each potential action might lead to economic growth.

Challenge Estimate the costs and the benefits of each action. Which actions would have the most lasting positive effect on the economy?

375

4 Assess & Reteach

Assess Discuss questions 1–5 and 7–9 as a whole class activity. Give students the choice of answering question 6 or question 10 in an extended piece of writing. Have students work in pairs to complete the activity in Economics in Practice.

Unit 5 Resource Book
- Section Quiz, p. 29

Interactive Review @ ClassZone.com
- Section Quiz

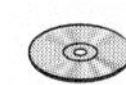
Test Generator CD-ROM
- Section Quiz

Reteach Hold a "Future Conference," a gathering of economists meeting in the year 2020. Divide the class into three groups. The first will make a presentation as if in the year 2020, covering the idea of economic growth (pages 368–369), with projections about how both GDP and population will have grown by then. The second group will make a presentation covering the role of the four factors and productivity on economic growth (pages 370–372) in the years between now and 2020. The third group will make a presentation on what lies ahead in the more distant future, touching on topics covered on pages 373–374.

Unit 5 Resource Book
- Reteaching Activity, p. 30

SECTION 3 ASSESSMENT ANSWERS

Reviewing Key Concepts

1. a. *economic growth*, p. 368; *real GDP per capita*, p. 369
   b. *capital deepening*, p. 371; *labor input*, p. 371
2. real GDP
3. natural resources, human resources, capital, and technology and innovation
4. They are directly related: when productivity increases, so does economic growth.
5. Malthus hypothesized that population growth would outpace growth in agricultural productivity, leading to poverty and famine.
6. See page 368 for an example of a completed diagram. Answers will vary, but look for an understanding of the key concepts with specific information from this section of the chapter.

Critical Thinking

7. Answers will vary, but look for an understanding of market incentives applied to public goods.
8. Real GDP per capita shows economic growth per person and is used as a measure of standard of living. Real GDP does not include the number of people in a country. GDP per capita would not take price increases into account.
9. Global competition would likely spur innovation. To survive in a competitive marketplace, an enterprise needs new ideas and new technology.
10. Answers will vary, but look for an understanding of the factors cited.

Economics in Practice

Create a Healthy Economy (1) increase natural resources; (2) improve human resources; (3) increase capital resources; (4) incentive for creating new technology

Challenge Answers will vary but could include (1) costs: permanent loss of wilderness area, pollution; benefits: temporary supply of coal; (2) c: $10,000 per student; b: long-term improvement in human capital; (3) c: loss of tax revenue; b: improvements in capital; (4) c: enforcement of laws; b: more inventions. The scholarships or protecting inventors' rights would have the most lasting positive impact.

1 Plan & Prepare

Objectives

- Analyze sources to synthesize economic information.
- Understand the relationship between economic freedom and economic growth with Poland as an example.

2 Focus & Motivate

Ask students to picture the following scene set in Poland: *a man with a mustache plays table tennis with his chauffeur. The talk centers on politics, as usual, and the mustachioed man listens carefully but sends his own strong opinions across the table with the same force as the ball.* Then, ask students to choose from between the following to identify the mustachioed man:

- a member of the Communist party elite
- a man instrumental in bringing the Cold War to an end

The man is, of course, Lech Walesa who was the chairman of Solidarity, Poland's first independent trade union (formed in 1980). Solidarity was part of a coalition that wrested power from the Communists in 1989. Walesa himself became president of Poland in 1990. He symbolizes, among other things, the irony of the fall of communism, which came from within the labor movement—the same source as its rise.

3 Teach

A. What attractions does Wroclaw have for manufacturing businesses? *(semi-skilled workers, university students, workers who take pride in their work)*

B. Why is the farmer smiling? *(He is getting good benefits from Poland's membership in the EU.)*

C. Compare the sources of items A and C. What are the similarities and differences in the articles? *(Both articles are factual, but article C uses many statistics. A is written to appeal to a more general audience than C and uses more engaging language. C is targeted at business readers.)*

Economics Update

Go to **ClassZone.com** to find an update to this Case Study, including another article, an editable student worksheet, and an editable lesson plan.

Case Study

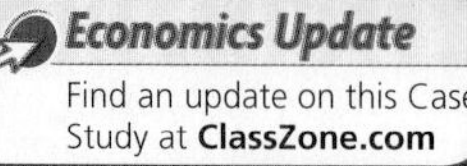

Find an update on this Case Study at **ClassZone.com**

Poland: Economic Freedom and Economic Growth

Background Communists ruled Poland and controlled its economy from 1948 to 1989. After holding its first free elections in 1990, Poland made rapid progress toward full democracy and a free market economy. Economic reforms included ending government price controls, privatizing industries formerly controlled by the government, and entering the international marketplace. As Poland moved away from government control of the economy, it experienced a surge in economic growth—outdistancing many other former Communist countries in eastern and central Europe. In 2004, Poland became a member of the European Union, further increasing its economic potential.

What's the issue? How successful is Poland's economy? Read these documents to learn about the challenges and rewards of the country's economic transition.

A. Online News Article

Wroclaw, a city in southwest Poland, offers one example of the country's success through embracing global capitalism. This article describes that phenomenon.

Wroclaw, Poland: Europe's Next Appliance Capital?

Appliance Manufacturers Pour into Southwest Poland

Money and companies are pouring in—not just the prestige nameplates like Bombardier, Siemens, Whirlpool, Toyota, and Volvo, but also the network of suppliers that inevitably follows them. At first, most of the new jobs were of the semi-skilled variety. Now they have been followed by design and engineering work that aims to tap into the largest concentration of university students in Eastern Europe.

"Everyone is coming, and they are coming very fast," reports Josu Ugarte . . . who heads the appliance manufacturing operations here of Mondragon, the giant Spanish industrial cooperative. He predicts, confidently, that the region around Wroclaw will soon surpass Northern Italy as Europe's appliance capital. . . .

The secret isn't just lower wages. It's also the attitude of workers who take pride and are willing to do what is necessary to succeed, even if it means outsourcing parts production or working on weekends or altering vacation schedules. . . .

Source: "Europe's Capitalism Curtain" WashingtonPost.com July 23, 2004

Many manufacturers have opened factories in Wroclaw, Poland. This Volvo factory produces buses.

Thinking Economically How has Poland's human capital contributed to the country's economic growth?

DIFFERENTIATING INSTRUCTION

Struggling Readers

2004 Economic Data for Poland

To grasp the many statistics in the third source and to see their relationships, have students use the data to create an economic database. You may wish to pair students for this activity, so they may talk through the data and the task. You may also start them with the following statistics: EU receipts €2.5 billion ($3.4 billion) ; EU payments €1.25 billion ($1.7 billion).

Inclusion

Use Government Sources

Unlike most private businesses, the U.S. government is required to provide accessible Web pages in compliance with section 508 of the Rehabilitation Act. If there is a lab with assistive technologies available, have students explore government Web sites for information to become familiar with locating them and using them. They are excellent sources of reliable information, especially on statistical matters.

B. Political Cartoon

Poland's farmers were sceptical about the benefits of European Union membership. This cartoon reflects their change of heart as agricultural exports increased and they received new subsidies from the European Union.

Thinking Economically Does the cartoon emphasize the free market benefits of the European Union or other benefits?

C. Magazine Article

Joining the European Union brought tremendous growth to Poland's economy. This article explains some of the elements that led to the success.

Reaping the European Union Harvest

How the new central European members learnt to stop worrying and love the European Union

After grumbling furiously about dangers to their sovereignty and their social values when they joined the European Union in May, Poles are discovering themselves now to be among the Union's most loyal citizens. Some three-quarters say they are happy with EU membership—and no wonder. In its first eight months of membership Poland got some €2.5 billion [€ is the euro, the currency of the European Union] ($3.4 billion) from the EU budget, or roughly twice what it paid in, according to the newspaper Rzeczpospolita. Rural incomes have risen by one-third for small farmers and two-thirds for big ones, reversing eight years of stagnation and decline, thanks to munificent EU subsidies and an influx of foreign buyers offering high prices for Polish meat and fruit.

Poland's total exports rose by more than 30% in the first nine months of 2004, helped by the abolition of customs formalities. EU rules have opened the skies to budget airlines, boosting tourist numbers by 20% last year. Higher-than-expected tax revenues have meant lower-than-expected budget deficits. . . .

Source: *The Economist*, January 8, 2005

Thinking Economically According to the document, how has membership in the EU helped Poland's economic growth?

THINKING ECONOMICALLY Synthesizing

1. Which economic measurements and indicators are evident in documents A and C? Explain what they convey about the strengths and weaknesses of Poland's economy.
2. What factors have driven Poland's economic growth?
3. Compare documents A and C, written about six months apart. What continued economic trends and new economic strengths do they describe?

More About . . .

Poland's Economic Freedom

In a 2006 study by the Heritage Foundation, Poland ranked 41st out of 157 nations in economic freedom. The economic freedom scale measures 10 factors, with 5 points being the worst possible score and 1 being the best. Students may be interested in the comparison with the U.S. rankings (overall the U.S. ranked 9th) below.

Factor	Poland	United States
trade policy	2.0	2.0
fiscal burden	2.4	3.9
government intervention	2.0	2.0
monetary policy	1.0	1.0
foreign investment	3.0	2.0
banking and finance	2.0	1.0
wages and prices	3.0	2.0
property rights	3.0	1.0
regulation	3.0	2.0
informal market	3.5	1.5

THINKING ECONOMICALLY—ANSWERS

A. *The positive attitude of Polish workers and the number of them with advanced degrees attract businesses.*

B. *It emphasizes the government subsidies available through the EU.*

C. *In its first eight months of membership, the EU spent about 2.5 billion euros on Polish projects. EU subsidies and open markets have increased farmers' incomes. Polish exports rose, as has tourism.*

Synthesizing

1. *A–building permits, manufacturing workweek, employment; all of these measures are up, thanks to investment from abroad. C–government spending, personal income, exports; membership in the EU has brought money to Poland through subsidies, exports, and tourism.*
2. *Joining the EU and encouraging foreign investment have driven Poland's economic growth.*
3. *Document C shows some of the effects of the foreign investment described in document A, namely, rising exports and tax revenues.*

Online Summary Answers

1. Gross domestic product (GDP)
2. national income accounting
3. Real gross domestic product
4. disposable personal income
5. business cycle
6. leading indicators
7. depression
8. economic growth
9. Capital deepening
10. real GDP per capita

Review this chapter using interactive activities at **ClassZone.com**

- Online Summary
- Quizzes
- Vocabulary Flip Cards
- Graphic Organizers
- Review and Study Notes

Online Summary

Complete the following activity either on your own paper or online at **ClassZone.com**

Choose the key concept that best completes the sentence. Not all key concepts will be used.

aggregate demand
aggregate supply
business cycle
capital deepening
coincident indicators
depression
disposable personal income (DPI)
economic growth
gross domestic product (GDP)
gross national product (GNP)
lagging indicators
leading indicators
macroeconomic equilibrium
national income (NI)
national income accounting
net national product (NNP)
nominal GDP
nonmarket activities
per capita real GDP
personal income (PI)
real GDP
recession
stagflation
underground economy

__1__, the market value of all goods and services produced in a nation, is one of the key measurements used in __2__. __3__ is especially useful because it gives the market value of all goods and services corrected for price level changes. Another very useful measurement is __4__, which shows the actual amount of money people have to spend.

The economy goes through regular changes called the __5__. Economists watch __6__, such as building permits issued and stock prices, to predict changes in the economy. Low points in the economy are usually self-correcting, but in times of a __7__, such as the one that happened in the 1930s, government intervention may be needed.

Several factors influence __8__, including an increase in capital. __9__, an increase in the ratio between capital and labor, increases productivity, helping the economy grow. Economists use __10__, real GDP divided by whole population, to distinguish an increase in population from a higher level of economic output.

CHAPTER 12 Assessment

REVIEWING KEY CONCEPTS

Gross Domestic Product and Other Indicators (pp. 350–357)

1. What is the purpose of national income accounting?
2. In what way is GDP a baseline for other economic indicators?

Business Cycles (pp. 358–367)

3. What do leading indicators say about the economy?
4. Explain how a business decision might have a ripple effect that would tilt the economy on a new phase of the business cycle.

Stimulating Economic Growth (pp. 368–377)

5. Explain how a country with few natural resources can still have economic growth.
6. What are the four key factors that influence economic growth?

APPLYING ECONOMIC CONCEPTS

The table below shows the size of the underground economies of selected countries.

FIGURE 12.17 UNDERGROUND ECONOMIES IN SELECTED COUNTRIES

Country	GDP Per Capita (in U.S. dollars)	Underground Economy as Percent of GDP
Egypt	3,900	69
Thailand	8,300	70
Russia	11,100	44
Chile	11,300	19
Singapore	28,100	14
Italy	29,200	27
Switzerland	32,300	9
United States	41,800	10

Sources: International Monetary Fund, U.S. Central Intelligence Agency, 1998-2005 data

7. Is there a relationship between GDP per capita and the size of a country's underground economy?
8. If a country incorporated its underground economy into the main economy, what would happen to its GDP per capita? Why?

CHAPTER 12 ASSESSMENT ANSWERS

Reviewing Key Concepts

1. to track the economy in order to make informed decisions about economic policies
2. Various items are subtracted from it or divided into it to arrive at other useful measurements.
3. They indicate whether the economy is likely to grow or shrink in the next six to nine months.
4. Answers will vary. Sample answer: If a business decides to cut back on the purchase of capital goods, then the producers of those goods might experience a slowdown. This in turn might lead to layoffs, which would leave consumers with less money to spend. The end result might be lower demand and cutbacks by other businesses.
5. A country with few natural resources can still innovate to make the most of the resources it has or export innovative products and import what it needs.
6. natural resources; human resources; capital; technology and innovation

Applying Economic Concepts

7. Generally, countries with lower GDP per capita have larger underground economies. (More developed countries tend to have more business opportunities, better legal systems to protect owners and investors, and less official corruption.)
8. GDP per capita would increase because there would be more economic resources for the same number of people.

CRITICAL THINKING

9. **Creating Graphs** Copy the blank graph onto your own paper. Then use the data in the table to create a line graph showing the percent change in U.S. real gross domestic product from 1999 through 2003.

   Use ***SMARTGrapher*** **@ ClassZone.com** to complete this activity.

FIGURE 12.18 PERCENT CHANGE IN REAL GDP FROM PRECEDING PERIOD

Year	Quarter 1	Quarter 2	Quarter 3	Quarter 4
1999	3.4	3.4	4.8	7.3
2000	1.0	6.4	–0.5	2.1
2001	–0.5	1.2	–1.4	1.6
2002	2.7	2.2	2.4	0.2
2003	1.7	3.7	7.2	3.6

Source: U.S. Bureau of Economic Analysis

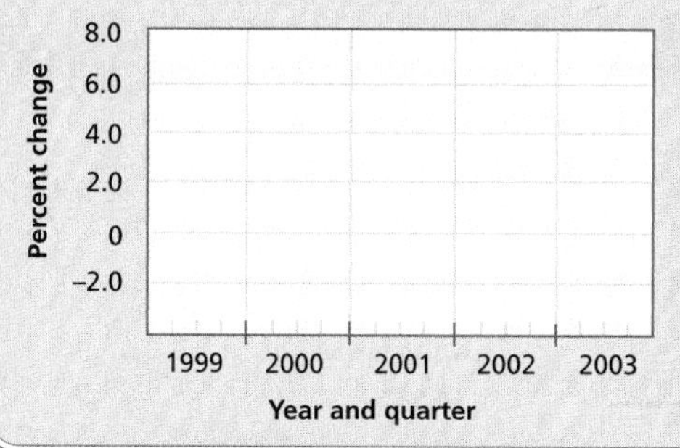

10. **Analyzing and Interpreting Data** Which year had the highest growth? The lowest?

11. **Analyzing Cause and Effect** The government enacted tax cuts and issued child tax credit refunds in 2003. What component of GDP would likely have increased because of these?

12. **Distinguishing Fact from Opinion** Does the graph support or counter the idea that the September 11, 2001 terrorist attacks caused a recession?

13. **Challenge** How could GDP grow by 5 percent a year but leave the economy no better off—or even worse off? Give two different explanations.

SIMULATION

Surveying Consumer Confidence

The Consumer Confidence Survey is one poll used to determine consumer expectations. Another is the ABC/Washington Post Consumer Comfort Index, which makes 1,000 phone calls to adults each month and asks the following questions:

- National Economy: "Would you describe the state of the nation's economy these days as excellent, good, not so good, or poor?"
- Personal Finances: "Would you describe the state of your own personal finances these days as excellent, good, not so good, or poor?"
- Buying Climate: "Considering the cost of things today and your own personal finances, would you say now is an excellent time, a good time, a not so good time, or a poor time to buy the things you want and need?"

To understand the consumer comfort index better, take a survey of your class.

Step 1. Break into five small groups and discuss each of the questions. The point is to share your thoughts, not to debate who is right or wrong.

Step 2. Return to your desk and write down your answers to each of the questions anonymously.

Step 3. Collect the anonymous answers from the whole class. Have one person tabulate the answers to each question on the board.

Step 4. Now calculate the consumer confidence of your class. For each question, add up the number of positive responses (either "excellent" or "good"). Then subtract the number of negative responses (either "not so good" or "poor"). Divide by the total number of students and multiply by 100.

Add the result from all three questions together, and then divide by three. That will yield an overall comfort level. A level of 100 would mean everyone is satisfied with everything. A level of –100 would mean that everyone felt negatively about everything.

Step 5. Discuss the result. Does it seem to accurately reflect the mood of the class? What would happen to the nation's GDP if all consumers felt as you do?

CHAPTER 12 • ASSESSMENT

McDougal Littell Assessment System

Assess

Online Test Practice
- Go to **ClassZone.com** for more test practice.

Unit 5 Resource Book
- Chapter Test, Forms A, B, & C, pp. 41–52

Test Generator CD-ROM
- Chapter Test, Forms (A, B, & C), in English and Spanish

Report

Use the McDougal Littell Assessment System to score assessments and receive customized reports.

Reteach

For activities customized for individual students, use the McDougal Littell Assessment System.

SMARTGrapher Students can create a line graph of real GDP using **SmartGrapher @ ClassZone.com**.

CHAPTER 12 ASSESSMENT ANSWERS

Critical Thinking

9. Look for a completed line graph showing the percent changes in growth of GDP. There should be four data points for each of the five years. The data points for negative quarters should appear below the 0 axis.
10. 1999 had the highest total growth; 2001 had the lowest.
11. consumer spending
12. The data suggest that the U.S. economy was already in a recession when the attacks happened. The third quarter of 2001, when the attacks occurred, was the last quarter in which real GDP was negative.
13. (1) If the country's population increased by 5 percent or more, GDP per capita would be the same or less. (2) If prices rose by 5 percent or more, real GDP would be the same or less.

Simulation Rubric

	Understanding of Concepts Involved	Presentation of Information
4	excellent	accurate, clear, and complete
3	good	mostly accurate and clear
2	fair	sometimes clear
1	poor	sketchy

CHAPTER 13: Addressing Economic Challenges
Planning Guide

Resources 2Go Complete print resources all on one USB drive allow you to customize lessons.

Section Titles and Objectives	Unit 5 Resource Book and Workbooks		Assessment Resources
1 Unemployment in Today's Economy pp. 382–387 • Explain how economists measure unemployment • Identify the different types of unemployment • Discuss the impact that unemployment has on the economy and on individuals	**Unit 5 Resource Book** • Reading Study Guide, pp. 53–54 • RSG with Additional Support, pp. 55–57 • RSG with Additional Support (Spanish), pp. 58–60	• Readings in Free Enterprise: The Relationship Between Inflation and Unemployment, pp. 85–86 • Economic Simulations: Wage-Price Spiral, pp. 89–90	**Unit 5 Resource Book** • Section Quiz, p. 61 • Reteaching Activity, p. 62 **Test Generator CD-ROM** **Daily Test Practice Transparencies,** TT43
2 Poverty and Income Distribution pp. 388–395 • Explain how economists measure poverty • Discuss the causes of poverty • Describe how economists measure income inequality • Identify what antipoverty programs are available	**Unit 5 Resource Book** • Reading Study Guide, pp. 63–64 • RSG with Additional Support, pp. 65–67 • RSG with Additional Support (Spanish), pp. 68–70 • Economic Skills and Problem Solving Activity, pp. 83–84	**NCEE Student Activities** • Poverty and Income Distribution, pp. 49–52	**Unit 5 Resource Book** • Section Quiz, p. 71 • Reteaching Activity, p. 72 **Test Generator CD-ROM** **Daily Test Practice Transparencies,** TT44
3 Causes and Consequences of Inflation pp. 396–405 • Explain how economists measure inflation • Identify what causes inflation • Describe how inflation affects the economy	**Unit 5 Resource Book** • Reading Study Guide, pp. 73–74 • RSG with Additional Support, pp. 75–77 • RSG with Additional Support (Spanish), pp. 78–80 • Math Skills Worksheet: Calculating the Rate of Inflation, p. 91 • Case Study Resources: What Inflation Means For . . . , pp. 87–88	**Test Practice and Review Workbook,** pp. 47–48	**Unit 5 Resource Book** • Section Quiz, p. 81 • Reteaching Activity, p. 82 • Chapter Test, (Forms A, B, & C), pp. 93–104 **Test Generator CD-ROM** **Daily Test Practice Transparencies,** TT45

Integrated Technology

No Time? To focus students on the most important content in this chapter, use Economics Concepts Transparencies, CT45, "Inflation and Unemployment," available in Resources 2Go.

Teacher Presentation Options

Presentation Toolkit

Power Presentation DVD-ROM

- Lecture Notes
- Media Gallery
- Review Game
- Interactive Review
- Animated Economics

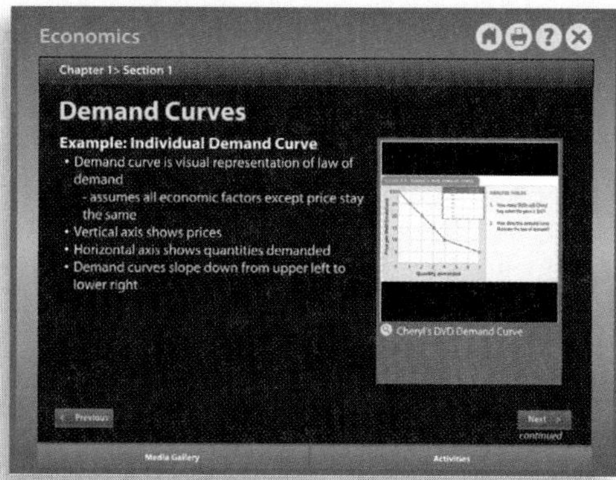

Economics Concepts Transparencies

- Types of Unemployment, CT43
- Income Distribution in the United States, 2004, CT44
- Inflation and Unemployment: 1980 to 2005, CT45

Electronic Books

eEdition DVD-ROM

eEdition Online

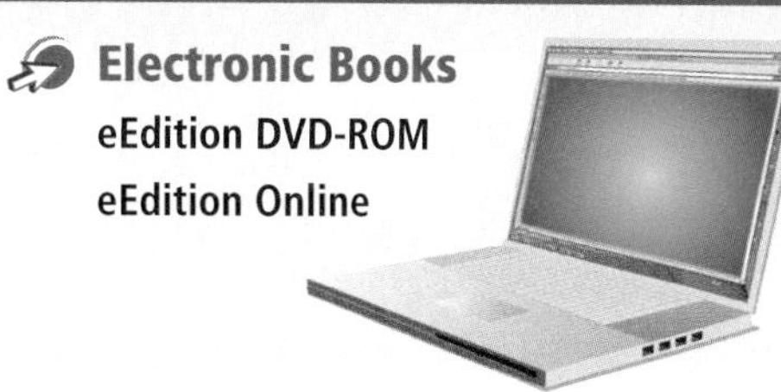

Daily Test Practice Transparencies, TT43, TT44, TT45

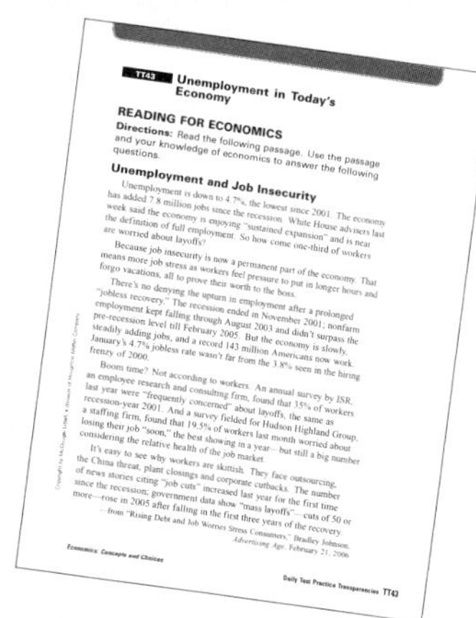

TT43 Unemployment in Today's Economy

READING FOR ECONOMICS

Unemployment and Job Insecurity

SMARTGrapher

- Create Aggregate Supply and Demand Curves, p. 403
- Create a Bar Graph, p. 407

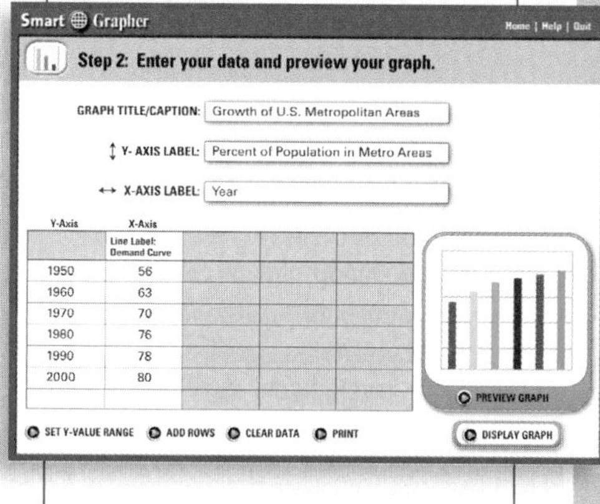

Online Activities at ClassZone.com

Economics Update

- U.S. Unemployment Rate, p. 383
- U.S. Poverty Rate, p. 389
- Hernando de Soto, p. 394
- U.S. Consumer Price Index, p. 397
- The Effects of Inflation in the 1970's, p. 404

Activity Maker

- Vocabulary Flip Cards
- Review Game

Research Center

- Graphs and Data

Interactive Review

- Online Summary
- Quizzes
- Vocabulary Flip Cards
- Graphic Organizers
- Review and Study Notes

SMARTGrapher

- Create Aggregate Supply and Demand Curves, p. 403
- Create a Bar Graph, p. 407

Teacher-Tested Activities

Name: Michael D. Bruce

School: William Fremd High School

State: Illinois

Teacher-Tested Activities

At the beginning of this chapter, look for my classroom-proven idea for teaching economics concepts and thinking.

Resources for Differentiated Instruction

Struggling Readers

Teacher's Edition Activities

- Follow Continuous Text, p. 384
- Activate Prior Knowledge, p. 390
- Summarize, p. 394
- Use Illustrations to Understand, p. 400
- Use the Reading Process, p. 404

Unit 5 Resource Book

- Reading Study Guide with Additional Support, pp. 55–57, 65–67, 75–77 **A**
- Reteaching Activities, pp. 62, 72, 82 **B**
- Chapter Test (Form A), pp. 93–96 **C**

ClassZone.com

- Animated Economics
- Interactive Review

Test Generator CD-ROM

- Chapter Test (Form A)
- Chapter Test (Form A), in Spanish

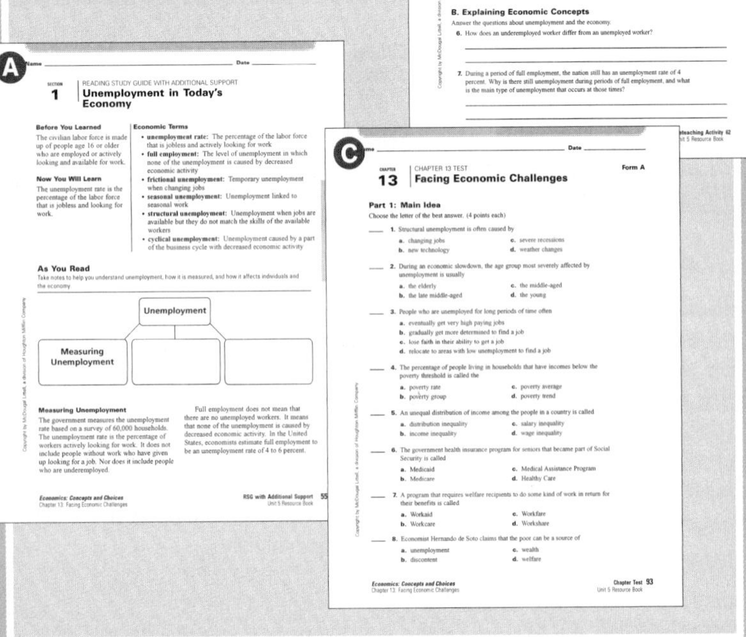

English Learners

Teacher's Edition Activities

- Distinguish Between Words, p. 386
- Research and Report Cooperatively, p. 392
- Use Prefixes to Understand, p. 398
- Use Conversation to Personalize Learning, p. 402

Unit 5 Resource Book

- RSG with Additional Support (Spanish), pp. 58–60, 68–70, 78–80 **A**

Test Generator CD-ROM

- Chapter Test (Forms A, B, & C), in Spanish **B**

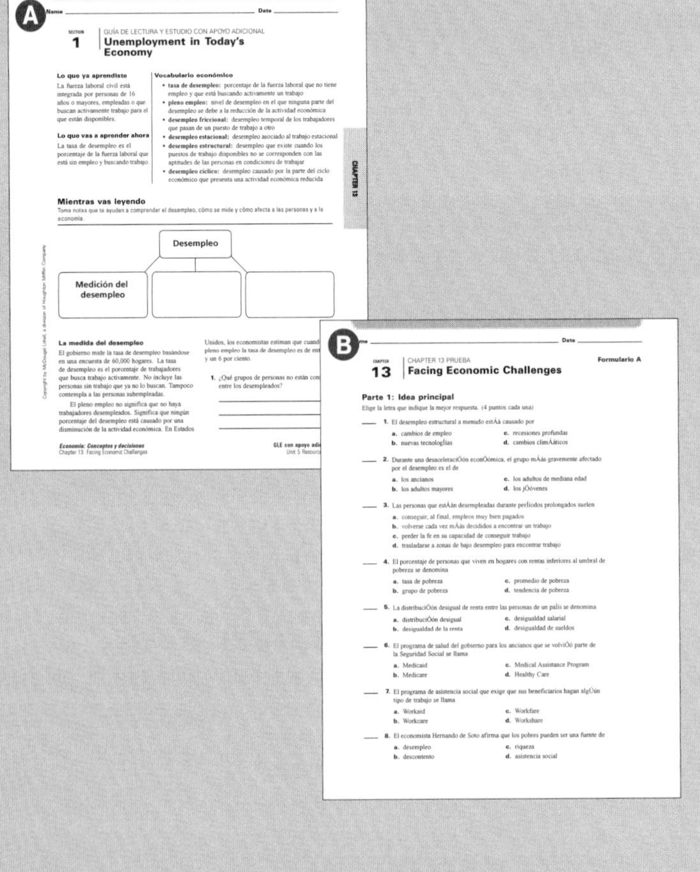

Inclusion

Teacher's Edition Activities

- Illustrate Types of Unemployment, p. 384
- Answer Questions While Reading, p. 390
- Listen for Understanding, p. 394
- Work in Pairs, p. 400
- Focus on Key Points, p. 404

Lesson Plans

- Modified Lessons for Inclusion, pp. 43–45 (A)

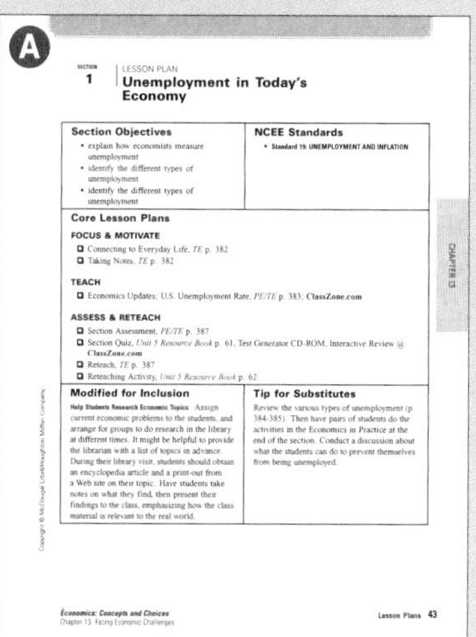
A

SECTION 1 | LESSON PLAN
Unemployment in Today's Economy

Section Objectives	NCEE Standards
• explain how economists measure unemployment • identify the different types of unemployment • identify the different types of unemployment	• Standard 19: UNEMPLOYMENT AND INFLATION

Core Lesson Plans

FOCUS & MOTIVATE
- ❑ Connecting to Everyday Life, *TE* p. 382
- ❑ Taking Notes, *TE* p. 382

TEACH
- ❑ Economics Updates: U.S. Unemployment Rate, *PE/TE* p. 383; **ClassZone.com**

ASSESS & RETEACH
- ❑ Section Assessment, *PE/TE* p. 387
- ❑ Section Quiz, *Unit 5 Resource Book* p. 61, Test Generator CD-ROM, Interactive Review @ **ClassZone.com**
- ❑ Reteach, *TE* p. 387
- ❑ Reteaching Activity, *Unit 5 Resource Book* p. 62

Modified for Inclusion	Tip for Substitutes
Help Students Research Economic Topics Assign current economic problems to the students, and arrange for groups to do research in the library at different times. It might be helpful to provide the librarian with a list of topics in advance. During their library visit, students should obtain an encyclopedia article and a print-out from a Web site on their topic. Have students take notes on what they find, then present their findings to the class, emphasizing how the class material is relevant to the real world.	Review the various types of unemployment (p. 384-385). Then have pairs of students do the activities in the Economics in Practice at the end of the section. Conduct a discussion about what the students can do to prevent themselves from being unemployed.

CHAPTER 13

Copyright © McDougal Littell/Houghton Mifflin Company.

Economics: Concepts and Choices
Chapter 13 Facing Economic Challenges

Lesson Plans 43

Gifted and Talented

Teacher's Edition Activities

- Research and Present, p. 386
- Debate Welfare Programs, p. 392
- Analyze Cause and Effect, p. 398
- Create Comparative Graphs, p. 402

Unit 5 Resource Book

- Readings in Free Enterprise: The Relationship Between Inflation and Unemployment, pp. 85–86 (A)
- Case Study Resources: What Inflation Means For . . . , pp. 87–88 (B)

NCEE Student Activities

- Poverty and Income Distribution, pp. 49–52 (C)

ClassZone.com

- Research Center

Test Generator CD-ROM

- Chapter Test (Form C)
- Chapter Test (Form C), in Spanish

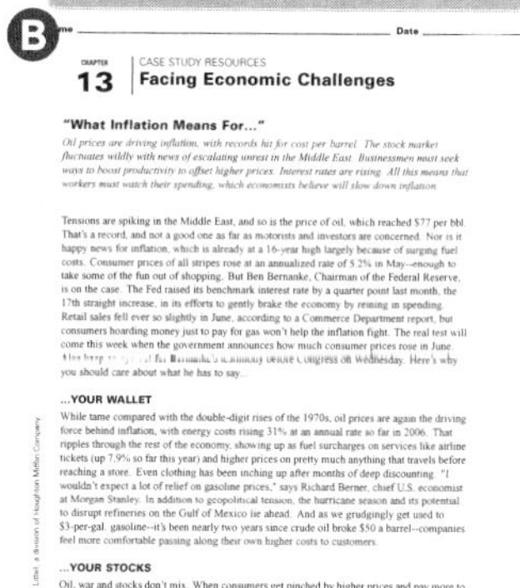
B

Name ______ Date ______

CHAPTER 13 | CASE STUDY RESOURCES
Facing Economic Challenges

"What Inflation Means For..."

Oil prices are driving inflation, with records hit for cost per barrel. The stock market fluctuates wildly with news of escalating unrest in the Middle East. Businessmen must seek ways to boost productivity to offset higher prices. Interest rates are rising. All this means that workers must watch their spending, which economists believe will slow down inflation.

Tensions are spiking in the Middle East, and so is the price of oil, which reached $77 per bbl. That's a record, and not a good one as far as motorists and investors are concerned. Nor is it happy news for inflation, which is already at a 16-year high largely because of surging fuel costs. Consumer prices of all stripes rose at an annualized rate of 5.2% in May--enough to take some of the fun out of shopping. But Ben Bernanke, Chairman of the Federal Reserve, is on the case. The Fed raised its benchmark interest rate by a quarter point last month, the 17th straight increase, in its efforts to gently brake the economy by reining in spending. Retail sales fell ever so slightly in June, according to a Commerce Department report, but consumers hoarding money just to pay for gas won't help the inflation fight. The real test will come this week when the government announces how much consumer prices rose in June. [illegible] Bernanke's testimony before Congress on Wednesday. Here's why you should care about what he has to say...

...YOUR WALLET

While tame compared with the double-digit rises of the 1970s, oil prices are again the driving force behind inflation, with energy costs rising 31% at an annual rate so far in 2006. That ripples through the rest of the economy, showing up as fuel surcharges on services like airline tickets (up 7.9% so far this year) and higher prices on pretty much anything that travels before reaching a store. Even clothing has been inching up after months of deep discounting. "I wouldn't expect a lot of relief on gasoline prices," says Richard Berner, chief U.S. economist at Morgan Stanley. In addition to geopolitical tension, the hurricane season and its potential to disrupt refineries on the Gulf of Mexico lie ahead. And as we grudgingly get used to $3-per-gal. gasoline--it's been nearly two years since crude oil broke $50 a barrel--companies feel more comfortable passing along their own higher costs to customers.

...YOUR STOCKS

Oil, war and stocks don't mix. When consumers get pinched by higher prices and pay more to borrow, investors are worried that they'll have less to spend, thus lowering overall demand for [illegible]

Case Study Resources 87
Unit 5 Resource Book

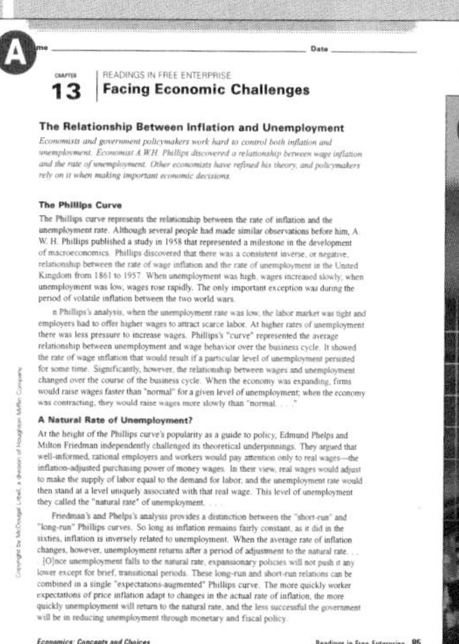
A

Name ______ Date ______

CHAPTER 13 | READINGS IN FREE ENTERPRISE
Facing Economic Challenges

The Relationship Between Inflation and Unemployment

Economists and government policymakers work hard to control both inflation and unemployment. Economist A.W.H. Phillips discovered a relationship between wage inflation and the rate of unemployment. Other economists have refined his theory, and policymakers rely on it when making important economic decisions.

The Phillips Curve

The Phillips curve represents the relationship between the rate of inflation and the unemployment rate. Although several people had made similar observations before him, A. W. H. Phillips published a study in 1958 that represented a milestone in the development of macroeconomics. Phillips discovered that there was a consistent inverse, or negative, relationship between the rate of wage inflation and the rate of unemployment in the United Kingdom from 1861 to 1957. When unemployment was high, wages increased slowly; when unemployment was low, wages rose rapidly. The only important exception was during the period of volatile inflation between the two world wars.

n Phillips's analysis, when the unemployment rate was low, the labor market was tight and employers had to offer higher wages to attract scarce labor. At higher rates of unemployment there was less pressure to increase wages. Phillips's "curve" represented the average relationship between unemployment and wage behavior over the business cycle. It showed the rate of wage inflation that would result if a particular level of unemployment persisted for some time. Significantly, however, the relationship between wages and unemployment changed over the course of the business cycle. When the economy was expanding, firms would raise wages faster than "normal" for a given level of unemployment; when the economy was contracting, they would raise wages more slowly than "normal. . . ."

A Natural Rate of Unemployment?

At the height of the Phillips curve's popularity as a guide to policy, Edmund Phelps and Milton Friedman independently challenged its theoretical underpinnings. They argued that well-informed, rational employers and workers would pay attention only to real wages—the inflation-adjusted purchasing power of money wages. In their view, real wages would adjust to make the supply of labor equal to the demand for labor, and the unemployment rate would then stand at a level uniquely associated with that real wage. This level of unemployment they called the "natural rate" of unemployment. . . .

Friedman's and Phelps's analysis provides a distinction between the "short-run" and "long-run" Phillips curves. So long as inflation remains fairly constant, as it did in the sixties, inflation is inversely related to unemployment. When the average rate of inflation changes, however, unemployment returns after a period of adjustment to the natural rate. . . . [O]nce unemployment falls to the natural rate, expansionary policies will not push it any lower except for brief, transitional periods. These long-run and short-run relations can be combined in a single "expectations-augmented" Phillips curve. The more quickly worker expectations of price inflation adapt to changes in the actual rate of inflation, the more quickly unemployment will return to the natural rate, and the less successful the government will be in reducing unemployment through monetary and fiscal policy.

Copyright by McDougal Littell, a division of Houghton Mifflin Company.

Economics: Concepts and Choices
Chapter 13 Facing Economic Challenges

Readings in Free Enterprise 85
Unit 5 Resource Book

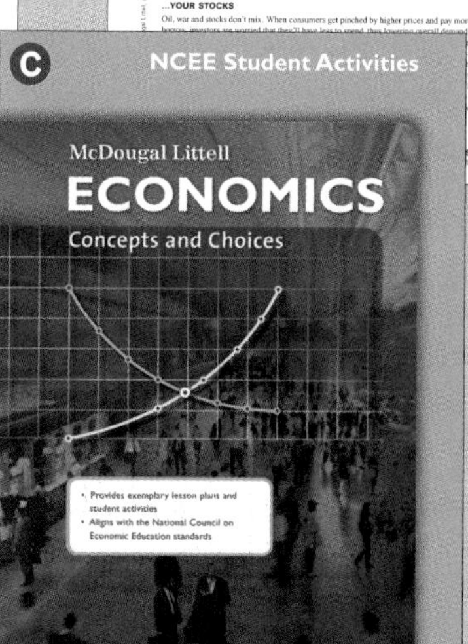

Focus & Motivate

Objective

Explain some of the challenges facing the economy, their causes, and possible solutions.

Why the Concept Matters

Give students several minutes to preview this chapter by looking at the headings and the illustrations. Then, ask them why it is important to learn about the challenges facing the economy. *(Possible answers: How the challenges are addressed can have a positive or negative impact on huge numbers of people; elections often turn on differing approaches to solving economic problems, so the stakes are high.)* Ask students if they can think of any examples in U.S. history in which economic challenges led to serious political or social problems. *(Possible answers: Revolutionary War, Civil War, Great Depression)* Understanding economic challenges and how to address them is a critical part of life in a democracy.

Analyzing the Photograph

Ask students to explain why they think that this photograph of mountain climbers was chosen for this chapter. *(Possible answer: to represent the effort involved in taking on challenges)* Also ask students to give personal examples of how they might face an uphill climb to join the workforce after leaving high school.

Economic Challenges
The national economy faces many challenges. Economics can help us understand and cope with these challenges.

380

CONTENT STANDARDS

NCEE STANDARDS

Standard 19: Unemployment and Inflation

Students will understand that

Unemployment imposes costs on individuals and nations. Unexpected inflation imposes costs on many people and benefits some others because it arbitrarily redistributes purchasing power. Inflation can reduce the rate of growth of national living standards because individuals and organizations use resources to protect themselves against the uncertainty of future prices.

Students will be able to use this knowledge to

Make informed decisions by anticipating the consequences of inflation and unemployment.

Benchmarks

Students will know that

Unemployment exists when people who are willing and able to work do not have jobs. *(page 382)*

The unemployment rate is the percentage of the labor force that is willing and able to work, does not currently have a job, and is actively looking for work. *(page 382)*

Unemployment can be caused by people changing jobs, by seasonal fluctuations in demand, by changes in the skills needed by employers, or by cyclical fluctuations in the level of national spending. *(pages 384–385)*

Explain why some people are unemployed when the economy is said to be functioning at full employment. *(page 383)*

Inflation is an increase in most prices; deflation is a decrease in most prices. *(pages 396–398)*

The Consumer Price Index (CPI) is the most commonly used measure of price-level changes. It can be used to compare the price level in one year with price levels in earlier or later periods. *(pages 396–397)*

Expectations of inflation may lead to higher interest rates. *(page 402)*

CHAPTER

13

Facing Economic Challenges

CONCEPT REVIEW

Business cycle is the series of growing and shrinking periods of economic activity, measured by increases or decreases in real gross domestic product.

CHAPTER 13 KEY CONCEPT

Unemployment has a variety of causes. Some level of unemployment is expected, even when an economy is healthy.

WHY THE CONCEPT MATTERS

As the nation's economy goes through business cycles, it will face the twin problems of unemployment and inflation. You may find yourself unemployed at some point during your working years, if only for a short period. For some people, persistent unemployment leads to poverty. During periods of inflation, you may have a job but your wages may buy less.

Online Highlights

More at ClassZone.com

Economics Update

Go to **ECONOMICS UPDATE** for chapter updates and further information on inflation in the 1970s. (See Case Study, pp. 404–405.) ▶

SMARTGrapher

Go to **SMART GRAPHER** to complete graphing activities in this chapter.

Interactive Review

Go to **INTERACTIVE REVIEW** for concept review and activities.

How did inflation in the 1970s affect people and businesses? See the Case Study on pages 404–405.

From the Classroom

Michael Bruce, William Fremd H.S.

Poverty and Social Differences

To demonstrate the idea that economic class influences one's life, I hold a "birth lotto."

I find census data that shows the percentage of households living in various income categories in the United States. I figure out how many students should represent each income category, making sure there will be at least one student in each income group.

As students enter class, they choose a number off of my desk. I write the income categories on the board and show how many students will represent each group. I tell them that today we will have a "birth lotto" that will randomly place them into income groups. I announce which income group we will start with—saving the extremes of wealth and poverty for the end—then choose numbers from a bag.

After all the numbers have been chosen, we discuss how their lives might be different if they had been born into this new income group. Students might also write a brief essay on the same topic.

Previewing Chapter Technology at ClassZone.com

Economics Update Students will find updates to information in the pupil edition on pages 383, 389, 394, 397, and 404.

Interactive Review Students will find additional section and chapter assessment support for materials on pages 387, 395, 403, and 406.

TEACHER MEDIA FAVORITES

Books

- Solow, Robert M., and John B Taylor. *Inflation, Unemployment, and Monetary Policy.* Cambridge, MA: MIT Press, 1999. A lively exchange of views by leading economists on public policy matters.
- Bernanke, Ben S., Thomas Laubach, Frederic S. Mishkin, and Adam S. Posen. *Inflation Targeting: Lessons from the International Experience.* Princeton, NJ: Princeton UP, 2001. Case studies of nations with inflation problems.
- Mangum, Garth L., Stephen L. Mangum, and Andrew M. Sum. *The Persistence of Poverty in the United States.* Baltimore, MD: Johns Hopkins UP, 2003. Overview of poverty in the United States.

Videos/DVDs

- *Unemployment, Inflation, and National Output.* 28 minutes. Films for the Humanities & Sciences, 1993. This film explains how unemployment and inflation are measured and their relation to business cycles.
- *Outsourcing: White Collar Exodus.* 51 minutes. Films for the Humanities & Sciences, 2005. This film examines the pros and cons of outsourcing and includes many real-life examples, including India's call centers.

Internet

Visit **ClassZone.com** to link to
- a variety of chapter-specific, content-reviewed sites
- updates on data and topics presented throughout the chapter sections and Case Study
- updates to the Power Presentations

1 Plan & Prepare

Section 1 Objectives

- explain how economists measure unemployment
- identify the different types of unemployment
- discuss the impact that unemployment has on the economy and on individuals

2 Focus & Motivate

Connecting to Everyday Life Point out that about two-thirds of Americans aged 16–24 are part of the labor force in the summers. Ask students to review what labor force means. *(people 16 or older actively looking for work or working)* Ask students to discuss why a summer job is so important, especially to students who have just graduated from high school. *(to bolster college funds; to gain experience; to get started in a vocation)* Also ask students to consider what would happen if they were not able to find work. Point out that the unemployment rate is directly tied to opportunity for advancement and that young people are often the hardest hit when unemployment is high.

Taking Notes Remind students to take notes as they read by completing a cluster diagram on unemployment. They can use the Graphic Organizer at **Interactive Review @ ClassZone.com**. A sample is shown below.

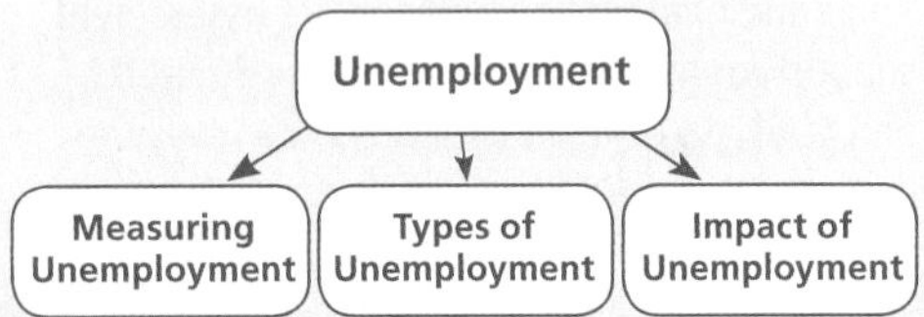

SECTION 1

Unemployment in Today's Economy

OBJECTIVES

In Section 1, you will
- explain how economists measure unemployment
- identify the different types of unemployment
- discuss the impact that unemployment has on the economy and on individuals

KEY TERMS

unemployment rate, *p. 382*
underemployed, *p. 383*
full employment, *p. 383*
frictional unemployment, *p. 384*
seasonal unemployment, *p. 384*
structural unemployment, *p. 384*
cyclical unemployment, *p. 384*

TAKING NOTES

As you read Section 1, complete a cluster diagram like the one below to record and organize what you learn about unemployment. Use the Graphic Organizer at **Interactive Review @ ClassZone.com**

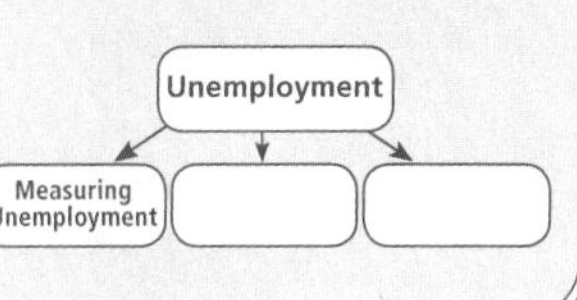

Measuring Unemployment

KEY CONCEPTS

In November 2005, General Motors Corporation announced that it would close or scale back about a dozen plants and lay off about 30,000 workers. The impact of a decision like that on the towns where the factories are located can be extensive. Because the unemployed cannot buy as many goods and services as they did when they had a paycheck, other area businesses might decrease output, and they might even lay off some of their own workers. If businesses across the country decide to stop hiring or to cut back, the decreased production might reduce gross domestic product (GDP), the leading measure of a country's economic health. Economists use unemployment figures to judge the performance of the economy. The measure they use most is the **unemployment rate**, the percentage of the labor force that is jobless and actively looking for work.

QUICK REFERENCE

The **unemployment rate** is the percentage of the labor force that is jobless and looking for work.

Unemployment Job fairs allow people looking for work to meet with many potential employers.

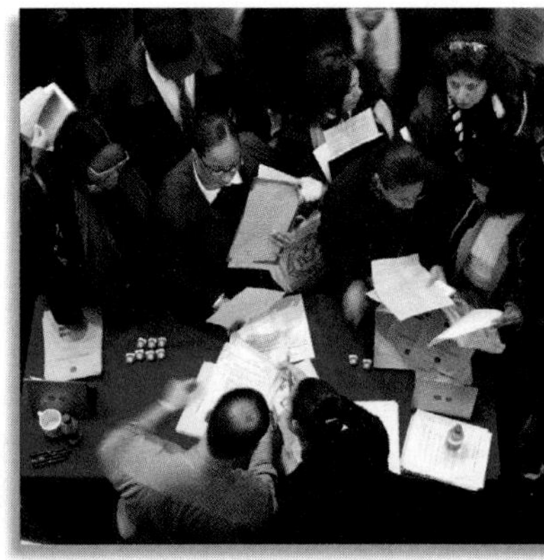

The Unemployment Rate

The civilian labor force, as you learned in Chapter 9, is made up of people over the age of 16 who are employed or actively looking and available for work. It does not include people in the military or those in schools, prisons, or other institutions. To determine the unemployment rate, the U.S. Bureau of Labor Statistics (BLS) surveys the labor

SECTION 1 PROGRAM RESOURCES

ON LEVEL

Lesson Plans
- Core, p. 43

Unit 5 Resource Book
- Reading Study Guide, pp. 53–54
- Economic Simulations, pp. 89–90
- Section Quiz, p. 61

STRUGGLING READERS

Unit 5 Resource Book
- Reading Study Guide with Additional Support, pp. 55–57
- Reteaching Activity, p. 62

ENGLISH LEARNERS

Unit 5 Resource Book
- Reading Study Guide with Additional Support (Spanish), pp. 58–60

INCLUSION

Lesson Plans
- Modified for Inclusion, p. 43

GIFTED AND TALENTED

Unit 5 Resource Book
- Readings in Free Enterprise: The Phillips Curve, pp. 85–86

TECHNOLOGY

eEdition DVD-ROM
eEdition Online
Power Presentation DVD-ROM
Economics Concepts Transparencies
- CT43 Types of Unemployment

Daily Test Practice Transparencies, TT43
ClassZone.com

FIGURE 13.1 U.S. UNEMPLOYMENT RATE

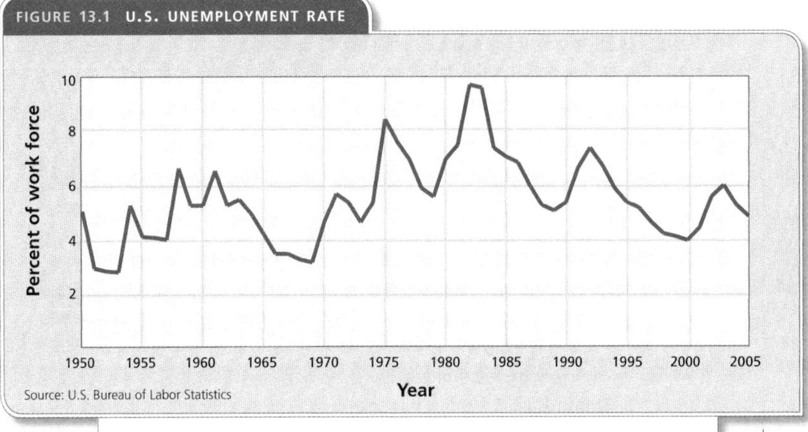

ANALYZE GRAPHS

1. From 1950 to 2005, when was the unemployment rate the highest?
2. From 1950 to 2005, when was the unemployment rate the lowest?

Economics Update

Find an update on the U.S. unemployment rate at **ClassZone.com**

force in 60,000 households each month. Workers over the age of 16 who are not working but are able to work and who have looked for work sometime during the previous four weeks are considered unemployed. The BLS then divides the number of unemployed persons by the total number of workers in the civilian labor force to arrive at the unemployment rate. While very useful, the unemployment rate does not account for discouraged workers who have stopped looking for work. Nor does it count the **underemployed**, those who work part-time when they want full-time employment or those who work at a job below their skill level. These include recently laid-off workers who may be in a temporary, lower-paying job.

QUICK REFERENCE

The **underemployed** are part-time workers who want to work full-time or people working below their skill level.

Full employment means no unemployment caused by decreased economic activity.

Full Employment

Despite its name, **full employment** does not mean a zero unemployment rate. Instead, it means a level of unemployment in which none of the unemployment is caused by decreased economic activity. Even in a healthy economy there is always some level of unemployment. Sometimes people become unemployed when they relocate or when they leave one job to try to find another job that suits them better. Sometimes the available jobs do not match up with the skills of the available workers. In other words, some amount of unemployment is inevitable.

Economists generally agree that an unemployment rate of four to six percent indicates full employment in the United States. In other countries, with different labor markets and economic policies, full employment may occur at higher or lower rates of unemployment.

APPLICATION Explaining an Economic Concept

A. Explain why the unemployment rate is based on a country's civilian labor force, not its entire population. Some segments of the population, such as children younger than 16, the retired, and those incapable of working, are not considered unemployed.

3 Teach

Measuring Unemployment

Discuss

- What does the unemployment rate measure? *(percentage of the job force that wants to work but cannot find a job)* What does it not measure? *(discouraged workers and the underemployed)* Why do economists measure unemployment? *(It reflects the overall performance of the economy.)*
- What does full employment mean? *(that nobody is unemployed because of decreased economic activity)* Why is a small amount of unemployment inevitable? *(people change jobs; poor match between available jobs and skills of available workers; relocation)*

Analyze Graphs: Figure 13.1

Have students review the graph on page 366 and explain the unemployment rate curve in terms of GDP and business cycles. *(Generally, decreases in unemployment correspond to increases in GDP.)*

Answers

1. *1982 (9.7 percent)*
2. *1953 (2.9 percent)*

Economics Update

At **ClassZone.com** students will see updated information on the U.S. unemployment rate.

LEVELED ACTIVITY

Understanding Business Cycles

Time 30–45 Minutes 

Objective Students will demonstrate an understanding of the cause-and-effect chains in economic challenges. (Concepts involved in this activity are covered in all three sections of this chapter.)

Basic

Choose one of the following topics: unemployment, poverty, or inflation. Identify a cause-and-effect chain (at least three causes and effects) related to the topic chosen and represent it in a flow chart. Then, write a paragraph explaining how the effect of the first cause becomes a cause for the next effect, and so on.

On Level

Choose one of the following topics: unemployment, poverty, or inflation. Identify a cause-and-effect chain (at least three causes and effects) in your topic, as well as one cause-and-effect chain that connects that topic with another. Then, write a brief essay explaining the cause-and-effect chains on both the economy and on individuals.

Challenge

Create a graphic representation of a chain or cycle of causes and effects that tie together the following topics: unemployment, poverty, and inflation. Then, write an essay explaining how a change in one cause on your graphic (higher unemployment, for example) would spread through the rest of the chain or cycle.

Types of Unemployment

Discuss

- Why might frictional unemployment be called that? *(Possible answer: It refers to people moving from job to job. When there is movement, there is often also friction.)*
- Which type of unemployment seems the most serious? Which the least serious? Why? *(Answers will vary on which is the most serious—look for well-reasoned answers. Frictional unemployment is the least serious and may be interpreted as a sign of economic freedom.)*

Technomics

Unemployment Statistics

The U.S. Bureau of Labor Statistics (BLS) gathers, maintains, and makes public a vast amount of information about unemployment. The BLS publishes current data on a regular basis and maintains archives of data on previous years. In addition to state and national statistics, BLS also—through a partnership with state governments—gathers monthly unemployment information on over 7,000 local areas, including census regions and divisions and all metropolitan areas with 25,000 people or more.

The BLS publishes unemployment data in periodic bulletins and on its Web site. The BLS Web site includes copies of the print publications as well as databases that can be used to create customized maps and tables.

Presentation Options

Review the four types of unemployment by using the following presentation options:

 **Power Presentations DVD-ROM**

Using the Display Tool, you can highlight the types of unemployment recognized by economists, and see how they impact an increasing number of people.

 **Economics Concepts Transparencies**

- CT43 Types of Unemployment

Types of Unemployment

QUICK REFERENCE

Frictional unemployment is temporary unemployment of people changing jobs.

Seasonal unemployment is unemployment linked to seasonal work.

Structural unemployment is when jobs exist but do not match the skills of available workers.

Cyclical unemployment is unemployment caused by a part of the business cycle with decreased economic activity.

KEY CONCEPTS

Economists pay attention not only to the unemployment statistics, but also to the reasons for unemployment. Economists recognize four types of unemployment:

- **Frictional unemployment**, temporary unemployment experienced by people changing jobs
- **Seasonal unemployment**, unemployment linked to seasonal work
- **Structural unemployment**, a situation where jobs exist but workers looking for work do not have the necessary skills for these jobs
- **Cyclical unemployment**, unemployment caused by a part of the business cycle with decreased economic activity

TYPE 1 Frictional Unemployment

Frictional unemployment refers to the temporary unemployment of workers moving from one job to another. The frictionally unemployed might include a parent who has spent time at home raising children and decides to move back into the work force; a magazine designer who leaves his job to seek work as a designer at a book publisher; or a recent college graduate who is looking for her first full-time job. Frictional unemployment is a reflection of workers' freedom to find the work best suited for them at the highest possible wage. Economists consider frictional unemployment normal and not a threat to economic stability.

TYPE 2 Seasonal Unemployment

Demand for some jobs changes dramatically from season to season, resulting in seasonal unemployment. Demand for construction workers, for example, typically falls in the winter months when construction activities are more difficult. Tourism peaks at certain times of the year, and different regions have different tourist seasons. Migrant farm workers, who move from one area to another following the growing schedules of the crops, are hard hit by seasonal unemployment. The winter months are especially slow, resulting in economic hardship for many migrant families.

Seasonal Unemployment Demand for lifeguards is high during the warmer months.

TYPE 3 Structural Unemployment

Structural unemployment results when the available jobs do not match up well with the skills and experience of the available workers. A dynamic economy will often create structural unemployment as businesses become more efficient and require fewer workers to create the same amount of output. There are a number of possible triggers for structural unemployment. New technology can replace human workers or require workers to retrain. New industries requiring specialized education can leave less well-educated workers

DIFFERENTIATING INSTRUCTION

Struggling Readers

Follow Continuous Text

Have students explain where they continue reading when they get to the end of page 384. If they say that they go to the continuation of the paragraph on page 385, ask why. Try to elicit the answer that the regular text continues there, even though a feature at the top of the page interrupts it. Ask students to discuss why their reading of "A Global Perspective" will be somewhat different from their reading of the continuous text.

Inclusion

Illustrate Types of Unemployment

Direct students to design a page with four distinct sections on it. Then, have them illustrate the different types of unemployment in those sections. The style of illustration—hand drawing, computer-generated graphics, clip art—should be determined by the students' strengths and preferences.

A GLOBAL PERSPECTIVE

Offshore Outsourcing: Scourge or Boon?

Many American workers fear losing their jobs to offshore outsourcing—the contracting of work to suppliers in other countries. But the likelihood of offshore outsourcing varies widely from one occupation to the next. According to a report issued by the McKinsey Global Institute in 2005, about 11 percent of all service jobs in the United States have the potential to be outsourced to another country. Jobs in information technology, engineering, and accounting are much more likely to be outsourced than jobs in health care, retail sales, and other fields that require direct personal interaction.

The offshore outsourcing trend has created some structural unemployment, as laid-off workers seek new jobs. But ultimately, it should make the U.S. economy more efficient. The firms that save money by outsourcing will be more competitive. As these businesses grow, they will hire more U.S. workers.

Office worker in India

For some U.S. workers, outsourcing may offer unique opportunities. India has been so successful in securing business outsourced by other countries that it has a shortage of qualified labor. Because many jobs outsourced to India require workers to be fluent in English or European languages, one study predicts that 120,000 Europeans, Americans, and Australians will be working in India by 2010.

CONNECTING ACROSS THE GLOBE

1. **Synthesizing Economic Information** Explain how outsourcing might change the American economy.
2. **Evaluating** What career do you want to pursue? Explain whether it has the potential to be outsourced.

out of work. A change in consumer demand—from compact discs to computer music files, for example—can shift the type of workers needed. Offshore outsourcing, when jobs once held by Americans are staffed overseas, is another cause of structural unemployment.

TYPE 4 Cyclical Unemployment

Cyclical unemployment results when the economy hits a low point in the business cycle and employers decide to lay off workers. Workers who lose their jobs during a recession can have trouble finding new jobs because the economy as a whole is scaling back, and the demand for labor declines. When the economy picks up again, many workers are again able to find jobs.

The duration of unemployment in these four types ranges widely, but the average duration of unemployment is relatively short. More than a third of the unemployed are out of work for five weeks or less.

APPLICATION Making Inferences

B. If you owned a clothing factory, how would a high rate of unemployment affect your business?

High unemployment would make it easier to find workers, but it might also reduce the demand for clothing.

A Global Perspective

Offshore Outsourcing: Scourge or Boon?
Offshore outsourcing often has little impact on unemployment in the countries that receive the new jobs. Although some jobs once filled in the United States are now outsourced to other countries, unemployment in those countries remains a problem.

In India, for example, about 90 percent of the labor force works in parts of the economy not covered by such regulations as the minimum wage. Even though many new jobs have been created in India since the late 1900s, population growth has outstripped the increase in new jobs.

Answers

1. *Outsourcing creates some structural unemployment, but ultimately makes the economy more efficient.*
2. *Answers will vary, but look for an understanding of pertinent concepts.*

More About . . .

Measuring Unemployment
The key measure of unemployment is the number of jobless claims received by the U.S. Department of Labor.

Another measure approaches the data from a different angle—that of the employer. A non-profit organization, The Conference Board, keeps a Help-Wanted Advertising Index as a way of assessing how many businesses are hiring workers.

SMALL GROUP ACTIVITY

Understanding Types of Unemployment

Time 30 Minutes

Task Understand the human impact of the various types of unemployment

Materials Needed paper and pens

Activity

- Divide students into four groups, one for each type of unemployment on these pages. Have each group choose an example that demonstrates that kind of unemployment.
- Ask each group to create a fictional person who is experiencing the type of unemployment they have chosen.
- Instruct them to collaborate in preparing a letter that their person would write to a friend. The letter should explain how the person became unemployed, what it is like to be unemployed, and what the person plans to do about it.
- Have each group read its letter to the class, and allow a brief discussion after each presentation.

Rubric

	Understanding of Types of Unemployment	Presentation of Information
4	excellent	original and complete
3	good	clear and complete
2	fair	mostly clear and complete
1	poor	unclear and incomplete

The Impact of Unemployment

Discuss

- Inefficiency clearly affects the economy as a whole. But how do inequality and discouraged workers affect the whole economy, not just the individuals involved? *(Both affect efficiency, since workers who might otherwise be able to add productively to the economy are shut out.)*
- What other social impact might unemployment have? *(Possible answers: It can lead to civil unrest, as it did in France in 2005 among unemployed and mainly minority youths. Also, it can draw down such government resources as unemployment insurance.)*

Analyzing Graphs: Figures 13.2 and 13.3

Help students practice drawing conclusions by asking them to write comparative statements using the information in these charts. That is, each statement should include a comparison of at least two of the groups identified in the charts. For example: *A slightly higher percentage of people age 35 to 44 are unemployed than people age 45 to 54.* Have students think of as many comparative statements as possible. As a class, check each one for accuracy.

Answers

1. *people 16 to 19 years old*
2. *Generally, it goes down.*
3. *Retired people are not counted as part of the work force because they are not actively looking for work.*

The Impact of Unemployment

KEY CONCEPTS

Although some unemployment is unavoidable, excessive or persistent unemployment hurts the economy in several ways. It reduces efficiency; it hurts the least economically secure; and it damages workers' self-confidence.

Efficiency Unemployment is inefficient. It wastes human resources, one of the key factors of economic growth.

Inequality Unemployment does not follow equal opportunity rules. In an economic slowdown, those with the least experience lose their jobs first—usually minorities and the young (see the graphs below). Also, with fewer jobs available, people on the lower rungs of the employment ladder have less opportunity to advance.

Discouraged Workers People who are unemployed—or underemployed—for long periods of time may begin to lose faith in their abilities to get a job that suits their skills. Potentially productive workers may give up their search for work. If they are underemployed, they may not be motivated to do their best work.

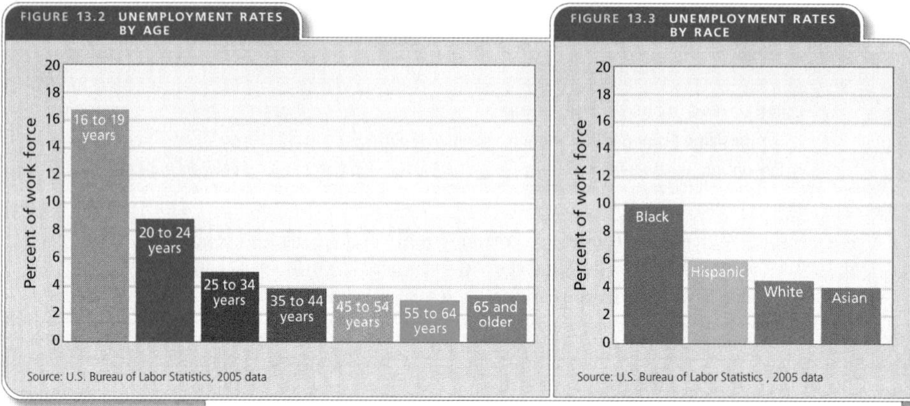

ANALYZE GRAPHS

1. Which group, either age or race, has the highest rate of unemployment?
2. What happens to the unemployment rate as people get older?
3. If the majority of people aged 65 and older are retired, why is the unemployment rate for that group so low?

APPLICATION Writing About Economics

C. In 1889, Jane Addams founded the Hull House Association in Chicago to help newly arrived immigrants adjust to the challenges of city life. In 1910, she wrote that "of all the aspects of social misery nothing is so heartbreaking as unemployment." Write a paragraph explaining the impact of unemployment on immigrants.

Look for paragraphs that include the impact of unemployment on efficiency, inequality, and self-esteem.

DIFFERENTIATING INSTRUCTION

English Learners

Distinguish Between Words

Point out the last sentence in the paragraph headed by "Inequality." Ask a volunteer to read it aloud. Then have students infer the difference between the words *fewer* and *less*. *(*Fewer *refers to specific numbers of things and means "not as many."* Less *refers to something in the aggregate and means "not as much.")* Give students the following words and ask them whether *fewer* or *less* would be the correct choice—dollars *(fewer)*, money *(less)*, inflation *(less)*, and injuries *(fewer)*.

Gifted and Talented

Research and Present

Direct students to research cultural references to the value of work (or the cost of unemployment). For example, Mark Twain said, "What work I have done I have done because it has been play." Ask students to find comments about work made by other cultural icons. Then, have them create a presentation in the style of the person they chose that draws some conclusions about the value our culture places on work.

SECTION 1 Assessment

REVIEWING KEY CONCEPTS

1. Explain the relationship between the terms in each of these pairs.
   a. *frictional unemployment* *structural unemployment*
   b. *seasonal unemployment* *cyclical unemployment*
2. Explain how the unemployment rate is calculated.
3. Why are economists interested in the unemployment rate?
4. Name a job that might be affected by structural unemployment. Explain why it might be affected.
5. What is full employment?
6. **Using Your Notes** Write a brief summary of this section, covering measuring unemployment, types of unemployment, and the impact of unemployment. Refer to your completed cluster diagram.

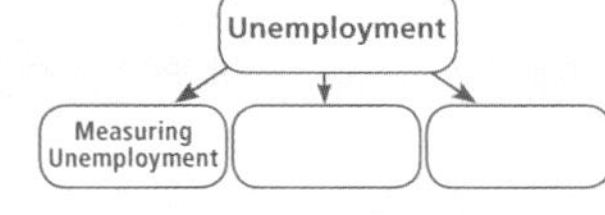

Use the Graphic Organizer at **Interactive Review @ ClassZone.com**

CRITICAL THINKING

7. **Solving Economic Problems** Unemployment insurance provides money to workers who have lost their jobs through no fault of their own. In most states, the insurance is funded entirely by employers. What else might business and government do to help unemployed workers?
8. **Analyzing Cause and Effect** In June 2005, claims for unemployment insurance in Illinois from construction workers made up about 14 percent of all claims. In December 2005, they made up about 21 percent. Why might more construction workers file for unemployment benefits in December than in June? What type of unemployment best explains the difference?
9. **Applying Economic Concepts** Give specific examples from the Great Depression of the 1930s of ways in which the widespread unemployment (1) affected efficiency, (2) was distributed unequally, and (3) eroded self-esteem.
10. **Challenge** Think about the type of career you hope to have when you are finished with your education. Do you think it is more likely or less likely than others to be affected by each of the various types of unemployment? Explain each of your answers.

ECONOMICS IN PRACTICE

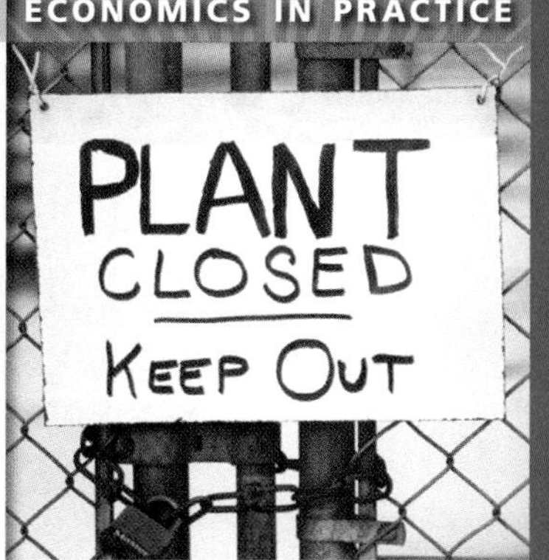

Identifying Types of Unemployment
Read the following descriptions of unemployment scenarios.

Categorize Economic Information Decide which of the four types of unemployment each scenario describes.

- Because of reduced demand, an appliance company temporarily closes one of its factories and lays off workers.
- In September, a part-time student at the University of Central Florida in Orlando loses his job at a theme park.
- A newspaper journalist leaves her job to make a switch into television journalism. She has been looking for a new job for several months.
- A local travel agency has to close down because of the widespread availability of direct online booking options.

Challenge Young people are two to three times more likely than older people to be unemployed. Why is this?

4 Assess & Reteach

Assess Discuss the first six questions as a whole class. For questions 7–10, pair students and have each pair work together to answer the questions. Allow time for each pair to present their question and answers to the class.

Unit 5 Resource Book
- Section Quiz, p. 61

Interactive Review @ ClassZone.com
- Section Quiz

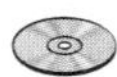

Test Generator CD-ROM
- Section Quiz

Reteach To review this section, have students share with the rest of the class the work they completed on the Leveled Activity on page 383.

Unit 5 Resource Book
- Reteaching Activity, p. 62

Economics in Practice
Categorize Economic Information
1. cyclical
2. seasonal
3. frictional
4. structural

Challenge Answers will vary but may include that young workers have less experience, skills, and education than older workers.

SECTION 1 ASSESSMENT ANSWERS

Reviewing Key Concepts
1. a. *frictional unemployment*, p. 384; *structural unemployment*, p. 384
   b. *seasonal unemployment*, p. 384; *cyclical unemployment*, p. 384
2. the BLS divides the number of unemployed persons by the total number of workers in the civilian labor force
3. because it reflects changes in economic activity
4. Sample answers: A TV repair person who only knows how to work on CRTs might lose their job as flat-screen TVs become the norm. The employees of a local grocery store might lose their jobs after a large chain opens nearby and drives the shop out of business.
5. the employment rate at which there is no unemployment as a result of decreased economic activity (about 4 to 6 percent)
6. See page 382 for an example of a completed diagram. Answers will vary, but should show an understanding of the measurement, types, and impact of unemployment.

Critical Thinking
7. Answers will vary but are likely to include job retraining or other kinds of education.
8. Less construction is done in the winter months; seasonal unemployment.
9. Sample answers: (1) Economic output declined by about a third, leaving many valuable resources unused. (2) People with jobs that fulfilled everyday needs—such as schoolteachers and transportation workers—survived better than others; the poorest were the hardest hit. (3) Millions of people who had been self-sufficient had to resort to handouts and soup lines to survive.
10. Answers will vary, but look for a well thought out response that reflects an understanding of the various types of unemployment.

Economics in Practice
See answers in side column above.

1 Plan & Prepare

Section 2 Objectives

- explain how economists measure poverty
- discuss the causes of poverty
- describe how economists measure income inequality
- identify what antipoverty programs are available

2 Focus & Motivate

Connecting to Everyday Life Tell students that in a speech in 2006, Louise Arbour, the UN's High Commissioner for Human Rights, identified poverty as the world's "most serious . . . and widespread human rights violation." She believes it denies people of their full range of rights—from political and social to civil, cultural, and economic. Engage students in a discussion of how poverty relates to human rights. If students disagree with Arbour's assertion, encourage them to explain.

Taking Notes Remind students to take notes as they read by completing a summary chart. They can use the Graphic Organizer at **Interactive Review @ ClassZone.com**. A sample is shown below.

What Is Poverty?	Problem of Poverty	Antipoverty Programs	Hernando de Soto
poverty threshold	factors affecting poverty	programs for low-income households	property rights
poverty rate	income distribution	general programs	poor as source of wealth

SECTION 2

Poverty and Income Distribution

OBJECTIVES

In Section 2, you will
- explain how economists measure poverty
- discuss the causes of poverty
- describe how economists measure income inequality
- identify what antipoverty programs are available

KEY TERMS

poverty, *p. 388*
poverty threshold, *p. 388*
poverty rate, *p. 389*
income distribution, *p. 390*
income inequality, *p. 390*
Lorenz curve, *p. 391*
welfare, *p. 392*
workfare, *p. 393*

TAKING NOTES

As you read Section 2, complete a summary chart like the one below to pull together the most important ideas about poverty and income distribution. Use the Graphic Organizer at **Interactive Review @ ClassZone.com**

What Is Poverty?			

What Is Poverty?

QUICK REFERENCE

Poverty is the condition where a person's income and resources do not allow him or her to achieve a minimum standard of living.

Poverty threshold is the minimum income needed to pay for the basic expenses of living.

KEY CONCEPTS

Persistent unemployment sometimes leads to **poverty**, a situation in which a person lacks the income and resources to achieve a minimum standard of living. This minimum standard varies from country to country because different countries have different ways of life. Someone who herds sheep and lives in a hut would probably be considered poor in the United States. But such a person might be thought to have a comfortable life in some other countries. Because of such disparities, there is no universal standard for what constitutes poverty.

The U.S. government has established its own standard for poverty based on income levels. This **poverty threshold** is the official minimum income needed for the basic necessities of life in the United States.

The Poverty Threshold

The poverty threshold, also called the poverty line, is the amount of income the government has determined to be necessary for meeting basic expenses. People with incomes below that threshold are considered to live in poverty. The threshold, first formulated in the early 1960s, was calculated by finding the cost of nutritionally sound food and then multiplying by three, on the assumption that food costs are about a third of a person's expenses.

The threshold differs according to the size of the household and is adjusted annually to reflect changing prices. In 2005, the poverty threshold for a family of four in the United States was about $20,000. That same year, the median income for a family of four was over $65,000.

SECTION 2 PROGRAM RESOURCES

ON LEVEL

Lesson Plans
- Core, p. 44

Unit 5 Resource Book
- Reading Study Guide, pp. 63–64
- Economic Skills and Problem Solving Activity, pp. 83–84
- Section Quiz, p. 71

STRUGGLING READERS

Unit 5 Resource Book
- Reading Study Guide with Additional Support, pp. 65–67
- Reteaching Activity, p. 72

ENGLISH LEARNERS

Unit 5 Resource Book
- Reading Study Guide with Additional Support (Spanish), pp. 68–70

INCLUSION

Lesson Plans
- Modified for Inclusion, p. 44

GIFTED AND TALENTED

NCEE Student Activities
- Poverty and Income Distribution, pp. 49–52

TECHNOLOGY

eEdition DVD-ROM

eEdition Online

Power Presentation DVD-ROM

Economics Concepts Transparencies
- CT44 Income Distribution in the United States, 2004

Daily Test Practice Transparencies, TT44

ClassZone.com

The Poverty Rate

The **poverty rate** is the percentage of people living in households that have incomes below the poverty threshold. Unlike the unemployment rate, the poverty rate is based on the population as a whole. Through census information, the poverty rate can be estimated for individuals, households, or specific segments of the population, such as African-American children or single-parent households.

The overall poverty rate in the United States declined between 1993 and 2000 to a low of 11.3 percent. It began to rise in 2000 and by 2004 had climbed to 12.7 percent, with 37 million people living below the poverty line. (See Figure 13.4.)

Poverty, like unemployment, does not hit all sectors of society equally. Children are especially at risk. Children made up more than half of the 1.3 million increase in the number of people living in poverty between 2002 and 2003. The number of families below the poverty line that are headed by a single mother also rose. Minorities and families that live in either an inner city or a rural area tend to have higher than average poverty rates. While the numbers tell the statistical story of poverty, only personal voices can convey the toll of being poor. James Baldwin, an African-American writer born in poverty, wrote that "anyone who has ever struggled with poverty knows how extremely expensive it is to be poor."

QUICK REFERENCE

The **poverty rate** is the percentage of people living in households that have incomes below the poverty threshold.

FIGURE 13.4 U.S. POVERTY RATE, 1959–2004

Percent of total population: 0, 5, 10, 15, 20, 25

Years: 1960, 1965, 1970, 1975, 1980, 1985, 1990, 1995, 2000, 2005

Source: U.S. Census Bureau

ANALYZE GRAPHS

1. From 1959 to 2004, when was the poverty rate the highest? When was it lowest?
2. What decade saw the largest drop in the rate of poverty?

Economics Update

Find an update on the U.S. poverty rate at **ClassZone.com**

APPLICATION Drawing Conclusions

A. Why is the poverty rate based on the entire population, while the unemployment rate is based on the civilian work force?

Poverty affects everyone, but unemployment only affects those with the potential to have a job.

3 Teach

What Is Poverty?

Discuss

- Does the way the poverty threshold was originally determined seem reasonable? Why or why not? *(Answers will vary, but encourage students to determine if they spend one-third of their income on basic foods.)*
- What might James Baldwin have meant by saying it is "expensive" to be poor? *(Answers will vary, but will probably focus on the cost in terms of human potential—how much energy needs to be expended on the basics of life rather than on developing full potential.)*

Analyze Graphs: Figure 13.4

Ask students how recent business cycles might explain the falling and then rising poverty in the years from 1990 to 2004. *(expansion from 1991 to 2001, then a contraction, which match the shape of the line)* Have students compare this graph to the graph of unemployment on page 383 and draw conclusions about their relationship. *(Unemployment and poverty appear to be related.)*

Answers

1. *highest–1959; lowest–1973-74, or 2000*
2. *the 1960s*

Economics Update

At **ClassZone.com** students will see updated information on the U.S. poverty rate.

SMALL GROUP ACTIVITY

Considering Careers

Time 30 Minutes 

Task Identify a career that would help fight poverty.

Materials Needed paper and pens, several career encyclopedias or other career-cataloging books to share

Activity

- Have students work in pairs to identify a career that would either help fight poverty or help people living in poverty.
- Encourage students to imagine careers beyond social work that would still directly impact poverty (for example, starting a business in an impoverished neighborhood).
- Direct students to describe the career, as well as the requirements for the job.
- Instruct students also to summarize what they think the best and worst parts of the job would be.
- Have each pair present their career to the class.

Rubric

	Understanding of Poverty Fighting Careers	Presentation of Information
4	excellent	creative ideas, original presentation
3	good	interesting, good presentation
2	fair	standard ideas, acceptable presentation
1	poor	incomplete or careless

The Problem of Poverty

Discuss

- Is a lower level of education a cause of poverty or a result? *(Both answers are possible: It is a cause of poverty because it keeps workers out of better paying jobs; it is a result of poverty because many people have to work to support a family and cannot afford to go to college or to seek other post-secondary education.)*
- Why is income inequality of interest to economists and policymakers? *(To the extent that the government seeks to redress economic inequality, economists and policymakers must track it to develop sound programs. Also, lawmakers are accountable to the electorate and are charged with representing the interests of their constituents, including those who live in poverty.)*

More About . . .

Income Inequality

While working on a doctoral degree at the University of Wisconsin, Max O. Lorenz wrote a paper on the inequality of wealth. In it, he developed what has become known as the Lorenz curve, a graphical representation of income distribution. Lorenz developed it as a way to describe the extent of inequality in a society. Since the paper was published in 1905, the Lorenz curve has become the foundation of much research into income inequality.

Lorenz, an economist, worked for the federal government for a number of years, including service at the Census Bureau, the Bureau of Railway Economics, the Bureau of Statistics, and the Interstate Commerce Commission.

The Problem of Poverty

KEY CONCEPTS

Across the globe, about half of the world's 6 billion people live in poverty. In the United States, one of the world's wealthiest countries, almost 40 million people live below the poverty level. Even good economic times, such as the boom that the United States experienced in the 1990s, do little to move large numbers of people out of poverty. Why is an adequate income out of reach for so many people?

Factors Affecting Poverty

Four major factors have the strongest influence on who lives in poverty in the United States: education, discrimination, demography, and changes in the labor force.

Education As you learned in Chapter 9, usually there is a direct relationship between level of education and income: the higher the level of education, the higher the income. In the United States, the poverty rate of people who did not complete high school is 12 times higher than that of people with a college education.

Discrimination White males tend to have higher incomes than racial minorities and women, even when there are no differences in education or experience. Certain groups sometimes face wage discrimination or occupational segregation and may find it difficult to move beyond low-paying jobs. Government initiatives, as well as the pressures of the competitive marketplace, have helped to reduce job discrimination.

Demographic Trends In the 1950s, about one-fourth of all marriages ended in divorce. Now, almost half of all marriages end in divorce. Over the same period, births to unmarried mothers jumped from about 5 percent of all births to over 30 percent. Such demographic trends lead to higher poverty rates because single-parent families are more likely to have economic problems than two-parent families.

Changes in the Labor Force The shift in the labor force from mainly manufacturing to mainly service industries is one of the changes that affects the distribution of poverty. When manufacturing jobs were plentiful, even relatively low-skilled workers were able to earn a good wage. As the jobs shifted from manufacturing to service, the wages did not always follow. Workers in many service jobs, such as fast-food clerks, tend to earn lower wages than similarly skilled workers in manufacturing.

Income Distribution

The United States has one of the highest median family incomes in the world, yet millions of Americans live below the poverty line. This disparity is reflected in the country's **income distribution**, the way income is divided among people in a nation.

All countries have some degree of **income inequality**, an unequal distribution of income. Unless everyone earns the same amount, there will always be a difference between the incomes of the wealthiest citizens and those of the poorest. Compared to other advanced nations, the United States has relatively high income inequality. However, less advanced countries tend to have the most extreme differences between what the rich earn and what the poor earn.

QUICK REFERENCE

Income distribution is the way income is divided among people.

Income inequality is the unequal distribution of income.

DIFFERENTIATING INSTRUCTION

Struggling Readers

Activate Prior Knowledge

Reinforce for students the importance of pre-reading to aid comprehension. Model the process for this lesson. Begin by activating prior knowledge—tell students what you know about the distribution of poverty already, what you would still like to know, and ideally some vivid examples of encounters with poverty or the contrast between poverty and wealth. When you have finished, ask students to do the same, to build connections with their own knowledge and experience before reading.

Inclusion

Answer Questions While Reading

Divide students into pairs. Give each pair the following questions to guide their reading of this lesson. Have them jot answers to the questions as they read.

- How does education affect poverty?
- How does discrimination affect poverty?
- How do changing social patterns affect poverty?
- How did the switch from manufacturing to service industries affect poverty?

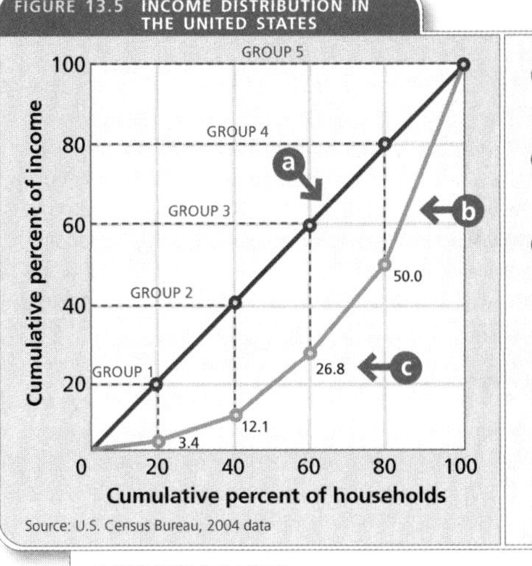

Source: U.S. Census Bureau, 2004 data

a If income were evenly divided, a line of income equality would result.

b The actual income distribution is reflected by the **Lorenz curve**.

c Each point reflects the cumulative income of that cumulative percent of households.

ANALYZE GRAPHS

1. According to the graph, about how much of the total income in the United States is earned by the lowest 60 percent of households?
2. How would the graph change if the lower groups earned a greater percent of the nation's total income?

A **Lorenz curve** graphically illustrates the degree of income inequality in a nation. The Lorenz curve in Figure 13.5, for example, plots income distribution in the United States. If income were distributed equally, then 20 percent of the population would receive 20 percent of the income, 40 percent would receive 40 percent, and so on. That distribution would be represented with a diagonal line.

However, income is not equally divided. The Lorenz curve in Figure 13.5 shows that the lowest 20 percent of the population (Group 1) receives only about 3.4 percent of the nation's total income. The lowest 40 percent (Group 2)—which includes the lowest 20 percent plus the next 20 percent—receive about 12.1 percent of the nation's total income. The more the Lorenz curve dips away from the diagonal line of equality, the greater the level of income inequality.

In the United States, the income gap between the lower 80 percent of the population and the top 20 percent grew steadily throughout the late 1900s. In 1970, the richest 20 percent of Americans earned on average 9 times more than the poorest. By 1997, they were earning 15 times more. Households are not stuck in one group. When people gain experience and education, their incomes tend to increase. When they retire or make poor economic decisions, their incomes decrease.

QUICK REFERENCE

Lorenz curve is a curve that shows the degree of income inequality in a nation.

APPLICATION Applying Economic Concepts

B. In 2004, the richest 20 percent of households in the United States received about 50 percent of the nation's income. Based on that proportion, if $100 was shared among five people, how much would the richest one receive? How much would each of the other four get if they shared the rest equally?

The richest one would get $50; the others would each get $12.50.

Analyze Graphs: Figure 13.5

Point out that the diagonal line in the Lorenz curve shows what perfect income equality would look like—if everyone got the same share of the income. To help students understand the graphic fully, ask them to identify what a line representing perfect inequality would look like. Begin by having them explain what perfect inequality would mean. *(that one person has all the income and everyone else has none)* From that point, students should be able to see that the curve would be a straight vertical line along the right side of the graph.

Answers

1. *26.8 percent*
2. *The Lorenz curve would be closer to the line of income equality (closer to diagonal).*

More About . . .

The Pay Gap

In the United States in 2005, the average corporate chief executive officer (CEO) earned more in a day than the average worker earned in a year. The compensation for CEOs was 262 times the compensation for average workers. The gap in 2005 was the second highest in the 40 years that the figures have been tracked.

SMALL GROUP ACTIVITY

Understanding Factors Affecting Poverty

Time 30 Minutes

Task Create a fictional profile of someone in the United States and determine his or her likelihood of poverty

Materials Needed paper and pens

Activity

- Divide the class into five groups, with each group creating a "profile" for an American adult. The profile should include level of education, race or ethnic group, gender, family situation, and a recent job change.
- Have students refer to the material under "Factors Affecting Poverty" on page 390, as they create their profile.
- Ask each group to write the profile, in the first person (e.g., "I am a Hispanic single mother with a college degree and have recently changed jobs from...") and present it to the class.
- After the presentations, have the groups meet again to rank the profiles in order of least to most likely to live in poverty and to give reasons why.

Rubric

	Understanding of Factors Affecting Poverty	Presentation of Information
4	excellent	polished, clear, and complete
3	good	clear and complete
2	fair	rough presentation but clear ideas
1	poor	rough and unclear

Antipoverty Programs

Discuss

Compare and contrast the government's approach to fighting poverty in the 1960s and 1970s with its approach in the 1990s and 2000s. *(Earlier efforts provided direct assistance to people in poverty in the form of transfer payments. Later efforts focused on helping people find a place in the work force.)*

- What are some programs that are designed to prevent poverty? *(Social Security, unemployment insurance)* What are some programs that are designed to help people already in poverty? *(food stamps, Medicaid, earned-income tax credit, programs aimed at communities rather than individuals, such as the community services block grants and Empowerment Zones programs)*

International Economics

Antipoverty Programs in Other Nations

Antipoverty programs in the United States reduce the extent and duration of poverty and provide medical care to the needy. But programs in other developed nations are more effective, especially in lifting children out of poverty.

According to a recent study, U.S. programs succeed in lifting one out of nine children out of a low-income bracket to half the national median income. Antipoverty programs in Canada, in contrast, lift one out of three children to that level. In some European nations, the figure is one out of two children. Also, the poorest children in the United States are poorer than the poorest children in Canada, Germany, and most other developed nations.

Antipoverty Programs

KEY CONCEPTS

QUICK REFERENCE

Welfare is government economic and social programs that provide assistance to the needy.

In 1964, in his first State of the Union Address, President Lyndon Johnson pledged: "This administration today, here and now, declares unconditional war on poverty in America." Johnson's antipoverty programs were among many that the U.S. government has tried in an effort to close the income gap. These programs are often referred to as **welfare**, government economic and social programs that provide assistance to the needy. Some of these programs, however, have been criticized for wasting government funds and for harming rather than helping the recipients. During the 1980s and 1990s, the government changed its approach, and it now uses tax breaks, grants, job training, and other "self-help" initiatives in addition to cash benefits.

Programs for Low-Income Households

The national food stamp program, which was established by the Food Stamp Act of 1964, helps ensure that no one will go hungry. Qualifying individuals and families receive electronic benefit transfers, which have replaced the paper food stamps that had been used originally. Recipients are given a card tied to an account into which the government makes monthly deposits of food benefits. The card can be used only to purchase food at grocery stores. Since 1975, the number of food stamp recipients has fluctuated from year to year from about 16 million to about 27 million. In 2005, almost 26 million people participated in the program.

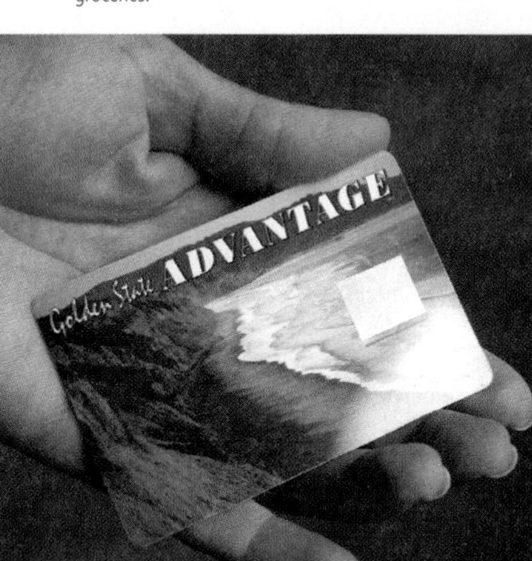

Food Stamps The food stamp program helps those with low incomes to buy groceries.

The Medicaid program is another antipoverty measure for low-income households. Medicaid offers health care for the poor and is funded by both the federal and state governments. The expense to each state is often as much as 25 percent of the state budget. Medicaid is the only health care coverage for about 40 million Americans, nearly half of them children.

Another antipoverty program is the earned-income tax credit. This program provides the working poor a refund of payroll taxes and other taxes deducted from their paychecks. About 21 million people received these credits in 2004. One benefit of the program is that the money refunded to the recipients generally gets spent in their own communities. This spending helps to boost the economies of poor neighborhoods.

General Programs

The U.S. government's Social Security program—which pays benefits to retirees, survivors, and the disabled—is the largest government program in the world. In the year 2004 alone, it paid out $500 billion, and that amount is expected to increase as people born during the baby boom after World War II reach retirement age. It was established in 1935 by the Social Security Act.

DIFFERENTIATING INSTRUCTION

English Learners

Research and Report Cooperatively

Have students work in small groups to research the benefits available to legal immigrants to the United States and to develop a presentation on that subject for the rest of the class. Point out that studies have shown that the so-called safety net for this group of Americans is weaker than for other groups. Encourage students in the group to clarify the roles each student will take in researching and presenting the information.

Gifted and Talented

Debate Welfare Programs

Have pairs research recent studies and findings from any of the following organizations: National Poverty Center at the University of Michigan; Institute of Research on Poverty at the University of Wisconsin-Madison; University of Kentucky Poverty Research Center; West Coast Poverty Research Center. Using the Web sites of these organizations, have pairs develop a debatable topic, take opposing sides, and debate in front of the class.

The Social Security program is funded through a special payroll tax. At retirement, all workers—rich and poor alike—are entitled to monthly checks to help with living expenses. Another payroll tax helps to fund Medicare, a government health insurance program for seniors. Medicare became part of the Social Security program in 1965. These benefits have been key in reducing the number of older Americans in poverty. From 1960 to 1995, the poverty rate of those aged 65 and over fell from about 35 percent to about 10 percent.

The Social Security Act also established a system of unemployment insurance administered through state governments. People who lose their jobs through no fault of their own are eligible to receive income while they look for work. Each state administers its own unemployment insurance program. Most of the programs are funded by taxes paid by employers, but in a few states employees contribute too. These benefits, which usually last no more than 26 weeks, help people avoid financial problems while they seek new employment.

Other Programs

Other antipoverty programs supplement the largest programs. One is the Community Services Block Grant program, which provides blocks of federal money to local communities to address such issues as employment, education, and housing. Job training is another. One such program provides grants to community colleges to develop training for high-tech, high-growth jobs. Another way to provide jobs for the unemployed and at the same time boost the economy of a struggling neighborhood is through Empowerment Zones. The government tries to attract businesses to these specially designated neighborhoods by not charging them certain taxes. Businesses that operate in Empowerment Zones provide needed services and offer employment opportunities to area residents.

Job Training Job training helps unemployed people to learn new skills.

In 1996, the federal welfare program underwent substantial revision in a series of changes often referred to as welfare-to-work. These changes included new incentives for working, which older welfare programs often did not provide. **Workfare**, for example, is a program that requires welfare recipients to do some kind of work in return for their benefits. Their work provides a useful service and also helps prepare the workers for future jobs. Direct financial aid, now called Temporary Assistance for Needy Families (TANF), now has a limit of five years.

QUICK REFERENCE

Workfare is a program that requires welfare recipients to do some kind of work.

APPLICATION Explaining an Economic Concept

C. In terms of government spending, what is a fundamental difference between the food stamp program and the Empowerment Zone initiative?
The first is a direct transfer payment; the second is indirect, using market forces to create benefits.

More About . . .

Fighting Welfare Fraud
While the majority of benefits recipients are honest, some recipients—and even some workers at government welfare agencies—have found ways to defraud the government through dishonest reporting. A newspaper investigation in Boston in 2006 revealed that agencies administering welfare programs often have a difficult time tracking those who cheat and following up on court orders for restitution.

An organization called United Council on Welfare Fraud helps train government workers to identify and prevent welfare fraud. Such efforts can be costly, but the savings can be even more substantial.

More About . . .

TANF
TANF's purposes include
- assisting needy families so that children can be cared for in their own homes
- reducing the welfare dependency of needy parents by promoting job preparation, work, and marriage
- preventing out-of-wedlock pregnancies
- encouraging the formation of two-parent families

TANF also addresses teens:
- Unmarried minor parents must participate in education and training and live with a responsible adult.
- States find adult-supervised settings for teens who cannot live at home.

WHOLE CLASS ACTIVITY

Holding an Election

Time 60 Minutes ●

Task Create an electorate, hear campaign speeches about government assistance, and vote.

Materials Needed paper and pens

Activity
- Divide students into five equal groups, each of which represents one of the income groups from the Lorenz curve.
- Select one "candidate" from the wealthiest group and one from the middle group. Have one candidate develop a campaign speech supporting government assistance to those in poverty. Have the other advocate alternatives to government assistance.
- While the candidates are developing their speeches, ask the other students to create a profile for themselves as part of their income group.
- Have the candidates present their speeches, then hold a vote.
- Ask students to explain their profile and their vote.

Rubric

	Understanding of Government Anti-Poverty Programs	Presentation of Information
4	excellent	creative profile and clear reasoning
3	good	believable profile and clear reasoning
2	fair	acceptable profile and reasoning
1	poor	sketchy, incomplete

Hernando de Soto

More About . . .

Hernando de Soto
The son of a Peruvian diplomat, de Soto spent the first seven years of his life in his native country. The overthrow of Peru's government in 1948 forced his family to flee. They settled in Switzerland. De Soto later returned to Peru for graduate studies. His experience as a diplomat's son may have helped prepare him for the global diplomacy that he has engaged in as he has spread his ideas about property throughout the world.

De Soto has helped effect significant changes in his home country. About 400 laws and other kinds of programs and regulations that modernized Peru's economy are credited to de Soto and his Institute for Liberty and Democracy.

More About . . .

The Other Path
The title of de Soto's first major book is a direct reference to an organization called the Shining Path, a Marxist terrorist group active in Peru when de Soto was advising the Peruvian president on economic matters.

Because of terrorism, security is very tight at the Institute for Liberty and Democracy. After a bomb killed several people at the site, armed soldiers have kept watch. However, Shining Path has all but disappeared after the capture of key leaders and military defeats in the 1990s.

Economics Update

ClassZone.com includes links to more information on Hernando de Soto.

ECONOMICS PACESETTER

Hernando de Soto: Another Path out of Poverty

Peruvian economist Hernando de Soto has attacked the problem of poverty by redefining it: "The poor . . . are essentially the biggest source of wealth within [a] country." According to de Soto, the poor have numerous assets—but in most countries they lack the basic property rights they need to grow economically. "They have houses but not titles; crops, but not deeds; businesses, but not statutes of incorporation." In short, their wealth is not protected by the rule of law.

FAST FACTS

Hernando de Soto

Title: President and Chief Executive Officer of the Institute for Liberty and Democracy

Born: 1941 in Arequipa, Peru

Major Accomplishments: Founded Institute for Liberty and Democracy

Major Publications: *The Other Path* (1986); *The Mystery of Capital: Why Capitalism Triumphs in the West and Fails Everywhere Else* (2000)

Reputation: "The poor man's capitalist"—*New York Times Magazine*

One of the "100 most influential people in the world"—*Time Magazine*

Prosperity Through Property Rights

As a young man, de Soto was struck by the sharp contrast between the poverty in Peru's shantytowns and the energetic industry of the people. These thoughts led him, in time, to establish the Institute for Liberty and Democracy (ILD), which addresses this contrast in Peru and throughout the world.

De Soto estimates that 4 billion of the world's 6 billion people are shut out of the formal economy. Antiquated and needlessly complex laws make it difficult for these people to gain legal ownership of their homes and businesses, assets that are recognized as theirs in the informal economy.

Hernando de Soto
De Soto developed innovative ideas about the origins of poverty.

De Soto estimates that the assets of the world's poor add up to about $10 *trillion.* He argues that until legal systems change to accommodate the poor, they will continue to prefer to operate in the informal economy—at the cost of lost economic opportunity for everyone. If the resources of the poor could be brought into the formal economy and developed, the wealth they would create could lift struggling nations out of poverty into prosperity.

De Soto's critics point to his non-scholarly approach, but he says that he purposely "closed the books and opened his ears" as he traveled throughout the world listening to the voices of the poor. Former U.S. President Bill Clinton echoed the sentiments of many world leaders when he described de Soto's ILD as "the most promising antipoverty initiative in the world."

Economics Update
Find an update on Hernando de Soto at **ClassZone.com**

APPLICATION Writing About Economics

D. De Soto said: "Capitalism . . . allowed the people that came from humble origins of the world to have economic rights the way only nobility . . . had it before. So capitalism is essentially a tool for poor people to prosper." Do you agree with that explanation? Write a paragraph to explain your answer.
Answers will vary but should include that the marketplace welcomes anyone who has something to exchange and that ease of market entry can lead to prosperity.

DIFFERENTIATING INSTRUCTION

Struggling Readers

Summarize
Direct students to write a one- or two-sentence summary in their own words as they finish each paragraph of this feature. Then, pair students and have them share their summaries with one another, comparing what they found to be the most important point in each paragraph and checking each other for possible inaccuracies.

Inclusion

Listen for Understanding
Pair a mainstream student with an inclusion student and have the mainstream student read aloud the material on page 394. After the selection is read, have the inclusion student retell the reading, with the reader taking notes about points included. Then, ask the reader to go back over the material with the listener for anything important that was left out.

SECTION 2 Assessment

REVIEWING KEY CONCEPTS

1. Explain the relationship between the terms in each of these pairs.
   a. *poverty threshold* *poverty rate*
   b. *income distribution* *income inequality*
   c. *welfare* *workfare*
2. Why is it difficult to determine a universal poverty threshold?
3. What groups are especially hard hit by poverty?
4. What four factors help explain the distribution of poverty?
5. What does the Lorenz curve show?
6. **Using Your Notes** Describe five different antipoverty programs and the problems each combats. Refer to your completed summary chart.

What Is Poverty?			

Use the Graphic Organizer at **Interactive Review @ ClassZone.com**

CRITICAL THINKING

7. **Making Inferences and Drawing Conclusions** A number of antipoverty programs are targeted specifically at children:
   - State Children's Health Insurance Program (SCHIP) provides health insurance to low income children who do not qualify for Medicaid and have no health insurance
   - National School Lunch Program provides free or reduced price lunches to eligible children
   - School Breakfast Program provides cash to schools for offering breakfasts to more than 8 million children nationally

   What are the economic benefits of antipoverty programs aimed at children?
8. **Solving Economic Problems** Antipoverty programs in the United States are least effective for immigrant families and for non-elderly people without children. Why might this be so?
9. **Analyzing Cause and Effect** How does the earned income tax credit aid both the working poor and their communities?
10. **Challenge** In 2005, the poverty threshold for a family of four was an annual income of just over $19,800. Based on this income, devise a monthly budget for a family of four. Assume that no taxes or payroll deductions will reduce the family's income. Also assume that the family lives in an apartment that costs $700 per month. Provide a detailed account of your estimated allowances for food, clothing, and other expenses.

Online Quiz ClassZone.com

ECONOMICS IN PRACTICE

Food aid from the United States and other nations assists those in extreme poverty.

Understanding World Poverty Different parts of the world have different levels of poverty.

FIGURE 13.6 PERCENT OF POPULATION IN POVERTY

Region	Percent
Sub-Saharan Africa	75
South-Central Asia	75
World	53
China	47
North Africa	29
Latin America / Caribbean	26
Eastern Europe	14

Source: World Bank, 2004 data

Analyze and Interpret Data Use the information in the table to answer these questions.

1. The table uses a poverty threshold of living on less than $2 a day. Why doesn't North America appear?
2. China has a population of about 1.3 billion people. About how many of them, in millions, live in poverty?

Challenge Do the same factors that affect poverty in the United States apply to the rest of the world?

4 Assess & Reteach

Assess Discuss questions 1–9, and the Economics in Practice activity as a class. For the Challenge question, divide students into groups and have them compare results when they are finished.

Unit 5 Resource Book
- Section Quiz, p. 71

Interactive Review @ ClassZone.com
- Section Quiz

Test Generator CD-ROM
- Section Quiz

Reteach Divide the class into three groups. Assign each group part of Section 2 to report on to the class. Reports should include main ideas, a summary of any graphics, and key details.

Unit 5 Resource Book
- Reteaching Activity, p. 72

Economics in Practice
Analyze and Interpret Data

1. An extremely low percentage of people in North America live on less than $2 a day.
2. about 600 million (47 percent of 1.3 billion = 611 million)

Challenge No, because the U.S. has a superabundance of material goods. The problem in the U.S. is how best to channel the excess in order to help the poor and how to help the poor become self-supporting. Many other countries truly face the problem of scarcity—there are simply not enough resources to adequately feed, clothe, and house all of the country's people.

SECTION 2 ASSESSMENT ANSWERS

Reviewing Key Concepts

1. a. *poverty threshold*, p. 388; *poverty rate*, p. 389
   b. *Income distribution*, p. 390; *income inequality*, p. 390
   c. *welfare*, p. 392; *workfare*, p. 393
2. Different countries have different standards about what constitutes poverty.
3. children, women, minorities, families headed by a single mother
4. education, discrimination, demographic trends, changes in the labor force
5. income distribution in a nation and how far away it is from equal distribution
6. See page 388 for an example of a completed diagram. Five of the following: Social Security—retirees, disabled, survivors; Medicare—health care for seniors; Medicaid—health care for the poor; food stamps—food for the poor; Community Services Block Grants—needs based on particular locality; earned income tax credit—working poor; Workfare—chronically unemployed; TANF—poor families; Job training—employable workers; Empowerment Zones—low-income neighborhoods

Critical Thinking

7. Preventing disease and malnourishment gives poor children a better chance to become productive adults.
8. Answers will vary but may include the difficulty of immigrant documentation and having benefits reach recipients. The non-elderly without children are people from which work is expected, so less direct aid is available.
9. Reduced taxes make work more profitable. The money from EIC tax refunds are spent in the recipient's neighborhood.
10. Answers will vary. Point out that people in poverty often earn significantly less than this.

Economics in Practice
See answers in side column above.

1 Plan & Prepare

Section 3 Objectives

- explain how economists measure inflation
- identify what causes inflation
- describe how inflation affects the economy

2 Focus & Motivate

Connecting to Everyday Life Ask students to consider a person who puts $1,000 in a certificate of deposit that earns 5 percent per year. After ten years, the CD is worth over $1,600. Has that person gained money in terms of purchasing power? Can the person buy more with the $1,600 ten years later than could be bought with the $1,000 ten years before? Lead the discussion to the main point: without knowing how much prices changed in those ten years, it is impossible to answer the question. If prices have risen by more than 5 percent annually, then the person would be worse off. If prices rose by less than 5 percent per year, the person would be better off.

Taking Notes Remind students to take notes as they read by completing a cluster diagram. They can use the Graphic Organizer at **Interactive Review @ ClassZone.com**. A sample is shown below.

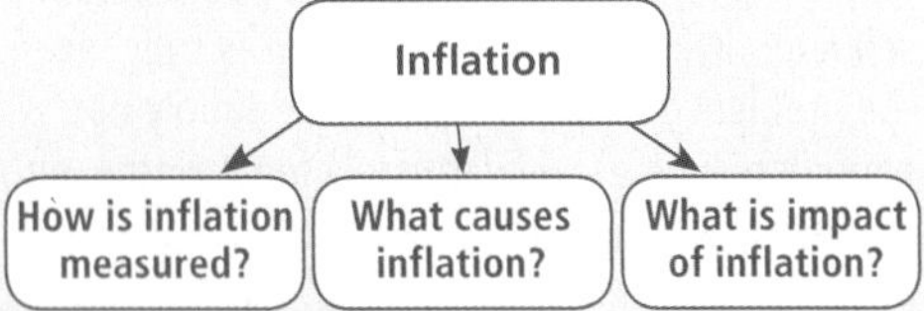

SECTION 3

Causes and Consequences of Inflation

OBJECTIVES

In Section 3, you will
- explain how economists measure inflation
- identify what causes inflation
- describe how inflation affects the economy

KEY TERMS

inflation, *p. 396*
consumer price index (CPI), *p. 396*
producer price index (PPI), *p. 397*
inflation rate, *p. 397*
hyperinflation, *p. 398*
deflation, *p. 398*
demand-pull inflation, *p. 399*
cost-push inflation, *p. 399*
wage-price spiral, *p. 400*

TAKING NOTES

As you read Section 3, complete a cluster diagram like the one below to record what you learn about inflation. Use the Graphic Organizer at **Interactive Review @ ClassZone.com**

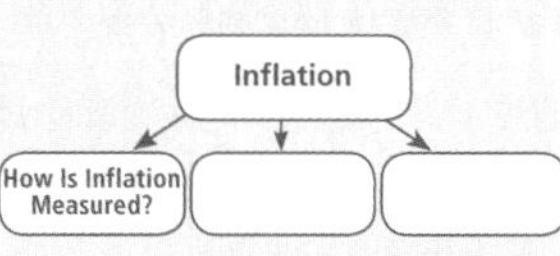

What Is Inflation and How Is It Measured?

KEY CONCEPTS

In 2006, militants attacked many of Nigeria's oil installations, demanding that more of the country's oil wealth be shared with the Nigerian people. Before the attacks, Nigeria produced about 2.5 million barrels of oil a day, and the country was the fifth largest source of oil imported by the United States. On news of the attacks, the price of oil rose by almost 20 percent. Some economists predicted that if oil stayed at those price levels, manufacturers might raise the prices of their products to compensate for higher fuel costs. They suggested that the high oil prices might ultimately lead to **inflation**, a sustained rise in the level of prices generally or a sustained fall in the purchasing power of money. Economists have several instruments for measuring inflation.

QUICK REFERENCE

Inflation is a sustained rise in the general price level or a fall in the purchasing power of money.

Consumer price index (CPI) is a measure of changes in the prices of goods and services commonly purchased by consumers.

Consumer Price Index

One tool for gauging inflation is the **consumer price index (CPI)**, a measure of changes in the prices of goods and services commonly purchased by consumers. Creating the index requires many different steps, but the following describes the basic process. The U.S. government surveys thousands of people across the country to find out what goods and services they buy on a regular basis. The government then creates a "market basket" of about 400 different

SECTION 3 PROGRAM RESOURCES

ON LEVEL

Lesson Plans
- Core, p. 45

Unit 5 Resource Book
- Reading Study Guide, pp. 73–74
- Math Skills Worksheet, p. 91
- Section Quiz, p. 81

STRUGGLING READERS

Unit 5 Resource Book
- Reading Study Guide with Additional Support, pp. 75–77
- Reteaching Activity, p. 82

ENGLISH LEARNERS

Unit 5 Resource Book
- Reading Study Guide with Additional Support (Spanish), pp. 78–80

INCLUSION

Lesson Plans
- Modified for Inclusion, p. 45

GIFTED AND TALENTED

Unit 5 Resource Book
- Case Study Resources: What Inflation Means for . . . , pp. 87–88

TECHNOLOGY

eEdition DVD-ROM

eEdition Online

Power Presentation DVD-ROM

Economics Concepts Transparencies
- CT45 Inflation and Unemployment: 1980 to 2005

Daily Test Practice Transparencies, TT45

ClassZone.com

goods and services purchased by a typical household. The basket is adjusted to account for how much of a household's budget goes to purchase each type of item. For example, families tend to spend more on food than on lawn care, so the market basket is balanced to reflect this.

Each month, government workers research the current prices of the items in the market basket. What consumers spend to fill the basket can then be compared to prices in the reference base, which reflects the level of prices in the three years 1982 to 1984. Those numbers are given the value of 100. See the Connect to Math sidebar for more information.

Economics Update

Find an update about the U.S. consumer price index at **ClassZone.com**

FIGURE 13.7 **U.S. CONSUMER PRICE INDEX**

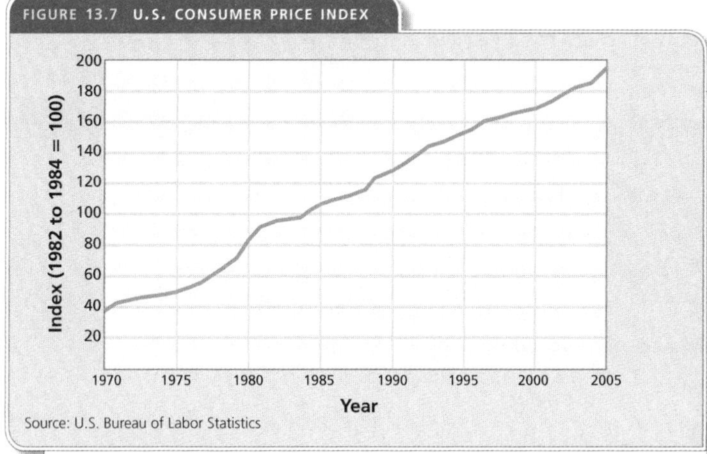

Source: U.S. Bureau of Labor Statistics

ANALYZE CHARTS

1. If you paid $500 to fill the market basket in 1984, about how much would you pay to fill the basket in 2005?
2. Prices doubled from 1971 to 1980. How long did it take them to double again after 1980?

CONNECT TO MATH

Suppose the original value of the market basket was $500 and the current year's value is $550. To determine CPI, you divide the new value by the original value and multiply by 100. The current CPI, then, is 110.

$550 / $500 x 100 = 110

Producer Price Index

The CPI shows the level of inflation experienced by consumers, but producers also experience inflation. The tool that gauges that kind of inflation is the **producer price index (PPI)**, a measure of changes in wholesale prices. The PPI is constructed in roughly the same way as the CPI, but it reflects the prices producers receive for their goods rather than the prices consumers pay. The difference between consumer prices and producer prices lies in all the additional fees consumers pay, such as sales taxes or shipping charges. Like the CPI, the PPI is tied to a reference base of producer prices. More than 10,000 PPIs for individual products and groups of products are available. The indices are grouped either by stage of production (finished goods, intermediate goods, and raw materials, for example) or by industry. Index changes from period to period are calculated in the same general way as the CPI.

Because producers tend to encounter inflation before consumers, PPI tends to lead CPI as an indicator of inflation. Economists use CPI and PPI to calculate the **inflation rate**, the rate of change in prices over a set period of time.

QUICK REFERENCE

Producer price index (PPI) is a measure of changes in wholesale prices.

Inflation rate is the rate of change in prices over a set period of time.

3 Teach

What Is Inflation and How Is It Measured?

Discuss

- Ask students to imagine a concrete example to show why hyperinflation is so serious. *(Possible answer: If the inflation rate is 50 percent per month, then someone who spends $1,000 per month would need $1,500 the next to buy the same amount of goods. If the inflation rate continued at that level, then $2,250 the next month. The increased costs would far outpace the possibility of making that much more money.)*

Analyze Graphs: Figure 13.7

Point out that to factor out the most volatile areas of the economy, economists also use the "core index" to track inflation, which eliminates food and energy from the market basket. The core index tends to rise at a considerably slower pace than the CPI.

Answers

1. *$1,000*
2. *16 years*

Economics Update

At **ClassZone.com** students will see updated information on the U.S. consumer price index.

SMALL GROUP ACTIVITY

Analyzing CPI Issues

Time 30 Minutes

Task Recognize limitations in CPI measurements and suggest solutions

Materials Needed paper and pens

Activity

- Have students work in small groups.
- Explain that one criticism of CPI measurement is that the current prices do not take product improvements into sufficient account.
- Offer the refrigerator as an example. A model bought in 1982 might cost less in real dollars than a 2007 model, but the later model may last longer, be more energy efficient, and actually save the owner money.
- Ask groups to suggest another example to illustrate the CPI problem and propose a solution to make the CPI more accurate.
- Instruct the groups to present their examples and proposals to the class in an interesting and original way.

Rubric

	Understanding of the CPI	Presentation of Information
4	excellent	original ideas, well thought through
3	good	interesting, mostly thought through
2	fair	basically correct but incomplete
1	poor	incorrect or off-base

Math Challenge: Figure 13.8

Help students approach the CPI from another angle by giving them the following problems:

If a new coat costs $110 in a year when the CPI is 110, what did the coat cost in the base year? *(The answer to this may be obvious to many students. But use the following equation to help any students that might struggle with math:*

$\frac{\$110}{\$x} = \frac{110}{100}$ $x = \$100$)

If a laptop computer costs $1,000 in a year when the CPI is 115, what did the laptop computer cost in the base year? *(To solve this, use the following equation:*

$\frac{\$1000}{\$x} = \frac{115}{100} = \$869.57$)

International Economics

Hyperinflation in Zimbabwe

In the 2000s, the African nation of Zimbabwe had the highest inflation rate in the world. In 2000, the annual rate of inflation was about 55 percent. By 2003, it had risen to about 260 percent per year. In 2006, the annual rate of inflation was estimated to have risen to over 1,000 percent.

Once considered the breadbasket of Southern Africa, Zimbabwe turned to foreign aid for food donations. Experts estimated that about 4 million of the nation's 13 million people required aid.

MATH CHALLENGE

FIGURE 13.8 Calculating the Rate of Inflation

To calculate the rate of inflation, economists evaluate the prices of many different goods. This hypothetical example uses a simplified market basket consisting of prices for milk, bread, and juice. The table shows that the prices of milk and bread increased from Year B to Year C, but the price of juice decreased. To see the general trend in prices, you must look at the total price of the market basket of milk, bread, and juice. The steps below show how to use this simplified market basket to calculate the rate of inflation for Year C. The base year is Year A.

Price of a Market Basket

	Year A	Year B	Year C
1 gallon milk	$2.50	$2.40	$2.60
1 loaf bread	$1.00	$1.35	$1.53
1 gallon juice	$2.00	$2.30	$2.20
Price of basket	$5.50	$6.05	$6.33
CPI, base: Year A	100	110	115

Step 1: Calculate each year's consumer price index (CPI).

Calculations for Year C

$$\frac{\text{Price of market basket}}{\text{Price of basket in base year}} \times 100 = \text{CPI} \qquad \frac{\$6.33}{\$5.50} \times 100 = 115$$

Step 2: Use the CPI to calculate the rate of inflation.

$$\frac{\text{CPI} - \text{CPI for preceding year}}{\text{CPI for preceding year}} \times 100 = \text{Rate of Inflation} \qquad \frac{115 - 110}{110} \times 100 = 4.5$$

The rate of inflation in Year C was about 4.5 percent.

Choosing a market basket To calculate the rate of inflation, economists use a complicated market basket of hundreds of goods. The market basket is intended to represent the goods that are purchased by a typical urban consumer.

Types of Inflation

QUICK REFERENCE

Hyperinflation is a rapid, uncontrolled rate of inflation in excess of 50 percent per month.

Deflation is a decrease in the general price level.

The different types of inflation are defined according to the degree or level of the inflation rate. Rates below 1 percent are negligible, and those between 1 and 3 percent are moderate. If a moderate rate continues over a period of time, the result is *creeping inflation*. A rapid increase in price level is known as *galloping inflation*. If galloping inflation gets out of hand, the result is **hyperinflation**—a rapid, uncontrolled rate of inflation in excess of 50 percent per month. One of the most dramatic episodes of hyperinflation happened in Germany in 1922 and 1923. At the height of the crisis, prices rose at a rate of about 322 percent per month. **Deflation**, a decrease in the general price level, happens more rarely. The Great Depression of the 1930s in the United States was marked by deflation.

APPLICATION Applying Economic Concepts

A. If the price of milk goes up, is that inflation? Why or why not?
Not necessarily. Inflation is an increase in prices generally.

DIFFERENTIATING INSTRUCTION

English Learners

Use Prefixes to Understand
Point out the word *hyperinflation* on this page. Ask students to name or infer the meaning of the prefix *hyper (over).* Then, have students use a dictionary to find at least five commonly used words that begin with that prefix and to note them and the definitions in their personal dictionaries. Also, ask students to look up the prefix *hypo (under),* and have them find and note five common words beginning with that prefix.

Gifted and Talented

Analyze Cause and Effect
Direct students to develop a specific example that demonstrates clearly why deflation causes people to become poorer, even though lower prices appear to be a good thing. Suggest that students represent their example in the visual way of their choice—a flow chart, an illustrated poster, a cartoon, and so on.

What Causes Inflation?

KEY CONCEPTS

Economists generally distinguish between two kinds of inflation, each with a different cause. When the inflationary forces are on the demand side of the economy, the result is **demand-pull inflation**, a situation where total demand is rising faster than the production of goods and services. When the forces that lead to inflation originate on the supply side of the economy, the result is **cost-push inflation**, a situation where increases in production costs push up prices.

QUICK REFERENCE

Demand-pull inflation results when total demand rises faster than the production of goods and services.

Cost-push inflation results when increases in the costs of production push up prices.

Demand-Pull Inflation

In demand-pull inflation, total demand rises faster than the production of goods and services, creating a scarcity that then drives up prices. Suppose, for example, that consumers gain confidence in the economy and decide they want to buy more durable goods—new refrigerators, stoves, second cars, and so on. It takes producers some time to recognize this rise in demand and to gear up for higher production. During this lag period, consumer demand pushes up prices on the currently available goods. Figure 13.9 illustrates how demand-pull inflation happens.

As you will learn in Chapter 16, the U.S. government creates and controls money through the Federal Reserve Bank. If the government creates too much money during the lag period before an increase in production makes more goods available, there will be too much money chasing too few goods, and prices will rise. The creation of excess money is the main reason for demand-pull inflation.

FIGURE 13.9 **Demand-Pull Inflation**

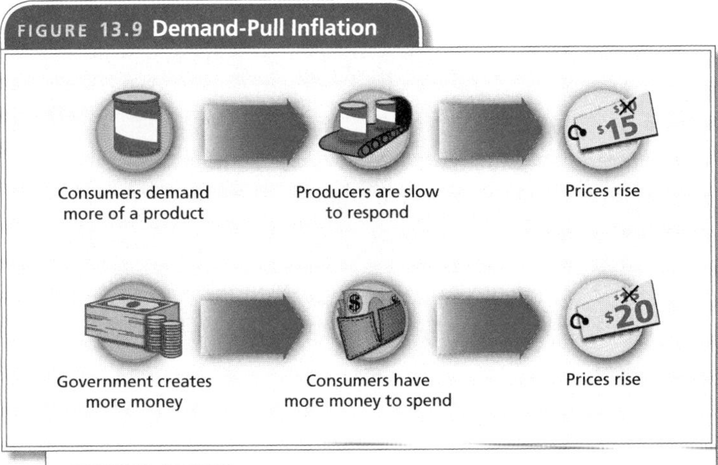

Consumers demand more of a product
Producers are slow to respond
$15
Prices rise
Government creates more money
Consumers have more money to spend
$20
Prices rise

ANALYZE CHARTS

1. In the first scenario, did the demand curve shift or the supply curve?
2. In the second scenario, which curve shifts when the supply of money increases?

What Causes Inflation?

Discuss

- What is the relationship between cost-push inflation and the wage-price spiral? *(Part of the wage-price spiral is a type of cost-push inflation: when higher wages push up the cost of production.)*

Economics Illustrated

To remember demand-pull inflation, think of a hand pulling up a shopping bag, which pulls up the inflation rate on a graph.

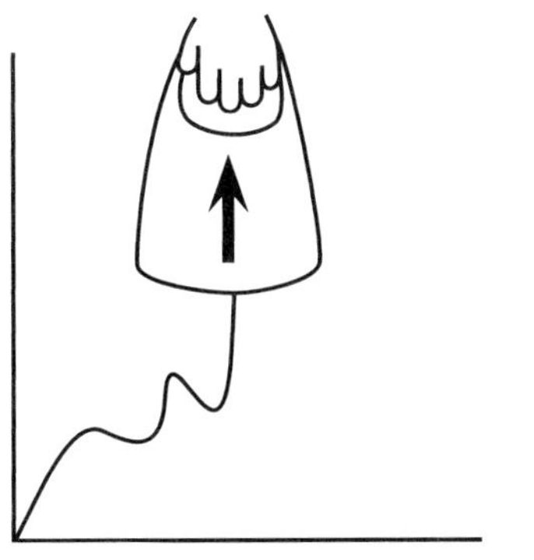

Analyzing Charts: Figure 13.9

Ask students what needs to be coordinated to avoid demand-pull inflation. *(Producers must coordinate supply with demand; the government must coordinate the amount of money in circulation with the amount of consumer spending.)*

Answers

1. *demand curve*
2. *demand curve*

INDIVIDUAL ACTIVITY

Understanding Personal Inflation Rate

Time 30 Minutes ◑

Task Adjust the CPI weightings to reflect personal spending to see how individual inflation rates may differ from the published norm.

Materials Needed paper and pens

Activity

- Put the following weightings assigned to each category of the 2001 CPI on a chart on the board: food and beverages 15.7; housing 40.9; apparel 4.4; transportation 17.1; medical care 5.8; recreation 6.0; education and communication 5.8; other goods and services 4.3; total all items, 100.0
- Explain that the weightings show the relative importance of each category.
- Ask students to write their monthly budget based on each of these categories and figure out the weightings according to what they spend.
- Then, have students write a few paragraphs explaining how their personal CPI differs from the published CPI.

Rubric

	Understanding of Personal CPI	Presentation of Information
4	excellent	complete budget, accurate and well-written composition
3	good	well-developed and complete
2	fair	adequate but sometimes off-target
1	poor	sketchy, incomplete

Cost-Push Inflation

In cost-push inflation, prices are pushed upward by rising production costs. When production costs increase, producers make less of a profit. If consumer demand is strong, producers may raise their prices in order to maintain their profits. A general trend of rising prices leads to inflation.

Cost-push inflation is often the result of supply shocks—sharp increases in prices of raw materials or energy. For example, in 1973 and 1974, many members of the Organization of Petroleum Exporting Countries (OPEC) limited the amount of oil they sold to the United States and other Western countries. The resulting rapid rise in the price of oil led to cost-push inflation.

Cost-Push Inflation Shortages of raw materials or energy can lead to cost-push inflation.

Wages are a large part of the production costs for many goods, so rising wages can lead to cost-push inflation. A **wage-price spiral** is a cycle in which increased wages lead to higher production costs, which in turn result in higher prices, which then lead to demands for higher wages. You can see the wage-price spiral in motion in Figure 13.10.

QUICK REFERENCE

A **wage-price spiral** is a cycle that begins with increased wages, which lead to higher production costs, which in turn result in higher prices, which result in demands for even higher wages.

FIGURE 13.10 Wage-Price Spiral

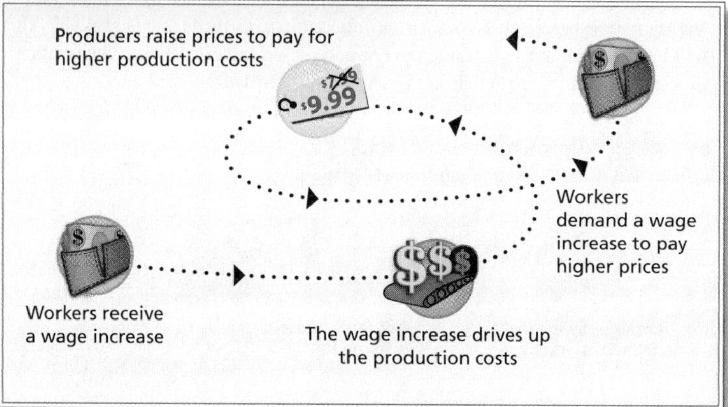
Producers raise prices to pay for higher production costs
$9.99
Workers demand a wage increase to pay higher prices
Workers receive a wage increase
The wage increase drives up the production costs

ANALYZE CHARTS

1. Using the cotton industry as an example, explain how the cycle might proceed. Use the cotton workers, cotton growers, textile mills, and other intermediate industries in your explanation.
2. Do employers grant wage increases whenever employees ask for a raise? What economic principles determine wage levels?

APPLICATION Categorizing Economic Information

B. What type of inflation would result if bad weather hit farmers hard over a long stretch of time?

Cost-push—food producers would have to pay more for scarcer agricultural goods.

Economics Illustrated

To remember cost-push inflation, think of a worker holding an inflation curve chart above his head like a barbell, pushing it up from his shoulders.

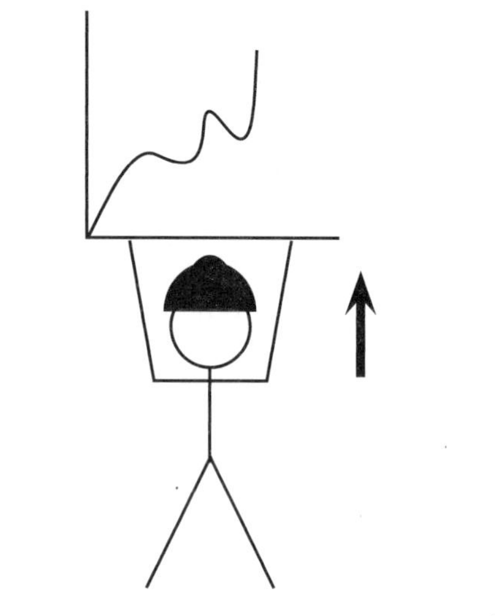

Analyze Charts: Figure 13.10

Ask students why wage-price inflation is called a "spiral." *(because one increase leads to another)* Ask if the spiral must start with demands for higher wages. *(No—it could start with higher prices, leading to demands for higher wages.)* Wherever it starts, the next step is not a foregone conclusion. An employer might find a way to compensate for higher production costs other than raising prices. And employers certainly don't raise wages every time their employees ask for an increase.

Answers

1. *Possible answer: Cotton workers receive a wage increase; growers raise cotton prices to pay for increase; mills raise price of textiles to pay for increase in price of cotton; manufacturers raise price of clothes to pay for more expensive textiles; cotton workers need more money to pay for more expensive clothes.*
2. *no—supply and demand*

DIFFERENTIATING INSTRUCTION

Struggling Readers

Use Illustrations to Understand
Have students use the photo at the top of this page to explain how scarcity of oil might lead to cost-push inflation. Suggest that students create a mental photograph of each stage of the process.

Inclusion

Work in Pairs
Pair an inclusion student with a mainstream student to ask each other questions and provide answers about the following key points in the first lesson. Each student should ask at least one question on each of the following topics: what inflation is; CPI and PPI; types of inflation; causes of demand-pull; causes of cost-push.

What Is the Impact of Inflation?

KEY CONCEPTS

Since the 1960s, the impact of inflation on the United States economy has been significant. Inflation has raised interest rates, limited the growth of the stock market, forced agricultural bankruptcies, and slowed production. It has also had a huge impact on politics. More than half of those who voted for Ronald Reagan in 1980 said that his promise to stop the long-running inflation of the 1970s was the decisive factor. Inflation is a major challenge to economic stability. For the economy as a whole and for individual consumers, inflation has an especially strong impact on the purchasing power of the dollar and on interest rates.

EFFECT 1 Decreasing Value of the Dollar

With inflation, today's dollar buys less than last year's. The consumer price index, illustrated in Figure 13.7, shows that the real value of a dollar has declined steadily. The rising index represents the declining value of the dollar.

Consider how this declining value affects people who are on a fixed income. Suppose, for example, that your cousin started college with a savings of $10,000 to see him through. He planned to spend $2,500 a year on carefully budgeted expenses. However, because of inflation, each of those dollars bought less each year. To pay for exactly the same things he bought in his freshman year for $2,500, by the time he was a senior he needed $2,750. Inflation had pushed prices up by 10 percent over the four-year period. Senior citizens living on a fixed retirement income—as well as anyone else with a fixed income—are especially vulnerable to the decreasing value of the dollar through inflation.

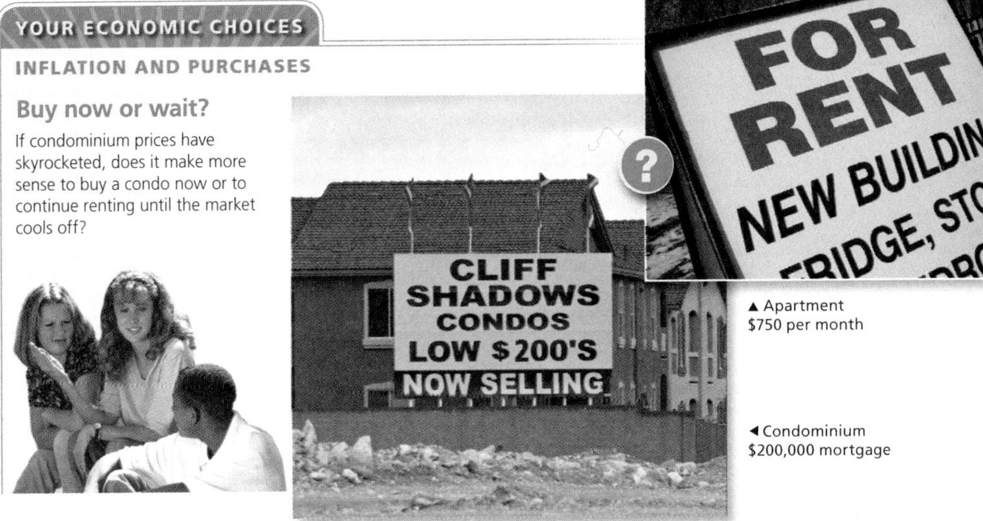

YOUR ECONOMIC CHOICES
INFLATION AND PURCHASES
Buy now or wait?
If condominium prices have skyrocketed, does it make more sense to buy a condo now or to continue renting until the market cools off?
?
FOR RENT
NEW BUILDIN
CLIFF SHADOWS
CONDOS
LOW $200'S
NOW SELLING

▲ Apartment $750 per month

◄ Condominium $200,000 mortgage

What Is the Impact of Inflation?

Discuss

- If inflation was guaranteed to be 9 percent per year forever, would it still be a problem? *(Help students understand that the uncertainty of the inflation rate creates problems, because it complicates economic decisions. A known rate of inflation could be accounted for, especially if wages increased along with prices.)*

Your Economic Choices

INFLATION AND PURCHASES

Buy now or wait?
This is a very complicated question. Financial considerations include income (ability to make mortgage payments), savings (down payment), mortgage interest rates, and how long you expect to stay in the home. However, there are almost always other factors than strictly financial ones in economic decisions. Those other factors can be just as important to consider as the raw numbers.

Activity Have students work in small groups to brainstorm a list of other factors that might affect the decision to buy a house now or to continue to rent. Have each group give weights to the various factors and explain the decision they would make. Ask each group to share their decision and reasoning with the rest of the class.

SMALL GROUP ACTIVITY

Defining the Effect of Inflation on Fundamental Principles of the Economy

Time 30 Minutes ◑

Task Illustrate defining principles in the U.S. economy and ways in which inflation affects them.

Materials Needed illustration sources, such as magazines or online clip art, construction or poster paper, pens and markers

Activity

- Organize students into small groups.
- Direct students to identify the ethical values that underlie the U.S. economy, such as hard work, equal opportunity, and so on.
- Then, instruct the groups to consider how inflation affects each of those principles.
- Have each group choose three principles and the effect of inflation on them and illustrate the impact of inflation on their chosen principles.
- Display the completed illustrations.

Rubric

	Understanding of the Impact of Inflation	Presentation of Information
4	excellent	creative, complete, and accurate
3	good	complete and accurate
2	fair	missing a principle
1	poor	incomplete and poorly presented

More About . . .

Increasing Rates on Student Loans
Why were college students and parents of college students rushing to lock in interest rates on loans for college education as July 1, 2006 approached? On July 1st of each year, the rates for the popular government Stafford and Parent PLUS loans are readjusted in relation to the 91-day Treasury Bill rate. From 7/05 to 7/06, that rate had risen by 2 percentage points. So, students and families were eager to avoid higher than necessary interest rates.

In recent past years, variable rates were offered on these semester-by-semester loans, because interest rates were at a historic low level. However, with the expectation that those levels will not be seen again for some time, the government loans are now set at a fixed rate.

More About . . .

Taxes and Inflation
Inflation can create distortions in the market. One example was during the inflationary 1970s. In that period, the rise in housing prices—and interest rates—increased the tax deduction for homeowners and fueled a real estate boom.

During the boom, many sawmills, anticipating increased demand, decided to expand production. However, their decision was based on a distortion—the real estate boom could not last forever. Some sawmills suffered severe losses when inflation subsided in the 1980s.

APPLICATION
Answer *Answers will vary. Students who argue that inflation is the more serious problem might cite any of the three effects discussed in this subsection. Students who argue that unemployment is the more serious problem might cite the effects discussed on page 386.*

Increasing Interest Rates Higher interest rates make borrowing more expensive.

Conversely, inflation can help borrowers. With inflation, those who borrow at a fixed rate of interest can repay their debts with dollars that are worth less, making their repayments smaller than they would have been without inflation. Suppose someone borrows $100 at 5 percent interest, promising to pay the lender $105 after a year. If inflation rises at 5 percent, the $105 the borrower pays the lender will have the same purchasing power as the $100 of the original loan. The borrower essentially paid no real interest on the money he borrowed.

EFFECT 2 Increasing Interest Rates

As prices increase, interest rates also tend to increase. Lenders raise their interest rates to ensure they earn money on their loans despite inflation. Higher interest rates mean that borrowing money becomes more expensive. For example, a $10,000 loan at 10 percent interest to be repaid over the course of five years would have a monthly payment of $212.47. At 5 percent interest, the monthly payment would be only $188.71. At the end of five years, you would have paid over $1,425 more for the loan at the higher rate. When interest rates are high, businesses are less likely to borrow to expand or to make capital improvements. Consumers are less likely to make purchases of high-priced items that they would need to finance. People carrying debt on credit cards have to make higher monthly payments as their rates rise.

EFFECT 3 Decreasing Real Returns on Savings

Inflation also has a significant effect on savings. People who save at a fixed interest rate get a lower rate of return on their savings. While the interest paid on savings tends to increase during inflationary times, the difference between the rate of return and the rate of inflation still leaves them at a disadvantage.

For example, if someone puts $100 in a savings account that pays 5 percent interest per year, they will have $105 at the end of a year. But if the rate of inflation for the year was 10 percent, that $105 will buy only about what $95 bought when they deposited their money. Although they have more dollars, that money will buy less. Inflation, then, can discourage savings, leading more people to make purchases today rather than saving for tomorrow.

Inflation is the most commonly used economic term in the popular media, far outpacing the distant second, *unemployment*. Inflation worries many people, especially those who remember the volatile 1970s. Much of the worry centers on a person's individual standard of living: Will my wages keep up with rising prices? Will my savings see me through retirement? Fear of inflation has contributed to the shift away from the traditional American belief in saving over consumption.

APPLICATION Writing About Economics

C. According to opinion polls, most Americans feel inflation is a more serious problem than unemployment. Write a paragraph stating your view on which is more serious. Use convincing reasons and examples.
See Teacher's Edition for possible answers.

DIFFERENTIATING INSTRUCTION

English Learners

Use Conversation to Personalize Learning
Have students work in pairs made up of one English speaker and one English learner. Direct the pairs to have a relaxed conversation about how they believe inflation will affect them—or already has affected them—in relation to choices about their future.

Gifted and Talented

Create Comparative Graphs
Direct students to research unemployment rates, interest rates, inflation rates, and patterns in savings and investment in the years between 1970 and today. Have them create one or more graphs to correlate the various patterns. Then, ask them to write their conclusions in a brief composition about the relationship among these trends.

SECTION 3 Assessment

Online Quiz
ClassZone.com

REVIEWING KEY CONCEPTS

1. Explain the relationship between the terms in each of these pairs.
   a. *consumer price index* / *producer price index*
   b. *hyperinflation* / *deflation*
   c. *demand-pull inflation* / *cost-push inflation*
2. What are the stages in a wage-price spiral?
3. Use a specific example to explain cost-push inflation.
4. Use a specific example to explain demand-pull inflation.
5. What are three effects of inflation?
6. **Using Your Notes** If you were a business owner, what decisions might you make on news of a steady rise in inflation? Refer to your completed cluster diagram and provide specific examples.

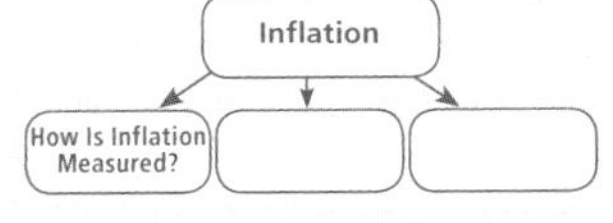

Use the Graphic Organizer at **Interactive Review @ ClassZone.com**

CRITICAL THINKING

7. **Analyzing Cause and Effect** Why would producers tend to experience inflation before consumers? What type of inflation would the producers experience?
8. **Explaining an Economic Concept** How does the creation of excess money cause a demand-pull inflation? Refer to Figure 13.9 to help you answer this question.
9. **Applying an Economic Concept** Imagine that union leaders are meeting with the owners of a steel manufacturer to negotiate a new five-year contract for union employees. Explain how both sides of the union-management negotiation team must take the unpredictability of future inflation into account.
10. **Challenge** The cost of attending college has been rising faster than the inflation rate, at times twice as fast. For proof, ask your school guidance counselor for a catalog from a private college that shows prices from several years ago. Compare the old prices to the current prices shown on the college website. Calculate the percentage increase for this school.

ECONOMICS IN PRACTICE

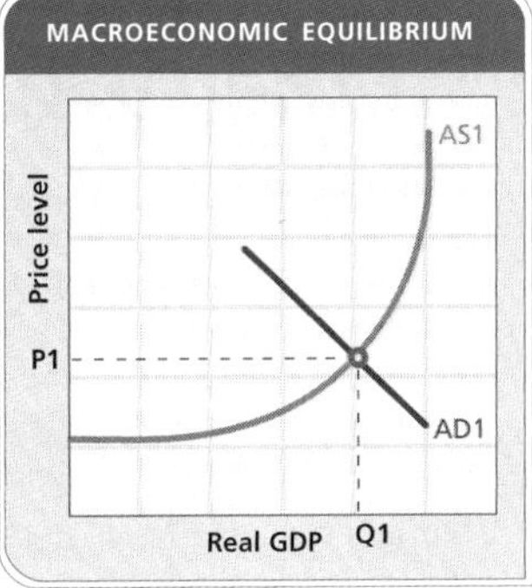

Estimating the Effects of Inflation Suppose that a natural disaster disrupts the production of oil so dramatically that prices for oil and related products double in a short period of time. In this graph of macroeconomic equilibrium, P1 shows the price level before the natural disaster.

Draw Aggregate Supply and Demand Curves On your own paper, recreate the graph of macroeconomic equilibrium. Then draw the new aggregate supply curve that would result from the natural disaster scenario, and indicate where P2 would fall.

Challenge Explain what will happen to total economic output because of the change in prices. How does the new graph show this?

Use **SMARTGrapher @ ClassZone.com** to complete this activity.

4 Assess & Reteach

Assess Assign questions 1-6 and Economics in Practice as written work for each student. Discuss questions 7–9 as a whole class.

Unit 5 Resource Book
- Section Quiz, p. 81

Interactive Review @ ClassZone.com
- Section Quiz

Test Generator CD-ROM
- Section Quiz

Reteach Divide the class into four teams and play a game to review Section 3. For every illustration in Section 3, ask the teams to think of one factual statement that relates to the material near the illustration. For example, relevant statements about the photo of the changing gas prices might include "Energy prices are figured into the CPI" or "A supply shock could drive prices up."

Unit 5 Resource Book
- Reteaching Activity, p. 82

Economics in Practice
Draw Aggregate Supply and Demand Curves Aggregate supply curve would shift to the left, causing the price level (P2) to rise.

Challenge Output will decline because the economy has added no new factors of production to offset the decrease in the purchasing power of money.

SMARTGrapher Students can create aggregate supply and demand curves using **SmartGrapher @ ClassZone.com**.

SECTION 3 ASSESSMENT ANSWERS

Reviewing Key Concepts

1. a. *consumer price index*, p. 396; *producer price index*, p. 397
   b. *hyperinflation*, p. 398; *deflation*, p. 398
   c. *demand-pull inflation*, p. 399; *cost-push inflation*, p. 399
2. increased wages, higher production costs, higher prices, demands for higher wages
3. Answers will vary, but look for understanding of the supply side roots of cost-push inflation.
4. Answers will vary, but look for understanding of the demand side roots of demand-pull inflation.
5. decreasing value of the currency, higher interest rates, lower real returns on savings
6. See page 396 for an example of a completed diagram. Answers will vary but might include securing a loan (to be repaid with lower-valued dollars); improving productivity; and purchasing supplies in advance (to avoid price increases).

Critical Thinking

7. Producers would experience inflation when buying raw materials; in response, they might increase product prices. Producers would experience cost-push inflation.
8. Each new dollar pumped into the economy, beyond what the productivity level can support, lowers the value of the other dollars, making inflation worse.
9. Answers will vary but may include the idea that workers must try to achieve a pay increase that will keep pace with inflation or, ideally, exceed it; while management will try to avoid a wage level that would limit their profits along with the erosion that inflation causes.
10. Answers will vary, but look for application of this formula:
    current prices / old prices x 100 = percentage increase

Economics in Practice

See answers in side column above.

1 Plan & Prepare

Objectives

- Analyze sources to synthesize economic information.
- Explain the role of government in controlling inflation.

2 Focus & Motivate

To help students understand the importance of fighting inflation, ask them to comment on the role of inflation in Hitler's rise to power in Germany. Point out that prices skyrocketed from 1914 to 1923. The price of an egg, for example, rose from a few pfennigs (1/100 of a mark) to over 300 million marks. People burned money in their fireplaces because it was cheaper than firewood. Inflation had thrown the economy into a tailspin. When Hitler began to blame the Jews for the country's economic troubles, many Germans were eager to find a scapegoat. When a country's economy is in such bad shape, people can be frightened into terrible changes.

3 Teach

Using the Sources

Discuss

A. What two conditions exacerbated the inflation of the 1970s in the United States? *(slowed economic growth and reduced productivity)*

B. How valid economically is the father's argument? *(Increasing a child's allowance would have little or no effect on inflation.)*

C. Could both the economists and the consumer be correct in their view of the economic situation? Explain. *(For the government economists, a downward change in the rate of inflation indicates that the economy is headed in the right direction. For the consumer, any increase in the rate of inflation has a negative effect on purchasing power.)*

Economics Update

Go to **ClassZone.com** to find an update to this Case Study, including another article, an editable student worksheet, and an editable lesson plan.

Case Study

Economics Update Find an update on this Case Study at **ClassZone.com**

The Effects of Inflation in the 1970s

Background Periods of high inflation can wreak havoc with a country's economy. In the 1970s, for example, the United States experienced the biggest and most sustained period of inflation in the country's history. By 1979, inflation had risen into the "double digits," that is, to 10 percent per year or higher. The prices of consumer goods—everything from food and gas to cars and houses—rose dramatically. Those on fixed incomes were particularly hard-hit, because as prices rose their limited budgets bought less.

What's the issue? How did inflation affect people and businesses in the 1970s? Study these sources to discover what it was like to live with a high rate of inflation.

A. Economic Analysis

In the late 1960s, the rate of inflation began rising in many countries. This article explains inflation's effects on the U.S. economy.

The Industrialized World and Inflation

How inflation affected the U.S. economy

For the years 1967 through 1978, the U.S. inflation rate averaged 6.1 per cent a year, compared with an average of 2 per cent for the years 1952 through 1967. Even during the 1973–74 recession, unlike most previous recessions, the inflation rate continued at a relatively high rate. In the late 1970s inflation speeded up again, reaching unprecedented levels.

Inflation would not be so bad, in the opinion of some economists, if it were accompanied by substantial increases in output and employment. But economic growth in the United States slowed during the high-inflation 1970s, bringing on a condition that economists describe as "stagflation." Another measure of economic health—productivity, or output per worker—also slowed dramatically in [those] years throughout the industrialized world, and in the United States and Great Britain for a time failed to increase at all. For the United States, a country long accustomed to ever-increasing material wealth, the fall-off in economic growth and the constantly eroding value of the dollar were traumatic developments. If the trends continued, the average American could no longer anticipate a constantly rising standard of living.

Source: *The Search for a New Economic Order*, The Ford Foundation, 1982

Thinking Economically Explain how the effects of inflation might be offset by increases in output and employment.

DIFFERENTIATING INSTRUCTION

Struggling Readers

Use the Reading Process

Point out that the structure of the case studies reflects a reading process that students will find useful in all reading. Discuss the purpose of the "Background" paragraph and how it activates prior knowledge by bringing to mind what they already know about the subject. "What's the issue?" parallels the focusing experienced readers do before beginning reading. Ask students to apply this process to the next reading assignment, and then reflect on how it affected their comprehension.

Inclusion

Focus on Key Points

Encourage students to make a template, such as the following, for reading the sources in the case studies.

Source: (Title, author, and type of source)
Main idea:
Detail 1:
Detail 2:
Detail 3:
Summary:

B. Cartoon

In this cartoon by Larry Katzman, a father offers an early lesson in economics.

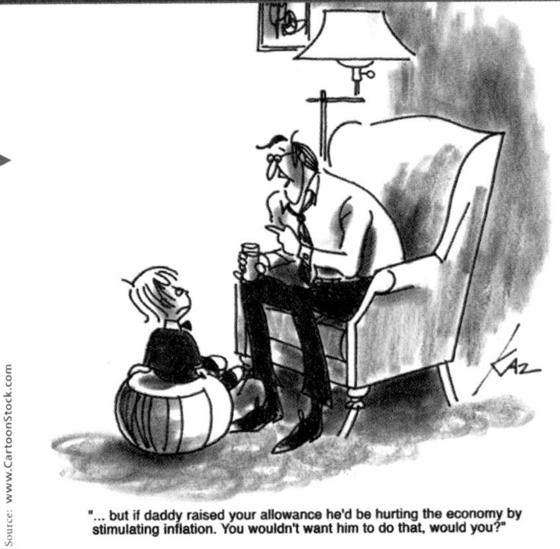

"... but if daddy raised your allowance he'd be hurting the economy by stimulating inflation. You wouldn't want him to do that, would you?"
KAZ
Source: www.CartoonStock.com

Thinking Economically Which type of inflation does the cartoon reflect? Explain your answer.

C. Newspaper Editorial

Prices rose dramatically during the 1970s. This editorial reflects the anger many consumers felt about the situation.

Protesting Inflation

Consumers grew impatient with the government's inability to control inflation.

Here we are, spending more and getting less, but the [government] economists are optimistic. What makes them so happy? The rate of inflation may have dropped 1 per cent. Just suppose the rate of inflation had gone down from 5 per cent to 4 per cent. . . . To me this is another increase of four cents, and a further shrinkage of my dollar.

Obviously this type of economics is good for someone. It certainly isn't good for me, or my friends, or my relatives. Everyone is complaining, but the experts are satisfied.

I have a family of meat eaters. . . . Long ago I discovered a marvelous cut of meat called skirt steak. It used to cost 89 cents a pound. It has inched its way up and has recently taken a leap to $1.59 and overtaken sirloin steak. Chopped meat is now where my skirt steak used to be. . . . Even the lowly onion is no longer cheap. A weekly trip to the supermarket, which in 1969 cost $50, now costs $70.

Source: *The New York Times*, September 29, 1972

Thinking Economically Why might a small decrease in a large rate of inflation satisfy government economists but frustrate consumers?

THINKING ECONOMICALLY Synthesizing

1. Name one example from each document that shows how inflation has a negative impact on the economy.
2. Inflation is a general rise in price levels. Are the examples of price increases in documents B and C symptoms of inflation or isolated price increases?
3. Compare the tone of documents A and C. Do economists care as much about inflation as consumers? Explain your answer.

Thinking Economically

Answers

A. *If higher prices led to more goods produced and more people employed to produce those goods, then more people would have more money to spend. Under those circumstances, people would not feel the effects of inflation to the extent that they did in the 1970s.*

B. *demand-pull inflation; increasing the allowance would fuel demand*

C. *Government economists would like that inflation was going down. Consumers would still face a large rate of inflation.*

Synthesizing

1. **A.** *slow economic growth, low productivity, reduced expectations;* **B.** *wages not keeping up with prices;* **C.** *consumer anger, expensive groceries*
2. **B.** *isolated;* **C.** *symptoms*
3. *Answers will vary. Yes, economists care because they are consumers, too. No, they do not care because they just look at the numbers.*

TECHNOLOGY ACTIVITY

Creating a Movie or Slide Show

Time 60 Minutes ●

Task Create a computerized movie or slide show, illustrating the inflation of the 1970s, its impact, and the effect of efforts to control it.

Materials Needed computer with software for creating slide shows or movies; previously researched illustrations and audio clips; computer projection system for final presentation

Activity

- Divide students into four groups.
- Direct each group to identify illustrations online that could be used in the slide show and save them to a disk. Have them do the same for music or speeches for the audio portion.
- Give each group one period to access classroom computers and compile their slide show.
- Remind students to use titles and other text tools, as needed.
- When the slide shows are finished, have each group present theirs to the class.

Rubric

	Understanding of Inflation	Presentation of Information
4	excellent	compelling, accurate, rich in multimedia
3	good	well-designed, accurate, good multimedia
2	fair	acceptable design, a few multimedia elements
1	poor	carelessly designed, no multimedia elements

Online Summary Answers

1. Frictional unemployment
2. Structural unemployment
3. full employment
4. poverty threshold
5. welfare
6. workfare
7. Inflation
8. consumer price index
9. producer price index
10. inflation rate

Interactive Review

Review this chapter using interactive activities at ClassZone.com
- Online Summary
- Quizzes
- Vocabulary Flip Cards
- Graphic Organizers
- Review and Study Notes

Online Summary

Complete the following activity either on your own paper or online at ClassZone.com

Choose the key concept that best completes the sentence. Not all key concepts will be used.

consumer price index (CPI)
cost-push inflation
cyclical unemployment
deflation
demand-pull inflation
frictional unemployment
full employment
hyperinflation
income distribution
income inequality
inflation
inflation rate
Lorenz curve
poverty
poverty rate
poverty threshold
producer price index (PPI)
seasonal unemployment
structural unemployment
underemployed
unemployment rate
wage-price spiral
welfare
workfare

There are different types of unemployment. __1__ represents workers changing jobs to increase their working satisfaction or to accommodate a move to another region. __2__ results from significant changes in the economy and in the way work is done. Even during periods of __3__ about 4 to 6 percent of the work force is still unemployed.

Nearly 40 million people in the United States have incomes below the __4__, even though the nation has one of the highest median incomes in the world. The poorest receive assistance through __5__. In recent years __6__, which requires an exchange of labor for government benefits, has replaced some direct cash payments.

__7__, a rise in the general level of prices, is another economic challenge. To monitor it, government economists developed the __8__, which tracks what consumers pay for a market basket of items, and the __9__, which tracks prices from the producers' point of view. They monitor the __10__ using these indices.

CHAPTER 13 Assessment

REVIEWING KEY CONCEPTS

Unemployment in Today's Economy (pp. 382–387)

1. What are the four main kinds of unemployment and how do they differ from one another?
2. What are three negative impacts of unemployment?

Poverty and Income Distribution (pp. 388–395)

3. Which of the following persons is most likely to live in poverty: a senior citizen, a disabled adult, a college graduate, or a child? Explain your answer with specific facts and reasons.
4. Describe three antipoverty programs you feel are most useful and give reasons for your position.

Causes and Consequences of Inflation (pp. 396–405)

5. Describe two causes of inflation.
6. Which consequence of inflation would be the most troublesome to you personally? Explain your answer.

APPLYING ECONOMIC CONCEPTS

The table below shows employees laid off from selected industries in 2004. It also shows how many of these jobs were replaced by outsourcing.

7. What type of unemployment is it when an industry lays off workers but outsources their jobs? Name an example from the table.
8. Which industries' job cuts are probably due to changes in the business cycle?

FIGURE 13.11 LAYOFFS AND OUTSOURCING

Industry	Employees Laid Off	Replaced by Outsourcing
Mining	6,123	0
Apparel Manufacturing	11,583	4,102
Computer and Electronic Products	14,979	6,481
Transportation Equipment	40,634	6,223
Retail Trade	143,660	5,298
Transportation and Warehousing	59,098	2,090
Educational Services	1,429	0
Health Care and Social Assistance	44,212	621

Source: U.S. Census Bureau, 2004 data

CHAPTER 13 ASSESSMENT ANSWERS

Reviewing Key Concepts

1. frictional—people voluntarily looking for a new job;
structural—people out of work because of changes in the economy or the way of producing something;
cyclical—people out of work because of a slowdown in economic activity;
seasonal—people out of work because their jobs can only be done in certain seasons of the year
2. It takes a toll on efficiency, since the nation's productive resources are underutilized; it affects people unequally, having a greater impact on people at the lower rung of the economic ladder; it affects workers' self-esteem and motivation.
3. A child. Social Security helps combat poverty in the elderly and disabled, and college graduates have good earning power.
4. Answers will vary but look for well-supported views.
5. An increase in demand that precedes an increase in production; too much money chasing too few goods; higher production costs.
6. Answers will vary but look for an understanding of the consequences of inflation (lower purchasing power of dollar, higher interest rates, lower return on savings).

Apply Economic Concepts

7. structural—the best examples are apparel manufacturing, computer and electronic products, furniture and related products
8. mining, retail trade, transportation and warehousing, educational services, health care and social assistance

Critical Thinking

9. Look for an accurate graphic representation of the figures.
10. Answers will vary but are likely to include the basic ideas that there is considerable income mobility and that the chances of staying in the lowest quintile are actually slightly smaller than moving to the highest.

CRITICAL THINKING

9. **Creating Graphs** The population can be divided into five equal groups—or quintiles—according to income. Income mobility means moving from one quintile to another. A study done by the U.S. Treasury Department between 1979 and 1988 showed the following about taxpayers who started out in the lowest quintile:
   - 14.2 percent of the taxpayers in the bottom quintile in 1979 were still there in 1988
   - 20.7 percent had moved to the next higher quintile
   - 25 percent had moved to the middle quintile
   - 25.3 percent had moved to the second highest quintile
   - 14.4 percent of those who started in the lowest quintile had moved into the highest quintile

   Create a bar graph that illustrates these facts about income mobility in the United States.
   Use ***SMARTGrapher*** **@ ClassZone.com** to complete this activity.

10. **Analyzing and Interpreting Data** What conclusions can you draw about income mobility based on the above data?

11. **Analyzing Cause and Effect** Think of three possible reasons a person might be able to move from one level of income to another.

12. **Explaining an Economic Concept** Which antipoverty programs use market forces to achieve their goals? Explain your answer.

13. **Analyzing and Interpreting Data** Consider the following data:

    Consumer Price Index: up by 6 percent
    Unemployment Rate: up to 7 percent
    Gross Domestic Product: up by 1 percent

    What's the economic problem? To correct the problem, which of these measures would you address first and why?

14. **Challenge** Which economic challenge—unemployment, poverty, or inflation—represents the greatest threat to social stability, in your opinion? Explain your answer with reasons and examples.

SIMULATION

The Pursuit of Happiness

Do you need money to be happy? Since income alone does not tell the whole story of someone's quality of life, some people think other measures besides income should be used to determine a household's well-being. Many elements beyond material possessions also affect a person's quality of life.

To better understand the relationship between wealth and happiness, create a quality-of-life threshold by following the steps below.

Step 1. As a whole class, discuss the differences between income and quality of life.

Step 2. Break into five small groups and devise a quality-of-life threshold, a standard below which a person would be considered seriously impoverished.

Step 3. Try to find a measure for each of your criteria. For example, if one standard is "lives in warm climate," define the temperature range that qualifies as warm.

Step 4. Report your criteria to the rest of the class and explain how you would measure each.

Step 5. With the whole class, debate the relative merits of each quality-of-life threshold and its measurement.

Challenge Write a paragraph explaining how the quality-of-life threshold you developed relates to Hernando de Soto's ideas about property and prosperity (see page 394).

McDougal Littell Assessment System

Assess

Online Test Practice
- Go to **ClassZone.com** for more test practice.

Unit 5 Resource Book
- Chapter Test, Forms A, B, & C, pp. 81–92

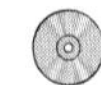

Test Generator CD-ROM
- Chapter Test, Forms (A, B, & C), in English and Spanish

Report

Use the McDougal Littell Assessment System to score assessments and receive customized reports.

Reteach

For activities customized for individual students, use the McDougal Littell Assessment System.

CHAPTER 13 ASSESSMENT ANSWERS

11. Age—youngest earn more as they grow older and retirees earn less; change in marital status—married couples benefit from two incomes; more education leads to better income opportunities; serious injury or disability might reduce earning capability.
12. The Earned Income Tax Credit, Empowerment Zones, and workfare.
13. Inflation. Controlling consumer prices should help businesses, which would reduce unemployment and increase GDP.
14. Answers will vary, but look for an understanding of chapter concepts.

Simulation Rubric

	Understanding of Concepts Involved	Presentation of Information
4	excellent	accurate, clear, and complete
3	good	mostly accurate and clear
2	fair	sometimes clear
1	poor	sketchy

CHAPTER 14: Government Revenue and Spending
Planning Guide

Resources 2Go Complete print resources all on one USB drive allow you to customize lessons.

Section Titles and Objectives	Unit 6 Resource Book and Workbooks		Assessment Resources
1 How Taxes Work pp. 410–419 • Explain why the government establishes taxes • Identify the principles and structure of taxes • Examine the incidence of taxes • Describe how taxes affect the economy	**Unit 6 Resource Book** • Reading Study Guide, pp. 1–2 • RSG with Additional Support, pp. 3–5 • RSG with Additional Support (Spanish), pp. 6–8 • Math Skills Worksheet: Calculating Progressive Taxes, p. 49	**NCEE Student Activities** • Fair Taxes and Citizen Responses, pp. 53–56	**Unit 6 Resource Book** • Section Quiz, p. 9 • Reteaching Activity, p. 10 **Test Generator CD-ROM** **Daily Test Practice Transparencies,** TT46
2 Federal Taxes pp. 420–427 • Describe the process of paying individual income taxes • Explain taxes for Social Security, Medicare, and unemployment • Identify other taxes that are collected by the federal government	**Unit 6 Resource Book** • Reading Study Guide, pp. 11–12 • RSG with Additional Support, pp. 13–15 • RSG with Additional Support (Spanish), pp. 16–18 • Economic Skills and Problem Solving Activity, pp. 41–42	**NCEE Student Activities** • Fair Taxes and Citizen Responses, pp. 53–56	**Unit 6 Resource Book** • Section Quiz, p. 19 • Reteaching Activity, p. 20 **Test Generator CD-ROM** **Daily Test Practice Transparencies,** TT47
3 Federal Government Spending pp. 428–433 • Compare the two types of government expenditures • Explain how the federal budget is developed • Describe how government payments are made • Identify the impact that federal spending has on the economy	**Unit 6 Resource Book** • Reading Study Guide, pp. 21–22 • RSG with Additional Support, pp. 23–25 • RSG with Additional Support (Spanish), pp. 26–28 • Readings in Free Enterprise: A Quiz for Capitalists, pp. 43–44	• Economic Simulations: Economic Impact Presentation, pp. 47–48 **Test Practice and Review Workbook,** pp. 49–50	**Unit 6 Resource Book** • Section Quiz, p. 29 • Reteaching Activity, p. 30 **Test Generator CD-ROM** **Daily Test Practice Transparencies,** TT48
4 State and Local Taxes and Spending pp. 434–441 • Identify the major sources of revenue for both state and local governments • Examine the concept of a balanced budget • Describe the major categories of state and local expenditures	**Unit 6 Resource Book** • Reading Study Guide, pp. 31–32 • RSG with Additional Support, pp. 33–35 • RSG with Additional Support (Spanish), pp. 36–38 • Economic Simulations: Economic Impact Presentation, pp. 47–48	• Case Study Resources: Online Tax Debate Heats Up, p. 45; Online Sales Tax Debate Rages On, p. 46 **Test Practice and Review Workbook,** pp. 49–50	**Unit 6 Resource Book** • Section Quiz, p. 39 • Reteaching Activity, p. 40 • Chapter Test, (Forms A, B, & C), pp. 51–62 **Test Generator CD-ROM** **Daily Test Practice Transparencies,** TT49

Integrated Technology

No Time? To focus students on the most important content in this chapter, use the chart, "The Federal Budget," that appears on page 431.

Teacher Presentation Options

Presentation Toolkit

Power Presentation DVD-ROM

- Lecture Notes
- Media Gallery
- Review Game
- Interactive Review
- Animated Economics

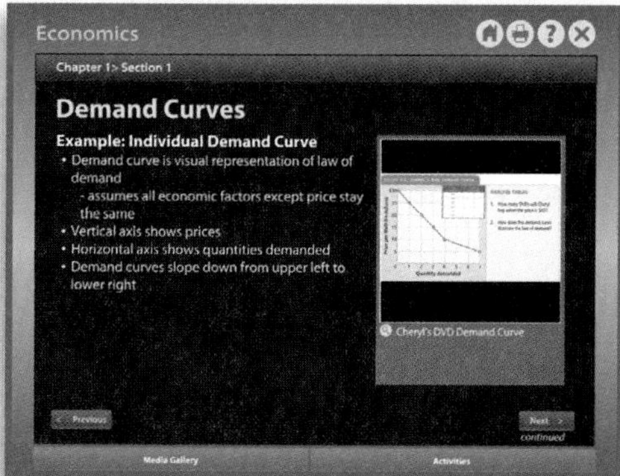

Economics Concepts Transparencies

- Tax Structures, CT46
- Percent of Federal Receipts by Source, CT47
- Federal Budget Receipts and Outlays, CT48
- Federal, State, and Local Revenue and Expenditures, CT49

Electronic Books

eEdition DVD-ROM

eEdition Online

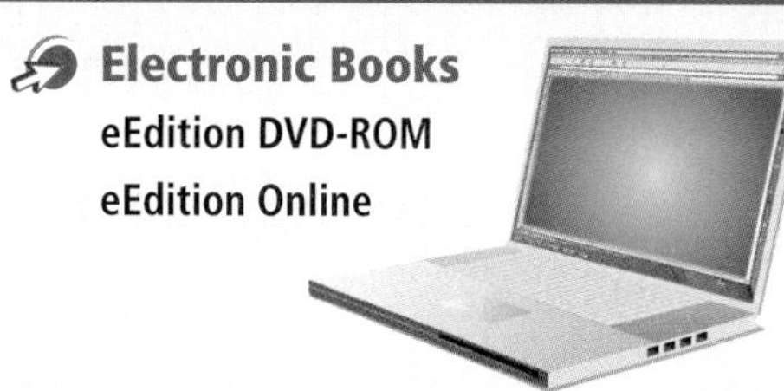

Daily Test Practice Transparencies, TT46, TT47, TT48, TT49

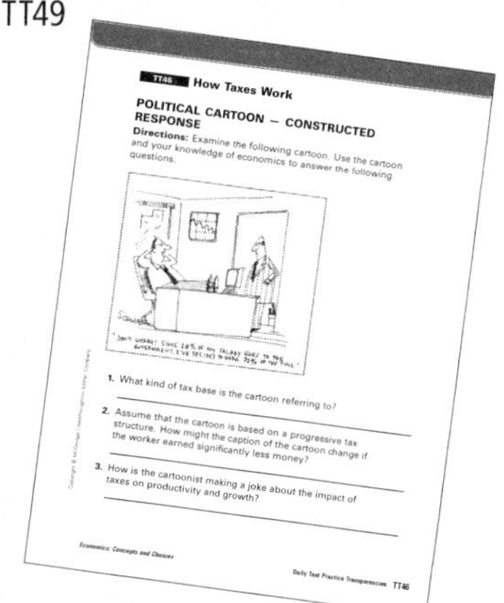

TT46 How Taxes Work
POLITICAL CARTOON — CONSTRUCTED RESPONSE
Directions: Examine the following cartoon. Use the cartoon and your knowledge of economics to answer the following questions.
1. What kind of tax base is the cartoon referring to?
2. Assume that the cartoon is based on a progressive tax structure. How might the caption of the cartoon change if the worker earned significantly less money?
3. How is the cartoonist making a joke about the impact of taxes on productivity and growth?
Economics: Concepts and Choices
Daily Test Practice Transparencies TT46

Animated Economics

- Interactive Demand Elasticity, p. 415

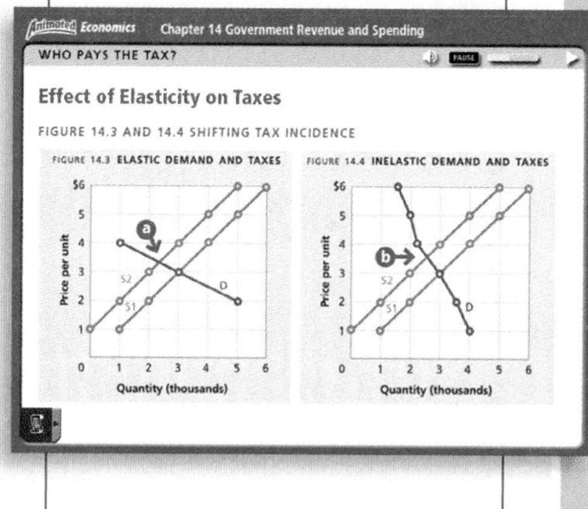

Online Activities at ClassZone.com

Economics Update

- Taxation, p. 411
- Tax Schedules, p. 422
- Maya MacGuineas, p. 426
- Social Security, p. 429
- State Sales Taxes, p. 434
- Should Online Sales Be Taxed? P. 440

Animated Economics

- Interactive Graphics

Activity Maker

- Vocabulary Flip Cards
- Review Game

Research Center

- Graphs and Data

Interactive Review

- Online Summary
- Quizzes
- Vocabulary Flip Cards
- Graphic Organizers
- Review and Study Notes

SMARTGrapher

- Create a Supply and Demand Curve, p. 419
- Create Supply and Demand Curves, p. 443

Teacher-Tested Activities

Name: Tim O'Driscoll (ret.)

School: Arrowhead High School

State: Wisconsin

Teacher-Tested Activities

At the beginning of this chapter, look for my classroom-proven idea for teaching economics concepts and thinking.

Chapter 14: Government Revenue and Spending

Resources for Differentiated Instruction

Struggling Readers

Teacher's Edition Activities

- Use Reciprocal Teaching, p. 412
- Diagram Cause and Effect, p. 416
- Use a Table, p. 422
- Compare Economic Information, p. 430
- Use Popcorn Reading, p. 436
- Summarize Visually, p. 438

Unit 6 Resource Book

- RSG with Additional Support, pp. 3–5, 13–15, 23–25, 33–35 (A)
- Reteaching Activities, pp. 10, 20, 30, 40 (B)
- Chapter Test (Ford A), pp. 51–54 (C)

ClassZone.com

- Animated Economics
- Interactive Review

Test Generator CD-ROM

- Chapter Test (Form A)
- Chapter Test (Form A), in Spanish

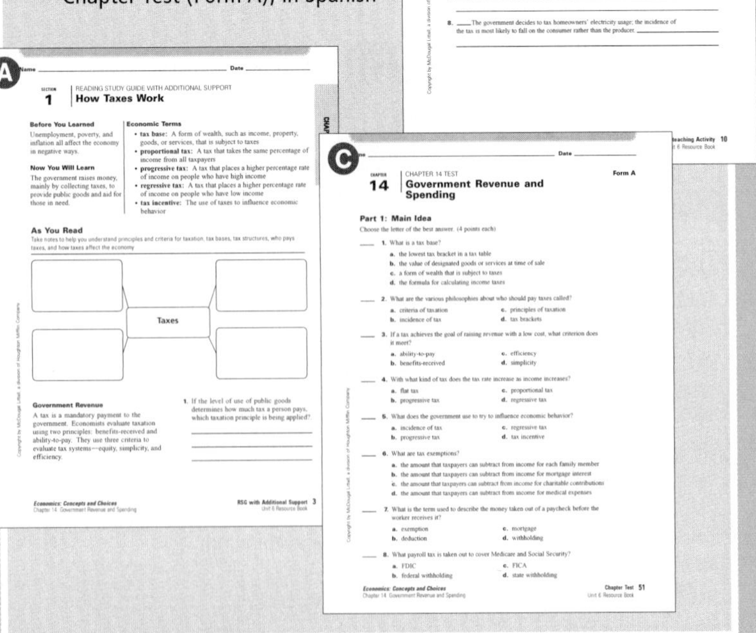

English Learners

Teacher's Edition Activities

- Build Economic Vocabulary, p. 412
- Understand Colloquial English, p. 416
- Analyze Word Forms, p. 422
- Understand Multiple-Meaning Words, p. 424
- Compare Nouns and Verbs, p. 432
- Provide Background Knowledge, p. 440

Unit 6 Resource Book

- RSG with Additional Support (Spanish), pp. 6–8, 16–18, 26–28, 36–38 (A)

Test Generator CD-ROM

- Chapter Test (Forms A, B, & C), in Spanish (B)

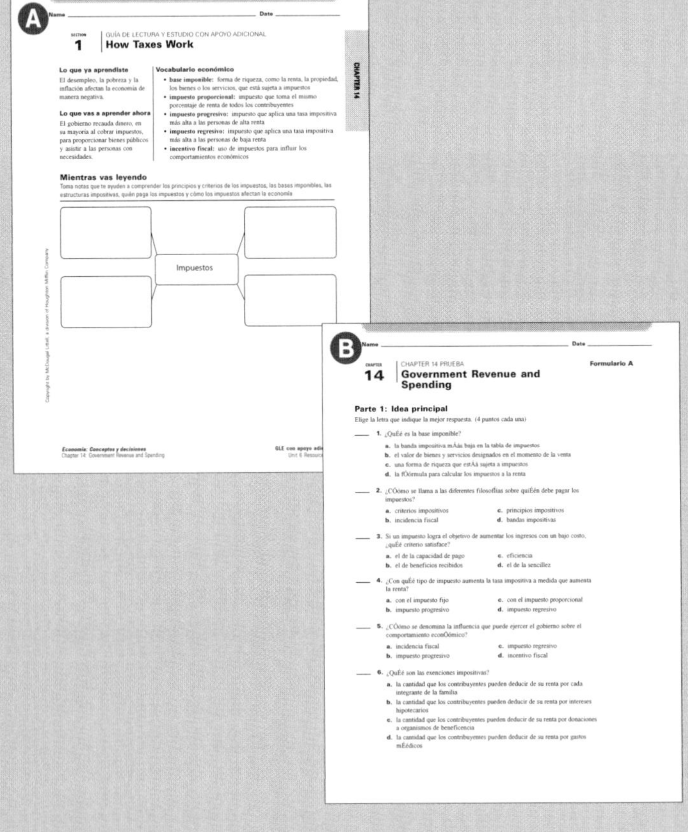

Inclusion

Teacher's Edition Activities

- Complete a Chart, p. 414
- Enlarge the Text, p. 418
- Explain Visuals, p. 424
- Create Line Graphs, p. 426
- Create a Quiz, p. 436
- Listen to the Case Study, p. 440

Lesson Plans

- Modified Lessons for Inclusion, pp. 46–49 (A)

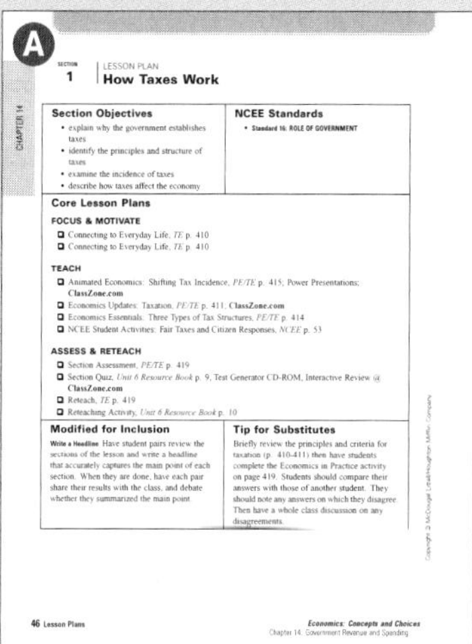

A

SECTION 1 | LESSON PLAN
How Taxes Work

CHAPTER 14

Section Objectives	NCEE Standards
• explain why the government establishes taxes • identify the principles and structure of taxes • examine the incidence of taxes • describe how taxes affect the economy	• Standard 16: ROLE OF GOVERNMENT

Core Lesson Plans

FOCUS & MOTIVATE

- ❑ Connecting to Everyday Life, *TE* p. 410
- ❑ Connecting to Everyday Life, *TE* p. 410

TEACH

- ❑ Animated Economics: Shifting Tax Incidence, *PE/TE* p. 415; Power Presentations; **ClassZone.com**
- ❑ Economics Updates: Taxation, *PE/TE* p. 411; **ClassZone.com**
- ❑ Economics Essentials: Three Types of Tax Structures, *PE/TE* p. 414
- ❑ NCEE Student Activities: Fair Taxes and Citizen Responses, *NCEE* p. 53

ASSESS & RETEACH

- ❑ Section Assessment, *PE/TE* p. 419
- ❑ Section Quiz, *Unit 6 Resource Book* p. 9, Test Generator CD-ROM, Interactive Review @ **ClassZone.com**
- ❑ Reteach, *TE* p. 419
- ❑ Reteaching Activity, *Unit 6 Resource Book* p. 10

Modified for Inclusion	Tip for Substitutes
Write a Headline Have student pairs review the sections of the lesson and write a headline that accurately captures the main point of each section. When they are done, have each pair share their results with the class, and debate whether they summarized the main point.	Briefly review the principles and criteria for taxation (p. 410-411) then have students complete the Economics in Practice activity on page 419. Students should compare their answers with those of another student. They should note any answers on which they disagree. Then have a whole class discussion on any disagreements.

Copyright © McDougal Littell/Houghton Mifflin Company

46 Lesson Plans

Economics: Concepts and Choices
Chapter 14: Government Revenue and Spending

Gifted and Talented

Teacher's Edition Activities

- Write an Editorial, p. 414
- Develop a Research Guide, p. 418
- Role-Play an Interview, p. 426
- Graph Spending Trends, p. 430
- Write a News Story, p. 432
- Research Local Government, p. 438

Unit 6 Resource Book

- Readings in Free Enterprise: A Quiz for Capitalists, pp. 43–44 (A)
- Case Study Resources: Online Tax Debate Heats Up; Online Sales Tax Debate Rages On, pp. 45–46 (B)

NCEE Student Activities

- Fair Taxes and Citizen Responses, pp. 53–56 (C)

ClassZone.com

- Research Center

Test Generator CD-ROM

- Chapter Test (Form C)
- Chapter Test (Form C), in Spanish

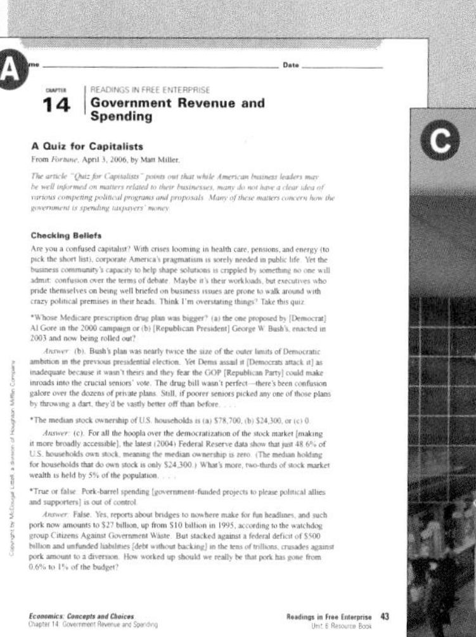

A

Name ______ Date ______

CHAPTER 14 | READINGS IN FREE ENTERPRISE
Government Revenue and Spending

A Quiz for Capitalists

From *Fortune*, April 3, 2006, by Matt Miller.

The article "Quiz for Capitalists" points out that while American business leaders may be well informed on matters related to their businesses, many do not have a clear idea of various competing political programs and proposals. Many of these matters concern how the government is spending taxpayers' money.

Checking Beliefs

Are you a confused capitalist? With crises looming in health care, pensions, and energy (to pick the short list), corporate America's pragmatism is sorely needed in public life. Yet the business community's capacity to help shape solutions is crippled by something no one will admit: confusion over the terms of debate. Maybe it's their workloads, but executives who pride themselves on being well briefed on business issues are prone to walk around with crazy political premises in their heads. Think I'm overstating things? Take this quiz.

*Whose Medicare prescription drug plan was bigger? (a) the one proposed by [Democrat] Al Gore in the 2000 campaign or (b) [Republican President] George W. Bush's, enacted in 2003 and now being rolled out?

Answer: (b). Bush's plan was nearly twice the size of the outer limits of Democratic ambition in the previous presidential election. Yet Dems assail it [Democrats attack it] as inadequate because it wasn't theirs and they fear the GOP [Republican Party] could make inroads into the crucial seniors' vote. The drug bill wasn't perfect—there's been confusion galore over the dozens of private plans. Still, if poorer seniors picked any one of those plans by throwing a dart, they'd be vastly better off than before. . . .

*The median stock ownership of U.S. households is (a) $78,700, (b) $24,300, or (c) 0.

Answer: (c). For all the hoopla over the democratization of the stock market [making it more broadly accessible], the latest (2004) Federal Reserve data show that just 48.6% of U.S. households own stock, meaning the median ownership is zero. (The median holding for households that do own stock is only $24,300.) What's more, two-thirds of stock market wealth is held by 5% of the population. . . .

*True or false: Pork-barrel spending [government-funded projects to please political allies and supporters] is out of control.

Answer: False. Yes, reports about bridges to nowhere make for fun headlines, and such pork now amounts to $27 billion, up from $10 billion in 1995, according to the watchdog group Citizens Against Government Waste. But stacked against a federal deficit of $500 billion and unfunded liabilities [debt without backing] in the tens of trillions, crusades against pork amount to a diversion. How worked up should we really be that pork has gone from 0.6% to 1% of the budget?

Copyright by McDougal Littell, a division of Houghton Mifflin Company

Economics: Concepts and Choices
Chapter 14: Government Revenue and Spending

Readings in Free Enterprise 43
Unit 6 Resource Book

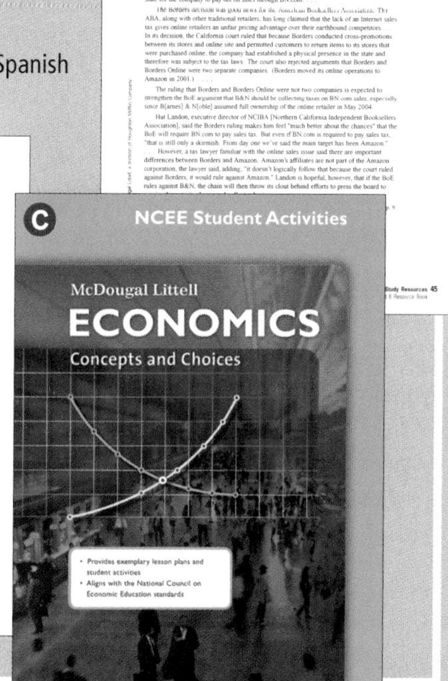

B

Name ______ Date ______

CHAPTER 14 | CASE STUDY RESOURCES
Government Revenue and Spending

Online Tax Debate Heats Up

The first article reports that bookstore giant Borders has been ordered to pay sales tax on its online sales by the California Appeals court.

Internet Sales Tax

The California Appeals court ruling late last month that Borders had a sufficient presence in the state to force the chain to charge and collect tax on online sales is expected to be only the first of several decisions that will move the debate on online taxes forward. Next up is expected to be a ruling by the California Board of Equalization [BoE], the state's tax collection arm, on whether Barnes & Noble has enough of a physical nexus [center] in the state for the company to pay tax on sales through BN.com. . . .

The Borders decision was good news for the American Booksellers Association. The ABA, along with other traditional retailers, has long claimed that the lack of an Internet sales tax gives online retailers an unfair pricing advantage over their earthbound competitors. . . . In its decision, the California court ruled that because Borders conducted cross-promotions between its stores and online site and permitted customers to return items to its stores that were purchased online, the company had established a physical presence in the state and therefore was subject to the tax laws. The court also rejected arguments that Borders and Borders Online were two separate companies. (Borders moved its online operations to Amazon in 2001.) . . .

The ruling that Borders and Borders Online were not two companies is expected to strengthen the BoE argument that B&N should be collecting taxes on BN.com sales, especially since B[arnes] & N[oble] assumed full ownership of the online retailer in May 2004.

Hut Landon, executive director of NCIBA [Northern California Independent Booksellers Association], said the Borders ruling makes him feel "much better about the chances" that the BoE will require BN.com to pay sales tax. But even if BN.com is required to pay sales tax, "that is still only a skirmish. From day one we've said the main target has been Amazon." . . . However, a tax lawyer familiar with the online sales issue said there are important differences between Borders and Amazon. Amazon's affiliates are not part of the Amazon corporation, the lawyer said, adding, "it doesn't logically follow that because the court ruled against Borders, it would rule against Amazon." Landon is hopeful, however, that if the BoE rules against B&N, the chain will then throw its clout behind efforts to press the board to

Focus & Motivate

Objective

Describe how government uses taxation to raise revenue in order to provide public goods.

Why the Concept Matters

Explain that taxes are the means by which citizens pay for public goods. Government sets up a system for collecting taxes in order to raise revenue. Elected officials then decide how the revenue should be spent, based on input from citizens. Government services are so familiar that we may not always think about how important they are.

Analyzing the Photograph

Have students study the photograph and read the caption. Invite volunteers to suggest who benefits from the government programs shown in the photograph. *(Possible response: Citizens and foreign visitors may enjoy the national park. Society benefits from protecting natural areas in the parks.)*

Ask students what they can infer from the photograph about how goods provided by the government are different from goods provided by the market. *(Possible response: Government provides goods that benefit large numbers of people and that are not sold on an individual basis.)*

Conclude by noting that Chapter 14 describes why and how government uses various kinds of taxes to raise revenue to provide such public goods.

Macroeconomics

Unit 6

The Role of Government in the Economy

Government Spending

Government funds pay for national parks such as the Grand Canyon National Park. Government raises the money for such services through taxation.

408

CONTENT STANDARDS

NCEE STANDARDS

Standard 16: Role of Government

Students will understand that

There is an economic role for government in a market economy whenever the benefits of a government policy outweigh its costs. Governments often provide for national defense [and] address environmental concerns. . . . Most government policies also redistribute income.

Students will be able to use this knowledge to

Identify and evaluate the benefits and costs of alternative public policies, and assess who enjoys the benefits and who bears the costs.

Benchmarks

Students will know that

- Governments pay for the goods and services they use or provide by taxing or borrowing from people. *(pages 410–417, 420–426, 434–435, 437)*
- If a good or service cannot be withheld from those who do not pay for it, providers expect to be unable to sell it and, therefore, will not produce it. In market economies, governments provide some of these goods and services. *(pages 410–411, 428–432, 436, 438)*
- Governments provide an alternative method to markets for supplying goods and services when it appears that the benefits to society of doing so outweigh the costs to society. Not all individuals will bear the same costs or share the same benefits of those policies. *(pages 410–411, 428–432)*
- Governments often redistribute income directly when individuals or interest groups are not satisfied with the income distribution resulting from markets; governments also redistribute income indirectly as side-effects of other government actions that affect prices or output levels. *(pages 416–417, 428–429, 432)*

CHAPTER

14

Government Revenue and Spending

CONCEPT REVIEW

A **modified free enterprise economy** is an economic system, like that of the United States, that includes some government involvement that influences the free enterprise system.

CHAPTER 14 KEY CONCEPT

A **tax** is a mandatory payment to a local, state, or national government, while **revenue** is government income from taxes and other nontax sources.

WHY THE CONCEPT MATTERS

Taxes are a part of your everyday life—from the income tax withheld from your paycheck to the sales tax you pay on the snack you bought at the sandwich shop. The revenues raised from these taxes fund programs that are familiar to you. For example, the highways you drive on, the police that protect you, and the parks that you use are all paid for by government revenues.

Online Highlights

More at ClassZone.com

Economics Update

Go to **ECONOMICS UPDATE** for chapter updates and current news on sales taxes on Internet purchases. (See Case Study, pages 440–441.)

Animated Economics

Go to **ANIMATED ECONOMICS** for interactive lessons on the graphs and tables in this chapter. ▶

Interactive Review

Go to **INTERACTIVE REVIEW** for concept review and activities.

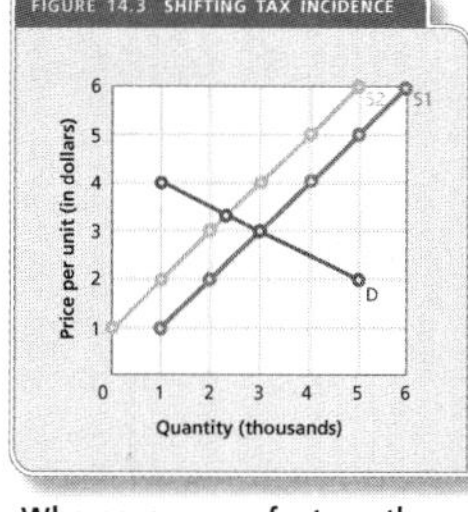

Who pays more of a tax—the consumer or the producer? See Figures 14.3 and 14.4 on page 415.

From the Classroom

Tim O'Driscoll, Arrowhead H.S. (retired)

Taxes and Government Services

All levels of government—local, state and federal—collect taxes from citizens. The types and amounts of taxes collected are determined by elected politicians. They also decide how the money collected, called tax revenue, is used to pay for public goods and services.

Some students may be unaware of the wide variety of taxes that they and their parents pay. Other students may be opposed to taxes because they do not like the idea of the government taking their money. Many students may not have given any thought to the benefits that citizens receive from government expenditures of tax dollars.

To start students thinking about taxes and government spending, put them into small groups and have them fill out two tables. One table should list taxes and fees collected at each level of government. The other should list programs and services provided by each level of government.

After students have been given 10 to 15 minutes to fill out the chart, use the board or the overhead to record their responses.

Previewing Chapter Technology at ClassZone.com

Economics Update Students will find references to online articles or statistics that update information in the pupil edition on pages 411, 422, 426, 429, 434, and 440.

Animated Economics Students will find interactive lessons related to materials on page 415.

Interactive Review Students will find additional section and chapter assessment support for materials on pages 419, 427, 433, 439, and 442.

TEACHER MEDIA FAVORITES

Books for the Teacher

- Gelfand, David M. et al. *State and Local Taxation and Finance in a Nutshell.* 2d ed. St. Paul: West Group, 2000. Detailed summary of state and local revenue sources and expenditures.
- Santow, Leonard J., and Mark E. Santow, *Social Security and the Middle-Class Squeeze: Fact and Fiction about America's Entitlement Programs.* Westport, CT: Praeger, 2005. An economist and a historian provide a primer on the three largest entitlement programs and how to improve them.
- Slemrod, Joel, and Jon Bakija. *Taxing Ourselves: A Citizen's Guide to the Debate over Taxes.* 3rd ed. Cambridge, MA: MIT Press, 2004. A clear overview of the U.S. tax system and an unbiased guide to the key tax reform issues.
- Wiseman, Alan E. *The Internet Economy: Access, Taxes, and Market Structure.* Washington, D.C.: Brookings Institution Press, 2002. Explores economic issues and the role of government in the Internet economy.

Videos/DVDs

- *How People Are Paid: Understanding Salaries and Benefits.* 19 Minutes. Learning Seed. Explains paychecks and deductions, including FICA and the Social Security benefits it covers.

Software

- *Virtual Economics® Version 3.0.* New York: National Council on Economic Education, 2005. Provides a complete resource library for teaching and understanding basic economic concepts.

Internet

Visit **ClassZone.com** to link to

- a variety of chapter-specific, content-reviewed sites
- updates on data and topics presented throughout the chapter sections and Case Study
- updates to the Power Presentations

1 Plan & Prepare

Section 1 Objectives

- explain why the government establishes taxes
- identify the principles and structure of taxes
- examine the incidence of taxes
- describe how taxes affect the economy

2 Focus & Motivate

Connecting to Everyday Life Explain that this section focuses on the reasons government imposes taxes and how they work. Invite students to discuss why it is important for taxes to be fair and to suggest some things that need to be done to make them fair.

Taking Notes Remind students to take notes as they read by completing a cluster diagram on taxes. They can use the Graphic Organizer at **Interactive Review @ ClassZone.com**. A sample is shown below.

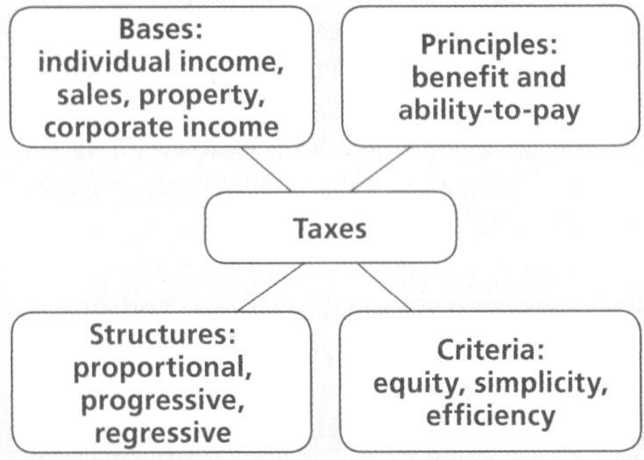

SECTION 1

How Taxes Work

OBJECTIVES

In Section 1, you will

- explain why the government establishes taxes
- identify the principles and structure of taxes
- examine the incidence of taxes
- describe how taxes affect the economy

KEY TERMS

tax, *p. 410*
revenue, *p. 410*
tax base, *p. 412*
individual income tax, *p. 412*
corporate income tax, *p. 412*
sales tax, *p. 412*
property tax, *p. 412*
proportional tax, *p. 412*
progressive tax, *p. 412*
regressive tax, *p. 412*
incidence of a tax, *p. 415*
tax incentive, *p. 417*

TAKING NOTES

As you read Section 1, complete a cluster diagram, using the key concepts and other helpful words and phrases. Use the Graphic Organizer at **Interactive Review @ ClassZone.com**

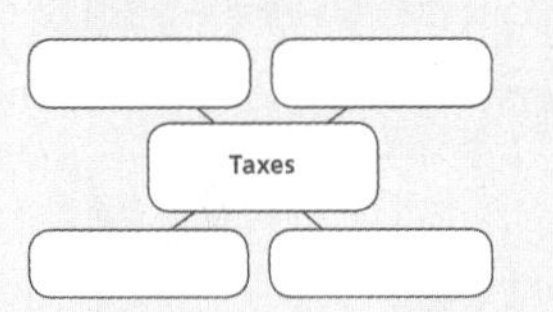

Government Revenue

KEY CONCEPTS

QUICK REFERENCE

A **tax** is a mandatory payment to a government.

Revenue is government income from taxes and other sources.

Governments provide certain public goods that generally are not provided by the market, such as street lighting, highways, law enforcement, and the court system. Government also provides aid for people in need. Where does the money come from to pay for such goods and services? The most important source is taxes. A **tax** is a mandatory payment to a local, state, or national government. **Revenue** is government income from taxes and nontax sources. Nontax sources include borrowing and lotteries. The rights of government to tax are set down in the U.S. Constitution and in state constitutions.

Principles of Taxation

When Chelsea started her 20-hour-per-week job at the local library, she expected to receive $120 in her weekly paycheck. However, she was surprised to see that some money was deducted from her pay for various taxes. She wondered why she had to pay these taxes.

Economists use certain principles and criteria to evaluate whether or not taxes should be paid and who should pay them. These principles most often are based on the benefits taxpayers receive from taxes and their ability to pay.

SECTION 1 PROGRAM RESOURCES

ON LEVEL

Lesson Plans

- Core, p. 46

Unit 6 Resource Book

- Reading Study Guide, pp. 1–2
- Math Skills Worksheet, p. 49
- Section Quiz, p. 9

STRUGGLING READERS

Unit 6 Resource Book

- Reading Study Guide with Additional Support, pp. 3–5
- Reteaching Activity, p. 10

ENGLISH LEARNERS

Unit 6 Resource Book

- Reading Study Guide with Additional Support (Spanish), pp. 6–8

INCLUSION

Lesson Plans

- Modified for Inclusion, p. 46

GIFTED AND TALENTED

NCEE Student Activities

- Fair Taxes and Citizen Responses, pp. 53–56

TECHNOLOGY

eEdition DVD-ROM

eEdition Online

Power Presentation DVD-ROM

Economics Concepts Transparencies

- CT46 Tax Structures

Daily Test Practice Transparencies, TT46

ClassZone.com

Benefits-Received Principle The benefits-received principle of taxation holds that people who benefit directly from public goods should pay for them in proportion to the amount of benefits received. One example of this principle is the financing of road construction and maintenance through taxes on gasoline. However, it is difficult for governments to assess exactly how much different taxpayers benefit from services like national defense, national parks, local police and fire protection, and public education.

Ability-to-Pay Principle The ability-to-pay principle of taxation holds that people should be taxed on their ability to pay, no matter the level of benefits they receive. According to this principle, people with higher incomes will pay more than people with lower incomes. The level of benefits received is not a consideration. Yet, income alone might not completely determine someone's ability to pay taxes. Other questions also arise. For example, should everyone pay the same percentage of income, which still results in wealthier people paying more in taxes, or should those with higher incomes pay a higher percentage of their income in taxes?

Criteria for Taxation

Tax systems attempt to meet three criteria: equity, simplicity, and efficiency. However, the criteria are sometimes in conflict, and a given tax may not meet all of the criteria equally well.

Simplicity One criticism of the U. S. tax code is that it is too complicated.

Equity The equity, or fairness, of a tax is established by how uniformly the tax is applied. Equity requires that people in similar situations pay a similar amount of taxes. For example, everyone who buys gasoline pays the same tax, or all people with the same level of income pay the same amount in taxes. In addition, some believe that equity requires that people with higher incomes pay more than people with lower incomes.

Simplicity The simplicity of a tax is determined by how easy it is for the taxpayer to understand and how easy it is for the government to collect. In addition, there should be no confusion about the time the tax is due and the amount to be paid. The sales tax, which you'll read about on the next page, meets the criterion of simplicity. A set percentage of the price of a taxed item is collected every time that item is purchased.

Efficiency The efficiency of a tax can be judged by how well the tax achieves the goal of raising revenue for the government with the least cost in terms of administration. From the taxpayers' viewpoint, tax efficiency can be judged by the amount of effort and expense it takes to pay the tax. Of all the types of taxes levied, the individual income tax—which you'll learn more about on the next page—best meets the criterion of efficiency.

Economics Update

Find an update on taxation at **ClassZone.com**

APPLICATION Drawing Conclusions

A. Businesses and homeowners both benefit from police protection. How does this statement show the limitations of the benefits-received principle of taxation?

See Teacher's Edition for answer. ▶

3 Teach

Government Revenue

Discuss

- What is the difference between the two principles of taxation? *(One is based on who receives benefits from taxes, and the other is based on the ability of people to pay the taxes.)*
- How might the criterion of equity conflict with the criteria of simplicity and efficiency? *(Possible answer: A tax that is simple and efficient for taxpayers and the government may not be the fairest, which may need to be more complex to account for different situations.)*

Economics Update

At **ClassZone.com** students will see updated information on criteria for taxation.

APPLICATION

Answer *It would be difficult to quantify the benefit each business and homeowner receives from police protection. Therefore, it is impossible to fairly set the amount of tax each business and homeowner should pay for the service.*

LEVELED ACTIVITY

Analyze the Role of Government

Time 30 Minutes

Objective Students will demonstrate an understanding of the importance of public goods and of taxation as the means to finance them. (Draws on material from all sections.)

Basic

Develop a list of goods and services provided by government rather than by the market. List how the government raises money to pay for these goods and services. Write a paragraph describing how life would be different if government had no power to tax. Include your opinion about the value of public goods.

On Level

Read the preamble to the U.S. Constitution. Note the phrases that describe the roles of government. Create a graphic organizer showing specific examples of public goods that the government provides to fulfill each of these roles. Write a caption explaining why taxation is important in achieving these goals.

Challenge

Read the preamble to the U.S. Constitution. Consider what you have learned about government revenue and spending for public goods and services. Write a speech using key concepts from the chapter to express your philosophy of taxation as it relates to government's fulfilling its roles as outlined in the preamble.

Tax Bases and Structures

Discuss

- What is the difference between individual income and corporate income as tax bases? *(Individual income refers to the money earned by individuals through work or investment. Corporate income refers to the profits that businesses make from providing goods and services.)*
- Why are sales and property taxes considered regressive rather than proportional? *(because low-income earners pay a higher percentage of their income in these taxes than do high-income earners, even though the tax rate is the same for all taxpayers)*

International Economics

Value Added Tax

In most developed nations, a major source of government revenue is the value added tax (VAT). This tax is similar to a national sales tax. But instead of being levied only on retail sales, it is levied on all stages of production. All businesses collect taxes on their sales but are able to deduct taxes paid on purchases. So, the net tax at each stage of production is on the value added at that stage. The final consumer pays the total tax.

Tax Bases and Structures

KEY CONCEPTS

Government imposes taxes on various forms of income and wealth in order to raise the revenue to provide public goods and various other services. Each type of wealth subject to taxes is called a **tax base.** The four most common tax bases are individual income, corporate income, sales, and property.

QUICK REFERENCE

A **tax base** is a form of wealth—such as income, property, goods, or services—that is subject to taxes.

Individual income tax is based on an individual's income from all sources.

Corporate income tax is based on a corporation's profits.

Sales tax is based on the value of goods or services at the time of sale.

Property tax is based on the value of an individual's or a business's assets.

A **proportional tax** takes the same percentage of income from all taxpayers.

A **progressive tax** places a higher percentage rate of taxation on high-income people.

A **regressive tax** takes a larger percentage of income from low-income people.

Tax Bases

Individual income tax is a tax based on an individual's income from all sources: wages, interest, dividends, and tips. All taxes are ultimately paid from income, but using income as a tax base means that the amount of tax is directly linked to a person's earnings. For most individuals, income is earned mainly from work in the form of wages or tips. It may also come from savings and investment in the form of interest and dividends. Corporations pay income tax too. **Corporate income tax** is a tax based on a corporation's profits.

Sales tax is a tax based on the value of designated goods or services at the time of sale. Generally, sales taxes are imposed on a wide range of goods and services. The tax usually is a percentage of the posted price of the good or service and is included in the final price that the buyer pays. The seller then passes the tax revenue collected from customers on to the government that has imposed the tax.

Property tax is a tax based on the value of an individual's or business's assets, generally real estate. Homeowners and business owners pay property taxes based on the value of their buildings and the land on which the buildings stand. Property tax is generally included in the rents charged by property owners to individuals or businesses that rent the property, whether it is an apartment, an office, a factory, or a retail store. Property tax may also be imposed on other assets such as automobiles.

You may have heard references to a particular government's tax base growing or shrinking. Such statements refer to the amount of wealth that is available to be taxed. If overall personal income rises, the individual income tax base grows. If there are fewer homes or businesses in a certain locality or if their value declines, the property tax base shrinks because there is less wealth for the government to tax.

Tax Structures

The way in which taxes are imposed on the different tax bases gives rise to three different tax structures. These tax structures are distinguished from one another based on the percentage of income that a particular tax takes. A **proportional tax** takes the same percentage of income from all taxpayers regardless of income level. A **progressive tax** places a higher percentage rate of taxation on high-income earners than on low-income earners. A **regressive tax** takes a larger percentage of income from people with low incomes than from people with high incomes.

Proportional Tax A proportional tax is sometimes called a flat tax, because the rate of tax is the same for all taxpayers. For example, all taxpayers in a given country or state might be charged a flat 15 percent tax on their income, no matter how much

DIFFERENTIATING INSTRUCTION

Struggling Readers

Use Reciprocal Teaching

Have pairs of students take turns reading paragraphs out loud and asking their partners to summarize what they have just heard. Students who are reading may also ask their partners questions about what they have read. Ask students to discuss the Application questions together and agree on answers.

English Learners

Build Economic Vocabulary

Help students understand the different tax bases and structures. Organize students into pairs and direct them to make vocabulary cards for each key term on page 412. Encourage students to break the compound nouns into the word *tax* and the other words that it modifies (*base*) or is modified by, such as *individual income.* Have students write a definition for each term on the cards. Partners may quiz each other on term meanings.

MATH CHALLENGE

FIGURE 14.1 Understanding a Progressive Tax

Step 1: Study the table to the right, which shows income tax brackets for a progressive tax. Each marginal tax rate is applied only to the income in that tax bracket. For example, for a taxable income of $12,000, $10,000 is taxed at 10 percent and the remaining $2,000 is taxed at 15 percent.

Income Bracket	Marginal Tax Rate
$0–$10,000	10%
$10,000–$30,000	15%
$30,000–$50,000	25%

Step 2: Assume you have a taxable income of $40,000. The table to the right shows how much of that income is in each tax bracket.

Income in Each Bracket	Tax Bracket
$10,000	10%
$20,000	15%
$10,000	25%

Step 3: Calculate the marginal tax for the income in each bracket. Add these figures to get the total tax for a taxable of income of $40,000. The total tax on $40,000 of taxable income is $6,500.

Income in bracket	×	Marginal tax rate	=	Marginal tax
$10,000	×	10%	=	$1,000
$20,000	×	15%	=	$3,000
$10,000	×	25%	=	$2,500
				Total tax: $6,500

More Calculations Repeat calculations for taxable incomes of $25,000 and $45,000.

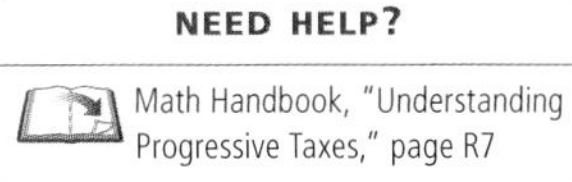

NEED HELP?

Math Handbook, "Understanding Progressive Taxes," page R7

their income is. An individual who earns $20,000 would pay $3,000 in taxes, and an individual who earns $50,000 would pay $7,500 in taxes. In the United States, some state and local governments have proportional taxes on individual income. For example, the state of Michigan has a flat income tax rate of 3.9 percent, while the state of Massachusetts has a 5.3 percent rate. Similarly, the city of Bowling Green, Ohio, collects a flat rate of 1.92 percent on its residents' incomes.

Progressive Tax As you saw above, even with a proportional tax, the amount of tax increases as income increases. A progressive tax is one in which the tax rate also increases as a person's income increases. In other words, under a progressive tax structure, a high-income person not only pays more in the amount of taxes but also pays a higher percentage of income in taxes. Figure 14.1 shows how a progressive income tax works. You can see that a progressive tax is most closely linked to the ability-to-pay principle.

In the United States, the federal income tax is a progressive tax, because the tax rate increases as income increases. (You'll learn more about the federal income tax in Section 2.) Many states, including California, Kansas, New York, and South Carolina, also have progressive income taxes.

Math Challenge: Figure 14.1

Understanding a Progressive Tax
Explain that a tax bracket refers to a grouping of income that is subject to a specific tax rate. The rate is called a marginal rate because it only applies to a portion of the income, as shown in the tables. Taxpayers may be labeled as being in a particular tax bracket, referring to the highest rate that applies to any of their income. To say that someone is in the 25 percent bracket does not mean that all income is taxed at that rate.

Ask students to calculate the overall tax rate for the example by dividing $6,500 by $40,000 (*16.25%*) to reinforce this point. Allow them to practice calculating the tax for different levels of income by following the example.

Math Handbook
Understanding Progressive Taxes, p. R7.

INDIVIDUAL ACTIVITY

Creating a Graphic Organizer

Time 20 Minutes

Task Create an Economics Essentials graphic organizer on tax bases.

Materials Needed paper and pens or markers

Activity

- Have students review the material on page 412 describing the four most common tax bases.
- Invite students to create a graphic organizer to summarize the information.
- Encourage them to use Figure 14.2 on page 414 as a model, pointing out that they should include visuals and captions in their graphic organizers.
- Allow students to share their graphic organizers in small groups.
- Call on volunteers from different groups to describe how different tax bases are represented and to explain how each illustrates the concept of a tax base.

Rubric

	Understanding of Concepts	Presentation of Information
4	excellent	clear and accurate
3	good	mostly accurate
2	fair	somewhat accurate
1	poor	sketchy

Economics Essentials: Figure 14.2

Explain that the diagram summarizes how the different tax structures affect low-income earners and high-income earners.

- Which type of tax structure reflects the ability-to-pay principle of taxation? Why? *(progressive, because the tax rate increases as income increases and those who can afford more pay more)*

Analyze

Explanations will vary. Students should demonstrate an understanding that flat taxes such as some state and local income taxes are proportional, the federal and some state income taxes are progressive, sales and property taxes are regressive. Corporate income taxes may be proportional or progressive, depending on how they are structured.

Economics Illustrated

To help students better understand the impact of the three tax structures, draw a simple graph on the board. Label the horizontal axis as "Income" and the vertical axis as "% of income taken as taxes." Draw a line on the graph, sloping upwards from lower left to upper right and say, "Progressive taxes take a greater percentage of income as income rises." Erase the line, then draw a line sloping downwards from upper left to lower right, saying, "Regressive taxes take a smaller percentage of income as income rises." Erase the line, then draw a horizontal line from left to right, saying, "Proportional taxes take the same percentage of income regardless of income level."

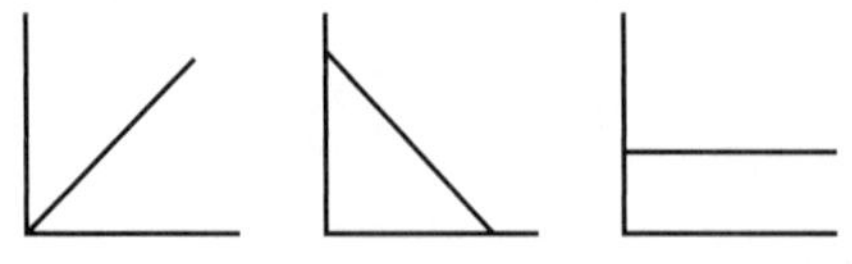

APPLICATION

Answer *Proportional and regressive taxes that rely on flat tax rate are simpler than progressive taxes that have different rates for different income levels, but proportional and regressive taxes may not be as equitable as progressive taxes.*

ECONOMICS ESSENTIALS

FIGURE 14.2 Three Types of Tax Structures

What is the impact of each of the tax structures?

Proportional Tax A proportional tax takes the same percentage of income from all taxpayers, regardless of income level.

Progressive Tax A progressive tax is based on income level. It takes a larger percentage of income from high-income earners and a smaller percentage of income from low-income earners.

Regressive Tax A regressive tax hits low-income earners harder than it hits high-income earners. This is because the proportion of income that goes to taxes falls as income rises.

ANALYZE CHARTS

Look again at the description of the various tax bases on page 412. Consider which kind of tax structure applies to each of these tax bases. Write a brief paragraph explaining your choices.

Regressive Tax With a regressive tax, the percentage of income paid in taxes decreases as income increases. Some taxes are regressive because they are applied to sales, not income. For example, although a sales-tax rate is applied equally to all items subject to the tax, the tax as a percentage of income is regressive. This is because low-income earners tend to spend a higher proportion of income than do high-income earners. Suppose that a state charges 5 percent sales tax on certain goods sold in the state. If the Jones family earns $20,000 and spends $15,000 on taxable goods, they pay $750 in sales taxes (5 percent of $15,000), or 3.75 percent of their income. If the Smith family earns $50,000 and spends $25,000 on taxable goods, they pay $1,250 in sales tax (5 percent of $25,000), or 2.5 percent of their income.

For similar reasons, property taxes on homes are also considered regressive. Low-income homeowners usually spend a higher percentage of their income on housing than do high-income homeowners. Therefore, property taxes take a higher percentage of their income. In addition, poorer communities often charge a higher tax rate, because the property has a lower value and therefore the property tax base is smaller. Even those who do not own homes are subject to the regressive property tax, because property taxes are generally passed on to renters. Figure 14.2 above shows the impact of each type of tax structure on low-income earners and high-income earners.

APPLICATION Comparing and Contrasting

B. How do proportional, progressive, and regressive taxes meet the criteria of simplicity and equity? ◀ See Teacher's Edition for answer.

DIFFERENTIATING INSTRUCTION

Inclusion

Complete a Chart

Help students understand the example of regressive sales taxes described on page 414 by working with them to complete this chart.

	Jones	Smith
Earns		
Spends		
Sales Tax		
% of income		

Gifted and Talented

Write an Editorial

Invite students to reflect on what they have learned about the principles and criteria of taxation, tax bases, and tax structures. Encourage them to write an editorial expressing their opinion on some aspect of taxation. They might choose topics such as: whether a flat tax should replace the progressive federal income tax, whether property taxes should be reduced or eliminated, or what tax bases the community should use. Allow volunteers to share their editorials with the class.

Who Pays the Tax?

KEY CONCEPTS

The impact of a tax can also be measured by who actually pays it. The **incidence of a tax** is the final burden of that tax. In other words, it is the impact of the tax on a taxpayer. For example, taxes imposed on businesses may get passed on to the consumer in the form of higher prices or rents. To understand this, you need to apply the concepts of supply and demand.

QUICK REFERENCE

The **incidence of a tax** is the final burden of the tax.

Effect of Elasticity on Taxes

Suppose that the government imposes a $1 tax on a product. Demand elasticity influences the incidence of this tax. If a product has elastic demand, the seller pays more of the tax, because the seller faces decreased quantity demanded if prices rise. If the product has inelastic demand, the consumer pays more of the tax in the form of higher prices. The seller recognizes that quantity demanded will go down only slightly for goods or services that have inelastic demand, because they are less price-sensitive. Figures 14.3 and 14.4 illustrate the difference in tax incidence between products with elastic and inelastic demand.

FIGURES 14.3 AND 14.4 SHIFTING TAX INCIDENCE

FIGURE 14.3 ELASTIC DEMAND AND TAXES

FIGURE 14.4 INELASTIC DEMAND AND TAXES

When a $1 tax is imposed, the supply curve (S1) shifts to the left (S2) by the amount of the tax.

a In Figure 14.3, the equilibrium price increases to $3.40, and the seller pays more of the tax.

b In Figure 14.4, the equilibrium price rises to $3.80, and the consumer pays more of the tax.

ANALYZE GRAPHS

1. In Figure 14.3, how does quantity demanded at equilibrium change?
2. Which producer's revenues would be least affected by the $1 tax?

Animated Economics Use interactive demand elasticity curves at **ClassZone.com**

APPLICATION Applying Economic Concepts

C. Who would bear the greater incidence of these taxes: a. $1 tax on movie tickets? b. $1 tax on gasoline? Give reasons for your answers.

See Teacher's Edition for answer. ▶

Who Pays the Tax?

Discuss

- Why do businesses not always increase their prices by the full amount of taxes? *(because demand will decrease significantly if prices rise too high on products that have elastic demand)*

Analyzing Graphs: Figures 14.3 and 14.4

Ask students how the graphs reflect a factor that decreases supply. *(when production costs rise for any reason, supply decreases.)* Have them compare and contrast what happens to equilibrium price in the two graphs. *(The tax causes equilibrium price to rise, but it increases more when demand is inelastic.)*

Answers

1. *It decreases from 3,000 to about 2,200.*
2. *the producer of the product with inelastic demand, because most of the tax would be passed on to the consumer*

Animated ***Economics*** These graphs show how changes in supply caused by a tax increase affect equilibrium price for goods with elastic and inelastic demand. They will help students understand the relationship between elasticity of demand and tax incidence.

APPLICATION

Answer ***a.*** *producers, because demand is elastic, so producer pays most of tax;* ***b.*** *consumers, because demand is inelastic, so consumers pay most of the tax.*

CLASS ACTIVITY

Role-Playing Tax Incidence

Time 30 minutes

Task Create and act out scenarios showing how elasticity of demand affects tax incidence.

Materials Needed paper and markers to create simple props or paper money

Activity

- Organize students into two groups. Explain that one group represents a producer and consumers of a product with elastic demand and the other represents a product with inelastic demand.
- Encourage members of each group to choose a specific product with appropriate elasticity and discuss how a new $1 tax will affect them.
- Direct groups to create scenarios showing relative incidence of the tax on producers and consumers.
- Allow groups to present their scenarios. Invite volunteers to summarize the cause and effect relationships of tax incidence for different types of products.

Rubric

	Understanding of Concepts	Presentation of Information
4	excellent	clear, creative
3	good	somewhat creative
2	fair	a few creative elements
1	poor	unoriginal

Impact of Taxes on the Economy

Discuss

- How might taxes affect people's desire to work and save? *(Possible answer: If taxes are too high on income from work, interest, or dividends, people might be less inclined to work or save money.)*
- Why might government give tax rebates to new businesses in economically depressed areas? *(Possible answer: to encourage businesses to locate in those areas in order to boost the economy there)*

Presentation Options

Review the impact of taxes on the economy by using the following presentation options:

Power Presentations DVD-ROM
Using the Display Tool, you can highlight the areas of the economy that are impacted by taxes.

Impact of Taxes on the Economy

KEY CONCEPTS

Taxes do more than provide government with the revenue that allows it to provide public goods and other programs. Taxes have an economic impact on resource allocation, productivity and growth, and the economic behavior of individuals and businesses. Government chooses what to tax and how to tax based on the amount of income it wants to raise and the other economic effects it wants to achieve.

IMPACT 1 Resource Allocation

A tax placed on a good or service will increase the costs of production and therefore shift the supply curve to the left. If the demand remains the same, the price of the good or service will go up. This shift will likely result in a shift in resources. Recall what you learned about tax incidence earlier. If a supplier is not able to pass increased costs along to the consumer in the form of higher prices, the supplier may choose to shift production to another good that will be more profitable.

For example, if the government imposed a 10 percent tax on luxury yachts, which have elastic demand, the producer of the yachts would not be able to raise prices enough to cover the full cost of the tax. If it were no longer profitable to sell the yachts because of the extra cost of the tax, the producer might decide to shift resources to producing small fishing boats or go into a different business.

IMPACT 2 Productivity and Growth

When taxes on interest and dividends are high, people tend to save less than when taxes on this source of income are low. Therefore, taxes also have an impact on the amount of money available to producers to invest in their businesses. Some economists also believe that high taxes reduce incentives to work. They suggest that people may spend more time on activities other than work if a large percentage of their income goes to taxes.

Other economists suggest that the underground economy is a result of high taxes. The underground economy refers to jobs, services, and business transactions conducted by word of mouth and, for the most part, paid for in cash to avoid paying taxes. For example, Bob has a part-time landscaping business. He works on the weekends, charges lower prices than larger landscaping companies, and insists that his customers pay him in cash. Since there are no records of Bob's business transactions, it is difficult for the government to tax his income.

Underground Economy Bob avoids paying taxes on his landscaping business by working on a cash-only basis.

DIFFERENTIATING INSTRUCTION

Struggling Readers

Diagram Cause and Effect
Mention that impact has the same meaning as effect. Model how to create a cause-and-effect chain for the topic of resource allocation. Point out that the tax is the cause that leads to multiple results.

- Have students work in pairs to create similar chains for the topics of productivity and growth and behavior incentives.
- Ask volunteers to summarize their diagrams for the class. Discuss how different taxes have similar effects, such as encouraging or discouraging actions.

English Learners

Understand Colloquial English
Explain that there are certain phrases in the text that should not be taken literally. Encourage students to use context clues to figure out the meaning of *underground economy, word of mouth*, and *sin tax*. Lead them to understand that *underground* means "hidden from tax collectors," *word of mouth* refers to informal referrals from customers, and *sin taxes* refer to taxes on activities disapproved of in some way, but which may or may not be considered immoral by different people.

IMPACT 3 Economic Behavior

A **tax incentive** is the use of taxes to encourage or discourage certain economic behaviors. By providing tax credits or rebates, the government may encourage behavior that it believes is good for the economy and for society. For example, it may give tax rebates to businesses for opening new factories, offices, and stores in economically depressed areas. Or government may give tax credits to consumers for activities such as recycling or using energy more efficiently. The positive tax incentive with the widest impact is perhaps the home mortgage interest deduction, which is designed to encourage home ownership. (You'll learn more about tax deductions later in this chapter.)

So-called sin taxes are often imposed on products or activities considered to be unhealthful or damaging to society, such as gambling, alcohol, and cigarettes. These taxes are generally levied on products or activities for which there is relatively inelastic demand, so that the incidence of the tax will fall on the consumer. Yet because demand for such products is relatively inelastic, the government knows that decline in quantity demanded will not cause tax revenues to decrease dramatically. (Figure 14.5 shows how the quantity demanded of cigarettes changes when states enact higher cigarette taxes.) Demand for sin-tax products becomes somewhat more elastic as tax increases get steeper. For example, cigarette sales in Washington fell by nearly 19 percent in the year after the state imposed a 60-cents-per-pack tax increase in 2002. Even so, since the tax increase was so large, cigarette tax revenues went up by more than 40 percent.

QUICK REFERENCE

A **tax incentive** is the use of taxes to influence economic behavior.

FIGURE 14.5 THE EFFECT OF CIGARETTE TAXES ON QUANTITY DEMANDED

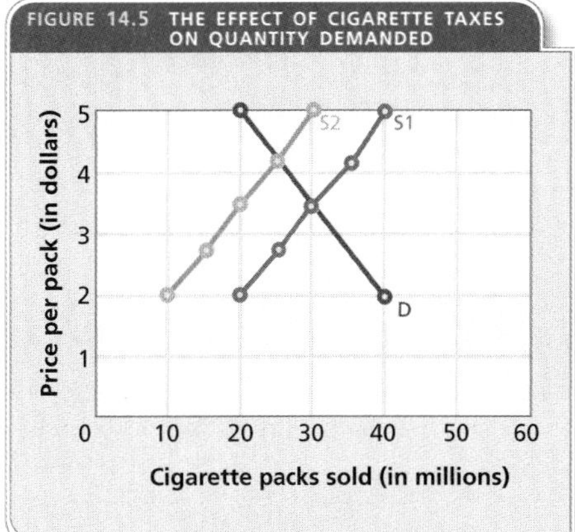

When a tax is imposed on cigarettes, the supply curve shifts to the left by the amount of the tax. On this graph, a 75-cent tax shifts the supply curve from $3.40 per pack to $4.15 per pack. The increased price results in less demand.

ANALYZE GRAPHS

1. How does the quantity demanded of cigarettes change when the price rises from $3.40 to $4.15 per pack?
2. How does this graph illustrate the concept of tax incentives?

APPLICATION Analyzing Effects

D. What effect does the underground economy have on government revenue?
It decreases the amount of revenue the government receives from taxes.

More About . . .

Cigarette Taxes

In 2004, the average state cigarette tax was 96 cents per pack, with lower taxes in tobacco-growing states. The lowest tax was 7 cents per pack in South Carolina, the highest, $2.58 in New Jersey.

Studies in high-income countries estimate that a 10 percent increase in price decreases demand by about 4 percent, reflected in fewer new smokers and current smokers quitting or smoking less. Younger people and lower-income people are most sensitive to price increases.

Analyzing Graphs: Figure 14.5

Explain that the graph illustrates a tax increase, but any increase in price would produce a similar shift in the supply curve. Ask students what they can infer about the tax incidence of cigarette taxes based on the graph. *(Consumers pay most of the tax increases because the demand curve shows that demand is inelastic.)*

Answers

1. *It decreases from about 30 million to about 25 or 26 million packs.*
2. *It shows that higher taxes on cigarettes discourage some people from buying cigarettes and decreases smoking, the desired effect of the tax.*

SMALL GROUP ACTIVITY

Researching Tax Incentives

Time 45 Minutes 

Task Gather information about tax incentives and present findings in oral reports.

Materials Needed computer with Internet access

Activity

- Organize students into small groups and have each one research a different type of tax incentive. Assign topics or allow groups to choose.
- Make sure that both positive and negative incentives are included. For example, positive incentives may include tax deductions for home mortgage expenses or tax credits for things such as cleaning up pollution, restoring historic properties, or buying a fuel-efficient vehicle. Sin taxes are examples of negative incentives meant to discourage certain behavior.
- Allow groups to present their findings in oral reports. Discuss the effects of various tax incentives.

Rubric

	Understanding of Concepts	Presentation of Information
4	excellent	clear and complete
3	good	mostly clear
2	fair	sometimes clear
1	poor	sketchy

Using the Internet for Research

❶ Plan & Prepare

Objectives

- Analyze some types of information available on the Internet for research.
- Make inferences about taxes on student wages from a government Web site.

❷ Focus & Motivate

Encourage students to think about the following questions as they review the material shown in the screen shot.

- Why do you think the Treasury Department might include this "Question" on its Web site? *(Possible answer: because it gives them an opportunity to address an opinion that many students may have)*
- What does the "Answer" reveal about how the federal government sets up its tax system? *(Congress passes all federal tax laws that determine who must pay taxes.)*

❸ Teach

- Explain that FAQs, a common Web site feature, are a good way to learn basic information.
- Point out links give an outline of the information available on the Web site. In the left column, you can see that FAQs are one link under Education, and taxes are a broad category under FAQs. Tax topics are shown on the right.

For additional practice see **Skillbuilder Handbook**, page R28.

THINKING ECONOMICALLY Answers

1. *Paying taxes to the Crown of England, while they didn't have voting rights to determine how they were governed, was one of the reasons that the colonists rebelled and fought the Revolutionary War. The student identifies with the idea because he pays taxes through his paycheck, but is not old enough to vote.*
2. *Possible answer: Click on the Press Room item in the left hand column of the Web page. On this page, check under Latest Press Releases to see if there is an item about the new tax legislation.*
3. *According to Oliver Wendell Holmes, former Justice of the U.S. Supreme Court, "Taxes are what we pay for a civilized society."*

ECONOMICS SKILLBUILDER

For more information on evaluating sources, see the Skillbuilder Handbook, page R28.

Using the Internet for Research

The Internet is a powerful tool for researching information. The Web site of the U.S. Treasury Department, for example, provides information on government revenue and spending.

RESEARCHING ON THE INTERNET Below is an example of FAQs, or "frequently asked questions." Use the following tips to help you navigate this and similar Internet Web sites that you might use for research.

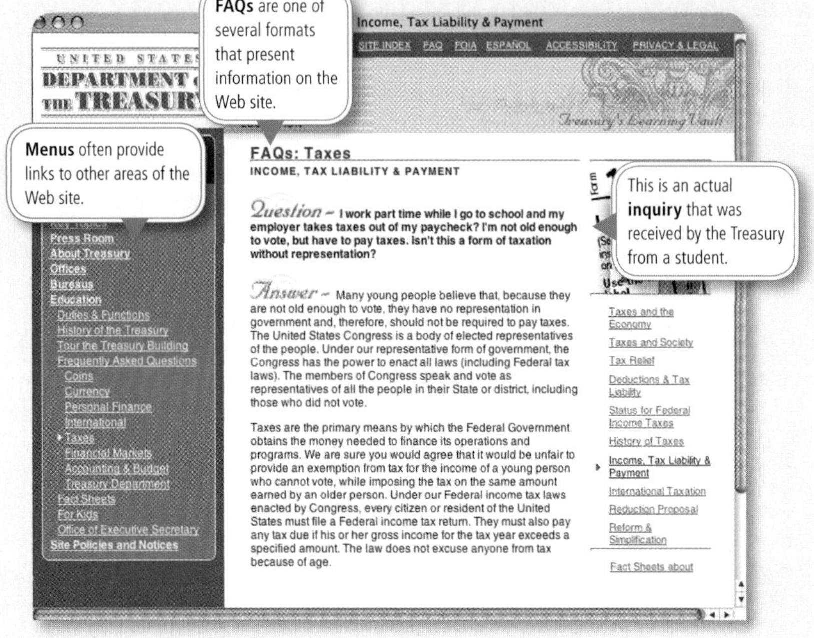

Source: U.S. Department of the Treasury

THINKING ECONOMICALLY Using the Internet

1. Why do you think the student used the phrase "taxation without representation"? (If you are unfamiliar with the phrase, use a search engine to research its origin.)
2. How might you navigate this page of the U. S. Department of the Treasury Web site to locate a press release on new tax legislation?
3. Access this Web site and use the FAQs to discover how the Treasury Department answers the question: Why do I have to pay taxes?

DIFFERENTIATING INSTRUCTION

Inclusion

Enlarge the Text

Students with visual impairments may benefit from enlarging text on a Web page. This process can be followed for any Web site. Looking under "View" on their main browser menu, students will find a way to increase text size on the screen. Options may be labeled Text Size, Text Zoom, Text Magnification, or Font Size. Once they have a size that works for them, they should follow the path to the specific FAQ *(www.treasury.gov> FAQ > Taxes > Income, Tax Liability & Payment)*.

Gifted and Talented

Develop a Research Guide

Allow interested students to examine the U.S. Treasury Web site in more depth. Invite students to choose a section of the Web site that might be useful to economics students. Encourage them to develop a research guide that outlines some questions that might be studied on the site and that summarizes the kinds of information available. Have students share their research guides with their classmates.

SECTION 1 Assessment

Online Quiz
ClassZone.com

REVIEWING KEY CONCEPTS

1. Explain the difference between the terms in each of these pairs.
   a. *tax* / *revenue*
   b. *sales tax* / *property tax*
   c. *progressive tax* / *regressive tax*
2. Why do governments collect taxes?
3. What are the four most used tax bases?
4. How does demand elasticity influence the incidence of a tax?
5. What is the purpose of a tax incentive?
6. **Using Your Notes** What are the major criteria for a good tax system? Refer to your completed cluster diagram.

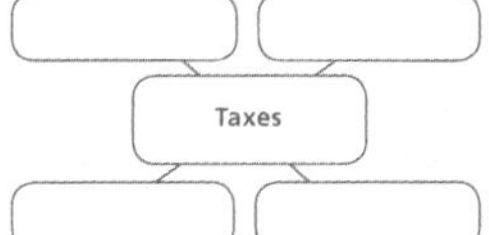

Use the Graphic Organizer at **Interactive Review @ ClassZone.com**

CRITICAL THINKING

7. **Categorizing Economic Information** Colorado has a state income tax of 4.63 percent on all income and a sales tax of 2.9 percent. Are these taxes proportional, progressive, or regressive? Give reasons for your answers.
8. **Drawing Conclusions** In 2005, Hurricane Katrina destroyed many homes and businesses along the Gulf Coast of the United States. How did this natural disaster affect the tax bases in communities in that region?
9. **Analyzing Effects** Where does the burden of an increase in a sin tax usually fall? Illustrate your answer with supply and demand curves.
   Use ***SMARTGrapher*** **@ ClassZone.com** to complete this activity.
10. **Applying Economic Concepts** Demand for insulin is highly inelastic. Would the government be likely to use a tax on insulin as a tax incentive? Why or why not?
11. **Challenge** Pennsylvania and Illinois each have state income taxes of about 3 percent of income. In Illinois, the first $2,000 of individual income is exempt from taxation. Pennsylvania has no similar individual tax exemptions. Is one state's tax more progressive than the other? Why or why not? (You'll learn more about tax exemptions in Section 2.)

ECONOMICS IN PRACTICE

Driver's license

Evaluating Taxes
Review what you have learned about the principles and criteria used to evaluate the effectiveness of a tax, and then complete the following activities.

Draw Conclusions Evaluate the effectiveness of each tax listed in the chart below by indicating with a checkmark whether it meets each principle and criterion.

Tax	Principles		Criteria		
	Benefits received	Ability to pay	Equity	Simplicity	Efficiency
Fee for driver's license					
Sales tax					
Flat rate income tax					
Progressive income tax					
Highway tolls					
Property tax					
Corporate income tax					

Challenge How would you evaluate a tax to support public education that was imposed only on families with children?

4 Assess & Reteach

Assess Have pairs of students work together to write the answers to questions 2–9 on index cards. Tell students not to identify which question they are answering. Then have pairs exchange cards and match the answers with the correct question.

Unit 6 Resource Book
- Section Quiz, p. 7

Interactive Review @ ClassZone.com
- Section Quiz

Test Generator CD-ROM
- Section Quiz

Reteach Write each of the key terms from the section on a small piece of paper. Place the papers in a box. Call on volunteers to draw a piece of paper from the box and use the chosen term in a sentence that illustrates the meaning of the term.

Unit 6 Resource Book
- Reteaching Activity, p. 8

Economics in Practice
Draw Conclusions Students' completed charts should reflect an understanding of the principles and criteria of taxation.

Challenge Such a tax would be unfair because it is not only the families with children who benefit from the education. The country benefits from having educated citizens, and employers benefit from having educated workers.

SECTION 1 ASSESSMENT ANSWERS

Reviewing Key Concepts

1. a. *tax*, p. 410; *revenue*, p. 410
   b. *sales tax*, p. 412; *property tax*, p. 412
   c. *progressive tax*, p. 412; *regressive tax*, p. 412
2. in order to generate some of the revenue needed to provide goods and services not provided by the market economy, e.g., national defense, highways, police and fire protection, education, courts
3. individual and corporate income, sales, and property
4. When demand is elastic, tax incidence falls mostly on the producer. When demand is inelastic, the incidence of the tax falls mostly on the consumer.
5. to encourage or discourage certain behaviors
6. See page 410 for an example of a completed cluster diagram: equity, simplicity, efficiency.

Critical Thinking

7. Income tax: proportional; same percentage of tax taken no matter the level of income. Sales tax: regressive; low-income people pay higher percentage of income in tax than high-income people, because low-income people spend more of their income.
8. All tax bases shrunk. Destroyed homes and businesses: less property to tax; fewer businesses to create jobs: less income to tax; fewer businesses: fewer sales to tax; fewer sales would mean lower profits: less corporate income to tax.
9. Supply and demand curves should indicate that burden of an increase in a sin tax falls on the producer when demand is elastic and on the consumer when demand is inelastic
10. The government would not likely tax insulin even though demand is inelastic because a tax incentive is meant to encourage or discourage certain behavior. Many diabetics need insulin, and the tax would neither encourage nor discourage its use. Taxing a needed medicine would be unfair to those who could not afford to pay more for the medicine..
11. The Illinois tax is slightly more progressive because the exemption means that people pay no tax on the first $2,000 of income in Illinois.

Economics in Practice
See answers in side column above.

1 Plan & Prepare

Section 2 Objectives

- describe the process of paying individual income taxes
- explain taxes for Social Security, Medicare, and unemployment
- identify other taxes that are collected by the federal government

2 Focus & Motivate

Connecting to Everyday Life Explain that this section focuses on taxes paid to the federal government. Invite students to think about which tax bases the federal government is most likely to use.

Taking Notes Remind students to take notes as they read by completing a cluster diagram. They can use the Graphic Organizer at **Interactive Review @ClassZone.com**. A sample is shown below.

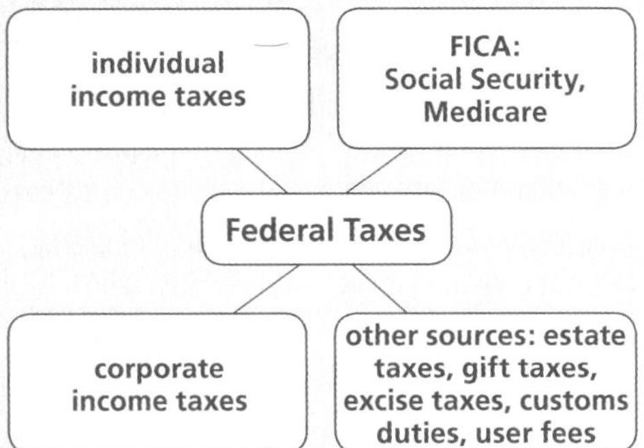

SECTION 2

Federal Taxes

OBJECTIVES

In Section 2, you will

- describe the process of paying individual income taxes
- explain taxes for Social Security, Medicare, and unemployment
- identify other taxes that are collected by the federal government

KEY TERMS

withholding, *p. 421*
taxable income, *p. 421*
tax return, *p. 421*
FICA, *p. 423*
Social Security, *p. 423*
Medicare, *p. 423*
estate tax, *p. 425*
gift tax, *p. 425*
excise tax, *p. 425*
customs duty, *p. 425*
user fee, *p. 425*

TAKING NOTES

As you read Section 2, complete a cluster diagram using the key concepts and other helpful words and phrases. Use the Graphic Organizer at **Interactive Review @ ClassZone.com**

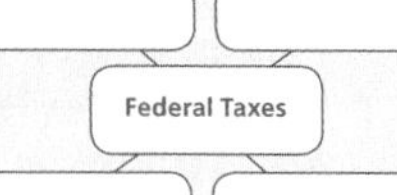

Individual Income Tax

KEY CONCEPTS

The federal government takes in around $2.5 trillion in revenue each year. This money comes from several sources, including individual income tax, social insurance taxes, corporate income taxes, estate taxes, gift taxes, excise taxes, and customs taxes. The largest source of taxes for the federal government is the individual income tax. (You can see the contribution of the various taxes to total revenue in Figure 14.8 on page 425.) The government began using the income tax after the Sixteenth Amendment to the U.S. Constitution, which recognized this type of direct taxation on individuals, was ratified in 1913. Prior to that time, excise taxes and customs duties were the main sources of federal revenue. (Figure 14.8 shows that today only a very small portion of federal tax revenue comes from excise taxes and customs duties.) Social insurance taxes are the second largest source of federal tax revenue. Workers and employers share the burden of these taxes.

EXAMPLE **Paying Your Taxes**

If taxpayers had to pay their income taxes in one lump sum at the end of each year, some people would have difficulty coming up with all the money at once. Also, receiving revenue just once a year would create problems for the government. Drawing up a budget for the year would be very difficult, and developing sound economic plans for the future would be almost

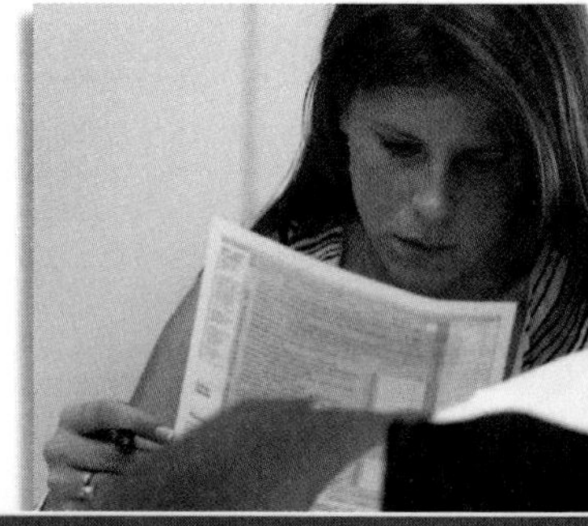

SECTION 2 PROGRAM RESOURCES

ON LEVEL

Lesson Plans
- Core, p. 47

Unit 6 Resource Book
- Reading Study Guide, pp. 11–12
- Economic Skills and Problem Solving Activity, pp. 41–42
- Section Quiz, p. 19

STRUGGLING READERS

Unit 6 Resource Book
- Reading Study Guide with Additional Support, pp. 13–15
- Reteaching Activity, p. 20

ENGLISH LEARNERS

Unit 6 Resource Book
- Reading Study Guide with Additional Support (Spanish), pp. 16–18

INCLUSION

Lesson Plans
- Modified for Inclusion, p. 47

GIFTED AND TALENTED

NCEE Student Activities
- Fair Taxes and Citizen Responses, pp. 53–56

TECHNOLOGY

eEdition DVD-ROM

eEdition Online

Power Presentation DVD-ROM

Economics Concepts Transparencies
- CT47 Percentage of Federal Receipts by Source, 1960 to 2005

Daily Test Practice Transparencies, TT47

ClassZone.com

impossible. Therefore, to make it easier for taxpayers and the government, a payroll tax—a tax that is taken from a worker's paycheck—is collected. The payroll tax is deducted from a paycheck as **withholding**, or money taken from a worker's pay before the worker receives it.

To see how this works, let's look at the example of Scott, who works part-time during the school year and full-time during the summer at the Main Street Grocery Store. For every hour Scott works, he earns $6. Because of withholding for taxes, the amount he receives in his paycheck is less than the total amount he earns. In this way, he pays his taxes as he earns income, and the government receives a steady stream of revenue. The Main Street Grocery Store forwards the money withheld from Scott's paycheck to the Internal Revenue Service (IRS). The IRS is the government agency that collects the money for the federal government and administers the federal tax system.

The federal income tax is a progressive tax based on the ability-to-pay principle of taxation. This means that people with higher incomes not only pay more in total taxes but also pay a higher percentage of their income in taxes. The amount owed is based on **taxable income**, the portion of income subject to taxation. Under federal income tax laws, taxpayers may take certain exemptions and deductions from their total earned income to reduce the amount of their taxable income. Exemptions are allowed for each individual adult and child, so larger families reduce their taxable income by a greater amount than do smaller families. In addition, taxpayers may take a standard deduction or itemize deductions, such as interest paid on a home mortgage, state and local taxes, charitable contributions, and a certain portion of medical expenses. Figure 14.6 below provides information on some of the itemized deductions taken by taxpayers in 2004.

Each year, taxpayers must complete a **tax return**, a form used to report income and taxes owed to various levels of government. The federal tax return shows how much income has been earned, the exemptions being claimed, and how much tax has been paid through withholding. State and local tax returns show similar, but less detailed, information. Taxpayers who have too much tax withheld receive a refund for overpayment. Taxpayers who have not had enough withheld must then pay any additional taxes owed directly to the IRS or to state or local revenue departments.

QUICK REFERENCE

Withholding is money taken from pay before the worker receives it.

Taxable income is the portion of income subject to taxation.

A **tax return** is a form used to report income and taxes owed to government.

FIGURE 14.6 SELECTED ITEMIZED DEDUCTIONS ON INDIVIDUAL INCOME TAX RETURNS

Deduction	Number of Returns	Amount Claimed (in $)
Interest Paid	37,961,584	346.0 billion
State and Local Sales and Income Taxes	44,685,865	217.2 billion
Charitable Contributions	40,594,576	156.2 billion
Medical and Dental Expenses	9,458,443	61.3 billion

Source: Internal Revenue Service, 2004 figures

About 132.4 million individual income tax returns were filed in 2004. Some 46.2 million—or 35 percent—of these returns claimed itemized deductions to taxable income. Total itemized deductions equaled close to $972 billion, or just over $21,000 for each return.

ANALYZE GRAPHS

1. Which was the largest deduction taken in terms of the dollar amount claimed?
2. What percentage of total deductions taken in 2004 did state and local sales and income taxes represent?

3 Teach

Individual Income Tax

Discuss

- What is the relationship between payroll taxes and withholding? *(Payroll taxes are taken from workers' paychecks as withholding, so that workers pay their taxes as they earn income.)*
- How is withholding related to a tax return? *(On their tax returns, taxpayers figure out how much tax they owe and then compare it to their withholding to see if they need to pay more or will receive a refund.)*

Analyzing Charts: Figure 14.6

Explain that all taxpayers may take a standard deduction on their tax return. In 2005, that amount was $5,000 for a single person. Taxpayers claim itemized deductions when the total exceeds the standard deduction. The deductions reduce the amount of taxable income. Ask students how much greater the average itemized deductions per return were than the standard deduction. *(about $16,000)*

Answers

1. *home mortgage interest*
2. *about 22 percent*

CLASS ACTIVITY

Creating a Living Time Line

Time 30 minutes

Task Create a living time line on the history of federal taxes.

Materials Needed computer with Internet access, paper and markers

Activity

- Assign small groups to research information about a tax-related date or time period mentioned in this section. The earliest item should be prior to 1913 when customs taxes were the main source of federal revenue. Bring the time line up to the present by having students research current tax provisions.
- Have students note their date and its significance on a sheet of paper.
- Invite students to form a living time line and present the information they have learned to their classmates.
- Discuss how the federal tax system has changed over time and how it affects individuals and businesses now.

Rubric

	Understanding of Concepts	Presentation of Information
4	excellent	clear and complete
3	good	mostly clear
2	fair	sometimes clear
1	poor	sketchy

More About . . .

Indexing

According to the IRS, there are more than three dozen tax benefits that were adjusted for inflation in 2006. Not all parts of the tax system are adjusted equally. Personal and dependent exemptions, the standard deduction, and tax brackets each rose by about 3 percent in 2006.

However, the exemption on the gift tax (see page 425) rose from $11,000 to $12,000, an increase of about 9 percent, well above the rate of inflation. The Alternative Minimum Tax (AMT), first aimed at high-income earners in the 1970s, was not indexed for inflation. Until 2000, it affected about 1 percent of taxpayers but could affect 20 percent by 2010 unless changes are made.

Economics Update

At **ClassZone.com** students will see updated information on tax schedules.

EXAMPLE Indexing

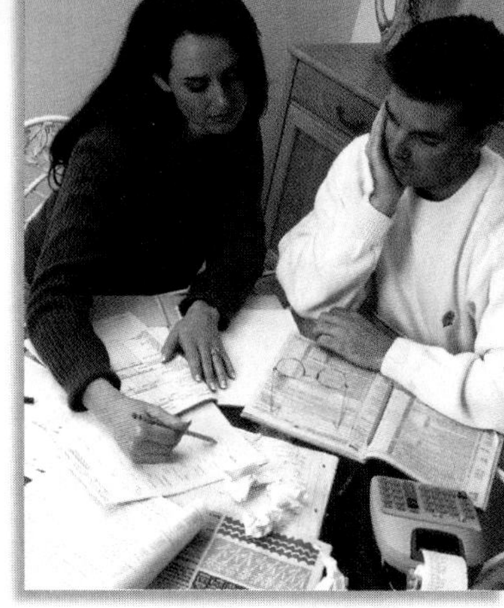

Tax Return Checking your taxable income against the various tax brackets is an important step in completing your tax return.

Because the federal income tax is a progressive tax, the tax rate increases as taxable income increases. The level of income that causes someone to pay a higher rate of tax is the dividing point between tax brackets. The tax bracket is identified by the tax rate for that income span. For example, the tax schedule at the bottom of this page shows that in 2006 a single taxpayer with $7,550 or less in taxable income is in the 10 percent tax bracket. Someone with taxable income between $7,550 and $30,650 is in the 15 percent tax bracket, someone with taxable income between $30,650 and $74,200 would be in the 25 percent bracket, and so on.

Look again at the tax schedule below. Suppose that Scott has $7,000 in taxable income. He is in the 10 percent bracket and pays 10 percent, or $700, in taxes. If, however, he had $8,000 in taxable income, he would be in the 15 percent tax bracket. He would pay 10 percent on the first $7,550 of his earnings and 15 percent on the remaining $450. His total taxes would be $822.50 ($755 + $67.50) or about 10.3 percent of his income.

Indexing is a revision of tax brackets to prevent workers from paying more taxes due to inflation. For example, suppose Scott's taxable income rises from $8,000 to $8,320—a 4 percent increase—due to inflation. Without indexing, $770 of his income is taxed at the 15 percent rate and he pays $870.50 in taxes, or about 10.5 percent of his income. With indexing, the beginning level of the 15 percent bracket is adjusted by 4 percent to $7, 852. So Scott continues to pay 10.3 percent of his income in taxes. Indexing, therefore, combats the effect of inflation and keeps the rate of taxation relatively constant.

Economics Update

Find an update on tax schedules at **ClassZone.com**

2006 Tax Rates: Schedule X—Single

If your taxable income is: *Over—*	*But not over—*	The tax is:
$0	$7,550	**10% of the amount over $0**
7,550	30,650	**$755 plus 15% of the amount over $7,550**
30,650	74,200	**$4,220 plus 25% of the amount over $30,650**
74,200	154,800	**$15,108 plus 28% of the amount over $74,200**
154,800	336,550	**$37,676 plus 33% of the amount over $154,800**
336,550	No limit	**$97,653 plus 35% of the amount over $336,550**

APPLICATION Analyzing Effects

A. How much of Scott's income of $8,320 would be taxed at 15 percent if the 10 percent tax bracket were indexed and increased to $7,780? What effect would this have on his overall tax rate?
$540 would be taxed at 15 percent and his overall tax rate would remain at about 10.3 percent of his total income.

DIFFERENTIATING INSTRUCTION

Struggling Readers

Use a Table

Help students understand the principle of indexing by referring back to Figure 14.1 on page 413. Have students work in pairs to set up tables based on the model, using the income and tax rates described on page 422. Encourage them to perform the calculations themselves to see how indexing helped Scott when his income rose. Call on volunteers to explain the concept of indexing in their own words.

English Learners

Analyze Word Forms

Help students understand the terms *FICA* and *Medicare.* Explain that FICA is an acronym (pronounced FY-kuh), and ask them to see how it was formed (*from the first letters of Federal Insurance Contributions Act*). Have them consider what two words were combined to form *Medicare* (*medical care*). Explain that government and businesses may make up such terms in order to create a distinctive word that is easy to remember.

FICA: Taxes to Ease Hardships

KEY CONCEPTS

FICA is the Federal Insurance Contributions Act, a payroll tax that provides coverage for the elderly, the unemployed due to disability, and surviving family members of wage earners who have died. Also known as social insurance, FICA encompasses Social Security and Medicare. Both employees and employers make payments into FICA accounts.

Social Security **Social Security** is a federal program to aid older citizens who have retired, children who have lost a parent or both parents, and people with disabilities. The program began during the Great Depression of the 1930s as a way to help people who were in desperate need of economic assistance. The employer and employee each pay 6.2 percent of the employee's income up to an annual maximum. In 2006, Social Security tax was applied to $94,200 of earned income. The limit generally rises each year.

Medicare Introduced in 1966, **Medicare** is a national health insurance program for citizens over 65 and certain other groups of people. Employers and employees each pay 1.45 percent of employee income. There is no limit on the amount of income subject to the tax for Medicare.

Unemployment Taxes Unemployment compensation is a program funded by federal and state taxes and administered by the states. It provides benefits for a certain period of time to employees who lose their jobs through no fault of their own. Unemployment tax applies to the first $7,000 earned by an employee and, for the most part, is paid only by employers.

QUICK REFERENCE

FICA is the Federal Insurance Contributions Act.

Social Security is a federal program to aid older citizens, children who have lost a parent, and the disabled.

Medicare is a national health insurance program mainly for citizens over 65.

I.R.S.
"SURELY YOU CAN EARN MORE THAN THIS! SOMEONE HAS to SUPPORT MEDICARE AND SOCIAL SECURITY."
Source: www.CartoonStock.com

FICA Accounts As the American population ages, fears are growing that there will not be enough workers to fund FICA.

APPLICATION Applying Economic Concepts

B. How would the employee portion of total FICA taxes for an individual earning $100,000 be split between Social Security and Medicare? Show your calculations.
Social Security: .062 × $94,200 = $5,580; Medicare: .0145 × $100,000 = $1,450

FICA: Taxes to Ease Hardships

Discuss

- What is the difference between Social Security and Medicare taxes? *(Social Security tax does not apply to all income and has a higher tax rate than the Medicare tax.)*
- How is the unemployment tax different from the FICA taxes? *(Unemployment tax only applies to the first $7,000 of income and, for the most part, is paid only by the employer. FICA taxes apply to higher levels of income and are paid by both employees and employers.)*

INDIVIDUAL ACTIVITY

Calculating Taxes

Time 20 Minutes

Task Calculate federal income and FICA taxes and create a chart.

Materials Needed paper and pencil

Activity

- Write different amounts of taxable income on individual slips of paper and place them in a box. Have each student draw a slip of paper from the box.
- Direct students to refer to the tax table on page 422 and the FICA tax rates on page 423 to calculate the income and FICA taxes paid on the amount of income on the paper. Have them calculate the amount of each tax paid as a percentage of income. Allow students to use calculators.
- Combine information into a single chart on the board. Arrange income from lowest to highest. Invite volunteers to state conclusions about the tax structure of these federal taxes.

Rubric

	Understanding of Concepts	Presentation of Information
4	excellent	clear and complete
3	good	mostly clear
2	fair	sometimes clear
1	poor	sketchy

Corporate Income and Other Taxes

Discuss

- Why do most corporations pay less than the stated 35 percent tax rate? *(because they are able to take deductions for things like investing in buildings, equipment, and research)*
- Compare and contrast excise taxes and sales taxes. *(Both are taxes on the sale of goods and services, but excise taxes apply to specific products and sales taxes apply to a broad range of products.)*

Analyzing Charts: Figure 14.7

Point out that although corporate income tax receipts have increased steadily since 1950, their percentage of the total tax revenue has declined. *(from $185,406 millions to $2,189,162 millions, and from 27.5% to 10%)* Ask students what is significant about corporate income tax receipts as a percentage of GDP since 1980. *(The percentage has remained relatively stable during that period.)*

Answers

1. *Corporate income tax receipts are declining as a percentage of total federal tax revenue and as a percentage of GDP.*
2. *1990–1999; during this decade corporate income tax receipts grew as a percentage of total federal tax revenue and as a percentage of GDP*

Corporate Income and Other Taxes

KEY CONCEPTS

The federal government collects more than individual income and FICA taxes. It also uses corporate income, estate, gift, and excise taxes, as well as customs duties and user fees, to finance its operations.

Corporate Income Taxes

As you recall from earlier in this chapter, corporate income tax is tax on corporate profits. This tax is the third largest source of tax revenue for the federal government. Between 1941 and 1968, corporate income tax was the second largest source of revenue. Since that time, however, it has been surpassed by social insurance taxes. As Figure 14.7 shows, corporate income tax receipts have increased in total dollars since the mid-1900s, but have decreased relative both to total federal tax revenues and to the overall size of the economy.

Only certain types of corporations are subject to corporate income tax. These corporations are about 8 percent of all businesses that file tax returns. While the tax rate for most corporations is 35 percent of profits, most pay only about 26 percent of their profits in taxes. Like individuals, corporations can deduct certain expenses from their profits to reduce their taxable income. Some of the most important tax breaks for corporations include deductions for investment in buildings, equipment, and research, and rules that benefit multinational corporations.

A common criticism of the corporate income tax is that corporate profits are subject to double taxation. Profits are taxed at the corporate level and again at the individual level, since shareholders pay taxes on the income they receive in the form of dividends or capital gains. In recent years, the tax rate on capital gains has decreased in answer to this criticism.

FIGURE 14.7 CORPORATE INCOME TAX RECEIPTS, 1950–2009

	Receipts (in millions of $)	As Percentage of Total Federal Tax Revenue	As Percentage of GDP
1950–59	185,406	27.5	4.8
1960–69	262,891	21.3	3.8
1970–79	437,564	15.0	2.7
1980–89	675,358	9.3	1.7
1990–99	1,434,246	10.5	1.9
2000–09*	2,189,162	10.0	1.8

Source: The Budget of the United States, FY 2007

*Reflects government budget estimates for 2006–2009

ANALYZE GRAPHS

1. What overall trend is shown in the chart?
2. Which decade diverges from this overall trend? How does it differ from the overall trend?

DIFFERENTIATING INSTRUCTION

English Learners

Understand Multiple-Meaning Words

Explain that *duty* and *fee* are not always synonymous with *tax*. *Duty* is used in that sense when it refers to taxes on imports. It is most commonly used in the phrases *customs duty* or *duty free*. The latter is used to describe goods that may be brought into a country without being taxed. *Fee* means "tax" when it is charged by a government. Businesses or nonprofit organizations may also charge user fees but they are not taxes.

Inclusion

Explain Visuals

Help students understand Figure 14.8 in a more concrete way. Explain that percentages may be thought of as the part of every dollar of revenue that comes from a particular kind of tax. Model sentences such as "Forty-five cents of every tax dollar the government receives comes from individual income tax." Show students 100 pennies. Invite volunteers to place them in stacks to represent each source of federal tax revenue. Ask volunteers to explain what each stack represents.

Other Taxes

Several miscellaneous taxes provide a small part of total federal revenue, as you can see in Figure 14.8 below. The **estate tax** is a tax on property that is transferred to others on the death of the owner. Most estates are not subject to this tax, because the government only taxes large estates. In 2006, estates valued at less than $2 million were not subject to this tax. The **gift tax** is a tax on money or property given by one living person to another. As with the estate tax, there are exemptions to the gifts that are subject to the tax. For the most part, these exemptions allow family members to give money to other family members tax-free.

The **excise tax** is a tax on the production or sale of a specific product, such as gasoline or telephone service. The sin taxes discussed earlier in this chapter are other examples of excise taxes. In general, the government places excise taxes on goods or services for which there is relatively inelastic demand in order to maintain a steady stream of revenue. The **customs duty** is a tax on goods imported into the United States from another country. Customs duties are basically excise taxes on imports and are also known as tariffs. (You'll read more about tariffs in Chapter 17.)

The **user fee** is money charged for the use of a good or service. These fees are based on the benefits-received principle of taxation. For example, the federal government charges entrance, parking, and camping fees to visitors to national parks. So the people enjoying the parks the most pay for the benefits provided by the parks.

QUICK REFERENCE

The **estate tax** is a tax on property transferred to others on the death of the owner.

The **gift tax** is a tax on assets given by one living person to another.

The **excise tax** is a tax on the production or sale of a specific good or service.

Customs duty is a tax on goods imported into the United States.

A **user fee** is money charged for the use of a good or service.

FIGURE 14.8 SOURCES OF FEDERAL TAX REVENUE

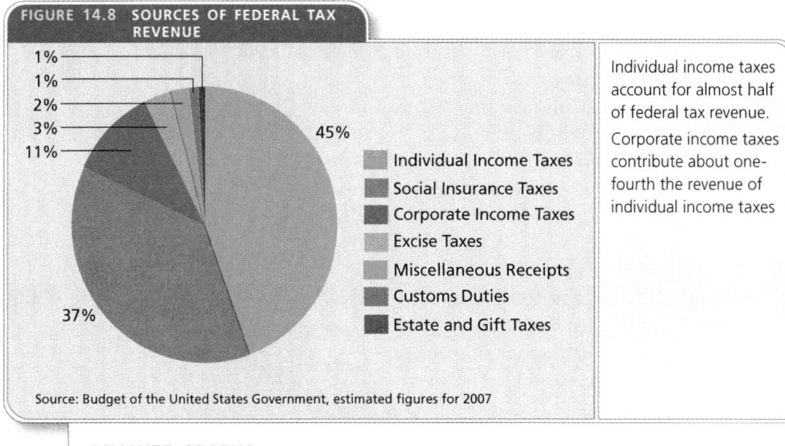

Individual income taxes account for almost half of federal tax revenue.

Corporate income taxes contribute about one-fourth the revenue of individual income taxes

ANALYZE GRAPHS

1. What percentage of federal tax revenue comes from individual income taxes and social insurance taxes combined?
2. If total tax revenue for 2007 is estimated to be about $2.35 trillion, about how much revenue will come from individual income taxes?

APPLICATION Drawing Conclusions

C. There are plans to eliminate the estate tax. Who will benefit most from this?
Heirs of wealthy people whose estates are worth more than $2 million.

More About . . .

Estate Tax Repeal

Congress voted to repeal the estate tax in 2000, but President Clinton vetoed the measure. President Bush's 2001 tax cut package included provisions to increase the size of estates exempt from taxation, leading to complete repeal of the tax in 2010. However, in 2011, the estate tax would revert to the levels of 2000. In 2006, plans by Congress to permanently repeal the tax were shelved.

At one time, a majority of Americans favored repeal of the so-called "death tax." They believed that many small businesses and family farms would be subject to large taxes. After learning that this was not the case, support for repeal slipped to 23 percent in 2006.

Analyzing Graphs: Figure 14.8

Explain that this pie graph summarizes how each of the federal taxes contributes to overall federal revenue. Ask students how these taxes relate to the four most common tax bases. *(Federal income and social insurance taxes: individual income; corporate income tax: profits of certain corporations; excise taxes and customs taxes: sales; estate and gift taxes: property)*

Answers

1. *82 percent*
2. *about $1.1 trillion; 45 percent x $2.42 trillion = $1.089 trillion*

SMALL GROUP ACTIVITY

Creating a Poster

Time 30 minutes ◑

Task Gather information about a specific federal tax and create a poster.

Materials Needed computer with Internet access, poster board and markers

Activity

- Have small groups focus on one of the taxes described on pages 424–425. Direct students to use the Internet or library resources to research more specific information about these taxes.
- Invite groups to create posters using their own drawings or copies of images from their research to communicate how these taxes are used and the revenue that they contribute to the running of the federal government.
- Display the posters in the classroom and call on volunteers from each group to answer questions from their classmates about the particular tax.

Rubric

	Understanding of Concepts	Presentation of Information
4	excellent	clear and complete
3	good	mostly clear
2	fair	sometimes clear
1	poor	sketchy

Maya MacGuineas

More About . . .

Maya MacGuineas
Maya MacGuineas considers herself a "budget watchdog." She spends her workday conducting research, writing about policy issues, and speaking before various groups. Another important component of her work is meeting with members of Congress and their staffs to promote the ideas of her organization.

MacGuineas also appears at Congressional Committee hearings to comment on pending legislation. Noted for her candor, she once told a committee that its bill was filled "with expensive, unnecessary and unjustified corporate handouts, and any pretense that [it] constitutes good tax policy was lost long ago."

More About . . .

The Committee for a Responsible Federal Budget (CRFB)
The CRFB, which McGuineas heads, is a policy program of the New America Foundation, a nonpartisan public policy institute. CRFB provides Congress, the media, and the public with nonpartisan analyses of federal budget issues. To educate the public, CRFB provides policy recommendations on responsible budgeting, entitlement reform, and tax reform.

Economics Update
At **ClassZone.com** students will find an article about Maya MacGuineas.

APPLICATION
Answer *Answers may vary. Most students probably will argue that education and housing should not be taxed as consumption. In support of their view, some students might point out that education and housing are necessities and should not be taxed. Others might suggest that these items are really investments and therefore should not be taxed as consumption.*

ECONOMICS PACESETTER

Maya MacGuineas: Reforming the Tax System

For the most part, tax reform measures of the last few years have involved tinkering with tax rates, exemptions, and deductions. Maya MacGuineas, a tax policy analyst, thinks that it's time for far more dramatic change—a complete overhaul of the U.S. tax system, in fact.

FAST FACTS

Maya MacGuineas

Title: President, Committee for a Responsible Federal Budget: Program Director, New American Foundation

Born: February 21, 1968

Previous Positions Held: Senior Research Analyst, Brookings Institution; Policy Analyst, Concord Coalition; Researcher, PaineWebber

Board Memberships: Common Cause (government watchdog group); Centrists.Org and Third Millennium (nonpartisan policy think tanks)

Publications: Articles published in *Atlantic Monthly, Boston Globe, New York Times, Washington Post, Los Angeles Times, Financial Times*

A Tax Revolution?

Why does MacGuineas think that such drastic action is needed? The present tax system, she says, is complicated, inefficient, and unfair, and doesn't raise the revenue to fund all of the government's programs. The new tax system, she argues, ought to be based on simplicity, efficiency, equity, and responsible budgeting.

To this end, MacGuineas suggests that the income tax should be simplified by ending most tax deductions and exemptions. This, she says, would also make the system more equitable, since taxpayers in higher marginal tax brackets gain the greatest benefit from these measures. In part for reasons of efficiency, MacGuineas believes that the corporate income tax should be phased out. She also supports new environmental taxes, a different approach to how the estate tax is levied, and a complete restructuring of the nation's entitlement programs.

Perhaps MacGuineas's most revolutionary measure involves FICA taxes, which she thinks should be replaced with a progressive consumption tax. Such a tax would be tied to total spending rather than income, with rates rising as spending levels rise. For example, the first $20,000 spent would be tax-free, spending between $20,000 and $50,000 would be taxed at 10 percent, spending between $50,000 and $175,000 would be taxed at 15 percent, and so on. In other words, people who spend more would face progressively higher marginal tax rates. A progressive consumption tax would not only be simpler and fairer, MacGuineas argues, it would also provide tremendous incentives to save.

Tax Reform Maya MacGuineas wants to make the tax system more equitable and less complex.

Economics Update
Find an update on Maya MacGuineas at **ClassZone.com**

APPLICATION Making Inferences

D. Should spending on education and housing be exempt from MacGuineas's consumption tax? Why or why not?
◀ See Teacher's Edition for answer.

DIFFERENTIATING INSTRUCTION

Inclusion

Create Line Graphs
Help students understand the trend in corporate income tax receipts since 1950. Use overhead transparencies to create line graphs from the data in Figure 14.7. Call on volunteers to explain the differences in the two graphs, summarize the trend common to both, and state the implications of it. *(One shows corporate taxes as a share of all federal revenue; the other, as a share of the total economy. Because these taxes have declined, the government must raise money from other sources.)*

Gifted and Talented

Role-Play an Interview
Invite students to work in pairs to find out more about Maya MacGuineas's work on tax reform, discussed on page 426. Encourage them to develop a list of questions they might ask her in an interview, along with possible answers based on their research. Allow partners to role-play an interview with her for the class. Discuss how her ideas reflect current concerns about the federal tax system.

SECTION 2 Assessment

REVIEWING KEY CONCEPTS

1. Explain the relationship between the terms in each of these pairs.
   a. *taxable income* / *tax return*
   b. *FICA* / *Social Security*
   c. *estate tax* / *gift tax*
2. Why is indexing important to taxpayers?
3. What is the role of the IRS in relationship to federal taxes?
4. How are excise taxes and customs duties similar? How are they different?
5. How are payroll taxes and user fees different?
6. **Using Your Notes** What two programs are financed by FICA? Refer to your completed cluster diagram. Use the Graphic Organizer at **Interactive Review @ ClassZone.com**

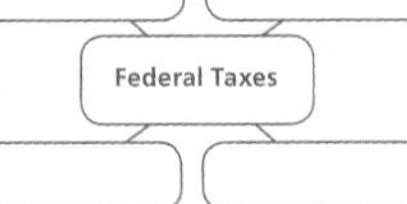

CRITICAL THINKING

7. **Analyzing and Interpreting Data** In 2005, the 10 percent tax bracket limit was $7,300. In 2006, it increased to $7,550. By what percentage did the tax bracket limit increase? How does this example illustrate the concept of indexing?
8. **Applying Economic Concepts** The Social Security tax rate for employees is 6.2 percent, and the Medicare tax rate is 1.45 percent. Are both parts of the FICA tax proportional? Give reasons for your answer.
9. **Drawing Conclusions** Study these two statements about tax payments for the 2005 tax year:
   - On average, an individual with $100,000 in taxable income paid about 29.5 percent in combined income and FICA taxes.
   - On average, an individual with $150,000 in taxable income also paid about 29.5 percent in combined taxes.

   Why were the combined tax rates the same for these two taxpayers?
10. **Challenge** Review the data in Figure 14.7. As a share of federal tax revenue and as a share of GDP, by what percentage have corporate income taxes declined between the 1950s and the first decade of the 21st century?

ECONOMICS IN PRACTICE

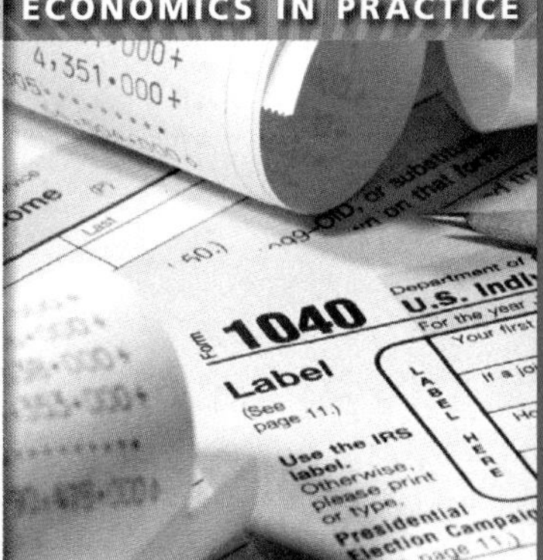

Analyzing Tax Schedules
The IRS provides tax schedules, or tables, to help taxpayers calculate their taxes.

Calculate Taxes Suppose that you work for a tax preparation company. Use the tax schedule on page 422 to answer the questions about the taxpayers described below.

a. Chris has $8,500 in taxable income. What is her tax bracket, how much tax does she pay, and what is her actual tax rate?

b. Miguel earned $35,000 in taxable income this year. How much more does he pay in taxes than if he had earned $30,000?

c. Meredith had $125,000 in taxable income and had $30,000 in taxes withheld. Will she receive a refund or owe money? How much?

Challenge Calculate the FICA taxes and tax rates for each of the above taxpayers.

427

4 Assess & Reteach

Assess Have students answer the two review questions that they find most challenging. Students should refer to the text to clarify details. Ask students to share their responses to their chosen questions.

Unit 6 Resource Book
- Section Quiz, p. 19

Interactive Review @ ClassZone.com
- Section Quiz

Test Generator CD-ROM
- Section Quiz

Reteach Call on volunteers to describe each of the federal taxes shown in Figure 14.8. Invite other class members to contribute additional information.

Unit 6 Resource Book
- Reteaching Activity, p. 20

SECTION 2 ASSESSMENT ANSWERS

Reviewing Key Concepts

1. a. *taxable income*, p. 421; *tax return*, p. 421
   b. *FICA*, p. 423; *Social Security*, p. 423
   c. *estate tax*, p. 425 *gift tax*, p. 425
2. because it protects them from the effects of inflation and keeps their tax rate relatively constant
3. It receives federal tax money for the government and administers the tax system.
4. They are both taxes placed on specific products. Excise taxes are placed on the production or sale of a product; customs duties are imposed on products imported into the country.
5. payroll tax: based on income; user fee: based on usage of a product
6. See page 420 for an example of a completed cluster diagram: Social Security, Medicare

Critical Thinking

7. 3.4 percent; it shows how tax brackets are revised so that taxpayers don't pay higher tax rates if their income rises due to inflation.
8. The Medicare tax is proportional but the Social Security tax is regressive because there is a limit on the amount of income subject to Social Security tax and therefore the tax rate decreases as income increases.
9. because the FICA tax is regressive; the taxpayer who earns $150,000 pays a lower rate of FICA taxes than does someone who earns $100,000 because the limit on Social Security tax is $94,200
10. as share of federal tax revenue, declined by about 65%; as share of GDP, also declined by about 65%

Economics in Practice

Calculate Taxes

a. 15% bracket, $897.50, 10.6% tax rate
b. $1,185 (taxes on $30,000 = $4,122.50 and taxes on $35,000 = $5,307.50)
c. She will receive a refund of $668.50 (taxes on $125,000 = $29, 331.50).

Challenge

a. $650.25, 7.65 percent
b. $2,677.50, 7.65 percent
c. $7,652.90, 6.12 percent

1 Plan & Prepare

Section 3 Objectives

- compare the two types of government expenditures
- explain how the federal budget is developed
- describe how government payments are made
- identify the impact that federal spending has on the economy

2 Focus & Motivate

Connecting to Everyday Life Explain that this section focuses on how the federal government spends the money that it receives in taxes. Encourage students to discuss how they think the government might change its spending patterns.

Taking Notes Remind students to take notes as they read by completing a hierarchy diagram. They can use the Graphic Organizer at **Interactive Review @ ClassZone.com**. A sample is shown below.

Federal Spending
- Federal Expenditures
  1. mandatory spending
  2. discretionary spending
- The Federal Budget and Spending
  1. Congress acts on the budget
  2. methods of federal spending
  3. impact of federal spending

SECTION 3

Federal Government Spending

OBJECTIVES

In Section 3, you will
- compare the two types of government expenditures
- explain how the federal budget is developed
- describe how government payments are made
- identify the impact that federal spending has on the economy

KEY TERMS

mandatory spending, *p. 428*
discretionary spending, *p. 428*
entitlements, *p. 428*
Medicaid, *p. 429*
federal budget, *p. 431*
fiscal year, *p. 431*
appropriations, *p. 431*
transfer payments, *p. 432*
grant-in-aid, *p. 432*
private sector, *p. 432*

TAKING NOTES

As you read Section 3, complete a hierarchy diagram to track main ideas and details. Use the Graphic Organizer at **Interactive Review @ ClassZone.com**

Federal Spending
- main idea — details
- main idea — details

Federal Expenditures

QUICK REFERENCE

Mandatory spending is required by law.

Discretionary spending has to be authorized each year.

Entitlements are social welfare programs with specific requirements.

KEY CONCEPTS

As you have seen, the federal government takes in a huge amount of money in taxes. The programs and services the federal government funds with this revenue are divided into two categories. These are **mandatory spending**, or spending that is required by current law, and **discretionary spending**, or spending that the government must authorize each year. For example, the law requires that the government spend money to fund the Social Security and Medicare programs. However, the federal government can decide to fund or not fund highway construction or maintenance of national parks. The federal government, then, has certain expenses that must be paid under current law, while other expenses are covered with what is left after those required expenses have been met.

TYPE 1 Mandatory Spending

Mandatory spending makes up well over half of all federal spending. Most of this spending is in the form of **entitlements**, which are social welfare programs with specific requirements. Social Security and Medicare are entitlement programs that provide payments to anyone who is eligible based on age or disability. Many

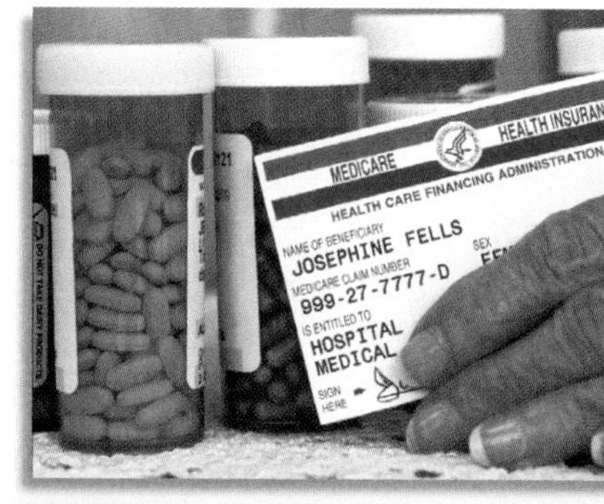

Medicare About 42 million Americans are enrolled in the Medicare program.

SECTION 3 PROGRAM RESOURCES

ON LEVEL

Lesson Plans
- Core, p. 48

Unit 6 Resource Book
- Reading Study Guide, pp. 21–22
- Economics Simulations, pp. 47–48
- Section Quiz, p. 29

STRUGGLING READERS

Unit 6 Resource Book
- Reading Study Guide with Additional Support, pp. 23–25
- Reteaching Activity, p. 30

ENGLISH LEARNERS

Unit 6 Resource Book
- Reading Study Guide with Additional Support (Spanish), pp. 26–28

INCLUSION

Lesson Plans
- Modified for Inclusion, p. 48

GIFTED AND TALENTED

Unit 6 Resource Book
- Readings in Free Enterprise: A Quiz for Capitalists, pp. 43–44

TECHNOLOGY

eEdition DVD-ROM
eEdition Online
Power Presentation DVD-ROM
Economics Concepts Transparencies
- CT48 Federal Budget Receipts and Outlays, 1960 to 2004

Daily Test Practice Transparencies, TT48
ClassZone.com

of these programs are not "means tested." In other words, anyone who meets the eligibility requirements receives the benefits, regardless of income level. For some other programs, however, income level is part of the requirement.

Social Security The Social Security program takes the largest amount of federal spending. It provides benefits to older retired workers, disabled workers with limited incomes, and survivors of workers who have died. Social Security is financed through a payroll tax. Therefore, workers must have worked for a certain period of time before they are eligible to receive full benefits under the program.

As the population of the United States has gotten older and more people have retired, costs for Social Security have increased. To help control costs, the government has gradually raised the age of full retirement—the point at which a worker is eligible to receive maximum benefits. Full retirement age ranges from 65 to 67, depending on the person's year of birth. Retirement benefits are not means tested. However, if retirees have additional income, benefits may be subject to withholding. For example, in 2006 retirees could earn $1,040 a month and still receive full Social Security benefits. However, retirees who earned more than this amount had their benefits reduced by $1 for every $3 over the income limit.

Economics Update
Find an update on Social Security at ClassZone.com

Medicare The Medicare program was introduced in 1966 as an additional old-age benefit under Social Security. Originally, Medicare provided hospital insurance, funded by a payroll tax, for people over 65, as well as optional medical coverage for items such as doctor bills. This part of Medicare is funded by premiums paid by those choosing the coverage and by general tax revenues.

Because of increasing numbers of retirees and increasing health care costs, Medicare costs have risen dramatically since the program began. Beginning in 2006, reforms to the program required Medicare to compete with private health insurance providers. Means testing was added for all but the lowest-income group of senior citizens. In addition, some coverage was added for prescription drugs.

QUICK REFERENCE

Medicaid is a government medical insurance program for low-income people.

Medicaid Established at the same time as Medicare, **Medicaid** is a joint federal-state medical insurance program for low-income people. The federal government funds about 63 percent of the costs of the program, and the states pay about 37 percent. In recent years, states have tightened their eligibility requirements for Medicaid in an effort to control costs.

Other Mandatory Spending Programs There are a variety of other mandatory spending programs that define eligibility requirements and are then funded based on an estimate of how many people meet those requirements. The Food Stamp program provides funds for about 26 million low-income people to purchase food. Veterans' benefits include health care coverage and disability payments for service-related illness or injury. People who have served in the military are also eligible for education assistance. The federal government spends about $50 billion a year on veterans' benefits.

Payments for the federal portion of unemployment insurance are also part of mandatory spending. In addition, the federal government pays its workers some retirement benefits. Federal employees hired after 1983 are also eligible for some Social Security retirement benefits.

Services for Veterans The Veterans Administration serves the needs and represents the interests of some 26 million veterans and their dependents.

3 Teach

Federal Expenditures

Discuss

- What are the similarities and differences between Medicare and Medicaid? *(Both are government health care programs. Medicare is mostly for people over 65, while Medicaid is a federal-state program for low-income people.)*
- How are mandatory spending programs funded? *(Congress defines eligibility requirements and then allocates funds based on how many people are expected to meet the requirements.)*

Economics Update

At **ClassZone.com** students will see updated information on Social Security.

Technomics

Social Security Online

The Social Security Administration Web site <www.socialsecurity.gov> contains a wealth of useful and interesting information, ranging from the history of Social Security and Medicare to an annual survey of the most popular baby names. FAQs are searchable by 24 broad subject categories.

The site also features material in 15 languages, ranging from Arabic to Vietnamese. Information for kids and families includes FAQs that provide an overview of the Social Security program. Information for the press includes a collection of fact sheets and statistics.

LEVELED ACTIVITY

Investigating Social Security

Time 30 Minutes

Objective Students will demonstrate an understanding of Social Security benefits and financing. (This activity also draws on material from Section 2.)

Basic

Review the information in the textbook about the Social Security and Medicare programs. Create a diagram to explain how the programs are financed through taxes and what kinds of benefits they provide. Compare the percentages of federal revenue and spending that are related to these two programs.

On Level

Choose one of these questions about Social Security to research: Why was the program established? How does the program work? Who pays for the benefits? The FAQs on the "Kids and Families" page of the Social Security Web site are a good source of information. Write a one-page summary of your research.

Challenge

Use the Internet to research the current debate on Social Security reform. Discover what challenges the system faces and analyze at least two different proposals for addressing them. Summarize your research and draw conclusions from it about possible solutions to the problem.

International Economics

Defense Spending
A 2004 report by the Congressional Research Service compared the military spending of the United States and 168 foreign countries for 2002, based on public sources. According to this report, U.S. defense spending for that year was $348.5 billion. This amount was greater than the next 12 countries combined.

U.S. defense spending was about 3.3 percent of GDP. By this measure the United States ranked at 47. North Korea had the highest ratio at 25 percent of GDP.

Your Economic Choices

DISCRETIONARY SPENDING

How will you assign discretionary spending funds?

- Why might the government want to improve math and science education? *(Possible answer: to provide students with skills that will help them in a technology-based economy; to keep the United States competitive with other countries)*
- Why might the government undertake toy-safety research rather than toy companies? *(Possible answer: because the toy companies would rather not increase their costs of production and reduce their profits)*

Activity Organize students into small groups. Have each group discuss the question, considering the costs and benefits of each program. Ask them to think about who benefits directly and indirectly from each program. Encourage them to think about whether there are alternatives to government funding for the programs. Invite volunteers from each group to report on the conclusions reached by their group.

APPLICATION
Answer *Mandatory: medical coverage for low-income people, retirement benefits for older workers. Discretionary: AIDS prevention programs, air traffic regulation, pollution control.*

TYPE 2 Discretionary Spending

More than one-third of federal revenue is devoted to discretionary spending. The programs covered by discretionary spending fall into several different categories. These categories include

- interstate highway system and transportation programs, such as Amtrak;
- natural resources and the environment, including conservation programs, pollution clean-up, and national parks;
- education, most notably college tuition assistance;
- science, space, technology, and other research programs;
- justice administration, including enforcement agencies, such as the Federal Bureau of Investigation (FBI), and the federal court system.

The largest discretionary expenditure category, however, is national defense, which takes up about 50 percent of the total discretionary budget. National defense includes a large amount of the nation's military spending, including the salaries of military personnel, weapons, and the construction and maintenance of military bases. Not all national defense spending is discretionary. Some spending on homeland security—border protection and the enforcement of some immigration laws, for example—falls in the mandatory expenditures category. In addition, certain military spending, such as additional funding requests for the wars in Iraq and Afghanistan, is outside the basic federal budget.

YOUR ECONOMIC CHOICES

DISCRETIONARY SPENDING

How will you assign discretionary spending funds?

Two programs are competing for $100 million in discretionary funds—an initiative to improve math and science education in high schools and a research project to test new developments in toy safety. How will you advise officials to assign the funds and why?

Math class

Safer toys

APPLICATION Categorizing Economic Information

A. Categorize the following items as either mandatory spending or discretionary spending: AIDS prevention programs, air traffic regulation, medical coverage for low-income people, pollution control, retirement benefits for older workers.

◀ See Teacher's Edition for answer.

DIFFERENTIATING INSTRUCTION

Struggling Readers

Compare Economic Information
Encourage students to relate the bulleted list on page 430 to Figure 14.9. *(All items listed except for education are included in "Other.")* Point out that national defense is 17 percent of the total budget but about 50 percent of the discretionary portion. Have them compare Figure 14.9 with Figure 14.8 on page 425. How do social insurance taxes compare to spending on Social Security and Medicare? *(These taxes are 37 percent of revenue and the two programs are 36 percent of spending.)*

Gifted and Talented

Graph Spending Trends
Invite students to research the federal budget in more depth. The Office of Management and Budget Web site <www.whitehouse.gov/omb/budget/> includes the current fiscal year's budget along with historical tables tracking spending since 1940. Encourage students to choose three categories of spending to track over a period of time. Invite them to summarize the results of their research in graphs and present their graphs to the class along with conclusions about spending trends.

The Federal Budget and Spending

KEY CONCEPTS

Each year the President and Congress work together to establish the **federal budget**, a plan for spending federal tax money. The budget is prepared for a **fiscal year**, a 12-month period for which an organization plans its expenditures. The federal government's fiscal year runs from October 1 through September 30. The President's budget is prepared by the Office of Management and Budget (OMB) and takes into account estimated tax receipts and requests by all federal departments and agencies. Figure 14.9 shows the OMB budget estimate for fiscal year 2007.

QUICK REFERENCE

The **federal budget** is a plan for spending federal tax money.

A **fiscal year** is a 12-month period for which an organization plans its expenditures.

Appropriations are specific amounts of money set aside for specific purposes.

Congress Acts on the Budget

The Congressional Budget Office helps the House and Senate develop guidelines for different **appropriations**, which are set amounts of money set aside for specific purposes. Members of Congress often make deals to gain votes for appropriations that they support. Congress votes on the final budget and sends it to the president for approval. If the budget is not approved by the beginning of the new fiscal year, Congress passes resolutions to keep the government running on a day-to-day basis.

Methods of Federal Spending

After budget approval, the funds are spent in several ways. One way is direct spending, by which the government buys goods and services that it needs to operate, such as military equipment and office supplies. Paying the salaries of government

FIGURE 14.9 THE FEDERAL BUDGET

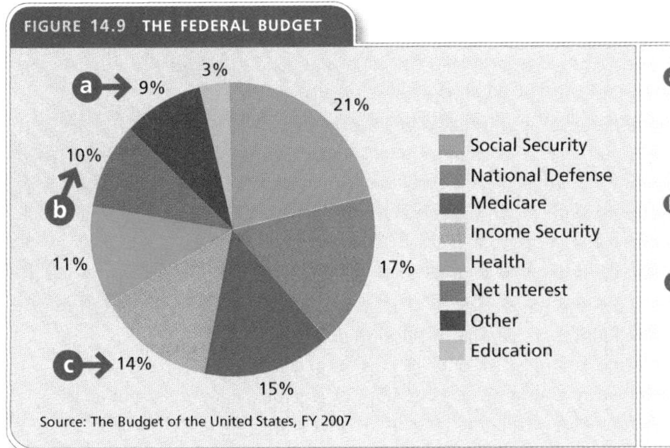

Source: The Budget of the United States, FY 2007

a This category includes spending for veterans' benefits, energy, the environment, transportation, and other government programs.

b Net interest is the interest that the federal government pays on loans it has taken out.

c Income security includes retirement for certain government employees and housing and food programs for low-income people.

ANALYZE GRAPHS

1. What is the largest category of spending in the federal budget?
2. Approximately how much of the federal budget goes to health and education?

The Federal Budget and Spending

Discuss

- What is the difference between the Office of Management and Budget and the Congressional Budget Office? *(The OMB prepares a budget for the president, while the CBO helps Congress decide how much to spend on different budget categories.)*
- How is direct government spending different from transfer payments? *(Direct spending refers to government purchases, salaries, and projects. Transfer payments are government payments to individuals who do not provide any goods or services in return.)*

Analyzing Graphs: Figure 14.9

Explain that this pie graph summarizes the main categories of government spending. Note that payment of interest on the debt is part of mandatory spending, because the government must keep up interest payments in order to maintain good credit and be able to borrow in the future. Ask students to identify the categories that reflect discretionary spending. *(national defense, education, other, and some health spending)*

Answers

1. *Social Security*
2. *14 percent goes to Health and Education combined.*

CLASS ACTIVITY

Researching the Budget Process

Time 45 Minutes

Task Gather information on the federal budget process and create a bulletin board display.

Materials Needed computer with Internet access, paper and markers

Activity

- Assign small groups to research different aspects of the budget process. Some may research the roles of the Office of Management and Budget, Congressional Budget Office, and the main committees in Congress responsible for developing the budget.
- Others may research the general timetable for preparing the annual budget or examples of the negotiations and compromises that occur during the process.
- Direct students to collaborate on creating a bulletin board display based on their research.
- Invite volunteers to explain the details of the budgeting process.

Rubric

	Understanding of Concepts	Presentation of Information
4	excellent	clear and complete
3	good	mostly clear
2	fair	sometimes clear
1	poor	sketchy

More About . . .

Methods of Federal Spending
National defense is the largest category of direct federal spending. In 1960, national defense accounted for about 52 percent of all federal outlays. Payments for individuals, including direct transfer payments and grants to state and local governments, amounted to about 26 percent. By 2007, those percentages had changed to about 17 percent and 64 percent respectively.

Direct transfer payments to individuals accounted for about $1,357 billion in 2007, and grants for individuals through state and local governments equaled about $304 billion. All other grants totaled $139 billion, about 5 percent of all federal outlays.

Technomics

The Catalog of Federal Domestic Assistance
The CFDA Web site <www.cfda.gov> is a centralized resource for state and local governments and other institutions looking for federal assistance. The site provides access to a database of many kinds of assistance programs, especially grants and loans.

Visitors to the site may use a keyword search or may see the programs that are generating the most interest from other users (Top 10% Program List). Information on new programs is located in one place, and the site is updated every two weeks with new information from federal agencies.

QUICK REFERENCE

Transfer payments are money distributed to individuals who do not provide anything in return.

A **grant-in-aid** is a transfer payment from the federal government to state or local governments.

The **private sector** is the part of the economy owned by individuals or businesses.

employees is another type of direct spending. A second way the government spends the money is through **transfer payments**—money distributed to individuals who do not provide goods or services in return. A **grant-in-aid** is a transfer payment from the federal government to state or local governments.

Transfer Payments These payments are generally part of the mandatory spending you learned about earlier. For example, Social Security retirement or disability benefits and health care benefits from Medicare or veterans' programs are transfer payments from the government to individuals. The individuals do not provide specific goods or services in exchange for these government funds.

Grants-in-aid These grants are transfer payments between levels of government. The federal government makes grants to states, local governments, and regions. The grants are designated for specific categories of activities such as highway construction, certain school services, or Medicaid funding.

The Impact of Federal Spending

Because the federal government spends trillions of dollars, it is a big factor in the economy. The federal government influences the economy in three ways: resource allocation, income redistribution, and competition with the **private sector**, which is that part of the economy owned by individuals or businesses.

Resource Allocation The federal government makes choices concerning where to spend money and on what to spend it, and that influences how resources are allocated. For example, if money goes to urban transit, it cannot go to fix rural roads. Similarly, money spent on weapons systems for the military cannot be spent on some other program, such as environmental protection.

Income Redistribution Government spending affects the incomes of families, individuals, and businesses. Transfer payments for health care, retirement, and Food Stamp benefits, for example, provide income support for many low-income earners. How the government awards work contracts can also influence the distribution of income. For example, if the government awards a contract to build several submarines to a shipyard in the Northeast, workers there will be assured work and an income. However, workers at a California shipyard that failed to get the contract may lose their jobs. In turn, they will not have income to spend at local businesses.

Government Contracts A government contract, such as one to build submarines, has a huge impact on local, state, and regional economies.

Competition with the Private Sector The government may produce goods or services that are also produced in the private sector. Examples include veterans' hospitals that compete with privately owned hospitals, or federal housing that competes with homes and apartments provided by private developers and landlords.

APPLICATION Drawing Conclusions

B. How are transfer payments related to income redistribution?
Transfer payments are the method used by the federal government to redistribute income, e.g. from higher-income taxpayers to low-income earners.

DIFFERENTIATING INSTRUCTION

English Learners

Compare Nouns and Verbs
Explain that the impact of federal spending is described on page 432 in the form of three noun phrases. Invite students to identify the verb form of each of the nouns *(allocate, redistribute, and compete)*. Remind students that the prefix *re-* means "again." Check student understanding of these different parts of speech by writing fill-in-the-blank sentences on the board. Call on volunteers to insert the correct noun or verb in the blank.

Gifted and Talented

Write a News Story
Invite students to explore the Catalog of Federal Domestic Assistance Web site <www.cfda.gov> to find out about new programs available for state and local governments or other institutions. Once students find general information about a program of interest on that Web site, they might do an Internet search for the program name to learn additional information, such as the amount of funding available. Encourage students to write a news story about the program they have selected.

SECTION 3 Assessment

Online Quiz
ClassZone.com

REVIEWING KEY CONCEPTS

1. Explain the relationship between the terms in each of these pairs.
   a. *mandatory spending* *entitlement*
   b. *federal budget* *fiscal year*
   c. *transfer payment* *grant-in-aid*
2. What is the difference between mandatory spending and discretionary spending?
3. Why is Medicaid an example of an entitlement program?
4. What does Congress do when it decides on appropriations?
5. How does the government compete with the private sector?
6. **Using Your Notes** How is the federal budget established? Refer to your completed hierarchy diagram. Use the Graphic Organizer at **Interactive Review @ ClassZone.com**

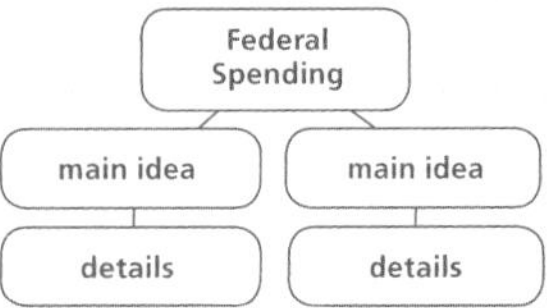

CRITICAL THINKING

7. **Making Inferences** Between 2007 and 2009, spending on Social Security is projected to remain at 21.5 percent of the federal budget, while spending on education is projected to decline from 3.4 percent to 3.1 percent of the budget. How does this show the difference between mandatory and discretionary spending?
8. **Categorizing Economic Information** Categorize each of these examples of federal spending as direct spending, transfer payment, or grant-in-aid:
   - computers for IRS
   - disability benefits
   - flood control in Gulf Coast region
   - highway funds for states
   - medical care for elderly
   - money for urban housing
   - price supports for farmers
   - repair of space shuttle
   - salaries for national park rangers
9. **Challenge** Molly's grandmother was born in 1943. If she retires in 2005, she'll receive $750 per month in Social Security benefits. If she waits until 2009, she will receive $1,000, and if she waits until 2010, her monthly benefit increases to $1,080. Why do you think Congress structured the Social Security benefit payments program in this way?

ECONOMICS IN PRACTICE

Military base entrance

Studying Economic Impact Consider what you have learned about the impact of federal spending on the economy. The chart below shows information on the impact of a hypothetical military base on an area's economy.

Direct military base employment	27,400 jobs, $1 billion payroll
Additional related jobs	19,500 jobs, $800 million payroll
Payments to private health care providers	$19 million
Contracts for goods and services	$115 million
State and local taxes	$102.8 million

Analyze Data Study the chart to answer these questions:

- What is the total number of jobs attributable to the military base?
- How much does the base spend on health care?

Challenge Write a summary of the economic impact of the military base.

4 Assess & Reteach

Assess Have students answer the questions individually and then gather in groups to review and discuss their responses.

Unit 6 Resource Book
- Section Quiz, p. 29

Interactive Review @ ClassZone.com
- Section Quiz

Test Generator CD-ROM
- Section Quiz

Reteach Have pairs of students write three multiple-choice questions about the section. Then allow pairs to quiz one another.

Unit 6 Resource Book
- Reteaching Activity, p. 30

Economics in Practice
Analyze Data
- 46,900
- $19 million to private health care providers

Challenge Summary should reflect an understanding that the base has a large impact on the local economy through a large number of jobs directly and indirectly attributable to the base. Additional impacts include payments for rental housing, contracts for goods and services needed by the base, and health care for military personnel. These personnel also contribute to the local and state tax bases and result in federal aid to the local schools, which educate their children.

SECTION 3 ASSESSMENT ANSWERS

Reviewing Key Concepts
1. a. *mandatory spending*, p. 428 *entitlements*, p. 428
   b. *federal budget*, p. 431; *fiscal year*, p. 431
   c. *transfer payment*, p. 432; *grant-in-aid*, p. 432
2. Mandatory spending is spending that is required by current law, and discretionary spending is spending that must be authorized by the government each year.
3. because it is a social welfare program with specific requirements, specifically it's a health care program for low-income people
4. It decides how much money to allocate to specific government programs.
5. by providing goods and services that may have parallels in the private sector, such as housing or hospitals
6. See page 428 for an example of a completed hierarchy diagram. The OMB prepares a budget, which is submitted to Congress for review. Congress develops specific appropriations, which it then votes on. The president signs the final budget.

Critical Thinking
7. Social Security is a mandatory program and the government must provide funding to provide benefits to all people who meet the program requirements. Education is a discretionary category and Congress must make choices about which programs to fund each year. If mandatory programs require more money there is less available for discretionary programs.
8. direct spending: computers for the IRS, repair of space shuttle, salaries for national park rangers; transfer payment: disability benefits, medical care for the elderly, price supports for corn farmers; grant-in-aid: flood control in the Gulf Coast region, highway funds for the states, money for urban housing
9. Congress provides incentives to encourage people to retire later in order to stretch the money for the entitlement program, which must be funded every year and which has increased expenses as the population ages and more people reach retirement age.

Economics in Practice
See answers in side column above.

❶ Plan & Prepare

Section 4 Objectives

- identify the major sources of revenue for both state and local governments
- examine the concept of a balanced budget
- describe the major categories of state and local expenditures

❷ Focus & Motivate

Connecting to Everyday Life Explain that this section focuses on how state and local governments collect taxes and provide public goods. Encourage students to brainstorm a list of public goods and services provided by their state and local governments.

Taking Notes Remind students to take notes as they read by completing a chart. They can use the Graphic Organizer at **Interactive Review @ ClassZone.com**. A sample is shown below.

State Government		Local Government	
Revenue	Spending	Revenue	Spending
Intergovernmental revenue; sales tax; individual and corporate income taxes	Public welfare; higher education; aid to local school districts; public safety	Intergovernmental revenue; property tax; sales tax	Public schools; public safety; public welfare; public utilities

At **ClassZone.com** students will see updated information on state sales taxes.

SECTION 4

State and Local Taxes and Spending

OBJECTIVES

In Section 4, you will
- identify the major sources of revenue for both state and local governments
- examine the concept of a balanced budget
- describe the major categories of state and local expenditures

KEY TERMS

balanced budget, *p. 436*
operating budget, *p. 436*
capital budget, *p. 436*
tax assessor, *p. 437*

TAKING NOTES

As you read Section 4, complete a chart using the key concepts and other helpful words and phrases. Use the Graphic Organizer at **Interactive Review @ ClassZone.com**

State Government		Local Government	
Revenue	Spending	Revenue	Spending

State Revenues

KEY CONCEPTS

As you recall from earlier in this chapter, all levels of government may impose taxes to raise revenue to support their activities. The federal government has the broadest tax base, while the smallest tax base is at the local level. There are thousands of local governmental units, from towns, cities, and counties to districts set up to handle a specific problem such as mosquito control or sewage treatment.

State revenues come from a variety of sources, the largest of which is intergovernmental revenue, mostly grants-in-aid from the federal government. States also raise funds from state sales taxes and from state income tax, both on individuals and on corporations. (See Figure 14.11 on page 437.)

Economics Update

Find an update on state sales taxes at **ClassZone.com**

TYPE 1 Sales and Excise Taxes

All states except Alaska, Delaware, New Hampshire, Montana, and Oregon levy a state sales tax. Rates range from 2.9 percent in Colorado to 7.25 percent in California. These taxes generally are applied to most goods and services sold within the state. However, many states exempt food and prescription drugs from sales tax. Some other states tax these goods, over-the-counter drugs, and certain other medical supplies at a lower rate. In addition, charitable, religious, and educational organizations are often exempt from paying sales taxes.

All states also have excise taxes on cigarettes, alcohol, gasoline, and diesel fuel. Certain government organizations, volunteer fire-fighting companies, and farmers may be exempt from fuel taxes. Many states also have special sales taxes that mostly affect tourists, such as taxes on car rentals and hotel and motel room rates.

SECTION 4 PROGRAM RESOURCES

ON LEVEL

Lesson Plans
- Core, p. 49

Unit 6 Resource Book
- Reading Study Guide, pp. 31–32
- Section Quiz, p. 39
- Economic Simulations, pp. 47–48

STRUGGLING READERS

Unit 6 Resource Book
- Reading Study Guide with Additional Support, pp. 33–35
- Reteaching Activity, p. 40

ENGLISH LEARNERS

Unit 6 Resource Book
- Reading Study Guide with Additional Support (Spanish), pp. 36–38

INCLUSION

Lesson Plans
- Modified for Inclusion, p. 49

GIFTED AND TALENTED

Unit 6 Resource Book
- Case Study Resources: Online Tax Debate Heats Up, p. 45; Online Sales Tax Debate Rages On, p. 46

TECHNOLOGY

eEdition DVD-ROM

eEdition Online

Power Presentation DVD-ROM

Economics Concepts Transparencies
- CT49 Federal, State, and Local Revenue and Expenditures, 2000

Daily Test Practice Transparencies, TT49

ClassZone.com

TYPE 2 Income Tax and Other Revenue Sources

Income taxes account for some 16 percent of states' total revenue. Most states levy taxes on both individual and corporate income. However, Alaska, Florida, and Texas have no individual income tax. And Nevada, South Dakota, Washington, and Wyoming levy neither individual nor corporate income taxes. Most states have progressive tax rates on individual income and flat tax rates on corporate income. Individual income tax rates range from a low of 0.36 percent for the lowest tax bracket in Iowa to 9.5 percent for the highest tax bracket in Vermont. Figure 14.10 below compares average individual income tax rates and sales tax rates for several states.

FIGURE 14.10 COMPARING STATE TAXES

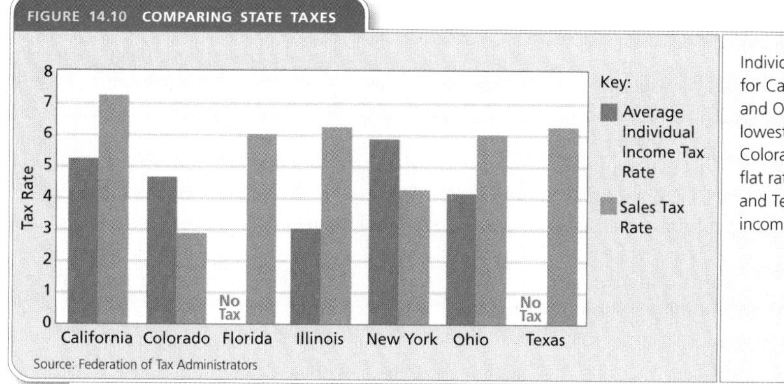

Individual income tax rates for California, New York, and Ohio are averages of lowest and highest brackets. Colorado and Illinois have a flat rate income tax. Florida and Texas have no state income tax.

ANALYZE GRAPHS

1. Which state has the highest income tax rate? Which has the highest sales tax rate?
2. Which state has the heaviest tax burden?

The average state corporate tax rate is about 6.8 percent, ranging from a low of 1 percent for the lowest brackets in Alaska and Arkansas to Pennsylvania's flat rate of 9.99 percent. Many state governments structure their corporate tax rates to attract businesses to the state. These governments have used billions of dollars in tax cuts and incentives for businesses to promote economic development. However, states receive benefits from these tax practices in the increased economic activity that development brings.

States also raise revenue from several other sources. Many of these sources, including estate taxes and user fees, are the same as those used by the federal government. (See Figure 14.8 on page 425.) Most states also levy property taxes. In addition, most states charge several fees related to business operations. These include registration fees for certain types of businesses and license fees for doctors, dentists, lawyers, and accountants.

APPLICATION Comparing Economic Information

A. How do state income tax rates compare to federal income tax rates?

They are much lower.

3 Teach

State Revenues

Discuss

- How do some states make their sales taxes less regressive? *(by exempting food and medications from the tax or applying a lower tax rate to these necessities)*
- What type of tax structure do most states use for individual and corporate income taxes? *(progressive for individual income and proportional for corporate income)*

Analyzing Graphs: Figure 14.10

Have students read the caption to make sure they understand that some of the income tax rates shown are average rates from a progressive tax structure and others are actual rates from a proportional tax structures. Ask students to identify the state with the lowest sales tax rate. *(Colorado)*

Answers

1. *New York, California*
2. *California, because its combined tax rates are the highest among states shown*

SMALL GROUP ACTIVITY

Promoting Business Incentives

Time 45 Minutes 

Task Gather information on state or local business tax incentives and create a storyboard.

Materials Needed computer with Internet access, paper and markers

Activity

- Have small groups of students research state or local government tax incentives for businesses. Direct students to use their state or city and business tax incentive as keywords.
- Encourage each group to create a storyboard for a TV commercial that the government might use to promote these incentives to potential businesses.
- Students may focus on a particular type of incentive or on the overall business climate.
- Allow each group to present its storyboard to the class. Discuss why the government uses tax incentives to attract businesses.

Rubric

	Understanding of Concepts	Presentation of Information
4	excellent	clear, complete, creative
3	good	mostly clear
2	fair	sometimes clear
1	poor	sketchy and unoriginal

State Budgets and Spending

Discuss

- Which kind of state budget must be balanced and why? *(operating budgets because they are used for day-to-day expenses and are funded by taxes rather than by borrowing, which is used to fund capital budgets)*
- Why is education a bigger part of state budgets than of the federal budget? *(Possible answer: because states provide funds for state colleges and universities as well as public schools, while the federal government has less direct responsibility for education)*

State Budgets and Spending

KEY CONCEPTS

All states except Vermont are required to have a **balanced budget**, in which total government revenue from all sources is equal to total government spending. However, balanced-budget requirements usually apply only to certain kinds of spending. Further, nearly every state has a reserve fund or may run a surplus, both of which can be used to balance the budget in subsequent years.

QUICK REFERENCE

A **balanced budget** requires that total government revenue is equal to total government spending.

An **operating budget** is a plan for day-to-day expenses.

A **capital budget** is a plan for major expenses or investments.

State Budgets

States actually work with two types of budgets—an **operating budget,** a plan for day-to-day expenses, and a **capital budget**, a plan for major expenses or investments. The operating budget generally covers expenses that occur each year, such as salaries for state government employees, payments for health and welfare benefits, and funds for education systems. Capital budgets provide funds for large construction and maintenance projects on state buildings, roads, and bridges, as well as for land acquisition for state construction needs or state parks. Usually, operating budgets are subject to balanced-budget requirements. Capital budgets are not, because they are usually funded through borrowing. In fact, capital budgets often are run at a deficit, meaning that more is spent than is collected in revenues.

Deficit Spending Both federal and state governments practice deficit spending—spending more than they collect in revenues—to cover their expenses.

State Expenses

Education is a major expense for the states, which not only support community colleges and state university systems but also provide assistance to local school districts. For example, state assistance accounted for about 49 percent of public school funding in 2002. Public safety, too, is a significant state expense. Spending on public safety includes state police, crime labs, and prisons and other correctional facilities. States also support a court system.

Public welfare expenses involve funds for state-run hospitals as well as cash assistance and medical care payments to the needy. States also fund programs that help citizens with problems related to housing, disability, unemployment, and job training. Other expenses include state government administration, retirement funds for state employees, natural resources, and economic development.

APPLICATION Categorizing

B. Would a grant to a city to build a new sewage treatment plant be part of the city's operating budget or capital budget? capital budget

DIFFERENTIATING INSTRUCTION

Struggling Readers

Use Popcorn Reading
Have students read the material on pages 436–438 together in small groups. Assign one student to read aloud while the others follow. The reader should stop suddenly and call out another student's name. The named student should begin to read from the point where the first reader left off. Group members should repeat the process until they have finished the material.

Inclusion

Create a Quiz
Have groups of students read Section 4 together. Have each group, as they read, write two questions (with answers) about the content of each of the three main subsections. Encourage students to collaborate orally about the questions and answers. One student can write the final questions and answers on a sheet of paper. Have groups quiz each other orally.

Local Revenue and Spending

KEY CONCEPTS

Local government units include counties, cities, towns, villages, townships, school districts, and other special districts. They have fewer options for raising revenue than do other levels of government. Their major revenue sources are intergovernmental revenue—or transfers—from state and federal governments and property taxes. Local governments also tap other sources, many of which are similar to the state tax base. Figure 14.11 shows revenue sources for state and local governments.

Property Tax

Recall that you read about property tax in the first section of the chapter. This tax can be levied on real estate and on personal property such as motor vehicles, boats, expensive jewelry, or computers. Local governments rely on a **tax assessor**, a government official who determines the value of the property. They then enact a tax based on a percentage of the property's value.

QUICK REFERENCE

A **tax assessor** determines the value of property.

Other Taxes

Local governments also use sales taxes, sin taxes on activities such as gambling, hospitality taxes on hotels and restaurants, entertainment taxes on tickets or entrance fees, and payroll taxes. The local payroll tax is a tax on people who work in a city but live outside the city. Such a tax is often used in large metropolitan areas where workers from the suburbs benefit from city services such as police and fire protection.

FIGURE 14.11 SOURCES OF STATE AND LOCAL GOVERNMENT REVENUE

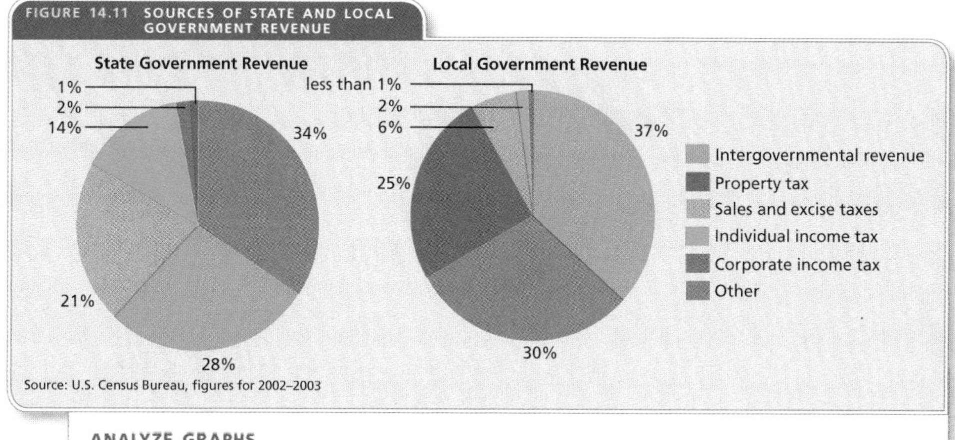

Source: U.S. Census Bureau, figures for 2002–2003

ANALYZE GRAPHS

1. What are the two largest sources of revenue for both state and local governments?
2. Which type of government gets a larger percentage of its revenue from sales and excise taxes?

Local Revenue and Spending

Discuss

- Why do some cities levy payroll taxes on people who work in the city but live in the suburbs? *(because workers benefit from city services such as streets, police and fire protection, and trash removal)*
- Why do local governments employ more people than state governments do? *(because local governments provide more direct services to people)*

Analyzing Graphs: Figure 14.11

Explain that these pie graphs summarize the main categories of state and local government revenue. Call on volunteers to identify the percentage of each type of revenue for state and local governments and to note the main differences. *(State governments get more revenue from sales taxes and income taxes, while local governments get more revenue from property taxes.)* Encourage students to compare these graphs to Figure 14.8 on page 425. Note that the federal government is a source of intergovernmental revenue but not a recipient of it.

Answers

1. *Intergovernmental revenue and Other*
2. *state government*

INDIVIDUAL ACTIVITY

Analyzing Government Support of Education

Time 30 Minutes

Task Reflect on government spending on education and write an essay.

Materials Needed paper and pen or computer with word processing software

Activity

- At the end of Section 4, encourage students to review what they have learned about how different levels of government provide support for education.
- Have students reflect on the costs and benefits of public support for education. Are they aware of any problems with the system?
- Direct students to write a one- or two-page essay on the topic, including an analysis of the effects on individuals and society as a whole.
- Invite volunteers to share their essays with the class. Discuss how society would be different without this government support.

Rubric

	Understanding of Concepts	Presentation of Information
4	excellent	clear and complete
3	good	mostly clear
2	fair	sometimes clear
1	poor	sketchy

More About . . .

Public School Funding

The trend toward less reliance on local property taxes to fund public education began in the 1970s and 1980s. There is wide variation among the states in how much they continue to rely on local funding sources. For example, in Pennsylvania, New Jersey, and Illinois local revenue accounted for 50 to 60 percent of funding in 2004.

At the same time, Michigan and California schools received only 30 to 35 percent of their funds from local sources. The national average is about 43 percent. Recent studies show that while funding may be more equitable it is still often inadequate to meet educational goals.

Local Spending

Local governments provide most of the direct services that citizens receive. To deliver these services, local governments employ almost three times the number of workers as state governments do. Some of the most important areas of local spending are described below.

Public Schools Local governments have the main responsibility for elementary and secondary schools. About 46 percent of local government spending goes to education. Government funds pay for construction and maintenance of school buildings, salaries for teachers, administrators, and other personnel, as well as for items such as textbooks and computers. Reliance on the property tax has led to difficulties for many local governments, since communities with lower property values have smaller tax bases to finance education.

Public Safety Local governments provide police and fire protection to secure lives and property in their communities. They are also responsible for emergency medical equipment and personnel to provide on-site treatment and transportation to medical facilities. Local governments maintain the 911 emergency telephone number system. Other expenditures in this category include animal control, consumer protection, and preparation for and response to natural disasters.

Public Safety Ensuring the safety of life and property in the community—by providing fire protection, for example—is the responsibility of local government.

Public Welfare Local governments spend less than state governments on direct payments for medical care and assistance to the needy. However, many local governments maintain public health departments, and some own and operate their own hospitals. Local health departments are concerned with immunization programs, environmental health, and maintaining birth and death records. They also are responsible for making sure that restaurants meet health standards.

Other Responsibilities Local governments also have primary responsibility for providing most public utilities such as water, public transit, sewage systems, and trash removal. They maintain local highways, roads, and streets, including traffic control lights and signs, snow removal, and pothole repair. Finally, local governments provide many kinds of recreational and cultural facilities including parks, recreation centers, swimming pools, and libraries.

APPLICATION Drawing Conclusions

B. Why do local governments rely more on property taxes as a source of revenue than do state governments? because local governments provide most of the services that directly benefit property owners such as schools, public utilities, and local roads and streets

438 Chapter 14

DIFFERENTIATING INSTRUCTION

Struggling Readers

Summarize Visually

Have pairs of students use text and graphics to summarize the important ideas about local revenue and spending. You may wish to assign pairs to work on specific topics covered on pages 437 and 438. One approach might be to have students arrange their text and graphics on a large poster-sized map of your city or county. Have students present their visual summaries to their classmates.

Gifted and Talented

Research Local Government

Invite interested students to research the public goods provided by their local government. Encourage them to find out what tax bases the local government uses as well. Students may use Internet resources or interview government officials. Suggest that students create a brochure for newcomers highlighting the benefits of living in the community that are a result of government spending. They may include information about the types of taxes that citizens pay that provide funding for these services.

SECTION 4 Assessment

REVIEWING KEY CONCEPTS

1. Use each of the three terms below in a sentence that illustrates the meaning of the term.
   a. *balanced budget* **b.** *capital budget* **c.** *tax assessor*
2. What is the difference between an operating budget and a capital budget?
3. How is an operating budget related to a balanced budget?
4. What is the largest revenue source for state governments? What is the largest source for local governments?
5. Why do local governments need tax assessors?
6. **Using Your Notes** What kinds of education do state and local governments spend money on? Refer to your completed chart. Use the Graphic Organizer at **Interactive Review @ ClassZone.com**

State Government		Local Government	
Revenue	Spending	Revenue	Spending

CRITICAL THINKING

7. **Comparing and Contrasting** What are the similarities and differences in the sources of revenue for state and local governments?
8. **Analyzing Effects** Which level of government would be most affected if the federal government decided to limit the amount of money that it spent on the Medicaid program? Give reasons for your answer.
9. **Making Inferences** Voters in your city must decide whether to raise revenue by increasing the rate of property tax for owners of homes and businesses or by placing a new tax on motel and hotel room rates and car rentals. Which tax are voters more likely to choose? Give reasons for your answer.
10. **Challenge** Between 1992 and 2002, average state funding for public schools increased from 46 percent of all state expenditures to 49 percent of all state expenditures. At the same time, local government funding of public schools decreased from 47 percent to 43 percent. Why do you think the source of school funding has changed in this way?

ECONOMICS IN PRACTICE

School board meeting

Using a Decision Making Process Suppose that you are on a local school board. Total budget for the school district is $25,000,000. The chart below lists the items to be funded out of this budget.

Spending Category	Priority
Administrative salaries	
Classroom computers	
School lunch program	
Special education programs	
Teacher salaries	
Textbooks and other instructional materials	
Utilities	

Decide on Funding Priorities Use a decision-making process to decide how to allocate the budget. Complete the chart by ranking the items from 1 to 7, from most important to least important.

Challenge Based on your priorities, allocate a percentage of the budget to each category.

④ Assess & Reteach

Assess Have students present their answers to the Critical Thinking questions in graphic organizers.

Unit 6 Resource Book
- Section Quiz, p. 39

Interactive Review @ ClassZone.com
- Section Quiz

Test Generator CD-ROM
- Section Quiz

Reteach Call on volunteers to use the chart they created while taking notes to summarize the main ideas and details about state and local taxes and spending.

Unit 6 Resource Book
- Reteaching Activity, p. 40

Economics in Practice

Decide on Funding Priorities Accept all reasonable answers that can be supported by the student's decision-making choices and goals.

Challenge Percentages should match priorities and total 100 percent.

SECTION 4 ASSESSMENT ANSWERS

Reviewing Key Concepts

1. **a.** *balanced budget*, p. 436
   b. *capital budget*, p. 436
   c. *tax assessor*, p. 437
2. An operating budget is for recurring, day-to-day expenses such as salaries and ongoing programs. A capital budget is for large expenses and investments such as buildings and land.
3. It is generally the state operating budget that must be balanced so that revenue and expenditures are equal.
4. state: "other" sources of revenue; local: intergovernmental revenue
5. because property taxes account for 25 percent of local tax revenue, and the tax assessor determines the value of property to be taxed
6. See page 434 for an example of a completed chart. state: colleges, universities, support for local schools; local: elementary, secondary schools

Critical Thinking

7. For both, intergovernmental revenue and "other" are the largest sources of funding. States rely primarily on sales taxes and individual income taxes for other revenue, while local governments rely on property taxes.
8. state government, because it is the states that are primarily responsible for public welfare such as medical care for needy people
9. Answers will vary. Some students may select the tax on motel and hotel room rates and car rentals because the tax will affect tourists more than the people who live in the city. Other students may select the property tax because it will raise more money.
10. Possible response: The funding of education primarily through local property taxes leads to inequality of educational opportunity. Wealthy communities will have better schools than poor communities because they have a stronger tax base and can raise more money for schools. Increased state funding is intended to equalize schools throughout the state.

Economics in Practice

See answers in side column above.

1 Plan & Prepare

Objectives

- Compare arguments for and against taxing Internet sales.
- Draw conclusions about the costs and benefits of taxing Internet sales.

2 Focus & Motivate

Invite students to describe times when they pay sales tax. Explain that this Case Study explores arguments about whether online purchases should be subject to sales tax.

3 Teach

Using the Sources

Encourage students to examine each source to discover arguments for and against taxing online purchases.

A. Why might taxes on digital goods harm the growth of a new market? *(Taxes make the goods more expensive for consumers and less profitable for suppliers.)*

B. Why would states look favorably upon Internet sales as a potential source of tax revenue? *(Online purchases have increased dramatically since 2000.)*

C. Why did the states develop uniform sales tax rules? *(to make it easier for online businesses that sell to customers in many states to collect sales taxes)*

International Economics

European Internet Taxation
The European Union (EU) has always considered Internet sales to be taxable. Customers living in the EU who buy goods online from a company based outside the EU pay their country's value added tax (VAT) and customs duties on these products. Goods valued at less than about $27 are exempt from the taxes.

Buyers who pay to download music or software from a European company over the Internet are taxed on these purchases because they are considered services, which are taxed at the place where they are provided.

Case Study

Economics Update
Find an update on this Case Study at ClassZone.com

Should Online Sales Be Taxed?

Background In 1992 the Supreme Court upheld a law making Internet retailers exempt from collecting most sales taxes. The ruling was based on the fact that, at the time, the various state and local rules for tax collection varied widely. The differing rules would have placed a heavy burden on Internet retailers charged with having to collect taxes on what they sold.

Today, however, tax collection is becoming simpler and more streamlined. In addition, Internet purchases have become commonplace, with shoppers buying everything from computers to airplane tickets. Many online shoppers fail to realize that they are required to pay sales tax for Internet purchases at their home state's rate. To date, most states have tried to collect Internet sales tax on a voluntary basis. Needless to say, results have been poor. Given this and other considerations, Internet sales tax once again is a subject for debate.

What's the issue? Should there be sales tax on Internet purchases? Study these sources to discover arguments for and against taxing purchases online.

A. Online News Story

This news story on whether to impose the "iPod tax"—a tax on digital products—illustrates the differences of opinion on online sales tax.

Entertainment Lovers May Soon Pay Tax on Downloads

Wisconsin governor and legislators disagree over "iPod" tax.

Wisconsin Gov. Jim Doyle now wants his state to start collecting taxes on digital music, videos and software. Key Republicans in the GOP-dominated legislature say they will block the proposal, but administration officials say they're just trying to make things fair.

"It's an issue of tax equity," said Jessica Iverson, a spokeswoman for the Wisconsin Department of Revenue. "If you go into a Main Street business and purchase a CD, you are paying tax. . . ."

Economists are split . . . as to whether adding these kinds of taxes is a good idea. Some say that taxes on digital goods will hamper the growth of a potentially vibrant new marketplace, while others say that having taxes only on offline versions of the same goods distorts the operation of free markets.

Source: News.com, March 10, 2005

Thinking Economically What do you think economists mean when they say that taxing only offline versions of the same goods "distorts the operation of free markets"?

DIFFERENTIATING INSTRUCTION

English Learners

Provide Background Knowledge
Help students understand this Case Study by providing background information about how the different branches of government work together. Explain that on both the state and federal levels it is the legislative branch that passes laws. Document A describes a disagreement between the executive branch (the governor) and the legislature. The governor and the majority in the legislature are from two different political parties and have different attitudes toward this issue.

Inclusion

Listen to the Case Study
Pair students who have vision impairments with those who do not. The students who do not have impairments can read the Case Study aloud, stopping to ask each Thinking Economically question. The partners should work together to find the answers. Encourage students with vision impairments to orally summarize each section of the Case Study.

B. Graph

This graph shows the growth of online purchases during the 2000s.

FIGURE 14.12 U.S. ONLINE PURCHASES

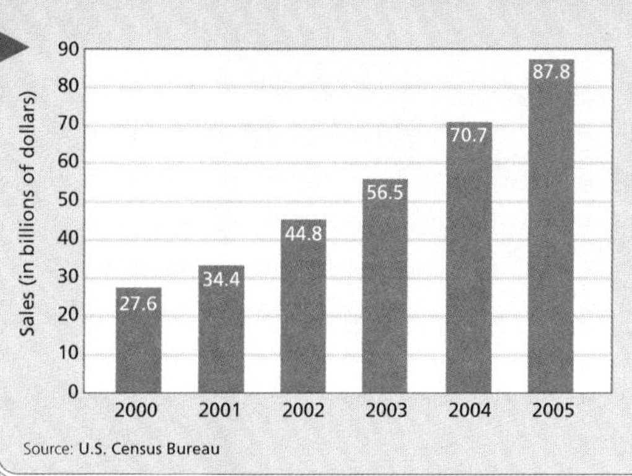

Source: U.S. Census Bureau

Thinking Economically How might state and local governments use the information in the graph to support their demand to levy sales taxes on online purchases?

C. Newspaper Editorial

Some states are becoming pro-active in their efforts to promote Internet sales tax. This newspaper editorial describes one multistate project to facilitate the collection of the tax.

Internet Sales Tax

Eighteen states agree to establish uniform sales tax rules.

Last week, 18 state tax collectors met in Chicago to announce an interstate agreement establishing uniform sales tax rules. Starting in October, the group will offer free software that will allow any business to easily collect the required taxes online.

The states' demonstration project will drive home the point that online sales-tax collection can be done nationwide. Many retailers already collect the taxes. Now Congress should step up and pass a law overturning the court's exemption in states that have streamlined their tax systems. That would allow hard-pressed states to take in roughly $20 billion a year in annual sales tax revenue that is rightfully theirs, and perhaps much more, depending on the growth in online shopping. It would also help level the playing field between local and online retailers.

Source: "Internet Sales Tax," *New York Times*, July 5, 2005

Thinking Economically What impact has Internet shopping had on state and local revenues? Explain your answer.

THINKING ECONOMICALLY Synthesizing

1. Summarize the arguments for and against an Internet sales tax as presented in the documents.
2. Who is most likely to benefit from Internet sales tax revenue? Explain your answer, using information from the documents.
3. How has government responded to e-commerce—the selling of goods and services online? Use information from the documents in your answer.

Thinking Economically

Answers

A. *Possible answer: Taxing offline purchases but not those made online places an undue burden on the offline seller. It "distorts" the market by giving a cost advantage to the non-taxed item.*

B. *Possible answer: They would look at the increase in online purchases as lost revenue for their constituents. If the purchases were made offline, the sales taxes could be funding important state programs.*

C. *Revenues have gone down due to customers buying online goods and not paying state and local sales tax.*

Synthesizing

1. *For: correct unfair advantage that online sellers have over local retailers, increase revenue to state and local government Against: hinder growth of new market*
2. *state and local governments, who generate sales tax; and indirectly, the constituents who benefit from the services provided by those governments*
3. *At this time the question is being handled at the state and local government level, although some are calling for Congress to step in.*

Economics Update

Go to **ClassZone.com** to find an update to this Case Study, including another article, an editable student worksheet, and an editable lesson plan.

TECHNOLOGY ACTIVITY

Creating a Database

Time 45 Minutes 

Task Research articles about online sales taxes and create a database.

Materials Needed computer with Internet access, database software (optional)

Activity

- Organize students into groups to find online articles about Internet sales taxes. Groups may focus on topics such as the Streamlined Sales Tax Project, Congress and online sales tax, or arguments for or against Internet taxation.
- Invite groups to find two or three articles on their topic, noting the title, name and URL of the source, and date. Have them write a brief summary of the main idea of the article.
- Have groups combine their information into a database that is searchable by topic or date.
- Call on volunteers to describe how researchers might use the database.

Rubric

	Understanding of Concepts	Presentation of Information
4	excellent	clear and complete
3	good	mostly clear
2	fair	sometimes clear
1	poor	sketchy

Online Summary Answers

1. Tax
2. Revenue
3. ability-to-pay principle of taxation
4. tax base
5. proportional tax
6. progressive tax
7. regressive tax
8. incidence of tax
9. Withholding
10. indexing
11. entitlement
12. mandatory spending
13. balanced budget

Interactive Review

Review this chapter using interactive activities at ClassZone.com

- Online Summary
- Quizzes
- Vocabulary Flip Cards
- Graphic Organizers
- Review and Study Notes

Online Summary

Complete the following activity either on your own paper or online at **ClassZone.com**

Choose the key concept that best completes the sentence. Not all key concepts will be used.

ability-to-pay principle of taxation	proportional tax
balanced budget	regressive tax
benefit principle of taxation	revenue
capital budget	tax
discretionary spending	tax base
entitlement	tax incentive
incidence of tax	tax return
indexing	taxable income
mandatory spending	transfer payment
progressive tax	withholding

__1__ is a mandatory payment to a government. __2__ is government income. The __3__ holds that people should be taxed on their ability to pay, no matter the level of benefits they receive.

A __4__ is the income, property, goods or services subject to taxes. A __5__ takes the same percentage of income from all taxpayers. A __6__ places a higher rate of taxation on high-income people, and a __7__ takes a larger percentage of income from low-income people. The __8__ is the final burden of tax.

__9__ is money taken from a worker's pay before the worker receives it. __10__ is a revision of tax brackets to prevent workers from paying more taxes due to inflation. Social Security is an example of an __11__, a social welfare program with specific requirements. Such programs make up most of federal __12__, which is spending that is required by law.

States are required to have a __13__, in which government revenue and spending are equal.

CHAPTER 14 Assessment

REVIEWING KEY CONCEPTS

How Taxes Work (pp. 410–419)

1. What is the relationship between tax and revenue?
2. Identify three ways that taxes affect the economy.

Federal Taxes (pp. 420–427)

3. What is the largest source of federal revenue?
4. Which tax pays for Social Security and Medicare?

Federal Government Spending (pp. 428–433)

5. What are three programs that make up most mandatory spending?
6. How does federal spending affect the economy?

State and Local Taxes and Spending (pp. 434–441)

7. What are the two types of state budgets?
8. What tax base are tax assessors concerned with?

APPLYING ECONOMIC CONCEPTS

Look at the chart below showing average combined city and state tax rates for families with different incomes in several cities.

FIGURE 14.13 STATE AND LOCAL TAXES FOR A FAMILY OF FOUR

City	Total taxes paid as a percent of income				
	$25,000	$50,000	$75,000	$100,000	$150,000
Atlanta	8.1	10.3	11.4	11.5	11.7
Chicago	9.3	9.5	10.0	9.7	9.3
Houston	6.2	6.0	6.3	5.9	5.5
Jacksonville	4.3	4.6	5.0	4.8	4.6
Los Angeles	8.6	8.7	10.3	11.2	12.3
New York	5.6	10.8	12.7	13.4	14.1
Philadelphia	11.0	13.2	13.0	12.6	12.2

Source: *Statistical Abstract of the United States, 2002 figures*

9. Which city has the lowest tax rate for the lowest-income families? Which has the lowest tax rate for the highest-income families?
10. Which combined city and state tax structures are progressive and which are regressive?

CHAPTER 14 ASSESSMENT ANSWERS

Reviewing Key Concepts

1. Governments use a variety of taxes to raise revenue to pay for government services.
2. resource allocation, productivity and growth, and incentives to affect economic behavior
3. individual income tax
4. FICA
5. Social Security, Medicare, and Medicaid
6. resource allocation, income redistribution, competition with the private sector
7. operating budget and capital budget
8. property, including real estate and personal property

Applying Economic Concepts

9. Jacksonville
10. Progressive: Atlanta, Los Angeles, New York, Regressive: Chicago, Houston, Jacksonville, Philadelphia

Critical Thinking

11. All graphs should show a decrease in supply after the tax: supply curve shifts to the left. Graphs for gasoline and local telephone service should reflect inelastic demand with most of the tax paid by consumers; graphs for ice cream and sports cars should show elastic demand with most of the tax paid by the producers.

SMARTGrapher Students can create supply and demand curves using **SmartGrapher @ ClassZone.com.**

CRITICAL THINKING

11. **Creating Graphs** The state legislature proposes new 10 percent excise taxes on the following goods and services: gasoline, ice cream, local telephone service, and sports cars. For each good or service create supply and demand curves showing the supply curve before the tax and how the supply curve shifts after the tax. Under each graph, write a caption explaining who will pay more of the tax—the consumer or the producer—and why.
    Use *SMARTGrapher* @ **ClassZone.com** to complete this activity.

12. **Analyzing Data** Shandra earns $30,000 per year from her job as a radiology technician. She takes a personal exemption of $3,200 and the standard deduction of $5,000 to reduce her taxable income.
    a. If she pays 10 percent tax on the first $7,300 of taxable income and 15 percent on the rest, how much does she pay in income tax?
    b. Shandra's FICA tax rate is 7.65 percent. What are her FICA taxes?
    c. How much total tax does Shandra pay? What is her effective tax rate as a percentage of her taxable income and of her total income?

13. **Making Inferences** When Rajiv goes shopping for a new MP3 player, he notices that he pays 7.35 percent sales tax on the purchase. He knows that the state sales tax rate is 4.22 percent. What accounts for the difference?

14. **Comparing and Contrasting** All states have excise taxes on cigarettes and gasoline. What are the similarities and differences in the reasons why states tax these two items?

15. **Challenge** In 2003, Congress reduced the tax rate paid by individual investors on dividends and capital gains to 15 percent. Previously the rate for dividends had been as high as 38.6 percent, and capital gains had been taxed at 20 percent. Which of these changes addressed the charge that corporate income is subject to double taxation? Give reasons for your answer.

SIMULATION

Develop a Federal Budget

Step 1 Choose a partner. Imagine that you are members of Congress who must determine the discretionary spending portion of the federal budget. The table below shows the categories of spending. You have a total of $960 billion to spend. Determine your spending priorities by deciding what percent of the budget to allocate to each category.

FEDERAL DISCRETIONARY SPENDING CATEGORIES

Administration of justice	Health (non-Medicaid)
Agriculture	International affairs
Community & regional development	National defense
Education	Natural resources & environment
Energy	Science, space & technology
General government	Transportation

Step 2 Form a group with two or three other pairs of students so that there are now a total of four groups in the class. Compare your budgets, noting areas of agreement and disagreement. Negotiate to develop a single budget proposal for your group.

Step 3 Present your group's budget proposal to the class. Include a list of reasons to support your budget choices.

Step 4 As a class, decide on a final recommendation that resolves any differences among the four budget proposals.

Step 5 Present your final budget to your teacher, who is acting as the President. Make necessary changes to the budget to resolve any differences between the Congress and the President.

McDougal Littell Assessment System

Assess

Online Test Practice
- Go to **ClassZone.com** for more test practice.

Unit 6 Resource Book
- Chapter Test, Forms A, B, & C, pp. 51–62

Test Generator CD-ROM
- Chapter Test, Forms (A, B, & C), in English and Spanish

Report

Use the McDougal Littell Assessment System to score assessments and receive customized reports.

Reteach

For activities customized for individual students, use the McDougal Littell Assessment System.

CHAPTER 14 ASSESSMENT ANSWERS

12. **a.** $730 + $2,175 = $2,905
    b. $1,667.70
    c. $4,572.70, 21 percent, 15 percent
13. sales tax charged by the local government
14. Both are taxed because they have inelastic demand. Tax on gasoline is levied to raise money for roads. Tax on cigarettes is an incentive to cut down cigarette smoking.
15. Reduction of the tax rate on dividends addressed the charge. Dividends are paid out of corporate profits that are subject to the corporate income tax.

Simulation Rubric

	Understanding of Concepts	Presentation of Information
4	excellent	clear, persuasive
3	good	somewhat clear
2	fair	somewhat disorganized
1	poor	unfocused , incomplete

CHAPTER 15: Using Fiscal Policy
Planning Guide

Resources 2Go Complete print resources all on one USB drive allow you to customize lessons.

Section Titles and Objectives	Unit 6 Resource Book and Workbooks		Assessment Resources
1 What Is Fiscal Policy? pp. 446–453 • Examine the tools used in fiscal policy • Determine how fiscal policy affects the economy • Identify the problems and limitations of fiscal policy	**Unit 6 Resource Book** • Reading Study Guide, pp. 63–64 • RSG with Additional Support, pp. 65–67 • RSG with Additional Support (Spanish), pp. 68–70 • Economic Simulations: Fiscal Policy and Human Behavior, pp. 99–100	**NCEE Student Activities** • Taking the Fiscal Route, pp. 57–60	**Unit 6 Resource Book** • Section Quiz, p. 71 • Reteaching Activity, p. 72 **Test Generator CD-ROM** **Daily Test Practice Transparencies,** TT50
2 Demand-Side and Supply-Side Policies pp. 454–461 • Describe how demand-side fiscal policy can be used to stimulate the economy • Describe how supply-side fiscal policy can be used to stimulate the economy • Identify the role that fiscal policy has in changing the economy	**Unit 6 Resource Book** • Reading Study Guide, pp. 73–74 • RSG with Additional Support, pp. 75–77 • RSG with Additional Support (Spanish), pp. 78–80 • Math Skills: Applying the Spending Multiplier, p. 101	**NCEE Student Activities** • Taking the Fiscal Route, pp. 57–60	**Unit 6 Resource Book** • Section Quiz, p. 81 • Reteaching Activity, p. 82 **Test Generator CD-ROM** **Daily Test Practice Transparencies,** TT51
3 Deficits and the National Debt pp. 462–469 • Examine the difference between the deficit and the debt • Explain why national deficits occur • Describe how deficits are financed • Identify the impact of the national debt on the economy	**Unit 6 Resource Book** • Reading Study Guide, pp. 83–84 • RSG with Additional Support, pp. 85–87 • RSG with Additional Support (Spanish), pp. 88–90 • Economic Skills and Problem Solving Activity, pp. 93–94 • Readings in Free Enterprise: A Dangerous Legacy, pp. 95–96 • Case Study Resources: Federal Deficit Estimate Down to $296B, p.97; A Small Deficit: Worth a Bronx Cheer, p. 98	**Test Practice and Review Workbook,** pp. 51–52	**Unit 6 Resource Book** • Section Quiz, p. 91 • Reteaching Activity, p. 92 • Chapter Test, (Forms A, B, & C), pp. 103–114 **Test Generator CD-ROM** **Daily Test Practice Transparencies,** TT52

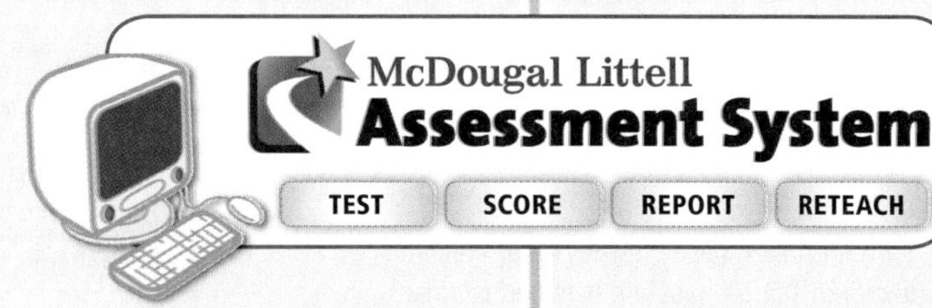

Integrated Technology

No Time? To focus students on the most important content in this chapter, use Animated Economics, "Effects of Fiscal Policy," available in Resources 2Go.

Teacher Presentation Options

Presentation Toolkit

Power Presentation DVD-ROM

- Lecture Notes
- Media Gallery
- Review Game
- Interactive Review
- Animated Economics

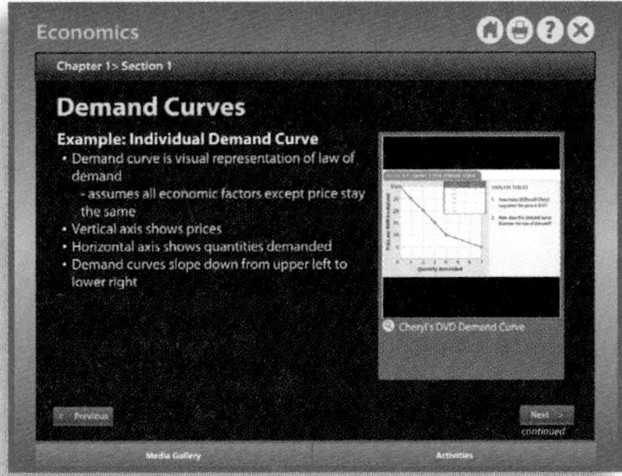

Economics Concepts Transparencies

- Fiscal Policy Tools, CT50
- Demand-Side Versus Supply-Side Policies, CT51
- Debt and Deficit as Percentages of GDP, CT52

Electronic Books

eEdition DVD-ROM

eEdition Online

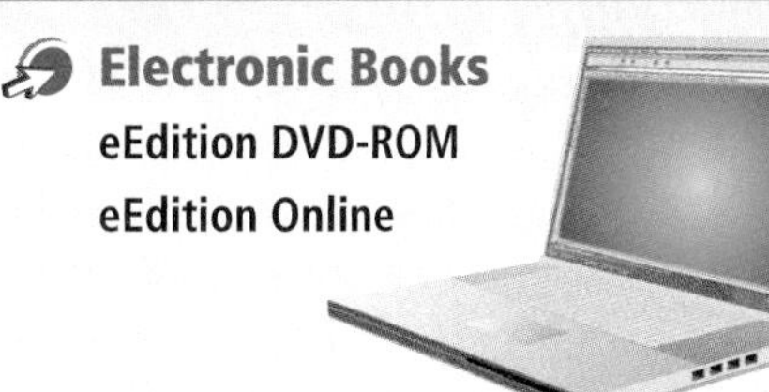

Daily Test Practice Transparencies, TT50, TT51, TT52

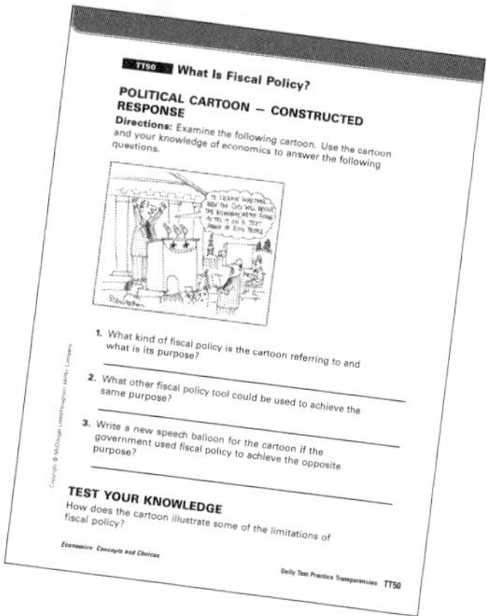

Animated Economics

- Effects of Fiscal Policy, p. 449

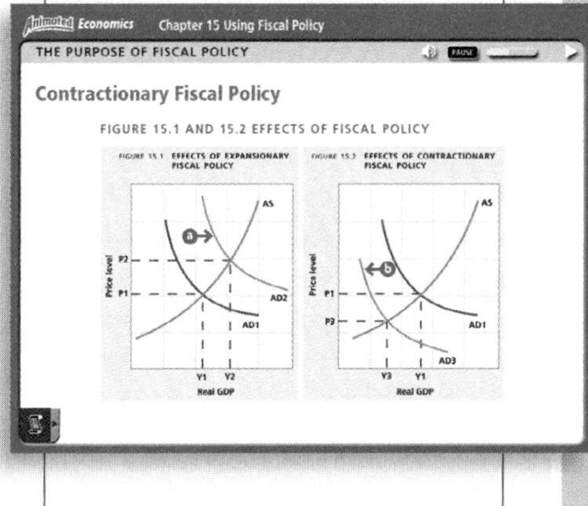

Online Activities at ClassZone.com

Economics Update

- Automatic Stabilizers, p. 447
- John Maynard Keynes, p. 456
- National Debt, p. 465
- Is The Federal Deficit Too Large?, p. 468

Animated Economics

- Interactive Graphics

Activity Maker

- Vocabulary Flip Cards
- Review Game

Research Center

- Graphs and Data

Interactive Review

- Online Summary
- Quizzes
- Vocabulary Flip Cards
- Graphic Organizers
- Review and Study Notes

SMARTGrapher

- Creating Graphs, p. 461

Teacher-Tested Activities

Name: Bill Smiley (ret.)
School: Leigh High School
State: California

Teacher-Tested Activities

At the beginning of this chapter, look for my classroom-proven idea for teaching economics concepts and thinking.

Resources for Differentiated Instruction

Struggling Readers

Teacher's Edition Activities

- Access Prior Knowledge, p. 448
- Analyze Political Influences, p. 452
- Create a Venn Diagram, p. 458
- Compare Economic Information, p. 466
- Summarize the Case Study, p. 468

Unit 6 Resource Book

- RSG with Additional Support, pp. 65–67, 75–77, 85–87 (A)
- Reteaching Activities, pp. 72, 82, 92 (B)
- Chapter Test (Form A), pp. 103–106 (C)

ClassZone.com

- Animated Economics
- Interactive Review

Test Generator CD-ROM

- Chapter Test (Form A)
- Chapter Test (Form A), in Spanish

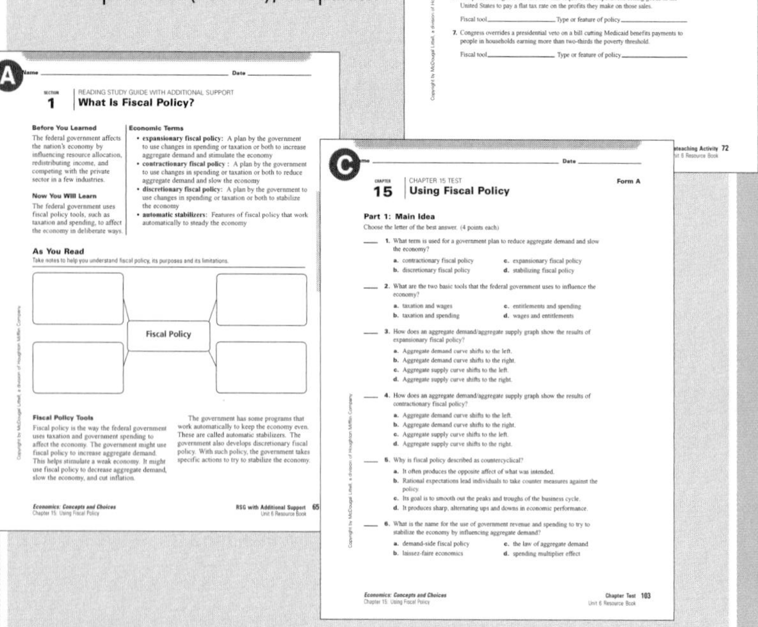

(B) Name ___ Date ___
SECTION 1 | RETEACHING ACTIVITY
What Is Fiscal Policy?

A. Categorizing Fiscal Policy Tools

(A) Name ___ Date ___
SECTION 1 | READING STUDY GUIDE WITH ADDITIONAL SUPPORT
What Is Fiscal Policy?

Before You Learned
Economic Terms
Now You Will Learn
As You Read
Fiscal Policy
Fiscal Policy Tools

(C) Name ___ Date ___
CHAPTER 15 | CHAPTER 15 TEST
Using Fiscal Policy — Form A

Part 1: Main Idea
Choose the letter of the best answer. (4 points each)

English Learners

Teacher's Edition Activities

- Build Economic Vocabulary, p. 448
- Sequence Events, p. 456
- Formulate Questions, p. 460
- Interpret the Pie Chart, p. 464

Unit 6 Resource Book

- RSG with Additional Support (Spanish), pp. 68–70, 78–80, 88–90 (A)

Test Generator CD-ROM

- Chapter Test (Forms A, B, & C), in Spanish (B)

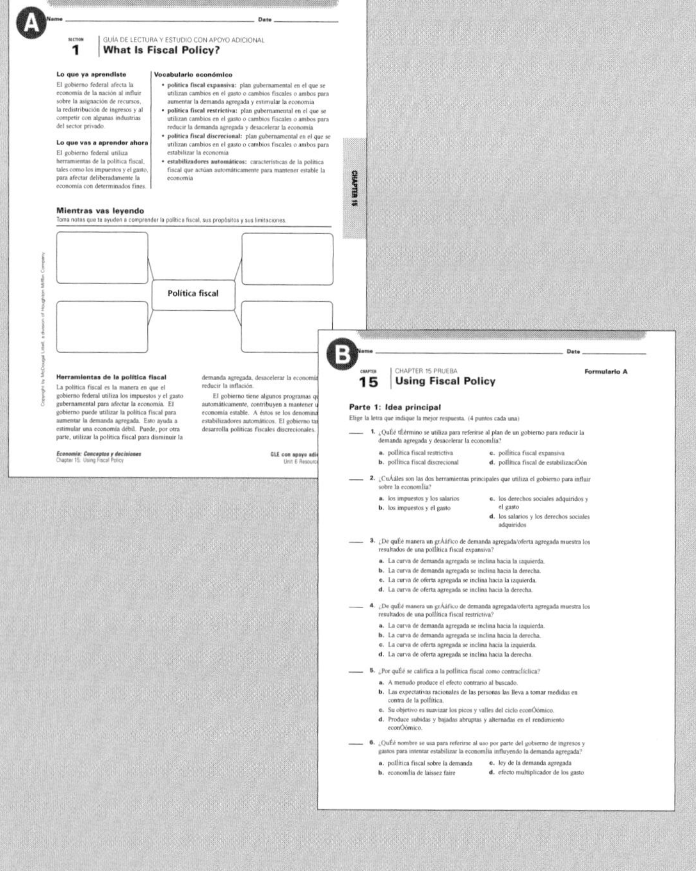

(A) Name ___ Date ___
SECTION 1 | GUÍA DE LECTURA Y ESTUDIO CON APOYO ADICIONAL
What Is Fiscal Policy?

Lo que ya aprendiste
Vocabulario económico
Lo que vas a aprender ahora
Mientras vas leyendo
Política fiscal
Herramientas de la política fiscal

(B) Name ___ Date ___
CHAPTER 15 | CHAPTER 15 PRUEBA
Using Fiscal Policy — Formulario A

Parte 1: Idea principal

Inclusion

Teacher's Edition Activities

- Explain the Visual, p. 450
- Use Examples, p. 458
- Explain the Numbers, p. 464

Lesson Plans

- Modified Lessons for Inclusion, pp. 50–52 (A)

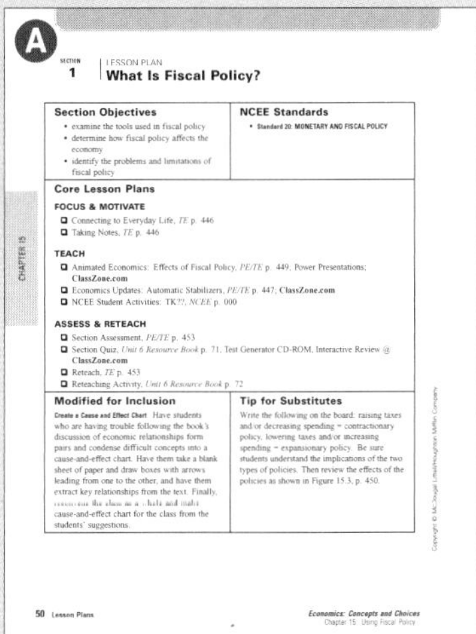

Gifted and Talented

Teacher's Edition Activities

- Conduct Research, p. 450
- Investigate the Council of Economic Advisers, p. 452
- Analyze Primary Sources, p. 456
- Hold a Panel Discussion, p. 460
- Create Fact Sheets, p. 466
- Graph Deficit Trends, p. 468

Unit 6 Resource Book

- Readings in Free Enterprise: A Dangerous Legacy, pp. 95–96 (A)
- Case Study Resources: Federal Deficit Estimate Down To $296B, p. 97; A Small Deficit: Worth A Bronx Cheer, p. 98 (B)

NCEE Student Activities

- Taking the Fiscal Route, pp. 57–60 (C)

ClassZone.com

- Research Center

Test Generator CD-ROM

- Chapter Test (Form C)
- Chapter Test (Form C), in Spanish

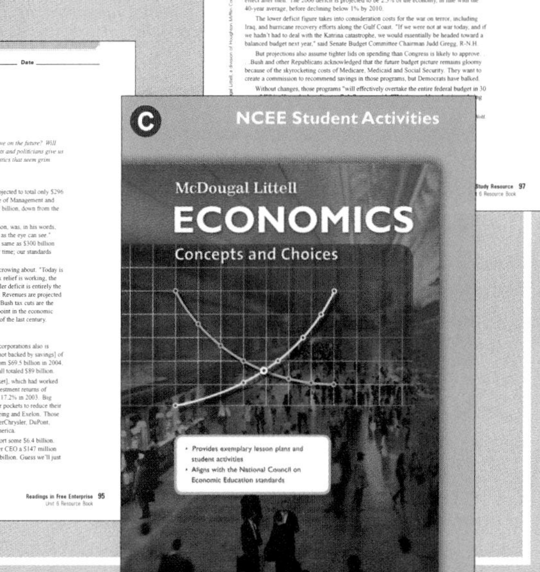

Focus & Motivate

Objective

Explain how government uses taxation and government spending to stabilize the economy.

Why the Concept Matters

Invite students to recall what they learned in Chapter 14 about how taxes and government spending affect the economy. Explain that fiscal policy is the way that government can use those tools to achieve specific results when the economy is out of balance.

Analyzing the Photograph

Have students study the photograph and read the caption. Invite a volunteer to describe what the photograph shows and what particular branch of government it represents. *(the U. S. Capitol, which is where Congress, the legislative branch, meets)*

Ask students how they can relate the photograph to the federal budget process that they studied in Chapter 14. *(Possible answer: Congress initiates legislation on taxation and also agrees on appropriations for government spending after the president submits a budget.)* Ask how the caption expands their understanding of this process. *(It explains that these actions may contribute to economic stability.)* Explain that when taxation and government spending are used to stabilize the economy the government is implementing fiscal policy, which is the subject of Chapter 15.

Government
Federal government actions in the areas of taxing and spending are designed to enhance the nation's economic stability.

444

CONTENT STANDARDS

NCEE STANDARDS

Standard 20: Monetary and Fiscal Policy

Students will understand that
Federal government budgetary policy and the Federal Reserve System's monetary policy influence the overall levels of employment, output, and prices.

Students will be able to use this knowledge to
Anticipate the impact of federal government and Federal Reserve System macroeconomic policy decisions on themselves and others.

Benchmarks
Students will know that

- Fiscal policies are decisions to change spending and tax levels by the federal government. These decisions are adopted to influence national levels of output, employment, and prices. *(pages 446–447, 448–451, 454–460)*
- The federal government's annual budget is balanced when its revenues from taxes and user fees equal its expenditures. The government runs a budget deficit when its expenditures exceed its revenues. The government runs a surplus when its revenues exceed its expenditures. *(pages 462–463, 468–469)*
- When the government runs a budget deficit, it must borrow from individuals, corporations, or financial institutions to finance that deficit. *(pages 464, 468–469)*
- The national debt is the total amount of money the federal government owes. This is the accumulated sum of its annual deficits and surpluses. The government pays interest on the money it borrows to finance the national debt. *(pages 462, 465–466, 468–469)*

CHAPTER 15

Using Fiscal Policy

CONCEPT REVIEW

The **business cycle** is the series of growing and shrinking periods of economic activity.

CHAPTER 15 KEY CONCEPT

Fiscal policy uses taxes and government spending in an effort to smooth out the peaks and troughs of the business cycle.

WHY THE CONCEPT MATTERS

In history classes, you've probably read about instances of rampant inflation when people needed bags and bags of cash to pay for their groceries. Or you might have read about periods of economic depression when millions of workers lost their jobs. By using a combination of spending and taxation, the federal government tries to reduce the impact of such economic extremes.

Online Highlights

More at ClassZone.com

Economics Update Go to ECONOMICS UPDATE for chapter updates and current news on the federal deficit. (See Case Study, pp. 468–469.) ▶

Animated Economics Go to ANIMATED ECONOMICS for interactive lessons on the graphs and tables in this chapter.

Interactive Review Go to INTERACTIVE REVIEW for concept review and activities.

BUREAU OF SPENDING INCREASES AND DEFICIT REDUCTION
"WAIT A MINUTE! HOW CAN THAT BE?"

Source: www.CartoonStock.com

How big a problem is the federal deficit? See the Case Study on pages 468–469.

CHAPTER 15

From the Classroom

Bill Smiley, Leigh High School (retired)

Dealing with Budget Deficits

In this activity, students play the role of economic advisors to the president. Their task is to decide how the federal government should deal with a large budget deficit ($350 billion).

Break the class into groups of White House advisors, and ask each group to examine the alternatives. They could decide to take no action to reduce the deficit, to decrease government spending by $350 billion, to increase taxes by $350 billion, or to use some combination of these options. In evaluating the alternatives, students should consider the following criteria:

(1.) How will this affect aggregate demand and the level of GDP?
(2.) How will this affect inflation and unemployment?
(3.) How will this affect the national debt?
(4.) How will this affect government services?
(5.) How politically feasible is the alternative?

Each group will then present their recommendations and rationale to the class for reaction and discussion.

Previewing Chapter Technology at ClassZone.com

Economics Update Students will find references to online articles or statistics that update information in the pupil edition on pages 447, 456, 465, and 468.

Animated Economics Students will find interactive supply and demand curves related to materials on page 449.

Interactive Review Students will find additional section and chapter assessment support for materials on pages 453, 461, 467, and 470.

TEACHER MEDIA FAVORITES

Books

- Buchholz, Todd G. *New Ideas from Dead Economists: An Introduction to Modern Economic Thought.* Rev. ed. New York: Plume, 1999. Analyzes strengths and weaknesses of major economists by applying their ideas to contemporary problems.
- Kopcke, Richard, et al., eds. *The Macroeconomics of Fiscal Policy.* Cambridge, MA: MIT Press, 2006. Examines the history of fiscal policy since World War II.
- Rivlin, Alice M., and Isabel Sawhill, eds. *Restoring Fiscal Sanity, 2005: Meeting the Long-Run Challenge.* Washington, DC: Brookings Institution Press, 2005. Explores the challenge of bringing federal spending in line with revenue.
- Skidelsky, Robert. *John Maynard Keynes, 1883–1946: Economist, Philosopher, Statesman.* New York: Penguin, 2005. A revised edition of the biography, which also analyzes Keynesian economic philosophy.

Videos/DVDs

- *John Maynard Keynes/Fiscal Policy.* Two 30-minute programs. Economics USA, 1987. TV-news format addresses issues relevant to students' lives.
- *Productivity/Federal Deficits.* Two 30-minute programs. Economics USA, 1986/2003. Explores key topics and issues through a TV-news format.

Software

- *Virtual Economics® Version 3.0.* New York: National Council on Economic Education, 2005.

Internet

Visit **ClassZone.com** to link to

- a variety of chapter-specific, content-reviewed sites
- updates on data and topics presented throughout the chapter sections and Case Study
- updates to the Power Presentation

1 Plan & Prepare

Section 1 Objectives

- examine the tools used in fiscal policy
- determine how fiscal policy affects the economy
- identify the problems and limitations of fiscal policy

2 Focus & Motivate

Connecting to Everyday Life Explain that this section focuses on the ways government uses taxation and spending to smooth out the business cycle. Invite students to discuss some of the economic indicators that help identify where the economy is in the business cycle.

Taking Notes Remind students to take notes as they read by completing a cluster diagram about fiscal policy. They can use the Graphic Organizer at **Interactive Review @ ClassZone.com**. A sample is shown below.

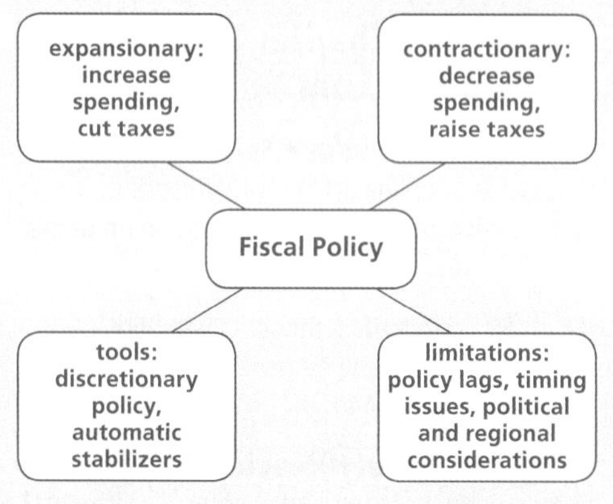

SECTION 1

What Is Fiscal Policy?

OBJECTIVES

In Section 1, you will
- examine the tools used in fiscal policy
- determine how fiscal policy affects the economy
- identify the problems and limitations of fiscal policy

KEY TERMS

fiscal, *p. 446*
fiscal policy, *p. 446*
expansionary fiscal policy, *p. 446*
contractionary fiscal policy, *p. 446*
discretionary fiscal policy, *p. 446*
automatic stabilizers, *p. 447*
rational expectations theory, *p. 452*
Council of Economic Advisers, *p. 452*

TAKING NOTES

As you read Section 1, complete a cluster diagram that organizes the main ideas about fiscal policy. Use the Graphic Organizer at **Interactive Review @ ClassZone.com**

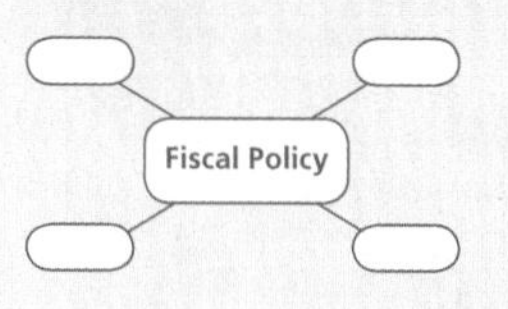

Fiscal Policy Tools

QUICK REFERENCE

Fiscal refers to government revenue, spending, and debt.

Fiscal policy uses taxes and government spending to affect the economy.

Expansionary fiscal policy is a plan to increase aggregate demand and stimulate the economy.

Contractionary fiscal policy is a plan to reduce aggregate demand and slow the economy.

Discretionary fiscal policy refers to actions selected by the government to stabilize the economy.

KEY CONCEPTS

In Chapter 14, you learned that the government puts the tax dollars it collects to a variety of uses. The term **fiscal** refers to anything related to government revenue, spending, and debt. **Fiscal policy** is the federal government's use of taxes and government spending to affect the economy. Fiscal policy has one of two goals: to increase aggregate demand or to fight inflation.

To stabilize or strengthen the economy, the government may use one of two basic policies. When the economy slows, the government may use **expansionary fiscal policy**, a plan to increase aggregate demand and stimulate a weak economy. When the economy is in an inflationary period, the government may use a **contractionary fiscal policy**, a plan to reduce aggregate demand and slow the economy in a period of too-rapid expansion. The federal government has two basic fiscal tools to influence the economy: taxation and government spending.

Discretionary Fiscal Policy

As you learned in Chapter 14, discretionary spending is spending that the government must authorize each year. In other words, the government must make a choice about this type of spending. Similarly, **discretionary fiscal policy** involves actions taken by the government by choice to correct economic instability. This type of policy involves an active government response, through choices about taxes or government spending, to help stabilize the economy. Congress must enact legislation for these policies to be implemented. This type of fiscal policy is discussed in more depth later in this section and in Section 2.

446 Chapter 15

SECTION 1 PROGRAM RESOURCES

ON LEVEL

Lesson Plans
- Core, p. 50

Unit 6 Resource Book
- Reading Study Guide, pp. 63–64
- Economics Simulation, pp. 99–100
- Section Quiz, p. 71

STRUGGLING READERS

Unit 6 Resource Book
- Reading Study Guide with Additional Support, pp. 65–67
- Reteaching Activity, p. 72

ENGLISH LEARNERS

Unit 6 Resource Book
- Reading Study Guide with Additional Support (Spanish), pp. 68–70

INCLUSION

Lesson Plans
- Modified for Inclusion, p. 50

GIFTED AND TALENTED

NCEE Student Activities
- Taking the Fiscal Route, pp. 57–60

TECHNOLOGY

eEdition DVD-ROM

eEdition Online

Power Presentation DVD-ROM

Economics Concepts Transparencies
- CT50 Fiscal Policy Tools

Daily Test Practice Transparencies, TT50

ClassZone.com

Automatic Stabilizers

Unlike discretionary fiscal policy, **automatic stabilizers** are features of fiscal policy that work automatically to steady the economy. Both of these approaches use taxes and government spending to influence the economy. Discretionary fiscal policy involves government choices about whether an expansionary or contractionary policy is needed and how the chosen policy should be put into action. Automatic stabilizers, such as public transfer payments and progressive income taxes, may work in an expansionary or contractionary manner, but they work automatically rather than through active policy choices.

QUICK REFERENCE

Policy features called **automatic stabilizers** work automatically to steady the economy.

Public Transfer Payments As you recall from Chapter 14, public transfer payments include programs such as unemployment compensation, food stamps, and other entitlements. These payments automatically set up a flow of money into the economy. Therefore, this form of government spending helps stabilize the economy automatically.

For example, during a recession more people are unemployed and qualify to receive unemployment compensation and other government benefits, such as food stamps or welfare payments. When people receive these benefits, they gain a certain amount of income to spend, and the effects of the recession are less severe than they would be without the transfer payments.

Automatic Stabilizers Unemployed workers wait to register for unemployment compensation, a program designed to stabilize the economy by providing temporary replacement wages.

When the economy improves, fewer people qualify for food stamps, unemployment compensation, and other entitlements, and government spending automatically decreases. This automatic decrease keeps the economy from growing too fast. By helping to control aggregate demand, this automatic stabilizer keeps prices from rising too quickly and leading to inflation.

Progressive Income Taxes The individual income tax is progressive. As income increases, so do the tax rate and the amount of taxes paid. The progressive nature of the income tax allows it to act as an automatic stabilizer to the economy without additional government action.

For example, during prosperous times, individual incomes rise, and some individuals move into higher tax brackets. These taxpayers pay more in taxes and do not have all of their increased income to spend or save. By preventing some of the increased income from entering the economy, this automatically higher taxation keeps the economy from growing too quickly and helps keep inflation in check. On the other hand, during a recession, individuals earn less income and may move into lower tax brackets. Therefore, lower incomes result in lower taxes, which automatically reduce the impact of the recession.

Economics Update

Find an update on automatic stabilizers at **ClassZone.com**

APPLICATION Applying Economic Concepts

A. Programs such as unemployment insurance ensure that people experiencing economic hardship have a basic level of income. How does this help to stabilize the economy?
See Teacher's Edition for answer. ▶

3 Teach

Fiscal Policy Tools

Discuss

- What are the two goals of fiscal policy? *(to increase demand or fight inflation)*
- How do automatic stabilizers work to counteract problems in the economy? *(They are designed to automatically pump money into a weak economy through transfer payments or lower taxes as income falls. In a strong economy, they take money out of the economy through a decrease in transfer payments or higher taxes.)*

Economics Update

At **ClassZone.com** students will find an article on automatic stabilizers.

APPLICATION

Answer *Such programs keep the economy steady by providing some income to people when they are unemployed, thus preventing a precipitous drop in demand when people's financial circumstances change.*

LEVELED ACTIVITY

Applying Fiscal Policy

Time 45 Minutes

Objective Students will demonstrate an understanding of the goals, tools, purposes, and limitations of fiscal policy. (Fiscal policy is introduced in Section 1.)

Basic

Create a two-column chart. Label one column *increase aggregate demand* and the other *fight inflation.* List under each heading the type of fiscal policy required and the ways that fiscal policy tools are used to achieve each goal. Describe the problems that limit the effectiveness of fiscal policy.

On Level

Develop two newspaper headlines, one reflecting an economic recession and the other pointing to high inflation. Write appropriate news stories for each headline, describing how the government will use fiscal policy to improve the economy. Mention reasons why the policy actions may not achieve their goal.

Challenge

Research the key economic indicators that reveal the current state of the economy. Write a briefing report for Congress, outlining your recommendations for using fiscal policy to improve the situation. Include awareness of issues that may limit the effectiveness of your proposals.

The Purpose of Fiscal Policy

Discuss

- Which type of fiscal policy is needed to reduce unemployment? Why? *(expansionary, because it increases aggregate demand and causes businesses to hire workers to increase output to meet the demand)*
- How would the government use taxation to fight inflation? *(It would increase taxes to take money out of the economy.)*

Presentation Options

Review the different purposes of fiscal policy by using the following presentation options:

Power Presentations DVD-ROM
Using the Display Tool, you can highlight the major features and desired outcomes of expansionary and contractionary fiscal policy.

Economics Concepts Transparencies
- CT50 Fiscal Policy Tools

More About . . .

Automatic Stabilizers
Automatic stabilizers work because they are linked to changes in GDP. When GDP decreases in a recession, automatic stabilizers pump money into the economy through decreased taxes and increased transfer payments, such as food stamps, welfare benefits, and unemployment compensation. They have the opposite effect during inflation.

The more progressive the tax system, the more stability is built into the economy because such a tax system is more closely linked to changes in GDP. Many economists now recommend reliance on automatic stabilizers and monetary policy (see Chapter 16) rather than discretionary fiscal policy to keep the economy on track.

The Purpose of Fiscal Policy

KEY CONCEPTS

Fiscal policy can be used for expansionary or contractionary purposes. The choice of policy depends on whether the economy is weak or strong. Expansionary fiscal policy is designed to stimulate a weak economy to grow. Contractionary fiscal policy is used to slow the economy down in order to control inflation.

POLICY 1 Expansionary Fiscal Policy

Government may use expansionary policy to increase the level of aggregate demand so that growth occurs in the economy. As you recall from Chapter 13, increased aggregate demand causes prices to rise, providing incentives for businesses to expand and causing GDP to increase. Expansionary fiscal policy also reduces the rate of unemployment, as there are more jobs available when businesses are expanding. Expansionary fiscal policy may involve increased government spending, decreased taxes, or both.

For example, suppose the economy is in recession and, in response, the government decides to increase spending for highways. The government spends the money by contracting with private firms in many cities to build new roads. This spending creates additional jobs as the contractors hire more and more construction workers to complete the projects. If employment increases, more people will have income to spend, and aggregate demand increases for all goods and services in the economy.

The government may also choose to cut taxes to stimulate the economy. By lowering individual and corporate income tax rates, the government allows individuals and businesses to have more income left after taxes. Individuals may spend their increased income and thereby increase demand for numerous goods and services. Increased income may allow them to increase their savings, which makes more money available to businesses to invest. Lower taxes also leave businesses with more money to invest in new equipment or plants, or in additional workers to produce more goods and services to meet increased demand.

Whether the government increases spending, decreases taxes, or uses some combination of the two, the result is somewhat similar. As Figure 15.1 on the opposite page shows, expansionary fiscal policy leads to an increase in aggregate demand (the curve shifts to the right) and, therefore, economic growth.

Expansion Increased construction of new housing is an indication that the economy is expanding.

DIFFERENTIATING INSTRUCTION

Struggling Readers

Access Prior Knowledge
Explain that students will need to remember key concepts from previous chapters to understand fiscal policy. Write *aggregate demand, aggregate supply, GDP,* and *demand-pull inflation* on the board. Call on volunteers to define each. Write the definitions on the board for students to refer to as they read. Encourage students to pause in their reading whenever the text refers to concepts from an earlier chapter and see if they can recall and state the concept in their own words.

English Learners

Build Economic Vocabulary
Help students understand *expansionary* and *contractionary* by beginning with the verbs *expand* and *contract*. Encourage students to look for words in the text that have similar meanings, such as *grow, increase,* and *stimulate* (*expand*) and *decrease, slow down,* and *less* (*contract*). Point out that the *d* in *expand* is changed to *s* before adding the suffix *–ion* to create a noun and then *–ary* to make an adjective.

POLICY 2 Contractionary Fiscal Policy

The federal government may use contractionary policy to decrease the level of aggregate demand so that inflation is reduced. When the economy is growing too rapidly, aggregate demand may increase faster than aggregate supply, leading to demand-pull inflation. This type of inflation, which you read about in Chapter 13, is characterized by a steadily rising price level and a decrease in the purchasing power of people's incomes.

When the government faces such an economy, it may employ contractionary fiscal policy and use spending and taxes in ways opposite to expansionary fiscal policy. In other words, it may choose to decrease government spending or increase taxes in order to control inflation.

FIGURES 15.1 AND 15.2 EFFECTS OF FISCAL POLICY

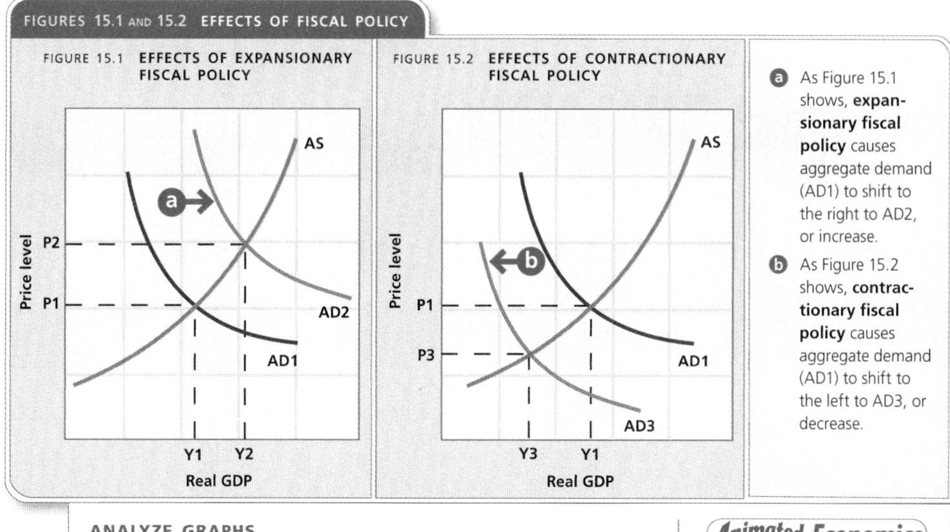

ⓐ As Figure 15.1 shows, **expansionary fiscal policy** causes aggregate demand (AD1) to shift to the right to AD2, or increase.

ⓑ As Figure 15.2 shows, **contractionary fiscal policy** causes aggregate demand (AD1) to shift to the left to AD3, or decrease.

ANALYZE GRAPHS

1. In Figure 15.1, what happens to real GDP as a result of expansionary fiscal policy?
2. In Figure 15.2, what happens to the price level as a result of contractionary fiscal policy?

Animated Economics

Use interactive aggregate demand and aggregate supply curves at **ClassZone.com**

For example, if the economy is growing too rapidly, the government may cut its spending on a variety of programs such as highway construction, education, and health care. By cutting spending, the government takes money out of the economy. This decreased government spending results in less income for individuals or businesses that are directly affected by the cuts in government programs. So these individuals have less money to spend on goods and services, and aggregate demand decreases. Businesses may cut production in response to decreased aggregate demand. As aggregate demand decreases, the rise in the price level is stopped, and inflation is brought under control.

Analyzing Graphs: Figures 15.1 and 15.2

Ask students where they have seen similar graphs and what they show. *(when they studied the different parts of the business cycle through the concepts of aggregate supply and demand; show changes in demand)* Have them compare and contrast what happens to equilibrium price in the two graphs. *(Expansionary policy causes equilibrium price to rise, and contractionary policy causes equilibrium price to fall.)*

Answers

1. *It increases as aggregate demand increases.*
2. *Prices fall as aggregate demand decreases.*

Animated Economics These graphs show how fiscal policy shifts the aggregate demand curve. They will help students understand the impact of expansionary and contractionary fiscal policy.

SMALL GROUP ACTIVITY

Comparing Fiscal Policies

Time 30 Minutes

Task Create a graphic comparison of expansionary and contractionary fiscal policies.

Materials Needed paper and pens or markers

Activity

- Direct students to work in pairs and discuss the similarities and differences between the two types of fiscal policy.
- Have partners select a way to graphically compare the two policies. They may choose to use a poster or a graphic organizer, such as a Venn diagram or cause and effect chain.
- Suggest one partner focus on expansionary policy and the other on contractionary policy.
- Allow students to share their work in small groups. Invite them to summarize when and how each fiscal policy is used.

Rubric

	Understanding of Concepts	Presentation of Information
4	excellent	clear and complete
3	good	mostly clear
2	fair	sometimes clear
1	poor	sketchy

Economics Essentials: Figure 15.3

Explain that the diagram graphically summarizes the tools and purposes of fiscal policy.

- Which of the tools listed are used for expansionary fiscal policy and which are used for contractionary fiscal policy? *(expansionary: automatic stabilizers, increase spending, cut taxes, and tax breaks and incentives for business; contractionary: automatic stabilizers, decrease spending, and raise taxes)*
- What is the difference in the effect on aggregate demand of the two types of policies? *(expansionary: aggregate demand increases; contractionary: aggregate demand decreases)*

Answers

Answers will depend on the state of the economy. Students should understand that if the economy is contracting or in a trough, expansionary policy is needed, and if the economy is expanding or at a peak, contractionary policy is needed.

Economics Illustrated

To help students better understand the difference between expansionary fiscal policy and contractionary policy, you might blow up and deflate a balloon. Point out that the balloon represents economic activity; the air your blow into the balloon represents expansionary fiscal policy. Then blow up the balloon and note that the policy has caused economic activity to increase. Next, release some air from the balloon and note that this action is like applying contractionary fiscal policy, causing economic activity to decrease, or deflate.

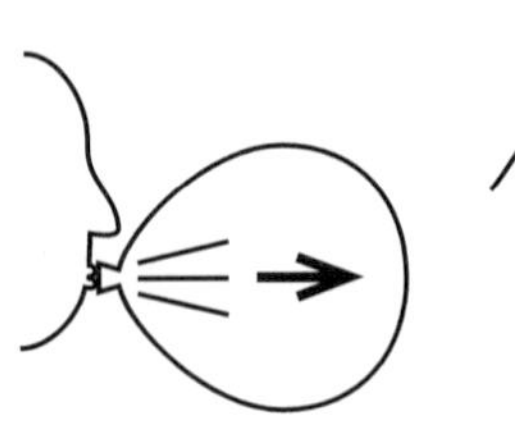

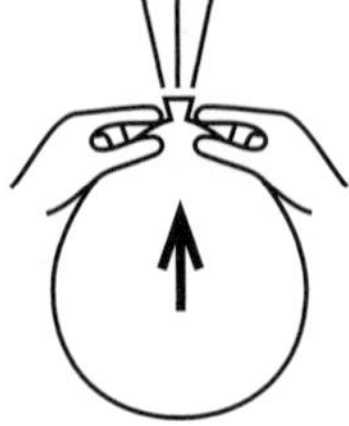

Rather than cut spending, the government may choose to increase taxes. This leads to a decrease in consumer spending and, therefore, a slowdown in the rate of inflation. In other words, when individuals and businesses have to pay higher taxes, they have less income left over to spend or invest. As a result, aggregate demand will decrease. As aggregate demand decreases, businesses may cut back production and lay off workers. This will cause a further decrease in aggregate demand, because workers will have less to spend on goods and services. And as aggregate demand falls, so will the price level.

Whether the government decreases spending or increases taxes or uses some combination of the two, the impact of contractionary fiscal policy on aggregate demand and inflation is somewhat similar. Turn back to Figure 15.2 on page 449. Notice that contractionary fiscal policy results in the aggregate demand curve shifting to the left. This indicates that aggregate demand is decreasing. This decline in aggregate demand, in turn, helps control inflation. (The major fiscal policy tools, and their impact on the economy, are reviewed in Figure 15.3.)

ECONOMICS ESSENTIALS

FIGURE 15.3 Effects of Fiscal Policy on the Economy

Fiscal Policy Tools

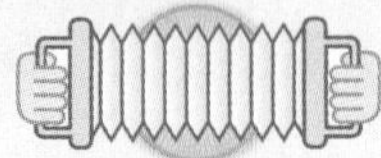

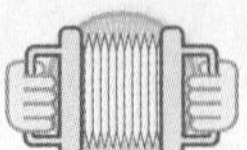

Expansionary Effects
- Economic activity increases as businesses increase production, hire more workers, and increase investment
- More workers have more income to spend on goods and services
- Aggregate demand increases, resulting in economic growth

- Automatic stabilizers
- Raising or cutting taxes; offering tax breaks and incentives to businesses
- Increasing or decreasing government spending

Contractionary Effects
- Economic activity decreases as businesses cut production and lay off workers
- Workers have less income to spend on goods and services
- Aggregate demand decreases, bring inflation under control

ANALYZE CHARTS

The government can use a combination of taxing and spending policies to stimulate a sluggish economy or to slow down an overheated economy. At what point in the business cycle do you think the economy is today? What type of fiscal policy do you think the government should apply at this time?

APPLICATION Analyzing Cause and Effect

B. What effect does expansionary fiscal policy have on consumer spending? Explain your answer. Consumer spending increases as a result of increased income available from increased government spending or decreased taxes.

DIFFERENTIATING INSTRUCTION

Inclusion

Explain the Visual

It may be helpful for students to split the list of tools in Figure 15.3 into two columns to clearly differentiate which ones are used for expansionary policy and which for contractionary policy. Ask volunteers to give more specific examples of each and to state in their own words how these tools achieve the specific effects. Lead them to understand that the list of effects is a chain of events, with change in aggregate demand as the final result.

Gifted and Talented

Conduct Research

Interested students might like to conduct research on the uses of expansionary fiscal policy and contractionary fiscal policy in recent U.S. history. Suggest that students select either form of fiscal policy and then research the topic on the Internet or in history textbooks. Encourage students to present their findings in a written report on the historical episode, including reasons why the policy was followed and how effective it proved to be.

Limitations of Fiscal Policy

KEY CONCEPTS

The purpose of fiscal policy is to reduce economic slowdowns, which result in unemployment, and to curb inflation. The success of fiscal policy, however, is limited by a number of issues, including policy lags and timing.

LIMITATION 1 Policy Lags

Fiscal policy lags behind the economic conditions it is designed to address. This situation is often related to identifying the problem and getting Congress to move on the issue. Months of debate may precede policy change. The lag also may be related to how quickly the change in policy takes effect. For example, the time for tax changes to take effect is shorter than that for government spending. In particular, it may take a long time for public spending programs to get started and money to begin flowing into the economy. Therefore, tax changes may be more effective than policy changes in dealing with short-term recessions.

LIMITATION 2 Timing Issues

The goal of fiscal policy is to provide a stable economic environment. This means that it should coordinate with the business cycle. Fiscal policy is described as countercyclical because the goal is to smooth out the peaks and troughs of the business cycle. If the timing of the policy is good, fluctuations in the business cycle will be less severe, as Figure 15.4 illustrates. If the timing is bad, however, it could make matters worse. For example, if the economy is already moving out of a recession when an expansionary fiscal policy takes effect, the result could be inflation.

FIGURE 15.4 FISCAL POLICY AND THE BUSINESS CYCLE

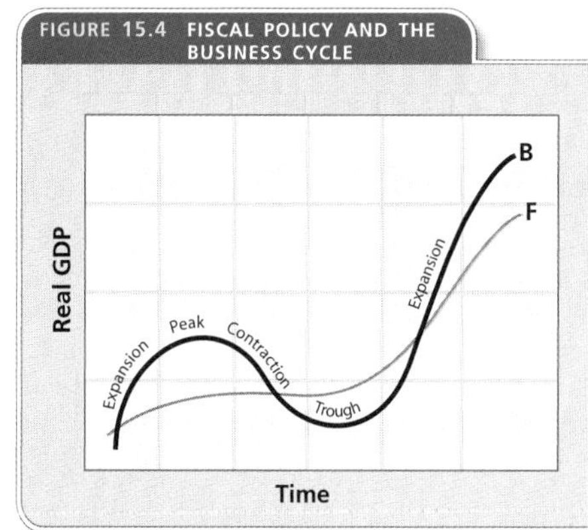

Line B shows how the economy fluctuates during the normal business cycle if fiscal policy actions are not used. Line F shows economic fluctuations if fiscal policy actions are effective.

ANALYZE GRAPHS

1. What kind of fiscal policy might be used to address rapid movement toward a trough?
2. How does this diagram illustrate that fiscal policy is countercyclical?

Limitations of Fiscal Policy

Discuss

- What are the two ways that policy lags limit the effectiveness of fiscal policy? *(It takes time to recognize a problem and agree on a solution and it takes time for the policy to take effect.)*
- How do you think political concerns may affect policy lags? *(Possible answer: Members of Congress may want to rush through or slow down certain policy decisions, depending on how they think the decision will affect their chances of getting reelected.)*

Analyzing Graphs: Figure 15.4

Ask students to recall what they learned in Chapter 12 about the business cycle. Call on volunteers to explain it in their own words and describe how Figure 15.4 shows changes in aggregate demand. *(In the expansion phase, GDP or aggregate demand increases, and in the contraction phase, it decreases.)*

Answers

1. *expansionary fiscal policy*
2. *Countercyclical actions tend to smooth out the peaks and troughs of the business cycle. On line F, which shows the business cycle with fiscal policy implemented, peaks and troughs are much less severe.*

INDIVIDUAL ACTIVITY

Creating a Graphic Organizer

Time 20 Minutes

Task Create an Economics Essentials graphic organizer on the limitations of fiscal policy.

Materials Needed paper and pens or markers

Activity

- Have students review the material on page 451 describing the limitations of fiscal policy and invite them to create a graphic organizer to summarize the information.
- Encourage students to use Figure 15.3 on page 450 as a model, pointing out that they should include visuals and captions in their graphic organizers.
- Allow students to share their graphic organizers in small groups.
- Call on volunteers from different groups to describe how students chose to represent each limitation. Discuss how these limitations show the importance of the automatic stabilizers in keeping the economy steady.

Rubric

	Understanding of Concepts	Presentation of Information
4	excellent	clear and complete
3	good	mostly complete
2	fair	somewhat complete
1	poor	sketchy

More About . . .

Council of Economic Advisers
The Council of Economic Advisers (CEA) was established by the Employment Act of 1946. Its purpose was to provide the president with objective economic analysis and advice on the development and implementation of domestic and international economic policy issues. Since its founding, it has played an important role in setting national economic policy.

Some of the nation's most distinguished economists have served on the CEA. Several later won the Nobel Prize for Economics, including George Akerlof, James Tobin, Joseph Stiglitz, and Robert M. Solow.

LIMITATION 3 Rational Expectations Theory

QUICK REFERENCE

The **rational expectations theory** states that people anticipate that changes in fiscal policy will affect the economy in a particular way and that, as a result, people will take steps to protect their interests.

A second phenomenon affecting timing is explained by the **rational expectations theory**, which states that individuals and business firms expect that changes in fiscal policy will have particular outcomes, and they take actions to protect their interests against those outcomes. These actions may limit the effectiveness of fiscal policy. For example, expansionary fiscal policy attempts to stimulate aggregate demand to increase employment. An increase in aggregate demand might also pull up the price level, causing inflation. In anticipation of rising inflation, people spend more to keep their buying power from decreasing. However, this increased spending causes more inflation and defeats the aims of the expansionary policy.

LIMITATION 4 Political Issues

QUICK REFERENCE

The **Council of Economic Advisers** is a group of economic advisors to the president.

Fiscal policy decisions are not always based on economic considerations. Sometimes, political considerations, most notably enhancing the chances of reelection, may influence the kind of fiscal policy that a government follows. The **Council of Economic Advisers** is a three-member group that advises the President on fiscal policy and other economic issues. Because of political pressures, however, the President may not always follow their advice. Even if the President does accept the council's guidance, members of Congress—again because of political considerations—may not agree with proposed policies. This is an important issue, since the House of Representatives is where all tax bills originate.

Fiscal Policy and Politics Decisions on economic policy often are influenced by politics.

LIMITATION 5 Regional Issues

Another limitation of the effectiveness of fiscal policy is related to geography. Not every state or region of the country may be experiencing the same economic issues. For example, the Gulf Coast region may be recovering from the economic effects of hurricane damage. At the same time, the West Coast may be experiencing a high tech boom that is causing inflation. The Gulf Coast might benefit from expansionary policies, while contractionary policies might be best for the West Coast. In such circumstances, broad fiscal-policy solutions may not be appropriate.

APPLICATION Making Inferences

C. How do policy lags and timing issues work together to limit the effectiveness of fiscal policy? ◀ See Teacher's Edition for answer.

APPLICATION
Answer *Government leaders need time to assess what is happening in the business cycle and agree on fiscal policies to address the problems. These time lags may mean that by the time the policy is implemented the business cycle has moved to a different phase and the policy is less effective in combating the initial problem.*

DIFFERENTIATING INSTRUCTION

Struggling Readers

Analyze Political Influences
Read the first two sentences under Limitation 4. They explain how political considerations often affect decisions on economic policy. Ask a volunteer to restate the sentences in his or her own words. Then, have students work in pairs to discuss this concept and to suggest an instance where they think that political considerations may play a role in the government's economic decisions. Review student work and clarify understanding as needed.

Gifted and Talented

Investigate the Council of Economic Advisers
Invite interested students to use the Internet to research the Council of Economic Advisers. Some students may learn about the three current members and the economists who support them, including information on their background and points of view. Others may explore the different jobs the Council performs or various publications or speeches given by the members. Allow students to present their findings in oral reports to the class.

SECTION 1 Assessment

Online Quiz
ClassZone.com

REVIEWING KEY CONCEPTS

1. Use each of the three terms below in a sentence that illustrates the meaning of the term.
   a. *expansionary fiscal policy*
   b. *discretionary fiscal policy*
   c. *rational expectations theory*
2. What are the two basic goals of fiscal policy?
3. How do expansionary fiscal policy and contractionary fiscal policy use the same fiscal policy tools in different ways?
4. What is the difference between discretionary fiscal policy and automatic stabilizers?
5. What is the role of the Council of Economic Advisers?
6. **Using Your Notes** What are the limitations of fiscal policy? Refer to your completed cluster diagram.

   Use the Graphic Organizer at **Interactive Review @ ClassZone.com**

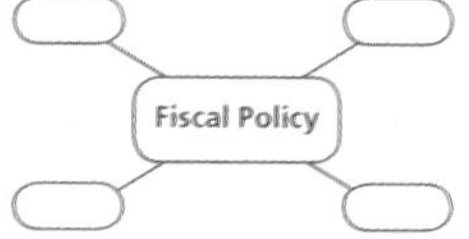

CRITICAL THINKING

7. **Making Inferences** Between 2001 and 2004, Congress passed a series of tax cuts and increased government spending. Do these actions reflect expansionary or contractionary fiscal policy? Explain your answer.
8. **Applying Economic Concepts** Agricultural price supports provide farmers with government subsidies when market prices of certain crops are low. What kind of fiscal policy is at work in this situation and how does it work?
9. **Drawing Conclusions** Federal government officials want to prevent a slowing economy from going into recession. They debate whether to increase spending on new public transit systems or decrease individual and corporate income tax rates.
   a. How would an understanding of policy lags help them decide which government action would be most effective?
   b. What other issues might affect their decision?
10. **Challenge** Make a copy of Figure 15.4 on page 451 and label the part of line F that might represent expansionary fiscal policy and the part that might represent contractionary fiscal policy.

ECONOMICS IN PRACTICE

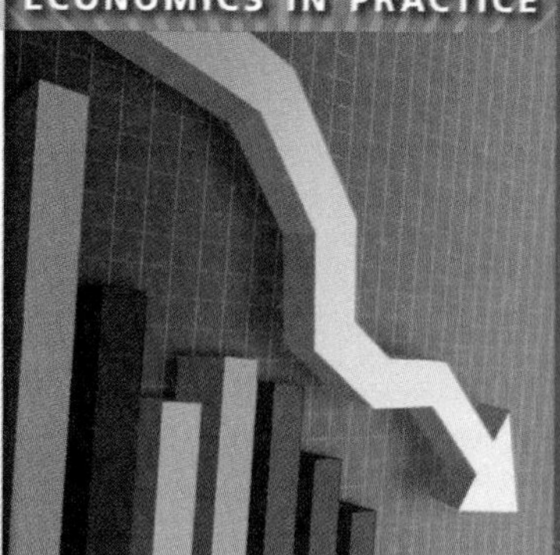

Analyzing Economic Conditions Consider what you've learned about economic instability and fiscal policy. Then complete the following activities.

Propose Fiscal Policies For each situation listed in the chart, identify the problem and decide whether the fiscal policy should be expansionary or contractionary.

Economic Situation	Problem/Fiscal Policy Needed
Business investment spending declines for six straight months	
Consumer Price Index rises for four straight months	
Unemployment rate increases from 4% to 6.5% over six months	
Consumer confidence falls for five straight months	

Challenge Choose one situation and give examples of how fiscal policy might be applied to it.

4 Assess & Reteach

Assess Have students review the questions individually and then quiz each other in pairs.

Unit 6 Resource Book
- Section Quiz, p. 71

Interactive Review @ ClassZone.com
- Section Quiz

Test Generator CD-ROM
- Section Quiz

Reteach Have students work individually on the Reading Study Guide for this lesson. Ask them to share their responses in small groups.

Unit 6 Resource Book
- Reteaching Activity, p. 72

Economics in Practice
Propose Fiscal Policies recession, expansionary; inflation, contractionary; recession, expansionary; recession, expansionary

Challenge Examples should reflect an understanding that expansionary fiscal policy uses increased government spending and reduced taxes, while contractionary fiscal policy uses decreased government spending and increased taxes to achieve their goals.

SECTION 1 ASSESSMENT ANSWERS

Reviewing Key Concepts
1. a. *expansionary fiscal policy*, p. 446
   b. *discretionary fiscal policy*, p. 446
   c. *rational expectations theory*, p. 452
2. to increase aggregate demand and fight inflation
3. Expansionary fiscal policy uses increased government spending and tax decreases, while contractionary fiscal policy uses decreased government spending and tax increases.
4. Discretionary fiscal policy requires government action through Congress to make changes in spending or taxation; automatic stabilizers use spending in the form of transfer payments and taxation in the form of progressive income taxes to steady the economy automatically.
5. to advise the president on economic matters such as fiscal policy
6. See page 446 for a sample of a completed cluster diagram. policy lags, timing issues, political considerations, and regional differences

Critical Thinking
7. expansionary because it involved tax reduction and increased government spending
8. Agricultural price supports are a form of transfer payments. They serve as automatic stabilizers by keeping farm income from dropping too low and by lessening the effects of a slow farm economy.
9. a. Government leaders might decide that tax cuts would be more effective because they impact the economy more quickly. Since public transit systems require time to plan and build, money from transit system projects would enter the economy more slowly.
   b. Political leaders might have different opinions about public transit depending on how useful it would be to their constituents. Not all regions of the country might benefit from this kind of government spending.
10. The part under the peak represents contractionary fiscal policy. The part above the trough represents expansionary fiscal policy.

Economics in Practice
See answers in side column above.

1 Plan & Prepare

Section 2 Objectives

- describe how demand-side fiscal policy can be used to stimulate the economy
- describe how supply-side fiscal policy can be used to stimulate the economy
- identify the role that fiscal policy has in changing the economy

2 Focus & Motivate

Connecting to Everyday Life Explain that this section focuses on two approaches to fiscal policy, one focused on demand and one focused on supply. Ask students to suggest which policy focuses on consumers and which on producers.

Taking Notes Remind students to take notes as they read by completing a chart on demand-side and supply-side policies. They can use the Graphic Organizer at **Interactive Review @ ClassZone.com**. A sample is shown below.

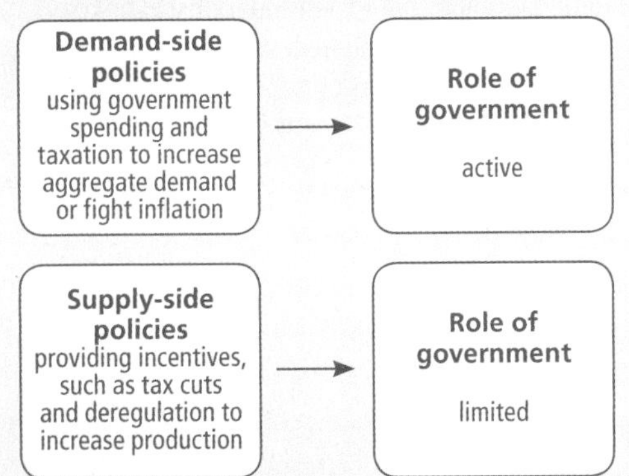

SECTION 2

Demand-Side and Supply-Side Policies

OBJECTIVES

In Section 2, you will

- describe how demand-side fiscal policy can be used to stimulate the economy
- describe how supply-side fiscal policy can be used to stimulate the economy
- identify the role that fiscal policy has in changing the economy

KEY TERMS

Keynesian economics, *p. 454*
demand-side fiscal policy, *p. 454*
spending multiplier effect, *p. 455*
supply-side fiscal policy, *p. 458*
Laffer Curve, *p. 459*

TAKING NOTES

As you read Section 2, complete a chart to show the major features of demand-side and supply-side policies. Use the Graphic Organizer at **Interactive Review @ ClassZone.com**

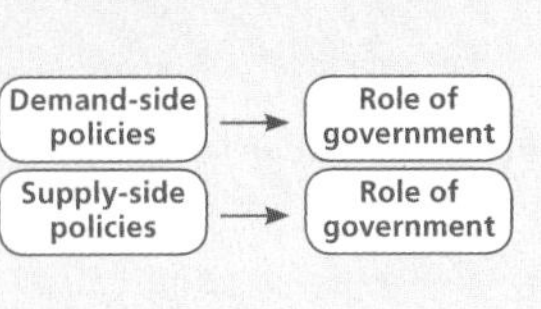

Demand-Side Economics

KEY CONCEPTS

Economists have not always supported the idea of discretionary fiscal policy. Historically, most think that the national government should have a limited role in the economy. When the country experienced financial panics and depressions, the government did little to help the economy get back on track.

The Great Depression of the 1930s changed many people's minds about the role of the government. High unemployment and low production persisted for several years. Many economists concluded that the old ways were ineffective in this situation. One economist, John Maynard Keynes, proposed a new way to address the problem.

The theories that Keynes put forward are called **Keynesian economics**, the idea that in times of recession aggregate demand needs to be stimulated by government action. Keynes believed that such an approach would lower unemployment. Keynesian economics forms the basis of **demand-side fiscal policy**, fiscal policy to stimulate aggregate demand.

QUICK REFERENCE

Keynesian economics states that aggregate demand needs to be stimulated by government action.

Demand-side fiscal policy is a plan to stimulate aggregate demand.

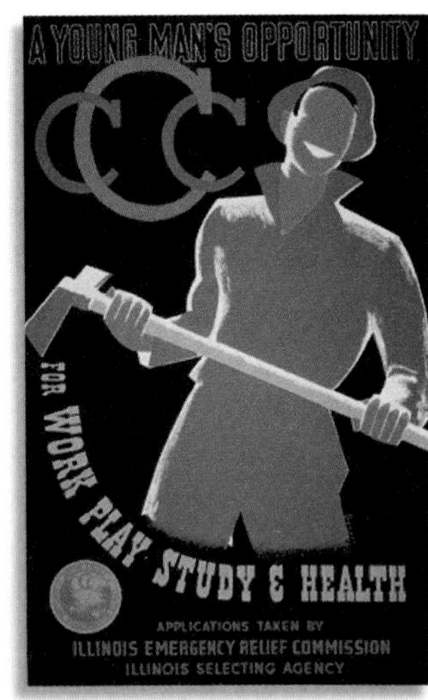

Demand-Side Policies The Civilian Conservation Corps (CCC), an employment program for young men, was one government action aimed at stimulating the economy during the Great Depression.

SECTION 2 PROGRAM RESOURCES

ON LEVEL

Lesson Plans
- Core, p. 51

Unit 6 Resource Book
- Reading Study Guide, pp. 73–74
- Section Quiz, p. 81
- Math Skills Worksheet, p. 101

STRUGGLING READERS

Unit 6 Resource Book
- Reading Study Guide with Additional Support, pp. 75–77
- Reteaching Activity, p. 82

ENGLISH LEARNERS

Unit 6 Resource Book
- Reading Study Guide with Additional Support (Spanish), pp. 78–80

INCLUSION

Lesson Plans
- Modified for Inclusion, p. 51

GIFTED AND TALENTED

NCEE Student Activities
- Taking the Fiscal Route, pp. 57–60

TECHNOLOGY

eEdition DVD-ROM

eEdition Online

Power Presentation DVD-ROM

Economics Concepts Transparencies
- CT51 Demand-Side Versus Supply-Side Policies

Daily Test Practice Transparencies, TT51

ClassZone.com

Keynesian Theory

Keynes argued that changes in aggregate demand influence the business cycle, and he expressed this idea in an equation. His equation states that the GDP equals the total market value of all consumer goods (C), investment goods (I), government goods (G), and net exports (F). The equation looks like this: GDP = C + I + G + F.

Keynes believed that net exports played only a small role in the economy and that government and consumer expenditures were fairly stable. He reasoned that it was investment that caused the economy to fluctuate and that investment creates a greater than one-for-one change in national income. That is, one dollar spent in investment has a **spending multiplier effect**, meaning that a change in spending is multiplied into a larger change in GDP. (See Figure 15.5.)

QUICK REFERENCE

The **spending multiplier effect** states that a small change in spending causes a much larger change in GDP.

MATH CHALLENGE

FIGURE 15.5 Spending Multiplier Effect

If Zain receives a $100 raise and spends $60 of it to buy products from Joan, Joan's income increases too. Similarly, if Joan uses $36 of her increased income to buy products from Ravi, Ravi's income increases. Ravi then buys from Sarah, and so on. Each increase in income contributes to the GDP, so the total effect of Zain's spending is multiplied. To quantify how spending increases GDP, economists use the spending multiplier.

NEED HELP?

Math Handbook, "Calculating and Using Percents," page R4

Step 1: Determine the percentage of the money that is spent on domestic goods and services each time the money is reused. In the example, this is 60 percent.

Step 2: Use this equation, where A is the percentage, to calculate the spending multiplier.

Sample Calculations

$$\frac{1}{1-A} = \text{Spending multiplier} \qquad \frac{1}{1-60\%} = \frac{1}{1-0.60} = 2.5$$

Step 3: Use the spending multiplier to calculate the total increase in GDP.

$$\text{Initial investment} \times \text{Spending multiplier} = \text{Total increase in GDP} \qquad \$100 \times 2.5 = \$250$$

If businesses invest less, the spending multiplier effect means that the decrease in overall spending is greater than the initial decrease in business investment. Because this effect touches the entire economy, the government may need to step in to offset changes in investment. This idea became the basis of demand-side fiscal economics, which favors the use of fiscal policy to stimulate aggregate demand.

APPLICATION Making Inferences

A. How did Keynes's equation help him conclude that if investment declined, government needed to increase spending or cut taxes to stimulate aggregate demand?

See Teacher's Edition for answer. ▶

3 Teach

Demand-Side Economics

Discuss

- What is the basic idea of Keynesian economics? *(that government action is needed to stimulate aggregate demand)*

Math Challenge: Figure 15.5

Spending Multiplier Effect

This formula is somewhat simplified. In addition to going to savings and spending on imported goods, some part of additional income is used to pay taxes. The Council of Economic Advisors estimates that the actual spending multiplier in the United States is about 2. Therefore, the percentage spent on domestic goods would be 50 percent rather than 60 percent as shown in the example.

Point out that Step 3 allows economists to estimate how increases in government spending might affect GDP. For example, using this formula, the government would need to increase spending by $2 billion to increase GDP by $5 billion.

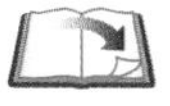

Math Handbook
Calculating and Using Percents, p. R4

APPLICATION

Answer *If investment declines the equation cannot remain balanced unless government goods or consumer goods increase. Increased government spending or decreased taxes will achieve those results.*

CLASS ACTIVITY

Demonstrating the Spending Multiplier Effect

Time 30 Minutes ◑

Task Track increases in income throughout the class, based on the spending multiplier effect.

Materials Needed paper and pencil

Activity

- Create a chart on a sheet of paper with enough rows for each student in the class.
- Assume that the amount spent on domestic goods is 50 percent.
- Allow one student to start with an initial investment of $100. Have that student write his or her name on the first row of the chart, fill in the correct amounts, and then pass the chart to another student to fill in.
- Continue the process until all students have filled in the chart.
- Total the increase in income and see how close it comes to the total amount that GDP would increase, namely $200.

Rubric

	Understanding of Concepts	Presentation of Information
4	excellent	clear and complete
3	good	mostly clear
2	fair	sometimes clear
1	poor	sketchy

John Maynard Keynes

More About . . .

John Maynard Keynes
John Maynard Keynes followed in the footsteps of his father, John Neville Keynes, who was a prominent economist of his time. J. M. Keynes received a degree in mathematics from Kings College at Cambridge University in 1905. He studied economics for another year under Alfred Marshall and Arthur Pigou.

Keynes returned to teach at Cambridge after working for the British civil service and representing the British Treasury during the peace conference after World War I. By 1942, Keynes's work had gained him wide recognition, and he received the title Baron Keynes of Tilton.

More About . . .

Keynesian Economists
Keynesian economics refers to the theories of macroeconomics based on Keynes's writings. A group of young economists at Cambridge formed a study group when Keynes published his *Treatise on Money*. Their reading and critique influenced Keynes's later work. One of them, Richard Kahn, wrote the article on the spending multiplier that was a key idea in *The General Theory*.

Other members of the group, such as Joan Robinson (see page 212), wrote articles that helped explain and clarify Keynes's work. In general, younger economists supported Keynes's ideas and older ones opposed them. Keynes's original ideas were significantly revised and expanded by many economists over the years.

At **ClassZone.com** students will find more information on John Maynard Keynes.

ECONOMICS PACESETTER

John Maynard Keynes: Architect of Demand-Side Policy

Many Americans are accustomed to the idea that the government plays an active role in the market economy. However, when John Maynard Keynes proposed his ideas in the 1930s, they were considered revolutionary. He questioned the principles of economics that had been accepted since the time of Adam Smith. How did Keynes's work change the way that people viewed the role of government in the economy?

FAST FACTS

John Maynard Keynes

Career: British academic and government economist

Born: June 5, 1883, in Cambridge, England

Died: April 21, 1946

Major Accomplishment: Introduced the idea of using government action to stimulate aggregate demand

Books: *A Treatise on Money* (1930); *The General Theory of Employment, Interest, and Money* (1936)

Famous Quotation: *The difficulty lies, not in the new ideas, but in escaping from the old ones.*

Jobs: Lecturer in economics, Cambridge University; editor of the *Economics Journal*; positions with the British Treasury office during World Wars I and II

Learn more about John Maynard Keynes at **ClassZone.com**

Using Government Action to Stimulate Demand

The economic situation of the 1920s led John Maynard Keynes to question the classical economic theories of supply and demand. Classical economists believed that a free market would eventually correct any imbalances. However, as aggregate demand fell, businesses invested and produced less, which led to layoffs. As a result, consumers had even less money to spend, and businesses cut back production even further.

As early as 1929, Keynes proposed that the British government spend money on public works projects to help ease unemployment. However, he had no theoretical backing for his proposal until he read an article in 1931 about the spending multiplier. This concept proved to be the key to his new economic theory, which he published in *The General Theory of Employment, Interest, and Money* (1936). This ground-breaking book marked the beginning of the field of macroeconomics.

Keynes's first revolutionary idea was to define aggregate demand as the sum of investment, consumer spending, government spending and net exports. He further stated that only government intervention could break the business cycle patterns that caused so much economic suffering. Even more revolutionary, however, was his argument that it was better for the government to spend money to help stabilize the economy than to have a balanced budget.

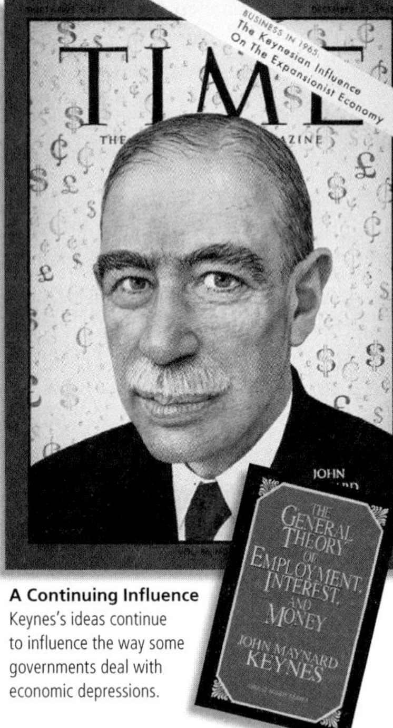

A Continuing Influence Keynes's ideas continue to influence the way some governments deal with economic depressions.

APPLICATION Contrasting Economic Information

B. What made Keynes's ideas different from those of classical economists?
He thought that government should intervene in the market economy to help smooth out the business cycle rather than waiting for the market to self-correct.

DIFFERENTIATING INSTRUCTION

English Learners

Sequence Events
Help students understand the significance of Keynes's ideas by working with them to sequence events described on page 456. Draw a time line on the board. Write Adam Smith's name at one end and Keynes's at the other. Allow students to refer to Chapter 1 for information on Smith. Have students add dates mentioned in Keynes's biography. Lead them to conclude that Keynes overturned long-held ideas and changed the way people thought about government and the economy.

Gifted and Talented

Analyze Primary Sources
Invite interested students to analyze some of Keynes's writing. Explain that even economists find *The General Theory* difficult to read. The book is readily available in paperback. Robert L. Heilbroner's anthology *Teachings from the Worldly Philosophy* includes an excerpt from Keynes's work. Have students write a summary of their reading.

Government and Demand-Side Policies

KEY CONCEPTS

Discretionary fiscal policy involves choices about how to use government spending and taxation to increase aggregate demand or control inflation. Demand-side policies advocate use of these fiscal policy tools to control aggregate demand and stabilize the economy.

The Role of Government

Keynes proposed an active role for government in the economy. He argued that the federal government ought to step into the economy using expansionary fiscal policy to promote full employment. The Great Depression had shown that the economy could reach equilibrium with less than full employment and that business was unable to break out of this cycle because of insufficient aggregate demand. Therefore, Keynes advocated increased government spending and decreased taxation to end recessions. Increased government spending helps create jobs and increases income, and decreased taxation encourages consumers to spend more, which prompts businesses to invest more. Such actions help increase aggregate demand.

On the other hand, Keynes thought that when inflation was high the government should use contractionary fiscal policy to keep prices from rising. The government would take an active role through decreasing government spending or increasing taxes. Both of these actions help decrease aggregate demand and control inflation.

Wartime Spending Massive government spending on wartime industries brought the United States out of economic depression.

Demand-Side Policies—Analysis

In some circumstances, an increase in government spending may lead to economic recovery. For example, government spending on public works programs and on production related to World War II brought the United States out of the Great Depression. However, it is not easy to limit such spending to times of recession, because federal programs seem to take on a life of their own and are difficult to terminate. Politicians are often reluctant to discontinue programs that are popular.

Excessive aggregate demand due to government or consumer spending can lead to inflation. Contractionary fiscal policy requires decreases in government spending or increases in taxation. Just as it is difficult to decrease government spending, it is difficult to enact the tax increases. Politicians must often choose between doing what is best for the economy and doing what is most likely to ensure their reelection. Furthermore, when the economy experiences stagflation—slow economic growth with high unemployment and inflation—as it did in the 1970s, demand-side policies seem to be ineffective.

APPLICATION Drawing Conclusions

C. Why are demand-side policies more effective against recession than against inflation?
See Teacher's Edition for answer. ▶

Government and Demand-Side Policies

Discuss

- How do political considerations limit the effectiveness of demand-side fiscal policy? *(Demand-side fiscal policy requires government spending cuts and increased taxes to fight inflation, yet politicians may be reluctant to use these measures because they are generally unpopular.)*

More About . . .

Fiscal Policy in the 1970s

In 1971, President Nixon remarked, "We are all Keynesians now." Republicans generally favored a smaller role for government in the economy, but Nixon felt the need to take action. He increased spending and instituted wage and price controls to stabilize the economy before his reelection bid in 1972. The measures were initially successful.

However, inflation rose with increases in oil and food prices. When Nixon cut spending, the economy went into recession. Presidents Ford and Carter had some success in reducing unemployment, but when oil prices rose again, Carter's spending cuts caused unemployment to rise and did little to curb inflation.

APPLICATION

Answer *because the expansionary practices of increased government spending and decreased taxes are more politically popular and easier to enact than the contractionary practices of cutting spending or increasing taxes*

CLASS ACTIVITY

Creating a Classroom Display

Time 60 Minutes ●

Task Gather information on Keynesian economics and the Great Depression and create a classroom display.

Materials Needed computer with Internet access, poster board and markers

Activity

- Organize students into groups and assign each to research some aspect of how Keynesian economics was used to solve the problems of the Great Depression.
- Some groups may focus on President Roosevelt's New Deal programs that reflected Keynes's ideas. Others may research how policies related to American entry into World War II showed Keynes's influence. Others may track unemployment and inflation rates during the period.
- Direct groups to collaborate to create a classroom display that presents a coherent story of how demand-side policy helped resolve this economic crisis.

Rubric

	Understanding of Concepts	Presentation of Information
4	excellent	clear, complete, creative
3	good	mostly clear, somewhat creative
2	fair	sometimes clear, some creative elements
1	poor	sketchy and unoriginal

Supply-Side Economics

Discuss

- How might supply-side policies make the tax structure less progressive? *(by lowering the highest tax brackets to reduce the tax burden on higher income taxpayers)*
- Why do supply-side economists favor less government regulation of business? *(because less regulation will reduce businesses' production costs and allow them to produce more, which will allow the economy to grow)*

Analyzing Charts: Figure 15.6

Encourage students to read each column to summarize each type of fiscal policy. Then have students read each bullet point for both types of policies in order to compare them. Ask students what is the common goal of both kinds of policy. *(to reduce unemployment and help the economy to grow)*

Answers

1. *Both are designed to stimulate the economic activity.*
2. *Supply-side economics states that government's role is to remove obstacles to business investment and growth.*

Supply-Side Economics

QUICK REFERENCE

Supply-side fiscal policy provides incentives to producers to increase aggregate supply.

KEY CONCEPTS

Some economists believe that the best way to influence the economy is through the supply side rather than through the demand side. **Supply-side fiscal policy** is designed to provide incentives to producers to increase aggregate supply. In other words, demand-side economics uses fiscal policy to encourage consumers to spend more, while supply-side economics focuses on cutting the cost of production to encourage producers to supply more. Figure 15.6 compares supply-side economics to demand-side economics.

The Role of Government

As you have learned, the role of the government in the economy falls into three categories: taxation, spending, and regulation. For the most part, supply-side economists favor less government involvement in these three areas.

Supply-side economists favor cutting the tax rates on individual and corporate income because they believe that high tax rates slow economic growth by discouraging working, saving, and investing. Lower tax rates, on the other hand, encourage individuals and businesses to work, save, and invest more. Specifically, reducing the highest tax brackets provides more available income to the people most likely to invest in new business activities. Spending cuts are another way that supply-side economics seeks to stimulate aggregate supply. Cuts in spending are related to tax cuts. If the government spends less, it needs to take in less in revenue and, therefore, is able to lower taxes. Finally, decreased government regulation can also stimulate business production. Government regulations add to the costs of production and make it harder for businesses to grow. Deregulation, however, cuts costs and leads to increases in aggregate supply.

FIGURE 15.6 Supply-Side and Demand-Side Economics

Supply-Side Economics	Demand-Side Economics
• Focuses on stimulating production (supply) to increase business output • Lower taxes + decreased government spending + deregulation = greater incentives for business investment • Businesses expand and create jobs; people work, save, and invest more • Greater investment and productivity cause businesses to increase output	• Focuses on stimulating consumption (demand) to increase business output • Increased government spending results in more money in people's hands • People spend more • Increased demand causes business to increase output

ANALYZE CHARTS

1. What is similar about supply-side and demand-side tax policies?
2. Which system favors less government involvement in the economy?

DIFFERENTIATING INSTRUCTION

Struggling Readers

Create a Venn Diagram

Have students work in pairs to compare and contrast supply-side and demand-side economics. Point out that Figure 15.6 is set up with parallel statements for easy comparison. Encourage partners to read the chart carefully to note where similar phrases are used and where there are differences. Have them create a Venn diagram to graphically show similarities and differences between the two policies. Call on volunteers to use their diagrams to summarize the similarities and differences.

Inclusion

Use Examples

Help students understand that supply-side tax cuts do not always encourage people to work more. Suppose a worker is in the highest tax bracket, and each additional dollar earned is taxed at 50 percent. If the worker earns $200 more by working 10 hours of overtime, take-home pay will be $100. If the tax rate is reduced to 28 percent, the worker could work 10 hours of overtime and take home $144, or 7 hours and take home $100.80.

The Laffer Curve

Supply-side economists refer to the **Laffer Curve**, a graph developed by economist Arthur Laffer, to illustrate how tax cuts affect tax revenues and economic growth. As Figure 15.7 shows, Laffer theorized that tax revenues increase as tax rates increase up to a certain point. After that point, higher tax rates actually lead to decreased tax revenues. The reasoning behind the curve is that higher taxes discourage people from working, saving, and investing. So, at a tax rate of 100 percent, the government would theoretically collect no tax revenues, because people would have no incentive to earn income if it all went to the government for taxes.

In other words, the higher the tax rate, the likelier it is that people will take some type of action to avoid paying more taxes. When people find alternatives to income-producing activity, total taxable income declines, tax revenues decrease, aggregate supply falls, and economic growth slows. Conversely, as tax rates fall, people are more inclined to undertake income-producing activity because less of their income will go to taxes. Further, they are more likely to save and invest this extra income, which will lead to increasing aggregate supply and greater economic growth.

QUICK REFERENCE

The **Laffer Curve** is a graph that illustrates the economist Arthur Laffer's theory of how tax cuts affect tax revenues.

FIGURE 15.7 THE LAFFER CURVE

ⓐ There is a tax rate between 0 and 100 percent (point R0) at which maximum revenue is collected.

ⓑ Tax rates higher than R0, such as R1, will not bring in more revenue (T1), because higher taxes discourage productive activity and shrink the tax base.

ⓒ When tax rates are higher than R0, lowering the tax rate (R2) will lead to higher tax revenue (T2). Lower tax rates tend to encourage productive activity and increase the tax base.

ANALYZE GRAPHS

1. There is no tax revenue at two points on the graph—when the tax rate is 0 percent and when it is 100 percent. Why is this so?
2. How does this graph support the ideas of supply-side economists?

Supply-Side Policies—Analysis

When the principles of the Laffer Curve were applied in the United States in the 1980s, the results were much as Laffer had predicted. Legislation passed in that decade reduced federal income tax rates substantially. For example, the top bracket went from 70 percent to around 30 percent. At the same time, federal government receipts from income taxes over the whole decade were about 13 percent higher than

Analyzing Graphs: Figure 15.7

Mention that it appears that point R0, the tax rate that yields maximum revenue, is 50 percent. However, this is not necessarily the case for the U.S. economy. As the text indicates, it is difficult to know where an economy is located on the curve. Many economists now think that the U.S. economy is located to the left of point R0. Therefore, cutting tax rates would decrease tax revenue.

Answers

1. *At 0 percent, there is no tax collected; at 100 percent, there is no income on which to collect taxes because there is no incentive to work.*
2. *It provides a model that supports the idea that lower taxes can generate as much revenue as higher taxes because there will be more incentive for people to invest in productive activity.*

More About . . .

Reaganomics

It was President Ronald Reagan (1981–1989) who first applied the Laffer Curve to fiscal policy. Therefore, supply-side economics is often referred to as Reaganomics or trickle-down economics. The latter term comes from the idea that tax incentives that benefit higher income taxpayers and businesses will stimulate the economy in such a way that all taxpayers benefit.

SMALL GROUP ACTIVITY

Creating a Poster

Time 30 Minutes ◑

Task Review and assess analyses of different types of fiscal policy and create a poster.

Materials Needed poster board and markers

Activity

- Have students work in pairs. Encourage them to review the analyses of demand-side policies on page 457 and supply-side policies on pages 459–460.
- Ask partners to consider the analyses of each type of policy and discuss how they would like to summarize the information graphically.
- Instruct pairs to create a poster that summarizes the analyses of the two types of fiscal policy.
- Allow students to share their posters in small groups and discuss what they consider the strengths and weaknesses of each policy.

Rubric

	Understanding of Concepts	Presentation of Information
4	excellent	clear, complete, creative
3	good	mostly clear and somewhat creative
2	fair	sometimes clear and creative
1	poor	sketchy and unoriginal

Your Economic Choices

DEMAND-SIDE POLICIES VS. SUPPLY-SIDE POLICIES

Which candidate will you choose?

- Which candidate represents supply-side policies? How do you know? *(the second, because the candidate favors less government spending and regulation)*
- Why do you think individual taxpayers have different opinions about cutting taxes? *(Possible answer: Their opinion depends on how the particular type of tax cut affects them and whether there are related cuts in government programs that they think are important.)*

Activity Invite students to write a letter to a political candidate saying why they agree or disagree with the candidate's position on taxes and government spending. Students may write to a fictional candidate based on the information in the textbook or an actual local or national politician. Allow volunteers to share their letters with the class.

they had been in the 1970s. Inflation and unemployment rates both fell during the decade. Further, the economy grew steadily in the 1980s, with real GDP increasing by about 3 percent each year.

Even so, some of Laffer's predictions did not hold true. The supply-side approach suggests that with lower tax rates, people will work more. However, while some people did choose to work more, others chose to work less, since they could earn the same amount of after-tax income by working fewer hours. In addition, supply-side theory states that lower tax rates encourage people to save and invest. In fact, the savings rate declined during the 1980s.

Some economists have suggested that the success of supply-side policies depends on where the economy is located on the Laffer Curve. Look again at Figure 15.7 on page 459. Find the tax rate R0 on the horizontal axis and trace the broken line from that point to where the line intersects the curve. Tax revenue is maximized at this point. If the economy is not at this point on the curve, then tax rate cuts will decrease tax revenue rather than increase it. Supply-side theory offers no measures for establishing where on the curve an economy might be. Other economists have argued that it is difficult to isolate the effects of supply-side incentives from demand-side results to determine what caused unemployment and inflation rates to fall and the economy to grow during the 1980s. They suggest that tax cuts and increased government spending on defense drove up aggregate demand, resulting in economic growth. This increased spending was fueled by deficits, which you'll learn more about in Section 3.

YOUR ECONOMIC CHOICES

DEMAND-SIDE POLICIES VS. SUPPLY-SIDE POLICIES

Which candidate will you choose?

In an upcoming congressional election, one candidate favors tax cuts and increased government spending. The other favors more substantial tax cuts, decreased government spending, and less government regulation of the economy. For which candidate will you cast your vote? Why?

▲ Supply-side supporter

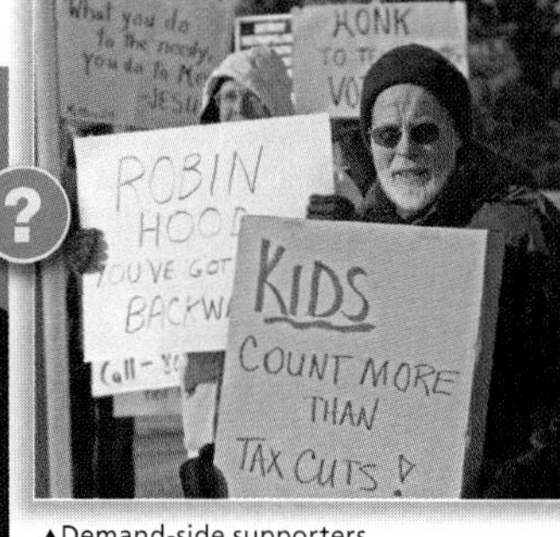

▲Demand-side supporters

APPLICATION Analyzing Causes

D. What fiscal policy techniques do supply-side economists advocate to reduce unemployment and fight inflation at the same time?

Reduce taxes; decrease government spending, especially on social programs; and reduce government regulations in order to stimulate production.

DIFFERENTIATING INSTRUCTION

English Learners

Formulate Questions

Model how to identify important details from the text to formulate, ask, and respond to questions. Example: How did supply-side economics affect the automatic stabilizers in the economy? *(Possible answer: It reduced their effectiveness by limiting transfer payments and making the tax system less progressive.)* Have students work in pairs to apply this skill to the section. Encourage them to use the following question forms: Who? What? When? Where? Why? How?

Gifted and Talented

Hold a Panel Discussion

Invite students to use the Internet or library resources to find out more information about the application of supply-side economics in the United States in the 1980s. Encourage students to learn more specific details about how the policy was applied, as well as different points of view about the effectiveness of the policies. Allow students to hold a panel discussion on the topic based on their research. Ask students to draw conclusions about the success of these policies.

SECTION 2 Assessment

Online Quiz
ClassZone.com

REVIEWING KEY CONCEPTS

1. Explain the relationship between the terms in each of these pairs.
   a. *Keynesian economics* *demand-side fiscal policy*
   b. *supply-side fiscal policy* *Laffer Curve*
2. How did the Great Depression influence Keynesian economics?
3. How is the spending multiplier effect related to demand-side economics?
4. How are supply-side and demand-side economics different?
5. Which fiscal policy tool does the Laffer Curve address?
6. **Using Your Notes** How does the role of government differ in demand-side and supply-side economics? Refer to your completed flow chart.

   Demand-side policies → Role of government
   Supply-side policies → Role of government

   Use the Graphic Organizer at **Interactive Review @ ClassZone.com**

CRITICAL THINKING

7. **Creating Graphs** Create a graph showing aggregate demand and aggregate supply in the economy. Then add new curves to show the expected shifts based on expansionary demand-side policies and supply-side policies. What happens to price level and GDP as a result of each type of policy?
   Use ***SMARTGrapher*** **@ ClassZone.com** to complete this activity.
8. **Applying Economic Concepts** Suppose that the federal government decides to increase its spending on highway construction by $5 billion to keep the economy from falling into a recession. Explain the real impact on GDP of this spending.
9. **Analyzing Effects** Tom, Cia, and Julie were all in the 50 percent tax bracket. When a tax cut program reduced their tax bracket to 28 percent, they all made changes in their lives. Tom decided to work fewer hours so he could begin training to run in a marathon. Cia bought the new sports car she'd been wanting. Julie chose to work more hours so she could save extra money for her daughter's college education. Explain the effects of the tax cut for each individual. Use supply-side or demand-side economics reasoning in your answer.
10. **Challenge** Why is it difficult for demand-side economics to solve the problems of high unemployment and high inflation when they occur at the same time?

ECONOMICS IN PRACTICE

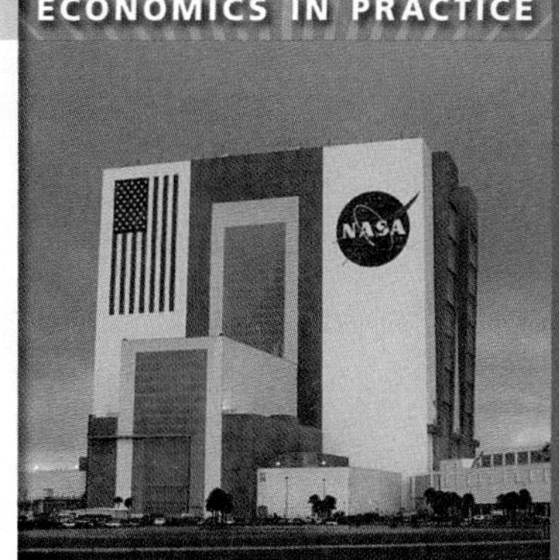

Space research center

Categorizing Economic Information Consider what you've learned about demand-side or supply-side fiscal policy. Then complete the following activities.

Identify Policies Complete the chart by indicating whether each action reflects a demand-side or a supply-side policy.

Government Action	Demand-Side or Supply-Side
Cut capital gains tax rates to encourage investment	
Expand government spending on space exploration	
Increase federal grants for education	
Reduce safety rules that businesses must follow	

Challenge Why is it difficult to tell if a cut in individual income tax rates is the result of a demand-side or a supply-side policy?

4 Assess & Reteach

Assess Ask students what questions they think the section assessment should include. Discuss assessment questions as a class; then answer any of the students' remaining questions.

Unit 6 Resource Book
- Section Quiz, p. 81

Interactive Review @ ClassZone.com
- Section Quiz

Test Generator CD-ROM
- Section Quiz

Reteach Write the key terms on the board and ask students to use the terms in a summary of the section.

Unit 6 Resource Book
- Reteaching Activity, p. 82

Economics in Practice

Identify Policies supply-side; demand-side; demand-side; supply-side

Challenge because both types of policy may advocate tax cuts to stimulate the economy, but in different ways; demand-side policy stimulates production indirectly by first increasing consumer demand, whereas supply-side policy wants the tax cuts to serve as incentives for greater productive activity such as more work, savings, and investment

SECTION 2 ASSESSMENT ANSWERS

Reviewing Key Concepts

1. a. *Keynesian economics*, p. 454; *demand-side fiscal policy*, p. 454
   b. *supply-side fiscal policy*, p. 458; *Laffer Curve*, p. 459
2. For many economists, it showed that the old way of thinking was not effective. Keynesian economics proposed that government spending be used to get the economy moving.
3. It explains why demand-side fiscal policies will add more to the GDP than just the amount of the government funds involved.
4. Supply-side: stimulate production to increase aggregate supply; demand-side: stimulate consumption to increase aggregate demand.
5. It focuses on taxation, namely the way in which higher tax rates may decrease tax revenues.
6. See page 454 for an example of a completed diagram. Demand-side economics advocates a more active role for government, using government spending and taxation to increase aggregate demand. Supply-side economics advocates that government focus on incentives such as tax cuts and deregulation to increase production.

Critical Thinking

7. Demand-side graph shows a shift in aggregate demand to the right, price level would rise and GDP would increase; supply-side graph shows a shift in aggregate supply to the right, price level would fall and GDP would increase
8. Calculations should follow the model of Figure 15.5 and show the spending multiplier effect of an increase in GDP greater than $5 billion.
9. Julie's decision reflects the desired effect of supply-side policies. Tom's decision shows that supply-side economics does not always result in more productive work. He can earn the same after-tax income by working fewer hours. Cia's actions show a demand-side result of a tax cut as she has more after-tax income and chooses to spend it.
10. because high unemployment requires expansionary policy; high inflation requires contractionary policy

Economics in Practice

See answers in side column above.

1 Plan & Prepare

Section 3 Objectives

- examine the difference between the deficit and the debt
- explain why national deficits occur
- describe how deficits are financed
- identify the impact of the national debt on the economy

2 Focus & Motivate

Connecting to Everyday Life Explain that this section focuses on the results of the government spending more than it receives in tax revenue. Invite students to discuss what they know about how families deal with trying to balance spending and income.

Taking Notes Remind students to take notes as they read by completing a comparison chart on federal deficits and the national debt. They can use the Graphic Organizer at **Interactive Review @ ClassZone.com.** A sample is shown below.

Federal Deficits	National Debt
• Government spends more than it takes in • refers to one year • 4 causes: emergencies, demand for public goods, fiscal policy, government social programs • every year except 1998–2001	• sum of all deficits and surpluses • more than one-third held by government trust funds • grew faster than inflation since 1980s • crowding-out effect drives up interest rates

SECTION 3

Deficits and the National Debt

OBJECTIVES

In Section 3, you will
- examine the difference between the deficit and the debt
- explain why national deficits occur
- describe how deficits are financed
- identify the impact of the national debt on the economy

KEY TERMS

budget surplus, *p. 462*
budget deficit, *p. 462*
deficit spending, *p. 462*
national debt, *p. 462*
Treasury bills, *p. 464*
Treasury notes, *p. 464*
Treasury bonds, *p. 464*
trust funds, *p. 465*
crowding-out effect, *p. 466*

TAKING NOTES

As you read Section 3, complete a comparison chart to show the similarities and differences between federal deficits and the national debt. Use the Graphic Organizer at **Interactive Review @ ClassZone.com**

Federal Deficits	National Debt

The Federal Deficit and Debt

QUICK REFERENCE

A **budget surplus** occurs when the government takes in more than it spends.

A **budget deficit** occurs when government spends more than it takes in.

Deficit spending is a government practice of spending more than it takes in for a specific budget year.

The **national debt** is the money that the government owes.

KEY CONCEPTS

Governments have frequently made efforts to balance their budgets so that spending equals the revenues collected. In reality, however, all levels of government often struggle to achieve a balanced budget. As you recall, Congress and state legislatures make budget decisions with both economic and political considerations in mind.

Federal government spending falls into one of three categories: a balanced budget; a **budget surplus**, when the government takes in more than it spends; or a **budget deficit**, when government spends more than it takes in. In recent years, the federal government has rarely achieved a budget surplus. Since 1970, a surplus was recorded only between 1998 and 2001. Figure 15.8 on the opposite page shows the pattern of budget deficits and surpluses since 1980.

It is important to note that a budget surplus or budget deficit refers to only one year. **Deficit spending** occurs when a government spends more than it collects in revenue for a specific budget year. Annual deficits contribute to the **national debt**, which is the total amount of money that the government owes. In effect, the national debt is equal to the sum of annual budget deficits minus any budget surpluses or other payments against the debt.

Source: www.CartoonStock.com

Controlling the Deficit This cartoon suggests one way to deal with a budget deficit.

SECTION 3 PROGRAM RESOURCES

ON LEVEL
Lesson Plans
- Core, p. 52

Unit 6 Resource Book
- Reading Study Guide, pp. 83–84
- Economic Skills and Problem Solving Activity, pp. 93–94
- Section Quiz, p. 91

STRUGGLING READERS
Unit 6 Resource Book
- Reading Study Guide with Additional Support, pp. 85–87
- Reteaching Activity, p. 92

ENGLISH LEARNERS
Unit 6 Resource Book
- Reading Study Guide with Additional Support (Spanish), pp. 88–90

INCLUSION
Lesson Plans
- Modified for Inclusion, p. 52

GIFTED AND TALENTED
Unit 6 Resource Book
- Readings in Free Enterprise: A Dangerous Legacy, pp. 95–96
- Case Study Resources: Federal Deficit Estimate Down to $296B, p. 97; A Small Deficit: Worth a Bronx Cheer, p. 98

TECHNOLOGY
eEdition DVD-ROM
eEdition Online
Power Presentation DVD-ROM
Economics Concepts Transparencies
- CT52 Debt and Deficit as a Percentage of GDP, 1960–2004

Daily Test Practice Transparencies, TT52
ClassZone.com

Causes of the Deficit

There are four main causes of deficit spending: national emergencies, a desire for more public goods, stabilization of the economy, and the role of government in society. Many times a budget deficit may be the result of more than one of these causes.

National Emergencies Generally speaking, national emergencies are wars in which the United States is involved. Deficit spending has been used in wartime from the Revolutionary War to the war in Iraq that began in 2003. The terrorist attacks of September 11, 2001, and catastrophic weather events are other examples of national emergencies. All may require massive spending beyond the normal outlay of funds.

Need for Public Goods and Services Public goods and services benefit many different people and groups. The interstate highway system, dams, flood-control projects, and airports are examples of public goods. Building such infrastructure is expensive and lasts many years. The public expects the government to provide these goods to facilitate commerce, agriculture, and transportation.

Stabilization of the Economy As you learned earlier in this chapter, fiscal policy can include government spending to stimulate the economy. The classic example of this occurred during the Great Depression. The government spent money on a variety of public works projects to build roads, bridges, schools, and parks, putting millions of unemployed people to work. This government spending led to budget deficits.

Role of Government in Society As you have seen, people have also come to depend on government programs such as Social Security, Medicare, Medicaid, and unemployment insurance to provide help for those in need. These programs are expensive, and because they are entitlement programs, they require funding each year.

FIGURE 15.8 BUDGET DEFICITS AND SURPLUSES

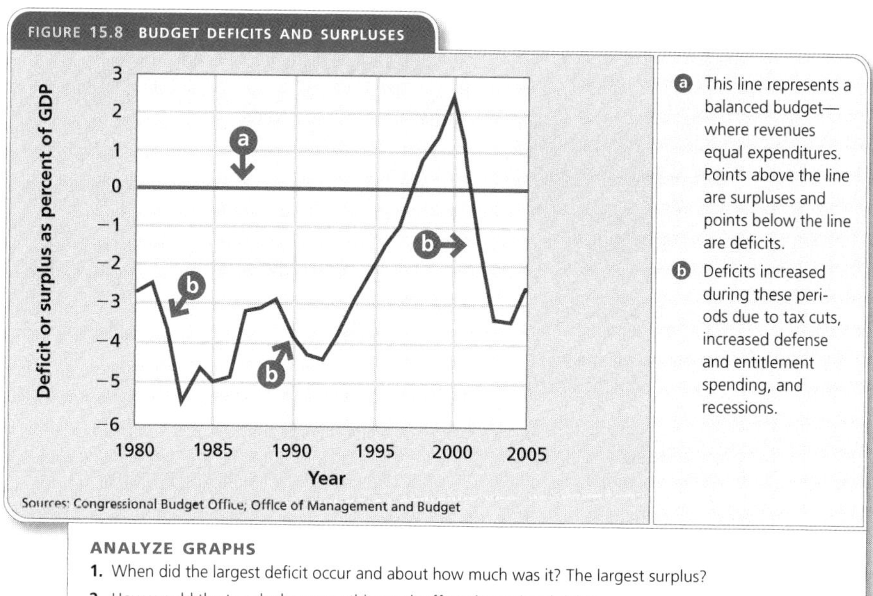
Deficit or surplus as percent of GDP
3
2
1
0
−1
−2
−3
−4
−5
−6
1980
1985
1990
1995
2000
2005
Year
a
b
a This line represents a balanced budget—where revenues equal expenditures. Points above the line are surpluses and points below the line are deficits.
b Deficits increased during these periods due to tax cuts, increased defense and entitlement spending, and recessions.
Sources: Congressional Budget Office; Office of Management and Budget

ANALYZE GRAPHS

1. When did the largest deficit occur and about how much was it? The largest surplus?
2. How would the trends shown on this graph affect the national debt?

3 Teach

The Federal Deficit and Debt

Discuss

- What is the difference between a budget deficit and the national debt? *(A deficit refers to only one fiscal year; the national debt is the cumulative amount the government owes.)*
- Why does the government sell bonds? *(in order to raise money through borrowing to cover deficit spending)*

Analyzing Graphs: Figure 15.8

Explain that this line graph shows annual budget deficits or surpluses from 1980 to 2005. Point out that measuring deficits or surpluses as a percent of GDP provides a clearer picture by factoring out inflation and the growth of the national economy. In nominal dollar figures, the deficits and surpluses of the 1990s were larger than ever before—but so was the size of the economy. Ask students how budget deficits changed from 1992 to 2000 *(went from −4.5 to +2.5).*

Answers

1. *1983, −5.6%; 2000, +2.5%*
2. *The national debt would increase in every year except 1998–2001.*

SMALL GROUP ACTIVITY

Researching Causes of the Deficit

Time 45 Minutes 

Task Investigate a certain time period to discover causes of deficits or surpluses and give an oral presentation.

Materials Needed computer with Internet access

Activity

- Organize students into groups. Assign each group one of the following time periods to research: 1940s, 1970s, 1980s, 1990s, 2000-present.
- Direct students to research information about their assigned period in order to draw conclusions about the causes of increasing or decreasing budget deficits during the period.
- Allow each group to present its conclusions to the class.
- Encourage students to discuss whether they think the government could have made different choices to prevent growing budget deficits.

Rubric

	Understanding of Concepts	Presentation of Information
4	excellent	clear and complete
3	good	mostly clear
2	fair	sometimes clear
1	poor	sketchy

International Economics

Foreign Holders of U.S. Debt
In March 2006, three countries held about 55 percent of the Treasury securities held by foreigners. Japan held about $640 billion or 31 percent, China accounted for about $320 billion or 15 percent, and the United Kingdom held about $180 billion or 9 percent.

In February 1998, the top three holders were the United Kingdom (24 percent), Japan (23 percent), and Germany (7 percent). China was in 7th place with 4 percent. Foreign official institutions—central banks, for example—held 63 percent of the total held by foreigners in March 2006. Foreign lenders financed about 80 percent of the growth in the debt since 2001.

Analyzing Graphs: Figure 15.9

Explain that this pie graph shows the investors who lend money to the Federal government. The types of investors are listed from largest to smallest percentage and are shown in clockwise order around the pie graph. Point out that individual investors may buy savings bonds or other Treasury securities individually or through mutual funds. Ask students why investors choose to lend money to the U.S. government. *(because Treasury securities are a very safe investment that pays a predictable rate of interest)*

Answers

1. *55.4 percent; 44.6 percent*
2. *Only 4.5 percent of government borrowing is through savings bonds; most is through Treasury bills, notes, and bonds.*

Raising Money for Deficit Spending

QUICK REFERENCE

Treasury bills mature in less than one year.

Treasury notes mature between two and ten years.

Treasury bonds mature in 30 years.

When the federal government does not receive enough revenue from taxes to finance its spending, it can borrow money to expand the economy. In effect, the government pays for its present needs by borrowing money that it will have to repay at some future date. It does this by issuing government bonds, through the Department of the Treasury.

Perhaps the best known type of bond issued by the government is the savings bond. Savings bonds mature in 20 years and are available in both small and large denominations—from $25 up to $10,000. The Department of the Treasury issues three other types of bonds. **Treasury bills** (T bills) are short-term bonds that mature in less than one year. **Treasury notes** are bonds that mature between two and ten years. And finally, **Treasury bonds** are issued for 30 years. Interest is paid on all these bonds, with higher interest rates sometimes being paid on instruments with longer maturity dates.

Individuals, state and local governments, insurance companies, pension funds, financial institutions, the Federal Reserve banks, and foreign investors hold these bonds. Figure 15.9 shows the percentage of federal debt held by different types of investors. A trend in recent years has been an increase in the percentage of the federal debt owned by foreign investors. Most foreign investors in U.S. Treasury bonds are the central banks of other countries. Japan and China hold the largest amount of foreign investors' share of the debt.

FIGURE 15.9 CREDITORS OF THE FEDERAL GOVERNMENT

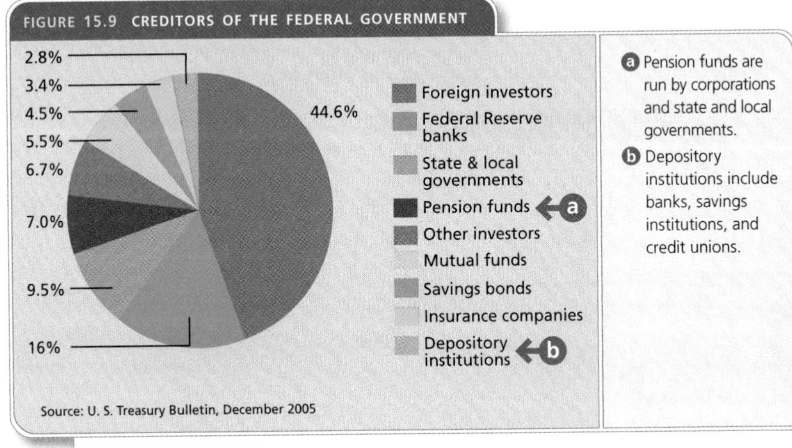

Source: U. S. Treasury Bulletin, December 2005

ⓐ Pension funds are run by corporations and state and local governments.

ⓑ Depository institutions include banks, savings institutions, and credit unions.

ANALYZE GRAPHS

1. What percentage of the federal debt is owed to U.S. investors? What percentage is owed to foreign investors?
2. How do savings bonds compare to other government bonds as a form of government borrowing?

APPLICATION Drawing Conclusions

A. Why do all levels of government often struggle to achieve balanced budgets or budget surpluses? Because citizens expect the government to take care of many needs, and it is not easy for the government to increase taxes as much as may be required to meet those needs.

DIFFERENTIATING INSTRUCTION

English Learners

Interpret the Pie Chart
Model sentences that describe the information shown in Figure 15.9, such as: "Almost half the money lent to the federal government comes from foreign investors" or "Federal Reserve banks hold 16 percent of the federal debt." Have students work in pairs to practice making statements about the information in the chart. One partner can make a statement orally, while the other writes it down and reads it back. Students should take turns speaking and writing.

Inclusion

Explain the Numbers
Help students understand the large numbers used to express budget deficits and surpluses and the national debt by building up from 10 to 1 trillion. Write 10 on the board and underneath it add a zero to form 100. Continue adding one zero at a time up to the 12 zeros that represent 1 trillion. Point out that commas are inserted after every third place. Show them that 1 million is the same as 1,000 thousands, 1 billion is 1,000 millions, and 1 trillion is 1,000 billions.

The National Debt

KEY CONCEPTS

As you have seen, the national debt consists of the total accumulation of government deficits and surpluses over time. The money is owed to savers for the bonds they purchase and the interest paid on them. However, the actual debt situation is somewhat more complicated. The government also borrows from **trust funds**, which are funds being held for specific purposes to be expended at a future date. Examples of government trust funds include Social Security, Medicare, Medicaid, and government pension funds. When the trust funds accumulate surpluses by taking in more tax revenue than is needed for annual benefit payments, the surplus is invested in government bonds until the specific programs need the funds. In essence, therefore, the government borrows from itself to cover some deficit spending.

Some economists do not consider this to truly be debt. The money is transferred from one part of the government to another. This borrowing does not place a burden on the current economy because the current budget is not used to pay for it.

QUICK REFERENCE

Trust funds are held for specific purposes to be expended at a future date.

The Size of the National Debt

In August 2006, the total national debt was about $8.4 trillion. About $4.8 trillion was privately owned by the creditors shown in Figure 15.9, and about $3.6 trillion was in government trust funds.

There were only five years from 1962 to 2005 in which the federal government had a surplus of funds. In all the other years of that period, the government borrowed money to cover its deficits. Each time it borrowed money, it increased the size of the national debt. From 1980 to 1994 alone, the national debt grew by more than five times, from about $930 billion in 1980 to about $4.7 trillion in 1994.

Economists often look at the country's debt as a percentage of GDP. That perspective allows them to see how the burden of borrowing compares to the strength of the overall economy. The national debt was 33 percent of GDP in 1981. By 2006, it had doubled to nearly 68 percent of GDP. However, in 1981 about 80 percent of the debt was privately owned. In 2006, less than 60 percent was privately owned.

Economics Update

Find an update about the national debt at **ClassZone.com**

More About the National Debt

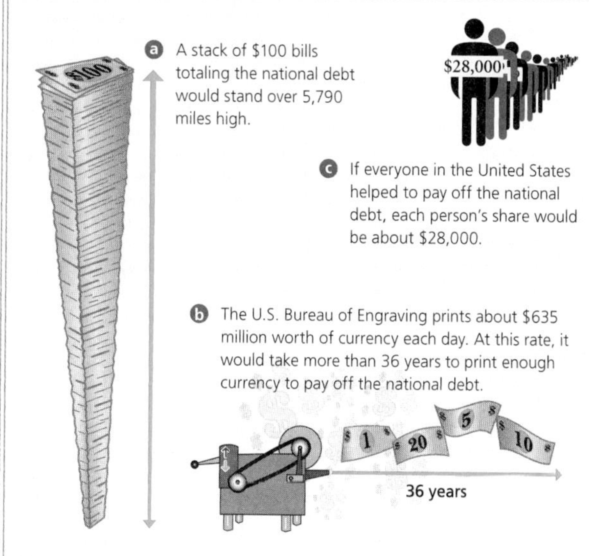

a A stack of $100 bills totaling the national debt would stand over 5,790 miles high.
$28,000
c If everyone in the United States helped to pay off the national debt, each person's share would be about $28,000.
b The U.S. Bureau of Engraving prints about $635 million worth of currency each day. At this rate, it would take more than 36 years to print enough currency to pay off the national debt.
36 years

The National Debt

Discuss

- Why do some economists not consider the money borrowed from government trust funds to be debt? *(because money is basically moved from one part of the government to another)*
- What are some positive effects that government debt can have on the economy? *(Deficit spending by the government can stimulate the economy, which can create jobs and improve the infrastructure.)*

Economics Update

At **ClassZone.com** students will see updated information on the national debt.

Technomics

Bureau of the Public Debt

The Bureau of the Public Debt is part of the Department of the Treasury. Its Web site <www.publicdebt.treas.gov> updates the amount of the national debt each day, showing the amounts in public and intragovernmental holdings. It also shows current interest rates for T-bills and savings bonds, as well as information on other government securities.

A link from the home page to "The Public Debt" provides updated daily and monthly totals as well as historical information on the debt dating back to 1791. Much of this information may be downloaded in a variety of formats.

INDIVIDUAL ACTIVITY

Expressing an Opinion about Deficits and the Debt

Time 30 Minutes

Task Review information about budget deficits and the national debt and express an opinion about the topic.

Materials Needed paper and pens, pencils, or markers

Activity

- Have students review information about budget deficits and the national debt on pages 462–466.
- Invite them to create a personal expression of their opinion on the topic, such as a political cartoon, editorial, story, or poem.
- Allow volunteers to share their creations with the class. Encourage them to provide supporting evidence from the text that informed their opinion.
- Discuss the opinions expressed and explore whether there are points of consensus.

Rubric

	Understanding of Concepts	Presentation of Information
4	excellent	clear, complete, creative
3	good	mostly clear, somewhat creative
2	fair	sometimes clear, some creative elements
1	poor	sketchy and unoriginal

More About . . .

The Crowding-Out Effect

The ideas behind the crowding-out effect are generally accepted in principle by economists. However, there is no conclusive evidence that government borrowing significantly changes the actual amount of spending and investment by businesses.

Some of the government spending financed by borrowing goes to improve the nation's infrastructure or human capital and this may offset any declines in private capital. In addition, some government spending may cause growth in private sector businesses that are complementary to it. For example, a new federal office complex may lead to the opening of new stores, restaurants, and other businesses nearby.

More About . . .

The Budget Enforcement Act

The Budget Enforcement Act (BEA) of 1990 represented a different approach to deficit reduction in light of the failure of the Gramm-Rudman-Hollings Act of 1985 to achieve its goals. The caps on discretionary spending and the pay-as-you-go financing provision were budgeting procedures agreed to by the president and Congress.

These provisions were extended in the later deficit reduction acts of 1993 and 1997 and were effective in controlling spending until surpluses began to accumulate in 1998. BEA provisions expired in 2002, just as the federal budget once again returned to deficit spending.

The Effect of the Debt on the Economy

The national debt can have positive or negative effects on the economy. When government spending stimulates the economy, jobs are created and public goods such as the infrastructure may be improved. These improvements benefit everyone. However, when the government competes with the private sector to raise money by paying higher interest rates to get the savers' dollars, the results often are negative. The **crowding-out effect** is what happens when the government outbids private bond interest rates to gain loanable funds. Money leaves the private sector, and interest rates increase.

QUICK REFERENCE

The **crowding-out effect** is the result of the government's outbidding private bond interest rates.

Repaying the interest on government bonds, or servicing the debt, also can have a negative impact on the economy. The 2007 federal budget estimate showed interest payments to be nearly 10 percent of all federal spending. Constant borrowing raises the amount of interest to be paid. This, in turn, increases the need for taxes to service the debt. Higher taxes mean less spending by consumers and less investment by businesses, both of which may hurt the economy.

FIGURE 15.10 Actions to Control Deficits and Debt

Budget Action	Goal	Key Points	Analysis
Gramm-Rudman Hollings (1985)	Eliminate the deficit by 1991	Set annual deficit targets; automatic spending cuts	Unrealistic goals; deficits increased
Budget Enforcement Act (1990)	Ensure new laws do not increase deficits	Caps on discretionary spending; "pay-as-you-go" financing	Deficits declined after 1992
Omnibus Budget Reconciliation Act (1993)	Cut deficit by $500 billion over 5 years	Make income tax more progressive; some spending cuts	Deficits declined significantly; strong economy
Balanced Budget Agreement (1997)	Balance the budget by 2002	Cut some entitlement spending; increase education spending; targeted tax cuts	Budget surpluses 1998–2001

Attempts To Control Deficits and Debt

Sharp increases in deficits and the debt in the 1980s led government officials to look for ways to control deficit spending. (These efforts are summarized in Figure 15.10 above.) One measure set annual deficit targets with the goal of eliminating the deficit completely within five years. Another set limits on discretionary spending and mandated that new spending required cuts elsewhere in the budget, an approach known as "pay-as-you-go" financing. A third attempted to trim the deficit with a combination of tax increases and spending cuts. Still another sought to balance the budget through spending cuts in entitlement programs. Some of these measures failed, and deficits actually increased. Others enjoyed only limited success. As a result, the government continues to struggle to control the national debt.

APPLICATION Making Inferences

B. Why is paying interest on the national debt considered mandatory spending?
Because the government must pay interest to the bondholders in order to maintain its good credit and to continue its ability to borrow.

DIFFERENTIATING INSTRUCTION

Struggling Readers

Compare Economic Information

Make sure that students understand that Figure 15.10 presents more detailed information about the deficit reduction efforts described in general in the paragraph that follows it. Encourage students to look for key phrases in the paragraph that are repeated in the chart in order to understand which budget acts are being described. Call on volunteers to summarize each of the budget actions in their own words.

Gifted and Talented

Create Fact Sheets

Encourage interested students to use the Internet to research more information about actions to control deficits and the debt, such as those described in Figure 15.10. Invite them to find out details about specific provisions of each law and reasons for its success or failure. Some may wish to see if there have been other measures taken since the return to deficit spending in 2002. Suggest that students create fact sheets on the law(s) they researched to share with the class.

Online Quiz
ClassZone.com

REVIEWING KEY CONCEPTS

1. Explain the difference between the terms in each of these pairs.
   a. *budget surplus* *budget deficit*
   b. *national debt* *deficit spending*
   c. *Treasury bills* *Treasury bonds*
2. How do budget deficits affect the national debt? Why?
3. What do Treasury bills, Treasury notes, and Treasury bonds have in common?
4. Why is government borrowing from trust funds different from privately-owned debt?
5. How is the crowding-out effect related to the national debt?
6. **Using Your Notes** What are the four causes of budget deficits? Refer to your completed chart.

Federal Deficits	National Debt

Use the Graphic Organizer at **Interactive Review @ ClassZone.com**

CRITICAL THINKING

7. **Applying Economic Concepts** In 2007, the federal government was expected to have tax revenue of $2,350.8 billion. Total federal spending was estimated at $2,592.1 billion. Would the government have a budget deficit or a budget surplus that year? How much would it be?
8. **Analyzing Causes** Each of the following headlines reflects an example of deficit spending. Which of the causes of budget deficits is suggested by each headline?
   a. President Proposes Tax Cut Extensions to Keep Economy on Track
   b. Baby Boomers' Retirement Will Strain Social Security and Medicare
   c. Hurricane Recovery Effort to Require Massive Federal Aid
9. **Analyzing Data** Assume that the privately-owned part of the debt is $4,900 billion and the amount held by government trust funds is $3,500 billion. Use the percentages shown in Figure 15.9 to calculate the dollar amounts held by different creditors.
10. **Challenge** The Social Security Administration estimates that annual revenue from payroll taxes will be insufficient to meet annual benefit payments beginning in 2018. The Social Security trust fund will be used to make up the difference. How will this change affect the nature of the national debt?

ECONOMICS IN PRACTICE

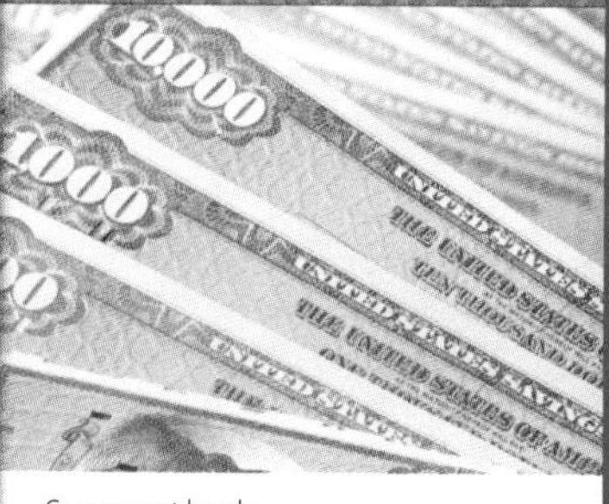

Government bonds

Applying Economic Concepts Recall what you learned about the crowding-out effect and then complete the following activities.

Analyze the Crowding-Out Effect The graph below shows the crowding-out effect in terms of supply and demand. Why would some private bond issuers be crowded out as a result of government borrowing?

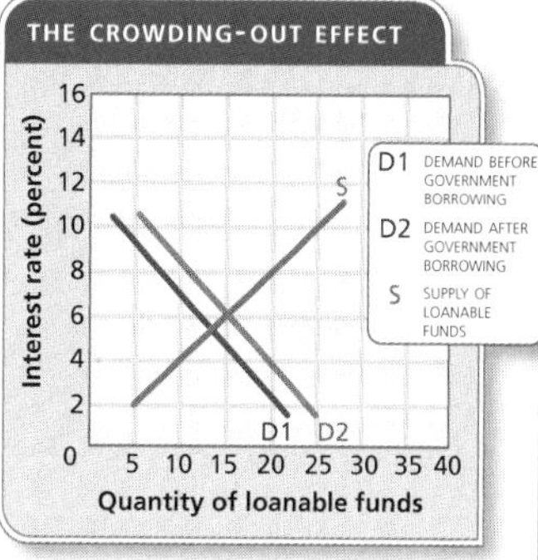

Challenge What part of the national debt might cause the crowding-out effect, the public-owned portion, the portion in government trust funds, or both? Explain your answer.

❹ Assess & Reteach

Assess Have students answer the questions in pairs, with one student responding to a question orally while his or her partner writes down the answer. Students switch roles and repeat the activity until all of the questions are answered.

Unit 6 Resource Book
- Section Quiz, p. 91

Interactive Review @ ClassZone.com
- Section Quiz

Test Generator CD-ROM
- Section Quiz

Reteach Have students write a question and answer that brings out an important idea from the section. Invite students to take turns asking their questions of the class.

Unit 6 Resource Book
- Reteaching Activity, p. 92

Economics in Practice

Analyze the Crowding-Out Effect They may be unable to pay the higher interest rate to bondholders and still remain solvent.

Challenge the portion held by the public, because that is the part that competes with private bond issuers for savers' dollars, although the portion held by government trust funds might lead to crowding out later when the trust funds cash in their debt

SECTION 3 ASSESSMENT ANSWERS

Reviewing Key Concepts

1. a. *budget surplus*, p. 462; *budget deficit*, p. 462
   b. *national debt*, p. 462; *deficit spending*, p. 462
   c. *Treasury bills*, p. 464; *Treasury bonds*, p. 464
2. Budget deficits add to the national debt because the debt is the sum of all budget deficits.
3. They are all types of federal government bonds that allow the government to borrow money.
4. It reflects surpluses in the trust funds that are invested in government securities, so it is more like transferring money from one part of the government to another rather than true borrowing.
5. As the national debt grows through increased borrowing there is more likelihood that government competition with the private sector for loanable funds will raise interest rates and crowd some private bond issuers out of the market.
6. See page 462 for an example of a completed chart. emergencies, demand for public goods, fiscal policy, government social programs

Critical Thinking

7. a deficit of $241.3 billion
8. a. using fiscal policy requiring deficit spending to stabilize the economy
   b. government's role as a provider of social programs that require large expenditures
   c. national emergencies that require government expenditure beyond the normal outlay of funds
9. Federal Reserve banks: $752 bil; Depository institutions: $131.6 bil; Savings bonds: $211.5 bil; Pension funds: $329 bil; Insurance companies: $159.8 bil; Mutual funds: $258.5 bil; State & local governments: $446.5 bil; Foreign investors: $2,068 bil; Other investors: $314.9 bil; Government trust funds: $3,400 bil
10. The share of the debt held by trust funds will decrease and the share held by the public will increase, as the government will need to borrow from the public to refinance the debt formerly held by the trust funds.

Economics in Practice
See answers in side column above.

1 Plan & Prepare

Objectives

- Evaluate various opinions about the size of the federal budget deficit.
- Draw conclusions about the size of the federal budget deficit.

2 Focus & Motivate

Invite students to discuss problems that can arise when an individual or a government lives beyond its means. Explain that this Case Study explores various opinions about the size of the federal budget deficit.

3 Teach

Using the Sources

Encourage students to examine each source to distinguish between facts and opinions about the budget deficit.

A. What is the major concern of economists with the government's continued deficit spending? *(that economic activity will slow because of higher borrowing costs for consumers and companies)*

B. What do you think the cartoonist's opinion is about how the government is handling the budget deficit? *(Possible answer: He thinks that government wants to look like it is reducing the deficit, but it keeps increasing spending.)*

C. Why do you think Secretary Snow says that the administration will not reconsider its tax policies? *(Possible answer: because raising taxes would be a way to reduce the deficit but is politically unpopular)*

Economics Update

Go to **ClassZone.com** to find an update to this Case Study, including another article, an editable student worksheet, and an editable lesson plan.

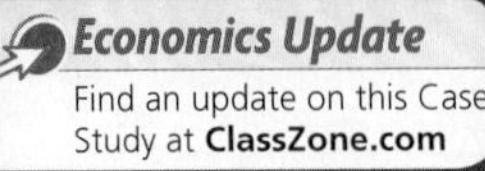

Case Study

Economics Update
Find an update on this Case Study at **ClassZone.com**

Is the Federal Deficit Too Large?

Background The federal deficit is a matter of interest not only to economists but also to the average American, because it is the taxpayer who ultimately pays the interest on the country's debt. This debt was created by pursuing a policy of deficit spending that requires the government to borrow money to make up the difference between how much it takes in and the amount it spends.

There are several reasons for using deficit spending. One major reason is the need to deal with national emergencies, such as the September 11 terrorist attacks or natural disasters like Hurricane Katrina. Another is to implement expansionary fiscal policies during periods of recession. Regardless of the reasons for deficit spending, the larger the deficit grows, the more controversial it becomes.

What's the issue? Is the federal deficit too large? Study these sources offering various opinions regarding what is a manageable federal deficit.

A. Online News Story

This article discusses a major problem that could arise from the government's continued deficit spending.

Federal Budget Deficit Sparks Worries

Higher Borrowing Costs Could Slow Economic Activity

. . . Here's the worry: Persistent deficits will lead to higher borrowing costs for consumers and companies, slowing economic activity. As Uncle Sam seeks to borrow . . . to finance those deficits, rates on Treasury securities would rise to entice investors. That would push up other interest rates, such as home mortgages, many auto loans, some home equity lines of credit and some credit cards. . . . For businesses, rates on corporate bonds would climb. It would become more expensive to borrow to pay for new plants and equipment and other capital investments.

Economists are troubled by the prospects of budget deficits as far as the eye can see and want to see them trimmed. But the size of the current budget deficits, while unwelcome, do not signal that a crisis is imminent. . . .

[But] there is more concern about higher borrowing costs over time crimping business investment and ultimately the production of goods and services. . . .

Yearly deficits add to the country's growing national debt.

Source: "Federal Budget Deficit Sparks Worries," Associated Press, January 15, 2006.

Thinking Economically What negative impact of deficit spending is discussed in this article?

DIFFERENTIATING INSTRUCTION

Struggling Readers

Summarize the Case Study
Have students work in pairs to write a short summary of what they have learned from this Case Study. Encourage students to write down the main ideas they want to include before composing their sentences. Ask students to share their summaries.

Gifted and Talented

Graph Deficit Trends
Encourage interested students to use online resources from the Office of Management and Budget or the Congressional Budget Office to research trends in the deficit since 2002. Ask students to create graphs showing the amount of the annual deficit in current and constant dollars (adjusted for inflation) and as a percentage of GDP. Allow students to present their graphs to the class. Ask them to assess how successful were government attempts to reduce the deficit.

B. Political Cartoon

Cartoonist Harley Schwadron made this comment about government spending.

BUREAU OF SPENDING INCREASES AND DEFICIT REDUCTION
SCHWADRON
"WAIT A MINUTE! HOW CAN THAT BE?"

Source: www.CartoonStock.com

Thinking Economically In what way is the statement on the bureau door contrary to valid economic principles?

C. Online News Story

In this article, former Secretary of the Treasury John Snow outlines the Bush administration's fiscal policy designed to reduce the federal deficit.

Setting Sights on the Deficit

Reducing the Deficit by Controlling Spending

The Bush administration's highest economic priority for its remaining three years is to control the growth of federal spending and bring down the U.S. budget deficit, John Snow, [former] U.S. Treasury secretary, said.

"The clear priority of the administration right now is the deficit, making sure that we achieve the president's objective of cutting the deficit in half by the time he leaves office," he said . . . This would put the deficit below 2 per cent of gross domestic product, low by historical standards. . . .

When he came to office in 2001, the president inherited a projected 10-year surplus of $5,600 billion. But tax cuts and growing spending for the military and homeland security have contributed to a sharp reversal, with the Congressional Budget Office now predicting a $2,100 billion deficit over the next decade. The annual deficit has been falling, however, from $413 billion in the 2004 fiscal year to $316 billion this year, according to CBO figures . . .

Mr. Snow made it clear that, in spite of the focus on the deficit, the administration would not reconsider its low tax policies.

Source: "U.S. Sets its Sights on Deficit," by Edward Alden, Andrew Balls and Holly Yeager. *Financial Times*, November 4, 2005.

Thinking Economically How does the Bush administration plan to cut the deficit by half in three years? What other steps might it take to control the deficit?

THINKING ECONOMICALLY **Synthesizing**

1. Identify the economic cause-and-effect relationships described in Documents A and C.
2. How does Document B illustrate the challenge facing the Bush administration in its efforts to carry out the plan discussed in Document C?
3. Do you think the Bush administration shares the concerns about the deficit expressed in Document A? Use information from the documents to explain your answer.

Thinking Economically

Answers

A. *crowding-out effect*

B. *As spending increases, the effect is likely to be an increase, rather than a reduction, in the deficit.*

C. *The plan is to control the growth of government spending. Other possible measures include mandatory spending cuts, "pay-as-you-go" spending, tax reforms, and tax increases.*

Synthesizing

1. *Document A: Financing deficits will drive up interest rates and make borrowing to pay for capital investment more expensive. Document C: Tax cuts and growing spending for the military and homeland security resulted in deficits.*
2. *The name of the office—Bureau of Spending Increases and Deficit Reduction—seems to describe the Bush Administration plan of continued tax cuts and increased military spending while making attempts to cut the deficit.*
3. *Answers will vary, but most students will suggest that the Bush Administration does not share these concerns because, in Document C, former Secretary of the Treasury John Snow seems convinced that the administration can bring federal spending under control in order to cut the deficit to historically low levels.*

TECHNOLOGY ACTIVITY

Creating a Multimedia Presentation

Time 45 Minutes

Task Research opinions about the federal budget deficit and create a multimedia presentation.

Materials Needed computer with Internet access, presentation software (optional)

Activity

- Assign groups of students to research various opinion pieces about the federal deficit. Suggest that students use the keywords "US budget deficit" to conduct online searches.
- Students may focus on mainstream print media, political cartoons, features from broadcast media, or postings from bloggers.
- Have groups collaborate on a multimedia presentation on the deficit. Encourage students to include critical analysis of the pieces that they research.

Rubric

	Understanding of Concepts	Presentation of Information
4	excellent	clear and complete
3	good	mostly clear
2	fair	sometimes clear
1	poor	sketchy

Online Summary Answers

1. Fiscal policy
2. Expansionary fiscal policy
3. Contractionary fiscal policy
4. Discretionary fiscal policy
5. automatic stabilizers
6. Keynesian economics
7. demand-side fiscal policy
8. spending multiplier effect
9. Supply-side fiscal policy
10. Laffer Curve
11. budget surplus
12. budget deficit
13. national debt
14. crowding-out effect

Interactive Review

Review this chapter using interactive activities at **ClassZone.com**

- Online Summary
- Quizzes
- Vocabulary Flip Cards
- Graphic Organizers
- Review and Study Notes

Online Summary

Complete the following activity either on your own paper or online at **ClassZone.com**

Choose the key concept that best completes the sentence. Not all key concepts will be used.

automatic stabilizers	fiscal policy
budget deficit	Keynesian economics
budget surplus	Laffer Curve
contractionary fiscal policy	national debt
Council of Economic Advisers	spending multiplier effect
crowding-out effect	supply-side fiscal policy
deficit spending	Treasury bills
demand-side fiscal policy	Treasury bonds
discretionary fiscal policy	Treasury notes
expansionary fiscal policy	trust funds

__1__ is the government's use of taxes and government spending to affect the economy. __2__ is a plan to stimulate a weak economy. __3__ is a plan to slow the economy when it is expanding too rapidly. __4__ refers to actions chosen by the government to stabilize the economy. Public transfer payments and progressive income taxes are examples of __5__.

__6__ is the idea that aggregate demand needed to be stimulated by government action. It forms the basis of __7__. The __8__ means that small changes in income cause a larger change in spending.

__9__ is fiscal policy that provides incentives to producers to increase aggregate supply. The __10__ illustrates how tax cuts affect tax revenues and economic growth.

A __11__ occurs when the government takes in more than it spends. When it spends more than it takes in __12__ occurs. The __13__ is the total amount of money owed to federal bondholders. The __14__ results when the government outbids private bond interest rates.

CHAPTER 15 Assessment

REVIEWING KEY CONCEPTS

What Is Fiscal Policy? (pp. 446–453)

1. What is the difference between expansionary fiscal policy and contractionary fiscal policy?
2. How do automatic stabilizers avoid the limitations that affect discretionary fiscal policy?

Demand-Side and Supply-Side Policies (pp. 454–461)

3. Why does Keynesian economics advocate government spending during a recession?
4. What economic problems does supply-side economics try to address simultaneously?

Deficits and the National Debt (pp. 462–469)

5. How does government finance deficit spending?
6. How does deficit spending contribute to the national debt?

APPLYING ECONOMIC CONCEPTS

Look at the bar graph below showing national debt as a percentage of GDP in several countries.

7. Which European countries on this graph have lower ratios of debt to GDP than the United States?
8. How does U.S. debt compare to Japan's debt as a percentage of GDP?

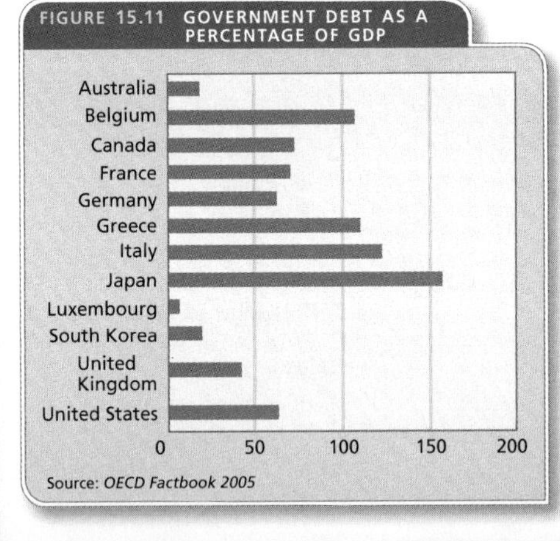

Source: *OECD Factbook 2005*

CHAPTER 15 ASSESSMENT ANSWERS

Reviewing Key Concepts

1. The goal of expansionary fiscal policy is to stimulate the economy and increase aggregate demand; the goal of contractionary fiscal policy is to slow the economy and fight inflation.
2. Automatic stabilizers work without the need of government action to counter the effects of the business cycle so there are no policy lags, timing issues, or political or regional considerations that delay their taking effect.
3. because the government is the only entity able to counteract decreased consumer and business spending in order to increase aggregate demand
4. high unemployment and high inflation
5. by borrowing money through the sale of government bonds
6. Each year that there is a budget deficit the national debt increases.

Applying Economic Concepts

7. United Kingdom and Luxembourg
8. It is less than half that of Japan's as a percentage of GDP.

Critical Thinking

9. Supply-side economics would expect tax revenues to fall less than the amount of the tax cut due to stronger incentives to work and invest. It is also possible that supply-side economics would expect the tax cut to increase tax revenues.
10. Answers will vary and should reflect an understanding of the multiplier effect as it applies to each student's spending patterns.
11. Since it takes several months to recognize that there is a problem and more time to agree on a plan and implement changes in government spending or taxes, the recession is likely to be ending by the time discretionary fiscal policy comes into play.

CRITICAL THINKING

9. **Analyzing Cause and Effect** In early 2001, the federal budget had shown surpluses for the previous three fiscal years and was predicted to continue to do so. The President and Congress thought the best thing to do was to return some of the surplus to taxpayers through tax cuts. How would supply-side economics describe the expected outcome of these tax cuts?
10. **Applying Economic Concepts** Suppose that you got a better job that increased your take-home pay each week from $250 to $300. Assume that you spent 80 percent of that increase. Give specific examples to show how your spending would create a multiplier effect.
11. **Drawing Conclusions** Recessions in 1990–1991 and in 2001 lasted about eight months each and were relatively mild in their effects on the overall economy. Why would policy lags limit the effectiveness of discretionary fiscal policy in bringing the country out of such recessions?
12. **Making Inferences** Between 1998 and 2001, the annual federal budgets showed surpluses, and the amount of national debt held by the public decreased by about $450 billion, yet the total federal debt grew by about $400 billion during that same time period. What do you think accounts for this difference?
13. **Challenge** In 1997, some members of Congress proposed a constitutional amendment that would require the federal budget to be balanced each year. Opponents argued that such an amendment would make recessions worse by requiring the government to use contractionary fiscal policy during such times. Why would a balanced budget require that kind of fiscal policy?

SIMULATION

Advise the President

Step 1 Form a team with two other students. Imagine that you are the Council of Economic Advisers whose job is to advise the president on the best fiscal policy to use in different economic situations. The current state of the economy is indicated by the following facts:

a. The unemployment rate has risen from 4.5 percent to 6 percent.

b. Automobile dealers, home improvement stores, and computer retailers have noted that their sales have dropped off sharply from the previous year.

c. Fewer houses and commercial buildings are being built.

Decide whether an expansionary or contractionary fiscal policy is needed.

Step 2 Develop some specific government spending and taxation recommendations to follow through with your decision in Step 1. Think about what kinds of federal spending you would increase or decrease and what kinds of taxes you would cut or increase to achieve your objectives.

Step 3 Some economic indicators have improved. However, the unemployment rate has not changed, and high energy costs have led to rapid increases in the Consumer Price Index. In light of this new information, recommend changes in fiscal policy to solve these problems.

Step 4 The economy seems to be back on track. However, annual budget deficits are getting larger each year, and there is concern about the growing national debt. Recommend some ways to control deficit spending without harming the economy.

Step 5 Present your policy suggestions to the rest of the class. As a class, discuss the differences and similarities among the plans offered by various groups.

McDougal Littell Assessment System

Assess

Online Test Practice
- Go to **ClassZone.com** for more test practice.

Unit 6 Resource Book
- Chapter Test, Forms A, B, & C, pp. 103–114

Test Generator CD-ROM
- Chapter Test, Forms (A, B, & C), in English and Spanish

Report

Use the McDougal Littell Assessment System to score assessments and receive customized reports.

Reteach

For activities customized for individual students, use the McDougal Littell Assessment System.

CHAPTER 15 ASSESSMENT ANSWERS

12. The government trust fund surpluses grew by about $850 billion during that same period and increased the part of the debt held by those funds.
13. A balanced budget amendment would require decreased government spending or increased taxes to try to counter the effects of less tax revenue that would come in during a recession. This contractionary fiscal policy would be the opposite of what is needed to bring the economy out of recession, which requires a budget deficit.

SIMULATION

Step 1 The economy is entering a recessionary period, so an expansionary fiscal policy is needed.

Step 2 Answers may vary. Most responses will involve some combination of demand-side policies, such as increased government spending and tax cuts.

Step 3 Answers may vary. Most responses will focus on some combination of supply-side policies, such as cuts in government spending, tax cuts, and deregulation of business.

Step 4 Answers may vary. Most responses will suggest some cuts in government spending and cautious tax increases.

Simulation Rubric

	Understanding of Concepts Involved	Presentation of Information
4	excellent	accurate, clear, and complete
3	good	mostly accurate and clear
2	fair	sometimes clear
1	poor	sketchy

Chapter 16: The Federal Reserve and Monetary Policy
Planning Guide

Resources 2Go Complete print resources all on one USB drive allow you to customize lessons.

Section Titles and Objectives	Unit 6 Resource Book and Workbooks	Assessment Resources
1 The Federal Reserve System pp. 474–479 • Examine the purpose and duties of a central bank • Identify the distinctive features of the Federal Reserve System • Explain the structure of the Federal Reserve System	**Unit 6 Resource Book** • Reading Study Guide, pp. 115–116 • RSG with Additional Support, pp. 117–119 • RSG with Additional Support (Spanish), pp. 120–122 • Economic Skills and Problem Solving Activity, pp. 155–156 • Readings in Free Enterprise: Gentle Ben, pp. 157–158	**Unit 6 Resource Book** • Section Quiz, p. 123 • Reteaching Activity, p. 124 **Test Generator CD-ROM** **Daily Test Practice Transparencies,** TT53
2 Functions of the Federal Reserve pp. 480–489 • Identify the services the Fed provides for the banking system • Explain how the Fed acts as a banker for the federal government • Describe the creation of money • Discuss what factors influence the money supply	**Unit 6 Resource Book** • Reading Study Guide, pp. 125–126 • RSG with Additional Support, pp. 127–129 • RSG with Additional Support (Spanish), pp. 130–132 • Math Skills Worksheet: Applying the Deposit Expansion Multiplier, p. 163 • Readings in Free Enterprise: Gentle Ben, pp. 157–158	**Unit 6 Resource Book** • Section Quiz, p. 133 • Reteaching Activity, p. 134 **Test Generator CD-ROM** **Daily Test Practice Transparencies,** TT54
3 Monetary Policy pp. 490–497 • Examine the Fed's tools for monetary policy • Explain how the Fed's monetary policy promotes growth and stability • Analyze the challenges the Fed faces in implementing its policy	**Unit 6 Resource Book** • Reading Study Guide, pp. 135–136 • RSG with Additional Support, pp. 137–139 • RSG with Additional Support (Spanish), pp. 140–142 • Economic Simulations: Monetary Policy: Balancing Short- and Long-Term Goals, pp. 161–162 **NCEE Student Activities** • The Federal Reserve System and Its Tools, pp. 61–64	**Unit 6 Resource Book** • Section Quiz, p. 143 • Reteaching Activity, p. 144 **Test Generator CD-ROM** **Daily Test Practice Transparencies,** TT55
4 Applying Monetary and Fiscal Policy pp. 498–505 • Describe how monetary and fiscal policy can coordinate to improve the economy • Understand how monetary and fiscal policy can work against each other • Identify other measures that can be used to manage the economy	**Unit 6 Resource Book** • Reading Study Guide, pp. 145–146 • RSG with Additional Support, pp. 147–149 • RSG with Additional Support (Spanish), pp. 150–152 • Economic Simulations: Monetary Policy: Balancing Short- and Long-Term Goals, pp. 161–162 • Case Study Resources: Misreading His Lips, pp. 159–160 **Test Practice and Review Workbook,** pp. 53–54	**Unit 6 Resource Book** • Section Quiz, p. 153 • Reteaching Activity, p. 154 • Chapter Test, (Forms A, B, & C), pp. 165–176 **Test Generator CD-ROM** **Daily Test Practice Transparencies,** TT56

Integrated Technology

No Time? To focus students on the most important content in this chapter, use Animated Economics, "Interactive Money Supply Curve," available in Resources 2Go.

Teacher Presentation Options

Presentation Toolkit

Power Presentation DVD-ROM

- Lecture Notes
- Interactive Review
- Media Gallery
- Animated Economics
- Review Game

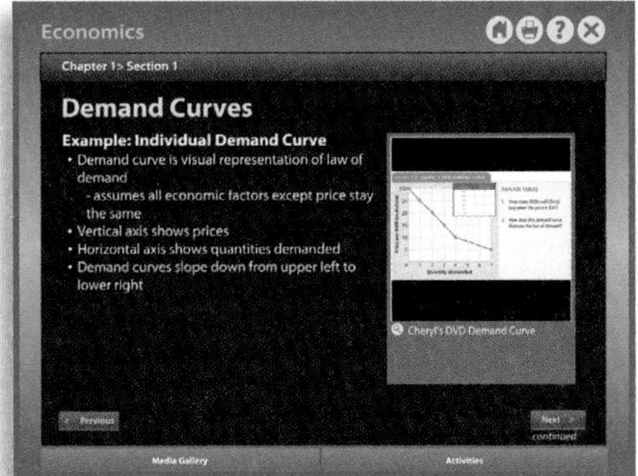

Economics Concepts Transparencies

- Federal Reserve System Structure CT53
- How the Fed Creates Money, CT54
- The Fed's Monetary Policy Tools, CT55
- How Monetary Policy Contributed to the Great Depression, CT56

Electronic Books

eEdition DVD-ROM

eEdition Online

Daily Test Practice Transparencies, TT53, TT54, TT55, TT56

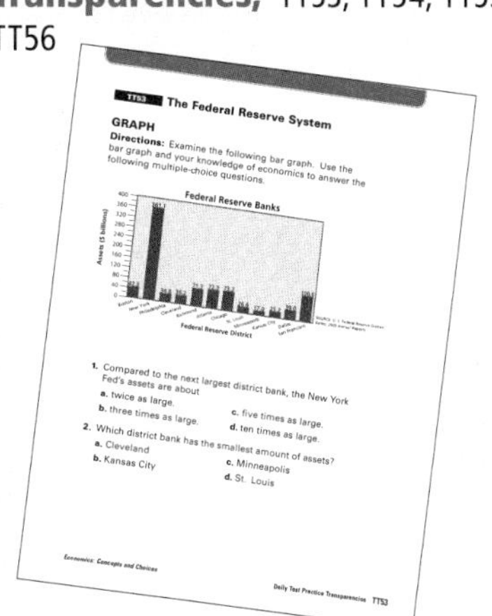

TT53 The Federal Reserve System

GRAPH

Directions: Examine the following bar graph. Use the bar graph and your knowledge of economics to answer the following multiple-choice questions.

1. Compared to the next largest district bank, the New York Fed's assets are about
   a. twice as large.
   b. three times as large.
   c. five times as large.
   d. ten times as large.
2. Which district bank has the smallest amount of assets?
   a. Cleveland
   b. Kansas City
   c. Minneapolis
   d. St. Louis

Economics: Concepts and Choices

Daily Test Practice Transparencies TT53

Animated Economics

- Interactive Money Supply Curve, p. 495

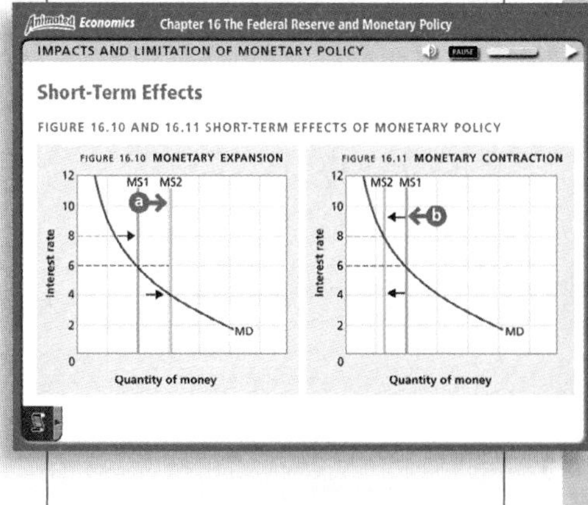

Online Activities at ClassZone.com

Economics Update

- Duties of the Fed, p. 475
- Fed's Role in the Sale of Government Securities, p. 482
- Alan Greenspan, p. 494
- Interpreting Signals from the Fed, p. 504

 Animated Economics

- Interactive Graphics

 Activity Maker

- Vocabulary Flip Cards
- Review Game

Research Center

- Graphs and Data

 Interactive Review

- Online Summary
- Quizzes
- Vocabulary Flip Cards
- Graphic Organizers
- Review and Study Notes

Teacher-Tested Activities

Name: Bill Smiley (ret.)
School: Leigh High School
State: California

Teacher-Tested Activities

At the beginning of this chapter, look for my classroom-proven idea for teaching economics concepts and thinking.

CHAPTER 16: The Federal Reserve and Monetary Policy

Resources for Differentiated Instruction

Struggling Readers

Teacher's Edition Activities

- Use Jigsaw Reading, p. 478
- Adjust Reading Rates, p. 482
- Locate Cause-and-Effect Words, p. 486
- Create a Venn Diagram, p. 488
- Diagram Cause and Effect, p. 492
- Identify Main Ideas, p. 496
- Organize Information, p. 502

Unit 6 Resource Book

- RSG with Additional Support, pp. 117–119, 127–129, 137–139, 147–149 (A)
- Reteaching Activities, pp. 124, 134, 144, 154 (B)
- Chapter Test (Form A), pp. 165–168 (C)

ClassZone.com

- Animated Economics
- Interactive Review

Test Generator CD-ROM

- Chapter Test (Form A)
- Chapter Test (Form A), in Spanish

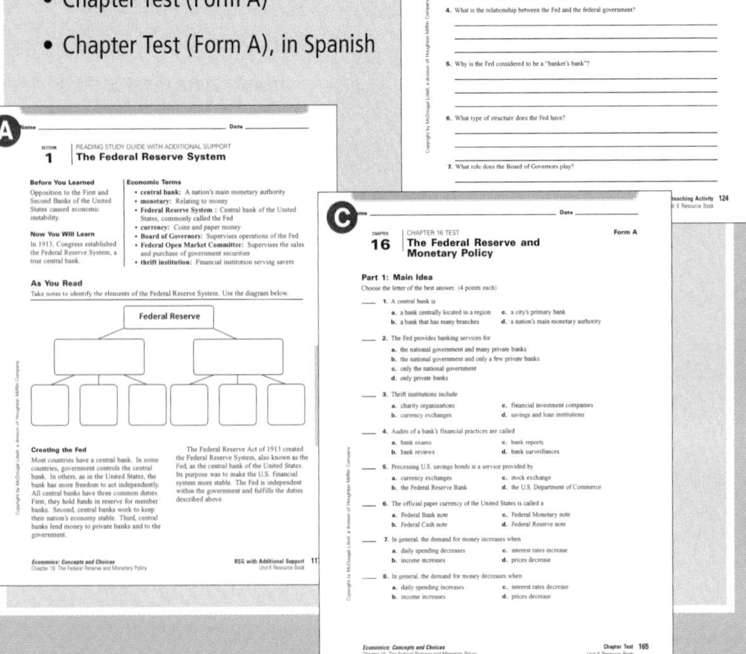

(A) Section 1 — Reading Study Guide with Additional Support — The Federal Reserve System

(C) Chapter 16 Test — The Federal Reserve and Monetary Policy — Form A

English Learners

Teacher's Edition Activities

- Understand Multiple Meaning Words, p. 476
- Build Economics Vocabulary, p. 484
- Summarize Information, p. 492
- Take Notes, p. 500
- Understand Colloquial English, p. 504

Unit 6 Resource Book

- RSG with Additional Support (Spanish), pp. 120–122, 130–132, 140–142, 150–152 (A)

Test Generator CD-ROM

- Chapter Test (Forms A, B, & C), in Spanish (B)

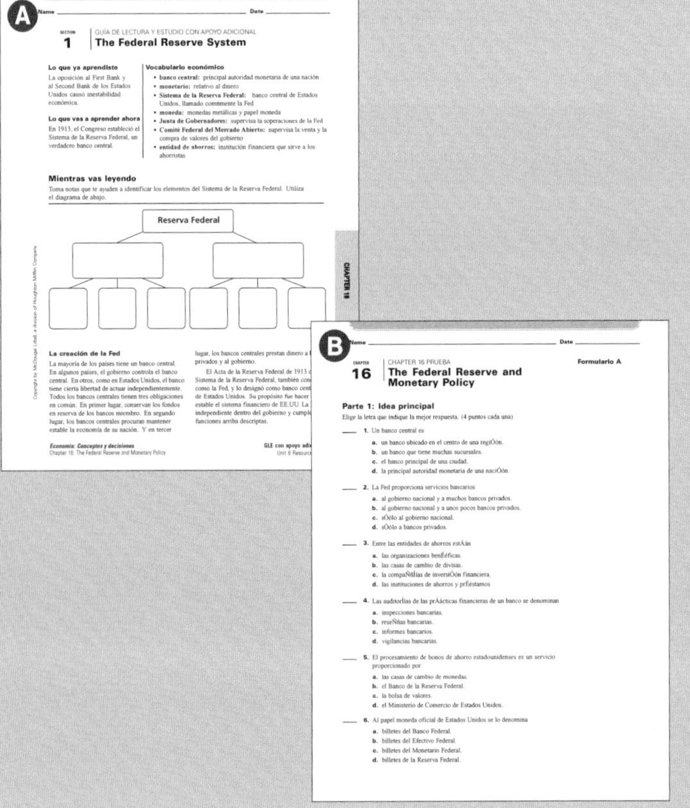

(B) Section 1 — Reteaching Activity — The Federal Reserve System

(A) Section 1 — Guía de lectura y estudio con apoyo adicional — The Federal Reserve System

(B) Capítulo 16 Prueba — The Federal Reserve and Monetary Policy — Formulario A

Inclusion

Teacher's Edition Activities

- Read the Map, p. 476
- Enlarge the Visual, p. 484
- Summarize Orally, p. 486
- Illustrate the Biography, p. 494
- Use Flash Cards, p. 496
- Manipulate Visuals, p. 500

Lesson Plans

- Modified Lessons for Inclusion, pp. 53–56 (A)

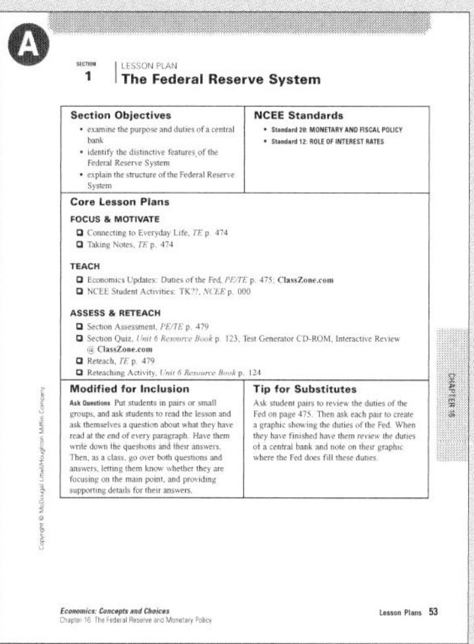

A

SECTION 1 | LESSON PLAN
The Federal Reserve System

Section Objectives
- examine the purpose and duties of a central bank
- identify the distinctive features of the Federal Reserve System
- explain the structure of the Federal Reserve System

NCEE Standards
- Standard 20: MONETARY AND FISCAL POLICY
- Standard 12: ROLE OF INTEREST RATES

Core Lesson Plans

FOCUS & MOTIVATE
- ❑ Connecting to Everyday Life, *TE* p. 474
- ❑ Taking Notes, *TE* p. 474

TEACH
- ❑ Economics Updates: Duties of the Fed, *PE/TE* p. 475; **ClassZone.com**
- ❑ NCEE Student Activities: TK??, *NCEE* p. 000

ASSESS & RETEACH
- ❑ Section Assessment, *PE/TE* p. 479
- ❑ Section Quiz, *Unit 6 Resource Book* p. 123, Test Generator CD-ROM, Interactive Review @ **ClassZone.com**
- ❑ Reteach, *TE* p. 479
- ❑ Reteaching Activity, *Unit 6 Resource Book* p. 124

Modified for Inclusion

Ask Questions Put students in pairs or small groups, and ask students to read the lesson and ask themselves a question about what they have read at the end of every paragraph. Have them write down the questions and their answers. Then, as a class, go over both questions and answers, letting them know whether they are focusing on the main point, and providing supporting details for their answers.

Tip for Substitutes

Ask student pairs to review the duties of the Fed on page 475. Then ask each pair to create a graphic showing the duties of the Fed. When they have finished have them review the duties of a central bank and note on their graphic where the Fed does fill these duties.

CHAPTER 16

Economics: Concepts and Choices
Chapter 16 The Federal Reserve and Monetary Policy
Lesson Plans 53

Gifted and Talented

Teacher's Edition Activities

- Research the Structure of the Fed, p. 478
- Develop Handouts, p. 482
- Create an Organizational Chart, p. 488
- Evaluate Greenspan's Policies, p. 494
- Analyze Policies, p. 502
- Write a Biography, p. 504

Unit 6 Resource Book

- Readings in Free Enterprise: Gentle Ben, pp. 157–158 (A)
- Case Study Resources: Misreading His Lips, pp. 159–160 (B)

NCEE Student Activities

- The Federal Reserve System and Its Tools, p. 61–64 (C)

ClassZone.com

- Research Center

Test Generator CD-ROM

- Chapter Test (Form C)
- Chapter Test (Form C), in Spanish

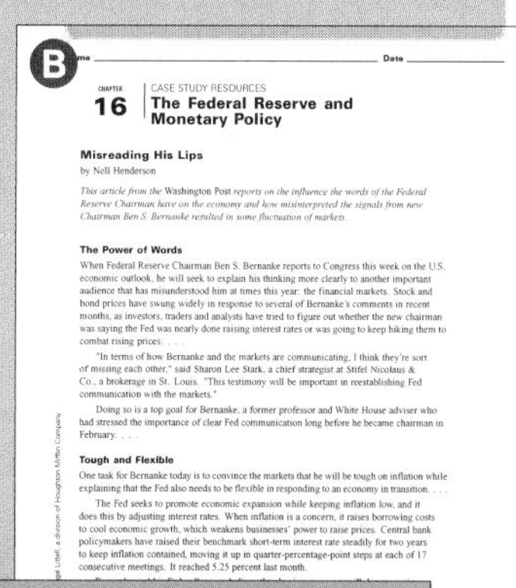

B

Name ______________________ Date ____________

CHAPTER 16 | CASE STUDY RESOURCES
The Federal Reserve and Monetary Policy

Misreading His Lips
by Nell Henderson

This article from the Washington Post *reports on the influence the words of the Federal Reserve Chairman have on the economy and how misinterpreted the signals from new Chairman Ben S. Bernanke resulted in some fluctuation of markets.*

The Power of Words

When Federal Reserve Chairman Ben S. Bernanke reports to Congress this week on the U.S. economic outlook, he will seek to explain his thinking more clearly to another important audience that has misunderstood him at times this year: the financial markets. Stock and bond prices have swung widely in response to several of Bernanke's comments in recent months, as investors, traders and analysts have tried to figure out whether the new chairman was saying the Fed was nearly done raising interest rates or was going to keep hiking them to combat rising prices. . . .

"In terms of how Bernanke and the markets are communicating, I think they're sort of missing each other," said Sharon Lee Stark, a chief strategist at Stifel Nicolaus & Co., a brokerage in St. Louis. "This testimony will be important in reestablishing Fed communication with the markets."

Doing so is a top goal for Bernanke, a former professor and White House adviser who had stressed the importance of clear Fed communication long before he became chairman in February. . . .

Tough and Flexible

One task for Bernanke today is to convince the markets that he will be tough on inflation while explaining that the Fed also needs to be flexible in responding to an economy in transition. . . .

The Fed seeks to promote economic expansion while keeping inflation low, and it does this by adjusting interest rates. When inflation is a concern, it raises borrowing costs to cool economic growth, which weakens businesses' power to raise prices. Central bank policymakers have raised their benchmark short-term interest rate steadily for two years to keep inflation contained, moving it up in quarter-percentage-point steps at each of 17 consecutive meetings. It reached 5.25 percent last month.

Study Resources 159
6 Resource Book

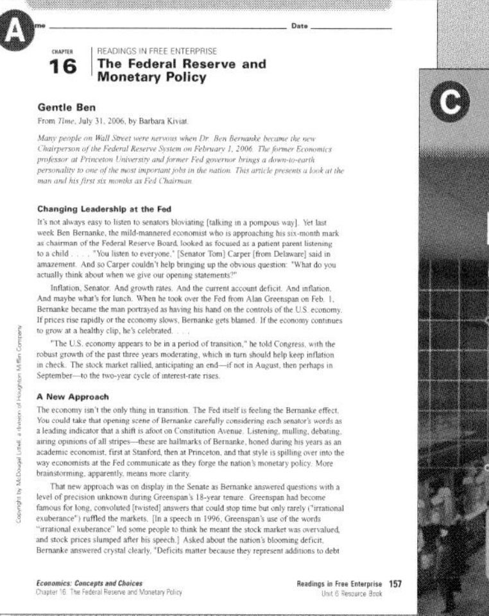

A

Name ______________________ Date ____________

CHAPTER 16 | READINGS IN FREE ENTERPRISE
The Federal Reserve and Monetary Policy

Gentle Ben
From *Time*, July 31, 2006, by Barbara Kiviat.

Many people on Wall Street were nervous when Dr. Ben Bernanke became the new Chairperson of the Federal Reserve System on February 1, 2006. The former Economics professor at Princeton University and former Fed governor brings a down-to-earth personality to one of the most important jobs in the nation. This article presents a look at the man and his first six months as Fed Chairman.

Changing Leadership at the Fed

It's not always easy to listen to senators bloviating [talking in a pompous way]. Yet last week Ben Bernanke, the mild-mannered economist who is approaching his six-month mark as chairman of the Federal Reserve Board, looked as focused as a patient parent listening to a child . . . . "You listen to everyone," [Senator Tom] Carper [from Delaware] said in amazement. And so Carper couldn't help bringing up the obvious question: "What do you actually think about when we give our opening statements?"

Inflation, Senator. And growth rates. And the current account deficit. And inflation. And maybe what's for lunch. When he took over the Fed from Alan Greenspan on Feb. 1, Bernanke became the man portrayed as having his hand on the controls of the U.S. economy. If prices rise rapidly or the economy slows, Bernanke gets blamed. If the economy continues to grow at a healthy clip, he's celebrated. . . .

"The U.S. economy appears to be in a period of transition," he told Congress, with the robust growth of the past three years moderating, which in turn should help keep inflation in check. The stock market rallied, anticipating an end—if not in August, then perhaps in September—to the two-year cycle of interest-rate rises.

A New Approach

The economy isn't the only thing in transition. The Fed itself is feeling the Bernanke effect. You could take that opening scene of Bernanke carefully considering each senator's words as a leading indicator that a shift is afoot on Constitution Avenue. Listening, mulling, debating, airing opinions of all stripes—these are hallmarks of Bernanke, honed during his years as an academic economist, first at Stanford, then at Princeton, and that style is spilling over into the way economists at the Fed communicate as they forge the nation's monetary policy. More brainstorming, apparently, means more clarity.

That new approach was on display in the Senate as Bernanke answered questions with a level of precision unknown during Greenspan's 18-year tenure. Greenspan had become famous for long, convoluted [twisted] answers that could stop time but only rarely ("irrational exuberance") ruffled the markets. [In a speech in 1996, Greenspan's use of the words "irrational exuberance" led some people to think he meant the stock market was overvalued, and stock prices slumped after his speech.] Asked about the nation's blooming deficit, Bernanke answered crystal clearly. "Deficits matter because they represent additions to debt

Economics: Concepts and Choices
Chapter 16 The Federal Reserve and Monetary Policy
Readings in Free Enterprise 157
Unit 6 Resource Book

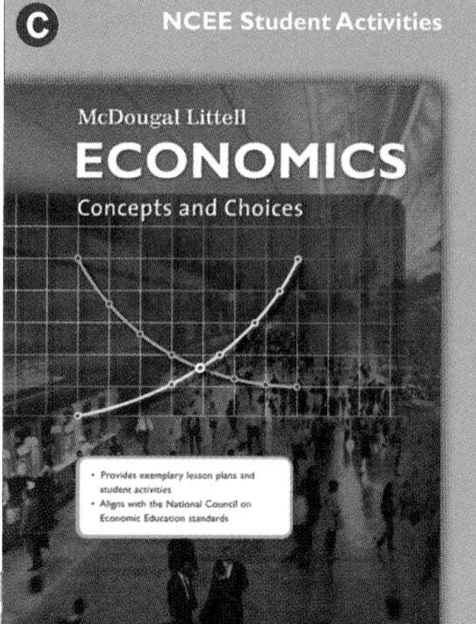

CHAPTER 16

Focus & Motivate

Objective

Describe the role of the Federal Reserve in stabilizing the economy.

Why the Concept Matters

Invite students to recall what they learned in Chapter 15 about extremes in the business cycle and how the government uses fiscal policy to moderate these extremes. Explain that monetary policy seeks to achieve similar goals through controlling the money supply.

Analyzing the Photograph

Have students study the photograph and read the caption. Invite a volunteer to describe what the photograph shows. *(Possible answer: large bundles of $100 bills worth $10,000 each)*

Ask students what the caption tells them about the Federal Reserve. *(Possible response: It distributes currency and controls the money supply.)* Explain that distributing currency is just one of many jobs performed by the Federal Reserve to help the economy operate smoothly. In Chapter 16, students will also learn about the other duties the Federal Reserve performs and how its management of the money supply helps control inflation and promote economic growth.

The Money Supply
Paper currency—an important part of the money supply—is distributed by the Federal Reserve.

472

CONTENT STANDARDS

NCEE STANDARDS

Standard 20: Monetary and Fiscal Policy

Students will understand that
Federal government budgetary policy and the Federal Reserve System's monetary policy influence the overall levels of employment, output, and prices.

Students will be able to use this knowledge to
Anticipate the impact of federal government and Federal Reserve System macroeconomic policy decisions on themselves and others.

Benchmarks
Students will know that

- The major monetary policy tool that the Federal Reserve System uses is open market purchases or sales of government securities. Other policy tools used by the Federal Reserve System include increasing or decreasing the discount rate charged on loans it makes to commercial banks and raising or lowering reserve requirements for commercial banks. *(pages 477–478, 482, 484–485, 490–493, 498–500, 502)*
- Monetary policies are decisions by the Federal Reserve System that lead to changes in the supply of money and the availability of credit. Changes in the money supply can influence overall levels of spending, employment, and prices in the economy by inducing changes in interest rates charged for credit, and by affecting the levels of personal and business investment spending. *(pages 490–496, 498–502)*

CHAPTER

16

The Federal Reserve and Monetary Policy

CONCEPT REVIEW

Fiscal policy is the federal government's use of taxes and government spending to affect the economy. It has one of two goals: to decrease unemployment or to fight inflation.

CHAPTER 16 KEY CONCEPT

Monetary policy includes all the Federal Reserve actions that change the money supply in order to influence the economy. Its purpose is to curb inflation or to reduce economic stagnation or recession.

WHY THE CONCEPT MATTERS

All economies experience the business cycle, a series of periods of growing and shrinking economic activity. Sometimes, these ups and downs become extreme, and the government takes action to even out the business cycle. The government has many tools available to do this—monetary policy is one of the most important.

Online Highlights

More at ClassZone.com

Economics Update

Go to ECONOMICS UPDATE for chapter updates and current news on monetary policy. (See Case Study, pp. 504–505).

Animated Economics

Go to ANIMATED ECONOMICS for interactive lessons on the graphs and tables in this chapter. ▶

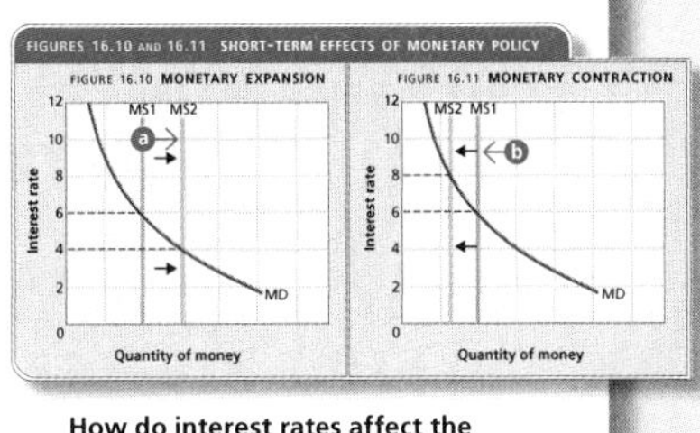

How do interest rates affect the demand for money? See Figures 16.10 and 16.11 on page 495.

Interactive Review

Go to INTERACTIVE REVIEW for concept review and activities.

From the Classroom

Bill Smiley, Leigh High School (retired)

Determining Monetary Policy

Divide students into small groups in which they assume the role of the Board of Governors of the Federal Reserve. Explain that they must decide what actions to take in response to an increase in inflation during a period of continued unemployment. They should use the following criteria to assist them in determining the appropriate monetary policy: How will their policy affect inflation? unemployment? commercial banks and other financial institutions? the American consumer? Ask the groups to record the specific effects of their monetary policy on the American economy and the reasons why their policy would be effective in addressing the problem. Finally, have each group report its conclusions to the entire class.

Previewing Chapter Technology at ClassZone.com

Economics Update Students will find references to online articles or statistics that update information in the pupil edition on pages 475, 482, 494, and 504.

Animated Economics Students will find interactive lessons related to material on page 495.

Interactive Review Students will find additional section and chapter assessment support for materials on pages 479, 489, 497, 503, and 506.

TEACHER MEDIA FAVORITES

Books

- Langdana, Farrokh K. *Macroeconomic Policy: Demystifying Monetary and Fiscal Policy*. New York: Springer, 2002. Connections between monetary and fiscal policy explained in news stories.
- Mayer, Martin. *The Fed: The Inside Story of How the World's Most Powerful Financial Institution Drives Markets*. New York: Free Press, 2001. Overview of the history and workings of the Fed.
- Rockoff, Hugh. *Drastic Measure: A History of Wage and Price Controls in the United States*. New York: Cambridge UP, 1984. Examines the effects of wage and price controls and their relationship to monetary policy.
- Sicilia, David B., and Jeffery L. Cruikshank. *The Greenspan Effect: Words That Move the World's Markets*. New York: McGraw-Hill, 2000. Analysis of Alan Greenspan's speeches and writings that tracks their effects on the stock market.

Videos/DVDs

- *Monetary Policy/Stabilization Policy*. Two 30-minute programs. Economics USA, 2002. Addresses concepts and issues using a TV-news format.
- *The Federal Reserve/Stagflation*. Two 30-minute programs. Economics USA, 2002. Explores key topics and issues.

Software

- *Virtual Economics® Version 3.0*. New York: National Council on Economic Education, 2005.

Internet

Visit **ClassZone.com** to link to

- a variety of chapter-specific, content-reviewed sites
- updates on data and topics presented throughout the chapter sections and Case Study
- updates to the Power Presentation

1 Plan & Prepare

Section 1 Objectives

- examine the purpose and duties of a central bank
- identify the distinctive features of the Federal Reserve System
- explain the structure of the Federal Reserve System

2 Focus & Motivate

Connecting to Everyday Life Explain that this section focuses on the central bank of the United States, which is called the Federal Reserve System. Ask students to suggest some reasons why a country might want to have a central bank.

Taking Notes Remind students to take notes as they read by completing a cluster diagram on the Federal Reserve System. They can use the Graphic Organizer at **Interactive Review @ ClassZone.com**. A sample is shown below.

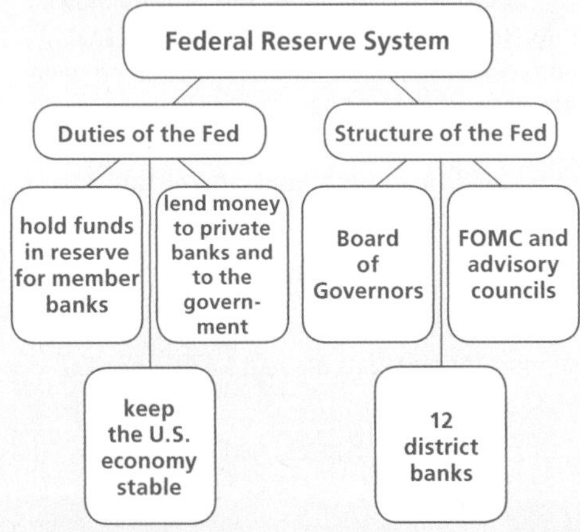

SECTION 1

The Federal Reserve System

OBJECTIVES

In Section 1, you will
- examine the purpose and duties of a central bank
- identify the distinctive features of the Federal Reserve System
- explain the structure of the Federal Reserve System

KEY TERMS

central bank, *p. 474*
monetary, *p. 474*
Federal Reserve System, *p. 474*
currency, *p. 475*
Board of Governors, *p. 476*
Federal Open Market Committee, *p. 477*
thrift institution, *p. 478*

TAKING NOTES

As you read Section 1, complete a cluster diagram to identify the major characteristics of the Federal Reserve System. Use the Graphic Organizer at **Interactive Review @ ClassZone.com**

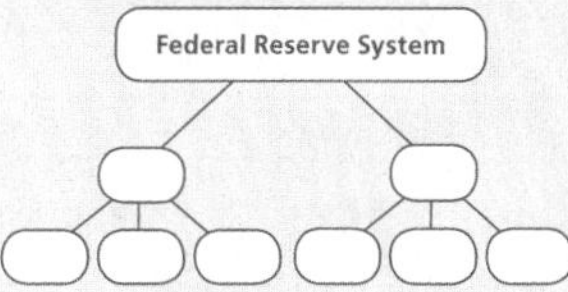

Creating the Fed

QUICK REFERENCE

A **central bank** is a nation's main monetary authority.

Monetary is a term that means "relating to money."

The **Federal Reserve System** is the central bank of the United States.

KEY CONCEPTS

As you recall from Chapter 10, there were times when the U.S. economy suffered from panics and banking was very unstable. The government made many efforts to address this problem, but had only limited success. Perhaps the most far-reaching of these efforts to stabilize the American financial system was the passage of the Federal Reserve Act in 1913. This act created a central bank for the United States. A **central bank** is a nation's main monetary authority, which is able to conduct certain monetary practices. (**Monetary** means "relating to money.") The **Federal Reserve System** is the central bank of the United States and is commonly called the Fed. The Fed is an independent organization within the government, which has both public and private characteristics.

The Duties of a Central Bank

Most countries have a central bank to oversee their banking system. The central bank may be owned and controlled by the government or it may have considerable political independence. There are three common duties that all central banks perform: holding reserves, assuring stability of the banking and monetary systems, and lending money to banks and the government.

Holding Reserves Central banks are sometimes called reserve banks. You learned in Chapter 10 that banks lend only a part of their funds to individuals and businesses and keep the rest in reserve. The central bank holds these reserves to influence the amount of loanable funds banks have available. This allows the central bank to control the money supply.

SECTION 1 PROGRAM RESOURCES

ON LEVEL

Lesson Plans
- Core, p. 53

Unit 6 Resource Book
- Reading Study Guide, pp. 115–116
- Economic Skills and Problem Solving Activity, pp. 155–156
- Section Quiz, p. 123

STRUGGLING READERS

Unit 6 Resource Book
- Reading Study Guide with Additional Support, pp. 117–119
- Reteaching Activity, p. 124

ENGLISH LEARNERS

Unit 6 Resource Book
- Reading Study Guide with Additional Support (Spanish), pp. 120–122

INCLUSION

Lesson Plans
- Modified for Inclusion, p. 53

GIFTED AND TALENTED

Unit 6 Resource Book
- Readings in Free Enterprise: Gentle Ben, pp. 157–158

TECHNOLOGY

eEdition DVD-ROM

eEdition Online

Power Presentation DVD-ROM

Economics Concepts Transparencies
- CT53 The Structure of the Federal Reserve System

Daily Test Practice Transparencies, TT53

ClassZone.com

Assuring Stability The central bank also acts to assure stability in the national banking and monetary systems. For example, it is one of the banking regulatory agencies that regulate and supervise banks to make sure that they act in ways that serve the interests of depositors and of the economy. Also, by controlling the way money is issued and circulated, the central bank attempts to avoid the confusion that might result when individual banks issue their own bank notes.

Lending Money The final duty of the central bank involves one of the primary functions of all banks—it lends money. Its lending practices are unlike those other banks, however. It does not seek to make a profit through lending, and it serves private banks and the government rather than individual customers and businesses.

Creating the Fed President Woodrow Wilson proposed the Federal Reserve Act, in part, to break the power of the nation's biggest banks.

The Duties of the Fed

With the passage of the Federal Reserve Act of 1913, Congress created the first national bank in the United States that could truly fulfill the duties of a central bank. The Fed supervises banking in the United States by providing regulation and oversight to make sure that banks follow sound practices in their operations. The Fed also takes steps to ensure that banks do not defraud customers and works to protect consumers' rights as they relate to borrowing money.

Like all central banks, the Fed provides banking services for both private banks and the national government. It accepts and holds deposits in the form of cash reserves, transfers funds between banks or between banks and the government, and makes loans to these institutions. Because it performs such functions, the Fed is sometimes referred to as the bankers' bank.

This responsibility of the Fed is especially important in times of emergency. Shortly after the Fed was created, it played a major role in financing U.S. involvement in World War I by purchasing government war bonds. The Fed also took emergency action after the terrorist attacks on New York City and Washington, D.C. in 2001. It issued $45 billion in loans to banks throughout the United States in order to ensure that there would be as little disruption to the banking system as possible in light of the destruction in these cities.

The Fed also distributes **currency**, which is coins and paper money, and regulates the supply of money. The supply of money does not mean actual cash but all available sources of money. Specifically, the amount of money that banks have available to lend has important effects on the whole economy. You will learn more about these functions of the Fed in Section 2.

Economics Update

Find an update on the duties of the Fed at **ClassZone.com**

QUICK REFERENCE

Currency is coins and paper money.

APPLICATION Comparing and Contrasting

A. Recall what you learned about the structure and functions of commercial banks in Chapter 10. What are the similarities and differences between the Federal Reserve and a commercial bank? All banks take deposits and make loans. However, Fed does not seek to make profit as commercial bank does; Fed's customers are other banks and government,

3 Teach

Creating the Fed

Discuss

- Why did Congress pass the Federal Reserve Act of 1913? *(to create a central bank that could help stabilize the financial system)*
- Why is the Federal Reserve called the bankers' bank? *(because it holds reserves for banks, transfers funds between banks, and lends money to banks)*

Technomics

The Federal Reserve Online

The home page of the Federal Reserve Board of Governors Web site <www. federalreserve.gov> is the best place to start when researching information about the Fed. The page contains links to recent speeches and other breaking news along with recent statistical releases.

The link "About the Fed" leads to in-depth information about the Federal Reserve Board, including FAQs, the Federal Reserve System, and other central banks. Links connect to the Web sites of each of the Federal Reserve district banks and to educational sites sponsored by the Fed. There are also links to related U.S. government Web sites.

Economics Update

At **ClassZone.com** students will see updated information on the duties of the Fed.

LEVELED ACTIVITY

Analyzing the Federal Reserve

Time 45 Minutes

Objective Students will demonstrate an understanding of how the Federal Reserve fulfills the purpose and duties of a central bank. (This activity also draws on material from Sections 2 and 3.)

Basic

Use the information in the textbook to answer the following questions: Who runs the Federal Reserve? What are its main duties? When was it established? Where is the Fed located? Why does the Fed act to control the money supply? How does the Fed do that? Present the information in a graphic organizer.

On Level

Locate a news story about Federal Reserve decisions that affect interest rates. Write a background article that explains which part of the Fed structure is taking the action. Discuss how the Fed's actions show that it is fulfilling its purpose as a central bank and describe how these actions affect the economy.

Challenge

Research the history of the Federal Reserve System. Write an essay tracing important changes in the central bank over time. Give special emphasis to changes in the Fed's approach to monetary policy and periods when the Fed's actions had an especially significant impact on economic stability.

The Structure of the Fed

Discuss

- What is the role of the Board of Governors of the Federal Reserve? *(It sets Fed policy and makes up 7 of the 12 members of the Federal Open Market Committee.)*
- How do member banks provide funding for the Fed? *(They purchase stock in their Federal Reserve district bank.)*

Analyzing Charts: Figure 16.1

Point out how the FOMC is made up of the whole Board of Governors plus 5 of the 12 district bank presidents at any one time. Explain that the president of the New York Fed is always one of the members, but the other four places are rotating positions. Ask students how they think member banks play a role in Fed policy. *(Possible answer: Officers of member banks may serve on advisory councils or communicate their concerns to their district bank president, who in turn provides input on the FOMC.)*

The Structure of the Fed

KEY CONCEPTS

The Fed is different from most countries' central banks because it is not a single national bank but has both a national and a regional structure. This structure represents a compromise between power resting at the regional level and at the national level. As you may recall from Chapter 10, many U.S. citizens were hesitant to give too much power to a national bank. In addition, the United States is a large and economically diverse country with a complex banking system.

Elements of the Fed

The elements that make up the Fed reflect this balance between national and regional authority. An appointed board sets national Fed policy, and a regional system of district banks carries out this policy and performs the duties of the central bank. This approach gives the Fed some independence from political influence. Even so, the Fed is ultimately accountable to Congress. Figure 16.1 shows how the Fed is organized.

QUICK REFERENCE

The **Board of Governors** supervises the operations of the Fed.

Board of Governors The **Board of Governors** is a board of seven appointed members who supervise the operations of the Fed and set policy. The president appoints members for a single 14-year term, with the approval of the Senate. One board member's term expires every two years, and the president may also appoint replacements to fill vacancies created by members who leave before the end of their terms. The president chooses the chairman and vice-chairman, who serve four-year terms, from among

FIGURE 16.1 STRUCTURE OF THE FED

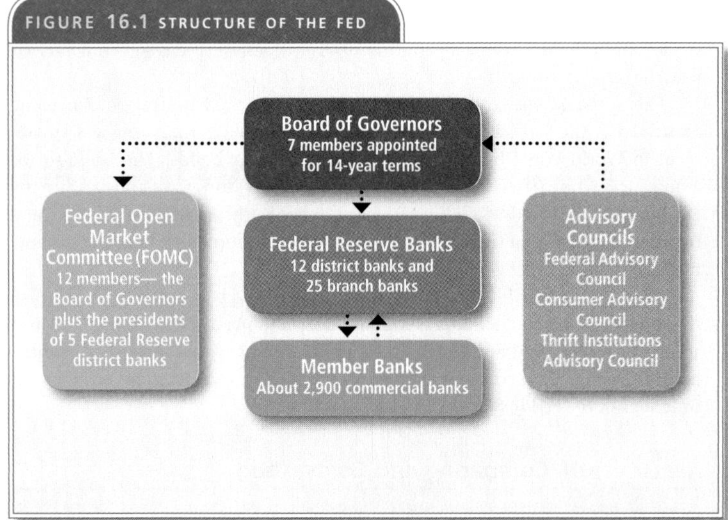

DIFFERENTIATING INSTRUCTION

English Learners

Understand Multiple Meaning Words

Invite students to use context clues to understand the meaning of the word *board,* as it relates to the Federal Reserve. Call on volunteers to state the meaning in their own words. Explain that this word is frequently used by various organizations to refer to a group of people who oversee the organization and set policy. Point out that this word commonly refers to a piece of sawed wood, generally longer than it is wide.

Inclusion

Read the Map

Have pairs study the map of the Federal Reserve System on page 477. Suggest that students compare the map to the United States political map on pages A2–A3 in the Atlas at the front of their textbook to help them answer the following questions: In what city is the Board of Governors located? *(Washington, D.C.)* The district headed by what city covers the most states? *(San Francisco)* How many states does that district serve? *(nine states)* Discuss results as a group.

the seven members. The chairman is considered the most influential member and is the spokesperson for the board. Alan Greenspan, who held the position for nearly 20 years, was so influential as Fed chairman that he almost came to personify the institution. (You can read more about Alan Greenspan on page 494.)

Twelve District Banks The Federal Reserve System is organized into 12 districts. Figure 16.2 shows these districts and the cities where the Federal Reserve district banks and the offices of the Board of Governors are located. While the district banks are responsible for carrying out the national policy set forth by the Board of Governors, each one also serves the needs of its particular region.

FIGURE 16.2 FEDERAL RESERVE DISTRICTS

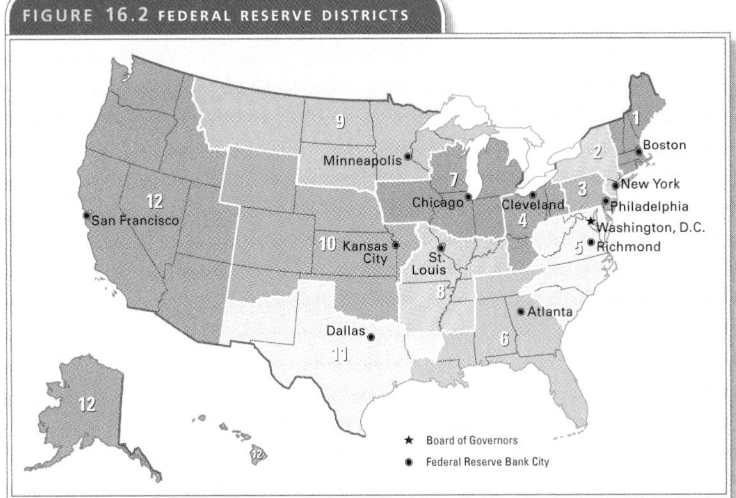

Member Banks All nationally chartered banks automatically are members of the Federal Reserve System. State-chartered banks, if they wish, may apply to join the Fed. In 2004, there were about 2,000 national bank members and 900 state bank members, about 37 percent of all commercial banks.

Each member bank must purchase stock in its Federal Reserve district bank. However, this stock ownership is not the same as ownership of stock in a private corporation or a commercial bank. It may not be bought or sold on the open market. Member banks earn a set dividend rate on the stock they hold. This helps to make up for the interest they do not earn on the reserves that the Fed requires them to hold. (See the information on reserve requirements on page 484.)

Federal Open Market Committee The **Federal Open Market Committee (FOMC)** is a board of the Fed that supervises the sale and purchase of federal government securities. The term *open market* refers to the way that government securities are bought and sold. The FOMC consists of 12 voting members, including the Board of Governors, the president of the Federal Reserve Bank of New York, and four other Fed district bank presidents who take turns serving one-year terms. All Fed bank presidents attend the meetings and provide input even when they have no vote.

QUICK REFERENCE

The **Federal Open Market Committee (FOMC)** supervises the sales and purchase of government securities.

Analyzing Maps: Figure 16.2

Have students identify the locations of Federal Reserve headquarters and the 12 district banks. Point out that the sizes of the districts reflect the distribution of population and banking activity when the Fed was created. For example, in 1913, the San Francisco district held fewer people than the Boston district. Now, the San Francisco district is the most populous district, with almost four times as many people as the Boston district. District banks have added branches to serve their increased populations.

More About . . .

The Federal Reserve Bank of New York

The New York Fed carries out the same duties as the other district banks but also has some unique responsibilities. The Open Market Trading Desk monitors bank reserves and carries out the necessary open market trades in U.S. Treasury securities to ensure that the federal funds rate target set by the FOMC is met. (See page 490.)

For this reason, the New York Fed president is a permanent member of the FOMC and usually is its vice chairman. The New York Fed also carries out foreign exchange operations for the Federal Reserve, the U.S. Treasury, and other central banks. It stores monetary gold for more than 60 countries, about one-fourth of the world's supply.

SMALL GROUP ACTIVITY

Creating Posters

Time 45 Minutes

Task Research a Federal Reserve district bank and create a poster.

Materials Needed computer with Internet access, poster board and markers

Activity

- Organize students into 12 groups and assign each to research one Federal Reserve district bank. Each bank maintains a Web site that provides information about the bank and the services it provides.
- Advise students to define the area served, find out the main duties performed by the bank, and determine how it serves its region. Encourage them to look for something that is unique about their bank.
- Display the posters in the classroom and invite volunteers from each group to present information on their district.
- Discuss the similarities and differences among the banks.

Rubric

	Understanding of Concepts	Presentation of Information
4	excellent	clear and complete
3	good	mostly clear
2	fair	sometimes clear
1	poor	sketchy

A Global Perspective

Comparing Central Banks
The Bank for International Settlements (BIS) serves as a bank for central banks and other international financial organizations. The BIS, established in 1930, is headquartered in Basel, Switzerland. Other offices are located in Hong Kong and Mexico City. It helps its customers carry out international transactions and provides a forum to discuss issues of interest to the international financial community.

The central banks of 55 countries, plus the European Central Bank, hold the capital for the BIS. The Federal Reserve Chairman is one of 20 members of the board of directors. The BIS Web site provides links to the world's central banks.

Answers

1. *Possible answer: because the countries recognize the benefits of having a central monetary authority that can help stabilize the economy and serve as a bankers' bank*
2. *The Bank of England produces currency, but the Federal Reserve distributes currency produced by the U.S. Treasury Department.*

More About . . .

Advisory Councils
Each Federal Reserve district bank chooses a commercial banker to represent it on the Federal Advisory Council (FAC). Each representative serves three one-year terms. The FAC meets at least four times a year.

The Fed Board of Governors (BOG) appoints 10 members annually to the Consumer Advisory Council (CAC). Members serve staggered three-year terms during which they represent the concerns of consumers, financial services institutions, and their communities.

The BOG also appoints the 12 members of the Thrift Institutions Advisory Council (TIAC), who represent different thrift institutions and serve two-year terms. The CAC and the TIAC meet three times per year in Washington, D. C.

A GLOBAL PERSPECTIVE

Comparing Central Banks

Chinese bank note

British bank note

Today, more than 160 nations have central banks. These banks function as the main monetary authority for their respective nations. They also serve the same purpose—maintaining economic stability. Further, they use similar tools to fulfill this purpose. Even so, these central banks do have several differences. One difference is historical. The Federal Reserve, for example, was established by an act of Congress in 1913. The Bank of England, Great Britain's central bank, claims a royal pedigree, having been established in 1694 during the reign of William and Mary. In China, the People's Bank of China (PBC) began as a commercial bank in 1948. It functioned as a central bank and a commercial bank until 1983, when it was reorganized solely as a central bank.

Another difference lies in the production of money. The central banks of Great Britain and China both produce and distribute currency. In the United States, the Treasury produces currency and the Federal Reserve distributes it.

CONNECTING ACROSS THE GLOBE

1. Why do you think central banks are common to countries that have very different forms of government, such as the United States and China?
2. In terms of money production, how does the Bank of England differ from the Federal Reserve?

The sale and purchases of federal government bonds on the open market are the principal tools used by the Fed to promote a stable, growing economy. At the end of each of its meetings, the FOMC issues a public statement to explain its assessment of the economy and its latest actions. You will learn more about the functions of the FOMC in Section 3.

Advisory Councils Three committees provide advice directly to the Board of Governors. The 12 members of the Federal Advisory Council, one from each Fed district, represent the commercial banking industry. The Consumer Advisory Council advises the board on matters concerning the Fed's responsibilities in enforcing consumer protection laws related to borrowing. Its 30 members, for the most part, are drawn from consumer groups and the financial services industry.

QUICK REFERENCE

A **thrift institution** is a financial institution that serves savers.

The Federal Reserve Board created the Thrift Institutions Advisory Council in 1980 to provide advice about the needs of this important segment of the financial services industry. **Thrift institutions** are savings and loan institutions, savings banks, or other institutions that serve savers. While the Fed does not regulate thrift institutions, the thrifts must conform to the Fed's reserve requirements and may borrow from the Fed.

APPLICATION Making Inferences

B. How does the 14-year term of members of the Board of Governors help make the Fed an independent government agency?
Longevity and job security allow them to act in the best interests of the economy rather than being concerned about short-term politics.

DIFFERENTIATING INSTRUCTION

Struggling Readers

Use Jigsaw Reading
Organize students into home groups of five and assign each student a number from one to five. Then, organize students into new groups, based on their number. Have each new group read about one element of the Fed described on pages 476–478. Encourage students to take notes and discuss how to present the material to their home groups. Direct students to reassemble in their home groups. Allow each student a few minutes to present the topic to their home group.

Gifted and Talented

Research the Structure of the Fed
Invite students to use the Federal Reserve Web site to research the Federal Reserve System structure. Students may focus on the Board of Governors, district banks, the FOMC, or Advisory Councils. Suggest that students researching the district banks focus on their structural elements and the role of the banks' board of directors. Encourage students to find out who is currently serving in these positions and to learn more about their roles. Have students present their research in oral reports.

SECTION 1 Assessment

Online Quiz
ClassZone.com

REVIEWING KEY CONCEPTS

1. Explain the relationship between the terms in each of these pairs.
   a. *central bank* / *Federal Reserve System*
   b. *monetary* / *currency*
   c. *Board of Governors* / *Federal Open Market Committee*
2. What are the three duties of a central bank?
3. How is the Fed different from other central banks?
4. How does the composition of the Federal Open Market Committee reflect the blend of national and regional power in the Fed?
5. What do all thrift institutions have in common?
6. **Using Your Notes** What are the five elements of the Fed? Refer to your completed cluster diagram.

   Federal Reserve System

   Use the Graphic Organizer at **Interactive Review @ ClassZone.com**

CRITICAL THINKING

7. **Analyzing Causes and Effects** If all members of the Board of Governors served 14-year terms, no president would appoint more than four members during two terms in office. However, many board members do not serve full terms, and vacancies occur on average more than once every two years. How does this situation affect a president's influence on the Board?
8. **Drawing Conclusions** The four rotating members on the Federal Open Market Committee are chosen from these groups:
   - Boston, Philadelphia, and Richmond
   - Cleveland and Chicago
   - Atlanta, St. Louis, and Dallas
   - Minneapolis, Kansas City, and San Francisco

   Why does the Fed mandate that one of the rotating members must come from each of these four groups?
9. **Challenge** The Federal Reserve Act of 1913 created the Federal Advisory Council. The Consumer Advisory Council was not created until 1976. How does this difference reflect changes in the duties of the Fed?

ECONOMICS IN PRACTICE

Analyzing Information

Refer to Figure 16.2 on page 477 to answer the following questions about the creation and present alignment of the Fed.

Analyze Maps Complete the chart below by indicating your answer to each question in the space provided.

Question	Response
Which region of the country has the most Fed district banks?	
How does the size of Fed districts 1–5 compare with districts 9–12?	
Where is the Board of Governors located?	
In which Fed district is your community located?	
How do the Federal Reserve Districts reflect U.S. geographic and economic diversity?	

Challenge How might the Federal Reserve districts be different if they were created today?

4 Assess & Reteach

Assess Have pairs of students write the answers to one or two of the questions on index cards. Collect the cards. Read aloud the answers to the class, one at a time. Have students identify the questions to which the responses belong.

Unit 6 Resource Book
- Section Quiz, p. 123

Interactive Review @ ClassZone.com
- Section Quiz

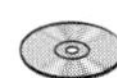

Test Generator CD-ROM
- Section Quiz

Reteach Call on volunteers to use Figure 16.1 to explain how the structure of the Federal Reserve System allows it to fulfill the purpose and duties of a central bank.

Unit 6 Resource Book
- Reteaching Activity, p. 124

SECTION 1 ASSESSMENT ANSWERS

Reviewing Key Concepts

1. a. *central bank*, p. 474; *Federal Reserve System*, p. 474
   b. *monetary*, p. 474; *currency*, p. 475
   c. *Board of Governors*, p. 476; *Federal Open Market Committee*, p. 477
2. hold cash reserves, stabilize the banking system, lend money to other banks and government
3. It is not just one national bank but a system of regional banks with a national policy board.
4. It's made up of the Board of Governors, which is the national authority, and presidents of five of the district banks, which represent the regional authority.
5. They serve the needs of savers.
6. See page 474 for a sample of a completed cluster diagram. Board of Governors, 12 District Banks, member banks, FOMC, advisory councils

Critical Thinking

7. The president might appoint a majority of members to the board during a particular administration. However, the board members may still serve longer than the president who appointed them so the Fed is still somewhat independent of politics.
8. so that there is representation for all regions of the country and no one region can dominate or unduly influence the committee
9. When the Fed was created it was focused on stabilizing the banking system and serving its needs. As consumer credit became more common the Fed became more directly involved in protecting consumers in their relationships with banks.

Economics in Practice

Analyze Maps East Coast; Districts 1–5 cover a much smaller geographical areas; Washington, D.C.; answers will vary; each district covers one or more major cities and also reflects the particular economic base of its region

Challenge Some of the southern and western districts might be split to reflect the increased population in those regions, while some of the eastern and Midwestern districts might be combined to reflect population decreases.

1 Plan & Prepare

Section 2 Objectives

- identify the services the Fed provides for the banking system
- explain how the Fed acts as a banker for the federal government
- describe the creation of money
- discuss what factors influence the money supply

2 Focus & Motivate

Connecting to Everyday Life Explain that this section focuses on the ways that the Federal Reserve System serves the banking system and the government. Invite students to brainstorm ideas of services that the Fed might provide based on what they learned about central banks.

Taking Notes Remind students to take notes as they read by completing a chart on the major functions of the Federal Reserve. They can use the Graphic Organizer at **Interactive Review @ ClassZone.com**. A sample is shown below.

Functions of the Federal Reserve		
Serving the banking system	Serving the federal government	Creating money
check clearing, lending money, regulating and supervising banks	paying government bills, selling government bonds, distributing currency	adjusting the RRR to influence the amount of money created

SECTION 2

Functions of the Federal Reserve

OBJECTIVES

In Section 2, you will

- identify the services the Fed provides for the banking system
- explain how the Fed acts as a banker for the federal government
- describe the creation of money
- discuss what factors influence the money supply

KEY TERMS

check clearing, *p. 480*
bank holding company, *p. 481*
bank exams, *p. 481*
required reserve ratio, *p. 484*
deposit multiplier formula, *p. 485*

TAKING NOTES

As you read Section 2, complete a chart to identify the major functions of the Federal Reserve. Use the Graphic Organizer at **Interactive Review @ ClassZone.com**

Functions of the Federal Reserve		
Serving the banking system	Serving the federal government	Creating money

Serving the Banking System

KEY CONCEPTS

As the banker's bank, the Fed has the responsibility of helping banks do their jobs. The Fed serves the banking system in a variety of ways, including providing check clearing and other services that facilitate the transfer of funds, lending money, and regulating and supervising banking activity.

QUICK REFERENCE

Check clearing is a service offered by the Fed to record receipts and expenditures of bank clients.

SERVICE 1 Check Clearing

One of the services that the Fed offers to banks is **check clearing**, a process in which banks record the receipts and expenditures of their clients. Each Fed district processes millions of checks every day, but most checks clear in two days or less. Figure 16.3 on the next page shows how a check is cleared by following its path from the time it is written until the money is taken from the check writer's account. Electronic-payment methods, such as credit and debit cards, have begun to replace checks. Further, more private companies are involved in the check-clearing process. As a result, check clearing has become a less important function of the Fed.

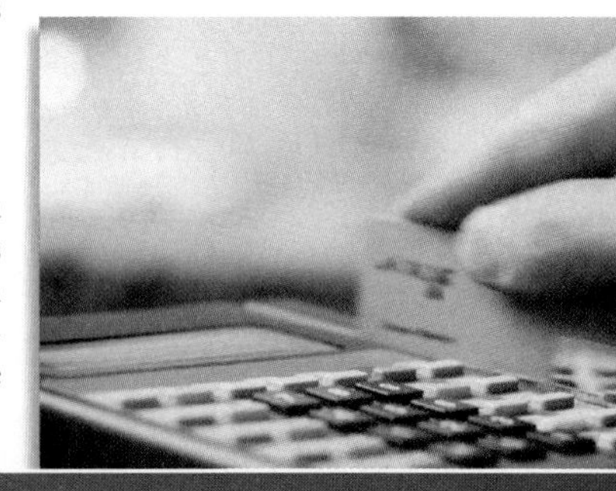

SERVICE 2 Lending Money

Banks often loan each other money on a short-term basis. Sometimes all the banks in a region are faced with short-term cash flow issues, usually during natural disasters. At such times, the Fed will provide

SECTION 2 PROGRAM RESOURCES

ON LEVEL

Lesson Plans

- Core, p. 54

Unit 6 Resource Book

- Reading Study Guide, pp. 125–126
- Math Skills Worksheet, p. 163
- Section Quiz, p. 133

STRUGGLING READERS

Unit 6 Resource Book

- Reading Study Guide with Additional Support, pp. 127–129
- Reteaching Activity, p. 134

ENGLISH LEARNERS

Unit 6 Resource Book

- Reading Study Guide with Additional Support (Spanish), pp. 130–132

INCLUSION

Lesson Plans

- Modified for Inclusion, p. 54

GIFTED AND TALENTED

Unit 6 Resource Book

- Readings in Free Enterprise: Gentle Ben, pp. 157–158

TECHNOLOGY

eEdition DVD-ROM

eEdition Online

Power Presentation DVD-ROM

Economics Concepts Transparencies

- CT54 How the Federal Reserve Creates Money

Daily Test Practice Transparencies, TT54

ClassZone.com

FIGURE 16.3 **The Federal Reserve and Check Clearing**

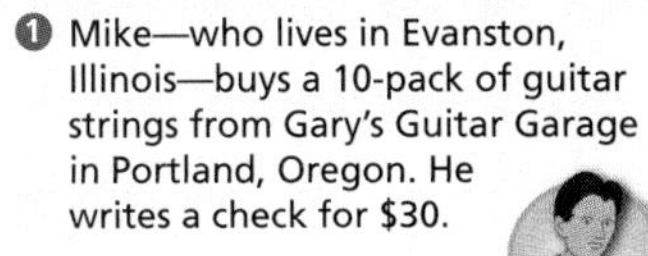

1 Mike—who lives in Evanston, Illinois—buys a 10-pack of guitar strings from Gary's Guitar Garage in Portland, Oregon. He writes a check for $30.
2 Gary, the store owner, deposits the check at his bank.
GARY'S GUITAR GARAGE
3 Gary's bank credits his account with $30 and then sends Mike's check to the Federal Reserve Bank of San Francisco—the Fed district bank that serves Portland.
GARY'S BANK
4 The Federal Reserve Bank of San Francisco credits $30 to Gary's bank's reserve account and then sends Mike's check to the Federal Reserve Bank of Chicago—the Fed district bank that serves Evanston.
5 The Federal Reserve Bank of Chicago transfers $30 from its reserves to the San Francisco Fed district bank and then sends Mike's check to his bank in Evanston.
6 Mike's bank transfers $30 from its reserve to the Federal Reserve Bank of Chicago and deducts $30 from Mike's account. This transaction is reflected on Mike's next bank statement.
MIKE'S BANK
MIKE'S BANK

ANALYZE CHARTS

This diagram illustrates the steps in the check-clearing process for a typical check transaction. Note how many banks handle Mike's check during the process. What is the importance of the Fed's role in clearing Mike's check?

loans to banks and may charge reduced interest rates. Banks must have sufficient assets and capital to qualify for Fed loans. In addition, smaller banks that have seasonal cash flow needs due to the nature of their local economy may borrow from the Fed. The Fed also acts as the lender of last resort to prevent a banking crisis.

SERVICE 3 Regulating and Supervising Banks

Each Federal Reserve Bank supervises the practices of state-chartered member banks and bank holding companies in its district. A **bank holding company** is a company that owns, or has a controlling interest in, more than one bank. This supervision includes **bank exams**, which are audits of the bank's financial practices. These exams make sure that banks are not engaged in risky or fraudulent practices, especially in lending. The Fed monitors bank mergers to ensure that competition is maintained and enforces truth-in-lending laws to protect consumers in such areas as home mortgages, auto loans, and retail credit.

QUICK REFERENCE

A **bank holding company** owns, or has a controlling interest in, more than one bank.

A **bank exam** is an audit of the bank's financial practices.

APPLICATION Making Inferences

A. Why might the Fed help a small bank in an agricultural region stabilize its cash flow?

See Teacher's Edition for answer. ▶

3 Teach

Serving the Banking System

Discuss

- What are two reasons that check clearing is becoming a less important function of the Fed? *(Fewer checks are being written; private companies also offer check-clearing services.)*

Analyzing Charts: Figure 16.3

Explain that crediting an account means adding money to it. Ask students which bank has a decrease in checkable deposits *(Mike's)* and which has an increase in checkable deposits *(Gary's)*. Essentially the funds get transferred from Mike's bank to Gary's through each bank's reserve account at the Fed.

Answer

The check is handled by four banks (two private banks and two Fed district banks). It facilitates the movement of funds from Mike's bank to Gary's bank and, therefore, makes the economic exchange between Mike and Gary's Guitar Garage possible.

APPLICATION

Answer *because the bank has seasonal demands for money, for example, high demand for loans at the beginning of the growing season and a lower demand at the end of the season when farmers have income from crops to repay the loans*

SMALL GROUP ACTIVITY

Researching Federal Reserve Services to Banks

Time 45 Minutes

Task Gather information about Federal Reserve services to banks and present an oral report.

Materials Needed computer with Internet access

Activity

- Organize students into small groups and assign each one to research a service that Federal Reserve district banks provide to banks.
- Encourage students to find out more details about the specific services, including information about how the Fed is paid for providing these services.
- Allow groups to present their findings in oral reports to the class. Discuss how Fed services help banks serve their customers and keep the banking system stable.

Rubric

	Understanding of Concepts	Presentation of Information
4	excellent	clear and complete
3	good	mostly clear
2	fair	sometimes clear
1	poor	sketchy

Serving the Federal Government

Discuss

- Which services provided by the Fed are related to its fiscal responsibilities? *(It accepts deposits of tax revenues and then manages accounts for government agencies, so that they can use the revenue for transfer payments and direct spending.)*
- What are two reasons that the Fed sells government securities? *(to allow the government to raise money and to stabilize the economy)*

 **Economics Update**

At **ClassZone.com** students will see updated information on the Fed's role in the sale of government securities.

Presentation Options

Review the functions of the Federal Reserve by using the following presentation options:

 **Power Presentations DVD-ROM**
Using the Display Tool, you can highlight the banking services the Fed provides to the government.

 **Economics Concepts Transparencies**

- CT54 How the Federal Reserve Creates Money

Serving the Federal Government

KEY CONCEPTS

A second function of the Fed is to serve as the federal government's banker. As you learned in Chapter 14, the federal government receives billions of tax dollars each year and uses this money on a variety of programs through direct spending and transfer payments. In its role as the federal government's banker, the Fed also fulfills certain fiscal responsibilities by helping the government to carry out its taxation and spending activities.

SERVICE 1 Paying Government Bills

When the IRS collects tax revenues, the funds are deposited with the Fed. The Fed then issues checks or makes electronic payments, via the U.S. Treasury, for such programs as Social Security, Medicare, and IRS tax refunds. When these funds are deposited in the recipient's bank account or the check is cashed, the Fed deducts that amount from the government's account.

Including military personnel, the federal government employs about 4.6 million people, and their wages and benefits are processed through the Fed. Direct government spending also comes from accounts at the Fed. Whether the government is buying office supplies or military equipment or paying contractors to maintain federal highways, the money is funneled through the Fed. The Fed also processes food stamps, which are issued by the Department of Agriculture, and postal money orders, which are issued by the U.S. Postal Service. The Fed, therefore, facilitates government payments in a way that is similar to the way it clears checks and processes electronic payments in the private sector.

Economics Update

Find an update on the Fed's role in the sale of government securities at **ClassZone.com**

SERVICE 2 Selling Government Securities

As you learned in Chapter 15, the federal government has different kinds of securities that it sells when it wants to borrow money. (Remember that securities are another name for bonds and stocks.) The Fed processes U.S. savings bonds and auctions other kinds of securities for the U.S. Treasury to provide funds for various government activities.

The Fed has many roles in this process. It provides information about the securities to potential buyers, receives orders from customers, collects payments from buyers, credits the funds to the Treasury's account, and delivers the bonds to their owners. It also pays the interest on these bonds on a regular basis or at maturity. Many of these transactions are now handled electronically. Even when individuals purchase government securities on the Treasury Department's Web site, the Fed transfers funds between the purchaser and the Treasury and pays the interest when it is due. The Fed does not charge fees for these services.

In addition to selling government securities to raise money to fund government activities, the Federal Open Market Committee supervises the sales and purchases of government securities as a way to stabilize the economy. You'll learn more about this aspect of the Fed's work in Section 3.

DIFFERENTIATING INSTRUCTION

Struggling Readers

Adjust Reading Rates
Have partners read the text together, stopping after every paragraph to ask and answer *who, what, where, when,* and *why* questions about the material. If students have difficulty answering the questions, suggest that they read more slowly and concentrate on details. Students can also reread text, as needed, to find answers to their questions.

Gifted and Talented

Develop Handouts
Invite interested students to use Internet resources to learn more about Fed services to the government. Some may focus on the Fed's role in the auction of Treasury securities. Others may investigate the Fed's role in circulating currency. The New York Fed has published Fedpoint articles that provide information on these topics. Related information may be found on the Federal Reserve and Treasury Department Web sites. Encourage students to create handouts for classmates that summarize their research.

SERVICE 3 Distributing Currency

One of the important functions of a central bank is to issue a standard currency that is used throughout the economy. In the United States, Federal Reserve notes are the official paper currency. These notes are fiat money backed by the confidence of the federal government and managed by the Federal Reserve. The government's backing is made plain by the statement on each note: "This note is legal tender for all debts, public and private." Figure 16.4 highlights several important features of Federal Reserve notes.

The Department of the Treasury's Bureau of Engraving and Printing prints Federal Reserve notes, which are distributed by the Fed to its district banks. The notes are then moved on to depository institutions and finally into the hands of individuals and businesses. The Fed makes sure that bills are distributed to banks in the amounts that they need. Paper money has a life span of between two and five years. Smaller denomination bills tend to have a shorter life span. Larger denomination bills stay in circulation longer. When bills get worn out, they are taken out of circulation, destroyed, and replaced with new ones. In a similar way, the Fed distributes coins that are produced by the U.S. Mint.

FIGURE 16.4 A FEDERAL RESERVE NOTE

ⓐ Federal Reserve Notes are the official U.S. paper **currency**.

ⓑ Code indicates to which Federal Reserve Bank the Treasury issued the note. For example, B2 is New York, E5 is Richmond, and K11 is Dallas.

ⓒ Each note has a unique serial number. The second letter identifies the Fed district to which the note was issued.

ⓓ The Federal Reserve seal is on the left, the Treasury Department seal on the right.

ⓔ The signature of the Treasurer is on the left, the signature of the Secretary of the Treasury on the right.

ⓕ In 1955, Congress required that the phrase "In God We Trust" be used on all currency and coins.

ANALYZE

1. To which Federal Reserve Bank was this bill issued?
2. How might serial numbers help the authorities detect counterfeit bills?

APPLICATION Comparing Economic Information

B. How are the banking services the Fed provides to the government similar to the services it provides to banks?

It clears checks and transfers funds to facilitate payments.

Analyzing Graphs: Figure 16.4

You may want to use an actual bill or use the enlarged version of the visual available at **ClassZone.com**, in order to allow students to see the features more clearly. Invite students to compare different denomination bills to see that all except the one-dollar bill are designed in a similar way.

Answers

1. *Dallas*
2. *Counterfeiters might not use unique numbers for each bill or know the details of the Treasury's system of numbering.*

More About . . .

The Fed and Currency

Each year the Fed estimates how much paper currency will be demanded and places an order with the Bureau of Engraving and Printing. In December 2005, about 26 billion bills, totaling almost $759 billion, were in circulation.

Fed district banks supply currency directly to about half of the depository institutions in the United States. These are larger banks that maintain reserve accounts with the Fed. Banks pay for their currency by having the Fed debit their reserves for the amount of currency they receive. Smaller banks receive currency through these larger banks and pay them a fee for it.

INDIVIDUAL ACTIVITY

Creating a Flow Chart

Time 20 Minutes

Task Illustrate Federal Reserve services to the federal government in a flow chart.

Materials Needed paper and pens or markers

Activity

- Assign students one of the three services described on pages 482–483, or allow students to choose.
- Direct students to review the material on their specific service.
- Then, ask them to create a flow chart to illustrate how the Federal Reserve interacts with various government agencies, other banks, consumers, and businesses in its role as the federal government's banker.
- Allow students to share their work in small groups with students who have worked on different services. Encourage them to discuss how the Federal Reserve helps the government do its job and serve its citizens.

Rubric

	Understanding of Concepts	Presentation of Information
4	excellent	clear and complete
3	good	mostly clear
2	fair	sometimes clear
1	poor	sketchy

Creating Money

Discuss

- How do banks determine how much of their deposits they can lend? *(They can lend anything in excess of the required reserve ratio.)*
- What happens to the amount of money in the economy when the Federal Reserve lowers the required reserve ratio? Why? *(It increases because banks have more money to lend.)*

Analyzing Charts: Figure 16.5

Point out that the $10,000 deposited in Bank A is shown as the total of the two bars representing loans and the RRR. Ask students how the two bars shown for Bank B are related to the bars for Bank A and why. *(The two bars for Bank B equal the purple bar for Bank A because the purple bar represents the amount that Bank A lent to Kecia that was deposited in Bank B.)* Read the paragraphs on money creation and have students follow each transaction on the chart. Encourage them to use the text to get the exact dollar amounts needed to answer the question below the chart.

Answer

At 20 percent, Bank D must hold $1,024 in reserve and can lend $4,096 of the $5,120 that Bank C could lend. At 10 percent, Bank D must hold $729 in reserve and can lend $6,561 of the $7,290 that Bank C could lend.

Creating Money

KEY CONCEPTS

Creating money does not mean printing paper currency and minting coins. It refers to the way money gets into circulation through deposits and loans at banks. (You learned briefly about this process in Chapter 10.) Because the United States has a fractional reserve banking system, banks are not allowed to loan out all the money they have in deposits. The Fed establishes a **required reserve ratio (RRR)**, which is the fraction of the bank's deposits that must be kept in reserve by the bank, to control the amount a bank can loan. Money on deposit in excess of the required reserve amount can be loaned out. The money in reserve may be stored as cash in the bank's vault or deposited with the Fed.

QUICK REFERENCE

Required reserve ratio (RRR) is the fraction of a bank's deposits that it must keep in reserve.

EXAMPLE Money Creation

The banking system creates money whenever banks receive deposits and make loans. The level of the RRR determines how much money may be loaned and, therefore, how much money gets created. Let's see how this works by studying Figure 16.5. At the top of the chart, the RRR is set at 20 percent. If Bank A has $10,000 in deposits, it must keep 20 percent, or $2,000, on reserve. It lends the remaining $8,000 to Kecia's Fitness Studio, which Kecia deposits in Bank B. Bank B keeps 20 percent of the $8,000, or $1,600, on reserve as required. Bank B lends the remaining $6,400 to Juan's Computer Repair, and Juan deposits it in Bank C. At this point, the money supply has increased by $14,400, the total of the loans made. The process could continue until there was nothing left to lend.

FIGURE 16.5 The Fed Creates Money

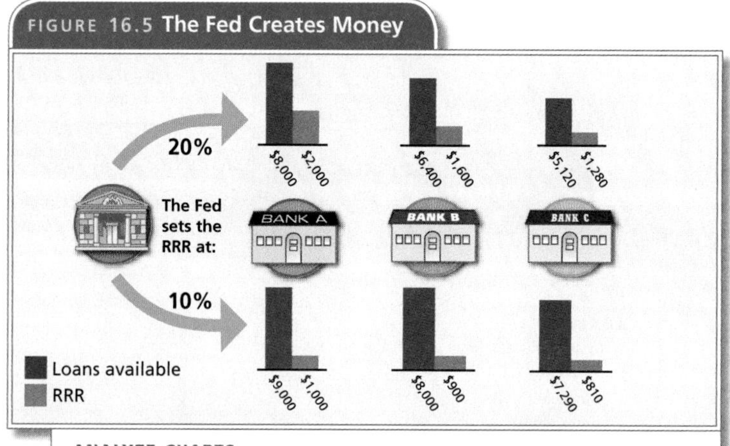

ANALYZE CHARTS

Remember that the amount of money that each bank can loan is limited by the RRR. Suppose that Bank C loaned its available funds to Miles and Miles deposited the money in Bank D. How much money would Bank D have to hold in reserve and how much would it have available for loans if the RRR is set at 20 percent? What would these figures be if the RRR were set at 10 percent?

DIFFERENTIATING INSTRUCTION

English Learners

Build Economics Vocabulary

Explain that *ratio* and *fraction* are synonyms because they both refer to a relationship of two numbers expressed as a part of a whole—in this case, which part of the total deposits must be held in reserve and which part can be loaned. Invite students to explain in their own words what they know about fractions from math class. Ask them to point to the words in the definition of *required reserve ratio* that refer to each part of the phrase *(fraction, must be kept in reserve)*.

Inclusion

Enlarge the Visual

Students with visual impairments may benefit from working with an enlarged version of Figure 16.5, available at **ClassZone.com**. Allow students to work with a partner without visual impairments to read the text related to the chart. Encourage partners to work together on the answer to the question. Students may record their answers orally, or the student without impairments may write them down as the other student describes the calculations.

Now look at what happens if the Fed reduces the RRR to 10 percent. The change is shown at the bottom of Figure 16.5. Bank A can now lend $9,000 to Kecia and Bank B can lend $8,100 to Juan. In this scenario, the money supply would increase by $17,100. The decrease in the RRR allowed the money supply to increase by an additional $2,700.

How do you figure out how much the money supply will increase after all possible loans have been made? The **deposit multiplier formula** is a mathematical formula that tells how much the money supply will increase after an initial cash deposit in a bank. The formula is 1/RRR. For example, if the RRR is 10 percent the deposit multiplier equals 10. Figure 16.6 illustrates how the deposit multiplier formula is used to determine the amount of increase in the money supply from an initial deposit of $100 and a reserve requirement of 10 percent.

QUICK REFERENCE

Deposit multiplier formula tells how much the money supply will increase after an initial cash deposit.

MATH CHALLENGE

FIGURE 16.6 Deposit Expansion Multiplier

Step 1: Study the table below, which shows how an initial deposit of $100 can increase the money supply. To quantify the total amount of money that can be created from this initial deposit, economists use the deposit expansion multiplier.

	Money deposited	=	10% held as reserves	+	90% loaned out
Bank A	$100.00	=	$10.00	+	$90.00
Bank B	$90.00	=	$ 9.00	+	$81.00
Bank C	$81.00	=	$ 8.10	+	$72.90
Bank D	$72.90	=	$ 7.29	+	$65.61
---	---		---		---
	Total		$100.00		$900.00

Step 2: Calculate the deposit expansion multiplier.

$$\frac{1}{\text{Required reserve ratio}} = \text{Deposit expansion multiplier}$$

Sample Calculations

$$\frac{1}{10\%} = \frac{1}{0.10} = 10$$

Step 3: Use the deposit expansion multiplier to calculate the total money that can be loaned.

$$\text{Initial deposit} \times \left[\text{Deposit expansion multiplier} - 1\right] = \text{Total available for loans}$$

$$\$100 \times [10-1] = \$100 \times 9 = \$900$$

APPLICATION **Analyzing Effects**

C. If the Fed raised the RRR from 10 percent to 12 percent, how would it affect the money supply and by approximately how much, if the initial deposit was $5,000? Show your calculations. decrease by $9,500 [$5,000 x (10-1) = $45,000 vs. $5,000 x (8.3-1) = $36,500]

Math Challenge: Figure 16.6

Deposit Expansion Multiplier

It may be helpful for students to review the concept of fractional reserve banking as outlined in Figure 10.5 on page 305. Help students see that the example shown here follows the same pattern described in the example of money creation and illustrated in Figure 16.5. However, it begins with $100 instead of $10,000, in order to simplify the calculations. Allow students to practice using the formula with different RRRs. Remind them that the larger the denominator, i.e. the higher the RRR, the smaller the result will be. Lead them to conclude that a lower RRR leads to a larger deposit expansion multiplier and, thus, more money available for loan.

Math Handbook
Using Ratios, p. R5

CLASS ACTIVITY

Creating a Bulletin Board Display

Time 45 Minutes 

Task Create a bulletin board display on the three functions of the Federal Reserve.

Materials Needed paper or poster board and markers, computer with Internet access (optional)

Activity

- Encourage students to review the material on the three functions of the Federal Reserve on pages 480–485.
- Direct them to collaborate on a bulletin board display that presents information on these three functions in a coherent way. Students may wish to work in three groups to develop preliminary ideas on how to represent each topic. They may create their own visuals or use images found on the Internet.
- Invite volunteers to describe each function and how they are interrelated. Discuss how the functions relate to the purpose and duties of a central bank.

Rubric

	Understanding of Concepts	Presentation of Information
4	excellent	clear, complete, creative
3	good	mostly clear, somewhat creative
2	fair	sometimes clear, with some creative elements
1	poor	sketchy and unoriginal

Factors Affecting Demand for Money

Discuss

- How would the increase in electronic payments, such as debit and credit cards, affect the demand for money that makes up M1? *(There would be less demand for currency but more demand for checkable deposits to cover the electronic payments.)*
- How would inflation affect the demand for money? *(Possible answer: It would increase the demand, because rising costs of consumer goods means that buyers need more money to buy them.)*

More About . . .

Demand for Currency
The demand for currency varies not only by the season but also by time of the month and day of the week. For example, there is more cash circulating on Mondays because many people use ATMs to withdraw cash over the weekend. Growth in the number of ATMs has increased the demand for currency overall, since people are no longer limited to bank hours to withdraw cash.

Federal Reserve data indicates that the value of paper currency in circulation increased 89 percent between 1995 and 2005. During that same period, the number of bills in circulation grew by 48 percent. The greatest increase was in the number of 100-dollar bills, which increased by 125 percent.

Factors Affecting Demand for Money

KEY CONCEPTS

The Fed monitors two major indicators of the money supply, namely M1 and M2. Recall that you learned in Chapter 10 that M1 includes cash and checkable deposits, while M2 includes M1 plus savings deposits and certain time deposits. The Fed needs to know how large each type of money is in order to act appropriately to manage the supply of money. Four factors influence how much money individuals and businesses need—cash on hand, interest rates, the cost of consumer goods and services, and the level of income.

FACTOR 1 Cash on Hand

Individuals and businesses need cash to complete certain financial transactions. Recall that M1, which includes cash and checkable deposits, is also called transactions money. Consumers use this money to pay for things such as food, clothing, transportation costs such as gasoline and bus or train fares, and entertainment. Businesses also use cash and checks for many day-to-day expenses. The fastest growing form of payment is the debit card, which was used for more than 23 billion transactions in 2005. While a debit card is not money, it is linked to a checking account, and the funds in the account are considered money.

The Fed understands that there are certain times when people need more cash. It routinely increases the amount of cash at banks during the holiday season because people want more money to buy gifts. Similarly, during the summer months the Fed ensures that banks in areas popular with tourists have more cash. Natural disasters also influence the amount of cash the Fed puts into circulation. In response to Hurricane Katrina's devastation of the Gulf Coast in 2005, the Fed shipped large amounts of currency to banks in several nearby districts because of the immediate demand for more cash by residents. Since many parts of the Gulf Coast were without electricity, people were not able to use debit cards and credit cards as they ordinarily would.

Cash on Hand Portable ATMs dispensed much-needed cash to evacuees from the Gulf Coast after Hurricane Katrina.

FACTOR 2 Interest Rates

When interest rates are high, individuals and businesses may place excess cash in savings instruments, such as bonds, stocks, or savings accounts. This of course pulls cash out of circulation. The money then exists as a part of M2. Figure 16.7 shows how the demand for money is affected by interest rates. When interest rates are high, the demand for money is lower because there is less incentive for individuals and businesses to spend and more incentive to save and earn interest. When interest rates are lower, however, more money is demanded because people have less incentive to save and more incentive to spend.

DIFFERENTIATING INSTRUCTION

Struggling Readers

Locate Cause-and-Effect Words
Explain that factors that affect demand are causes that lead to different effects or results. For example, consumers want to buy things and the result is a greater demand for cash. Causes might be signaled by words such as *when, since, because of,* or *in response to*. An effect might be signaled by the word *then*. Have pairs read pages 486–487 and look for words that signal cause and effect relationships. Encourage them to formulate direct cause-and-effect statements.

Inclusion

Summarize Orally
Have students work in pairs to read the material on each factor aloud or silently. Then have partners take turns summarizing the important ideas about each factor in one or two sentences. Students may wish to write these summaries in their notes. Consider having students use this technique for other material in the section.

FIGURE 16.7 DEMAND FOR MONEY

Interest rate

Quantity of money demanded

Here, the term *money* refers to M1. Note that when interest rates are high the quantity demanded of money is lower. Conversely, when interest rates decrease the quantity demanded of money increases.

Analyzing Graphs: Figure 16.7

Help students relate this graph to other demand curves they have seen by explaining that the interest rate is equivalent to the price. In this case, they can think of it as the opportunity cost of having money in cash or checkable deposits rather than in savings. When the price (interest rate) is high, there is a smaller quantity of M1 demanded. Remind them that moving along the demand curve shows changes in quantity demanded not change in demand.

FACTOR 3 Cost of Consumer Goods and Services

As the cost of consumer goods or services increases, buyers may wish to have more money available. Suppose that adverse weather conditions and higher energy prices have driven up the prices of fresh fruits and vegetables. People may need to have more cash when they buy groceries at the supermarket than they did before the prices increased. They might also find that it takes more cash to buy gasoline than it used to.

Businesses face the same challenges. They would also wish to have more cash to purchase the goods and services they need for their operations. Of course, when businesses pay more for goods and services, production costs increase and the higher costs are often passed on to consumers. This, in turn, may lead consumers to want to have more money available.

FACTOR 4 Level of Income

As income increases, individuals and companies have a tendency to hold more cash. Recall that level of income is one of the factors that affect demand. Suppose that Bob has a part-time job cooking at a restaurant. When he gets a raise, he notices that he keeps more money in his wallet because he feels he can afford to spend more on clothes and DVDs. The same holds true for businesses. When their income increases, they will keep more cash because they are able to spend more on the goods and services that they need to pay for operations. In general, when income levels rise, so will the demand for money.

The Fed can take several actions to change the money supply in response to changes in demand for money. More important, the Fed can use these methods of increasing or decreasing the money supply to stabilize the economy. In the next section, you'll learn about the nature of these methods and how they are used to establish economy stability.

APPLICATION Analyzing Effects

D. Which factor is likely to increase the size of M2? Why?

See answer in Teacher's Edition. ▶

APPLICATION

Answer *Interest rates, because when interest rate are higher, more money will move into M2 as people seek to earn interest on some of their money rather than spending it all.*

INDIVIDUAL ACTIVITY

Creating a Graphic Organizer

Time 20 Minutes

Task Create an Economics Essentials graphic organizer on the factors that affect the demand for money.

Materials Needed paper and pens or markers

Activity

- Have students review the material on pages 486–487, describing the factors that affect the demand for money.
- Invite students to create a graphic organizer to summarize the information.
- Encourage students to use an Economics Essentials diagram, such as Figure 15.3 on page 450 as a model, pointing out that they should include visuals and captions.
- Allow students to share their graphic organizers in small groups.
- Call on volunteers from different groups to describe how students chose to represent each factor. Discuss how these factors relate to the Fed's need to monitor the money supply.

Rubric

	Understanding of Concepts	Presentation of Information
4	excellent	clear and complete
3	good	mostly complete
2	fair	somewhat complete
1	poor	sketchy

Comparing the Treasury and the Fed

1 Plan & Prepare

Objectives

- Describe similarities and differences between the U.S. Treasury and the Federal Reserve System.
- Identify the roles of the U.S. Treasury and the Federal Reserve System in the U.S. economy.

2 Focus & Motivate

Suggest that students identify whether each highlighted word in the passage signals a similarity or a difference. Have them consider the following questions as they read.

- What is the primary focus of each organization's responsibilities? *(Possible answer: Treasury—managing the government's finances; Fed—the stability of the nation's financial system)*

3 Teach

- Encourage students to notice how the passage is organized, with each paragraph being primarily focused on one of the two organizations. As the Treasury is described first, there is more comparison in the second paragraph, which refers back to the first.
- Explain that students will need to make inferences about some of the similarities and differences between the two organizations based on the description of their responsibilities.

For additional practice see **Skillbuilder Handbook**, page R19.

THINKING ECONOMICALLY Answers

1. *both created by an act of Congress; both essential to the functioning of the economy*
2. *Fed: central bank, sets monetary policy, structure consists of a governing body and member banks; Treasury: federal department, manages federal finances, structure consists of main treasury and a number of bureaus*
3. *the Fed, because it is concerned with setting monetary policy*

ECONOMICS SKILLBUILDER

For more information on comparing economic information, see Skillbuilder Handbook, page R19

Comparing the Treasury and the Fed

The following passage provides information about the U.S. Treasury and the Federal Reserve System. Compare the two by looking for similarities and differences between them. This will help you understand the role that each plays in the nation's economy.

TIPS FOR COMPARING Use the following tips to help you compare economic information.

The U.S. Treasury and the Federal Reserve System

Although the U.S. Treasury and the Federal Reserve are both essential to the functioning of the nation's economy, they differ in many ways. The U.S. Treasury Department was established by an act of Congress in 1789. It is the primary federal agency responsible for the economic prosperity of the United States. As such, it is responsible for managing federal finances, including the collection of taxes, duties, and other monies due to the United States; the paying of the nation's bills; and the management of government accounts and the public debt. In addition, the Treasury Department produces stamps, currency, and coinage.

The Federal Reserve System similarly was established by an act of Congress but much later, in 1913. Unlike the U.S. Treasury, which is a department of the federal government, the Fed is the nation's central bank. According to its mission statement, the purpose of the Federal Reserve is "to provide the nation with a safer, more flexible, and more stable monetary and financial system."

The duties of the Federal Reserve fall into four general areas: conducting the nation's monetary policy in pursuit of maximum employment and economic stability; supervising and regulating the nation's banking institutions; maintaining the stability of the financial system; and providing financial services such as check clearing and short-term loans to member banks. The Fed consists of a board of governors and 12 regional banks, a structure that varies considerably from that of the Treasury.

Look for words that signal similarities, such as *both, similarly,* and *also.*

Look for words that signal differences, or contrasts, such as *unlike, differ,* and *varies.*

THINKING ECONOMICALLY Analyzing

1. In what ways are the Treasury and the Fed similar?
2. What are some important differences between the Fed and the Treasury?
3. Which do you think is more policy oriented, the Fed or the Treasury? Explain why you think so.

DIFFERENTIATING INSTRUCTION

Struggling Readers

Create a Venn Diagram
Allow students to work in pairs to create a Venn diagram to help them summarize the similarities and differences between the two organizations. Suggest that they use the highlighted clue words to help them determine where to place information on their diagram. Remind them that only things that are common to both organizations should be placed in the overlapping area of the diagram. Encourage them to summarize each paragraph in their own words.

Gifted and Talented

Create an Organizational Chart
Have interested students explore the different structures of the U.S. Treasury and the Fed. Encourage students to research the organizational chart of the Treasury and compare it with the structure of the Fed as shown in Figure 16.1. Suggest that students learn where each of these organizations fits into the overall structure of the federal government and what their connection is to the president and Congress. Invite students to create an organizational chart that shows these relationships.

SECTION 2 Assessment

Online Quiz ClassZone.com

REVIEWING KEY CONCEPTS

1. Use each of the three terms below in a sentence that illustrates the meaning of the term.
   a. *check clearing* b. *bank holding company* c. *required reserve ratio*
2. Why are bank exams an important way for the Fed to help create a sound banking system?
3. What is the relationship between the required reserve ratio and the deposit multiplier formula?
4. How does the Fed's check-clearing service help the banking system?
5. How does the deposit multiplier formula allow the Fed to create money through the banking system?
6. **Using Your Notes** What are the three services that the Fed provides to the federal government? Refer to your completed chart.

   Use the Graphic Organizer at **Interactive Review @ ClassZone.com**

Functions of the Federal Reserve		
Serving the banking system	Serving the federal government	Creating money

CRITICAL THINKING

7. **Applying Economic Concepts** Daniel is a high school senior living in California. He receives a check from his grandmother in Florida as a graduation gift. How is the Federal Reserve involved in transferring the money from Daniel's grandmother's bank account to his account? Illustrate your answer with a flow chart.
8. **Applying Economic Concepts** You've been planning your college finances and you know that you'll have to take a bank loan to cover tuition costs. You read that the Fed intends to raise the RRR from 10 percent to 20 percent. How will this change affect the money supply and your ability to borrow money for college tuition?
9. **Analyzing Data** The Fed sets the required reserve ratio at 10 percent. What is the initial deposit if the money supply increases by $40,000? Use the deposit multiplier formula to determine your answer and show your calculations.
10. **Challenge** Banks do not earn interest on the funds they hold as reserves. How does this provide an incentive to banks to create money by making loans rather than to deposit excess funds in a Fed bank?

ECONOMICS IN PRACTICE

Buying school supplies

Evaluating Demand for Money Consider the factors that affect the demand for money and then complete the following activities.

Identify Changes in Demand The chart below shows some scenarios that would cause demand for money to change. For each example, note if demand is increasing or decreasing.

Factor Affecting Demand for Money	Increasing or Decreasing?
Back-to-school shopping begins	
Banks lower the interest rate on CDs from 6% to 3%	
Energy costs for home heating are up by 20%	
Interest rates on savings deposits increase from 1% to 4.5%	

Challenge What type of potential economic instability is suggested by rising prices? How might the Fed adjust the money supply in such a situation? You will learn more about this topic in Section 3.

489

4 Assess & Reteach

Assess Have students jot down notes in response to the Critical Thinking Questions. Formulate answers to the questions as a class.

Unit 6 Resource Book
- Section Quiz, p. 133

Interactive Review @ ClassZone.com
- Section Quiz

Test Generator CD-ROM
- Section Quiz

Reteach Call on volunteers to use their notes from their charts on the Functions of the Federal Reserve to summarize the main ideas and details in each part of the section for the class.

Unit 6 Resource Book
- Reteaching Activity, p. 134

Economics in Practice
Identify Changes in Demand increasing, increasing, increasing, decreasing
Challenge inflation, decrease the money supply

SECTION 2 ASSESSMENT ANSWERS

Reviewing Key Concepts

1. a. *check clearing*, p. 480
   b. *bank holding company*, p. 481
   c. *required reserve ratio*, p. 484
2. The Fed uses the exams to see how well the banks are following regulations and to make sure they are not engaged in risky or fraudulent practices that would undermine the stability of the banking system and hurt consumers.
3. multiplier formula = 1/required reserve ratio
4. It allows banks an easy way to transfer funds between check writers and check recipients by keeping track of receipts and expenditures.
5. Because of the deposit multiplier formula, an initial deposit in a bank creates money through lending that is greater than the initial deposit. The amount of the RRR determines the size of the deposit multiplier and the amount of money that can be created.
6. See page 480 for a sample of a completed chart. paying the government's bills, selling government securities, distributing currency

Critical Thinking

7. Daniel's bank credits the money to his account when he deposits the check and sends the check to the Fed in his district, which sends it to the Fed in his grandmother's district, which sends it to Daniel's grandmother's bank, which subtracts the money from her account. See p. 481 for a model for the flow chart.
8. The money supply decreases, interest rates rise, and borrowing money is more difficult.
9. With an RRR of 10 percent the deposit multiplier will be 10 and the Fed must make an initial deposit of $4,000 in order to increase the money supply by $40,000.
10. Banks will generally hold only the required amount of reserves so they can lend the rest and earn interest on the loans. This interest income is an incentive to the banks to create money by lending the maximum amount possible. Loans of excess reserves are what create money in the banking system.

Economics in Practice

See answers in side column above.

1 Plan & Prepare

Section 3 Objectives

- examine the Fed's tools for monetary policy
- explain how the Fed's monetary policy promotes growth and stability
- analyze the challenges the Fed faces in implementing its policy

2 Focus & Motivate

Connecting to Everyday Life Explain that this section focuses on monetary policy, which is the way that the Fed influences the economy. Ask students to suggest economic problems caused by the business cycle that the Fed may try to solve.

Taking Notes Remind students to take notes as they read by completing a hierarchy diagram with information on monetary policy. They can use the Graphic Organizer at **Interactive Review @ ClassZone.com**. A sample is shown below.

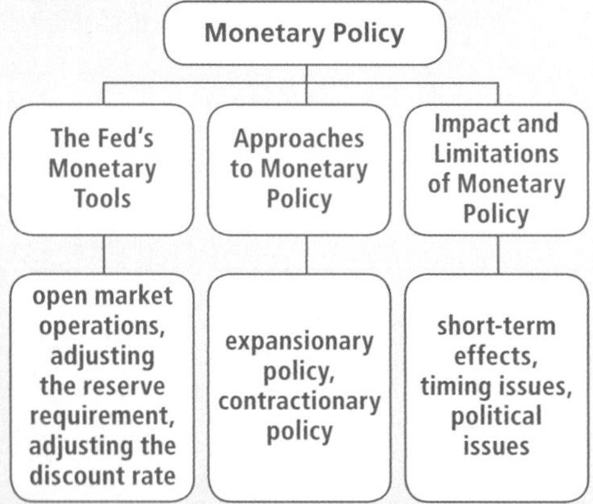

SECTION 3

Monetary Policy

OBJECTIVES

In Section 3, you will
- examine the Fed's tools for monetary policy
- explain how the Fed's monetary policy promotes growth and stability
- analyze the challenges the Fed faces in implementing its policy

KEY TERMS

monetary policy, *p. 490*
open market operations, *p. 490*
federal funds rate, *p. 490*
discount rate, *p. 491*
prime rate, *p. 491*
expansionary monetary policy, *p. 492*
contractionary monetary policy, *p. 492*
easy-money policy, *p. 492*
tight-money policy, *p. 493*
monetarism, *p. 496*

TAKING NOTES

As you read Section 3, complete a hierarchy diagram to track main ideas and supporting details about monetary policy. Use the Graphic Organizer at **Interactive Review @ ClassZone.com**

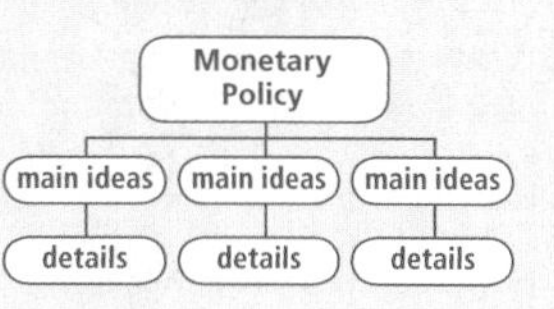

The Fed's Monetary Tools

QUICK REFERENCE

Monetary policy includes the Fed's actions that change the money supply in order to influence the economy.

Open market operations are the sales and purchase of federal government securities.

The **federal funds rate (FFR)** is the interest rate that banks charge one another to borrow money.

KEY CONCEPTS

Monetary policy involves Federal Reserve actions that change the money supply in order to influence the economy. There are three actions the Fed can take to manage the supply of money: open market operations, adjusting the reserve requirement, and adjusting the discount rate. They may be taken individually or in combination with one another. The impact of these actions is shown in Figure 16.8.

ACTION 1 Open Market Operations

Open market operations are the sales and purchase of marketable federal government securities. This is the monetary policy tool most used by the Fed to adjust the money supply. When the Fed wants to expand the money supply, it buys government securities. The Fed pays for the bonds it buys from commercial banks or the public by writing checks on itself. When sellers receive the funds from the Fed, they deposit them in banks. The banks can then lend their new excess reserves. When the Fed wants to contract the money supply, it sells government bonds on the open market. The purchasers of the bonds transfer funds to the Fed to pay for the bonds. These funds are taken out of circulation, and the reserves available for loans decrease.

The Fed communicates its intention to buy or sell bonds by announcing a target for the federal funds rate. The **federal funds rate (FFR)** is the interest rate at which a depository institution lends immediately available funds (balances at the Federal Reserve) to another depository institution overnight. When the Fed lowers the target for the FFR, it buys bonds. When it raises the target, it sells bonds. The Fed does not set the rate directly but influences it through its actions.

SECTION 3 PROGRAM RESOURCES

ON LEVEL

Lesson Plans
- Core, p. 55

Unit 6 Resource Book
- Reading Study Guide, pp. 135–136
- Economic Skills and Problem Solving Activity, pp. 155–156
- Economics Simulation, pp. 161–162
- Section Quiz, p. 143

STRUGGLING READERS

Unit 6 Resource Book
- Reading Study Guide with Additional Support, pp. 137–139
- Reteaching Activity, p. 144

ENGLISH LEARNERS

Unit 6 Resource Book
- Reading Study Guide with Additional Support (Spanish), pp. 140–142

INCLUSION

Lesson Plans
- Modified for Inclusion, p. 55

GIFTED AND TALENTED

NCEE Student Activities
- The Federal Reserve System and Its Tools, pp. 61–64

TECHNOLOGY

eEdition DVD-ROM

eEdition Online

Power Presentation DVD-ROM

Economics Concepts Transparencies
- CT55 The Fed's Monetary Policy Tools

Daily Test Practice Transparencies, TT55

ClassZone.com

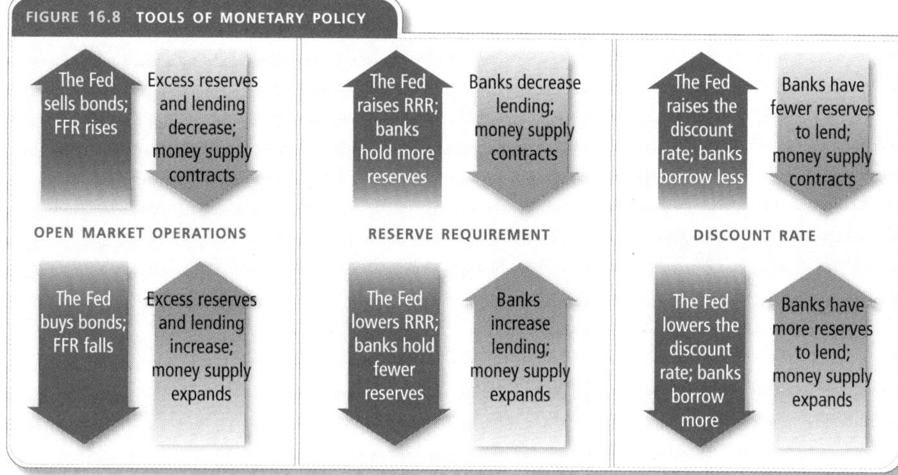
The Fed sells bonds; FFR rises
Excess reserves and lending decrease; money supply contracts
The Fed raises RRR; banks hold more reserves
Banks decrease lending; money supply contracts
The Fed raises the discount rate; banks borrow less
Banks have fewer reserves to lend; money supply contracts
OPEN MARKET OPERATIONS
RESERVE REQUIREMENT
DISCOUNT RATE
The Fed buys bonds; FFR falls
Excess reserves and lending increase; money supply expands
The Fed lowers RRR; banks hold fewer reserves
Banks increase lending; money supply expands
The Fed lowers the discount rate; banks borrow more
Banks have more reserves to lend; money supply expands

FIGURE 16.8 TOOLS OF MONETARY POLICY

ACTION 2 Adjusting the Reserve Requirement

As you recall from Section 2, the Fed sets the required reserve ratio (RRR) for all depository institutions. The RRR affects the money supply through the deposit multiplier formula. Increasing the RRR can reduce the money supply; decreasing the RRR can expand the money supply. Since the early 1990s, the RRR has been between 10 and 12 percent for transaction deposits and between 0 and 3 percent for time deposits.

ACTION 3 Adjusting the Discount Rate

The **discount rate** is the interest rate that the Fed charges when it lends money to other banks. The discount rate affects the money supply because it sets the reserves that banks have available to lend. When the Fed increases the discount rate, banks tend to borrow less money from the Fed. They must then use their existing funds to meet reserve requirements and have less excess reserves to lend. Therefore, the money supply decreases. The opposite happens when the discount rate is lowered. Banks borrow more money from the Fed and increase their reserves. When this happens, they have more money to lend, and the money supply increases.

The Fed's actions also impact businesses and individuals who borrow. The **prime rate** is the interest rate that banks charge their best customers. Interest rates for other borrowers tend to be two or three percentage points above prime. To make a profit on the loans they make, banks need to charge higher rates than they pay to borrow. So when the discount rate increases, so does the prime rate and, therefore, the cost of business and consumer credit.

QUICK REFERENCE

The **discount rate** is the interest rate that the Fed charges when it lends money to other banks.

The **prime rate** is the interest rate that banks charge their best customers.

APPLICATION Analyzing Causes

A. Which open market operation causes the money supply to expand? Why?
When the Fed buys bonds, it increases the reserves in the banking system, which causes the supply of money to expand.

3 Teach

The Fed's Monetary Tools

Discuss

- Why is it inaccurate to say that the Fed sets the federal funds rate? *(because the Fed does not set the rate directly but influences it through open market operations)*
- What is the relationship between the discount rate and the prime rate? *(The prime rate tends to rise and fall as the discount rate does, because banks charge their customers more than it costs them to borrow money from the Fed.)*

More About . . .

The Federal Funds Rate

The term *federal funds* refers to excess reserves that banks have on deposit at the Federal Reserve. These reserves do not earn interest, so banks have an incentive to lend this money to other banks, usually on an overnight basis. Banks most frequently borrow from one another in this way in order to meet their reserve requirements.

Daily transactions may not leave every bank with the exact amount of reserves it needs. The Fed does not set the rate but is able to control it because it is the only supplier of bank reserves. The Fed announces a target for the FFR but the actual rate may vary slightly from that target based on the exact open market operations for the day.

SMALL GROUP ACTIVITY

Writing a Report

Time 45 Minutes

Task Research one of the Fed's monetary policy tools and write a report.

Materials Needed computer with Internet access, paper and pen

Activity

- Organize students into three or more groups. Assign each one to use the Internet to learn more about one of the Fed's monetary policy tools. You may choose to assign more than one group to research the more complex tools.
- Suggest that they use Federal Reserve Web sites or other resources on monetary policy.
- Encourage students to learn more detail about how the Fed implements each of these tools.
- Direct groups to create written reports on their topics and to include visuals, such as charts or graphs, in their reports, if needed.
- Have volunteers from each group share their reports with the class.

Rubric

	Understanding of Concepts	Presentation of Information
4	excellent	clear and complete
3	good	mostly clear
2	fair	sometimes clear
1	poor	sketchy

Approaches to Monetary Policy

Discuss

- When and why does the Fed use expansionary monetary policy? *(when the economy is in recession, because increasing the money supply at that time will help stimulate demand)*
- Why does expansionary monetary policy using open market operations lower interest rates? *(because the Fed buys bonds, which increases demand for them, causing bond prices to rise and interest rates to fall)*
- Why does the Fed sometimes want to make it harder for individuals and businesses to borrow money? *(Possible answer: because too much borrowing contributes to inflation by providing money that fuels demand)*

Economics Illustrated

To help students better understand the impact of monetary policy on the money supply, you might suggest that they think of the money supply as a concertina. When expansionary fiscal policy is applied, the money supply, like a concertina, expands. When contractionary monetary policy is applied, the money supply, again like a concertina, contracts.

Expansionary Policy

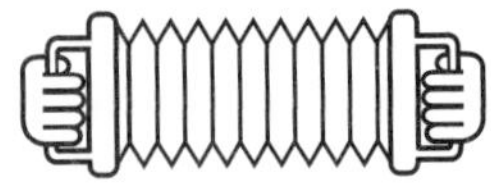

Contractionary Policy

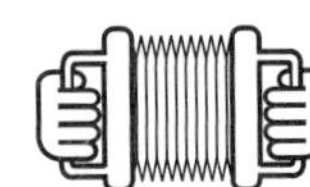

Approaches to Monetary Policy

QUICK REFERENCE

Expansionary monetary policy is a plan to increase the money supply.

Contractionary monetary policy is a plan to reduce the money supply.

Easy-money policy is another name for expansionary monetary policy.

KEY CONCEPTS

The most important job of the Fed is to promote growth and stability in the American economy. The purpose of monetary policy is to curb inflation and reduce economic stagnation or recession. By focusing on these goals, the Fed tries to promote full employment and growth without rapid increases in prices or high interest rates.

The Fed uses two basic policies—expansionary or contractionary monetary policy. **Expansionary monetary policy** is a plan to increase the amount of money in circulation. **Contractionary monetary policy** is a plan to reduce the amount of money in circulation. When the economy slows, the Fed uses expansionary monetary policy to pump more money into the economy. When the economy is overheated, the Fed uses a contractionary policy to reduce the amount of money in the economy.

POLICY 1 Expansionary Policy

In Chapter 15 you studied expansionary policy as it related to the federal government's fiscal-policy actions. This type of fiscal policy is used during a slowdown in economic activity. The Fed's expansionary monetary policy is used at the same point in the business cycle. It is sometimes called the **easy-money policy** because it puts more money into circulation by making it easier for borrowers to secure a loan.

During a recession, when unemployment is high, the Fed wants to have more money circulating in the economy to stimulate aggregate demand. When it is easier to borrow money, consumers will take out more loans to buy homes, automobiles, and other goods and services. In response, businesses then produce more, which creates jobs and decreases unemployment. An easy-money policy allows businesses to borrow funds to help them expand. When more loans are made, more money is created in the banking system.

The Fed enacts an easy-money policy by buying bonds on the open market, by decreasing reserve requirements, by decreasing the discount rate, or by some combination of these tools. The Fed's most common action in this situation is to buy bonds on the open market. When the Fed decides to buy more bonds, it increases the demand for them, which raises their price. Recall that bond prices have an inverse, or opposite, relationship to interest rates. When bond prices rise, interest rates fall. Lower interest rates will encourage more lending. More lending increases consumer spending and investment. This, in turn, increases aggregate demand, resulting in the growth of GDP and lower unemployment. If the Fed expands the money supply too much, however, aggregate demand may increase to a level that causes inflation.

Monetary Policy The Fed's monetary policy must be well-timed and well-balanced to have the required effect.

DIFFERENTIATING INSTRUCTION

Struggling Readers

Diagram Cause and Effect

Have students work in pairs to understand cause-and-effect relationships involved in expansionary and contractionary monetary policy. Draw a cause-and-effect chain on the board that starts with the economy slowing down. Show the result as being increased GDP growth and lower unemployment. Invite pairs to fill in intermediate effects and causes. Have them complete a similar chain, beginning with high inflation and ending with decreased GDP growth and lower prices.

English Learners

Summarize Information

Model how to summarize information and list key details in a cluster web. Revisit the text with students. Monitor students as they work in pairs to create a cluster web that summarizes what they have learned about expansionary monetary policy. Have them share their summaries in small groups. To conclude, have students write summaries that tell about contractionary monetary policy.

POLICY 2 Contractionary Policy

In Chapter 15, you also studied the federal government's contractionary fiscal policy, used during an expansionary period. The Fed's contractionary monetary policy also is used when economic activity is rapidly increasing. It is sometimes called a **tight-money policy** because it is designed to reduce inflation by making it more difficult for businesses and individuals to get loans.

Suppose that aggregate demand is increasing faster than aggregate supply, leading to higher prices and concerns about inflation. The Fed would want to have less money circulating because more money fuels demand and may lead to inflation in wages and prices. In other words, the Fed would want to make it harder for businesses and individuals to borrow money. Therefore, it would decrease the money supply by decreasing reserves available for loans.

The Fed enacts a tight-money policy by selling bonds on the open market, increasing reserve requirements, or increasing the discount rate. As with easy-money policy, the Fed's most likely action involves open market operations. Selling bonds causes bond prices to fall and interest rates to increase. Higher interest rates discourage lending. Less lending decreases aggregate demand, which decreases growth in GDP, and lowers the general price level. If the Fed contracts the money supply too much, however, aggregate demand may decrease to a level where unemployment increases. Figure 16.9 summarizes how the Fed uses expansionary and contractionary monetary policies.

QUICK REFERENCE

Tight-money policy is another name for contractionary monetary policy.

ECONOMICS ESSENTIALS

FIGURE 16.9 Approaches to Monetary Policy

How does the Fed use its monetary policy tools?

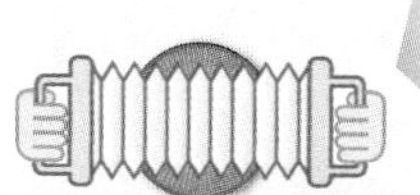

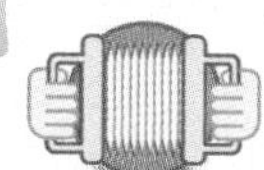

Expansionary Policy
- Buy bonds on the open market
- Lower the reserve requirement
- Reduce the discount rate

Contractionary Policy
- Sell bonds on the open market
- Raise the reserve requirement
- Increase the discount rate

ANALYZE CHARTS

Monetary policy is designed to even out the extremes of the business cycle by expanding or contracting the money supply. Explain how the actions listed under Expansionary Policy increase the supply of money and those under Contractionary Policy decrease the supply of money.

APPLICATION Comparing and Contrasting

B. What are the similarities and differences between expansionary fiscal policy and expansionary monetary policy? See Teacher's Edition for answer. ▶

Economics Essentials: Figure 16.9

Explain that the diagram graphically summarizes how the Fed uses its monetary policy tools to expand or contract the money supply.

- Which open market action would be used to fight inflation? *(sell bonds)*
- How would the Fed change the discount rate to fight recession? *(decrease it)*

Analyze

Possible answer: Expansionary policy actions increase the amount of bank reserves so that banks have more money to lend. When banks make more loans, the money supply increases. Contractionary policy actions decrease reserves and loans and shrink the money supply.

APPLICATION

Answer *Both have the same goal: to bring the economy out of recession, but they use different tools. Fiscal policy stimulates demand by increasing government spending or cutting taxes. Monetary policy uses tools that increase the money supply to make it easier for consumers and businesses to borrow money to buy goods and services.*

CLASS ACTIVITY

Role-Playing Approaches to Monetary Policy

Time 45 Minutes 

Task Create and act out skits to illustrate different approaches to monetary policy.

Materials Needed paper and pens or markers

Activity
- Direct students to review the descriptions of expansionary and contractionary monetary policy on pages 492–493.
- Have them brainstorm ideas for two skits that show how each policy is implemented using open market operations.
- Encourage students to consider how to portray the Fed's actions, as well as their effects on consumers and businesses.
- Some students may focus on writing scripts, others may make simple props, and others may perform various roles.
- Allow students to present their two skits. Discuss the different open market operations used and the effects of each approach to monetary policy on the economy.

Rubric

	Understanding of Concepts	Presentation of Information
4	excellent	clear, complete, creative
3	good	mostly clear, somewhat creative
2	fair	sometimes clear, some creative elements
1	poor	sketchy and unoriginal

Alan Greenspan

More About . . .

Alan Greenspan
Alan Greenspan, the son of a stockbroker and a saleswoman, showed a talent for solving mathematical puzzles as a child. Although he briefly studied music at the Julliard School in New York City after high school, he soon turned to economics. He received bachelor's (1948), master's (1950), and doctoral (1977) degrees in economics from New York University.

Greenspan's corporate consulting and board work provided valuable experience in and connections to the private sector. His years as chairman of the Council of Economic Advisers under President Ford (1974–1977) exposed him to Washington politics. Both proved useful during his terms at the Fed.

More About . . .

Greenspan's Fed
While Greenspan became famous for his obscure language, he also made Fed operations more transparent to the financial community. In February 1994, the FOMC, for the first time, announced its intentions regarding the federal funds rate to the public immediately after a meeting.

As Fed chairman, Greenspan analyzed mountains of financial data and worked with sophisticated computer models. Yet, he also relied on his gut instincts about the economy. Greenspan preferred a flexible approach to monetary policy, based on managing risks rather than one bound by strict rules.

At **ClassZone.com** students will see an article about Alan Greenspan.

ECONOMICS PACESETTER

Alan Greenspan: Fighting Inflation

During his 18-plus years as chairman of the Fed, Alan Greenspan came to personify the institution. The worldwide financial community and the media waited eagerly to hear what he would say after each meeting of the FOMC. Why did so many people come to believe that one man's decisions could have such a profound impact on everything from the performance of the stock market to mortgage rates?

FAST FACTS

Alan Greenspan

Title: Chairman of the Federal Reserve Board (1987–2006)

Born: March 6, 1926, New York City

Major Accomplishment: Controlled inflation while supporting unprecedented economic growth

Presidents Served Under: Ronald Reagan, George H. W. Bush, Bill Clinton, George W. Bush

Time as Fed Chairman: 18 years, 5 months (second longest tenure)

Notable Quotation: *I guess I should warn you, if I turn out to be particularly clear, you've probably misunderstood what I've said.*

Managing Monetary Policy

President Ronald Reagan appointed Alan Greenspan chairman of the Federal Reserve Board of Governors in 1987. He had a reputation as a committed inflation fighter and fulfilled that role with great success. The core inflation rate was 3.9 percent when he became chairman and was 2 percent in 2005.

Although the chairman has only one vote on the FOMC, Greenspan's economic insight and persuasiveness gave him much greater power. He led the Fed in using open market operations to help raise interest rates to cool down the economy when it experienced inflationary periods. At other times, for example, when the stock market crash of October 1987 threatened to lead the economy into a severe recession, Greenspan responded by expanding the money supply as needed to cushion the shock. Then, in the late 1990s, he pushed the Fed to edge up interest rates, and the economy experienced a period of unprecedented growth without inflation.

Greenspan's success was due to his clear understanding of the tools of monetary policy and how to apply them, as well as in-depth knowledge of a wide range of economic indicators. Also, throughout his years as chairman, he developed a sense of timing, knowing just when to direct the Fed to expand the money supply and when to contract it.

A Celebrity During his tenure as Fed chairman, Alan Greenspan practically achieved celebrity status.

Economics Update

Find an update about Alan Greenspan at **ClassZone.com**

APPLICATION Making Inferences

C. Did Greenspan advocate a tight-money policy or an easy-money policy in the late 1990s? How do you know?
An easy-money policy because he wanted to keep interest rates from rising so it would be easier for businesses to borrow money, promoting economic growth.

DIFFERENTIATING INSTRUCTION

Inclusion

Illustrate the Biography
Allow students who learn best through visuals to work in pairs to create a comic strip version of the Greenspan biography on page 494. Encourage students to identify key events in Greenspan's tenure as Fed chairman. Then have them create drawings to illustrate them. Taken together, student drawings should communicate the main ideas of the biography.

Gifted and Talented

Evaluate Greenspan's Policies
Invite interested students to use Internet or library sources to investigate the role of the Fed's monetary policy in promoting economic growth during the high-tech boom of the 1990s. Give special emphasis to Greenspan's role. Suggest that they look for different points of view about Greenspan's actions relative to the dot-com bubble and its aftermath, including the housing bubble of the early 2000s. Encourage students to present their assessment of his actions in an informal debate.

Impacts and Limitation of Monetary Policy

KEY CONCEPTS

As you recall, the purpose of monetary policy is to curb inflation and to halt recessions, which result in unemployment. But what impact does monetary policy have on the economy, and how successful is it in fulfilling its purpose?

IMPACT 1 Short-Term Effects

Adjustments to monetary policy have both short-term and long-term effects. The short-term effect is change in the price of credit—in other words, the interest rates on loans. The Fed's open market operations influence the FFR fairly quickly by increasing or decreasing the level of reserves that banks have available to lend. Figure 16.10 shows that when the Fed uses an easy-money policy to expand the money supply, interest rates decline. When the Fed uses a tight-money policy, as shown in Figure 16.11, interest rates rise.

FIGURES 16.10 AND 16.11 SHORT-TERM EFFECTS OF MONETARY POLICY

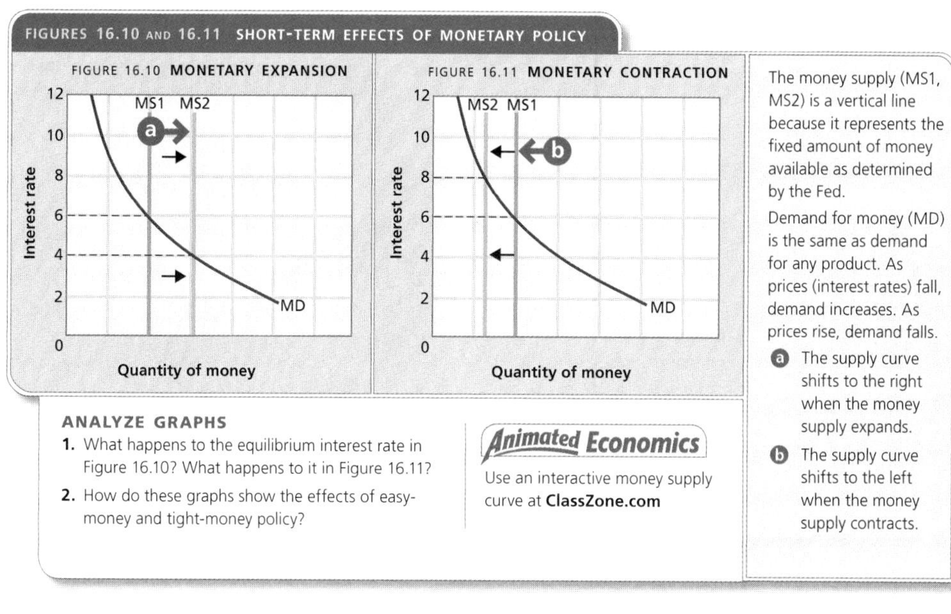

The money supply (MS1, MS2) is a vertical line because it represents the fixed amount of money available as determined by the Fed.

Demand for money (MD) is the same as demand for any product. As prices (interest rates) fall, demand increases. As prices rise, demand falls.

ⓐ The supply curve shifts to the right when the money supply expands.

ⓑ The supply curve shifts to the left when the money supply contracts.

ANALYZE GRAPHS

1. What happens to the equilibrium interest rate in Figure 16.10? What happens to it in Figure 16.11?
2. How do these graphs show the effects of easy-money and tight-money policy?

Animated **Economics** Use an interactive money supply curve at **ClassZone.com**

IMPACT 2 Policy Lags

Some lags, or delays, that affect monetary policy are related to identifying the problem. The Fed needs specific information and statistics in order to identify the problem and take action. Other lags have to do with how quickly the change in policy

Impacts and Limitation of Monetary Policy

Discuss

- Why do monetarists often disagree with monetary policy actions? *(Possible answer: because they believe these actions are likely to make the economy worse because they change the money supply too quickly)*

Analyzing Graphs: Figures 16.10 and 16.11

Explain that these graphs show the effects of changes in the money supply on interest rates for loans. Ask students how these money supply curves are different from other supply curves they have seen. *(The quantity of money supplied does not increase as interest rates increase but stays constant. Therefore, the supply curve is a straight line rather than a sloping line.)*

Answers

1. *It decreases from 6 percent to 4 percent. It increases from 6 percent to 8 percent.*
2. *They show that an easy-money policy expands the money supply and lowers interest rates, while a tight-money policy contracts the money supply and raises interest rates.*

Animated **Economics** These graphs show how changes in the money supply caused by monetary policy actions affect interest rates for loans. They will help students understand the short-term effects of monetary policy.

INDIVIDUAL ACTIVITY

Graphing the Effects of Monetary Policy

Time 20 Minutes

Task Create supply and demand curves showing the effects of different monetary policy actions.

Materials Needed graph paper and pencils or computer with graphing software

Activity

- Assign students one or more of the six possible Federal Reserve monetary policy actions (outlined in Figure 16.9).
- Direct them to create supply and demand curves that show the short-term effects of each action on the money supply and interest rates. They may use Figures 16.10 and 16.11 as models. Have them write a caption for each graph explaining what is shown.
- Allow students to share their graphs in small groups. Encourage them to summarize the short-term effects of expansionary and contractionary policy.

Rubric

	Understanding of Concepts	Presentation of Information
4	excellent	clear and complete
3	good	mostly complete
2	fair	somewhat complete
1	poor	sketchy

More About . . .

Monetarism

Monetarism began as a critique of Keynesian economics. It became more influential in the 1960s and 1970s after Milton Friedman and Anna Schwartz published *A Monetary History of the United States, 1867–1960* (1963). In 1979, the Federal Reserve became more focused on targeting the money supply, reflecting a monetarist approach.

In the early 1980s, other central banks also set targets for money supply growth. However, economists then discovered that the link between money supply and inflation was not as strong as monetarists had predicted. Since 1990, economists who once favored a strict monetary rule are more likely to focus on setting targets for inflation.

takes effect. Many economists suggest that it may take as long as two years for adjustments in monetary policy to take full effect. This may have long-term effects on the economy. For example, businesses often delay plans for expansion if interest rates are too high. Because policies designed to lower rates may take some time to take effect, actual investment in expansion may lag months or years behind the plans.

IMPACT 3 Timing Issues

As with fiscal policy, monetary policy must be coordinated with the business cycle in order to provide a stable economic environment. If the policy is correct and the timing is good, extremes in the business cycle will be evened out. If the timing is bad, a business cycle phase may be exaggerated. For example, high interest rates in 1990 that were intended to help fight inflation actually took effect as the economy was going into a recession, worsening the effects of that recession.

Supporters of monetarism cite such situations to show that using monetary policy to influence short-term changes in the business cycle can create major problems. **Monetarism** is a theory that suggests that rapid changes in the money supply are the main cause of economic instability. Milton Friedman is the most prominent monetarist. (You can read more about Friedman on page 76.) He studied how changes in the growth rate of the money supply affected prices and concluded that inflation is always accompanied by rapid monetary growth. Conversely, he noted that there has been little or no inflation when the money supply has grown slowly and steadily.

QUICK REFERENCE

Monetarism is a theory that holds that rapid changes in the money supply cause economic instability.

Monetarists do believe that monetary policy is an important tool. However, they argue that best way to ensure economic growth and stability is to allow the money supply to grow slowly and steadily—by around 3 percent a year. They disapprove of the Fed's use of monetary policy to constantly tinker with the money supply.

Monetarism According to monetarists, a slow, steady growth in the amount of money in circulation is the best monetary policy.

Other Issues

The use of the monetary policy tools is just one way the economy can be corrected. It is more effective if it is coordinated with fiscal policy. In addition, the goals of the Fed may clash with those of Congress or the president. Since members of the Fed's Board of Governors serve for 14-year terms, they are not as susceptible to political pressure as are politicians, who are elected every two to six years.

APPLICATION Analyzing Causes

D. What will happen to interest rates when the Fed sells bonds in open market operations? Why? They will rise because the Fed's bond sales cause the money supply to contract, which results in higher interest rates.

DIFFERENTIATING INSTRUCTION

Struggling Readers

Identify Main Ideas

The concepts under the headings "Policy Lags" and "Timing Issues" may be challenging for some students. Have small groups read each paragraph aloud and explain what they have read in their own words. Then, encourage students to come to a consensus on the main ideas and write them down in their notebooks before moving to the next paragraph.

Inclusion

Use Flash Cards

Have students make three large cards bearing the letters *A, B,* and *C*. To test students' understanding of the text, ask them simple questions about important concepts, each with three response choices. The questions may also be written on large cards. For each question, students should hold up the card with the letter signifying the correct response.

SECTION 3 Assessment

Online Quiz
ClassZone.com

REVIEWING KEY CONCEPTS

1. Explain the difference between the terms in each of these pairs.
   a. *monetary policy* *monetarism*
   b. *easy-money policy* *tight-money policy*
   c. *discount rate* *prime rate*
2. How should a contractionary monetary policy affect interest rates and the rate of inflation? Why?
3. How should an expansionary monetary policy affect interest rates and the unemployment rate? Why?
4. How does the Fed use open market operations as a monetary policy tool?
5. What is the main short-term effect of monetary policy?
6. **Using Your Notes** Which monetary policy tool does the Fed use least often? Refer to your completed hierarchy diagram.

   Monetary Policy → main ideas / main ideas / main ideas → details / details / details

   Use the Graphic Organizer at **Interactive Review @ ClassZone.com**

CRITICAL THINKING

7. **Analyzing Causes** To curb inflation, why is it easier for the Fed to use monetary policy to raise interest rates than it is for Congress to implement contractionary fiscal policy?
8. **Making Inferences** What are the Fed's underlying assumptions about the state of the economy, based on these Fed actions?
   a. The Fed's open market operations caused the FFR to drop from 6.25 percent to 1 percent.
   b. The FFR rose from 1 percent to 4.25 percent.
9. **Applying Economic Concepts** In 2005, the Fed set the discount rate for banks in good financial condition at 1 percent above the targeted FFR.
   a. Would these banks be more likely to borrow short-term funds from another bank or from the Fed? Why?
   b. How does this policy help keep the federal funds rate close to the target set by the Fed?
10. **Challenge** Explain how the Fed buying bonds affects interest rates, aggregate demand, price level, and GDP. Illustrate your answer using two graphs, one showing the money market and one showing aggregate supply and aggregate demand.

ECONOMICS IN PRACTICE

Durable goods—washing machines

Applying Economic Concepts Think about the ways monetary policy is used to address economic problems. Then complete the following activities.

Determine Monetary Policy The chart below lists several economic situations. For each one, decide whether an easy-money or tight-money policy is needed.

Economic Situation	Monetary Policy Needed
Consumer spending on durable goods rises faster than production	
Rising energy prices are pushing prices of many products higher	
Unemployment rate increases from 5.4% to 6.8% over six months	

Challenge Choose one example that requires an easy-money policy and one that requires a tight-money policy and explain how open market operations would be used in each case.

497

④ Assess & Reteach

Assess Group students and have the students in each group number off. Ask a question from the Section Assessment, and allow group members to agree on an answer. Then call out a number for a student from each group to give the group's answer.

Unit 6 Resource Book
- Section Quiz, p. 143

Interactive Review @ ClassZone.com
- Section Quiz

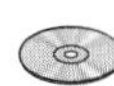

Test Generator CD-ROM
- Section Quiz

Reteach Work with the class to outline the parts of the section on an overhead transparency. Ask students to use their textbooks to contribute information to the outline. Have students copy the outline into their notes.

Unit 6 Resource Book
- Reteaching Activity, p. 144

Economics in Practice

Determine Monetary Policy tight-money policy; tight-money policy; easy-money policy

Challenge Tight-money: Fed will sell bonds on the open market. This will cause interest rates to increase, discouraging lending. This will decrease aggregate demand, slow GDP growth, and lower the general price level. Easy-money: Fed will buy bonds on the open market. This will cause interest rates to fall, encouraging lending. This will increase spending and investment, increase aggregate demand, speed GDP growth, and lower unemployment.

SECTION 3 ASSESSMENT ANSWERS

Reviewing Key Concepts

1. a. *monetary policy*, p. 490; *monetarism*, p. 496
   b. *easy-money policy*, p. 492; *tight-money policy*, p. 493
   c. *discount rate*, p. 491; *prime rate*, p. 491
2. Interest rates will rise, inflation rate will fall. Higher interest rates discourage lending, which will decrease aggregate demand, slow GDP growth, and lower general price level.
3. Interest rates will fall, unemployment will fall. Lower interest rates encourage lending, which will increase spending and investment, increase aggregate demand, and speed GDP growth.
4. By buying and selling government securities the Fed affects the amount of reserves in the banking system, which in turn determines whether the money supply will expand or contract.
5. It affects the price of credit, i.e. interest rates. Tight-money policy causes interest rates to rise, and easy-money policy causes them to fall.
6. See page 490 for a sample of a completed hierarchy diagram. changing the reserve requirement

Critical Thinking

7. Because Fed members are appointed, rather than elected, they are more willing to do what is best for the economy rather than what is politically popular.
8. a. Economy was in recession.
   b. Economy was showing signs of inflation.
9. a. from another bank because the federal funds rate charged by banks is lower than the discount rate charged by the Fed
   b. Banks would be unwilling to raise the federal funds rate above the discount rate because it would discourage banks from borrowing from one another.
10. Buying government bonds would cause the aggregate demand curve to shift to the right. Aggregate supply and demand and real GDP would increase. Bond prices would rise and interest rates would fall and the money supply curve moves to the right, indicating an increase in the money supply.

Economics in Practice

See answers in side column above.

❶ Plan & Prepare

Section 4 Objectives

- describe how monetary and fiscal policy can coordinate to improve the economy
- understand how monetary and fiscal policy can work against each other
- identify other measures that can be used to manage the economy

❷ Focus & Motivate

Connecting to Everyday Life Explain that this section focuses on the ways that monetary policy and fiscal policy affect one another. Ask students to review the effects of expansionary and contractionary fiscal and monetary policies.

Taking Notes Remind students to take notes as they read by completing a cause-and-effect chart. They can use the Graphic Organizer at **Interactive Review @ ClassZone.com**. A sample is shown below.

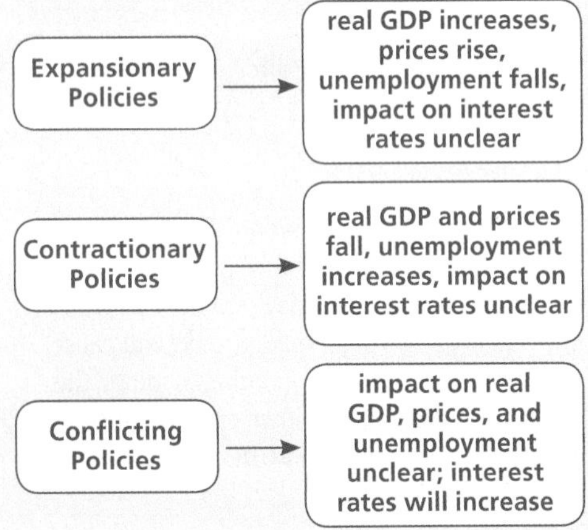
Expansionary Policies
real GDP increases, prices rise, unemployment falls, impact on interest rates unclear
Contractionary Policies
real GDP and prices fall, unemployment increases, impact on interest rates unclear
Conflicting Policies
impact on real GDP, prices, and unemployment unclear; interest rates will increase

SECTION 4

Applying Monetary and Fiscal Policy

OBJECTIVES	KEY TERMS	TAKING NOTES
In Section 4, you will • describe how monetary and fiscal policy can coordinate to improve the economy • understand how monetary and fiscal policy can work against each other • identify other measures that can be used to manage the economy	wage and price controls, *p. 501*	As you read Section 4, complete a cause-and-effect chart using the key concepts and other helpful words and phrases. Use the Graphic Organizer at **Interactive Review @ ClassZone.com** Expansionary Policies → results Contractionary Policies → results Conflicting Policies → results

Policies to Expand the Economy

KEY CONCEPTS

The goals of both fiscal and monetary policy are to stabilize the economy by easing the effects of recession and controlling inflation. Fiscal policy relies on government spending and taxation to achieve its goals. Monetary policy uses open market operations, the discount rate, and reserve requirements as its tools.

These policies, as well as affecting the economy, also have an impact on each other. As you recall, both monetary and fiscal policy have limitations. These include policy lags, political constraints, and timing issues. Policy lags relate to the time it takes to identify the problem and for policy actions to take effect. Political considerations may limit government's ability to do what is best for the economy. Timing, too, is important because to be effective government actions must counteract the negative effects of the business cycle. Intervention at the wrong time may skew the cycle and make the problem worse.

A second phenomenon affecting timing is explained by the rational expectations theory. As you recall from Chapter 15, this states that individuals and business firms learn, through experience, to anticipate changes in monetary and fiscal policy and take steps to protect their interests. For example, if there is debate in Congress about tax cuts, individuals and businesses may take actions before the legislation is even passed, based on their expectations that tax cuts will increase their income. Individuals may decide to purchase durable goods, such as automobiles, refrigerators, and washing machines. Similarly, businesses may decide to expand their operations by building new factories and hiring more workers. On the other hand, if individuals and businesses think the tax cuts will be temporary, they may choose not to spend as the policy intended.

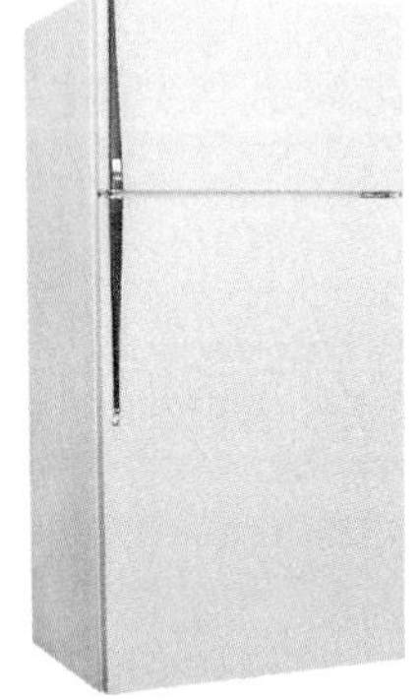

Rational Expectations Expectations that tax cuts will increase their incomes may cause people to buy "big-ticket" items such as refrigerators.

498 Chapter 16

SECTION 4 PROGRAM RESOURCES

ON LEVEL

Lesson Plans
- Core, p. 56

Unit 6 Resource Book
- Reading Study Guide, pp. 145–146
- Economic Simulations, pp. 161–162
- Section Quiz, p. 153

STRUGGLING READERS

Unit 6 Resource Book
- Reading Study Guide with Additional Support, pp. 147–149
- Reteaching Activity, p. 154

ENGLISH LEARNERS

Unit 6 Resource Book
- Reading Study Guide with Additional Support (Spanish), pp. 150–152

INCLUSION

Lesson Plans
- Modified for Inclusion, p. 56

GIFTED AND TALENTED

Unit 6 Resource Book
- Case Study Resources: Misreading His Lips, pp. 159–160

TECHNOLOGY

eEdition DVD-ROM

eEdition Online

Power Presentation DVD-ROM

Economics Concepts Transparencies
- CT56 How Monetary Policy Contributed to the Great Depression

Daily Test Practice Transparencies, TT56

ClassZone.com

People who disagree with the use of most discretionary policy often support their argument with the rational expectations theory. They suggest that rather than fiddling with fiscal and monetary policy, the government should aim for a stable monetary policy so that business decisions are made for economic reasons and not in anticipation of new policies.

EXAMPLE Expansionary Monetary and Fiscal Policy

The goal of expansionary policy is to stimulate the economy by reducing unemployment and increasing investment. As you recall, expansionary fiscal policy involves increased government spending or tax cuts. Also, to enact expansionary monetary policy, the Fed buys government bonds or reduces the discount rate or the reserve requirement.

For example, suppose that the unemployment rate is 9.5 percent and the Consumer Price Index (CPI) is at 2 percent. The economy is in recession and inflation is a minimal concern. In order to increase the money supply, the Fed buys bonds on the open market and lowers the discount rate. The federal government also cuts personal income taxes and increases government spending. These expansionary policies are designed to increase aggregate demand and decrease unemployment. Real GDP will expand and prices will rise as aggregate demand increases. Figure 16.12 shows how expansionary policies affect these key economic indicators.

Expansionary fiscal policy is likely to raise interest rates, while expansionary monetary policy should decrease interest rates. Therefore, the actual change in interest rates will depend on the relative strength of the two policies. The amount of investment spending will depend on what happens with interest rates.

FIGURE 16.12 Effects of Expansionary Policies

Policies

(a) **Monetary Policy** The Fed buys bonds and lowers the discount rate to increase money supply

Fiscal Policy Increased spending/ tax cuts to increase aggregate demand

Effects

(b) **Real GDP** increases and **prices** rise

Unemployment falls

(a) Here, fiscal and monetary policies work together to expand the economy.

(b) These policies tend to increase aggregate demand, increase real GDP, and lower unemployment.

ANALYZE CHARTS

1. According to the chart, what are the goals of expansionary policies?
2. Which indicator in the chart suggests that expansionary policy might lead toward inflation?

APPLICATION Analyzing Effects

A. What effect would government borrowing to finance increased spending have on interest rates and why? It would tend to increase interest rates because it increases government demand for credit and would raise its price, i.e. interest rates.

3 Teach

Policies to Expand the Economy

Discuss

- What are the tools used in applying expansionary fiscal and monetary policy? *(increase government spending, cut taxes, buy bonds, decrease the discount rate or reserve requirement)*
- Why is it difficult to determine how expansionary policies will affect interest rates? *(because fiscal policy and monetary policy have opposite effects on interest rates)*

Analyzing Charts: Figure 16.12

Point out that the two up arrows indicate that monetary policy and fiscal policy are both working to expand the economy. Ask students what the chart shows about the relationship of GDP and unemployment. *(It shows that they have an inverse relationship; as GDP increases, unemployment falls.)*

Answers

1. *increases in the money supply and aggregate demand*
2. *rising prices*

INDIVIDUAL ACTIVITY

Writing a News Story

Time 30 minutes ◑

Task Write a news story based on an example of applying monetary and fiscal policy.

Materials Needed paper and pens

Activity

- Allow students to choose an example of the application of monetary and fiscal policy to solve an economic problem, such as those on pages 499–502.
- Have each student write a news story based on the example.
- Encourage students to add details about the economic situation and government and Federal Reserve actions in order to tell the story in a journalistic style.
- Recommend that students also include reasons why the policies may be limited in their effectiveness.
- Invite volunteers to share their stories. Discuss how monetary and fiscal policies affect the economy and one another.

Rubric

	Understanding of Concepts	Presentation of Information
4	excellent	clear and complete
3	good	mostly clear
2	fair	sometimes clear
1	poor	sketchy

Policies to Control Inflation

Discuss

- What economic indicator is most important in determining the need for contractionary policies? *(a high CPI that indicates the economy is experiencing inflation)*
- How effective were wage and price controls at controlling inflation in the 1970s? *(They were not effective; the rate of inflation more than doubled during the period they were in effect.)*

Analyzing Charts: Figure 16.13

Point out that the two down arrows under Policies show that monetary and fiscal policy are working together to tighten the economy. Ask students how the Effects shown on this chart compare to those in Figure 16.12. *(The charts show opposite effects because the policies have opposite goals.)*

Answers

1. *decreases in the money supply and aggregate demand*
2. *It is leading to lower interest rates, and increased borrowing might lead to inflation.*

Policies to Control Inflation

KEY CONCEPTS

The goal of contractionary monetary policy is to tighten up the economy by decreasing inflation and increasing interest rates. Contractionary fiscal policy tools include decreased government spending or tax increases. The Fed will sell bonds on the open market or raise the discount rate or the reserve requirement as contractionary monetary policy tools.

EXAMPLE Contractionary Monetary and Fiscal Policy

Suppose that the unemployment rate is 4.5 percent and the CPI is running in excess of 10 percent. The economy is operating at or above a sustainable level of output, and inflation is very high. In order to decrease the money supply, the Fed sells bonds on the open market and raises the discount rate. The federal government cuts spending on government programs. It also may raise taxes. These contractionary policies are designed to decrease aggregate demand and bring inflation under control. Real GDP will decrease, and prices will fall as aggregate demand decreases. Further, unemployment tends to rise as real GDP decreases. Figure 16.13 shows how contractionary monetary and fiscal policies affect the key economic indicators of unemployment and real GDP.

Contractionary fiscal policy is likely to lower interest rates because decreased government spending will decrease demand for loans. Contractionary monetary policy should raise interest rates. Therefore, the actual change in interest rates will depend on the relative strength of the two policies. The amount of investment spending depends on what happens with interest rates.

FIGURE 16.13 Effects of Contractionary Policies

Policies
a
Monetary Policy The Fed sells bonds and raises the discount rate to cut money supply
Fiscal Policy Decreased spending/ tax increases to decrease aggregate demand
Effects
b
Real GDP and prices fall
Unemployment increases

a Here, fiscal and monetary policies work together to contract the economy.

b These policies decrease aggregate demand, control inflation, and raise unemployment.

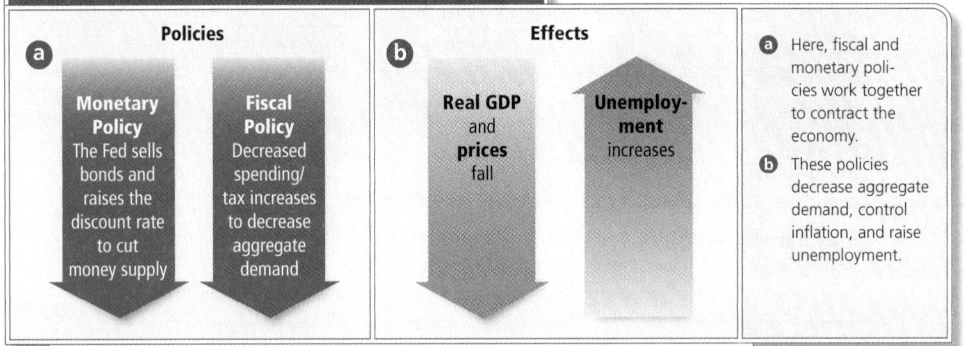

ANALYZE CHARTS

1. According to the chart, what are the goals of contractionary policies?
2. In what way might the fiscal policy shown here not help to control inflation?

DIFFERENTIATING INSTRUCTION

English Learners

Take Notes

Write the heading *Expansionary Monetary and Fiscal Policy* on the board and reread the three paragraphs in the text on page 499. Model how to write key details or facts that explain expansionary policies. Remind students that note-taking only includes key details or information. Have students practice taking notes on the material on pages 500–502 and then retelling the information on one topic to a classmate.

Inclusion

Manipulate Visuals

Work with students to create enlarged arrows as shown in Figures 16.12, 16.13, and 16.14. You may draw the arrows on large index cards or poster board or cut out arrow shapes and label them. Then, work with students to help them understand what arrows belong together to show policies working together or policies in conflict. For example, you might show them the up arrow for expansionary monetary policy and ask which fiscal policy arrow would show policies working together.

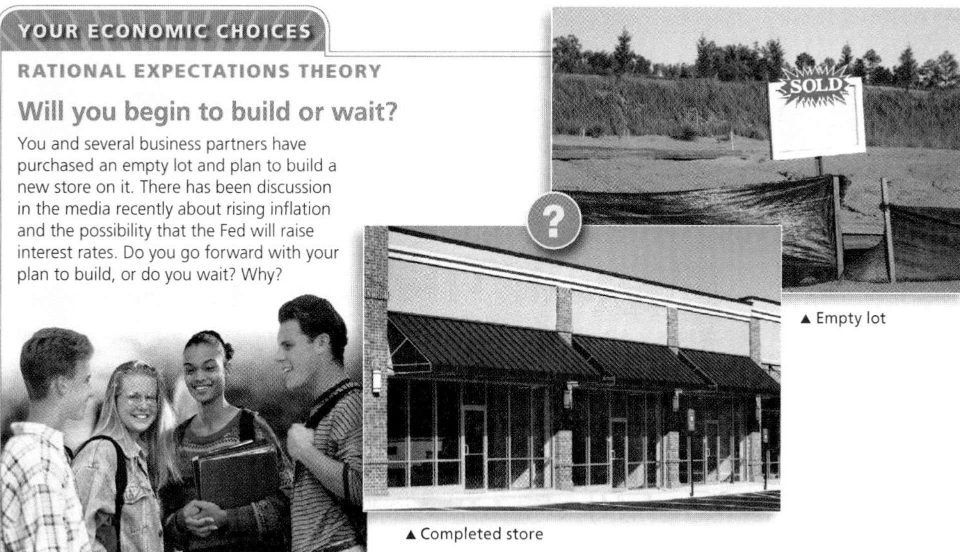

YOUR ECONOMIC CHOICES

RATIONAL EXPECTATIONS THEORY

Will you begin to build or wait?

You and several business partners have purchased an empty lot and plan to build a new store on it. There has been discussion in the media recently about rising inflation and the possibility that the Fed will raise interest rates. Do you go forward with your plan to build, or do you wait? Why?

▲ Empty lot

▲ Completed store

EXAMPLE Wage and Price Controls

At times in the past, the government has taken extreme measures to control the economy, especially during wartime. For example, the government may establish a set of wage and price guidelines that are not mandatory. **Wage and price controls** are limits, established by the government, on increases in certain wages and prices. These controls, unlike wage and price guidelines, are mandatory and enforced by the government.

World War II led to increased production of goods needed by the military. This situation created shortages of many consumer goods as well as a labor shortage, which tended to drive up prices and wages. In an effort to control inflation, President Franklin D. Roosevelt established the Office of Price Administration (OPA) in 1942. This agency set strict wage and price controls on all sectors of the economy. These measures had some, but not total, success. They were phased out almost immediately after the end of the war.

In 1971, President Richard M. Nixon was faced with stagflation, a situation in which rising unemployment is accompanied by rising inflation rates. In August of that year, Nixon announced a 90-day freeze on wages and prices to try to control inflation. The program was renewed several times and lasted until April 1974. Even so, it had little impact. From late 1971 to early 1974, the inflation rate actually rose from about 4 percent to 11 percent.

QUICK REFERENCE

Wage and price controls are government limits on increases in wages and prices.

APPLICATION Comparing and Contrasting

B. What are the similarities and differences between contractionary monetary policy and wage and price controls? See answer in Teacher's Edition. ▶

Your Economic Choices

RATIONAL EXPECTATIONS THEORY

Will you begin to build or wait?

- What expectation did you have when you and your partners purchased the lot and made your plans? *(Possible answer: that it was a good location for a profitable business and that the investment would pay off)*
- What do you expect will happen if the Fed raises interest rates? *(It will cost more to borrow money in the future.)*

Activity Have students work in small groups to do a cost-benefit analysis of the two choices. Encourage them to consider direct costs involved in building now vs. waiting, as well as the opportunity costs involved in each situation. Invite volunteers to share their analyses with the class. Discuss how this scenario illustrates rational expectations theory.

APPLICATION

Answer *Both have goal of controlling inflation. Monetary policy affects wages and prices indirectly by raising interest rates and contracting money supply; wage and price controls set government limits directly on wages and prices.*

SMALL GROUP ACTIVITY

Reporting on Wage and Price Controls

Time 45 Minutes 

Task Research information on wage and price control measures and present an oral report.

Materials Needed computer with Internet access

Activity

- Organize students into groups and have each one research an example of wage and price guidelines or controls.
- Suggest groups focus on World War II or the Korean War, Nixon's price controls, or voluntary programs under the Ford and Carter administrations.
- Encourage students to find out how serious the problem of inflation was, how the controls or guidelines were established, and how effective they were.
- Allow groups to present the results of their research in oral reports. Discuss why these policies are now rarely used.

Rubric

	Understanding of Concepts	Presentation of Information
4	excellent	clear and complete
3	good	mostly clear
2	fair	sometimes clear
1	poor	sketchy

Policies in Conflict

Discuss

- Why are coordinated policies more effective than conflicting policies? *(Possible answer: because coordinated policies have common goals, while conflicting policies are focused on different goals)*
- How might political considerations lead to conflicting policies? *(Possible answer: It is difficult for the president and Congress to institute contractionary fiscal policy when the Fed is using contractionary monetary policy. The reason is that such fiscal policy is politically unpopular.)*

Analyzing Charts: Figure 16.14

Point out that the different directions of the two policy arrows show that they are in conflict. Ask students which policy would need to be stronger in order to fight inflation. *(contractionary monetary policy)*

Answers

1. *expansionary fiscal policy*
2. *Contractionary monetary policy limits consumer spending by making it more expensive to borrow money; expansionary fiscal policy in the form of tax cuts gives consumers more money to spend.*

APPLICATION

Answer *When government cuts taxes, it needs to borrow more money to cover the same amount of spending, thus increasing the demand for credit and its price, namely interest rates.*

Policies in Conflict

KEY CONCEPTS

As you have seen, coordinated policies are, for the most part, effective in reaching a mutually agreed upon goal—that is, a stable but growing economy with little inflation. When fiscal and monetary policies are not coordinated, however, one policy can counter the effect of the other and thwart this goal, creating economic instability instead.

EXAMPLE Conflicting Monetary and Fiscal Policies

Suppose that the unemployment rate is 7 percent and the CPI stands at 6 percent and is steadily rising. The Fed may decide that the most pressing problem for the economy is rising inflation. So, to cool down the economy it follows a contractionary monetary policy, selling bonds on the open market and raising the discount rate. At the same time, the federal government may decide that rising unemployment needs is a bigger problem. To stimulate aggregate demand, it follows an expansionary fiscal policy, cutting personal taxes and increasing spending on public works programs.

The only clear result of these conflicting policies is that interest rates will increase. Because the policies are in conflict, the effects on GDP, prices, and unemployment cannot be predicted. This is illustrated in Figure 16.14.

FIGURE 16.14 Effects of Conflicting Policies

Policies
a
Monetary Policy The Fed sells bonds and raises the discount rate to cut money supply
Fiscal Policy Tax cuts/ increased spending to increase aggregate demand
Effects
b
Real GDP and prices may rise or fall
Unemployment may rise or fall

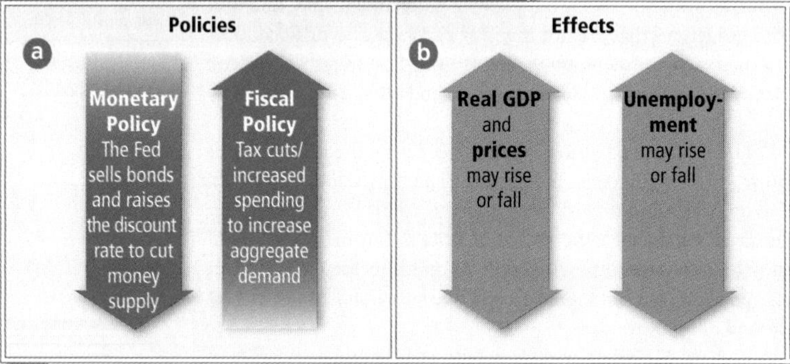

a This shows that the policies are working against each other in efforts to stabilize the economy.

b Here, conflicting policies make it impossible to predict the effects on GDP, prices, and unemployment.

ANALYZE GRAPHS

1. According to the chart, which policy is designed to increase GDP?
2. How do you think conflicting monetary and fiscal policies, like those described above, will affect consumer spending? Why?

APPLICATION Analyzing Causes

C. Why do tax cuts and increased government spending result in a rise in interest rates?

◄ See answer in Teacher's Edition.

DIFFERENTIATING INSTRUCTION

Struggling Readers

Organize Information

Ask partners or small groups to read through the section one heading at a time, stopping after each subsection to jot down main ideas. Bring the groups together to compare and discuss main ideas. Help students identify supporting details.

Gifted and Talented

Analyze Policies

Have students use the Internet to find out what current fiscal and monetary policies are being used by the government and the Fed. Students should look for trends in government spending, taxation, and the federal funds rate. Ask them to determine whether the policies are coordinated or conflicting and what effect they are having. Suggest students write their point of view about how effective these policies are, including supporting evidence.

SECTION 4 Assessment

Online Quiz
ClassZone.com

REVIEWING KEY CONCEPTS

1. Use the term below in a sentence that illustrates the meaning of the term.
   wage and price controls
2. How is rational expectations theory related to the limitations of fiscal and monetary policy?
3. Why does rational expectations theory oppose most discretionary fiscal and monetary policy?
4. Does monetary policy or fiscal policy most directly affect the economy? Why?
5. Why might an expansionary fiscal policy and a contractionary monetary policy work against each other?
6. **Using Your Notes** What are the effects of expansionary fiscal and monetary policies? Refer to your completed diagram.

Expansionary Policies	→	results
Contractionary Policies	→	results
Conflicting Policies	→	results

   Use the Graphic Organizer at **Interactive Review @ ClassZone.com**

CRITICAL THINKING

7. **Drawing Conclusions** What happens to interest rates if the Fed implements a contractionary monetary policy when Congress and the president cut taxes and increase government spending? What effect do you think this would have on the economy? Why?
8. **Applying Economic Concepts** When President Nixon imposed wage and price controls in the 1970s in an attempt to control inflation, he felt he could then use expansionary fiscal policy to decrease unemployment. These policies helped him win reelection in 1972, but inflation rose sharply over the next three years. Use the economic concepts you have learned in this section to explain what happened.
9. **Challenge** Many economists argue that the economy is better off when monetary policy is used most often to stabilize the economy, with fiscal policy being used primarily as a backup to bring the economy out of longer recessions. Do you agree or disagree with this assessment? Why or why not?

ECONOMICS IN PRACTICE

Applying Economic Concepts Recall what you have learned about the effectiveness of monetary policy, then complete the activities below.

Interpreting Economic Models Which graph shows poor timing of monetary policy in relation to the business cycle? What is the effect of monetary policy on the business cycle shown on each graph?

Challenge How do these graphs reflect rational expectations theory?

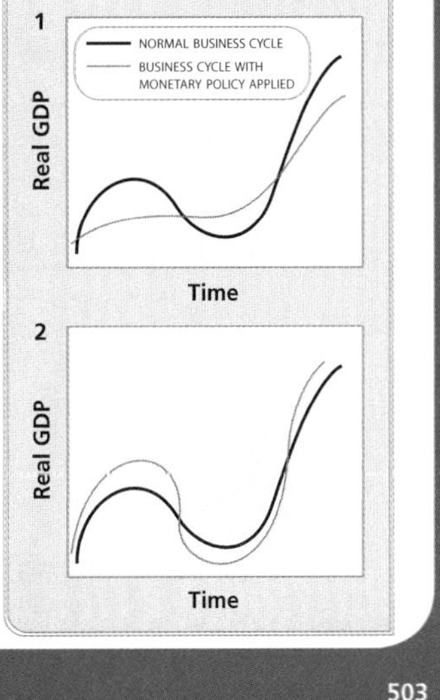

4 Assess & Reteach

Assess Have students write answers to all the review questions. Then ask them to pick out the questions that they find the most challenging and would like to discuss in class.

Unit 6 Resource Book
- Section Quiz, p. 153

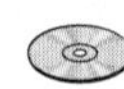

Interactive Review @ ClassZone.com
- Section Quiz

Test Generator CD-ROM
- Section Quiz

Reteach Have students write summaries of the section. Each summary should include at least three paragraphs, one for each major heading of the text. Call on volunteers to share their summaries with the class.

Unit 6 Resource Book
- Reteaching Activity, p. 154

Economics in Practice

Interpreting Economic Models Graph 2; Graph 1 shows that well-timed monetary policy can minimize the effects of the business cycle. Graph 2 shows that poorly timed monetary policy can make the effects of the business cycle worse.

Challenge They show that given time the economy will self-correct and that at best monetary policy may slightly mitigate the effects of the business cycle. If the timing is off, monetary policy makes the economy worse off than it would be if it were left alone.

SECTION 4 ASSESSMENT ANSWERS

Reviewing Key Concepts

1. *wage and price controls*, p. 501
2. Rational expectations theory is related to the timing issues that affect fiscal and monetary policy because over time individuals and firms come to expect certain results from these policies and adapt their actions to further their interest, thus limiting the effectiveness of these policies.
3. because it believes that the economy will self-correct without intervention and that due to the limitations of the policies they may actually make economic problems worse
4. Monetary policy, because it tends to take effect quicker than fiscal policy
5. because one is designed to stimulate economic activity and the other is designed to slow economic activity
6. See page 498 for a completed diagram. increased GDP, higher prices, lower unemployment, uncertain on interest rates and investment

Critical Thinking

7. The combination of expansionary fiscal policy and contractionary monetary policy definitely leads to higher interest rates. However, expansionary fiscal policy leads to higher prices; if it is stronger than the monetary policy, it could contribute to inflation in spite of higher interest rates. If the monetary policy is stronger it might send the economy into recession by stifling economic growth.
8. The goals of the policy were in conflict, and the expansionary policy tended to raise prices. The wage and price controls created shortages and tended to raise prices in spite of their intention to check inflation. Because they did not affect the money supply, the controls did not help to raise interest rates to check inflation.
9. Agree: monetary policy can be enacted quickly with less political pressure and is more effective in controlling inflation, contractionary fiscal policy is too politically unpopular. Disagree: policy lags and timing issues limit the effectiveness of both policies.

Economics in Practice
See answers in side column above.

1 Plan & Prepare

Objectives

- Describe how the Fed sends signals to financial markets.
- Understand how Fed actions affect financial markets.

2 Focus & Motivate

Invite students to consider times when their actions have been influenced by someone's words. Explain that this Case Study explores how statements by the Fed chairman may affect the actions of investors.

3 Teach

Using the Sources

Encourage students to examine each source to learn how having a new Fed chairman affected financial markets.

A. Why might Ben Bernanke be brushing up on his communication techniques? *(Possible answer: because he wants to make sure that he communicates in a way that will not be misinterpreted)*

B. In what way might Bernanke be following in Greenspan's footsteps? *(Possible answer: Bernanke is communicating in a similar, difficult-to-understand way.)*

C. How would you summarize the state of the economy based on Bernanke's statements? *(Possible answer: The economy is starting to slow down but inflation is a more important problem.)*

Economics Update

Go to **ClassZone.com** to find an update to this Case Study, including another article, an editable student worksheet, and an editable lesson plan.

Case Study

Find an update on this Case Study at **ClassZone.com**

Interpreting Signals from the Fed

Background The Federal Reserve is a powerful institution, so people pay attention to the Fed chairman's comments. A hint that the Fed might raise the discount rate can lead to a great deal of activity in the stock market. Some people might buy stock because they are confident that the Fed will keep inflation low. Others might sell stock because they are worried that the economy is slowing down. Over the 18 years that Alan Greenspan was Fed chairman, economists and financial observers scrutinized his every word in an attempt to predict how his statements would affect the economy. When Ben Bernanke was appointed as Fed chairman in 2006, observers had to learn a new language.

What's the issue? How much does the market rely on signals from the Fed to make economic decisions? Read the following to see what happened when the status quo changed and the signals were different.

A. Internet Article

This article demonstrates how Fed Chairman Ben Bernanke had to carefully review his public comments.

Crossed Economic Signals

Fed Expected to Boost Key Interest Rates

After nearly two decades of decoding Alan Greenspan's famously opaque speaking style, financial markets are having to learn to interpret his successor Ben Bernanke. So far, the results have been a little rocky. . . .

Some economists believe the Fed will stop with the funds rate at 5 percent, up significantly from the 46-year low of 1 percent in effect before the rate increases began. Others think the Fed will only pause for a meeting or two and then raise rates one or two more times. And still a third group thinks there won't be any pause as the Fed continues a steady march toward higher rates.

Part of the blame for the confusion is being assigned to Bernanke, who took over as Fed chairman on Feb. 1. He roiled markets over the past two weeks, first with testimony before the Joint Economic Committee on April 27 that the markets read as a strong signal that the Fed was going to pause in its string of rate increases, and then the next week when he told a reporter that the markets had misinterpreted his comments.

Economists said that the incident showed that there is a new Fed chairman with a different speaking style. . . . In any event, forecasters predicted Bernanke will be brushing up on his communication techniques.

Source: **"Fed Expected to Boost Key Interest Rates," by Martin Crutsinger. Associated Press, May 10, 2006.**

Thinking Economically Why does the Fed chairman need to develop strong communication techniques ?

DIFFERENTIATING INSTRUCTION

English Learners

Understand Colloquial English

Explain that writers use phrases not meant to be understood literally but that are used to communicate in a vivid way. Allow students to work with partners to use context clues to determine the meaning of phrases such as "a little rocky," "string of rate increases," and "brushing up on." Encourage students to restate the sentences where these phrases appear in their own words to make sure they understand. Discuss images that come to mind when students see these phrases.

Gifted and Talented

Write a Biography

Encourage interested students to research information about Ben Bernanke, including his background and qualifications for the role of Fed chairman and his approach to monetary policy. Suggest that students write a brief biography about Bernanke that focuses on how he will tackle the job of fighting inflation while promoting economic growth. Students may use the Greenspan biography on page 494 as a model. Allow students to share their biographies with the class.

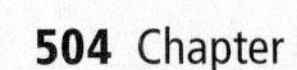

B. Political Cartoon

Harley Schwadron drew this cartoon about the new Fed chairman following in his predecessor's footsteps.

I THINK IT WAS A SUCCESSFUL MEETING. THEY DIDN'T UNDERSTAND A WORD I SAID.
ECONOMIC HEARING TODAY
SCHWADRON
Source: www.CartoonStock.com

BERNANKE FOLLOWS IN GREENSPAN'S FOOTSTEPS.

Thinking Economically What message does this cartoon convey about how the Fed has been known to give information?

C. Newspaper Article

This article reports on a speech Chairman Bernanke made at an international financial conference and the reaction that followed.

Open to Analysis

Bernanke Talks Tough on Inflation

Ben S. Bernanke, chairman of the Federal Reserve, warned Monday that recent inflation trends were "unwelcome developments," indicating that he was far less worried about signs of weaker economic growth than about the danger of higher prices.

In his toughest comments yet about the risks of inflation, Mr. Bernanke said consumer prices were rising faster than he would like. . . . Investors, increasingly convinced that the central bank will raise rates . . . immediately began selling stocks.

The Dow industrials and the broader Standard & Poor's 500-stock index each fell about 1.75 percent, and the Nasdaq index tumbled more than 2 percent. . . .

Speaking to a conference . . . on international monetary issues with other central bankers, Mr. Bernanke said inflation had climbed to the upper limits of his acceptability.

"Core inflation, measured over the past three to six months, has reached a level that, if sustained, would be at or above the upper range that many economists, including myself, would consider consistent with price stability," Mr. Bernanke said. . . .

Mr. Bernanke made clear that he thought the economy was now in a "transition" to slower economic growth. . . . Instead of highlighting signs of a cooling economy, which would ease inflationary pressures, Mr. Bernanke placed top emphasis on the need for vigilance against rising prices.

Source: "Bernanke Talks Tough on Inflation," by Edmund L. Andrews. *New York Times*, June 6, 2006

Thinking Economically What kind of monetary policy did investors expect Bernanke to follow—expansionary or contractionary policy? Explain your answer.

THINKING ECONOMICALLY Synthesizing

1. How do articles A and C illustrate the rational expectations theory?
2. Based on these three sources and your own knowledge, how would you describe the differences and similarities between Greenspan and Bernanke and their impact on the market?

Thinking Economically

Answers

A. *If the Fed chairman is not completely clear when making statements, the markets may respond in a negative way.*

B. *The Fed has not been completely clear in the way it delivers information.*

C. *contractionary policy, to combat inflation*

Synthesizing

1. *The articles suggest that investors decided that Bernanke's statements signaled that he would take particular actions and they took steps to protect their investments.*
2. *Bernanke's speaking style seems to be somewhat more forthright than Greenspan's, and the markets are having trouble working out exactly how to react to what Bernanke says.*

TECHNOLOGY ACTIVITY

Analyzing Fed Communications and the Markets

Time 45 Minutes 

Task Use the Internet to research communications by the Fed and prepare a written report on their effects on the financial markets.

Materials Needed computer with Internet access, word processing software (optional)

Activity

- Have groups research some communications from the Fed, such as speeches by the chairman, testimony before Congress, or statements released after meetings of the FOMC.
- Assign groups different types of communication or different time periods.
- Ask students to find related news stories that focus on the stock or bond market's reaction to the communication.
- Direct each group to prepare a report of its findings.
- Allow groups to share reports with the class. Discuss the effects of the Fed's statements.

Rubric

	Understanding of Concepts	Presentation of Information
4	excellent	clear and complete
3	good	mostly clear
2	fair	sometimes clear
1	poor	sketchy

Online Summary Answers

1. Federal Reserve System
2. central bank
3. Board of Governors
4. Federal Open Market Committee
5. required reserve ratio
6. deposit multiplier formula
7. Monetary policy
8. discount rate
9. open market operations
10. federal funds rate
11. Expansionary monetary policy
12. easy-money policy
13. Contractionary monetary policy
14. tight-money policy

Interactive Review

Review this chapter using interactive activities at **ClassZone.com**

- Online Summary
- Quizzes
- Vocabulary Flip Cards
- Graphic Organizers
- Review and Study Notes

Online Summary

Complete the following activity either on your own paper or online at **ClassZone.com**

Choose the key concept that best completes the sentence. Not all key concepts will be used.

bank holding company	Federal Reserve System
Board of Governors	monetarism
central bank	monetary policy
contractionary monetary policy	open market operations
deposit multiplier formula	prime rate
discount rate	required reserve ratio
easy-money policy	thrift institution
expansionary monetary policy	tight-money policy
federal funds rate	wage and price controls
Federal Open Market Committee	

The __1__ is the __2__ of the United States and is commonly known as the Fed. The __3__ supervises the operations of the Fed. The __4__ supervises the sales and purchase of federal government securities.

The Fed controls the amount of money a bank can loan through the __5__. The __6__ tells how much the money supply will increase after an initial cash deposit.

__7__ is actions by the Fed that change the money supply in order to influence the economy. The three tools used by the Fed to change the money supply are reserve requirements, the __8__, which is the rate the Fed charges when it lends money to banks, and __9__. The last tool allows the Fed to influence the __10__, the rate banks charge one another to borrow funds overnight.

__11__ seeks to increase the amount of money in circulation and is also known as __12__. __13__ seeks to decrease the amount of money in circulation and is also known as __14__.

CHAPTER 16 Assessment

REVIEWING KEY CONCEPTS

The Federal Reserve System (pp. 474–479)

1. What are the three duties of the Federal Reserve?
2. What are the different responsibilities of the Board of Governors and the Federal Open Market Committee?

Functions of the Federal Reserve (pp. 480–489)

3. What are the three functions of the Federal Reserve?
4. How does the size of the RRR affect the banking system's ability to create money?

Monetary Policy (pp. 490–497)

5. What is the Fed's most frequently used monetary policy tool?
6. What is the purpose of monetary policy?

Applying Monetary and Fiscal Policy (pp. 498–505)

7. What tools would be used to implement contractionary monetary and fiscal policy?
8. Why might it be important to coordinate monetary and fiscal policy?

APPLYING ECONOMIC CONCEPTS

Look at the line graph below showing the FFR and the prime rate over several years.

FIGURE 16.15 SHORT-TERM INTEREST RATES

Source: *Federal Reserve*

9. What is the relationship of the prime rate to the FFR as shown on this graph?
10. What conclusion can you draw about the U.S. economy based on interest rates in 2002–2004?

CHAPTER 16 ASSESSMENT ANSWERS

Reviewing Key Concepts

1. holding reserves, assuring stability, and lending money
2. The Board of Governors sets policy and supervises the Fed's operations, and the Federal Open Market Committee supervises the sales and purchase of government securities to manage the money supply.
3. serve the banking system, serve the federal government, create money
4. The amount of money the banking system can create is inversely proportional to the RRR.
5. open market operations
6. to promote high employment and stable economic growth with low inflation
7. monetary: sell bonds, increase the discount rate, raise the reserve requirements; fiscal: cut spending, raise taxes
8. because coordinated policies make it easier to achieve the goal of stable growth with little inflation

Applying Economic Concepts

9. The prime rate is directly related to the federal funds rate and is about 3 percentage points higher.
10. Low rates show that the economy was in recession and the Fed was pursuing an easy-money policy.

CRITICAL THINKING

11. **Making Inferences** Eight times per year the Fed collects economic information from each of its districts and compiles a report to help the FOMC make its decisions. How does this practice reflect the benefits of the Fed's structure?

12. **Applying Economic Concepts** In response to the terrorist attacks of September 11, 2001, the Fed started lowering the FFR target the following week. Congress was unable to agree on a program to help stimulate the economy until March 2002. How does this situation illustrate the effects of policy lags on monetary and fiscal policy?

13. **Analyzing Causes and Effects** Suppose that the Fed buys a $10,000 T-bond from the First National Bank. What effect will this have on First National's reserves and on the FFR? Why?

14. **Drawing Conclusions** In 2001, Congress approved a major tax cut package, while the Fed lowered the FFR target. In January 2006, the president asked Congress to make the tax cuts permanent, and the Fed raised the FFR target. When were fiscal and monetary policies working together, and when were they in conflict?

15. **Challenge** The FOMC issued the following statement after one of its meetings:

> *Although recent economic data have been uneven, the expansion in economic activity appears solid. Core inflation has stayed relatively low in recent months, and longer-term inflation expectations remain contained. Nevertheless, possible increases in resource utilization as well as elevated energy prices have the potential to add to inflation pressures.*
>
> *The Committee judges that some further policy firming may be needed to keep the risks to the attainment of both sustainable economic growth and price stability roughly in balance.*

Did the committee raise, lower, or maintain the target for the FFR? Cite evidence from the statement to support your answer.

SIMULATION

Stabilize the Economy

Step 1 Choose a partner. Imagine that you are advisers to the president of your Federal Reserve District bank. Your job is to prepare the president for the next FOMC meeting. The current state of the economy is shown in column A of the Key Economic Indicators table below. Decide whether an expansionary or contractionary monetary policy is needed. Recommend the type of open market operations needed as well as a target for the FFR. Give reasons for your recommendation and outline what you expect to happen to the other indicators as a result of this policy.

KEY ECONOMIC INDICATORS (IN PERCENT)

Indicator	A	B	C
GDP	+3.00	+2.00	+6.50
CPI	+6.25	+3.00	+1.50
Unemployment Rate	5.60	7.50	4.50
Federal Funds Rate	7.75	4.75	5.25

Step 2 The state of the economy two years later is shown in column B. Develop a new recommendation based on this data, with the same kind of details you included in Step 1.

Step 3 The economy has experienced several years of growth as indicated by the information in column C. Develop a new recommendation based on your evaluation of this situation.

Step 4 Share your three recommendations with the class. As a class, decide on a final monetary policy recommendation for each scenario.

Step 5 Consider what would happen if the government used a coordinated fiscal policy for the data in columns A and B and a conflicting fiscal policy with the data in column C. Discuss as a class what would happen to the three key indicators when fiscal policy effects are considered.

McDougal Littell Assessment System

Assess

Online Test Practice
- Go to **ClassZone.com** for more test practice.

Unit 6 Resource Book
- Chapter Test, Forms A, B, & C, pp. 165–176

Test Generator CD-ROM
- Chapter Test, Forms (A, B, & C), in English and Spanish

Report

Use the McDougal Littell Assessment System to score assessments and receive customized reports.

Reteach

For activities customized for individual students, use the McDougal Littell Assessment System.

CHAPTER 16 ASSESSMENT ANSWERS

Critical Thinking

11. The district banks provide regional information to ensure that national Fed policy is based on the economic needs of all sectors of the economy. District banks are closer to local problems; the national Board of Governors sets policy for the economy as a whole.

12. Both identified the problem rapidly, but the Fed's greater political independence allowed it to respond to the problem more quickly than Congress could. The time lag for monetary policy is shorter than for fiscal policy.

13. It will increase reserves and lower the federal funds rate, because the Fed added $10,000 to the money supply. More loanable funds results in lower interest rates.

14. In 2001, policies were both expansionary and worked together. In 2006, expansionary fiscal policy conflicted with contractionary monetary policy.

15. The committee raised it, based on concerns about possible future inflation. The need for continued policy firming suggests contractionary policy.

Simulation Rubric

	Understanding of Concepts	Presentation of Information
4	excellent	accurate, clear, complete
3	good	mostly accurate, clear
2	fair	sometimes clear
1	poor	sketchy

Planning Guide

Resources 2Go Complete print resources all on one USB drive allow you to customize lessons.

Section Titles and Objectives	Unit 7 Resource Book and Workbooks		Assessment Resources
1 Benefits and Issues of International Trade pp. 510–519 • Determine why nations choose to specialize their economies • Examine the difference between absolute and comparative advantage • Explain how international trade impacts prices and quantity	**Unit 7 Resource Book** • Reading Study Guide, pp. 1–2 • RSG with Additional Support, pp. 3–5 • RSG with Additional Support (Spanish), pp. 6–8 • Economic Simulations: Comparative Advantage in the Workplace, pp. 47–48	**NCEE Student Activities** • Why Do People Buy Foreign Goods?, pp. 65–68	**Unit 7 Resource Book** • Section Quiz, p. 9 • Reteaching Activity, p. 10 **Test Generator CD-ROM** **Daily Test Practice Transparencies,** TT57
2 Trade Barriers pp. 520–525 • Identify barriers to trade • Examine the economic consequences of trade barriers • Describe protectionism and the arguments for it	**Unit 7 Resource Book** • Reading Study Guide, pp. 11–12 • RSG with Additional Support, pp. 13–15 • RSG with Additional Support (Spanish), pp. 16–18	• Economic Skills and Problem Solving Activity, pp. 41–42 • Case Study Resources: Sugar Tariff Fails to Yield Sweet Results for Anyone, p. 45	**Unit 7 Resource Book** • Section Quiz, p. 19 • Reteaching Activity, p. 20 **Test Generator CD-ROM** **Daily Test Practice Transparencies,** TT58
3 Measuring the Value of Trade pp. 526–531 • Describe how nations determine the value of their currency in a world market • Explain why nations want a favorable balance of trade	**Unit 7 Resource Book** • Reading Study Guide, pp. 21–22 • RSG with Additional Support, pp. 23–25 • RSG with Additional Support (Spanish), pp. 26–28 • Math Skills Worksheet: Using Exchange Rates, p. 49	• Readings in Free Enterprise: Emerging Giants, pp. 43–44	**Unit 7 Resource Book** • Section Quiz, p. 29 • Reteaching Activity, p. 30 **Test Generator CD-ROM** **Daily Test Practice Transparencies,** TT59
4 Modern International Institutions pp. 532–539 • Describe what agreements were made to start the free trade movement • Identify international and regional trade groups • Explain what role multinationals play in world trade	**Unit 7 Resource Book** • Reading Study Guide, pp. 31–32 • RSG with Additional Support, pp. 33–35 • RSG with Additional Support (Spanish), pp. 36–38 • Economic Skills and Problem Solving Activity, pp. 41–42	• Case Study Resources: Sugar Tariff Fails to Yield Sweet Results for Anyone, p. 45; CAFTA Barely Passes, p. 46 **Test Practice and Review Workbook,** pp. 55–56	**Unit 7 Resource Book** • Section Quiz, p. 39 • Reteaching Activity, p. 40 • Chapter Test, (Forms A, B, & C), pp. 51–62 **Test Generator CD-ROM** **Daily Test Practice Transparencies,** TT60

Integrated Technology

No Time? To focus students on the most important content in this chapter, use Animated Economics, "The Effects of International Trade," available in Resources 2Go.

Teacher Presentation Options

Presentation Toolkit

Power Presentation DVD-ROM

- Lecture Notes
- Interactive Review
- Media Gallery
- Animated Economics
- Review Game

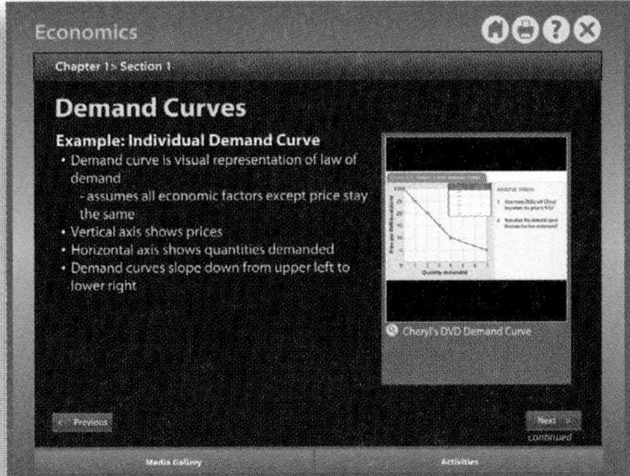

Economics Concepts Transparencies

- No Specialization v. Specialization, CT57
- Trade Barriers, CT58
- Leading U.S. Trade Partners, CT59
- Members of the European Union, CT60

Electronic Books

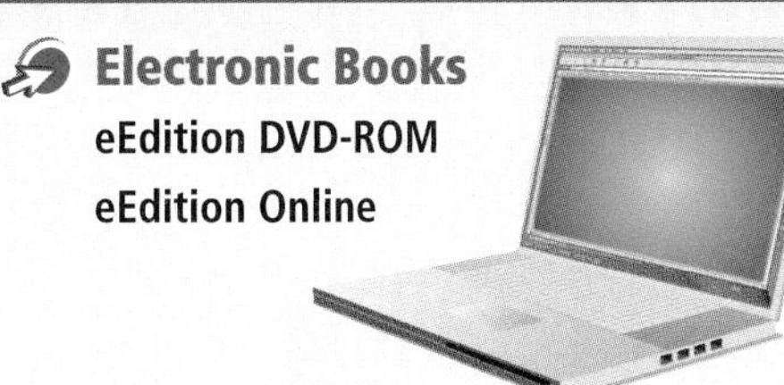

eEdition DVD-ROM

eEdition Online

Daily Test Practice Transparencies, TT57, TT58, TT59, TT60

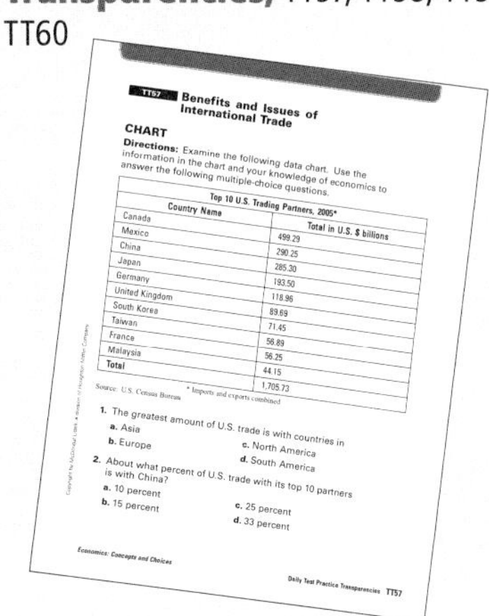

TT57 **Benefits and Issues of International Trade**

CHART

Directions: Examine the following data chart. Use the information in the chart and your knowledge of economics to answer the following multiple-choice questions.

Top 10 U.S. Trading Partners, 2005*	
Country Name	**Total in U.S. $ billions**
Canada	499.29
Mexico	290.25
China	285.30
Japan	193.50
Germany	118.96
United Kingdom	89.69
South Korea	71.45
Taiwan	56.89
France	56.25
Malaysia	44.15
Total	1,705.73

Source: U.S. Census Bureau

* Imports and exports combined

1. The greatest amount of U.S. trade is with countries in
   a. Asia
   b. Europe
   c. North America
   d. South America
2. About what percent of U.S. trade with its top 10 partners is with China?
   a. 10 percent
   b. 15 percent
   c. 25 percent
   d. 33 percent

Economics: Concepts and Choices

Daily Test Practice Transparencies TT57

Animated Economics

- The Effects of International Trade, p. 517

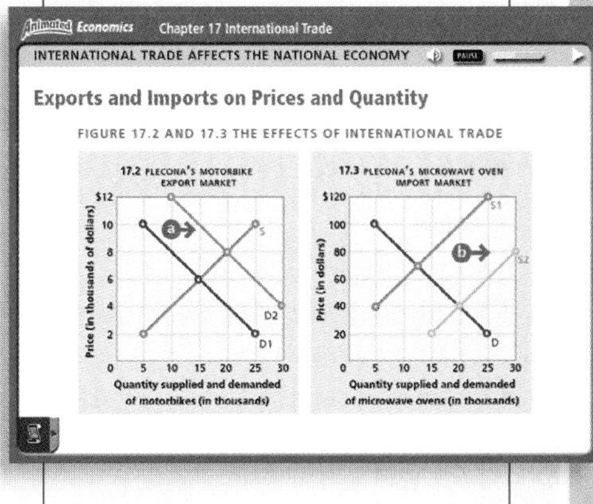

Online Activities at ClassZone.com

Economics Update

- Costa Rica's Economy, p. 511
- David Ricardo, p. 512
- U.S. Imports, p. 518
- U.S. Balance of Trade, p. 530
- Analyzing Tariffs—Who Wins and Who Loses?, p. 538

Animated Economics

- Interactive Graphics

Activity Maker

- Vocabulary Flip Cards
- Review Game

Research Center

- Graphs and Data

Interactive Review

- Online Summary
- Quizzes
- Vocabulary Flip Cards
- Graphic Organizers
- Review and Study Notes

SMARTGrapher

- Create a Graph, p. 541

Teacher-Tested Activities

Name: Sandra K. Wright

School: Adlai E. Stevenson High School

State: Illinois

Teacher-Tested Activities

At the beginning of this chapter, look for my classroom-proven idea for teaching economics concepts and thinking.

Resources for Differentiated Instruction

Struggling Readers

Teacher's Edition Activities

- Make Notes to Understand, p. 514
- Compare Text and Graphic, p. 518
- Relate to Personal Experience, p. 524
- Isolate Concepts, p. 530
- Generalize from an Example, p. 534

Unit 7 Resource Book

- RSG with Additional Support, pp. 3–5, 13–15, 23–25, 33–35 (A)
- Reteaching Activities, pp. 10, 20, 30, 40 (B)
- Chapter Test (Form A), pp. 51–54 (C)

ClassZone.com

- Animated Economics
- Interactive Review

Test Generator CD-ROM

- Chapter Test (Form A)
- Chapter Test (Form A), in Spanish

B

Name ____________ Date ____________

SECTION 1 RETEACHING ACTIVITY
Benefits and Issues of International Trade

A. Finding Main Ideas
The following questions deal with international trade. Answer them in the space provided.

1. Is specialization to a nation's economic advantage? Support your answer with information from the text.
2. How does specialization increase economic interdependence?
3. When does a nation have an absolute advantage over another?
4. When does a nation have a comparative advantage over another?
5. How do countries benefit from free trade?
6. What effect do exports have on prices and quantity?
7. How can domestic producers benefit from imports?

Reteaching Activity 10

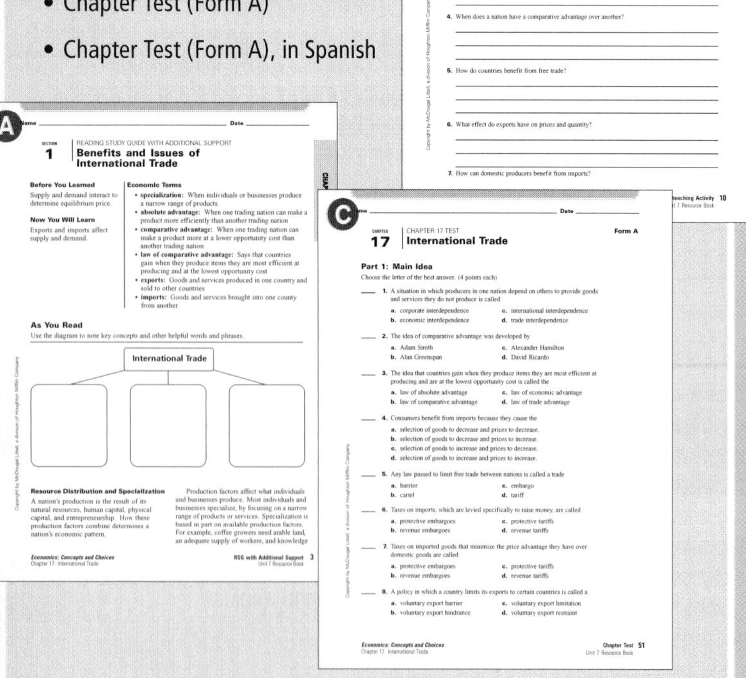

A

Name ____________ Date ____________

SECTION 1 READING STUDY GUIDE WITH ADDITIONAL SUPPORT
Benefits and Issues of International Trade

Before You Learned
Supply and demand interact to determine equilibrium price.

Now You Will Learn
Exports and imports affect supply and demand.

Economic Terms
- **specialization:** When individuals or businesses produce a narrow range of products
- **absolute advantage:** When one trading nation can make a product more efficiently than another trading nation
- **comparative advantage:** When one trading nation can make a product at a lower opportunity cost than another trading nation
- **law of comparative advantage:** Says that countries gain when they produce items they are most efficient at producing and at the lowest opportunity cost
- **exports:** Goods and services produced in one country and sold to other countries
- **imports:** Goods and services brought into one country from another

As You Read
Use the diagram to note key concepts and other helpful words and phrases.

International Trade

Resource Distribution and Specialization

Economics: Concepts and Choices
Chapter 17 International Trade

RSG with Additional Support 3
Unit 7 Resource Book

C

Name ____________ Date ____________

CHAPTER 17 TEST
17 International Trade Form A

Part 1: Main Idea
Choose the letter of the best answer. (4 points each)

___ 1. A situation in which producers in one nation depend on others to provide goods and services they do not produce is called
a. corporate interdependence c. international interdependence
b. economic interdependence d. trade interdependence

___ 2. The idea of comparative advantage was developed by
a. Adam Smith c. Alexander Hamilton
b. Alan Greenspan d. David Ricardo

___ 3. The idea that countries gain when they produce items they are most efficient at producing and are at the lowest opportunity cost is called the
a. law of absolute advantage c. law of economic advantage
b. law of comparative advantage d. law of trade advantage

___ 4. Consumers benefit from imports because they cause the
a. selection of goods to decrease and prices to decrease.
b. selection of goods to decrease and prices to increase.
c. selection of goods to increase and prices to decrease.
d. selection of goods to increase and prices to increase.

___ 5. Any law passed to limit free trade between nations is called a trade
a. barrier c. embargo
b. cartel d. tariff

___ 6. Taxes on imports, which are levied specifically to raise money, are called
a. protective embargoes c. protective tariffs
b. revenue embargoes d. revenue tariffs

___ 7. Taxes on imported goods that minimize the price advantage they have over domestic goods are called
a. protective embargoes c. protective tariffs
b. revenue embargoes d. revenue tariffs

___ 8. A policy in which a country limits its exports to certain countries is called a
a. voluntary export barrier c. voluntary export limitation
b. voluntary export hindrance d. voluntary export restraint

Economics: Concepts and Choices
Chapter 17 International Trade

Chapter Test 51
Unit 7 Resource Book

English Learners

Teacher's Edition Activities

- English Language Learners, p. 514
- Use Root Words to Understand, p. 516
- Use Conversation to Understand, p. 524
- Relate to One's Culture, p. 528
- Recognize Parallel Structure, p. 534

Unit 7 Resource Book

- RSG with Additional Support (Spanish), pp. 6–8, 16–18, 26–28, 36–38 (A)

Test Generator CD-ROM

- Chapter Test (Forms A, B, & C), in Spanish (B)

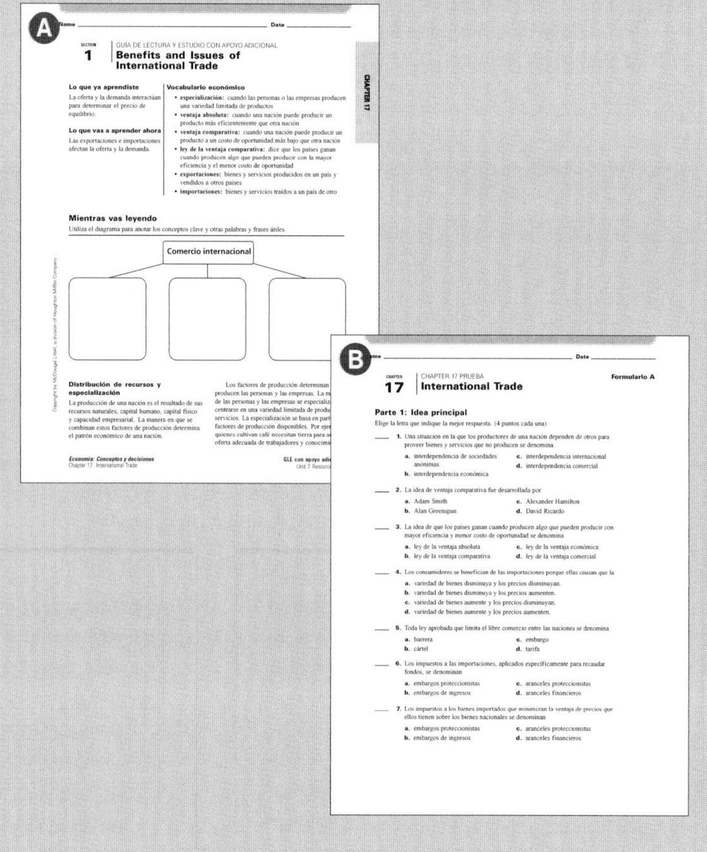

A

Nombre ____________ Fecha ____________

SECCIÓN 1 GUÍA DE LECTURA Y ESTUDIO CON APOYO ADICIONAL
Benefits and Issues of International Trade

Lo que ya aprendiste
La oferta y la demanda interactúan para determinar el precio de equilibrio.

Lo que vas a aprender ahora
Las exportaciones e importaciones afectan la oferta y la demanda.

Vocabulario económico
- **especialización:** cuando las personas o las empresas producen una variedad limitada de productos
- **ventaja absoluta:** cuando una nación puede producir un producto más eficientemente que otra nación
- **ventaja comparativa:** cuando una nación puede producir un producto a un costo de oportunidad más bajo que otra nación
- **ley de la ventaja comparativa:** dice que los países ganan cuando producen algo que pueden producir con la mayor eficiencia y el menor costo de oportunidad
- **exportaciones:** bienes y servicios producidos en un país y vendidos a otros países
- **importaciones:** bienes y servicios traídos a un país de otro

Mientras vas leyendo
Utiliza el diagrama para anotar los conceptos clave y otras palabras y frases útiles.

Comercio internacional

Distribución de recursos y especialización

Economics: Conceptos y decisiones
Chapter 17 International Trade

B

Nombre ____________ Fecha ____________

CAPÍTULO 17 PRUEBA
17 International Trade Formulario A

Parte 1: Idea principal
Elige la letra que indique la mejor respuesta. (4 puntos cada una)

___ 1. Una situación en la que los productores de una nación dependen de otros para proveer bienes y servicios que no producen se denomina
a. interdependencia de sociedades anónimas c. interdependencia internacional
b. interdependencia económica d. interdependencia comercial

___ 2. La idea de ventaja comparativa fue desarrollada por
a. Adam Smith c. Alexander Hamilton
b. Alan Greenspan d. David Ricardo

___ 3. La idea de que los países ganan cuando producen algo que pueden producir con mayor eficiencia y menor costo de oportunidad se denomina
a. ley de la ventaja absoluta c. ley de la ventaja económica
b. ley de la ventaja comparativa d. ley de la ventaja comercial

___ 4. Los consumidores se benefician de las importaciones porque ellas causan que la
a. variedad de bienes disminuya y los precios disminuyan.
b. variedad de bienes disminuya y los precios aumenten.
c. variedad de bienes aumente y los precios disminuyan.
d. variedad de bienes aumente y los precios aumenten.

___ 5. Toda ley aprobada que limita el libre comercio entre las naciones se denomina
a. barrera c. embargo
b. cártel d. tarifa

___ 6. Los impuestos a las importaciones, aplicados específicamente para recaudar fondos, se denominan
a. embargos proteccionistas c. aranceles proteccionistas
b. embargos de ingresos d. aranceles financieros

___ 7. Los impuestos a los bienes importados que minimizan la ventaja de precios que ellos tienen sobre los bienes nacionales se denominan
a. embargos proteccionistas c. aranceles proteccionistas
b. embargos de ingresos d. aranceles financieros

Inclusion

Teacher's Edition Activities

- Create Icons to Understand, p. 512
- Draw a Trade Map, p. 518
- Develop a Concrete Example, p. 522
- Provide Verbal Descriptions, p. 530
- Describe the Illustrations, p. 536
- Monitor Learning, p. 538

Lesson Plans

- Modified Lessons for Inclusion, pp. 57–60 (A)

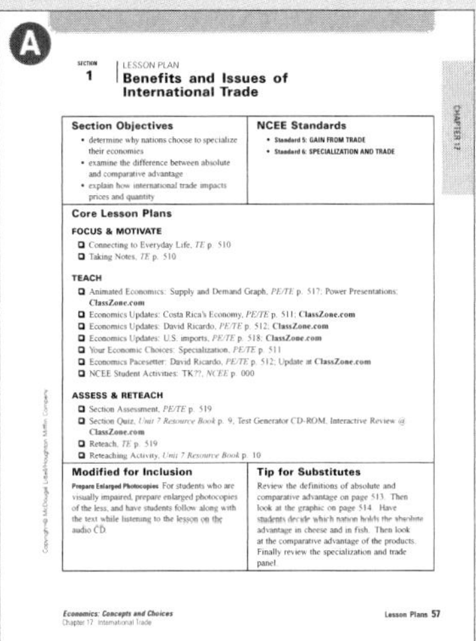

A

SECTION 1 | LESSON PLAN
Benefits and Issues of International Trade

Section Objectives	NCEE Standards
• determine why nations choose to specialize their economies • examine the difference between absolute and comparative advantage • explain how international trade impacts prices and quantity	• Standard 5: GAIN FROM TRADE • Standard 6: SPECIALIZATION AND TRADE

Core Lesson Plans

FOCUS & MOTIVATE
- Connecting to Everyday Life, *TE* p. 510
- Taking Notes, *TE* p. 510

TEACH
- Animated Economics: Supply and Demand Graph, *PE/TE* p. 517; Power Presentations; **ClassZone.com**
- Economics Updates: Costa Rica's Economy, *PE/TE* p. 511; **ClassZone.com**
- Economics Updates: David Ricardo, *PE/TE* p. 512; **ClassZone.com**
- Economics Updates: U.S. imports, *PE/TE* p. 518; **ClassZone.com**
- Your Economic Choices: Specialization, *PE/TE* p. 513
- Economics Pacesetter: David Ricardo, *PE/TE* p. 512; Update at **ClassZone.com**
- NCEE Student Activities: TK??, *NCEE* p. 000

ASSESS & RETEACH
- Section Assessment, *PE/TE* p. 519
- Section Quiz, *Unit 7 Resource Book* p. 9; Test Generator CD-ROM; Interactive Review @ **ClassZone.com**
- Reteach, *TE* p. 519
- Reteaching Activity, *Unit 7 Resource Book* p. 10

Modified for Inclusion	Tip for Substitutes
Prepare Enlarged Photocopies For students who are visually impaired, prepare enlarged photocopies of the text, and have students follow along with the text while listening to the lesson on the audio CD.	Review the definitions of absolute and comparative advantage on page 513. Then look at the graphic on page 514. Have students decide which nation holds the absolute advantage in cheese and in fish. Then look at the comparative advantage of the products. Finally review the specialization and trade panel.

CHAPTER 17

Economics: Concepts and Choices
Chapter 17 International Trade

Lesson Plans 57

Copyright © McDougal Littell/Houghton Mifflin Company

Gifted and Talented

Teacher's Edition Activities

- Debate in Character, p. 512
- Develop a Trade Proposal, p. 516
- Identify Key Players, p. 522
- Determine Cause and Effect, p. 528
- Write a Press Release, p. 536
- Research the American Sugar Alliance, p. 538

Unit 7 Resource Book

- Readings in Free Enterprise: Emerging Giants, pp. 43–44 (A)
- Case Study Resources: Sugar Tariff Fails to Yield Sweet Results for Anyone, p. 45; CAFTA Barely Passes, p. 46 (B)

NCEE Student Activities

- Why Do People Buy Foreign Goods?, pp. 65–68 (C)

ClassZone.com

- Research Center

Test Generator CD-ROM

- Chapter Test (Form C)
- Chapter Test (Form C), in Spanish

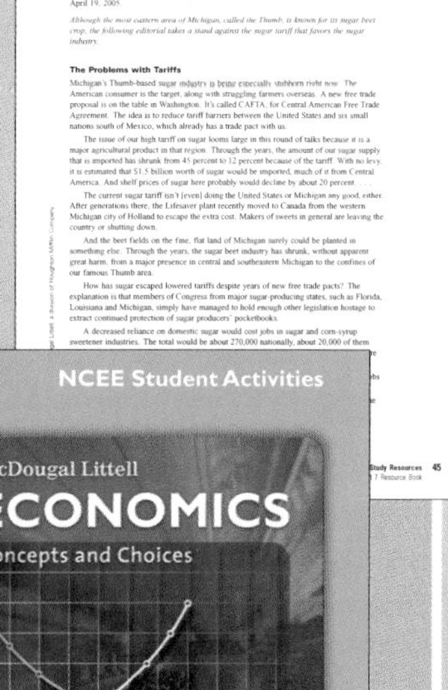

B

Name ______________________ Date ____________

CHAPTER 17 | CASE STUDY RESOURCES
International Trade

Sugar Tariff Fails to Yield Sweet Results for Anyone

From "Sugar Tariff Fails to Yield Sweet Results for Anyone," *The Daily Oakland* (MI) *Press*, April 19, 2005.

Although the most eastern area of Michigan, called the Thumb, is known for its sugar beet crop, the following editorial takes a stand against the sugar tariff that favors the sugar industry.

The Problems with Tariffs

Michigan's Thumb-based sugar industry is being especially stubborn right now. The American consumer is the target, along with struggling farmers overseas. A new free trade proposal is on the table in Washington. It's called CAFTA, for Central American Free Trade Agreement. The idea is to reduce tariff barriers between the United States and six small nations south of Mexico, which already has a trade pact with us.

The issue of our high tariff on sugar looms large in this round of talks because it is a major agricultural product in that region. Through the years, the amount of our sugar supply that is imported has shrunk from 45 percent to 12 percent because of the tariff. With no levy, it is estimated that $1.5 billion worth of sugar would be imported, much of it from Central America. And shelf prices of sugar here probably would decline by about 20 percent. . . .

The current sugar tariff isn't [even] doing the United States or Michigan any good, either. After generations there, the Lifesaver plant recently moved to Canada from the western Michigan city of Holland to escape the extra cost. Makers of sweets in general are leaving the country or shutting down.

And the beet fields on the fine, flat land of Michigan surely could be planted in something else. Through the years, the sugar beet industry has shrunk, without apparent great harm, from a major presence in central and southeastern Michigan to the confines of our famous Thumb area.

How has sugar escaped lowered tariffs despite years of new free trade pacts? The explanation is that members of Congress from major sugar-producing states, such as Florida, Louisiana and Michigan, simply have managed to hold enough other legislation hostage to extract continued protection of sugar producers' pocketbooks.

A decreased reliance on domestic sugar would cost jobs in sugar and corn-syrup sweetener industries. The total would be about 270,000 nationally, about 20,000 of them . . .

Case Study Resources 45
Unit 7 Resource Book

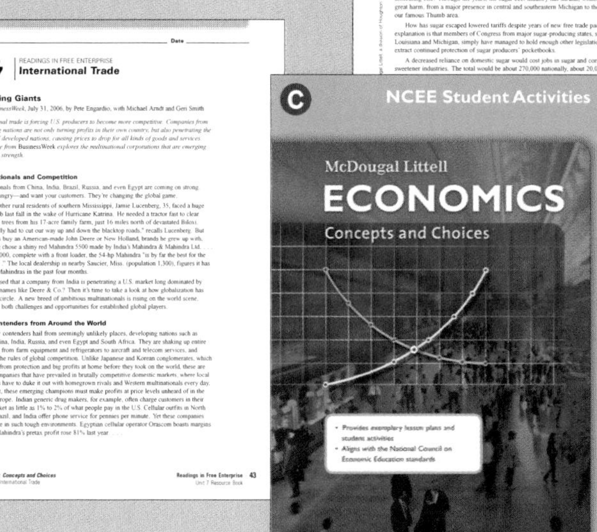

A

Name ______________________ Date ____________

CHAPTER 17 | READINGS IN FREE ENTERPRISE
International Trade

Emerging Giants

From *BusinessWeek*, July 31, 2006, by Pete Engardio, with Michael Arndt and Geri Smith

International trade is forcing U.S. producers to become more competitive. Companies from developing nations are not only turning profits in their own country, but also penetrating the markets of developed nations, causing prices to drop for all kinds of goods and services. This article from BusinessWeek *explores the multinational corporations that are emerging with great strength.*

Multinationals and Competition

Multinationals from China, India, Brazil, Russia, and even Egypt are coming on strong. They're hungry—and want your customers. They're changing the global game.

Like other rural residents of southern Mississippi, Jamie Lucenberg, 35, faced a huge cleanup job last fall in the wake of Hurricane Katrina. He needed a tractor fast to clear debris and trees from his 17-acre family farm, just 16 miles north of devastated Biloxi. "We literally had to cut our way up and down the blacktop roads," recalls Lucenberg. But rather than buy an American-made John Deere or New Holland, brands he grew up with, Lucenberg chose a shiny red Mahindra 5500 made by India's Mahindra & Mahindra Ltd. . . . [F]or $27,000, complete with a front loader, the 54-hp Mahindra "is by far the best for the money. . . ." The local dealership in nearby Saucier, Miss. (population 1,300), figures it has sold 300 Mahindras in the past four months.

Surprised that a company from India is penetrating a U.S. market long dominated by venerable names like Deere & Co.? Then it's time to take a look at how globalization has come full circle. A new breed of ambitious multinationals is rising on the world scene, presenting both challenges and opportunities for established global players.

New Contenders from Around the World

These new contenders hail from seemingly unlikely places, developing nations such as Brazil, China, India, Russia, and even Egypt and South Africa. They are shaking up entire industries, from farm equipment and refrigerators to aircraft and telecom services, and changing the rules of global competition. Unlike Japanese and Korean conglomerates, which benefited from protection and big profits at home before they took on the world, these are mostly companies that have prevailed in brutally competitive domestic markets, where local companies have to duke it out with homegrown rivals and Western multinationals every day. As a result, these emerging champions must make profits at price levels unheard of in the U.S. or Europe. Indian generic drug makers, for example, often charge customers in their home market as little as 1% to 2% of what people pay in the U.S. Cellular outfits in North Africa, Brazil, and India offer phone service for pennies per minute. Yet these companies often thrive in such tough environments. Egyptian cellular operator Orascom boasts margins of 49%; Mahindra's pretax profit rose 81% last year. . . .

Economics: Concepts and Choices
Chapter 17 International Trade

Readings in Free Enterprise 43
Unit 7 Resource Book

Copyright © by McDougal Littell, a division of Houghton Mifflin Company

Focus & Motivate

Objective

Explain the issues and institutions related to international trade.

Why the Concept Matters

The world of work that students will be entering upon graduation from high school or college has changed dramatically in the last generation. Globalization has forever altered the economy of individual countries and their economic relationships with other nations. Understanding international trade and the global economy will provide insight into the economic marketplace that these students will enter as employees and consumers. It will also help them as citizens to evaluate the positions of politicians and the policies of their government.

Analyzing the Photograph

Ask students to identify aspects of the photograph that suggest this location is a hub of trade. *(Possible answer: waterway, port facilities, shipping containers)* Ask students to use what they know about goods that are imported and exported and tell a hypothetical story about what is taking place at this port. What goods are arriving from where? Where and how will they be delivered?

Unit 7

The Global Economy

A Global Marketplace

International trade allows nations to produce some items and trade them for other items. How do they decide what to produce and what to trade for?

508

CONTENT STANDARDS

NCEE STANDARDS

Standard 5: Gain from Trade

Students will understand that

Voluntary exchange occurs only when all participating parties expect to gain. This is true for trade among individuals or organizations within a nation and . . . in different nations.

Students will be able to use this knowledge to

Negotiate exchanges and identify the gains to themselves and others. Compare the benefits and costs of policies that alter trade barriers between nations, such as tariffs and quotas. *(pages 515–518, 520–524, 529–530)*

Standard 1: Specialization and Trade

Students will understand that

Nations specialize in what they can produce at the lowest cost and then trade with others, both production and consumption increase.

Students will be able to use this knowledge to

Explain how they can benefit themselves and others by developing special skills and strengths. *(pages 510–514)*

CHAPTER 17

International Trade

CONCEPT REVIEW

The **global economy** is the sum of all economic interactions that cross international boundaries.

CHAPTER 17 KEY CONCEPT

Economic interdependence involves producers in one nation that depend on producers in other nations to supply them with certain goods and services.

WHY THE CONCEPT MATTERS

Japan is a world-class producer of automobiles, in spite of the fact that it has few mineral resources. How can this be? The answer lies in the realm of international trade, where nations choose to produce some things and trade for others. In the case of Japan, it must trade for the raw materials it uses in order to produce automobiles. It then turns around and trades the automobiles for other goods.

Online Highlights

More at ClassZone.com

Economics Update
Go to **ECONOMICS UPDATE** for chapter updates and current news on how tariffs and subsidies affect the sugar market. (See Case Study, pp. 538–539). ▶

Animated Economics
Go to **ANIMATED ECONOMICS** for interactive lessons on the graphs and tables in this chapter.

Interactive Review
Go to **INTERACTIVE REVIEW** for concept review and activities.

Why do many people believe that U.S. government subsidies to sugar producers are a problem? See the Case Study on pages 538–539.

From the Classroom

Sandra Wright, Adlai E. Stevenson H.S.

International Trade

1. Get one brown paper bag for each student, and number the bags 1–6, resulting in groups of 1s, 2s, etc. Sort six different kinds of prizes into the numbered bags (e.g. candy bars in bags labeled 1).

2. Pass out the bags, and have students rate their satisfaction with their items on a scale of 1–5. Add up students' scores and calculate the average.

3. Tell students that they can trade in the following pairs: 1 & 2, 3 & 4, 5 & 6. Have students again rate their satisfaction. Add up their scores and calculate the average.

4. Allow all odds to trade together and all evens to trade together. Have students rate their satisfaction, and calculate the average. Point out that the average satisfaction has increased.

5. Allow students to trade with anyone, then rate their satisfaction and calculate the average.

6. Ask students which scenario best allowed them to maximize their satisfaction. Ask students which scenario most resembles the world today. Prompt students to see that free trade in a global economy results in making the most people satisfied.

Previewing Chapter Technology at ClassZone.com

Economics Update Students will find updates to information in the pupil edition on pages 511, 512, 518, 530, and 538.

Animated Economics Students will find interactive graphs related to material on page 517.

Interactive Review Students will find additional section and chapter assessment support for materials on pages 519, 525, 531, 537, and 540.

TEACHER MEDIA FAVORITES

Books

- Schott, Jeffrey, ed. *Free Trade Agreements: US Strategies and Priorities.* Washington, DC: Institute for International Economics, 2004. An exploration of U.S. trade initiatives with nations all over the world.
- Greider, William, Margaret Eleanor Atwood, and Ralph Nader. *The Case Against Free Trade: GATT, NAFTA, and the Globalization of Corporate Power.* Berkeley, CA: North Atlantic Books, 1993. A critical look at the effects of globalization and the free trade movement.
- Irwin, Douglas *A. Free Trade Under Fire: Second Edition.* Princeton, NJ: Princeton UP, 2005. A readable defense of free trade by a prominent economist.

Videos/DVDs

- *International Trade/Exchange Rates.* 30 minutes each. Annenberg/CPB Collection, 2002, 2003. These videos present the topics in an engaging television-news format.

Software

- *The Global Economics Game.* Ronald Shuelke. 2004. Online economics game that simulates the economic performance and policies of countries in the global economy. [http://www.worldgameofeconomics.com/]

Internet

Visit **ClassZone.com** to link to

- a variety of chapter-specific, content-reviewed sites
- updates on data and topics presented throughout the chapter sections and Case Study
- updates to the Power Presentation

1 Plan & Prepare

Section 1 Objectives

- determine why nations choose to specialize their economies
- examine the difference between absolute and comparative advantage
- explain how international trade impacts prices and quantity

2 Focus & Motivate

Connecting to Everyday Life Pose this scenario to students: Suppose that you and a friend are responsible for providing costumes and making the set for a play. Your friend owns a sewing machine and is able to design clothes. You are handy with tools and have a workshop in your basement. Should you divide the work for both tasks equally or divide it so that your friend does all the sewing and you build the set? Ask students to give reasons for their answers. Point out that nations face similar decisions when they consider trade with other nations.

Taking Notes Remind students to take notes as they read by completing a diagram. They can use the Graphic Organizer at **Interactive Review @ ClassZone.com**. A sample is shown below.

International Trade

- resource distribution and specialization
  - specialization—increase efficiency by producing a narrow range of products
  - economic interdependence—producers rely on one another
- absolute and comparative advantage
  - absolute advantage—make a product more efficiently
  - comparative advantage—make a product at a lower opportunity cost
- international trade and the national economy
  - exports are sold to other countries
  - imports are brought into a country to be sold
  - exports and imports affect price and quantity
  - trade affects employment

SECTION 1

Benefits and Issues of International Trade

OBJECTIVES	KEY TERMS	TAKING NOTES
In Section 1, you will • determine why nations choose to specialize their economies • examine the difference between absolute and comparative advantage • explain how international trade impacts prices and quantity	specialization, *p. 510* economic interdependence, *p. 510* absolute advantage, *p. 513* comparative advantage, *p. 513* law of comparative advantage, *p. 514* exports, *p. 516* imports, *p. 516*	As you read Section 1, complete a diagram that shows how the concepts in the section relate to international trade. Use the Graphic Organizer at **Interactive Review @ ClassZone.com**

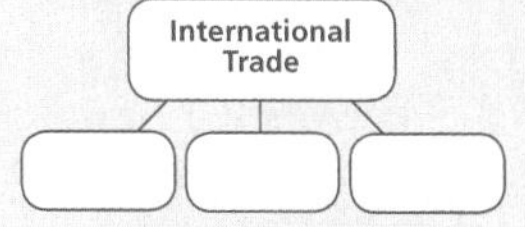

Resource Distribution and Specialization

KEY CONCEPTS

A nation's economic patterns are based on its unique combination of factors of production: natural resources, human capital, physical capital, and entrepreneurship. For example, a nation rich in arable land but lacking well-educated workers is less likely to develop a strong technology sector than a country with better-educated citizens and diverse natural resources. Economic patterns may also change over time. The United States, for example, once relied heavily on its agricultural sector, but the U.S. economy is now also extremely high-tech and highly skilled.

Because each nation has certain resources and cannot produce everything it wants, individuals and businesses must decide what goods and services to focus on. The result is **specialization**, a situation that occurs when individuals or businesses produce a narrow range of products. Through specialization, businesses can increase productivity and profit—the driving force of world trade. Specialization also leads to **economic interdependence**, a situation in which producers in one nation depend on others to provide goods and services they do not produce.

QUICK REFERENCE

Specialization is a situation that occurs when individuals or businesses produce a narrow range of products.

Economic interdependence is a situation in which producers in one nation depend on others to provide goods and services they do not produce.

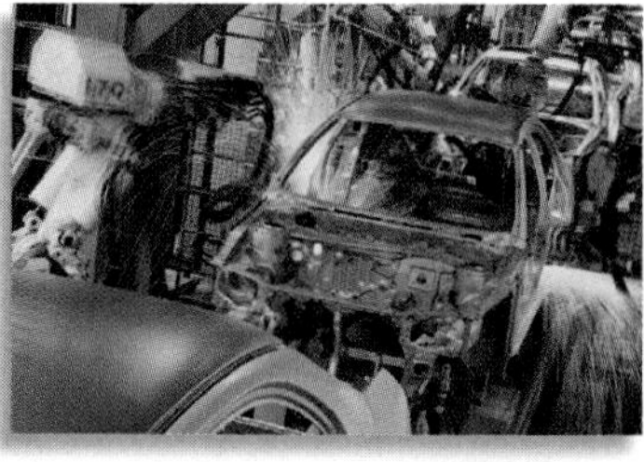

Specialization A coal-rich nation that lacks advanced technology can trade its coal for manufactured goods, such as automobiles, from nations with higher levels of technology.

510 Chapter 17

SECTION 1 PROGRAM RESOURCES

ON LEVEL

Lesson Plans
- Core, p. 57

Unit 7 Resource Book
- Reading Study Guide, pp. 1–2
- Economic Simulations, p. 47–48
- Section Quiz, p. 9

STRUGGLING READERS

Unit 7 Resource Book
- Reading Study Guide with Additional Support, pp. 3–5
- Reteaching Activity, p. 10

ENGLISH LEARNERS

Unit 7 Resource Book
- Reading Study Guide with Additional Support (Spanish), pp. 6–8

INCLUSION

Lesson Plans
- Modified for Inclusion, p. 57

GIFTED AND TALENTED

NCEE Student Activities
- Why Do People Buy Foreign Goods?, pp. 65–68

TECHNOLOGY

eEdition DVD-ROM

eEdition Online

Power Presentation DVD-ROM

Economics Concepts Transparencies
- CT57 No Specialization Versus Specialization and Trade

Daily Test Practice Transparencies, TT57

ClassZone.com

YOUR ECONOMIC CHOICES

SPECIALIZATION

Will you specialize in lawn mowing or babysitting?

Do you have a lawn mower? Do you know children that need to be watched? What other questions might you ask yourself before deciding what you will specialize in?

Mow lawns

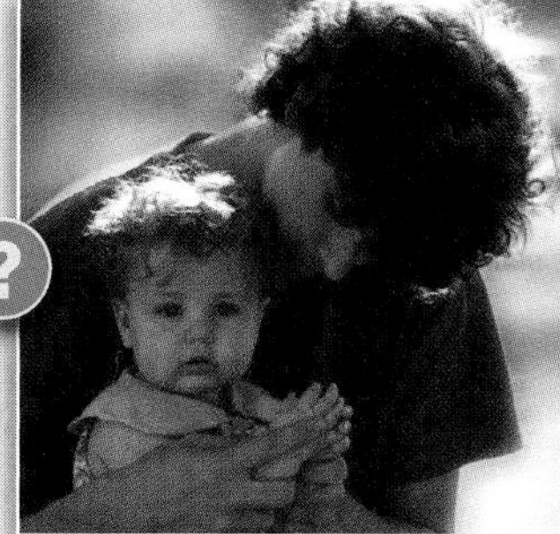

Babysit

EXAMPLE Specialization

The concept of specialization can be illustrated by looking at the agricultural production of two nations: Costa Rica and New Zealand. The climate, the labor conditions, and the level of technology of each nation have made some agricultural products more important than others. In other words, each nation has decided to specialize in certain agricultural areas because they have an advantage in doing so.

For Costa Rica, the product of choice is bananas. It is the world's seventh-largest producer and second-largest exporter of bananas. For New Zealand, the product of choice is sheep. It is the world's third-largest producer and second-largest exporter of wool and is responsible for about 50 percent of the world's lamb and mutton exports. What explains each nation's specialization?

Costa Rica has the necessary climate for bananas—warm and wet. In addition, agricultural wages are relatively low, an important point as banana production is quite labor intensive.

On the other hand, New Zealand has the temperate climate, water resources, and vast expanses of open grasslands to support the grazing of millions of sheep. (Today, there are about 10 sheep for every person in New Zealand.) Raising sheep is not nearly as labor intensive as banana production, and this suits the fairly low population density of this remote island nation. Also, scientific breeding practices and mechanized wool- and meat-processing operations are available to a developed nation such as New Zealand.

It makes sense for each nation to specialize as it does and to trade for the things it cannot produce as efficiently.

Economics Update

Find an update on Costa Rica's economy at **ClassZone.com**

APPLICATION Drawing Conclusions

A. Why should nations specialize in what they produce most efficiently and trade for the rest?
It makes sense to take advantage of what you produce efficiently and use it for trade, rather than producing things inefficiently. Since both producers in this relationship are efficient, the traded items end up costing less overall.

3 Teach

Resource Distribution and Specialization

Discuss

- Think of a fresh example of two nations and two products that parallels the Costa Rica/New Zealand example. *(Answers should discuss two nations, the products they have chosen for specialization, and the reasons why.)*

Your Economic Choices

SPECIALIZATION

Will you specialize in lawn mowing or babysitting?

Discuss the following question with students:

What would the student have to give up by choosing one job instead of the other? In other words, what is the opportunity cost of the choice?

Activity Write a detailed job description for each—lawn mowing and babysitting. That is, write out all the tasks involved in each job. Then, prepare a detailed resume showing your experience and interests. Match the resume with appropriate job and write a paragraph explaining why that job is the better fit.

Economics Update

At **ClassZone.com** students will see updated information on Costa Rica's economy.

LEVELED ACTIVITY

Understanding Key Issues

Time 30–45 Minutes

Objective Students will demonstrate an understanding of the key issues in the debate about world trade.

Basic

Identify at least three issues related to international trade that generate debate. For each one, write three to four sentences explaining the issue in more detail and the positions people take on the issues. Finally, write three to four sentences about the World Trade Organization: its members, its purpose, and its problems.

On Level

Identify at least three issues related to international trade that generate debate. Free write or brainstorm about each issue until you have explored everything you know about each. Then, write an essay about one issue. The essay can be informative (that is, "these are the issues...") or persuasive (that is, "I believe that because...").

Challenge

Research the Doha round of WTO talks. Write an essay about the talks that illuminates the following: the key players in the Doha round; the key areas of disagreement; your position on the areas of disagreement and suggestions for a possible resolution; and the outcome of the talks.

David Ricardo

More About . . .

David Ricardo

The break with his family at the time of his marriage did little to slow Ricardo's extraordinary ability to make money. Known for both his skill and his integrity, he soon became a successful dealer in government securities. By the age of 41, Ricardo had made so much money that he was able to retire from city life and became a country gentleman, living at Gatcombe Park.

In 1819, at the urging of a friend, Ricardo turned to public life and was elected to the British Parliament, representing a borough in Ireland. He was also a good friend of the economist Thomas Malthus, though the two differed strongly on a number of points.

More About . . .

The Work of David Ricardo

From the perspective of a modern reader, it is hard to recreate the world of thought in which Ricardo worked. He had the uncanny ability to analyze complex theoretical problems without the use of the mathematical equations that are so important to economics today.

Modern economist David Friedman wrote: "The modern economist reading Ricardo's *Principles* feels rather as a member of one of the Mount Everest expeditions would feel if, arriving at the top of the mountain, he encountered a hiker clad in T-shirt and tennis shoes."

Economics Update

ClassZone.com includes links to sites about David Ricardo's life and works. These links will help students appreciate the context in which Ricardo worked and his contribution to modern economics.

ECONOMICS PACESETTER

David Ricardo: The Theory of Comparative Advantage

FAST FACTS

David Ricardo

Title: Economist, stockbroker

Born: 1772

Died: 1823

Major Accomplishment: Brilliantly thinking through economic principles and laying the foundation for free trade

Major Work: *On the Principles of Political Economy and Taxation* (1817)

Famous Quotation: *"The labor of 100 Englishmen cannot be given for that of 80 Englishmen, but the produce of the labor of 100 Englishmen may be given for the produce of the labour of 80 Portuguese, 60 Russians, or 120 East Indians."*

Many things about London-born economist David Ricardo make him a memorable figure. He was one of 17 children in a Jewish family. At age 14, he went to work in his father's stockbrokerage. He married a Quaker at age 21 and broke from the Jewish faith, at which time his father disinherited him. And finally, when he died at age 51, he left a $126 million fortune.

Ricardo is most remembered, however, for the idea that has become the backbone for free trade—comparative advantage. It states, in short, that a trading nation should produce a certain product if it can do so at a lower opportunity cost than that of another trading nation.

EXAMPLE Trading in Opportunity

The prevailing view about international trade in Ricardo's time was based on the idea of absolute advantage, the ability of one trading nation to make a product more efficiently than another trading nation. Most people believed that if Portugal, for example, could make grape juice more efficiently than England, and if England could make cloth more efficiently than Portugal, then trade would be beneficial to both.

Ricardo, however, set up a different problem, one that challenged this outlook. What if, he thought, Portugal makes both products more efficiently than England? Would trade, at least for Portugal, no longer be beneficial? His surprising answer was that trade would indeed still be beneficial. He based his conclusion on the opportunity costs each nation spends to make its products.

Suppose that in Portugal, it takes two hours of labor to produce a jug of grape juice, while in England, it takes four hours. Suppose also that in Portugal, a yard of cloth takes six hours to make; in England it takes eight hours. Ricardo reasoned that in Portugal, every yard of cloth costs three jugs of grape juice in lost opportunity. In England, however, every yard of cloth costs only two jugs of grape juice. Portugal, then, would be wise to buy cloth from England and to specialize in grape juice. This understanding has become known as the law of comparative advantage: countries gain when they produce items they are most efficient at producing and that have the lowest opportunity cost.

David Ricardo

Learn more about David Ricardo at **ClassZone.com**

APPLICATION Applying Economic Concepts

B. Does the law of comparative advantage apply only to nations, or does it apply to individuals as well? Explain your answer.

It applies to individuals as well; there are opportunity costs involved in many of the decisions they make every day.

DIFFERENTIATING INSTRUCTION

Inclusion

Create Icons to Understand

Help students create icons for grape juice, cloth, and hours to map out Ricardo's ideas about comparative advantage. Specifically, direct them to the final paragraph of the feature and have them create a graphic with their icons that represents comparative advantage for Portugal and England.

Gifted and Talented

Debate in Character

Invite interested students to research the relationship between David Ricardo and Thomas Malthus and their differences over economic theory. Have them work in groups of two to develop a script for a debate between the two thinkers. Allow them to present the debate to the class, each playing one of the parts.

Absolute and Comparative Advantage

KEY CONCEPTS

Absolute advantage is the ability of one trading nation to make a product more efficiently than another trading nation. Some regions or nations have absolute advantage in producing certain products or services because of the uneven distribution of production factors.

Comparative advantage, in contrast, is the idea that a nation will specialize in what it can produce at a lower opportunity cost than any other nation. When determining comparative advantage, you look not for the absolute cost of a product, but for its opportunity cost.

QUICK REFERENCE

Absolute advantage is the ability of one trading nation to make a product more efficiently than another trading nation.

Comparative advantage is a trading nation's ability to produce something at a lower opportunity cost than that of another trading nation.

EXAMPLE Absolute Advantage

Consider the trade relations between two countries on the Pacific Rim today, China and Australia. Both countries produce iron ore; both also produce steel. Suppose that every week, Australia produces 5,000 tons of iron ore and 1,000 tons of steel. In the same period of time, and with the same amount of labor, China produces 2,700 tons of iron ore and 900 tons of steel. In this case, Australia has an absolute advantage over China in both areas.

Before Ricardo, the standard logic held that, in this situation, the nation that held the absolute advantage for both commodities would trade for neither. But, as you've read, when the important factor of opportunity cost is considered, this logic doesn't stand up. Why would it benefit Australia to import steel from China, in spite of its absolute advantage? The answer is comparative advantage.

What Does Opportunity Cost? Should Australia specialize in mining iron ore (left) and leave the steel production (right) to China? Where does the comparative advantage lie?

Absolute and Comparative Advantage

Discuss

- For a trading relationship to be beneficial, does one nation need to produce the traded product more efficiently than the other? *(No. As long as the nation has a comparative advantage—a lower opportunity cost—in producing the traded product, trade is still beneficial.)*
- What are some advantages of free trade? *(improved production ratios, increased world output, ability to get things otherwise unavailable, economic growth)*

More About . . .

Comparative Advantage
Inform students that they should not feel frustrated if it takes them time to understand comparative advantage. Paul Samuelson, author of the best-selling economics textbook of all time, was once challenged by famous mathematician Stanislaw Ulam to name one proposition in the social sciences that was both true and non-trivial. It took him some 30 years to come up with an answer, and it was comparative advantage.

Samuelson wrote, "That it is logically true need not be argued before a mathematician; that it is not trivial is attested by the thousands of important and intelligent men who have never been able to grasp the doctrine for themselves or to believe it after it was explained to them."

SMALL GROUP ACTIVITY

Understanding Comparative Advantage

Time 30 Minutes ◑

Task Develop an example that shows the concept of comparative advantage.

Materials Needed paper and pens

Activity

- Have students work in pairs.
- Direct them to develop an example, such as the one Ricardo created with Portugal and England or the one in this text about China and Australia.
- Instruct them that the example should include two nations, each with two products. Tell them to make up the relative costs of producing each item, the production ratios.
- Then, have students suggest a trade pattern between the two nations that would be advantageous to both.
- Ask each pair to present their example to the class.

Rubric

	Understanding of Comparative Advantage	Presentation of Information
4	excellent	original and complete
3	good	clear and complete
2	fair	incomplete, but clear ideas
1	poor	incomplete, unclear

More About . . .

Australia-China Trade

On April 18, 2005, Australian Prime Minister John Howard and Chinese Premier Wen Jiabao agreed to begin negotiations on a Free Trade Agreement (FTA) between their two nations. This decision followed upon a cooperative feasibility study.

In a statement, the Australian government said that it had concluded that the FTA would create Australian jobs and raise standards of living. It also had forecast that the agreement would boost Australia's real GDP from 2006 to 2015 by US$18 billion and would increase China's real GDP during the same period by US$64 billion.

Presentation Options

Review the law of comparative advantage by using the following presentation options:

 **Power Presentations DVD-ROM**
Using the Display Tool, you can highlight how efficient production and low opportunity cost comprise the law of comparative advantage.

 **Economics Concepts Transparencies**

- CT57 No Specialization Versus Specialization and Trade

More About . . .

Fair Trade

In debates about world trade, lines are usually drawn between supporters of free trade and supporters of fair trade. Yet, most people on both sides support an overall goal of trade: alleviation of poverty and improved living conditions. Free trade supporters believe the goal is best accomplished without intrusions into free market mechanisms; fair traders desire restrictions that assure that trade agreements are just.

Fair trade supporters believe that the developed nations and developing nations come to trade agreements on an uneven playing field. To even that playing field, the interests of the developing nations should be considered even at the expense of free market exchanges.

EXAMPLE Comparative Advantage

Let's start with a simple example of comparative advantage. After years as an office manager at a law firm by day and a law student by night, Ellen becomes a lawyer and starts her own practice. She charges $150 per hour for her legal services. She hires Miguel to run her office, and she pays him $25 per hour. Although Miguel works hard and is good at his job, Ellen soon realizes that, due to her years of experience, she could run her own office better than Miguel. Should she take over these duties? The answer lies in opportunity cost. Every hour that Ellen spends engaged in the duties that are worth $25 per hour costs her an hour that could be spent doing work that is worth $150 per hour. Clearly it makes sense for her to employ an office manager and concentrate on the legal end of her practice.

> **QUICK REFERENCE**
>
> The **law of comparative advantage** states that countries gain when they produce items they are most efficient at producing and are at the lowest opportunity cost.

Back to our previous example of Australia and China, we see that Australia's production ratio of steel to iron ore is 1:5. In other words, Australia's opportunity cost for one ton of steel is five tons of iron ore. Applying the same logic to China, we find that its production ratio of steel to iron ore is 1:3. Its opportunity cost for one ton of steel is three tons of iron ore. So, in the production of steel, China has a comparative advantage. Australia would benefit by trading for Chinese steel. This is the **law of comparative advantage**: countries gain when they produce items that they are most efficient at producing and that are at the lowest opportunity cost.

FIGURE 17.1 Specialization and Trade

No Specialization

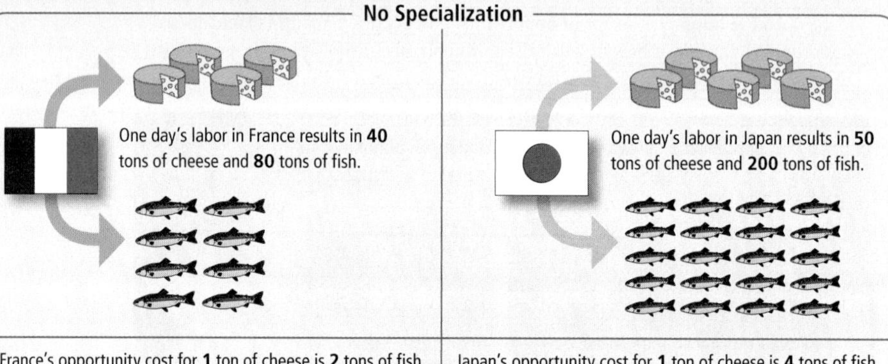

One day's labor in France results in 40 tons of cheese and 80 tons of fish.
One day's labor in Japan results in 50 tons of cheese and 200 tons of fish.

France's opportunity cost for 1 ton of cheese is 2 tons of fish. | Japan's opportunity cost for 1 ton of cheese is 4 tons of fish.

Specialization and Trade

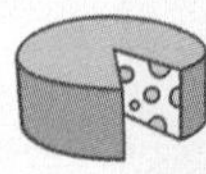

France trades 1 ton of cheese.

Japan trades 3 tons of fish.

It used to cost France 1 ton of cheese to get 2 tons of fish; now it trades 1 ton of cheese for 3 tons of fish.

It used to cost Japan 4 tons of fish for 1 ton of cheese; now it trades only 3 tons of fish for 1 ton of cheese.

DIFFERENTIATING INSTRUCTION

Struggling Readers

Make Notes to Understand

The text under the heading "Comparative Advantage" requires great concentration to read with understanding. Point out that while some kinds of texts can be skimmed to get the main idea, this kind of passage, in which readers are asked to suppose various things and hold them in their minds, requires studious attention. Model how making notes after each sentence or after several sentences can help students keep the details—and the argument they support—straight.

English Learners

Understand Not Only / But Also

Help students understand the relationship between the phrases *not only* and *but also.* Direct students to the heading "Advantages of Free Trade" on page 515. In particular, show them the construction of the first sentence of paragraph two under that heading. Point out that *not only* is rarely, if ever, used without *but also.* Ask students to think of other phrases that express the same relationship between ideas. *(Possible answer: "This is true and even that is true.")*

A GLOBAL PERSPECTIVE

Economic Success with Few Natural Resources

The headquarters of the Industrial Development Agency of Ireland, in Dublin

Some economies thrive as a direct result of natural resources—Saudi Arabia and its oil, for instance. But, many nations, such as the Republic of Ireland, thrive economically in spite of a relative lack of natural resources.

It is not rich in mineral resources and relies on imports for the majority of its energy supply. However, it has formulated and carried out certain policies that have helped to produce today's dynamic economy.

In the mid-1950s, Ireland began a continuing process of reversing protectionist tariff and quota policies. The Programmes for Economic Expansion (1958 and 1963) attracted large amounts of foreign direct investment through financial grants and tax concessions. Levels of human capital were increased through educational reforms in the 1960s. It was also an original member of the EU and took advantage of EU funds to shore up its infrastructure. These and other policies set the stage for Ireland's economic boom of the 1990s. During this decade, it became a major manufacturer of high-tech electronics, computer products, chemicals, and pharmaceuticals. It has also become an important center for banking and finance.

CONNECTING ACROSS THE GLOBE

1. **Drawing Conclusions** What specialization has, for the most part, driven Ireland's economic boom?
2. **Applying Economic Concepts** Why might an economy like Ireland's be more desirable than one that relies solely on natural resources?

EXAMPLE Advantages of Free Trade

If China and Australia decide to specialize and trade, they can improve their ratio of return. Previously, China's ratio of steel production to iron ore production was 1:3 and Australia's was 1:5. If the two nations establish a trade ratio of 1:4 (China trades one ton of its steel for four tons of Australian iron ore), both countries win. China now gets four tons of iron ore for a ton of steel; it got three before. Also, one ton of steel now costs Australia only four tons of iron ore; it previously cost five.

When countries specialize and trade, they not only improve their production ratios but they also increase world output. If China specializes in steel and Australia in iron ore, each can make more of their products than the two nations could have made together if they had not specialized. Increased output is a mark of economic growth, which is a factor in raising standards of living.

APPLICATION Interpreting Tables

C. Use the example in Figure 17.1 to explain how output for both nations increases through specialization and trade. *By specializing in what it produces more efficiently, each nation can produce more of that product and trade a more efficient output for what it has given up.*

A Global Perspective

Economic Success with Few Natural Resources

The relationship between natural resources and economic growth does not always apply. Some nations with abundant resources are still struggling. Tanzania is one example of a country that is rich in resources (hydropower, tin, phosphates, iron ore, coal, diamonds, gemstones, gold, natural gas, and nickel) but burdened by extreme poverty nonetheless.

Agriculture still accounts for about half of Tanzania's GDP and employs about 80 percent of the workforce. Most of the nation's exports are also agricultural, though since 2005 the mineral output has increased and the economy has grown by 6 percent.

Answers

1. *manufacturing*
2. *An economy focused solely on natural resources could be negatively affected by changes in the resources' supply or demand.*

SMALL GROUP ACTIVITY

Understanding Trade Advantages

Time 30 minutes

Task Identify items in U.S. trade flow and draw conclusions about the advantages.

Materials Needed paper and pens

Activity

- Divide students into small groups.
- Have each group identify at least five items that are either imported to or exported from the United States.
- For each item, have the group posit an advantage to Americans reflected in this traded item, as well as advantages to the trading partner.
- Have each group present their items and advantages to the class.

Rubric

	Understanding of Trade Advantages	Presentation of Information
4	excellent	original and complete
3	good	clear and complete
2	fair	incomplete but clear ideas
1	poor	incomplete and unclear

International Trade Affects the National Economy

Discuss

- How do consumers benefit from trade? *(They benefit from imports because they create a greater selection and lower prices.)* How do producers benefit from trade? *(They benefit from exports because they increase demand and raise prices for their products.)*
- What is the relationship between trade and employment? *(As trade leads to economic growth, more jobs are created. However, some jobs may be eliminated or change as imported goods replace domestic goods.)*

More About . . .

Microwave Ovens and Imports
Microwave ovens were first marketed in 1947. They were enormous in size. They stood over 5 feet high and weighed about 750 pounds. The price tag was enormous, too; they sold for about $5,000. Understandably, the "Radarange" did not sell well.

Microwave technology, however, improved rapidly. By the 1970s, inexpensive imports from Japan flooded the market. This helped to lower the price of the now much smaller-in-size microwave ovens to under $500.

International Trade Affects the National Economy

QUICK REFERENCE

Exports are goods and services produced in one country and sold to other countries.

Imports are goods and services produced in one country and purchased by another.

KEY CONCEPTS

Because of the law of comparative advantage, nations gain through trading goods and services. Goods and services produced in one country and sold to other countries are called **exports**. Goods and services produced in one country and purchased by another are called **imports**.

The costs and benefits of international trade vary by nation. To understand how trade affects a nation's economy, economists use supply and demand analysis. They look at the impact of exports and imports on prices and quantity.

IMPACT 1 Exports on Prices and Quantity

Suppose that a county called Plecona existed and that it did not trade with other countries. Figure 17.2 shows the equilibrium price for Plecona's motorbikes.

What would happen to prices and demand if Plecona decided to become a trading nation and export its motorbikes? In some countries, such as Nepocal, people would give up their bicycles and begin to buy Pleconese motorbikes. This results in an increase in demand for Pleconese motorbikes, shifting the demand curve to the right and establishing a new equilibrium price. Motorbikes will now cost more in Plecona too. However, the greater demand resulting from exporting offsets this by creating more jobs and more income in Plecona, as the motorbike producer invests its profits to expand production and hire more workers.

IMPACT 2 Imports on Prices and Quantity

Now suppose that Nepocal and Plecona agree that Nepocal may sell its major product, microwave ovens, in Plecona. Instead of having only Pleconese-made microwaves, consumers in Plecona may now purchase ovens imported from Nepocal. This change adds to the number of microwave oven producers in the Pleconese market. Adding producers shifts the supply curve of microwave ovens to the right and thereby establishes a new, lower equilibrium price. (See Figure 17.3.)

In other words, there are now more microwave ovens in Plecona, and the consumers are paying a lower price for them. However, because of the lower price, Pleconese producers of microwave ovens will choose to offer fewer microwaves for sale. So imports have the effect of initially increasing supply and of providing consumers with greater selection and lower prices. The competition also establishes incentives for domestic producers to become more efficient in production, improve worker productivity, and enhance customer service.

Both consumers and producers, then, benefit from international trade. Consumers benefit from imports because the selection of goods increases and prices decrease. Producers benefit from exports by gaining a new market for their products, and thereby giving them the opportunity to increase revenues and earn a profit.

DIFFERENTIATING INSTRUCTION

English Learners

Use Root Words to Understand
Have students use a dictionary to find the meaning of the root *-port* in the words *import* and *export*. *(to carry* or *to carry in)* Then have them list at least five words, with definitions, that also have this root in them. Point out that the word *importance,* though not directly related to *imports*, nonetheless has the idea of "something that carries or conveys meaning."

Gifted and Talented

Develop a Trade Proposal
Invite interested students to decipher the scrambled names Plecona and Nepocal *(no place)* and then make up products these nations might produce. Suggest students also think of names for these products by scrambling words related to *no place*. (Example: a hingnot, which unscrambled is *nothing,* might be a type of vacuum.) Next, have students draw up a trade proposal with the invented products, showing benefits of trade to both nations.

FIGURES 17.2 AND 17.3 THE EFFECTS OF INTERNATIONAL TRADE

17.2 PLECONA'S MOTORBIKE EXPORT MARKET

Price (in thousands of dollars): $12, 10, 8, 6, 4, 2, 0

Quantity supplied and demanded of motorbikes (in thousands): 5, 10, 15, 20, 25, 30

a, S, D2, D1

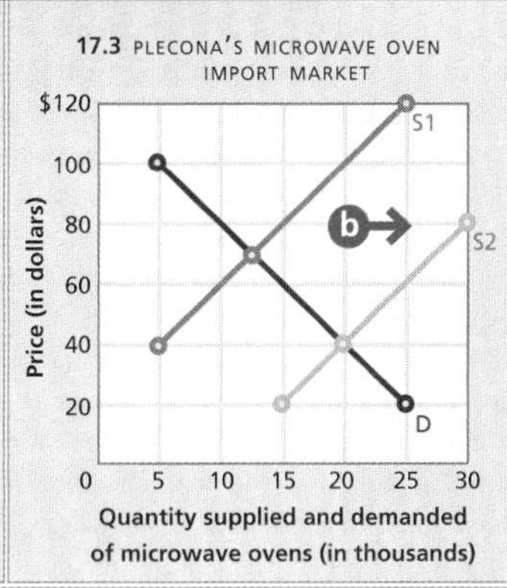

a Increased demand causes the demand curve to shift to the right.

b Increased supply causes the supply curve to shift to the right.

ANALYZE GRAPHS

What are the initial and then post-shift equilibrium prices for motorbikes in Figure 17.2? for microwaves in Figure 17.3?

Animated Economics

Use an interactive supply and demand graph at **ClassZone.com**

IMPACT 3 Trade Affects Employment

As nations specialize in their changing areas of strength, the availability of certain jobs can undergo dramatic changes. For example, if Australia specializes in producing iron ore or providing educational services (another area of strength for that nation) at the expense of making steel, then some Australian steelworkers may lose their jobs. At the same time, however, the overall number of Australian jobs may increase significantly. The Australian Trade Commission estimates that a ten percent increase in exports results in 70,000 new jobs for workers in Australia.

In the United States, manufacturing output increased 600 percent between 1950 and 2000. During the same period, however, employment in manufacturing, as a share of total employment, declined by nearly two-thirds. The United States was shifting its specialization from manufacturing to technology. In the process, it became a world leader in technology exports. So, while many manufacturing jobs in some sectors were lost, the shift in specialization and the resulting trade had positive effects on U.S. employment in general. During the 1990s, for example, U.S. exports were responsible for about 25 percent of the nation's economic growth, supporting about 12 million jobs. About 20 percent of all U.S. factory jobs depend on trade. Also, jobs in plants that export their products pay an average of 18 percent higher wages than jobs in non-exporting plants.

Biotech Jobs The U.S. economy's move to the technology sector has meant a sharp rise in biotechnology employment.

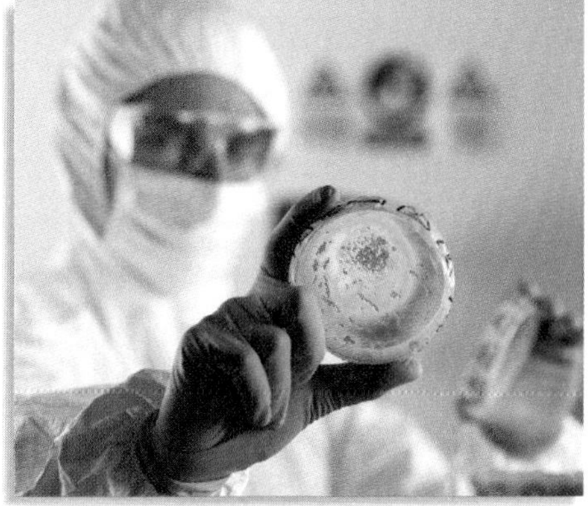

Analyzing Graphs: Figures 17.2 and 17.3

Ask students to explain what would happen to production and prices at the point nearest **b** on Figure 17.3. *(Quantity demanded exceeds supply, so the price is high. Supply then increases in response to demand and prices drop.)*

Answers

Figure 17.2: *initial, $6,000; post-shift, $8,000*

Figure 17.3: *initial, $70; post-shift, $40*

International Economics

Reopening the Silk Roads

The Silk Roads were ancient networks of trails used for Chinese trade with India, western Asia, and Europe. In recent times, stretches of the border between China and India have been disputed territory between these two giant nations. A key route along the Silk Roads, the Nathu La pass in the Himalayan Mountains, was closed as a result of border tensions.

Diplomacy has made little progress in settling the disputes. But the economic opportunity of resumed trade between these nations via this land route proved too tempting to pass up. In July 2006, the route was reopened. Trade through this section of the Silk Roads is projected to reach $3 billion by 2015.

SMALL GROUP ACTIVITY

Understanding Impact of Trade

Time 30 minutes

Task Create a two-country, two-product trade model and do a supply and demand analysis.

Materials Needed paper and pens

Activity

- Divide students into small groups.
- Instruct each group to create a basic scenario such as that involving Plecona and Nepocal, using either real or imaginary countries.
- Direct groups to select two products other than motorbikes and microwaves.
- Then, have students do a supply and demand analysis, creating a series of graphs like Figures 17.2 and 17.3.
- Have each group present its trade scenario and analysis to the class.

Rubric

	Understanding of Impact of Trade	Presentation of Information
4	excellent	original and complete
3	good	clear and complete
2	fair	incomplete but clear ideas
1	poor	incomplete and unclear

More About . . .

International Trade

The "containerization" system of transport was a breakthrough in shipping costs and efficiencies and supports the explosion of international trade. In this system, a single container can be loaded and sealed at its point of origin, transported by truck, and moved onto a railroad car. It is then transported by rail to a shipping dock, loaded onto an ocean liner, and exported.

When the container reaches its destination, it remains sealed and is transported as before until it is finally opened by the importer. Today, more than a quarter of all containers shipped originate in China.

Economics Update

At **ClassZone.com** students will see updated information on U.S. imports.

Analyzing Graphs: Figure 17.4

Ask students if the fact that the United States imports about 500,000 industrial supplies and materials while it exports only about 230,000 of such goods means that other nations can produce those goods more efficiently. Why or why not? *(It does not mean that. It only means that the exporting nations have a comparative advantage—a lower opportunity cost.)*

Answers

1. *capital goods; food and beverages*
2. *They indicate that the U.S. specializes most in capital goods and food and beverages, and largely trades for other goods.*

The United States in the World Economy

The United States is a leading nation in a number of aspects of the world economy. It is the largest exporter in the world, selling more than $900 billion in goods and services in 2005. The United States mostly exports capital goods (computers, machinery, civilian aircraft, and so on), automobiles, industrial supplies, consumer goods, and agricultural products. It is also the world's largest importer, buying nearly $1.7 trillion worth of goods and services from all over the world. It imports mainly crude oil and refined petroleum products, machinery, automobiles, consumer goods, and industrial raw materials.

Economics Update

Find an update on U.S. imports at **ClassZone.com**

While the United States imports more goods than it exports, it exports more services than it imports. Such services as travel and tourism, transportation, architecture and construction, and information systems find ready customers in Europe, Japan, Canada, and Mexico. The four most important trading partners for the United States in goods and services are Canada, accounting for 20 percent of trade, China (12 percent), Mexico (11 percent), and Japan (7 percent). Trade with these four partners accounts for half of U.S. foreign trade.

FIGURE 17.4 U.S. INTERNATIONAL TRADE IN GOODS BY CATEGORY

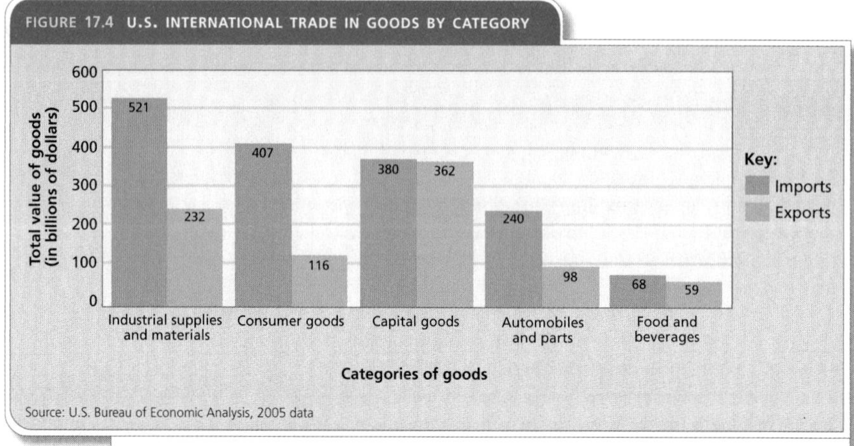

Source: U.S. Bureau of Economic Analysis, 2005 data

ANALYZE GRAPHS

1. In what two areas do U.S. export totals approach import totals?
2. What do these graphs show about the United States and specialization?

In recent years, as shown in Figure 17.4, the United States has imported an increasingly larger amount than it has exported. You will learn more about this in Section 4 of this chapter.

APPLICATION Interpreting Graphs

D. In what category of goods is the difference between imports and exports the greatest? Why do you think this is so?
Consumer goods; the United States doesn't specialize in consumer-goods manufacturing anymore, choosing to trade for these goods instead.

DIFFERENTIATING INSTRUCTION

Struggling Readers

Compare Text and Graphic

Point out that the textual material in the first two paragraphs conveys information about U.S. trade, and that the chart in Figure 17.4 also presents trade information. Ask students to think about and then discuss how the different methods of conveying information leave different impressions. In other words, what do readers take away and remember from the written information as compared to the graphic presentations? *(Possible answer: The graphics make relationships clearer.)*

Inclusion

Draw a Trade Map

Help students use the information in the second paragraph to create a map and/or other graphic showing which countries are the most important trading partners of the United States. Be sure that the varying percentages of trade are represented somewhere on the finished product.

SECTION 1 Assessment

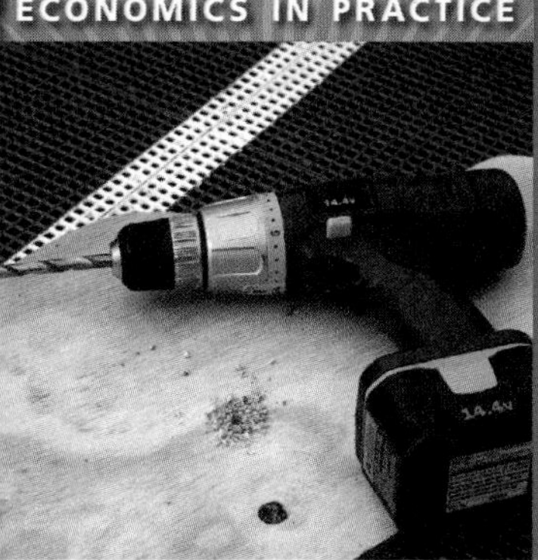

REVIEWING KEY CONCEPTS

1. Explain the difference between the terms in the following pairs:
   a. *specialization* and *economic interdependence*
   b. *absolute advantage* and *comparative advantage*
   c. *export* and *import*
2. What principle explains why nations specialize and trade?
3. Explain why trade is good for nations that produce exports as well as buy imports.
4. What effect do imports have on price and supply? Why?
5. What effect do exports have on price and demand? Why?
6. **Using Your Notes** Write a speech for the president of Australia, explaining why your nation should specialize in the production of iron ore and trade for steel. Use the Graphic Organizer at **Interactive Review @ ClassZone.com**

CRITICAL THINKING

7. **Analyzing Cause and Effect** You have just learned that high-quality electric guitars made in South Korea will soon be exported to the United States. Should you buy a new guitar now or wait until after the imports begin arriving? Explain your answer.
8. **Making Inferences and Drawing Conclusions** Why does the law of comparative advantage explain that all people and nations can trade?
9. **Explaining an Economic Concept** How does international trade help create jobs? How does it shift jobs?
10. **Challenge** Shelley started her own comedy improvisation club right after college, and at first she did everything: developed new material, starred in the show, handled publicity, and sold tickets. As the enterprise grew, however, she hired an assistant to handle publicity and sell tickets, even though she was better at doing those things than he was. Explain why that was a good idea, using terms from this lesson.

ECONOMICS IN PRACTICE

Figuring Absolute and Comparative Advantage

Review the following scenario that describes cordless drill and drill bit production in the fictional nations of Freedonia and Sylvania.

Freedonia and Sylvania both produce cordless drills and drill bits. Over the span of a month, Freedonia can produce 3,000 cordless drills and 21,000 drill bits. During this same period, Sylvania can produce 2,000 cordless drills and 10,000 drill bits.

Drawing Conclusions Use what you've learned in this section to answer the following questions:

1. For each product, which nation has the absolute advantage?
2. What are the production ratios for each nation? What is each nation's opportunity cost for each cordless drill produced?
3. Which country has the comparative advantage in cordless drill production?

Challenge Draw up and explain a scenario whereby Freedonia and Sylvania agree to trade, and each gets a better deal by adjusting its trade ratio.

4 Assess & Reteach

Assess Assign half of the class the even-numbered items and half the odd-numbered items. Follow up with a class discussion so that each side benefits from the other's answers.

Unit 7 Resource Book
- Section Quiz, p. 9

Interactive Review @ ClassZone.com
- Section Quiz

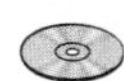
Test Generator CD-ROM
- Section Quiz

Reteach Have the class work in four groups, one for each heading in this section. Each group should ask and then answer these questions, by way of reviewing and synthesizing the material:
- What is the "economic way of thinking" underlying the material under this heading?
- What has personal relevance to me?

Each group should develop a presentation to convey its answers to the rest of the class.

Unit 7 Resource Book
- Reteaching Activity, p. 10

Economics in Practice
Drawing Conclusions
1. Freedonia has the absolute advantage in both.
2. Freedonia: 7 to 1, Sylvania: 5 to 1; Freedonia's opportunity cost is 7 drill bits per drill, and Sylvania's is 5 bits per drill.
3. Sylvania

Challenge If they agree to trade at a ratio of 6 to 1, they both benefit as explained in Figure 17.1.

SECTION 1 ASSESSMENT ANSWERS

Reviewing Key Concepts

1. a. *specialization*, p. 510; *economic interdependence*, p. 510
   b. *absolute advantage*, p. 513; *comparative advantage*, p. 513
   c. *export*, p. 516, *import*, p. 516
2. the law of comparative advantage
3. Exporting and importing points to a nation that is specializing and trading. When nations do this they operate at the lowest opportunity cost.
4. Imports lower prices and increase supply; they put more goods into the home market.
5. Exports decrease supply and raise prices, but at the new prices producers may produce more, hire more workers, and create more jobs.
6. See page 510 for an example of a completed diagram. Answers will vary, but look for an understanding of the benefits of trade for all participants.

Critical Thinking

7. You should wait, because by increasing the supply, the imported guitars will also lower prices.
8. The examples on page 515 show that both nations and individuals can benefit when they specialize and trade with opportunity cost as the focus.
9. It can help create jobs when higher prices for exported goods motivate producers to produce more, leading to economic expansion. It shifts jobs by requiring, for efficiency, that nations specialize. The areas in which nations specialize often change over time. This causes shifts in the industries that are offering employment.
10. Shelley has an absolute advantage over her assistant, but her assistant has a comparative advantage in the lower-level jobs he is performing. In other words, he has a lower opportunity cost to perform those jobs, giving up less valuable things than Shelley would have to give up if she continued to do them.

Economics in Practice

See answers in side column above.

1 Plan & Prepare

Section 2 Objectives

- identify barriers to trade
- examine the economic consequences of trade barriers
- describe protectionism and the arguments for it

2 Focus & Motivate

Connecting to Everyday Life Ask students to relate what they know about tariffs. Most will probably remember them from history classes. If the class does not know what a tariff is, ask a student to find the definition of tariff on page 521 and read it to the class. Point out that although tariffs may seem somewhat distant from students' everyday experiences, they have a profound impact. Because of tariffs, people in South Korea, for example, pay 10 times more for food than people in other parts of the world.

Taking Notes Remind students to take notes as they read by completing a chart. They can use the Graphic Organizer at **Interactive Review @ClassZone.com**. A sample is shown below.

Cause	Effect
Quota	limit on imports
	higher prices
	dumping
	some jobs protected

SECTION 2

Trade Barriers

OBJECTIVES

In Section 2, you will
- identify barriers to trade
- examine the economic consequences of trade barriers
- describe protectionism and the arguments for it

KEY TERMS

trade barrier, *p. 520*
quota, *p. 520*
dumping, *p. 521*
tariff, *p. 521*
revenue tariff, *p. 521*
protective tariff, *p. 521*
voluntary export restraint, *p. 521*
embargo, *p. 521*
trade war, *p. 522*
protectionism, *p. 523*
infant industries, *p. 523*

TAKING NOTES

As you read Section 2, complete a chart that shows the causes and effects of trade barriers. Use the Graphic Organizer at **Interactive Review @ ClassZone.com**

Cause	Effect
quota	higher prices

Barriers to Trade

KEY CONCEPTS

In order to offer some short-term protection to jobs and industries located within their borders, almost all nations pass some sort of laws that limit trade. These laws lead to higher prices on the restricted items or to economic retaliation by other nations. In the end, these industries and the jobs they provide can only be saved by becoming more competitive. The issue of trade restrictions is basically political in nature, and governments struggle to find the best policies to enact.

QUICK REFERENCE

A **trade barrier** is any law that limits free trade between nations.

A **quota** is a limit on the amount of a product that can be imported.

Types of Trade Barriers

A **trade barrier** is any law passed to limit free trade among nations. There are five basic types of trade barriers. Most are mandatory, but some are voluntary.

Quota Lifted Chinese textiles cross the Great Wall on their way to markets in the United States and the EU.

Quotas Nations often impose **quotas**, limits on the amount of a product that can be imported. For example, the United States had quotas on the amount of textiles allowed to be imported. These quotas limited supply and kept textile prices relatively high. These quotas expired on January 1, 2005. Chinese producers then flooded the United States (and the European Union) with low-priced textiles. Prices for Chinese textiles

SECTION 2 PROGRAM RESOURCES

ON LEVEL

Lesson Plans
- Core, p. 58

Unit 7 Resource Book
- Reading Study Guide, pp. 11–12
- Economic Skills and Problem Solving Activity, pp. 41–42
- Section Quiz, p. 19

STRUGGLING READERS

Unit 7 Resource Book
- Reading Study Guide with Additional Support, pp. 13–15
- Reteaching Activity, p. 20

ENGLISH LEARNERS

Unit 7 Resource Book
- Reading Study Guide with Additional Support (Spanish), pp. 16–18

INCLUSION

Lesson Plans
- Modified for Inclusion, p. 58

GIFTED AND TALENTED

Unit 7 Resource Book
- Case Study Resources: Sugar Tariff Fails to Yield Sweet Results for Anyone, p. 45

TECHNOLOGY

eEdition DVD-ROM

eEdition Online

Power Presentation DVD-ROM

Economics Concepts Transparencies
- CT58 Trade Barriers

Daily Test Practice Transparencies, TT58

ClassZone.com

increased, however, in other nations. This practice of **dumping**, the sale of a product in another country at a price lower than that charged in the home market, hurts domestic producers but provides consumers a lower price.

Tariffs Another trade barrier is the **tariff**, a fee charged for goods brought into a country from another country. There are two types of tariffs: revenue and protective. **Revenue tariffs**, taxes on imports specifically to raise money, are rarely used today. In the past, however, nations regularly used them as a source of income. Today nations use **protective tariffs**, taxes on imported goods, to protect domestic goods. Protective tariffs raise prices on goods produced more cheaply elsewhere, thereby minimizing the price advantage the imports have over domestic goods. Tariff rates have fallen worldwide since the late 1980s. (See Figure 17.5.)

Voluntary Export Restraint Sometimes, to avoid a quota or a tariff, a country may choose to limit an export. This is called a **voluntary export restraint (VER)**. It usually comes about when a trade ambassador from one nation makes appeals to a counterpart, warning of possible consequences without the VER.

Embargoes An **embargo** is a law that cuts off most or all trade with a specific country. It is often used for political purposes. Since the early 1960s, for example, the United States has had an embargo on trade with Communist Cuba.

Informal Trade Barriers Other trade restrictions are indirect. Licenses, environmental regulations, and health and safety measures (such as a ban on the use of certain herbicides) are, in effect, trade barriers.

QUICK REFERENCE

Dumping is the sale of a product in another country at a price lower than in the home market.

A **tariff** is a fee charged for goods brought into one country from another.

A **revenue tariff** is a tax levied on imports specifically to raise money.

A **protective tariff** is a tax on imported goods to protect domestic goods.

A **voluntary export restraint (VER)** is a country's self-imposed restriction on exports.

An **embargo** is a law that cuts off trade with a specific country.

FIGURE 17.5 TARIFF RATES ARE FALLING

Source: United Nations Human Development Report, 2005

APPLICATION Categorizing Economic Information

A. Aside from imposing an embargo, how might one nation limit the import of a product from another nation?

It could apply a high tariff or mandate that the item needs to be licensed (with the license having a large pricetag).

3 Teach

Barriers to Trade

Discuss

- In 2006, U.S. Ambassador to South Korea, Alexander R. Vershbow quoted 19th-century journalist and economist Henry George, saying:

  Protective tariffs are as much applications of force as are blockading squadrons, and their objective is the same: to prevent trade. The difference between the two is that blockading squadrons are a means whereby nations seek to prevent their enemies from trading; protective tariffs are a means whereby nations attempt to prevent their own people from trading.

  Ask students to comment on this comparison and explain how tariffs prevent a nation's own people from trading. *(Answers will vary, but some students may recognize that if a high tariff is imposed on imports, then exports to that country are likely to face a similarly high tariff in retaliation, limiting trading options.)*

Analyzing Graphs: Figure 17.5

Point out to students that this graph shows that tariffs rates have fallen significantly throughout the world since the late 1980s. Ask them where the greatest drop in rates has occurred. *(in South Asia)* Then ask which nations have the lowest tariff rates? *(developed nations)*

LEVELED ACTIVITY

Understanding Trade Barriers

Time 30 Minutes ◑

Objective Students will demonstrate an understanding of types of trade barriers, their impact, and arguments for protectionism.

Basic

Use the section's headings to help you add subheads to the following sentence outline.

A. Barriers to trade restrict market forces.

B. Trade barriers have an impact on both trading economies.

C. There are several arguments for protectionism.

On Level

Prepare some type of graphic—poster, collage, chart, short video—expressing ideas about trade barriers, their impact on the economy, and issues related to protectionism. Use text in your graphic to include definitions of words in this section and to explain the ideas behind some of your graphic representations.

Challenge

Take a position on protectionism and develop a campaign speech expressing your views. Be sure to anticipate the opposition's arguments and include refutations of those positions in your speech. Use visual aids as needed.

The Impact of Trade Barriers

Discuss

- Was the tariff on the Korean computer chip a good idea? Ask students to give reasons for their answers. *(Answers will vary. Those who think it was a good idea will likely argue on the basis of fairness. Those who do not think it was a good idea will likely point to the higher prices and disincentive to be efficient.)*
- Do you think that the European Union was justified in banning hormone-treated U.S. beef? *(Answers will vary. Some students may say yes because of the health concerns raised by the beef. Some students may be aware that domestically raised beef is often treated with hormones and that the U.S. government says it is safe to eat.)*

Analyzing Graphs: Figure 17.6

Point out to students that tariffs reduce supply. Ask them what the effect will be on prices, if demand stays the same. *(Higher prices will result.)*

The Impact of Trade Barriers

QUICK REFERENCE

trade war succession of increasing trade barriers between nations

KEY CONCEPTS

Trade barriers have numerous effects. They may temporarily save domestic jobs in certain industries, but without competition, those industries might continue to operate inefficiently. In the end, consumers pay higher prices. Further, limits on trade sometimes lead to a **trade war**, a succession of trade barriers between nations.

IMPACT 1 Higher Prices

Trade barriers raise prices or keep them high. For example, in the early 2000s, the United States and Japan, who both produce semiconductor chips, imposed tariffs on chips from South Korea. The reason for the tariff was that the Korean government had subsidized the chip maker, allowing the chips to be sold at a very low price. The result was a higher price in U.S. and Japanese markets for both the Korean chips (up 27 to 44 percent) as well as for those produced domestically. (See Figure 17.6.)

FIGURE 17.6 THE EFFECT OF AN IMPORT TARIFF ON PRICE

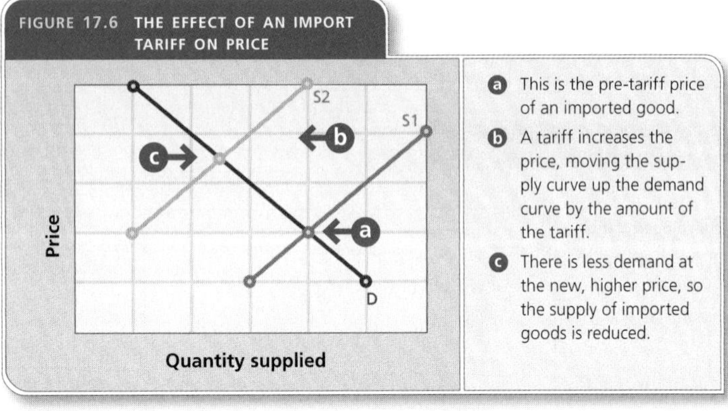

ⓐ This is the pre-tariff price of an imported good.
ⓑ A tariff increases the price, moving the supply curve up the demand curve by the amount of the tariff.
ⓒ There is less demand at the new, higher price, so the supply of imported goods is reduced.

IMPACT 2 Trade Wars

Trade wars often occur when nations disagree on quotas or tariffs. One recent trade war, however, came about in 1999 when the European Union banned the importation of hormone-treated U.S. beef. Many U.S. ranchers treat their cattle with hormones, which cause the animals to develop muscle faster than untreated animals. But EU scientists, citing health concerns, helped push through a ban. In response, the United States levied 100 percent tariffs on a range of EU products, including ham, onions, mustard, chocolate, and Roquefort cheese.

APPLICATION Applying an Economic Concept

B. Boeing, a U.S. airplane producer, and Airbus, its European competitor, each claim the other receives unfair governmental support. Why does each object to the alleged unfair support?
Because it would lower production costs for the maker, who could then offer a lower price to customers and drive out the competition.

DIFFERENTIATING INSTRUCTION

Inclusion

Develop a Concrete Example
Have students work in pairs to develop a concrete example to explain the events represented in the graph above. That is, ask them to think of a product, a reason for a tariff, and the effects of the tariff on prices for that product. Specifically, have students use their example to explain: the situation at point **a**; the reason for the shift in the supply curve; and the situation at point **c**.

Gifted and Talented

Identify Key Players
Interested students might like to research the Steel Tariff of 2002. Suggest that they focus on who the various stakeholders were in the decision to levy and then, later, lift the tariff on imported steel. Encourage them to create a "cast of characters" of these players, including organizations, and to briefly describe the position each would hold on the tariff issue and why.

Arguments for Protectionism

KEY CONCEPTS

Considering all the disadvantages of trade barriers, why would a country enact such laws? The answer lies in the concept of **protectionism**, the use of trade barriers between nations to protect domestic industries. Protectionists argue that trade barriers protect domestic jobs, promote **infant industries** (new industries that are often unable to compete against larger, more established competitors), and protect national security.

QUICK REFERENCE

Protectionism is the use of trade barriers between nations to protect domestic industries.

Infant industries are new industries that are often unable to compete against larger, more established competitors.

ARGUMENT 1 Protecting Domestic Jobs

Between 2000 and 2003, Stark County, Ohio, lost ten percent of its manufacturing jobs, including hundreds at a plant that makes Hoover vacuum cleaners. Imports from Asia and Mexico forced a ten percent drop in the price of vacuum cleaners. The U.S. workers, many of whom earned high wages to do their skilled work, were understandably upset by the shift of their jobs to overseas facilities.

In Ohio and elsewhere, people argue that trade barriers are needed to protect domestic jobs, even though, in reality, these actions generally protect inefficient production and result in higher prices for everyone. Voters in industrial areas bring their voices to the national debate about foreign trade. By doing so, they have helped bring about federal job training programs for workers who find themselves unemployed as a result of the movement of jobs to places where the per unit cost of labor is lower.

Irish Success Bono suggested that Ireland's ability to protect its industries helped the Irish economy become stronger.

ARGUMENT 2 Protecting Infant Industries

What was an Irish rock star, Bono, doing at the 2006 World Economic Conference in Davos, Switzerland? For one thing, this performer, known for his commitment to Africa, was arguing that African infant industries should be protected. Referring to the history of his own country, he said that Irish infant industries were protected in their day but that such protection is "denied . . . to the poorest countries in the world."

The idea behind protecting infant industries is to assist newly developing industries in their growth process until they are able to compete with better-developed foreign rivals. This argument is often used by newly developing nations to keep out goods from economically well developed nations. In Africa, for example, Uganda has received protection for its infant industries in the form of tariffs on exports from neighboring Kenya. However, even with these protective tariffs, Ugandan industry has not yet found a way to become competitive on its own and continues to request extensions of the tariff.

This example points to a potential problem. Critics say that, provided with a sheltered existence that is free from the need to compete on equal terms, these industries settle into perpetual infancy. And a perpetual infant needs perpetual support.

Arguments for Protectionism

Discuss

- What are the trade-offs in using protectionist policies to protect domestic jobs and infant industries? *(higher prices for consumers, continued inefficiencies)*
- In the examples on page 524 of the Chinese bid for an energy company and a bid by a Dubai company for port facility control, was the outcome one you would support? Why or why not? *(Answers will vary and will divide between those with strong concerns about national security and those with strong feelings about free trade. Look for good reasoning.)*

More About . . .

Live 8

Bono's colleague in bringing world attention to poverty in developing nations is Sir Bob Geldof. He was the organizer of the Live Aid fundraising concerts in 1985 that brought relief efforts to famine-stricken Ethiopia. Live 8 was another day of simultaneous worldwide concerts in 2006, held just before a meeting of leaders of the G8 nations.

This time, however, the organizers were collecting names, not money. About 38 million people have signed a petition supporting the eradication of poverty. In response to public pressure, G8 leaders agreed to $50 billion more in aid by 2010, debt cancellation for 38 countries, and free primary education and basic healthcare for all children.

SMALL GROUP ACTIVITY

Understanding Trade Wars

Time 30 Minutes ◑

Task Develop a game that uses the principles of world trade.

Materials Needed paper and pens

Activity

- Tell students that in the early days of computing, the first multiplayer game was called Trade Wars. Players had to trade effectively, manage scarce resources, and develop strategic relationships.
- Direct student groups to devise their own game (board game, card game, or computer game). The game must use principles and practices of international trade, including tariffs and other trade barriers.
- Then, have each group write a set of directions for playing their game.
- Each group should present its game to the class.

Rubric

	Understanding of Trade Wars	Presentation of Information
4	excellent	original and accurately presented
3	good	clear and accurate
2	fair	some key trade ideas missing or presented ideas inaccurately
1	poor	incomplete, unclear

A Global Perspective

Non-Economic Trade Barriers
Cultural protectionism affects the U.S. entertainment industry greatly. American-made films and television programs are shown in all parts of the world. Americans are able to make television programs and films more efficiently than many other nations. So, they are attractive overseas because they are often more affordable than home-grown productions.

However, government leaders in many nations, even those much like the United States in many ways, such as Australia and France, worry about the domination of U.S. culture. As a result, they have set quotas on the percentage of airtime or screen time given to foreign-made entertainment.

Answers

1. *Answers may vary. Students may say that since barriers are almost always politically motivated, they lack sound economic reasoning.*
2. *argument 2, because French and Canadian fear of domination by U.S. media giants resembles the arguments for infant industry protection*

More About . . .

Trade and National Security
The agency responsible for determining whether a foreign investment poses a national security risk is the Committee on Foreign Investment in the United States. It is chaired by the Secretary of the Treasury and includes representatives from several U.S. agencies including the departments of State, Defense, Commerce, Homeland Security, and Justice.

Non-member U.S. agencies are sometimes brought into the process of reviewing the proposed transaction. During this 30-day review process, each committee member conducts a separate investigation. Decisions are made by consensus.

A GLOBAL PERSPECTIVE

Non-Economic Trade Barriers

French movie poster

Some nations impose trade barriers for religious reasons. Iran, for instance, has banned any Western movies that portray secularism, feminism, and other activities deemed unethical. Western popular music has also been deemed indecent and "un-Islamic" and, therefore, banned. These barriers have driven demand for Western movies and music underground, where they can be found on the black market.

Some nations enact trade barriers based on more general notions of culture. During the 1994 round of negotiations related to the Global Agreement on Tariffs and Trade (GATT), the French movie industry won a victory on a principal close to its heart.

It's known as the cultural exception, and it basically states that cultural goods are different from other goods and should not be covered by trade agreements. The cultural exception has been used, notably by France and Canada, to boost domestic television and film industries (through subsidies and quotas) and limit foreign competition, mostly from the United States.

Without these protections, the exception's proponents say, a handful of U.S. media multinationals would be able to dominate the area of audiovisual entertainment, thereby overwhelming the traditional cultures of other nations.

CONNECTING ACROSS THE GLOBE

1. **Explaining an Economic Concept** Some would argue that all trade barriers lack sound, economic reasoning. Do you agree? Why?
2. **Making Inferences and Drawing Conclusions** Which one of the three arguments for protectionism most resembles the actions taken by France and Canada? Explain.

ARGUMENT 3 Protecting National Security

National security affects the trade of industries that nations consider to be vital to their safety. The energy industry is considered vital by most. In 2005, a government-run Chinese company bid on U.S. oil company UNOCAL. Many in Congress and elsewhere in the United States warned against allowing a foreign government to take over an important U.S. energy supplier. After the House of Representatives voted 398 to 15 to ask President Bush to step in, the Chinese company withdrew its bid.

But sharp political differences exist over what industries are truly vital to national security. In 2006, a company from Dubai, which had purchased the rights to operate port facilities in New York, Miami, New Orleans, and elsewhere, was forced to abandon the deal in light of political pressure over port security. Many analysts were skeptical of the security concerns, however, and worried more about the implications of interference in free international trade for purely political reasons.

APPLICATION Making Inferences and Drawing Conclusions

C. Do you think that political pressure for protectionist trade barriers rises or falls during a recession? Explain your answer. It would likely rise in an effort to protect already threatened jobs.

DIFFERENTIATING INSTRUCTION

English Learners

Use Conversation to Understand
Pair an English learner with an English speaker. Have students discuss the relationship between trade barriers and politics. They can begin their discussion with the two examples provided on this page.

Struggling Readers

Relate to Personal Experience
Divide students into small discussion groups. Instruct them to focus their talk on the information in the Global Perspective on this page. Have students discuss specific ways in which popular entertainment has influenced them, if at all, and encourage them to imagine its effect on a more traditional culture.

SECTION 2 Assessment

REVIEWING KEY CONCEPTS

1. Explain the relationship between the terms in the following pairs:
   a. *trade barrier* / *quota*
   b. *tariff* / *voluntary export restraint*
   c. *trade war* / *protective tariff*
   d. *infant industries* / *protectionism*
2. Why would a country engage in dumping?
3. How does a trade war get started? What effects does it have?
4. Why do some people feel that barriers to free trade are essential for national security?
5. Who benefits from trade barriers, inefficient or efficient producers?
6. **Using Your Notes** Take a position on free trade vs. protectionism and explain your position in a brief essay. Refer to your completed cause-and-effect chart. Use the Graphic Organizer at **Interactive Review @ ClassZone.com**

Cause	Effect
quota	higher prices

CRITICAL THINKING

7. **Analyzing Cause and Effect** In 1996, the United States expanded the embargo against Cuba, declaring that any foreign corporation that engaged in trade with Cuba would lose its privilege of trading with the United States. Give two possible effects of this embargo expansion.
8. **Solving Economic Problems** If you were the CEO of a manufacturing company facing stiff foreign competition, what are some ways you could adjust your business to stay competitive? What are the advantages and disadvantages of these changes?
9. **Applying Economic Concepts** Give three examples of U.S. citizens earning an income by selling products domestically that were made in other countries. Give three examples of U.S. citizens earning an income by selling products or services that are ultimately purchased by people in other countries.
10. **Challenge** A trade agreement between Kenya and some nations in Europe requires Kenyan farmers, most of whom have small peasant farms, to comply with 400 conditions before they can export their produce to European countries. They must be able to document the fertilizers, pesticides, and other additives used in the growing of their crops. How would you categorize this trade restriction? What impact do you think it will have on Kenyan exports and prices in the European nations?

Online Quiz
ClassZone.com

ECONOMICS IN PRACTICE

Analyzing Tariff Rates
Look at the graph below showing selected U.S. tariff rates for nations with which it has "Normal Trade Relations" (NTR), also known as the "most-favored nation" (MFN) status.

Item	NTR/MFN Tariff (%)
Ceramic tableware	4.5
Cars	2.5
Trucks	25.0
Most bicycles	11.0
Sports footwear	10.5

Analyzing and Interpreting Data How much does the cost of a $32,000 truck increase because of the tariffs? If you pay $245.31 for a bicycle, what amount is the tariff?

Challenge Suppose a pair of imported running shoes costs $10. With the tariff added, the importer has to pay $11.50. The importer, however, has to raise the price of the shoes to cover the expense of selling and shipping them to retailers, and retailers have to raise the price to cover their expenses in selling the shoes. Assuming the price increases by 50 percent at each stage of the process, what amount does the initial $1.50 tariff grow into?

4 Assess & Reteach

Assess Have students write definitions in their own words for all the key terms in question 1. Then have them read only their definition and ask the rest of the class to name the word being defined. Discuss the remaining key concept questions as a class activity. Divide the class into five groups for the remaining work and assign items 7–10 and Economics in Practice, one item per group. Have each group present its answers to the rest of the class.

Unit 7 Resource Book
- Section Quiz, p. 19

Interactive Review @ ClassZone.com
- Section Quiz

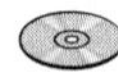

Test Generator CD-ROM
- Section Quiz

Reteach Have students imagine they are members of a galactic trade federation. Divide the class into three groups, one for each heading in this section. Ask each group to develop and then to present a discussion among members of this trade federation that is tied to the issues dealt with under each heading. To get them in the mood, you might want to read the opening crawl from The Phantom Menace, Episode 1 of the Star Wars series, which is found at http://www.starwars.com.

Unit 7 Resource Book
- Reteaching Activity, p. 20

SECTION 2 ASSESSMENT ANSWERS

1. **Reviewing Key Concepts**
   a. *trade barrier*, p. 520; *quota*, p. 520
   b. *tariff*, p. 521; *voluntary export restraint*, p. 521
   c. *trade war*, p. 522; *protective tariff*, p. 521
   d. *infant industries*, p. 523; *protectionism*, p. 523
2. to compete for limited quota opportunities
3. Trade wars usually start as the result of a tariff or other trade barrier enacted by one of the trading countries. They result in a decline in trade.
4. Trade barriers can help keep nations from depending too heavily on imported necessities so that they can be self-sufficient in times of crisis.
5. inefficient producers who are unable to compete in the open market with foreign competitors
6. See page 520 for an example of a completed diagram. Answers will vary, but look for an accurate use of the terms and concepts in the section.

Critical Thinking

7. Sample answers: Nations will choose to do business with the United States over Cuba; a trade war involving the United States and nations that wish to trade with Cuba.
8. Answers will vary but may include layoffs, outsourcing, increased technology to improve productivity. Advantages may include greater profitability and the ability to compete; disadvantages may include worker displacement.
9. Sample answers: importers—ethnic grocery store workers; salesperson for appliance company; auto mechanic; exporters—software engineer; citrus grower; wheat farmer
10. This is an informal trade barrier. It is likely to significantly reduce trade between Kenya and EU because of the difficulty of compliance, and EU prices will likely remain high.

Economics in Practice

Using Prices as Incentives $8,000; $26.98

Challenge The tariff grows to $3.38 (1.50 + 50% = 2.25; 2.25 + 50% = 3.375).

1 Plan & Prepare

Section 3 Objectives

- describe how nations determine the value of their currency in a world market
- explain why nations want a favorable balance of trade

2 Focus & Motivate

Connecting to Everyday Life Paint the following two scenes for students: *In the middle of the night, a man in Tokyo hunts for bargains on the foreign exchange market. He buys and sells Brazilian reals and Swedish kroners. On the other side of the world, in your neighborhood, shoppers hunt for bargains at the superstore.* Then ask students what the man in Tokyo has to do with the shoppers in your neighborhood? Let the discussion go where it will. If the question does not get answered directly, tell students to keep it in mind as they read this section.

Taking Notes Remind students to take notes as they read by completing a cluster diagram. They can use the Graphic Organizer at **Interactive Review @ ClassZone.com.** A sample is shown below.

Measuring Trade
- foreign exchange: foreign exchange market; foreign exchange rate; fixed rate of exchange; flexible exchange rate
- calculating exchange rates
- strong and weak currencies: trade-weighted value of the dollar
- balance of trade: balance of payments; trade surplus, trade deficit

SECTION 3

Measuring the Value of Trade

OBJECTIVES

In Section 3, you will
- describe how nations determine the value of their currency in a world market
- explain why nations want a favorable balance of trade

KEY TERMS

foreign exchange market, *p. 526*
foreign exchange rate, *p. 526*
fixed rate of exchange, *p. 526*
flexible rate of exchange, *p. 527*
trade weighted value of the dollar, *p. 528*
balance of trade, *p. 529*
balance of payments, *p. 529*
trade surplus, *p. 529*
trade deficit, *p. 529*

TAKING NOTES

As you read Section 3, complete a cluster diagram summarizing key information about measuring trade. Use the Graphic Organizer at **Interactive Review @ ClassZone.com**

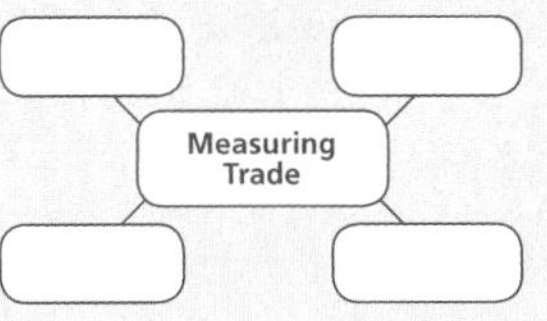

Foreign Exchange

QUICK REFERENCE

In the **foreign exchange market**, the currencies of different countries are bought and sold.

The **foreign exchange rate** is the price of a currency in the currencies of other nations.

With a **fixed rate of exchange**, the currency of one nation is fixed, or constant, in relation to other currencies.

KEY CONCEPTS

If a certain good costs $100, how many euros does it cost? How many Mexican pesos? Or Russian rubles? International trade requires some way to establish the relative value of the different currencies of the nations doing the trading. So nations have worked out systems that facilitate the exchange of currencies between buyers and sellers. One key element is the **foreign exchange market**, a market in which currencies of different countries are bought and sold. This market is a network of major commercial and investment banks that link the economies of the world. Another key element in facilitating international trade is the **foreign exchange rate**, the price of one currency in the currencies of other nations.

Rates of Exchange

During the 1800s and early 1900s, gold was the standard against which the value of a nation's currency was determined. Nations traded on the basis of a **fixed rate of exchange**, a system in which the currency of one nation

Currency Exchange The Mexican peso, the Australian dollar, and the Chinese yuan are all bought and sold on the foreign exchange market.

SECTION 3 PROGRAM RESOURCES

ON LEVEL

Lesson Plans
- Core, p. 59

Unit 7 Resource Book
- Reading Study Guide, pp. 21–22
- Math Skills Worksheet, p. 49
- Section Quiz, p. 29

STRUGGLING READERS

Unit 7 Resource Book
- Reading Study Guide with Additional Support, pp. 23–25
- Reteaching Activity, p. 30

ENGLISH LEARNERS

Unit 7 Resource Book
- Reading Study Guide with Additional Support (Spanish), pp. 26–28

INCLUSION

Lesson Plans
- Modified for Inclusion, p. 59

GIFTED AND TALENTED

Unit 7 Resource Book
- Readings in Free Enterprise: Emerging Giants, pp. 43–44

TECHNOLOGY

eEdition DVD-ROM
eEdition Online
Power Presentation DVD-ROM
Economics Concepts Transparencies
- CT59 Leading U.S. Trade Partners

Daily Test Practice Transparencies, TT59
ClassZone.com

is fixed, or constant, in relation to other currencies—in this case to gold. After the profound economic disruption of World War II, other currencies were "pegged" to the stable U.S. dollar. That is, their currency was valued according to its relation to the U.S. dollar. The price of an ounce of gold was fixed at $35.

The volatile 1970s brought another change. As the United States ran up a trade deficit and the dollar declined in value, the standard of $35 per ounce of gold was no longer sustainable, and the **flexible rate of exchange**, also called the floating rate, became predominant. This is a system in which the exchange rates for currencies change as the supply of and demand for the currencies change. For example, suppose that one British pound (GBP) is worth two U.S. dollars (USD). If an American importer wants to buy 100 British-made watches valued at 100 GBP each, then the importer would sell 20,000 USD in the foreign exchange market to obtain the necessary 10,000 GBPs. As the supply of dollars increases, their relative value drops. So the next time the importer wants to buy watches, the exchange rate might be 1 GPB:2.5 USD, and the watches would cost 25,000 U.S. dollars, making them less attractive as imports. Over time, the flexible exchange rate acts as a regulator on foreign exchange, balancing imports and exports.

QUICK REFERENCE

The **flexible rate of exchange** is a system in which the exchange rate for currency changes as supply and demand for the currency changes.

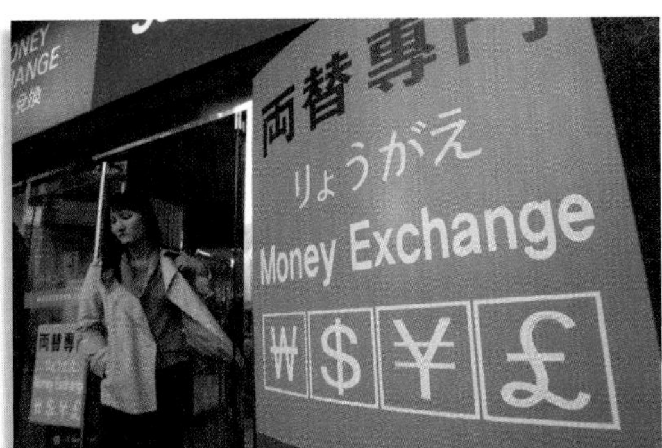

MATH CHALLENGE

FIGURE 17.7 Calculating Exchange Rates

Suppose you want to buy a book in Germany, where the currency is the euro (€). The book costs €25, and the seller wants you to pay in euros, but you have U.S. dollars. To buy the book you must first buy euros.

To find out how much €25 costs in U.S. dollars, you must know the exchange rate. In this case, let's say the exchange rate is 1.25, which means that one euro costs $1.25. Now use the following formula.

Amount of currency you want to buy	×	Exchange rate	=	Cost in currency you have	Example Calculation
					€25 × 1.25 $/€ = $31.25

To buy €25, you must pay $31.25.

Reciprocal exchange rate The exchange rate 1.25 can be written as a fraction: $1.25/€1. You can use this fraction to find the exchange rate a German must use to buy U.S. dollars with euros. First take the reciprocal of the fraction by swapping the numerator and the denominator; then use a calculator to write the fraction as a decimal.

The reciprocal of $\frac{\$1.25}{€1}$ is $\frac{€1}{\$1.25}$, which is 0.80 €/$

So to convert from U.S. dollars to euros, multiply by the exchange rate 0.80.

3 Teach

Foreign Exchange

Discuss

- What causes the supply of currency to vary? *(One cause is the purchase of foreign goods; other causes include the Fed's printing more money; foreign investment; and speculators who buy and sell currencies.)*

Math Challenge: Figure 17.7

Calculating Exchange Rates

Another way to see the relative value of currencies is the Big Mac Index, published annually in *The Economist*. The index uses the Big Mac as the only item in a market basket and compares prices in dollars and other currencies. Using those figures and the market exchange rates, economists can determine what exchange rate would be needed to make the Big Mac cost the same with two currencies.

For example, in 2006, a Big Mac cost an average of $3.10 in the United States, while costing S$3.60 in Singapore. Using the standard conversion formula (3.60/3.10) the exchange rate calculates to 1.16. But the actual exchange rate at that time was 1.59. So, the purchasing power of the Singapore dollar was undervalued.

SMALL GROUP ACTIVITY

Understanding Foreign Exchange Markets

Time 30 Minutes 

Task Develop a flow chart showing the course and impact of a foreign exchange.

Materials Needed paper and pens

Activity

- Have students work in small groups.
- Direct students to create a flow chart that begins with this event: "A U.S. importer wants to buy goods from Sweden, where the currency is called the kroner."
- Instruct students to include as many steps as they can in the process.
- Instruct them to include steps that show both what the individual trader does and the impact of those decisions on foreign exchange rates.
- Each group should present and explain its chart to the class.

Rubric

	Understanding of Foreign Exchange	Presentation of Information
4	excellent	outstanding use of graphic format, accurate
3	good	clear and accurate
2	fair	some key ideas missing or inaccurate
1	poor	incomplete, unclear

Analyzing Graphs: Figure 17.8

With the class, talk through the events in this graphic, using a concrete example of a product with a starting price before the events in the graphic. Have students answer the following questions:

- What might cause the value of the U.S. dollar to rise? *(exchanges in the currency markets; the Fed's printing more money; foreign investment; and speculation)*
- Why do U.S. imports become less expensive? *(Each dollar can buy more as the value rises.)*
- Why do exports become more expensive? *(because the buyers would have to spend more of their currency relative to the dollar to buy the goods)*

Your Economic Choices

STRONG DOLLAR AND WEAK DOLLAR

Which sweater will you buy?
Ask students how they would know the relative value of the Hong Kong and U.S. currencies. *(They probably would not have checked the exchange rates that day, but the difference should show up in the pricing.)* In that case, the economic choice boils down to saving money or supporting U.S. producers.

Activity Invite students to compare prices for some fairly simple item, such as a cotton T-shirt in their size. Tell them to try to find comparable products, one made in a foreign country and the other made in the United States. Have them note the foreign country and the two prices and then research the foreign exchange rates at any of the many Web sites with that information. Ask them to explain whether or not the exchange rates are consistent with the pricing.

Strong and Weak Currencies

QUICK REFERENCE

The **trade-weighted value of the dollar** is a measure of the international value of the dollar.

The Federal Reserve keeps a measure of the international value of the dollar called the **trade-weighted value of the dollar**. It determines if the dollar is strong or weak as measured against another currency. Because of the flexible exchange rate, as currencies are traded, some increase or decrease in value when measured against another currency.

For example, if the U.S. dollar becomes stronger in comparison to the Mexican peso, then the U.S. dollar buys more Mexican pesos than it could previously. What this means is that imports from Mexico now cost less. As you can see in Figure 17.8, importers in the United States benefit because they are able to buy foreign goods and services relatively cheaply.

At the same time, however, goods made in the United States may have a hard time competing with these inexpensive imports in the U.S. domestic market. Also, the strong dollar has a negative effect on U.S. exporters, since goods made here would be more costly to purchase abroad at the strong dollar rate. The weak dollar has the same effects but in reverse, as imported goods become more expensive and exporters are able to sell relatively cheaply.

FIGURE 17.8 THE STRONG DOLLAR AND U.S. TRADE

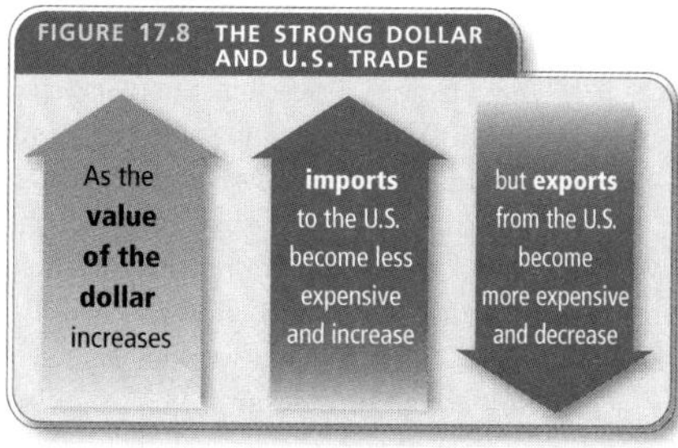

As the **value of the dollar** increases
imports to the U.S. become less expensive and increase
but **exports** from the U.S. become more expensive and decrease

YOUR ECONOMIC CHOICES

STRONG DOLLAR AND WEAK DOLLAR

Which sweater will you buy?

The U.S. dollar is very weak versus the Hong Kong dollar (HKD). How might this influence your decision to buy a new sweater made in the United States, or one imported from Hong Kong?

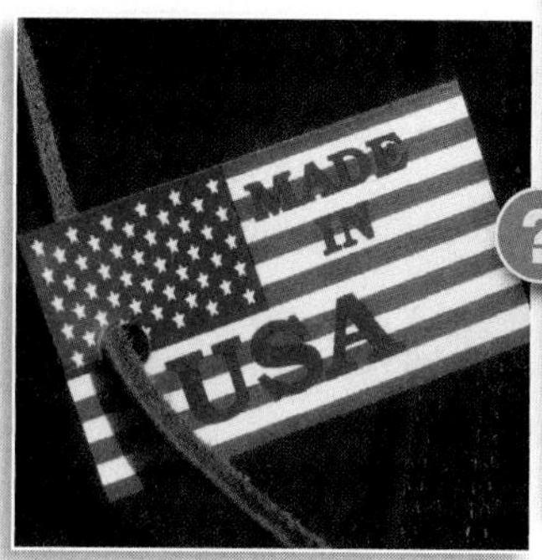

Domestically produced

Imported from overseas

APPLICATION Applying Economic Concepts

A. If you are an American exporter, does a strong dollar help your business? Explain.
No. Foreign consumers would have to give up more of their currency to make purchases in US dollars.

DIFFERENTIATING INSTRUCTION

English Learners

Relate to One's Culture
Help students understand currencies by having them prepare a report on the currency of the country (or one of the countries) to which they trace their roots. Encourage students to have their reports include an explanation of the values of the various coins and bills, as well as the current exchange rate with the U.S. dollar.

Gifted and Talented

Determine Cause and Effect
Invite interested students to write a paragraph or create a flow chart or some other graphic representation showing the relationship between a trade deficit and a decrease in the value of a dollar. Suggest that the relationship be shown through a chain of causes and effects.

Balance of Trade

KEY CONCEPTS

In Chapter 12, you read about net exports as an economic measure. Another name for the difference between the value of a country's imports and exports is its **balance of trade**. It is tallied through the **balance of payments**, a record of all the transactions that occurred between the individuals, businesses, and government units of one nation and those of the rest of the world. The U.S. balance of payments includes the goods and services traded between it and other nations, as well as the investments foreign interests make in the United States and those made by Americans in a foreign country. A nation is said to have a favorable balance of trade if it has a **trade surplus**—that is, it exports more than it imports. If a nation imports more than it exports it has a **trade deficit**, also known as an unfavorable balance of trade.

QUICK REFERENCE

A nation's **balance of trade** is the difference between the value of its imports and exports.

The **balance of payments** is a record of all the transactions that occurred between the individuals, businesses, and government units of one nation and those of the rest of the world.

A nation with a **trade surplus** exports more than it imports.

A nation with a **trade deficit** imports more than it exports.

EXAMPLE U.S.-China Trade

In recent years, China has undergone one of the most rapid industrializations in history. In addition to its fast-growing output of manufactured goods, the Chinese currency, the RenMinBi (RMB), or yuan, has also been weak compared to the U.S. dollar. The yuan's weakness versus the dollar resulted from China's decision to peg its value at a fixed rate versus the dollar, beginning in 1994. This artificially weak position helped make the United States the number-one destination for Chinese exports. By 2005, China had a record trade surplus of just over $200 billion with the United States. The surplus helps China fuel its continued manufacturing growth.

FIGURE 17.9 BALANCE OF U.S. TRADE WITH CHINA

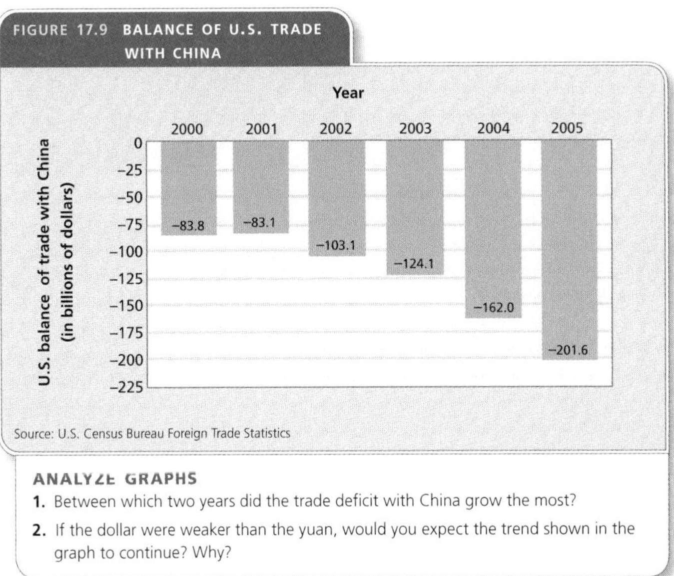

Source: U.S. Census Bureau Foreign Trade Statistics

ANALYZE GRAPHS

1. Between which two years did the trade deficit with China grow the most?
2. If the dollar were weaker than the yuan, would you expect the trend shown in the graph to continue? Why?

Balance of Trade

Discuss

- How would Adam Smith feel about a trade deficit? (Refer students to page 30 for a reminder of his views.) *(He would—and in fact did—dismiss it, arguing that a nation's ability to produce wealth, through specialization and efficiency, is the critical issue.)*
- What are an advantage and a disadvantage of a trade deficit? Which is more important, in your opinion? Give reasons for your answers. *(advantage—lower prices for consumers; disadvantage—need to borrow money, sell off assets, or tap into reserves of foreign currencies. Answers will vary on which is more important. Those favoring lower prices will likely focus on free trade benefits; others may favor greater national financial security and independence.)*

Analyzing Graphs: Figure 17.9

Ask students to discuss why China has been slow to adjust its currency. *(As long as it is undervalued compared to the dollar, exports to the United States will be very attractive.)* Point out that in 2005, under pressure from the United States and the World Trade Organization, China revalued its currency, pegging it to a market basket that included other currencies besides the U.S. dollar. Its value immediately appreciated.

Answers

1. *between 2004 and 2005*
2. *No, because U.S. imports would then cost less than Chinese imports.*

SMALL GROUP ACTIVITY

Negotiating Trade Issues

Time 30 Minutes ◑

Task Develop a response to China's currency valuation.

Materials Needed paper and pens

Activity

- Have students work in small groups.
- Direct students to think of ways that the U.S. government could pressure China to increase the value of its currency.
- Instruct students to develop a proposed plan of action and to write a brief description.
- Then have each group present its plan to the class.
- Follow each presentation with a brief discussion of the effectiveness of the ideas.

Rubric

	Understanding of Responses to Trade Issues	Presentation of Information
4	excellent	creative and effective
3	good	clear and effective
2	fair	few effective ideas or ideas presented inaccurately
1	poor	incomplete, unclear

Analyzing Graphs: Figure 17.10

Ask students to compare this graph on the balance of trade with the graph on page 529. What similarities do they see? *(same decreasing deficit from 2000 to 2001 and same increasing deficits from 2002 to 2005)* Also ask students to use the two charts to estimate the percentage of the trade deficit represented by trade with China in each year from 2000 to 2005. *(For example, out of about a $416 billion deficit in 2000, the trade deficit with China was about $84 billion, or approximately 20 percent.)*

Answers

1. *2001*
2. *falling prices*

More About . . .

The Trade Deficit and the Economy
Those who worry about the trade deficit fear that it is a sign of a weakening economy. In fact, rising trade deficits correspond to a growing economy. Critics also worry about the effect of a trade deficit on domestic jobs. However, in years when the trade deficit increases, manufacturing output increases as well.

Many analysts believe that trade deficits are actually a sign of economic strength. But this is only true as long as the economy is investing in future productivity.

Economics Update

At **ClassZone.com** students will see updated information on the U.S. balance of trade. The information will help students recognize trade patterns.

EXAMPLE The U.S. Trade Balance

The balance of trade in the United States has gone through roughly five phases. From about 1770 to 1870, the young nation had a deficit in goods and services but a surplus in capital investment from foreign countries that recognized the nation's potential for growth. Between 1870 and 1920, the nation was paying back foreign debts from the previous phase, but it was also exporting more goods and services than it was importing. In the years between 1920 and 1945, the United States had a surplus in exports but a deficit in foreign investments, as the nation sought to help rebuild Europe after World War I. From 1945 to 1980, the nation had a deficit in merchandise and continued its deficit in foreign investments as large amounts of money went to post–World War II reconstruction.

In the current phase, the United States has a large surplus of foreign investment, which is attracted by a relatively low inflation rate and a generally stable economy. However, high rates of consumer spending (versus low rates of saving), as well as high oil prices (which significantly increased the dollar value of U.S. imports) have helped create a very large merchandise deficit. An advantage of this deficit is that it allows U.S. consumers to buy low-priced imports. A disadvantage is that financing the deficit may require borrowing money from the rest of the world, selling off assets, or tapping into foreign currency reserves.

Economics Update
For an update on the U.S. balance of trade go to **ClassZone.com**

FIGURE 17.10 U.S. BALANCE OF TRADE

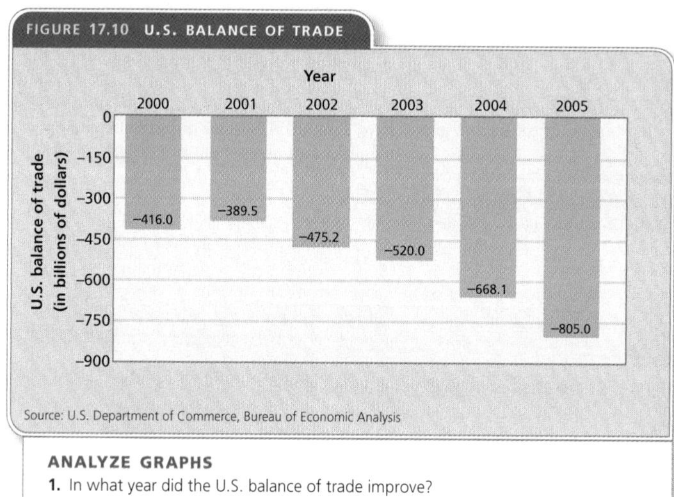

ANALYZE GRAPHS

1. In what year did the U.S. balance of trade improve?
2. Does this overall trend point to rising or falling prices for U.S. consumers?

APPLICATION Analyzing Cause and Effect

B. Between 1870 and 1920, the United States was exporting more goods and services than it imported. What does this say about the relative strength of the dollar during this period? The dollar was relatively strong because, as we see in Figure 17.8, a strong dollar results in increased exports.

DIFFERENTIATING INSTRUCTION

Inclusion

Provide Verbal Descriptions
Pair a student with a visual impairment with a student with no visual impairment. Ask that student to read aloud the text on this page, encouraging questions from the listening student. Then, have the student without impairment describe Figures 17.9 and 17.10 as accurately as possible. Give the visually impaired student the opportunity to repeat the description or, at least, the main points.

Struggling Readers

Isolate Concepts
The second paragraph on this page contains a substantial amount of information. Have students work in pairs to break down each sentence into its separate concepts and make new sentences. Model the first sentence for students. *(The United States has a large surplus of foreign investment. The foreign investment is attracted by low inflation. It is also attracted by a generally stable economy.)* Note that this strategy can be used to improve comprehension.

SECTION 3 Assessment

Online Quiz
ClassZone.com

REVIEWING KEY CONCEPTS

1. Explain the differences between the terms in each of these pairs:
   a. *foreign exchange market* / *foreign exchange rate*
   b. *fixed rate of exchange* / *flexible rate of exchange*
   c. *trade surplus* / *trade deficit*
2. What is an advantage of a trade surplus? A disadvantage?
3. What is an advantage of a trade deficit? A disadvantage?
4. How does the value of the U.S. dollar affect the U.S. trade surplus or deficit?
5. How does a flexible exchange rate help to stabilize trade balances?
6. **Using Your Notes** Write a brief essay arguing for or against a single world currency. Refer to your completed cluster and use the section's key words.

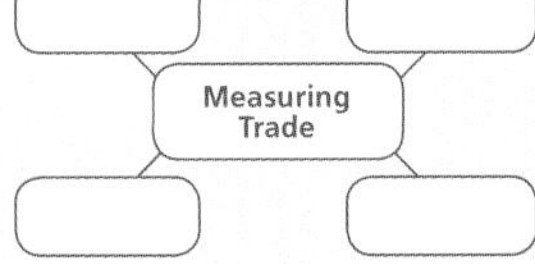

Use the Graphic Organizer at **Interactive Review @ ClassZone.com**

CRITICAL THINKING

7. **Analyzing Cause and Effect** In July 2005, the Chinese RMB became fixed to a "market-basket" of currencies, including the U.S. dollar and the Japanese yen, removing a decade-long peg to the U.S. dollar alone. The new formula slightly raised the value of the RMB. If China's trade surpluses continue, what will happen to the value of the RMB?
8. **Applying an Economic Concept** While you are in France on a business trip, you find out that the euro has gained strength against the U.S. dollar. Will your hotel room and food now be more or less expensive? Why? What about the goods you're trying to sell on your trip; will they be more or less expensive to your customers in France? Why?
9. **Making Inferences and Drawing Conclusions** Japan has the world's largest foreign currency reserves, followed by China. State two conclusions you can draw about the economies of these two nations based on their foreign currency reserves.
10. **Challenge** What are the advantages of a large supply of foreign investment in a domestic economy? What are the disadvantages?

ECONOMICS IN PRACTICE

Understanding Exchange Rates Just as there are stock markets for trading company shares, there are currency markets for trading currencies. The picture shows the prices of three currencies in dollars and how the prices have changed.

	One			
Buys	U.S. Dollar	Euro	Chinese Yuan	Indian Rupee
U.S. Dollar	1.00	1.32	0.13	0.02
Euro	0.76	1.00	0.10	0.02
Chinese Yuan	7.82	10.33	1.00	0.18
Indian Rupee	44.48	58.72	5.69	1.00

Average rates, December 2006

Analyze Data Use this exchange rate table to answer the following questions.

- How much of each of the other currencies will $5 U.S. purchase?
- If the exchange rate from euros to dollars changed from 1.32 to 1.40, which currency has gotten weaker?
- How would that affect EU businesses that export to the United States?

Challenge Why might businesses need to buy foreign currencies?

❹ Assess & Reteach

Assess Go over all the questions except question 5 as a whole group activity. Have each student read his or her essay on a single world currency to the class.

Unit 7 Resource Book
- Section Quiz, p. 29

Interactive Review @ ClassZone.com
- Section Quiz

Test Generator CD-ROM
- Section Quiz

Reteach Use the graphics and special features as the focus points for a discussion to review the material in this section.

Unit 7 Resource Book
- Reteaching Activity, p. 30

SECTION 3 ASSESSMENT ANSWERS

Reviewing Key Concepts

1. a. *foreign exchange market*, p. 526; *foreign exchange rate*, p. 526
   b. *fixed rate of exchange*, p. 526; *flexible exchange rate*, p. 527
   c. *trade surplus*, p. 529; *trade deficit*, p. 529
2. advantage—potentially large reserves of foreign currency; disadvantage—domestic consumers do not get to enjoy products' lower prices
3. advantage—consumers enjoy lower prices of imports; disadvantage—may need to borrow or sell off assets to pay foreign debt
4. When the dollar is strong, the trade deficit is likely to increase; when the dollar is weak the trade surplus will likely increase.
5. Because of the relationship between price and quantity demanded, the flexible exchange rate will help lead to an equilibrium level of trade.
6. See page 526 for an example of a completed diagram. The essay should show an understanding of the Key Terms and concepts discussed in Section 3.

Critical Thinking

7. It will continue to rise.
8. more expensive—it now costs more U.S. money to buy a euro; less expensive—a weaker dollar means the cost of U.S. exports decreases
9. Answers will vary but may include the following: (1) that Japan and China have a trade surplus; (2) that Japanese and Chinese consumers may pay higher prices for goods than consumers in the nations they export to
10. Possible answers: advantages—money to pay off debts or grow businesses; disadvantages—foreign ownership of domestic concerns and the loss of independence that goes with that

Economics in Practice

Analyze Data Five dollars buy 3.80 euro, 39.10 yuan, or 222.40 rupee.
The dollar has gotten weaker.
There might be less demand for their products.

Challenge Businesses that buy goods from other countries need foreign currencies to make their purchases.

1 Plan & Prepare

Section 4 Objectives

- describe what agreements were made to start the free trade movement
- identify international and regional trade groups
- explain what role multinationals play in world trade

2 Focus & Motivate

Connecting to Everyday Life Explain to students that a trade agreement such as NAFTA has had real effects that can be seen every day. Prices, wages, job shifts—these are everyday things that NAFTA has had an impact on since it was instituted.

Taking Notes Remind students to take notes as they read by completing a summary chart. They can use the Graphic Organizer at **Interactive Review @ ClassZone.com**. A sample is shown below.

Regional	International
EU	WTO
NAFTA	G8
Mercosur	
ASEAN	
APEC	
SADC	

SECTION 4

Modern International Institutions

OBJECTIVES

In Section 4, you will

- describe what agreements were made to start the free-trade movement
- identify international and regional trade groups
- explain what role multinationals play in world trade

KEY TERMS

free-trade zone, *p. 532*
customs union, *p. 532*
European Union, *p. 532*
euro, *p. 533*
NAFTA, *p. 533*
OPEC, *p. 535*
cartel, *p. 535*
WTO, *p. 535*

TAKING NOTES

As you read Section 4, complete a summary chart like the one shown, using the key concepts and other helpful words and phrases. Use the Graphic Organizer at **Interactive Review @ ClassZone.com**

Regional	International

Regional and World Trade Organizations

QUICK REFERENCE

A **free-trade zone** is a specific region in which trade between nations takes place without protective tariffs.

A **customs union** is an agreement that abolishes trade barriers among its members and establishes uniform tariffs for non-members.

The **European Union**, the EU, is an economic and political union of European nations established in 1993.

KEY CONCEPTS

Following the failed protectionist policies of the 1930s, nations have sought to expand trade and reduce or eliminate trade barriers. They have organized regional trading groups to create **free-trade zones**, specific regions in which trade between nations takes place without protective tariffs. Some have created **customs unions**, agreements that abolish trade barriers among the members and establish uniform tariffs for non-members. Some of these organizations are called common markets. As a result of these efforts, global tariffs have dropped by about one-third.

GROUP 1 The European Union

In 1957, six European nations recognized the benefits of abolishing trade barriers and formed a customs union called the European Economic Community. It was widely known as the Common Market. In 1993 the Common Market evolved into the **European Union**, or EU , which tightly bound its member nations to one another both economically and politically. The political nature of the EU, the fact that its members surrender some sovereignty in specified areas, makes it unique among

EU Expansion Lithuanians celebrate their nation's admission to the EU in 2004.

SECTION 4 PROGRAM RESOURCES

ON LEVEL

Lesson Plans

- Core, p. 60

Unit 7 Resource Book

- Reading Study Guide, pp. 31–32
- Economic Skills and Problem Solving Activity, pp. 41–42
- Section Quiz, p. 39

STRUGGLING READERS

Unit 7 Resource Book

- Reading Study Guide with Additional Support, pp. 33–35
- Reteaching Activity, p. 40

ENGLISH LEARNERS

Unit 7 Resource Book

- Reading Study Guide with Additional Support (Spanish), pp. 36–38

INCLUSION

Lesson Plans

- Modified for Inclusion, p. 60

GIFTED AND TALENTED

Unit 7 Resource Book

- Case Study Resources: Sugar Tariff Fails to Yield Sweet Results for Anyone, p. 45; CAFTA Barely Passes, p. 46

TECHNOLOGY

eEdition DVD-ROM

eEdition Online

Power Presentation DVD-ROM

Economics Concepts Transparencies

- CT60 Members of the European Union

Daily Test Practice Transparencies, TT60

ClassZone.com

trading groups. The Treaty on European Union had monetary union and a common foreign policy as key goals. Monetary union was established in 2002, as 12 member states adopted the **euro**. (See "The Euro as Common Currency" on p. 292.)

The six original members were Belgium, France, Germany, Italy, Luxembourg, and the Netherlands. In 1973, Denmark, Ireland, and the United Kingdom became members. Greece joined in 1981, and Portugal and Spain in 1986. In 1995, after the Common Market became the European Union, Austria, Finland, and Sweden joined. In 2004, ten nations became members: Cyprus, the Czech Republic, Estonia, Hungary, Latvia, Lithuania, Malta, Poland, Slovakia, and Slovenia. In 2007, Bulgaria and Romania joined, raising the total number of members to 27.

The EU accounts for about 20 percent of global exports and imports, making it the world's biggest trader. It has removed barriers to free trade among member nations, with the ultimate goal that Europe's national borders will be no more a barrier to free trade than are the borders of U.S. states.

QUICK REFERENCE

The **euro** is the currency of the European Union.

GROUP 2 NAFTA

In 1990, negotiations began on a free-trade agreement among the United States, Canada, and Mexico. The result of these negotiations, the North American Free Trade Agreement, or **NAFTA**, created the largest free-trade zone in the world. When it went into effect on January 1, 1994, it immediately eliminated tariffs on half of the goods exported to Mexico from the United States. The agreement called for an eventual phase-out of all trade barriers on goods and services. It also called for improved protection of intellectual property rights, stronger environmental and worker protections, and standardized investment policies.

The advantages of NAFTA include specialization and increased efficiency, a competitive advantage over the EU and Japan, expanded markets, and new jobs. And while some object to NAFTA on a number of political, social, and even environmental grounds, the economic results appear robust. (See Figure 17.11.) Between 1993 and 2003, Mexico and Canada experienced economic gains as well. Two-way agricultural

QUICK REFERENCE

NAFTA, the North America Free Trade Agreement, is designed to ensure trade without barriers between Canada, Mexico, and the United States.

FIGURE 17.11 NAFTA'S FIRST TEN YEARS

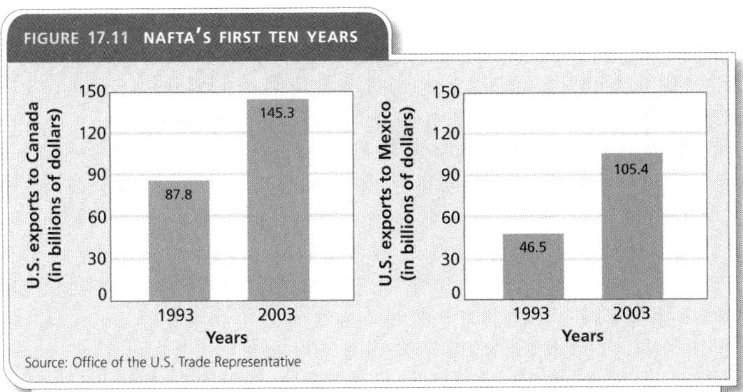

Source: Office of the U.S. Trade Representative

ANALYZE GRAPHS

1. Which nation, Canada or Mexico, increased its trade with the United States by a larger percentage?
2. Is an increase in trade typically beneficial for nations? Explain.

3 Teach

Regional and World Trade Organizations

Discuss

- Why would nations form trading associations? *(Possible answers: specialization, efficiency, expanded markets, more jobs, competitive strength against other trade organizations)*
- In what important way are NAFTA nations, in relation to each other, different from nations in the EU? *(The level of economic development of Mexico is different from that of the U.S. or Canada, while the nations in the EU are at similar development levels.)* What challenges does this difference pose? *(Developing nations have different trade issues to promote, such as protection of infant industries and fair trade.)*

Analyzing Graphs: Figure 17.11

To encourage students to look closely at the bar graphs, ask them which increased by the greatest percentage, exports to Canada or exports to Mexico? *(Mexico)* Ask students why this may be so. *(Possible answer: Exports to Canada were already well established.)*

Answers

1. *Mexico*
2. *Typically yes, because of the laws of comparative advantage explained previously.*

SMALL GROUP ACTIVITY

Developing a Common Currency

Time 30–45 Minutes 

Task Design a currency for a trade group.

Materials Needed paper and pens, pictures of currency from member nations (available online)

Activity

- Begin with a discussion of the social and cultural issues that may arise through membership in a trade organization.
- Then, have each group choose a trade group mentioned in the text (but not EU) for which to design a common currency.
- Instruct students to keep the discussion points about social and cultural issues in mind as they design the currency.
- Direct groups to obtain front and back images of the basic currency denomination of each member country.
- Have them design both front and back of the new currency and give it a value in relation to the original currencies.
- Allow each group to describe its new currency to the class.

Rubric

	Understanding Organizations	Presentation of Information
4	excellent	creative solution
3	good	solid solution
2	fair	attempted solution that lacks focus
1	poor	incomplete, does not address issues

More About . . .

World Trade Blocs

Regional trade blocs are a subject of controversy. To free-trade advocates, they seem to serve protectionist purposes, operating at the regional rather than the international level. Indeed, strengthening a region in relation to the rest of the world is a key part of regional trade organizations. While trade barriers between member nations are lowered, regional organizations often impose high tariffs on outsiders.

Economic ties also provide strong political ties. As a result, a regional trade group can unify the nations in a region and help create stability.

Analyzing Maps: Figure 17.12

Ask students to look closely at the map of the world. What can be said about the extent of regional trade groups? *(There are regional trade groups in most regions of the world.)* Why have so many regions formed trade groups? *(Possible answer: to stay competitive with other regions)*

Answers

The U.S. and Canada belong to the G8, APEC, and NAFTA. As developed nations, both nations produce and trade a lot. Being part of multiple organizations helps them trade easily in different parts of the world.

trade between Mexico and the United States increased 125 percent—from $6.2 billion in 1993 to $14.2 billion in 2003. Productivity in Mexico increased a remarkable 55 percent. Canada's exports to its NAFTA partners increased by 104 percent, and its overall economy grew by over 30 percent. Overall trade between the three partners more than doubled during this period, from $289.3 billion in 1993 to $623.1 billion in 2003.

GROUP 3 Other Regional Trade Groups

Throughout the world, nations are forming trade organizations to specialize, promote free trade, and stay competitive with other trade groups. Descriptions of a number of these agreements from all parts of the world follow:

Mercosur (*Mercado Comun del Cono Sur*) This group promotes the movement of goods and people in South America. Formed in 1995, Mercosur eliminated tariffs on 90 percent of goods traded between the group's full members (Argentina, Brazil, Paraguay, and Uruguay). Venezuela became a full member in July of 2006. Counting associate members Mexico, Chile, Bolivia, and Peru, Mercosur has become the world's fourth-largest trade association.

ASEAN The Association of Southest Asian Nations was formed in 1967 to accelerate economic growth, social progress, and cultural development in the region, and to promote regional peace and stability. Its members include Indonesia, the Philippines, Singapore, Thailand, Vietnam, Laos, Cambodia, and others.

FIGURE 17.12 **Some Regional Trade Groups**

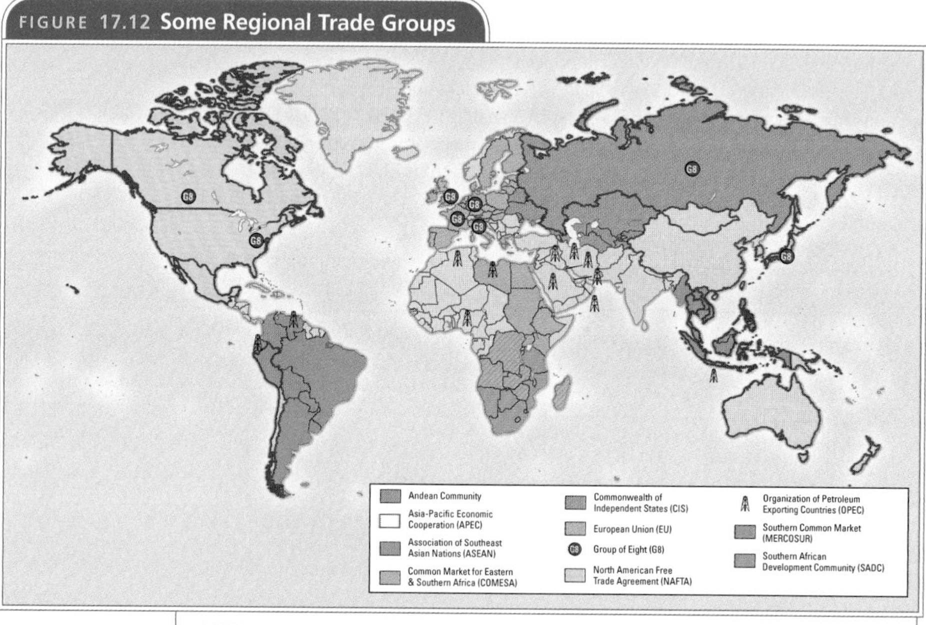

ANALYZE MAPS

How many trading groups do the United States and Canada belong to? Why does it make sense for such developed nations to be part of multiple trading groups?

DIFFERENTIATING INSTRUCTION

Struggling Readers

Generalize from an Example

Direct students to "A Multinational Telecom Company" on page 536. Have students identify the words that set this passage up as an example. *(Consider the case . . .)* Then, have students discuss what they can infer about multinationals generally from the one example given. *(may own an enterprise in a foreign country for getting raw materials; may have a manufacturing center in another country; may market the product in a foreign region; may outsource customer service to another country)*

English Learners

Recognize Parallel Structure

Direct students' attention to the first sentence of the second paragraph under Group 4 (page 535). Point out the use of *–ing* (participial) endings:

- negotiating and administering
- resolving
- monitoring
- providing

Explain that when a construction is used repeatedly, students can expect the information in one item to parallel that in another. This may boost comprehension.

534 Chapter 17

APEC The Asia-Pacific Economic Cooperation group is a trade organization of nations on the Pacific Rim—those that are adjacent to or within the Pacific Ocean. It includes developed nations such as Australia, Japan, and the United States, transitional economies such as Russia and China, as well as less developed countries such as Thailand, Papua New Guinea, and Chile. The group has set ambitious goals for trade liberalization throughout the region by 2020. However, since all APEC decisions require a unanimous vote, progress toward its goals has been slow.

OPEC The Organization of Petroleum Exporting Countries is a **cartel**—a group of producers who regulate the production, pricing, and marketing of a particular product. In OPEC's case, that product is petroleum, or oil. It has had mixed results in controlling the oil market since its formation in 1960. However, surging demand, from nations such as China and the United States, and periods of regional political instability have strengthened OPEC's position in recent years.

QUICK REFERENCE

OPEC is the Organization of Petroleum Exporting Countries.

A **cartel** is a group of producers that regulates the production, pricing, and marketing of a product.

SADC Founded in 1979, the South African Development Community's original goal was to act as a counterbalance to the region's main economic power—South Africa. (After South Africa finally abandoned minority white rule—the apartheid system—it also became a member in 1994.) A regional free-trade zone was established in 2000.

Dedication to free trade is a key element in boosting the region's economies. However, corruption, political instability, various health issues (most importantly, AIDS), substandard education, and poor infrastructure consistently hamper development. (You'll learn about these and other development issues in Chapter 18.)

GROUP 4 World Trade Organization

In 1944, the Allied nations met to plan for recovery after World War II. Among other important outcomes, they produced the General Agreement on Tariffs and Trade (GATT), which laid out rules and policies for international trade. In 1995, the GATT principles were incorporated into a new organization, the **World Trade Organization**, or WTO. At the end of 2005, the WTO had 149 member nations.

QUICK REFERENCE

The **World Trade Organization**, or **WTO**, is a group of nations that adhere to the policies of the General Agreement on Tariffs and Trade.

The purposes of the WTO include negotiating and administering trade agreements, resolving trade disputes, monitoring the trading policies of member nations, and providing support for developing countries. The principles underlying these purposes are that trade rules should apply equally to domestic and imported products. To that end all member nations should extend one another Normal Trade Relation (NTR) status, formerly known as Most Favored Nation (MFN) status. This means that no nation should extend more favorable trade terms to one WTO member than it does to another. Members should also work toward lowering trade barriers of all kinds and support fair trade as well as free trade.

To varying degrees, the WTO has been successful. It has helped reduce tariffs on manufactured goods, lower trade barriers in agriculture, and promote intellectual property rights. It has also resolved disputes among members while maintaining each nation's sovereignty, and promoted stability among member nations.

APPLICATION Making Inferences and Drawing Conclusions

A. Why do you think the term *most favored nation* has been replaced by *normal trade relations*? Since the WTO has 149 members, each a separate nation that is to be traded with on equal terms, none should be more "favored" than any other.

International Economics

The Creation of OPEC

In the 1950's, the price of oil was controlled by the world's largest multinational oil companies, not by the countries that produced the oil. These countries were all developing nations whose economic well-being depended on revenues generated by the sale of their petroleum resources.

Iraq, Iran, Kuwait, Saudi Arabia, and Venezuela joined together to form OPEC in 1960. Their purpose was to gain greater control over oil prices by coordinating their production and export policies. Today, there are 11 members.

More About . . .

WTO Regulations

There is controversy in the United States over food imports and WTO regulations. The WTO's "concept of equivalency" says that even if an exporting country's health standards are different from the importing country's, government officials can determine them to be equivalent in the interest of free trade.

In the United States, officials at the Food Safety and Inspection Service or the Department of Agriculture can make this determination. Critics argue that this practice is not in keeping with U.S. law. Imports needed to be compliant with U.S. laws before the WTO issued its "equivalency" ruling.

INDIVIDUAL ACTIVITY

Creating New Trade Blocs

Time 30 Minutes

Task Redraw the trade blocs of the world for creative interactions.

Materials Needed blank world maps, colored pencils or markers

Activity

- Have students review what they know about developing vs. developed nations and about political tensions in the world today.
- Instruct students to create four or five new trade groups, promoting unusual alliances that may have beneficial results.
- Direct students to give each group a name and draw the members on the map in the same colors.
- Ask them to write a paragraph explaining the new trading blocs and their potential benefit.

Rubric

	Understanding of Trade Blocs	Presentation of Information
4	excellent	creative and neat
3	good	mostly clear and neat
2	fair	at times clear and neat
1	poor	unclear, messy

Multinationals Bring Changes to International Trade

Discuss

- What benefits do multinationals have? *(Possible answers: efficiency; creation of jobs in foreign nations that may spur economic development)*
- According to the United Nations, multinationals produce more than half the world's trade. What impact, if any, may this have on the economy of developing nations or on small businesses? *(Possible answers: on developing nations—introduction of new ways of doing things and new cultural patterns; on small businesses—more difficult to compete effectively)*

More About . . .

Multinationals
Most of the largest multinational corporations are American or Japanese. They account for more than half of the top 500 multinationals. France, Germany, and the United Kingdom are next on the list of countries with the largest number of multinational corporations. Only one developing country, China, has any of the largest multinationals.

These 500 multinationals had revenues of $11.4 trillion and total assets of $33.3 trillion in 1996. They also employed about 36 million persons worldwide. Intrafirm trade plays a large role in the operations of multinational corporations. For U.S. multinationals, this trade consists predominantly of shipments from American parent companies to their overseas affiliates.

Multinationals Bring Changes to International Trade

KEY CONCEPTS

Multinational corporations (see Chapter 8) cross many borders and must deal with tariffs, labor restrictions, and taxes in different nations. They often bring jobs and technology to developing nations, while boosting overall levels of international trade—something that benefits everyone involved.

International Trade Within Multinationals

As multinationals have become more prevalent, trade between the various divisions of multinationals has become an area of increasing interest. Intrafirm trade, as it is known, can simply be the exchange of goods between two parts of a multinational. But international intrafirm trade also covers the coordination of production between parts of a multinational. This means, for instance, that when a U.S. parent company sends parts to an overseas affiliate to assemble, that is counted in the export column for U.S. statistics on trade. Likewise, when the assembled goods are shipped back to the U.S. parent from its overseas affiliate, that is counted in the import column. In general, intrafirm imports account for about 40 percent of total U.S. imports. Intrafirm exports account for about one-third of total U.S. exports.

EXAMPLE A Multinational Telecom Corporation

Consider the case of Worldwide Cellular, a U.S.-based multinational that makes, markets, and services cellular phones. It imports an essential raw material from its mining arm in Australia, manufactures the phones at its facility in South Korea, markets the phones in Europe, and then directs customers who have questions or complaints to technical support and customer service representatives in India. Throughout the process, the people and the economies of each nation benefit.

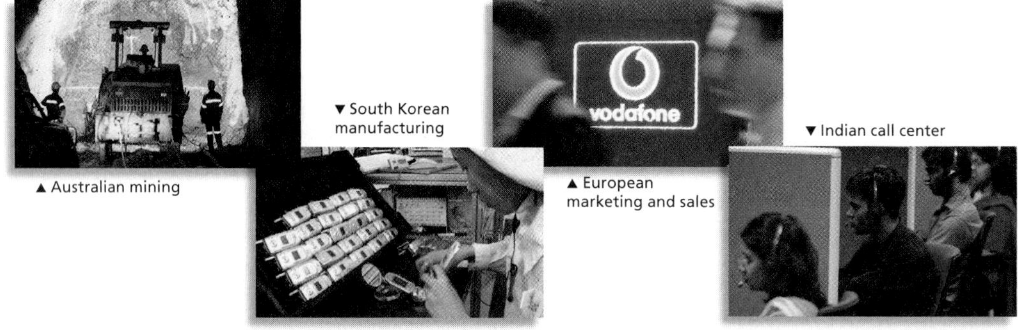

▲ Australian mining
▼ South Korean manufacturing
▲ European marketing and sales
▼ Indian call center

APPLICATION to come

B. In 1969, there were about 7,200 known multinationals. By 2000, that number had grown to more than 63,000. Give three possible contributing reasons for that growth.
Sample answers: relaxed trade restrictions; globalization trend; efficiency of specialization.

DIFFERENTIATING INSTRUCTION

Inclusion

Describe the Illustrations
Pair a student with a visual impairment with a student volunteer who does not have one. Ask the volunteer to read the Example text on page 536 to the partner. Direct the reader to pause in the reading where appropriate to describe the photograph that illustrates each multinational affiliate and to try to answer any questions that the partner may ask. Clarify, if needed.

Gifted and Talented

Write a Press Release
Invite interested students to explore the Internet to find out more about the 500 largest multinational corporations. Suggest that they select one of these multinationals for further research. Once they have found general information on their selection, encourage them to write a press release, highlighting the corporation's activities. Allow them to read what they have written to the class.

SECTION 4 Assessment

Online Quiz
ClassZone.com

REVIEWING KEY CONCEPTS

1. Explain the relationship between the terms in each of these pairs:
   a. *free-trade zone* *customs union*
   b. *EU* *NAFTA*
   c. *OPEC* *cartel*
2. What circumstances led to a liberalization in global trading?
3. How do customs unions help member nations?
4. How is the EU different from other regional trading groups?
5. What are some advantages of NAFTA?
6. **Using Your Notes** Write a brief summary of the major regional and international trade organizations. Refer to your completed summary chart and use the section's key words. Use the Graphic Organizer at **Interactive Review @ ClassZone.com**

Regional	International

CRITICAL THINKING

7. **Making Inferences and Drawing Conclusions** Some regional trade associations are viewed as an attempt by less developed countries to protect themselves and their regions from globalization's aggressive momentum. Explain how regional groups might have that effect.
8. **Analyzing Cause and Effect** Many multinationals grew out of exporting businesses. How might the exporting business prepare a company to become a multinational?
9. **Predicting Economic Trends** Before NAFTA was passed, some experts predicted a reduction in illegal immigration from Mexico to the United States. In fact, in the first few years after NAFTA went into effect, illegal immigration increased. What reasoning might have explained the prediction that illegal immigration would decline? What reasons might explain the increase?
10. **Challenge** At the Hong Kong gathering of the World Trade Organization in 2005, Supachai Panitchpakdi, secretary general of the United Nations Conference on Trade and Development (UNCTAD) said: "Rich countries will have to reject not just protectionism, but populism, too. They will have to speak honestly to their people about the changing economies of the 21st century, and about global interdependence and the fact that prosperity elsewhere means prosperity and jobs at home." Write a brief essay that "speaks honestly" to the rich countries about the changing economies of the 21st century.

ECONOMICS IN PRACTICE

The Effects of NAFTA
Between 1993 and 2002, the total trade among Canada, the United States, and Mexico more than doubled. The table below shows export figures for NAFTA members Canada and Mexico in each of those years.

	Exports (in billions of dollars)	
Nation	1993	2002
Canada		
to United States	113.6	213.9
to Mexico	.9	1.6
Mexico		
to United States	31.8	136.1
to Canada	2.9	8.8

Analyzing and Interpreting Data Canada has a higher export amount than Mexico, but did its level of trade increase more than Mexico's in the interval? Explain.

Challenge Can Canadian companies produce, package, and market products for both of its NAFTA partners in the same way? Explain why or why not.

4 Assess & Reteach

Assess Assign questions 1–5 to one group in the class and questions 7 and 8 and the Economics in Practice activity to a second group. Have students share their answers in a class review of these questions. You may wish to have basic students complete question 6 as a written composition; on-level students complete question 8 as a written composition; and advanced students write a response to question 9.

Unit 7 Resource Book
- Section Quiz, p. 39

Interactive Review @ ClassZone.com
- Section Quiz

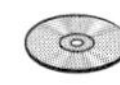

Test Generator CD-ROM
- Section Quiz

Reteach Divide the class into four groups. One will research and report on matters of debate in the EU; a second will do the same for NAFTA; a third, the other regional trade groups named on pages 534–535; and the fourth, the WTO.

Unit 7 Resource Book
- Reteaching Activity, p. 40

SECTION 4 ASSESSMENT ANSWERS

Reviewing Key Concepts

1. **a.** *free trade zone*, p. 532; *customs union*, p. 532
   b. *European Union*, p. 532; *NAFTA*, p. 533
   c. *OPEC*, p. 535; *cartel*, p. 535
2. economic recession following protectionist policies of the 1930s
3. They reduce or eliminate trade barriers.
4. The EU is a political as well as a commercial entity. It has a foreign policy and the majority of its members use a common currency, the euro.
5. specialization and increased efficiency; a competitive advantage over EU and Japan; expanded markets; new jobs; economic growth
6. See page 532 for an example of a completed diagram. Answers will vary but should show knowledge of the trading groups discussed in Section 4.

Critical Thinking

7. They can impose tariffs on non-member imports, for example, or set trade standards high enough to limit trade.
8. Sample answer: company might gain experience and key contacts in a foreign market.
9. Sample answers—prediction that illegal immigration would decline: more jobs in Mexico; reasons for increase: even more jobs, with better pay, in the United States
10. Answers will vary but look for an understanding of international and domestic issues associated with free trade.

Economics in Practice

Analyzing and Interpreting Data It did not. Canada's level of trade did not quite double, while Mexico's more than quadrupled.

Challenge Packaging and marketing may have to be changed because of the language difference between its two NAFTA partners, Mexico and the United States.

❶ Plan & Prepare

Objectives

- Analyze sources to synthesize economic information.
- Analyze the marginal costs and benefits of tariffs.

❷ Focus & Motivate

Ask students to tell you what they typically eat during the day. As the answers come from the class, jot them down on the board. After items from breakfasts, lunches, dinners, and snacks have been added, direct students to look over the list and determine which of those have sugar in them. (Students may be interested to know that U.S. cereal makers are the nation's largest users of sugar. Their products account for about 20 percent of U.S. sugar consumption.) Point out that every time they buy one of these items, students are paying about three times more for sugar than do people in other parts of the world.

❸ Teach

Using the Sources

Discuss

A. Does this article have a bias? That is, does it do more than report facts? How can you tell? Does it interpret the facts and draw conclusions? If so, what are those conclusions? *(Possible answers: has a bias; it shows through word choice, such as "prop up" the price; draws the conclusion that the sugar supports have a negative impact on the national interest)*

B. What does the chart indicate about raw sugar prices? *(that U.S. raw sugar prices are significantly higher than world prices)*

C. How does the American Sugar Alliance make its case that the sugar industry is an important part of the U.S. economy? *(Possible answer: It gives statistics that show the industry's revenue generation and the number of workers who are employed in the industry.)*

Economics Update

Go to **ClassZone.com** to find an update to this Case Study, including another article, an editable student worksheet, and an editable lesson plan.

Case Study

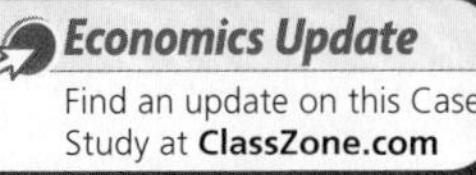

Find an update on this Case Study at **ClassZone.com**

Analyzing Tariffs—Who Wins and Who Loses?

Background Tariffs on foreign sugar have been around almost as long as the United States itself. Although early tariffs were a form of revenue, their purpose expanded in the 19th century to provide protection for the domestic sugar industry. That protection continues to this day.

Globalization, however, is having a direct impact on the way nations trade. Agricultural subsidies and tariffs have become a point of contention in recent WTO talks, with less-developed countries unhappy about the lack of market access for their goods and about their price disadvantage.

What's the issue? How do the trade barriers set up by the U.S. government affect producers (both foreign and domestic) and consumers?

A. Online Article

This article describes how the U.S. government supports sugar prices. Note that sugar subsidies are paid to the processor, rather than the farmer. The farmer receives a share once the sugar is processed.

Sugar Interests Harm the National Interest

USDA loan rates set floor on price of sugar.

The [government] program allows sugar processors to take out loans from the USDA [U.S. Department of Agriculture] by pledging sugar as collateral. The loan rates—18 cents per pound for cane sugar, 22.9 cents per pound for beet sugar—are significantly higher than average world sugar prices. These loans must be repaid within nine months, but processors also have the option of forfeiting their sugar to the government in lieu of repaying their debt.

This arrangement effectively guarantees that the processors receive a price for their sugar that is no lower than the loan value: If prices fell below that level, they would simply forfeit their sugar and keep the government's money.

In order to avoid that scenario, the USDA must prop up the domestic price of sugar. It does this by controlling supply through two mechanisms. First, it sets quotas on how much foreign sugar can be imported without facing prohibitive tariffs; second, it regulates the amount of sugar that domestic processors can sell.

Source: Jason Lee Steorts, *National Review*, July 18, 2005

CANE LOADING AREA AHEAD

Thinking Economically In your own words, describe the mechanisms by which the U.S. government props up domestic sugar prices.

DIFFERENTIATED INSTRUCTION

Inclusion

Monitor Learning

Tell students that as they approach the end of this book they should not only have learned a great deal about the subject of economics but also about the ways in which they can best learn. Ask them to write or in some other way present a reflection on the strategies that worked especially well for them and those that should be avoided or modified in the future because they did not work as well.

Gifted and Talented

Research the American Sugar Alliance

Direct students to research the trade organization that is promoting the interest of U.S. sugar producers to discover their arguments for maintaining the governmental sugar supports. Have student write a brief summary of the ASA's position and another brief statement indicating what they think about it and why.

B. Government Report

This information from the U.S. Department of Agriculture charts U.S. raw sugar prices versus raw sugar prices for the rest of the world.

FIGURE 17.13 U.S. AND WORLD RAW SUGAR PRICES

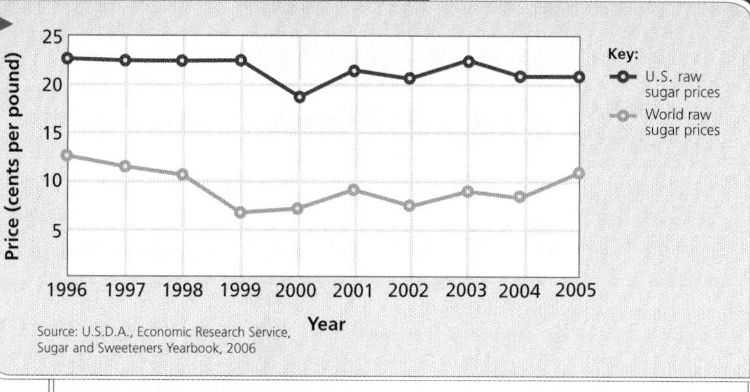

Source: U.S.D.A., Economic Research Service, Sugar and Sweeteners Yearbook, 2006

Thinking Economically On average, how much greater are U.S. raw sugar prices than those for the rest of the world?

C. Trade Association Web Page

The American Sugar Alliance's Web site makes the case that the U.S. sugar industry is an important part of the overall U.S. economy.

Sweetener's Impact on the U.S. Economy

The American sweetener industry has a significant impact on the nation's economy.

- Economic impact: $21.1 billion of economic activity in 42 states is generated in the U.S. each year by the sugar and corn sweetener industries.
- Beet sugar industry: Over 1,400,000 acres of sugarbeets are grown in 12 states and are processed in 25 sugarbeet factories. The industry creates 88,200 full time direct and indirect jobs for people across the nation.
- Cane sugar industry: Seven cane refineries and 22 mills process sugar cane raised in four states: Florida, Hawaii, Louisiana and Texas. The production and processing of sugarcane creates 71,900 full time direct and indirect jobs.
- Jobs: 372,000 jobs in the U.S. rely on a strong U.S. sweetener industry.

Source: www.sugaralliance.org

Thinking Economically Why does the American Sugar Alliance want to emphasize the economic impact of the sugar industry?

THINKING ECONOMICALLY Synthesizing

1. Which argument for protection does document C seem to make? Use the document and pages 523 and 524 to formulate your answer. Is this argument economically valid? Explain.
2. Is the difference in price shown in document B an unavoidable outcome of the program outlined in document A? Explain your answer.
3. How does U.S. government intervention in the sugar industry limit the functioning of the economy as a free market? Use examples from the documents in your answer.

More About . . .

The Flight of the Big Three

All three of the major U.S. candy makers—Mars, Inc.; Tootsie Roll Industries, Inc.; and Hershey Foods Corp.—have moved many of their plants to Mexico. The chief reason for the move to Mexico is the price of raw sugar. Mexico pays the going world rate for raw sugar. Mexico also has a significant youth population, and the large candy makers are looking to expand their markets.

Thinking Economically

Answers

A. *The government sets tariffs on sugar imports and controls the amount of sugar exports.*

B. *about 12 cents per pound*

C. *They want to convince the government to continue supporting the industry.*

Synthesizing

1. *argument one, "Protects Domestic Jobs?"; no, because what's really being protected is inefficient production, and the jobs will eventually be lost anyway*
2. *yes because the program is a price floor that keeps sugar prices in the United States artificially high*
3. *It has set a price floor, it gives subsidies to sugar growers, it sets quotas on sugar imports, and imposes tariffs. The results of these actions can be clearly seen in document B.*

TECHNOLOGY ACTIVITY

Creating a Power Presentation

Time 60 Minutes 

Task Create a Power Presentation to argue for or against the government's sugar supports.

Materials Needed computer with software for creating Power Presentations, previously researched information and illustrations, computer projection system for final presentation

Activity

- Divide students into three groups. Have each group discuss the issues and decide upon a position to present in their Power Presentation.
- Instruct students to research information and illustrations to support their position. If necessary, tell them that they may put them on a diskette to be brought to school.
- If you do not have access to three computers simultaneously, give each group one period to access the classroom computer and compile their presentation.
- Have each group give their presentation to the class.

Rubric

	Understanding of Sugar Tariff	Presentation of Information
4	excellent	very well-designed and persuasive
3	good	well-designed and structured
2	fair	carelessly designed
1	poor	sketchy

Online Summary Answers

1. absolute advantage
2. comparative advantage
3. economic interdependence
4. protectionism
5. trade barriers
6. quotas
7. tariffs
8. foreign exchange market
9. balance of trade
10. trade surplus
11. trade deficit
12. free-trade zones
13. NAFTA

Interactive Review

Review this chapter using interactive activities at **ClassZone.com**

- Online Summary
- Quizzes
- Vocabulary Flip Cards
- Graphic Organizers
- Review and Study Notes

Online Summary

Complete the following activity either on your own paper or online at **ClassZone.com**

Choose the key concept that best completes the sentence. Not all key concepts will be used.

absolute advantage	NAFTA
balance of trade	protectionism
comparative advantage	quota
economic interdependence	revenue tariffs
embargo	tariff
exports	trade barrier
foreign exchange market	trade deficit
foreign exchange rate	trade surplus
free trade zone	trade war
imports	WTO

When nations can produce something at a lower cost than other nations, they are said to have a(n) __1__. This is different from a(n) __2__, which means that goods or services are produced at a lower opportunity cost. Through trade, nations develop __3__, relying on one another.

Policies of __4__ have created __5__ between nations, including __6__—limits on imports—and __7__—fees charged on goods brought into a country.

International trade would not be possible without the __8__, where currencies of different countries are bought and sold. Nations keep track of their __9__, the difference between their exports and their imports. With a __10__, large reserves of foreign currency accumulate. With a __11__, domestic consumers enjoy lower prices.

The trend since the end of World War II has been toward free trade. Nations have formed regional __12__ that abolish trade barriers among members. In 1994 the United States became part of a trading organization with Mexico and Canada known as __13__.

CHAPTER 17 Assessment

REVIEWING KEY CONCEPTS

Benefits and Issues of International Trade (pp. 510–519)

1. How do nations gain by specializing in products for which they have a comparative advantage?
2. How does trade affect a national economy?

Trade Barriers (pp. 520–525)

3. Name and describe four trade barriers.
4. What three reasons are protectionists likely to offer to support their position?

Measuring the Value of Trade (pp. 526–531)

5. Explain how an importer purchases a foreign product and what effect those actions would have on the value of each currency.
6. What does the term *strong dollar* mean?

Modern International Institutions (pp. 532–539)

7. What agreements helped launch the free trade movement?
8. Create a fictional multinational and explain how it might operate from raw materials all the way through marketing the finished product.

APPLYING ECONOMIC CONCEPTS

Look at the graph below showing U.S. imports and exports to and from various trading regions.

9. To which group does the United States export the lowest dollar value of goods and services?
10. With which group does the United States have the largest trade deficit? the smallest trade deficit?

FIGURE 17.14 U.S. TRADE WITH REGIONAL GROUPS

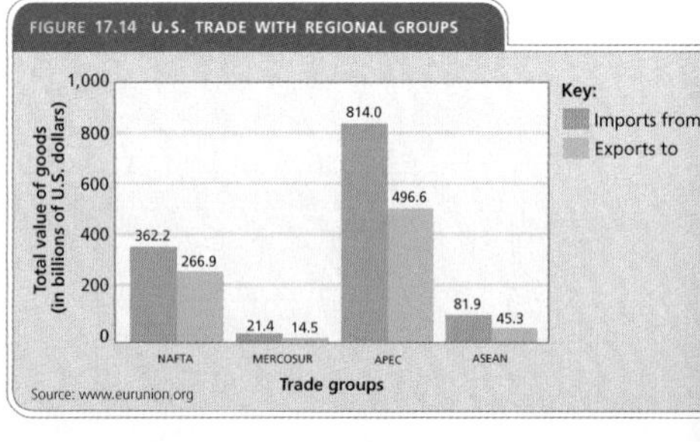

CHAPTER 17 ASSESSMENT ANSWERS

Reviewing Key Concepts

1. They can devote their resources to their most productive enterprises.
2. It affects prices and quantity of products and services (imports increase quantity and lower prices; exports increase production, possibly creating more jobs, and raise prices). It also affect domestic jobs—disrupting some, creating other new ones.
3. Possible answers: quotas—limits on imports; tariffs—fees charged for bringing something into the country; voluntary export restraints—arrangements to limit trade made through diplomacy to avoid retaliation; embargos—limits on trade for political reasons.
4. Jobs need to be protected; infant industries need to be protected; and national security cannot be compromised by being overly dependent on foreign supplier.
5. Importer would exchange domestic currency for currency of nation from which the purchase will be made. That would lower the value of the domestic currency and raise the value of the other one.
6. *Strong dollar* means that the US dollar can buy more goods in a foreign country than the currency of that foreign country can buy in the United States.
7. GATT, EU, NAFTA, WTO
8. Answers will vary but look for an understanding of how different divisions of multinationals function in different nations and how products move between these divisions and nations.

Applying Economic Concepts

9. Mercosur
10. APEC; Mercosur

CRITICAL THINKING

11. **Creating Graphs** Create a bar graph to illustrate the following trade data for selected regions. The EU25 is made up of the 15 countries that were members of the European Union in 2003 and the 10 that would become members in 2004.

FIGURE 17.15 IMPORTS AND EXPORTS FOR SELECTED REGIONS

Country or region	United States	EU25	Japan
Total imports (billions of U.S. dollars)	1,517	1,047	477
Total exports (billions of U.S. dollars)	1,021	1,250	597
World import share (percent)	22.9	14.0	6.8
World export share (percent)	13.8	13.1	8.5

Source: Eurostat, 2003 data

Use SMARTGrapher @ ClassZone.com to complete this activity.

12. **Analyzing and Interpreting Data** Which two of the three trading entities in the table above are likely to have good reserves of foreign currency?

13. **Synthesizing Economic Data** In which trading entity in the table above are imports the highest percent of total trade value? The lowest?

14. **Comparing and Contrasting Economic Information** What are developed nations hoping to gain through reduced global trade barriers? What are developing nations hoping to gain?

15. **Challenge** The World Trade Organization, unlike GATT, has an organizational structure to implement its principles. However, it has no authority to force a nation to do something against its own laws. How is it able, then, to resolve disputes among members?

SIMULATION

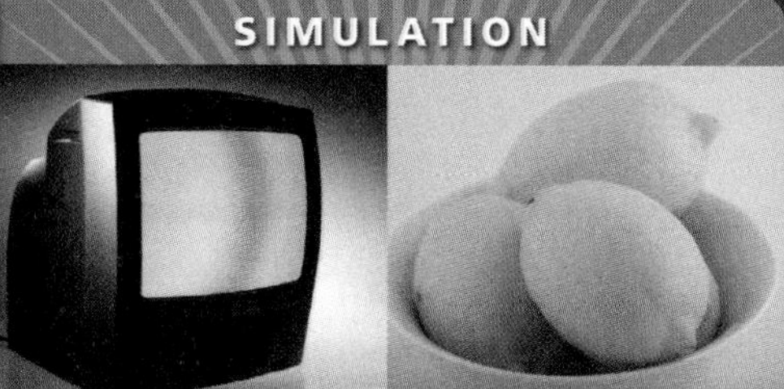

The Advantages of International Trade

The concept of comparative advantage explains why specialization and international trade are so important to economic success. Complete this exercise with a partner to help further your understanding.

Each of you will represent a trading nation. One of you will be El Estado, and the other will be Lichtenbourg. Both countries produce lemons and televisions. The following table shows monthly production by each nation.

	El Estado	Lichtenbourg
Lemons (in pounds)	20,000	9,000
Televisions	4,000	3,000

Step 1 Decide whether El Estado or Lichtenbourg has the absolute advantage for each product. Explain why this is so.

Step 2 Each student should calculate what his or her nation's production ratio is. Express your ratio in terms of opportunity cost. How many pounds of lemons does it cost to make one TV?

Step 3 With your ratios calculated, decide which nation has the comparative advantage in the production of TVs. On this basis, decide which nation should specialize in the production of each product.

Step 4 Now that you've decided to specialize and trade, calculate a trade ratio that makes trade between your two nations even more advantageous. Explain how the new ratio achieves this goal.

McDougal Littell **Assessment System**

Assess

Online Test Practice
- Go to **ClassZone.com** for more test practice.

Unit 1 Resource Book
- Chapter Test, Forms A, B, & C, pp. 51–62

Test Generator CD-ROM
- Section Quiz

Report

Use the McDougal Littell Assessment System to score assessments and receive customized reports.

Reteach

For activities customized for individual students, use the McDougal Littell Assessment System.

SMARTGrapher Students can create the graph of their choice for question 11 by using **SmartGrapher @ ClassZone.com.**

CHAPTER 17 ASSESSMENT ANSWERS

Critical Thinking

11. Answers will vary, but look for an accurate graphic representation of the figures.
12. Japan and the EU25
13. highest-United States; lowest-Japan
14. Answers will vary but may include the ideas that developed nations want markets for their goods, cheap labor and raw materials; developing nations want, generally, a road into development through industry and technology as well as markets for their goods.
15. Possible answer: since the WTO has so many members (149), pressure can be exerted through economic means to get countries to follow the organization's dispute-resolution process.

SIMULATION

Step 1 El Estado has the absolute advantage in both TV and lemon production.

Step 2 It costs El Estado 5 pounds of lemons to make 1 TV; it costs Lichtenbourg 3 pounds of lemons to make 1 TV.

Step 3 Lichtenbourg has the comparative advantage in TV production; it should produce TV and El Estado should produce lemons.

Step 4 The two nations could trade 4 pound of lemons for every TV. This is advantageous to both. It used to cost El Estado 5 pounds of lemons to make a TV, but now it trades only 4 pounds of lemons for a TV; for Lichtenbourg, it used to produce 3 pounds of lemons for 1 TV, now it trades 1 TV for 4 pounds of lemons.

Planning Guide

Resources 2Go Complete print resources all on one USB drive allow you to customize lessons.

Section Titles and Objectives	Unit 7 Resource Book and Workbooks		Assessment Resources
1 Definitions of Development pp. 544–551 • Determine how economic development is defined • Explain how certain indicators can illustrate the level of economic development of a nation	**Unit 7 Resource Book** • Reading Study Guide, pp. 63–64 • RSG with Additional Support, pp. 65–67 • RSG with Additional Support (Spanish), pp. 68–70 • Economic Skills and Problem Solving Activity, pp. 93–94	• Readings in Free Enterprise: The Costs of World Poverty, p. 95	**Unit 7 Resource Book** • Section Quiz, p. 71 • Reteaching Activity, p. 72 **Test Generator CD-ROM** **Daily Test Practice Transparencies,** TT61
2 A Framework for Economic Development Objectives pp. 552–561 • Evaluate the importance of developing human and physical capital • Examine the importance of stability and opportunity in economic development • Describe how developing nations raise money for development programs	**Unit 7 Resource Book** • Reading Study Guide, pp. 73–74 • RSG with Additional Support, pp. 75–77 • RSG with Additional Support (Spanish), pp. 78–80 • Math Skills Worksheet: Constructing and Analyzing Data from Bar Graphs, p. 101 • American Free Trade: Is Ricardo Still Right?, pp. 95–96	**NCEE Student Activities** • Investing Internationally, pp. 69–72	**Unit 7 Resource Book** • Section Quiz, p. 81 • Reteaching Activity, p. 82 **Test Generator CD-ROM** **Daily Test Practice Transparencies,** TT62
3 Transition to a Market Economy pp. 562–571 • Identify problems that emerge when an economy goes from command to market • Describe the transitions to a market economy in the former Soviet Union and nations it dominated • Discuss the transitions to a market economy in China	**Unit 7 Resource Book** • Reading Study Guide, pp. 83–84 • RSG with Additional Support, pp. 85–87 • RSG with Additional Support (Spanish), pp. 88–90 • Economic Simulations: Negotiate International Economic Ties, pp. 99–100 • Case Study Resources: China: Rich Country, Poor Country, pp. 97–98	**Test Practice and Review Workbook,** pp. 57–58	**Unit 7 Resource Book** • Section Quiz, p. 91 • Reteaching Activity, p. 92 • Chapter Test, (Forms A, B, & C), pp. 103–114 **Test Generator CD-ROM** **Daily Test Practice Transparencies,** TT63

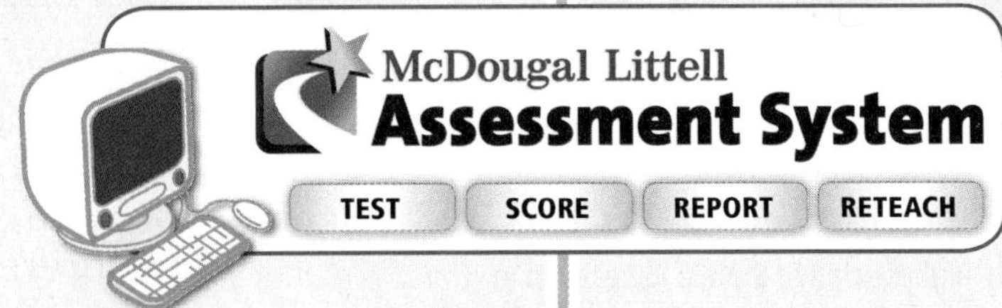

Integrated Technology

No Time? To focus students on the most important content in this chapter, use Economics Concepts Transparencies CT62, about economic development, which is available in Resources 2Go.

Teacher Presentation Options

Presentation Toolkit

Power Presentation DVD-ROM

- Lecture Notes
- Interactive Review
- Media Gallery
- Animated Economics
- Review Game

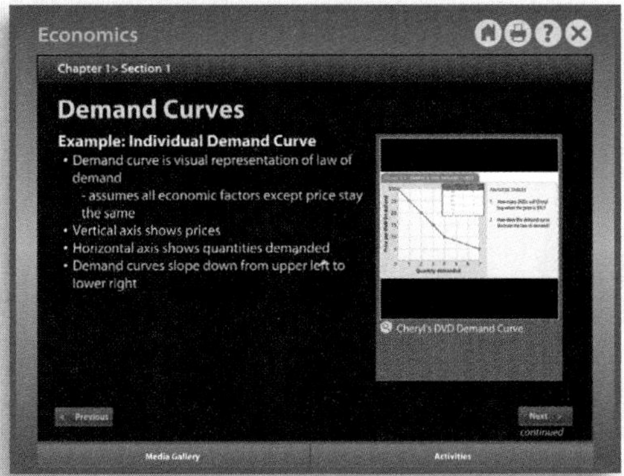

Economics Concepts Transparencies

- Developed v. Low-Income LDCs, CT61
- Elements that Contribute to Economic Development, CT62
- Post-Soviet States, CT63

Electronic Books

eEdition DVD-ROM

eEdition Online

Daily Test Practice Transparencies, TT61, TT62, TT63

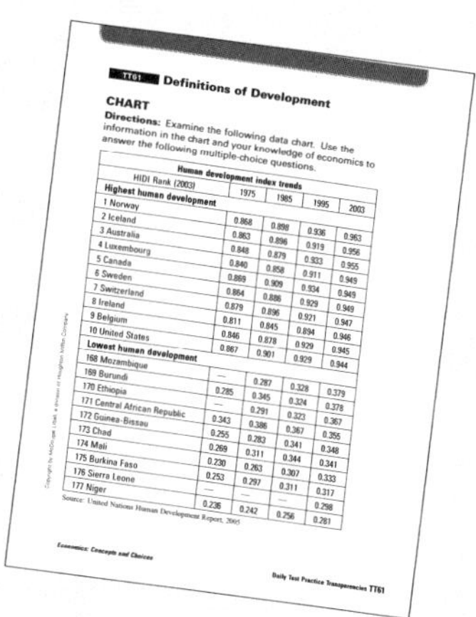

TT61 Definitions of Development

CHART

Directions: Examine the following data chart. Use the information in the chart and your knowledge of economics to answer the following multiple-choice questions.

SMARTGrapher

- Create a Graph, p. 573

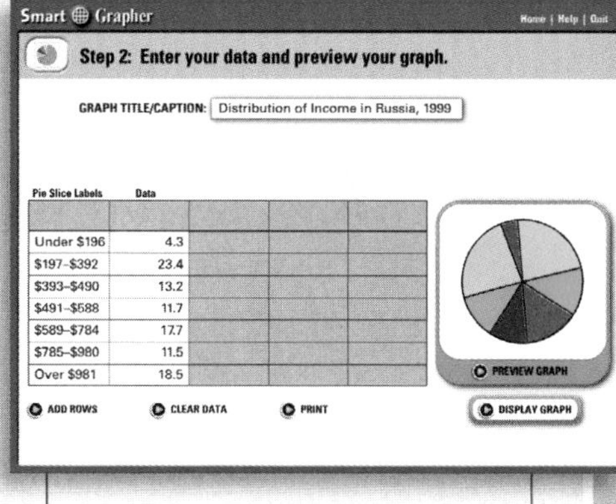

Online Activities at ClassZone.com

Economics Update

- Health Statistics in LDCs, p. 545
- Women in the Workplace in LDCs, p. 556
- Anne Krueger, p. 560
- China's Special Economic Zones, p. 567
- China's Campaign for Economic Power, p. 570

Activity Maker

- Vocabulary Flip Cards
- Review Game

Research Center

- Graphs and Data

Interactive Review

- Online Summary
- Quizzes
- Vocabulary Flip Cards
- Graphic Organizers
- Review and Study Notes

SMARTGrapher

- Create a Graph, p. 573

Teacher-Tested Activities

Name: Tim O'Driscoll (ret.)

School: Arrowhead High School

State: Wisconsin

Teacher-Tested Activities

At the beginning of this chapter, look for my classroom-proven idea for teaching economics concepts and thinking.

Chapter 18: Issues of Economic Development
Resources for Differentiated Instruction

Struggling Readers

Teacher's Edition Activities

- Modify Strategies, p. 548
- Activate Prior Knowledge, p. 556
- Generalize from Details, p. 560
- Recognize Organizational Cues, p. 564
- Recognize Signal Words, p. 568

Unit 7 Resource Book

- RSG with Additional Support, pp. 65–67, 75–77, 85–87 (A)
- Reteaching Activities, pp. 72, 82, 92 (B)
- Chapter Test (Form A), pp. 103–106 (C)

ClassZone.com

- Animated Economics
- Interactive Review

Test Generator CD-ROM

- Chapter Test (Form A)
- Chapter Test (Form A), in Spanish

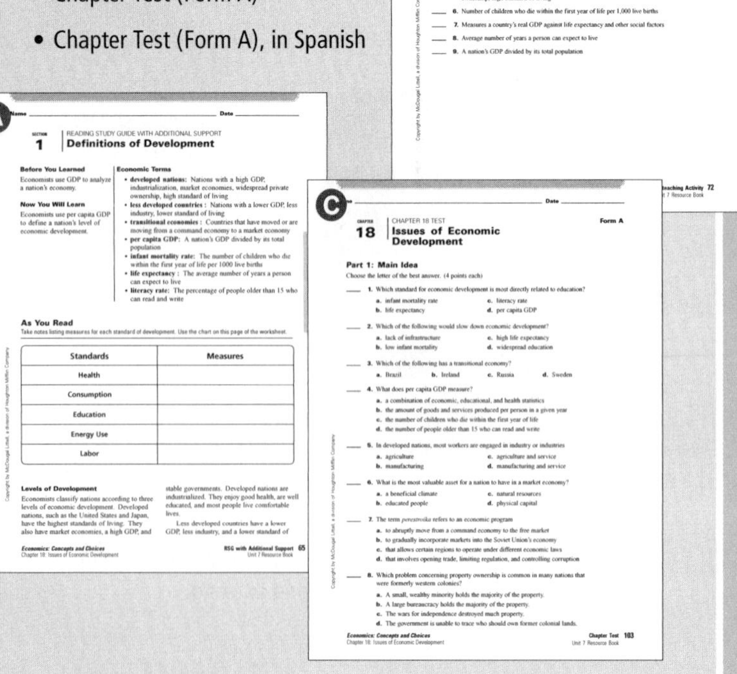

B
Name ______ Date ______
SECTION 1 | RETEACHING ACTIVITY
Definitions of Development

A. Explaining Economic Concepts
Find the term that best matches the description. Then write the letter of your answer on the line.

a. developed nations
b. less developed countries
c. infrastructure
d. transitional economies
e. GDP per capita
f. infant mortality rate
g. life expectancy
h. literacy rate
i. human development index

____ 1. Roads and other basic systems that support an economy
____ 2. Nations with a lower GDP, less industry, lower standard of living
____ 3. Countries that have moved or are moving from a command economy to a market economy
____ 4. Percentage of people older than 15 who can read and write
____ 5. Nations with a high GDP, industrialization, market economies, widespread private ownership, high standard of living
____ 6. Number of children who die within the first year of life per 1,000 live births
____ 7. Measures a country's real GDP against life expectancy and other social factors
____ 8. Average number of years a person can expect to live
____ 9. A nation's GDP divided by its total population

Reteaching Activity 72

A
Name ______ Date ______
SECTION 1 | READING STUDY GUIDE WITH ADDITIONAL SUPPORT
Definitions of Development

Before You Learned
Economists use GDP to analyze a nation's economy.

Now You Will Learn
Economists use per capita GDP to define a nation's level of economic development.

Economic Terms
- developed nations: Nations with a high GDP, industrialization, market economies, widespread private ownership, high standard of living
- less developed countries: Nations with a lower GDP, less industry, lower standard of living
- transitional economies: Countries that have moved or are moving from a command economy to a market economy
- per capita GDP: A nation's GDP divided by its total population
- infant mortality rate: The number of children who die within the first year of life per 1000 live births
- life expectancy: The average number of years a person can expect to live
- literacy rate: The percentage of people older than 15 who can read and write

As You Read
Take notes listing measures for each standard of development. Use the chart on this page of the worksheet.

Standards	Measures
Health	
Consumption	
Education	
Energy Use	
Labor	

Levels of Development
Economists classify nations according to three levels of economic development. Developed nations, such as the United States and Japan, have the highest standards of living. They also have market economies, a high GDP, and stable governments. Developed nations are industrialized. They enjoy good health, are well educated, and most people live comfortable lives.
Less developed countries have a lower GDP, less industry, and a lower standard of

Economics: Concepts and Choices
Chapter 18: Issues of Economic Development
RSG with Additional Support 65
Unit 7 Resource Book

C
Name ______ Date ______
CHAPTER 18 | CHAPTER 18 TEST
Issues of Economic Development
Form A

Part 1: Main Idea
Choose the letter of the best answer. (4 points each)

____ 1. Which standard for economic development is most directly related to education?
a. infant mortality rate c. literacy rate
b. life expectancy d. per capita GDP

____ 2. Which of the following would slow down economic development?
a. lack of infrastructure c. high life expectancy
b. low infant mortality d. widespread education

____ 3. Which of the following has a transitional economy?
a. Brazil b. Ireland c. Russia d. Sweden

____ 4. What does per capita GDP measure?
a. a combination of economic, educational, and health statistics
b. the amount of goods and services produced per person in a given year
c. the number of children who die within the first year of life
d. the number of people older than 15 who can read and write

____ 5. In developed nations, most workers are engaged in industry or industries
a. agriculture c. agriculture and service
b. manufacturing d. manufacturing and service

____ 6. What is the most valuable asset for a nation to have in a market economy?
a. a beneficial climate c. natural resources
b. educated people d. physical capital

____ 7. The term *perestroika* refers to an economic program
a. to abruptly move from a command economy to the free market
b. to gradually incorporate markets into the Soviet Union's economy
c. that allows certain regions to operate under different economic laws
d. that involves opening trade, limiting regulation, and controlling corruption

____ 8. Which problem concerning property ownership is common in many nations that were formerly western colonies?
a. A small, wealthy minority holds the majority of the property.
b. A large bureaucracy holds the majority of the property.
c. The wars for independence destroyed much property.
d. The government is unable to trace who should own former colonial lands.

Economics: Concepts and Choices
Chapter 18: Issues of Economic Development
Chapter Test 103
Unit 7 Resource Book

English Learners

Teacher's Edition Activities

- Understand Idioms, p. 548
- Develop Academic Language, p. 556
- Read and Discuss, p. 560
- Frame Questions, p. 564
- Rephrase in a New Framework, p. 568

Unit 7 Resource Book

- RSG with Additional Support (Spanish), pp. 68–70, 78–80, 88–90 (A)

Test Generator CD-ROM

- Chapter Test (Forms A, B, & C), in Spanish (B)

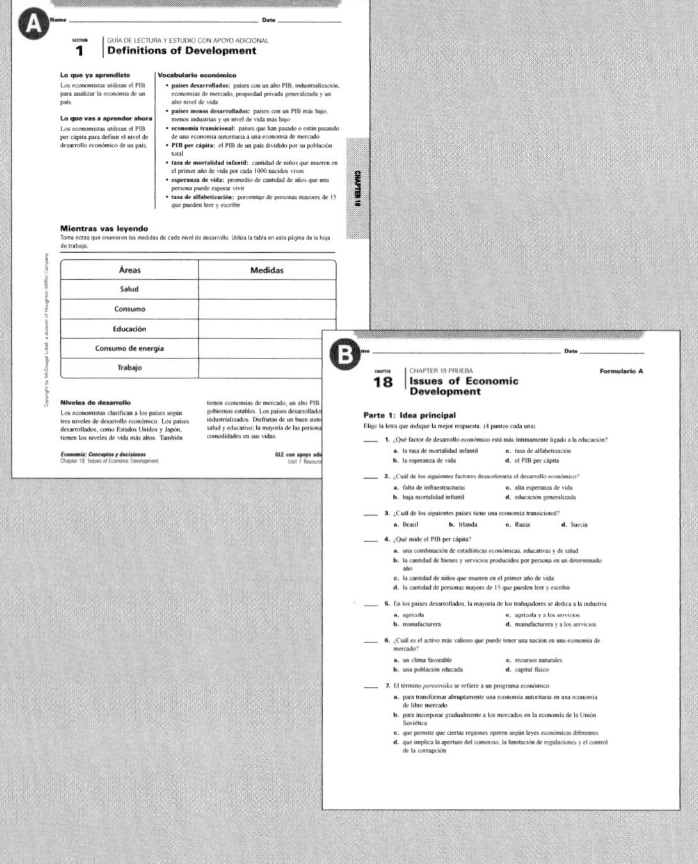

A
Name ______ Date ______
SECCIÓN 1 | GUÍA DE LECTURA Y ESTUDIO CON APOYO ADICIONAL
Definitions of Development

Lo que ya aprendiste
Los economistas utilizan el PIB para analizar la economía de un país.

Lo que vas a aprender ahora
Los economistas utilizan el PIB per cápita para definir el nivel de desarrollo económico de un país.

Vocabulario económico
- países desarrollados: países con un alto PIB, industrialización, economías de mercado, propiedad privada generalizada y un alto nivel de vida
- países menos desarrollados: países con un PIB más bajo, menos industrias y un nivel de vida más bajo
- economía transicional: países que han pasado o están pasando de una economía autoritaria a una economía de mercado
- PIB per cápita: el PIB de un país dividido por su población total
- tasa de mortalidad infantil: cantidad de niños que mueren en el primer año de vida por cada 1000 nacidos vivos
- esperanza de vida: promedio de cantidad de años que una persona puede esperar vivir
- tasa de alfabetización: porcentaje de personas mayores de 15 que pueden leer y escribir

Mientras vas leyendo
Toma notas que enumeren las medidas de cada nivel de desarrollo. Utiliza la tabla en esta página de la hoja de trabajo.

Áreas	Medidas
Salud	
Consumo	
Educación	
Consumo de energía	
Trabajo	

Niveles de desarrollo
Los economistas clasifican a los países según tres niveles de desarrollo económico. Los países desarrollados, como Estados Unidos y Japón, tienen los niveles de vida más altos. También tienen economías de mercado, un alto PIB, gobiernos estables. Los países desarrollados están industrializados. Disfrutan de un buen estado de salud y educativo; la mayoría de las personas tienen comodidades en sus vidas.

Economía: Conceptos y decisiones
Chapter 18: Issues of Economic Development

B
Name ______ Date ______
CAPÍTULO 18 | CHAPTER 18 PRUEBA
Issues of Economic Development
Formulario A

Parte 1: Idea principal
Elige la letra que indique la mejor respuesta. (4 puntos cada una)

____ 1. ¿Qué factor de desarrollo económico está más íntimamente ligado a la educación?
a. la tasa de mortalidad infantil c. tasa de alfabetización
b. la esperanza de vida d. el PIB per cápita

____ 2. ¿Cuál de los siguientes factores desacelerará el desarrollo económico?
a. falta de infraestructuras c. alta esperanza de vida
b. baja mortalidad infantil d. educación generalizada

____ 3. ¿Cuál de los siguientes países tiene una economía transicional?
a. Brasil b. Irlanda c. Rusia d. Suecia

____ 4. ¿Qué mide el PIB per cápita?
a. una combinación de estadísticas económicas, educativas y de salud
b. la cantidad de bienes y servicios producidos por persona en un determinado año
c. la cantidad de niños que mueren en el primer año de vida
d. la cantidad de personas mayores de 15 que pueden leer y escribir

____ 5. En los países desarrollados, la mayoría de los trabajadores se dedica a la industria
a. agrícola c. agrícola y a los servicios
b. manufacturera d. manufacturera y a los servicios

____ 6. ¿Cuál es el activo más valioso que puede tener una nación en una economía de mercado?
a. un clima favorable c. recursos naturales
b. una población educada d. capital físico

____ 7. El término *perestroika* se refiere a un programa económico
a. para transformar abruptamente una economía autoritaria en una economía de libre mercado
b. para incorporar gradualmente a los mercados en la economía de la Unión Soviética
c. que permite que ciertas regiones operen según leyes económicas diferentes
d. que implica la apertura del comercio, la limitación de regulaciones y el control de la corrupción

Inclusion

Teacher's Edition Activities

- Profile a Nation, p. 546
- Focus on Key Ideas, p. 550
- Find Key Information, p. 554
- Create Tactile Graphics, p. 558
- Make a Time Line, p. 566
- Make Drawings, p. 570

Lesson Plans

- Modified Lessons for Inclusion, pp. 61–63 (A)

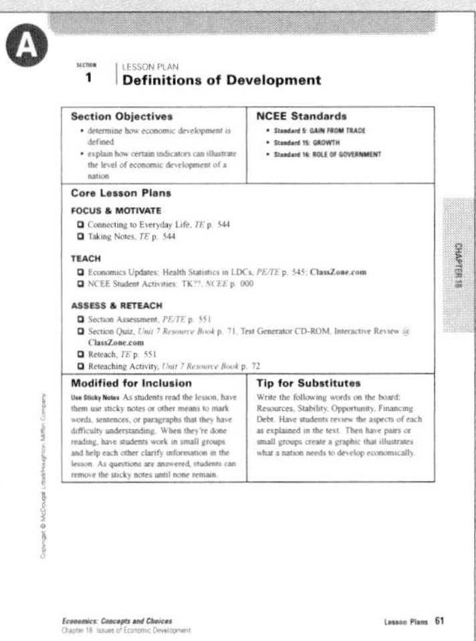

A

SECTION 1 | LESSON PLAN
Definitions of Development

Section Objectives	**NCEE Standards**
• determine how economic development is defined • explain how certain indicators can illustrate the level of economic development of a nation	• Standard 5: GAIN FROM TRADE • Standard 15: GROWTH • Standard 16: ROLE OF GOVERNMENT

Core Lesson Plans

FOCUS & MOTIVATE
- ❑ Connecting to Everyday Life, *TE* p. 544
- ❑ Taking Notes, *TE* p. 544

TEACH
- ❑ Economics Updates: Health Statistics in LDCs, *PE/TE* p. 545; **ClassZone.com**
- ❑ NCEE Student Activities: TK??, *NCEE* p. 000

ASSESS & RETEACH
- ❑ Section Assessment, *PE/TE* p. 551
- ❑ Section Quiz, *Unit 7 Resource Book* p. 71, Test Generator CD-ROM, Interactive Review @ **ClassZone.com**
- ❑ Reteach, *TE* p. 551
- ❑ Reteaching Activity, *Unit 7 Resource Book* p. 72

Modified for Inclusion	**Tip for Substitutes**
Use Sticky Notes As students read the lesson, have them use sticky notes or other means to mark words, sentences, or paragraphs that they have difficulty understanding. When they're done reading, have students work in small groups and help each other clarify information in the lesson. As questions are answered, students can remove the sticky notes until none remain.	Write the following words on the board: Resources, Stability, Opportunity, Financing Debt. Have students review the aspects of each as explained in the text. Then have pairs or small groups create a graphic that illustrates what a nation needs to develop economically.

CHAPTER 18

Copyright © McDougal Littell/Houghton Mifflin Company

Economics: Concepts and Choices
Chapter 18 Issues of Economic Development

Lesson Plans 61

Gifted and Talented

Teacher's Edition Activities

- Make a World Map of HDI, p. 546
- Evaluate and Persuade, p. 550
- Research Positive and Negative Liberty, p. 554
- Identify Pros and Cons, p. 558
- Research and Present, p. 566
- Prepare a Speech, p. 570

Unit 7 Resource Book

- Readings in Free Enterprise: The Costs of World Poverty, p. 95; American Free Trade: Is Ricardo Still Right?, p. 96 (A)
- Case Study Resources: China: Rich Country, Poor Country, pp. 97–98 (B)

NCEE Student Activities

- Investing Internationally, p. 69–72 (C)

ClassZone.com

- Research Center

Test Generator CD-ROM

- Chapter Test (Form C)
- Chapter Test (Form C), in Spanish

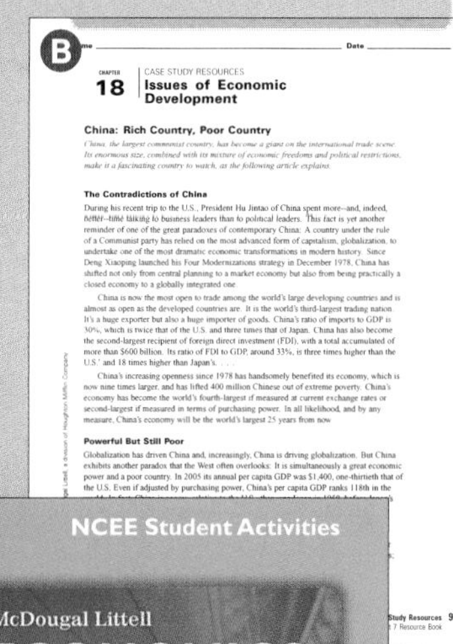

B

Name ______ Date ______

CHAPTER 18 | CASE STUDY RESOURCES
Issues of Economic Development

China: Rich Country, Poor Country

China, the largest communist country, has become a giant on the international trade scene. Its enormous size, combined with its mixture of economic freedoms and political restrictions, make it a fascinating country to watch, as the following article explains.

The Contradictions of China

During his recent trip to the U.S., President Hu Jintao of China spent more--and, indeed, better--time talking to business leaders than to political leaders. This fact is yet another reminder of one of the great paradoxes of contemporary China: A country under the rule of a Communist party has relied on the most advanced form of capitalism, globalization, to undertake one of the most dramatic economic transformations in modern history. Since Deng Xiaoping launched his Four Modernizations strategy in December 1978, China has shifted not only from central planning to a market economy but also from being practically a closed economy to a globally integrated one.

China is now the most open to trade among the world's large developing countries and is almost as open as the developed countries are. It is the world's third-largest trading nation. It's a huge exporter but also a huge importer of goods. China's ratio of imports to GDP is 30%, which is twice that of the U.S. and three times that of Japan. China has also become the second-largest recipient of foreign direct investment (FDI), with a total accumulated of more than $600 billion. Its ratio of FDI to GDP, around 33%, is three times higher than the U.S.' and 18 times higher than Japan's. . . .

China's increasing openness since 1978 has handsomely benefited its economy, which is now nine times larger, and has lifted 400 million Chinese out of extreme poverty. China's economy has become the world's fourth-largest if measured at current exchange rates or second-largest if measured in terms of purchasing power. In all likelihood, and by any measure, China's economy will be the world's largest 25 years from now.

Powerful But Still Poor

Globalization has driven China and, increasingly, China is driving globalization. But China exhibits another paradox that the West often overlooks: It is simultaneously a great economic power and a poor country. In 2005 its annual per capita GDP was $1,400, one-thirtieth that of the U.S. Even if adjusted by purchasing power, China's per capita GDP ranks 118th in the

Study Resources 97
7 Resource Book

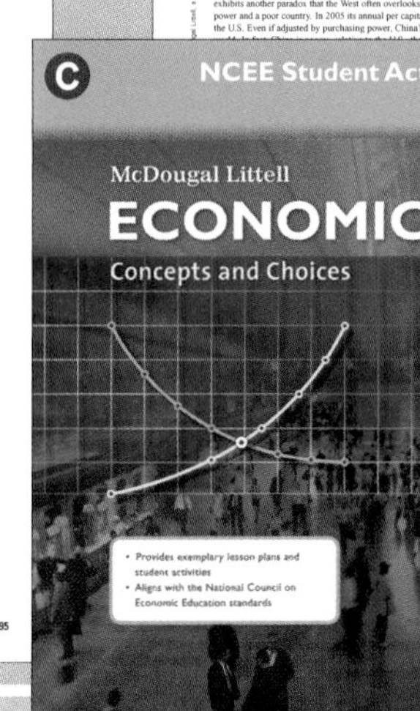

Focus & Motivate

Objective

Explain the issues and institutions related to economic development and how they have been applied in several cases.

Why the Concept Matters

Explain that the economic stability and prosperity of a nation has an impact on the nations around it and, increasingly, on the global economy.

Analyzing the Photograph

Direct students to study the photograph and read the caption. Call on volunteers to describe what is being depicted by the photograph. *(Possible answer: The photograph shows two Arab men looking out over a major city, probably somewhere in an oil producing nation in Southwest Asia.)*

Ask students what the photograph indicates about the nation's stability, resources, and level of economic development. *(Possible answers: The city is well-developed and appears to have been built in the not too distant past. This indicates a level of political stability and significant economic wealth.)*

Point out to students that these factors are important to economic development.

Economic Development
Issues of economic development are as much about the basic building blocks of societies as they are about money. When governments are stable and help to provide their people with resources and opportunities, economic development can become a reality.

542

CONTENT STANDARDS

NCEE STANDARDS

Standard 15: Growth

Students will understand that

Investment in factories, machinery, new technology, and in the health, education, and training of people can raise future standards of living.

Students will be able to use this knowledge to

Predict the consequences of investment decisions made by individuals, businesses, and governments.

Benchmarks

Students will know that

Economic growth is a sustained rise in a nation's production of goods and services. It results from investments in human and physical capital, research and development, and technological change, and from improved institutional arrangements and incentives. *(page 544–547)*

The rate of productivity increase in an economy is strongly affected by the incentives that reward successful innovation and investments (in research and development, and in physical and human capital). *(pages 552–553)*

18 Issues of Economic Development

CONCEPT REVIEW

Free enterprise system is another name for capitalism, an economic system based on private ownership of productive resources.

CHAPTER 18 KEY CONCEPT

A **transitional economy** is a country that has moved (or is moving) from a command economy, such as communism, to a market economy.

WHY THE CONCEPT MATTERS

The development of the world's less developed countries has grown increasingly important as globalization has taken hold. Promoting development also promotes good government and economic opportunity in less developed countries. When a nation's government is democratic and stable and its citizens are prosperous, the benefits reach beyond that emerging economy to the world community, which gains a new economic and political partner.

Online Highlights

More at ClassZone.com

Economics Update

Go to ECONOMICS UPDATE for chapter updates and current news on trade and China's transition to a market economy. (See Case Study, pp. 570–571.) ▶

SMARTGrapher

Go to SMART GRAPHER to complete graphing activities in this chapter.

Interactive Review

Go to INTERACTIVE REVIEW for concept review and activities.

How has international trade helped China make the transition to a market economy? See the Case Study on pages 570–571.

From the Classroom

Tim O'Driscoll, Arrowhead H.S. (retired)

Benefits of Private Ownership

Market economies depend on the protection of property rights—the rights to use property you own as you wish, to sell or transfer your property, to keep others from using your property, and to use the legal system to enforce property rights.

Put students into small groups and ask them to list items that they own and, therefore, take care of. Lead a discussion about how ownership creates incentives to take care of things.

Previewing Chapter Technology at ClassZone.com

Economics Update Students will find updates to information in the pupil edition on pages 545, 556, 560, 567, and 570.

Interactive Review Students will find additional section and chapter assessment support for materials on pages 551, 561, 569, and 572.

TEACHER MEDIA FAVORITES

Books

- Moran, Theodore H. *Beyond Sweatshops: Foreign Direct Investment and Globalization in Developing Nations.* Washington, DC: Brookings Institution Press, 2002. A top scholar looks at the effect of foreign investment on the lives of workers and average citizens in the developing world.
- Chow, Gregory C. *China's Economic Transformation.* Malden, MA: Blackwell Publishing, Inc., 2002. A discussion of China's economic output, predicting it will equal that of the United States.
- Klein, Lawrence R., and Marshall Pomer (eds.). *The New Russia: Transition Gone Awry.* Stanford, CA: Stanford UP, 2001. Essays on balancing free-market forces and government involvement in the Russian economy.

Videos/DVDs

- *Economic Development: A Global Challenge.* 36 minutes. Films for the Humanities and Sciences, 2007. This video explores geographic, historical, and political reasons for underdevelopment, viewing the topics with a global perspective.

Software

- The Economics Web Institute includes a number of interactive tools for exploring world trade issues.

Internet

Visit **ClassZone.com** to link to

- a variety of chapter-specific, content-reviewed sites
- updates on data and topics presented throughout the chapter sections and Case Study
- updates to the Power Presentation

1 Plan & Prepare

Section 1 Objectives

- determine how economic development is defined
- explain how certain indicators can illustrate the level of economic development of a nation

2 Focus & Motivate

Connecting to Everyday Life Ask students to think about how long they might expect to live. Ask how they determined their answers. Also, ask them to imagine the possibility of having children in the future. Will they be healthy? Will they be educated? Then ask students to discuss what relationship there is between the answers to these questions and a nation's level of economic development. Point out that in this section, students will learn how such factors as life expectancy and levels of education help define a nation's level of development.

Taking Notes Remind students to take notes as they read by completing a summary table. They can use the Graphic Organizer at **Interactive Review @ ClassZone.com**. A sample is shown below.

Definitions of Development	
Levels of Development	Standards of Economic Development
developed nations	per capita GDP
transitional economies	health education
less developed countries	consumption of goods and services
	energy use
	labor force

SECTION 1

Definitions of Development

OBJECTIVES

In Section 1 you will
- determine how economic development is defined
- explain how certain indicators can illustrate the level of economic development of a nation

KEY TERMS

developed nations, *p. 544*
transitional economies, *p. 545*
less developed countries (LDC), *p. 545*
infrastructure, *p. 545*
per capita GDP, *p. 546*
infant mortality rate, *p. 547*
life expectancy, *p. 547*
literacy rate, *p. 547*
human development index (HDI), *p. 547*

TAKING NOTES

As you read Section 1, complete a summary table like the one shown. Use the Graphic Organizer at **Interactive Review @ ClassZone.com**

Definitions of Development	
Levels of Development	Standards of Economic Development

Levels of Development

KEY CONCEPTS

Do you have at least $1 in your pocket at the moment? If so, you have more money than over a billion of the world's people have for food, shelter, and clothing for today. Economists gather this type of data to compare the economies of nations and the impact of those economies on people's standard of living. They use the data to measure the nations' level of economic development.

QUICK REFERENCE

Developed nations have a market economy, a relatively high standard of living, a high GDP, industrialization, widespread private ownership of property, and stable and effective governments.

Developed Nations

Economists have defined three major levels of economic development. The nations with the highest standards of living are known as **developed nations**. In addition to a relatively high standard of living, these nations have a market economy, a high GDP, industrialization, widespread private ownership of property, and stable and effective governments. The nations of Western Europe, the United States, Canada, Australia, New Zealand, Japan, and South Korea are all developed nations.

You can identify some of the features of a developed nation by looking around you. Most people live fairly comfortable lives and enjoy such consumer goods as television sets, washing machines, and cars. You will also see that most people live in urban areas, where they have jobs in service and industrial enterprises: banks, insurance companies, auto parts manufacturing, and so on. Even though few people work in agriculture, the nation produces a surplus of agricultural products using advanced science and technology and highly efficient farming methods. You will also see that, on the whole, people are generally healthy and well-educated. They have political and economic freedom, and they exercise those freedoms in pursuit of well-being. You will see exceptions to all of these features—poverty, unemployment, poor living conditions—but they are not the prevailing features of the society.

SECTION 1 PROGRAM RESOURCES

ON LEVEL

Lesson Plans
- Core, p. 61

Unit 7 Resource Book
- Reading Study Guide, pp. 63–64
- Economic Skills and Problem Solving Activity, pp. 93–94
- Section Quiz, p. 71

STRUGGLING READERS

Unit 7 Resource Book
- Reading Study Guide with Additional Support, pp. 65–67
- Reteaching Activity, p. 72

ENGLISH LEARNERS

Unit 7 Resource Book
- Reading Study Guide with Additional Support (Spanish), pp. 68–70

INCLUSION

Lesson Plans
- Modified for Inclusion, p. 61

GIFTED AND TALENTED

Unit 7 Resource Book
- Readings in Free Enterprise: The Costs of World Poverty, p. 95

TECHNOLOGY

eEdition DVD-ROM

eEdition Online

Power Presentation DVD-ROM

Economics Concepts Transparencies
- CT61 Developed Versus Low-Income, Less Developed Countries

Daily Test Practice Transparencies, TT61

ClassZone.com

Transitional Economies

Economists have also defined the development that occurs in **transitional economies**. These are countries that have moved (or are moving) from a command economy to a market economy. China, Russia, and a number of Eastern European countries are considered to be transitional economies.

Poland, in Eastern Europe, is in transition and categorized as a less developed country. Like other transitional economies, however, it is on a clear path toward improving standards of living. As democracy and economic freedom begin to take hold, Poland's economy and its citizens' quality of life have steadily improved.

QUICK REFERENCE

A **transitional economy** is a country that has moved (or is moving) from a command economy to a market economy.

In Transition A developed economy, such as the United States (left), generally has greater access to technology than a transitional economy, such as China (right).

Less Developed Countries

Less developed countries (LDCs), such as many African, South American, and Eastern European countries, have a lower GDP, less well developed industry, and a lower standard of living. Often, these nations have ineffective or even outright corrupt governments that fail to protect private property rights. LDCs are sometimes called emerging economies, but some have emerged, so to speak, more than others. As a result, they can be divided into middle-income nations, such as Brazil and Thailand, and low-income nations, such as Mozambique and Cambodia.

The picture in the low-income nations is starkly different from what you see when you look around the United States. A high percentage of people live in substandard housing. Few families own televisions or washing machines. Even if they owned cars, there are few good roads to drive them on, since developing nations often lack infrastructure. **Infrastructure** is the basic set of support systems needed to keep an economy going. It includes such things as power, communications, transportation, water, sanitation, and education systems.

In these economies, a relatively high percentage of the people work at subsistence farming and have little savings. Often, even children toil with the rest of the family. Some go to school for only three or four years; some children receive no schooling. Health conditions are substandard, as medical care is hard to come by in rural areas. In many developing nations, political freedom is still a dream.

QUICK REFERENCE

A **less developed country** (LDC) has a lower GDP, less well developed industry, and a lower standard of living.

Infrastructure is the basic support systems needed to keep an economy going, including power, communications, transportation, water, sanitation, and education systems.

 **Economics Update**

Find an update on health statistics in LDCs at **ClassZone.com**

APPLICATION Economies

A. What role does technology play in economic development?
It is a vital ingredient in industrialization, which is a vital ingredient of economic development.

3 Teach

Levels of Development

Discuss

- What are two major differences between a developed economy and a transitional economy? *(Possible answers: Transitional economies are moving from a command system to a market system and have improving standards of living; developed nations have a stable system and high standards of living.)*
- What are some of the key concerns in a developing economy? *(Possible answers: high percentage of people in poverty, with inadequate health care and education; lack of infrastructure to support industry; political instability)*

Economics Update

At **ClassZone.com** students will see updated information on health statistics in LDCs.

LEVELED ACTIVITY

Understanding Levels of Development

Time 30–45 Minutes 

Objective Students will demonstrate an understanding of the various levels of development and their effect on people's lives.

Basic

Make a 3-column chart such as the following, with explanatory comments in each section.

Feature	Developed	Transitional	LDC
Health			
Education			
Consumption			
Energy use			

On Level

Tell students to imagine what their lives would be like if they lived in a transitional economy or a less developed country. Have them write about how a typical day might be different in those settings. Their days should incorporate many of the main points that differentiate these countries from their own.

Challenge

Write an essay explaining the various levels of development and answering these questions: In what ways are the features of each level of economic development both causes and effects? What does your answer suggest about how to maintain or improve the level of economic development?

Standards of Economic Development

Discuss

- What other ways might there be to measure a nation's level of economic development? *(Possible answers: poverty rate; distribution of income; technology sector; level of environmental protection)*
- The quote on page 547 from the World Education Forum includes the term *sustainable development.* What might this mean? *(development at a pace that does not deplete resources or cause harm; a rate of development that can be maintained over time, rather than temporarily)*

Analyzing Maps: Figure 18.1

Point out that this map shows per capita gross domestic product for each country in the world. Ask students to look closely at the map. What can be said about which areas of the world have the highest per capita GDP? *(They are the developed nations, including the United States and Canada in North America, most of countries of Western Europe, Australia, New Zealand, and Japan in Asia.)*

Answers

1. *Africa*
2. *Africa and South America*

Standards of Economic Development

KEY CONCEPTS

How is it possible to compare economies when each country may have its own ideas of what is valuable? For example, the number of television sets per thousand households yields valid information about the economic conditions in most nations. However, not every culture values television ownership to the same extent. Such statistics need to be used in conjunction with others, so that a more nuanced image of a nation's overall level of development can be obtained. Economists use the following standards of development to bring this detailed image into focus.

QUICK REFERENCE

Per capita gross domestic product is a nation's GDP divided by its total population.

Per Capita Gross Domestic Product

The most popular measure of economic development is **per capita gross domestic product**, a nation's overall GDP divided by its total population. This statistic is informative because it estimates the amount of goods and services produced per person in a given year. These figures can be used to compare one country to another. (See Figure 18.1.) For example, the per capita GDP of the United States is among the world's highest—over $40,000. In Tanzania, in east Africa, it is $700—among the lowest. Often these figures are adjusted to take into account the idea that a dollar may go further in some less developed countries where goods and services are less costly.

FIGURE 18.1 World Per Capita GDPs

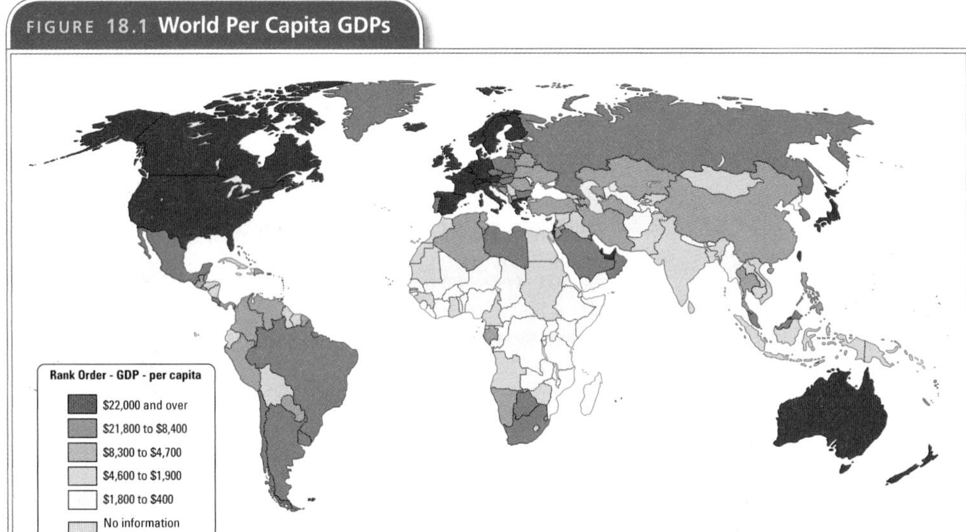

ANALYZE MAPS

1. Which continent is the least developed?
2. Which continents have no countries in the top per capita GDP bracket?

DIFFERENTIATING INSTRUCTION

Inclusion

Profile a Nation

Have students choose a nation to profile, that is, to gather key information about that would show the nation's level of economic development. Refer students to the *CIA Factbook* found online at www.cia.gov. This publication is in the public domain and has a fully accessible text-only version that complies with Section 508 of the Rehabilitation Act.

Gifted and Talented

Make a World Map of HDI

Direct interested students to use a blank world map to create a colored map that shows the Human Development Index of various representative nations. Tell them they can find the HDI at http://hdr.undp.org. Countries are classified high, medium, or low human development; tell students to use a different color for countries in each level. Suggest that the representative nations should include all of North America and at least five nations each in South America, Africa, Europe, and Asia.

Health

Statistics showing various aspects of health and health care are also useful in determining economic development. Especially indicative are statistics on the survival rate of babies. This measure is called the **infant mortality rate**, the number of children who die within the first year of life per 1,000 live births.

Dangerous Water More than a billion people worldwide use unsafe drinking water sources. Disease and death can be real consequences of this fact.

The infant mortality rate in Japan is 3. In China it is 23. In Angola it is 185. What can economists learn from these figures? The answer lies in understanding the conditions in which infants thrive. These conditions include a safe and sanitary birth environment with access to needed emergency care, adequate nutrition, an adequately fed mother who has access to clean drinking water and acceptable shelter, and protection from disease in the form of early-childhood vaccinations. A subsistence society, or one in extreme poverty, is unlikely to be able to provide these conditions. Less developed economies may be able to provide them to some degree, but in developed economies, these conditions are the norm.

Another useful standard is **life expectancy**, the average number of years a person could expect to live if current mortality trends were to continue for the rest of that person's life. For example, people born today in Japan can expect to live to age 82, in China, to age 72, while in Angola, only to age 39.

Education

The World Education Forum declares in its Framework for Action that "education is . . . the key to sustainable development and peace and stability within and among countries, and thus an indispensable means for effective participation in the societies and economies of the twenty-first century. . . ." Since education is so clearly tied into the economy, education statistics are tracked as useful indicators of the development level of a nation. One key education figure is the **literacy rate**, the percentage of people older than 15 who can read and write. Japan's literacy rate is 99 percent; Somalia's is 38 percent. Another useful statistic is student enrollment at all levels. This figure tells the percentage of school-age individuals who are actually going to school. In Belgium and Japan, for example, primary-school enrollment is 100 percent. In Niger, it is about 40 percent.

In 1990, another standard was introduced that combines some of these other statistics. It is the **human development index** (HDI)—the brainchild of Pakistani economist Mahbub ul Haq. A nation's HDI is a combination of its real GDP per capita, life expectancy, adult literacy rate, and student enrollment figures. Its measures are an important indicator of what life is like in a specific country.

QUICK REFERENCE

Infant mortality rate is the number of children who die within the first year of life per 1,000 live births.

Life expectancy is the average number of years a person can expect to live if current mortality trends were to continue for the rest of that person's life.

Literacy rate is the percentage of people older than 15 who can read and write.

The **human development index** (HDI) uses targeted economic, education, and health statistics to assess a nation's level of development.

International Economics

Infant Mortality Rates

The United States is not even in the top 30 nations for lowest infant mortality rates. In 2006, the top ten nations with the lowest rates, starting with the lowest infant mortality rate, were: Singapore, Sweden, Hong Kong, Japan, Iceland, Finland, Norway, Malta, Czech Republic, and Andorra.

One reason for the low ranking of the United States is the heterogeneous U.S. population and the wide disparity in infant mortality rates among the country's many racial and ethnic groups. For example, there are more than twice as many infant deaths in the first year of life among African Americans than there are among white Americans.

More About . . .

Unclean Water

According to Global Water, a nonprofit organization that works to provide access to clean water for those most in need, almost 40,000 people die every day from diseases directly related to unclean water. Further, four out of five fatal childhood diseases are caused by contaminants in water.

Global Water and organizations similar to it work to enable people to tap into the water resources already at hand to develop a clean water supply that will last forever.

SMALL GROUP ACTIVITY

Seeing Relationships Among Economic Standards

Time 30–45 Minutes 

Task Research and compare various standards of economic development looking for correlations.

Materials Needed paper and pens, computer with Internet access for research, or library materials with basic factual information about the nations of the world

Activity

- Organize students into three or four groups.
- Direct each group to choose a country and research as many of the standards of economic development as they can—per capita GDP, infant mortality rate, life expectancy, literacy rate, consumption of goods and services, and energy use.
- Tell students their task is to compile their findings in a graphic that highlights the relationships among these standards, especially the degree to which they are correlated positively.
- Have each group present and explain its graphic to the class.

Rubric

	Understanding of Relationships Among Economic Standards	Presentation of Information
4	excellent	original and complete
3	good	clear and complete
2	fair	incomplete, but clear ideas
1	poor	incomplete, unclear

More About . . .

Consumer Goods in China
Entrepreneur Wang Gouduan, once manager of a run-down state-owned factory for making rice cookers, has helped build one of China's most dynamic manufacturers of consumer goods, Kelon. When he and a few partners saw their first refrigerator in 1983, they knew they could turn the business around.

The partners got a small loan from the government, about $11,000. With those funds, they bought a Japanese-made refrigerator, took it apart, and then figured out how to make one from scratch. From that modest beginning, the company went public in 1996 and raised $100 million dollars from shareholders. To continue its growth, Kelon is now also developing air conditioners.

Presentation Options

Review the characteristics of consumerism in a developing economy by using the following presentation options:

Power Presentations DVD-ROM
Using the Display Tool, you can highlight the consumption patterns of less developed countries.

Economics Concepts Transparencies
- CT61 Developed Versus Low-Income, Less Developed Countries

Consumption of Goods and Services

In the mid-1990s, home appliances were still relatively rare in less developed countries like China. By the year 2000, however, the refrigerator had become a familiar part of Chinese city life; three out of four dwellings in major urban areas had one. Refrigerators have even begun to reach the secondary cities and rural areas, though they are still so rare there that they are sometimes displayed proudly in the living room rather than hidden away in the kitchen. Washing machines are also becoming increasingly commonplace. China's consumption of cell phones has risen rapidly in recent years too. At the beginning of 2001, there were approximately 65 million cell phones in use in China; by 2004, there were about 335 million—more than in any other country. The number of personal computers owned in China is doubling every 28 months.

What do these statistics say about China's economic development? These data show how people choose to spend their income after they have food and shelter. When consumption of such big-ticket items as refrigerators, automobiles, and washing machines increases, an economy is growing and developing. This indicates that people's living standards are rising. Goods that once were available only to the rich are now purchased by middle- and even low-income families.

In the less developed nations of China and India, 16 percent of the population is following this consumption pattern, compared with 89 percent of the population in Europe. The less developed nations therefore have the greatest room for growth in the consumption of consumer goods and services. For now, however, consumers in North America and Western Europe, whose population is about 12 percent of the global total, are responsible for 60 percent of the global total of consumption of goods and services. The 30 percent of the world population that lives in South Asia and sub-Saharan Africa, on the other hand, spends only 3.2 percent. Comparisons like the one below in Figure 18.2 offer another way to measure relative growth.

FIGURE 18.2 Ownership of Typical Consumer Goods

(per thousand residents)

Country	Television Sets	Telephone Mainlines
United States	835	659
Ukraine	456	212
India	83	40

Source: The State of the World, 2004

DIFFERENTIATING INSTRUCTION

Struggling Readers

Modify Strategies
Have students take turns reading the three paragraphs on page 548. Then, ask them to comment on which parts of the passage seemed easiest to understand and which were more difficult. Most students will probably find the final paragraph the most challenging. Ask them to explain why it may be more difficult to read. *(because of its many statistics)* Also ask why the other sections seemed easier. Point out that readers adjust their strategies as they encounter different kinds of text.

English Learners

Understand Idioms
Help students understand the use of idioms by pointing out the term "big-ticket" in paragraph two. Ask students what they think that means based on the context. Inquire whether they know any other idioms related to the cost of something. *(Possible answers: it cost "an arm and a leg," "sticker shock," "dirt cheap.")* Suggest that students keep notes in their personal dictionaries about the idioms they encounter.

Energy Use

Of the roughly 6.5 billion people in the world, as many as 2 billion are without electricity. Since electricity and other forms of energy contribute to economic development, statistics on energy use can reveal an aspect of a nation's economic development. Energy use is not spread evenly throughout the population. Asia, with 50 percent of the world's people, accounts for just over 21 percent of annual energy consumption. For another example, the average global consumption of electricity is 2,744 kilowatt hours (KWh) per capita. Japan's annual per capita consumption of electricity, like that of other industrialized nations, is well over 7,000 KWhs. Colombia's annual rate of about 820 KWh per capita is typical of LDCs, which average about 750 KWh per capita each year.

How the energy is put to use is another revealing statistic, especially the amount used for commercial purposes. The United States, for example, uses the equivalent energy of 8,148 kilograms of oil per person in commercial enterprises. India uses the equivalent of about 494 kilograms of oil per person for commercial activities. The amount of energy used for commercial purposes correlates to a nation's level of technological achievement and other economic measures.

Projected energy use to the year 2025 follows the same pattern as the projected consumption of consumer goods and services, with LDCs outpacing developed nations. The LDCs are expected to increase their energy use by about 3.2 percent a year. In Asia, including China and India, the demand for energy is expected to double between 2002 and 2025. The relatively rapid increase in energy use coincides with the move toward industrialization and technological advances. In fact, transportation and industry account for nearly all of the projected increase in the use of fossil fuels.

Wind Power Wind farms, such as this one in northwest China, contribute a small but growing part of the world's electricity.

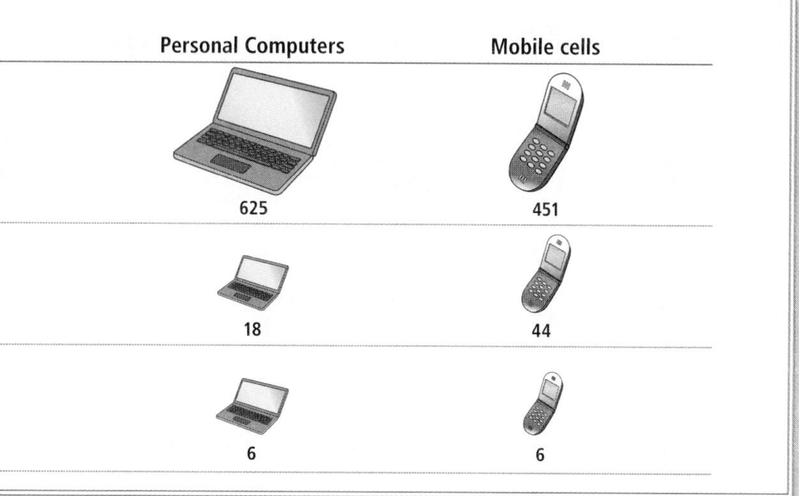

Personal Computers
Mobile cells
625
451
18
44
6
6

More About . . .

Energy Intensity

Energy intensity refers to the relationship between GDP and energy use. In LDCs, the energy intensity level is high, meaning that the demand for energy rises at about the same pace as the growth of GDP. In many developed nations, however, the link between the two is weaker.

In the more stable developed nations, consumers have been buying energy-using goods for so long that they are now buying replacements. These replacements are often more energy efficient than the earlier products. So, a rise in GDP in a developed nation does not always mean that energy use will rise at an equivalent rate.

International Economics

China's Wind Power

Among its many other first-place claims, China is the first in the world in the number of off-grid wind turbine generators. These are generators that supply power to remote regions rather than link up with the conventional power grid.

China has developed its wind power through partnerships with other countries, especially Denmark and Germany, which, like other European nations, have a commitment to developing wind power and other renewable energy sources. The Chinese government has been offering incentives and other support to make wind power account for more than the very small percent of energy it now produces.

SMALL GROUP ACTIVITY

Analyzing Ownership of Consumer Goods Worldwide

Time 45 minutes

Task Research and analyze ownership of consumer goods in selected nations, expanding upon data in Figure 18.2.

Materials Needed paper and pens, computer with Internet access for research, or library materials with basic factual information about the nations of the world

Activity

- Divide students into four groups, one for each of the following areas: the Americas, Europe, Asia, and Africa.
- Direct each group to research levels of ownership of typical consumer goods in three countries in their area (other than those in Figure 18.2).
- Tell students to use the same categories listed in Figure 18.2, if possible.
- Have the groups present their findings to the class, explaining what the consumption patterns reveal about the level of economic development in each country.

Rubric

	Analyzing of Ownership of Consumer Goods	Presentation of Information
4	excellent	clear and complete
3	good	mostly clear
2	fair	sometimes clear
1	poor	sketchy

A Global Perspective

Botswana's Growing Economy

One industry being developed as part of Botswana's attempt at economic diversification is tourism. Though it provides a far smaller percentage of GDP than diamonds (4.5 percent compared to about 33 percent), it employs more people than diamond mining (about 10,000 compared to 6,000).

Botswana has the highest percentage of land dedicated to nature preserves (17 percent) of any nation, and its wildlife is a chief attraction for tourists who come to Botswana for safaris. Many safari owners are expatriates and revenue is sent to their new homeland, usually in Europe or South Africa. However, more of Botswana's citizens are learning the business side of tourism, which will lead to revenue being directed into the Botswana economy.

Answers

1. *It has remained stable, managed mining income wisely, bolstered human capital and the nation's infrastructure, and sought to diversify the economic activities beyond mining alone.*
2. *It has a "stable and responsible governmental system" and it has an A credit rating from Moody's and Standard and Poor's.*

More About . . .

Human Development and Public Services in Botswana

Botswana's sound economic policies have made it possible to direct significant funds toward human development and public services. Since independence in 1966, the population has become significantly better educated, with females now representing more than half of school enrollments. Infant mortality has dropped dramatically.

One scourge, however, has been hard to eradicate—HIV/AIDS. The rate of people infected with HIV/AIDS is one of the highest in the world, one in every three persons. The widespread problem with AIDS has dropped life expectancy rates in Botswana to under the age of 40.

In contrast, the developed nations are projected to increase their energy use by only 1.1 percent a year. Developed economies use fuel more efficiently, which accounts in part for their slower rate of increase in energy use. Transitional economies are expected to increase their energy use by 1.6 percent each year as they face the challenges of moving to a market economy.

Labor Force

In what kind of job do most of a nation's workers find themselves employed? The answer to this question reveals one aspect of a nation's level of development. According to the World Bank, this measure includes all the economically active people between the ages of 15 and 65 in a country—including the employed, the unemployed, and soldiers, but excluding students and unpaid caregivers. The fewer workers there are engaged in agriculture, and the greater the number of workers in manufacturing and service industries, the more developed the nation.

A GLOBAL PERSPECTIVE

Botswana's Growing Economy

Since it became independent in 1966, Botswana's per capita income growth has been among the fastest of any nation in the world. This small African country transformed itself from one of the world's poorest countries to a middle-income nation in under 50 years. In 2004, Botswana received an A credit rating from Moody's and from Standard and Poor's.

Botswana has succeeded largely by maintaining a stable and responsible governmental system. The government has managed the income from large-scale mining operations wisely, reinvesting it in the nation's physical and human infrastructure. In recent years, the development of the financial services and tourism industries has been stressed. Together, they now represent about one-quarter of the nation's GDP.

Botswana still faces a number of social and economic challenges, including high unemployment, low manufacturing output, and one of the world's highest rates of HIV/AIDS infection. But through its moves to diversify the economy, the government has put the nation on a solid development track.

CONNECTING ACROSS THE GLOBE

1. How has the government of Botswana helped keep the nation's economy growing?
2. In the article, what tells investors that Botswana is a relatively safe place to invest?

APPLICATION Drawing Conclusions

B. Would you expect a positive or negative correlation between literacy rates and infant mortality rates? Explain. Negative: the higher the literacy rate, the lower the infant mortality rate. Better educated parents can more effectively protect their children from disease and harm.

DIFFERENTIATING INSTRUCTION

Inclusion

Focus on Key Ideas

Have students review the standards of economic development. Write the following headings on the board, leaving space between them: Per Capita Gross Domestic Product, Health, Education, Consumption of Goods and Services, Energy Use, and Labor Force. Then, work with students to write two sentences about each that crystallize the key ideas.

Gifted and Talented

Evaluate and Persuade

Invite students to review the various standards of economic development covered in this section and decide which is the most telling in representing a nation's level of development. Then, suggest that they write a persuasive essay arguing for or against a nation's using that standard as a goal for improvement. For example, should a nation focus on improving its GDP (if that seems the most telling), or should it strive to improve its human-development index, or some other standard?

SECTION 1 Assessment

Online Quiz
ClassZone.com

REVIEWING KEY CONCEPTS

1. Explain the relationship between the terms in each of these pairs:
   a. *developed nations* / *less developed countries*
   b. *human development index* / *infant mortality rate*
2. What does the state of a nation's infrastructure say about the country's level of economic development?
3. Why is per capita GDP a more useful statistic than overall GDP when comparing nations?
4. What does an analysis of the labor force and energy usage tell economists about a nation?
5. Why are health and longevity statistics useful in determining a nation's level of development?
6. **Using Your Notes** Pick one example of a developed nation, one of a transitional economy, and one of a less developed nation. Use your notes to explain why you chose each.

Definitions of Development	
Levels of Development	Standards of Economic Development

Use the Graphic Organizer at **Interactive Review @ ClassZone.com**

CRITICAL THINKING

7. **Comparing and Contrasting** Compare and contrast three characteristics of a developed nation and a less developed nation.
8. **Making Inferences and Drawing Conclusions** One measure of economic development is the extent to which a nation buys big-ticket consumer goods. Does the production of those goods also indicate a level of economic development? Explain your answer.
9. **Writing About Economics** Some economists argue that GDP does not give an accurate picture of a nation's well-being. They point out that GDP reflects economic activity that pollutes the environment and depletes resources as well as economic activity that counteracts the pollution. In other words, it shows both the polluting enterprises and the cost of cleaning up the pollution on the plus side of the balance sheet. Write a paragraph speculating on how to revise GDP figures to reflect this concern.
10. **Challenge** In poorer countries, where does the money for development initiatives come from?

ECONOMICS IN PRACTICE

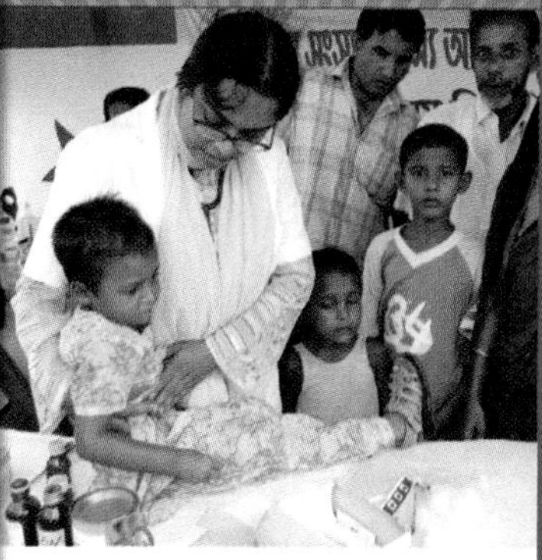

Health care in Bangladesh

Understanding Levels of Development
The chart below shows life expectancy, infant mortality rates, and literacy rates for five countries.

Country	Life Expectancy (years)	Infant Mortality (per 1,000 live births)	Literacy Rate (%)
Bolivia	65.8	51.8	87.2
Germany	78.8	4.1	99.0
Moldova	65.7	38.4	99.1
Philippines	70.2	22.8	92.6
Bangladesh	62.5	60.8	43.1

Source: *CIA World Factbook, 2006*

Drawing Conclusions Which nation is probably the most developed? Which nation is probably the least developed? Which nation is more developed, Bolivia or the Philippines? Explain your answers.

Challenge If you were "weighting" the various measures used to show economic development, which would you consider most meaningful: life expectancy, infant mortality, or literacy rate? Explain your answer.

4 Assess & Reteach

Assess Assign the first six items to the entire class as a written activity, and go over the answers in class. For the Critical Thinking questions, have the class work in four groups, one for each question, and report their answers to the rest of the class. Use the Economics in Practice as a whole class activity.

Unit 7 Resource Book
- Section Quiz, p. 71

Interactive Review @ ClassZone.com
- Section Quiz

Test Generator CD-ROM
- Section Quiz

Reteach A number of the suggested activities have had students applying the information to hypothetical though realistic people. Continue with that theme as you reteach this lesson. Ask students to comment on the personal impact that the subject of each of the headings in this lesson may have.

Unit 7 Resource Book
- Reteaching Activity, p. 72

SECTION 1 ASSESSMENT ANSWERS

Reviewing Key Concepts

1. a. *developed nations*, p. 544; *less developed countries*, p. 545
   b. *human development index*, p. 547; *infant mortality rate*, p. 547
2. The infrastructure indicates the level of industrialization a nation has, since without good infrastructure industrialization will falter. It also indicates a competence on the part of the government to oversee and pay for such improvements.
3. It puts nations of varying population sizes on an equal, individual level of measurement.
4. They indicate the degree of industrialization.
5. Good health and longevity both require a developed economy to support them—through good medical care and a safe, healthy environment.
6. See page 544 for an example of a completed diagram. Answers will vary, but should include accurate definitions of standards of economic development.

Critical Thinking

7. Sample answers: Developed—high GDP, industrialization, high standard of living; developing—lower GDP, less well developed industry, lower standard of living.
8. It portrays economic development by showing the amount of industrialization in an economy.
9. Students might suggest that GDP figures be revised by subtracting from the total GDP for activities that are harmful enough to the environment to warrant expensive cleanup efforts.
10. Answers will vary. Students may speculate that the more developed nations provide aid.

Economics in Practice

Drawing Conclusions Germany is probably the most developed because it is strong in each statistic. Bangladesh is probably the least developed because it scores lowest in each category. The Philippines is probably more developed than Bolivia because it shows strength over Bolivia in each statistic.

Challenge Possible answer: life expectancy, because it takes into account a wide range of factors that affect a person over the span of a lifetime

1 Plan & Prepare

Section 2 Objectives

- evaluate the importance of developing human and physical capital
- examine the importance of stability and opportunity in economic development
- describe how developing nations raise money for development programs

2 Focus & Motivate

Connecting to Everyday Life Facilitate a discussion based on the familiar adage, "It's not what you know, it's who you know." Ask students to comment on how it applies to the opportunities that await them after high school, such as college or a job. Help students understand the importance of social networking. Ask them, however, to take it to an extreme and imagine the effects. If favoritism and other forms of exclusive networks were widespread, how would that affect their chances of tapping into opportunities? Point out that a stable government with little corruption is a key factor in economic development.

Taking Notes Remind students to take notes as they read by completing a cluster diagram. They can use the Graphic Organizer at **Interactive Review @ ClassZone.com**. A sample is shown below.

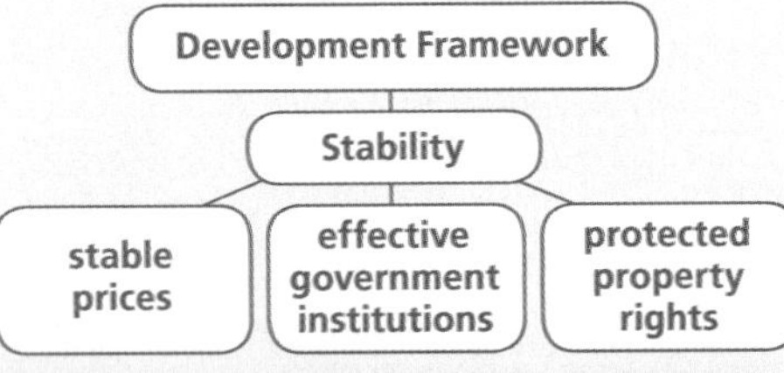

SECTION 2

A Framework for Economic Development Objectives

OBJECTIVES

In Section 2 you will
- evaluate the importance of developing human and physical capital
- examine the importance of stability and opportunity in economic development
- describe how developing nations raise money for development programs

KEY TERMS

capital flight, *p. 558*
default, *p. 559*
World Bank, *p. 559*
International Monetary Fund (IMF), *p. 559*
debt restructuring, *p. 559*
stabilization program, *p. 559*

TAKING NOTES

As you read Section 2, complete a cluster diagram like the one shown for each major concept. Include key concepts and other helpful words and phrases. Use the Graphic Organizer at **Interactive Review @ ClassZone.com**

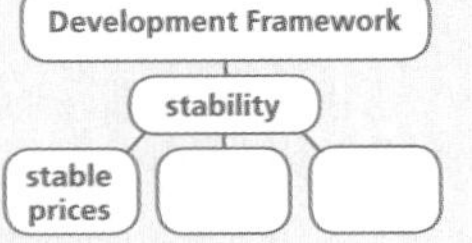

Resources

KEY CONCEPTS

What does a nation need to develop economically? Natural resources such as minerals and fossil fuels play a role in economic development. A nation's climate and the amount of land suited for agriculture are also factors. Each nation uses the resources it has. However, natural resources are not enough. Investing in human capital and physical capital, for example, are ways that many nations promote economic expansion.

High Levels of Human Capital

People are the most valuable resources in a market economy. One element of a healthy and growing market economy is a commitment to make the most of its human resources through education and training. Education and training help people develop the skills to enter into and function productively in the economy.

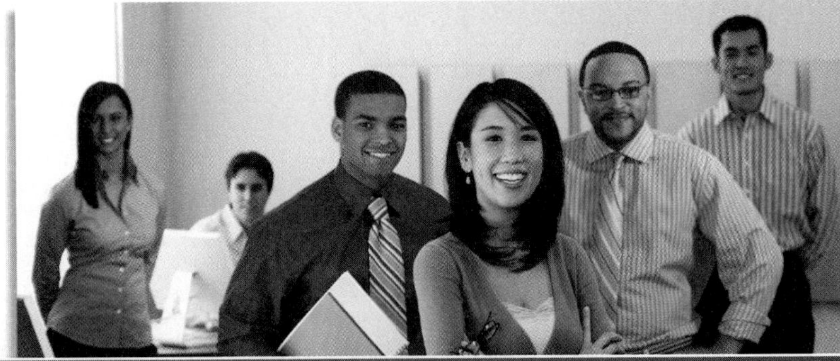

Human Capital Societies benefit in many ways when their citizens are well educated.

552 Chapter 18

SECTION 2 PROGRAM RESOURCES

ON LEVEL

Lesson Plans
- Core, p. 62

Unit 7 Resource Book
- Reading Study Guide, pp. 73–74
- Math Skills Worksheet, p. 101
- Section Quiz, p. 81

STRUGGLING READERS

Unit 7 Resource Book
- Reading Study Guide with Additional Support, pp. 75–77
- Reteaching Activity, p. 82

ENGLISH LEARNERS

Unit 7 Resource Book
- Reading Study Guide with Additional Support (Spanish), pp. 78–80

INCLUSION

Lesson Plans
- Modified for Inclusion, p. 62

GIFTED AND TALENTED

Unit 7 Resource Book
- Readings in Free Enterprise: American Free Trade: Is Ricardo Still Right?, p. 96

NCEE Student Activities
- Investing Internationally, pp. 69–72

TECHNOLOGY

eEdition DVD-ROM
eEdition Online
Power Presentation DVD-ROM
Economics Concepts Transparencies
- CT62 Elements That Contribute to Economic Development

Daily Test Practice Transparencies, TT62
ClassZone.com

Investing in education also affects other aspects of a society. Educated citizens are able to make informed decisions about health matters. Educated parents are likely to vaccinate their children and invest in their children's education. Furthermore, educated citizens are likely to vote, participate in civic affairs, rise above poverty, and avoid criminal activity.

FIGURE 18.3 RATES OF PRIMARY SCHOOL COMPLETION AND SECONDARY SCHOOL ENROLLMENT

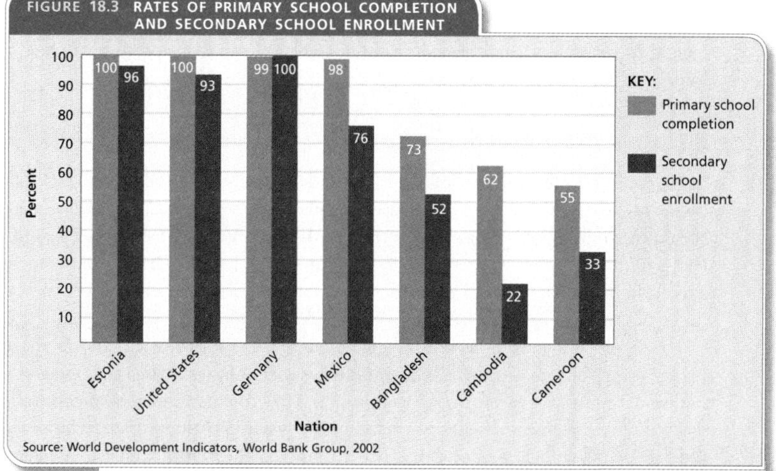

Source: World Development Indicators, World Bank Group, 2002

ANALYZE GRAPHS

1. What nation shows the largest drop-off between the percentage of students that complete primary school and the percentage who go on to secondary school?
2. Do you think the amount of drop-off between education levels is a clue to a nation's level of development? Explain your answer.

High Levels of Physical Capital

Physical capital is also an important factor contributing to economic growth. As you read in Chapter 1, physical capital consists of the human-made goods—machines—that are used in the production of other goods and services. Investments in physical capital make people more productive.

Fortunately, LDCs do not have to reinvent the wheel. Technology and other innovative capital resources are always being refined in developed nations. LDCs need only copy or import the technology. The desire to copy or import technologies points to the link between human and physical capital. Copying technology requires educated and well-trained people. Importing technology requires money, which is generally in short supply in LDCs, so these nations look to foreign investment. However, a country that lacks human capital is less attractive to investors that might supply this money.

APPLICATION Explaining an Economic Concept

A. Think of your own examples to explain the ripple effect that education has on a society and economy.

Answers will vary, but look for an understanding of the "virtuous circle" in which one improvement makes many others possible.

3 Teach

Resources

Discuss

- Which would be more beneficial to a developing economy, a large quantity of physical capital, most of which is outdated, or a smaller supply of higher efficiency physical capital? Give reasons for your answer. *(Answers will vary. Those recommending large quantities of outdated physical capital might argue that the more widely that even dated equipment is spread through the economy, the more productive the economy will be. Those arguing for small amounts of higher efficiency physical capital may point to more opportunities to keep developing efficient technologies.)*

Analyzing Graphs: Figure 18.3

Refer students back to Figure 9.4 in Chapter 9, page 261, which shows the pay differences in median earnings by education level. Have students use that graph and this one to explain the effect of a poorly educated citizenry on an economy in strictly financial terms.

Answers

1. *Cambodia, a drop-off of 40 percent*
2. *Yes it is; since the amount and quality of education is a marker of a developed society, a low number of citizens enrolling in secondary school does not bode well for present or future development.*

LEVELED ACTIVITY

Understanding Levels of Capital

Time 30 Minutes

Objective Students will demonstrate an understanding of the various levels of investment in human and physical capital.

Basic

Using photo pairs from magazines or the Internet, create a poster showing differences between high levels and low levels of human capital investment and of physical capital investment. For example, you may use photos of an advanced agricultural machine for the high level of investment in physical capital and of a simple shovel for the low level.

On Level

Using specific examples, write a brief description of the level of investment in human and physical capital in your community and/or state. Include at least five examples of each kind of capital investment.

Challenge

Consider the level of investment in human and physical capital in your community and/or state. What concrete steps can be taken to increase those levels? Write a proposal for lawmakers suggesting several practical ways in which the levels of both human and physical capital could be raised.

Stability

Discuss

- How would your day-to-day life be different if we did not have the rule of law in the United States? *(Answers will vary, but may include such things as not feeling assured of justice in a dispute, having to do things against your will, and possibly being shut out of opportunities.)*
- Review what you read about the causes and consequences of inflation in Section 3 of Chapter 13. Using one of the specific examples you learned, explain why economic development is hindered in a nation with unchecked inflation. *(Answers will vary. Possible answer: People would lose money rapidly, panic would set in, and the situation would be ripe for an authoritarian takeover. This sort of political instability often scares away foreign investment.)*

More About . . .

Amartya Sen

Born in India, Amartya Sen is currently a professor of economics at Harvard University. He came to write his 1981 book *Poverty and Famines: An Essay on Entitlement and Deprivation,* in part, through personal experience.

As a boy of nine, Sen witnessed the disastrous Bengal famine of 1943. Three million people perished, even though Sen was later to show that food supplies themselves were not inadequate. Instead, he determined that the people's inability to access the food supplies, through unemployment, poor distribution systems, and rising prices, among other factors, was at the heart of the problem.

Stability

KEY CONCEPTS

While such inputs as human capital and physical capital are necessary for increased output, they are only part of the framework for economic growth. The overall governmental and economic environments must be stable enough to support growth before those inputs can best be put to use.

Effective Government Institutions

In the United States, the rule of law is so fundamentally a part of the culture that it may be taken for granted. We are used to laws made by a legislature that we elect according to the principles laid out in the Constitution. We take for granted that the laws will then be made public for all to know and follow. We expect those laws to be applied fairly. When there are disputes, we trust that our legal system will sort out the differences according to the law, not by bribery or intimidation.

In many countries, however, the rule of law is still out of reach, and in those places, economic growth suffers. Business investment always carries risk, even in a nation with effective government institutions. That risk rises sharply in countries where the enforcement of laws is unpredictable, where private property rights are unprotected, where a bureaucracy is corrupt or bloated or both, and where judges can be bought and sold. The rule of law provides a foundation of predictability and certainty that reduces economic risk.

Democracy itself is a key factor of economic growth. Democratic nations have a higher rate of economic growth than nations with a different form of government. In nations where people can choose their representatives in free and open elections, they can promote their economic self-interest with the same degree of power as other citizens. When the press is uncensored, views that oppose government policy can be aired and debated. In a famous study, one Nobel Prize–winning economist, Amartya Sen, concluded that crop failures are not the chief cause of famines: political systems are. He points out that no widespread famine has ever occurred in a democratic nation. India has had famines, but none since it became a democracy in 1947. The democratic process reduces the likelihood that the government will interfere with the self-correcting market forces that could prevent widespread famine.

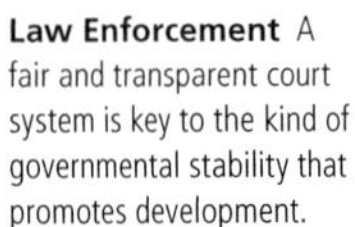

Law Enforcement A fair and transparent court system is key to the kind of governmental stability that promotes development.

DIFFERENTIATING INSTRUCTION

Inclusion

Find Key Information

Have student pairs complete the following sentences with information from the text: The rule of law makes economic risk-taking _____. *(acceptable)* Democracy assures that people can promote their economic _____. *(self-interest)* Investors do not want to take a chance in a location where _____ rights are not guaranteed. *(property)*

Gifted and Talented

Research Positive and Negative Liberty

Invite interested students to research Isaiah Berlin's concepts of positive and negative liberty (*Two Concepts of Liberty,* 1958). Then, suggest that they relate them in a short essay to Sen's findings about the role of democracy in preventing famines.

Stable Prices

In areas where prices are stable and where the governments' fiscal and monetary policies are sound, economic growth can take root. Investors in such an environment know what to expect. They do not see volatile changes in interest rates, prices, or the level of the government debt.

With price stability, businesses can make long-term plans with some assurance that conditions will not change too dramatically and that the government will not go bankrupt. In contrast, in nations with a high inflation rate or with unstable interest rates, investors run a high risk. Many will choose to avoid investing in such an environment in the first place. And even if they do take a chance, they are likely to withdraw their investment at the first sign of trouble. That leaves the unstable country further behind, since the funds it could use for economic expansion are placed in more stable nations.

Monetary Stability Runaway prices in post–World War I Germany made money into children's toys (left). A stable currency and stable prices create real purchasing power (right).

Protected Property Rights

Guaranteed protection of private property provides an incentive for economies to grow. If businesses have no way to assert ownership of their enterprises, they will have little incentive to take economic risks, since they will have no guarantee of reaping the rewards if they succeed. Assured property rights give investors confidence and stimulate entrepreneurship.

Business owners also need private property rights to prevent the government from interfering with or restricting their operations. In such unstable nations as Haiti, Kazakhstan, and Indonesia, where corruption and favoritism are widespread, private property rights are insecure. This lack of stability is more than enough to cause investors to look elsewhere to locate their enterprises.

In some LDCs, especially former colonies of Western nations, land ownership is in the hands of a very small percentage of the population—usually the descendants of the colonists. In some cases, this land is seized by the government for redistribution to the majority population. Foreign investors are wary of locating businesses in countries that threaten private property.

APPLICATION Drawing Conclusions

B. Why is the rule of law a stabilizing force that promotes development?
It drastically reduces destabilizing activities, such as bribery, intimidation, and theft, that increase the level of risk associated with business investment.

More About . . .

The Rule of Law and Chinese Economic Growth
Some analysts have argued that China may be a counterexample to the idea that economic growth depends on the rule of law. By some measures, the Chinese have relatively weak institutions to support the rule of law and/or enforcement of the rules that exist (for example, bankruptcy laws). Yet, the Chinese economy by all accounts has achieved dramatic growth.

However, economists who have carefully studied the relationship suggest that while initial economic growth can take place amidst weak institutions, a sustained growth will depend on strong institutions that support and enforce the rule of law.

More About . . .

Monetary Instability
Zimbabwe is an object lesson in the problems of unstable prices and unprotected property rights. In 2000, the government of President Robert Mugabe began to expropriate white-owned land, suppress opposition, and limit freedom of the press.

By 2006, Zimbabwe was in the midst of an economic collapse. It had the highest inflation rate in the world—1,000 percent. Millions of acres of farmland were unused, since only about 40 percent of the black landowners occupied their land. About 4 million people, one-fourth of Zimbabwe's population, had fled the country. Many of those who remained survived only because they received aid.

SMALL GROUP ACTIVITY

Researching Foreign Business Climates

Time 30–45 Minutes ◑◕

Task Research a foreign nation as to its suitability as a location for opening a business.

Materials Needed paper and pens, computer with Internet access for research, or library materials with basic factual information about the nations of the world

Activity

- Organize students into four groups, one for each of the following nations: Malaysia, Argentina, Cambodia, and Cote d'Ivoire.
- Direct each group to research the business climate of their nation online or in library books.
- Tell students their task is to write a position statement about whether or not investing in that country is a good idea. The statement should contain very specific reasons and examples to support the position.
- Have each group present and explain its recommendation to the rest of the class.

Rubric

	Understanding of Business Climates	Presentation of Information
4	excellent	original and complete
3	good	clear and complete
2	fair	incomplete, but some clear ideas
1	poor	incomplete, unclear

Opportunity

Discuss

- How does the upward mobility of people help an economy grow? *(The more money people have, the more they can buy and invest.)*
- What political systems seem most likely to be riddled with corruption? Why? *(Any system that does not hold officials accountable by open elections will be prone to corruption. Examples include dictatorships and planned economies.)*

International Economics

Social Mobility in Singapore
Industrial growth and economic expansion in Singapore in the 1970s and 1980s allowed for significant upward mobility. During 1953–54, for example, 19 percent of citizens were said to be living in absolute poverty—without even money to provide food, clothing, and shelter.

By 1982–83, the number of people living in absolute poverty had fallen to 0.3 percent. During this period of economic expansion, the nation's income was distributed relatively evenly, with educational level being the key determinant of income.

At **ClassZone.com** students will see updated information on women in the workplace in LDCs.

Opportunity

KEY CONCEPTS

Economic opportunity depends on a number of functions that fall to the government. These include opening international trade, helping people move up the income ladder, controlling corruption, and limiting regulations.

Open International Trade

The government can also create opportunities for economic growth by lowering restrictions on international trade. As you read in Chapter 17, trade benefits the trading nations by allowing them to produce what they are most efficient at producing and trading for the rest. Partners in a trading relationship produce more than they would without trade, leading to economic growth.

However, in less developed countries, governments have imposed high tariffs on imports and instituted other protectionist measures in an effort to give local producers an advantage. Governments often justify these protections as a short-term effort to help local industries until they grow strong enough to compete with foreign competitors. Protectionist measures come with costs, though. Consumers have to pay more for goods than they would in a market open to imports. Also, government protections may reduce incentives for producers to become more efficient. Industries may become dependent on tariffs and other trade barriers.

Increase Social and Economic Mobility

Economic opportunity leads to the most vigorous economic growth when that opportunity is open to the entire population. If all citizens have an equal opportunity under the law to engage in economic enterprise, many will be motivated to lift themselves into a higher income bracket. A number of studies have found that in the United States, for example, about 25 to 33 percent of the population moves into a new income quintile each year. Over a ten-year period, that number rises to 60 percent. In the process of seeking personal economic reward, these people are also helping the economy to grow.

In some traditional cultures, however, social conditions do not promote equal opportunity. For example, in some LDCs with a traditional culture, the lower status of women keeps half the labor force from developing its full potential. Further, an entrenched class structure in some nations hampers growth, since the rich do not want changes that could deprive them of their wealth. Governmental changes that promote equal opportunity will help create a successful framework for economic growth.

Economics Update
Find an update on women in the workplace in LDCs at **ClassZone.com**

Economic Potential In many traditional societies, women are an untapped resource that could give development a boost.

DIFFERENTIATING INSTRUCTION

Struggling Readers

Activate Prior Knowledge
Ask students to recall what they know about each of the topics on this spread before reading each part. For example, ask students what they can remember about international trade, especially as it relates to opportunity, from the previous discussions of it in this text or from their own knowledge and experience. Tell students that calling to mind what they know about a subject before they read about it creates a context for that subject, which aids understanding.

English Learners

Develop Academic Language
To help English-language learners acquire the academic language skills that they need to succeed in school, model how you would write a formal summary of the information on pages 556–557, paragraph by paragraph. During the next several weeks, gradually release responsibility to students for writing their own formal summaries.

Control Corruption

Corruption, the abuse of public office for private gain, is an especially urgent problem that helps explain why some nations are able to develop and others are not. When government officials are at liberty to enrich themselves and others—by taking bribes and kickbacks, funneling lucrative government jobs and contracts to relatives and allies, skimming aid and loan money, and so on—the rest of the nation, especially the poor, pays the price. (See Figure 18.4.) Although there is not an exact correlation between corruption and per capita GDP, much more often than not, countries with less corruption have higher per capita GDPs.

FIGURE 18.4 Corruption and Per Capita GDP

Country	Corruption Index*	Per Capita GDP (in U.S. dollars)
Finland	9.6	31,000
Australia	8.7	31,600
Chile	7.3	11,900
United States	7.3	41,600
Slovenia	6.4	21,500
Bhutan	6.0	1,400
South Korea	5.1	22,600
South Africa	4.6	12,200
Turkey	3.8	8,400
Bolivia	2.7	2,900
Uganda	2.7	1,800
Albania	2.6	5,300
Russia	2.5	11,000
Kyrgyzstan	2.2	2,000
Cambodia	2.1	2,500

*10=least corrupt; 0=most corrupt
Sources: Transparency International; CIA World Factbook; 2006 and earlier data

Limit Regulation

Governments with reasonable tax levels and business regulations help to create economic opportunity. Businesses and other investors are more likely to be attracted to nations with relatively little "red tape."

Even in the United States, which has relatively few regulations on business, it is estimated that companies with 20 or fewer employees have to pay over $7,500 per employee each year to comply with government regulations. In many LDCs, the number of regulations is significantly higher. In a climate of instability, the high number of regulations can lead to corruption. Rather than comply with all the regulations, businesses are tempted to bypass them through payoffs. As you have read, a corrupt environment removes economic incentive and slows economic growth.

APPLICATION Applying Economic Concepts

C. Nations with the highest corruption index tend to have their wealth distributed less evenly, with a large percentage of people living in poverty. Why might this be so? Wealth and power become concentrated in the hands of an elite that is connected to the government, so little money ever makes its way to other parts of the society.

More About . . .

Corruption in Indonesia

Transparency International, a group that monitors corruption worldwide, has determined that former president Suharto of Indonesia embezzled more money from his nation than any modern leader. They estimate that in his 31 years of power he defrauded the Indonesian people of $15 to $35 billion.

The Indonesian government filed formal charges against Suharto, but his attorneys have argued over the years that his health was too poor to let him stand trial. In 2006, all charges against Suharto were dropped because of health reasons.

Analyzing Tables: Figure 18.4

Ask students if there seems to be a correlation between corruption and GDP per capita. *(Generally, wealthier countries have less corruption.)* Ask them to find an example of a country with low GDP per capita and low corruption. *(Chile, Bhutan)* Lead a discussion on this question: Does corruption cause economic problems or is it a symptom of economic problems? *(Possible answers: Symptom: Corruption can arise when a country's economy is struggling and people try to pad their legal incomes. Cause: Corruption leads to problems by diverting money from the economy.)*

SMALL GROUP ACTIVITY

Understanding the Role of Opportunity in Development

Time 30 Minutes ◑

Task Explain how the strategies presented on pages 556–557 will help meet the UN Millennium Development Goals.

Materials Needed paper and pens

Activity

- Divide students into eight groups, one for each of the Millennium goals. They can be found online. Direct each group to consider how the four ways to increase opportunity presented on pages 556–557 would help a nation achieve the millennium goal their group has been assigned.
- Instruct students to use very specific examples to explain their points.
- Have each group present its analysis to the rest of the class and allow a brief discussion after each presentation.

Rubric

	Understanding of Opportunity and Development	Presentation of Information
4	excellent	original and complete
3	good	clear and complete
2	fair	incomplete, but some clear ideas
1	poor	incomplete, unclear

Financing Development

Discuss

- What are both the positive and negative aspects of foreign investment and loans and aid? *(foreign investment—positive: pumps foreign money into economy and often creates jobs; negative: can lead to dependence on foreign nations who invest; loans and aid—positive: can supply much needed funds for crucial projects; negative: may be impossible to repay)*
- What negatives, if any, are associated with taking money and other kinds of aid from international help agencies? *(Answers will vary, but may include the idea that the help agencies can set conditions on how the money is used that may run counter to the culture of the borrowing nation.)*

More About . . .

Sony International

In 2006, to commemorate both the 10th anniversary of Sony (China) Limited and the 60th anniversary of Sony Corporation, the company invited 10 high school students from Beijing and 10 from Shanghai to come to Japan.

The students' schedule included visits with Japanese high school students and multinational employees of Sony. They were also scheduled to take part in envisioning an "Eco-City" of the future, one that would address energy concerns. Such development efforts are aided by mutual understanding among nations.

Economics Illustrated

To better understand where foreign aid from the United States goes and at what levels, you might visualize 100 pennies distributed in six stacks, using the percentages in Figure 18.5. For example, the stack for Africa would contain 31 pennies, and so on.

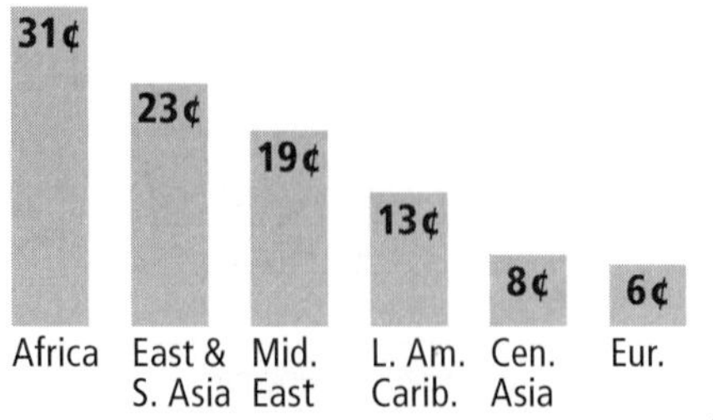

Financing Development

KEY CONCEPTS

Nations seeking to finance economic development can look to four main sources: internal investment, foreign investment, aid from foreign governments, or investments from international agencies. A developing nation must consider both the positive and negative aspects of each source.

Internal Investment

Investment funds for economic development can come from both public and private internal investment. Banks within the nation invest in economic enterprises, such as roads, bridges, and other infrastructure. Egypt, for example, has a goal to make domestic savings the key force in development and has been working toward increasing the savings rate to 25 percent of GDP. To do so, it has an initiative to bolster the insurance industry, which is successful at pooling and channeling savings.

In poorer nations, personal savings are very low, so banks have little to invest. Compounding the problem, the wealthy citizens of these countries sometimes invest their funds in developed countries rather than their own country, a problem known as **capital flight**. If private banks lack the funds to invest, the country's government may provide funds. It might also seek foreign investment from multinational corporations of through sales of government bonds.

> **QUICK REFERENCE**
>
> **Capital flight** occurs when capital from a country is invested outside that country.

Foreign Investment

There are several ways in which foreign interests can invest in an economy. One is foreign direct investment (FDI), the establishment of a business enterprise in a foreign country. A second is foreign portfolio investment, through which foreign investors take part in a nation's stock and other financial markets. Foreign investment in less developed countries increased from $44 billion in 1990 to $226 billion in 2000. One reason for the increase is that less developed nations had created a more attractive business climate for investors. Multinationals that open manufacturing plants in foreign nations provide jobs and training to the local population and reap the benefits of cheaper labor.

Foreign Direct Investment Multinational corporations bring employment, training, and new technology to less developed countries. This factory in Beijing is a joint venture between a Chinese company and DaimlerChrysler.

DIFFERENTIATING INSTRUCTION

Inclusion

Create Tactile Graphics

If possible, obtain a Tactile Graphics Starter Kit from the American Printing House for the Blind. This kit is designed for people with no experience in creating tactile graphics. Train students with no visual disabilities to create a tactile version of Figure 18.5 to be used by students with visual impairment. Alternatively, have both groups of students work together to create a 3-D version of Figure 18.5, using modeling clay or heavy paper for the various wedges of the pie.

Gifted and Talented

Identify Pros and Cons

Invite interested students to select one of the multinationals represented in the illustration on this page. Then, encourage them to conduct research on that corporation to find examples of both positive and negative impacts on nations in which it has made direct foreign investment. Encourage students to find a creative way to present their examples to the rest of the class.

Loans and Aid

Developing nations have also turned to loans to help finance their economic development. External debt, money borrowed from foreign banks or governments, has become an issue of great concern in some LDCs. Some countries, especially in South America and Africa, have more debt than they can pay back. When a nation cannot pay interest or principle on a loan, it is said to be in **default**.

Nations may also seek foreign aid—money from other nations. (See Figure 18.5 for aid figures from the U.S. Agency for International Development [USAID]).

FIGURE 18.5 USAID ALLOCATIONS BY REGION

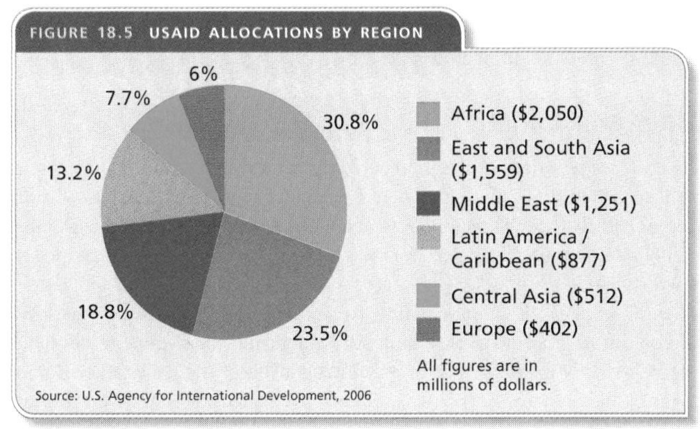

Source: U.S. Agency for International Development, 2006

International Help Agencies

LDCs also receive aid from several important international organizations. The World Bank, the International Monetary Fund, and the United Nations Development Program are the main international organizations devoted to economic development.

- **World Bank** is a financial institution that provides loans, policy advice, and technical assistance to low- and middle-income countries to reduce poverty.
- **International Monetary Fund (IMF)** is an international organization established to promote international monetary cooperation, foster economic growth, and provide temporary financial assistance to countries to help ease balance of payments adjustment. The IMF helps nations overloaded with debt to develop **debt restructuring**, a method used by countries with outstanding debt obligations to alter the terms of the debt agreements in order to achieve some advantage. It often oversees **stabilization programs**, in which it requires these troubled nations to carry out reforms—reducing foreign trade deficits and external debt, eliminating price controls, closing inefficient public enterprises, and slashing budget deficits.
- **United Nations Development Program** (UNDP) is a United Nations agency working to fight poverty. In 2006 it had active programs in 174 nations.

APPLICATION Making Inferences and Drawing Conclusions

D. Why would Kuwait, a developing nation, offer aid to countries in its region?

Answers will vary but are likely to note the improved stability of Kuwait with economically stable countries nearby.

QUICK REFERENCE

Default is when a nation cannot pay interest or principle on a loan

The **World Bank** is a financial institution that provides loans, policy advice, and technical assistance to low- and middle-income countries to reduce poverty.

The **International Monetary Fund (IMF)** promotes international monetary cooperation, fosters economic growth, and provides temporary financial assistance to countries to help ease balance of payments adjustment.

Debt restructuring is a method used by countries to alter the terms of their debt agreements in order to achieve some advantage.

A **stabilization program** is a required program of reforms imposed by the IMF to steady the economy of a debtor nation in danger of default.

More About . . .

Odious Debt

Odious debt is a legal concept that holds that if a debt was incurred by a despotic regime and used for that regime's good, not the nation's good, then it should fall when the regime falls. In other words, it cannot be collected from the successor government.

Many in South Africa are seeking to have the concept applied to the enormous debt amassed by the apartheid government of South Africa, which held power for nearly a half century in the 1900s. These South Africans say that the foreign debts incurred by this government were used to suppress black South Africans and should, therefore, be declared odious and written off.

Analyzing Graphs: Figure 18.5

Have students look at the levels of aid allocated by USAID versus the per capita GDPs shown in the map on page 546 (Figure 18.1). Do the levels of aid for regions in 18.5 seem to match the level of need shown by the map? *(It would seem that the Middle East receives a large share of funds for the size of the region and its level of development—especially in comparison to Central Asia.)* Why might the Middle East receive comparatively greater funding? *(because it is an economically important area that has more than its share of political instability and military conflict)*

SMALL GROUP ACTIVITY

Understanding Motivation to Provide Aid

Time 30 Minutes

Task Explain how providing aid to foreign nations serves the self-interest of the United States.

Materials Needed paper and pens, computer with Internet access for research, or current library materials

Activity

- Divide students into six groups, one for each of the regions represented in the pie chart showing U.S. aid allocations by regions.
- Direct each group to research the reasons why the United States gave aid to their region. Be sure students go beyond the humanitarian explanation and probe the national self-interest of the United States.
- Tell students to use very specific examples to explain their points.
- Have each group present their findings to the class.

Rubric

	Understanding of Motivation to Provide Aid	Presentation of Information
4	excellent	original and complete
3	good	clear and complete
2	fair	incomplete, but clear ideas
1	poor	incomplete, unclear

Anne Krueger

More About . . .

Anne Krueger
Krueger was the first woman to hold a senior position at the IMF. One of her colleagues at Stanford University had said this when he learned of her appointment to the IMF, "You really need a hard-nosed, experienced person who knows the ropes and is not a shrinking violet. She is assertive, she is articulate, and she is used to taking strong policy positions in settings where most of the other participants are male."

More About . . .

Anne Krueger at the IMF
Krueger left her position at the IMF when her five-year contract expired in August 2006. IMF Managing Director Rodrigo de Rato praised his colleague upon her departure.

"Anne brought to the Fund an impressive array of contacts among policymakers and academia around the world. This, together with her strong analytical mind and in-depth knowledge of country and policy issues has made her a highly effective representative of the Fund. . . ."

Economics Update

At **ClassZone.com** students can find an update on where Anne Krueger's career has taken her since she left the IMF.

ECONOMICS PACESETTER

Anne Krueger: Reforming IMF Development Policy

On September 1, 2001, Anne Krueger became First Deputy Director of the International Monetary Fund. Ten days later, the terrorist attacks on the United States sent shockwaves through the global economy. Three months later, Argentina suspended payments on its $132 billion foreign debt. At the time, this was the biggest default in history. All the while, there were significant economic upheavals as well as international protests over the burden of debt in developing nations. Clearly, she didn't have the luxury of easing into her new position.

FAST FACTS

Anne O. Krueger

Title: First Deputy Managing Director of the IMF, September 2001 to August 2006

Born: February 12, 1934, New York City

Major Publications Edited:

Reforming India's Economic, Financial, and Fiscal Policies. Edited with Sajjid Z. Chinoy, 2003

Latin American Macroeconomic Reform: The Second Stage. Edited with Jose Antonion Gonzales, Vittorio Corbo, and Aaron Tornell, 2003

Selected Awards:

- Distinguished Fellow and past President of the American Economic Association
- Frank E. Seidman Distinguished Award in political economy (1993)
- Bernard Harms Prize awarded by the Kiel Institute of World Economics (1990)

Economics Update

Find an update on Anne Krueger at **ClassZone.com**

A New Role for IMF

Luckily, Krueger came very well prepared for her new job. In addition to her professorships at Stanford University, Duke University, and the University of Minnesota, Krueger had also been Director of the Center for Research on Economic Development and Policy Reform, at Stanford, and the Vice President of Economics and Research at the World Bank.

In November 2001, anticipating Argentina's default, Krueger put forward a proposal for the role of the IMF in debt restructuring and dispute resolution. In her proposal, the IMF would oversee the restructuring of the debt rather than simply providing bailout funds. The reform effort also called for collective action clauses, measures that let a supermajority of creditors overrule a creditor who is holding out for more repayment than may be possible. In fact, after several years of negotiations, most of Argentina's creditors accepted 35 cents on the dollar in early 2005, and Argentina's credit rating climbed once again.

Even 35 cents on the dollar, however, seems too high to many critics, who believe that debt in most developing nations should be forgiven 100 percent so the money used to service the debt can be put to use providing such needed human services as health care and education. Krueger has disagreed: ". . . Unless there is radical change from past behavior on the part of the debtors, their priorities for the use of released resources are not likely to be on education, health, or other expenditures that will enable the poor to improve their lot." Nonetheless, the IMF is part of a plan to forgive debt completely in 18 of the most heavily indebted poor nations in exchange for economic policies that favor trade liberalization and other development goals.

Anne Krueger

APPLICATION Solving Economic Problems

C. Krueger believes that direct aid to nongovernmental organizations working in health or education are more effective than debt cancellation. Critics argue that grants with conditions show the IMFs desire to control nations' economies. Who do you agree with? Give reasons for your answers.

DIFFERENTIATING INSTRUCTION

Struggling Readers

Generalize from Details
Direct students' attention to the feature's first paragraph. Ask them if they can identify a topic sentence. Some may say the first sentence, however, the real topic sentence is implied. Have students identify events in the paragraph and note them on the board. Then, ask them what the events have in common. *(They all signal significant disruptions in the global economy.)* Help students frame a topic sentence using that idea.

English Learners

Read and Discuss
Have an English speaker and English learner work together, reading and discussing each paragraph of this feature. Point out that there is at least one word and one phrase in the feature that may need some special explanation: *bailout* and *cents on the dollar.* Have the English learner tell the English speaker what those words are in his or her first language.

SECTION 2 Assessment

Online Quiz
ClassZone.com

REVIEWING KEY CONCEPTS

1. Explain the relationship between this pair of terms:
   a. *International Monetary Fund*
   b. *stabilization program*
2. What are four key sources of funding for development?
3. How can a nation develop its human capital?
4. How can a nation improve its business climate?
5. What roles do foreign nations play in a country's development?
6. **Using Your Notes** Use your completed cluster diagram to help you explain how the economic development of one nation might be an opportunity for growth for another nation. Use the Graphic Organizer at **Interactive Review @ ClassZone.com**

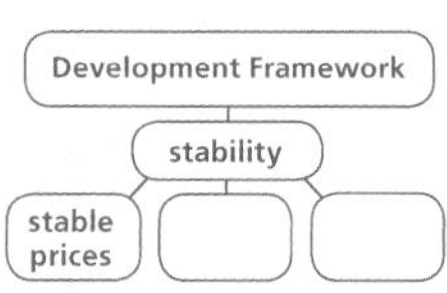

CRITICAL THINKING

7. **Analyzing Cause and Effect** How might the bailout by an international agency of a nation that has defaulted on foreign debt lead to more corruption in the future?
8. **Writing About Economics** Many economists believe that a country that is rich in a particular natural resource may actually be at a developmental disadvantage. They point out that nations such as these tend to put all of their resources into this one industry. Write a paragraph about how you, as leader of a nation, would use the large income from your nation's natural resource to take other avenues to developing your economy.
9. **Applying Economic Concepts** Look again at Figure 18.5. The United States grants aid money each year to nations in the developing world. Do you think Anne Krueger would think this aid money should come with certain terms or conditions? Explain.
10. **Challenge** If you were in charge of development efforts for a poor nation, which source of development funds would you focus on? Why?

ECONOMICS IN PRACTICE

Understanding the Path to Development
Read the following scenarios of fictional less developed countries:

- In nation A, there is a democratically elected government, but a corrupt law enforcement system has made property rights shaky. There is little foreign trade, and few foreign firms have set up manufacturing facilities. However, a foreign nation gives nation A hundreds of millions of dollars in aid each year.
- In nation B, the move toward democracy has begun. A system of fair and transparent law enforcement is in place, and international trade and foreign direct investment are on the rise. High levels of foreign debt, however, could pose a problem in the future.

Categorizing Economic Information Is nation A or nation B more likely on a path to successful development? Explain why you think so.

Challenge What's more beneficial to development— a connection to a large amount of foreign aid money or a plan to increase social, political, and economic stability? Why?

4 Assess & Reteach

Assess Have students answer questions 1–5 on paper. Discuss them as a class. As a class, discuss the issues that are brought up in items 7–10 and the Economics in Practice before having the students attempt to answer them on paper. Go over these questions as a class as well when the students complete their responses.

Unit 7 Resource Book
- Section Quiz, p. 81

Interactive Review @ ClassZone.com
- Section Quiz

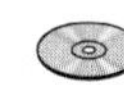

Test Generator CD-ROM
- Section Quiz

Reteach Use the metaphor implied in the title of Section 2 as a way to reteach the material. Work with students to construct a visual "framework" for development incorporating the key elements included in each lesson (Resources, Stability, Opportunity, and Financing). For examples, these may be pillars holding up a structure called Economic Development. Make several notes for each element in the framework, so that students can use the visual to review the material on their own. Create the collaborative framework on the board, but have students copy it onto their own papers.

Unit 7 Resource Book
- Reteaching Activity, p. 82

SECTION 2 ASSESSMENT ANSWERS

Reviewing Key Concepts

1. a. *International Monetary Fund*, p. 559
   b. *stabilization program*, p. 559
2. internal investment; foreign private investment, foreign aid or loans from another nation; aid from an international organization
3. by focusing resources on health care and education
4. by reducing trade barriers and corruption, having fair tax structures, and securing property rights
5. They can invest, through bonds or through multinational corporations; they can provide aid in the form of grants and loans.
6. See page 552 for an example of a completed diagram. Answers will vary, but should show a general understanding of the benefits both nations might receive through trade and investment.

Critical Thinking

7. It may encourage the sort of corruption that got the country in trouble to begin with.
8. The paragraph should stress the importance of investing in human and physical capital and in infrastructure. It might also touch on using the money made from the natural resource to develop other segments of the economy.
9. She would say that recipient nations must make changes that guarantee the money will be put toward useful development projects. She also might press the nations to liberalize trade.
10. Answers will vary, but should show an understanding of the benefits of the chosen source. Possible answer: foreign investment, because it helps the greatest number of people by providing technology, training, and jobs.

Economics in Practice

Categorizing Economic Information Nation B is on the more successful path. In spite of its possible problem with foreign debt, it is putting together the important governmental institutions (democracy, law enforcement, courts) that have already begun to attract foreign investment.

Challenge The plan to increase stability is more beneficial because it will benefit society as a whole. Aid money is often misappropriated and can be taken away by the donor.

1 Plan & Prepare

Section 3 Objectives

- identify problems that emerge when an economy goes from command to market
- describe the transitions to a market economy in the former Soviet Union and nations it dominated
- discuss the transitions to a market economy in China

2 Focus & Motivate

Connecting to Everyday Life Facilitate a discussion about times in students' lives when they faced big changes. Ask them to discuss whether they approached the changes with gradual adjustments or if they were able to adjust quickly. Have students consider the pros and cons of each approach. Then, point out that this section will discuss how the changes in former command economies are being handled.

Taking Notes Remind students to take notes as they read by completing a cluster diagram. They can use the Graphic Organizer at **Interactive Review @ Classzone.com**. A sample is shown below.

Transition to a Market Economy
new challenges
- poor infrastructure: A market economy needs a strong infrastructure to move goods, communication, and people.
- privatization: Moving from state owned to private is a difficult process.
- rise in prices: Shock therapy to a command economy causes prices to rise.

SECTION 3

Transition to a Market Economy

OBJECTIVES

In Section 3 you will
- identify problems that emerge when an economy goes from command to market
- describe the transitions to a market economy in the former Soviet Union and nations it dominated
- discuss the transitions to a market economy in China

KEY TERMS

privatization, *p. 563*
shock therapy, *p. 563*
perestroika, *p. 564*
special economic zone (SEZ), *p. 567*

TAKING NOTES

As you read Section 3, complete a cluster diagram like the one shown, using the key concepts and other helpful words and phrases. Use the Graphic Organizer at **Interactive Review @ ClassZone.com**

Transition to a Market Economy
new challenges

New Challenges

KEY CONCEPTS

In Chapter 2, you read about different economic systems, including a command, or centrally planned, economy in which all economic decisions are made by the society's leaders, usually government officials acting in a central location. For a while, much of the world's population lived in a command economy. However, China, the nations that formerly made up the Soviet Union, and many Eastern European countries have taken steps toward a market economy. The transition requires new answers to the basic economic questions that central planners used to answer. Both the government and private individuals and companies face a number of challenges.

CHALLENGE 1 Poor Infrastructure

A market economy needs a solid infrastructure to facilitate the production and distribution of goods and services. In a command economy, transportation, communications, banking, and education—the infrastructure of an industrialized nation—are as inefficient as other industries tend to be. With no competition there is little incentive to create a more robust physical and institutional infrastructure. Modernized airports, phone systems, roads, harbors, bridges, and computer connections help a transitional economy support and spread the goods and services it produces.

Bridging the Gap Transportation infrastructure is vital to develop a successful market economy.

SECTION 3 PROGRAM RESOURCES

ON LEVEL

Lesson Plans
- Core, p. 63

Unit 7 Resource Book
- Reading Study Guide, pp. 83–84
- Economic Simulations, pp. 99–100
- Section Quiz, p. 91

STRUGGLING READERS

Unit 7 Resource Book
- Reading Study Guide with Additional Support, pp. 85–87
- Reteaching Activity, p. 92

ENGLISH LEARNERS

Unit 7 Resource Book
- Reading Study Guide with Additional Support (Spanish), pp. 88–90

INCLUSION

Lesson Plans
- Modified for Inclusion, p. 63

GIFTED AND TALENTED

Unit 7 Resource Book
- Case Study Resources: China: Rich Country, Poor Country, pp. 97–98

TECHNOLOGY

eEdition DVD-ROM
eEdition Online
Power Presentation DVD-ROM
Economics Concepts Transparencies
- CT63 Post-Soviet States

Daily Test Practice Transparencies, TT63
ClassZone.com

CHALLENGE 2 Privatization

Under communism, the government owns all property. As transitional nations move toward a market economy, they have all undertaken the challenges of **privatization**, the process of transferring state owned-property and businesses to individuals. A major problem with privatization is how to sell the property. It can, for example, be auctioned off, but command economies have little private savings, and few people have the needed finances. Also, as you'll read later, these auctions can sometimes be rigged to benefit those close to the ruling elites. A second method is to sell shares of businesses through a vehicle like the stock market. A third way is to give vouchers to people to purchase shares of a business, making cash unnecessary.

> **QUICK REFERENCE**
>
> **Privatization** is the process of transferring state owned property and businesses to individuals.

CHALLENGE 3 Rise in Prices

In a command economy, some goods may have artificially low prices. Part of the switch to a market economy is the removal of price controls, allowing the market to operate. On January 1, 1990, Poland's government gave the go-ahead for an economic program referred to as **shock therapy,** involving the abrupt shift from a command to a free-market economy. The initial result indeed shocked consumers; the inflation rate that first month was 78 percent. However, this inflationary "correction" eased as the free-market policies were allowed to take hold. (See Figure 18.6.)

> **QUICK REFERENCE**
>
> **Shock therapy** is an economic program involving the abrupt shift from a command economy to a free-market economy.

FIGURE 18.6 POLAND'S INFLATION RATE AFTER SHOCK THERAPY

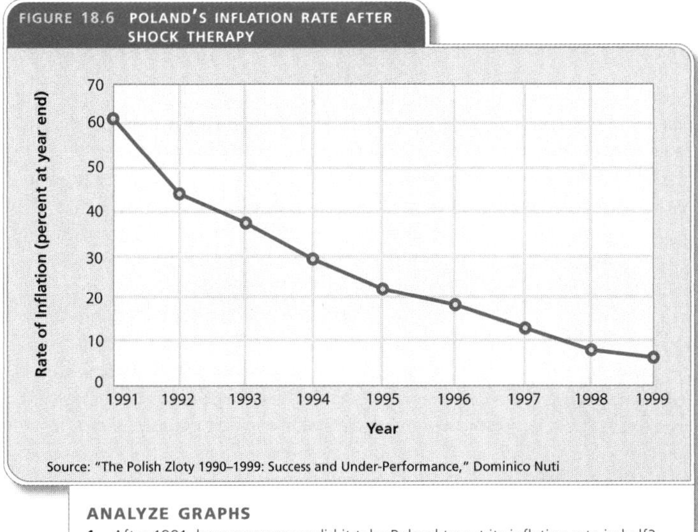

Source: "The Polish Zloty 1990–1999: Success and Under-Performance," Dominico Nuti

ANALYZE GRAPHS

1. After 1991, how many years did it take Poland to cut its inflation rate in half?
2. Why did the inflation rate consistently decrease after the initial "shock" of 1991?

APPLICATION Making Inferences and Drawing Conclusions

A. Which of the challenges above do you think is the most serious? Give reasons for your answer. Sample answers: privatization, because it marks a total shift in the way an economy operates; poor infrastructure, since fixing this requires large amounts of cash that these economies don't have

3 Teach

New Challenges

Discuss

- How might workers need to adjust their attitudes during a transition from a command to a market economy? *(In a command economy, with no competition for their labor, workers have little incentive to increase productivity. They are given production quotas that focus only on the number of items produced, not their quality. The results are sometimes shoddy. With the change to a market economy, workers can no longer continue with poor work habits—a market economy will drive such workers out of their jobs.)*

Analyze Graphs: Figure 18.6

Ask students to explain why the biggest drop in the inflation rate occurred in the first year. *(Possible answers: The inflation rate was high as a result of the shock therapy. So, when market forces had a chance to regulate the economy, the drop was dramatic.)*

Answers

1. *three*
2. *Free market policies were instituted, and as they took hold, inflation decreased.*

LEVELED ACTIVITY

Understanding Approaches to Transition

Time 30–45 Minutes 

Objective Students will demonstrate an understanding of the range of approaches that nations have taken in the transition to a market economy.

Basic

Briefly describe the approach China, Russia, Poland, and other Eastern European nations have taken as they make a transition from a command to a market economy. Write at least three sentences about each one. Focus especially on the pace of change during the transition period.

On Level

Write an essay on the transition from a command to a market economy. Use the examples of China, Russia, Poland, and other Eastern European nations to show the issues involved and the different approaches. Begin with an introduction that contains a thesis statement and end with a conclusion that draws your ideas together.

Challenge

In a persuasive essay, evaluate the approaches to transition that China, Russia, Poland, and other Eastern European nations have taken. Put forward an opinion about which approach seems best, and support it with solid examples and reasoning. Be sure to define the qualities that make one approach better than another.

Economic Change in the Former Soviet Bloc

Discuss

- Although they might be present in varying degrees, what characteristics of a transitional economy do Russia, the former Soviet Republics, and the nations of Eastern Europe have in common? *(inflation, poor infrastructure, an underground economy, poor protection of property rights, unemployment)*
- What effect do you think Western franchises, such as a McDonald's and IKEA, are having on the economy of Poland? *(Possible answer: providing jobs and expertise in running businesses)*

More About . . .

Mikhail Khodorkovsky

After foreign investors lost money when the ruble collapsed in 1998, Russians found it very difficult to attract Western business investment in Russian enterprises. To improve the situation, Khodorkovsky took the unprecedented step of creating transparency in the petroleum company Yukos.

Khodorkovsky revealed his controlling stake in the company and the identity of other shareholders, started paying taxes, hired Westerners in prominent positions, and started following international business standards. As a result, Westerners began investing in Russia again. However, after Khodorkovsky was arrested, possibly for political reasons, the business climate was once again tainted by the arbitrary application of laws.

Economic Change in the Former Soviet Bloc

QUICK REFERENCE

Perestroika was a gradual plan to incorporate markets into the Soviet Union's command economy.

KEY CONCEPTS

In the 1980s, Soviet leader Mikhail Gorbachev introduced **perestroika**, a plan to gradually incorporate markets into the Soviet Union's command economy. People began to push for political freedom as well, and in 1991 the Soviet Union dissolved. The collapse of the Soviet Union caused a period of dramatic transition throughout Eastern Europe and Central Asia.

EXAMPLE 1 Russia

The transition has been a turbulent time for Russia. Like Poland and several other Eastern European nations, it pursued a program of economic "shock therapy." The resulting inflation was devastating. Supplies of goods were very low, and many industries were forced into bankruptcy when faced with the need to become "self-financing." Further, the state was poorly equipped to carry out even the most basic functions of government, such as tax collection. As a result, with little revenue to work with, it could not offer welfare services to cover the disruptions of the economic shift, and the burden of government debt began to rise.

Amid the upheaval, some market forces began to exert themselves. Without directives from central planners, regional business initiatives could address the real demands of consumers. In 1992, a program of privatization began to put the means of production into private ownership, introducing incentives for success.

The privatization process, however, was fixed in favor of certain individuals. As a result, a small group of politically well-connected business people snapped up many of Russia's former public assets through a series of rigged auctions. These oligarchs, as they're known, went on to build massive corporations and became the most powerful economic force in modern Russia.

At Will Oligarchs? The prosecution of Khodorkovsky was seen by many as a warning to Russia's oligarchs: the price of opposition to Putin's government may be your freedom.

The best-known oligarch, Mikhail Khodorkovsky, has recently been sentenced to nine years in prison on fraud and tax evasion charges. In addition, his giant oil company, Yukos, was taken over by the government. It is widely believed that the charges against him were motivated by his support for political parties that were opposed to Russia's president, Vladimir Putin. Many saw this case and others as symptoms of Putin's reluctance to truly adopt democratic reforms and a market economy. Taken together, Putin's actions, the power of Russian organized crime, and the persistence of widespread corruption threatened to undermine Russia's successful development.

DIFFERENTIATING INSTRUCTION

Struggling Readers

Recognize Organizational Cues

Direct students to the first paragraph on this page. Have a volunteer read the paragraph aloud. Then ask what students think they can expect from the remaining portions of text. Point out that the first paragraph contains a map of what is to follow, especially the final sentence in the paragraph. It also gives cues about the order in which topics will be covered. Explain that readers can use these cues to prepare themselves for what is to come.

English Learners

Frame Questions

For practice in writing and interpreting academic English, pair students for this activity. Have each student write a question about the material on pages 564–565 that would be suitable for a brief essay-type answer. Then, have pairs exchange questions and write a response to their partner's question. When they have finished, have them read their responses and discuss them.

EXAMPLE 2 Former Soviet Republics

The transition of the former Soviet Republics has been varied. The Baltic Republics—Latvia, Lithuania, and Estonia—have fared better than others, experiencing a 45 percent inflation rate while Ukraine had a 400 percent rate and Kazakhstan in Central Asia had a rate higher than 1,000 percent. Of all the former republics, only the Baltic Republics, Armenia, Belarus, and Kazakhstan have a higher output now than they did before the collapse of the Soviet Union. Nevertheless, many economists believe the quality of goods and services produced is higher. In the other republics, poor infrastructure, complicated bureaucracies, undeveloped property laws, and corruption have interfered with economic growth.

Vilnius Since independence, the capital of Lithuania has thrived. It accounts for one-third of the nation's GDP and attracted 2.815 billion euros in FDI in 2005.

EXAMPLE 3 Eastern Europe

The formerly Communist nations of Eastern European have faced some of the same challenges as their neighbors and had similarly varying degrees of success. The largest nations, the Czech Republic, Hungary, and Poland, are now much like Western countries. They are members of the European Union, but some experts believe they will need until 2035 to catch up economically with other member nations. Nonetheless, progress is apparent. Since the transition, Poland's economy has been growing at an average rate of 6 percent annually, industrial productivity has increased by more than 20 percent, and the private sector is responsible for more than 70 percent of the national income. There are more than 2.5 million small- or medium-sized businesses operating today, and Western franchises, such as the McDonald Corporation and the IKEA Group, have become entrenched.

However, Poland also has problems that are common across the nations of Eastern Europe. Its infrastructure is out of date, and telephone and internet services are very costly. The laws for registering to do business in the Polish market are confusing, and the patent process that protects property rights is slow. The health care and pension systems have weakened, and unemployment is high. Averaged throughout the country, the unemployment rate is about 18 percent, but in some regions it is as high as 40 percent, and workers are discouraged. In Hungary, the illegal "hidden economy" may account for up to 30 percent of GDP.

APPLICATION Comparing and Contrasting Economic Information

B. Which of the three regions—Russia, the former Soviet Republics, or Eastern European nations—has had the hardest transition? Explain your answer. Students will probably choose Russia's transition as the most difficult, noting the troubles after shock therapy, the complete collapse in 1998, and the reduced output.

International Economics

Post-Soviet Organization

After the collapse of the Soviet Union, the former Soviet republics sought ways to cooperate regionally to improve their economic conditions. The challenge was to determine with which region to cooperate.

One attempt resulted in creation of the Commonwealth of Independent States. This organization failed to coalesce. But its members, including Russia, Belarus, Ukraine, and Kazakhstan, agreed to form a new customs union, the Common Economic Space (CES). Meanwhile, the Baltic states of Lithuania, Latvia, and Estonia forged alliances with Western European nations and joined the European Union in 2004.

More About . . .

Vilnius

Recent surveys by the French Geographical Institute have placed the exact center of Europe very close to the city of Vilnius at 54°54′ N, 25°19′ E. As a result, Lithuania undertook the building of a monument to its centrality—the Geographical Centre of Europe monument.

The history of Vilnius dates back to medieval times, but city planners have developed a bustling new city center dominated by the Europa Tower. This modern landmark is 423 feet high, has 33 floors, and is the tallest high-rise building in the Baltic states. It was opened as part of the celebrations to mark Lithuania's joining the European Union in 2004.

SMALL GROUP ACTIVITY

Filing a Field Report

Time 45 Minutes

Task Create a news report from a region within the former Soviet Union or a country in Eastern Europe telling what you see as signs of the transition.

Materials Needed paper and pens

Activity

- Divide students into three groups, one for Russia, one for the former Soviet republics, and one for Eastern Europe.
- Instruct each group to use the information on these pages, from elsewhere in the book, or in some other source at hand (a geography text, for example) and write an "eyewitness" news report on economic conditions today.
- Instruct students to divide the reporting duties, so that everyone gets "camera time."

Rubric

	Understanding of Changes in the Soviet Bloc	Presentation of Information
4	excellent	creative, thoughtful, and accurate
3	good	clear and accurate
2	fair	unclear or inaccurate
1	poor	unclear, inaccurate

China Moves Toward a Market Economy

Discuss

- Why do you think the "household responsibility system" was effective? *(It provided an incentive for efficiency.)*
- Do you think a gradual, scattered program like China's would have been a better idea than the shock therapy in places like Poland and Russia? Explain your answer. *(Answers will vary. Look for an understanding of the high toll of shock therapy, as well as its effectiveness over time, and an understanding of the scattered approach China took, with its pluses and minuses.)*

More About . . .

China's Urban/Rural Divide
At the annual meeting of the National People's Congress in China in 2006, government officials promised reforms aimed at creating a "new socialist countryside." This resulted from growing numbers of rural uprisings. One report lists 87,000 "mass incidents" involving peasants and other rural workers in 2005.

These incidents were protests—often with fatalities—against the government takeover of land for factories, the resulting environmental degradation, and the huge income gap between urban and rural China, estimated to be at a 3:1 ratio. Since about 60 percent of China's population lives in rural areas, the image of China's modernization and rapid economic growth is only part of the picture.

China Moves Toward a Market Economy

KEY CONCEPTS

China became a Communist country in 1949, but it began a transition to a free market economy in 1978. At that time, its leader, Deng Xiaoping, introduced free market economic principles to stimulate China's economy. The result was a vastly changed and rapidly growing economy.

EXAMPLE Rapid but Uneven Growth

In the early years of China's Communist economy, central planners focused on redistributing land, developing heavy industry, and improving China's transportation system. In 1958, the government introduced the Great Leap Forward. This plan focused on the building of huge collective farms and the development of the steel industry. For a while, both agricultural and steel output increased. However, the gains were short-lived. Poor economic planning and a series of natural disasters led to stark times. Millions of people died in famines.

When Deng Xiaoping came to power in the late 1970s, hundreds of millions of Chinese villagers lived in poverty, sometimes sharing one pair of trousers among a whole family. Deng brought hope and practical programs to the people. "It is time to prosper. . . . To get rich is glorious," he said. Deng began a far-reaching but gradual program to relax government control over the economy and let market forces drive economic growth.

In agriculture, farmland that had been confiscated was returned to the farmers in household units. Under this "household responsibility system," farms still had to supply a quota of staple goods to the government at set prices, but beyond that the farmers could grow what they wanted and sell any surplus on the open market. China reported a ten percent annual growth in agricultural output between 1979 and 1984. Brick homes began to replace thatched huts as farmers' income soared.

A Growing Divide Modernization has come at breakneck speed in many of China's urban centers, while life in rural China can seem to be in a different century.

DIFFERENTIATING INSTRUCTION

Inclusion

Make a Time Line
To help students keep the information on these pages clearly in mind, work with them to make a time line of the events discussed. Point out that they can easily start this process by simply looking for the dates in the text and making notations regarding what happened at each point along the time line. Use the board to make a large, easy-to-read time line that students can copy in their notebooks.

Gifted and Talented

Research and Present
Direct students to use the Internet or other current sources to research a region of China—a special economic zone, a city, or a rural area. Have them develop a detailed picture of the daily life of the people living there—their clothing, food, education, health-care options, work, and future outlook. Then, have students share the written pictures of their region with others and discuss the similarities and differences between regions.

In the mid-1980s, Deng focused his reform effort on industry, where two-thirds of the manufacturing plants were still state-owned. Deng moved slowly and cautiously. Instead of privatizing suddenly or making drastic, uniform changes, he scattered the reforms among different industries. In one industry, local managers might have more decision-making power. In another, workers might get raises based on the profits of the factory. Deng's reforms also called for localities to invest in the industries they thought would thrive. In this process, resources were re-allocated from heavy to light industry, a key factor in China's rapid growth.

Deng also created **special economic zones (SEZs)**, regions that have economic laws that are different from a country's usual economic laws, with the goal of increasing foreign investment. The first four were begun in 1979 as an experiment. In 1984, fourteen more were created in cities along the coast, including Shanghai; now there are hundreds. The SEZs have tax incentives for foreign investment, and the economic activities are driven entirely by market forces. Further, when capitalist Hong Kong was returned to China in 1997 after a 99-year lease by the United Kingdom, it was reunified under the "one country, two systems" framework. The government did not interfere with its economy; in fact, it became a model for the nation.

Areas with high foreign investment have raced ahead of other parts of the country economically, contributing to China's annual growth in GDP of between 5 and 15 percent since the reforms began. Some people, encouraged by Deng's proclamation, have become very rich. However, in 2003, the number of people living in extreme poverty (on less than $77 a year) rose for the first time in 25 years, to about 3 percent of the population. In some villages of western China, 90 percent of the people live on government welfare and do not have indoor plumbing or telephones.

QUICK REFERENCE

A **special economic zone (SEZ)** is a geographical region that has economic laws that are different from a country's usual economic laws, with the goal of increasing foreign investment.

Economics Update

Find an update on China's special economic zones at **ClassZone.com**

FIGURE 18.7 ANNUAL ECONOMIC GROWTH RATE, CHINA AND SELECTED DEVELOPED NATIONS

KEY: China, Ireland, Japan, United States

Annual economic growth rate (percent)

Year

Source: CIA World Factbook

APPLICATION **Explaining an Economic Concept**

C. What role do the SEZs play in China's transition to a market economy?

They contain the impact of market forces so there is no shock as there was in Russia, and they also set a model of development for the rest of the nation.

More About . . .

Hong Kong's Economic Significance

The importance of Hong Kong in the Chinese economy is hard to overstate. The 11th largest trading economy in the world, Hong Kong is also the most important distribution center for the Chinese mainland. Further, at the end of 2005, fully 45 percent of foreign direct investment in China was localized in Hong Kong.

China is also one of the most important investors in the Hong Kong economy, accounting for about 29 percent of Hong Kong's domestic investment. Hong Kong also ranks second in the world in per capita holdings of foreign exchange reserves.

Economics Update

At **ClassZone.com** students will see updated information on China's special economic zones.

Analyzing Graphs, Figure 18.7

Ask students to pose questions that are suggested by the dramatic movements in the lines on this graph. They may include: Why did the GDP of Japan drop so sharply between 1996 and 1998? What happened between 2000–2001 that might explain the sudden drop in GDP in the United States? Tell students that, in the age of Internet search engines, answers to these questions can be found using fairly general search terms. An example might be *recession Japan 1996–1998*.

INDIVIDUAL ACTIVITY

Researching Special Economic Zones

Time 60 Minutes 

Task Choose an SEZ and write a report covering basic information about it.

Materials Needed research sources, pens and paper, or computer with printer

Activity

- Instruct students to do preliminary research on China's SEZs and then choose one that interests them. Their choice of SEZ must also have sufficient information available to use in a report.
- Tell students that the following topics must be covered in their reports: the location of the SEZ, the specialty of the SEZ, the history of the SEZ, the role of the SEZ in China's economy, and a representative sample of its daily life.
- Encourage students to choose a means of presenting their information that will make it clear and engaging.
- Have students present the results of their research to the rest of the class.

Rubric

	Understanding of SEZs in China	Presentation of Information
4	excellent	thorough, creative
3	good	mostly complete, creative
2	fair	less than complete, somewhat creative
1	poor	incomplete, uncreative

Using a Decision-Making Process

1 Plan & Prepare

Objectives

- Use a decision-making process.
- Analyze an application of the decision-making process.

2 Focus & Motivate

Facilitate a discussion about the kinds and number of decisions students make every day. Ask them to articulate what process they use to make decisions and to give examples. As students offer their thoughts, you may wish to note various stages of the decision-making process on the board to be compared to those offered in the Skillbuilder.

3 Teach

After having students read through this Skillbuilder, review the four stages of the decision-making process and compare them to those you noted during the students' discussion.

For additional practice see **Skillbuilder Handbook**, page R17.

THINKING ECONOMICALLY Answers

1. *The Chinese government had to decide how to handle the flooding of the Chang, or Yangtze, River, which had killed over a million people over the previous 100 years. They decided that damming the river was their best decision.*
2. *The large amount of hydropower generated and the ability of large, ocean-going ships to sail 1,500 miles inland likely helped make damming the government's choice.*
3. *Over a million people have to be resettled. This may cause overpopulation or large-scale migration; either could be economically damaging. Also, pollution and extinctions can have serious consequences and point to other damage yet to come.*

ECONOMICS SKILLBUILDER

For more on using a decision-making process, see the Skillbuilder Handbook, page R17.

Using a Decision-Making Process

Making decisions in complicated situations can be extremely difficult. Having a plan, or process, in place can be quite helpful.

TECHNIQUES USED IN MAKING DECISIONS Making decisions involves (1) gathering information to identify the situation in question, (2) identifying options, (3) predicting consequences, and (4) implementing a decision. The following passage describes the problem of flooding on China's Chang River. It illustrates the decision-making process.

Look for information that points to a situation that requires a decision. Figures on the deadly toll of flooding show that a decision on damming was needed.

Predict possible consequences. The positive and negative results of the dam are listed.

Controlling the Chang River

In the past 100 years, more than 1 million people have died as a result of flooding along China's Chang (Yangtze) River. After devastating floods in the 1950s, Chinese leader Mao Zedong ordered studies to see whether damming the river was feasible. Finally, in the 1990s, construction began on the Three Gorges Dam, which—when completed—will be the largest dam in the world. In addition to providing flood control, the dam will be a source of hydropower. Its turbines are expected to produce up to one-ninth of China's electricity. The dam's series of locks will allow ocean-going ships to sail 1,500 miles inland.

Nevertheless, the project has serious drawbacks. For one thing, it will require the resettlement of an estimated 1.2 million people. Environmentalists warn of water pollution, as well as the eradication of migratory fish and rare plants. The dam is scheduled for completion in 2009. In the meantime, the Chinese government has already begun to address the problem of pollution with the building of at least one comprehensive sewage treatment plant.

Look for any options that are offered. Here, only the option of damming the river is considered.

Decide what the result was. The dam is scheduled to be completed in 2009.

THINKING ECONOMICALLY Making Decisions

1. What choice did the government have regarding the flooding of the Chang River?
2. What economic incentives do you think may have added to the government's decision?
3. What consequences of the decision might be contrary to economic growth? Explain your answer.

568 Chapter 18

DIFFERENTIATING INSTRUCTION

Struggling Readers

Recognize Signal Words

Ask students to make a two-column chart of the positive and negative outcomes of the dam. Then, have them review the text to find words that signal to the reader what kind of information is to follow and write them on their papers. For example, in the first paragraph, the phrase *In addition* signals that more of the same ideas (positive effects in this case) are to follow. In the second paragraph, *nevertheless* signals the change to the drawbacks.

English Learners

Rephrase in a New Framework

Ask students to write the four stages of the decision-making process on a sheet of paper, leaving plenty of space after each one. Then, have them use the passage about the Chang River to show how each part of the process was handled. For example, under the first step—gathering information—students should write something such as the following: The facts show that more than 1 million people have died from flooding in 100 years.

SECTION 3 Assessment

REVIEWING KEY CONCEPTS

1. 1. Explain the difference between these terms:
   a. *shock therapy* b. *perestroika*
2. What makes privatization a challenge in transitional economies?
3. What role does infrastructure play in transitional economies?
4. Why are special economic zones important to the growth of the Chinese economy?
5. In what way(s) is privatization an element of China's shift to a market economy?
6. **Using Your Notes** Write a summary of the challenges of economic transitions and explain how they have been addressed in the former Soviet bloc and in China. Refer to your completed cluster diagram.

   Use the Graphic Organizer at **Online Review @ ClassZone.com**

CRITICAL THINKING

7. **Comparing and Contrasting Economic Information** What are three key differences between the economic transitions of the former Soviet bloc and China?
8. **Making Inferences and Drawing Conclusions** While China has welcomed western economic principles, it has continued to come down hard on political freedoms. For example, Deng crushed protesters in Tiananmen Square in 1989. Why do you think capitalism can grow in China under a restrictive government when in the former Soviet bloc it went hand in hand with political freedom?
9. **Applying Economic Concepts** Explain how life in the former Soviet bloc changed for each of the following during a transition to a market economy.
   a. factory worker **b.** farmer **c.** consumer **d.** factory manager
10. **Challenge** Do businesses from foreign nations with strong anti-pollution laws have a responsibility to voluntarily limit pollution when located in a less developed country with less developed pollution laws? Give reasons for your answer.

ECONOMICS IN PRACTICE

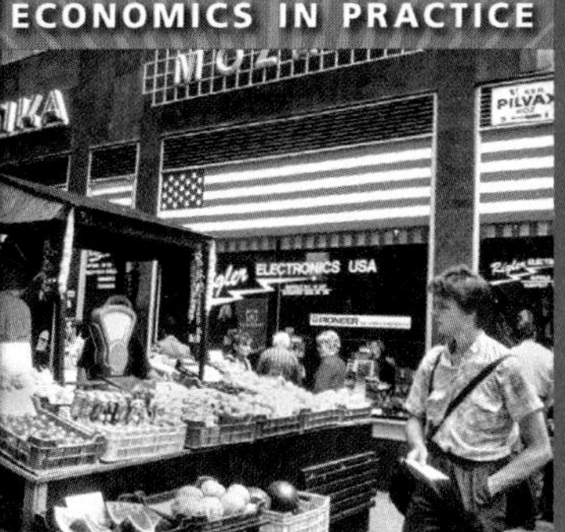

Budapest, Hungary

Assessing Development
The chart below shows statistics from 2004 for Kyrgyzstan and Tajikistan, in Central Asia, and Hungary and Romania, in Eastern Europe.

	Kyrgyzstan	Tajikistan	Hungary	Romania
Gross national income ($ per capita)	268	154	4,913	1,729
Real GDP growth rate	6.0	10.5	3.9	8.1
Industrial production growth rate	6.0	8.2	9.6	4.0
Human development index (HDI)*	0.702	0.652	0.862	0.792

* Highest HDI is 1.0; lowest is 0.0.
Sources: CIA World Factbook; UNDP

Compare and Contrast Economic Information Write a paragraph comparing and contrasting the transition to a market economy in the selected Central Asian and Eastern European countries. Use the figures from the chart to explain the similarities and differences.

Challenge Why might the nation with the highest HDI, Hungary, also have the lowest real GDP growth?

4 Assess & Reteach

Assess You may wish to go over all the questions, except question 6 and question 10, in a whole class discussion. You may want to use question 10 as the subject of a class debate. The Economics in Practice activity is a good opportunity for students to practice comparison and contrast in writing.

Unit 7 Resource Book
- Section Quiz, p. 91

Interactive Review @ ClassZone.com
- Section Quiz

Test Generator CD-ROM
- Section Quiz

Reteach In a class discussion, review the three challenges outlined on pages 562–563 and discuss how they apply to Russia, the former Soviet Republics, Eastern Europe (especially Poland), and China.

Unit 7 Resource Book
- Reteaching Activity, p. 92

Economics in Practice
Comparing and Contrasting Economic Information Answers may reflect these main points: Central Asia nations have low per capita incomes; they still have a lower HDI than Eastern European nations. Hungary's GDP growth rate is low, while Tajikistan is showing high rates of growth.

Challenge Hungary must have outscored the other four countries in some or all of the other indicators (life expectancy, literacy, education) that the HDI reflects.

SECTION 3 ASSESSMENT ANSWERS

Reviewing Key Concepts
1. **a.** *shock therapy*, p. 563
   b. *perestroika*, p. 564
2. how to sell businesses in a country lacking wealth; inefficient old enterprises have trouble competing; possibility of a corrupt process, as in Russia.
3. The poor infrastructure left behind by the command economy inhibits economic growth by making it hard to transport everything, find educated workers, or handle financial transactions.
4. Their special economic laws attracted foreign investment and spurred economic growth.
5. It provided an incentive for people to work to improve their own material well-being, which increased productivity.
6. See page 562 for an example of a completed diagram. Writings should summarize the main points addressed in Section 3.

Critical Thinking
7. Possible answers: China's gradual change versus Russia and Eastern Europe's abrupt one, China's use of SEZs, Russia's problems with oligarchs and organized crime.
8. Answers will vary but may include the idea that the gradual changes in China afforded people a way to work the changes into their political ideology; also, the Chinese government crushed attempts to protest.
9. Sample answers: factory worker—might have lost job as factories went bankrupt; will have to learn new attitudes about productivity on the job; farmer—had more freedom of choice about what to produce and where and how to sell the produce; consumer—faced extremely high prices, though eventually had more consumer goods available for purchase; factory manager—may have had an opportunity for "insider" purchasing as part of privatization program.
10. Answers will vary; look for good reasons.

Economics in Practice
See answers in side column above.

1 Plan & Prepare

Objectives

- analyze sources to synthesize economic information
- examine the domestic and international effects of China's growth

2 Focus & Motivate

Suggest to students that the next time they go to a mid- to low-priced department store they should check a sampling of clothing for the labels that tell where an item was made. It is probable that they will find more made in China than anywhere else. Ask students to discuss why that should matter to them. *(Possible answers: Any future job that they have may be affected by China's economic position in relation to the United States; as a consumer, they will have lower prices.)*

3 Teach

Using the Sources

Encourage students to examine each source to learn more about China's campaign for economic power.

A. What are two reasons for China's growing impact on the global economy? *(China has a vast supply of cheap labor, and it is unusually open to foreign trade and investment.)*

B. What is the impact of expressing the idea of China's volume of exports graphically compared to a simple text description? *(It makes a stronger impression by showing how dominating China's presence is, especially with the ominous red (for Communist) depiction of the shipping container.)*

C. What problems has China's economic expansion brought to the country? *(Answers may vary, but should include the unequal distribution of wealth and the corruption.)*

Economics Update

Go to **ClassZone.com** to find an update to this Case Study, including another article, an editable student worksheet, and an editable lesson plan.

Case Study

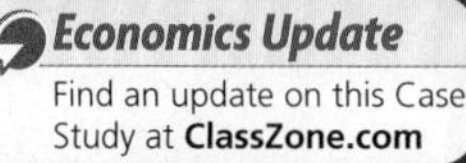

Find an update on this Case Study at **ClassZone.com**

China's Campaign for Economic Power

Background Since 1978, when China's former leader, Deng Xiaoping, made the decision to adopt free-market reforms, China's economy has been steadily gaining momentum. Deng's "four modernizations" (agriculture, industry, science and technology, and defense) have helped China become a player in the global economy in less than a generation.

Its success is based in part on its encouragement of foreign investment, the establishment of a number of special economic zones, and the opening of 14 coastal cities to foreign investment in 1984. Also, in 2001, China joined the World Trade Organization. Today, China's economic impact is too big to ignore.

What's the issue? What accounts for China's successful transition to a market economy? Study these sources to discover what fuels China's economic growth and how it affects the rest of the world.

A. Magazine Article

This article discusses some of the underlying reasons for China's growing impact on the global economy.

The Dragon Awakes

China is changing the dynamics of the global economy.

[China's] contribution to global GDP growth since 2000 has been almost twice as large as that of the next three biggest emerging economies, India, Brazil and Russia, combined. Moreover, there is [a] crucial reason why China's integration into the world economy is today having a bigger global impact than other emerging economies, or than Japan did during its period of rapid growth from the mid-1950s onwards. Uniquely, China combines a vast supply of cheap labor with an economy that is (for its size) unusually open to the rest of the world, in terms of trade and foreign direct investment. The sum of its total exports and imports of goods and services amounts to around 75% of China's GDP; in Japan, India and Brazil the figure is 25–30%. . . . As a result, the dragon's awakening is more traumatic for the rest of the world.

Source: *The Economist*, July 28, 2005

Thinking Economically Identify the aspect of China's economy that, according to the article, has had the most significant impact on the global economy, and explain why its impact has been so great.

570 Chapter 18

DIFFERENTIATING INSTRUCTION

Inclusion

Make Drawings
Read the first and third source aloud. Then, discuss with students how the second source represents the idea without words. Have students create a drawing that represents the ideas in the first source and another drawing that represents the ideas in the third source. After they finish, ask them to explain their drawings to the class or to a small group.

Gifted and Talented

Prepare a Speech
Invite interested students to assume the role of a government official and prepare a speech explaining China's successes, challenges, and specific plans for building on successes and addressing challenges. Suggest to students that they research actual speeches by Chinese leaders to pick up the tone and ideas that underlie the speeches before they write their own. Encourage students to deliver their speeches before the rest of the class.

B. Political Cartoon

The volume of China's exports has gotten a lot of attention in recent years.

Thinking Economically Why is it worth pointing out that China's exporting power seems to outstrip that of other nations?

C. Online News Story

China's economic growth frequently is referred to as an "economic miracle." The miracle, however, is not without problems.

China's Economic Miracle: the High Price of Progress

China's progress is uneven and sometimes problematic.

[China's] GDP is growing by 10 percent a year. Industrial production is galloping ahead at an annual rate of 17 percent. Its economy is now the second-biggest in the world, behind only the U.S., and there are predictions it will assume the top spot as early as 2020. . . .

China's explosive growth has come at a price. The economic gains have not been shared equally. Millions have become richer. But hundreds of millions have not. More than 60 percent of the population still toils in agriculture; the country's "economic miracle" has yet to make an appearance in much of the country. Corruption also remains well entrenched . . . [and] millions of workers have lost their jobs in the restructuring, prompting frequent protests. . . .

Source: CBC News Online, April 20, 2005

Thinking Economically Will China's economic growth alone increase the incomes of its poorest people? Why or why not?

THINKING ECONOMICALLY Synthesizing

1. All three documents point to China's success in international trade. What key element of financing development does document A cite as a component of China's success?
2. Documents A and B hint that the rest of the world is uneasy with China's economic growth, while document C discusses some of China's problems at home. Discuss these fears and problems in the context of what you've learned throughout Chapter 18.
3. Which factors do you think are most significant relative to China's economic growth? Explain why you think so. Use evidence from the documents in your answer.

Thinking Economically

Answers

A. *It does a huge business in importing and exporting, and this has a direct impact on trading partners.*

B. *Possible answers: balance of trade issues are important to other nations; it may signal China beginning to surpass other nations in other ways; other nations may see China as a threat.*

C. *no, because those in China who still work in agriculture don't necessarily benefit from the boom in trade*

Synthesizing

1. *It cites two: openness to international trade and to foreign direct investment.*
2. *Answers will vary. They may take into account the effects China's growth may have on other developing economies. China's manufacturing sector may draw investments away from other less developed countries. China's successful development under an authoritarian regime may also encourage other countries to follow the same path. China's internal problems may be discussed in terms of labor force, development of human capital, or increase in mobility.*
3. *Open international trade and foreign investment are most significant. Documents A and B point directly to these elements. GDP growth, as shown in Documents A and C, is also significant as a marker of China's growth.*

TECHNOLOGY ACTIVITY

Creating an Interactive Map

Time 60 Minutes ●

Task Create a map of China with clickable areas.

Materials Needed computer with software for advanced graphics and web development tools that allow popups and/or mouseovers, previously researched information about key areas in China, computer with access to a projection system for final presentation

Activity

- Organize three student groups.
- Ask group members to share what they learned in their research about areas of China.
- Have students divide the tasks (obtaining an outline map of China; adding color for various regions; writing text for popups or mouseovers; making map clickable) and carry them out.
- Direct students to provide information that will appear in popups or mouseovers on the clickable areas of the map.
- Have each group present its map to the class.

Rubric

	Understanding China's Economy	Presentation of Information
4	excellent	great design, content
3	good	good design, content
2	fair	acceptable design, content
1	poor	little design, incorrect content

Online Summary Answers

1. less developed countries
2. developed nations
3. per capita GDP
4. default
5. debt restructuring
6. privatization
7. shock therapy

Review this chapter using interactive activities at **ClassZone.com**

- Online Summary
- Quizzes
- Vocabulary Flip Cards
- Graphic Organizers
- Review and Study Notes

Online Summary

Complete the following activity either on your own paper or online at **ClassZone.com**

Choose the key concept that best completes the sentence. Not all key concepts will be used.

debt restructuring	per capita GDP
default	"shock therapy"
developed nations	stabilization program
infant mortality rate	privatization
International Monetary Fund (IMF)	World Bank
less developed countries (LDC)	

Nations with little industry and relatively low GDP are said to be __1__, while nations with a market economy and higher standard of living are known as __2__. Economists measure the level of a nation's development through such statistics as __3__, which allows for easy comparison with other countries because it shows the nation's output in relation to its population.

When nations set a course for development, they often seek loans from other nations. Some heavily indebted nations have gone into __4__ on their loans, being unable to pay them back. In those cases, nations can negotiate a __5__ plan to extend the payback and/or lower the payback rate.

Some economies are moving from central planning to an open market. These nations face a number of challenges. For example, there are questions about how to carry out __6__, the transfer of public property into individually owned property. There are also questions about the pace of change. __7__ involved suddenly removing governmental restrictions on the economy.

CHAPTER 18 Assessment

REVIEWING KEY CONCEPTS

Definitions of Development (pp. 544–551)

1. What are some features of a developed nation?
2. Name five measures economists use to gauge a nation's level of development.

A Framework for Economic Development Objectives (pp. 552–561)

3. Describe the internal and external goals a developing nation may set for itself.
4. In what ways can developing nations receive aid from other countries?

Transition to a Market Economy (pp. 562–571)

5. Name five challenges nations face when moving from a command economy to a market economy.
6. Briefly summarize the transition to a market economy in the former Soviet bloc and in China.

APPLYING ECONOMIC CONCEPTS

Look at the graph below showing life expectancy in various countries and regions from 1980 to 2003.

7. What explanation can you offer for the regions in which life expectancy declined?
8. In 2003, how much longer could someone living in a country that belongs to OECD expect to live than someone living in sub-Saharan Africa?

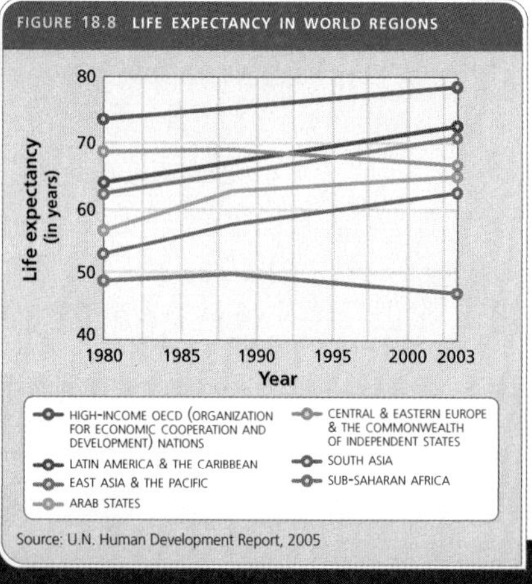

Source: U.N. Human Development Report, 2005

CHAPTER 18 ASSESSMENT ANSWERS

Reviewing Key Concepts

1. high GDP, industrialization, high standard of living, market economy, private property, stable and effective government
2. Possible answers: per capita GDP, human development index, energy use, consumption of goods and services, infant mortality rate, life expectancy, education
3. internal: improve human resources and the business climate; external: attract foreign capital or seek loans or grants
4. loans or grants from individual nations and/or international organizations such as the World Bank or the UNDP
5. privatization, poor infrastructure, rise in prices, poor work attitudes, dealing with political change, unemployment, poor distribution of wealth
6. Possible answer: In the former Soviet bloc, changes were introduced suddenly and were accompanied by political change as well. The economic disruption in the form of inflation, unemployment, and scarcity was significant and the countries are only now beginning to grow again. In China, the changes were more gradual and were not accompanied by political freedom. Market forces were implemented slowly and confined to special economic zones, which have done extremely well.

Applying Economic Concepts

7. Answers should make reference to high versus low levels of development as reflected in standards of development from Section 1.
8. about 32 years

Critical Thinking

9. Graphic should accurately represent the information on the table.
10. East Asia and the Pacific; Europe and Central Asia and Sub-Saharan Africa
11. the economic crises of the countries of the former Soviet Union and Eastern Europe
12. Answers will vary but are likely to touch on the need for protection from terrorist attacks and the promotion of democratic and capitalist

CRITICAL THINKING

9. Creating Graphs Create a graphic of your choice to show the figures below on the percentage of people living on $1 a day or less between 1981 and 2001.

Region	1981	1990	2001
East Asia & Pacific	56.7	29.5	14.3
Europe & Central Asia	0.8	0.5	3.5
Latin America & Caribbean	10.1	11.6	9.9
Middle East & North Africa	5.1	2.3	2.4
South Asia	51.5	41.3	31.9
Sub-Saharan Africa	41.6	44.5	46.4
World	40.4	26.3	20.7

Source: U.N. Human Development Report, 2005

Use SMARTGrapher @ ClassZone.com to complete this activity.

10. Analyzing and Interpreting Data Refer to the graph you created. In which region was the improvement in poverty most dramatic? In which regions did the situation worsen?

11. Analyzing Cause and Effect What might explain why this measure of poverty increased in Europe and Central Asia during this time period?

12. Making Inferences and Drawing Conclusions For each dollar spent on foreign aid by members of OECD, $10 is spent on the military. What can you conclude about the OECD member nations' concerns for the future?

13. Challenge A recent study found that an increase of ten mobile phones per 100 people raised GDP growth in a developing nation by ten percent. What might explain this? What does it suggest as a way to speed development?

SIMULATION

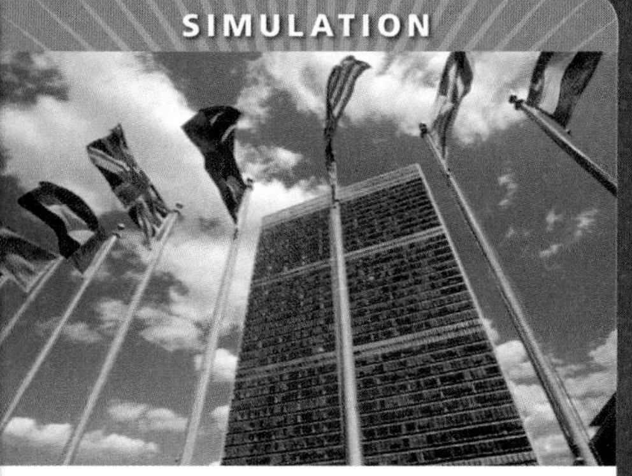

Work Toward Development Goals

In 2005, all the 191 members of the United Nations voted to adopt the Millennium Development Goals, with a target date of 2015 to have the goals realized.

Step 1 As a whole class, discuss the following eight goals that are part of this program:

1. Eradicate extreme poverty and hunger
2. Achieve universal primary education
3. Promote gender equality and empower women
4. Reduce child mortality
5. Improve maternal health
6. Combat HIV/AIDS, malaria, and other diseases
7. Ensure environmental sustainability
8. Develop a global partnership for development

Step 2 Break into eight small groups, one for each of the goals.

Step 3 Meet with your group and discuss concrete ways that the international community (either through such organizations as the IMF or World Bank or United Nations Development Program or through the efforts of individual nations or trading entities) can meet your goal and why it is important that it be met.

Step 4 Present your recommendations to the rest of the class.

Step 5 Follow up on the presentations with a discussion of how many different ways of approaching the problem surfaced and which seem most likely to lead to success.

McDougal Littell **Assessment System**

Assess

Online Test Practice
- Go to **ClassZone.com** for more test practice.

Unit 6 Resource Book
- Chapter Test, Forms A, B, & C, pp. 103–114

Test Generator CD-ROM
- Chapter Test, Forms (A, B, & C), in English and Spanish

Report

Use the McDougal Littell Assessment System to score assessments and receive customized reports.

Reteach

For activities customized for individual students, use the McDougal Littell Assessment System.

CHAPTER 18 ASSESSMENT ANSWERS

allies in developing regions.

13. Answers will vary but may include the idea that cell phones can serve as very cheap computers, letting even isolated fishers or farmers get information on weather reports and prices and other business matters that may help them make decisions that improve their productivity. It suggests that affordable technology that provides self-help is a fruitful avenue for boosting development.

SIMULATION

Encourage discussion that focuses on concrete and specific development ideas and that also recognizes the political challenges involved in issues of global economic development.

Simulation Rubric

	Understanding of Development Goals	Presentation of Information
4	excellent	ideas are well thought out, workable
3	good	ideas are useful, generally workable
2	fair	ideas at times useful, workable
1	poor	ideas will not work

1 Plan & Prepare

Section 1 Objectives

- describe the purpose and process of setting up a budget
- explain how a checking account is useful for managing money
- compare the risk and return of saving and investment options
- identify the three rules for building wealth

2 Focus & Motivate

Connecting to Everyday Life Explain that this section focuses on the importance of budgeting and money management. Invite students to discuss challenges they have had with managing money.

3 Teach

1.1 Budgeting

Discuss

- Why is it important to have a budget? *(because it helps you use your limited funds wisely—to meet present needs without sacrificing future goals)*
- What is the difference between fixed and flexible expenses? *(Fixed expenses must be paid every month in roughly the same amount. Flexible expenses involve choices and may be more or less each month.)*

1 Budgeting and Money Management

1.1 Budgeting

As an independent adult you have the freedom to make your own financial decisions. But with freedom comes responsibility. It takes planning and practice to learn how to use your income wisely, to pay your bills on time, and to have money left to save for the future.

QUICK REFERENCE

A **budget** is a plan for allocating income for saving and spending.

What Would a Budget Do for Me?

Everyone has a limited amount of money. A **budget**—a plan for how to save and spend your income—can help you focus your limited financial resources on what's most important to you. It will help you pay for basics like food, clothing, and shelter. After those expenses are met, it can include optional items such as travel or entertainment. And with savings as part of your budget, you will be on the path to achieve your long-term financial goals.

How Do I Set Up a Budget?

Determine Your Income Make a list of all the steady income you receive, including your pay from after-school and summer jobs and occasional work such as mowing lawns. List only the money you take home after taxes have been withheld from your paycheck.

Track Your Expenses To learn where your money goes, keep a record of all your expenses for a month. Save your receipts, and carry a small notebook to jot down purchases when you make them. The list should cover a full month, because not all expenses occur every week.

Categorize Expenses When you have a record of your expenses, put them into categories, such as transportation, food, clothing, savings, and entertainment. Figure CPF 1 shows how monthly expenses might be categorized to help set up a budget.

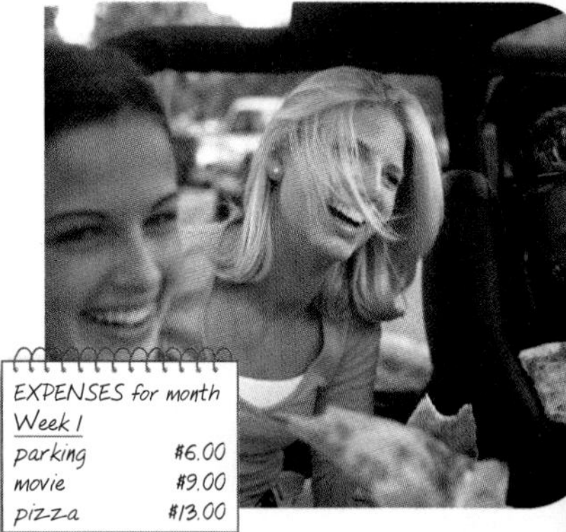

EXPENSES for month
Week 1
parking $6.00
movie $9.00
pizza $13.00

BUDGETING AND MONEY MANAGEMENT PROGRAM RESOURCES

1.1 BUDGETING

Consumer and Personal Finance Activities Book
- Reteaching Activity: Applying Economic Concepts, p. 1
- Applying Personal Finance Skills: Making a Budget, p. 2

1.2 CHECKING ACCOUNTS

Consumer and Personal Finance Activities Book
- Reteaching Activity: Explaining Economic Concepts, p. 3
- Applying Personal Finance Skills: Opening a Checking Account, p. 4

1.3 SAVING AND INVESTING

Consumer and Personal Finance Activities Book
- Reteaching Activity: Explaining Economic Concepts, p. 5
- Applying Personal Finance Skills: Choosing a Savings Account, p. 6

Figure CPF 1 Creating a Budget

(a) **Fixed Expenses** Your car payment and auto insurance are examples of fixed expenses.

(b) **Spending Wisely** Food is a necessity. But packing a lunch, cutting back on snacks, or eating out less often can help your budget.

(c) **Savings** Pay yourself each month. Limiting fixed expenses and reducing flexible expenses will help you meet your savings goals.

(d) **Flexible Expenses** Make room in the budget for entertainment, travel, and other fun stuff.

Monthly Expenses		
Category	**Current Expenses**	**Budget**
(a) **Transportation**		
Car payment	$200	$200
Insurance	70	70
Gas	60	40
Parking	6	0
Maintenance	50	25
(b) **Food**		
School lunches	$85	$80
Snacks	35	30
Eating out	30	15
(c) **Savings**	20	50
Clothing	100	50
(d) **Entertainment**		
Movie tickets	$27	$18
Movie rentals	12	12
Recorded music	20	20
TOTALS	$715	$610

CONSUMER & PERSONAL FINANCE

Determine Fixed and Flexible Expenses Identify which expenses must be paid every month and determine what portion of your income they take. Savings should be a fixed amount, not a flexible amount. Money from savings pays for emergencies, large insurance bills that only come due once or twice a year, and major investments such as cars or real estate. What's left is available for flexible expenses like entertainment.

Set Up a Spending Plan Now look at your income and expenses. Set out a plan for fixed expenses. Look at the amount left over and allocate it to cover the flexible expenses. If your flexible expenses are cutting into your savings or leading to debt, look for ways to cut your spending. For example, you might eat more meals at home instead of at restaurants, or rent DVDs to watch with friends instead of going out to the movies.

Check It Out!

- ✔ Create an emergency fund for unexpected expenses.
- ✔ Save in advance for holiday or birthday gifts.
- ✔ Resist the temptation of impulse buying.

APPLICATION Budgeting

1. Which of the expenses in Step 3 will be monthly bills?
2. **Planning a Budget** Suppose you have a job that brings in $1,150 a month after taxes. You contribute $350 toward rent and utilities each month for an apartment you share with two other people. You put $100 each month into a savings account, and you spend about $50 per month for a cell phone. Of course, you also eat, wear clothes, and go out with friends. You want to buy a car that will cost $300 per month for payments and insurance. Can you afford it? Plan a budget to see if you can take on this new fixed expense.

Analyzing Charts: Figure CPF 1

Explain that this budget reflects a student who is still living at home. Ask what other fixed expenses someone living independently might have. *(housing and utilities)* Have students compare the budget line by line to see where current expenses are greater than the amount budgeted. Discuss ways that expenses might be brought in line with the budget. Suggest that students calculate the totals for each category and see what percentage each is of the total budget. Ask students if they agree or disagree with these spending priorities.

APPLICATION Answers

1. *car payment, savings, possibly insurance*
2. *Answers will vary, depending on allowances for food, clothing, etc.*

FROM THE CLASSROOM

Steve Lueck, Park Hill South High School

The Real World: Monthly Budget for Living on Your Own

You are 18 and right out of high school. Explain the basic expenses you have living on your own. Can you survive?

Find a job appropriate for your age and education. Explain your job and how much you make each month. Subtract 1/3 for taxes.

Explain where you live—apartment, condo, or house—and how much you pay for rent or a mortgage. Don't forget about utilities and cable bills.

Assume you buy a used car. Explain what kind and the monthly payments (divide cost of car by 36). Include auto insurance ($100 per month for girls and $150 per month for guys).

Add budget entries for food, clothing, and entertainment, and explain each. Be sure to include an amount—regardless of how small or large—to deposit to savings each month.

Add up all your expenses and subtract them from your income. Does it balance?

1.2 Checking Accounts

Discuss

- What are the benefits of having a checking account? *(a safe place to keep money, an easy way to pay bills, a way to use ATM or debit cards for electronic banking)*
- How are ATM and debit cards similar? *(Both can be used to access a checking account through ATM machines and to make purchases conveniently.)*

Analyzing Charts: Figure CPF 2

Explain each of the steps in writing a check as indicated in the callouts. Point out that it is also important to enter the date on the check and that businesses will not accept a check that is dated in the future. Some people try to use this practice so that the check will not be cashed until a later date when enough money is available in the account to cover the check. Ask students why they should never sign a blank check. *(because someone could enter a payee name or amount that would not be what the check writer intended and the amount might exceed the money available in the account and result in an overdraft)*

1.2 Checking Accounts

Banks offer two basic types of accounts: checking and savings. Checking accounts are for immediate expenses. They can help you manage your expenses and pay your bills. The bank records deposits and withdrawals on your checking account, whether they are in the form of paper checks, automated teller machine (ATM) transactions, debit card purchases, or electronic transactions.

What Are the Benefits of Checking Accounts?

When you earn money on a regular basis, you should have a place to put it. Most people use checking accounts. Not only is your money safe in the bank, but a checking account makes it easy to pay your bills. In order to use electronic banking and ATMs, you need a checking account.

If you keep all your money as cash, your cash may be lost or stolen. It's also difficult to pay bills with cash. A checking account is safe and convenient.

QUICK REFERENCE

A **minimum balance requirement** is the amount needed in an account to avoid fees.

An **overdraft** is a check that exceeds the account balance.

Opening an Account By shopping around, you can find an account that suits your situation. Ask questions about fees, interest rates paid on the checking account, charges for printing checks, and any restrictions on the number or size of checks you write. Find out the bank's **minimum balance requirement**, which is the amount of money you must keep in the account in order to avoid fees. Most banks charge a high fee for an **overdraft**, a check or other withdrawal for more than the existing account balance.

You'll need several documents to open an account. Most banks require two forms of identification, one of which should have your photo on it. You must provide your Social Security number, address, and phone number. The bank may also ask for a personal or work reference. The money for an initial deposit may be in the form of cash or a check.

Figure CPF 2 Writing a Check

ⓐ Write the full name of the person or business receiving the check.

ⓑ Enter the amount in numbers and then in words on the next line.

ⓒ Sign the check to make it valid. Never sign a blank check.

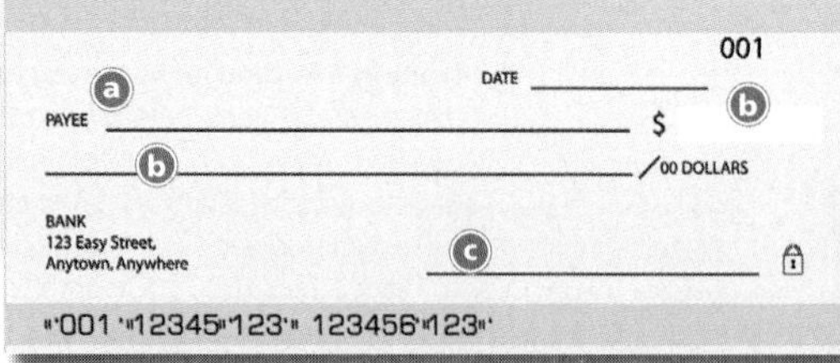

DIFFERENTIATING INSTRUCTION

Struggling Readers

Develop Questions
Help students to understand the types of questions they should ask when opening a bank account. Model a question such as, What kind of fees do you charge for a checking account? Have pairs write out questions on other topics suggested in the paragraph "Opening an Account." Invite volunteers to share their questions with the class and to explain why it is important to find out the answers before choosing to open an account. Clarify understanding as needed.

English Learners

Understand Multiple-Meaning Words
Help students to understand the special meanings of *tell* and *draw* as they relate to banking. Explain that a *teller* may mean someone who speaks, such as a storyteller, but in banking it means "someone who handles transactions." The word *draw* in banking does not mean "to create pictures" but means "to take money out of an account." We also say *withdraw* money from an account. *Overdraw* means "to take out too much money."

What's the Difference Between an ATM Card and a Debit Card?

Once you have a checking account, you have several options for making deposits and withdrawals. You could go to the bank, but that can be time-consuming, and some banks charge a fee for using a human teller. Instead, automated teller machines (ATMs) give you access to your checking account.

At ATMs Both ATM cards and debit cards allow you to use an ATM to access your checking account. You can withdraw cash, deposit cash or checks, or transfer money between linked accounts. Both cards require that you enter your personal identification number (PIN) when you use the ATM.

Using an ATM can cost you money. Most ATMs charge a service fee unless you have an account with that bank. Fees range from $1 to $3 or more. To avoid this expense, learn where your bank has ATMs near your home, school, and workplace.

At Stores You can also use ATM and debit cards at businesses to purchase goods and services. However, debit cards can be used like a credit card—the business swipes your card and you sign for the purchase. With an ATM card, the business must have a keypad for you to enter your PIN. In either case, the money comes directly out of your account. Some stores let you get cash back—with no additional charge—when you make a purchase. For example, if you buy $20 worth of groceries, you can charge your ATM or debit card $50 and receive the $30 difference in cash.

Register all the transactions you make with your ATM or debit card in your checkbook. These transactions will be recorded on the monthly account statement that the bank will send to you, but keep track of them as you go along to avoid overdrawing your account.

Check It Out!

- ✔ Research banking services at several banks.
- ✔ Immediately record your deposits and withdrawals—including checks, cash withdrawals, and purchases—in your checkbook register.
- ✔ Review your bank statement every month.

CONSUMER & PERSONAL FINANCE

APPLICATION Checking Accounts

1. How is a debit card different from an ATM card?
2. **Finding a bank** Using the Internet, research checking accounts at three banks in your neighborhood. Create a table comparing the services offered and fees charged by the banks. Then write a paragraph identifying the bank you would choose if you wanted to open an account and why you would choose it.

More About . . .

Debit Card Usage

Young adults are the age group that most prefers to use debit cards. In 2005, about 28 percent of purchases by those aged 18–24 were made with debit cards, compared to about 7 percent by those over 45. Younger consumers also use credit cards for about 22 percent of their purchases. Cash and checks accounted for about 41 percent. Overall, there were about 23 billion debit card transactions in 2005, totaling $872 billion.

Credit cards accounted for about 20 billion transactions, totaling $1.75 trillion. Many banks have developed special card programs aimed at young adults, and the preferences of younger consumers are leading more merchants to accept debit and credit cards.

APPLICATION Answers

1. *A debit card can be used wherever credit cards are accepted.*
2. *Answers will vary. Tables should list the banks as a header row and the services and fees down the left-most column (or vice versa). The explanation for why a student would choose a bank should cite information from the table, although other reasons are also acceptable.*

CHECK IT OUT!

Prepare a class discussion by asking students to talk to their parents about their checking accounts. Have them find out where their parents bank, how long they have banked there, why they chose that bank, and why they stick with that bank. Have them ask their parents about how they keep track of transactions and how they balance their checkbook. After students have collected this information, lead a discussion on these topics.

1.3 Saving and Investing

Discuss

- Why do financial advisors recommend that you have savings equal to at least three to six months of expenses? *(so that you have funds available to cover expenses in case of emergencies, including inability to work)*
- Why is it important to start investing early? *(to allow more time for wealth to build through the power of compounding and reinvesting)*

Analyzing Charts: Figure CPF 3

Explain that this chart shows the three basic types of government-insured savings accounts. Standard savings accounts are sometimes called statement savings or passbook accounts. Money market accounts pay somewhat higher interest. They allow access through writing checks, but only a limited number per month. They should not be confused with money market mutual funds, which invest in securities with maturity dates of about one year or less and which are offered by brokers and mutual fund companies. Certificates of deposit, despite their name, rarely involve actual certificates. Invite volunteers to summarize the benefits and limitations of each type of savings vehicle.

1.3 Saving and Investing

What are your dreams? Do you want to go to college, to travel, to own a car and a home, or perhaps to retire early? Saving some of your income each month can help you achieve your dreams. Accidents and unforeseen problems happen to everyone, so it is good to have an emergency fund, too. When you save your money at a bank or invest in a company, they pay you for the privilege of using your funds. If you save and invest wisely, your money will grow, and you won't have to work as hard to achieve your dreams.

What Are the Benefits of Savings Accounts?

Savings accounts allow you to save money for future expenses. Your money grows in a savings account because banks pay **interest**, a fee for the use of your money. To open a savings account, you'll need the same kinds of identification and other information that you needed to open a checking account.

QUICK REFERENCE

Interest is the price paid for the use of money.

Types of Accounts Banks and credit unions offer a variety of savings accounts including standard accounts, money market deposit accounts, and certificates of deposit (CDs). The minimum balance, interest rates, and other features vary by type of account. Some banks offer better rates than others, so it's important to shop around for the best deal.

Deposits in these accounts are insured by the government. If the bank should fail, the Federal Deposit Insurance Corporation (FDIC) would make sure you got your money back. The FDIC insures each depositor up to $100,000 at each bank. Retirement accounts are insured up to $250,000.

Unlike stocks, bonds, and many other investments, you are guaranteed to get a positive return on your money in a government-insured account. Figure CPF 3 summarizes the features of the most common types of accounts used for savings.

Figure CPF 3 Government-Insured Accounts

Standard Savings Account	Money Market Account	Certificate of Deposit
A standard savings account requires a small initial deposit and allows you the most access to your money. However, it pays the lowest rate of interest.	A money market account pays higher interest and allows you to write a limited number of checks. But it also requires a higher minimum balance.	Certificates of Deposit (CDs) usually offer the highest interest rates. But you pay a penalty if you withdraw any money before the CD matures.

DIFFERENTIATING INSTRUCTION

Inclusion

Create a Living Graph

Write each type of investment in Figure CPF 4 on a separate large index card. Distribute cards to students. Ask them to arrange themselves in order with lowest risk/return investment on the left and highest risk/return investment on the right. Invite each student to compare the risk and return of the investment on his or her card to those on the cards of adjacent students and explain the reasons why it carries that level of risk and return.

Gifted and Talented

Interview a Financial Planner

Invite interested students to interview a financial planner in their community. Students may use the telephone directory or Internet to find names of advisors. Encourage students to ask the planners what services they offer and how they are paid for their services. Explain that financial planners charge fees for advice and may also earn commissions on products that they sell, such as stocks or insurance. Have students write summaries of their interviews. Allow volunteers to share them with the class.

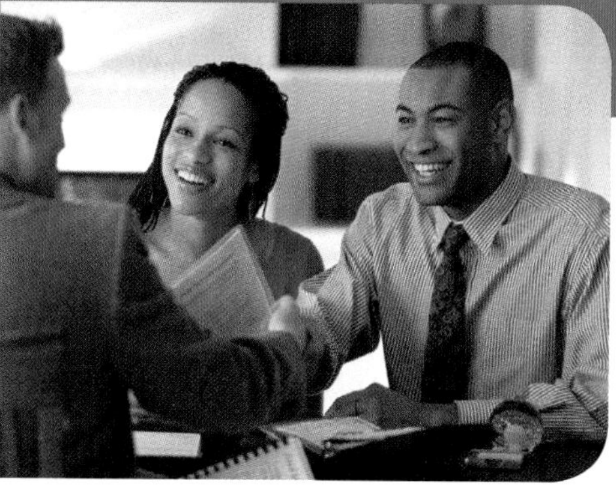

When Should I Start Investing?

The purpose of saving is to accumulate readily available cash. Most financial advisors recommend saving an emergency fund that would cover three to six months of expenses. After you have created your emergency fund, you can begin saving for short-term goals such as buying a car or paying for college tuition.

The purpose of investing is to build wealth—that is, to acquire assets that will grow in value over time and give you a pool of assets beyond the income you earn from a job. Building wealth comes from making your money work for you over a long period of time. It is never too early to start this process, even if you can only allocate a small portion of your income to investment. Investing even small amounts on a regular basis over a long period of time can lead to significant growth.

Before saving or investing, pay off any credit card debt. It is almost impossible to earn more from your investments than you are paying in interest on your debt. For example, if you are paying 15 percent interest on a loan, it doesn't make sense to put some of your money in a savings account that only pays 3 percent interest. Pay off the expensive loan first, then start saving.

Determining Risk As you learned in Chapter 11, there is an inverse relationship between risk and return—the riskier the investment, the greater the potential return. Figure CPF 4 shows this relationship, with the least risky investments at the bottom of the graph and the riskiest ones at the top. Savings accounts and CDs carry little or no risk because the government insures the principal, and they pay a guaranteed rate of interest. Treasury bonds carry little risk because the U.S. government backs them. Corporate bonds carry greater risk because a company may go bankrupt and be unable to repay its creditors. Stocks offer higher possible returns but are subject to market risks and may decrease rather than increase in value.

Figure CPF 4 Risk and Return

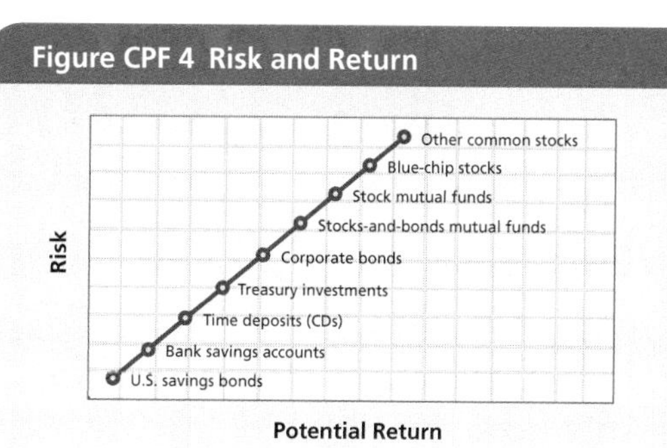

CONSUMER & PERSONAL FINANCE

More About . . .

Financial Advisors
There are four types of financial advisors:

1. Registered representatives, also known as stockbrokers, must be SEC licensed and must work for a licensed NASD broker/dealer. They are primarily compensated through commissions.
2. Registered Investment Advisors, also known as independent financial advisors, must be registered as or work for an RIA. They are primarily compensated through fees and have a fiduciary duty to the client (i.e., must put client's best interest in front of the RIA's).
3. Certified Financial Planners must be certified by the CFP Board of Standards. Certification conveys a specified level of education and experience, ongoing education, and compliance with the CFP code of ethics. May be employed by a broker/dealer, an RIA, or other business.
4. Other. Anyone can call themselves a financial advisor. Many CPA's, attorneys, and agents do so. However, they are not certified or regulated.

Analyzing Charts: Figure CPF 4

Emphasize that investments with a high potential to make money also have a high risk of losing money. Ask students why mutual funds that contain a mix of stocks and bonds are less risky than mutual funds that contain only stocks. *(because bonds are less risky than stocks and, therefore, decrease the risk of the overall investment)*

LEVELED ACTIVITY

Describing Steps Toward Financial Independence

Time 45 minutes

Objective Students will demonstrate an understanding of the steps needed to achieve financial independence. (Draws on material from all four sections of 1.3.)

Basic

Consider the steps you will take after graduation toward achieving financial independence. Create a list of ten guidelines to help achieve that goal, based on what you learned in section 1.3. Include material from each of the four sections that is relevant to your life situation.

On Level

Consider the steps you will take after graduation toward achieving financial independence. Write an essay describing how you will apply the lessons learned in section 1.3. Discuss how ideas from each section are important to your becoming a financially independent adult.

Challenge

Write a series of four advice columns aimed at young adults interested in becoming financially independent. Begin each one with a question from a reader focused on one of the main topics of section 1.3, as indicated by the section titles. Summarize each main idea in your responses.

1 Budgeting and Money Management

International Economics

Mutual Funds

Mutual funds around the world held about $17.77 trillion in assets in 2005. Funds based in the United States held about half of the total. European funds held about a third of the assets, with funds based in Luxembourg and France accounting for the second and third largest amount of assets, respectively. About one-tenth of the assets were in funds based in Africa and the Asia-Pacific region. (Note that these statistics reflect where the mutual fund companies were based, not where they invested their assets.)

Funds in the United States tend to be larger than those in other regions. There were about 8,000 U.S. mutual funds compared to more than 30,000 in Europe and about 12,000 in Asia-Pacific. About 40 percent of all funds were stock funds.

Analyzing Charts: Figure CPF 5

Explain that the first column of the chart lists investment options that may be used by investors to achieve many kinds of investment objectives. The second and third columns are both focused on retirement. Options in column two are mainly offered by employers. IRAs are open to all workers, including those who are self-employed. Ask students the similarities and differences between the two kinds of IRAs. *(Both allow workers to save for retirement with some tax benefits. Traditional IRA contributions may be tax deductible, but you pay taxes when you withdraw the money. Roth IRA contributions are not tax deductible, but withdrawals are tax-free.)*

How Should I Invest?

Consider your investment objective when choosing the type of investment. If you want to use the money to buy a house in five years, you would choose a different type of investment than if you are investing for your retirement. Generally, the sooner you plan to use the money, the more conservatively you should invest. Conversely, the longer you have before you need the money, the easier it will be to recover from any downturns. Figure CPF 5 shows different ways of investing to reach long-term goals.

There are three basic rules for building wealth: start early, buy and hold, and diversify.

Start Early By starting to invest early you have a longer time for wealth to build. A longer investment time frame also allows you to take more risks, because you can ride out the fluctuations in the market.

Buy and Hold The phrase "buy and hold" describes a disciplined approach to investing. Do research and talk to a financial adviser to make wise decisions, and then hold the investments you make for a long enough period of time to allow your wealth to build. Jumping in and out of the market can lead to significant losses of potential return.

Diversify Diversifying helps you maximize your returns and limit risks. You've probably heard the saying "Don't put all your eggs in one basket." Putting your money in different types of investments allows you to choose different levels of risk.

Figure CPF 5 Investment Options

Stocks, Bonds, and Mutual Funds	Employer-Sponsored Retirement Plans	Individual Retirement Accounts (IRAs)
• Stocks let you share in corporate profits. • Government and corporate bonds pay a fixed rate of interest. • Mutual funds are an easy way to invest in a large number of different stocks or bonds. • See Chapter 11 for more information.	• 401(k) plans let workers invest money for retirement and defer taxes. Employers may also contribute. • Pension plans are controlled by employers. • Employers may fund employee retirement benefits through profit sharing or stock ownership plans.	• Workers may invest money each year for retirement, tax deferred. • Traditional IRA contributions may be tax deductible. • Roth IRA contributions are not tax deductible but earn tax-free income. • Funds must be held until age 59½—with some exceptions.

DIFFERENTIATING INSTRUCTION

Inclusion

Expand the Chart

Help students understand the power of compounding by working with them to expand Figure CPF 6. Write the following equation on the board: previous balance + annual investment + return = new balance. Have partners create a four-column chart with the parts of the equation as headings. Explain that the previous balance refers to the new balance at the end of the previous year. The previous balance for year 1 would be zero. Have pairs complete their charts using data from the figure.

Gifted and Talented

Analyze Investment Options

Invite students to use the Internet to find out more about the different investment options outlined in Figure CPF 5. Have students focus on one option listed in columns two and three and discover how it is related to the options listed in column one. Encourage students to learn how much investing in the United States is in the context of saving for retirement. Allow students to hold a panel discussion for the class based on the results of their research.

Figures CPF 6 and 7 The Benefits of Investing Early

FIGURE CPF 6 THE POWER OF COMPOUNDING

Year	Annual Investment (in dollars)	5 Percent Return (in dollars)	Year-end Balance (in dollars)
1	2,000.00	100.00	2,100.00
2	2,000.00	205.00	4,305.00
3	2,000.00	315.25	6,620.25
4	2,000.00	431.01	9,051.26
5	2,000.00	552.56	11,603.82
6	2,000.00	680.19	14,284.01
7	2,000.00	814.20	17,098.21
8	2,000.00	954.91	20,053.12
9	2,000.00	1,102.66	23,155.78
10	2,000.00	1,257.79	26,413.57

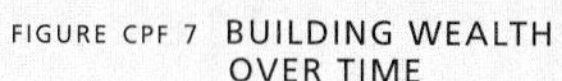

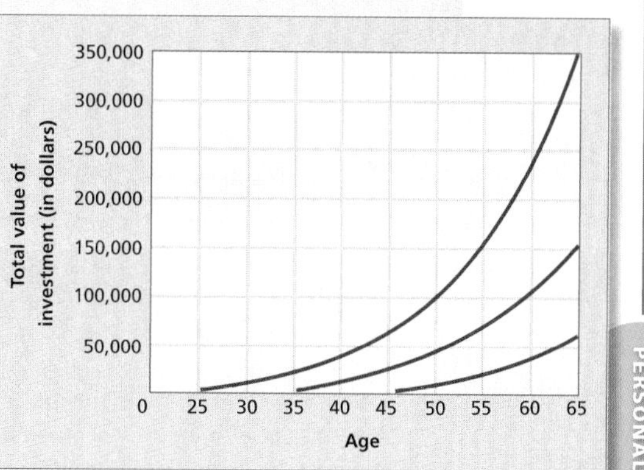

CONSUMER & PERSONAL FINANCE

What Are the Benefits of Starting Early?

Figures CPF 6 and CPF 7 graphically illustrate the benefits of starting your investment program when you are young. The table, Figure CPF 6, shows how a savings account that pays 5 percent interest would grow. Investing $2,000 each year for 10 years—a total of $20,000—yields a balance of more than $26,000 through the benefits of compounding and reinvesting the earnings. If the investments continued at the same pace for 45 years, the total balance would reach almost $1 million.

The graph, Figure CPF 7, shows the benefits of starting to save for retirement early. The graph shows what happens to three people who invest $100 per month in a retirement account. It assumes they receive a return on their investments of 8 percent, which approximates the historical average return for the stock market. Someone who begins investing $100 per month at age 25 has over twice as much at retirement as someone who waits until age 35 and almost six times as much as someone who waits until age 45.

Check It Out!

- ✔ Make regular contributions to your savings account.
- ✔ Commit to investing for the long term.
- ✔ Diversify your investments.

Review Budgeting and Money Management using interactive activities at **ClassZone.com**

APPLICATION Saving and Investing

1. Suppose you have saved $1,000 toward the purchase of a car. Which type of savings plan would be best for this money until you are ready to use it? Why?
2. **Listing Financial Goals** Make a list of financial goals you might want to reach by the time you are 30 years old, then 50 years old, then at retirement age. Think about a plan that might help you achieve these goals. What sort of investments will you make? Write a summary paragraph describing your goals and plans.

Analyze Tables & Graphs: Figures CPF 6 and 7

Remind students that compounding means that interest is paid on the value of the previous interest as well as on the amount of principal invested. Review Figure 11.2 Calculating Interest on page 321, if necessary. Ask students how much the investor in Figure CPF 6 would have earned in the second year if interest had not been compounded. *($200)* Explain that the table and the graph show not only the benefit of compounding but of adding to the principal on a regular basis. The earlier the money is invested, the earlier it benefits from compounding.

More About . . .

Automatic Investing

One of the best ways for investors to build wealth is to invest a small amount of money on a regular basis. Most mutual funds allow investors to set up Automatic Investing plans through which they purchase a set dollar amount of shares monthly or quarterly by transferring money from a checking or money market account.

Mutual funds also encourage investors to reinvest their dividends or capital gains. Many corporations offer Dividend Reinvestment Plans or Drips that allow investors not only to reinvest dividends but also to purchase small amounts of stock on a regular basis.

APPLICATION Answers

1. *A money market account or certificate of deposit would be the best options. Since you will use the money in the near future, you should not put it in risky investments.*
2. *Answers will vary, but should reflect an understanding of chapter concepts.*

CHECK IT OUT!

Set up a spreadsheet that lets students experiment with savings decisions and outcomes. The spreadsheet should allow students to plug in different monthly or yearly contributions and rates of return. The spreadsheet might also have a column for projected "fun money" withdrawals, to show their effect. The spreadsheet can be used for either government insured accounts or riskier investments. But to simulate the stock market, returns should fluctuate—sometimes 15 percent, sometimes 2 percent, etc. Many Internet sites have similar simulations.

1 Plan & Prepare

Section 2 Objectives

- outline the three criteria for qualifying for credit
- learn how to use credit cards responsibly
- discuss what a credit report is and how it is used
- describe common forms of identity theft and explain how to protect against them

2 Focus & Motivate

Connecting to Everyday Life Explain that this section focuses on the use of credit as a way to buy goods and services now and pay for them in the future. Encourage students to discuss reasons that they might have for borrowing money.

3 Teach

2.1 Types of Credit

Discuss

- Compare and contrast loans and credit cards. *(Both are ways of borrowing money, and both must be repaid. Loans are usually for large purchases, such as a car, home, or education. Credit cards are used for smaller purchases and usually charge higher rates of interest than loans.)*
- What is the APR for a credit card? *(an expression of the annual rate of interest charged for balances that are not paid in full each month)*

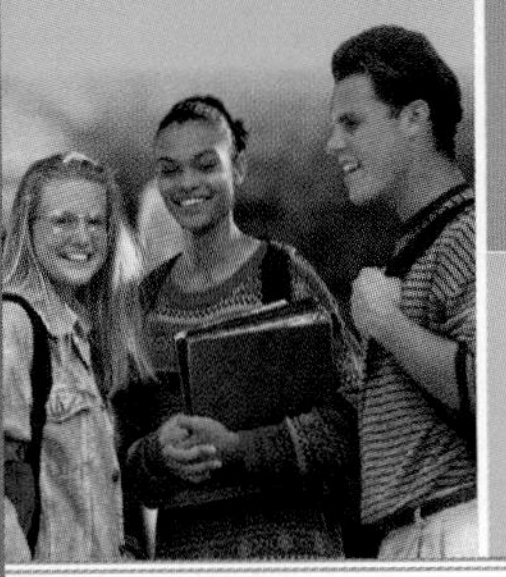

2 Credit

2.1 Types of Credit

If you budget wisely and save your money, you will be able to buy what you need most of the time. But sometimes, waiting to accumulate the money to achieve a goal is not the best economic choice. Using credit to make important purchases, such as a college education or a home, often has economic benefits. If you decide to finance a purchase by using credit, you first need to decide what type of credit to use.

QUICK REFERENCE

Credit is the practice of making a purchase now and paying for it in the future.

A **loan** is borrowed money repaid with interest.

What Is Credit?

Credit is the practice of buying goods or services now and paying for them in the future. One form of credit is a **loan**, which is borrowed money that must be repaid with interest. Just as banks pay you interest for the use of your money in a savings account, you have to pay them interest if you want to use their money to buy something. Loans are usually used for large purchases such as a home, automobile, or school tuition.

Credit cards are like short-term loans, because they allow you to buy things without having the cash at the time of purchase. But you will be charged interest if the credit card balance is not paid in full each month, and credit cards usually charge higher interest rates than other loans.

QUICK REFERENCE

The **finance charge** is the total cost of the loan.

The **annual percentage rate (APR)** is the amount of interest charged per year.

How Much Does Credit Cost?

The cost of credit is called the **finance charge**. It includes the total amount of interest you will pay plus any service charges. The amount of interest you pay depends on the **annual percentage rate (APR)**, the length of the loan, and how often you make payments. With all of these variables, it can be challenging to figure out how much a loan actually costs. But all lenders are

CREDIT PROGRAM RESOURCES

2.1 TYPES OF CREDIT

Consumer and Personal Finance Activities Book

- Reteaching Activity: Making Inferences, p. 7
- Applying Personal Finance Skills: Applying for a Loan, p. 8

2.2 CREDIT REPORTS

Consumer and Personal Finance Activities Book

- Reteaching Activity: Explaining Economic Concepts, p. 9
- Applying Personal Finance Skills: Understanding Credit History, p. 10

2.3 IDENTITY THEFT

Consumer and Personal Finance Activities Book

- Reteaching Activity: Distinguishing Fact from Opinion, p. 11
- Applying Personal Finance Skills: Responding to Identity Theft, p. 12

Figure CPF 8 Costs of Borrowing $10,000

Loan	APR (in percent)	Length of Loan (in months)	Monthly Payment (in dollars)	Total Payments (in dollars)	Finance Charge (in dollars)
A	4	36	295.24	10,628.63	628.63
B	8	36	313.36	11,281.11	1,281.11
C	8	60	202.76	12,165.89	2,165.89

required to tell you the total finance charges and the APR. This information should allow you to understand how much a loan will cost and to compare offers from different lenders.

For example, suppose you want to borrow $10,000 to purchase a car. The finance charge will vary depending on the length of the loan and the interest rate. As you can see in Figure CPF 8, a longer loan might have a lower monthly payment, but it will also have the highest total cost.

How Do Lenders Decide If I Can Get Credit?

Lenders use three basic criteria to determine if you are creditworthy and can be trusted to repay a loan. The criteria—character, capacity, and capital—are often referred to as the three Cs. These three criteria are based on your past, present, and future financial situation.

Character refers to your past record of paying your bills on time. Lenders want to know if you can live within your means, which makes it more likely that you will be able to repay the loan. When you make car payments on time or pay off a department store charge card each month, you build a positive credit history. These actions show that you are financially responsible.

Capacity refers to your level of income relative to the size of the loan. A lender will check to see if you have a steady income and if the amount of your income is enough to make the loan payments. The lender may look at your past employment history to see if you are likely to keep your current job or may check with your employer to see if your income will remain steady over the projected term of the loan.

Capital—specifically, financial capital—includes your income, savings, and other investments. Lenders will consider how much money you have in the bank as well as assets such as a car or house. If you fail to repay the loan, the lender may be able to take these assets to recover the cost of the loan.

If you are weak on any of these criteria a lender might ask for a cosigner for the loan. A **cosigner** is a person who will assume responsibility for the debt if you fail to repay the loan. Taking out a loan with a cosigner but repaying it yourself is one way you can build up a positive credit history.

QUICK REFERENCE

A **cosigner** assumes responsibility for debt if a borrower doesn't repay.

CONSUMER & PERSONAL FINANCE

More About . . .

Cosigning for a Loan
Someone who cosigns for a loan takes on a serious obligation. The cosigner is liable for the entire debt if the primary borrower does not pay it. Banks or collections agencies may choose to go after the cosigner first because they have the right to decide who seems most likely to repay the debt. Therefore, cosigning for a loan can affect the cosigner's credit rating or make it harder for the cosigner to borrow in the future.

Some financial advisors suggest that a parent be the primary holder of a credit card with the young adult child as an authorized user. The primary cardholder is the one who receives the bills and can, therefore, monitor the account to see if debt is accumulating.

Analyzing Tables: Figure CPF 8

Point out to students that Figure CPF 8 shows the costs of borrowing $10,000 at different APRs and for different lengths of time. The cost to the borrower for 36 months at 4 percent is less than half the finance charge at 8 percent. *($628.63 compared to $1,281.11)* Ask them what the difference in borrowing cost is at 8 percent when the loan takes 60 rather than 36 months to repay. *($884.78 more)*

FROM THE CLASSROOM

Bill Smiley, Leigh High School (retired)

Applying for a Business Loan
This role-play helps students to understand the 3 Cs of credit: character, capacity, and capital. Banks use the three Cs when they decide whether to loan money to individuals.

Create profiles for three or four loan applicants who wish to start new businesses. Provide information on the type of business each wishes to start, the amount of start-up capital needed, their education, previous business experience, assets, credit history, etc.

Develop specific questions that a loan officer will ask each applicant. These questions should focus on character, capacity, and capital: Is the borrower trustworthy? Does he or she have a record of honesty and follow-through? Does the borrower have the resources to repay the loan if the business should fail?

Select students to play the applicants and loan officers. After they have reviewed the profiles and questions, hold the mock interviews. After each interview, have the class discuss whether to grant the loan.

More About . . .

Young Adults and Credit Cards
Credit cards have been aggressively marketed to college students since the 1990s. Recently, high school students have been increasingly targeted. Some estimate that about 30 percent of high school seniors and 75 percent to 85 percent of college students have credit cards.

A Federal Reserve study in 2004 found that about half of those ages 20–29 had credit card debt. The median balance was $1,400, but over 3 percent of those in that age group owed $10,000 or more on credit cards.

2 Credit

What Should I Consider When Choosing a Credit Card?

Credit card companies are eager to get young adults to use their cards. But these companies offer a variety of terms, and some of them can be costly. Before you apply for a credit card, carefully examine the terms.

Annual Fee Many cards have no annual fee, but some charge $60 per year or more for membership.

Interest Rate The Truth in Lending Act requires that credit card companies state the interest rate in the form of an annual percentage rate (APR). Rates may be fixed, meaning that they will stay the same, or variable, meaning that they are tied to an index and likely to change frequently.

Grace Period The grace period is the time between your billing date and the date your payment is due. Late payments may result in stiff fees.

Minimum Payment The minimum payment may be a flat amount or a certain percentage of your balance. Paying this amount allows you to avoid paying penalties, but not interest.

Credit Limit The credit limit is the maximum amount you can charge. Your available credit is your credit limit minus any outstanding balance.

Other Fees There are usually fees for paying late or for spending over your credit limit. There may be a minimum finance charge or amount of interest due, or transaction fees for cash advances.

Bonuses Many credit cards offer to give you a bonus based on how much you charge as an incentive to use the card. Some cards offer "cash back"—a refund of a small percentage of your total purchases. Others offer discounts on merchandise or air travel.

WHAT SHOULD I DO IF MY CREDIT CARD IS LOST OR STOLEN?

1. Notify your bank or credit card companies immediately to limit your liability.
2. Report the loss to authorities or law enforcement officials.
3. Keep a list of account numbers and toll-free phone numbers in a safe place.

What Should I Know About My Credit Card Statement?

When you pay by credit card, you will receive a record of what you have spent each month called a statement. It will also show any payments or credits to your account. Check your credit card statement right away to make sure all the purchases shown are ones that you made. Also check to be sure the credit card company received your last payment.

Figure CPF 9 points out some of the important information to notice on your credit card statement. Your new balance is the amount you must pay by the due date to avoid paying interest. The finance charge is the interest due on any unpaid balance from your last statement. Notice that the minimum payment is only a small percentage of your new balance. Credit card companies make money if you pay less than the full balance, because they charge you interest on the rest of your balance.

DIFFERENTIATING INSTRUCTION

Struggling Readers

Create a Chart
Help students compare the features of ATM, debit, and credit cards by completing a three-column chart. Have partners review the relevant material on pages 577 and 585. Encourage them to list the details about each type of card in the appropriate column. Suggest that they use their charts to write a paragraph summarizing the similarities and differences among the cards. Call on volunteers to share their paragraphs with the class. Clarify understanding as needed.

English Learners

Compare and Contrast
Tell students that the word *both* can be used to compare two things, while *but* can be used to contrast two things. Invite students to review material on credit and debit cards on page 585 and look for these clue words. Then, call on volunteers to summarize what they have read with statements that use *but* or *both.* You may want to encourage students to use this strategy to compare and contrast credit cards and loans (page 582) and ATM and debit cards (page 577).

Figure CPF 9 Understanding Your Credit Card Statement

(a) The new balance includes all of your purchases for the month, plus any unpaid balance from the last month and interest, plus any fees. To avoid finance charges, pay the entire balance by the due date.

(b) If you cannot pay the entire balance, pay at least the minimum balance by the due date to avoid late fees. The minimum balance may be only a small percentage of your total balance but is usually at least $10.

(c) The periodic rate is the daily interest rate, that is, the APR divided by the number of days in the year.

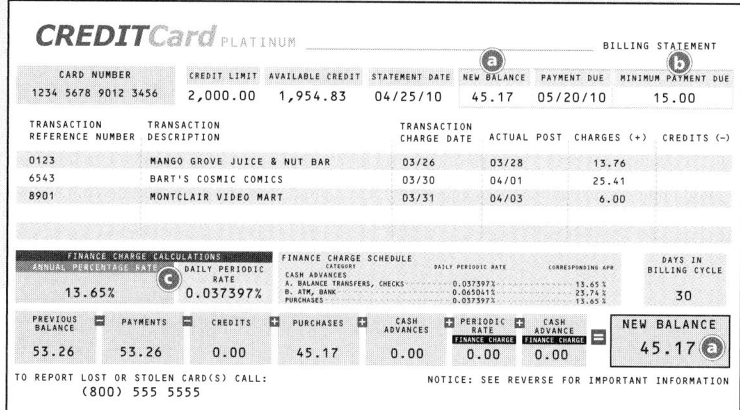

CREDITCard PLATINUM — BILLING STATEMENT

CARD NUMBER	CREDIT LIMIT	AVAILABLE CREDIT	STATEMENT DATE	NEW BALANCE (a)	PAYMENT DUE	MINIMUM PAYMENT DUE (b)
1234 5678 9012 3456	2,000.00	1,954.83	04/25/10	45.17	05/20/10	15.00

TRANSACTION REFERENCE NUMBER	TRANSACTION DESCRIPTION	TRANSACTION CHARGE DATE	ACTUAL POST	CHARGES (+)	CREDITS (–)
0123	MANGO GROVE JUICE & NUT BAR	03/26	03/28	13.76	
6543	BART'S COSMIC COMICS	03/30	04/01	25.41	
8901	MONTCLAIR VIDEO MART	03/31	04/03	6.00	

FINANCE CHARGE CALCULATIONS

ANNUAL PERCENTAGE RATE	DAILY PERIODIC RATE (c)
13.65%	0.037397%

FINANCE CHARGE SCHEDULE

CATEGORY	DAILY PERIODIC RATE	CORRESPONDING APR
CASH ADVANCES		
A. BALANCE TRANSFERS, CHECKS	0.037397%	13.65%
B. ATM, BANK	0.065041%	23.74%
PURCHASES	0.037397%	13.65%

DAYS IN BILLING CYCLE: 30

PREVIOUS BALANCE	– PAYMENTS	– CREDITS	+ PURCHASES	+ CASH ADVANCES	+ PERIODIC RATE FINANCE CHARGE	+ CASH ADVANCE FINANCE CHARGE	= NEW BALANCE
53.26	53.26	0.00	45.17	0.00	0.00	0.00	45.17 (a)

TO REPORT LOST OR STOLEN CARD(S) CALL: (800) 555 5555

NOTICE: SEE REVERSE FOR IMPORTANT INFORMATION

Pay at least the minimum balance by the due date. Most credit card companies charge high fees for late payments. Allow time for your payment to arrive and be processed before the due date.

How Is a Credit Card Different from a Debit Card?

Both cards can be used to make purchases. But when you use a credit card you create a loan to repay, while a debit card takes money directly from your checking account. You can use your debit card to get cash from your checking account at an ATM. But if you use your credit card to get cash, you are essentially taking out a loan. Interest begins accruing right away on the amount of the cash advance, and most cards charge an additional transaction fee. It is a very expensive way to get cash.

Check It Out!

- ✔ Determine all costs and fees for a credit card or loan.
- ✔ Check your statement every month for unauthorized expenses.
- ✔ Pay on time.

APPLICATION Types of Credit

1. What are the three Cs, and who uses them?
2. **Determining the Best Offer** Suppose you have offers from three credit card companies. Company A offers a fixed APR of 12 percent and has an annual fee of $60.00. Company B has no annual fee and offers an introductory rate of 9 percent—but it rises to 18 percent after the first 3 months. Company C offers a fixed APR of 15 percent with an annual fee of $30. If you pay off your balance each month, which offer is best for you?

CONSUMER & PERSONAL FINANCE

Analyzing Charts: Figure CPF 9

Encourage students to read the credit card statement line by line from top to bottom and left to right. Make sure that they understand each term and the amount, date, or percentage listed. The terms described in the text on page 584 may help them clarify items that they are not sure about. For example, ask them how the available credit amount is calculated *(subtract the current balance from the credit limit)* and what the grace period is *(the time between the statement date of 4/25 and the payment due date of 5/20)*. Explain that it is important to check transactions on the statement to make sure they are ones that you made, preferably by comparing them to receipts you saved.

APPLICATION
Answers

1. *character, capacity, capital; used by lenders*
2. *company B, because there are no annual fees—the interest rate is irrelevant if you pay off your balance each month*

CHECK IT OUT!

Lead a discussion about the costs and benefits of living without a credit card. Make a list of each on the board. Assign each student one of the costs or benefits to research. For example, is there an alternative way to buy things over the Internet without a credit card? Are people who don't have credit cards less likely to go bankrupt? After the students have done their research, have them report their findings to the class and discuss.

2.2 Credit Reports

Discuss

- What kind of information is contained in a credit report? *(information on bank accounts, employment, credit history, and financial problems for a period of 7 to 10 years)*
- What does it mean to say that the best cure for credit problems is prevention? *(It is better to avoid credit problems in the first place by managing money wisely than to create problems that need to be fixed.)*

More About . . .

Credit Scores
Many lenders use software developed by Fair Isaac Corporation (FICO) to arrive at a consumer's credit score. FICO scores range from 300 to 850, but most are in the low 700s. Different factors are weighted to determine the score, especially past bill paying history, outstanding debts, and length of credit history.

In 2006, the three major credit bureaus introduced a competitive system known as VantageScore. While the system was designed to make the companies' scores more consistent, it did not solve the problem of incorrect or incomplete information on the credit reports themselves.

2.2 Credit Reports

How you handle your finances can determine your ability to qualify for a loan or credit card, to be hired for a job, or to rent an apartment. Your credit report contains much of the information on the three Cs discussed earlier.

What's a Credit Report?

A **credit report** is a statement by a credit bureau that details a consumer's credit record. Equifax, Experian, and Trans Union are the three companies that handle most credit reporting. The report includes information on your employment, bank accounts, and credit history. It will also indicate if you've had any legal problems regarding your finances, such as bankruptcy. The report shows how well you have handled your financial obligations over the previous 7 to 10 years so lenders can determine if you are a good credit risk.

Credit agencies use the information in your credit report to assign you a **credit score**, a number that rates your credit worthiness. Different agencies use different scoring systems, but higher scores indicate a better credit history. Lenders may charge a lower interest rate to someone with a high credit score.

QUICK REFERENCE

A **credit report** describes a consumer's credit record.

A **credit score** is a number that summarizes your credit worthiness.

Credit Report Users Lenders evaluate your credit report when you apply for a loan or a credit card. Buying the report from one of the three major companies saves them the time of contacting all your creditors to see how well you've paid your bills. Landlords may also check your credit report before agreeing to rent you an apartment. Some employers check credit scores before hiring people. Because so many people rely on these reports, you should verify the accuracy of the information in the report. Checking your credit reports also helps guard against identity theft. (See 2.3 Identity Theft for more information on this topic.)

Where Do I Get My Credit Reports?

online:	www.annualcreditreport.com
phone:	1-877-322-8228
mail:	Annual Credit Report Request Service P.O. Box 105281 Atlanta, GA 30348-5281 (print form at www.annualcreditreport.com)

Do not contact the three nationwide consumer credit reporting companies directly for free reports.

How Do I Get a Copy of My Credit Report?

The Fair Credit Reporting Act makes it easy to access your credit reports (see "Where Do I Get My Credit Reports?" sidebar). By law, you may use this service to order one free copy from each company every 12 months. You provide your name, address, Social Security number, and date of birth. You may be asked other questions to verify your identity.

The government is the only legitimate source for free credit reports.

DIFFERENTIATING INSTRUCTION

Struggling Readers

Use Reciprocal Teaching
Have pairs of students take turns reading paragraphs out loud and asking their partners to summarize what they have just heard. Students who are reading may also ask their partners questions about what they have read. Direct students to discuss all the Application questions together and to agree on answers.

Gifted and Talented

Research Credit Bureaus
Encourage students to use the Internet to research information about one of the three main credit bureaus—Equifax, Experian, or TransUnion. Suggest that students use company Web sites and other sources to prepare an oral report on the company selected. They should provide a company profile, as well as information on what kinds of products and services the companies sell. Allow students to present their reports to the class and to answer questions from classmates about these credit reporting companies.

Figure CPF 10 How Does Your Credit History Rate?

Good Rating
- You pay bills in full
- You pay bills on time
- You can cover payments in case of emergency
- You can make payments if you lose your job

Danger
- More than 25 percent of your take-home pay goes to pay off debt
- You only make minimum payments
- You make payments after the due date
- You open new accounts because the old ones are maxed out
- Creditors harass you

Overextended
- Creditors repossess (take back) what you bought on credit
- Creditors garnish your wages (take money from your paycheck before you get it)
- You must declare bankruptcy

Avoid other sources that claim to offer free credit reports. Some of them want to sell you unnecessary services, and others want to steal your identity. Also avoid firms that promise to fix your credit rating. Only you can do that.

How Do I Solve Credit Problems?

The best cure is prevention. You can avoid credit problems by following your budget and paying off your bills on time. But if you recognize any of the signs of danger or overextension shown in Figure CPF 10, you can take action to avoid financial problems.

Self-Help These are the first steps for restoring your credit rating.
- Talk to your creditors and explain your situation and your desire to correct it.
- Cut up your credit cards and pay off your debts as soon as possible.
- Create a strict budget and follow it.

Professional Help If you are unable to resolve the problems yourself, see a professional counselor. Try nonprofit agencies first. The National Foundation for Credit Counseling can provide referrals. These agencies will provide services and help you to straighten out your debt problems.

Check It Out!

- ✔ Check your credit report yearly.
- ✔ Pay your bills on time.
- ✔ Watch for the danger signs, and act promptly to correct the problem.

APPLICATION Credit Reports

1. What groups might use your credit score?
2. **Paying Off Your Bills** Suppose you have a student loan, a car payment, and a credit card with debt. The student loan debt is $4,000 with interest at APR 8 percent. The car loan is $8,000 with APR of 4 percent. The credit card debt is $1,500 with APR of 18 percent. Your grandmother sends you a check for $1,000 for graduation. Which bill would you put the money towards?

Analyzing Charts: Figure CPF 10

Explain that people with a good rating as reflected by the behavior on the chart will have better credit scores than those in the danger category. They will have an easier time borrowing at the best rates and may also have an easier time renting an apartment or getting a good job. Ask students why it is dangerous to open up new accounts when old ones have reached their credit limits. *(Opening a new account just builds up more debt. Instead, recognize that you have reached a limit and work to pay off your debts before spending more with credit.)*

More About . . .

National Foundation for Credit Counseling

The National Foundation for Credit Counseling (NFCC) is an organization of nonprofit credit counseling agencies. In 2006, it had more than 100 member agencies, with more than 900 offices nationwide. Many members use the name Consumer Credit Counseling Service.

Creditors, such as banks and credit card companies, founded the NFCC in 1951 as the National Foundation for Consumer Credit. It changed its name in 2000. The NFCC provides educational programs and individual counseling services that are either free or at low cost. NFCC members are recognized for their high ethical standards.

APPLICATION Answers

1. *lenders, landlords, employers*
2. *the credit card debt, because it has the highest interest rate*

CHECK IT OUT!

Print out a sample credit report from the Internet. Make copies for the class or make an overhead transparency. Review the report in detail and discuss each section. Ask students what control they have over each item. Emphasize that their day-to-day spending decisions have long-term implications.

2.3 Identity Theft

Discuss

- How can identity theft affect your credit rating? *(Possible answer: Someone might steal personal information and run up debts in your name. This would damage your credit rating.)*
- How are spamming, phishing, and hacking similar? *(They are all ways that identity thieves use technology to steal personal information.)*

International Economics

Identity Theft
Identity theft is a worldwide problem. Information stolen from consumers in one country may be used to withdraw cash or make purchases in another. However, identity theft has been less common in Europe than in the United States, partly because European countries do not rely on a single identification number that is similar to the U.S. Social Security number.

Credit card usage is also lower in Europe. Fraud related to phishing has increased in Britain and Japan in recent years. There have also been instances of information being stolen by employees at customer service centers abroad that affected consumers in several countries.

Economics Update

At **ClassZone.com** students will find updated information on identity theft.

2.3 Identity Theft

Your bank accounts, credit cards, and other financial tools are all tied to your name. You've seen what can happen if your credit report shows a poor credit history. What if a poor credit rating is not your fault?

What Is Identity Theft?

QUICK REFERENCE

Identity theft is the use of someone else's personal information for criminal purposes.

Identity theft is the use of personal information—such as Social Security numbers, credit card or bank account numbers—to commit fraud and other crimes. Identity thieves steal personal information to run up charges on existing accounts or to open new ones. They may withdraw money from your bank accounts, apply for loans, or use your telephone calling card. It takes victims weeks, months, and sometimes years to correct the damage done after their identity has been stolen.

How Can I Protect Myself?

If you know how these thieves operate, you can take measures to protect yourself. While some victims lose their identity through loss or theft of their wallet or purse, almost half of the victims don't know how the thief obtained their information. Here are some of the most common techniques.

Shoulder Surfing Identity thieves may watch you as you punch in a calling card or credit card number or your PIN. They might overhear you giving out an account number over the phone. Be conscious of those around you when you use an ATM or give out personal financial information.

Dumpster Diving Thieves look through the trash to find discarded credit card statements or other documents with financial information. Put such documents through a shredder before throwing them away.

Economics Update

Find an update on identity theft at **ClassZone.com**

Spamming or Phishing Identity thieves may send unsolicited e-mail (spam) that appears to be from a legitimate source. Or they may telephone and say there is a problem with your account or offer you some benefit if you confirm information.

Hacking Sometimes identity thieves will use programs that invade your computer

DIFFERENTIATING INSTRUCTION

English Learners

Understand Colloquial English
Explain to students that terms used to describe identity theft techniques are colloquial terms that have special meanings in this context. *Shoulder surfing* is related to *surfing* as it refers to browsing the Internet or television channels. *Dumpster diving* does not literally mean people jump into trash containers but that they look in them for documents or other useful items. *Phishing* refers to fishing for information through password harvesting. *Hacking* suggests strong computer skills and does not always have negative connotations.

Inclusion

Illustrate Problems and Solutions
Help students to understand the common techniques used by identity thieves that are described on page 588. Allow them to work in pairs to create problem-solution illustrations for each of the techniques described. Have students share their drawings with the class. Discuss ways that people can protect themselves from each of these kinds of identity theft.

and find your personal data. Or they might direct you to a fake Web site set up to look like that of a bank or other business. Security software can help prevent hacking, but you must pay attention when you give out credit card and other personal information over the Internet. Confirm that the site you visit is legitimate.

Where Do I Get More Information?

Department of Justice	www.usdoj.gov
Federal Trade Commission	www.consumer.gov or 1-877-ID-THEFT 1-877-(438-4338)
Consumer Action Web Site	www.consumeraction.gov

What If I Become a Victim?

If you learn that your personal information has been stolen, act immediately to limit the damage. Keep good records of all the steps you take. First, contact one of the three credit reporting companies to place a fraud alert on your credit report. The fraud alert will make it necessary for creditors to contact you before opening new accounts in your name. The Federal Trade Commission and Department of Justice Web sites (see "Where Do I Get More Information?" sidebar) provide toll-free phone numbers and Web site addresses for the credit reporting companies. When you notify one company it will notify the others to place a similar alert on their reports. Once you have placed such an alert, you may order free copies of your report to check for fraudulent activity.

Contact your creditors or banks to close out accounts that have been accessed by thieves or that have been opened without your permission. The FTC Web site also provides a form to dispute new accounts that you did not authorize. You may want to stop payment on any checks that have not cleared and change your ATM account and PIN number.

File a report with the police and get a copy of the report or the report number. Provide as much information as you can. The report will provide proof to your creditors or financial institutions that a crime has been committed. Also file a report with the FTC, which maintains a database of reported cases of identity theft.

Check It Out!

Remember the word SCAM.

- ✔ Be **S**tingy. Only give personal information to people you trust.
- ✔ **C**heck your bank and credit card statements regularly.
- ✔ **A**sk for your credit report every 12 months.
- ✔ **M**aintain careful records of all your financial accounts.

Interactive Review

Review Credit using interactive activities at **ClassZone.com**

APPLICATION Identity Theft

1. What are some ways that identity theft can occur?
2. **Planning a Response** Take a look in your wallet or purse. What items there could be the source of identity theft? How do you protect yourself from having these items stolen? Review how you would respond if these items were stolen.

More About . . .

Identity Theft Statistics

In 2003, the Federal Trade Commission released a study of the impact of identity theft in the United States. From 1998 to 2002, businesses—including financial institutions—lost about $48 billion to identity theft. Over the same period, according to the study, consumer losses totaled about $5 billion.

The Bureau of Justice Statistics estimated that during the last half of 2004 about 3.6 million households had been victims of identity theft. About half of these were unauthorized use of credit cards. People 18 to 24 years of age, those in cities or suburban areas, and those with incomes above $75,000 a year were the most likely victims.

CONSUMER & PERSONAL FINANCE

APPLICATION

Answers

1. *shoulder surfing, dumpster diving, spamming, phishing, hacking*
2. *driver's license, ATM card, debit card, credit card, check book, cell phone, PDA, or any other items that contain significant personal details; keep them with you or in a secure place at all times; photocopy cards; back up PDA info; do not carry passport (unless outside the country) or social security card*

CHECK IT OUT!

Have students use the Internet to find recent stories about identity theft. To avoid duplication, ask different students, or groups of students, to research different topics: a personal account of identity theft; an example of each of the types discussed in section 2.3; statistics on how common the problem is; etc. After they have collected their information, have each student or group discuss their findings.

1 Plan & Prepare

Section 3 Objectives

- describe the process of buying a car
- explore options in higher education and ways to finance it
- explain the importance of insurance and how it works
- outline the things to consider when signing a contract

2 Focus & Motivate

Connecting to Everyday Life Explain that this section focuses on information that will help students make better choices as consumers. Ask students to suggest some important consumer choices that they will face after graduation from high school.

3 Teach

3.1 Buying a Car

Discuss

- What are the main advantages and disadvantages of new and used cars? *(Possible answers: new—covered by warranties, but expensive and depreciate quickly; used—less expensive, but may have hidden problems)*
- What should you beware of if you finance a car through a car dealer? *(Low APR financing for a car at full price might be more expensive than a good deal at a higher APR. Also, be careful to understand all the terms of the loan.)*

3 Wise Choices for Consumers

3.1 Buying a Car

A car is a symbol of freedom and independence. It is convenient to be able to travel where and when you want. Yet owning a car includes financial obligations. Since it's expensive to own a car, first consider whether you really need one. Is good public transportation, such as a bus or a train, available to get you to work or school? Do you live close enough to ride a bike or to walk? If you don't need a car most of the time, would it make sense to rent a car occasionally or to join a car sharing plan?

What Should I Consider When Buying a Car?

If a vehicle is definitely in your future, take your time before you make a purchase. A car is a major investment, so it makes sense to do some research. Use the information in Figure CPF 11 as a starting point.

One decision is whether to buy a new car or a used car. New cars cost a lot and **depreciate**, or decrease in value, quickly. On average a new car loses 10 percent of its value as soon as you drive it off the lot. The biggest advantage new cars have is that they are covered by warranties. If something goes wrong, you probably won't have to dip into your savings to pay repair bills.

QUICK REFERENCE

Depreciate means to decrease in value.

A used car will cost less but may be less reliable. Many experts suggest that cars that are two to three years old offer the best value. Certified used cars come with limited warranties to cover certain major repairs.

How Can I Finance the Purchase of a Car?

If you have not saved enough for the total purchase price of a car, you might consider applying for a car loan. Investigate loans before you shop for the car, so that you will know how much you can afford to spend. Call banks and credit unions and check out online banks to find the best interest rate. Find out the length of available loans, total finance charges, and the amount of your monthly payment. Most lenders will require that you have a down payment on the loan. You may also need a cosigner for your loan.

Beware of financing packages offered by car dealers. Combining price negotiations with financing terms generally results in a good deal for the dealer, not for you.

WISE CHOICES FOR CONSUMERS

3.1 BUYING A CAR

Consumer and Personal Finance Activities Book

- Reteaching Activity: Distinguishing Fact from Opinion, p. 13
- Applying Personal Finance Skills: Considering a Car Purchase, p. 14

3.2 FINANCING YOUR EDUCATION

Consumer and Personal Finance Activities Book

- Reteaching Activity: Clarifying, p. 15
- Applying Personal Finance Skills: Making a Decision About Higher Education, p. 16

3.3 GETTING INSURANCE

Consumer and Personal Finance Activities Book

- Reteaching Activity: Explaining Economic Concepts, p. 17
- Applying Personal Finance Skills: Making Insurance Decisions, p. 18

3.4 CONTRACTS: READING THE FINE PRINT

Consumer and Personal Finance Activities Book

- Reteaching Activity: Clarifying, p. 19
- Applying Personal Finance Skills: Getting the Right Contract for Your Needs, p. 20

Figure CPF 11 Buying a Car

Research

- Decide what kind of vehicle best suits your needs and budget.
- Use Internet or library resources to find out such information as gas mileage, repair costs, safety record, and prices.
- If it's a new car, find out what the dealer paid for the car so you can negotiate a good price.
- If it's a used car, look up the average resale value in a "blue book" (used car price guide).

Looking for cars

- Visit dealer lots when they are closed to get an idea of what's available without sales pressure.
- Ask family and friends about their car-buying experiences. See if they know a reliable dealer or anyone selling a car.
- Check out "for sale" ads in newspapers, on local bulletin boards, or on Web sites.
- Look for dealer ads in newspapers or on the Internet.

Used cars

- Check the odometer. Avoid cars with an average of 15,000 miles per year or more.
- Look for rust, dents, and signs of the car having been in an accident.
- Review the vehicle's repair record. Check for regular maintenance such as oil changes.
- Find the vehicle identification number (VIN), and use it to research the car's history through an Internet service.
- Take a test drive. Test the air conditioner, heater, radio, and other equipment.
- Pay a mechanic you trust to examine the car and to list what needs to be repaired.

The buying experience

- Always go prepared with the information you have gathered.
- Know which options you want and which ones you can live without.
- Get any offer in writing. That way you are very clear on the exact costs.

CONSUMER & PERSONAL FINANCE

Check It Out!

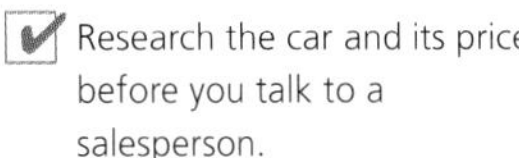

- ✔ Consider whether you really need a car.
- ✔ Research the car and its price before you talk to a salesperson.
- ✔ Be sure you have all the necessary legal documents.

What Should I Do After I Buy a Car?

Each state has laws about vehicle titles, taxes, registration, and insurance. You can learn what is required from a car dealership or your state's motor vehicle department. Call several insurance agencies to find out how much insurance for your vehicle will cost (also see 3.3 Getting Insurance). Keep the title, sales receipts, and other important documents in a safe place—not in the glove compartment. Only the registration and proof of insurance should be carried in the vehicle.

APPLICATION Buying a Car

1. Why should you do research on vehicles before you talk to a dealer?
2. **Planning a Purchase** Choose a particular model of car, new or used. Go to the library or look on the Internet and find information about the car from at least three different sources. Try to learn as much as you can about the car's features, reliability, and pricing, and write down what you learn.

Analyzing Charts: Figure CPF 11

Have students read the bulleted lists under each step, then call on volunteers to summarize the steps in their own words. Ask students why it's best to avoid used cars with 15,000 miles or more per year. *(because that indicates the car has been driven more than average and may not last as long as other cars of the same age)*

APPLICATION Answers

1. *to develop some knowledge of available cars and options so that you can have a more informed conversation*
2. *Answers will vary, but should include details that would help the student make an informed decision.*

FROM THE CLASSROOM

Doug Young, Croton-Harmon High School

Buying a New Vehicle

Buying a motor vehicle involves numerous costs beyond the purchase price. Have students choose a new car or truck and estimate how much it would cost to get it on the road.

(1) Ask students to go online to find the cost of the vehicle with all the options they want.

(2) Then ask them to use a Web site to calculate the costs of a vehicle loan. Have them report the loan amount, interest rate, length, and monthly payments.

(3) Ask students to research the vehicle sales tax in your area and to calculate the tax on their chosen vehicle.

(4) Have students research the fees for title, registration, and license plates. Have them report how much they would pay in fees for the vehicle they selected.

(5) Ask students to call an insurance company to get a quote on insurance for their vehicle.

(6) Have students list the one-time costs, monthly costs, and annual costs of owning this vehicle.

CHECK IT OUT!

Have students research car ownership experiences. If they do not own a car, have them talk with their parents or friends who do. Ask them to learn about the experience of owning a car: How often does the car need oil changes or other regular maintenance? How often does it break down or need other unscheduled repairs? How often have drivers gotten speeding tickets? Have they ever been in an accident? After they have done their research, hold a class discussion.

3.2 Financing Your Education

Discuss

- Why is paying for additional education after high school a good investment? *(because more education generally leads to better jobs and higher earnings)*
- Why do most students need some type of financial aid for higher education? *(because most students are unable to cover all the costs from current income and savings alone)*

More About . . .

Education and Earnings
According to the Bureau of Labor Statistics, higher education significantly increases earnings. In 2003, high school graduates earned a median $554 weekly. Those with an associate's degree earned $672, or 21 percent more; those with a bachelor's degree earned $900, or 62 percent more. Holders of advanced degrees ranged from about $1,060 for those with masters degrees to about $1,350 for those with doctorates. The College Board determined that a college graduate's career earnings were about 73 percent higher than a high school graduate's.

3.2 Financing Your Education

Choosing to go on to college or vocational or technical school after graduation from high school is one of the biggest economic decisions you will make. Getting more schooling will cost you money, but it will pay off in higher salaries and a greater lifetime income. As you learned in Chapter 9, each additional amount of education you receive increases your chances of earning a higher income. More highly educated workers are also less likely to be unemployed. Although the costs of higher education can be daunting, there are many alternatives to help finance your education.

How Do I Decide About Higher Education?

What type of higher education do you want? Choices include college, vocational school, and technical school. Costs at different types of schools vary widely and may influence the type of education you choose. Generally, public colleges are less expensive than private ones, and community colleges are less expensive than four-year schools. Consider your career goals, interests, and aptitudes, and think about what type of school offers the best value that meets your needs.

Do you want to start right after high school? If you want to take a year off, think about what you will do and who will provide your financial support. Consider your income and expenses during that time and what kind of help your parents might give you. Postponing education postpones your future higher earnings and may lead to increased education costs.

Where do you want to go for schooling? Are there schools in your state that would meet your needs? Out-of-state tuition is significantly higher than tuition at a public college in your own state. Going away to school generally means higher costs for housing, food, and travel, but it may be important for other reasons.

DIFFERENTIATING INSTRUCTION

Struggling Readers

Write Study Notes
Organize students into groups of four or five. Provide students with the same number of index cards as there are members of the group. Have each student write the main ideas from one or two of the main question headings in section 3.2. Then have students copy those notes onto their other cards to distribute to the group members. Each student should end up with four or five index cards that identify the important ideas about financing higher education.

English Learners

Analyze Verb Phrases
Some students may have difficulty distinguishing the meaning of verb phrases used on pages 592–595. Write the following on the board: *go on to, go to, go away to, go off to, pay off, pay for.* Read the text with students, including the cartoon on page 594, and pause when you encounter one of the phrases. Point out that different forms of the verbs *go* and *pay* may be used. Have volunteers state the meaning of sentences containing the phrases.

What Will Be the Total Cost of Going to School?

Paying for tuition to cover the costs of your coursework is just the beginning of school expenses. A variety of fees to cover student activities, connection to the school's computer network, and other costs are added to tuition. In the 2005–2006 school year, average tuition and fees ranged from about $2,200 at a public two-year college to about $5,500 at a public four-year college and more than $21,200 at a private four-year college. Room and board costs cover housing and food and average more than $6,600 per year at a public four-year college. You must also buy your textbooks, which may cost as much as $1,000 per year. Transportation for visits home as well as other personal expenses are also part of the costs of going to school.

Economics Update

Find an update on the cost of higher education at **ClassZone.com**

Where Can I Get the Money for Higher Education?

Once you have determined the costs of going to school, you can begin to make decisions about how to pay for your education. Here are some things to think about: Do I have the money to pay for it myself? Will my parents or family help me out? Can I work and study at the same time? Answers to these questions will help you decide if you need financial aid to go on to school.

All the costs of going to school can be daunting. Over 60 percent of students find that they need some financial help. In fact, most students pay much less than the published costs because of financial aid. There are three basic types of financial aid: grants and scholarships, loans, and work-study programs. Figure CPF 12 outlines the characteristics of each type of aid.

Figure CPF 12 Financial Aid Options

Grants	Scholarships	Loans	Work-Study Programs
• do not need to be repaid • usually based on need • sometimes based on academic merit • given by federal and state governments and colleges	• do not need to be repaid • usually based on academic merit or athletic or artistic ability • awarded by colleges, private groups, and the U.S. military	• must be repaid • federal loans for students • federal and private loans for parents • subsidized—based on need, some interest paid by government • unsubsidized—student pays all interest	• college helps student find a job • federal government helps pay the salary • earnings do not need to be repaid • students who work part-time often do better in school

CONSUMER & PERSONAL FINANCE

More About . . .

Rising College Costs

According to the College Board, college costs grew faster than inflation during 1995–2005, and the trend was expected to continue. For the 2004–2005 and 2005–2006 school years, tuition and fees at private four-year colleges rose by almost 6 percent. Costs at public universities grew even more, increasing by more than 10 percent in the 2004–2005 school year and by about 7 percent in 2005–2006.

At the same time, grants accounted for a smaller percentage of federal aid, decreasing from 23 percent in 1995 to 20 percent in 2005. Federal tax credits and deductions account for 9 percent of aid.

Economics Update

At **ClassZone.com** students will see updated information on the cost of higher education.

Analyzing Charts: Figure CPF 12

Have students read the chart column by column to learn the characteristics of each type of financial aid. Then ask them to read across the columns to understand the similarities and differences among the different aid options. Ask students how loans are different from the other forms of aid. *(Loans must be repaid but other aid does not need to be repaid.)*

SMALL GROUP ACTIVITY

Researching Schools and Colleges

Time 45 Minutes

Task Gather information about higher education options and create fact sheets

Materials Needed paper and pens, computer with Internet access

Activity

- Have groups use the Internet or library resources to research different types of higher education institutions in your community or state. Include vocational and technical schools as well as public and private two-year and four-year colleges.
- Depending on the number of institutions in your region, you may assign groups to research individual schools or categories of institutions.
- Direct students to create fact sheets that provide brief summaries of the schools, with special emphasis on costs and financial aid options.
- Compile the fact sheets into a folder or binder for student use.

Rubric

	Understanding of Educational Options	Presentation of Information
4	excellent	clear and complete
3	good	mostly clear
2	fair	somewhat clear
1	poor	sketchy

More About . . .

Student Loan Debt
Rapidly rising college costs and greater reliance on loans as a source of financial aid have left more students with larger amounts of debt. About two-thirds of students had loans in 2000; the average loan balance for undergraduates was almost $19,000 in 2002. In the early 1990s, only about half of students borrowed money, and the average amount owed was about $9,000.

Federal Reserve statistics from 2004 indicate that about 30 percent of people in their 20s had student loan debt, with a median amount owed of $9,200. Almost 20 percent of graduates from colleges and professional schools indicate that the amount of their debt has influenced their career choices.

How Much Aid Can I Get?

In general, the amount of aid you receive is determined by the difference between the cost of attending school and the amount you and your family can contribute. Schools consider the following when awarding financial aid:

- Income—yours and your parents. This is the single most important factor in determining financial aid based on need. Students and families with higher incomes are expected to contribute more.
- Number of higher education students in your family. A family with more than one student in college would be expected to contribute less for each one.
- Family assets and expenses. Students are expected to contribute a higher percentage of their savings than parents are, so it's better to have more savings in parents' accounts. In general, schools do not consider the value of retirement funds, a home, or personal assets such as automobiles in figuring out a family's contribution. Some schools do consider these assets, so it's important to know how the schools you are interested in figure their aid awards. Unusual medical expenses and other large expenses may be considered in determining a family's contribution.

- Pool of aid dollars at the school you want to attend. Schools award aid based on a combination of federal, state, and school funds. A wealthy private school may have more funds available than a state school.
- Number of students applying for aid at the school you want to attend. Since each school has a limited amount of funds available for aid, if more students apply for aid there may be less available for each student. The level of need of the students applying might also affect how much individual students receive.

How Do I Apply?

Start Early Meet with your guidance counselor and request financial aid information from schools at least a year before you plan to start school. Begin to research scholarships. Make note of all application deadlines.

Get a PIN A personal identification number (PIN) allows you to submit your Free Application for Federal Student Aid (FAFSA) online for faster results. Go to www.pin.ed.gov.

DIFFERENTIATING INSTRUCTION

Inclusion

Read in Pairs
Have students work in pairs to read each section of the text. Partners should alternate reading passages aloud and then retelling in their own words what they have read. As students read and retell, they should note any questions that they have. Discuss these questions with the class.

Gifted and Talented

Develop Handouts
Invite students to research one of the Web sites listed in the sidebar on page 595. Encourage them to summarize the types of information available on the site that would be useful to other students. Have students develop handouts about the Web sites to share with their classmates.

Gather All the Documents You Need You'll need income tax returns and W-2 forms for you and your parents, as well as information on nontaxable income. You'll also need your Social Security number and driver's license number, along with bank statements and information on mortgage payments and investments.

Complete the FAFSA Fill out a paper form or go to www.fafsa.ed.gov to apply online. Follow the instructions carefully. You only need to complete one form, which will be used by all the schools to which you are applying.

Fill Out Any Additional Aid Forms These forms may be required for some nonfederal aid such as state and school aid or private scholarships. Ask for recommendations from your teachers and other adults who know you well at least a month before scholarship application deadlines. Provide them any necessary forms and a stamped envelope for the recommender to send to the school.

Where Do I Get More Information?	
Federal Student Aid Information Center	studentaid.ed.gov 1-800-4-FED-AID (1-800-433-3243)
FAFSA on the Web	www.fafsa.ed.gov
The College Board	www.collegeboard.com
SallieMae® loans	www.salliemae.com
Your school guidance counselor and the financial aid offices of the schools you are considering also have information.	

Review Your Student Aid Report (SAR) This report is the result of your FAFSA application. Make sure all the information is accurate. Your SAR shows your Expected Family Contribution (EFC), which determines your eligibility for federal student aid based on need.

Contact Schools' Financial Aid Offices Make sure all schools you've applied to received all the information they need.

Compare Your Aid Awards After you receive responses, decide which school's aid package offers the best combination of grants, scholarships, loans, and work-study.

Check It Out!

- ✔ Get forms in on time.
- ✔ Photocopy all information or print copies of online applications.
- ✔ Make sure information is consistent on all forms.

CONSUMER & PERSONAL FINANCE

APPLICATION Financing Your Education

1. What criteria are used to determine who gets financial aid?
2. **Using a Decision-Making Grid** Using the questions on page 592 and a decision-making grid, determine which type of schooling makes the most economic sense for you.

More About . . .

Federal Student Aid

Federal aid is the largest source of financial aid for higher education for U.S. students. In 2006, more than 10 million students received about $82 billion in federal aid. The Federal Student Aid office of the Department of Education provides the Free Application for Federal Student Aid (FAFSA) as a single application for all forms of federal aid, including grants, loans, work-study funds, and many forms of state and private aid.

About 14 million FAFSAs are processed each year. By providing FAFSA online, the government has made it easier to complete the application accurately and shortened the processing time.

APPLICATION
Answers

1. *income, number of students in family, family assets, school's aid dollars, number of students applying for aid*
2. *Answers will vary, but look for application of section ideas.*

CHECK IT OUT!

Print out a copy of the FAFSA, make copies of it, and distribute. Use an overhead transparency to review the form as a class. Discuss how much time it might take to fill out the form, and when the form is due. If any students have already filled out the FAFSA, get their hints on how to make the process easier.

3.3 Getting Insurance

Discuss

- How and why is the size of the deductible related to the amount of insurance premiums? *(Higher deductibles lead to lower premiums because the insured carries a larger portion of the risk.)*
- Why is insurance that covers full replacement cost more expensive than current value coverage? *(because it covers the cost of buying a new item to replace an older item that was damaged or stolen)*

More About . . .

Insuring Young Drivers

The two most important factors in determining car insurance premiums are the age of the driver and the type of car. Young drivers may pay 25 to 50 percent more for insurance than their parents do because they are more likely to get into an accident. Drivers aged 15 to 20 are only 6.4 percent of all drivers but account for 14 percent of all driver deaths.

Premiums for a young driver with a new car range from $1,000 to $5,000 per year. Premiums usually decrease at ages 21, 25, and 30. Young drivers may have lower premiums if their car is included on their parents' policy. Discounts may also be offered for good grades or completing a driver's education course.

3.3 Getting Insurance

Insurance protects people from the financial effects of unexpected losses. When you buy insurance coverage, your money joins a pool of money from many different people who face similar risks. The system works because the risk is spread over a large group of people. The chances of any one individual suffering a loss are small.

What Are the Benefits of Insurance?

Most people take out insurance for problems that may be unlikely but would be expensive if they happened: medical treatment for a serious illness or accident, repairing a car damaged in an accident, or replacing valuables stolen from your residence. Such losses are potentially so large that it would be difficult to save enough in an emergency fund to pay for them. Insurance protects you financially against those kinds of losses.

What Kinds of Insurance Should I Get?

QUICK REFERENCE

A **premium** is amount paid for insurance.

A **deductible** is an amount paid by the insured before the insurance company pays.

A **co-pay** is an amount due when an insured receives health care.

A **claim** is a request for payment on an insured loss.

When you buy an insurance policy you purchase a certain amount of protection or coverage. Your payment for this protection is called an insurance **premium**. Many types of insurance require you to pay a **deductible**, which is the amount you pay before the insurance company pays on a loss. Some health insurance requires a **co-pay**, an amount you must pay each time you receive health care under your policy. When you have a loss you submit a **claim**, which is a request for payment, to the insurance company.

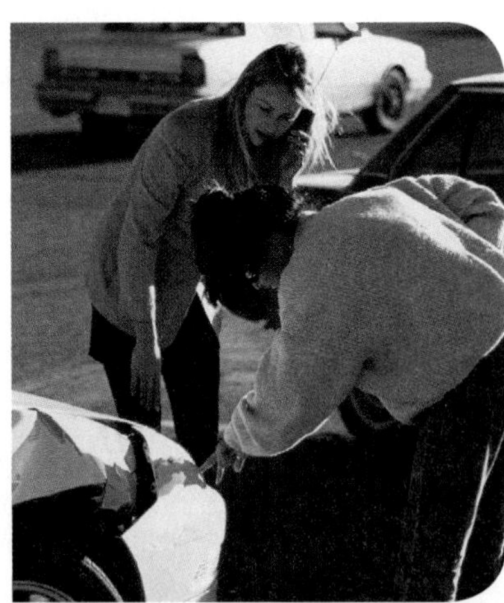

Most people start out with car insurance, health insurance, and renter's or personal property insurance. There are other options as well. See Figure CPF 13 for an overview of the basic types of insurance.

Most states require that you carry at least a minimum amount of car insurance in case of injury or property damage caused by your car. Premiums are based on the type of vehicle, your age, your driving record, and other related information. The more coverage you have the more the insurance will cost. If you carry a high deductible, it will reduce the premium.

DIFFERENTIATING INSTRUCTION

English Learners

Interpret the Photograph

Read the text on page 596 with students. Then, ask them to describe what is shown in the photograph. Invite them to imagine how each young woman feels about the situation and how insurance will help them. Have students write a caption for the photograph that summarizes the importance of car insurance. Invite volunteers to share their captions with the class.

Inclusion

Sequence Events

Help students understand how insurance works. Write each of the following statements on an index card: *States require car insurance. Talk to insurance agents. Buy an insurance policy. Pay premiums. Have a car accident. Submit an insurance claim. Receive payment from the insurance company. Fix my car.* Shuffle the cards and distribute them to students. Ask them to arrange them in the proper sequence, as shown above. Invite volunteers to summarize how insurance works in their own words.

Figure CPF 13 Types of Insurance

Type of Insurance	Protects	Pays
Car	vehicle in case of accident or theft; occupants in case of accident	for property damage and bodily injury, legal costs, and related expenses
Health	policyholder in the event of illness or injury	for doctor and hospital visits, prescription drugs
Homeowner's	structures, land, and personal property	for damage due to fire, theft, or natural disaster
Renter's	personal property	for loss of or damage to personal items
Disability	income when a person cannot work	a percentage of income when a person is out of work due to injury or illness
Life	family when a wage-earner dies	money to the family to meet expenses after death

Health insurance is very costly. Your employer or school may offer insurance plans to cover some or all of your needs. In some states, you may be covered by your parents' health insurance until you graduate from college or reach age 25.

If you live in rented housing, you may want to protect your belongings with renter's insurance or with personal property insurance. Some policies cover the full replacement cost of insured items; others cover only the current value of the items. For example, actual cash value coverage will not cover the full cost of replacing a three-year-old bike that gets stolen.

Check It Out!

- ✔ Find out if you have insurance coverage at work or through your educational institution.
- ✔ See if your insurance covers the current value or the full replacement cost.
- ✔ Determine how much you can afford in deductibles.

What Questions Should I Ask an Insurance Agent?

- How much does the policy cover? Are there limits each year or for each accident or illness? Are there maximums for certain kinds of losses?
- What levels of deductibles are available? Higher deductibles lower the premiums.
- Are claims paid on actual cash value or on replacement value? The former may cost less, but you will receive less in the event of a loss.
- How often are premiums due—monthly or once or twice per year?

APPLICATION Getting Insurance

1. What reasons do people cite for getting insurance?
2. **Selecting Insurance** Explain how having insurance could help in each of the following situations. Case A: Your CD player and 10 CDs are stolen from your car. Case B: You have to have emergency surgery for a fractured leg. Case C: Your car is smashed up by a hit-and-run driver. The damage is well over $2,000.

CONSUMER & PERSONAL FINANCE

Analyzing Tables: Figure CPF 13

Explain that the headings on the chart show the similarities among all kinds of insurance. They all protect against certain losses and pay money to the insureds based on the type of coverage. Encourage students to read each row of the chart using complete sentences to understand each type of insurance. Ask students to compare homeowner's and renter's insurance. *(Both protect personal property; homeowner's also covers the structures and land.)* Why might someone need both health insurance and disability insurance? *(because health insurance only covers medical bills but does not replace income if an illness or accident keeps you from working)*

More About . . .

Health Insurance for Young Adults
Several studies show that young adults under 30 are the largest group of uninsured adults. According to the Federal Reserve, in 2004 about 32 percent of families in their 20s had no health insurance, compared to 21 percent in their 30s, 17 percent in their 40s, and 13 percent in their 50s.

The College Board found that entry-level workers with college degrees were about twice as likely to have employer-sponsored health insurance as were workers with high school diplomas (68 percent compared to 35 percent).

APPLICATION Answers

1. *coverage for expensive risks, such as medical treatment, car accidents, or loss of or damage to property*
2. *A—insurance might pay to replace the CD player and CDs; B—insurance might help pay the medical bills; C—insurance might pay to repair the damage.*

CHECK IT OUT!

Have students ask their parents about the different kinds of insurance the family has. Conduct a discussion about each of the six types of insurance listed in Figure CPF 13, and ask students to contribute what they learned.

3.4 Contracts: Reading the Fine Print

Discuss

- What does the saying "Experience is what you get when you don't read the fine print" mean? *(If you don't read a contract carefully, you may have a bad experience that will teach you to be more careful in the future.)*
- Why might companies put the terms and conditions of a contract in the fine print? *(So they can fulfill legal requirements to provide the information but make it difficult for people to find it.)*

More About . . .

The FTC Cooling-Off Rule

In general, consumers are bound by contracts once they sign them. The FTC regulation known as the Cooling-Off Rule does allow consumers to change their minds about certain purchases. The rule gives consumers three business days after a purchase to cancel the sale or contract for sales over $25 that occurred in certain places.

These places include the buyer's home, workplace, or dormitory or at any facilities temporarily rented by the seller, such as motel rooms, convention centers, or fairgrounds. Exceptions to this rule include sales that were entirely by mail or phone and sales of motor vehicles, real estate, insurance, securities, or arts and crafts sold in public places.

3.4 Contracts: Reading the Fine Print

QUICK REFERENCE

A **contract** is a legally binding agreement.

Buying insurance, taking out a loan, signing up for a credit card—all of these involve a formal, legally binding agreement known as a **contract**. The contract may be in the form of a signed document or may be executed on a Web site when you download something from the Internet. These terms and conditions are called the "fine print" because they are often set in small type.

Why Should I Read the Fine Print?

There's an old saying: "Education is when you read the fine print. Experience is what you get when you don't." By reading the fine print, you will understand exactly what you are agreeing to when you sign a contract. The fine print often contains information about extra charges and fees that may not be displayed in marketing brochures or advertisements.

Consider Michele, a student who signed a cell phone service contract without reading it. When the first bill arrived, it was over $1,000. She checked the contract and found fine print stating that all text messaging both sent and received was subject to a charge. Even though Michele hadn't read these terms, she had signed the contract, and she had to pay the bill.

What Should I Do Before Signing a Contract?

- First, actually read the contract. If it is long or complicated, ask for a copy and take it home to read.
- Clarify all terms or provisions you don't understand. In a cell phone contract, for example, be clear on peak and off-peak hours, roaming charges, and the cancellation policy. Ask questions until you understand everything clearly. If there are parts you can't figure out, get advice from a friend before signing.
- Check all figures in the contract. Bring a calculator and figure the costs yourself—don't depend on the salesperson's math.
- Make sure any mistakes or omissions are corrected on the contract and initialed by the salesperson.

"Sign here to indicate you have no idea what you've signed."

DIFFERENTIATING INSTRUCTION

Struggling Readers

Summarize Information

Have students work in pairs to write a short summary of what they have learned about contracts. Direct students to create a "dos" and "don'ts" list in which they restate each bullet point on pages 598–599 in their own words. Encourage students to use their list to help them formulate the sentences that they want to include in their summaries. Remind students that a summary focuses on main ideas.

Gifted and Talented

Paraphrase Terms and Conditions

Invite students to use their own cell phone contracts or to find one on the Internet that lists terms and conditions. Challenge students to simplify the language in the terms and conditions while retaining the legal agreements. Allow students to share their paraphrased documents with the class and to conduct a tutorial on how to read the terms and conditions in a contract.

Figure CPF 14 A Cell Phone Contract

(a) Note how many minutes are included in the basic monthly price.

(b) Asterisks or footnotes often lead to small print that provides important information.

(c) If you exceed the allotted number of text messages, you pay a fee for each one.

(d) If you want to end your contract before it expires, you pay the cancellation fee.

(e) Your signature here shows that you have read and agree to the fine print.

CellPhone — Service Agreement

Monthly calling plan	$24.95
Total minutes/month (peak)	400 (a)
Unlimited off-peak	$5.95
Voice mail	Included* (b)
Additional minutes	$0.40/minute
Roaming charges (See coverage map and terms for details)	$1.00/minute
Text messaging	$3.95
Total outgoing messages/month	100
Additional outgoing messages	$0.10/each (c)
Incoming messages	Unlimited Free
Plus federal, state, and local taxes and fees	
Contract length	24 months
Cancellation fee	$150.00 (d)

(b) *Accessing voice mail through cellular phone accrues minutes like any other call.

I acknowledge that I have read and agree to the company's Terms and Conditions

(e) (your signature)

What Should I Beware of?

- Don't let the salesperson rush you. Take your time and make sure you are certain of the terms of the contract. Even if the salesperson says certain desirable terms are about to expire, you should not sign anything you do not thoroughly understand and agree to.
- Never sign a contract with blank spaces. Make sure every blank on the contract is either filled in or marked through as being not applicable. If you leave blanks, someone might enter something after you sign that you did not want to agree to.
- Don't agree to verbal contracts. Make sure everything is in writing. If you agree to a verbal contract and run into a problem, you have no evidence of what the agreement was. Business agreements are generally too complex for either side to remember all the details.
- Don't leave without getting a copy of the contract. Keep the contract in a safe place. Check your first bill carefully to make sure everything matches the contract. If you have questions, call the company to resolve your concerns.

Check It Out!

- ✔ If it seems too good to be true, it probably is.
- ✔ Check all figures on the contract.
- ✔ Never sign a contract with blanks not filled in or crossed out.

Interactive Review

Review Wise Choices for Consumers using interactive activities at **ClassZone.com**

APPLICATION Contracts

1. Why shouldn't you agree to a verbal contract?
2. **Evaluating an Offer** Study the ads or commercials for cell phone service. Suppose you are ready to sign a contract for cell phone service. Make a list of the questions you will ask before you sign the contract.

CONSUMER & PERSONAL FINANCE

Analyzing Charts: Figure CPF 14

Have students read the contract line by line and note any areas that might lead to unexpected charges, such as extra minutes, roaming charges, or extra text messages. Ask students how the asterisk modifies the terms of the contract. *(Possible response: There is no extra charge for voice mail but checking voice mail uses up the minutes in the contract.)* What are some terms that a buyer might want to clarify before signing this contract? *(Possible response: What times are included in peak and off-peak? Where do roaming charges apply?)*

APPLICATION
Answers

1. *Verbal contracts provide no evidence of what the details were.*
2. *Possible answers: What is the base monthly fee? How much are additional minutes? How long is the contract? What happens if I cancel? Can I continue to use my old number?*

CHECK IT OUT!

Break students into groups and have each group create a humorous contract between student and teacher, student and parent, or student and another authority figure. Have them make one contract for the student to sign, another for the authority figure to sign. Let each group present its mock-contract to the class, making sure to point out the details in the fine print.

1 Plan & Prepare

Section 4 Objectives

- explore the steps to follow to get a job
- identify the forms needed to file taxes
- explain how to fill out a tax form and file taxes
- describe the process of renting an apartment

2 Focus & Motivate

Connecting to Everyday Life Explain that this section focuses on information that will help students live as independent adults. Invite students to discuss some of the differences between living with their parents and getting out on their own.

3 Teach

4.1 Getting a Job

Discuss

- Why is it important to look in multiple places for job leads? *(because the more sources you explore the better chance you have of finding the best job for you)*
- How might preparing a resumé and list of references help you fill out a job application? *(You will have the information you need in an organized form that is easy to reference.)*

4 Getting Out on Your Own

4.1 Getting a Job

An important step to becoming an independent adult is getting a job. A job allows you to earn money, gain experience, and learn new skills. A career is more than a job. It is a work path that provides satisfaction, challenge, and opportunities for self-expression. Your first jobs help you learn about the world of work and what kind of career you might enjoy.

Where Can I Look for a Job?

Finding a job that suits your skills and helps advance you along your career path can be challenging. There are many sources of information about jobs, and the more you use, the better your chances of finding a good fit.

Friends and Family Talk to them to find out if they know of any job openings. They are the beginning of your network—people who will support you in what you attempt, and whom you support in turn.

School Guidance Counselor, or Career Planning or Placement Office These offices have listings of jobs and intern positions. You can also learn about different careers.

Internet Many Web sites offer job listings, places to post your resumé, and other services. America's Job Bank, managed through a partnership between federal and state governments, allows you to tap into career resources, look at job listings all over the country, and post a resumé.

Newspaper Want Ads Your local newspaper is a good source for jobs in your area.

Employment Agencies Your state and local governments may offer employment services. These public agencies often offer job counseling and training as well as job listings. Private agencies also offer job listings and placement, but they sometimes charge a fee for their services.

Job Fairs Job fairs offer the opportunity to talk to many employers in an area or a specific job category in a very short period of time.

Are you between the ages of 15 to 24 years of
You are invited to a
YOUTH CAREER AND JOB FAIR
Use technology to find job openings • Interview for jobs • Learn about Careers
Saturday, May 3
9 a.m. to Noon
Employment Development Department
1325 Pine Street
Redding, CA
Explore Career Options in...
• Construction
• Auto Body and Repair
• Health Care
• Hospitality and Tourism
• Arts and Communication
• Natural Resources

GETTING OUT ON YOUR OWN PROGRAM RESOURCES

4.1 GETTING A JOB

Consumer and Personal Finance Activities Book
- Reteaching Activity: Sentence Completion, p. 21
- Applying Personal Finance Skills: Applying for a Job, p. 22

4.2 PAYING TAXES

Consumer and Personal Finance Activities Book
- Reteaching Activity: Distinguishing Fact from Opinion, p. 23
- Applying Personal Finance Skills: Filing an Income Tax Return, p. 24

4.3 FINDING AN APARTMENT

Consumer and Personal Finance Activities Book
- Reteaching Activity: Clarifying, p. 25
- Applying Personal Finance Skills: Living with Roommates, p. 26

What Do I Need to Apply for a Job?

Before you apply for a job, you will need to prepare materials that introduce you to potential employers and tell them about your qualifications. You will need a resumé, a cover letter, and a list of references. References are people who know you and your work habits and are willing to talk to potential employers. Many jobs will also require that you fill out an application form.

Resumé A resumé is a record of your job history and education. It should be truthful and succinct—no more than one page long. Since employers judge you by your resumé, be sure it is visually appealing and free of errors. Figure CPF 15 shows a sample resumé for a recent high school graduate. If you apply for different kinds of jobs, you may want to develop more than one resumé.

Cover Letter A cover letter briefly explains why you want the job and how you are qualified for it. Address your letter to the specific individual who is

CONSUMER & PERSONAL FINANCE

Cheryl A. Miller (a)
1909 E. Walnut St.
Long Beach, CA 90811
310-555-5678
camiller89@isp.net

(b) **Objective** To obtain an entry-level customer service position

Education Jefferson High School, 2003-2007

(c) **Experience**
September 2006–Present
Sales Associate, Electronics Super Center
- Advised customers on product features and helped them choose the ones that best met their needs
- Met or exceeded weekly sales quotas
- Developed promotional materials for in-store use

Summer 2006
Administrative Assistant, Oceanside Computer Center
- Tracked customer sales and repair orders to improve response time
- Responded to customer questions by phone and email
- Provided office support for staff of six

September 2005–June 2006
User support, Jefferson High computer lab
- Developed an orientation program for incoming students
- Helped students use a variety of software applications
- Led a workshop on Web page design

(d) **Other Skills**
- Proficient in a wide range of application software, including word processing, spreadsheet, database, and presentations
- Internet research

(e) **Activities and Honors**
- Member of varsity girls' track team
- Captain of debate team

References available upon request

Figure CPF 15
Writing a Resumé

(a) Include all the information an employer might need to contact you.

(b) Make your objective specific and succinct. Tailor it to the job you are applying for.

(c) List your work experience in reverse chronological order. Include volunteer work if you have little paid work experience. Focus on skills and accomplishments.

(d) List other skills you have that might be useful on the job, even if you have not been able to use them in previous jobs.

(e) Include a section that lists activities, honors, and community service.

Analyzing Charts: Figure CPF 15

Invite students to skim the bold headings to get an idea of how the resumé is organized before they read the content. Ask students how this organization might be helpful to potential employers. *(It allows them to skim the information quickly to see if the candidate is qualified for a particular job.)* Point out how the bullet-points in the experience section support Cheryl's objective. Note that each one begins with a verb.

INDIVIDUAL ACTIVITY

Starting a Job Search

Time 45 Minutes 

Task Gather information about jobs of interest and create a database or chart

Materials Needed computer with Internet access, database or word processing software (optional), paper and pens

Activity
- Have students use the sources of information described on page 600 to explore jobs of interest. Some may be jobs they would like to apply for now, while others may be ones for a future career.
- Encourage them to organize information about three to five jobs in a database or table, including notes about why the job appeals to them, their current qualifications, and additional training required.
- Invite students to write a brief summary of the process, including what they learned and follow-up steps they plan to take.

Rubric

	Understanding of Job Search Process	Presentation of Information
4	excellent	clear and complete
3	good	mostly clear
2	fair	somewhat clear
1	poor	sketchy

More About . . .

Cover Letters

While Internet resources and books provide samples of a variety of cover letters, it is important that job seekers learn to write cover letters that are personal and that reflect their ability to communicate in a professional, persuasive, and succinct way.

As much as possible, letters should be tailored to both the specific company and job. Therefore, research begins at this stage, well before the interview. The applicant should try to learn the name of the hiring manager for the particular job. If this is not possible, it is acceptable to address the letter "Dear Hiring Manager." It is essential that the cover letter be free from errors.

designated to receive applications. Open your letter with a strong statement of your interest in this particular job. In the body of the letter, use information from your resumé to explain why you are the best candidate. Close by restating your interest and indicate your intention to follow up to request an interview. Internet and library resources can give you samples of strong cover letters.

Figure CPF 16 References

Cheryl A. Miller
1909 E. Walnut St.
Long Beach, CA 90811
310-555-5678
camiller89@isp.net

References

Barry Woods **Assistant Manager** **Electronics Super Center** 1234 Main St. Long Beach, CA 90811 310-555-1357 bwoods@esc.com	**Cynthia North** **Director** **Jefferson High Computer Lab** 461 Grand Oak Boulevard Long Beach, CA 90811 310-555-1234 c_north@jefferson.lb.ca.edu
Danielle Curran **Office Manager** **Oceanside Computer Center** 4916 Oceanside Road Long Beach, CA 90812 310-555-2468 dmcurran@occ.com	**Julie Barnes** **Moderator** **Jefferson High Debate Team** 461 Grand Oak Boulevard Long Beach, CA 90811 310-555-1345 j_barnes@jefferson.lb.ca.edu

References Before you list someone as a reference, talk with him or her about your job hunt and ask their permission. The list of references should include the person's name, address (either business or home), telephone number, and an e-mail address, if they have one. It's also a good idea to indicate the person's position or relationship to you.

The people you choose as references should know you well enough to be able to describe your skills, experiences, and work habits. Choose people who will be enthusiastic about your abilities based on their experience with you. Typical references include former or current employers, teachers or coaches, or family friends who can vouch for your personal character. Stay in touch with your references during your job hunt. Let them know when they might expect to hear from an employer, and discuss what you would like them to emphasize when they are contacted.

How Can I Ace the Interview?

If an employer gets a good impression of you from your resumé and cover letter, they may invite you to come in for an interview. The interview is a chance for the employer to learn more about you and for you to learn more about the job and the company.

The Company and the Job Do some research on the company to which you are applying. A company's Web site will tell you more about the organization, but you might also find newspaper articles with information about the company. This research will help you to confirm that you are interested in working for the company. It will also show the company that you cared enough about the job to do some investigating before the interview.

DIFFERENTIATING INSTRUCTION

Inclusion

Take Audio Notes

Students who are visually impaired can take notes by making an audiotape or digital recording with a partner. First, have each student's partner read section 4.1 aloud. Then, students should prepare notes for the section, having his or her partner reread as necessary to confirm the details. Encourage students to organize their notes, so that they include a brief summary answer to the question posed in each of the subheads in the section.

Gifted and Talented

Prepare a Resource List

Invite interested students to use the Internet and the library to find resources that will help young adults in their job search process. Students may locate Web sites or books on choosing a career, finding a job, researching companies, writing resumés and cover letters, and developing interview skills. Have students compile their information into one-page lists to share with classmates. Encourage them to include one- or two-sentence annotations saying why they think each resource is a valuable one.

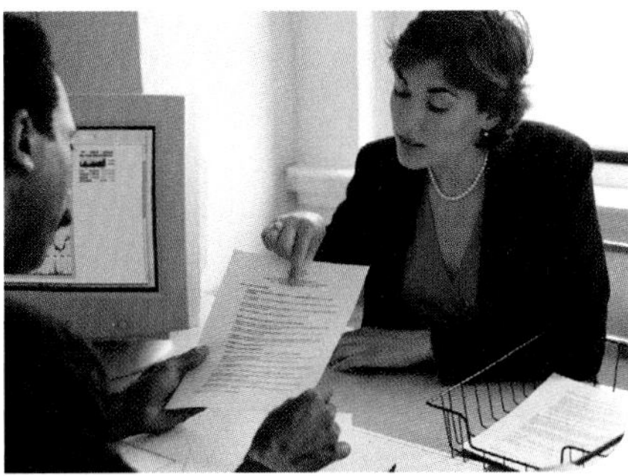

Use your research to prepare a set of questions about the organization and the job. Find out as much as you can about the job requirements and responsibilities before discussing such things as pay, hours, or benefits. In some cases, those topics may not come up until a later interview. Remember that both you and the employer want to confirm that you are a good fit for the job and the organization.

Presenting Yourself Be ready to answer questions about your qualifications and about how you will fit into the company. You may want to practice answering questions in front of a mirror or with a friend or family member. Make sure your answers are clear and succinct. Take time to think about your responses to unexpected questions. Books and online resources can provide examples of many common interview questions.

Dress appropriately for the job you are seeking. Don't show up to the interview in business attire if you are applying to work where you will get very dirty. By the same token, don't go to an interview for an office job dressed in jeans and a T-shirt. Always appear neat, clean, and well groomed.

Determine how long it will take to get to the interview. Plan to arrive about ten minutes early. Take weather conditions and traffic into consideration. If you are delayed, be sure to call and explain that you will be late.

Bring extra copies of your resumé and list of references. You may want to bring a pad of paper to take notes during the interview. Be sure to get the name and title of each person who interviews you.

Check It Out!

- ✔ Learn about the company where you are applying.
- ✔ Prepare a list of questions about the job and the company.
- ✔ Bring extra copies of your resumé and your list of references.
- ✔ Be on time for your interview.

Follow-Up Write a short thank-you note immediately after the interview to each interviewer. Thank the interviewer for spending time with you. If you still want the job, restate your interest in it. Refer to something you learned in the interview. Express your desire to learn more about the position.

APPLICATION Getting a Job

1. What is the purpose of a resumé?
2. **Writing Your Resumé** Study the resumé in this section. Prepare a personal resumé based on the model. Also assemble a list of people whom you might want to use as references.

More About . . .

The Hiring Process

The hiring process varies by industry, by size of company, and even by individual department. Large organizations have a separate department that manages the hiring process. This department is sometimes referred to as the human resources or personnel department. It may recruit candidates, screen applicants, and schedule interviews.

There may be hundreds of candidates for an individual job. The manager of the department where the candidate will work may screen resumés and usually conducts interviews and makes the hiring decision. This person is referred to as the hiring manager, although that is not an official job title.

APPLICATION Answers

1. *to summarize your career objective and your qualifications for potential employers*
2. *Resumés should reflect concepts discussed in this section: contact info, career objective, work experience described with active verbs, skills, activities and honors.*

CHECK IT OUT!

Print a variety of sample resumés from the Internet to give students a better idea of the range of resumé options. Make copies for students, and make an overhead slide of each. Discuss the resumés as a class. Point out the different styles, but note that they all share basic elements: contact information, job history, education.

4.2 Paying Taxes

Discuss

- What is the difference between the W-4 and W-2 forms? *(The W-4 is filled out when you start a job and determines how much tax is withheld from your paycheck. The W-2 is an annual summary of earnings and taxes withheld.)*
- Why do you need to file a tax return even if you do not owe any money? *(because the IRS requires that everyone who earns above a certain amount of income file a return so that it can verify earnings and taxes paid; if you have had too much withheld you must file a return to get a refund)*

Analyzing Charts: Figure CPF 17

Have students read the form line by line to see the kind of information that is required. Point out that the top part of the form, which is not shown completely, is a worksheet with instructions to help people fill in the form. Ask students why someone might want to have additional money withheld from their paycheck. *(to avoid having to pay additional taxes when the tax return is filed)* Why would someone choose to be exempt from withholding if they meet the criteria in line 7? *(because they would rather have the money during the year than have to wait to get it all back when they file a return)*

4.2 Paying Taxes

Benjamin Franklin once said, "In this world nothing is certain but death and taxes." As you learned in Chapter 14, taxes provide the government with revenue to provide needed services. Recall that the Internal Revenue Service (IRS) is the government agency that collects the federal taxes owed by Americans. Most states also collect taxes. Taxes for the previous year must be paid by April 15 of the current year. For example, taxes for income earned in 2010 would need to be paid by April 15, 2011.

How Are My Taxes Determined?

QUICK REFERENCE

Filing status is based on your marital status or support of dependents.

Taxable income is the income subject to taxation after exemptions and deductions.

The amount you pay in taxes is determined by your filing status and your taxable income. **Filing status** is based on your marital status or whether you have any dependents. A dependent is a child or relative in your household whom you support. People with more dependents have less tax withheld. Employers use the W-4 form, shown in Figure CPF 17, to determine your filing status for withholding taxes from your paycheck. You fill out a W-4 form when you begin a job. As long as you are still dependent on your parents, you claim only one withholding allowance.

The second determinant is your **taxable income**, which is the amount of income subject to taxation after all exemptions and deductions. The higher your income, the higher your taxes will be. Certain income may not be taxed. For example, money can be deducted from your paycheck before taxes to pay for health insurance. Income above a certain level is not subject to Federal Insurance Contributions Act (FICA) taxes for Social Security.

Figure CPF 17 The W-4 Form

ⓐ Instructions help you determine how many allowances to claim. A single person with one job who is claimed as a dependent gets one allowance.

ⓑ Your Social Security number is required on all IRS forms.

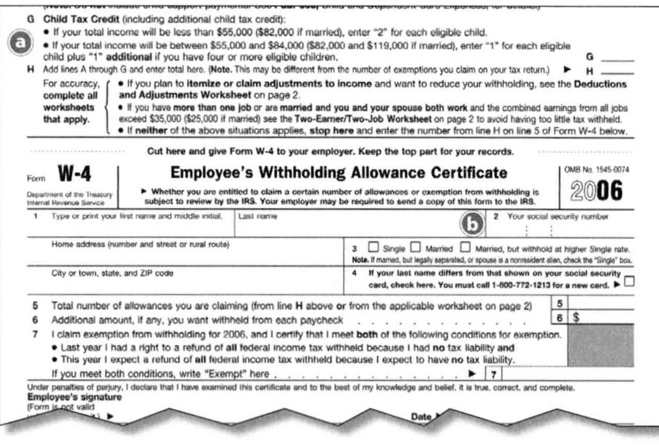

G **Child Tax Credit** (including additional child tax credit):
- If your total income will be less than $55,000 ($82,000 if married), enter "2" for each eligible child.
- If your total income will be between $55,000 and $84,000 ($82,000 and $119,000 if married), enter "1" for each eligible child plus "1" **additional** if you have four or more eligible children. G ____

H Add lines A through G and enter total here. (**Note.** This may be different from the number of exemptions you claim on your tax return.) ▶ H ____

For accuracy, complete all worksheets that apply.
- If you plan to **itemize or claim adjustments to income** and want to reduce your withholding, see the **Deductions and Adjustments Worksheet** on page 2.
- If you have **more than one job** or are **married and you and your spouse both work** and the combined earnings from all jobs exceed $35,000 ($25,000 if married) see the **Two-Earner/Two-Job Worksheet** on page 2 to avoid having too little tax withheld.
- If **neither** of the above situations applies, **stop here** and enter the number from line H on line 5 of Form W-4 below.

Cut here and give Form W-4 to your employer. Keep the top part for your records.

Form **W-4** — Department of the Treasury, Internal Revenue Service

Employee's Withholding Allowance Certificate

▶ **Whether you are entitled to claim a certain number of allowances or exemption from withholding is subject to review by the IRS. Your employer may be required to send a copy of this form to the IRS.**

OMB No. 1545-0074 **2006**

1 Type or print your first name and middle initial. | Last name | 2 Your social security number

Home address (number and street or rural route) | 3 ☐ Single ☐ Married ☐ Married, but withhold at higher Single rate. **Note.** If married, but legally separated, or spouse is a nonresident alien, check the "Single" box.

City or town, state, and ZIP code | 4 **If your last name differs from that shown on your social security card, check here. You must call 1-800-772-1213 for a new card.** ▶ ☐

5 Total number of allowances you are claiming (from line **H** above **or** from the applicable worksheet on page 2) 5

6 Additional amount, if any, you want withheld from each paycheck . . . . 6 $

7 I claim exemption from withholding for 2006, and I certify that I meet **both** of the following conditions for exemption.
- Last year I had a right to a refund of **all** federal income tax withheld because I had **no** tax liability **and**
- This year I expect a refund of **all** federal income tax withheld because I expect to have **no** tax liability.

If you meet both conditions, write "Exempt" here . . . . ▶ 7

Under penalties of perjury, I declare that I have examined this certificate and to the best of my knowledge and belief, it is true, correct, and complete.

Employee's signature
(Form is not valid ▶ Date ▶

DIFFERENTIATING INSTRUCTION

Struggling Readers

Access Prior Knowledge

Have students review what they learned about taxes in Chapter 14. In particular, call on volunteers to explain what is meant by a progressive tax, withholding, tax deductions and exemptions, and FICA taxes. Summarize student information on the board, so that students may refer to it as they study section 4.2.

English Learners

Use a Calendar

Help students understand the time sequence involved in paying taxes by using a calendar to show important dates. Start with June, and use the example of a student starting a job and filling out a W-4 form. Explain that taxes would be withheld the rest of the year. Then, indicate that in January the student could pick up tax forms and would receive a W-2 form. Finally, point to April 15 as the date by which tax forms must be filed.

Where Do I Get Tax Forms?

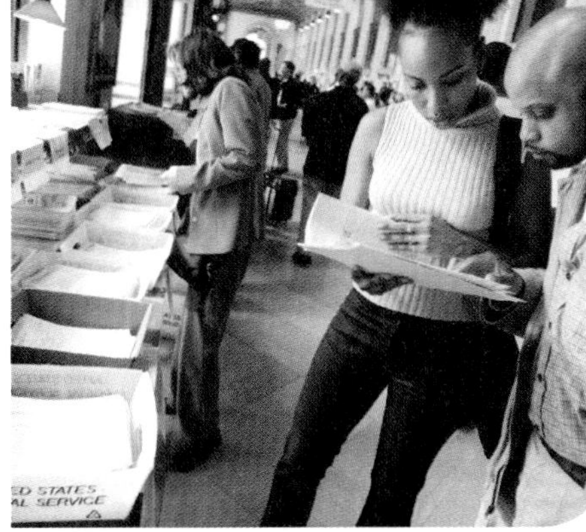

Federal and state tax forms are available starting in January each year at post offices (federal forms only), libraries, banks, and IRS or state tax offices. They are also available through official Web sites, or you can order forms through the mail or by phone. The first year you file taxes, you will need to find the forms yourself. After that, you should receive forms in the mail from the state and federal governments at the end of each year. If your tax situation changes significantly from the previous year, you may need to pick up additional forms.

Form 1040 Most young adults do not have to file complicated tax forms. Generally, the 1040EZ form should be sufficient for your federal taxes. This is a one-page form that has only 12 lines to fill out. The back of the form explains who is eligible to use it. See Figure CPF 18 for a sample of a 1040EZ form.

If you receive more than $1,500 in interest, you cannot use the 1040EZ form. Likewise, if you receive any dividends or other income from stocks, bonds, or similar investments, you cannot use 1040EZ. Instead, you will need to use form 1040A or 1040. These forms have related forms, known as schedules, for reporting investment income.

Most state tax forms are simple because they are based on the results you obtain from filling out your federal forms.

The W-2 Form The W-2 form shows how much you earned during the year and how much you paid in taxes through withholding. The form shows your total gross earnings and the amount of earnings subject to taxation. The amount withheld for each type of tax is also shown, including federal income tax, Social Security and Medicare taxes, and state and local taxes.

At the end of each year, any employer that you have worked for that year must send you a W-2 form. Employers must send the forms in time to arrive at your home by January 31. The W-2 will include copies to file with your federal, state, and local tax returns, as well as one copy for your files.

Other Forms When you have savings or investments, your bank or financial institution will send you other forms. Form 1099-INT for savings interest and form 1099-DIV for investment gains should arrive about the same time as your W-2.

More About . . .

Tax Forms and Schedules

There are three versions of the primary income tax form: 1040, 1040A, and 1040EZ. Which version you use depends on the complexity of your financial situation.

Both 1040EZ and 1040A are limited to taxpayers who have taxable income under $100,000. Those who use 1040EZ must have no dependents and less than $1,500 in taxable interest income. Form 1040A has schedules for interest and dividend income and dependent care expenses. Taxpayers with higher incomes or who are self-employed and those who want to itemize deductions or take advantage of various tax credits file Form 1040.

SMALL GROUP ACTIVITY

Designing a Tax Help Web Page

Time 45 Minutes

Task Organize information about paying taxes and design a Web page

Materials Needed computer with Internet access, Web design software or paper and pens

Activity

- Have groups review the material in section 4.2 about paying taxes.
- Direct groups to use the information to design a Web page that might help new taxpayers understand the income tax system and how to file taxes.
- Encourage students to include links to IRS and state tax department Web sites that provide information and the forms needed to file federal and state income taxes.
- Allow groups to present their Web page designs to the class. Discuss what features make the Web pages most useful to new taxpayers.

Rubric

	Understanding of Paying Taxes	Presentation of Information
4	excellent	clear and complete
3	good	mostly clear
2	fair	somewhat clear
1	poor	sketchy

Analyzing Charts: Figure CPF 18

Have students skim the headings in the left margin of the 1040EZ form to see how the tax form is organized. Then have them review the form line by line to see the types of information required. Ask students what kinds of income are shown on a W-2 form. *(wages, salaries, and tips)* If students have questions about the form, refer them to the worksheet on the back of the form or the instructions, available at the IRS Web site.

How Do I Fill Out a Tax Form?

Instruction booklets are available in most locations where you find tax forms. You may also download them for free from the IRS or state tax Web sites or request them by mail or phone. The instructions will take you through the steps to fill out the form line by line. They will also provide additional background information that may be helpful, as well as telling you where to go if you need help. Perhaps most important, the instructions contain the tax tables that will tell you how much tax you have to pay once you have determined your taxable income.

Follow the step-by-step instructions to complete each form. Always use correct and verifiable numbers. Making up numbers is considered tax fraud, which can be punishable with severe penalties. Figure CPF 18 shows a sample of a 1040EZ form.

Figure CPF 18 Filling Out the 1040EZ

- **a** Use your W-2 form(s) to find the amount to enter here.
- **b** The 1099-INT form shows how much interest you earned.
- **c** The amount you enter here depends on your filing status. If you are a dependent, you get the standard deduction but not the personal exemption.
- **d** The amount of tax withheld is found on your W-2 form along with earnings.
- **e** If you had more withheld than you owe in taxes, you will get money back in the form of a refund. If you didn't have enough withheld, you will have to pay the amount you still owe to the IRS.

Form **1040EZ** — Department of the Treasury—Internal Revenue Service — **Income Tax Return for Single and Joint Filers With No Dependents** (99) **2005** — OMB No. 1545-0074

Label (See page 11.) **Use the IRS label.** Otherwise, please print or type. — Your first name and initial | Last name | **Your social security number**; If a joint return, spouse's first name and initial | Last name | **Spouse's social security number**; Home address (number and street). If you have a P.O. box, see page 11. | Apt. no. | You **must** enter your SSN(s) above.; City, town or post office, state, and ZIP code. If you have a foreign address, see page 11.

Presidential Election Campaign (page 12) — Check here if you, or your spouse if a joint return, want $3 to go to this fund? ☐ You ☐ Spouse — Checking a box below will not change your tax or refund.

Income — Attach Form(s) W-2 here. Enclose, but do not attach, any payment.

1 Wages, salaries, and tips. This should be shown in box 1 of your Form(s) W-2. Attach your Form(s) W-2. (a)
2 Taxable interest. If the total is over $1,500, you cannot use Form 1040EZ. (b)
3 Unemployment compensation and Alaska Permanent Fund dividends (see page 13).
4 Add lines 1, 2, and 3. This is your **adjusted gross income.**
5 If someone can claim you (or your spouse if a joint return) as a dependent, check the applicable box(es) below and enter the amount from the worksheet on back. ☐ You ☐ Spouse If someone cannot claim you (or your spouse if a joint return), enter $8,200 if **single;** $16,400 if **married filing jointly.** See back for explanation. (c)
6 Subtract line 5 from line 4. If line 5 is larger than line 4, enter -0-. This is your **taxable income.**

Payments and tax

7 Federal income tax withheld from box 2 of your Form(s) W-2. (d)
8a **Earned income credit (EIC).**
b Nontaxable combat pay election. 8b
9 Add lines 7 and 8a. These are your **total payments.**
10 **Tax.** Use the amount on **line 6 above** to find your tax in the tax table on pages 24–32 of the booklet. Then, enter the tax from the table on this line.

Refund — Have it directly deposited! See page 18 and fill in 11b, 11c, and 11d.

11a If line 9 is larger than line 10, subtract line 10 from line 9. This is your **refund.** (e)
b Routing number — c Type: ☐ Checking ☐ Savings
d Account number

Amount you owe

12 If line 10 is larger than line 9, subtract line 9 from line 10. This is the **amount you owe.** For details on how to pay, see page 19. (e)

Third party designee — Do you want to allow another person to discuss this return with the IRS (see page 19)? ☐ Yes. Complete the following. ☐ No — Designee's name | Phone no. ( ) | Personal identification number (PIN)

Sign here — Joint return? See page 11. Keep a copy for your records. — Under penalties of perjury, I declare that I have examined this return, and to the best of my knowledge and belief, it is true, correct, and accurately lists all amounts and sources of income I received during the tax year. Declaration of preparer (other than the taxpayer) is based on all information of which the preparer has any knowledge. — Your signature | Date | Your occupation | Daytime phone number ( ); Spouse's signature. If a joint return, **both** must sign. | Date | Spouse's occupation

Paid preparer's use only — Preparer's signature | Date | Check if self-employed ☐ | Preparer's SSN or PTIN; Firm's name (or yours if self-employed), address, and ZIP code | EIN | Phone no. ( )

For Disclosure, Privacy Act, and Paperwork Reduction Act Notice, see page 23. Cat. No. 11329W Form **1040EZ** (2005)

DIFFERENTIATING INSTRUCTION

Inclusion

Enlarge the Visual

Students with visual impairments may benefit from working with larger versions of Figures CPF 17 and CPF 18. These images are available online at **ClassZone.com** or in the Forms and Publications section of the IRS Web site. IRS forms are available as pdf files that may be enlarged by 800 percent or more. If desired, allow students to work with a partner without visual impairments to help them understand the forms.

Gifted and Talented

Record a Public Service Announcement

Encourage students to use the IRS Web site or other Internet resources to learn more about e-filing options that allow taxpayers to file their tax returns and make payments electronically. Then, have students record a 60-second public service announcement that briefly outlines the benefits of e-filing and tells taxpayers how to learn more about it. Allow students to play or perform their announcements for the class. Discuss whether the announcements make students more interested in exploring these options.

How Do I File My Taxes?

Everyone who receives more than a certain amount of income during the year must file a tax return. Check the tax form instructions or the IRS Web site to determine if you are required to file. Even if you don't owe money, you must file a form if you meet the requirements. And, of course, you will not receive a refund for excess taxes withheld unless you file a tax return. See the "What if I get stuck?" sidebar to find out how to receive help with your taxes.

Before you send in your forms, double check your work. Confirm that you have entered the correct Social Security number; that your income, withholding, and tax figures are correct; and that you have signed your forms. Then make a photocopy of the forms for your own records.

When everything is ready, you can mail all the paperwork to the IRS service center listed on your form. You can also file your tax forms electronically. Electronically filed returns are generally more accurate, and refunds are processed more quickly. The IRS has formed a partnership with several tax software companies to offer the Free File service that allows most taxpayers to prepare and file their taxes electronically for free. You can find more information and instructions on e-filing options on the IRS Web site.

After you file your return, be sure to keep all your forms and copies in a safe place. Keep your tax returns and all related documents for at least three years—the limit if the IRS wants to contest your return.

WHAT IF I GET STUCK?

- Ask a parent or other trusted adult. Most have many years of experience filling out tax forms.
- For federal tax help, go to the IRS Web site. For state tax help use the name of your state and the key words *tax help* to find the Web site.
- For additional help, call the local IRS office (1-800-829-1040) or your state tax office.

Mistakes The IRS and state tax auditors usually catch simple math mistakes and inform you of them. They then recalculate your taxes and adjust the amount of your refund or taxes owed. If you discover a major error or omission on your form after you submit it, file an amended return as soon as possible. You must file an amended return within three years of the time when the original return was filed. You may have to pay a penalty depending on the type of error involved.

Check It Out!

- ✔ The filing deadline is April 15, every year.
- ✔ Check everything on your form carefully before submitting it.
- ✔ Save your forms and copies for at least three years.

APPLICATION Paying Taxes

1. Where can you go to get tax forms?
2. **Preparing to Do Your Taxes** Make a list of the documents and information you will need to file federal and state income tax forms. Decide on a location where you will keep the list and the information until it is time to file your taxes.

More About . . .

Electronic Tax Filing

The IRS has offered electronic tax filing since 1986, and professional tax preparers have been the largest users of the system. In 2005, for the first time, more than half of individual taxpayers filed returns electronically, including about 20 million who filed returns from their home computers using tax preparation software. The IRS estimated that in 2006, 93 million taxpayers, with adjusted gross incomes under about $50,000 could take advantage of the Free File program available at the IRS Web site.

APPLICATION Answers

1. *post office, library, bank, tax office, Internet*
2. *W-2; 1099-INT; 1099-DIV; paycheck stubs*

CHECK IT OUT!

Make copies of a 1040EZ form and a state tax form. Ask students to fill out the forms as though they had earned $20,000 after taxes and other withholding, and as though they had paid $2,000 in federal taxes and $500 in state taxes through payroll deductions. After they have attempted to fill out the form, go through it line by line and discuss any trouble spots.

4.3 Finding an Apartment

Discuss

- What are some advantages and disadvantages of living with roommates? *(Roommates can help pay the bills and provide companionship, but there might be conflicts if they are unreliable or have a different lifestyle.)*
- Why is it necessary to have more than one month's rent available when you rent an apartment? *(because you often have to pay additional money such as the last month's rent, security deposit, and other fees)*

More About . . .

Rental Housing
Rents in the United States declined during 2001–2005 but then began to increase. Supply decreased as fewer new apartments were built and many older units were converted into condominiums. Affordable housing was especially scarce. In 2005, about one-third of Americans spent more than 30 percent of their income on housing, and about one-seventh spent more than 50 percent.

According to the Department of Housing and Urban Development, households with one full-time worker earning minimum-wage could not afford a two-bedroom apartment anywhere in the country. Growth in the number of young adults was expected to keep demand for rental housing strong into 2015.

4.3 Finding an Apartment

Most young adults will rent an apartment when they start out on their own because apartments are an affordable type of housing. Moving out of your parents' home or out of a college dormitory into an apartment will give you more freedom. But it also means more responsibilities. You will have to pay monthly bills, shop for groceries, fix meals, clean your apartment, and do laundry. With a little effort, you can find an apartment that suits you.

What Should I Consider About Renting an Apartment?

How much should I spend? Your housing expenses should amount to no more than about one-fourth to one-third of your take-home pay. These expenses include not only your rent, but also utilities, cable, and any other housing costs. Spending a higher proportion of your income on housing may not leave you enough to meet your other expenses or to have the money you want to enjoy life.

Should I live by myself or with roommates? If one-third of your take-home pay only pays rent for a storage locker, you may want to consider sharing a larger apartment with one or more roommates. Roommates can make living in an apartment cheaper and more fun, but they can become a problem if they are irresponsible or have a lifestyle that clashes with your own. Think about how to balance the desire for privacy and your own space with the desire for companionship and help with household expenses and chores. If you decide to live with roommates, consider looking for an apartment together. That way, everyone can commit to the same place, and people will be less likely to grow dissatisfied and leave.

How do I choose roommates? Look for individuals you are compatible with, whose personalities and lifestyles are similar to your own. Roommates should be people you can count on, whether it's to pay their share of the rent or to do their share of household chores. Living with other people can bring up conflicts about how to share expenses, use the living space, and keep it clean. You and your roommates will need to communicate to resolve such issues. Consider drawing up an agreement together that spells out the rules that everyone must obey and the responsibilities that each roommate accepts.

DIFFERENTIATING INSTRUCTION

Struggling Readers

Do Popcorn Reading
Have students read section 4.3 on finding an apartment together in small groups. Assign one student to read aloud while the others follow. The reader should stop suddenly and call out another student's name. The named student should begin to read from the point where the first reader left off. Group members should repeat the process until they have finished the selection.

English Learners

Make Vocabulary Cards
Have students read section 4.3 on finding an apartment and jot down all the words that they do not know. Give them time to look up those words and write down the definitions on index cards. Tell them to reread the section slowly, referring to the index cards as needed. Explain any phrases or sentences that they still have trouble understanding.

Figure CPF 19 Looking for an Apartment

Location
- Is it convenient to where you work?
- Is there nearby public transportation or parking?
- Are there grocery stores, self-service laundries, or other stores you need nearby?
- Is the neighborhood safe?

The Building
- Is it clean and well taken care of?
- Do the other tenants seem friendly?
- Are the lobby and stairwells safe?
- Are there sufficient parking spaces, laundry facilities, or bike rooms?

Space
- Is there enough room for the number of people living in the apartment?
- Is it suitable for your way of life?
- Are all the roommates happy with the living space and available storage?

Furnished or Unfurnished
- Do you want it furnished with furniture or do you want to use your own furniture?
- Can you get used furniture from family or friends or purchase inexpensive furniture?
- Does the apartment include appliances, such as a stove and refrigerator?

What Do I Need to Know About Signing a Lease?

- A **lease** is a contract for renting an apartment for a specific period of time. The contract is between you and your **landlord**, who is the owner of the rental property. A lease is a legal document that obligates you to pay rent and to follow certain rules for a specific period of time. The landlord has responsibilities as well. If you have roommates, whoever signs the lease is responsible even if other roommates fail to pay their part of the rent.
- You may be asked for the first and last months' rent, a security deposit, and possibly cleaning and key fees. When you move out, the landlord will inspect the property and return some or all of the security deposit and fees, depending on what repairs need to be done.
- You may need to provide character references—name, address, and phone number. Generally you should use three people who are not relatives, such as teachers, employers, or supervisors of volunteer work, who can vouch for you.
- You must provide your Social Security number and bank information. If you are employed you will provide employment information.
- If this is your first apartment or you are not employed, you may be asked to have a responsible adult act as a cosigner. This ensures that the landlord will be paid the rent due if you fail to pay.

QUICK REFERENCE

A **lease** is a contract for renting an apartment.

A **landlord** is the owner of rental property.

Check It Out!

- ✔ Provide a list of references.
- ✔ Be prepared for up-front costs such as a security deposit.
- ✔ Look at several places before committing to an apartment.

APPLICATION Finding an Apartment

1. What is a lease?
2. **Analyzing Your Needs** Decide if you would prefer to live alone or with others. If you prefer to live alone, write a paragraph explaining your decision. If you would like to live with others, create a list of roommate rules and responsibilities.

Interactive Review

Review Getting Out on Your Own using interactive activities at **ClassZone.com**

Analyzing Charts: Figure CPF 19

Call on volunteers to read the bulleted lists in each section of the chart. Invite students to discuss why these are important questions to consider. Ask students if they have additional questions to add on any of the topics based on their knowledge of their community or their own lifestyle considerations.

More About . . .

Tenant Rights

Tenant rights vary from place to place, but there are certain federal regulations that apply to most rental housing. Of greatest importance is that the landlord may not discriminate based on race, color, religion, national origin, sex, family status, or physical or mental disability.

This prohibition against discrimination applies to advertising as well as to landlord statements and actions. These regulations do not apply to owner-occupied buildings that have fewer than four rental units. Tenants have the right to a dwelling that is safe and free from vermin. The landlord may not enter the rental unit without notice except in the case of emergency such as fire or flood.

APPLICATION Answers

1. *a contract for renting an apartment for a specific length of time*
2. *Answers will vary but should reflect understanding of section concepts.*

CHECK IT OUT!

Have students choose a nearby neighborhood and look for an apartment. They can use newspapers, the Internet, and community bulletin boards. Ask them to bring the following information about three possible apartments: location, number of bedrooms, monthly rent, what utilities are included, special facilities or amenities (such as weight rooms or laundry facilities). Prompt each student to share what they have found, and lead a class discussion on what to do when visiting a potential apartment.

Reference Section

McDougal Littell

ECONOMICS

Concepts and Choices

Table of Contents

Refer to the Math Handbook when you need help with the mathematical concepts that you might encounter in your study of economics.

MATH HANDBOOK

Math Handbook **R1**

1.1 Working with Decimals and Percents

Understanding the Skill

A decimal is a number that uses the base-ten value system where a decimal point separates the ones' and tenths' digits. Each place value is ten times the place value to its right. For example, 5.2 is five and two tenths and 12.45 is twelve and forty-five hundredths.

The word *percent* means "per hundred." For example, 5 percent means "5 per 100," or 5/100. If 5 percent of the population is unemployed, then, on average, 5 out of 100 people are unemployed.

To write a decimal as a percent, multiply by 100 percent. To write a percent as a decimal, divide by 100 percent.

Example 1: A company's February sales were 0.125 of its total annual sales. Express this as a percentage.

$0.125 = 0.125 \times 100\%$	*Multiply by 100 percent.*
$= 12.5\%$	*Move the decimal point two places to the right.*

Check your answer: 12.5 should be larger than 0.125 because you multiplied by 100.

Example 2: A company's workforce was 105 percent of what it was a year earlier. Express this as a decimal.

$105\% = \frac{105\%}{100\%}$	*Divide by 100 percent.*
$= \frac{105}{100}$	*Cancel the % signs.*
$= 1.05$	*To divide by 100, move the decimal point 2 places to the left.*

Check your answer: 1.05 should be smaller than 105 because you divided by 100.

Applying the Skill

1. In 2002, the total personal income in the United States was $8.922 trillion and the total personal taxes were $1.112 trillion. What percent of income were taxes? Round your answer to the nearest hundredth.
2. The GDP of the United States is $11.750 trillion and the GDP of the world is $55.500 trillion. What percent of the world's GDP is from the United States? Round your answer to the nearest tenth.

R2 Math Handbook

Answers

1. *about 12.46%*
2. *about 21.2%*

1.2 Calculating Averages

Understanding the Skill

There are three ways to express the average of a group of numbers. The most common way is to divide the total by the number of values. This kind of average is called the *mean*.

Mean, Median, and Mode Notice that, in Example 1, most workers earn much less than the mean of $27,000; the mean doesn't describe typical earnings well. Typical earnings are often described better by the two other kinds of average: the mode and the median. To determine the mode and the median of a group of numbers, write the numbers in order from smallest to largest. The *mode* is the most common value. The *median* is the middle value. If the number of values is even, the median is the mean of the two middle values.

Example 1: The annual earnings of five workers are shown below. Calculate the mean earnings.

$14,000 $18,000 $14,000 $75,000 $14,000

Solution

Divide the total by the number of values. There are five numbers to average, so the number of values is 5.

$\text{Mean} = \frac{\text{Total}}{\text{Number of values}}$

$= \frac{135{,}000}{5}$ — *Simplify the numerator.*

$= \$27{,}000$ — *Divide.*

The workers have mean earnings of $27,000 — *Answer the question.*

Example 2: Find the mode and the median of the earnings in Example 1.

Solution

Write the values in order from smallest to largest.

$14,000 $14,000 $14,000 $18,000 $75,000

The most common value is $14,000, so the mode is $14,000.

$14,000 $14,000 **$14,000** $18,000 $75,000

The middle value is also $14,000, so the **median** is $14,000.

Applying the Skill

Calculate the mean, the median, and the mode of each group of numbers.

1. $40,000 $32,000 $38,000 $40,000 $40,000
2. $80,000 $50,000 $35,000 $35,000 $40,000 $60,000

Answers

1. *mean: $38,000; median: $40,000; mode: $40,000*
2. *mean: $50,000; median: $45,000; mode: $35,000*

1.3 Calculating and Using Percents

Understanding the Skill

As you recall, the term *percent* means "per hundred." For example, 25% is 25/100. To change a decimal to a percent, move the decimal point two places to the right and add the % symbol.

0.253 = 25.3%   1.63 = 163%

To calculate and use percents, first write a question. Then rewrite your question as an equation. Replace "percent" with /100, "of" with ×, and "is" with =. Replace the unknown value with a variable, like *x*.

Example 1: Sweden's gross domestic product (GDP) is $255,400,000,000. Agriculture accounts for about $5,108,000,000 of the GDP. What percent of the GDP is from agriculture?

Solution

What **percent of** the GDP **is** from agriculture?	*Write a question.*
What percent of $255,400,000,000 **is** $5,108,000,000?	*Substitute numbers.*
x/100 × $255,400,000,000 = $5,108,000,000	*Rewrite as an equation.*
$x = \frac{\$5{,}108{,}000{,}000}{\$255{,}400{,}000{,}000} \times 100$	*Solve the equation.*
x = 2	*Use a calculator.*
Two percent of Sweden's GDP is from agriculture.	*Answer the question.*

Example 2: Sweden's unemployment rate is 5.6% and its labor force is 4.46 million. About how many people are unemployed?

Solution

5.6 **percent of** the labor force **is** how many people?	*Write a question.*
5.6 **percent of** 4.46 million **is how many**?	*Substitute numbers.*
5.6/**100** × 4,460,000 = x	*Rewrite as an equation.*
249,760 = x	*Use a calculator.*
About 250,000 people are unemployed.	*Round your answer.*

Applying the Skill

1. What is 10% of $65?

2. What is 150% of 256,000?

3. $3.75 is 15% of how much?

Answers

1. *$6.50*

2. *384,000*

3. *$25*

1.4 Using Ratios

Understanding the Skill

A ratio compares two numbers that have the same units of measure. For example, if Tina runs 8 miles per hour and Maria runs 7 miles per hour, the ratio of their speeds is 8 to 7, or 8:7. A ratio can also be written as a fraction: $\frac{8}{7}$.

You can simplify ratios in the same way that you simplify fractions.

Example 1: Raul runs 8 miles per hour and his little brother Ben runs 4 miles per hour. What is the ratio of Raul's speed to Ben's speed?

Solution

$\frac{\text{Raul's speed}}{\text{Ben's speed}} = \frac{8}{4}$	*Write a fraction.*
$= \frac{8 \div 4}{4 \div 4}$	*To simplify the fraction, divide both the top and the bottom by 4.*
$= \frac{2}{1}$	$\frac{2}{1}$ *means the same as* 2:1 *and* "2 to 1."

The ratio of Raul's speed to Ben's speed is 2 to 1.

Ratios are sometimes written as decimals. For example, a company's price-earnings ratio is the ratio of the price of a share of the company's stock to the earnings per share.

Example 2 Suppose a share of a company's stock costs $54.75 and the earnings per share are $2.73. What is the company's price-earnings ratio?

Solution

Price-earnings ratio = $\frac{\text{Price of a share of stock}}{\text{Earnings per share}}$	*Write a fraction.*
$= \frac{\$55.75}{\$2.73}$	*Substitute numbers.*
$= 20.421245$	*Use a calculator.*
≈ 20.4	*Round your answer.*
The company's price-earnings ratio is about 20.4.	*Answer the question.*

Applying the Skill

1. The GDP of the world is about $55 trillion and the GDP of the United States is about $11 trillion. What is the ratio of the GDP of the world to the GDP of the United States?
2. Suppose a share of a company's stock costs $26.24 and the earnings per share are $3.19. What is the company's price-earnings ratio?

Answers

1. *5 to l; other acceptable answers include 5:l and* $\frac{5}{l}$.
2. *8.2*

1.5 Calculating Compound Interest

Understanding the Skill

For some savings instruments, interest is calculated and paid multiple times each year. To calculate the amount of each interest payment, you can use the following formula.

$$\text{Interest} = \frac{\text{Balance} \times \text{Interest rate}}{\text{Number of times calculated each year}}$$

If interest on your savings is *compounded,* that means the interest you earn is added to your total savings, and is included in future calculations of interest.

Notice that the interest for the second half of the year is greater than the interest for the first half of the year. In the second half of the year, you earn interest not only on your original balance, but also on the interest you earned in the first half of the year.

Compound interest on loans works the same as compound interest on savings. But for loans, if interest is compounded, you must *pay* interest on interest you haven't yet paid.

Example: If interest on $1,000 is compounded biannually with an interest rate of 5 percent, how much interest do you earn for each compounding period in the first year?

Solution

If interest is compounded *biannually,* that means it is calculated **two** times a year and each compounding period is a half of a year. Calculate the interest for each half.

First half of year $\text{Interest} = \frac{\text{Balance} \times \text{Interest rate}}{\text{Number of times calculated each year}}$

$= \frac{\$1{,}000 \times 5\%}{2}$ *Substitute numbers.*

$= \frac{\$1{,}000 \times 0.05}{2}$ *Convert the percent to a decimal.*

$=$ **$25.00** *Use a calculator.*

Second half of year

First, calculate the new balance by adding the interest to the old balance.

New balance $=$ Old balance $+$ Interest on old balance

$= \$1{,}000 +$ **$25.00**

$=$ **$1,025.00**

$\text{Interest} = \frac{\textbf{New balance} \times \text{Interest rate}}{\text{Number of times calculated each year}} = \frac{\textbf{\$1,025.00} + 5\%}{2} \approx \$25.63$

The interest for the first half of the year is $25.00 and for the second half is $25.63.

Applying the Skill

1. If interest on $2,000 is compounded biannually with a rate of 6 percent, what is the interest for each compounding period in the first year? What is the total interest for one year?
2. If interest on $2,000 is compounded four times a year with a rate of 6 percent, what is the interest for each compounding period in the first year? What is the total interest?
3. Look at your answers to Questions 1 and 2. Do you earn more if the interest is compounded twice a year or if it is compounded four times a year?

Answers

1. *First half of year: $60.00; second half of year: $61.80; total: $121.80*
2. *First quarter: $30.00; second quarter: $30.45; third quarter: $30.91; fourth quarter: $31.37; total: $122.73*
3. *Four times a year*

1.6 Understanding Progressive Taxes

Understanding the Skill

The federal income tax is progressive: a person with a low income is taxed at a lower rate than a person with a higher income. The table at the bottom of the page shows the 2006 income tax brackets for a single person. If you file as single and your taxable income is **$7,125,** you are in the **10 percent** tax bracket because $7,125 is between **$0** and **$7,550.** If your taxable income is **$7,750,** then you are in the 15 percent tax bracket, but your tax is not 15 percent of $7,750. Instead, you pay 10 percent on the first $7,550 of your income. You pay 15 percent on the rest.

Example 1: Calculate tax in the 10 percent tax bracket on $7,125.

Tax = Tax rate x Income in bracket

= **10%** × **$7,125** *Substitute numbers.*

= 0.10 × $7,125 *Write 10 percent as a decimal.*

= $712.50 *Multiply.*

The tax on $7,125 is $713. *Answer the question. Round to the nearest dollar.*

Example 2: Calculate tax in the 15 percent tax bracket on $7,550.

Pay **10 percent** on the first **$7,550.**

Tax = Tax rate x Income in bracket = **10%** × **$7,550** = **$755.00**

Pay 15 percent on the rest of the income.

Income in 15% bracket = Total income – **Income in 10% bracket**

= **$7,750** – **$7,550**

= **$200**

Tax = Tax rate x Income in bracket = **15%** × **$200** = **$30.00**

Add the tax from the two brackets together to find the total tax.

$755.00 + **$30.00** = **$785.00**

Applying the Skill

Using the tax bracket table on the right, calculate the taxes on the following taxable incomes:

A. $7,175 **B.** $17,225
C. $74,100 **D.** $98,975

2006 Federal Income Tax Brackets (Single)

Income Bracket	Tax Rate
$0–$7,550	10%
$7,550–$30,650	15%
$30,650–$74,200	25%
$74,200–$154,800	28%

Answers

A. *$718*

B. *$2,584*

C. *$18,525*

D. *$27,713*

1.7 Creating Line Graphs

Understanding the Skill

A line graph is useful for showing how a value changes over time. You can use a spreadsheet or graphing software to make a line graph. In the example, type the years and inflation rates into the software. The software will do most of the above steps for you. See the software's tutorials or help feature for guidance.

United States Inflation Rate (in percent)									
1970	1971	1972	1973	1974	1975	1976	1977	1978	1979
5.7	4.4	3.2	6.2	11.0	9.1	5.8	6.5	7.6	11.3

Source: U.S. Bureau of Labor Statistics

1. Write the title of the graph and make a grid under it.
2. Write numbers along the left side, or verticle axis, of the grid with 0 at the bottom. The top number should be larger than the largest rate in the table. Label the axis.
3. Write years from the table evenly along the bottom line, or horizontal axis, of the grid. Label the axis.
4. Graph each point where the horizontal line from the **inflation rate** meets the vertical line from the **year.**
5. Draw a straight line to connect each point to the point for the next year.

Example: Make a line graph showing the rate of inflation from 1970 to 1979. Find the largest rate in the table. It is **11.3.**

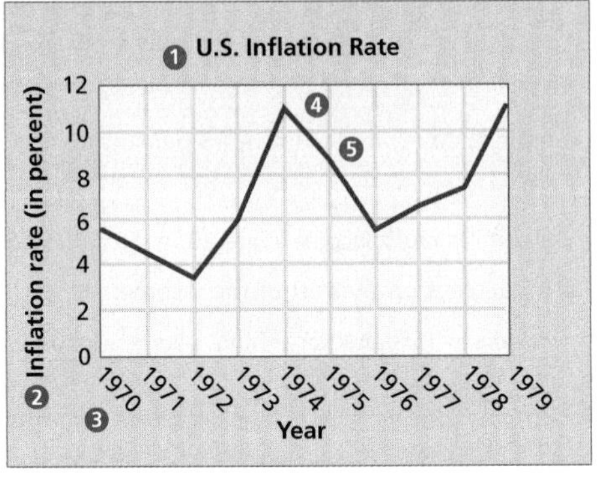

Applying the Skill

Make a line graph to show the unemployment rate from 1993 to 2002.

Unemployment Rate (in percent)									
1993	1994	1995	1996	1997	1998	1999	2000	2001	2002
6.9	6.1	5.6	5.4	4.9	4.5	4.2	4.0	4.7	5.8

Source: U.S. Bureau of Labor Statistics

Answers

1. *Graphs may vary. For example, students may use different scales on the axes. A sample graph appears at right.*

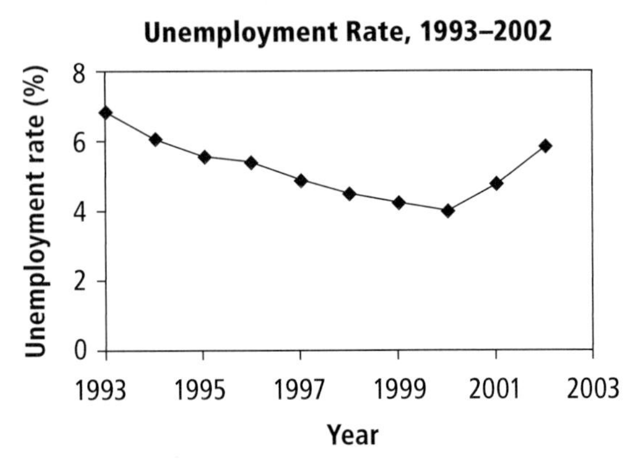

1.8 Creating Bar Graphs

Understanding the Skill

A bar graph is useful for comparing different values. You can use a spreadsheet or graphing software to make a bar graph. In the example, type the oil consumption information into the software. The software will do most of the above steps for you. See the software's tutorials or help feature for guidance.

Leading Oil Consumers (in millions of barrels per day)							
United States	European Union	China	Japan	India	Brazil	Russia	Canada
20.0	14.6	6.4	5.6	2.3	2.1	2.8	2.2

Source: CIA World Factbook, 2005 data

1. Write the title of the graph. Draw a box under it.
2. Write numbers evenly along the vertical axis. The largest number should be larger than 20.0 and the smallest number should be 0. Label the axis.
3. Write the names evenly along the horizontal axis. Label the axis.
4. Draw each bar. Find the **oil consumption** on the vertical axis. Imagine a horizontal line from the oil consumption to directly above the **name.** Draw the bar as shown. Each bar should be the same width.

Example: Make a bar graph of the oil consumption of the three greatest oil consumers: the United States, the European Union, and China

Solution

Begin by finding the highest level of oil consumption—the United States with 20 million barrels a day. Then complete the following steps.

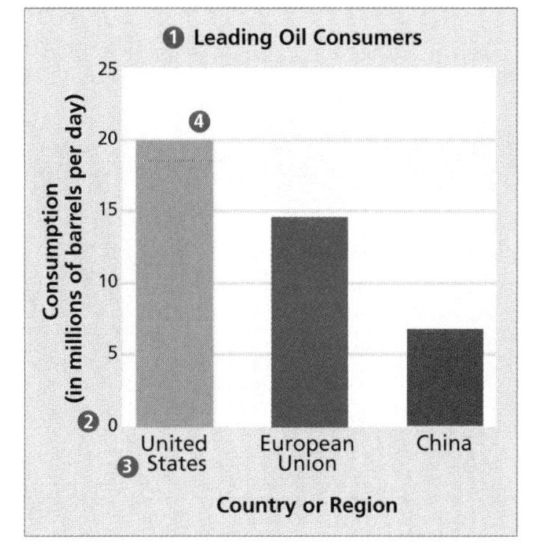

Applying the Skill

Use the information in the table at the top of the page to make a bar graph of the oil consumption of the three leading oil consumers in Asia: China, Japan, and India.

Answers

1. *Graphs may vary. For example, students may use different scales on the axes. A sample graph appears at right.*

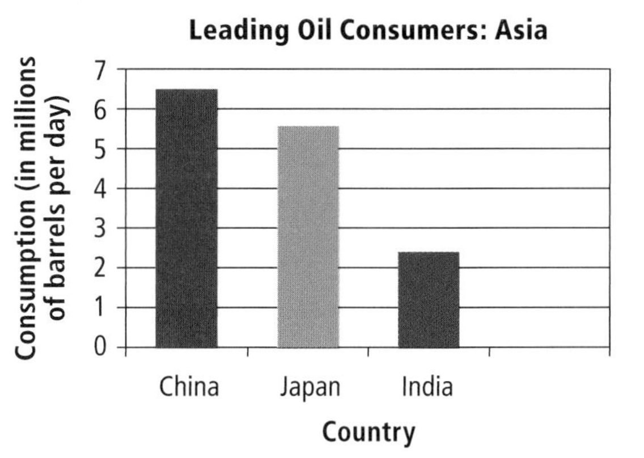

1.9 Creating Pie Graphs

Understanding the Skill

A pie graph is useful for showing the relationship of parts to the whole. The table at the right and the pie graph below show the GDP for various countries and the European Union. The graph makes it easy to see how each GDP contributes to the world's total GDP. The example shows how to make the pie graph.

GDP (trillions of U. S. dollars) and Population (millions of people) of Various Countries and the European Union					
Country	GDP	Population	Country	GDP	Population
United States	11.8	296	Russia	1.4	143
European Union	11.7	457	Canada	1.0	33
China	7.3	1,306	Mexico	1.0	106
Japan	3.7	127	South Korea	0.9	49
India	3.3	1,080	Indonesia	0.8	242
Brazil	1.5	186	Other	11.1	2,421

Source: CIA World Factbook, 2005 data

Example

1. Write a title for the pie graph.
2. Draw a circle. This represents the total GDP of all countries, or $55.5 trillion.
3. Draw a wedge to represent each country or group of countries. Calculate the angle for each wedge using this formula:

   $$\text{Angle} = \frac{\text{Country's GDP}}{\text{World GDP}} \times 360°$$

4. Label each wedge with the country name and the amount of GDP. Wedges too small to draw easily can be grouped together and labeled "Other."

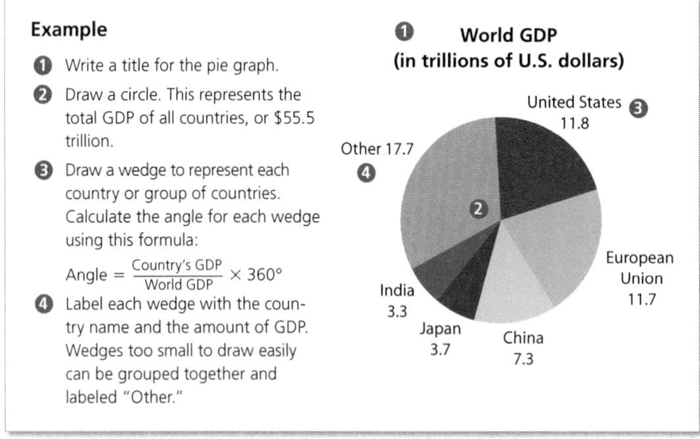

Applying the Skill

Use the information in the table at the top of the page to make a pie graph of the populations of the world. Include wedges for the five largest countries, and one for all others.

Answers

1. *Graphs may vary. For example, some students may order the wedges differently. A sample graph appears at right.*

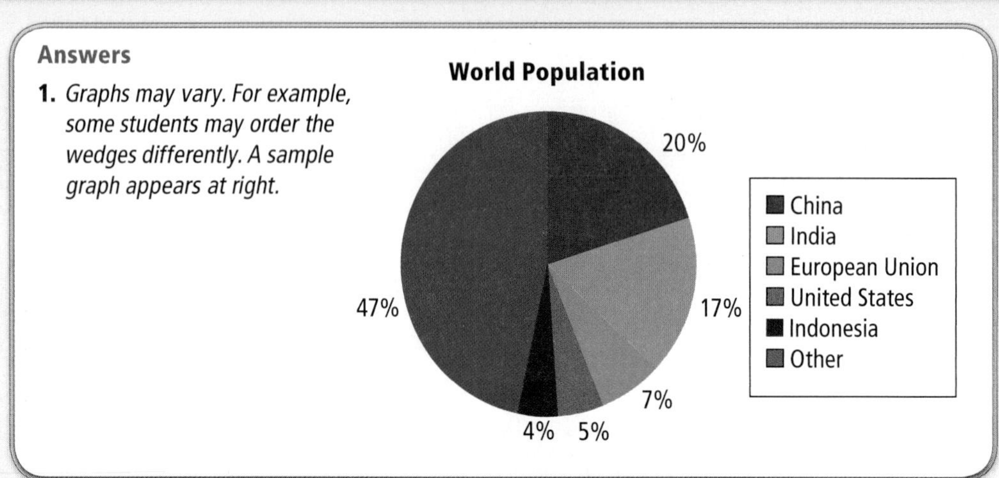

1.10 Creating a Database

Understanding the Skill

A database is a large collection of information that can be organized and searched. You can use a spreadsheet to make a database. First enter information into the spreadsheet. Label each row and column, including units of measure. You can use the spreadsheet software to manipulate the information and answer questions.

Example Which country has the largest per capita oil consumption?

	A	B	C	D	E	F	G
1		United States	European Union	Japan	Russia	Canada	Mexico
2	Oil Consumption (**millions** of barrels per day)	**20.0**	14.6	5.6	2.8	2.2	1.8
3	Population (**millions** of people)	**296**	457	127	143	33	106

Solution

Per capita oil consumption is **oil consumption** divided by **population.** For the U.S. it is

$$\frac{\textbf{20.0}\ \cancel{\text{million}}\ \text{barrels per day}}{\textbf{296}\ \cancel{\text{million}}\ \text{people}} = \frac{\textbf{20.0}\ \text{barrels per day}}{\textbf{296}\ \text{people}} \approx 0.07 \text{ barrels per person per day.}$$

1. Divide row 2 by row 3. Put the answer in row 4.
2. Sort the whole database by row 4, from largest to smallest.

	A	B	C	D	E	F	G
1		**United States**	**Canada**	Japan	European Union	Russia	Mexico
2	Oil Consumption (**millions** of barrels per day)	**20.0**	2.2	5.6	14.6	2.8	1.8
3	Population (**millions** of people)	**296**	33	127	457	143	106
4	Per capita oil consumption (barrels/person/day)	**0.07**	**0.07**	0.04	0.03	0.02	0.02

Once the database is sorted, the United States and Canada are the first in the new order. So the United States and Canada are the countries in the database that have the greatest per capita oil consumption, with consumptions of 0.07 barrels per person per day.

Applying the Skill

Make a database of the information in the table on page R10, by entering the information into spreadsheet software. Multiply each GDP by 1 trillion so the units are "dollars" instead of "trillions of dollars." Multiply each population by 1 million so the units are "people" instead of "millions of people".

Answers

1. *Answers may vary. A sample answer is given (rows and columns may be swapped).*

	A	B	C	D	E	F	G
1		United States	European Union	China	Japan	India	Brazil
2	GDP (U. S. dollars)	11,800,000,000,000	11,700,000,000,000	7,300,000,000,000	3,700,000,000,000	3,300,000,000,000	1,500,000,000,000
3	Population (people)	296,000,000	457,000,000	1,306,000,000	127,000,000	1,080,000,000	186,000,000

	H	I	J	K	L	M
1	Russia	Canada	Mexico	South Korea	Indonesia	Other
2	1,400,000,000,000	1,000,000,000,000	1,000,000,000,000	900,000,000,000	800,000,000,000	11,100,000,000,000
3	143,000,000	33,000,000	106,000,000	49,000,000	242,000,000	2,421,000,000

Contents

Refer to the Economics Skillbuilder Handbook when you need help in answering Application questions or questions in Section Assessments and Chapter Assessments. In addition, the handbook will help you answer questions about charts, graphs, databases, and economic models.

Skills for Understanding Economics

Using Print, Visual, and Technology Sources

1.1 Explaining an Economic Concept

EXPLAINING ECONOMIC CONCEPTS involves clarifying and communicating the basic ideas of economics. Some of these concepts are simple, while others are complex. Three basic steps will help you develop an explanation of a concept, regardless of its complexity.

Understanding the Skill

STRATEGY: Use the steps in the concept-explanation process. The following passage provides information on economic recessions. The table below that provides an analysis of the concept of economic recession based on the concept-explanation process.

1 Identify and define the economic concept.

2 Describe the impact of the concept on the economy.

3 Give an example of the concept. Providing an illustrative example will help underscore your explanation of the concept.

1 An economic recession may be defined as a downturn in the business cycle. During a recession, both production and employment decline. 2 As a result, the economy experiences little, if any, growth. 3 In 1990 and 1991, the United States experienced the greatest recession since the Great Depression. According to some economic analysts, the 1990–1991 recession caused the loss of 1.9 million jobs in 1992.

Make a Table

Use a table like the one shown here to help you explain an economic concept with the three-step process.

Explaining an Economic Concept	
Concept	*Economic recession*
Definition	*A downturn in the business cycle, characterized by a decline in production and employment*
Impact	*Slows economic growth*
Example	*U.S. recession of 1990-1991*

Applying the Skill

Turn to Chapter 7, Section 4, and read about deregulation on page 218. Use a table to explain the economic concept of deregulation with the three-step process.

1.2 Analyzing and Interpreting Data

DATA, or factual information, is the most basic tool of the economist. Economic data is most often in the form of statistics. Economists **ANALYZE** data to learn about economic conditions and trends. They **INTERPRET** data to draw conclusions or make predictions based on their analysis.

Understanding the Skill

STRATEGY: Analyze and interpret the data. Data usually is presented in visual form as a graph or a table like the one below.

1 Read the title. The title provides a good indication of the kind of data shown. Here, the data concerns average food expenditures for several large cities in the Midwest of the United States.

2 Determine how the data is organized. Here, data in each horizontal row provides information on a category of food expenditure. Each vertical column shows expenditures by food category for one of five metropolitan areas.

3 Ask what kinds of questions may be answered from the data. Answering such questions helps in the analysis and interpretation of the data.

1 Average Annual Household Food Expenditures in Selected Midwestern Metropolitan Areas, 2003–2004 (in dollars)

	Chicago	Detroit	Milwaukee	Minneapolis-St. Paul	Cleveland
Cereals and Bakery	472	470	460	509	388
Meats, Fish, and Eggs	855	863	837	779	854
Dairy	366	339	309	431	310
Fruits and Vegetables	606	542	506	610	449
Other Foods at Home	1,128	1,073	950	1,236	822
Food Away from Home	2,597	2,439	2,126	2,983	1,765

Source: Consumer Expenditure Survey, 2003–2004, U.S. Bureau of Labor Statistics

Write a Summary

Summarize your analysis and interpretation of the data in the table

Data in the above table reflects average annual household food expenditures for one year (2003-2004) for 5 Midwestern metropolitan areas. Food expenditures are shown according to type of food purchased: a food at home versus food away from home. The data may be analyzed and interpreted in a number of ways, including the following: comparing expenditures in different cities for foods in a single category or comparing expenditures for two or more food categories within a city; computation of percentages of total expenditure spent on specific food categories.

Applying the Skill

Turn to Chapter 14, Section 2, page 421, and study the table showing data on itemized tax deductions. Write a summary of your analysis and interpretation of data in the table.

1.3 Applying Economic Concepts

When attempting to understand complex economic behavior, economists make constant use of fundamental economic concepts, such as supply, demand, and price. By **APPLYING ECONOMIC CONCEPTS** to everyday situations, economists develop a better understanding of how the economy works.

Understanding the Skill

STRATEGY: Examine the information carefully. The news story below describes a fall in the price of crude oil. The supply and demand curves beneath it graphically illustrate this shift.

1 Look for economic concepts as you read. Such words as *prices, supplies, inventories,* and *capacity* indicate that the topic of this story is the relationship between supply and price.

2 Look for relationships among concepts. The story states that OPEC, the oil-producing cartel, has decided not to curtail production. It also notes that BP could restore lost oil production. So, even if demand remains constant, an increase in supply will cause the equilibrium price to fall.

3 Express the relationship in graphic form. Supply and demand curves provide a vivid picture of the impact of increased supply on price.

Crude Oil Prices Sink Below $66 a Barrel

1 Oil prices fell below $66 a barrel Monday as concerns over 1 supplies eased in expectation that 2 OPEC ministers would not change their production targets. . . .

1 Supplies remain ample. . . . OPEC maintains about 2 million barrels a day of spare 1 capacity, and stocks are high elsewhere; the U.S. Department of Energy said last week that 1 inventories have hit their highest levels since 1998. . . .

2 The possibility that [British Petroleum] could restore 180,000 barrels per day of lost Alaskan production at Prudhoe Bay by the end of October also calmed the market.

Source: Associated Press, September 11, 2006

Draw Demand and Supply Curves

Draw demand and supply curves to illustrate the situation described in the news story. Assume that demand stays constant. The increased supply shifts the supply curve to the right (from S1 to S2), causing prices to fall (from P1 to P2).

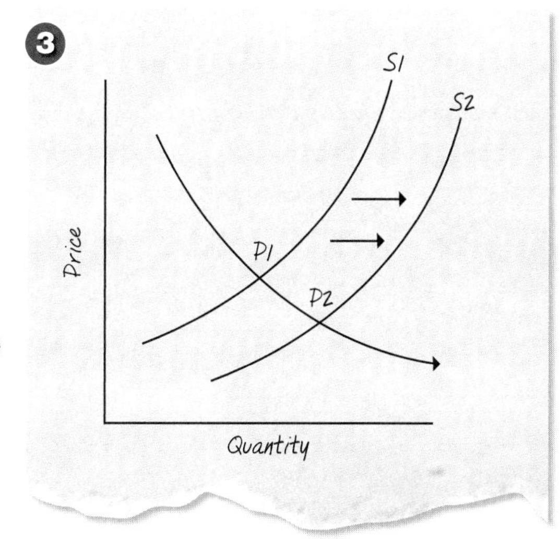

Applying the Skill

In the business section of a newspaper, find a story about a change in price. Analyze the information in the story to determine why the price changed. Then draw supply and demand curves that illustrate the shifts that caused such a change.

1.4 Creating and Interpreting Economic Models

CREATING an economic model involves using information and ideas to show an economic concept or situation in a visual way. An **ECONOMIC MODEL** might be a graph, a diagram, a three-dimensional representation, or a computer program. **INTERPRETING AN ECONOMIC MODEL** involves carefully studying the model in order to draw conclusions or make predictions based on the information it provides.

Understanding the Skill

STRATEGY: Create an economic model. The model below is a circular flow diagram. Economists use the circular flow model to help understand and describe how a market-based economy operates. Use the following steps to create an economic model.

1 Gather the information you need to create an economic model. In this case, you need to show the rules that govern the relationships between economic actors and economic markets in a market economy.

2 Visualize and sketch an idea of your model. The creator of this economic model used a circular diagram to convey the relationships between economic markets and economic actors.

3 Think of symbols you may want to use. Here, different colored arrows indicate the flow of money and the flow of resources and products.

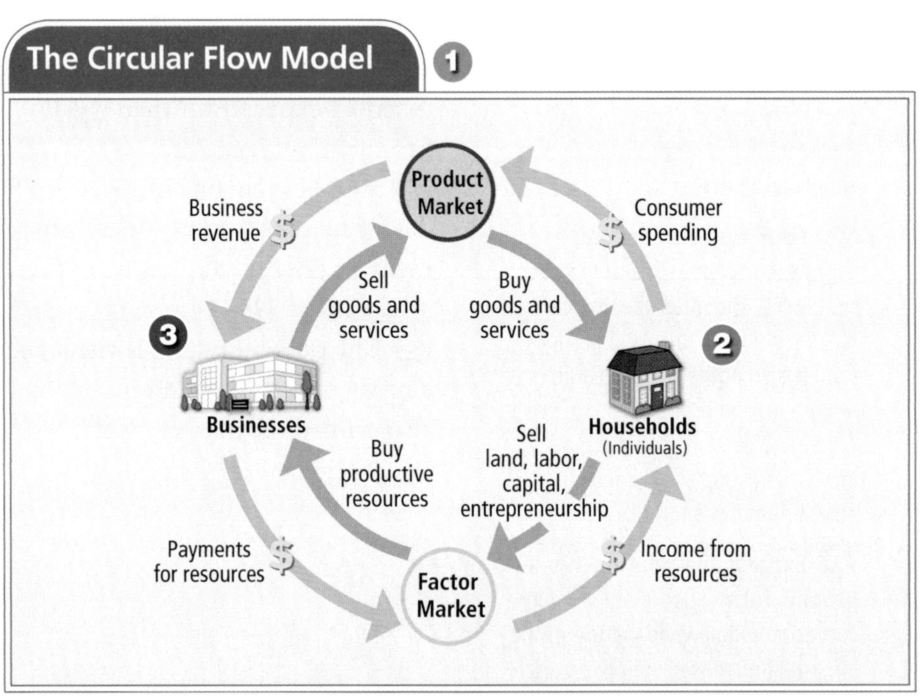

Interpret the Model

Write a summary of your interpretation of the information in the model.

This model illustrates the interactions between businesses and individuals in the economy. The two main economic decision makers, businesses and households, are shown on the left and right of the model. The two main economic markets, product and factor, are shown at the top and bottom. The green arrows represent the flow of money between actors and through the markets. The blue arrows represent the flow of resources and products through the economy.

Applying the Skill

Turn to Chapter 7, Section 1, and read the information on perfect competition on pages 192–194. Create an economic model that shows the relationship between two actors—buyers and sellers—in a perfectly competitive market.

1.5 Using a Decision-Making Process

USING A DECISION-MAKING PROCESS involves choosing between two or more options or courses of action. Organized decision-making involves four steps: 1) identify the problem or situation that requires a decision; 2) identify options; 3) predict possible consequences of the decision; 4) put the decision into effect.

Understanding the Skill

STRATEGY: Use the steps in the decision-making process. The following passage describes how a Polish food producer used a decision-making process to introduce a new product into Poland's convenience food market. The flow chart organizes the elements of the process that was used.

1 **Identify the decision that needs to be made.** In this passage, the title offers a clue to the problem, which is stated more fully in the text.

2 **Identify options.** The company might have chosen to stay out of the convenience food market because most Poles did not own microwave ovens.

3 **Identify possible consequences of the decision.** Remember that there can be more than one possibility. Also look for factors that could affect the consequences.

4 **Note what decision was made and the impact it had.**

1 Polish Meals in the Microwave?

At the beginning of the current millennium, Pudliszki, a Polish firm owned by Heinz, was faced with a decision. 1 Should the company introduce full-course microwaveable meals into Poland's market for convenience foods? Poland's accession into the European Union promised to have a positive effect on both employment and disposable income. And with Polish workers averaging 40 hours on the job, projected demand for convenience foods appeared promising—a strong indication for the product's success. 2 However, households owning microwaves were very much in the minority, which could result in the product's failure. 3 Perhaps banking on an increase in household microwaves, Pudliszki introduced Meals from the Four Corners of the World. According to Euromonitor, an international market research firm, 4 Pudliszki's four full-course meals were "reasonably priced and accepted rather well by the market."

Source: Adapted from "Poland's EU Membership Presents Packaging Opportunities" by Chris Mercer. *Food Industry News*, February 2, 2005.

Make a Flow Chart

In a flow chart, state the decision to be made, its possible consequences, the actual decision, and the actual consequences of the decision.

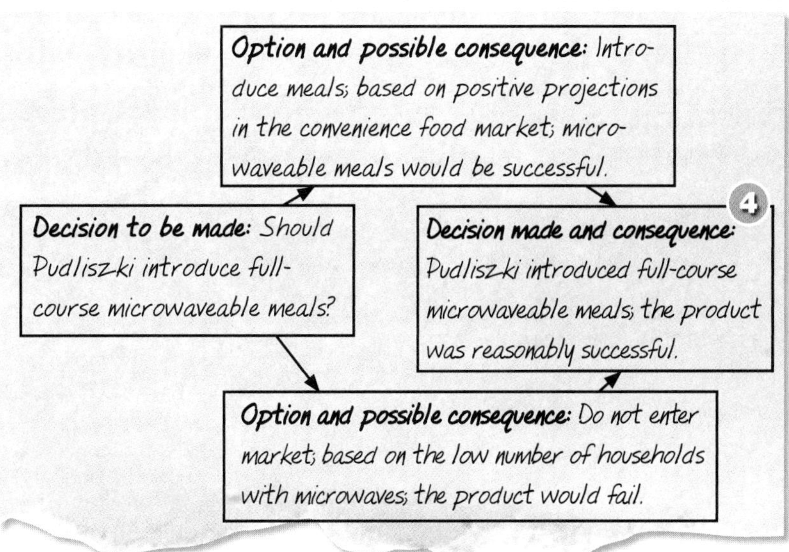

Option and possible consequence: Introduce meals; based on positive projections in the convenience food market; microwaveable meals would be successful.
Decision to be made: Should Pudliszki introduce full-course microwaveable meals?
4
Decision made and consequence: Pudliszki introduced full-course microwaveable meals; the product was reasonably successful.
Option and possible consequence: Do not enter market; based on the low number of households with microwaves; the product would fail.

Applying the Skill

Read the Chapter 1 Case Study, "The Real Cost of Expanding O'Hare Airport," on pages 32–33. From this information, identify the four steps of the decision-making process. Present your findings in a flow chart like the one shown at the right.

1.6 Conducting Cost-Benefit Analyses

A **COST- BENEFIT ANALYSIS** involves determining the economic costs and benefits of an action and then balancing the costs against the benefits.

Understanding the Skill

STRATEGY: Look for the trade-offs that are a part of every economic decision.
The passage below describes the costs and benefits of a government-subsidized business development in Hong Kong. The decision-making grid beneath it summarizes the trade-offs in the project.

1 **Identify the decision that is being made.** The article notes that the Hong Kong government signed an agreement with a large private company to construct a new business.

2 **Note the potential benefits of the decision.** Here, government officials provide estimates of the economic benefits—jobs and money pumped into the economy.

3 **Note the potential costs of the decision.** The article focuses on the huge cost of the project to the government.

4 **Determine if the decision is beneficial.**

1 Hoping to jump-start their economy, government officials in Hong Kong inked an agreement with Walt Disney to build the U.S. company's third overseas theme park. . . . Government officials estimate that 2 construction of Hong Kong Disneyland will create 16,000 jobs. Another 18,400 jobs will be created once the park opens in 2005. Further, they hope that the park will draw millions of tourists to this city every year, raising more than US $1 billion a year.

Few doubt that the project will provide the city with a shot of confidence. Yet John Whaley, a Virginia-based economist, says the construction jobs provided by the project will be short-term positions, with little long-term economic impact. Also, since many tourists to Hong Kong are people of modest means from China, there is no guarantee that they will spend the money to go to the park.

3 Nevertheless, much of the costs for the new park will be paid by the Hong Kong government, which is spending more than US $2.83 billion to build the park. Estimates suggest the government is spending about US $100,000 for every new job it will create when the park is running.

Source: Adapted from "Disney-Park Deal May Not Wave A Magic Wand Over Hong Kong" by Jon E. Hilsenrath and Zach Coleman. *The Wall Street Journal*, November 4, 1999.

Make a Diagram

Summarize the costs and benefits of the Hong Kong government's decision in a diagram. Consider the wisdom of the decision by analyzing these costs and benefits.

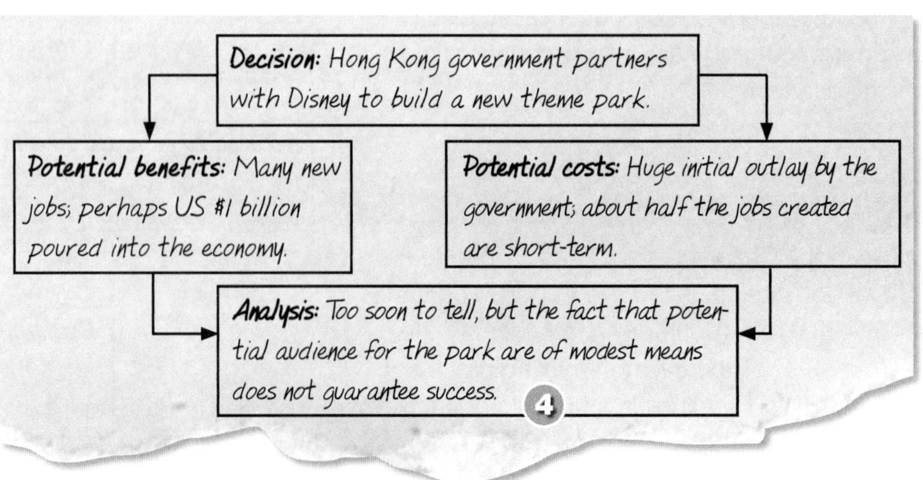

Decision: Hong Kong government partners with Disney to build a new theme park.
Potential benefits: Many new jobs; perhaps US $1 billion poured into the economy.
Potential costs: Huge initial outlay by the government; about half the jobs created are short-term.
Analysis: Too soon to tell, but the fact that potential audience for the park are of modest means does not guarantee success.
4

Applying the Skill

Turn to page 125 and read the article titled "The Year of the Hybrid." Based on the information you find there, conduct a cost-benefit analysis of buying a hybrid automobile.

1.7 Comparing and Contrasting Economic Information

Economists compare and contrast economic programs, concepts, and trends in order to understand them better. **COMPARING** involves finding both similarities and differences between two or more things. **CONTRASTING** means examining only the differences between them.

Understanding the Skill

STRATEGY: Look for similarities and differences. The following passage describes pension reform in Chile and in Britain. The Venn diagram that follows the passage shows some of the similarities and differences between the two economic programs.

1 **Compare: Look for features that two subjects or ideas have in common.** Here, you learn that both Chile and Britain needed to reform their pension systems.

2 **Compare: Look for clue words indicating that two things are alike.** Clue words include *all, both, as, likewise,* and *similarly.*

3 **Contrast: Look for clue words that show how two things differ.** Clue words include *different, however, unlike,* and *except.*

4 **Contrast: Look for ways in which two things are different.** Here you learn that the structure and the administration of the two programs were different.

Pension Reform in Chile and Britain

In the late 20th century, Chile and Britain faced 1 the same problem: how to reform their overburdened pension systems. 2 Both countries had social welfare budgets that were stretched to the limit. And both had pension systems that were nearly bankrupt. To provide for their aging population, Chile and Britain chose privatization as the means to reform their pension programs.

3 However, 4 the structure and administration of the two programs were very different. For example, in Chile a monthly payroll deduction became mandatory for all employees. The payments are administered by one of six private pension funds. In Britain, however, the plan was voluntary. Six million people chose the plan when it was first offered. They received a government rebate, along with responsibility for managing their own retirement money.

Source: Adapted from "In Britain and in Chile, Lessons for Social Security" by Mark Rice-Oxley and Jennifer Ross. *The Christian Science Monitor*, March 14, 2005

Make a Venn Diagram

Summarize similarities and differences in a Venn diagram like the one shown here. In the overlapping area, list characteristics shared by both subjects. Then, in one oval, list the characteristics of one subject not shared by the other. In the other oval, list characteristics unique to the second subject.

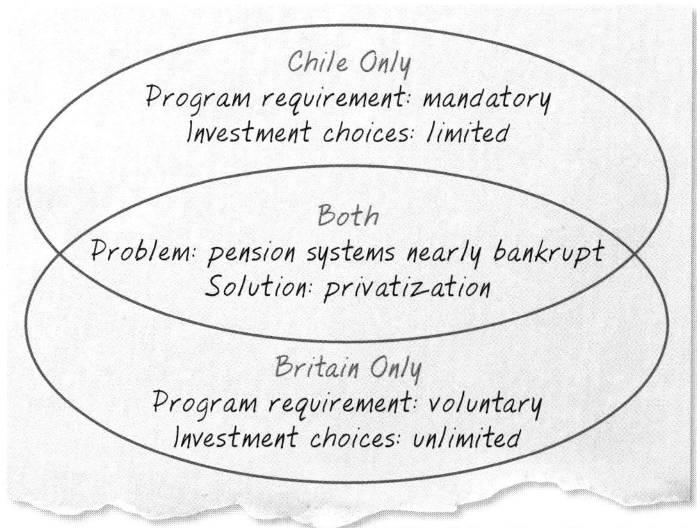

Applying the Skill

Turn to Chapter 8 and read Sections 1 and 2, pages 226–235. Construct a Venn diagram comparing and contrasting sole proprietorships and partnerships.

1.8 Analyzing Cause and Effect

CAUSES are the events, factors, and other reasons that lead to an event or condition. Causes happen before the event in time; they explain why it happened. **EFFECTS** are the results or consequences of the event. One effect often becomes the cause of other effects, resulting in a chain of events. Causes and effects can be both short-term and long-term.

Understanding the Skill

STRATEGY: Keep track of causes and effects as you read. The passage below describes factors leading to a shortfall of qualified staff in India's call centers. The diagram that follows the passage summarizes the economic chain of causes and effects.

1 **Causes: Look for clue words that show cause.** These include *due to, cause,* and *therefore.*

2 **Look for multiple causes and multiple effects.** Increased outsourcing to India caused the series of effects discussed in the rest of the article.

3 **Effects: Look for results or consequences.** Sometimes these are indicated by clue words such as *as a result* and *consequence.*

4 **Notice that an effect may be the cause of another event.** This begins a chain of causes and effects.

Each year, three thousand English speakers graduate from India's universities. 1 Largely due to this pool of job seekers fluent in English, India has been able to establish a highly successful business process outsourcing industry. 2 As businesses in more and more countries outsourced to India, call centers there have become increasingly successful. As a result, salaries for entry-level positions have continued to rise. An unintended 3 consequence of the 4 higher salaries has been a greater tendency of workers to job hop. Increasing success also has created increasing stress, as employees often are required to work long hours. Therefore, employment in call centers, once considered glamorous, has begun to lose its appeal. Analysts claim that such conditions will cause a shortfall of as many as 260,000 qualified workers by 2009.

Source: Adapted from "Busy Signals," *The Economist,* September 10, 2005

Make a Cause-and-Effect Diagram

Summarize cause-and-effect relationships in a diagram. Starting with the first cause in a series, fill in the boxes until you reach the end result.

Cause →	Effect / Cause →	Effect / Cause →	Effect / Cause →	Effect
Many of India's college graduates speak English.	Outsourcing industry enjoys success.	• Pay improves for entry-level jobs. • On-the-job stress increases.	• Workers change jobs often. • Fewer people apply.	There will soon be a shortage of qualified workers.

Applying the Skill

Turn to Chapter 2 and read "Under Pressure to Change" on page 40. Construct a Cause-and-Effect diagram summarizing the information you find.

1.9 Making Inferences and Drawing Conclusions

MAKING INFERENCES involves reading between the lines to extend the information provided. **DRAWING CONCLUSIONS** involves analyzing what has been read and forming an opinion about its meaning.

Understanding the Skill

STRATEGY: Develop inferences from the facts. Use the facts to draw conclusions. The passage below describes the U.S. trade deficit in 2005. The diagram that follows shows how to organize the facts and inferences to draw conclusions.

1 **Read carefully to understand all the facts.** Fact: The U.S. trade deficit rose almost 18 percent in 2005.

2 **Use the facts to make an inference.** Inference: It's unlikely that the United States will see a trade surplus in the foreseeable future.

3 **Read between the lines to make inferences.** Inference: Continued dependence on foreign oil will continue to increase the deficit.

4 **Ask questions of the material.** How can the United States reduce its trade deficit?

5 **Use all this information to draw a conclusion.** Conclusion: In order to reduce the deficit, the United States will need to reduce its dependence on foreign oil.

1 The U.S. trade deficit jumped nearly 18 percent in 2005, the government reported Friday, hitting its fourth consecutive record as consumer demand for imports increased, energy prices soared and the dollar strengthened against other currencies.

The $725.8 billion gap, 1 which is almost exactly twice the deficit in 2001, was driven by a 12 percent jump in imports and a more muted 10 percent increase in exports, the Commerce Department reported in Washington. 2 The nation last had a trade surplus, of $12.4 billion, in 1975.

3 The nation's deficit in trade for petroleum products accounted for 29 percent of the total gap, up from 25 percent in 2004. 4 Imports of petroleum goods climbed 39 percent, to $251.6 billion, after rising by 39 percent in 2004. Excluding oil and other petroleum products, the trade deficit would have grown 10 percent, to $537 billion.

Source: "The U.S. Trade Deficit Hit Record High in 2005" by Vikas Bajaj. *The New York Times,* February 10, 2006

Applying the Skill

Read the online news story "China's Economic Miracle; the High Price of Progress" on page 571. Use the chart at the right as a model for organizing facts, inferences, and conclusions about the passage.

Facts	Inferences	Conclusion about Passage
The U.S. trade deficit rose almost 18 percent in 2005. The deficit nearly doubled between 2001 and 2005.	The deficit is growing at a marked rate.	5 In order to reduce the deficit, the United States will need to reduce its dependence on foreign oil.
Last trade surplus was in 1975.	Trade surplus is unlikely in foreseeable future.	
Trade in petroleum products accounted for 29 percent of deficit.	Continued dependence on foreign oil will continue to increase the deficit.	

1.10 Evaluating Economic Decisions

EVALUATING ECONOMIC DECISIONS means making judgments about decisions that individuals, businesses, and governments make on economic matters. Economists evaluate a decision based on its outcome and the choices available when that decision was made.

Understanding the Skill

STRATEGY: Look for choices and reasons. The following passage describes the marketing decisions Joe Sillett made to promote a cricket bat he had begun to manufacture. As you read the passage, look for alternative decisions he could have made.

1 Look at decisions made by individuals or by groups. Identify the decision Sillett made to market his company's product.

2 Look at the outcome of the decisions.

3 Analyze a decision in terms of the choices that were possible. Sillett could have chosen a marketing strategy that was less expensive and therefore less risky. Make a simple chart of your analysis.

Marketing Woodworm

When Joe Sillett formed his company, Woodworm, to make cricket bats, he was up against stiff competition. . . Sillett had to decide how to break into the market. Should he utilize traditional marketing techniques, such as the development and purchase of print and media ads, to introduce his product? Or should he try something bolder? 1 Sillett decided to risk most of his marketing budget on a single idea: the sponsorship of two English heavy hitters—Andrew Flintoff and Kevin Pietersen. Sillett's idea proved to be a winner. 2 In just three years, Woodworm bats succeeded in capturing ten percent of the cricket bat market.

3 Sillett knew that a less expensive approach would have allowed him to grow his company over a more extended period of time. But because he believed that linking Woodworm bats with high profile players would quickly create brand recognition, Sillett risked the future of his company on a single marketing idea and won.

Source: Adapted from "The Benefits of Woodworm." *The Economist*, September 8th, 2005

3

Sillett's Choices	Pros	Cons	Evaluation
Sponsor popular players	Possible to gain market share quickly	Risky and expensive	In your opinion, which was the better choice? Why?
Pursue a less expensive marketing strategy	Less risky	Market share likely to grow slowly	

Applying the Skill

Pages 234–235 of Chapter 8 describe Bart's decision to open his comic store as a partnership rather than a sole proprietorship. Make a chart like the one shown to summarize the pros and cons of his decision and your evaluation of that decision.

1.11 Synthesizing Economic Data

SYNTHESIZING ECONOMIC DATA is the skill economists use to develop interpretations of past economic events. Like detective work, synthesizing involves putting together clues from data to form an overall picture of an economic event.

Understanding the Skill

STRATEGY: Build an interpretation as you read. The passage below describes the collapse of Enron, a giant American energy company. Note how combining different data leads to a synthesis—an overall picture of Enron's fall and its significance.

1 **Read carefully to understand the data.** These statements explain why Enron borrowed money and how it succeeded in hiding $600 million in debt.

2 **Look for variables in the data that need an explanation.** Here, the data in the two statements present a puzzling picture. They lead one to question how a large company that tripled its profits could experience a loss of $638 million less than a year later.

3 **Form a synthesis based on the data.** This interpretation brings together the different pieces of data to arrive at a new understanding of the subject. Summarize your synthesis in a graphic organizer, such as a table or a cluster diagram.

Enron's Downfall

1 Enron began to borrow money to invest in new projects. Enron then created partnerships to keep the debt off its books. One partnership . . . allowed Enron to keep $600 million in debt off the books it showed to the government and to people who own Enron stock.
2 In December 2000, Enron claimed to have tripled its profits in two years.
2 The collapse began in October [2001], when Enron announced a loss of $638 million. In November, Enron said that it had overstated earnings for the past four years and it now owed over $6 billion. With these announcements, Enron's stock price took a dive.
3 Since Enron had made deals based on the assumption that the stock would go up, it suddenly had to repay lots of money. When Enron could not come up with the cash, it declared bankruptcy.
3 [One] consequence of [Enron's] failure may be new laws that change how much money big businesses can give politicians. Enron gave over $5 million to [political] campaigns since 1998. Lawmakers [also] are considering whether to make new laws to better regulate accounting practices.

Source: "Not Business as Usual," by Elisabeth Bauman. Online NewsHour Extra, January 30, 2002 (www.pbs.org)

Applying the Skill

Read the information on income distribution and income inequality on pages 390–391. Look for data to support a synthesis about the effectiveness and limitations of measuring income inequality. Organize your findings in a table or cluster diagram.

R23

1.12 Generalizing from Economic Information

GENERALIZING involves making broad judgments based on information from more than one source. When you form generalizations, you need to be sure they are based on sufficient evidence and that they are consistent with the information given.

Understanding the Skill

STRATEGY: Look for common themes. The following three excerpts reflect concern regarding the economic deprivation of the elderly during the Great Depression.

1 **Determine what information the sources have in common.** All the sources suggest the need for a government program to provide pensions to the elderly.

2 **Form a generalization about the common information.**

3 **State your generalization in sentence form.** A generalization often needs a qualifying word, such as *most, many,* or *some,* to make it valid.

Plight of the Elderly

1 We also propose to give the old-age pensions to the old people . . . so that the people who reach the age of sixty can be retired from the active labor of life and given an opportunity to have surcease [rest] and ease for the balance of the life that they have on earth.

—Governor Huey Long of Louisiana

1 "Old age dependent pensions . . . are not gifts from charity. They are for compensation well earned."

—Flyer attached to a letter written to President Franklin D. Roosevelt by a woman asking for help for her 81-year-old mother

1 "It is estimated that the population of the age of 60 and above in the United States is somewhere between nine and twelve millions. I suggest that the national government retire all who reach that age on a monthly pension of $200 a month or more."

—Francis E. Townsend

Make a Web Diagram

Using a diagram can help you make generalizations. The diagram below records relevant information from the three statements that leads to a valid generalization.

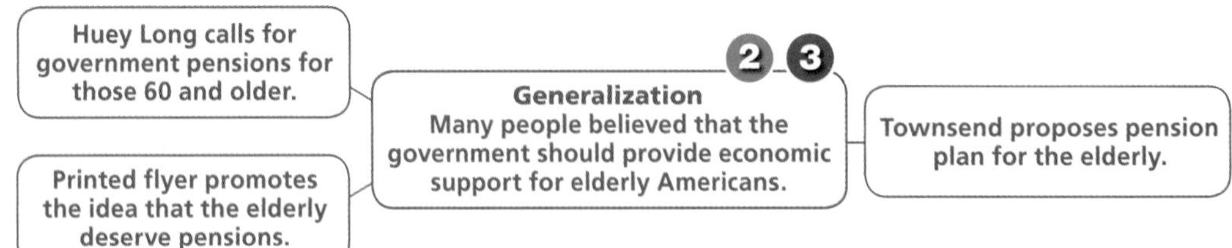

Huey Long calls for government pensions for those 60 and older.
Printed flyer promotes the idea that the elderly deserve pensions.
2 3
Generalization
Many people believed that the government should provide economic support for elderly Americans.
Townsend proposes pension plan for the elderly.

Applying the Skill

Read the information under the headings "Changing Occupations" and "Changes in the Way People Work" on pages 268–271. Use a diagram like the one above to make a generalization about technology and work in the United States today.

1.13 Predicting Economic Trends

PREDICTING ECONOMIC TRENDS involves projecting the outcome or the continuation of an economic condition or trend. Economists use their knowledge of past economic events and conditions and related decisions to predict the outcome of current economic events and conditions.

Understanding the Skill

STRATEGY: Identify decisions. The following passage describes how the United States government, under the leadership of President Franklin D. Roosevelt, dealt with a nationwide banking crisis during the Great Depression.

1. **To help you identify decisions, look for clue words.** These words include *decide, decision,* and *chose.*
2. **Notice how one economic decision often leads to others.**
3. **Notice that decisions may have positive or negative impacts.**
4. **Consider alternatives to the decisions that were made.**
5. **Make a chart to record decisions, suggest alternative decisions, and predict a possible outcome for each alternative decision.**

During the Great Depression, many banks in the United States failed. In 1933 Americans, fearing the loss of their money, created "runs" on banks throughout the country. A bank run occurs when large numbers of people attempt to withdraw money within a short period of time. Banks did not have enough money to meet the demand.

In response, President Roosevelt (1) decided to temporarily shut down the nation's banks by proclaiming a bank holiday. (2) Congress (1) chose to pass a law in support of Roosevelt's decision. The law also provided for the rehabilitation of the nation's banking facilities. To avoid an epidemic of bank failures, (3) it was decided not to reopen all the banks at the same time. Instead, banks would open once they had been examined and judged to be sound. In addition, the government made the (1) decision to issue new currency—based on sound assets—so that banks, once reopened, would have enough currency to meet increased demand. Finally, it was decided to include state banks that were not members of the Federal Reserve in the rehabilitation process. The government response to the banking crisis served to stabilize the U.S. banking system.

Source: Franklin D. Roosevelt's First Fireside Chat, March 12, 1933

Applying the Skill

Read the document titled "Two American Entrepreneurs Start Out in a Garage" on page 252 and identify three business decisions that "the two Steves" made. Record them in a chart similar to the one shown for the passage above, along with an alternative decision for each. Then predict a possible outcome for each alternative decision.

(5)

Decisions	Alternative Decisions (4)	Prediction of Outcome
FDR proclaimed a nationwide bank holiday.	FDR did not proclaim a bank holiday.	The run on banks continued.
Congress passed a law to rehabilitate banking facilities.	Congress passed no law to rehabilitate banking facilities.	Banks were not rehabilitated.
New currency was issued.	New currency was not issued.	There was not enough money to meet depositors' demands.
State banks would receive assistance.	Fed did not assist non-member state banks.	State banks failed to reopen.

2.1 Analyzing Political Cartoons

POLITICAL CARTOONS are drawings that express the artist's point of view about a local, national, or international situation or event. They may criticize, show approval, or draw attention to a particular issue, and may be either serious or humorous. Political cartoonists often use symbols as well as other visual clues to communicate their message.

Understanding the Skill

STRATEGY: Examine the cartoon carefully. The cartoon below was drawn as a comment on the process of globalization.

1. **Look at the cartoon as a whole to determine the subject.**
2. **Look for symbols, which are especially effective in communicating ideas visually.** Here, the cartoonist uses symbols that stand for a global economy. The arm in a suit stands for big business. The globe stands for Earth and its resources. The people represent consumers.
3. **Analyze the visual details, which help express the artist's point of view.** The Western-style house and clothing suggest that the people are Americans or Europeans. The people are smiling, indicating that they are happy about what is being offered to them.

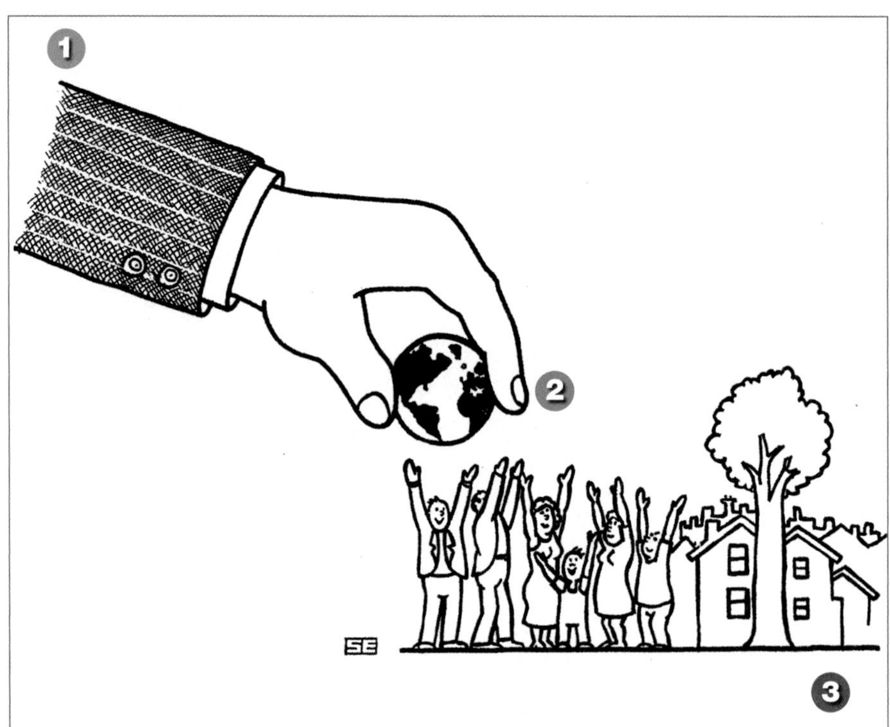

Make a Chart

Summarize your interpretation in a chart. Look for details and interpret their significance. Then decide on the message of the cartoon.

Symbols and Visual Details	Significance	Message
Oversized arm in business suit	Corporations	Big business is the driving force behind globalization.
Disproportionately small Earth	Earth as the property of big business	
Happy people reaching out	Consumers	

Applying the Skill

Turn to page 283 and study the political cartoon. Note the clothing and apparent attitudes of the figures in the cartoon, as well as how they relate to one another. Then analyze the cartoon by making a chart like the one to the left.

2.2 Distinguishing Fact from Opinion

FACTS are events, dates, statistics, or statements that can be proved to be true. Facts can be checked for accuracy. **OPINIONS** are judgments, beliefs, and feelings of the writer or speaker.

Understanding the Skill

STRATEGY: Find clues in the text. The following excerpt describes economist Sir William Beveridge's 1942 recommendations for creating a welfare state in Great Britain.

1 **Facts: Look for specific names, dates, statistics, and statements that can be proved.** The first paragraph gives a factual account of the government's plan.

2 **Opinion: Look for assertions, claims, hypotheses, and judgments.** Beveridge expresses his opinion regarding provision for old age and for medical care.

3 **Opinion: Look for judgment words that the writer uses to describe policies and events.** Judgment words are often adjectives that are used to arouse a reader's emotions.

1 The coalition British Government has unveiled plans for a welfare state offering care to all from the cradle to the grave. The Beveridge report proposes a far-reaching series of changes designed to provide a financial safety net to ensure a "freedom from want" after the war is over. Everyone of working age would be expected to pay a weekly national insurance contribution. In return benefits would be paid to the sick, widowed, retired, unemployed and there would also be an allowance for families.

The architect of the report, economist Sir William Beveridge, drew on advice from various government departments. 2 He found provision for old age represented one of the most pressing problems. But there were other failings too. Medical provision was not universally available to all and Britain's achievement, in his words, "fell seriously short" compared with other countries of the world.

At a time when the war was destroying landmarks of every kind, [Beveridge] said, it was a 3 "revolutionary moment in the world's history, a time for revolutions, not for patching."

Source: BBC News

Make a Chart

Divide facts and opinions in a chart. Summarize and separate the facts from the opinions expressed in the passage.

Facts	*Opinions*
In 1942 the British government unveiled plans for a welfare state. The plan was based on a report by Sir William Beveridge and was designed to provide British citizens with a financial safety net.	• *The British government's provision for old age represented one of the most pressing problems.* • *Britain's medical provision fell seriously short as compared to that of other countries.* • *It was a revolutionary moment in history.*

Applying the Skill

Read "Government and Demand-Side Policies" on page 457. Using a chart like the one to the left, summarize the facts, opinions, and judgments stated. Look carefully at the language used in order to separate one from the other.

2.3 Evaluating Online Sources

EVALUATING ONLINE SOURCES involves making judgments about sites that are available on the Internet—a network of computers associated with universities, libraries, news organizations, government agencies, and other information providers. Each location on the Internet has a home page with its own address, or URL. The international collection of home pages, known as the **WORLD WIDE WEB,** is a good source of up-to-the-minute information as well as in-depth research on economic subjects.

Understanding the Skill

STRATEGY: Explore and evaluate the elements on the screen. The computer screen below shows "Treasury's Learning Vault," the education page of the United States Department of the Treasury.

1 Go directly to a Web page. Access the Internet using your Internet Service Provider (ISP). If you know the address of the Web site you want, type it in the address box at the top of your computer screen, then press ENTER or RETURN. (To access the page shown here, type in www.ustreas.gov/education.)

2 Explore the features and links. Click on any one of the images or topics to find out more about a specific subject. These links take you to other pages at this Web site. Some links take you to related information that can be found at other places on the Internet.

3 Evaluate the Web site. Use the information you gathered in Step 2 to evaluate the Web site. Ask yourself the following questions: Is the information provided by the site useful to an economist or a student of economics? How reliable is this information?

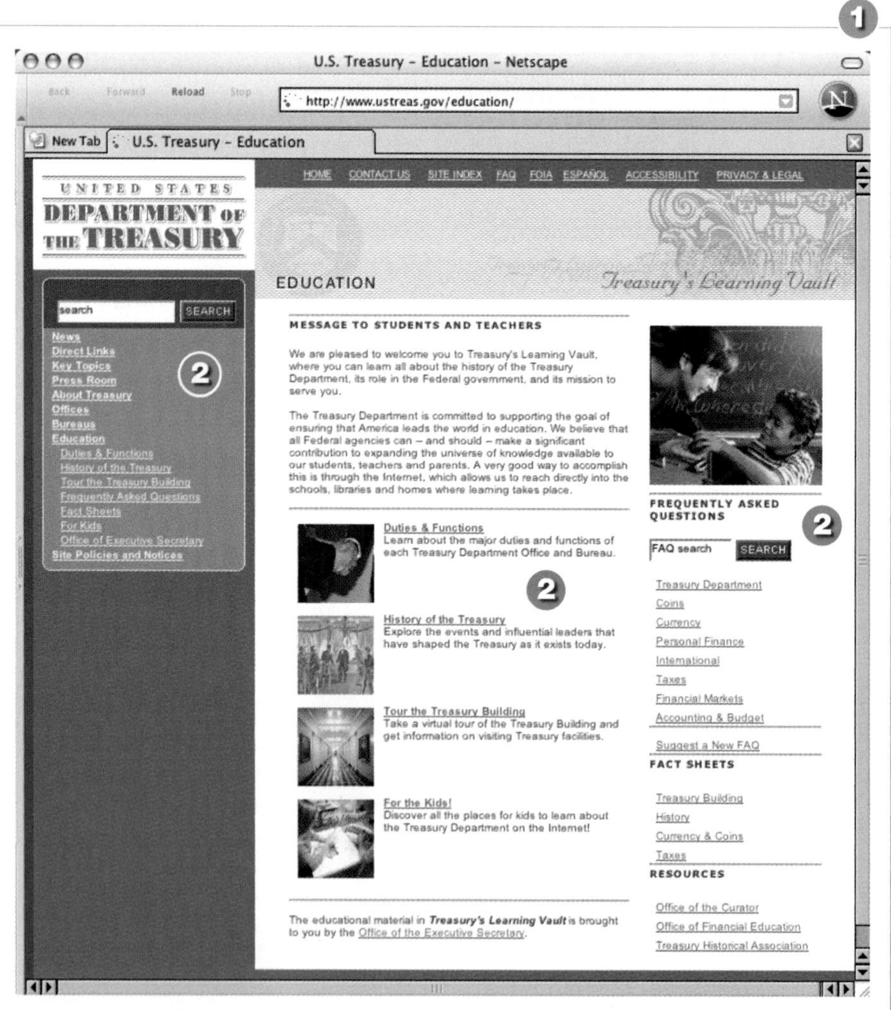

Applying the Skill

Access the Bureau of Labor Statistics (www.bls.gov) and the Census Bureau (www.census.gov) Websites through ClassZone.com. How useful do you think these sites might be to economists? How might economists use the information on these sites?

2.4 Interpreting Graphs

GRAPHS show statistical information in a visual manner. Economists use graphs to show comparative amounts, ratios, trends, and changes over time. Interpreting graphs will increase your understanding of economic trends and data. **LINE GRAPHS** can show changes over time, or trends. Usually, the horizontal axis shows a unit of time, such as years, and the vertical axis shows quantities. **PIE GRAPHS** are useful for showing relative proportions. The circle represents the whole, such as the entire population, and the slices represent the different groups that make up the whole. **BAR GRAPHS** compare numbers or sets of numbers. The length of each bar indicates a quantity. With bar graphs, it is easy to see at a glance how different categories compare.

Understanding the Skill

STRATEGY: Study all the elements of the graph. This double line graph shows the number of new firms started and the number of firm closures from 1994 to 2005.

1 **Read the title to identify the content of the graph.** Here, the title explicitly states the content of the graph—new firms and firm closures.

2 **Read the vertical and horizontal axes.** The vertical axis shows the number of firms, and the horizontal axis shows years.

3 **Look at the legend to understand what colors and symbols represent.** In this graph, different colored lines are used to represent new firms and firm closures.

4 **Summarize the information shown in each part of the graph.** What trend does each line show?

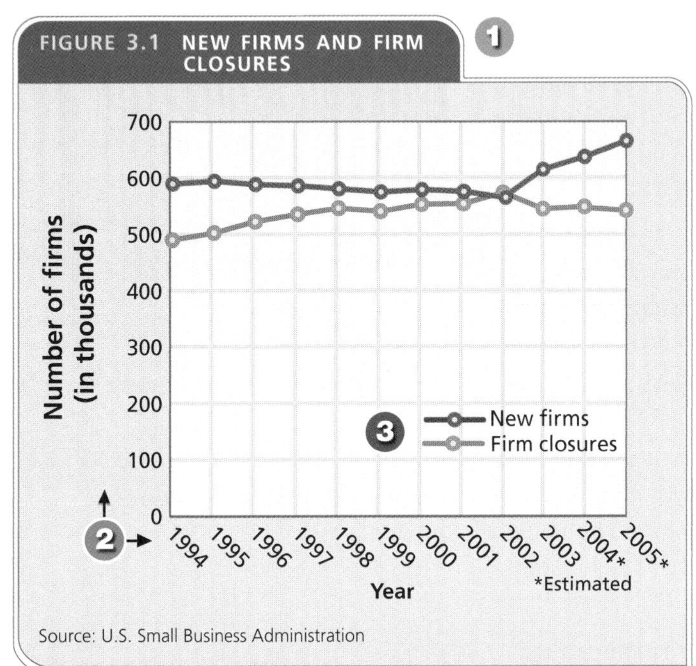

Write a Summary

Write a summary paragraph to show what you have learned from the graph.

4 *Each year from 1994 to 2005, about 600,000 new firms opened in the United States. During the same time period, anywhere from 500,000 to about 575,000 firms closed. In 2002, there actually were more firm closures than new firm openings. The overall trend shows that nearly as many firms close as open each year.*

Applying the Skill

Turn to page 267 and study Figure 9.7, a graph that provides information on the U.S. labor force. Write a paragraph summarizing what you learn from the graph.

R29

2.5 Interpreting Tables

TABLES present information in a visual form. Tables are created by simplifying, summarizing, and organizing information into a format that is easy to understand. Tables are the most commonly used charts in Economics books.

Understanding the Skill

STRATEGY: Study all the elements of the table. The table shown here provides statistical information about employment in the United States.

1 **Read the title to identify the main idea of the table.** This table provides information on selected aspects of the United States labor force during 2006.

2 **Read the headings to determine how the table is organized.** In this table, data is organized by category and by month.

3 **Study the data in the table to understand what the table was designed to show.** This table shows economic data regarding employment in the United States during a six-month period in 2006.

4 **Be sure to read any footnotes provided with the table. Footnotes clarify information.** For example, (P) indicates that a statistic is preliminary rather than final.

5 **Summarize the information shown in each part of the table.** Use the title and side headings to help you focus on what information the table is presenting.

Selected Labor Force Statistics, February to July, 2006 1

2 Month	Unemployment Rate (percent)	New Jobs Added (thousands)	Average Hourly Earnings[1] (in dollars)
February	4.8	200	16.47
March	4.7	175	16.51 3
April	4.7	112	16.61
May	4.6	100	16.62
June	4.6	124[P]	16.69[P]
July	4.8	113[P]	16.76[P]

Footnotes:
(P) Preliminary 
(1) For production and nonsupervisory workers, in dollars and cents
Source: Bureau of Labor Statistics

5 *The table provides statistical information about employment in the United States. Statistics are given for each of six months, from February through July 2006. The unemployment rate fluctuated between 4.6 and 4.8 percent. There was an increase in the number of jobs each month, with the greatest increase occurring in June and the smallest in May. Average hourly earnings rose fairly steadily from $16.47 in February to $16.76 July.*

Applying the Skill

Turn to page 79 and study Figure 3.3. Then write a paragraph summarizing the information presented in the table.

2.6 Analyzing Databases

A **DATABASE** is a collection of data, or information, that is organized so that you can find and retrieve information on a specific topic quickly and easily. You can search for specific information without going through the entire database. A database provides a list of all information related to a specific topic.

Understanding the Skill

STRATEGY: Study the elements of the database. First identify the topic. The title "World's Top Oil Consumers" indicates the criterion for listing the six nations in the database. Look at the categories shown and pose questions about what you can learn from them. For example, in this database you could search for "countries consuming more than 10 million bbls (barrels) per day" and discover that the United States and the European Union fall into that category.

1 Determine the order of presentation of information. The six countries in this database are listed according to the amount of oil they consume, from most to least.

2 Identify the entries included under each heading. Here, the data in each row relates to one of the six countries listed.

3 Determine how the categories in the database relate to one another. This database includes the categories "oil production" and "proved oil reserves." Both relate to oil consumption. These related categories enable you, for example, to determine which countries, if any, produce less oil than they consume.

4 Read any labels or footnotes that clarify the nature of the data. In this database, the figures represent barrels (bbl) of oil. Also note that for purposes of providing statistical information, the EU is considered to be one country.

5 Note the source of the data. Is the source reliable? The source of data here is The CIA World Factbook, a respected and reliable source of data on the countries of the world.

World's Top Oil Consumers (3)

Country	Oil Consumption (Millions of bbl[1] / day)	Oil Production (Millions of bbl[1] / day)	Proved Oil Reserves (Billions of bbl[1])
(2) United States	20.0 (1)	7.6	22.5
European Union[2]	14.6	3.4	7.3
China	6.4	3.5	18.3
Russia	2.8	9.1	69.0
Saudi Arabia	1.8	9.5	262.7
Iran	1.4	4.0	133.3

Footnotes: 

(1) Barrels

(2) For data presentation, treated as a single country

Source: The CIA World Factbook, 2005 data (5)

Analyze the Database

Consider the kinds of information that you could quickly find from the database. For example, you can search for countries that produce or consume more or less oil than a specific number of barrels per day. Make a list of the kinds of information you could search for in this database.

Applying the Skill

Turn to page A12 in the Economic Atlas and Statistics and review the information in the two sets of graphs. Create a database for United States industry using statistics for the most recent year shown. Consider the steps listed above when creating your database.

Glossary

A

absolute advantage *n.* the ability of one trading nation to make a product more efficiently than another trading nation (p. 513)

aggregate demand *n.* the sum of all the demand in the economy (p. 360)

aggregate supply *n.* the sum of all the supply in the economy (p. 360)

antitrust legislation *n.* laws that define monopolies and give government the power to control or dissolve them (p. 214)

appropriations *n.* set amounts of money put aside for specific purposes (p. 431)

authoritarian *adj.* requiring absolute loyalty and obedience to authority (p. 43)

automated teller machine (ATM) *n.* an electronic device that allows bank customers to make transactions without seeing a bank officer (p. 308)

automatic stabilizer *n.* a feature of fiscal policy that works automatically to steady the economy (p. 447)

B

balanced budget *n.* a budget in which total government revenue is equal to total government spending (p. 436)

balance of payments *n.* a record of all the transactions that occurred between the individuals, businesses, and government units of one nation and those of the rest of the world (p. 529)

balance of trade *n.* the difference between the value of a country's imports and exports (p. 529)

bank exam *n.* an audit, conducted by the Federal Reserve, of a bank's financial practices (p. 481)

bank holding company *n.* a company that owns more than one bank (p. 481)

barrier to entry *n.* anything that hinders a business from entering a market (p. 198)

barter *n.* the exchange of goods and services without using money (p. 288)

bear market *n.* a situation in which stock market prices decline steadily over time (p. 335)

binding arbitration *n.* a process by which an impartial third party resolves disputes between management and unions (p. 280)

black market *n.* the illegal business of buying or selling goods or services in violation of price controls or rationing (p. 183)

Board of Governors *n.* the board of seven appointed members that supervises the operations of the Federal Reserve System and sets monetary policy (p. 476)

bond *n.* a contract a corporation issues that promises to repay borrowed money, plus interest, on a fixed schedule (p. 240)

bounced check *see* overdraft

break-even point *n.* a situation in which total costs and total revenues are the same (p. 142)

budget *n.* a plan for allocating income for saving and spending (p. 574)

budget deficit *n.* a situation in which the government spends more than it takes in (p. 462)

budget surplus *n.* a situation in which the government takes in more than it spends (p. 462)

bull market *n.* a situation in which stock market prices rise steadily over time (p. 335)

business cycle *n.* the series of growing and shrinking periods of economic activity, measured by increases or decreases in real gross domestic product (p. 358)

business organization *n.* an enterprise that produces goods or provides services, usually to make a profit (p. 226)

business structure *see* business organization

C

capital *n.* all the resources people make and use to produce and distribute goods and services (p. 8)

capital budget *n.* a plan for major expenses or investments (p. 436)

capital deepening *n.* an increase in the ratio of capital to labor (p. 371)

capital flight *n.* a situation in which capital from a country is invested outside the country (p. 558)

capital gain *n.* the profit made from the sale of securities (p. 330)

capitalism *n.* an economic system based on private ownership of the factors of production (p. 49)

capital market *n.* a market in which long-term financial assets are bought and sold (p. 322)

cartel *n.* a formal organization of sellers or producers who regulate the production, pricing, and marketing of a product (pp. 198, 535)

cease and desist order *n.* a ruling requiring a firm to stop an unfair business practice (p. 217)

central bank *n.* a nation's main monetary authority (p. 474)

centrally planned economy *n.* a system in which the society's leaders make all economic decisions (p. 42)

change in demand *n.* a situation in which a change in the marketplace prompts consumers to buy different amounts of a good or service at every price (p. 109)

change in quantity demanded *n.* a change in the amount of a product that consumers will buy because of a change in price (p. 108)

change in quantity supplied *n.* an increase or decrease in the amount of a good or service that producers are willing to sell because of a change in price (p. 146)

change in supply *n.* a situation in which a change in the marketplace prompts producers to offer different amounts for sale at every price (p. 148)

check clearing *n.* a service provided by the Federal Reserve to record receipts and expenditures of bank clients (p. 480)

circular flow model *n.* a visualization of all interactions in a market economy (p. 52)

civilian labor force *n.* people age 16 or older who are employed or actively looking for and available to do work (p. 266)

claim *n.* a request to an insurance company for payment on an insured loss (p. 596)

closed shop *n.* a business in which an employer can hire only union members (p. 279)

coincident indicators *n.* measures of economic performance that usually change at the same time as real gross domestic product changes (p. 364)

collective bargaining *n.* the process of negotiation between a business and its organized employees to establish wages and improve working conditions (p. 280)

command economy *n.* an economic system in which the government makes all economic decisions (p. 39)

commodity money *n.* money that has intrinsic value based on the material from which it is made (p. 291)

common stock *n.* a share of ownership in a corporation that gives the holder voting rights and a share of profits (p. 331)

communism *n.* an economic system in which there is no private ownership of property and little or no political freedom (p. 43)

comparative advantage *n.* the ability of one trading nation to produce something at a lower opportunity cost than that of another trading nation (p. 513)

competition *n.* the effort of two or more people acting independently to get business by offering the best deal (p. 49)

competitive pricing *n.* a situation in which producers sell goods and services at prices that best balance the twin desires of making the highest profit and luring customers away from rival producers (p. 174)

complements *n.* products that are used together, so the increase or decrease in demand for one will result in an increase or decrease in demand for the other (p. 112)

conglomerate *n.* a business composed of companies that produce unrelated goods or services (p. 243)

consumer *n.* a person who buys goods or services for personal use (p. 5)

consumer price index (CPI) *n.* a measure of changes in the prices of goods and services that consumers commonly purchase (p. 396)

consumer sovereignty *n.* the idea that consumers have the ultimate control over what is produced because they are free to buy what they want and refuse products they do not want (p. 50)

contingent employment *n.* temporary or part-time work (p. 270)

contract *n.* a formal, legally binding agreement (p. 598)

contraction *n.* a decrease in economic activity (p. 359); *see* business cycle

contractionary fiscal policy *n.* a plan to reduce aggregate demand and slow down the economy during a period of too-rapid economic expansion (p. 446)

contractionary monetary policy *n.* a plan to reduce the amount of money in circulation; also called tight-money policy (p. 492)

cooperative *n.* a type of business operated for the shared benefit of the owners, who are also its customers (p. 250)

co-pay *n.* an amount the insured owes when an insured receives health care (p. 596)

corporate income tax *n.* a tax based on a corporation's profits (p. 412)

corporation *n.* a business owned by shareholders, also called stockholders, who own the rights to the company's profits but face only limited liability for the company's debts and losses (p. 238)

cosigner *n.* a person who assumes responsibility for the debt if the borrower fails to repay the loan (p. 583)

cost-benefit analysis *n.* the practice of examining the costs and the expected benefits of a choice as an aid to decision making (p. 15)

cost-push inflation *n.* a situation in which increases in production costs push up prices (p. 399)

R33

Council of Economic Advisers *n.* the three-member group that advises the President on fiscal policy and other economic issues (p. 452)

coupon rate *n.* the interest rate a bond-holder receives every year until the bond matures (p. 338)

craft union *n.* an organization of workers with similar skills who work in different industries for different employers (p. 274)

credit *n.* the practice of buying goods or services now and paying for them in the future (p. 582)

credit report *n.* a statement by a credit bureau that details a consumer's credit record (p. 586)

credit score *n.* a number that summarizes a consumer's creditworthiness (p. 586)

crowding-out effect *n.* a situation in which the government outbids private bond interest rates to gain loanable funds (p. 466)

currency *n.* paper money and coins (pp. 293, 475)

customs duty *n.* a tax on goods imported into the United States (p. 425)

customs unions *n.* agreements that abolish trade barriers among the members and establish uniform tariffs for non-members (p. 532)

cyclical unemployment *n.* unemployment caused by the part of the business cycle with decreased economic activity (p. 384)

D

debit card *n.* a card one can use like an ATM card to withdraw cash or like a check to make purchases (p. 308)

debt restructuring *n.* a method countries with outstanding debt obligations use to alter the terms of debt agreements to achieve some advantage (p. 559)

deductible *n.* the amount the insured pays before the insurance company pays (p. 596)

default *n.* the condition that occurs when a nation cannot pay interest or principle on a loan (p. 559)

deficit spending *n.* the government practice of spending more than it collects in revenue for a specific fiscal year (p. 462)

deflation *n.* a decrease in the general price level (p. 398)

demand *n.* the desire to have some good or service and the ability to pay for it (p. 98)

demand curve *n.* a graph that shows a demand schedule, or how much of a good or service an individual is willing and able to purchase at each price (p. 102)

demand deposits *n.* checking accounts, so called because checking accounts can be converted into currency "on demand" (p. 293)

demand-pull inflation *n.* a condition that occurs when total demand rises faster than the production of goods and services (p. 399)

demand schedule *n.* a table that shows how much of a good or service an individual is willing and able to purchase at each price (p. 100)

demand-side fiscal policy *n.* a plan to stimulate aggregate demand (p. 454)

deposit multiplier formula *n.* a mathematical formula that tells how much the money supply will increase after an initial cash deposit in a bank (p. 485)

depreciate *v.* to decrease in value (p. 590)

depression *n.* an extended period of high unemployment and reduced business activity (p. 359)

deregulation *n.* the reduction or elimination of government oversight and control of business (p. 218)

derived demand *n.* a demand for a product or resource based on its contribution to the final product (p. 259)

developed nations *n.* nations that have a market economy, a relatively high standard of living, a high GDP, industrialization, widespread private ownership of private property, and stable and effective governments (p. 544)

differentiated product *see* product differentiation

diminishing returns *n.* a situation in which new workers cause marginal product to grow but at a decreasing rate (p. 139)

discount rate *n.* the interest rate that the Federal Reserve charges when it lends money to other banks (p. 491)

discretionary fiscal policy *n.* actions taken by the federal government by choice to correct economic instability (p. 446)

discretionary spending *n.* spending that the government must authorize each year (p. 428)

disequilibrium *n.* a situation in which quantity supplied and quantity demanded are not in balance (p. 169)

disposable personal income (DPI) *n.* personal income minus taxes (p. 355)

diversification *n.* the practice of distributing investments among different financial assets to maximize return and limit risk (p. 327)

dividend *n.* the part of a corporation's profit that the company pays the stockholders (p. 238)

dumping *n.* the sale of a product in another country at a price lower than that charged in the home market (p. 521)

Dumpster diving *n.* technique used by identity thieves to gather personal information in the garbage (p. 588)

E

easy-money policy *see* expansionary monetary policy

economic cycle *see* business cycle

economic growth *n.* an increase in a nation's real gross domestic product (p. 358)

economic interdependence *n.* a situation in which producers in one nation depend on others to provide goods and services they do not produce (p. 510)

economic model *n.* a simplified representation of economic activities, systems, or problems (p. 18)

economics *n.* the study of how individuals and societies satisfy their unlimited wants with limited resources (p. 4)

economic system *n.* the way in which a society uses its scarce resources to satisfy its people's unlimited wants (p. 38)

economies of scale *n.* a situation in which the average cost of production falls as the producer grows larger (p. 201)

economize *v.* to make decisions according what is believed to be the best combination of costs and benefits (p. 12)

efficiency *n.* the condition in which economic resources are used to produce the maximum amount of goods and services (p. 20)

elastic *adj.* referring to a situation in which a change in price, either up or down, leads to a relatively larger change in the quantity demanded or the quantity supplied (pp. 117, 154)

elasticity of demand *n.* a measure of how responsive consumers are to price changes in the marketplace (p. 117)

elasticity of supply *n.* a measure of how responsive producers are to price changes in the marketplace (p. 154)

embargo *n.* a law that cuts off most or all trade with a specific country (p. 521)

entitlement *n.* a social welfare program with specific eligibility requirements (p. 428)

entrepreneurship *n.* the combination of vision, skill, ingenuity, and willingness to take risks that is needed to create and run new businesses (p. 9)

equilibrium price *n.* the price at which the quantity demanded equals the quantity supplied (p. 164)

equilibrium wage *n.* the wage at which the quantity of workers demanded equals the quantity of workers supplied; the market price for labor (p. 258)

estate tax *n.* a tax on the assets of a person who has died (p. 425)

European Union (EU) *n.* the economic and political union of European nations that was established in 1993 (p. 532)

euro *n.* the single currency of the European Union (p. 533)

excise tax *n.* a tax on the production or sale of a specific good or service (pp. 149, 425)

expansion *n.* an increase in economic activity (p. 358); *see* business cycle

expansionary fiscal policy *n.* a plan to increase aggregate demand and stimulate a weak economy (p. 446)

expansionary monetary policy *n.* a plan to increase the amount of money in circulation; also called easy-money policy (p. 492)

exports *n.* goods or services produced in one country and sold to other countries (p. 516)

externality *n.* a side effect of a transaction that affects someone other than the producer or buyer (p. 87)

F

factor market *n.* the market for the factors of production—land, labor, capital, and entrepreneurship (p. 52)

factors of production *n.* the economic resources needed to produce goods and services (p. 8)

federal budget *n.* a plan for spending federal tax money (p. 431)

federal funds rate (FFR) *n.* the interest at which a depository institution lends available funds to another depository institution overnight (p. 490)

Federal Insurance Contributions Act (FICA) *n.* a payroll tax that provides coverage for the elderly, the unemployed due to disability, and surviving family members of wage earners who have died (p. 423)

Federal Open Market Committee (FOMC) *n.* the Federal Reserve System board that supervises the sale and purchase of federal government securities (p. 477)

Federal Reserve System *n.* the central bank of the United States; commonly called the Fed (p. 474)

fiat money *n.* money that has no tangible backing but is declared by the government and accepted by citizens to have worth (p. 291)

filing status *n.* for filing taxes, based on marital status or support of dependents (p. 604)

financial asset *n.* a claim on a borrower's property (p. 319)

financial intermediary *n.* an institution that collects funds from savers and invests these funds in financial assets (p. 319)

financial market *n.* a situation in which buyers and sellers exchange financial assets (p. 319)

financial system *n.* all the institutions that help transfer funds between savers and investors (p. 318)

fiscal *adj.* of or relating to government revenue and spending (p. 446)

fiscal policy *n.* the federal government's use of taxing and spending to affect the economy (p. 446)

fiscal year *n.* a 12-month period for which an organization plans its expenditures (p. 431)

fixed costs *n.* expenses that business owners incur no matter how much they produce (p. 140)

fixed rate of exchange *n.* a system in which the currency of one nation is fixed or constant in relation to other currencies (p. 526)

flexible exchange rate *n.* a system in which the exchange rate for currency changes as supply and demand for the currency changes; also called the floating rate (p. 527)

focus group *n.* a moderated discussion with small groups of consumers (p. 208)

foreign exchange market *n.* a market in which currencies of different countries are bought and sold (p. 526)

foreign exchange rate *n.* the price of one currency in the currencies of other nations (p. 526)

franchise *n.* a business made up of semi-independent businesses that all offer the same products or services (p. 248)

franchisee *n.* a semi-independent business that pays a fee for the right to sell the parent company's products or services in a particular area (p. 248)

free contract *n.* a situation in which people decide for themselves which legal agreements to enter into (p. 73)

free enterprise system *n.* another name for capitalism, an economic system based on private ownership of productive resources (p. 70)

free rider *n.* a person who does not pay for a good or service but who benefits from it when it is provided (p. 85)

free-trade zone *n.* a specific region in which trade between nations takes place without protective tariffs (p. 532)

frictional unemployment *n.* the temporary unemployment of workers moving from one job to another (p. 384)

full employment *n.* a level of unemployment in which none of the unemployment is caused by decreased economic activity; generally marked by an unemployment rate of 4 to 6 percent (p. 383)

future *n.* a contract to buy or sell a stock on a specified future date at a preset price (p. 333)

G

general partnership *n.* a partnership in which each partner shares the management of the business and is liable for all business debts and losses (p. 233)

geographic monopoly *n.* a monopoly that exists because there are no other producers or sellers within a certain region (p. 201)

gift tax *n.* a tax on money or property given by one living person to another (p. 425)

glass ceiling *n.* an unseen, artificial barrier to advancement that women and minorities sometimes face (p. 262)

global economy *n.* all the economic interactions that cross international boundaries (p. 61)

gold standard *n.* a system in which the basic monetary unit is equal to a set amount of gold (p. 299)

goods *n.* physical objects, such as food, clothing, and furniture, that can be purchased (p. 5)

government monopoly *n.* a monopoly that exists because the government either owns and runs the business or authorizes only one producer (p. 201)

grant-in-aid *n.* a transfer payment from the federal government to state or local governments (p. 432)

gross domestic product (GDP) *n.* the market value of all final goods and services produced within a nation in a given time period (p. 350)

gross national product (GNP) *n.* the market value of all final goods and services produced by a country in a given time period (p. 355)

H

hacking *n.* technique used by identity thieves to gather personal information using computers and related technology (p. 588)

horizontal merger *n.* the joining of two or more companies that offer the same or similar products or services (p. 243)

human capital *n.* the knowledge and skills that enable workers to be productive (p. 261)

human development index (HDI) *n.* a combination of a nation's real GDP per capita, life expectancy, adult literacy rate, and student enrollment figures that indicates what life is like in a specific country (p. 547)

hyperinflation *n.* a rapid, uncontrolled rate of inflation in excess of 50 percent (p. 398)

I

identity theft *n.* the use of someone else's personal information for criminal purposes (p. 588)

imperfect competition *n.* a market structure that lacks one or more of the conditions needed for perfect competition (p. 195)

imports *n.* goods or services produced in one country and purchased by another (p. 516)

incentive *n.* a benefit offered to encourage people to act in a certain way (pp. 12, 176)

incidence of a tax *n.* the final burden of a tax (p. 415)

income distribution *n.* the way income is divided among people in a nation (p. 390)

income effect *n.* a change in the amount of a good or service a consumer will buy because his or her income (and therefore purchasing power) changes (p. 107)

income inequality *n.* the unequal distribution of income (p. 390)

increasing returns *n.* a situation in which hiring new workers cause marginal product to increase (p. 139)

independent contractor *n.* someone who sells his or her services on a contract basis (p. 270)

individual income tax *n.* a tax based on an individual's income from all sources (p. 412)

industrial union *n.* an organization of workers with many different skills who work in the same industry (p. 274)

inelastic *n.* a situation in which quantity demanded or quantity supplied changes little as price changes (pp. 117, 155)

infant industries *n.* new industries that are often unable to compete against larger, more established competitors (p. 523)

infant mortality rate *n.* the number of children who die within the first year of life per 1,000 births (p. 547)

inferior goods *n.* goods that consumers demand less of when their incomes rise (p. 110)

inflation *n.* a sustained rise in the general price level, or a sustained fall in the purchasing power of money (p. 396)

inflation rate *n.* the rate of change in prices over a set period of time (p. 397)

infrastructure *n.* the basic set of support systems—such as power, communications, transportation, water, sanitation, and education systems—needed to keep an economy and society going (pp. 86, 545)

input costs *n.* the price of the resources needed to produce a good or service (p. 148)

insourcing *n.* the practice of foreign companies establishing operations in, and therefore bringing jobs to, the United States (p. 269)

interest *n.* a fee a bank pays for the use of money (p. 578)

International Monetary Fund (IMF) *n.* the international organization established to promote international monetary cooperation, foster economic growth, and provide temporary financial assistance to countries to help ease balance-of-payments adjustment (p. 559)

investment *n.* the use of income today in a way that allows for a future benefit (p. 318)

investment objective *n.* a financial goal that is used to determine if an investment is appropriate (p. 324)

J

junk bond *n.* a high-risk, high-yield corporate bond (p. 339)

K

Keynesian economics *n.* the idea, first advanced by John Maynard Keynes, that the government needs to stimulate aggregate demand in times of recession (p. 454)

L

labor *n.* all the human time, effort, and talent used to produce goods and services (p. 8)

labor input *n.* the size of the labor force multiplied by the length of the workweek (p. 371)

labor productivity *n.* the amount of goods and services a person can produce in a given time (p. 149)

labor union *n.* an organization of workers that seeks to improve wages, working conditions, fringe benefits, job security, and other work-related matters for its members (p. 274)

Laffer Curve *n.* a graph that illustrates how tax cuts affect tax revenues and economic growth (p. 459)

lagging indicators *n.* measures of economic performance that usually change after real gross domestic product changes (p. 364)

laissez faire *n.* the principle that the government should not interfere in the economy (p. 49)

land *n.* all the natural resources on or under the ground that are used to produce goods and services (p. 8)

landlord *n.* the owner of rental property (p. 609)

law of comparative advantage *n.* the law stating that countries gain when they produce items that they are most efficient at producing and that are at the lowest opportunity cost (p. 514)

law of demand *n.* states that when the price of a good or service goes down, quantity demanded increases, and when the prices go up, quantity demanded falls (p. 99)

law of diminishing marginal utility *n.* states that the marginal benefit from using each additional unit of a good or service during a given time period tends to decline as each is used (p. 106)

law of increasing opportunity costs *n.* states that as production switches from one product to another, increasingly more resources are needed to increase the production of the second product, which causes opportunity costs to rise (p. 21)

law of supply *n.* states that producers are willing to sell more of a good or service at a higher price than they are at a lower price (p. 131)

leading indicators *n.* measures of economic performance that usually change before real gross domestic product changes (p. 364)

lease *n.* a contract for renting an apartment, vehicle, or other item for a specific period of time (p. 609)

legal equality *n.* a situation in which everyone has the same economic rights under the law (p. 73)

less developed countries (LDCs) *n.* countries with lower GDPs, less well-developed industry, and lower standards of living; sometimes called emerging economies (p. 545)

life expectancy *n.* the average number of years a person could expect to live if current mortality trends were to continue for the rest of that person's life (p. 547)

limited liability *n.* a situation in which a business owner's liability for business debts and losses is limited (p. 240)

limited liability partnership (LLP) *n.* a partnership in which all partners are not responsible for the debts and other liabilities of the other partners (p. 233)

limited life *n.* a situation in which a business ceases to exist if the owner dies, retires, or leaves (p. 228)

limited partnership *n.* a partnership in which at least one partner is not involved in running the business and is liable only for the funds he or she invested (p. 233)

literacy rate *n.* the percentage of people older than 15 who can read and write (p. 547)

loan *n.* borrowed money that is usually repaid with interest (p. 582)

Lorenz curve *n.* a curve that shows the degree of income inequality in a nation (p. 391)

M

macroeconomic equilibrium *n.* the point where aggregate demand equals aggregate supply (p. 361)

macroeconomics *n.* the study of the behavior of the economy as a whole; concerned with large-scale economic activity (p. 27)

mandatory spending *n.* government spending that is required by current law (p. 428)

marginal benefit *n.* the benefit or satisfaction gained from using one more unit of a good or service (p. 16)

marginal cost *n.* the additional cost of producing or using one more unit of a good or service (pp. 16, 140)

marginal product *n.* the change in total output that results from adding one more worker (p. 138)

marginal revenue *n.* the money made from each additional unit sold (p. 142)

market *n.* any place or situation in which people buy and sell goods and services (p. 48)

market allocation *n.* an agreement among or between competing businesses to divide up a market (p. 216)

market demand curve *n.* a graph that shows data from a market demand schedule, or how much of a good or service all consumers are willing and able to purchase at each price (p. 102)

market demand schedule *n.* a table that shows how much of a good or service all consumers are willing and able to purchase at each price in a market (p. 100)

market division *see* market allocation

market economy *n.* an economic system based on individual choice and voluntary exchange (p. 39)

market equilibrium *n.* a situation in which the quantity supplied and the quantity demanded at a particular price are equal (p. 164)

market failure *n.* a situation in which people who are not part of a marketplace interaction benefit from it or pay part of its costs (p. 84)

market research *n.* the gathering and evaluation of information about consumer preferences for goods and services (p. 208)

market share *n.* a company's percent of total sales in a particular market (p. 209)

market structure *n.* an economic model of competition among businesses in the same industry (p. 192)

market supply curve *n.* a graph that shows data from a market supply schedule (p. 134)

market supply schedule *n.* how much of a good or service all producers in a market are willing and able to offer for sale at each price (p. 132)

maturity *n.* the date when a bond is due to be repaid (p. 338)

Medicaid *n.* a government-run medical insurance program for low-income people (p. 429)

Medicare *n.* a government-run, national health insurance program mainly for citizens over age 65 (p. 423)

medium of exchange *n.* a means through which goods and services can be exchanged (p. 288)

merger *n.* the combining of two or more companies to form a single company (p. 214)

microeconomics *n.* the study of the behavior of individual players—such as individuals, families, and businesses—in an economy (p. 27)

minimum balance requirement *n.* the amount of money needed in an account to avoid fees (p. 576)

minimum wage *n.* the lowest amount, established by law, that an employer may pay a worker for one hour of work (pp. 182, 262)

mixed economy *n.* an economic system that has elements of traditional, command, and market economies; the most common economic system (p. 58)

modified free enterprise economy *n.* a mixed economic system that includes some government protections, provisions, and regulations to adjust the free enterprise system (p. 80)

monetarism *n.* an economic theory that suggests that rapid changes in the money supply are the main cause of economic instability (p. 496)

monetary *adj.* of or relating to money (p. 474)

monetary policy *n.* the Federal Reserve's actions that change the money supply to influence the economy (p. 490)

money *n.* anything that people will accept as payment for goods and services (p. 288)

money market *n.* a market in which short-term financial assets are bought and sold (p. 322)

monopolistic competition *n.* a market structure in which many sellers offer similar, but not standardized, products to consumers (p. 206)

monopoly *n.* a market structure in which only one seller sells a product for which there are no close substitutes (p. 198)

monopsony *n.* market structure in which there are many sellers but only one large buyer (p. 212)

multifactor productivity *n.* the ratio between an industry's economic output and its labor and capital inputs (p. 372)

multinational corporation *n.* a corporation with branches in several countries (p. 243)

mutual fund *n.* an investment company that gathers money from individual investors and uses the money to purchase a range of financial assets (p. 320)

N

NAFTA *n.* the North America Free Trade Agreement, which ensures free trade throughout the continent and constitutes the largest free-trade zone in the world (p. 533)

national accounts *see* national income accounting

national bank *n.* a bank chartered by the national government (p. 299)

national debt *n.* the total amount of money that the federal government owes (p. 462)

national income (NI) *n.* the total income earned in a nation from the production of goods and services in a given time period (p. 355)

national income accounting *n.* a way of analyzing a country's economy using statistical measures of its income, spending, and output (p. 350)

nationalize *v.* to change from private ownership to government or public ownership (p. 61)

natural monopoly *n.* a market situation in which the costs of production are lowest when only one firm supplies a product or service (p. 201)

near money *n.* savings accounts and other similar time deposits that can be converted into cash relatively easily (p. 293)

needs *n.* things such as food, clothing, and shelter that are necessary for survival (p. 4)

negative externality *n.* an externality that costs people who were not involved in the original economic activity (p. 87)

R39

net national product (NNP) *n.* the gross national product minus depreciation of capital stock—in other words, the value of final goods and services less the value of capital goods that became worn out during the year (p. 355)

nominal GDP *n.* the gross domestic product stated in terms of the current value of goods and services (p. 352)

nonmarket activities *n.* services that have potential economic value but are performed without charge (p. 354)

nonprice competition *n.* the use of factors other than price—such as style, service, advertising, or giveaways—to try to convince customers to buy from one producer rather than another (p. 207)

nonprofit organization *n.* an institution that acts like a business but exists to benefit society rather than to make a profit (p. 250)

normal goods *n.* goods that consumers demand more of when their incomes rise (p. 110)

normative economics *n.* a way of describing and explaining what economic behavior ought to be, not what it actually is (p. 29)

not-for-profit *see* nonprofit organization

O

oligopoly *n.* a market structure in which only a few sellers offer a similar product (p. 209)

OPEC *n.* the Organization of Petroleum Exporting Countries, a regional trade group (p. 535)

open market operations *n.* the Federal Reserve's sale and purchase of federal government securities; the monetary policy tool most used by the Federal Reserve to adjust the money supply (p. 490)

open opportunity *n.* the ability of everyone to enter and compete in the market of his or her own free choice (p. 73)

operating budget *n.* a plan for day-to-day expenses (p. 436)

opportunity cost *n.* the value of something that is given up by choosing one alternative over another (p. 14)

option *n.* a contract giving an investor the right to buy or sell stock at a future date at a preset price (p. 333)

outsourcing *n.* the practice of contracting with an outside company, often in a foreign country, to provide goods or services (p. 269)

overdraft *n.* a check or other withdrawal that exceeds the existing account balance (p. 576)

P

par value *n.* the amount that a bond issuer promises to pay the buyer at maturity (p. 338)

partnership *n.* a business co-owned by two or more people, or "partners," who agree on how responsibilities, profits, and losses should be divided (p. 232)

patent *n.* a legal registration of an invention or a process that gives the inventor the exclusive property rights to that invention or process for a certain number of years (p. 202)

peak *n.* the end of an expansion in the economy (p. 359); *see* business cycle

per capita gross domestic product *n.* a nation's GDP divided by its total population (p. 546)

perestroika *n.* Russian leader Mikhail Gorbachev's plan to gradually incorporate markets into the Soviet Union's command economy (p. 564)

perfect competition *n.* the ideal model of a market economy; the market structure in which none of the many well-informed and independent sellers or buyers has control over the price of a standardized good or service (p. 192)

personal income (PI) *n.* the annual income received by a country's people from all sources (p. 355)

phishing *n.* technique used by identity thieves to gather personal information through deceptive telephone calls (p. 588)

PIN *n.* personal identification number (p. 577)

positive economics *n.* a way of describing and explaining economics as it is (p. 29)

positive externality *n.* an externality that benefits people who were not involved in the original economic activity (p. 87)

poverty *n.* the situation in which a person's income and resources do not allow him or her to achieve a minimum standard of living (p. 388)

poverty line *see* poverty threshold

poverty rate *n.* the percentage of people living in households that have incomes below the poverty threshold (p. 389)

poverty threshold *n.* the official minimum income needed to pay for the basic expenses of living (p. 388)

predatory pricing *n.* the setting of prices below cost for a time to drive smaller competitors out of a market (p. 216)

preferred stock *n.* a share of ownership in a corporation giving the holder a share of profits but, in general, no voting rights (p. 331)

premium *n.* an amount paid for insurance (p. 596)

price ceiling *n.* an established maximum price that sellers may charge for a product (p. 180)

price fixing *n.* conspiring among or between businesses to set the prices of competing products (p. 216)

price floor *n.* an established minimum price that buyers must pay for a product (p. 182)

price maker *n.* a business that does not have to consider competitors when setting its prices (p. 198)

price taker *n.* a firm that must accept the market price set by the interaction of supply and demand (p. 193)

primary market *n.* a market for buying newly created financial assets directly from the issuing entity (p. 322)

prime rate *n.* the interest rate that banks charge their best customers (p. 491)

private company *n.* a corporation that controls who can buy or sell its stock (p. 238)

private property rights *n.* the rights of individuals and groups to own resources and businesses (p. 48)

private sector *n.* the part of the economy that is owned by individuals or businesses (p. 432)

privatization *n.* the process of transferring state-owned property and businesses to individuals (p. 563)

privatize *v.* to change from government or public ownership to private ownership (p. 61)

producer *n.* a person who makes goods or provides services (p. 5)

producer price index (PPI) *n.* a measure of changes in wholesale prices (p. 397)

product differentiation *n.* the attempt to distinguish a product from similar products (p. 206)

product market *n.* the market in which goods and services are bought and sold (p. 52)

production possibilities curve (PPC) *n.* a graph used to illustrate the impact of scarcity on an economy (p. 18)

productivity *n.* the amount of output produced from a set amount of inputs (p. 372)

productivity, labor *see* labor productivity

profit *n.* the financial gain a seller makes from a business transaction (p. 49); the money left over after the costs of producing a product are subtracted from the income gained by selling that product (p. 78)

profit-maximizing output *n.* the point in production at which a business has reached its highest level of profit (p. 143)

profit motive *n.* the incentive that encourages people and organizations to improve their material well-being by seeking to gain from economic activities (p. 73)

progressive tax *n.* a tax that places a higher percentage rate of taxation on high-income earners than on low-income earners (p. 412)

property tax *n.* a tax based on the value of an individual's or a business's assets (p. 412)

proportional tax *n.* a tax that takes the same percentage of income from all taxpayers regardless of income level (p. 412)

protectionism *n.* the use of trade barriers between nations to protect domestic industries (p. 523)

protective tariff *n.* a tax on imported goods to protect domestic goods (p. 521)

public company *n.* a corporation that issues stock that can be freely traded (p. 238)

public disclosure *n.* a policy requiring businesses to reveal product information to consumers (p. 217)

public goods *n.* goods and services provided by the government and consumed by the public as a group (p. 84)

public transfer payment *n.* a transfer payment in which the government transfers income from taxpayers to recipients who do not provide anything in return (p. 89)

pure competition *see* perfect competition

Q

quota *n.* a limit on the amount of a product that can be imported (p. 520)

R

rational expectations theory *n.* the theory that states that individuals and business firms expect changes in fiscal policy will have particular effects and take action to protect their interests against those effects (p. 452)

rationing *n.* a system in which the government allocates goods and services using factors other than price (p. 183)

real GDP *n.* the gross domestic product corrected for changes in prices from year to year (p. 352)

real GDP per capita *n.* the real gross domestic product divided by total population (p. 369)

recession *n.* a prolonged economic contraction lasting two or more quarters (six months or more) (p. 359)

regressive tax *n.* a tax that takes a larger percentage of income from low-income earners than from high-income earners (p. 412)

regulation *n.* a set of rules or laws designed to control business behavior (pp. 150, 214)

representative money *n.* paper money that is backed by something tangible (p. 291)

required reserve ratio (RRR) *n.* the fraction of a bank's deposits, determined by the Federal Reserve, that it must keep in reserve so that it can loan out money (p. 484)

return *n.* the profit or loss made on an investment (p. 327)

revenue *n.* government income from taxes and nontax sources (p. 410)

revenue tariff *n.* a tax on imports specifically to raise money; are rarely used today (p. 521)

right-to-work laws *n.* legislation that makes it illegal to require workers to join unions (p. 279)

risk *n.* the possibility for loss on an investment (p. 327)

S

safety net *n.* government programs designed to protect people from economic hardships (p. 89)

sales tax *n.* a tax based on the value of goods or services at the time of sale (p. 412)

savings *n.* income not used for consumption (p. 318)

scarcity *n.* a situation that exists when there are not enough resources to meet human wants (p. 4)

seasonal unemployment *n.* unemployment linked to seasonal work (p. 384)

secondary market *n.* a market in which financial assets are resold (p. 322)

service *n.* work that one person does for another for payment (p. 5)

shadow economy *see* underground economy

share *n.* part of the stock of a corporation (p. 238); *see* stock

shock therapy *n.* an economic program involving the abrupt shift from a command economy to a free-market economy (p. 563)

shortage *n.* a situation in which demand is greater than supply, usually the result of prices being set too low (p. 167)

shoulder surfing *n.* technique used by identity thieves to gather personal information as you disclose private information in public (p. 588)

socialism *n.* an economic system in which the government owns some or all of the factors of production (p. 43)

Social Security *n.* a federal program to aid older citizens, orphaned children, and the disabled (p. 423)

sole proprietorship *n.* a business owned and controlled by one person (p. 226)

spamming *n.* technique used by identity thieves to gather personal information through deceptive e-mails (p. 588)

special economic zone (SEZ) *n.* a geographic region that has economic laws that are different from a country's usual economic laws, with the goal of increasing foreign investment (p. 567)

specialization *n.* a situation that occurs when individuals or businesses concentrate their efforts in the areas in which they have an advantage for increased productivity and profit (pp. 50, 138, 510)

spending multiplier effect *n.* a situation in which a small change in spending eventually results in a much larger change in GDP (p. 455)

stabilization programs *n.* programs that require troubled nations to carry out reforms such as reducing foreign trade deficits and external debt, eliminating price controls, closing inefficient public enterprises, and slashing budget deficits (p. 559)

stagflation *n.* a period during which prices rise at the same time that there is a slowdown in business activity (p. 359)

standardized product *n.* a product that consumers consider identical in all essential features to other products in the same market (p. 192)

standard of value *n.* the yardstick of economic worth in the exchange process (p. 289)

start-up costs *n.* the expenses that a new business must pay to enter a market and begin selling to consumers (p. 209)

state bank *n.* a bank chartered by a state government (p. 296)

statistics *n.* numerical data (p. 24)

stock *n.* shares of ownership in a corporation (p. 238)

stockbroker *n.* an agent who buys and sells securities for customers (p. 332)

stock exchange *n.* a secondary market where securities are bought and sold (p. 330)

stock index *n.* an instrument used to measure and report the change in prices of a set of stocks (p. 334)

stored-value card *n.* a card that represents money that the card holder has on deposit with the card issuer (p. 308)

store of value *n.* something that holds its value over time (p. 289)

strike *n.* a work stoppage used to gain negotiating power while attempting to convince an employer to improve wages, working conditions, or other work-related matters (p. 274)

structural unemployment *n.* unemployment that exists when the available jobs do not match the skills of available workers (p. 384)

subsidy *n.* a government payment that helps cover the cost of an economic activity that can benefit the public as a whole (p. 88)

substitutes *n.* products that can be used in place of other products to satisfy consumer wants (p. 112)

substitution effect *n.* the pattern of behavior that occurs when consumers react to a change in price of a product by buying a substitute product that offers a better relative value (p. 107)

supply *n.* the willingness and ability of a producer to produce and sell a product (p. 130)

supply curve *n.* a graph that shows data from a supply schedule (p. 134)

supply schedule *n.* a table that shows how much of a good or service an individual producer is willing and able to offer for sale at each price (p. 132)

supply-side fiscal policy *n.* a plan designed to provide incentives to producers to increase aggregate supply (p. 458)

surplus *n.* a situation in which supply is greater than demand, usually the result of prices being set too high (p. 167)

T

tariff *n.* a fee charged for goods brought into a country from another country (p. 521)

tax *n.* a mandatory payment to a government (p. 410)

taxable income *n.* the portion of income subject to taxation after all deductions and exemptions (pp. 421, 604)

tax assessor *n.* a government official who determines the value of property to be taxed (p. 437)

tax base *n.* a form of wealth—such as income, property, goods, or services—that is subject to taxes (p. 412)

tax incentive *n.* the use of taxes to encourage or discourage certain economic behaviors (p. 417)

tax return *n.* a form used to report income and taxes owed to the government (p. 421)

technological monopoly *n.* a monopoly that exists because a firm controls a manufacturing method, invention, or type of technology (p. 201)

technology *n.* the application of scientific methods and innovations to production (p. 149)

telecommuting *n.* the practice of doing office work in a location other than the office (p. 270)

telework *see* telecommuting

temp, temps, temping *see* contingent employment

thrift institution *n.* a financial institution that serves savers (p. 478)

tight-money policy *see* contractionary monetary policy

total cost *n.* the sum of fixed and variable costs (p. 140)

total revenue *n.* the income a business receives from selling its products (pp. 122, 142)

total revenue test *n.* a method of measuring elasticity by comparing the total revenue a business would receive when offering its product at various prices (p. 122)

trade barrier *n.* any law passed to limit free trade between nations (p. 520)

trade deficit *n.* an unfavorable balance of trade that occurs when a nation imports more than it exports (p. 529)

trade-off *n.* the alternative someone gives up when making an economic choice (p. 14)

trade surplus *n.* a favorable balance of trade that occurs when a nation exports more than it imports (p. 529)

trade union *see* labor union

trade war *n.* a succession of trade barriers between nations (p. 522)

trade-weighted value of the dollar *n.* a measure of the international value of the dollar that determines if the dollar is strong or weak as measured against another currency (p. 528)

traditional economy *n.* an economic system in which people make economic decisions based on customs and beliefs that have been handed down from one generation to the next (p. 38)

transfer payment *n.* money distributed to individuals who do not provide goods or services in return (pp. 89, 432)

transitional economy *n.* a country that has moved (or is moving) from a command economy to a market economy (p. 545)

Treasury bill (T bill) *n.* a short-term bond that matures in less than one year (p. 464)

Treasury bond *n.* a long-term bond that matures in 30 years (p. 464)

Treasury note *n.* an intermediate-term bond that matures in between two and ten years (p. 464)

trough *n.* the end of a contraction in the economy (p. 359); *see* business cycle

trust *n.* a group of firms combined in order to reduce competition in an industry (p. 214)

trust fund *n.* a fund held for a specific purpose to be expended at a future date (p. 465)

U

underemployed *n.* people employed part-time who want to work full-time, or those who work at a job below their skill level (p. 383)

underground economy *n.* market activities that go unreported because they are illegal or because those involved want to avoid taxation (p. 354)

underutilization *n.* the condition in which economic resources are not being used to their full potential, resulting in fewer goods and services (p. 20)

unemployment rate *n.* the percentage of the labor force that is jobless and actively looking for work (p. 382)

union *see* labor union

union shop *n.* a business in which workers are required to join a union within a set time period after being hired (p. 279)

unit elastic *adj.* relating to a situation in which the percentage change in price and quantity demanded are the same (p. 118)

unlimited liability *n.* a situation in which a business owner is responsible for all the losses and debts of a business (p. 228)

unlimited life *n.* a situation in which a corporation continues to exist even after a change in ownership (p. 240)

user fee *n.* money charged for the use of a good or service (p. 425)

utility *n.* the benefit or satisfaction gained from using a good or service (p. 12)

V

variable costs *n.* business costs that vary with the level of production output (p. 140)

vertical merger *n.* the combining of two or more businesses involved in different steps of producing or marketing a product or service (p. 243)

voluntary exchange *n.* a trade in which the parties involved anticipate that the benefits will outweigh the cost (p. 49)

voluntary export restraint (VER) *n.* a self-imposed limit on exports to certain countries to avoid quotas or tariffs (p. 521)

W

wage and price controls *n.* government limits on increases in wages and prices (p. 501)

wage-price spiral *n.* a cycle that begins with increased wages, which lead to higher production costs, which in turn result in higher prices, which result in demands for even higher wages (p. 400)

wage rate *n.* the established rate of pay for a specific job or work performed (p. 261)

wages *n.* the payments workers receive in return for work (p. 258)

wants *n.* desires that can be satisfied by consuming a good or service (p. 4)

welfare *n.* government economic and social programs that provide assistance to the needy (p. 392)

withholding *n.* the money taken from a worker's pay before the worker receives the pay (p. 421)

workfare *n.* a program that requires welfare recipients to do some kind of work in return for their benefits (p. 393)

World Bank *n.* a financial institution that provides loans, policy advice, and technical assistance to low and middle income countries to reduce poverty (p. 559)

World Trade Organization (WTO) *n.* an organization that negotiates and administers trade agreements, resolves trade disputes, monitors trading policies, and supports developing countries (p. 535)

Y

yield *n.* the annual rate of return on a bond (p. 338)

Spanish Glossary

A

absolute advantage [ventaja absoluta] *n.* capacidad de un país para hacer un producto más eficientemente que otro país (pág. 513)

aggregate demand [demanda agregada] *n.* suma de las demandas totales existentes en la economía (pág. 360)

aggregate supply [oferta agregada] *n.* suma de las ofertas totales existentes en la economía (pág. 360)

antitrust legislation [legislación antimonopolio] *n.* leyes que definen los monopolios y dan al gobierno el poder de controlarlos o disolverlos (pág. 214)

appropriations [asignaciones] *n.* cantidades fijas de dinero destinadas a fines determinados (pág. 431)

authoritarian [autoritario] *adj.* lo que exige una lealtad y una obediencia absolutas ante la autoridad (pág. 43)

automated teller machine (ATM) [cajero automático (ATM)] *n.* dispositivo electrónico que permite a los clientes de un banco hacer transacciones sin ver al personal del banco (pág. 308)

automatic stabilizer [estabilizador automático] *n.* característica de la política fiscal que actúa automáticamente para mantener estable la economía (pág. 447)

B

balanced budget [presupuesto balanceado] *n.* presupuesto en el que el total de ingresos del gobierno es igual al total de gastos del gobierno (pág. 436)

balance of payments [balanza de pagos] *n.* registro de todas las transacciones ocurridas entre las personas, las empresas y las unidades gubernamentales de un país y las del resto del mundo (pág. 529)

balance of trade [balanza de comercio] *n.* diferencia entre el valor de las exportaciones y el de las importaciones de un país (pág. 529)

bank exam [inspección bancaria] *n.* auditoría, realizada por la Reserva Federal, de las prácticas financieras de un banco (pág. 481)

bank holding company [compañía tenedora de acciones bancarias] *n.* compañía que posee más de un banco (pág. 481)

barrier to entry [barrera de entrada] *n.* todo factor que impide que una empresa entre en un mercado (pág. 198)

barter [trueque] *n.* intercambio de bienes y servicios sin utilizar dinero (pág. 288)

bear market [mercado a la baja (mercado "oso")] *n.* situación en la que los precios del mercado de valores bajan constantemente con el tiempo (pág. 335)

binding arbitration [arbitraje vinculante] *n.* proceso por el que un tercero imparcial resuelve los conflictos entre la dirección de una empresa y los sindicatos (pág. 280)

black market [mercado negro] *n.* compra o venta ilegal de bienes o servicios, violando los controles de precios o el racionamiento (pág. 183)

Board of Governors [Junta de Gobernadores] *n.* junta de siete miembros nombrados que supervisa las operaciones del Sistema de la Reserva Federal y establece la política monetaria (pág. 476)

bond [bono] *n.* contrato emitido por una sociedad anónima que promete reembolsar el dinero prestado, más intereses, según las fechas establecidas (pág. 240)

bounced check [cheque rebotado] véase overdraft [sobregiro]

break-even point [punto de equilibrio] *n.* situación en la que el total de costos y el total de ingresos son iguales (pág. 142)

budget [presupuesto] *n.* plan para asignar el ahorro y el gasto del ingreso (pág. 574)

budget deficit [déficit presupuestario] *n.* situación en la que los gastos del gobierno son mayores que los ingresos (pág. 462)

budget surplus [superávit presupuestario] *n.* situación en la que los ingresos del gobierno son mayores que los gastos (pág. 462)

bull market [mercado alcista (mercado "toro")] *n.* situación en la que los precios del mercado de valores suben constantemente con el tiempo (pág. 335)

business cycle [ciclo económico] *n.* serie de períodos de ascenso y descenso de la actividad económica, medida por los aumentos o las disminuciones del producto interior bruto real (pág. 358)

business organization [organización comercial] *n.* empresa que produce bienes o presta servicios, generalmente para obtener ganancias (pág. 226)

business structure [estructura comercial] véase business organization [organización comercial]

C

capital [capital] *n.* todos los recursos que se crean y utilizan para producir y distribuir bienes y servicios (pág. 8)

capital budget [presupuesto de capital] *n.* plan referente a los principales gastos o inversiones (pág. 436)

capital deepening [intensificación del uso del capital] *n.* aumento de la razón entre el capital y el trabajo (pág. 371)

capital flight [fuga de capitales] *n.* situación en la que capitales de un país se invierten fuera de dicho país (pág. 558)

capital gain [ganancias de capital] *n.* ganancias obtenidas de la venta de valores (pág. 330)
capitalism [capitalismo] *n.* sistema económico basado en la propiedad privada de los factores de producción (pág. 49)
capital market [mercado de capitales] *n.* mercado en el que se venden y compran activos financieros a largo plazo (pág. 322)
cartel [cártel] *n.* organización formal de vendedores o productores que regulan la producción, la fijación de precios y la comercialización de un producto (págs. 198, 535)
cease and desist order [orden de cese de actividades comerciales] *n.* decisión judicial que obliga a una compañía a dejar de realizar una práctica comercial injusta (pág. 217)
central bank [banco central] *n.* principal autoridad monetaria de un país (pág. 474)
centrally planned economy [economía de planificación centralizada] *n.* sistema en el que los dirigentes del país toman todas las decisiones económicas (pág. 42)
change in demand [cambio en la demanda] *n.* situación en la que un cambio en el mercado incita a los consumidores a comprar una cantidad diferente de un bien o de un servicio a cada precio (pág. 109)
change in quantity demanded [cambio en la cantidad demandada] *n.* cambio en la cantidad de un producto que los consumidores comprarán debido a un cambio en el precio (pág. 108)
change in quantity supplied [cambio en la cantidad ofertada] *n.* aumento o disminución de la cantidad de un bien o de un servicio que los productores están dispuestos a vender debido a un cambio en el precio (pág. 146)
change in supply [cambio en la oferta] *n.* situación en la que un cambio en el mercado incita a los productores a ofrecer para su venta una cantidad diferente a cada precio (pág. 148)
check clearing [compensación de cheques] *n.* servicio proporcionado por la Reserva Federal para registrar las entradas y las salidas de los clientes de los bancos (pág. 480)
circular flow model [modelo de flujo circular] *n.* visualización de todas las interacciones de una economía de mercado (pág. 52)
civilian labor force [fuerza laboral civil] *n.* personas de 16 años o mayores que trabajan o que buscan activamente un trabajo y están en condiciones para trabajar (pág. 266)
claim [reclamación] *n.* petición presentada ante una compañía de seguros para recibir un pago sobre una pérdida asegurada (pág. 596)
closed shop [compañía de sindicación obligatoria] *n.* compañía en la que el empleador sólo puede contratar miembros del sindicato (pág. 279)
coincident indicators [indicadores coincidentes] *n.* medidas del rendimiento económico que generalmente cambian al mismo tiempo que cambia el producto interior bruto real (pág. 364)
collective bargaining [negociación colectiva] *n.* proceso de negociación entre una empresa y sus empleados sindicalizados para establecer los salarios y mejorar las condiciones de trabajo (pág. 280)
command economy [economía autoritaria] *n.* sistema económico en el que el gobierno toma todas las decisiones económicas (pág. 39)
commodity money [dinero-mercancía] *n.* dinero que tiene un valor intrínsico basado en el material del que se compone (pág. 291)
common stock [acciones ordinarias] *n.* participación en la propiedad de una sociedad anónima que da al titular derecho a voto y parte de las ganancias (pág. 331)
communism [comunismo] *n.* sistema económico en el que no existe la propiedad privada y hay poca o ninguna libertad política (pág. 43)
comparative advantage [ventaja comparativa] *n.* capacidad de un país para producir algo a un costo de oportunidad más bajo que el de otro país (pág. 513)
competition [competencia] *n.* esfuerzo de dos o más personas que actúan independientemente por obtener clientes ofreciéndoles la mejor opción (pág. 49)
competitive pricing [fijación de precios competitivos] *n.* situación en la que los productores venden bienes y servicios a precios que intentan el mejor equilibrio entre dos deseos: obtener las mayores ganancias y atraer a los clientes de los productores rivales (pág. 174)
complements [complementarios] *n.* productos que se usan conjuntamente, de manera que el aumento y la disminución de la demanda de uno produzca el aumento o la disminución de la demanda del otro (pág. 112)
conglomerate [conglomerado] *n.* empresa compuesta de compañías que producen bienes o servicios no relacionados (pág. 243)
consumer [consumidor] *n.* persona que compra bienes o servicios para su uso personal (pág. 5)
consumer price index (CPI) [índice de precios al consumo (IPC)] *v* medida porcentual de los cambios en los precios de una cesta de los bienes y los servicios que los consumidores compran frecuentemente (pág. 396)
consumer sovereignty [soberanía del consumidor] *n.* idea de que los consumidores tienen el control definitivo sobre lo que se produce ya que son libres para comprar lo que quieren y para rechazar productos que no quieren (pág. 50)

contingent employment [empleo contingente] *n.* trabajo temporal o a tiempo parcial (pág. 270)

contract [contrato] *n.* acuerdo formal con fuerza jurídica (pág. 598)

contraction [contracción] *n.* reducción de la actividad económica (pág. 359); *véase* business cycle [ciclo económico]

contractionary fiscal policy [política fiscal restrictiva] *n.* plan para reducir la demanda agregada y desacelerar la economía durante un período de expansión económica demasiado rápido (pág. 446)

contractionary monetary policy [política monetaria restrictiva] *n.* plan para reducir la cantidad de dinero en circulación; también llamada política de dinero escaso (pág. 492)

cooperative [cooperativa] *n.* tipo de negocio dirigido a favor del beneficio compartido de los propietarios, que son también los clientes (pág. 250)

co-pay [copago] *n.* cantidad que el asegurado debe pagar cuando una persona asegurada recibe atención médica (pág. 596)

corporate income tax [impuesto de sociedades anónimas] *n.* impuesto basado en las ganancias de una sociedad anónima (pág. 412)

corporation [sociedad anónima] *n.* empresa que pertenece a los titulares de acciones, o accionistas, que poseen los derechos a las ganancias de la compañía pero cuya responsabilidad es limitada respecto a las deudas y pérdidas de la compañía (pág. 238)

cosigner [cofirmante, aval, avalista] *n.* persona que asume la responsabilidad de la deuda si el prestatario no reembolsa el préstamo (pág. 583)

cost-benefit analysis [análisis costo-beneficio] *n.* práctica de examinar los costos y los beneficios previstos de una opción, como ayuda en la toma de decisiones (pág. 15)

cost-push inflation [inflación de costos] *n.* situación en la que el aumento de los costos de producción hace subir los precios (pág. 399)

Council of Economic Advisers [Consejo de Consejeros Económicos] *n.* grupo de tres miembros que aconseja al Presidente sobre la política fiscal y otros asuntos económicos (pág. 452)

coupon rate [tasa de cupón] *n.* tasa de interés que el titular de un bono obtiene cada año hasta que vence el bono (pág. 338)

craft union [sindicato gremial] *n.* organización de trabajadores con aptitudes similares que trabajan en diferentes industrias para diferentes empleadores (pág. 274)

credit [crédito] *n.* práctica de comprar bienes o servicios en el presente y pagarlos en el futuro (pág. 582)

credit report [informe crediticio] *n.* documento emitido por una agencia de informes crediticios que explica detalladamente el historial de crédito de un consumidor (pág. 586)

credit score [calificación del riesgo crediticio] *n.* número que resume la reputación crediticia de un consumidor (pág. 586)

crowding-out effect [efecto de exclusión] *n.* situación en la que el gobierno supera la oferta de las tasas de interés de bonos privados para obtener fondos prestables (pág. 466)

currency [moneda] *n.* papel moneda y monedas metálicas (págs. 293, 475)

customs duty [derecho arancelario] *n.* impuesto aplicado en Estados Unidos a los bienes importados (pág. 425)

customs unions [uniones aduaneras] *n.* acuerdos que eliminan las barreras al comercio entre los miembros y establecen aranceles uniformes para los no miembros (pág. 532)

cyclical unemployment [desempleo cíclico] *n.* desempleo causado por la parte del ciclo económico que presenta una actividad económica reducida (pág. 384)

D

debit card [tarjeta de débito] *n.* tarjeta que se puede usar como tarjeta de cajero automático (ATM) para retirar dinero o como cheque para hacer compras (pág. 308)

debt restructuring [reestructuración de la deuda] *n.* método que utilizan los países con obligaciones de deuda pendientes para alterar los términos de los acuerdos de la deuda, a fin de conseguir alguna ventaja (pág. 559)

deduction [deducible] *n.* cantidad que el asegurado paga antes de que pague la compañía aseguradora (pág. 596)

default [incumplimiento] *n.* condición que se presenta cuando un país no puede pagar los intereses o el capital sobre un préstamo (pág. 559)

deficit spending [gastos deficitarios] *n.* práctica del gobierno de gastar más de lo que obtiene en ingresos en un determinado año fiscal (pág. 462)

deflation [deflación] *n.* disminución del nivel general de precios (pág. 398)

demand [demanda] *n.* deseo de obtener algún bien o servicio y la capacidad para pagarlo (pág. 98)

demand curve [curva de la demanda] *n.* gráfica que muestra una tabla de demanda, o la cantidad de un bien o de un servicio que una persona puede y está dispuesta a comprar a cada precio (pág. 102)

demand deposits [depósitos a la vista] *n.* cuentas corrientes, llamadas así porque las cuentas corrientes pueden convertirse en dinero "a la vista" (pág. 293)

demand-pull inflation [inflación de demanda] *n.* condición que se presenta cuando la demanda total sube más rápido que la producción de bienes y servicios (pág. 399)
demand schedule [tabla de demanda] *n.* tabla que muestra la cantidad de un bien o de un servicio que una persona puede y está dispuesta a comprar a cada precio (pág. 100)
demand-side fiscal policy [política fiscal sobre la demanda] *n.* plan para estimular la demanda agregada (pág. 454)
deposit multiplier formula [fórmula del multiplicador de depósitos] *n.* fórmula matemática que indica cuánto aumentará la oferta monetaria tras realizar un depósito inicial de dinero en un banco (pág. 485)
depreciate [depreciar] *v.* disminuir de valor (pág. 590)
depression [depresión] *n.* período prolongado con un alto nivel de desempleo y una reducción de la actividad económica (pág. 359)
deregulation [desregulación] *n.* reducción o eliminación de la vigilancia y el control de las empresas por parte del gobierno (pág. 218)
derived demand [demanda derivada] *n.* demanda de un producto o un recurso que se basa en su aportación al producto final (pág. 259)
developed nations [países desarrollados] *n.* países que tienen una economía de mercado, un nivel de vida relativamente alto, un PIB alto, industrialización, propiedad privada generalizada y un gobierno estable y efectivo (pág. 544)
differentiated product [producto diferenciado] véase product differentiation [diferenciación de productos]
diminishing returns [rentabilidad decreciente] *n.* situación en la que nuevos trabajadores hacen que el producto marginal aumente pero a un ritmo decreciente (pág. 139)
discount rate [tasa de descuento] *n.* tasa de interés que aplica la Reserva Federal cuando presta dinero a otros bancos (pág. 491)
discretionary fiscal policy [política fiscal discrecional] *n.* medidas que toma el gobierno federal a voluntad para corregir la inestabilidad económica (pág. 446)
discretionary spending [gastos discrecionales] *n.* gastos que el gobierno debe autorizar cada año (pág. 428)
disequilibrium [desequilibrio] *n.* situación en la que la cantidad ofertada y la cantidad demandada no se encuentran en equilibrio (pág. 169)
disposable personal income (DPI) [renta personal disponible (RPD)] *n.* renta personal menos los impuestos (pág. 355)
diversification [diversificación] *n.* práctica de distribuir las inversiones entre diferentes activos financieros para maximizar la rentabilidad y limitar el riesgo (pág. 327)
dividend [dividendo] *n.* aquella parte de las ganancias de una sociedad anónima que la compañía paga a los accionistas (pág. 238)
dumping [dumping] *n.* venta de un producto en otro país a un precio más bajo del que tiene en el mercado de origen (pág. 521)
Dumpster diving [buceo en la basura] *n.* técnica utilizada por los ladrones de identidad para recoger información personal en la basura (pág. 584)

E

easy-money policy [política de dinero barato] véase expansionary monetary policy [política monetaria expansiva]
economic cycle [ciclo económico] véase business cycle [ciclo económico]
economic growth [crecimiento económico] *n.* aumento del producto interior bruto real de un país (pág. 358)
economic interdependence [interdependencia económica] *n.* situación en la que los productores de un país dependen de otros para conseguir bienes y servicios que ellos no producen (pág. 510)
economic model [modelo económico] *n.* representación simplificada de las actividades, sistemas o problemas económicos (pág. 18)
economics [economía] *n.* estudio de cómo las personas y la sociedad satisfacen sus deseos ilimitados con recursos limitados (pág. 4)
economic system [sistema económico] *n.* forma en que la sociedad utiliza sus recursos escasos para satisfacer los deseos ilimitados de su población (pág. 38)
economies of scale [economías de escala] *n.* situación en la que el costo promedio de producción disminuye al crecer el productor (pág. 201)
economize [economizar] *v.* tomar decisiones según lo que se cree la mejor combinación de costos y beneficios (pág. 12)
efficiency [eficiencia] *n.* condición en la que los recursos económicos se utilizan para producir la cantidad máxima de bienes y servicios (pág. 20)
elastic [elástica] *adj.* situación en la que un cambio en el precio, ya sea para más o para menos, produce un cambio relativamente más grande en la cantidad demandada o en la cantidad ofertada (págs. 117, 154)
elasticity of demand [elasticidad de la demanda] *n.* medida de la reacción de los consumidores ante los cambios de los precios en el mercado (pág. 117)
elasticity of supply [elasticidad de la oferta] *n.* medida de la reacción de los productores ante los cambios de los precios en el mercado (pág. 154)

embargo [embargo] *n.* ley que prohíbe la mayor parte o todo el comercio con un país determinado (pág. 521)
entitlement [derechos sociales adquiridos] *n.* programa de asistencia social que tiene determinados requisitos de admisión (pág. 428)
entrepreneurship [capacidad empresarial] *n.* combinación de visión, aptitud, ingenio y disposición de asumir riesgos, necesaria para crear y dirigir nuevas empresas (pág. 9)
equilibrium price [precio de equilibrio] *n.* precio al que la cantidad demandada equivale a la cantidad ofertada (pág. 164)
equilibrium wage [salario de equilibrio] *n.* salario en el que la cantidad de trabajadores demandados equivale a la cantidad de trabajadores ofertados; precio de mercado de la mano de obra (pág. 258)
estate tax [impuesto de sucesiones] *n.* impuesto aplicado a los activos de una persona que ha muerto (pág. 425)
European Union (EU) [Unión Europea (UE)] *n.* unión económica y política de los países europeos, establecida en 1993 (pág. 532)
euro [euro] *n.* moneda única de la Unión Europea (pág. 533)
excise tax [impuesto sobre consumos] *n.* impuesto aplicado a la producción o a la venta de un bien o un servicio determinado (págs. 149, 425)
expansion [expansión] *n.* aumento de la actividad económica (pág. 358); *véase* business cycle [ciclo económico]
expansionary fiscal policy [política fiscal expansiva] *n.* plan para aumentar la demanda agregada y estimular una economía débil (pág. 446)
expansionary monetary policy [política monetaria expansiva] *n.* plan para aumentar la cantidad de dinero en circulación; también llamada política de dinero barato (pág. 492)
exports [exportaciones] *n.* bienes o servicios producidos en un país y vendidos a otros países (pág. 516)
externality [externalidad] *n.* efecto secundario de una transacción que afecta a alguien que no sea el productor o el comprador (pág. 87)

F

factor market [mercado de factores] *n.* mercado para los factores de producción: tierra, trabajo, capital y capacidad empresarial (pág. 52)
factors of production [factores de producción] *n.* recursos económicos necesarios para producir bienes y servicios (pág. 8)
federal budget [presupuesto federal] *n.* plan para gastar los ingresos obtenidos mediante los impuestos federales (pág. 431)
federal funds rate (FFR) [tasa de interés para fondos federales (TFF)] *n.* interés al que una institución de depósitos presta por un día fondos disponibles a otra institución de depósitos (pág. 490)
Federal Insurance Contributions Act (FICA) [Ley de Contribuciones al Seguro Federal] *n.* impuesto sobre nóminas que proporciona cobertura a las personas mayores, a los desempleados por incapacidad y a los familiares supervivientes de asalariados que han muerto (pág. 423)
Federal Open Market Committee (FOMC) [Comité Federal del Mercado Abierto] *n.* junta del Sistema de la Reserva Federal que supervisa la venta y la compra de valores del gobierno federal (pág. 477)
Federal Reserve System [Sistema de la Reserva Federal] *n.* banco central de Estados Unidos, llamado comúnmente la Fed (pág. 474)
fiat money [dinero fiduciario] *n.* dinero que no tiene respaldo tangible pero cuyo valor es declarado por el gobierno y aceptado por los ciudadanos (pág. 291)
filing status [estado personal] *n.* para la declaración de impuestos, se basa en el estado civil o en las cargas familiares (pág. 604)
financial asset [activo financiero] *n.* derecho de la propiedad del prestatario (pág. 319)
financial intermediary [intermediario financiero] *n.* institución que reúne fondos de los ahorradores e invierte estos fondos en activos financieros (pág. 319)
financial market [mercado financiero] *n.* situación en la que los compradores y los vendedores intercambian activos financieros (pág. 319)
financial system [sistema financiero] *n.* todas las instituciones que ayudan a transferir fondos entre los ahorradores y los inversionistas (pág. 318)
fiscal [fiscal] *adj.* lo relacionado a los ingresos y a los gastos del gobierno (pág. 446)
fiscal policy [política fiscal] *n.* uso que hace el gobierno federal de los impuestos y los gastos para afectar a la economía (pág. 446)
fiscal year [año fiscal] *n.* período de 12 meses en el que una organización planifica sus gastos (pág. 431)
fixed costs [costos fijos] *n.* gastos en los que incurren los propietarios de empresas, independientemente de cuánto produzcan (pág. 140)
fixed rate of exchange [tasa de cambio fija] *n.* sistema en el que la divisa de un país es fija o constante respecto a las otras divisas (pág. 526)

R49

flexible exchange rate [tasa de cambio flexible] *n.* sistema en el que la tasa de cambio para una divisa fluctúa al fluctuar la oferta y la demanda de la divisa; también llamada tasa flotante (pág. 527)
focus group [grupo focal] *n.* discusión dirigida por un moderador y realizada con pequeños grupos de consumidores (pág. 208)
foreign exchange market [mercado de divisas] *n.* mercado en el que se compran y venden divisas de diferentes países (pág. 526)
foreign exchange rate [tasa de cambio de divisas] *n.* precio de una divisa expresado en las divisas de otros países (pág. 526)
franchise [franquicia] *n.* negocio formado por negocios parcialmente independientes que ofrecen todos los mismos productos o servicios (pág. 248)
franchisee [franquiciado] *n.* negocio parcialmente independiente que paga un cargo por el derecho a vender en una determinada zona los productos o servicios de la compañía matriz (pág. 248)
free contract [contrato libre] *n.* situación en la que las personas deciden por sí solas qué contratos legales aceptar (pág. 73)
free-enterprise system [sistema de libre mercado] *n.* otro nombre del capitalismo, sistema económico basado en la propiedad privada de los recursos productivos (pág. 70)
free rider [beneficiario gratuito] *n.* persona que no paga un bien o un servicio pero que se beneficia de él cuando se le da (pág. 85)
free-trade zone [zona de libre comercio] *n.* determinada región en la que el comercio entre los países se realiza sin aranceles proteccionistas (pág. 532)
frictional unemployment [desempleo friccional] *n.* desempleo temporal de los trabajadores que pasan de un puesto de trabajo a otro (pág. 384)
full employment [pleno empleo] *n.* nivel de desempleo en el que ninguna parte del desempleo se debe a la reducción de la actividad económica; por lo general, está marcado por una tasa de desempleo del 4 al 6 por ciento (pág. 383)
future [futuro] *n.* contrato para comprar o vender acciones en una fecha futura determinada y a un precio establecido (pág. 333)

G

general partnership [sociedad colectiva] *n.* sociedad en la que cada socio participa en la dirección de la empresa y es responsable de todas las deudas y pérdidas de la empresa (pág. 233)
geographic monopoly [monopolio geográfico] *n.* monopolio que existe debido a la ausencia de otros productores o vendedores en cierta región (pág. 201)
gift tax [impuesto sobre donaciones] *n.* impuesto aplicado al dinero o a las propiedades que una persona viva le da a otra (pág. 425)
glass ceiling [techo de cristal] *n.* barrera artificial e invisible que a veces afrontan las mujeres y las minorías y que les impide avanzar profesionalmente (pág. 262)
global economy [economía global] *n.* todas las interacciones económicas que cruzan las fronteras internacionales (pág. 61)
gold standard [patrón oro] *n.* sistema en el que la unidad monetaria básica es igual a una cantidad de oro establecida (pág. 299)
goods [bienes] *n.* objetos físicos, como los alimentos, la ropa y los muebles, que pueden comprarse (pág. 5)
government monopoly [monopolio gubernamental] *n.* monopolio que existe debido a que el gobierno posee y dirige esa empresa o autoriza un solo productor (pág. 201)
grant-in-aid [donativo del gobierno federal] *n.* pago de transferencia del gobierno federal a gobiernos estatales o locales (pág. 432)
gross domestic product (GDP) [producto interior bruto (PIB)] *n.* valor de mercado de todos los bienes y servicios finales producidos en un país durante un determinado período de tiempo (pág. 350)
gross national product (GNP) [producto nacional bruto (PNB)] *n.* valor de mercado de todos los bienes y servicios finales producidos por un país durante un determinado período de tiempo (pág. 355)

H

hacking [hacking] *n.* técnica empleada por los ladrones de identidad para recoger información personal mediante computadoras y tecnología relacionada (pág. 588)
horizontal merger [fusión horizontal] *n.* unión de dos o más compañías que ofrecen productos o servicios iguales o similares (pág. 243)
human capital [capital humano] *n.* conocimientos y aptitudes que permiten a los trabajadores ser productivos (pág. 261)
human development index (HDI) [índice de desarrollo humano (IDH)] *n.* combinación del PIB real per cápita, la esperanza de vida al nacer, la tasa de alfabetización de adultos y la tasa de matriculación de los estudiantes de un país y todo esto indica cómo es la vida en un país determinado (pág. 547)

hyperinflation [hiperinflación] *n.* tasa de inflación acelerada y no controlada superior al 50 por ciento (pág. 398)

I

identity theft [robo de identidad] *n.* uso de la información personal de otra persona con fines criminales (pág. 588)
imperfect competition [competencia imperfecta] *n.* estructura de mercado que carece de una o más de las condiciones necesarias para la competencia perfecta (pág. 195)
imports [importaciones] *n.* bienes o servicios producidos en un país y comprados por otro (pág. 516)
incentive [incentivo] *n.* beneficio ofrecido para estimular a las personas a que actúen de cierta manera (págs. 12, 176)
incidence of a tax [incidencia fiscal] *n.* carga final de un impuesto (pág. 415)
income distribution [distribución de la renta] *n.* forma en que la renta se divide entre las personas de un país (pág. 390)
income effect [efecto renta] *n.* cambio en la cantidad de un bien o de un servicio que un consumidor comprará debido a la variación de su renta (y por ello su poder adquisitivo) (pág. 107)
income inequality [desigualdad de la renta] *n.* distribución desigual de la renta (pág. 390)
increasing returns [rentabilidad creciente] *n.* situación en la que la contratación de nuevos trabajadores hace aumentar el producto marginal (pág. 139)
independent contractor [contratista independiente] *n.* alguien que vende sus servicios mediante un contrato (pág. 270)
individual income tax [impuesto sobre la renta personal] *n.* impuesto basado en las rentas que una persona recibe de todas las fuentes (pág. 412)
industrial union [sindicato industrial] *n.* organización de trabajadores con muchas y diversas aptitudes y que trabajan en la misma industria (pág. 274)
inelastic [inelástica] *n.* situación en la que la cantidad demandada o la cantidad ofertada cambia poco al cambiar el precio (págs. 117, 155)
infant industries [industrias nacientes] *n.* nuevas industrias que frecuentemente son incapaces de competir contra los competidores más grandes y establecidos (pág. 523)
infant mortality rate [tasa de mortalidad infantil] *n.* número de niños que mueren durante el primer año de vida por 1,000 nacimientos (pág. 547)
inferior goods [bienes inferiores] *n.* bienes que tienen menos demanda por parte de los consumidores cuando aumentan sus ingresos (pág. 110)
inflation [inflación] *n.* aumento persistente del nivel general de precios, o disminución persistente del poder adquisitivo del dinero (pág. 396)
inflation rate [tasa de inflación] *n.* tasa de variación de los precios durante un período de tiempo establecido (pág. 397)
infrastructure [infraestructuras] *n.* conjunto básico de los sistemas de soporte, como los sistemas energéticos, de comunicaciones, de transporte, de agua, sanitarios y de educación, que se necesitan para el funcionamiento de la economía y la sociedad (págs. 86, 545)
input costs [costos de los insumos] *n.* precio de los recursos necesarios para producir un bien o un servicio (pág. 148)
insourcing [uso de recursos internos] *n.* práctica de las compañías extranjeras que establecen operaciones en Estados Unidos y por lo tanto crean puestos de trabajo en este país (pág. 269)
interest [interés] *n.* cargo que paga un banco por el uso del dinero (pág. 578)
International Monetary Fund (IMF) [Fondo Monetario Internacional (FMI)] *n.* organización internacional establecida para promocionar la cooperación monetaria internacional, fomentar el crecimiento económico y proporcionar apoyo financiero temporal a los países para ayudar a mitigar el ajuste de la balanza-de-pagos (pág. 559)
investment [inversión] *n.* uso actual de la renta de manera tal que permita obtener un beneficio futuro (pág. 318)
investment objective [objetivo de inversión] *n.* meta financiera utilizada para determinar si una inversión es apropiada (pág. 324)

J

junk bond [bono basura] *n.* bono de empresa que es de alto riesgo y de alto rendimiento (pág. 339)

K

Keynesian economics [economía keynesiana] *n.* idea, propuesta inicialmente por John Maynard Keynes, de que el gobierno necesita estimular la demanda agregada en períodos de recesión (pág. 454)

L

labor [trabajo] *n.* todo el tiempo, esfuerzo y talento humano usado para producir bienes y servicios (pág. 8)
labor input [factor trabajo] *n.* magnitud de la fuerza laboral multiplicada por la duración de la semana laborable (pág. 371)
labor productivity [productividad del trabajo] *n.* cantidad de bienes y servicios que una persona puede producir en un tiempo determinado (pág. 149)

labor union [sindicato laboral] *n.* organización de trabajadores que trata de mejorar para sus miembros los salarios, las condiciones laborales, los beneficios suplementarios, la seguridad en el empleo y otros asuntos relacionados con el trabajo (pág. 274)
Laffer Curve [curva de Laffer] *n.* gráfica que ilustra cómo afecta la reducción de los impuestos a los ingresos fiscales y al crecimiento económico (pág. 459)
lagging indicators [indicadores retrasados] *n.* medidas del rendimiento económico que suelen cambiar después de cambiar el producto interior bruto real (pág. 364)
laissez faire [laissez faire] *n.* principio según el cual el gobierno no debe interferir en la economía (pág. 49)
land [tierra] *n.* todos los recursos naturales sobre o bajo el suelo que se utilizan para producir bienes y servicios (pág. 8)
landlord [propietario de una propiedad] *n.* dueño de una propiedad de alquiler (pág. 609)
law of comparative advantage [ley de la ventaja comparativa] *n.* ley según la cual los países se benefician cuando producen artículos cuya fabricación realizan con la mayor eficiencia y con el menor costo de oportunidad (pág. 514)
law of demand [ley de la demanda] *n.* establece que cuando el precio de un bien o de un servicio baja la cantidad demandada aumenta, y cuando los precios suben la cantidad demandada disminuye (pág. 99)
law of diminishing marginal utility [ley de la utilidad marginal decreciente] *n.* establece que el beneficio marginal obtenido al consumir cada unidad adicional de un bien o de un servicio durante un determinado período de tiempo tiende a disminuir tras el consumo de cada una (pág. 106)
law of increasing opportunity costs [ley de costos de oportunidad crecientes] *n.* establece que al pasar de fabricar un producto a fabricar otro, se necesitan cada vez más recursos para aumentar la fabricación del segundo producto, lo cual hace aumentar los costos de oportunidad (pág. 21)
law of supply [ley de la oferta] *n.* establece que los productores están dispuestos a vender más de un bien o de un servicio a un precio más alto que a un precio más bajo (pág. 131)
leading indicators [indicadores principales] *n.* medidas del rendimiento económico que generalmente cambian antes de que cambie el producto interior bruto real (pág. 364)
lease [contrato de arrendamiento financiero] *n.* contrato para alquilar un apartamento, vehículo u otro objeto durante un determinado período de tiempo (pág. 609)
legal equality [igualdad legal] *n.* situación en la que todo el mundo tiene los mismos derechos económicos bajo la ley (pág. 73)
less developed countries (LDCs) [países menos desarrollados (PMD)] *n.* países con un PIB más bajo, menos industrias bien desarrolladas y un nivel de vida menor; a veces, se llaman economías emergentes (pág. 545)
life expectancy [esperanza de vida al nacer] *n.* promedio de años que se prevé que una persona vivirá si las tendencias de mortalidad actuales continúan durante el resto de la vida de esa persona (pág. 547)
limited liability [responsabilidad limitada] *n.* situación en la que la responsabilidad del propietario de una empresa respecto a las deudas y a las pérdidas de la empresa es limitada (pág. 240)
limited liability partnership (LLP) [sociedad de responsabilidad limitada (SRL)] *n.* sociedad en la que no todos los socios son responsables de las deudas y de otras obligaciones de los otros socios (pág. 233)
limited life [vida limitada] *n.* situación en la que una empresa deja de existir si el propietario muere, se jubila o abandona la empresa (pág. 228)
limited partnership [sociedad limitada] *n.* sociedad en la que hay al menos un socio que no participa en la gestión de la empresa y es responsable sólo de los fondos que invirtió (pág. 233)
literacy rate [tasa de alfabetización] *n.* porcentaje de personas mayores de 15 años que saben leer y escribir (pág. 547)
loan [préstamo] *n.* dinero prestado que se reembolsa generalmente con intereses (pág. 582)
Lorenz curve [curva de Lorenz] *n.* curva que muestra el grado de desigualdad de la renta de un país (pág. 391)

M

macroeconomic equilibrium [equilibrio macroeconómico] *n.* punto donde la demanda agregada equivale a la oferta agregada (pág. 361)
macroeconomics [macroeconomía] *n.* estudio del comportamiento de la economía en su conjunto; lo relacionado a la actividad económica a gran escala (pág. 27)
mandatory spending [gastos obligatorios] *n.* gastos que debe realizar el gobierno según las leyes actuales (pág. 428)
marginal benefit [beneficio marginal] *n.* beneficio o satisfacción obtenido al consumir una unidad adicional de un bien o de un servicio (pág. 16)
marginal cost [costo marginal] *n.* costo adicional de producir o consumir una unidad adicional de un bien o de un servicio (págs. 16, 140)
marginal product [producto marginal] *n.* cambio en el producto total que es resultado de añadir un trabajador más (pág. 138)

marginal revenue [ingreso marginal] *n.* dinero obtenido al vender cada unidad adicional (pág. 142)
market [mercado] *n.* cualquier lugar o situación en que las personas compran y venden bienes y servicios (pág. 48)
market allocation [reparto de mercado] *n.* acuerdo entre dos o más empresas competidoras por el que se divide un mercado (pág. 216)
market demand curve [curva de demanda de mercado] *n.* gráfica que muestra datos de una tabla de demanda de mercado, o la cantidad de un bien o de un servicio que todos los consumidores pueden y están dispuestos a comprar a cada precio (pág. 102)
market demand schedule [tabla de demanda de mercado] *n.* tabla que muestra la cantidad de un bien o de un servicio que todos los consumidores pueden y están dispuestos a comprar a cada precio de un mercado (pág. 100)
market division [repartición de mercado] *véase* market allocation [reparto de mercado]
market economy [economía de mercado] *n.* sistema económico basado en la elección individual y el intercambio voluntario (pág. 39)
market equilibrium [equilibrio del mercado] *n.* situación en la que la cantidad ofertada y la cantidad demandada a un precio determinado son iguales (pág. 164)
market failure [fallo del mercado] *n.* situación en la que personas no participantes de una interacción del mercado se benefician de ella o pagan parte de sus costos (pág. 84)
market research [investigación de mercados] *n.* recogida y evaluación de información sobre las preferencias de los consumidores respecto a bienes y servicios (pág. 208)
market share [cuota de mercado] *n.* porcentaje del total de ventas de una empresa en un mercado determinado (pág. 209)
market structure [estructura de mercado] *n.* modelo económico de competencia entre las empresas de la misma industria (pág. 192)
market supply curve [curva de oferta de mercado] *n.* gráfica que muestra datos de una tabla de oferta de mercado (pág. 134)
market supply schedule [tabla de oferta de mercado] *n.* tabla que muestra la cantidad de un bien o de un servicio que todos los productores de un mercado pueden y están dispuestos a ofrecer para su venta a cada precio (pág. 132)
maturity [vencimiento] *n.* fecha en la que un bono debe reembolsarse (pág. 338)
Medicaid [Medicaid] *n.* programa de seguro médico gubernamental destinado a las personas de baja renta (pág. 429)
Medicare [Medicare] *n.* programa de seguro de salud nacional y gubernamental destinado principalmente a los ciudadanos mayores de 65 años (pág. 423)
medium of exchange [medio de intercambio] *n.* medio por el que se pueden intercambiar bienes y servicios (pág. 288)
merger [fusión] *n.* unión de dos o más compañías para formar una sola compañía (pág. 214)
microeconomics [microeconomía] *n.* estudio del comportamiento de los participantes individuales de una economía, como las personas, las familias y las empresas (pág. 27)
minimum balance requirement [requisito de saldo mínimo] *n.* cantidad de dinero que se debe mantener en una cuenta para evitar los cargos (pág. 576)
minimum wage [salario mínimo] *n.* la menor cantidad, según establece la ley, que un empleador puede pagar a un trabajador por una hora de trabajo (págs. 182, 262)
mixed economy [economía mixta] *n.* sistema económico que presenta elementos de las economías tradicional, autoritaria y de mercado; sistema económico más común (pág. 58)
modified free enterprise economy [economía de libre mercado modificada] *n.* sistema económico mixto que incluye algunas medidas protectoras, disposiciones y reglamentos del gobierno, para ajustar el sistema de libre mercado (pág. 80)
monetarism [monetarismo] *n.* teoría económica que sugiere que los cambios rápidos en la oferta monetaria son la causa principal de la inestabilidad económica (pág. 496)
monetary [monetario] *adj.* lo relacionado al dinero (pág. 474)
monetary policy [política monetaria] *n.* medidas de la Reserva Federal que cambian la oferta monetaria para influir en la economía (pág. 490)
money [dinero] *n.* todo lo que las personas aceptan como pago de bienes y servicios (pág. 288)
money market [mercado monetario] *n.* mercado en el que se compran y venden activos financieros a corto plazo (pág. 322)
monopolistic competition [competencia monopolista] *n.* estructura de mercado en la que un gran número de vendedores ofrecen a los consumidores productos similares pero no estandarizados (pág. 206)
monopoly [monopolio] *n.* estructura de mercado en la que un único vendedor vende un producto para el que no existen sustitutos adecuados (pág. 198)
monopsony [monopsonio] *n.* estructura de mercado en la que existe gran número de vendedores pero sólo un comprador grande (pág. 212)

multifactor productivity [productividad multifactorial] *n.* razón entre la producción económica de una industria y los factores trabajo y capital (pág. 372)
multinational corporation [empresa multinacional] *n.* sociedad anónima que tiene establecimientos en varios países (pág. 243)
mutual fund [fondo de mercado monetario, fondo mutual] *n.* compañía de inversión que reúne dinero de inversionistas individuales y lo utiliza para comprar una variedad de activos financieros (pág. 320)

N

NAFTA [NAFTA] *n.* Tratado de Libre Comercio con América del Norte, convenio que asegura el libre comercio por todo el continente y constituye la zona de libre comercio más grande del mundo (pág. 533)
national accounts [cuentas nacionales] *véase* national income accounting [contabilidad nacional]
national bank [banco nacional] *n.* banco autorizado por el gobierno nacional (pág. 299)
national debt [deuda pública] *n.* cantidad total de dinero que debe el gobierno federal (pág. 462)
national income (NI) [renta nacional (RN)] *n.* renta total percibida en un país por la producción de bienes y servicios durante un determinado período de tiempo (pág. 355)
national income accounting [contabilidad nacional] *n.* método de analizar la economía de un país usando medidas estadísticas de los ingresos, los gastos y la producción (pág. 350)
nationalize [nacionalizar] *v.* pasar de la propiedad privada a la propiedad gubernamental o pública (pág. 61)
natural monopoly [monopolio natural] *n.* situación del mercado en la que los costos de producción son más bajos cuando una única empresa proporciona un producto o un servicio (pág. 201)
near money [cuasidinero] *n.* cuentas de ahorro y otros depósitos a plazo similares que pueden convertirse en dinero de manera relativamente fácil (pág. 293)
needs [necesidades] *n.* objetos como los alimentos, la ropa y los lugares de vivienda, que son necesarios para la vida (pág. 4)
negative externality [externalidad negativa] *n.* externalidad que supone un costo para personas no participantes en la actividad económica original (pág. 87)
net national product (NNP) [producto nacional neto (PNN)] *n.* producto nacional bruto menos la depreciación del capital social. Es decir, es el valor de los bienes y los servicios finales menos el valor de los bienes capitales que quedaron desgastados durante el año (pág. 355)
nominal GDP [PIB nominal] *n.* producto interior bruto expresado en función del valor actual de los bienes y los servicios (pág. 352)
nonmarket activities [actividades no comerciales] *n.* servicios que tienen un valor económico en potencia pero que se prestan sin cobrar (pág. 354)
nonprice competition [competencia no basada en el precio] *n.* uso de factores distintos al precio, como el estilo, el servicio, la publicidad o los regalos, para tratar de convencer a los clientes para que compren algo de un productor y no de otro (pág. 207)
nonprofit organization [organización sin fines de lucro] *n.* institución que actúa como empresa pero que existe para beneficiar a la comunidad en lugar de obtener ganancias (pág. 250)
normal goods [bienes normales] *n.* bienes que tienen más demanda por parte de los consumidores cuando aumentan sus ingresos (pág. 110)
normative economics [economía normativa] *n.* forma de describir y explicar cómo debería ser el comportamiento económico y no cómo es en realidad (pág. 29)
not-for-profit [sin fines de lucro] *véase* nonprofit organization [organización sin fines de lucro]

O

oligopoly [oligopolio] *n.* estructura de mercado en la que un número reducido de vendedores ofrecen un producto similar (pág. 209)
OPEC [OPEP] *n.* Organización de Países Exportadores de Petróleo, grupo comercial regional (pág. 535)
open market operations [operaciones de mercado abierto] *n.* compraventa por parte de la Reserva Federal de valores del gobierno federal; instrumento de política monetaria de mayor uso por la Reserva Federal para ajustar la oferta monetaria (pág. 490)
open opportunity [oportunidad abierta] *n.* capacidad para que todo el mundo pueda entrar y competir en el mercado según su libre elección (pág. 73)
operating budget [presupuesto de operación] *n.* plan para los gastos diarios (pág. 436)
opportunity cost [costo de oportunidad] *n.* costo de elegir una alternativa económica en lugar de otra (pág. 14)
option [opción] *n.* contrato por el que se da al inversionista el derecho a comprar o vender acciones en una fecha futura y a un precio establecido (pág. 333)
outsourcing [subcontratación] *n.* práctica de contratar una empresa externa, a menudo en un país extranjero, para que proporcione bienes y servicios (pág. 269)

overdraft [sobregiro] *n.* cheque u otra forma de retirar fondos que excede del saldo existente en la cuenta (pág. 576)

P

par value [valor a la par] *n.* cantidad que el emisor de un bono promete pagar al comprador en la fecha de vencimiento (pág. 338)

partnership [sociedad] *n.* empresa que pertenece a dos o más personas, o "socios", que acuerdan la forma de repartir las responsabilidades, las ganancias y las pérdidas (pág. 232)

patent [patente] *n.* inscripción legal de un invento o de un proceso que da al inventor los derechos exclusivos de la propiedad sobre ese invento o proceso durante cierto número de años (pág. 202)

peak [punto máximo, pico] *n.* fin de una expansión de la economía (pág. 359); *véase* business cycle [ciclo económico]

per capita gross domestic product [producto interior bruto per cápita] *n.* PIB de un país, dividido por la población total (pág. 546)

perestroika [perestroika] *n.* plan del dirigente ruso Mijaíl Gorbachov de incorporar de forma gradual mercados en la economía autoritaria de la Unión Soviética (pág. 564)

perfect competition [competencia perfecta] *n.* modelo ideal de una economía de mercado; estructura de mercado en la que ninguno de los numerosos vendedores y compradores independientes y bien informados tiene control sobre el precio de un bien o un servicio estandarizado (pág. 192)

personal income (PI) [renta personal (RP)] *n.* renta anual recibida por el conjunto de personas de un país y procedente de todas las fuentes (pág. 355)

phishing [phishing] *n.* técnica empleada por los ladrones de identidad para recoger información personal mediante llamadas telefónicas engañosas (pág. 588)

PIN [PIN] *n.* número de identificación personal (pág. 577)

positive economics [economía positiva] *n.* forma de describir y explicar la economía tal como es (pág. 29)

positive externality [externalidad positiva] *n.* externalidad que beneficia a personas no participantes en la actividad económica original (pág. 87)

poverty [pobreza] *n.* situación en la que la renta y los recursos de una persona no le permiten obtener un nivel de vida mínimo (pág. 388)

poverty line [línea de pobreza] *véase* poverty threshold [umbral de pobreza]

poverty rate [tasa de pobreza] *n.* porcentaje de personas que viven en hogares cuya renta es inferior a la del umbral de pobreza (pág. 389)

poverty threshold [umbral de pobreza] *n.* renta mínima oficial necesaria para pagar los gastos básicos de la vida (pág. 388)

predatory pricing [establecer precios predatorios] *n.* fijar los precios por debajo del costo durante un tiempo para excluir de un mercado a los competidores de menor tamaño (pág. 216)

preferred stock [acciones preferentes] *n.* participación en la propiedad de una sociedad anónima que da al titular parte de las ganancias pero generalmente no da derecho a voto (pág. 331)

premium [prima] *n.* cantidad que se paga por un seguro (pág. 596)

price ceiling [precio máximo] *n.* precio máximo establecido que los vendedores pueden cobrar por un producto (pág. 180)

price fixing [imposición de precios] *n.* pactos entre dos o más empresas por los que fijan los precios de productos competidores (pág. 216)

price floor [precio mínimo] *n.* precio mínimo establecido al que los compradores deben pagar un producto (pág. 182)

price maker [fijador de precio] *n.* empresa que no tiene que tomar en cuenta a los competidores cuando fija sus precios (pág. 198)

price taker [tomador de precio] *n.* compañía que debe aceptar el precio de mercado fijado por la interacción de la oferta y la demanda (pág. 193)

primary market [mercado primario] *n.* mercado de valores para comprar activos financieros directamente del emisor (pág. 322)

prime rate [tasa preferencial] *n.* tasa de interés que los bancos aplican a sus mejores clientes (pág. 491)

private company [compañía privada] *n.* sociedad anónima que controla quién puede comprar o vender sus acciones (pág. 238)

private property rights [derechos a propiedad privada] *n.* derechos de las personas y de los grupos a poseer recursos y empresas (pág. 48)

private sector [sector privado] *n.* parte de la economía que pertenece a las personas o a las empresas (pág. 432)

privatization [privatización] *n.* proceso de transferir a las personas propiedades y empresas públicas (pág. 563)

privatize [privatizar] *v.* pasar de la propiedad gubernamental o pública a la propiedad privada (pág. 61)

producer [productor] *n.* persona que produce bienes o presta servicios (pág. 5)

producer price index (PPI) [índice de precios al por mayor (IPM)] *n.* medida de los cambios en los precios al por mayor (pág. 397)

product differentiation [diferenciación de productos] *n.* intento de distinguir un producto de otros productos similares (pág. 206)

product market [mercado de productos] *n.* mercado en el que se compran y venden bienes y servicios (pág. 52)
production possibilities curve (PPC) [curva de posibilidades de producción (CPP)] *n.* gráfica utilizada para ilustrar el efecto de la carencia sobre una economía (pág. 18)
productivity [productividad] *n.* cantidad de producto obtenido a partir de una cantidad establecida de insumos (pág. 372)
productivity, labor [productividad, trabajo] *véase* labor productivity [productividad del trabajo]
profit [ganancias] *n.* ganancias financieras que obtiene un vendedor al realizar una transacción comercial (pág. 49); dinero que queda tras restar los costos de fabricar un producto a los ingresos obtenidos al vender ese producto (pág. 78)
profit-maximizing output [nivel de producción de máxima ganancia] *n.* punto de la producción en el que una empresa ha alcanzado su mayor nivel de ganancias (pág. 143)
profit motive [afán de lucro] *n.* incentivo que estimula a las personas y a las organizaciones para que mejoren su bienestar material buscando obtener ganancias de actividades económicas (pág. 73)
progressive tax [impuesto progresivo] *n.* impuesto que aplica una tasa impositiva más alta a las personas de alta renta que a las personas de baja renta (pág. 412)
property tax [impuesto sobre la propiedad] *n.* impuesto basado en el valor de los activos de una persona o de una empresa (pág. 412)
proportional tax [impuesto proporcional] *n.* impuesto que extrae el mismo porcentaje de renta a todos los contribuyentes, independientemente de su nivel de renta (pág. 412)
protectionism [proteccionismo] *n.* uso de barreras al comercio entre los países para proteger las industrias nacionales (pág. 523)
protective tariff [arancel proteccionista] *n.* impuesto aplicado a los bienes importados para proteger los bienes nacionales (pág. 521)
public company [empresa que cotiza en Bolsa] *n.* sociedad anónima que emite acciones que pueden negociarse libremente (pág. 238)
public disclosure [divulgación pública] *n.* política que exige que las empresas revelen a los consumidores información sobre sus productos (pág. 217)
public goods [bienes públicos] *n.* bienes y servicios proporcionados por el gobierno y consumidos por el público como grupo (pág. 84)
public transfer payment [pago de transferencia público] *n.* pago de transferencia por el que el gobierno transfiere ingresos de los contribuyentes a los beneficiarios sin que éstos den nada a cambio (pág. 89)
pure competition [competencia pura] *véase* perfect competition [competencia perfecta]

Q

quota [cuota] *n.* límite sobre la cantidad de un producto que puede importarse (pág. 520)

R

rational expectations theory [teoría de las expectativas racionales] *n.* teoría según la cual las personas y las empresas prevén que los cambios en la política fiscal tendrán efectos determinados y actúan para proteger sus intereses contra esos efectos (pág. 452)
rationing [racionamiento] *n.* sistema en el que el gobierno asigna bienes y servicios aplicando factores distintos al precio (pág. 183)
real GDP [PIB real] *n.* producto interior bruto corregido respecto a los cambios en los precios de un año a otro (pág. 352)
real GDP per capita [PIB real per cápita] *n.* producto interior bruto real dividido por la población total (pág. 369)
recession [recesión] *n.* contracción económica prolongada que dura dos o más trimestres (seis meses o más) (pág. 359)
regressive tax [impuesto regresivo] *n.* impuesto que extrae un mayor porcentaje de renta a las personas de baja renta que a las personas de alta renta (pág. 412)
regulation [regulación] *n.* serie de reglas o leyes diseñadas para controlar el comportamiento comercial (págs. 150, 214)
representative money [dinero representativo] *n.* papel moneda respaldado por algo tangible (pág. 291)
required reserve ratio (RRR) [coeficiente de reservas exigidas (CRE)] *n.* fracción de los depósitos de un banco, tal como lo determina la Reserva Federal, que debe tener en forma de reservas para poder dar préstamos de dinero (pág. 484)
return [rentabilidad] *n.* ganancias o pérdidas derivadas de una inversión (pág. 327)
revenue [ingresos] *n.* renta gubernamental procedente de los impuestos y de fuentes no impositivas (pág. 410)
revenue tariff [arancel financiero] *n.* impuesto aplicado a las importaciones específicamente para recaudar fondos; actualmente se usa muy poco (pág. 521)

right-to-work laws [leyes de libertad de sindicación] *n.* legislación que hace ilegal exigir que los trabajadores se asocien a los sindicatos (pág. 279)
risk [riesgo] *n.* posibilidad de sufrir pérdidas en una inversión (pág. 327)

S

safety net [red de protección] *n.* programas gubernamentales diseñados para proteger a las personas de las dificultades económicas (pág. 89)
sales tax [impuesto sobre las ventas] *n.* impuesto basado en el valor de los bienes o los servicios en el momento de la venta (pág. 412)
savings [ahorros] *n.* ingresos que no se utilizan para el consumo (pág. 318)
scarcity [carencia] *n.* situación en la que los recursos no son suficientes para satisfacer los deseos humanos (pág. 4)
seasonal unemployment [desempleo estacional] *n.* desempleo asociado al trabajo estacional (pág. 384)
secondary market [mercado secundario] *n.* mercado en el que los activos financieros se venden de nuevo (pág. 322)
service [servicios] *n.* trabajo que una persona realiza para otra a cambio de un pago (pág. 5)
shadow economy [economía sumergida] *véase* underground economy [economía subterránea]
share [acción] *n.* unidad del conjunto de acciones de una sociedad anónima (pág. 238); *véase* stock [acciones]
shock therapy [terapia de choque] *n.* programa económico en el que se pasa abruptamente de una economía autoritaria a una economía de libre mercado (pág. 563)
shortage [escasez] *n.* situación en la que la demanda es mayor que la oferta y la causa suele ser la fijación de precios excesivamente bajos (pág. 167)
shoulder surfing [navegar por el hombro] *n.* técnica utilizada por los ladrones de identidad para recoger información personal cuando se revela información privada en público (pág. 588)
socialism [socialismo] *n.* sistema económico en el que el gobierno posee algunos o todos los factores de producción (pág. 43)
Social Security [Seguridad Social] *n.* programa federal que proporciona ayuda a los ciudadanos mayores, a los niños huérfanos y a los incapacitados (pág. 423)
sole proprietorship [empresa unipersonal] *n.* empresa que pertenece a una sola persona y que es controlada por esa persona (pág. 226)
spamming [spamming] *n.* técnica utilizada por los ladrones de identidad para recoger información personal mediante correos electrónicos engañosos (pág. 588)
special economic zone (SEZ) [zona económica especial (ZEE)] *n.* región geográfica que tiene leyes económicas diferentes de las leyes económicas normales de un país, con el objetivo de aumentar las inversiones extranjeras (pág. 567)
specialization [especialización] *n.* situación en la que las personas o las empresas centran sus esfuerzos comerciales en los campos en que presentan una ventaja para una mayor productividad y mayores ganancias (págs. 50, 138, 510)
spending multiplier effect [efecto multiplicador de los gastos] *n.* situación en la que un pequeño cambio en los gastos acaba produciendo un cambio mucho más grande en el PIB (pág. 455)
stabilization programs [programas de estabilización] *n.* programas en los que los países en dificultades se ven obligados a realizar reformas, como reducir el déficit comercial exterior y el endeudamiento externo, eliminar los controles de precios, cerrar las empresas públicas ineficientes y bajar radicalmente el déficit presupuestario (pág. 559)
stagflation [estanflación] *n.* períodos durante los que suben los precios a la vez que se reduce la actividad económica (pág. 359)
standardized product [producto estandarizado] *n.* producto que los consumidores consideran idéntico en todas sus características esenciales a otros productos del mismo mercado (pág. 192)
standard of value [patrón de valor] *n.* forma de medir el valor económico en el proceso de cambio de divisas (pág. 289)
start-up costs [costos de puesta en marcha] *n.* gastos que una nueva empresa debe pagar para entrar en un mercado y empezar a vender a los consumidores (pág. 209)
state bank [banco estatal] *n.* banco autorizado por el gobierno de un estado (pág. 296)
statistics [estadísticas] n. datos numéricos (pág. 24)
stock [acciones] *n.* participaciones en la propiedad de una sociedad anónima (pág. 238)
stockbroker [agente de bolsa] *n.* agente que compra y vende valores para los clientes (pág. 332)
stock exchange [bolsa de valores] *n.* mercado secundario donde se venden y compran valores (pág. 330)
stock index [índice bursátil] *n.* instrumento utilizado para medir e informar sobre el cambio en los precios de un conjunto de acciones (pág. 334)
stored-value card [tarjeta de valor almacenado] *n.* tarjeta que representa dinero que el titular tiene en forma de depósito con la compañía emisora (pág. 308)

store of value [depósito de valor] *n.* algo que conserva su valor con el paso del tiempo (pág. 289)
strike [huelga] *n.* paralización del trabajo utilizada para ejercer presión en las negociaciones mientras se trata de convencer al empleador de que mejore los salarios, las condiciones laborales u otros asuntos relacionados con el trabajo (pág. 274)
structural unemployment [desempleo estructural] *n.* desempleo que existe cuando los puestos de trabajo disponibles no se corresponden con las aptitudes de las personas en condiciones de trabajar (pág. 384)
subsidy [subsidio] *n.* pago gubernamental que ayuda a cubrir el costo de una actividad económica que puede beneficiar al público en su conjunto (pág. 88)
substitutes [sustitutos] *n.* productos que se pueden usar en lugar de otros productos, para satisfacer los deseos de los consumidores (pág. 112)
substitution effect [efecto sustitución] *n.* patrón de comportamiento que se presenta cuando los consumidores, al reaccionar ante un cambio en el precio de un producto, compran un producto sustitutivo que ofrece un mejor valor relativo (pág. 107)
supply [oferta] *n.* disponibilidad y capacidad para producir y vender un producto (pág. 130)
supply curve [curva de la oferta] *n.* gráfica que muestra los datos de una tabla de oferta (pág. 134)
supply schedule [tabla de oferta] *n.* tabla que muestra la cantidad de un bien o de un servicio que un productor individual puede y está dispuesto a ofrecer para su venta a cada precio (pág. 132)
supply-side fiscal policy [política fiscal sobre la oferta] *n.* plan diseñado para ofrecer incentivos a los productores para que aumenten la oferta agregada (pág. 458)
surplus [excedente] *n.* situación en la que la oferta es mayor que la demanda y la causa suele ser la fijación de precios excesivamente altos (pág. 167)

T

tariff [arancel] *n.* cargo aplicado a los bienes transferidos a un país procedentes de otro país (pág. 521)
tax [impuesto] *n.* pago obligatorio a un gobierno (pág. 410)
taxable income [renta gravable] *n.* aquella parte de la renta sujeta a impuestos después de descontar todas las deducciones y exenciones (págs. 421, 604)
tax assessor [asesor fiscal] *n.* funcionario gubernamental que determina el valor de una propiedad sujeta a impuestos (pág. 437)
tax base [base imponible] *n.* forma de riqueza, como la renta, la propiedad, los bienes o los servicios, que está sujeta a impuestos (pág. 412)
tax incentive [incentivo fiscal] *n.* uso de impuestos para estimular o desalentar ciertos comportamientos económicos (pág. 417)
tax return [declaración de la renta] *n.* formulario utilizado para declarar la renta y los impuestos que deben pagarse al gobierno (pág. 421)
technological monopoly [monopolio tecnológico] *n.* monopolio que existe debido a que una empresa controla un método de fabricación, un invento o un tipo de tecnología (pág. 201)
technology [tecnología] *n.* aplicación de métodos e innovaciones científicos a la producción (pág. 149)
telecommuting [trabajo a distancia] *n.* práctica de realizar el trabajo de oficina en un lugar distinto a la propia oficina (pág. 270)
telework [teletrabajo] *véase* telecommuting [trabajo a distancia]
temp, temps, temping [trabajo temporal] *véase* contingent employment [empleo contingente]
thrift institution [entidad de ahorros] *n.* institución financiera que sirve a los ahorradores (pág. 478)
tight-money policy [política de dinero escaso] *véase* contractionary monetary policy [política monetaria restrictiva]
total cost [costo total] *n.* suma de los costos fijos y variables (pág. 140)
total revenue [ingreso total] *n.* ingreso que recibe una empresa al vender sus productos (págs. 122, 142)
total revenue test [prueba del ingreso total] *n.* método para medir la elasticidad comparando el ingreso total que obtendría una empresa al ofrecer su producto a diferentes precios (pág. 122)
trade barrier [barrera al comercio] *n.* toda ley aprobada para limitar el libre comercio entre los países (pág. 520)
trade deficit [déficit comercial] *n.* balanza de comercio desfavorable que se produce cuando un país importa más de lo que exporta (pág. 529)
trade-off [compensación] *n.* alternativa que se rechaza al tomar una decisión económica (pág. 14)
trade surplus [superávit comercial] *n.* balanza de comercio favorable que se produce cuando un país exporta más de lo que importa (pág. 529)
trade union [sindicato] *véase* labor union [sindicato laboral]
trade war [guerra comercial] *n.* serie de barreras al comercio entre los países (pág. 522)

trade-weighted value of the dollar [valor ponderado del dólar] *n.* medida del valor internacional del dólar que determina si el dólar es fuerte o débil al compararse con otra divisa (pág. 528)
traditional economy [economía tradicional] *n.* sistema económico en el que las personas toman decisiones económicas basándose en costumbres y creencias que se han pasado de una generación a la siguiente (pág. 38)
transfer payment [pago de transferencia] *n.* dinero enviado a personas que no dan bienes o servicios a cambio. (págs. 89, 432)
transitional economy [economía transicional] *n.* país que ha pasado (o está pasando) de una economía autoritaria a una economía de mercado (pág. 545)
Treasury bill (T bill) [letra del Tesoro] *n.* bono a corto plazo cuyo vencimiento es de menos de un año (pág. 464)
Treasury bond [bono del Tesoro a largo plazo] *n.* bono a largo plazo cuyo vencimiento es de 30 años (pág. 464)
Treasury note [pagaré del Tesoro] *n.* bono a medio plazo cuyo vencimiento es de entre dos y diez años (pág. 464)
trough [punto mínimo] *n.* fin de una contracción de la economía (pág. 359); *véase* business cycle [ciclo económico]
trust [grupo de empresas] *n.* grupo de compañías que se combinan para reducir la competencia en una industria (pág. 214)
trust fund [fondo fiduciario] *n.* fondo creado para un fin determinado y para un uso futuro (pág. 465)

U

underemployed [subempleados] *n.* personas que trabajan a tiempo parcial pero que quieren trabajar a tiempo completo, o personas que tienen un trabajo que requiere una capacidad inferior a la suya (pág. 383)
underground economy [economía subterránea] *n.* actividades de mercado que no se declaran por ser ilegales o porque los participantes quieren evitar pagar impuestos (pág. 354)
underutilization [infrautilización] *n.* condición en la que los recursos económicos se usan por debajo de su potencia total, dando lugar a menos bienes y servicios (pág. 20)
unemployment rate [tasa de desempleo] *n.* porcentaje de la fuerza laboral que no tiene empleo y que está buscando activamente un trabajo (pág. 382)
union [sindicato] *véase* labor union [sindicato laboral]
union shop [compañía de exclusividad sindical] *n.* empresa en la que los trabajadores están obligados a asociarse a un sindicato durante un período de tiempo establecido después de ser contratados (pág. 279)
unit elastic [elasticidad unitaria] *n.* situación en la que el cambio porcentual del precio y el de la cantidad demandada son iguales (pág. 118)
unlimited liability [responsabilidad ilimitada] *n.* situación en la que el propietario de una empresa es responsable de todas las pérdidas y deudas de la empresa (pág. 228)
unlimited life [vida ilimitada] *n.* situación en la que una sociedad anónima continúa existiendo aun después de un cambio de propietario (pág. 240)
user fee [cargo de usuario] *n.* cantidad de dinero que se cobra por el uso de un bien o servicio (pág. 425)
utility [utilidad] *n.* beneficio o satisfacción obtenido del consumo de un bien o un servicio (pág. 12)

V

variable costs [costos variables] *n.* costos comerciales que varían con el nivel de producción (pág. 140)
vertical merger [fusión vertical] *n.* combinación de dos o más empresas relacionadas con diferentes fases de la producción o de la comercialización de un producto o un servicio (pág. 243)
voluntary exchange [intercambio voluntario] *n.* intercambio en el que las partes participantes prevén que los beneficios serán más importantes que el costo (pág. 49)
voluntary export restraint (VER) [retricción voluntaria a la exportación (RVE)] *n.* autolimitación sobre las exportaciones a ciertos países para evitar cuotas o aranceles (pág. 521)

W

wage and price controls [controles de precios y salarios] *n.* limitaciones gubernamentales sobre el aumento de los precios y los salarios (pág. 501)
wage-price spiral [espiral de precios y salarios] *n.* ciclo que empieza con el aumento de los salarios, lo cual da lugar a costos de producción más altos, que a su vez produce precios más altos; esto provoca la demanda de salarios incluso más altos (pág. 400)
wage rate [escala de salarios] *n.* salario establecido para un determinado puesto de trabajo o tarea realizada (pág. 261)
wages [salarios] *n.* pagos que reciben los trabajadores a cambio de su trabajo (pág. 258)
wants [deseos] *n.* deseos que pueden satisfacerse mediante el consumo de un bien o un servicio (pág. 4)
welfare [asistencia social] *n.* programas económicos y sociales del gobierno que proporcionan ayuda a los necesitados (pág. 392)

R59

withholding [retención] *n.* dinero descontado del pago de un trabajador antes de que reciba ese pago (pág. 421)
workfare [programa de empleo público] *n.* programa que obliga a los beneficiarios de la asistencia social a realizar algún tipo de trabajo a cambio de sus beneficios (pág. 393)
World Bank [Banco Mundial] *n.* institución financiera que proporciona préstamos, consejos relacionados con la política y ayuda técnica a países de ingresos bajos o medios, para reducir la pobreza (pág. 559)
World Trade Organization (WTO) [Organización Mundial del Comercio (OMC)] *n.* organización que negocia y gestiona acuerdos comerciales, resuelve conflictos comerciales, supervisa las políticas comerciales y apoya los países en vías de desarrollo (pág. 535)

Y

yield [rendimiento] *n.* tasa de rentabilidad anual sobre un bono (pág. 338)

Index

Page numbers in **bold** indicate that the term is defined on that page. Page numbers in *italics* indicate an illustration. A letter after a number indicates a specific kind of illustration: *c* – chart; *i* – photograph; *m* – map. An *a* after an italicized page number indicates an Animated Economics feature.

C

R63

R65

F

J

K

N

O

P

R73

T

Y

Z

Acknowledgments

Text Acknowledgments

Chapter 1, page 32: Excerpts from "O'Hare International Airport (ORD/KORD), Chicago, IL, USA," from the Airport-Technology Web site. Reprinted by permission of SPG Media Limited.

Chapter 1, page 33: Excerpt from "Organization and Introduction," from the AReCO Web site. Reprinted by permission of The Alliance of Residents Concerning O'Hare, Inc. (AReCO).

Chapter 2, page 64: Excerpt from "The North Korean Famine," from *Peace Watch,* June 2002. Reprinted by permission of the United States Institute of Peace.

Chapter 2, page 65: Excerpt from "Masters of the Digital Age," by Rana Foroohar and B. J. Lee, *Newsweek,* October 18, 2004. Copyright © 2004 *Newsweek,* Inc. All rights reserved. Reprinted by permission.

Chapter 3, page 92: Excerpt from "The Industry: Message in a Bottle" by Matt Lee and Ted Lee, *The New York Times,* June 28, 2005. Copyright © 2005 by The New York Times Co. Reprinted with permission.

Chapter 3, page 93: Excerpt from "Growing Occupation: Being Your Own Boss" by Stacey Hirsh, *Baltimore Sun,* April 21, 2006. Copyright © 2006 The Baltimore Sun. Reprinted by permission.

Chapter 4, page 124: Excerpts from "Volkswagen Tries 12 Months of Free Car Insurance to Lure Buyers" by Jeff Green, December 31, 2004, Bloomberg Web site. Copyright © 2004 Bloomberg L.P. All rights reserved. Reprinted by permission of Bloomberg L.P.

Chapter 4, page 125: Excerpt from "2005 – The Year of the Hybrid," from the InvoiceDealers Web site. Reprinted by permission of Dealix Corporation, a Division of The Cobalt Group.

Chapter 5, page 144: Excerpt from "Why is the Supply of Cement Falling Short of Demand?" from the Portland Cement Association Web site. Reprinted by permission of the Portland Cement Association.

Chapter 5, 158: Excerpts from "Robots for Babies: Toyota at the Leading Edge" by Burritt Sabin, Japan Inc. Web site. Reprinted by permission of Japan Inc.

Chapter 5, page 159: Excerpt from "Cake Decorating" from the EPSON Robots Web site. Reprinted by permission of EPSON America Inc.

Chapter 6, page 187: Figure 1 from "The Economics of Real Superstars: The Market for Concerts in the Material World" by Alan B. Krueger, *Journal of Labor Economics,* 23(1), 2005. Reprinted by permission of The University of Chicago Press.

Chapter 7, page 220: Excerpts from "Anyone for Telly?," The Economist, September 10, 2005. The Economist Newspaper Ltd. All rights reserved. Reprinted with permission. Further reproduction prohibited. www.economist.com.

Chapter 7, page 221: Excerpt from "Gartner Says Mobile Phone Sales Will Exceed One Billion in 2009," from the Gartner Web site. Reprinted with permission.

Chapter 8, page 248: "World's Leading Franchises," from Franchise Facts. Copyright © International Franchise Association. Reprinted by permission of the International Franchise Association.

Chapter 8, page 252: Excerpt from "Steve Jobs and Steve Wozniak: The Personal Computer" from the Lemelson-MIT Program Web site. Courtesy of Inventor of the Week, Lemelson-MIT Program, http://web.mit.edu/invent.

Chapter 8, page 253: Excerpts from "Interview with Evelyn Richards" by Wendy Marinaccio, appearing on the "Making the Mac/Technology and Culture in Silicon Valley" Web page, Stanford University Library. Reprinted by permission of the Stanford University Library.

Chapter 8, page 253: "Highlights in Apple Company History" adapted from Apple timeline appearing in *Macworld,* February 2004. Copyright © 2004 Mac Publishing LLC. All rights reserved. Reprinted by permission.

Chapter 8, page 255: "Mergers in the United States" *MergerStat Review,* 2004. Copyright © 2004 Mergerstat Holdings, LLP. Reprinted by permission of FactSet Mergerstat LLC.

Chapter 9, page 282: Excerpt from "Subcontinental Drift" by Nandini Lakshman, *Business Week,* January 16, 2006. Copyright © 2006 by The McGraw-Hill Companies, Inc. Reprinted by special permission.

Chapter 9, page 283: Excerpt from "Foreign Firms Come Bearing Jobs" by Mike Meyers, *Star Tribune,* September 5, 2004. Copyright © 2004 Star Tribune. All rights reserved. Reprinted by permission of the Star Tribune, Minneapolis – St. Paul, Minnesota.

Chapter 10, page 312: Excerpts from "Congress Cuts Funding for Student Loans" by Anne Marie Chaker, *The Wall Street Journal,* December 22, 2005. Copyright © 2005 The Wall Street Journal. Reprinted by permission.

Chapter 10, page 313: Excerpts from "It's Payback Time" by Jonathan D. Glater, *The New York Times,* April 23, 2006. Copyright © 2006 by The New York Times Co. Reprinted with permission.

Chapter 11, page 334: "Dow Jones Industrial Average, 1929-2006," from Yahoo! Finance Web site. Copyright © 2006 Yahoo! Inc. YAHOO! and the YAHOO! logo are trademarks of Yahoo! Inc. Reprinted by permission of Yahoo! Inc.

Chapter 11, page 342: "Apple Computer (AAPL-Q)," from *The Globe and Mail,* April 19, 2006. Reprinted by permission of the Globe and Mail

Chapter 11, page 344: "Kozmo.com," from the Wikipedia Web site. Reprinted by permission.

Chapter 11, page 345: Excerpt from "The Bubble Bowl" by David M. Ewalt, Forbes Web site, January 27, 2005. Copyright © 2005 Forbes.com Inc. Reprinted by permission.

Chapter 12, page 364: "U.S. Leading Economic Indicators (LEI) and Real GDP". The Conference Board, United States Bureau of Economic Analysis, National Bureau of Economic Research. Reprinted by permission of The Conference Board Inc.

Chapter 12, page 376: Excerpts from "Europe's Capitalism Curtain" by Steve Pearlstein, *The Washington Post,* July 23, 2004. Copyright © 2004, The Washington Post. Excerpted with permission.

Chapter 12, page 377: Excerpts from "Reaping the European Union Harvest," *The Economist,* January 8, 2005. The Economist Newspaper Ltd. All rights reserved. Reprinted with permission. Further reproduction prohibited. www.economist.com.

Chapter 13, page 404: Excerpt from "The Search for a New Economic Order" by Robert Tolles, *Ford Foundation,* New York, 1982, p. 24. Reprinted by permission of the Ford Foundation.

Chapter 13, page 405: Excerpts from "Open Editorial" by Bernice Davidson, *The New York Times,* September 29, 1972. Copyright © 1972 by The New York Times Co. Reprinted with permission.

Chapter 14, page 440: Excerpts from "iPod Tax Planned for Music Downloads?" from the CNET Web site, March 10, 2006. Copyright © 2006 CNET Networks, Inc. All rights reserved. Reprinted by permission of Reprint Management Services.

Chapter 14, page 441: Excerpt from "Internet Sales Tax," from *The New York Times,* July 5, 2005. Copyright © 2005 by The New York Times Co. Reprinted with permission.

Chapter 15, page 468: Excerpts from "Federal Budget Deficit Sparks Worries," *The Associated Press,* January 15, 2006. Copyright © 2006 The Associated Press. All rights reserved. Reprinted by permission of Reprint Management Services.

Chapter 15, page 469: Excerpt from "Snow Sets Sights on Deficits" by Edward Alden, Andrew Balls, and Holly Yeaser, *Financial Times,* November 4, 2005. Copyright © The Financial Times Ltd. 2005. Reprinted with permission.

Chapter 16, page 504: Excerpts from "Fed Expected to Boost Key Interest Rates," *The Associated Press,* May 10, 2006. Copyright © 2006 The Associated Press. All rights reserved. Reprinted by permission of Reprint Management Services.

Chapter 16, page 505: Excerpts from "Bernanke Talks Tough on Inflation" by Edmund L. Andrews, *The New York Times,* June 6, 2006. Copyright © 2006 by The New York Times Co. Reprinted with permission.

Chapter 17, page 521: "Tariffs are Falling," from the *Human Development Report,* 2005, United Nations Development Programme. Reprinted by permission of the United Nations Publications Department.

Chapter 17, page 538: Excerpt from "Sugar Daddies" by Jason Lee Steorts, *National Review,* July 18, 2005. Copyright © 2005 National Review. Reprinted by permission.

Chapter 17, page 539: Excerpts from "Sweetener Impact on US Economy," from the American Sugar Alliance Web site. Copyright © 2005 American Sugar Alliance. Reprinted by permission.

Chapter 18, page 570: Excerpt from "From T-shirts to T-bonds," *The Economist,* July 28, 2005. The Economist Newspaper Ltd. All rights reserved. Reprinted with permission. Further reproduction prohibited. www.economist.com.

Chapter 18, page: Excerpts from "China's Economic Miracle: The High Price of Progress," from CBC News, April 20, 2006, Canadian Broadcasting Corporation Web site. Copyright © CBC 2006. Reprinted by permission.

Skillbuilder Handbook

Page R15: Excerpts from "Crude Oil Prices Sink Below $66 a Barrel," *The Associated Press,* September 11, 2006. Copyright © 2006 The Associated Press. All rights reserved. Reprinted by permission of Reprint Management Services.

Page R21: Excerpt from "U.S. Trade Deficit Hit Record High in 2005"by Vikas Bajaj, *The New York Times,* February 10, 2006. Copyright © 2006 by The New York Times Co. Reprinted with permission.

Page R23: Excerpt from "Not Business as Usual" by Elizabeth Bauman, *Online NewsHour Extra,* January 30, 2002. Copyright © 2002 MacNeil-Lehrer Productions. Reprinted by permission.

Page R27: Excerpt from "1942: Beveridge Lays Welfare Foundations," from BBC Web site. Copyright © BBC. Reprinted by permission.

Art Credits

Frontmatter

cov *top* © Randy Faris/Corbis; *bottom left* © Peter Horree/Alamy Images; *top right* © Scott Olson/Getty Images; *center right* © Jochem D. Wijnands/Getty Images; *bottom right* © ShutterStock; **iii** *top* © Mark Lewis/Getty Images; *second from top* © Paul A. Souders/Corbis; *third from top* © Veer; *third from bottom* © Joeseph Sohm-Visions of America/Getty Images; *second from bottom* © Jack Dagley Photography/ShutterStock; *bottom* © Jose Luis Pelaez, Inc./Corbis; **iv** *Sally Meek* Photo courtesy of Isaac Portrait Photography, Dallas, Texas, isaacphotography.com; *Mark Schug* Photo courtesy of Diana Johnson, Northwestern University; *John Morton* Photo courtesy of Kathryn S. Morton; **4** © Getty Images.

Unit 1

2–3 © Charles Gupton/Corbis; **5** AP/Wide World Photos; **6** AP/Wide World Photos; **7** *left* © Peter Dean/Grant Heilman Photography; *right* © Grant Heilman/Grant Heilman Photography; **8** © Karen Kasmauski/Corbis; **11** © PictureQuest; **12** © Michelle Pedone/zefa/Corbis; **13** *right* © GDT/Getty Images; *center* © RNT Productions/Corbis; *left* © Getty Images; **14** © Nancy Ney/Getty Images; **16** *left* © Getty Images;*center* © Corbis; *right* © Peter Mason/Getty Images; **17** © Bryan Bedder/Getty Images; **18** © C Squared Studios/Getty Images; **21** *left* © Frank Rossoto Stocktrek/Getty Images; *right* © David Hancock/Alamy Images; **23** AP/Wide World Photos; **25** AP/Wide World Photos; **27** © Baerbel Schmidt/Getty Images; **29** © Matthew Mcvay/Corbis; **30** *left* The Granger Collection, New York; *right* The Granger Collection, New York; **31** © Bettmann/Corbis; **32** © Lawrence Manning/Corbis; **33** © CartoonStock; **36** © Keren Su/Corbis; **39** *left* © Frans Lanting/Corbis; *center* © Peter Turnley/Corbis; *right* © Burt Glinn/Magnum Photos; **40** © Frank Herholdt/Alamy Images; **41** © Robert Harding Picture Library Ltd/ Alamy Images; **44** *bottom* © Dagli Orti/The Art Archive; *center* The Granger Collection, New York; **46** *left* © Thomas Hoepker/Magnum Photos; *right* © Wolfgang Kaehler/Corbis; **47** © Peter Turnley/Corbis; **48** © Rolf Bruderer/ Corbis; **50** *left* © Getty Images; *center* © Tim Boyle/Getty Images; *right* © Mario Tama/Getty Images; **52** © Juan Silva/Getty Images; **54** © Sue Cunningham Photographic/Alamy Images; **55** © image100/Getty Images; **57** © Stockbyte/ Getty Images; **59** © David Woods/Corbis; **61** © Martin Guhl/CartoonStock; **62** © Rubberball/Jupiter Images; **63** © Fotosearch Stock Photography; **64** Lasse Norgaard/Red Cross/AP/Wide World Photos; **67** © Cathrine Wessel/ Corbis; **68–69** © Cohen/Ostrow/Getty Images; **70** Photo courtesy of Monica Ramirez; **72** © Russell Gordon/Danita Delimont; **73** © Al Freni/Getty Images; **75** *center* © Jeff Greenberg/age fotostock america, inc.; *right* © Susan Van Etten/PhotoEdit; *left* © Getty Images; **76** *bottom* © Roger Ressmeyer/Corbis; *book image* © John Labbe/Getty Images; *book cover Free to Choose,* © 1980 by Milton Friedman and Rose Friedman, reproduced by permission of Harcourt, Inc. This material may not be reproduced in any form or by any means without prior written permission of the publisher.; **77** © Veer Wild Bill Melton/Getty Images; **78** © Creatas/Alamy Images; **83** © Time Life Pictures/Getty Images; **84** © Seth Joel/Getty Images; **85** © Joe Drivas/Getty Images; **86** *left* © Getty Images; *center* © Gideon Mendel/Corbis; *right* © David McNew/Getty Images; **87** © Ashley Cooper/Corbis; **88** © LADA/Photo Researchers, Inc.; **89** © David Young-Wolff/PhotoEdit; **91** © Gabe Palmer/Corbis; **92** © Ben Stechschulte/ Redux; **95** © Niall McDiarmid/Alamy Images.

Unit 2

96-97 © Ryan McVay/Getty Images; **97** © Issei Kato/Reuters/Corbis; **98** © Jupiter Images; **99** © Getty Images; **102** © Scott Barbour/Getty Images; **104** *bottom* © Matthew Peyton/Getty Images; *center* Thomas Iannaccone/ Fairchild Publications/AP/Wide World Photos; **107** © Getty Images; **108** © Getty Images; **110** *left* © Getty Images; *center* © Getty Images; *right* © Ron Kimball/Ron Kimball Stock; **112** *left* © Getty Images; *center* © Benjamin Rondel/Corbis; *right* © Martyn Goddard/Corbis; **114** © Kevin Kallaugher, www.kaltoons.com; **115** © Corbis; **116** © Vehbi Koca/Alamy Images; **117** *left* © Getty Images; *bottom inset* © Corbis; *bottom right* © Wayne Eastep/Getty Images; **119** *left* © Altrendo images/Getty Images; *center* © Getty Images; *right* Photograph by Tricia Bauman/Clik Photography; **123** © Mark E. Gibson; **124** © David Young-Wolff/Getty Images; **125** *top* © Brian Duffy/The Des Moines Register; *center* © Issei Kato/Reuters/Corbis; **128-129** © AFP/Getty Images; **129** © Lucas Schifres/Corbis; **130** © Mason Morfit/Getty Images; **131** © Jupiter Images; **132** © Chris Thomaidis/Getty Images; **136** © Martin Thiel/Getty Images; **137** © Spencer Grant/PhotoEdit; **138** © David A. Barnes/Alamy Images; **140** *clockwise from top left* © Michael Goldman/Getty Images; © Brownie Harris/Corbis; © Corbis; © Danish Khan/ShutterStock; © Todd S. Holder/ShutterStock; © Image Source/Getty Images; **142** © C Squared Studios/Getty Images (Royalty-Free); **145** © David McNew/Getty Images; **146** *left* © James L. Amos/Corbis; *right* © David Young-Wolff/ PhotoEdit; **149** *left* © Albo/ShutterStock; *right* © Doug Priebe/ShutterStock; **152** *bottom* AP/Wide World Photos; *center* Stephen Chernin/AP/Wide World Photos; **153** © Getty Images; **154** AP/Wide World Photos; **156** *left* © Getty Images; *center* © David Joel/Getty Images; *right* © Jupiter Images; **157** © Thinkstock; 158 © Lucas Schifres/Corbis; 159 © John Morris/CartoonStock; **162–163** © Peter M. Fisher/Corbis; **163** © Tim Mosenfelder/Getty Images; **164** © Eric Futran/FoodPix/Jupiter Images; **168** AP/Wide World Photos; **171** © Danny Lehman/Corbis; **173** © Dennis Wise/Getty Images; **174** © Tom Stewart/Corbis; **177** *center* © Yoshikazu Tsuno/AFP/Getty Images; *right* © Getty Images; *left* © Getty Images; **178** *top* Harry Cabluck/AP/Wide World Photos; *center* © Bob Riha, Jr./Dell/Handout/Reuters/Corbis; *bottom* © Elipsa/Corbis; **179** © Sally and Richard Greenhill/Alamy Images; **180** © David Bergman/Corbis; **183** © Corbis; **184** © Forrest Anderson/Getty Images; **185** © Robert Barclay/Grant Heilman Photography; **186** © Tim Mosenfelder/Getty Images; **190–191** © Chuck Pefley/ Alamy Images; **191** Kai-Uwe Knoth/AP/Wide World Photos; **193** © Veer; **195** © Sandra Ivany/Botanica/Jupiter Images; **197** © Brigitte Sporrer/zefa/Corbis; **198** © Dave G. Houser/Post-Houserstock/Corbis; **201** © Will & Deni McIntyre/Corbis; **202** *top left* © Getty Images; *top right* © BananaStock/Alamy Images; *top center* © Dynamic Graphics Group/i2i/Alamy Images; *bottom right* © istockphoto.com; **203** © Rob Leiter/MLB Photos via Getty Images; **204** © Harley Schwadron/ CartoonStock; **205** © Royalty-Free/Corbis; **206** © Judy Griesedieck/Corbis; **207** © Matt Bowman/Foodpix/Jupiter Images; **208** © Justin Kase/Alamy Images; **209** © Chuck Savage/Corbis; **210** © Sue Cunningham Photographic/Alamy Images; **212** © Peter Lofts Photography; **213** © Royalty-Free/Corbis; **214** © Stock Montage/Getty Images; **215** Caleb Jones/AP/Wide World Photos; **218** © 2006 by R. J. Matson/Caglecartoons.com. All rights reserved.; **219** © Joseph Sohm/Visions of America/Corbis; **220** Kai-Uwe Knoth/AP/Wide World Photos; **221** © Richard Sly/CartoonStock; **223** © Hans-Peter Merten/Digital Vision/Getty Images.

Unit 3

224–225 © Comstock Images/Jupiter Images; **225** Paul Sakuma/AP/Wide World Photos; **226** © Getty Images; **227** © Stockbyte Platinum/Alamy Images; **228** © Brand X Pictures/Alamy Images; **230** Photo courtesy of Mary Kay Inc.; **231** © Viviane Moos/Corbis; **232** © Yuri Arcurs/ShutterStock; **233** © Arthur Tilley/Getty Images; **235** © Creasource/Corbis; **237** © Michael Keller/Corbis; **241** © Chris Wildt/CartoonStock; **244** © John Morris/CartoonStock; **246** © Lynn Goldsmith/Corbis; **247** © LWA-Dann Tardif/Corbis; **249** *top left* © Getty Images; *top right* © Thinkstock/Alamy Images; *top center* © Douglas Freer/ShutterStock; **250** *bottom* Courtesy of Salvation Army; *top* Reprinted with permission © 2007 American Lung Association. For more information about the American Lung Association or to support the work it does, call 1-800-LUNG-USA (1-800-586-4872) or log on to www.lungusa.org; **251** Alan Diaz/AP/Wide World Photos; **252** Paul Sakuma/AP/Wide World Photos; **253** © Bernard Gotfryd/Getty Images; **255** © Dave G. Houser/Post-Houserstock/Corbis; **256–257** © Bruce Avres/Getty Images; **257** © Andrew Toos/CartoonStock; **258** © Ariel Skelley/Corbis; **262** © Roger Ressmeyer/ Corbis; **264** *right* Joshua Lott/AP/Wide World Photos; *left* Human Capital: A Theoretical and Empirical Analysis with Special Reference to Education, by Gary S. Becker. © 1993. Reprinted with permission of The University of Chicago Press.; **265** © Brenda Prince/Photofusion Picture Library/Alamy Images; **266** © Getty Images; **269** *top right* © Robert Llewellyn/Corbis; *top left* © H. Armstrong Roberts/Corbis; **270** *bottom left* © Getty Images; *bottom center* © David Sacks/Getty Images; *bottom right* © Terry McCormick/Getty Images; **271** © Charles Thatcher/Getty Images; **273** © Alamy Images; **275** © Time Life Pictures/Getty Images; **276** *left* © Hulton Archive/Getty Images; *second from right* © Bettmann/Corbis; *right* The Granger Collection, New York; *second from left* The Granger Collection, New York; **277** *left* © Ted Streshinsky/Corbis; *right* © Roger Ressmeyer/Corbis; **280** © Jeff Kowalsky/AFP/Getty Images; **281** © H. P. Merten/zefa/Corbis; **282** © Jagadeesh/Reuters/Corbis; **283** © Andrew Toos/CartoonStock.

Unit 4

286–287 © George Diebold Photography/Getty Images; **287** © Ralph Hagen/CartoonStock; **288** © Comstock Images/Alamy Images; **290** © Lowell Georgia/Corbis; **291** © W. Perry Conway/CORBIS; **292** © Dennis Galante/ Corbis; *all flags this page* © FOTW Flags of the World website at http:// flagspot.net/flags; **295** © Klaus Hackenberg/zefa/Corbis; **296** Counting House (about 1375–1400). British Library, London. Photo © HIP/Art Resource, New York; **297** *center* © Archivo Iconografico, S.A./Corbis; *bottom right* The Granger Collection, New York; **298** *top left* © The Granger Collection, New York; *bottom right* The Granger Collection, New York; *top right* © The British Museum; *right* The Granger Collection, New York; **299** *left* © Getty Images; *top* © Bettmann/Corbis; *right* © Wally McNamee/Corbis; 300 © Marty Katz/Time Life Pictures/Getty Images; **303** © Don Smetzer/PhotoEdit; **307** *bottom left* © Bettmann/Corbis; *bottom right* © Getty Images; **308** © Brandtner & Staedeli/Getty Images; **309** *right* © Chuck Savage/Corbis; *bottom left* © Altrendo images/Getty Images; *center* © Chuck Savage/Corbis; **310** © Michael Keller/Corbis; **311** © Ryan McVay/Getty Images; **313** © Ralph Hagen/CartoonStock; **315** © Antonio M. Rosario/The Image Bank/Getty Images; **316–317** © Jean Miele/Corbis; **317** © Andrew Toos/CartoonStock; **318** © Graca Victoria/ShutterStock; **320** © Free Agents Limited/Corbis; **322** © Susan Van Etten/PhotoEdit; **323** © White Packert/Getty Images; **324** © Marc Romanelli/Getty Images; **325** *top left* © Getty Images; *top center* © Peter Adams/zefa/Corbis; *top right* © Chuck Savage/Corbis; **326** © Peter Kramer/Getty Images; **328** *top left* © Altrendo images/Getty Images; *top* *center* © Royalty-Free/Corbis; *top right* © Alan Schein/zefa/Corbis; **329** © Robert Mizerek/ShutterStock; **330** © Alan Schein/zefa/Corbis; **331** © Harley Schwadron/CartoonStock; **332** © Scott Barrow, Inc./SuperStock; **333** © Tonis Valing/ShutterStock; **335** © J. McGillen/CartoonStock; **336** © The Cover Story/Corbis; **337** © Ethan Miller/Getty Images; **339** *right* © Glowimages/Getty Images; *top* © Peter Bowater/Alamy Images; *center* © Zina Seletskaya/ShutterStock; **341** © Jim Sizemore/CartoonStock; **343** © Kai Hecker/ShutterStock; **344** © Erik Freeland/Corbis; **345** © Andrew Toos/ CartoonStock; **347** © Royalty-Free/Corbis.

Unit 5

348–349 © Royalty-Free/Corbis; **349** © Wojtek Laski/East News via Getty Images; **350** © Jason Hawkes/Corbis; **354** © Ariel Skelley/Corbis; **357** © Royalty-Free/Corbis; **358** © Best of Latin America/Caglecartoons.com; **362** © Andersen Ross/Getty Images; **363** © Stan Honda/AFP/Getty Images; **365** *top* © Archive Holdings Inc./Getty Images; *bottom* The Granger Collection, New York; **371** © Ed Kashi/Corbis; **374** The Granger Collection, New York; **375** © Gary Braasch/Corbis; **376** © Wojtek Laski/East News via Getty Images; **377** © Peter Schrank; **380–381** © David Trood/Getty Images; **381** © Time & Life Pictures/Getty Images; **382** © Chris Hondros/Getty Images; **384** © Adam Crowley/Getty Images; **385** © AFP/Getty Images; **387** © Cleo Photography/ PhotoEdit; **392** © Justin Sullivan/Getty Images; **393** © Photofusion Library/ Alamy Images; **394** *top* © Cecilia Durand/*El Comercio,* Lima, Peru; *bottom* © Getty Images; **395** © Khaled El Fiqui/epa/Corbis; **396** © Dave Einsel/Getty Images; **400** © Stephanie Davis/ShutterStock; **401** *right* © Danny Bailey/ istockphoto.com; *center* © James Leynse/Corbis; *left* © Getty Images; **402** © James Leynse/Corbis; **404** © Time & Life Pictures/Getty Images; **405** © Larry Katzman/CartoonStock; **407** © David Lees/Getty Images.

Unit 6

408–409 © Tom Bean/Getty Images; **411** Frank and Ernest reprinted with permission of Thaves; **416** © Ljupco Smokovski/ShutterStock; **419** Phil Coale/AP/Wide World Photos; **420** © Tim Boyle/Getty Images; **422** © Myrleen Ferguson Cate/PhotoEdit; **423** © Harley Schwadron/CartoonStock; **426** Photo courtesy of Sarah Brennan; **427** © Elizabeth Simpson/Getty Images; **428** © George Mattei/Photo Researchers, Inc.; **429** © Spencer Platt/Getty Images; **430** *left* © Getty Images; *center* © Jose Luis Pelaez, Inc./Corbis; *right* © Mark Wilson/Getty Images; **432** © Royalty-Free/Corbis; **433** Rachel Denny Clow/Corpus Christi Caller-Times/AP/Wide World Photos; **436** © Mike Lane/Caglecartoons.com; **438** © Dan Brandenburg/istockphoto.com; **439** © Michael Newman/PhotoEdit; **440** © G. Schuster/zefa/Corbis; **444–445** © I. Vanderharst/Getty Images; **445** © Harley Schwadron/www.CartoonStock. com; **447** © Joel Stettenheim/Corbis; **448** © John Humble/Getty Images; **452** © Larry Wright/Caglecartoons.com; **453** © Jeff Metzger/ShutterStock; **454** The Granger Collection, New York; **456** From *The General Theory of Employment, Interests, and Money,* by John Maynard Keynes (1997), book cover. (Amherst, NY: Prometheus Books). Book cover © 1997 by Prometheus Books. Reprinted with permission of the publisher.; *Time cover* © Time Life Pictures/Getty Images; **457** © Hulton-Deutsch Collection/Corbis; **460** *left* © Altrendo images/Getty Images; center Mel Evans/AP/Wide World Photos; *right* © Jim West/Alamy Images; **461** © Charles Luzier/Reuters/Corbis; **462** © Harley Schwadron/www.CartoonStock.com; 467 © Peter Beck/Corbis; **468** © Stan Honda/AFP/Getty Images; **469** © Harley Schwadron/www.CartoonStock. com; **472–473** © Brooks Kraft/Corbis; **475** The Granger Collection, New York; **478** *bottom* © Kitt Cooper-Smith/Alamy Images; *top* © James Leynse/Corbis; **479** © Louie Psihoyos/Corbis; **480** © Janis Christie/Getty Images; **483** *top* U. S. Treasury/AP/Wide World Photos; *bottom* U. S. Treasury/AP/Wide World Photos; **486** David Zalubowski/AP/Wide World Photos; **489** © Jim Pathe/Star Ledger/Corbis; **492** Frank and Ernest reprinted with permission of Thaves.; **494** © Time & Life Pictures/Getty Images; **496** © James Leynse/Corbis; **497** © Don Mason/Corbis; **498** © Royalty-Free/Corbis; **501** *left* © Getty Images; *center* © Greg Henry/istockphoto.com; *right* © Sharon Meredith/istockphoto.com; **503** © Stocksearch/Alamy Images; **504** © J. Scott Applewhite/AP/Wide World Photos; **505** © Harley Schwadron/www.CartoonStock.com.

Unit 7

508–509 © Paul Chesley/Getty Images; **509** © Jack Kurtz/ZUMA/Corbis; **510** *left* © KCNA/epa/Corbis; right © Benelux Press/Getty Images; **511** *left* © Altrendo images/Getty Images; *center* © Tom Stewart/Corbis; *right* © Anita Patterson Peppers/ShutterStock; **512** The Granger Collection, New York; **513** *left* © Robert Garvey/Corbis; *right* © Royalty-Free/Corbis; **515** © Barry Mason/Alamy Images; **517** © Andrew Brookes/Corbis; **519** © Gordon Swanson/ShutterStock; **520** © Stephane Peray/Caglecartoons.com; **523** © Pierre Verdy/AFP/Getty Images; **524** © images-of-france/Alamy Images; **525** © Karl Weatherly/Getty Images; **526** *top* © Danita Delimont/Alamy Images; *center* © B.A.E. Inc./Alamy Images; *bottom* © Pacific Press Service/Alamy Images; **527** © You Sung-Ho/Reuters/Corbis; **528** *left* © Getty Images; *center* © Blue Line Pictures/Getty Images; *right* © Jerry Arcieri/Corbis; **531** © Alan Schein Photography/Corbis; **532** Mindaugas Kulbis/AP/Wide World Photos; **535** *right* Gautam Singh/AP/Wide World Photos; *second from right* © Ralph Orlowski/Getty Images; *second from left* © Chung Sung Jun/Getty Images; left Newscast/AP/Wide World Photos; **537** © PhotoLink/Getty Images; **538** © Jack Kurtz/ZUMA/Corbis; **541** *left* © Royalty-Free/Corbis; *right* © Steven Collins/ShutterStock; **542–543** © Mark Daffey/Getty Images; **543** © Best of Latin America/Caglecartoons.com; **545** *left* © Ed Kashi/ Corbis; *right* © Justin Guariglia/Corbis; **547** © Caroline Penn/Corbis; **549** © Bob Sacha/Corbis; **550** © Juda Ngwenya/Reuters/Corbis; **551** © Rafiqur Rahman/Reuters/Corbis; **552** © Royalty-Free/Corbis; **554** © Bill Fritsch/Age Fotostock America, Inc.; **555** *right* © SW Productions/Getty Images; *left* © Three Lions/Hulton Archive/Getty Images; **556** © Penny Tweedie/Alamy Images; **558** © AP/Wide World Photos; **560** © Dieter Nagl/AFP/Getty Images; **561** © James Marshall/Corbis; **562** © Javier Larrea/Age Fotostock; **564** © Christo Komarnitski/Caglecartoons.com; **565** © Jon Hicks/Corbis; **566** *left* © Panorama Media (Beijing) Ltd./Alamy Images; *right* © Raymond Gehman/ NGSImages.com; **569** © Directphoto.org/Alamy Images; **570** © Best of Latin America/Caglecartoons.com; **571** © Best of Latin America/Caglecartoons. com; **573** © Bob Krist/Corbis; **574** © George Shelley/Corbis; © Getty Images; **576** © Tara Urbach/ShutterStock; **577** © Digital Vision/Getty Images; **579** © Ariel Skelley/Corbis; **582** *top left* © Getty Images; *bottom right* © Mike Lane/Caglecartoons.com; **588** © BananaStock/Jupiter Images; **590** *top left* © Getty Images; *right* © Gabe Palmer/Corbis; **591** © Alexander Walter/Getty Images; **592** © David Young-Wolff/PhotoEdit; **594** © Mike Lane/Caglecartoons. com; **596** © Colorstock/Getty Images; **598** © John Morris/www.CartoonStock. com; **600** *top left* © Getty Images; *bottom right* Reprinted with permission of the Employment Development Department, State of California; **603** © Creatas Images/Jupiter Images; 605 © Mario Tama/Getty Images; **606** © Ken Reid/Getty Images; **608** © PM Images/Getty Images.

Backmatter

R26 © Stan Eales/CartoonStock.

Maps (except Economic Atlas and Statistics maps)

© GeoNova Group.

Trademark Acknowledgments

ADIDAS and the Adidas design are registered trademarks of Adidas AG Joint Stock Company
AMERICAN RED CROSS design is a trademark of American Red Cross Inc.
AMOCO design is a registered trademark of Amoco Oil Company
BET.COM design is a trademark of Black Entertainment Television, Inc.
COCA-COLA and the Coca-Cola design are registered trademarks of The Coca-Cola Company
DELL design is a registered trademark of Dell Inc.
FANTASTIC SAM'S is a registered trademark of Fantastic Sam's Franchise Corporation
HABITAT FOR HUMANITY design is a registered trademark of Habitat for Humanity International, Inc.
INTERNATIONAL MONETARY FUND design is a trademark of The International Monetary Fund
KOZMO.COM design is a registered trademark of of Kozmo.com, Inc.
MASTERCARD design is a registered trademark of MasterCard International Incorporated
MICROSOFT is a registered trademark of Microsoft Corporation
NASDAQ is a registered trademark of NASDAQ Stock Exchange, Inc.
NEWSWEEK is a registered trademark of Newsweek, Inc.
NOKIA is a registered trademark of Nokia Corporation
NYSE is a registered trademark of New York Stock Exchange, Inc.
PIONEER is a registered trademark of Pioneer Kabushiki Kaisha DAB Pioneer Electronic Corporation
SALVATION ARMY design is a registered trademark of The Salvation Army
SAMSUNG is a regisered trademark of Samsung Electronics Co., Ltd.
The **SHELL** emblem is a trademark of Shell International Limited
SONY is a registered trademark of Sony Kabushiki Kaisha TA Sony Corporation
TIME design is a registered trademark of Time, Inc.
TYCO is a trademark of Mattel, Inc.
U.S. NEWS & WORLD REPORT design is a registered trademark of U.S. News & World Report, L.P.
VAIO design is a registered trademark of Sony Kabushiki Kaisha TA Sony Corporation
VISA design is a registered trademark of Visa International Service Association
VOLVO is a registered trademark of Volvo Trademark Holding AB Corporation
WWF design is a registered trademark of World Wide Fund for Nature

All other trademarks are property of their respective owners and are in no way affiliated with, connected to or sponsored by McDougal Littell, a division of Houghton Mifflin Company. Trademarks, trade names, logos and graphics are shown in this book strictly for illustrative purposes.

R81